SCHOOL DIVISION

PRENTICE HALL

The
quality
choice
for
today's
classrooms

Prentice Hall can help you build a bridge.

TEACHER'S EDITION

PRENTICE HALL

AMERICA
PATHWAYS
— TO THE —
PRESENT

America: Pathways to the Present ©1995
America in the Twentieth Century

The Student Edition starts with a simple idea: history is not predictable.

History's decision makers—whether famous or ordinary citizens—never knew how things were going to turn out. But the consequences of their decisions helped determine how we arrived where we are today. Tracing these pathways makes students active participants in the unfolding of history.

In developing the narrative for each chapter, our authors utilized the concept of the "big idea." The "big idea" organizes and focuses the chapter, helping students better see the connections between the diverse peoples and stories of a period.

Students' understanding is strengthened by focusing on turning points in history, events that changed the course of history and have lasting impact on our contemporary lives.

Equally important, the textbook's design appeals to the video generation, guiding them more easily through the information.

A Teacher's Edition that organizes and focuses instruction.

Every historical period is a complex web of events, influences, and relationships. But in each era there is a main trend, a big idea, that can be used pedagogically to cut through the clutter and help students understand, focus, and master this important subject matter.

Each chapter of the Teacher's Edition is "jump started" by discussing the relevance of the big idea that organizes chapter content. The lesson plan that follows is structured around that big idea, too.

Our Teacher's Edition employs a wraparound style in which comments, answers to questions, program resources, and background notes occur when you need them. It is the teaching equivalent of perfect timing.

Teaching Resources based on real-world strategies.

We provide you with every bit of mortar and steel you need to build a bridge to your students. One of the teaching resources that you won't want to be without is the Teacher-to-Teacher Network File. Based on their actual classroom experience, teachers across the country offer strategies that they've found absolutely successful in giving U.S. history relevance . . . strategies that make history come alive.

Arranged on a chapter-by-chapter basis, the extensive Teaching Resources package combines everything you need in one place.

The Transparencies recognize that *some* students learn better visually.

The visual medium of the transparencies is perfect for showing historical change. For example, you can use **Pathways'** set of overlay transparencies to follow the evolution of a theme across the span of U.S. history.

This medium is also ideal for cutting away the outer skin of technological processes. For example, you can show students how an auto factory operates or how the Brooklyn Bridge was constructed.

Multimedia Resources that recognize your need for flexibility.

Prentice Hall is the first and only publisher to develop an original multimedia package specifically designed to work simultaneously with a new U.S. History program. Finally you will have the opportunity to merge print and other media together easily. For those who have access to videotape, videodisc, or computer equipment, **Pathways** provides this optional level of integrated classroom technology.

Imagine a learning tool that combines motion, sound, photography, graphics, and text to immerse students in a period, topic, or theme. Each of the 7 textbook units has a video montage as irresistible as a music video. The turning points examined in the text are also extended through video presentations.

In addition, you can take advantage of our:
- Computer Test Bank (Macintosh and DOS)
- Social Studies Update
- Guided Reading Audiotapes (Spanish and English)

Pathways Makes History Relevant . . .

1 Through a Dramatic Narrative

Political and Social History. *America: Pathways to the Present* offers a balance of political and social history, telling the stories of key people and events as well as capturing what life was like for ordinary Americans. *(See the Table of Contents, pages vi–xxi.)*

Primary Sources. Primary sources and first-person accounts are interspersed throughout the narrative, adding a human face to far-off events. These accounts are not in secluded boxes to be skipped by students, but are core content, with questions related to them in the chapter reviews. *(See pages 372, 448, 482, and 541 for examples.)*

❋ SOURCE READINGS

Source Readings. *America: Pathways to the Present* ends each chapter with Source Readings—a collection of primary sources and literature that relates to chapter content. *(See pages xiii–xiv for a complete list.)*

In Depth
Multicultural Perspectives

America: Pathways to the Present recognizes that diversity has given the United States its special character. Multicultural content is embedded in the narrative—not set off in a box or treated as an afterthought. In-Depth notes in the **Teacher's Edition** offer additional information for teachers to share with students. *(For examples in the **Student Edition**, see pages 355, 411, and 548. For examples in the **Teacher's Edition**, see pages 630, 657, and 798.)*

2 By Looking in Depth at Pivotal Moments in Our Past

TURNING POINTS

Certain events—turning points— have shifted the direction of American society and had immediate consequences on political, economic, and social life. Each of these turning points also had a lasting impact that can still be felt today. Once per unit, *America: Pathways to the Present* devotes an entire section to an in-depth look at a critical event in our history. Following each "Turning Point" section, a two-page feature examines its lasting impact, a discussion of the historical event's contemporary significance. *(See pages 355, 457, 518, and 748 for examples.)*

RESOURCE DIRECTORY

In the **Teaching Resources** box you will find extension activities that further explore the lasting impact of each "Turning Point" event.

Videodiscs/Videotapes

Visions of America, the program's multimedia component, includes "Turning Point" stories that dramatize the "Turning Points" with archival footage.   In addition, *Visions of America* includes "Roundtable Discussions" in which historians and prominent social commentators debate and discuss the turning point's meaning. Barcodes in the **Teacher's Edition** correlate videodisc segments to **Student Edition** content.

3 By Encouraging Students to Become Active Learners

MAKING CONNECTIONS

Questions in the middle of each section ask students to connect what they have just read with something they read earlier or with something in their own lives. *(See pages 323, 351, 538, and 655 for examples.)*

4 By Emphasizing Decision Making

History *might not have* Happened This Way

"History Might Not Have Happened This Way" focuses on key decisions, exploring the background of the decision makers, both famous and ordinary, and the consequences of their decisions. By emphasizing that people's decisions influence the course of history, students come to see that they, too, can play a part in shaping the present and future. *(See pages 290, 408, and 634 for examples.)*

 RESOURCE DIRECTORY

In the **Teaching Resources** box are decision-making extension activities that focus on a contemporary decision related to each "History Might Not Have Happened This Way" topic in the **Student Edition**.

Computer Software

Visions of America includes a software game that allows students to explore pivotal decisions in United States history.

5 By Appealing to Today's Visual Learners

Maps, Graphs, Charts and Tables

The **Student Edition** includes maps, graphs, charts, tables, and graphic organizers designed to meet the needs of visual learners. These illustrations, along with photographs, provide opportunities for visual learners to study U.S. history. *(See pages 322, 354, 445, 733, and 768 for examples.)*

Teaching Resources

"Visual Learning Activities" in the **Teaching Resources** utilize cartoons, advertisements, posters, and photographs to illustrate main ideas, summarize chapter content, and spark discussion. *(See pages 102 and 103 of the Unit 4 folder in the **Teaching Resources** for examples.)*

Transparencies

A collection of 170 color overhead transparencies with lesson suggestions includes fine art, maps, charts, tables, political cartoons, and photographs—to help you teach and enrich main ideas. *(See the Transparency Sampler in the **Teaching Resources** box.)*

 American Album

Pictorial essays in each unit teach history through artifacts from the exhibitions and collections of the Smithsonian Institution's National Museum of American History. *(See pages 294, 430, 554, and 738 for examples.)*

 Videodiscs/Videotapes

Visions of America videodiscs and videotapes include video montages, "Scenes of an Era," for each unit that capture students' interest with sounds and images as exciting as music videos.

"Here's what matters to me: What has the publisher done to help me cut down on planning time? I want to spend my time teaching— not hunting and gathering."

— *Pittsburgh United States history teacher*

Pathways Makes Instruction Manageable ...

1 By Focusing on Big Ideas

THE BIG IDEA

Every chapter in *America: Pathways to the Present* was written with a "big idea" in mind. These big ideas help students focus on key ideas in United States history to see how we as a nation got where we are today. To help manage instruction, lesson plans in the **Teacher's Edition** are structured around the big ideas. Before each chapter, a graphic organizer in the **Teacher's Edition** highlights the chapter's big idea and shows how each section of the chapter relates to it. *(See pages 470B and 650B for examples.)*

 **Connecting to the Big Idea**

At the beginning of each section in the **Teacher's Edition** is a suggestion for "Connecting to the Big Idea" to help you focus instruction. *(See page 472 for an example.)* Concluding the section is a suggestion for "Reinforcing the Big Idea" to help you close instruction. *(See page 478 for an example.)* In addition, the **Teaching Resources** includes an alternate lesson plan, "Demonstrating the Big Idea," for every chapter. *(See pages 89, 94, 105, and 117 of the Alternate Lesson Plans folder in the **Teaching Resources** box for examples.)*

2 By Addressing the Needs of Different Types of Learners

Instructional Options. *America: Pathways to the Present* offers a variety of instructional options. In the **Teacher's Edition** you will find a modified Madeline Hunter— Focus, Instruct, Assess, Close—lesson plan in the side columns. *(See pages 472–478 of the **Teacher's Edition** for an example.)* In addition, in the **Teaching Resources**, each section has an alternate lesson plan in one of three categories: Critical Thinking, Cooperative Learning, and Learning Styles. *(See pages 118, 119, and 120 of the Alternate Lessons Plans folder in the **Teaching Resources** for examples.)*

Assessment Options. In the **Teaching Resources** box you will find traditional methods of assessment, such as chapter and unit tests, as well as information about the Computer Test Bank.

 Alternative Assessment

Because many teachers are becoming interested in alternative methods of assessment, the **Teacher's Edition** of *America: Pathways to the Present* offers an alternative assessment activity for every chapter, including suggestions for setting up, monitoring, and evaluating each activity. *(See pages 471, 478, and 491 in the **Teacher's Edition** for examples.)*

RESOURCE DIRECTORY

A separate handbook in the **Teaching Resources** box discusses how to construct alternative assessments such as portfolio and performance assessments for your United States history classes. It also provides scoring rubrics and evaluation forms for both students and teachers.

3 By Organizing Teaching Resources Chapter by Chapter

Unit Folders

America: Pathways to the Present **Teaching Resources** are organized the way you teach — chapter by chapter, arranged in unit folders. All core resources for the chapter are housed in a convenient file folder, eliminating the need for "hunting and gathering."

4 By Offering Technology Options That Fit Your Requirements

Videodiscs/Videotapes

Visions of America, the multimedia component custom-made for *America: Pathways to the Present,* is a flexible technology package of videodiscs, videotapes, and software.

5 By Clearly Referencing All Program Resources at Point of Use

RESOURCE DIRECTORY

America: Pathways to the Present **Teacher's Edition** brings all these resources together. In the Resource Directory at the bottom of each page all program resources— activity sheets, transparencies and multimedia— are referenced at the point of use. It's the teaching equivalent of perfect timing. *(See pages 470–489 for examples.)*

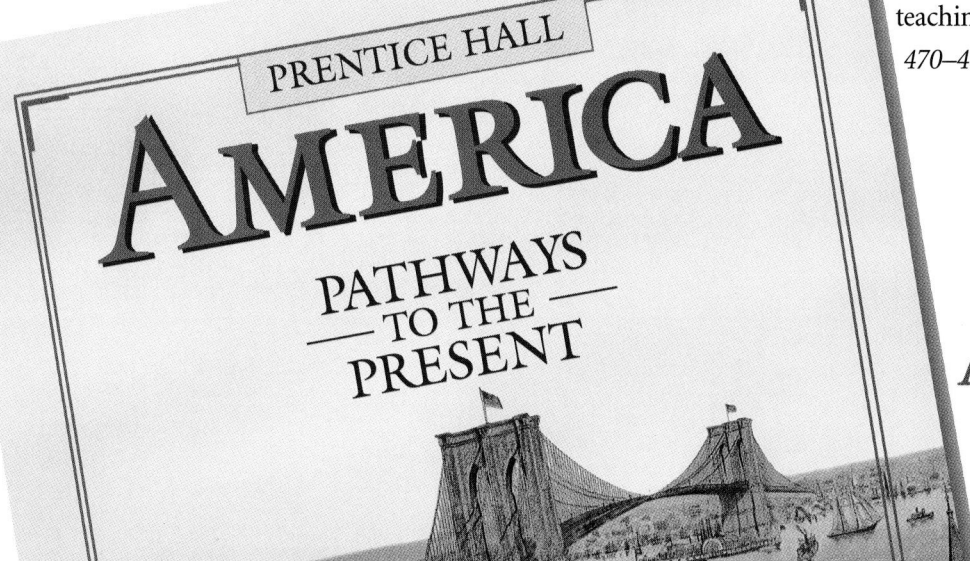

PRENTICE HALL

AMERICA

PATHWAYS —TO THE— PRESENT

A Bridge to Today

PRENTICE HALL

AMERICA

PATHWAYS
— TO THE —
PRESENT

America in the Twentieth Century

Program Reviewers and Advisers

Teacher Reviewers

Pamela Lee Gray
Tustin High School
Tustin, California

Rita Geiger
Social Studies Specialist
Oklahoma City, Oklahoma

Phillip James
Lincoln-Sudbury Regional High School
Sudbury, Massachusetts

Jerome L. Ruderman
Social Studies Department Head
Frankford High School
Philadelphia, Pennsylvania

Limited English Proficiency

Lynn Hall
English as a Second Language Teacher
Board of Cooperative Educational Services
Spencerport, New York

Alternative Assessment

Hannah Kruglanski
Director of Curriculum and Assessment
Edunetics Corporation
Arlington, Virginia

Photo Credits
Page T10 *Stone axes* Richard Alexander Cooke III; **T11** *Student at archeological dig* Courtesy, Shaun P. Bresnahan; **T11** *Pueblo bowl* Eric Long, Smithsonian Institution, Courtesy of the Museum of Indian Arts and Culture, Laboratory of Anthropology Collection, Santa Fe; **T17** *Classroom* Ken Karp; **T18** *Disks* David Dennis/Tom Stack & Associates; **T19** *Monitor* Ken O'Donoghue; **T19** *Computer screen image* James Karales; **T19** *Student at computer* FPG International; **T22–T23** *Student discussion* Larry Lawfer

PRENTICE HALL
A Division of Simon and Schuster
Upper Saddle River, New Jersey 07458

ISBN 0-13-803495-8

Printed in the United States of America

2 3 4 5 6 7 8 9 02 01 00 99 98 97 96 95

HISTORY EDUCATOR'S HANDBOOK

Making History Relevant

han was
National
Studies
r of the
1992.
been
g
States
in
town,
chusetts,
nty-five

RELEVANCE:
The Ultimate Challenge

by Shaun Bresnahan

If there is one single challenge that history teachers face continually, it is the challenge of making history relevant to our students. Every year we find it getting harder and harder. We are often asked what spells we use to entice our students to learn. What do we do to challenge our students' intellectual curiosity, encourage self-motivation, and foster critical thinking skills? Each and every one of you has your own methods and ideas. There is no one magical method or technique waiting to be discovered in some dusty tome. I'd like to share with you some of the ways that I try to meet the challenge and teach United States history to my high school class.

Meeting the Challenge

Over the last twenty-five years, I have designed activities that use a discovery approach to education. I have found that one of the most accessible routes to participation in the study of history is through the study of material culture. The study of material culture, or artifact analysis, has been a tool in anthropology and archeology for some time now. By examining objects from the past, students take on the roles of researcher, archeologist, and detective. They explore not only the physical remains of past societies but also the thoughts and feelings of people in the period they are studying. Primary sources abound in the form of architecture, music, tools, and toys; and they can be found in every town and community throughout the country. Artifacts in all forms, from a bowl or button to a computer or church window, offer students a glimpse of the past, a puzzle to solve, and a problem to analyze in their continuing efforts to bridge the historical past and connect it to their own lives.

Here are some of the strategies that I use to make history meaningful to my students and to teach them the critical thinking and evaluative skills that are so necessary in the world today.

Role-Play

I walk into the classroom and say, "I pledge you, I pledge myself, to a new deal for the American public." Or I bring in an apple, write on the chalkboard, "There were 6,000 apple sellers in New York City in 1931," and recite a song, "I don't want your millions, mister. I don't want your diamond ring. All I want is the right to live, mister. Give me back my job again." "Who are these characters?" I ask my students. "What are they talking about, and why?" I stay in character and answer students' questions.

Artifact Analysis

When examining the cultural diversity of the indigenous peoples of the Atlantic World, I conduct a simulated archeological dig. Using a soccer or baseball field, I section off the field into a number of "sites" and cover each one with a plastic trash bag. On top of each trash bag are artifacts representing cultures we studied in class. These include vegetables, broken pottery, pictures of Native American masks, animal skins, and burnt ash. Students probe and investigate a number of sites and reconstruct information from that period. During the course of the archeological dig, students participate in games, listen to music, and eat foods that represent the cultures being studied. I've done this activity in my classroom on a smaller scale covering almost every time period in United States history.

History Alive

I have my students choose a time period, event, or society that they would like to explore in greater detail. Then they re-create that time or event by using primary source documents, artifacts, and role-playing. The history of our local community has always been a favorite topic. I have used our high school gym to stage the re-creation of our community as it was two hundred years ago. Through dance, music, art, and a little carpentry, students become members of our eighteenth-century town. This is the stuff that cultural history is made of. Students soon begin to discover what makes history; they personalize it, and they undertake the reassembling of history in order to bring it to life.

The Mystery of History

Not all my classes are devoted to creating Federalist villages or archeological digs. I have students focus on how a particular event in history has influenced their lives. Or I ask them to consider what their lives might have been like if the incident had happened differently. How might our societies have been affected? Why did the participants in a particular historical event make the decisions they did? The process of answering these questions helps students understand that history is not, as they often think, a predetermined straight line connecting the past to the present. The people involved in an event did not know how things would turn out. As students come to recognize the uncertain and dramatic quality of the past for those who lived through it, they can begin to see that they, too, are participants in history.

These strategies may not cast a magic spell. But I do believe that they arouse curiosity. They prompt students to be active in learning history, convey to them that their decisions, too, play a part in determining how the present will be remembered, and above all give them a sense that history is a great adventure.

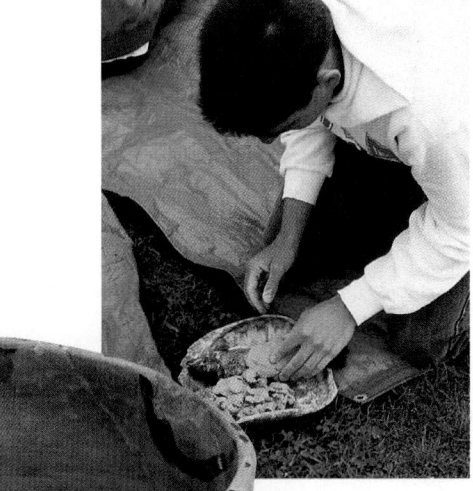

Artifacts— from a bowl or button to a computer or church window— offer students a glimpse of the past, a puzzle to solve, and a problem to analyze in their continuing efforts to bridge the historical past and connect it to their own lives.

ng
, Jr.
utive
esident,
dary
ion,
ount
ning.

Multicultural Education:
A Road to United States History

by Irving Hamer, Jr.

In classrooms around the country the issue of multiculturalism is of central importance. In part, this emphasis is a consequence of the current political and social landscape: high schools reflect the growing diversity in the general U.S. population. But there is more to it. Teachers want more and better multicultural content because students are *interested* in people like themselves. Teachers see multiculturalism as a means of making history relevant.

A Multicultural Focus

No course of study has more potential to honor our pluralistic tradition than American history when that history is viewed through a lens with a multicultural focus.

Over the past thirty years the body of knowledge called American history has evolved in revolutionary ways. People and events that were ignored have become integral to our understanding of history, and events long considered historical milestones have taken on new interpretations. Research from many disciplines has given validity to the experiences and contributions of racial and ethnic minorities and of women.

Let's consider some examples. The "discovery of the New World" by Christopher Columbus is now

> *"I would like to see multiculturalism in the complete course. It brings about divisions as long as we keep separating it. It really should be taught as part of history. If I'm going to keep saying we're a multicultural nation, why do we keep dividing it?"*
>
> Memphis teacher

seen as the first invasion by Europeans of a continent with well-established populations, and what we are now discovering about the intricate cultures and environmental knowledge that pre-Columbian Native Americans possessed is changing an old misconception that they had no meaningful cultures. Similarly, historians are now acknowledging that enslaved Africans made important and creative contributions to the development of this country, and old ideas about their merely subordinate and subservient roles are changing. The essential and significant contributions of women to every aspect of the nation's history were rarely acknowledged in textbooks of earlier decades, but now they are beginning to receive the recognition they have always deserved.

Teaching United States History from Multicultural Points of View

The writing of United States history has been sometimes criticized as a one-dimensional discipline, chronicling only the experiences of famous white men. The only images of history-makers presented to students were the heroic, virtuous, and only rarely scandalous, white, male immigrants from Western Europe. As reported in textbooks of past decades, these men apparently built the United States all by themselves. Of course, there were famous exceptions such as the Wampanoag who fed the starving Pilgrims, and Sacajawea, whose role in guiding the Lewis and Clark expedition is often romanticized.

The best way to instruct students about our multicultural traditions is to look at the historical narrative from the points of view of *all* its peoples. The compelling, and often dramatic, chronicle of our past offers enormous opportunity to enrich and enliven the study of history. Students can acquire critical thinking skills that will enable them to peel back the many layers of what once were one-dimensional approaches. For example, in *America: Pathways to the Present*, Chapter 8, "Cultural and Social Transformations," begins: "Along with the growth of industry and urban areas in the late 1800s came a host of other changes. More children began to attend school, and college became an attainable goal for a growing number of students. A recreation industry, which borrowed heavily from African American culture, emerged to meet the needs of the new urban workers. Yet some segments of society remained mired in the mud of old discriminatory attitudes, refusing to grant such groups as women and African Americans an equal chance at success." One whole section in the chapter is devoted to post-Reconstruction discrimination against African Americans. Another section discusses the woman question, which focused on the social role of women. Chapter 5 looks at Mexican immigration into the southwest from the Mexicans' point of view. After the rebellions in Mexico between 1911 and 1915, many Chicanos saw themselves as returning to New Spain rather than to Texas, Arizona, New Mexico, or California.

Besides a narrative that presents United States history from the points of view of all its peoples, features in the **Student Edition** such as "American Profiles," "Links Across Time," "Viewpoints," "Time and Place," and "History Might Not Have Happened This Way," profile people and issues from diverse racial, ethnic, and gender groups.

The **Teacher's Edition** offers specific help to teachers for heightening student awareness of cultural diversity. Of special interest are the "In Depth" notes titled "Multicultural Perspectives" and "Biography," found in the wraparound. These notes offer teachers high-interest

"I want to be able to teach multiculture as if it happened in history in the chronological approach. I don't want to talk about an event and then say, 'Oh, by the way, there's John Doe and he was there, looking around the corner.' I want it to fit into the course, and we have a difficult time finding that. I want it integrated in the content."

Pittsburgh teacher

background information on multicultural aspects of history and people from many racial and ethnic groups within the chronological framework; not as afterthoughts.

In **Teaching Resources**, the unit folders contain Primary Source Activities, Viewpoints, Literature Activities, Visual Learning, Turning Points Extension Activities, and History Might Not Have Happened This Way that often have multicultural content as appropriate in the chronological study of the historical period.

Above all else, you, the teacher, and your students must be active and aggressive in your pursuit of multicultural perspectives. Such engagement, more than anything else, will make your teaching and your students' study of United States history truly multicultural.

The Elements of a Multicultural History Education

An excellent history education honors the pluralistic tradition of the United States by presenting the expanding knowledge of our country's multicultural past. A good multicultural history education can achieve many worthy goals, although achieving them all through one vehicle is an overwhelming task. Nevertheless, no discipline has more potential to meet the goals of multicultural education than United States history. A good multicultural course will include the following elements.

★ **Critical Thinking** A multicultural history education requires an evaluation of the many dimensions, perspectives, and experiences of history that compete with and complement one another. Therefore, a multicultural history education requires the use of critical thinking skills as well as helping to develop these skills.

★ **Connections** It is the connections between people, places, events, and things that shaped the character and traditions of the United States. Focusing on these connections highlights the roles of cultural, racial, ethnic, and religious groups whose accomplishments contributed to the legacy of the United States.

★ **Active Participation** Multicultural education informs and inspires students to become active participants in the civic, social, political, economic, and cultural life of the United States.

★ **Inclusiveness** The voices heard in a multicultural history are inclusive of the many people who actively participated in shaping the United States. Because many earlier treatments of United States history rendered so many people invisible, multicultural history gives voice to those who were formerly voiceless.

★ **Identification with the Past** Because multicultural history broadens the range of voices students hear beyond famous white men, *all* students have the opportunity to identify with aspects of the country's development and character.

★ **Vision** Relating the multicultural history of the United States provides students with pictures and profiles of the aspirations, struggles, collaborations, and contributions that are the foundation of the pursuit of democracy. A multicultural chronicle is essential to students shaping a democratic vision for tomorrow and taking responsibility for creating our country's future.

avin has
red or co-
red more
40 articles
4 books,
ling
erative
ing: Theory,
rch, and
ice (Prentice
1990);
ational
ology:
y and
ice (Allyn &
n, 1994);
tive
ams for
nts at Risk
& Bacon,
; Preventing
School
e (Allyn &
n, 1994);
School and
room
nization
aum, 1989).

Cooperative Learning

Prentice Hall Interviews Robert Slavin

Cooperative learning is being used now more than ever before. But what is cooperative learning, and why should you incorporate it into your classroom activities?

For a clearer picture, we talked with Dr. Robert E. Slavin, Director of the Early and Elementary School Program at the Center for Research on Effective Schooling for Disadvantaged Students at the Johns Hopkins University Center for Social Organization of Schools. He is one of the nation's leading researchers on the use of cooperative learning in the classroom.

Q What are we talking about when we say "cooperative learning"?

A Cooperative learning actually refers to a wide range of different methods. What is common to all of them is the idea that kids of the same age are working together to help each other learn.

Q How does that happen? How does cooperative learning reinforce or expand learning?

A One of the things that cooperative learning does is motivate students to be concerned about each other's learning, so that students feel that their peers are supporting their learning efforts.

Another benefit is that students, in the process of discussing material presented by the teacher, get to voice their own current understanding. This helps them because people learn by teaching. Cooperative learning also helps kids by filling in gaps in their understanding. Explaining ideas to each other helps kids grasp ideas that they may have only dimly understood at the end of the teacher's lesson.

Q Why should cooperative learning be used in the classroom? For example, what are its benefits?

A The main benefit of cooperative learning is that it improves student achievement. Many studies that have compared it to traditional learning have found that cooperative learning improves the achievement of high, average, and low achievers in many different circumstances.

Cooperative learning also fosters improved intergroup relations, including acceptance of mainstreamed academically handicapped kids. Since kids enjoy working

cooperatively, they feel good about a class in which they are able to work together in this way.

Q What is the ideal group size?

A Four is an ideal group size. It allows for activities in pairs and activities as a total team.

Q How should groups be assigned?

A They should be assigned by the teacher. Have a high and a low achiever and a couple of average achievers in each group. Be sure that there's some kind of balance of sex and ethnicity. Take into account which kids are likely to work together—you know, which kids were dating but have now broken up and the personalities involved.

Q What are some specific ways cooperative learning can be used in the social studies classroom?

A There are many forms of cooperative learning that have been successfully used. It is important to use the right methods for the objective being pursued. For example, one method is for students to study together to make sure that everyone has learned a given body of knowledge. Students are then quizzed on the material, and groups earn certificates based on the average of the quiz scores. This is excellent for teaching facts and concepts of history, geography, and economics. Another method, well adapted to learning from texts, requires each student in a group to become an expert on some aspect of a text and to meet with experts from other groups. The experts return to their groups and teach their groupmates what they have learned. A third method involves students working together on group projects, each student being responsible for one portion of the project. The chosen method should include some evaluation of students' individual work and evaluation of the project based on the performance of all group members.

Q How can cooperative learning be structured so that one student doesn't do all the work?

A The group has to work to earn certificates or some recognition based on the learning of all its members. What this means is that the only way for the group to succeed is if everybody learns. There's no way that one student can do all the work. You rarely want to give the group a single activity that everyone has to do, because then it *is* possible for one student to do all the work.

Q You've said that group success should depend on individual learning. How does that work?

A The success of the group must be dependent on the individual learning of each student. There must be something that can be traced back to each person. For example, teams might earn certificates if the average score on quizzes or essays completed individually by all group members is higher than 80 percent. The idea here is that if students want their groups to succeed, they need to do a good job of teaching each other, of making sure that every group member has learned.

Q Some people are opposed to using rewards and certificates. How do you feel about that?

A There are some kinds of objectives for which they may not be necessary, such as composition, because kids enjoy that anyway; but for most school subjects, some kind of a group reward is necessary. It doesn't have to be big, just something to communicate to the kids that the activity is important. Without that, the students don't see as clearly the need to help each other. There has to be something that they're trying to work toward as a group. However, simple recognition is often enough.

Q How often should cooperative learning be used?

A It should be used pretty extensively. Even when you're using cooperative learning, the kids are not working in groups all day or all the time. There's a cycle of activities that includes instruction, individual assessment, and may include some individual work. There are many classrooms where cooperative learning is used all year. But it also makes sense to use it for shorter periods, as long as

you're not using it on, say, every other Thursday when it's raining. It's important to use it consistently for a period of time, maybe six weeks, rather than to do it just from time to time.

Q Should the groups be constant over that period?

A Yes. A group should stay together for about six weeks. There is a major benefit to having a group that kids can identify with and think is important. If you're changing groups every day, that's not going to happen.

America: Pathways to the Present provides teachers with many cooperative learning resources. The **Teacher's Edition** wraparound includes a cooperative learning activity for every chapter. The **Teaching Resources** package contains an extended essay by Dr. Slavin in the To the Teacher folder, and the Alternate Lesson Plans folder offers a number of cooperative learning lesson plans.

How It Works	
Group Size	4–5 students
Group Make-Up	Combination of high, average, and low achievers, with a balance of sex, ethnicity, and personalities.
Duration of Groups	Change after about six weeks.
Frequency of Use	As often as practical; consistency is important.
Accountability	Group success should depend on individual learning—measured by one evaluation, or by improvement over time.
Recognition	Something small to show that group success is valued—praise and public recognition are often enough; bonus points or small prizes such as stickers or pins are good, too.

rah
n taught
studies
English for
en years.
s now
tor of
iction for
arland
nunity
ols,
onsin.

Accommodating Individual Learning Styles

by Deborah K. Larson

The task of accommodating a broad range of student abilities, interests, and needs is greater than ever before. This essay is designed to help you meet the task of creating a learning environment in which all students can thrive.

Each student has a personal set of strategies for taking in, storing, and retrieving information. In some cases the strategy is easily observable, such as in the behavior of good spellers. When in doubt, they may close their eyes or write the word on a scrap of paper in order to visualize the word. In other cases, however, the strategy isn't quite so easy to see. Therefore, teachers should use a screening tool to help students determine whether their preferred learning style is *visual, auditory,* or *tactile/kinesthetic.* Most of these diagnostic instruments are checklists and take only a few minutes to administer and interpret.

Some learners have a very strong preference for a specific learning style, while others use a more balanced combination. The ideal situation exists when a student knows his or her strength, employs a variety of strategies to maximize that strength, and has the ability to tap into other styles as well. To increase student achievement, many of the alternate lesson plans in the **Teaching Resources** for *America: Pathways to the Present* target specific learning styles. Each of the alternate lesson plans is described in the Resource Directory at the bottom of the **Teacher's Edition** pages.

THE MAIN TYPES OF LEARNING STYLES

The Visual Learner

Visual learners enjoy reading and writing. Strong visual learners are able to reconstruct a mental image of the information when attempting to remember something. They benefit by highlighting text as they read, recopying their notes, creating graphic organizers, making lists, and viewing all sorts of visual stimuli—including graphs,

charts, works of art, political cartoons, comics, and videotapes.

The Auditory Learner

Auditory learners retain information they have heard better than information they have only read. Strong auditory learners learn best by listening intently; and they may resist the distraction of taking notes. They benefit from listening to videotapes, television or audiotapes; reading or chanting aloud when studying; interviewing people; studying with others and discussing their notes; and repeating information aloud after hearing it.

The Tactile/Kinesthetic Learner

Tactile/kinesthetic learners are sensitive to touch. In many classrooms they are the most neglected group of learners, for their preferred strategies are usually incorporated in active, hands-on projects and go beyond reading, writing, discussing, and listening. They like to handle, manipulate, and change their environment. Frequently, they are good at building things and may show talent for movement, dance, or athletics. They benefit from constructing models, finding and examining artifacts, sketching and drawing, physically enacting an event through role-playing, visiting a place they're learning about (or constructing a model of it), moving around while studying, and solving problems with objects that they can move, such as maps cut out as puzzles and games that require moving pieces.

Projects

Undertaking projects, a common practice in many social studies classes, offers a practical means for tailoring the curriculum to individual learning styles and for making history meaningful and immediate. Complex projects and activities usually require the application of many skills and present opportunities for students to exercise a degree of choice. Projects give students chances to act as historians, anthropologists, sociologists, economists, and geographers by collecting and analyzing data (including primary sources and artifacts), interviewing, debating, constructing models, and creating maps and other graphics. The Resource Directory in the **Teacher's Edition**, the enrichment activities in the wraparound, the Teacher-to-Teacher Network folder, and the Alternate Lesson Plans folder in the **Teaching Resources** are rich sources of strategies and activities based on actual classroom experiences that can be adapted to suit specific classes or individuals.

The Role of the Arts

Art, music, drama, and literature are powerful sources for making history come alive and for giving students a forum for individual expression. Visual learners can interpret and personalize an event through art, literature, and film. Through drama and music, auditory learners connect with a historical event in a way that it is impossible for them to do through text alone. Drama and other forms of role-playing, finding and interviewing real people, and constructing dioramas and other models are all activities that help tactile/kinesthetic learners absorb difficult concepts and enable them to share their special talents.

For those who have access to videotape, videodisc, and computer equipment, *America: Pathways to the Present*'s multimedia resource package, *Visions of America*, combines motion, sound, photography, graphics, and text to immerse students in a period, theme, or topic. Each of the seven textbook units has a video montage, and the "Turning Points" examined in the text are also extended through video presentations.

"We're given only one textbook and we're given twenty-five abilities. We often encounter four or five different learning styles . . . "

Classroom teacher in Detroit, Michigan

Group Work

Teachers who frequently use cooperative learning strategies are adept at structuring groups in a variety of ways. One consideration in setting up a group can be the learning styles of the participants. A variety of styles within a group will broaden the outlook and lead to a richer end product. The combining of students' learning styles in cooperative learning groups teaches students to appreciate the differing talents of their classmates and challenges them to build on their strengths and strengthen their weaknesses. For example, the most verbal student should not always be the one to speak for the group, and the best reader should not always be the one to search for information or interpret a chart. The activities in *America: Pathways to the Present* frequently suggest group discussion, analysis, or problem solving and offer many opportunities to use cooperative learning skills.

For an expanded discussion of learning styles, please see the lengthier essay in the To the Teacher folder. For alternate lesson plans that address different learning styles, please see the Alternate Lesson Plans folder. These folders are in your **Teaching Resources** package.

an November
a social
dies teacher
d national
chnology
nsultant. He
vises for the
enbrook High
hools in
nois.

Technology in the Classroom

by Alan November

O ur society has a great capacity to invent new products to make our lives more productive and entertaining, and easier to manage. The classroom is no exception. In the last few years, we have seen the introduction there of the computer, the VCR, the videodisc player, and the CD-ROM drive. All these devices help teachers and students do their work better. The new technologies also offer us another, perhaps greater, benefit—a new ability to innovate, to explore, and to create new learning opportunities for teachers and students.

Applying Technology

When a new technology is introduced, we often end up using it in ways that were not imagined by its inventor. The application of technology is constantly changing. For example, when Alexander Graham Bell set out to design the telephone he thought he was designing a tool to help deaf people communicate. Instead, most of us now have phones and use them for calling our friends and relatives or accessing computer networks. As time goes on, new uses for the phone are still evolving.

Similarly, the first computer software programs for the schools were electronic workbooks—more, better, and faster ways to "drill and kill." The first software also offered us familiar but easier ways to administer, grade, and record the results for traditional tests. Today we see new computer programs that offer simulations, explorations, innovative ways to collect and store information, and student authoring systems. Eventually, new computer programs may be introduced that are as different from the first software as the modern telecommunications network is from Bell's original telephone.

These examples illustrate that there are two ways to think about applying any technology. One is *automating*; the other can be called *informatting*.

Automating

The first stage of thinking about applying technology is to improve current reality, or to automate. When you automate, you look at what is currently happening at school or at home and you apply technology to make things easier to do or more comfortable, cheaper, or faster.

Let's apply the concept of automation to something familiar—the refrigerator. We can add a water cooler, an ice maker, and a defroster. Automating these features saves us time. Now, we don't need to store containers of water, fill and empty ice cube trays, or chip ice away.

Informatting

What if we built a kitchen network around our refrigerator that could monitor all the nutrient and calorie information in our foods? We could add a barcode reader to the inside of the refrigerator that automatically reads nutrient information on all the foods we put in. The data could be stored in a kitchen computer. We then would have an accurate record of the nutrient and calorie flow into our bodies. We could use this information to lead healthier lives.

This refrigerator has added more than convenience. It is now providing a health service. Typically, informatting leads to new roles for old inventions and new roles for the people using them.

The Difference Between Automating and Informatting

The difference between automating and informatting is a difference in how we think. The first requires knowledge about the current situation; the second requires the ability to make connections between activities—connections that currently do not exist. When we automate, we keep the same relationships and jobs. When we informat, there can be changes in relationships and jobs.

In our refrigerator example, when we informat the kitchen, the repair person's job changes significantly. He or she is still required to use a dolly to move the refrigerator, but now he or she must also know something about computers. The repair person learns a whole new set of skills. The end user's, or eater's, role in this situation also changes. The user can use the informatted refrigerator to lead a healthier life.

How do we know if a system has been automated or informatted? There is one critical question that needs to be asked: Have the roles changed? In an automated system, the roles do not change. We use new technology to do what we have always done, but better. In an informatted system, new roles are created and skills need to be learned. Informatting means that many more of us—like the repair person—will need to develop more complex problem-solving skills.

New Uses for Technology in the Schools

In the classroom, we have used the overhead projector, the slide projector, the filmstrip, the VCR, the CD-ROM drive, the computer, and the videodisc player. In an automated classroom, you would use a videodisc player, for example, as a presentation tool. Students would still receive information, conduct research, and present reports in much the same way as they have always done. In this example, the videodisc becomes a powerful automation tool and the classroom has more interesting visual elements. The roles of you and your students stay the same, with improvement in learning.

To informat the videodisc or any other technology tool in the classroom, we would have to examine the roles of those closest to the learning—you and the student. For example, in the informatted version of

the videodisc, a team of students combines the visuals on existing videodisc products with their own research and commentary to create new information products that can be recorded on videotape or on a computer. The subjects of these student-produced information products can range from a comprehensive study of acid rain to background and commentary on new legislation that is being considered by your state legislature. The information product can be used by the community outside the classroom to help make decisions.

Informatting the videodisc in the classroom might also change the roles of teachers and students in the following ways:

- Students would have a sense of owning and defining problems rather than just being given assignments.
- The teacher becomes a facilitator for students who are learning new skills.
- Students would work in teams with other students, members of the community, and even people from around the world across electronic networks.
- Students' success could be assessed in new ways.
- Students with different skill levels could successfully pursue projects at their own pace and level of sophistication.
- Students would become experienced problem solvers.

As educators, we have options. We can automate with technology and improve the current reality. We can create new and innovative learning opportunities for students. With technology we have a new, powerful tool that enables our students to become critical thinkers, better problem solvers, and producers of useful information products.

ah
lanski is
ntly the
tor of
culum and
ssment,
etics
oration,
gton,
iia.

New Trends in Assessment

by Hannah Kruglanski

When closely examining alternative assessments—tests that differ from the traditional multiple-choice, true-false, and matching assessments—social studies teachers usually find them both familiar and unfamiliar. The essays, presentations, constructions, and portfolios used in alternative assessments seem familiar because they have long been a part of the social studies classroom. They appear unfamiliar primarily because teachers are asked to use these activities in unaccustomed ways.

The Importance of Testing

We know that tests play a major role in the lives of students—and teachers. Tests signal to students what is important; students then make adjustments in their efforts to get the best possible grades. Tests determine students' placement in programs and "track" future schooling paths. Test scores affect schools as well by indicating the quality of programs to district administrators and legislators. Furthermore, tests communicate educational standards and signal to the community—students, teachers, and parents—what the community considers important to teach and to learn.

Too often the tests used in our schools reward only the memorization of facts. Thus, students gear their learning and teachers focus their instruction on the bits of information needed for the test. If we choose to emphasize reasoning, problem solving, and application of knowledge over memorization, we need to provide assessments that measure these outcomes and foster their learning. This goal—improving critical thinking and the ability to apply knowledge—is why the new forms of assessment are important.

What Is Alternative Assessment?

All forms of alternative assessments require students to construct answers, generate information, or create products in response to test assignments. They tap higher-order thinking skills and challenge students to apply their knowledge in problem-solving situations that foster active learning. The various forms of alternative assessments foster conceptual understanding and the making of connections to students' own lives. They frequently mirror the processes of learning by asking students to reflect on their work, periodically assess their own knowledge, and seek feedback from peers and experts. Alternative assessments allow for a broader, more comprehensive measurement of diverse learning experiences than do the limited responses to standardized tests.

Teachers do not need to throw out traditional tests when adopting alternative assessments. For subjects such as geography, where the amassing of a knowledge base is an important instructional outcome, traditional tests offer a good measurement of this outcome. However, students need to learn how to evaluate the knowledge they acquire—to apply it, to use it to solve problems, and to link that new knowledge to their old knowledge and their lives. Alternative assessments provide a means for meeting these goals.

How to Carry Out Alternative Assessments

The most frequently used forms are performance, portfolio, essay, and exhibition assessments. Examining performance assessment and portfolio assessment in more detail will provide examples of how to carry out alternative assessments in the classroom.

Performance Assessment

This method consists of open-ended and multistep tasks that are designed to demonstrate how students can apply and use their learning in solving problems and making decisions. The tasks usually reflect authentic, or real-life, problems and issues. They focus on the "big ideas," or important concepts. Student responses could be in the form of written or oral presentations or in a visual form such as videotapes or posters.

Social studies performance assessments could require students to analyze an issue, form an opinion, debate various points of view, or consider causes and effects.

Performance assessment tasks link students' prior knowledge and provide opportunities for new connections to be made. Although tasks do not target facts or formulas, students are still expected to use and apply knowledge of facts when appropriate.

Portfolio Assessment

This assessment tool is designed to measure growth in student performance over time by keeping a systematic record of progress as demonstrated in samples of students' work. Before students begin assembling their portfolios, teachers should determine:

- *Its Purpose*—Will it be used for instruction, assessment, or both?
- *How It Will Be Used*—Will it be the sole measurement of students' work for that course? Will it be used for the entire year or for a specific time period?
- *Criteria for Selection of Items*—Will it be the students' best work, their typical work, or an assortment of their work?
- *Ownership*—Who decides what goes in the portfolio—the teacher, the student, or both?
- *Scoring Criteria*—Will the entire portfolio, the separate components, or a composite be scored?

Once these decisions have been made, the teacher should next focus on the contents of the portfolios. A valid portfolio includes a variety of evidence and a range of students' work. Evidence in a portfolio needs to relate directly to the outcomes it is intended to measure. Use the following guidelines to help ensure that portfolios meet those criteria:

- *Work Biographies*—To demonstrate student development, collect samples of students' work from different points in time but on a specific topic or type of activity. For example, several drafts of a writing assignment constitute a work biography.
- *Range of Work*—To demonstrate growth, collect samples across different types of work. For example, work in different areas of social studies constitutes a range of work.
- *Self-Assessment*—To show changes in students' awareness about their performance and perspective in relation to their previous work, collect evidence that shows how students react to the contents of their own portfolios.

Scoring Alternative Assessments

Alternative assessments are scored in a way that reflects the desired outcomes and are closely linked with instruction. The procedure for scoring involves developing a rubric—a pre-established criterion for a scoring scale and sample performances to illustrate each point on the scale. To begin developing the rubric, the teacher explains the characteristics of an outstanding performance; this is the top scoring point. The teacher then spells out the criteria for an unacceptable or limited performance; this is the bottom point on the scale. Generally, the rubric contains two scoring points between unacceptable and outstanding—one for an acceptable performance and one for an extensive or commendable performance.

There are several methods of scoring—the two major strategies being holistic and analytic.

- *Holistic Scoring*—This strategy rates a task on one criterion and a single score is given for the overall quality of the task. It provides general information about the performance.
- *Analytic Scoring*—This strategy rates the task by multiple criteria. Scores are given for each criterion. They reflect the relative contribution of each criterion and can provide a diagnosis of the performance.
- *Modified Holistic Scoring*—This strategy combines elements from holistic and analytic scoring. A single score is given, but the relative contribution of each criterion can be isolated.

The **Teacher's Edition** of *America: Pathways to the Present* provides alternative assessment project strategies for each chapter in the wraparound. For more in-depth information on scoring criteria, strategies for alternative methods of assessment, as well as sample evaluation forms for teachers and student self-evaluation, see the Alternative Assessment Handbook in the **Teaching Resources**.

Symcox,
nt director
National
for
y in the
ls at UCLA,
assistant
r of the
nal History
ards
t.

Using Themes in Teaching U.S. History

by Linda Symcox

"*All those dates, and what do they really mean in the end? History puts me to sleep!*"
—a common student complaint

Generations of American high school students have bemoaned the enormous scope and detail of history classes. A thematic approach to the study of history allows students to overcome their sense that historical events are no more than unconnected trivia. Teaching with attention to themes makes the study of history more than the recapitulation of endless facts. It shifts the focus of inquiry from *who, what, when* to *how* and *why*. By tracing broad themes over time, students can move beyond memorizing information to understanding the patterns of history and their connections to the present.

Themes Show Relevance

"It all happened so long ago, and what does it have to do with the way we live today?"—another student complaint

Students often see the past as being remote and irrelevant. Teaching thematically enables students to see that the forces governing their lives, such as pressures for reform movements, changes in technology, ethnic diversity, or debates over the nature of democracy, also guided the lives of previous generations. Themes expressed as ideas and issues are the principles underlying a continuous process of historical development that did not end yesterday, leaving the students suspended in an unconnected present. By following these threads through history, students can bridge the gulf that separates them from their past, root themselves in their history, and ultimately create a thematic view of the past and the present.

Themes Organize Information

Students graduating from high school need to understand the fundamental themes and developments that defined their nation's past. Although each era of United States history has its unique character, defined by specific moments, peoples, and ideals, students must also understand that a number of unifying themes weave their way through all the eras and continue to define their lives today. The thematic approach provides a way to bring order to the seeming chaos of a rapidly evolving and increasingly complex society.

A thematic approach gives students an intellectual tool kit that allows them to organize information in a rational, coherent, and meaningful way. Armed with the analytical tools that a thematic organization gives them, students learn how to establish relationships between events, to separate the insignificant from the significant, to relate parts to wholes. Students can then understand the importance of major turning points in American history.

Putting Themes to Work

How does teaching thematically work in practice? *America: Pathways to the Present* has identified ten broad themes for teaching the American story. (See box.) Teachers may select several relevant themes, combining them wherever thematic interaction offers a richer fabric for discussion. Chapter 12, for example, addresses the rise of a shared national culture during the 1920s. Teachers can emphasize how the expansion of the economy, new communications technology, and the diversity of the American population converged to drive the burst of creativity and optimism expressed in the Harlem Renaissance, the Jazz Age, and the new styles of behavior and dress that became parts of a shared national culture.

Teachers might also consider a single theme with students, and trace its development over time. This would be an especially illuminating exercise for review at the close of a quarter, semester, or year.

Let's examine one theme—diversity—and briefly trace its unfolding in the pages of *America: Pathways to the Present*. Chapter 1 sets the stage with the Native Americans, the only inhabitants of the continent until the arrival of Europeans and Africans from the late fifteenth to the eighteenth centuries. The chapter shows how these three groups collided and converged. In Unit 2, *America: Pathways to the Present* shows how the successive waves of new immigrants who flocked to the U.S. in the nineteenth and twentieth centuries added to the nation's diversity and changed the very fabric of American cities. Unit 6 explores the late twentieth-century aspects of diversity in the United States: nonviolent confrontation, the challenge of Black Power, ethnic minorities seeking equality, and the women's movement.

This unfolding story of "a gathering of many peoples" is itself profoundly dramatic, but it has fundamental political, social, and economic implications that link it to other themes that *America: Pathways to the Present* develops: it explains the reserves of strength and the constant self-renewal that is the secret of this country's dynamism, and it is, at the same time, a story of political conflicts and social tensions. As students follow this dramatic theme throughout American history, they will better understand America's continual efforts to remake and transform itself, to profit from the strengths that diversity imparts, while transcending the tensions it inevitably generates. A thematic approach can involve students in the unfolding story that is theirs: history, instead of remaining remote and impersonal, becomes *their* history.

Tools for Teaching Thematically

America: Pathways to the Present provides resources for teachers who want to use a thematic approach in their teaching. The **Student Edition** feature, "Links Across Time," asks students to consider issues and themes in history that people have had to consider in every era. For example, in Chapter 20 the feature is subtitled "Equal Rights Movements," and points out that the civil rights movement of the 1960s inspired other groups, such as Latinos, women, the elderly, Asian Americans, and people with disabilities, to organize for equal rights.

In the **Teacher's Edition**, four themes are featured in the wraparound at the beginning of every unit.

The **Teaching Resources** provide "Themes in American History" posters that illustrate historical events visually along a time line.

Themes in *America: Pathways to the Present*

Reform Movements
People in the United States have frequently taken action in grass roots movements to right perceived wrongs and to secure improvements in the quality of life.

Values
A variety of religious, ethical, and moral beliefs have propelled and guided Americans on their quest for a just and ordered society.

Economics
Americans have searched for new and better ways to make a living and have struggled to define government's role in this pursuit.

Technology
Americans' ability to develop new skills and tools and to increase their knowledge of the physical world has greatly affected the way they live and work, and has led to a high standard of living.

Environment
The geography and available resources of the continent have affected the actions of Americans. Similarly, the actions of Americans have affected the environment and physical landscape.

Diversity
Throughout its history, America has been made up of a gathering of many peoples from around the world. Americans have both benefited from and encountered problems with this diversity.

Unity and Conflict
Americans have developed unique political systems and laws that affirm a shared commitment to certain goals, such as individual rights and equality. Nevertheless, groups with differing views on how to achieve these goals have often clashed.

American Democracy
The concepts of democratic representation, equality under the law, and freedom from discrimination have been gradually broadened to include previously excluded groups.

American Culture
In every period of their history, Americans gave special expression to their views through art, literature, films, music, manners, and morals.

The United States and the World
America's relationships with other countries have been influenced at different times by a sense of mission, by values, and by self-interest.

Critical Thinking: Correlation Guide

America: Pathways to the Present teaches, reinforces, and applies seventeen types of critical thinking skills, which are listed in the table below. Each critical thinking skill is taught in the "Historian's Toolbox" feature in the **Student Edition** and is reinforced and applied through questions and activities in the **Student Edition**, **Teacher's Edition**, and **Teaching Resources**. The page numbers in the chart list where these critical thinking skills are covered in each of the three components. (ALP denotes Alternate Lesson Plan.)

SKILL	STUDENT EDITION on pages	TEACHER'S EDITION on pages	TEACHING RESOURCES on pages
Expressing problems clearly To succinctly describe a complex situation or body of information	47, 58, 293, 325, 391, 407, 463, 525, 563, 565, 571, 582, 607, 700, 737, 781, 784, 819	18, 45, 58, 60, 67, 93, 121, 273, 282, 286, 293, 325, 389, 391, 407, 463, 524, 549, 563, 564, 570, 578, 582, 607, 697, 698, 700, 737, 781, 791, 819	Unit 1: 67, 119, 138, 141 Unit 2: 39, 110 Unit 3: 33 Unit 5: 25, 145 Unit 6: 20 Unit 7: 71, 133
Identifying central issues To identify the main ideas in a piece of information	33, 97, 203, 250, 289, 317, 323, 329, 342, 347, 359, 362, 363, 393, 445, 453, 478, 489, 517, 565, 633, 689, 703, 751, 803, 833, 859	24, 33, 37, 53, 81, 82, 87, 97, 202, 204, 233, 249, 253, 289, 313, 317, 322, 327, 341, 347, 358, 362, 363, 393, 426, 441, 453, 455, 478, 488, 517, 562, 564, 632, 668, 688, 703, 751, 803, 833, 859	Unit 1: 82, 97 Unit 2: (ALP 75), 36 Unit 3: 8, 10, 12, 14, 31, 32, 33, 34, 35, 43, 45, 47, 49, 68, 69, 70, 71, 72, 81, 83, 85, 87, 89, 93, 95, 104, 105, 107, 109, 113, 114, 115 Unit 4: 9, 11, 13, 15, 17, 34, 35, 36, 37, 38, 39, 47, 49, 51, 53, 55, 65, 74, 75, 76, 77, 78, 79, 85, 87, 89, 104, 105, 107, 108, 110, 111, 113, 114, 115 Unit 5: (ALP 124, 128), 8, 10, 12, 14, 31, 32, 33, 34, 35, 36, 43, 45, 47, 49, 64, 65, 66, 67, 68, 69, 76, 78, 80, 82, 88, 97, 98, 99, 100, 101, 102, 109, 111, 113, 115,134, 135, 137, 138, 140, 141, 142, 143, 144, 145

SKILL	STUDENT EDITION on pages	TEACHER'S EDITION on pages	TEACHING RESOURCES on pages
Identifying central issues (continued)			Unit 6: (ALP 151), 7, 9, 11, 28, 29, 31, 32, 40, 42, 44, 63, 64, 65, 66, 67, 68, 75, 77, 79, 81, 89, 99, 101, 102, 103, 111, 113, 115, 117, 119, 128, 135, 136, 137 Unit 7: 8, 10, 12, 31, 32, 33, 34, 35, 36, 43, 47, 66, 67, 68, 70, 71, 78, 80, 82, 84, 95, 102, 103, 104, 105, 112, 114, 116, 131, 132, 133, 134, 135, 136
Making comparisons To identify how different ideas, objects, historic figures, or situations are alike and/or different	45, 117, 126, 129, 156, 166, 172, 179, 180, 183, 211, 234, 243, 265, 284, 293, 316, 323, 325, 329, 361, 385, 390, 417, 421, 450, 475, 490, 491, 509, 515, 553, 565, 582, 583, 599, 615, 638, 643, 644, 645, 661, 676, 686, 700, 719, 721, 755, 793, 811, 815, 833, 851	29, 38, 43, 45, 81, 117, 125, 128, 161, 166, 179, 183, 191, 243, 265, 277, 279, 284, 287, 292, 309, 314, 316, 322, 323, 325, 326, 329, 339, 356, 361, 385, 390, 416, 417, 421, 430, 449, 450, 458, 475, 490, 501, 509, 515, 553, 560, 563, 564, 568, 574, 582, 583, 590, 599, 602, 603, 609, 614, 622, 638, 642, 644, 645, 661, 684, 686, 687, 700, 719, 721, 725, 735, 746, 750, 755, 793, 794, 811, 815, 833, 851	Unit 1: (ALP 66), 22, 33, 36, 48, 59, 67, 94, 97, 138 Unit 2: 73, 95, 99, 107, 127, 136, 142, 145 Unit 3: (ALP 92), 16, 20, 36, 70, 112, 115 Unit 4: (ALP 108), 20, 32, 36, 39, 93, 103, 112, 115 Unit 5: (ALP 138), 33, 36, 63, 106, 107, 139 Unit 6: (ALP 149), 17, 84, 100, 136, 139 Unit 7: (ALP 173), 18, 30, 103, 125
Determining relevance To decide if and how events, situations, or items are related to one another	57, 113, 137, 139, 206, 239, 256, 263, 273, 289, 324, 326, 347, 349, 376, 378, 387, 420, 446, 452, 464, 465, 548, 576, 580, 611, 632, 633, 635, 645, 673, 689, 707, 725, 728, 735, 759, 770, 788, 789, 833, 845, 859	56, 89, 137, 139, 238, 256, 263, 273, 289 306, 324, 326, 336, 347, 349, 376, 378, 387, 411, 416, 420, 421, 451, 464, 470, 548, 575, 580, 596, 611, 625, 632, 633, 635, 645, 673, 684, 688, 725, 728, 735, 750, 759, 770, 788, 789, 796, 829, 842, 845	Unit 1: 23, 83, 118, 122, 141 Unit 2: (ALP 80), 17 Unit 3: (ALP 96), 36, 91, 106 Unit 4: 30, 76 Unit 5: 102, 125, 142 Unit 6: (ALP 143), 15, 17, 25, 27, 94, 139 Unit 7: (ALP 167), 30, 68, 71, 98, 103, 125, 136
Formulating questions To create questions that seek answers to specific objectives and lead to a deeper understanding of an issue	22, 91, 136, 181, 219, 265, 327, 414, 456, 512, 523, 535, 665, 667, 737 825	21, 30, 91, 136, 181, 219, 265, 276, 328, 381, 414, 456, 479, 511, 523, 535, 536, 604, 633, 665, 677, 696, 700, 737, 788, 825, 840	Unit 1: (ALP 50, 61), 29, 94 Unit 2: (ALP 25), 21, 107, 129 Unit 3: 18, 73, 90 Unit 4: (ALP 115), 90 Unit 6: 25, 57 Unit 7: 57, 106

SKILL	STUDENT EDITION on pages	TEACHER'S EDITION on pages	TEACHING RESOURCES on pages
Distinguishing fact from opinion To separate those statements that can be proven to be true from those that reflect a personal viewpoint	111, 331, 483, 484, 516, 550, 569, 599, 677, 690, 732	27, 111, 403, 482, 484, 516, 549, 550, 569, 599, 677, 732	Unit 2: (ALP 74), 110 Unit 3: 106 Unit 4: 94 Unit 5: 28, 122, 123 Unit 7: 52, 88
Checking consistency To compare two or more items or ideas and determine whether they agree or disagree with each other	30, 63, 65, 71, 95, 197, 217, 344, 373, 380, 389, 393, 460, 483, 717, 726, 803	65, 71, 95, 107, 131, 197, 217, 344, 373, 380, 389, 393, 460, 482, 514, 515, 717, 726, 803	Unit 1: 53 Unit 3: 33, 112 Unit 4: 79, 109 Unit 5: 69, 99, 136 Unit 6: 30, 33, 124 Unit 7: 33, 53
Distinguishing false from accurate images To examine a widely held belief about a person, place, or thing and determine whether or not the belief is based in fact	24, 27, 183, 284, 429, 453, 460, 525, 725, 773	26, 183, 284, 429, 453, 461, 524, 725, 773	Unit 2: (ALP 81), 25, 55, 97 Unit 3: 59, 109 Unit 4: 64, 76, 79 Unit 5: 58, 66, 89 Unit 6: 85, 100 Unit 7: 17
Identifying assumptions To recognize unstated beliefs that may underlie a statement, action, or event	45, 73, 97, 265, 329, 351, 445, 539, 545, 553, 581, 689, 730, 753, 786	45, 73, 97, 139, 246, 265, 309, 329, 351, 445, 539, 545, 553, 575, 688, 730, 786, 859	Unit 1:19 Unit 2: 18, 27, 92, 137 Unit 3: 55 Unit 4: 28, 39, 60, 79, 106 Unit 5: 51, 99, 128, 131 Unit 6: 33, 89, 136, 139 Unit 7: (ALP 163), 125, 133
Recognizing bias To identify a stated or unstated viewpoint or slant that is designed to promote one set of beliefs over another	119, 190, 241, 255, 279, 419, 481, 539, 544, 595, 605, 690, 695	119, 241, 255, 278, 356, 419, 539, 544, 549, 595, 605, 690, 694	Unit 1: (ALP 55), 54, 59, 88, 123, 125 Unit 2: 60, 142 Unit 3: (ALP 90), 36, 54, 109 Unit 4: 39, 101 Unit 5: 19, 20, 61 Unit 6: 88, 90
Recognizing ideologies To identify underlying beliefs from actions or statements	35, 109, 183, 219, 239, 342, 359, 387, 393, 418, 425, 429, 491, 607, 641, 654, 705, 723, 794, 853	35, 54, 89, 109, 183, 219, 239, 253, 341, 344, 358, 387, 393, 418, 425, 429, 490, 607, 641, 654, 666, 705, 723, 794, 853	Unit 1: 78, 117, 121 Unit 2: 22, 39, 70, 132 Unit 3: 33 Unit 4: 36, 95, 112 Unit 5: (ALP 132), 17, 62, 95, 102, 121, 136 Unit 6: 121 Unit 7: (ALP 172), 33, 56, 87, 92, 103, 106
Drawing conclusions To find an answer or to form an opinion based on available information	66, 73, 157, 235, 239, 280, 285, 293, 309, 311, 322, 331, 359, 363, 371, 372, 385, 414, 478, 502, 503, 507, 533, 542, 564, 565, 583, 598, 615, 627, 639, 663, 671, 675, 707, 750, 766, 798, 822, 850	66, 73, 83, 122, 156, 235, 238, 279, 285, 292, 309, 311, 322, 331, 351, 363, 371, 372, 385, 406, 414, 425, 439, 477, 502, 503, 507, 520, 533, 542, 564, 565, 583, 598, 614, 627, 639, 663, 671, 675, 693, 707, 750, 766, 798, 822, 850	Unit 1: 18 Unit 2: 70, 96, 126 Unit 3: 22, 103, 112, 115 Unit 4: 21, 61, 71, 76, 106, 109 Unit 5: (ALP 139), 56, 83, 124, 145 Unit 6: 24, 125 Unit 7: (ALP 165), 28, 60, 90, 91, 106, 117, 122

SKILL	STUDENT EDITION on pages	TEACHER'S EDITION on pages	TEACHING RESOURCES on pages
Recognizing cause and effect To examine how one event or idea causes other events or ideas to occur	65, 153, 202, 229, 255, 260, 291, 331, 353, 392, 393, 423, 445, 465, 522, 525, 538, 551, 554, 566, 571, 593, 594, 665, 676, 703, 751, 799, 814, 831, 842, 850	64, 168, 175, 255, 291, 309,331, 353, 392, 393, 405, 413,423, 445, 449, 464, 522, 525,534, 536, 538, 550, 554, 566,570, 593, 600, 665, 676, 703, 751, 765, 799, 814, 831, 842,850	Unit 1: 49, 138, 141 Unit 2: (ALP 31), 47, 88, 93, 106, 109, 110, 115, 118, 142 Unit 3: (ALP 103), 28, 70, 112, 115 Unit 4: (ALP 106), 12, 27, 36 Unit 5: 33, 66, 69, 87, 94, 102, 119, 136, 139, 142 Unit 6: (ALP 156), 19, 80, 100, 136 Unit 7: (ALP 170), 36, 79, 133
Predicting consequences To determine the likely effect of an event or action on the outcome of future events or actions	42, 61, 123, 173, 219, 232, 237, 275, 409, 465, 503, 543, 553, 601, 613, 615, 645, 833, 856, 857	34, 41, 68, 73, 108, 123, 125, 172, 219, 237, 275, 409, 416, 424, 464, 503, 519, 543, 553, 601, 613, 615, 645, 722, 746, 773, 827, 856, 857	Unit 1: 89 Unit 2: (ALP 29), 16, 56 Unit 3: 62, 96, 109 Unit 4: (ALP 113), 31 Unit 5: 22, 36, 59, 84, 86 Unit 6: 14, 95, 128, 130 Unit 7: 22, 36, 121
Identifying alternatives To identify one or more methods to achieve a goal or solve a problem; to recognize the possibility of other goals	73, 97, 374, 378, 447, 521, 583, 677, 781	34, 73, 97, 153, 236, 374, 378, 447, 521, 583, 638, 677, 714, 760, 781, 789, 827	Unit 2: (ALP 70), 62, 145 Unit 3: 73, 98 Unit 4: 59 Unit 5: (ALP 125), 36, 55 Unit 6: 21, 120 Unit 7: 55, 120
Testing conclusions To examine a conclusion and determine whether or not it is supported by known facts	86, 195, 292, 347, 354, 505, 517, 626, 689, 716, 773, 803	24, 85, 114, 194, 292, 347, 354, 376, 505, 517, 602, 626, 684, 689, 716, 773, 803	Unit 1: 85 Unit 2: (ALP 86), 107 Unit 3: 17, 58, 106 Unit 4: 25, 90, 112 Unit 5: 18, 120, 139, 145 Unit 6: (ALP 160), 103 Unit 7: 68, 71
Demonstrating reasoned judgment To present evidence or reasoning that supports a given opinion or statement	73, 94, 159, 163, 279, 331, 363, 371, 377, 383, 418, 427, 429, 453, 481, 491, 521, 615, 626, 642, 643, 655, 657, 668, 670, 702, 716, 737, 763, 764, 773, 784, 803, 820, 831, 833	94, 137, 159, 161, 231, 279, 319, 326, 331, 363, 370, 377, 383, 384, 404, 416, 417, 427, 429, 438, 443, 453, 481, 490, 502, 521, 562, 591, 608, 614, 629, 633, 642, 643, 655, 657, 660, 670, 684, 701, 702, 707,716, 718, 728, 746, 763, 764, 773, 784, 796, 820, 821, 831, 833	Unit 1: 33, 36, 67, 84, 88, 94 Unit 2: 36, 65, 70, 73, 145 Unit 3: 65, 115 Unit 4: (ALP 119), 23, 115 Unit 5: (ALP 129), 33, 50, 66, 69, 99 Unit 6: (ALP 151), 30, 33, 54, 103 Unit 7: 30, 33, 36, 91, 136

PRENTICE HALL

AMERICA

PATHWAYS
—TO THE—
PRESENT

America in the
Twentieth Century

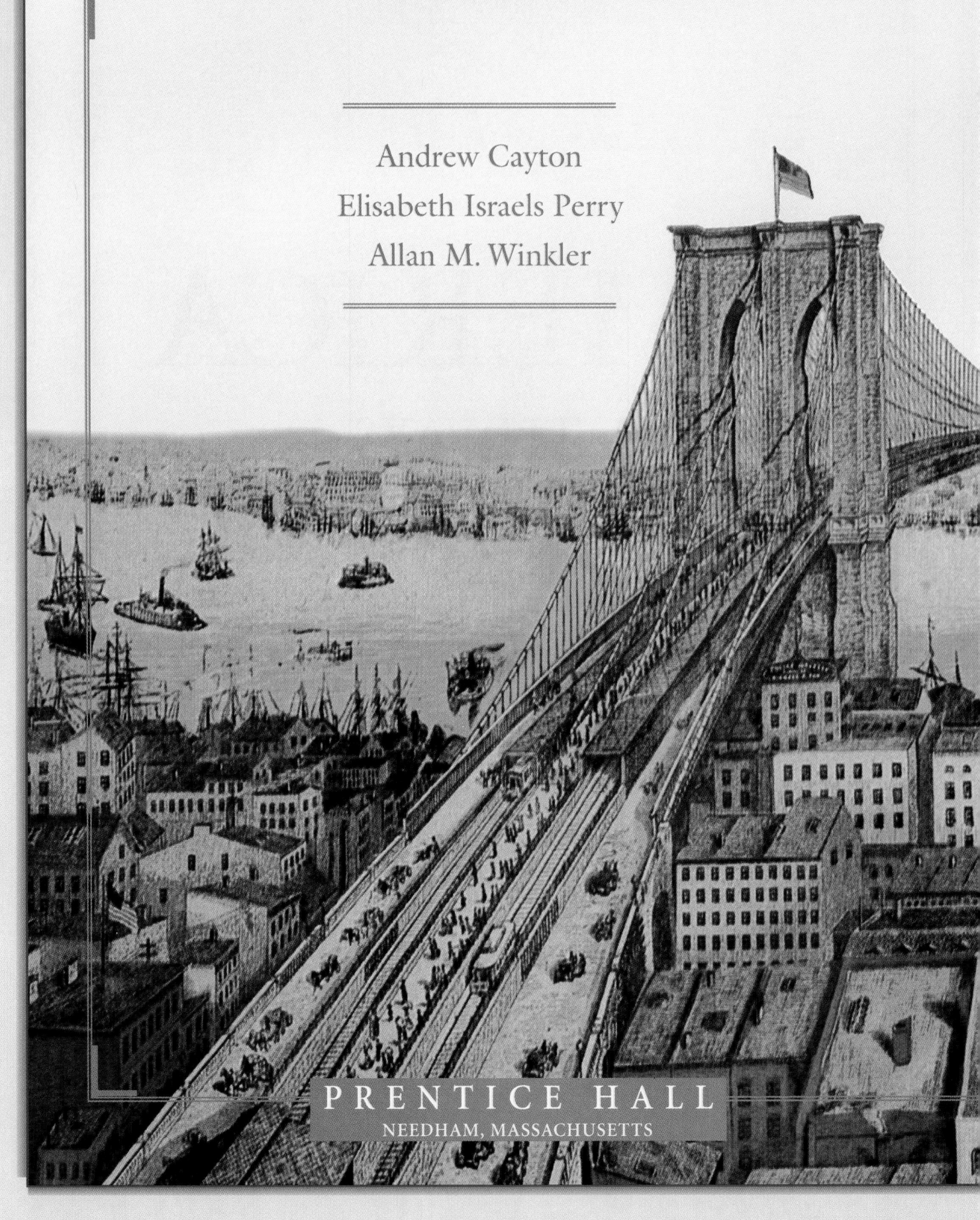

Andrew Cayton

Elisabeth Israels Perry

Allan M. Winkler

PRENTICE HALL
NEEDHAM, MASSACHUSETTS

AMERICA

PATHWAYS
—TO THE—
PRESENT

America in the
Twentieth Century

About the Authors

Andrew Cayton, Ph.D.

Andrew Cayton is Professor of History at Miami University in Oxford, Ohio. Born in Cincinnati, Ohio, he is the grandson of a high school history teacher. Dr. Cayton received his B.A. with high honors from the University of Virginia and his M.A. and Ph.D. from Brown University.

Dr. Cayton is an early American historian, whose specialization is political and social history. He is the author of *The Frontier Republic: Ideology and Politics in the Ohio Country, 1780–1825* and coauthor of *The Midwest and the Nation: Rethinking the History of an American Region.*

Dr. Cayton received the 1993 Outstanding Teacher Award from the Ohio Academy of History and the 1992 Distinguished Educator Award from the College of Arts and Sciences at Miami University. He lives in Hamilton, Ohio, with his wife, Mary Kupiec Cayton, and daughters, Elizabeth and Hannah.

Elisabeth Israels Perry, Ph.D.

Elisabeth Israels Perry serves as the Director of the Graduate Program in Women's History at Sarah Lawrence College, in Bronxville, New York. She previously taught U.S. women's history at Vanderbilt University, in Nashville, Tennessee. She received her B.A. and Ph.D. in history from the University of California at Los Angeles.

Dr. Perry's period of specialization is the late nineteenth and early twentieth centuries. Her greatest scholarly interests are women's history and reform movements. She is the author of *Belle Moskowitz: Feminine Politics and the Exercise of Power in the Age of Alfred E. Smith.* She is the coeditor of *The Challenge of Feminist Biography: Writing the Lives of Modern American Women.*

Dr. Perry has received major grants from Fulbright, the National Endowment for the Humanities, and the American Council of Learned Societies. She has directed three NEH Summer Seminars for secondary school history and literature teachers.

Allan M. Winkler, Ph.D.

Allan M. Winkler chairs the Department of History at Miami University of Ohio. He received his B.A. from Harvard University, his M.A. from Columbia University, and his Ph.D. from Yale University.

Dr. Winkler's specialization is twentieth-century social and political history. He is the author of eight books, including *The Politics of Propaganda: The Office of War Information, 1942–1945; Modern America: The United States from the Second World War to the Present; The Recent Past: Readings on America Since World War II;* and *Home Front U.S.A.: America During World War II.* His most recent book, published in 1993, is *Life Under a Cloud: American Anxiety About the Atom.*

Dr. Winkler began his teaching career in the Peace Corps in the Philippines, where he worked at the elementary and secondary level as well as at the college level. He has taught at Yale University and the University of Oregon, and has also held the Bicentennial Chair in American Studies in Helsinki, Finland and the John Adams Chair in American Civilization in Amsterdam, in the Netherlands.

PRENTICE HALL

A Division of Simon & Schuster
Upper Saddle River, New Jersey 07458

© Copyright 1995 by Prentice-Hall, Inc.

ISBN 0-13-802570-3

Printed in the United States of America

2 3 4 5 6 7 8 9 02 01 00 99 98 97 96 95

iv

Program Reviewers

Teacher Advisory Panel

Alfred B. Cate, Jr. Central High School, Memphis, Tennessee
Pamela Gray Tustin High School, Orange County, California
Robert Durkin Washington Irving High School, New York, New York
Richard Hryniewicki Cudahy High School, Wisconsin
Phillip James Lincoln-Sudbury High School, Sudbury, Massachusetts
Gerald F. Krows Moore High School, Moore, Oklahoma
Jayne Rotsko Ipswich High School, Ipswich, Massachusetts
Gloria S. Sesso Half Hollow Hill East, Dix Hills, New York
Jerome L. Ruderman Frankford High School, Philadelphia, Pennsylvania

Student Review Board

Brenda Borchardt Cudahy High School, Cudahy, Wisconsin
Rebecca A. Day Moore High School, Moore, Oklahoma
Lena K. Franks Frankford High School, Philadelphia, Pennsylvania
Phillip Payne Moore High School, Moore, Oklahoma
Brooke J. Peterson Lincoln-Sudbury High School, Sudbury, Massachusetts
Jeramogi Carreé Todd Central High School, Memphis, Tennessee

Historian Reviewers

Parentheses indicate area of specialization.

Elizabeth Blackmar Department of History, Columbia University,
New York, New York (social and urban history)
Donald L. Fixico Department of History, Western Michigan University, Kalamazoo,
Michigan (American Indian history, American history Reconstruction to the present)
Mario Garcia Department of History, University of California,
Santa Barbara, California (Latino history)
Gerald Gill Department of History, Tufts University, Medford,
Massachusetts (African American history, twentieth-century history)
William M. King Afroamerican Studies, Center for Studies of Ethnicity and
Race in America, University of Colorado at Boulder, Boulder, Colorado
(Afroamerican history, twentieth-century U.S. society and culture)
Huping Ling Division of Social Science, Northeast Missouri State University,
Kirksville, Missouri (Asian American history)
Melton A. McLaurin Department of History, The University of North Carolina
at Wilmington, Wilmington, North Carolina (nineteenth-century social history)
Roy Rosenzweig Department of History, George Mason University,
Fairfax, Virginia (nineteenth and twentieth-century social and cultural history)
Susan Smulyan Department of American Civilization, Brown University,
Providence, Rhode Island (twentieth-century history)

*Prentice Hall and the authors are grateful to our reviewers, who provided valuable assistance in making
this textbook one that meets the needs of American history teachers and students. Teacher and student reviewers
read chapter manuscript. Historian reviewers read chapters with content that corresponded to their
areas of specialization.*

The *Pathways* Team

*The editors, designers, marketers, managers, electronic publishing specialists, copyeditor, production and manufacturing buyers, page production
manager, and advertising and production manager who made up the* Pathways *team are listed below.*

Alison Anholt-White, Gabriella Della Corte, Robert G. Dunn, David Graham, Barbara Flockhart, Jeffrey M. Ikler, Dorshia I. Johnson,
Linda D. Johnson, Russell Lappa, David Lippman, Nancy Rogier, Luess Sampson-Lizotte, Holly Schuster, Amit Shah, Virginia Shine,
Diane Shohet, Marisa Sibio Shuff, Martha G. Smith, L. Christopher Valente, Pearl B. Weinstein, Naomi Y. Wilsey, David R. Zarowin

CONTENTS

UNIT **3** **The United States on the Brink of Change, 1890–1920** **304**

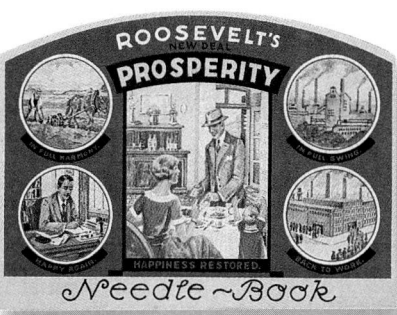

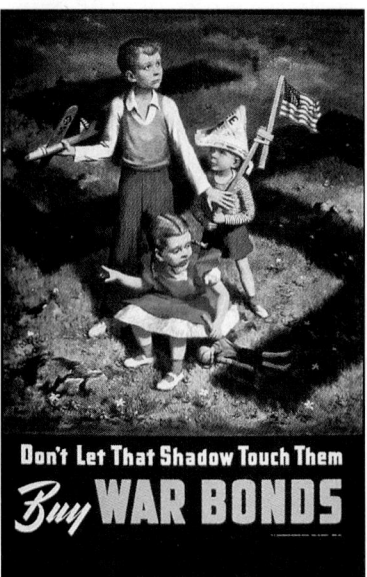

Don't Let That Shadow Touch Them
Buy **WAR BONDS**

GIVE EARTH A CHANCE

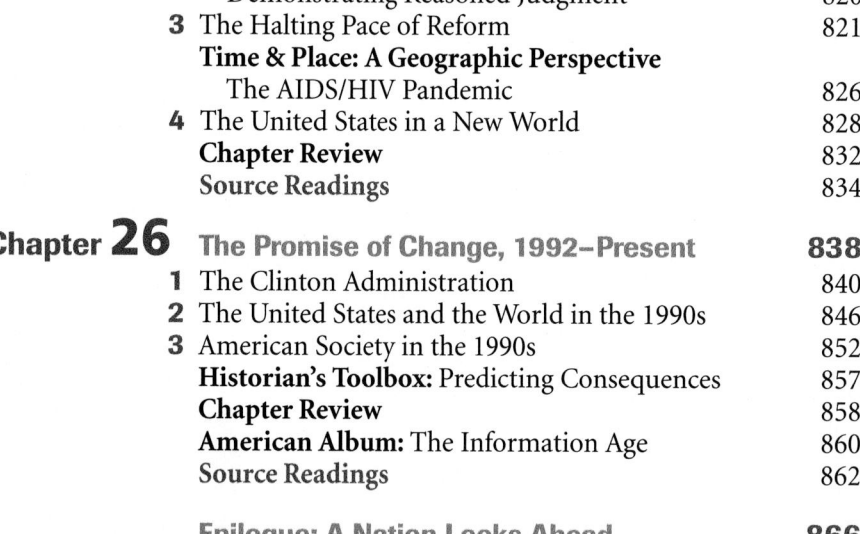

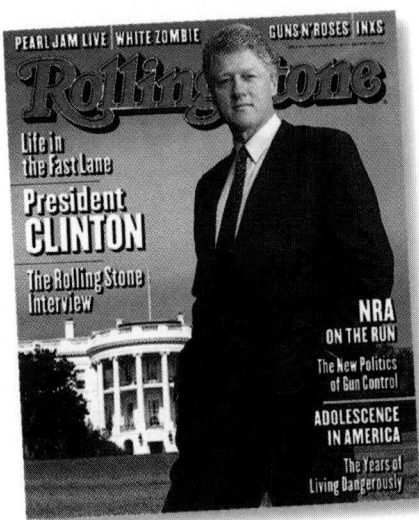

SPECIAL FEATURES

✳ SOURCE READINGS

**A collection of literature and primary source readings
that provide thoughtful insights into our nation's history**

 Literature

*Primary
Sources*

Viewpoints

**Two opposing or contrasting viewpoints
on major historical topics**

TIME & PLACE: A GEOGRAPHIC PERSPECTIVE

**An in-depth look at the links between
geography and history**

History might not have Happened This Way

AMERICAN PROFILES

**Biographical sketches of both famous and
ordinary Americans and their impact on society**

American Album

**Artifacts from the exhibitions and collections at the
Smithsonian Institution National Museum of American History**

The Way It Works

Detailed drawings that illustrate key historical events
and advances in technology

105-horsepower,
six-cylinder engine

Driver

Commander

One of four Lewis
machine guns

One of two 57-mm
pedestal-mounted
guns

Armor
plating

Pressed steel
track plate

HISTORIAN'S TOOLBOX

 Maps

Maps (continued)

Graphs, Charts, and Tables

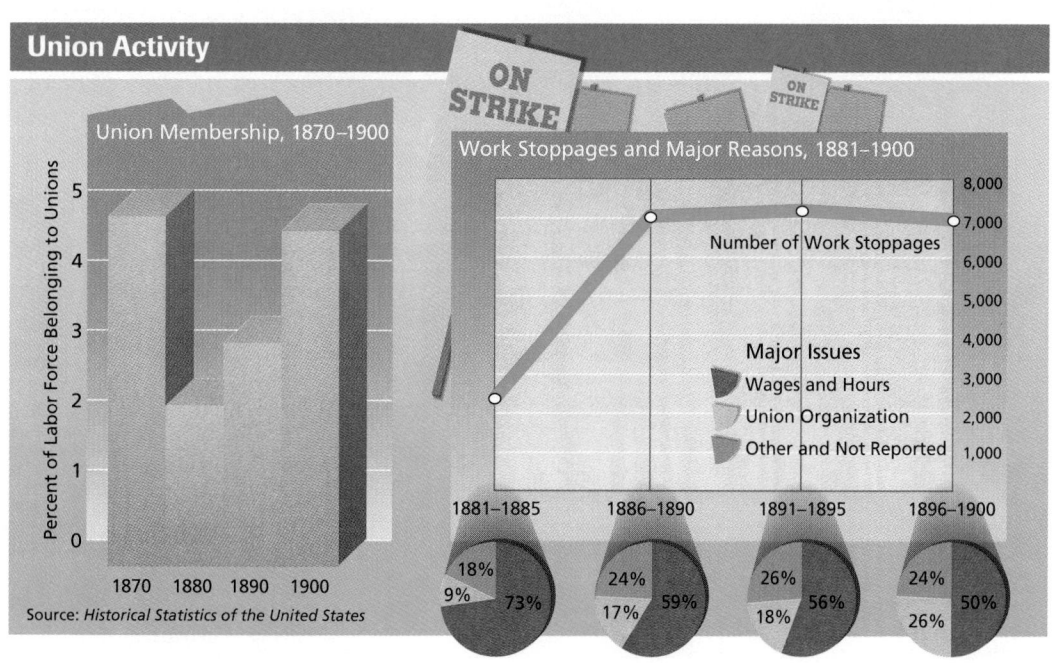

Union Activity

Union Membership, 1870–1900

Work Stoppages and Major Reasons, 1881–1900

Source: *Historical Statistics of the United States*

Bridging Past and Present

The construction of the Brooklyn Bridge between 1869 and 1883 is one of America's great stories. The story of this bridge also tells us a lot about the subject of history and why this subject is so fascinating and important.

Because other, shorter suspension bridges had failed before the Brooklyn Bridge was begun, the outcome of this project remained in doubt until its completion. Two engineers check the progress of the bridge's construction in 1881 (above), and workers cut and tie cables in 1882 (right).

HISTORY IS FULL OF UNEXPECTED OUTCOMES

John A. Roebling designed the Brooklyn Bridge and began its construction. He never knew the results of his effort, however. At the very beginning of the construction in 1869, a boat crushed his foot, and two weeks later he died from tetanus.

John Roebling's unfortunate story illustrates something about history that we may overlook. We know what John Roebling never knew—that his plan succeeded and that the Brooklyn Bridge still stands today. When we read about the events of the past, we can easily forget that the participants in the drama did not know how things would turn out. They had no more idea about the outcome of events than you now have about the outcome of today's events.

John A. Roebling

HISTORY REVEALS THE CAUSES OF EVENTS

People knew they needed a bridge to connect Manhattan Island with Brooklyn for more than half a century. Why was the bridge not begun until 1869, and why was it begun by John Roebling? History does not always give one sure answer about how and why an event took place. But historians can tell us about important earlier incidents that led to the event.

The East River, which the Brooklyn Bridge would eventually cross, flows swiftly and runs deep. The river served as a major route for large ocean-going ships and could not be blocked with a low bridge. The best type of bridge to span this river would be a suspension bridge, and it had to be almost 1,600 feet long. No one had ever constructed a long-span suspension bridge until John Roebling built one in 1846 across the Ohio River at Wheeling, West Virginia. The bridge that made him famous and captured the public's imagination, however, was the one that stretched more than 1,000 feet across Niagara Falls.

Roebling's technical success was not the only reason the Brooklyn Bridge got built when it did. Residents of Manhattan had used ferry boats to travel back and forth between Brooklyn and Manhattan. Although traveling by ferry took much longer than crossing a bridge, a bridge would cost the taxpayers more money than they wished to invest. In the winter of 1866 to1867, however, the cold weather halted ferry service and isolated Manhattan. The residents now were ready to pay for their bridge.

Fireworks mark the opening of the Brooklyn Bridge on May 24, 1883 (below). The bridge, which was completed by Washington Roebling (inset) after his father's death, marked a turning point in history. It began an era of bridge building that greatly improved transportation in the United States.

History reveals that many key events of the past have had a lasting impact on the present.

Emily Roebling, Washington Roebling's wife, carried his instructions to work crews at the bridge when an accident disabled Washington.

History Might Not Have Happened This Way

What happened when John Roebling died only a few weeks after beginning the bridge? Was only one outcome possible? When you turn the pages of a history book, you may feel that historical events were destined to turn out a certain way; in other words, history had to have happened the way that it did. But, if people had made different decisions and taken different actions, history might not have happened that way. Historians examine the options people had and the reasons they chose a certain path. From the study of history, we learn that many individuals, making personal choices and selecting among options, determine the course of events.

With the sudden death of the most-respected bridge builder of the time, the fate of the bridge—which many doubted could be built—was in question. The project might have been abandoned, or the corrupt political leader of New York, Boss Tweed, might have put one of his cronies in charge. Instead, John Roebling's son, Washington Roebling, carried on after his father's death.

Washington Roebling proved an able successor to his father, although an 1872 accident disabled him physically. Washington Roebling spent the last eleven years of the project confined to his apartment in a wheelchair. He watched the progress of the construction through his apartment window, while his wife, Emily Roebling, carried his instructions to the work crews at the bridge.

History Is Everyone's Story

The Roeblings did not build the bridge alone. The muscle, sweat, and skill of hundreds of laborers, many of them foreign born, were crucial. These workers toiled under hard and dangerous conditions. Some died in the process. Bankers and financiers, together with national and city politicians, also played major roles in building the bridge.

Historians, however, cannot tell everyone's story. They must focus on the people and events they feel are most important. Some historians choose to tell the story of a few famous people—political, military, and industrial leaders. *America: Pathways to the Present* chooses instead to weave the stories of ordinary women and men from many backgrounds and occupations together with the stories of the famous.

History Helps Us Understand the Present

The building of the Brooklyn Bridge was a turning point in history. Its success led to a boom in bridge building that made the crossing of major waterways a casual, everyday event throughout the country. The Brooklyn Bridge is an important path to the present, but it is only one of many events that, when studied historically, can lead us to a better understanding of the United States today. History reveals that many key events of the past have had a lasting impact on the present.

Obviously, most of the people you will read about in this book died long ago. As a result, their dreams and actions may seem remote to you. But the people of the past once walked and talked, hoped and dreamed, cried and laughed like you. And many of the things they did—from the bridges they built to the games they played—still affect us today.

To understand who you are, you first have to know about those people whose beliefs and experiences shaped your life.

The Brooklyn Bridge (in the foreground above and in the inset) remains an important part of the life of New Yorkers today.

THE PAST IS DIFFERENT FROM THE PRESENT

Studying the past is like studying a foreign country; the people there often do things differently from us. In America's past, its people sometimes did things quite differently than we do today. For example, Americans once had a very different view of what *equality* meant.

When historians examine our country's past, they focus on the realities of people's lives at that time. They try to help us understand why people in the past made the choices they did. History is not always pleasant or uplifting. The stories of the past do not always have happy endings. Sometimes they are very violent and disturbing.

We need to be honest about these events, and also to try to understand them and assess their meaning. Your job as a history student is to make a connection with them, to find out what you do and do not share with them and to engage them in conversation as a means of gaining a better understanding of both them and yourself.

WHY STUDY HISTORY?

Knowing about the past can help you understand the present. You know this from personal experience. To understand who you are, you first have to know about those people whose beliefs and experiences shaped your life.

History also reminds us of the continuity of the human experience. We may dismiss the past as irrelevant, to conclude that dead people and past events have little to do with us. But that would be a mistake. The present is linked to the past. History is not about memorizing a series of dates and events; it is an active, imaginative journey during which you share experiences with people from the past. These people may speak, think, and dress differently from you, but they still share universal concerns and a wish for

a better future. To study history is in a very real sense to participate in history itself.

America: Pathways to the Present will be an important tool as you study the story of our great nation. In it you will read about the many outstanding achievements of this nation, along with the challenges that face it still. Most of all, you will read about the people of America, the people who made the nation what it is today and the people who have a continual stake in preserving, protecting, and defending our freedoms.

As you will discover, this nation was built on the principles of liberty and self-government. As a result of the efforts of Americans who fought for their freedom more than 200 years ago, we today are guaranteed many rights, such as freedom of speech and worship, the right to assemble in groups and to petition the government, and the right to a fair trial. The efforts of earlier Americans also ensure our right to live under a government based on the will of the majority of citizens, expressed through elected representatives.

The United States has grown great because of its leaders and its people. Remarkable leaders like Washington and Lincoln have served our country well in times of pressing crisis. Still other leaders have made possible our progress in business, in science and invention, and in education. But the United States has also grown strong from the hard work and dedicated effort of countless others who have made use of the opportunities offered by our free way of life.

And that is what makes this textbook different from any other. In many books, the spotlight of history shines only on the great leaders. In *America: Pathways to the Present* the stage is illuminated to include the story of all Americans—women as well as men, nonwhites as well as whites, the little-known as well as the famous. They have always been there, of course, but in this book the stage is lit with their story, the story of all Americans as they seek to preserve freedom while facing the challenges of the future.

A Century of Change

The Transformation of America in the Twentieth Century

This textbook focuses on America in the twentieth century. In these ninety-plus years, our country has experienced sweeping changes in everyday life—perhaps more changes than in the three centuries before. Today's population is much more diverse than in 1900. In 1900, fast food restaurants were unknown. Cars were a novelty. Television had not yet been invented. But once these things became part of the national scene, the American people quickly made them fixtures of life. As you look at these pages, notice how the rate of change has increased after 1945 and think about how much—and how fast—life in the future may change.

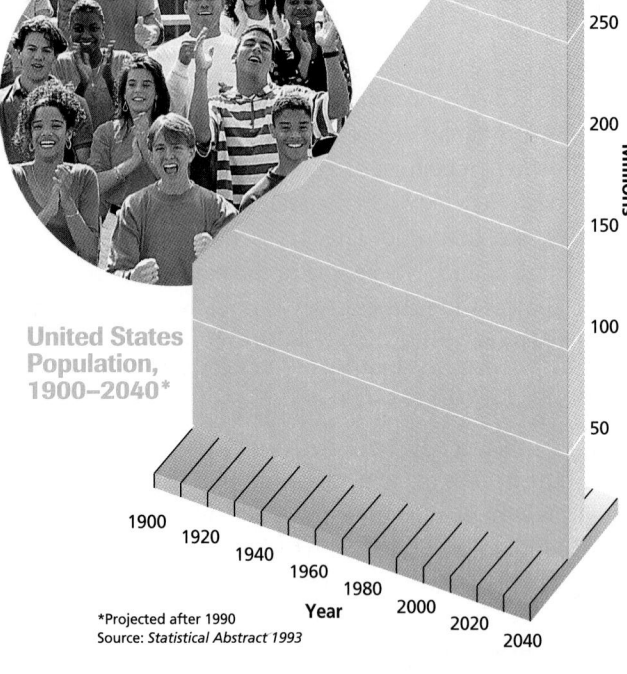

United States Population, 1900–2040*

*Projected after 1990
Source: *Statistical Abstract 1993*

The nation's population surged after World War II, as shown in the graph above. So did the numbers of Americans living in urban areas (below). *See pages 592–593 to find out what contributed to these population changes.*

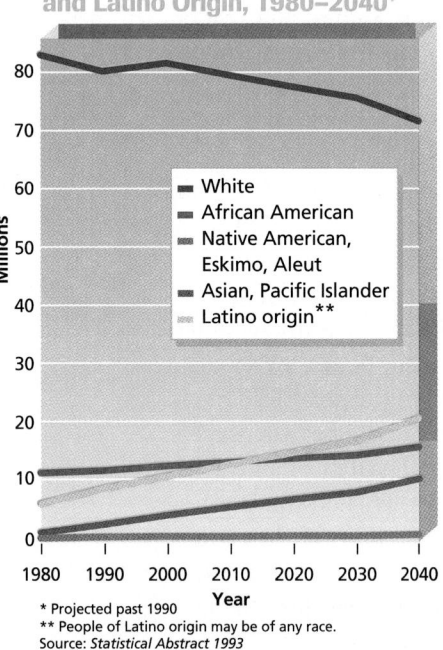

United States Population: Race and Latino Origin, 1980–2040*

Legend:
- White
- African American
- Native American, Eskimo, Aleut
- Asian, Pacific Islander
- Latino origin**

* Projected past 1990
** People of Latino origin may be of any race.
Source: *Statistical Abstract 1993*

The United States has always been made up of people from a rich variety of backgrounds—but the rate at which its diversity is growing is truly remarkable. The Bureau of the Census projects that in about the year 2020, the number of Latino Americans will be greater than the number of African Americans. *See pages 852–856 to find out what factors combined to change the ethnic composition of the United States.*

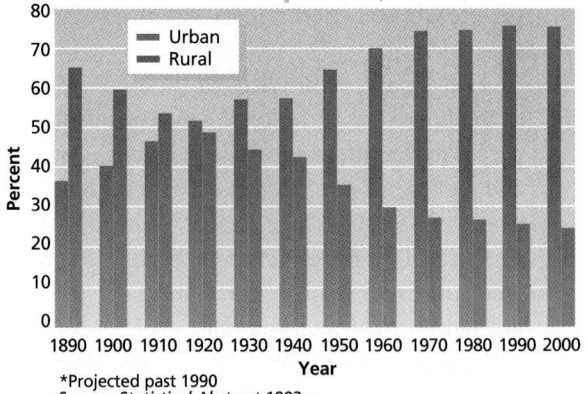

United States: Urban and Rural Population, 1890–2000*

Legend:
- Urban
- Rural

*Projected past 1990
Source: *Statistical Abstract 1992*

More Urban and Racially Diverse: The Nation's Population

Plugged In: Home Entertainment

Percent of Households with Television

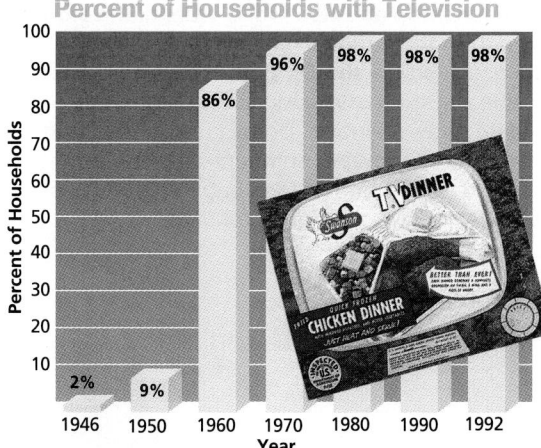

- 1946: 2%
- 1950: 9%
- 1960: 86%
- 1970: 96%
- 1980: 98%
- 1990: 98%
- 1992: 98%

Source: Bureau of the Census

Television is part of the American way of life—and it has been since the 1950s, when the number of households with televisions skyrocketed. Today virtually every family in the country has a television set, and well over half of American homes have two or more sets. In the 1990s, at least one TV is on in each household an average of seven hours per day. *See page 591 to find out how much TV the average American family watched per day in 1955.*

One of the most dramatic changes in home entertainment since 1980 has been the rise of the compact disc and the decline of the phonograph record. Record manufactures have plummeted since 1980, and in the 1990s compact discs had all but taken their place. *What do you think might replace compact discs in the future?*

Manufacture of Records, Compact Discs, and Cassettes (millions of units)

Year	Phonograph Records	Compact Discs*	Audiotape Cassettes
1980	487.1	0	110.2
1990	39.3	286.5	442.2
1991	26.8	333.3	360.1

* Compact discs were not manufactured and shipped until 1983.
Source: *Statistical Abstract 1993*

It's for You: Growth in Telephone Use

A new age of communication dawned at the close of the nineteenth century, thanks to Alexander Graham Bell and his invention of the telephone. Twentieth-century Americans embraced the new technology, and telephone use grew rapidly, especially after World War II. Today, nearly every household owns a telephone, and the American people talk on the phone more than 200 million times each day. *See page 230 to see a picture of an early telephone.*

Average Daily Telephone Conversations, 1890–1980

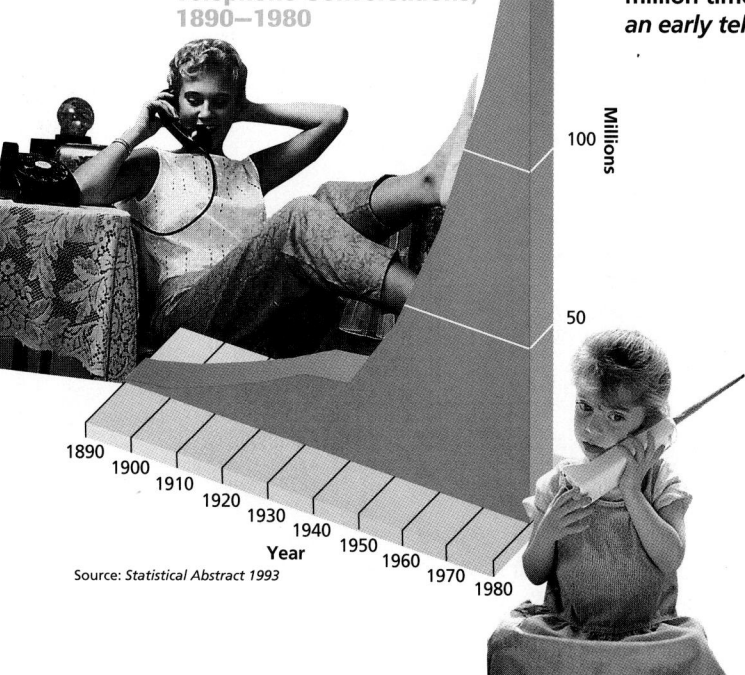

Source: *Statistical Abstract 1993*

Percent of Households with Telephones

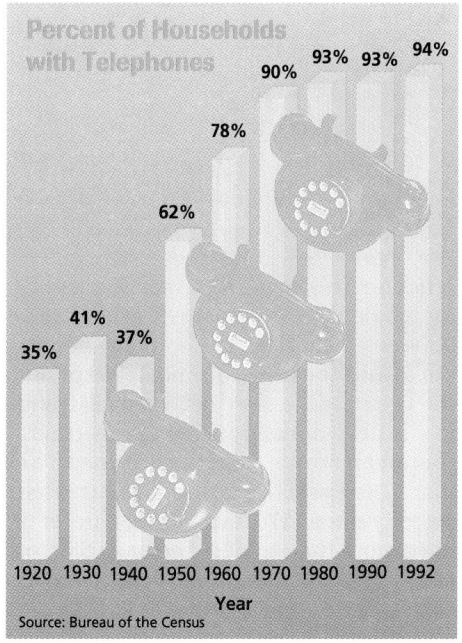

- 1920: 35%
- 1930: 41%
- 1940: 37%
- 1950: 62%
- 1960: 78%
- 1970: 90%
- 1980: 93%
- 1990: 93%
- 1992: 94%

Source: Bureau of the Census

Cars, Trucks, and Planes: From Novelty to Necessity

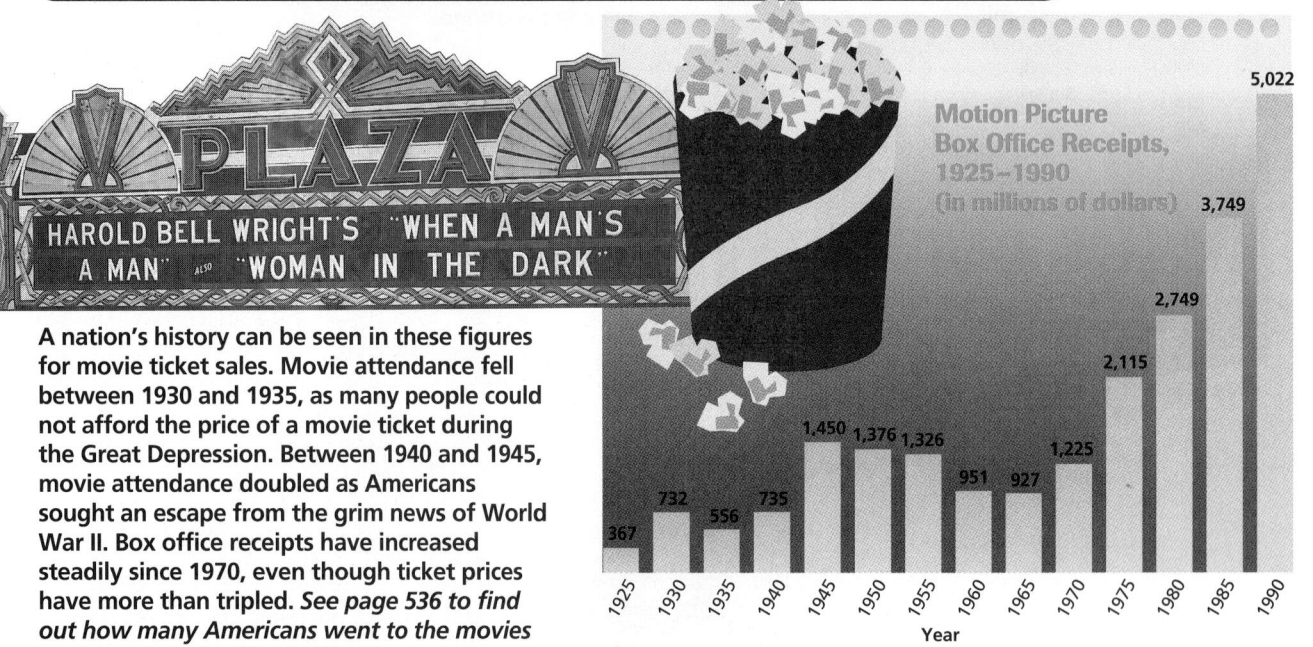

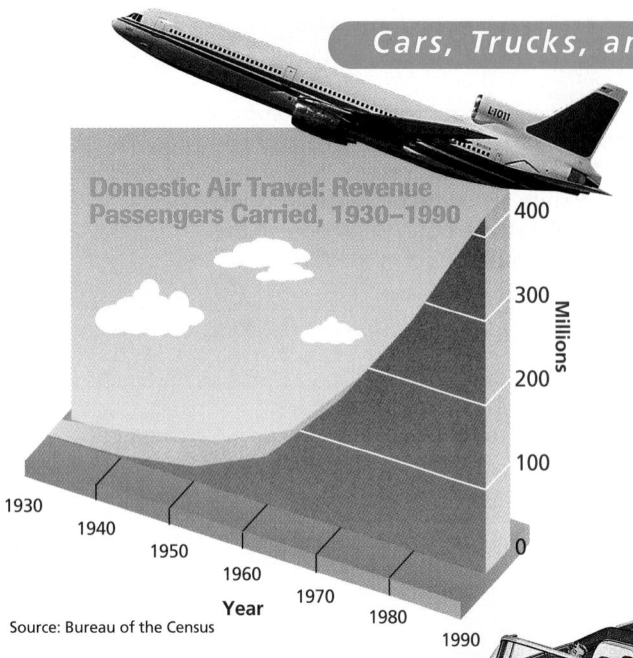

Domestic Air Travel: Revenue Passengers Carried, 1930–1990
400
300
200
100
0
Millions
1930
1940
1950
1960
1970
1980
1990
Year
Source: Bureau of the Census

An economic depression and two world wars didn't slow the rapid growth of the nation's reliance on cars and trucks, as the graph below shows. With the rising numbers of vehicles came a system of roadways and highways—and the problem of air pollution. Domestic air travel (left) took off after 1960, as growing numbers of Americans held jobs that required them to travel. ***See page 600–601 to find out how cars affected the growth of suburbs.***

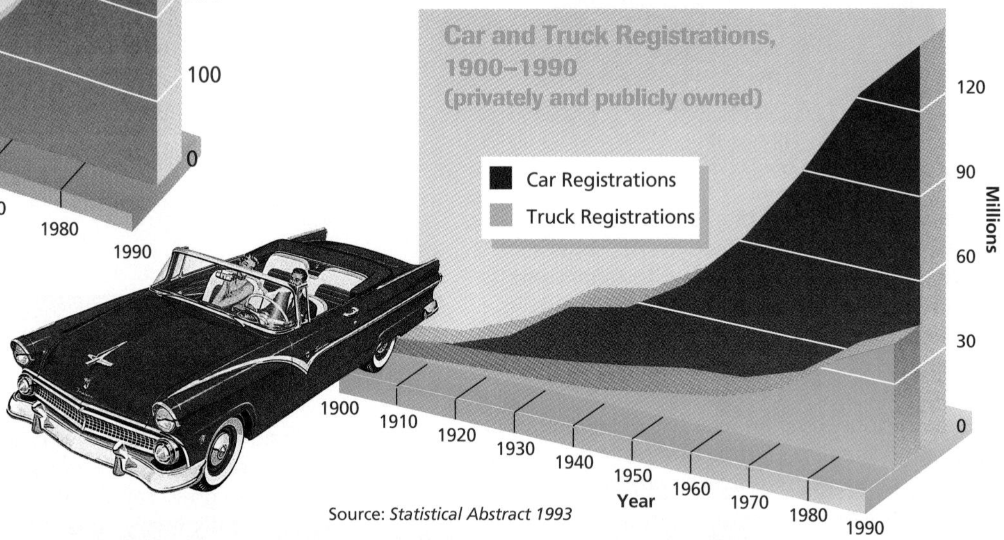

Car and Truck Registrations, 1900–1990 (privately and publicly owned)
Car Registrations
Truck Registrations
120
90
60
30
0
Millions
1900
1910
1920
1930
1940
1950
1960
1970
1980
1990
Year
Source: Statistical Abstract 1993

History at the Movies: Americans and Motion Pictures

PLAZA
HAROLD BELL WRIGHT'S "WHEN A MAN'S A MAN" ALSO "WOMAN IN THE DARK"

A nation's history can be seen in these figures for movie ticket sales. Movie attendance fell between 1930 and 1935, as many people could not afford the price of a movie ticket during the Great Depression. Between 1940 and 1945, movie attendance doubled as Americans sought an escape from the grim news of World War II. Box office receipts have increased steadily since 1970, even though ticket prices have more than tripled. ***See page 536 to find out how many Americans went to the movies each week during World War II.***

Motion Picture Box Office Receipts, 1925–1990 (in millions of dollars)
367
732
556
735
1,450
1,376
1,326
951
927
1,225
2,115
2,749
3,749
5,022
1925
1930
1935
1940
1945
1950
1955
1960
1965
1970
1975
1980
1985
1990
Year

Source: Bureau of the Census, *Historical Statistics of the United States* and *The Universal Almanac*

Per Capita Consumption of Soft Drinks, 1955–1990 (in gallons)

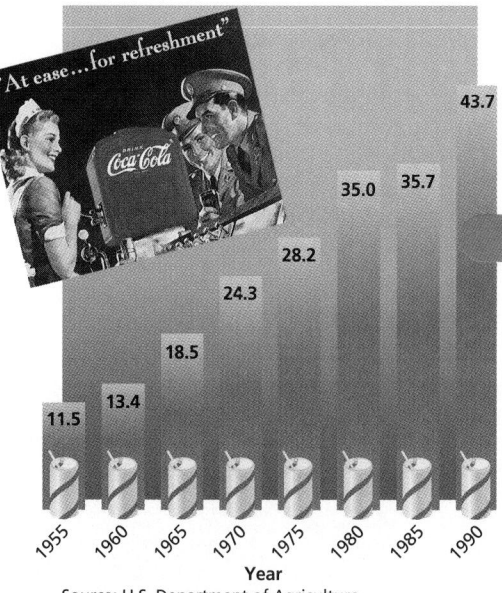

Year	Gallons
1955	11.5
1960	13.4
1965	18.5
1970	24.3
1975	28.2
1980	35.0
1985	35.7
1990	43.7

Year

Source: U.S. Department of Agriculture, Economics Research Service

Soft drinks have been around since about the mid-1800s, but until the 1950s they were served mostly at soda fountains like the one in this World War II–era Coke ad. Soft drink consumption increased rapidly after the 1950s due to new packaging methods such as the aluminum can. By the end of the 1990s, per capita consumption of soft drinks will exceed 50 gallons, which equals 533 twelve-ounce cans. *How does this figure compare to how much soda you drink?*

What's for Dinner?: American Eating Habits

Sales from Full-Service Restaurants and Fast-Food Restaurants, 1970–1994

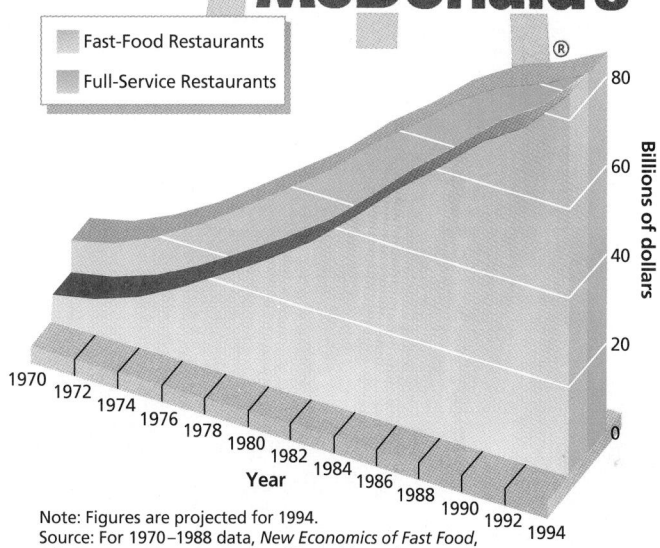

- Fast-Food Restaurants
- Full-Service Restaurants

Billions of dollars (0, 20, 40, 60, 80)

Year (1970, 1972, 1974, 1976, 1978, 1980, 1982, 1984, 1986, 1988, 1990, 1992, 1994)

Note: Figures are projected for 1994.
Source: For 1970–1988 data, *New Economics of Fast Food*, John Emerson (Van Nordstrom Rhinehold, 1990). For 1990–1994 data, National Restaurant Association.

With rising numbers of working couples, Americans have less time for home cooking and have come to rely on faster ways to have a meal. In response, more and more supermarkets sell ready-to-eat takeout food. As the graph at right shows, the restaurant industry has seen a steady increase in sales, especially fast-food restaurants, which offer affordable prices, speedy service, and a family-friendly atmosphere. By the mid-1990s, for the first time, sales of fast-food restaurants surpassed those of full-service restaurants. *See pages 590–591 to find out how a former milkshake mixer salesman created industry giant McDonald's.*

Sales from Eating and Drinking Places, 1935–1990

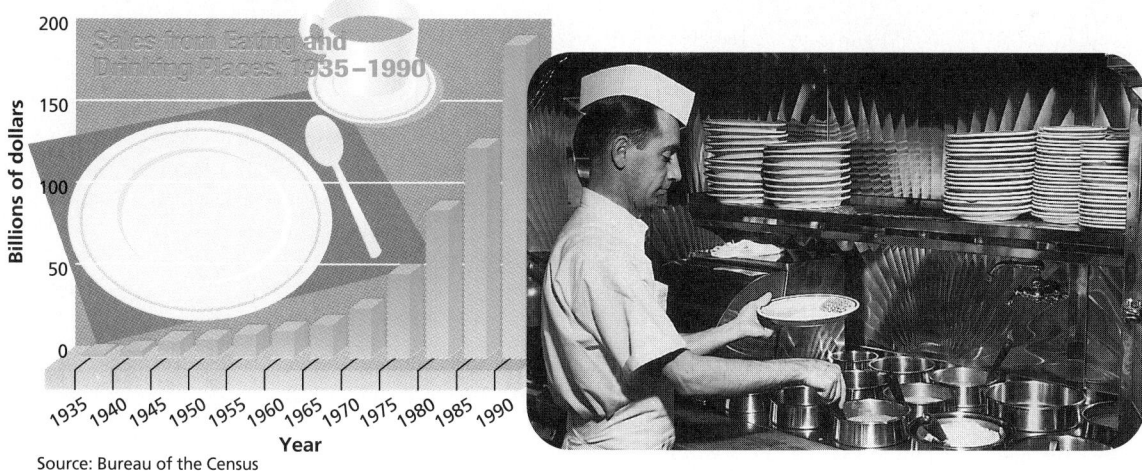

Billions of dollars (0, 50, 100, 150, 200)

Year (1935, 1940, 1945, 1950, 1955, 1960, 1965, 1970, 1975, 1980, 1985, 1990)

Source: Bureau of the Census

Themes in American History

M uch of what you learn about American history can be better understood if you view events as part of a larger pattern. The themes listed on page 11 apply to all periods of American history and can help you link events across time.

A jazz band poses for a photograph in the 1930s (above). A huge audience listens closely to rock and folk music at Woodstock in 1969 (inset). American culture—the special expression of ideas, attitudes, and feelings through various art forms, manners, and morals—is one of the important themes in American history.

REFORM MOVEMENTS

People in the United States have frequently taken action in grass-roots movements to right perceived wrongs and to secure improvements in the quality of life.

VALUES

A variety of religious, ethical, and moral beliefs have propelled and guided the quest of Americans for a just and ordered society.

ECONOMICS

Americans have searched for new and better ways to make a living and have struggled to define government's role in this pursuit.

TECHNOLOGY

Americans' ability to develop new skills and tools and to increase their knowledge of the physical world has greatly affected the way they live and work, and has led to a high standard of living.

ENVIRONMENT

The geography and available resources of the continent have affected the actions of Americans. Similarly, the actions of Americans have affected the environment and physical landscape.

DIVERSITY

The United States throughout its history has been made up of a gathering of many peoples from throughout the world. Americans have both benefited from and encountered problems with this diversity.

UNITY AND CONFLICT

Americans have developed unique political systems and laws that affirm a shared commitment to certain goals, such as individual rights and equality. Nevertheless, groups with differing views on how to achieve these goals have sometimes clashed.

AMERICAN CULTURE

In every period of their history, Americans gave special expression to their views in forms such as art, literature, films, music, manners, and morals.

AMERICAN DEMOCRACY

The concepts of democratic representation, equality under the law, and freedom from discrimination have been gradually broadened to include previously excluded groups.

THE UNITED STATES AND THE WORLD

America's relationships with other countries have been influenced at different times by a sense of mission, by values, and by self-interest.

Introducing the Unit

Interpreting the Visual After settling on North American shores and casting off British rule, the American people sought to win European approval by imitating the British lifestyle. But after the War of 1812 Americans began to take pride in developing a unique American character.

German-born painter John Lewis Krimmel (1729–1821), like other artists in the United States at the time, contributed to the development of a national character by selecting subjects and styles that were uniquely American, rather than British. In the painting shown on pages 8–9, Krimmel depicts the American passion for a good political fight.

Divide the class into small groups. The members of each group should take turns writing one sentence that describes Krimmel's painting until they have exhausted their ideas. Have a volunteer from each group read the collective description to the class. Then ask: What do you think Krimmel would include in an election-day painting today?

Establishing Chronology The unit opens with the encounter between Native Americans, Europeans, and Africans in the 1500s and 1600s and the Europeans' eventual rise to power. It describes the formation of a new American society and its struggle for independence from Great Britain, won in 1783. The unit then addresses the formation of the United States government, beginning with the writing of the Constitution in 1787 and then continuing with the presidencies from Washington to Jackson. It also includes a discussion of the social changes in the nation from 1789 to 1860.

UNIT 1

The Nation's Beginnings to 1840

"A people without a history is like wind on the buffalo grass."
–Proverb, Teton Sioux

*T*he rich and varied histories of several groups of people shaped the growth and direction of our nation. When the colonists overthrew British rule in the American Revolution, the new nation they created was already a multicultural society. As the nation grew, it struggled to achieve a balance between liberty and order. The pace of growth was rapid and by the early 1800s the United States seemed to be a nation in constant motion. As changes occurred the economic and political focus of the nation shifted from the local to the national level.

 RESOURCE DIRECTORY

Teaching Resources

Local History Activity "Publick Times in Colonial Williamsburg," "When Washington Was a Wilderness," and the Local Focus research topic sugestions, found in the Local History Resources folder, pp. 3–8, are designed to help students understand how history affects all lives.

★ **Themes in American History Posters** Wall-size, illustrated posters, found in the Teaching Resources package, illustrate the four unit themes.

Unit Test Forms A and B are found in the Unit 1 folder, pp. 139–144.

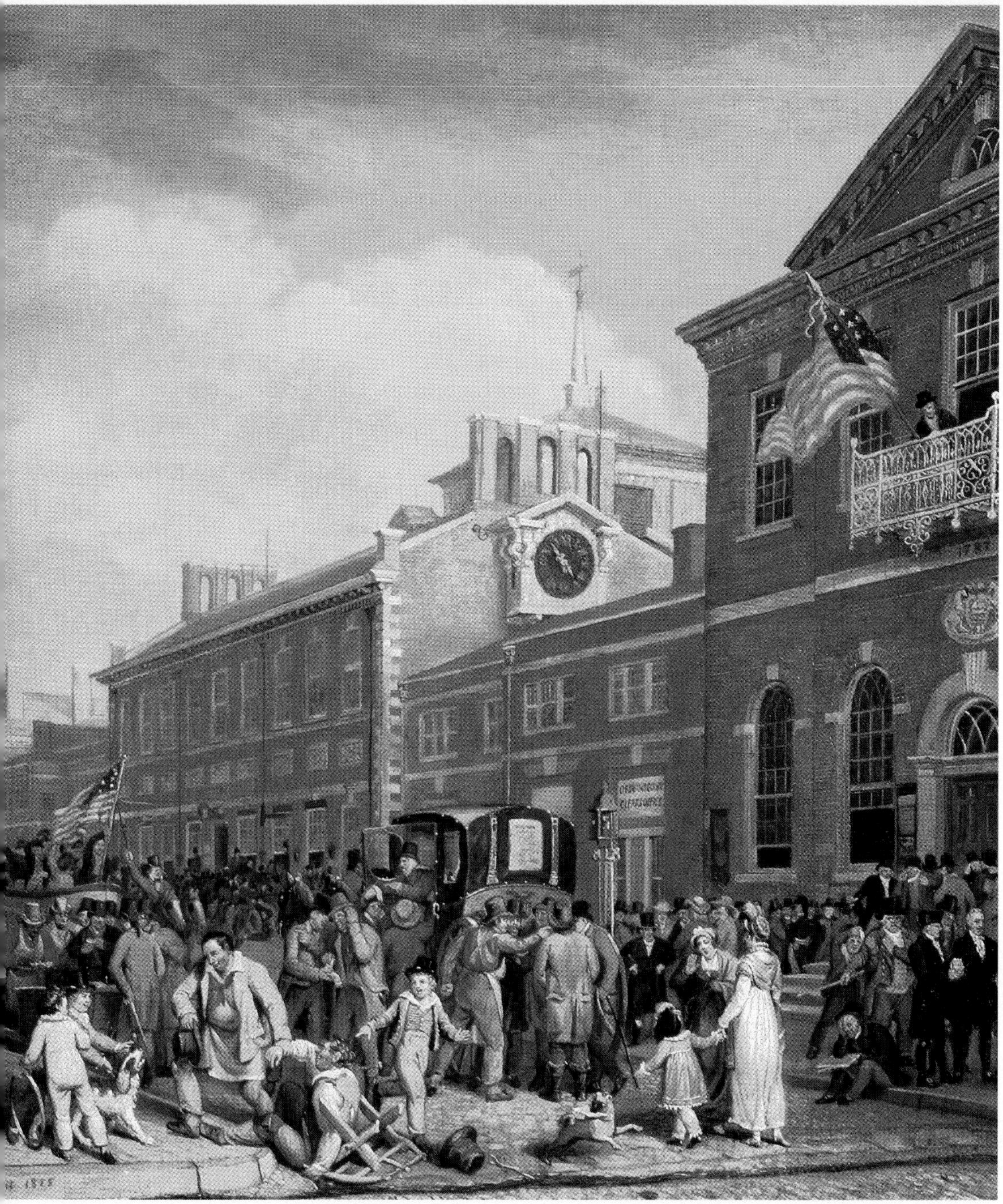

The excitement of government by the people is captured in this 1815 painting of Independence Hall, titled "Election Day in Philadelphia," by John L. Krimmel.

Media and Technology

 **Visions of America: Scenes of an Era** To introduce students to the main ideas and events covered in this unit, play the following "Scenes of an Era" (length: 2.5 minutes each): "Origins of a New Society" and "Balancing Liberty and Order" (side 1 of videodiscs; videotape 1); and "An Emerging New Nation" (side 2 of the videodiscs; videotape 2). Lesson plans

Side 1, Chapter 2

Side 1, Chapter 5

Side 1, Chapter 10

can be found in the Visions of America Teacher's Guidebook.

Using Multimedia Technology This folder contains instructional tools and strategies for using technology in the classroom.

Transparency Binder Contains full-color transparencies with lesson suggestions. From a large collection divided into twelve categories, specific transparencies are referenced throughout the chapters at appropriate points of use.

Chapter 1 Encounters and Colonies
To 1754

📁 Teaching Resources (See Unit 1 Folder)

	Instruction	Enrichment
Section 1 **Three Lands on the Atlantic** (pp. 16–22)	Reproducible Lesson Plan, p. 3 Alternate Lesson Plan, p. 50 Guided Reading and Review, p. 7 Quiz, p. 8	Literature Activity, Corn Mother, pp. 26–27 Critical Thinking Activity, Determining Relevance, p. 23 Visual Learning Activity, Slave Factories, p. 29
Section 2 **The Atlantic World Is Born** (pp. 23–27)	Reproducible Lesson Plan, p. 4 Alternate Lesson Plan, p. 51 Guided Reading and Review, p. 9 Quiz, p. 10	Primary Source Activity, Europeans Encounter Native Americans, pp. 24 Viewpoints Activity, On Celebrating Columbus Day, pp. 20–21
Section 3 **European Settlement and Native American Resistance** (pp. 28–33)	Reproducible Lesson Plan, p. 5 Alternate Lesson Plan, p. 52 Guided Reading and Review, p. 11 Quiz, pp. 12–13	American Profiles Activity, Popé, Medicine Man of the Pueblos, p. 18 Literature Activity, The Fate of an Indentured Servant, p. 28 History Might Not . . . Activity, Using Chinese Laborers to Build the Transcontinental Railroad, pp. 16–17
Section 4 **Life in Colonial America** (pp. 36–42)	Reproducible Lesson Plan, p. 6 Alternate Lesson Plan, p. 53 Guided Reading and Review, p. 14 Quiz, p. 15 Chapter Test, Forms A & B, pp. 31–36	Primary Source Activity, A Marriage Agreement, p. 25 Visual Learning Activity, Education as a Step Toward Freedom, p. 30 American Profiles Activity, Hannah Callowhill Penn, p. 19 Historian's Toolbox Activity, Making Comparisons, p. 22

📁 Additional Chapter Resources

Resource Organizer, p. 2
Alternate Lesson Plan, p. 49
Answer Keys, pp. 145–157

Bibliography

For the Teacher
Catton, Bruce. *The Bold and Magnificent Dream: America's Founding Years, 1492–1815.* Doubleday, 1978. (Account of the nation's history from colonial settlement to the early years of independence.)
Thornton, John. *Africa and Africans in the Making of the Atlantic World, 1400–1680.* Cambridge University Press, 1992.

Prentice Hall Literature Excerpts from *The American Experience,* 1994, including "Native American Voices," "Explorers," and Edwards, Jonathan. "Sinners in the Hands of an Angry God," from Faust, Clarence H., and Thomas H. Johnson.

Media and Technology

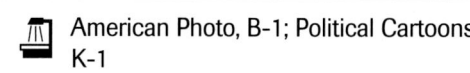 Time Lines, E-1; Fine Art, D-1; Our Multicultural Heritage, C-4; The Way It Works, H-1

American Photo, B-1; Political Cartoons, K-1

Cause and Effect, F-1

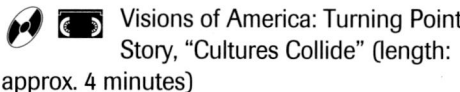 Visions of America: Turning Point Story, "Cultures Collide" (length: approx. 4 minutes)

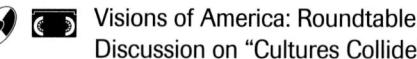 Visions of America: Roundtable Discussion on "Cultures Collide"

Visions of America: History Might Not Have Happened This Way Game

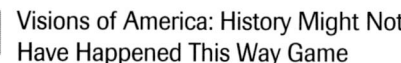 Historical Maps, L-1; Time Lines, E-2; Our Multicultural Heritage, C-1, C-6; Links Across Time, J-1; Graphic Organizer, G-2

Guided Reading Audiotapes (English and Spanish)

Computer Test Bank

For the Student
Digging Up America's Past: North America Before Columbus. National Geographic Society. Filmstrip.

Irving, Washington. "Philip of Pakanoket." In *Rip Van Winkle, The Legend of Sleepy Hollow and Other Stories.* Easton Press, 1967. (A moving account of King Philip's War.)

THE BIG IDEA

The Big Idea for the chapter and how the main ideas in each section relate to the Big Idea are graphically displayed below. Comprehension of this chapter's Big Idea is critical to students' understanding of United States history and how we as a nation got where we are today.

CHAPTER 1

When Europeans arrived on the shores of North America in the late 1400s, they encountered people who had been living there for thousands of years. Conflict between the groups soon developed, and after years of fighting and struggle, the Native Americans were forced to give up their lands and yield power to the Europeans. African Americans torn from their homelands and taken to North America were kept in slavery and not allowed to defend themselves in any way.

SECTION 1

Native Americans, Africans, and Europeans had each developed a distinct culture before they began interacting with one another in the late 1400s. Some of their beliefs and values were similar; others were very different.

SECTION 2

Beginning with the first voyage of Columbus, regular exchanges among the peoples of the Americas, Europe, and Africa created the Atlantic World. These contacts brought new trading opportunities, as well as the spread of slavery and a violent clash of values and beliefs.

SECTION 3

Each group of Europeans in North America during the sixteenth and seventeenth centuries formed a distinct society, and each group disrupted the Native American societies it encountered. By the end of the seventeenth century, Native American resistance in New England finally gave way to the English.

SECTION 4

Colonial society was organized into a hierarchy. At the top were powerful landowners who were almost always white men. Women had little legal power, but their work was vital to the success of the colonies. Enslaved African Americans were allowed no rights at all.

14B

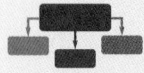

The Relevance of the Big Idea

Five hundred years ago, the different cultures of the Americas, Europe, and Africa all came into contact—and conflict. This contact was maintained in what is today the United States. By the mid-1700s, growth and prosperity came to many in the developing American colonies. Yet that in itself spelled loss and decline to others. Colonial society was defined by intolerance, strong class and ethnic distinctions, and inequality among races.

Point out that throughout American history phrases such as *melting pot* have been used to characterize the association of diverse cultures in American society. Discuss with students how they view American society today.

In Depth

Global Connections

Discovery of a fast route to Asia was a top priority for fifteenth-century European explorers. Many believed that Asia lay just beyond the western coast of North America, and that they had only to find a water passage through the continent to reach it. In 1513, after leading a hazardous trail across what is now called the Isthmus of Panama, the Spanish explorer Balboa was the first European to see the Pacific Ocean. While these explorations excited curiosity among Europeans, the Native Americans had to contend with Europeans who plundered their land for wealth and spread Christianity.

14 REVIEW UNIT

Encounters and Colonies
To 1754

Five hundred years ago, a few frail ships crossing the waters of the Atlantic Ocean first brought Europeans to Native American shores. Africans torn from their homelands soon followed. After a period during which Native Americans and Europeans alternately dominated and resisted one another, the Europeans overwhelmed Native Americans and took hold in North America.

Events in the United States

800–1000 Navahos migrate to the Southwest from the fringes of North America.

1000 Norsemen under Leif Ericson land on the coast of North America.

| 800 | 900 | 1000 | 1100 | 1200 |

Events in the World

800 Charlemagne crowned emperor of Romans.

1095 European Christians set out on the First Crusade to capture Palestine from the Muslims.

▶ RESOURCE DIRECTORY

Teaching Resources

Alternate Lesson Plan: Demonstrating the Big Idea found in the Alternate Lesson Plans folder, p. 49, provides a lesson strategy to instruct students about the Big Idea that the collision of cultures from America, Europe, and Africa led to the destruction of existing societies and the development of a new society and culture in the American colonies.

Alternative Assessment Handbook provides information, guidance, and strategies for alternative methods of assessment. It includes an essay on new trends in assessment, guidance and strategies for developing performance tasks and portfolios, scoring rubrics, and sample evaluation forms.

Pages 16–22
Three Lands on the Atlantic

Each of the three main culture areas around the Atlantic Ocean had a long history of its own before they all began to interact with one another in the late 1400s. Though these cultures had many similar customs and beliefs, certain differences among them would later lead to a violent clash of values.

Pages 23–27
The Atlantic World Is Born

The voyage of an Italian navigator was the prelude to centuries of trade and tragic conflict among Native Americans, Europeans, and Africans. In these years new societies would be built and old ones swept aside.

Pages 28–33
European Settlement and Native American Resistance

After 1492, the Spanish, English, French, and Dutch invaded the Americas, devising various ways to exploit its natural wealth. Meanwhile, Native Americans fought against them, determined to preserve their way of life.

Pages 36–43
Life in Colonial America

For England in the mid-1600s and early 1700s, the colonies were a reliable source of raw materials and a prime place to sell English goods. Eventually, however, the colonies grew and prospered with little direct interference from the English government. As they grew, a distinct colonial culture emerged— one in which the wealthy few dominated the majority of people.

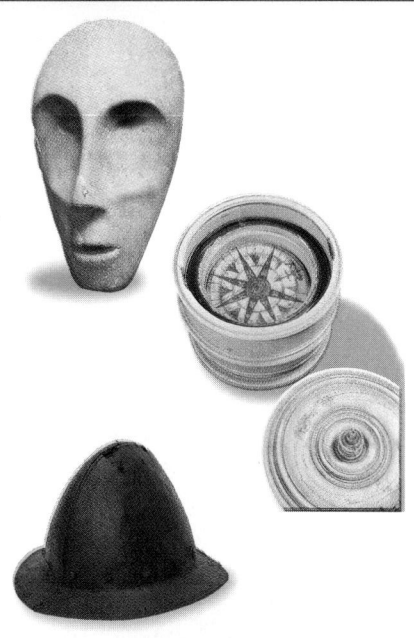

1492 Columbus sails from Spain and lands on islands in the Caribbean.

1598 Spain claims territory of New Mexico.

1630 European settlers found the Massachusetts Bay Colony.

1680 Pueblo people expel the Spanish from New Mexico.

1750 Number of enslaved African Americans in the British colonies passes 236,000.

1300	1400	1500	1600	1700

1271 Marco Polo journeys to China.

1591 End of the Songhai Empire in West Africa.

1648 The Taj Mahal is completed in India.

1762 Catherine the Great becomes ruler of Russia.

Alternative Assessment

As an ongoing chapter project, students can assume the role of an English traveler returning to London in 1754 from a trip to the colonies. Students could produce an account of their travels demonstrating knowledge of the Native Americans, Europeans, and Africans inhabiting North America at that time. Students could include information on the collision of the three cultures affected each, the struggle between Native Americans and Europeans in various parts of the colonies, the colonies' economic activities, the organization of colonial society, the institution of slavery, and the lives of enslaved African Americans in various regions. Suggested formats are to:

● Prepare a written document such as a travel diary, arranged by colonial region.

● Prepare a series of articles, illustrated with maps and pictures, for a London newspaper, each dealing with one of the suggested topics. Explain that finished projects will be assessed according to the following criteria:

● **Unacceptable** Projects are not attempted or fail to meet requirements outlined.

● **Limited/Acceptable** Projects are based on material from the textbook and reflect some effort to show the interaction of cultures in America and the growth of the colonies.

● **Extensive/Commendable** Projects are based on some outside research and indicate a comprehensive understanding of our cultural and colonial background.

● **Extraordinary/Outstanding** Projects are based on considerable outside research and reflect in-depth knowledge, specific as well as general, of the struggle among the various groups in North America and the development of the colonies.

For information on alternative assessment trends and strategies, see the Alternative Assessment Handbook in the Resource Directory on page 14.

1. FOCUS

Connecting to the Big Idea

See page 14B. Explain to students that in the 1400s, three very different societies were thriving on three separate continents—America, Europe, and Africa. All three groups shared a coastline on the Atlantic Ocean. Have students think about other similarities and differences that existed among these cultures.

Objectives

- Understand both the diversity of Native American cultures, as reflected by regional variations, and the importance of Native American trade across North America.
- Explain how the hierarchically organized Europeans competed for trade and why they were eager to find new markets.
- Describe society in the West African kingdoms and the extensive trading system in the region.

Bellringer

Have students recall the most recent item they or some family members have purchased. Ask them to jot down where they think the item originated and what kind of route it might have taken to reach them.

Reading Strategy

Reading for Evidence Ask students to find evidence that the three worlds on the Atlantic had fully developed and flourishing cultures. Have students write down one fact about each of the cultures discussed and indicate how each differed from the others.

Three Lands on the Atlantic

SECTION PREVIEW

Each of the three main culture areas around the Atlantic Ocean had a long history of its own before they all began to interact with one another in the late 1400s. Though these cultures had many similar customs and beliefs, certain differences among them would later lead to a violent clash of values.

Key Concepts

- By the 1400s, the region that would become the United States was inhabited by many diverse cultural groups linked by trade.
- Competition among the highly structured societies of Europe encouraged the people of that region to look overseas for trading opportunities in the 1400s.
- The kingdoms of West Africa were complex and wealthy cultures, with an extensive trading system that stretched from the Guinea coast to North Africa.

Key Terms, People, and Places
kinship network, clan, hierarchy, patriarchal society, lineage; Guinea, Songhai

Native American artists in what is now Gallatin County, Kentucky, sculpted in stone the spare, crisp lines and curves of this face.

A rchaeologists theorize that beginning as much as 40,000 years ago, people migrated eastward from Asia to a land where humans had never lived before—the Americas. The people who descended from these migrants are today generally referred to as Native Americans, because their ancestors were the first to be native to, or born on, the American continents. In fact, the Native Americans' own legends say that their people have lived in the Americas since the creation of the earth.

Over the centuries after their arrival, Native Americans grew in number and fanned out across North and South America. As they went, they gained hard-won knowledge about how to

live on the land, weaving new societies and building on old traditions to meet the demands of their times. Their language branched and evolved until groups who spoke its separate offshoots often could not understand one another. Empires rose and fell among them; skills and crafts sprang into being, only to vanish and revive again.

During these thousands upon thousands of years, the wide Atlantic and Pacific oceans generally isolated the Americas from people elsewhere in the world. Those other people, too, were forging societies and building cultures. Then, in the late 1400s A.D., the Atlantic Ocean ceased to be a barrier and became instead a highway on which the three main cultures around the Atlantic Ocean—Native American, European, and African—came into contact with one another. The similarities and differences among their beliefs and their ways of life at once began to profoundly affect the interaction among them. This section compares and contrasts the beliefs and the ways of life of these three cultures before contact.

America: A Flourishing World

By the late 1400s, when the encounter among the Atlantic cultures began, some eight to ten million people may have lived in what is now the United States. Some scholars contest these figures, claiming they should be as low as 700,000 to 800,000. The map on page 17 shows that whatever the size of this population, it included a dazzling number of distinct groups. The map also indicates how these groups can be categorized by region, reflecting differences in the way they adapted their way of life to the local environment.

Social Organization and Spiritual Life No matter how Native Americans adapted to the land in which they lived, whether they hoed the soil in the dry Southwest or stalked buffalo on the Great Plains, they generally looked to the

RESOURCE DIRECTORY

Teaching Resources

Reproducible Lesson Plan found in the Unit 1 folder, p. 3, provides a summary of the Section 1 lesson plan content.

Alternate Lesson Plan: Critical Thinking Formulating Questions, found in the Alternate Lesson Plans folder, p. 50, helps students apply this skill in thinking about the differences between the three lands on the Atlantic.

Guided Reading and Review found in the Unit 1 folder, p. 7, provides a structure for reading and mastering the key concepts and reviewing the key terms for Section 1. (Guided Practice)

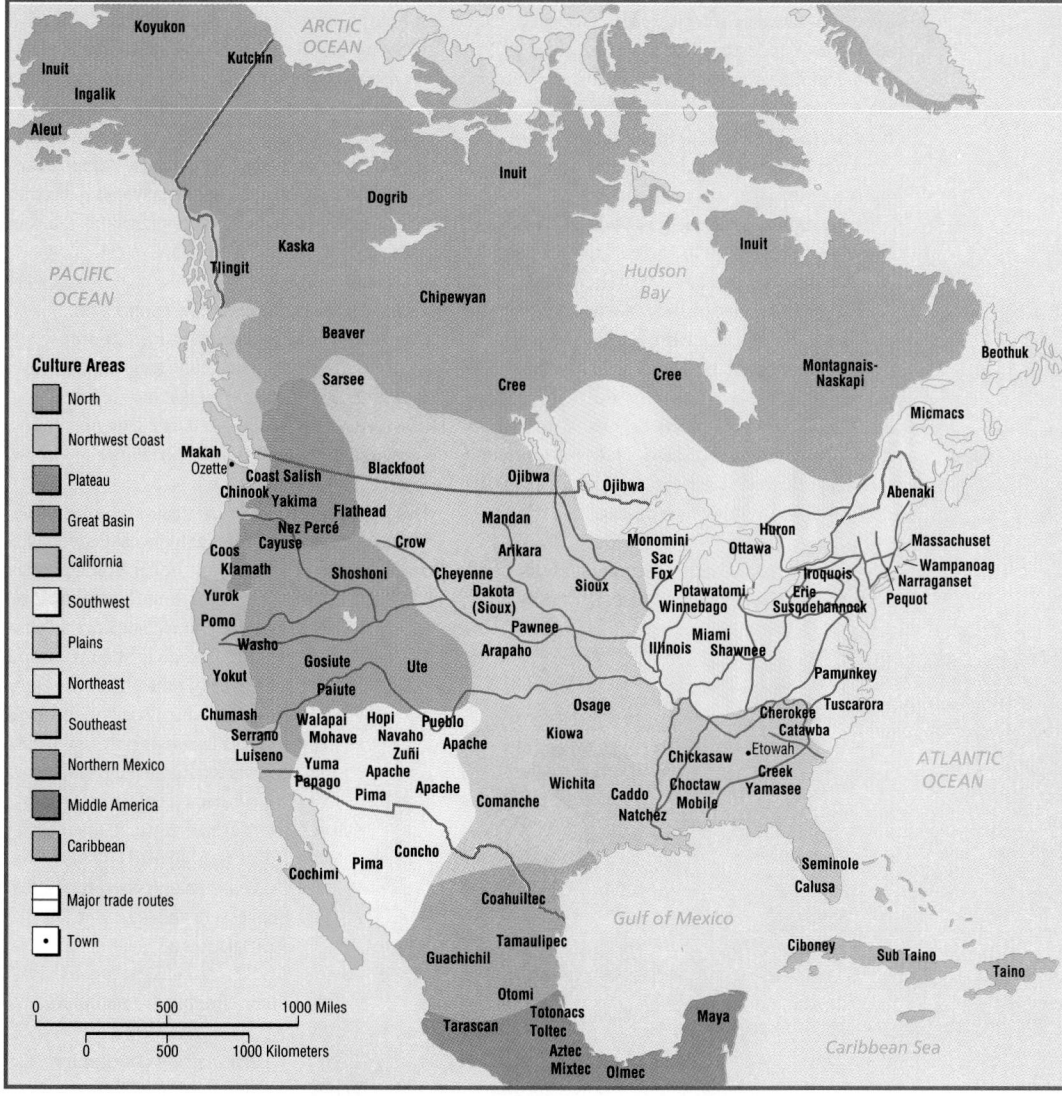

Culture Areas

- North
- Northwest Coast
- Plateau
- Great Basin
- California
- Southwest
- Plains
- Northeast
- Southeast
- Northern Mexico
- Middle America
- Caribbean
- Major trade routes
- • Town

 Geography and History: Interpreting Maps
The map shows only some of the groups thriving in North America in the 1400s. The trade routes, too, are only a selection; nearly any waterway or path served as a potential path for trade. *In which region is a small number of culture groups spread out over a large area? Why?*

family to fulfill many of their social needs. Their families provided them with many of the services we expect today from governments, churches, and private organizations, including medical care, child care, settlement of disputes, and education.

For the Native American, the family usually meant not just parents and children, but a **kinship network**. This was a group of relatives, or kin, such as parents, children, grandparents, aunts, uncles, cousins, and those who had married into the family.

Media and Technology

 Transparencies
Time Lines, E-1; Fine Art, D-1

Explain

Explain that the cultures in the three continents had fully developed kinship networks, established religious and social practices, and methods of trading with their neighbors. Different Native American groups shared many common elements of social organization such as kinship networks, but developed distinct characteristics in adapting to mountains, desert, coastal or other environments. European society was hierarchical and used land as a basis for wealth. West African societies were complex communities engaged in trading and farming.

 In Depth

Did You Know?

The experience of the Navaho demonstrates the relationship between culture and the environment. When the Navaho lived in eastern Alaska, they adapted to snow and cold by gathering wild food and hunting. Later, they migrated to the more temperate Southwest, where they grew corn to survive. The Navaho chose the plant as a symbol of their vitality and incorporated it into their religious beliefs. Because they needed a word for *seed,* they adapted their old word for *snowflake.*

Discuss

Have students describe the land use patterns of the three cultural groups discussed in this section. Ask why different attitudes about land might lead to conflict when these groups interacted.

 Activity

(The clock icon indicates an activity that can be successfully conducted within a class period. Each chapter has at least one such activity.)

Teaching Heterogeneous Groups

In order for all students to understand that *where* we live affects *how* we live, brainstorm a list of categories that help define how we live. (*clothing, food, housing, etc.*) Divide students into groups representing America, Europe, and coastal West Africa. Using the categories they developed, have each group prepare a Where We Live/How We Live chart for their region. **LEP**

 In Depth

Then and Now

Native Americans believe that displaying skeletal remains and burial relics is sacrilegious. Under the Native American Graves Protection and Repatriation Act of 1990, museums in the United States were given until 1995 to catalogue all Native American sacred artifacts in their collections. "It's about time. We're going to be made to know what the museums have that belongs to us," says William Tallbull, chairman of the Northern Cheyenne's cultural commission in Lame Deer, Montana. Tallbull wants the return of as many as 3,500 Cheyenne burial objects believed to be in various museums scattered across the United States.

One kind of kinship network is today referred to as a **clan.** A clan was formed of groups of families who were all descended from a common ancestor. The Lenape people of the mid-Atlantic seaboard, for example, had at least three clans. The diagram below illustrates how the Lenape clans gathered together for ceremonies that had social, religious, and political significance.

Ceremonies such as these, which reinforced social ties, were vital to the social organization of Native Americans. Furthermore, like Africans and Europeans, Native Americans believed that misfortunes, such as military defeat, disease, or bad harvests, happened to people who ignored rituals. For this reason, whether they were planting crops, falling in love, or burying their dead, Native Americans strictly followed traditional rituals. Failure to do so was an invitation to disaster.

Peaceful Trade One traditional activity of all Native American groups, no matter how large or small, was trade for food or goods within their group and outside it. They traded not only for items they needed or wanted, but also to demonstrate hospitality and friendliness. Even basic economic transactions took on a social dimension, because sharing was a sign of respect. Such trading customs began thousands of years before the collision of the Atlantic cultures and continued long afterward. A French priest, Father Joseph François Lafitau, noted in 1724 that the Native Americans

have traded with each other from time immemorial. . . . The feasts and dances which they have when they go to deal with other tribes [groups] make their trade an agreeable diversion. . . . Their way of engaging in trade is by an exchange of gifts.

The Native American View of Land Use
Although Native Americans might give away possessions as gifts, they never traded away land. In their view, the land could not be owned. They believed that people had a right to use land and could grant others the right to use it too. But to sell land outright, as people in other countries did at the time and as we do today, was unthinkable to Native Americans. Chief Joseph, a leader of the Nez Percé people in the late 1800s, expressed the age-old Native American view:

T*he country was made without lines of demarcation [boundary lines], and it is no man's business to divide it. . . . The earth and myself are of one mind. The measure of the land and the measure of our bodies are the same. . . . I never said the land was mine to do with it as I chose. The one who has the right to dispose of it is the one who has created it.* ⭐

Central post This post was a symbolic link to the sky, home of the Creator.

Carvings These carvings represented twelve sky spirits.

Entry at east This entry symbolized birth.

Oval Floor The shape represented the back of the turtle that was believed to form the earth.

Wolf clan

Drummers

Turtle clan

Turkey clan

Circle of men

Circle of women

Exit at west This exit symbolized death.

In a ceremony woven of prayer, chanting, and dance, clans of the Lenape gave thanks to the Creator. The longhouse and all within it reflected relationships in the universe. For example, men sat within a circle of women, who headed the clans.

RESOURCE DIRECTORY

Teaching Resources

⭐ **Literature Activity** "Corn Mother," found in the Unit 1 folder, pp. 26–27, uses a Penobscot folktale to portray Native American attitudes toward the land.

This difference in views about how land should be used would lead to violent disagreement between Native Americans and Europeans when the two cultures met.

The Nations of Europe

The meeting of the three Atlantic cultures was brought about by the Europeans, who were the first to cross the Atlantic Ocean. One aim in particular motivated them to do so: the desire to win wealth through trade. Their trade, however, was very different from Native American trade, and arose in the context of a very different society.

The Importance of Land Europeans in the 1400s depended heavily on farming for survival, but land was scarce and people were numerous. In fact, for centuries Europe had had more people than it could feed with the crops it grew at that time. Thus land was valued because owning land meant being powerful. Relatively few people owned and controlled land; these few—the wealthy—did little work. Instead, they made the people who farmed their land pay rent or give over part of their crops.

By contrast, the working poor made up about 50 percent of the total population of Europe; the very poorest group varied between 10 and 20 percent. Most of the working poor were farmers, or peasants, growing crops such as wheat on land they did not own. Halfway between the rich and the poor was a middle class of craftspeople, who made goods, and merchants, who exchanged goods for money.

A World of Ordered Levels Europeans explained this world of contrasts—of great wealth, middling wealth, and enduring poverty—as part of a **hierarchy**, or system of many levels in which each level has power over the levels beneath it. Europeans believed that everything, from the universe to the average household, was ordered in hierarchies. At the head of most European hierarchies was a father figure. In the Christian religion, the most common faith in Europe at that time, God was considered the supreme Father. Most governments, too, had a parentlike ruler at their head—sometimes a queen, but most often a king. In European families, whether wealthy landowners or poor peasants, each individual father ruled over his dependents—his wife, children, and, in some cases, servants or apprentices. This type of male-dominated social organization is called a **patriarchal society**, or patriarchy. By contrast, Native American societies were often led by men and women together, and few were organized into hierarchies.

The Household Kinship provided the focus for the daily life of Europeans, as it did for Native Americans and Africans. In England, for example, the most important social unit was the family and its household. In the English household, at least at the level of farmers and tradespeople, everyone performed economic activities for the good of the whole. Unlike most modern

Using Historical Evidence For Europeans in the 1400s, the household was a center of production. In this household workshop, a family works together. *How do the tasks the family is engaged in serve their common good?*

Media and Technology

Transparencies
Our Multicultural Heritage, C-4; The Way It Works, H-1

Enrichment

The field of archeology has provided us with much of the information we have about earlier societies. Have students choose one of the groups discussed in this section and find out about specific archeological discoveries related to their chosen group.

Caption Answer to ...

Using Historical Evidence

The man and the boy are producing some type of woodwork, probably for sale; the woman is producing thread for use in making clothing or for sale.

Answers will vary but may cite the presence of foreign products in the United States market or the prevalence of news covering trade negotiations with other nations.

American homes, the primary purpose of the English household was production rather than consumption. In other words, people worked long hours in and around the house to provide for their basic needs. They did not consider the house as simply a place where they could use and enjoy products made elsewhere.

The survival of the household depended upon the willingness of all its members to put aside their individual interests for the good of the whole. In this respect, European households were like Native American families.

Europe's Traders Look Outward During the 1400s, competition for trade grew more intense in Europe, encouraging queens, kings, and merchants to look outward for new sources of wealth. England offers a good example of the increasing energy of European trade. The people of this nation developed an extensive trade with the rest of Europe during the 1300s and 1400s. They shipped lead and tin from English mines, and hides, wool, honey, and butter from English farms. Furthermore, they added value to raw materials by turning them into more finished goods. Increasingly, traders shipped out woolen cloth produced by English spinners and weavers instead of raw wool. During the two centuries after 1350, the percentage of total wool exports shipped in the form of cloth surged from 4 percent to 60 percent. In the bustling ports of Spain, France, and Portugal, English traders exchanged these goods for wines, fruit, silk, spices, silver, and gold.

The English were not alone. Merchants from all over Europe were scouting for new markets. Around 1520 an anonymous English poet gave this pessimistic assessment:

> We Englishmen behold
> Our ancient customs bold
> more preciouser than gold
> be clean cast away,
> And other new be found, the which
> (you may understand)
> that causeth all your land
> So greatly to decay. . . .
> Other lands advanced be,
> And buy and sell among us free;
> And thus our own commodity

> Doth clean undo our self . . .
> French ware hither is brought,
> And English handcraft goeth to nought.

This fierce competition illustrates a crucial difference between the way Europeans and Native Americans conducted trade. Unlike Native Americans, Europeans tended to see trade as a simple material exchange that did not create further social obligations between people. As in the case of many other differences between cultures, neither view was right or wrong. In this particular case, however, just as in the case of varying views about land use, the difference would lead to bitter misunderstandings when Europeans and Native Americans finally encountered one another across the Atlantic. ★

MAKING CONNECTIONS

What evidence do you see in your own life of nations competing for trade?

The Trading Kingdoms of Africa

With so much pressure for new markets and new products, it was no wonder that Europeans began to look overseas for trading opportunities. Africa had always been the major source of gold for Europeans, and India offered exotic spices that fetched a good profit. The Portuguese, under the direction of Prince Henry the Navigator, began raiding and trading on the western coast of Africa as early as 1434. One of their navigators, Bartolomeu Dias, rounded the southernmost cape of Africa in 1488, and by 1498 another, Vasco da Gama, had forged beyond Africa and on to India. At this time, trade in the area of the most contact between Europeans and Africans, West Africa, was concentrated in two areas: the coastal forests and the drier region beyond the coast. ★

The Forest Kingdoms The coastal region of West Africa that became the focus of trade between Europeans and Africans stretched from Morocco in the north to the Congo River in the south. In the center of this long swath was the area of heaviest interaction, generally called

RESOURCE DIRECTORY

Teaching Resources

★ **Critical Thinking Activity** Determining Relevance: Solving an Archeological Puzzle, found in the Unit 1 folder, p. 23, is designed to help students apply this skill by analyzing a tool of Neanderthal, or Stone Age, times.

★ **Visual Learning Activity** Slave Factories, found in the Unit 1 folder, p. 29, is designed to enhance students' understanding of slavery's beginnings through an illustration of a West African slave "factory."

Guinea. In the 1400s, Guinea was home to three energetic forest kingdoms: Oyo, Ife, and Benin.

Trade was vital to Guinea long before interaction began across the Atlantic Ocean. In Benin, for instance, merchants traded farm products, works of art, and goods forged from African iron, which at that time was probably superior to any in the world. Trade was controlled by the Oba, or king, who had a very high status among his people. From a central city, also called Benin, he ruled all of the surrounding forest land, waging war, directing agriculture, and regulating commerce through administrators and local leaders.

The ruling classes in Guinea were generally groups made up of people who identified closely with one another because they shared a common ancestor. This type of kinship network is called a **lineage.** (Native American clans are a form of lineage group.) These leaders dealt with their people primarily through local headmen, who usually were also the heads of similar kinship networks.

In fact, lineages were the major social units in this part of Africa. Most societies in Guinea were made up of people who lived in towns and supported themselves primarily through farming. Usually, most of the people in a town in Guinea belonged to the same lineage. Even in larger urban areas, people probably lived close to their families, since the lineage provided them with social support when they needed it.

For spiritual support, the people of Guinea relied on religious beliefs that varied considerably from one group to another. Generally their beliefs included a Supreme Being who created other, lesser gods or spirits. These spirits inhabited everything, from animals to trees and stones. The people of Guinea believed that humans, too, were living spirits both before and after death. In short, the world was full of spirits of all kinds. Like Native Americans and Europeans, Africans believed that the goodwill of more-than-human forces must be won through prayer and ceremony.

A Golden Empire South of the Sahara Beyond the coastal forests, in the grasslands south of the Sahara, lay another area of African trade in the late 1400s. Called **Songhai,** it was one of the largest empires in the world at the time. Its capital city alone, Tombouctou, had a population of some 100,000. Leo Africanus, an African who visited Songhai at this time, enthused about its trading power, saying, "It is a wonder to see what plentie of Merchandize is daily brought hither and how costly and sumptious all things be."

Songhai's traders obtained goods such as gold and ivory from the forest kingdoms. The forests also supplied another popular trade item, kola nuts, used to flavor a beverage that was the first version of the colas people drink today. The traders carried these goods north across Songhai, paying heavy fees to Songhai's ruler, and then on across the Sahara in caravans of as many as 12,000 camels. On their return trip from North Africa, Songhai's traders brought salt, weapons, cloth, horses, books, and paper. The books were often destined for Tombouctou, with its world-renowned university and some 150 schools, or for the other cities of Songhai that boasted university centers— Gao, Walata, and Jenné.

The person who profited most from this trade was Askia Muhammad, the ruler of Songhai. To rule over his domain, which extended over much of western Africa, Askia directed a highly developed system of paid officials. This hierarchy made the organization of Songhai society similar to that in Europe but unlike the family-centered Native Americans. Askia's officials administered laws, kept the peace, collected taxes, and monitored

The Oba, attended by servants holding symbols of power, is offered trade goods by Portuguese traders (background) in a bronze plaque of the 1500s.

The Baule people of West Africa made this pendant, over three inches long, from the gold for which their region was well known.

3. ASSESS

Section 1 Review Answers

1. (a) kinship network, see p. 17, (b) clan, see p. 18, (c) hierarchy, see p. 19, (d) patriarchal society, see p. 19, (e) lineage, see p. 21

2. (a) Guinea, see p. 21, (b) Songhai, see p. 21

3. To gain items they needed or wanted and to demonstrate hospitality and friendliness.

4. Competition for trade grew more intense in Europe, with pressure for new markets and new products.

5. The Oba of Benin directed war, agriculture, and trade through administrators; Benin merchants traded farm products, works of art, and goods forged from African iron, creating wealth that supported the large capital city of Benin.

6. Answers will vary but may include the following: Who handles interaction between the household and others? Are there specific areas in which the husband makes all decisions and others in which the wife makes all decisions? Who manages money? Who owns or rents the household's land?

Reteach

Have students write the headings Native Americans, Europeans, and West Africans on a piece of paper. Ask them to write details under each heading to support the statement that these groups had a long history of their own before they began to interact with one another in the late 1400s.

4. CLOSE

Reinforcing the Big Idea

In spite of the many similarities among these cultures, as stated in the text, "certain differences among them would later lead to a violent clash of values." The next section describes how the three lands on the Atlantic interacted to form the Atlantic World.

An engraving from the 1800s captures a moment repeated countless times through the centuries: a caravan arrives at the city of Tombouctou.

diplomatic exchanges with other nations of the world. Under Askia's direction, they ran a sophisticated banking system. They also oversaw great royal estates that produced food or manufactured goods.

Slavery in Africa As in some parts of Europe and North America, a more grim item of trade than food and goods could be found in Africa as well. This was human life—in the form of people kidnapped from one region of Africa to another and enslaved. In a sense, the entire trading system was built on enslaved people, not only because they were sold as goods themselves, but also because they produced or gathered many of the other goods that were exchanged,

from gold to kola nuts. They also carried goods through parts of West Africa where animals were not an effective means of transport.

In Africa, people who had been cut off from their lineage were the most likely to be enslaved. They included prisoners of war (probably the greatest source), orphans, criminals, or other people torn from their homes or rejected by society. Generally, slaves were adopted into existing kinship networks.

In their new lineages, enslaved people filled a wide variety of positions, playing a major role in African life. After the collision of the Atlantic cultures, they would also be forced to go to the Americas, where they would take part in creating the new societies that would someday arise there.

SECTION 1 REVIEW

Key Terms, People, and Places

1. Define (a) kinship network, (b) clan, (c) hierarchy, (d) patriarchal society, (e) lineage.

2. Identify (a) Guinea, (b) Songhai.

Key Concepts

3. Give two reasons Native Americans traded goods.

4. Why did Europe look overseas for trading opportunities in the 1400s?

5. Give evidence to show that Benin was a complex and wealthy kingdom.

Critical Thinking

6. Formulating Questions What questions would you have asked of an English couple in the 1400s to determine how well their household fit the patriarchal model?

▶ RESOURCE DIRECTORY

Teaching Resources

Quiz found in the Unit 1 folder, p. 8, covers the main ideas in this section as well as the key terms.

The Atlantic World Is Born

SECTION PREVIEW

The voyage of an Italian navigator was the prelude to centuries of trade and tragic conflict among Native Americans, Europeans, and Africans. In these years new societies would be built and old ones ruthlessly swept aside.

Key Concepts

• For Native Americans, one effect of contact with Europeans was death from disease.
• Europeans competed among themselves to settle and exploit the Americas.
• After interaction began among the Atlantic cultures, millions of West Africans were transported against their will to the Americas.

Key Terms, People, and Places

Atlantic World; Christopher Columbus

S hortly before sunrise on Friday, August 3, 1492, three ships set sail from the seaport of Palos, in the Spanish kingdom of Castile. Before the crews lay the ocean and a great enterprise—"the Enterprise of the Indies," as their commander called it—the challenge of finding a new route to the Indies, or Asia.

A Voyage of Encounter

The expedition was Spanish, but its commander, **Christopher Columbus,** was not. He had been born into a family of woolen weavers in Genoa, Italy. Stubborn and moody, he had devoted most of his forty-one years to mastering the craft of navigation and to dogging European monarchs to win financing for this very voyage.

Going West to Reach the East Not until January 1492 had Isabella, Queen of Castile, finally granted Columbus his wish. Dubbing him High Admiral of the Ocean Sea, Isabella autho-

rized him to make contact with the people of "the lands of India." As the admiral later explained, Isabella and her husband, King Ferdinand, had "ordained that [Columbus] should not go eastward by land in the usual manner but by the western way which no one about whom we have positive information has ever followed."

Columbus knew that the earth was a sphere. As daunting as the trip was, he was not afraid of falling off the planet when he sailed westward, as later legend suggested. However, Columbus *was* gambling when he assumed he could reach the Indies, or Asia, by sailing west across the vast expanse of the ocean. It was a gamble he would have lost, because he had underestimated the size of the planet. The expedition had neither food nor water enough to sail all the way to Asia.

The Encounter Begins Fortunately for Columbus and his crew, in mid-October he encountered the islands of the Caribbean Sea and the Native Americans on them, the Tainos. The Tainos greeted the newcomers with gifts— much astonishing Columbus, who was not familiar with the Native American view of trade as an exchange of gifts. In 1493 Columbus wrote about the Tainos to Isabella and Ferdinand:

T hey are so ingenuous [innocent] and free with all they have, that no one would believe it who has not seen it; of anything that they possess, if it be asked of them, they never say no; on the contrary, they invite you to share it and show as much love as if their hearts went with it.

Technology developed for long sea voyages, like this compass of 1580, guided Columbus west across the uncharted Atlantic Ocean.

Discuss

Remind students that the creation of the Atlantic World was based on elements from each of the three interacting cultures—Native American, European, and West African. Ask them to describe the contributions of each culture to the interchange.

Discuss with students the ways in which disease and technology allowed Europeans to dominate the interaction. Ask why the Europeans wanted to conquer the Americas.

Activity

Conducting a Debate

Divide the class into groups to debate the following proposition: Resolved, that the most important result of the development of the Atlantic World was the enrichment of the European economy. Allow students to work in groups to brainstorm and list reasons that either support or refute the proposition. Have one volunteer from each group present the group's position.

Answer to ...

MAKING   CONNECTIONS

Answers may vary but should suggest that the Atlantic World has been subsumed by a larger "Global World." This question prepares students to consider the features of the Atlantic World that can now be seen in the "Global World," including the continued clash of cultures, transmission of disease, exchange of goods through trade, and mixing of populations.

Whales and flying fish, suggesting the hazards of the Atlantic, alarm the crew of a lively Portuguese caravel in this painting from 1594.

Columbus's voyage was significant because it was one of encounter, not discovery. After all, the Americas had long since been discovered by others, the Native Americans. Centuries earlier, other little-known explorers had also found their way across the waters to the Americas and had even settled there.

But with Columbus's crossing in 1492, a regular, permanent exchange began among the people of the Americas, Africa, and Europe, involving goods and people, ideas and diseases. This exchange brought into existence a world of encounter—the **Atlantic World.**

MAKING   CONNECTIONS

Is it still accurate to speak of an Atlantic World today? Why or why not?

The Impact of the Encounter on the Native Americans: Disease

For the people of the early Atlantic World—whether Native Americans, Europeans, or Africans—life expectancy was much lower than it is today. In their era, minor illnesses or wounds could suddenly become fatal due to poor hygiene and medical practices. Exchange across the Atlantic only made this problem worse, for it brought together people who had been isolated from one another and had no resistance to one another's diseases.

Diseases Struck Native Americans Europeans had already experienced a severe decline in their population due to plague and other diseases. They brought a similar disaster with them when they arrived on the American continents. Passing germs through even the most casual contact, explorers and soldiers infected Native Americans with smallpox, typhus, measles, and other deadly diseases.

The Effects of Disease Once Europeans reached the Americas, disease spread ahead of them, carried by the extensive Native American trading system. Inca Garcilaso, the son of a Native American woman and a Spanish captain, described what explorers found in 1540 when they first reached Talomeca, a town of the Creek Native American group in what is now Georgia. It had five hundred houses, a temple with eight separate halls, and was ringed with outlying towns—all vacant. Garcilaso explained:

The Castilians found the town of Talomeco without any people at all, because the recent pestilence [disease] had raged with more virulence [strength] and cruelty in this town than in any other of the entire province. [Near] the rich temple, it is said they found four longhouses filled with bodies from the plague.

As people of European descent pushed westward across the North American continent over the next three hundred years, the diseases they brought repeatedly ravaged Native Americans.

The Impact of the Encounter on Europeans: Struggle and Exchange

"God saw fit to send the Indians smallpox," said one European about 1525. The diseases that struck Native Americans seemed to some Europeans to be a sign that God intended Europeans to conquer the Americas. And conquest was exactly what Europeans planned, for

three reasons. The first was to obtain land, which was scarce in Europe. The second was to convert the vast natural resources of the Americas into goods that could be traded. The third reason was to "bring to the worship of [Christ] and the profession of the Catholic faith [the] residents and inhabitants" of the Americas, in the words of Pope Alexander VI in 1493.

Competing for Empire At the urging of Pope Alexander, in 1494 Portugal and Spain agreed to the Treaty of Tordesillas. Under the treaty, any lands not already claimed by other Christians would be divided between the two countries by an invisible line around the world. Spain was assigned rule over what lay west of the line, including most of the Americas. Portugal was left with control over the rest, including Brazil and its route around Africa.

For centuries, Spain and Portugal were able to control and exploit much of the regions they claimed. Soon, however, the people of other nations grew eager for their share of the wealth. France, England, and the Netherlands began to move into North America in the 1500s and 1600s (see Section 3). Although these nations fought bitterly among themselves for control of

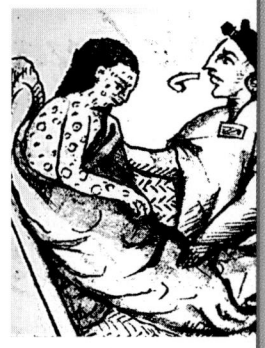

A Native American in Mexico drew this picture of a victim of smallpox comforted by a healer. The squiggle symbolizes spoken words.

| 1650 | 1700 | 1750 | 1800 | | | 1850 | 1900 | 1950 | 2000 |

Links Across Time

Navigating the Ocean

Early sailors sighted the sun on an astrolabe to find their latitude (above). Today they rely on a geopositioning instrument that reads signals from satellites to give a ship's position by night or day (left). *What advantage does the new technology offer?*

Enrichment

Ask students to research some of the celebrations and demonstrations held to mark the five-hundredth anniversary of Columbus's first voyage to the Americas. Students may write plans to mark a future anniversary in a way they find appropriate. See Viewpoints on page 27.

Answer to ...

Links Across Time

It allows sailors to find their position even if the sun is not visible.

In Depth

Historical Misconceptions

Educated Europeans in the 1400s accepted the estimates of Eratosthenes that put the circumference of the earth at what we would calculate today as 25,000 miles. The danger in sailing west, they believed, was not falling off the edge of the world but having to sail too long without fresh water and food before reaching Asia. Columbus took a calculated risk because he believed the less accurate figures of the ancient Egyptian Ptolemy, who estimated the world to be only 18,000 miles around. When Columbus found land, therefore, he believed that the islands of the West Indies lay off the coast of Asia. He died without understanding that he had encountered an entirely separate landmass.

Section 2 Review Answers

1. Atlantic World, see p. 24

2. Christopher Columbus, see p. 23

3. European disease caused a severe decline in Native American population similar to the decline that had previously occurred in Europe.

4. Contact with the Americas resulted in a struggle among European powers for control of Native American lands. It encouraged Europeans' belief that their culture was superior to any in the world. The potato put an end to repeated famine in Europe, and gold and silver from the Americas made Europe's economy the richest on earth.

5. The slave trade brought millions of West Africans as enslaved people to the Americas. It also caused disturbances in West African society, including the destruction of some groups and wars in which new empires rose and old ones fell.

6. Students should point out that the Americas had already been discovered by Native Americans tens of thousands of years before the arrival of Columbus. He, however, began the permanent contact between Europe and the Americas; in that sense he can be said to have "discovered" the Americas for Europeans.

In Depth

Multicultural Perspectives

Muslim scholars made significant contributions in the sciences. Until the seventeenth century, Arab textbooks on diseases were considered the best in their fields. Muslims established one of the first systems of medical training, including exams for doctors and pharmacists. Muslim scientists made important advances in chemistry. They invented the beakers and crystallizing dishes still used in laboratories today.

Native American lands, on the whole they felt confirmed in the certainty that European culture was superior to any in the world, and that Europeans were meant to rule all others.

The Exchange of Cultures The culture that Europeans brought to the Americas included languages, laws, and customs. Europeans also introduced crops, such as wheat, and domesticated animals, such as the cow and the horse. The settlers who followed the conquerors brought with them European technologies, including the firearm and the wheel.

But exchange across the Atlantic was not one-sided, as the chart below shows. One American plant, the potato, quickly became the

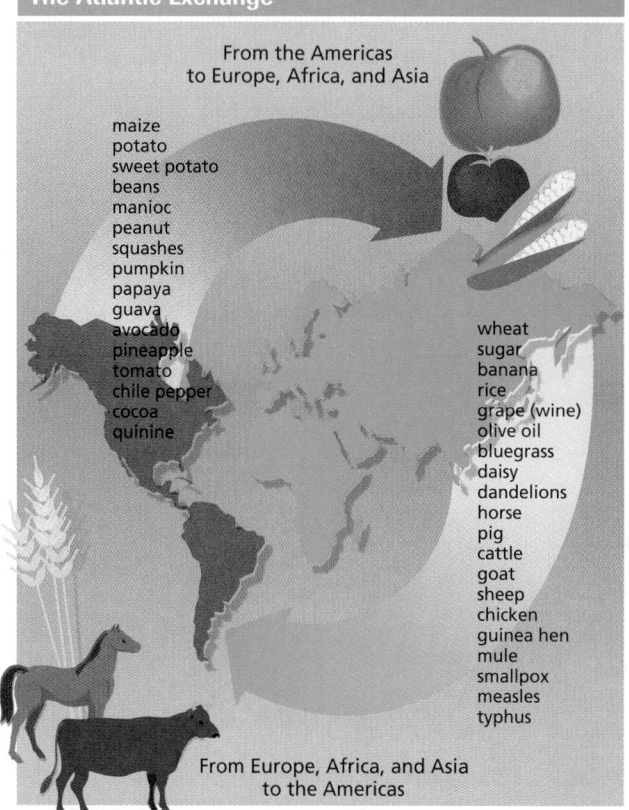

The Atlantic Exchange

From the Americas to Europe, Africa, and Asia

maize
potato
sweet potato
beans
manioc
peanut
squashes
pumpkin
papaya
guava
avocado
pineapple
tomato
chile pepper
cocoa
quinine

wheat
sugar
banana
rice
grape (wine)
olive oil
bluegrass
daisy
dandelions
horse
pig
cattle
goat
sheep
chicken
guinea hen
mule
smallpox
measles
typhus

From Europe, Africa, and Asia to the Americas

 **Interpreting Charts**
Exchanges across the Atlantic went both ways and included valued crops, domesticated animals, and diseases. *In which direction did the listed diseases move?*

new food of the poor in Europe, bringing an end to the repeated famines Europe had suffered. Another, manioc, became the chief food throughout much of Africa.

Europe's wealthy also benefited from the exchange. In the first century after Columbus's voyage, the amount of gold and silver in Europe's economy increased eight times over, boosted by ore from the mines of the Americas. This new wealth ignited Europe's economy and quickly made it the richest on earth. ★

The Impact of the Encounter on Africans: Slavery

When Europeans began to exploit the natural resources of the Americas, they found they needed a large amount of labor to do so. They turned to West Africa to supply it, and West Africans soon were swept into their own encounter with the Americas, suffering violence and displacement for centuries after Columbus's voyage.

The Independence of West Africa Regular interaction between Europeans and Africans had begun even before the voyage of Columbus. Throughout the late 1400s, the Portuguese had been moving down the African coast in search of new markets. They found that from Songhai to the forest kingdoms, West Africans had a well developed economy, and could control European trade within their countries. Furthermore, the Africans were able to defeat virtually all European efforts to conquer them, both then and over the next four centuries.

As time went on, Europeans realized that although they could not seize the land of Africa, they could seize another valuable resource—the West Africans themselves. Settlers in the Americas were beginning to grow crops such as sugar and tobacco to send to Europe. European slave traders supplied the labor needed on large farms by tapping into the existing West African slave trade.

As early as the 1400s, Europeans took up stations on the West African coast. To these outposts European governments and trading companies shipped various goods to be exchanged for enslaved people.

▶ RESOURCE DIRECTORY

Teaching Resources

★ **Primary Source Activity** Europeans Encounter Native Americans, found in the Unit 1 folder, p. 24, contrasts the views of Christopher Columbus with those of Spanish nobleman Juan Gines de Sepulveda to illustrate the thinking of the day.

The Growth of the Slave Trade Facts and figures on the impact of slavery on West Africa remain a matter of controversy. Some researchers estimate that during the 1500s some 275,000 West Africans were transported involuntarily across the Atlantic Ocean. By contrast, they say, the 1700s saw 6,050,000 transported. Estimates of the total number of West Africans abducted from their homeland and taken to North and South America range from 9,300,000 to 11,500,000 or more. The removal of such a huge number of people over several centuries seriously affected some African societies. The Aja-speaking people in Guinea, for example, were completely destroyed. Europeans also set in motion grim wars between African societies to obtain slaves to sell. New empires equipped with guns sprang up and overran the old kingdoms.

Mere numbers, however, cannot portray the full horror of slavery for West Africans. Slavery had existed in Africa before the encounter of the Atlantic cultures, but Europeans gave it a very different face in the Americas. African slavery was based on the belief that people who had been enslaved were inferior to their masters because they were not connected with their master's lineage. Among Africans (and Native Americans), captives taken in war might later be adopted into a lineage and regain at least some freedom. Such adoption shows that the basic humanity of enslaved people was recognized in Africa. In the Americas, European masters believed that enslaved people were inferior simply because they were of a different race. Because slavery was based on race, enslavement in the Americas usually offered enslaved people no hope of regaining

their freedom. Thus their masters forever denied that enslaved people were humans, with desires and dreams of their own.

In the aftermath of the encounter across the Atlantic Ocean, vast changes tested the ways of life and the values of people on four continents. Out of that collision the society of the United States would eventually emerge—a society still struggling to understand cultural differences that had their origin on separate continents hundreds of years ago.

Viewpoints
On Celebrating Columbus Day

The five-hundredth anniversary of Columbus's voyage to the Americas inspired a spirited debate over whether a celebration was appropriate to mark the event. *What broader issue, other than the celebration of Columbus Day, is revealed in the viewpoints below?*

For a Celebration of Columbus Day

"Celebrate Columbus? Not if that simply means backslapping and flag waving. But it can mean more: taking stock of the long, fascinating record, noting that inevitable conflict resulted in losers as well as winners and produced a mixture of races, customs, and habits never before seen in the world."

Journalist Paul Gray, *Time*, October 7, 1991

Against a Celebration of Columbus Day

"Yes, Christopher Columbus was the first European to sail to America in recorded history. But Columbus set into motion a sequence of greed, cruelty, slavery and genocide that, even in the bloody history of mankind, has few parallels. He organized an extermination of Native Americans."

Essayist Hans Koning, *The New York Times*, August 14, 1990

SECTION 2 REVIEW

Key Terms, People, and Places
1. Define Atlantic World.
2. Identify Christopher Columbus.

Key Concepts
3. How did European disease affect Native Americans?
4. What changes did contact with the Americas bring to Europe?

5. What effect did the Atlantic slave trade have on West Africans?

Critical Thinking
6. **Distinguishing False from Accurate Images** Is it true or false to say that Columbus discovered the Americas? Explain your answer.

 Viewpoints Activity On Celebrating Columbus Day, found in the Unit 1 folder, pp. 20–21, provides additional viewpoints and perspectives on Christopher Columbus and the spirit of the times.

Quiz found in the Unit 1 folder, p. 10, covers the main ideas in this section as well as the key terms.

Media and Technology

Transparencies
American Photo, B-1; Political Cartoons, K-1

Answer to ...

Viewpoints

Both viewpoints recognize the broader issue of the impact of European exploration and settlement on both Europeans and the peoples of the Americas. For a more thorough examination of the controversy surrounding Columbus Day, see the Resource Directory below.

Caption Answer to ...

 Interpreting Charts

(See page 26) Toward the Americas.

Reteach

Ask students to either trace an outline map of the world or use an existing one to draw lines representing the major interactions among the cultures of the Atlantic World. Have them use symbols to show the major items that were interchanged: disease; foodstuffs and cash crops; slaves; gold and silver.

 Alternative Assessment

Mid-Point Monitoring
Ask students if they have
• Decided on the format of their travel accounts
• Begun their outside research
• Started drafting portions of their accounts

 **Reinforcing the Big Idea**

Interactions among the diverse cultures of Native Americans, Europeans, and West Africans began the creation of the Atlantic World. The three cultures that formed the Atlantic World had much in common, but they were also differentiated by features that would lead to lasting conflict among them. The next section focuses on the conflict between Europeans and Native Americans.

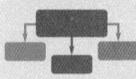

1. FOCUS

Connecting to the Big Idea

See page 14B. Point out that in the wake of the Atlantic World's creation, Spanish, English, French, and Dutch colonists all established settlements in what is now the United States. Ask students how each of these groups interacted with the Native Americans in the territories they claimed.

Objectives

● Describe Native American resistance to the Spanish in New Mexico and Florida and describe how the Spanish settlement pattern changed in response to it.
● Explain the effect of Native American resistance on English settlement.
● Demonstrate that the French and Dutch colonies were based on trade with Native Americans but that the English in New England tried to replace Native American culture with their own.

Bellringer

Ask students to consider what might happen if a new teacher took over their history class at mid-semester, abandoning all the things they liked about the class and establishing expectations and evaluations totally unfamiliar to them.

Reading Strategy

Problem Solving Ask students to imagine that it is the mid-1600s and that they are coming from abroad to settle in a colony in North America. Which colony would they choose? Ask students to pose questions about the colonies and to look for answers to them as they read the section.

European Settlement and Native American Resistance

SECTION PREVIEW

After 1492, the Spanish, English, French, and Dutch invaded the Americas, devising various ways to exploit its natural wealth. Meanwhile, Native Americans fought against them, determined to preserve their way of life.

Key Concepts

• Native Americans experienced some success in slowing the Spanish invasion of New Mexico.
• The Native Americans of the Chesapeake Bay area resisted English settlement during the 1600s, but were sharply reduced in number.
• The French and Dutch colonies in the Northeast were based on mutual trade with Native American groups, but in New England the English fought to replace the Native American way of life with their own.

A silent witness to the Spanish attempt to conquer Florida, this soldier's helmet was lost in the 1500s at Palm Beach and discovered in recent times.

Key Terms, People, and Places

conquistador, *encomienda* system, colony, presidio, *congregacion*, indentured servant, Reformation, religious toleration; Popé, Powhatan, Puritans, Metacom

---

A fter the American, European, and African cultures collided in the 1400s, the Spanish were the first to invade the Americas. They had three reasons for conquest: to spread the Christian religion, to gain wealth, and to win fame or improved social standing. In short, they fought for God, gold, and glory—and perhaps the love of gold most of all. The thirty-four-year-old Hernán Cortés, one of the **conquistadores,** as the Spanish conquerors were

called, spoke for many when he said in 1519: "I and my companions suffer from a disease of the heart which can be cured only by gold."

The Spanish Settle in the Americas

The Spanish conquistadores ruthlessly destroyed much of the culture they found in the Americas. They did not try to replace it completely, however, by driving out the Native Americans. Instead, they attempted to force Native Americans into Spanish culture. One method the Spanish employed to accomplish this was known as the *encomienda* **system.** Under this system, Native Americans were required to farm, ranch, or mine for the profit of an individual Spaniard. In return, the Spaniard was supposed to see to their wellbeing. The *encomienda* system was a version of the social system of Europe, where the wealthy controlled land worked by the poor.

By the 1550s, the Spanish had numerous well-established **colonies.** Colonies are areas settled by immigrants who continue to be the subjects of their parent country. These Spanish colonies formed a large empire on the islands of the Caribbean Sea, and in Mexico, Central America, and South America. In order to protect the colonies, the Spanish built defensive bases in Florida—for instance, at St. Augustine—and in what they called New Mexico. (Spanish New Mexico included parts of what is now Arizona and Texas. See the map on page 29.)

The settlements that dotted the south and west of the land that is now part of the United States were really just **presidios,** or forts, manned by a few soldiers. But the survival of these Spanish outposts was due not to the soldiers, but to the faith of a few dozen Franciscans. These priests, members of a Catholic order dedicated to the work of St. Francis of Assisi, settled

---

▶ RESOURCE DIRECTORY

Teaching Resources

Reproducible Lesson Plan found in the Unit 1 folder, p. 5, provides a summary of the Section 3 lesson plan content.

Alternate Lesson Plan: Cooperative Learning found in the Alternate Lesson Plans folder, p. 52, is designed to help groups of students to examine and describe Native American resistance to the Spanish.

Guided Reading and Review found in the Unit 1 folder, p. 11, provides a structure for reading and mastering the key concepts and reviewing the key terms for Section 3. (Guided Practice)

American Profiles Activity Popé, Medicine Man of the Pueblos, found in the Unit 1 folder, p. 18, profiles the charismatic man who united the Pueblo and eventually organized a successful revolt against the Spanish.

Geography and History: Interpreting Maps
An adviser to the Spanish king in the 1500s remarked: "It is towards the south, not towards the frozen north, that those who seek their fortune should bend their way; for everything at the equator is rich." *Cite evidence from the map to show that Spanish settlers followed this policy.*

throughout Florida and New Mexico. They established dozens of missions—headquarters for their work of converting Native Americans to Christianity. With the help of soldiers, the priests forced the Native Americans into settled villages called *congregacions,* where they were made to farm and worship like Catholic Europeans.

MAKING CONNECTIONS

The Spanish combined force and persuasion to settle Native Americans in *congregacions.* How would you expect the Native Americans to react?

Native American Resistance to the Spanish

Fighting by Native Americans against the Spanish was generally disorganized. But in New Mexico, following years of drought that weakened Spanish power, the Pueblo people united and expelled the Spanish in what is called the Revolt of 1680.

The Background of the Revolt The Spanish had established outposts along the Rio Grande, including a capital at Santa Fe in 1610. By the 1670s, widespread sickness and drought had reduced the Pueblo population to 17,000 people. Seeking to reverse this decline, the Pueblo began to turn back to their traditional religious practices, which the Spanish denounced as witchcraft and tried to stamp out. Then a brilliant medicine man named **Popé** rallied the disheartened Pueblos and some Apaches. Popé blamed the Spanish for all the Native Americans' miseries. One Pueblo witness, Jeronimo, later reported Popé's claim that when the Europeans were gone, the Pueblo

Media and Technology

 Transparency
Cause and Effect, F-1

Explain/Discuss

Remind students that European Christians thought it was their duty to spread their religion throughout the world. Discuss how this belief affected the dealings of different European colonists with Native Americans. Ask students how the Spanish pattern of conquest compared with that pursued by the English.

Analyze

Analyze the role of geography in the European settlement of North America. Why did the different groups settle where they did?

Answer to ...

MAKING CONNECTIONS

Answers should suggest that Native Americans would most likely resist the imposition of Spanish culture in the move to *congregacións.*

Caption Answer to ...

 Interpreting Maps

No settlement shown is farther north than about 35° north latitude.

In Depth

Interdisciplinary

The economic system set up by the Spanish in Latin America—the *encomienda* system—was based on the labor of a specific population and depended upon nearly absolute control of that labor. The *encomienda* system enslaved the native peoples until most had died of disease or ill treatment. Examples of similar systems include the plantation system of the American South before the Civil War.

Activity

(The clock icon indicates an activity that can be successfully conducted within a class period. Each chapter has at least one such activity.)

Conducting an Interview

Ask students to stage a panel interview with Native American leaders Popé, Powhatan, and Metacom. Each student should prepare one question for each leader about his interaction with colonists. Have volunteers then take turns answering in the roles of these leaders.

In Depth

Did You Know?

John Smith's iron will and his ability to make friends with the Native Americans were crucial to the success of the small Jamestown settlement. According to legend, Smith was saved from execution at the hands of Powhatan's warriors by the chief's young daughter, Pocahontas. She also brought food to the hungry settlers and was, according to Smith, "the instrument to preserve this Colony from death, famine, and utter confusion." Later, Pocahontas married settler John Rolfe, and the two of them took Virginia's first tobacco crop to London.

---

would gather large crops of grain, maize [corn] with large and thick ears, many bundles of cotton, many calabashes [squash] and watermelons.

The Revolt Drives Out the Spanish In August 1680, the 2,350 Spaniards in New Mexico suddenly were confronted with a well-coordinated revolt by more than 8,000 warriors. The Native Americans killed 375 colonists and 21 of 33 priests outright, destroyed missions, and drove the Spanish out of Santa Fe. By early September, when the surviving Spanish gathered near El Paso, they numbered around 1,500.

It took the Spanish years to reestablish themselves along the Rio Grande. They did not retake Santa Fe until 1696. During this time, however, the Pueblo still declined rapidly in number, under increasing attack by the neighboring Apache and Navaho people. By 1706 the Pueblo population had shrunk to only 9,000. In the 1700s they accepted Spanish rule to gain protection.

In forming this new connection, however, both sides compromised. The Pueblo became Catholics who continued to practice traditional rituals. They acknowledged Spanish authority, but governed their own local affairs. The *encomienda* system was abolished altogether. Ultimately, the Spanish and Pueblo forged a new bond in which their dependence on each other overcame mutual distrust.

The Jamestown Settlement

The English arrived in the Americas with an attitude toward conquered peoples that was even more harsh than that of the Spanish. Believing it was best to remake completely any culture they conquered, they did not practice the forced blending of European and Native American societies that was taking place in the Spanish colonies. For the English, conquest would be all—or nothing.

A Colony near the Chesapeake Bay In 1607 the English established their first successful settlement, Jamestown, about 60 miles from the mouth of the James River in the Chesapeake Bay region, in a colony they called Virginia. Unfortunately, the site they chose was a mosquito-infested swamp, and the settlement was very nearly a complete disaster. In its first decade, disease and starvation were common; the settlers even resorted to cannibalism. By 1624, of the approximately 6,000 Europeans who had migrated to Virginia over the preceding sixteen years, only about 1,300 remained alive.

Native American Reaction The Native Americans in the Chesapeake region, who numbered about 8,000, did not stand by idly while foreigners invaded their land. Shortly after the arrival of the English, about 200 Native Americans attacked. Only an English cannon forced them to retreat.

The leader of the Native Americans in the region, **Powhatan,** had every reason to distrust the settlers' intentions. The Spanish had captured his brother, Opechancanough, in the 1560s. Opechancanough had visited Spain twice, lived for a time in the capital of Spanish Mexico, and accompanied Spanish expeditions to the Chesapeake area. In 1570 he returned to his own people. During his years with the Spanish, Opechancanough came to know and despise the goals of European settlers—which included exploiting the labor of the Native Americans and the natural wealth of their land.

In spite of initial conflicts and continuing mutual suspicion, an uneasy peace was eventually established between the Native Americans and the English. Both sides tried to keep this peace. In fact, during the times of the settlers' worst problems, the Native Americans saved the newcomers by supplying them with food and fresh water. But in March 1622, relations between the two peoples broke down altogether. At that time Opechancanough planned and led a brilliantly coordinated surprise attack on Jamestown. It was only partially successful. Still, 347 of the English lost their lives—more than 10 percent of the population of the settlement at that time. Within days, the settlers killed as many or more Native Americans in retaliation.

Powhatan's people mounted their last major act of armed resistance against the English in the Chesapeake area in 1644. It failed. During the attack, Opechancanough, still active and defiant at nearly 100 years of age, was shot through the back in the streets of Jamestown.

RESOURCE DIRECTORY

Teaching Resources

Literature Activity "The Fate of an Indentured Servant," found in the Unit 1 folder, p. 28, uses Englishman James Revel's poem to illustrate the harsh life of indentured servitude.

Two years later, the Native Americans agreed to make a regular payment to the English in return for a guarantee of some land. By 1669, however, there were only 2,000 Native Americans left in the Chesapeake region.

The Tobacco Colony

During the early years of their settlement, only one thing saved the Virginia colonists from failing altogether: growing tobacco for sale. In 1616, Virginians sent 2,500 pounds of the weed to England; by 1640, Virginia and its neighboring colony Maryland, which had been established in 1632, were sending home 3 million pounds a year.

 To produce tobacco, planters needed people to work the fields. During the first sixty years after the founding of the colony, they turned primarily to **indentured servants** from England. These were people who had to work for a master for a period of time, usually seven years, under a contract called an indenture. In return for their work, their master paid the cost of their voyage to Virginia and gave them food and shelter. Some indentures promised a piece of land to the servant at the end of the indenture period. Historians estimate that between 100,000 and 150,000 men and women came as servants to work in the fields of Virginia and Maryland during the 1600s. Most of them were eighteen to twenty-two years of age, unmarried, and poor.

Few of the indentured servants lived long enough to claim their land at the end of their service. Exposure to the climate and diseases of the Chesapeake Bay killed them in horrendous numbers. Just as discouraging was the fact that it became harder to make a fortune after the first years of the tobacco boom. Early and wealthy settlers had taken the most fertile and easily accessible land. Driven by this land shortage, in 1676 a man named Nathaniel Bacon raised an unauthorized force of planters and indentured servants to drive the Native Americans farther west. His action quickly evolved into a rebellion against the established government, and was put down forcefully.

After Bacon's Rebellion, those in power saw that they needed a more controllable source of labor. Accordingly they began to buy enslaved West Africans brought across the Atlantic Ocean by slave traders. As discussed in Section 4, these enslaved Africans had a major effect on the culture and economy of the Southern Colonies, beginning in the 1700s.

Europeans and Native Americans in the Northeast

In 1608 a French explorer, Samuel de Champlain, founded the town of Quebec on the St. Lawrence River in what is now Canada. Perched on heights above a narrow stretch of the river, Quebec was a prime location for a trading settlement. Similarly, the Dutch—people from the Netherlands—established New Amsterdam

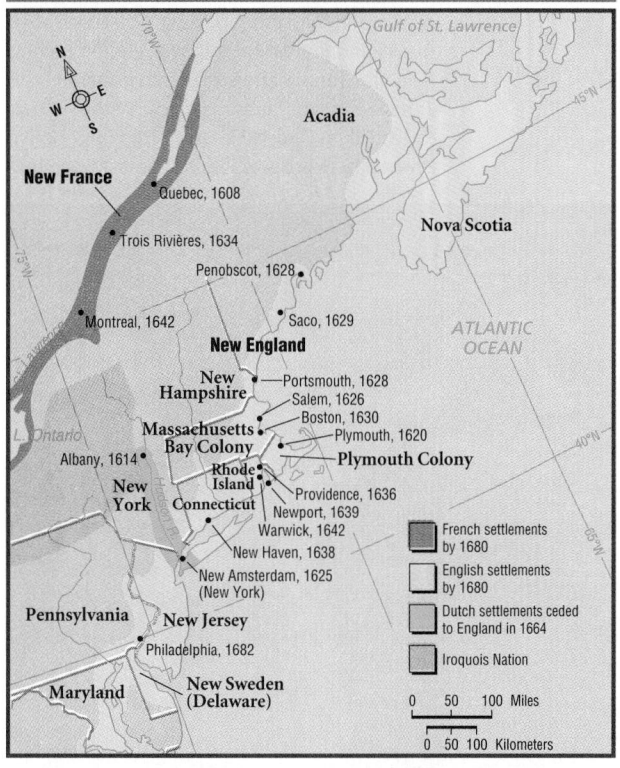

Northeast and Middle Colonies Before 1680

French settlements by 1680

English settlements by 1680

Dutch settlements ceded to England in 1664

Iroquois Nation

 Geography and History: Interpreting Maps
Native Americans and Europeans quickly became dependent upon one another. While Native Americans controlled vast stretches of woodland, European settlement was at first limited to coastal and river areas. *How did the location of the Iroquois help make them powerful?*

Media and Technology

 **Visions of America: Turning Point Story** To enhance students' understanding of the Turning Point topic, play "Cultures Collide," a story about the contemporary resonances of King Philip's War (length: approximately 4 minutes). This selection can be located on side 1 of the videodiscs. This selection can also be located on videotape 1. Lesson plans for Turning Point stories can be found in the Visions of America Teacher's Guidebook.

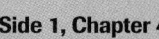
Side 1, Chapter 3

 **Visions of America: Roundtable Discussion** To introduce students to different and differing viewpoints on the Turning Point topic, play all or part of the Roundtable Discussion on "Cultures Collide," remarks by respected historians and social commentators. This selection can be found on side 1 of the videodiscs. This selection can also be located on videotape 1.

Side 1, Chapter 4

Enrichment

Ask students to research and report on the Iroquois League, or Iroquois Confederacy, specifically its origin and effect on Iroquois life.

Caption Answer to ...

Interpreting Maps

Controlling the land immediately adjacent to French, Dutch, and English settlement areas, the Iroquois acted as a strategic buffer between one and the others.

In Depth

Biography

Jacques Marquette (1637–1675) was sent to the French colonies in North America by the Jesuits. He befriended the Native Americans with whom he lived and quickly learned several of their languages. In 1672, Marquette joined fur trader Louis Jolliet and five traders in mapping a route down the Wisconsin River to the Mississippi River. Marquette and Jolliet sought precious metals as well as a water passage to the Pacific Ocean. When Native Americans told them that the Mississippi emptied into the Gulf of Mexico, not to the west or to the east, they returned north. Marquette and Jolliet are believed to have been the first Europeans to explore the upper Mississippi and parts of Illinois and Wisconsin.

Section 3 Review Answers

1. (a) conquistador, see p. 28,
(b) *encomienda* system, see p. 28,
(c) colony, see p. 28, (d) presidio, see
p. 28, (e) *congregación*, see p. 29,
(f) indentured servant, see p. 31,
(g) Reformation, see p. 32, (h) religious
toleration, see p. 33

2. (a) Popé, see p. 29, (b) Powhatan, see
p. 30, (c) Puritans, see p. 33, (d) Metacom, see p. 33

3. The Native Americans adopted only
those parts of Christianity they chose,
and then only on their own terms. In
New Mexico they gathered forces and
expelled the Spanish and their religion.

4. They responded initially by attacking
the settlers. After an uneasy and temporary peace, Powhatan's people mounted
their last major act of armed resistance
against the English in the Chesapeake
in 1644.

5. The French and Dutch were involved
in the fur trade, which depended on
maintaining ties with the Native Americans and did not interfere with Native
Americans' traditional use of land. The
English did not see Native Americans as
partners but rather as a hindrance to
their goal of establishing agricultural
colonies, thus leading to discord and
conflict between them.

6. Answers may suggest that Europeans
primarily expected wealth from their
settlements in North America. Many
also moved to North America to spread
the Christian religion or to escape poor
economic conditions in Europe.

Caption Answer to ...

Using Historical Evidence

Well-made and elaborate clothing;
accessories, such as the cane and
jewelry.

(now New York City) in 1626 to control trade along the Hudson River. Later, Fort Orange (Albany), founded in 1624, became the center of their trade with the Native Americans.

The Fur Trade Both the French and the Dutch traded knives, beads, and guns for furs that could be sold in Europe. These furs were to the French what tobacco was to the English in Virginia and Maryland. As the Dutchman Adriaen Van der Donck noted in 1655,

> The Indians, without our labour or
> trouble, bring to us their fur trade,
> worth tons of gold, which may be
> increased, and is like goods found.

Unlike tobacco growing, the fur trade did not require elaborate farms or towns. Rather, it depended on forming trading ties with Native American hunters and trappers, and on leaving alone the forests and streams that formed the animals' natural habitats. Because the French depended on Native American trapping, Native Americans in areas of French contact remained

Using Historical Evidence David, Joanna, and Abigail Mason posed for this portrait about 1670. Like other Puritan children, they could expect to live twice as long as children in colonies where life was harder. *What evidence of prosperity do you see in this painting?*

---

more powerful than those in Virginia. Yet they were greatly weakened by disease and by wars they fought to control the fur hunting grounds.

One group, the Iroquois, was particularly successful at both war and trade. In the mid- to late 1600s, the Iroquois engaged in a series of struggles called the Beaver Wars, in which they pushed the Hurons and other Native American groups out of their homelands to an area west of the Great Lakes. The Iroquois occupied the area between the French to the north and the Dutch and the English to the east and south. The Iroquois were thus in a perfect position to tip the balance of power among European colonists in the Northeast. For instance, the Iroquois were allies of both the English and the Dutch even after 1633, when the English entered the region that is now Connecticut and New York and began to compete with the Dutch for control of the area. And the Iroquois retained their powerful position into the early 1700s, finding it easy to accept the transition when the English took over the Dutch colony of New Netherlands completely.

Puritans in New England In 1630, while the French and Dutch were building trade links with Native Americans, the Great Migration—a wave of English migration across the Atlantic Ocean—began to reach the shores of New England. Immigrants had come to New England before then—the most familiar today is the group known as the Pilgrims, who settled at Plymouth, Massachusetts, in 1620. The Pilgrims, however, numbered only 102 people when they landed. By contrast, a total of 1,000 settlers braved the Atlantic crossing in 1630 to found the new Massachusetts Bay Colony. By 1643 the colony's population had increased to 16,000 people living in twenty towns, including its capital, Boston.

The Great Migration had its origin in a major change in Christianity that began a century earlier. At that time a powerful religious movement, the **Reformation,** swept over Europe in a protest against what was seen as the corruption and inadequacy of the Catholic church. The Reformation gave birth to a new form of the Christian religion, known as Protestantism. In England, most of the population became members of a new Protestant national church, the Church of England.

RESOURCE DIRECTORY

Teaching Resources

Despite this change in the English church, some people still believed that its worship remained too similar to Roman Catholic worship. They wanted to "purify" the English church from within, and so they were called **Puritans.**

The term *Puritan* has come to be associated with cheerlessness and hypocritical morality. Contrary to this image, Puritans were people capable of affection and merriment as well as deep religious devotion. They did, however, insist that social order begins with personal order. Well-ordered families in well-ordered towns in well-ordered colonies: that was the Puritan ideal. Though the Puritans came from England to escape persecution, or harassment, for their beliefs, they themselves did not believe in the principle of **religious toleration**—the idea that people of different religions should live in peace. This would have run counter to their ideal of an ordered society, and to their belief that they alone possessed the truth. They punished dissidents—people who disagree with a political or religious system—by banishing or hanging them.

King Philip's War In order to create their dream of an ordered society, Puritans transformed the landscape of New England. They replaced forests with fields, cultivated wheat, barley, and corn, and raised domestic animals like cows and pigs rather than relying on wild deer or beaver. Their population grew rapidly: by the 1670s they totaled some 45,000 people living in about ninety towns. All of these changes threatened the livelihood of the Native American groups in the Northeast. Most of these people belonged to the Algonquian culture and lived by hunting game, gathering plants for food, and growing crops—a way of life that required sixteen to twenty times as much land per person as the way of life practiced by Puritan farmers.

"You know," recalled Miantonomo, leader of the Narraganset people, in 1642,

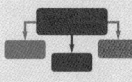

> Our fathers had plenty of deer and skins, our plains were full of deer, as also our woods, and of turkies, and our coves full of fish and fowl. But these English having gotten our land, they with scythes cut down the grass, and with axes fell the trees; their cows and horse eat the grass, and their hogs spoil our clam banks, and we shall be starved.

In the spring of 1675, the leader of the Wampanoag people, **Metacom**—also known by his English name, King Philip—could no longer bear seeing the newcomers destroy the world of his people. He rallied Native Americans throughout southern New England and defended the Native American way of life—much as the Pueblos were doing in the Southwest and Powhatan's people had done in the Virginia colony.

In proportion to the number of people involved and their possessions, no war in American history cost more in lives and property than King Philip's War, as the conflict was called. In the end, however, the Puritans won. With the final defeat of Metacom and his allies, the English conquest of New England was virtually complete.

Native Americans fought on both sides in the war that sprang up in 1675. This medal was presented to those who helped the English.

Reteach
List with students three problems faced by settlers of the Virginia colony in its early days. Ask students to review the section to find a cause for each of the problems and the ultimate resolution of the problem.

4. CLOSE

 Reinforcing the Big Idea

The European colonists who came to America in the 1600s brought with them different goals and methods with which they hoped to exploit the wealth of the continent. In doing so they all exploited the Native Americans in their colonies, who often fought against them as invaders. The next section discusses the life and culture of the developing English colonies.

SECTION 3 REVIEW

Key Terms, People, and Places

1. Define (a) conquistador, (b) *encomienda* system, (c) colony, (d) presidio, (e) *congregacion*, (f) indentured servant, (g) Reformation, (h) religious toleration.
2. Identify (a) Popé, (b) Powhatan, (c) Puritans, (d) Metacom.

Key Concepts

3. What was the effect of Native American resistance in New Mexico?

4. How did the Native Americans of the Chesapeake Bay area respond to invasion by the English?
5. How did the French and Dutch in the Northeast differ from the English in their relationship with Native Americans?

Critical Thinking

6. **Identifying Central Issues** North America was a difficult, dangerous place for both the Spanish and the English. Why did they want to move there?

Quiz found in the Unit 1 folder, pp. 12–13, covers the main ideas in this section as well as the key terms.

In Depth

Then and Now

By 1675, tuberculosis and smallpox had reduced the southern New England population of Native Americans to about 20,000, while approximately 50,000 settlers displaced them. This shift put the Native Americans at a disadvantage before King Philip's War had even begun, and one present-day writer regards King Philip's defeat as "America's first war of ethnic cleansing." Today there are approximately 12,000 Wampanoag living in Massachusetts, many on Cape Cod and on the Gay Head reservation on Martha's Vineyard.

The Decision to Use Enslaved Africans for Labor

Focus Few decisions have affected the history of the United States as completely as the decision to use enslaved Africans for labor in the Virginia Colony. This was not a decision made once by a central authority. In the late 1600s, individual planters in the Chesapeake Bay area chose to buy enslaved Africans. Their decisions contributed to a number of future events that shaped the country. This decision about labor changed the population and culture of the future United States and ultimately led the country into a civil war, a period of bitter Reconstruction, and an ongoing movement for civil rights that spread from African Americans to other groups in U.S. society. Students are asked to evaluate the decision to purchase enslaved Africans and to recognize some of the assumptions of the planters who made it.

Instruct Tell students that the first Africans in the Virginia Colony were treated as indentured servants, in part because they had Spanish names and were thought to have been baptized into Christianity.

Read aloud the following list of factors and ask students to indicate to what extent they think each added to the likelihood of establishing slavery:
- West Africans did not speak English.
- West Africans were immune to European diseases.
- West Africans could survive in semitropical climates.
- It cost less to purchase and support enslaved Africans than to bring indentured servants from England.
- American colonists did not respect Africans or their culture.

Ask students to explain their reasoning.

Extend You might ask students to propose alternatives to using enslaved Africans in the Virginia colony. What other crops might they have planted? What else could they have done with the land?

The Decision to Use Enslaved Africans for Labor

Time Frame:	Mid to late 1600s
Place:	The Chesapeake Bay area
Key People:	English gentlemen planters
Situation:	In the 1600s, planters in the Chesapeake Bay searched for a steady source of labor to work their fields. Their decision about where to obtain that labor would have a profound effect on the future United States.

To English colonists in early Virginia, the possibilities for making money seemed almost limitless. They had nearly all of what we now call the three factors of production. Backers in England had put up one of these factors, the investment money, or capital, needed to begin the settlement. Virginia offered the second, abundant land. Only one factor was missing: someone to do the work of clearing forests, plowing fields, and harvesting crops.

Labor Options

As gentlemen, the planters had no intention of performing physical labor, since in the social structure with which they were familiar, such labor was a badge of lower social status. They wanted to create a society in which they could live off the labor of others.

Nor did the planters consider simply hiring workers, the way we would today. The notion of laborers working for a certain number of hours for a wage is a fairly modern one. People in the 1600s generally did not view labor itself as something that could be bought or sold.

What other choices did the planters have? In the beginning, they planned to use Native Americans. They knew that the Spanish had successfully forced Native Americans to work in mines to the south. Moreover, Native Americans already were living in Virginia and knew the land and climate. The English had great confidence in their ability to persuade Native Americans to work for them in exchange for the advantages offered by the supposedly superior civilization of Europe.

Another potential source of labor was indentured servants from England. They proved inexpensive, because disease and grim working conditions killed close to two thirds of them before they could take possession of the land promised in their indentures.

Planters discovered a third option when a ship landed a group of enslaved Africans in Jamestown in 1619, an event that is depicted in the painting below. But it was not an option they seized on immediately. Forty years later, fewer than 1,700 Africans lived in Virginia and Maryland; sixty years later, in the 1680s, Africans totaled only around 4,000.

Weighing the Choices

The decision about which form of labor to use was not made suddenly and dramatically. Over the decades the choice grew clear. Native Americans demonstrated by an active resistance that they would have no part in the plans of the English. Moreover, European disease soon severely reduced Native American populations, conclusively canceling that option.

▶ RESOURCE DIRECTORY

Teaching Resources

History Might Not ... Activity Using Chinese Laborers to Build the Transcontinental Railroad, found in the Unit 1 folder, pp. 16–17, reflects the historical trend that kept disadvantaged and immigrant populations on the lowest rungs of the economic ladder.

GOALS	Find a cheap and reliable source of labor to exploit the natural resources of the Chesapeake Bay area.		
POSSIBLE ACTIONS	Use Native Americans	Use English indentured servants	Use enslaved Africans
ADVANTAGES/ DISADVANTAGES	• Difficulty in obtaining and controlling laborers due to resistance • Failure of labor supply due to decrease in Native American population	• In the early and mid 1600s, low cost of labor due to short life of indentured servants; need for constant supply because of high death rate • Ease of communication and interaction due to shared language and customs • In the late 1600s, increased cost due to increased life span • Possible political disturbances	• In the late 1600s, a lower cost than indentured servants to obtain and maintain • Steady supply due to immunity to European disease and hardiness to warm climate • Problems in communication and interaction due to language and customs different from English

At first, English landowners clearly preferred the second option—English indentured servants. Indentured labor cost landowners little, especially if the servants died young. Furthermore, indentured servants already shared the language and customs of the planters. By contrast, enslaved Africans were expensive to purchase and came from a culture unfamiliar to the English. For this reason slavery contributed such a small part to the Chesapeake labor force that the practice was not legally recognized until 1660.

In the last few decades of the 1600s, however, English gentlemen began to buy large numbers of slaves from Africa. By 1700, there were 20,000 enslaved Africans in Virginia. Another 100,000 were imported by 1750. What brought about this reversal in established practice? Why did so many individual planters make the conscious decision, at approximately the same time, to replace indentured servants with enslaved Africans?

Part of the answer is strictly economic. By the middle of the 1600s, better diets and improved working conditions meant that white servants were living longer—and demanding their promised 50 acres. The high early death rate that had made indentured servitude cheaper than slavery was disappearing. At the same time, many planters were increasingly able to afford enslaved Africans. It became cheaper to buy and support an African laborer for the duration of his or her lifetime than it was to support an indentured servant for seven years and then give him 50 acres.

Part of the reason for the shift was political. Bacon's Rebellion revealed the tensions between rich planters in the Chesapeake area and those who were less fortunate. The gentry began to see enslaved Africans as a more stable and less unruly source of labor than indentured servants.

They imagined enslaved people simply would become a permanent part of the lower order in the hierarchical society of the colonies. Their assumption was that Africans would never expect their freedom, would never expect any land, and would never expect to have any say in running the colony.

During the 1700s, slavery became well established throughout the English colonies. It had never been inevitable, however. It was a deliberate choice among three options made by powerful men in order to secure their economic and political position.

EVALUATING DECISIONS

1. Why were planters forced to give up the idea of using Native Americans for labor?
2. Why did planters in the Chesapeake Bay area prefer indentured labor in the early years?

Critical Thinking
3. **Recognizing Ideologies** Summarize the key assumptions made by wealthy planters in deciding to use African labor.

Media and Technology

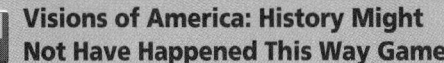 **Visions of America: History Might Not Have Happened This Way Game**

To encourage students to explore pivotal moments in United States history, have students use the Visions of America software. Refer to the Visions of America Teacher's Guidebook for viewing objectives, activities, game instructions, and discussion questions.

Answers to Evaluating Decisions

1. Native Americans resisted English attempts to use their labor. They were also severely reduced in number by European diseases.

2. Indentured labor was cheaper than slave labor, and indentured servants understood the language and customs of the planters.

3. Answers should include mention of the planters' basic assumption that others should provide them with a living; that Native Americans would benefit from the supposedly superior culture of Europe; and that Africans would take a low place in the established hierarchy without protest.

Life in Colonial America

SECTION 4

Life in Colonial America

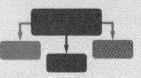

Connecting to the Big Idea

See page 14B. Under a policy of salutary neglect from their parent country, the colonies prospered and developed distinct economies and societies. Ask students who held power in colonial America. What governed the lives of most people?

Objectives

● Define *mercantilism* and explain its consequences for the colonies.
● Identify and describe the economies and societies of the three colonial regions.
● Define the fundamental belief in inequality that governed the way colonists organized their society.
● Delineate the tensions created among Native Americans, the French, and the British as the settlers migrated west.
● Describe how the Great Awakening indirectly challenged the colonial belief in inequality.

Bellringer

Ask students to brainstorm a list of industries or commercial activities important to their region's economy. Then name a very different region of the country and ask students if they can list important economic activities there. Ask students why the lists may differ. Does economic activity help shape social organization? Are regional economic interests important today?

Reading Strategy

Question Writing Ask students to skim the section, read each of the headings and subheadings, and turn each heading into a question. Then have them jot down answers to the questions they have created as they read.

SECTION PREVIEW

For England in the mid-1600s and early 1700s, the colonies were a reliable source of raw materials and a prime place to sell English goods. Eventually, however, the colonies grew and prospered with little direct interference from the English government. As they grew, a distinct culture emerged—one in which the wealthy few dominated the majority of people.

Playing their part in trade by buying finished goods from the parent country, customers in the colonies ordered English cloth from this sample book.

Key Concepts

· Although England flirted with the idea of strictly regulating its colonies in order to increase its power and wealth, on the whole it let them develop on their own in the early 1700s.
· As they grew, the colonies in each region developed very different economies and societies.
· Colonial Americans organized their society according to a belief in inequality.
· As British settlers migrated west, tension increased among Native Americans, the French, and the British, as all competed for the same territory.
· A religious movement called the Great Awakening indirectly challenged the colonial acceptance of inequality.

Key Terms, People, and Places

mercantilism, balance of trade, salutary neglect, triangular trade, gentry, Middle Passage, Great Awakening

---

B
y the late 1600s and early 1700s, English-speaking people had established a cluster of colonies on the Atlantic coast of North America, as shown in the map on page 37. England prized these colonies for two reasons: they were suppliers of food and raw materials such as tobacco, rice, and lumber, and they were avid buyers of English goods. These activities—supplying raw materials and buying goods—dovetailed neatly with a new European economic theory called **mercantilism,** which supposedly explained how a nation could increase its wealth and thus its power.

Mercantilism at Work

According to the theory of mercantilism, a country should get and keep as much bullion, or gold and silver, as possible. For England, France, and other countries without mines like those Spain controlled in the Americas, the only way to obtain more bullion was to have a favorable **balance of trade**—that is, to export more goods than were imported.

To boost its balance of trade, mercantilists believed, a nation should have colonies where it could buy raw materials and sell products. The colonies should not be allowed to manufacture goods. The right to make goods for sale was reserved exclusively for the parent country, since manufacturing was a major source of profit. In 1660 the English king, Charles II, approved a stronger version of a previous law called the Navigation Act, which, together with other legislation, brought the colonial policy in line with these mercantilist goals.

However, after the rule of the next king, James II, had ended, the British government rarely tried to interfere directly in colonial business. By the 1700s legislative bodies, such as the House of Burgesses in Virginia or assemblies in other colonies, had gained extensive power over local affairs. Most of these colonial assemblies consisted of an upper house of prominent colonists appointed by the king and a lower house elected by voting landowners. Even in colonies owned by the king, laws could not go into effect without the consent of the free men of the colony or their chosen representatives.

Why did the British government allow its colonies such freedom in governing themselves—

▶ RESOURCE DIRECTORY

Teaching Resources

📁 **Reproducible Lesson Plan** found in the Unit 1 folder, p. 6, provides a summary of the Section 4 lesson plan content.

📁 **Alternate Lesson Plan: Learning Styles** found in the Alternate Lesson Plans folder, p. 53, helps students understand colonial life by focusing particularly on the nature of work and is especially effective for visual learners.

📄 **Guided Reading and Review** found in the Unit 1 folder, p. 14, provides a structure for reading and mastering the key concepts and reviewing the key terms for Section 4. (Guided Practice)

far more than was found in Spanish or French colonies? Part of the answer lies in the English tradition of strong local government and weak central power; part lies in the fact that the British government lacked the resources and the bureaucracy to enforce its wishes. Then, too, colonists recognized the authority of the king and Parliament without being forced to; most were proud to be British subjects.

Finally, the economy and the politics of the colonists served the interests of Great Britain very well. The British realized that the most salutary, or beneficial, policy was to neglect their colonies. Thus, later historians would call British colonial policy during the early 1700s **salutary neglect**.

MAKING CONNECTIONS

Can you think of ways in which the policy of salutary neglect might backfire on the British and harm their interests in the colonies?

The Expanding and Diverse Economies of the Colonies

While the Spanish colonies continued to rely on mining silver and growing sugar, and New France still focused on the fur trade, the British regions of eastern North America—the Southern, Middle, and New England colonies—developed diverse economies.

Staple Crops in the Southern Colonies In the Southern Colonies—Virginia, Maryland, South Carolina, North Carolina, and Georgia—the economy was based on growing crops that were in constant demand. Such crops are called staples. In Virginia and North Carolina, the staple crop was tobacco; in the warm and wet coastal regions of South Carolina and Georgia, it was rice. In the early 1730s, these two colonies were exporting 16.8 million pounds of rice per year; by 1770, the number was 76.9 million. Meanwhile, the number of pounds of tobacco exported per year by Virginia, Maryland, and Delaware rose from 32 million in 1700 to 83.8 million in 1770.

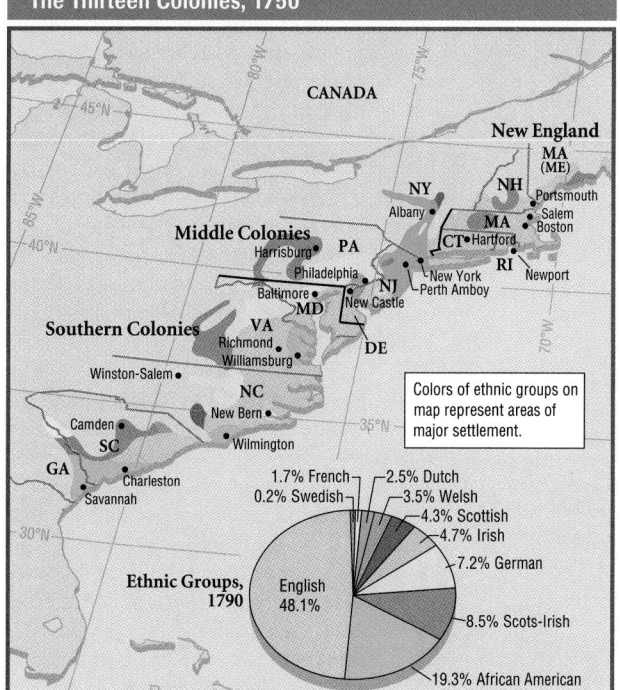

The Thirteen Colonies, 1750

Ethnic Groups, 1790
English 48.1%
1.7% French
0.2% Swedish
2.5% Dutch
3.5% Welsh
4.3% Scottish
4.7% Irish
7.2% German
8.5% Scots-Irish
19.3% African American

Colors of ethnic groups on map represent areas of major settlement.

 Geography and History: Interpreting Maps
English settlements in North America in the 1700s generally clung to the Eastern seaboard and its rivers. In this narrow band, however, lived a wide variety of ethnic groups. *Which was the largest group after the English?*

To produce staple crops, planters needed huge amounts of land and labor but very little else. As a result, the Southern Colonies remained a region of plantations strung out along rivers and coastlines. Except for Charles Town (Charleston), in South Carolina and Williamsburg in Virginia, the South had few towns and only a small group of people who could be called merchants.

A Mixture in the Middle Colonies From Maryland north to New York, the economy of the Middle Colonies was a mixture of farming and commerce. The length of the Delaware and Hudson rivers and the tributaries that fed them allowed colonists to move into the interior and establish farms on rich, fertile soil. There they specialized in growing grains.

But commerce was just as important as agriculture in the Middle Colonies. New York

Media and Technology

 Transparencies
Historical Maps, L-1; Time Lines, E-2

2. INSTRUCT

Explain/Discuss
Explain to students that colonial society was basically unequal. Ask students to describe the gentry and to identify symbols that defined their class. Ask students why the gentry were considered "the gentle folk."

Discuss with students the lives, rights, and duties of colonial women. Ask what right adult single women possessed that married women and underage daughters did not.

Answer to ...
MAKING CONNECTIONS

Possible answers: Colonists might develop independent institutions and a tradition of operating without interference, making it difficult for the British to assert their authority when they wished to do so.

Caption Answer to ...

 Interpreting Maps

African Americans

In Depth

Did You Know?

By the 1700s, it was said that in the colony of Virginia "the Establishment is indeed Tobacco," because this staple was the crop around which much of Virginia's economy revolved. Clergymen, for example, were paid in tobacco rather than in hard currency. In 1695, the annual salary of a clergyman was legally fixed at 16,000 pounds of tobacco, and the money value of the minister's salary depended solely on the quality of the local crop. Ministers, often recruited from England, were more easily lured to the colony by offers from regions growing the higher-priced "Sweet Scented" tobacco.

In Depth

Then and Now

Enslaved Africans brought with them to the United States the ancient tradition of storytelling. Alex Haley, who grew up listening to his grandmother's stories about an African ancestor, Kunta Kinte, journeyed to West Africa to research his family's origins. The trip led Haley to write his best-selling novel, *Roots*, which was viewed by a record 130 million people when it was dramatized for television in 1977. *Roots* awakened a popular interest in African American history and culture and, by the 1980s, in fiction written by African Americans. In 1993, Toni Morrison, whose works include the Pulitzer Prize–winning novel *Beloved*, was awarded the Nobel Prize in Literature and became the first African American to be so honored.

and Philadelphia were already among the largest cities in North America. Home to growing numbers of merchants, traders, and artisans—craftspeople such as printers, bakers, and furniture makers—the streets of these cities teemed with people in the business of buying and selling goods. As the map on page 37 shows, the Middle Colonies had many different ethnic groups. In contrast, most of the residents of Massachusetts were still of English descent, and almost everyone in the South was either of African or of English descent.

Agriculture and Trade in New England In the 1700s, the New England Colonies were a region of small, relatively self-sufficient farms and of towns dependent on long-distance trade. Unlike the merchants of Philadelphia and New York, those in Boston, Salem, and Newport in Rhode Island did not rely heavily on local crops for their commerce. Instead, they had long since developed a business of carrying crops and goods from one place to another—a "carrying trade." They might haul china, books, and cloth from England to the West Indies in the Caribbean Sea; transport sugar back to New England, where it was usually distilled into rum; trade rum and firearms for slaves in West Africa; and then carry slaves to the West Indies for more sugar. This trade between three points in the Atlantic World—the Americas, Europe, and Africa—was called the **triangular trade.**

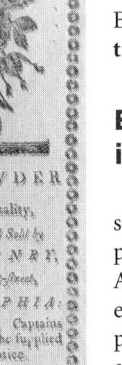

In the unequal society of the colonies, a white wig, or hair powdered to look like one, was the hallmark of a gentleman.

Everyday Life in the Colonies

In general, colonial American society was dedicated to the belief that people were not equal. Almost all Americans of European descent, for example, accepted slavery as a normal part of life. Nearly all colonists also assumed that women were not equal to men. Some may not have liked these assumptions, but colonial society offered little opportunity for debate over such issues. In the words of one New Englander, "ranks and degrees" were as much a part of this world as "Mountains and Plains, Hills and Vallies."

The Gentle Folk Colonial clothes, houses, and manners offer the best evidence of this belief in inequality. **Gentry**, or men and women wealthy enough to afford others to work for them, set themselves apart by their clothing: wigs, silk stockings, lace cuffs, and the latest fashions in suits, dresses, and hats. Ordinary people wore plain breeches and shirts or dresses. Wigs were an unmistakable sign of status, power, and wealth. "Gentle folk," a colonial term for the gentry class, were the most important members of colonial society; to be considered "gentle," one had to be wealthy. For English colonists, the foundation of real wealth was land. Although adult single women and free African Americans could legally own land, almost all landowners were white men.

From New Hampshire to the Carolinas and Georgia, small groups of landowning men in each colony dominated politics. Lawyers, planters, and merchants held most of the seats in the colonial assemblies, or lawmaking bodies.

Women in Colonial America The colonial belief in inequality defined the status of colonial women, including the wives and daughters of gentlemen. Within the households of colonial America, husbands exercised nearly unlimited power. English law, for example, permitted men to beat their wives without fear of prosecution. Divorces, although legal, were extremely rare. Most women, either as underage daughters or as wives, were legally the dependents of men, could not own land, and thus could not vote or hold office or serve on a jury. Even adult single women—widows, for instance, who took over the ownership of land from their late husbands—did not have any political rights, although they could conduct business.

In practice, however, men and women depended heavily on one another. In colonial America, women juggled a number of duties

RESOURCE DIRECTORY

Teaching Resources

Primary Source Activity A Marriage Agreement, found in the Unit 1 folder, p. 25, illustrates issues relating to family life as well as the nature of legal arrangements in the colonies.

that contributed to the well-being of the household and also of the community. Women took chief responsibility for the tasks that kept a household operating, such as cooking, gardening, washing, spinning thread, weaving cloth, cleaning, and sewing. They supported one another by helping in childbirth, sharing equipment and tools, and applying community pressure on offenders in cases of domestic abuse. Women also assisted in whatever work their husbands did, from planting crops to managing the business affairs of the family. And they trained their daughters in the traditional responsibilities of women.

The Nature of Work in Colonial America By the mid-1700s, life was better for most Europeans in North America than it would have been in Europe. American colonists ate better, lived longer, and had more children to help them with their work than their European counterparts. Still, working people had to labor very hard to keep themselves and their families alive.

Everyone in a household—husbands, wives, children, and servants—worked to maintain the household by producing food and goods. In fact, the basic goal of the household was to maintain itself. While men grew crops or made goods such as shoes, guns, or candles, the rest of the household was equally busy. Many women sewed and spun cloth, made butter, and tended small gardens and animals. Children helped both parents from an early age. Almost all work was performed in or around the home; the separation between work and home with which we are familiar today did not develop until the 1800s. Even artisans worked out of shops in the front of their houses.

African Americans in the Colonies

Not counting Native Americans, about one out of every five people living in British North America by the middle of the 1700s was of African descent. For many African men,

Using Historical Evidence Prudence Punderson, a Connecticut housewife, created this symbolic view in needlework of the life of a colonial woman. The symbols, from right to left, indicate birth, work, and death. *What three symbols would you choose to sum up your own life? How do they differ from the symbols Punderson chose?*

Media and Technology

Transparencies
Our Multicultural Heritage, C-8, Links
Across Time, J-1

Ask students to prepare a report about the lives of children in colonial times, answering questions such as the following: What types of schools were there for children? What was the apprentice system and how did it work? Who went to school and what subjects did they learn? What games and toys did children play with? How did they dress? How were children expected to behave?

In Depth

Multicultural Perspectives

Paul Cuffe (1759–1817), the son of an ex-slave father and a Native American mother, went to sea at the age of sixteen. He became a successful shipowner, hiring only African American crews. Cuffe, who joined the Quakers in 1808, became convinced that African Americans should resettle in Africa. In 1811 he took the first African American recruits to Africa. He died before he could carry out his plans to settle many more African Americans in the land of their ancestors.

women, and children, interaction with colonial society began when they were uprooted from their homeland and sold into slavery. One African who later told his story from the beginning was Olaudah Equiano.

AMERICAN PROFILES
Olaudah Equiano

Olaudah Equiano was born around 1745 in the country of Benin. He wrote in his autobiography decades later that the land of his youth was "uncommonly rich and fruitful" and "a nation of dancers, musicians, and poets." As a child, he learned "the art of war" and proudly wore "the emblems of a warrior" made by his mother. When Equiano was ten, his world was shattered. Two men and a woman kidnapped him and one of his sisters while their parents were working. Separated from his sister, Equiano was enslaved to a series of African masters. About six months after he was kidnapped, Equiano found himself facing a still greater trial. Taken to the coast, he was sold again and put aboard a British slave ship bound for the Americas.

During the **Middle Passage,** the name given to the part of the triangular trade that went between Africa and the Americas bearing enslaved Africans, Equiano witnessed many scenes of brutality. Although historians differ on the actual figures, from 10 to 40 percent of the Africans on a slave ship might perish in a crossing. Sick with fear about where they were being taken, they were forced to endure chains, heat, disease, and the overpowering odor caused by the lack of sanitation and their cramped, stuffy quarters. As Equiano wrote, "Many a time we were near suffocation from the want of fresh air, which we were often without for whole days together."

Occasionally enslaved Africans physically resisted during the Middle Passage by staging what the slavers called "mutinies." The heavily

Continuing traditions established in Africa, enslaved African Americans made and played this banjo and fiddle in North America.

armed and manned slave ships were evidence that the slavers lived in continual fear of Africans striking out for their freedom. No mutiny took place aboard Equiano's ship, although statistics about the British slave trade show that a rebellion occurred every two years on the average. Many of these were successful.

Equiano's ship finally arrived at a port on the island of Barbados, in the West Indies, where the crew put up the Africans for sale at a public auction. Most went to work and die in the sugar plantations of the West Indies. Equiano noted how the sale separated families, leaving people grief-stricken and alone.

In 1766 Equiano was taken to Virginia, where he was eventually able to buy his freedom. Migrating to Great Britain, he found work as a barber and a personal servant and became active in the antislavery movement.

Africans in South Carolina and Georgia
Much of the seaboard region of South Carolina and Georgia is formed by a coastal plain called the low country. Planters found the low country excellent for the cultivation of rice and indigo. Enslaved people there labored under particularly brutal conditions.

African Americans in South Carolina and Georgia made up the majority of the population, and they generally had regular contact with only a handful of colonists. As a result, they were able to exercise greater control over their day-to-day existence than those enslaved in other colonies and to preserve many of their cultural traditions. Many had come to South Carolina and Georgia directly from Africa. Perhaps the most vital tradition that enslaved people tried to preserve was the strong kinship network found in West Africa. They also continued practicing the crafts and making the music of their homeland. In some cases, they kept their culture alive in their speech.

African Americans had superior knowledge of cattle herding and fishing, as well as great skill in the use of semitropical herbs. Because many had grown rice extensively in their homelands, they generally had vital, practical know-how about its cultivation. Without this knowledge, to

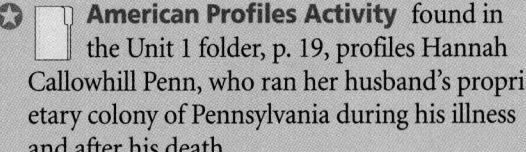
RESOURCE DIRECTORY

Teaching Resources

Visual Learning Activity Education as a Step Toward Freedom, found in the Unit 1 folder, p. 30, is designed to promote students' understanding of differing views on slavery in the colonies.

American Profiles Activity found in the Unit 1 folder, p. 19, profiles Hannah Callowhill Penn, who ran her husband's proprietary colony of Pennsylvania during his illness and after his death.

say nothing of African American labor, it is doubtful that the colonies that came to depend on rice as a staple could have survived.

Africans in Virginia and Maryland The way enslaved people lived in the tobacco colonies of Virginia, Maryland, and to some extent North Carolina differed sharply from the way of life of African Americans in South Carolina and Georgia. The work they performed was different. Cultivating tobacco, the major crop, did not take as much time as growing rice, so slave-owners put enslaved African Americans to work at a variety of other tasks. And, African Americans in Virginia and Maryland had more regular contact with European Americans. The result was greater integration of the two cultures than in South Carolina and Georgia.

Slavery in New England and the Middle Colonies About 400,000 African Americans lived in the Southern Colonies by the late 1700s, compared to about 50,000 in the New England and Middle colonies combined. Most of the enslaved people in the northern colonies worked on farms, either in the fields or as cooks, housekeepers, or artisans. They also worked in the forests as lumberjacks. Because shipbuilding and shipping were major economic activities in the New England and Middle colonies, some African American men worked along the seacoast. Others, men and women, worked in cities, in manufacturing and trading or as servants in the homes of wealthy families.

The First Movement West

Less than 150 years after the times of starvation and trouble at Jamestown, the British colonies in North America had become economic successes. Colonial settlers, with the forced cooperation of enslaved African Americans, had transformed the Atlantic colonies into a world of prosperous farms, towns, and plantations. Though it may be hard to believe, British colonists had begun to feel crowded, especially in New England.

By the middle of the 1700s, European settlers began moving into the interior of North

America. Scots-Irish (Scottish people who had lived in Ireland) and Germans settled in central Pennsylvania and the Shenandoah Valley of Virginia. Farther to the north, people were spreading into the Mohawk River valley in New York and the Connecticut River valley in what is now Vermont.

Just ahead of the English migrants were Native Americans, including the Delaware and the Shawnee. They were moving west, too. Though heavily involved in trade with the Europeans, they preferred forest life to farm life. By the mid-1700s, disease and war over trade had taken a toll on Native American cultures; the Iroquois, for example, were no longer as strong militarily as they had been in the 1600s. Native Americans nonetheless remained powerful players in the development of American colonial society.

The relentless intrusion of the English alarmed the French as well as the Native Americans. By the early 1750s, it was clear that some kind of explosion was rapidly approaching. The most likely setting was western Pennsylvania. Whoever controlled the forks of the Ohio River, the place where the Allegheny and Monongahela rivers meet to form the Ohio, would have a considerable strategic advantage over everyone else. ✪

Religious Tensions Within the Colonies

While tensions built along the outer edges of the British colonies, unrest was also increasing within them. Nowhere was this more obvious than in colonial religious life.

In the early 1700s, many ministers believed that the colonists had fallen away from the faith of their ancestors. In the 1730s and 1740s, they led a series of revivals that especially touched women of all ages and young men. This revival of religious feeling is now known as the **Great Awakening.**

The purpose of the preachers who brought about the Great Awakening was to remind people of the power of God and—at least in the beginning—of the authority of their ministers. In a well-known fiery sermon, "Sinners in the Hands of an Angry God,"

Section 4 Review Answers

1. (a) mercantilism, see p. 36, (b) balance of trade, see p. 36, (c) salutary neglect, see p. 37, (d) triangular trade, see p. 38, (e) gentry, see p. 38, (f) Middle Passage, see p. 40, (g) Great Awakening, see p. 41

2. To help the parent country have a favorable balance of trade by providing raw materials and buying manufactured products.

3. The Southern Colonies' economy was based on growing staple crops such as tobacco and rice, using enslaved Africans for labor. The economy in the Middle Colonies was a mixture of farming and commerce. The New England Colonies developed an economy based on the "carrying trade," or long-distance trade, as well as small family farms.

4. Colonial American society was based on a belief in inequality. It continued the hierarchical society that had originated in Europe, in which most power was held by white, upper-class men who owned land.

5. They were alarmed by the expansion; it became clear that some kind of explosion was likely, probably at the forks of the Ohio River.

6. It raised the suggestion that ordinary people, since they could worship God on their own, could also figure out how to govern themselves.

7. Possible answers: The economic growth of the colonies might have been hampered by the requirement both to pay duties in England and to transport all goods there first. For example, the triangular trade would have been much more difficult if the Navigation Act had been enforced.

Reteach

Ask students to imagine that they are advising the king of England in 1700 and must report to him on the economic and social conditions of the colonies. They must first describe the current English policy toward the colonies, next report on its success, and then describe the economies and lifestyles of the three colonial regions.

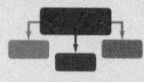 **Reinforcing the Big Idea**

While England ruled its colonies from a distance, the colonies themselves developed distinctly different economies. However, they shared a hierarchical social organization in which male landowners dominated and African Americans were disenfranchised.

Known for their "pathetical," or emotional, style, preachers such as George Whitefield (left) encouraged ordinary people to believe that they, too, could reach out to God.

revivalist Jonathan Edwards appealed to the individuals in his congregation in Northampton, Massachusetts:

> *O sinner! Consider the fearful danger you are in: it is a great furnace of wrath, a wide and bottomless pit, full of the fire of wrath, that you are held over in the hand of that God, whose wrath is provoked and incensed as much against you, as against many of the damned in hell. You hang by a slender thread.*

As time went on, however, the Great Awakening did more than revive people's religious conviction. It energized them to speak for themselves and to reject the traditional authority of ministers and books. As George Whitefield, one of the most famous and popular revivalists, said,

> *The Generality of Preachers talk of an unknown, unfelt Christ. And the Reason why Congregations have been so dead, is because dead Men preach to them.*

People flocked not to the established ministers but to wandering preachers, often poorly educated, who told of the ability of all people to have a personal relationship with Jesus Christ. According to these preachers, the infinitely great power of God did not put Him beyond the reach of ordinary people. The message these ministers spread was that faith and sincerity were the major requirements needed to understand the Gospel.

In the end, the Great Awakening became a challenge to the social and political order of British North America. If ordinary people did not need a hierarchy of ministers to help them know God, perhaps the hierarchy of gentle folk was not so necessary either. And if people could figure out how to worship God on their own, couldn't they figure out how to govern themselves as well?

SECTION 4 REVIEW

Key Terms, People, and Places
1. Define (a) mercantilism, (b) balance of trade, (c) salutary neglect, (d) triangular trade, (e) gentry, (f) Middle Passage, (g) Great Awakening.

Key Concepts
2. What were the English colonies supposed to do for the parent country, according to mercantilist theory?
3. Describe the economies of the Southern Colonies, the Middle Colonies, and the New England Colonies.
4. Describe the basic belief on which colonial American

society was based and its effect on society.
5. How did Native Americans and the French react to westward expansion by British settlers?
6. Why was the Great Awakening an indirect challenge to fundamental colonial beliefs?

Critical Thinking
7. **Predicting Consequences** How might the growth of the American colonies have been affected if the British had strictly enforced the Navigation Act of 1660?

Making Comparisons

Making comparisons means examining two or more ideas, objects, events, activities, or people to discover how they are alike and how they are different. When studying history, being able to make comparisons allows you to more fully evaluate historical periods.

One way to evaluate a historical period is to compare the economic activities in that period. By the mid-1700s, clear patterns of economic activity were emerging among the British colonies in North America. This map uses symbols and a color-coded key to present basic information about land use in the colonies. Use the following steps to compare the economic activities in the different colonies.

1. Identify the basis on which you will make the comparison. It is not possible to compare two or more items that are fundamentally different. (a) What did the colonies have in common? (b) What purpose would a comparison of the colonies serve?

2. Determine the ways in which the colonies were alike. Making comparisons includes finding similarities between items. Were the economic activities in the colonies similar in any way? If so, in what ways were they similar?

3. Determine the ways in which the colonies were different. Making comparisons also includes finding any differences that may exist between items. In what fundamental ways did the regions differ from one another?

4. Summarize your comparison of the colonies and evaluate your findings. Complete the comparison based on similarities and differences. (a) What were the main economic activities in each region? (b) In your opinion, how would the economic activities in each region have influenced daily life?

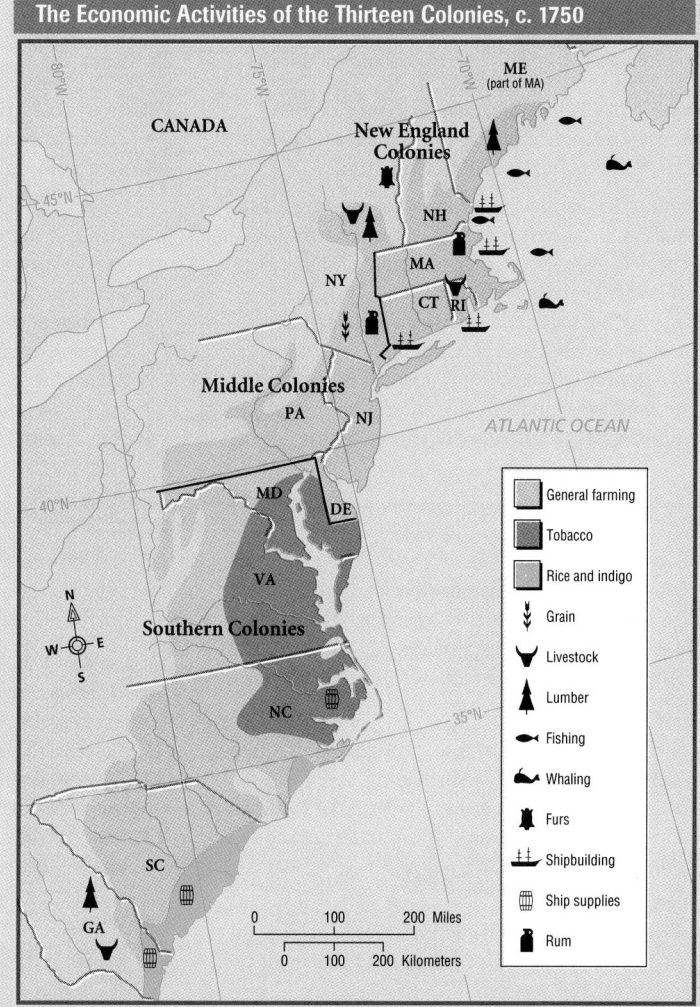

The Economic Activities of the Thirteen Colonies, c. 1750

General farming
Tobacco
Rice and indigo
Grain
Livestock
Lumber
Fishing
Whaling
Furs
Shipbuilding
Ship supplies
Rum

Historian's Toolbox Activity Expressing Problems Clearly, found in the Unit 1 folder, p. 22, helps students apply this skill by examining the petition for relief from taxes from a group of African Americans in Massachusetts.

Critical Thinking
Making Comparisons

Focus Compare economic activities on a map to learn more about a time period.

Instruct Before reading the feature, have students brainstorm a list of reasons explaining why it is important to be able to make good comparisons. Explain that making comparisons allows people to evaluate historical periods, specific events, or differing viewpoints. After answering the questions, students should find current economic activity maps in a geography textbook or encyclopedia showing the same regions. Ask students to compare the maps and name at least three things that have changed.

Extend See Historian's Toolbox Activity in the Resource Directory below.

Answers

1. (a) All the colonies were located on the east coast. They all had agriculture as a main economic activity. (b) By comparing the economic activities in the colonies around 1750, students can gain a better understanding of daily life in the colonies.

2. There were some activities that were similar. All of the colonies were supported by general farming.

3. The Middle Colonies and Southern Colonies were supported mainly by agriculture—including tobacco, rice, and indigo. The New England Colonies relied on fishing, whaling, shipbuilding, and lumber. There was more industry in the North. Farming was more diverse in the South.

4. (a) The New England Colonies had fishing, whaling, shipbuilding, lumber, rum, livestock, furs, and general farming. The Middle Colonies had grain, rum, livestock, and general farming. The Southern Colonies had ship supplies, lumber, livestock, general farming, tobacco, rice, and indigo. (b) Answers will vary. The tobacco, rice, and indigo industries in the South required larger farms or plantations. The New England colonies had a variety of economic activities that were dependent on one another. Lumber production enabled the New England colonists to build ships that could be used for fishing and whaling.

Understanding Key Terms, People, and Places

Terms
Students should refer to the definitions of the key terms in the chapter to write sentences that show the relation of each word to the cultures of the Native Americans or to the colonization of the Americas.

Matching
1. hierarchy
2. *encomienda* system
3. clan
4. gentry

True or False
1. false, the Atlantic World
2. true
3. true
4. false, Metacom

Reviewing Main Ideas

1. Native Americans believed that the land could not be owned. They believed that people had a right to use land and could grant others that right, but to sell the land outright was unthinkable. It was also unthinkable to change the land so that it could no longer support the Native American way of life.

2. Land was controlled by a relatively few wealthy landowners; beneath them was a class of craftspeople and merchants; at the bottom of the hierarchy were peasant farmers.

3. Songhai lay between the forest kingdoms, with their extensive trading network, and North Africa and thus played a major part in the flow of trade in West Africa in the late 1400s.

4. Native Americans had not built up immunities to the new diseases.

5. Under the terms of the treaty, any land not already claimed by other Christians would be divided between Spain and Portugal by an invisible line around the world. Spain was assigned to rule over what lay west of the line; Portugal was left with control over the rest.

6. Among Africans (and Native Americans), the enslaved person could be adopted into a lineage, a practice that recognized the basic humanity of enslaved people. In the Americas, Europeans based slavery on race, thus making it an irrevocable condition.

7. The Franciscans were a powerful presence; they established missions to convert Native Americans to Christianity and make them conform to European customs.

Chapter Review

Understanding Key Terms, People, and Places

Key Terms
1. kinship network
2. clan
3. hierarchy
4. patriarchal society
5. lineage
6. conquistador
7. *encomienda* system
8. colony
9. presidio
10. *congregacion*
11. indentured servant
12. Reformation
13. religious toleration
14. mercantilism
15. balance of trade
16. salutary neglect
17. triangular trade
18. gentry
19. Middle Passage
20. Great Awakening

People
21. Christopher Columbus
22. Popé
23. Powhatan
24. Puritans
25. Metacom

Places
26. Guinea
27. Songhai
28. Atlantic World

Terms For each term above, write a sentence that explains its relation to the culture of the Native Americans or to the colonization of the Americas.

Matching Review the key terms in the list above. If you are not sure of a term's meaning, review its definition in the chapter. Then choose a term from the list that best matches each description below.
1. a system of many levels in which each level has power over the levels beneath it
2. a system in which Native Americans were required to work for an individual Spaniard, who was supposed to care for their well-being in return
3. groups of Native American families descended from a common ancestor
4. men and women in the colonies wealthy enough to afford others to work for them

True or False Determine whether each statement is true or false. If it is true, write "true." If it is false, change the underlined person or place to make the statement true.
1. The people of Guinea included Native Americans, Europeans, and Africans.
2. Askia Muhammad ruled the empire of Songhai.
3. Popé led a revolt against the Spanish in 1680.
4. New England settlers defeated Wampanoag leader Powhatan and his allies in King Philip's War.

Reviewing Main Ideas

Section 1 (pp. 16–22)
1. How did Native Americans view land use?
2. How was European society organized in the 1400s?
3. Describe how the empire of Songhai participated in African trade in the late 1400s.

Section 2 (pp. 23–27)
4. Why were European diseases brought to the Americas so deadly to Native Americans?
5. What was the significance of the Treaty of Tordesillas?
6. How did attitudes toward slavery differ among Africans and Europeans?

Section 3 (pp. 28–33)
7. What was the role of the Franciscans in helping the Spanish outposts in North America to succeed?

8. Describe the Pueblo Revolt of 1680.
9. How did the attitude of English settlers toward conquered peoples differ from that of the Spanish?

Section 4 (pp. 36–43)
10. What was the British government's policy toward the colonies after the rule of King James II ended?
11. Describe the colonial view regarding equality.
12. Why did English settlers begin moving into the interior of North America by the middle of the 1700s?
13. How did the employment of enslaved African Americans in the New England and Middle colonies reflect the geography and economy of the North?
14. What attracted people to wandering preachers during the Great Awakening?

---

8. In 1680, a Pueblo medicine man named Popé organized a successful revolt against the Spanish, whom he blamed for widespread sickness and drought. After the war, it took the Spanish years to reestablish themselves along the Rio Grande.

9. The English developed a harsh attitude toward conquered people. Unlike the Spanish, they did not practice the forced blending of cultures. For the English, conquest would be all or nothing.

10. Relying on the policy of salutary neglect, Parliament rarely tried to interfere in the affairs of the colonies.

11. Most colonists accepted slavery as a normal part of life. Most also assumed that women were not equal to men. In addition, the landed gentry set themselves apart from ordinary people by their superior clothes, houses, and manner.

12. By the middle of the 1700s, the English settlers were already beginning to feel crowded on the eastern coast of North America. Sons of families who owned land were given enough to start their own farms; soon, there was simply not enough to go around.

Thinking Critically

1. **Expressing Problems Clearly** The birth of the Atlantic World represented the collision of three distinct cultures. What values, beliefs, and customs differed among the cultures? Choose one way in which the cultures differed, and explain why this difference might have led to misunderstanding and conflict.

2. **Identifying Assumptions** What the Spanish settlers called rebellions by Native Americans, some modern historians call armed struggles for liberation. What assumptions underlie each of these terms?

3. **Making Comparisons** During the 1700s, the gentry class in the English colonies set themselves apart from other people by their clothes, houses, and manners. Is there a gentry class in the United States today? If so, does this group set itself apart in its dress, manners, and possessions?

Making Connections

1. **Evaluating Primary Sources** Review the primary source excerpt on page 23. What does Columbus's statement reveal about the differences between Native American and European views of trade?

2. **Understanding the Visuals** The needlework on page 39 presents a symbolic view of the life of a colonial woman. Examine the needlework to discover the symbols it includes. Based on your reading of Section 4, what additional symbols would you add that represent the status of women in colonial America?

3. **Writing About the Chapter** Write a diary entry from the point of view of one of the following people in colonial America: (a) a member of the gentry, (b) an enslaved African American, (c) a woman, (d) an ordinary worker. First, make a list of the ways in which you might spend a typical day. Note any feelings you might have toward the way you spend your day, as well as reasons for why you live as you do. Next, write a draft of your entry, in which you explain your typical day in as much detail as possible. Revise your entry, making sure that your details reflect the times in which your character is writing. Proofread your entry and draft a final copy.

4. **Using the Graphic Organizer** This graphic organizer uses webs to compare and contrast characteristics of Native American, European, and African societies. (a) Using the right side of the graphic organizer, summarize the view of land held by each society. (b) Using the left side, determine the two societies in which the family fulfilled a social function. (c) Working on a separate sheet of paper, create your own graphic organizer comparing and contrasting Native Americans, Europeans, and Africans in terms of religion and trade.

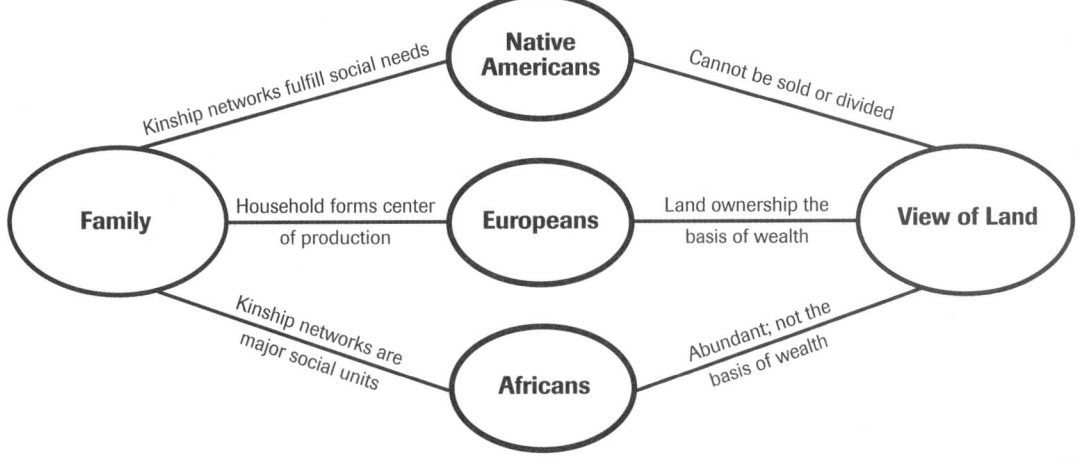

Making Connections

1. For Native Americans, trade represented an exchange of gifts and was a gesture of hospitality. For Europeans, trade carried no social obligations and was merely a business transaction.

2. Answers will vary but should indicate an understanding that women had few legal rights in colonial America and were not considered equal to men.

3. Answers will vary. Students' diary entries should reveal a grasp of their character's station in colonial society and the expectations surrounding that station.

4. (a) Native Americans viewed land as something that could be used but not owned and, therefore, not sold. Europeans associated land ownership with wealth. Since land was an abundant commodity in Africa, it was not associated with the wealthy. (b) In Native American and African societies, the family fulfilled a social function. (c) Students' graphic organizers should reflect an understanding of the role of religion and trade in each of the three cultures.

 Alternative Assessment

Final Evaluation

Use the following guidelines to evaluate student projects:

- **Evidence of thoughtfulness** Do projects cover the issues listed on page 15?
- **Evidence of outside research** To what extent did students use outside research materials for their project?
- **Evidence of synthesis** Do projects demonstrate that students understand how topics are related?
- **Communication style** Do the projects convey their purpose to an audience in a clear, appealing way?

Allow interested students to present their finished travel accounts to the class.

---

13. In the North, enslaved people worked in the forests and on the seacoast. Others worked in manufacturing or as domestic servants.

14. The wandering preachers spread the message that God was not beyond the reach of ordinary people and that faith and sincerity were the major requirements for salvation.

Thinking Critically

1. Possible answers: different views toward trade, slavery, and land use; as an example of possible consequences, different views of land use might lead to a clash over land itself.

2. The term *rebellion* implies simply a resistance to authority, which the Spanish would have seen as legitimate authority. The phrase "armed struggle for liberation" clearly assumes the legitimacy of the Native Americans' desire to free themselves from Spanish domination.

3. Answers will vary. Students may note that although American society today is far more egalitarian than in colonial times, it is not classless. Dress is less of an indicator of wealth than in the past, but wealth and power still often overlap.

FOCUS

Connecting Literature and History

Between the 1400s and the early 1700s, the area that is now the United States changed dramatically. In the 1400s the land was peopled with varied and distinct Native American groups who farmed and hunted, conducted their own governments, and traded with one another. In the late 1400s, when Europeans began arriving, conflicts arose between settlers and Native Americans, two groups who had very different ways of viewing the world. By the early 1700s the presence of European colonists had largely supplanted that of Native Americans along the coast of North America. Tell students that the three source readings chronicle this series of changes.

INSTRUCT

Ask students to compare the values and beliefs revealed in the reading from the Teton Sioux with those revealed in the William Byrd piece. As they do so, ask students whether they see any reasons that Native Americans and Europeans had trouble understanding one another. Point out that events such as that experienced by Mary Rowlandson were often the result of misunderstanding and lack of toleration.

Tell students that it has only been in recent years that more balanced and comprehensive information about the role of Native Americans in United States history has been included in textbooks. Ask students why it might be that information on Native Americans had been so sparse in the past. Point out that the Native American tradition of passing knowledge and history from generation to generation by word of mouth led to a lack of written accounts like William Byrd's. This in turn made it difficult for historians to trace the events and lives of Native Americans.

Song Concerning a Dream of the Thunderbirds

Literature

Teton Sioux

INTRODUCTION As Native Americans, Africans, and Europeans came into contact beginning in the late 1400s, each group began to learn about the culture and traditions of the others. All three groups shared, to some extent, an oral tradition, or the passing down of sayings, songs, tales, and myths from one generation to the next by word of mouth. A poem such as the Native American one below was probably sung or chanted on special occasions, perhaps with a drum as accompaniment.

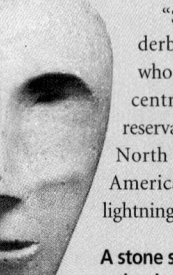

"Song Concerning a Dream of the Thunderbirds" originates from the Teton Sioux, who once lived in the northeastern and north central part of the country and now live on reservations in Minnesota, Nebraska, Montana, North Dakota, and South Dakota. In Native American myth, the thunderbird causes the lightning and thunder that precede the storm.

A stone sculpture made by Native American artists in what is now Gallatin County, Kentucky.

*F*riends, behold!
Sacred I have been made.
Friends, behold!
In a sacred manner
I have been influenced
At the gathering of the clouds.
Friends, behold!
Sacred I have been made.

THINKING ABOUT THE SELECTION

1. To what does the "gathering of the clouds" refer?
2. To whom might the "friends" in the poem refer?

Critical Thinking
3. **Determining Relevance** Native American groups place a strong emphasis on the importance of nature and find much spirituality in the natural world. How does this poem relate to the influence of nature on Native Americans?

ANSWERS TO

Thinking About the Selection
1. The "gathering of the clouds" refers to the beginning of a thunderstorm.
2. The "friends" are probably members of the author's kinship network or clan.
3. The poem is about the power of nature and describes a storm as an event that can give the observer a feeling of sacredness, or holiness.

Finally, ask students to consider what role prejudice against Native Americans, begun in part by such accounts as Mary Rowlandson's, might have played in keeping Native Americans out of history textbooks.

The Captivity of Mary Rowlandson

 *Primary Source*

INTRODUCTION One of the most famous victims of King Philip's War was Mary Rowlandson, the wife of the minister of the town of Lancaster, which was attacked in February 1676. Mrs. Rowlandson spent eleven weeks as a captive of the Narrangansett. After her release, she returned to Lancaster where she recorded her experiences. Her narrative, *A True History of the Captivity and Restoration of Mrs. Mary Rowlandson,* published in 1682, may have been the first American best-seller.

VOCABULARY Before you read the selection, find the meaning of these words in a dictionary: doleful, ravenous, barbarous, vexation.

On the tenth of February, 1675, came the *Indians* with great number upon Lancaster. Their first coming was about Sun-rising. Hearing the noise of some guns, we looked out; several Houses were burning, and the smoke ascending to Heaven. . . .

At length they came and beset our own House, and quickly it was the dolefullest day that ever mine eyes saw. The House stood upon the edge of a Hill; some of the *Indians* got behind the Hill, others into the Barn, and others behind any thing that would shelter them from all which Places they shot against the House, so that the Bullets seemed to fly like Hail. . . .

I had often before this said, that if the *Indians* should come, I would chuse rather to be killed by them than taken alive; but when it came to the trial my mind changed; their glittering Weapons so daunted my spirit, that I chose rather to go along with those (as I may say) ravenous Bears, than that moment to end my daies. And that I may the better declare what happened to me during that grievous Captivity, I shall particularly speak of the several Removes we had up and down the Wilderness.

The first Remove.—Now away we must go with those Barbarous Creatures, with our bodies wounded and bleeding, and our hearts no less than our bodies. About a mile we went that night; up upon a hill, within sight of the Town, where they intended to lodge. . . . This was the dolefullest night that ever my eyes saw: oh the roaring, and singing, and dancing, and yelling. . . . And as miserable was the waste that was there made of Horses, Cattle, Sheep, Swine, Calves, Lambs, Roasting Pigs, and Fowls, (which they had plundered in the Town,) . . . to feed our merciless Enemies. . . .

The second Remove.—But now (the next morning) I must turn my back upon the Town, and travel with them into the vast and desolate Wilderness, I know not whither. It is not my tongue or pen can express the sorrows of my heart and bitterness of my spirit that I had at this departure: but God was with me in a wonderful manner, carrying me along, and bearing up my Spirit, that it did not quite fail. One of the *Indians* carried my poor wounded Babe upon a horse: it went moaning all along, I shall die, I shall die! I went on foot after it, with sorrow that cannot not be exprest. . . .

The twelfth Remove.—It was upon a Sabbath-day morning that they prepared for their Travel. This morning, I asked my Master, whether he would sell me to my Husband? he answered, *Nux,* which did much rejoyce my spirit. My Mistress, before we went, was gone to the burial of a *Papoos*; and returning, she found me sitting and reading in my Bible; she snatched it hastily out of my hand, and threw it out of doors; I ran out and catcht it up, and put it into my pocket, and never let her see it afterward. Then they packed up their things to be gone, and gave me my load; I complained it was too heavy, whereupon she gave me a slap. . . .

Ask students to research your local area to learn about the Native Americans who inhabited it at one time. Students can begin their search at the local library, asking the librarian for help in finding materials on the history of the town or region. In addition, students can check local historical societies and town halls for further information. Students should try to determine what Native American group lived in the area, what their relationship was to the white settlers there, and what happened to them. Do any aspects or reminders of Native American culture exist in the area today? Have students write their findings in a report that they present to the class.

SOURCE READINGS

The twentieth Remove.—I was with the Enemy eleven weeks and five days; and not one Week passed without the fury of the Enemy, and some desolation by fire and sword upon one place or other. . . . They would boast much of their Victories; saying, that in two hours time, they had destroyed such a Captain and his Company in such a place . . . and boast how many Towns they had destroyed, and then scoff, and say, they had done them a good turn to send them to Heaven so soon. . . .

But to return again to my going home; where we may see a remarkable change of Providence: At first they were all against it, except my Husband would come for me; but afterwards they assented to it, and seemed much to rejoyce in it; some asking me to send them some Bread, others some Tobacco, others shaking me by the hand, offering me a Hood and Scarf to ride in; not one moving hand or tongue against it. . . . In my Travels an Indian came to me, and told me, if I were willing, he and his Squaw would run away, and go home along with me. I told him, No, I was not willing to run away, but desired to wait God's time, that I might go home quietly, and without fear. And now God hath granted me my desire. . . .

I have seen the extreme vanity of this World; one hour I have been in health and wealth, wanting nothing; but the next hour in sickness, and wounds, and death, having nothing but sorrow and affliction. . . .

It is good for me that I have been afflicted. The Lord hath shewed me the vanity of these outward things, that they are the vanity of *vanities, and vexation of spirit*; that they are but a shadow, a blast, a bubble, and things of no continuance; that we must rely on God himself, and our whole dependence must be upon him. If trouble from smaller matters begin to arise in me, I have something at hand to check myself with, and say when I am troubled, it was but the other day, that if I had had the world, I would have given it for my Freedom, or to have been a Servant to a *Christian*. I have learned to look beyond present and smaller troubles, and to be quieted under them, as *Moses* said, *Exod.* xiv. 13, *Stand still, and see the salvation of the Lord.*

THINKING ABOUT THE SELECTION

1. What were some of Mrs. Rowlandson's experiences during captivity?
2. How did her eleven weeks in captivity change Rowlandson?

Critical Thinking

3. **Predicting Consequences** Mrs. Rowlandson's narrative became one of the popular books of the seventeenth century, both in the colonies and in Britain. What effect do you think the book might have had on relations between British settlers and Native Americans?

The Diary of a Colonial Gentleman

 **Primary Source**

William Byrd

INTRODUCTION Colonial society was dominated by the gentry, or the wealthy class. In the early 1700s, gentry devoted much of their time to displaying their status and perfecting their "gentle" manners. William Byrd, whose diary is excerpted here, owned several plantations in the colony of Virginia. Although he had to keep track of his plantations, his was a world of leisure. His diary records that he spent much of his time reading Greek and Latin,

saying his prayers, and "dancing his dance" (performing a series of exercises). Like many other colonial gentlemen, Byrd wished to demonstrate his refinement and to prove that he deserved the respect of others.

VOCABULARY Before you read the selection, find the meaning of these words in a dictionary: infallibility, hogshead.

ANSWERS TO

Thinking About the Selection

1. Rowlandson describes injuries from the fighting in Lancaster, much walking, the celebrations of the Native Americans when they did well in battle, being separated from her baby, not being allowed to ride in the canoe, having her Bible taken roughly away, being slapped, being offered help to escape by a Native American, and finally being allowed to return home.
2. During her captivity, Rowlandson realized that small misfortunes or discomforts are noth-
ing compared with how difficult and painful life can become. She learned to trust in God and appreciate small things.
3. The book paints an unfavorable picture of Native Americans, referring to them as "ravenous," "barbarous," and "boastful," and telling of many instances in which they treated her cruelly. Thus, the book most likely inflamed anti–Native American sentiments and contributed to the British settlers' negative perception of Native Americans.

May 1709

1 . . . . I endeavored to learn all I could from Major Burwell who is a sensible man skilled in matters relating to tobacco. In the evening we talked about religion and my wife and her sister had a fierce dispute about the infallibility of the Bible. . . .

4. . . . Captain Berkeley came to see us, who is a very good-humored man. We walked in the garden about an hour; then we went to dinner and I ate boiled beef. In the afternoon we danced a minuet and then took our leave and returned over the river again to Major Burwell's where we found Colonel Bassett and his lady who are very good people. In the evening we saw a great ship sail up the river. The Major sent on board for his letters which brought no news. . . .

6. . . . In the afternoon Colonel Ludwell . . . brought us the bad news that Captain Morgan had lost his ship in Margate Roads by a storm as likewise had several others. My loss was very great in this ship where I had seven hogsheads of skins and 60 hogsheads of heavy tobacco. The Lord gives and the Lord has taken away—blessed be the name of the Lord. In the evening Mr. Clayton and Mr. Robinson came and confirmed the same bad news. However I ate a good supper of mutton and asparagus. Then we went to dance away sorrow. I had good health, good thoughts, and good humor, notwithstanding my misfortune, thanks be to God Almighty.

12. . . . I proceeded to the Falls and went to see my uncle who was much better than he had been. I gave him the best advice I could and then went to view my plantation. The people were all planting because it was a rainy day. Everything was in good order but because I would not hinder the people's planting I returned to Falling Creek, and by the way called on my uncle and there ate bacon and eggs. I likewise called on the Dutchman who I understood was sick,

A colonial gentlewoman and gentleman perform a dance. Colonial gentry had the leisure time to spend on such social activities.

but I found him not at home. . . . About 4 o'clock I returned home but did not find Mr. Anderson, who was gone to Tom the tailor's wedding. I found all well at home, thank God. I had good health, good thoughts, but was out of humor. . . .

13. . . . I rose at 6 o'clock and read a chapter in Hebrew and some Greek in Josephus. I said my prayers and ate milk for breakfast. I danced my dance and settled my accounts. I ate red herring and sallet for dinner. In the afternoon I settled my accounts again. . . .

27. . . . When we were at dinner Mr. Will Randolph came from Williamsburg and brought me two letters from England, one of which told me a sad story of the misfortune of our last fleet by the storm but there are some hopes that the Perry and Lane is not last as we had been informed, thought she was in great danger. . . .

31. . . . This day we sheared the sheep. My man Jack was better and the swelling of his foot abated. We began to shear the sheep but the rain interrupted us. I read some Latin. I ate roast chicken for dinner and green peas. . . . I read more Latin and Greek and wrote on articles of faith. In the evening I walked about the plantation and went to see them hang the tobacco. . . .

THINKING ABOUT THE SELECTION

1. Based on the excerpts from William Byrd's diary, describe how colonial gentry lived.
2. Why was Byrd upset by the news that "Captain Morgan had lost his ship"?

Critical Thinking

3. **Drawing Conclusions** What can you determine about the speed of communications in colonial days from Byrd's diary? Give evidence from the excerpt to support your answer.

ANSWERS TO

Thinking About the Selection

1. Based on Byrd's diary, students should surmise that colonial gentlemen had a good deal of leisure time, during which they engaged in such activities as discussing religion, visiting other colonial gentry, walking on their property, dancing, exercising, reading Greek and Latin, and praying. They did perform some work, such as paying bills or "settling" their accounts, and it seems Mr. Byrd helped with the sheep shearing.

2. Byrd was upset because he had a good deal of skins and tobacco aboard the ship that were to be sold in England. He lost his merchandise and thus the chance of making any profit from it.

3. Students should surmise that communications were very slow in colonial times, based on the fact that Byrd first heard rumors of the loss of the ship Perry and Lane on May 6th, but it was not until May 27th that a letter actually arrived from England that told him of the loss. Even then, the exact extent of the damage was not yet known.

Chapter 2 The Revolutionary Era
1754–1783

📁 Teaching Resources (See Unit 1 Folder)

	Instruction	Enrichment
Section 1 **Colonial Issues and Independent Ideas** (pp. 52–57)	Reproducible Lesson Plan, p. 38 Alternate Lesson Plan, p. 55 Guided Reading and Review, pp. 41–42 Quiz, p. 43	Primary Source Activity, Braddock's Defeat, p. 54 Visual Learning Activity, The American Rattlesnake, p. 61 Visual Learning Activity, Boycotting Tea, p. 60 Literature Activity, To the King, p. 57 Historian's Toolbox Activity, Expressing Problems Clearly, p. 52
Section 2 **The War for Independence** (pp. 59–65)	Reproducible Lesson Plan, p. 39 Alternate Lesson Plan, p. 56 Guided Reading and Review, p. 44 Quiz, p. 45	Critical Thinking Activity, Checking Consistency, p. 53 American Profiles Activity, Deborah Sampson Gannett, p. 48 Primary Source Activity, War Diary of Margaret Hill Morris, pp. 55–56
Section 3 **Government by the States** (pp. 66–71)	Reproducible Lesson Plan, p. 40 Alternate Lesson Plan, p. 57 Guided Reading and Review, p. 46 Quiz, p. 47 Chapter Test, Forms A&B, pp. 62–67	Viewpoints Activity, On the United States as an Independent Nation. pp. 50–51 American Profiles Activity, Daniel Shays, p. 49 Literature Activity, The Contrast, pp. 58–59

📁 Additional Chapter Resources

Resource Organizer, p. 37
Alternate Lesson Plan, p. 54
Answer Keys, pp. 145–157

Bibliography

For the Teacher
DePauw, Linda Grant. *Founding Mothers: Women in America in the Revolutionary Era.* Houghton Mifflin, 1975. (Narrative accounts of women's contributions during the Revolutionary period.)
Harling, Frederick, and Martin Kaufman, eds. *The Ethnic Contribution to the American Revolution.* Historical Journal of Western Massachusetts, 1976. (Documents illustrating the contributions to the Revolution made by various minority groups.)
Smith, Page. *A New Age Now Begins: A People's History of the American Revolution.* McGraw-Hill, 1976. (Fast-paced, comprehensive account of the Revolutionary period.)

Prentice Hall Literature Excerpts from *The American Experience,* 1994, "The Revolutionary Period, 1750–1800," including Henry, Patrick. "Speech in the Virginia Convention."

The Big Idea for the chapter and how the main ideas in each section relate to the Big Idea are graphically displayed below. Comprehension of this chapter's Big Idea is critical to students' understanding of United States history and how we as a nation got where we are today.

Media and Technology

 Critical Thinking, I–10, The Way It Works, H–4,

 Fine Art, D-4, D–5

 Graphic Organizer, G-2

 Visions of America: History Might Not Have Happened This Way Game

 Guided Reading Audiotapes (English and Spanish)

 Computer Test Bank

For the Student

America. Part 4, *Inventing a Nation.* Time-Life. Filmstrip. (Alistair Cooke investigates the Independence Hall debates.)

Lagguth, A. J. *Patriots: The Men who Started the American Revolution.* Simon & Schuster, 1988. (Well-illustrated biographical sketches of some of the most important male figures of the Revolution.)

Meltzer, Milton. *The American Revolutionaries: A History in Their Own Words.* Crowell, 1987. (Includes an exchange of letters between Abigail and John Adams.)

CHAPTER 2

The American Revolution was more than a war for independence. The struggle reflected the development of a unique American identity that was fueled by colonists' personal definition of democracy and equality. This new consciousness inspired a war that led to independence from Great Britain and the creation of a radically new society.

SECTION 1

Many colonists were deeply angered by British attempts to make them pay taxes, which they felt robbed them of their personal liberty and reduced them to slavery. Important new beliefs, including the ideas that people were born equal and could rule themselves, also helped fuel the War for Independence.

SECTION 2

The War for Independence established the American colonies' independence from Great Britain and laid the foundation for a new society based on principles of equality and democracy.

SECTION 3

Many Americans were happy with the country's highly democratic government after the War for Independence; but economic and political problems caused other Americans to worry that the nation would be destroyed if the national government was not strengthened.

The Revolutionary Era
1754–1783

The Relevance of the Big Idea

Before the American Revolution, the thought of establishing a society based on the principles of liberty, equality, and the pursuit of happiness was almost unimaginable. At that time, most people in the world were governed by some form of absolute ruler. But even as the rhetoric of the Revolution was being written down, it became clear that the Founders did not necessarily equate principles with actions. Liberty and equality were neither guaranteed nor universally enjoyed. The application of such principles to all groups in society would be gradual and ongoing throughout American history.

Ask students to provide examples from their own experiences or knowledge of history in which principles have not been practiced.

In Depth

Global Connections

By the mid-eighteenth century, Britain and France had emerged as the two main contenders in the struggle for world empire. Their rivalry dominated the Seven Years' War (1756–1763), a global conflict involving nine European nations that was fought in Europe, Asia, and North America. In North America it was known as the French and Indian War. In the end, the British were victorious in India and, with the help of American colonists, in North America, thus gaining an empire and moving into a position of global supremacy.

The Revolutionary Era
1754–1783

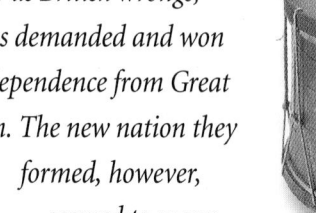

Struggling for their rights and protesting against what they saw as British wrongs, colonists in the Americas demanded and won their independence from Great Britain. The new nation they formed, however, seemed to many Americans to be prone to disorder and instability. Thus, in the 1780s a group of well-educated, well-organized men worked to establish a powerful central government under a written constitution.

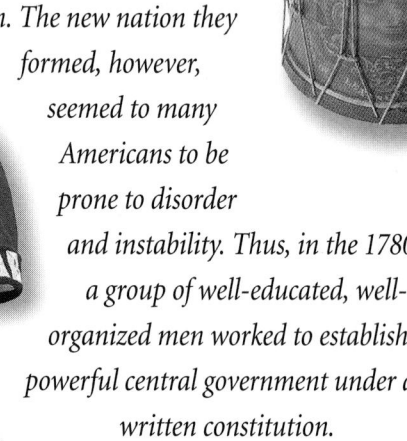

Events in the United States	1754 The French and Indian War begins.		1759 The British defeat the French at Quebec.		1766 Colonists protest the Stamp Act.	1770 The Boston Massacre increases British-colonial tensions.
	1754	**1758**	**1762**	**1766**		**1770**
Events in the World		1756 The French and Indian War spreads to Europe.	1762 Catherine the Great becomes ruler of Russia.			1769 Scotland's James Watt makes a steam engine capable of running other machines.

RESOURCE DIRECTORY

Teaching Resources

Alternate Lesson Plan: Demonstrating the Big Idea found in the Alternate Lesson Plans folder, p. 54, provides a lesson strategy to instruct students about the main political, economic, and ideological issues that led to the conflict between Britain and the American colonies.

Alternative Assessment Handbook provides information, guidance, and strategies for alternative methods of assessment. It includes an essay on new trends in assessment, guidance and strategies for developing performance tasks and portfolios, scoring rubrics, and sample evaluation forms.

Pages 52–57
Colonial Issues and Independent Ideas

Under the pressure of new debts from a war between France and Britain, the British government tried to make its colonies pay what it cost to govern and protect them. In doing so, the British sparked deep anger and resentment among many colonists.

Pages 59–65
The War for Independence

Americans won their independence militarily by outlasting the British in one of the longest and costliest wars in American history. It was a true people's war—though not all Americans fought on the same side.

Pages 66–71
Government by the States

Many Americans were pleased with the highly democratic state created during the American Revolution. But a sizable number of citizens lobbied hard for a stronger national government.

1776 The War for Independence rages.
• The Continental Congress signs the Declaration of Independence.

1781 British general Lord Cornwallis surrenders at Yorktown.

1787 Shays's Rebellion put down.
• The Constitutional Convention is held in Philadelphia.

1774	1778	1782	1786	1790

1778 English explorer James Cook lands on Hawaii.

1781 Peruvian leader Tupac Amaru II leads a revolt against Spanish rule in Peru.

1789 The French Revolution begins, taking its inspiration from the American Revolution.

Alternative Assessment

As an ongoing chapter project, have students assume the role of an adviser to King George III on colonial affairs conducting an investigation into the unrest in the American colonies. Encourage students to collect information and to analyze its significance in terms of its threat to Great Britain's authority. Presentations should contain a minimum of three of the following:

• Copies of political pamphlets outlining radical beliefs
• Letters to British citizens from relatives in the colonies with information about the political mood of the colonies
• Reports from British spies on rebel activities and rebel leaders
• Maps showing areas of rebel activity, such as towns with militias, and specific locations of weapon storehouses
• Interviews with high-ranking British officers regarding the political situation in the colonies

Explain that finished projects will be assessed according to the following guidelines:

• **Unacceptable** Projects are not attempted or fail to meet requirements outlined.
• **Limited/Acceptable** Projects are completed and an attempt is made to understand and interpret the data in terms of how seriously they might affect Great Britain.
• **Extensive/Commendable** Projects are completed, the data are plausibly interpreted, and the seriousness of their implications is well judged.
• **Extraordinary/Outstanding** Data are compiled from more than three sources, thoroughly interpreted, and specifically assessed for their relative importance to Great Britain's position.

For information and guidance on alternative assessment trends and strategies, see the Alternative Assessment Handbook in the Resource Directory on page 50.

Colonial Issues and Independent Ideas

1. FOCUS

Connecting to the Big Idea

See page 50B. Tell students that the War for Independence was fueled by both British actions and new ideas. To increase tax revenues, Great Britain tried to tighten its control over the fiercely independent colonies. Ask students what specific events caused Americans to think that their freedom was threatened. Meanwhile, powerful new ideas were inspiring Americans to challenge authority in hopes of creating a completely different kind of society. Ask students what these new ideas were.

Objectives

● Describe the series of events between 1763 and 1775 that led Americans to believe they were being deprived of their rights.

● Describe the ideas contained in *Common Sense* and the Declaration of Independence.

Bellringer

Write the word *idealistic* on the chalkboard. Ask students to provide a brief definition of the word and to list some attributes of an idealistic person.

Reading Strategy

Reinforcing Key Ideas Draw students' attention to this sentence on page 54: "By 1770, growing numbers of Americans were convinced that British politicians were engaged in nothing less than a deliberate plot to rob them of their personal independence through taxation." As they read, students should list and briefly describe specific British actions that led so many Americans to feel this way.

SECTION PREVIEW

Under the pressure of new debts from a war between France and Britain, the British government tried to make its colonies pay what it cost to govern and protect them. In doing so, the British sparked deep anger and resentment among many colonists, who thought they were being treated like enslaved people rather than free men and women.

Key Concepts

• The pattern of events between 1763 and 1775 led many Americans to believe that the British were using taxation as an excuse to deprive them of their rights.

         • Writings of the 1770s established new and radical principles of freedom and equality in American government and society.

Key Terms, People, and Places

American Revolution, War for Independence, depression, boycott, Declaration of Independence, popular sovereignty; minuteman, George Washington, King George III, Thomas Paine, Thomas Jefferson, Abigail Adams

Colonists who poured their tea from this pot bolstered their resistance to the Stamp Act, a British tax law that led to the War for Independence.

On the morning on April 19, 1775, about 70 men stood on the green in the center of Lexington, Massachusetts. They were **minutemen**—local residents organized as a defensive force who had pledged to respond in a matter of minutes when called to action. They had been waiting since 2 A.M. for the British force that was to march through Lexington on its way to destroy a store of military supplies in neighboring Concord.

A little after dawn, British major John Pitcairn led between 700 and 800 British regulars into Lexington, outnumbering the minutemen ten times over. Pitcairn took a position behind the Americans and ordered them to give up their guns. The captain of the minutemen told

---

his men to go home. Some began to leave; others stood their ground.

Exactly what happened next will never be known. Both British and Americans denied shooting at each other first. In any case, the British soldiers were soon firing into the American ranks and using their bayonets. Within minutes, eight dead Americans lay on Lexington Green and another nine were wounded. The victorious British regrouped and marched on toward Concord.

This brief encounter was the beginning of an eight-year war between the British government and thirteen of its North American colonies. To win their independence, the colonies would organize themselves into a loose confederation called the United States of America. The war and the political and social changes that accompanied it are called the **American Revolution**. The war itself is called the **War for Independence**. But before you read about the Revolution, you must first understand what motivated several dozen farmers and artisans to stand on a green in the middle of the night and defy the authority of their king.

The Background to Revolution

The background to the War for Independence includes an earlier war that had broken out in 1754 and lasted until 1763. Called the French and Indian War, the British and their colonists waged it against the French and their Native American allies for control of eastern North America. It ended in a British victory. With the Treaty of Paris, signed in 1763, the French turned over all of Canada to the British. ⭐ Though a success for the British and their colonies, the French and Indian War had several bad side effects that severely strained British-American relations. For example, the arrogance of many royal officers insulted colonial gentlemen like colonial leader **George Washington**. And it seemed to ordinary colonists that the

---

▶ RESOURCE DIRECTORY

Teaching Resources

📄 **Reproducible Lesson Plan** found in the Unit 1 folder, p. 38, provides a summary of the Section 1 Lesson Plan content.

📄 **Alternate Lesson Plan: Critical Thinking** Recognizing Bias, found in the Alternate Lesson Plans folder, p. 55, helps students to recognize bias clearly by writing editorials on a prewar event from the British and American perspectives.

📄 **Guided Reading and Review** found in the Unit 1 folder, pp. 41–42, provides a structure for reading and mastering the key concepts and reviewing the key terms for Section 1. (Guided Practice)

📄 **Primary Source Activity** Braddock's Defeat, found in the Unit 1 folder, p. 54, focuses on Benjamin Franklin's account of the disastrous defeat of British general Edward Braddock's forces in the French and Indian War.

British were dealing with their colonial governments and local merchants in a high-handed manner—suggesting that the British considered the colonists to be inferior. This angered Americans, who felt they had every right to be treated like full-fledged citizens of a great empire, especially while they were helping protect that empire.

The Issues That Led to the War for Independence

In protecting Americans with troops and ships during the French and Indian War, Great Britain had built up huge debts. It only made sense that the colonists should pay their share of the cost of running the Empire so that Britain could pay off those debts. Besides, the British knew that the colonists were well off; their collective standard of living was higher than any in Europe. Britain, in particular, was in the midst of a serious **depression,** or economic slump.

An End to Salutary Neglect In early 1764, under the leadership of George Grenville, the chief minister under the British king, **George III,** the British Parliament passed a law called the Sugar Act. It was intended to raise money from the colonies by a change in the tax on molasses, a product that was widely used at that time. The act signaled an end to Britain's salutary neglect of its colonies. Now it would deliberately interfere in local matters, disrupting old traditions and accepted customs. Colonists who were involved in overseas commerce, including southern tobacco and rice planters as well as northern merchants, were especially displeased with the change in policy.

The Stamp Act Crisis The growing anger over British government interference finally exploded in 1765 after Parliament's passage of the Stamp Act. Grenville intended this law in part to raise money for the defense and support of the American colonies. It required that all legal documents and printed materials—newspapers, for example—should have an attached paper stamp bought from the government. The stamp simply showed that a required fee had been paid. The modern practice of putting a paper stamp on a piece of mail is similar.

News of the Stamp Act created a firestorm of protest in the colonies. Merchants and artisans joined together in a **boycott**—a form of protest in which people refuse to buy goods or services. Colonial legislatures, and a special Stamp Act Congress, met to argue that colonists were freeborn Englishmen and Parliament could not tax them without their consent. They had no representatives in Parliament, they pointed out, and so Parliament had no right to decide what kind of taxes they should pay. In other words, there should be no taxation without representation.

British merchants, too, howled in protest as they saw their trade with the colonies threatened by the boycott. In the face of such a torrent of opposition and the virtual refusal of colonists to buy the stamps, Parliament backed down. Grenville was forced from power, and new British leaders repealed the Stamp Act in 1766.

The Colonists Resist "Slavery" The triumphant colonists quieted down. But the issues raised by the Stamp Act would not go away. Could Parliament tax Americans without representation in Parliament? Did the rights that English law gave to free men in England also belong to free men in the American colonies?

In 1767 Parliament reasserted its authority by placing taxes on certain imported goods, including lead, glass, and tea. These Townshend

Using Historical Evidence By distorting space and time, the painter of this view of the British attack on Quebec in 1759 was able to illustrate several events at once. *What British actions are shown?*

Media and Technology

 Transparency
Critical Thinking, 1–10

Explain/Discuss

Review British policy toward the colonies until the 1760s. Ask why Great Britain felt justified in exerting more political and economic control over the colonies after the French and Indian War. Why did the colonists react so strongly?

Discuss the growing tension between the colonists and Great Britain. Ask why the passage of the Sugar Act was significant. Why did the Stamp Act inspire such strong American protest? What measures led Americans to believe that the British were trying to take away their freedom?

Caption Answer to ...

Using Historical Evidence

The advance over water, the British troops scaling the heights, and the final battle.

 In Depth

Did You Know?

Women played a central role in the movement to boycott British goods. Instead of tea, Patriot women served coffee and herbal brews. Refusing to buy British cotton, they dressed themselves and their families in homespun. At times women took more direct action. One Boston man described a "Female Riot" in which a large mob of women attacked a merchant who was overcharging for coffee "and demanded the Keys to his Store, which he refusing to deliver, they immediately placed him in a Cart and threatened to Cart him out of Town."

Explain to students that ideas played an important role in the War for Independence. Ask students to discuss the war in terms of the ideas of thinkers like Thomas Paine and Thomas Jefferson. Why might these men be considered idealists? You might want to refer to the attributes students listed in the Bellringer activity.

Discuss with students how the ideas that fueled the War for Independence also helped create a new society. Ask why *Common Sense* was important to the development of democracy. What important political ideas of foreign thinkers provided the foundation for the Declaration of Independence? What enduring principles of American government and society are included in it?

Caption Answer to ...

Interpreting Charts

1766, 1767, 1768; answers may also include 1770.

In Depth

Then and Now

Although tea, coffee, and chocolate were all introduced to North America in the seventeenth century, by the 1770s tea was the most popular nonalcoholic drink in the colonies. With the imposition of the tea tax and the Boston Tea Party, however, Americans developed a taste for coffee, a preference that is still apparent. Today the United States consumes about 70 percent of the world's coffee crop, an average of 15 to 16 pounds of coffee per person a year, or three cups of coffee a day.

Duties, named after the chief British financial official, Charles Townshend, also provoked protests and a boycott. Once again, Parliament eventually backed down, repealing all the taxes in 1770—all the taxes, that is, except for one that Parliament kept to save its pride: the tax on tea. As a result, tea became a symbol of British injustice, and many Americans refused to drink it.

⭐ By 1770, growing numbers of Americans were convinced that British politicians were engaged in nothing less than a deliberate plot to rob them of their personal independence through taxation. Protest groups that had formed throughout the colonies during the Stamp Act crisis—"Sons of Liberty" and "Daughters of Liberty"—complained that the British were taxing them in order to take away their property and make them into what amounted to slaves. This was something many people, whether gentlemen, farmers, or artisans, believed they simply could not tolerate. In the words of John Dickinson, a Pennsylvania lawyer,

> Those who are taxed without their own consent, expressed by themselves or their representatives, are slaves. We are taxed without our own consent, expressed by ourselves or our representatives. We are therefore—SLAVES.

More British actions followed. British troops occupied Boston in the late 1760s to protect officials enforcing the Townshend Duties. Tensions between soldiers and townspeople exploded in the Boston Massacre on March 5, 1770. An African American, Crispus Attucks, and four other colonists were killed.

⭐ Then, in 1773, the British government announced that it was going to sell millions of pounds of tea at discounted rates directly to the American public. To the colonists, the move seemed a way of trying to buy their acceptance of the detested tea tax. In harbors up and down the Atlantic seaboard, ships loaded with tea were turned away. Some residents of Boston, in a protest now known as the

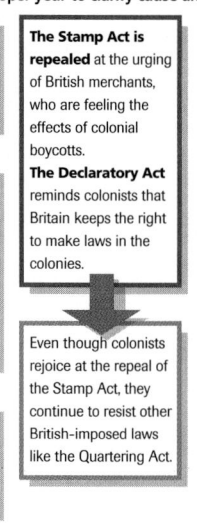
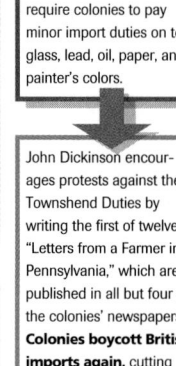

1764	1765	1766	1767	1768	1769

Some events are shown out of order within their proper year to clarify cause and effect.

Parliament passes and strictly enforces **the Sugar Act** to raise money to pay for the cost of administering the colonies.

Colonists respond with written protests, occasional boycotts, and cries of **"No taxation without representation."**

The Stamp Act requires the purchase of tax stamps, which are to be attached to all printed goods.

Colonists protest violently. Delegates of nine colonies meet in New York as **the Stamp Act Congress** and prepare a Declaration of Rights and Grievances. **Boycott** of British goods begins.

The Quartering Act requires the colonies to quarter, or provide food and lodging for, British soldiers.

The Stamp Act is repealed at the urging of British merchants, who are feeling the effects of colonial boycotts. **The Declaratory Act** reminds colonists that Britain keeps the right to make laws in the colonies.

Even though colonists rejoice at the repeal of the Stamp Act, they continue to resist other British-imposed laws like the Quartering Act.

The Townshend Duties require colonies to pay minor import duties on tea, glass, lead, oil, paper, and painter's colors.

John Dickinson encourages protests against the Townshend Duties by writing the first of twelve "Letters from a Farmer in Pennsylvania," which are published in all but four of the colonies' newspapers. **Colonies boycott British imports again,** cutting trade in half.

The New York Assembly is suspended for the colony's refusal to comply fully with Quartering Act.

The British government orders troops to be stationed in Boston to enforce the Townshend Duties.

Boston colonists refuse to quarter British troops.

The British governor of Virginia dissolves the Virginia Assembly for its resolution against British taxes and other protests.

Virginia, Maryland, and South Carolina agree not to import certain British goods.

| British Action |
| Colonial Action |

Most colonial legislatures refuse to pay for supplies required by the Quartering Act.

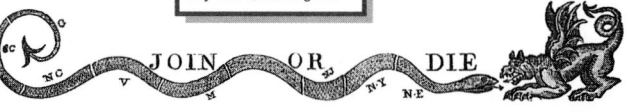

RESOURCE DIRECTORY

Teaching Resources

⭐ **Visual Learning Activity** The American Rattlesnake, found in the Unit 1 folder, p. 61, uses a cartoon depicting the rebellious colonies as a rattlesnake to emphasize the seriousness and strength of the colonists' position.

⭐ **Visual Learning Activity** Boycotting Tea, found in the Unit 1 folder, p. 60, focuses on the symbolic importance of the British Tea Act and the subsequent colonial boycott of British tea.

Boston Tea Party, threw the cargoes of several ships into the harbor.

Losing all patience, Parliament passed the Coercive Acts in 1774 to punish the colony of Massachusetts. Among other things, these acts—called the Intolerable Acts by colonists everywhere—virtually shut down individual town governments and the colonial legislature. These strong measures only confirmed American suspicions that the British were moving to take away their freedoms and their property.

Local Committees of Correspondence, groups formed to coordinate protest throughout the colonies, met to elect delegates to the First Continental Congress. The delegates discussed the proper reaction to the Coercive Acts. Their efforts to find a peaceful solution failed. In July 1775, after the war had erupted at Concord and Lexington, the Second Continental Congress agreed to a statement they called *A Declaration of the Causes and Necessities of Taking Up Arms.* It stated that the members were "resolved to die Free men rather than live Slaves."

The Continental Congress was only putting into words the belief that had brought the farmers and artisans of eastern Massachusetts to the green at Lexington that April. It was the conviction of the Congress and the minutemen alike that at some point they had to take a stand against the pattern of enslavement they saw in the actions of the British, whom they perceived as corrupt, immoral, and power hungry. They did not consider themselves radicals or revolutionaries; they were simply protecting their way of life, their land, and their households.

The Ideas That Led to the War for Independence

From the beginning, the American Revolution was more than a rebellion or a war for independence. The Revolution itself began long before the war and continued long after the war had ended. It announced the creation of a new society committed to such powerful ideas as equality and democracy. Although the

Colonists saw the "cursed stamp" as a symbol of enslavement to the British crown.

1770	1772	1773	1774	1775
In Boston, British troops come to the aid of a fellow soldier and fire into an angry mob. Five colonists are killed.	The British government orders that governors and judges in Massachusetts are now to be paid by Britain, removing them from the colony's control.	Parliament passes **the Tea Act** in an attempt to save the East India Company from bankruptcy and to reassert its right to tax.	The Coercive Acts, called **the "Intolerable Acts"** by the colonists, are passed in response to the Tea Party: • **The Port Bill** closes Boston's port until payment is made for the destroyed tea. • **The Massachusetts Government Act** effectively imposes a new form of government on the colony. • New provisions to **the Quartering Act** force colonists to quarter British soldiers in private homes, if necessary. • **The Administration of Justice Act** gives royal officials in Massachusetts the right to trial in a court outside the colony. Four thousand troops are sent to Boston to enforce these acts.	British troops march to Concord, Massachusetts, to seize and destroy colonial munitions being stored there.
Colonial propagandists quickly dub the riot the **"Boston Massacre."**	In response to the new salary arrangement, Samuel Adams forms the **Boston Committee of Correspondence** to alert Massachusetts and "the world" to the "infringements and violations" of the rights of colonists in Boston.	A group of Boston patriots destroy a shipment of tea in a protest known as **the Boston Tea Party.**		Colonial and British troops clash in the **Battle of Lexington.** The **Second Continental Congress** meets in Philadelphia to address revolutionary war aims and appoints George Washington commander-in-chief of the Continental Army.
British officials in Boston move troops to quarters outside the city to ease tensions.	**The *Gaspée*,** a British revenue cutter, aggressively patrols the Rhode Island coast in order to control colonial smuggling.	In response to British investigation of the *Gaspée* affair and to the aggressive British enforcement of customs regulations, Virginia's House of Burgesses appoints a **Provincial Committee of Correspondence** to inform all the colonial provinces of the actions of the British Parliament.		
Parliament repeals Townshend Duties, but retains tea tax.			In Philadelphia, delegates from all of the colonies except Georgia meet in the **First Continental Congress.** It creates the **Continental Association** to boycott British goods and sends a petition of grievances to the king, outlining what it considers the rights of the colonists and their assemblies.	
Colonists **end boycott** begun in 1767.	To protest the harsh treatment of legitimate traders as well as colonial smugglers, Rhode Island colonists burn the *Gaspée*.			

Media and Technology

Transparency
The Way It Works, H-4

Analyze

Have students analyze the American colonists' growing resentment of British authority. Have students explain the words *enslavement* and *slaves* as Americans like John Dickinson defined them. Why had many Americans come to take their freedom so seriously that they were willing to risk death for it?

Activity

Teaching Heterogeneous Groups

To demonstrate the British policy of forcing the colonists to share in the cost of running the colonies (and the colonists' reaction to it), have students list their most cherished privileges at home. Responses may include using the phone, driving the family car, watching television, and so on. Then announce to students that their parents will henceforth tax them for such privileges. Divide the class into two groups: parents (Tories) and students (colonists). Have the groups informally debate this new taxation policy.

Enrichment

Invite students to go back in time to the 1770s and hold an informal debate over the question of whether or not people are capable of self-rule. Different students should assume the respective roles of artisan, farmer, African American, woman, gentleman member of the leisure class, British supporter, or other individual from the Revolutionary period. Have students do research to prepare for their role in the debate.

Answer to ...

MAKING CONNECTIONS

(See page 56.) Some students may argue that ordinary people do run their own government through representatives; others may point out that interest groups wield power and influence over government unmatched by the ordinary citizen.

3. ASSESS

Section 1 Review Answers

1. (a) American Revolution, see p. 52, (b) War for Independence, see p. 52, (c) depression, see p. 53, (d) boycott, see p. 53, (e) Declaration of Independence, see p. 56, (f) popular sovereignty, see p. 56

2. (a) minuteman, see p. 52, (b) George Washington, see p. 52, (c) King George III, see p. 53, (d) Thomas Paine, see p. 56, (e) Thomas Jefferson, see p. 56, (f) Abigail Adams, see p. 56

3. Such actions include the occupation of Boston, the Boston Massacre, and a series of controversies that arose between the British and individual colonies.

4. Paine attacked the whole idea of government by kings and aristocrats.

5. Answers should suggest that the American colonists would act in the same way whether or not the conspiracy was real.

In Depth

Biography

Elizabeth Freeman (1744–1829) was a Massachusetts slave who in 1781 sued for her freedom under the new state constitution that declared all people "free and equal" under the law. Represented by a lawyer, she won her case and went free, setting a legal precedent that would help to end slavery in Massachusetts. Freeman, who lived into her eighties, became widely admired. Her lawyer once said of her, "Having known this woman, I cannot believe in the moral or physical inferiority of the race to which she belonged."

immediate accomplishment of the Revolution was simply to preserve the power of white men of the "gentle" class, its long-term significance lay in changing people's thinking about the world. ✪

Two Documents Spread Democratic Ideas
One of the chief documents that expressed and developed the ideas of the Revolution was *Common Sense,* published in 1776. Written by **Thomas Paine,** a recent immigrant from England, this pamphlet reached hundreds of thousands of readers of all social classes. Democratic in both style and substance, it was a direct assault on the whole idea of government by kings and aristocrats. What good were kings? asked Paine bluntly. "Of more worth is one honest man to society, and in the sight of God," he said, "than all the crowned ruffians that ever lived."

The other great democratic document of 1776 was written by an American aristocrat, or member of the gentle class, named **Thomas Jefferson.** In June 1776, after the colonies had been at war with Britain for over a year, the Continental Congress decided that it was high time to issue a statement declaring that the colonies were cutting their ties with their parent country. This is the document we now call the **Declaration of Independence.**

Jefferson drew largely on a theory of government devised by earlier European political thinkers, including the Englishman John Locke. According to this theory, originally people had been completely free of government. In order to gain increased safety and comfort, they had joined together in a community. They had then given certain individuals the power to govern the community, forming a social contract. If a ruler failed to act in the best interests of those he governed, he was breaking the social contract. In that case, the people had the right to revolt against his unjust rule and choose a new form of government.

Jefferson wrote that governments get their power from "the consent of the governed," implying that ordinary people can and should govern themselves. This idea is now called **popular sovereignty,** although the term did not come into use until later.

MAKING CONNECTIONS

Do you think the United States today is a nation in which ordinary citizens run their own government? Explain your thinking.

What the Declaration Accomplished On July 4—the date Americans now celebrate as Independence Day—all thirteen colonies joined in accepting the declaration. With that vote, they ceased being colonies and officially became a new nation, the United States.

But the Declaration achieved more than just proclaiming the existence of the United States of America. It also announced that both popular sovereignty and equality were basic principles of American government and society. As the declaration stated:

> We hold these truths to be self-evident, that all men are created Equal, that they are Endowed By their Creator with Certain unalienable rights [rights that cannot be taken away], that among these are Life, Liberty, and the pursuit of happiness.

Despite these stirring words, Jefferson, like most members of the Continental Congress, had no intention of surrendering power to people who were not like him. Though he condemned slavery in theory, he was a slaveholder himself, and he could not have imagined a society in which African Americans were treated as his equals. Nor could he have understood how women might share in the rights and responsibilities of government. The "Founding Fathers"—the men who approved the Declaration and those who later created the federal government—were just that: patriarchs, heads of households with many dependents. When they talked about equality and popular sovereignty, they meant equality and sovereignty for gentlemen of property and high standing in society. But once these ideas were let loose, neither the Founders nor later generations of white men could control them. Immediately, both African Americans and white women began to apply the idea of equality to themselves. One of the women who did so was **Abigail Adams.**

▶ RESOURCE DIRECTORY

Teaching Resources

✪ **Literature Activity** "To the King," found in the Unit 1 folder, p. 57, uses a Phillis Wheatley poem to illustrate a popular colonial sentiment toward King George III in pre-Revolutionary times

AMERICAN PROFILES
Abigail Adams

Born on November 22, 1744, Abigail Smith grew up in a Massachusetts household. Abigail's youth was a comfortable one; she devoted much of her time to religion and reading. Shortly before her twentieth birthday, she married twenty-nine-year-old John Adams.

In the 1770s, John Adams—a stubborn and outspoken lawyer—became one of the leaders of the opposition to British colonial policy. While Abigail remained shut off from the public debate because she was a woman, she did not hesitate to express her opinions to her husband. Abigail saw the Revolution as an opportunity for Americans to rethink domestic as well as public relationships. Several months before the signing of the Declaration of Independence, Abigail sent a letter to John, who was attending the Continental Congress.

I long to hear that you have declared an independency—and by the way in the new Code of Laws which I suppose it will be necessary for you to make I desire you would Remember the Ladies, and be more generous and favorable to them than your ancestors. Do not put such unlimited power into the hands of the Husbands.

Remember all Men would be tyrants if they could. If particular care and attention is not paid to the Ladies we are determined to foment [stir up] a Rebellion, and will not hold ourselves bound by any Laws in which we have no voice, or Representation.

Part of Abigail's intention was to tease John by implying that he was included in her negative representation of husbands. The two had an affectionate relationship and truly respected each other. She was serious, however, in her complaints about how men in general treated women. As she explained, she wanted husbands to change their relationships with their wives by giving up "the harsh title of Master for the more tender and endearing one of Friend."

The humor and friendship that lighted Abigail and John's letters remained a part of their marriage until her death in 1818. Together they weathered the War for Independence and eventually became the first presidential couple to live in the White House.

Abigail Adams's questioning of the existing order was just part of the revolution begun by men such as Jefferson and Paine. The next section shows that before any Americans could enjoy the fruits of that revolution, they had a difficult war to win.

Abigail Adams advised her husband to "Remember the Ladies" when declaring independence for the new nation.

SECTION 1 REVIEW

Key Terms, People, and Places
1. Define (a) American Revolution, (b) War for Independence, (c) depression, (d) boycott, (e) Declaration of Independence, (f) popular sovereignty.
2. Identify (a) minuteman, (b) George Washington, (c) King George III, (d) Thomas Paine, (e) Thomas Jefferson, (f) Abigail Adams.

Key Concepts
3. Describe three British actions the colonists interpreted as signs of a British intention to take away their liberty.
4. What ideas did Thomas Paine attack in his great democratic document, *Common Sense?*

Critical Thinking
5. **Determining Relevance** By 1770 many Americans thought the British were trying to take away their freedoms. Did it matter whether or not they were right? Explain your thinking.

Quiz found in the Unit 1 folder, p. 43, covers the main ideas in this section as well as the key terms.

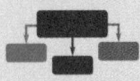

In Depth
Multicultural Perspectives

In 1767 a Caribbean landowner traveled to London with his slave, Jonathon Strong, whom he beat viciously in a fit of rage. Strong was found and befriended by a white Englishman, Granville Sharp, who helped him to escape. In 1772 Sharp took the issue of slavery before the British lord chief justice, who ruled, "Is not a Negro a Man? . . . As soon as any slave sets foot on English soil he shall be free." Sharp also helped organize the British Anti-Slavery Movement. In 1807 Parliament voted to halt Britain's slave trade, but it did not abolish slavery in the British colonies, where it existed.

Critical Thinking

Expressing Problems Clearly

Focus Clearly express the dispute between supporters of the Stamp Act and its opponents.

Instruct Provide students with the following facts: (1) Most Patriot politicians had never lobbied to send representatives to the British Parliament. (2) Americans were being treated no differently from their British counterparts in being taxed without representation, since a majority of British adult males were not entitled to vote because they did not own enough property.

Ask students how this information might change their perception of the dispute between supporters and opponents of the Stamp Act.

Extend See Historian's Toolbox Activity in the Resource Directory below.

Answers

1. (a) The tax imposed under the Stamp Act was not legal. (b) To be considered British subjects, the American colonists must share in the payment of Britain's tax burden.

2. (a) To keep the colonists from being subjected to a tax that violated their rights as British citizens. (b) That the colonists acknowledge Parliament's authority and pay a fair share of Britain's taxes.

3. (a) No. This characterization is essentially an interpretation of the problem. (b) Excerpt A: The characterization of the situation as a calamity and the feelings of concern and alarming apprehension; the reference to a "fiction of law." Excerpt B: the statement about squandering away blood and treasure in the colonies' defense.

4. The Stamp Act's supporters wanted the colonists to recognize the authority of Parliament and abide by its resolutions. They wanted the colonists to pay the taxes imposed by the Stamp Act and to acknowledge the fairness of those taxes. Opponents wanted the Stamp Act nullified in recognition of the fact that it was imposed illegally, in violation of the colonists' rights as British subjects.

Expressing Problems Clearly

The ability to express a problem clearly means being able to describe the nature of a situation or a question that is difficult, puzzling, or open to debate. When you express a problem clearly, you are taking the first step toward understanding and solving it.

Following Parliament's passage of the Stamp Act in 1765, articles like those excerpted on this page appeared in American and British newspapers.

Use the following steps to practice expressing problems clearly.

1. Analyze the information. When you are confronted with a problem, study the information involved. Read excerpts A and B. (a) What was the nature of the case made by the American colonist in excerpt A? (b) What information was given by the British writer in excerpt B?

2. Identify the basic concepts involved. Problems usually arise out of a specific set of circumstances. However, they often revolve around a general principle, such as fairness. To identify this concept, try to express the problem in terms of what each side wants for itself. (a) What benefit did the American writer want to achieve for the colonists? (b) What did the British writer want?

3. Identify the function of the supporting details. In any problem, details often are presented that may not be basic to the problem itself. (a) The British writer characterizes the colonists' opposition to an act of Parliament as "an alarming crisis." Is this a basic part of the problem? Why or why not? (b) What other details in these excerpts did not relate to the basic issue of disagreement?

4. Express the problem clearly. Now that you have identified the main area of dispute and stripped away irrelevant details, you are ready to express the problem clearly. How would you describe the dispute between the British supporters of the Stamp Act and its American opponents?

A "In all the calamities which have ever befallen this country, we have never felt so great a concern, or such alarming apprehensions, as on this occasion. . . . We [find] this tax to be unconstitutional. We have always understood it to be a grand and fundamental principle of the [British] constitution, that no freeman should be subject to any tax to which he has not given his own consent, in person or by proxy [representation]. And . . . that no freeman can be separated from his property but by his own act or fault. We take it clearly, therefore, to be inconsistent with the spirit of the . . . principles of the British constitution, that we should be subject to any tax imposed by the British Parliament; because we are not represented in that assembly in any sense, unless it be by a fiction of law."

John Adams, *Instructions of the Town of Braintree Massachusetts on the Stamp Act,* October 14, 1765

B "The question now is, Whether those American subjects are, or are not, bound by the resolutions of a British parliament? If they are not, they are entirely a separate people from us. On the other hand, if the people of America are bound by the proceedings of the English legislature, . . . [then] the present crisis . . . is really an alarming one. The people of the colonies know very well that the taxes of the Mother country are every day increasing; and can they expect that no addition whatsoever will be made to theirs? . . . In assisting the colonies we had an eye to our own interest. It would be ridiculous otherwise to squander away our blood and our treasure in their defense. But surely the benefit was mutual; and consequently the disadvantage [of taxes] should be mutual too."

"William Pym" to the *London General Evening Post,* August 20, 1765, reprinted in the *Newport Mercury,* October 28, 1765

 **RESOURCE DIRECTORY**

Teaching Resources

Historian's Toolbox Activity Expressing Problems Clearly, found in the Unit 1 folder, p. 52, helps students apply this skill by examining various opinions about the issue of increased taxes.

The War for Independence

SECTION PREVIEW

Americans won their independence militarily by outlasting the British in one of the longest and costliest wars in American history. It was a true people's war—though not all Americans fought on the same side.

Key Concepts

· Despite the size and experience of the British military, the British did not have a superior position at the start of the war any more than the Americans did.

· The forces of the United States continued to fight against the British despite repeated losses.

· The Americans, with the help of the French, ended the war by trapping Cornwallis's army at Yorktown.

· Many American groups, including Native Americans and African Americans, experienced violence and hardship during the war.

Key Terms, People, and Places

Treaty of Paris, inflation; Patriots, Loyalists, Tories, Marquis de Lafayette, Baron von Steuben

A s important as all the talk of self-government was, it would remain only talk if Americans could not win their independence. The British were not willing to let thirteen colonies go their way without a fight, especially when those colonies were prosperous. It took the Americans eight years, from 1775 to 1783, to accomplish their goal of freedom. Not only was the War for Independence the longest war in United States history after the Vietnam War, but it was the only one to be fought throughout the entire nation.

Advantages and Disadvantages

⭐ After scattering the rebels—or **Patriots,** as the Americans preferred to call themselves—

from Lexington Green on April 19, 1775, the British forces continued on to Concord. (See Section 1.) There they fulfilled their mission by burning some rebel war supplies. As the British returned to Boston, however, Patriots from nearby towns gathered along the route and sniped at them from behind stone walls and other cover by the roadside. The easy British victory at dawn had become an exhausting and costly defeat by evening, as the British tallied 273 wounded or killed, compared to only 95 Patriots.

Still, the British had several reasons for believing that they would easily crush the rebellion in their American colonies. After all, Great Britain was the most powerful nation on earth. It had the richest economy, the largest navy, and an experienced and confident military. Almost a decade earlier, its armies and ships had defeated France in North America and Europe and added India as well as Canada to its Empire.

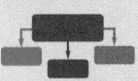

American Disadvantages The Americans, on the other hand, had no navy, no army, and no real government. They were not only disorganized, they were divided by state, by region, and by differing political goals. They even were split along racial lines. In the South, the British offered freedom to enslaved African Americans who would fight against the rebels. Throughout the colonies, Native Americans were outraged by American attacks against them and believed that their best interests lay in supporting the British, who were trying to prevent settlement in the West.

Furthermore, a great many colonists, called **Loyalists**—or **Tories,** after the majority party in Britain's Parliament—preferred to remain loyal to King George, even if they disagreed with the policies of his officials. John Adams estimated that one third of Americans were rebels, one third Tories, and one third neither. Tories tended

In a gesture symbolizing America's self-reliance, George Washington, the commander of the United States forces, declined to accept these elegant silver pistols captured from British major John Pitcairn.

SECTION 2

1. FOCUS

Connecting to the Big Idea

See page 50B. Explain to students that the War for Independence was a long and costly war that caused people great hardship. In the end, Americans won their independence from Great Britain. Ask students why the Americans were victorious.

Objectives

● Explain why neither the British nor the Americans had an advantage over the other at the start of the war.

● Describe how American forces continued to fight despite repeated losses.

● Explain how American forces, with the help of the French, finally ended the war.

● Identify how the war affected Native Americans and African Americans.

Bellringer

Ask students if they can recall a time in their life when they felt hopelessly defeated but kept going in spite of their feelings and were eventually successful. What techniques did they use to boost their morale?

Reading Strategy

Predicting Content Ask students to skim Section 2, list the main headings and subheadings, and write a sentence or phrase to predict the content listed under each one. Then have them review their predictions after they have finished reading the section, testing them against the actual text.

📋 **The Reproducible Lesson Plan** found in the Unit 1 folder, p. 39, provides a summary of the Section 2 Lesson Plan content.

📋 **Alternate Lesson Plan: Learning Styles** found in the Unit 1 folder, p. 56, especially effective for auditory and kinesthetic learners, helps students to identify and explain the significance of key battles of the War for Independence through preparation of mock press briefings.

📋 **Guided Reading and Review** found in the Unit 1 folder, p. 44, provides a structure for reading and mastering the key concepts and reviewing the key terms for Section 2. (Guided Practice)

⭐📋 **Critical Thinking Activity** Checking Consistency: Lexington and Concord, found in the Unit 1 folder, p. 53, helps students apply this skill by presenting two differing accounts of which side fired the first shot of the Revolutionary War.

Explain/Discuss

Explain to students that Americans made great sacrifices during the long, hard, and costly war. Why were they willing to sacrifice so much?

Discuss the course of the war and ask why it took the colonists so long to win. What kinds of hardships did Americans suffer during the war? How did they finally win?

In Depth

Historical Misconceptions

The first major conflict of the Revolutionary War, and the one that has become synonymous with the fight for American independence, is the Battle of Bunker Hill. The battle, however, was actually fought a few thousand feet away from Bunker Hill, at a mound known as Breed's Hill. Though colonial officers were ordered to fortify Bunker Hill against possible British attack in an effort to control Boston Harbor, the officers, for reasons still unknown, fortified Breed's Hill. Today Breed's Hill is known as Bunker Hill, and the original site of Bunker Hill has houses built on it.

A minuteman using shoot-and-run tactics killed the British officer who carried this sword during the retreat from the Battle of Concord on April 19, 1776.

to be either merchants or well-established people with connections to the British government. They might also be freed slaves, Scots-Irish people in the backcountry, and other people who preferred to be ruled by the British rather than by colonial gentlemen. About 80,000 people left the United States during the war rather than give up their allegiance to the British Crown.

British Disadvantages The British had their own problems, however. The war was not popular in Great Britain. Many of the British resented paying taxes to fight the war and sympathized with the Americans. In addition, the British had to fight against an enemy that was thousands of miles away across an ocean, spread out over a huge territory, difficult to identify, and without any visible organization that could be attacked. As Americans would discover two centuries later in Vietnam, winning battles and having superiority in training are not enough when your opponent constantly shifts ground—and will not give up.

The Battle of Bunker Hill

The British began the war assuming that they could crush the rebellion by simply "showing the flag." They would remind people in New England of the power and authority of their government. They would intimidate them into surrender. The best example of this strategy was the battle for Breed's Hill near Boston in June 1775. (It has come to be called the Battle of Bunker Hill, after a nearby hill.)

After pursuing the British on their return from Concord in April, the Patriots—a varied group of white and African American artisans, farmers, and others—had surrounded Boston. But they were so disorganized that they could not agree on what to do next; in fact, they were unable to feed themselves and keep their camps around Boston in order.

Meanwhile, the British under General Thomas Gage sat in Boston, well supplied and protected by the British navy in the harbor. In early June, the Americans extended their lines north of Boston to the hills in Charlestown. General Gage decided to take advantage of

this move to overawe the rebels and send them home. He ordered a massive frontal assault by some 2,200 troops on the Patriot camp at the top of Breed's Hill.

After landing by ship, the British had to march uphill for about a mile. They began their attack at about 3 P.M. on a sunny day. It was a magnificent sight. Hundreds of soldiers in scarlet coats moved forward up the slope, accompanied by drums and bagpipes and carrying battle flags in an impressive display of discipline and power.

When the British neared the American line, the rebels fired a ragged but deadly volley into their ranks. Without cover on the open hillside, the British were an easy target for this withering fire. Their proud army staggered and retreated. According to one anonymous Englishman,

> *Our light-infantry were served up in companies against the grass fence* [a defensive barrier], *without being able to penetrate. . . . Most of our grenadiers and light-infantry . . . lost three fourths, and many nine tenths of their men. Some had only eight or nine men a company* [about 100 men] *left; some only three, four, and five.*

Embarrassed but still determined, the British troops attacked again. Again, the rebels stopped them. Again, the British attacked. This time the rebels, out of ammunition, retreated in disarray. The British troops, having picked their way through the bodies of dozens of wounded and dead comrades, overran the American position and took the hill.

The Battle of Bunker Hill was a British victory. But it came at too high a price. Of the 2,200 men Gage sent into battle that day, 226 were killed and another 828 were wounded. In other words, the number of casualties, or dead and wounded combined, was close to 50 percent, more than the British could bear. Above all, the battle demonstrated that the Americans would not be intimidated easily.

In early July, the general appointed by Congress, George Washington, assumed command of the American troops and brought greater discipline to the army. The siege of Boston continued throughout the fall and winter until the

▶ RESOURCE DIRECTORY

Teaching Resources

BOSTON

Americans dragged cannon they had captured in New York into position on the hills south of Boston. Faced with the possibility of deadly bombardment, the new British general, William Howe, evacuated Boston on March 17, 1776.

MAKING   CONNECTIONS

Even in this early period of the war, the British and Americans constantly alternated between attacking and retreating. As you read on, notice how this general pattern continues. Who would be most likely to win such a war, and why?

War for Morale, 1776 to 1778

The British fleet took General Howe, his army, and thousands of Loyalists to Halifax, Nova Scotia, where they regrouped. In late summer, Howe launched an attack on New York City. The British had decided to concentrate on the Middle Colonies because the population of those colonies included more Tories, who could support them. In a series of large and small battles, Howe trounced Washington's poorly trained, poorly equipped, and poorly organized army.

An American volunteer, Michael Graham, later recalled one of these battles in August 1776.

> I t is impossible for me to describe the confusion and horror of the scene that ensued: the artillery flying with the chains [of the gun carriages] over the horses' backs, our men running in almost every direction, and run which way they would, they were almost sure to meet the British. . . . And the enemy huzzahing when they took prisoners made it truly a day of distress to the Americans.

The Crisis By October the British had captured New York City and driven Washington's army all the way to Pennsylvania. Men were deserting Washington in droves; between the summer and winter of 1776, Washington's army shrank from 20,000 to about 6,000. The entire cause was on the verge of collapse.

In December 1776, Thomas Paine issued a paper he called *The Crisis*, which began with these words:

> T hese are the times that try men's souls. The summer soldier and the sunshine patriot will, in this crisis, shrink from the service of their country; but he that stands it NOW, deserves the love and thanks of man and woman. Tyranny, like hell, is not easily conquered; yet we have this consolation with us, that the harder the conflict, the more glorious the triumph. What we obtain too cheap, we esteem [value] too lightly: It is dearness [expensiveness] only that gives every thing its value.

The Surprise Attack on Trenton Although the "summer soldiers" may have deserted, Washington still had some Patriots to form an army that next winter. He had the daring to put them to good use, too, as he broke the rules of

In a costly attempt to over-awe American forces, waves of British troops climb Breed's Hill toward the waiting enemy.

Analyze
Have students analyze why the war can be considered "a people's war." Why did so many different kinds of people become involved? What might African Americans have hoped to gain by participating in it? Why do you suppose so many Americans sided with the British?

Answer to ...

MAKING   CONNECTIONS

Answers should suggest that the Americans had the advantage in a war in which prudent retreat was always an option; they could simply outwait the British and strike when circumstances were most favorable. Fighting on home soil would inevitably require less expenditure of manpower and funds than the British would incur fighting 3,000 miles from home.

Media and Technology

 Transparencies
Fine Art, D-4, D-5

Activity

(The clock icon indicates an activity that can be successfully conducted within a class period. Each chapter has at least one such activity.)

Writing a Letter

Have students assume the roles of both an American soldier and a British soldier fighting in the Battle of Bunker Hill. Ask them to write letters home from the battlefront describing the war experience from each point of view. Encourage them to include details about the battle, their reactions to it, and the overall morale of the British army or militia, as the case may be.

Caption Answer to ...

 Interpreting Maps

1775: Concord, Lexington, Bunker Hill, Ticonderoga; 1777: Germantown, Brandywine; 1781: Cowpens, Guilford Court House, Yorktown.

 In Depth

Did You Know?

The Journal of Nicholas Cresswell, 1774–1777, chronicles the travels of a young English Loyalist who said of Trenton: "Six weeks ago . . . [the Americans thought] all was gone, all was lost. But now the scale is turned and Washington's name is extolled to the clouds. Alexander, Pompey, and Hannibal were pygmy Generals, in comparison with the magnanimous Washington. Poor General Howe is ridiculed in all companies and all my countrymen abused. I am obliged to hear this daily and dare not speak a word in their favor. It is the damned Hessians that has caused this, curse the scoundrel that first thought of sending them here."

war by ordering a surprise attack on the enemy in their winter quarters. On Christmas Eve, 1776, Massachusetts fishermen rowed Washington and 2,400 men across the Delaware River to New Jersey. At dawn, they attacked Trenton, as shown on the map below, and captured the mercenaries, or hired soldiers, whom Great Britain had brought from the German state of Hesse; a few days later, the Patriots fought a small battle at Princeton. Then Washington retreated to Pennsylvania.

The significance of Trenton was immense, as it boosted American morale and persuaded many of Washington's soldiers to re-enlist. It was hardly a great military victory—in fact, Washington lost most of the battles he fought during the war. He was, however, a great leader. He inspired people to follow him, and he recognized when to act boldly and decisively. Furthermore, he gradually came to understand that winning individual battles meant little compared to just hanging on and being ready to strike when the British made a mistake. Despite all the victories the British won in 1776, they could not win the war because they could not put Washington out of business.

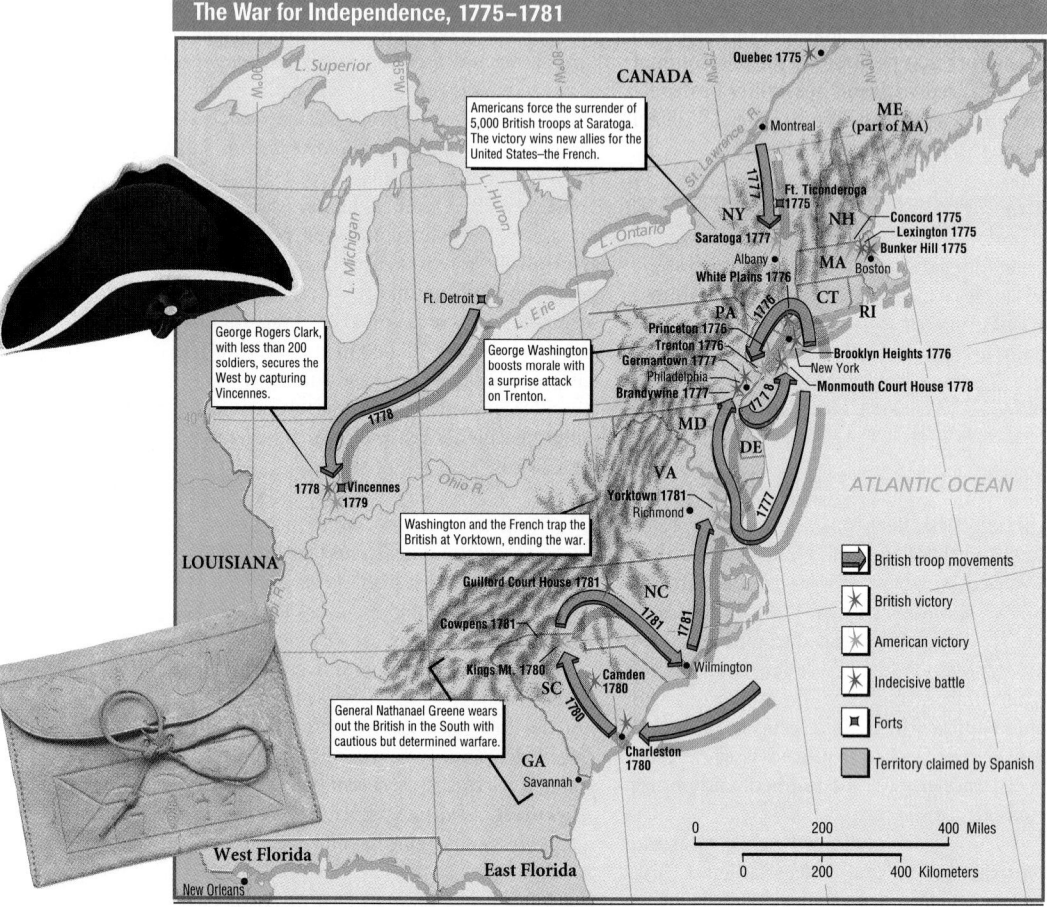

The War for Independence, 1775–1781

Americans force the surrender of 5,000 British troops at Saratoga. The victory wins new allies for the United States–the French.

George Rogers Clark, with less than 200 soldiers, secures the West by capturing Vincennes.

George Washington boosts morale with a surprise attack on Trenton.

Washington and the French trap the British at Yorktown, ending the war.

General Nathanael Greene wears out the British in the South with cautious but determined warfare.

- ▶ British troop movements
- ✶ British victory
- ✶ American victory
- ✶ Indecisive battle
- ▣ Forts
- Territory claimed by Spanish

0   200   400 Miles
0   200   400 Kilometers

Geography and History: Interpreting Maps
Because the movements of United States forces were so often a reaction to British advances or retreats, only British movements are shown here. The major battles of the early part of the war took place in the North, but the focus shifted gradually southward. *Locate battles that took place in 1775, 1777, and 1781.*

The War Turns at Saratoga The next summer brought only mixed success for the Americans. Howe brushed aside Washington's army and captured the American capital of Philadelphia. But at Saratoga in upstate New York, a hastily organized army of Americans defeated a British army moving south from Canada in October 1777. Many historians call this victory the turning point of the war, for it convinced many people that the Americans would win if they could just hold on.

Among those persuaded was the French government. At the urging of Ambassador Benjamin Franklin, the French joined sides with the Americans. Not only did this mean money and supplies, it also meant that the British had to protect themselves in Europe. The French officer the **Marquis de Lafayette,** who fought alongside the Americans, later persuaded the French to assist with an army of 6,000 men.

Another European was also vital to the American cause: the Prussian officer **Baron von Steuben.** During a bitter winter at Valley Forge, Pennsylvania, he drilled Washington's troops and wrote a book of regulations that brought much-needed discipline to the Continental Army.

In the same year, 1778, the British abandoned Philadelphia and marched back across New Jersey toward New York City. At Monmouth Court House in New Jersey, Washington's army, now better equipped and better trained, caught up with the rear guard of the British and fought them to a standstill. After years of disorganization, the American army now had the discipline that made it a unit fit to be reckoned with.

Fighting the War to an End

While they continued to occupy New York, the British turned their primary attention to the South. There they hoped to demoralize the Americans by freeing slaves and laying waste the countryside. In 1780 the British captured Charleston, South Carolina. They then used the city as a base of operations, winning several battles.

The war, always an ugly business, was especially vicious in the South. Most of the southern war was fought by Americans against Americans, as Tories and Patriots clashed. At the battle of King's Mountain in South Carolina in 1780, where the Tories suffered a defeat, all the combatants were Americans. Elsewhere in the western part of the South, other Patriot forces dealt the British several losses.

Meanwhile, the British general Lord Cornwallis marched from South Carolina toward New York. Harassed but not defeated by small American armies commanded by Nathanael Greene and the Marquis de Lafayette, Cornwallis decided to transport his army to New York by ship in the summer of 1781. Marching his forces to the Virginia coast, he took up a position at Yorktown, near the point where the York River enters the Chesapeake Bay.

Washington, who was in camp near New York City, again acted boldly; he left the middle states and moved his army quickly south. There, together with the recently arrived French army, he laid siege to Yorktown in September. Luckily for the Americans, a French fleet turned back a British fleet off the coast of Virginia, and Cornwallis was trapped by a force twice the size of his own. On October 19, 1781, he had the "mortification," as he put it in a later letter to his superior, of surrendering his army to Washington and the French.

As the war moved into the southern states, it became increasingly hard fought. The commander of the British troops in this cavalry skirmish, Colonel Banastre Tarleton, was known as "the Butcher" for killing his prisoners.

Enrichment
Tell students that while the men were away fighting, many women took over the responsibility of running the family farm. Have students research information about these women and write a diary entry describing a day in the life of one of them.

In Depth

Interdisciplinary

From the beginning of the war, geography helped the American cause by making it impossible for Britain to control the American seacoast. Blockade-running colonists needed to go no farther than the Caribbean to beat the blockade and find a market. Since the trade winds from Europe led directly to the Caribbean Islands, many other countries found them an ideal location for trading with America. The neutral port of the Dutch-held island St. Eustasius—where traders could buy anything from tea to gunpowder, guns to sugar—was especially crowded with American ships. In 1780 the admiral of the British fleet wrote that "this rock of only six miles in length and three in breadth has done more harm than all the arms of her most potent enemies, and alone supported the infamous American rebellion."

Alternative Assessment

Mid-Point Monitoring

Ask students if they have
● Selected the activities they will include in their project
● Begun to research the issues for each

This woodcut was published in 1779 with a poem in which a Daughter of Liberty described civilian hardships during the War for Independence.

A wife of one of the American soldiers, Sarah Osborn, was present at the surrender. Over fifty years later, she recalled that the British forces

> *marched out beating and playing a melancholy [sad] tune, their drums covered with black handkerchiefs and their fifes with black ribbons tied around them, into an old field and there grounded their arms and then returned into town again to await their destiny.*

The "melancholy tune" the British played was a song popular at the time called "The World Turned Upside Down." And that it was; the world would never be the same again. Faced with rising opposition at home, a new British government began negotiations that resulted in the signing of the **Treaty of Paris** in September 1783. Under this treaty, George III was no longer sovereign, or ruler, in his thirteen former colonies. Instead, the people were sovereign, although exactly which people that meant and how they would rule remained to be determined. In any case, it was not just white men, but all kinds of people who had fought the War for Independence.

A People's War

The British lost their colonies because Americans—or at least some Americans—had the determination to outlast them, even in the face of repeated military defeats. Like all wars, the War for Independence affected many people. Perhaps 200,000 men or more served at one time or another in the American cause.

The American Soldier's Experience Most of the fighting was carried out by young, relatively poor men. They and their officers were paid badly, if at all, and poorly fed and clothed. Washington wrote: "You might have tracked the army . . . to Valley Forge by the blood of their feet." In 1780 a soldier named Joseph Plumb Martin described their situation:

> T he men were . . . *exasperated* [irritated] *beyond endurance; they could*

> *not stand it any longer. . . . What was to be done? Here was the army starved and naked, and there their country sitting still and expecting the army to do notable things while fainting from sheer starvation.*

Occasionally their various frustrations boiled over into unrest, as in the case of the brief mutiny in January 1781 by a unit known as the Pennsylvania Line.

African American men—about five thousand of them—also experienced the life of a soldier, in the fighting on both sides. Women, too, both white and African American, served the cause they believed in, whether rebel or Tory. Many followed husbands, lovers, or fathers into battle, cared for them, and nursed them. These women formed an unofficial but vital part of the army, which could not have functioned without them. And a few actually fought side by side with men. The most famous was Deborah Sampson, who disguised herself as a man, took the name Robert Shurtleff, and served in the Continental Army from May 1782 to October 1783. Her husband later became the only man to be granted a pension as the "widow" of a veteran. ✪

The Civilian Experience of the War The war affected civilians too. The British navy blockaded the seacoast and severely disrupted American commerce. Measured in the British monetary unit of pounds sterling, the combined value of American imports and exports fell from about £4,600,000 in 1775 to £200,000 in 1777. Exports of tobacco and rice in particular fell markedly. Occupation by British soldiers damaged cities such as New York. In fact, half of the 21,000 people who lived in New York before the war left the city.

✪ Nearly everyone felt the pinch during the war. Often needed goods were scarce. Even when goods were available, it was not always possible to purchase them, due to **inflation,** or a steady increase in prices over a period of time that reduces people's ability to buy goods. In Massachusetts, for example, the price of a bushel of corn rose from less than one dollar in 1777 to almost eighty dollars in 1779. Congress issued paper money (called Continental

dollars) to pay for military expenses. But inflation soon made the money of little value. In 1777 it took three Continental dollars to equal one dollar in gold; by 1778, it took seven; one hundred in 1780; and almost a hundred and fifty in 1781. This decline in value gave rise to the expression "not worth a Continental." In the long run, the War for Independence stimulated economic development. But its short-term impact was harsh.

The Native American Experience of the War
Not all of the pain of the war was economic. In the middle and southern states especially, rebels and Tories treated each other savagely; they harassed each other, destroyed property, and killed hundreds of people. But the group most hurt by the war was the Native American population. At first, the Iroquois tried to stay out of what Mohawk sachem Little Abraham called "a family affair" between Britain and its colonies. The war, however, provided an excuse for Americans on the New York frontier to settle the question of control in the region. Angered by American attacks on their villages, the Iroquois joined the British in 1777. Under the able leadership of another Mohawk sachem, Joseph Brant, they launched several devastating raids in New York and Pennsylvania. In 1779, Americans under

Despite the brilliant leadership of Joseph Brant (above) and others, Native Americans suffered great hardships during the long war.

the command of General John Sullivan retaliated with raids of their own. Meanwhile, in the South, Virginians and Carolinians sent repeated expeditions to attack the Cherokee for supporting the British. For most Native Americans, the American victory in 1783 was a serious blow, the meaning of which would only become clear in the next two to three decades.

The War for Independence was a long and brutal war, complete with betrayals and corruption, torture and terrible violence. But it confirmed the commitment of many white Americans to the cause of independence. Now that they had won, however, they faced the difficult challenge of defining exactly what their victory meant.

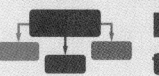
Georgia's Nancy Hart was said to have shot one of the six Tories who broke into her home, wounded another, and held the rest prisoner until her husband returned— to help her hang them.

Quiz found in the Unit 1 folder, p. 45, covers the main ideas in this section as well as the key terms.

SECTION 2 REVIEW

Key Terms, People, and Places
1. Define (a) Treaty of Paris, (b) inflation.
2. Identify (a) Patriots, (b) Loyalists, (c) Tories, (d) Marquis de Lafayette, (e) Baron von Steuben.

Key Concepts
3. Give two advantages and two disadvantages of the British at the beginning of the War for Independence.

4. Explain how the victory at Saratoga led to final victory at Yorktown.
5. What was the overall effect of the war on Native Americans?

Critical Thinking
6. **Checking Consistency** Analyze George Washington's qualities of leadership.

Section 2 Review Answers
1. (a) Treaty of Paris, see p. 64, (b) inflation, see p. 64
2. (a) Patriots, see p. 59, (b) Loyalists, see p. 59, (c) Tories, see p. 59, (c) Marquis de Lafayette, see p. 63, (d) Baron von Steuben, see p. 63
3. Possible answers: Among its advantages, Great Britain was the most powerful nation on earth; it had the world's largest navy and an experienced military. Among the disadvantages of the British, many resented paying taxes to fight the war; they had to fight against an enemy thousands of miles away.
4. The American victory convinced the French that the Americans might be able to win the war. The French then provided troops and supplies to the American forces, making possible the final success at Yorktown.
5. For most Native Americans, the American victory in 1783 was a serious blow.
6. Washington was not a great general, since he lost most of the battles he fought during the war. He was, however, a great leader, since he inspired people to follow him and recognized when the time had come to act boldly and decisively.

Reteach
Have students make a list of the major battles between the British and the Americans and indicate beside each entry who won. Then have them write one or two sentences summarizing the reasons for the Americans' final victory.

Reinforcing the Big Idea
Having won their independence, Americans faced the challenge of establishing a new society based on their ideals. The next section describes the years immediately after the War for Independence.

SECTION 3

Government by the States

1. FOCUS

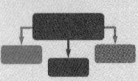

Connecting to the Big Idea

See page 50B. Explain to students that the years after the War for Independence were difficult ones for the United States. The new country was disorganized and suffered from economic and political problems. Some Americans, known as Nationalists, began to demand a stronger national government. Ask students why the Nationalists felt that a stronger national government would be beneficial.

Objectives

• Describe government in the United States before 1788.
• Explain why the Nationalists believed there should be a strong national government.
• Explain the reaction of the Nationalists to Shays's Rebellion.

Bellringer

Ask students when or why people turn to the federal government. For example, why do people expect the federal government to help after natural disasters?

Reading Strategy

Question Writing Have students first read the section's main headings, next write a question about each heading, and then look for the answers to their questions as they read.

Answer to . . .

MAKING CONNECTIONS

Answers may suggest that a dictatorship might be able to decree solutions to some problems if it was so inclined, whereas the conflicting interests represented in a democracy often hinder decision and swift action. Dictatorships, however, often bring problems of reduced personal freedom, police terror, and increased inequalities between classes.

SECTION PREVIEW

Many Americans were pleased with the highly democratic state and national governments created during the American Revolution. But a sizable number of citizens, worried that there was too much social disorder in the new nation, lobbied hard for a stronger national government.

A testimony to changed attitudes, this bowl made by diehard revolutionary Paul Revere honors a general who crushed a rebellion against increased taxes in 1787.

Key Concepts

• Before 1788 the national government was weak and the state constitutions were powerful.
• The Nationalists believed that the new nation's many problems could only be solved by a strong national government.
• Shays's Rebellion persuaded many that the United States was on the brink of dangerous disorder.

Key Terms, People, and Places

confederation, Articles of Confederation, legislative branch, executive branch, judicial branch, unicameral legislature, bicameral legislature; Nationalists

---

O n December 23, 1783, a month after watching the British army leave New York forever, George Washington performed perhaps the most remarkable act of his life: he voluntarily gave up power. Having helped Americans achieve their freedom from a king, he did not want to become another ruler over them. In an act of formal resignation that astonished the world, he gave up his commission as commander of the American army.

Washington's resignation highlighted a new dilemma for the American people. Could they enjoy their freedom without the strong, unified, national government symbolized by Washington's leadership? Could they keep their new liberty and maintain order at the same time? In short, what kind of government should a free people have?

MAKING CONNECTIONS

Would a dictatorship—the very government Washington was afraid of creating—be able to solve the problems of the United States today more easily than a democracy? Explain.

Government in the Early United States

George Washington had become powerful in large part because a single military authority was needed to win the War for Independence. The Congress that approved the Declaration of Independence in 1776 was nothing more than a loose collection of representatives from thirteen separate states. Almost no one imagined creating a powerful national government. After all, Americans were rebelling against an imperial government that had tried repeatedly to strengthen its power over them.

Instead, many people saw Congress as only a necessary wartime inconvenience. The white men who had a voice in government thought of themselves as citizens of individual states rather than as citizens of a nation. It is significant that in referring to the United States, most Americans in those times wrote "the united States are" rather than "the United States is," as people do today. They believed that the nation as a whole was less important than its thirteen parts. It was not a nation as much as it was a **confederation**—an alliance of states formed to coordinate their defense and their relations with foreign governments.

The Articles of Confederation To govern the United States, the Continental Congress created a set of laws called the **Articles of Confederation.** Although written in 1776, the Articles were not approved until 1781. Under the Articles, the government consisted of a legislature, or group of representatives from the states who gathered

---

▶ RESOURCE DIRECTORY

Teaching Resources

📁 **The Reproducible Lesson Plan** found in the Unit 1 folder, p. 40, provides a summary of the Section 3 lesson plan content.

📁 **Alternate Lesson Plan: Learning Styles** found in the Alternate Lesson Plans folder, p. 57, helps students chart the weaknesses of the Articles of Confederation and is especially useful for visual learners.

📄 **Guided Reading and Review** found in the Unit 1 folder, p. 46, provides a structure for reading and mastering the key concepts and reviewing the key terms for Section 3. (Guided Practice)

Both the stern general and his officers were overcome by emotion on the day Washington left the army. With his resignation, the nation was left without strong leadership.

to conduct business. The gathering of the legislature was called a Congress. This Continental Congress passed laws and tried to make sure they were enforced. Thus it combined the functions of a **legislative branch**—the part that makes laws—and an **executive branch,** the part that executes or puts into action the laws passed by a legislature. The Articles made no attempt to create a **judicial branch,** the part of government that judges whether laws have been broken; that job was left to the states.

Under the Articles, states could send as many representatives to Congress as they wished. But each state had only one vote in Congress. It took nine votes, not just a simple majority, to pass any measure dealing with money and unanimous approval to amend or change the Articles. Congress also did not have the power to tax—a serious disadvantage that forced the national government to beg funds from the states. Nor did Congress have any coercive power, the power to force the states to do what it wanted.

These and other defects in the Articles made the United States government weak. But that was exactly what most Americans wanted their national government to be. As late as 1783, the author of the Declaration of Independence, Thomas Jefferson, put forth the argument that "the constant session [meeting] of Congress cannot be necessary in time of peace." Congressional representatives, Jefferson stated, should "separate and return to [their] respective states, leaving only a Committee of the states, [and thus] destroy the strange idea of their being a permanent body."

State Constitutions
Far more important than the Articles in the country's early years were the individual state constitutions—the sets of laws that established the governments of the states. Not every state adopted a new constitution during the Revolution, but most did. The most revolutionary was the

Weaknesses in the Articles of Confederation

- One vote for each state, regardless of size
- Congress powerless to impose and collect taxes or duties
- Congress powerless to regulate foreign and interstate commerce
- No separate executive to enforce acts of Congress
- No national court system to interpret laws
- Amendment only with consent of all the states
- A 9/13 majority required to pass laws
- Articles only a "firm league of friendship"

 Interpreting Tables
The weaknesses of the Articles aroused concern both at home and abroad. "All respect for our government is annihilated [destroyed]," Thomas Jefferson reported from France. "The present is justly considered an alarming crisis," added an observer in the states. *Choose one weakness listed in the chart and explain why it would hurt the nation.*

Discuss
Review with students the ideas that fueled the American Revolution. Ask them to explain how the government of the United States before 1788 reflected these ideas. Why were many Americans happy with a weak national government?

Discuss the problems faced by the United States after the War for Independence. What role did government play in these problems? What were the defects of the Articles of Confederation? Why were some Americans critical of the new state constitutions? What kind of government did the Nationalists propose? Why?

Caption Answer to ...

Interpreting Tables

Possible answers: The lack of power to regulate commerce would result in conflicting regulations by different states and an inability to respond when foreign nations heavily taxed American imports.

In Depth

Then and Now

In 1786 the United States national debt totaled over $50 million. The debt forced state governments to print cheap paper money to allow people to repay their loans. In 1992 the national debt was over $4 trillion, and some economists estimate that by the year 2000 the deficit will reach $13 trillion, more than 260,000 times what it was a little more than two hundred years ago.

Pennsylvania Constitution of 1776. Under this state constitution, all white men twenty-one or older who paid taxes—not just gentlemen—were allowed to vote. In itself this was a radical innovation.

The writers of the Pennsylvania constitution went still further, however. They took care to make the legislature the most powerful part of the government, because the legislature was the body most directly responsible to the people. The representatives in the legislature were very responsive to the people's wishes, since they stood for election every year. Their terms of office—like those of officers in the executive branch—were limited, so that no one could hold power too long. Furthermore, the representatives served in a **unicameral legislature**—that is, a legislature with just one house, or group of representatives. No other house balanced its power, as is the case in a **bicameral legislature,** a legislature with two houses. Thus the voters of Pennsylvania had great control over their own government. This was a truly radical government structure in a time when most nations were still ruled by kings and queens.

While other state constitutions did not go as far as Pennsylvania's, most made popular sovereignty a central principle of government. The men who wrote these early constitutions believed it was more important to protect the people from their government than it was to protect the government from the people.

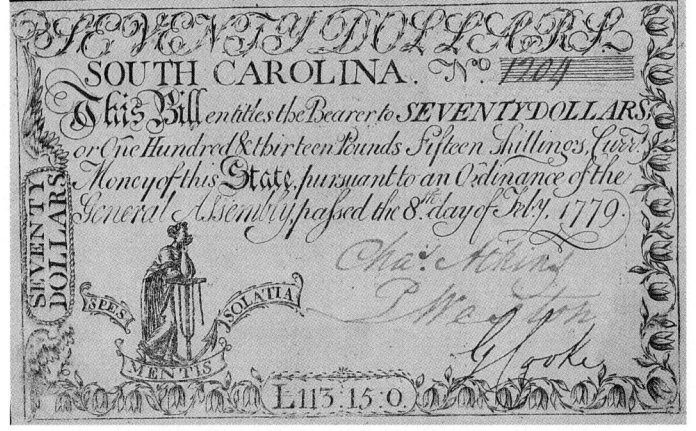

Are you in debt? Print money to pay your bills. Many states resorted to this tactic during the War for Independence and the years afterward.

Criticism of the New Constitutions

Some Americans did not like either the Articles of Confederation or the new state constitutions. Their numbers increased as the years passed. More and more gentlemen worried that the American Revolution had given too much power to the "people"—in other words, those who were not of their own class. As a general rule, democracy involves more conflict of opinion and apparent disorder than other systems of government, and these critics worried that such freedom was incompatible with an orderly, smoothly functioning society.

They had plenty of disorder to point to. By 1786, three years after Washington's resignation, the nation still owed about $50 million—a huge sum at that time—to foreign countries and to its own citizens for the expenses of the War for Independence. Debt everywhere was such a problem that some state governments were distributing cheap paper money to help their citizens pay off their loans. This was creating economic chaos.

All the states were desperately looking for ways to raise money. States with good seaports heavily taxed goods bound for neighboring states—whose citizens were outraged at the taxes. Land sales also became an issue. In the Treaty of Paris in 1783, the United States had gained political control over the vast area between the Appalachian Mountains and the Mississippi River. The states, disregarding the rights of Native Americans in the territory, quarreled bitterly among themselves over which should be able to profit by the sale of this land.

A considerable number of American gentlemen believed that much of this disorder had arisen because the people had too much power in their state legislatures. As noble as this kind of democracy might be, these critics thought, it was not always the best way to run a government or a society.

The Nationalists Fear That the Government Is Too Weak By the early 1780s, a group of men called **Nationalists** were working to make the national government stronger, so that it could counterbalance what they saw as the unpredictable behavior of the states. The Nationalists were former military officers, members of Congress, merchants, planters, and lawyers, and many whose names are now familiar: George Washington, Benjamin Franklin, James Madison, and Alexander Hamilton.

In the 1780s, Nationalists expressed their views about the dangers of a weak national government and too much democracy both in private correspondence and in letters written for publication in newspapers. They pointed out that Congress sometimes did not have enough members in attendance to do anything. They warned that the lack of a national court system and national economic policies would create tension and chaos. They feared that the United States would not command respect from the rest of the world and that Americans would be treated badly abroad.

Most of all, however, they worried that Americans' fondness for challenging authority and for asserting individual rights was getting out of hand. For this reason, the Nationalists called the years from 1781 to 1787 the Critical Period—which they perceived as a time of social disorder and indecision about how to govern the new nation. Fisher Ames of Massachusetts put it this way:

> Every man of sense must be convinced that our disturbances have arisen more from the want of [government] power than the abuse of it.

Most Americans did not agree with this view. The new state constitutions and the Articles of Confederation were doing exactly what they were supposed to be doing: keeping government close to the people. So what if government was disorderly? So what if mistakes were made? Better to have mistakes under the government of the people than efficiency under the rule of tyrants. Besides, Congress under the Articles had won the War for Independence and worked out a treaty with Great Britain. Those were no small accomplishments.

The Nationalists Argue from History
Because the Nationalists, a relatively small

Though the Revolution was over, many Americans were still challenging authority. In this engraving, a crowd puts an end to a county meeting by throwing a government official into a brook.

group, were generally successful men with a standing in society that they wanted to protect, some historians have concluded that they were essentially looking after their own interests when they called for a stronger national government. To a certain extent, that is exactly what they were doing. But they were also well educated in European history. They knew that nearly every European nation of any size that had tried a republican government—a government of the people—had failed, ending in chaos and then tyranny. This had happened to the Roman Republic, over 1800 years before their time; it might, the Nationalists reasoned, happen to the United States as well. They believed history had demonstrated that people were not naturally wise enough to have so much power over their own affairs. Concluded George Washington as he surveyed what he considered the disorder of the times: "We have . . . had too good an opinion of human nature in forming our confederation."

The Nationalists See America as a Model
Finally, the Nationalists agreed with Thomas Paine that America was a model for the world. It would be irresponsible, they believed, to allow the nation to fall into disagreement and

Activity
Teaching Heterogeneous Groups

In 1776, a loose confederation of thirteen states met to establish the Articles of Confederation. This attempt to centralize government was resisted by state governments. To demonstrate this struggle, divide the class into thirteen "states," each of which should develop its own constitution of three laws. Then have all states send a representative to the "First Continental Congress" to establish ten federal laws that do not conflict with their state constitutions.

In Depth
Then and Now

In 1787 rumors circulating about the drafting of a constitution were met with fear by many American citizens. The new government, it was said, would have powers to tax and regulate their lives. The discussion of federalism did not end with the Founders. In the late 1980s a senator joked, "There are two ways to empty a room in Washington: Hold a fundraiser for a defeated candidate or a debate on federalism."

Viewpoints

Andrew Burnaby, the British clergy-man, is concerned that the colonists, coming from different parts of Europe with varying customs and religions, could never become unified into a stable political entity. He is, in fact, predicting how regional differences would eventually lead the country into civil war. For a more thorough examination of American independence, see the Resource Directory below.

Enrichment

Historians have sometimes described the participants in Shays's Rebellion as "rabble." Yet out of those indicted for treason as a result of the uprising, a number were referred to in court records as "gentlemen." Have students research the social backgrounds and characters of the leaders of the rebellion.

In Depth

Did You Know?

Referring to Shays's Rebellion, George Washington said to James Madison, "If there exists not a power to check them, what security has a man for life, liberty, or property?" Thomas Jefferson, on the other hand, saw it differently: "A little revolution now and then is a good thing; the tree of liberty must be refreshed from time to time with the blood of patriots and tyrants."

Viewpoints
On the United States as an Independent Nation

Long before the Critical Period, the question of the United States' future was debated on both sides of the Atlantic. **What major concern is expressed in the British viewpoint below?**

European Opinion

"I [see] insurmountable causes for weakness that will prevent America from being a powerful state. . . . In short, such is the difference of character, manners, religion and interest of the different colonies that if they were left to themselves, there would soon be a civil war from one end of the continent to another."
Andrew Burnaby, British clergyman, in *Burnaby's Travels Through North America*, 1775

Colonial Opinion

"Let us view [America] as it now is—AN INDEPENDENT STATE that has taken an equal station amid the nations of the earth. . . . It is a vitality [living thing] liable, indeed, to many disorders, many dangerous diseases; but it is young and strong, and will struggle . . . against those evils and surmount them. . . . Its strength will grow with its years."
Thomas Pownall, former governor of Massachusetts, in *A Memorial Most Humbly Addressed to the Sovereigns of Europe on the Present State of Affairs, Between the Old and the New World*, 1780

violence. If they did, wrote Englishman Richard Price in 1785,

> the fairest experiment ever tried in human affairs will miscarry; and . . . a REVOLUTION which had revived the hopes of good men and promised an opening to better times, will become a discouragement to all future efforts in favor of liberty, and prove only an opening to a new scene of human degeneracy and misery.

Indeed, as you have seen, it was Washington's profound understanding of history and his regard for this greater cause that led him to give up his command to civilian authorities so promptly. He did not want to play the role of Julius Caesar of ancient Rome—a general who became a symbol of tyranny by replacing a republican government with a dictatorship.

Shays's Rebellion

⭐ In 1786, Nationalists managed to arrange a meeting of the representatives of the states in Annapolis, Maryland, to discuss the economic problems caused by the Articles of Confederation. But only twelve delegates from five states attended. There simply was not much interest in revising the Articles. All that the Nationalist leaders could obtain was a promise to try again. They called for another meeting in Philadelphia in the summer of 1787.

Between the time of the convention in Annapolis and that in Philadelphia, dramatic changes occurred—including the outbreak of armed rebellion in Massachusetts. The uprising became known as Shays's Rebellion after its leader, Captain Daniel Shays, a veteran of the War for Independence.

The Causes of the Rebellion At its root, Shays's Rebellion was a struggle over debts and taxes. In the 1780s, Massachusetts was in a serious economic depression, yet it owed money both to private lenders and to the national government for the expenses of the War for Independence. In 1786 the legislature voted the heaviest direct tax in the history of Massachusetts to that time. Furthermore, the legislature decreed that the tax had to be paid in specie, or gold or silver coin, which was scarce, rather than in paper money. In taxing their citizens so heavily, public officials were driven by a desire to honor the state's debts and by pressure from merchants to whom much of the money was owed.

Already suffering hard times, citizens now had to come up with specie to pay heavy taxes. Many refused to do so, and the rebellion was under way. Throughout rural areas of Massachusetts, but especially in the west, citizens drove off tax collectors and protested the new taxes with petitions and public meetings. When the courts rejected their petitions, the rebels closed them down. Crowds of protesters reacted violently when the state legislature refused to repeal the taxes.

⭐ Historians argue about exactly who supported the rebellion. In fact, people often chose sides for purely personal or local reasons. Still,

---

 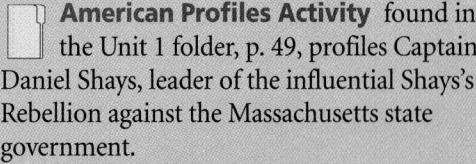

RESOURCE DIRECTORY

Teaching Resources

📄 **Viewpoints Activity** On the United States as an Independent Nation, found in the Unit 1 folder, pp. 50–51, uses opposing European views of the United States' likelihood of long-term survival to help students understand the challenges that the nation faced in its infancy.

⭐ 📄 **American Profiles Activity** found in the Unit 1 folder, p. 49, profiles Captain Daniel Shays, leader of the influential Shays's Rebellion against the Massachusetts state government.

⭐ 📄 **Literature Activity** The Contrast, found in the Unit 1 folder, pp. 58–59, uses Royall Tyler's social comedy to help students understand some contemporary views of Shays's Rebellion.

it is safe to say that in Shays's Rebellion many citizens were reacting violently to the direct interference of merchants and politicians in their lives. They were very mindful that part of the reason they had fought the American Revolution was to keep a distant government from imposing taxes after an expensive war. Unlike the government and the merchants they fought, they believed that the growth of state power was a bad development.

The Aftermath of the Rebellion Even in this case of open rebellion, Congress could only look on helplessly, unable to provide any assistance. It had no money to raise an army and no way to force the states to give it money. Finally the government of Massachusetts managed to gather an army and send it to the western part of the state, where it dispersed the rebels in January 1787. The unrest soon quieted down. Many rebels and their families left Massachusetts for Vermont, New York, or Ohio.

The significance of Shays's Rebellion lived on, however. This significance was twofold. From the perspective of the rebels, the rebellion demonstrated a continuing commitment to defy the authority of any government when that government acted against the people's wishes. From the perspective of the Nationalists, Shays's Rebellion was an example of the kind of civil unrest that was coming if they did not act soon. It confirmed their worst fears that Americans would sacrifice social order for individual liberty. A Pennsylvania doctor, Benjamin Rush, wrote after Shays's Rebellion:

The same enthusiasm now pervades all classes in favor of government that actuated us [put us in action] *in favor of liberty in the years 1774 and 1775.*

The rebellion did indeed convince many well-educated and prominent Americans that they had to act. In May 1787, delegates began to arrive in Philadelphia—in a trickle at first, but after a week or so in sufficient number to begin the business at hand. In the words of one key participant, James Madison, that business was to "decide forever the fate of republican government."

Liberty and order clashed in Shays's Rebellion, as protesters—shown here blocking a courthouse—refused to pay taxes, and the government insisted that laws be obeyed.

SECTION 3 REVIEW

Key Terms, People, and Places
1. Define (a) confederation, (b) Articles of Confederation, (c) legislative branch, (d) executive branch, (e) judicial branch, (f) unicameral legislature, (g) bicameral legislature.
2. Identify Nationalists.

Key Concepts
3. What were three weaknesses of the Articles of Confederation?

4. Why did the Nationalists call the years between 1781 and 1787 the Critical Period?
5. What is the twofold significance of Shays's Rebellion?

Critical Thinking
6. **Checking Consistency** Why did the Nationalists believe that disorder during Shays's Rebellion was not justified, although disorder was justified during the American Revolution?

 Quiz found in the Unit 1 folder, p. 40, covers the main ideas in this section as well as the key terms.

 Chapter Test Forms A and B are found in the Unit 1 folder, pp. 62–67.

 Answer Keys found in the Unit 1 folder, pp. 145–157, provide answers to all student activities.

Media and Technology

Transparency
Graphic Organizer, G-2

Guided Reading Audiotapes
(English and Spanish)

Computer Test Bank

3. ASSESS

Section 3 Review Answers

1. (a) confederation, see p. 66, (b) Articles of Confederation, see p. 66, (c) legislative branch, see p. 67, (d) executive branch, see page 67, (e) judicial branch, see p. 67, (f) unicameral legislature, see p. 68, (g) bicameral legislature, see p. 68

2. Nationalists, see p. 68

3. The executive and legislative functions were combined. There was no judicial branch. Amending the Articles required unanimous approval. Congress had no coercive power and no power to tax.

4. The Nationalists considered these years a time of social disorder and indecision about how to govern the new nation.

5. From the perspective of the rebels, the rebellion was significant because it demonstrated a continuing commitment to defy the authority of any government that acted against the people's wishes. From the perspective of the Nationalists, Shays's Rebellion confirmed their worst fears that Americans would sacrifice social order for individual liberty.

6. Answers should state that the Nationalists believed that disorder in the name of liberty was no longer allowed once liberty from Great Britain had been achieved.

Reteach

Have students create a time line of the events that led to the Constitutional Convention discussed in this section.

4. CLOSE

 **Reinforcing the Big Idea**

After the War for Independence, the United States suffered from severe political and economic problems caused by a weak national government. To save the new nation, a small group of Americans made plans to restructure the government.

Understanding Key Terms, People, and Places

Terms
Students should refer to the definitions of the key terms in the chapter to write sentences that show the relation of each word to the War for Independence or to the events leading up to the Constitutional Convention of 1787.

Word Relationships
1. (c) does not belong. The Treaty of Paris ended the War for Independence, which had been fought for the right of a new nation to exist as stated in the Declaration of Independence. A bicameral legislature is a legislature with two houses.

2. (d) does not belong. Loyalists and Tories were colonists who preferred to remain loyal to King George III. Thomas Paine developed and expressed the ideas of the Revolution in a pamphlet called *Common Sense.*

3. (a) does not belong. The legislative branch of a government makes the laws, the executive branch puts the laws into action, and the judicial branch judges whether laws have been broken. A minuteman was a colonist who fought British forces in the American Revolution. He pledged to volunteer military service at a minute's notice.

True or False
1. false, minutemen
2. false, Marquis de Lafayette
3. true
4. true

Reviewing Main Ideas
1. The British passed the Sugar Act, the Proclamation of 1763, the Stamp Act; they closely regulated colonial trade.

2. Delegates from several colonies—the Stamp Act Congress—gathered in New York to declare that their rights as British subjects had been violated. Other colonists forced stamp distributors to resign and attacked officials who supported the policy.

3. The Intolerable Acts seemed to confirm the colonists' suspicions that the British intended to take away their freedoms.

4. *Common Sense* and the Declaration of Independence expounded the principles of freedom and equality in American government and society.

5. The Patriots had no organized military and no real government. African Americans and Native Americans had no incentives to fight the British. Also, many

---

Chapter Review

Understanding Key Terms, People, and Places

Key Terms
1. American Revolution
2. War for Independence
3. depression
4. boycott
5. Declaration of Independence
6. popular sovereignty
7. Treaty of Paris
8. inflation
9. confederation
10. Articles of Confederation
11. legislative branch
12. executive branch
13. judicial branch
14. unicameral legislature
15. bicameral legislature

People
16. minuteman
17. George Washington
18. King George III
19. Thomas Paine
20. Thomas Jefferson
21. Abigail Adams
22. Patriots
23. Loyalists
24. Tories
25. Marquis de Lafayette
26. Baron von Steuben
27. Nationalists

Terms For each term above, write a sentence that explains its relation to the War for Independence or to the events leading up to the Constitutional Convention of 1787.

Word Relationships Three of the terms in each of the following sets of terms are related. Choose the term that does not belong and explain why it does not belong.
1. (a) Declaration of Independence, (b) Treaty of Paris, (c) bicameral legislature, (d) War for Independence
2. (a) Loyalists, (b) Tories, (c) King George III, (d) Thomas Paine
3. (a) minuteman, (b) executive branch, (c) judicial branch, (d) legislative branch

True or False Determine whether each statement is true or false. If it is true, write "true." If it is false, change the underlined name to make the statement true.
1. Organized as a defensive force of local residents, <u>Tories</u> pledged to respond quickly when called to action.
2. The French officer <u>Thomas Paine</u> played a part in getting France to help the Americans.
3. The Prussian officer <u>Baron von Steuben</u> brought discipline to George Washington's army at Valley Forge, Pennsylvania.
4. The <u>Nationalists</u> advocated a strong national government to control the states.

Reviewing Main Ideas

Section 1 (pp. 52–57)
1. What policies did the British begin during the 1760s in order to deal with debts from the French and Indian War?
2. What actions did the colonists take to protest the Stamp Act?
3. Describe the effect of the Intolerable Acts on the colonists' perception of the British.
4. What basic principles were defined in Thomas Paine's pamphlet *Common Sense* and in the Declaration of Independence?

Section 2 (pp. 59–65)
5. What were some of the disadvantages that the Patriots had to face at the beginning of the American Revolution?

6. What did the Battle of Bunker Hill and Washington's attack on Trenton demonstrate about American troops?
7. Describe how the French helped the Americans win the war.
8. What groups were most severely affected by the American Revolution?

Section 3 (pp. 66–71)
9. Give evidence to prove that before 1788 the national government was weak while the state governments were powerful.
10. What were the goals of the Nationalists?
11. What effect did Shays's Rebellion have on the 1787 Philadelphia Convention?

---

colonists remained loyal to King George.

6. The Battle of Bunker Hill demonstrated that American troops could not be easily intimidated and would continue to fight even if the odds were against them. Trenton showed that at least some Americans would continue fighting despite losses; it also demonstrated the Americans' daring.

7. The French offered money, supplies, troops, and the assistance of the Marquis de Lafayette. At Yorktown, the French turned back a British fleet off the coast of Virginia, trapping Cornwallis.

8. Young, poor men, including African Americans, did most of the fighting. Many women accompanied them. Native Americans suffered the most because, hoping to keep control of their lands, they sided with

the British.

9. Congress before 1788 was only a loose collection of separate states; people in fact wrote "the United States are" rather than "the United States is." Congress did not have the power to force the states to do what it wanted.

10. The Nationalists wanted to make the United States government stronger and avoid too much democracy, which they felt led to disorder.

11. Shays's Rebellion convinced many people of the necessity of attending the Philadelphia Convention in order to avoid the civil unrest that the rebellion seemed to foreshadow.

1. She wanted men to give up the harsh title of master for the tender one of friend. Abigail saw the Revolution as an opportunity for Americans to rethink domestic relationships. She used the language of the Revolution to express her ideas.

2. The painting tries to convey the feelings of loss the people felt when Washington resigned. Without Washington as a leader, Americans had to make a decision about what kind of government a free people should have.

3. Letters should reflect an understanding of the British policies that led to the Revolution and of the colonists' new ideas about freedom and equality.

4. (a) Both the British and Americans took pride in the empire and were allied against the French. (b) The British attitude contributed to the war by treating the colonists as inferior; the colonists' view contributed by discouraging reconciliation. (c) Students' graphic organizers should reflect an understanding of the advantages and disadvantages of both sides in the war.

 **Alternative Assessment**

Final Evaluation
Use the following guidelines to evaluate student projects:

● **Evidence of mastery of content** To what extent do projects demonstrate knowledge and understanding of chapter content?

● **Evidence of thoughtfulness** To what extent do projects demonstrate the British perspective regarding colonial affairs?

● **Evidence of outside research** To what extent do projects demonstrate students' outside research?

Thinking Critically

1. Demonstrating Reasoned Judgment The colonists resented the restrictions that the British placed on their freedoms. On what grounds would you feel justified in rebelling against government restrictions?

2. Identifying Alternatives In America today the media—television in particular—significantly influence public opinion. In the absence of television in the late 1700s, newspapers, pamphlets, and documents like the Declaration of Independence informed and incited the colonists. Do you think the Revolution would have taken place without these writings? Explain your reasoning.

3. Identifying Assumptions What was the long-term significance of the assumption in the Declaration of Independence that both popular sovereignty and equality were basic principles of American government and society?

4. Drawing Conclusions You have read that after their defeat at Yorktown, the British played a song called "The World Turned Upside Down." In what ways was this an appropriate title for the times?

Making Connections

1. Evaluating Primary Sources Review the words of Abigail Adams on page 57. How did she want men to change their relations to women? In what ways were her words a revolutionary statement?

2. Understanding the Visuals Examine the painting of George Washington's resignation on page 67. What sentiments does the painting seek to evoke?

3. Writing About the Chapter It is 1776. You are writing a letter to your cousin in England explaining why you support, or do not support, the colonists' decision to rebel against Britain. First, list what you see as the reasons for your support or lack of support. Mention any ways in which you can sympathize with the other side's point of view. Then write a draft of your letter in which you explain your position. Revise your letter, making sure that each idea is expressed clearly. Proofread your letter and draft a final copy.

4. Using the Graphic Organizer This graphic organizer uses a double web to compare and contrast British and American self-images during the French and Indian War. (a) What did the British and the Americans have in common? (b) How did their views of one another contribute to the American Revolution? (c) On a separate piece of paper, create your own graphic organizer comparing and contrasting the advantages and disadvantages of the British and Americans at the start of the War for Independence.

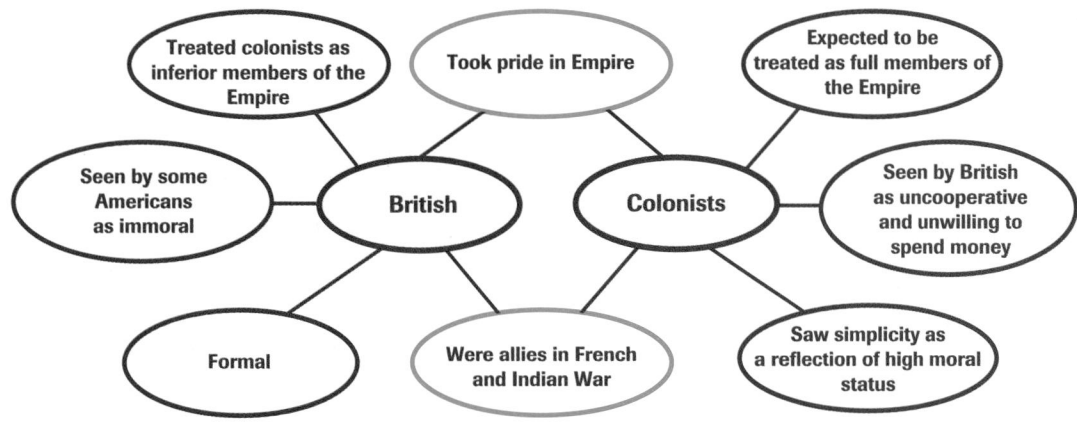

Thinking Critically

1. Answers should center on restrictions that are arbitrary and unnecessary. Most students will feel that rebellion against unnecessary restrictions can be justified.

2. Answers should show an awareness that the Revolution was provoked not only by specific actions like the Stamp Act but also by the spread of new beliefs about freedom and equality. These beliefs were explained in the writings that circulated among the colonists before and during the Revolution.

3. Answers should indicate that the United States is still struggling with issues of equality for all of its people, notably minorities and women.

4. The world must have felt turned upside down for the British, who entered the war feeling that their superior strength could easily put down the colonists' rebellion. The outcome of the Revolution also upset the British belief in an unchanging hierarchy. In addition, this song symbolizes the fact that many groups who took up the ideas of the American Revolution, including women and African Americans, would not earlier have spoken out for these ideas.

When learning the important dates and names of the War for Independence, it is easy for students to overlook the drama and tension of those days. The two source readings, excerpts from Howard Fast's *April Morning* and the diary that a young girl kept during the war, will bring home to students the fact that the war affected individual lives in a very personal way. Students will come to understand that the War for Independence was more than just some long-ago struggle; it was a fight that took the lives of loved ones and turned people's lives on end for several years.

INSTRUCT

Ask students to imagine that they are either the boy in *April Morning* or Sally Wister, the young diarist in the second selection. Have students write either another chapter to Fast's book or another day's entry in Wister's diary. If they choose to write as though they are the boy revolutionary, they should focus on the aftermath of the Battle at Lexington Green. In so doing, they should draw on their knowledge of those events from the chapter content.

Students who choose to take on the role of Sally Wister should explore in their diary entries whether or not the Wister family ever encounters the British army, how long the British army remains in Philadelphia, and what course the war takes following the British occupation of that city. Again, students should draw on the information presented in the chapter to write their diary entries.

After students finish their writing, have several of them read their work aloud to the class. Then hold a discussion about the similarities and differences between those pieces that have been read aloud.

CHAPTER 2
SOURCE READINGS

April Morning

 Literature

Howard Fast

INTRODUCTION The military engagements at Lexington and Concord on April 19, 1775, marked the beginning of the War for Independence. In the following excerpt from his novel *April Morning*, author Howard Fast captures the sights and sounds of the tense skirmish at Lexington Green. Through his vivid imagery, we catch a glimpse of the feelings of some Americans as the enormity of what they were attempting dawned on them in the early light of an April morning.

VOCABULARY Before you read the selection, find the meaning of these words in a dictionary: dissipate, jubilation.

When the British saw us, they were on the road past Buckman's[1]. First, there were three officers on horseback. Then two flag-bearers, one carrying the regimental flag and the other bearing the British colors. Then a corps of eight drums. Then rank after rank of the redcoats, stretching back on the road and into the curtain of mist, and emerging from the mist constantly, so that they appeared to be an endless force and an endless number. It was dreamlike and not very believable, and it caused me to turn and look at the houses around the common, to see whether all the rest of what we were, our mothers and sisters and brothers and grandparents, were watching the same thing we watched. My impression was that the houses had appeared by magic, for I could only remember looking around in the darkness and seeing nothing where now all the houses stood—and the houses were dead and silent, every shutter closed and bolted, every door and storm door closed and barred. Never before had I seen the houses like that, not in the worst cold or the worst storms.

And the redcoats did not quicken their pace or slow it, but marched up the road with the same even pace, up to the edge of the common; and when they were there, one of the officers held up his arm—and the drums stopped and the soldiers stopped, the line of soldiers stretching all the way down the road and into the dissipating mist. They were about one hundred and fifty paces from us.

The three officers sat on their horses, studying us. The morning air was cold and clean and sharp, and I could see their faces and the faces of the redcoat soldiers behind them, the black bands of their knapsacks, the glitter of their buckles. Their coats were red as fire, but their light trousers were stained and dirty from the march.

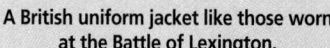

A British uniform jacket like those worn at the Battle of Lexington.

[1] a tavern near Lexington Green

Then, one of the officers sang out to them, "Fix bayonets!" and all down the line, the bayonets sparkled in the morning sun, and we heard the ring of metal against metal as they were clamped onto the guns. . . .

Then another British officer—I discovered afterward that he was Major Pitcairn—called out orders: "Columns right!" and then, "By the left flank," and, "Drums to the rear!" The drummers stood still and beat their drums, and the redcoats marched past them smartly, wheeling and parading across the common, while the three mounted officers spurred over the grass at a sharp canter, straight across our front and then back, reining in their prancing horses to face us. Meanwhile, the redcoats marched onto the common, the first company wheeling to face us when it was past our front of thirty-three men, the second company repeating the exercise, until they made a wall of red coats across the common, with no more than thirty or forty paces separating us. Even so close, they were unreal; only their guns were real, and their glittering bayonets too—and suddenly, I realized, and I believed that everyone else around me realized, that this was not to be an exercise or a parade or an argument, but something undreamed of and unimagined.

I think the Reverend was beginning to speak when Major Pitcairn drove down on him so that he had to leap aside. My father clutched the Reverend's arm to keep him from falling, and wheeling his horse, Major Pitcairn checked the beast so that it pawed at the air and neighed shrilly. The Reverend was speaking again, but no one heard his words or remembered them. The redcoats were grinning; small, pinched faces under the white wigs—they grinned at us. Leaning over his horse, Major Pitcairn screamed at us:

"Lay down your arms . . . Disperse, do you hear me! Disperse, you lousy peasant scum! Clear the way, do you hear me! Get off the King's green!"

At least, those were the words that I seem to remember. Others remembered differently; but the way he screamed, in his strange London accent, with all the motion and excitement, with his horse rearing and kicking at the Reverend and Father, with the drums beating again and the fixed bayonets glittering in the sunshine, it's a wonder that any of his words remained with us.

Yet for all that, this was a point where everything appeared to happen slowly. Abel Loring clutched my arm and said dryly, "Adam, Adam, Adam." He let go of his gun and it fell to the ground. "Pick it up," I said to him, watching Father, who pulled the Reverend into the protection of his body. Jonas Parker turned to us and cried at us:

"Steady! Steady! Now just hold steady!"

We still stood in our two lines, our guns butt end on the ground or held loosely in our hands. Major Pitcairn spurred his horse and raced between the lines. Somewhere, away from us, a shot sounded. A redcoat soldier raised his musket, leveled it at Father, and fired. My father clutched at his breast, then crumpled to the ground like an empty sack and lay with his face in the grass. I screamed. I was two. One part of me was screaming; another part of me looked at Father and grasped my gun in aching hands. Then the whole British front burst into a roar of sound and flame and smoke, and our whole world crashed at us, and broke into little pieces that fell around our ears, and came to an end; and the roaring, screaming noise was like the jubilation of the damned.

I ran. I was filled with fear, saturated with it, sick with it. Everyone else was running. The boys were running and the men were running. Our two lines were gone, and now it was only men and boys running in every direction that was away from the British, across the common and away from the British.

THINKING ABOUT THE SELECTION

1. Judging from the excerpt, how did the British force at Lexington compare with the colonists' force?

2. According to the excerpt, who fired the first shot? How does this compare with the information in the chapter?

Critical Thinking

3. **Distinguishing False from Accurate Images** Based on the facts in the chapter about the Battle of Lexington, do you think that Fast's fictional description of the event is reasonably accurate? Explain your answer.

ANSWERS TO

Thinking About the Selection

1. The British greatly outnumbered the colonists and were better trained and equipped.

2. The excerpt does not specify who fired the first shot, but says only that it came from "[s]omewhere, away from us." According to the chapter information, no one knows who fired the first shot, so this vague description is consistent with the facts.

3. Answers will vary, but should show an understanding of the battle's events and the role of dramatization in fiction. In addition, however, students should realize that the drama presented here is appropriate for describing the events of the battle.

Remind students that following the Battle at Lexington, the Second Continental Congress met in Philadelphia and chose George Washington as commander in chief. In June, the Americans and the British fought the Battle of Bunker Hill. Thomas Paine published *Common Sense* in January of 1776, and the Declaration of Independence was signed in July of that year. The British abandoned Philadelphia in 1778 and were attacked by the Americans as they moved toward New York City. The war then shifted toward the south and finally ended with the British surrender at Yorktown in October 1781. Students may find the time line on pages 104–105 helpful in understanding the events that preceded the Battle at Lexington.

Point out to students that the American Revolution could never have happened without individuals who were independent thinkers and who had strong personalities. Ask students to find a person who contributed to the revolution in some way. The person can be either a famous figure, such as Samuel Adams, Benjamin Franklin, or Patrick Henry, or a little-known figure, such as Sally Wister, who nonetheless contributed to the American effort in some way. Then have students collect information and write a one-page biography about the person's life and involvement in the American Revolution. To choose a subject, students could use their textbooks or sources such as *The Ethnic Contribution to the American Revolution*, edited by Frederick Harling and Martin Kaufman, or *Patriots: The Men who Started the American Revolution*, by A. J. Languth. To write their biographies, students should look for other biographies on the person they have chosen, or read materials written by that person. Students should be sure their biographies answer the following questions: Who is the person? How was he/she involved in the American Revolution? What thoughts and beliefs did this person have about the revolution? What happened to the person after the war was won?

SOURCE READINGS

A Young Woman's War-Time Diary

 *Primary Source*

Sally Wister

INTRODUCTION In 1777, in the midst of the War for Independence, fifteen-year-old Sally Wister and her family left Philadelphia and went to a relative's country house. They hoped to avoid the British army, who they believed were about to occupy the city. The following excerpts are from a diary Wister kept during the time. She wrote the entries as though she were addressing letters to her friend Deborah Norris.

VOCABULARY Before you read the selection, find the meaning of these words in a dictionary: dispel, chintz, kenton.

September, 1777.

Yesterday, which was the 24th of September, two Virginia officers called at our home, and informed us that the British army had crossed the Schuylkill[2]. Presently after, another person stopped, and confirmed what they had said, and that General Washington and army were near Pottsgrove. Well, thee may be sure we were sufficiently scared; however, the road was very still till evening. About seven o'clock we heard a great noise. To the door we all went. A large number of waggons, with about three hundred of the Philadelphia militia. They begged for drink, and several pushed into the house. One of those that entered was a little tipsy, and had a mind to be [rude]. I then thought it time for me to retreat; so figure me (mightily scared, as not having presence of mind enough to face so many of the military) running in at one door, and out at another, all in a shake with fear; but after a little, seeing the officers appear gentlemanly and the soldiers civil, I called reason to my aid. My fears were in some measure dispelled, tho' my teeth rattled, and my hand shook like an aspen leaf. They did not offer to take their quarters with us; so, with many blessings, and as many adieus, they marched off.

Fifth Day, September 26th.

About 12 o'clock cousin Jesse heard that General Howe's army had moved down towards Philadelphia. Then, my dear, our hopes and fears were engaged for you. However, my advice is, summon up all your resolution, call Fortitude to your aid, don't suffer your spirits to sink, my dear; there's nothing like courage; 'tis what I stand in need of myself, but unfortunately have but little of it in my composition.

I was standing in the kitchen about 12, when somebody came to me in a hurry, screaming, "Sally, Sally, here are the light horse!"[3] This was by far the greatest fright I had endured. . . . I ran immediately to the western door, where the family were assembled, anxiously waiting for the event. They rode up to the door and halted, and enquired if we had horses to sell; he answered negatively. "Have not you, sir," to my father, "two black horses?"— "Yes, but have no mind to dispose of them." My terror had by this time nearly subsided. The officer and men behaved perfectly civil; the first drank two glasses of wine, rode away, bidding his men to follow, which, after adieus in number, they did. The officer was Lieutenant Lindsay, of Blands's regiment, Lee's troop. The men, to our great joy, were Americans, and but 4 in all. What made us imagine them British, they wore blue and red, which with us is not common.

December 5th, Sixth Day.

Oh, gracious Debby, I am all alive with fear. The English have come out to attack (as we imagine) our army, three miles this side. What will become of us,

---

[2] a tributary of the Delaware River

[3] calvary

only six miles distant? We are in hourly expectation of an engagement. I fear we shall be in the midst of it. Heaven defend us from so dreadful a sight. The battle of Germantown, and the horrors of that day, are recent in my mind. It will be sufficiently dreadful, if we are only in hearing of the firing, to think how many of our fellow creatures are plung'd into the boundless ocean of eternity, few of them prepar'd to meet their fate. But they are summon'd before an all-merciful judge, from whom they have a great deal to hope.

Sixth Day, June 5th, Morn, 11 o'clock.

Last night we were a little alarm'd. I was awaken'd about 12, with somebody's opening the chamber door. I observ'd cousin Prissa talking to mamma. I asked what was the matter. "Only a party of light horse." "Are they Americans?" I quickly said. She answer'd in the affirmative, (which dispell'd my fears), and told me Major Jameson commanded, and that Captains Call and Nixon were with him. With that intelligence she left us. . . . This morning I rose by, or near seven, dress'd in my light chintz, which is made gown-fashion, kenton handkerchief, and linen apron. . . .

Dress'd as above, down I came, and went down to our kitchen, which is a small distance from the house. As I came back, I saw Jameson at the window. He met me in the entry, bow'd: — "How do you do, Miss Sally?" . . . I invited him into our parlour. He followed me in. We chatted very sociably. . . .

Woodcut, 1779

I ask'd him whether Dandridge was on this side the Delaware [river]. He said, "Yes." I wanted sadly to hear his opinion, but he said not a word. The conversation turn'd upon the British leaving Philadelphia. He firmly believ'd they were going. I sincerely wish'd it might be true, but was afraid to flatter myself. I had heard it so often that I was quite faithless. . . . He smiled and assur'd me they were going away.

He was summon'd to breakfast. I ask'd him to stay with us. He declin'd the invitation with politeness, adding that he was in a hurry,—oblig'd to go to camp as soon as he could. He bow'd, "Your servant, ladies," and withdrew immediately. After breakfast they set off for Valley Forge, where Gen'l Washington's army still are.

THINKING ABOUT THE SELECTION

1. What is Wister afraid will happen near the house where she is staying?
2. Based on this excerpt and on the information in the chapter, who won the battle when the British finally did attack Philadelphia?

Critical Thinking

3. **Drawing Conclusions** What events in Wister's recent experience might help explain her fear of encountering the British army?

ANSWERS TO

Thinking About the Selection

1. She is afraid to see more destruction and suffering from a nearby battle.
2. Based on Wister's discussion with Jameson ("The conversation turn'd upon the British leaving Philadelphia. He firmly believ'd they were going. I sincerely wish'd it might be true, but was afraid to flatter myself. I had heard it so often that I was quite faithless. . . . He smiled and assur'd me they were going away.") and the information in the text, students should know that the British won the battle.

3. Wister refers to the "the battle of Germantown, and the horrors of that day" and wishes to be spared such a sight again. Thus, her own negative experience has led her to fear the British and the war.

Chapter 3 The Constitution of the United States
1783–1789

📁 Teaching Resources (See Unit 1 Folder)

	Instruction	Enrichment
Section 1 **The Constitutional Convention** (pp. 80–86)	Reproducible Lesson Plan, p. 69 Alternate Lesson Plan, p. 59 Guided Reading and Review, p. 72 Quiz, p. 73	Literature Activity, On America, p. 89 Primary Source Activity, Hamilton and Jefferson, p. 84 Critical Thinking Activity, Determining Relevance, p. 83 Historian's Toolbox Activity, Identifying Central Issues, p. 82
Section 2 **Ratifying the Constitution** (pp. 88–91)	Reproducible Lesson Plan, p. 70 Alternate Lesson Plan, p. 60 Guided Reading and Review, p. 74 Quiz, p. 75	Primary Source Activity, A Department of Peace, p. 86 Visual Learning Activity, The First United States Coins, p. 90 Viewpoints Activity, For and Against the Bill of Rights, pp. 80–81 American Profiles Activity, Richard Allen, p. 79
Section 3 **The New Government** (pp. 92–95)	Reproducible Lesson Plan, p. 71 Alternate Lesson Plan, p. 61 Guided Reading and Review, p. 76 Quiz, p. 77 Chapter Test, Forms A & B, pp. 92–97	Visual Learning Activity, A Portrait of a President, p. 91 Primary Source Activity, Meeting President and Mrs. Washington, p. 85 American Profiles Activity, Benjamin Banneker, p. 78

📁 Additional Chapter Resources

Resource Organizer, p. 68
Alternate Lesson Plan, p. 58
Answer Keys, pp. 145–157

Bibliography

For the Teacher
Hentoff, Nat. *The First Freedom: The Tumultuous History of Free Speech in America.* Delacorte, 1988. (A historical account of the interpretation and application of the First Amendment.)

Lessons on the Federalist Papers: Supplement to High School Courses in American History, Government and Civics. Organization of American Historians, 1987. (Core concepts from *The Federalist* such as the separation of powers, limited government, and the rights of individuals. Ten lessons.)

Prentice Hall Literature Excerpts from *The American Experience,* 1994, including Wheatley, Phillis. "To His Excellency, General Washington," from *The Poems of Phillis Wheatley.* University of North Carolina, 1966.

The Big Idea for the chapter and how the main ideas in each section relate to the Big Idea are graphically displayed below. Comprehension of this chapter's Big Idea is critical to students' understanding of United States history and how we as a nation got where we are today.

Media and Technology

 Critical Thinking, I-6; The Way It Works, H-5

 Graphic Organizer, G-1

 Guided Reading Audiotapes (English and Spanish)

 Computer Test Bank

For the Student

Bowen, Catherine D. *Miracle at Philadelphia: The Story of the Constitution., May to September, 1787.* Little, Brown, 1986 edition.

Lindop, Edmund. *Birth of the Constitution.* Enslow, 1987. (An easy-to-read description of the Constitutional Convention, including the text of the Constitution and the amendments.)

America: A Personal History of the United States, No. 4—Inventing a Nation. Color film, 16mm, 52 minutes, Time-Life Films, 1972. (An investigation of the Independence Hall debates, narrated by Alastair Cooke.)

CHAPTER 3

A group of powerful men succeeded in writing and winning approval of the federal Constitution and in establishing a powerful central government. The conflict generated by their efforts resulted in safeguards in the form of the Bill of Rights to protect Americans' liberty from government infringement.

SECTION 1

Delegates gathered at the Constitutional Convention to restructure the country's government. After a great deal of compromise, they came up with a new plan for government that blended popular sovereignty with a strong national government.

SECTION 2

Many Americans opposed the Constitution because they were afraid it meant the end of liberty, and it was narrowly ratified only when the Federalists agreed to add the Bill of Rights.

SECTION 3

With the framework for the new government finally in place, the Federalists set about making their vision of a great "republican empire" come true.

78B

The Constitution of the United States

1783–1789

CHAPTER 3

The Constitution of The United States

1783–1789

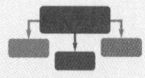

The Relevance of the Big Idea

The struggle to resolve the two points of view that led to the creation of the Constitution—a plan for government that combined strong national powers with a respect for and protection of individual liberty—is debated even after more than two hundred years. Issues such as gun control, states' rights regarding death penalties, seat-belt laws, and reproductive rights are all part of the same debate.

Explain to students that many people feel that institutions have too much power over individuals. Have students generate a list of possible institutions—school, family, clubs, or other organizations to which they may belong—and explain how they feel about the level of power of those institutions.

In Depth

Global Connections

After the success of the American Revolution, many British people blamed King George III, whose irascible nature and inability to compromise, they felt, provoked the American colonies to rebel. Also, the aftermath of the war with America left the British economy severely strained. Within a few years, however, the British economy greatly improved, as trade with the United States became a more lucrative enterprise than it had ever been between Britain and its American colonies.

*C*oncerned about disorder among the people and worried about the stability of the new nation, a group of well-educated, well-organized men worked in the 1780s to save the United States. They succeeded in writing and winning approval of the Constitution and in establishing a powerful central government. By century's end a new capital, a symbol of their hopes for an American empire, was rising on the banks of the Potomac River.

Events in the United States

1781 The Articles of Confederation are approved.

1783 George Washington resigns as commander of the American army.

1781	1782	1783	1784	1785

Events in the World

1783 Simón Bolívar, later hero of South American war for independence, is born in Venezuela.

1785 Edward Cartwright invents the power loom in Britain.

▶ RESOURCE DIRECTORY

Teaching Resources

Alternate Lesson Plan: Demonstrating the Big Idea found in the Alternate Lesson Plans folder, p. 58, provides a lesson strategy to instruct students about the Big Idea that the United States Constitution was the result of much conflict and debate among the powerful political leaders of the time.

Alternative Assessment Handbook provides information, guidance, and strategies for alternative methods of assessment. It includes an essay on new trends in assessment, guidance and strategies for developing performance tasks and portfolios, scoring rubrics, and sample evaluation forms.

Pages 80–86
The Constitutional Convention
During the long summer of 1787, delegates to a convention in Philadelphia fashioned a Constitution that forever sealed the people's right to direct their government—with some restrictions.

Pages 88–91
Ratifying the Constitution
With a combination of political skill and persuasive argument, the Federalists managed to win narrow approval of the Constitution. Their key concession to their opponents was the Bill of Rights.

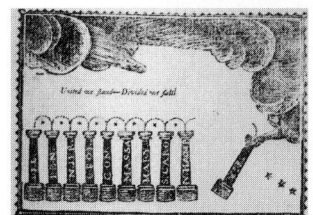

Pages 92–95
The New Government
In the first years under the Constitution, Federalists labored to make the United States government as impressive as possible. They chose talented officials, opted for high ceremony, and made plans for an elaborate national capital.

1786	1787	1788	1789	1790	1791
1786 The Annapolis Convention takes place. • Shays's Rebellion begins.	*1787* The Constitutional Convention is held in Philadelphia.	*1788* The Constitution is approved by the states and goes into effect.	*1789* George Washington becomes the first President of the United States.	*1790* Rhode Island becomes the last of the original 13 states to ratify the Constitution.	*1791* The Bill of Rights is ratified and becomes part of the Constitution.
	1787 Turkey declares war on Russia.		*1789* The French Revolution begins.		*1791* Austrian composer Wolfgang Amadeus Mozart dies. • Haitians revolt against French rule.

Alternative Assessment

As an ongoing chapter project, students can create a museum exhibition on the creation of the Constitution of the United States titled Forging a Lasting Foundation. Suggestions for contributions to the exhibition follow.

● Create a newspaper page for the day after the Constitution was ratified. The page can include a political cartoon, letters to the editor, an editorial, and background on the document's evolution.

● Make an audiotape to guide visitors through the exhibition that also provides background information about exhibits.

● Write the script for and act in a "living" exhibit, such as the gathering many years later of a group of aged Federalists and Anti-Federalists remembering the days of the debate over the Constitution.

Explain that finished projects will be assessed according to the following criteria:

● **Unacceptable** Projects are not attempted or fail to meet requirements outlined.

● **Limited/Acceptable** Projects are based on material from the textbook and reflect some effort to show the intensity and conflict behind the creation of the Constitution.

● **Extensive/Commendable** Projects are based on some outside research and indicate a comprehensive understanding of the struggle behind our Constitution.

● **Extraordinary/Outstanding** Projects are based on considerable outside research and reflect in-depth knowledge, specific as well as general, of the struggle behind the Constitution's creation.

For information on alternative assessment trends and strategies, see the Alternative Assessment Handbook in the Resource Directory on page 78.

The Constitutional Convention

SECTION 1

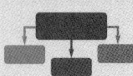

1. FOCUS

Connecting to the Big Idea

See page 78B. Explain that restructuring the United States government was a difficult task. Delegates to the Constitutional Convention struggled over the issue of how much power should remain with the states and how much should be given to the national government. Ask students how the new government was structured.

Objectives

● Describe James Madison's contributions to the Constitutional Convention.
● Explain the debate over how states would be represented in the legislature.
● Describe how the Constitution blended popular sovereignty with restrictions that limited the power of the people.

Bellringer

Ask students to define the word *compromise* and recall a time in their life when they compromised on an important issue.

Reading Strategy

Structured Overview Have students write the following section headings on a piece of paper: James Madison, Divisions and Compromises at the Convention, The Outlines of the New Government. Then ask them to scan the section for subheadings under each of these headings and to fill in details from the text as they read.

The Constitutional Convention

SECTION PREVIEW

During the long summer of 1787, delegates to a convention in Philadelphia fashioned a Constitution that forever sealed the people's right to direct their government—with some restrictions.

Key Concepts

• James Madison was a central figure in the gathering of Nationalists at the Constitutional Convention.
• A key question in the debate about the new government was whether each state would have equal representation in the legislature or whether larger states would have more power than smaller states.
• The founders of the Constitution blended popular sovereignty with restrictions that limited the power of the people.

Key Terms, People, and Places

Virginia Plan, veto, New Jersey Plan, Great Compromise, Three-fifths Compromise, separation of powers, system of checks and balances, Electoral College; James Madison

During the Constitutional Convention, Benjamin Franklin often wondered if the decoration on the chair in which Washington sat represented a sunset or a sunrise—and whether the convention would be an end or a new beginning for the United States.

T he delegates to the convention in the summer of 1787—that is, most of them—did not leave Philadelphia until they had written a new set of rules by which the nation was to be governed, rules which today Americans refer to simply as the Constitution. It begins with this Preamble:

W e the People of the United States, in Order to form a more perfect Union, establish Justice, insure domestic Tranquility, provide for the common defence, promote the general Welfare, and secure the Blessings of Liberty to ourselves and our Posterity, do ordain and establish this Constitution for the United States of America.

Over the years, Americans have come to see the first three words of the Constitution, "We the People," as the most important. Everything else in the document follows from the basic assumption that in the United States the people will govern themselves.

The men who wrote the Constitution, however, were not as interested in protecting popular sovereignty as they were in restraining it. Notice that among their purposes they listed forming "a more perfect union," because the union of states was far from perfect. They wanted to "insure domestic tranquility," or peace within the nation, because Shays's Rebellion had shown how weak the safeguards of tranquility were. Finally, they wanted "to secure the blessings of liberty" for themselves and for those who would come after them, because they were afraid they might lose their liberty if chaos broke out.

The Constitutional Convention was by no means a gathering to make the final refinement of a successful government; instead it was a rescue mission for one that might well be failing. According to the most influential member of the convention, **James Madison,** the idea was to find a way to "at once support . . . the national authority, and leave in force the local authorities" only to the extent that the local authorities could be useful without interfering with the national government.

AMERICAN PROFILES

James Madison

Madison, like many of the fifty-five men who attended the convention in Philadelphia during the summer of 1787, was a relatively

---

RESOURCE DIRECTORY

Teaching Resources

Reproducible Lesson Plan found in the Unit 1 folder, p. 69, provides a summary of the Section 1 lesson plan content.

Alternate Lesson Plan: Learning Styles found in the Alternate Lesson Plans folder, p. 59, helps students create presentations on issues of debate at the Constitutional Convention and is especially effective for kinesthetic learners.

Guided Reading and Review found in the Unit 1 folder, p. 72, provides a structure for reading and mastering the key concepts and reviewing the key terms for Section 1. (Guided Practice)

young man. He was only thirty-seven; half of the delegates were over forty-two. Aside from being gentlemen of about the same age, the delegates had little in common. They were from a wide variety of backgrounds. A few were very rich, but some had no more than a comfortable living. Many were well educated and familiar with the theories of European political thinkers. Few, however, had spent as much time on the specifics of a possible government as had Madison. In his home at the foot of the Blue Ridge Mountains he spent evening after evening poring over books of history, government, and law. By the time of the convention, Madison had already invested a year of thought in the form of new government.

The "Father of the Constitution," as Madison came to be called, grew up on a plantation in Orange County, Virginia, where he studied European political thought under a Scottish tutor. Although Madison was an unassuming man, he always retained something of an intellectual edge over his peers due to natural inclination and his intensive training.

Madison's studies of philosophy had led him to believe that people are naturally selfish creatures driven by powerful emotions and personal interests. That did not mean there was no hope for order in society, however. European theorists had argued that through proper government, humans could take control of themselves and their world and improve the condition of both. Constitutions established political structures that encouraged the best in people while restraining their worst tendencies. A dream of devising just such a constitution was exactly what would bring James Madison to the Philadelphia Convention.

Even after he entered public life, Madison was never comfortable with crowds and their politics. He did not marry until he was forty-

three, but when he did he found a good match in the lively and cheerful Dolley Todd, a twenty-six-year-old widow. They were happily married for forty-two years.

Supporting his life of productive leisure and domestic happiness, however, were several dozen enslaved people. Madison, like many of the Framers of the Constitution who owned slaves, considered slavery immoral. And like them, he was unable to bring himself to do anything about this contradiction. Madison knew that if he had been born a slave, he could not have become a successful public man. He would not have had the opportunity to accomplish what he did in the Virginia legislature and the Continental Congress, or at the convention itself.

James Madison (above) looked like a boy even at age thirty-seven. The Nationalist Fisher Ames described him as "little and ordinary," but added, "his language is very pure . . . and to the point."

Madison made it his business to attend every meeting of the convention. During these sessions, he could be seen busily taking the notes that later would become our best record of the proceedings. The delegates were intentionally secretive; they allowed no reporters to attend and kept silent when questioned by outsiders. They even posted sentries to keep curious onlookers away from the windows of the room where they met. Only in secrecy, they believed, could they speak their minds freely.

Inside that room, the Assembly Room of the Pennsylvania State House (now called Independence Hall), was a colorful and exciting scene. There sat the members of the convention, representing every state except Rhode Island, which had declined to send delegates. All the summer long, the members came to Philadelphia and went away again; never were the full fifty-five participants present at once. They stayed until family or business called them home—or until the sweltering heat of the city summer, with its smell and its infinite number of flies, drove them away.

Explain/Discuss

Explain to students that although delegates to the Constitutional Convention shared the same basic beliefs about government, crafting a workable and lasting national government was an arduous process of debate and compromise. Ask students why compromise was so important to the successful outcome of the convention.

Discuss the divisive issues and important compromises of the Constitutional Convention. Encourage discussion with questions such as the following: What was the major division at the Constitutional Convention? What role did James Madison play at the convention? How did the Virginia Plan differ from the New Jersey Plan? What was the Great Compromise? the Three-fifths Compromise?

Analyze

Have students analyze the Constitution and the new government it created. How did the Constitution combine popular sovereignty with a strong national government? Why did delegates to the convention impose limits on presidential power? Are there problems today that the Constitution fails to address?

Divisions and Compromises at the Convention

The major division at the Constitutional Convention in 1787 was between those who wanted to abandon the Articles of Confederation and those who merely wanted to amend them. Nearly everyone agreed on the need for a stronger national government, but some saw no need to start from scratch. Madison and others who wanted truly significant changes were able to dominate the proceedings by bringing a plan with them. Their **Virginia Plan** became the focus of discussion against which all other ideas were weighed.

The Convention Is Divided The Virginia Plan called for the creation of a bicameral, or two-house, national legislature. Each state would send representatives in proportion to the number of its citizens. A state with a large population would have more representatives in both houses than a state with a small population—and thus have more voting power in the legislature. The proposed government would also have an executive branch and a judicial branch, as well as the right to tax its citizens, thus correcting serious shortcomings of the Articles of Confederation. It would also have the power to **veto,** or overturn, any act of a state legislature—an idea that frightened some because it would give the national government greater power than the states.

Opponents of the Virginia Plan, many of whom were from smaller states, were afraid they would have no power in the new government. So they proposed an alternative, the **New Jersey Plan.** Like the Virginia Plan, this plan would give Congress the power to tax and would create executive and judicial branches. It preserved a feature of the Articles of Confederation that the big states did not like, however: every state would continue to have an equal vote in a unicameral Congress, no matter how large the state population. The New Jersey Plan ensured that the states would remain the most powerful governments in America.

The Convention Compromises On July 2, the convention voted on whether representation in the legislature should be based on population. The vote was split and the convention deadlocked. For a while, matters seemed hopeless. Then, over a period of several days, a solution emerged, one that is now called the **Great Compromise.** The legislative branch would be made up of two houses, as called for in the Virginia Plan. But in one house—the House of Representatives—each state would have a number of representatives that corresponded to the size of its population. In the other house, the Senate, every state would have an equal number of representatives.

⭐ An observer noted that the streets outside the Pennsylvania State House during the convention were filled with people of "every rank and condition in life, from the highest to the lowest, male and female, of every age and every color. . . . There seemed to be some of every nation under heaven."

▶ RESOURCE DIRECTORY

Teaching Resources

⭐ 📄 **Literature Activity** On America, found in the Unit 1 folder, p. 89, uses a poem by the "Poet of the American Revolution," Philip Freneau comparing America and Europe.

⭐ 📄 **Primary Source Activity** Jefferson and Hamilton, found in the Unit 1 folder, p. 84, presents Hamiltonian and Jeffersonian views on popular sovereignty and human nature.

As they signed the Constitution on September 17, 1787, the delegates put an end to the divisions of opinion that had made the work of the convention difficult.

 Activity

(The clock icon indicates an activity that can be successfully conducted within a class period. Each chapter has at least one such activity.)

An Eyewitness Account
Ask students to imagine that they have found a spot where they can observe the proceedings at the Constitutional Convention unnoticed. Have them write a description of the event.

Answer to ...

MAKING   CONNECTIONS

Possible answers: widespread violence, conflict over social issues such as prayer in schools, and foreign ownership of American businesses.

The Great Compromise, approved on July 16, included the answer to another crucial question. How should the enslaved people who were so numerous in the southern states be counted? If they were all included in the count of the general population, the southern states would have great power in the House of Representatives. If they were not counted at all, the southern states would be weak in the House. The delegates adopted a formula that became known as the **Three-fifths Compromise.** Under this plan, all enslaved people would be counted, but then the total would be multiplied by three fifths.

The Three-fifths Compromise did not mean that enslaved African Americans would be allowed to vote, however, or that their interests would be represented in Congress. They, like Native Americans, were excluded from participating in the government, although in this early period some free African Americans in some states could vote.

Although many features of Madison's plan survived these compromises, the delegates never went as far in strengthening the national government as Madison would have

liked. For example, they refused to give Congress the right to veto state legislation. So upset with such revisions was Alexander Hamilton, a key Nationalist delegate from New York, that he left the convention. Madison, too, was disappointed, but he stayed in Philadelphia.

MAKING   CONNECTIONS

Slavery became an increasingly divisive issue in the United States, eventually becoming one of the causes of the Civil War—a period when the Constitution failed to hold the nation together. What problems do we face today that the Founders were unable to foresee?

The Outlines of the New Government

After further debate over the exact provisions of the Constitution, the convention turned the document over to a Committee on Style on September 9. It then approved the final draft on September 17, 1787. Although the delegates provided a way to change the Constitution,

In Depth

Multicultural Perspectives

That slaves, indentured servants, women, Native Americans, and men without land were not protected under the Constitution was forcefully pointed out by Charles Beard (1874–1948). In *An Economic Interpretation of the Constitution* (1913) he reviewed the backgrounds of the fifty-five white men who drew up the Constitution in 1787. Finding most of them to be wealthy landowners, Beard stirred passions pro and con by suggesting that they established a system of government to protect their own economic interests.

Some historians have suggested that delegates to the Constitutional Convention to some extent created the Constitution to protect their own financial interests. Other historians reject the idea that the delegates put self-interest before principle. Ask students to research the life of one delegate to the convention and then to write a short paper discussing his motives for taking part in the convention.

Caption Answer to ...

 Interpreting Charts

It appoints federal judges and grants pardons to federal offenders.

 In Depth

Did You Know?

The separation of powers so prized by the Founders was inspired by the high regard many of them held for the love of liberty and patriotism of the ancient Romans. Of course they viewed the subsequent decline of that republic as cause for great alarm. After independence, therefore, they tried to create a system of government that would avoid the pitfalls that cost the Romans their liberty. The root of Rome's decline, said James Otis, was that the Romans "never had a proper balance between the Senate and the people."

The American System of Checks and Balances

Judicial Branch

Checks on Legislative Branch:
• Can declare acts of Congress unconstitutional

Checks on Judicial Branch:
• Creates lower federal courts
• Can impeach and remove judges
• Can propose amendments to overrule judicial decisions
• Approves appointments of federal judges

Supreme Court Interprets the Law

Legislative Branch

BILL

Congress Makes the Law

Checks on Executive Branch:
• Can declare executive actions unconstitutional

Checks on Executive Branch:
• Can override presidential veto
• Confirms executive appointments
• Ratifies treaties
• Can declare war
• Appropriates money
• Can impeach and remove President

Executive Branch

Checks on Judicial Branch:
• Appoints federal judges
• Can grant pardons to federal offenders

Checks on Legislative Branch:
• Can propose laws
• Can veto laws
• Can call special sessions of Congress
• Makes appointments to federal posts
• Negotiates foreign treaties

President Carries Out the Law

 Interpreting Charts
"You must first enable the government to control the governed," wrote Madison, "and in the next place, oblige it to control itself." The control Madison meant is found in the system of checks and balances in the Constitution. *How does the executive branch check the judicial branch?* ⭐

which has been amended twenty-seven times, this written plan of government has remained basically the same for over two hundred years.

The delegates created what some began to call a federal government, in which power was shared among state and national authorities.

The Constitution called for a **separation of powers** among the three branches. That is, powers of government at the national level would be divided among legislative, executive, and judicial branches. In addition, each branch would be able to check, or stop, the others in

▶ RESOURCE DIRECTORY

Teaching Resources

⭐ **Critical Thinking Activity** Determining Relevance: Checks and Balances, found in the Unit 1 folder, p. 83, enhances students' understanding of complex issues through identification of relationships.

certain ways. For instance, the President, as the head of the executive branch, could veto acts of Congress. This executive power was balanced, however, by Congress's power to overturn the veto with a two-thirds vote of both houses. This government structure is known today as the **system of checks and balances,** illustrated in the chart on page 84.

The New Congress By dividing power between the state and national governments and among the three branches of the national government, the delegates had ingeniously constructed a government that both preserved and limited popular sovereignty. A comparison of the House of Representatives and the Senate further demonstrates their aims.

Because voting in the House of Representatives was based on population, the House was the part of government most directly responsible to the people. Therefore, its members were all to be chosen every two years. If the people wished, they could change the membership of the House quickly.

They could not do the same with the Senate. According to the process outlined in the Constitution (later changed), members of state legislatures would elect senators for six-year terms. Only one third of the Senate would come up for reelection every two years. Thus it was harder for the people to have a direct and sudden impact on the membership of the Senate.

Why did the convention make the Senate more removed from the people? The authors of the Constitution felt that in this way the Senate would be less likely to follow the whims of the crowd. Because no law could be passed unless approved by this more elite body of representatives, the people could not force the passage of bad laws. Furthermore, the writers of the Constitution wanted to make sure that the Senate could be trusted with certain powers, such as giving advice and consent to the President, a responsibility they did not grant to the House of Representatives. They did, however, decide that bills about raising and spending money should be introduced in the House of Representatives alone, because the large states were afraid of losing their influence over money matters.

The House of Representatives and the Senate, when combined as the Congress of the United States, became the most powerful legislative body in the nation. Only the Congress could coin money, deal with other nations, declare war, raise an army, provide for a navy, and regulate commerce. In a sweeping statement now known as the Elastic Clause because it fits so many situations, the Constitution declares that the Congress can

make all Laws which shall be necessary and proper for carrying into Execution the foregoing Powers, and all other Powers vested by this Constitution in the Government of the United States, or in any Department or Officer thereof.
Article 1, Section 8, Clause 18

The President of the United States The Constitution created a strong executive officer, the President of the United States. His term was to be only four years, but he could be reelected as many times as the people wished.

Again, the writers of the Constitution placed a shield between the government and the people by making the election of the President complicated. Voters were to choose electors to do their electing for them. Each state would have as many electoral votes as it had members of Congress. Whoever received the majority of the votes in the meeting of the electors—the **Electoral College**—would become President.

Members of the convention knew that George Washington was likely to be the nation's first President. They believed, however, that it would be difficult for presidential candidates after him to win the required majority—Washington was unique in being popular nationally. Thus the convention provided for the House of Representatives to be the final decision makers. If the Electoral College failed to produce a clear majority for one candidate, the choice would go to the House of Representatives. There each state would have one vote, and the representatives would continue to vote until one of the candidates received a majority.

The Electoral College was a device to allow the people to feel as if they were participating in the choice of their President, while ensuring that

Section 1 Review Answers

1. (a) veto, see p. 82, (b) the Great Compromise, see p. 82, (c) Three-fifths Compromise, see page 83, (d) system of checks and balances, see p. 85, (e) Electoral College, see p. 85

2. James Madison, see p. 80

3. Madison's studies of philosophy had led him to believe that people are naturally selfish creatures driven by powerful emotions. That did not mean that there was no hope for order in society, however. European theorists had argued that through proper government, humans could take control of themselves and their world and improve the condition of both. Constitutions established political structures that encouraged the best in people while restraining their worst tendencies.

4. The Virginia Plan called for the creation of a bicameral national legislature. Each state would send representatives in proportion to the number of its citizens. The New Jersey Plan proposed a unicameral legislature in which every state would continue to have an equal vote.

5. They made the election of the President complex. Voters were to choose electors to do their electing for them. Each state would have as many electoral votes as it had members of Congress. Whoever received a majority of the votes in the meeting of the electors—the Electoral College—would become President.

6. Possible answers: the possibility of amending the Constitution, the Elastic Clause, and the deliberate absence of specifics on the judicial branch.

Media and Technology

Transparencies
Critical Thinking, I-6; The Way It Works, H-5

Tell students that the Constitution has often been called a "bundle of compromises." Ask them to identify specific examples of compromise as outlined in the section.

4. CLOSE

Reinforcing the Big Idea

Writing the Constitution was an important step in creating a lasting nation. But before the document could become law, it had to be approved by the states. The next section describes how the Constitution was ratified.

In Depth

Historical Misconceptions

Those who wrote and supported the Constitution are often thought of as wise old men. But the nine leading Federalists were, on average, ten to twelve years younger than the Anti-Federalists. Fifty-five-year-old George Washington was the oldest of the leading Federalists in 1787. James Madison, "father of the Constitution," was just thirty-six, and Alexander Hamilton was only thirty. Anti-Federalist leaders reflected the generational split among the Founders. Samuel Adams, for example, was sixty-seven in 1787.

The Framers expected that Washington would be the only future candidate for President who would be nationally known and thus able to be elected by a clear majority of the voters.

electors or members of Congress would make the actual selection. Or so the writers of the Constitution thought. As it turned out, a deadlock of the electors has only occurred twice in American history—in the elections of 1800 and 1824. But in 1787 many assumed that it would happen often.

The Constitution gave the President enormous powers. He was to be commander-in-chief of the armed forces. In the system of checks and balances, he also had the power to veto acts of Congress.

Federal Courts The President, again with the advice and consent of the Senate, would also choose judges for the national court system. These judges would hold office for life, as long as they did not act dishonorably. The choice of judges was one step removed from the people—that is, the President, indirectly chosen by the people, chose the judges. In addition, removing judges was made difficult so that the people could not directly control them. Although the Constitution called for one Supreme Court and several lesser ones, the details were left purposely vague. In later years, Congress developed the court system to fit the nation's needs.

This, then, was the outline of the new government as set forth in the Constitution, completed by the delegates in three months of intense work during the summer of 1787. They agreed to submit their new document to state conventions for approval rather than directly to the people. And they required the approval of only nine of thirteen states to make the Constitution legal. Supporters of the new Constitution knew that winning approval for it would not be easy. The following section tells the story of their struggle to make sure that the document they had crafted in debate and compromise became the law of the land.

SECTION 1 REVIEW

Key Terms, People, and Places
1. Define (a) veto, (b) the Great Compromise, (c) Three-fifths Compromise, (d) system of checks and balances, (e) Electoral College.
2. Identify James Madison.

Key Concepts
3. Describe James Madison's view of government.
4. What were the differences between the Virginia Plan and the New Jersey Plan?

5. How did the authors of the Constitution keep the people from directly electing the President?

Critical Thinking
6. **Testing Conclusions** A commentator in the late 1800s said that in making the Constitution, the Founders built "a machine that would go of itself." Cite some features of the structure of the Constitution that have made it adaptable to the changing needs of the nation.

RESOURCE DIRECTORY

Teaching Resources

Quiz found in the Unit 1 folder, p. 75, covers the main ideas in this section as well as the key terms.

Identifying Central Issues

Identifying central issues means recognizing the problems at the core of a piece of information. Usually, all the problems a writer discusses are connected in some way with the central issues. Thus it is vital to be able to recognize central issues—and to be able to judge them without being swayed by the way they are expressed.

The excerpt below is part of an article that appeared in a newspaper in Rhode Island, the only state that did not send delegates to the Constitutional Convention. It is a parable—a story in which a lesson is set forth in symbols. In a parable, the symbols are chosen specifically to influence the reader's understanding of the central issues being discussed.

First read the excerpt and then use the following steps to identify the story's central issues.

1. Identify the subject of the excerpt. Refer to the excerpt to answer these questions. (a) What is the subject of the excerpt? (b) On what date did the parable appear in the newspaper? (c) Given the subject and the date of the excerpt, to what historical period or event do you think the writer of the parable is referring?

2. Examine the excerpt to determine the meaning of its symbols. A symbol is something that stands for or suggests something else. Review the excerpt then answer these questions. (a) Who or what do you think

the parents and the sons in the parable represent? (b) What historical period or event is represented by the events in the parable that occur between the building of the house and the addition to the house? (c) Who or what do you think the three rooms of the dwelling represent? (d) Who or what do you think the "thirteenth son" represents?

3. Summarize the message or main idea and identify the central issue of the excerpt. (a) What central issue does the excerpt from a 1787 newspaper article address? (b) Explain how the parable illustrates this point. (c) What point does the parable make about the consequences of failing to participate in a common effort?

Philadelphia, August 25, 1787

The conduct of the United States, with respect to their governments, may be illustrated by the following story:—An old man arrived, after a long and dangerous voyage, upon the coast of America, with a family consisting of a wife, a few choice old servants, and *thirteen* sons. As soon as they landed, they joined and built a large and commodious dwelling-house, where they lived in safety for several years. The sons, however, grew weary of the company of their parents, and each of them built a cabin for himself, at a distance from the family mansion-house. They had not lived long in this way, before they began to suffer many difficulties and wants. . . . At last *twelve* of them met by agreement upon a plain, and agreed to petition their father to be admitted again under his protection. The venerable [honorable] old man opened his doors to them, and they again became members of his family. They first joined in repairing and fortifying the old mansion-house. They, moreover, added *two* more rooms to it, for the separate use of the old man and his wife, in order thereby to preserve their dignity and authority. From this time the whole family became respectable, happy, and prosperous . . . .

The *thirteenth* son, who refused to accompany his brothers to his father's house, after living a miserable life . . . by himself in the woods, was found *hanging* . . . to the limb of a tree near his cabin.

—*Providence Gazette and Country Journal,* Vol. 24 (Saturday, September 8, 1787), p. 2

📄 **Historian's Toolbox Activity** Identifying Central Issues: Statehood for Washington, D.C., found in the Unit 1 folder, p. 82, encourages students to apply this skill by writing a parable reflecting the political status of the District of Columbia.

Critical Thinking
Identifying Central Issues

Focus Students will interpret a parable to identify the central issues.

Instruct Before you introduce this lesson, you might explain to students that a symbol is a word or sign that stands for something other than itself. Then ask students to read the parable and discuss the symbols in it.

When students have identified the central issue, ask them why they think the writer chose to use these particular symbols and how they contribute to communicating the central issue.

Extend See the Historian's Toolbox Activity in the Resource Directory below.

Answers

1. (a) The behavior of the states toward their government. (b) The parable was first printed on September 8, 1787. (c) The Constitutional Convention.

2. (a) The parents represent a strong central government. The thirteen sons represent the thirteen states. (b) The Critical Period, the Constitutional Convention, and the twelve states' recommitment to the concept of a unified national government. (c) Possible answer: The three rooms symbolize the three branches of government. (d) The thirteenth son represents the state of Rhode Island, which refused to send delegates to the Constitutional Convention.

3. (a) The need for a successful government to be a strong, unified, national government. (b) It illustrates the point by comparing the states to sons who learned the lesson that to be "respectable, happy, and prosperous," they must live and work together as a unit, under one roof. (c) Those who fail to participate could expect to suffer dire consequences. This retribution is illustrated by the thirteenth son, who "refused to accompany his brothers to his father's house" and suffered misery, loneliness, and death as a result.

SECTION 2

Ratifying the Constitution

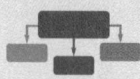

Connecting to the Big Idea

See page 78B. Explain to students that at the time the Constitution was written it was a highly controversial document. The Anti-Federalists, representing a significant number of Americans, were afraid that it meant the end of liberty. The Constitution was approved by only a narrow margin. Ask how the Federalists finally managed to get the Constitution ratified.

Objectives

● State the Federalists' argument in favor of the Constitution.
● Explain why the Anti-Federalists opposed the Constitution.
● State why the Bill of Rights was created.

Bellringer

Ask students if they think the United States government infringes too much on individual liberty. Possible examples of infringement include taxes or military service. Have them justify their answers.

Reading Strategy

Question Writing Ask students to scan the section and formulate *who, what, when, where,* and *why* questions about the text. Have them exchange papers and answer the questions as they read.

SECTION PREVIEW

With a combination of political skill and persuasive argument, the Federalists managed to win narrow approval of the Constitution. Their key concession to their opponents was the Bill of Rights.

As the debate on the new Constitution spread across the land, its supporters rallied around a new symbol—a ship with full sails, ready to ride the winds of the future.

Key Concepts

• The Federalists based their argument in favor of the Constitution on the nation's need for a strong, energetic government.
• The Anti-Federalists feared strong government under the proposed Constitution more than they feared the direct rule of the people.
• The Bill of Rights was designed to protect Americans against the power of the national government.

Key Terms, People, and Places

faction, ratify, Bill of Rights; Federalists, Anti-Federalists

---

Today, many Americans seem to assume that approval of the Constitution was a foregone conclusion. In actuality, the proposed government was highly controversial. Had the Constitution been put to a vote in 1787, it is extremely doubtful that a majority of Americans would have voted for it.

Federalists: For the Constitution

Supporters of the Constitution were called **Federalists** because they stood for a strong federal government. They had all been Nationalists, but not all Nationalists were now Federalists. The Federalist leaders included Washington, Madison, and Alexander Hamilton of New York—the man who had left the Convention in disgust, but now had decided to throw his

support behind the Constitution. Federalists argued that even if there were problems with the document, it had to be approved.

The most influential statement of their reasoning was a series of eighty-five essays now called *The Federalist,* published in a New York City newspaper. The authors were Hamilton, Madison, and John Jay, a Nationalist from New York. The purpose of *The Federalist* essays was simply to convince the members of the New York state convention to agree to the Constitution.

In the papers, Hamilton and Madison explained the need for the Constitution and how the federal government would work. They called for "a republican empire." In the 1700s the word *republican* did not refer to a political party. It referred to a government by the people. Because most previous empires had been governed by lone rulers, an empire governed by the people was a striking idea.

Indeed, because the country was so big, wrote Madison in *The Federalist* Number Ten, no one **faction**—what we call a "special interest group" today—would be able to control the government. Instead, the United States would referee the conflict of interests that could not be avoided in a democracy. Madison argued that the strength of the federal system was not in preventing regional or economic or religious interests from fighting with each other, but in keeping any one of them from getting the upper hand for long. Without the Constitution, argued the Federalists, the United States would degenerate into anarchy—lack of government—and civil war.

Anti-Federalists: Against the Constitution

By contrast with the Federalists, the opponents of the Constitution, who were called **Anti-Federalists,** were certain that the new government would be the death of American liberty. They were led by older revolutionary

---

RESOURCE DIRECTORY

Teaching Resources

Reproducible Lesson Plan found in the Unit 1 folder, p. 70, provides a summary of the Section 2 lesson plan content.

Alternate Lesson Plan: Learning Styles found in the Alternate Lesson Plans folder, p. 60, uses a talk show format to help students understand and participate in the constitutional debate and is particularly useful for auditory learners.

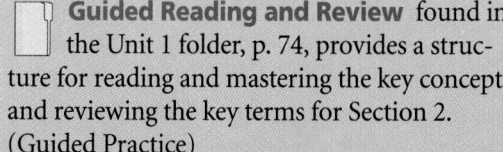

Guided Reading and Review found in the Unit 1 folder, p. 74, provides a structure for reading and mastering the key concepts and reviewing the key terms for Section 2. (Guided Practice)

figures, such as Patrick Henry of Virginia, and had widespread support in the areas that had less commerce, particularly the lands distant from the Atlantic Ocean and major rivers. People in these areas had less need for the leadership and laws of a strong national government.

The Anti-Federalists condemned the Constitution as a betrayal of the American Revolution. What was the President but a king? Had people fought and died in the long war against Great Britain to create a faraway government that could tax them and regulate their affairs even more than the British had ever attempted to do?

While the Federalists feared the people more than government, the Anti-Federalists feared government more than the people. Many objected not only to the presidency, but to the new federal court system. They also worried that those governments closest to the people—the local and state governments—would be crushed by this new giant of a federal government.

MAKING CONNECTIONS

Think over what you know about the federal government today. Were the Anti-Federalists right to be afraid that it would gain too much power? If you answered yes, suggest additions to the Constitution to protect the people. If you disagree, give evidence to support your answer.

How the Federalists Won Ratification

Most Americans probably agreed with the Anti-Federalists. But the Federalists had several advantages in their campaign for ratification of the Constitution. First, they played on the feeling of many that the Articles of Confederation needed to be reformed. Second, they made the Anti-Federalists look as if they were merely negative critics with no constructive plan of their own to offer. Third, the Federalists were a well-organized *national* group in regular contact with each other. The Anti-Federalists tended to be men with only local and state power who could not coordinate their activities on the national level. Fourth, the Federalists had George Washington.

It is easy to dismiss the influence of one man. But the fact that so many people admired and trusted Washington was of critical importance. Everyone expected him to be the first President, and that made them more willing to accept the idea of the new government. They knew he was a leader; he had proved that in a long war, despite repeated defeat and discouragement. More significant, he had given up his power at the end of the war, demonstrating his willingness to act within the law.

For the Constitution to replace the Articles of Confederation, nine states had to **ratify,** or approve, it. Several states—Delaware, New Jersey, and Connecticut—ratified it quickly. They were relatively small states and their citizens expected advantages in being part of a large federal structure. Georgia, too, approved the Constitution promptly. The Georgians feared a war with Native Americans and wanted a national government to ensure they would have federal help. In Pennsylvania, conservatives had won power and were revising the state constitution of 1776; they readily agreed to the new federal government. These states acted in December 1787 and January 1788. Then Massachusetts narrowly voted to ratify. Maryland and South Carolina soon fell into line. The honor of being the ninth state went to New Hampshire, although the Federalists there had to delay the vote until they had a majority.

Even with the approval of nine states, everyone knew the new nation would not be able to succeed unless the highly populated states of Virginia and New York joined in. Loud debates and shady maneuvers during the summer of 1788 produced Federalist victories by slim margins in the voting in both these key states. North Carolina had rejected the Constitution but finally reversed itself and agreed to ratify it in November 1789. In May 1790 Rhode Island similarly reversed an earlier vote of rejection and became the last of the original thirteen states to say yes.

The Bill of Rights

The states did adopt the Constitution—but the voting was close, and they might easily have rejected it. What turned the tide in close states like

Enrichment

Ask students to research the ideas behind the French Revolution of 1789 and to identify similarities between them and the ideas of freedom reflected in the Bill of Rights.

Answer to ...

Viewpoints

Brutus is concerned that a fundamental principle that protects the people from those who govern them is being left out of the Constitution. Alexander Hamilton is concerned that the inclusion of a bill of rights would allow the government to claim more rights than are granted to it by the Constitution.

3. ASSESS

Section 2 Review Answers

1. (a) faction, see p. 88, (b) ratify, see p. 89, (3) Bill of Rights, see p. 90

2. (a) Federalists, see p. 88, (b) Anti-Federalists, see p. 88

3. They believed that it was a betrayal of the Revolution, that the President would be just another king, and that the government would tax them and regulate their affairs even more than had the British.

4. They played on the widespread agreement that there was a need for reform of the Articles of Confederation. They kept their opponents on the defensive, making them look as if they were merely negative critics with no plan of their own. The Federalists were a well-organized national group whose members maintained regular contact with one another and had the prestige of George Washington's support.

Viewpoints
For and Against the Bill of Rights

A fierce debate raged over whether or not to include a Bill of Rights in the new Constitution. *What is the main concern expressed by each writer below?*

For a Bill of Rights

"I need say no more, I presume, to an American, than, that this principle is a fundamental one, in all the constitutions of our own states; there is not one of them but what is either founded on a declaration or bill of rights. . . . It is therefore the more astonishing, that this grand security, to the rights of the people, is not found in this constitution."

From "The Essays of Brutus," published in *The New York Journal* between October 1787 and April 1788

Against a Bill of Rights

"I go further, and affirm that bills of rights . . . are not only unnecessary in the proposed constitution, but would even be dangerous. They would contain various exceptions to powers which are not granted; and on this very account, would afford a colourable pretext to claim more than were granted. For why declare that things shall not be done which there is no power to do?"

Alexander Hamilton in *The Federalist* Number 84, May 28, 1788

Nine states had to approve the new Constitution before it became law. This cartoon shows the states as pillars, with nine upright and a tenth being raised.

Massachusetts, Virginia, and New York? While the persuasive skills of men such as Madison and Hamilton had an impact, by far the most important factor was the Federalist offer to adopt immediately several changes in the Constitution. Congress proposed them in September 1789.

United we stand—Divided we fall.

And in December 1791 the resulting ten amendments became part of the document. They are known today as the **Bill of Rights.**

The Argument Against the Bill of Rights Most Federalists saw no need for these amendments. Members of the Constitutional Convention had talked about protecting freedom of speech, the press, and religion. But they decided such provisions were unnecessary, largely because they were establishing a government of, for, and by the people. Under the Constitution, the people and the government were the same. So why did the people need to protect their rights from themselves? In *The Federalist* Number 84, Hamilton quoted the Preamble of the Constitution and argued that under the proposed new system "the people surrender nothing"—that is, they keep all power for themselves. "Here is a better recognition of popular rights," he asserted, than any added list of rights. Most Americans, however, did not buy this clever argument.

The Argument for the Bill of Rights To many Americans, the new federal government seemed a potentially tyrannical force in their lives. They wanted protection from it. Thomas Jefferson, who generally approved of the Constitution, urged Madison to agree to explicit protection for freedom of religion and of the press as well as from armies and unjust courts. ✪

A bill of rights is what the people are entitled to against every government on earth . . . and what no government should refuse, or rest on inference [leave unstated].

So strong was the Anti-Federalist demand for a Bill of Rights that Madison and other Federalists gave in to it. In fact, it was this concession of the Federalists—their agreement to amend the Constitution to protect certain basic freedoms—that was the key to their victory. Without the promise of a Bill of Rights, several states probably would not have ratified the Constitution.

Thus the Bill of Rights, the most significant guarantee of individual freedoms to American citizens, came about in part because Federalist leaders traded it for approval of the Constitution. These ten amendments, shown in the

RESOURCE DIRECTORY

Teaching Resources

📁 **Viewpoints Activity** For and Against the Bill of Rights, found in the Unit 1 folder, pp. 80–81, offers several contemporary arguments for and against the Bill of Rights.

✪📁 **Primary Source Activity** A Department of Peace, found in the Unit 1 folder, p. 86, uses an excerpt from Benjamin Rush's "Plan of a Peace-Office for the United States" to help

show the ideals people had for the development of their new country.

✪📁 **Visual Learning Activity** The First United States Coins, found in the Unit 1 folder, p. 90, displays the design of the first coin minted as United States currency.

✪📁 **American Profiles Activity** found in the Unit 1 folder, p. 79, profiles Richard Allen, a brilliant African American minister who founded the African Methodist Episcopal Church.

The Bill of Rights

1st Amendment	Guarantees freedom of religion, speech, press, assembly, and petition
2nd Amendment	Guarantees the individual states the right to maintain a militia
3rd Amendment	Restricts the manner in which the federal government may house troops in the homes of citizens
4th Amendment	Protects individuals against unreasonable searches and seizures
5th Amendment	Provides that a person can be tried for a serious federal crime only if he or she has been accused of that crime by a grand jury; protects individuals against self-incrimination and against being tried twice for the same crime; prohibits unfair, arbitrary actions by the federal government; prohibits the federal government from taking private property for public use without paying a fair price for the property taken
6th Amendment	Guarantees persons accused of crime the right to a swift and fair trial
7th Amendment	Guarantees the right to a jury trial in cases of civil suits heard in federal courts
8th Amendment	Protects against cruel and unusual punishment and excessive bail
9th Amendment	Establishes that the people have rights beyond those stated in the Constitution
10th Amendment	Establishes that all powers not guaranteed to the federal government and not prohibited to the states are held by each of the states, or the people of each state

Interpreting Tables
The Bill of Rights was intended to protect Americans from the powerful government the Constitution created. The Third Amendment, for instance, ensured that the government could not put citizens on trial without a jury drawn from the people themselves. *Which amendment protects the people from government interference in their religion?*

table above, protect Americans from their government.

Jefferson wished the Bill of Rights had been more explicit in protecting the rights of citizens. For instance, he wanted it to specify the number of days a person could be held under arrest without a trial. He also believed it was important to ensure that the army would disband immediately after its service. But even as it was written, the Bill of Rights became the foundation of American liberty. If the Anti-Federalists lost the war over ratification, they nonetheless won a major victory for freedom in the process.

 The Bill of Rights was one of the first items on the agenda of the new government. A truly new government Americans made of it, too, as the next section shows.

SECTION 2 REVIEW

Key Terms, People, and Places
1. Define (a) faction, (b) ratify, (c) Bill of Rights.
2. Identify (a) Federalists, (b) Anti-Federalists.

Key Concepts
3. Explain why Anti-Federalists objected to the Constitution.
4. What advantages did the Federalists have in their efforts to win approval of the Constitution?

5. Why did Federalists think the Bill of Rights was unnecessary?

Critical Thinking
6. **Formulating Questions** If you had been trying to decide whether to ratify the Constitution, what questions would you have asked the Federalists? Explain how the questions you suggest reveal your view of government.

Quiz found in the Unit 1 folder, p. 75, covers the main ideas in this section as well as the key terms.

---

5. They believed that under the Constitution, the people and the government were the same. The people therefore had no need to protect their rights from themselves.

6. Possible questions: Why do the people not elect the President directly? What guarantee do the people have that the legislature will not pass laws that restrict their liberties? What guarantee do the people have that the courts will not be cruel and unfair? Students should note that the questions reveal the same concerns the Federalists and Anti-Federalists had about the conflict between liberty and order.

Caption Answer to ...

 **Interpreting Tables**

The First Amendment.

Reteach

Have students create a two-column chart with the headings Federalists and Anti-Federalists. Under each heading have students list the relative positions of each and the milestones in the ratification process.

Alternative Assessment

Mid-Point Monitoring
Ask students if they have
• Chosen a format for their project
• Outlined the main ideas
• Begun outside research and preparation of the exhibition.

 **4.** CLOSE

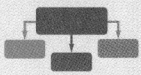 **Reinforcing the Big Idea**

With the ratification of the Constitution, the United States created a government that combined a powerful central government with a respect for individual liberty. In the next section, students will read about the leaders and policies of the new government.

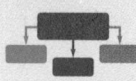

Connecting to the Big Idea

See page 78B. Explain to students that with the ratification of the Constitution, the work of strengthening the central government had only just begun. Now the Federalists had to get down to the business of making the new plan work. Ask how they did this.

Objectives

● Describe the political differences between Thomas Jefferson and Alexander Hamilton.

● Explain how the government under George Washington tried to make the new government impressive.

● Show how Washington, D.C., fulfilled the Federalist dream of an imposing capital of the United States.

Bellringer

Ask students to recall magazine, newspaper, or television pictures of Washington, D.C. What are their impressions of the capital?

Reading Strategy

Reading for Evidence Ask students to find evidence as they read the section that the government under Washington was either sensitive or insensitive to the American need for a government that was both powerful and democratic.

The New Government

SECTION PREVIEW

In the first years under the Constitution, Federalists labored to make the United States government as impressive as possible. They chose talented officials, opted for high ceremony, and made plans for an elaborate national capital.

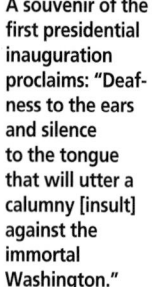

A souvenir of the first presidential inauguration proclaims: "Deafness to the ears and silence to the tongue that will utter a calumny [insult] against the immortal Washington."

Key Concepts

• Washington chose as two of his key officials Jefferson and Hamilton—men who had very different views of the role of government.

• The first Congress and the executive branch under Washington tried to set an impressive tone for the new government.

• Washington, D. C., is the product of Federalist dreams for an imposing capital for the "republican empire" of the United States.

Key Terms, People, and Places
cabinet, administration; Alexander Hamilton; District of Columbia, Washington

I n the elections that took place in the fall of 1788, most of those elected to Congress were Federalists. George Washington of Virginia and John Adams of Massachusetts were chosen as President and Vice President. The selection of Washington was unanimous. But the work of strengthening the government had only just begun.

Few groups have ever had grander plans for the United States than the Federalists. Having created a Constitution to secure the republic from too much influence by the people at large, they moved to make their vision of a great "republican empire" come true.

The Leaders of the New Republic

Washington became President in New York City on April 30, 1789. He was dressed in a brown broadcloth suit made in Hartford, Connecticut, and white silk stockings. His hair was freshly powdered. A committee of newly elected members of Congress escorted him to Federal Hall. There, on a small porch in front of thousands of people crowding nearby streets and rooftops, he took the oath of office and kissed a Bible. The crowd roared their approval. "Never," wrote a French ambassador,

has sovereign reigned more completely in the hearts of his subjects than did Washington in those of his fellow-citizens. . . . He has the soul, look and figure of a hero united in him. ◐

In addition to great popularity, Washington also had formidable tasks. The United States had a huge debt, no permanent capital, and no federal officers beyond the elected members of Congress and the President and Vice President. Immediately, Washington began to appoint officials, including the **cabinet**—the heads of the major departments of the executive branch. For attorney general, he chose Edmund Randolph of Virginia; for secretary of war, the able Henry Knox. The choices to head the state and treasury departments were even more crucial.

Secretary of State Thomas Jefferson Washington chose Thomas Jefferson to be secretary of state—the official who would manage the nation's relations with other countries. Jefferson was not particularly well known in 1789, despite the fact that he had been the principal author of the Declaration of Independence. Jefferson had been the American ambassador to France from 1785 to 1789, in touch with events in the United States only through correspondence with friends like James Madison. Though in France when the Constitution was drafted and adopted, Jefferson supported the Constitution and the addition of a Bill of Rights. He would one day become the third President of the United States.

RESOURCE DIRECTORY

Teaching Resources

Reproducible Lesson Plan found in the Unit 1 folder, p. 71, provides a summary of the Section 3 lesson plan content.

Alternate Lesson Plan: Critical Thinking Formulating Questions, found in the Alternate Lesson Plans folder, p. 61, helps students apply this skill to identify the nation's early leaders and their concerns.

Guided Reading and Review found in the Unit 1 folder, p. 76, provides a structure for reading and mastering the key concepts and reviewing the key terms for Section 3. (Guided Practice)

Visual Learning Activity A Portrait of a President, found in the Unit 1 folder, p. 91, uses a 1789 print of George Washington, surrounded by symbols of the United States, to illustrate some images and ideals of that time.

Many years later, when John F. Kennedy was hosting a supper at the White House for Nobel Prize winners, the President joked that his guests were the greatest gathering of talent ever to dine in the building, except when Thomas Jefferson ate there by himself. He *was* a man of many talents. Not only a planter, lawyer, and diplomat, Jefferson was also a violinist and an inventor. Perhaps his greatest passion was architecture. Jefferson built several homes for himself. The most famous was Monticello, an intricately planned house on a small mountain outside of Charlottesville, Virginia.

Jefferson had a passionate commitment to human rights—and yet he owned slaves. Jefferson well knew that slavery was wrong. Few white planters wrote more eloquently about it as a moral evil; and yet he could never bring himself to free more than a few slaves. As a planter, his livelihood depended on their labor. He would not discard his prejudices and risk losing the personal comfort that slave labor brought him, even for the principle of democratic equality.

Washington chose Jefferson to be secretary of state because he had experience dealing with France, still the closest ally of the new republic. But in the bargain he also got a man who would become one of the President's most ardent critics. While Jefferson approved of the Constitution, he never trusted the new government.

Treasury Secretary Alexander Hamilton
Like Jefferson, Treasury Secretary **Alexander Hamilton** was relatively young (only thirty-four) and intellectually brilliant. The son of a West Indies planter, Hamilton was raised by aunts and then sent to King's College (now Columbia University) in New York City. By his early twenties, Hamilton was already writing political pamphlets and seeking power.

He soon displayed a talent for making himself indispensable to powerful people. As an officer in the United States Army during the War for Independence, Hamilton became an aide and private secretary to General Washington.

Now Washington entrusted the young Hamilton with control of the largest department in the government and with responsibility

With enthusiastic hopes for their new government, Americans cheered the inauguration of Washington on April 29, 1789.

for finding a way to pay off the huge debt the nation still owed from the War for Independence. In contrast to Jefferson, who never really trusted government and remained idealistic about the people, Hamilton was a practical fellow who believed that governmental power, properly used, could accomplish great things. He had every intention of making his time in the federal government an active one.

Jefferson and Hamilton were on a collision course. But in the first months, even years, of the new government, matters went fairly smoothly. The adoption of the Constitution occurred at the same time as a general recovery from the economic problems brought on by the war. Americans were happy to have the question of their national government resolved. They were eager to move on to other things.

Formalities of the New Government

During the first four years of Washington's **administration,** or term in office, the government was preoccupied with matters both large and small. Washington and his officials were doing things no one else had done before. No one knew exactly what the Supreme Court was supposed to do. No one knew exactly how

Explain/Discuss

Explain to students that although the Constitution provided a framework for the new government, it had never before been implemented. Washington and the members of Congress were charting completely new territory when they took office. Ask students to name the unique challenges faced by the first government of the United States.

Discuss the new government with students in terms of its grand designs. Ask questions such as the following: How did Washington choose his cabinet members? Was there provision for a cabinet in the Constitution? What impression did government officials hope to give the people about the government? What elements of design made the new capital a symbol of a powerful national government?

In Depth

Biography

As a young twenty-nine-year-old adviser to General George Washington, Alexander Hamilton (1755–1804) saw the need for a strong central government to unify the thirteen states. He insisted that the states convene at a larger meeting to discuss the matter—the successful Constitutional Convention of 1787. As an army captain who helped turn back British General Cornwallis at Yorktown, an influential attorney, and a political theorist who wrote most of the influential *Federalist,* Hamilton was one of the fathers of the Republic. He died in 1804 in a dramatic duel with political rival Aaron Burr.

Analyze

Have students analyze the Federalists' vision of a great "republican empire" as it was realized during Washington's presidency. What fueled the Federalist dreams for a government characterized by ceremony and grandeur?

Activity

Cooperative Learning

Time: One class period.
Activity: Designing a capital.
Grouping: Four to six students.
Purpose: To design a capital that reflects the Anti-Federalist view of government. The plan should contrast with that of the French architect Pierre L'Enfant, whom the Federalists commissioned to design Washington, D.C., as a city that would symbolize a strong republic with noble roots. He produced a plan for a magnificent city, with classical buildings and broad boulevards radiating outward from the center of government.
Roles: Building architects, landscape architects, artists, contractors.
Outcome: Students will understand how the design of Washington, D.C., reflects the philosophy of government of the early Federalists.

Enrichment

Just as the role of women has changed since the American Revolution, so has the position of the President's wife. Ask students to compare the role of Martha Washington with that of a modern First Lady, such as Hillary Rodham Clinton.

Answer to ...

Links Across Time

(See page 95.) Answers will vary but should indicate an awareness of the changes in the capital's size, grandeur, and population from the 1800s to today.

Caption Answer to ...

Using Historical Evidence

The grandness and formality shown represent exactly what the Federalists wanted in their new government.

Using Historical Evidence This painting of a reception during the Washington administration is titled "The Republican Court." *How does the scene reflect Federalist plans for the new government?*

The campaign buttons of modern times are the offspring of these buttons commemorating Washington's inauguration.

Congress and the President should deal with each other.

Typical of this sense of newness and experimentation was the debate in the Senate over what to call the President. Should something like "Your Majesty" be used? Or would "Mr. Washington" be more appropriate? A Senate committee recommended "His Highness the President of the United States of America and Protector of the Rights of the Same." The House of Representative refused to endorse that title, however, and the issue died. Today we simply use the more democratic form of address: "Mr. President." ✪

President Washington was doing what he could to make his government impressive. His appearance and personality helped. Washington was tall (over six feet) and physically imposing, especially on horseback. He was also solemn and reserved, a very private man. During the Constitutional Convention, some members had dared Gouverneur Morris of Pennsylvania to put his hand on Washington's shoulder. According to an account of the incident,

> Washington withdrew his hand, stepped suddenly back, [and] fixed his eye on Morris for several minutes with an angry frown, until the latter retreated abashed, and sought refuge in the crowd.

The President lived in a formal, if not extravagant, manner, believing that it was necessary to command the respect of the citizens of the United States as well as the rest of the world. Soldiers escorted his carriage, which was pulled by six horses. He and his wife Martha held regular Friday afternoon parties, or levees, to entertain government officials and ambassadors. Every year, government officials celebrated the President's birthday with elaborate ceremonies and pageantry. To many, such parties and ceremonies made Washington seem like a king with a court.

Odd as such controversy over presidential behavior may seem, it reveals just how experimental the new republic was. Americans were sailing on uncharted waters. No wonder they found it difficult to balance the need to make their government appear both powerful and democratic at the same time. In fact, only a few American Presidents have succeeded in this balancing act.

MAKING CONNECTIONS

Too much ceremony in government can result in an expensive spectacle that only irritates taxpayers. Does government ceremony today, such as the inauguration of the President, impress you or strike you as excessive? Explain your reaction.

Planning a Capital City

The efforts to make the new government awe inspiring went beyond recruiting talented officials and holding formal ceremonies. The United States needed an impressive capital, too. It got one, as a result of the Residence Act of 1790, which specified that the capital would be a 10-square-mile tract of land on the Potomac River near Washington's home at Mount Vernon. ✪ This federally governed area was to be called by the grand name of the **District of Columbia.** (The name **Washington** was not used for the capital city itself until 1799, after President Washington had died.) On Jefferson's recommendation, George Washington appointed an African American mathematician and inventor, Benjamin Banneker, to the

▶ RESOURCE DIRECTORY

Teaching Resources

✪ **Primary Source Activity** Meeting President and Mrs. Washington, found in the Unit 1 folder, p. 85, provides a personal viewpoint on George and Martha Washington.

✪ **American Profiles Activity** found in the Unit 1 folder, p. 78, profiles Benjamin Banneker, an African American member of the team that surveyed the land prior to construction of the nation's capital.

Changes to the Capitol

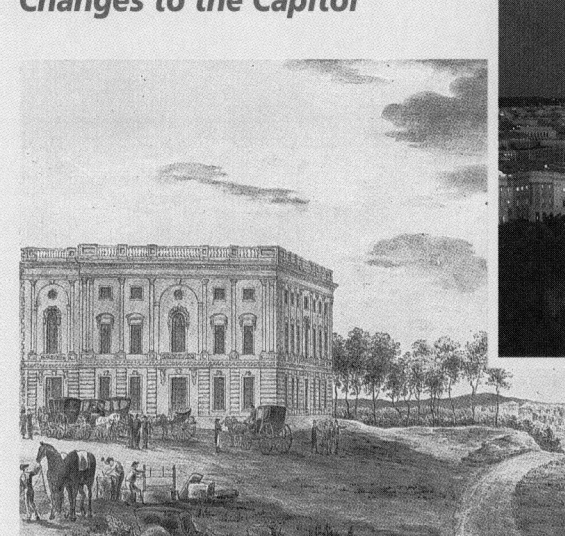

The Capitol in 1800 was no more than one wing in a muddy wilderness (left). Today, with two wings and a dome, the Capitol dominates the Washington skyline (above). *Describe in your own words the impression the Capitol gives today.*

commission in charge of surveying the city. Pierre Charles L'Enfant, a French artist and architect who had fought for the United States during the War for Independence, developed the city plan. L'Enfant designed a capital with broad streets, public walks, a mansion for the President, a pedestrian mall, and the Capitol. Although the federal government moved to the District in 1800, it took decades longer to realize the L'Enfant plan in its entirety.

Washington, D.C., with its great boulevards, marble buildings in the Roman style, and public monuments, is the most obvious legacy of the Federalists' grand plans for the United States. They meant to display the power and majesty of their new national government. Washington, D.C., was the symbol of the strong federal government they had lobbied for throughout the 1780s and outlined in the Constitution.

Some Americans, however, found the Federalists' interest in ceremony and grandeur disturbing, not to mention expensive. And in the 1790s, they would unite in growing numbers behind Secretary of State Thomas Jefferson to protect what they believed was the true legacy of the American Revolution—liberty.

SECTION 3 REVIEW

Key Terms, People, and Places
1. Define (a) cabinet, (b) administration.
2. Identify Alexander Hamilton.
3. Identify (a) District of Columbia, (b) Washington.

Key Concepts
4. How did Jefferson and Hamilton differ?
5. Why did Washington promote formality in his administration?

6. What impression were the Federalists hoping for when they approved L'Enfant's design for Washington, D.C.?

Critical Thinking
7. **Checking Consistency** In an empire, a central government has control over extensive territory and many different peoples. How might an empire be inconsistent with the ideal of popular sovereignty?

 Quiz found in the Unit 1 folder, p. 77, covers the main ideas in this section as well as the key terms.

 Chapter Test Forms A and B are found in the Unit 1 folder, pp. 92–97.

 Answer Keys found in the Unit 1 folder, pp. 145–157, provide answers to all student activities.

Media and Technology

Transparency
Graphic Organizer, G-1

Guided Reading Audiotapes
(English and Spanish)

Computer Test Bank

---

3. ASSESS

Section 3 Review Answers
1. (a) cabinet, see p. 92, (b) administration, see p. 93

2. Alexander Hamilton, see p. 93

3. (a) The District of Columbia, see p. 94, (b) Washington, see p. 94

4. Jefferson possessed an abiding faith in liberty and progress; he trusted the people more than government. Hamilton was far more pragmatic and focused than Jefferson, he preferred structure and order to liberty and freedom.

5. To set a tone for his government that would command the respect of the citizens of the United States as well as the rest of the world.

6. They were hoping to display the power and majesty of their new national government.

7. Answers should point out that empire is inconsistent with the idea of rule by the people insofar as it does not necessarily give the people a voice in the central government.

Reteach

Ask students to write two paragraphs summarizing Section 3 but leaving important ideas, key terms, people, or places blank. Then have pairs of students exchange their papers and fill in the missing words.

4. CLOSE

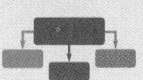 **Reinforcing the Big Idea**

Federalists worked hard in the first few years under the Constitution to make the United States government as impressive as possible. A growing number of Americans were disturbed by their taste for ceremony and expensive displays of power. They worried that the real ideals of the Revolution were being lost.

Understanding Key Terms, People, and Places

Terms
Students should refer to the definitions of the key terms in the chapter to write sentences that show the relation of each word to the Constitutional Convention of 1787, ratification of the Constitution, or the United States government in its first years.

Matching
1. the Great Compromise
2. veto
3. cabinet
4. Bill of Rights
5. system of checks and balances
6. administration
7. Virginia Plan

True or False
1. false, Anti-Federalists
2. true
3. true

Reviewing Main Ideas

1. Madison envisioned a constitution that would encourage the best in people while restraining their tendencies toward selfishness.

2. The Great Compromise provided for a bicameral legislature in one house of which each state would have a number of votes based on the size of its population, while in the other of which each state would have an equal number of votes.

3. The Constitution limits popular sovereignty by dividing power between the state and national governments and among the three branches of the national government; it also gives the Electoral College the final say in a presidential election in case of a deadlock.

4. Americans have come to see the first three words of the Constitution as the most important because the rest of the document flows from this basic assumption that in the United States the people govern themselves.

5. The Federalists feared that without the Constitution, the country would degenerate into anarchy and civil war.

6. The Federalists' greatest fear was that democracy would lead to anarchy; the Anti-Federalists' greatest fear was that a more powerful government would mean the end of American liberty.

7. The Anti-Federalists wanted a list of certain guaranteed rights that would protect the people's basic freedoms. In this way, they felt that the power of the strong

---

Chapter Review

Understanding Key Terms, People, and Places

Key Terms
1. Virginia Plan
2. veto
3. New Jersey Plan
4. Great Compromise
5. Three-fifths Compromise
6. separation of powers
7. system of checks and balances
8. Electoral College
9. faction
10. ratify
11. Bill of Rights
12. cabinet
13. administration

People
14. James Madison

15. Federalists
16. Anti-Federalists
17. Alexander Hamilton

Places
18. District of Columbia
19. Washington

Terms For each term above, write a sentence that explains its relation to events leading to the Constitutional Convention of 1787, ratification of the Constitution, or the United States government in its first years.

Matching Review the key terms in the list above. If you are not sure of a term's meaning, review its definition in the chapter. Then choose a term from the list that best matches each description below.
1. the solution to the issue of whether representation in the legislature should be based on population
2. the power to overturn an act of legislature
3. the heads of the major departments of the executive branch
4. the ten amendments that became part of the Constitution in 1791
5. the system of government where each branch can check the other branches
6. a President's term in office
7. the first plan introduced at the Constitutional Convention

True or False Determine whether each statement is true or false. If it is true, write "true." If it is false, change the underlined name to make the statement true.
1. <u>Federalists</u> opposed the Constitution as a betrayal of the American Revolution.
2. By the time the Constitutional Convention took place, <u>James Madison</u> had already devised a plan for a new Constitution.
3. <u>Alexander Hamilton</u> believed that government power could accomplish great things if used properly.

Reviewing Main Ideas

Section 1 (pp. 80–86)
1. Describe the kind of constitution that James Madison envisioned when he came to Philadelphia.
2. How was the question of whether larger states would have more power than smaller ones finally resolved?
3. How does the Constitution limit popular sovereignty?
4. Explain why Americans have come to see the first three words of the Constitution, "We the People," as the most important.

Section 2 (pp. 88–91)
5. Why did the Federalists support the Constitution?
6. Explain the following statement: "While the Federalists feared people more than government, the Anti-Federalists feared government more than people."
7. Why did the Anti-Federalists insist that a Bill of Rights be included in the Constitution?

Section 3 (pp. 92–95)
8. Which cabinet member became a critic of the new government, Alexander Hamilton or Thomas Jefferson? Explain your answer.
9. Describe the tone that President Washington set for the new government.
10. What features of Washington, D.C., suggest the power and dignity of the federal government?

---

national government created by the Constitution would be kept in check.

8. Thomas Jefferson. He distrusted government and did not want it to become too powerful.

9. Washington set a tone of formality and dignity.

10. Features that suggest power and dignity include the city's great boulevards, marble buildings in the Roman style, and public monuments.

Thinking Critically

1. The Three-fifths Compromise suggested that the Framers thought that African American slaves counted for less than other citizens.

2. Answers will vary. Students' responses should discuss the advantages and disadvantages of a strong central government.

3. Answers will vary. Some students may choose to preserve the grandeur of the capital as it is now, believing that government must remain formal and dignified in order to be respected. Others may opt for a less formal style, believing that government should reflect the styles of those whom it represents.

- **Evidence of thoughtfulness** Do projects include the main topics from the chapter?
- **Evidence of outside research** To what extent did students use outside research materials for their projects?
- **Evidence of synthesis** Do projects demonstrate an understanding of how topics are related?
- **Communication style** Do projects convey their purpose to an audience in a clear, appealing way?

Allow interested students to present their finished projects to the class.

Thinking Critically

1. **Identifying Assumptions** What did the Three-fifths Compromise suggest about how the Framers of the Constitution viewed enslaved African Americans?
2. **Identifying Central Issues** Imagine that you had been a delegate to the Constitutional Convention. Would you have been a Federalist or an Anti-Federalist? Explain your choice.
3. **Identifying Alternatives** If you were commissioned to design a new United States capital, how would it be similar to or different from L'Enfant's plans for Washington, D.C.? Explain your thinking.

Making Connections

1. **Evaluating Primary Sources** Review the primary source excerpt on page 90. Why did Thomas Jefferson think that no government should refuse to accept a bill of rights?
2. **Understanding the Visuals** Contrast the painting of Washington's resignation on page 67 with the description of Washington's character on page 94. Does the painting support Washington's reputation as a reserved man? Explain your answer.
3. **Writing About the Chapter** The year is 1789. Write a letter to one of the Framers in which you express your opinion on the Constitution. First, create a list of what you see as the positive aspects of the document. Then, list the negative features. Note any suggestions you have for improvements. Next, write a draft of your letter in which you offer your ideas. Revise your letter, making certain that each idea is clearly explained. Proofread your letter and draft a final copy.
4. **Using the Graphic Organizer** This graphic organizer uses a tree map to organize information about reasons for the Constitutional Convention. (a) How is the problem of a weak Continental Congress related to Shays's Rebellion? (b) What was the main source of tension between the states? (c) On a separate sheet of paper, create your own tree map about the new government in the first years after the Constitution was written, using this graphic organizer as an example.

Reasons for the Constitutional Convention

Continental Congress Is Weak	Individual States Unable to Work Together to Solve Problems	Nationalists Fear Failure and Disorder	Shays's Rebellion Erupts
• No power to tax despite huge war debt • No coercive power • Need nine votes to make a decision rather than a simple majority	• States each issue their own paper money • States tax goods shipped to other states in a desperate attempt to raise money • States quarrel over who will profit from sale of western land	• Warn of dangers of weak government • Fear that Americans' fondness for challenging authority will get out of hand • Want the United States to be a model of successful revolution • See the years 1781–1787 as a "Critical Period" that tests the Revolution's success	• Shows that Americans will continue their commitment to defy government • Fuels fears of growing civil unrest

Making Connections

1. Jefferson was a strong believer in government by the people and in protecting them from a tyrannical government. His words on page 90 reflect these beliefs; if a government is reluctant to state basic rights explicitly, then it is not to be trusted by the people.

2. The painting indicates that although Washington appeared reserved, according to this painter he was capable of feeling and exhibiting strong emotion.

3. Students' responses should take into account such issues as fair representation, whether or not the Constitution grants the states and the national government too much or too little power, and the wisdom of the elastic clause, the amendments procedure, and the Electoral College.

4. (a) Because the Continental Congress had no coercive power, it was unable to gather troops to put down the rebellion. (b) The main source of tension between the states was vying for ways to raise money. (c) Students' graphic organizers should include information about Jefferson and Hamilton, the tone of the new administration, and the planning of Washington, D.C.

Ask students to scan the American Album display After the Revolution. Point out the gridiron on page 99 and read about its function. Then ask students what the word *gridiron* has to do with the sport of football. *(It refers to the playing field, which has lines every ten yards.)* Ask students to speculate how the word came to be used to describe the playing field.

Ask students to study the other artifacts and to read the accompanying captions. Using the images as a basis for discussion, ask students what the artifacts reveal about the working life of early Americans. Note the images that indicate the work that young people performed.

Ask students to note the picture and caption for the "freedom suit." Ask what a young man or woman who completed job training today might receive instead of a suit of clothes.

To connect the artifact display to the chapter content, have students look again at the engraving in the bottom right corner. Ask volunteers what *venerate* means *(revere, respect, honor)* and what "venerate the plough" might mean. Why might this engraving be considered a romanticized depiction of farm life? What impact did this idealized view of farming have on the settlement of the United States?

Ask students to list the chores that they and other family members have to do around the house. Do any of them sew, care for animals, or tend a garden? Have volunteers read their lists and compare and contrast their chores with those of people in the early republic. What artifacts and symbols would they use in a display depicting life in the 1990s?

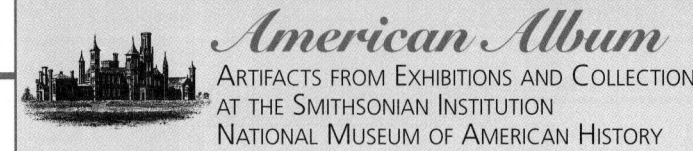

AFTER THE REVOLUTION

Life was not the same for everyone following the Revolution. How people lived their life varied depending on where they lived, their wealth, their ethnic background, their gender, and whether they were free or enslaved. This diversity can be seen in the familiar objects of everyday life. *What do these objects tell you about people's lives?*

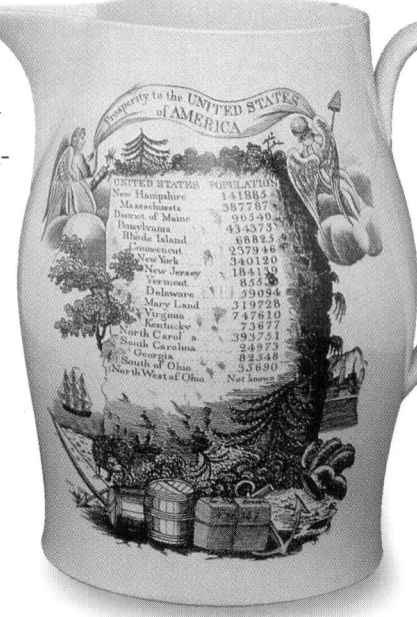

◀ LIBERTY JUG This practical creamware jug celebrates the nation by listing the populations of the new American states.

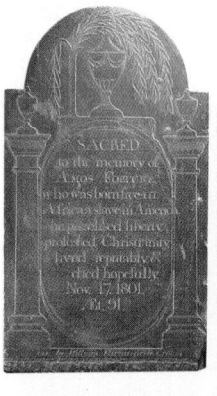

◀ BLACKSMITH'S ANVIL AND HAMMER Most everyday objects were handmade by artisans using fairly simple tools, such as an anvil and hammer. A blacksmith heated metal until it was glowing and soft, then shaped it with a hammer on the anvil.

▼GRAVESTONES These matching stones mark the graves of a husband and wife who were born in Africa. Brought to America to work as slaves, they eventually purchased their own freedom.

◀ GRIDIRON One of the most common household objects, a gridiron was used to broil foods over coals in an open fireplace. Almost all cooking utensils were designed for use in a fireplace.

▶ SAMPLER A sampler recorded the decorative stitches learned by well-off young girls. Poor girls used sewing to earn money for the family.

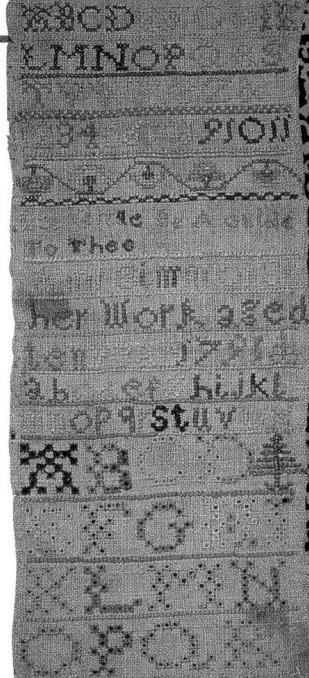

▲ DAIRYING This engraving titled "Straining and Skimming" shows an idealized view of two women preparing dairy products from whole milk.

◀ FREEDOM SUIT A young man learned a craft by apprenticing to a master craftsman. Because apprentices were bound for years to one master, the new clothes that some received at the end of training were called a "freedom suit."

◀ NATIVE AMERICAN OBJECTS This cradle board and dolls were made by Iroquois people, a group in upstate New York. White settlers overran most of the Iroquois lands shortly after the Revolution.

▶ RESPECT FOR THE LAND This engraving from an 1876 magazine shows the popular link between American liberty and hardworking farmers.

VENERATE THE PLOUGH

The formation of the government of the United States and the early days of that new government were fraught with uncertainty, and the delegates to the convention had the distinct feeling that the nation was watching them. Indeed it was; the citizens of the country kept a keen eye on the doings of the Constitutional Convention and the new government that followed. After all, such proceedings were hardly the norm in the late eighteenth century. In addition, many other countries in the world paid close attention to the proceedings, some in the hope that their predictions about the incompetence of the new nation would be proved true, others in the hope that they, too, could achieve the independence won by the United States.

The source readings for this chapter focus on those early formative days. Students will read about the strict rule of secrecy during the Constitutional Convention and how it was regarded by the delegates. They will read Benjamin Franklin's address to the delegates following the close of the debates and the writing of the Constitution. Finally, they will read the words of a senator addressing the first Congress ever to sit in the United States and learn of yet another viewpoint on the new government.

INSTRUCT

Have students use their textbooks to create a time line of the events between the signing of the Treaty of Paris in 1783 and President Washington's inauguration in 1789. Then have them illustrate the various events on their time lines using images photocopied from the textbook or from other sources that they find in the library. Display the time lines in the classroom for students to use to review the key events of those years.

CHAPTER 3
SOURCE READINGS

Miracle at Philadelphia

 *Literature*

Catherine Drinker Bowen

INTRODUCTION Despite the stifling heat of Philadelphia in the summer of 1787, delegates to the Constitutional Convention often sat with the windows of the east chamber of the State House tightly closed. They did so in order that passers-by on the street or eavesdroppers from local newspapers could not hear the debates raging inside. The excerpt below, from the book *Miracle at Philadelphia*, describes the delegates' struggle to avoid discussing the Convention with outsiders and the seriousness with which they took their promise of secrecy and their task of developing a new plan of government.

VOCABULARY Before you read the selection, find the meaning of these words in a dictionary: convivial, entreat, repose, dissipate.

It must have been difficult to maintain the rule of secrecy. Delegates were questioned on all sides; one meets it in their letters. [Delegate] Pierce of Georgia was apt to be talkative, especially when he went over to the meetings of Congress in New York. As for old Dr. Franklin, it seemed impossible to keep him quiet; it is said a discreet member attended the Doctor's convivial dinners, heading off the conversation when Franklin in one of his anecdotes threatened to reveal secrets of the Convention.

There was criticism of the secrecy rule; Jefferson did not like it when he heard. Yet it is difficult to see how a Constitution could have evolved had the Convention been open to abuse and suggestion from the public. Sentries were placed at the State House doors; members could not copy the daily journal without permission. . . .

One anecdote, . . . from [delegate] Pierce, shows the seriousness with which the secrecy rule was regarded, shows also the awe in which delegates held their chairman, the President of the Convention.[1] As the meeting rose one afternoon, a member dropped a paper on the floor. It was picked up and handed to Washington. Pierce tells how, next day, when debate was over and the question for adjournment called for, the General rose from his seat. "Gentlemen!" he said. "I am sorry to find that some one member of this body has been so neglectful of the secrets of the Convention as to drop in the State House a copy of their proceedings, which by accident was picked up and delivered to me this morning. I must entreat gentlemen to be more careful, lest our transactions get into the newspapers and disturb the public

---
[1] George Washington

"Independence Hall," by William Birch, 1790.

repose by premature speculations. I know not whose paper it is, but there it is [throwing it down on the table], let him who owns it take it."

"At the same time he bowed," Pierce's notes continue, "picked up his hat and quitted the room with a dignity so severe that every person seemed alarmed; for my part I was extremely so, for putting my hand in my pocket I missed my copy of the same paper, but advancing up to the table my fears soon dissipated; I found it to be in the handwriting of another person. When I went to my lodgings at the Indian Queen, I found my copy in a coat pocket which I had pulled off that morning. It is something remarkable that no person ever owned the paper."

THINKING ABOUT THE SELECTION

1. Based on what you know about the compromises that were hammered out at the Convention, why do you think the delegates decided to keep the proceedings secret until a final document was crafted?
2. Why was Pierce especially alarmed when Washington reprimanded the group for finding some notes of the proceedings on the floor?

Critical Thinking
3. **Identifying Alternatives** What other courses of action might the delegates have agreed upon, other than secrecy, for keeping public speculation and opinions from influencing their work?

Benjamin Franklin Campaigns for the Constitution

 *Primary Source*

INTRODUCTION "It is much easier to pull down a government . . . than to build up, at such a season as the present," wrote John Adams early in 1787. Considering the chaos that seemed to have descended on the United States in those days and the differences in background and intent of the delegates to the Constitutional Convention, many would have agreed with Adams. Yet on September 17, 1787, the completed Constitution of the United States was put before the delegates for their signatures. It was fitting that Benjamin Franklin, who for so long had been part of the revolutionary changes sweeping the nation, should rise at that point and urge the delegates to approve the document, despite all its faults and imperfections.

VOCABULARY Before you read the selection, find the meaning of these words in a dictionary: sect, infallible, despotism, constituents, partisan, salutary, manifest, vicisitude.

Monday, September 17, 1787: In Convention:

The engrossed[2] Constitution being read, Doctor FRANKLIN rose with a speech in his hand, which he had reduced to writing for his own conveniency, and which Mr. Wilson read in the words following.

Mr. President

I confess that there are several parts of this constitution which I do not at present approve, but I am not sure I shall never approve them: For having lived long, I have experienced many instances of being obliged by better information, or fuller consideration, to change opinions even on important subjects, which

I once thought right, but found to be otherwise. It is therefore that the older I grow, the more apt I am to doubt my own judgment, and to pay more respect to the judgment of others. Most men indeed as well as most sects in Religion, think themselves in possession of all truth, and that wherever others differ from them it is so far error. Steele, a Protestant, in a Dedication tells the Pope that the only difference between our Churches in their opinions of the certainty of their doctrines is, the Church of Rome is infallible and the Church of England is never in the wrong. But though many private persons think almost as highly of their own infallibility as of that of their sect, few express it so

---

[2]formally written out, on parchment

ANSWERS TO

Thinking About the Selection
1. So many possible forms of government were considered during the convention that if the public had been aware of the specific debates they might have become alarmed at something that was only considered briefly by the convention and then discarded. In addition, the delegates might have been overly influenced by the opinions of those who were not part of the proceedings or been subject to the harsh criticism of those who did not agree with their decisions.

2. Pierce could not find his own notes and thought that those given to Washington might have belonged to him.
3. The delegates might have agreed to release daily reports to the press which included only those details they deemed appropriate. They might also have sequestered the delegates completely, allowing them no contact with the public at all.

Using newspaper accounts and books on the subject, have students compare the inauguration of President Washington in 1789 to that of President Clinton in 1993. The comparisons should examine the role of the federal government in relation to those of the states at the time of the two inaugurations, public opinion about the two men, the backgrounds of the two men, and public attitudes toward the presidency in general.

As another part of this exercise, students could interview family members, neighbors, and other teachers about their views on the presidency. Students could draft a list of questions that they wish to ask interviewees, such as: Do you think the President of the United States has too much power? Too little power? Why do you think so? Do you think the President is in touch with the needs and desires of ordinary people of the United States? What one thing would you want to tell President Clinton if you could meet with him today?

After having their questions reviewed and approved, students can conduct their interviews, tape recording or videotaping them if possible. The interviews can then be played back to the classroom or read aloud from a transcript. Discuss with students the differing views on the presidency and the issues that people are concerned about today. Ask them what issues the people of the United States might have been concerned about in Washington's day.

naturally as a certain french lady, who in a dispute with her sister, said "I don't know how it happens, Sister but I meet with no body but myself, that's always in the right—Il n'y a que moi qui a toujours raison."

In these sentiments, Sir, I agree to this Constitution with all its faults, if they are such; because I think a general Government necessary for us, and there is no form of Government but what may be a blessing to the people if well administered, and believe farther that this is likely to be well administered for a course of years, and can only end in Despotism, as other forms have done before it, when the people shall became so corrupted as to need despotic Government, being incapable of any other. I doubt too whether any other Convention we can obtain, may be able to make a better Constitution. For when you assemble a number of men to have the advantage of their joint wisdom, you inevitably assemble with those men, all their prejudices, their passions, their errors of opinion, their local interests, and their selfish views. From such an assembly can a perfect production be expected? It therefore astonishes me, Sir, to find this system approaching so near to perfection as it does; and I think it will astonish our enemies, who are waiting with confidence to hear that our councils are confounded like those of the Builders of Babel; and that our States are on the point of separation, only to meet hereafter for the purpose of cutting one another's throats. Thus I consent, Sir, to this Constitution because I expect no better, and because I am not sure, that it is not the best. The opinions I have had of its errors, I sacrifice to the public good. I have never whispered a syllable of them abroad. Within these walls they were born, and here they shall die. If every one of us in returning to our Constituents were to report the objections he has had to it, and endeavor to gain partizans in support of them, we might prevent its being generally received, and thereby lose all the salutary effects & great advantages resulting naturally in our favor among foreign Nations as well as among ourselves, from our real or apparent unanimity. Much of the strength & efficiency of any Government in procuring and securing happiness to the people,

depends, on opinion, on the general opinion of the goodness of the Government, as well as of the wisdom and integrity of its Governors. I hope therefore that for our own sakes as a part of the people, and for the sake of posterity, we shall act heartily and unanimously in recommending this Constitution (if approved by Congress & confirmed by the Conventions) wherever our influence may extend, and turn our future thoughts & endeavors to the means of having it well administered.

On the whole, Sir, I can not help expressing a wish that every member of the Convention who may still have objections to it, would with me, on this occasion doubt a little of his own infallibility, and to make manifest our unanimity, put his name to this instrument. . . .

Whilst the last members were signing it Doctor FRANKLIN looking towards the President's Chair, at the back of which a rising sun happened to be painted, observed to a few members near him, that Painters had found it difficult to distinguish in their art a rising from a setting sun. I have, said he, . . . often in the course of the Session, and the vicisitudes of my hopes and fears as to its issue, looked at that behind the President without being able to tell whether it was rising or setting: But now at length I have the happiness to know that it is a rising and not a setting Sun.

A detail of the sun decoration from the chair in which George Washington sat during the Constitutional Convention.

The Constitution being signed by all the members except Mr. [Edmund] Randolph [of Virginia], Mr. Mason, and Mr. Gerry who declined giving it the sanction of their names, the Convention dissolved itself by an Adjournment sine die—

THINKING ABOUT THE SELECTION

1. Why does Franklin believe the Constitution should be approved?

2. What does Franklin mean when he urges the delegates to "doubt a little of [their] own infallibility"?

Critical Thinking

3. **Identifying Assumptions** What assumption was Franklin making about the delegates when he wrote this speech?

ANSWERS TO

Thinking About the Selection

1. Franklin believes that government is necessary for the new nation to succeed and that no other group is likely to write a document is that is any more satisfactory than that of the Convention.

2. He refers to each person's belief that they are right and the others wrong, and he asks them to consider that perhaps other viewpoints are also valid.

3. Franklin was assuming that some delegates were undecided about whether or not they would sign the Constitution.

Journal of a Senator

Primary Source

INTRODUCTION In the early days after the Constitution was approved, the new government found itself at sea in uncharted waters. How should it conduct itself? What rules should govern it? One senator, William Maclay of Pennsylvania, kept a journal detailing those early days and debates. If those in the highest positions took very seriously the task of shaping a government that would be followed for centuries, Maclay saw in the painstaking proceedings a bit of the ridiculous. The excerpts below from his journal provide an unforgiving look at the debate over how the President should be received when he came to Congress to be administered the oath of office.

VOCABULARY Before you read the selection, find the meaning of these words in a dictionary: profane, sagacious, mace.

30th April

This is a great, important day. Goddess of etiquette, assist me while I describe it. The Senate stood adjourned to half after eleven o'clock. About ten dressed in my best clothes; went for Mr. [Robert] Morris' lodgings, but met his son, who told me that his father would not be in town until Saturday.

Turned into the Hall. The crowd already great. The Senate met. The Vice-President rose in the most solemn manner. This son of Adam seemed impressed with deeper gravity, yet what shall I think of him? He often, in the midst of his most important airs—I believe when he is at loss for expressions (and this he often is, wrapped up, I suppose, in the contemplation of his own importance) suffers an unmeaning kind of vacant laugh to escape him. This was the case to-day, and really to me bore the air of ridiculing the farce he was acting.

"Gentlemen, I wish for the direction of the Senate. The President will, I suppose, address the Congress. How shall I behave? How shall we receive it? Shall it be standing or sitting?"

Mr. Lee began with the House of Commons (as is usual with him), then the House of Lords,[2] then the King and then back again. The result of his information was that the Lords sat and the Commons stood on the delivery of the King's speech.

Mr. Izard got up and told how often he had been in the Houses of Parliament. He said a great deal of

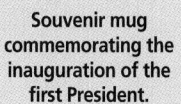

Souvenir mug commemorating the inauguration of the first President.

what he had seen there. He made, however, this sagacious discovery, that the Commons stood because they had no seats to sit on.

Mr. Carrol got up to declare that he thought it of no consequence how it was in Great Britain; they were no rule to us. But all at once the Secretary, who had been out, whispered to the Chair that the Clerk from the Representatives was at the door with a communication.

Gentlemen of the Senate, how shall he be received?

Mr. Lee brought the House of Commons before us again. He declared that the Clerk should not come within the bar of the House; that the proper mode was for the Sergeant-at-Arms, with the mace on his shoulder, to meet the Clerk at the door and receive his communication; we are not, however, provided for this ceremonious way of doing business, having neither mace nor sergeant.

Here we sat an hour and ten minutes before the President arrived.

[2] the houses of Parliament in London

THINKING ABOUT THE SELECTION

1. What issue are the delegates discussing?
2. Are such issues important to the running of a government? Explain your answer.

Critical Thinking

3. **Determining Relevance** Why do the delegates who speak on the subject refer to the houses of Parliament in their examples?

ANSWERS TO

Thinking About the Selection

1. They are discussing how to receive the President when he comes to the Senate chamber to take the oath of office and how to receive the messenger who announces the President's arrival.

2. Answers will vary, but students should recognize that rules of etiquette and behavior are important in keeping order and in running any meeting efficiently and effectively.

3. The delegates' backgrounds are all in the English system of government. Therefore, they relate the present circumstance to an event in their own experiences.

Chapter 4 From Jefferson Through Jackson
1789–1840

📁 Teaching Resources (See Unit 1 Folder)

	Instruction	Enrichment
Section 1 **The Election of 1800: A Turning Point in History** (pp. 106–109)	Reproducible Lesson Plan, p. 99 Alternate Lesson Plan, p. 63 Guided Reading and Review, p. 104 Quiz, p. 105	Critical Thinking Activity, Recognizing Bias, p. 123 Turning Points Extension Activity, The Lasting Impact of the Election of 1800, pp. 114–115 Visual Learning Activity, Honoring Thomas Jefferson, p. 131
Section 2 **Life in the New Nation** (pp. 112–117)	Reproducible Lesson Plan, p. 100 Alternate Lesson Plan, p. 64 Guided Reading and Review, p. 106 Quiz, p. 107	Primary Source Activity, Moving West, pp. 124–125 Time and Place Activity, Moving the City to the Country, pp. 116–117
Section 3 **Changing Households and New Markets** (pp. 120–123)	Reproducible Lesson Plan, p. 101 Alternate Lesson Plan, p. 65 Guided Reading and Review, p. 108 Quiz, p. 109	Literature Activity, The Life of Washington, pp. 128–129 American Profiles Activity, Sarah Todd Astor, p. 118 Literature Activity, Preacher to the World, p. 130
Section 4 **Sectional Divisions Arise** (pp. 124–129)	Reproducible Lesson Plan, p. 102 Alternate Lesson Plan, p. 66 Guided Reading and Review, p. 110 Quiz, p. 111	Primary Source Activity, New England Mill Women, pp. 126–127 Viewpoints Activity, On Slavery, pp. 120–121
Section 5 **The Age of Jackson** (pp. 130–136)	Reproducible Lesson Plan, p. 103 Alternate Lesson Plan, p. 67 Guided Reading and Review, p. 112 Quiz, p. 113 Chapter Test, Forms A & B, pp. 133–138	Visual Learning Activity, The Jackson Ticket, p. 132 American Profiles Activity, Sequoyah, p. 119 Historian's Toolbox Activity, Determining Relevance, p. 122

📁 Additional Chapter Resources

Resource Organizer, p. 98
Alternate Lesson Plan, p. 62
Answer Keys, pp. 145–157

Bibliography

For the Teacher

Kutler, Stanley I., ed. *John Marshall.* Prentice Hall, 1972. (Selected essays by Marshall's contemporaries and others assessing the famous Chief Justice's place in history.)

Walker, Juliet E. K. *Free Frank: A Black Pioneer on the Antebellum Frontier.* University of Kentucky Press, 1983. (An account of an African American couple who worked to buy their own freedom and that of their family members.)

Prentice Hall Literature Excerpts from *The American Experience,* 1994, including Crèvecoeur, Michel-Guillaume Jean de. *Letters from an American Farmer.* Matthew Carey, 1793.

Media and Technology

 Visions of America: Turning Point Story, "Natural Aristocracy" (length: Approx. 4 minutes)

 Visions of America: Roundtable Discussion on "Natural Aristocracy"

 Critical Thinking, I–14; Historical Maps, L–2

 Our Multicultural Heritage, C–8

 Geographic Setting, M–2, M–3, M–4; The Way It Works, H–8

 Graphic Organizer, G–2

 Guided Reading Audiotapes (English and Spanish)

 Computer Test Bank

For the Student

Ehle, John. *Trail of Tears: The Rise and Fall of the Cherokee Nation.* Anchor, 1988. (Compact account of the forced removal of the Cherokee.)

Electing the President. Encyclopedia Britannica. Film/Video. (Portrays the development of the electoral process from the beginning of the Republic to the present day.)

THE BIG IDEA

The Big Idea for the chapter and how the main ideas in each section relate to the Big Idea are graphically displayed below. Comprehension of this chapter's Big Idea is critical to students' understanding of United States history and how we as a nation got where we are today.

CHAPTER 4

In the years following the ratification of the Constitution, American leaders fought passionately over the formation of the new government. Meanwhile, tremendous change struck the twenty-four states of the nation in the early nineteenth century. Expanding markets and thriving industries transformed American life in what is called the Market Revolution. Making money became a chief goal of many Americans, but divisions emerged between the poor and the wealthy, and between different regions of the country.

SECTION 1

Two parties quickly formed: the Federalists, focusing on order, and the Democrats, focusing on liberty. Democrat Thomas Jefferson was elected President in the rancorous election of 1800.

SECTION 2

The dramatic population growth and movement, as well as new technology, brought both opportunities and uncertainties to the people of the new republic.

SECTION 3

The Market Revolution changed the way Americans conducted their economic lives—what they produced, how they sold goods, and why they bought what they did.

SECTION 4

In the Northeast, new industries developed to supply the needs of expanding cities. The South developed a thriving economy based on commercial agriculture and supported by the labor of enslaved African Americans.

SECTION 5

Economic issues moved to the forefront of American politics and created a deep split, leading to the second American party system and the 1828 election of Andrew Jackson.

104B

From Jefferson Through Jackson
1789–1840

CHAPTER 4

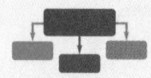 **The Relevance of the Big Idea**

In 1799 an Englishman traveling through the United States commented on the conversations he heard in taverns and inns: "It is scarcely possible for a dozen Americans to sit together without arguing about politics." Americans are still arguing about politics and the roles political parties play.

Discuss with students the influence politics and political parties can have on economic conditions in the United States. Ask students what they think would constitute another "market revolution" changing the relationship of work and home.

From Jefferson Through Jackson
1789–1840

During the early republic, the nation grew dramatically, and its jostling, young population faced new challenges on every side. In national politics, people who had a say in government continued to focus on the question of how much power the national government should have. In economic matters, a revolution transformed the way Americans worked, lived, and bought and sold products. Meanwhile, settlers were streaming constantly over the Appalachian Mountains, creating new states in lands that had been home to Native Americans.

Events in the United States

1790s Native Americans form alliances to resist encroachment onto their land.

1801 The House of Representatives elects Thomas Jefferson as the nation's third President.

1810s A Second Great Awakening revives religion in the United States.

1820 The Missouri Compromise forbids slavery in certain areas of the nation.

1789	1796	1803	1810	1817

Events in the World

1791 Haitians revolt against French rule.

1802 Nguyen Anh unites a country in Asia and calls it Vietnam.

1815 Brazil declares its independence.
• Napoleon is defeated at Waterloo.

 ## In Depth

Global Connections

In the wake of the French Revolution in 1789, France hoped to spread republican fervor. The first ambassador of the French Republic, Edmond Genêt, arrived in 1793 urging the United States to join France in war against Britain. He went as far as to arm ships himself, threatening the neutrality declared by Washington. Resentment against Genêt's intrusion solidified support for the anti-French Federalists and weakened the position of Jeffersonian Republicans, who had championed the French cause.

▶ RESOURCE DIRECTORY

Teaching Resources

Alternate Lesson Plan: Demonstrating the Big Idea found in the Alternate Lesson Plans folder, p. 62, provides a lesson strategy to instruct students about the Big Idea that after the War for Independence Americans still had to fight to determine what kind of government they would have at home.

Alternative Assesment Handbook provides information, guidance, and strategies for alternative methods of assessment. It includes an essay on new trends in assessment, guidance and strategies for developing performance tasks and portfolios, scoring rubrics, and sample evaluation forms.

Pages 106–109

The Election of 1800: A Turning Point in History

With the election of 1800, American leaders peacefully accomplished the nation's first transfer of power from one party to another.

Pages 110–111

The Lasting Impact of the Election of 1800

Pages 112–117

Life in the New Nation

During the first part of the 1800s, Americans pushed westward, and they knit the land together in a network of refreshed religion, new communication, and commerce fueled by bold inventions.

Pages 120–123

Changing Households and New Markets

In colonial times, people had focused on how to keep their households operating. For many people in the early republic, that focus gave way to a determination to make money—as much and as quickly as possible.

Pages 124 – 129

Sectional Divisions Arise

The North remained largely a land of farmers, now producing cash crops for the city market. In the South, much of the region's wealth was built on a peculiar relationship between capitalists and their workers—slavery.

Pages 130 – 136

The Age of Jackson

During his presidency, Andrew Jackson became the symbol for an age in which Americans first began to believe that elected officials should act according to the views of the voters.

1837 The United States government forces the Cherokee to move west.

1840 New England mills produce 323 million yards of cotton cloth.

1850 The population of New York City reaches half a million.

1828 Andrew Jackson wins the presidency.

1824	1831	1838	1845	1852

1824 Simón Bolívar becomes emperor of Peru.

1835 English becomes the language of government in India.

1839 The first photographs are taken in France and Britain.

1848 German Karl Marx publishes The Communist Manifesto.

Media and Technology

Transparency
Time Lines, E-3

Alternative Assessment

As an ongoing chapter project, students can create a work of historical fiction—a short story, a play or skit, or an episode of a TV drama—that looks at life in an American town in about 1830. The dramatization can span a day, a week, or longer. The content should depict family life, society, and the impact of migration, technology, and religion on the town. The setting should be clearly described and identified as being in the North or South, and either east or west of the Appalachians. Students may choose to tell the story through a narrator, an omniscient writer, or a resident of the town. More ambitious works will incorporate outside research to create a more accurate contemporary atmosphere.

Explain that finished projects will be evaluated according to the following guidelines:
- **Unacceptable** Projects are not attempted or fail to meet the requirements outlined.
- **Limited/Acceptable** Projects give an accurate picture of some social aspects of American life in the 1830s.
- **Extensive/Commendable** Projects integrate the required criteria into a work that is accurate and lively.
- **Extraordinary/Outstanding** Projects show evidence of outside research in an integrated, accurate, and lively presentation.

 For more information and guidance on alternative assessment trends and strategies, see the Alternative Assessment Handbook in the Resource Directory on page 104.

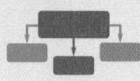

1. FOCUS

Connecting to the Big Idea

See page 104B. As the Federalists tried to institute their vision of the American government, their opponents organized to stop them, creating a new political party in the process. The election between these parties in 1800 was bitter and raucous, but in the end power was peacefully transferred from the Federalists to the Jeffersonians. Ask what were the major differences between the parties and how the peaceful transition was accomplished.

Objectives

● Explain how the national government won support by assuming the debts of the states.
● Describe the Federalist laws that restricted freedoms and explain the Jeffersonian reaction to those laws.
● Identify the result of the election of 1800 and explain the significance of the transfer of power from one party to another.

Bellringer

Ask students if they consider themselves Republicans, Democrats, Independents, or members of a minor political party. Why do we have political parties? Have students define the political goals of different parties.

Reading Strategy

Predicting Content Have students predict before they read the section who won the election of 1800. Ask them to check their prediction as they read the section.

The Election of 1800: A Turning Point in History

SECTION PREVIEW

With the election of 1800, American leaders peacefully accomplished the nation's first transfer of power from one party to another.

Key Concepts
• Under the program of Treasury Secretary Alexander Hamilton, the national government won increased support by taking over the debts of the states.
• Spurred on by a fear of war, the Federalists passed laws restricting freedoms—and the Jeffersonians reacted angrily.
• White American men had a choice between liberty and order in 1800, and they exercised it by electing Thomas Jefferson as President.

Key Terms, People, and Places
political party, first American party system, excise, tariff, Whiskey Rebellion, precedent; Jeffersonian Republicans

In 1800, during widespread enthusiasm over a turn away from Federalism and back to the republican principles of 1776, an unknown artist painted Liberty feeding the American eagle.

T oday politics in the United States is dominated by two major **political parties.** These are groups actively involved in the political process of the nation, which run candidates for offices in order to establish and control government policies. One party is the Republican party; the other is the Democratic party. The Republican party came into being in the 1850s, but the first form of the Democratic party became active in the United States in the 1790s, when Thomas Jefferson and other critics of George Washington's administration formed an alliance of widely different people to oppose the Federalists. Originally these critics were called Republicans or Democratic Republicans because they stood for a more democratic republic. To avoid confusing them with the modern Republican party, historians call them **Jeffersonian Republicans.** This group, along with the Federalists, formed what today is known as the **first American party system.**

Hamilton Acts to Strengthen the Government

In an effort to expand the role of government under the Constitution, Hamilton won congressional approval for the national government to take on the debts incurred by the states during the War for Independence. This decision may seem strange at first. The United States already had a huge debt of about $50 million. Why would Congress want to add to this burden?

The Reasons Behind Hamilton's Program
The answer is simpler than one might think. Most of the state and national debt was owed to European banks and American merchants and speculators, or people who take a financial risk in the hope of future profit. Hamilton knew that these creditors, or lenders, were interested in keeping alive and well whatever government owed them money. If the individual states owed them money, Hamilton reasoned, they would care about the states. But if the United States government owed them the money, they would be less interested in the individual states and more concerned with the future of the United States as a whole.

RESOURCE DIRECTORY

Teaching Resources

Reproducible Lesson Plan found in the Unit 1 folder, p. 99, provides a summary of the Section 1 lesson plan content.

Alternate Lesson Plan: Learning Styles found in the Alternate Lesson Plans folder, p. 63, focuses on the election of 1800 by creating campaign materials and is especially helpful for visual and auditory learners.

Guided Reading and Review found in the Unit 1 folder, p. 104, provides a structure for reading and mastering the key concepts and reviewing the key terms for Section 1. (Guided Practice)

Critical Thinking Activity Recognizing Bias: The Seeds of Nationalism, found in the Unit 1 folder, p. 123, is designed to help students apply this skill by analyzing a patriotic song written in the 1800s.

Creditors accepted this plan because Hamilton outlined a regular budget and set up a regular payment scheme. Two measures would help to raise money to pay off the debts. In 1791 Congress made whiskey the target of a new **excise,** which is a tax on a product manufactured within a country. Then, in 1792, Congress created a tax on foreign goods imported into the country, a type of tax called a **tariff.** Hamilton put some of this tax money into a special fund used to pay creditors. He did not intend to pay them off right away; if he did, they would have no reason to care what happened to the United States. Instead, the government paid them interest—a percentage of the money they were owed. To handle these complicated financial matters, Congress also established the Bank of the United States in 1791.

Hamilton thus transformed the debts of all American governments into what amounted to a long-term investment in the United States government. The national debt had been a weakness in the 1780s. Now, even though it totaled over $80 million, it had become a source of strength.

Opposition to Hamilton's Plan Many believed the Federalist program, coupled with the elegant style of Washington's presidency, smacked of aristocracy and monarchy, an all-out assault on the hard-won liberty of the American people. Secretary of State Jefferson had fierce arguments with Hamilton over the treasury secretary's plans. At the end of 1793, Jefferson formally resigned. From his home at Monticello, however, he remained involved in politics by corresponding with other critics of the administration.

Resistance to Hamilton's economic program was growing beyond the small group of men active in national politics. As early as 1793, artisans and professional men were forming what were called Democratic Societies to oppose the Federalists. These Jeffersonian or Democratic Republicans included slaveholders, planters, commercial farmers, and people distant from urban areas. They objected to the interference of the national government in local and state affairs. And they disliked taxes.

In western Pennsylvania and other frontier areas, many people took their dislike a step further and refused to pay the excise tax on whiskey. Whiskey was not just a traditional beverage—it was one of the only products farmers could make out of corn that could be transported to market without spoiling. In 1794, farmers who opposed the whiskey tax in western Pennsylvania closed courts and harassed tax collectors. But President Washington and Secretary Hamilton were determined to crush what was called the **Whiskey Rebellion.** In the summer of 1794, they marched 12,000 soldiers across the Appalachian Mountains as a show of force. The rebellion quickly dissolved.

MAKING CONNECTIONS

Contrast the response of the national government during the Whiskey Rebellion with its response during Shays's Rebellion. What accounts for the difference?

Liberty vs. Order

From the very beginning of the United States, international politics intruded on life in the new nation. In 1789 the people of France started a revolution of their own, overthrowing their king and establishing a new government. Frightened that the lower classes in their own nations might also revolt, European governments, led by that of Great Britain, rallied against the French. The French fought back. In 1793 a full-scale war broke out, beginning a series of conflicts called the Wars of the French Revolution, which continued off and on until 1815.

Impact of the French Revolution The issue of the French Revolution sharply divided Americans. Federalists tended to oppose it, seeing it as an example of a democratic revolution gone wrong. The Jeffersonians generally embraced the French Revolution as an extension of the American Revolution. Controversy raged over which side the new nation should support—its old enemy, Britain, or its old ally, France. In 1794 the Federalist government, believing that the long-term interests of the United States would be served better by an

2. INSTRUCT

Explain/Discuss

Explain that Jefferson called the election of 1800 "as real a revolution in the principles of our government as that of 1776 was in its form." The Federalists moved out and the Jeffersonians moved in.

Discuss whether the young United States would be more inclined to favor France or Great Britain. Ask students to summarize the reasons behind the Federalist Alien and Sedition Acts and the effects of those laws. Then have them describe the Jeffersonian response to those acts.

Answer to ...

MAKING CONNECTIONS

The national government under the Articles of Confederation was unable to respond to Shays's Rebellion; by contrast, the national government under the Constitution was empowered to execute a very effective military response to the Whiskey Rebellion. The difference can be accounted for by the form of national government in each case: one weak, the other strong.

In Depth

Interdisciplinary

The federal government may manipulate money in order to produce a desired economic effect within the American economy. In the 1790s the government sought to pay off completely war debts from the Revolution; by assuming the debts of the states, it aimed to restore national credit, create wealth, and promote new business. During the Great Depression the government, following Keynesian economics, purposely ran up large deficits to get money into circulation, promote private spending, and hasten the return of prosperity. (See Chapter 13, pp. 436–466.)

Media and Technology

Visions of America: Turning Point Story To enhance students' understanding of the Turning Point topic in this section, play "Natural Aristocracy," a story about party politics prior to the election of 1800 (length: approximately 4 minutes). This selection can be located on side 1 of the videodiscs. This selection can also be located on videotape 1. Lesson plans for Turning Point stories can be found in the Visions of America Teacher's Guidebook.

Visions of America: Roundtable Discussion To introduce students to different and differing viewpoints on the Turning Point topic in this section, play all or part of the Roundtable Discussion on "Natural Aristocracy," remarks by respected historians and social commentators. This selection can be located on side 1 of the videodiscs. This selection can also be located on videotape 1.

Analyze

Tell students that Adams won all electoral votes of the New England states. Jefferson took the southern votes. Ask students to speculate about the future effects of such sectional division.

Activity

Analyzing Points of View

Assign volunteers one of the following roles: a farmer from western Pennsylvania, a French revolutionary, a Dutch banker, George Washington, John Marshall, the wife of a Virginia tobacco planter, a wealthy Boston merchant, or a tavern keeper from upper New York state. Ask students to state their point of view (Federalist or Jeffersonian), giving two reasons in support.

Enrichment

Tell students that in 1969 President Richard Nixon announced a new policy that he called the "New Federalism." Ask students to write a description, based on what they have learned about Federalist beliefs and programs, of what such a policy might entail.

In Depth

Historical Misconceptions

It is often assumed that because women could not vote (except in New Jersey for a couple of decades after the American Revolution), they had no interest in politics. But diaries and letters of middle-class women in the early 1800s reveal strong opinions about the struggles of the Federalists and the Jeffersonian Republicans. Rosalie Siters Calvert of Maryland wrote: "Our politics are going badly. Jacobinism and democracy increase every day. [President Jefferson] really is a fool, full of vanity and desire to pass himself off as a philosopher and a great man."

alliance with Britain than with France, reached an agreement called the Jay Treaty with Great Britain. Many Americans saw it as a betrayal of revolutionary ideals.

In the midst of this storm of bitter feelings, President Washington chose not to run for a third term. He thus set a **precedent**—a custom followed in later times though not a written law. Washington's precedent was followed until 1940, when President Franklin D. Roosevelt ran for a third term.

Washington's Vice President, John Adams, ran for President against Thomas Jefferson in 1796. Adams gained a majority of electoral votes; Jefferson finished second. In accordance with the election system established by the Constitution, Jefferson became the new Vice President. President Washington left office in a bit of a huff, warning the nation about the dangers of factionalism—the struggle between factions, or parties.

The War Crisis and the Election From the beginning of the Adams administration, the United States began to drift toward war with France. By 1798 France and the United States were involved in what amounted to an undeclared war, firing on and seizing one another's ships on the high seas.

The Federalists took advantage of the war crisis to press even stronger measures through Congress. Among these were an increase in the size of the army, higher taxes to support the army and navy, and the Alien and Sedition Acts of 1798. Under the Alien Act, the President gained the right to imprison or deport citizens of other countries residing in the United States. Under the Sedition Act, persons who wrote, published, or said anything "of a false, scandalous, and malicious" nature against the government of the United States or its agents were subject to heavy fines and imprisonment. The Federalists used the Sedition Act to muzzle their critics.

John Adams (above), an outspoken and decisive Federalist President, was driven out of office after only one term when the Federalists and Jeffersonian Republicans clashed in the election of 1800.

Both Federalists and Jeffersonian Republicans were angry by the late 1790s. Congressmen were physically assaulting each other in the House of Representatives. Crowds taunted President Adams, forcing him to enter the presidential residence in Philadelphia through the back door. In Virginia, Jeffersonians drank a toast calling for "a speedy death to General Washington."

As the presidential election loomed, pitting John Adams against Thomas Jefferson and other candidates, many people believed that the future of the nation was at stake. Would the nation tilt toward what Jefferson called "the Spirit of 1776," the ideal of liberty found in the Declaration of Independence, or toward the Spirit of 1787, the emphasis on order stated in the Constitution? ⭐

The Election of 1800

The personal attacks and negative campaigning of elections today are nothing new. The election of 1800 was truly a nasty campaign. When the dust had settled and the balloting was over in December 1800, Jefferson won the popular vote. He was unable to get a majority in the Electoral College, however. Despite the fact that the Jeffersonians had won most of the seats in the new Congress, the old House of Representatives—which was mostly Federalist—had to decide who would be President. Even before the voting began in the House on February 11, 1801, it was clear that no candidate could get a majority immediately. Margaret Bayard Smith, the wife of a newspaper editor, later described both the scene at the Capitol and her own feelings as she awaited the news:

*I*t was an awful crisis. The people, who with such an overwhelming majority had declared their will, would never peaceably have allowed the man of their choice to be set aside. . . . A

RESOURCE DIRECTORY

Media and Technology

⭐ 📄 **Visual Learning Activity** Honoring Thomas Jefferson, found in the Unit 1 folder, p. 131, features a picture of Thomas Jefferson's monument, which reveals the accomplishments for which Jefferson most wanted to be remembered.

civil war must have taken place. . . . Crowds . . . from the adjacent county and cities thronged to the seat of government and hung like a thunder cloud over the Capitol. . . . That night I never lay down or closed my eyes. As the hour drew near its close, my heart would almost audibly beat.

On February 17, only a few days before the end of Adams's term, the House of Representatives finally elected Jefferson as the third President of the United States on the thirty-sixth ballot. Wrote Margaret Smith: "The dark and threatening cloud which had hung over the political horizon rolled harmlessly away."

New Jersey law allowed women to vote until 1808. During the crucial election of 1800, they helped Jefferson win the state and sent a full slate of Jeffersonian Republicans to Congress. When the election had to be decided in the House of Representatives, New Jersey was one of eight states that stood by Jefferson throughout the balloting.

A Revolution Without Violence

Washington, D.C., in 1801 seemed very much like the Federalists' plans in general: grand and unfinished. The new capital designed by L'Enfant with broad boulevards and Roman buildings was little more than a swamp with muddy, rutted roads and half-completed structures. Here, on March 4, 1801, Thomas Jefferson took the oath of office administered by Adams's appointee, Chief Justice John Marshall.

With this inauguration, the Federalist leaders of the young republic proved that they could do what so many leaders in other times and places have found so difficult. Although few on either side could forget their bitter disagreements and personal hatreds, the Federalists did step down and let the Jeffersonian Republicans take over. Whether they stood for the Spirit of 1776 or the Spirit of 1787, Americans had proved that they could transfer power from one party to another—and do it peacefully.

SECTION 1 REVIEW

Key Terms, People, and Places
1. Define (a) political party, (b) first American party system, (c) excise, (d) tariff, (e) Whiskey Rebellion, (f) precedent.
2. Identify Jeffersonian Republicans.

Key Concepts
3. What was the major goal of Hamilton's financial program?
4. Why did the Federalists pass the Alien and Sedition Acts, and what did they use the Sedition Act for?
5. Why was the election of 1800 a turning point in the history of the United States?

Critical Thinking
6. **Recognizing Ideologies** How does the Sedition Act reflect the Federalists' position in the controversy between those who favored liberty and those who favored order?

📄 **Quiz** found in the Unit 1 folder, p. 105, covers the main ideas in this section as well as the key terms.

---

3. ASSESS

Section 1 Review Answers
1. (a) political party, see p. 106, (b) first American party system, see p. 106, (c) excise, see p. 107, (d) tariff, see p. 107, (e) Whiskey Rebellion, see p. 107, (f) precedent, see p. 108

2. Jeffersonian Republicans, see p. 106

3. The goal of Hamilton's financial program was to strengthen outside support for the national government by having it assume the states' war debts, thus transforming the debt into a long-term investment in the United States.

4. The Federalists passed the Alien and Sedition Acts to gain greater control during a period of undeclared war with France. They used the Sedition Act to muzzle their critics.

5. The election of 1800 was a significant victory for the political system that was emerging in the United States. Rather than relying on violence to make their point, citizens turned the presidential election into a decision on the very nature of their government.

6. It showed that the overall good of the national government was of more importance to the Federalists than the right of the individual to speak freely.

Reteach
Ask students to answer each of the following questions:
• Who were the candidates in the election of 1800?
• What parties did they represent?
• Which party focused on social order, and which on individual liberty?
• Who won the election?
• Why was the election significant?

---

4. CLOSE

 **Reinforcing the Big Idea**

The Election of 1800 marked a political turning point for the United States. The next section shows that the country was on the brink of social change as well, with the young republic growing dramatically and facing new challenges on every side.

The Lasting Impact of the Election of 1800

Focus The election of 1800 was the first in which two strong political factions opposed each other. Although some predicted that the result of the election of 1800 would be civil war rather than a new President, Jefferson finally did become the new chief executive, marking the defeat of the Federalists and the rise of the Jeffersonians. What has been the lasting impact of the election of 1800?

Instruct Tell students that during the election of 1800, one pamphlet put out by the Jeffersonians asked, "Is it not high time for a CHANGE?" Although we are used to the challenging party insisting on the value of change from the incumbent party, in 1800 the idea of such a change was unprecedented.

Ask students how the peaceful transfer of power allowed politics to flourish. Once the voters and the nation's leaders showed that they could use ballots and abide by their results, dissent became less charged.

Ask students to use a list of Presidents to count how many times the nation has transferred the office of President from one political party to another.

Discuss with students what might have happened if the Federalists had somehow managed to invalidate the election results or rig the election to remain in power. What options would have been open to the Anti-Federalists to remove them from office? Would there have been an election of 1804?

Extend Ask students to create a political cartoon about the election of 1800. The cartoon may support either Adams or Jefferson, or it may celebrate the peaceful transfer of power from one party to another.

The Lasting Impact of the Election of 1800

What were the long-term consequences when the Jeffersonian Republicans won the election of 1800 and took office? The answer lies in the peaceful transfer of power from one group to another and the gradual understanding that diversity could strengthen, rather than destroy, the nation.

The Transfer of Power

The real winner of the election of 1800 was the Constitution of the United States, simply because it survived. As late as February 16, several representatives were heard to proclaim they would "go without a constitution and take the risk of civil war" rather than vote for "such a wretch as Jefferson." The governors of Virginia and Pennsylvania, both Jeffersonians, were on alert, probably intending to respond with troops if the Federalists acted against the will of the people. Had that happened, it is impossible to know what the consequences would have been on the United States of today.

Jefferson himself described the crisis and its significance in a letter shortly after his election.

*W*e can no longer say there is nothing new under the sun. For this whole chapter in the history of man is new. . . . The order & good sense displayed in this recovery from delusion, and in the momentous crisis which lately arose, really bespeak a strength of character in our nation which augurs well [foretells a good future] for the duration of our Republic; & I am much better satisfied now of its stability than I was before it was tried.

With this example of a peaceful exchange of power to look back upon, American democracy gained a maturity that today we take for granted.

1800 Despite Federalists' fears, "Mad Tom" Jefferson does not pull down the federal government, as this cartoon predicts.

1880s–1890s Candidates for President continue to broaden their appeal to the people.

| 1800 | 1840 | 1880 |

1824 A smooth transfer of power occurs even though the House of Representatives elects John Quincy Adams as President in defiance of the popular vote for Andrew Jackson.

RESOURCE DIRECTORY

Teaching Resources

 Turning Points Extension Activity
The Lasting Impact of the Election of 1800, found in the Unit 1 folder, pp. 114–115, allows students to discover the relevance of the principles of order and liberty in their lives through a mock council election and debate.

A Political Revolution

Another consequence of the election was that the nation turned from the Federalist interest in order to the Jeffersonian insistence upon liberty. In later years, Jefferson called the election of 1800 "as real a revolution in the principles of our government as that of 1776 was in its form."

The Federalists, too, felt the force of the change. A Federalist newspaper in Boston printed this obituary notice in a black border:

> YESTERDAY EXPIRED
> *Deeply regretted by MILLIONS of grateful*
> *Americans,*
> *And by all GOOD MEN,*
> *The Federal Administration*
> *of the*
> *GOVERNMENT of the United States*

A Lesson in Party Politics

The contest between liberty and order would later resume, but first another party besides that of the Federalists would have to arise. Although the Federalists attempted a comeback in the next few

elections, they had little chance of success. As the observer Noah Webster remarked at the time, "They have attempted to resist the force of current public opinion, instead of falling into the current with a view to direct it." The long-term result? Never again would a political party hope to gain power by telling the people it was wiser than they were. From then to modern times, politicians have appealed to the people, no matter whose interests they actually represented.

It can be argued that the most enduring change brought by the election of 1800 was the one that was slowest to take effect. Gradually, as the decades passed, Americans would take to heart the lesson of the election—learning that differences of opinion would not destroy the nation, and that no matter what politics Americans profess, they are still Americans united under the Constitution. As Jefferson himself said in his inaugural address,

> *Every difference of opinion is not a difference of principle. . . . We are all republicans; we are all federalists.*

REVIEWING THE FACTS

1. What was the "real winner" of the election of 1800?
2. How did the failure of the Federalists influence later politics?

Critical Thinking

3. **Distinguishing Fact from Opinion** When Jefferson called the election of 1800 a revolution, was he stating a fact or voicing an opinion? Explain your reasoning.

1941 Demonstrating continued national unity despite party differences, Congress approves President Roosevelt's call for a declaration of war.

1920   1960   2000

1992 The forty-second change of Presidents follows the pattern for a smooth transition set after the election of 1800.

TURNING POINTS

SECTION 2

Life in the New Nation

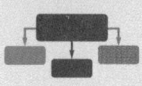

1. FOCUS

Connecting to the Big Idea

See page 104B. Explain that the original thirteen states had only a fraction of the population of the twenty-four states in the Union by 1830. The dramatic population growth and movement brought both opportunities and uncertainties to the people of the new republic. Americans responded with growing confidence in material progress and religious salvation. Ask students what effect this had on the original inhabitants of the country.

Objectives

● Describe the settling of the trans-Appalachian region.
● Explain how technology changed the economic, social, and political life of the new nation.
● Describe how the idea of religious equality was practiced.

Bellringer

Have students list ways in which they or other people try to change either their own lives or society in general. Do people always respond favorably to efforts toward change? Why or why not?

Reading Strategy

Question Writing Ask students to skim the section, noting the headings and subheadings. Then have them turn the headings into questions and answer the questions as they read the section.

SECTION PREVIEW

During the first part of the 1800s, Americans pushed westward, and they knit the land together in a network of refreshed religion, new communication, and commerce fueled by bold inventions.

Key Concepts
• Americans settled and transformed the trans-Appalachian region of the United States with unprecedented speed and thoroughness.
• Inventions such as the cotton gin and improvements in transportation allowed rapid economic development, while a revolution in communication changed the social and political life of the new nation.
• A new awakening of religious life encouraged the participation of all—men and women, rich and poor, and people of all races. Thus, religion became more democratic.

Key Terms, People, and Places
Northwest Territory, black codes, Missouri Compromise, Industrial Revolution, Second Great Awakening, evangelical movement; Andrew Jackson, Eli Whitney

The main reason that the United States grew explosively during its early years was that Americans had so many babies. One of them lay in this cradle about 1800.

 hile Jeffersonians and Federalists debated the proper role of the national government, ordinary Americans were rapidly developing the new nation.

Tens of thousands of people migrated west of the Appalachian Mountains in search of better living conditions. Others came up with inventions that dramatically improved production, transportation, and communication. Still others focused on improving their spiritual life by bringing a new democratic liveliness to religion. But alongside this booming expansion and change there remained the continued enslavement of African Americans and the ongoing devastation of Native Americans.

The Settlement of Trans-Appalachia

⭐ The population of the United States grew explosively during the period before 1830, as the graph on page 113 shows. About 2.7 million people lived in the original thirteen states in 1780. By 1830 there were 12 million people in 24 states. During the 1780s, the population increased by more than 40 percent, the greatest increase by percentage in the country's history. The number of Americans was roughly doubling about every twenty years.

Starting in the 1770s, Americans of both European and African descent migrated over the Appalachians into the Ohio, Mississippi, Tennessee, and Cumberland river valleys. In a matter of years, cities developed at key points such as Cincinnati, St. Louis, Memphis, and Chicago. Territories became states, and farms appeared in place of forests and meadows.

In 1787, when the Constitution was being written, only a few hundred Europeans were living north of the Ohio River. By 1830 there were hundreds of thousands of Americans living in the three states and two territories in the region.

National Policy and the West

In the late 1700s, the United States government had tried to influence the nature of western expansion. The Land Ordinance of 1785 provided for the regular survey and sale of

---

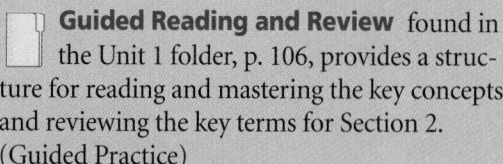

RESOURCE DIRECTORY

Teaching Resources

📄 **Reproducible Lesson Plan** found in the Unit 1 folder, p. 100, provides a summary of the Section 2 lesson plan content.

📄 **Alternate Lesson Plan: Cooperative Learning** found in the Alternate Lesson Plans folder, p. 64, provides a format for groups of students to prepare oral presentations on the changes described in the section.

📄 **Guided Reading and Review** found in the Unit 1 folder, p. 106, provides a structure for reading and mastering the key concepts and reviewing the key terms for Section 2. (Guided Practice)

📄 **Primary Source Activity** Moving West, found in the Unit 1 folder, pp. 124–125, uses excerpts from artist John James Audubon's *Audubon's America* to help students visualize the life of a Kentucky settler.

Native American land northwest of the Ohio River, called the **Northwest Territory,** or the Old Northwest, to distinguish it from the present-day Northwest. The Northwest Ordinance of 1787 established a process by which territories could become states.

Under President Jefferson, the national government continued to play a key role in the development of the trans-Appalachian west. More dramatic was the Louisiana Purchase of 1803. Although he had doubts about whether the Constitution permitted him to do so, Jefferson accepted when French emperor Napoleon Bonaparte offered to sell France's claim to a vast area of Native American land (see the map on page 897). The purchase nearly doubled the size of the United States. But its most immediate impact was to give American settlers unrestricted access to both the most important waterway in the center of North America—the Mississippi River—and the most important city, New Orleans.

(see the map on page 897)

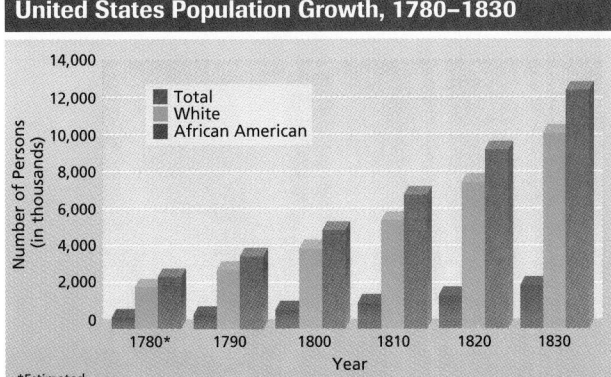

United States Population Growth, 1780–1830

Legend:
- Total
- White
- African American

Y-axis: Number of Persons (in thousands) — 0, 2,000, 4,000, 6,000, 8,000, 10,000, 12,000, 14,000
X-axis: Year — 1780*, 1790, 1800, 1810, 1820, 1830

*Estimated
Source: *Historical Statistics of the United States*

 Interpreting Graphs

The census, a national head count taken every ten years, recorded the startling population growth of the United States. *Which group grew more rapidly, white or African American? About how much did the total population increase between 1780 and 1830?*

MAKING CONNECTIONS

The migration into the trans-Appalachian region has been called a repopulation or resettlement. Why?

The War of 1812

The War of 1812, declared in June of that year, also had a great impact on trans-Appalachia. Interference with American shipping by the British navy was the direct cause of the war. Western Americans were also irritated by British support of Native American resistance; many dreamed of conquering Canada.

With only a small army and navy, the United States was in no position to challenge Britain, which was then one of the strongest nations in the world. A planned invasion of Canada from Michigan failed in the summer of 1812. In 1814 a virtually unopposed British army burned most of Washington, D.C., including the Capitol and the White House.

American forces had more success in the western region. In the summer of 1813, Master Commandant Oliver Hazard Perry and a small fleet of ships defeated a British flotilla in the

Battle of Lake Erie and gained control of the Great Lakes. In October 1813, William Henry Harrison defeated a combined force of Native Americans and British soldiers at the Battle of the Thames. In Alabama, **Andrew Jackson** won the Battle of Horseshoe Bend in March 1814 against the Creeks and other Native Americans.

The greatest American victory, the Battle of New Orleans, took place in January 1815. Ironically, this occurred after the United States and Great Britain had negotiated the Treaty of Ghent, bringing the War of 1812 to an end. Still, the victory of Jackson's 4,500 volunteers over 11,000 British regulars greatly boosted American morale. The Battle of New Orleans ended the war on a high note—and made a national hero out of Andrew Jackson.

Native American Resistance

The battles of the Thames and Horseshoe Bend basically brought to an end the Native American resistance to American expansion east of the Mississippi River. These battles formed the final chapter in a long struggle dating back to the early 1790s, when many Miami, Delaware, Shawnee, and others had come together and created a sizeable opposition in this region. Led by warriors such as Little Turtle

2. INSTRUCT

Explain/Discuss

Point out to students that the ideas of rapid change, progress, and improvement of humankind are concepts most Americans take for granted today. This was not always the case. Ask students how they think new ideas, inventions, and improvements in production, communication, and transportation relate to the rapid expansion westward of the United States in the late 1700s and early 1800s.

Answer to ...

MAKING CONNECTIONS

The region had originally been populated or settled by Native Americans; later population and settlement of the region thus can accurately be referred to as a repopulation or resettlement.

Caption Answer to ...

Interpreting Graphs

The white population grew more rapidly; by about nine or ten million.

Analyze

Ask students why it could be said that the country became more united at the end of the 1700s and in the early 1800s. Have them consider the effect of ideas as well as technology.

Caption Answer to ...

Using Historical Evidence

Shawanoes (Shawnee), Ottawas (Ottawa), Chipawas (Chippewa), Putawatames (Potawatomi), Putawatames of the River St. Joseph, Putawatames of Huron, Miamis (Miami).

In Depth

Historical Misconceptions

No image is more associated with American history than that of the move westward toward the frontier—perpetuated in popular stories and films as the triumph of cowboys over Native Americans, settlers over hunters. Now some claim that the very word *frontier* masks the facts of European conquest and exploitation of Native Americans. Some historians are sympathetic to such criticism and would like to redefine the term. Historian Richard White, for instance, describes the frontier as a zone, a middle ground, a place of relatively equal interaction among different people where no particular group is dominant.

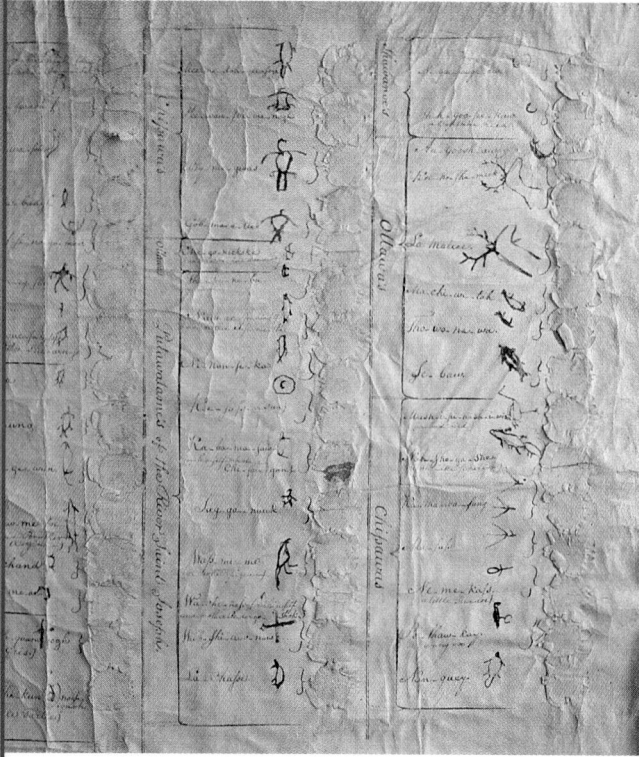

Using Historical Evidence Forced to sign away their rights to Ohio in the Treaty of Greenville (above), Native Americans made their mark beside the English spelling of their names. *What Native American groups are identified in the vertical headings?*

and Blue Jacket, they smashed a United States army at Miamitown (now Fort Wayne, Indiana) in 1790. Then they overran an expedition commanded by Northwest Territory governor Arthur St. Clair, inflicting one of the biggest defeats ever suffered by a United States army.

The Native American alliance, however, soon was deserted by the British. Worse still, they now faced a tougher foe in General "Mad Anthony" Wayne, who trained and equipped a new national force, the Legion of the United States. In 1794 Wayne led the Legion to victory over the Native Americans at the Battle of Fallen Timbers in what is now northwestern Ohio. As a result of this battle, in the next year the Miami, Delaware, Shawnee, and other Native Americans were forced to accept the Treaty of Greenville, in which they lost the southern two thirds of Ohio.

The treaty also compelled them to acknowledge that the Ohio River was no longer a permanent boundary between their lands and lands settled by Americans of European descent.

African Americans and Slavery in the Trans-Appalachian West

Not all of the Americans moving west of the Appalachians were of European heritage. One recent historian has estimated that owners forcibly relocated some 98,000 enslaved African Americans from Virginia and Maryland between 1790 and 1810. When the people brought directly from Africa or from the West Indies are added in, some 194,000 African Americans were among the multitudes of people who settled Kentucky, Tennessee, and the Gulf Coast states. Another 144,000 followed between 1810 and 1820.

North of the Ohio River, slavery was technically illegal, in accordance with the Northwest Ordinance of 1787. But laws called **black codes** kept African Americans there under the authority of white Americans. Indentured servitude, too, was used as a means to exploit African American labor without resorting to enslavement.

More powerful than the willingness to exploit African Americans, however, was the prejudice that led new settlers to try to keep African Americans out of their territories and states altogether. Many Americans of European descent living in Ohio, Indiana, and Illinois did not want African Americans in their states, not only because of bias, but because of their fear that African Americans would take up land and take away jobs. As a result, stiff requirements for African American settlers kept the African American population north of the Ohio River very small.

The Missouri Compromise

Americans in the early republic agreed that slavery was legal south of the Ohio River and illegal north of it. But by 1819 the case of Missouri, which did not lie on either side of that river, led to a lengthy debate in Congress.

The issue seemed simple: should Missouri be admitted to the Union as a slave state—a state where slavery was legal? Several members of Congress from the North objected to this. They were not simply concerned about the liberty of African Americans; they also worried that another slave state might increase the power of the southern states in the national government. Members of Congress from the South replied that the national government had no business dictating to states what they could and could not do. They feared that if the United States could forbid slavery in Missouri, it would soon do so elsewhere.

After months of bitter debate, Congress reached what is now called the **Missouri Compromise,** which was signed into law in 1820. Under the agreement, slavery would be permitted in Missouri; at the same time, Maine was carved out of what had been northern Massachusetts and admitted to the union as a free, or nonslave, state. This arrangement would balance power in the Senate between North and South. Furthermore, Congress agreed that as the United States expanded westward, states north of 36° 30' N latitude would be free states, and states south of that line would be slave states, as shown on the map to the right.

Improvements of All Kinds

While many Americans were conquering and developing the West, others were finding ways to conquer distances and save time. Many of their inventions stemmed from a development in Great Britain known as the **Industrial Revolution.** This revolution was a major change in the economy due to the increased use of machines powered by sources other than humans or animals. The British guarded this new technology, making it illegal for anyone knowledgeable in the design of industrial machines to emigrate to another country.

Textile Improvements In 1789, however, an English textile worker named Samuel Slater defied British law and brought the Industrial Revolution to the United States. Working from memory, he duplicated British machinery that quickly and efficiently spun cotton fibers into thread. Slater's water-powered spinning mill at Pawtucket, Rhode Island, was only the first of many. Throughout the 1790s and into the 1800s, New Englanders were building mills at the many waterfalls of their region.

The boom in milling cotton was fed by another new invention, the cotton gin. Devised by New Englander **Eli Whitney** while visiting a Georgia plantation in 1793, the gin easily separated the seeds from cotton fiber. A worker could clean 1 pound of cotton per day without a gin; with a gin operated by water power, he could clean 1,000 pounds. Profit per pound of cotton skyrocketed, and with it the amount of cotton planted for harvest. The bales of cotton produced in the South rose from 6,000 in 1792 to 146,000 by 1805 and 334,378 by 1820. As profits grew, so did the demand for slave labor. The cotton gin, shown on page 116, was largely responsible for the continued growth and

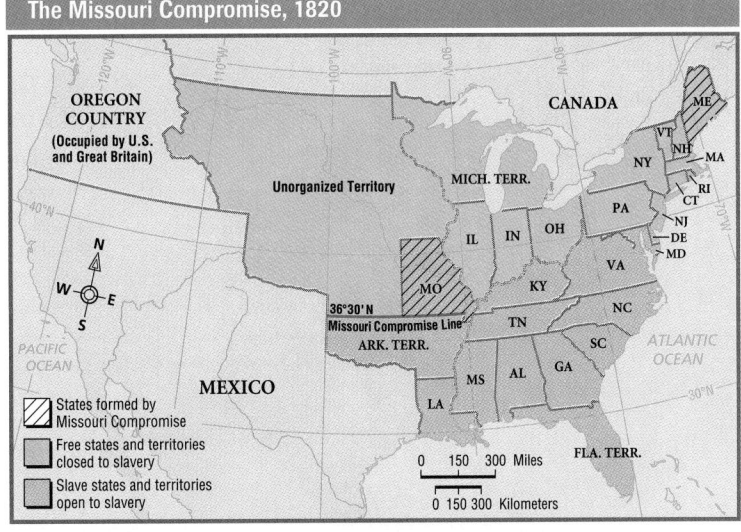

The Missouri Compromise, 1820

Geography and History: Interpreting Maps
Under the terms of the Missouri Compromise, a new free state, Maine, was carved out of Massachusetts to balance the new slave state, Missouri. Congress also agreed that in the future, only states south of 36° 30' N latitude would be slave states. Southerners figured that cotton would not grow north of this line. *Which would cover more land under the compromise, the new free states or the new slave states?*

Activity

(The clock icon indicates an activity that can be successfully conducted within a class period. Each chapter has at least one such activity.)

Teaching Heterogeneous Groups
Constant migration turned the early republic into a nation of strangers. To ease their loneliness, many Americans turned to church and social organizations to establish relationships, social contact, and a sense of community. To demonstrate the importance of community and social relationships, have students identify communities of which they feel a part. These could be neighborhoods, schools, religious groups, clubs, or their town or city. Ask what needs are filled by their community and what qualities its members have in common. The information might be recorded on a group chart, then placed on a "gallery walk." When all charts are on the wall, students can examine them and list on a piece of paper the key recurring themes.

Caption Answer to ...

 Interpreting Maps

The new free states.

In Depth

Multicultural Perspectives

As early as 1651, an African American couple were landowners in Virginia. Anthony and Mary Johnson had been indentured servants. After earning their freedom in 1651, the Johnsons began planting corn and tobacco on their own land. They prospered until a fire destroyed their home and forced them to seek tax relief from the courts. On reviewing the Johnsons' hardship, the court ruled that they no longer had to pay taxes.

economic success of the slave labor system. It also fed the southern fever to move to undeveloped lands in the West, where sure wealth was the reward of anyone who put large acreage into producing cotton.

Steam Power The boom in cotton was helped by another innovation, the steamboat—a boat driven by the power of steam produced by burning coal or wood. By the 1820s, dozens of steamboats traveled on American rivers, reducing the costs of transportation and commerce.

People today are so used to rapid travel that they may find it hard to understand the significance of the steamboat. Before this invention, the speed at which humans could travel had not changed much in centuries. Now the steam engine created a revolution in transportation. Soon it would be adapted for travel on land— by railroads—and for use as a power source in factories and mills.

Canals People were not only overcoming river currents; they were creating their own rivers in the form of canals. If rapids or waterfalls inter-

rupted the easy flow of commerce, or if moving goods from one river to another was vital, the solution was to build a canal. In the early 1800s, there was a virtual frenzy of canal building, much of it by states, some by private investors.

The most successful of these projects was the Erie Canal, which opened in 1825. Built by the state of New York, this 363-mile ditch linked the Hudson River and Lake Erie. But it affected an even wider area. Farmers in the Great Lakes region could now ship their products to markets as far away as New York City and beyond.

Communications Americans in the early republic also enjoyed improvements in communication. Here the federal government took the lead. There were only 75 post offices in the United States in 1790; by 1830 there were 8,450. Regular mail delivery made communication with distant places more efficient than ever before. It also created a national network of information, since the mail carried newspapers, magazines, and books. Newspapers in themselves made information available to large numbers of people; they were to the early 1800s what television was to the late 1900s. The way Americans experienced their world would never be the same again.

The Democratization of American Religion

In the early 1800s, a new wave of religious revivals called the **Second Great Awakening** swept the United States. Like the First Great Awakening in the 1730s and 1740s, this revival was an **evangelical movement,** stressing preaching instead of rituals, and emphasizing that people could be saved for a happy life after death if they believed in Christ and the Bible. This movement was democratic—its members believed that anyone could participate and experience salvation if he or she chose to do so.

Among the denominations, or religious subgroups, that experienced the most growth during the Second Great Awakening were Baptists, Methodists, and Disciples of Christ. Methodists in particular attracted large numbers of converts in the late 1700s and early 1800s. With a well-developed organization and an insistence on the idea that anyone could achieve salvation,

Planters had been looking for a way to clean the seeds from the short-fiber cotton that grew well in the South, and Eli Whitney's cotton gin filled that need.

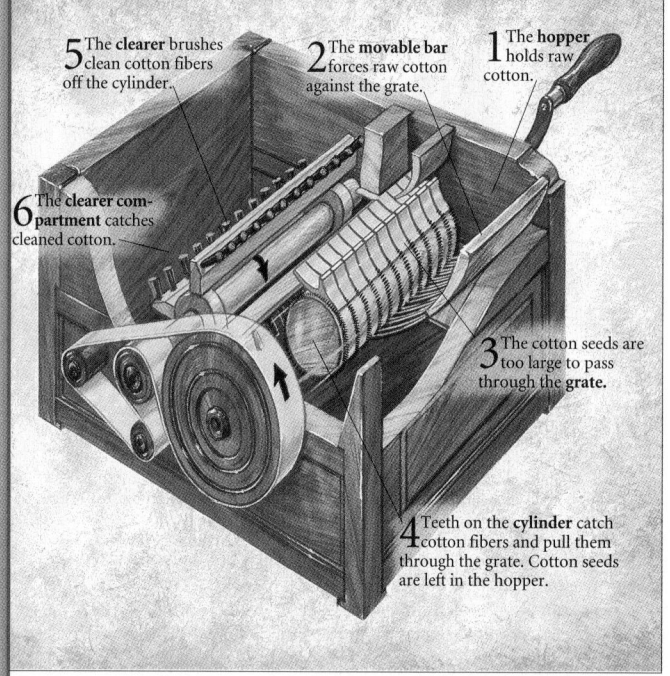

5 The **clearer** brushes clean cotton fibers off the cylinder.

2 The **movable bar** forces raw cotton against the grate.

1 The **hopper** holds raw cotton.

6 The **clearer compartment** catches cleaned cotton.

3 The cotton seeds are too large to pass through the **grate.**

4 Teeth on the **cylinder** catch cotton fibers and pull them through the grate. Cotton seeds are left in the hopper.

Methodists grew into one of the largest Christian denominations in the United States in the 1800s.

Women and children were the main participants in the religious awakening of the early 1800s. Within the new church community, women organized sewing circles and women's auxiliaries, or clubs. They also formed local and regional reform societies to help widows and orphans, to convert people to Christianity, and to improve the living conditions for mothers.

In addition to participating in this enlarged community, women exercised increasing power over the selection of ministers within the churches. Through religion, women shared a sense of spiritual equality with men, even if their political power was limited. Religious work gave them wide outlets for their talents, offering them an opportunity to influence the moral development of their communities.

African Americans and Democratic Religion

In the 1700s, Methodist and other evangelical congregations were often multiracial; Americans of both European and African heritage often worshiped God together. Indeed, American Protestantism owes much to African religious traditions, such as the call-and-response, in which the congregation responded as a whole to a statement made by one member.

In many communities of enslaved people, a rich combination of Christian and African spiritual traditions was emerging. Along the coast of South Carolina, enslaved African Americans transformed Christian worship services into a mutual activity of both preachers and congregations. When they incorporated their own traditional African beliefs, such as the belief in possession by spirits, they gave an entirely new dimension to the worship.

Enslaved people also adopted Christian ideas and stories that condemned their bondage and offered some hope of rescue. African American hymns, or spirituals, became powerful testaments to the confidence of enslaved people that some day, in heaven if not on earth, they would be liberated.

Although some white Methodists and others in the late 1700s did attack slavery, most whites were uncomfortable with multiracial worship, especially as African Americans became more assertive about sharing in democratic liberty. In the North, this tension produced another distinctively American denomination, the African Methodist Episcopal Church (AME).

Like other Americans, great numbers of African Americans turned to evangelical religion because they believed their souls were at risk. But Methodism and other Protestant denominations also offered the framework of community and assurance that what mattered in the United States was not wealth or color, but what civil rights leader Martin Luther King, Jr., would later call "the content of one's character."

The democratic power of evangelical Christianity was enormous. This power did not overcome prejudice based on race or establish real equality. Still, revivals reinforced in the field of religion what the American Revolution had begun in the world of politics. Though the United States was far from achieving full social equality and popular sovereignty, there was no getting away from the fact that Americans were defining themselves as a nation in those very terms.

This lantern lit the way to a meeting at a religous camp during the great reawakening of religious life that took place during the early 1800s.

SECTION 2 REVIEW

Key Terms, People, and Places
1. Define (a) Northwest Territory, (b) black codes, (c) Missouri Compromise, (d) Industrial Revolution, (e) evangelical movement.
2. Identify (a) Andrew Jackson, (b) Eli Whitney.

Key Concepts
3. What area did Americans settle in the early 1800s?

4. Describe improvements in communication in the new nation.
5. Why was the Second Great Awakening democratic?

Thinking Critically
6. **Making Comparisons** Compare and contrast the First Great Awakening and the Second Great Awakening.

 Quiz found in the Unit 1 folder, p. 107, covers the main ideas in this section as well as the key terms.

Media and Technology

Transparencies
Critical Thinking, I-14
Historical Maps, L-2

---

3. ASSESS

Section 2 Review Answers

1. (a) Northwest Territory, see p. 113, (b) black codes, see p. 114, (c) Missouri Compromise, see p. 115, (d) Industrial Revolution, see p. 115, (e) evangelical movement, see p. 116

2. (a) Andrew Jackson, see p. 113, (b) Eli Whitney, see p. 115

3. The trans-Appalachia area, including the Ohio, Mississippi, Tennessee, and Cumberland river valleys

4. The federal government increased the number of post offices by more than a hundred times. Newspapers and magazines were also carried through regular mail delivery, linking the nation.

5. Its followers believed that anyone could participate and experience salvation if he or she chose to do so.

6. Possible answers: The First Great Awakening (of the 1730s and 1740s) energized people to reject the traditional authorities of ministers and books; the Second Great Awakening (in the early 1800s) likewise promised salvation to anyone who was willing to believe in the authority of Christ and the Bible. Both democratized religion, although the Second Great Awakening carried this trend further.

Reteach

Ask students to list the changes highlighted in this section in the following categories: population, territory, technology, and religion.

4. CLOSE

Reinforcing the Big Idea

The new nation began to define itself politically and spiritually, spreading itself over the continent through migration aided by technology. The next section examines ordinary life and the emphasis on economics that ensued.

Moving the East to the West

Focus In this section students will examine how the location of Marietta, Ohio, the first settlement in the western lands of the United States, contributed to its success and how the characteristics of the New Englanders who built the new town endured.

Instruct Ask students if any of them have lived in, or visited, another part of the country. Discuss the types of distinct differences that exist between their former and present communities. Ask students what might account for such differences.

Before students read the feature, you might want to review the descriptions of New England society and New England towns given in Chapter 1. Point out that in some ways, Marietta became just like a New England town.

Explain that Marietta was the first of a number of Ohio towns begun by New Englanders. As a first step, prospective settlers formed covenants with one another that resembled those made by their ancestors upon first reaching the shores of Massachusetts. The New England settlers of Oberlin, Ohio, for example, pledged one another to "a life of simplicity, to special devotion to church and school, and to earnest labor in the missionary cause." (Quoted in Smith, Page. *The Shaping of America, A People's History of the Young Republic,* Vol. III. McGraw-Hill, 1980, p. 735.) Similarly, when twenty-four members of the Congregational Church of Granville, Massachusetts, decided to emigrate to Ohio, they first signed a covenant. They took a minister and church deacons to what became Granville, Ohio.

Like Granville, many towns in Ohio were named for New England towns (which themselves were often named for places in England). Ask students to use road maps (or other detailed maps) of New England and Ohio to find other places in Ohio whose names recall place names in New England. Students can then consult a geographical atlas to find out when these Ohio

Moving the East to the West

Marietta, Ohio, was the first major United States settlement on the western frontier. How did settlers go about remaking the wilderness of Ohio into the kind of land they knew?

After the American Revolution, the Continental Congress gained control of the vast lands between the Appalachian Mountains and the Mississippi River. Eager to pay off its war debts, Congress cast about for a systematic way to sell the public lands northwest of the Ohio River—the land known as the Northwest Territory, shown in the map on page 119. The success of the first settlement on western lands depended on three geographical factors: the location of the land chosen, the imprint of humans on the land, and the characteristics humans brought to the place.

Location

The Appalachian Mountains had always formed a barrier between the original British colonies and the land to the west. By the time of the American Revolution, however, settlers had pierced this barrier by making use of military roads that linked Pennsylvania with the Ohio River.

For this reason, Congress chose a tract of land on the Ohio River as the first to be sold in the Northwest Territory. (The tract, about 5 million acres in size, is labeled "Area of First Survey" on the map on page 119.) The Ohio Company—the organization that bought the land—quickly founded the town of Marietta where the Muskingum River flows into the Ohio River. Marietta grew rapidly because it was a magnet for new settlers. Furthermore, the town was a jumping-off point to lands farther west and so carried on a thriving trade with travelers. Between 1788 and 1790 alone, nearly nine hundred boats carrying a total of twenty thousand settlers passed along Marietta's shores on their way west.

The Human Imprint on the Land

Under the terms of the Land Ordinance of 1785, western lands had to be surveyed according to a particular system before they could be sold. This system was based on principles used in laying out New England towns. The survey system had a tremendous impact on the geography of the West, because it was adopted, with modifications, throughout that region.

Marietta became a pocket of New England beliefs and attitudes in the Northwest Territory.

The major unit of this system was the township, which was a square, six miles on a side and thirty-six square miles in area. Under the New England–style survey system, townships were to be measured off in tiers from an intersecting Principal Meridian and Base Line. Every other township was to be subdivided into thirty-six lots (now called sections), each lot being a square mile (640 acres) in size, with lot number 16 set aside for maintaining a public school in the township. Lots were to be the smallest sized unit offered for sale, and the minimum price was to be $1.00 per acre. The idea was that lots could be purchased by individual farmers who could afford them, and undivided townships might be purchased by homogeneous groups wishing to start communities in the New England tradition, or by people pooling their resources to acquire a township for division into individual farm units.

RESOURCE DIRECTORY

Teaching Resources

Time and Place Activity Moving the City to the Country, found in the Unit 1 folder, pp. 116–117, focuses on the city of Reston, Virginia, a modern example of planned community development.

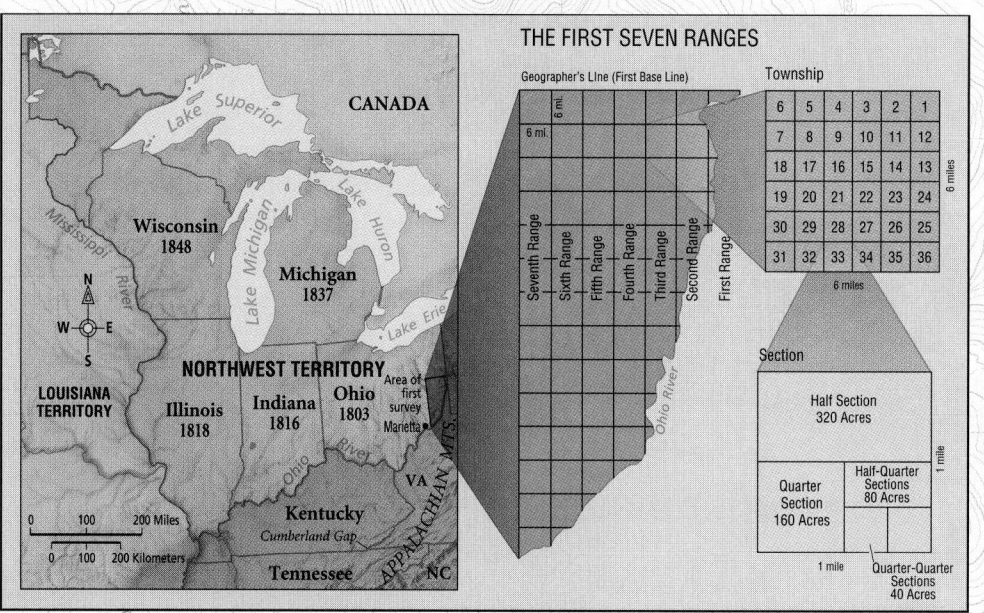

THE FIRST SEVEN RANGES

Geographer's Line (First Base Line)

Township

6	5	4	3	2	1
7	8	9	10	11	12
18	17	16	15	14	13
19	20	21	22	23	24
30	29	28	27	26	25
31	32	33	34	35	36

6 miles

Section

Half Section
320 Acres

Quarter Section
160 Acres

Half-Quarter Sections
80 Acres

1 mile

Quarter-Quarter Sections
40 Acres

Seventh Range · Sixth Range · Fifth Range · Fourth Range · Third Range · Second Range · First Range

CANADA

Lake Superior

Wisconsin 1848

Michigan 1837

Lake Michigan

Lake Huron

Lake Erie

NORTHWEST TERRITORY

Mississippi River

LOUISIANA TERRITORY

Illinois 1818

Indiana 1816

Ohio 1803

Area of first survey
Marietta

Ohio River

VA

Kentucky
Cumberland Gap

Tennessee

APPALACHIAN MTS.

NC

0   100   200 Miles
0   100   200 Kilometers

Human Characteristics of Place

The type of people who settle a place may largely determine whether the settlement will succeed. Even the word *frontier* brings to mind colorful figures who seem larger than life. White settlement west of the Appalachians, however, owed more to land companies and those who founded them. The Ohio Company was started by speculators—investors who hoped to resell the land for a profit. But they were not just little-known business people. "No colony in America," declared George Washington of the first settlement, "was ever settled under such favorable [sponsorship]. . . . Information, property, and strength will be its characteristics. I know many of the settlers personally, and there never were men better calculated to promote the welfare of such a community."

Although the character of the founders of the Ohio Company was vital in its success, they might well have come from any part of the United States, north or south. As it happened, they were New Englanders and persuaded people from that region to move to Ohio with them. And this New England background distinguished the place from surround-

ing territory settled by people from other parts of the United States. Marietta became a pocket of New England beliefs and attitudes in the Northwest Territory. This is reflected in the voting patterns of the settlers and their descendants in national elections until well into the nineteenth century. Marietta's residents voted as New Englanders did, rather than as did the inhabitants of the surrounding areas of Ohio and Kentucky. The human characteristics of the original settlement—like its location and the human imprint left by land division—endured into modern times.

GEOGRAPHIC CONNECTIONS

1. How did the location of the Ohio Company land contribute to its success?
2. How did settlers in the Ohio Company land affect the way the West was settled?

Critical Thinking
3. **Recognizing Bias** Is there anything in Washington's statement about the prospects of Marietta to suggest that his assessment might not have been an objective one?

towns were founded. If they were established in the late 1700s or early 1800s, they may indeed have been named by emigrating New Englanders.

The Marietta region of Ohio and the Western Reserve region, which was heavily populated by emigrants from Connecticut, voted with New England on many matters, especially against any extension of slavery. In many presidential elections, the Marietta and Western Reserve regions supported candidates other than those favored by the rest of the state.

Tell students that Congress applied the principles of the Northwest Ordinance to other areas of the growing United States. Britain also adopted similar policies in Canada, Australia, and New Zealand.

Extend Ask students to suppose that a small group of settlers from their community is emigrating to an undeveloped, extremely isolated section of Alaska. Ask each student to make a list of at least ten major principles or institutions that they would expect to see replicated in the new settlement.

Answers

1. The land was located on one of the major routes west, and western settlement began in earnest during this time.

2. Settlers of the Ohio Company land came from New England and established a land survey system based on the New England town and on the principle that only surveyed land would be granted to settlers. This system was then used throughout the West.

3. Washington's statement, "I know many of the settlers personally. . ." suggests that his assessment was not entirely objective.

In the early 1800s the banking industry was a powerful force that helped bring changes to the way things were made and sold. One such change—illustrated on this bank note—was that people began to work for a living outside their homes.

SECTION PREVIEW

In colonial times, people had focused on how to keep their households operating. For many people in the early republic, that focus gave way to a determination to make money—as much and as quickly as possible.

Key Concepts

· During this period, the meaning of work changed. Instead of an activity that kept households running, labor became something to be bought and sold.
· The growing power of banks reflected the increasing importance of credit and money.
· As manufacturing increased, more and more households purchased goods that once had been produced in the household.

Key Terms, People, and Places

Market Revolution, entrepreneur, capitalism, capital, household economy, commodity, centralize

W ith a growing population, expanding territory, and constantly improving transportation and communication, the United States in the early 1800s was experiencing a vast change and increase in its market for goods. Americans purchased more and more goods, rather than making those goods themselves. And rather than trading one kind of goods for another, Americans used money—both cash and credit—to get what they needed. This change in the way people made, bought, and sold goods is now called the **Market Revolution.**

☆ With enormous enthusiasm, American men during this period began to devote themselves to the business of making money. Everywhere, north and south, they went in pursuit of what they called "the main chance"—their opportunity to strike it rich. Among the most successful of these go-getters was industrialist Samuel Slater.

AMERICAN PROFILES

Samuel Slater

Samuel Slater arrived in New York City in November 1789 with a head full of technological information. He had been born in Derbyshire, England, in 1768, the son of farmers. Slater's father died when Slater was 14. Before his death, his father arranged for Slater to become an apprentice to Jedediah Strutt. As an apprentice, Samuel Slater spent almost seven years learning a trade from Strutt.

Strutt was a pioneer in the development of English cotton mills, or textile factories. Other men, including Richard Arkwright, James Hargreaves, and Samuel Compton, had developed new water-powered machines that spun cotton fibers into thread. Slater worked in Strutt's mills as a manager. Supervising laborers, he learned how the machinery operated and how it was built and repaired. When Slater's apprenticeship ended, he decided to migrate to the United States. He hoped that his experience and knowledge would help him make a lot of money in the new nation, where textile technology was not as advanced as it was in England.

It was illegal for either textile workers or information about textile machinery to leave England. So Slater had to travel in disguise and memorize as much of the workings of English textile machinery as he could. In 1790, he agreed to build cotton-spinning machines for a textile business in Providence, Rhode Island. Athough the machinery was complicated, Slater reproduced it by memory alone. He soon became a partner in this business. In 1793, Slater and his partners built a mill in Pawtucket, Rhode Island. They chose the spot because of a waterfall in a river, which produced the power to operate the mill.

Samuel Slater was a pioneer in the nation's cotton textile industry.

In 1798, Slater and his wife's father and brothers established Samuel Slater and Company. The new firm made its own machines and built another mill in Pawtucket. Within a few years, Slater was expanding his operations throughout New England. When he died in 1835, he owned all or part of thirteen textile mills. His business made him a rich man by the standards of the time. In 1829, forty years after he had arrived in the United States, Slater estimated his worth at between $800,000 and $1 million.

Other men eager to get rich quickly copied Slater's methods. By 1814, there were about 240 mills operating in the United States, most of them in Pennsylvania, New York, and New England.

More than hard work and a good memory made Slater wealthy. He took advantage of the potential of the young United States. The United States was producing more and more cotton to meet the needs of a growing population and it had many rivers with waterfalls. No wonder Slater succeeded. He gave Americans exactly what they needed when they needed it.

The Nature of Work Changes

Samuel Slater was a businessman who devoted his life to finding that competitive edge that would bring him a profit. This type of person—known as an **entrepreneur**—was becoming much more common in the United States at that time. An entrepreneur is someone who takes on business risks for the sake of profit. Entrepreneurs thrived in the economic system beginning to flourish during this time. In this system, known as **capitalism,** manufacturing is controlled by private corporations and by individuals competing for profit. This system takes its name from the term *capital*. **Capital** is a supply of wealth that can be used to produce goods and make money. Capitalism was not new, strictly speaking, but during the early 1800s, it rapidly expanded. And as it did so, the nature of work itself began to change.

The Household Economy Declines In the 1600s and 1700s, the **household economy** had dominated North American life outside the major seaports. In this type of economy, people's business consists of simply keeping their households running. Colonial Americans grew their own food and made their own clothes, soap, and other necessities. Their goal was not to get rich but to have enough property to be able to live comfortably and independently.

To be sure, most Americans in the 1600s and 1700s sold products—from extra crops to eggs to cloth; and many bought items they could not make for themselves, such as books and glass. But such buying and selling did not dominate their lives. Work was something done for and within the household. It was not at that time a **commodity,** something to be bought and sold.

When most Americans work today, they are essentially selling their time and labor. Their employers buy their services. To a great extent, the idea of selling labor in order to earn money dates from the early nineteenth century. As more and more people moved and then moved again, as the United States became a nation of strangers, Americans changed their economic habits. Whether they labored in workshops, mills, or offices, people started to work for a specific number of hours each day and for a specific amount of money.

As time passed, families produced fewer and fewer of the things they needed; instead, they bought those items from stores or other individuals. By 1830, goods such as soap and

Discuss

Review the characteristics of the American economy during colonial times. Ask what factors led to economic change during the early 1800s.

Discuss the expansion of capitalism and the changes it created. Ask students to describe the Market Revolution. How did the relationship between Americans and their work change as a result of the Market Revolution? What role did banks play in fueling the new economy? Why is Mason Weems an appropriate symbol of his time?

Analyze

Have students analyze how the Market Revolution affected American society. How did it alter both the role of the family within society and relationships within the family? What impact do you think it had on the status of women?

Answer to ...

Links Across Time

The new jobs allow people to participate in the increased productivity of the centralized workplace while enjoying the advantages of working in the home.

Enrichment

Before the Market Revolution, specialized goods, such as clocks and guns, were made by skilled craftspeople. Ask students to research the accomplishments of Eli Terry, Eli Whitney, and Samuel Colt and to explain in a short paper why it might be said that the achievements of these entrepreneurs brought to an end the era of craftsmanship.

Answer to ...

MAKING CONNECTIONS

Students may describe items that would be eliminated because they could not be made at home. They might also focus on the change in lifestyle that would occur if basic needs were supplied by home production rather than by making money to purchase goods.

3. ASSESS

Section 3 Review Answers

1. (a) Market Revolution, see p. 120, (b) entrepreneur, see p. 121, (c) capitalism, see p. 121, (d) capital, see p. 121 (e) household economy, see p. 121, (f) commodity, see p. 121, (g) centralize, see p. 122

2. Families began to produce fewer and fewer of the things they needed; instead, they bought those items from stores or other individuals.

3. Banks fueled the development of the American economy by providing loans that allowed people to buy land and investments. Banks were also the source of problems that came with debt and depression.

4. Homes became much more elaborately decorated and furnished as Americans purchased items such as china, paintings, and silverware.

Changing the Workplace

When entrepreneurs centralized work during the early 1800s, they drastically changed the way most Americans spent their days. Rather than working at home or on the farm to keep their households running, people increasingly reported to a factory or mill each day where they labored in exchange for a wage.

Today, the workplace for the majority of American workers is neither the factory nor the farm, but the office. A small but increasing number of these office workers, however, are opting to turn back time. Instead of leaving their homes for the workplace each day, they are working for their employers at home—or telecommuting—as part of what some people describe as "a work-at-home revolt." Personal computers, modems, FAX machines, answering machines, and copiers are only some of the high-tech tools that permit workers to perform their jobs from their homes. Today it is estimated that 3 to 6 million people telecommute at least one day a week. That number is expected to increase to some 25 million by the year 2000. *What features of the household economy of the 1700s and the market economy of the 1800s are combined in the new work-at-home jobs?*

---

clothes were commonly made outside the homes where they were used. The people who made goods—whether in their own homes, in workshops, or in factories—were not the same as the people who used them.

Centralizing Work Making goods in workshops and factories was a logical development of changes in the way things were made. Increasingly entrepreneurs would **centralize** manufacturing by making all tasks involved in producing something happen in one place. Centralizing work dramatically increased production. One centralized industry in New England, the cloth-making mills, produced 4 million yards of cotton cloth in 1817; by 1840 the amount was 323 million yards. Often, however, entrepreneurs hired noncentralized workers—women working at home—to cut and sew the cloth into clothing.

MAKING CONNECTIONS

How would our lives in the United States today be different if households still produced most of what they needed?

Banks Spark Economic Growth

The Market Revolution brought new businesses to the forefront of American life. Banks quickly rose to the top as the most influential of the new organizations, because they provided the credit and the cash necessary for entrepreneurs to buy land or to invest in moneymaking schemes.

The first real banks appeared in the United States in the 1780s and 1790s. By the 1830s, hundreds of them had cropped up. Banks could be found in remote rural areas as well as in the middle of cities. Some Americans favored them because banks meant money, available to borrow. Others saw banks as the source of the problems that came with debt and economic depression.

Banks generally were started by groups of private investors. Although states had to give banks legal standing by issuing each of them a charter, they did not strictly control the banks. As a result, many banks made bad loans—loans to people who could not repay them—and most banks did not have additional money on hand to back up their transactions. Still, as long as they had the confidence of their customers, banks sparked economic growth by putting money into people's pockets.

Money in the early republic was not what it is today. The United States government did not issue paper money. Most people preferred to deal in specie, or coin, mainly of gold or silver. Specie was scarce, however, and difficult to carry around. The most common form of money was bank notes—pieces of paper that

---

▶ RESOURCE DIRECTORY

Teaching Resources

Literature Activity Preacher to the World, found in the Unit 1 folder, p. 130, features excerpts from the journals of Ralph Waldo Emerson to give students a glimpse of other reactions to American materialism.

American Profiles Activity found in the Unit 1 folder, p. 118, profiles Sara Todd Astor, whom many consider to have been the entrepreneurial power behind her husband, fur magnate John Jacob Astor.

banks issued to their customers, who then used the notes to pay for goods and services. Similar to modern-day checks, bank notes were promises to pay specie on demand. The problem with these notes was that their value was unpredictable. Imagine selling something and receiving in payment a $100 check that might really be worth anything from $50 to $200, depending on the time and place you tried to cash it.

Despite the shortcomings of their notes, banks fueled the development of the American economy. They provided the loans that allowed Americans to buy millions of acres of federal land in the West and to invest in various money-making schemes. Although people continued to rely on money borrowed from private individuals, they turned increasingly to banks. And banks—because they tended to act together—caused wild economic booms and severe depressions such as the Panic of 1819.

Americans Learn to Buy

As the Market Revolution continued, Americans began to buy more and more goods. In colonial America, only the houses of the wealthiest planters and merchants had been full of goods. But in the 1800s, the relatively simple homes of the 1700s gave way to much more elaborately decorated and furnished homes. In many ways, families were defined more by what they bought than what they sold.

By the middle of the 1800s, the homes of middle-class Americans were positively cluttered with purchased items. Middle-class families bought reproductions of paintings to hang on their walls; china and silverware to eat with; fine materials and silks to make clothing; and more

expensive furniture. Parlors—rooms similar to modern living rooms—became a necessity in every home. Families entertained guests in their parlors, which were filled with knick knacks and furniture, in order to display their good taste and material comfort. When they did not have guests in the house, many people preferred to spend time in their kitchens. How could anyone relax in chilly parlors stuffed with goods?

★ Some Americans avoided or resisted the Market Revolution. But whether they liked it or not, Americans were affected by a growing acceptance of the idea that making money was a good thing. This straightforward pursuit of capital set Americans of the 1800s apart from their colonial ancestors.

A general commitment to capitalism did not mean economic development was the same everywhere, however. By the 1830s, different sections of the United States were developing in different ways. In particular, the economy and societies of the North and South were growing more and more distinct.

Using Historical Evidence The well-to-do city merchant and his wife who posed for the painting from which this 1843 engraving was taken wanted to be shown in their "best room"—the parlor. *What objects in the engraving reveal the new American passion for buying goods?*

 SECTION 3 REVIEW

Key Terms, People, and Places
1. Define (a) Market Revolution, (b) entrepreneur, (c) capitalism, (d) capital, (e) household economy, (f) commodity, (g) centralize.

Key Concepts
2. What was the impact of the Market Revolution on households?

3. What positive effect and what negative effect did banks have on the United States between 1815 and 1845?
4. What changes did increased purchasing of goods bring to American homes?

Critical Thinking
5. **Predicting Consequences** How might bringing workers into one central place affect family life?

Quiz found in the Unit 1 folder, p. 109, covers the main ideas in this section as well as the key terms.

Media and Technology

Transparency
Our Multicultural Heritage, C-8

---

5. It is likely that family life would suffer because workers had to work away from their homes and families; family members would spend less time together.

Caption Answer to ...

Using Historical Evidence

The extensive library, carpets, lamp, and other ornate furnishings.

Reteach

Ask students to use the following key terms and people in a short essay describing how the American economy changed in the early 1800s: Market Revolution, entrepreneur, capitalism, capital, household economy, commodity, centralize, Mason Weems.

 ### Alternative Assessment

Mid-Point Monitoring
Ask students if they have
● Determined the location for their fictional American town
● Decided on a point of view from which the story will be told
● Constructed a rough outline for the plot that includes at least some of the key people or elements

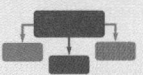 **4. CLOSE**

Reinforcing the Big Idea

The Market Revolution radically altered life throughout the United States. The next section explains how this revolution affected the northern and southern regions of the country differently.

SECTION 4

Sectional Divisions Arise

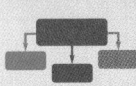
Connecting to the Big Idea

See page 104B. Point out that the Market Revolution affected regions of the country in different ways. Although most northerners remained farmers, the region underwent significant economic and social changes. The southern economy still centered on commercial agriculture, yet the South became a dynamic, capitalist society. Ask students what changes reshaped the North. What made the southern economy flourish?

Objectives

• Explain how farmers in the Old Northwest both encouraged the growth of cities and developed an increasingly complicated system for supplying them with food.

• Explain how agriculture in the South was different from agriculture in the North.

• Describe the ways in which enslaved people resisted slaveholders.

Bellringer

Ask students if they can name words particular to their own or another region of the country. (For example, in New England a drinking fountain is often called a bubbler.) Next ask them to explain the phrase *regional difference.* Then ask students what regional differences exist between the North and the South today.

Reading Strategy

Structured Overview Ask students to write the following headings on a piece of paper: Northern Farms and Factories, The Cotton Kingdom, The Slavery System and Resistance. Have students fill in details from the text under the appropriate heading as they read.

SECTION PREVIEW

The North remained largely a land of farmers, now producing cash crops for the city market. In the South, much of the region's wealth was built on a peculiar relationship between capitalists and their workers—slavery.

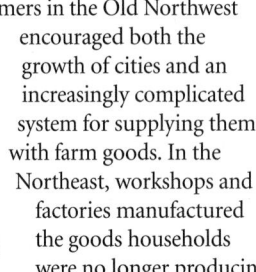

A woman going to work in one of the busy mills of the North carried her noonday meal in this tin and wood lunch pail.

Key Concepts

• Farmers in the Old Northwest encouraged both the growth of cities and an increasingly complicated system for supplying them with farm goods. In the Northeast, workshops and factories manufactured the goods households were no longer producing.

• Like the North, the South was a dynamic, capitalist society, but its staple crops required little processing or handling before they were shipped directly to markets outside of the South.

• Enslaved people occasionally rebelled as a group, but most resistance consisted of small rebellions in daily relationships.

Key Terms, People, and Places

section, capitalist; Denmark Vesey, Nat Turner; North, Northeast, Old Northwest, South

---

I n the early 1800s, Americans became more and more aware that their nation was divided into **sections,** regions distinguished from one another by economic and cultural differences. The two main sections during this period were the North and the South.

The Northern Section

The **North** itself was made up of two parts. One was the **Northeast,** composed of New England, New York, New Jersey, and Pennsylvania—an area that had once been the New England and Middle colonies. The other was the region north and west of the Ohio River, called the **Old Northwest** to distinguish it from the Northwest of today. It included land that is now Ohio, Indiana, Illinois, Michigan, Wisconsin, and part of Minnesota.

The Old Northwest Farmers in the Old Northwest produced large quantities of corn, wheat, and other grains for sale as far away as Europe. Mostly they worked with the assistance of family members or young men hired to help out during harvests.

Grains were profitable crops, but they tended to spoil. Farmers had to deliver them to market quickly or turn them into a product that would not go bad. For example, corn could be used to raise pigs. Pigs could then be slaughtered and sold not just for meat, but also for fat—which was used to make soap—and bristles, which were useful in brushes. Similarly, wheat and other crops could be fed to cattle.

To process and market farm products, farmers depended on urban centers and specialized personnel, including bankers, operators of slaughterhouses and distilleries, and merchants. From Pennsylvania west into Iowa, small towns dotted the landscape, ringing the central urban areas they supplied, such as Cincinnati, St. Louis, and later Chicago.

In the early 1800s, farmers sent flour, meal, pork products, whiskey, and other products by river to New Orleans to be sold in the islands of the Caribbean Sea, the eastern United States, and Europe. The market for these goods expanded even more during the 1820s and 1830s, when canals created an economic lifeline through the Great Lakes to New York City.

⊙ **The Mills of the Northeast** The pork, beef, and beer of the Old Northwest were sold into a market where many people no longer raised

---

RESOURCE DIRECTORY

Teaching Resources

📄 **Reproducible Lesson Plan** found in the Unit 1 folder, p. 102, provides a summary of the Section 4 lesson plan content.

📄 **Alternate Lesson Plan: Critical Thinking** Making Comparisons, found in the Alternate Lesson Plans folder, p. 66, helps students apply this skill by explaining how the economy of the South differed from that of the North.

📄 **Guided Reading and Review** found in the Unit 1 folder, p. 110, provides a structure for reading and mastering the key concepts and reviewing the key terms for Section 4. (Guided Practice)

⭐ 📄 **Primary Source Activity** New England Mill Women, found in the Unit 1 folder, pp. 126–127, uses a discussion between two Lowell, Massachusetts, millworkers to examine the pros and cons of factory life.

their own food. Although most people in the Northeast still lived on farms, many others now worked in the factories supplying the goods that households had once made for themselves.

After the War of 1812, businessmen in Boston financed huge new mills with water-driven power looms in Waltham and Lowell, Massachusetts. To operate these mills, they hired young unmarried women from New England farms, promising them a regulated and moral environment as well as a predictable income. The women were generally pleased to be able to earn money to put aside before they married. Part of the reason the mill owners hired women laborers was because they could be persuaded to work for about half the pay that men would have demanded. Women made up the bulk of factory employees until the 1840s, when immigrant Irish men, unable to find better-paying jobs, took their places.

Women millworkers usually lived in boarding houses run by the mill owners. Six days a week, twelve hours a day, from dawn till seven at night, they tended the clattering machines. In the evening they might attend lectures, or gather in sewing or reading circles. Although the work was boring, the women valued the friendships they developed with their co-workers.

Into the Cities The Northeast was full of young people looking for work. Unable to support themselves as farmers in the Northeast, where the population had outgrown the available land, some went west. But thousands went to cities. In 1810 about 6 percent of Americans lived in cities. By 1840 about 12 percent lived in cities, as shown in the graph on page 126.

The largest cities in colonial North America had had no more than 30,000 residents. By contrast, in the early United States, the population of New York City (meaning Manhattan only) increased sharply—from about 33,000 in 1790 to about 124,000 in 1820, and then to about 516,000 by 1850.

Work had changed in the northern cities, and with it an entire way of life. Colonial households had been more than the homes of families; they had also served as schools, hospitals, welfare centers, and support agencies. Many Americans may not realize that the government services of today were first established to help fill the gap left when the household lost importance. As the household economy broke

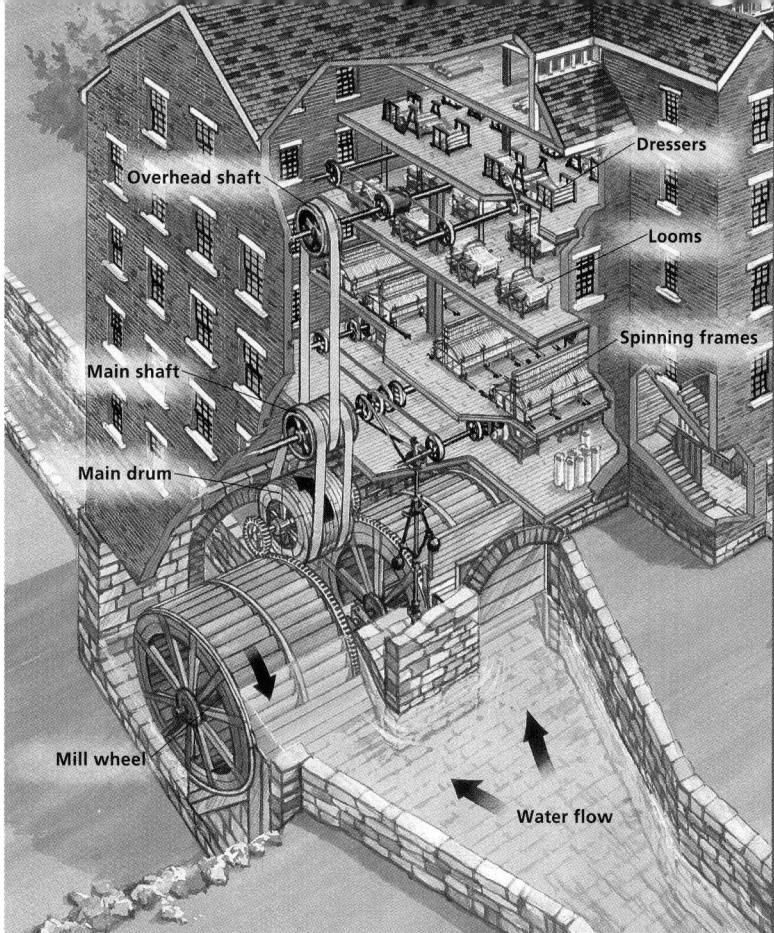

Clean, cheap power drove the textile mills of New England. Though at first mill builders relied on a system of huge wooden gears to harness river power, they soon adopted the system of belts shown here. On the first floor, cotton was spun into thread; on the second, thread was woven into cloth; on the third, the cloth was dressed or finished.

Labels on image: Overhead shaft, Dressers, Looms, Spinning frames, Main shaft, Main drum, Mill wheel, Water flow

Media and Technology

Transparencies
Geographic Setting, M-2, M-3, M-4; The Way It Works, H-8

2. INSTRUCT

Discuss

Discuss the economies of the North and South. Ask how agriculture in the South differed from agriculture in the North. How did the changing nature of work affect the entire way of life in northern cities? In what ways were southern planters and farmers as capitalistic as their northern counterparts?

Analyze

Have students analyze the role enslaved people played in the southern economy. Would commercial agriculture as practiced in the South have been possible without slavery?

Answer to ...

MAKING CONNECTIONS

Answers may cite features mentioned in the text. Some services, such as welfare, sewer, and firefighting services, have improved.

Caption Answer to ...

 Interpreting Graphs

1830: about 1,100,000; 1850: about 3,500,000; increase: about 2,400,000.

In Depth

Then and Now

The growth of cities meant the segregation of economic classes. Many members of the middle class chose to live far away from their places of work. Residing some distance from the downtown urban areas, lawyers, managers, and merchants commuted into town to work. In the 1990s, most members of the middle and upper classes live in suburbs. (See Chapter 18, Section 2.)

down, people no longer supplied the same care to their families within the home. Thus, the residents of northern cities were largely on their own, without households to support them in times of trouble.

In the cities, the growing number of poor people were concentrated in areas where housing was cheap. The Five Points area in lower Manhattan, for example, was notorious for its run-down buildings divided into apartments by the 1830s. Two decades later, a group of middle-class Methodist women described Five Points as

> miserable-looking buildings, liquor-stores innumerable, neglected children by scores, playing in rags and dirt, squalid-looking women, brutal men with black eyes and disfigured faces proclaiming drunken brawls and fearful violence.

Cities were simply unable to handle the tremendous increase in their populations. They lacked sewage systems and reliable supplies of fresh water. Police and fire services were primitive at best. When disease struck,

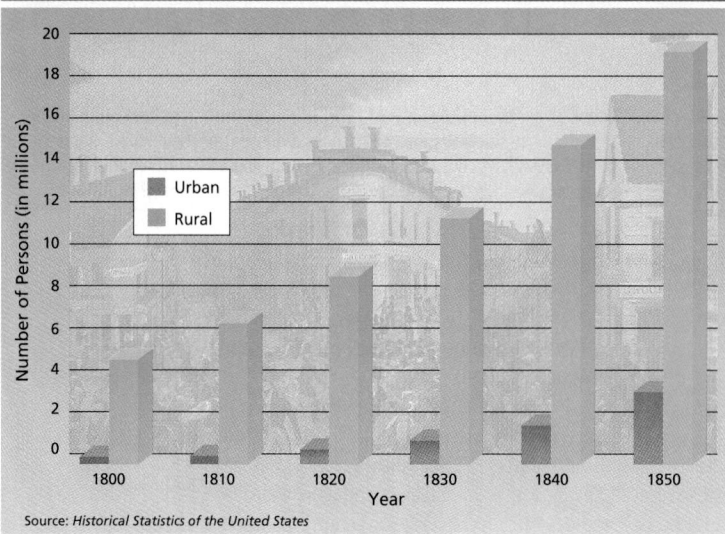

Urban and Rural Populations of the United States, 1800–1850

Source: *Historical Statistics of the United States*

Interpreting Graphs
The scene in the background of this graph is the Five Points area of Manhattan **about 1830.** *How many Americans lived in cities in 1830? In 1850? What was the increase in urban population during the years 1830 to 1850?*

disaster followed. In 1832 and 1833, cholera, an intestinal disease carried by contaminated water, swept along the rivers and canals of the United States, leaving thousands dead or weakened in its wake.

MAKING CONNECTIONS

Were the problems of cities in the early 1800s similar to those of cities today? If so, how?

Owners and Workers Clash

Owners of factories and businessmen in general began to see the relationship between themselves and their employees in strictly economic terms. As **capitalists,** they supplied the capital that built the factory or started the business. They then paid for the labor of the people who worked for them. Beyond that, the employees were on their own. The Lowell mill owners were the exception. Most employers believed that if workers lived in poor housing, had little to eat, or dressed in rags, it was of no concern to the employer. In a society where buying and selling goods and labor determined so much, human welfare mattered little.

Workers had a different viewpoint. Work was no longer a rewarding focus of personal life, as it had been for most colonial Americans. People looked instead for increased wealth to take the place of that reward. And rather than attacking capitalism itself, workers focused on problems that arose in their specific situations, including long hours and low wages. In 1834, for example, one out of every six women in Lowell went on strike when employers announced a 15 percent wage cut in response to poor sales.

Such strikes were the only real weapon workers had. They had become an American tradition as early as the 1700s, when sailors and dockworkers went on strike. But between 1834 and 1836, 168 strikes took place in the United States, mainly for shorter hours and higher pay.

In 1834, during this period of intense labor activity, the first national labor organization, the National Trades Union (NTU), was formed. Close to 300,000 people belonged to the NTU and other unions in the 1830s, a large number for that period.

The early flowering of unions was short-lived, however—killed by economic depression and court rulings that outlawed labor organizations. All the same, the stage was set for later labor activity. By the 1840s, the North had a booming and complex economy. It was increasingly a region of cities and towns, banks and factories, a place with growing tensions between middle- and working-class people. More and more, the market linked people together or pushed them apart. The market was redefining northern society.

The Southern Section

Like the North, the South remained overwhelmingly agricultural. The area considered the **South** consisted of what is now Delaware, Maryland, Virginia, West Virginia, North Carolina, South Carolina, Georgia, Kentucky, Tennessee, Alabama, Mississippi, Louisiana, and Arkansas. Its primary products were staple crops such as cotton, tobacco, sugar, and rice. Cotton especially was immensely profitable, by far the most valuable single product of the United States in the 1800s.

Most of the staple crops of the South did not require the same kind of processing that was needed to transport the grains of the Old Northwest long distances. Properly cared for, cotton and tobacco would not spoil before they reached distant markets in the Northeast and Europe. In 1860 King Cotton made up two thirds of the total value of American exports; tobacco made up one tenth.

A Dynamic Farm Economy The South had an economy not unlike that of a colony. Its residents produced staple crops and raw materials that were processed and sold elsewhere. They did not develop as many towns and industries as did northerners. The region remained one of farms and open countryside.

Yet the South had as active an economy as any part of the United States. White southern men saw in cotton what Parson Weems saw in his biography of George Washington—a ticket to wealth. Southern farmers and planters were just as much developers and entrepreneurs as the factory owners and business people of the North.

Southern Cities Although it was not as town-centered as the North, the South did have cities. New Orleans in Louisiana, Charleston in South Carolina, and Richmond in Virginia had many of the same problems that troubled New York City and Boston. Southern cities, however, were fewer in number, smaller in population, and were growing more slowly. They served the needs of plantations.

The southern cities were also home to large numbers of free African Americans. By 1850, of the 3.7 million African Americans in the United States, 12 percent were free. Some lived in the North, but most resided in southern cities or rural areas away from the large plantations. Generally, free African Americans were older and better educated than enslaved African Americans.

Whether in the North or South, free blacks were usually very poor. Excluded from better-paying jobs, they worked as laborers, servants, cooks, laundresses, and barbers. And although they had their freedom, they enjoyed almost none of the privileges of American citizenship. They could not vote or hold office, for example.

The Slavery System

A planter had to have three things in order to profit from growing cotton, tobacco, sugar, and other agricultural products. The first was land—lots of it. The second was relatively easy and inexpensive access to markets. Finally, white southerners needed labor to grow crops such as cotton. Enslaved African Americans often supplied this labor.

Most white southerners did not own enslaved people. In 1830, slaveholders made up only 36 percent of the white population. All the

In Depth

Did You Know?

Desperate economic conditions in New York City, where fifty thousand people—about one third of the working population—were unemployed, resulted in the Flour Riot of 1837. The *New York Commercial Register* reported on the riot: "Barrels of flour, by dozens, fifties and hundreds were tumbled into the street . . . thrown in rapid succession from the windows. . . . [And] numbers of women were engaged . . . filling . . . their aprons with flour and making off with it."

Section 4 Review Answers

1. (a) section, see p. 124, (b) capitalist, see p. 126

2. (a) Denmark Vesey, see p. 128, (b) Nat Turner, see p. 128

3. (a) North, see p. 124, (b) Northeast, see p. 124, (c) Old Northwest, see p. 124, (d) South, see p. 127

4. The crops grown in the Old Northwest needed to be processed and marketed by the specialized personnel who lived in cities.

5. Southern planters and farmers were just as much developers and entrepreneurs as were the factory owners and businesspeople of the North.

6. Some ran away; others refused to work at the pace demanded by owners, pretending not to hear or understand; still others rebelled by stealing or destroying property.

7. Answers should suggest that the southern economy was like that of a colony in that it produced mainly raw materials to be shipped elsewhere for processing. The North produced, processed, and often sold goods within the region.

In Depth

Historical Misconceptions

A common misconception is that the South had its own economic system, including slavery, which was quite independent of the North. "With us every branch and pursuit of life, every trade, profession, and occupation, is dependent upon the North," an Alabama newspaper complained. "In northern vessels (the southerner's) products are carried to market, his cotton is ginned in northern gins, his sugar is crushed and preserved by northern machinery; his rivers are navigated by northern steamboats . . . and a Yankee clock sits upon his mantelpiece."

same, because of their wealth, slaveholders did possess great influence in politics, society, and of course, the economy. And the South would have been very poor without the African American workers who built its economy. They made up more than half of the population of South Carolina and Mississippi in 1860.

Life on Small and Large Farms The life of enslaved Americans varied depending on circumstances. The typical slaveholder owned only a few African Americans. On small farms, enslaved people often worked side by side with their owners and their families. They sometimes ate together and slept in the same house. Close personal relationships sometimes developed; but, just as often, enslaved workers endured all manner of cruelties without a larger community to turn to for support and protection.

Most enslaved Americans, however, lived on plantations. There they had the benefits of a sizeable community of people, usually including twenty or more African Americans. But plantation life had serious drawbacks in contrast to life on a small farm. Labor could be harsher, for example. Plantation workers frequently toiled in gangs under the supervision of foremen and slave drivers.

For enslaved women in particular, life could be extremely difficult. In addition to bearing and caring for their own children and taking care of their households, they cooked and served food, cleaned houses and clothes, and labored in the fields. Especially hard work was required of them at harvest time in the late summer and fall. In addition to the drudgery of plantation life, they also had to endure rape or the threat of rape by slave owners.

Slavery as an Economic Relationship Whether enslaved people lived closely with their owners or not, their relationship was always affected by the fact that slavery was based on economics. Owners exploited enslaved humans in order to get work done; they saw enslaved people as property that performed labor. In a bill of sale from 1811, an enslaved woman named Eve and her child, at a price of $156.00, are listed between a plow for $1.60 and "Eight Fancy Chairs" for $9.25. Such treatment of humans as property was the essence of slavery.

Enslaved African Americans Resist

Like working-class people in the North, enslaved people in the South fought back on occasion. One open resistance in the early 1820s was led by **Denmark Vesey**, an African American in Charleston, South Carolina. Having bought his freedom with a lottery jackpot, he supported himself as a carpenter. A preacher at the local African Methodist Episcopal Church, Vesey was well read and determined in his principles. He was impatient with African Americans who would not stand up to whites. According to the report of his conspiracy, when he saw an enslaved person step aside to allow a white man to pass him on the street, Vesey

> would rebuke him, and observe that all men were born equal, and that he was surprised that anyone would degrade himself by such conduct; that he would never cringe to the whites, nor ought anyone who had the feelings of a man. When answered, We are slaves, he would sarcastically and indignantly reply, "You deserve to remain slaves."

Vesey and several allies, including the African-born Gullah Jack, planned to take over Charleston in July 1822. About eighty participants were to act in six units arranged by African origins.

But Vesey was betrayed by some of his followers. The governor of South Carolina called out five companies of troops in June, and the rebellion was smashed before it could get started. Before the end of the summer, thirty-five African Americans were hanged, including Vesey, and another thirty-seven were banished from South Carolina.

Nat Turner, a well-educated, thirty-one-year-old African American preacher who believed he acted with divine inspiration, also planned a rebellion. In 1831 he led about seventy enslaved people in southeastern Virginia in an uprising. The rebels killed fifty-five whites. Eventually, local militia captured most of the

RESOURCE DIRECTORY

Teaching Resources

rebels. The state of Virginia hanged about twenty of them, including Turner. Crowds of frightened and angry whites rioted and slaughtered about a hundred African American bystanders who had no part in the plot.

The aborted Vesey and Turner rebellions led to harsher slave laws. Virginia and North Carolina passed laws against teaching enslaved people to read. Criticizing slavery in speech or writing was forbidden. Whites throughout the South became extremely frightened of possible rebellions. In South Carolina, Edwin C. Holland wrote that enslaved African Americans were

the barbarians who would, IF THEY COULD, become the DESTROYERS of our race.

Yet rebellions of enslaved people in the region were rare. More commonly, enslaved people resisted slavery in less dramatic fashion. Some ran away, though when caught, they might be forcibly returned. Others refused to work at the pace established by their owners, pretending not to hear or understand. Yet another form of resistance was stealing or destroying property.

Though slavery was based on a need for labor, like the relationship between entrepreneurs and workers in the North, it obviously encouraged different attitudes toward labor. The separation between work and home transforming the North did not occur in the South because most people, enslaved or not, continued to work at or near home. Thus, the Market Revolution took different forms in the North and South. Both regions were expanding capitalistic societies. But the North was a world of farms and cities, banks and factories, while the South was a world of farms and plantations producing cotton and other staples. The North adopted new technologies eagerly, the South more slowly. These differences laid the foundation for conflict in the 1850s and 1860s.

Viewpoints
On Slavery

Because the economy of the South depended on slave labor, southerners began to defend the institution against a growing antislavery movement. *In the quotations below, how does the viewpoint of the formerly enslaved man conflict with the southerner's viewpoint?*

In Defense of Slavery

"A merrier being does not exist on the face of the globe than the Negro slave of the United States. They are happy and contented, and the master is much less cruel than is generally imagined. Why then . . . should we attempt to disturb his contentment by planting in his mind a vain and indefinite desire for liberty—something which he cannot understand?"

Professor Thomas R. Dew, William and Mary College, address to the Virginia legislature, 1832

In Opposition to Slavery

"I thank God I am not property now, but am regarded as a man like yourself. . . . You may perhaps think hard of us for running away from slavery, but as for myself, I have but one apology to make for it, which is this: I have only to regret that I did not start at an early period."

Henry Bibb, who escaped from slavery with his family, in a letter to his former master, 1844

Viewpoints Activity On Slavery, found in the Unit 1 folder, pp. 120–121, provides extended quotations from both sides of the debate over slavery in the early nineteenth century.

Quiz found in the Unit 1 folder, p. 111, covers the main ideas in this section as well as the key terms.

SECTION 4 REVIEW

Key Terms, People, and Places

1. Define (a) section, (b) capitalist.
2. Identify (a) Denmark Vesey, (b) Nat Turner.
3. Identify (a) North, (b) Northeast, (c) Old Northwest, (d) South.

Key Concepts

4. How did agriculture in the Old Northwest encourage the growth of cities?
5. Explain why, despite the South's use of slave rather than free labor, that region can be considered as capitalist as the North.
6. Describe the most common forms of rebellion among enslaved people.

Critical Thinking

7. **Making Comparisons** You have read that the economy of the South was like that of a colony. Was the economy of the North also like that of a colony? Explain your response.

Answer to . . .

Viewpoints

Dew states that enslaved people cannot grasp the concept of liberty; Bibb makes it clear that he understands and treasures his freedom very well. For a more thorough examination of the slavery issues, see the Resource Directory below.

Reteach

Ask students to write one-paragraph summaries of the economy of the North and of the South from the perspective of either a northern factory owner, a factory laborer, a plantation owner, or an enslaved African American.

4. CLOSE

Reinforcing the Big Idea

As the economies of the two regions developed differently, northerners and southerners began to feel that their interests were not compatible. The next section covers the hectic politics of the second American party system and the Age of Jackson.

The Age of Jackson

SECTION 5

The Age of Jackson

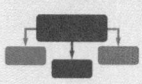

Connecting to the Big Idea

See page 104B. Explain to students that Andrew Jackson's term in office was marked by a commitment to minimize the role of national government in an effort to clear a path to success for the ordinary citizen. Ask what events characterized Jackson's two terms in office.

Objectives

● Describe how National Republicans and Jacksonian Democrats viewed the role of national government in the economic development of the United States.
● Explain why Jackson opposed South Carolina's attempt to strike down a federal law.
● Describe Jackson's response to the Cherokee when the state of Georgia seized their land.

Bellringer

Ask students to write a statement indicating their position on an issue such as raising the legal driving age, censoring or rating music and movies, or imposing a town curfew for teenagers. Students should indicate how they might organize to support their position.

Reading Strategy

Relating to Topic Have students answer the following question as they read: What were the political differences between the Democratic and the National Republican parties, and what role did these differences play in getting candidates elected to office?

SECTION PREVIEW

During his presidency, Andrew Jackson became the symbol for an age in which Americans first began to believe that elected officials should act according to the views of the voters.

Key Concepts
• National Republicans such as John Quincy Adams and Henry Clay argued that government power should be used to promote economic development. Jacksonian Democrats strongly opposed this role for the national government.
• Despite his opposition to a strong national government, President Andrew Jackson opposed one state's attempt to strike down a federal law.
• Jackson refused to support the Cherokee when the state of Georgia seized their land.

Key Terms, People, and Places
American System, second American party system, secede, Trail of Tears; John C. Calhoun, Henry Clay, National Republicans, Jacksonian Democrats

A new clash between political parties began in the election of 1824. During the campaign, supporters of candidate John Quincy Adams distributed this decorated box.

O n July 4, 1826—the fiftieth anniversary of the Declaration of Independence—Thomas Jefferson and John Adams both died. This remarkable coincidence was just one among many signs that the generation that had brought the United States into being no longer was leading administrations and holding membership in Congress. Two years before, in 1824, James Monroe had ended his second term in office. In 1824, for the first time in the brief history of the nation, none of the presidential candidates could boast of having been a leader during the Revolution.

The Election of 1824

The four main candidates in the election of 1824 were John Quincy Adams of Massachusetts, John C. Calhoun of South Carolina, Henry Clay of Kentucky, and Andrew Jackson of Tennessee.

The Accomplishments of Adams The son of Abigail and John Adams, John Quincy Adams had become a Jeffersonian Republican nearly twenty years earlier when he was a senator. He had made his reputation as a diplomat, a role that suited him. While he was well educated and highly ethical, he was also considered to be cold and formal. While serving as secretary of state under Monroe, he had negotiated the Adams-Onís Treaty of 1819, by which the United States acquired Florida from Spain.

Another legacy of Adams's diplomatic career was the Monroe Doctrine of 1823, which Adams largely wrote. During the 1820s, every Spanish colony in the Western Hemisphere except Cuba and Puerto Rico had won its independence. The Monroe Doctrine warned European governments to stay out of the Americas and allow the new nations to develop on their own.

But neither the government nor the merchants of the United States had any intention of leaving the former Spanish colonies alone. The new countries possessed huge markets that attracted Americans. Moreover, the United States did not have the armed forces necessary to make the Monroe Doctrine anything but a paper declaration of policy. Still, the policy was a bold one for a young nation whose Capitol had been burned to the ground by a foreign army only a decade earlier. And much of the credit went to John Quincy Adams.

Calhoun and Clay: South and West Born in South Carolina, **John C. Calhoun** had served in the United States Congress and as Monroe's

---

RESOURCE DIRECTORY

Teaching Resources

Reproducible Lesson Plan found in the Unit 1 folder, p. 103, provides a summary of the Section 5 lesson plan content.

Alternate Lesson Plan: Learning Styles found in the Alternate Lesson Plans folder, p. 67, provides a setting for students to "grade" the Jackson administration and is especially useful for visual or auditory learners.

Guided Reading and Review found in the Unit 1 folder, p. 112, provides a structure for reading and mastering the key concepts and reviewing the key terms for Section 5. (Guided Practice)

secretary of war. A brilliant man, Calhoun had been an early supporter of national economic policies. But in the 1820s, he was beginning to shift toward defending southern sectional interests, which required protection of both slavery and the agricultural exports the slavery system produced, especially cotton. He withdrew from the race when he saw a chance to become Vice President. Besides, another candidate, William H. Crawford of Georgia, was already representing southern interests.

Henry Clay, a former speaker of the House of Representatives and a United States senator from Kentucky, was the most dynamic and colorful politician of his generation. "Harry of the West," as he was called, was a slaveholder and a man of great passions. He wanted to be President, and he was willing to make a political deal if it would improve his chances at a later time.

Jackson's Candidacy Catches Fire Finally, there was the wild card—Andrew Jackson. Jackson had served in the Senate in the 1790s and was a wealthy plantation owner near Nashville, Tennessee. Yet his fame rested not on these eminent positions in government or society, but mainly on military exploits like his victory at New Orleans in 1815. Jackson's iron will and his impulsive, passionate personality made him enormously popular. Those same characteristics also worried many people who saw him as a poorly educated and ill-tempered military chieftain.

As 1824 progressed, Jackson's candidacy caught fire. Like Jefferson, Jackson believed in the common people, whose support he rapidly gained. The general won the majority of the people's votes, but neither he nor any other candidate received a majority of votes in the Electoral College. Thus the House of Representatives had to choose a President from among the top vote-getters. That left Jackson and Adams as the main rivals—and Adams won a majority of votes in the House.

But Jackson and his followers believed that Adams's victory was the result of what they called "a corrupt bargain" with Clay. They charged that Clay, in return for giving Kentucky's votes to Adams, had been given the post of secretary of state. Adams and Clay

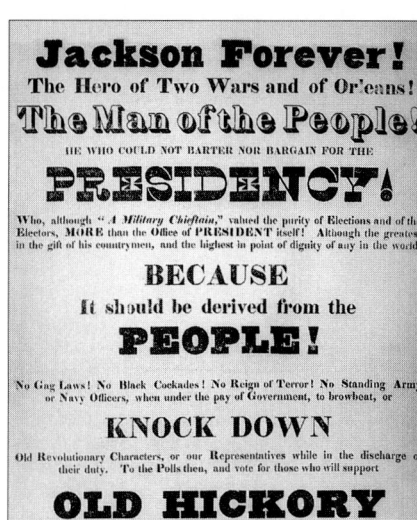

both denied the accusation, but a great many Americans believed it.

Using Historical Evidence This poster praises Andrew "Old Hickory" Jackson for honoring the constitutional election system in 1824 even though it cost him the presidency. *How does the poster describe Andrew Jackson?*

MAKING CONNECTIONS

In the election of 1824, the candidate chosen by the majority of American voters was denied the presidency. Such a result is still possible today. Do you think the Constitution should be changed so this can no longer happen? Why or why not?

Two New Parties Face Off

While Jackson plotted to get his revenge in the next election, President Adams and Secretary of State Clay tried to establish a federal policy of actively intervening in the economy of the nation. In 1825 Adams said:

> The spirit of improvement is abroad upon the earth. . . . Let us not be unmindful that liberty is power; and that the tenure [holding] of power by man is . . . upon condition that it shall be exercised . . . to improve the condition of himself and his fellowmen.

To Improve the Nation Simply put, Adams believed that the national government should

2. INSTRUCT

Explain/Discuss

Explain that Jackson's actions as President were consistent with the political views he expressed before his election. Ask how these views gave the common man hope and encouraged the spirit of capitalism. Discuss why Jackson's veto of the rechartering of the Bank of the United States was considered a defining moment in his presidency. What was the eventual effect of this decision?

Caption Answer to . . .

Using Historical Evidence

As "The Hero of Two Wars and [New] Orleans" and as "The Man of the People."

Answer to . . .

MAKING CONNECTIONS

Reform of the Electoral College is a complex issue with many pros and cons; students may support either the principle of majority vote by the people or the existing Electoral College system.

Interpreting Tables

The National Republican government wanted the federal government to support such improvements; the Jacksonian Democrats wanted the individual states to be responsible for them.

Analyze

Analyze the role of specific economic interests in the second American party system. How does the debate over the role of the national government in the economy continue in politics today?

Second American Party System

National Republicans/Whigs	Jacksonian Democrats
Example: John Quincy Adams	Example: Andrew Jackson
Federal government should take a leadership role	Federal government should remain as inactive as possible
Federal government should support internal improvements, such as roads and bridges	The individual states should be responsible for internal improvements
For national bank	Against national bank
Tended to be middle-class or well-established Protestants	Tended to be ambitious slave-holders, small farmers, non-Protestants, and working class

Interpreting Tables
Both National Republicans and Jacksonian Democrats agreed on the goals of the American system, but disagreed on how to reach those goals. *How did each party want to bring about internal improvements?*

take the lead in developing the economy. The new administration was proposing what Secretary Clay called an **American System.** Under this system, the government would support internal improvements, including roads, canals, bridges, lighthouses, universities, and many other projects. The purpose of the improvements was to encourage the development of American industries. In addition, the government would put a high tariff, or import tax, on goods brought into the United States. This tariff would make foreign goods more expensive and encourage Americans to buy goods manufactured in the United States.

The Election of 1828 Few politicians quarreled with the goal of making American industries stronger. But many believed, as did Andrew Jackson, that the United States government had no business taking such an active role in the economic development of the nation. They argued that Americans wanted the national government to leave them alone, and that society and the economy actually would work better without government interference.

Both Jackson and Adams had once been Jeffersonian Republicans, the party that had quarreled with Federalists, largely over constitutional issues. Now the stupendous changes of the Market Revolution were pushing economic issues to the forefront of the debate, and once again politicians were choosing sides.

The supporters of Adams and Clay began to call themselves **National Republicans.** They believed they were true to the Jeffersonian spirit of improvement. The followers of Jackson called themselves Democrats, a shortened form of Democrat-Republicans, the old name of the Jeffersonian Republicans. Historians often refer to them as **Jacksonian Democrats.** Members of this party believed that they were true to the Jeffersonian commitment to frugal, or minimal, government. This new face-off in politics, in which the National Republicans challenged the Jacksonian Democrats, is now known as the **second American party system.** It is summarized in the table at left. ☉

Some clever state politicians, including New York senator Martin Van Buren, agreed with Jackson's opposition to a powerful national government. They joined together in supporting Jackson when the election of 1828 rolled around. In this election, voters realized that their choice would determine the role the national government would play in their lives. As a result, more than twice as many men voted in 1828 than had voted in 1824, and most of these new voters threw their support to the man of the people, Andrew Jackson. With this sizable following, Jackson trounced Adams.

Federal Policy in the Age of Jackson

Like Jefferson, Andrew Jackson tried not to do much as President. He used his veto power to keep the government as inactive as possible, rejecting more acts of Congress than the six previous Presidents combined. Typical was the Maysville Road Veto of 1830. Congress had voted money to build a road from the Ohio River at Maysville across Kentucky to Lexington, but Jackson vetoed the bill. He did not object to the road; he just thought the state of Kentucky, not the national government, should build it.

Jackson Defends the Spoils System For many years, victorious office seekers had appointed their friends and supporters to public office in their administrations. This practice, known as patronage, became official when

RESOURCE DIRECTORY

Teaching Resources

☉ **Visual Learning Activity** The Jackson Ticket, found in the Unit 1 folder, p. 132, uses election tickets from 1828 to show the images used to win support for the Democratic candidates.

Andrew Jackson took office. He dismissed more than two hundred previous presidential appointees and nearly two thousand other officeholders and replaced them with Jacksonian Democrats.

Patronage under Jackson became known as the spoils system. In this case, the spoils, or booty taken from a conquered enemy, were government jobs for party supporters. Jackson defended the system on the grounds that any intelligent person could perform the duties required and that "rotation in office" would prevent a small group from controlling the government. His support for the spoils system contributed to Jackson's image as the champion of the common man.

The Bank War The defining moment of Jackson's presidency came in 1832. The President had a deep personal hatred of the Bank of the United States. He had lost money to the first bank in the 1790s, and he had never agreed with the establishment of the second bank in 1816. Like many Americans, Jackson believed the Bank of the United States was a "monster" institution. He held it responsible for the Panic of 1819 and the hard times that had followed.

Under law, the Bank of the United States could only operate until 1836, unless Congress extended the life of the bank by issuing it a new charter. Supporters of the bank, including Senator Henry Clay, Senator Daniel Webster of Massachusetts, and the president of the bank, Nicholas Biddle, decided to recharter it four years early, partly to embarrass Jackson. They expected that he would offend his followers by allowing the bank to continue.

The Bank of the United States already had survived one challenge. In a complicated scheme to hinder the bank, the state of Maryland had tried unsuccessfully to make the bank pay a tax, and then imposed a large penalty when it failed to do so. The national government claimed the fine was illegal, and the dispute reached the Supreme Court in 1819. In *McCulloch* v. *Maryland*, Chief Justice John Marshall went to the heart of the issue by declaring the fine illegal and the bank itself constitutional. The powers of the federal government were greater than those spelled out in the Constitution, Marshall said. He based his argument on Article I, Section 8, which states that Congress has the right "to make all laws necessary and proper" for carrying out the powers granted it under the Constitution. Thus Congress had the power to create such a bank if it wished. Furthermore, Chief Justice Marshall stressed that

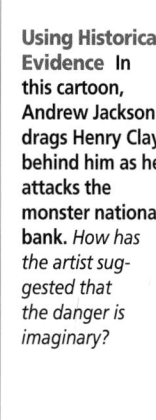

Using Historical Evidence In this cartoon, Andrew Jackson drags Henry Clay behind him as he attacks the monster national bank. *How has the artist suggested that the danger is imaginary?*

Activity

(The clock icon indicates an activity that can be successfully conducted within a class period. Each chapter has at least one such activity.)

Creating a Campaign Slogan
Ask students to create a campaign slogan for the 1828 election for either John Quincy Adams or Andrew Jackson, based on the candidate's view of the role of government in the economy. **LEP**

Caption Answer to ...

Using Historical Evidence

The artist has shown the battle taking place at night in Jackson's bedroom, as if it were just a bad dream.

In Depth

Biography

Born to privilege and power, Nicholas Biddle (1786–1844) led the attempt to recharter the Bank of the United States in 1832. After being reelected President, a furious Jackson ordered all government deposits removed from the bank. Biddle then refused to extend credit for existing loans and withdrew credit for new loans. Jackson blamed the ensuing economic downturn on Biddle, whose supporters claimed that he "used the great power of the institution effectively to serve the financial needs of a growing country."

because the national government had created the bank, no state had the power to tax it. "The power to tax is the power to destroy," he pointed out. No state could destroy by taxes what the federal government under the Constitution had created.

In 1832 the supporters of the Bank of the United States acted without understanding the popularity of the President or the unpopularity of the bank. Jackson vetoed the act of Congress that rechartered the bank, dooming it to close in 1836. The President justified his action as a protection of the rights of ordinary citizens. In a lengthy veto message, he attacked the bank as a tool of greedy aristocrats:

*I*t is to be regretted that the rich and powerful too often bend the acts of government to their selfish purposes. Distinctions in society will always exist under every just government . . . but when the laws undertake . . . to make the rich richer and the potent more powerful, the humble members of society—the farmers, mechanics, and laborers—who have neither the time nor the means of

securing like favors to themselves, have a right to complain of the injustice of their Government.

The National Republicans thought they could use the issue of Jackson's veto against him in the election of 1832. They changed their name to the Whigs, after the party in the British Parliament that had opposed the king during the 1700s, and ran Henry Clay for President. Criticizing Jackson's veto, however, was a mistaken strategy. As in 1828, Jackson won the election by a huge margin.

The Nullification Crisis

During his second administration, Jackson proved equal to yet another challenge. Supporters of the American System had passed the Tariff of 1828, which put a high tax on imports in order to encourage manufacturing within the United States. Most manufacturers, however, were in the North, and southerners did not like paying higher prices for goods to help northerners make a profit. They called the Tariff of 1828 the Tariff of Abominations, after the term *abomination*

The issue of nullification burst on the national scene in 1830, in a debate on the subject between Massachusetts senator Daniel Webster (standing) and South Carolina senator Robert Hayne (seated, hands before him). Webster rejected nullification, claiming it would make the Constitution "a rope of sand" that would not hold the states together.

 **RESOURCE DIRECTORY**

Teaching Resources

American Profiles Activity found in the Unit 1 folder, p. 119, profiles Sequoyah, the Cherokee who developed an original system for writing the Cherokee language.

used in the Bible for something especially horrible or monstrous. In 1832, after passage of yet another tariff act, South Carolina declared the tariffs "null, void, and no law, nor binding upon this State, its officers or citizens." In doing so, it raised the question of nullification: did a state have the right to nullify, or declare illegal, a law passed by Congress? South Carolina also went further by threatening to **secede,** or withdraw, from the United States if its nullification was not respected.

You might expect that Jackson would be sympathetic to South Carolina. After all, he was a supporter of "negative" government, or using government power to protect the people from the government itself. He had put federal power to work attacking politicians he considered corrupt and laws that he thought would prevent the people from fully enjoying their liberty. Thus he had acted to destroy the Bank of the United States. Furthermore, he understood southern issues; he was a slaveholder himself. Yet South Carolina's nullification outraged him.

Why would a believer in negative government take offense when a state asserted its rights? The explanation of this seeming contradiction is simple. President Jackson believed that in defying the laws of the United States, South Carolina was defying the will of the people. That he would never allow.

At Jackson's urging, Congress passed the Force Bill in 1833, which compelled the state of South Carolina to collect the Tariff Act duties. The President threatened to send 50,000 troops to the defiant state. But Henry Clay engineered a compromise that ended the crisis. Congress reduced some of the import duties, and South Carolina cancelled its Nullification Act—although as an act of continued defiance it nullified the Force Bill at the same time.

The Trail of Tears

⭐ President Jackson also used federal power negatively to support the relocation of the Cherokee, Choctaw, Creek, Chickasaw, and Seminole peoples to what is now Oklahoma. He had a deep prejudice against Native Americans and believed that they would prevent white people from moving west and opening up land for cotton production.

Many Americans shared Jackson's prejudice against Native Americans. In 1829 Georgia seized Cherokee land for cotton growers. After appealing to the United States Senate with little result, the Cherokee appealed directly to the American people in 1830. In that appeal, the Cherokee said:

A navy ship bore this figurehead of Andrew Jackson in 1834. In an action typical of the strong political feelings of the time, someone sawed off the head soon after the carving was fastened in place.

The people of the United States will have the fairness to reflect, that all the treaties between them and the Cherokee were made . . . for the benefit, of the whites. . . . We wish to remain on the land of our fathers. We have a perfect and original right to remain without interruption. . . . The treaties with us and laws of the United States made in pursuance of treaties, guaranty our residence. . . . It cannot be that the community we are addressing, remarkable for its intelligence and religious sensibilities, and preeminent [admired] for its devotion to the rights of man, will lay aside this appeal.

Two years later, Chief Justice Marshall, in the case *Worcester* v. *Georgia,* ruled that Georgia's action was unconstitutional and should not be allowed. But Jackson and Georgia ignored the Supreme Court, which had no power to enforce its decision. In 1837 and 1838, the United States Army gathered about fifteen thousand Cherokee and forced them to migrate west.

On this nightmare journey, which has come to be called the **Trail of Tears,** about one out of every four Cherokees died of exposure or disease. In an added outrage, the $6 million spent by the federal government to relocate the Cherokee was charged against the $9 million

In Depth

Multicultural Perspectives

Sequoyah, a citizen of the Cherokee nation, spoke no English. But he admired the way that some English-speaking people could make marks on sheets of paper—"leaves" Sequoyah called them—and make the marks "talk" back to them. In 1809 he began making a set of symbols for the sounds in the Cherokee language. When he was finished, he had an syllabary of eighty-six characters. (See American Profiles Activity in the Resource Directory at left.)

Section 5 Review Answers

1. (a) American System, see p. 132, (b) second American party system, see p. 132, (c) secede, see p. 135, (d) Trail of Tears, see p. 135

2. (a) John C. Calhoun, see p. 130, (b) Henry Clay, see p. 131, (c) National Republicans, see p. 132, (d) Jacksonian Democrats, see p. 132

3. National Republicans believed that government should take the lead in developing the American economy. Jacksonian Democrats believed that they were being true to the Jeffersonian commitment to minimal government.

4. Jackson believed that in defying the laws of the United States, South Carolina was defying the will of the people.

5. Jackson held a deep prejudice against Native Americans who, he believed, would prevent white people from moving west and opening up land for cotton production.

6. Questions should focus on internal improvements or federal interference in the economy, for example: "Do you support a national bank?" "Do you support 'negative' government?"

Reteach

Ask students to explain the term *negative government* and to give examples of its application during Jackson's two terms in office.

4. CLOSE

Reinforcing the Big Idea

The Market Revolution created a split in American politics that resulted in the development of two distinct parties. In 1828, the people elected Andrew Jackson as their new leader. Jackson's presidency was marked by a commitment to the interests of the common man and the belief that it was the right of every white American male to compete and make money.

William Henry Harrison was known as "Tippecanoe" because he had fought in the battle by that name. Whigs in 1840 campaigned for him and running mate John Tyler with the slogan "Tippecanoe and Tyler too."

that the Cherokee had been forced to accept for their lands.

The Age of Jackson Ends

Jackson's presidency was marked by his strong personality, his unsinkable courage—and his quick temper. To many Americans, he seemed a larger-than-life figure, a tough, stubborn man who embodied the spirit of the frontier.

After two terms, Andrew Jackson left the presidency. The next President, Martin Van Buren, whom Jackson had supported as a candidate, was not as popular as the general. The Panic of 1837 struck during his term. In this severe depression, caused in part by the end of the national bank, thousands of people lost their jobs and poverty grew worse in American cities.

When the next election year arrived in 1840, the depression was still dragging on. The Whigs did what they could to imitate the Democrats. They chose William Henry Harrison as their candidate for President, a military hero like Jackson. They boasted that Harrison, too, was a plain man of the people, and that he had lived in a log cabin. In fact, he was the son of an aristocratic family and had grown up in a mansion. It was a fierce campaign, and over 80 percent of eligible voters cast ballots. Many voted in hopes that a change might end the depression.

Harrison defeated President Van Buren, only to be defeated in turn by illness. He caught a cold while giving a lengthy inaugural speech and died of pneumonia a month later. Vice President John Tyler, who took over as President, was more of a Jacksonian Democrat than a Whig, and his term was largely one of fruitless quarreling between the parties.

Much as Whigs and Jacksonians quarreled, however, they almost all agreed that an essential ingredient of American liberty was the right to compete and to make money. Politicians argued about the effects and the course of the Market Revolution. But rare was the political leader who did not believe that it had brought unparalleled economic and social progress to the United States of America.

SECTION 5 REVIEW

Key Terms, People, and Places
1. Define (a) American System, (b) second American party system, (c) secede, (d) Trail of Tears.
2. Identify (a) John C. Calhoun, (b) Henry Clay, (c) National Republicans, (d) Jacksonian Democrats.

Key Concepts
3. What was the main difference in outlook between National Republicans and Jacksonian Democrats?

4. Why did Jackson oppose nullification?
5. Why did Jackson fail to support the Cherokee when Georgia took their land?

Critical Thinking
6. **Formulating Questions** What questions would you have asked a politician during the Age of Jackson to determine whether he was a Whig or a Jacksonian Democrat?

 RESOURCE DIRECTORY

Teaching Resources

 Quiz found in the Unit 1 folder, p. 113, covers the main ideas in this section as well as the key terms.

 Chapter Test Forms A and B are found in the Unit 1 folder, pp. 133–138.

 Answer Keys found in the Unit 1 folder, pp. 145–157, provide answers to all student activities.

Media and Technology

Transparency
Graphic Organizer, G-2

Guided Reading Audiotapes
(English and Spanish)

Computer Test Bank

Determining Relevance

Determining relevance means discovering whether a logical connection exists between one item of information and another. If relevance does exist, you can use one item to learn about the other. For instance, you have seen that the Market Revolution led to increased opportunities for making money. You have also seen that a new political party system developed in the 1820s because politicians and voters were keenly interested in the role government should play in improving ways to make money. So you know that the Market Revolution is relevant to an understanding of American politics during this period.

Use the tables on this page and the following steps to practice determining the relevance of different pieces of information.

1. Identify the main purpose of each table. Study each table, including titles and headings. (a) What purpose does Table A serve? (b) What is the purpose of Table B? (c) What is the purpose of Table C?

2. Determine the relevance of the tables. Examine each table in the light of a specific need. (a) Imagine you want to find out how people who favored slavery voted in 1828. Which tables would be relevant? (b) Imagine you want to know which candidates in 1824 favored tariffs. Which tables would be most relevant? (c) Imagine you have used Table A to find the total votes cast for Jackson and Adams

in 1828. Now, however, you want to know how each section of the country voted in that election. Which table would now be relevant to your needs?

3. Use your understanding of the relevance of the tables to support an observation. (a) Using the relevant tables, support the statement that western states tended to be against the national bank. (b) Generally speaking, northerners favored the American System of tariffs and internal improvements more than southerners because the North had more industry. Explain how the tables support this generalization. (c) Imagine that you want to demonstrate to someone that in an election the popular vote is often closer than the vote in the Electoral College. Explain how the tables could be used to demonstrate this.

A. Presidential Elections, 1824 and 1828

			Votes Cast		
Year	Candidate	Political Party	Popular	Electoral	House of Representatives
1824	John Quincy Adams	No distinct party designations	108,740	84	13
	Andrew Jackson		153,544	99	7
	Henry Clay		47,136	37	0
	W. H. Crawford		46,618	41	4
1828	Andrew Jackson	Democratic	647,826	178	No vote needed
	John Quincy Adams	National Republican	508,064	83	

Source: *World Almanac & Book of Facts, 1993; Historical Statistics of the United States*

B. State Electoral Votes Cast for President, 1828

	Slave States		Free States		
	South	West	North	West	Total
Number of States	9	3	9	3	24
Number of Electoral Votes	86	28	123	24	261
Number of Democratic Electoral Votes	77	28	49	24	178
Number of National Republican Electoral Votes	9	0	74	0	83

Source: *Historical Statistics of the United States*

C. Candidate Profiles

Issue	Adams	Jackson
Slavery	Against	For
National Bank	For	Against
Protective Tariffs	For	Generally against
Federally Funded Internal Improvements	For	Against
Voting Rights for Propertyless Workers	Against	For

Historian's Toolbox Activity Determining Relevance, found in the Unit 1 folder, p. 122, uses tables of party affiliation and opinion from the 1990s to provide further practice with this skill.

Critical Thinking
Determining Relevance

Focus Determine the relevance of three tables of political information to specific questions about the Market Revolution.

Instruct Ask students to identify the information presented in each table. For example, ask students to identify the title and headings in Table A. Then have them summarize the information in the table. Repeat this process for Tables B and C. Finally, ask students how these three tables relate to one another and to the Market Revolution.

Extend See Historian's Toolbox Activity in the Resource Directory below.

Answers

1. (a) To describe the voting and results of the elections of 1824 and 1828; (b) to describe how different states voted for President in 1828; (c) to show the respective views of Adams and Jackson on various topics.

2. (a) A, B, and C (b) A and C (c) B

3. (a) Table B shows that all the western states voted for Jackson; Table A shows that the Democrat was Andrew Jackson; Table C shows that Jackson was against the national bank. (b) Table C shows that Adams was for federally funded internal improvements and protective tariffs; Table B shows that the North favored Adams over Jackson by a vote of 74 to 28 in the Electoral College. (c) Table A shows that the popular vote in 1828 was far closer than the electoral vote.

Understanding Key Terms, People, and Places

Terms
Students should refer to the definitions of the key terms in the chapter to write sentences that explains their meanings.

Matching
1. evangelical movement
2. political party
3. capital
4. commodity

True or False
1. false, Eli Whitney
2. true
3. true

Reviewing Main Ideas

1. Hamilton transformed the debts of all the states into a long-term investment in the United States government for the country's creditors.

2. The election of 1800 was a significant victory for the new political system in the United States. Despite a fierce campaign, power was peacefully transferred from the Federalists to the Jeffersonians.

3. The Louisiana Purchase allowed westward expansion all the way to Oregon.

4. With the new steam engines, boats could now easily travel against the current. Steamboats reduced the cost of transportation and commerce and increased the speed at which people could travel.

5. Work changed from being an activity centered on keeping the household running to something that could be bought and sold.

6. Banks provided the credit and cash necessary for entrepreneurs to invest or to buy land.

7. Products included flour, meal, pork products, and whiskey.

8. Manufacturers were supplying the goods that households had traditionally supplied for themselves.

9. Factory owners treated workers as a commodity; workers rebelled against long hours and low wages.

10. Jackson's veto was a victory for those who opposed a strong national government.

11. Jackson supported "negative government" and opposed laws that he thought would curtail liberty; he was also a slave owner. He was outraged at South Carolina's nullification, however, because he believed that the state was defying the will of the people.

Chapter Review

Understanding Key Terms, People, and Places

Key Terms.
1. political party
2. first American party system
3. excise
4. tariff
5. Whiskey Rebellion
6. precedent
7. Northwest Territory
8. black codes
9. Missouri Compromise
10. Industrial Revolution
11. Second Great Awakening
12. evangelical movement
13. Market Revolution
14. entrepreneur
15. capitalism
16. capital
17. household economy
18. commodity
19. centralize
20. section
21. capitalist
22. American System
23. second American party system
24. secede
25. Trail of Tears

People
26. Jeffersonian Republicans
27. Andrew Jackson
28. Eli Whitney
29. Denmark Vesey
30. Nat Turner
31. John C. Calhoun
32. Henry Clay
33. National Republicans
34. Jacksonian Democrats

Places
35. North
36. Northeast
37. Old Northwest
38. South

Terms For each term above, write a sentence that explains its meaning.

Matching Review the key terms in the list above. If you are not sure of a term's meaning, review its definition in the chapter. Then choose a term from the list that best matches each description below.
1. a new wave of religious revivals that took place in the early 1800s
2. group that runs candidates for political offices
3. a supply of wealth that can be used to produce goods
4. something that can be bought and sold

True or False Determine whether each statement is true or false. If it is true, write "true." If it is false, change the underlined name to make the statement true.
1. Denmark Vesey invented the cotton gin.
2. Nat Turner led an uprising of enslaved people in Virginia in 1831.
3. Andrew Jackson supported the spoils system.

Reviewing Main Ideas

Section 1 (pp. 106–109)
1. How was Alexander Hamilton able to change the national debt from a weakness to a strength?
2. Briefly explain the significance of the election of 1800.

Section 2 (pp. 112–117)
3. What was the effect of the Louisiana Purchase on the westward expansion of the United States?
4. Describe how steam power improved transportation in the first half of the 1800s.

Section 3 (pp. 120–123)
5. How did the meaning of work change during the first half of the 1800s?
6. Why were there more banks in 1830 than in 1780?

Section 4 (pp. 124–129)
7. What products did the farmers of the Old Northwest produce in the early 1800s?
8. What did the growth of factories and textile mills suggest about the role of the household?
9. Why did factory owners and workers clash during the early 1800s?

Section 5 (pp. 130–136)
10. What was the importance of Jackson's veto of the rechartering of the Second Bank of the United States?
11. Why might one expect Jackson to be sympathetic to South Carolina's attempt to nullify federal tariffs?
12. Describe the situation that led to the Trail of Tears.

---

12. In 1829, Georgia seized Cherokee land for cotton growers. Jackson, ignoring the Supreme Court's decision that Georgia's action was unconstitutional, sent the United States Army to force about fifteen thousand Cherokee to move west.

Thinking Critically

1. The election of 1800 was the first time that the United States had experienced a change in power. Under European monarchies, such a change had often been accompanied by violence. Americans were therefore unsure whether a peaceful transfer of power could actually be accomplished.

2. Answers will vary. Students should recognize that although population growth and migration have slowed significantly, many people today are separated from their families. Many people also still move frequently and are searching for a sense of connection among strangers.

Final Evaluation
Use the following guidelines to evaluate student activities:
● **Evidence of thoughtfulness** Do projects include the main ideas from the chapter?
● **Evidence of outside research** To what extent do projects reflect outside research?
● **Evidence of synthesis** Do projects demonstrate that students understand how topics are related?
● **Communication style** Do students convey their purpose to an audience in a clear, appealing way?

Thinking Critically

1. Identifying Assumptions Today we expect a peaceful transfer of power when Americans vote to change political parties in a presidential election. Why were people unable to make this assumption in the election of 1800?

2. Determining Relevance During the early republic, rapid population growth and constant migration created a nation of strangers. Are we a nation of strangers today?

Making Connections

1. Evaluating Primary Sources Review the primary source excerpt on page 134. Give evidence from the quotation that Jackson deserved his reputation as a "man of the people."

2. Understanding the Visuals Describe in your own words how the cotton gin on page 116 operates.

3. Writing About the Chapter It is 1830, and you are visiting the United States from abroad. You have visited once before, in 1783. Write a letter to your family at home describing the changes that you observe in American society. Create a list of the changes that you have observed between the two visits, as well as the things that have remained the same. Next, divide your lists into categories, such as "changes in the role of women," "new inventions," and "life for African Americans." Write a draft of your letter in which you compare your observations from your two visits, organized according to the categories you have chosen. Revise your letter, making certain that each idea is clearly explained. Proofread your letter and draft a final copy.

4. Using the Graphic Organizer This graphic organizer uses a web to organize information about the Market Revolution. Webs often can describe the attributes of a historical era. In this web, dotted lines show connections among these attributes. (a) Explain the connection between the development of centralized work and the decline of the household economy. (b) Create your own web map about Section 5, using this graphic organizer as an example.

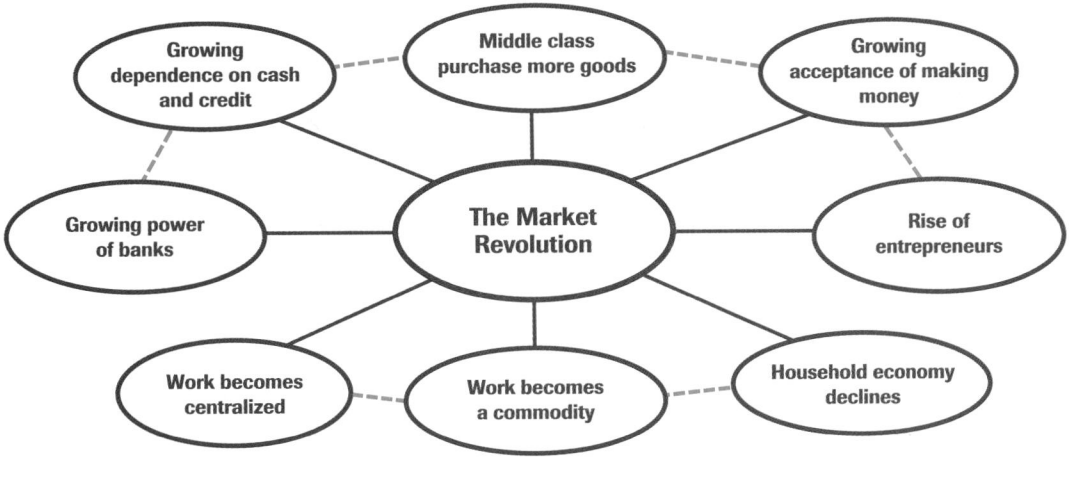

Making Connections

1. In the quotation Jackson speaks against the "rich and powerful" and on behalf of the "humble members of society."

2. Answers will vary but should mention what the cotton gin does and some of the steps involved.

3. Students' letters should show an understanding of the social and technological developments that took place during the early years of the Republic.

4. (a) Centralized manufacturing was a logical outgrowth of the decline of the household economy that resulted from the manufacture of goods outside the home. (b) Students' graphic organizers should show the Age of Jackson at the center of the web and include such attributes as a commitment to minimal government, Jackson's extensive use of the veto power, the prevalence of the spoils system, and Jackson's image as champion of the common man.

Connecting Literature and History

It is astonishing that the United States, barely half a century old, would hold a figurative hand in the face of the ancient, powerful, and aggressive European powers. Yet, with the issuing of the Monroe Doctrine in 1823, the United States dared to do just that.

Americans had already stood up to Great Britain twice—during the War for Independence and the War of 1812. In some sense, then, it is not surprising that President Monroe and John Quincy Adams felt it appropriate to issue the Monroe Doctrine. But at the same time, the boldness of the doctrine's wording leaves the reader who possesses some hindsight to question the wisdom of such a move. As students read the text of the Monroe Doctrine, remind them of the United States' position at the time as a relative newcomer to world affairs, and point out the dangers inherent in the strong language used in the doctrine.

Students will also find strong language used in President Jackson's letter to the Seminole. The remarkable feature of this excerpt, however, is the fact that the President was threatening not an outside aggressor, but people residing within its own borders. Students should focus on this fact as they read the letter.

Finally, in Walt Whitman's poem students will find a passionate expression of the invigorating growth of the United States during this period that is unparalleled by any mere recounting of facts and figures.

INSTRUCT

Divide the class into groups of five students each. Assign each group one of the source readings for this chapter. Tell students to analyze the excerpt they have been assigned. Have them begin by carefully reading the excerpt several times. Then ask

---

CHAPTER 4

SOURCE READINGS

The Monroe Doctrine

 *Primary Source*

INTRODUCTION One of the strong contenders in the election of 1824 was John Quincy Adams, who had won some measure of fame through his work as a diplomat and secretary of state. In 1823 he advised President James Monroe to issue a statement declaring that the United States would not stand idly by if European nations tried to interfere in the affairs of North or South America. The speech below was written in large part by Adams and given to Congress by President Monroe as part of his annual message to Congress. The policy eventually came to be known as the Monroe Doctrine.

VOCABULARY Before you read the selection, find the meaning of these words in a dictionary: comport, menace, candor, dependency.

The occasion has been judged proper for asserting, as a principle in which the rights and interests of the United States are involved, that the American continents, by the free and independent condition which they have assumed and maintain, are henceforth not to be considered as subjects for future colonization by any European powers. . . .

Of events in that quarter of the globe, with which we have so much intercourse and from which we derive our origin, we have always been anxious and interested spectators. The citizens of the United States cherish sentiments the most friendly in favor of the liberty and happiness of their fellow-men on that side of the Atlantic. In the wars of the European powers in matters relating to themselves we have never taken any part, nor does it comport with our policy so to do. It is only when our rights are invaded or seriously menaced that we resent injuries or make preparation for our defense.

With the movements in this hemisphere, we are of necessity more immediately connected, and by causes which must be obvious to all enlightened and impartial observers. The political system of the [European] powers is essentially different in this respect from that of America. . . . We owe it, therefore, to candor and to the amicable relations existing between the United States and those powers to declare that we should consider any attempt on their part to extend their system to any portion of this

This 1901 political cartoon illustrates the lasting impact of the Monroe Doctrine. In it, the Monroe Doctrine is a chicken coop in which European nations are caged, while the United States is the rooster that watches over Latin American countries.

hemisphere as dangerous to our peace and safety. With the existing colonies or dependencies of any European power we have not interfered and shall not interfere. But with the Governments who have declared their independence and maintained it, and whose independence we have, on great consideration and on just principles, acknowledged, we could not view any interposition[1] for the purpose of oppressing them, or controlling in any other manner their destiny, by any European power in any other light than as the manifestation of an unfriendly disposition toward the United States.

[1] intervention

THINKING ABOUT THE SELECTION

1. Why, according to the Monroe Doctrine, should the American continents no longer be open to European colonization?
2. Under what circumstances would the United States oppose European involvement in the affairs of South America?

Critical Thinking

3. **Identifying Assumptions** What assumption about the nations of North and South America does the Monroe Doctrine make?

President Jackson's Letter to the Seminole

Primary Source

INTRODUCTION One of Andrew Jackson's goals as President was to move all Native Americans west of the Mississippi River. Jackson was willing to go to great lengths to accomplish this goal. He wrote the letter below to the Seminole in 1835, advising them to move west voluntarily. In it, Jackson hinted at the measures he was prepared to take if the Seminole refused to leave. The Seminole did refuse to go, and a bloody seven-year war followed. The Second Seminole War ended in 1842 with most of the Seminole surrendering.

VOCABULARY Before you read the selection, find the meaning of these words in a dictionary: counsel, plunder, kindred, annuity.

My Children—
I am sorry to have heard that you have been listening to bad counsel. You know me. You know that I would not deceive nor advise you to do anything that was unjust or harmful. Open your ears and attend to what I shall now say to you. They are the words of a friend and the words of truth.

The white people are settling around you. The game has disappeared from your country. Your people are poor and hungry. All this you have known for some time. I tell you that you must go and that you will go. Even if you had a right to stay, how could you live where you now are? You have sold all your country. You have not a piece as large as a blanket to sit down upon. What is to support yourselves, your women, and children?

The tract you have given up will soon be surveyed and sold. Immediately afterwards, it will be occupied by a white population. You will soon be in a state of starvation. You will be forced to rob and plunder the property of our citizens. You will be resisted, punished, perhaps killed.

Jackson Forever!
The Hero of Two Wars and of Or'eans!
The Man of the People!
HE WHO COULD NOT BARTER NOR BARGAIN FOR THE
PRESIDENCY!
Who, although " A Military Chieftain," valued the purity of Elections and of the Electors, MORE than the Office of PRESIDENT itself! Although the greatest in the gift of his countrymen, and the highest in point of dignity of any in the world,
BECAUSE
It should be derived from the
PEOPLE!
No Gag Laws! No Black Cockades! No Reign of Terror! No Standing Army or Navy Officers, when under the pay of Government, to browbeat, or
KNOCK DOWN
Old Revolutionary Characters, or our Representatives while in the discharge of their duty. To the Polls then, and vote for those who will support
OLD HICKORY
AND THE ELECTORAL LAW.

A poster from the 1828 presidential campaign, in which Andrew Jackson defeated National Republican candidate John Quincy Adams.

them to discuss in their groups the language used in the piece. Is it angry? Thoughtful? Threatening? Then have students make a list of the words that contribute to the overall feel of the piece. Finally, ask students to turn to Chapter 4 in their textbooks and to find passages that are supported by their particular source reading. For example, students assigned either the Jackson letter or the Whitman poem might list the following excerpt from Section 3 of Chapter 4: "alongside this booming expansion and change there remained the continued enslavement of African Americans and the ongoing devastation of Native Americans." Students assigned the Monroe Doctrine might list this passage from Section 5: "The Monroe Doctrine warned European governments to stay out of the Americas and allow the new nations to develop on their own."

After students have finished, have them share their lists with the rest of the class. Discuss the fact that primary sources such as speeches and letters are used as evidence by historians when they are piecing together the events of the past. Pieces of literature such as Walt Whitman's poem often provide further evidence of the mood of the nation and the events that unfolded at a particular time.

ANSWERS TO

Thinking About the Selection

1. The American continents should no longer be open to European colonization because those nations that have won their independence wish to maintain it.
2. If a European nation attempted to take control of a nation in which it did not presently exert control and which had declared itself independent, that action would be opposed by the United States.
3. The Monroe Doctrine assumes that the nations of North and South America would welcome or accept United States intervention in their affairs.

Have students write a poem or short story that relates to the issuing of the Monroe Doctrine in 1823 or to President Jackson's goal to move all Native Americans west of the Mississippi. Encourage students to research those events further in such sources as *Hunted Like a Wolf: The Story of the Seminole War* by Milton Meltzer or *The Making of the Monroe Doctrine* by E. R. May. Read some of the students' work to the class.

SOURCE READINGS

Now is it not better peaceably to move to a fine, fertile country, occupied by your own kindred, where you can raise all the necessities of life, and where game is yet abundant? The annuities payable to you and the other arrangements made in your favor will make your situation comfortable. They will enable you to increase and improve.

If, therefore, you had a right to stay where you now are, still every true friend would advise you to move. But you have no right to stay, and you must go. I am very desirous that you should go peaceably and voluntarily. You shall be comfortably taken care of and kindly treated on the road. When you arrive in your new country, supplies will be issued to you for a year so that you can have ample time to provide for your future support.

But in case some of your rash young men should forcibly oppose your arrangements for removal, I have ordered a large military force to be sent among you. I have directed that one-third of your people, as provided for in the treaty, be removed during the present season. If you listen to the voice of friendship and truth, you will go quietly and voluntarily. But should you listen to the bad birds that are always flying about you and refuse to move, I have then directed the commanding officer to remove you by force. This will be done. I pray the Great Spirit, therefore, to incline you to do what is right.

Your friend,
A. Jackson
Washington, February 16, 1835

THINKING ABOUT THE SELECTION

1. According to President Jackson, why should the Seminoles leave?
2. If the Seminoles refuse to leave, what does Jackson warn them he will do?

Critical Thinking
3. **Distinguishing False from Accurate Images** Jackson signs this letter "Your friend." Do you think Jackson was the Seminoles' friend? Why or why not?

To a Locomotive in Winter 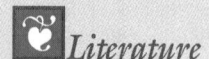Literature

Walt Whitman

INTRODUCTION Walt Whitman gave Americans poetry that was uniquely theirs. He departed from the traditional European style of writing in favor of a freer form that would give voice to the vastness and energy of the new United States. At first, his work was not popular, but by the time the poem below was written, in 1881, he was revered as one of the foremost literary figures in the world. "To a Locomotive in Winter" celebrates the railroads, which, with their expansion in the later part of the 1800s, gave a new excitement and urgency to the movement of the people of the United States.

VOCABULARY Before you read the selection, find the meaning of these words in a dictionary: recitative, panoply, ponderous, metrical, Muse, debonair, glib, unpent.

> Thee for my recitative,
> Thee in the driving storm even as now, the snow, the winter-day declining,
> Thee in thy panoply, thy measur'd dual throbbing and thy beat convulsive,
> Thy black cylindric body, golden brass and silvery steel,
> Thy ponderous side-bars, parallel and connecting rods, gyrating, shuttling at thy sides,
> Thy metrical, now swelling pant and roar, now tapering in the distance,
> Thy great protruding head-light fix'd in front,

ANSWERS TO

Thinking About the Selection
1. Jackson thinks the Seminole should leave because their lands are being taken over by white people and the game on which the Seminole depend for food and other necessities is disappearing. They will soon be starving and forced to steal in order to survive.
2. Jackson warns that if the Seminole refuse to leave he will send the military to forcibly remove them.

3. Jackson does not seem to be a friend to the Seminole. He seems to be acting in his own self-interest and what he perceives to be the interest of the white people of the United States. If he were indeed a friend, he would probably sit down with the Seminole and try to help them work out a way to coexist peacefully with the white people in the location of their choice.

"Lazell, Perkins and Co., Bridge-water, Ma." painted in 1858 by J.P. Newell.

Thy long, pale, floating vapor-pennants, tinged with delicate purple,
The dense and murky clouds out-belching from thy smoke-stack,
Thy knitted frame, thy springs and valves, the tremulous twinkle of thy wheels,
Thy train of cars behind, obedient, merrily following,
Through gale or calm, now swift, now slack, yet steadily careering;
Type of the modern—emblem of motion and power—pulse of the continent,
For once come serve the Muse and merge in verse, even as here I see thee,
With storm and buffeting gusts of wind and falling snow,
By day thy warning ringing bell to sound its notes,
By night thy silent signal lamps to swing.

Fierce-throated beauty!
Roll through my chant with all thy lawless music, thy swinging lamps at night,
Thy madly-whistled laughter, echoing, rumbling like an earthquake, rousing all,
Law of thyself complete, thine own track firmly holding,
(No sweetness debonair of tearful harp or glib piano thine,)
Thy trills of shrieks by rocks and hills return'd,
Launch'd o'er the prairies wide, across the lakes,
To the free skies unpent and glad and strong.

THINKING ABOUT THE SELECTION

1. What image of the railroad does Whitman's poem evoke? Give examples of words or phrases from the poem that help to convey this image.

2. How might a Native American writer of the late 1800s have described the railroad? Would the description likely be similar to Whitman's or different? Explain your answer.

Critical Thinking

3. Demonstrating Reasoned Judgment This poem was written in 1881, at the time when the railroads were relatively new in the United States. How does this poem describe the railroad and other aspects of the United States at the time?

ANSWERS TO

Thinking About the Selection

1. Whitman's poem evokes an image of the railroad as powerful and full of energy. Words and phrases used include: "throbbing," "ponderous," "pant and roar," "protruding," "dense," "emblem of motion and power," "pulse of the continent," "fierce-throated beauty," "earthquake," "strong."

2. One possible answer is that a Native American writer might see the railroad as an unwelcome intruder that brings noise and dirt into the natural world. The description and tone would likely differ from Whitman's.

3. The poem conveys the sense of newness, energy, and motion that was characteristic of the United States at the time.

The Nation's Beginnings to 1840

Using the Unit Summary

This textbook contains two units that review United States history before the twentieth century. Unit 1 provides a review of United States history to 1840. The Unit 1 Summary provides a four-page synopsis of Unit 1 that focuses on the key ideas covered in the review unit.

Listed below are some of the possible uses for the Unit 1 Summary.

To Review Unit 1 When students have completed Unit 1, you might want to assign the Unit 1 Summary as a tool for review.

To Set the Stage for Unit 2 The Unit 1 Summary may also be used to set the stage for Unit 2, which reviews United States history from 1815 to 1915.

To Omit Unit 1 If you wish to skip Unit 1, it may be helpful to assign the Unit 1 Summary to students as a review before starting the next unit.

The Nation's Beginnings to 1840

Most Americans think of our early history as remote, far removed from the issues and concerns we face today. What could Native Americans, European settlers, and enslaved Africans who lived hundreds of years ago—people long since dead and in most cases forgotten—have to do with our lives now?

The people who lived hundreds of years ago established the character of American society and developed the basic principles that define the United States.

The answer is: a great deal. The people who lived on this continent hundreds of years ago established the character of American society. They developed the basic principles that define our country. They shaped the environment and economic structures in fundamental ways. Focusing only on the recent past is like watching the last few moments of a movie: you miss the excitement that comes from understanding who the characters are and why they are in the situation in which you see them.

Cultural Encounters Through the 1700s

Long before Europeans and Africans arrived in North America, Native Americans occupied the continent. They were not all alike. They were divided into societies that spoke different languages, wore different kinds of clothing, ate different foods, and lived in different kinds of shelters. These Native American groups traded with one another and sometimes fought one another. Like all human societies, they were intent on protecting themselves and their way of life.

The Europeans Arrive The arrival of Spanish, English, French, and Dutch settlers in the 1500s and 1600s disrupted Native American societies. New diseases killed tens of thousands of Native Americans, and increased trade and complicated new political pressures sparked devastating wars between settlers and Native Americans and among Native Americans themselves.

The establishment of European colonies, however, also continued and strengthened the cultural diversity long present in North America. European nationalities were different from one another just as Native American groups were. For example, different European nationalities had different expectations about what their colonies should become. The English were interested in transforming, or completely changing, the environment into a version of their homeland. The Dutch and the French, on the other hand, tended to concentrate on extracting natural resources like fish and furs. These different expectations go a long way toward explaining why Europeans dealt with Native Americans in different ways.

Diverse Societies By the early 1700s, distinctive societies had emerged in North America. In some areas they were unique combinations of European and Native American ways of life. In New Mexico, the armed resistance of the Pueblo people had forced the Spanish to accept a mixed culture. In Canada, the French had established a colony dependent upon the fur trade, which could not operate without the cooperation of Native Americans.

In New England, English Puritans had worked to create a stable world, built around patriarchal households, religious devotion, and intense soul-searching. In the place of Native American villages and hunting grounds, the Puritans had established fields, cattle pastures, small towns, and even a few sizable cities.

In the Southeast, other groups of people from England had fashioned colonies structured around the production of staples, or key crops, such as tobacco and rice. But instead of small farms and towns, they had developed plantations, or large, relatively self-sufficient farms, to produce quantities of their staple crops for European markets.

The English people in the Southern Colonies needed labor to work their plantations, and this need brought another diverse group of people into the land that would someday become the United States. These new arrivals, West Africans, did not choose to migrate. They were enslaved and brought by force to the Americas. Though they had to endure exploitation and degradation, they brought economic success to the Southern Colonies and made outstanding contributions to American agriculture, architecture, music, and religion.

A New Nation Emerges, 1754–1800

In the second half of the 1700s, colonists of British descent emerged as the most powerful group in North America, in part because they were also the most numerous. Even as early as the mid-1700s, British colonists had felt increasingly crowded along the Atlantic seacoast and wanted to expand into the interior of the continent. In 1754 the colonists' need for more land led to a war between Great Britain and France for the control of their territories in North America. This conflict—the French and Indian War—was settled in 1763, several years after a decisive British victory. Although French-speaking people remained in Canada and the Great Lakes region, after the war the French government was no longer directly involved in North America.

The Colonists Demand Equal Treatment British colonists were jubilant at defeating the French, but they were also disturbed at the way British officials and soldiers had behaved toward them during the war. They were even more upset during the remainder of the 1760s and during the early 1770s when the British government tried to tax them to offset the cost of defending and governing the North American colonies.

Colonial gentlemen were particularly angry. Many of them thought the British were not allowing them the full rights of Englishmen—that the British were treating them as inferiors. Some colonists believed the British government intended to tax them into slavery, making them completely dependent on Great Britain.

These fears made sense in British colonial society. Most colonists believed that human beings were fundamentally unequal and that some people were more important than others. White gentlemen—men with enough property to be independent—dominated colonial societies. Women, servants, and enslaved people were considered to be secondary to white gentlemen. They had roles to play in society, but no real power.

Respected at home, colonial gentlemen saw no reason they should be slighted by the British government. When it seemed to colonists that government was treating them much as they themselves treated their women and enslaved workers, the colonists reacted at first by petitioning for their rights and finally by fighting for them. After a year of armed clashes with the British, in 1776 the colonists declared their independence and created a new nation—the United States.

In the course of a war that lasted until 1783, the people of the United States did indeed win their independence. But they faced even greater challenges than that. In bringing about the American Revolution, they had broken away from Britain, and now they had to define what kind of a nation they were. What would their basic principles be, the beliefs they shared that made them into one nation?

As this early seal shows, the United States promised a *novus ordo seclorum*— "a new order for the ages"— and a new era of liberty.

New Principles As it turned out, the American Revolution was a rejection of many of the basic principles of colonial society. In key documents such as the

Declaration of Independence and Thomas Paine's *Common Sense*, Americans announced their commitment to new ways of organizing and governing their society. Some of their new ideas came from the protests of ordinary people. Some came from religious and intellectual traditions. Still others were formed in the heat of the Revolution. Wherever those ideas came from, they became the new principles of American society. They included popular sovereignty, which was the idea that governments get their power and authority from the consent of the governed: in the United States, "We, the People" rule. Another basic principle was social equality, the idea that people are on some level fundamentally equal to one other. As Thomas Jefferson wrote in the Declaration of Independence, "All men are created equal" and "are endowed by their Creator with certain inalienable rights," including the right to "life, liberty, and the pursuit of happiness."

These were ideals, and most of them were not put into practice at the time. But Americans have been raising questions about the meaning and application of these ideals ever since. For instance, in a society based on equality, why was slavery still allowed? And what was the place of women in this new world of consent and equality?

Liberty vs. Order In the late 1700s and early 1800s, the meaning of these revolutionary ideals was hotly debated in the emerging arena of American politics. Over and over again, they returned to the question of how to balance liberty and order, freedom and stability. How far should Americans carry their new principles?

One group in the 1780s, called Federalists, were concerned that the Revolution had gone too far. In the Constitution of the United States, written in 1787 and ratified in 1788, they tried to emphasize order. They gave the country a strong national government, with a President, Congress, and court system, in order to ensure "a more perfect union." Many people criticized the Constitution for making the national government too powerful. In fact, to overcome this criticism, the Federalists had to agree to a set of amendments to the Constitution, called the Bill of Rights, guaranteeing specific freedoms.

In the 1790s Federalists tried to turn the United States into an orderly and prosperous empire. They took over the debts of the states, strengthened the military, raised taxes, and followed a generally pro-British foreign policy. Many Americans objected to the strong actions of the Federalists. Led by Thomas Jefferson of Virginia, they organized what would become the Democratic party and attacked the Federalists as men who preferred order to liberty.

In 1800 Jefferson and his followers won a key presidential election. The victory of the Jeffersonian Democrats meant that the Federalists would never control the national government again. For the next sixty years, despite the efforts of such diehard Federalists as Supreme Court Chief Justice John Marshall, the United States would have a relatively weak national government.

A Time of Rapid Change, 1800–1840

Nowadays Americans like to think that they are living in times of change unlike anything in the history of the nation. But in the first half of the 1800s, too, change was rapid, bewildering, upsetting, and exciting. Part of this change was due to simple expansion. The United States doubled its claims to North American territory when it completed the Louisiana Purchase in 1803. When Native Americans became Great Britain's allies against the United States during the War of 1812, the young nation defeated them and forced them to give up a vast expanse of land. Continuing the process of conquest and development, by the mid-1800s Americans had extended their claims from the Appalachian Mountains to the Great Plains and from the Great Lakes to the Gulf of Mexico.

Other changes were equally swift. The population of the United States had been doubling every twenty years towards the end of the 1700s. During the early 1800s, it continued to grow at a wild rate. Society and the economy were transformed by the Market Revolution. In this gradual but drastic change, the United States moved away from a household economy—one centered around keeping the household going—to a money economy centered on buying and selling goods in the marketplace. People came up with hundreds of money-making, labor-saving inventions, such as the cotton gin and the steamboat. Transportation and communication improved dramatically as Americans

The Market Revolution transformed the nation's society and economy. As shown on this bank note from the early 1800s, the nation moved away from a household economy to a money economy centered on people working for a living outside their homes—in factories and workshops.

built canals, roads, and railroads. Cities such as New York and Philadelphia suddenly became huge metropolises. The United States was full of hustle and bustle, overrun with people moving around in search of better places to live or developing new ways to do things or make a living.

The Contradictions of Equality

Despite all this change, the United States remained a nation torn by serious problems and contradictions. Of these, slavery was the most obvious. Although African Americans lived in a republic committed to equality and popular sovereignty, most of them were still subjected to the unequal conditions of slavery. African Americans themselves were fully aware of this contradiction and pointed it out at every opportunity.

The problem was that the Constitution gave enslaved people no rights. In fact, it suggested that an enslaved African American was only three fifths of a human being and that liberty was something reserved for white men. Yet this was contradicted by the language of the Declaration of Independence, which said that all men were created equal.

As for Native Americans, it had become clear by the 1830s that whites would not allow them a place in American society. After decades of resistance and some efforts at accommodation, worn down by disease and by the sheer number of white settlers, Native Americans in the East were forced by the United States government to relocate west of the Mississippi River. In the West, the Native Americans of the Plains, such as the Sioux, would continue to resist United States expansion for decades.

The Market Revolution and the Age of Jackson

By the 1830s the effect of the Market Revolution was clear. Americans were devoting themselves eagerly to making money and building the economy. Politicians argued about what role governments, both at the national and state level, should play in guiding economic development. But very few questioned whether or not the ongoing commercial and territorial expansion of the United States was a good thing.

Expansion and the Market Revolution did not affect all regions of the country in the same way. By the middle of the 1800s the North and South had become contradictions of one another in many ways. The South continued to rely on slave labor and on staple agricultural crops such as cotton and rice, the North on free labor and a combination of agriculture and industry. The South, with fewer people, remained overwhelmingly rural, while the North grew increasingly urban.

To a great extent, President Andrew Jackson symbolized the contradictions of the United States in the 1830s, an era often called the Age of Jackson. Hot-tempered and ambitious, Jackson was an energetic individualist from a poor background who had become famous and powerful. He had made his reputation as a frontier warrior, fighting both the British and the Native Americans. And yet this powerful champion of democratic rights was also a slaveholder and a strong advocate of removing Native Americans across the Mississippi River. His career reflected the situation of the nation at that time. Despite its impressive principles and its astonishing expansion, the United States in the 1830s had not yet come to terms with either its cultural diversity or the ideals expressed in its founding documents.

Introducing the Unit

Interpreting the Visual After the devastation of the Civil War and the slow mending of the nation during Reconstruction, the American people forged ahead with dramatic inventions that radically changed life in the nation.

Ask students to study the photograph shown on pages 148–149. Then write two column headings on the chalkboard, Rewards and Costs. Ask students first to list the rewards that the railroad brought to the nation. Then ask them to identify the environmental costs of the railroad construction visible in the photograph. Next, expand the discussion by having students form hypotheses to list the rewards and costs of the following topics: the territorial expansion of the United States as a result of war with Mexico, the Civil War, and increased immigration and the accompanying growth of cities.

Establishing Chronology This unit begins by exploring the period of reform that the United States entered in the early 1800s and the territorial expansion that occurred during that time. Next, it outlines the growing tensions between North and South that led to Civil War by 1861. The unit then chronicles the war and the bitter period of Reconstruction that followed. The dramatic technological changes that transformed the nation are examined, along with westward expansion and immigration and urban life from the late 1800s to the early 1900s. The unit ends with the cultural and social changes that affected the nation during this period.

"Mark the spirit of invention everywhere, thy rapid patents, Thy continual workshops, foundries, risen or rising, See, from their chimneys how the tall flame-fires stream."
–Walt Whitman, from "Song of the Exposition," 1872

*T*he explosive growth that Whitman celebrates in these lines describes a transformation in the United States that began with the expansion to newly acquired territories in the West. Despite the devastation of the Civil War, and the bitterness and resentment felt during the period of Reconstruction, the United States continued to flourish. After the war, the promise of new opportunities attracted thousands of settlers to the West and set off a dramatic wave of immigration. Unfortunately, the rewards of expansion came with a heavy price. Urban poverty, child labor, and the displacement of Native Americans were only some of those costs.

▶ RESOURCE DIRECTORY

Teaching Resources

📄 **Local History Activity** "Student Life at Boston High, 1820s Style," "Rebel Belles in Old New Orleans," "St. Louis, Missouri: 'Meet Me at the Fair,'" and the Local Focus research topic suggestions, found in the Local History Resources folder, pp. 9–17, are designed to help students understand how history affects all lives.

★ **Themes in American History Poster** Wall-size, illustrated posters, found in the Teaching Resources package, illustrate the four unit themes.

📄 **Unit Test** Forms A and B are found in the Unit 2 folder, pp. 146–151.

This photo of an excursion party at Devil's Gate Bridge in Utah captures both rewards and costs of the nation's growth

Teachers may wish to discuss specific historical events in the context of historical themes. Here are four suggestions for Unit 2.

Reform Movements *People in the United States have frequently taken action in grass-roots movements to right perceived wrongs and to secure improvements in the quality of life.*
- Middle-class reform movements pressed for public education, temperance, and other improvements.
- The antislavery and women's rights movements sought greater equality for women and African Americans.
- Labor unions fought for workers' rights.

Technology *Americans' ability to develop new skills and tools and to increase their knowledge of the physical world has greatly affected the way they live and work, and has led to a high standard of living.*
- Electric power transformed life at home and in factories.
- Railroads and telegraph lines connected the nation in elaborate networks.

Unity and Conflict *Americans have developed unique political systems and laws that affirm a shared commitment to certain goals, such as individual rights and equality. Nevertheless, groups with differing views on how to achieve these goals have often clashed.*
- The federal government removed most Native Americans from their homelands east of the Mississippi River.
- Debate over slavery reached an impasse and eventually erupted into civil war.

Environment *The geography and available resources of the continent have affected the actions of Americans. Similarly, the actions of Americans have affected the environment and physical landscape.*
- The mechanization of farm machines allowed more western lands to be farmed and thus changed the landscape.
- Rapid urban growth resulted in slums, air and water pollution, and disease.

Media and Technology

 **Visions of America: Scenes of an Era** To introduce students to the main idea covered in this unit, play the following "Scenes of an Era" (length: 2.5 minutes each): "An Emerging New Nation" (side 1 of videodiscs; videotape 2); "Division and Uneasy Reunion" (side 2 of the videodiscs; videotape 2); and "Expansion:

Rewards and Costs" (side 2 of the videodiscs; videotape 3). Lesson plans can be found in the Visions of America Teacher's Guidebook.

Using Multimedia Technology This folder contains instructional tools and strategies for using technology in the classroom.

Transparency Binder Contains full-color transparencies with lesson suggestions. From a large collection divided into twelve categories, specific transparencies are referenced throughout the chapters at appropriate points of use.

Side 1, Chapter 10

Side 2, Chapter 13

Side 2, Chapter 16

Chapter 5 Reform and Expansion
1815–1860

Teaching Resources (See Unit 2 Folder)

	Instruction	Enrichment
Section 1 **Reform and Abolitionism** (pp. 152–157)	Reproducible Lesson Plan, p. 3 Alternate Lesson Plan, p. 69 Guided Reading and Review, p. 7 Quiz, p. 8	Critical Thinking Activity, Recognizing Ideologies, p. 22 Primary Source Activity, Protecting Society's Outcasts, pp. 23–24 Visual Learning Activity, Countrymen in Chains, p. 32 Time and Place Activity, The Sanctuary Movement in the United States, pp. 15–16
Section 2 **Women and the Working Class** (pp. 160–166)	Reproducible Lesson Plan, p. 4 Alternate Lesson Plan, p. 70 Guided Reading and Review, p. 9 Quiz, p. 10	Literature Activity, Advice on Marriage, p. 28 American Profiles Activity, Maria Mitchell, p. 17 Primary Source Activity, Plantation Life, p. 25
Section 3 **Beyond the Mississippi** (pp. 167–173)	Reproducible Lesson Plan, p. 5 Alternate Lesson Plan, p. 71 Guided Reading and Review, p. 11 Quiz, p. 12	American Profiles Activity, York, p. 18 Literature Activity, Native American Legends: Hiawatha, p. 29 Literature Activity, What Happened in Texas, p. 30
Section 4 **The Conquest of the West** (pp. 174–180)	Reproducible Lesson Plan, p. 6 Alternate Lesson Plan, p. 72 Guided Reading and Review, p. 13 Quiz, p. 14 Chapter Test, Forms A & B, pp. 34–39	Literature Activity, Song of the Pioneers, p. 31 Primary Source Activity, Traveling West, pp. 26–27 Visual Learning Activity, The Annexation of Texas, p. 33 Viewpoints Activity, On Expanding into Mexican Territory, pp. 19–20 Historian's Toolbox Activity, Formulating Questions, p. 21

Additional Chapter Resources

Resource Organizer, p. 2
Alternate Lesson Plan, p. 68
Answer Keys, pp. 152–165

Bibliography

For the Teacher
Hill, William E. *The Oregon Trail: Yesterday and Today.* Caxton Printers, 1990. (Selections from the diaries of travelers going west.)

Prentice Hall Literature Excerpts from *The American Experience,* 1994, including Emerson, Ralph Waldo. *Nature.* Beacon, 1989 and *Self-Reliance.* Peter Pauper, 1967.

The Big Idea for the chapter and how the main ideas in each section relate to the Big Idea are graphically displayed below. Comprehension of this chapter's Big Idea is critical to students' understanding of United States history and how we as a nation got where we are today.

Media and Technology

 Our Multicultural Heritage, C-5

 Visions of America: Turning Point Story, "Speak Out" (length: approx. 4 minutes)

 Visions of America: Roundtable Discussion on "Speak Out"

 Our Multicultural Heritage, C-13

 Fine Art, D-7, D-8, D-13; Our Multicultural Heritage C-10

Cause and Effect, F-4; Historical Maps, L-2; Our Multicultural Heritage, C-10; The Way It Works, H-10; Graphic Organizer, G-1

 Guided Reading Audiotapes (English and Spanish)

 Computer Test Bank

For the Student

Jeffery, J. *Frontier Women: The Trans-Mississippi West, 1840–1880.* Hill & Wang, 1979. (Diaries and letters of ordinary women who crossed the country in the mid-1800s.)

Katz, William Loren. *The Black West.* Open Hand, 1987. (Pictorial history of the African American experience on the frontier.)

CHAPTER 5

A growing and dynamic reform movement urged Americans to seek both personal and social improvements, shaping society and the nation for generations to come. Other Americans pushed westward into Texas, New Mexico, California, and Oregon in search of new opportunities. As their numbers grew, however, tensions developed between the new settlers and the peoples who already claimed these lands as their home.

SECTION 1

Middle-class Americans took part in a variety of reform movements, including the antislavery movement.

SECTION 2

Participation in the antislavery movement inspired many women to consider their own role in society and to press for new reforms. Their efforts stirred resentment among Americans of other regional and economic groups.

SECTION 3

The lives of Native American groups living on the Great Plains had already been affected by European contact by the time white Americans arrived. Meanwhile, a steady steam of white settlers moving into the Mexican lands of Texas, New Mexico, and California created tension with the Mexican government.

SECTION 4

Beginning in the 1830s, thousands of settlers traveled westward as white Americans set about fulfilling their dream of a nation that stretched from the Atlantic to the Pacific. Open conflict developed between the groups who already lived on these lands and the new arrivals.

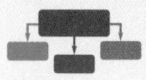

The Relevance of the Big Idea

The pace of social change is always too fast for some people, too slow for others. In the early 1800s, some Americans sought major reforms in their society, while some resisted change. Still others forced change by moving west into territories already settled by Native Americans and Hispanics. Conflict and tension developed as people with different ways of life came into contact with one another. The struggle between forces for and against change continues today. Issues such as environmental regulation, education, and health concerns are debated, and sometimes fought over, in the 1990s.

Ask students to identify current social problems that have been caused by new technology or other rapid changes. Then discuss how these problems pit people in various regions or cultures against one another. Ask students to consider why people often respond adversely to change.

In Depth

Global Connections

In the years that followed the War of 1812, the United States and Britain peacefully settled a number of outstanding issues. After the Oregon Country had been opened to trade, people from both the United States and Britain settled there. In 1846 the two countries finally divided the Oregon Country and agreed on another border—one that reached from the Rockies to the Pacific.

CHAPTER 5

Reform and Expansion
1815–1860

*I*nspired by religious revivals that emphasized the importance of character and the possibility of personal change, in the early 1800s many Americans participated in a variety of reform movements. Meanwhile, thousands of Americans began pushing westward into Texas, New Mexico, California, and Oregon—invading land where Native Americans and Mexicans had lived for centuries. The tensions that resulted from these encounters led eventually to conflict with Native Americans and a war with Mexico.

Events in the United States

1815	1820	1825	1830	1835

1817 The American Colonization Society forms to return African Americans to Africa.

1821 Stephen Austin founds a colony of American settlers in Texas.

1831 Abolitionist William Lloyd Garrison founds The Liberator, an antislavery newspaper.

Events in the World

1816 Argentina declares its independence.

1822 The American Colonization Society founds the West African nation of Liberia.

1830 Greece becomes an independent state.

▶ RESOURCE DIRECTORY

Teaching Resources

Alternate Lesson Plan: Demonstrating the Big Idea found in the Alternate Lesson Plans folder, p. 68, provides a lesson strategy to instruct students about the major social reform movements of the 1800s as well as the movement toward the west.

Alternative Assessment Handbook provides information, guidance, and strategies for alternative methods of assessment. It includes an essay on new trends in assessment, guidance and strategies for developing performance tasks and portfolios, scoring rubrics, and sample evaluation forms.

Pages 152–157
Reform and Abolitionism

Dismayed by a wide variety of social problems, many middle-class Americans banded together in the mid-1800s in an effort to improve life in the United States. Among these activities was an antislavery movement.

Pages 160–166
Women and the Working Class

Although middle-class women were expected to devote their energies to home, family, and community in the early 1800s, many women were not content with this work. Meanwhile, many people resented interfering reformers who told them how to live their lives.

Pages 167–173
Beyond the Mississippi

During the 1700s and 1800s, powerful new forces transformed the lives of Native Americans and Hispanics in what is now the West. For Native Americans, the introduction of the horse brought dramatic changes. For Hispanics, the pressure of new settlers and traders from the United States led to the creation of some settlements and the loss of others.

Pages 174–180
The Conquest of the West

The Mexican War extended the nation's boundaries from the Atlantic to the Pacific. At war's end, the discovery of gold in California transformed a stream of western-moving settlers into a flood, resulting in growing tensions with many Native American groups.

1841 Catharine Beecher publishes A Treatise on Domestic Economy.

1848 A gold rush begins in California.
• The Mexican War ends.

1851 Maine bans the manufacture and sale of all alcoholic beverages.

1861 Kansas becomes a state.

1865 Maria Mitchell becomes the first professor of astronomy at Vassar College.

1840	1845	1850	1855	1860	1865

1840 Female delegates are excluded from the World Anti-Slavery Convention in London.

1845 Irish potato famine spurs immigration to the United States.

1859 Charles Darwin publishes The Origin of Species.

Media and Technology

Transparency
Time Lines, E-4

SECTION 1

Reform and Abolitionism

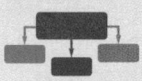

Connecting to the Big Idea

See page 150B. Many Americans were concerned about the problems that accompanied the sudden growth and development of the United States, as well as the ongoing existence of slavery. Ask students how Americans reacted to these problems. What new tensions did the reform efforts create?

Objectives

● Characterize the reformers' view of the relationship between the individual and society.
● Describe the role of African Americans in the antislavery movement.
● Explain why the antislavery movement caused political tension between the North and South.

Bellringer

Ask students to describe their ideal society. Would it have rules and standards? If so, what kinds of values might it seek to promote among its members?

Reading Strategy

Predicting Content Ask students to read the section preview and the first paragraph on page 152 and to predict what steps Americans took in response to society's ills. Have students check the accuracy of their predictions as they read the section.

SECTION PREVIEW

Dismayed by a wide variety of social problems, many middle-class Americans banded together in the mid-1800s in an effort to improve life in the United States. Among these activities was an antislavery movement.

This banner celebrates the founding of William Lloyd Garrison's famous antislavery newspaper, *The Liberator.*

Key Concepts

• Middle-class reformers believed that improving individual character was the first step in improving society as a whole.
• Free African Americans, at the forefront of the antislavery movement, began to build momentum against slavery during the early 1800s.
• The antislavery movement increasingly divided the North and South.

Key Terms, People, and Places

Transcendentalism, temperance movement, abolition, gag rule; Lyman Beecher, Henry David Thoreau, Horace Mann, Dorothea Dix, William Lloyd Garrison, Frederick Douglass, Harriet Tubman; Liberia

---

A s the United States moved through the Great Awakening in the early decades of the 1800s, Americans began to look at the nation they were creating and take action to guide its growth.

Religion and Philosophy Inspire Reformers

The impulse to reform what exists grows out of a vision of a better way of life. For early reformers, religion and philosophy supplied this new vision.

Evangelical Reformers The evangelical ministers of the Second Great Awakening preached that humans have the power to choose to act rightly, not only in accepting Jesus Christ but in other personal decisions. In their view, those who correctly use this power to choose have "character," meaning they exercise self-restraint and follow God's laws. As reformers, these ministers sought to end all practices that worked against self-restraint.

One such minister was **Lyman Beecher.** The son of a blacksmith, Beecher attended Yale University and became a popular preacher in Boston. In 1832 he moved to Cincinnati to become president of the Lane Theological Seminary. Beecher, like other revivalists, feared that "the vast extent of territory, our numerous and increasing population, . . . diversity of local interests, the power of selfishness, and the fury of sectional jealousy and hate" threatened the future of the United States. How, he wondered, could such a huge, loosely organized nation survive the rapid and far-reaching changes of the Market Revolution? The answer, he and others believed, lay in the work of improving the individual. In other words, people of good character would make a country of good character.

The Transcendentalists Another group of reformers was more philosophical than religious in outlook. Relatively few in number—and centered mainly in New England—the followers of **Transcendentalism** believed that the most important truths in life went beyond, or "transcended," human understanding. Transcendentalists prized self-reliance and the questioning of authority—ideal qualities for reformers. One Transcendentalist, Ralph Waldo Emerson, went so far as to ask, "What is man born for but to be a Reformer?" Another Transcendentalist, **Henry David Thoreau,** demonstrated the importance of individuals reforming their own lives. In 1846, Thoreau refused to pay taxes to support the Mexican War because he

---

▶ RESOURCE DIRECTORY

Teaching Resources

Reproducible Lesson Plan found in the Unit 2 folder, p. 3, provides a summary of the Section 1 lesson plan content.

Alternate Lesson Plan: Learning Styles found in the Alternate Lesson Plans folder, p. 69, especially useful for auditory learners, will help students identify the goals of the various reform movements by creating public speeches explaining their causes.

Guided Reading and Review found in the Unit 2 folder, p. 7, provides a structure for reading and mastering the key concepts and reviewing the key terms for Section 1. (Guided Practice)

Critical Thinking Activity Recognizing Ideologies: Transcendentalism, found in the Unit 2 folder, p. 22, helps students identify a writer's or speaker's point of view by analyzing an excerpt from Henry David Thoreau's "Higher Laws."

saw the war as a government plan to extend slavery. Rather than be a part of that plan, he went to jail, which was the penalty for not paying taxes.

The Major Reform Movements

The young United States had many ills that attracted the attention of reformers—widespread use of alcohol, a crying need for a system of basic education, and the problems of crime and mental illness. The first of these, consumption of alcohol, was the target of the most successful middle-class reform of the era.

The Temperance Movement Americans were drinking more alcoholic beverages per person during the early 1800s than at any other time in American history. And reformers believed that only Americans who did *not* drink—who were "temperate," or moderate, in their habits—could be in control of themselves and thus be free to develop their character and contribute to their nation. In 1842 a thirty-three-year-old lawyer named Abraham Lincoln illustrated this viewpoint clearly when he said he looked forward to the

> *happy day when . . . the victory shall be complete—when there shall be neither a slave nor a drunkard on the earth. . . . How nobly distinguished that people who shall have planted and nurtured to maturity both the political and moral freedom of their species.*

The campaign against alcohol began about 1815 and became known as the **temperance movement.** By 1834 the American Temperance Society boasted 7,000 local organizations with 1,250,000 members. They urged people to take pledges to abstain from alcohol, lobbied distillers and distributors of alcohol, established alcohol-free hotels and boat lines, encouraged employers to require their workers to sign antidrinking pledges, and worked for political candidates who promised to ban the sale of alcohol.

The temperance movement had a significant impact on Americans' drinking habits. Between the 1830s and the 1860s, the per capita, or per person, consumption of distilled spirits in the United States dropped dramatically, as the table at right shows.

Improving Public Education The failure of individual character, reformers believed, was partly due to a lack of good public education. Beginning in the 1820s, many working-class and middle-class citizens started to demand tax-supported schools. Despite opposition from some taxpayers, the movement for educational reform gained strength in the 1830s. It owed much of its eventual success to **Horace Mann,** a Massachusetts lawyer who became that state's first secretary of the Board of Education in 1837. Under Mann's leadership, Massachusetts pioneered school reform. He began a system of graded schools, uniform curricula, and teacher training. Using Massachusetts as a model, educational reformers led movements to establish public schools in other states. By the 1850s most northern states had established free public elementary schools, and by the beginning of the next decade the number of public high schools in the United States had risen to three hundred. Progress toward public education lagged far behind in the South, however. In addition, access to public education tended to be better in urban than in rural areas.

Even where public schools did exist, some groups remained blocked from using them. Girls, for example, often were discouraged from attending school, particularly if they wished to continue their education after learning to read and write. More frequently, towns and cities barred free African Americans from entering local public schools. In places where African Americans could attend public schools, such as Boston and New York, they often were segregated in inferior schools.

Opportunities for women and African Americans in higher education were even more

Alcohol Consumption in the United States, 1800–1860

Year	Gallons Consumed Per Capita
1800	6.6
1810	7.1
1820	6.8
1830	7.1
1840	3.1
1850	1.8
1860	2.1

Source: *The Alcoholic Republic: An American Tradition,* by W. J. Rorabaugh

Interpreting Tables
Per capita, or per person, consumption of alcohol in the United States is shown on this table. *What evidence of the impact of the temperance movement does this table illustrate?*

2. INSTRUCT

Explain/Discuss

Explain to students that during this period some reformers attempted to create utopian communities—small societies that would achieve ideal social and political conditions. Like the utopianists, some social reformers wanted to get away from society's ills, while others wanted to change them. Ask students to identify people or groups of people in each category. What values or ideas did these people all share?

Analyze

Ask students to identify people or groups of people who favored immediate abolition, gradual abolition, and the continuation of slavery respectively. Then have them analyze which approach they think would have been best for the nation at the beginning of the nineteenth century and explain their meaning.

Interpreting Graphs

Probably white males.

Activity
Writing an Editorial

Ask students to write an editorial for the abolitionist newspaper of either William Lloyd Garrison or Frederick Douglass. Students should first consider the likely audience for the newspaper and tailor their arguments accordingly. The editorials should attempt to stir readers to specific actions. **LEP**

 In Depth

Then and Now

In the 1990s there are more women than men in both undergraduate institutions and graduate schools in the United States. Yet in early 1994, the Gender Equity in Education Act was introduced in Congress. It calls for educators to treat the sexes equally from kindergarten through twelfth grade, supports textbooks that eliminate sexist assumptions, and allows federal funding for such instruction. Supporters of the bill justify the need for it by citing factors like females' lower scores on national achievement tests and the channeling of males and females into gender-oriented roles. "Last year there were 18,000 boys eligible for National Merit Scholarships," notes Elizabeth T. Kennan, president of Mount Holyoke College, and a supporter of the bill, "and there were only 8,000 girls. So something is happening, and I think it needs to be urgently addressed."

This 1857 photograph shows a class at a school in Massachusetts. Teachers of the time tended toward strict discipline and drill to teach their students.

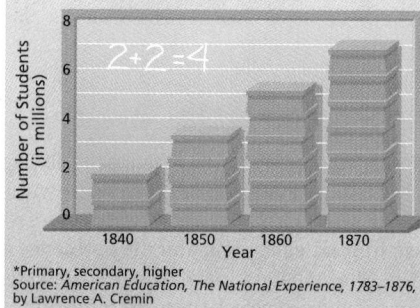

School* Enrollment, 1840–1870

*Primary, secondary, higher
Source: *American Education, The National Experience, 1783–1876,* by Lawrence A. Cremin

Interpreting Graphs
Thanks to the efforts of Horace Mann and other educational reformers, school enrollment in the United States increased rapidly in the mid-1800s. *What group do you think is most represented by these figures?*

limited. Although sixteen states funded some kind of higher education by 1860, few students at these schools were female or African American. Several private colleges, such as Oberlin, Amherst, and Dartmouth, did open their doors to a small number of African American students, and three black colleges—Avery, Lincoln, and Wilberforce—were founded during this period. In addition, Oberlin, Grinnell, and several other private colleges were coeducational. For the most part, however, white males were the only students welcome at public universities.

The Work of Dorothea Dix A Boston schoolteacher named **Dorothea Dix** paid a visit to a Massachusetts jail in 1841. She discovered men and women, young and old, sane and insane, first-time offenders and hardened criminals all crowded together in deplorable conditions. Many of the inmates she met were dressed in rags, poorly fed, and living in unheated cells.

Shocked, Dix spent the next two years visiting every prison and poorhouse—a place where very poor people lived supported by public funds—in Massachusetts. In the report she prepared for the Massachusetts legislature, Dix

"I come to present the strong claims of suffering humanity," wrote Dorothea Dix in her report to the Massachusetts legislature.

related in vivid detail the appalling conditions and mistreatment she had witnessed. Her powerful testimony convinced Massachusetts lawmakers to pass legislation to improve conditions in prisons and poorhouses. Dix also persuaded them to establish a separate public institution for the mentally ill, arguing that "To confine the insane to persons whose education and habits do not qualify them for this charge is to condemn them to mental death."

As a result of Dix's campaign to have the mentally ill treated as patients rather than criminals, fifteen states established special hospitals for the mentally ill. Few individual reformers in United States history have been as effective as Dix. ✪

The Antislavery Movement

Of the many reform movements that sprang up between 1820 and 1860, the **abolition,** or antislavery, movement created the most widespread controversy, both outside the movement and within it. ✪

Colonization Typical of this controversy was the reaction to one abolitionist proposal, colonization, a program to return free blacks and emancipated slaves to Africa.

RESOURCE DIRECTORY

Teaching Resources

✪ **Primary Source Activity** Protecting Society's Outcasts, found in the Unit 2 folder, pp. 23–24, highlights the inhumane treatment of prisoners and the insane through an excerpt from Dorothea Dix's testimony to the Massachusetts legislature.

✪ **Visual Learning Activity** Countrymen in Chains, found in the Unit 2 folder, p. 32, uses a popular abolitionist poster to illustrate the sentiment against slavery.

Convinced that African Americans would never achieve full participation in American society, in 1822 some antislavery advocates founded the country of **Liberia** in West Africa as a homeland for African Americans.

Although a free African American named Paul Cuffe had been one of the originators of the idea of colonization, the plan offended most African Americans. They were interested in improving their lives in the land they considered their home, the United States, not moving to a continent they had never seen. At an 1817 meeting in Philadelphia, three thousand free African Americans shouted their opposition to such schemes with a roar that threatened to "bring down the walls of the building," according to one report. Thanks largely to such opposition, colonization was a failure. As of 1831, only about 1,400 African Americans had migrated to Liberia.

Radical Abolition As they demonstrated in rejecting colonization, African Americans wanted not to dodge the issue of slavery but to end the practice immediately. For African Americans, the movement to end slavery had a personal dimension and an urgency that white people could never fully understand. By 1829, nearly fifty African American antislavery groups had formed throughout the nation. In that year, a forty-four-year-old free African American named David Walker captured their sentiments in his *Appeal to the Colored Citizens of the World.*

Walker's essay was an eloquent and angry denunciation of slavery and the nation that tolerated it. He did not mince words. White Americans had made African Americans into "the most wretched, degraded and abject set of beings that ever lived since the world began." Throwing the words of the Declaration of Independence in the faces of whites, Walker not only demanded equality but also spoke of the right of revolution.

Walker wanted neither charity nor condescension, but to be treated as a human entitled to the opportunities the United States had to offer. He hoped that white people would cooperate so that all Americans could "live in peace and happiness together." But if they would not

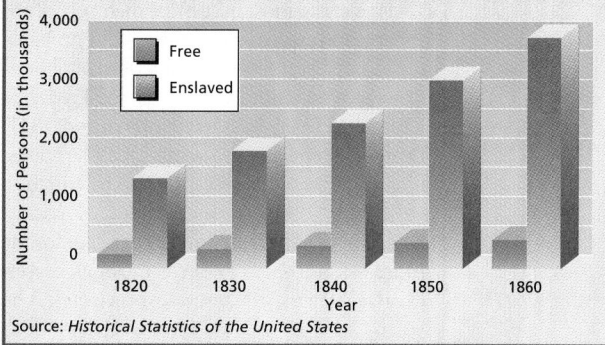

Free and Enslaved African American Population, 1820–1860

Source: *Historical Statistics of the United States*

 Interpreting Graphs
The population of both free and enslaved African Americans rose sharply in the early 1800s. *Which rose more rapidly?*

listen, he warned them, then "we must and shall be free I say, in spite of you . . . for America is as much our country, as it is yours."

Although David Walker died in the streets of Boston in 1830, possibly murdered by poisoning, his *Appeal* marked a shift in the antislavery movement to a more aggressive tone and approach. During the 1830s, many African American and white members of the movement embraced this more militant form of abolitionism. One was a white Bostonian named **William Lloyd Garrison,** who in 1831 began publishing *The Liberator,* an antislavery newspaper supported largely by free African Americans. Garrison denounced moderation in the fight against slavery. He proclaimed to the world his commitment to ending slavery:

I am in earnest— I will not equivocate—I will not excuse—I will not retreat a single inch—AND I WILL BE HEARD.

With the support of both white and African American abolitionists, Garrison also founded the American Anti-Slavery Society in 1833. As the decade progressed, more middle-class northern whites became sympathetic to the cause of the immediate abolition of slavery. By 1835 the American Anti-Slavery Society had some 1,000 local chapters with roughly 150,000 members. Agents traveling throughout the North for the society distributed more than

Enrichment

Ask students to research the history of United States prisons in the early 1800s, exploring the criminal justice system, prison conditions, and efforts toward reform.

In Depth

Historical Misconceptions

It is a mistake to assume that segregation and racial bigotry were peculiar to the South. In 1842 Charles Lenox Remond (1810–1873), a friend of fellow abolitionist William Lloyd Garrison and a vocal critic of northern segregation policies, was the first African American to address the Massachusetts legislature in Boston. "[I]n this country, this State, aye, this city, the Athens of America," declared Remond, "the rights, privileges and immunities of its citizens are measured by complexion."

Answer to ...

MAKING CONNECTIONS

Participants in the sanctuary movement broke laws to protect a vulnerable group of people from being returned to a place where they would be mistreated, persecuted, and possibly killed. Also, the sanctuary movement comprised a network of individuals who took risks to hide people who were in danger from the authorities. In these ways, it was similar to the underground railroad. (See the Time and Place Activity on page 158.)

3. ASSESS

Section 1 Review Answers

1. (a) Transcendentalism, see p. 152, (b) temperance movement, see p. 153, (c) abolition, see p. 154, (d) gag rule, see p. 157

2. (a) Lyman Beecher, see p. 152, (b) Henry David Thoreau, see p. 152, (c) Horace Mann, see p. 153, (d) Dorothea Dix, see p. 154, (e) William Lloyd Garrison, see p. 155, (f) Frederick Douglass, see p. 156, (g) Harriet Tubman, see p. 156

3. Liberia, see p. 155

4. Many middle-class Americans believed that individual character was the key to social order in a democratic society. People with good character were people who had voluntarily decided to control their passions and behave in a respectable fashion.

5. They wanted to be treated as citizens of the United States, not as misfits to be shipped back to a place they had never known. Colonization was a potential remedy to slavery but it was also seen as coercive, paternalistic, and racist.

6. Answers may include the refusal of southern postmasters to deliver abolitionist literature, or the imposition by southern congressmen of a gag rule on antislavery petitions in the U.S. Congress.

7. It suggests that in the mid-1800s few Americans foresaw the day when whites and blacks would have equal rights.

one million antislavery tracts, or informational pamphlets, every year.

One of the most influential members of the American Anti-Slavery Society—and probably the most powerful African American abolitionist—was a self-educated man named **Frederick Douglass.** Born in Maryland around 1817, Douglass spent the first twenty-one years of his life in slavery before escaping to the North in 1838. After settling in New Bedford, Massachusetts, Douglass became a full-time agent for the American Anti-Slavery Society. Douglass condemned slavery in eloquent speeches that he delivered in both the United States and Great Britain. In 1847 he parted ways with Garrison and founded his own antislavery newspaper, called *The North Star.*

Once enslaved, Frederick Douglass often denounced the "murderous traffic" of the slave trade in his abolitionist speeches.

The Underground Railroad Given the intense passions stirred by the issue of slavery and the fierce commitment of many abolitionists, it is not surprising that divisions appeared in the antislavery movement. Some abolitionists favored indirect action to end slavery and some favored direct action, whether legal or illegal. The underground railroad, for instance, was daringly illegal. It was actually not a railroad at all, but a network of men and women "conductors" who helped runaway enslaved persons escape to the North and then into Canada. (See "Time and Place: Routes to Freedom," on pages 158–159.) African Americans made up the majority of the railroad's volunteers. One of them was a courageous formerly enslaved woman named **Harriet Tubman,** who repeatedly risked her life to lead runaway enslaved persons to freedom. She was known as "the Black Moses" among African Americans

because her calling, like that of Moses in the Bible, was to lead her people to freedom. Tubman boasted later in life: "I never run my train off the track, and I never lost a passenger." Her work enraged southern slave owners, who offered a $40,000 reward for her capture.

MAKING CONNECTIONS

Individuals and religious groups that participated in a "sanctuary movement" in the 1980s ignored immigration laws in order to prevent Central American political refugees from being returned to countries where they might be tortured, imprisoned, or murdered. Was this activity comparable to the underground railroad? Explain your thinking.

Resistance to Abolitionism

Abolitionists, though vocal, remained a minority in the early 1800s. In the North, merchants worried that the antislavery movement would further sour relations between North and South and consequently hurt trade between the two regions. White workers and labor leaders feared competition from free African American workers willing to accept lower wages. Even northerners who opposed slavery did not necessarily want free African Americans, whom they viewed as socially inferior, living in their communities.

Northern opposition to the antislavery movement sometimes became violent. Hostile opponents often booed abolitionists to drown out their messages or used physical threats to prevent them from speaking. William Lloyd Garrison narrowly escaped death in 1835 at the hands of an angry Boston crowd. Abolitionist editor Elijah P. Lovejoy was not so lucky. When he tried to prevent the members of a hostile mob from destroying his printing press in Alton, Illinois, in 1837, they shot and killed him. Many who were not normally sympathetic to the abolitionist cause were angered by Lovejoy's brutal murder.

Not surprisingly, most southerners were outraged by the criticisms the antislavery

▶ RESOURCE DIRECTORY

Teaching Resources

movement leveled at the institution of slavery. Attacks by northern abolitionists such as Garrison, together with Nat Turner's 1831 rebellion, made many southerners even more determined to defend the institution of slavery. During the 1830s, it became increasingly rare and dangerous for southerners to speak out in favor of freeing enslaved people.

Public officials in the South also joined in the battle against abolitionism. Southern postmasters, for example, refused to deliver abolitionist literature. In 1836, moreover, southern representatives in Congress succeeded in passing the so-called **gag rule,** which for the next eight years automatically tabled all antislavery petitions and thus prevented them from being read in the House.

In provoking these responses, abolitionism was gradually building a fire that would sear both North and South. It had other unexpected consequences too, as the next section shows, for it inspired women to reach out for new freedoms of their own.

"There's two things I've got a right to . . . death or liberty." So said Harriet Tubman (far left), shown here with a group of formerly enslaved people whom she led to freedom.

SECTION 1 REVIEW

Key Terms, People, and Places
1. Define (a) Transcendentalism, (b) temperance movement, (c) abolition, (d) gag rule.
2. Identify (a) Lyman Beecher, (b) Henry David Thoreau, (c) Horace Mann, (d) Dorothea Dix, (e) William Lloyd Garrison, (f) Frederick Douglass, (g) Harriet Tubman.
3. Identify Liberia.

Key Concepts
4. Why did middle-class reformers of the early 1800s

place so much emphasis on individual character?
5. Why did most free African Americans reject the idea of colonization?
6. What steps did white southerners take to resist abolitionism?

Criticial Thinking
7. **Drawing Conclusions** What does the northern response to the abolition movement suggest about racial attitudes in American society as a whole during this era?

 Quiz found in the Unit 2 folder, p. 8, covers the main ideas in this section as well as the key terms.

Media and Technology

 Transparency
Our Multicultural Heritage, C-5

Reteach

Have students review the key facts about reform and abolitionism by answering these questions:
• *Who* were the reformers and abolitionists?
• *What* did they hope to accomplish?
• *When* did the reform movement take hold?
• *Why* did these people think change was necessary?
• *How* did they try to bring about change?
• *Where* did they meet the most resistance?

4. CLOSE

 **Reinforcing the Big Idea**

A few decades into the nineteenth century, movements for social change and reform developed significant power. The next section examines the role of women in the public sphere during this period.

In Depth

Biography

Born into slavery, Harriet Tubman (1821–1913) was one of eleven children. She ran away to the North alone, later saying, "There was no one to welcome me to the land of freedom. I was a stranger in a strange land." By the beginning of the Civil War in 1861, Tubman had escorted over three hundred slaves to freedom, including her brothers, sisters, and parents. Then, as a scout and spy for the Union Army, she helped free more than 750 slaves. In 1896, Tubman founded the National Association of Colored Women.

Routes to Freedom

Routes to Freedom

On a map, the routes of the underground railroad look like a confused tangle of lines streaming from the slave states of the South to the freedom of Canada. What logic lies behind that apparent confusion?

The underground railroad was not strictly a railroad, nor was it underground: it was a network of routes, including paths, roads, rivers, and real railways, that led fugitives out of slavery in the South. Geography can help explain the routes marked out by the railroad.

Geographers use themes in their study, much as a workman uses tools. Two of these themes are place—including the physical characteristics of the land—and regions. The routes of the underground railroad depended on certain physical features and regional attitudes in the United States.

"It is evident that there exist some eighteen or nineteen thoroughly organized thoroughfares through the State of Ohio for the transportation of runaway and stolen slaves."

Physical Features Lead Out of the South

Several physical features of the South provided relatively protected routes for fugitives traveling to underground railroad connections in the free states. In the West, the valley of the Mississippi River was a natural escape route. Some enslaved people even managed to book riverboat passage northward and reach the underground railroad routes of western Illinois. The Mississippi pathway was dangerous, however, because it constantly brought fugitives into contact with potentially hostile white people.

The east coast, by contrast, boasted a physical feature that offered protection from human pursuers, but posed serious natural dangers. This was the string of low-lying swamps stretching along the Atlantic coast from southern Georgia to southern Virginia. Fugitives who traveled north through the swamps—and survived the hazards of poisonous snakes and disease-bearing mosquitoes—linked up with one of the eastern underground railroad routes to Canada shown on the map on page 159.

But the physical feature that had the greatest impact on the choice of a southern route was the Appalachian mountain chain. Its narrow, steep-sided valleys, separated by forested ridges, stretch from northern Georgia into Pennsylvania. The Appalachians affected the routes to freedom in two ways. First, their forests and limestone caves sheltered fugitives as they avoided capture on their way north. Second, the Appalachians acted as a barrier that deflected western runaways northward into a region of intense underground railway activity.

Regional Attitudes

This busy region was formed by Ohio and parts of the states on either side of it, Indiana and Pennsylvania. As a whole, the region shared a long boundary with two slave states, Virginia and Kentucky.

Once the fugitives crossed into Ohio, they found themselves in a region with an attitude toward

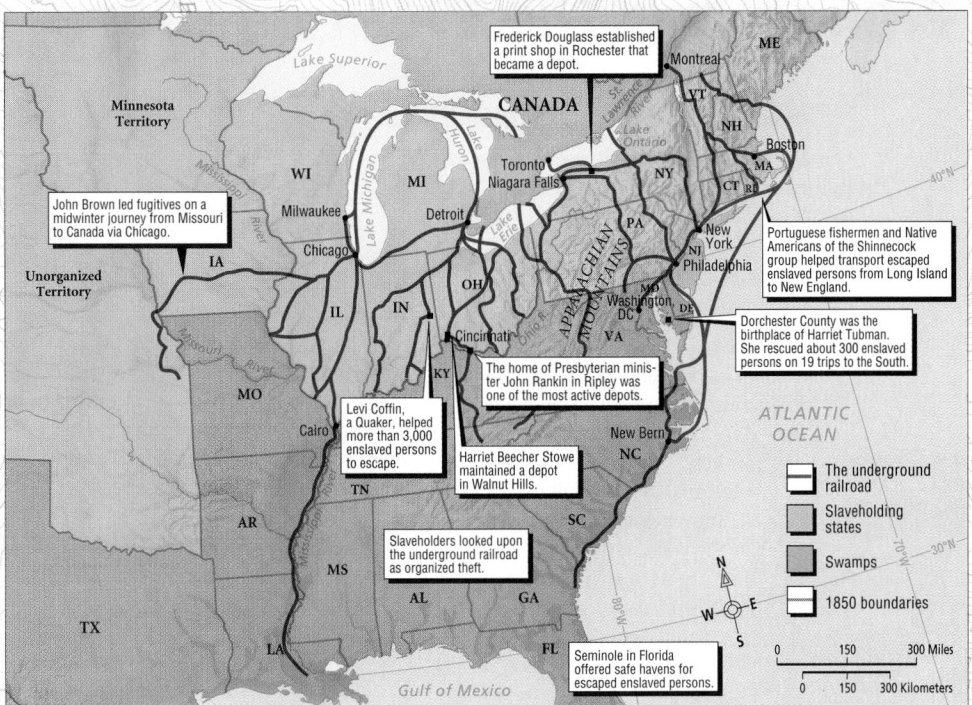

1. The forested ridges of the Appalachian mountain chain; limestone caves in the Appalachian Mountains; the string of low-lying swamps stretching along the Atlantic coast from southern Virginia to southern Georgia. Dangers included poisonous snakes and disease-bearing mosquitoes.

2. Many Ohioans were friendly to the antislavery cause.

3. Answers may be based on any of the three options but should explain the advantages and disadvantages of the choice made.

slavery very different from the one in the region they had left behind. Southern Ohio was home to many Quakers, Covenanters, and others who volunteered their houses as depots, or stations, on religious principles. There, too, lived free African Americans, as well as whites who had moved out of the South because they opposed slavery. In the north and east of the state, many whites had roots in New England and shared its antislavery views. The photograph on page 158 shows the sort of lengths such people took to aid African Americans. This cupboard slid back to reveal a hiding place where several fugitives might conceal themselves if necessary.

The sympathetic attitude of residents throughout much of the Ohio region caused a headache for southern slave owners. "It is evident," an anonymous writer declared indignantly in 1842, "that there exist some eighteen or nineteen thoroughly organized thoroughfares through the State of Ohio for the transportation of runaway and stolen slaves." To the east of Ohio, regional attitudes were similar.

Southern Illinois, however, was a dangerous region for fugitives, because it had been settled by southerners and remained proslavery. Often sympathizers in that area simply ticketed fugitives on a real railroad, the Illinois Central, for swift transit to Chicago. From there they continued on toward Canada, following the North Star as it shone in the night sky and marked their route to freedom.

GEOGRAPHIC CONNECTIONS

1. What physical features in the South offered fugitives protection from pursuers? What dangers also lurked in those areas?
2. Why did so many of the underground railroad routes run through Ohio?

Critical Thinking

3. **Demonstrating Reasoned Judgment** If you had been an enslaved person escaping from the South, which route to freedom would you have taken? Explain your reasoning.

1. FOCUS

Connecting to the Big Idea

See page 150B. Women in the early 1800s were expected to dedicate themselves to tending a home and family. Many women, however, were not content with this role and society's expectations. The reform movement provided both an outlet for their ambitions and fuel for the fight for greater equality. Yet they and other middle-class reformers were resented by people in some segments of society. Ask students why the reformers and their efforts caused such resentment and bitterness.

Objectives

● Explain how reform movements of the 1830s and 1840s increased the visibility of women.
● Identify the connection between the abolitionist movement and the early women's movement.
● Explain why working-class people resented the efforts of reformers.

Bellringer

Have students speculate on how a woman of the early 1800s would react if she were somehow transported to the present day. Which aspects of society might she enjoy? Which might she dislike?

Reading Strategy

Structured Overview Have students construct a chart entitled "Cultural Differences" with the following four column headings: Middle Class, Working Class, Northerners, and Southerners. As students read the section, they should list each group's attitude toward reform in the appropriate column.

Women and the Working Class

SECTION PREVIEW

Although middle-class women were expected to devote their energies to home, family, and community in the early 1800s, many women were not content with this work. Meanwhile, many people resented interfering reformers who told them how to live their lives.

Key Concepts
• The reform movements of the 1830s and 1840s provided American women with new opportunities to speak and act publicly.
  • Inspired in part by the abolitionist movement, some American women started a women's rights movement in the 1840s.
  • More concerned with economic survival than social reform, working-class people resented reformers' efforts to impose values with which they did not necessarily agree.

Key Terms, People, and Places
suffrage, cult of domesticity; Catharine Beecher, Lucretia Mott, Elizabeth Cady Stanton, Sojourner Truth; Seneca Falls

Awareness of the plight of women who were enslaved, as shown in this antislavery logo, made many white abolitionist women begin thinking about women's rights.

W omen played a prominent role in almost every reform movement of the first half of the nineteenth century, from temperance to antislavery. In spite of the enormous contribution they made to these movements, their participation was often highly controversial. Middle-class women at this time were expected to raise and educate their children, create a nurturing home, entertain guests, serve their husbands, do community service, and engage in such genteel activities as needlework. Participating in politics or public meetings with men was considered shocking and unladylike. Even a successful public figure like

Dorothea Dix found it necessary for a man to present her findings to legislatures.

✪ The cultural attitudes of the period were reinforced by laws. For example, women did not enjoy **suffrage,** or the right to vote, at this time. In most states in the early 1800s, moreover, married women could not own property, make a will, or keep the wages they earned outside the home. During the 1840s, some women began to be angered by these forms of legal discrimination, as well as by attempts to block their participation in public life. Others, however, continued to promote a role for women as reformers in the home.

AMERICAN PROFILES

Catharine Beecher

One of the most visible advocates of a domestic role for women was **Catharine Beecher** (1800–1878), who tried to win respect for women's contributions as wives, mothers, and teachers. Daughter of the revivalist Lyman Beecher and sister of both the novelist Harriet Beecher Stowe and the prominent Presbyterian minister Henry Ward Beecher, Catharine Beecher grew up in a family devoted to moral improvement and public service.

Born on Long Island in New York, Beecher attended school in Connecticut and began teaching in 1821. Teaching was considered a proper occupation for a young woman because it was an extension of the role of mother. In 1823, a year after her fiancé was drowned at sea, Catharine and her sister Mary Beecher started the Hartford Female Seminary.

While teaching, Catharine Beecher also started writing about and lobbying for the education of females. Beecher's most popular and influential work was *A Treatise on Domestic Economy,* first published in 1841. In the *Treatise,* Beecher sought to help middle-class women adjust to a new world where they were

---

RESOURCE DIRECTORY

Teaching Resources

Reproducible Lesson Plan found in the Unit 2 folder, p. 4, provides a summary of the Section 2 lesson plan content.

Alternate Lesson Plan: Critical Thinking Identifying Alternatives, found in the Alternate Lesson Plans folder, p. 70, helps students apply this skill by studying the perspectives of women in the early 1800s, the views of

supporters of women's rights, and the attitudes of working class toward reformers.

Guided Reading and Review found in the Unit 2 folder, p. 9, provides a structure for reading and mastering the key concepts and reviewing the key terms for Section 2. (Guided Practice)

✪ **Literature Activity** Advice on Marriage, found in the Unit 2 folder, p. 28, uses a contemporary magazine article to demonstrate the popular values of the early 1800s.

consumers more than producers and where they were having fewer children. Aside from offering practical advice and household tips, she wrote on a positive note about the contributions that women could make in a capitalistic society.

Beecher did not believe that women should move beyond the realms of family and education. In her view, being a mother and a wife should give women their focus in life. Women's work remained as central to the overall economy as it had been in the 1600s, but in different ways. Although middle-class women no longer milked cows or planted vegetables, they were not supposed to become idle or lazy. In fact, it was precisely because they had primary responsibility for the home and the family, Beecher argued, that women were so important.

Everyone knew, wrote Beecher in her *Treatise*, that "the success of democratic institutions . . . depends upon the intellectual and moral character of the mass of the people." Everyone also agreed that "the formation of the moral and intellectual character of the young is committed mainly to the female hand." Here, then, was the reason why women were so critically important to the welfare of the United States:

T*he mother forms the character of the future man; . . . the wife sways the heart, whose energies may turn for good or for evil the destinies of a nation. . . . Let the women of a country be made virtuous and intelligent, and the men will certainly be the same. The proper education of a man decides the welfare of an individual; but educate a woman, and the interests of a whole family are secured.*

Catharine Beecher helped to establish notions about the role of American women that continue to be held by some segments of American society today. Women were powerful, but

In her *Treatise on Domestic Economy*, Catharine Beecher argued that women should play the central role in managing the household and raising children.

only privately, in their duties as mothers and wives. Some historians refer to this as the **cult of domesticity**, or the belief in the importance of women's role in the home.

Beyond the Private Sphere

As influential as Catharine Beecher was, many northern middle-class American women in the first half of the 1800s did not limit themselves to the home and charitable work. Increasingly, women challenged traditional attitudes by becoming involved in political activities. They joined a variety of reform movements, including those advocating temperance and abolitionism; they marched in parades to support their causes and participated in economic boycotts; they gave lectures at public assemblies. Even while Beecher was writing her popular books, northern middle-class women were having fewer children and becoming more visible in areas in which they had long been invisible.

Perhaps the most important development for women in this period was a growing sense of what one historian has called "the bonds of womanhood." By participating in reform movements, many northern middle-class women became more conscious of—and consequently more vocal about—their inferior position in American society. At the same time, they formed strong intellectual and emotional ties with other women in similar positions.

Abolitionism was the primary vehicle through which women, both African American and white, emerged from the domestic world of home and family into the public world of politics. By the 1840s, some women were actively protesting their subordinate position within both the antislavery movement and American society in general.

Women who participated in the abolition movement saw obvious parallels between the plight of enslaved African Americans and the

2. INSTRUCT

Explain/Discuss

Explain to students that radical reform often comes about slowly through a series of gradual changes in people's lifestyles or attitudes. Sometimes people achieve breakthroughs that in their day seem huge; subsequent generations accept the old breakthroughs as the norm and even amplify and improve on them.

Discuss with students how some of Catharine Beecher's peers might have considered her views "radical." Then compare her views with those of reformer Elizabeth Cady Stanton. In what ways do Stanton's views represent a further development of Beecher's ideas about women?

Analyze

Ask students to analyze the growing differences between North and South, and between the middle class and the working class. How did these differences affect each group's interest in social reform, including women's rights?

Visions of America: Turning Point Story To enhance students' understanding of the Turning Point topic in this section, play "Speak Out," a story about Harriet Jacobs's escape from slavery and her role in the abolition movement (length: approximately 4 minutes). This selection can be located on side 1 of the videodiscs. This selection can also be located on videotape 2. Lesson plans for Turning Point stories can be found in the Visions of America Teacher's Guidebook.

Visions of America: Roundtable Discussion To introduce students to different and differing viewpoint on the Turning point topic in this section, play all or part of the Roundtable Discussion on "Speak Out," remarks by respected historians and social commentators. This selection can be located on side 1 of the videodiscs. This selection can also be located on videotape 2.

Activity

(The clock icon indicates an activity that can be successfully conducted within a class period. Each chapter has at least one such activity.)

Creating Needs Pyramids

Ask students to work in groups to create two pyramid lists—lowest priorities at the bottom, the highest priority level having only one or two items. One should reflect the needs and priorities of the working class of the early 1800s, the other the needs and priorities of middle-class women at this time. Each pyramid should have six to eight levels. Students can first brainstorm ideas and then coordinate responses for each level. **LEP**

Enrichment

Have students design a logo that might have been used by women and African Americans to illustrate their common bonds in the fight against oppression.

In Depth

Then and Now

The struggle for women's rights and the cessation of double standards based on gender is an important issue in the 1990s. The National Organization for Women, or NOW (see pages 686–687), is one of the most active organizations for women's rights in the 1990s. "We lead public opinion, we do not follow it," says Patricia Ireland, who has led the organization since 1991. "Taking a leadership position makes people uncomfortable. But my ultimate value isn't comfort. My ultimate value is progress for women."

status of women. Neither group could vote or hold office, and both were denied the full rights of American citizens. Although white and African American women had been aware of these constraints for decades, the religious revivals and reform movements of the early 1800s heightened their sense of women's potential and power.

In addition to raising their consciousness, abolitionism provided women with a political platform from which they could assert their power. In 1836, for example, South Carolina–born abolitionist Angelina Grimké demanded that the women of the South fight slavery. Although women could not make laws, she said, they could still influence those who do: "If you really suppose you can do nothing to overthrow slavery, you are greatly mistaken. . . . You can read. . . . You can pray. . . . You can speak. . . . You can act." Both black and white women began to attend meetings, gather petitions, give public talks, and write pamphlets and books.

The Seneca Falls Convention In the 1840s, two American abolitionists, **Lucretia Mott** and **Elizabeth Cady Stanton,** took their search for human rights one step further by organizing the first convention in history to discuss the question of women's rights. Held at **Seneca Falls,** New York, in 1848, the convention issued a *Declaration of*

Elizabeth Cady Stanton (left) issued a manifesto declaring that "all men and women are created equal."

Sojourner Truth is pictured on the right. Her commanding presence and powerful speaking style captured people's attention at many antislavery and women's rights meetings.

Sentiments signed by sixty-eight women and thirty-two men. Only one African American, Frederick Douglass, was present.

The *Declaration,* written by Stanton, deliberately echoed the form and language of the Declaration of Independence. In addition to protesting women's lack of legal and political rights, it also attacked the double standard that society held for men and women:

> *The history of mankind is a history of repeated injuries and usurpations* [violent seizing of power] *on the part of man toward woman, having in direct object the establishment of an absolute tyranny over her. . . . Because women do feel themselves aggrieved* [offended], *oppressed, and fraudulently deprived of their most sacred moral rights, we insist that they have immediate admission to all the rights and privileges which belong to them as citizens of the United States.*

Although the vast majority of Americans ignored or dismissed the Declaration, the Seneca Falls convention marked the beginning

RESOURCE DIRECTORY

Teaching Resources

American Profiles Activity found in the Unit 2 folder, p. 17, profiles Maria Mitchell, who received many academic distinctions as America's first woman astronomer.

In addition to discovering a new comet in 1847, astronomer Maria Mitchell was the first woman elected to the American Academy of Arts and Sciences.

Answer to ...

MAKING CONNECTIONS

In both the 1840s and 1960s, women active in movements for racial justice became aware of the parallels between the plight of African Americans and their own inequality. This awareness inspired them to work for equal rights and full participation in society for women. In both instances, women also gained experience in how to run effective reform movements.

of the organized movement for women's rights in the United States.

Sojourner Truth Speaks Out for Women
African American women also were inspired and empowered by the movement for abolition. Among the most famous of these were three former enslaved women: Harriet Tubman, famous for her activities in the underground railroad; Harriet Brent Jacobs, author of the 1861 book *Incidents in the Life of a Slave Girl;* and **Sojourner Truth.**

Truth, whose original name was Isabella Baumfree, was born in Ulster County, New York, in 1797. Freed in 1827, she initially found work as a domestic servant in New York City but soon became involved in a variety of religious and reform movements of her day. She took the name Sojourner Truth in the early 1840s because she believed her life mission was to travel around the nation telling the truth about slavery and God.

Although she never learned to read or write, Sojourner Truth became a powerful spokesperson in the antislavery cause. She also became one of a small number of African American women in the 1840s and 1850s who were active in the movement for women's rights. No black women attended the Seneca Falls convention, and only a handful came to most other women's rights conventions. For most black women, abolition was the more pressing issue. Truth, however, was often in attendance at these meetings, reminding white women that their African American sisters also had a place in the movement for women's rights.

MAKING CONNECTIONS

Just as the women's movement of the 1840s was inspired by the abolitionist movement, the women's movement of the 1960s was inspired by the civil rights movement. Why do you think these two movements for racial justice, separated by more than a century, encouraged the rise of movements for women's rights?

A Foundation for Change

The activities of such reformers as Elizabeth Cady Stanton and Sojourner Truth did not bring about a sudden, fundamental change in the status of American women. Nevertheless, reformers did succeed in gradually expanding the opportunities available to American women outside the home.

Whereas no seminary or college in the United States admitted women in 1820, by 1890 more than 2,500 women a year were graduating

In Depth

Interdisciplinary

Astronomer Maria Mitchell (1818–1889) was born in the busy whaling port of Nantucket, Massachusetts. As a child, she helped her father record an eclipse of the sun and was encouraged to use his telescope. In 1847, she discovered a comet, which was later named for her. As a teacher, she advised her students to question everything: "We especially need imagination in science. It is not all mathematics, nor all logic, it is somewhat beauty and poetry." (See the American Profiles Activity in the Resource Directory.)

from American colleges and universities. Thanks in part to the benefits of education, women began appearing in professions from which they previously had been excluded. After becoming the first woman to earn a medical diploma, Elizabeth Blackwell began practicing medicine in New York City in 1850 and seven years later founded the first school of nursing in the United States. Astronomer Maria Mitchell, pictured on page 163, was not only a member of the American Academy of Arts and Sciences but also became the first professor of astronomy at newly founded Vassar College for women in 1865.

Women also excelled as writers, editors, and publishers. Margaret Fuller, the editor of an important philosophical journal, also wrote an 1845 book *Woman in the Nineteenth Century,* in which she criticized cultural traditions that restricted women's roles in society. And as editor of the popular magazine *Godey's Lady's Book,* Sarah Josepha Hale published articles about women's issues for almost fifty years.

In spite of fierce opposition, the women struggling for equal rights would not be silenced. In the piercing words of Sojourner Truth:

⭐ The patriarchal character of plantation life is apparent in this painting, in which the plantation owner's presence overshadows his wife as well as his servant.

The women are coming up, blessed be God, and a few of the men are coming up with them. But man is in a tight place, the poor slave is on him, woman is coming on him, and he is surely between a hawk and a buzzard.

The Lives of Southern Women

Just as southerners bitterly resented the criticisms and activities of the abolitionists, they did not welcome the advice of northern reformers who prodded them to give more rights to women. The reasons behind this were both economic and social.

While the North became increasingly industrial and urban in the early 1800s, the South remained primarily agricultural and rural. In fact, the great majority of southern whites in the 1830s and 1840s were farmers who depended on the cash crop of cotton for their living. In most areas of the South, the household remained an important economic unit. Less affected by the Market Revolution that was changing the character of the North, many southern families, both rich and poor, continued to blend work and family activities. They saw little need for restructuring family life. Furthermore, because farms and plantations were often miles apart, opportunities to participate in public organizations and community meetings were rare.

Social relationships remained quite traditional in the South, especially with regard to matters of gender. Whether small farmers or wealthy planters, southern males viewed themselves as the rulers of their domains. Southern plantations, in particular, were classic examples of patriarchal systems. The master of the plantation exercised power over all of his dependents, including women, children, and enslaved African Americans.

A few southern white women saw parallels between their position in this patriarchal system and that of the enslaved. South Carolina's Mary Boykin Chesnut confided to her diary that her husband was "master of the house. To hear is to obey. . . . All the comforts of my life depend upon his being in a good humor." Chesnut went so far as to comment that "there is no slave . . . like a wife."

Although southern men idealized their women, there women were less likely to have the moral influence and public role of their northern counterparts. The wives of small farmers often worked with their husbands in the fields, while planters' wives supervised large households and sometimes helped manage the plantation. Many

▶ **RESOURCE DIRECTORY**

Teaching Resources

⭐ **Primary Source Activity** Plantation Life, found in the Unit 2 folder, p. 25, presents excerpts from Anne Kemble's *Journal of a Residence on a Georgian Plantation in 1838–39,* in which she comments on differences between paid laborers of the North and enslaved laborers of the South, a well as on the nature of southern chivalry.

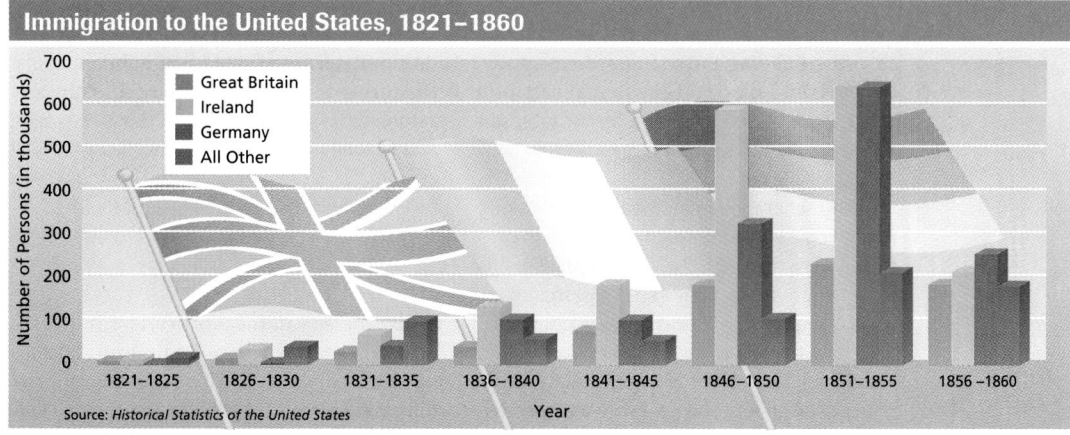

Immigration to the United States, 1821–1860

Number of Persons (in thousands)

- Great Britain
- Ireland
- Germany
- All Other

700
600
500
400
300
200
100
0

1821–1825   1826–1830   1831–1835   1836–1840   1841–1845   1846–1850   1851–1855   1856–1860

Year

Source: *Historical Statistics of the United States*

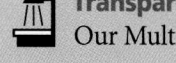 **Interpreting Graphs**
Seeking to escape famine and revolution in Europe, several million immigrants came to the United States in the 1840s and 1850s, changing the character of the United States population in the process. *Which nation sent the largest number of immigrants to the United States in the period from 1846 to 1855?*

of these women, rich and poor, oversaw their children's education. Because farms and plantations were often miles apart, opportunities to participate in public organizations and community meetings were rare. While in the urban North, women such as Elizabeth Cady Stanton and Sojourner Truth attempted to redefine the position of women in American society, in the rural South, women remained locked in traditional roles and activities.

The traditional nature of southern society was also apparent in its inhabitants' highly developed sense of honor. Southern men, in particular, were sensitive about their public reputations. The great emphasis that southern culture put on honor makes it easier to understand the intense anger with which southerners responded to criticism by northern reformers.

Reform and the Working Class

Like southerners, working class people viewed reformers as meddlers and moralists who had no business interfering in the lives of others. The large size of this working class was a result of the Market Revolution of the early 1800s. Some members of the working class were people born in the United States who had moved from farms to cities to find factory jobs. Many, however, were immigrants who came to the United States

during the dramatic surge in immigration that took place between 1830 and 1860. The graph above shows this increase.

Although some of the new immigrants arrived from Scandinavia and England, most came from Ireland and Germany. Because the system of slave labor in the South limited economic opportunities in that region, the great majority of these immigrants settled in the North. Forced out of their homeland by the disastrous potato famine of the mid-1840s, Irish immigrants tended to settle in northeastern cities and take manual labor jobs in factories or on canals or railroads. German immigrants, on the other hand—many of whom had fled political oppression after the failure of the European revolutions of 1848—bought farmland in the Midwest or settled in northern cities such as New York, Philadelphia, Cincinnati, Chicago, and Milwaukee.

Religious differences immediately created tension between middle-class reformers and working-class immigrants. Nearly all of the Irish immigrants and many of the German immigrants were Roman Catholic. Reformers strongly disapproved of the Catholic religion. They believed that the emphasis Catholicism placed on ritual and the authority of the Pope and bishops made it impossible for individuals to think for themselves and to find their own salvation.

Media and Technology

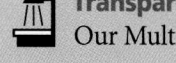 **Transparency**
Our Multicultural Heritage, C-13

Caption Answer to ...

 Interpreting Graphs

Ireland

Reteach

Ask students to list the major steps in the development of the women's movement. Then have them list three types of conflict during the early 1800s caused by cultural differences and three types caused by regional differences.

 Alternative Assessment

Mid-Point Monitoring
Ask students if they have
- Selected the activities they will include in their project
- Begun to research information for each

 In Depth

Multicultural Perspectives

In 1828 a *New York Evening Post* reporter complained about "large groups of men and boys playing ball and filling the air with their shouts and yells." But the noise over baseball was just beginning. In June 1846 the first organized game of baseball was played in New York, and by 1876 a National League was formed. African Americans, however, were largely excluded from playing in the major leagues until 1947, when Jackie Robinson played for the Brooklyn Dodgers, helped win the pennant, and was named Rookie of the Year. (See pages 608–609 and 612–613.)

Section 2 Review Answers

1. (a) suffrage, see p. 160, (b) cult of domesticity, see p. 161

2. (a) Catharine Beecher, see p. 160, (b) Lucretia Mott, see p. 162, (c) Elizabeth Cady Stanton, see p. 162, (d) Sojourner Truth, see p. 163

3. Seneca Falls, see p. 162

4. They opened women's eyes to injustices they themselves were suffering and gave them experience and knowledge of organizing and working for reform.

5. Lucretia Mott and Elizabeth Cady Stanton.

6. They clashed mostly because working-class people spent their leisure time enjoying sports, drinking in taverns, and gambling. Middle-class evangelicals denounced these activities as idle and self-indulgent. They believed that people should spend their time in more uplifting ways.

7. Both the antislavery and women's rights movements succeeded in making their causes part of the public debate and in winning some important advances. On the other hand, it was more than a century before African Americans and women began to win substantial victories in their struggle for full political and civil rights and full participation in American society.

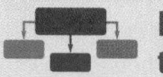 CLOSE

Reinforcing the Big Idea

Inspired by the antislavery movement, women began fighting for equality. Their demands for reform of all kinds met with bitter resistance among some groups and regions in the United States. Southerners and working-class people felt particularly under siege by these reformers. The next section turns to the situation of the Native Americans of the plains at the start of the nineteenth century.

For their part, working-class immigrants found that the evangelical Protestant version of character-building and self-improvement were unnecessary luxuries. They were much more concerned with putting food on the table and keeping a roof over their heads than with debating issues of morality.

Whether immigrant or native born, working-class people valued different things from most middle-class reformers. Because they had so little power in their working lives, working people wanted to do as they pleased in their leisure time. Alcohol often played an important role in their social lives. Men drank in taverns that were the center of neighborhood society. Women bought beer to enjoy with neighbors on the steps of tenements. The idea that drinking alcohol was an inherently immoral act was a strange one in their view, and they resented temperance activists who preached to them about its evils.

Organized sports played an increasingly important role in working-class lives in the 1840s and 1850s. People who spent much of their lives working in poorly paying, unsatisfying jobs took pleasure in boxing matches, horse races, and newly emerging team sports such as baseball. Gambling and drinking were sometimes part of the fun. Most middle-class reformers were dismayed by these activities. They denounced them as examples of idle behavior and moral weakness and wondered whether working people had the character necessary to become good citizens.

In the end, what many middle-class reformers wanted, particularly evangelical reformers, was for working-class people to become like them. They sought an end to drinking and gambling, a celebration of hard work, and a form of religion that encouraged self-improvement rather than devotion to tradition. Reformers hoped that public schools, together with laws that restricted drinking and gambling, would transform working-class men and women into the middle-class idea of model citizens. What working people wanted was to be left alone to live their lives as they wished.

Worlds Apart

By the 1840s, the North and South were rapidly moving apart, not only economically, but culturally as well. These growing cultural differences clearly contributed to the rising tension between the two regions, which were quickly becoming like two different worlds.

An armed conflict between the North and South would happen, in part, because northern middle-class reformers found southern behavior so unacceptable that they demanded change. And white southerners would eventually decide to leave the union because they would never submit to northern middle-class definitions of morality and social relationships. Although the reform movements of the early 1800s strained relations between North and South, it was ultimately the question of how to develop the vast lands west of the Mississippi River that brought this relationship to the breaking point.

Thus, in the 1840s tensions increased between the middle class and the working class, as well as between North and South. For the time being, the existing political system was capable of containing these strains and stresses. But another factor would soon heighten tensions still further and put the nation at risk: ongoing expansion to the West.

SECTION 2 REVIEW

Key Terms, People, and Places
1. Define (a) suffrage, (b) cult of domesticity.
2. Identify (a) Catharine Beecher, (b) Lucretia Mott, (c) Elizabeth Cady Stanton, (d) Sojourner Truth.
3. Identify Seneca Falls.

Key Concepts
4. How did the reform movements of the 1830s and 1840s advance the cause of women's rights?
5. Who organized the Seneca Falls convention?
6. Why did the working class and reformers clash?

Critical Thinking
7. **Making Comparisons** Compare and contrast the achievements and failures of the antislavery and the women's rights movements.

 RESOURCE DIRECTORY

Teaching Resources

Quiz found in the Unit 2 folder, p. 10, covers the main ideas in this section as well as the key terms.

Beyond the Mississippi

SECTION PREVIEW

During the 1700s and 1800s, powerful new forces transformed the lives of Native Americans and Hispanics in what is now the West. For Native Americans, the introduction of the horse brought dramatic changes. For Hispanics, the pressure of new settlers and traders from the United States led to the creation of some settlements and the loss of others.

Key Concepts

- Nomadic cultures tended to increase the power of Native American men and weaken the influence that women had exercised in more settled villages.
- Spain tried to strengthen its northern colonies in California, New Mexico, and Texas in the late 1700s.
- The American immigrants who moved into Texas established an independent republic in 1836.

Key Terms, People, and Places

nomad, secularize; Meriwether Lewis, William Clark, Sacajawea, Stephen Austin, Sam Houston; Great Plains

E ven before the United States had completed the purchase of Louisiana from France in 1803, President Jefferson was making plans to send an expedition west to explore the nation's new territory. Jefferson hoped this expedition would both establish the political boundaries of Louisiana and gather information about the territory's natural resources that might prove useful for future economic development. Jefferson added another reason in an 1806 speech that revealed much about his attitude toward Native Americans:

I . . . sent our beloved man, Captain Lewis, . . . to go up the Missouri river to get acquainted with all the Indian nations in its neighborhood, to take them by the hand, deliver my talks to them, and to inform us in what way we could be useful to them.

⭐ Explorers **Meriwether Lewis** and **William Clark** set out from St. Louis, Missouri, in May 1804 with a small "Corps of Discovery." The roughly fifty men who participated in the expedition journeyed up the Missouri River. Their course took them over the Continental Divide, which is the ridge of the Rocky Mountains that separates rivers that flow west from rivers that flow east. They then journeyed down the Columbia River to the Pacific Ocean, returning east more than two years later. The nation received with much interest the scientific samples, maps of the mountains and rivers of the territory, and information about the Native Americans in the region that the group brought back.

Lewis and Clark's well-organized expedition was a remarkable achievement, but it was not a journey into unsettled territory. Hundreds of thousands of Native Americans lived west of the Mississippi River in the early 1800s. In fact, the expedition owed some of its success to one of these Native Americans—a Shoshone woman named **Sacajawea,** who served as translator and guide for the two explorers.

Lewis and Clark were by no means the first white people whom Native Americans west of the Mississippi had encountered. Spaniards had been living in New Mexico and Texas for decades and had moved into California not long before the Corps of Discovery set out. In the early 1800s, however, both Native Americans and Hispanics faced the enormous challenge

The flags and horses on this Sioux beaded vest indicate increasing contract among Native Americans, Europeans, and the United States.

📘 **Reproducible Lesson Plan** found in the Unit 2 folder, p. 5, provides a summary of the Section 3 lesson plan content.

📘 **Alternate Lesson Plan: Cooperative Learning** found in the Alternate Lesson Plans folder, p. 71, helps students interpret key events in the lands beyond the Mississippi.

📘 **Guided Reading and Review** found in the Unit 2 folder, p. 11, provides a structure for reading and mastering the key concepts and reviewing the key terms for Section 3. (Guided Practice)

⭐📘 **American Profiles Activity** York, found in the Unit 2 folder, p. 18, profiles William Clark's slave, who proved invaluable on Lewis and Clark's epic journey.

1. FOCUS

Connecting to the Big Idea

See page 150B. Explain that the lives of Native Americans living on the Great Plains were significantly altered by contact with the Spanish long before the arrival of white American settlers. The continued westward movement of settlers and traders into Texas, New Mexico, and California increased tension with both the Native Americans and the Mexican government. Ask how Mexico reacted to these new immigrants.

Objectives

- Explain how nomadic cultures increased the power of Native American men and decreased the influence of women.
- Explain how Spain tried to strengthen its northern colonies in the late 1700s in California, New Mexico, and Texas.
- Explain how American immigrants who moved into Texas established an independent republic in 1836.

Bellringer

Provide a map of the United States and ask students to list at least five cities in California, Texas, and New Mexico with names that are Spanish in origin. Ask them if, based on what they know, Mexican and American cultures would be likely to clash.

Reading Strategy

Reading for Evidence Ask students to find evidence as they read the section that European animals and technology affected Native American societies of the Great Plains.

Explain/Discuss

Discuss the effect of the introduction of the horse. Ask how the horse changed the traditional life of some groups of Native Americans living on the Great Plains. How did the horse affect the relationship between nomadic and village peoples?

Discuss the American settlement of Hispanic North America. Ask questions such as the following: What was Spain trying to do by establishing missions in California? How did Mexico unwittingly encourage the eventual American takeover of Texas?

Analyze

Ask students to analyze the tension caused by the American settlement of Mexico's northern territories. What role might cultural differences have played in the conflict? How do these differences continue to be a source of conflict today in Texas, New Mexico, and California?

Alfred Jacob Miller's painting illustrates the nomadic life many Native Americans of the plains adopted after the arrival of the horse. Using the *travois* shown, dogs could pull 40-pound loads five or six miles a day.

posed by the tens of thousands of Americans who were migrating into their worlds. But the animals and technology imported from Europe had already been affecting Native American societies of the **Great Plains**—the vast grasslands that lie between the Mississippi River and the Rocky Mountains—for almost two centuries.

The Coming of the Horse

One of these European animals, the horse, had a profound impact on the everyday lives of the Native Americans of the plains. The Spanish brought horses to their colonies in New Mexico, and Native Americans acquired them through trading, raids, and occasional carelessness on the part of the Europeans. By the mid-1700s, horses had spread as far north as the Missouri Valley, the Dakotas, and parts of what are now Oregon and Washington.

Before the arrival of the horse, Native Americans had generally utilized only one domesticated four-legged animal—the dog, which was useful for hunting and fighting. Many Native Americans took advantage of the horse without allowing it to transform their cultures. The Pawnee, Mandan, and other Native American nations continued to live primarily as farmers, hunters, and gatherers. As in most Native American societies, the women in these villages did most of the farming, while the

men were responsible for the hunting. Other Native Americans rode the horse to an entirely new way of life. They became **nomads**—people who migrate constantly instead of living permanently in a particular place. Carrying their possessions on the backs of horses, they followed the vast herds of buffalo that crisscrossed the Great Plains.

The Uses of the Horse By 1800 the Native Americans of the Great Plains had used horses to hunt the buffalo for more than half a century. During that time they discovered a multitude of purposes for the buffalo. According to James R. Walker, a doctor who lived for a time among the Oglala Lakota, after butchering the buffalo, those people used

> *their hair for making ropes and pads and for ornamental and ceremonial purposes; the horns and hoofs for making implements and utensils; the bones for making soup and articles to be used in their various occupations and games; the sinews for making their sewing thread and their stronger cords such as bowstrings; the skins for making ropes, tipis, clothing . . . ; the flesh and viscera [intestines] for food.*

Most of the nomads who lived on the Great Plains in the early 1800s were recent immigrants to that region. The Crow had long lived

▶ RESOURCE DIRECTORY

Teaching Resources

Literature Activity Native American Legends: Hiawatha, found in the Unit 2 folder, p. 29, uses an excerpt from Henry Wadsworth Longfellow's "Song of Hiawatha" to illustrate his views on the Native American hero.

on the plains, but the Cheyenne, the Sioux, the Comanche, and the Blackfeet all migrated to that area after horses made it possible for them to live on the move. Although the seemingly endless herds of buffalo drew them to the plains, these Native Americans also moved westward to avoid the great wave of settlers who were pushing toward and beyond the Mississippi River.

Changing Roles for Men and Women While there were significant variations from group to group, the nomadic Native Americans of the plains did share some characteristics. Because they depended heavily on skilled riding, hunting, and fighting, which only men learned formally, nomadic societies granted men higher status than women. Men had to be aggressive in dealing with other Native Americans as well as in hunting buffalo. In the early 1800s, Native Americans often conducted raids on one another to obtain horses or to subdue rivals.

Men also benefited because in nomadic life, social and political structures tended to be more fluid than in farming villages. Wealth was determined by the number of horses one had, and power by the skill and daring one showed in battle or during the hunt.

A young Cheyenne named Wilkis remembered when his uncle taught him how to hunt buffalo and gave him the following advice:

R*ide your horse close up to the buffalo, as close as you can, and then let fly the arrow with all your force. If the buffalo turns to fight, your horse will take you away from it; but, above all things, do not be afraid; you will not kill buffalo if you are afraid to get close to them.*

Eventually Wilkis became exactly what a grown man was supposed to be according to Cheyenne culture: "I was a good hunter; I had a herd of horses, and had been to war, and been well spoken of by the leaders whose war parties I went with."

Women were generally less influential and less well off in nomadic cultures. Because these Native Americans rarely stayed in one place long enough to farm the land, women's responsibilities now involved activities created by a horse-centered culture. For the most part, women spent their time either preparing for the hunt or drying buffalo meat and tanning buffalo hides after it was over.

Female influence in agricultural villages had rested, in part, on the fact that women remained at home and ran the village when the men left for long periods of hunting and fighting. After Native American nations such as the Sioux and Comanche had adopted a nomadic way of life, however, women followed their husbands and fathers on an endless buffalo hunt. Power that had previously resided in the female-oriented village now rested in the male-dominated hunting parties.

The Decline of Village Societies Before the arrival of the horse, the various Native American nations of the Great Plains lived in relative harmony. But as the 1700s wore on, the nomadic Native Americans engaged in a series of destructive raids on more settled Native American groups. To the south, the Comanche drove the Apache and Navaho west into New Mexico. In the North, the Sioux—in alliance with the Arapaho and Cheyenne—emerged as the dominant Native American group by the early 1800s.

Caught between white Americans who were pushing from the east and their nomadic neighbors to the west, agricultural Native Americans suffered greatly. The diseases brought by white settlers added to the tragic effects.

By the mid-1800s, about 75,000 nomadic

Artist George Catlin lived with observed the Native Americans of the plains for many years, producing more than 500 sketches and painting of the Native American way of life. The painting below is entitled *Buffalo Chase—Single Death.*

Activity
(The clock icon indicates an activity that can be successfully conducted within a class period. Each chapter has at least one such activity.)

Teaching Heterogeneous Groups
With the introduction of the horse, the lifestyle of many Native Americans on the Great Plains became nomadic rather than agricultural. To help students understand how the introduction of new technology can radically alter people's lives, have them consider how much their lives would change if there were no cars. Have students list five ways in which their lives would change if their community outlawed cars to prevent further pollution. **LEP**

Enrichment
Tell students that while Native Americans in California allowed Spanish missions to flourish, New Mexico's Native Americans made the establishment of missions there difficult. Ask students to research and compare the cultures of the Native Americans in these two territories and to explain the characteristics that either contributed to or undermined Spanish colonization.

In Depth

Then and Now

Before the arrival of white settlers, about one million Native Americans lived in the continental United States. By the early 1900s, that number had been reduced to a mere 300,000. By 1960, the numbers had climbed back up to about 800,000—half of whom lived on reservations. In the 1990s, nearly two million Native Americans live in the United States; according to the Census Bureau, about four in ten are either Cherokee, Sioux, Navaho, or Chippewa.

Yesterday's trails were carved in the most easily navigable routes from place to place, for example, in the place where the mountains are lower and the rivers narrowest. When modern highways were put in, they often took the same route as had the old trails, and for the same reason. The more accessible a route was, the less expensive it was to put a road there.

1650 1700 1750 1800 **Links Across Time** 1850 1900 1950 2000

Yesterday's Trails, Today's Highways

The trails that Native Americans, fur traders, missionaries, and others carved in the landscape (left) became today's superhighways. The photo above shows a group of would-be pioneers who recently reconstructed the journey along the Santa Fe Trail. **Why do you think yesterday's trails have become today's highways?**

Native Americans dominated the Great Plains. In addition, roughly 84,000 Native Americans from the East, forced to relocate by the United States government, lived in what is now Oklahoma. These two groups constituted about 40 percent of the Native American population of North America.

Until the 1840s, their relationship with white Americans had been uneasy but distant, consisting mainly of occasional contacts with fur traders or explorers. But that was about to change. The revolutionary impact of the horse on the people of the Great Plains seems slight when compared with the changes brought by wave after wave of white settlers from the East.

Hispanic Settlements

In the 1700s, surrounded by increasingly powerful nomadic Native Americans, the Spanish remained confined to a string of small towns along the Rio Grande and throughout present-day Texas. Spanish weakness in New Mexico and Texas reflected the larger weakness of the empire as a whole. No longer the most powerful nation in Europe, Spain in the late 1700s faced growing threats to its North American territory, from the British and the French

These Spanish mission bells were rung at religious services to indicate key points in the Mass.

and from the Russians on the northern Pacific Coast.

To confront these various threats, the Spanish government attempted to establish better relations with the Comanche and Apache. Their efforts won them a somewhat fitful peace with these Native American groups.

Securing California The Spanish expended still more effort to secure the area that is now the state of California, which they feared would fall into the hands of either the British or the Russians. In the late 1700s, Spanish soldiers and priests established a network of missions and presidios, or forts, along the rugged California coastline. Eventually they created a chain of twenty-one missions running north from San Diego to San Francisco.

From the Spanish perspective, the colonizing efforts in California were a great success. While their settlements in New Mexico and Texas remained small, the presidios and missions in California were dynamic, thriving places. The missions thrived largely as a result of Native American labor, however, and the priests who ran these communities were often harsh taskmasters. Because whippings and confinement in irons awaited those who refused to work, some Native Americans chose to leave when opportunities to escape arose. Moreover, the Native Americans who tended the cattle and sheep, farmed the land, built the missions, and wove clothing usually received only food, clothing, and shelter in return for their efforts. Poor living conditions and inadequate medical care contributed to devastating epidemics among the Native Americans on the missions. Between 1769 and 1848, the population of Native Americans in California fell from about 300,000 to about 150,000.

While the number of Native Americans declined, the number of Mexicans grew. Settling along the coast, usually around the missions and presidios, these Mexican colonists re-created the strong extended families that were often found in Spain and Mexico at that time. Monterey was the capital of the territory of California, although important settlements also were located at Santa Barbara, San Diego, and Los Angeles.

New Mexico Grows Meanwhile, change also had come to New Mexico. Thanks to long stretches of peace and increased attention from Spain, the Mexican population in the region increased from 3,800 in 1750 to 19,000 by 1800. Unlike eastern North America, however, New Mexico had a harsh landscape. This setting and the powerful nomadic Native Americans made it impossible for large numbers of people to spread out over the countryside in small farms. As a result, many people earned a living as craftspeople and traders in large settlements such as Albuquerque.

Women in this region enjoyed considerable independence. Wives were able to run businesses, divorce their husbands, own property, and sue in courts of law. In fact, women actually lost rights and influence when New Mexico became part of the United States in 1848.

Mexican Independence Leads to American Control

Mexico won its independence from Spain in 1821, after thirteen years of war and economic devastation. Although California, New Mexico, and Texas (then part of Mexico) were far from the fighting, independence still had an effect on their residents. As citizens of Mexico, the men in these territories were now free to elect representatives to the new government in Mexico City.

Because Mexico's new government was hostile to the Roman Catholic church, it **secularized** the missions, meaning it put them under the control of the state rather than the church. By the 1830s, only a handful of priests remained in northern Mexico. In addition, economic reforms designed to bolster the Mexican economy actually widened the gap between rich and poor in Mexico's northern territories. But these reforms also encouraged trade with the United States.

In 1821 William Becknell, a nearly bankrupt American, brought a load of goods from Missouri to the New Mexican capital of Santa Fe, where he sold them for mules and silver coins. Other Americans followed, taking advantage of the commercial opening created by Mexican independence and economic reforms. The high quality and low prices of American goods virtually destroyed New Mexico's trade with the rest of Mexico. By the early 1830s, caravans of wagons traveled regularly between Independence, Missouri, and New Mexico along the Santa Fe Trail.

American fur traders and merchants exploited economic openings in other parts of Mexico's northern territories. New Englanders who sailed around South America to reach the West soon dominated the trade with California in fur, cattle hides, and tallow, a waxy substance used to make candles. In return, Californians bought finished goods from the New Englanders. According to one resident of Monterey in the 1840s, "There is not a yard of tape, a pin, or a piece of domestic cotton or even thread that does not come from the United States."

Long before the United States conquered the Mexican provinces of Texas, New Mexico, and California militarily, it had conquered them economically. By loosening the regulations affecting trade with American merchants, the Mexican government ensured that the commercial ties of its northern provinces would be with the United States, rather than with its own merchants. More important, stronger commercial ties encouraged some

In Depth

Biography

At fifteen, Sam Houston (1793–1863) ran away to live with the Cherokee, returning home three years later with a Native American name: "The Raven." After studying law, Houston became a member of the United States Congress in 1823; and in 1827 was elected governor of Tennessee. He then left public life and returned to the Cherokee until 1832. In 1835 Andrew Jackson made him leader of the Texan forces against Mexico; he reentered public life as Texas's president, then as the state's United States senator, and later as its governor. In 1861, when Texas withdrew from the Union, Houston resigned, saying, "I love Texas too well to bring civil strife and bloodshed upon her."

Americans who moved into Texas in the 1820s were looking for economic opportunities and a new life, the same goals that draw Mexicans into the United States today.

Reteach

List the following terms on the chalkboard and ask students to use each one in a sentence that relates to the section content: Continental Divide, Great Plains, nomad, village society, mission, Santa Fe Trail, William Travis, the Alamo, General Antonio López de Santa Anna.

3. ASSESS

Section 3 Review Answers

1. (a) nomad, see p. 168, (b) secularize, see p. 171

2. (a) Meriwether Lewis, see p. 167, (b) William Clark, see p. 167, (c) Sacajawea, see p. 167, (d) Stephen Austin, see p. 172, (e) Sam Houston, see p. 173

3. Great Plains, see p. 168

In Depth

Historical Misconceptions

The story that the defense of the Alamo symbolizes a struggle of brave white settlers against despotism is under close scrutiny by a new generation of historians. They regard it more as a symbol of United States imperialism and racism toward Mexicans and Native Americans. According to University of Texas history professor Cynthia Orozco, "The Euro-Americans wanted to distinguish themselves from people who were here before them."

Bowing to his father's dying wish, Stephen Austin established the first colony of American settlers in Texas in 1822.

Americans to seek new opportunities in Mexico's northern territories.

Texas Wins Independence

Nowhere was the influx of Americans into Mexican territory more apparent in the 1820s than in Texas. **Stephen Austin,** carrying out the plan begun by his father, Moses Austin, received permission from the Mexican government to found a colony of about 300 settlers in east Texas. Austin, twenty-nine years old and a member of the Missouri territorial legislature, led the first organized group of American settlers into Texas in 1822. By 1824 some 2,000 immigrants were living in Austin's colony.

By 1830 about 7,000 Americans lived in Texas, more than twice the number of Mexicans in the territory. Worried that they were losing Texas through immigration, Mexico passed a law in 1830 prohibiting any more

Americans from settling there. Equally important, they outlawed the importation of enslaved people. Still, Americans continued to flow across the border.

Many Americans in the 1820s and 1830s migrated to Texas following reports of fertile soil for growing crops. Today, many Mexicans attempt to immigrate to the United States. Do these two groups of people share similar reasons for wanting to settle in a new land?

Tension Erupts into War By 1835 more than 30,000 Americans and 3,000 enslaved African Americans lived in Texas. As their numbers swelled, these Americans demanded more political freedom. In particular, they wanted slavery to be guaranteed under Mexican law. When the vain and ambitious General Antonio López de Santa Anna declared himself dictator of Mexico, supporters of an independent Texas became even more determined to break away. American settlers united in the cause of independence, and in March 1836, they formally declared the founding of the Republic of Texas.

⭐ Santa Anna responded to this defiance of Mexican authority by leading an army of several thousand men north to subdue the rebellion. The Mexican leader won early victories at the Alamo, a fortress built on the ruins of a Spanish mission in San Antonio, and at Goliad. At the Alamo, fewer than 200 Texans defended an abandoned Spanish mission for twelve days while inflicting heavy casualties on 4,000 Mexican troops. Before his death, the Texans' leader, a hot-tempered lawyer from Alabama named William Travis, sent this plea for help "to the People of Texas and all the Americans in the World":

> Fellow citizens & compatriots, I am besieged by a thousand or more of the Mexicans under Santa Anna. . . . I call on you in the name of Liberty, of patriotism & everything dear to the American character to come to our aid, with all dispatch. . . . If this call is neglected, I am determined to

▶ RESOURCE DIRECTORY

Teaching Resources

 Literature Activity What Happened in Texas, found in the Unit 2 folder, p. 30, uses an excerpt from Walt Whitman's "Song of Myself" to demonstrate the popularity of the Alamo in American folklore.

*sustain myself as long as possible & die like
a soldier who never forgets what is due to
his own honor or that of his country.*

The deaths of the courageous Alamo defenders—including Travis and the legendary frontiersman Davy Crockett—and the massacre of 371 prisoners captured by the Mexicans at Goliad, enraged and energized Texans to mighty actions for their cause.

Texas Fighters Turn the Tables Still confident of victory, Santa Anna divided his force to finish off the Texan rebels, thousands of whom were fleeing eastward in what became known as the Runaway Scrape. Just when all seemed lost, more than 900 Texans regrouped at the San Jacinto River under **Sam Houston,** a strong-willed former governor of Tennessee. There they surprised the careless Santa Anna. Rallying to cries of "Remember the Alamo!" they routed the Mexican troops in a matter of minutes. The map on this page illustrates the war for independence.

In retaliation for the Alamo and Goliad, the Texans killed several hundred of their prisoners and forced Santa Anna to sign a treaty recognizing the Republic of Texas. The Mexican government later denounced that treaty but did not contest it militarily. In the fall of 1836, the citizens of Texas elected Sam Houston as their first president.

By the end of the 1830s, with almost no help from the United States government, American traders and settlers had established a firm presence from Texas to California. They

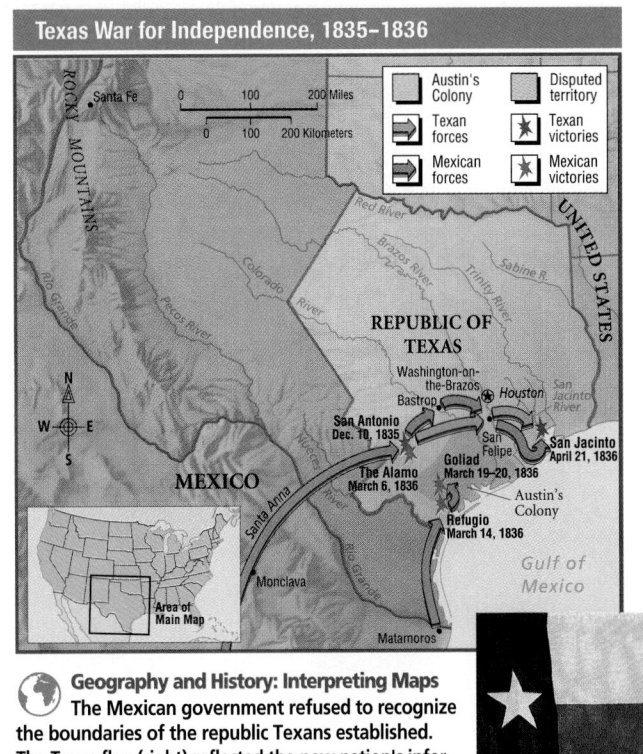

Texas War for Independence, 1835–1836

Austin's Colony
Texan forces
Mexican forces
Disputed territory
Texan victories
Mexican victories

Geography and History: Interpreting Maps
The Mexican government refused to recognize the boundaries of the republic Texans established. The Texas flag (right) reflected the new nation's informal name: the Lone Star Republic. *What formed the southernmost edge of the disputed territory?*

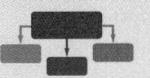

also had succeeded in prying away a large piece of territory from Mexico. As Americans continued to push west during the next decade—and the Mexican government continued to fume over the loss of Texas—tensions between Mexico and the United States grew to the point that war once again became a possibility.

SECTION 3 REVIEW

Key Terms, People, and Places
1. Define (a) nomad, (b) secularize.
2. Identify (a) Meriwether Lewis, (b) William Clark, (c) Sacajawea, (d) Stephen Austin, (e) Sam Houston.
3. Identify Great Plains.

Key Concepts
4. Why did Native American women lose power in Native American societies that became nomadic?
5. Why did the Spanish try to reform their empire and

colonize California in the late 1700s?
6. Why did Americans in Texas want their independence from Mexico?

Critical Thinking
7. **Predicting Consequences** In making it easier for the Native Americans of the plains to follow and kill buffalo, how did the arrival of the horse also make their way of life more vulnerable?

 Quiz found in the Unit 2 folder, p. 12, covers the main ideas in this section as well as the key terms.

Media and Technology

 Transparency
Our Multicultural Heritage, C-10

---

4. One source of women's influence in settled societies was their control over agriculture. But in nomadic societies, the buffalo was the primary source of food and wealth. This put a greater premium on hunting rather than agriculture.

5. To defend their empire from other Europeans from the Pacific or from Americans from the east.

6. They greatly outnumbered Mexicans in the territory and demanded more political freedom and the guarantee of slavery.

7. By encouraging Native Americans of the plains to focus their entire way of life around a single animal, the introduction of the horse also made them vulnerable to devastating loss in the event that the buffalo was eradicated.

Caption Answer to ...

Interpreting Maps

The Rio Grande.

4. CLOSE

Reinforcing the Big Idea
By the time white Americans began to explore the territory west of the Mississippi River, contact with the Spanish had already changed traditional Native American life in the Great Plains region. As more settlers pushed into Mexican territories, tensions developed between Mexico and the United States. The next section discusses Americans' push westward over the Oregon Trail and the conflict that arose between the new arrivals and those who already lived there.

SECTION 4

The Conquest of the West

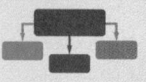

1. FOCUS

Connecting to the Big Idea

See page 150B. Attracted by stories of a beautiful and fertile land beyond the Rocky Mountains, settlers began to travel west to the Oregon Country. As settlers streamed into the West, more and more Americans began to believe it was the destiny of the United States to extend from the Atlantic to the Pacific. Ask how the United States realized its dream of a continental empire.

Objectives

● Describe the journey west made by thousands of settlers to Oregon and California in the late 1840s.
● Explain what the United States gained from its war with Mexico.
● Describe how western migration after the Mexican War and the discovery of gold in California increased tensions between Native Americans and white settlers.

Bellringer

Write the word *destiny* on the chalkboard. Ask students to jot down a definition and to think about what the word might have to do with the expanding United States in the mid-1840s.

Reading Strategy

Predicting Content Before they read the section, have students predict the problems that could arise from westward migration and American expansion. Ask students to look for data to support their predictions as they read.

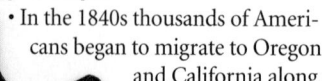

SECTION PREVIEW

The Mexican War extended the nation's boundaries from the Atlantic to the Pacific. At war's end, the discovery of gold in California transformed a stream of western-moving settlers into a flood, resulting in growing tensions with many Native American groups.

Key Concepts

• In the 1840s thousands of Americans began to migrate to Oregon and California along a variety of long and difficult western trails.
• After a war with Mexico, the victorious United States received about two fifths of Mexico's territory.
• The push of western migration after the Mexican War and the discovery of gold in California increased friction between Native Americans and white settlers.

This journal recorded the adventures of one pioneer who braved the western trails to find a new home and a new life.

Key Terms, People, and Places

Oregon Trail, manifest destiny, Gadsden Purchase, Wilmot Proviso; Joseph Smith, Brigham Young

W hile some Americans were pushing into Texas in the early 1820s, others were drawn by stories they heard of a beautiful land beyond the Rocky Mountains. This vast territory, known as the Oregon Country (now called the Pacific Northwest), stretched from northern California to the southern border of Alaska.

To the Oregon Country

Although a variety of Native American groups had lived in Oregon for centuries, by the early 1800s four different nations—the United States, Great Britain, Russia, and Spain—claimed rights to the territory. Ignoring the Native Americans who already lived there, the United States and Britain signed a treaty in 1818 agreeing to joint occupation of the territory. Distracted by other problems, Russia and Spain withdrew their claims to the area in the mid-1820s. By that time, the small but growing number of Americans who had made their way into Oregon were beginning to spread the word of what they had found there.

Routes to Oregon Merchants from New England, traveling by ship, first traded for furs with the Native Americans of Oregon in the late 1700s. After Lewis and Clark completed their expedition in 1806, fur traders began to roam the Rocky Mountains in search of animal pelts. Dubbed mountain men, these hardy trappers discovered Native American trails that led through the Rockies to California and Oregon, including the route that came to be known as the **Oregon Trail,** shown on the map on page 175. 🌐

Starting in 1843, groups of mainly white families from the midwestern states met at a small town in western Missouri called Independence—the beginning of the Oregon Trail. From there they began a grueling, 2,000-mile trek across the Great Plains and the Rocky Mountains.

Although the average time of their journeys was 121 days if they were heading for California and 139 days if they were going to Oregon, the trip west sometimes took as long as 6 months. It was an expensive journey as well, costing a typical family between $500 and $1,000.

Normally, the pioneers traveled along the Platte River in present-day Nebraska and through the South Pass in what is now Wyoming. People heading for California would turn southwest at the Snake River, follow the Humboldt River across the Sierra Nevada, and descend into the Central Valley of California

RESOURCE DIRECTORY

Teaching Resources

📄 **Reproducible Lesson Plan** found in the Unit 2 folder, p. 6, provides a summary of the Section 4 lesson plan content.

📄 **Alternate Lesson Plan: Learning Styles** found in the Alternate Lesson Plans folder, p. 72, especially useful for kinesthetic and auditory learners, helps students focus on the preparation for making the journey west on the Oregon Trail.

📄 **Guided Reading and Review** found in the Unit 2 folder, p. 13, provides a structure for reading and mastering the key concepts and reviewing the key terms for Section 4. (Guided Practice)

⭐📄 **Literature Activity** Song of the Pioneers, found in the Unit 2 folder, p. 31, uses the popular wagon song "Sweet Betsy from Pike" to illustrate both the hardships and the spirit of humor that existed along the trail to the West.

The Overland Trails to the West, 1840s

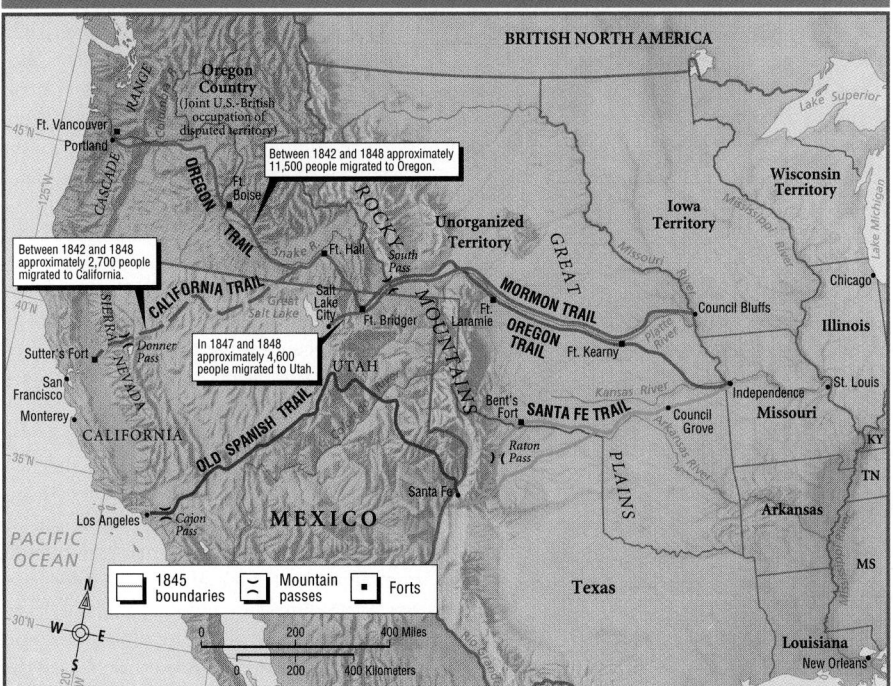

Between 1842 and 1848 approximately 11,500 people migrated to Oregon.

Between 1842 and 1848 approximately 2,700 people migrated to California.

In 1847 and 1848 approximately 4,600 people migrated to Utah.

1845 boundaries | Mountain passes | Forts

 Geography and History: Interpreting Maps
Thousands of settlers headed west along various overland trails in the 1840s, facing dry, barren country in some parts of the journey and tall, rugged mountains in others. *Along what important river did the final leg of the Oregon Trail run?*

near Sacramento. Those bound for Oregon would continue to the northwest along the Snake River until they reached the settlements along the Columbia and Willamette Rivers.

The beauty of the plains and mountains impressed many pioneers, but it made the trip no less long and difficult. Getting the heavy covered wagons across rivers, through muddy bogs, and up steep hills was exhausting, back-breaking work. And conditions for travel were often terrible in other ways as well, as an anonymous 1852 pioneer made clear:

> To enjoy such a trip along with such a crowd of emigration, a man must be able to endure heat like a Salamander, mud and water like a muskrat, dust like a toad, and labor like a jackass. He must learn to eat with his unwashed fingers, drink out of the same vessel with his mules, sleep on the ground when it rains, and share his blanket with vermin, and have patience with musketos. . . . It is a hardship without glory, to be sick without a home, to die and be buried like a dog.

Movies and television westerns would have us believe that pioneers and Native Americans were constantly fighting with each other. In fact, they spent more time trading than fighting. White travelers received food and other necessities from Native Americans in return for clothing and tools. It was not until the 1850s that serious conflict developed. Far more deadly to white settlers than any threats from Native Americans were diseases such as cholera, which killed as many as 10,000 pioneers—or about 4 percent of the total—between 1840 and 1860.

Media and Technology

 Transparency
Cause and Effect, F-4

---

2. INSTRUCT

Explain/Discuss

Explain that the national policy of manifest destiny expressed on a larger scale the goals of individual American families to find a better life for themselves. Both national and individual behavior reflected courage and tenacity, along with greed and a sometimes narrow-minded sense of superiority.

Discuss with students the reasons individuals headed west and why the government pushed west and south. Why did Americans feel justified in their expansion, despite the cost to other people and nations? How did the westward migration of American settlers affect Native Americans?

In Depth

Did You Know?

J. M. Shively's 1846 guidebook for travelers to Oregon gives a glimpse of the nature of the journey. "Take as much tea, coffee, sugar and spices as you please; but above all take plenty of flour and well cured side bacon to last you through if you can. Let each man and lad be provided with . . . two very wide-brimmed hats, wide enough to keep the mouth from the sun. For the want of such hat, thousands suffer nearly all the way to Oregon with their lips ulcerated, caused by sun-burn."

Caption Answer to ...

Interpreting Maps

Students should infer that the Americans won the war, because the map shows far more American battle victories than Mexican victories.

Analyze

Ask students to analyze the effect of territorial expansion on other concerns of the country, especially the issue of slavery and the differences between regions.

Activity

Cooperative Learning

Time: One class period.
Activity: Pioneers moving west over the Oregon Trail faced perilous risks. Have groups develop a skit about one challenge pioneers might have faced while crossing the Oregon Trail.
Grouping: Four to six students.
Purpose: To help students understand the types of challenges pioneers faced while moving west.
Roles: Skit writers, director, actors.
Outcome: Students will empathize with the experience and hardship of the Oregon Trail. **LEP**

Oregon Becomes United States Territory By 1845 more than 5,000 Americans had moved to the Oregon Country. When American settlers in the territory began to outnumber the British in 1843, they drew up a temporary government to be used until Oregon came under the jurisdiction of the United States. In the Treaty of 1846, the United States and Great Britain agreed to divide the Oregon Country along the 49th parallel. ⭐

War with Mexico

As the surge of migrants from the United States into western territories gained momen-tum in the 1830s and 1840s, some Americans began to dream of a continental empire stretching from the Atlantic to the Pacific. These Americans believed that the United States had a divine mission to spread liberty across the continent. John L. O'Sullivan, a New York journalist, coined the phrase **manifest destiny** for this idea of continental expansion. He said that it was the nation's manifest, or obvious, destiny "to overspread and to possess the whole of the continent." Soon manifest destiny became a rationalization for expansion. Unfortunately, Americans were not the only ones who believed that it was their destiny to possess the West, as quickly became clear when the United States added Texas to its growing list of states.

Annexation of Texas After winning independence from Mexico in 1836, many Texans assumed that the United States would quickly absorb their new republic. Americans were far from united on the question of annexing Texas, however. Southerners and supporters of slavery were eager to carve one or more slave states out of the Texas territory. Northerners feared that the addition of even one slave state would shift the balance of power in Congress and the Electoral College to the South. Many people in both the North and South worried that annexation would lead to war with Mexico.

In the early 1840s, northerners held up the annexation of Texas while southerners tried to push it through Congress. When Democrat James K. Polk, running on an expansionist platform, won the presidency in 1844, the tide began to shift. In February 1845, before Polk even took the oath of office, Congress approved annexation. After Texas voters added their approval in December of that year, Texas became the twenty-eighth state in the Union. ❌

War for Territory Years before the United States annexed Texas, the steady influx of Americans into Mexico's northern territories had led to growing friction between the two nations. After Congress approved annexation in early 1845, Mexico immediately broke off diplomatic relations with the United States. Continuing disagreements about the southern border of Texas signaled further trouble ahead.

The Mexican War, 1846–1848

Oregon Country

Unorganized Territory

ROCKY MOUNTAINS

IA

Ft. Leavenworth

MO

Bear Flag Revolt
June 14, 1846

San Francisco

Monterey
occupied July 7, 1846

Santa Fe
occupied Aug. 18, 1847

UNITED
STATES

San Gabriel
Jan. 8, 1847

AR

San Diego

San Pasqual
Dec. 6, 1846

El Brazito
Dec. 25, 1846

LA

MEXICO

TEXAS

Sacramento
Feb. 28, 1847

Corpus Christi

Palo Alto
May 8, 1846

PACIFIC
OCEAN

Matamoros

Buena Vista
Feb. 22–23, 1847

Monterrey
Sept. 20–25, 1846

Tropic of Cancer

Mazatlán

Santa Anna

Gulf of
Mexico

Tampico

Mexico City
entered Sept. 14, 1847

0   200   400 Miles

0   200   400 Kilometers

Chapultepec
Sept. 13, 1847

Cerro Gordo
April 18, 1847

Veracruz
March 29, 1847

Disputed territory	American victories
American forces	Mexican victories
Mexican forces	

 **Geography and History: Interpreting Maps**
Many Americans, including President Polk, viewed the Mexican War as an opportunity for the United States to expand its boundaries across the continent. *Looking at this map, what information can you use to make a judgment about who probably won the war?*

▶ **RESOURCE DIRECTORY** ❌

Teaching Resources

⚙ 📄 **Primary Source Activity** Traveling West, found in the Unit 2 folder, pp. 26–27, contains excerpts from the diaries of women traveling west along wagon trails in the mid-1800s and helps students visualize the hardships pioneer families endured.

📄 **Visual Learning Activity** The Annexation of Texas, found in the Unit 2 folder, p. 33, presents a pamphlet opposing the annexation of Texas to demonstrate the controversy surrounding this issue.

President Polk and other southern Democrats wanted much more from Mexico than Texas. Polk had dreams of acquiring the entire territory stretching from Texas to the Pacific. In a final attempt to avoid war, he sent Ambassador John Slidell to Mexico City in November 1845 with an offer to buy California and New Mexico for $30 million. But the Mexican government refused even to receive Slidell, let alone consider his offer.

Determined to have his way, Polk sent two thousand American troops under General Zachary Taylor into southern Texas to support the American claim that the Rio Grande was the official American-Mexican border. Since the Mexican government claimed that the Nueces River, located quite a few miles further north, was the border, it considered Taylor's movements an invasion of Mexican territory. Tensions between the two nations escalated rapidly. Meanwhile, an American expedition under the command of Captain John C. Frémont moved into California, probably under orders from the President to stir up trouble.

When Mexican troops engaged in a skirmish with Taylor's forces in early May 1846, Polk had the excuse for which he had long been waiting. Expressing outrage at the loss of "American blood on American soil," the President pushed for an immediate declaration of war. Despite some opposition, Congress gave it to him on May 13, 1846.

The Bear Flag Revolt Before news of the war had reached California, a group of American settlers took matters into their own hands. Led by William B. Ide, these settlers launched a surprise attack on the town of Sonoma on June 14 and proclaimed the California Republic, or Bear Flag Republic—named for their flag, which pictured a grizzly bear and a single star. Frémont quickly assumed control of the rebel forces and drove the Mexican army out of northern California.

Meanwhile, United States troops under the command of General Stephen Kearny crossed into New Mexico. Meeting little or no resistance, American forces occupied Santa Fe by mid-August (see the map on page 176). Kearny then took part of his army and marched west to California to join Frémont. Although the Mexican army won several victories in the fighting that followed, Kearny and Frémont eventually were able to subdue all opposing forces in the territory. By January 1847, the United States had taken control of New Mexico and California.

Fighting in Mexico While Frémont and Kearny were securing Mexico's northern territories for the United States, General Taylor had taken the war into Mexico itself. After crossing the Rio Grande, Taylor won a series of victories, leading finally to the Battle of Buena Vista in February 1847. Here he met Santa Anna, who had brought an army of 20,000 Mexican troops north from Mexico City. Although Taylor won the battle, Santa Anna chose to declare victory and return to Mexico City rather than continue

Viewpoints
On Expanding into Mexican Territory

Strained relations between North and South intensified when the United States annexed vast Mexican territories in 1848. *How is the spirit of the times reflected in the following viewpoints?*

Pro-Annexation

"The pretense that the annexation has been unrightful and unrighteous is wholly untrue and unjust to ourselves. If Texas became peopled with an American population, it was on the express invitation of Mexico herself. . . .What, then, can be more preposterous than all this clamor by Mexico against annexation as a violation of any rights of hers, any duties of ours?"

John L. O'Sullivan, editorial in *United States Magazine and Democratic Review*, 1845

Anti-Annexation

"They [who favor the Mexican War] have succeeded in robbing Mexico of her territory. And they are rejoicing over their success under the hypocritical pretense of a regard for peace. Had they not succeeded in robbing Mexico of the most important and most valuable part of her territory, many of those now loudest in their cries of favor for peace would be loudest and wildest for war. . . . We are not the people to rejoice. We ought rather blush and hang our heads for shame."

Frederick Douglass, African American leader of the antislavery movement, editorial in *North Star*, March 17, 1848

Expansion of the United States, 1800–1860	
Year	Square Miles
1800	888,811
1810	1,716,003
1820	1,788,006
1830	1,788,006
1840	1,788,006
1850	2,992,747
1860	3,022,387

Source: *Historical Statistics of the United States*

Interpreting Tables The United States more than tripled in size between 1800 and 1860. *During what decade did the largest expansion occur?*

the struggle, which might well have resulted in victory for the Mexicans.

Santa Anna abandoned northeastern Mexico to Taylor, in part because of a more serious threat, this time to his capital. Pressing for complete victory, Polk dispatched forces under General Winfield Scott to take Mexico City. Having captured the port city of Vera Cruz in March 1847, Scott marched his army of 10,000 men toward Mexico City along the route once taken by Spanish conquistador Hernando Cortés. After fierce fighting, Scott defeated Santa Anna's forces and captured the Mexican capital on September 14, bringing the war to an end.

The Treaty of Guadalupe Hidalgo

With the defeat of its troops and the fall of their country's capital, the Mexican government was at the mercy of the United States. Although some Americans now had visions of annexing most of Mexico, negotiations produced more limited results. Still, by the 1848 Treaty of Guadalupe Hidalgo, Mexico not only recognized the Rio Grande as the border of Texas but also gave up New Mexico and California—more than two fifths of its territory—to the United States. In return, the United States government paid Mexico $15 million and agreed to cover debts owed to United States citizens.

Five years later, in 1853, the Mexican government sold 30,000 square miles of what is now southern New Mexico and Arizona to the United States for $10 million. Known as the **Gadsden Purchase,** this land eventually provided a route for the southern transcontinental railroad. The table on this page shows the square miles added to United States territory from 1800 to 1860. The Illustrated Data Bank in the reference section shows the territories that were gradually added to the United States from 1787 to 1899.

Although the Mexican War is often seen as a minor footnote in the history of the United States, the American victory over Mexico had important consequences. The Treaty of Guadalupe Hidalgo, together with the 1846

division of Oregon and the Gadsden Purchase, established the boundaries of the continental United States as we now know them. Referred to by Mexicans as the North American Invasion, the war also left many Mexicans deeply bitter toward the United States and led to decades of poor relations and misunderstandings between the two nations. Finally, the acquisition of a vast expanse of territory in the West opened the doors for a new and even larger wave of western migration.

The Wilmot Proviso Possibly the most important consequence of the Mexican War was the role it played in bringing the question of slavery to the forefront of American politics. The central issue that confronted Congress was what to do with the vast territory acquired by the United States from Mexico. Northerners did not want the balance of power in the United States to tip to the South and did not want to compete with plantation owners moving west, whose use of slavery drove wages down. As a result, northerners' fear of additional slave states was strong. Partly in response to Whig criticisms of the war, Pennsylvania Democrat David Wilmot attached an amendment to a military appropriations bill in 1846. The **Wilmot Proviso** stated that slavery would not be permitted in any of the territory acquired from Mexico.

Although Congress defeated the proviso, Wilmot laid bare tensions between the North and South. Eventually, the issue of slavery in the western territories would prove to be one of the most important causes of the Civil War. Americans could sidestep the question of slavery within existing states, but they had to confront the issue directly whenever they created new territories and new states.

Mormons Settle Utah

At the time of the Mexican War, the Mormons, one of the largest groups of migrants to head west in the 1840s, were finding a new home in present-day Utah. Mormons, or members of the Church of Jesus Christ of Latter-day Saints, had been looking for a permanent home ever since **Joseph Smith** founded the religion in western New York in 1830. Harrassed by neighbors who were suspicious of their beliefs, the Mormons moved to Ohio, then to Missouri, and finally to Nauvoo, Illinois.

Although the Mormons initially prospered in Illinois, relations with neighbors deteriorated after Smith revealed in 1843 that the Mormons accepted polygyny, a practice in which a family includes one husband and several wives. After a hostile mob killed Smith and his brother in 1844, the Mormons were forced to move on once again.

The religion's new leader, **Brigham Young,** decided that the Mormons' only hope was to live beyond the borders of the United States of that time. He and other leaders chose the Great Salt Lake Basin as the Mormons' new home, largely because it was located nearly a thousand miles from other Americans. As Young said in an 1862 sermon:

> We are not going to wait for the angels, . . .to come and build up Zion [the promised land], *but we are going to build it up. We will raise our wheat, build our houses, fence our farms, plant our vineyards and orchards, and produce everything that will make our bodies comfortable and happy and in this manner we intend to build up Zion on the earth, and purify and cleanse it from all pollutions.*

Starting in 1847, hundreds of Mormons left their temporary camps in Iowa for new homes near the Great Salt Lake. Within three years, more than 11,000 Mormons had settled in the region. By 1860, about 30,000 Mormons lived in Salt Lake City and more than ninety other towns in present-day Utah.

Despite many difficulties, these settlements were orderly and prosperous. The Mormons skillfully irrigated their desert region and devoted themselves primarily to farming.

At first the leaders of the Mormon church established their own system of government. With the end of the Mexican War, however, Utah became an official territory of the United States and Brigham Young its first governor. Utah eventually entered the Union in 1896 as the forty-fifth state.

This gold miner was one of many who traveled to California to find his fortune.

MAKING CONNECTIONS

How was the Mormons' decision to establish a settlement in Utah in the 1840s similar to the Puritans' decision to found the Massachusetts Bay Colony in the 1620s?

The Gold Rush in California

Though settlers moving west like the Mormons often dreamed of fertile farmlands, others dreamed of instant wealth, especially after the discovery of gold at Sutter's Mill in California in January 1848. As the lumps of gold were displayed from town to town, they began to realize what the discovery meant. Walter Colton, mayor of Monterey, describes how the news affected his community:

> The family who had kept house for me caught the moving fever. Husband and wife were both packing up; the blacksmith dropped his hammer, the carpenter his plane, the mason his trowel, the farmer his sickle, the baker his loaf, and the tapster his bottle. All were off for the mines. . . .

3. ASSESS

Section 4 Review Answers

1. (a) Oregon Trail, see p. 174
(b) manifest destiny, see p. 176,
(c) Gadsden Purchase, see p. 178,
(d) Wilmot Proviso, see p. 178

2. (a) Joseph Smith, see p. 178,
(b) Brigham Young, see p. 179

3. Disease posed the greatest threat, resulting in far more deaths than occurred from Native American attacks.

4. Mexico ceded about two fifths of its territory for under $20 million. It had little choice, given the reality of an American occupying army.

5. It brought hundreds of thousands of people to the state, transformed San Francisco into a major commercial center, and destroyed much of what remained of Native American cultures.

6. In both cases the government's attitude, spurred by a sense of cultural superiority, was that no nation should be allowed to keep the United States from fulfilling its destiny of occupying the entire continent and that any action toward that end was justifiable.

 In Depth

Interdisciplinary

The worst disappointment for gold prospectors was mistaking pyrite, also known as fool's gold, for the real thing. Pyrite, which is not a metal, can be distinguished from gold by pounding it. Real gold will not break when hammered, but pyrite, whose name comes from the Greek word for fire, gives off large sparks when struck hard. In fact it was used by some Native American groups to make fire.

Reteach

Have students write two column headings, Cause and Effect, on a piece of paper. In the first column, have them list the following: American migration to Oregon Country; annexation of Texas; Mexican War; Mormon migration to Utah; discovery of gold at Sutter's Mill, California; American settlement in Native American lands. Then have them list in the second column the consequences resulting from each action or event.

 **4.** CLOSE

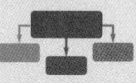 **Reinforcing the Big Idea**

By 1845 thousands of pioneers had survived the trip west over the Oregon Trail and settled in the Oregon Country, which soon became part of the United States. Tensions grew between American settlers and the Mexicans and Native Americans who already lived in the West, but the United States was determined to let nothing stop it from fulfilling its dream of having its territory stretch from the Atlantic to the Pacific.

 In Depth

Multicultural Perspectives

The land disputes between Native Americans and settlers in California have not completely vanished. In late 1993, the Acagchemem, who claim their origins in the San Juan Capistrano region of California, won a temporary injunction halting all construction by California State University, Long Beach, for a faculty housing project on a 22-acre sacred site. "Our ancestors must know we haven't forsaken them," said an Acagchemem spokesperson. "In order to survive, many of my people . . . called themselves Mexicans."

Newspapers in the eastern United States were soon full of the exciting news, and people touched by gold fever rushed west by the thousands. California had 14,000 residents in 1848. Within a year, 100,000 people were living in the state, and by 1852 that number had reached 200,000.

A majority of the new immigrants were unmarried men. In fact, only 5 percent of the "forty-niners" who went to California in the 1849 gold rush were women or children. African Americans, both enslaved and free, were also part of the gold rush. Enslaved people worked as servants or searched for gold on their owners' work crews. Some free African Americans became independent miners.

Western Migration and Native Americans

The gold rush had a tremendous impact on life in California. For Native Americans, the influx of thousands of white immigrants was a disaster. The tens of thousands of miners forced Native Americans to work—the men in the mines, the women in their households. Disease and forced labor reduced the Native American population in California from roughly 150,000 in 1848 to 35,000 by 1860.

The Native Americans in California were not alone in their fate. Until the Mexican War, the United States had proclaimed all land west of the 95th meridian to be "Indian Country." Along the so-called Permanent Indian Frontier, running from Minnesota to Louisiana, the United States Army built a series of forts. As growing numbers of Americans migrated beyond this frontier line, however, the United States established military posts farther and farther west.

Other government groups also dealt with Native Americans. The Bureau of Indian Affairs (1824), or BIA, became part of the newly created Department of the Interior in 1849. The Bureau attempted to "extinguish" Native American land claims through treaties and annuities, or yearly payments. In the 1850s the government increasingly championed the idea of reservations as the ultimate solution to the "Indian problem."

In California, these policies led to the creation of eight reservations by 1858. Native Americans in Oregon and Washington fought back in an 1855 war led by the Yakima chief Kamiakin. But there, too, treaties eventually led to the confinement of thousands of people on eight reservations.

Nomadic Native Americans proved to be the most successful at resisting the government's efforts to control them. Despite treaties of peace signed in the early 1850s, tension increased with every group of white settlers that crossed the Mississippi. By the end of the 1850s, both the United States government and the Plains Indians saw military action as their only option for dealing with each other.

Little did the Native Americans of the plains know that another impasse was ahead—one between northerners and southerners of the United States. As the debate over slavery in the western territories grew shriller and political solutions became increasingly less likely, the nation sped toward war. By 1860, decades of tension and debate would erupt in armed conflict between the North and South.

SECTION 4 REVIEW

Key Terms, People, and Places
1. Define (a) Oregon Trail, (b) manifest destiny, (c) Gadsden Purchase, (d) Wilmot Proviso.
2. Identify (a) Joseph Smith, (b) Brigham Young.

Key Concepts
3. What posed the greatest threat to those American settlers who migrated to California and Oregon on the western trails?

4. What did Mexico give up in the Treaty of Guadalupe Hidalgo?
5. What was the impact of the gold rush on California?

Critical Thinking
6. **Making Comparisons** How was the attitude of the United States government toward Mexico's northern territories similiar to its attitude toward the area designated as "Indian Country"?

 **RESOURCE DIRECTORY**

Media and Technology

Teaching Resources

 Quiz found in the Unit 2 folder, p. 14, covers the main ideas in this section as well as the key terms.

 Chapter Test Forms A and B are found in the Unit 2 folder, pp. 34–39.

 Answer Keys found in the Unit 2 folder, pp. 152–165, provide answers to all student activities.

Transparency
Graphic Organizer, G-1

Guided Reading Audiotapes (English and Spanish)

Computer Test Bank

Formulating Questions

An important aspect of critical thinking is being able to formulate questions as you read. Asking questions about what you read helps you to focus on the facts. Formulating questions can help you gain insight into the material you read and thus sharpen your understanding of that material.

To formulate good questions, keep in mind the question words used by reporters: *Who? What? When? Where? Why?* and *How?* The first four words help you gather the basic facts. The last two help you to interpret those facts.

The box to the right shows a selection of epitaphs, or inscriptions, found on gravestones along the Oregon Trail. Estimates of the number of people who died range from 20,000 to 45,000. Use the following steps to formulate questions about the epitaphs. By asking questions, you can discover when people lived, how long they lived, and sometimes how they died.

1. Identify the topic. Identify the people, the years in which they lived, and, if possible, how they met their death. To guide your understanding, first think about who would be traveling on an overland trail. (a) What questions can you formulate about the ages of the people who died on the Oregon Trail? (b) What questions can you ask to identify the causes of death?

2. Identify a point of view. Who do you think wrote the epitaphs? Evaluate how people were remembered by those who knew them. (a) What questions can you formulate about the Winslow epitaph? (b) What questions can you formulate about the Martess marker?

3. Locate the important details. Study the grave markers to see what clues they offer about the historical period. Use the information about the time period, how the people died, and how those they left behind felt to help you understand what life was like on the Oregon Trail. (a) What questions can you ask to discover the dangers of traveling on the Oregon Trail? (b) What questions would you ask the people who survived?

Died: Of Cholera

(This was the most frequent epitaph found on grave sites along the way.)

Mary Ellis
Died May 7th, 1845
Aged two months

(This epitaph was found on a piece of plank standing up from a grave site, its letters traced by a red-hot piece of iron.)

Marlena Elizabeth Martess
Died Aug. 9th, 1863
Born July 7th, 1862
Friends nor physician could save her
from the grave

(This epitaph was followed by a plea to all who might pass to keep the grave in good repair.)

IN MEMORY OF GEORGE WINSLOW
who died on this great highway June 8, 1849
and was buried here by his comrades. . . . This
tablet is affectionately placed by his sons,
George Edward and Orrin Henry Winslow.

Rachel E. Pattison
Aged 18
June 19, '49

(This was a rock, hand-lettered.)

Rebecca Winters,
age 50 years

(This was crudely carved on a wagon wheel, which served as the grave's headstone.)

In Memory
of Charles Hatch HO
Died June 12, 1850

(Scratched on this carved tombstone is "Killed by Indians.")

Pioneer Grave of
John D. Henderson
Died of Thirst
August 9, 1852
Unaware of Nearness of the Malheur River
Leaving Independence, Missouri, in May
1852, Mr. Henderson and Companion
Name Unknown, Had completed Only Part
of the Journey When Their Team Died. They
were Compelled to Continue on Foot Carry-
ing Their Few Possessions. The Twenty Miles
of Desert Separating the Snake and Maleur
Rivers Proved too Great a Struggle for the
Weary Travelers

(This marker replaced a stone that gave Henderson's name and date of death.)

📄 **Historian's Toolbox Activity**
Formulating Questions, found in the Unit 2 folder, p. 21, helps students understand what information about a society can be gleaned from death notices.

TOOLBOX

Critical Thinking
Formulating Questions

Focus Analyze epitaphs using questions that demonstrate critical thinking skills.

Instruct Explain to students that just as detectives ask thoughtful questions and make careful observations when attempting to solve a crime, readers need to ask careful questions about the material they are studying. Only then can they determine what kind of information is available from the selection and whether or not the information is reliable or useful.

Extend See the Historian's Toolbox Activity in the Resource Directory below.

Answers

1. Possible questions: (a) How many graves were for children? Why was it difficult for children to survive the Oregon Trail? (b) What was the epidemic that plagued the Oregon Trail? How did a lack of water affect some pioneers? What was the result of conflicts with Native Americans?

2. Possible questions: (a) How do you know George Winslow was well remembered? Who placed the marker in honor of Winslow? (b) Who would have left the marker? How do you think her family felt at her loss?

3. Possible questions (a) What could happen to pioneers if their horses died? How did the Native Americans react to the settlers moving west? Why was it hard to find good drinking water? What roles did illness and accidents play? (b) Did you know it would be so difficult before you started on your journey? Were the hardships too much of a price to pay for the end result?

Understanding Key Terms, People, and Places

Terms

Students should refer to the definitions of key terms in the chapter to create sentences that show an understanding of their relation to the reform movements from 1815 to 1860 or to the settlement of lands beyond the Mississippi River.

Matching

1. cult of domesticity
2. suffrage
3. manifest destiny
4. secularize
5. Wilmot Proviso

True or False

1. true
2. true
3. false, William Lloyd Garrison
4. false, Sam Houston
5. false, Great Plains
6. false, Joseph Smith

Reviewing the Main Ideas

1. Reforms included prohibiting the use of alcohol, improving conditions for prison inmates and the mentally ill, and making education available for all Americans.

2. Abolitionists favored a moderate approach of phasing out slavery; a small minority favored colonization.

3. Women did not have suffrage; in most states married women could not own property, make a will, or keep earned wages.

4. Women joined reform movements, became involved in political activities, and became more visible members of society.

5. Both groups resented the interference of reformers. Southerners had economic and social reasons; the rural agricultural environment prevented women from participating in community meetings. Working-class people held different moral and cultural values. For example, many working-class people were more concerned about feeding their families and keeping a roof over their heads than they were about debating issues of morality.

6. Men in nomadic societies acquired greater status than women because only they were taught the important skills of riding, hunting, and fighting.

Chapter Review

Understanding Key Terms, People, and Places

Key Terms
1. Transcendentalism
2. temperance movement
3. abolition
4. gag rule
5. suffrage
6. cult of domesticity
7. nomad
8. secularize
9. Oregon Trail
10. manifest destiny
11. Gadsden Purchase
12. Wilmot Proviso

People
13. Lyman Beecher
14. Henry David Thoreau
15. Horace Mann
16. Dorothea Dix
17. William Lloyd Garrison
18. Frederick Douglass
19. Harriet Tubman
20. Catharine Beecher
21. Lucretia Mott
22. Elizabeth Cady Stanton
23. Sojourner Truth
24. Meriwether Lewis
25. William Clark
26. Sacajawea
27. Stephen Austin
28. Sam Houston
29. Joseph Smith
30. Brigham Young

Places
31. Liberia
32. Seneca Falls
33. Great Plains

Terms For each term above, write a sentence that explains its relation to the reform movements from 1815 to 1860 or to the settlement of lands beyond the Mississippi River.

Matching Review the key terms in the list above. If you are not sure of a term's meaning, review its definition in the chapter. Then choose a term from the list that best matches each description below.

1. the belief in the importance of women's role at home
2. the right to vote
3. the belief that the United States had a divine mission to spread liberty across the continent
4. to transfer control from the church to the state
5. the amendment that prohibited slavery in the territory acquired from Mexico.

True or False Determine whether each statement is true or false. If it is true, write "true." If it is false, change the underlined person or place to make the statement true.

1. Under the leadership of <u>Horace Mann</u>, Massachusetts pioneered school reform.
2. <u>Lucretia Mott</u> and <u>Elizabeth Cady Stanton</u> organized a women's rights convention at Seneca Falls, New York.
3. <u>Frederick Douglass</u> published an antislavery newspaper called *The Liberator*.
4. <u>Stephen Austin</u> became the first president of the Republic of Texas.
5. The vast grasslands that lie between the Mississippi River and the Rocky Mountains are known as <u>Liberia.</u>
6. <u>William Clark</u> founded the Mormon religion in 1830.

Reviewing Main Ideas

Section 1 (pp. 152–157)
1. What were some of the social reforms undertaken by reform-minded citizens?
2. What approaches were favored by abolitionists before 1830?

Section 2 (pp. 160–166)
3. Give examples to show that the cultural attitudes toward women in the United States were reinforced by laws in the early 1800s.
4. In what ways did women begin to challenge traditional values in the period between 1815 and 1860?
5. How were the reactions of southerners to reformers similar to those of working class people?

Section 3 (pp. 167–173)
6. How did men acquire greater status than women in Native American nomadic societies?
7. Give two reasons that help explain why Native American village societies declined in the early 1800s.
8. Why were the California missions able to thrive?
9. What was the ultimate effect of the increasing immigration of Americans into Texas?

Section 4 (pp. 174–180)
10. Briefly describe a typical overland journey to Oregon during the period of western expansion.
11. What were three consequences of the Mexican War?

---

7. Village societies were attacked by nomadic groups and devastated by European diseases.

8. They thrived largely as a result of the work of Native Americans, who were treated as a pool of cheap labor.

9. Americans in Texas demanded more freedom from the Mexican government and eventually succeeded in breaking away from Mexico.

10. Students' descriptions should include evidence demonstrating that the journey was long, difficult, and dangerous.

11. The Treaty of Guadalupe Hidalgo, together with the 1846 division of Oregon and the Gadsden Purchase, established the boundaries of the continental United States as we know them; many Mexicans were left with bitter feelings toward the United States; the acquisition of the vast new territory opened the door for a large westward migration.

Thinking Critically

1. **Making Comparisons** How did the views of Catharine Beecher differ from those of other women, such as Lucretia Mott and Elizabeth Cady Stanton, in the women's rights movement? What different voices can you identify in the women's movement today?

2. **Distinguishing False from Accurate Images** Briefly describe the popular image of the Native American as portrayed in television westerns and movies. What groups of Native Americans is this image based on? What groups does it ignore?

3. **Recognizing Ideologies** While the United States referred to the conflict with Mexico as the Mexican War, Mexicans called the war the North American Invasion. What do these different names suggest about each country's perspective on the war? Was the war in fact an act of aggression on the part of the United States?

Making Connections

1. **Evaluating Primary Sources** Review the primary source excerpt on page 162. Explain how the excerpt attacks the double standard that society held for men and women. What other groups in American society have sometimes been treated with a double standard?

2. **Understanding the Visuals** Look at the table on page 178. Why might John O'Sullivan see this table as visual evidence that the nation was following his concept of manifest destiny?

3. **Writing About the Chapter** It is 1849. You have just received a letter from your cousin in California urging you to come west. Write a response in which you explain why you will or will not make the journey. First, make a list of the reasons that support your decision. Also note the reasons that support the opposite point of view and why they fail to persuade you. Next, write a draft of your response in which you explain your intention to travel or to remain at home; use examples from the chapter to support your decision. Revise your response, making sure that you have clearly and persuasively explained your ideas. Proofread your response and draft a final copy.

4. **Using the Graphic Organizer** This graphic organizer uses a web map to organize information about nomadic groups of Native Americans on the Great Plains. In this web, dotted lines are used to show connections between ideas. (a) Why does the graphic organizer show a connection between the two animals central to nomadic culture, the horse and the buffalo? (b) Explain the other connections suggested by this graphic organizer. (c) On a separate sheet of paper, create your own web map about Spanish missions in California, using this graphic organizer as an example.

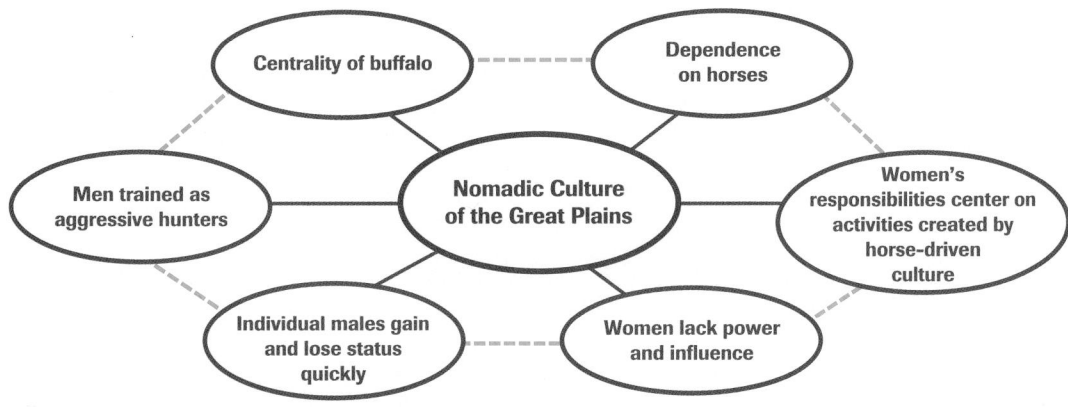

Making Connections

1. Although the Constitution guarantees citizens of the United States many rights and freedoms, these rights and freedoms had not been extended to women. Other groups with similar experiences are African Americans and Native Americans.

2. O'Sullivan believed that it was the United States' inevitable fate to occupy the entire continent. This table details the nation's rapid and seemingly unstoppable expansion from a strip of thirteen colonies along the eastern seaboard to a vast nation of over three million square miles stretching from the Atlantic to the Pacific.

3. Students' letters should weigh the prospects offered by the California gold rush, opportunities in the West, the hardships of the journey, and the spirit of adventure required to undertake such a journey.

4. (a) The horse allowed Native Americans to follow and hunt buffalo. (b) As hunters, men became more aggressive and concerned with status; women consequently lost status. (c) Students' graphic organizers should include information both about the purpose of the California missions and about their negative impact on Native American culture.

 ### Alternative Assessment

Final Evaluation

Use the following guidelines to evaluate student projects:

• **Evidence of outside research** To what extent did students use outside research materials for their project?

• **Evidence of synthesis** Do projects demonstrate that students understand how topics are related?

• **Communication style** Do the projects convey their purpose to an audience in a clear, appealing way?

Thinking Critically

1. Catharine Beecher believed that although women could make important contributions to the newly emerging capitalist society, their duties as wives and mothers should provide their primary focus in life. Other women were more militant in their demands for equal rights. Students may identify similar trends today.

2. The stereotypical Native American is vindictive, bloodthirsty, and usually on horseback. This exaggerated image is based on the behavior of the more warlike nomadic groups, which differed sharply from that of agricultural groups. The latter seldom appear in popular imagery, however, partly because popular culture favors violence and partly because white settlers probably had the most conflict and interaction with the nomadic groups.

3. The United States saw the war as an opportunity to exercise the doctrine of manifest destiny rather than an as act of aggression, while Mexico saw it as an act of imperialism. Most students will probably agree that the war was an act of aggression.

One of the gravest crimes of slavery was that it treated the enslaved as though they were less than human. Thus, even the kindest and most solidly moral slave owners would treat an enslaved person in ways they would never consider treating a white person—and never recognize the contradiction in their actions. The source reading from Harriet Ann Jacobs reveals such treatment in a very personal way. The excerpt will help students understand both the subtle and the blatant abuses that slave owners dealt to the enslaved.

In the second selection, students can see the California gold rush of the mid-1800s through the eyes of Chinese immigrants. The view presented reveals a bit about American society at that time, and the picture it paints is not necessarily attractive. Have students read with an eye toward weighing the validity of the viewpoint presented.

Divide the class into two groups and have each group make a list of the similarities and differences between the experiences described by Harriet Ann Jacobs and those described by Betty Lee Sung. Then reconvene as a whole and have the two groups take turns filling in items under the headings "Similarities" and "Differences" on the chalkboard. Use the list as an impetus for discussing the various challenges and difficulties faced by Americans in the mid-1800s.

Incidents in the Life of a Slave Girl

Primary Source

Harriet Ann Jacobs

INTRODUCTION Harriet Ann Jacobs was born into slavery in Edenton, North Carolina, in 1813 and achieved freedom in 1852. Her long and remarkable road to freedom began in 1835, when she and her two young children went into hiding in her hometown. In 1842, Jacobs escaped to New York with her son and daughter. There, she made a home for her children and was eventually purchased by the Colonization Society and freed in 1852. Shortly afterward she wrote her autobiography, which provides a personal account of what it was like to be enslaved in the 1800s. These excerpts describe parts of her early childhood and the circumstances that were forced upon her and her family.

VOCABULARY Before you read the selection, find the meaning of these words in a dictionary: indebted, toilsome, bequeath, chattel, defrauded.

I was born a slave; but I never knew it till six years of happy childhood had passed away. My father was a carpenter, and considered so intelligent and skillful in his trade, that, when buildings out of the common line were to be erected, he was sent for from long distances, to be head workman. On condition of paying his mistress two hundred dollars a year, and supporting himself, he was allowed to work at his trade, and manage his own affairs. His strongest wish was to purchase his children; but, though he several times offered his hard earnings for that purpose, he never succeeded.

I was so fondly shielded that I never dreamed I was a piece of merchandise, trusted to them for safe keeping, and liable to be demanded of them at any moment. . . .

Antislavery logo symbolizing the link between the women's rights movement and the abolitionist movement.

Such were the unusually fortunate circumstances of my early childhood. When I was six years old, my mother died; and then, for the first time, I learned, by the talk around me, that I was a slave. My mother's mistress was the daughter of my grandmother's mistress. She was the foster sister of my mother; they were both nourished at my grandmother's breast. In fact, my mother had been weaned at three months old, that the babe of the mistress might obtain sufficient food. They played together as children; and, when they became women, my mother was a most faithful servant to her white foster sister. On her deathbed her mistress promised that her children should never suffer for any thing; and during her lifetime she kept her word. They all spoke kindly of my dead mother, who had been a slave merely in name, but in nature was noble and womanly. I grieved for her, and my young mind was troubled with the thought who would now take of me and my little brother. I was told that my home was now to be with her mistress; and I found it a happy one. No toilsome or disagreeable duties were imposed upon me. My mistress was so kind to me that I was always glad to do her bidding, and proud to labor for her as much as my young years would permit. . . .

When I was nearly twelve years old, my kind mistress sickened and died. As I saw the cheek grow paler, and the eye more glassy, how earnestly I prayed in my heart that she might live! I loved her; for she had been almost like a mother to me. My prayers were not answered. She died, and they buried her in the little churchyard, where, day after day, my tears fell upon her grave.

I was sent to spend a week with my grandmother. I was now old enough to begin to think of the future; and again and again I asked myself what they would do with me. I felt sure I should never find another mistress so kind as the one who was gone. She had promised my dying mother that her children would never suffer for any thing; and when I remembered that, and recalled her many proofs of attachment to me, I could not help having some hopes that she had left me free. . . .

After a brief period of suspense . . . we learned that she had bequeathed me to her sister's daughter, a child of five years old. So vanished our hopes. My mistress had taught me the precepts of God's Word: "Thou shalt love thy neighbor as thyself." "Whatsoever ye would that men should do unto you, do ye even so unto them." But I was her slave, and I suppose she did not recognize me as her neighbor. I would give much to blot out from my memory that one great wrong. As a child, I loved my mistress; and, looking back on the happy days I spent with her, I try to think with less bitterness of this act of injustice. While I was with her, she taught me to read and spell; and for this privilege, which so rarely falls to the lot of a slave, I bless her memory. . . .

My grandmother's mistress had always promised her that, at her death, she should be free; and it was said that in her will she made good the promise. But when the estate was settled, Dr. Flint told the faithful old servant that, under existing circumstances, it was necessary she should be sold.

On the appointed day, the customary advertisement was posted up, proclaiming that there would be a "public sale of negroes, horses, &c." Dr. Flint called to tell my grandmother that he was unwilling to wound her feelings by putting her up at auction, and that he would prefer to dispose of her at private sale. My grandmother saw through his hypocrisy; she understood very well that he was ashamed of the job. She was a very spirited woman, and if he was base enough to sell her, when her mistress intended she should be free, she was determined the public should know it. She had for a long time supplied many families with crackers and preserves; consequently, "Aunt Marthy," as she was called, was generally known, and every body who knew her respected her intelligence and good character. Her long and faithful service in the family was also well known, and the intention of her mistress to leave her free. When the day of sale came, she took her place among the chattels, and at the first call she sprang upon the auction-block. Many voices called out, "Shame! Shame! Who is going to sell you, Aunt Marthy? Don't stand there! That is no place for you." Without saying a word, she quietly awaited her fate. No one bid for her. At last, a feeble voice said, "Fifty dollars." It came from a maiden lady, seventy years old, the sister of my grandmother's deceased mistress. She had lived forty years under the same roof with my grandmother; she knew how faithfully she had served her owners, and how cruelly she had been defrauded of her rights; and she resolved to protect her.

THINKING ABOUT THE SELECTION

1. What skill did Jacobs' former mistress teach her? How important was this skill to Jacobs?
2. Why did Dr. Flint want to sell Jacobs' grandmother at a private auction?

Critical Thinking

3. **Formulating Questions** What questions might you ask of Jacobs to learn more about her life?

ANSWERS TO

Thinking About the Selection

1. Jacobs's mistress taught her how to read and write. The skill proved to be quite important both to Jacobs and to history because she used it to write of her life as an enslaved person.
2. Because he knew that the community would be enraged at the idea of selling her at all and wanted to do it secretly.
3. Questions might include: What sort of work did you do as an enslaved person? How did white children treat you? What books did you read and what did you learn from them? How did you escape from slavery?

Have students research the daily life of an enslaved person on a southern plantation, a Chinese immigrant working in the gold mines of California, or some other figure from Chapter 5. Students might use such sources as *Six Women's Slave Narratives* by William Andrews or *Asian American Experiences in the United States* by Joann F. Lee. Students should each then prepare a ten-minute, one-person skit that will demonstrate what the daily life of their chosen person was like. Afterwards, discuss with the class what the skit revealed about the person and the history of the time. If possible, videotape the skits for viewing by other classes.

SOURCE READINGS

The Pioneer Chinese

Literature

Betty Lee Sung

INTRODUCTION The California gold rush, which began in 1848, attracted huge numbers of people who hoped to strike it rich mining gold. Among these were thousands of Chinese who were lured to California by tales of unimaginable riches. In the following excerpt from her book, *Mountain of Gold: The Story of Chinese in America,* Betty Lee Sung describes the experience of one Chinese pioneer, a nineteen-year-old man named Fatt Hing. As the excerpt begins, Fatt Hing is aboard a Spanish ship headed for California—a ship filled with other young Chinese men journeying for the same reason as he.

VOCABULARY Before you read the selection, find the meaning of these words in a dictionary: imperative, hoodwinked, compatriot, queues, disconcerting, laborious, disgorge.

Fatt Hing recognized no familiar face when he came aboard. As his surname was Chin, he quickly sought out others with the same name, for presumably a Chin was related to another Chin regardless of how many generations back they may have shared a common ancestor. Those without name relations sought out others from the same vicinity or district. . . .

The fears of some that they had been hoodwinked and were being transported to a foreign land to be sold as slaves proved unfounded. Toward dusk on the ninety-fifth day, the hills of San Francisco rose over the horizon. The captain ordered the holds opened and the men swarmed out onto the decks. None slept that night as they watched the ship inch in toward the harbor.

When the ship docked the next day, a delegation of Chinese was on hand to greet the new arrivals. "Come with us," said the spokesman for the group, "and we will take you to the Chinese Street."

After the new arrivals were fed and refreshed with cups of strong hot tea, the leader spoke again.

"I am Wong Wing Dock, chairman of the Six Companies," he said. "We came as you came on board one of those ships, and we came for the same purpose—to seek gold. When we set foot on these shores, however, there were no Chinese faces to greet us, for we were among the first to arrive. Weak and wearied from our long journey, we were bewildered and lost. We did not know where to turn for shelter or food. Fortunately, there were enough of us so that some set

to putting up these houses while others looked for food. We followed the white men into the hills and found out how they sifted the sands for gold and we did the same.

"One valuable lesson we have learned and which you will soon appreciate is that we must stick together and help one another, even though we are not kin. That is why we have formed this organization called the Six Companies representing the six districts which most of us come from. Our compatriots have honored me by choosing me chairman. . . .

These miners were photographed in 1852, three years after the California gold rush began. The four Chinese Americans at right worked with picks and shovels to dig dirt which was then washed down the chute to reveal gold.

"We are Chinese in a land of foreigners. Their ways are different from our ways. Their language is different from our language. Most of them are loud and rough. We are accustomed to an orderly society, but it seems as if they are not bound by any rules of conduct. It is best, if possible, to avoid any contact with them.

"Try not to provoke the foreigners. But you will find that they like to provoke us. We are comfortable in our loose cotton jackets and trousers and we are used to going barefooted. They like to wear rough coarse clothing with high-laced boots. They cut their hair short and let the hair grow on their faces. We wear our hair long and braided and we shave the hair from our faces. Since we all want to return to our homeland, we cannot cut off our queues.

"Be patient and maintain your dignity. If you are lucky you may not have to stay here long. Some of us and many white men have made rich finds. They need workers to help them. As new arrivals you may want to work for these men, or you may choose to prospect on your own.

"You will need a pick, a shovel and a few supplies," continued Chairman Wong. "You may take what you need from our headquarters now, and the sum will be entered in the company books against your name."

As soon as Chairman Wong had finished speaking, some of the men hastily asked where they should go for their pick and shovel. Though the strangeness of their environment was disconcerting, and though they were weak from their confinement in the ship's hold, they were impatient to be off into the hills.

Fatt Hing held back. As one of the younger men, he did not want to push ahead of his elders, but he also wanted time to think. "What do I know about mining?" he wondered. "Where should I start looking? Perhaps it would be better if I hired myself out until I get to know more about this new land."

The thoughts of Fatt Hing's shipmates ran in the same vein. Chairman Wong had received many requests for Chinese workers and he knew exactly where to send them. The terms were generous. Each workers was to receive half of the gold he mined.

Early next morning, the men set out on foot for the hills. When they arrived at their destination, Fatt Hing saw that hundreds of his fellow countrymen who had come previously had set up camp. It was comforting for him to know that he would be among his own people—people who spoke his own language and observed his own customs—though he was thousands of miles away from home.

Dig and sift, dig and sift. Fatt Hing and his fellow workers pecked at the mountainsides, in the ravines and gulches, working loose the earth and washing out the fine gold particles which sank to the bottom of the pan. It seemed as if other miners had worked the claim before, taking out the larger pieces while scorning the fine gold particles which required more laborious work. To Fatt Hing, however, the glitter of the gold dust in the loose earth drove him to work with unrelenting fury. "Truly, these are mountains of gold," he cried. "I must write my brothers and my cousins and tell them to come."

Thus each boatload brought more Chinese and more. Brothers sent for brothers and even distant kin so that Chinese immigration snowballed. No sooner had a ship disgorged its passengers than they were off to the mines. Although Canton, China, was 7,000 miles and a three months' journey away, it was a less hazardous and quicker trip than the overland route across the American continent or the boat trip around Cape Horn. From Canton also came lumber for the houses, cottons and silks, and even bundles of clean laundry which had been sent clear across the Pacific for washing.

THINKING ABOUT THE SELECTION

1. What was one fear of the men on the ship headed for California?
2. Who welcomed the Chinese to their new home?

Critical Thinking

3. **Drawing Conclusions** The excerpt describes the terms of employment as "generous. Each worker was to receive half of the gold he mined." Based on information in the excerpt, do you agree that these terms were generous? Explain why or why not.

ANSWERS TO

Thinking About the Selection

1. The men feared that they had been tricked and were really being taken to California to be sold as slaves.

2. A group of Chinese who had been among the first to arrive in the United States welcomed them.

3. Answers will vary, but students should note that the Chinese were assigned to the more time-consuming work of collecting the finer traces of gold while the big pieces had already been mined. It is likely that for the number of hours that the Chinese worked, their compensation was relatively low.

Chapter 6 The Civil War and Reconstruction
1848–1877

📁 **Teaching Resources** (See Unit 2 Folder)

	Instruction	Enrichment
Section 1 **The Coming of the Civil War** (pp. 190–195)	Reproducible Lesson Plan, p. 41 Alternate Lesson Plan, p. 74 Guided Reading and Review, p. 45 Quiz, p. 46	Visual Learning Activity, Anthony Burns and the Fugitive Slave Law, p. 66 Literature Activity, An Antislavery Best-Seller, pp. 63–64 Primary Source Activity, An Interview with John Brown, p. 61 History Might Not . . . Activity, Can Separate Be Equal? pp. 53–54
Section 2 **The First Two Years of the Civil War** (pp. 198–203)	Reproducible Lesson Plan, p. 42 Alternate Lesson Plan, p. 75 Guided Reading and Review, p. 47 Quiz, p. 48	Literature Activity, The Battle of Manassas, p. 65 Critical Thinking Activity, Recognizing Bias, p. 60 American Profiles Activity, General Robert E. Lee, p. 55 Historian's Toolbox Activity, Using Letters as Primary Sources, p. 59
Section 3 **War Brings Change** (pp. 205–211)	Reproducible Lesson Plan, p. 43 Alternate Lesson Plan, p. 76 Guided Reading and Review, p. 49 Quiz, p. 50	American Profiles Activity, Mary Elizabeth Bowser, p. 56 Visual Learning Activity, Defending Atlanta, p. 67
Section 4 **Reconstruction** (pp. 212–217)	Reproducible Lesson Plan, p. 44 Alternate Lesson Plan, p. 77 Guided Reading and Review, p. 51 Quiz, p. 52 Chapter Test, Forms A & B, pp. 68–73	Primary Source Activity, A Bleak Future for Freedmen, p. 62 Viewpoints Activity, On Voting Rights for African Americans, pp. 57–58

📁 **Additional Chapter Resources**

Resource Organizer, p. 40
Alternate Lesson Plan, p. 73
Answer Keys, pp. 152–165

Bibliography

For the Teacher
Catton, Bruce. *The Coming Fury.* Washington Square Press, 1972. (Traces the split between the North and the South from the election of 1860 through the first Battle of Bull Run.)

Prentice Hall Literature Excerpts from *The American Experience,* 1994, including "Division, War, and Reconciliation, 1855–1865."

The Big Idea for the chapter and how the main ideas in each section relate to the Big Idea are graphically displayed below. Comprehension of this chapter's Big Idea is critical to students' understanding of United States history and how we as a nation got where we are today.

Media and Technology

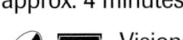

Cause and Effect, F-5; Historical Maps, L-3

Visions of America: History Might Not Have Happened This Way Game

Fine Art, D-10; The Way It Works, H-11, H-12

The Way It Works, H-13; Geographic Setting, M-3, M-4; Fine Art, D-11

Visions of America: Turning Point Story, "Mississippi Siege" (length: approx. 4 minutes)

Visions of America: Roundtable Discussion on "Mississippi Siege"

Political Cartoons, K-4; Graphic Organizer, G-4

Guided Reading Audiotapes (English and Spanish)

Computer Test Bank

For the Student
The Civil War. PBS Video. (Acclaimed, multi-part series that combines scholarly analysis and primary sources.)

Holzer, Harold, ed. *Dear Mr. Lincoln: Letters to the President.* Addison-Wesley, 1993. (Letters from ordinary people.)

CHAPTER 6

The growing differences and distrust between North and South finally became insurmountable when Abraham Lincoln was elected President without carrying a single southern state. Civil war erupted, bringing death and devastation to the nation. After a long and bitter war, the Union was saved and African Americans won their freedom. Reconstruction followed as the people of both North and South strove to adjust to new social and political conditions.

SECTION 1

The mid-nineteenth century was a time of deep distrust and escalating hostility between the North and the South. Many Americans no longer believed that the federal government could settle their differences, and the Union, the unified nation, finally shattered.

SECTION 2

During the first two years of the war, the Union put its Anaconda Plan into action by blockading the coasts of the Confederacy and taking control of its midwestern part. Union troops failed to take the Confederate capital, however.

SECTION 3

During the war, national government in both the North and the South became more powerful. As the conflict wore on, the Confederacy suffered major defeats at Vicksburg and Gettysburg. The Union Army battered the South until the Confederate commander, General Lee, surrendered at Appomattox Court House.

SECTION 4

In the aftermath of the Civil War Reconstruction policies strained to help the nation cope with new conditions. While African Americans obtained their liberty and southern society was transformed, Reconstruction redefined social, economic, and political relationships between the North and South as well as between the races.

The Civil War and Reconstruction
1848–1877

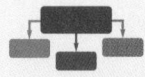

The Relevance of the Big Idea

In the mid-1800s, the northern and southern regions of the United States were so deeply divided that Americans embarked on a bloody civil war. Ask students what regions they think exist within the United States today. How do these regions differ? What conditions might convince one region to separate from the rest of the United States?

After the war was over, the Reconstruction era (1863–1877) transformed American society and brought African Americans some measure of social equality and justice. Yet even this degree of progress proved temporary, and full equality remained elusive. Discuss with students the problems the United States faces in the 1990s that could be regarded in some measure as legacies of the Civil War.

In Depth

Global Connections

In the 1850s the southern states thought that cotton could bring them success as a separate nation. More than 80 percent of Britain's cotton came from the South, but by mid-1861 there was a 50 percent oversupply of cotton in the British market. Also, in May 1861 Britain declared its "strict and impartial neutrality" in what was termed the contest between the "Government of the United States of America and certain states styling themselves the Confederate States of America."

The Civil War and Reconstruction
1848–1877

*U*nder the strain of conflict between North and South in the 1850s, the great web of law, compromise, and tradition that had held the United States together for over seventy years snapped. During the four years that the Civil War raged between the North and the South, hundreds of thousands of Americans were killed or maimed and billions of dollars worth of property was destroyed. In the end, African Americans won their freedom, the Union was preserved, and the federal government became for the first time a powerful presence in the lives of the people.

Events in the United States

1848	**1852**	**1856**	**1860**

- **1850** Congress passes the Compromise of 1850.
  - Senator John Calhoun dies.
- **1856** Debate over slavery erupts into violence in Kansas.
- **1860** Republican Abraham Lincoln is elected United States President.
  - South Carolina secedes from the Union.

Events in the World

- **1848** Revolutions sweep Europe.
  - Franz Josef becomes Emperor of Austria.
- **1851** The Great Exhibition is held at the Crystal Palace in London.
- **1860** English novelist George Eliot publishes The Mill on the Floss.

▶ RESOURCE DIRECTORY

Teaching Resources

Alternate Lesson Plan: Demonstrating the Big Idea found in the Alternate Lesson Plans folder, p. 73, provides a lesson strategy to instruct students about the Big Idea that, with the election of Abraham Lincoln to the presidency, the conflict between the North and South escalated to a civil war. Through a series of radio talk shows students can demonstrate their understanding of the war and its aftermath.

Alternative Assessment Handbook provides information, guidance, and strategies for alternative methods of assessment. It includes an essay on new trends in assessment, guidance and strategies for developing performance tasks and portfolios, scoring rubrics, and sample evaluation forms.

Pages 190–195

The Coming of the Civil War

Between 1850 and 1860, the failure of political compromise and the breakdown of basic law and order over the issue of slavery brought emotions to the flashpoint. When Abraham Lincoln, a candidate known to oppose slavery, won the presidency, secession spread like wildfire through the southern states. The nation broke into separate sections—North and South—and plunged into war.

Pages 198–203

The First Two Years of the Civil War

In the first two years of the war, Union armies tried again and again to capture the Confederate capital but were driven back by bolder and more skillful generals. Union forces did succeed, however, in blockading the coasts of the South and seizing control of the great river valleys of its midwestern states.

Pages 205–211

War Brings Change

During the Civil War, the national government became a powerful presence in the lives of ordinary people. In this and other ways, the conflict turned out to be more than a struggle over the Union. It became instead a redefinition of the American nation.

Pages 212–217

Reconstruction

The meaning of freedom was clear to the freed people of the South. For Congress, however, the end of the Civil War raised many difficult questions about how to rebuild the nation. The result was a series of acts and amendments that redefined citizenship and attempted to create a new social order in the South. But after some mixed success, political leaders turned from this dream and focused on economic expansion instead.

1863 Lincoln proclaims freedom for enslaved people in the Confederacy.	1865 Lincoln is assassinated. • Lee surrenders to Grant at Appomattox. • The 13th Amendment abolishes slavery.		1872 President Ulysses S. Grant wins reelection.	1875 Congress passes a Civil Rights Act.	1877 The Compromise of 1877 ends military occupation of the South.
1864	**1868**	**1872**	**1876**		**1880**
1863 The International Red Cross is founded in Switzerland.	1867 The Dominion of Canada is established.		1873 Slave markets and exports of enslaved people are abolished in Zanzibar in Africa.	1876 Korea becomes an independent nation. • Serbia declares war on Turkey.	

As an ongoing chapter project, students can create a two-volume series for elementary school students. The first volume should be a description of the growing tension and hostility leading the nation toward civil war. Volume II should explain some of the major events of the Civil War. Students should illustrate their books with maps, drawings, or photocopies of photographs. Each book should contain chapters on at least three of the following topics:

- The differences between the northern and southern economies
- John Brown's raid
- The election of 1860
- The first two years of the war, including a discussion of the Anaconda Plan and the struggle for the capitals
- The generals and soldiers who fought the war
- The effect of the war on African Americans
- The last two years of the war

Explain that finished projects will be assessed according to the following standards:

- **Unacceptable** Projects are not completed or fail to meet requirements outlined.
- **Limited/Acceptable** Projects are based on material from the textbook and correctly describe the events leading the nation to war and the war itself.
- **Extensive/Commendable** Projects incorporate some outside research, correctly describe the major events of the period, and are attractively illustrated.
- **Extraordinary/Outstanding** Projects are based on considerable outside research, summarize and show relationships among events, and are written clearly and vividly. Books are well illustrated with a variety of visual material.

For more information on alternative assessment trends and strategies, see the Alternative Assessment Handbook in the Resource Directory on page 188.

SECTION 1

The Coming of the Civil War

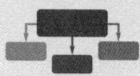

1. FOCUS

Connecting to the Big Idea

See page 188B. Explain that in the 1850s, differences between the North and the South increasingly polarized the two regions. Ask what the key differences between them were.

Objectives

● Describe the Kansas-Nebraska Act of 1854.
● Identify Abraham Lincoln's views on slavery.
● Explain why the southern states left the Union.

Bellringer

Ask students to discuss what they know about differences that may exist among regions in the United States today. What effect might these differences have on the nation as a whole?

Reading Strategy

Predicting Content Ask students to skim the section, list the main headings and subheadings, and write a sentence or phrase next to each one predicting the content of that portion. Then have students test their predictions against the actual text.

SECTION PREVIEW

Between 1850 and 1860, the failure of political compromise and the breakdown of basic law and order over the issue of slavery brought emotions to the flashpoint. When Abraham Lincoln, a candidate known to oppose slavery, won the presidency, secession spread like wildfire through the southern states. The nation broke into separate sections—North and South—and plunged into war.

CHARLESTON

MERCURY

EXTRA:

Passed unanimously at 1.15 o'clock, P. M. December 20th, 1860,

AN ORDINANCE

To dissolve the Union between the State of South Carolina and other States united with her under the compact entitled "The Constitution of the United States of America."

We, the People of the State of South Carolina, in Convention assembled, do declare and ordain, and it is hereby declared and ordained,

That the Ordinance adopted by us in Convention, on the twenty-third day of May, in the year of our Lord one thousand seven hundred and eighty eight, whereby the Constitution of the United States of America was ratified and also all Acts and part of Acts of the General Assembly of this State, ratifying amendments of the said Constitution, are hereby repealed; and that the union now subsisting between South Carolina and other States, under the name of "The United States of America," is hereby dissolved.

THE

UNION
IS
DISSOLVED!

Proudly declaring its independence, South Carolina was the first state to secede from the Union.

Key Concepts

· The Kansas-Nebraska Act of 1854 established that the people of those territories could decide for themselves whether they would allow slavery when they became states.

· During a senatorial campaign in Illinois in 1858, the North gained a new spokesperson for its antislavery views, Abraham Lincoln.

· Finding that the North was able to elect an antislavery President despite his complete rejection by the South, southern states left the Union one after another.

Key Terms, People, and Places

Civil War, Union, Compromise of 1850, Kansas-Nebraska Act, *Dred Scott* v. *Sandford*; Democratic party, Republican party, John Brown, Abraham Lincoln; Border States, Lower South, Upper South

B etween 1861 and 1865, the southern and northern states clashed with one another in a violent conflict that Americans call the **Civil War.** The result of the war would decide whether the **Union,** as the unified nation was called, would continue unbroken or be shattered forever.

The Causes of the Civil War

Many events contributed to the start of the Civil War. Though the war had many causes, the direct cause was the inability of politicians to resolve the question of whether or not slavery would be allowed in the territories. This does not mean the troops that struggled on both sides when the Civil War began were fighting to end slavery or to save it. They were fighting about whether the South would remain part of the United States. Yet the issue of slavery was one of the main differences between North and South that brought on the war.

Other differences contributed as well. During the 1850s, the North was becoming increasingly more populous and urban than the South. Irish and German immigrants helped swell the population of the North to a figure two and a half times that of the South. By 1860, nine of the ten largest cities in the United States were in the North. Technological improvements, too, were affecting the North more than the South. In 1860 the North had 70 percent of the railroad tracks in the United States. It also had more telegraph wires strung along those railroads, carrying instant communication by means of electric signals.

Finally, the North was more industrialized. In 1860 the North had 110,000 factories, compared to 20,000 in the South; it produced $1.5 billion worth of goods, compared to the South's $155 million. In fact, in terms of numbers, the South outdid the North in only two notable ways: it had more enslaved people and it had more cotton.

MAKING CONNECTIONS

Suggest how the North might use the Declaration of Independence to argue for ending slavery and the South might use it to argue for resisting northern interference.

 RESOURCE DIRECTORY

Teaching Resources

Reproducible Lesson Plan found in the Unit 2 folder, p. 41, provides a summary of the Section 1 lesson plan content.

Alternate Lesson Plan: Critical Thinking Distinguishing Facts from Opinion, found in the Alternate Lesson Plans folder, p. 74, helps students apply this skill by writing brief newspaper articles following a headline.

Guided Reading and Review found in the Unit 2 folder, p. 45, provides a structure for reading and mastering the key concepts and reviewing the key terms for Section 1. (Guided Practice)

Visual Learning Activity Anthony Burns and the Fugitive Slave Law, found in the Unit 2 folder, p. 66, features contemporary sketches depicting the escape of Anthony Burns and his subsequent return to slavery as a result of the Fugitive Slave Act of 1850.

The Compromise of 1850

After the United States acquired a large part of Mexico in the Mexican War, many northerners were unwilling to accept the boundary established by the Missouri Compromise. They feared that the new territory would be divided into several slave states, thus giving the South a majority vote in the United States Senate and perhaps in the Electoral College. Southerners were equally firm in insisting that the national government had no business telling its free citizens they could not take their property to the territories if they wanted to.

⭐ In 1850 Congress put together a compromise that was designed to balance the demands of both North and South. According to this package of laws, called the **Compromise of 1850,** California became a free state; in return, the people of the territories of New Mexico and Utah were to decide for themselves whether slavery would be legal. Congress also abolished the sale of enslaved people, but not slavery itself, in Washington, D.C. In exchange, the Compromise called for Congress to pass the Fugitive Slave Act, which ordered all citizens to assist in the return of enslaved people who had escaped from their owners. The act also denied a jury trial to enslaved people who had escaped.

The Kansas-Nebraska Act

⭐While the Compromise of 1850 kept slavery out of national politics for a few years, sectional tensions continued to escalate. Particularly influential was a novel by Harriet Beecher Stowe, *Uncle Tom's Cabin.* Middle-class northerners were horrified by Stowe's description of the impact of slavery on families (both African American and white), while southerners denounced the novel as abolitionist propaganda.

Then, in 1854, a Democratic politician, Senator Stephen Douglas of Illinois, again raised the dangerous issue of slavery in the territories. Douglas had two conflicting ambitions. He wanted Chicago to benefit from the development of the West. The sooner the territories of Kansas and Nebraska became states, the sooner railroads could be built across them to link Chicago with the West.

But Douglas also wanted to run for President. To do that, he needed the support of southern Democrats. Pushing statehood for Kansas and Nebraska was not the way to gain supporters in the South, because under the terms of the Missouri Compromise of 1820, Kansas and Nebraska would create free states. The North would then become still more powerful, and southerners would see Douglas as an enemy.

So Douglas tried to score points with both northerners and southerners. His **Kansas-Nebraska Act,** introduced in the United States Senate in January 1854, proclaimed that the people in a territory should decide whether slavery would be allowed there. What Douglas was saying, basically, was that the nation should forget the boundary of 36° 30' N established by the Missouri Compromise and rely on popular sovereignty.

Douglas knew that the Kansas-Nebraska Act would please southerners, because it raised the possibility that Kansas and Nebraska might become slave states. But he also figured that northerners would not object to relying on popular sovereignty to make the decision. He was positive that because agriculture on the Great Plains would not support cotton or slavery, the people of Kansas and Nebraska would peacefully choose to be free states.

Instead of applauding the bill, as Douglas expected, northerners were outraged by it. Northern members of Douglas's own party, the Democrats, denounced Douglas for what they saw as a sellout to the Slave Power—the South. And after Congress passed the Kansas-Nebraska Act, Douglas found out just how wrong he was about a peaceful vote in the territories.

The Rise of the Republican Party

Today's **Democratic party,** which was formed by Jefferson and carried on through the Age of Jackson, was still popular in the United States in the 1860s.

Stephen Douglas champions popular sovereignty in this 1858 cartoon. Douglas believed that slavery in the territories no longer would be a national issue if it were decided by voters in the territories themselves.

⭐ **Literature Activity** An Antislavery Best-Seller, found in the Unit 2 folder, pp. 63–64, uses an excerpt from Harriet Beecher Stowe's novel *Uncle Tom's Cabin* to show how a work of popular literature can influence public opinion.

Media and Technology

 Transparency
Cause and Effect, F-5

Explain/Discuss

Review the economies of the North and the South as discussed in Chapter 4. Ask students to compare the two regions in terms of their economic and material differences.

Discuss the way in which slavery divided the North and the South. Ask why so many northerners found slavery morally offensive. Why did southerners accuse northerners of hypocrisy regarding slavery?

Analyze

Have students analyze the roots of the conflict between North and South. Why might it be said that slavery was a lightning rod for larger issues between the two regions? Despite their differences, did Americans living in the North and the South share enough basic values, such as the belief in democracy and capitalism, to have been able to avoid the Civil War had the political leadership of the nation been more effective? Explain.

 In Depth

Then and Now

The Fugitive Slave Law angered and terrified free African Americans in the North. It permitted the capture not only of newly escaped slaves but of anyone who had ever fled from slavery. Any African American accused of being a fugitive slave had to stand trial before a special commissioner, not a judge. No jury heard the case, and the accused could not testify. Furthermore, the commissioner received a $10 fee for sending the accused back to slavery and only $5 for freeing the person.

Links Across Time

The slavery system might have collapsed by itself had southern planters not been dependent on slave labor to produce profits.

Activity

(The clock icon indicates an activity that can be successfully conducted within a class period. Each chapter has at least one such activity.)

Teaching Heterogeneous Groups
In 1852, the publication of *Uncle Tom's Cabin* ignited the antislavery movement. The author, Harriet Beecher Stowe, created one character who evoked sympathy and a contrasting, despicable character. To assist students in understanding both sides of the Civil War issue, divide the class into small groups. Ask each group to come up with a theme for a book and to create two main characters who would evoke the reader's sympathies toward the South. **LEP**

In Depth

Then and Now

The telegraph made it possible for American newspapers to pool their resources into the first wire service: the Associated Press of New York, now known as the Associated Press. During the Civil War telegraph lines were often cut or news transmissions replaced by military bulletins. To get their stories across before interruption, reporters would stack a complete summary of the story in the lead paragraph. This style of news writing, called the *inverted pyramid,* is still in modified use today.

| 1650 | 1700 | 1750 | 1800 | **Links Across Time** | 1850 | 1900 | 1950 | 2000 |

Picking Cotton: Humans vs. Machines

Picking cotton by hand (immediate right, in a photograph from the 1800s) required many workers. Modern mechanical cotton harvesters (far right) need only a few operators. *How might the slavery system have been affected if harvesting machines had been available to pick cotton in the early 1800s?*

The other major party that still exists today, the **Republican party,** grew out of the uproar over the Kansas-Nebraska Act. It drew its support almost entirely from the North and from Protestant middle-class and working-class voters. Farmers, professionals, small business owners, craftworkers, hardworking middle-class people—these were the Republicans. This new party tended to appeal to the same kind of voters as their chief rivals, the American party.

The American party had been formed from a secret organization whose members responded that they "knew nothing" when asked about their society. Thus the party was also called the Know Nothing party. It was part of the nativist movement, which worked to ensure that people born in the United States, who considered themselves "natives," received better treatment than immigrants. Nativism had appeared in the early 1850s in response to the huge influx of largely Catholic immigrants into the United States. Nativists feared that immigrants would take jobs, create disorder, and make the Pope a powerful political presence. Indeed, some northerners saw "Papal Power" as a threat to the American republic equal to that of the Slave Power.

In the mid-1850s, Know Nothings and Republicans struggled to see who would succeed the Whigs as the opposition to the Democrats.

The Republicans succeeded, in part by adopting the nativist ideas of the American party. They drew voters away from the American party, making their own party a single powerful force opposed to both slavery and Catholicism.

Neither the American party nor the Republican party, however, won the election for President in 1856. The Democratic candidate, James Buchanan, became President, with the backing of southerners. To repay the South for its support, he pledged to stop "the agitation of the slavery issue" in the North.

The Republicans did receive many votes from northerners fearful about the slavery issue and about what was now going on in the Kansas Territory. People there were quarreling about whether Kansas would become a free state or a slave state. And they were not just talking about it—they were shooting at each other.

The System Fails

Tension in Kansas began in 1854 when the Kansas-Nebraska bill became law. Antislavery organizations in the Northeast then decided to take action. If the question of slavery in the territories was going to be resolved by voting, they would have to make sure antislavery forces were in the majority there. They set up so-called

RESOURCE DIRECTORY

Teaching Resources

Primary Source Activity An Interview with John Brown, found in the Unit 2 folder, p. 61, uses a contemporary newspaper interview to provide students with an explanation for John Brown's raid.

Emigrant Aid societies and in 1854 and early 1855 sent some 1,200 New Englanders to Kansas to fight against the Slave Power. Like others who were committed to making the territories free, the new settlers were called free soilers.

Meanwhile, proslavery settlers in Missouri organized secret societies to oppose the free soilers. Many crossed into Kansas to vote illegally in territorial elections. By 1855 Kansas had—only twenty miles apart—an antislavery capital at Topeka and a proslavery capital at Lecompton.

 In May 1856 tensions escalated into open violence. A group of proslavery southerners looted Lawrence, Kansas, a center of free-soiler activity. In response, a group of antislavery northerners led by abolitionist **John Brown** killed five men in a proslavery settlement near Pottawatomie Creek. These actions sparked a summer of murderous raids and counterraids throughout Kansas that won the territory a grim nickname: "Bleeding Kansas."

In late May, the violence spread into the halls of Congress. A South Carolina congressman named Preston Brooks beat a Republican senator, Charles Sumner of Massachusetts, with his cane while Sumner sat at his desk on the Senate floor. Brooks was retaliating for the fiery speech given by Sumner titled "The Crime Against Kansas." Sumner survived the caning, but it took him four years to return to the Senate.

Northerners were outraged by Brooks's action. To them it seemed that if a southern member of Congress could beat a United States senator in the middle of the Senate without punishment, then the North was at the mercy of the South. Southerners, however, saw the caning as a justified response to a terrible insult against their honor.

A Decision and a Debate

In March 1857, the Supreme Court added to the growing tension with its decision in the case of *Dred Scott v. Sandford.* (See History Might Not Have Happened This Way: The Dred Scott Decision, on page 196.) Scott, an enslaved man living in Missouri, had filed suit against his owner. He argued that because he and his wife, Harriet, had once been taken into states and territories where slavery was illegal, the couple was in fact free.

By a vote of seven to two, the justices ruled against the Scotts. Chief Justice Roger Taney stated that as an African American, Dred Scott was inferior and without rights. Thus, he was not a citizen of the United States and could not sue anyone. In any case, Scott could not be considered free simply because he had once stood on free soil. As an enslaved person, Scott was property. Taney noted that "the right of property

Political Parties of the 1850s

Party	Views	Supporters
Democrats (North)	Favored deciding issue of slavery in the territories by popular sovereignty	A variety of backgrounds, but particularly northern voters in urban areas and Catholics; some of those born in South who had moved to Old Northwest
Democrats (South)	Favored expanding slavery in territories	Those living in southern areas undergoing growth in economy and population
Republicans	Opposed to slavery, supported nativist movement	People in New England and people born in New England living in the Old Northwest; Protestant English, Scots-Irish immigrants; former American party followers
American Party	Known as "Know Nothings"; anti-Catholic, fearing "Papal Power"; nativist, favoring a longer naturalization period for immigrants; antislavery	Supporters were generally middle-class, northern Protestants born in the United States

 Interpreting Tables
During the 1850s, three major parties jostled for power in the North, but only one major party represented the South. *Why did the Republicans lack support in the South? What views did the Republican party share with the American party that enabled it to win over American party members?*

Media and Technology

Transparency
Historical Maps, L-3

 In Depth

Historical Misconceptions

Because more than 80 percent of African Americans today favor Democratic candidates, they are strongly identified with that party. But until the 1930s, African Americans in the North generally voted Republican. As far back as 1856, a gathering of voters resolved: "That we, the colored citizens of Boston, will support with our voices and our votes, John C. Frémont, of California, as President of the United States. . . . [That] while we regard the Republican party as the people's party . . . and while we are willing to unite with them to resist the aggressions of the Slave Power, we do not pledge ourselves to go further with the Republicans than [they] will go with us."

Section 1 Review Answers

1. (a) Civil War, see p. 190, (b) Union, see p. 190, (c) Compromise of 1850, see p. 191, (d) Kansas-Nebraska Act, see p. 191, (e) *Dred Scott* v. *Sandford*, see p. 193

2. (a) Democratic party, see p. 191, (b) Republican party, see p. 192, (c) John Brown, see p. 193, (d) Abraham Lincoln, see p. 194

3. (a) Border States, see p. 194, (b) Lower South, see p. 195, (c) Upper South, see p. 195

4. It proposed sovereignty.

5. Lincoln hoped that if slavery was confined to the states in which it already existed, it would eventually die out.

6. North Carolina and the Lower South generally voted for Breckinridge; three Border States voted for Bell; Missouri voted for Douglas; and most of the North voted for Lincoln.

7. Answers should point out that the existing political system, with its party and sectional divisions, was unable to find a compromise that was acceptable in the long term to the majority of Americans. The illegal actions of both proslavery and antislavery forces are proof of this failure.

In Depth

Did You Know?

In December 1860, Congress made some last-ditch efforts to hold the Union together. Kentucky Senator John J. Crittenden proposed a series of "unamendable amendments" to the Constitution, one of which would stretch the Missouri Compromise (see pages 114–115) to California as the dividing line between slavery and free soil. President Lincoln's Republicans, however, stood firm in refusing to allow slavery to extend into new territories, and the so-called Crittenden Compromise was narrowly defeated in the Senate on March 2, 1861.

During his 1858 campaign for the Senate, Abraham Lincoln told one audience that he was driven "by something higher than an anxiety for office," a desire to defend the principle of equality established by the Declaration of Independence.

in a slave is distinctly and expressly affirmed in the Constitution." This meant that Congress had no power to ban slavery anywhere, including the territories. Needless to say, northerners were horrified by this decision.

The issues raised by the Kansas-Nebraska Act and the *Dred Scott* decision found a forum for national attention in 1858, when Illinois senator Stephen Douglas debated Republican lawyer **Abraham Lincoln** during a tough campaign for one of Illinois's Senate seats. The debates intensified the clash between those who thought slavery immoral and those who tolerated it. They also made the relatively unknown Lincoln a national figure, though he lost the Senate election.

Lincoln had concluded that slavery was wrong, and thus it was a moral as well as a political issue that the United States had to deal with. In a speech in June 1858, Lincoln insisted:

> A house divided against itself cannot stand. I believe this government cannot endure, permanently half slave and half free. I do not expect the Union to be dissolved—I do not expect the house to fall—but I do expect it will cease to be divided. It will become all one thing, or all the other.

John Brown's Raid

On October 16, 1859, John Brown and twenty-two men attacked the federal arsenal at Harpers Ferry, Virginia (now West Virginia). They planned to give the weapons in the arsenal to enslaved people and start an uprising that would end slavery and lead the United States to moral renewal.

Alerted to the attack, federal troops surrounded Brown and his men in the arsenal, killing about half of them. Convicted of treason against the state of Virginia, Brown left a prophetic message before he was executed:

> I John Brown am now quite certain that the crimes of this guilty land will never be purged away; but with Blood.

The Election of 1860

Differences between northern Democrats and southern Democrats finally ripped the Democratic party apart in the summer of 1860. Northerners nominated Stephen Douglas of Illinois, and southerners chose John C. Breckinridge, the current Vice President. He was committed to an aggressive policy of expanding slavery in the territories that even northern Democrats like Douglas could not tolerate.

Republicans nominated Abraham Lincoln, in part because he was considered relatively moderate on the slavery issue. But most southerners had heard too much extreme language from the Republican party to trust anyone it nominated.

Appalled by the increasingly radical positions of the southern Democrats and the Republicans, some moderates formed the Constitutional Union party. They were mostly southerners who had belonged to the Whig party, along with a few politicians from the **Border States**—Delaware, Maryland, Kentucky, and Missouri. They chose John Bell of Tennessee, a moderate slaveholder, as their presidential nominee.

The November election was essentially two elections, one in the South between Bell and Breckinridge and one in the North between Lincoln and Douglas. Lincoln received the majority he needed to win the presidency by picking up 180 electoral votes out of a possible 303. But while he won a majority of the popular vote in the North, he received only 40 percent of the popular vote in the nation as a whole. Contributing to Lincoln's failure to achieve a national majority was the fact that he received virtually no votes in most of the South.

The War Starts

Southerners were outraged that a President could be elected with so few of their votes. They feared that the national government had passed

RESOURCE DIRECTORY

Teaching Resources

completely out of their hands. Planters and others who backed slavery refused to remain in a Union run by the antislavery Republicans. Secessionists—those who wanted the South to secede—argued that since the states had voluntarily joined the United States, they also could choose to leave it.

The Lower South Secedes South Carolina officially left the Union on December 20, 1860. The six other states of the **Lower South**—Texas, Louisiana, Mississippi, Alabama, Florida, and Georgia—soon followed. In early February 1861, delegates from the seven states met in Montgomery, Alabama. There they created a new nation, the Confederate States of America, also called the Confederacy, shown on the map to the right.

Fort Sumter, Symbol of the Union As Lincoln took the oath of office on March 4, 1861, the attention of the nation was on Fort Sumter, a federal fort on an island in the harbor of Charleston, South Carolina. Cut off by Confederate forces, federal soldiers at the fort were fast running out of supplies. Initially the fort's commander refused to give up. But when the Confederates opened fire on April 12, 1861, he surrendered after a twenty-four-hour bombardment.

By firing on federal property, the Confederate states had committed an undeniable act of

open rebellion. When Lincoln called for volunteers to put down the rebellion, southerners saw his action as an act of war against them. The **Upper South**—Virginia, North Carolina, Tennessee, and Arkansas—now joined the Lower South in the Confederacy.

Eighty-four years after the Continental Congress had declared the independence of the United States of America, the nation had come apart. Union with slavery was no longer possible.

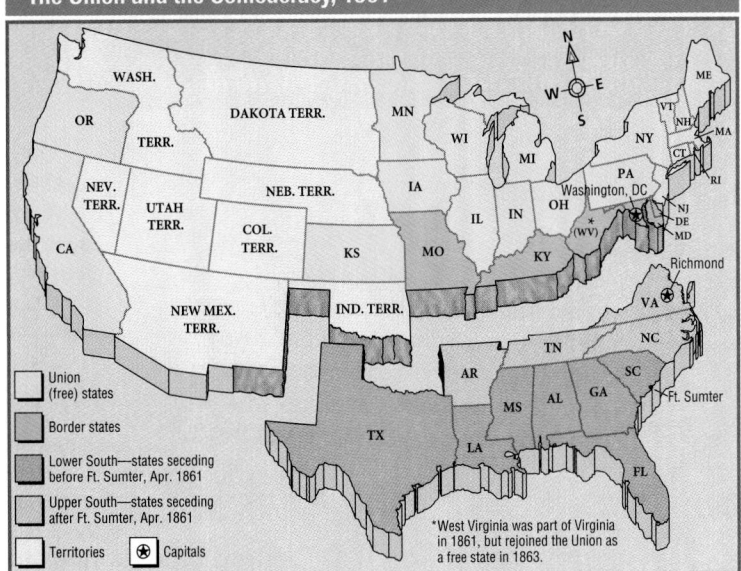

The Union and the Confederacy, 1861

*West Virginia was part of Virginia in 1861, but rejoined the Union as a free state in 1863.

Key:
- Union (free) states
- Border states
- Lower South—states seceding before Ft. Sumter, Apr. 1861
- Upper South—states seceding after Ft. Sumter, Apr. 1861
- Territories
- ✪ Capitals

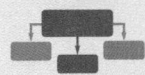 **Geography and History: Interpreting Maps**
When South Carolina seceded, one Unionist sarcastically observed that the state was "too small for a republic and too big for a lunatic asylum." South Carolina was soon joined by other states, however—making the Confederate republic one of the largest in the world. *Name the states that seceded after the surrender of Fort Sumter.*

SECTION 1 REVIEW

Key Terms, People, and Places
1. Define (a) Civil War, (b) Union, (c) Compromise of 1850, (d) Kansas-Nebraska Act, (e) *Dred Scott* v. *Sandford*.
2. Identify (a) Democratic party, (b) Republican party, (c) John Brown, (d) Abraham Lincoln.
3. Identify (a) Border States, (b) Lower South, (c) Upper South.

Key Concepts
4. How did the Kansas-Nebraska Act propose to settle the issue of slavery in the territories?
5. What was Abraham Lincoln's position on slavery?
6. Summarize the results of the election of 1860.

Critical Thinking
7. **Testing Conclusions** Explain why one of the headings in this chapter is "The System Fails."

Quiz found in the Unit 2 folder, p. 46, covers the main ideas in this section as well as the key terms.

The Dred Scott Decision

Focus The Supreme Court had the opportunity to reexamine laws about slavery in the Dred Scott case. Instead, by denying Dred Scott and his wife, Harriet, their freedom in 1857, it chose to support the fragile web of compromise that had so far kept the North and South out of a civil war. Like other efforts on the part of the federal government to avoid direct confrontation over the slavery question, the decision increased tensions between North and South. Students are asked to evaluate the ruling and to investigate some of the consequences of other options available to the Court.

Instruct To check students' understanding of the facts of the case, ask them to summarize in a few sentences why Dred Scott felt he and his wife should be freed. Then review the arguments for and against both a narrow and a broad ruling against Scott. Ask students why the Court never really had the option of setting Scott and his wife free. Ask students to write their own ruling in this case.

Extend To extend the activity, have students research the Fourteenth Amendment to explore how and when African Americans were finally granted United States citizenship.

The Dred Scott Decision

Time Frame:	March 1857
Place:	Washington, D.C.
Key People:	Dred and Harriet Scott, Chief Justice Roger Taney
Situation:	In the 1850s, as controversy raged over slavery, the Supreme Court was faced with a tough question: Did enslaved people become free when they were taken into territories where slavery was against the law?

I n the 1830s, a white man from Missouri named Emerson took Dred Scott, an enslaved African American, into the state of Illinois and the federal territory of Wisconsin. In Wisconsin, Scott met and married his wife, Harriet. Under the Missouri Compromise of 1820, slavery was illegal in both places. After living with their owner in these free areas, the Scotts returned to the slave state of Missouri. The husband, Dred Scott—shown in the painting on this page—sued for his family's freedom in 1846. He argued that residence in a free state and then in a free territory had ended his enslavement.

The Court's Options

When the Court finally began considering the case, the justices had to decide between two approaches to the question. They could issue what is called a *narrow ruling*, responding to the legal arguments Dred Scott had made and stating simply whether or not he was free. Or they could issue a *broad ruling*, in which they considered whether the laws involved in the case were constitutional.

Only One Option in a Narrow Ruling The Court could not really use a narrow ruling to declare Scott free. Too many issues would be left unresolved if they did so. After all, the Constitution and federal laws had always upheld the rights of property owners. The Court could not inter-

fere with that right without reexamining the Constitution at length.

The Court could, however, use a narrow ruling to declare that Scott was still enslaved. This decision had already been made by the lower courts that had considered the case. The Supreme Court could simply support their decision.

The Broad Ruling Options The justices did not *have* to make a broad ruling. But throughout its history, the Supreme Court has used certain cases to examine laws and determine if they are constitutional. The justices might well believe it was time to reexamine laws about slavery. Their broad ruling might declare Scott free or declare him enslaved.

Weighing the Options

By setting Scott free, the Court would place human rights above the right of slaveholders to own human property. African Americans and abolitionists would have enthusiastically welcomed this decision. But for

▶ **RESOURCE DIRECTORY**

History Might Not... Activity Can Separate Be Equal? found in the Unit 2 folder, pp. 53–54, highlights the case of Homer Adolph Plessy and his attempt to sit in a whites-only railroad car.

1. Too many issues would be left unresolved.

2. Only citizens can sue. Taney claimed that African Americans were not citizens under the Constitution.

3. It was Taney's responsibility to protect the Constitution and the federal laws, which he believed had always upheld the rights of the owners of enslaved people.

GOALS	Determine whether Dred Scott was free; make a decision about the larger issue of slavery		
POSSIBLE ACTIONS	**Rule broadly for Scott**	**Rule narrowly against Scott**	**Rule broadly against Scott**
POSSIBLE RESULTS	• Will place human rights above the right of whites to own enslaved people • Will please African Americans and abolitionists • Will make it easier for enslaved people to escape slavery • Will anger southerners	• Will please southerners and slave holders • Will probably not surprise the majority of northern white people • Will keep the compromises in place, reducing chance of violence	• Will jar compromises over slavery • Might extend slavery into the territories • Would win wide support among white southerners • Might alarm large numbers of white northerners

many whites in the 1850s, the choice was not so clear.

A majority of the Court justices, including Chief Justice Roger Taney, were southerners. Taney himself hated slavery—and proved it by setting free the enslaved people he owned. But he knew that setting Scott free would make it easier for enslaved African Americans everywhere to win their freedom. This would cause a violent backlash from southern slaveholders threatened with the loss of their labor force. And Taney also knew that the Constitution and federal laws had always upheld the right to own property. Setting Scott free would be interfering with that right. So the real question was not whether the Court would rule for Scott. Instead, the question was whether the Court would rule narrowly, or whether it would rule broadly and reconsider federal laws about slavery.

If the Court ruled against Scott narrowly, it would please southerners and slaveholders by making it impossible for slaves to become free simply by entering free territory. And most northern whites would not be surprised by one more court decision that supported slavery. A narrow ruling would not disturb the compromises made over the years between slave states and free states, such as the Missouri Compromise and the Compromise of 1850.

If the Court ruled against Scott broadly, reexamining previous laws, they might jar that fragile web of compromise. They might even use the power of the Court to extend slavery into places where it was not currently legal. Southerners would approve of this, but northerners would be outraged.

When the Court decided the case on March 6, 1857, all nine justices wrote separate statements of their opinions. Taney's was the most influential, however, and the majority of the justices agreed with him. He did not set Scott free. And he combined both a narrow and a broad ruling in his statement on the case.

In the narrow part of his ruling, Taney pointed out that only citizens could sue others. Scott, Taney claimed, could not sue anybody because the Framers of the Constitution had never intended African Americans to be considered citizens.

In the broad part of his ruling, Taney emphasized that the Constitution protected the right to own property, and no federal law could break the Constitution. The Missouri Compromise of 1820 was a federal law that interfered with the right to own property—that is, enslaved people—in certain parts of the United States. Therefore the Missouri Compromise was unconstitutional.

Taney and his colleagues may have hoped that their bold ruling would end the controversy over slavery once and for all. Unfortunately, it only increased tensions.

EVALUATING DECISIONS

1. Why could a narrow ruling not free Scott?

2. Why did Taney decide Dred Scott could not sue?

Critical Thinking

3. Checking Consistency If Taney hated slavery, why did he not declare Dred Scott a free man?

Media and Technology

Visions of America: History Might Not Have Happened This Way Game

To encourage students to explore pivotal moments in United States history, have students use the Visions of America software. Refer to the Visions of America Teacher's Guidebook for viewing objectives, activities, game instructions, and discussion questions.

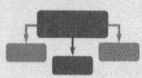

1. FOCUS

Connecting to the Big Idea

See page 188B. Explain that during the first two years of the Civil War, each side tried without success to capture the other's capital. Ask why the war looked like a stalemate by 1863.

Objectives

● Explain how new technology and political pressure affected the tactics of the war.
● Describe Union strategy in the western part of the Confederacy.
● Describe the unsuccessful attempts by northern and southern generals to invade each other's territory.

Bellringer

Ask students to think about how new technologies have influenced their lives. Which of these technologies were developed by the military? How have such technologies changed the nature of war? How did technology change the nature of warfare during the Civil War?

Reading Strategy

Structured Overview Ask students to write the following column headings on a piece of paper: Union Tactics, Confederate Tactics, Union Victories, Confederate Victories. As they read, students should fill in details from the text in the appropriate column.

The First Two Years of the Civil War

SECTION PREVIEW

In the first two years of the war, Union armies tried again and again to capture the Confederate capital but were driven back by bolder and more skillful generals. Union forces did succeed, however, in blockading the coasts of the South and seizing control of the great river valleys of its midwestern states.

Key Concepts
• Both new technology and political pressure greatly affected the tactics of the war.
• In the western part of the Confederacy, northern forces captured most of Kentucky, Tennessee, and the Mississippi Valley.
• Both the North and South resisted attempts to invade their territory in the East.

Key Terms, People, and Places
shell, canister, war of attrition, Anaconda Plan, gunboat; Stonewall Jackson, George McClellan, Ulysses S. Grant, Robert E. Lee; Manassas, Shiloh, Antietam

More than 90 percent of all battle wounds in the Civil War were caused by bullets—many of them by the new, more accurate type shown here.

F orward to Richmond! Forward to Richmond!" thundered the *New York Tribune* in July 1861. With the secession of the Upper South from the Union, the Confederate states had shifted their capital from Montgomery, Alabama, to Richmond, Virginia. Now northern newspapers demanded immediate action from the volunteers assembled after the surrender of Fort Sumter.

Southerners were just as eager to fight. Like northern troops, southern soldiers had volunteered for short periods of service. And like their brothers in the North, they were in a hurry to get the war over.

The Battle of Manassas

⭐ Public pressure for action had its effect in July 1861, when a large Union army tried to march to Richmond and collided with a Confederate army. This first major battle of the war was called both **Manassas**—the name of a nearby town—and the First Battle of Bull Run, after a small river in the area. Many Civil War battles have two names, one given by the South and the other given by the North. The South tended to connect a battle with the nearest town, the North with some physical feature close by the battlefield.

General Irvin McDowell had brought 30,000 Union troops about 30 miles west from Washington, D.C., to attack a southern army under General P.G.T. Beauregard—the officer who had captured Fort Sumter. On the morning of July 21, McDowell sent thousands of poorly trained men on a 10-mile march to strike at the left side of the Confederate army.

Confederate spies, including several women, sighted the Union troops, whose advance was no secret anyway. A huge crowd of civilians had traveled out from Washington behind the army to picnic and watch the battle.

The Confederates were well prepared. Although at first the Union troops nearly broke Beauregard's army, the southerners held their positions. The fighting was fierce: by the time it was over, nearly 5,000 men were killed, wounded, or missing.

In the afternoon, fresh Confederate troops were brought in by railroad—a technology now used in war for the first time—and streamed into the fight. Exhausted, the Union soldiers quit the battle. McDowell ordered a retreat.

But the day was not over. As they turned back, the Union soldiers ran into the crowds of sightseers who had followed them. The result was total confusion. Soldiers and civilians were caught in a tangle of wagons and horses on the narrow road. Terrified that Confederate forces would catch them, troops and picnickers broke into a panic. The army disintegrated; by nightfall it had become a mass of men running headlong for the safety of Washington.

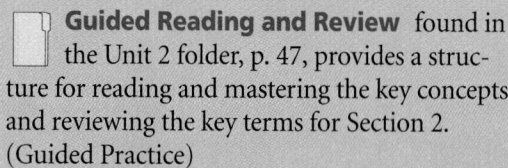

RESOURCE DIRECTORY

Teaching Resources

Reproducible Lesson Plan found in the Unit 2 folder, p. 42, provides a summary of the Section 2 lesson plan content.

Alternate Lesson Plan: Critical Thinking, Identifying Central Issues, found in the Alternate Lesson Plans folder, p. 75, helps students apply this skill by understanding the strategies and outcomes of key battles of the Civil War.

Guided Reading and Review found in the Unit 2 folder, p. 47, provides a structure for reading and mastering the key concepts and reviewing the key terms for Section 2. (Guided Practice)

⭐ **Literature Activity** The Battle of Manassas, found in the Unit 2 folder, p. 65, features poems by Herman Melville describing the famous author's impressions of the battle.

The Tactics of the War

Battles are not always won or lost by dramatic chance events, split-second decisions, or the skill and heroism of one or two individuals. On some occasions, however, such factors do matter. At Manassas, for example, an intensely religious and energetic Confederate officer named Thomas Jonathan Jackson made his troops stand as solidly as a stone wall during a Union attack. He stopped the Union advance and earned the nickname **Stonewall Jackson**.

Though armies need extraordinary soldiers like Stonewall Jackson, more often victory depends on two less colorful factors—organization and training. At Manassas, both armies were poorly organized and trained, and the generals soon realized it. For example, neither McDowell nor Beauregard had a good staff of officers to deliver orders to the battlefield quickly and efficiently. And once the soldiers received their orders, they did not always have the training to know what to do.

Technology Influences Tactics Though both sides quickly learned their lesson about organization and training, they failed to learn that the old ways of fighting a war did not work anymore. Europeans had fought wars for centuries by attacking the enemy's capital city or gathering their forces for one big battle that would decide everything. Cannons and muskets in early times were neither accurate nor capable of repeating fire very quickly. To overwhelm the enemy, generals relied on masses of men moving across open fields.

Almost all the generals of the Civil War had shared a belief in the old-fashioned tactics of gathering their forces in one place, attacking a position with massed troops, and driving the enemy away. The most vital position to attack, they believed, was the enemy's capital.

In the Civil War, however, American generals gradually had to confront a new technology that had made this strategy suicidal. Gun makers had learned that a long piece of lead with a rounded tip—a bullet—did not drift as it flew, like the older type of lead ball ammunition. They also had discovered that a spiral groove—called rifling—cut on the inside of a gun barrel would make a fired bullet pick up spin and travel in a nearly straight line. These new, more accurate rifles also could be reloaded rapidly. Cannons, too, had been improved. Instead of relying on simple iron cannon balls to smash their targets, gunners had more deadly options. They could fire a cannon **shell** that exploded in the air over the enemy or burst after it hit, or a **canister**—a special shell filled with lead balls about the size of bullets. To cross an open field against such weapons was an act of madness. Some Union and Confederate officers never realized this, though it was clear as early as the first battle at Manassas. Others eventually realized that it was slaughter to send soldiers against bullets, shells, and canister fire, but they continued to do so anyway.

Politics Influences Tactics Why did Civil War generals continue to use the old tactics? The reason is that Americans in both North and South were impatient; they wanted to win quickly. The people demanded instant results from their politicians, and the politicians demanded instant results from their generals.

The Confederacy would have had the greatest chance of success if it had worn down the Union in a **war of attrition**. In this kind of war, a weaker army inflicts continuous losses of soldiers and material that gradually add up to an unbearable burden for the other side. The table on page 200 shows that the North had tremendous resources. But such an advantage does not always mean victory, as the British had learned during the American Revolution.

Although Confederate president Jefferson Davis apparently recognized the wisdom of waging a war of attrition, his citizens would not let him adopt it. To fight a war of attrition, the army of the weaker side often has to avoid direct confrontations. It has to be able to retreat out of the enemy's way, even if it means giving up territory temporarily. Southerners, however, insisted that their government defend the entire Confederacy. The result was that the South had to stretch its precious soldiers and equipment in a thin line from Virginia to Texas. Its war goal was basically to keep attacking armies out of the Confederacy.

The goal of the North was to conquer the South, but northerners, too, would have been

Explain/Discuss

Discuss with students how the expectations of both sides were called into question in the early days of the war. Why did each side wish to capture the other's capital? Ask students to point out the capitals on a map. How far apart were they? *(About 100 miles.)* How did the results of the Battle of Manassas affect those calling for a short war?

Ask students to discuss the tactics of the war. How did tactics lag behind technology? What caused the lag?

Display a wall map and ask students to use it to describe the Anaconda Plan. What sorts of forces did this plan require? Ask students to predict which locations were vital to the success of the Anaconda Plan as they study the map. *(Major ports and river towns such as New Orleans and Vicksburg.)*

Ask students to point out the areas of stalemate in the East and West in 1863 and to predict how these would be broken.

In Depth

Interdisciplinary

Hot-air balloons, first employed in warfare by France in 1794, were used by American balloonist Thaddeus Lowe to provide the Union army with information on Confederate troop movements. Lowe conducted the first airborne operation of the recently invented telegraph. He also brought aloft cameras, which were just coming into popular use, to provide panoramic shots of military positions.

Interpreting Tables

Greater population, greater financial resources, and more industries.

Analyze

Ask students to analyze Grant's victory at Shiloh. Grant himself said that the Battle of Shiloh convinced him that the Confederacy would not collapse after a decisive Union victory but would require "complete conquest." In what ways did Shiloh cause each side to reassess its commitment to the war?

 Activity

(The clock icon indicates an activity that can be successfully conducted within a class period. Each chapter has at least one such activity.)

The Game of Generals

Ask each student to select four generals discussed in this section, write a first-person statement describing each general on one side of an index card, and then list the general's name on the other side. An example might be, "My soldiers stopped the Union advance at Manassas"; Stonewall Jackson. When students have completed their clues, hold a brief contest to see how many leaders students can identify. **LEP**

Advantages and Disadvantages of the North and South		
	Northern States*	**Southern States**
Population	21.5 million	9 million
Railroad Mileage	21.7 thousand miles	9 thousand miles
Manufacturing		
Number of Factories	110.1 thousand	20.6 thousand
Number of Workers	1.17 million	111 thousand
Value of Products	$1.62 billion	$155 million
Finance		
Bank Deposits	$207 million	$47 million
Specie	$56 million	$27 million
Agriculture		
Corn (bushels)	446 million	280 million
Wheat (bushels)	132 million	31 million
Oats (bushels)	150 million	20 million
Cotton (bales)	4 thousand	5 million
Tobacco (pounds)	229 million	199 million
Rice (pounds)	50 thousand	187 million
Livestock		
Horses	4.2 million	1.7 million
Donkeys and Mules	300 thousand	800 thousand
Milch Cows	5.7 million	2.7 million
Beef Cattle	6.6 million	7 million
Sheep	16 million	5 million
Swine	16.3 million	15.5 million
* Includes border states		

Source: *The American Heritage Picture History of the Civil War,* edited by Richard M. Ketchum

 **Interpreting Tables**
Northerner William T. Sherman warned a southern friend in 1860, "You are bound to fail." *Which advantages would allow the North to raise a larger, better equipped army than the South?*

better off avoiding direct confrontations. General Winfield Scott, the hero of the Mexican War and the commander of the United States Army in 1861, knew this well. Scott called for Union forces to surround the Confederacy and squeeze it to death. Northern ships could cut the South off from the rest of the world, especially cotton markets in Europe. Union riverboats and armies could cut the Confederacy in two at the Mississippi. This plan would make the best use of the North's advantages—its superiority in population and industry, its more extensive railroads, and its navy.

In the end, the North did make use of Scott's plan. But when word of the strategy was leaked to northern newspapers, they ridiculed it, calling it the **Anaconda Plan**, after a type of snake that coils around its victims and crushes them to death. In 1861 and 1862, most Americans still had dreams of a short war. Much as Manassas horrified soldiers and humbled officers, the political pressure for a quick victory remained strong.

The North Begins to Strangle the South

The day after Manassas, President Lincoln appointed **George McClellan** to command the major Union army in the East. General McClellan was a master organizer. He spent months preparing his men for battle and ensuring that they would have enough food and weapons. McClellan was a favorite with his men because he watched out for their welfare, but he was unpopular with Lincoln and northern politicians, who wanted results. ✪

Though McClellan took no action, other Union officers did. Along the Confederate seacoasts, the United States Navy succeeded in retaking several important federal forts and in setting up a blockade of enemy ports. The great industrial and economic strength of the North came into play as the government built and bought the first of more than six hundred ships it would add to its navy. The anaconda had begun to flex its muscles.

The War on the Rivers In order for the North to squeeze the South, however, Union forces had to gain control of the midwestern part of the Confederacy. Conflict did take place even farther west, in Missouri, Texas, and Oklahoma, which was then called the Indian Territory, but the war in the midwest of the Confederacy is generally referred to as the war in the West. This region, shown on the map on page 201, includes Tennessee, Arkansas, Mississippi, and Louisiana. It was a land of waterways, all leading to the Mississippi River. Whoever controlled the rivers would control commerce and military movements throughout the region. Knowing this full well, Confederate forces built Fort Henry on the Tennessee River and Fort Donelson on the Cumberland River, both in the state of Tennessee.

▶ **RESOURCE DIRECTORY**

Teaching Resources

✪ **Critical Thinking Activity** Recognizing Bias: Six Months on the Potomac, found in the Unit 2 folder, p. 60, encourages students to practice identifying points of view and bias using an 1862 cartoon that depicts General McClellan and his Confederate counterpart encamped along the Potomac.

✪ **American Profiles Activity** General Robert E. Lee, found in the Unit 2 folder, p. 55, profiles the Confederacy's brilliant military commander.

But this type of fort was a leftover from an older time. A new and deadly technology, the **gunboat**, made such forts largely useless. The typical gunboat was basically a small floating fort fitted with rifled cannons. Built to navigate even shallow rivers, driven by steam power, and often protected by iron armor, it brought the destructive power of Union cannon shells deep into the Confederacy.

Under the command of a tough Union general, **Ulysses S. Grant,** gunboats quickly pounded Fort Henry into surrender in February 1862. Not long after, following three days of shelling by gunboats, Fort Donelson surrendered unconditionally—earning U. S. Grant the nickname "Unconditional Surrender" Grant.

The Cumberland and Tennessee rivers now formed Union highways into the heart of the midwestern Confederate states. Nashville soon fell to the Union, and by April General Grant had pushed south nearly to Mississippi and Alabama.

The Slaughter at Shiloh On April 6, however, a southern army unexpectedly struck Grant's forces near Shiloh Church in Tennessee. The Confederates won the first day of this Battle of **Shiloh,** driving the Union troops back nearly into the Tennessee River. But Grant, displaying the determination that would see him through many a crisis in the years ahead, refused to give up. "Retreat?" he scoffed to his doubting officers after the first day. "No. I propose to attack at daylight and whip them."

With the help of reinforcements, Grant was as good as his boast. The North won the battle on April 7. But some 13,000 Union men and 10,000 Confederates had been killed, wounded, or captured. Wrote one Tennessee soldier after Shiloh:

> I never realized the "pomp and circumstance" of the thing called glorious war until I saw this. Men . . . lying in every conceivable position; the dead . . . with their eyes open, the wounded begging piteously for help.

The Battle of Shiloh showed northern civilians once again that the Confederacy would not collapse overnight. But it also stopped the

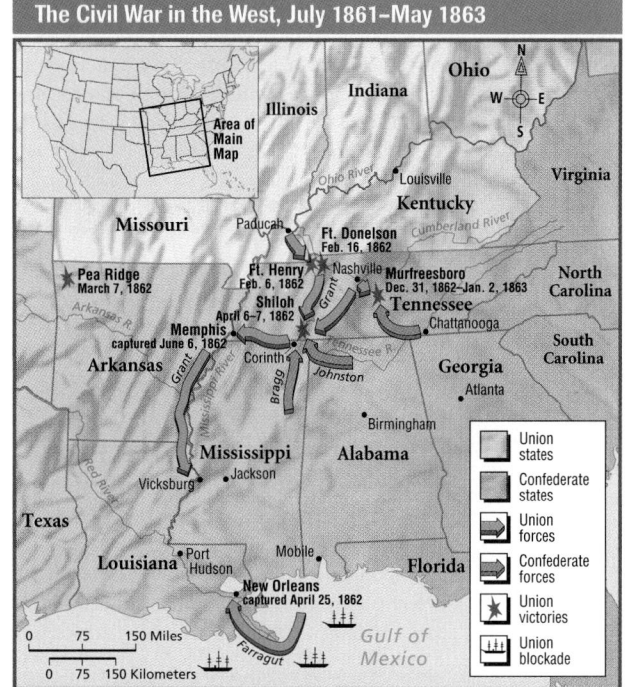

The Civil War in the West, July 1861–May 1863

Union states

Confederate states

Union forces

Confederate forces

Union victories

Union blockade

Geography and History: Interpreting Maps
Union generals in the West such as Grant (shown below) focused their attention on the Mississippi River. "That Mississippi ruins us, if lost," worried southern observer Mary Boykin Chesnut in 1862. *What two key cities on the Mississippi had the Union captured by the summer of 1862?*

South from regaining western Tennessee and its river highways. ★

Action on the Mississippi While Grant was breaking into the Confederacy in Kentucky and Tennessee, Union gunboats and troops were taking many of the Confederate posts on the Mississippi River. In late April 1862, a naval squadron commanded by sixty-year-old Captain David Farragut forced the surrender of New Orleans, Louisiana. Less than two months later, on June 6, the Union navy also seized Memphis, Tennessee.

Slowly, in battle after battle, the Union was putting the Anaconda Plan into operation. In early 1862, Union forces had captured 50,000 square miles, taken control of 1,000 miles of navigable rivers, and seized New Orleans.

Ulysses S. Grant

Media and Technology

Transparencies
Fine Art, D-10; The Way It Works, H-12

In Depth

Biography

Mary Boykin Chesnut (1823–1886) is the best known of the Confederate women diarists. A member of a prominent political family, Chesnut's husband, James Chesnut, Jr., was a wealthy senator, and her social circle included President Jefferson Davis. The time in which she lived was one of stress for the entire country, but she limited her observations to what was going on around her. It was her eye for daily life under wartime conditions that makes her diary so valuable. In July 1861 she wrote: "They brought me a Yankee soldier's portfolio from the battlefield. . . . One might shed tears over some of the letters. Women, wives and mothers, are the same everywhere."

The South would be unable to ship large quantities of cotton from its midwestern region; this would drastically affect its ability to earn money to pay for desperately needed supplies.

Caption Answer to …

 Interpreting Maps

He moved northward across Virginia into Maryland.

3. ASSESS

Section 2 Review Answers

1. (a) shell, see p. 199, (b) canister, see p. 199, (c) war of attrition, see p. 199, (d) Anaconda Plan, see p. 200, (e) gunboat, see p. 201

2. (a) Stonewall Jackson, see p. 199, (b) George McClellan, see p. 200 (c) Ulysses S. Grant, see p. 201, (d) Robert E. Lee, see p. 202

3. (a) Manassas, see p. 198, (b) Shiloh, see p. 201, (c) Antietam, see p. 203

4. New technology such as bullets, rifle guns, cannons, exploding shells, and canisters turned the tactic of attacking a position with massed troops into an act of madness. Political pressures from both northerners and southerners who wanted instant results from the war, however, drove generals to keep using this tactic.

5. Union forces took control of the Cumberland and Tennessee rivers, pushed nearly to Mississippi and Alabama, and captured New Orleans and Memphis.

6. Huge Union armies had failed four times to reach Richmond.

7. Possible answers: Follow the more elastic defense used by George Washington, concentrate on defending a more limited part of the Confederacy, or concentrate forces to break the naval blockade or Union control of the Mississippi River at specific points. Students may also observe that these options probably would not have succeeded.

Only two major posts on the Mississippi River now remained in Confederate hands—Vicksburg, Mississippi, and Port Hudson, Louisiana. If northern forces could find some way to capture them, the entire Mississippi River valley would be under Union control.

MAKING   CONNECTIONS

You have read in previous chapters that the South was dependent on its rivers, especially the Mississippi River, to transport cotton for sale abroad. What effect would closing the Mississippi to Confederate boats have on the South's effort to win the war?

The War for the Capitals

Though Union action on the seas and in the western river valleys was actually far more sig-

nificant than capturing Richmond, the North was still obsessed with making a quick end of the war by taking the enemy capital. By the spring of 1862, George McClellan had built a huge, well-equipped army. But he was reluctant to move. President Lincoln supposedly became so frustrated with his commander that he quipped: "I will hold McClellan's horse if he will only bring us success."

McClellan's Troops Invade Virginia McClellan thought that going to Richmond through Manassas again would be a mistake. So in the spring of 1862, he moved the Army of the Potomac by ship to the peninsula near Yorktown, Virginia. He inched his troops forward until, by the end of May, he was within a few miles of Richmond (see the map below).

McClellan had about 100,000 soldiers—twice as many as the Army of Northern Virginia, the Confederate force near Richmond. But the South had two brilliant military leaders.

The first was General **Robert E. Lee**—the man who had captured John Brown at Harpers Ferry in 1859. Lee took over as the leader of the Confederate forces when General Joseph Johnston was wounded in late May. Lee was an experienced officer and a leader of great courage and intelligence. Like all great generals, Lee wanted well-trained men and well-thought-out plans. But he also understood that victory often depends on a willingness to take chances.

The other brilliant leader was General Stonewall Jackson. He drove his men hard and could move his army with a speed that baffled the enemy. While McClellan was creeping close to Richmond, Jackson dashed north of the capital and carried out a series of lightning attacks on Union forces in the Shenandoah Valley in the Blue Ridge Mountains of Virginia. Lincoln was alarmed. Would Jackson attack Washington?

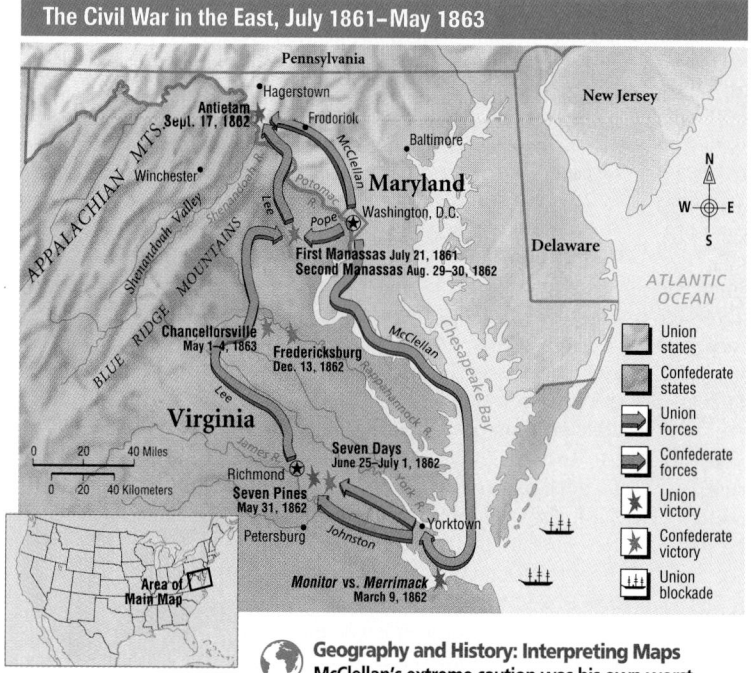

The Civil War in the East, July 1861–May 1863

Geography and History: Interpreting Maps
McClellan's extreme caution was his own worst enemy. "No one but McClellan would have hesitated to attack," said Confederate general Joe Johnston during McClellan's slow advance toward Richmond before the Seven Days' Battles. *What action did Lee take after winning the Seven Days' Battle?*

▶ RESOURCE DIRECTORY

Teaching Resources

The Union secretary of war, Edwin M. Stanton, ordered 50,000 Union troops to pursue Jackson instead of joining McClellan. After Jackson had thoroughly confused and alarmed the enemy, he slipped his forces away to help General Lee.

A Union general with the determination of Grant might well have taken the Confederate capital. But McClellan was not Grant. In the Seven Days' Battles, fought from June 25 through July 1, 1862, the outnumbered southerners wore out McClellan's great army. Again the human cost was nearly unbelievable: some 30,000 Americans were killed or wounded.

The Confederacy Attacks Now that Richmond had been saved, Lee tried to exploit the situation by invading the North. Any show of southern strength could have great benefits, because Great Britain was watching events closely, waiting for a sign that the Confederacy could stand on its own two feet. If Britain could be persuaded to recognize the Confederate States as an independent nation, its assistance in the war would be enormous. Furthermore, a successful invasion of the Northeast might force the United States to end the war.

For a few months, as Lee, Jackson, and other excellent Confederate generals fought their way into Maryland, the Confederacy seemed about to win its independence. But that hope faded on September 17, near Sharpsburg, Maryland, when McClellan's reorganized army met Lee's forces in the Battle of **Antietam.** It was the bloodiest day of the entire war: close to 6,000 soldiers were killed and 17,000 wounded. Neither side won a clear victory. All the same, Lee's heavy losses forced him to turn back to Virginia.

The War Becomes a Stalemate After Antietam, McClellan was replaced. The Union army again tried to take Richmond. In December 1862, General Ambrose Burnside led 110,000 men against Lee's 75,000 men, who were well entrenched along the Rappahannock River near Fredericksburg, Virginia. The Union forces were soundly defeated.

In early May 1863, another Union general, Joseph Hooker, clashed with Lee at Chancellorsville, Virginia. Outnumbered as usual, Lee broke two rules of good generalship: he divided his forces, and he attacked a larger army, rather than waiting to be attacked. He sent Stonewall Jackson and his men on a long, risky march to strike Hooker from behind. The strategy worked brilliantly. Lee thrashed the Union army, though it was twice the size of his own.

Among the many Confederate dead was Stonewall Jackson, who was wounded by his own men in the confusion and died a week later. The North lost about 17,000 men and gave up its lingering hopes for a short war.

In fact, it seemed to northerners that the war had reached a stalemate. In the East, huge Union armies had now failed four times to reach Richmond. In the West, Grant was stuck in the Mississippi Valley, trying to find some way to capture Vicksburg and open up the Mississippi River to Union warships.

But the stalemate would not last long. Ulysses S. Grant was indeed a determined man—as determined as Lee was brilliant.

SECTION 2 REVIEW

Key Terms, People, and Places
1. Define (a) shell, (b) canister, (c) war of attrition, (d) Anaconda Plan, (e) gunboat.
2. Identify (a) Stonewall Jackson, (b) George McClellan, (c) Ulysses S. Grant, (d) Robert E. Lee.
3. Identify (a) Manassas, (b) Shiloh, (c) Antietam.

Key Concepts
4. Give examples of the way in which new technology and political pressure affected the Civil War.

5. What gains did Union forces make in the western part of the Confederacy in the first two years of the Civil War?
6. Why did the war in the East seem like a stalemate by early 1863?

Critical Thinking
7. **Identifying Central Issues** If you had been the president of the Confederacy, how would you have defended your nation against the Anaconda Plan?

 Quiz found in the Unit 2 folder, p. 48, covers the main ideas in this section as well as the key terms.

Media and Technology

 Transparency
The Way It Works, H-11

Reteach
Ask students to correct each of the following incorrect statements:
• The Battle of Manassas was a Union victory that fed the notion that the war would be won quickly.
• The Confederacy tried to wage a war of attrition against the Union.
• The goal of the Anaconda Plan was to capture Richmond and demand that the Confederates surrender.
• By 1863 the Union was clearly on its way to capturing Richmond and ending the war.

 **Alternative Assessment**

Mid-Point Monitoring
Ask students if they have
● Selected the chapters they plan to include
● Begun their outside research
● Located maps and other illustrations

4. CLOSE

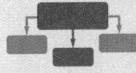 **Reinforcing the Big Idea**
The first two years of the Civil War were terribly bloody and in some ways indecisive. The Union victories in the West, however, were crucial. In the next section, students will see that the war changed the lives of Americans on both sides of the conflict.

In Depth

Then and Now

Before the Civil War, Richmond, Virginia, was a major center for the slave trade. A century later, in 1977, African Americans won five of the nine seats on the Richmond city council, and Henry L. Marsh III was elected Richmond's first African American mayor. In 1982, Marsh was succeeded as mayor by another African American, Roy A. West.

TOOLBOX

Historical Evidence

Using Letters as Primary Sources

Focus Students analyze letters as a source of historical evidence.

Instruct After students have read the feature, discuss how the information in letters such as those in the feature contributes to our understanding of the Civil War. Discuss how different sorts of letters provide different sorts of historical evidence. Ask students what types of evidence might take the place of letters in the future.

Extend See the Historian's Toolbox Activity in the Resource Directory below.

Answers

1. (a) Letter A refers to a husband and children and to farm matters; clearly it is from a wife and mother living on a farm. Letter B refers to nursing work on the battlefield; clearly the letter is from a woman who is a nurse. (b) Letter A was written to a husband; Letter B was written to a cousin. (c) Letter A was written on June 1, 1862; Letter B was written on July 8, 1863. (d) Letter A: Lowndes County, Alabama (the South); Letter B: Gettysburg, Pennsylvania (the North). (e) Letter A discusses crops, children, farm animals, and the writer's sadness about the absence of her husband. The topics of letter B include the conditions of wounded men and the duties of the writer.

2. (a) She mentions that a hired worker has quit and that a horse has gone blind and lame. (b) She gives food and drink to the wounded and writes letters for them.

3. (a) They had difficulties tending the crops and livestock without help in addition to their usual task of raising children. (b) They suffered intensely, lying on the grounds in rags with only biscuits to eat, and many had to have their limbs amputated. (c) Women assisted both by maintaining farm operations and by nursing the wounded.

HISTORIAN'S TOOLBOX

GEOGRAPHY | GRAPHS & CHARTS | CRITICAL THINKING | HISTORICAL EVIDENCE

Using Letters as Primary Sources

When people write letters, they report firsthand about something of interest to them. For this reason, letters are a valuable source of historical evidence. Not only do they present factual information about a subject, but they also give clues to the attitudes of people in a particular historical period.

Use the following steps to analyze the historical evidence in the letters on this page.

1. Lay the groundwork for analyzing the letters by asking who, when, where, and what. (a) What clues do the letters give about the identity of the writers? (b) To whom were the letters written? (c) When were they written? (d) Where were they written? (e) What are the topics of the letters?

2. Analyze the information in each letter. Study the letters to identify their main points. (a) What specific problems does the writer of Letter A describe? (b) What tasks does the writer of Letter B perform?

3. Study each letter to see what it reveals about conditions and attitudes during the period in which it was written. (a) What general difficulties did farm wives face when their husbands were away at war? (b) Summarize what conditions were like for the wounded after Civil War battles. (c) Generalize about the contribution to the war effort made by women during the Civil War.

A *Lowndes County, Alabama, June 1, 1862*
Dear husband, I now take my pen in hand [to] drop you a few lines to let you know that we are all well as common and I am in about the same health that I was when you left. I hopes these lines may find you the same. The boys [her sons] has come home to see me on a furlough [leave from the army] and stayed 10 days. They started back yesterday to the camp. . . . John, my corn is out now and I have not drawed [harvested] any thing yet but I hope I will. My crop is nice but Pane [a hired man] has quit and left my crop in bad fix, but the neighbors says they will help us. You said you wanted me to pray for you. As for prayers, I pray for you all of the time. I pray for you nearly every breath I draw. . . . Your baby is the prettyest thing you ever saw in your life. She can walk by herself and your little grandson is pretty as a pink and grows the fastest in the world. You must come home and see all of your babies and kiss them. I have got the rye cut. . . . Your old mare is gone blind in one eye and something is the matter with one of her feet so she can't hardly walk. Your hogs and cows is coming on very well. I want you to come home for I want to see you so bad I don't know what to do. I must come to a close by saying I remain your loving wife until death. You must write to me as soon as you get this letter. Goodbye to you.
   Lucy Lowe to John P. Lowe
        Adapted from Katharine M. Jones, *Heroines of Dixie*, 1955

B *Gettysburg, Pennsylvania, July 8th, 1863*
My Dear Cousin, I am very tired tonight; have been on the field all day. . . . There are no words in the English language to express the sufferings I witnessed today. The men lie on the ground; their clothes have been cut off them to dress [bandage] their wounds; they . . . have nothing but hardtack [biscuit] to eat only as Sanitary Commissions, Christian Associations [volunteer workers], and so forth give them. . . . To give you some idea of the extent and numbers of the wounds, four surgeons, none of whom were idle fifteen minutes at a time, were busy all day amputating legs and arms. I gave to every man that had a leg or arm off a gill [measure] of wine, to every wounded in the Third Division, one glass of lemonade, some bread and preserves and tobacco—as much as I am opposed to the latter. . . . I would get on first rate [remain in good spirits] if they would not ask me to write to their wives; that I cannot do without crying, which is not pleasant to either party.
   Cornelia
        Cornelia Hancock, *South After Gettysburg*, 1956

RESOURCE DIRECTORY

Teaching Resources

Historian's Toolbox Activity Using Letters as Primary Sources, found in the Unit 2 folder, p. 59, provides further opportunity to examine historical evidence with letters to and from soldiers in Vietnam.

War Brings Change

SECTION PREVIEW

During the Civil War, the national government became a powerful presence in the lives of ordinary people. In this and other ways, the conflict turned out to be more than a struggle over the Union. It became instead a redefinition of the American nation.

Key Concepts
- Republicans in Congress passed legislation that later allowed the United States to become a major economic power.
- During the Civil War, many African Americans set themselves free, and many also fought to free others.
- In the Gettysburg Address, Lincoln redefined the United States, emphasizing that democracy existed to preserve freedom and equality.
- Lee, finally hemmed in by Union forces, surrendered to Grant at Appomattox, Virginia.

Key Terms, People, and Places
draft, Emancipation Proclamation, contraband, total war, Gettysburg Address; Vicksburg, Appomattox Court House

B oth the central government of the Confederate states and the federal government of the United States dramatically increased their power in the course of the Civil War. Though all the changes in Confederate power were temporary, as were some of the changes in federal power, many new laws introduced during the war continue to have an impact on the nation today.

Increases in Federal Power

Both governments passed laws to establish a **draft**—a legal means of forcing people to serve in the armed forces. These were the first draft laws in American history, and they set a powerful precedent—and provoked an angry response, especially in the North. In July 1863, mobs in New York City vented their rage at the law in one of the worst riots in American history. At least 105 people died during four days of looting and destruction.

As the head of the federal government, Lincoln had many critics, not only in the streets, but in the press and Congress—including antiwar Democratic politicians called Copperheads, after a type of poisonous snake. Lincoln responded to some of these critics by using government power to deny them their basic rights. He sent the army to shut down newspapers that criticized the policies of his administration. He also had some 13,000 Americans who objected to federal policies put into prisons and held without trial during the war.

Government Grows Bigger Most of the critics of Republican policies—southern Democrats—had left Congress before the war started. Many Republicans, including Lincoln, were former Whigs and as such had supported a strong national government that would promote business. Faced with the need to raise money to pay for the war, the Republican-controlled Congress passed a tariff that not only would bring in cash, but also would protect American industries from foreign competition.

The Republicans also created other taxes, including the first federal tax on income in American history, and taxes on items such as liquor, tobacco, medicine, and newspaper ads. Although almost all of the taxes ended with the war, the Bureau of Internal Revenue created by Republican legislation became a permanent part of the federal government. It is now known as the Internal Revenue Service (IRS) and is responsible for collecting taxes from individuals and corporations.

During the war, President Lincoln also signed several laws that had a powerful impact

Through their own efforts, including outstanding courage in battle, Americans brought dramatic changes to their lives during the Civil War. Medals of Honor like this one were awarded to many, including twenty-one African Americans.

1. FOCUS

Connecting to the Big Idea

See page 188B. Explain that the Civil War brought many changes to the lives of both northerners and southerners. Its turning point came in 1863 with the battles of Vicksburg and Gettysburg. Explain that the war ended when General Lee finally surrendered at Appomattox Court House, Virginia, in April 1865. Ask students to consider the costs of the Civil War. What were its major results?

Objectives
- Identify legislation passed during the Civil War that later allowed the United States to become a major economic power.
- Explain how many African Americans freed themselves during the war and fought to free others.
- Explain how Lincoln's Gettysburg Address redefined the United States.
- Describe the terms under which the war ended.

Bellringer

Ask students if they can remember being without electricity for any length of time. If so, ask them to describe how they spent that time. Then ask them to imagine how that experience would compare to living in a cave for several months while an enemy army shelled their city.

Reading Strategy

Reinforcing Key Ideas Ask students to write the main headings from the section on a sheet of paper and to take notes about each as they read. When students have finished reading the section, ask them to use their notes to write a paragraph that summarizes the section content.

The Republican policy created a stronger, more centralized federal government that overshadowed the states more than it had done before the war. The states declined in both political and popular importance. Thus, Americans today are likely to feel a stronger loyalty to the nation than to a particular state.

"All that has been said by orators and poets since the creation of the world in praise of women ... would not do them justice for their conduct during the war," said Abraham Lincoln. This woman cared for her children and her soldier husband in a Union camp in 1862.

In Depth

Then and Now

Students in the 1990s can see the story of the 54th Massachusetts Regiment retold in the film *Glory*. The film, which won three Academy Awards in 1989, also won praise for its attention to historical detail. Historian Peter Burchard wrote: "It took great heart . . . to tell the story of the Fifty-fourth as it is told in *Glory*—from the point of view of the regiment's rank and file."

on the nation's expansion. The Pacific Railroad Act of 1862 permitted the federal government to offer public land and money to several companies in return for the construction of a railroad from Nebraska to the Pacific Coast. As a result of this act, transcontinental railways would soon link East and West. The Homestead Act of 1862 granted 160 acres of federal land to settlers who lived on the grant and improved it for a period of five years. Under the Morrill Act of 1862, money from the sale of public land was to be used to fund an agricultural college in each state. Many of these colleges later developed into the great universities of the Midwest. The Morrill Act also established the Department of Agriculture to promote farming in the nation.

With this legislation, the Republicans made the Civil War Congresses among the most active in American history. They laid the political and economic foundations for the emergence of the United States as the most powerful industrial and agricultural nation in the world. They also, however, created a cozy relationship between capitalists and the United States government that would become a target of reformers in years to come.

After the Civil War, people seldom used the term Union or used expressions such as "the United States *are*." They were more likely to refer to "the nation" and to say "the United States *is*." Explain how the Republican policy of making government bigger and more powerful helped bring about this change in attitude.

African Americans Free Themselves

During the early part of the war, President Lincoln continued to insist that the struggle was about the Union, not about emancipation, or freeing enslaved people. Eventually, however, he realized that he could not achieve his purpose without emancipating the enslaved people of the South. On September 22, 1862, he moved toward this goal by issuing the **Emancipation Proclamation.** It stated that as of January 1, 1863, all enslaved people in the areas in open rebellion against the government would "be then, thenceforward, and forever free."

The Emancipation Proclamation had no immediate effect on enslaved people because they were still under southern control. But it was a promise that they would be free when the North won the war. Thus, the war was no longer just about the political question of whether the Union would survive. It was about the moral question of whether slavery would fail.

Actually, African Americans had been setting themselves free by the thousands since the beginning of the war. All they had to do was to

RESOURCE DIRECTORY

Teaching Resources

American Profiles Activity Mary Elizabeth Bowser, found in the Unit 2 folder, p. 56, profiles a former slave and important spy for the Union.

move to territory controlled by Union troops, where they were designated to be **contraband,** a legal term that means property seized by the government. The federal government, as their legal owner, could then declare them free.

Once freed, African Americans could fight to free others who were still enslaved. Some 85 percent of those eligible to fight did so. These African Americans in the armed forces eventually totalled nearly 180,000 soldiers, almost 10 percent of the Union fighting force. During the war, more than 68,000 were killed or wounded, and 21 won the Medal of Honor, the nation's highest award for courage in combat. One of these was William Harvey Carney, a member of the 54th Massachusetts Regiment.

AMERICAN PROFILES
William Harvey Carney

Carney was born in 1840, but no one is sure where. About his family the record is silent. When the Civil War began, he was just another unknown American. It is documented, however, that in February 1863 Carney enlisted in Company C of the 54th Massachusetts Regiment. Hundreds of African American men from all over the northern states signed up with the regiment at the same time.

Carney soon rose to the rank of sergeant. He could not rise higher because, with few exceptions, only whites could be officers. Even though they wore the blue uniform of the United States, Carney and his fellow soldiers had to endure all kinds of insults. Not only were they paid less than white troops, they were denied adequate supplies and equipment. Overcoming these challenges, the 54th became a disciplined and proud unit.

The Charge on Fort Wagner On July 18, 1863, as part of the Union attack on the city of Charleston, the 54th Massachusetts led the assault on Fort Wagner on Morris Island. The regiment was assigned to charge the fort under cover of darkness. When the attack began, the soldiers came under heavy fire. All the same, they hurled themselves through or over one obstacle after another, including a ditch filled

Many years after his heroic actions in the Civil War, William Harvey Carney posed for a photographer. He achieved widespread fame for his refusal to let the American flag touch the ground during battle.

with 4 feet of water. Then they climbed the main defensive wall of the fort in the darkness and set the flag of their regiment at the top.

The Confederate defenders, however, met them in full force. Color Sergeant John Wall, whose job it was to carry the flag of the United States, was struck down. But before the symbol of liberty could touch the ground, Sergeant Carney seized it and planted it next to the regimental flag.

Defenders and attackers were now locked together in fierce hand-to-hand combat, which raged along the wall for close to an hour. Carney was wounded in both legs, his right arm, and his chest. But he refused to stop fighting or to let the enemy cut down the flag. When the remaining members of the regiment were ordered to pull back from the fort to a position some 700 yards away, Carney carried the flag with him.

The Aftermath of the Assault Of the 600 members of the 54th who had charged Fort Wagner, 259 were dead, wounded, or missing. Sergeant Carney was taken to the field hospital.

2. INSTRUCT

Explain/Discuss

Discuss with students the strengths and weaknesses of the Confederate government. Ask students in what ways it resembled the federal government during the Revolution.

Ask students to list the ways the federal government increased its power during the war. Tell students that Lincoln took on extraordinary power, interfering with freedom of the press and suspending the writ of *habeas corpus* to hold Maryland and the other Border States within the Union. Do students think that Lincoln was justified? What might have happened if he had not acted decisively to hold the Border States?

Ask students to list the permanent increases in federal power described in the section. Ask why the Civil War provided the opportunity for these increases.

In Depth
Multicultural Perspectives

When African American soldiers joined the Union Army they were paid only seven dollars a month, compared with the thirteen dollars a month paid other soldiers. James Gooding, an African American soldier, wrote to President Lincoln, "We have done a soldier's duty. Why can't we have a soldier's pay?"

Analyze

Ask students to speculate about what might have happened if General Meade had pursued Lee's forces after the Battle of Gettysburg. Ask students to create a time line showing events from Gettysburg to the end of the war.

Activity

Cooperative Learning

Time: One class period.

Activity: Have students plan the itinerary of a research tour through the major battlefields and historic sites of the Civil War.

Grouping: Groups of four students.

Purpose: To identify the significance of specific sites, routes, and battles of the war.

Roles: Members of the research project's travel department, including travel agents, tour planners, guides.

Outcome: Students will identify important battlefields and sites of the Civil War.

In Depth

Historical Misconceptions

Over 620,000 soldiers lost their lives in the Civil War—but not all died in battle. Around twice as many soldiers died from disease as were killed or mortally wounded in combat. In the 1860s scientists were just beginning to understand the role of bacteria in disease. Doctors did not understand, for example, the close connection between unsterilized surgical instruments and infections.

Other wounded soldiers saw the flag he still carried in his hands and broke into a ragged cheer. "The old flag never touched the ground, boys," he assured them.

Not much is known about Sergeant Carney's life after the charge on Fort Wagner. He reappears in history only once, in 1900. In that year he was awarded the Congressional Medal of Honor for his bravery on the evening of July 18, 1863.

The attack on Fort Wagner was a military failure. But the exploits of the 54th Regiment, widely publicized in the North, had a dramatic impact on white attitudes toward African American soldiers. Wrote a reporter for the *New York Herald:*

> I saw them [African Americans] *fight at Wagner as none but splendid soldiers, splendidly officered, could fight, dashing through shot and shell, grape, canister and shrapnel, and showers of bullets, and . . . when they did retreat [it was] by command and with choice white troops for company.*

The Battle of Gettysburg

Before the assault on Fort Wagner, one of the most decisive battles of the war had taken place not in the South, but in the North. After Lee had defeated Hooker at Chancellorsville, he

Confederate troops in George Pickett's charge at Gettysburg temporarily broke the Union line in the action shown here, at a crook in a stone wall called the Angle. After the charge, General Lee told Pickett to re-form his division to repel a possible counterattack. "General Lee," exclaimed Pickett, "I have no division now."

spent May and June of 1863 organizing and moving his troops into the North once again. This time he pushed as far as Pennsylvania. His plan was to cut off Washington, D.C., from the rest of the Union and win recognition for Confederate independence.

Once again, the Union army pursued Lee's forces. On July 1, just west of the little village of Gettysburg, Pennsylvania, Union troops clashed with the advance units of the Confederate army as it began to concentrate in the vicinity of the town. Within hours, tens of thousands of Union and Confederate troops poured into the area. So began the Battle of Gettysburg, a struggle that would drag on through three terrible days.

On July 1, the first day of the battle, the Confederates pushed the Union troops through Gettysburg and into defensive positions along a ridge south of the town. The new Union commander, General George G. Meade, decided to defend this high ground and force the Confederates to attack.

On July 2, Lee sent repeated shock waves at one part of the Union battle line after another. He tried to capture high ground in two places—Little Round Top and Culp's Hill—so that he could fire down on the enemy. Both of these efforts were pushed back by the Union troops. Though the Union line stretched for miles along the ridge, Lee could not break it.

On July 3, Lee ordered a direct attack on the center of the Union line. Known as Pickett's Charge after George Pickett, one of the generals who led the attack, it was a classic confrontation between the old and the new kind of warfare. More than 14,000 Confederates marched the better part of a mile across open ground under fire from Union cannons firing shells and canisters. Then they charged up a rise toward the Union guns. Only a few reached the federal lines and fought hand-to-hand with Union troops; most were cut down, and the survivors were captured or forced to retreat.

 RESOURCE DIRECTORY

Teaching Resources

The next morning, July 4, Lee's army, which had suffered 28,000 casualties, left the battlefield and headed south. The exhausted Army of the Potomac, which had 23,000 men dead, wounded, or missing, did not follow the Confederates. Lee and his men escaped, but they would never go on the offensive again.

Vicksburg

Meanwhile, a Union army under General Grant struggled for months to capture the city of **Vicksburg,** Mississippi. Along with another fortress at Port Hudson, Louisiana, this Confederate stronghold prevented the Union from taking complete control of the Mississippi River.

Vicksburg seemed safe from attack. A Union officer later described the location as

a long line of high, rugged, irregular bluffs, clearly cut against the sky, crowned with cannon which peered ominously [threateningly] from embrasures [openings] to the right and left as far as the eye could see. . . . The approaches to this position were frightful.

In April 1863 Grant finally settled on a clever but dangerous plan. Though he was camped on the opposite side of the Mississippi River and to the north of Vicksburg, he now sent his army south of the city, where he ferried them across the river to attack from the land side. By mid-May, Grant's troops were at Vicksburg's doorstep, chasing the Confederates into the safety of the town.

Grant soon found he could not take the city by direct attack. A siege would be necessary—a form of prolonged attack in which a city is surrounded and starved into surrender. The conflict between the North and South now became **total war.** In this form of war, opponents strike not only against one another's soldiers, but against civilians and the entire economic system of the enemy.

The residents of Vicksburg endured forty-seven days of increasing hunger and relentless shelling. On July 3—as Pickett's men were charging the Union lines at Gettysburg—the Confederate officer in command at Vicksburg,

General John C. Pemberton, met with Grant to discuss the terms of a surrender of the city. The next day, the Fourth of July, 1863, Vicksburg was turned over to the Union.

Five days later, Confederate forces at Port Hudson, Louisiana, surrendered the last Confederate post on the Mississippi River. Though the war would continue for two more years, the Mississippi River would remain under the control of the Union navy. The Confederacy had been cut in two.

A New Birth of Freedom

On November 19, 1863, President Lincoln spoke at the dedication of a cemetery at the Gettysburg battlefield. In his short speech, Lincoln simply and eloquently explained the meaning of the Civil War—and redefined the meaning of the United States.

Lincoln began his speech, now known as the **Gettysburg Address,** by reminding his listeners that in 1776 the American people had

brought forth upon this continent a new nation conceived in liberty and dedicated to the proposition that all men are created equal.

The Civil War, said Lincoln, was a test of whether any nation dedicated to freedom and equality can survive. Freedom and equality, he stressed, were what the Union dead had been fighting for. Americans should now resolve that

these dead shall not have died in vain; this nation, under God, shall have a new birth of freedom; and that government of the people, by the people, for the people, shall not perish from the earth.

Lincoln spoke with a wisdom ahead of his time. Americans in 1863 did not like his speech; they thought it was too short and simple. But in the years since then, people have come to appreciate that Lincoln's words marked a dramatic new definition of the United States. Freedom and equality no longer belonged to a few, as they had in 1776. They were the right of everyone. Democracy and the

Enrichment

Ask students to prepare an oral reading of one of the following: the Gettysburg Address, selections from Stephen Vincent Benet's "John Brown's Body," or Walt Whitman's poem "O Captain! My Captain!" mourning the death of Lincoln.

3. ASSESS

Section 3 Review Answers

1. (a) draft, see p. 205, (b) Emancipation Proclamation, see p. 206, (c) contraband, see p. 207, (d) total war, see p. 209 (e) Gettysburg Address, see p. 209

2. (a) Vicksburg, see p. 209, (b) Appomattox Court House, see p. 210

3. Possible answer: The Pacific Railroad Act provided for the construction of transcontinental railways that linked East and West.

4. African Americans abandoned southern plantations, which depended on their labor, severely weakening the South; they also fought in the Union army in large numbers.

5. He described it as a test of whether any nation dedicated to freedom and equality can survive.

6. His supplies were cut off, his men were starving and deserting, and he was in danger of being surrounded.

7. Possible answer: During Washington's first term as President, the political system was just setting out on the road to freedom for all; by the end of Lincoln's presidency, the system was taking steps to include African Americans in the political process. In both cases the Union was intact, although obviously damaged in 1865; sectional differences were not so stark during Washington's presidency.

Ask students to identify the significance of the following in relation to the end of the Civil War and the redefinition of the nation: Gettysburg Address, Thirteenth Amendment, Appomattox Court House.

Union did not exist to serve the interests of white men; they existed to preserve freedom for all. Lincoln's speech marked a great milestone in the gradual expansion of liberty to all people in the United States—an expansion that still continues today.

Sherman Burns and Grant Hammers

Grant's success in 1863 convinced Lincoln that he had found a leader who could win battles. The President called the general to Washington to assume overall command of the northern armies.

Grant brought with him a new plan for winning the war. He would fight Lee's army repeatedly until he exhausted it. And he would send General William Tecumseh Sherman into Georgia to do the same to the other major Confederate army there.

Sherman's March to the Sea As it turned out, Sherman could not catch the army he was sent after. Instead he beseiged Atlanta, Georgia, and captured it in September 1864. His victory

persuaded many in the North that Lincoln was pursuing the right course, and voters gave him 212 out of 233 electoral votes.

By reelecting Lincoln, voters showed their approval not only of his war policy, but of his stand against slavery. Three months later, in February 1865, members of Congress joined him in that stand and passed the Thirteenth Amendment to the Constitution. It was ratified by the states and became law on December 6, 1865. In a few simple words, the amendment ended slavery in the United States forever.

Meanwhile, with Atlanta in flames behind him, Sherman set out to carry total war across Georgia. Cutting a 60-mile-wide swath across the red earth of the state, he burned the harvest, plundered plantations, uprooted railroad tracks, and smashed bridges, factories, and mills. By December 22, 1864, he had reached the coast and captured Savannah. He had succeeded in his purpose—to make the people of Georgia "so sick of war that generations would pass away before they would again appeal to it." But his march would also make the hatred between North and South still more difficult to heal. ⊗

Though Sherman issued orders that civilians were not to be harmed during his march to the sea, one of the soldiers who followed him wrote: "The cruelties practiced on this campaign toward the citizens have been enough to blast a more sacred cause than ours."

Grant Hammers at Lee While Sherman was loose in Georgia, Grant and the Army of the Potomac were pressing toward Richmond, relentlessly hammering at Lee's force, the Army of Northern Virginia. Outnumbered nearly two to one, Lee fought a series of defensive battles that held back the Union advance. Each time Lee stopped him, Grant simply moved his army to the left and attacked again.

A bloody standoff at Petersburg continued through March 1865. Then Lee was cut off from his supplies. Hemmed in by Union forces and with no other alternative, Lee sent word that he wanted to discuss surrender.

On Sunday, April 9, 1865, Grant and Lee met in the town of **Appomattox Court House,** Virginia. Lee was as dignified in defeat as he had

▶ RESOURCE DIRECTORY

Teaching Resources

⊗ **Visual Learning Activity** Defending Atlanta, found in the Unit 2 folder, p. 67, promotes understanding of the new weapons technology and strategies of the Civil War through photographs of the fortifications built to counter them.

been courageous and skillful in battle. Grant proved as generous in victory as he had been relentless in war. The two men agreed to the terms of the surrender and were enemies no more.

What Was Lost and What Was Won

Five days later, President Lincoln was shot by a young actor and southern sympathizer named John Wilkes Booth. When Lincoln perished on April 15, the South lost not only its most powerful opponent, but also the man who would probably have become its most powerful friend and protector. Lincoln had already begun to insist that the reunion of the nation after the war should be based on fairness and mercy, not hatred and vengeance.

Like Lincoln, many of the soldiers on both sides did not live to return home. Some 360,000 Union and 258,000 Confederate soldiers died of disease, wounds, or poor medical treatment. Few other wars in history have had so great a human cost.

Neither side could truly win such a terrible war. The South did not win the independence for which it struggled. The North did not achieve the easy victory that it had hoped for. Instead both sides suffered bitterly.

But if both North and South lost by the war, they both also gained by it. They gained an undivided nation that would go on to become the most powerful country in the world, a democracy that would continue to seek the equality

Lincoln had promised for it. And they gained new fellow citizens—the African Americans who had broken the bonds of slavery and claimed their right to be free and equal, every one.

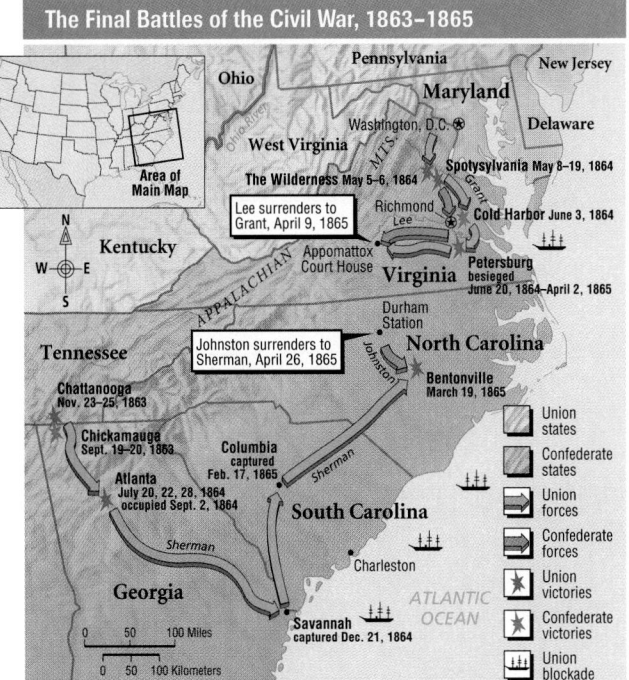

The Final Battles of the Civil War, 1863–1865

Area of Main Map

Lee surrenders to Grant, April 9, 1865

Johnston surrenders to Sherman, April 26, 1865

The Wilderness May 5–6, 1864
Spotsylvania May 8–19, 1864
Cold Harbor June 3, 1864
Petersburg besieged June 20, 1864–April 2, 1865
Durham Station
Bentonville March 19, 1865
Chattanooga Nov. 23–25, 1863
Chickamauga Sept. 19–20, 1863
Columbia captured Feb. 17, 1865
Atlanta July 20, 22, 28, 1864 occupied Sept. 2, 1864
Charleston
Savannah captured Dec. 21, 1864

Union states
Confederate states
Union forces
Confederate forces
Union victories
Confederate victories
Union blockade

0   50   100 Miles
0   50   100 Kilometers

Geography and History: Interpreting Maps
After one Civil War battle, a Union general said about the Confederate troops: "I doubt if any soldiers in the world ever needed so much cumulative evidence to convince them they were beaten." The same could be said of the South as a whole. *What were the two main movements of Union forces that brought the war to an end?*

Caption Answer to ...

 Interpreting Maps

Sherman's march through the South and Grant's movement toward Richmond and Petersburg.

 **4. CLOSE**

Reinforcing the Big Idea

During the Civil War, the governments of both the North and the South took steps that increased their power. The turning point of the war came with Union victories at Vicksburg and Gettysburg. The war finally ended in 1865, after Sherman's brutal march through Georgia and Grant's fierce hammering of Lee's exhausted troops. The nation emerged from the war an undivided democracy, with slavery abolished. The next section describes the time of Reconstruction that followed the war.

SECTION 3 REVIEW

Key Terms, People, and Places
1. Define (a) draft, (b) Emancipation Proclamation, (c) contraband, (d) total war, (e) Gettysburg Address.
2. Identify (a) Vicksburg, (b) Appomattox Court House.

Key Concepts
3. Give an example of Republican legislation, and explain how it gave permanent support to economic development.
4. How did African Americans help to bring slavery to

an end?
5. How did Lincoln describe the Civil War in the Gettysburg Address?
6. Why did Lee finally surrender?

Critical Thinking
7. **Making Comparisons** Compare and contrast the condition of the United States at the time of President Lincoln's death with its condition at the time of Washington's first presidency.

Quiz found in the Unit 2 folder, p. 50, covers the main ideas in this section as well as the key terms.

Media and Technology

Transparencies
The Way It Works, H-13; Geographic Setting, M-3, M-4; Fine Art, D-11

Reconstruction

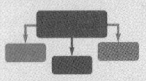

Connecting to the Big Idea

See page 188B. Explain that the passage of the Thirteenth Amendment in 1865 brought great changes to the southern way of life. African Americans were no longer property at the mercy of their white masters but free human beings. Meanwhile, the federal government struggled with the issue of how to put the nation back together again. For a while, the Republicans were able to impose their Reconstruction plan on the South, bringing radical changes. Ask what gains the Republicans were able to make in the South and how white southerners finally acted to reverse them.

Objectives

● Explain what freedom meant to formerly enslaved African Americans.
● Describe the different groups that supported the Republican party in the South.
● Describe the kinds of labor that replaced the slave system in the South.

Bellringer

Ask students to imagine themselves newly freed citizens after the Civil War. What is the first thing they would want to do to celebrate their freedom?

Reading Strategy

Reading for Evidence Ask students to look for evidence as they read the section that African Americans still had many struggles for equality and fair treatment in the years following the Civil War.

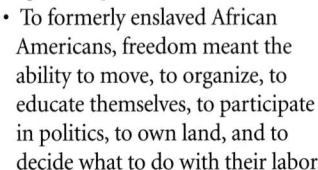

Reconstruction

SECTION PREVIEW

The meaning of freedom was clear to the freed people of the South. For Congress, however, the end of the Civil War raised many difficult questions about how to rebuild the nation. The result was a series of acts and amendments that redefined citizenship and attempted to create a new social order in the South. But after some mixed success, political leaders turned from this dream and focused on economic expansion instead.

Key Concepts

• To formerly enslaved African Americans, freedom meant the ability to move, to organize, to educate themselves, to participate in politics, to own land, and to decide what to do with their labor.
• A combination of different groups, including African Americans as well as white northerners and southerners, provided support for the Republican party in the South.
• New forms of enforced labor replaced the slave system in the South.

Key Terms, People, and Places

Reconstruction, Freedmen's Bureau, impeach, debt peonage; Andrew Johnson, carpetbagger, scalawag, sharecropper, tenant farmer, Ku Klux Klan, Rutherford B. Hayes

---

Freedom for African Americans meant— among other things—the freedom to worship. After the Civil War, African American churches in the South gained hundreds of thousands of new members. This photograph shows a woman ready to preach.

I n 1865 the states ratified the Thirteenth Amendment to the Constitution, thereby abolishing slavery. Long before this amendment had been written, however, African Americans had begun to anticipate its arrival. During the war, African Americans in the South often simply ceased paying any attention to the authority of their owners as soon as Union troops were reported to be nearby. They

had no doubt they were free. Indeed, the Emancipation Proclamation and the Thirteenth Amendment merely made legal what was already fact throughout the South. But African Americans did not have an opportunity to explore the full meaning of freedom until **Reconstruction** began—the period of United States history in which the nation tried to adjust to the new conditions created by the Civil War.

What Freedom Meant to African Americans

To the "freed people," as they were called, freedom meant the basic things that whites took for granted. It meant, for example, the freedom to go wherever they wanted. Thus, free African Americans often traveled away from the plantations on which they had worked and lived. In the end, many freed people returned to live on or near their old plantations. Yet the excitement of being able to move freely was memorable.

The movement of freed people was not aimless; many traveled with a purpose, for freedom also meant reuniting families. Freed people sometimes walked hundreds of miles looking for relatives separated by the slave trade. Many were successful in their quest. Reconstruction brought together families that had been broken apart by slavery and testified to the deep emotional ties among African Americans.

Freedom also encouraged the formation of new African American organizations. The most visible of these were churches. Across the South, freed people withdrew from congregations with both white and African American members and formed their own churches. They also started thousands of voluntary organizations, including mutual aid societies, trade associations, temperance clubs, debating clubs, and drama societies.

Freedom meant education, too. Historians estimate that 90 percent of adult freed people

---

RESOURCE DIRECTORY

Teaching Resources

Reproducible Lesson Plan found in the Unit 2 folder, p. 44, provides a summary of the Section 4 lesson plan content.

Alternate Lesson Plan: Learning Styles found in the Alternate Lesson Plans folder, p. 77, especially useful for auditory learners, helps students understand the experience of formerly enslaved African Americans during Reconstruction.

Guided Reading and Review found in the Unit 2 folder, p. 51, provides a structure for reading and mastering the key concepts and reviewing the key terms for Section 4. (Guided Practice)

were illiterate in 1860. Slave codes, or laws, had often prohibited teaching enslaved people to read and write. After the war, freed people continued eagerly to seek reading and writing skills. African Americans also organized to set up and support schools for higher education. Between 1865 and 1870, thirty African American colleges were founded.

Finally, freedom for African Americans meant control of land and labor. It meant the right to own property, the ability to pursue whatever line of work they chose, and the power to determine what they produced. A white northern visitor to the South in the fall of 1865 gave this summary of what owning land meant to freed people:

> The sole ambition of the freedman at the present time appears to be to become the owner of a little piece of land, there to erect a humble home, and to dwell in peace and security at his own free will and pleasure. If he wishes to cultivate the ground in cotton on his own account, to be able to do so without anyone to dictate to him hours or system of labor, if he wishes instead to plant corn or sweet potatoes—to be able to do that free from any outside control. . . . That is their idea, their desire and their hope.

In spite of unrelenting prejudice against African Americans, many whites were committed to helping freed people build new lives. It was in this spirit that Congress established the **Freedmen's Bureau** in March 1865. The bureau gave out clothing, medical supplies, and millions of meals to refugees of the war, both African American and white. Its most significant work, however, came in the establishment of schools for African Americans.

Lincoln and Johnson's Reconstruction Plans

Meanwhile, politicians in Washington, D.C., were struggling with the many questions raised by the defeat of the Confederacy. On what terms should the United States be reunited?

Symbols of the new working relationships between African and white Americans after the Civil War, these two cowhands posed side by side in the 1860s.

In December 1863 President Lincoln had proposed a moderate Reconstruction policy. Lincoln offered a pardon—an official forgiveness of a crime—to most Confederates who would swear allegiance to the Union and accept the end of slavery. He also made it relatively easy for the states that had seceded to return to the Union. They would have to endorse the Thirteenth Amendment but they were not required explicitly to ensure African American rights.

Radical Republicans wanted terms that would be much more difficult for southern whites to accept. They wanted to change southern society in order to ensure the rights of African Americans. They also wanted to punish the white South severely for its secession. But when they passed the radical Wade-Davis Bill in July 1864, Lincoln refused to sign it, creating a stalemate.

The assassination of Lincoln in April 1865 raised Vice President **Andrew Johnson** to the presidency. To the dismay of Radical Republicans, President Johnson was quite forgiving of former Confederates. He made most Confederates eligible for pardons in return for taking an oath of loyalty to the United States. He also favored easy terms under which the Confederate states could return to the Union.

2. INSTRUCT

Explain/Discuss

Discuss with students the impact of freedom on African Americans. Encourage discussion with questions such as the following: How did African Americans define freedom? In what ways did African Americans use their new freedom? Why did they so eagerly pursue education? What was the significance of owning their own land?

Discuss Reconstruction with students. Ask them to summarize and compare the three Reconstruction plans. What was the main intent of the Radical Republican plan for Reconstruction? How did it differ from what Lincoln and Johnson hoped to accomplish with their plans? What did southern states do to undermine Reconstruction? How did the South's refusal to accept Johnson's moderate plan hurt white southerners even more? What important acts and amendments were passed in response to southern resistance to Reconstruction?

In Depth

Then and Now

A century after the Civil War, African Americans continued to struggle for equal access to education in the South. In 1956, after years of court battles, twenty-seven-year-old Autherine Lucy was admitted to the University of Alabama—only to be expelled a few days later because of violent protests. In 1988, the university revoked its resolution of expulsion and invited Lucy to enroll again. "The University of Alabama is still my alma mater. I just stayed there for three days, but it is still my alma mater," says Lucy. "I did not feel evil toward them because I didn't think they were fighting me. They were fighting tradition and change. It just wasn't my time."

Possible answer: No. The South traditionally defied northern attempts to
outlaw slavery and to impose northern
values on its way of life.

Caption Answer to ...

 Interpreting Maps

Tennessee; Virginia, Georgia, Mississippi, and Texas

Analyze

Have students analyze the motives
behind the feelings and actions of
southerners and northerners regarding Reconstruction. Why were so
many northerners eager to punish
the South? Why did white southerners feel justified in resisting efforts to
reshape southern society?

In Depth

Then and Now

In the mid-1990s, about 130
years after Robert E. Lee's surrender at Appomattox, the rebel
emblem is still saluted across the
old Confederacy. In 1994, for
example, African American legislators in Jackson, Mississippi,
joined the National Association
for the Advancement of Colored
People (NAACP) in writing bills
and filing lawsuits to remove the
Confederate emblem from the
state flag. Beatrice Branch, president of the Mississippi NAACP,
explained: "We want to have the
Confederate battle flag taken off
the corner of our state flag. We
object to it because it signifies to
us racism and hatred."

Once southern state governments were
established, they acted to weaken Johnson's
plan. For example, they quickly enacted black
codes, laws that severely restricted the rights of
freed people. In effect, the black codes reestablished slavery by a different name. Some southern whites also used violence in an effort to
regain power over African Americans. In addition to countless individual acts of violence,
serious riots erupted in several cities.

Are you surprised by the South's defiant rejection of efforts at Reconstruction? Explain why
or why not.

The Radical Plan for Reconstruction

President Johnson and Congress disagreed
about how to respond to southern resistance to
Reconstruction. In March 1866, Congress
passed a Civil Rights Act in order to ensure
equal rights for African Americans in spite of
the black codes. Johnson vetoed it. Congress

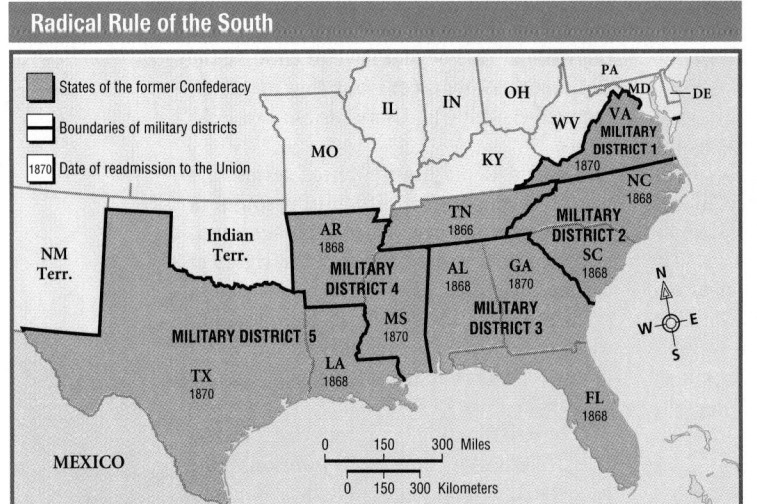

Radical Rule of the South

- States of the former Confederacy
- Boundaries of military districts
- 1870 Date of readmission to the Union

NM Terr. · Indian Terr. · MEXICO · MO · IL · IN · OH · PA · MD · DE · WV · VA MILITARY DISTRICT 1 1870 · KY · NC 1868 · TN 1866 · MILITARY DISTRICT 2 · SC 1868 · AR 1868 · MILITARY DISTRICT 4 · AL 1868 · GA 1870 · MILITARY DISTRICT 3 · MS 1870 · MILITARY DISTRICT 5 · LA 1868 · TX 1870 · FL 1868

0   150   300 Miles
0   150   300 Kilometers

Geography and History: Interpreting Maps
In April of 1865, Abraham Lincoln expressed a wish that the nation should put
the southern state governments "in successful operation, with order prevailing and the
Union reestablished, before . . . December." Under Radical rule, however, many of the
former Confederate states did not rejoin the Union for years. *Which state was the first to
rejoin the Union? Which states rejoined in 1870?*

---

overrode his veto. It then switched course and
proposed the Fourteenth Amendment to the
Constitution, which became law two years later.

The Fourteenth Amendment said that
everyone born or naturalized in the United
States was a citizen and that no state could
restrict his or her rights. More specifically, no
state could

*deprive any person of life, liberty, or prop-
erty, without due process of law, nor deny
to any person within its jurisdiction the
equal protection of the laws.*

The amendment also provided for the punishment of states that did not permit African
Americans to vote.

The Acts of the Radical Congress White
southern defiance contributed to significant
Republican gains in the 1866 congressional
elections. As a result, Radicals now had enough
strength to impose their own conditions—and
inflict punishment—on the white South.

The new Congress passed the Military
Reconstruction Act of 1867. This legislation
divided the South into five military districts that were to be governed by northern generals, as
shown in the map to the left. All
qualified voters, including African
American men, but excluding voters who had supported the Confederacy, had to be allowed to vote
for delegates to create new state
constitutions. Southern states had
to guarantee equal rights to all citizens, permit African Americans to
vote, and ratify the Fourteenth
Amendment.

At the same time, Congress
attempted to limit the power of
President Johnson. It passed the
Tenure of Office Act, which dealt
with the President's power to hire
and fire government officials. The
act said that if a President wanted
to fire an official who had earlier
been approved by the Senate, the
Senate had to agree to the firing.

▶ RESOURCE DIRECTORY

Teaching Resources

⭐ **Primary Source Activity** A Bleak
Future for Freedmen, found in the Unit 2
folder, p. 62, provides an example, through a
formerly enslaved man's letter to the editor in
Nashville's Weekly *Anglo-African*, of African
Americans' difficulties during Reconstruction.

Johnson and the Congress quickly came into conflict over the Tenure of Office Act. When the President tried to fire Secretary of War Edwin Stanton, the House of Representatives voted to **impeach** him—to charge him formally with wrongdoing in office. Under the Constitution, officials impeached by the House are then tried by the Senate, which by a two-thirds majority can convict the official and remove him or her from office. The Senate tried Johnson in the spring of 1868. But the Radicals fell one vote short of the two-thirds majority needed to convict.

The Last Reconstruction Legislation The final major piece of Reconstruction legislation was the Fifteenth Amendment, proposed in February 1869 and ratified in March 1870. The Fifteenth Amendment stated that no citizen could be denied the right to vote "by the United States or by any State on account of race, color, or previous condition of servitude." The table on page 216 shows this amendment as well as other Reconstruction legislation.

The Fifteenth Amendment was inspired in part by the presidential election of 1868. Republican Ulysses S. Grant won a narrow victory that was made possible by the votes of African Americans in the South. The Fifteenth Amendment aimed at ensuring that African Americans would be free to vote in future elections—presumably for Republican candidates. As Chapter 8 reveals, however, southern states eventually found ways to deny African Americans the vote. ⭐

Republican Activity in the South

In order for Reconstruction in the South to be effective, two conditions had to be met. First, Republicans had to hold office on the state level. Second, federal officials had to be willing to use their power to support them. For a while, these conditions existed, and Republicans were able to bring about significant change in the South. In the end, however, that success led to a violent resistance that reversed many of the gains of Reconstruction.

Republicans depended for their support in the South on African Americans and on people

Viewpoints
On Voting Rights for African Americans

The effort by Radical Republicans to extend voting rights to African Americans in the South was hotly debated in the 1860s. *Summarize the main arguments given in the two viewpoints below.*

In Favor of Voting Rights for African Americans

"If impartial suffrage is excluded in rebel States, then every one of them is sure to send a solid rebel representative delegation to Congress, and cast a solid rebel electoral vote. They . . . would always elect the President and control Congress. . . . I am for negro suffrage in every rebel State. If it be just, it should not be denied; if it be necessary, it should be adopted; if it is a punishment to traitors, they deserve it."
Thaddeus Stevens, Radical Republican (Pennsylvania), speech in the House of Representatives, January 3, 1867

Against Voting Rights for African Americans

"Most of the whites are disenfranchised [not legally able to vote] and ineligible for office, whilst the Negroes are invested with [granted] the right of voting. The political power is therefore thrown into the hands of a mass of human beings who, having just emerged from a state of servitude [slavery], are ignorant of the forms of government and totally unfit to exercise this, the highest privilege of a free people."
Henry William Ravenel, South Carolina planter, journal entry for February 24, 1867

who are now known as carpetbaggers and scalawags. **Carpetbaggers** were northern Republicans who moved to the South after the Civil War. Their name referred to a kind of suitcase, and it implied that these northerners had hastily migrated into the region to take advantage of the political situation. **Scalawags,** a term that means "rascals," were southern whites who became Republicans.

Republican Policies State governments controlled by Republicans did bring some change to the South. They committed state governments to systems of public education, although these systems were divided along racial lines. They passed civil rights legislation that guaranteed African Americans access to transportation and hotels, though this legislation was

📖 **Viewpoints Activity** On Voting Rights for African Americans, found in the Unit 2 folder, pp. 57–58, demonstrates the pros and cons raised in the debate over the granting of suffrage to African American males during the 1860s.

Viewpoints

Stevens argues for extension of suffrage because a solid bloc of white southern representatives would not serve northern interests; Ravenel is afraid of the political power of the newly freed slaves, so he attacks them on the grounds of their ignorance. For a more thorough examination of the issue of voting rights for African Americans, see the Resource Directory below.

Activity
Writing About Hopes for the Future

Ask each student to imagine living in the year 1865, first as a poor African American sharecropper and then as a white southern planter whose plantation lies in ruins. Students should write two brief essays in each of which the character describes hopes of what life will be like ten years later. **LEP**

In Depth
Multicultural Perspectives

In her book *The Dispossessed*, historian Jacqueline Jones writes that the sharecropping system had a "superficial simplicity," behind which "lay an intense power struggle between planter and field hand, a struggle that went to the heart of power relations in the rural South." One aspect of that struggle was the practice of fining sharecroppers up to a dollar a day for "time lost" if they refused to devote all their time to field work, as they had been forced to do when they were enslaved.

Enrichment

Ask students to watch the film *Gone with the Wind* and then write an essay comparing Reconstruction as portrayed in the film with its depiction in historical sources. Students may do additional research on Reconstruction to write the essay if they wish.

3. ASSESS

Section 4 Review Answers

1. (a) Reconstruction, see p. 212, (b) Freedmen's Bureau, see p. 213, (c) impeach, see p. 215, (d) debt peonage, see p. 216

2. (a) Andrew Johnson, see p. 213, (b) carpetbagger, see p. 215, (c) scalawag, see p. 215, (d) sharecropper, see p. 216, (e) tenant farmer, see p. 216, (f) Ku Klux Klan, see p. 217, (g) Rutherford B. Hayes, see p. 217

In Depth

Biography

Born enslaved in Virginia, Blanche K. Bruce (1841–1898) fled north to freedom when the Civil War began. After pursuing his education at Oberlin College, he returned to the South. In 1871, while running as a Republican candidate for sheriff in Mississippi, Bruce rebutted the insults of opponents: "It is true that I was a house slave. But I freed myself, educated myself, and raised myself up in the world. If my opponent had started out where I did, he would still be there." Bruce won the election and later served in the Senate from 1875 to 1881.

Reconstruction Legislation

Legislation	Date	Purpose
13th Amendment	Submitted and ratified 1865	Abolishes slavery in the United States
Freedmen's Bureau	1865 and 1866	Provides services for war refugees and freed people, including food, medical aid, education
Civil Rights Act of 1866	1866	Gives citizenship to African Americans; gives federal government the power to protect African American rights
14th Amendment	Submitted 1866, ratified 1868	Defines citizenship to include African Americans; guarantees due process of law and equal protection under law
Reconstruction Acts	1867	Establish Radical Reconstruction
15th Amendment	Submitted 1869, ratified 1870	Guarantees that voting rights will not be denied on the basis of race
Ku Klux Klan Acts	1871	Seek to outlaw organizations aimed at denying African Americans their rights
Civil Rights Act of 1875	1875	Protects African American rights in public places

 **Interpreting Tables**
During Reconstruction, the federal government struggled to create a new social and political order in the South. *Which amendment ended slavery? Which guaranteed that voting rights would not be denied on the basis of race?*

largely unenforced. In addition, they repealed black codes and removed restrictions on African American workers.

Republicans focused much of their effort on economic development. Advocating "the gospel of prosperity," they contended that the key to better times was more railroads, banks, and businesses. Southern governments aided in this development with grants, paid for out of higher taxes. But while thousands of miles of railroad track were laid, government aid did little to improve general economic conditions. Most African Americans, and not a few whites, remained mired in poverty.

Changes in Southern Agriculture

Devastated by the Civil War, southern planters never recovered the dominance that they had enjoyed before the war. Some sought to re-create the past by finding ways to preserve slavery in a new form.

Debt Peonage To achieve this end, planters signed former slaves to labor contracts. Under the terms of these contracts, planters advanced money to laborers in return for signed promises from the workers that they pay all debts before they moved on. Planters then found ways to increase workers' debts while keeping them ignorant of any escape. Year after year, laborers remained bound to work off debts that always got larger. Though slavery was dead, in **debt peonage,** as this system of forced labor came to be called, the South brought some aspects of the slave system back to life.

Sharecropping Many freed people wanted no part of contract agreements for their labor. In order to make money from their fields, white landowners began to rent their land to African Americans and poor whites. In one common system, farmers called **sharecroppers** grew a crop on land owned by someone else. In return for the use of the land and supplies such as seed and fertilizer, the farmer gave one third to one half of the annual crop to the landowner. Others, called **tenant farmers,** paid cash for the rental of land. They typically agreed to sell their crop to a local merchant, who gave them use of tools and supplies in advance of harvest.

African American sharecroppers and tenant farmers enjoyed more practical freedom than they had possessed as enslaved people. They controlled their own schedules, determined where they lived, and worked without white supervision. On the other hand, low cotton prices made it hard for sharecroppers to earn enough money to survive. Many had to borrow from local stores for food and supplies, creating debts that grew larger and larger every year. Thus sharecroppers and tenant farmers were trapped in a continuous effort to pay off their debts, just like farmers working under the system of debt peonage.

 ### RESOURCE DIRECTORY

Teaching Resources

Reconstruction Comes to an End

From 1868 through 1871, many southern whites launched a counterrevolution against the changes of Reconstruction. The intensity of their violence was a tribute to how far the changes brought by the Republicans had gone.

The Ku Klux Klan At the forefront of the campaign was the **Ku Klux Klan,** an organization that began as a social club in Tennessee in 1866. Although Klan members often wore elaborate disguises, including white hoods and robes, members were well known locally. Leaders included planters, merchants, lawyers, and occasionally ministers. Many were former Confederate officers. The oath each member took included a promise to "defend the social and political superiority" of whites, to vote only for white candidates, and to protect whites against what the Klan called the "aggressions of an inferior race."

The goal of the Klan during Reconstruction was to intimidate both African Americans and sympathetic whites so that they became silent and submissive. To keep freed people from voting or asserting themselves, hooded men surrounded the homes of prominent African Americans and harassed and abused them. Whippings were common. So was murder.

As northern anger mounted against southern violence, Congress passed the Enforcement Acts, or the Ku Klux Klan Acts, in 1871. In the next year, the United States used its considerable military and judicial power to break the Klan. But by that time, southern whites had already achieved much of their goal of "redeeming," or winning back, the South from Republican rule by thoroughly intimidating scalawags, African Americans, and carpetbaggers.

The Compromise of 1877 For southern whites, final "redemption" came in 1877. In the presidential election of 1876, Republican **Rutherford B. Hayes** lost the popular vote to Democrat Samuel Tilden. Because of the way election results were reported, however, the electoral vote was in dispute, and a political deal, the Compromise of 1877, was worked out to clear the way for Hayes's victory. Under this agreement, Hayes promised that as President, he would remove federal troops from all southern states. Southern Democrats would regain complete control of the region. In return, Democrats allowed Hayes to claim a victory he had not clearly won.

The Significance of Reconstruction With the Compromise of 1877, Reconstruction came to an end. In most respects, it had been a tragic failure. Despite the many positive changes that took place, the nation had squandered the opportunity to achieve true equality and social justice. As an African American woman noted, "There is no redress [help] for us from a government that promised to help all under its flag." It would be close to a century before African Americans and whites would truly achieve the legal and political freedoms that were supposedly guaranteed by the legislation of the Reconstruction period.

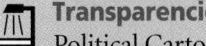

SECTION 4 REVIEW

Key Terms, People, and Places
1. Define (a) Reconstruction, (b) Freedmen's Bureau, (c) impeach, (d) debt peonage.
2. Identify (a) Andrew Johnson, (b) carpetbagger, (c) scalawag, (d) sharecropper, (e) tenant farmer, (f) Ku Klux Klan, (g) Rutherford B. Hayes.

Key Concepts
3. What did freedom mean to African Americans after the end of the Civil War?

4. What groups formed the basis of support for the Republican party in the South during Reconstruction?
5. In what ways were debt peonage, sharecropping, and tenant farming alike?

Critical Thinking
6. **Checking Consistency** The text states that African Americans had many political rights, yet they still lacked power. Explain this apparent inconsistency.

Quiz found in the Unit 2 folder, p. 52, covers the main ideas in this section as well as the key terms.

Chapter Test Forms A and B are found in the Unit 2 folder, pp. 68–73.

Answer Keys found in the Unit 2 folder, pp. 152–165, provide answers to all student activities.

Media and Technology

Transparencies
Political Cartoons, K-4; Graphic Organizer, G-4

Guided Reading Audiotapes (English and Spanish)

Computer Test Bank

---

3. It meant mobility; the opportunity to learn; and the chance to form new institutions and organization such as churches, colleges, and self-help groups. In addition, it meant a chance to receive payment for work and to own land.

4. The groups included carpetbaggers (northern Republicans who came South during Reconstruction), scalawags (southern whites who became Republicans), and African Americans.

5. Each of these systems is a way of keeping landowners in power while making use of the labor of others. All three systems use debt to keep the laborer in subjugation.

6. Possible answer: African Americans represented such a small (and poor) portion of the population that they alone could not achieve any political power. Without the support of other large groups, they would remain powerless.

Reteach

Have students review the section and write ten true/false statements about the section content. Students should then exchange their papers with a partner and indicate whether their partner's statements are true or false.

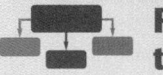

4. CLOSE

Reinforcing the Big Idea

African Americans took up their new freedom with great enthusiasm. Meanwhile, Radical Republicans in Congress gained enough strength to impose their plan for Reconstruction on the South, which resulted in great changes in that region. White southerners, however, resented these changes and finally struck back violently to reverse them. Reconstruction ended in 1877, with many of its goals for social justice and equality unmet.

Understanding Key Terms, People, and Places

Terms
Students should refer to the definitions of key terms in the chapter to create sentences that show an understanding of their relation to the Civil War, Reconstruction, or the post–Civil War period.

Matching
1. Kansas-Nebraska Act
2. canister
3. gunboat

True or False
1. false, John Brown
2. true
3. false, Robert E. Lee

Reviewing the Main Ideas

1. The two main issues were slavery and immigration.

2. Douglas argued for the absolute right of white citizens to choose the kind of society and government they wanted; he therefore condoned slavery. Lincoln, although sharing Douglas's views of African Americans as inferior to white Americans, believed that slavery was morally wrong.

3. Lincoln was an antislavery President elected by northerners. The South felt that it no longer had a voice in government.

4. Northerners demanded instant results; southerners did not want to wait for the results of a war of attrition or give up territory even temporarily. The public on both sides demanded direct confrontation.

5. The plan began by capturing key parts of the western region of the Confederacy, including the vital waterways that led to the Mississippi, in an effort to strangle the South.

6. Union troops under Irvin McDowell were repulsed at Manassas in 1861; troops under McClellan were repulsed by Lee in 1862; troops under Burnside were beaten in Fredericksburg in 1862; troops under Hooker were beaten at Chancellorsville in 1863.

7. Republicans passed legislation that laid the economic foundations for the United States to become a major world power.

8. Many enslaved African Americans set themselves free by crossing Union lines; Union troops, including African Americans; and Abraham Lincoln.

Chapter Review

Understanding Key Terms, People, and Places

Key Terms
1. Civil War
2. Union
3. Compromise of 1850
4. Kansas-Nebraska Act
5. *Dred Scott* v. *Sandford*
6. shell
7. canister
8. war of attrition
9. Anconada Plan
10. gunboat
11. draft
12. Emancipation Proclamation
13. contraband
14. total war
15. Gettysburg Address
16. Reconstruction
17. Freedmen's Bureau
18. impeach
19. debt peonage

People
20. Democratic party
21. Republican party
22. John Brown
23. Abraham Lincoln
24. Stonewall Jackson
25. George McClellan
26. Ulysses S. Grant
27. Robert E. Lee
28. Andrew Johnson
29. carpetbagger
30. scalawag
31. sharecropper
32. tenant farmer
33. Ku Klux Klan
34. Rutherford B. Hayes

Places
35. Border States
36. Lower South
37. Upper South
38. Manassas
39. Shiloh
40. Antietam
41. Vicksburg
42. Appomattox Court House

Terms For each term above, write a sentence that explains its relation to the Civil War, Reconstruction, or the post–Civil War period.

Matching Review the key terms in the list above. If you are not sure of a term's meaning, review its definition in the chapter. Then choose a term from the list that best matches each description below.
1. legislation allowing the people in a territory to decide whether slavery would be allowed there
2. shell filled with lead balls about the size of bullets
3. a small floating fort fitted with cannons

True of False Determine whether each statement is true or false. If it is true, write "true." If it is false, change the underlined person to make the statement true.
1. A group of northerners led by abolitionist <u>George McClellan</u> killed five men in a proslavery settlement in Kansas.
2. <u>Stonewall Jackson</u> held his troops solidly at Manassas and stopped the Union advance.
3. <u>Ulysses S. Grant</u> took over as the leader of the Confederate forces in May of 1862.

Reviewing Main Ideas

Section 1 (pp. 190–195)
1. What issues helped the Republicans in the 1850s?
2. How did Lincoln and Douglas differ in their views?
3. Why did Lincoln's election prompt secession?

Section 2 (pp. 198–203)
4. Why did Civil War generals use outmoded tactics?
5. How was the Anaconda Plan put into action?
6. Briefly summarize Union efforts to capture the southern capital of Richmond.

Section 3 (pp. 205–211)
7. What was the permanent effect of the absence of Southern Democrats from Congress during the war?

8. Who set enslaved persons free during the Civil War?
9. Explain how the Gettysburg Address redefined the concept of freedom for Americans.
10. Briefly describe the events of 1865 that led to Lee's surrender.

Section 4 (pp. 212–217)
11. How did freedom affect the travel and education of formerly enslaved African Americans?
12. Give evidence to show that African Americans made significant political contributions in the South after the Civil War.
13. In what ways did white southerners try to replace the slave system?

---

9. The speech reflected the idea that freedom and equality no longer belonged to a few white men but were the rights of all.

10. Sheridan cut off Lee's supplies, forcing him to abandon Petersburg and Richmond. Then, hemmed in by Union forces, Lee surrendered at Appomattox Court House.

11. Many newly freed African Americans traveled away from the plantations where they had lived, often in order to be reunited with family members. Newly freed people also eagerly sought education, which had been denied them before the Civil War.

12. Almost one third of the men who attended state constitutional conventions in the South were African Americans. African Americans also held high office and were members of various state legislatures.

13. They created new forms of enforced labor—including debt peonage, sharecropping, and tenant farming.

Thinking Critically

1. **Predicting Consequences** What economic difficulties would the South have faced if Lincoln had allowed it to leave the Union peacefully?
2. **Formulating Questions** Create three questions to ask William Harvey Carney that could lead to a greater understanding of the role of African Americans during the Civil War.
3. **Recognizing Ideologies** Imagine that you could interview an enslaved African American and a white slave owner living during the Civil War. Describe how their visions of what the South should be like after the war might differ.

Making Connections

1. **Evaluating Primary Sources** Review the primary source excerpt on page 194. Why did Lincoln believe that the United States could not endure if it was half slave and half free?
2. **Understanding the Visuals** Examine the painting of Pickett's Charge on page 208. How can you tell that the Confederate forces are about to overrun the enemy lines?
3. **Writing About the Chapter** You are a newspaper reporter filing a story about one of the following events of the Civil War: the Battle of Manassas, the Battle of Vicksburg, the dedication ceremony at Gettysburg, or the surrender at Appomattox Court House. First, make a list of your observations at the event you have chosen. Include your perceptions of the physical setting of the event, the people involved, and the event's significance. Next, write a draft of your story in which you describe the event as you observed it. Revise your story, making sure that details are vividly and clearly described. Proofread your story and draft a final copy.
4. **Using the Graphic Organizer** This graphic organizer uses a flow map to show causes and effects of the Civil War. (a) According to the organizer, what forces clashed in the 1860s? (b) Explain the connection between the Declaration of Independence and the results of the Civil War. (c) On a separate sheet of paper, create your own graphic organizer about the events of 1861–1865, using this graphic organizer as an example.

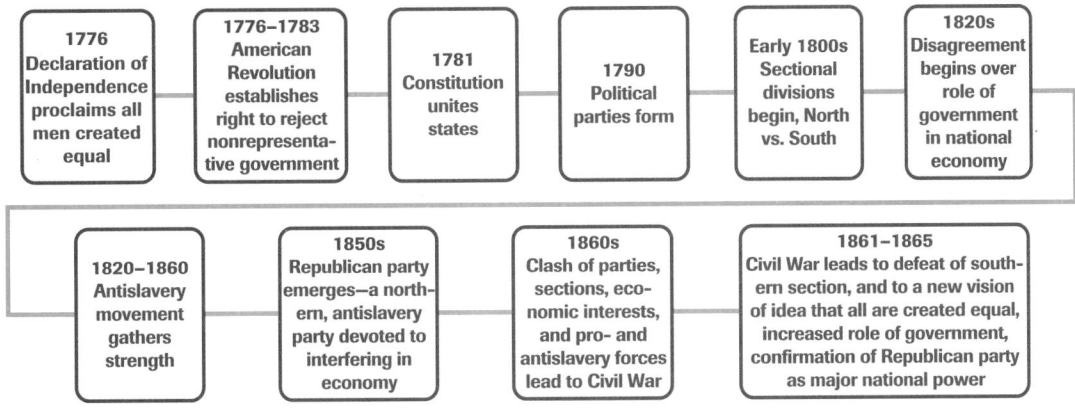

| 1776 Declaration of Independence proclaims all men created equal | 1776–1783 American Revolution establishes right to reject nonrepresentative government | 1781 Constitution unites states | 1790 Political parties form | Early 1800s Sectional divisions begin, North vs. South | 1820s Disagreement begins over role of government in national economy |

| 1820–1860 Antislavery movement gathers strength | 1850s Republican party emerges—a northern, antislavery party devoted to interfering in economy | 1860s Clash of parties, sections, economic interests, and pro- and antislavery forces lead to Civil War | 1861–1865 Civil War leads to defeat of southern section, and to a new vision of idea that all are created equal, increased role of government, confirmation of Republican party as major national power |

 Alternative Assessment

Final Evaluation
Use the following guidelines to evaluate student projects:
● **Evidence of mastery of content** To what extent do projects show knowledge and understanding of the chapter content?
● **Evidence of thoughtfulness** To what extent do projects show an understanding of the importance and significance of events?
● **Evidence of outside research** To what extent did students use outside research materials for their projects?
● **Communication style** To what extent do projects vividly portray the events leading up to and including the Civil War in a way appropriate for elementary school students?

Thinking Critically

1. Answers should acknowledge that the South lacked industry and much new technology. It also had a colonial-style economy, which would have limited economic growth.

2. Possible questions: Why were you willing to fight for the United States despite discrimination? What was your regiment trying to prove besides its courage? What impact did the bravery of your regiment have on white attitudes toward African American soldiers?

3. The enslaved African American would picture a society in which everyone was regarded as equal. The slave owner would picture a society in which he or she still had a superior status.

Making Connections

1. Slavery was too explosive and divisive an issue. Compromises had already been tried without success.

2. They are overrunning a cannon that is pointed directly at them.

3. Student's stories should reveal an understanding of the setting, the people involved, and the importance of the event that they have chosen.

LIFE AT WAR

When Union and Confederate soldiers set off to war in 1861, both sides expected it to last only a short time. They soon realized that the struggle would not be settled quickly and that they would have to adapt to long months at war. As in most wars, much of what the soldiers did was boring and uncomfortable. Their routine consisted mainly of training for battle, securing food, idling with their fellow soldiers, and traveling. Soldiers far preferred these daily discomforts and boredoms, however, to the deadly horrors they faced from fierce battles, diseases, and infections. More than 600,000 died—the most Americans ever to die in a war. Four of every ten men who went off to the Civil War were killed or wounded. *Why do you think soldiers were willing to pay such a high cost for their side's cause?*

▲ BOWIE KNIFE Many Confederate soldiers carried Bowie knives—named after frontiersman Jim Bowie.

▲ CONFEDERATE UNIFORM John Mosby, a Confederate scout and guerrilla leader, wore this jacket. Mosby and his Partisan Rangers often operated behind enemy lines in Virginia and Maryland.

▲ BULLET IN SHOULDER BELT PLATE
The soldier who wore this shoulder plate was very lucky. The plate saved his life by stopping a musket bullet.

▲ CIVIL WAR MUSKET
Many soldiers during the war used a musket, but the rifle soon replaced it as the standard army weapon. A rifle was easier to load, more accurate over long distances, and misfired less often.

▲ MESS TINS A soldier carried his own eating implements with him. These mess tins took up little space when put away and could be carried easily inside a soldier's pack.

▲ FIELD CUTLERY Soldiers carried utensils like these with their mess tins. Getting food to the soldiers was a problem that slowed down both armies.

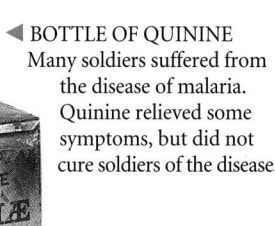

◀ BOTTLE OF QUININE Many soldiers suffered from the disease of malaria. Quinine relieved some symptoms, but did not cure soldiers of the disease.

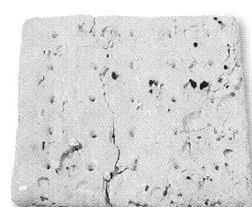

◀ HARD TACK Although not very tasty, this chewy bread was very nourishing, lasted a long time without spoiling, and was easy to carry.

▶ REGIMENTAL FLAG This flag commemorates some important battles by an African American regiment. About 180,000 of the 2,000,000 Union soldiers were African Americans.

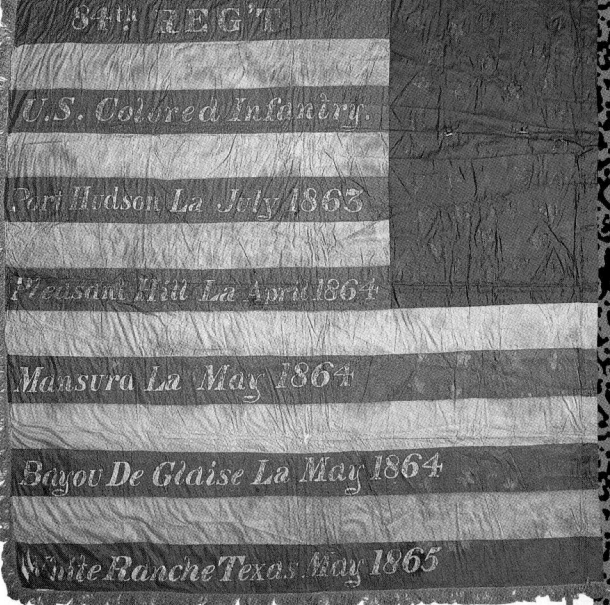

▲ FIELD HOSPITAL More soldiers died from disease and from infections caused by wounds than were killed in battles. Many women served their cause by working in field hospitals.

The course of a nation from the exhilarating days just after the declaration of war to a bittersweet tribute to those who died fighting—this is a path that can be compared to the growth of a child from the innocence of infancy to the full knowledge and awareness of adulthood. Explain to students that many people, both northerners and southerners, embarked on the Civil War with little realization of the horrors that they had invited into the nation's cities, countrysides, and, indeed, into the hearts of its citizens.

INSTRUCT

Ask students to consider how it might have affected the South's decision to secede from the Union if southerners had read the text of Lincoln's Gettysburg Address beforehand. Then have students write a short speech that might have been given by one of the following personalities after the war ended that either defends or attacks the decision to declare war: a Confederate soldier, a Union soldier, an enslaved woman whose son fought in the war, a southern woman whose husband fought in the war, a female nurse on the battlefields. Have students give their speeches before the class. Discuss the role of hindsight in our understanding of history and in our judgments about the decisions made in the past.

Choose a current event and discuss with students how that event might be viewed one hundred years from now.

CHAPTER 6

SOURCE READINGS

Diary of a Southern Woman 🖋 *Primary Source*

Mary Boykin Chesnut

INTRODUCTION The days before the start of the Civil War were strange times in the history of the nation. As North and South readied themselves for war, both sides were uncertain and fearful of what lay ahead. They were also brave and flamboyant about the prospect of fighting for something in which they strongly believed. Mary Boykin Chesnut of South Carolina was a well-to-do southerner who kept a diary during those days. Her crisp writing style and keen observations of her fellow southerners offer a sharp picture of the atmosphere of the time, as well as an account of plantation life. Unlike most slaveholders in the South, the Chesnuts owned hundreds of slaves. Because her husband, James Chesnut, Jr., served as an aide to Jefferson Davis, president of the Confederacy, Mary Boykin Chesnut knew members of the Confederate cabinet and many of the Confederacy's most important generals, including Robert E. Lee.

VOCABULARY Before you read the selection, find the meaning of these words in a dictionary: forestall, stagnant, clandestine, prowess, sanguine, extirpation.

June 10, 1861

The war is making us all tenderly sentimental. No casualties yet, no real mourning, nobody hurt; so it is all parade, fuss and fine feathers. There is no imagination here to forestall woe, and only the excitement and wild awakening from everyday stagnant life is felt; that is, when one gets away from the two or three sensible men who are still left in the world. . . .

In Charleston, a butcher has been clandestinely supplying the Yankee fleet outside of the Bar with beef. They say he gave the information which led to the capture of the *Savannah*. They will hang him. Mr. Petigru alone, in South Carolina, has not seceded. When they pray for our President, he gets up from his knees. He might risk a prayer for Mr. Davis, though I doubt if it would do Mr. Davis any good. Mr. Petigru is too clever to think himself one of the righteous, whose prayers avail so overly much. Mr. Petigru's disciple, Mr. Bryan, followed his example. Mr. Petigru has such a keen sense of the ridiculous, he must be laughing in his sleeve at the hubbub this untimely trait of independence has raised. . . .

Harper's Ferry has been evacuated, and we are looking out for a battle at Manassas Station. I am always ill. The name of my disease is a longing to get away from here, and go to Richmond. Good Lord, forgive me! Your commandment I cannot keep. How can I honor what is so dishonorable, or respect what is so little respectable, or love what is so utterly unlovely. Then I must go, indeed; go away from here[1]. . . .

June 28, 1861

In Mrs. Davis's drawing-room last night, the President[2] took a seat by me on the sofa where I sat. He talked for nearly an hour. He laughed at our faith in our own prowess. We are like the British; we think every Southerner equal to three Yankees at least, but we will have to be equivalent to a dozen now. After his experience of the fighting qualities of Southerners in Mexico, Mr. Davis believes that we will do all that can be done by pluck and muscle, endurance and dogged courage, dash and red-hot patriotism, and yet his

---

[1] At this time, Chesnut was living with her husband's parents. These lines convey her unhappiness with living with her in-laws.
[2] Jefferson Davis, President of the Confederate States.

tone was not sanguine. There was a sad refrain running through it all. For one thing, either way, he thinks it will be a long war. That floored me at once. It has been too long for me already. Then he said that before the end came we would have many a bitter experience. He said only fools doubted the courage of the Yankees, or their willingness to fight when they saw fit. And now we have stung their pride, we have roused them till they will fight like devils. . . .

October 7, 1861

An appalling list of foreigners in the Yankee army, just as I feared; a rush of all Europe to them, as soon as they raised the cry that this war is for the extirpation of slavery. If our people had read less of Mr. Calhoun's works, and only read the signs of the times a little more; if they had known more of what was going on around them in the world.

October 13, 1861

I was shocked to hear that dear friends of mine refused to take work for the soldiers because their seamstresses had their winter clothes to make. I told them true patriotesses would be willing to wear the same clothes until our siege was raised. They did not seem to care. They have seen no ragged, dirty, sick and miserable soldiers lying in the hospital, no lack of woman's nursing, no lack of woman's tears, but an awful lack of a proper change in clean clothes. They know nothing of the horrors of war. One has to see to believe. They take it easy, and are not yet willing to make personal sacrifices. The time is coming when they will not be given a choice in the matter.

This picture of the bombardment of Fort Sumter in South Carolina on April 12, 1861, appeared in the pages of *Harper's Weekly* magazine. The artist showed how residents of Charleston watched the attack from the rooftops of buildings.

THINKING ABOUT THE SELECTION

1. What is Jefferson Davis's opinion of the fighting abilities of the northerners?
2. Why does Chesnut wish that southerners had paid more attention to what was going on in the world before the Civil War?

Critical Thinking

3. **Drawing Conclusions** What can you determine about the mood of some southerners from Chesnut's diary? Give examples to support your answer.

ANSWERS TO

Thinking About the Selection

1. He thinks that they are able and courageous fighters.
2. They would have been aware of the antislavery climate in much of the world. The North, aware of this sentiment, was able to use it to recruit foreigners to help fight for its cause.

3. Their mood is "tenderly sentimental," "all parade, fuss and fine feathers." They feel "excitement and wild awakening." According to Davis, the southerners think highly of their own fighting abilities and are of a low opinion of the northerners' abilities. Finally, Chesnut reveals that some southerners are not yet aware of the sacrifices and hardship that the war will entail.

Have students watch one of the many documentaries on the Civil War, such as Ken Burns's *The Civil War* or *Civil War: 1863–1865* produced by Coronet Films. Then have students write a brief essay describing how the film showed or did not show the nation's journey from innocence to awareness during the Civil War. Alternatively, have students read one of the many works of fiction about the Civil War, such as *The Red Badge of Courage,* and analyze it for evidence of the same journey to awareness.

SOURCE READINGS

The Gettysburg Address

 *Primary Source*

Abraham Lincoln

INTRODUCTION Edward Everett, a former United States senator from Massachusetts and known as one of the greatest orators of his day, spoke for two hours at the ceremony dedicating the cemetery at Gettysburg. When President Lincoln rose after Everett to give his dedication, the crowd fell silent in anticipation. At just 267 words, the speech was short, so short that a photographer who meant to take a picture of Lincoln delivering the speech did not have time to focus his camera. Later Everett wrote to Lincoln, "I should be glad if I could flatter myself that I came as near to the central idea of the occasion in two hours as you did in two minutes." Indeed, Lincoln's address, criticized at the time for its brevity, encapsulated an ideal that citizens continue to cherish today.

VOCABULARY Before you read the selection, find the meaning of this word in a dictionary: consecrate.

Four score and seven years ago our fathers brought forth on this continent, a new nation, conceived in Liberty, and dedicated to the proposition that all men are created equal.

Now we are engaged in a great civil war, testing whether that nation, or any nation so conceived and so dedicated, can long endure. We are met on a great battlefield of that war. We have come to dedicate a portion of that field, as a final resting place for those who here gave their lives that that nation might live. It is altogether fitting and proper that we should do this.

But, in a larger sense, we can not dedicate—we cannot consecrate—we can not hallow—this ground. The brave men, living and dead, who struggled here, have consecrated it, far above our poor power to add or detract. The world will little note nor long remember what we say here, but it can never forget what they did here. It is for us the living, rather, to be dedicated here to the unfinished work which they who fought here have thus far so nobly advanced. It is rather for us to be here dedicated to the great task remaining before us—that from these honored dead we take increased devotion to that cause for which they gave the last full measure of devotion—that we here highly resolve that these dead shall not have died in vain—that this nation, under God, shall have a new birth of freedom—and that government of the people, by the people, for the people, shall not perish from the earth.

This framed photograph of Abraham Lincoln shows the President before the start of the Civil War.

THINKING ABOUT THE SELECTION

1. How does Lincoln describe the soldiers who died at Gettysburg?
2. Why does Lincoln say that the people attending this ceremony cannot really dedicate the cemetery?

Critical Thinking

3. **Determining Relevance** What are some of the ideals expressed in the Gettysburg Address that we still find relevant today?

ANSWERS TO

Thinking About the Selection
1. He describes them as "brave," noble, and "honored."
2. He says that the deaths of the men who fought in the battle have dedicated it more than can those who gather to honor them.
3. The ideal that all are created equal, that those who fight for their country should be honored, and that a government of the people, by the people, and for the people is worth fighting for.

Saving the Union

Primary Source

Abraham Lincoln

INTRODUCTION President Lincoln wrote this letter to Horace Greeley, the editor of the *New York Tribune,* on August 22, 1862, in reply to a signed editorial in which Greeley had criticized Lincoln for not making the end of slavery the chief goal of the Civil War. Since the early part of the war, Lincoln had maintained that his chief aim was to save the Union and not to free enslaved people. His reply to Greeley is one of the clearest statements of the objective of this war policy. When Lincoln wrote this letter, however, he had already decided he could not achieve his purpose without freeing those enslaved in the South. He issued the Emancipation Proclamation on September 22, 1862.

Dear Sir:

I have just read yours of the 19th, addressed to myself through the *New York Tribune.* If there be in it any statements or assumptions of fact which I may know to be erroneous, I do not now and here controvert them. If there be in it any inferences which I may believe to be falsely drawn, I do not now and here argue against them. If there be perceptible in it an impatient and dictatorial tone, I waive it in deference to an old friend, whose heart I have always supposed to be right.

As to the policy I "seem to be pursuing," as you say, I have not meant to leave anyone in doubt.

I would save the Union. I would save it the shortest way under the Constitution. The sooner the national authority can be restored, the nearer the Union will be "the Union as it was." If there be those who would not save the Union unless they could at the same time save slavery, I do not agree with them. If there be those who would not save the Union unless they could at the same time destroy slavery, I do not agree with them. My paramount objective in this stuggle is to save the Union, and is not either to save or destroy slavery. If I could save the Union without freeing any slave, I would do it; and if I could save it by freeing all the slaves, I would do it; and if I could do it by freeing some and leaving others alone, I would also do that.

What I do about slavery and the colored race I do because I believe it helps to save this Union; and what I forbear I forbear because I do not believe it would help save the Union. I shall do less whenever I shall believe what I am doing hurts the cause, and I shall do more whenever I shall believe doing more will help the cause. I shall try to correct errors when shown to be errors; and I shall adopt new views so fast as they shall appear to be true views.

I have here stated my purpose according to my view of official duty, and I intend no modification of my oft-expressed personal wish that all men, everywhere, could be free.

THINKING ABOUT THE SELECTION

1. What did President Lincoln see as his official duty in regards to his war policy?
2. According to the letter, how did Lincoln's official duty differ from his personal viewpoint about slavery?

Critical Thinking

3. **Checking Consistency** In this letter, Lincoln stated that "What I do about slavery and the colored race I do because I believe it helps to save this Union." Review page 206 of Chapter 6. How was the issuing of the Emancipation Proclamation consistent with this statement?

ANSWERS TO

Thinking About the Selection

1. Lincoln saw that his duty was to save the Union by the fastest means available under the Constitution.

2. Lincoln declared that his paramount purpose and official duty was to save the Union, that the issue of slavery was relevant only in terms of whether its existence would aid or harm the Union, and that he would maintain his personal beliefs regardless of the actions he needed to take as President to save the Union.

3. Lincoln believed he could not preserve the Union without freeing the enslaved, so he issued the Emancipation Proclamation.

Chapter 7 Changing Frontiers
1860–1910

📁 Teaching Resources (See Unit 2 Folder)

	Instruction	Enrichment
Section 1 **The Expansion of American Industry** (pp. 228–234)	Reproducible Lesson Plan, p. 75 Alternate Lesson Plan, p. 79 Guided Reading and Review, p. 80 Quiz, p. 81	Primary Source Activity, Working on the Railroad, p. 98 Visual Learning Activity, Home of the Trusts, p. 103 Historian's Toolbox Activity, Drawing Conclusions, p. 96
Section 2 **The Great Strikes: A Turning Point in History** (pp. 236–241)	Reproducible Lesson Plan, p. 76 Alternate Lesson Plan, p. 80 Guided Reading and Review, p. 82 Quiz, p. 83	Literature Activity, Sister Carrie, pp. 100–101 Viewpoints Activity, On Labor Unions, pp. 94–95 American Profiles Activity, Mary Kenney O'Sullivan, p. 92 Turning Points Extension Activity, The Lasting Impact of the Great Strikes, pp. 90–91
Section 3 **Moving West** (pp. 244–250)	Reproducible Lesson Plan, p. 77 Alternate Lesson Plan, p. 81 Guided Reading and Review, p. 84 Quiz, p. 85	Visual Learning Activity, The Farmers' Complaint, p. 104 American Profiles Activity, Nat Love, Alias Deadwood Dick, p. 93
Section 4 **Politics in the Gilded Age** (pp. 251–256)	Reproducible Lesson Plan, p. 78 Alternate Lesson Plan, p. 82 Guided Reading and Review, p. 86 Quiz, p. 87	Critical Thinking Activity, Distinguishing False from Accurate Images, p. 97
Section 5 **Immigration and Urban Life** (pp. 257–263)	Reproducible Lesson Plan, p. 79 Alternate Lesson Plan, p. 83 Guided Reading and Review, p. 88 Quiz, p. 89 Chapter Test, Forms A & B, pp. 105–110	Literature Activity, The Statue of Liberty, p. 102 Primary Source Activity, New York Gangs, p. 99

📁 Additional Chapter Resources

Resource Organizer, p. 74
Alternate Lesson Plan, p. 78
Answer Keys, pp. 152–165

Bibliography

For the Teacher
McKelvey, Blake. *The Urbanization of America, 1860–1915.* Rutgers, 1963. (Detailed discussion of the growth of American cities in the late 1800s and early 1900s.)
Takaki, Ronald. *Strangers from a Different Shore: A History of Asian Americans.* Little, Brown, 1989. (A comprehensive account of the Asian American immigrant experience.)

Prentice Hall Literature Excerpts from *The American Experience,* 1994, including Twain, Mark. *Life on the Mississippi.* HarperCollins, 1939 edition.

Media and Technology

 The Way It Works, H-11, H-14

  Visions of America: Turning Point Story, "Company Town" (length: approx. 4 minutes)

  Visions of America: Roundtable Discussion of "Company Town"

 The Way It Works, H-15; Cause and Effect, F-4

 Links Across Time, J-7

 Our Multicultural Heritage, C-2, C-15; Graphic Organizer, G-3

 Guided Reading Audiotapes (English and Spanish)

 Computer Test Bank

For the Student

Addams, Jane. *Twenty Years at Hull-House.* University of Illinois Press, 1989. (The reformer's autobiography, first published in 1910.)

Dakota Wars and Reservation Life. University of Nebraska. Film. (Depicts the lives of Native Americans of the plains and their struggle, including Custer's last stand.)

THE BIG IDEA

The Big Idea for the chapter and how the main ideas in each section relate to the Big Idea are graphically displayed below. Comprehension of this chapter's Big Idea is critical to students' understanding of United States history and how we as a nation got where we are today.

CHAPTER 7

After the Civil War, industrial progress transformed the nation, but workers faced poor conditions in the new factories. They formed labor unions to demand change, but met limited success. Immigrants from abroad and migrants from within the country crowded into cities, which became collections of political factions, ghettos, ethnic enclaves, and extremes of rich and poor. Meanwhile, other Americans were moving west, creating conflict with the Native Americans who already lived there.

SECTION 1

New technology revolutionized the way Americans worked, lived, and conducted business. But workers were paid low wages for laboring long hours in poor conditions.

SECTION 2

Labor unions promised some hope of improving conditions for workers, but fierce opposition from big business slowed the growth of organized labor.

SECTION 3

After the Civil War, Americans moved west of the Mississippi River, taking over the land for farms, ranches, and mines and forcing out the original Native American inhabitants.

SECTION 4

Political turmoil marked the years from 1876 to 1900. Neither of the two major parties could capture the loyalty of the people for very long. The parties were often more concerned with their own agendas than with a single national one.

SECTION 5

Newcomers from overseas and migrants from the nation's rural areas swelled America's cities. Some wished to control immigration; others worked to improve conditions.

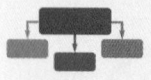

Changing Frontiers
1860–1910

The Relevance of the Big Idea

After the Civil War, Americans discovered several new frontiers. In the old cities of the Northeast new technologies allowed goods to be made in startling new ways that had an enormous impact on the way people lived and worked. In the American West wide open spaces beckoned weary factory workers and tired farmers of the East. At the same time, thousands of new immigrants from abroad poured into the country , while migrants from the nation's rural areas moved into cities. This enormous influx of people provided new workers for the growing factories.

Point out to students that there are disadvantages resulting from new growth or new conquests. Ask students to list one possible negative outcome of each of these frontiers: the development of industrial America, the movement west, the growth of the nation's cities.

In Depth

Global Connections

Between 1847 and 1860, over a million Irish immigrants entered the U.S. through the port of New York City alone. The Irish came in large part because a blight destroyed their country's entire potato crop, which was the mainstay of their diet. Eventually over one million died in Ireland from starvation and disease during the potato famine. America seemed a far cry from the disaster. One new arrival wrote, "Every day [in America] is like Christmas Day."

Changing Frontiers
1860–1910

After the Civil War, settlers from the East continued to push the frontiers of the United States westward. But the nation grew on other frontiers, too. New technologies sparked a business boom, and workers spoke out for a larger share of the nation's wealth. As immigrants poured into the cities, government and social reform struggled to meet their challenge. All of this new growth brought remarkable rewards. But those rewards came with a price that included urban poverty, child labor, and the displacement of Native Americans.

Events in the United States

1862 Congress passes the Morrill Land-Grant Act and the Homestead Act to give away public land.

1869 The transcontinental railroad is completed.

1877 The railroad strike of 1877 erupts in Pittsburgh, Pennsylvania.

1883 Railroads adopt standard time zones.
• The Brooklyn Bridge is opened.

1860	1866	1872	1878	1884

Events in the World

1861 Charles Dickens publishes Great Expectations.

1868 Imperial capital of Japan moves to Tokyo.
• Bones of Cro-Magnon are found in France.

1881 Czar Alexander II of Russia is assassinated by revolutionaries.

RESOURCE DIRECTORY

Teaching Resources

Alternate Lesson Plan: Demonstrating the Big Idea found in the Alternate Lesson Plans folder, p. 78, provides a lesson strategy to instruct students about the Big Idea that industrial progress after the Civil War transformed the nation, resulting in both positive and negative consequences.

Alternative Assessment Handbook provides information, guidance, and strategies for alternative methods of assessment. It includes an essay on new trends in assessment, guidance and strategies for developing performance tasks and portfolios, scoring rubrics, and sample evaluation forms.

Pages 228–234
The Expansion of American Industry

The late 1800s saw the emergence of giant industries built on new technologies. These business produced great wealth for their owners. But for millions of people, industrialization was a curse as well as a blessing.

Pages 236–241
The Great Strikes: A Turning Point in History

Many American workers sought relief from their difficulties through labor unions. What they found in the late 1800s was strong resistance from big business and only fleeting success.

Pages 242–243
The Lasting Impact of the Great Strikes

Pages 244–250
Moving West

The West was home for thousands of years to Native Americans. But modern farming methods, discovery of mineral deposits, and ranching soon made the West attractive to many others, including big business.

Pages 251–256
Politics in the Gilded Age

In the years after Reconstruction, the United States changed from a nation of farms into one of growing businesses, factories, and cities. Yet despite such changes—and sometimes because of them—many problems festered.

Pages 257–263
Immigration and Urban Life

As immigrants from Europe and Asia arrived on American shores, most pinned their hopes on the nation's cities. Bustling, noisy, and straining at the seams, the cities were places where the new became neighbors with the old and where progress lived next door to poverty.

1890 Congress passes the Sherman Antitrust Act.	1894 Coxey's army of the unemployed marches on Washington.	1901 President William McKinley is assassinated by an anarchist.				
1890	**1896**	**1902**	**1908**	**1914**	**1920**	
			1905 Albert Einstein develops his special theory of relativity.		1918 A worldwide influenza epidemic kills more than twenty million people.	

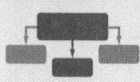

The Expansion of American Industry

SECTION 1

The Expansion of American Industry

1. FOCUS

Connecting to the Big Idea

See page 226B. Review with students that inventions and technology led to the growth of big business in the late 1800s. Explain that in addition to technology and financial backing, workers were needed to make new products for market. Ask students how this increased demand for labor would affect life for most Americans.

Objectives

- Identify some of the inventions that transformed American life in the decades following the Civil War.
- Show how big business tried to control competition.
- Describe the toll that industrial growth took on workers.

Bellringer

Write the following inventions on the chalkboard: typewriter, phonograph, telegraph, telephone. Ask students to decide which they consider the most important and why.

Reading Strategy

Reinforcing Key Ideas Tell students that they will read about daily life in the United States between 1865 and 1900. Then ask them to list, as they read, the ways in which the United States changed during those thirty-five years.

Electricity provided power that made postwar industrial development possible. In turn, electric companies such as General Electric, whose ad appears here, grew into large industrial corporations.

SECTION PREVIEW

The late 1800s saw the emergence of giant industries built on new technologies. These businesses produced great wealth for their owners. But for millions of people, industrialization was a curse as well as a blessing.

Key Concepts
- Technological change and an explosion of new ideas transformed American life in the post–Civil War years.
- Big business sought to control competition through various forms of consolidation.
- Industrial growth depended on the labor of millions of workers, who toiled under harsh conditions that inflicted physical and emotional harm.

Key Terms, People, and Places
social Darwinism, monopoly, cartel, trust, horizontal consolidation, vertical consolidation; Andrew Carnegie

 mericans today flip a switch for light, turn a faucet for hot running water, and use many devices to communicate with people they may never meet face to face. It is hard to imagine life without these conveniences. In 1865, however, people experienced such a life firsthand.

New Technology Transforms Daily Life

In 1865 indoor electric lighting did not exist. Instead the rising and setting of the sun dictated the rhythm of work and play. After dark, people lit candles or oil lamps if they could afford them; if not, they simply went to sleep, to rise with the first light. People endured summer heat without the benefits of refrigeration. Ice, sawn out of frozen ponds during the winter, was available, but only at great cost. Communications were agonizingly slow. In 1860, most mail from the East Coast took ten days to reach the Midwest and three weeks to get to the West. An immigrant living on the frontier would wait months for news from relatives in Europe.

By 1900, a number of factors had combined to change this picture of daily life. After the Civil War, new ideas and inventions had flooded the nation. Between 1790 and 1860, the Patent and Trademark Office of the federal government issued just 36,000 patents. In contrast, in the thirty years between 1860 and 1890, the office issued 500,000 patents for new inventions, including the typewriter, the phonograph, and many new manufacturing processes as well.

Using profits gained during the Civil War, European investors and American business leaders began to invest heavily in these inventions. This combination of ingenuity and financial backing created new industries and expanded old ones. By 1900, the industrial productivity and overall standard of living in the United States had risen considerably.

New Fuels, New Power New fuels and sources of power also transformed daily life. Researchers began developing new uses for petroleum, including fuels such as gasoline that would eventually power new forms of transportation. Electricity advanced the nation's industrial development. It also changed people's eating, working, and even sleeping habits. Thanks to the work of inventors such as Thomas Alva Edison, George Westinghouse, and Lewis Latimore in the 1870s and 1880s, nearly three thousand power stations were lighting two million light bulbs across the land by 1898. Electricity made refrigeration possible too, reducing food spoilage.

Electricity also created new job opportunities. Electrified in 1886, sewing machines

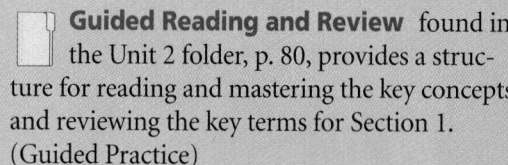

RESOURCE DIRECTORY

Teaching Resources

Reproducible Lesson Plan found in the Unit 2 folder, p. 75, provides a summary of the Section 1 lesson plan content.

Alternate Lesson Plan: Learning Styles found in the Alternate Lesson Plans folder, p. 79, especially useful for visual learners, focuses on the inventions and ideas that resulted in the post–Civil War technological revolution.

Guided Reading and Review found in the Unit 2 folder, p. 80, provides a structure for reading and mastering the key concepts and reviewing the key terms for Section 1. (Guided Practice)

Primary Source Activity Working on the Railroad, found in the Unit 2 folder, p. 98, introduces students to the hard life of an 1880s worker with a folk song by Thomas Casey.

enabled the rapid expansion of the ready-made clothing industry. Many of the country's new immigrants, especially women and children, found work making clothing in factories powered by electricity. Because clothing was now inexpensive and readily available, many women stopped making their own at home.

Electricity's benefits were not evenly distributed, however. Rural areas especially went without electricity for many decades. Even where electricity was available, many could not afford its conveniences.

Improving Transportation Systems As the Civil War ended, steam-powered ships still provided much of the nation's transportation. During the mid-1800s, improvements in railroad travel created interconnecting links on land. Shrewd industrialists seized upon the opportunities offered by the railroads to make money and stimulate industrial growth.

Before the Civil War, most of the nation's 30,000 miles of track were in short lines, almost all of them east of the Mississippi River. Lines were generally not connected because track width, or gauge, varied among railroad lines.

After the Civil War, thanks to massive government loans, railroad building projects multiplied, as shown on the map below. To do this work, immigrant laborers were brought in. Irish and Chinese workers used picks, shovels, and dynamite to build railroads across deserts and mountain ranges. In 1869, they completed the first transcontinental link. ★

Over time, train travel improved. Steel rails replaced iron rails, and track gauges and

Caption Answer to ...

 Interpreting Maps

Railroads opened vast new regions for American settlement and allowed manufacturers to ship more raw materials and goods to more places.

Time Zones and the Growth of the Railroads, 1870–1890

Geography and History: Interpreting Maps
Following the Civil War, railroads expanded rapidly across the United States. Workers such as those pictured here performed the dangerous, backbreaking construction. The growth of the railroads made necessary the introduction of standard time zones. *In what ways did the nation's growing transportation system help promote industrial growth?*

In Depth

Did You Know?

Not everyone greeted the improvements in railroad transportation and travel with enthusiasm. The *Boston Courier* printed the following assertion as part of an editorial in 1827: "The project of a railroad from Boston to Albany is impracticable, as every one knows who knows the simplest rule of arithmetic, and the expense would be little less than the market value of the whole of Massachusetts; and which, if practicable, every person of common sense knows would be as useless as a railroad from Boston to the moon."

Links Across Time

Answers will vary but might include the following: A company can save money by eliminating the need for its employees to travel to a common site for meetings and discussions. Employees from various parts of the country, and even abroad, can meet by punching a few buttons. Picture telephones usually offer graphic display capabilities so that everyone in a meeting can view a document simultaneously.

In Depth

Biography

African American engineer Elijah McCoy (1843–1929) was born in Canada to parents who had escaped slavery. He studied in Edinburgh, Scotland, before settling in the United States. In 1872, while working for the Michigan Central Railroad, McCoy invented the lubricating cup — a device that continuously oiled the moving parts of a machine. Over the years he adapted his invention to many other machines. It is sometimes said that the expression "the real McCoy," meaning the genuine article, came into use as people insisted that the machinery they buy be equipped with McCoy's invention.

signals became standardized. George Westinghouse developed more effective air brakes. Granville Woods invented a telegraph system for communications to and from moving trains, thus reducing collision risks. Standardized time zones, introduced in 1883, improved scheduling.

Rail improvements led to lower costs for businesses that shipped goods. In 1865, shipping a barrel of flour from Chicago to New York cost $3.45; by 1895, it cost only 68 cents.

The Power to Communicate Samuel F. B. Morse's invention of the telegraph began a communications revolution. Using a code of short and long electrical impulses to represent letters of the alphabet, Morse sent his first message in 1844. The Western Union Telegraph Company was formed after the Civil War. In 1870 it sent 9 million telegraph messages over 112,000 miles of wire. By 1900 it was sending 63 million messages a year over its 933,000 miles of wire. Like many companies born in the late 1800s, Western Union still operates today.

In 1876 Alexander Graham Bell of Scotland, an instructor of the hearing impaired, invented a "talking telegraph"—the first telephone. In 1884 Bell and a group of partners set up the American Telephone and Telegraph Company, another company that is still a powerful player in the communications field. By 1900 about 1.5 million telephones were in use, linking homes and businesses in entire cities through central switchboards staffed by operators.

The Power to Build Things Until the mid-1800s, the nation depended on iron for railroads and for the framework of most of its large buildings. Then in the 1850s, an affordable process was developed for making steel, a metal that is lighter, stronger, and more flexible than iron. A new age of building was dawning. Perhaps no construction project so exemplified that new age as the building of the Brooklyn Bridge.

The bridge became necessary when New York City's status as a business center had risen, along with the number of its residents, many of whom settled in nearby Brooklyn. But the only way to travel between the two areas was by ferry across a river often impassable in winter. Could a bridge high enough to clear river traffic be built across such a great distance? Engineer John A. Roebling, a German immigrant, thought it could.

| 1650 | 1700 | 1750 | 1800 | **Links Across Time** | 1850 | 1900 | 1950 | 2000 |

New Ways to Communicate

When Alexander Graham Bell patented the first model of his telephone in 1876, businesses everywhere flocked to buy the new invention. As technology moves into the twenty-first century, a new communications revolution is taking place. The picture telephone technology shown here allows modern businesses to speak with and to see the party whom they have called. *How might a company benefit from picture telephones?*

 **RESOURCE DIRECTORY**

Teaching Resources

Roebling envisioned a suspension bridge with thick steel cables suspended from high towers to hold up the span. At 1,595 feet long, his Brooklyn Bridge—which was completed in 1883 by his son Washington—was the longest bridge built up to that time. Its opening confirmed the nation's ingenuity for all the world.

The Growth of Big Business

In addition to inventions, faster transportation, and daring construction projects, the late 1800s also was a time of new thinking and action in the business world. Business success in this era required large outlays of money for the building of large factories and the marketing of products on a mass scale. Business leaders pooled funds and resources to form large companies. Thus was born the age of "big business."

Robber Barons or Captains of Industry?
Historians have adopted the terms *captains of industry* and *robber barons* to describe the powerful industrialists who established large businesses in this era. Each term conjures up strikingly different images, and debate still rages over which is more fitting.

Captains of industry suggests that the business leaders served their nation in a positive way. They increased the availability of goods and created more jobs, thus enabling more Americans to buy the new goods. They also founded and funded many of the nation's great museums, libraries, and universities.

The term *robber barons* implies that the business leaders built their fortunes by stealing from the public. According to this view, they drained the country of its natural resources and bribed public officials to interpret laws in their favor. They also drove their competitors to ruin and paid meager wages while forcing their workers to toil under dangerous and unhealthy conditions.

Andrew Carnegie, the steel magnate, and John D. Rockefeller, who made millions of dollars in the oil industry, are two examples of industrialists of this era. Both men felt that they were improving conditions for all Americans. They also gave large amounts of money to

Andrew Carnegie's success in business enabled him to surround himself with comfort. Here he relaxes at his private golf cottage.

found many public institutions. In one essay, Carnegie wrote:

> It will be a great mistake for the community to shoot the millionaires, for they are the bees that make the most honey, and contribute most to the hive even after they have gorged themselves full.

In statements such as these, Carnegie revealed support for **social Darwinism,** a popular theory of the late 1800s. This theory applied to society Charles Darwin's theory of evolution, first published in 1859. According to Darwin, all animal life had evolved by a process of "natural selection" through which only the fittest survived to reproduce.

Applying this idea to the struggle between workers and employers, social Darwinism held that society should do as little as possible to interfere with the process by which people succeed or fail. If government and other institutions would stay out of the affairs of business, those who were most "fit" would survive—that is, succeed and become rich. Society as a whole would benefit from the success of the fit and the weeding out of the unfit.

Many Americans agreed with the great industrialists that the nation's prosperity depended on a laissez-faire, or "hands-off," approach to the economy by the government. As a result, government neither taxed the profits of businesses nor regulated their relations with their workers.

Media and Technology

Transparencies
The Way It Works, H-11, H-14

2. INSTRUCT

Explain
Point out to students that conditions in the United States were ideal for the great surge in industrial activity that occurred. Business leaders had capital to invest, the labor supply was adequate, and abundant forests and mines provided raw materials. Changes in the means of production, including mechanization and electrification, provided the last ingredient needed for the expansion of industry.

Help students to visualize the differences between working in a small, owner-operated blacksmith shop in a small town and working as a blacksmith in one of Andrew Carnegie's steel plants. What sort of relationship did worker and employer have in the small smithy? How did industrialization change that relationship?

Discuss
Discuss with students the probability that the powerful industrialists of the late 1800s were *both* captains of industry and robber barons. Ask students to explain how that could be. Next, discuss with students why millions of workers either migrated from the nation's farms or came from abroad to work in the great industries that developed after the Civil War. Ask why workers tolerated the poor pay and conditions of most industrial jobs.

In Depth

Did You Know?

John Roebling, the engineer who built the Brooklyn Bridge, died six months after construction began. His son Colonel Washington Roebling took over, but he contracted "the bends," or caisson disease, in 1872 and was confined to his bed. His wife, Emily, acted as his messenger, and many consider her to have been, in effect, the chief engineer during the final phases of construction.

Answer to ...

MAKING CONNECTIONS

Students should predict that less powerful businesses would go out of business or be purchased by more powerful enterprises. Assist students as they explore how an abstract concept functions in reality.

Activity

Cooperative Learning

Time: One class period.
Activity: Create a demonstration of a piece-work system.
Grouping: Groups of four to six students.
Purpose: To demonstrate how a piecework system favors the employer. Each worker must perform a task, such as the making of a paper hat or airplane, chosen by the group. Provide the students with the following information to incorporate into their skits: pay per task accomplished; pay scale according to job held, marketability of the product, maintenance of quality control, evaluation of the product.
Roles: Workers, foreman or boss, manager, quality control supervisor, factory owner.
Outcome: Students will portray the frustrations experienced by workers in a piecework system. **LEP**

Enrichment

To illustrate the delicate balance between economic development and fair treatment of workers, ask students to consider how industrialists like Andrew Carnegie and labor leaders like Samuel Gompers might have expressed their ideas through mass media in the 1800s. Have students create public service announcements for either industrialists or laborers. Suggest that students brainstorm a list of features that they would want to highlight in their announcements.

MAKING CONNECTIONS

Based on your understanding of the laissez-faire approach of government, what do you predict might have happened to those business owners who were less powerful?

Competition in the Age of Big Business

Despite the *laissez-faire* attitude of many Americans, taxes and regulation eventually became necessary. Industrialists used any means, fair or foul, against their rivals. They paid as little as they could for raw materials, labor, and shipping. The new forms of business they created to gain control over competition—monopolies, cartels, and trusts—soon got out of hand.

Monopolies, Cartels, and Trusts In order to create a **monopoly,** a business bought out its competitors and all of their patents. The business could then charge any price for its product that it wished. In the late 1800s, political leaders passed laws to prevent certain monopolistic practices, but most politicians were unwilling to attack powerful business leaders.

Cartels are loose associations, usually formed in secret, of businesses making the same product. Members agree to limit the supply of their product because when supply is low, a product's price remains high. During hard times, however, cartels tended to fall apart. To achieve a more reliable arrangement, Samuel Dodd, a lawyer for oil magnate John D. Rockefeller, invented the **trust** in 1882.

Rockefeller had made enough money in the oil business to buy out his competitors. But state laws prohibited one company from owning the stock of another, since such practices reduced competition and "restrained" free trade.

Samuel Dodd was able to convince the companies bought by Rockefeller to turn over their assets to a board of nine trustees. In return, they received a share of the profits of the new conglomerate. The board of trustees, which Rockefeller controlled, managed the companies as a single unit called a trust. This

Standard Oil Trust soon controlled most of the nation's oil-refining capacity.

Since trusts limit competition and keep prices high for consumers, many Americans began to favor the breakup of the giant conglomerates. In 1890, the federal government passed the Sherman Antitrust Act to combat restraint of trade caused by trusts. The act was rarely enforced, however, and its vague wording made it hard to apply in court. When officials did invoke the act, they often used it against labor unions on the grounds that their actions restrained trade.

Methods of Industrial Control Rockefeller's approach to consolidation—the creation of one giant business from many smaller enterprises—was **horizontal consolidation.** Other industrialists practiced **vertical consolidation,** in which one business gained control of all phases of a product's development. Carnegie used this method in the steel business. By controlling all phases of steel production, Carnegie lowered his costs and drove competitors out of business.

Public Reaction to Big Business Most people recognized that the trusts and other large businesses did not have consumer or worker interests at heart. When markets became glutted with goods, businesses lowered prices but also cut wages and laid off workers. Sudden panics, or widespread fears that heavily indebted businesses might not be able to pay their debts, also caused strain. When investors rushed to sell stock in affected businesses, stock prices fell and companies went bankrupt. Depressions, or periods of severe shrinking of economic growth, factory closings, and unemployment, usually followed such panics.

Industrialization and Workers

Fourteen million people arrived in the United States from abroad between 1860 and 1900. In a population shift almost as dramatic as this immigration, some eight or nine million native-born Americans fled poor economic conditions on the nation's farms to move to its cities. Most came in the hope of finding factory

---

▶ RESOURCE DIRECTORY

Teaching Resources

Visual Learning Activity Home of the Trusts, found in the Unit 2 folder, p. 103, uses an antitrust cartoon by noted political cartoonist Thomas Nast to assist students in analyzing political imagery.

work in the booming industrial centers of the United States.

A Hard Life for the Factory Laborer For those who labored in the factories, work was a family affair. Because wages were low, no one person could earn enough to sustain a household. Children often left school at the age of twelve or thirteen to work. Girls sometimes took factory jobs so that their brothers could stay in school. If a mother could not make some money working at home, she might also take a factory job, leaving babies with older siblings or neighbors.

Other than private charities, there were no government welfare programs for families in need. Unemployment insurance—payments for workers who are laid off from their jobs—did not exist. When economic crises arose, legislators resisted the idea of creating broad programs of public work to relieve distress.

Increasing Efficiency In the 1860s, the ordinary work day was about twelve hours, and the work week was six days or longer. By the turn of the century, a ten-hour day prevailed but not in all industries. In many industries, employers paid workers a fixed amount for each finished piece they produced—for example, a few cents for a garment or a number of cigars. This piecework system meant that those who worked fastest and produced the most pieces earned the most money. Piecework favored young and strong workers; older or less able workers suffered.

In the 1880s, management engineer Frederick Winslow Taylor developed time-and-motion studies to get workers to produce more in less time. Taylor's idea was to make the most efficient use of all motion and activity. Many workers hated and resisted Taylor's ideas because they imposed an outside control on the way they did their work. They also feared that any increased efficiency caused by Taylor's methods would result in layoffs or a lower rate of pay for each piece of work.

By the early years of the twentieth century, Taylor had used his studies as the basis of an entire system of so-called scientific management in which

The work of every workman is fully planned out by the management at least one day in advance, and each man receives in most cases complete written instructions, describing in detail the task which he is to accomplish, as well as the means to be used in doing the work . . . and the exact time allowed for doing it.

Frederick Winslow Taylor, *The Principles of Scientific Management*, 1911

Taylor's ideas were just one method of improving efficiency. Employers often increased the speed of factory machines or added to workers' loads, especially in hard times. Yet workers' pay did not increase, and their health and safety suffered. For instance, a Fall River, Massachusetts, textile company increased the number of its looms, but not the number of its

Industrial growth created jobs for African Americans, though opportunities were limited. For example, these three men were hired for the low-paying job of carrying bricks. White men got the higher-paying jobs as masons.

Section 1 Review Answers

1. (a) social Darwinism, see p. 231, (b) monopoly, see p. 232, (c) cartel, see p. 232, (d) trust, see p. 232, (e) horizontal consolidation, see p. 232, (f) vertical consolidation, see p. 232.

2. Andrew Carnegie, see p. 231.

3. Factors include the discovery of new uses for the nation's raw materials and the financial backing of wealthy business leaders.

4. To eliminate competition.

5. The government did not have relief or public works programs to help the poor and jobless.

6. The statements suggest a view of workers as machines.

Reteach

Have students describe life in the United States before 1865, focusing on transportation, daily schedules, and types of food available. Then ask them to describe how life had changed by the 1900s and to cite the inventions that helped to bring about the changes. Finally, ask students how the nature of work changed during this period.

In Depth

Multicultural Perspectives

Many workers came from China to California during the gold rush of the mid-1800s. The Chinese workers caught the attention of railroad owners who recruited them when they found it difficult to attract other workers to the hard labor and low wages that were offered. Of the 12,000 men who worked to build the Central Pacific Railroad, 10,000 were Chinese. They were paid $26 a month—less than the other workers—and out of this sum they paid Central Pacific for their food and lodging. All other workers were paid $35 a month and given free food and lodging.

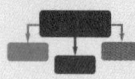
Reinforcing the Big Idea

The inventions and discoveries of the late 1800s required entrepreneurs to bring them to market. Businesses grew and consolidated, becoming huge corporations and monopolies. Workers, however, were poorly paid and worked under harsh conditions. They soon took action through labor unions. The next section describes the intensity of the struggle between labor and management.

In Depth

Interdisciplinary

Jacob Riis was a New York City police reporter who used his camera to document the squalid conditions of the working poor. Although newspapers lacked the equipment needed to print his photographs, in 1888 the *New York Sun* published twelve drawings from his pictures. The photographs in his 1890 book *How the Other Half Lives* proved to be powerful tools in the campaign for social reform.

---

workers. As one woman put it, when "they gave us twelve looms I didn't see that we could make it out alive."

Hardships of Factory Work Bosses seldom visited the factory floor where their workers toiled. Workers seldom saw a finished product. Called hands or operatives, they were viewed as cogs in a huge system performing only a small piece of the system's work. One factory manager in 1883 declared,

> I regard my people as I regard my machinery. So long as they can do my work for what I choose to pay them, I keep them, getting out of them all I can. What they do or how they fare outside my walls I don't know, nor do I consider it my business to know.

Discipline was strict. A worker could be fined or fired for being late, answering back, refusing to do a task, talking, or other minor offenses. The noise of the machines was deafening. Lighting and ventilation were poor. Fatigue, faulty equipment, and careless training resulted in frequent fires and accidents. The courts in the late 1800s held that a worker who sued an employer over an injury had to show that the employer was responsible for causing it. This was usually impossible.

Despite the harsh conditions, employers suffered no shortage of labor. Thousands of Irish, German, and Italian immigrants, for example, built the Brooklyn Bridge. The nation's factories were likewise jammed with men, women, and children, many desperate for the opportunity to earn even meager wages.

Industry's Impact on Women and Children Employers in industry excluded women from the most skilled and highest-paid jobs, assigning to them the operation only of simple machines. More complex machines required machinists and engineers. These were almost always men, for only they had access to training in such fields.

Women enjoyed almost no chances for advancement in factory work. In the garment industry, for example, running the machines that cut out patterns from large stacks of fabric was defined as a man's job. It paid much more than work reserved for women, which usually consisted of performing only one part of the process of sewing a garment.

Children also suffered in the factory system. Today, the use of child labor is strictly regulated by law. In the 1880s, however, children made up more than 5 percent of the industrial labor force. In many households, children's wages meant the difference between going hungry or having food on the table.

Children especially suffered from the hazards of the workplace. Working in unhealthful factories or mines, living on inadequate diets, and performing monotonous, dangerous work, many children became stunted in both body and mind. The practice of child labor would come under attack in the early 1900s. By 1912, three fourths of the states would have laws limiting the presence of children in the workplace.

SECTION 1 REVIEW

Key Terms, People, and Places
1. Define (a) social Darwinism, (b) monopoly, (c) cartel, (d) trust, (e) horizontal consolidation, (f) vertical consolidation.
2. Identify Andrew Carnegie.

Key Concepts
3. What were some of the factors that helped spur economic development after the Civil War?

4. Why did manufacturers form cartels and trusts?
5. What made life for working people so difficult in times of economic hardship?

Critical Thinking
6. **Identifying Central Issues** Review the quotations by Taylor and the factory manager in this section. What do their statements reveal about their views of working men and women?

▶ RESOURCE DIRECTORY

Teaching Resources

Quiz found in the Unit 2 folder, p. 81, covers the main ideas in this section as well as the key terms.

Drawing Conclusions

Drawing conclusions means finding out an answer or forming an opinion based on information that is suggested but not stated directly. When you read about history or any subject, it is important to be able to draw conclusions. Then you can go beyond what is presented in textbooks and other sources and form new insights about a historical period or event.

Use the following steps and the political cartoon from the late 1800s that appears on this page to practice drawing conclusions.

1. Study the facts and ideas that the cartoonist presents. Review the cartoon, and then answer the fol-

lowing questions. (a) Who do the men on the top represent? (b) Who are the people holding up the men on the top? (c) What does the water represent?

2. Make a summary statement as a conclusion about a group of details. A statement that summarizes the major point of the cartoon is one type of conclusion. Clarify the cartoonist's position by summarizing the basic information contained in the drawing. Then answer the following questions. (a) What can you conclude about the relationship between the workers and the business leaders? Explain your answer. (b) Who do you

think the cartoonist is criticizing? Why?

3. Decide whether or not you can draw a conclusion based on what is provided. If the information is not sufficient, it is possible to jump to a faulty conclusion. As you answer these questions, you are deciding whether you have enough information to draw conclusions. (a) Has the cartoonist provided enough information to draw a fair conclusion? (b) What do you think a cartoon drawn from the opposite point of view might look like? (c) How do you think industry leaders would have reacted to this cartoon?

PUCK.

THE PROTECTORS OF OUR INDUSTRIES.

Historian's Toolbox Activity Drawing Conclusions, found in the Unit 2 folder, p. 96, uses contrasting maps designed to enhance students' application of this skill.

TOOLBOX

Critical Thinking
Drawing Conclusions

Focus Examine a political cartoon from the late 1800s to practice drawing conclusions.

Instruct Present students with these statements: "Workers in factories in the late 1800s labored under the best of conditions. Clean, well-lit work areas, more than adequate safety equipment, and humane policies of worker's compensation, sick days, and hours were the norm." Ask students for their opinions of these statements. Students should say that the statements are false and inaccurately describe working conditions in the late 1800s. Then ask students why the ability to draw conclusions is important.

Extend See the Historian's Toolbox Activity in the Resource Directory below.

Answers

1. (a) business leaders (b) workers (c) The water represents "hard times."

2. The cartoonist believes that business leaders take advantage of workers and ride on their backs while the workers suffer hard times and poor pay. He or she ridicules the idea that business leaders are "the protectors of our industries." (a) The relationship is an unequal one, because the workers toil and suffer while the business leaders ride along in luxury and wealth. (b) The cartoonist is criticizing the business leaders who enjoy the fruits of the workers' labors but do not consider whether or not they are treating those workers fairly.

3. (a) No, the cartoonist is presenting only one side of the issue, and that information is colored by his or her own perspective. (b) Answers will vary but students should show an understanding of the point of view of the business leader. (c) Some industry leaders would probably have been angered by the cartoon, feeling that it did not fairly represent conditions in their factories or their attitudes toward their workers. Others, for example those who considered their workers no more than machinery, might not have been concerned about the cartoon at all.

SECTION 2

The Great Strikes: A Turning Point in History

1. FOCUS

Connecting to the Big Idea

See page 226B. Explain to students that the late nineteenth century was a period of intense struggle between big business and workers. Workers organized themselves to change working conditions, while management did everything in its power to prevent their success. Explain to students that they will be examining how effective the labor unions formed in the late nineteenth century were in changing working conditions.

Objectives

● Explain why the gap between rich and poor widened in the late 1800s.
● Identify the aims of labor unions to improve workers' wages and working conditions.
● Describe how violent strikes marked relations between labor unions and business owners in the late 1800s.

Bellringer

Have students work in pairs to brainstorm several possible courses of action in the following situation: Workers at a fast-food restaurant are told on Monday that unless they agree to work four additional evening hours each week for no additional pay, they will be fired. As students read the section, have them list on a separate sheet of paper any option that uses the concept of collective bargaining as defined on page 238.

Reading Strategy

Reinforcing Key Ideas Ask students to make two columns on their paper, headed Successes and Failures. As they read, ask students to note the successes and failures of labor unions in the appropriate column.

SECTION PREVIEW

Many American workers sought relief from their difficulties through labor unions. What they found in the late 1800s was strong resistance from big business and only fleeting success.

Key Concepts
• The gap between rich and poor widened in the late 1800s.
• Labor unions organized to improve the wages and working conditions of workers.
• Violent strikes marked relations between labor unions and business owners in the late 1800s.

Key Terms, People, and Places
socialism, collective bargaining, scab, anarchist; Pinkerton; Haymarket Square, Homestead, Pullman strike

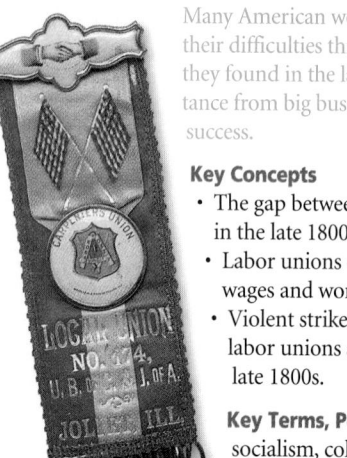

Workers in many industries formed unions in the late 1800s.

I ndustrialization brought changes and great wealth to the United States. These changes, however, did not bring contentment or prosperity to the nation's working people. Indeed, as the rich grew richer during this era, these workers became increasingly bitter over their own daily struggle for a decent standard of living. During the last quarter of the nineteenth century, working men and women began to take their complaints directly and forcefully to their employers. The resulting turmoil marked a turning point in American history.

The Widening Gulf Between Rich and Poor

The 1890 census revealed that the richest 9 percent of Americans held nearly 75 percent of the national wealth. The nation's workers, however, did not need the census to tell them that they were poor. Able in the best of times to earn only a few hundred dollars a year, workers were well aware of how the elite lived, and they resented it. ✪

Poor families had little hope of relief when hard times hit. Some suffered in silence, trusting that tomorrow would be better; others became politically active in an effort to improve their difficult lives. A few of these individuals were drawn to the idea of socialism then gaining popularity in many European industrialized countries.

Socialism in the Industrial Age

Socialism is an economic and political philosophy that advocates collective or government ownership of factories and property. One goal of socialism is to distribute broadly a society's wealth. In the late 1800s, socialism was strongly influenced by the ideas of Karl Marx, a German philosopher who criticized the capitalist economic system and predicted its eventual overthrow by workers.

Endorsing socialism in the late 1800s was dangerous, however. Most Americans disagreed with socialist theory. They felt that socialism threatened the deeply rooted American ideals of private property and free enterprise—the right of people to compete freely and succeed to whatever extent they can. Most wealthy people also rejected socialism. They would not give up what they owned without a fight. Even though workers had numbers on their side, wealthy Americans knew that if workers tried to bring socialism to the United States by force, the federal government would respond with military action to preserve the nation's economic and political system.

▶ RESOURCE DIRECTORY

Teaching Resources

Reproducible Lesson Plan found in the Unit 2 folder, p. 76, provides a summary of the Section 2 lesson plan content.

Alternate Lesson Plan: Critical Thinking Determining Relevance, found in the Alternate Lesson Plans folder, p. 80, is designed to help students apply this skill by using a classification system for arranging the section.

Guided Reading and Review found in the Unit 2 folder, p. 82, provides a structure for reading and mastering the key concepts and reviewing the key terms for Section 2. (Guided Practice)

Literature Activity *Sister Carrie*, found in the Unit 2 folder, pp. 100–101, introduces students to factory life in the late 1800s with an excerpt from Theodore Dreiser's novel.

Using Historical Evidence Many workers lived in crowded boarding houses, such as the one shown at left. Many wealthy industrialists, on the other hand, enjoyed great personal wealth and luxurious comforts. *How would you expect workers to respond to the contrast between rich and poor?*

Caption Answer to ...

Using Historical Evidence

Many workers were outraged at the contrast between the enormous wealth of the few industrialists and their own poverty.

The Return of Labor Unions

Socialism itself never achieved a significant following in the United States in the nineteenth century. But the limited appeal of its themes did reflect a growing discontent among the nation's workers. Many of these men and women looked instead to labor unions as a way to improve their standard of living.

Early Labor Unions The early years of industrialization had spawned a few labor unions, organized among workers in certain trades, such as construction and textile manufacturing. But these early unions had not lasted long.

Unions resurfaced after the Civil War. These groups were initially designed to provide help for their members in bad times. Soon they became the means for channeling workers' demands for shorter workdays, higher wages, and better working conditions. The increasing emphasis on protest led to growing opposition to unions among employers.

Unions grew significantly in the 1860s and 1870s. Indeed, labor activists began trying to organize nationally based unions. One, the National Labor Union formed in Baltimore in 1866, nominated a candidate for the presidential election of 1872. This union, however, failed to survive an economic downturn that began the following year. Indeed, unions in general suffered a steep decline in membership as a result of the depression.

The Knights of Labor Another early national union, The Noble Order of the Knights of Labor, was formed in Philadelphia in 1869. The Knights hoped to organize virtually all working men and women into a single union. Membership included farmers, factory workers, and white-collar workers. The union actively recruited African Americans, of whom sixty thousand joined.

Under the dynamic leadership of former machinist Terence Powderly, the Knights pursued broad social reforms. These included equal pay for equal work, the eight-hour day, and an end to child labor.

The leadership of the Knights did not generally advocate the use of strikes, and they did not emphasize higher wages as their primary goal. The majority of members, however, often differed with the leadership. In fact, it was a strike that helped the Knights achieve their

In Depth

Multicultural Perspectives

Fifteen African Americans were inducted into a British Chartered Lodge of Freemasons at Boston Harbor in 1775. After the American Revolution, the group was chartered as African Lodge No. 459. Out of these organizations, and their auxiliary activities such as insurance and burial societies, arose the founders of the first African American–owned insurance companies and banks. Around the turn of the century, John Merrick and Alonzo F. Herndon, both formerly enslaved and barbers, each founded an insurance company. Merrick started North Carolina Life, and Herndon formed Atlanta Life.

Media and Technology

Visions of America: Turning Point Story To enhance students' understanding of the Turning Point topic in this section, play "Company Town," a story about the Pullman Strike of 1894 (length: approximately 4 minutes). This selection can be located on side 2 of the videodiscs. This selection can also be located on videotape 3. Lesson plans for Turning Point stories can be found in the Visions of America Teacher's Guidebook.

Visions of America: Roundtable Discussion To introduce students to different and differing viewpoints on the Turning Point topic in this section, play all or part of the Roundtable Discussion on "Company Town," remarks by respected historians and social commentators. This selection can be located on side 2 of the videodiscs. This selection can also be located on videotape 3.

Side 2, Chapter 17

Side 2, Chapter 18

Answer to ...

Viewpoints

The labor leader wants more government protection for workers; the factory manager wants less government involvement with labor. For a more thorough examination of views about labor unions, see the Resource Directory below.

2. INSTRUCT

Explain

Ask students to consider what ingredients were required for the nation's tremendous industrial surge following the Civil War. Point out that workers were in abundant supply. Ask students to describe how workers were treated by employers.

Discuss

Discuss with students how socialism, anarchism, and labor unions were all political movements that aimed to solve the problems of workers. Ask them to identify how socialism promised to improve workers' lives. Then ask what American ideals run counter to the goals of socialism. Ask students to describe public reaction to the incidents at Haymarket and Homestead. What pattern of events did the Pullman strike set in motion for many years to come?

TURNING POINTS

greatest strength. In 1885, when unions affiliated with the Knights forced railroad owner Jay Gould to give up a wage cut, membership quickly soared to 700,000. Yet a series of failed strikes quickly followed, dampening enthusiasm in the Knights. They had largely disappeared as a national force by the 1890s.

The American Federation of Labor A third national union, the American Federation of Labor (AFL) followed the leadership of Samuel Gompers, a London-born cigar maker. Formed in 1886, the AFL differed from the Knights of Labor by seeking to organize only skilled workers in a network of smaller unions, each devoted to a specific craft. Between 1886 and 1892, the AFL gained some 250,000 members. Yet they still represented only a tiny portion of the nation's labor force.

In theory the AFL was open to African Americans. Local unions, however, often found ways to exclude African Americans from their membership. Gompers also opposed women members because he believed that their participation in the work force drove wages down.

> We know to our regret that too often are wives, sisters and children brought into the factories and workshops only to reduce the wages and displace the labor of men—the heads of families.
>
> Samuel Gompers, *Labor and the Employer*, 1887

Gompers and the AFL were primarily interested in issues of wages, hours, and working conditions—so-called bread-and-butter unionism. They sought to force employers to participate in **collective bargaining,** in which workers nego-

---

Viewpoints
On Labor Unions

The Senate Committee on Education and Labor held a series of hearings concerning the relationships between workers and management in 1883. The committee heard these opposing views about the need for labor unions. **What is the major argument presented in each of the two viewpoints below?**

Testimony of a Labor Leader

"The laws written [by Congress] and now in operation to protect the property of the capitalist and the moneyed class generally are almost innumerable, yet nothing has been done to protect the property of the workingmen, the only property that they possess, their working power, their savings bank, their school, and trades union."

Samuel Gompers, founder of the American Federation of Labor in 1886

Testimony of a Factory Manager

"I think that . . . in a free country like this . . . it is perfectly safe for at least the lifetime of this generation to leave the question of how a man shall work, and how long he shall work, and what wages he shall get to himself."

Thomas L. Livermore, manager for the Amoskeag Manufacturing Company, Manchester, New Hampshire

---

tiate as a group with employers. The Federation believed that workers acting as a group had more power than a worker acting individually. To strengthen its collective bargaining power, the Federation advocated a "closed shop" that employed only Federation members.

Growing Friction Between Labor and Employers

Not surprisingly, employers disliked and feared unions. They preferred to deal with employees as individuals instead of in powerful groups. Employers took measures to stop unions, such as forbidding union meetings and firing union organizers. They even forced new employees to sign "yellow dog" contracts that exacted a promise never to join a union or to participate in a strike. Some business leaders refused to recognize unions as the workers' legitimate representatives. Wrote one company president:

RESOURCE DIRECTORY

Teaching Resources

Viewpoints Activity On Labor Unions, found in the Unit 2 folder, pp. 94–95, provides additional viewpoints and perspectives on the responsibilities of labor, business, and government in an industrial age.

---

*R*ights and interests of the laboring man will be protected and cared for—not by the labor agitators, but by the Christian men to whom God has given control of the property interests of the country.

> George F. Baer, mining
> company president, 1902

Unions, of course, demanded more than recognition. The competing interests of labor and employers would not be easily reconciled.

MAKING CONNECTIONS

Consider the statement above by George F. Baer. How does it relate to the idea of social Darwinism discussed in Section 1?

The Railroad Strike of 1877

The nation's first major episode of labor unrest occurred in the summer of 1877 in the railroad industry. The strike began when the Baltimore and Ohio Railroad announced a wage cut of 10 percent, the second cut in eight months. Railroads elsewhere imposed similar cuts, along with orders to run "double headers," trains with two engines, twice as many cars—and an increased risk of accident and worker layoffs. Violent reactions against these moves among railway workers spread rapidly across Pennsylvania and Ohio and on to Chicago, Illinois, and St. Louis, Missouri. When the local militia in Pittsburgh refused to stop the unrest, employers called in troops from Philadelphia, who fired on the demonstrators, killing and wounding many. A crowd of twenty thousand angry men and women reacted to the shootings by setting fire to railroad company property. President Rutherford B. Hayes then sent in federal troops, a move that stopped the riots but caused more deaths.

From the 1877 strike on, employers relied on federal and state troops to repress labor unrest. A new and violent era in labor relations had begun.

Strikes Rock the Nation

The period 1881–1900 was one continuing industrial crisis in the United States. An amazing

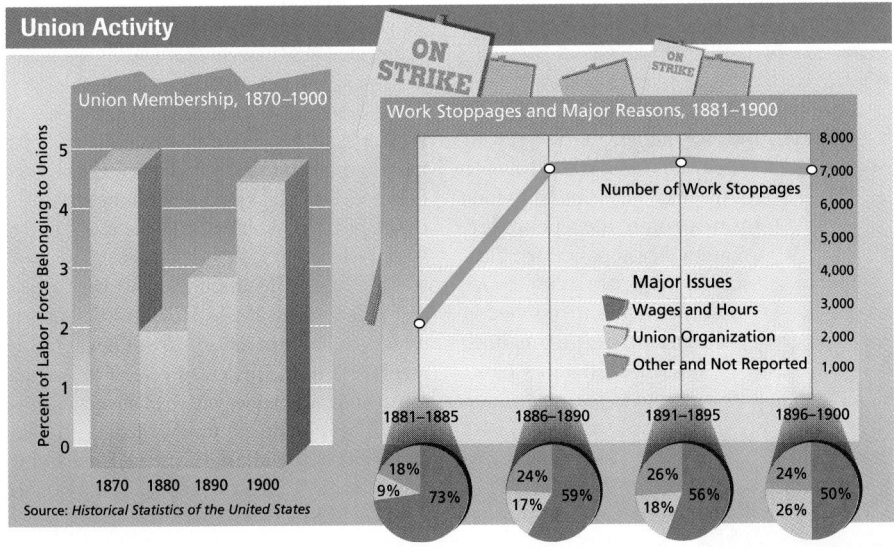

Union Activity

Union Membership, 1870–1900

Work Stoppages and Major Reasons, 1881–1900

Interpreting Graphs
A severe economic depression helped cause a steep decline in union membership in the 1870s. But the 1880s and 1890s saw growth in the numbers of members and in work stoppages. *What trends can you identify in the causes of work stoppages in the late 1800s?*

Source: *Historical Statistics of the United States*

Answer to ...
MAKING CONNECTIONS

Answer to ...
MAKING CONNECTIONS

Answers will vary but may point out that the speaker expresses the belief that one group—the employers—has a special power or ability to take care of the workers, who by implication are less fit. Encourage students to see how attitudes and actions reflect a certain idea or belief.

Caption Answer to ...

 Interpreting Graphs

As a percentage of work stoppages, disputes over union organization increased, while strikes over wages and hours decreased.

In Depth

Historical Misconceptions

Though the cost of manufactured consumer goods dropped because of industrialization, working-class women had difficulty affording these finished goods. Women's wages and advancement opportunities were far below those of men. African American women were even worse off, being excluded from most factory positions until World War I. Consider the average earnings of a working woman and the price of consumer goods: Factories paid the average woman worker $5 a week; department stores paid $2 a week plus 5 percent commission; and families paid domestic servants $3 a week plus board. A ready-made blouse cost $1, a skirt $2, and a pair of shoes $1.50. Carfare for sales clerks was a nickel each way, and a dormitory bed cost $2.50 a week.

Activity

(The clock icon indicates an activity that can be successfully conducted within a class period. Each chapter has at least one such activity.)

Teaching Heterogeneous Groups

To enable all students to understand the different perspectives of the parties involved in labor disputes of the late nineteenth century, assign students the following roles: Pinkerton, strikebreaker or scab, anarchist, laborer (skilled and unskilled), recent immigrant, business owner, union leader. Based on their reading, have students write a description of their roles and what they hope to achieve in an industrial dispute.

Enrichment

Ask students to research both socialism and Andrew Carnegie's theories of wealth. Then have them work in pairs to write a dialogue between a socialist and Andrew Carnegie, in which both discuss their respective beliefs on wealth.

TURNING POINTS

24,000 strikes erupted in the nation's factories, mines, mills, and yards during those two decades alone. Out of this ongoing turmoil, three major incidents of industrial warfare overshadow the rest. ★

Haymarket, 1886 On May 1, 1886, several workers' groups mounted a national demonstration for an eight-hour work day. "Eight hours for work, eight hours for rest, eight hours for what we will," ran the cry. Strikes then broke out in a number of cities. At Chicago's McCormick reaper factory, police broke up a fight between strikers and **scabs,** strikebreakers who replace striking workers and allow a company to continue operating. The police action caused several casualties among the workers.

In protest, **anarchists** called a rally for the evening of May 4 in Chicago's **Haymarket Square.** Anarchists are political radicals who oppose all government on the grounds that it limits individual liberty and acts in the interests of the wealthy, ruling classes. In an effort to whip up the anger of the workers, anarchist newspaper editor August Spies wrote

The violence of the Haymarket incident, depicted here, troubled many Americans.

> Y ou have endured the pangs of want and hunger; your children you have sacrificed to the factory-lords. In short, you have been miserable and obedient slaves all these years. Why? To satisfy the insatiable greed, to fill the coffers of your lazy thieving master!

At the May 4 event, someone threw a bomb into a police formation. Seven policemen died, and in the ensuing riot, police and citizen gunfire resulted in dozens of deaths on both sides. Investigators never found the bomb thrower, yet eight anarchists were tried for conspiracy to commit murder. Four were hanged. Another committed suicide in jail. In the belief that the convictions were the result of public hysteria rather than evidence, Governor John P. Altgeld of Illinois later pardoned the remaining three anarchists.

To many unionists, the Haymarket anarchists forever would be heroes. To employers, they remained vicious criminals determined to overthrow law and order. In many people's minds, unions were associated with violence and radical ideas. The Knights of Labor especially suffered from this public reaction.

Homestead, 1892 Continued labor unrest renewed fears of social revolution. It was in this environment that labor strife struck Andrew Carnegie's enterprise.

A union of iron and steel workers associated with the American Federation of Labor had negotiated a labor contract with Andrew Carnegie's steel company. In the summer of 1892, while Carnegie was in Europe, his partner Henry Frick tried to cut wages for company workers. The union at the Carnegie plant in **Homestead,** Pennsylvania, called a strike.

Frick, perhaps with Carnegie's support, was intent on crushing the union. On July 1, Frick called in the **Pinkertons,** a private police force known for its ability to break strikes. Under cover of darkness, three hundred Pinkertons moved up the Monongahela River on barges. When strikers fired on them from the shore, deaths and injuries occurred on both sides.

At first many Americans sympathized with the workers. Then anarchist Alexander Berkman tried and failed to assassinate Frick. Although Berkman was unconnected with the strike, the public associated his act with the rising tide of labor violence.

Eventually, the union acknowledged defeat and called off the strike. Homestead reopened under militia protection. "I will never recognize the Union, never, never!" Frick cried. Meanwhile, Carnegie, who had always claimed to support nonviolent unions, remained silent about the entire affair. Carnegie Steel and its successor (U.S. Steel) remained nonunionized until the late 1930s.

Pullman, 1894 Like the strike of 1877, the last of the great strikes also involved the railroad industry. This strike also completed a turning

▶ RESOURCE DIRECTORY

Teaching Resources

American Profiles Activity found in the Unit 2 folder, p. 92, profiles Mary Kenney O'Sullivan, who campaigned for legislation to regulate and improve working conditions in factories.

point in the federal government's involvement with labor-employer relations.

Sleeping-car maker George Pullman considered himself one of the era's most benevolent industrialists. He built a town for his workers near Chicago that boasted a school, bank, water and gas systems, and comfortable homes.

Conditions in the town, however, took a turn for the worse during a depression in 1893. Pullman laid off workers and cut wages 25 to 40 percent. Meanwhile, he kept rent and food prices in his town at the same levels. In May 1894, a delegation of workers went to him to protest. Pullman's response was to fire three of the workers. When the American Railway Union called a strike, Pullman refused to negotiate and shut down the plant.

The founder of the American Railway Union was Eugene V. Debs, a popular labor organizer from Indiana. By June 1894, Debs had encouraged 120,000 railway workers throughout the region to join in the **Pullman strike.** Though Debs had instructed strikers not to interfere with the nation's mail, the strike led to the complete disruption of western railroad traffic, including the delivery of the mail.

Railroad owners turned to the federal government for help. Arguing that the mail had to get through—and citing the Sherman Antitrust Act—Attorney General Richard Olney won court orders forbidding all union activity that halted railroad traffic. President Grover Cleveland sent in troops to ensure that strikers obeyed the court orders. Twelve deaths and many arrests resulted from ensuing violence.

Debs, who refused to obey the court orders, was jailed for six months. Its leadership in disarray, the American Railway Union and its strike fell apart.

The Pullman strike and its outcome set an important pattern. In the years ahead, factory owners appealed frequently for court orders against unions. The federal government regularly responded to these appeals, denying unions recognition as legally protected organizations. This official government opposition helped limit union gains for over thirty years.

Eugene Debs was a tremendously successful labor organizer in the late 1800s. Later, Debs would combine his energetic style and his belief in socialism to conduct several unsuccessful presidential campaigns as the leader of the Socialist party.

TURNING POINTS

SECTION 2 REVIEW

Key Terms, People, and Places
1. Identify (a) socialism, (b) scab, (c) anarchist, (d) collective bargaining.
2. Identify (a) the Pinkertons, (b) Haymarket Square, (c) Homestead, (d) Pullman strike.

Key Concepts
3. How did industrial growth in the late 1800s affect the distribution of wealth?

4. Explain the purpose and goals of labor unions.
5. How successful were labor unions in the late 1800s?

Critical Thinking
6. **Recognizing Bias** Many labor unions did not include or effectively represent the concerns of women or minorities. What does this fact suggest about their view of worker rights?

Quiz found in the Unit 2 folder, p. 83, covers the main ideas in this section as well as the key terms.

---

3. ASSESS

Section 2 Review Answers

1. (a) socialism, see p. 236, (b) scab, see p. 240, (c) anarchist, see p. 240, (d) collective bargaining, see p. 238,

2. (a) Pinkertons, see p. 240, (b) Haymarket Square, see p. 240, (c) Homestead, see p. 240, (d) Pullman strike, see p. 241.

3. Wealth was heavily concentrated in the hands of a few.

4. Labor unions sought strength in numbers through collective bargaining. Their main goals were to improve wages and working conditions.

5. Labor was generally not successful in the large strikes of the late 1800s.

6. These policies reflect a belief that white men were superior to women and minorities and therefore deserved to have their rights protected first.

Reteach

Ask students to create a chart titled Labor Movement with the following two column headings: Causes and Effects. Have students then list in the appropriate column the causes and effects of the development of the labor movement in the 1800s.

4. CLOSE

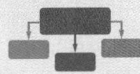 **Reinforcing the Big Idea**

Industrial growth in the late 1800s resulted in a more uneven distribution of wealth, with a widening gap between rich industrialists and poor laborers. Although unions were organized to improve workers' conditions, opposition from employers resulted in violent strikes and enormous suffering. The next section describes the movement to the West and the conflicts that resulted from it.

The Lasting Impact of the Great Strikes

Focus The Great Strikes of the late 1800s caused the federal government to intervene in business-labor disputes, a change from its former "hands off" policy. Since that time, the government has regularly set guidelines and policies for unions and businesses. At the turn of the century, government policy favored business; at other times, government action furthered the cause of labor. Ask students what the lasting impact of government intervention in business-labor disputes has been.

Instruct Divide the class into two groups. Assign one group the year 1890 and the other the year 1990. Ask each group to decide the probable government policy for that date in the following hypothetical situation: The nation's electrical workers go out on strike seeking higher wages and stricter safety regulations. Some other unions, including transportation and communications workers, strike in sympathy with the electrical workers. Soon the nation's communications and transportation will be at a standstill. How does the government act to help resolve the situation?

Review with students the reason that federal policy began to favor workers during the Great Depression and moved to restrict union activity in the late 1940s.

Ask students to work in small groups to discuss what they consider the ideal government approach to business-labor disputes. Should government policy favor one side or the other? Is a perfectly balanced approach possible or desirable? What do people do if they do not agree with the government's labor policy?

The Lasting Impact of the Great Strikes

The federal government adopted a hands-off approach to business and its relations with its employees throughout much of the 1800s. By the turn of the century, however, government had become a central player in the ongoing struggle between business and labor unions.

The Great Strikes of the late 1800s marked the turning point for this fundamental change in government policy. Since that time, the federal government has regularly involved itself in business-labor relations. The government's position has been either more probusiness or prolabor, depending on the changing circumstances of the day. Over time, while supporting law and order, it has tried more and more often to encourage the two sides to negotiate their grievances.

After the Great Strikes

After the strikes of the late 1800s, many business owners felt little need to deal with unions. They were confident that in the event of labor unrest, government would come to their aid with guns or court orders. Labor, meanwhile, continued its struggle without any government protection. Unions enjoyed no legal right to strike, picket, bargain collectively, or recruit members without interference or threat of losing their jobs.

Some employers did conclude that it was better to work with unions than to fight them. Most, however, remained hostile, while continuing to enjoy the support of the federal government for the first three decades of the twentieth century.

1903 The Women's Trade Union League forms to urge women to join unions, since male-dominated unions seldom recruit women members.

1932 As the economy crumbles and millions lose their jobs, the government begins to consider offering more support to workers.

1900   1920   1940

1935 With President Roosevelt's support, the Wagner Act is passed, guaranteeing workers' rights to join unions and bargain collectively.

▶ RESOURCE DIRECTORY

Teaching Resources

Turning Points Extension Activity
The Lasting Impact of the Great Strikes, found in the Unit 2 folder, pp. 90–91, aims to extend students' understanding of the long-term impact of the Great Strikes by contrasting the views of labor with those of business, and by profiling a case study of a business today.

How the Depression, the New Deal, and World War II Affected Labor

In the 1930s, the federal government again intervened in labor-business relations. Now, however, government took a more prolabor position.

The Great Depression of the 1930s had a deep impact on American attitudes toward business and labor. Sympathy for the cause of labor—and distrust of business—increased among the public and in the federal government. In 1932, Congress passed the Norris-LaGuardia Act, which included provisions that limited the power of the federal courts when acting against unions.

President Franklin Roosevelt's administration also supported several prolabor laws. The most significant was the Wagner Act of 1935, which protected labor's right to organize and to bargain collectively. After more than thirty years of hostility, the federal government was now officially recognizing unions as legitimate organizations.

The federal government again adjusted its position on labor issues following World War II. Postwar prosperity in the United States led labor to seek a greater share of the nation's wealth. The result was a record number of strikes, which aroused national concern. In 1947, the Taft-Hartley Act introduced a number of new restrictions on union activity. For example, the law set guidelines for government response to strikes that involved matters of public health and safety.

Government and Labor in Recent Years

In recent years, the federal government has continued to regulate and monitor the activities of labor unions. In 1981, President Ronald Reagan ordered the firing of striking members of the Professional Air Traffic Controllers Organization, whose walkout violated federal law. And, in the late 1980s, the Justice Department pursued racketeering charges against the Teamsters' Union in response to allegations of widespread corruption and links to organized crime in that union. In settling the charges in 1989, the Teamsters agreed to reform the process by which the union elects its leaders.

REVIEWING THE FACTS

1. For what reason did business choose not to negotiate with unions in the early 1900s?
2. What events helped shape government's approach to labor in the 1900s?

Critical Thinking

3. **Making Comparisons** Summarize the difference between the federal government's approach to labor in 1900 and today.

1947 Unions seek a greater share of the enormous postwar prosperity in a wave of strikes. Congress passes Taft-Hartley Act to curb union power.

1960   **1980**   **2000**

1962 President John F. Kennedy issues an executive order that protects federal employees' right to organize and bargain collectively, but not to strike.

1993 The Teamsters union hopes to begin a new era following settlement of its dispute with the federal government over charges of corruption.

Extend Ask students to use the indices to newspapers and the *Readers' Guide to Periodical Literature* or Infotrac to find stories about strikes or threats of strikes by health professionals, teachers, and other vital workers. Ask students to summarize the stories and post their summaries in the classroom, along with a statement saying whether or not the group should strike.

Answers

1. They knew they could count on government support in the event of unrest.

2. The Great Depression and World War II had an impact on public opinion and government attitudes.

3. Answers will vary but may include the following: Government essentially sided with employers in 1900, taking the position that unions did not have a legitimate right to act in a way that was unacceptable to their employers. Today, government has assumed a greater role in mediating between labor and business and in setting some of the ground rules by which disputes are resolved.

Moving West

Moving West

Moving West

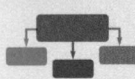

1. FOCUS

Connecting to the Big Idea

See page 226B. Tell students that after the Civil War, large numbers of Americans and Europeans continued to move into "the West," the area between the settled West Coast and the Mississippi River. Explain that these new settlers took over land that had been home to Native Americans for many generations. Ask students what happened to the Native Americans of the West when the settlers moved in.

Objectives

- Identify the ways in which settlers acquired land in the West and describe the demands of their new lives.
- Explain how American expansion into the West led to the near destruction of the Native American nations there.
- Describe how modernization, mechanization, and big business methods transformed agriculture, mining, and ranching in the West.
- Explain why farmers were in financial difficulty at the close of the century and describe how they began to protest their economic plight.

Bellringer

Ask students what they would do if they were moving to another part of the country. What difficulties would they face in leaving their old home and settling into a new one? Why might they choose to face these difficulties?

Reading Strategy

Problem Solving Ask students to list solutions to the following problems as they read the section: how to obtain land, how to locate water, how to work prairie sod.

SECTION PREVIEW

The West was home for thousands of years to Native Americans. But modern farming methods, the discovery of mineral deposits, and ranching soon made the West attractive to many others, including big business.

Key Concepts

- After settlers from the United States acquired land in the West—usually from big business or government grants—they quickly found that their new life meant difficult work and required cooperation with others.
- American expansion into the West led to the near destruction of the Native American nations there.
- Modernization, mechanization, and big business methods transformed agriculture in the West, and also came to dominate mining and ranching industries.
- Farmers began to protest their plight at the close of the century.

Key Terms, People, and Places

Morrill Land-Grant Act, Homestead Act, bonanza farms, deflation; George Armstrong Custer, Chief Joseph, Populists, William Jennings Bryan, Frederick Jackson Turner; Wounded Knee

Only the settlers' most cherished possessions made the trip west.

By the time of the Civil War, Americans already had settled areas west of the Mississippi and along parts of the West Coast. Following the war, Americans and Europeans hoping for a new start in life began filling in the areas in between—the Great Plains, the Pacific Northwest, and the Southwest. To most people in the United States, this land was "the West." It was also the home of Native Americans who had lived there for centuries before.

Seeking Opportunity in the West

Much of the western lands to which people flocked belonged to big businesses—railroad, road and canal, timber, and mining companies. These companies had received huge land grants from the federal government, which they then sold to settlers at a profit.

Settlers also obtained land as a result of the **Morrill Land-Grant Act** of 1862. This act gave 140 million acres of western lands to state governments, which they used to fund agricultural colleges. The states sold their land at fifty cents an acre to bankers and land speculators, who in turn sold it to others at five to ten dollars an acre.

The government also gave land directly to settlers through the 1862 **Homestead Act.** This act offered American citizens and immigrants who planned to be citizens 160 acres of public land each for a ten-dollar registration fee. After building a house and living and farming on the land for five consecutive years, the settler could claim ownership. Thousands benefited from the Homestead Act. By 1900, individual families had filed 600,000 claims for 80 million acres. Meanwhile, however, over six times as much public land had gone to business interests.

No matter how they obtained their land, settlers usually found that life was a struggle in the West. Water was scarce and not always pure. Working the tough prairie sod required backbreaking labor. Men often had to travel far afield to earn cash while waiting for crops to come in. Women produced most of the articles that families needed, such as clothing, soap, candles, dairy products, and preserved foods.

Settlers had to rely heavily on each other. Families cooperated in raising houses and barns, sewing quilts, husking corn, and providing many other forms of mutual support. "Occasionally a new comer has a 'bee'," noted Howard Ruede about his experience on a Kansas homestead in 1877, adding

---

RESOURCE DIRECTORY

Teaching Resources

Reproducible Lesson Plan found in the Unit 2 folder, p. 77, provides a summary of the Section 3 lesson plan content.

Alternate Lesson Plan: Critical Thinking Distinguishing False from Accurate Images, found in the Alternate Lesson Plans folder, p. 81, is designed to help students apply this skill by writing letters from different points of view.

Guided Reading and Review found in the Unit 2 folder, p. 84, provides a structure for reading and mastering the key concepts and reviewing the key terms for Section 3. (Guided Practice)

*T*he neighbors for miles around gather at his claim and put up his house in a day. Of course there is no charge for labor in such cases. The women come too, and while the men lay up the sod walls, they prepare dinner for the crowd, and have a very sociable hour at noon.

MAKING CONNECTIONS

Can you identify and describe similar examples of cooperation in your community today?

The Conquest of the Native Americans

For generations, many Americans envisioned the West as a wild, empty expanse, freely avail-able to those brave enough to tame it. But the West was not empty. Others had laid claim to it centuries before. After the Civil War, as the railroads pushed their way deeper into the West, the Plains began to swarm with settlers. The chances for Native American survival became bleaker.

Some Native Americans resisted the settlers violently. Others initiated friendly contacts. Some tribal leaders signed treaties that sold their lands and accepted government demands that they live within reservations set aside for them. But these agreements tended to fall apart, sometimes because not all members of a particular Native American group supported them. In addition, the Native American concept of land ownership differed from that of settlers. When Native Americans signed treaties, they often did not realize that settlers would not let them continue to use the land. Isolated acts of violence by both settlers and

Answer to ...
MAKING CONNECTIONS

Answers will vary depending on location and experiences. Encourage students to investigate local organizations for such examples .

Caption Answer to ...

 Interpreting Maps

Most of the reservation land is located in the central portion of the continent. Much of this was land that American settlers were not interested in at that time.

Native American Territory and Major Battles, 1860–1900

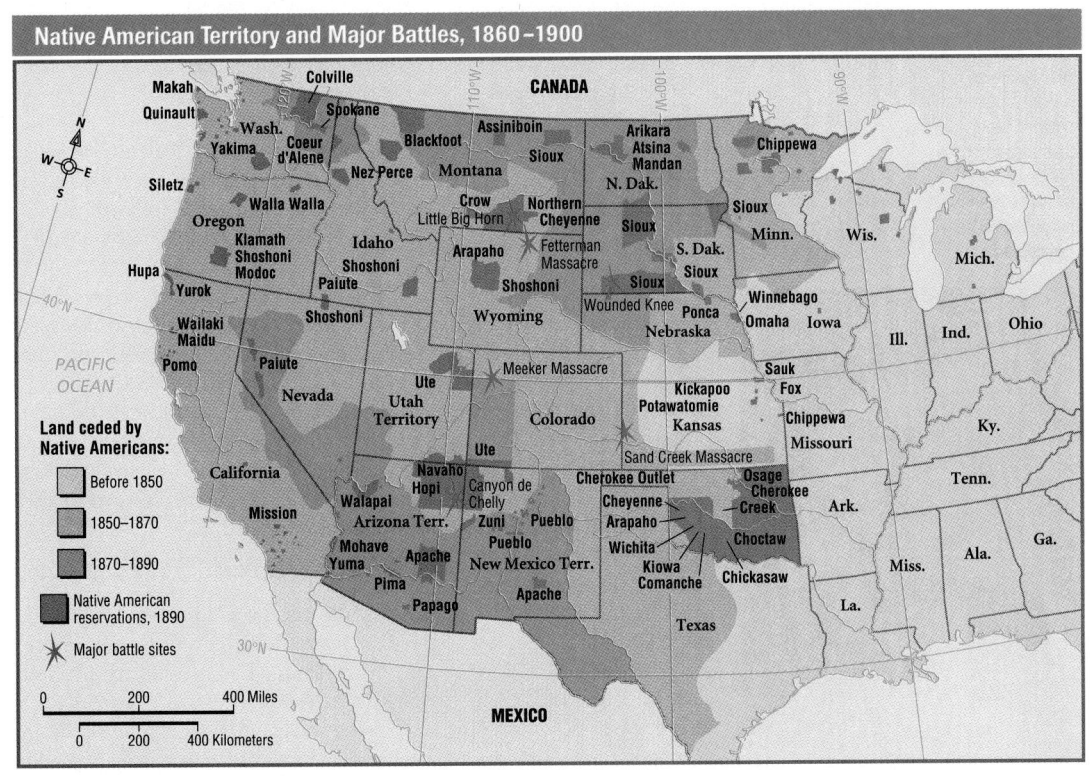

Land ceded by Native Americans:
- Before 1850
- 1850–1870
- 1870–1890
- Native American reservations, 1890
- ✴ Major battle sites

0   200   400 Miles
0   200   400 Kilometers

 Geography and History: Interpreting Maps
Though Native Americans won occasional victories in isolated battles, they were vastly outnumbered and defeat was sure to follow. *What pattern can you see in the location of the remaining Native American reservations in 1890?*

Media and Technology

Transparencies
The Way It Works, H-15; Cause and Effect, F-4

In Depth

Multicultural Perspectives

The town of Wounded Knee has become a continuing symbol of Native American suffering. In March 1973 more than two hundred members of the American Indian Movement (AIM) seized the trading post at Wounded Knee in an attempt to draw national attention to their platform. AIM leaders wanted reforms in the tribal government and demanded Senate hearings on United States treaties with Native American nations. In response, federal law officers surrounded the area. "You have here," said one government official, "an arguable case of treason." The AIM occupation ended in surrender to the federal authorities, but it mobilized other Native American groups and focused attention on recovering title to their tribal territories.

Explain/Discuss

Explain that conditions in parts of the United States and Europe inspired people to head west. Many veterans of the Civil War from New England sought larger, more fertile fields. Many African Americans wanted to leave the restrictive South and obtain land of their own.

Discuss with students some of the rationalizations used to justify taking Native American territory and violating agreements made with Native American groups. Ask students to respond to each rationalization.
• White settlers produced more food and wealth for the country.
• White settlers needed to exact revenge for settlers and soldiers killed by Native Americans.
• Native Americans should be concentrated on a few reservations for their own safety.

Analyze

Explain that pressure for a homestead law began long before 1862. Why did northerners oppose such a law until the Civil War? Ask students to consider the factors that might have made life easier for African Americans in the West.

Ask students what allowed the ranching frontier to flourish. What caused its decline?

Activity

Teaching Heterogeneous Groups

In order for all students to understand the role of organizations such as the Grange, divide students into at least two groups. Members of one group should role-play reporters from an eastern newspaper in 1870; members of the other should act as Grange members. Now pair "reporters" and "Grangers" and ask the reporters to interview the Grangers about why they joined the Grange, what they like about it, and what has disappointed them. **LEP**

Chief Joseph led his Nez Percé on a dramatic flight from United States troops. To his great sadness, he never returned to his homeland.

Native Americans set off cycles of revenge and counter-revenge.

One by one, Native American groups fell. (See the map on page 245 and the table on pages 894–895.) From the 1860s to the 1880s, the Navaho and the Apache of the Southwest were forced onto reservations, starved, or killed in battle. After wars during the 1860s and 1870s, the Cheyenne finally surrendered.

After battling the Cheyenne, Lieutenant Colonel **George Armstrong Custer** attempted to break the power of the Sioux. In June 1876, he moved his cavalry toward the Little Bighorn River in what is now Montana, where he met a larger-than-expected Sioux force. In the clash that followed—the Battle of Little Bighorn—Custer and an entire unit of more than 260 men were killed. This Native American victory did not put an end to the conflict, however. After the death of the Sioux leader, Sitting Bull, more than 200 unarmed Sioux were massacred by soldiers at **Wounded Knee** in 1890. The experience of Sitting Bull and the Sioux was paralleled by that of another Native American leader, Chief Joseph, and his people, the Nez Percé.

AMERICAN PROFILES

Chief Joseph

The Nez Percé inhabited a large area in what is now Idaho and the eastern sections of Washington and Oregon. In the 1850s and 1860s, some Nez Percé signed treaties agreeing to sell their lands to the government. But the largest group, which lived in the Wallowa Valley at the crossroads of the three states, refused. As the chief of this group lay dying in 1871, he made his son and successor, Joseph, swear never to sell their homeland.

Fulfilling that promise proved impossible. After pressuring **Chief Joseph** (1840–1904) for five years, General Oliver Otis Howard finally ordered him and his people to leave Wallowa Valley for a reservation in Idaho. Faced with the threat of superior force, Chief Joseph felt he must give in. Before he could do so, however, a group of Nez Percé youths attacked some settlers who had been accused of stealing Nez Percé horses. The Nez Percé and the United States government were now at war.

Chief Joseph wanted to stay and fight, but his advisory council thought that they could escape. Pursued by soldiers, the Nez Percé fled. Eventually Chief Joseph's group reached Montana. Exhausted, they set up camp at Big Hole Basin, but in a surprise 4:30 A.M. raid, United States soldiers attacked, killing men, women, and children.

The Nez Percé who escaped looked to Canada as their last hope for freedom. On September 30, 1877, less than 40 miles from Canada, Colonel Nelson Miles's cavalry charged them. Heavily outnumbered, Chief Joseph had no choice but to surrender. "I am tired of fighting," he is reported to have said.

> *The old men are dead. The children are freezing to death. Hear me, my chiefs! My heart is sick and sad. From where the sun now stands, I will fight no more forever.*

The government sent Chief Joseph's people to Indian Territory. There, due to heat and malaria, many more Nez Percé died, including all of Joseph's children. In 1885 Chief Joseph and the remaining Nez Percé were allowed to leave the territory for a reservation in present-day Washington state, but the federal government did not allow them to return to their beloved Wallowa Valley.

As white culture gradually overwhelmed the West, many aspects of Native American culture disappeared. The peoples of the Great Plains had relied on the buffalo for food, clothing, shelter, fuel, and tools. By the 1870s, the great buffalo herds began to vanish, hunted by the railroads to feed workers and by settlers to clear the range, to satisfy a craze for hides, and for sport.

Even those whites who protested these events believed that Native Americans needed to be "civilized." This meant, in part, to conform to American farming practices. With the Dawes Act of 1887, the government broke up communal villages and gave separate plots to each Native American family headed by a male. Many sold their lands to speculators: between 1887 and 1934, the amount of land owned by Native Americans shrank by 65 percent.

Farming, Mining, and Ranching

As white settlers spread into the West, they found it a challenge to bring into this different environment the kind of agriculture with which they were familiar. Inventors and industrialists met this challenge and reaped great riches as a result.

Modernization of Farming on the Great Plains The Great Plains was not a farmer's paradise. In addition to unpredictable rainfall and the tough prairie grass, there were grasshoppers, locusts, and boll weevils that ruined crops. In many of the best farming areas of the East, 80 acres of farmland could provide a farmer with a living. In the West, a farmer needed 360 acres to survive. Thus, farmers welcomed any mechanical means to reduce the time and effort needed to work their land.

During the 1870s, improvements in farm implements multiplied. Soon farmers were riding behind a plow rather than walking beside it, and were plowing several furrows at once. By 1880, they were using automatic grain binders. Steam-powered threshers arrived by 1875 and cornhuskers and cornbinders by the 1890s. The new machines did not always lead to farm prosperity, however. They could not protect farmers against insect plagues or bad weather. Moreover, once farmers had invested in machines, they had to produce only the crop for which the machines were designed. If prices for that crop dipped, farmers could not pay off their debts.

All the same, entrepreneurs were willing to invest in new machines and agricultural knowledge, hoping to reap a "bonanza" by supplying food to the rising populations of the East. They applied to farming the same organizational ideas then taking hold in industry. **Bonanza farms,** controlled by large businesses and managed by professionals, specialized in single cash crops. These farms made huge profits, but they had their down side. When the market became glutted with the food they produced, prices fell. Small-scale farmers suffered the most, but even corporate giants felt the blow.

Business Takes Over Mining in the West "Gold!" The word alone conjures up the image of a lucky prospector striking it rich. In reality, such individuals were rare and largely a phenomenon of short periods when people swarmed over gold deposits that were unusually easy to mine, as in the California gold rush of 1849. By the late 1850s and early 1860s, most of the precious metals that remained in the West lay deeply buried. Only huge companies could afford the large investments in machinery, mine shafts, and tunnels required to reach these riches. Like so many other industries, mining became the realm of big business.

The Cattle Frontier American settlers in Texas learned the cattle ranching ways of the Mexicans living there. During the 1860s and 1870s, cattle ranching boomed. The destruction of the buffalo and removal of Native Americans to reservations made room for grazing cattle, and railroads that shipped the cattle to markets across the country made large profits possible.

Looking for wealth, entrepreneurs developed large-scale cattle businesses, complete from cattle ranges to stockyards. But the cattle boom ended in the mid-1880s. One reason was Joseph Glidden's 1874 invention of barbed wire, which allowed farmers to fence their land and keep out grazing cattle. Cold winters, dry summers, and cattle fever also destroyed herds and bankrupted many ranchers. Cattle ranching survived, but only on a much smaller scale.

Farmers Protest Government Policies

While cattle ranchers were struggling, farmers all over the nation in the late 1800s were

By the late 1800s, machines such as those shown in this detail from an advertisement of the time performed many harvesting tasks.

Enrichment

Ask students to compare and contrast the following views of the Great Plains in an essay.

Beret, a Norwegian immigrant in O. E. Rolvaag's novel *Giants in the Earth*, reacts to the stillness and bareness of the Great Plains: "How *could* existence go on, she thought desperately. If life is to thrive and endure, it must at least have something to hide behind!"

Chief Ten Bears, a Comanche from Texas, speaks to a group of government commissioners: "I was born upon the prairie, where the wind blew free and there was nothing to break the light of the sun." [Quoted in *I Have Spoken: American History Through the Voices of the Indians*, compiled by Virginia Irving Armstrong, Ohio U. Press, 1971.]

In Depth

Did You Know?

More than eight hundred diaries written by women who journeyed west between 1840 and 1870 have been published or catalogued in library archives. The writings offer a glimpse into the pioneer woman's point of view and the particular challenges of being a woman homesteader. Although they seldom mention the fact, about one in five women was pregnant or gave birth during the journey. Taboos against discussions of a personal nature prevented women from writing about childbirth, even in their diaries. A comprehensive collection of pioneer women's diaries is found in Johanna L. Stratton's *Pioneer Women, Voices from the Kansas Frontier*. Simon & Schuster, 1981.

In Depth

Interdisciplinary

Songs have always played an important part in American history, and from the 1870s to the turn of the century, popular songs of the agricultural Grange movement contributed to this tradition. There were even special Grange songbooks with song titles such as "The Dear Old Farm," "As We Go Forth to Labor," and "Plow Deep's the Motto." The following verse and refrain from "The Farmer Is the Man," was composed by an unknown writer who agreed with Thomas Jefferson that the farmer is the most important person in society:

When the farmer comes to town
With his wagon broken down,
Oh, the farmer is the man who
        feeds them all!
If you'll only look and see,
I think you will agree,
That the farmer is the man who
        feeds them all!
Refrain:
The farmer is the man,
The farmer is the man,
Lives on credit til the fall;
Then they take him by the hand,
And they lead him from the land,
And the middleman's the one
        who gets it all.

suffering from a long-term decline in crop prices. New farm machinery and agricultural technologies had increased yields, but overproduction had glutted markets. Farmers began trying to solve their problems by changing the government's economic policies.

Farmers and Tariffs One policy farmers protested was the the tariff policy. Tariffs impose duties, or taxes, on imported goods. The purpose of these taxes is to promote the purchase of goods produced within that country. Americans in the late 1800s were divided on the benefit of tariffs. Industrialists claimed that protecting American-made goods protected factory jobs. But tariffs also raised the prices of goods that workers had to buy. Farmers resented the high prices of manufactured goods, but they opposed the "duty free" entry of foreign farm produce into the United States. On the other hand, tariffs on farm imports prevented foreigners from earning the American currency they needed to buy American crops. Thus, tariffs hurt American farmers in two ways: by raising their living expenses at home and by lowering what they could earn abroad. ⭐

Goldbugs, Greenbackers, and Silverites Much as farmers disliked tariffs, in the late 1800s, they became even more concerned about the government's money policy. After the Civil War, the nation's money supply shrank as the federal government took out of circulation the paper money issued during the war. The nation experienced a prolonged period of dropping prices called **deflation.**

Deflation hurt farmers, whose income and ability to pay off their debts depended on high prices for crops. Deflation helped bankers and other lenders, however, because the dollars repaid to them could buy more goods than the dollars they had lent out. Currency policy—the government's plan for the makeup and quantity of the nation's money supply—emerged as a major issue in national politics.

In 1873 the supporters of deflation won a victory when Congress put the nation's currency on a gold standard, which means they made gold the material of value that backed the nation's money. So-called "goldbugs," many of them big lenders, liked the idea of being repaid in currency backed by gold. "Silverites," mostly silver-mining interests and western farmers, were furious. They claimed that the end of silver as a monetary standard would bring down farm produce prices. "Greenbackers" also entered the debate. Hoping for inflation, they argued in favor of more paper money, which was not redeemable in gold or silver.

Economists at the time were vague about the impact of currency amounts and standards on crop prices. Nevertheless, farmers' protests after the 1870s revolved increasingly around the call for "free silver"—by which they meant the unlimited coining of silver dollars as a means of increasing the money supply.

Using Historical Evidence Farmers' Alliances provided an important channel for farmer protest and political action in the late 1800s. This illustration comes from a book of songs for these organizations. *What do the images on this songbook cover reveal about the ideals of the Farmers' Alliances?*

 RESOURCE DIRECTORY

Teaching Resources

⭐ **Visual Learning Activity** The Farmers' Complaint, found in the Unit 2 folder, p. 104, uses an 1875 poster to illustrate the plight of the American farmer.

Organizing Farmer Protest In the late nineteenth century, several farm protest groups formed. The first was the Patrons of Husbandry, or the Grange. Founded in 1867, it helped farmers form cooperatives with the intent of buying goods in large quantities to save money. It also pressured lawmakers to regulate the businesses important to farmers, such as grain elevators and railroads.

Another organization was the Farmers' Alliances, formed in the 1880s. The Alliances attacked monopolies, especially those that controlled the railroads, and favored a greater circulation of currency, state departments of agriculture, antitrust laws, and farm credit.

Federal officials responded weakly to farmers' concerns, including the natural disasters (floods, droughts, and blizzards) that struck the West in the late 1800s, causing widespread misery. Democratic President Grover Cleveland expressed a then commonly held view that "though the people support the government, the government should not support the people." He did, however, sign the Interstate Commerce Act of 1887, which regulated the charges paid to move freight, such as farmers' crops, between states. Cleveland's successor, Republican Benjamin Harrison, approved the Sherman Antitrust Act in 1890. But this act, meant to curb the power of trusts and monopolies, received lax enforcement during its first decade.

Populists Push the Farmers' Program

In 1892 the Farmers' Alliances founded the People's party, which demanded radical economic and social reform. The **Populists,** as the new party's followers were known, called for an increased circulation of money, a silver standard, and a graduated income tax. The Populist party also called for government ownership of the country's transportation and communications systems.

Although populism generated great excitement during the 1892 campaign, the party's presidential candidate barely won a million votes. Democratic candidate Grover Cleveland returned to the presidency.

In the 1896 election, which focused mainly on currency issues, the Republicans ran William McKinley on a gold-standard platform. **William Jennings Bryan,** a former silverite congressman from Nebraska and a powerful speaker, overwhelmed the Democratic party's convention with a plea for free silver. Using images from the Bible, he stood with head bowed and arms outstretched and cried out at the climax of his speech, "You shall not press down upon the brow of labor this crown of thorns. You shall not crucify mankind upon a cross of gold!"

Although Bryan's speech brought him both the Democratic and Populist party nominations, he lost the election. He carried the Democratic West and South but not one of the urban and industrial Midwest and northern states.

By 1897 McKinley's administration had raised the tariff to new heights. In 1900, after new gold finds added more than $100 million worth of gold to the world's supply, Congress again passed a gold standard. To the surprise of many farmers, crop prices began a slow rise that would last until 1920. The silver movement died, as did populism. Yet in the decades ahead, other political thinkers applied populist ideas to urban and industrial problems. In

THE SACRILEGIOUS CANDIDATE.

Using Historical Evidence This cartoon shows William Jennings Bryan wielding the crown of thorns and cross of gold—images that he used in a famous speech. *Is this cartoon presenting Bryan in a positive or a negative light?*

Section 3 Review Answers

1. (a) Morrill Land-Grant Act, see p. 244, (b) Homestead Act, see p. 244, (c) bonanza farms, see p. 247, (d) deflation, see p. 248.

2. (a) George Armstrong Custer, see p. 246, (b) Chief Joseph, see p. 246, (c) Populists, see p. 249, (d) William Jennings Bryan, see p. 249, (e) Frederick Jackson Turner, see p. 250.

3. Wounded Knee, see p. 246.

4. They lived in sod houses and had difficulty finding water; men had to leave home to earn cash, and women had to provide all day-to-day needs. For all settlers, work never stopped.

5. Native Americans were forced onto reservations, and reformers tried to make them adopt the ways of white Americans.

6. The operation of large-scale farms owned by corporations, run according to systems, and managed by professionals.

7. Farmers protested through Granges and Farmers' Alliances, and through the Populists, who nominated William Jennings Bryan for President in 1896.

8. Possible answers: Mechanization increased productivity. High productivity also caused prices to decline hurting farmers. Mechanization also reduced the need for farm labor, increased start-up costs for farmers, and necessitated crop specialization.

Reteach

Ask students to correct each of the following statements:
• Settling on the Great Plains was a relatively easy undertaking.
• Once they had the proper equipment, small farmers prospered on the Great Plains.
• Native Americans and new settlers lived in peace and cooperation in the West.
• Big business played a minor role in the mining frontier, where individual prospectors worked to strike it rich.

Using Historical Evidence

Cody presented white people as being in conflict with Native Americans. Both are depicted with weapons.

Alternative Assessment

Mid-Point Monitoring

Ask students if they have
● Decided on a format for their projects
● Visited the library to begin their outside research
● Started drafting portions of their handbooks

4. CLOSE

Reinforcing the Big Idea

Homesteaders and other settlers moved to the West hoping to build new lives. The Native Americans who already lived there lost access to traditional hunting lands and their traditions. Farmers formed organizations to solve problems. The next section describes politics in the Gilded Age.

In Depth

Then and Now

In the 1870s, store owner Levi Strauss and tailor Jacob David answered the need for stronger, heavier, work clothes. The used white tent canvas to make pants with double-stitched seams and small copper rivets pounded into the corners of the front and back pockets. The new clothes were an immediate success and became even more popular when Strauss and David switched from canvas to tougher, softer, dyed-blue denim.

In the 1950s and 1960s, blue jeans were seen as the symbol of restless, idealistic youth. By the 1990s, international designers had turned them into high-fashion clothing.

---

doing so, they launched new reform programs that shifted the course of United States history.

Frontier Myths and Realities

Using Historical Evidence William F. "Buffalo Bill" Cody became famous by playing up the myths of the American West. This 1890 poster promoted his "Wild West" show. *What does the poster tell you about Cody's presentation of the West?*

As the 1800s came to a close, the opportunities of the American frontier seemed to be disappearing. By 1880 the number of tenant farmers—who rented rather than owned land—had risen, along with the number of large farms owned by corporations. Many farmers were deep in debt. "Free" lands were harder to find. In 1890 the superintendent of the census announced the end of the frontier. Three years later, a young historian named **Frederick Jackson Turner** delivered a speech in which he discussed the end of the frontier and claimed that it had played a central role in forming the American character. The West had forced settlers to shed their old ways and adapt, innovate, and invent, he said.

Historians have since taken some exception to the views of the superintendent and Turner.

They have pointed out that homesteading continued into the twentieth century. In addition, the West had hardly been a land of unlimited opportunity. Boom had inevitably led to bust, especially when prices fell for the commodities settlers relied on to succeed. Rare among those who made it big were African Americans, Asians, Mexicans, or single women. ✪

Other realities included the displacement and destruction of Native Americans and, on the West Coast, the discriminatory treatment of Asian immigrants. Finally, by acting as though the vast natural resources of the West were limitless, settlers and big business had exacted a high toll on the environment.

Despite these realities, frontier myths linger on. Through literature, film, and song, they continue to influence how Americans think about themselves. The myth of the American cowboy began developing as early as the 1870s, popularized by novels and after 1883 by William F. ("Buffalo Bill") Cody's Wild West shows. These shows drew thousands of spectators to rodeos and staged battles between "good" cavalry regiments and "bad" Native Americans.

Frontier myths have left permanent marks on the nation's character. Many classic American songs were inspired by the cowboy era. Songs like "Home on the Range," where the buffalo roamed, and "Don't Fence Me In" gave rise to enduring images of wide open spaces and freedom from the confines of civilization. Although the reality was different, myths fed the spirit of a nation.

SECTION 3 REVIEW

Key Terms, People, and Places
1. Define (a) Morrill Land-Grant Act, (b) Homestead Act, (c) bonanza farms, (d) deflation.
2. Identify (a) George Armstrong Custer, (b) Chief Joseph, (c) Populists, (d) William Jennings Bryan, (e) Frederick Jackson Turner.
3. Identify Wounded Knee.

Key Concepts
4. Describe some of the hardships homesteaders endured.

5. What was the result of United States expansion into Native American lands?
6. What was bonanza farming? Who made use of it?
7. By what means did farmers organize to protest and present their views?

Critical Thinking
8. **Identifying Central Issues** Briefly describe the benefits and drawbacks of new farm machinery and knowledge.

 **RESOURCE DIRECTORY**

Teaching Resources

✪ **American Profiles Activity** found in the Unit 2 folder, p. 93 profiles Nat Love, Alias Deadwood Dick, the legendary African American cowboy.

Quiz found in the Unit 2 folder, p. 85, covers the main ideas in this section as well as the key terms.

Politics in the Gilded Age

SECTION PREVIEW

In the years after Reconstruction, the United States changed from a nation of farms into one of growing businesses, factories, and cities. Yet despite such changes—and sometimes because of them—many problems festered.

Key Concepts
- Unfair business practices led to new government regulations.
- Republicans and Democrats were divided on issues such as tariffs, the currency question, and political reform.
- Political leaders instituted reforms to end corrupt government practices, but these proved largely ineffective.

Key Terms, People, and Places
Gilded Age, laissez-faire, blue laws, Pendleton Act, Interstate Commerce Act; Jacob S. Coxey

---

Many labels have been used to describe the post-Reconstruction era (1877–1900) in the United States. The most famous is the **Gilded Age,** a term coined by writer Mark Twain that implies a thin layer of glitter over a cheap base. Other labels for the period included the Tragic Era and the Dreadful Decades. All of these terms present an unflattering picture of this era. The decades earned their reputation because of widespread corruption in government and business, as well as the failure of the era's Presidents to solve the persistent economic, social, and political problems plaguing the nation. ★

The Political Landscape in the Late 1800s

The United States faced great challenges as it emerged from Reconstruction. Industrial expansion raised factory and farm productivity,

but economic cycles of boom and bust, low wages for workers, and rising farmer debt contributed to feelings of deep discontent among most working people. Others, such as speculators in stocks and land, quickly rose "from rags to riches." Corruption tempted business and political leaders, who also hoped to achieve such dreams of power and wealth. A dissatisfied public demanded reform.

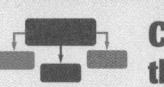

Political campaigns such as William McKinley's presidential bid aroused wide interest in the late 1800s.

Laissez-Faire Policies In the late 1800s, businesses operated largely without government regulation. This **laissez-faire**, or hands-off, approach to economic matters holds that government should play only a very limited role in business. Supporters of this theory maintain that if government doesn't interfere, the strongest businesses will succeed and bring wealth to the nation as a whole.

In the late nineteenth century, most Americans accepted this philosophy in theory. In practice, however, many supported government involvement when it benefited business. For example, champions of the laissez-faire approach favored high tariffs on imported goods. They argued that raising the prices of imported goods discouraged people from buying them, thus helping American businesses, and eventually the economy, to grow. American businesses also willingly accepted government land grants and subsidies—payments made by the government to encourage the development of certain key industries, such as railroads.

Business giants during the Gilded Age supported friendly politicians with both legal and illegal contributions of money. Between 1875 and 1885, the Central Pacific Railroad (CPR) reportedly budgeted $500,000 annually for bribes. CPR cofounder Collis P. Huntington explained, "If you have to pay money to have

1. FOCUS

Connecting to the Big Idea

See page 226B. Explain that national politics during the Gilded Age were uninspired at best. Reformers tried without much success to end the widespread corruption in politics and business. Ask students what national problems plagued the nation during the Gilded Age and why reformers were unable to end corruption.

Objectives
- Identify business practices that led to new government regulations.
- Describe the respective positions of Democrats and Republicans on issues such as tariffs, currency questions, and political reform.
- Explain why the reforms to end corrupt government practices were largely ineffective.

Bellringer

Ask students to list ideas they associate with the word *reformer.* In what areas of American life are reformers trying to make changes today? What factors work against them?

Reading Strategy

Structured Overview Ask students to copy the following Section 4 headings on a piece of paper: The Political Landscape in the Late 1800s, Presidents and Reforms, Railroad Abuses Lead to New Regulations, Efforts to Regulate Tariffs. Then have them scan the section and create subheadings for each of these headings, adding details from the text as they read.

Reproducible Lesson Plan found in the Unit 2 folder, p. 78, provides a summary of the Section 4 lesson plan content.

Alternate Lesson Plan: Learning Styles found in the Alternate Lesson Plans folder, p. 82, is especially helpful for kinesthetic learners and is designed to guide students in enacting a Gilded Age time line.

Guided Reading and Review found in the Unit 2 folder, p. 86, provides a structure for reading and mastering the key concepts and reviewing the key terms for Section 4. (Guided Practice)

Critical Thinking Activity Distinguishing False from Accurate Images: Honest Graft, found in the Unit 2 folder, p. 97, is designed to help students apply this skill by examining a politician's attempted justification of "honest graft."

In Depth

Did You Know?

The corruption of this period is illustrated in the story of the Johnstown Flood of 1889. The developer who purchased the South Fork Dam and its reservoir from Pennsylvania in 1879 had the right friends and political connections. He turned the property into an exclusive fishing and hunting club that counted among its members the entrepreneurs Andrew Mellon and Andrew Carnegie. Officials in the nearby industrial center of Johnstown, about 12 miles east of Stony Creek, persistently warned that the reservoir lake, which could hold approximately 5 billion gallons of water, was unsafe. "You and your people are in no danger from our enterprise," they were assured by the club's owners. However, on May 31, 1889, the South Fork Dam collapsed. One witness described the scene: "In an instant the deserted street became black with people running for their lives. The flood came and licked them up with one eager and ferocious lap." More than two thousand people died in the Johnstown Flood.

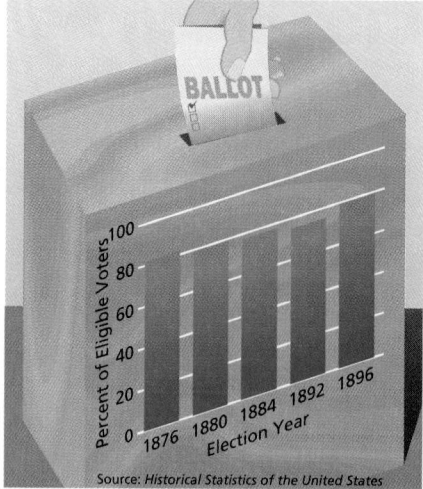

Voter Participation in Presidential Elections, 1876–1896

Percent of Eligible Voters

Source: *Historical Statistics of the United States*

Interpreting Graphs
Voter turnout was high in the late 1800s compared to earlier eras. By 1920, it had dropped below 50 percent and never again rose as high as 65 percent. *What factors might help explain the high turnout in the late 1800s?*

the right thing done, it is only just and fair to do it."

The Spoils System Another controversial practice in American politics at the time was the spoils system. Under the spoils system, those who were elected to public office were free to appoint friends and supporters to government jobs, regardless of their qualifications—or their honesty. The use of this system became widespread during the presidency of Andrew Jackson, and by the Gilded Age its impact on government had reached a crisis point.

The spoils system appealed to many politicians because it ensured a flock of supporters in future elections. Both Democrats and Republicans handed out jobs to pay off the people who had helped them get elected. But the system led to corruption when dishonest appointees used their jobs for personal profit.

Political Parties During the Gilded Age, the numbers of Democrats and Republicans in the United States were about equal, but the characteristics of their members were quite different. The two parties also held starkly different positions on the major issues of the day.

Republicans controlled New York state, New England, and the upper Midwest. In general, they favored a tight money supply backed by gold, high tariffs to protect American business, generous pensions for Union soldiers, and government aid to the railroads. They also wanted to restrict immigration and enforce **blue laws**, which prohibited certain personal behaviors, such as drinking alcoholic beverages on Sundays.

As a rule, the Democratic party attracted those in American society who felt—and sometimes were—less privileged. These groups included northern urban immigrants, laborers, and southern planters and western farmers. Democrats claimed to represent the interests of ordinary people and favored free silver as a means of increasing the money supply and raising farm prices. Democrats typically opposed blue laws.

Presidents and Reforms

Because the two parties had roughly equal numbers of supporters during the Gilded Age, presidential candidates needed almost total support of the members of their party in order to win an election. Candidates generally avoided taking strong stands on political issues in order not to offend potential supporters. They preferred, instead, to "wave the bloody shirt," which meant they focused on their Civil War records. Once in office, however, each of the era's Presidents did exercise a degree of leadership on the major issues of the day. Indeed, the era witnessed some important reforms of the spoils system, the railroads, and trusts.

Hayes Addresses Currency and Patronage
After his election in 1876, the honest and practical Rutherford B. Hayes faced the money supply debate. Those who favored soft money—the term used to describe an increase in the currency supply—supported the passage of the Bland-Allison Act of 1878. This act favored those with high debts, such as farmers and business owners who had borrowed money. It required

the federal government to purchase and coin more silver, increasing the currency supply and causing inflation. If prices went up, farmers would make more money for their goods and would more easily pay off debts incurred earlier.

Although Congress passed the act, Hayes vetoed it because he opposed the inflation it would create. Congress overrode Hayes's veto. Nevertheless, Hayes's Treasury Department limited the effectiveness of the act by buying only the minimum silver it required. The Treasury also refused to circulate the silver dollars that the law required it to mint.

Hayes was the first President to turn away from the practice of patronage. He did not have congressional support for his actions, even from members of his own Republican party, but he did what he could through executive orders and appointments. Hayes appointed qualified political independents to cabinet posts, outlawed the practice of forcing federal employees to make campaign contributions, and fired those employees who were not needed.

Garfield Assassinated in Office In 1880 the Republican party had three factions. The Stalwarts, followers of New York senator Roscoe Conkling, defended the spoils system. The Half-Breeds followed Maine senator James G. Blaine and tried to balance the need for reform of the spoils system with loyalty to the party. Independents opposed the spoils system altogether. They were sometimes called "googoos," a derisive term that was short for *good government*. In the 1880s, when independents left the party to support a Democrat, they also became known as *Mugwumps*. An Algonquin word for "renegade chief," the term stuck when a newspaper editor joked that it really meant "unreliable Republicans," men whose "mugs" were on one side of the fence and "wumps" on the other.

Hayes had announced at the beginning of his presidency that he would not seek a second term. In 1880, Republicans selected James A. Garfield, a member of Congress from Ohio, as their presidential candidate. Because Garfield was linked to the Half-Breeds, who were only somewhat loyal to old-time Republican policies, the vice-presidential slot went to Chester A. Arthur, a Stalwart.

In the 1880 election, Garfield won a narrow victory against Democratic candidate General Winfield S. Hancock. His term was cut short, however, by an assassin's bullet. On July 2, 1881, a deranged lawyer named Charles Guiteau shot Garfield as the President walked through the Washington, D.C., railroad station. When he fired his fatal shot, Guiteau cried out, "I am a Stalwart and Arthur is President now!" Garfield suffered for nearly three months before dying.

It turned out that Guiteau was a loyal Republican and a disappointed office seeker. He felt that his loyalty had earned him a job under the spoils system, and he became enraged when Garfield passed him over. Guiteau's violent act aroused public outrage at the spoils system.

Arthur Ends Patronage With Garfield's death, Vice President Chester Arthur succeeded to the nation's highest office. During the Hayes

President Garfield's assassination by a disappointed office seeker roused the nation to the need for reform of the spoils system.

A GREAT NATION IN GRIEF

PRESIDENT GARFIELD SHOT BY AN ASSASSIN.

THOUGH SERIOUSLY WOUNDED HE STILL SURVIVES.

THE WOULD-BE MURDERER LODGED IN PRISON.

THE PRESIDENT OF THE UNITED STATES ATTACKED AND TERRIBLY WOUNDED BY A FANATICAL OFFICE-SEEKER ON THE EVE OF INDEPENDENCE DAY—THE NATION HORRIFIED AND THE WHOLE CIVILIZED WORLD SHOCKED—THE PRESIDENT STILL ALIVE AND HIS RECOVERY POSSIBLE.

2. INSTRUCT

Explain/Discuss

Review with students the reasons some Americans demanded reforms after Reconstruction. (*Economic cycles of boom and bust, low wages for workers, rising farm debt, corruption in politics and business.*)

Discuss with students the positions of the two major political parties. Which party was favored by wealthy Americans? (*Republican*) Which party generally attracted the less privileged in society and opposed blue laws? (*Democratic*)

Ask students to list the efforts of Presidents Hayes and Arthur to end patronage. How did President Garfield's assassination contribute to the end of patronage?

Analyze

Ask students to explain why the passage of the Interstate Commerce Act was a hollow victory for those who wished to stop the abuses of the railroads.

Discuss the motives President Harrison might have had for supporting large veterans' pensions.

Cooperative Learning

Time: One class period.
Activity: Present a portion of an evening news broadcast dealing with one political event described in the section.
Grouping: Four to six students.
Purpose: To increase students' understanding of American politics during this period. Students should work in small groups to create a segment for the evening news. Assign each group one of the following events: Congress overrides Hayes's veto of the Bland-Allison Act; Garfield is assassinated; Cleveland wins the presidential election of 1884; Coxey's Army marches on Washington.
Roles: Anchors, newsroom staff, including scriptwriter and editor, and reporters on location.
Outcome: Students will identify and present the key issues related to a political event.

Enrichment

Invite students to research the lives of the very wealthy during the Gilded Age. Students may present their findings in a report or skit that presents some of the details of a day in the life of a wealthy New York socialite.

administration, Arthur had benefited from the practice of patronage. He had been appointed to a high-paying job in the New York Customs House because of his support of Senator Roscoe Conkling. Once in office, however, he urged Congress to support reform of the spoils system. With Garfield's assassination fresh in the nation's mind, President Arthur was able to garner legislative support for his ideas, and the **Pendleton Act** became law in 1883.

The act empowered three civil service commissioners to classify government jobs and test applicants' fitness for them. It also stated that federal employees could not be required to contribute to campaign funds and could not be fired for political reasons.

Democrats Take Over In the 1884 presidential campaign, the key issues were high tariffs, unfair business practices, and unregulated railroads. The Republicans nominated the eloquent James G. Blaine, a former secretary of state and senator from Maine. The Democratic party chose the genial Grover Cleveland, former mayor of Buffalo and governor of New York. In spite of the serious economic issues of the day, the campaign focused mostly on scandals.

Had James G. Blaine received railroad stock options in return for favorable votes while he was in Congress? No one could prove it. Had Cleveland fathered an illegitimate child when a bachelor in Buffalo? Cleveland admitted it was true. Republicans jeered, "Ma, Ma, where's my Pa?" to which the Democrats responded, "Going to the White House, ha, ha, ha!" In spite of his admission, Cleveland won the election, thereby becoming the first Democrat elected to the presidency since 1856. Cleveland did appoint Democrats to office but avoided giving in to the spoils system. He tried to ensure that his appointments were based on merit.

An advocate of tight money, Cleveland was acceptable to most business interests. Yet he opposed generous pensions and high tariffs, and he took back from the railroads and other interests 81 million acres of land grants on which they had failed to fulfill their obligations. Cleveland also supported regulation of the powerful railroads. He believed that fierce competition among the various railroad lines led to practices, such as secret rebates to high-volume shippers, that hurt small businesses.

Railroad Abuses Lead to New Regulations

Railroad regulation had begun in 1869, when Massachusetts officials investigated rate abuses in that state. By 1880, fourteen states had railroad commissions to look into complaints against railroad practices. Such practices included awarding stock to legislators in return for favors and manipulating the state legal system to win court challenges against rate abuses. In 1877 the Supreme Court decision in *Munn* v. *Illinois* allowed states to regulate certain enterprises within their boundaries. Lawyers for the railroads responded with the argument that, under the Constitution, states could not regulate interstate commerce. Because railroad traffic often crossed state lines, only the federal government could regulate their activities. With this argument the railroads were successful and continued to pursue their disputed practices.

Pressure mounted on Congress to take action to curb railroad company abuses. In 1887 the legislature passed the **Interstate Commerce Act.** The act required that rates be set in proportion to the distance traveled and that rate schedules be made public. The act also outlawed the practice of giving rebates and favors to powerful customers. It set up the nation's first regulatory board, the Interstate Commerce Commission (ICC), to enforce the act.

Unfortunately, the act failed to give the commission the power necessary to set rates, rendering it largely ineffective. To enforce its rulings, the ICC had to take the railroads to court. But of the sixteen cases involving the ICC that came before the Supreme Court between 1887 and 1905, the Court ruled against the ICC fifteen times. Still, the creation of the ICC established the precedent that private enterprise was subject to government control.

How did the passing of the Interstate Commerce Act weaken the policy of laissez-faire?

Efforts to Regulate Tariffs

The White House again found itself with a new tenant when Cleveland lost the 1888 election to Republican Benjamin Harrison. Tariffs provided a focal point for the campaign. Cleveland favored a minor reduction; Harrison campaigned for an increase, a position that won him much business support and, ultimately, the presidency.

Among President Harrison's achievements was the signing of the Sherman Antitrust Act in 1890, described in Section 1. Like the Interstate Commerce Act, however, this seemingly bold action failed to curb the power of the largest corporations until well after the turn of the century.

Meanwhile, Harrison also took actions that favored business. In 1890 he approved a huge tariff increase, and he supported legislation on behalf of special business interests. Although he was considered a conservative regarding the public treasury, he was liberal when it came to veterans' pensions. He ate up the last federal surplus in United States history with huge new pensions for the dependents of Civil War soldiers.

In the election of 1892, with many new immigrants swelling Democratic party rolls, and campaigning for lower tariffs, Grover Cleveland was returned to the presidency. By the time his term was over, however, many people were more disillusioned with government than ever before.

Cleveland's Second Term Cleveland's second term started badly. To begin with, he inherited Harrison's treasury deficit. Also, Americans were experiencing the worst depression the country had yet seen. Millions of people lost their jobs or had their wages slashed, yet government offered no help to those out of work. In 1894 **Jacob S. Coxey**, a wealthy Ohio quarry owner turned Populist, demanded that government create jobs for the unemployed. He then called for a march on Washington. "We will

Using Historical Evidence This cartoon expresses the widespread concern about the harmful effects of monopolies in the late 1800s. *How do the images in this cartoon communicate such a message?*

send a petition to Washington with boots on," he declared.

Many small "armies" started out on the protest march, but only Coxey's arrived. Police arrested him and a few others for illegally carrying banners on the Capitol grounds and for trampling the grass. Based on the tune of "The Star-Spangled Banner," a song created by Coxey's supporters mocked their government's vigilance in protecting the lawns of the Capitol while ignoring the pleas of the nation's poor.

Oh, say, can you see, by the dawn's early light
That grass plot so dear to the hearts of us all?
Is it green yet and fair, in well-nurtured plight,
Unpolluted by the Coxeyites' hated foot-fall?
Midst the yells of police, and swish of clubs through the air,
We could hardly tell if our grass was still there.
But the green growing grass does in triumph yet wave,
And the gallant police with their buttons of brass
Will sure make the Coxeyites keep off the grass.

Anonymous, 1894

5. The people who won elections could appoint their friends to government jobs. Through these acts of patronage, they were guaranteed supporters in future contests. The Pendleton Act empowered civil service commissioners to classify government jobs and test applicants' fitness for them. The act also prevented politicians from either requiring federal employees to contribute to their campaign funds, or from firing them for political reasons.

6. Possible answer: Officeholders would be appointed on the basis of merit, and appointees would have to prove their fitness for the duties of the job. There would no longer be political favors that had to be repaid.

Reteach

Ask students to correct any of the following statements that are incorrect:
- Government regulations such as the Interstate Commerce Act stopped unfair business practices.
- During the Gilded Age, the positions of the Republicans and Democrats were more or less interchangeable.
- The assassination of President Garfield led to the end of patronage.

4. CLOSE

Reinforcing the Big Idea

During the Gilded Age, a series of ineffective Presidents failed to deal with economic problems and corruption in business and politics. The next section describes the lives of the many immigrants entering the United States during this period and the changes in the nation's cities resulting from their expanding populations.

Coxey's Army, shown above, marched through many villages on its way to Washington to demand federal action to resolve the nation's economic problems.

In his second term, Cleveland managed to anger not only the unemployed, but almost every group in his party. He angered labor when he sent federal troops to Chicago at the time of the Pullman strike of 1894. He angered farmers by repealing the Silver Purchase Act and returning the country to a gold standard. Having alienated so many fellow Democrats, Cleveland failed to win his party's nomination in 1896.

A Republican Returns to the White House
The Populists had emerged as a political power during the economic hard times of the early 1890s and had made gains in the elections of 1894. But in 1896 William Jennings Bryan, the presidential candidate they shared with the Democrats, lost to Republican William McKinley. Supported by urban workers and the middle class, McKinley won the election with ease.

A new tariff and the gold standard brought Republicans an even more decisive victory against Bryan in 1900. As the economic depression of the 1890s began to loosen its grip, the Republicans claimed credit with their slogan, "A Full Dinner Pail."

McKinley did not live long enough to enjoy the effects of the growing prosperity. On September 6, 1901, a mentally ill, unemployed anarchist named Leon Czolgosz hid a gun in a bandaged hand and shot President McKinley as he greeted the public at the Pan-American Exposition in Buffalo. When McKinley died a few days later, national hysteria followed.

In the public mind, dangerous ideas, many of them associated with foreign people—or those with foreign names such as Czolgosz—were threatening the country. Those blossoming fears would have a profound impact on the nation's huge and growing immigrant population, as the next section describes.

SECTION 4 REVIEW

Key Terms, People, and Places
1. Identify (a) Interstate Commerce Act, (b) Jacob S. Coxey.
2. Define (a) laissez-faire, (b) blue laws.

Key Concepts
3. For what reason(s) is the post–Reconstruction period in national politics referred to as the Gilded Age?
4. Describe the business practices that led to government regulation. What regulations were passed in the Gilded Age, and how effective were they?
5. Describe how the spoils system worked and what action the government took to control it.

Critical Thinking
6. **Determining Relevance** For what reasons do you think political reformers believed that a civil service law could help wipe out corrupt government practices?

 **RESOURCE DIRECTORY**

Media and Technology

 Transparency
Links Across Time, J-7

Teaching Resources

Quiz found in the Unit 2 folder, p. 87, covers the main ideas in this section as well as the key terms.

Immigration and Urban Life

SECTION PREVIEW

As immigrants from Europe and Asia arrived on American shores, most pinned their hopes on the nation's cities. Bustling, noisy, and straining at the seams, the cities were places where the new became neighbors with the old and where progress lived next door to poverty.

Key Concepts

• Economic hardship and political and religious persecution led immigrants to the United States in the late 1800s.
• American cities expanded upward and outward with the arrival of tremendous numbers of new residents.
• The growth of American cities contributed to corrupt political practices at the local level.
• One reform movement sought to limit immigration into the United States; another focused on helping the needy by providing charity and social services.

Key Terms, People, and Places

suburb, political machine, political boss, Tammany Hall, social gospel movement; William Marcy Tweed, Jane Addams, Ellen Gates Starr; Ellis Island, Angel Island, Hull House

A s politicians steered their way through the nagging economic and political problems of the late nineteenth century, human dramas were unfolding far from Washington, D.C. Played out in the nation's gritty ports and grimy back streets, these dramas were tales of triumph and tragedy, with millions of heroes and more than a few villains. These were the stories of the nation's immigrants.

Migration to and Within the United States

In the late 1800s, people in many parts of the world were on the move, from farms to cities and then on to other countries. They were fleeing crop failures, land and job shortages, rising taxes, and famine. Some were also escaping religious or political persecution. The United States received a huge portion of this migration. In 1860 the resident population of the United States was 31.5 million people. Between 1865 and 1920, close to 30 million additional people entered the country. Some of these newcomers dreamed of making fortunes, or at least of getting free government land through the Homestead Act. Others yearned for more personal freedom. In the United States, they had heard, everyone could go to school, young men were not forced to serve long years in the army, and democratic government meant equality and participation for more people.

In the late 1800s, steam-powered ships could cross the Atlantic Ocean in two to three weeks. By 1900 the crossing took just one week. Even this brief journey, however, could be an ordeal for those who could not afford cabins, and most could not. The majority of immigrants traveled in steerage, a large open area beneath the ship's deck. Because steerage had inadequate toilet facilities, no privacy, and poor food, tickets for this section cost as little as $15.

Immigrants from Europe Historians estimate that about 10 million immigrants, mostly northern Europeans from countries such as England and Germany, arrived between 1865 and 1890. In the 1890s, the pattern of immigration shifted. Most people now came from southern and eastern Europe and the Middle East. Between 1890 and 1920, about 10 million Italians, Greeks, Slavs, Eastern European and Russian Jews, and Armenians arrived.

Cities such as Chicago, pictured on this postcard, grew upward and outward in the late 1800s.

1. FOCUS

Connecting to the Big Idea

See page 226B. Point out to students that immigrants and migrants flocked to the nation's cities during the Gilded Age. Explain that this rapid population growth led to many urban problems. Reformers worked to improve social, economic, and political conditions in the cities. Ask students what the goals of reformers were. How successful were they in reaching their goals?

Objectives

● Identify the reasons that immigrants came to the United States in the late 1800s.
● Demonstrate that American cities expanded with the arrival of millions of immigrants.
● Describe how the growth of cities contributed to corrupt political practices at the local level.

Bellringer

Ask students to imagine they are immigrants entering the United States in 1900. What are their thoughts as they see the Statue of Liberty for the first time? Ask students to explain why the Statue of Liberty remains a potent symbol today, despite the fact that few immigrants now arrive in this country by sailing into New York harbor.

Reading Strategy

Reading for Evidence Ask students to find evidence to support the statement on page 260, "The arrival of large numbers of newcomers radically changed the face of the nation's cities."

📑 **Reproducible Lesson Plan** found in the Unit 2 folder, p. 79, provides a summary of the Section 5 lesson plan content.

📑 **Alternate Lesson Plan: Critical Thinking** Testing Conclusions found in the Alternate Lesson Plans folder, p. 83, is designed to help students test conclusions by identifying sentences that support or refute a given statement.

📑 **Guided Reading and Review** found in the Unit 2 folder, p. 88, provides a structure for reading and mastering the key concepts and reviewing the key terms for Section 5. (Guided Practice)

Explain/Discuss

Ask students why immigrants left their homelands to come to the United States. What might motivate a person, possibly someone with very little money, to go to a country where a different language is spoken?

Discuss the events and trends that made some Americans wary of increased immigration. Examples include the assassination of McKinley by an anarchist with a foreign name, corruption in city governments, and poor conditions in slums and ghettos.

In Depth

Then and Now

Arrivals at Ellis Island were carefully screened for medical problems. For example, a would-be immigrant with trachoma, a highly contagious eye infection that can cause blindness, would not be admitted. Passengers who failed immediate clearance were kept in detention centers, and those with suspected health problems had initials chalked on their clothing to identify the possible problems: *E* for eyes, *L* for lameness, *X* for mental disability. "Their stolid faces hide frightened, throbbing hearts," wrote one observer of arrivals going through the screening process. The steamship companies were responsible for the return of the 2 percent—often as many as one thousand people per month—who were denied immigrant status. Ellis Island officially closed in November 1954, but in September 1990 the Ellis Island Immigration Museum opened as a permanent memorial to the 12 million people who made it their first stop in America.

These recent arrivals on Ellis Island contemplate a bewildering yet promising future in their new homeland.

Immigrants entered the United States through several ports. Those from Europe might enter through Boston, Philadelphia, or Baltimore, but the most common port of entry was New York City, where more than 70 percent of all immigrants landed. It came to be called the "Golden Door." ✪

Before the 1880s, decisions about whom to allow into the country were left to the states. In 1891, the federal government created the Office of the Superintendent of Immigration to determine who was "fit" to enter. Applicants could be denied admission on medical or other grounds. In 1892 the government opened a huge reception center for steerage passengers on **Ellis Island** in New York Harbor, near where the Statue of Liberty had been built in 1886. The statue, a gift of France, celebrated "Liberty Enlightening the World." It became a world symbol of the United States as a place of refuge and hope.

Steerage immigrants who arrived at Ellis Island and were found to have contagious illnesses such as tuberculosis faced quarantine or even deportation. Those with trachoma, an eye disease that was common among immigrants, were automatically sent back to the country they had just left. Fiorello La Guardia, who later became mayor of New York City, worked as an interpreter at Ellis Island. "It was harrowing to see families separated," he remembered in the book *The Making of an Insurgent.*

> *S*ometimes, if it was a young child who suffered from trachoma, one of the parents had to return to the native country with the rejected member of the family. When they learned their fate, they were stunned. They . . . had no homes to return to.

After their physicals, immigrants showed their documents to officials and then collected their baggage. If they had the address of a friend or relative, they took a ferry, boat, or train to find them. Those who were on their own had a harder time. Crooks hung around ports with fake offers of lodgings and jobs, stealing money and baggage from the unwary.

Whether they landed at New York or some other city, immigrants often settled near their ports of entry. A significant number did move inland, however, often seeking communities established by previous settlers from their homelands. Large settlements of Poles and Italians formed in Buffalo, Cleveland, Detroit, and Milwaukee. Chicago—a port, railroad hub, and center for the garment, grain, lumber, and livestock industries—attracted a diverse group of immigrants. Some immigrants populated the mining towns of the West. Only 2 percent went to the South, primarily because the area did not offer newcomers enough jobs or land. Louisiana recruited Italian farm laborers, however, and Florida also sought foreign-born agricultural workers.

Once settled, immigrants looked for work. There were never enough jobs, and employers—often immigrants themselves—took

▶ RESOURCE DIRECTORY

Teaching Resources

Literature Activity The Statue of Liberty, found in the Unit 2 folder, p. 102, uses the poem inscribed on the pedestal of the Statue of Liberty to explore a symbolic view of nineteenth-century immigration.

advantage of the "greenhorns." They paid them less than other workers and paid women less than men. Men tailors, for example, working fourteen hours a day, six days a week, earned $6 to $10 a week. Women seamstresses, doing the same work, earned half that amount. Women domestic servants earned $4 to $10 a month, working sixteen hours or more a day and more than six days a week.

Immigrants from Asia Most immigrants who entered the United States on the West Coast came from Asia. In the 1800s, railroad companies recruited about a quarter of a million male workers from China. The men had to work for their companies until they had paid off the cost of their passage and upkeep. Many Chinese paid their debts, settled down to work in other fields, but had difficulty freeing themselves from ethnic stereotyping by whites.

In 1882 Congress passed the Chinese Exclusion Act, which prohibited Chinese laborers from entering the country. The act did not prevent entry by those who had previously established residence or who had family living in the United States. In 1910 the government built a detention center on **Angel Island** in San Francisco Bay, where immigrants' claims of prior residence or relationship to citizens received lengthy examination. The act was finally repealed in 1943.

Immigrants from Asia included those from Japan as well. By 1920, about 200,000 Japanese had arrived on the West Coast, many via Hawaii, which the United States annexed in 1898. Most Japanese settled in the Los Angeles area and soon were producing much of southern California's fruits and vegetables.

The success of Japanese immigrants aroused the jealousy of some, who gave them the derogatory nickname "The Yellow Peril." In 1905 California's political leaders urged, and two years later won, restrictions on Japanese immigration. This was accomplished when President Theodore Roosevelt made a so-called gentleman's agreement with Japanese officials, who agreed to limit Japanese emigration. In 1913 the California legislature passed an Alien Land Law, which banned noncitizen Asians from owning farmland.

Immigrants from Mexico In 1902 Congress passed the Newlands National Reclamation Act to stimulate the irrigation of southwestern lands. Over the next decade, irrigation turned millions of acres of desert into fertile farmland in Texas, Arizona, and California.

The new farmland meant new jobs. About 5 percent of Mexico's population, fleeing poverty and debt, entered the United States through El Paso, Texas. The 1909 Mexican Revolution increased the flow. By 1925 Los Angeles had the largest Spanish-speaking population in any North American city outside of Mexico.

Internal Migration At the same time that new immigrants were arriving, growing numbers of native-born Americans were leaving the economic hardship of farm life and seeking new opportunities in the cities. In 1880 about

Chinese immigrants brought distinctive styles and customs to the United States. Traditional dress and shops helped them feel at home—but also set them apart from other Americans, who often had little tolerance for differences.

Media and Technology

 Transparencies
Our Multicultural Heritage, C-2, C-15

Analyze

Ask students to analyze the role of fear and racism in discrimination against immigrants from Asia. How did Americans respond to Asian customs and traditions, their willingness to work for low wages, and their success in California agriculture?

Activity

Designing a City

Specialized areas such as business districts, retail districts, and industrial districts emerged as a result of urban expansion. Ask students to assume the role of city planner for a city of their choice. They should choose one of the specialized areas mentioned and create a drawing of it, trying to arrange it in the best interests of the city. **LEP**

 In Depth

Multicultural Perspectives

By the turn of the century, the largest Chinese community in the United States was in San Francisco; the second largest was in New York City. Racial prejudice drove many Chinese out of small towns and farming and forced them to work for other Chinese in service jobs in laundries and restaurants. Their neighborhoods, called Chinatowns, were tight enclaves built around small businesses such as cigar manufacturing, small grocery stores, barbershops, and Chinese restaurants. Scholar Ronald Takaki described the Chinatowns in American cities as "cultural islands, cut off from the mainland of American society, perceived by whites as strange places to visit as tourists."

By reducing the need for labor on the nation's farms, technology and mechanization left many farm laborers without work. Many of these people then came to the nation's cities in search of work.

In Depth

Biography

David Sarnoff (1891–1971) arrived in New York City from Russia in 1900 and exceeded the immigrant promise of America beyond the wildest dreams of most. Self-educated in Morse code, he got a job as a radio operator for the Marconi Wireless and Telegraph Company. By 1930 Sarnoff had become president of the Radio Corporation of America (RCA) and was the brains behind RCA's entry into radio broadcasting. By 1932 Sarnoff had added the National Broadcasting Corporation (NBC) to the ranks of RCA-owned companies. During World War II, Sarnoff postponed plans to expand the then-fledgling television industry to serve as General Eisenhower's communications consultant. After the war, Sarnoff aggressively promoted the color television industry for NBC.

72 percent of the population lived on farms. By 1910 that figure was down to 54 percent. Today it is about 3 percent.

Many African Americans were among the internal migrants. In 1870, less than a half million of the nation's 5 million African Americans lived outside the South. By 1890, partly as a result of increased segregation and racial violence in the South, 12 percent of the region's rural-dwelling African Americans had moved into nearby cities, and 150,000 had left the South altogether.

The Challenge to the Cities

The arrival of large numbers of newcomers radically changed the face of the nation's cities. Between the Civil War and 1900, many features of modern city life first appeared—noise, skyscrapers, traffic jams, slums, air pollution, and sanitation and health problems.

How Cities Grew Before the Civil War, cities were small in area—rarely more than 3 or 4 miles across. Most people lived at or near the place where they worked, and they moved about on foot. Public horse-drawn streetcars, introduced in the 1850s, changed this pattern somewhat. Those people who could afford the fares moved outside the cities, establishing new communities in the **suburbs,** or areas surrounding the cities. Cable cars and electric trolleys (first used in 1888 in Richmond, Virginia), elevated trains, automobiles (first appeared in 1893), and subways (first built in 1897 in Boston) made commuting much easier and speeded suburban growth.

Cities grew upward, too. Before the Civil War, no building stood more than five stories high. Iron and steel girders, as well as steam-driven elevators developed in 1861 by Elisha Graves Otis (and electrified by the 1890s), permitted the construction of skyscrapers. The first skyscraper, which was 535 feet high, appeared in Chicago in 1885.

As a result of expansion, cities developed specialized areas. Banks, financial offices, law firms, and government offices were located in one area and retail shops and department stores in another. Industrial, wholesale, and warehouse districts formed a ring around the center.

MAKING CONNECTIONS

Recall the discussion in Section 3 about the impact of technology on farms in the late 1800s. How might those same developments have contributed to the growth of cities?

Urban Living Conditions Some working-class city dwellers moved into housing especially built for them by mill and factory owners. The rest lived in buildings abandoned by middle-class residents and converted into multifamily units. Speculators also built cheap tenements that soon came to be identified as "slums." ✪

Through poverty, overcrowding, and neglect, the old residential neighborhoods of cities declined. Trees and grass disappeared. Soot from coal-fired steam engines and boilers darkened and befouled the air. Hundreds of families crammed into spaces meant only for a few. Open sewers and backyard privies attracted rats and other vermin. In 1905 journalist Eleanor McMain quoted a university student who visited a block of tenements in New Orleans' Italian district and described them as "death traps,"

> *closely built, jammed together, with no side openings. Twenty-five per cent of the yard space is damp and gloomy. . . . Where the houses are three or more rooms in depth, the middle ones are dark, without outside ventilator. . . . There is no fire protection whatever.*

Contagious diseases such as cholera, malaria, tuberculosis, diphtheria, and typhoid raged in such conditions. Children were especially vulnerable. In New York City, in one district of tenements, six out of ten babies died before their first birthday.

Political Divisions As the middle and upper classes left the cities for the suburbs beginning in the late 1800s, the gap between the well-to-do and the poor widened. Because many of the poor were foreign-born or people of color, the gap was not just economic, but ethnic and racial as well.

Urban political divisions stemmed from these social divisions. As cities expanded,

RESOURCE DIRECTORY

Teaching Resources

✪ **Primary Source Activity** New York Gangs, found in the Unit 2 folder, p. 99, uses excerpts from journalist Jacob Riis's book *How the Other Half Lives* to help students see some of the repercussions of urbanization.

pressure increased on officials to improve police and fire protection, sewage disposal, electrical and water service, transportation systems, and health care. To deliver these services, cities raised taxes and set up offices.

Various groups vied for control of these offices. Some groups represented the remaining middle and upper classes, who tended to be well educated and of old immigrant stock. Others were made up of new immigrant and working-class groups.

Out of these clashing interests, city **political machines** arose. These were unofficial organizations designed to keep a particular party or group in power. Usually a single, powerful **political boss** presided over them. One of the more notorious bosses of that period was **William Marcy Tweed.** Tweed was the most powerful politician of **Tammany Hall,** the political club that ran New York City's Democratic party.

Machines like Tammany Hall controlled not only political parties but jobs in all administrative offices. They gave their leaders access to graft, or money passed "under the table" in return for favors, such as the granting of a city contract for work.

Immigrants tended to vote for machine candidates, often because the machines made up for the lack of a public welfare system. Machine leaders doled out jobs, loans, and other favors to needy residents.

Ideas for Reform

The steady stream of people to the cities of the United States created serious urban problems that needed solutions. Some reform groups felt that these problems stemmed from the presence of so many immigrants. These reformers pursued their goals in two ways: by seeking limits on immigration and by trying to outlaw certain behaviors. In these ways, reformers hoped to return the nation to what they believed was a past of purity and virtue.

Nativism Nativism, a movement begun in the 1850s to restrict immigration, reappeared in the 1880s. The movement's first success came with the passage in 1882 of the Chinese Exclusion Act. In the Midwest, the American Protective Association called for the teaching of only the culture of the United States and only the English language in schools. It also demanded tighter rules on citizenship and employment of all "aliens."

In 1885, nativists won the repeal of the contract labor law, which had allowed businesses to

In the crowded cities, many immigrants were forced to live in cramped, unsafe apartments. Such conditions troubled many Americans.

In Depth

Historical Misconceptions

Daniel Patrick Moynihan, writing in the *New York Times* in May 1986, confronted a sentimental favorite of American history—the description of immigrants in the late nineteenth and early twentieth century as "the wretched refuse of your teeming shore." Moynihan argues that the majority of the 20 million or so immigrants who arrived in the United States between 1870 and 1910 were neither wretched nor refuse, at least no more than any other immigrant group, including the Pilgrims. These immigrants were energetic and enthusiastic, though most were uneducated and semiskilled. "They were an extraordinary, enterprising, and self-sufficient folk who knew exactly what they were doing, and doing it quite on their own, thank you very much."

Using Historical Evidence

The cartoon features Uncle Sam's face, composed of representatives of many different immigrant groups. The caption suggests that the combination gives Uncle Sam (the United States) strength and character. The cartoonist favors immigration.

3. ASSESS

Section 5 Review Answers

1. (a) suburb, see p. 260, (b) political machine, see p. 261, (c) political boss, see p. 261, (d) Tammany Hall, see p. 261, (e) social gospel movement, see p. 263.

2. (a) William Marcy Tweed, see p. 261, (b) Jane Addams, see p. 263, (c) Ellen Gates Starr, see p. 263.

3. (a) Ellis Island, see p. 258, (b) Angel Island, see p. 259, (c) Hull House, see p. 263.

4. The chief reason was economic. Many people were fleeing crop failures, land and job shortages, rising taxes, and famine. Some were escaping religious or political persecution.

5. With the introduction of streetcars and, later, cable cars, electric trolleys, automobiles, and subways, people began to move to the outskirts yet continue to work in the city. With the invention of elevators and the use of steel girders, cities grew upward, too.

6. Wide social and political divisions between classes and ethnic and racial groups encouraged the rise of political machines and the boss system. In the absence of welfare systems, these machines provided residents with important services in return for loyalty.

recruit workers from abroad. The practice continued illegally, however. During periods of labor unrest, companies often brought in foreign workers to replace striking employees. These actions increased antiforeign feelings among workers.

Upper-class nativism found expression in the Immigration Restriction League, organized in 1894 by some recent graduates of Harvard College. Republican senator Henry Cabot Lodge gave the League a voice in Congress. It hoped to exclude "unfit" immigrants by forcing them to pass literacy tests. Its main targets for exclusion were the so-called "new" immigrants from southern and eastern Europe, whose cultures differed significantly from that of League members.

Prohibition The temperance movement also saw a revival. Prohibitionists attacked drinking because it not only led to family tragedies but forged a link between saloons, immigrants, and political bosses. Immigrant

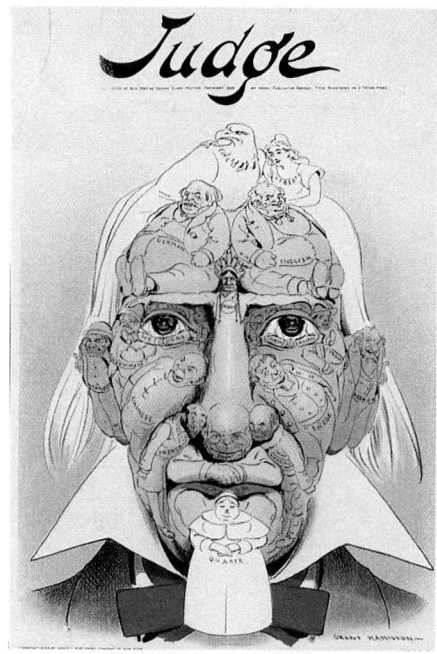

Using Historical Evidence The caption on this *Judge* cartoon reads "Uncle Sam is a man of strong features." *What does the cartoon suggest about the artist's view of immigration?*

men often used saloons as "social clubs" where they could pick up information about jobs as well as socialize. To prohibitionists, it seemed saloons formed the center of a foreign and subversive movement to take over the United States.

Purity Crusaders As urban populations grew, vice—whether in the form of drugs, gambling, or prostitution—became big business. Vice was not unique to cities, but large urban populations made vice highly visible and profitable.

"Purity crusaders" led the attack. In 1873 Anthony Comstock founded the New York Society for the Suppression of Vice. The following year he won passage of a law that prohibited sending through the United States mails materials deemed obscene, including those that described methods to prevent unwanted pregnancy.

Other purity crusaders attacked political machines on the grounds that machine-controlled police forces profited from vice. Corrupt police were known to demand payment from gamblers and prostitutes, for example, in return for ignoring illegal activities. Although purity crusaders were able to join with other reformers to throw machine politicians out of office, usually the machines returned to power in later elections.

Helping the Needy Other reformers, moved by social conscience or religious idealism, developed a quite different approach to social reform. They argued that the middle and upper classes should take responsibility for poverty and try to improve social conditions.

One of these reformers, Josephine Shaw Lowell, founded the New York Charity Organization Society (COS) in 1882. The COS tried to make charity "scientific" and kept detailed files on those who received help. In part, COS leaders wanted to prevent the duplication of efforts, but they also wanted to help only those they considered the "worthy" poor.

In the 1880s and 1890s, urban churches began to provide social services for the poor. They also tried to focus prohibition and

RESOURCE DIRECTORY

Teaching Resources

purity campaigns in new directions. Instead of blaming immigrants for drinking, gambling, and other destructive behaviors, they pointed out the circumstances that drove people into such activities.

Soon a **social gospel movement** developed within religious institutions. It sought to apply the gospel of Jesus directly to society. In 1908, followers of such views formed the Federal Council of the Churches of Christ, an organization that supported a larger share in the national wealth for all workers.

Thousands of young, educated women and men put the social gospel into practice in the social or neighborhood settlement movement. The chief idea behind it was for young people to "settle" in poor neighborhoods to witness the effects of poverty firsthand and to try to help the needy.

In 1889, inspired by a settlement in London, **Jane Addams** and **Ellen Gates Starr** bought the dilapidated Charles Hull mansion in Chicago, renovated it, and then opened its doors to their immigrant neighbors. At first, Starr and Addams simply wanted to get to know them, but over the decades that followed, the two reformers turned **Hull House** into a center of constructive activities and programs.

By 1910, more than four hundred settlements existed throughout the nation. Most were supported by donations and staffed by volunteers or people willing to work for low wages and free room and board. Except for leaders

such as Addams, most workers spent only a few years in these jobs. Many went on to professional careers in social work, education, or government, but few ever forgot their settlement experience. "I don't know that my attitude changed," wrote one former settlement worker, "but my point of view certainly did, or perhaps it would be more true to say that now I have several points of view." The settlements' ability to widen perspectives on social conditions and close the gap between social divisions may have been their most lasting contribution.

Judith Lathrop (left), Jane Addams (center), and Mary McDowell (right) were a few of the pioneers of the settlement house movement. *Inset:* Reformers helped newcomers by providing day care for working parents.

7. Nativism brought about the exclusion of the Chinese, called for teaching only "American" culture and language, and urged tighter rules on citizenship and the employment of "aliens." The social gospel movement developed to get church members to apply the gospel of Jesus Christ directly to contemporary society.

8. Both nativism and social Darwinism seek to promote the interests of those in power and to exclude the "weaker" members of society from achieving greater economic or political status.

Reteach

Ask students to make a two-column chart showing the goals and successes of the following reform movements: nativism, prohibition, purity crusades, the charity organization movement, the social gospel movement, the settlement movement.

4. CLOSE

Reinforcing the Big Idea

Immigrants from abroad and migrants from within the country flocked to the nation's cities in the late 1800s. The result was a strain on city services and a rise in political corruption. Reformers sought to address these issues, with some success.

SECTION 5 REVIEW

Key Terms, People, and Places
1. Define (a) suburb, (b) political machine, (c) political boss, (d) Tammany Hall, (e) social gospel movement.
2. Identify (a) William Marcy Tweed, (b) Jane Addams, (c) Ellen Gates Starr.
3. Identify (a) Ellis Island, (b) Angel Island, (c) Hull House.

Key Concepts
4. Why were so many people "on the move" in the late nineteenth century?

5. What inventions and developments contributed to the growth of cities?
6. How did the growth of cities and urban problems contribute to the rise of political machines and political bosses?
7. What were the goals of the followers of the nativism and social gospel movements?

Critical Thinking
8. **Determining Relevance** How does the idea of nativism relate to the concept of social Darwinism?

 Quiz found in the Unit 2 folder, p. 89, covers the main ideas in this section as well as the key terms.

 Chapter Test Forms A and B are found in the Unit 2 folder, pp. 105–110.

 Answers Keys found in the Unit 2 folder, pp. 152–165, provide answers to all student activities.

Media and Technology

Transparency
Graphic Organizer, G-3

Guided Reading Audiotapes
(English and Spanish)

Computer Test Bank

Understanding Key Terms, People, and Places

Terms
Students should refer to the definitions of the key terms in the chapter to write sentences that show the relation of each word to the technological revolution, the rise of big business in the late 1800s, the settlement of the West, or politics in the Gilded Age.

Matching
1. Morrill Land-Grant Act
2. laissez-faire
3. suburb

True or False
1. true
2. false, George Armstrong Custer
3. false, Angel Island

Reviewing Main Ideas

1. Problems included inconvenient schedules, discomfort, and distrust and fear of train travel. Developments included replacement of iron rails with steel, standardization of track gauges and signals, improved safety through more effective air brakes, and a telegraph system for intertrain communication.

2. During the late 1800s, businesses pooled their money and resources, creating giant conglomerates such as American Telephone and Telegraph, General Electric, and Westinghouse.

3. It made women's lives harder. In addition to devoting long hours to caring for their families, many women worked in factories, with almost no chance of advancement.

4. The first unions were "brotherhoods" or "orders" designed to help members through bad times. Later unions such as the Knights of Labor helped workers demand better conditions.

5. After the Great Strikes, the government remained opposed to unions for over thirty years.

6. The federal government responded to appeals for court orders by factory owners against labor unions. Unions were denied recognition as legally protected organizations.

7. Families cooperated in building houses and barns, making quilts, husking corn, and providing many other forms of support.

CHAPTER 7

Chapter Review

Understanding Key Terms, People, and Places

Key Terms
1. social Darwinism
2. monopoly
3. cartel
4. trust
5. horizontal consolidation
6. vertical consolidation
7. socialism
8. collective bargaining
9. scab
10. anarchist
11. Morrill Land-Grant

12. Homestead Act
13. bonanza farms
14. deflation
15. Gilded Age
16. laissez-faire
17. blue laws
18. Pendleton Act
19. Interstate Commerce Act
20. suburb
21. political machine
22. political boss

23. Tammany Hall
24. social gospel movement

People
25. Andrew Carnegie
26. Pinkerton
27. George Armstrong Custer
28. Chief Joseph
29. Populists
30. William Jennings Bryan
31. Frederick Jackson

Turner
32. Jacob S. Coxey
33. William Marcy Tweed
34. Jane Addams
35. Ellen Gates Starr

Places
36. Haymarket Square
37. Homestead
38. Pullman Strike
39. Wounded Knee
40. Ellis Island
40. Angel Island
41. Hull House

Terms For each term above, write a sentence that explains its relation to the technological revolution; the rise of big business in the late 1800s; the settlement of the West; or politics in the Gilded Age.

Matching Review the key terms in the list above. If you are not sure of a term's meaning, review its definition in the chapter. Then choose a term from the list that best matches each description below.
1. the act giving western lands to state governments
2. a hands-off approach to economic issues
3. the area surrounding a city.

True or False Determine whether each statement is true or false. If it is true, write "true." If it is false, change the underlined term to make the statement true.
1. Eugene V. Debs organized the <u>Pullman strike</u>.
2. <u>William Jennings Bryan</u> fought the Cheyenne.
3. Most Asian immigrants entered the United States at <u>Ellis Island</u>.

Reviewing Main Ideas

Section 1 (pp. 228–234)
1. Describe the problems that existed on the early railroads and five developments that helped solve them.
2. Explain what is meant by the age of big business.
3. How did the growth of industry affect women's lives?

Section 2 (pp. 236–241)
4. Describe the growth of early labor unions.
5. How did the federal government respond to the Great Strikes of the late 1800s?
6. How did the federal government respond to the unions in the years following the Pullman strike?

Section 3 (pp. 244–250)
7. Describe some of the ways settlers relied on each other.
8. By what means were Native American cultures destroyed in the late 1800s?
9. How did farmers protest their fate in the late 1800s?

Section 4 (pp. 251–256)
10. What practices bred corruption in American business and politics during the Gilded Age?
11. What important laws were passed at the national level during the Gilded Age?

Section 5 (pp. 257– 263)
12. What conditions in their homelands caused people to emigrate to the United States?
13. What were the advantages and disadvantages of political machines and bosses for urban residents?
14. How did the settlement houses help the poor?

---

8. The disappearance of the buffalo eventually destroyed Native Americans' ability to build lives on reservations. Many reformers attempted to "civilize" Native Americans. Also, much of the land given to Native Americans under the Dawes Act was unsuitable for farming; in addition, many Native Americans had no interest or experience in farming. Many therefore sold their land to speculators.

9. Several powerful farm protest groups, including the Grange and the Farmers' Alliances, were formed. Improved communication and transportation systems made united action easier and more practical for farmers.

10. The close relationship between business and government led to bribery. In addition, the spoils system led to abuses associated with patronage.

11. The Bland-Allison Act required the purchase and coining of silver. The Pendleton Act undermined the spoils system by instituting civil service exams. The Interstate Commerce Act enabled the federal government to regulate railroads. The Sherman Antitrust Act was an attempt to regulate trusts.

12. Immigrants were fleeing crop failures, land and job shortages, rising taxes, famine, and religious or political persecution in their homelands.

Thinking Critically

1. **Identifying Assumptions** During the late 1800s, many people began to associate labor unions with violence and radical political ideas. Why did people make this association?
2. **Formulating Questions** Based on what you have read in the chapter, write four questions to ask new homesteaders about their life in the West.
3. **Making Comparisons** Blue laws that restrict the operation of stores and the sale of liquor on Sundays are still enforced in some parts of the United States. Do you think that the arguments for and against these laws are the same as those used in the late 1800s?

Making Connections

1. **Evaluating Primary Sources** Review the primary source on page 263. What does the speaker mean by now having several points of view?
2. **Understanding the Visuals** Choose two visuals from the chapter that demonstrate the inequality of labor and business in the late 1800s and explain why you think they demonstrate the point.
3. **Writing About the Chapter** Imagine that the 1892 election is rapidly approaching. Create an informational flyer urging voters to support the Populist party. First decide why voters should support the Populists. Then write a draft of your flyer explaining your point of view. Anticipate and reply to any potential objections to the Populist platform. Revise your flyer, making certain that your writing is informative and persuasive, Proofread your flyer and draft a final copy.
4. **Using the Graphic Organizer** This graphic organizer uses a tree map to provide information about the developing West. (a) Based on what you have read in the chapter, how did mechanization and new agricultural knowledge lead to the growth of bonanza farms? (b) According to the graphic organizer below, what role did big business play in the development of the West? (c) On a separate sheet of paper, create your own graphic organizer, showing the effects of westward expansion on the Native American groups living in the West.

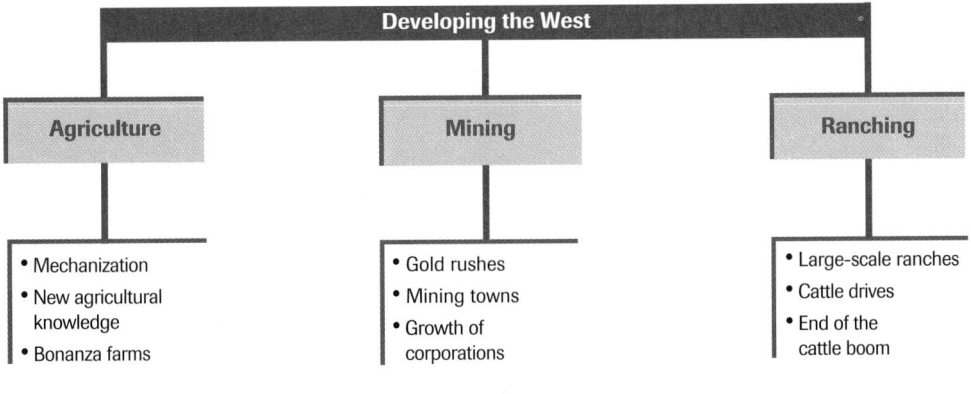

Developing the West

Agriculture
- Mechanization
- New agricultural knowledge
- Bonanza farms

Mining
- Gold rushes
- Mining towns
- Growth of corporations

Ranching
- Large-scale ranches
- Cattle drives
- End of the cattle boom

---

13. Disadvantages: Political machines and bosses were corrupt, surviving on bribery and graft. Advantages: They helped people and made up for the lack of a public welfare system.

14. Unlike other charity movements, settlements offered social services rather than money.

Thinking Critically

1. The public began to equate labor unions in general with the specific actions and violence of anarchists during some labor disputes. Although this violence turned many people against unions, of course not all strikes became violent.

2. Possible questions: Why did you move west? How did you purchase your land? What experience have you had with farming? How do the realities of life in the West fit with your expectations?

3. Arguments for in 1800s: Sunday is a holy day for Christians; everyone should have a day of rest; drinking should be restricted as much as possible. Arguments against in 1800s: Not everyone is Christian, so not everyone should be forced to rest; people who work all week need to be able to shop on Sundays; retailers need to be able to make a profit seven days a week. Arguments today probably place less stress on issues of morality and more emphasis on people's busy schedules than in the past.

Many people have the mistaken impression that Native Americans did little to resist white settlement of their lands other than attack pioneers and raid towns. In fact, Native Americans undertook many negotiations and made numerous trips to speak with members of the federal government regarding their position. Point out to students that when one is fighting a powerful opponent, it can be difficult to find any course of action that produces favorable results.

Throughout American history, a vast difference has existed between the idealized, popular view of United States and the reality that greeted immigrants. Ask students to think about whether the people who painted such glorified pictures of the United States in Anna Yezierska's excerpt were lying or simply focusing only on some aspects of society and not on others. Were Yezierska's dreams truly unattainable?

INSTRUCT

Assign several students to play the roles of the Otoe Chiefs and the federal government agent. Have them read the transcript of their talks in front of the class, using facial expressions and body language to portray their character's feelings. Then have the class discuss how each side must have felt during the conversations.

Then have one student read the excerpt from Anzia Yezierska's autobiography aloud. Ask students whether they have ever undertaken a new experience or venture, such as joining a new club, trying out for a part in a play, attending a new school, or going to a party where they know few people. Ask students to compare their expectations of the new experience to the reality. Ask them to describe their feelings after the first meeting of the club, the first

CHAPTER 7
SOURCE READINGS

Talks with Otoe Chiefs

Primary Source

INTRODUCTION As a result of the push westward, land was in great demand in the late 1800s. Vast areas controlled by Native Americans in the West were of increasing interest to settlers and the United States government. One Native American group, the Otoe of Nebraska, cultivated the land along the Platte River and hunted bison on the Great Plains. By the late 1800s, the United States government was interested in removing the Otoe from their land and selling the land to settlers. In 1873 a delegation of Otoe chiefs traveled from Nebraska to meet with Commissioner of Indian Affairs Edward P. Smith and the Otoe agent in Washington, D.C. The following is a condensation of a handwritten transcript of the conversations. A year after these conversations, one of the chiefs, Medicine Horse, attempted to lead fifty families on a flight to freedom from their Nebraska reservation into Kansas Territory, but he was captured and imprisoned before he could succeed.

VOCABULARY Before you read the selection, find the meaning of these words in a dictionary: render, annuity, appraise.

NOVEMBER 1, 1873, SECOND DAY

COMMISSIONER: Yesterday when we met you were tired and could not talk. I hope you have had a good sleep and can talk well now.

MEDICINE HORSE: My tribe has sent me down here to do the talking for them. I spoke to our Agent about it and I suppose you have heard about it, that we would sell our land. All our white brothers have big pieces of land, and get along much better than we do. We want the same. Some of the chiefs went with me to see another country. I like it and want to go there.

COMMISSIONER: There are two kinds of Indians there. Some are good and work, and others are very wild and bad. I should be very sorry to have you go from Nebraska so as to be able to go wild again like some now in Indian Territory. What you ought to do is get ready as fast as you can to be like white people, and know as much as they do. There are white men who live by roaming about, but they do not amount to much.

STAND BY: I made a Treaty and sold our lands—a large piece of it. We did not sell it for paper money but for hard money.

COMMISSIONER: I will tell you now for what purpose this money was promised to you. . . . The President decides whether to give the money or other things which he considers better for you. I will not take your money away but will spend it so as to do you good. Four hundred dollars will feed your tribe a month. It will fence a farm that will feed you and your children a hundred years. Is it not better for us to send money to your Agent to fence your farms than to send it to you to pass over to traders for trinkets?

STAND BY: We always raised something from the ground to support our families before we ever saw white men. But sometimes we get a good many furs and they bring us more money than we can get from what we raise. My Father told me if I wanted anything I should come here and get it. I know what kind of a treaty we made. I have it in my head.

COMMISSIONER: Things last longer on paper than they do in your head. Your grandchildren will be able to take from this paper what was agreed to be done with the money. When they couldn't tell at all from your head better than you can now.

STAND BY: How would these white men feel to have their property used in this way?

COMMISSIONER: If the white men are children and you are their guardian, you can do what you please with their money—provided you do what is good for them.

MEDICINE HORSE: We are not children. We are men. I never thought I would be treated so when I made the Treaty.

NOVEMBER 4, 1873, THIRD DAY

COMMISSIONER: You have had a long time to think about what we are to talk of today.

MEDICINE HORSE: Father, what you said to us the other day hurt our feelings very much and we could not sleep since. When we made a trade, they did not tell us we must use our money, as you told us the other day. Our Great Father owes us a great deal of money. I always thought I should draw my money. Your talk the other day takes our rights away. I will be ashamed to take home this news. . . .

COMMISSIONER: Our Great Father likes his children and does what is best for them when sometimes his children do not like it. You have received these annuities for nearly twenty years. You have had the best land in Nebraska. Just such land as your white brothers have made such good homes out of. Now why is it you have no houses, oxen, cows, horses, and homes like the white man? You have not been brought up that way. But there is a change coming over your life and it is hard for an old man to change his ways, but unless you change sometime, and it is hard for some old ones, it will be hard for the children to change.

STAND BY: We don't want to settle this business now. We want to go home and study about it. When white men want to make a plan, they get together and study about it two or three days. You want to put it all through at once, like drowning me in the river. We are not the only chiefs. There are some more at home. We will take the news home, and if it suits all, we will have to do so.

COMMISSIONER: There is no use to talk about half the land for that is settled. Congress passed a law and you all agreed to it, and men have been sent out to appraise the land, and if there is anyone to buy it, the land will be sold.

STAND BY: If you have a piece of land and I sell it, you would not like it.

COMMISSIONER: If you are my Agent and sell it, it is all right. You must remember there is a difference. You are the child of Government, and it must take care of you. . . .

BIG BEAR: We work all the time. We like to work. You want to bind us right down, and we don't like it. I have raised wheat, corn, potatoes, and pumpkins. We all work. But you cannot make white men of us. That is one thing you can't do.

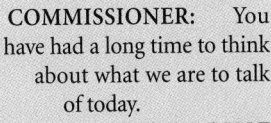

A chief's headress from the collection of the Pan-handle Plains Historical Society in Canyon, Texas.

THINKING ABOUT THE SELECTION

1. What did the Otoe chiefs hope to gain from their meeting in Washington?
2. How did the Otoe chiefs view the actions of the federal government?

Critical Thinking
3. **Recognizing Bias** How would you characterize the commissioner's attitude toward Native Americans?

ANSWERS TO

Thinking About the Selection
1. They hoped to be paid for the land that they had sold.
2. They viewed the actions of the federal government as unfair, dishonest, and humiliating.
3. The commissioner's attitude can be characterized as condescending. He is biased toward the ways of white people and does not consider that the ways of Native Americans are equally valid and valuable.

day at the new school, and so on. Then ask students to compare those feelings to those related by Anna Yezierska. How are they similar? How are they different?

Finally, have students write an essay, draw a picture, or compose a song comparing the situation of Native Americans and European immigrants to the United States during the late 1800s. Students can use their textbooks to help them understand the positions of these two groups of people.

EXTEND

Have students ask their parents or other relatives whether their ancestors immigrated to the United States from Europe during the late 1800s. If so, have students interview any living relative who remembers some details about the immigrant. Students should ask questions such as: Why did [relative] decide to leave his or her native country? How much did it cost to make the trip? What was the journey across the ocean like? Where did [relative] live on arriving in the United States? What did [relative] do for a living? Students can tape record their interviews and play them back to the class. Have them write a one-page paper describing the contents of the tape and what they learned about European immigrants in doing the interview. If a student does not have a relative who emigrated from Europe, have them check with neighbors or other people in the community to find someone who does. Students can then interview that person for memories about the immigrant.

SOURCE READINGS

Where Is America?

 *Literature*

Anzia Yezierska

INTRODUCTION Like many other immigrants who flooded into the nation's cities during the late 1800s, Anzia Yezierska and her family came to New York to escape ethnic persecution in their homeland. In her autobiography, *Hungry Hearts,* Yezierska describes what it was like to leave her Russian village and begin a new life in the United States.

VOCABULARY Before you read the selection, find the meaning of these words in a dictionary: Cossack, dilapidated, maw, galling.

Steerage—dirty bundles—foul odors—seasick humanity—but I saw and heard nothing of the foulness and ugliness around me. I floated in showers of sunshine. Vision upon vision of the new world opened before me. From everyone's lips flowed the golden legend of the golden country:

"In America you can say what you feel—you can join your friends in the open streets without fear of Cossack."

"In America is a home for everyone. The land is your land. Not like in Russia where you feel yourself a stranger in the village where you were born and lived—the village in which your father and grandfather lie buried." . . .

"Everybody can do what he wants with his life in America."

"There are no high or low in America. Even the President holds hands with Gedalyeh Mindel."

"Plenty for all. Learning flows free like milk and honey."

"Learning flows free."

The words painted pictures in my mind. I saw before me free schools, free colleges, free libraries, where I could learn and learn and keep on learning. . . .

"Land! Land!" came the joyous shout.

"America! We're in America!" cried my mother, almost smothering us in her rapture.

All crowded and pushed on deck. They strained and stretched to get the first glimpse of the "golden country," lifting their children on their shoulders that they might see beyond them.

Men fell on their knees to pray. Women hugged their babies and wept. Children danced. Strangers embraced and kissed like old friends. Old men and women had in their eyes a look of young people in love.

Age-old visions sang themselves in me—songs of freedom of an oppressed people.

America! America! . . .

Between buildings that loomed like mountains, we struggled with our bundles, spreading around us the smell of the steerage. Up Broadway, under the bridge, and through the swarming streets of the ghetto, we followed Gedalyeh Mindel.

I looked about the narrow streets of squeezed-in stores and houses, ragged clothes, dirty bedding oozing out of the windows, ash cans and garbage cans cluttering the sidewalk. A vague sadness pressed down my heart—the first doubt of America.

"Where are the green fields and open spaces in America?" cried my heart. "Where is the golden country of my dreams?"

A loneliness for the fragrant silence of the woods that lay beyond our mud hut welled up in my heart, a longing for the soft, responsive earth of our village streets. All about me was the hardness of brick and stone, the stinking smells of crowded poverty.

America, the destination of millions of immigrants in the late 1800s, is stamped in gold letters on the side of this steamer trunk.

"Here's your house with separate rooms like in a palace." Gedalyeh Mindel flung open the door of a dingy, airless flat.

"Oi weh!" my mother cried in dismay. "Where's the sunshine in America?"

She went to the window and looked out at the blank wall of the next house. "Gottuniu! Like in a grave so dark."

"It ain't so dark, it's only a little shady." Gedalyeh Mindel lighted the gas. "Look only." He pointed with pride to the dim gaslight. "No candles, no kerosene lamps in America, you turn on a screw and put to it a match and you got it light like with sunshine."

Again the shadow fell over me, again the doubt of America!

In America were rooms without sunlight, rooms to sleep in, to eat in, to cook in, but without sunshine. And Gedalyeh Mindel was happy. Could I be satisfied with just a place to sleep and eat in, and a door to shut people out—to take the place of sunlight? Or would I always need the sunlight to be happy?

And where was there a place in America for me to play? I looked out into the alley below and saw pale-faced children scrambling in the gutter. "Where is America?" cried my heart. . . .

"Heart of mine!" my mother's voice moaned above me. "Father is already gone an hour. You know how they'll squeeze from you a nickel for every minute you're late. Quick only!"

I seized my bread and herring and tumbled down the stairs and out into the street. I ate running, blindly pressing through the hurrying throngs of workers—my haste and fear choking each mouthful.

I felt a strangling in my throat as I neared the sweatshop prison[1]; all my nerves screwed together into iron hardness to endure the day's torture.

For an instant I hesitated as I faced the grated window of the old dilapidated building—dirt and decay cried out from every crumbling brick.

In the maw of the shop, raging around me the roar and the clatter, the clatter and the roar, the merciless grind of the pounding machines. Half maddened, half deadened, I struggled to think, to feel, to remember—what am I—who am I—why was I here?

[1] Factory where Yezierska worked

I struggled in vain—bewildered and lost in a whirlpool of noise.

"America—America—where was America?"

It cried in my heart.

The factory whistle—the slowing-down of the machines—the shout of release hailing the noon hour.

I woke as from a tense nightmare—a weary waking to pain.

In the dark chaos of my brain reason began to dawn. In my stifled heart feelings began to pulse. The wound of my wasted life began to throb and ache. My childhood choked with drudgery—must my youth too die—unlived?

The odor of herring and garlic—the ravenous munching of food—laughing and loud, vulgar jokes. Was it only I who was so wretched? I looked at those around me. Were they happy or only insensible to their slavery? How could they laugh and joke? Why were they not torn with rebellion against this galling grind—the crushing, deadening movements of the body, where only hands live and hearts and brains must die?

A touch on my shoulder. I looked up. It was Yetta Solomon from the machine next to mine.

"Here's your tea."

I stared at her, half hearing.

"Ain't you going to eat nothing?"

"Oi weh! Yetta! I can't stand it!" The cry broke from me. "I didn't come to America to turn into a machine. I came to America to make from myself a person. Does America want only my hands—only the strength of my body—not my heart—not my feelings—my thoughts?"

THINKING ABOUT THE SELECTION

1. What were Anzia Yezierska's expectations of life in the United States?
2. What did the author first miss about her village, once she had been shown the family's new residence?

Critical Thinking

3. **Identifying Central Issues** What was the author's biggest disillusionment with the United States?

ANSWERS TO

Thinking About the Selection

1. She expected to find freedom, choices, equality, and the opportunity to attend school and learn as much as she could.

2. She longed for the "fragrant silence of the woods" and the "soft, responsive earth of our village streets."

3. She was disillusioned when it seemed that the United States wanted only the labor of her hands, and was not interested in her thoughts or feelings.

Chapter 8 Cultural and Social Transformations
1870–1915

📁 Teaching Resources (See Unit 2 Folder)

	Instruction	Enrichment
Section 1 **The Expansion of Education** (pp. 272–275)	Reproducible Lesson Plan, p. 109 Alternate Lesson Plan, p. 85 Guided Reading and Review, p. 113 Quiz, p. 114	Literature Activity, The Promised Land, pp. 132–133 Visual Learning Activity, The Ideal Public School, p. 135 Primary Source Activity, The Washington– Du Bois Debate, p. 129
Section 2 **Recreation for the Masses** (pp. 276–280)	Reproducible Lesson Plan, p. 110 Alternate Lesson Plan, p. 86 Guided Reading and Review, p. 115 Quiz, p. 116	Critical Thinking Activity, Recognizing Cause and Effect, p. 128 American Profiles Activity, George M. Cohan, p. 123 Literature Activity, Around the World in 72 Days, p. 134
Section 3 **The World of Jim Crow** (pp. 281–284)	Reproducible Lesson Plan, p. 111 Alternate Lesson Plan, p. 87 Guided Reading and Review, p. 117 Quiz, p. 118	Primary Source Activity, Lynchings and Mob Law, pp. 130–131 Historian's Toolbox Activity, Reading a Political Cartoon, p. 127
Section 4 **The Woman Question** (pp. 286–289)	Reproducible Lesson Plan, p. 112 Alternate Lesson Plan, p. 88 Guided Reading and Review, p. 119 Quiz, p. 120 Chapter Test, Forms A & B, pp. 140–145	Visual Learning Activity, The New Woman and the New Man, p. 136 American Profiles Activity, Lucy Stone, p. 124 Viewpoints Activity, On the Woman Question, pp. 125–126 History Might Not . . . Activity, Promoting Women's Rights, pp. 121–122

📁 Additional Chapter Resources

Resource Organizer, p. 108
Alternate Lesson Plan, p. 84
Answer Keys, pp. 152–165

Bibliography

For the Teacher

Abrahams, Roger D. *Singing the Master: The Emergence of African Culture in the Plantation South.* Penguin USA, 1993. (Uses primary sources to trace the impact of plantation traditions and songs on African American performance styles in the nineteenth and twentieth centuries.)

Lewis, David Levering. *W. E. B. Du Bois: 1868–1919, Biography of a Race.* Holt, 1993. (The first fifty–one years of the life of the brilliant African American leader.)

Prentice Hall Literature Excerpts from *The American Experience,* 1994, including Chopin, Kate. "The Story of an Hour," from *The Awakening and Selected Short Stories.* Bantam, 1985 edition.

The Big Idea for the chapter and how the main ideas in each section relate to the Big Idea are graphically displayed below. Comprehension of this chapter's Big Idea is critical to students' understanding of United States history and how we as a nation got where we are today.

Media and Technology

 Critical Thinking, I-9

 Fine Art, D-14; Our Multicultural Heritage, C-9

 Visions of America: History Might Not Have Happened This Way Game

 Graphic Organizer, G-3

 Guided Reading Audiotapes (English and Spanish)

 Computer Test Bank

For the Student

Blacks and the Constitution. PBS Video, 1987.

Hymowitz, Carol, and Michaele Weissman. *A History of Women in America.* Bantam, 1978. (A discussion of women's roles from colonial times to the present.)

Washington, Booker T. *Up from Slavery.* Penguin, 1986 edition. (Classic autobiography of the famous civil rights leader.)

CHAPTER 8

The growth of industry and urban areas in the late 1800s brought many cultural and social transformations to the United States. At the same time, many Americans feared change and clung to old ideas about social roles, particularly those that affected women and African Americans.

SECTION 1

Educational opportunities expanded. A growing number of Americans, including African Americans, women, and immigrants, took advantage of these opportunities as a way toward economic and social success.

SECTION 2

Urban workers' demand for recreational activities led to new forms of entertainment that collided with traditional codes of behavior.

SECTION 3

Despite widespread discrimination, African Americans worked hard to rise above the hatred to reach high levels of achievement.

SECTION 4

Women's lives changed greatly, and in response they began to demand both an expanded social role and equal political and economic rights, demands that were contested by traditionalists.

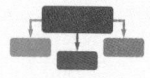

Cultural and Social Transformations
1870–1915

The Relevance of the Big Idea

In the period after the Civil War, Americans experienced dramatic cultural and social transformations—in fact, in many of the same areas as in the 1990s. Industrialization and urbanization brought changes in education, the makeup of society, recreational activities, and the role of women. These changes upset long-established patterns and often met with great resistance from certain segments of American society.

Structure a class discussion on the following topic: What social and cultural changes do Americans face in the 1990s? Have students generate a list of areas, such as the family, entertainment, education, the workplace, the roles of men and women, and the ethnic makeup of the United States, and ask students to explain their long-term significance.

In Depth

Global Connections

New methods of transportation, combined with an exploding American interest in travel and leisure, had a profound effect in the early twentieth century. These changes were symbolized by the British luxury liner, *Titanic,* which sank on its maiden voyage. About 1,500 passengers drowned, including many prominent Americans. As a result of the tragedy, the first International Convention for Safety of Life at Sea met in London in 1913 and agreed on stricter maritime laws—including more lifeboat space, more highly skilled crews, and updated communications equipment.

Cultural and Social Transformations
1870–1915

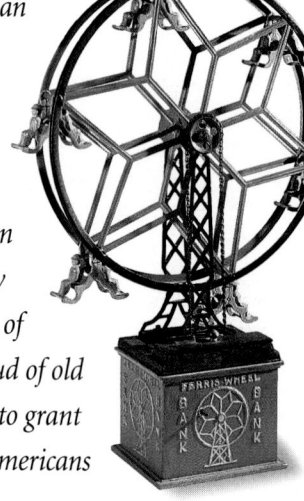

*A*long with the growth of industry and urban areas in the late 1800s came a host of other changes. More children began to attend school, and college became an attainable goal for a growing number of students. A recreation industry, which borrowed heavily from African American culture, emerged to meet the needs of the new urban workers. Yet some segments of society remained mired in the mud of old discriminatory attitudes, refusing to grant such groups as women and African Americans an equal chance at success.

Events in the United States

| 1870 Fewer than half of all American children attend school. | 1873 Boston University opens its doors to women professors. | 1883 Joseph Pulitzer buys the New York World. | 1890 National American Woman Suffrage Association is founded |

| **1870** | **1875** | **1880** | **1885** | **1890** |

Events in the World

1872 Japan begins universal military service.

RESOURCE DIRECTORY

Teaching Resources

Alternate Lesson Plan: Demonstrating the Big Idea found in the Alternate Lesson Plans folder, p. 84, provides a lesson strategy to instruct students about the Big Idea that in the late 1800s and early 1900s, many social and cultural changes transformed American society, but not all Americans could participate fully in these changes.

Alternative Assessment Handbook provides information, guidance, and strategies for alternative methods of assessment. It includes an essay on new trends in assessment, guidance and strategies for developing performance tasks and portfolios, scoring rubrics, and sample evaluation forms.

Pages 272–275

The Expansion of Education

Education was a lofty goal that was out of reach for most nineteenth-century Americans. As the century came to a close, however, more and more Americans, including women and minorities, gained the opportunity to learn and grow.

Pages 276–280

Recreation for the Masses

The growing urban working class took its recreation seriously in the late 1800s. Entertainment and sports became new industries that careened onto the American scene and collided with more restrained values.

Pages 281–284

The World of Jim Crow

White society proved quite resourceful at finding ways to repress African Americans in the years after Reconstruction. Yet many African Americans demonstrated an even greater will to rise above the discrimination and hate.

Pages 286–289

The Woman Question

Much had changed for women in the late 1800s—new jobs, new educational opportunities, new roles in the home. Yet much stayed the same, including continued economic and political inequality. This contradiction fueled great debate at the turn of the century.

1896 The Supreme Court legalizes segregation in Plessy v. Ferguson decision.

1903 The movie The Great Train Robbery is a huge popular success.

1910 The National Association for the Advancement of Colored People (NAACP) is founded.

1915 The Supreme Court declares grandfather clauses unconstitutional.

1895	1900	1905	1910	1915

1896 First modern Olympic Games take place in Athens.

1903 Emmeline Pankhurst founds the Women's Social and Political Union in Britain.

1910 The Mexican Revolution begins.

1913 Russian composer Igor Stravinsky revolutionizes music with The Rite of Spring.

Alternative Assessment

As an ongoing chapter project, students can create a project titled "A Changing World—The United States at the Turn of the Century." The objective is to illustrate the changes transforming the United States at the end of the 1800s. Research may include examination of documents or published sources. Students may design the project by following the suggestions below, or use an original format.

● Create a newspaper page, including photographs and illustrations with captions as well as short news items, that reflects the changes transforming the United States.

● Create a vaudeville-type show that portrays life at that time.

Explain that finished projects will be assessed according to the following standards:

● **Unacceptable** Projects are not attempted or fail to meet requirements outlined.

● **Limited/Acceptable** Projects are based on material from the textbook and reflect some effort to show connections among topics.

● **Extensive/Commendable** Projects are based on some outside research and demonstrate some connections among topics.

● **Extraordinary/Outstanding** Projects are based on considerable outside research, highlight specific as well as general relationships among topics, and reflect in-depth knowledge.

Students may choose to include finished projects in their portfolios.

For more information and guidance on alternative assessment trends and strategies, see the Alternative Assessment Handbook in the Resource Directory on page 270.

The Expansion of Education

1. FOCUS

Connecting to the Big Idea

See page 270B. Explain that as the United States became more industrialized and urbanized after the Civil War, Americans needed more education. Educational opportunities greatly increased. Ask students in what ways educational opportunities expanded and who benefited.

Objectives

● Describe how opportunities for public education expanded after the Civil War.

● Explain how opportunities for higher education increased in the late 1800s.

● Describe the impact the widening of educational opportunities had on women and African Americans.

Bellringer

Ask students if they think changes need to be made in American education in order to better prepare students for their future roles. Ask them to explain what they think these changes should be.

Reading Strategy

Reinforcing Key Ideas Ask students to list and briefly describe, as they read, the ways in which educational opportunities expanded in the late 1800s.

Answer to . . .

MAKING CONNECTIONS

(See page 273.) Possible answers: Today's lessons emphasize maintaining individual cultural heritage and valuing the diversity brought to the United States by different immigrant groups, whereas in the late 1800s the emphasis was on Americanization.

The Expansion of Education

SECTION PREVIEW

Education was a lofty goal that was out of reach for most nineteenth-century Americans. As the century came to a close, however, more and more Americans, including women and minorities, gained the opportunity to learn and grow.

Beginning in the late 1800s, a growing number of Americans sought the benefits of education.

Key Concepts

• Opportunities for public education expanded after the Civil War.
• Opportunities for higher education also expanded in the late 1800s.
    • The wider availability of higher education had a powerful impact on women and African Americans.

Key Terms, People, and Places

Booker T. Washington, W.E.B. Du Bois

A mericans had long understood that a democratic society functioned best when its citizens could read and write and communicate effectively. By the late 1800s, however, an education had become more than just a worthy goal. For a growing number of Americans, it was a necessary first step toward economic and social success. In recognition of this fact and in response to public demand, educational opportunities expanded.

Public Schools Gain More Students

By the time of the Civil War, more than half of the nation's white children were receiving some kind of formal education. A high school diploma was still the exception, however: even in 1870, only 2 percent of all seventeen-year-olds graduated from high school. Only a tiny elite went on to college. Because most children had to help their families earn a living, many left school at an early age.

The vast majority of American children had to make do with the basic skills acquired during a few school years, each of which lasted just a few months. As the United States became more industrialized and urbanized in the postwar era, young people began to realize that they needed more than basic skills to advance in life. Parents began pressuring local governments to increase school funding and lengthen the school year. At the same time, reformers pressured state governments to limit child labor. By 1900, thirty-two states had passed compulsory school laws that required children eight to fourteen years old to attend school.

Although unevenly enforced, these laws had a powerful effect. In 1870 overall school enrollment was less than 50 percent of all American children—including fewer than 1 in 10 African Americans. Fewer than 72,000 went to the nation's high schools. By 1910 enrollment was nearly 60 percent, and more than 1,000,000 students were studying in the nation's high schools.

Immigrants and Public Education Immigrants especially treasured American public education. In the mid-1890s, the Russian immigrant father of author Mary Antin was proud to send his children to a Boston public school, convinced "there was no surer way to their advancement and happiness." Adults attended school at night to learn English and civics to qualify for citizenship. ◉

In teaching American standards of cleanliness, thrift, patriotism, and hard work, public schools promoted assimilation of immigrants into the American way of life. In playing games like baseball or basketball or cooking traditional American foods in home economics classes, immigrant children became Americanized and began to forget their native cultures.

Some parents resisted Americanization. Many Greek Orthodox and Eastern European Jewish parents sent their children to religious schools to learn about their cultural heritage in their native languages. Polish parents in Chicago in the early 1900s sent their children to

---

▶ RESOURCE DIRECTORY

Teaching Resources

📘 **Reproducible Lesson Plan** found in the Unit 2 folder, p. 109, provides a summary of the Section 1 lesson plan content.

📘 **Alternate Lesson Plan: Critical Thinking** Identifying Assumptions, found in the Alternate Lesson Plans folder, p. 85, encourages students to apply this skill while comparing Booker T. Washington and W. E. B. Du Bois.

📘 **Guided Reading and Review** found in the Unit 2 folder, p. 113, provides a structure for reading and mastering the key concepts and reviewing the key terms for Section 1. (Guided Practice)

⭐📘 **Literature Activity** The Promised Land, found in the Unit 2 folder, pp. 132–133, an excerpt from the autobiography of Mary Antin, a Jewish immigrant living in Boston, shows the importance of education to immigrant families.

Roman Catholic schools where they learned about Polish history and religion in Polish but studied American history, bookkeeping, and algebra in English.

Immigrants also made their own contributions to American culture. As they shared customs and habits from their homelands, they enriched their new country. Thus, immigrants and Americans each benefited from exposure to one another.

Uneven Support for Schools Though state and local government support for education was expanding, not everyone benefited equally. Compared to white schools, schools for African Americans received less money—sometimes half as much. Writing of her upbringing in Durham, North Carolina, in the 1910s, civil rights activist Pauli Murray remembered vividly the contrast between "what we had and what the white children had."

W e got the greasy, torn, dog-eared books; they got the new ones. They had field day in the city park; we had it on a furrowed stubby hillside. They got wide mention in the newspaper; we got a paragraph at the bottom. . . . We came to know that whatever we had was always inferior.

African Americans were not the only group to receive a separate but unequal education. For example, beginning in the 1890s, Mexican Americans in parts of the Southwest were shuttled off to schools separate from and less well funded than those for white children. Many Asians in California were sent to separate schools. And by 1900, only a small percentage of Native American children were receiving any kind of formal schooling. ★

MAKING CONNECTIONS

What do today's students learn about the role of diverse cultures in American life? How are these lessons different from what students learned in the late 1800s?

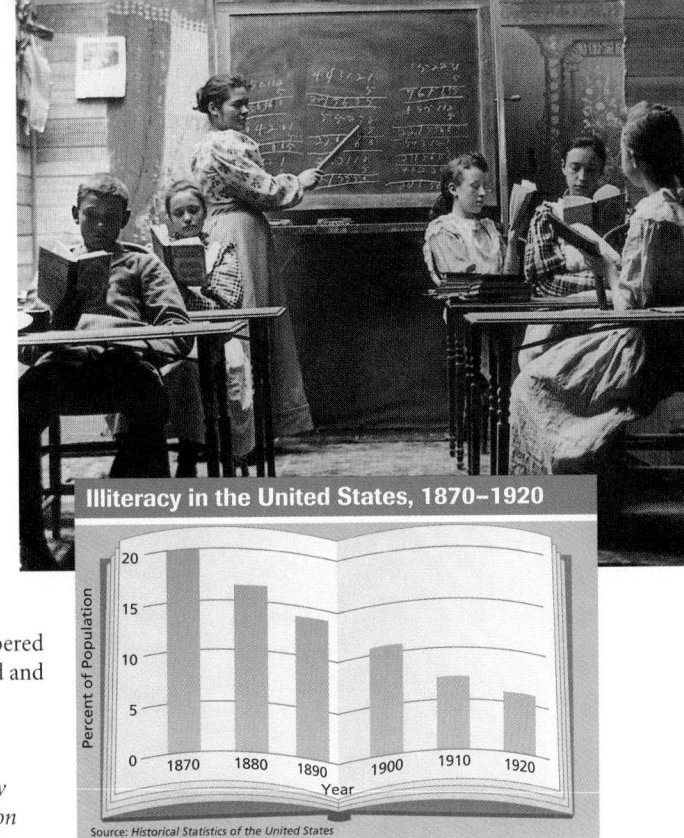

Illiteracy in the United States, 1870–1920

Percent of Population (y-axis: 0, 5, 10, 15, 20)
Year (x-axis): 1870, 1880, 1890, 1900, 1910, 1920

Source: Historical Statistics of the United States

 Interpreting Graphs
The expansion of education meant more students in classrooms, such as this one in Nebraska in 1895. It also meant jobs for women, who filled many teaching posts. *How does the change in the nation's literacy rate reflect the growth of education between 1870 and 1920?*

Higher Education Expands

Between 1880 and 1900, more than 250 new American colleges and universities opened, and college enrollment more than doubled. Wealthy capitalists often endowed institutions of higher learning. For example, in 1885 Leland Stanford, the entrepreneur who had helped build the transcontinental railroad, and his wife, Jane Lathrop Stanford, founded Stanford University. John D. Rockefeller made donations to the University of Chicago that eventually totaled $40 million.

After the Civil War, middle-class women called for greater educational opportunities. In response, educators and philanthropists established private women's colleges with high

 Visual Learning Activity The Ideal Public School, found in the Unit 2 folder, p. 135, uses an 1870 cartoon from *Harper's Weekly* to illustrate contemporary debates over public education.

Media and Technology

Transparency
Critical Thinking, I-9

2. INSTRUCT

Explain/Discuss
Discuss the demand for increasing educational opportunities as industrialization and urbanization increased in the United States. Why did young people need more education in the post–Civil War era? Discuss the increase in available educational opportunities. What was the result of compulsory school laws? How did education encourage immigrants to assimilate? Who benefited from increased opportunities for higher education?

Analyze
Analyze the impact of expanded educational opportunities for African Americans, women, and other minorities on these groups and on American society as a whole. Why was there such a difference between Booker T. Washington's and W. E. B. Du Bois's approach toward education for African Americans?

Caption Answer to ...

 Interpreting Graphs

The illiteracy rate dropped dramatically, from 20 percent to about 8 percent.

In Depth

Did You Know?

The Pledge of Allegiance, attributed to editor Francis Bellamy, first appeared in a magazine called *The Youth's Companion* on September 8, 1892. Bellamy's original Pledge stated, "I pledge allegiance to my Flag and the Republic for which it stands; one Nation indivisible with liberty and justice for all." In 1924, "my flag" was changed to "the Flag of the United States of America." Congress officially recognized the Pledge in 1942, and in 1954, the House of Representatives added "under God."

Interpreting Graphs

Not quite. Even though women saw a large increase in college and university attendance, they remained a minority of the overall student population.

Activity

Teaching Heterogeneous Groups

As a growing number of African Americans went on to higher education in the late 1800s, controversy existed regarding the goals of their education. To demonstrate the divergent goals expressed by Booker T. Washington and W. E. B. Du Bois respectively, divide students into two schools: the Washington School and the Du Bois School. Have each group design a day's class schedule to reflect the educational philosophy of their school.

Enrichment

American schools before and after the Civil War reflected the Protestant thinking of the white, male founders of the United States. A series of books by William H. McGuffey, used for teaching students how to read at the time, promoted these values. Locate one of McGuffey's readers and ask students to describe the values it advanced.

3. ASSESS

Section 1 Review Answers

1. (a) Booker T. Washington, see p. 275, (b) W. E. B. Du Bois, see p. 275

2. Most children learned only basic skills and dropped out of school early in order to earn a living. After the Civil War, communities increased funding for schools, lengthened the school year, and required children to stay in school up to age fourteen.

3. It provided the means for success and assimilation, although not all groups welcomed assimilation.

Women Enrolled in Institutions of Higher Learning, 1870–1920

- Number of Women Enrolled (in thousands)
- Percentage of All Students Enrolled

(y-axis: 0, 50, 100, 150, 200, 250, 300)
(x-axis: 1870, 1880, 1890, 1900, 1910, 1920 — Year)

Source: *A Century of Higher Education for American Women*

Interpreting Graphs
The women in this 1880 Smith College chemistry class were among the first to benefit from new higher education opportunities. *Did women achieve equality with men in the percentage of enrolled students?*

academic standards. The first was New York's Vassar College, which opened in 1865.

Pressure also increased on men's colleges to admit women in the 1880s and 1890s. Rather than do so, some schools founded separate institutions for women that were related to the men's schools. Tulane in Louisiana became the only major southern university to take this step when it established Sophie Newcomb College in 1886. Shortly thereafter, Columbia in New York opened Barnard (1889), Brown in Rhode Island started Pembroke (1891), and Harvard University in Massachusetts established Radcliffe (1894).

Opportunities for men and women to study together—coeducation—also increased. A number of religiously based colleges, including Oberlin, Knox, Antioch, Swarthmore, and Bates, had been coeducational since long before the Civil War. Some colleges also accepted African Americans. In the postwar years, they were joined by institutions such as Cornell and Boston University; the latter announced in 1873 that it welcomed women not only as students but also as professors.

Schools founded for African Americans after the Civil War, such as Fisk and Howard, accepted both women and men. Women's numbers remained small, however, because most of the scholarships that made college study possible went to men. Anna Julia Cooper, an Oberlin graduate who later became an educator, estimated that there were only thirty black college women studying in the United States in 1891.

Women had to fight for full access to most state-funded institutions. For example, in 1863 the coeducational University of Wisconsin required women to stand until all male students had found seats. After 1867 Wisconsin directed women into a "Female College." In 1873, however, when women refused to attend segregated classes, the university was forced to reestablish coeducation.

Who Went to College?

Even with the new opportunities, only a tiny proportion went to college at the turn of the century. Because in the 1890s annual family incomes averaged under a thousand dollars, parents were hard pressed to meet college costs. A few fortunate and gifted students won scholarships or worked their way through college.

Because most scholarships went to men, women had a harder time obtaining a college education. Even those who could afford the cost faced prejudice against educating women. Parents feared that college made daughters too "independent" or unmarriageable or brought them in contact with "unacceptable" friends. When Martha "Minnie" Carey Thomas finally

RESOURCE DIRECTORY

Teaching Resources

⭐ **Primary Source Activity** The Washington–Du Bois Debate, found in the Unit 2 folder, p. 129, uses an excerpt from W. E. B. Du Bois's *The Souls of Black Folk* to show how Du Bois took issue with the ideas of Booker T. Washington.

persuaded her Quaker father to allow her to take the Cornell University entrance exams, he said to her, "Well, Minnie, I am proud of thee, but this university is an awful place to swallow thee up."

African Americans and Higher Education

African Americans also had to fight prejudice in institutions of higher learning. In 1890 only 160 African Americans were attending white colleges. Many more were studying at the nation's African American institutions. By 1900, for example, more than 2,000 students had graduated from thirty-four African American colleges.

Foremost among these graduates was **Booker T. Washington.** Born into slavery in 1856, Washington began his studies at Hampton Institute in Virginia in 1872. His education there inspired him to develop a similar institution for African Americans in Tuskegee, Alabama. Washington taught his students skills and attitudes that he thought would help them succeed in an environment of increasing violence and discrimination. He told his students to prepare for productive, profitable work. Washington urged them to bring their intellect "to bear upon the everyday practical things of life, upon something that is needed to be done, and something which they will be permitted to do in the community in which they reside." African Americans could win white acceptance, he predicted, by succeeding in those occupations that whites needed them to fill.

Washington spelled out his approach in a speech he delivered in 1895 at the Atlanta Exposition. In addition to appealing to many African Americans, his ideas relieved those whites who had worried that educated blacks would be difficult to manage. Whites began to consult him on all issues concerning race rela-

tions, and President Theodore Roosevelt invited him to the White House in 1901. Washington's autobiography, *Up From Slavery* (1901), became a classic, and he became a dominant force in the African American community.

W.E.B. Du Bois led the next generation of African Americans in a different direction. Born free in Massachusetts, Du Bois graduated from Tennessee's Fisk University and then in 1895 became the first African American to earn a Ph.D. from Harvard.

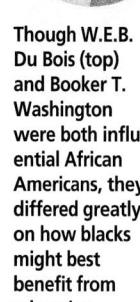

⭐ Du Bois rejected Washington's message, which he mockingly called the Atlanta Compromise. Instead, Du Bois argued that the brightest African Americans had to step forward to lead their people. He urged those future leaders to seek an advanced liberal arts education. Only when they had developed "intelligence, broad sympathy, knowledge of the world that was and is, and of the relation of men to it," he wrote, would they be equipped to lead "the Negro race." In writings such as *The Souls of Black Folk,* Du Bois urged blacks not to define themselves as whites saw them, but to take pride in both their African and their American heritages.

Expanding Opportunities

While the Washington–Du Bois debate raged, college opportunities continued to grow. By 1915 the college experience was still special but no longer unheard of for most Americans. Families of only middling income began to aspire to a college education for their children. This wide availability of advanced education would distinguish the United States from other industrialized countries.

Though W.E.B. Du Bois (top) and Booker T. Washington were both influential African Americans, they differed greatly on how blacks might best benefit from education.

---

4. Hundreds of new universities and colleges, some exclusively for women, opened. Coeducational opportunities for women increased. Women's college enrollment increased enormously. Scholarship and work opportunities meant that a college education in the United States would no longer be a privilege only of the elite.

5. Possible answer: Women and blacks would be better able to achieve gains of all sorts. At the same time, such skills would not enable them to overcome the discriminatory attitudes that had served to keep them down in the first place.

Reteach

Ask students to write one sentence describing how each of the following groups benefited from increased educational opportunities: women; African Americans; white, middle-class men; immigrants; and children.

---

 4. CLOSE

Reinforcing the Big Idea

As urbanization and industrialization increased in the late 1800s, a growing number of Americans took advantage of the country's expanding educational opportunities. The next section describes new opportunities for recreation and leisure time.

SECTION 1 REVIEW

Key Terms, People, and Places
1. Identify (a) Booker T. Washington, (b) W.E.B. Du Bois.

Key Concepts
2. What were the educational possibilities before the Civil War? How did this situation change after the war?
3. Why was education so important to many immigrants?

4. What kinds of higher educational opportunities were available after the Civil War, and with what results?

Critical Thinking
5. **Predicting Consequences** How would you expect the increase in educational opportunities to have affected women and African Americans?

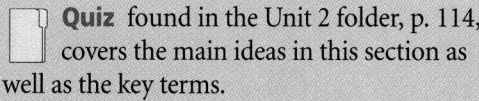 **Quiz** found in the Unit 2 folder, p. 114, covers the main ideas in this section as well as the key terms.

In Depth

Then and Now

Public education brought broad interest in new ideas on the treatment of children. Italian educator Maria Montessori devised her method, based on her belief in the child's right to be treated as an individual, in the early 1900s. Montessori schools were established around the world in countries as different as the United States and India. Today there are more than 450 Montessori schools in the United States.

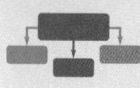

SECTION 2

Recreation for the Masses

1. FOCUS

Connecting to the Big Idea

See page 270B. Explain to students that urbanization and industrialization brought in their wake a new commercial entertainment industry. Ask students what the new forms of amusement were in the late 1800s. How did these clash with more traditional codes of behavior?

Objectives

• Describe the new forms of entertainment that emerged in the late nineteenth century.

• Explain the influence of African American musical styles on the new culture.

• Explain why popular amusements caused conflict between the working class and those who wanted to maintain existing codes of behavior.

Bellringer

Ask students how they like to entertain themselves during their free time and if any of their choices cause conflict with the wishes of their parents or other authority figures.

Reading Strategy

Question Writing Have students read the section's main headings. Then ask students to write a question about each heading and to look for answers to their questions as they read.

Basketball and other sports were popular forms of recreation at the turn of the century.

SECTION PREVIEW

The growing urban working class took its recreation seriously in the late 1800s. Entertainment and sports became new industries that careened onto the American scene and collided with more restrained values.

Key Concepts

• A new mass entertainment and recreation culture emerged in the late nineteenth century.

• The new culture borrowed heavily from African American musical styles.

• Popular amusements stimulated conflict between the working class and those who wanted to maintain existing moral codes.

Key Terms, People, and Places
vaudeville, yellow journalism, minstrel show, ragtime, jazz, Victorianism

I n rural America, time spent in play was considered time wasted. Only after the harvest was in or at times of special celebration would rural people allow themselves leisure activities, such as family and community get-togethers. These activities tended to be free—people provided their own food and music.

In contrast, working-class city residents worked by the clock. After long hours on the job, they wanted fun things to do. To meet the need for inexpensive entertainment for the masses, a commercial recreation industry emerged.

Popular Amusements in the Late 1800s

Of all the places where working people gathered in the late 1800s, saloons were the most popular. Denver (population 133,859) had nearly five hundred by 1900; New York City (population 3,437,202) had an estimated ten thousand. Besides providing entertainment, saloons served as places for forging neighborhood and ethnic ties and political alliances. Most of their customers were men. More popular with women were dance halls and cabarets, where patrons watched musical shows and danced the latest dances.

Trolley parks—amusement parks built at the end of trolley lines—were popular with the whole family. Moving pictures also appeared during this era. *The Great Train Robbery,* released in 1903, was a huge success and demonstrated very clearly the commercial possibilities of movies. By 1908 the nation had eight thousand nickelodeons—theaters set up in converted stores or warehouses that charged a nickel admission—showing slapstick comedies and other films to as many as 200,000 people daily.

Sports As leisure time expanded in the late 1800s, sporting events became a favorite pastime. Boxing and horse racing were widely enjoyed spectator sports, but baseball was by far the most popular. ⬤

By 1860, groups such as fire fighters, police officers, and teachers had formed baseball clubs in many American cities. When audiences for these games grew, entrepreneurs enclosed fields and charged admission. Teams formed into leagues and began to play championship games. In the 1870s, the sport's best players were paid. The most popular leagues, though open to Native Americans and white immigrants, excluded black players. Even the best African Americans had no alternative but to play in segregated leagues until the late 1940s.

What Americans loved most about baseball was the speed, daring, and split-second timing of the game. Pitcher Christy Mathewson commented, "The American public wants its excitement rolled up in a package and handed out quickly." Baseball fulfilled that desire. Popular writer Mark Twain remarked on the game's need for precision: "In baseball, you've got to do everything just right, or you don't get there."

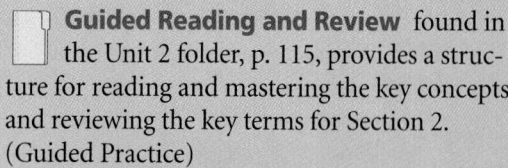

▶ RESOURCE DIRECTORY

Teaching Resources

Reproducible Lesson Plan found in the Unit 2 folder, p. 110, provides a summary of the Section 2 lesson plan content.

Alternate Lesson Plan: Cooperative Learning found in the Alternate Lesson Plans folder, p. 86, provides a strategy for students to work together to create a leisure guide or newspaper "Weekend" section describing recreational activities of the period.

Guided Reading and Review found in the Unit 2 folder, p. 115, provides a structure for reading and mastering the key concepts and reviewing the key terms for Section 2. (Guided Practice)

Critical Thinking Activity Recognizing Cause and Effect: America's Game, found in the Unit 2 folder, p. 128, focuses on the development of American baseball to help students apply this skill.

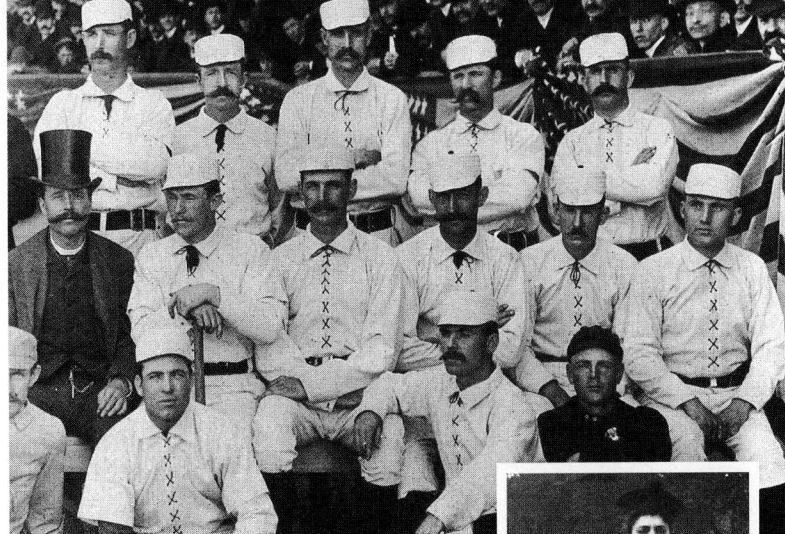

Baseball and football, another sport that achieved great popularity in the late 1800s, were exclusively men's games. Women, too, took up sports. Ice-skating had long been a favorite recreation of women. The national bicycling fad of the late 1800s also became popular among women. And because this sport required practical clothing, it helped to liberate women from some of the restrictive clothing styles of the day. "For muscle-play, freedom is the first requisite," a doctor advised in an 1896 article entitled "Bicycling for Women: The Puzzling Question of Costume." Women athletes had to abandon corsets, which wrapped tightly around their torsos and restricted breathing. Thanks to cycling, as well as to sports such as golf and tennis, shirtwaists—or ready-made blouses—that were tucked into shorter or split skirts, became socially acceptable.

Women students also played basketball, an indoor game invented in 1891 to keep athletes fit during winter. On the assumption that stiff competition and hard physical exertion were unhealthy for women, recreation specialists devised less demanding rules for them. Women athletes also learned gymnastics and swam, although social standards required them to wear black cotton stockings under short dresses or bloomers.

*S*uch words as Liar, Slob, Son-of-a-Gun, Devil, Sucker, . . . and all other words unfit for the ears of ladies and children, also any reference to questionable streets, resorts, localities, and bar-rooms, are prohibited under fine of instant discharge.

Like baseball, vaudeville came to be seen as typically American in character. It appealed to men and women of all ages and classes. Like much of what is on television today, vaudeville was entertainment for the masses.

Vaudeville Inexpensive theatrical performances attracted large crowds in this era. **Vaudeville,** a type of variety show that first appeared in the 1870s, was the most popular. Vaudeville performances consisted of comic sketches based on ethnic or racial humor, song-and-dance routines, and ventriloquists, jugglers, and trapeze artists.

Vaudeville was strictly for the family. Theater owners insisted on keeping everything on a "high plane of respectability and moral cleanliness." A "Notice to Performers" posted on the backstage wall of a prominent vaudeville house in 1899 stated that

Newspapers For city residents, newspapers always had been a vital source of information. In the late 1800s, they became a popular form of entertainment. Taking advantage of new production methods, publishers created larger and more interesting publications. They introduced new features, such as comics, sports sections, Sunday editions, women's pages, stories "hot off the wires," and graphic pictures.

Between 1870 and 1899, newspaper circulation soared from 2.8 to 24 million copies a day. Competing heatedly with one another, publishers urged reporters to discover fresh news

Sports were important to both men and women in this era. Baseball was a well-established spectator sport by 1886, when the picture of the team above was taken. Bicycling provided women with exercise, entertainment—and liberation from restrictive clothing.

American Profiles Activity found in the Unit 2 folder, p. 123, profiles George M. Cohan, the turn-of-the-century entertainer sometimes called "America's greatest showman."

2. INSTRUCT

Discuss

Discuss with students the kinds of popular amusements that emerged in the late 1800s. Ask what part sports played in mass entertainment. What was the role of African American art in popular entertainment?

Analyze

Analyze the conflict aroused by the new forms of entertainment. Contrast the kinds of behavior embraced by forms of entertainment like sports, vaudeville, and dance halls with the code of behavior followed by most middle- and upper-class Americans. In what ways are public amusements still a source of conflict today? You might want to refer to the Bellringer discussion regarding students' choices of entertainment.

In Depth

Biography

The game of basketball was invented in 1891 by Canadian American James A. Naismith (1861–1939). As head of the physical education department at Springfield College in Massachusetts, Naismith was asked to devise a safe indoor game for play during the cold winter months. Blending aspects of soccer, field hockey, football and other sports, and removing (in theory) physical contact, Naismith invented a basketball game for nine players on each side. He coached the game at the University of Kansas, Lawrence, until 1908.

Activity

Writing an Editorial

Ask students to assume the role of either a factory worker or an upper-class city resident and to write an editorial explaining that citizen's opinion of the new kinds of entertainment sweeping the city.

Enrichment

Many well-known American entertainers got their start in vaudeville. Have students research the early life of W. C. Fields, Charlie Chaplin, Will Rogers, Lillian Russell, or another star who began in vaudeville for a description of the performer's act.

Answer to ...

MAKING CONNECTIONS

(See page 279.) Possible answer: The humor of the minstrel show was based upon the notion that African Americans were not able to understand and function within white society. Such beliefs lay at the heart of white justifications for slavery and other forms of discrimination.

In Depth

Interdisciplinary

By 1905, the phonograph, another Edison invention, did for sound what the film projector did for film. Before radio, the phonograph gave the greatest impetus to the spread of popular music, much of it ragtime and jazz, and by 1914 more than half a million phonographs were manufactured each year. Ragtime was, according to African American writer LeRoi Jones (now known as Imamu Amiri Baraka), "a music the Negro came to in imitating white imitations of Negro music."

Newspapers such as the Chicago *Daily News* offered readers information—and entertainment. Magazines also expanded in this era, assisted by a grant of lower postal rates from Congress. ⭐

sources and lurid details of murders, vice, and scandal—anything to sell more papers. Such "sensational" news coverage came to be called **yellow journalism**, a reference to the yellow ink used in a popular comic strip of the era.

Several publishers became national figures. Hungarian-born Joseph Pulitzer, who owned the St. Louis *Post-Dispatch* and in 1883 bought the New York *World*, hoped to "expose all fraud and sham, fight all public evils and abuses." Californian William Randolph Hearst used his father's gold-mining millions to put out the even more sensational New York *Journal*.

Yellow journalism also troubled many. Critics charged that the "yellow press" intruded into private lives, invented facts, and sensationalized the ordinary with exaggeration.

Absorbing and Transforming African American Culture

As the mass entertainment culture expanded, it absorbed many forms of African American art. In the process, the culture transformed them in order to meet the tastes of white audiences.

The Negro Spiritual In 1871 nine Fisk University students went on a singing tour to raise money for their struggling school. When the Fisk Jubilee Singers began to concentrate solely on spirituals, they excited such interest that triumphal tours of the United States, England, and Europe resulted. Britain's Queen Victoria was so impressed that she had a group portrait of them painted.

In the process of making the spiritual acceptable to white audiences, the Fisk group and others like it transformed the musical form. It acquired characteristics of the European musical tradition with which whites were familiar. This new spiritual became identified as an American art form, as opposed to a purely African American one.

Minstrelsy Other forms of African American culture were also absorbed into the white entertainment world. The **minstrel show** began when white actors discovered they could captivate audiences with exaggerated imitations of African American music, dance, and humor. The shows perpetuated racist stereotypes, generally portraying African Americans as foolish imitators of a white culture they could not understand.

White actors in minstrel shows performed in "blackface"—they blackened their faces and hands and painted on wide grins. African Americans also performed in blackface, as minstrel jobs were often the only stage work they could get.

Minstrelsy peaked between the 1840s and 1870s, but even afterward every major town had a minstrel show. It survived long into the twentieth century, in vaudeville and the movies.

The music of ragtime composer Scott Joplin remains popular today.

Ragtime and Jazz A type of music known as **ragtime** originated among black musicians playing in saloons in the South and Midwest in the 1880s. Consisting of melodies with shifting accents over a steady, marching-band beat, it became a rage in the 1890s. Ragtime composer Scott Joplin, who came from St.

▶ RESOURCE DIRECTORY

Teaching Resources

 Literature Activity Around the World in 72 Days, found in the Unit 2 folder, p. 134, features a passage from the writings of Nellie Bly (Elizabeth Cochrane) describing how her record-breaking trip around the world originated.

Louis, Missouri, became famous for his "Maple Leaf Rag" of 1899.

Jazz grew out of the vibrant musical culture of New Orleans, a city with a popular marching-band tradition. After the Civil War, African American bands experimented with new styles of playing, including "raggy" rhythms and call-and-response forms in which singers or instruments respond to a single leader. They also played jazzed-up versions of familiar melodies, such as hymns or the mournful "blues" songs of southern sharecroppers.

New Orleans jazz styles from the 1890s slowly worked their way northward through towns along the Mississippi River. By 1915, thanks in part to the success of the phonograph, jazz—and the dances associated with it—was becoming a national passion.

MAKING CONNECTIONS

How do the attitudes about African Americans as reflected in minstrel shows relate to such issues as slavery and unequal government support for the education of African Americans?

Popular Amusements and Their Critics

Middle- and upper-class city residents had long found much that was offensive in popular amusements. Since well before the Civil War, for example, they had attacked saloons for wasting workers' time and money and helping to cause family abuse. Now, critics charged dance halls and trolley parks with promoting an unsupervised mixing of the sexes. Women especially were at risk of dire consequences associated with unrespectable amusements, critics worried.

Such concerns about the proper behavior of women are examples of **Victorianism,** a term that refers to moral ideas associated with Britain's Queen Victoria, who reigned from 1837 to 1901. Many middle- and upper-class Americans accepted the Victorian morals that dictated proper behavior. They believed that self-control was essential to social progress. Thus, they held personal behavior to a high standard, requiring perfect manners, hard work, sobriety, and, above all, restraint in relations between men and women.

Entertaining a Changing Nation

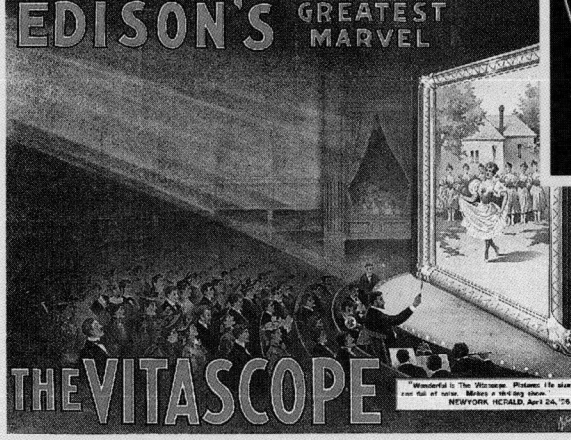

F ilms were just emerging as the hottest form of entertainment in the late 1800s. In today's newest form of entertainment, called virtual reality, computers feed images and sounds through a helmet like the one above. *Could virtual reality have the same impact on our culture as films? Explain your thinking.*

Media and Technology

Transparencies
Fine Art, D-14; Our Multicultural Heritage, C-9

3. ASSESS

Section 2 Review Answers

1. (a) vaudeville, see p. 277, (b) minstrel show, see p. 278

2. Urban residents sought activities to fill their newly acquired leisure time. Since the people had to pay for these activities, it was essential that they be affordable. Saloons, dance halls, trolley parks, and vaudeville were the most popular forms of entertainment.

3. Sports became a leading form of entertainment and recreation. Baseball and football became enormously popular, and Americans paid money to see professional and college teams play. Women skated, rode bicycles, and played other sports, leading to changes in styles of dress.

4. Emerging between the 1870s and 1890s, yellow journalism sensationalized news and attracted wide audiences, enabling it to have a major impact on public opinion.

5. Spirituals, ragtime, and jazz were all adopted by white culture.

6. Victorians, who believed above all in self-control, felt that public amusements were leading to a decline in public morality. Licensing and alternative amusements were introduced as a result.

7. Possible answer: Increasing population densities provided the audiences necessary for the success of organized entertainment and recreation.

Answer to ...

Links Across Time

Answers may suggest that virtual reality may someday be as widespread as films because the technology for its use by individuals or mass audiences is available; or answers may suggest that virtual reality will not catch on because people may not feel comfortable having their sensory input completely controlled by a computer.

Reteach

Ask students to list the key terms and then use them in a paragraph that summarizes the content of the section.

Alternative Assessment

Mid-Point Monitoring

Ask students if they have
- Chosen a format for their project
- Outlined the main ideas
- Begun outside research and preparation of the bibliography

4. CLOSE

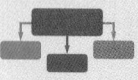

Reinforcing the Big Idea

In response to the demand of the urban working class for inexpensive recreational activities, a mass entertainment industry emerged in the late 1800s, challenging the established codes of moral and social behavior. The next section describes how African Americans confronted repression and discrimination.

The 1893 World's Columbian Exposition in Chicago reflected many aspects of American society during this era. The ferris wheel demonstrated a fascination with recreation and amusement. The White City, some of which appears at bottom right, represented an idealistic dream of urban perfection. In another example of social norms for the time, women had a separate building to showcase their accomplishments—it was segregated from the fair's other exhibits.

When critics raised alarms about the moral impact of places of popular amusement, some Victorians proposed extreme action, such as closing down all "evil resorts." Many working-class and immigrant people resisted such attempts. For them, such commercial "resorts" were often their sole sources of amusement. In the end, a compromise evolved.

After the turn of the century, city governments began to license public amusements, requiring them to adhere to health, safety, and liquor codes, and to uphold certain standards of behavior. Kansas City, for example, tried to ban "close dancing." A regulation from 1913 read, "The lady should place her right hand on her partner's arm and not on his shoulder, and partners should keep their bodies free from each other."

Other places tried to encourage moral behavior by providing "wholesome" recreational alternatives in carefully monitored social settings. Settlement houses and voluntary associations sponsored properly chaperoned dances. Educators added activities such as social dancing to their physical education programs. The urban park movement, which had begun in the 1850s, accelerated during this period. By the late 1800s, most cities had gardens for strolling, ponds for boating, baseball diamonds, skating rinks, and even dance pavilions.

By the turn of the century, a balance had emerged between the desires of the masses to amuse themselves and of more elite groups to preserve old codes of behavior. Public amusements, however, would remain a prime area of contention between diverse ethnic, racial, class, and generational groups in the decades ahead.

SECTION 2 REVIEW

Key Terms, People, and Places
1. Describe (a) vaudeville, (b) minstrel show.

Key Concepts
2. Why did mass entertainment and recreation emerge in the late 1800s, and what forms were most popular?
3. What was the role of sports in the entertainment of the masses in the late 1800s?
4. What was yellow journalism?

5. What forms of African American music were absorbed into white culture?
6. What was the basis for the criticism of public amusements, and what was the result of this criticism?

Critical Thinking
7. **Drawing Conclusions** How did the growth of cities help make possible the growth of the entertainment and recreation outlets discussed in this section?

 RESOURCE DIRECTORY

Teaching Resources

Quiz found in the Unit 2 folder, p. 116, covers the main ideas in this section as well as the key terms.

The World of Jim Crow

SECTION PREVIEW

White society proved quite resourceful at finding ways to repress African Americans in the years after Reconstruction. Yet many African Americans demonstrated an even greater will to rise above the discrimination and hate.

Key Concepts
• White society found a number of ways to discriminate against African Americans after Reconstruction.
• The African American community produced several responses to white discrimination.
• Many African Americans achieved great success in spite of the obstacles placed before them.

Key Terms, People, and Places
poll tax, literacy tests, grandfather clause, Jim Crow, lynching, de facto discrimination, National Association for the Advancement of Colored People (NAACP); Madam C. J. Walker

W ithin a few years after the end of Reconstruction in the 1870s, African Americans began to see many of their newly won freedoms disappear. In the South, they were prevented from exercising their voting rights and were subjected to segregation laws and random violence. Discrimination was also rampant in the North. Despite these developments, African Americans in this era reached high levels of achievement and founded powerful organizations for self-help and protest.

Post-Reconstruction Discrimination

At the same time that white Americans were claiming elements of black culture as their own, racial discrimination and violence were making life harder for African Americans. Booker T. Washington's belief that white Americans would accept hard-working African Americans into equal citizenship was proving too optimistic.

Southern whites, who in the past had always had slavery to repress African Americans, now faced a new situation—free blacks. Whites responded with increasingly vicious methods of oppression.

Voting Restrictions In many southern communities, whites were concerned about the possible impact of African American voters. To deny the vote to blacks—and many lower-class whites with whom African Americans might join forces—southern states employed several tactics during the 1890s. They required voters to own property and to pay a special fee, or **poll tax;** both requirements were beyond the financial reach of most African Americans. Voters also had to demonstrate minimum standards of knowledge by passing **literacy tests.** These tests were rigged to keep African Americans from voting. For example, blacks might be asked questions that were too difficult for most people to answer. White people were given much easier tests.

To ensure that the literacy tests did not keep too many whites from voting, states passed laws that exempted men from certain voting restrictions if they had ancestors who had been allowed to vote before black suffrage. Such laws are examples of **grandfather clauses,** by which groups are exempted from a law if they met certain conditions before that law was passed.

Segregation Also during this period, many states instituted a system of legal segregation that further degraded African Americans. This system was called **Jim Crow**, after a minstrel song-and-dance routine.

Although Jim Crow laws usually are associated with the South, they first appeared in the 1830s, when Massachusetts allowed railroad companies to separate black and white passengers. But it was in the South that Jim Crow became firmly established in many facets of

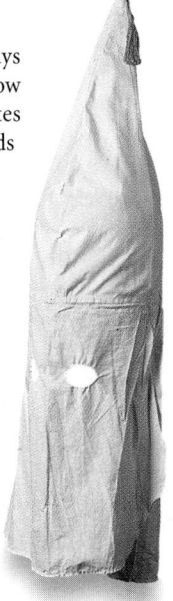

This hood was part of the costume of the Ku Klux Klan, an organization that began to terrorize African Americans in the late 1800s.

1. FOCUS

Connecting to the Big Idea

See page 270B. Tell students that although African Americans were free, white society found many ways to suppress them. Despite this, many African Americans reached high levels of achievement in the era after Reconstruction. Ask in what ways white society denied African Americans their freedom. How did African Americans rise above these injustices?

Objectives

● Describe the ways in which white society subordinated African Americans after Reconstruction.
● Explain how the African American community responded to discrimination.
● Describe the achievements African Americans made despite the obstacles placed in their way.

Bellringer

Ask students to define the words *discriminate* and *discrimination*. Ask how a discriminating person is different from a discriminatory one.

Reading Strategy

Making Predictions Ask students to skim the section, noting the headings and subheadings. Have them make predictions about the content. Have students verify or correct their predictions as they read.

📄 **Reproducible Lesson Plan** found in the Unit 2 folder, p. 111, provides a summary of the Section 3 lesson plan content.

📄 **Alternate Lesson Plan: Critical Thinking** Identifying Alternatives, found in the Alternate Lesson Plans folder, p. 87, provides a strategy for students to apply this skill in examining post-Reconstruction discrimination and the formation of the NAACP and other groups.

📄 **Guided Reading and Review** found in the Unit 2 folder, p. 117, provides a structure for reading and mastering the key concepts and reviewing the key terms for Section 3. (Guided Practice)

Discuss

Review with students discrimination against African Americans after Reconstruction. Ask what tactics whites used to oppress African Americans. Which tactics legally prohibited African Americans from doing certain things, and which inhibited them from exercising their full rights?

Analyze

Have students analyze the African American response to discrimination. What was the significance of "community" in furthering African American efforts to overcome discrimination?

Caption Answer to . . .

 Interpreting Tables

Louisiana, North Carolina, and Alabama adopted voting restrictions in all five categories shown. Virginia also adopted voting restrictions in five categories.

Answer to . . .

MAKING CONNECTIONS

Possible answer: White society adapted and sometimes mocked black culture for their own entertainment. Many whites were unable to tolerate free African Americans and introduced repressive means to put them into limited roles.

Adoption of Voting Restrictions in the South, 1889–1908

Year	Poll Tax	Literacy Test	Property Test	Grandfather Clause	Other*
1889	FL				TN, FL
1890	MI, TN	MI			MI
1891					AR
1892	AR				
1893					AL
1894					SC, VA
1895	SC	SC			SC
1896					
1897					LA
1898	LA	LA	LA	LA	
1899					NC
1900	NC	NC	NC	NC	
1901	AL	AL	AL	AI	
1902	VA, TX	VA	VA		VA
1903					TX
1904					
1905					
1906					
1907					
1908		GA	GA	GA	GA

*Registration, multiple-box, secret ballot, understanding clause
Source: *The American Record: Images of the Nation's Past,* Volume Two, edited by William Graebner and Leonard Richards

Interpreting Tables
As shown above, southern states began to adopt voting laws in the late 1800s. Though the laws varied in their techniques, the effect was always the same—African Americans were denied the vote. *Which states had the widest variety of voting restrictions?*

daily life. The laws began to appear in the South a few years after the end of Reconstruction and were solidly in place by 1900.

Jim Crow dominated almost every aspect of daily life by the early 1900s. The laws required the separation of blacks and whites in schools, parks, public buildings, hospitals, and on transportation systems. African Americans and whites could not use the same public toilets or water fountains. They could not sit in the same sections of theaters. Facilities designated for blacks were always inferior.

The Supreme Court legitimized Jim Crow. In 1883 the Court overturned the Civil Rights Act of 1875, ruling that the Fourteenth Amendment did not prevent private organizations from discriminating against others. *Plessy* v. *Ferguson* (1896) legalized separate facilities for African Americans, as long as they were considered to be equal to those provided to whites. The ruling in *Plessy* proved hard to enforce, and schools and other facilities in the South were rarely if ever made truly equal.

Violence The most horrible feature of the post-Reconstruction decline in conditions for African Americans was **lynching.** The term refers to a mob's illegal seizure and execution of a suspected criminal or troublemaker. Sometimes victims were merely individuals who were unlucky enough to be in the wrong place at the wrong time. The seizure sometimes included a mock trial, torture, and even mutilation before the victim—usually a man—was hanged and riddled with bullets. Those who carried out these horrors were rarely pursued or caught, much less punished. ✪

Conditions in the North Decline Many African Americans, though realizing that life in the North was not perfect, moved there in part to escape legal segregation. What they found instead was **de facto discrimination,** or discrimination in fact instead of by law. Through the widespread cooperation of whites, who enforced unwritten agreements to discriminate against African Americans, public areas, schools, housing, and employment were effectively segregated.

African Americans also experienced occasional lynchings in the North. In addition, bloody race riots occurred in 1900 in New York City and in 1908 in Springfield, Illinois—the city where Abraham Lincoln had practiced law in the early 1800s.

MAKING CONNECTIONS

White Americans seemed to be simultaneously repressing African Americans and embracing aspects of their music and culture. Give a possible explanation for how these two developments could have occurred at the same time.

 **RESOURCE DIRECTORY**

Teaching Resources

✪ **Primary Source Activity** Lynchings and Mob Law, found in the Unit 2 folder, pp. 130–131, provides students with a contemporary account of an Illinois lynching, written by Ida B. Wells.

African Americans Respond to Discrimination

As conditions for African Americans deteriorated, black leaders began to seek new approaches to race problems. For example, Bishop Henry M. Turner of the African Methodist Episcopal church advocated black pride and emigration to Africa. Others criticized Booker T. Washington and his silence on such issues as lynching. Such attacks ignored Washington's quiet support for legal cases against segregation and his financial support for civil rights and African American business activity.

In 1905 a number of outspoken African Americans came together under the leadership of W.E.B. Du Bois to denounce all political, civil, and economic discrimination against African Americans. Meeting in Niagara Falls, Canada, they vowed never to accept "inferiority," bow to "oppression," or apologize "before insult." "We do not hesitate to complain, and to complain loudly and insistently," they warned.

The Niagara Movement, as this group came to be called, gained only about four hundred members and won few concrete victories. But it formed the nucleus of a group that a few years later was joined by concerned whites, who were aroused into action by the 1908 Springfield riot.

Mary White Ovington, a white social worker who had worked in black neighborhoods, was among these concerned individuals. She helped organize a national conference on the "Negro Question" to be held on Lincoln's birthday in 1909. Niagara Movement leaders attended. The following year, this interracial group founded the **National Association for the Advancement of Colored People (NAACP).**

By 1914 the NAACP had fifty branches and six thousand members. Its magazine, the *Crisis*, edited by Du Bois, reached more than thirty thousand readers. The organization worked primarily through the courts. It won its first major victory when the Supreme Court declared grandfather clauses unconstitutional in 1915. In the decades ahead, the NAACP would remain a vital force in the fight for civil rights.

African American Achievement African American mutual aid and benefit societies

Lynching of African Americans, 1886–1920

Years	Number of Persons Lynched
1886–1890	392
1891–1895	639
1896–1900	493
1901–1905	407
1906–1910	345
1911–1915	279
1916–1920	275

Source: *Historical Statistics of the United States*

 Interpreting Tables
Violence against African Americans was an alarmingly frequent phenomenon in the late 1800s. In spite of vocal protests like the one shown below, mobs had killed more than 3,000 African Americans by the 1920s. *In which five-year period did the most lynchings occur?*

also multiplied in this period. Social workers and church groups founded settlement houses in black neighborhoods. The Young Men's and Young Women's Christian Associations developed separate recreational and guidance programs for African American youth. The National Urban League (1911) improved job opportunities and housing for blacks.

Also during this period, African American intellectuals began to publish literature, history, and path-breaking sociological studies. Black-owned businesses appeared everywhere. To help them, Booker T. Washington founded the National Negro Business League in 1900. By 1907 it had 320 branches.

Thanks to the determination and support of many individuals and institutions, African Americans survived the difficult post-Reconstruction era. Some, such as Madam C. J. Walker, actually thrived.

Caption Answer to ...

 Interpreting Tables

1891–1895

Activity
Creating a Slogan

Ask students to create a slogan, together with a logo, for the National Urban League, the National Negro Business Leagues, or another African American self-help organization.

Enrichment

The Supreme Court's decision in *Plessy* v. *Ferguson* introduced the "separate but equal" doctrine that maintained discrimination in the South for the next seventy years. Ask students to research the case and write summaries of the majority decision and the dissenting opinion.

In Depth

Multicultural Perspectives

African American demography has changed rapidly over the past century. In the mid-1870s, more than 90 percent of all African Americans lived in the rural South. In the 1990s, there are three major geographic centers of African American population: the rural South (about 15 percent), the urban South (more than 30 percent), and the urban Northeast, Midwest and West (55 percent).

3. ASSESS

Section 3 Review Answers

1. (a) poll tax, see p. 281, (b) literacy tests, see p. 281, (c) grandfather clause, see p. 281, (d) lynching, see p. 282

2. Madam C. J. Walker, see p. 284

3. Jim Crow laws constituted a system of legal segregation that was legitimized by the Supreme Court in 1883. De facto discrimination resulted in discrimination in practice but was not upheld by written law.

4. African Americans organized to promote black pride and to expose and denounce all forms of discrimination. In 1909, they formed the NAACP, which worked to improve civil rights.

5. African Americans formed their own mutual aid societies and the National Urban League. Intellectuals began to publish, and individuals such as Madam C. J. Walker started their own businesses.

6. Possible answer: African Americans were not truly free because they continued to suffer discrimination that denied them opportunities to improve economically and socially. Whites effectively denied them political rights, thus preventing them from seeking political redress.

Reteach

Ask students to write an agenda for the national conference on the "Negro Question" that Mary White Ovington helped to organize. The agenda should address strategies for surmounting discrimination.

4. CLOSE

Reinforcing the Big Idea

Despite the fact that African Americans were denied their most basic constitutional freedoms in the era following Reconstruction, they were able to reach high levels of achievement and founded powerful organizations. The next section discusses attitudes and changes regarding the status of women.

AMERICAN PROFILES

Madam C. J. Walker

In 1912 **Madam C. J. Walker** (1867–1919) asked Booker T. Washington to put her on the program of the annual meeting of the Negro Business League. He refused. But on the last day of the assembly, she spoke to the group anyway, saying:

> I am a woman who came from the cotton fields of the South. I was promoted from there to the washtub. Then I was promoted to the cook kitchen, and from there I promoted myself into the business of manufacturing hair goods and preparations. . . . I have built my own factory on my own ground.

Madam C. J. Walker was an inspiration to many African American women.

The mostly male audience was so impressed that they invited Walker back the next year as a keynote speaker.

Madam C. J. Walker is a stunning example of African American achievement in the turn-of-the-century era. Born Sarah Breedlove—the name *Walker* would come from a husband—she was the daughter of ex-slaves and share-croppers. Her first seven years were spent on a Louisiana cotton plantation. Then, after the death of her parents, she moved to Vicksburg, Mississippi, to work as a domestic servant. She later moved to St. Louis, where she worked for seventeen years laundering clothes.

"I got myself a start by giving myself a start," Walker would later say. She did so by deciding in her late thirties to develop her own preparations to style and strengthen the hair of African American women, many of whom suffered hair loss from poor diet, stress, scalp diseases, and damaging hair treatments. After experimenting with different formulas and trying them out on friends, Walker sold her products door to door.

Walker moved to Denver, Colorado, in 1905, where she married C. J. Walker, a newspaper sales agent. There she set up a prosperous mail-order business for her hair products. She also established a string of beauty parlors and training schools for "hair culturists."

Her business a great success, Walker bought property in Harlem, New York, an area that had begun to attract African American residents. Her Harlem town house and later her estate in Irvington-on-Hudson, New York, became gathering places for the country's African American leaders. Walker supported black welfare, education, and civil rights work with large contributions and made many speeches for the antilynching drives of the NAACP and for African American women's organizations.

Walker also created job opportunities for African Americans. In her keynote speech to the National Negro Business League in 1913, Walker summed up her life's work as having "made it possible for many colored women to abandon the washtub for a more pleasant and profitable occupation." By 1916 her company claimed twenty thousand employees.

"The girls and women of our race must not be afraid to take hold of business endeavor," she said in her 1913 speech. "I want to say to every Negro woman present, don't sit down and wait for the opportunities to come. . . . Get up and make them!"

SECTION 3 REVIEW

Key Terms, People, and Places

1. Define (a) poll tax, (b) literacy tests, (c) grandfather clause, (d) lynching.

2. Identify Madam C. J. Walker.

Key Concepts

3. How do Jim Crow laws and de facto discrimination differ?

4. How did African Americans respond to the growing repression following Reconstruction?

5. What are some examples of African American achievement and perseverance during this period?

Critical Thinking

6. **Distinguishing False from Accurate Images** To what extent did the end of slavery and the official granting of political rights bring freedom to African Americans? Explain.

RESOURCE DIRECTORY

Teaching Resources

Quiz found in the Unit 2 folder, p. 118, covers the main ideas in this section as well as the key terms.

Reading a Political Cartoon

Political cartoons can tell you a great deal about the past. For many years, cartoonists have tried to influence public feeling about important issues. To do so, they use visual images to exaggerate or highlight certain details about the facts. This is one reason why cartoons often can make a point more strongly than words alone can.

Study the cartoon below, which was published in 1892. Ask yourself what point about Jim Crow laws the cartoonist was trying to make. Then answer the following questions.

1. Identify the symbols used in the cartoon. Cartoons often use symbols, visual images that stand for some other idea or event. For exam-

ple, a skull and crossbones is a commonly used symbol for death. A dove is a symbol for peace. To understand a cartoon, you must be able to identify the symbols it uses.

Decide what the symbols in this cartoon stand for. (a) What is the figure on the left holding in his right hand? What are the men on the right holding? (b) What is the building at the right meant to be? (c) What is the significance of the cannon and the date printed on it? (d) Based on these symbols, what groups do these people represent?

2. Analyze the meaning of the symbols. Use your reading of this chapter and the cartoon to decide what the symbols refer to. (a) What

do the signs on the building say? (b) What practice is being referred to in this cartoon? (c) Based on your answers to a and b above, how would you interpret the meaning of the other symbols in the cartoon, which you identified earlier?

3. Interpret the cartoon. Draw conclusions about the cartoonist's point of view. (a) What do you think the cartoonist thought of Jim Crow laws? Give evidence to support your answer. (b) How is the cartoonist trying to influence the public's attitude toward the practice? (c) How does the cartoonist portray the white figures? Is this a sympathetic portrayal?

Historian's Toolbox Activity Reading a Political Cartoon, found in the Unit 2 folder, p. 127, focuses on a cartoon about the 1964 Civil Rights Act to enhance students' understanding of the power of cartoons.

SECTION 4

The Woman Question

The Woman Question

The Woman Question

1. FOCUS

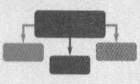

Connecting to the Big Idea

See page 270B. Explain that women's lives were undergoing rapid changes in the late 1880s. Yet many Americans were unwilling to acknowledge these changes and alter their view of women's roles. Ask what women's rights advocates wanted. Why were they opposed by people with more traditional views?

Objectives

- Describe the different attitudes Americans held regarding the role of women in society.
- Explain how women's lives were changing in the late 1800s.
- Identify the economic, political, and social changes women were demanding in the late 1800s.

Bellringer

Ask students if they think women have full equality with men in American society today. Encourage them to explain their answers.

Reading Strategy

Reading for Evidence Write the following statement on the chalkboard: Although much had changed for women in the late 1800s, many Americans were unwilling to acknowledge these changes. Ask students to find evidence to support this statement as they read.

Answer to ...

MAKING CONNECTIONS

Possible answers: Economic and political equality and domestic violence are both live issues today. Some new features of the woman question today include sexual freedom in general and reproductive rights in particular.

SECTION PREVIEW

Much had changed for women in the late 1800s—new jobs, new educational opportunities, new roles in the home. Yet much stayed the same, including continued economic and political inequality. This contradiction fueled great debate at the turn of the century.

Key Concepts

- Americans held conflicting attitudes about the status of women in society in the late 1800s.
- Women's lives were changing rapidly as a result of changes in technology, the workplace, and society in general.
- Many women demanded economic and political equality and promoted changes in women's lifestyles.

Many women at the turn of the century began seeking change in their traditional roles—and in their traditional clothing, such as the restrictive corsets advertised above.

Key Terms, People, and Places
woman question

W omen hain't no business a votin'," pronounced Josiah Allen, a fictional creation of the popular turn-of-the-century humorist Marietta Holley; "they had better let the laws alone, and tend to their housework. The law loves wimmin and protects 'em." Replied his wife, Samantha, "If the law loves wimmin so well, why don't he give her as much wages as men get for doin' the same work?" ✦

Most Americans around 1900 would have known exactly what Samantha and Josiah were arguing about. They would have called it the **woman question,** a wide-ranging debate about the social role of women that grew out of several major developments of the era. As a result of technological change, industrialization, the expansion of education, and the movement of

people into the cities, women's lives were undergoing rapid change. Yet many Americans were unwilling to acknowledge these changes and expand their view of women's status in society.

What Was the Woman Question?

For women like Samantha Allen, the woman question boiled down to a few key demands: Women should be able to vote. They should be paid the same as men for doing the same work. They should be able to control their own property and income. They should have equal access to higher education and professional jobs. And, they should be free from domestic violence.

Women's rights advocates were countered by traditionalists, who insisted that giving women economic and political power equal to that of men would upset the social order. Some argued that allowing women any public roles would destroy their femininity. As the reality of women's lives changed, however, such arguments against women's rights became increasingly difficult to justify.

MAKING CONNECTIONS

To what extent does the woman question still exist? What aspects of it continue from the past? What are some new features of today's woman question?

Women in the Economy and Society

What was the reality of women's lives at the turn of the century? Women worked in most sectors of the economy and in many areas of public life. Their unpaid work at home continued to be essential. At the same time, because new technologies such as running water and washing machines decreased the time spent doing housework, a growing number of women were earning advanced degrees and entering

RESOURCE DIRECTORY

Teaching Resources

Reproducible Lesson Plan found in the Unit 2 folder, p. 112, provides a summary of the Section 4 lesson plan content.

Alternate Lesson Plan: Learning Styles found in the Unit 2 folder, p. 88, is especially helpful for kinesthetic and visual learners, and helps all students identify conflicting viewpoints about the roles and status of women in the late 1800s.

Guided Reading and Review found in the Unit 2 folder, p. 119, provides a structure for reading and mastering the key concepts and reviewing the key terms for Section 4. (Guided Practice)

Visual Learning Activity The New Woman and the New Man, found in the Unit 2 folder, p. 136, uses a 1909 cartoon to illustrate a satirical point of view about women's suffrage.

professions. Others were building voluntary organizations that took leading roles in reforming education, labor relations, public health, and other areas of society.

Women's Work in the Home As they had for centuries, women continued to perform most of the jobs in the home. Thanks to the era's technological revolution (see Chapter 7), some aspects of this work became less time-consuming. Though technology was not available to all people, it did free many women for wage work, careers, and voluntary activity.

By 1900, fewer women were making their own bread or butchering and preserving their own meat. The number of foods available in tin cans increased fourfold between 1870 and 1880. Almost no one produced clothing from start to finish anymore. Patent medicines replaced remedies previously prepared at home. Even nursing the sick, once a special skill of women, was moving to the hospital and becoming professionalized.

Women still had much to do. In working-class households that could not afford the benefits of technology, housework continued to be strenuous. Many homes were without indoor plumbing. Even as late as 1917, only one quarter of American homes had electricity.

Working Outside the Home In 1870 nearly two million women—one in every eight over the age of ten—worked outside the home. Women worked in each of the 338 occupations listed in the United States census. Most of these women were single. But, in the decades that followed, a rising proportion of married women would go to work.

Most single female workers were between the ages of sixteen and twenty-four. Employers assumed they would leave upon marriage and rarely gave them supervisory jobs or advanced training. They also paid women three to five dollars a week less than men—about 30 to 60 percent less, on average.

Domestic work was an important source of income for many women. In 1900 about one in fifteen American homes employed live-in servants. Most were of foreign or African American origin. Working dawn to bedtime, six-and-a-half

days a week, these women cooked, cleaned, washed and ironed, and cared for children. Many supported their own families who lived elsewhere.

American society accepted the stereotype that women did not have the mental capacity for professional training. In 1873 retired Harvard Medical School professor Edward H. Clarke warned in his famous book *Sex in Education* that young women could not study and learn

and retain uninjured health and a future secure from [sickness], hysteria, and other derangements of the nervous system.

Three years before Clarke made this warning, the United States had 525 physicians, 67 ministers, and 5 lawyers who were women.

New technologies, such as this washing machine, helped lessen women's burdens. But women also had new responsibilities as household consumers as suggested in the ad above.

2. INSTRUCT

Discuss
Discuss with students the ways in which women's lives were different in the late 1890s than in the 1840s. What kinds of changes were women demanding? Why did women want more economic and political rights?

Analyze
Analyze why the demand for equal economic and political rights for women stirred up so much emotional controversy. Why did many men feel threatened by the demands of women's rights advocates? In what ways might some women also feel threatened? Why does the gender question continue to inspire emotional debate today?

In Depth

Historical Misconceptions

The notion that women should not depend on men for survival did not, as some believe, originate with the women's movements of the twentieth century. In her 1898 book, *Women and Economics,* Charlotte Perkins Gilman argued that, "If there should be built and opened. . . [an] apartment house for professional women with families, it would be filled at once. . . . It would be a home where the cleaning was done by [hired] workers . . . and [a] day nursery, and kindergarten, under well-trained professional nurses and teachers, would insure proper care of the children."

Activity

Cooperative Learning

Time: One class period.
Activity: Choose a club focus.
Grouping: Groups of four to six students.
Purpose: For many women in the late 1800s, club membership provided the means to involvement in public life for the first time. Have groups choose a focus for a club and develop an agenda of activities around that focus. Have a recorder from each group report to the class, and discuss common activities.
Roles: Members of a women's club.
Outcome: Students will portray the potential of clubs as a stepping-stone for women's broader participation in American society.

Enrichment

Debate was fierce over the issue of whether or not women should have equal rights with men. Have students research published viewpoints of the time, and write a position paper either for or against equal rights for women in the late 1880s.

3. ASSESS

Section 4 Review Answers

1. the woman question, see p. 286

2. They claimed that women were not capable of learning what they needed to know to play a greater role in society. Furthermore, they argued, women workers were likely to work only until they were married, so they did not deserve the same pay or training as men.

3. Women worked in factories, white-collar jobs, or as domestic servants. They had little chance of advancement and were paid 30 to 40 percent less than men doing the same work. Professional women found jobs primarily in institutions run by and for women.

4. Women joined voluntary associations that became vehicles for improving themselves and society. Women founded libraries, improved education for girls, and worked to achieve temperance, suffrage, and correction of political and social abuses.

During this era, women in growing numbers moved out of the home and into the workplace. Some, such as the telephone operators (top), worked in the new industries that came with industrialization. Domestic work employed many immigrants and minorities such as those in the bottom photograph.

Still, most Americans believed that careers and married life were incompatible. Self-supporting women were allowed to train for professions but discouraged from entering fields that put them in competition with men. Women professionals found opportunities mostly in female-dominated institutions, such as women's colleges, hospitals, and settlement houses.

Volunteering for a Larger Role in Society
Women in both the North and South had performed exemplary voluntary service during the Civil War. Afterward, there was an explosion of interest among middle-class women in voluntary associations.

Women joined these organizations primarily for intellectual stimulation and sociability.

They studied subjects of common interest, gave talks on selected topics, or heard lectures by distinguished guests. Some, such as the New England Woman's Club, founded in 1868, pursued specific causes such as temperance and girls' education. Others founded libraries or playgrounds. African American club women in Atlanta studied a national adult education program. The Chicago Woman's Club read Karl Marx's writings.

Whatever their focus, clubs gave women invaluable experience in speaking, writing, and financial skills. They helped women increase their self-confidence and take their first steps toward public life.

As the number of clubs for women expanded, the idea of forming them into national associations took hold. In 1873 the Association for the Advancement of Women came into being, and in 1890 the General Federation of Women's Clubs was formed. These groups took on increasingly ambitious and far-reaching projects, including suffrage and the correction of political abuses. In doing so, they joined with other groups founded to pursue specific reforms, such as the Woman's Christian Temperance Union, formed in 1874, and the National American Woman Suffrage Association, formed in 1890. This last group would carry the cause of woman suffrage to victory some thirty years later. ✪

▶ RESOURCE DIRECTORY

Teaching Resources

 American Profiles Activity found in the Unit 2 folder, p. 124, profiles Lucy Stone, a fervent abolitionist and pioneer in the struggle for women's rights.

New Women, New Ideas

During this period of change, women struggled to agree on a proper focus for their activities. By the early 1900s, the woman question had grown to include a number of issues besides economic and political rights.

One issue was the question of lifestyle: How should women dress and behave? As more women entered the work force or went to college, they took this matter into their own hands. In search of more convenient hair styles, they began to "bob" or shorten their hair. They raised hemlines and wore more practical skirts and blouses. The New England Woman's Club even opened a store where women could buy sensible clothing.

Courting and marriage customs also changed. For example, instead of entertaining a man at home, many women now went out on dates without supervision. New women, as they were sometimes called, still hoped to marry. Yet they seemed to have higher expectations of fulfillment in marriage. This expectation was evidenced by the divorce rate, which rose from one in twelve in 1900 to one in nine by 1916. Many married new women began to push for the legalized spread of information about birth control, a campaign led by New York nurse Margaret Sanger. Such developments were shocking to Americans who held on to Victorian morals.

What was the consensus among women on the woman question? At the turn of the century, most women rejected ideas for drastic social change, such as the demand of some that women be freed from all household duties. Though the majority agreed with the principle of greater rights, middle-class women still saw domestic

Viewpoints
On the Woman Question

In the late 1800s and early 1900s, debate over the social, political, and economic roles of women raged in the United States. *Summarize the arguments presented in the viewpoints below.*

For Women's Rights

"These things the women want to do and be and have are not in any sense masculine. They do not belong to men. They never did. They are departments of our social life, hitherto monopolized [until now controlled] by men, but no more made masculine by that use than the wearing of trousers by Turkish women makes trousers feminine. . . ."

Charlotte Perkins Gilman, "Are Women Human Beings?" *Harpers Weekly*, May 25, 1912

Against Women's Rights

"So I say deliberately that the so-called woman movement is an attempt to escape the function of woman, a revolt against the fact that woman is not a man, an attempt to enter the field of effort in which man's powers are properly exercised. It is a rising against nature. It is a revolt against God."

Dr. Cyrus Townsend Brady, from a sermon given October 17, 1915

fulfillment as their chief goal. Working-class women seldom had the time to debate the issue.

Voting rights was another matter. The issue of the vote prompted huge numbers of women to campaign or support the movement in some way. Even female workers got caught up in the suffrage movement. Soon the vote would be the one issue on which women from many walks of life would unite.

SECTION 4 REVIEW

Key Terms, People, and Places
1. Define the woman question.

Key Concepts
2. What arguments were used by those Americans who did not want to expand women's roles in the economy and society in the late 1800s?
3. What were the main characteristics of women's work outside the home in this period?

4. Describe women's involvement in volunteer work.
5. What was the general consensus among American women on the woman question?

Critical Thinking
6. **Determining Relevance** How did the growth in women's employment and volunteer activity outside the home support the demands by women for greater political and social roles?

 Viewpoints Activity On the Woman Question, found in the Unit 2 folder, pp. 125–126, provides additional viewpoints and perspectives on the woman question.

 Quiz found in the Unit 2 folder, p. 120, covers the main ideas in this section as well as the key terms.

 Chapter Test Forms A and B are found in the Unit 2 folder, pp. 137–142.

Answer Keys found in the Unit 2 folder, pp. 149–161, provide answers to all student activities.

Media and Technology

Transparency
Graphic Organizer, G-3

Guided Reading Audiotapes (English and Spanish)

Computer Test Bank

---

5. Most women rejected radical feminist ideas. Though agreeing generally on the need for more rights for women, most middle-class women held domestic fulfillment as their highest goal, while working women did not have time to debate these ideas. Many women did agree on the need for women's suffrage.

6. Possible answer: Women were assuming greater responsibilities and were proving that they could succeed in the male social and economic world. These achievements refuted the arguments used to deny women better pay, political rights, and so on.

Answer to . . .

Viewpoints

Gilman argues that the rights women are seeking belong to them by virtue of their being human beings and have been falsely denied to women on the grounds that these rights belong to men. Brady argues that men and women are different by nature, that society must therefore treat them differently, and that any attempt to do otherwise is sinful. For a more thorough examination of the woman question, see the Resource Directory below.

Reteach

Ask students to create a three-column chart using the section's three main headings and to enter important concepts and supporting details in each column.

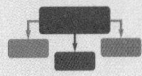
4. CLOSE

Reinforcing the Big Idea

The changing role of women at the turn of the century spurred women's rights advocates to demand greater economic and political rights for women. These demands were resisted by traditionalists, who were afraid of upsetting the social order.

The Decision to Rule Against Women's Suffrage

Focus The Supreme Court's decision to rule against women's suffrage illustrates the unwillingness of many Americans in the late 1800s to acknowledge that women's roles in society had changed and to grant them full economic and political rights. Students are asked to evaluate the Supreme Court decision to uphold the Missouri law that denied women the vote.

Instruct In order to give students more background regarding Virginia and Francis Minor's argument, ask them to read the Fourteenth and Fifteenth amendments. Review with them the definition of citizenship found in Section 1 of the Fourteenth Amendment.

To check student understanding of the arguments for and against women's suffrage, ask students these questions: According to Francis Minor, why did the Constitution give women the right to vote? On what grounds did the Court decide against Virginia Minor and women's suffrage? You might want to have students participate in a role-play of the Supreme Court hearing of the case *Minor v. Happersett.*

Extend To extend the activity, have students explore efforts to get the Equal Rights Amendment passed. Suggest that they research the history of the Amendment, the arguments for and against it, and the Amendment's current status.

The Decision to Rule Against Women's Suffrage

Time Frame:	1869–1875
Places:	St. Louis, Missouri; Washington, D.C.
Key People:	Virginia L. Minor and Francis Minor, Chief Justice Morrison R. Waite, and the Supreme Court
Situation:	Women's rights advocates believed the post-Civil War period to be right for winning the vote. Virginia Minor believed the Fourteenth Amendment made Missouri's ban against woman voters unconstitutional. She asked the Supreme Court to rule for women's suffrage.

I n the reform-minded atmosphere immediately after the Civil War, many women became more determined than ever to achieve woman suffrage, for which they had been fighting for decades. After all, new laws and the Fourteenth and Fifteenth amendments to the Constitution were granting rights and privileges, including citizenship and suffrage, to formerly enslaved African Americans. In view of these changes, suffragists reasoned, the nation must be ready to give women the vote.

In 1874, advocates of women's suffrage saw an opportunity to advance their cause. The Supreme Court had agreed to hear the case *Minor v. Happersett*. Depending on its ruling, the Court could make women's suffrage a reality.

Women Make a Move for Suffrage

In the aftermath of the Civil War, Congress passed and the states ratified the Fourteenth and Fifteenth amendments to the Constitution. These amendments were designed to protect the rights of African Americans who had recently been released from slavery. The Fourteenth Amendment extended the rights of citizenship to all Americans, while the Fifteenth guaranteed all races the right to vote.

These amendments split the woman suffrage movement, which had been formed in 1848 at the Seneca Falls Women's Rights Convention in New York. One faction, the National Woman's Suffrage Association (NWSA), refused to endorse the Fifteenth Amendment because it ignored women's voting rights. They continued lobbying for voting and other rights at the federal level. The other faction, known as the American Woman Suffrage Association, supported the Fifteenth Amendment as a step toward winning the vote for women.

Virginia Minor, the president of the Missouri chapter of NWSA, was convinced that women's status in the United States would not be raised until suffrage was won. Her husband, lawyer Francis Minor, enthusiastically supported her endeavors toward this end. In 1869 the couple devised an ingenious argument. They claimed that, of the "rights and privileges" that the Fourteenth Amendment guaranteed to all American citizens, including women, "chief among [them] is the elective franchise"—the right to vote. The NWSA enthusiastically endorsed the Minors' reasoning that embodied in the Constitution itself was the right of woman suffrage.

During the national elections of 1872, NWSA waged a campaign to challenge the ban on women voting. One hundred and fifty of its members tried to vote in ten states. In Missouri, Virginia Minor demanded that the St. Louis registrar, Reese Happersett, register her to vote. When he refused, citing the Missouri constitution, she sued on the basis of the Fourteenth Amendment.

The Logic Behind Minor's Case

Because Missouri state law made it impossible for Minor to bring suit independently of her husband, the Minors jointly took their case to the circuit court at St. Louis and then to the Missouri supreme court. Minor lost her case in the Missouri courts and then appealed to the Supreme Court in 1874. Francis Minor was one of the attorneys who presented the case before the Court. He and the other attorneys asserted that the Constitution gave women the right to vote because women are United States citizens and "there can be no half-way citizenship."

RESOURCE DIRECTORY

History Might Not . . . Activity
Decision Making: Promoting Women's Rights, found in the Unit 2 folder, pp. 121–122, focuses on Belva Lockwood's decision to push for her rights and become the first woman lawyer to practice before the U.S. Supreme Court.

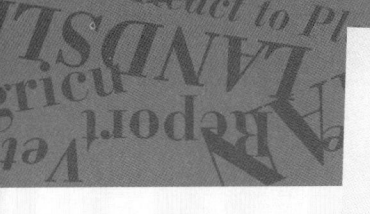

GOAL	Win women's suffrage	
POSSIBLE ACTIONS	The Supreme Court rules that under the Constitution the state of Missouri must allow Virginia Minor to vote	The Supreme Court rules that the state of Missouri has no obligation to allow Virginia Minor to vote
POSSIBLE RESULTS	• Women's suffrage is won under the Constitution.	• Women's suffrage can only be won through constitutional amendment.

Woman, as a citizen of the United States, is entitled to all the benefits of that position, and liable to all its obligations, or to none." Since citizens have the right to vote, and since the Fourteenth Amendment forbade the states from limiting the rights of citizens, then Missouri's ban on women voting was unconstitutional.

Supreme Court Chief Justice Morrison R. Waite, who sat listening to these arguments, was sympathetic to women's rights. Later, his personal physician would be a woman, and he would unsuccessfully argue for admitting women as members of the Supreme Court Bar. It seemed possible that Waite might be willing to embrace a broad reading of the Constitution, one that allowed him to infer women's suffrage from the vague wording of the Fourteenth Amendment.

Yet unfortunately for Minor and the NWSA, the Supreme Court had turned more cautious and respectful of precedent. The Court now tended to opt for more strict readings of the Constitution's language—readings that acknowledged only those rights specifically listed in the document. Realizing that their case had but a slim chance of victory, the Minors and the NWSA nevertheless remained hopeful that the Court would rule for women's suffrage.

The Response of the Supreme Court

The Supreme Court in 1875 decided unanimously that the state of Missouri had no obligation to allow Minor to vote. In the Court's opinion, written by Waite, the justices agreed that women were citizens entitled to the rights and privileges of citizenship, with or without the Fourteenth Amendment. Yet the Constitution and the Fourteenth Amendment never stated specifically that suffrage was one of those rights. Had that been so, they argued, the Fifteenth Amendment guaranteeing African Americans the right to vote would never have been necessary.

The Court further noted that the states always had determined the qualifications for voters. "When the Constitution of the United States was adopted," the justices continued, ". . . in no State were all citizens permitted to vote. Each State determined for itself who should have that power." If the framers of the Constitution meant all citizens to vote, the Court reasoned, they would have stated it explicitly. Waite's opinion concluded by remarking that the justices were not judging the merits of women's suffrage, but only determining the extent of women's constitutional rights.

After the Supreme Court's decision in *Minor* v. *Happersett,* those working for women's suffrage realized what a long road lay ahead. The only way to get a national vote for women would be through the long, difficult process of amending the Constitution. The two women's rights factions reunited in 1890 in the National American Woman Suffrage Association. Under a new generation of leaders, the group worked for thirty more years to achieve passage and ratification of the Nineteenth Amendment in 1920.

EVALUATING DECISIONS

1. (a) According to the Minors, how was women's suffrage implied in the Fourteenth Amendment? (b) Why was this argument attractive to the NWSA?
2. (a) What was the Supreme Court's reasoning in unanimously ruling against the Minors? (b) Why was 1874 an unlikely time to expect the Minors to win?

Critical Thinking
3. **Recognizing Cause and Effect** Waite was said to believe that the people, acting through their elected representatives, knew their own best interest. Explain how such a belief might have led Waite to a make a more strict reading of the Constitution.

Media and Technology

Visions of America: History Might Not Have Happened This Way Game
To encourage students to explore pivotal moments in United States history, have students use the Visions of America software. Refer to the Visions of America Teacher's Guidebook for viewing objectives, activities, game instructions, and discussion questions.

Answers

1. (a) The Fourteenth Amendment prohibits states from limiting the rights of citizens, including women. Since suffrage was a right of citizenship, states could not deny it to women. (b) The NWSA favored this argument, because it promised a quick national victory for women's suffrage.

2. (a) The Supreme Court found that the states, not the federal government, regulated voter qualifications. (b) By the 1870s, it was unlikely that the Court would have found in the Minors' favor as it followed the national consensus in backing away from radical social and legal experiments.

3. Possible answer: Waite believed that the people, through their legislators, could pass laws or amendments to achieve such goals as women's suffrage if that was what the people wanted. A strict reading of the Constitution— though not granting women's suffrage right away—would not prevent legislators from doing so if they so desired. On the other hand, a broad reading in which the Court offered its own interpretation of the Constitution would effectively make law regardless of what the people wanted.

Understanding Key Terms, People, and Places

Terms
Students should refer to the definitions of the key terms in the chapter to write sentences that show the relation of each word to the cultural and social transformations of the late 1800s and early 1900s.

Matching
1. Jim Crow
2. vaudeville
3. yellow journalism
4. woman question
5. Victorianism

True or False
1. false, Madam C. J. Walker
2. false, Booker T. Washington
3. true

Reviewing Main Ideas

1. As the United States became more industrialized and urbanized, people realized that they needed more education. To meet this need, school funding was increased, the school year was lengthened, and child labor laws were instituted, thus allowing more students to attend school.

2. Educators and philanthropists established private women's colleges, and pressure increased on men's colleges to admit women. Other opportunities for coeducation increased.

3. Both groups faced prejudice and limited opportunities.

4. Families could visit trolley parks, attend motion pictures and vaudeville shows, and participate in or watch sports such as baseball and football.

5. Ragtime originated among African American musicians playing in saloons in the South and Midwest. Jazz grew out of experiments with new styles of playing among African American musicians in New Orleans.

6. Victorians disapproved of the new forms of entertainment, finding them offensive and immoral.

7. Almost every aspect of the daily lives of African Americans in the South was affected by Jim Crow laws. The laws required the separation of blacks and whites in schools, parks, public buildings, hospitals, and many other facilities. The separate facilities for African Americans were almost always inferior.

Chapter Review

Understanding Key Terms, People, and Places

Key Terms
1. vaudeville
2. yellow journalism
3. minstrel show
4. ragtime
5. jazz
6. Victorianism
7. poll tax
8. literacy tests
9. grandfather clause
10. Jim Crow
11. lynching
12. de facto discrimination
13. National Association for the Advancement of Colored People (NAACP)
14. woman question

People
15. Booker T. Washington
16. W.E.B. Du Bois
17. Madam C. J. Walker

Terms For each term above, write a sentence that explains its relation to the cultural and social transformations of the late 1800s and early 1900s.

Matching Review the key terms in the list above. If you are not sure of a term's meaning, review its definition in the chapter. Then choose a term from the list that best matches each description below.
1. a system of legal segregation that degraded African Americans
2. a type of family entertainment consisting of comic sketches, song-and-dance routines, ventriloquists, jugglers, and trapeze artists
3. sensationalized news coverage
4. the wide-ranging debate about the social role of women that took place in the late 1800s
5. the beliefs associated with Britain's Queen Victoria, which include commitment to hard work, sobriety, and restraint in relations between men and women

True or False Determine whether each statement is true or false. If it is true, write "true." If it is false, change the underlined name to make the statement true.
1. Booker T. Washington was an African American who persevered through the post-Reconstruction era and established a successful business.
2. Madam C. J. Walker urged African Americans to win white acceptance by succeeding in occupations that whites needed them to fill.
3. W.E.B. Du Bois believed that the brightest African Americans had to step forward to seek advanced educations and lead their people.

Reviewing Main Ideas

Section 1 (pp. 272–275)
1. Why did public schools gain more students in the late 1800s?
2. Give evidence to show that opportunities for higher education increased for women during the late 1800s.
3. In what ways were the experiences of women and African Americans similar with regard to higher education?

Section 2 (pp. 276–280)
4. What kinds of amusements and entertainment were available for families to enjoy during the late 1800s?
5. Where and how did ragtime and jazz originate?
6. What did Victorians think of the new forms of entertainment that evolved during the late 1800s?

Section 3 (pp. 281–284)
7. In what ways did Jim Crow laws affect the daily lives of African Americans in the South?
8. How did the NAACP and the National Urban League help African Americans during the early 1900s?
9. What does the profile of Madam C. J. Walker reveal about the achievements of African Americans?

Section 4 (pp. 286–289)
10. What conflicting attitudes did Americans hold about the proper place of woman in the late 1800s?
11. How did women's lives change as a result of new technologies during this period?
12. Describe how women achieved greater social equality during the early 1900s.

---

8. The NAACP worked primarily through the courts to fight for African American civil rights. The National Urban League worked to improve job opportunities and housing.

9. The profile of Madam C. J. Walker proves that despite repression, some highly motivated and skilled African Americans were able to start their own businesses and achieve success.

10. Some Americans demanded equal economic and political equality for women, while others supported keeping women in traditional roles.

11. Housework for many women became less time-consuming, thus freeing them to work and volunteer outside the home.

12. Many women changed their dress and behavior, cutting their hair, wearing more practical clothing, and going on dates without supervision.

Thinking Critically

1. Students' responses should reflect the fact that in the period immediately following the Civil War, fewer than half of the nation's children were receiving formal education. Only a very small percentage graduated from high school, and even fewer went to college. Opportunities for African Americans and women were even scarcer.

2. Possible answer: Today activities for the family are still important, although theme parks have replaced trolley parks, and movies have replaced vaudeville.

Thinking Critically

1. **Drawing Conclusions** How might your education have been different if you had lived in the period immediately following the Civil War?
2. **Making Comparisons** As greater numbers of working-class people sought entertainment during the late 1800s, a commercial recreation industry emerged. How are the types of activities available today similar to the types of activities available during the late 1800s?
3. **Expressing Problems Clearly** Jim Crow required the segregation of whites and African Americans. Aside from the fact that facilities for African Americans were inferior, how might segregation have harmed African Americans?

Making Connections

1. **Evaluating Primary Sources** Review the primary source excerpt on page 276. Is Mathewson's assessment of the American public valid today? Give evidence to support your point of view.
2. **Understanding the Visuals** Review the quotations in the "Viewpoints" feature on page 289. Then, scan the chapter to find visuals that could be used to illustrate what each speaker believes is the proper role for women. Write a short paragraph explaining how each photograph supports the quotation.
3. **Writing About the Chapter** Imagine that you are living in the United States around the turn of the century. Write a letter to the editor of the local newspaper in which you take a stand on the woman question. Before you write your letter, draw up an outline of your argument. List several reasons for supporting or opposing expanded rights for women, and identify details or examples to support each of your reasons.

Next, write a draft of your letter. Begin by stating your position, and then present each of your reasons in a separate paragraph. Conclude by encouraging your readers to work for or against expanded women's rights. Read over your draft, carefully refining your arguments and correcting any errors. Then, make a final copy.

4. **Using the Graphic Organizer** This graphic organizer uses a tree map to organize information about the expansion of education in the late 1800s. (a) Based on what you have read in the chapter, how was the experience of higher education different for African Americans and minorities than it was for white males? (b) Describe the experience of higher education for women during the late 1800s. (c) On a separate sheet of paper, create your own graphic organizer about the changes in women's lives during the late 1800s.

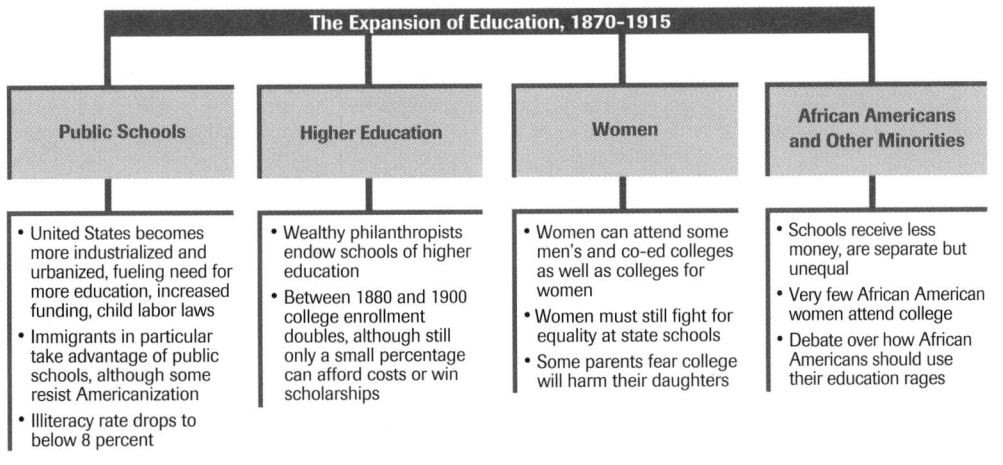

The Expansion of Education, 1870–1915

Public Schools	Higher Education	Women	African Americans and Other Minorities
• United States becomes more industrialized and urbanized, fueling need for more education, increased funding, child labor laws • Immigrants in particular take advantage of public schools, although some resist Americanization • Illiteracy rate drops to below 8 percent	• Wealthy philanthropists endow schools of higher education • Between 1880 and 1900 college enrollment doubles, although still only a small percentage can afford costs or win scholarships	• Women can attend some men's and co-ed colleges as well as colleges for women • Women must still fight for equality at state schools • Some parents fear college will harm their daughters	• Schools receive less money, are separate but unequal • Very few African American women attend college • Debate over how African Americans should use their education rages

3. Students' responses in favor of women's rights might mention the expanding role of women in the workplace and increasing levels of education. Arguments against women's rights might focus on disruption of the existing social order.

4. (a) Although meeting college costs was difficult for all families, including those headed by white males, African Americans faced the added burden of prejudice. (b) Women could attend some male or coeducational colleges or colleges for women, but had to fight for equal status at state-run colleges. Parents often discouraged their daughters from attending college. Very few African American women attended college. (c) Students' graphic organizers should include information about the changes in technology, the workplace, and society in general that affected women's lives in the late 1800s.

 **Alternative Assessment**

Final Evaluation
Use the following guidelines to evaluate student projects:
- **Evidence of thoughtfulness** Did the students include the main topics from the chapter?
- **Evidence of outside research** To what extent did students use outside research materials for their projects?
- **Evidence of synthesis** Do projects demonstrate that students understand how topics are related?
- **Communication style** Do the projects convey their purposes to an audience in a clear, appealing way?

Sports have played an important role in both eras. Many of today's activities, however, such as television viewing and video games, rely on advanced technology. Another difference is that many of these are individual rather than family pursuits.

3. Possible answer: By being forced to use separate public facilities, their self-esteem continued to be undermined. Blacks were effectively told that they were not as good as whites and that whites did not want to be associated with them.

Making Connections

1. Answers will vary. Students may point to the American public's taste for excitement and instant gratification and give examples from sports, movies, and television.

2. For the Charlotte Perkins Gilman quotation, students might choose the photograph of the woman graduate in the chapter opener, or the photograph of women students on page 274. For the Cyrus Townsend Brady quote, students might select the photograph of the woman teacher on page 273, the homemaker on page 287, or the workers on page 288. Explanations should show an understanding of the contrasting ideas each speaker holds on the proper role of women.

Recall with students that the popularity of sports at the turn of the century was a result of the increased availability of leisure time for Americans.

Ask students to study the artifacts and to read the captions on these pages. Using the artifacts and captions as a basis for discussion, ask students what changes in American society were indicated by the growing appeal of sports.

Ask students to examine the effect of technology, communications, and business on sports, and to compare the role of sports in popular culture at the turn of the century to the importance of sports in life today. Ask how technology, communications, and business affected the growth of sports. Is the influence of business on sports good or bad? Is sports of greater of lesser importance to the average American today than it was at the turn of the century? Is there as much criticism of sports today as there was at the turn of the century?

Ask students to make a list of the artifacts they would include in an American Album display about sports of the 1990s. Tell them to choose items that illustrate the wide variety of sports that Americans enjoy.

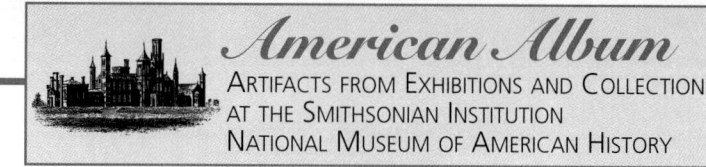

American Album
ARTIFACTS FROM EXHIBITIONS AND COLLECTIONS
AT THE SMITHSONIAN INSTITUTION
NATIONAL MUSEUM OF AMERICAN HISTORY

THE GROWTH OF SPORTS

The great rise in sports at the turn of the century reflected many other changes that were taking place in America at the same time. If not for the country's growing wealth, most adults would not have been free from their constant labor to seek excitement in games. The popularity of sports also signaled a change in the way that Americans viewed health and "idle" entertainments. Before this time, many Americans shunned activities that did not create wealth or improve character. It was now morally acceptable to spend time pursuing interests because they were just plain fun. *How do you think changes taking place in society, technology, communications, and business affected the growth of sports?*

Padded football pants

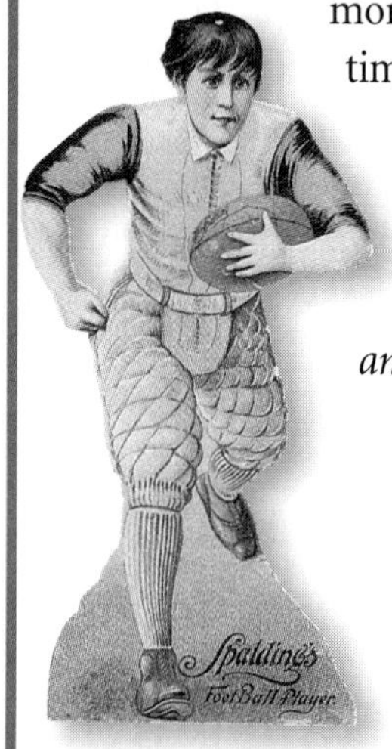

◄ FOOTBALL AT THE TURN OF THE CENTURY This football card shows that players wore much less protection than modern players. Notice the lack of shoulder pads and helmet. The only protection came from padded pants (also worn by some basketball players of the time), which protected players from leg bruises. A century ago, the game was also less violent.

▼ SKIING Skiing, as we know the sport today, began in Norway in the mid-1800s when the addition of bindings made it possible for skiers to turn and jump. Norwegian immigrants then brought the sport to Minnesota, from where it spread to other snowy areas in the United States. Skiing, however, did not become widely popular until the 1930s with the introduction of the ski tow.

◀ EARLY BASEBALL Baseball achieved its status as the great American pastime in the last third of the 1800s. Many songs celebrated the game's heroes, such as the polka tune shown on this sheet-music cover. Fans of Georgetown University's baseball team dyed the ball (in the mitt on the right) dark blue and painted in the score to honor their team's victory over Yale in 1899.

ICE SKATING A common winter sport before the 1800s, ice skating became even more popular in the late 1800s. One reason for the sport's growth in popularity was the introduction of low-priced "store-bought" skates. ▶

◀ WOMEN CYCLISTS Before the late 1800s, outdoor sports activities for women were limited. But women's steady struggle for legal and social rights, as well as improvements in bicycles, contributed to a change. By the 1890s, women had joined the bicycle craze and entered into active, public sport. The athletic demands of riding a bicycle required new, more practical clothing for women, which outraged many people.

◀ On this 1870 bicycle, the pedals connect directly to the front wheels at the axle. The introduction of a chain and foot brakes in the 1890s made pedaling much easier and gave the cyclist more control.

Explain to students that in some cases the decisions of the Supreme Court have a profound impact on the lives of every American. Tell them that one such decision was the *Plessy v. Ferguson* ruling. Point out that if the court had ruled differently, segregation would have been ended in the United States nearly sixty years sooner.

The decision in *Plessy* v. *Ferguson* legitimized the practice of Jim Crow. Ask students to think about a typical day in their lives. Discuss with students how the presence of Jim Crow would affect such a day. Students should realize during the course of this discussion that Jim Crow practices would have a dramatic effect on their lives. Still, students may not realize the subtleties and dangers of Jim Crow. The selection from Richard Wright will drive home to students the seriousness of living under Jim Crow.

INSTRUCT

Present students with the following scenario. Those whose last names begin with the letters *A* through *M* will be allowed to use the school's new, well-equipped gymnasium, but those whose last names began with the letters *N* through *Z* must use another facility. In the second facility, the roof leaks, and the only equipment is one basketball and one baseball. Have students write a paragraph on how they think this situation might affect them, both in their days at school and later in life. Students whose names begin with *A* through *M* should write assuming that they are allowed to use the new facility, while those whose last names begin with *N* through *Z* should assume they must use the "separate" facility.

Point out to students that this was the sort of unfair treatment that African Americans received under

---

Separate but Equal

Primary Source

INTRODUCTION The Fourteenth and Fifteenth amendments to the Constitution were passed after the Civil War to extend citizenship to formerly enslaved people and to protect African Americans' right to vote. A series of Supreme Court decisions in the late 1800s weakened the force of those amendments, however. One such case, *Plessy* v. *Ferguson* (1896), involved a Louisiana law that allowed separate accommodations for white and African American passengers on railroads in the state. Homer Plessy was arrested after refusing to sit in the car designated for African Americans. After being convicted in the state courts, he appealed to the Supreme Court. The Court's ruling in the case undercut the Fourteenth Amendment by upholding the idea that separate facilities for African Americans were acceptable, as long as those facilities were equal to those provided for white Americans. The Court's decision, delivered by Justice Henry Brown, denied the claim that separate facilities were, by nature, inferior and unequal. The excerpt below from the Court's decision details its reasoning on this matter and also includes a portion of the dissenting opinion.

VOCABULARY Before you read the selection, find the meaning of these words in a dictionary: commingle, competency, usage, conveyance, fallacy, plaintiff, relegate, acquiesce, affinity, beneficent, abridge, indissolubly, sanction, servitude.

MR. JUSTICE BROWN DELIVERED THE OPINION OF THE COURT:

The object of the [14th] amendment was undoubtedly to enforce the absolute equality of the two races before the law, but in the nature of things it could not have been intended to abolish distinctions based upon color, or to enforce social, as distinguished from political, equality, or a commingling of the two races upon terms unsatisfactory to either. Laws permitting, and even requiring their separation in places where they are liable to be brought into contact do not necessarily imply the inferiority of either race to the other, and have been generally, if not universally, recognized as within the competency of the state legislatures in the exercise of their police power. The most common instance of this is connected with the establishment of separate schools for white and colored children, which have been held to be a valid exercise of the legislative power even by courts of states where the political rights of the colored race have been longest and most earnestly enforced. . . .

So far, then, as a conflict with the 14th Amendment is concerned, the case reduces itself to the question whether the statute of Louisiana is a reasonable regulation, and with respect to this there must necessarily be a large discretion on the part of the legislature. In determining the question of reasonableness it is at liberty to act with reference to the established usages, customs, and traditions of the people, and with a view to the promotion of their comfort, and the preservation of the public peace and good order. Gauged by this standard, we cannot say that a law which authorizes or even requires the separation of the two races in public conveyances is unreasonable or more obnoxious to the 14th Amendment than the acts of Congress requiring separate schools for colored children in the District of Columbia, the constitutionality of which does not seem to have been questioned, or the corresponding acts of state legislatures.

We consider the underlying fallacy of the plaintiff's argument to consist in the assumption that the enforced separation of the two races stamps the colored race with a badge of inferiority. If this be so, it is not by reason of anything found in the act, but solely because the colored race chooses to put that construction upon it. The argument necessarily assumes that if, as has been more than once the case, and is not unlikely to be so again, the colored race should become the dominant power in the state legislature, and should enact a law in precisely similar terms, it would thereby relegate the white race to an inferior position. We imagine that the white race, at least, would not acquiesce in this assumption. The argument also assumes that social prejudices may be overcome by legislation, and that equal rights can not be secured to the negro except by an enforced commingling of the two races. We cannot accept this proposition. If the two races are to meet on terms of social equality, it must be the result of natural affinities, a mutual appreciation of each other's merits and a voluntary consent of individuals. . . .

MR. JUSTICE HARLAN DISSENTING . . .

The present decision, it may well be apprehended, will not only stimulate aggressions, more or less brutal and irritating, upon the admitted rights of colored citizens, but will encourage the belief that it is possible, by means of state enactments, to defeat the beneficent purposes which the people of the United States had in view when they adopted the recent amendments of the Constitution, by one of which the blacks of this country were made citizens of the United States and of the states in which they respectively reside and whose privileges and immunities, as citizens, the states are forbidden to abridge. Sixty millions of whites are in no danger from the presence here of eight millions of blacks. The destinies of the two races in this country are indissolubly linked together, and the interests of both require that the common government of all shall

Despite Supreme Court rulings that legitimized segregation, African Americans protested against the many forms of discrimination in the post-Reconstruction era, including lynching.

not permit the seeds of race hate to be planted under the sanction of law. What can more certainly arouse race hate, what more certainly create and perpetuate a feeling of distrust between these races, than state enactments which in fact proceed on the ground that colored citizens are so inferior and degraded that they cannot be allowed to sit in public coaches occupied by white citizens? That, as all will admit, is the real meaning of such legislation as was enacted in Louisana. . . .

If evils will result from the commingling of the two races upon public highways established for the benefit of all, they will be infinitely less than those that will surely come from state legislation regulating the enjoyment of civil rights upon the basis of race. We boast of the freedom enjoyed by our people above all other peoples. But it is difficult to reconcile that boast with a state of the law which, practically, puts the brand of servitude and degradation upon a large class of our fellow citizens, our equals before the law. The thin disguise of "equal" accommodations for passengers in railroad coaches will not mislead anyone, or atone for the wrong this day done.

THINKING ABOUT THE SELECTION

1. What does the decision state that the Fourteenth Amendment was meant to do? What was it not meant to do?
2. According to this decision, how does the Supreme Court determine the reasonableness of a particular law?

Critical Thinking

3. **Expressing Problems Clearly** What does the Court believe is wrong with the argument that separate facilities are unequal?

the "separate but equal" theory supported by the Supreme Court in the *Plessy* v. *Ferguson* case. Although the Court ruled that the facilities for African Americans and whites must be equal, they rarely were.

Finally, ask students to comment on the text of the decision. Do they think this ruling was consistent with the attitudes of the period? Ask students to consider what the Court would have risked if it had ruled in Plessy's favor. Tell students that it took people like Richard Wright to point out the real consequences that the decision had on the lives of African Americans.

ANSWERS TO

Thinking About the Selection

1. The Court's decision states that the Fourteenth Amendment was meant to "enforce the absolute equality of the two races before the law." The decision states that the amendment was not meant to "abolish distinctions based upon color, or to enforce social, as distinguished from political, equality, or a commingling of the two races upon terms unsatisfactory to either."

2. The Court uses established usage, customs, and traditions, keeping in mind the people's comfort and the preservation of the public peace and order.

3. The Court believes that separate does not necessarily mean unequal because if this were so, then a state legislature controlled by African Americans, acting under a similar law, would place white Americans in an unequal position. In addition, the Court does not believe that social prejudices can be overcome by legislation or that equal rights can be secured by forced commingling.

Ask students to think about how they would go about proving in a court of law that separate facilities are inherently unequal. Ask them to consider what evidence they would gather, whom they would call as witnesses, and how they would word their final argument. Then have students write a report explaining their approach.

Review students' reports and offer suggestions where needed. Then have students work in groups of five or six. One student should be the lawyer, one the judge, and the rest should be witnesses called to the stand by the lawyer. The students should then role-play for the class the trial of the separate but equal doctrine, acting out only the side of the prosecution (those attacking the doctrine).

The Ethics of Living Jim Crow: An Autobiographical Sketch 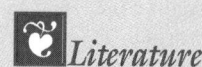 Literature

Richard Wright

INTRODUCTION Richard Wright, an African American writer born in 1908 in Mississippi, grew up during the height of Jim Crow. His books *Uncle Tom's Children*, *Native Son*, and *Black Boy* describe the degradation and danger of life under legal segregation. The excerpt below was taken from *The Ethics of Living Jim Crow*, originally published in 1937 as part of a Federal Writers' Project anthology.

VOCABULARY Before you read the selection, find the meaning of these words in a dictionary: unmolested, incriminating, subtly, dissemble, imbibe, fictitious, ingenuity.

Negroes who have lived South know the dread of being caught alone upon the streets in white neighborhoods after the sun has set. In such a simple situation as this the plight of the Negro in America is graphically symbolized. While white strangers may be in these neighborhoods trying to get home, they can pass unmolested. But the color of a Negro's skin makes him easily recognizable, makes him suspect, converts him into a defenseless target.

Late one Saturday night I made some deliveries in a white neighborhood. I was pedaling my bicycle back to the store as fast as I could, when a police car, swerving toward me, jammed me into the curbing.

"Get down and put up your hands!" the policemen ordered.

I did. They climbed out of the car, guns drawn, faces set, and advanced slowly.

"Keep still!" they ordered.

I reached my hands higher. They searched my pockets and packages. They seemed dissatisfied when they could find nothing incriminating. Finally, one of them said:

"Boy, tell your boss not to send you out in white neighborhoods after sundown."

As usual, I said:

"Yes, sir."

I had learned my Jim Crow lessons so thoroughly that I kept the hotel job till I left Jackson for Memphis. It so happened that while in Memphis I applied for a job at a branch of the optical company. I was hired. And for some reason, as long as I worked there, they never brought my past against me.

Here my Jim Crow education assumed quite a different form. It was no longer brutally cruel, but subtly cruel. Here I learned to lie, steal, to dissemble. I learned to play that dual role which every Negro must play if he wants to eat and live.

For example, it was almost impossible to get a book to read. It was assumed that after a Negro had imbibed what scanty schooling the state furnished he had no further need for books. I was always borrowing books from men on the job. One day I mustered enough courage to ask one of the men to let me get books from the library in his name. Surprisingly, he consented. I cannot help but think that he consented because he was a Roman Catholic and felt a vague sympathy for Negroes, being himself an object of hatred. Armed with a library card, I obtained books in the following manner: I would write a note to the librarian, saying: "Please let this nigger boy have the following books." I would then sign it with the white man's name.

When I went to the library, I would stand at the desk, hat in hand, looking as unbookish as possible. When I received the books desired I would take them home. If the books listed in the note happened to be out, I would sneak into the lobby and forge a new

The system of Jim Crow began after the end of Reconstruction and dominated almost every aspect of life by the early 1900s. This 1892 cartoon protests Jim Crow practices that kept African Americans from voting.

one. I never took any chances guessing with the white librarian about what the fictitious white man would want to read. No doubt if any of the white patrons had suspected that some of the volumes they enjoyed had been in the home of a Negro, they would not have tolerated it for an instant.

The factory force of the optical company in Memphis was much larger than that in Jackson, and more urbanized. At least they liked to talk, and would engage the Negro help in conversation whenever possible. By this means I found that many subjects were taboo from the white man's point of view. Among the topics they did not like to discuss with Negroes were the following: American white women; the Ku Klux Klan; France, and how Negro soldiers fared while there; French women; Jack Johnson[1]; the entire northern part of the United States; the Civil War; Abraham Lincoln; U.S. Grant; General Sherman; Catholics; the Pope; Jews; the Republican Party; slavery; social equality; Communism; Socialism; the 13th and 14th Amendments to the Constitution; or any topic calling for positive knowledge or manly self-assertion on the part of the Negro. The most accepted topics were sex and religion.

[1] Jack Johnson (1878–1946), an African American boxer who was heavyweight champion of the world from 1908 to 1915

There were many times when I had to exercise a great deal of ingenuity to keep out of trouble. It is a southern custom that all men must take off their hats when they enter an elevator. And especially did this apply to us blacks with rigid force. One day I stepped into an elevator with my arms full of packages. I was forced to ride with my hat on. Two white men stared at me coldly. Then one of them very kindly lifted my hat and placed it upon my armful of packages. Now the most accepted response for a Negro to make under such circumstances is to look at the white man out of the corner of his eye and grin. To have said: "Thank you!" would have made the white man think that you thought you were receiving from him a personal service. For such an act I have seen Negroes take a blow in the mouth. Finding the first alternative distasteful, and the second dangerous, I hit upon an acceptable course of action which fell safely between these two poles. I immediately—no sooner than my hat was lifted—pretended that my packages were about to spill, and appeared deeply distressed with keeping them in my arms. In this fashion I evaded having to acknowledge his service, and, in spite of adverse circumstances, salvaged a slender shred of personal pride.

THINKING ABOUT THE SELECTION

1. Why did African Americans in the South try to stay out of white neighborhoods after dark?
2. According to Wright, why could an African American not say "thank you" to a white man in a situation such as that described in the elevator?

Critical Thinking

3. **Recognizing Cause and Effect** How did the presence of Jim Crow laws lead Wright to forge a note in order to take books out of the public library?

ANSWERS TO

Thinking About the Selection

1. They tried to stay out of white neighborhoods after dark because their presence was viewed suspiciously and they were assumed to be guilty of wrongdoing. Some white people then would try to find evidence of wrongdoing even when none existed.

2. Doing so would imply that the white man had done a personal favor for the African American; the white man would see this as evidence of the African American thinking too highly of himself.

3. Because African Americans were not given schooling equal to that of white children, Wright had a need to get books from the public library. Jim Crow also meant that African Americans could not take books from the library themselves, but had to do so secretly through a white person.

The United States, 1815–1915

Using the Unit Summary

This textbook contains two units that review United States history before the twentieth century. Unit 1 provides a review of United States history to 1840. Unit 2 reviews United States history from 1815 to 1915. The Unit 2 Summary provides a four-page synopsis of Unit 2 that focuses on the key ideas covered in the review unit.

Listed below are some of the possible uses for the Unit 2 Summary.

To Review Unit 2 When students have completed Unit 2, you might want to assign the Unit 2 Summary as a tool for review.

To Set the Stage for Unit 3 The Unit 2 Summary may also be used to set the stage for Unit 3, which covers the nation's emergence as a world power, the era of progressive reform, and World War I.

To Omit Unit 2 If you wish to skip Unit 2, it may be helpful to assign the Unit 2 Summary to students as a review before beginning the next unit.

The United States, 1815–1915

In the last half of the nineteenth century, the United States became a unified nation in fact as well as in name. As has been true throughout American history, the varying groups that formed the nation each struggled to assert their values and promote their own way of life.

In the last half of the nineteenth century, the United States underwent dramatic and lasting change, as it experienced territorial expansion, civil war, industrialization, and population growth from increases in immigration.

The Rise of the Northern Middle Class, 1815–1860

One way of life grew increasingly visible in the North, where the Market Revolution of the early nineteenth century had helped create a growing middle class. In this class of society, men worked as lawyers, clerks, managers, or business people while their wives stayed home to care for their families. These people put enormous emphasis on individual character and the ability to restrain human desires. For example, they were opposed to excessive drinking. Growing numbers of them also opposed slavery. Though not interested in racial equality, they believed slavery was morally wrong because it destroyed family ties and kept individuals from making free choices. Their abolitionism—the desire to abolish or end slavery—put them in an increasingly dramatic confrontation with another group: powerful slave owners in the South.

Working-class Americans, often laboring in terrible conditions in the new cities, did not have the time or the money for middle-class morality. They had to concentrate on survival. When they did have a rest from work, they wanted to enjoy themselves, whether that was in drinking, gambling, watching boxing matches, or simply roving about the streets.

This behavior offended middle-class Americans, who had little tolerance for other ways of life. They expected all people to restrain themselves as they themselves did. But these reformers had little success instilling their middle class Protestant beliefs in the working class who simply wanted to be left alone. Their challenge grew even tougher when Irish Catholic and German Catholic immigrants began to arrive in large numbers in the 1830s and 1840s. The middle class now saw itself faced with two threats—one from the Slave Power in the South, and the other from the Papal, or Catholic, Power in the North.

The Conquest of the West and the Secession of the South, 1800–1865

The expansion of the nation eventually led to a clash between the values of various groups. By the 1830s, Americans were spreading across the continent. Not only had settlers moved into the Mexican provinces of Texas and California, but American merchants were active throughout the West, developing trails from Kansas to Santa Fe and from Missouri to Oregon. Convinced of their "manifest destiny" to rule from sea to shining sea, citizens of the United States were conquering a broad swath across the midsection of the North American continent.

Conquering Mexico In the mid-1840s, the United States formally annexed the Republic of Texas. This increased tensions in the region, which led in turn to war with Mexico in 1846. United States forces quickly took California and New Mexico. By late summer, 1847, the United States Army had captured Mexico City. In the Treaty of Guadalupe-Hidalgo, signed at the end of the war, the United States took from Mexico about a third of its land, including the territory from Texas to California.

The Slavery Question Arises The newly acquired Mexican territories brought to the forefront of American politics the clash between those who were for and those who were against slavery. Should slavery be allowed in new states carved out of this land? Supposedly the Missouri Compromise, which drew a line across the continent, had settled this question. But many northerners did not want any more slave states in the Union. Southern slave owners, on the other hand, claimed it was their right as free-born Americans to take their property—including enslaved people—wherever they wished, even into new states.

Politicians solved this disagreement temporarily in the Compromise of 1850. But in 1854 the ambitious Stephen Douglas, a Democratic senator from Illinois, reopened the issue. He said that according to the respected principle of American government—popular sovereignty, or the rule of the people—the residents of the Kansas and Nebraska territories should be allowed to vote on whether they wanted slavery. Northerners were outraged at this plan. In response, some formed an antislavery, anti-Southern political organization that became known as the Republican party. Opposed to immigration and Catholicism as well as slavery, it became the favored party of the northern middle class.

It was not long before new events increased tension still further. In Kansas, armed gangs on both sides of the issue killed their opponents. In the nation's capital, a southern member of Congress beat a Republican senator senseless in the Senate chamber. It seemed the nation's laws were unable to prevent disorder. Even the Supreme Court complicated matters. In the Dred Scott decision of 1857, the Court said that African Americans were not citizens and that the federal government could not keep slaveholders from taking

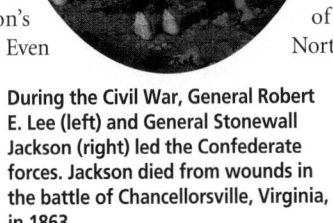

During the Civil War, General Robert E. Lee (left) and General Stonewall Jackson (right) led the Confederate forces. Jackson died from wounds in the battle of Chancellorsville, Virginia, in 1863.

their "property" into any part of the United States.

War Breaks Out The long-brewing clash between northern and southern values finally burst into open warfare after the Republican candidate, Abraham Lincoln of Illinois, won the presidency in 1860. Lincoln received a majority of the votes in the North but almost no votes in the South. Believing that the federal government no longer represented them or protected their rights, seven states in the Lower South seceded from, or left, the Union during the winter of 1860–1861 and formed a new nation, the Confederate States of America. They were later joined by the states of the Upper South.

Neither North nor South knew how the new President would respond until April 1861. In that month, Confederate forces bombarded Fort Sumter, a federal stronghold in the harbor of Charleston, South Carolina, and forced it to surrender. Lincoln labeled their action rebellion and called for troops to force the Confederate states back into the Union. The nation now plunged into the Civil War.

The Course of the War At first, the Civil War went badly for the North. The South had the advantage of being on the defensive. But in 1862, northern troops began to make progress in reconquering the Mississippi Valley. Meanwhile, the United States took back major ports and blockaded the South, preventing it from trading with Europeans.

In 1863, a Union army won a key victory at Vicksburg, Mississippi, bringing the Mississippi River under federal control. At Gettysburg, Pennsylvania, Union forces stopped a major Confederate invasion of the North. From that point on, the North simply wore the South down, taking full advantage of its own superiority in population and industrial production. The main Confederate armies surrendered in April 1865. In that month, too, President Lincoln was assassinated.

The Reconstruction of the Union

One of the major results of the Civil War was that the power and importance of the federal government was dramatically increased. During the war, the United States had censored newspapers, jailed critics of the government, and passed legislation increasing the role of the national government in economic development.

Other changes were made in the law of the land. For instance, the Thirteenth Amendment to the Constitution forever ended slavery. The United States now used its increased central authority to try to reconstruct the Union. Congress, still under northern control, passed amendments and laws to guarantee rights to African Americans and to force the South to change its social structure.

By the 1870s, many white northerners grew weary of the problems of Reconstruction, and many white southerners were finding new ways to continue their violent opposition. In 1877, southern Democrats agreed to allow Republican Rutherford B. Hayes to become president in a disputed election. In return, Republicans removed federal troops from the South and let the former Confederate states govern themselves again. Reconstruction was over. The Constitution now recognized African Americans as full and equal citizens. But it would be decades before those legal rights would become practical realities.

The Industrialization of the United States

The retreat from Reconstruction was in part due to a change in the values of political leaders, who became interested in promoting big business. Using profits gained during the Civil War, business leaders were beginning to invest heavily in new technical advances. Government helped entrepreneurs to develop new industries and expand old ones, sometimes through subsidies, more often by adopting a *laissez faire*, or "hands-off," policy toward business. By the late 1800s, giant industrial enterprises had emerged that controlled vast human and financial resources.

These new inventions and enterprises transformed daily life for millions of Americans, not just business leaders. Electricity and petroleum products brought new comforts to home life, increased economic opportunities, and speeded up transportation and communication. By 1900, railroads, steel bridges, telegraphs, and telephones had forged many new transportation and communication links across the nation.

Thus industrialists created jobs and increased the availability of goods for many Americans. They also took some of their profits and founded many of the nation's great cultural institutions. But some of their business practices prompted concern. Their monopolies, cartels, and trusts put competitors out of business. Their control over the economy led to periods of overproduction and dips in the market for goods, which in turn led to financial panics, depressions, and widespread unemployment.

Workers in this era had no protection against wage cuts, job-related injuries, or layoffs. To lobby for the things they valued, they formed labor unions. But the new unions provoked a harsh response from employers, who enlisted government power to put down worker demonstrations and strikes. This pattern was repeated in the Railroad Strike of 1877, the Haymarket riot in Chicago of 1886, the 1892 steel workers' strike at Homestead, Pennsylvania, and the strike of the workers on Pullman rail cars in 1894. All resulted in jail terms for workers and many injuries and deaths on both sides.

Moving West

Business and government expansion was linked to continued expansion of the nation into the Great Plains, the Pacific Northwest, and the Southwest. New settlers in these areas acquired land by buying it from large companies or state governments, which had obtained it cheaply from the federal government. In many cases, settlers took advantage of a law passed during the Civil War and received 160-acre parcels of land for free from the government.

The Costs of Growth This expansion, too, had its costs. Native Americans saw the West as their homeland and the settlers as invaders. As agreements between tribal leaders and settlers fell apart, violent exchanges erupted. Called in to protect settlers, the

United States army defeated and in some cases massacred large numbers of Native Americans. The remaining few were forced onto reservations.

Meanwhile, white settlers faced a great challenge in the West. The sod of the Great Plains was hard to work. Natural disasters occurred frequently. New mechanical implements introduced during the 1870s seemed likely to solve some of the difficulties facing farmers. But once farmers bought these labor-saving machines, they had to grow only the crop the machines could work. And if prices for the crop fell, farmers went into debt.

Other opportunities for settlers in the West were fast disappearing. By the early 1860s most of the deposits of gold and silver that remained were so deeply buried that only huge companies could afford to dig for them. Texas cattle ranching, which had boomed during the 1860s and 1870s, declined in the mid-1880s. Natural disasters destroyed many herds, and farmers were using newly invented barbed wire to fence their land against grazing cattle. As a result, many ranchers went bankrupt.

Farmers Call for Change In the late 1800s, farmers suffering from falling prices began to criticize government economic policies. They opposed tariffs, which raised their cost of living, and wanted the government to use silver rather than gold as money. This, they believed, would increase the money in circulation and help them pay their debts.

In the 1890s, farmer protest culminated in a "populist" movement that called for a silver monetary standard, graduated income tax, and government ownership of transportation and communications systems. Although the "People's party" lost at the polls, populist ideas survived and later were adopted by urban and industrial reform movements.

Immigration, Urbanization, and Reform

The pressure for reform increased as immigrants poured into the nation. Between 1865 and 1920, close to 30 million people entered the United States, almost doubling the population. About 10 million immigrants arrived between 1865 and 1890, coming mostly from northern European countries. In the 1890s, immi-grants began to arrive from southern and eastern Europe and the Middle East, as well as from Asia. These included railroad workers from China and Japanese farmers. In the early 1900s, thousands of Mexicans fled poverty, debt, and revolution in their homeland and settled in the southwest.

New Pressures on Cities Americans were also moving in this period—from the country into the cities. By 1900, many features of modern city life had appeared: slums, dirt, traffic jams, rising crime rates, and sanitation and public health problems. Middle- and upper-class urban residents began to flee to the suburbs, but still the cities swelled.

As city populations grew, local governments scrambled to set up new offices to provide services. The old and the new residential groups and ethnic divisions vied for control over city government. City political machines—unofficial organizations designed to keep a party or group in power—arose out of these contests. Some were completely corrupt; others made serious efforts to improve the quality of urban life.

Attempts at Reform Many ideas for solving urban social problems circulated in this era. Like the middle-class reformers of the 1830s, some people aimed at prohibiting undesirable social behaviors, such as drinking and other vices. Others argued that the middle and upper classes should assist those in poverty, leading to various movements to help the poor.

At the national level, cycles of economic boom and bust, declining wages, and rising farmer debt were causing deep discontent. Legislators took favors openly from big business. Government offices were given not to people fit for the work, but to those with political connections. Neither national party advanced distinguished candidates for office.

All the same, some reforms did take place. President Chester Arthur took a step toward ending corruption in government by introducing a merit-based civil service in 1883. Then President Grover Cleveland supported the Interstate Commerce Act of 1887, and President Benjamin Harrison signed the Sherman Anti-Trust Act of 1890. Though unevenly enforced at the time, these two acts formed the basis for reforming big business practices in later years.

Introducing the Unit

Interpreting the Visual Alfred Thayer Mahan, an American writer on naval affairs quoted on page 304, believed that a nation's greatness lay not in its buildings, factories, or crops but in a strong navy and merchant marine. Mahan's books influenced some of the key figures of his time, including Theodore Roosevelt and Kaiser Wilhelm I of Germany.

By the late 1880s, United States naval power was in decline, partly because investors were more attracted to other ventures, such as railroads and mining. In fact, in 1892 the United States still had more tonnage in sailing ships than in steamships.

Direct students to the photograph on pages 304–305 and point out the Brooklyn Bridge in the background. Ask students to list the kinds of transportation shown in the picture. Then divide the class into discussion groups and ask each group to explain why a vigorously expanding economy continually needs new markets. Ask students to identify the overseas market advertised by the steamship company in the picture.

Establishing Chronology Remind students that the previous chapters focused on the growth of American industry, the devastation of the Civil War, the bitterness of Reconstruction, the push toward the Western frontier, and the dramatic wave of immigration. This unit focuses on the nation's growing role as a world power from 1890 to 1920. From 1898 to 1899, the United States was at war with Spain. From 1917 to 1918, the nation fought in World War I. The progressive movement, which began around 1890, remained strong through the war years.

The United States on the Brink of Change
1890 – 1920

"Whether they will or not, Americans must now begin to look outward. The growing production of the country demands it."
—Alfred T. Mahan, 1890

The industrial boom at the turn of the century had far-reaching effects. In search of markets for its products, the United States joined the scramble for new territories, leading to international conflict and war. Meanwhile, the serious problems created by the boom inspired a reform movement known as progressivism. Both the ambitions of the imperialists and the ideals of the progressives contributed to the nation's growing role as a world power. This role eventually drew the United States into the horrors of World War I.

CHAPTER 9
Pages 306–331
Becoming a World Power
1890–1913

CHAPTER 10
Pages 336–363
The Era of Progressive Reform
1890–1920

CHAPTER 11
Pages 368–393
The World War I Era
1914–1920

 **RESOURCE DIRECTORY**

Teaching Resources

Local History Activity "The 'Newsies': A Chicago Street Scene" and the Local Focus research topic suggestions, found in the Local History Resources folder, pp. 18–20, are designed to help students understand how history affects all lives.

★ **Themes in American History Posters** Wall-size, illustrated posters, found in the Teaching Resources package, illustrate the four unit themes.

Unit Test Forms A and B are found in the Unit 3 folder, pp. 110–115.

New York City's docks were teeming with activity in the early 1900s as the United States reached across the Atlantic Ocean in its quest to become an economic and political world power.

Media and Technology

 **Visions of America: Scenes of an Era** To introduce students to the main idea and events covered in this unit, play "Scenes of an Era: The United States on the Brink of Change, 1890–1920" (length: 2.5 minutes). This selection can be located on side 2 of the videodiscs. This selection can also be located on videotape 3. Lesson plans for "Scenes of an Era" can be found in the Visions of America Teacher's Guidebook.

Using Multimedia Technology This folder contains instructional tools and strategies for using technology in the classroom.

Transparency Binder Contains full-color transparencies with lesson suggestions. From a large collection divided into twelve categories, specific transparencies are referenced throughout the chapters at appropriate points of use. For this unit, see American Photo, B-6; Fine Art, D-16; Cause and Effect, F-5; Links Across Time, J-6; Political Cartoon, K-6; and Geographic Setting, M-9.

Themes in American History

Teachers may wish to discuss specific historical events in the context of historical themes. Here are four suggestions for Unit 3.

Reform Movements *People in the United States have frequently taken action in grass-roots movements to right perceived wrongs and to secure improvements in the quality of life.*

• The seventy-year quest for women's suffrage ended in 1920 with the adoption of the Nineteenth Amendment.
• Progressivism took root in the late 1800s and led to major changes in urban, state, and federal laws and practices.

Values *A variety of religious, ethical, and moral beliefs have propelled and guided the quest of Americans for a just and ordered society.*

• The argument over American imperialism was shaped by moral, ethical, and religious ideals as well as racial and economic issues.
• The progressives argued that government had a moral responsibility for the welfare of citizens.

Unity and Conflict *Americans have developed unique political systems and laws that affirm a shared commitment to certain goals, such as individual rights and equality. Nevertheless, groups with differing views on how to achieve these goals have often clashed.*

• America's desire to expand its markets clashed with its reluctance to become involved in foreign entanglements and war.
• During World War I, the United States enacted many laws that censored the press and limited personal freedoms.

The United States and the World *America's relationships with other countries have been influenced at different times by a sense of mission, by values, and by self-interest.*

• America's desire to expand its markets led to conflict with Spain and several interventions in Latin America.
• President Wilson took the leading role in defining a vision of global peace after World War I, but Congress and the Allies kept his vision from being realized.

Chapter 9 Becoming a World Power
1890–1913

📁 Teaching Resources (See Unit 3 Folder)

	Instruction	Enrichment
Section 1 **The Pressure to Expand** (pp. 308–311)	Reproducible Lesson Plan, p. 3 Alternate Lesson Plan, p. 90 Guided Reading and Review, p. 7 Quiz, p. 8	Visual Learning Activity, Expansionism, p. 29

Section 2
Foreign Entanglements, War,
and Annexations
(pp. 312–317)
	Reproducible Lesson Plan, p. 4
	Alternate Lesson Plan, p. 91
	Guided Reading and Review, p. 9
	Quiz, p. 10
		Literature Activity, The Open Boat, pp. 26–27
		Critical Thinking Activity, Drawing
		  Conclusions, p. 22
		Visual Learning Activity, Wartime Propaganda,
		  p. 30
		Primary Source Activity, Teddy Roosevelt:
		  Letters Home, pp. 23–24
		American Profiles Activity, Walter Reed, p. 17
		Historian's Toolbox Activity, Using a Time
		  Zone Map, p. 21

Section 3
A Forceful Diplomacy
(pp. 319–323)
	Reproducible Lesson Plan, p. 5
	Alternate Lesson Plan, p. 92
	Guided Reading and Review, p. 11
	Quiz, p. 12
		Literature Activity, You're All Right, Teddy,
		  p. 28
		Primary Source Activity, The Panamanian
		  Revolution, p. 25
		Time and Place Activity, Building the Alaska
		  Pipeline, pp. 15–16

Section 4
The People's Response to
Imperialism
(pp. 326–329)
	Reproducible Lesson Plan, p. 6
	Alternate Lesson Plan, p. 93
	Guided Reading and Review, p. 13
	Quiz, p. 14
	Chapter Test, Forms A & B, pp. 31–36
		Viewpoints Activity, On the Race for Empire,
		  pp. 19–20
		American Profiles Activity, Juliette Gordon
		  Low, p. 18

📁 Additional Chapter Resources

Resource Organizer, p. 2
Alternate Lesson Plan, p. 89
Answer Keys, pp. 116–128

Bibliography

For the Teacher
Marks, George P., III, ed. *The Black Press Views American Imperialism (1898–1900).* Arno Press and The New York Times, Inc., 1971. (Includes source material on the annexation of Hawaii, the demand for African American officers, and the Spanish-American War.)
McCullough, David. *The Path Between the Seas: The Creation of the Panama Canal, 1870–1914.* Simon & Schuster, 1977. (Lively and full account contains excerpts from original sources and reads as an epic adventure.)

Prentice Hall Literature Excerpts from *The American Experience,* 1994, including "Realism and the Frontier, 1865–1915."

THE BIG IDEA

The Big Idea for the chapter and how the main ideas in each section relate to the Big Idea are graphically displayed below. Comprehension of this chapter's Big Idea is critical to students' understanding of United States history and how we as a nation got where we are today.

CHAPTER 9

By the 1890s, businesses and political leaders with dreams of empire were pushing into new markets and seizing control of territory abroad. Imperialism on the part of a country founded on freedom from colonialism troubled many United States citizens. The responsibilities of a world power brought conflicting domestic and international agendas of the government to the forefront.

SECTION 1

In the late 1800s, American farms and factories produced more than the nation could consume. The United States thus looked to expand its markets overseas. This drew it into conflicts on foreign soil.

SECTION 2

A swift American victory in the Spanish-American War confirmed the nation's status as a world power and obliged it to wrestle with how to govern newly acquired territories.

SECTION 3

President Theodore Roosevelt conducted an aggressive foreign policy that reflected the nation's new status as a world power. President William Howard Taft continued Roosevelt's policies with a more subtle approach.

SECTION 4

Following the Spanish-American War, anti-imperialists launched moral, political, and practical arguments against the country's foreign ventures. Most citizens, however, supported the interventionist policies of the United States.

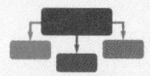

Becoming a World Power
1890–1913

CHAPTER 9

Becoming a World Power
1890–1913

The Relevance of the Big Idea

In the 1890s, United States business interests spread throughout the Western Hemisphere and the Pacific. In the 1990s, American multinational corporations operate throughout the world.

In order for students to understand the role of the United States in a global economy, ask them: "How far should the United States go to protect American companies that operate overseas?" Point out that the United States fought the Gulf War in 1991 in large part to protect the oil interests of the United States in Kuwait. Should the United States try to steer countries toward a type of government friendly to American businesses? Should it ever use force to do so?

*B*y the 1890s, farms and factories in the United States were producing more than the nation could consume. Soon, many business and political leaders began to pursue new markets abroad. Inspired by grand dreams of empire, some Americans pushed for new territory as well. As the nation grew into a world power, however, a troubling question arose in some citizens' minds: could a country born in a war for independence from colonial rule become a colonial power itself—without betraying the principles of liberty and equality on which it was founded?

In Depth

Global Connections

The peace that Teddy Roosevelt arranged between Russia and Japan haunted the United States later in the century. Even though the treaty may have "saved Japan from a beating," Japanese newspapers condemned it as cheating their country out of major territorial gains. Japan defied the terms of the treaty by annexing Korea in 1910. The spread of Japan's influence fueled the country's aspirations for empire in Asia, and its expansionist policies in the 1930s culminated in the bombing of Pearl Harbor and the entry of the United States into World War II.

Events in the United States

1890 Alfred Mahan publishes The Influence of Sea Power Upon History.	1893 American planters overthrow Queen Liliuokalani in Hawaii.	1896 William McKinley defeats William Jennings Bryan in presidential election.	1898 The Spanish-American War takes place. • The United States annexes Hawaii.
1890	**1893**	**1896**	**1899**

Events in the World

1885 Indian National Congress is founded.		1895 Japan defeats China in Sino-Japanese War. • Cubans rebel against Spanish rule.	1900 The Boxer Rebellion breaks out in China.

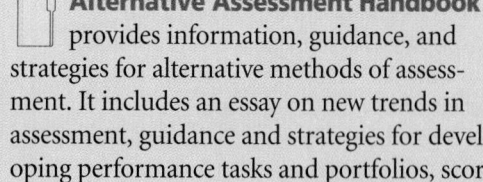
RESOURCE DIRECTORY

Teaching Resources

Alternate Lesson Plan: Demonstrating the Big Idea found in the Alternate Lesson Plans folder, p. 89, provides a lesson strategy to help students understand the issues that determine the roles the United States plays in the global economy.

Alternative Assessment Handbook provides information, guidance, and strategies for alternative methods of assessment. It includes an essay on new trends in assessment, guidance and strategies for developing performance tasks and portfolios, scoring rubrics, and sample evaluation forms.

Pages 308–311
The Pressure to Expand

In the late 1800s, the United States began bursting at the seams with more goods than the nation could consume. Soon other parts of the world beckoned to government and business leaders eager to sell those extra goods. This economic expansion, however, increasingly led the United States into conflicts on foreign soil.

ZULULAND

Pages 312–317
Foreign Entanglements, War, and Annexations

As the United States sought to increase its influence abroad, it frequently found itself feuding with other nations. A swift American victory in the Spanish-American War confirmed the nation's status as a world power, but it left some people arguing over how to govern newly acquired territories.

Pages 319–323
A Forceful Diplomacy

Whether people thought him a hero or a "wild man," most agreed that President Theodore Roosevelt conducted a vigorous foreign policy that suited the new status of the United States as a world power. Although President William Howard Taft continued Roosevelt's policies, he preferred a quieter, more subtle approach to influencing other nations.

Pages 326–329
The People's Response to Imperialism

After the Spanish-American War, the debate intensified over whether it was appropriate for the United States to continue to throw its net around other nations and drag them under American control. Anti-imperialists used a variety of arguments against the acquisition of territories.

1901 President McKinley is assassinated, and Theodore Roosevelt becomes President.

1908 William Howard Taft becomes President.

1910 Boy Scouts and Girl Scouts are introduced to the United States.

1914 Construction of the Panama Canal is completed.

1902	1905	1908	1911	1914	1917

1905 Japan defeats Russia in Russo-Japanese War.

1911 Revolution sweeps China.

1913 Second Balkan War erupts between Bulgaria, Serbia, and Greece.

◆ Alternative Assessment

As an ongoing chapter project, students can write two newspaper editorials that might have appeared in the 1890s. One should take a pro-imperialist stand; the other should be anti-imperialist.

Students might create a scenario involving the possible annexation of a fictional republic; or they might use other real historical examples. Editorials should reflect a firm knowledge of the arguments for or against United States expansionism.

The editorials should attempt to persuade by using reasoned arguments that address moral, economic, social, and political implications. They may be written in a yellow journalism style, employing exaggeration and appeal to jingoism. Students may choose to research and use actual quotations from political and business leaders of the time to help bolster their arguments.

Explain that projects will be evaluated according to the following guidelines:

• **Unacceptable** Editorials are not attempted or fail to meet the basic requirements.

• **Limited/Acceptable** Editorials reflect a basic understanding of the positions of imperialists and anti-imperialists, using information from the chapter.

• **Extensive/Commendable** Editorials reflect an in-depth understanding of the views and motives of imperialists and anti-imperialists, and demonstrate some outside research.

• **Extraordinary/Outstanding** Editorials employ arguments for each viewpoint, demonstrate a clear understanding of yellow journalism, show evidence of considerable outside research, and employ contemporary quotations.

For information and guidance in alternative assessment trends and strategies, see the Alternative Assessment Handbook in the Resource Directory on page 306.

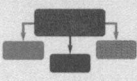

1. FOCUS

Connecting to the Big Idea

See page 306B. Explain that in the late 1800s, the United States needed new markets for its goods. Ask students how that economic problem led to political entanglements in foreign countries.

Objectives

● Explain why the United States needed to find new markets for its goods.

● Describe how increased European expansion affected United States foreign policy.

● List the main arguments used by those who favored expansion.

● Analyze why economic expansion led to political entanglements abroad.

Bellringer

Write the following saying on the chalkboard: "The sun never sets on the British Empire." Ask students what they think it means. Explain that in the late 1800s, when this saying was popular and accurate, the United States was beginning to build its own empire. Ask what an empire is.

Reading Strategy

Reinforcing Key Ideas As students read, they should list the pressures and attitudes that led the United States to adopt a policy of political and economic expansion overseas.

The Pressure to Expand

SECTION PREVIEW

In the late 1800s, the United States began bursting at the seams with more goods than the nation could consume. Soon other parts of the world beckoned to government and business leaders eager to sell those extra goods. This economic expansion, however, increasingly led the United States into conflicts on foreign soil.

Key Concepts

• Overproduction of industrial and agricultural goods threatened the United States economy and created a pressing need for foreign markets.

• The need of the United States for economic expansion occurred at a time when the major European powers were scrambling to seize new territories around the globe.

• Americans who favored expansion used economic, moral, and social Darwinist arguments to justify their position.

• Economic expansion involved the risk of foreign entanglements.

Key Terms, People, and Places

imperialism, annexation, most-favored nation, banana republic; Alfred T. Mahan, Henry Cabot Lodge, Albert J. Beveridge; Hawaii

Business leaders eagerly sought new markets abroad in which to sell goods such as this American-grown fruit.

B y the late 1800s, the industrialists, inventors, and laboring forces of the United States had built a powerful industrial economy. But the nation could not consume food and goods fast enough to prevent harmful cycles of financial panic and depression. Labor and farmers protested their plight, helping to convince business and political leaders that the United States must secure new markets abroad. Some people also began to believe that the United States had a responsibility to carry democratic values and Protestant Christianity to others around the globe.

The Growth of Imperialism Around the World

Meanwhile, Europe had reached new heights in its quest for territories to rule as shown on the map on page 309. Under **imperialism,** stronger nations attempt to create empires by dominating weaker nations—economically, politically, or militarily. This type of policy also has been called expansionism. Although Spain's once-great empire in the Americas and the Pacific had shrunk considerably by 1890, it still held on to a few remaining outposts in Cuba, Puerto Rico, and the Philippines. Meanwhile, developments in transportation and communication made it easier for Great Britain, France, and Russia—nations with long imperialist traditions—to maintain and extend their grip on far-flung lands.

Great Britain, in particular, acquired so much new territory in Africa, Asia, and the Pacific that the saying "The sun never sets on the British Empire" became popular. Competition for new territory grew even more intense when the powerful new German state, unified in 1871, also showed expansionist ambitions in Africa and Asia.

By 1890 the United States was eager to join the international competition for new territories. That year James G. Blaine, secretary of state under President Harrison from 1889 to 1892, summarized the situation as follows:

> W e have developed a volume of manufactures which, in many departments, overruns the demands of the home market. . . . Our great demand is expansion . . . of trade with countries where we can find profitable exchanges.

Blaine denied that the United States was seeking "annexation of territory." But **annexation**—the addition of a new territory to an existing country—did take place.

▶ RESOURCE DIRECTORY

Teaching Resources

Reproducible Lesson Plan found in the Unit 3 folder, p. 3, provides a summary of the Section 1 lesson plan content.

Alternate Lesson Plan: Critical Thinking Recognizing Bias, found in the Alternate Lesson Plans folder, p. 90, provides a structure for students to apply this skill in identifying factors in the drive for U.S. expansion and how it was justified with economic, moral, and social Darwinist arguments.

Guided Reading and Review found in the Unit 3 folder, p. 7, provides a structure for reading and mastering the key concepts and reviewing the key terms for Section 1. (Guided Practice)

The Tradition of Expansionism in the United States

Despite comments like Blaine's, the United States always had been an expansionist nation. In the 1840s, the concept of "manifest destiny" had captured the popular imagination. The seizure of new territories from Mexico and various Native American nations had followed.

As early as the 1820s, the chief principle of foreign policy in the United States had been the Monroe Doctrine. Under this doctrine, the United States had declared itself interested in anything that happened in the Western Hemisphere and warned European powers to keep out. United States secretaries of state continued to apply the principle after the Civil War. In 1866, for example, William H. Seward sent 50,000 federal troops, still in Texas after the Civil War, into Mexico. The display was meant to convince the French government to withdraw the puppet "emperor" they had placed on the Mexican throne. The following year, Seward bought Alaska from Russia. In addition to gaining more territory, Seward hoped that the presence of the United States on both sides of Canada would force the British out of that region.

Americans also had their eyes on the Pacific. By the 1860s, the United States had won **"most-favored nation"** status in China, which simply meant that it had the same access to trade with China as any other nation. The United States also had established a solid trading relationship with Japan. Now the United States government wanted control of some Pacific islands to use as refueling and repair stations for its naval vessels. To this end, Seward annexed the uninhabited Midway Islands in 1867. Eight years later, the United States government signed a treaty with **Hawaii,** an island nation in the Pacific, that allowed Hawaiians to sell sugar in the United States duty free, as long as they did not sell or lease territory to any foreign power.

Much closer to the United States, and therefore of greater concern, were the Caribbean islands and Latin America. In 1870 President Ulysses S. Grant announced that hereafter the Monroe Doctrine would protect all territories in these two regions from "transfer to a European power."

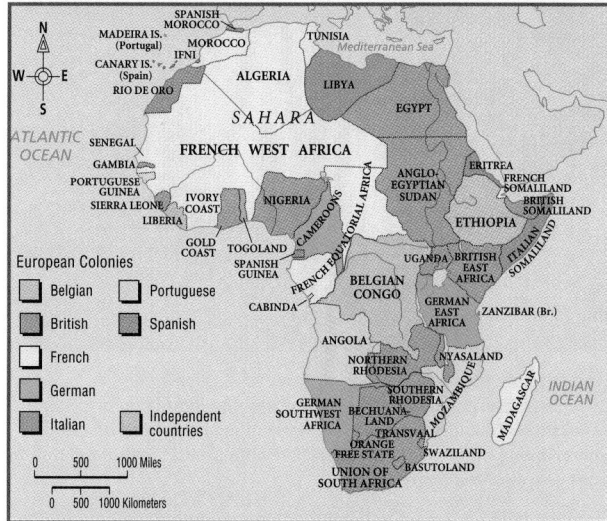

European Imperialism in Africa and Asia, c. 1900

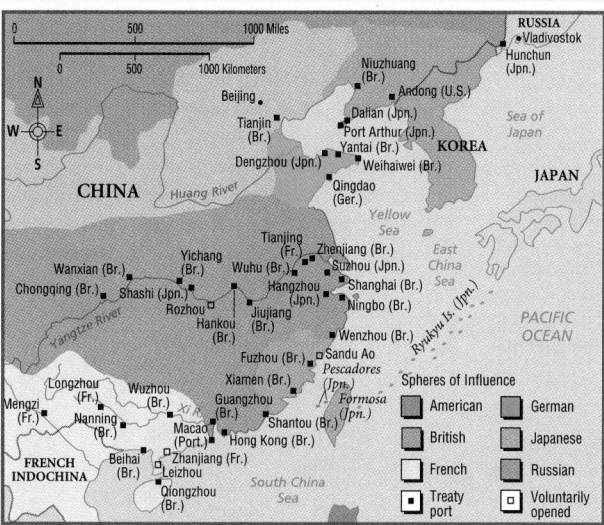

 Geography and History: Interpreting Maps
By 1900, European imperialist nations controlled vast amounts of territory in both Africa and Asia, as the above maps illustrate. *Which African nations retained their independence from imperialist control?*

MAKING CONNECTIONS

In what sense were the expansionist policies of the United States in the late 1800s simply a continuation of the concept of manifest destiny?

Discuss

Discuss with students why United States business leaders put so much pressure on the government to find new markets for their goods. Ask what happens when farms and factories cannot sell their products.

Ask students why the opening of new foreign markets and business ventures caused the United States to become politically involved in other countries' affairs.

Analyze

Have students read and compare the quotations by James G. Blaine on page 308 and by Albert J. Beveridge on page 311. Ask questions such as the following: What motives did each man have for United States expansion? What values and assumptions do their statements reflect? Whose interests did each have in mind?

Caption Answer to ...

Interpreting Maps

Only Ethiopia and Liberia remained free from imperialist control.

Answer to ...

MAKING CONNECTIONS

Just as many Americans in the 1820s believed that the United States had a divine destiny to take possession of the entire continent, many of those who favored expansionist policies in the 1890s believed that the United States had a divine mission to bring Protestant Christianity and democratic institutions to its newly acquired territories around the globe.

Interpreting Graphs

Markets in the United States could not consume the enormous amounts of goods being produced.

 Activity

Teaching Heterogeneous Groups

In the late 1800s, overproduction of goods in the United States created a need for American businesses to find foreign markets. Today the United States continues this search, just as other countries seek a place in the American market to sell their goods. For students to understand imports, exports, and the marketplace, have them list the names of the countries where their clothing and accessories originated. Conduct a survey to determine which country has the largest share of the classroom market.

Enrichment

Ask students to research and report on Minor Keith and the activities of his United Fruit Company. Students should find out how United Fruit was able to gain and maintain control of the Central American countries in which it did business.

3. ASSESS

Section 1 Review Answers

1. (a) imperialism, see p. 308 (b) annexation, see p. 308, (c) most-favored nation, see p. 309, (d) banana republic, see p. 310

2. (a) Alfred T. Mahan, see page 310, (b) Henry Cabot Lodge, see p. 311, (c) Albert J. Beveridge, see page 311

3. Hawaii, see p. 309

4. America's industrial and agricultural goods could not be consumed fast enough to prevent recurring cycles of panics and depression; foreign markets were needed to provide a place to sell the nation's surplus products.

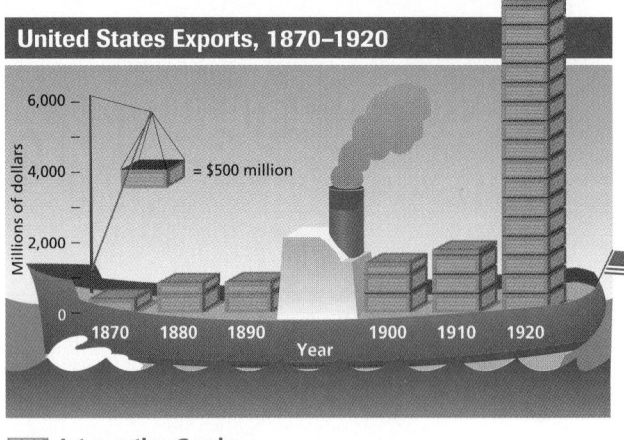

United States Exports, 1870–1920

= $500 million

Interpreting Graphs
The expansion of American businesses into international markets in the late 1800s and early 1900s led to the rapid rise in United States exports during this period. *Why did American businesses wish to sell their goods outside of the United States?*

Americans Debate Expansionism

As this 1901 political cartoon suggests, the United States relied on the Monroe Doctrine to block European involvement in Latin America.

A debate arose in the 1890s over what foreign policy would best serve the United States in its various interests abroad. Some argued that the country should become even more involved in international economic affairs. Others replied that the country had enough problems of its own without risking foreign entanglements.

Voices Supporting Expansion Many business leaders believed that the economic problems of

the nation could be solved by expanding its markets. Some American businesses already dominated international markets. In the 1880s and 1890s, Rockefeller's Standard Oil, McCormick reapers, American Telegraph and Telephone, Singer Sewing Machine, Kodak Camera, and Sherwin-Williams Paint all became international corporations. Southern cotton farmers and western wheat growers also were involved heavily in overseas trade.

Other business leaders had gone a step farther, by investing directly in the economies of other countries. This step led steadily toward increased political influence in those countries. In Central America, for example, an American named Minor C. Keith won long-term leases for lands and railroad lines by providing financial services to the Costa Rican government. By 1913 Keith's United Fruit Company not only exported 50 million bunches of bananas a year to ports in the United States, but also dominated the political and economic institutions of Costa Rica, Guatemala, and Honduras. As a result, some people began to refer to the Central American nations as **banana republics.**

Lobbyists who favored a strong United States Navy formed a second force pushing for expansion. By the 1880s, United States warships left over from the Civil War were rusting and rotting. Naval officers joined with business interests to convince Congress to build modern steam-powered, steel-hulled ships to protect overseas trade. The most influential of these officers was Captain (later Admiral) **Alfred T. Mahan.** In his 1890 book, *The Influence of Sea Power Upon History, 1660–1783,* Mahan asserted that the economic future of the nation depended on gaining new markets abroad and that a powerful navy would be essential to protect these markets from foreign rivals. Influenced by Mahan's arguments, Congress authorized the building of nine cruisers, including the U.S.S. *Maine,* in the 1890s. Battleships, gunboats, torpedo boats, and more cruisers followed. By 1900, the United States had one of the most powerful navies in the world.

▶ RESOURCE DIRECTORY

Teaching Resources

⭐ **Visual Learning Activity** Expansionism, found in the Unit 3 folder, p. 29, uses a political cartoon from the British magazine *Puck* to present a critical view of United States territorial expansion.

Political and cultural leaders also promoted expansionism. Among them were Massachusetts senator **Henry Cabot Lodge,** historian Frederick Jackson Turner, and a rising young politician from New York named Theodore Roosevelt. Although concerned about the need for new markets abroad, these men saw another purpose in expansionism. Worried about the effects of a closing frontier on the nation's spirit, they feared that the United States was on the brink of losing its vitality. They argued that a quest for empire might restore the country's pioneer spirit.

These and other leaders of the day also drew on the doctrine of social Darwinism to justify the conquest of new territories, just as they had done earlier to defend the treatment of Native Americans. In the opinion of such influential figures as Congregationalist minister Josiah Strong and Indiana senator **Albert J. Beveridge,** the "advanced" civilizations produced by Anglo-Saxon and Teutonic (Germanic) "races" were superior to the "primitive" societies they conquered. Thus, expansionism was not only inevitable but noble, for it introduced Protestant Christianity and modern civilization to those who might otherwise never have encountered such ideas. As Beveridge explained:

> I t is elemental. It is racial. God has not been preparing the English-speaking and Teutonic peoples for a thousand years for nothing but vain and idle self-contempla- tion and self-admiration. No! . . . He has marked the American people as His chosen Nation finally to lead in the regeneration [rebirth] of the world. . . . American law,

American order, American civilization, and the American flag will plant themselves on shores hitherto bloody and benighted [igno- rant], but by those agencies of God hence- forth to be made beautiful and bright.

Albert J. Beveridge, *The Meaning of the Times and Other Speeches,* 1908

This postcard of African Zulus with a Singer sewing machine illustrates the spread of Ameri- can products abroad in the late 1800s.

Public Opinion Leans Toward Expansion
Gradually public opinion warmed to the idea of expansionism. Most Americans did not see themselves as potential rulers of oppressed for- eign peoples, but they did want new markets abroad and favorable trade relations. What they soon discovered was that political and military entanglements tended to follow. To maintain a territory's political stability, intervention—and sometimes war—became necessary. When annexation of that territory followed, govern- ing those who resented American interference turned out to be difficult, bloody, and painful.

SECTION 1 REVIEW

Key Terms, People, and Places
1. Define (a) imperialism, (b) annexation, (c) most-favored nation, (d) banana republic.
2. Identify (a) Alfred T. Mahan, (b) Henry Cabot Lodge, (c) Albert J. Beveridge.
3. Identify Hawaii.

Key Concepts
4. Why did United States policy makers feel the need to secure new markets abroad in the late 1800s?

5. In addition to the potential economic benefits of expansion, what were some of the moral arguments that people who favored this policy used?
6. What risks did the United States take in attempting to find new foreign markets?

Critical Thinking
7. **Drawing Conclusions** How did the popular philos- ophy of social Darwinism make it easier for Ameri- cans to embrace imperialist policies in the late 1800s?

Quiz found in the Unit 3 folder, p. 8, cov- ers the main ideas in this section as well as the key terms.

Media and Technology

Transparency
Cause and Effect, F-7

---

5. They claimed that it would restore the country's pioneer spirit and bring Protestant Christianity and modern civ- ilization to "primitive" peoples.

6. Dangerous rivalries with other pow- erful countries; costly and disruptive wars; and involvement in the politics of weaker countries.

7. The social Darwinist notions helped many Americans to feel comfortable establishing American rule over colo- nial peoples.

Reteach
Have students write at least one cause for each of these effects:
● U.S. companies began to dominate the affairs of banana republics.
● Congress authorized an expansion of the United States Navy.
● Public opinion gradually warmed to the idea of expansionism.

4. CLOSE

Reinforcing the Big Idea
A search for new markets and com- petition for new territory led the United States to become heavily involved in the affairs of nations in Latin America and the Pacific. The next section describes how U.S. foreign policy would soon become even more aggressive, leading to deeper overseas entanglements— and even war.

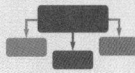

In Depth

Multicultural Perspectives

In 1909 a nationwide petition pleaded for an organized attempt to "improve the status of those Americans for whom the Civil War had been fought to set free." The petition helped form the National Association for the Advancement of Colored People (NAACP), one of the best-known organizations in the fight for civil rights. (See Key Events in the Ref- erence Section.)

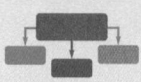

Foreign Entanglements, War, and Annexations

SECTION 2

Foreign Entanglements, War, and Annexations

Connecting to the Big Idea

See page 306B. An aggressive foreign policy brought the United States into conflict with several other nations. Ask what problems the United States faced as a new world power.

Objectives

• Explain how United States foreign policy at the turn of the century reaffirmed the aims of the Monroe Doctrine.
• List the main reasons that the United States went to war with Spain.
• Describe how the United States pursued its expansionist policies in the Pacific.

Bellringer

Write the word *sensationalism* on the chalkboard and ask students to define it. Ask how sensationalism can arouse public energy and response. Discuss types of news coverage that might be considered sensational.

Reading Strategy

Structured Overview Ask students to create a two-column chart entitled "United States Foreign Policy." Students should list countries where the United States pursued expansionist policies in the left-hand column, and the effects of United States policies on each of these countries in the remaining column.

SECTION PREVIEW

As the United States sought to increase its influence abroad, it frequently found itself feuding with other nations. A swift American victory in the Spanish-American War confirmed the nation's status as a world power, but it left some people arguing over how to govern newly acquired territories.

Key Concepts
• The United States took advantage of several incidents in Latin America to reaffirm the validity of the Monroe Doctrine.
• A rebellion in Cuba and the pressure for expansion led the United States into war with Spain.
• While pursuing its interventionist policies, the United States acquired new territories and influence in the Pacific.

Key Terms, People, and Places
guerrilla, jingoism, sphere of influence, Open Door policy; William Randolph Hearst, Joseph Pulitzer, George Dewey; Cuba, Philippine Islands, San Juan Hill

In its drive to become a world power, the United States increasingly became involved in the affairs of Latin American nations.

T hose in the United States who dreamed of expansion looked to three main areas of the world in the late 1800s: Latin America, the islands of the Pacific, and China. In the 1890s, the United States established a pattern of intervention in these three areas that changed its status in world politics. In the process of expanding and becoming a world power, however, the United States increasingly found itself in conflict with other nations.

Stirrings in Latin America

During the 1890s, the United States played an active role in three diplomatic and military conflicts in Latin America. In the first of these incidents, in 1891, the United States government forced Chile to pay $75,000 to the families of United States sailors who were killed or injured by an angry mob during the sailors' shore leave in Valparaíso. Two years later, when a rebellion threatened the friendly republican government of Brazil, President Cleveland ordered naval units to Rio de Janeiro to protect United States shipping. This show of force broke the back of the rebellion.

In the third and most important incident of the era, the United States confronted the nation then considered the most powerful in the world, Great Britain. Since the 1840s, Britain and Venezuela had disputed ownership of a piece of territory located at the border between Venezuela and British Guiana. In the 1880s, the dispute intensified when rumors surfaced of mineral wealth in this border area. When President Cleveland's secretary of state, Richard Olney, warned Britain in July 1895 that the United States would enforce the Monroe Doctrine, the British government replied that the doctrine had no standing in international law. Two years later, however, Britain backed down. Concerned about the rising power of Germany in Africa, the British government realized that it needed to stay on friendly terms with the increasingly powerful United States.

The Spanish-American War

By the mid-1890s, therefore, the United States had not only reaffirmed the Monroe Doctrine but also forced the world's most powerful nation to bow to its will. Encouraged by

RESOURCE DIRECTORY

Teaching Resources

Reproducible Lesson Plan found in the Unit 3 folder, p. 4, provides a summary of the Section 2 lesson plan content.

Alternate Lesson Plan: Learning Styles found in the Alternate Lesson Plans folder, p. 91, enhances students' understanding of the Monroe Doctrine and interventionist policies, and is especially helpful for auditory and visual learners.

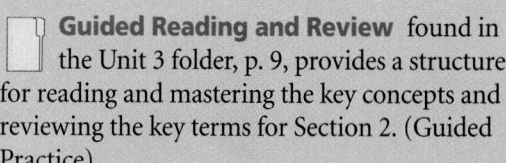

Guided Reading and Review found in the Unit 3 folder, p. 9, provides a structure for reading and mastering the key concepts and reviewing the key terms for Section 2. (Guided Practice)

Literature Activity "The Open Boat," found in the Unit 3 folder, pp. 26–27, describes the harrowing experience of author Stephen Crane, who survived the sinking of a munitions supply steamer returning from Cuba in 1897.

Sensational Newspapers

WOMAN TURNS INTO WILD DOG
WW2 BOMBER FOUND ON MOON
REAL AMERICAN MONSTERS AND DRAGONS
WONDERFUL RESULTS FROM MERELY
   HOLDING TUBES OF DRUGS NEAR
   ENTRANCED PATIENTS

Have you ever seen headlines like these while waiting in line at the supermarket? If so, you might be surprised to learn that the first two appeared in 1990, while the last two are from newspapers published in 1896.

Sensational newspapers are not a recent development. In the late 1800s, publishers engaged in fierce competition for the sale of popular daily newspapers. Yellow journalism attempted to attract customers by using sensational, though not necessarily true, photographs, stories, and headlines. If there was no startling news to report, editors would invent some.

One of William Randolph Hearst's editors described the logic behind the so-called "gee whiz" story: "We run our paper so that when the reader opens it, he says, 'Gee Whiz!'" Today's weekly tabloids refer to the same type of story as a "Hey, Martha."

It seems that many subjects are as popular today as they were one hundred years ago: miracle cures, harrowing escapes, gruesome crimes, controversial trials, tragic love stories, and supernatural occurrences. And as anyone can attest who has observed shoppers flipping through newspapers while waiting in today's supermarket lines, these stories still sell newspapers. *Can you think of any issues in the recent past that first surfaced in a tabloid like that described above?*

---

this development, expansionists soon spied an opportunity to make even more spectacular gains in Cuba.

The Cuban Rebellion An island nation off the coast of Florida, **Cuba** first rebelled against Spain in 1868. After ten years of fighting the rebels, Spain finally put in place a few meager reforms to appease the Cuban people. In 1895, after the island's economy had collapsed, Cubans who believed that Spanish rule was oppressive and incompetent rebelled again. This time Spain sent 150,000 troops and its best general, Valeriano Weyler, to put down the rebellion.

Cuban exiles led by journalist José Martí urged the United States to intervene. Even though public support for the rebels was on the rise, both Presidents Cleveland and McKinley refused, unwilling to spend the money that intervention would require and fearing the United States would be saddled with colonial responsibilities it could not handle. Frustrated, Cuban **guerrillas**—soldiers who fight using surprise tactics—turned to the one tactic they knew would attract the United States government's attention: the destruction of American sugar plantations and mills in Cuba. As a result, business owners increased their pressure on the government to act. Newspaper publishers

William Randolph Hearst and **Joseph Pulitzer** vied with one another to publish horrifying stories of "Butcher" Weyler and his barbed-wire concentration camps. Their sensational headlines and stories, known as yellow journalism, whipped up the American public in favor of the rebels. The intense burst of national pride and the desire for an aggressive foreign policy that followed came to be known as **jingoism.** The name came from a line from a British song of the 1870s: "We don't want to fight, yet by Jingo! if we do, We've got the ships, we've got the men, and got the money too."

Pressure for War Builds Early in 1898, riots erupted in Havana, the capital of Cuba. In response, President McKinley moved the U.S.S. *Maine* into the city's harbor to protect American citizens and property. A few months later, in early February 1898, United States newspapers published an intercepted letter from the Spanish ambassador that described McKinley as "weak and a bidder for the admiration of the crowd." War fever mounted.

⭐ Then, on February 15, an explosion on the *Maine* killed more than 250 American sailors.

Morning Journal Sales	
1895	30,000
1897	400,000
1898	1,000,000

Source: *American Heritage,* February 1957

Interpreting Tables Sales of William Randolph Hearst's *Morning Journal* soared in 1898 thanks to sensational stories before and during the Spanish-American War. *Why do you think people were attracted to such stories?*

⭐ **Critical Thinking Activity** Drawing Conclusions: The Explosion of the *Maine,* found in the Unit 3 folder, p. 22, presents contemporary reports about the mysterious explosion of the *Maine* to help students apply this skill.

Media and Technology

🗑 **Transparency** Critical Thinking, I-12

Ask students to compare José Martí of Cuba, Emilio Aguinaldo of the Philippines, and Queen Liliuokalani of Hawaii. Why did these strong nationalist leaders find themselves in conflict with the United States?

Activity

Staging a Campaign Debate

Have students stage a mock campaign debate for 1900 between candidates William McKinley and William Jennings Bryan. Ask students to consider how Bryan might have attacked McKinley's policies and how McKinley might have responded.

Caption Answer to ...

 Interpreting Maps

Major battles were fought on San Juan Hill in Santiago, Cuba; and in Manila, in the Philippine Islands.

DESTRUCTION OF THE WAR SHIP MAINE WAS THE WORK OF AN ENEMY

Headlines and pictures like these stirred the American public's anger following the explosion on the U.S.S. *Maine* **in early 1898.**

Even though it probably had been caused by a fire that set off ammunition, an enraged American public blamed the Spanish for the disaster and called for war. Still, McKinley hesitated.

On the other side of the world, the people of another of Spain's last remaining possessions, the **Philippine Islands,** also were rebelling. In the view of Theodore Roosevelt, then assistant secretary of the navy, the Philippines could become a key base from which the United States might protect its Asian trade. On February 25, while his boss, the secretary of the navy, was out of the office, Roosevelt cabled naval commanders in the Pacific to prepare for military action against Spain. When President McKinley discovered what Roosevelt had done, he ordered most of the cables withdrawn, but he made an exception in the case of the cable directed to Admiral **George Dewey.** Dewey was told to attack the Spanish fleet in the Philippines if war broke out with Spain.

Late in March, in a final attempt at a peaceful solution, McKinley sent a list of demands to Spain. These included compensation for the *Maine*, an end to the concentration camps, a truce, and Cuban independence. Although Spain accepted most of these demands and agreed to negotiate on the matter of Cuban independence, McKinley decided he could not resist the growing cries for war. On April 11, he sent a war message to Congress. A few days

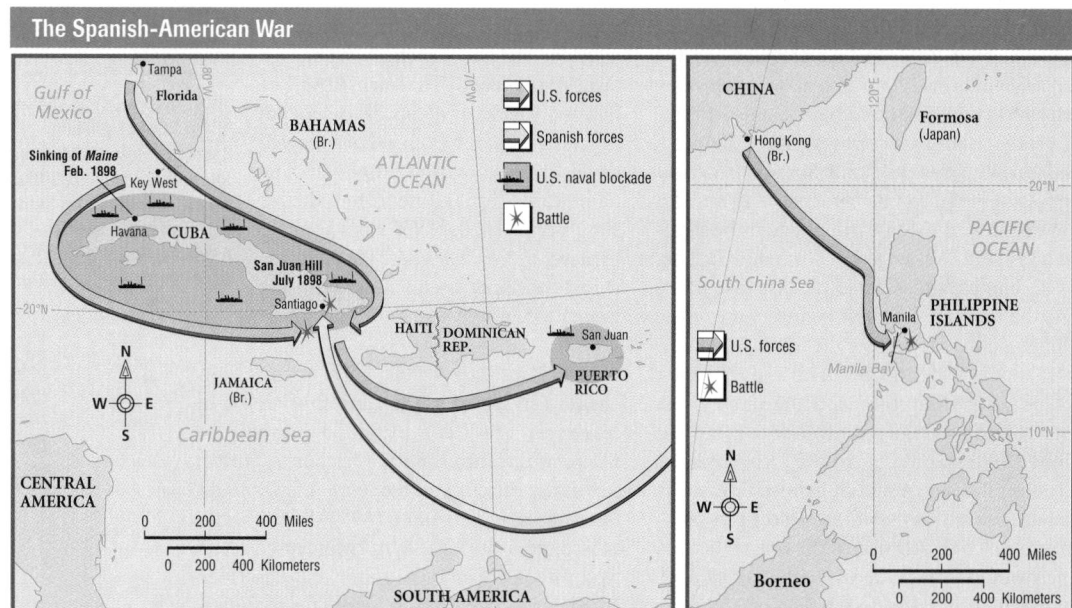

The Spanish-American War

Geography and History: Interpreting Maps
Although the Spanish-American War was fought in two locations on opposite sides of the world, the United States defeated Spain in just three months. *At what specific sites were the major battles of the war fought?*

▶ RESOURCE DIRECTORY

Teaching Resources

⭐ **Visual Learning Activity** Wartime Propaganda, found in the Unit 3 folder, p. 30, uses cartoons from Spanish and American newspapers to show how propaganda was used on both sides in the Spanish-American War.

⭐ **Primary Source Activity** Teddy Roosevelt: Letters Home, found in the Unit 3 folder, pp. 23–24, describes in vivid detail the hardships and harsh conditions facing the Rough Riders.

later, rallying to the cry of "Remember the *Maine!*" Congress recognized Cuban independence and authorized force against Spain.

"A Splendid Little War" The war's first action took place, not in Cuba, but in the Philippines as shown on the map on page 314. On May 1, 1898, Admiral Dewey launched a surprise attack on Spanish ships anchored in Manila Bay, destroying Spain's entire Pacific fleet in just seven hours. In Cuba, meanwhile, United States warships quickly bottled up Spain's Atlantic fleet in the harbor at Santiago. Two months later, Theodore Roosevelt led a group of hastily organized volunteers called the "Rough Riders" in a charge up **San Juan Hill,** which became the most famous incident of the war. Several units of African American troops, known as the "Buffalo Soldiers," also performed superbly in the land war. A white soldier later wrote the *Washington Post* that "if it had not been for the Negro cavalry, the Rough Riders would have been exterminated."

The Spanish fleet made a desperate attempt to escape the harbor on July 3. In the ensuing battle, the United States Navy sank every Spanish ship, setting off wild Independence Day celebrations back in the United States.

It had all seemed quite simple. Although 2,500 Americans had died in the short war, fewer than 400 died in battle. The remainder died from food poisoning, yellow fever, malaria, and inadequate medical care. Future secretary of state John Hay captured the public mood when he wrote his friend Teddy Roosevelt that it had been "a splendid little war."

Dilemma in the Philippines In the treaty the United States signed with Spain in December 1898, the Spanish government recognized Cuba's independence. In return for a payment of $20 million, Spain also gave up the Philippines, Puerto Rico, and the Pacific island of Guam to the United States. The United States government called these territories "unincorporated," which meant that their residents would not become American citizens.

Although many Americans supported the treaty, others were deeply troubled by it. How could the United States become a colonial power without violating the nation's most basic principle—that all people have the right to liberty? Forced to justify this departure from American ideals, President McKinley explained that rebels in the Philippines were on the edge of war with one another and that the Filipino people were "unfit for self-government." If the United States did not act first, moreover, European powers might seize the islands. After a heated debate, the Senate ratified the treaty in February 1899.

Filipino rebels had fought with American troops in the war against Spain with the expectation that victory would bring independence. But when rebel leader Emilio Aguinaldo issued a proclamation in January 1899 declaring the Philippines a republic, the United States government ignored him. Mounting tensions between the rebel forces and American soldiers finally erupted into war in February. In the bitter three-year war that followed, 4,200 Americans were killed and 2,800 more wounded. Fighting without restraint—and sometimes with great brutality—American forces killed some 16,000 Filipino rebels and hundreds of thousands of Filipino civilians. Occasional fighting continued for years. The Philippines did not gain complete independence until 1946.

The Fate of Cuba and Puerto Rico Although the Teller Amendment, attached to Congress's

African American soldiers in the Tenth United States Cavalry are shown below. Wrote one soldier from this regiment: "If I die on the shores of Cuba my earnest prayer to God is that when death comes to end all, I may meet it calmly and fearlessly."

In Depth

Biography

Puerto Rican nationalist Luis Muñoz Rivera (1859–1916) was elected head of a new liberal government in Puerto Rico only months before the United States invasion. In 1910, after sadly accepting the continuing U.S. presence, which he called "unworthy of the United States . . . and of the Puerto Ricans who have to endure it," Muñoz moved to Washington, D.C., as the island's representative in Congress. He died before the passage of the Jones Act of 1917, which granted United States citizenship to all Puerto Ricans who wanted it.

In both wars the United States swiftly defeated weak and disorganized enemies, and acquired important new territories from the defeated nations in the ensuing peace treaties.

3. ASSESS

Section 2 Review Answers

1. (a) guerrilla, see p. 313, (b) jingoism, see p. 313, (c) sphere of influence, see p. 317, (d) Open Door policy, see p. 317

2. (a) William Randolph Hearst, see p. 313, (b) Joseph Pulitzer, see p. 313, (c) George Dewey, see p. 314.

3. (a) Cuba, see p. 313, (b) the Philippine Islands, see p. 314, (c) San Juan Hill, see p. 315

4. In the 1890s, the American government forced Chile to pay an indemnity for the deaths of American sailors. Also, the United States intervened to prevent the overthrow of a friendly government in Brazil and forced Great Britain to accept its arbitration of a border dispute with Venezuela. Hostilities with Cuba and the explosion of the *Maine* also led to the war.

In Depth

Then and Now

Native Hawaiians waited a hundred years for the United States government to acknowledge its part in the overthrow of the Hawaiian monarchy in 1893. On November 16, 1993, the Congress admitted United States complicity in the 1893 overthrow of the Hawaiian monarchy and called for "reconciliation between the United States and the native Hawaiian people." Three weeks earlier, by a vote of 65–34, the Senate had backed the resolution that offered a formal apology to native Hawaiians.

Filipino civilians suffered the highest casualty rates during the three-year war between the United States and the Philippines.

1898 war resolution against Spain, promised Cubans their independence, United States involvement in Cuba did not end with the victory over Spain. In order to protect American business interests in the chaotic environment that followed the war, President McKinley installed a military government in Cuba that ruled for three years. This government organized a school system and restored economic stability. It also established a commission led by Major Walter Reed of the Army Medical Corps that found a cure for the deadly disease, yellow fever. ★

When Cubans began to draft a constitution in 1900, however, the United States government insisted that they include a document called the Platt Amendment. According to the provisions of this amendment, the Cuban government could not enter any foreign agreements, must allow the United States to establish two naval bases on the island, and must give the United States the right to intervene whenever necessary. The Platt Amendment remained in force until 1934.

Unlike Cuba, Puerto Rico never gained its independence. In an attempt to stem a growing independence movement, however, the United States government granted Puerto Ricans United States citizenship in 1917.

In what ways was the Spanish-American War similar to the war between the United States and Mexico in 1846?

Other Gains in the Pacific

The United States government was intervening in other parts of the Pacific at the same time that the Spanish-American War was brewing. This intervention eventually brought about changes in the United States' relationship with Hawaii, Samoa, and China.

Annexation of Hawaii Hawaii had become increasingly important to United States business interests in the late 1800s. When Hawaii and the United States renegotiated their trade treaty in 1887, Hawaii leased Pearl Harbor to the United States as a coaling and repair station for naval vessels. That same year, white Hawaiian-born planters forced the Hawaiian king, Kalakaua, to accept a new constitution that, in effect, gave them control of the government.

When the king died in 1891, his sister Liliuokalani came to the throne. A strong nationalist, Queen Liliuokalani opposed United States control of the islands and sought to reduce the power of foreign merchants. In 1893, with the help of the United States Marines, pineapple planter Sanford B. Dole removed Queen Liliuokalani from power, proclaimed a republic, and requested that Hawaii be annexed by the United States. In 1896, when William McKinley was elected President, he supported the annexation. "We need Hawaii just as much and a good deal more than we did California. It is manifest destiny," McKinley said in early 1898. After briefly considering whether the Hawaiian people wished to be annexed, Congress was swayed by arguments that the United States needed naval stations in Hawaii in order to be a world power. In 1898 Congress approved the annexation of Hawaii.

Samoa The Polynesian islands of Samoa represented another possible stepping-stone to the growing trade with Asia. Back in 1878, the United States had negotiated a treaty with

▶ RESOURCE DIRECTORY

Teaching Resources

 **American Profiles Activity** found in the Unit 3 folder, p. 17, profiles Walter Reed, the army physician whose scientific method led to the discovery of the cause and prevention of deadly yellow fever.

Samoa offering protection in return for a lease on their fine harbor at Pago Pago. When Britain and Germany began competing for control of these islands in the 1880s, tension between these European powers and the United States almost led to war. Eventually the three nations arranged a three-way protectorate of Samoa in 1889. The withdrawal of Great Britain from Samoa in 1899 left Germany and the United States to divide up the islands. A year after the annexation of Hawaii, the United States had acquired the harbor at Pago Pago as well.

Removed from power by American planters in 1893, Queen Liliuokalani was the last monarch of Hawaii.

An Open Door to China China's population was huge by the late 1800s, and its vast markets were increasingly important to American trade. But the United States was not the only nation interested in China. The Chinese monarchy was weakening, and many other countries—Russia, Germany, Britain, France, and Japan—were seeking **spheres of influence,** or areas of economic control, in China. In 1899 John Hay, now President McKinley's secretary of state, wrote notes to the major European powers trying to persuade them to keep an "open door" to China. He wanted to ensure through his **Open Door policy** that the United States would have equal access to China's millions of consumers.

Meanwhile, many Chinese resented foreign influence of any kind. A secret society called the Righteous and Harmonious Fists (the western press called them Boxers) started a rebellion in the spring of 1900 that led to the massacre of three hundred foreigners and Christian Chinese. Although the European powers eventually defeated the Boxers, Secretary Hay feared that these imperialist nations would use the rebellion as an excuse to seize more Chinese territory. Consequently, he issued a second series of Open Door notes. These notes reaffirmed the principle of open trade in China and made an even stronger statement about the intention of the United States to preserve it.

The Election of 1900

In the election of 1900, populist Democrat William Jennings Bryan and Republican William McKinley faced each other as they had in the election of 1896. McKinley named as his running mate Theodore Roosevelt, a man thoroughly identified with expansionism. American foreign policy had been so successful during McKinley's first term that the anti-imperialist Bryan had to drop the issue from his campaign speeches. Instead, he tried to emphasize the failures of Republican economic policies.

But by 1900, prosperity had returned to the nation. Bryan's complaints were ineffective, and McKinley won even more decisively than in 1896. A year later, however, he was dead—cut down by an assassin's bullet. Theodore Roosevelt, whom McKinley's friend Senator Marcus Hanna had once called a "wild man," was now President.

SECTION 2 REVIEW

Key Terms, People, and Places
1. Define (a) guerrilla, (b) jingoism, (c) sphere of influence, (d) Open Door policy.
2. Identify (a) William Randolph Hearst, (b) Joseph Pulitzer, (c) George Dewey.
3. Identify (a) Cuba, (b) the Philippine Islands, (c) San Juan Hill.

Key Concepts
4. What events led to the Spanish-American War?
5. What was the Open Door policy, and why was it important for the United States?

Critical Thinking
6. **Identifying Central Issues** What argument did anti-imperialists use to convince others that expansionism was wrong?

 Quiz found in the Unit 3 folder, p. 10, covers the main ideas in this section as well as the key terms.

Media and Technology

Transparency
Geographic Setting, M-9

5. The Open Door policy was drafted by John Hay, McKinley's secretary of state, who wanted to preserve access to China's mass markets and opposed the carving up of China by other imperialist nations. The policy ensured American participation in the lucrative China trade.

6. Anti-imperialists questioned the United States' ability to become a colonial power without violating the nation's basic principle of liberty for all.

Reteach
Ask students to list the countries mentioned in the section and to write one sentence for each that summarizes the outcome of United States expansionism in that country.

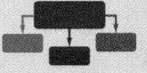 **Alternative Assessment**

Mid-Point Monitoring
Ask students if they have
● Decided on a format for their project and its focus
● Outlined and drafted some ideas
● Begun to identify sources for their project

 **4. CLOSE**

Reinforcing the Big Idea

In its bid to gain influence in Latin America and the Pacific, the United States seized territory and became enmeshed in complicated efforts to govern other peoples. The next section describes American foreign policy under Presidents Theodore Roosevelt and William Howard Taft.

Geography

Using a Time Zone Map

Focus Students will use a time zone map to calculate times in various locations in the world.

Instruct Ask students if they have seen pictures of the earth from space showing a clear dividing line between day and night. As areas of the earth pass out of the dark side and into the sun's light, people in these areas experience sunrise. We say that sunrise occurs at a specific time in a certain area, but that time is arbitrarily assigned, since sunrise is occurring on a continuous basis as the earth turns. For shuttle astronauts circling the earth many times in 24 hours, no specific time can be assigned for sunrise or sunset; these events cannot be guides for measuring days.

Ask why people on earth need agreed-upon times and time zones. Then guide students to follow steps 1 and 2.

Extend See the Historian's Toolbox Activity in the Resource Directory below.

Answers

1. (a) Moscow: 2:00 P.M.; Denver: 5:00 A.M. (b) 9:00 P.M.; 10:00 A.M. (c) You would have to set your watch back seven hours.

2. Answers will vary depending on students' time zones. Answers are given for the time zones labeled –5 through –10, which include those for the contiguous United States, Alaska, and Hawaii. (a) Zone –5: 11:00 A.M.; Zone –6: 12:00 noon; Zone –7: 1:00 P.M.; Zone –8: 2:00 P.M.; Zone –9: 3:00 P.M.; Zone –10: 4:00 P.M. (b) Zone –5: 10:00 A.M.; Zone –6: 9:00 A.M.; Zone –7: 8:00 A.M.; Zone –8: 7:00 A.M.; Zone –9: 6:00 A.M.; Zone –10: 5:00 A.M. (c) Zone –5: 12:00 noon on Thursday; Zone –6: 1:00 P.M. on Thursday; Zone –7: 2:00 P.M. on Thursday; Zone –8: 3:00 P.M. on Thursday; Zone –9: 4:00 P.M. on Thursday; Zone –10: 5:00 P.M. on Thursday.

Using a Time Zone Map

Until the late 1800s, communities around the world calculated local time by the sun. When railroads began providing rapid long-distance train service between many communities—each with its own version of local time—this method began to cause scheduling nightmares.

In 1884 delegates from twenty-seven nations met in Washington, D.C., to discuss the problem. They eventually agreed on a system of worldwide standard time. Under this system, the world is divided into twenty-four time zones, shown by colored bands on the map below. Time is the same throughout each zone.

The prime meridian, which passes through Greenwich, England at 0° longitude, is the starting point for calculating the time in each zone. The International Date Line—located in the Pacific Ocean at 180° longitude—is where the date changes. The calendar date to the east of this line is one day earlier than that to the west.

Use the following steps to read the time zone map below.

1. Study the information on the map. The numbers at the bottom of the map indicate the number of hours each time zone differs from Greenwich time at the prime meridian. For example, a value of +3 means that the time in that zone is three hours *later* than Greenwich time; –3 means it is three hours *earlier*. The numbers at the top of the map provide examples of how this system works. (a) If it is 12:00 noon, Greenwich time, what time is it in Moscow? In Denver? (b) If it is 2:00 P.M. in Abidjan, Côte d'Ivoire, what time is it in the zone labeled +7? In the zone labeled –4? (c) If you flew west from Cairo, Egypt, to Lima, Peru, how many hours forward or back would you have to set your watch?

2. Compare the time in your zone with others. Find your time zone on the map. (a) If it is 1:00 A.M. in the time zone where you live, what time is it in Karachi, Pakistan? (b) If it is 12:00 noon in São Paolo, Brazil, what time is it where you live? (c) If it is 9:00 P.M. on Wednesday where you live, what time and day is it in Brisbane, Australia?

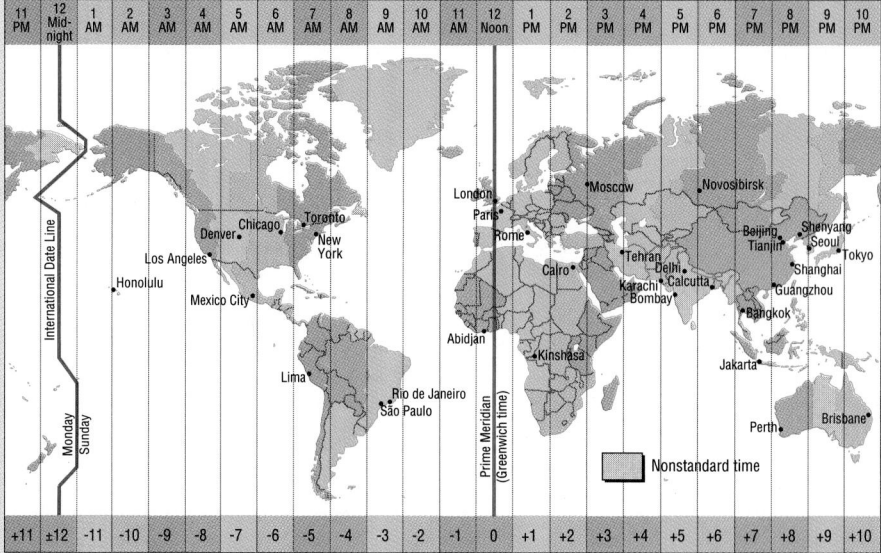

RESOURCE DIRECTORY

Teaching Resources

Historian's Toolbox Activity Using a Time Zone Map, found in the Unit 3 folder, p. 21, allows students to apply this skill by answering questions about global travel.

A Forceful Diplomacy

SECTION PREVIEW

Whether people thought him a hero or a "wild man," most agreed that President Theodore Roosevelt conducted a vigorous foreign policy that suited the new status of the United States as a world power. Although President William Howard Taft continued Roosevelt's policies, he preferred a quieter, more subtle approach to influencing other nations.

Key Concepts

• The forceful and sometimes high-handed manner in which President Theodore Roosevelt conducted foreign policy had the effect of increasing the power of the presidency.
• Under Roosevelt, the United States secured a strip of land in Panama on which it built a canal linking the Atlantic and Pacific oceans.
• President Roosevelt asserted the right of the United States to use military force to preserve stability and order in neighboring countries.
• President William Howard Taft preferred economic pressure to military force in the conduct of American foreign policy.

Key Terms, People, and Places

Roosevelt Corollary, dollar diplomacy; Theodore Roosevelt, William Howard Taft; Isthmus of Panama, Colombia

B y 1900 the United States had emerged as a genuine world power, in control of territories overseas. Presidents Theodore Roosevelt and William Howard Taft acknowledged the change by developing a foreign policy to support the nation's new role in the world. Under their leadership, the United States continued to intervene in the domestic affairs of weaker countries of economic and strategic interest to the nation. Roosevelt did so in an independent and sometimes high-handed manner. Taft took a less aggressive approach, preferring economic pressure to military intervention.

AMERICAN PROFILES

Theodore Roosevelt

Was **Theodore Roosevelt** (1858–1919) really a "wild man"? He certainly was energetic. Before becoming President, he was a historian, politician, cowboy, buffalo hunter, crime fighter, reformer, and cavalryman. His active and colorful lifestyle made him famous the world over. The initials of his name were enough to identify him: TR.

The Shaping of a President Born into a wealthy merchant family in New York, TR was raised to be a leader. Although he had asthma as a child, his father insisted that he overcome his illness with rigorous physical exercise. Eventually, he developed a stocky body and fighter's stance.

TR was also studious. In 1876 he entered Harvard College, where he became increasingly interested in history. After graduation, TR married Alice Hathaway Lee and began to study law.

In February 1884, in the course of a single day, TR lost both his wife, who died in childbirth, and his mother, who died of typhoid. To recover from these twin blows, TR went west. Living on a ranch in the Dakota Territory, he hunted, rode, and studied history. There he started work on his most important and popular work, *The Winning of the West*, a glorification of the frontier myth and the "strenuous life." In TR's view, only strong-willed action would save the United States from physical and moral flabbiness.

Like many of his contemporaries, TR also believed in the superiority of the Anglo-Saxon race. He used arguments of racial superiority to justify the destruction of Native Americans. As he explained in his history of the West: "The man who puts the soil to use must of right dispossess the man who does not, or the world will come to a standstill."

This 1904 campaign pin for Teddy Roosevelt consists of a "teddy" bear holding a soldier's hat and sword.

Reproducible Lesson Plan found in the Unit 3 folder, p. 5, provides a summary of the Section 3 lesson plan content.

Alternate Lesson Plan: Critical Thinking Making Comparisons, found in the Alternate Lesson Plans folder, p. 92, helps students identify similarities and differences in the foreign policies of TR and William Taft by charting their goals, initiatives, and methods.

Guided Reading and Review found in the Unit 3 folder, p. 11, provides a structure for reading and mastering the key concepts and reviewing the key terms for Section 3. (Guided Practice)

1. FOCUS

Connecting to the Big Idea

See page 306B. The foreign policies of Presidents Theodore Roosevelt and William Howard Taft were both crafted to suit America's new role as a world power. Ask students how their respective approaches differed.

Objectives

● Characterize the effect of President Theodore Roosevelt's foreign policy on the presidency.
● Describe how the Panama Canal came to be built.
● Explain Roosevelt's policy of preserving stability in neighboring countries.
● Analyze President William Howard Taft's approach to foreign policy.

Bellringer

Display a world map for students to observe. Ask students how much time they think it took a ship to travel from New York to San Francisco (a) before and (b) after the building of the Panama Canal. (*About three months and six weeks, respectively.*) Ask the approximate distance between the two cities.

Reading Strategy

Reading for Evidence Ask students to read this statement from the first paragraph of the section: "Under [Roosevelt's and Taft's] leadership, the United States continued to intervene in the domestic affairs of weaker countries of economic and strategic interest to the nation." Have students list specific facts from the section that support this statement.

Explain/Discuss

Point out to students that the United States did not colonize the territories it seized in the late 1800s and early 1900s. Americans did not move into these new acquisitions in large numbers as the British did in South Africa and other parts of the British Empire.

Why then did Roosevelt and Taft pursue policies that involved direct United States control of other countries? Discuss the motives and values of these two Presidents. Then evaluate their respective methods by comparing the Roosevelt Corollary with Taft's dollar diplomacy. What did each strategy hope to accomplish?

Analyze

Next to Washington, Jefferson, and Lincoln, the fourth stony face on the slopes of Mount Rushmore is that of Theodore Roosevelt. Why might people have wanted Roosevelt to be on this monument? Why might others feel that he did not belong?

In Depth

Did You Know?

In his book *The Path Between the Seas: The Creation of the Panama Canal, 1870–1914*, David McCullough wrote of the construction team: "They were to measure the heights of mountains and the depths of rivers and harbors. They were to gather botanical and geological specimens. They were to take astronomical observations, report on the climate, and observe the character of the Indians encountered." (See pages 324–325 and Key Events in the Reference Section.)

After spending time on the western frontier as a young man (top), Teddy Roosevelt went on to become a war hero and President of the United States (bottom).

Soon after his return to New York City in 1886, TR remarried, this time to a childhood sweetheart, Edith Carow. When President McKinley named him assistant secretary of the navy, he worked hard to build a two-ocean fleet. Like Senators Henry Cabot Lodge and Albert Beveridge, TR was an unapologetic imperialist, who favored war with Spain and the acquisition of new territories abroad. When the Spanish-American War began, he resigned his position in the navy department to organize the First United States Volunteer Cavalry Regiment, made up in part of men he had met out west. The charge of his Rough Riders up San Juan Hill to take a Spanish garrison brought TR lasting fame.

That fall TR narrowly won the New York governorship. Although he ran an impressive administration, he infuriated the conservative bosses of the state Republican party. They were delighted when McKinley asked him to run as his vice-presidential candidate in 1900. The vice presidency was a post of such weakness that they were sure it would bury TR's political career for good. But their celebration proved premature. In September 1901, an assassin's bullet put Theodore Roosevelt in the White House.

Roosevelt as President Roosevelt called the presidency "a bully pulpit," by which he meant that it gave him a wonderful stage from which to win public support for change. Frequently restricted by Congress and other legal checks, Roosevelt still managed to expand the President's powers, especially in foreign affairs.

When Roosevelt was sworn in as President, he was forty-two years old, the youngest man ever to hold the office. As in his own time, many people today consider Roosevelt a hero. He accomplished what most people could only dream of. ✪

The Panama Canal

The Spanish-American War brought home to Americans the need for a quick route between the Pacific and Atlantic oceans. The **Isthmus of Panama** was an ideal location for such a route. At that time Panama was a province of **Colombia,** a country in South America. In 1879 a French company headed by Ferdinand de Lesseps had bought a twenty-five-year concession from Colombia to build a canal across Panama. Defeated by yellow fever and mismanagement, the company abandoned the project ten years later. It offered its remaining rights to the United States for $100 million. When in 1901 the price fell to $40 million, Congress accepted, but a lease on the land still had to be obtained from Colombia.

Colombia, on the other hand, was waiting for the French concession to expire in 1904 so that it could offer the isthmus at a higher price. Roosevelt was enraged by this attempt by Colombian "bandits" to "rob" the United States. As a result, he conspired with an official of the French company to organize a Panamanian "revolution" against Colombia. ✪

The revolt took place in November 1903 with United States warships hovering offshore to provide support for the rebels. The United States immediately recognized an independent Panama and became its protector. In return, it

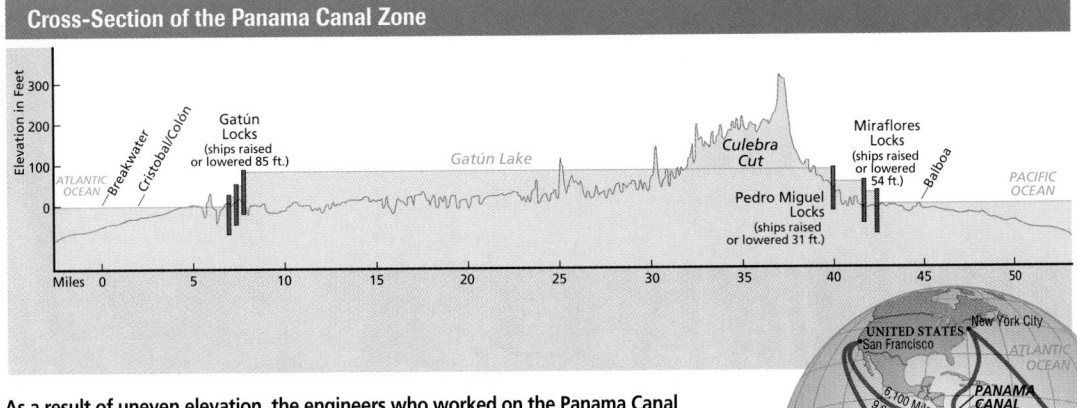

Cross-Section of the Panama Canal Zone

As a result of uneven elevation, the engineers who worked on the Panama Canal had to design a series of locks, pictured above, to raise and lower the ships that would pass through it. These locks added to the already considerable difficulty of constructing the canal. As the map at right shows, the Panama Canal cut thousands of miles off the sea journey from New York to San Francisco.

Activity
Creating a Political Cartoon

Ask students to create a political cartoon of TR. To help students come up with ideas, have them consider Roosevelt's colorful, aggressive character, his handling of Panama, his receipt of the Nobel Peace Prize, and the criticism of his opponents, such as William Randolph Hearst.

Enrichment

Ask interested students to study Theodore Roosevelt further in order to report on his handling of domestic issues. Encourage students to draw comparisons between TR's foreign and domestic policies, particularly his assault on the nation's big monopolies.

received a permanent grant of a ten-mile-wide strip of land for a Canal Zone.

Construction of the canal began in 1904. To complete this mammoth task, workers were brought in from several countries. Many of them had no construction experience whatsoever. Yet, after receiving proper training, the workers surpassed all expectations, finishing the canal in 1914, six months ahead of schedule and $23 million under budget.

Roosevelt's opponents did not appreciate the methods he had used to secure the Canal Zone. A newspaper published by William Randolph Hearst commented,

> Besides being a rough-riding assault upon another republic over the shattered wreckage of international law . . . it is a quite unexampled instance of foul play in American politics.

Most Americans, however, approved of President Roosevelt's gaining of the Canal Zone in Panama. Two years after leaving office, Theodore Roosevelt gave a speech at the University of California at Berkeley in which he justified his methods in the Canal Zone.

> If I had followed traditional, conservative methods I would have submitted a dignified State paper of probably 200 pages to Congress and the debates on it would have been going on yet; but I took the Canal Zone and let Congress debate; and while the debate goes on the canal does also.

Yet despite its success as a link between the Atlantic and Pacific oceans, the Panama Canal left a long heritage of ill will. In recognition of the illegal means used to acquire the Canal Zone, Congress voted a "guilt" payment of $25 million to Colombia in 1921, after TR had died.

Foreign Policy in the Early 1900s

In 1901 Roosevelt reminded an audience at the Minnesota State Fair of an old saying, "speak softly and carry a big stick; you will go far." In his view, the "big stick" was the American navy. Indeed, the threat of military force allowed Roosevelt to conduct an aggressive foreign policy.

In December 1904, Roosevelt issued a message to Congress that became known as the **Roosevelt Corollary** to the Monroe Doctrine. In this corollary, or extension of a previously accepted idea, Roosevelt denied that the United States was interested in acquiring any more territory. It wanted only "to see neighboring countries stable, orderly, and prosperous," he

In Depth

Then and Now

Secretary of State John Hay warned Colombia in 1903 that "something unpleasant would happen" if it rejected a treaty giving the United States sovereignty over the land strip desired for canal construction. Rejection led to the clear, though unofficial, United States support of rebels who wrested Panama from Colombian control. In the 1980s the U.S. Central Intelligence Agency covertly trained rebels known as *contras* to fight the Soviet-allied regime in Nicaragua, even though Congress had banned such military aid.

Possessions in the Pacific provided the United States with stepping-stones to the markets of Asia and stations for repair and coaling of their vessels.

3. ASSESS

Section 3 Review Answers

1. (a) Roosevelt Corollary, see p. 321, (b) dollar diplomacy, see p. 323

2. (a) Theodore Roosevelt, see p. 319, (b) William Howard Taft, see p. 323

3. (a) Isthmus of Panama, see p. 320, (b) Colombia, see p. 320

4. He increased the power of the presidency through his aggressive policies and activist, sometimes high-handed, approach.

5. It secretly encouraged a revolution in the Colombian province of Panama, sent military forces to protect it, and in return received a 10-mile strip (the Canal Zone) from Panama through which to build the canal.

6. The message was that the United States would act as an "international policeman" in the Western Hemisphere to maintain order and stability in neighboring countries and to keep powerful European nations out.

7. Both Roosevelt and Taft sought to influence other nations in a way that would advance America's economic, political, and strategic interests. Roosevelt relied on the threat of military force in pursuit of his foreign policy, whereas Taft relied more on economic pressure to influence other nations. On first view, Roosevelt's approach appears to have been more effective, but one could argue that his actions created more resentment toward the United States than did Taft's policy.

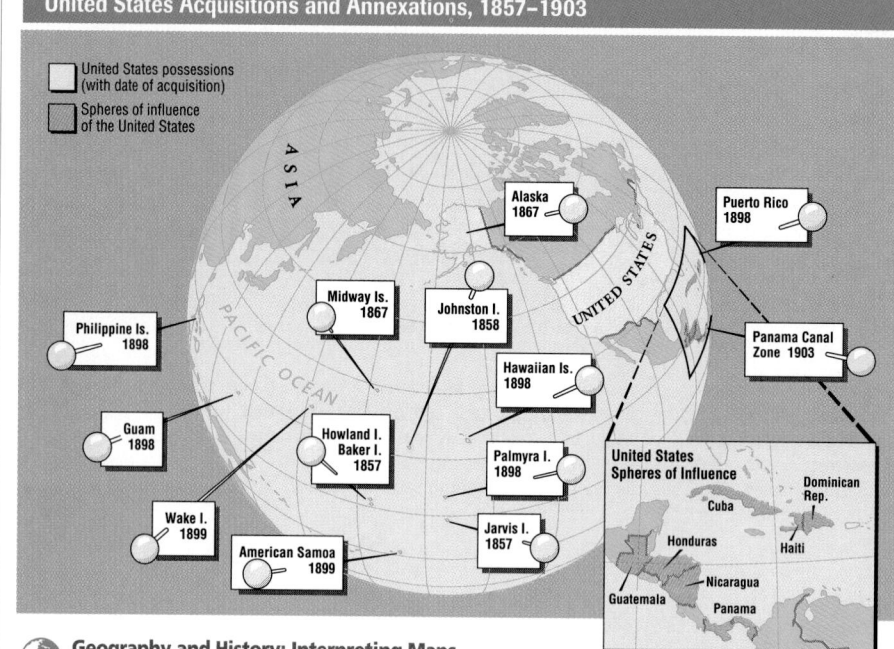

United States Acquisitions and Annexations, 1857–1903

United States possessions (with date of acquisition)

Spheres of influence of the United States

Alaska 1867 · Puerto Rico 1898 · Midway Is. 1867 · Johnston I. 1858 · Philippine Is. 1898 · Panama Canal Zone 1903 · Hawaiian Is. 1898 · Guam 1898 · Howland I. Baker I. 1857 · Palmyra I. 1898 · United States Spheres of Influence · Dominican Rep. · Cuba · Wake I. 1899 · Jarvis I. 1857 · Honduras · Haiti · American Samoa 1899 · Nicaragua · Guatemala · Panama

 Geography and History: Interpreting Maps
Between 1857 and 1903, the United States acquired many new territorial possessions around the globe. *Why do you think so many of these new possessions were islands located in the Pacific Ocean?*

said. But if the countries engaged in activities harmful to the interests of the United States or if their governments collapsed, inviting intervention from stronger nations, then the United States would be forced to exercise "an international police power." In other words, the United States government would intervene to prevent intervention from other powers.

The first test of the Roosevelt Corollary concerned the small Caribbean island republic of Santo Domingo (now the Dominican Republic). When the island went bankrupt, European nations threatened to intervene to collect their money. Quickly Roosevelt made an "executive agreement" with Santo Domingo's president. Bankers in the United States took over the country's finances and paid its European debt.

Under Roosevelt, United States intervention in Latin America became common. This development angered Western Hemisphere countries. Congress also was displeased, for Roosevelt's interventionism meant that presidential powers grew while those of the legislature shrank.

Roosevelt as Peacemaker

Roosevelt's chief concern in Asia was to preserve China's "open door." In order for this to

THE WORLD CONSTABLE.

Published after the announcement of the Roosevelt Corollary, this political cartoon depicts Teddy Roosevelt as the world's police officer, using his "big stick" to maintain order and stability in Latin America.

 **RESOURCE DIRECTORY**

Teaching Resources

happen, Roosevelt believed that both Japan and Russia had to be kept in check. To achieve this, he supported Japan in its war with Russia over supremacy in Asia, but he did not let the war drag on. Roosevelt mediated a peace agreement in 1905 before Japan crushed Russia completely. In this way, he ensured a balance of power in Asia. When Japan accepted the Open Door policy, he invited delegates from the two nations to Portsmouth, New Hampshire, where he persuaded Japan to be satisfied with small grants of land and control over Korea instead of a huge payment of money. He also secured a promise from Russia to vacate Manchuria. Roosevelt's role as mediator won this "war maker" the Nobel Peace Prize.

MAKING CONNECTIONS

How were Teddy Roosevelt and Andrew Jackson similar in the way they used the power of the presidency to achieve their policy goals?

Taft and "Dollar Diplomacy"

William Howard Taft, who succeeded Roosevelt in the White House, was not as aggressive in pursuing foreign policy aims. A distinguished lawyer from Ohio, Taft had served as Roosevelt's secretary of war and headed the commission that governed the Philippines.

Taft's main goals were to maintain the open door to Asia and preserve stability in Latin America. As for the rest, he preferred "substituting dollars for bullets." By this he meant maintaining orderly societies abroad by increasing United States investment in foreign economies. Such an approach, he said, "appeals alike to idealistic humanitarian sentiments, to the dictates of sound policy and strategy, and to legitimate commercial aims." In other words, it pleased public opinion and made money for investors in the United States. Although some of Taft's contemporaries mocked his approach, calling it **"dollar diplomacy,"** Taft himself later used this term with pride.

Although President William Howard Taft shared Teddy Roosevelt's policy goals, he adopted a less aggressive approach to foreign policy.

A Mixed Legacy

Dollar diplomacy did not succeed as well as Taft had hoped. Although it increased the level of United States financial involvement abroad, the results were not always profitable. For example, when Taft's secretary of state, Philander Knox, persuaded bankers to invest in railroad projects in China and Manchuria, Russia and Japan united in an effort to block the influence of the Americans. In addition, many United States investments in China were lost when the country collapsed in revolution in 1911. Dollar diplomacy also created enemies in Latin America, especially in the Caribbean and Central America where local revolutionary movements opposed United States influence. Although the United States reached new heights as an international power under Roosevelt and Taft, anti-colonialism abroad and anti-imperialism at home provided a growing check to further expansion.

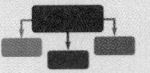
SECTION 3 REVIEW

Key Terms, People, and Places
1. Define (a) Roosevelt Corollary, (b) dollar diplomacy.
2. Identify (a) Theodore Roosevelt, (b) William Howard Taft.
3. Identify (a) Isthmus of Panama, (b) Colombia.

Key Concepts
4. What impact did Teddy Roosevelt have on the office of the presidency?

5. How did the United States secure the rights to build a canal through Panama?
6. What was the central message of the Roosevelt Corollary to the Monroe Doctrine?

Critical Thinking
7. **Making Comparisons** How was dollar diplomacy both similar to and different from the approach to foreign policy taken by Theodore Roosevelt?

Quiz found in the Unit 3 folder, p. 12, covers the main ideas in this section as well as the key terms.

Answer to ...

MAKING CONNECTIONS

Both were active Presidents who used aggressive and sometimes high-handed tactics in pursuit of their policy goals. For example, Jackson refused to enforce the Supreme Court's decision stating that the removal of the Cherokee people was illegal; and Roosevelt resorted to "executive agreements" with other nations to avoid the need to win congressional approval for treaties. Both men increased the power of the presidency by such actions.

Reteach

Ask students to make a two-column chart, heading one column Roosevelt and the other column Taft. Have them list major characteristics, attitudes, and accomplishments of each President in the appropriate column. Then ask them to assess which was the more effective President.

4. CLOSE

Reinforcing the Big Idea

Presidents Roosevelt and Taft pursued interventionist foreign policies that many people felt were appropriate to America's status as a world power. Eventually, however, many Americans would come to question United States interference in other countries' internal affairs.

The Building of the Panama Canal: A Geographic Perspective

Focus The building of the Panama Canal is all the more remarkable when one realizes that it was undertaken with the earliest types of earth-moving equipment and without aerial surveillance, computerized geological models, or even thorough knowledge of Panama's rugged jungle environment. In this feature students will identify and categorize some of the key geographic obstacles to building the canal.

Instruct Explain to students that the Panama Canal was the largest engineering accomplishment of its day. The project was far more daunting than the building of Egypt's Suez Canal. In fact, the French company that had built the Suez Canal was overwhelmed with difficulties in Panama. When the company finally ran out of money and abandoned the job, it had already moved enough earth to fill nearly 11,000 of today's Olympic-sized swimming pools.

Explain that the main challenges of the project fell into the categories of location, human-environmental interaction, and the movement of people and goods—three key factors in the study of geography.

Before they read, have students make a chart using these three factors as headings. Ask them to speculate about what specific challenges engineers might have faced and to write down their ideas under the appropriate heading.

Extend After they read, have students add to their chart by filling in factual information under each of the three headings and comparing it with their original, speculative answers.

The Building of the Panama Canal: A Geographic Perspective

On a world map, the Isthmus of Panama seems a mere thread of land. In reality, however, it is dozens of miles wide, formed of violent rivers, dense forests, and towering mountains. How did geographical issues affect the effort to build the canal?

When the United States set out to build the Panama Canal, three geographical factors affected the project. First, engineers had to decide where the canal should be located. Once construction began, the environment of the canal zone presented challenges to workers. Finally, to complete the project, massive amounts of earth had to be moved from one place to another.

Locating the Canal

When the construction team arrived in Panama in 1904, the end points of the canal already had been decided. It would begin at Colón on the Atlantic side and come out close to Panama City on the Pacific side, as the map on page 325 shows. In between lay two major obstacles. One was the Continental Divide, a ridge across Central America that separates rivers that flow west from rivers that flow east. The other obstacle was the wild and unpredictable Chagres River.

The French had never really solved the problem of how to tame the Chagres. The American solution, decided upon in 1906, was to "drown" the river. A vast earthen dam would be laid across the river valley at Gatún (see map opposite). The Chagres would then back up, creating the largest artificial lake in the world at that time. The Chagres would become the only river in the world to cross a continental divide and flow into two oceans at once.

It was not hard to see where the canal should cross the divide. In the 1880s, a French company had scooped out 19 million cubic yards of dirt and rock from the divide near Culebra. Neither the French nor the Americans guessed that this excavation, the Culebra Cut, would require another 96 million cubic yards of digging before it was finished.

This plan for locating the canal meant that from the entrance at Colón Harbor, ships using the canal would sail 7 miles up a channel and ascend through three locks to a height of 85 feet above sea level. Then they would cross the new and sprawling Gatún Lake for 24 miles, pass through the 9 miles of the Culebra Cut, and descend by one lock to a smaller lake about 1 mile long. Another set of two locks would bring them to sea level and the final 8-mile leg of the canal to the open Pacific.

Against the Environment

While engineers and Congress were wrestling with the location of the canal, army physician

▶ RESOURCE DIRECTORY

Teaching Resources

Time and Place Activity Building the Alaska Pipeline, found in the Unit 3 folder, pp. 15–16, encourages students to explore another, more modern example of humans tackling geographic barriers on a massive scale.

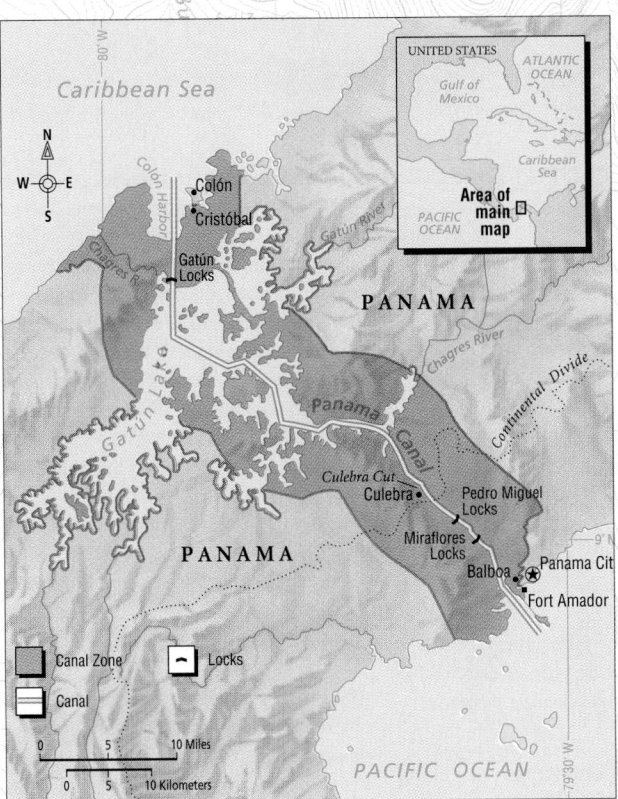

Caribbean Sea

PANAMA

PANAMA

Colón
Cristóbal
Gatún Locks
Culebra Cut
Culebra
Pedro Miguel Locks
Miraflores Locks
Balboa
Panama City
Fort Amador

Gatún Lake
Colon Harbor
Chagres River
Gatún River
Panama Canal
Continental Divide

UNITED STATES
Gulf of Mexico
ATLANTIC OCEAN
Caribbean Sea
PACIFIC OCEAN
Area of main map

PACIFIC OCEAN

Canal Zone
Locks
Canal

0   5   10 Miles
0   5   10 Kilometers

William Gorgas was wrestling with an insect. Medical science had learned only a few years before that two of the deadliest tropical diseases, yellow fever and malaria, were transmitted by mosquitoes. The secret of mosquito control, Gorgas found, was to cover, destroy, or drain every place where mosquitoes could lay their eggs—every tank, jar, hollow, and puddle, indoors or out. He divided the cities on the canal route into districts, each with an inspector who entered every house on a daily basis to check for uncovered or standing water. He also gave orders that any pools that could not be drained were to be covered with a film of oil or kerosene to kill the insects.

Gorgas's methods wiped out yellow fever before the end of 1905. Malaria, which was carried by a tougher mosquito, was not eliminated, but was much reduced.

A Problem in Movement

When it came to actually digging the canal, the chief engineer, John F. Stevens, viewed the project as a simple problem of movement: dirt—lots of it—had to be moved. As an experienced builder of railroads, he knew that the cheapest, fastest way to move anything on land was by rail.

Within a week after his arrival, the new chief engineer had ordered double tracks laid. To get the dirt from the ditch to the train cars, Stevens brought in monster steam shovels. President Theodore Roosevelt, on an inspection visit to Panama, wrote, "Now we have taken hold of the job. . . . The huge steam shovels are hard at it, scooping huge masses of rock and gravel and dirt." The shovels were so efficient they filled five hundred trains with debris every day.

The highly efficient railway system could not solve another problem, however. Since Panama could not provide enough supplies to keep tens of thousands of workers fed and busy, ships traveled frequently between Colón and the United States. Ships brought in workers as well, some 45,000 of them, from 97 different nations.

When the canal was completed in 1914, the geographical obstacles of location, interaction with the environment, and movement had been overcome.

GEOGRAPHIC CONNECTIONS

1. What two problems of movement did the building of the canal entail, and how were they solved?
2. How did Dr. Gorgas change the environment of Panama, and what effect did his work have?

Thinking Critically

3. **Making Comparisons** How was building the Panama Canal like building the transcontinental railroad?

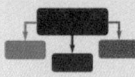

1. FOCUS

Connecting to the Big Idea

See page 306B. After the Spanish-American War, anti-imperialists launched heated debates over United States foreign policy. Ask what arguments these anti-imperialists used to support their case. How persuasive were they?

Objectives

● Describe the events that led to debate over United States imperialism.
● Summarize the key arguments of the anti-imperialists.
● Explain why imperialism continued to appeal to Americans at the turn of the century.

Bellringer

Write the following sentence on the chalkboard: The Constitution must follow the flag. Ask students to speculate on what it might mean in relation to the control of other nations by the United States.

Reading Strategy

Structured Overview Have students create a two-column chart with the headings Anti-Imperialists' Arguments and Appeal of Imperialism. Ask them to make entries under the appropriate headings as they read.

SECTION 4

The People's Response to Imperialism

SECTION PREVIEW

After the Spanish-American War, the debate intensified over whether it was appropriate for the United States to continue to throw its net around other nations and drag them under American control. Anti-imperialists used a variety of arguments against the acquisition of territories.

Key Concepts

• The annexation of the Philippines led to a spirited debate in the United States over imperialism.
• Anti-imperialists argued that taking over territories betrayed the principles on which the nation was founded.
• Economic benefits, pride in the nation's growing power, and the search for a new frontier made imperialism appealing to many Americans.

Key Terms, People, and Places

paradox of power; Juliette Low

This weathervane from about 1870 reflects national pride in the United States' emerging role as a world power.

B efore the Spanish-American War, United States citizens already were debating the consequences of an expanded role in world affairs. Walter Gresham, President Cleveland's secretary of state in 1894, was one government official who worried about the issue. He cautioned against "the evils of interference in affairs that do not specially concern us." Until the annexation of the Philippines in 1898, however, most citizens supported the idea of overseas involvement.

The Anti-Imperialists

After the annexation, opposition to imperialism grew. In November 1898, opponents of United States policy in the Philippines established the Anti-Imperialist League. Most of its organizers were upper-middle-class professionals, such as the prominent Republican and former senator Carl Schurz, editor E. L. Godkin, Democratic politician William Jennings Bryan, settlement house leader Jane Addams, charity reformer Josephine Shaw Lowell, novelist Mark Twain, and Harvard philosopher William James. Steel industrialist Andrew Carnegie contributed thousands of dollars to the cause.

Moral and Political Arguments The anti-imperialists used a variety of arguments to support their position. The strongest of these were moral and political in nature. "Any nation," wrote Boston pacifist Lucia Mead in 1900,

whether it be monarchy or republic, which buys or takes by conquest another people, and dominates them without promise of granting them independence or . . . guaranteeing future Statehood, has adopted an imperialist policy.

Such behavior, the anti-imperialists asserted, was a rejection of the nation's foundation of "liberty for all."

As Carl Schurz explained in 1899:

We regret that it has become necessary in the land of Washington and Lincoln to reaffirm that all men, of whatever race or color, are entitled to life, liberty, and the pursuit of happiness.

Others said it more concisely: "The Constitution must follow the flag," by which they meant that the United States flag and United States laws went together, and that people in territories controlled by the United States should be entitled to the guarantees in the United States Constitution.

RESOURCE DIRECTORY

Teaching Resources

Reproducible Lesson Plan found in the Unit 3 folder, p. 6, provides a summary of the Section 4 lesson plan content.

Alternate Lesson Plan: Learning Styles found in the Alternate Lesson Plans folder, p. 93, is particularly useful for auditory learners and directs students working in teams to identify conflicting viewpoints on imperialistic policies in the early 1900s.

Guided Reading and Review found in the Unit 3 folder, p. 13, provides a structure for reading and mastering the key concepts and reviewing the key terms for Section 4. (Guided Practice)

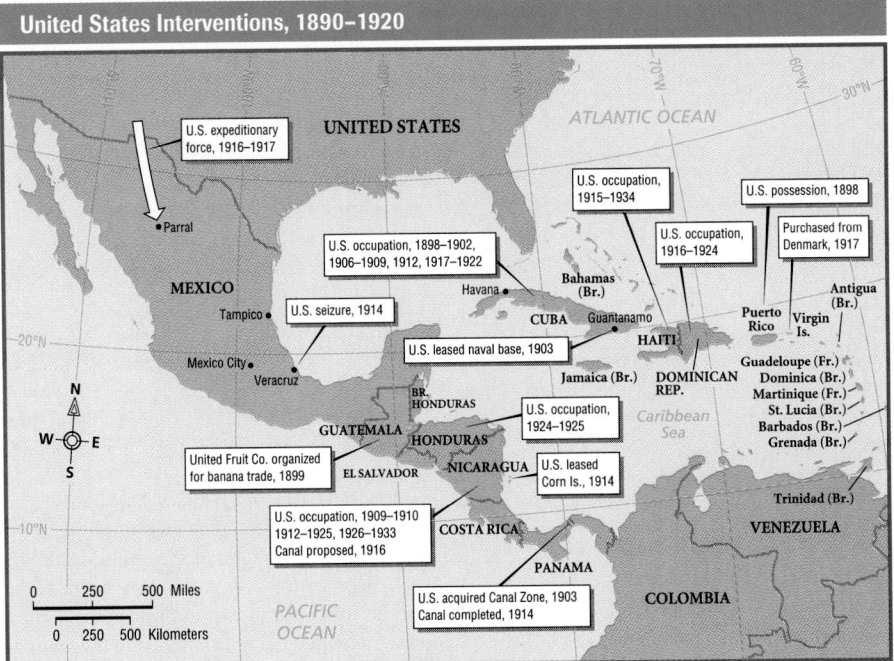

United States Interventions, 1890–1920

U.S. expeditionary force, 1916–1917

UNITED STATES

ATLANTIC OCEAN

30°N

Parral

MEXICO

Tampico

U.S. seizure, 1914

Mexico City

Veracruz

20°N

U.S. occupation, 1898–1902, 1906–1909, 1912, 1917–1922

Havana

Bahamas (Br.)

CUBA

Guantanamo

U.S. occupation, 1915–1934

U.S. occupation, 1916–1924

U.S. possession, 1898

Purchased from Denmark, 1917

HAITI

Puerto Rico

Virgin Is.

Antigua (Br.)

U.S. leased naval base, 1903

Jamaica (Br.)

DOMINICAN REP.

Guadeloupe (Fr.)
Dominica (Br.)
Martinique (Fr.)
St. Lucia (Br.)
Barbados (Br.)
Grenada (Br.)

BR. HONDURAS

GUATEMALA

HONDURAS

U.S. occupation, 1924–1925

Caribbean Sea

United Fruit Co. organized for banana trade, 1899

EL SALVADOR

NICARAGUA

U.S. leased Corn Is., 1914

Trinidad (Br.)

VENEZUELA

U.S. occupation, 1909–1910 1912–1925, 1926–1933 Canal proposed, 1916

COSTA RICA

PANAMA

COLOMBIA

N W E S

0   250   500 Miles
0   250   500 Kilometers

PACIFIC OCEAN

U.S. acquired Canal Zone, 1903 Canal completed, 1914

10°N

 Geography and History: Interpreting Maps
The above map illustrates how frequently the United States intervened in the affairs of Latin American countries in the early 1900s. The United States government defended these interventions as necessary for the protection of the nation's economic and political interests. *What economic interests were served by having influence in these nations?*

President of the American Federation of Labor Samuel Gompers objected to taking over countries in which United States labor laws did not apply. He pointed out that in Hawaii, half of the population consisted of "contract laborers, practically slaves," who did not benefit from the laws that protected American workers.

Expansionists replied that the people of the Caribbean and the Pacific were not ready for democracy and that the United States was preparing them for liberty. For example, Major General Arthur McArthur, military governor of the Philippines in 1900, said, "We are planting in those islands . . . the best traditions, the best characteristics of Americanism." The anti-imperialists responded that no people should be forced to wait to enjoy liberty.

Finally, anti-imperialists noted that imperialism endangered the nation's democratic institutions. Imperialist wars required large standing armies that could be used to crush dissent at home just as easily as to bring other nations under United States control.

A Race War? Other anti-imperialists saw racism at work in imperialism. Like Theodore Roosevelt, many Americans of this period believed that people of Anglo-Saxon heritage were superior to other races. The public officials who developed the country's imperialist policies shared these sentiments.

African Americans were at first torn about imperialistic issues. As United States citizens, they wanted to support their country in a time of war. But they recognized the racism that underlay imperialism. Bishop Alexander Walters of the A.M.E. Zion Church said in 1899,

Had the Filipinos been white and fought as bravely as they have, the war would have been ended and their independence granted a long time ago.

 Caption Answer to . . .

Interpreting Maps

The United States was able to gain new markets for its goods.

2. INSTRUCT

Discuss

Discuss with students why upper-middle-class professionals, southern Democrats, labor leaders, and African Americans opposed imperialism.

Ask students in what way racism entered into the arguments of both imperialists and anti-imperialists. Have them use examples from the text to support their explanations.

Analyze

Explain that a paradox is a statement that seems contradictory but may actually be true. How does the term "paradox of power" apply to the United States during the era of imperialism?

In Depth

Historical Misconceptions

The Filipino people were not blind to the irony of facing African American soldiers serving in the war against the Philippines (1898–1902). Joining the military was a way for African Americans to prove their patriotism, but as one African American soldier wrote from the Philippines, "I was struck by a question a little Filipino boy asked me, which ran this way: 'Why does the American Negro come . . . to fight us. . . ? Why don't you fight those people in America who burn Negroes?' "

Viewpoints

Sumner's point is that other people's customs and beliefs should be respected and that they should have the freedom to practice them; therefore, his statement is more in keeping with America's founding principles of equality and liberty. For a more thorough examination of imperialism, see the Resource Directory below.

Activity
Cooperative Learning

Time: One class period.
Activity: Role-play interviews on imperialism.
Grouping: Four to six students.
Purpose: One student conducts interviews with others playing various types of citizens to elicit their views on the subject of United States imperialism. Interviewees assume imperialist or anti-imperialist positions.
Roles: Reporter; interview subjects such as a Filipino immigrant, a social worker, a U.S. general, a coal miner, a cowboy, and a pineapple grower.
Outcome: Students will come to understand different perspectives regarding United States imperialism.

Enrichment

Students can read and evaluate excerpts from Theodore Roosevelt's *The Rough Riders*. They should state whether the book changed their opinion of Roosevelt or of United States imperialism, and if so, how.

3. ASSESS

Section 4 Review Answers

1. paradox of power, see p. 329

2. Juliette Low, see p. 329

3. Anti-imperialists objected to extending a protectorate over another country without also extending the protection and rights available to U.S. citizens under the Constitution. They believed that people in U.S. protectorates should not have to wait to enjoy the universal right of liberty. Imperialism was racist

Viewpoints
On the Race for Empire

The Spanish-American War heightened the debate between imperialist and anti-imperialist factions at home. ***Which of the following viewpoints do you think best represents the political ideals of liberty and equality on which the United States was founded?***

Anti-Imperialist

"We assume that what we like and practice, and what we think better, must come as a welcome blessing to Spanish-Americans and Filipinos. This is grossly and obviously untrue. They hate our ways. They are hostile to our ideas. Our religion, language, institutions, and manners offend them.
William G. Sumner, Yale University professor, in an 1898 speech

Pro-Imperialist

"Think of the thousands of Americans who will pour into Hawaii and Puerto Rico when the republic's laws cover those islands with justice and safety! Think of the tens of thousands of Americans who will invade mine and field and forest in the Philippines when a liberal government, protected and controlled by this republic, if not the government of the republic itself, shall establish order and equity there!"
Albert J. Beveridge, leading imperialist and later United States senator, in an 1898 speech

Although most southern Democrats also opposed imperialism, they did so for different reasons. Many southern politicians feared the effects of having to absorb more people of different races into the United States. Consequently, southern Democrats led the movement in the Senate against ratifying the treaty with Spain.

A number of anti-imperialists outside the South, including William Jennings Bryan and Samuel Gompers, also opposed imperialist policies because of the fear that they would encourage people of different racial backgrounds to move to the United States. Reformer Carl Schurz wrote about these concerns:

T*he prospects of the consequences which would follow the admission of the Spanish creoles and . . . the negroes . . . to participation in the conduct of our*

government is so alarming that you instinctively pause before taking the step.

Practical Objections Finally, anti-imperialists raised practical objections to expansionist policies. In the view of these thinkers, it was not a good time for the United States to expand. First, expansion involved too many costs. Maintaining the necessary armed forces required more taxation, debt, and possibly even compulsory military service. Second, as African American leader Booker T. Washington said, the United States already had enough difficulties at home. "Until our nation has settled the Negro and Indian problems I do not believe that we have a right to assume more social problems," he argued.

Samuel Gompers raised a third point. He argued that laborers coming to the United States from annexed territories would compete with American workers for jobs. Since these immigrants would work for lower wages, their presence would drive all wages down. Industrialists also pointed out that goods produced cheaply in annexed countries could be imported to the United States without customs duties, which would hurt many American industries in the process.

Imperialism's Appeal to the American Imagination

Despite the strength of many anti-imperialist arguments, imperialism maintained a powerful hold on the American imagination. The director of the census had declared the frontier "closed" in the 1890 census. The America of explorers and pioneers, who bravely charted unknown territories, overcome great obstacles, and accomplished great deeds, was fast disappearing into the shadows of memory. What would keep Americans from growing too soft, from losing their competitive edge? Some looked to a new frontier abroad to answer this question.

The growth and popularity of youth scouting programs during this period shows that many middle-class Americans shared a "frontier mentality." Sir Robert Baden-Powell, an army officer of the British Empire, had used scouting techniques (tracking, woodcraft, and

RESOURCE DIRECTORY

Teaching Resources

Viewpoints Activity On the Race for Empire, found in the Unit 3 folder, pp. 19–20, provides several contemporary speeches on the pros and cons of American imperialism.

American Profiles Activity found in the Unit 3 folder, p. 18, profiles Juliette Gordon Low, who founded the American Girl Scouts in 1912.

wilderness survival) to great success in a battle in South Africa. A few years after he returned to Britain as a war hero, Baden-Powell founded the Boy Scout movement. Scouting appeared in the United States in 1910 and soon became immensely popular. Two years later, **Juliette Low,** a close friend and admirer of Baden-Powell, founded the American Girl Scouts. Low hoped to use the program both to build moral character in girls and to teach them skills that would make them "hardy" and "handy."

In addition, the popular media glorified the accomplishments of imperialist frontier heroes. Theodore Roosevelt's book on his heroic charge, *The Rough Riders,* drew much praise. However, satirist Finley Peter Dunne's character, "Mr. Dooley," suggested the book should be called *Alone in Cuba* to emphasize Roosevelt's boastfulness. Another book of this era, *Conquest of the Tropics* (1914), describes the history of the United Fruit Company, portraying railroad entrepreneur Minor Keith as one of "the hardy American type which listens and responds eagerly to the call of the wild."

MAKING CONNECTIONS

How was the popular media's glorification of imperialist heroes such as Minor Keith similar to the often romantic portrayal of the men and women settlers of the American West?

The Paradox of Power

Having begun a pattern of international involvements, shown on the map on page 327,

THE·GIRL·SCOUT·PROMISE

On my honor, I will try:
To do my duty to God and my country,
To help other people at all times,
To obey the Girl Scout Laws.

the United States discovered that these actions frequently took on a life of their own. Unforeseen difficulties arose. In the Caribbean and Central America, for example, the United States often had to defend governments that were friendly to its economic and political interests but unpopular with local inhabitants. In Latin America, the cry "Yankee, Go Home!" began to be heard.

On the other hand, because the United States was quickly becoming so powerful, other countries—even those fearful about maintaining their independence—increasingly were turning to the United States government for help. This state of affairs illustrated the **paradox of power.** Both admired and hated, welcomed and rejected, the United States would spend the rest of the century trying to decide the best way to reconcile its growing power and national interests with its relationships with other nations and peoples.

As "The Girl Scout's Promise" suggests, founder Juliette Low (bottom) saw scouting as a way of teaching moral character as well as frontier skills. ⭐

and would result in the necessity of absorbing other races into an already complex and difficult racial system.

4. Now that the western frontier had been declared closed, an imperialist foreign policy gave Americans other opportunities to act in a forceful, heroic fashion in demanding circumstances. Imperialism also brought the United States economic rewards.

5. Imperialism led the United States into diplomatic conflicts and costly military engagements with other nations. By failing to extend the guarantees of the Constitution to peoples living in United States territories, the policy betrayed the democratic principles upon which the United States had been founded.

6. One can infer from the arguments of the anti-imperialists that they believed the United States should promote democratic principles and institutions around the world and that all peoples of the world deserved access to these rights, principles, and institutions.

Answer to ...

MAKING CONNECTIONS

Both emphasized brave, rugged individuals who had amazing adventures and overcame great obstacles while taming wild new frontiers.

Reteach

Ask students to create a newspaper advertisement that attempts to persuade Americans to support the anti-imperialists' arguments. Students should focus on these issues for their ad: anti-imperialist arguments; effective ways to counter the appeal of imperialism; and the effect of imperialism on the image of the United States in Latin America and the Pacific.

SECTION 4 REVIEW

Key Terms, People, and Places
1. Define paradox of power.
2. Identify Juliette Low.

Key Concepts
3. Name some of the major arguments of the anti-imperialists.
4. Explain why imperialism was so appealing to many United States citizens.

5. What were some of the disadvantages of imperialism for the United States?

Critical Thinking
6. **Identifying Assumptions** Based on the arguments they used against imperialism, what kind of role do you think the anti-imperialists believed the United States should play in world affairs?

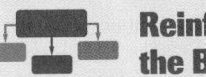
4. CLOSE

Reinforcing the Big Idea

After the Spanish-American War, the debate over United States imperialism intensified. Strong arguments by anti-imperialists, however, failed to dampen the appeal of imperialism to the American imagination.

Understanding Key Terms, People, and Places

Terms
Students should refer to the definitions of the key terms in the chapter to write sentences that show the relation of each word to the growth of the United States as a world power.

Matching
1. guerrillas
2. imperialism
3. annexation
4. dollar diplomacy
5. jingoism

Word Relationships
1. George Dewey was an admiral in the Spanish-American War, which was fought in the Philippine Islands and Cuba. William Howard Taft, President Roosevelt's successor, discouraged the use of military force.

2. William Randolph Hearst and Joseph Pulitzer published sensational stories that whipped up public sentiment in favor of the war against Spain, of which the charge up San Juan Hill was the most famous incident. The Isthmus of Panama was the site of the Panama Canal.

3. Alfred T. Mahan, Henry Cabot Lodge, and Theodore Roosevelt supported American expansionism. Juliette Low founded the American Girl Scouts in order to make American girls more hardy.

Reviewing Main Ideas

1. The economy was producing more than the nation could consume.

2. New developments in communication and transportation fueled intensified competition among nations with long traditions of imperialism, now joined by the newly unified Germany.

3. Mahan argued that the economic future of the United States depended on new markets abroad and a navy to protect these markets. Lodge worried about the effects of a disappearing frontier. Beveridge believed that expansionism was necessary because it introduced the ideas and customs of "superior" races to "primitive" societies.

4. The British government eventually backed down when warned that the United States would enforce the Monroe Doctrine.

5. Yellow journalism, which played on the human rights abuses taking place in Cuba and fanned public outrage over the destruction of American property in Cuba, was partly responsible for an

---

Chapter Review

Understanding Key Terms, People, and Places

Key Terms
1. imperialism
2. annexation
3. most-favored nation
4. banana republic
5. guerrilla
6. jingoism
7. sphere of influence
8. Open Door policy
9. Roosevelt Corollary
10. dollar diplomacy
11. paradox of power

People
12. Alfred T. Mahan
13. Henry Cabot Lodge
14. Albert J. Beveridge
15. William Randolph Hearst
16. Joseph Pulitzer
17. George Dewey
18. Theodore Roosevelt
19. William Howard Taft
20. Juliette Low

Place
21. Hawaii
22. Cuba
23. Philippine Islands
24. San Juan Hill
25. Isthmus of Panama
26. Colombia

Terms For each term above, write a sentence that explains its relation to the growth of the United States as a world power.

Matching Review the key terms in the list above. If you are not sure of a term's meaning, review its definition in the chapter. Then choose a term from the list that best matches each description below.
1. soldiers who fight using surprise tactics
2. the policy under which stronger nations attempt to create empires by dominating dominance over weaker nations
3. the addition of a new territory to an existing country
4. W. H. Taft's policy of "substituting dollars for bullets"
5. an intense burst of national pride and the desire for an aggressive foreign policy

Word Relationships Three of the terms in each of the following sets are related. Choose the term that does not belong and explain why it does not belong.
1. William Howard Taft, George Dewey, Philippine Islands, Cuba
2. William Randolph Hearst, Isthmus of Panama, Joseph Pulitzer, San Juan Hill
3. Alfred T. Mahan, Juliette Low, Henry Cabot Lodge, Theodore Roosevelt

Reviewing Main Ideas

Section 1 (pp. 308–311)
1. Describe the status of the United States economy in the late 1800s.
2. Why were the major European powers scrambling to seize new territory?
3. Briefly explain the arguments of Alfred T. Mahan, Henry Cabot Lodge, and Albert J. Beveridge regarding expansionism.

Section 2 (pp. 312–317)
4. Describe how the 1880 dispute between the United States and Great Britain reaffirmed the validity of the Monroe Doctrine.
5. Why did the American public favor war with Spain?
6. What new territories and influence did the United

States gain in the Pacific as a result of its interventionist policies?

Section 3 (pp. 319–323)
7. Describe Theodore Roosevelt's approach to foreign policy.
8. How did the Roosevelt Corollary affect United States policy in Latin America?
9. What were President Taft's main foreign policy goals and how did he plan to accomplish them?

Section 4 (pp. 326–329)
10. Explain why anti-imperialists believed that imperialism betrayed basic American principles.
11. What was the connection between imperialism and the closing of the American frontier?

---

intense burst of national pride in favor of war. In addition, the public blamed the Spanish for the explosion aboard the *Maine*.

6. The United States gained the Philippines, Puerto Rico, Guam, the harbor at Pago Pago, and Hawaii. It also gained influence in China.

7. Roosevelt conducted an aggressive and vigorous foreign policy. He often dealt with other countries in a high-handed manner, assuming that what he wanted for each country was necessarily in its best interests. He used his position as President to win public support for change, especially in foreign affairs.

8. The Roosevelt Corollary caused United States military intervention to become standard policy in Latin America.

9. Taft wanted to maintain the Open Door policy in Asia and to preserve stability in Latin America. He planned to accomplish these goals through economic rather than military pressure (dollar diplomacy).

10. Anti-imperialists believed that imperialism rejected the basic tenet of liberty for all peoples.

11. Many Americans saw expansion abroad as a way to continue the spirit and excitement of the frontier.

2. Pro-expansionism—students may choose any of the following visuals: the photograph on page 311, which shows that involvement in other countries would result in new markets for U.S. goods; the Panama Canal illustrations on page 321, which show that expansionism could have positive results such as this new route from the East to West coasts. Anti-expansionism—students may choose any of the following visuals: the painting and headline on page 314 or the photograph on page 316, which both show that involvement in the affairs of other nations can result in violence and bloodshed for Americans.

Thinking Critically

1. **Distinguishing Fact from Opinion** Future secretary of state John Hay referred to the Spanish-American War as "a splendid little war." Can you think of any Americans, in addition to anti-imperialists, who might disagree with Hay?

2. **Demonstrating Reasoned Judgment** You have read that although some people today question Teddy Roosevelt's militaristic and racial beliefs, in his own time many people considered him a hero. How can you account for this change in public perception?

3. **Drawing Conclusions** During the late 1800s, the press fanned the flames of the Spanish-American War by publishing sensational stories about Spanish cruelties in Cuba. On what current issues do you think the press has played a major role in influencing public opinion? Has sensationalism played a part in influencing the public?

3. Students' letters should take into account the imperialist and anti-imperialist arguments advanced in Sections 1 and 4.

4. (a) The primary negative effect of expansion was foreign entanglement. (b) Students' graphic organizers should show the main causes (including rebellion in Cuba and the pressure for expansion) and effects (acquisition of new territories and influence) of the Spanish-American War.

Making Connections

1. **Evaluating Primary Sources** Review the primary source excerpt on page 319. What does Roosevelt assume about Native American land use? Do you think that his assumption is accurate?

2. **Understanding the Visuals** Choose one visual from the chapter that provides an argument in favor of expansionism and one that provides an argument against expansionism. Explain how each visual argues its position.

3. **Writing About the Chapter** Imagine that you are living during the early 1900s. Write a letter to the editor of your local newspaper in which you argue either for or against an interventionist foreign policy. First, create a list of arguments that support your position. Note any opposing arguments to which you wish to reply. Next, write a draft of your letter in which you offer your ideas. Revise your letter, making sure that your opinions are well supported. Proofread your letter and draft a final copy.

4. **Using the Graphic Organizer** This graphic organizer uses a multi-flow map to show the causes and effects of American expansion during the late 1800s and early 1900s. (a) Based on the graphic organizer, what was the major negative effect of American expansion for Americans? (b) On a separate sheet of paper, create your own graphic organizer about the causes and effects of the Spanish-American War, using this graphic organizer as an example.

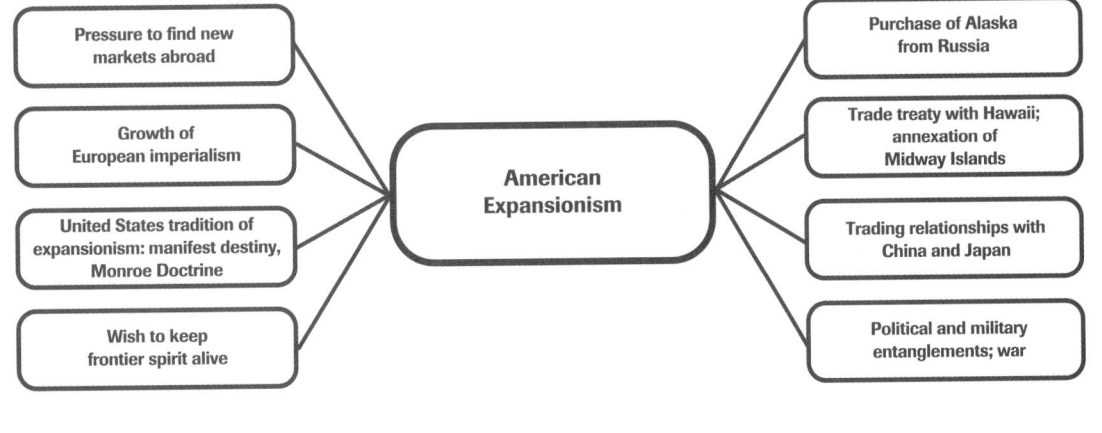

- Pressure to find new markets abroad
- Growth of European imperialism
- United States tradition of expansionism: manifest destiny, Monroe Doctrine
- Wish to keep frontier spirit alive

American Expansionism

- Purchase of Alaska from Russia
- Trade treaty with Hawaii; annexation of Midway Islands
- Trading relationships with China and Japan
- Political and military entanglements; war

Alternative Assessment

Final Evaluation
Use the following criteria to evaluate student projects:
- **Evidence of thoughtfulness** Are editorials well reasoned, making a strong claim and supporting it with appropriate facts and reasons?
- **Evidence of synthesis** Do editorials effectively use a combination of moral, economic, social, and political arguments?
- **Communication style** Are editorials logical, forceful, and persuasive?
- **Evidence of outside research** Do editorials use actual quotations from outside sources to support their claims?

Thinking Critically

1. The families of people who were injured or killed in the war would probably disagree with Hay, as would anyone who suffered as a result of the war.

2. Partly as a result of the civil rights movement, people today are more sensitive to the values of other races and cultures than was the case in the early part of the century. Also, expansionism is now viewed with disfavor, in part because Americans have experienced so much bloodshed as a result of foreign entanglements.

3. Answers will vary. Students might cite press coverage of any issue currently in the news. Students may point out that the degree of sensationalism usually depends on the source that is covering the story.

Making Connections

1. Roosevelt assumes that Native Americans made poor use of the land and that white Americans used the land to better advantage. Many students will disagree with Roosevelt's assumption, noting that Native Americans and white Americans simply used the land differently, but that this difference did not entitle white Americans to seize Native Americans lands.

INSTRUCT

Make copies of the following quotations from Senator Albert Beveridge of Indiana and William Jennings Bryan, presidential candidate in 1900. Then distribute the copies to the students. Beveridge: "American factories are making more than the American people can use; American soil is producing more than they can consume. Fate has written our policy for us; the trade of the world must and shall be ours. We will establish trading posts throughout the world as distributing points for American products. We will cover the ocean with our merchant marine. We will build a navy to the measure of our greatness. Great colonies governing themselves, flying our flag and trading with us, will grow about our posts of trade." Bryan: "It is not necessary to own people in order to trade with them. . . . We do not own Japan or China, but we trade with their people. We have not absorbed the republics of Central and South America, but we trade with them. Trade cannot be permanently profitable unless it is voluntary."

As students read the source readings from Alfred Mahan and Ruben Dario, have them compare the excerpts to these quotations. Then have students write two paragraphs describing whether Mahan and Dario would agree or disagree with

CHAPTER 9

SOURCE READINGS

The United States Looking Outward

Primary Source

Alfred T. Mahan

INTRODUCTION Naval historian and admiral Alfred T. Mahan believed that the United States should follow the example of Great Britain in order to gain dominance in world affairs. The most important act the country could undertake, according to Mahan, was to enlarge and strengthen its naval fleet so that no other nation could challenge it when trading overseas. In the excerpt below from "The United States Looking Outward," published in the *Atlantic Monthly* in 1890, Mahan explains his reasoning for such a policy. Mahan's writings led to the United States Navy becoming one of the most powerful in the world. For many years his books were standard reading for all naval officers.

VOCABULARY Before you read the selection, find the meaning of these words in a dictionary: temperament, ominous, prudent, inanition.

For nearly the lifetime of a generation, American industries have been protected[1] until the practice has assumed the force of a tradition. At bottom, however, the temperament of the American people is essentially alien to such a sluggish attitude. Independently of all bias for or against protection, it is safe to predict that, when the opportunities for gain abroad are understood, American enterprise will try to reach them. The importance of distant markets and their relation to our own production imply the recognition of the link that joins the products and the markets—that is, the carrying trade.[2] We need not follow far this line of thought before America's unique position becomes clear. Facing the older worlds of the East and West, America's shores are lapped by the oceans which touch the one or the other but which are common to her alone.

Together with these signs of change in our own policy there is a restlessness in the world at large which is deeply significant, if not ominous. There is no sound reason for believing that the world has passed into a period of peace outside the limits of Europe. Unsettled political conditions exist in Haiti, Central America, and many of the Pacific islands, especially the Hawaiian group. When combined with great military or commercial importance, these conditions contain dangerous germs of quarrel, against which it is at least prudent to be prepared.

Despite a superior geographical location, the United States is woefully unready to assert its influence in the Caribbean and Central America. We have not the navy. And, what is worse, we are not willing to have the navy that will weigh seriously in any disputes with those nations whose interests conflict with our own. We have not, and we are not anxious to provide, the defense of the Atlantic seaboard which will leave the navy free for its work at sea.

Whether they will or not, Americans must now begin to look outward. The growing production of the country demands it. An increasing volume of public sentiment demands it. The position of the United States, between the two Old Worlds and the

[1] Mahan is referring to protective tariffs that increase the price of imported goods so that American-made goods will be less expensive.

[2] The carrying trade refers to the fleets of merchant ships that carry products to markets overseas.

Mahan believed that a powerful navy was needed to protect the nation's "carrying trade," symbolized by this busy New York dock in the early 1900s.

two great oceans, makes the same claim, which will soon be strengthened by the creation of the new link joining the Atlantic and Pacific. The tendency will be increased by the growth of the European colonies in the Pacific, by the advancing civilization of Japan, and by the rapid peopling of our Pacific states.

The military needs of the Pacific states, as well as their supreme importance to the whole country, are yet a matter of the future. But this future is so near that provision should immediately begin to weigh their importance. To provide this, three things are needed: First, protection of the chief harbors by fortifications and coast-defense ships. Second, naval force, the arm of offensive power, which alone enables a country to extend its influence outward. Third, it should be an unshakeable resolution of our national policy that no European state should henceforth acquire a coaling position within 3,000 miles of San Francisco—a distance which includes the Sandwich and Galapagos

islands and the coast of Central America. For fuel is the life of modern naval war. It is the food of the ship. Without it the modern monsters of the deep die of ina- nition. Around it, therefore, cluster some of the most important considerations of naval strategy.

THINKING ABOUT THE SELECTION

1. For what geographical reasons does Mahan believe that the United States is in a unique position to become a powerful international trading force?
2. For what economic reasons does Mahan believe the United States must begin looking to distant markets for trading opportunities?

Critical Thinking

3. **Formulating Questions** What questions would you ask Mahan in order to understand how qualified he is to draw the conclusions stated in this excerpt?

ANSWERS TO

Thinking About the Selection
1. The United States is positioned geographi- cally between Europe and Asia and has coasts on both the Pacific and the Atlantic oceans, whereas Europe and Asia each have shores on only one of these oceans. In addition, the build- ing of the Panama Canal ("the new link joining the Atlantic and Pacific") will further strengthen the United States' position for engaging in international trade.

2. Mahan states that the "growing production of the country demands" that Americans begin to look outward. He refers to the surplus of goods that modern technology has allowed the United States to produce.
3. Questions might include: Describe your career in the navy. What studies have you made of the American economy? From where does your knowledge of foreign affairs come? Why do you believe that the United States should imitate British policy with regard to its navy?

Point out to students that Ruben Dario's poem expresses the anti-imperialist sentiments of the time. Ask students to write a poem that expresses the imperialist sentiments voiced by Alfred Mahan and Albert Beveridge. If they prefer, students can draw a political cartoon or other picture that illustrates in some way either the imperialist or the anti-imperialist side. Display students' work around the room and allow the class time to review the poems and drawings.

SOURCE
READINGS

1904

Literature

Ruben Dario

NTRODUCTION In 1904 President Theodore Roosevelt issued his "corollary" to the Monroe Doctrine. In it, Roosevelt declared that the United States had the right to intervene in Latin America to impose order and to "exercise our international police power." Not surprisingly, many Latin Americans were angered by what they saw as Roosevelt's arrogant use of power. The poem below was written in 1904 by Ruben Dario, a Nicaraguan poet and diplomat, to express his distaste for such actions and to voice a warning of sorts to the United States.

VOCABULARY Before you read the selection, find the meaning of these words in a dictionary: archaic, resonate, odorous.

> *Hunter, the only way to approach you*
> *is with a voice like that of the Bible, or poems like*
> *those of Walt Whitman.*
> *Archaic and modern, simple and involved,*
> *with something of Washington, and more of*
> *Nimrod.*
> *In fact you are the United States,*
> *you are the future invader*
> *of the naive American that still has native blood,*
> *that still prays to Jesus Christ, and still speaks*
> *Spanish.*
> *You are a magnificent and powerful example of*
> *your race:*
> *you are cultivated; you are efficient; you disagree*
> *Dominating horses or murdering tigers,*
> *with Tolstoy.*
> *you are an Alexander-Nebuchadnezzar.*
> *(You are a professor of energy,*
> *as the sports would say today.)*
>
> *You believe that to live is to burn,*
> *that progress is explosion,*
> *that where you place the rifle slug*
> *you place the future.*
> *   No.*
> *The United States is powerful and great.*
> *When the States shiver a deep shudder*
> *Moves down the enormous vertebrate of the Andes.*
> *If you shout, we hear it like a lion's roar.*
> *Hugo once said to Grant: "You own the stars."*
> *(Hardly visible, the Argentine sun is just rising,*

Two views of Theodore Roosevelt: as a young man dressed in hunting clothes (below) and as an exuberant President (next page).

and the star of Chile ascending . . .) You are rich.
You mingle the religion of Hercules with the
*   religion of Mammon;*
lighting up the road of easy domination of others,
Liberty raises her torch in New York.

But in the America we have, which has
*   produced poets*
since the ancient days of Netzahualocoyotl,which
has kept the footprints of the great Bacchus,
which even knew at one time the words of Pan,
which used to speak with the stars, which had
*   legends of Atlantis,*
whose name arrives to us, resonating, in Plato,
which since the most distant beginnings of its life,
lives out of light, out of fire, out of perfume, out of love,
America of the great Montezuma, of the Inca,
the odorous America of Christopher Columbus,
Catholic America, Spanish America,
America in which the aristocratic Guatemoc said:
"I do not find myself in a bed of roses"; that America
which is shaken by hurricanes and brought alive
*   by love:*
Men with Anglo-Saxon eyes and barbaric souls:
*   that America is alive,*
And it sleeps, and loves, and moves, and is the
*   daughter of the Sun.*
Be careful. Spanish America is alive!
The Spanish lion has wild cubs around.
Roosevelt, in order to take us in your iron claws
you would have to have been sent by God himself
as the terrifying Rifleman and the mighty Hunter.
It's all arranged, just one thing is missing: God!

THINKING ABOUT THE SELECTION

1. To what images does Dario compare Roosevelt and the United States? What message is he trying to convey by doing so?

2. What stylistic device does Dario use in his poem to emphasize how much he disagrees with Roosevelt and his policies?

Critical Thinking

3. **Drawing Conclusions** In what sense is the end of Dario's poem both a warning to and a criticism of Roosevelt?

ANSWERS TO

Thinking About the Selection

1. Dario uses images of the Hunter, the invader, the lion, iron claws, the Rifleman; these images all convey a sense of the United States and Roosevelt as a powerful and somewhat ruthless conqueror.

2. Dario interrupts the flow of the poem by placing a single word, "No," on a line by itself. This placement emphasizes the word and Dario's disagreement with Roosevelt's policies.

3. He warns Roosevelt that "The Spanish lion has wild cubs around," meaning that the Latin American people will not stand for his bullying and mistreatment without fighting back. He criticizes Roosevelt by implying that he thinks he is like God, but that in fact God is missing from his actions.

Chapter 10 The Era of Progressive Reform
1890–1920

📁 **Teaching Resources** (See Unit 3 Folder)

	Instruction	Enrichment
Section 1 **The Origins of Progressivism** (pp. 338–342)	Reproducible Lesson Plan, p. 38 Alternate Lesson Plan, p. 95 Guided Reading and Review, p. 42 Quiz, p. 43	Visual Learning Activity, A Different Kind of Wild West Show, p. 66 American Profiles Activity, Ida Tarbell, p. 54 Literature Activity, Horrors of the Meat-Packing Industry, pp. 63–64
Section 2 **Progressivism: Its Legislative Impact** (pp. 343–347)	Reproducible Lesson Plan, p. 39 Alternate Lesson Plan, p. 96 Guided Reading and Review, p. 44 Quiz, p. 45	Primary Source Activity, The Shame of the People, p. 60 Primary Source Activity, Giving the Child a Chance, pp. 61–62 History Might Not . . . Activity, Marching for Child Labor Laws, pp. 52–53
Section 3 **Progressivism: Its Impact on National Politics** (pp. 350–353)	Reproducible Lesson Plan, p. 40 Alternate Lesson Plan, p. 97 Guided Reading and Review, p. 46 Quiz, p. 47	Critical Thinking Activity, Distinguishing False from Accurate Images, p. 59 American Profiles Activity, Louis D. Brandeis, p. 55 Historian's Toolbox Activity, Testing Conclusions, p. 58
Section 4 **Suffrage at Last: A Turning Point in History** (pp. 355–359)	Reproducible Lesson Plan, p. 41 Alternate Lesson Plan, p. 98 Guided Reading and Review, p. 48 Quiz, p. 49 Chapter Test, Forms A & B, pp. 68–73	Literature Activity, The New Woman, p. 65 Viewpoints Activity, On the Nineteenth Amendment, pp. 56–57 Visual Learning Activity, When Women Have Rights, p. 67 Turning Points Extension Activity, The Lasting Impact of the Nineteenth Amendment, pp. 50–51

📁 **Additional Chapter Resources**

Resource Organizer, p. 37
Alternate Lesson Plan, p. 94
Answer Keys, pp. 116–126

Bibliography

For the Teacher
Cott, Nancy F. *Root of Bitterness: Documents of the Social History of American Women.* Dutton, 1972. (Examines the range and depth of women's experience through historical sources such as diaries, letters, and petitions.)

Prentice Hall Literature Excerpts from *The American Experience,* 1994, "Realism and the Frontier, 1865–1915."

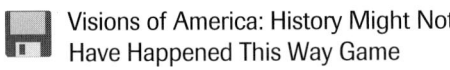

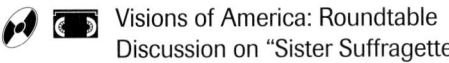
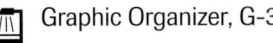

THE BIG IDEA

The Big Idea for the chapter and how the main ideas in each section relate to the Big Idea are graphically displayed below. Comprehension of this chapter's Big Idea is critical to students' understanding of United States history and how we as a nation got where we are today.

CHAPTER 10

At the turn of the century, many Americans hoped to change American society for the better. These reform-minded citizens, who were called progressives, worked for many different causes at the national, state, and local levels. Many of their reforms had lasting effects on American society.

SECTION 1

At the turn of the century, many educated, middle-class Americans began to think that the reforms needed in the nation were too great for private efforts. Progressives wanted the government to bring about reform.

SECTION 2

Progressives working at the federal, state, and local levels enacted many reform programs.

SECTION 3

In 1912, some progressives formed a political party. Although the Progressive party did not win the election, progressives continued to implement their reform programs until World War I focused the nation's attention on events in Europe.

SECTION 4

The Nineteenth Amendment was ratified in 1920, ending the long struggle of American women for enfranchisement.

The Era of Progressive Reform
1890–1920

The Relevance of the Big Idea

During the heady days of the progressive movement, muckraking journalists exposed corruption and scandal, stirring public opinion and supporting calls for reform.

One hundred years later, almost every major newspaper and television network employs an "investigative" team of reporters assigned to search out and report on scandals and corruption in government and industry. Some people think that investigative journalism has gone too far and that the media should exercise greater restraint.

Discuss with students the pros and cons of investigative journalism and how it does or does not help in reforming social and political ills.

In Depth

Global Connections

In 1905, as progressivism caught fire in the United States, Einstein's theory of relativity—the idea that space and time are connected and that nothing is absolute, that even the passage of time is not uniform but varies in relation to an object's velocity—set the stage for a major rethinking of scientific truth. Publication of the more sweeping theory of general relativity in 1916 brought with it a questioning of the status quo and justified, some felt, revolutionary calls for change.

The Era of Progressive Reform
1890–1920

GIVE YOUR CHILDREN EQUAL RIGHTS
VOTE YES Nov. 2
On the AMENDMENT ENABLING WOMAN TO VOTE

At the turn of the century, a spirit of reform known as progressivism took hold of many American people. Less a united movement than a loose collection of informal and unlikely alliances, progressivism targeted the massive problems of an urban, industrialized nation. In spite of opposition, progressives were able to redefine government's role in American life, make a serious run for the White House, and enact such lasting reforms as woman suffrage.

NO ONE CARES FOR ME
WORDS AND MUSIC BY TELL TAYLOR
COMPOSER OF "DOWN BY THE OLD MILL STREAM" "SOMEDAY" ETC.
VANDERSLOOT MUSIC PUB. CO. WILLIAMSPORT, PA.

Events in the United States

| | 1890 National American Woman Suffrage Association formed. • Yosemite declared a national park. | 1893 Illinois passes law prohibiting child labor. • A depression rocks the nation. | 1899 National Consumers League forms to investigate conditions under which goods are made. | 1903 Teddy Roosevelt proposes arbitration to end the United Mine Workers' strike. |

| 1890 | 1893 | 1896 | 1899 | 1902 |

Events in the World

| | 1890 Japan holds its first general elections. • Swiss government introduces social insurance. | 1894 Japan and Korea declare war on China. • British obtain control of Uganda. |

RESOURCE DIRECTORY

Teaching Resources

Alternate Lesson Plan: Demonstrating the Big Idea found in the Alternate Lesson Plans folder, p. 94, provides a lesson strategy to instruct students about the Big Idea that many of the reforms made during the progressive era had lasting effects on American society.

Alternative Assessment Handbook provides information, guidance, and strategies for alternative methods of assessment. It includes an essay on new trends in assessment, guidance and strategies for developing performance tasks and portfolios, scoring rubrics, and sample evaluation forms.

Pages 338–342

The Origins of Progressivism

In the twilight of the 1800s, many citizens could see that existing efforts to solve the massive problems of industrialization were failing. Could government heal the nation's ills?

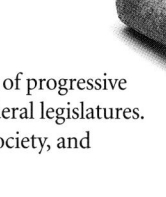

Pages 343–347

Progressivism: Its Legislative Impact

Driven by the rising tide of public demand, a torrent of progressive reform programs flowed through local, state, and federal legislatures. Targets for the proposed reforms included politics, society, and the economy.

Pages 350–353

Progressivism: Its Impact on National Politics

In 1912 several of the loosely allied interests that made up progressivism joined forces in a new political party. Hitching their campaign wagon to a bull moose named TR, they set a course for the White House. Though they lost, the victors promoted many progressive ideas—until a distant war cast a shadow across the country.

Pages 355–359

Suffrage at Last: A Turning Point in History

With a long, bitter campaign, women finally won the right to vote—and at the same time they demonstrated their skills as organizers and activists.

Pages 360–361

The Lasting Impact of the Nineteenth Amendment

1906 Upton Sinclair publishes The Jungle, an exposé of the meat-packing industry.	1908 The Supreme Court upholds an Oregon law limiting hours for women laundry workers.	1912 Massachusetts becomes the first state to adopt a minimum wage. • Woodrow Wilson is elected President.		1919 State legislatures ratify the 18th Amendment, enacting prohibition.	1920 Women win the vote with the ratification of the 19th Amendment.
1905	**1908**	**1911**	**1914**	**1917**	**1920**
1904 Ten-hour work day established in France.	1907 Universal direct suffrage instituted in Austria.	1911 Turkish-Italian war begins. • Mexican Civil War ends.			

◆ Alternative Assessment

As an ongoing chapter project, students can write an essay responding to the following analysis: The progressives had three basic goals: to end corruption and abuses of power in government and business; to reform social institutions so as to provide opportunity for every citizen; and to apply scientific principles to political and social institutions. Student essays should include information that either supports or challenges each of the three parts of the quotation and backs up their point of view with specific examples of progressive actions. Students may research the progressive movement and include in their essays information they discover.

Explain that finished projects will be assessed according to the following standards:

● **Unacceptable** Essays are not completed or fail to meet requirements outlined.

● **Limited/Acceptable** Essays are based on material from the textbook and provide a response to each of the three parts of the quotation.

● **Extensive/Commendable** Essays respond to each part of the quotation with a thoughtful stance of agreement or challenge, provide examples of progressive actions that support the students' opinions, and show evidence of some outside research.

● **Extraordinary/Outstanding** Essays respond to each part of the quotation, provide a variety of examples of progressive actions that support the students' opinions, and show evidence of extensive outside research.

For information and guidance on alternative assessment trends and strategies, see the Alternative Assessment Handbook in the Resource Directory on page 336.

SECTION 1

The Origins of Progressivism

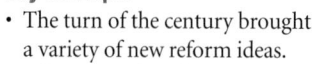

SECTION PREVIEW

In the twilight of the 1800s, many citizens could see that existing efforts to solve the massive problems of industrialization were failing. Could government heal the nation's ills?

One popular cause in the early 1900s was the campaign for pure food and medicine, referred to in the magazine cover above.

Key Concepts

• The turn of the century brought a variety of new reform ideas.
• The many plans for reform fed into a stream of ideas that came to be called progressivism.
• Though progressives did not all share the same ideas and beliefs, they often used similar methods.

Key Terms, People, and Places

home rule, progressivism, social welfare program, muckraker; Henry George, Edward Bellamy, Florence Kelley

B y the end of the 1800s, many citizens were aware of the massive problems resulting from rapid industrialization. Unemployment, unsafe working conditions, and political corruption were just a few of these concerns, which have been discussed in earlier chapters. Citizens also realized that private efforts to address these issues, such as charity or settlement-house work, were inadequate. These concerned citizens—most of them educated middle- and upper-class men and women—began to argue that government had to become more actively involved in addressing the nation's ills. Their ideas soon redefined the United States government's role in society.

A Spirit of Reform in the late 1800s

The 1880s and 1890s were filled with lively debates about how to reform society. The ideas of journalists Henry George and Edward Bellamy were among the most popular. Socialists, unionists, and city government reformers also had many followers.

Two Visionaries In 1879 **Henry George** had written the book *Progress and Poverty* in an effort to explain why an advanced civilization seemed to increase rather than eliminate poverty. He concluded that poverty arose because private interests—speculators—bought and held land until its price went up. This practice prevented others from using land productively.

George proposed to solve this problem by ending taxes on improvements on land, such as houses and cultivation. State and local governments raised much of their income from these taxes. Instead, George proposed only a single tax—on the value of land itself. Such a tax would make speculation in land less attractive by increasing the cost of holding land without using it.

George's ideas had a powerful effect. "Single-tax" clubs sprang up everywhere. In 1894, club members from Iowa, Ohio, Minnesota, and Pennsylvania migrated to Fairhope, Alabama, to establish a single-tax colony.

In 1888 newspaper editor **Edward Bellamy** published a novel called *Looking Backward.* In it, a man undergoes hypnosis in 1887 and wakes up in the year 2000. He finds the United States transformed. The harsh working conditions, gaps between social classes, and political corruption of the late 1800s have disappeared. The reason for the change was that government had nationalized the great trusts and organized industrial management to meet human needs rather than to make profits. Writes Bellamy,

> I n a word, the people of the United States concluded to assume the conduct of their own business, just as one hundred odd years before they had assumed the conduct of their own government.

Bellamy's novel was a phenomenal best seller. In response to its vision, hundreds of "Nationalist" clubs formed.

Socialists Bellamy's views were related to the widely discussed ideas of socialism, an economic and political system featuring collective or government ownership of a nation's wealth. (See Chapter 7.) Many American socialists in this era wanted to end the capitalist system, distribute wealth more equally, and nationalize American industries—but through the ballot box, not through revolution. In 1901 they formed a Socialist Party of America, which by 1912 had won more than one thousand municipal offices. Although the party never became a political force on the national level, many reform-minded Americans gave consideration to its ideas at some time.

The Labor Movement Like members of the Socialist party, union members also hoped for economic change for the masses. Unions, however, concentrated on hours, wages, and conditions in the workplace. Reformers around the turn of the century supported many union goals.

The union movement grew in the 1890s, but slowly. Union membership was risky. Big business easily got the courts to prohibit strikes with court orders called injunctions.

Municipal Reform The spirit of social reform was also felt at the municipal, or city government, level. Municipal reformers opposed the influence that political bosses wielded and sought honest, cost-efficient government through a professional, nonpolitical civil service. They also worked for **home rule,** under which cities exercise a limited degree of self-rule. At that time, home rule helped cities escape domination by state governments, which often were controlled by political machines or rural interests.

Municipal reformers sometimes appeared naive in their belief that they could abolish corruption. Some of them also held negative views of immigrants, whom they felt were responsible for many city problems. Still, their ideas formed an important element of the era's spirit of reform.

Progressivism Takes Hold

Aspects of all the reform visions and programs discussed above influenced citizens at the end of the century. Other movements were also influential at this time—including nativism, prohibitionism, the purity crusade, charity reform, social gospel, and the settlement house movement, all discussed in Chapter 7. Together these fed into the stream of ideas that became known as **progressivism.** The Populist movement formed another, though less central, current in the progressive movement.

Progressives did not agree on all points. The movement was made up of a series of temporary alliances among diverse interests pursuing different but related goals. Yet many reformers identified themselves as progressives, and for a number of years, many progressives organized themselves into a formal political party.

The Views of Progressives As mentioned before, many progressives were well-to-do Americans. They recognized that the nation's free enterprise system often could be unfair, but they did not want to lose the high standard of living and personal liberty it had given them, and they deeply feared the violence of revolution. Thus, progressives were faced with the question of how to preserve what was good about the United States while reforming the bad.

In spite of the obstacles facing unions, the International Ladies Garment Workers Union (ILGWU) formed in 1900. After the 1909 strike shown below, which included 20,000 New York City women garment workers, the ILGWU won the right to bargain collectively.

Media and Technology

Transparencies
Cause and Effect, F-3; Our Multicultural Heritage, C-13

2. INSTRUCT

Explain/Discuss

Discuss the theme of reform. In what ways does the progressive movement resemble the populist movement?

Ask students to compare the ideas of Henry George and Edward Bellamy. How did George want the government to act to eliminate poverty? What actions did Bellamy think the government should take to transform American society?

Discuss how the motives of progressive reformers were often mixed. How much self-interest was involved in the progressives' desire to maintain order and stability and the nation's high standard of living? Does self-interest on the part of reformers affect the value of their reforms?

Analyze

Discuss why American reformers were often wealthy or financially comfortable. Then ask students why women progressives tended to work for reforms that affected the lives of women and children.

In Depth

Then and Now

In the early 1920s, less than 10 percent of the nation's wage earners were organized into labor unions. By the 1940s and 1950s, over 30 percent of all working Americans were union members, and as recently as 1975 union membership still accounted for fully 25 percent of the labor force. In the 1990s, however, only about seventeen million Americans, less than 14 percent of the nation's labor force, belong to unions.

Activity

Teaching Heterogeneous Groups

While they did not have voting power, women often created ways to push progressive reform when legislators were slow to cooperate. Businesses that supported progressive social reform, for example, were placed on a list of places where women should do their shopping. In order to be named on this "White List," businesses needed to meet certain criteria in harmony with reform. Divide students into groups to create at least five criteria suitable for a White List of today. Then have the groups compare their lists and justify their choices. **LEP**

Enrichment

Ask students to research and report on the reforms suggested and implemented by progressive educator John Dewey. Ask students to identify progressive elements in their own education, such as "hands-on" math and science activities.

In Depth

Did You Know?

Progressive ideas were slow to gain acceptance in the world of literature. Theodore Dreiser's first novel, *Sister Carrie* (1900), with its gritty depiction of urban life and a heroine who goes unpunished for her sins, was apparently too shocking for its time. The book failed miserably at first, selling fewer than 700 copies. In 1981, the unedited original version was published by the University of Pennsylvania Press.

Progressives argued that government must play a larger role in regulating economic activity. This regulation would prevent businesses from treating workers and competing enterprises unfairly. Progressives opposed government control of businesses, except of those companies that supplied essential services such as water, electricity, and transportation. They wanted to allow other businesses the freedom to operate independently—as long as society's needs came first.

Progressives also believed that government ought to increase its responsibility for human welfare. Capitalism, progressives argued, often forced workers into poverty through no fault of their own. Workers had no protection against substandard wages, unemployment, or workplace hazards. Progressives proposed that government protect workers from such miseries. They also wanted government to develop more **social welfare programs,** which would help ensure a basic standard of living for all Americans. These programs might include unemployment and accident and health insurance, as well as a social security system to cover disability and old age. Progressives expected that government would rely on trained experts and scientists to plan efficient

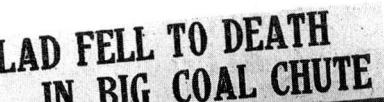

Workers of all ages enjoyed little protection against workplace hazards—and few benefits when an accident befell them on the job. The fate of injured or killed workers aroused public sympathy and demands for reform.

programs, which professionals, not politicians, would manage.

Suffrage and Progressivism The cause of votes for women was important to many progressives. As social worker Jane Addams explained in a 1910 *Ladies Home Journal* article, women had a special interest in the reform of American society.

> Women who live in the country sweep their own dooryards and may either feed the refuse [trash] of the table to a flock of chickens or allow it innocently to decay in the open air and sunshine. In a crowded city quarter, however, if the street is not cleaned by the city authorities no amount of private sweeping will keep the tenement free from grime; if the garbage is not properly collected and destroyed a tenement house mother may see her children sicken and die of diseases.

In short, Addams argued, women in cities could not care for their families without government help—so government had to allow women to make known their needs through voting.

Women activists did not all agree on how to change society. Many focused on outlawing alcohol, others on reforming conditions in the workplace. But whatever their focus, it was widely agreed that women were powerless without political rights.

Progressive Regulation and Control In order to protect vulnerable citizens, progressives accepted an increased level of government control over areas once considered private, such as housing, health care, and the content of the movies people watched or the dancing styles they enjoyed. This aspect of progressivism aroused resistance, often among the very people progressives hoped most to help. For example, progressives saw child labor laws as critical to social progress. Naturally, employers who relied on cheap child labor opposed the laws. But poor people who could not survive without sending their children out to work also objected. Such disputes added to the perception that typically well-to-do progressives were insensitive to the plight of the poor.

▶ RESOURCE DIRECTORY

Teaching Resources

Visual Learning Activity A Different Kind of "Wild West" Show, found in the Unit 3 folder, p. 66, depicts the goal of most progressives as the control of businesses, such as railroads, that affected the public interest.

American Profiles Activity found in the Unit 3 folder, p. 54, profiles Ida Tarbell, a muckraker for *McClure's* magazine, who exposed the coercion and ruthless business practices of John D. Rockefeller and Standard Oil.

Literature Activity Horrors of the Meat-Packing Industry, found in the Unit 3 folder, pp. 63–64, uses excerpts from Upton Sinclair's *The Jungle* to provide insight into the plight of immigrant workers in Chicago.

Progressive Methods

Progressives worked for reforms in a systematic manner. First, relying heavily on scientific data and expert testimony, they investigated issues of concern, such as slum or sweatshop conditions. Next, they publicized the results of their investigations and put pressure on legislators to get laws passed and enforced. Women's organizations, such as clubs and charitable groups, were a key means of increasing grass roots support and pressuring officials to take some action.

Using the new mass-circulation publications, journalists also alerted the public to wrongdoing on the part of political bosses or big business. Theodore Roosevelt called such writers **muckrakers,** an allusion to a character in John Bunyan's 1678 book *Pilgrim's Progress* who was too busy raking filth to look to heaven. While TR disapproved of those who whitewashed wrongdoing, he condemned those who "earn their livelihood by telling . . . scandalous falsehoods about honest men."

⭐ Despite Roosevelt's criticism, the muckrakers included respected writers who identified and exposed real abuses. Lincoln Steffens, for example, exposed political corruption in St. Louis and other cities. Ida Tarbell revealed the abuses committed by the huge Standard Oil trust. *The Jungle* (1906), a novel by Upton Sinclair, laid bare the horrors of the meat-packing industry. Wrote Sinclair of the nation's corrupt and filthy canneries,

> I t seemed they must have agencies all over the country, to hunt out old and crippled and diseased cattle to be canned. . . . It was stuff such as this that made the "embalmed beef" that had killed several times as many United States soldiers as all the bullets of the Spaniards [in the Spanish-American War].

Although it was meant to promote socialism, Sinclair's book did little for workers. Its revelations, however, turned people's stomachs and thus led to a federal meat inspection program. ⭐

This cartoon shows that TR himself was willing to wield the muckrake to attack difficult problems. Here, TR tries to clean up the nation's meatpacking industry.

AMERICAN PROFILES
Florence Kelley

When you shop for clothing, do you ever wonder under what conditions it was made? When you buy medicines or a package of meat, do you worry about possible harmful effects to your health? At the turn of the century, issues such as these bothered many consumers. Because women tended to be the shoppers for their families, they were often the most vocal in asking such questions.

Florence Kelley (1859–1932) became a leader in the search for answers. She came from a prominent Pennsylvania family. Her father, William Darrah Kelley, was a fifteen-term member of Congress. Her great-aunt, Sarah Pugh, had a strong influence on her. An abolitionist and suffragist, Pugh had once refused to use cotton and sugar because slave labor produced them.

After completing her education at Cornell and at the University of Zurich in Switzerland, Kelley became a resident in Jane Addams's Hull House in Chicago. When federal officials asked Addams to investigate labor conditions in the neighborhood, Addams recommended Kelley for the job.

Ask students to identify with the letter *P* all of the following statements that identify a belief or goal of progressive reformers at the turn of the century.

● Progressive reformers did not agree on all points.

● The progressive movement was part of the general world socialist movement.

● Progressives accepted an increased level of government control in the lives of citizens.

● Progressives used scientific methods and data and worked systematically for reform.

4. CLOSE

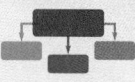

Reinforcing the Big Idea

At the turn of the century, a spirit of reform known as progressivism swept through the country, especially in the cities. In the next section, students will learn about the progressive bills passed by local, state, and federal legislatures.

Florence Kelley led the way in several areas of progressive reform, including workplace and municipal reform.

Kelley's Early Career "Hull-House was . . . surrounded in every direction by home work carried on under the sweating system," Kelley wrote later, referring to a system of labor featuring poor conditions and pay. "From the age of eighteen months few children able to sit in high chairs at tables were safe from being required to pull basting threads." Once, Kelley reported, a public official who was supposed to visit a sweatshop refused to enter, fearing contamination from one of the many diseases, such as tuberculosis, that raged through the tenements at that time.

Largely through her efforts, in 1893 Illinois passed a law prohibiting child labor, limiting working hours for women, and regulating sweatshop conditions. The governor put Kelley in charge of enforcing it. She became so frustrated by the district attorney's refusal to prosecute cases that she earned a law degree in order to take legal action herself.

In 1897 a new governor replaced Kelley as factory inspector with a political friend who did nothing to enforce the 1893 law. It was this experience that drew Kelley into municipal reform. Only a civil service based on merit instead of favors, she realized, would keep unqualified political appointees out of important regulatory jobs.

Leading Consumer Action In 1899 a National Consumers' League (NCL) was organized to unite local consumers' leagues that had formed in the 1890s across the country. The NCL's board invited Florence Kelley to become general secretary, a post she held until her death. Through the consumers' leagues, women around the country investigated the conditions under which goods were made and sold. Local leagues urged women to patronize only those shops on a "White List"— that is, shops that did not employ children or require overtime. Leagues also insisted that factories obey state factory inspection laws and, later, pay a minimum wage.

Under Kelley's leadership, the NCL spearheaded national movements to outlaw child labor and protect workers, especially women. When criticized over this issue, Kelley would ask why "seals, bears, reindeer, fish, wild game in the national parks, buffalo" and numerous other creatures were worthy of government protection, "but not the children of our race and their mothers."

Kelley's legacy lasted long after her death. In 1954 Supreme Court justice Felix Frankfurter said that Florence Kelley "had probably the largest single share in shaping the social history of the United States during the first thirty years of this century."

SECTION 1 REVIEW

Key Terms, People, and Places

1. Define (a) home rule, (b) social welfare program, (c) muckraker.
2. Identify (a) Henry George, (b) Edward Bellamy, (c) Florence Kelley.

Key Concepts

3. What were some of the reform ideas at the turn of the century?

4. Who were the progressives and what did they want?
5. Describe the special role of women in the progressive movement.
6. Describe the methods of progressives.

Critical Thinking

7. **Recognizing Ideologies** What beliefs about the proper role of government lie at the heart of the progressive movement?

RESOURCE DIRECTORY

Teaching Resources

Quiz found in the Unit 3 folder, p. 43, covers the main ideas in this section as well as the key terms.

Progressivism: Its Legislative Impact

SECTION PREVIEW

Driven by the rising tide of public demand, a torrent of progressive reform programs flowed through local, state, and federal legislatures. Targets for the proposed reforms included politics, society, and the economy.

Key Concepts
- The progressive era produced several different kinds of reforms.
- Reform took place at the urban, state, and federal levels.
- Reformers found unlikely allies in political machines.

Key Terms, People, and Places
direct primary, arbitration, holding company

T he unleashing of the progressive impulse led to a tremendous amount of legislation in the early 1900s. Reform took place at all levels of government—city, state, and federal.

Urban Reform

Much of the progressive reform began in the cities as opposed to the state or federal levels. In part this was because the less extensive the government, the easier it is to change that government. Also, cities were home to most of the settlement workers, club members, professionals, and business leaders who were pushing many of the reforms. Thus, they were on hand to maintain the pressure for change.

Attacking the Bosses Political machines and bosses sustained heavy criticism in the progressive period, but always seemed able to withstand such attacks. New York City provides a good example. In 1896 Columbia University president Seth Low ran for mayor, supported by municipal reformers and settlement work-

ers. To help his campaign against Tammany Hall's ward bosses, settlement houses sent out children with handbills to post in their neighborhoods. Low lost, but he tried again in 1901 and won, only to see the Tammany Hall machine return to power in the next election. Over the following decades, New York seesawed between turning to reform or sticking with the old political bosses.

In some cities, voter support for reforms prompted machine politicians to work with reformers. Together they registered voters, improved city services, established public health programs, and enforced tenement codes. Such alliances could bring about astonishing improvements in urban life.

Cities Take Over Utilities Reformers made efforts to regulate or dislodge the monopolies that provided city utilities such as water, gas, and electricity. Reform mayors Hazen S. Pingree of Detroit (1889–1897), Samuel M. "Golden Rule" Jones of Toledo (1897–1904), and Tom Johnson of Cleveland (1901–1909) pioneered city control or ownership of utilities, thus providing residents with more affordable services. By 1915, nearly two out of three cities had some form of city-owned utilities.

Providing Welfare Services Some reform mayors led movements for city-supported welfare services. Hazen Pingree provided public baths, parks, and, to combat the 1893 depression, a work-relief program. "Golden Rule" Jones opened playgrounds and free kindergartens and built lodging houses for the homeless. "Nobody has a right to rule anybody else," he once said. In his view, all people would be good if social conditions were good.

Progressive-era legislation resulted in the regulation of the meatpacking industry. This stamp was used by federal officials who inspected meat for freshness.

1. FOCUS

Connecting to the Big Idea

See page 336B. Progressives succeeded in passing many reform bills in local, state, and federal legislatures. Ask students what these laws were. What did they accomplish?

Objectives
- Describe the different kinds of reforms introduced during the progressive era.
- Give examples of progressive reform at the urban, state, and federal levels.
- Explain how progressives found unlikely allies in political machines.

Bellringer

Ask students to consider this statement by former Speaker of the House Thomas P. (Tip) O'Neill, Jr., "All politics are local [politics]." Do students agree or disagree with this view?

Reading Strategy

Structured Overview Ask students to write the following headings on a piece of paper: Urban Reforms; Reforms at the State Level; Reforms at the Federal Level. Have students then scan the section for subheadings and write them under the appropriate heading. Have students fill in details from the text as they read.

Possible answer: All three provisions allow voters to express their opinions directly about a specific issue or office-holder. Without these provisions, voters' only means of expressing their opinions is by voting for or against a particular candidate.

Answer to ...

MAKING CONNECTIONS

Possible answer: Since political machines often provided basic services for immigrants, the cooperation between machine politicians and urban reformers is not surprising.

2. INSTRUCT

Explain/Discuss

Discuss the accommodations made by machine politicians and progressive reformers in order for the two groups to work together. Do students think that reformers compromised their own ethics by working with the political machines?

Do students agree with "Golden Rule" Jones that people would be good if social conditions were good? How can that theory be proved or disproved?

Ask students whether progressives were justified in resorting to arguments about safeguarding mothers and prospective mothers in order to pass legislation protecting women workers. Why were such arguments successful? What harm did they do?

Explain that when the antitrust action against Northern Securities began, the head of Northern Securities, J. P. Morgan, said to President Roosevelt, "If we have done anything wrong, send your man to my man and they can fix it up." What attitude toward government does Morgan's statement reveal?

Gains Made by Voters During the Progressive Era

Referendum
Legislature refers measure to voters for approval or rejection

Initiative
Voters force placement of measure on the ballot

Sign Petitions → **Voters** ← Sign Petitions

Recall
Voters force elected officials to stand for reelection

 Interpreting Charts
Voters sought and won greater control over their state governments during the progressive era. By 1912, a dozen states had the initiative and referendum. Seven had recall. *Explain how these measures would help voters exert greater control over government.*

MAKING CONNECTIONS

Given what you read in Chapter 7 about political machines and immigrants, are you surprised to read about machines cooperating with progressive reformers? Explain.

Reforms at the State Level

⭐ Progressive governors and state legislators also were active. Governors Robert "Battling Bob" La Follette in Wisconsin and Hiram Johnson in California, among others, introduced reforms to make government more efficient and responsive to voters. They also championed state labor and factory legislation, motivated in part by the Triangle Shirtwaist Factory fire in New York City, in which inadequate and unenforced safety regulations contributed to 146 deaths (see "History Might Not Have Happened This Way," pages 348–349).

La Follette became a reformer out of disgust, after a Republican party boss offered him a bribe. In 1900 he won the Wisconsin governorship. By 1904 he had brought about a **direct primary,** an election in which voters cast ballots to select nominees for upcoming elections. Direct primaries replaced the handpicking of candidates by party leaders. By 1916 all but three states had direct primaries.

Reforms of the Workplace Activists also targeted the workplace. Applying the principle that employers and employees had to negotiate over differences, individual states established labor departments to provide information and dispute-resolution services to both sides.

States also worked toward ending exploitative and unsafe working conditions. They developed a workers' accident insurance and compensation system, and by 1920 all but five states had taken steps to make it easier for workers to collect payment for workplace accidents.

Government efforts to control working conditions met legal opposition at every turn. In a case known as *Lochner* v. *New York* (1905), for example, the Supreme Court struck down a law setting maximum hours for bakers on the ground that it "was an illegal interference with the rights of individuals . . . to make contracts."

Frustrated, reformers took another approach: they tried to convince the courts that government had to control conditions to protect women. This approach achieved a breakthrough in 1908, when in *Muller* v. *Oregon* the United States Supreme Court upheld an Oregon law that limited hours for women laundry workers to ten hours a day.

Labor reformers were successful on some other fronts as well. By 1907 the National Child Labor Committee had convinced some thirty states to abolish child labor—often defined as

---

RESOURCE DIRECTORY

Teaching Resources

Primary Source Activity The Shame of the People, found in the Unit 3 folder, p. 60, uses Lincoln Steffens's introduction to *The Shame of the Cities* to show the scope of graft and corruption found in the United States at the turn of the century.

Protecting Workers from Their Workplace

During the progressive era (left), reformers sought to eliminate the dangerous conditions of factories. Today (above), workers are protected by strict guidelines established by the Occupational Safety and Health Administration (OSHA). These guidelines require the use of protective clothing and equipment in the workplace. *What other reforms might progressives try to implement in today's workplaces?*

employment of children under age fourteen. Minimum wage legislation for women and children also made headway. Florence Kelley led the national campaign, and after Massachusetts adopted a minimum wage in 1912, eight other states followed.

The Paradox of Protective Legislation Laws that singled out particular groups for protection had both positive and negative results. Maximum hour and minimum wage legislation for women led some employers to replace women with men, who were willing to work longer hours for lower wages. Special protection for women also fostered beliefs about female weakness, hurting women's case for voting and work rights equal to those of men. In the *Muller* decision, for example, Justice David J. Brewer had said that

> *continuance for a long time on her feet at work, repeating this from day to day, tends to injurious effects upon the body, and, as healthy mothers are essential to vigorous offspring, the physical well-being of woman becomes an object of public interest.*

Many progressives believed that laws protecting women would eventually break down the opposition to protection for all workers. This prediction came true: over the following decades, most protective legislation came to apply to both sexes.

Reforms at the Federal Level

Progressivism appeared at the federal level in labor and industrial relations, in the regulation of business and commerce, in the preservation of the environment, and in social legislation.

Theodore Roosevelt's "Square Deal" As President, Theodore Roosevelt was determined to use his powers vigorously. He got his chance in May 1902, when the United Mine Workers called a strike because of their low wages. As winter approached and mine owners continued to refuse to talk to the union, TR decided to intervene. Without coal, he realized, the nation would be without a key source of heating fuel.

TR insisted that both sides submit to **arbitration,** a process in which an impartial third party decides on a legally binding solution.

Analyze
Read students the following comments by a Tammany Hall politician named George Washington Plunkitt: "A reformer can't last in politics. He can make a show for a while, but he always comes down like a rocket. Politics is as much a regular business as the grocery or dry goods or the drug business. You've got to be trained up to it or you're sure to fail." (Quoted in Riordan, William L. *Plunkitt of Tammany Hall.* Dutton, 1963, p. 19.) Ask students to agree or disagree with Plunkitt, explaining whether or not they think a newcomer to politics, an outsider, can make a difference.

Activity
Cooperative Learning
Time: One class period.
Activity: Students representing different sides in the 1902 coal miners' strike will discuss the issues and bargain for a solution with the help of (student) arbitrators.
Grouping: Groups of three to five students.
Purpose: To simulate the government arbitration of the 1902 coal miners' strike.
Roles: Miners, owners, government arbitrators.
Outcome: Students will learn the various issues and controversies involved in the 1902 coal miners' strike, and understand the government's response to the strike.

Most of these lands are in the western portion of the United States, a part of the country that has traditionally been sparsely populated.

Enrichment

Tell students that in 1905, after eighteen college players were killed playing football, President Roosevelt called a White House conference on the game. Ask students to research the results of this event and to present their findings in a report that examines the conference as a part of the progressive movement.

3. ASSESS

Section 2 Review Answers

1. (a) direct primary, see p. 344, (b) arbitration, see p. 345, (c) holding company, see p. 346

2. Examples include city control of or operation of utilities and provision of welfare services. When the machine politicians discovered that the reforms were popular with voters, in some cases they joined forces with reformers.

3. There were structural reforms, such as the direct primary and the initiative, referendum, and recall; workplace reforms such as child labor laws; and protective legislation for women.

4. Legislation designed to protect women and children interfered with private family life and stigmatized women as weak and unable to work outside the home. Yet without such legislation inhumane conditions would have persisted, and reformers might never have won protective laws for all workers.

5. TR was an aggressive regulator of trusts and of the nation's transportation system. He strengthened regulation of food and drugs. He also introduced a number of environmental reforms, though some conservationists disagreed with his willingness to use public land for mining, water projects, and logging. His "square deal" represented a compromise between business and labor interests.

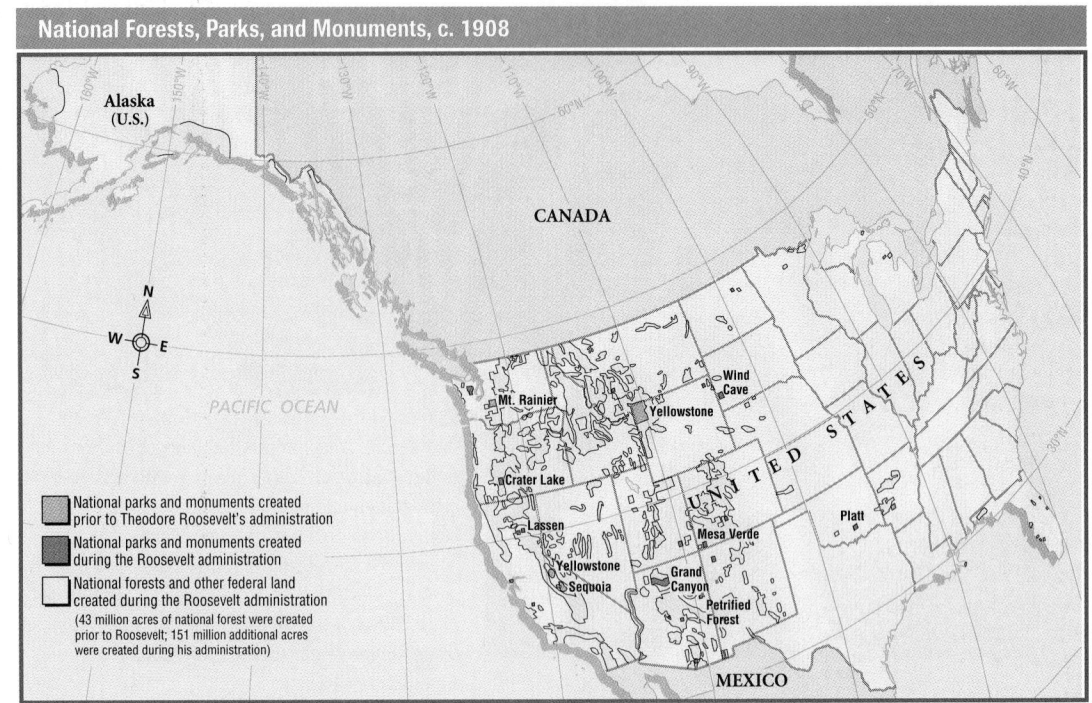

National Forests, Parks, and Monuments, c. 1908

Alaska (U.S.)

CANADA

PACIFIC OCEAN

UNITED STATES

Mt. Rainier
Wind Cave
Yellowstone
Crater Lake
Lassen
Yellowstone
Mesa Verde
Platt
Sequoia
Grand Canyon
Petrified Forest

MEXICO

☐ National parks and monuments created prior to Theodore Roosevelt's administration

■ National parks and monuments created during the Roosevelt administration

☐ National forests and other federal land created during the Roosevelt administration
(43 million acres of national forest were created prior to Roosevelt; 151 million additional acres were created during his administration)

Geography and History: Interpreting Maps
TR was convinced that "vigorous action must be taken" to save the nation's natural environment. Among the millions of acres of public land he set aside are sixteen national monuments and fifty-one wildlife refuges. *What do you notice about the location of the nation's parks, forests, and preserves?*

To encourage mine owners to accept this step, he threatened to use the army to seize and operate the mines. In 1903 arbitrators granted the miners a 10 percent raise and reduced their hours from ten to nine—but did not grant official recognition of their union. When TR called this a "square deal" for both sides, the phrase became a slogan of his presidency.

Reelected easily in 1904, TR focused on regulating railroads and food and drugs. In 1906 the Hepburn Act authorized the Interstate Commerce Commission to limit rates if shippers complained of unfair treatment. Also in 1906 the Pure Food and Drug Act and the Meat Inspection Act required accurate labeling of ingredients, strict sanitary conditions, and a rating system for meats.

Antitrust Activism Although the Sherman Antitrust Act (1890) was in place as a check on big business, it had never been vigorously enforced. Calling for an end to special privileges for capitalists, TR had his attorney general use the act to sue a huge holding company, the Northern Securities Company, which controlled railroads in the Northwest. **Holding companies** are corporations that hold the stocks and bonds of—and thus exert control over—numerous companies, thus achieving a monopoly. In 1904 the government won its case against Northern Securities in the Supreme Court.

By the time TR had completed his second term in 1909, the government had filed forty-two antitrust actions. The beef trust, Standard Oil, and the American Tobacco Company were either broken up or forced to reorganize. TR was not antibusiness. He did not wish to destroy trusts that he deemed "good," or not harmful to the public. But he believed that they should be supervised and controlled.

▶ RESOURCE DIRECTORY

Teaching Resources

Primary Source Activity Giving the Child a Chance, found in the Unit 3 folder, pp. 61–62, illustrates attempts made to stimulate interest in the crusade for children's rights using an article published in *Harper's Weekly*.

The Environment As settlement expanded into the West, people began to realize that the land, water, and forests there needed to be protected. At the urging of explorers and nature writers such as John Wesley Powell and John Muir, in 1872 Congress established Yellowstone in Wyoming as the nation's first national park and in 1890 made Yosemite in California a national park. Presidents Harrison and Cleveland preserved some 35 million acres of forest land.

In the early 1900s, reflecting the era's reliance on scientific data, the federal government called in experts to develop a workable policy for land and water use. In 1905 Roosevelt named Gifford Pinchot, a scientific forester, to head a new United States Forest Service. At his recommendation, TR set aside more than 200 million acres of land for national forests, mineral reserves, and water projects, shown on the map on page 346. A National Reclamation Act (1902) aimed at planning and developing irrigation projects aroused controversy between farmers and city residents in the Southwest over the use of scarce water resources that persist to this day.

Social Legislation Although most social legislation took place in the states, the federal government was active too. In response to pressure from women's clubs and labor organizations, in 1912 the government established a Children's Bureau within the Department of Labor, itself a new cabinet department. A Women's Bureau was formed in 1920. These two bureaus supported advocates of legislation that would benefit women and children. Both were headed by women, Julia Lathrop and Mary Anderson, the first female bureau heads at the federal level.

Progressive Era Amendments	
Amendment	**Result**
16th Amendment Gives Congress power to levy an income tax	Allowed government to raise more revenue from wealthy people's incomes and less from tariffs that hurt the working poor
17th Amendment Provides for direct election of senators	By taking the election of senators out of the hands of the legislature, voters were able to play a more direct role in government

 Interpreting Tables
   By 1913, the progressive era had produced the Sixteenth and Seventeenth amendments. *How did the Seventeenth Amendment relate to the initiative, referendum, and recall that had passed in many states?*

National Prohibition Although not all progressives favored prohibition, many thought it would protect society from the poverty and violence associated with drinking. Women's support for it prompted brewery and liquor interests to oppose woman suffrage.

A number of states had passed prohibition laws in the 1800s, though most soon repealed them. The expansion of prohibition increased in the early 1900s, however. The states of the South and West (except for California) had outlawed the sale and manufacture of liquor by the time national prohibition arrived with the ratification of the Eighteenth Amendment in 1919. Until its repeal in 1933, Americans could not legally make, sell, or import liquor. They could still drink, however, and they proved very resourceful at obtaining alcohol illegally.

Prohibition is but one of the many distinct interests that came under the banner of progressivism in the early 1900s. Eventually supporters of many of those interests joined forces in a national political party.

SECTION 2 REVIEW

Key Terms, People, and Places
1. Define (a) direct primary, (b) arbitration, (c) holding company.

Key Concepts
2. What kinds of reforms took place at the city level and how did political machines become involved?
3. Briefly describe state-level reforms.

4. What is the "paradox of protective legislation"?
5. Briefly describe TR's progressive record.

Critical Thinking
6. **Testing Conclusions** Progressivism was not a single, unified movement, but a collection of distinct causes and concerns. Find evidence in this section to support this conclusion.

Quiz found in the Unit 3 folder, p. 45, covers the main ideas in this section as well as the key terms.

Quiz found in the Unit 3 folder, p. 45,

---

6. Possible answer: Reforms were made at all levels of government—local, state, and federal. Areas covered included labor, public welfare, politics, and countless other unrelated ideas.

Caption Answer to ...

 Interpreting Tables

The Seventeenth Amendment also helped voters to express their opinions about their elected officials more directly.

Reteach

Ask students to complete all of the following statements and to label each as either an urban (U), state (S), or federal (F) reform.
- Machine politicians worked with progressive reformers in some cities because _____.
- The purpose of the direct primary was to _____.
- Reformers were first successful in passing legislation protecting _____ and _____ workers.
- President Roosevelt supported some antitrust actions because _____.

Alternative Assessment

Mid-Point Monitoring
Ask students if they have
- Started to outline their position on each part of the quotation
- Begun their outside research

 **4. CLOSE**

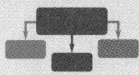 **Reinforcing the Big Idea**

Progressives were responsible for reforms being passed at the local, state, and federal level. In the next section, students will learn about the effect of the progressive movement on national politics.

The Decision to Lock the Doors at the Triangle Shirtwaist Company

Focus Before students read about the event, ask them to imagine that their community has few regulations for fire safety in public buildings such as schools, and existing regulations are not enforced. Ask them to further imagine that there is a terrible fire in a school located in a busy area, and 146 children are killed, many because they jumped from the burning building. The fire receives a great deal of publicity. What do students think would be the results of the fire?

Instruct Ask students to read the feature and to explain why the Triangle fire had such significant results.

Ask students to think of possible ways the Triangle owners might have met the fire regulations and continued to make money. Then divide the class into groups and ask the groups to consider some similar issues confronting business owners today. Many small business owners complain that if they comply with antipollution regulations they cannot make a profit and stay in business.

Ask each group to imagine that they are the owners of a small, barely profitable paper company. In order to meet new antipollution regulations, they must completely refit their main factory, requiring loans at high interest. Ask students to brainstorm choices they could make as factory owners in this situation. Then ask each group to select three possible choices and list the likely results of each course of action. Ask each group to try to arrive at a consensus.

Extend Tell students that Frances Perkins witnessed the Triangle fire. In 1933, President Franklin Roosevelt chose Perkins as his secretary of labor. Ask students to write a short biography of this interesting reformer.

The Decision to Lock the Doors at the Triangle Shirtwaist Company

Time Frame: 1909–1911
Place: The Asch Building in New York City's Greenwich Village
Key People: Max Blanck and Isaac Harris, owners of the Triangle Shirtwaist Company; Triangle workers
Situation: In New York's highly competitive garment manufacturing industry, the owners of the Triangle Shirtwaist Company had to decide how to cut spending in order to save money.

In the early 1900s, the Triangle Shirtwaist Company was one of the numerous garment manufacturing companies operating sweatshops in New York City. Seeking to boost profits, such manufacturers often tried to cut the costs involved in obeying the few existing fire safety laws. The Triangle Shirtwaist Company and others were able to take this approach in part because public officials failed to enforce safety and labor regulations adequately. The Triangle owners also tried to save money by preventing employees from leaving the workplace with materials supplied by the company—lace trims and fabric scraps, for example.

Sweatshop Conditions at Triangle

One of the largest garment manufacturers in New York, the Triangle company was also known as one of the hardest on its workers. Owners Max Blanck and Isaac Harris hired mostly immigrant women, who worked for less than men. Blanck and Harris also charged their workers for needles, the use of lockers and chairs, and any clothing that did not turn out right.

Avoiding the Costs of Meeting Fire Regulations

Aware that factories were hardly ever inspected for safety violations, the Triangle company routinely ignored local fire laws in an effort to save money. Like many of the sweatshops in downtown Manhattan, the ten-story Asch Building—and especially the top three floors that housed the Triangle Shirtwaist Company—was riddled with fire hazards. Blanck and Harris crammed as much equipment as possible into the factory, blocking access to fire hoses and stairways. They gave their employees no instruction in fire safety, nor did they hold fire drills.

Blanck and Harris were not alone in their willingness to avoid costs by ignoring fire safety standards. When the New York fire department tried to strengthen regulations and enforcement early in 1911, numerous local manufacturers blocked them at an emergency meeting on Wall Street. Claiming that the financial burden of the new regulations would be unreasonable, manufacturers convinced public officials that stricter fire laws should wait.

Locking Doors to Prevent Employee Theft Avoiding the costs of meeting fire regulations was not the only way Triangle's owners tried to save money. They also saved money by taking measures to prevent employee theft. According to a newspaper report, the owners of the company ordered two hall doors and a single fire escape door on each floor to be locked "to safeguard employers from the loss of goods by the departure of workers through fire exits." Workers

 **RESOURCE DIRECTORY**

Teaching Resources

History Might Not . . . Activity
Marching for Child Labor Laws, found in the Unit 3 folder, pp. 52–53, focuses on the decisions made by the reformer "Mother Jones" and others in an effort to establish child labor laws in the early 1900s.

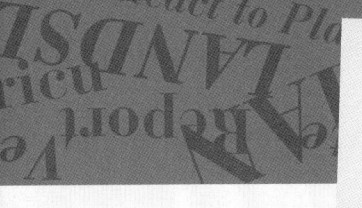

GOALS	Reduce business expenses and operating costs to save money and remain competitive in New York City's garment industry	
ACTIONS	Ignore fire safety standards or avoid the cost of meeting them.	Prevent employee theft of company goods.
OUTCOMES	• Block fire hoses and stairways with equipment. • Provide no fire drills or fire safety instruction. • Triangle employees are exposed to hazardous working conditions.	• Lock fire exits. • Have workers leave through one door. • Post a guard to check employees leaving work. • Triangle saves money.

left the company through one door, where a guard searched for stolen materials.

A Horrifying Disaster

Late in the afternoon on Saturday, March 25, 1911, tragedy struck. As about five hundred Triangle workers prepared to leave work, a carelessly tossed match or cigarette butt ignited some fabric cuttings on the eighth floor. Within seconds, a fire engulfed all three floors of the Triangle factory. A mere ten minutes later, more than 140 people lay dead.

The fire exposed the terrible potential of the Triangle company's violation of safety standards. As the flames spread, workers ran for the exits—and found most of them locked. A few dozen people made it to the elevator and reached the street before fire knocked the elevator out. There was one fire escape on the building, but those who were able to reach it found that the small, rusted structure could not support them. The fire escape collapsed to the ground, carrying people to their deaths. By the time firefighters could break down the factory's locked fire exits, scores of workers had burned to death, while many others had jumped to their deaths down the elevator shafts or out the windows. When it was all over, 146 workers were dead, and New York City had witnessed one of the most horrifying and tragic disasters in its history.

Response and Reform

The decision to lock the doors at Triangle was made without regard to the Triangle workers. The decisions that followed the blaze, however, helped to safeguard the lives, health, and welfare of workers throughout the state. The horror of the Triangle fire roused the public to immediate action. The day after the tragedy, the Women's Trade Union League and the Red Cross formed a committee to improve fire safety standards. It called on the city to appoint fire inspectors, to make fire drills compulsory, and to unlock and fireproof exits. The city building department declared the Asch Building unsafe, and fire officials began to improve the city's fire codes.

Labor unions demonstrated, calling on New York state to investigate factory conditions and enact stricter safety laws. In response, the state legislature formed a Factory Investigating Commission to look into working conditions. Its findings eventually prompted the state to redraft its entire labor code, making it the most ambitious in the nation.

EVALUATING DECISIONS

1. What actions did the Triangle Shirtwaist Company take that endangered its employees?
2. Why did the owners of the Triangle Shirtwaist Company decide to take those actions?

Critical Thinking

3. **Determining Relevance** The owners of the Triangle Shirtwaist Company were not alone in disregarding safety laws. How might this fact have affected their decisions?

Media and Technology

Visions of America: History Might Not Have Happened This Way Game

To encourage students to explore pivotal moments in United States history, have students use the Visions of America software. Refer to the Visions of America Teacher's Guidebook for viewing objectives, activities, game instructions, and discussion questions.

SECTION 3

Progressivism: Its Impact on National Politics

Connecting to the Big Idea

See page 336B. In 1912, many groups associated with the progressive movement established a formal political party. Although the Progressive party candidate did not win the presidential election, the new President, Woodrow Wilson, continued to institute progressive reforms. Ask what led the progressives to form a political party. What was the legacy of progressive reform?

Objectives

● Describe the progressive legislation enacted during Taft's administration.
● Explain why Roosevelt abandoned Taft and led the "Bull Moose" movement.
● Describe how Wilson continued progressivism until the approach of World War I.

Bellringer

Ask students to imagine an election for class president with four students running for office. What would happen if all the girls agreed to vote for one nominee and the boys voted for several? Who would win? Explain how the election of 1912 was determined by the Taft-Roosevelt split in a similar fashion.

Reading Strategy

Reinforcing Key Ideas Ask students to list the names of the presidential candidates in 1912—Debs, Taft, Roosevelt, and Wilson—at the top of a piece of paper. Ask students to make notes under each name as they read, identifying each candidate, his political party in 1912, and his claim to be called a progressive, even if he was not a member of the Progressive party.

SECTION PREVIEW

In 1912 several of the loosely allied interests that made up progressivism joined forces in a new political party. Hitching their campaign wagon to a bull moose named TR, they set a course for the White House. Though they lost, the victors promoted many progressive ideas—until a distant war cast a shadow across the country.

Many progressives joined forces in a new political party in 1912, taking as their symbol the mighty Bull Moose.

Key Concepts
• Taft's presidency was marked by progressive legislation—and a rebel movement within his own party.
• Roosevelt abandoned Taft and led the "Bull Moose" movement.
• Wilson continued progressivism—until the movement came to an end with the approach of World War I.

Key Terms, People, and Places
New Nationalism, Bull Moose party, New Freedom

The progressive movement had always been little more than a series of informal alliances. In 1912, however, a number of interests and groups associated with this movement came together into a formal political party. Though this party did not win the presidential election that year, its ideas continued to hold the attention of American voters and politicians—for a few more years, at least.

The Presidency After Roosevelt

The day after his election in 1904, TR announced he would not seek another presidential term. As the campaign of 1908 neared, he handpicked the next Republican presidential nominee—his secretary of war, William Howard Taft. On the Democratic side, William Jennings Bryan tried for a third (and last) time to win the office. Taft won easily.

President Taft had pledged to carry on TR's progressive program. He fulfilled that promise, pursuing some ninety antitrust cases and supporting numerous other reforms. Taft, however, had neither Roosevelt's energy nor strength of personality. He gave in to the Republican "old guard" that resisted many progressive programs. One such issue was tariff reduction, a favorite cause of progressives because tariffs favored business and hurt consumers. Taft's failure to reduce the tariff angered progressives in his own party, and an insurgent, or rebel, movement arose.

The Ballinger-Pinchot Affair A party crisis over conservation worsened matters for Taft. Ignoring the protests of conservationists, Taft's secretary of the interior, Richard A. Ballinger, allowed a private group to obtain several million acres of Alaskan public lands that contained rich coal deposits. Gifford Pinchot, TR's appointee to head the Forest Service, felt that Ballinger had shown special preference to the purchasing group and protested to a congressional committee. Taft fired Pinchot.

Upset over Taft's handling of the affair, insurgent House Republicans rebelled against their party leader. They joined with Democrats in a vote to investigate Ballinger. Although never found guilty of wrongdoing, Ballinger eventually resigned.

Insurgents also took action against the Republican old guard, who, by controlling the vital House Rules Committee, had blocked much reform legislation. The insurgents managed to change the committee's membership by making it elective and excluding powerful House Speaker, Joseph G. Cannon, a Republican reform opponent.

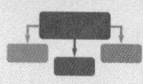 **RESOURCE DIRECTORY**

Teaching Resources

Reproducible Lesson Plan found in the Unit 3 folder, p. 40, provides a summary of the Section 3 lesson plan content.

Alternate Lesson Plan: Cooperative Learning found in the Alternate Lesson Plans folder, p. 97, organizes groups of students to write campaign speeches for each of the four presidential candidates in 1912.

Guided Reading and Review found in the Unit 3 folder, p. 46, provides a structure for reading and mastering the key concepts and reviewing the key terms for Section 3. (Guided Practice)

Critical Thinking Activity Distinguishing False from Accurate Images, found in the Unit 3 folder, p. 59, encourages students to apply this skill by analyzing a political cartoon.

The Midterm Elections of 1910 TR returned from a hunting trip in Africa to find a storm of protest rising against Taft. At first he kept clear of it, but soon he began speaking out in support of insurgent Republican candidates in the 1910 midterm elections. He called for more federal regulation of business, welfare legislation, and progressive reforms such as stronger workplace protections for women and children, income and inheritance taxes, direct primaries, and the initiative, referendum, and recall. TR called this program the **New Nationalism.**

In the election, the Republicans lost seats as the Democrats captured the House of Representatives. A progressive group of Democratic and Republican insurgents dominated the Senate. Roosevelt, back in the political picture, announced by early 1912 that he would oppose Taft for the Republican presidential nomination.

Taft's Record Taft did not have a bad record on progressive causes. He had reserved more public lands and brought more antitrust suits in four years than TR had in seven. He also had supported the Children's Bureau, the Sixteenth and Seventeenth amendments, and the Mann-Elkins Act (1910), which placed telephone and telegraph rates under the control of the Interstate Commerce Commission rather than big businesses. In the end, however, Taft never recovered from the Ballinger-Pinchot affair.

MAKING CONNECTIONS

How influential are the opinions of former Presidents who are alive today? Do Americans listen to them or seek their views? Give examples.

The Election of 1912

⭐ As TR and Taft vied for the nomination in the primaries of 1912, TR's challenge began to succeed. Still, Taft controlled the central party machinery. When the Republican national convention met in Chicago in June, the Taft group disqualified the delegates TR had won in the primaries. Charging Taft's group with fraud, TR's supporters marched out, vowing to form their own party. In August they held their own convention and formed the Progressive party. When TR was asked about his physical readiness for a campaign, he said, "I feel fit as a bull moose!" The **Bull Moose party** became the nickname of the Progressive party.

The Bull Moose platform included tariff reduction, woman suffrage, more regulation of business, an end to child labor, an eight-hour work day, a federal workers' compensation system, and the popular election of senators. Many women joined the party, campaigned for Progressive candidates, and in those states that already had won woman suffrage, ran for state and local offices. California's progressive crusader, Hiram Johnson, was TR's running mate.

TR ran a vigorous campaign that became legendary. For example, despite bleeding from a chest wound he suffered in an assassination attempt in Milwaukee, TR spoke for an hour and a half before seeking medical aid. "It takes more than this to kill a bull moose," he said as he showed the crowd his bloodstained shirt. Many Americans began to think of him as the people's champion and a hero.

A Four-Way Election Four men sought the presidency in 1912. Labor leader Eugene V. Debs ran on the Socialist ticket. Taft was the Republican candidate, and Roosevelt represented his Bull Moose progressives. Woodrow Wilson, a political newcomer and governor of New Jersey, headed the Democratic ticket. Wilson ran on a reform platform, too, but, unlike Roosevelt, he criticized both big business and big government.

Using Historical Evidence
In spite of his respectable record on progressive issues, Taft's presidency became entangled in controversy and conflict with Congress. *What does this cartoon suggest about TR's reaction to Taft's difficulties?*

Analyze

Ask students to analyze the election of 1912 in terms of the personalities of Taft, Roosevelt, and Wilson. How did the candidates' personalities affect the outcome of the election?

Activity

Name That Candidate

Ask each student to write two statements about each of the six candidates in the presidential election of 1912, following this format: "This candidate _____." Then invite pairs of students to exchange papers and identify the candidates described in each statement.

Enrichment

Ask students to research the background of Woodrow Wilson and explain how his education, experience, and religion influenced his political career.

In Depth

Multicultural Perspectives

Although they were mainly ignored by progressives, there were a few serious attempts to publicize the exclusion of African Americans from American society. The first movie extravaganza that became a box-office smash in 1915—D.W. Griffith's *The Birth of a Nation*—illustrated the depth of the exclusion. "It started people to thinking," one reviewer wrote. "The people of Chicago saw. . . the reason the South wants the Negro to 'keep in his place.' They saw in it a new conception of southern problems." (See page 353.)

Presidential Election of 1912			
Candidate and Party	**Popular vote**	**Percent**	**Electoral vote**
Woodrow Wilson/Democrat	6,296,547	41.8	435
Theodore Roosevelt/Progressive	4,118,571	27.4	88
William H. Taft/Republican	3,486,720	23.2	8
Eugene V. Debs/Socialist	900,672	6.0	–
Eugene Chafin/Prohibition	206,275	1.4	–
Arthur E. Reimer/Socialist Labor	28,750	0.8	–

Source: *Historical Statistics of the United States*

Interpreting Tables

In the 1912 election, progressive ideas played a part in the platforms of the Democrats, Progressives, Republicans, and Socialists. The button below shows Woodrow Wilson, the winner of the election. *What would have happened if TR had not run and Taft had received TR's votes?*

Calling his policy a **New Freedom,** he promised to enforce antitrust laws without threatening free economic competition.

Roosevelt trounced Taft, as the table above shows. But Wilson outdistanced them all, and the Democratic party took both houses of Congress.

Impact of the Wilson Victory An eloquent speaker and talented politician, Wilson could compromise when necessary—but also could hold unbendingly to his principles. As the governor of New Jersey, he had acquired a reputation as a reformer (see Section 2).

Wilson was not opposed to federal regulation, but he wanted to preserve as much free economic competition as possible. As he explained during the 1912 campaign, the world had become too interdependent for government to remain distant. "We used to think in the old-fashioned days," he said, "that all that government had to do was to put on a policeman's uniform, and say, 'Now don't anybody hurt anybody else.'" But life in the early 1900s had become so complex that Wilson believed government had "to step in and create new conditions."

Thus, following up on measures taken under TR, Wilson in 1914 created a Federal Trade Commission to be sure business complied with federal trade regulations. Also in 1914, the Clayton Antitrust Act spelled out specific activities big businesses could not do in restraint of trade, thus strengthening the nation's antitrust laws. Of great importance to labor unions, this act also exempted union activities from antitrust lawsuits, unless those activities led to "irreparable injury to property."

Wilson also lowered many tariffs and instituted major financial reforms. In 1913 he helped establish the Federal Reserve System. This system let banks borrow money to meet short-term demands, thus helping to prevent bank failures that occurred when large numbers of depositors withdrew funds during an economic panic. Such bank failures could cause widespread job loss and misery. Another Wilson financial reform was the establishment of the Federal Farm Loan Board in 1916, which made low-interest loans available to farmers.

Wilson was less active in social justice legislation. He allowed his cabinet officers to extend the Jim Crow practice of separating the races in federal offices—a practice that had begun under Taft. He also opposed a constitutional amendment on woman suffrage because his party platform had not endorsed it.

A Controversial Appointment Early in 1916 Wilson nominated progressive lawyer Louis D. Brandeis to the Supreme Court. Born in 1856 in Louisville, Kentucky, Brandeis was known for his brilliance and for fighting many public causes, often without fee. His work earned him the name "the people's lawyer." ✪

Brandeis supported Wilson in 1912 and advised him during the campaign. When Wilson nominated him to the Supreme Court, the action drew a storm of protest. Opponents, who included former President Taft, accused Brandeis of being too radical. Anti-Semitism also played a part in opposition to Brandeis, as he was the first Jewish Supreme Court nominee. Nevertheless, Brandeis won his seat on the Court and served with distinction until 1939. His appointment marked the peak of progressive reform at the federal level.

 **RESOURCE DIRECTORY**

Teaching Resources

✪ **American Profiles Activity** found in the Unit 3 folder, p. 55, profiles the progressive Supreme Court justice, Louis D. Brandeis.

Wilson Wins a Second Term Wilson ran for reelection in 1916. By then, the ties binding the Progressive party were weakening. TR did not want to run again. Instead, he endorsed Wilson's Republican opponent, Charles Evans Hughes, a former governor of New York and Supreme Court justice. Promising to keep the country out of war, Wilson won a narrow victory.

The Legacy of Progressive Reform

By the mid-1910s, progressives could take pride in the many changes they had helped bring about, such as redefining the role of government in business and politics.

A Limited View of Progress Progressives so identified themselves because they believed they were working toward progress. Usually this term has a positive meaning. But what seems progressive to one class, race, or region might seem regressive, even repressive, to another.

For example, many African Americans felt ignored by progressives. Only a tiny group of progressives, those who helped found the NAACP, concerned themselves with the worsening race relations of the era. At the 1912 Progressive party convention, Roosevelt declined to seat southern African American delegates for fear of alienating white southern supporters. In addition, some white southern progressives who favored the women's vote did so with the racist argument that the white vote would double if suffrage passed. African Americans, on the other hand, would fall further behind because of their lower population and the effectiveness of voting restrictions in the South.

EQUALITY

Progressives also focused narrowly on the problems of cities, ignoring the plight of tenant and migrant farmers and of nonunionized workers in general. Some supported immigration restriction and literacy tests.

Finally, many progressives uncritically supported the imperialistic adventures of the day. Just as they believed in the uplift of the slums and ghettos of American cities, they favored the "civilizing" of undeveloped nations, no matter what the residents of those countries wanted.

The End of the Progressive Coalition In August 1914, war began in Europe, and many nations began to assemble troops and supplies. Americans worried about how long they could remain uninvolved in the conflict. Soon, calls to prepare for war drowned out calls for reform in the United States. By the end of 1916 the reform spirit had sputtered out—with the exception of the drive for woman suffrage.

This lithograph trumpets one of the few bright spots in relations between African Americans and whites during this era: Booker T. Washington's visit to Teddy Roosevelt's White House in 1901.

SECTION 3 REVIEW

Key Terms, People, and Places
1. Identify (a) New Nationalism, (b) Bull Moose party, (c) New Freedom.

Key Concepts
2. In what ways did President Taft support the progressive agenda?
3. Why did an insurgent movement arise during Taft's presidency?
4. Who ran for President in 1912?

5. In what ways did Wilson support progressivism?
6. Did the progressives deserve the name *progressive*? Explain.

Critical Thinking
7. **Recognizing Cause and Effect** Consider what you have read about the nature of the progressive movement in the early 1900s. How does this help explain the failure of the Bull Moose challenge in 1912?

Quiz found in the Unit 3 folder, p. 47, covers the main ideas in this section as well as the key terms.

3. ASSESS

Section 3 Review Answers
1. (a) New Nationalism, see p. 351
(b) Bull Moose party, see p. 351,
(c) New Freedom, see p. 352

2. He pursued some ninety antitrust cases; supported the Sixteenth and Seventeenth amendments, the Children's Bureau, and the Mann-Elkins Act; and reserved many forest lands for public use.

3. Progressive Republicans were unhappy over the Ballinger-Pinchot affair.

4. Socialist Eugene V. Debs, Bull Moose Roosevelt, Republican Taft, and Democrat Woodrow Wilson.

5. He created the Federal Trade Commission, supported the Clayton Antitrust Act, lowered tariffs, and appointed reformist lawyer Louis Brandeis to the Supreme Court.

6. Answers will vary. Some students may agree that they deserved the name; others may argue that progressives did not believe in progress for all people.

7. Possible answer: The progressive movement was not a single-minded entity, but comprised diverse groups. No single political party, therefore, could hope to capture the loyalty of all progressives.

Reteach

Ask students to identify the leader described in the statements below.
- Although he chose not to run for President in 1908, he ran as a third-party candidate in 1912.
- This Democrat won the election of 1912.
- He began the practice of separating the races in federal offices.

4. CLOSE

Reinforcing the Big Idea

Although some progressives formed their own political party, Republican President Taft and Democratic President Wilson continued the flow of progressive reforms. The next section discusses a turning point in American life: women's suffrage.

Critical Thinking

Testing Conclusions

Focus Students test the validity of conclusions by checking to see if they are supported by known data.

Instruct Divide students into groups and ask each group to decide what kind of data they would need to test the validity of the following conclusions, each made by a prominent historian:

"The United States has had the bloodiest and most violent labor history of any industrial nation in the world." (Philip Taft and Philip Ross)

"The railroads . . . gave an enormous stimulus to industrial growth." (Page Smith)

"A good index of the industrial development of the Middle West is the rise of ship tonnage passing through the 'Soo' [Sault Ste. Marie] Canal between Lakes Superior and Huron." (Samuel Eliot Morison)

Compare responses from different groups.

Extend See the Historian's Toolbox Activity in the Resource Directory below.

Answers

1. (a) The work force, labor union membership, and earnings between 1900 and 1920. (b) Yes, the conclusions appear to be based on the data provided.

2. (a) Conclusion 1 requires data over a period of time because it is based on a trend. (b) no

3. (a) contradict (b) It is not valid—more information is needed. While students can conclude that builders had more union members than the other industries shown, they cannot conclude that builders had more union members than any other industry. (c) No. No data is given that indicates the earnings that were lost due to work stoppages. Therefore, conclusion 4 is not a valid conclusion.

Testing Conclusions

Testing conclusions means checking statements or opinions to see whether or not they are supported by known data. Data that is known to be valid can be used as criteria for testing a conclusion. If the data supports the conclusion, then you have reason to believe that the conclusion is sound. Use the following steps to test the validity of conclusions.

1. Study the conclusions to recognize the type of data that is necessary to verify them. If supporting data is provided, decide if it is useful for testing the conclusions. Read the conclusions at right, examine the data in the tables, and answer the following questions: (a) Upon what information are the conclusions based? (b) Is there a relationship between the conclusions and the evidence provided?

2. Decide on the criteria by which the conclusions could be tested most effectively. Some conclusions are based upon trends and must be tested against data that covers a period of time. Other conclusions are more specific and may need exact data for verification. (a) Does conclusion 1 deal with a trend or with a specific point in time? (b) Would data covering a period of time be needed to support conclusion 2?

3. Test the conclusions by comparing them with the data. Decide if the data supports or contradicts the conclusions and whether additional information is needed to determine the validity of some conclusions. (a) Do the facts support or contradict conclusion 3? (b) According to the data, is conclusion 5 valid or not? Why? (c) Do you agree with conclusion 4? Explain.

Conclusions:

1. The twenty-year period between 1900 and 1920 saw a steady and significant growth in union membership.

2. By 1920, union workers earned more money than nonunion workers while working fewer hours.

3. In terms of a percent of the work force, more workers were union members in 1910 than in 1920.

4. The reason why the vast majority of workers did not join labor unions in the early 1900s was that work stoppages led to pay stoppages and decreased earnings.

5. In 1900 builders claimed more union members than any other industry.

Work Force and Labor Union Membership

Year	Total Workers	Total Union Membership	Percentage of Work Force in Unions
1900	29,073,000	868,000	3.0
1910	37,371,000	2,140,000	5.7
1920	42,434,000	5,048,000	11.9

Union Membership by Industry

Year	Building	Textiles	Public Service
1900	153,000	8,000	15,000
1910	459,000	21,000	58,000
1920	888,000	149,000	161,000

Average Union and Nonunion Hours and Earnings in Manufacturing Industries

| Year | Union | | Nonunion | |
	Weekly Hours	Hourly Earnings	Weekly Hours	Hourly Earnings
1900	53.0	$0.341	62.1	$0.152
1910	50.1	$0.403	59.8	$0.188
1920	45.7	$0.884	53.5	$0.561

Source: *Historical Statistics of the United States*

RESOURCE DIRECTORY

Teaching Resources

Historian's Toolbox Activity Testing Conclusions, found in the Unit 3 folder, p. 58, provides further practice in interpreting quantitative data to examine conclusions.

Suffrage at Last: A Turning Point in History

SECTION PREVIEW

With a long, bitter campaign, women finally won the right to vote—and at the same time they demonstrated their skills as organizers and activists.

Key Concepts

• The quest for woman suffrage took more than seventy years and required great effort.
• The earliest victories for suffrage took place at the state level, and mostly in the western states.
• The campaign experienced internal division before finally achieving victory.

Key Terms, People, and Places
Carrie Chapman Catt, Alice Paul

I n August 1920, Tennessee's state legislature faced a tough issue. Thirty-five states had voted to ratify the Nineteenth Amendment, which established national woman suffrage. By the terms of the Constitution, the measure needed the approval of one more state in order to win ratification. Would Tennessee be the "perfect thirty-sixth"?

Gathered in the state capitol, the all-male Tennessee legislature made a rowdy spectacle. Despite prohibition, liquor flowed freely. Rumors of vote-buying circulated. Those on the suffrage side, the "suffs," wore yellow roses in their lapels. The "antis," or antisuffragists, wore red.

Both sides had supporters in hotels across the street. Suffrage leader Carrie Chapman Catt directed the lobbying effort for the suffs. "I've been here a month," she wrote a friend on August 15. "It is hot, muggy, nasty, and this last battle is desperate. . . . Even if we win, we who have been here will never remember it with anything but a shudder."

The Tennessee senate passed the amendment easily, voting 25 to 4. But the state house of representatives was bitterly divided. For day after sweltering day, the women and men who had fought for or against this moment anxiously followed every debate, every strategic move. Before learning the outcome, a review of the events preceding it will put the moment in perspective.

Suffrage at the Turn of the Century

Seventy-two years had passed since the 1848 meeting in Seneca Falls, New York, when activists formally demanded the vote for women. The struggle had cost a great deal of personal energy and money. People had grown old and died in the movement.

Divisions had plagued suffrage activists throughout. The movement had split in 1869 over different approaches to the goal. In 1890 a younger generation of leaders reconciled competing groups to form a united organization, the National American Woman Suffrage Association (NAWSA). ⭐

Women's Rights By the time of NAWSA's founding, women had won many rights. For example, married women could now buy, sell, and will property. Yet many challenges remained. Legal attempts to win suffrage had failed (see "History Might Not Have Happened This Way," a feature on *Minor* v. *Happersett,* pages 290–291). Perhaps more troubling to suffrage workers were the widely held attitudes about women and their proper

This deck of playing cards promotes the battle for woman suffrage—a battle that finally ended in 1920.

1. FOCUS

Connecting to the Big Idea

See page 336B. Women won the right to vote in 1920 after a long, bitter fight. Ask students how the suffrage campaign achieved success.

Objectives

● Describe the long campaign and great effort required to achieve women's suffrage.
● Identify the earliest victories for suffrage as occurring at the state level, mostly in western states.
● Describe the internal division in the campaign before victory was achieved.

Bellringer

Ask students if they intend to vote at every opportunity after they reach the age of eighteen. How would they feel if a constitutional amendment raised the minimum voting age to twenty-five?

Reading Strategy

Reinforcing Key Ideas Ask students to note these sentences on page 359: "Woman suffrage was not granted to women. They fought for it, long and hard." As they read, students should list and briefly describe the ways women fought for the right to vote.

📄 **Reproducible Lesson Plan** found in the Unit 3 folder, p. 41, provides a summary of the Section 4 lesson plan content.

📄 **Alternate Lesson Plan: Learning Styles** found in the Alternate Lesson Plans folder, p. 98, is especially suited for visual learners, encouraging students to think about the campaign for women's suffrage by creating slogans and posters for a demonstration.

📄 **Guided Reading and Review** found in the Unit 3 folder, p. 48, provides a structure for reading and mastering the key concepts and reviewing the key terms for Section 4. (Guided Practice)

⭐📄 **Literature Activity** The "New" Woman, found in the Unit 3 folder, p. 65, provides insight into the psychological and social oppression of women at the turn of the century with excerpts from Kate Chopin's novel, *The Awakening.*

MAKING CONNECTIONS

Possible answer: In spite of the fact that they did not enjoy suffrage, women were able to wield considerable political power through their involvement in various groups and causes.

2. INSTRUCT

Explain/Discuss

Explain to students that many progressives wanted women to vote because they thought that women would support reform measures. Ask students how the passage of prohibition affected the cause of women's suffrage?

Ask students to compare the tactics favored by Catt and the NAWSA with those adopted by Paul and the CU. How did the actions of both groups help the cause? Read students the following comment from a 1974 interview with Alice Paul, then eighty-nine years old: "I always feel . . . the movement is a sort of mosaic. Each of us puts in one little stone, and then you get a great mosaic at the end." (Quoted in Garraty, John A., ed. *Historical Viewpoints*, Vol. II. Harper & Row, 1983, p. 195.)

Analyze

Ask students to list arguments used against women's suffrage. Then ask for volunteers to refute each of the arguments.

Activity

Make a Time Line

Ask students to make a time line that shows the major events in the campaign for women's suffrage. Time lines should start in 1848 and end in 1920.

Caption Answer to ...

Using Historical Evidence

That the vote would cause women to misplace their attention and would undermine their childrearing role.

TURNING POINTS

social roles. When lawyer Myra Bradwell of Chicago was denied a state license to practice law in 1869, she took her case to the Supreme Court. In *Bradwell* v. *Illinois* (1873), the Court upheld the denial, reaffirming the "wide difference in the respective spheres and destinies of man and woman." Although Illinois had given Bradwell her license by 1890, for most Americans, woman's proper sphere remained the home, not the workplace.

By 1900, however, even larger numbers of traditional women were feeling justified in demanding the vote. Many women were participating in voluntary organizations that were investigating social conditions, publicizing their findings, suggesting reforms, lobbying officials, and monitoring enforcement of new laws. Working women were becoming more active in unions, picketing, and getting arrested. To many of these women, it seemed ridiculous to deny women the vote with arguments about "woman's proper sphere."

The Opposition Mobilizes As the suffrage movement became more energetic, an antisuffrage movement mobilized. Antis made two basic arguments. The first was that women were powerful enough without the vote. The second was the old notion that giving women the vote would blur the distinctions between the sexes and make women more masculine. Suffrage opponents also included liquor interests, who assumed that women voters would quickly establish prohibition.

MAKING CONNECTIONS

Consider what you read in Section 2 about the role of women in the progressive era. How does this information relate to the antisuffrage argument that women had enough power without the vote?

HUGGING A DELUSION

COPYRIGHTED BY LIFE PUBLISHING CO.

Using Historical Evidence Antisuffragists argued that suffragists were fooling themselves by expecting the vote to lead to fulfillment. *What does this cartoon suggest about how the vote would affect women?*

Suffragist Strategies

Suffragists followed two paths toward their goal. One path was to press for a constitutional amendment. The most commonly used method of amending the Constitution required two thirds of each house of Congress to pass a measure, which then had to be ratified by three fourths of the state legislatures.

The other path pursued by suffragists was to get individual states to permit women to vote. At first this approach was more successful (see the map on page 359), especially in the western states. There, survival on the frontier depended on the combined efforts of men and women—and thus encouraged a greater sense of equality.

Pushing for a federal amendment proved the more difficult approach. First introduced in Congress in 1868, a proposed amendment stalled. In 1878 it adopted the wording of suffrage leader Susan B. Anthony: "The right of citizens of the United States to vote shall not be denied or abridged by the United States or by any state on account of sex." With this language, the

▶ RESOURCE DIRECTORY

Teaching Resources

Viewpoints Activity On the Nineteenth Amendment, found in the Unit 3 folder, pp. 56–57, offers several contemporary arguments for and against women's suffrage.

proposed amendment received its first committee hearing. Elizabeth Cady Stanton described the experience:

I n the whole course of our struggle for equal rights, I never felt more exasperated than on this occasion, standing before a committee of men many years my junior, all comfortably seated in armchairs.

The chair of the committee, Senator Wadleigh of New Hampshire, was a picture of "inattention and contempt." "He stretched, yawned, gazed at the ceiling, cut his nails, sharpened his pencil, changing his occupation and position every two minutes."

Stalled again, the bill was not debated until 1887. It was then defeated in the Senate by a vote of 16 for, 34 against, and 26 absent. Supporters reintroduced the "Anthony Amendment," as the bill came to be called, every year until 1896. Then it disappeared, and did not resurface again until 1913.

The Movement Heats Up in the 1910s At the turn of the century, the idea of votes for women had become more acceptable to a wider proportion of the population. Prominent and working women supported it. Increasing numbers of men supported it. But the suffrage movement itself was in the doldrums. New leadership and new techniques were desperately needed to give it added momentum.

One of these new leaders was **Carrie Chapman Catt,** a former high school principal and superintendent of schools in Mason City, Iowa. A talented speaker and organizer, she headed NAWSA from 1900 to 1904, and then again after 1915. Catt systematized NAWSA techniques, insisting on close, precinct-by-precinct political work.

Alice Paul also came on the scene. She had experienced the aggressive English suffrage movement while she was a student in England. In January 1913, she and a friend, Lucy Burns, took over the NAWSA committee that was supposed to work on congressional passage of the federal amendment.

Two months later, the two women had organized a parade of five thousand women in

Viewpoints
On the Nineteenth Amendment

Woman suffrage had been a subject of debate in the United States since the mid-1800s. In the early 1900s, that debate heated up. *Summarize the arguments presented in the viewpoints below.*

Pro-Woman Suffrage
"The great doctrine of the American Republic that 'all governments derive their just powers from the consent of the governed' justifies the plea of one-half of the people, the women, to exercise the suffrage. The doctrine of the American Revolutionary War that taxation without representation is unendurable justifies women in exercising the suffrage."
Robert L. Owen, senator from Oklahoma, 1910

Anti-Suffrage
"In political warfare, it is perfectly fitting that actual strife and battle should be apportioned [given out] to man, and that the influence of woman, radiating from the homes of our land, should inspire to lofty aims and purposes those who struggle for the right. I am thoroughly convinced that woman can in no better way than this usefully serve the cause of political betterment."
Grover Cleveland, "Would Woman Suffrage Be Unwise?"
Ladies' Home Journal, October 1905

TURNING POINTS

Washington, D.C. Taking place on the day before Woodrow Wilson's inauguration, it drew so much attention that, when Wilson arrived at the train station, no crowd was there to greet him. Flushed with success, Paul transformed her committee into a new organization, the Congressional Union (CU).

A Collision over Strategy At this point, division tore the movement in two. Paul's CU called for an all-out national campaign for the constitutional amendment. She planned to enter different states, bypass the suffrage organizations there, and set up new ones.

The leadership of NAWSA felt that Paul's actions were premature, and in February 1914 expelled her group from the organization. When Paul adopted aggressive, militant protests—demonstrating in front of the White House, burning copies of President Wilson's speeches and even a life-size dummy made to look like Wilson—all attempts at smoothing

Answer to ...
Viewpoints

Owen: Women should be allowed to vote because the United States government gets its power from all its citizens and because all those who are taxed should be allowed to choose their representatives. Cleveland: In politics, as in war, women can best serve by supporting the men who participate. For a more thorough examination of women's suffrage, see the Resource Directory on page 356.

Enrichment

Ask students to use an almanac to find the percentage of eligible women voting in each of the presidential elections since 1920, and compare it with the percentage of eligible males voting. Students can show the statistics in a series of simple bar graphs or in a table.

In Depth
Biography

Born into slavery, Ida Bell Wells-Barnett (1862–1931) founded what was probably the first African American women's suffrage group, Chicago's Alpha Suffrage Club. As a journalist she was a strident crusader against the lynching of African Americans in the South, and in 1909 she helped organize the National Association for the Advancement of Colored People (NAACP). Her memoirs, *Crusade for Justice,* were published posthumously in 1970.

Section 4 Review Answers

1. (a) Carrie Chapman Catt, see p. 357, (b) Alice Paul, see p. 357

2. Tennessee was the thirty-sixth state to ratify women's suffrage. Under the Constitution, three fourths of the states (forty-eight at that time) had to approve suffrage in order for the Nineteenth Amendment to be ratified.

3. One strategy was to win suffrage for women in individual states. Another was to work for a constitutional amendment.

4. They felt that women had enough political power without the vote, and they worried that the vote would blur distinctions between men and women.

5. A number of states had enacted women's suffrage, increasing the political pressure; World War I demonstrated women's many contributions; and the fact that prohibition had already been passed meant that liquor interests no longer opposed votes for women.

6. They fought long and hard for it. Since announcing it as a goal in 1848, women waged hundreds of campaigns and spent countless hours lobbying legislators for state constitutional amendments and the federal amendment. They were not successful until 1920.

7. In both cases, women won the vote for making contributions to society that were similar in nature to those made by men.

A journalist covering a suffrage march in New York City in 1912 described "women striding five abreast" up Fifth Avenue. Such colorful parades became a favorite technique of suffragists in the 1910s.

"The question of woman suffrage is a very simple one," said Carrie Chapman Catt (left) in 1901. "The plea is dignified, calm, and logical."

over their differences failed. When CU members ended up in jail for their demonstrations, went on hunger strikes over prison conditions, and then were force-fed, NAWSA condemned them, not their treatment.

NAWSA's state campaigns continued. Hopes had centered on four eastern states, New York, Pennsylvania, Massachusetts, and New Jersey. In 1915 the suffrage campaigns failed in all four. At that point, Catt was put back at NAWSA's helm and was given free rein to bring about victory. Out of this challenge came her "Winning Plan."

This plan consisted of developing a large troop of totally committed, full-time leaders to work in "red-hot" campaigns for six years. The days of amateur dabbling were over. In addition, NAWSA decided to focus on getting Congress to propose the federal amendment.

By 1917, NAWSA had two million members. It was the largest voluntary organization in the country. In the fall, New York state finally voted in woman suffrage, raising to 172 the number of electoral votes from states with woman suffrage.

Impact of the War The United States entered World War I in April 1917. As women hastened to do their patriotic duty—volunteering for ambulance corps and medical work and taking up jobs left by men— their accomplishments came into the public eye. Talk about separate spheres for women and men seemed even more ridiculous. Moreover, in the spirit of national sacrifice inspired by the war, Congress adopted the prohibition amendment (the Eighteenth Amendment). Liquor interests no longer had reason to fight suffrage.

The Final Victory for Suffrage

In 1918 Congress formally proposed the suffrage amendment. Its members finally succumbed to the political forces of states that had passed suffrage and to the unrelenting work of NAWSA. They also had been keenly embarrassed and disturbed by the treatment the women of Paul's CU had received in jail.

Following the proposal of the amendment in Congress came the ratification battle. It would end in Tennessee.

Ratification Harry Burn, the Tennessee legislature's youngest member, had originally lined up with the antis. At the last moment he received a letter from his widowed mother. "Don't forget to be a good boy and help Mrs. Catt put the 'rat' in ratification," she wrote.

In deciding to vote "yes" for his mother, Burn broke a tie in the House. Realizing this, the speaker (an anti) voted *for* suffrage, and then called to reconsider the entire vote. (According to the legislature's rules, only by voting for a bill could a member move to

RESOURCE DIRECTORY

Teaching Resources

⭐ 📄 **Visual Learning Activity** When Women Have Rights found in the Unit 3 folder, p. 67, uses a 1913 cartoon to illustrate the antisuffrage argument that granting women the vote would make them more masculine.

reconsider it.) With this tactical move, the speaker hoped to gain time to rally the opposition.

The antis then took a daring step. They reasoned that if they left the capitol, the legislature would no longer have a quorum—the minimum number of members legally necessary to hold a vote. A large group of antis took a train to Alabama. The strategy backfired, however. When the house next met, the speaker claimed there was no quorum. But prosuffrage legislators held that the speaker was in violation of the rules and sent the suffrage bill to the governor.

On August 24, Tennessee's governor signed the suffrage bill. The news was rushed to Washington, D.C., and on August 26, the Nineteenth Amendment was declared ratified.

A Hard-Won Victory Woman suffrage was not granted to women. They fought for it, long and hard. When it was all over, Catt tried to calculate the effort. She counted

fifty-six campaigns of referenda to male voters; 480 campaigns to get Legislatures to submit suffrage amendments to voters; 47 campaigns to get State constitutional conventions to write woman suffrage into state constitutions; 277 campaigns to get State party conventions to include woman suffrage planks; 30 campaigns to get presidential party conventions to adopt woman suffrage planks in party platforms, and 19 campaigns with 19 successive Congresses.

Imagine the triumphant feelings after such an effort! Imagine, also, the bitterness at how long it had taken and the exhaustion of many women at its end. As Carrie Chapman Catt commented when the fight was all over, "It is doubtful that any man . . . ever realized what the suffrage struggle came to mean to women, . . . It leaves its mark on one, such a struggle."

The ratification of the Nineteenth Amendment marked the last major reform of the progressive era and was a turning point in American history. With suffrage finally won, women activists looked forward to a host of new battles in the long and difficult struggle to achieve true equality for women.

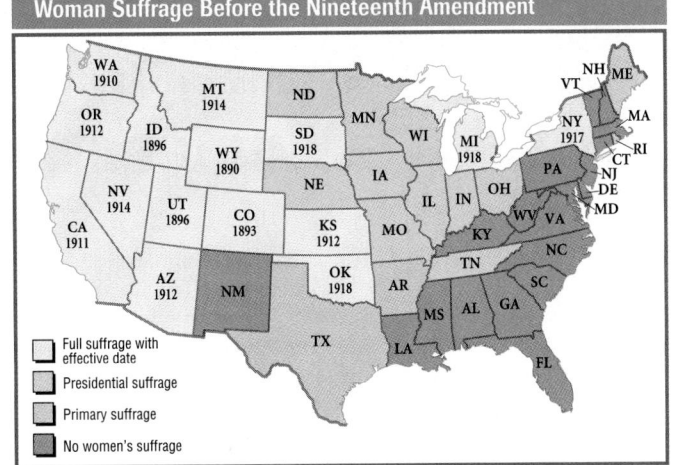
Woman Suffrage Before the Nineteenth Amendment

- Full suffrage with effective date
- Presidential suffrage
- Primary suffrage
- No women's suffrage

 Geography and History: Interpreting Maps
Suffrage was already a reality in many states by the time of the Nineteenth Amendment's ratification. *What pattern do you notice in the locations of states that did and did not pass suffrage at the state level?*

TURNING POINTS

Suffrage had been passed throughout nearly all of the West. The South and southeast, however, did not support it.

Reteach

Ask students to read and correct the following statements and to cite evidence from the text to support their correction.
- The campaign for suffrage began in 1920.
- Alice Paul founded the National American Woman Suffrage Association.
- Supporters of prohibition tended to oppose suffrage.
- The first states in which women won the right to vote were large eastern states.
- Predictions of a coming world war helped the passage of the suffrage amendment.

4. CLOSE

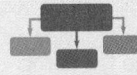 **Reinforcing the Big Idea**

The campaign for women's suffrage in the United States was a long, hard struggle. The passage of the Nineteenth Amendment marks a turning point in American history.

SECTION 4 REVIEW

Key Terms, People, and Places
1. Identify (a) Carrie Chapman Catt, (b) Alice Paul.

Key Concepts
2. What is the significance of the phrase "the perfect thirty-sixth"?
3. What were the two main strategies of the suffrage movement during the late 1800s and early 1900s?
4. On what grounds did people resist suffrage?

5. What factors finally turned the tide for suffrage?
6. Why is it incorrect to say that the vote was granted to women?

Critical Thinking
7. **Recognizing Ideologies** Recall what you have read about the reasons for the passage of suffrage in the West and at the national level. In the end, what seemed to "prove" women's fitness to vote?

 Quiz found in the Unit 3 folder, p. 49, covers the main ideas in this section as well as the key terms.

 Chapter Test Forms A and B are found in the Unit 3 folder, pp. 68–73.

 Answer Keys found in the Unit 3 folder, pp. 116–126, provide answers to all student activities.

Media and Technology

Transparency
Graphic Organizer, G-3

Guided Reading Audiotapes
(English and Spanish)

Computer Test Bank

The Lasting Impact of the Nineteenth Amendment

Focus In 1920 women won the vote. What has been the lasting impact of women's suffrage?

Instruct After students have read the feature, ask them to state the immediate results of the Nineteenth Amendment. Then ask them to list some of the long-term results of women's suffrage.

Discuss with students the great advantage the vote gave women in working for equality in other arenas such as careers, unions, and academic institutions.

Ask students to discuss why there is no consistent women's bloc among voters. Why do women vote along party lines rather than uniting as a political force?

Present students with the following quotations about the movement for women's rights. Ask students to guess the year each statement was made:

"NOW is a new national organization and has been formed 'To take action to bring women into full participation in the mainstream of American society NOW, exercising all the privileges and responsibilities thereof in equal partnership with men.'" (*1966*— National Organization for Women.)

"There are many discriminations in the laws against women. The discriminations show the need for the proposed equal rights amendment.

"The woman, even in the home— that place so often designated as her 'appropriate sphere'—does not share equally in the husband's authority." (*1931*—Testimony before the Senate of Burnita Matthews, chairwoman of the National Woman's Party Lawyer's Council.)

"The world will talk to you about the duties of wives & mothers & housekeepers, but all these incidental relations should ever be subordinated to the greater fact of womanhood. You may never be wives, or mothers, or housekeepers, but you will be women, therefore labor for the grander, more universal fact of your

360

TURNING POINTS

The Lasting Impact of the Nineteenth Amendment

The passage of woman suffrage was a turning point not just for American women but for men as well. Women's admittance into full citizenship (or almost full—some important rights remained to be won) changed everyone's lives, forever. After suffrage, women did not bring about dramatic improvements in American political and social life, and they made few inroads into political office until many decades later. But at least women now had the dignity of individual citizenship. Thus, suffrage is a central part of the larger story of the nation's gradual achievement of its democratic promise.

Concrete Impact Of course, the women's vote did have more than a symbolic impact. Although many doors remained closed to women for years to come,

the vote opened political and occupational opportunities previously unavailable to them. Women became eligible for posts within national party organizations, and public recognition and acceptance of women as professionals grew.

In addition, those who had been involved in the struggle were changed forever. Through participating in social reform movements, they had learned how to influence the making of social and public policy. The suffrage battle further honed their skills and made many of them even more aggressive in working for change. This experience helped women secure passage and state-by-state implementation of the Sheppard-Towner Act (1921), which allocated federal money for prenatal and infant health care. Later, women activists helped lead the fight for the repeal of prohibition.

1920 Suffragists celebrate ratification of the Nineteenth Amendment by painting in Tennessee on their suffrage map.

1933 Francis Perkins becomes the first woman to hold a cabinet post when Franklin Delano Roosevelt appoints her secretary of labor.

1900   1920   1940

1942 Women workers fill the nation's factories, making the planes, tanks, and other goods that help the United States win World War II.

SOLDIERS *without guns*

 RESOURCE DIRECTORY

Turning Points Extension Activity
The Lasting Impact of the Nineteenth Amendment found in the Unit 3 folder, pp. 50–51, provides a strategy for groups of students to explore gender equality issues that have been prominent in the public sphere since passage of the Nineteenth Amendment.

Continuing Divisions Another legacy of the suffrage movement was conflict. Almost immediately following the passage of the Nineteenth Amendment, the divisions over tactics that had marked the final years of the suffrage battle surfaced again. Alice Paul was less interested in pursuing the reforms of the progressive era than in achieving complete legal equality with men. In 1923 her National Woman's party launched a new constitutional amendment campaign, this time for an Equal Rights Amendment (ERA) that would make women and men equal before the law.

Because of the potential of ERA to make illegal all the protective legislation for working women that progressive reformers had struggled for since the 1890s, many former suffragists opposed it. The League of Women Voters, the successor organization to NAWSA, led the opposition of many women's groups, including the Women's Trade Union League and Florence Kelley's Consumers' League.

The struggle over ERA tore apart what remained of the suffrage movement in the 1920s. Although the two sides cooperated on some legislation, such as winning the right to jury service for women, for the most part they stood on opposite sides for several decades. It was only with the renewed women's movement of the 1960s and 1970s that the issue was resolved among those who worked for feminist causes. Even then, however, the rest of the nation was opposed to an ERA and refused to ratify it.

REVIEWING THE FACTS

1. In what sense was the Nineteenth Amendment a *symbolic* victory for the American people?
2. In what sense was the Nineteenth Amendment a *concrete* victory?

Critical Thinking

3. **Making Comparisons** Compare the divisions of the women's movement before and after suffrage.

1972 Congress passes the Equal Rights Amendment, touching off an unsuccessful ratification battle across the United States.

1992 Carol Mosely Braun becomes the first African American woman elected to the United States Senate. She is one of five women elected to the Senate that November.

1960   1980   2000

The famous bestseller that ignited women's liberation

BETTY FRIEDAN

THE FEMININE MYSTIQUE

1½ MILLION COPIES IN PRINT

1963 Feminist Betty Friedan's groundbreaking book The Feminine Mystique helps inspire a new generation of women activists in the 1960s and beyond.

existence." (*1870s*—Elizabeth Cady Stanton, lecture.)

(All quoted in Papachristou, Judith, ed. *Women Together: A History in Documents of the Women's Movement in the United States.* A Ms. Book, 1976.)

After students have heard all three quotes, ask them what generalizations they can make about the campaign for women's rights and the achievement of suffrage.

Extend Tell students that in 1902, Carrie Chapman Catt defined prejudice in her presidential address to the NAWSA:

"What is prejudice? An opinion, which is not based upon reason; a judgment, without having heard the argument; a feeling, without being able to trace from whence it came." (Quoted in Ravitch, Diane, ed. *The American Reader.* HarperCollins, 1990, p. 214.) Ask students in what way women defeated prejudice in 1920. What prejudices remain against women in American society?

Answers

1. Its passage did not have an immediate effect on the nature of American political and social life, or on the condition of women in the country.

2. The struggle to gain suffrage showed reformers, especially women, how they could influence social and public policy; suffrage opened the door a little further for women in politics and professions.

3. Before ratification of the amendment, the movement was divided over what kind of tactics to use to reach the common goal; after suffrage, the movement was divided over the goals themselves.

Understanding Key Terms, People, and Places

Terms
Students should refer to the definitions of the key terms in the chapter to write sentences that show the relation of each word to the era of progressive reform.

Matching
1. New Freedom
2. home rule
3. holding company
4. direct primary
5. arbitration

True or False
1. false, Florence Kelley
2. false, Edward Bellamy's
3. true

Reviewing Main Ideas

1. Bellamy proposed that government nationalize the nation's trusts and organize industry to meet human needs rather than to make a profit. Socialists similarly wanted to end capitalism, distribute wealth more equally, and nationalize industry.

2. Progressives valued the high standard of living and personal liberty of the free enterprise system. However, they wanted to change the unfair aspects of the system.

3. Progressives typically studied a social problem using scientific methods. Then they publicized their results to put pressure on lawmakers. Muckraking journalists helped publicize many progressive causes.

4. State reformers aimed at making government more responsive and efficient, for example, through direct primaries. They also championed labor and factory legislation. Urban reformers attacked political machines, took over utilities, and expanded welfare services.

5. The alliance accomplished many improvements in urban life, such as public health programs and enforcement of tenement codes.

6. TR went after certain "bad" trusts and sought to conserve the nation's natural resources. The federal government also established the Women's Bureau and the Children's Bureau.

Chapter Review

Understanding Key Terms, People, and Places

Key Terms
1. home rule
2. progressivism
3. social welfare program
4. muckraker
5. direct primary
6. arbitration
7. holding company
8. New Nationalism
9. Bull Moose party
10. New Freedom

People
11. Henry George
12. Edward Bellamy
13. Florence Kelley
14. Carrie Chapman Catt
15. Alice Paul

Terms For each term above, write a sentence that explains its relation to the era of progressive reform.

Matching Review the key terms in the list above. If you are not sure of a term's meaning, review its definition in the chapter. Then choose a term from the list that best matches each description below.
1. Woodrow Wilson's policy in which he promised to enforce antitrust laws without threatening free economic competition
2. the system under which cities exercise a limited degree of self-government
3. a corporation that owns the stocks and bonds of numerous companies
4. an election in which voters cast ballots to select nominees for upcoming elections
5. a process in which an impartial third party decides on a legally binding solution to a dispute

True or False Determine whether each statement is true or false. If it is true, write "true." If it is false, change the underlined name to make the statement true.
1. Under the leadership of <u>Edward Bellamy,</u> the National Consumers' League spearheaded national movements to outlaw child labor and protect workers.
2. In <u>Henry George's</u> novel, a man undergoes hypnosis and wakes up in the year 2000 to find the United States transformed.
3. The National American Woman Suffrage Association believed that the tactics of <u>Alice Paul</u> in trying to win the vote for women were too extreme.

Reviewing Main Ideas

Section 1 (pp. 338–342)
1. What reform programs did Edward Bellamy envision and how were they similar to the widely discussed ideas of socialism?
2. What did progressives see as good about the United States? What did they want to reform?
3. What were the typical methods of progressive reformers?

Section 2 (pp. 343–347)
4. Briefly describe progressive reforms at the state and municipal levels.
5. What did the alliance of progressive reformers and political machines accomplish?
6. Briefly describe progressive reforms at the national level.

Section 3 (pp. 350–353)
7. Briefly describe the successes and failures of the Taft presidency.
8. Why did progressivism—with the exception of the suffrage movement—come to an end?

Section 4 (pp. 355–359)
9. After the victory for woman suffrage, Carrie Chapman Catt made a count of the campaigns that achieved passage of the Nineteenth Amendment. What does her tally reveal?
10. Where did campaigns to achieve suffrage first meet with success?
11. How did the Congressional Union (CU) and the National American Woman Suffrage Association (NAWSA) differ in their strategies?

7. Taft achieved many progressive goals, such as increased prosecution of antitrust cases. Yet he lost progressive support because of events such as the Ballinger-Pinchot affair and his failure to lower the tariff.

8. Preparations for war began to occupy the nation.

9. Her tally reveals the enormous hard work that it took to achieve suffrage.

10. Early campaigns met with the greatest success on the state level, mostly in the West, since survival there depended on the efforts of both men and women.

11. The CU's strategy, calling for an all-out campaign for a constitutional amendment, was more militant than that of NAWSA, which planned long-term (six-year) campaigns focused on getting Congress to propose the amendment.

Thinking Critically

1. **Drawing Conclusions** What does the profile of Florence Kelley reveal about progressive concerns and methods?
2. **Identifying Central Issues** What does the fate of Taft's presidency suggest about the nature of the presidency and presidential leadership?
3. **Demonstrating Reasoned Judgment** Progressives were sometimes criticized for being insensitive to the needs of the poor. Do you think that this criticism was justified?

Making Connections

1. **Evaluating Primary Sources** Review the primary source excerpts quoting Elizabeth Cady Stanton on page 357. What bias is revealed by the behavior of Senator Wadleigh and the other committee members?
2. **Understanding the Visuals** What visual evidence can you find in the chapter to indicate that the efforts of the progressive era have had a positive impact on the nation today?
3. **Writing About the Chapter** You are running for student council on the progressive ticket. Write a progressive campaign statement for your school. Before you begin, create a list of the goals of the progressive era. Decide which of them you can apply or adapt to your school. Consider any areas in which you feel progressivism failed, and suggest changes

you think are necessary. Next, write a draft of your statement in which you explain your ideas. Revise your statement, making certain that each idea is clearly explained. Proofread your statement and draft a final copy.
4. **Using the Graphic Organizer** This graphic organizer uses a tree map to organize information about progressivism's legislative impact at the city, state, and federal levels. (a) What do the three levels of government have in common in terms of the types of reforms undertaken? (b) What were the four general areas of reform on the federal level? (c) On a separate sheet of paper, create your own tree map about the national political impact of progressivism (section 3), using this graphic organizer as an example.

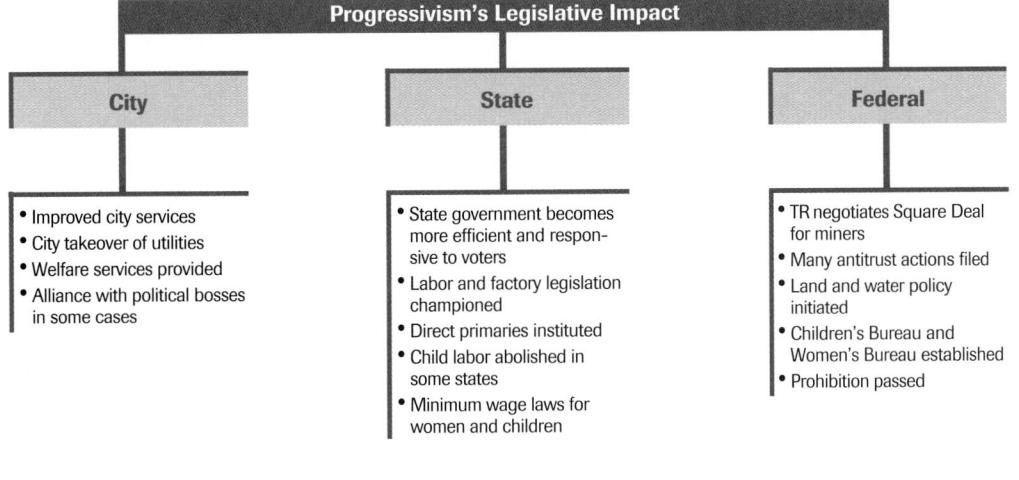

Progressivism's Legislative Impact

City
- Improved city services
- City takeover of utilities
- Welfare services provided
- Alliance with political bosses in some cases

State
- State government becomes more efficient and responsive to voters
- Labor and factory legislation championed
- Direct primaries instituted
- Child labor abolished in some states
- Minimum wage laws for women and children

Federal
- TR negotiates Square Deal for miners
- Many antitrust actions filed
- Land and water policy initiated
- Children's Bureau and Women's Bureau established
- Prohibition passed

Thinking Critically

1. The profile reveals Kelley's concerns about the general welfare of Americans, including child labor, consumers' rights, and workers' protection, especially for women. Kelley worked for reforms in a systematic manner, earning a law degree so that she could take legal action herself, and headed the consumers' leagues that investigated conditions under which goods were bought and sold.

2. Possible answer: Taft's fate suggests that a President must be able not only to achieve stated goals but to be perceived as an effective leader. Once a President loses political support, he is ineffective.

3. Possible answer: Some students might say that progressives worked to improve conditions for all people, and that they thus were not insensitive. Others might argue that progressive programs often hurt those they were designed to help, because progressives put their own goals ahead of the interests of the disadvantaged.

1. The behavior of Senator Wadleigh and his committee suggests that they feel smug, bored, and sure that the amendment before them is unworthy of their attention. They have no interest in its passage.

2. Possible answers: The chart on page 344 illustrates the initiative, referendum, and recall system, which gave voters greater power; Links Across Time on page 345 indicates improvements in worker protection; the table on page 347 summarizes the Sixteenth and Seventeenth amendments; the lithograph on page 353 depicts African American Booker T. Washington and white President Teddy Roosevelt sitting at a table called equality.

3. Statements should focus on reforms that guarantee greater equality and social welfare for students, show an awareness that progressivism failed to address the needs of some groups, such as African Americans, and include a strategy for avoiding these flaws.

4. (a) Each level focused on social welfare. (b) The four general areas of reform were labor and industrial relations, the regulation of business and commerce, the preservation of the environment, and social legislation. (c) Graphic organizers should contain information about the Taft presidency, the Bull Moose movement, and Wilson's attempts to continue progressivism.

 **Alternative Assessment**

Final Evaluation
Use the following guidelines to evaluate student projects:
- **Evidence of mastery of content** To what extent do essays show knowledge and understanding of chapter content?
- **Evidence of thoughtfulness** To what extent do essays show that students have formed an opinion about the goals of the progressives based on progressive actions?
- **Evidence of outside research** To what extent do projects use materials and information from outside research sources?
- **Communication style** Are the arguments clear and easy to follow?

Point out to students that in the early 1900s people their age had already been working for seven or eight years. Tell students that young people in those days worked in factories, mills, and coal mines, performing exhausting physical labor. Ask students to think about the differences between the lives of young people ninety years ago and their own lives today. Tell them that it was essentially the muckrakers who caused such differences by raising their voices against child labor until the federal government enacted laws against the practice.

Remind students that in a few years they will be eligible to vote. Point out that if they had lived in the early 1900s, the girls in the class would be watching their fellow male students prepare to go out and vote while they themselves would be prohibited from doing so. Tell students that suffragists such as Alice Paul, Doris Stevens, and Rosa Winslow endured much to win the vote for women.

INSTRUCT

Have students review the source reading about child miners, making a list of the various health and social problems that the author describes. Review the lists in class. Then ask students what other issues might arise in the child miners' lives as a result of their work in the mines. For example, as a result of sitting alone hour after hour when working as a "trap boy," a child would likely be stunted in his mental growth and social skills. As a result of working ten hours a day and receiving little schooling, child miners would not be able to gain the knowledge or skills that would enable them to find better work elsewhere. Lead students to realize that a description of the immediate horrors of the work in the

CHAPTER 10

SOURCE READINGS

Children in the Coal Mines 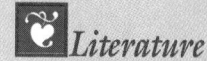 Literature

John Spargo

INTRODUCTION Although many of the muckrakers during the Progressive Era were talented writers, the conditions they reported often were so terrible that a mere recounting of the facts, with no elaboration or use of descriptive adjectives, was sufficient to horrify the reading public. In his 1906 book *The Bitter Cry of the Children*, muckraker John Spargo does a little of both: his descriptions of the work done by children in the coal mines are both factual and realistic. To readers of today as much as those of the early 1900s, they are shocking and disturbing.

VOCABULARY Before you read the selection, find the meaning of these words in a dictionary: refuse, consumption, pellucid, anthracite, bituminous, mantle, sanction.

Work in the coal breakers is exceedingly hard and dangerous. Crouched over the chutes, the boys sit hour after hour, picking out the pieces of slate and other refuse from the coal as it rushes past to the washers. From the cramped position they have to assume, most of them become more or less deformed and bent-backed like old men. When a boy has been working for some time and begins to get round-shouldered, his fellows say that "He's got his boy to carry round wherever he goes."

The coal is hard, and accidents to the hands, such as cut, broken, or crushed fingers, are common among the boys. Sometimes there is a worse accident: a terrified shriek is heard, and a boy is mangled and torn in the machinery, or disappears in the chute to be picked out later smothered and dead. Clouds of dust fill the breakers and are inhaled by the boys, laying the foundations for asthma and miners' consumption.

I once stood in a breaker for half an hour and tried to do the work a twelve-year-old boy was doing day after day, for ten hours at a stretch, for sixty cents a day. The gloom of the breaker appalled me. Outside the sun shone brightly, the air was pellucid, and the birds sang in chorus with the trees and the rivers. Within the breaker there was blackness, clouds of deadly dust enfolded everything, the harsh, grinding roar of the machinery and the ceaseless rushing of coal through the chutes filled the ears. I tried to pick out the pieces of slate from the hurrying stream of coal, often missing them; my hands were bruised and cut in a few minutes; I was covered from head to foot with coal dust, and for many hours afterwards I was expectorating some of the small particles of anthracite I had swallowed.

I could not do that work and live, but there were boys of ten and twelve years of age doing it for fifty and sixty cents a day. Some of them had never been inside of a school; few of them could read a child's primer. True, some of them attended the night schools, but after working ten hours in the breaker the educational results from attending school were practically nil. "We goes fer a good time, an' we keeps de guys wot's dere hoppin' all de time," said little Owen Jones, whose work I had been trying to do. . . .

As I stood in that breaker I thought of the reply of the small boy to Robert Owen.[1] Visiting an English coal mine one day, Owen asked a twelve-year-old lad if he knew God. The boy stared vacantly at his questioner: "God?" he said, "God? No, I don't. He must work in some other mine." It was hard to realize amid the danger and din and blackness of that Pennsylvania breaker that such a thing as belief in a great All-good God existed.

---
[1] British social reformer

mines really only scratched the surface of the problem—the work led to other, more far-reaching negative consequences.

For his book *The Bitter Cry of the Children,* muckraker John Spargo interviewed "breaker boys" like these, who were legally employed as laborers in the coal mines at ten years of age.

From the breakers the boys graduate to the mine depths, where they become door tenders, switch boys, or mule drivers. Here, far below the surface, work is still more dangerous. At fourteen or fifteen the boys assume the same risks as the men, and are surrounded by the same perils. Nor is it in Pennsylvania only that these conditions exist. In the bituminous mines of West Virginia, boys of nine or ten are frequently employed. I met one little fellow ten years old in Mt. Carbon, W. Va., last year, who was employed as a "trap boy." Think of what it means to be a trap boy at ten years of age. It means to sit alone in a dark mine passage hour after hour, with no human soul near; to see no living creature except the mules as they pass with their loads, or a rat or two seeking to share one's meal; to stand in water or mud that covers the ankles, chilled to the marrow by the cold draughts that rush in when you open the trap door for the mules to pass through; to work for fourteen hours—waiting—opening and shutting a door—then waiting again—for sixty cents; to reach the surface when all is wrapped in the mantle of night, and to fall to the earth exhausted and have to be carried away to the nearest "shack" to be revived before it is possible to walk to the farther shack called "home."

Boys twelve years of age may be legally employed in the mines of West Virginia, by day or by night, and for as many hours as the employers care to make them toil or their bodies will stand the strain. Where the disregard of child life is such that this may be done openly and with legal sanction, it is easy to believe what miners have again and again told me—that there are hundreds of little boys of nine and ten years of age employed in the coal mines of this state.

THINKING ABOUT THE SELECTION

1. How did Spargo fare when he attempted to do the work that a twelve-year-old boy was doing?
2. Why does Spargo's description strike the reader as believable?

Critical Thinking

3. **Predicting Consequences** How might a book such as *The Bitter Cry of the Children* change workers' lives?

ANSWERS TO

Thinking About the Selection

1. He could not keep up with the chute, he was covered with coal dust, his hands were bruised and cut, he coughed up small pieces of coal for hours afterward. In sum, he could not do the work and it made him ill.

2. Because it is clear that Spargo was an eyewitness. He attempted to do the work himself and he watched those who did the work and spoke with them about it.

3. The book might be read by a member of Congress, who would initiate legislation to restrict child labor or improve conditions in the mines. Greater public awareness might result in pressure on the coal companies to change their harsh policies and restrict child labor. One of the miners might read the book and begin a grass roots campaign to change conditions. A restriction in child labor, however, could adversely affect many families who depend on the income of their children to survive.

Have students look through newspapers or newsmagazines in order to find a current situation in the United States in which one group of people is treated unfairly or suffers unusually difficult circumstances. Then have students write a description of the situation to alert their classmates and the community in general about the situation and why they believe it must be rectified. Students might also contact the local office of their representative in Congress to see whether any legislation is currently pending that addresses the situation. If not, students might also write a letter to their representative, urging that the situation be looked into.

To extend the source reading on suffragist Rosa Winslow, have students check the percentage of women who voted in the most recent presidential election. Those figures can be found by calling the Federal Election Commission in Washington, D.C., or by checking the Statistical Abstract, which is available in most libraries. Then ask students to predict how the election might have been affected if women still were not allowed to vote.

SOURCE READINGS

Suffragists on a Hunger Strike

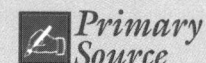
Primary Source

Doris Stevens

INTRODUCTION Following decades of marches, rallies, and speeches, some suffragists during the Progressive Era began to resort to more aggressive tactics to make their point about votes for women. Alice Paul was one such activist, as was Doris Stevens, the author of *Jailed for Freedom,* published in 1920. Her book, excerpted below, describes the fight of those who undertook such actions as hunger strikes in order to gain visibility for and considera-tion of the cause of woman suffrage. In her book, Stevens includes the notes of a fellow suffragist who was arrested for picketing, jailed, and subjected to force-feeding after going on a hunger strike.

VOCABULARY Before you read the selection, find the meaning of these words in a dictionary: picturesque, eloquent, prone, supine, insubordinate, desolate.

Among the prisoners who with Alice Paul led the hunger strike was a very picturesque figure, Rose Winslow (Rusa Wenclawska) of New York, whose parents had brought her in infancy from Poland to become a citizen of "free" America. At eleven she was put at a loom in a Pennsylvania mill, where she wove hosiery for fourteen hours a day until tuberculosis claimed her at nineteen. A poet by nature, she developed her mind to the full in spite of these disadvantages. When she was forced to abandon her loom she became an organizer for the Consumers' League, and later a vivid and eloquent power in the suffrage movement.

Her group preceded Miss Paul's by about a week in prison. These vivid sketches of Rose Winslow's impressions while in the prison hospital were written on tiny scraps of paper and smuggled out

A Massachusetts Woman Suffrage Association poster urges voters to "give your children equal rights" by voting for the Nineteenth Amendment on woman suffrage.

to us and to her husband during her imprisonment.

If this thing is necessary we will naturally go through with it. Force is so stupid a weapon. I feel so happy doing my bit for decency—for our war, which is after all, real and fundamental.

The women are all so magnificent, so beautiful. Alice Paul is as thin as ever, pale and large-eyed. We have been in solitary for five weeks. There is nothing to tell but that the days go by somehow. I have felt quite feeble the last few days—faint, so that I could hardly get my hair brushed, my arms ached so. But today I am well again. Alice Paul and I talked back and forth though we are at opposite ends of the building and a hall door also shuts us apart. But occasionally—thrills—we escape from behind our iron-barred doors and visit. Great laughter and rejoicing!

Alice Paul is in the psychopathic ward. She dreaded forcible feeding frightfully, and I hate to think how she must be feeling. I had a nervous time of it, gasping a long time afterward, and my stomach rejecting during the process. I spent a bad, restless night, but otherwise I am all right. . . . One feels so forsaken when one lies prone and people shove a pipe down one's stomach.

This morning but for an astonishing tiredness, I am all right. I am waiting to see what happens when the President realizes that brutal bullying isn't quite a statesmanlike method for settling a demand for justice at home. At least, if men are supine enough to endure, women—to their eternal glory—are not.

Never was there a sentence[1] like ours for such an offense as ours, even in England. No woman ever got it over there even for tearing down buildings. And during all that agitation we were busy saying that never would such things happen in the United States. The men told us they would not endure such frightfulness.

We still get no mail; we are "insubordinate." It's strange, isn't it; if you ask for food fit to eat, as we did, you are "insubordinate"; and if you refuse food you are "insubordinate." Amazing. I am really all right. If this continues very long I perhaps won't be. I am interested to see how long our so-called "splendid American men" will stand for this form of discipline.

All news cheers one marvelously because it is hard to feel anything but a bit desolate and forgotten here in this place.

All the officers here know we are making this hunger strike that women fighting for liberty may be considered political prisoners. We have told them.

<hr>

[1] The sentence was seven months for "obstructing traffic."

In addition to hunger strikes, suffragists used less aggressive tactics to demonstrate for their cause, such as this march, complete with elephants, held in New York City sometime in the 1910s.

God knows we don't want other women ever to have to do this over again.

THINKING ABOUT THE SELECTION

1. What causes Winslow's physical discomfort while she is in jail?
2. Why have the women gone on a hunger strike?

Critical Thinking
3. **Recognizing Cause and Effect** What elements of Rose Winslow's life might have affected her decision to fight for woman suffrage?

ANSWERS TO

Thinking About the Selection
1. At first, her discomfort is caused by lack of food; then it is caused by the force-feeding.
2. They went on a hunger strike so that the public would come to consider them political prisoners.
3. She was brought to the United States from Poland as a baby because her parents wanted her to become a citizen of free America. Instead of being truly free, however, she was denied suffrage because of her sex. She worked in the mills fourteen hours a day, and finally contracted tuberculosis, probably due to crowded and unsanitary living conditions. These early experiences and injustices may have contributed to her desire to fight for equal rights for women.

Chapter 11 The World War I Era
1914–1920

📁 Teaching Resources (See Unit 3 Folder)

	Instruction	Enrichment
Section 1 **The Road to War** (pp. 370–373)	Reproducible Lesson Plan, p. 75 Alternate Lesson Plan, p. 100 Guided Reading and Review, p. 80 Quiz, p. 81	Primary Source Activity, Thoughts on the War, p. 96 Historian's Toolbox Activity, Identifying Alternatives, p. 94
Section 2 **The United States Declares War** (pp. 375–378)	Reproducible Lesson Plan, p. 76 Alternate Lesson Plan, p. 101 Guided Reading and Review, p. 82 Quiz, p. 83	Critical Thinking Activity, Identifying Central Issues, p. 95 Visual Learning Activity, Uncle Sam's Pledge, p. 102 American Profiles Activity, Jeannette Rankin, p. 90
Section 3 **Americans on the European Front** (pp. 379–383)	Reproducible Lesson Plan, p. 77 Alternate Lesson Plan, p. 102 Guided Reading and Review, p. 84 Quiz, p. 85	Primary Source Activity, Women on the War Front, p. 97 Literature Activity, A War Song, p. 99 American Profiles Activity, Henry Johnson, p. 91 Literature Activity, A Poet Describes War, p. 101
Section 4 **On the Home Front** (pp. 384–387)	Reproducible Lesson Plan, p. 78 Alternate Lesson Plan, p. 103 Guided Reading and Review, p. 86 Quiz, p. 87	Literature Activity, Selling the War, p. 100 Visual Learning Activity, Women's Roles in World War I, p. 103
Section 5 **Global Peacemaker** (pp. 388–391)	Reproducible Lesson Plan, p. 79 Alternate Lesson Plan, p. 104 Guided Reading and Review, p. 88 Quiz, p. 89 Chapter Test, Forms A & B, pp. 104–109	Viewpoints Activity, On the League of Nations, pp. 92–93 Primary Source Activity, Mrs. Wilson's Role, p. 98

📁 Additional Chapter Resources

Resource Organizer, p. 74
Alternate Lesson Plan, p. 99
Answer Keys, pp. 116–126

Bibliography

For the Teacher
American Heritage editors. *American Heritage History of World War I.* American Heritage, 1964. (Richly illustrated coverage of the war.)
Rickards, Maurice. *Posters of the First World War.* Evelyn, Adams & Mackay, 1968. (Recruitment and propaganda posters, organized by their country of origin.)
Tuchman, Barbara W. *Guns of August.* Macmillan, 1962. (Chronicle of the events that resulted in World War I.)

Prentice Hall Literature *The American Experience,* 1994, including Hemingway, Ernest. "In Another Country" from *Men Without Women.* Charles Scribner's Sons, 1927.

Media and Technology

 Cause and Effect, F-8

 The Way It Works, H-17

 Critical Thinking, I-13

 Graphic Organizer, G-4

 Guided Reading Audiotapes
(English and Spanish)

 Computer Test Bank

For the Student

Remarque, Erich Maria. *All Quiet on the Western Front.* Fawcett, 1987. (Classic novel of the war from the German viewpoint; first published in 1929.)

Stallings, Laurence. *The Doughboys.* Harper & Row, 1963. (A first-person account of serving on the western front.)

Time-Life Books editors. *Time-Life Books: This Fabulous Century, Vol. 2. 1910–1920.* Time-Life, 1969. (Richly illustrated, comprehensive study of the era.)

THE BIG IDEA

The Big Idea for the chapter and how the main ideas in each section relate to the Big Idea are graphically displayed below. Comprehension of this chapter's Big Idea is critical to students' understanding of United States history and how we as a nation got where we are today.

CHAPTER 11

In the second decade of the twentieth century, a terrible war began in Europe, with the death toll eventually totaling an estimated eight million combatants—and many times more civilians. At first the United States vowed to maintain its neutrality. However, the nation finally declared war in order to support its allies and defend its commercial interests.

SECTION 1

When war broke out in Europe in 1914, the United States tried to maintain neutrality but also began to prepare for the possibility of war.

SECTION 2

Because of growing conflict between the two countries, the United States declared war on Germany and its allies to "make the world safe for democracy."

SECTION 3

Americans, serving in Europe in many capacities, helped the Allies to win the war.

SECTION 4

In its efforts to maintain order and preparedness during the war, the government took new responsibility for regulating the economy and controlling news and information. The government also repressed certain civil liberties for the sake of the war effort.

SECTION 5

The years immediately following the war were disillusioning for many Americans. Europeans rejected many of President Wilson's idealistic peace proposals, and he failed to secure Senate approval of the final treaty ending the war.

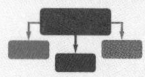

The Relevance of the Big Idea

The United States had been reluctant to enter World War I at first but later became involved, along with other nations, in a war that began in the Balkan Peninsula. In the 1990s, war in the Balkans once more captured the attention of the world, and the role of the United States was again questioned.

Ask students to locate the Balkans on a map of the world. If they were advisers to the President of the United States, what role would they recommend for the United States? Discuss the pros and cons of United States policy in Bosnia-Herzegovina.

In Depth

Global Connections

In 1918, a devastating, worldwide epidemic of influenza—the worst outbreak of disease since the Black Death more than five hundred years earlier—left some 20 million people dead, including more than 500,000 in the United States. All in all, the epidemic killed twice as many people in one year as did all four years of World War I.

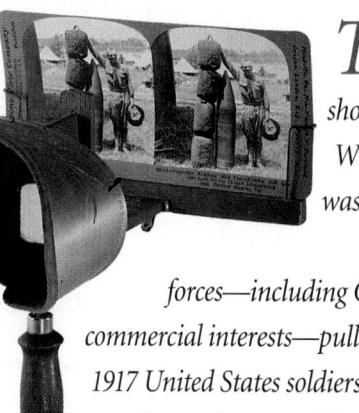

*T*he conflict began with a few shots fired by a single assassin. Within months, much of Europe was at war. Most Americans were reluctant to get involved, but powerful forces—including German submarines and American commercial interests—pulled the nation into the battle. By 1917 United States soldiers had joined Europeans in the trenches and terrors of the war. When the guns finally quieted, President Wilson launched a campaign for a treaty and a new international organization that would prevent such a tragedy from ever happening again. Meanwhile, the American people struggled to make peace in their own minds with the horrors of the war.

Events in the United States			
1914 The United States declares itself officially neutral in World War I.	**1915** Jane Addams and Carrie Chapman Catt organize the Woman's Peace party.	**1916** Woodrow Wilson is reelected United States President on a peace platform.	

1913	1914	1915	1916

Events in the World			
1914 The assassination of Archduke Francis Ferdinand sets off World War I.	**1915** German submarines sink the British Lusitania.	**1916** The Government of India Act gives Indians limited self-rule.	

 **RESOURCE DIRECTORY**

Teaching Resources

Alternate Lesson Plan: Demonstrating the Big Idea found in the Alternate Lesson Plans folder, p. 99, provides a strategy to instruct students about the Big Idea that although initially neutral, the United States was drawn by various factors into World War I, affecting life at home in spite of America's distance from the battle front.

Alternative Assessment Handbook provides information, guidance, and strategies for alternative methods of assessment. It includes an essay on new trends in assessment, guidance and strategies for developing performance tasks and portfolios, scoring rubrics, and sample evaluation forms.

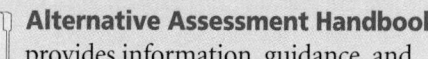

Pages 370–373
The Road to War
With the outbreak of war in Europe, Americans responded with claims of neutrality. Yet as the war dragged on, the need to defend American commercial and political interests drew the United States toward active involvement in the struggle.

 Pages 375–378
The United States Declares War
The United States struggled to avoid the horrors of World War I. But the nation could not prevent its slow slide into the conflict.

 Pages 379–383
Americans on the European Front
On entering the war, the United States saw itself merely as "associate" to the Allies. The Americans were quickly promoted to a leading role, however. Yankee soldiers and volunteers poured onto foreign battle-fields and served nobly in many capacities.

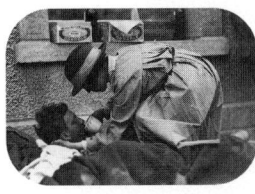

 Pages 384–387
On the Home Front
World War I was fought at home, too. To win that war, the government took control of the economy—and of people's minds—to an extent never before attempted.

 Pages 388–391
Global Peacemaker
President Wilson's lofty vision for peace was brought back to earth by contentious allies and Congress. Meanwhile, many Americans experienced keen disappointment over postwar conditions at home.

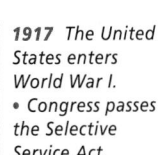

1917 The United States enters World War I.
• Congress passes the Selective Service Act.

1918 Congress passes the last of the Sedition and Espionage Acts.
• President Wilson announces his peace plan.

1919 The states ratify the Eighteenth Amendment, prohibiting the manufacture and sale of alcohol.

1920 Warren G. Harding is elected United States President.

| 1917 | 1918 | 1919 | 1920 | 1921 |

1917 The Russian Revolution ends the reign of the czars.

1918 Germany surrenders to the Allies.
• Women over 30 win the right to vote in Britain.

1919 The Versailles Treaty marks the official end of World War I.
• The Allies establish the League of Nations.

1920 Adolf Hitler helps organize the Nazi party in Germany.

Media and Technology

 Transparency
Time Lines, E-6

Alternative Assessment

As an ongoing chapter project, students can prepare an in-depth essay or oral report describing a particular diplomatic, political, or military event of World War I and explain how the event affected life in the United States during that time.

Explain that finished projects will be assessed according to the following standards:
• **Unacceptable** Projects are not attempted, or fail to meet requirements outlined.
• **Limited/Acceptable** Projects are based on material from the textbook and attempt to explain the importance of the events to the United States.
• **Extensive/Commendable** Projects are based on some outside research and provide clear explanation of the importance of the event to the United States.
• **Extraordinary/Outstanding** Projects are based on considerable outside research and thoroughly explain the importance of the event to the United States.

For more information and guidance on alternative assessment trends and strategies, see the Alternative Assessment Handbook in the Resource Directory on page 368.

The Road to War

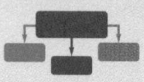

1. FOCUS

Connecting to the Big Idea

See page 368B. Explain that when war first broke out in Europe, most Americans wished to maintain strict neutrality. However, as the war continued, the United States moved toward more active involvement. Ask what prompted this change in direction.

Objectives

● Identify World War I as a conflict of global origins and dimensions.
● Describe the new weapons and military techniques used in the war.
● Explain how the United States responded to the war with calls for neutrality and for war preparedness.

Bellringer

Ask students to define the word *neutral*. Ask them to think of situations in which they chose to remain neutral and others in which they took a stand. What conditions encouraged them to take a stand rather than remain neutral?

Reading Strategy

Reading for Evidence Ask students to find evidence as they read the section that Americans responded to the war with "calls for neutrality and for war preparedness," as stated in the key concepts on page 370.

The Road to War

SECTION PREVIEW

With the outbreak of war in Europe, Americans responded with claims of neutrality. Yet as the war dragged on, the need to defend American commercial and political interests drew the United States toward active involvement in the struggle.

Key Concepts
• World War I was a conflict of global origins and dimensions.
• The war saw the introduction of destructive new weapons and techniques.
• Americans responded with calls for neutrality and for war preparedness.

Key Terms, People, and Places
Central Powers, Allies; Kaiser Wilhelm, autocrat

Soldiers in World War I wore gas masks such as this to protect themselves from poison gas, a horrible new weapon introduced in the war.

B y the early 1900s, war in Europe was hardly a new phenomenon. The Germans had fought often with France over Alsace-Lorraine, the coal- and iron-rich region near the border between the two countries. Austria-Hungary had fought to hold onto the many ethnic groups subject to its control. Russia's ancient quest for a warm-water port had led to frequent clashes on its frontiers. The French and British had warred repeatedly over territorial claims in Europe and in their colonies.

In 1914 all five of Europe's major powers went to war. The conflict—eventually known as World War I—divided them into two sides: Germany and Austria-Hungary made up the **Central Powers**; Russia, France, and Great Britain were called the **Allies**.

Archduke Francis Ferdinand: his assassination sparked the fighting.

Each side felt confident of swift victory. Six weeks, experts said, and it would all be over. The experts were wrong. Relatively equal in force and ability, the two sides quickly reached a bloody stalemate that would last more than four years and cost millions of lives. ★

What Caused World War I?

A complicated system of secret treaties had developed among the nations of Europe during the late nineteenth century. Designed to bolster each nation's security, the treaties bound the great powers to come to each other's aid in the event of attack. For many decades this system created a fragile balance of power that no nation dared disrupt. In 1914 the very system that had kept the peace led its creators into war.

The spark that ignited World War I was the June 28, 1914, assassination of the heir to the Austrian-Hungarian throne, Archduke Francis Ferdinand, and his wife, Sophie. They were gunned down during a visit to Sarajevo, the capital of Bosnia, a province within the Austrian-Hungarian Empire.

At the time of the assassinations, Bosnia was the focal point of a dispute between Austria-Hungary and the neighboring nation of Serbia. This dispute involved Serbia's efforts to achieve union with ethnic Serbs living in Bosnia by promoting Bosnian resistance to Austrian-Hungarian rule.

The Austrian-Hungarian government was convinced that Serbia was behind the assassinations, and used the event as an excuse to crush its small enemy. In late July Austria-Hungary insisted that Serbia apologize and made a number of other demands that interfered with Serbia's sovereignty. When Serbia refused to meet every one of the demands, Austria-Hungary declared war.

RESOURCE DIRECTORY

Teaching Resources

Reproducible Lesson Plan found in the Unit 3 folder, p. 75, provides a summary of the Section 1 lesson plan content.

Alternate Lesson Plan: Learning Styles found in the Alternate Lesson Plans folder, p. 100, helps students create a graphic organizer showing the steps leading to World War I and is particularly effective for visual learners.

Guided Reading and Review found in the Unit 3 folder, p. 80, provides a structure for reading and mastering the key concepts and reviewing the key terms for Section 1. (Guided Practice)

★ **Primary Source Activity** Thoughts on the War, found in the Unit 3 folder, p. 96, presents a passage written by Walter Hines Page, the United States ambassador to Great Britain, to show predictions about the consequences of World War I.

The Conflict Expands

The Austrian-Hungarian declaration of war set off a chain reaction that worked its way through Europe's complex web of alliances. Nation after nation became entangled. Serbia had the promise of protection from Russia, so Russia started amassing its troops. Two days later, Germany, Austria-Hungary's chief ally, demanded that Russia stop its mobilization. Russia refused. At that point, Russia's ally, France, began to ready its troops. Germany realized that soon it would be trapped between France attacking from the west and Russia from the east. So Germany too mobilized and, on August 1, declared war on Russia. Convinced that the French were ready to invade, Germany's military leaders decided to strike first. To reach France as fast as possible, however, they had to pass through Luxembourg and Belgium. This invasion brought Great Britain, Belgium's protector, into the conflict. A large proportion of the European continent was now at war.

Stalemate In earlier wars, a forceful offense led by a heroic cavalry often was enough to secure victory. Now, defensive forces could use modern firepower to stop such advances. In September 1914, German forces had advanced to within 30 miles of Paris. There, at the river Marne, a combined French and British force stopped their progress. Both sides then dug in. Holed up in a line of muddy, lice- and rat-infested trenches, the two sides faced each other across an empty "no man's land" (see the illustration on page 372). For months each side tried to reach the other's lines to destroy or at least push back the enemy. But neither side was able to gain more than a few miles, and that only at appalling human cost.

Meanwhile, an Austrian army was taking Belgrade, the Serbian capital. Combined German and Austrian-Hungarian forces were pushing the Russian lines back. At the end of 1914, the Ottoman Empire, centered in what is now Turkey, entered the war on the side of the Central Powers; and in the spring of 1915, Italy joined the Allies. Many more costly battles took place, but without significant gain for either side.

European Alliances in World War I

Geography and History: Interpreting Maps
Before the war, Europe was a land of empires and alliances. Thus when Austria-Hungary declared war on Serbia, much of the continent was drawn into the conflict. *Based on this map, which side, if any, had a geographical advantage in the war? Explain.*

Modern Warfare The number of soldiers killed or wounded was horrifying. Industrialization had produced new killing machines of terrible efficiency. In 1914 the youth of Europe had marched off to fight, eager for a chance at heroism. Ripped apart by machine guns, hand grenades, or artillery shells, and asphyxiated or disabled by poison gases, soldiers found that heroism came at a ghastly price.

"It was the machine gun that froze the front," one historian has written. If soldiers charging across no-man's land toward the enemy survived the shelling that rained down upon them, the enemy's machine guns, firing 450 rounds a minute, mowed them down. The generals, unaccustomed to the new weaponry, were confused. Again and again they gave the order to attack. But such tactics produced only a mounting pile of infantry dead. In one 1916 battle, for example, the British suffered 60,000 casualties in a single day of combat.

Morale sank. Desperate, troops began using any tactic available. They slaughtered prisoners of war. Erasing the distinction between soldier

SOURCE READINGS

 Source Readings on p. 396 will connect literature selections and primary source excerpts to historical events discussed in this section.

---

2. INSTRUCT

Explain/Discuss

Discuss the reasons why Serbia, Russia, Germany, France, Great Britain, and Austria-Hungary each became involved in the early days of the war. Then ask why the system of secret alliances that bound the nations of Europe to one another failed to maintain the peace. Ask in what way the system of alliances itself contributed to the war.

Discuss the possibility of being both neutral and prepared. Did building up arms and troops ensure that the United States would enter the war? Why or why not?

Analyze

Ask students to analyze why the United States was at first so removed from the conflict in Europe. Have students list the forces that beckoned the United States toward war and then to rank them in order of strength.

In Depth

Historical Misconceptions

Allied newspapers published graphic accounts of German atrocities in order to muster support. One common story was that German troops chopped off the hands of Belgian babies. After the war, when censorship was lifted, people learned that wartime propaganda had been efficient. Journalist William Shepherd reported: "I couldn't find atrocities . . . [or even] photographs of children whose hands had been cut off or who had been wounded or injured in other ways."

Trenches provided excellent defense. Combined with the machine gun, they neutralized the opponent's offense.

Answer to ...

Answers will vary but should indicate that students have thought carefully about the implications of foreign alliances.

Activity

Cooperative Learning

Time: One class period.

Activity: Prepare a briefing book on the countries of Europe for President Wilson.

Grouping: Groups of four to six students with each group being the expert on one nation.

Purpose: To prepare a document describing the major nations of Europe in June 1914, including sections on the head of state and form of government; major geographical features; economy, including major projects and trade partners; military leaders; and ethnic and religious composition of the population. Each student should assume responsibility for one section of the document for the group's assigned nation.

Roles: Researchers, writers.

Outcome: Students will identify and outline significant information on each of the major powers of Europe at the onset of World War I.

Enrichment

Britain's Queen Victoria, who reigned from 1837 to 1901, has been called "Europe's grandmother" because so many monarchs were descended from her five children. Ask students to make a family tree tracing Victoria's descendants up to 1920. Ask them to highlight the names of the cousins who reigned during World War I.

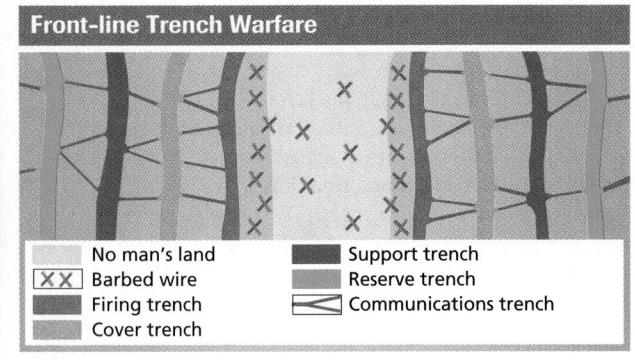

Front-line Trench Warfare

No man's land	Support trench
Barbed wire	Reserve trench
Firing trench	Communications trench
Cover trench	

Interpreting Charts
Trench networks allowed armies to fire on the enemy, get supplies and reinforcements, and find cover from enemy fire. But soldiers leaving the trench to press the battle faced deadly machine gun fire. *How did trench warfare contribute to a stalemate in World War I?*

and civilian, they burned fields and poisoned wells. On the seas, German submarines struck any ship they believed to be carrying arms to the Allies. A British naval blockade slowly starved the German people. Soon the war was one of attrition—meaning that each side tried to wear down the enemy gradually by inflicting enormous losses.

The United States today has many security alliances that are similar to those that drew so many countries into World War I. Do you think the United States should be willing to fight to protect the interests of its allies?

The American Response

July 29: AUSTRIA DECLARES WAR, RUSHES VAST ARMY INTO SERBIA; RUSSIA MASSES 80,000 MEN ON BORDER

August 2: GERMANY DECLARES WAR ON RUSSIA; FRANCE PREPARES TO JOIN HER ALLY

Americans read these 1914 headlines with mounting alarm. How could all these great countries of beauty, taste, and culture be at war with one another?

Some Americans felt personally involved. More than a third of the nation's 92 million people were first- or second-generation immi-

grants who still felt close ties to their old countries. About a quarter of these were German American, and another eighth were Irish American. Both groups harbored hostile feelings toward Great Britain due to past conflicts and the current war in Europe.

Most Americans favored the Allies, however. Germany, one of the Central Powers, was ruled by **Kaiser Wilhelm.** The Kaiser, or emperor, was an **autocrat**—a ruler with unlimited power. Americans saw the Germans as a people of frightening militarism and cold-blooded efficiency. Reporters who had rushed to Belgium in August 1914 to witness the German advance toward France fueled this view. Richard Harding Davis described the event for New York *Tribune* readers as "not men marching, but a force of nature like a tidal wave, an avalanche, or a river flooding its banks."

A t the sight of the first few regiments of the enemy we were thrilled. After, for three hours, they had passed in one unbroken steel-gray column, we were bored. But when hour after hour passed and there was no halt, no breathing time, no open spaces in the ranks, the thing became uncanny, unhuman.

Other Americans held a more neutral but cynical attitude. They looked at the European war as a great financial boon to the United States. One newspaper said that the war was "a

 RESOURCE DIRECTORY

Teaching Resources

supreme opportunity for American manufacturers to gain world-wide markets."

The United States Declares Neutrality In the end, the nation's business interests had a stronger impact on United States policy than the feelings of the American people. The war imperiled United States commercial investments overseas, which between 1897 and 1914 had increased fivefold, from $700 million to $3.5 billion. Now, German submarines and a British naval blockade of the North Sea were putting those investments at risk. To protect those investments, the United States declared itself officially neutral, protested the actions of both sides, and tried to act as peacemaker.

The Preparedness Movement At the same time that they pushed for neutrality, American business leaders who had strong commercial ties to Great Britain urged that the United States get ready for war. Their watchword was preparedness, and they wanted their country to be ready to aid Great Britain, if necessary. In December 1914, preparedness advocates organized a National Security League to "promote patriotic education and national sentiment and service among people of the United States."

By the late summer of 1915, the movement had won over President Wilson. The government set up camps to train American men for combat. By the summer of 1916, President Wilson and Congress had worked out an agreement for large increases in the armed forces.

The Peace Movement When world war broke out, a peace movement also swung into gear. In the early 1900s, peace advocates consisted primarily of former populists, midwest progressives, and social reformers.

Women were particularly active in the movement. On August 29, suffragists, dressed in black and carrying a banner of a dove, marched down New York City's Fifth Avenue to the slow beat of a muffled drum. In November 1915, a group of women and men social reformers founded the American Union Against Militarism.

Congress also had some peace advocates. Aiming to remind Americans of the costs of war, they insisted on paying for preparedness through a tax on the makers of arms and through higher income taxes. Claude Kitchin, member of Congress from North Carolina, predicted that when people discovered "that the income tax will have to pay for the increase in the army and navy, . . . preparedness will not be so popular with them as it now is."

Congress did increase taxes, but the preparedness movement remained strong. As you will read, the United States could not resist the forces pushing it toward entry into the conflict.

Jane Addams, second from the left in the front row, joined the delegation on this "peace ship," which journeyed to Europe in 1915 with hopes of ending the war.

SECTION 1 REVIEW

Key Terms, People, and Places
1. Define (a) Central Powers, (b) Allies,
2. Identify (a) Kaiser Wilhelm, (b) autocrat.

Key Concepts
3. Why did the dispute between Austria-Hungary and Serbia escalate?
4. For what reasons was this war so destructive?

5. What were the reactions in the United States to the outbreak of World War I?

Critical Thinking
6. **Checking Consistency** The alliance system in Europe in 1914 was designed to maintain peace. Yet it seemed to make the conflict worse once the fighting began. Explain this apparent inconsistency.

Quiz found in the Unit 3 folder, p. 81, covers the main ideas in this section as well as the key terms.

3. ASSESS

Section 1 Review Answers
1. (a) Central Powers, see p. 370, (b) Allies, see p. 370

2. (a) Kaiser Wilhelm, see p. 372, (b) autocrat, see p. 372

3. A system of mutual defense alliances brought Russia to Serbia's defense. This led Germany, Austria's ally, to mobilize for war against Russia and Russia's ally, France. The Germans' invasion of neutral Belgium on their way to invade France drew Great Britain, Belgium's ally, into the war.

4. Industrialization had produced more destructive weapons, namely machine guns. Thus, deaths rose and desperate troops began to use any tactics available including killing civilians.

5. Most Americans were pro-British. President Wilson decided on a position of neutrality. Both the preparedness movement, which urged the United States to get ready for war, and the peace movement were very active.

6. Possible answer: Once a war starts, alliances tend to widen the conflict by involving nations with no real interest in or concern with the issues that caused the war.

Reteach
Ask students to correct each of the following incorrect statements:
• World War I began with the assassination of a German archduke in Bosnia.
• Great Britain and Germany fought together against Russia and Austria-Hungary.

4. CLOSE

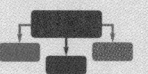

Reinforcing the Big Idea

When war began in Europe in 1914, the United States resolved to preserve its neutrality. Given the nation's commercial and personal interests abroad, this policy would be difficult to maintain. The next section describes how the nation finally joined the war.

TOOLBOX

Critical Thinking

Identifying Alternatives

Focus Students will identify and analyze alternatives, or possible solutions to a problem.

Instruct As a class, work through the question in steps 1 to 3. You might want to divide students into small groups for consideration of step 4. Ask each group to submit a sentence stating the goal of the United States regarding the war in Europe and at least three steps likely to achieve that goal. Have each group describe which of these steps the nation actually took.

Extend See the Historian's Toolbox Activity in the Resource Directory below.

Answers

1. (a) World War I and the United States' response to it. (b) No, they differ in their approach.

2. (a) Passage A proposes that the United States react without judgment and without acting for or against any power. (b) Passage B suggests that the United States act forcefully and swiftly for the side that it determines to be "right." (c) Passage A proposes caution and restraint; Passage B proposes swift action.

3. Possible answers: (a) It is difficult to expect people not to judge or feel strong sympathy with one side or another. (b) If the United States does not act in its own best interests, its interests may be injured. (c) Roosevelt does not clarify what he means by "[doing] ill." (d) Roosevelt does not give an answer to this question. It is presumed that this standard is clearly understood by all.

4. Possible answer: (a) A desirable goal is staying out of the war or joining the war on behalf of the side America feels is most worthy of its help. (b) Make sure students explain their answers.

GEOGRAPHY   GRAPHS & CHARTS

HISTORIAN'S TOOLBOX

CRITICAL THINKING   HISTORICAL EVIDENCE

Identifying Alternatives

Identifying alternatives means finding one or more possible solutions to a problem. In the previous section, you read about the conflict in the United States over how to react to the war raging in Europe. The passages on this page make the case for two responses the United States might have made. Passage A presents the views of then President Woodrow Wilson, as stated in August 1914. Passage B, which was published in January 1915, presents the thoughts of former President Theodore Roosevelt.

Use the following steps to identify and analyze the alternatives presented in the passages.

1. Identify the nature of the problem under discussion. Before you can identify alternative solutions to a problem, you must understand what the problem is. (a) What is the issue that both passages address? (b) Does each passage present the same approach to the problem?

2. Identify the solutions proposed in the two passages. (a) What does Passage A suggest is the proper response of the United States to the war raging in Europe? (b) How does Passage B propose that the United States respond to the war? (c) In what ways are these two viewpoints similar or different?

3. Evaluate the potential effectiveness of each view. Consider the strengths and weaknesses of each proposal. For example, you might ask the following questions about Passages A and B: (a) What difficulties do you see in Wilson's suggestion that the United States not judge the actions of other nations? (b) What might happen if the United States acts in a "disinterested" way, as Wilson suggests? (c) Does Roosevelt make clear what he means when he refers to a nation that "does ill"? (d) Does Roosevelt explain the basis by which nations should be judged "highly civilized" or "well behaved"?

4. Consider other alternatives. Recall the nature of the problem under discussion. Then, using insights you gained above, think of other possible solutions. Ask: (a) What should be the goal of the United States in responding to the war in Europe? (b) What steps are most likely to achieve that goal?

Passage A

"My thought is of America.... [T]his great country of ours ... should show herself in this time of peculiar trial a Nation fit beyond others to exhibit the fine poise of undisturbed judgment, the dignity of self-control, the efficiency of dispassionate [unemotional] action; a Nation that neither sits in judgment upon others nor is disturbed in her own counsels and which keeps herself fit and free to do what is honest and disinterested and truly serviceable for the peace of the world."

Woodrow Wilson, *Appeal for Neutrality*, August 19, 1914

Passage B

"Our true course should be to judge each nation on its conduct, unhesitatingly to antagonize every nation that does ill [at the point] it does ill, and equally without hesitation to act....

One of the greatest of international duties ought to be the protection of small, highly civilized, well-behaved and self-respecting states from oppression and conquest by their powerful military neighbors....

I feel in the strongest way that we should have interfered, at least to the extent of the most emphatic diplomatic protest and at the very outset—and then by whatever further action was necessary—[when Germany invaded Belgium]."

Theodore Roosevelt, *America and the World War*, 1915

 RESOURCE DIRECTORY

Teaching Resources

Historian's Toolbox Activity Identifying Alternatives, found in the Unit 3 folder, p. 94, extends students' opportunity to practice this skill by analyzing three 1993 policy proposals for United States response to the war in Bosnia-Herzegovina.

The United States Declares War

SECTION PREVIEW

The United States struggled to avoid the horrors of World War I. But the nation could not prevent its slow slide into the conflict.

Key Concepts

- Germany's unrestricted submarine warfare had a powerful impact on American attitudes toward the war.
- Wilson won reelection in 1916 based on his success at keeping the United States out of the war.
- A series of events finally pushed Congress to declare war on the Central Powers—an act that was met with mixed reactions by the American people.

Key Terms, People, and Places

U-boat, *Lusitania,* Zimmerman note

F rom 1915 to 1917, growing conflict between the United States and Germany increased the popularity of the preparedness position and intensified the pressure for war. Ultimately, both Congress and the President were pushed toward entering World War I on the side of the Allies.

German Submarine Warfare

One factor pushing the United States toward war was the German use of submarine warfare. This tactic was effective militarily, but it cost the Germans dearly in terms of American public opinion.

The German **U-boat,** short for *Unterseeboot,* or submarine, was a terrifying new weapon that changed the rules of naval warfare. Submarine attacks depended on the element of surprise, so unlike other naval ships, U-boats issued no warning to their targets. This situation troubled many Americans. Though the British blockade threatened freedom of the seas

and led to the slow starvation of the German people, the American public felt that such action was reasonable during wartime. In contrast, German attempts to break the blockade with submarines seemed unfair, even uncivilized.

The British encouraged such anti-German feeling. Shortly after the war began, the British cut the transatlantic cable connecting Germany and the United States. All news of the European front henceforth flowed through London. Its pro-Allied bias helped shape the opinion of the people in the United States in favor of punishing Germany for its alleged atrocities.

American public opinion of the Germans sank even lower on May 7, 1915, when a U-boat sighted the ***Lusitania,*** a British passenger liner, in the Irish Sea. Suspecting correctly that the ship carried weapons for the Allies, the U-boat fired on the liner. Eighteen minutes later the *Lusitania* disappeared beneath the waves along with its 1,198 passengers. Included among the dead were 128 Americans, who had boarded the *Lusitania* in spite of German warnings to stay off British ships. Nevertheless, the American press went wild over this German act of "barbarism."

Wilson counseled patience. He directed his secretary of state, William Jennings Bryan, to demand that Germany renounce unrestricted submarine warfare and make payments to the victims' survivors. Germany's reply that the ship carried small arms and ammunition did not quiet American anger.

Wilson ordered a second, stronger note. This time, however, Bryan refused to sign it, fearing it would lead to war. Bryan also insisted that Wilson send an equally strong note to

This German poster urges its U-boats on in their mission. The translation is, "Submarines: [come] out!"

1. FOCUS

Connecting to the Big Idea

See page 368B. Explain that from 1915 to 1917, relations between the United States and Germany deteriorated, and pressure for war increased. Ask why the United States finally declared war on the Central Powers.

Objectives

- Describe the impact of Germany's unrestricted submarine warfare on American attitudes toward the war.
- Identify President Wilson's avoidance of war as the key factor that helped him win the election of 1916.
- Explain why the United States Congress finally declared war on the Central Powers and describe the mixed reaction of the American people to the declaration.

Bellringer

Ask students what makes a country one of the great nations of the world. What domestic conditions and foreign alliances characterize a great nation? What countries are great nations today? Why?

Reading Strategy

Solving Problems Have students imagine that they are members of Congress in 1917. They must decide whether the United States should go to war with Germany and the other Central Powers. As they read the section, students should list the events that influence their decision.

Reproducible Lesson Plan found in the Unit 3 folder, p. 76, provides a summary of the Section 2 lesson plan content.

Alternate Lesson Plan: Cooperative Learning found in the Alternate Lesson Plans folder, p. 101, helps groups of students prepare and present interviews exploring different American opinions about the conflict in Europe.

Guided Reading and Review found in the Unit 3 folder, p. 82, provides a structure for reading and mastering the key concepts and reviewing the key terms for Section 2. (Guided Practice)

Media and Technology

 Transparency
Cause and Effect, F-8

Explain/Discuss

Discuss the reasons Germany said that submarines could not follow the traditions of international law. Ask students to respond to the German argument that the submarines should not be denied their weapon of surprise.

Ask students to list the options open to President Wilson in April 1917 in dealing with the war and to consider the consequences of each option.

Ask students to discuss whether President Wilson acted in good faith in the 1916 election when he campaigned on his success in maintaining the nation's neutrality. What evidence is there either to back up Wilson's assertion of neutrality or to show that he supported Great Britain?

Answer to ...

MAKING CONNECTIONS

The public perceived the Germans as militaristic and coldly efficient. Thus they judged German actions more cruel than those of the British, even though British actions had similarly harmful effects on noncombatants.

In Depth

Biography

In 1916, Jeannette Rankin of Montana (1880–1973) became the first woman elected to Congress. A staunch pacifist, she was in the minority in the House of Representatives in voting against the war resolution. "Little woman, you cannot afford not to vote," a veteran House member whispered to her prior to the vote. "You represent the womanhood of the country." When the roll call came, however, Rankin announced: "I want to stand by my country, but I cannot vote for war. I vote no."

American public opinion was extremely critical of Germany and its use of U-boats. The cartoon above right suggests that Germany felt no remorse for the loss of American lives. However, Germany did warn travelers—including passengers of the *Lusitania*—to stay out of the war zone (left).

Great Britain protesting its blockade. Wilson refused and Bryan resigned. His successor, Robert Lansing, signed the note to Germany. In response, Germany promised to stop sinking passenger ships without warning, as long as the ship's crew offered no resistance to German search or seizure.

Still, U-boats continued to sink British and French liners. The loss of American lives was small but infuriating. Wilson protested and, in response, Germany pledged restraint. Because Wilson could not threaten force without entering the war, however, he felt fairly powerless. But during this time, Wilson did embrace the concept of preparedness. He also authorized New York bankers to make a huge loan to the Allies. American neutrality was beginning to lose its meaning. ✪

MAKING CONNECTIONS

Consider public feelings about Germany discussed in Section 1. How might these feelings explain public condemnation of U-boat warfare—and public acceptance of the British blockade?

Moving Toward the Brink of War

On February 1, 1917, Germany once again began unrestricted submarine warfare. Wilson had been reelected in November of 1916 with the slogan "He kept us out of war." Now his hope of maintaining freedom of the seas—and American neutrality—was dashed. Two days later, the United States broke off diplomatic relations with Germany, and Wilson asked Congress for permission to arm American merchant ships.

The Zimmerman Telegram In the Senate, a group of antiwar senators tried to prevent action on Wilson's request by using a filibuster. A filibuster is a tactic in which senators take the floor, begin talking, and refuse to stop talking to permit a vote on a measure. While this was taking place, the British revealed the contents of an intercepted German telegram to Mexico. In it, Arthur Zimmerman, Germany's foreign secretary, wrote:

> We shall endeavor to keep the United States neutral. In the event of this not succeeding, we make Mexico a proposal of alliance. . . . : Make war together, make peace together, . . . and . . . Mexico is to

RESOURCE DIRECTORY

Teaching Resources

✪ **Critical Thinking Activity** Identifying Central Issues: Provocations of War, found in the Unit 3 folder, p. 95, encourages students to apply this skill in examining a 1917 political cartoon.

✪ **Visual Learning Activity** Uncle Sam's Pledge, found in the Unit 3 folder, p. 102, uses a Library of Congress drawing to show how symbols were used to promote public support for World War I.

reconquer the lost territory in Texas, New Mexico, and Arizona.

Neither Wilson nor Mexico took this telegram—the so-called **Zimmerman note**—seriously. Its release, however, scored another propaganda victory for Great Britain. War fever mounted.

Revolution in Russia By early 1917, Russia already had suffered enormous casualties in the war: 1.8 million killed, 2.4 million taken prisoner, and 2.8 million sick or wounded. Austrian and German forces had advanced deep into Russian territory. Ill-shod, ill-fed, and miserably equipped, the Russians fell back farther and farther into their interior.

Then, in March 1917, revolutionaries overthrew Czar Nicholas II, Russia's autocratic monarch, replacing him with a republican government. This event elated the prowar faction in the United States. Concern over being allied with the czar had helped slow the nation's move toward entry into the war. By overthrowing the czar, the Russian revolution removed a last stumbling block to a full American commitment to the Allies.

The War Resolution Meanwhile, between March 16 and March 18, Germany sank the United States ships *City of Memphis, Illinois,* and *Vigilancia.* On March 20 Wilson's cabinet voted unanimously for war. Casting the issue in idealistic terms, on April 2 Wilson told Congress that "The world must be made safe for democracy." ✪

I *t is a fearful thing to lead this great peaceful people into war, the most terrible and disastrous of all wars, civilization itself seeming to be in the balance. But the right is more precious than peace.*

Antiwar forces were devastated. Social worker Jane Addams used her considerable prestige to appeal directly to the President, but to no avail. An Emergency Peace Federation was formed to pressure Congress not to say yes to war. But a war resolution passed 82 to 6 in the Senate and 373 to 50 in the House. On April 6, the President signed it.

The United States entry into World War I broke some long-standing alliances among progressives.

President Woodrow Wilson reluctantly led the nation into World War I.

Making the World Safe for Democracy

A ccording to President Wilson, the United States entered World War I to make the world safe for democracy. By fighting its enemies, Wilson said, the United States would "bring peace and safety to all nations and make the world at last free." On a number of occasions since that time, the United States has followed a similar policy—using military action as well as diplomatic means in an attempt to achieve peace, security, and democracy.

After World War II, the United States, acting under this policy, committed itself to strong resistance to communism. This policy contributed to American involvement in several wars and military actions. In July 1950, for example, the United Nations Security Council backed the use of military action to combat the communists in North Korea who were trying to conquer South Korea. Led by the United States, the South Koreans received "assistance to repel armed attack and restore international peace and security in the area."

In the Vietnam War, the United States gave military and economic aid to the southeast Asian country of South Vietnam in an attempt to stop a takeover by communist North Vietnam. Despite the efforts of thousands of American troops, South Vietnam fell to communist forces in 1975.

More recently, President Bush echoed Wilson's policy in 1991 when he obtained Congress's approval to send American troops to liberate the Persian Gulf nation of Kuwait from an invasion by its neighbor Iraq. The action came after about six months of diplomatic pressures and economic sanctions against Iraq. *How successful do you think the United States has been in its policy of making "the world safe for democracy"?*

U-boat, see p. 375 · *Lusitania*, see p. 375 · Zimmerman note, see p. 377

Analyze

Ask students to analyze the reasons for declaring war against Germany and then to decide which was the most compelling. Have students explain their reasoning.

Activity

Writing Editorials

Ask students to assume the role of editor of a United States newspaper in early March 1917. Students should write an editorial either urging the United States into the war or cautioning the nation against further involvement in the conflict.

Enrichment

Ask students to research and report on either the Russian Revolution of 1917 or the Irish uprising of 1916. Reports should briefly describe the rebellion's goals, its leaders, the main events, and its effect on the United States.

Answer to ...

Links Across Time

Possible answers: Successful, because the United States' involvement in the Persian Gulf War let other countries know that the United States would not tolerate conflicts that threaten world peace; not successful, because as the century draws to a close, people in many countries are still struggling to achieve democracy.

3. ASSESS

Section 2 Review Answers

1. (a) U-boat, see p. 375, (b) *Lusitania,* see p. 375, (c) Zimmerman note, see p. 377

2. The United States broke off diplomatic relations with Germany, and President Wilson asked Congress for permission to prepare American merchant ships for war.

3. He ran on a combined peace and social reform platform. The party of his opponent, Charles Evans Hughes, did not present a unified platform. It was divided among advocates of preparedness, war, and social reform.

4. Russia was one of the Allies but a dictatorship. It had been difficult for Americans to think of joining the war on the Allied side as long as the Russian czar remained in power. When he was overthrown, Americans became much more sympathetic to Russia.

5. Feelings were divided. Fifty-six members of Congress, including Jeannette Rankin, voted against the war resolution. Most former progressives went along with the resolution, but some split off and continued to work in the peace movements. Many saw the war as an opportunity for the United States to enter a new age of peace and democracy.

6. Possible answer: The United States could have avoided the confrontations with Germany by keeping its commercial vessels out of waters patrolled by U-boats. This may have been politically impossible given that many commercial interests in the United States were at stake. It also may have been more costly to lose the commercial ties than to engage in war.

Reteach

Ask students to write the following events in chronological order:
- Germany begins unrestricted submarine warfare.
- A German U-boat sinks the *Lusitania*.
- Congress declares war.
- Bryan resigns as secretary of state.
- Wilson reveals the contents of the Zimmerman note.

 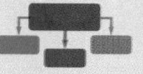
4. CLOSE

Reinforcing the Big Idea

Although the United States tried to maintain its neutrality, events pushed Congress into a declaration of war. The next section describes the role of Americans overseas in the war.

Jeanette Rankin of Montana, the first woman member of the House of Representatives, cast one of the few votes against the United States war resolution. She remained opposed to the war and lost her congressional seat in 1919.

Teddy Roosevelt pushed for war. La Follette favored peace. Settlement worker Lillian Wald resigned from the American Union Against Militarism, but Jane Addams stayed a member. Carrie Chapman Catt dedicated her suffrage association to serve the war effort, an act that prompted President Wilson to tell the Senate in 1918 that the passage of woman suffrage was "vital to the winning of the war."

Why Did the United States Go to War?

After years of reluctance, the United States was finally at war. Why? In the United States people believed that Germany's refusal to respect American claims to neutrality had forced the United States to retaliate. From Germany's perspective, however, its refusal was understandable. "Neutral noncombatant" hardly described the United States between 1914 and 1917. United States money and munitions had been flowing to the Allies long before its troops left for Europe.

⭐The decision also can be seen as the result of long-standing commercial interests. As Jeannette Rankin, the first woman member of Congress, said in defense of her vote against the war, "I knew we were asked to vote for a commercial war." Indeed, in 1912, Wilson had announced, "Our industries have expanded to such a point that they will burst their jackets if they cannot find a free outlet to the markets of the world." In addition, British propaganda had helped promote anti-German feeling. Finally, many believed that the world *could* be made safe for democracy. If the United States hoped to benefit from a new world of peace and freedom, then the nation would have to be a player in the drama.

Political commentator Walter Lippmann saw the war as an opportunity for the United States to tap "new sources of energy" in its people that would make "the impossible . . . possible." "We can dare to hope for things which we never dared to hope for in the past," he wrote. Lippmann was convinced that democracy would be realized not just abroad but at home as well. "We shall turn with fresh interest to our own tyrannies—to our Colorado mines, our autocratic steel industries, our sweatshops and our slums."

In short, many Americans felt that the United States was on the brink of greatness. Its participation in World War I would hasten progress toward that goal.

SECTION 2 REVIEW

Key Terms, People, and Places
1. Define (a) U-boat, (b) *Lusitania*, (c) Zimmerman note.

Key Concepts
2. What was the impact in the United States of Germany's unrestricted submarine warfare?
3. State the reason for Wilson's reelection in 1916.
4. Why did the March 1917 revolution in Russia push the United States toward war?

5. How did the American people respond to the declaration of war?

Critical Thinking
6. Identifying Alternatives Consider the causes that brought the United States into World War I. What would the United States have had to do to avoid the conflict altogether? For what reasons did the United States not take such steps?

▶ RESOURCE DIRECTORY

Teaching Resources

 American Profiles Activity found in the Unit 3 folder, p. 90, profiles Jeannette Rankin, the first woman elected to Congress and one of the fifty-six members to vote against United States entry into World War I.

Quiz found in the Unit 3 folder, p. 83, covers the main ideas in this section as well as the key terms.

Americans on the European Front

SECTION 3

Americans on the European Front

SECTION PREVIEW

On entering the war, the United States saw itself merely as "associate" to the Allies. The Americans were quickly promoted to a leading role, however. Yankee soldiers and volunteers poured onto foreign battlefields and served nobly in many capacities.

Key Concepts
• At first, Americans envisioned a limited role for themselves in World War I.
• The role of the United States quickly expanded, and millions of draftees and volunteers, both women and men, became part of the effort.
• American military involvement helped turn the tide of the war.

Key Terms, People, and Places
American Expeditionary Force, armistice; doughboy

The United States was now at war. Would Americans achieve greatness in the mighty conflict? Pacifists looked to the future and saw European battlefields strewn with American corpses. Enthusiastic patriots, anxious for an unrestrained American commitment to the war, saw glory for the nation. United States officials, however, focused on the present and took a more cautious approach.

The United States Slowly Gets Involved

At first, President Wilson envisioned Americans as "associates" in the war, rather than equal partners with the Allies. Congress therefore authorized $3 billion in loans, naval support, supplies, and arms—but did not send troops.

For the Allies, this contribution was not enough. They insisted on an armed force, even a token one, to boost morale. Thus, in June 1917 the United States War Department, which had no formal plans for a European military operation, sent over General John J. "Black Jack" Pershing, a cold, tough veteran of the Spanish-American War, and a contingent of 14,500 men. Pershing quickly realized that he needed more troops.

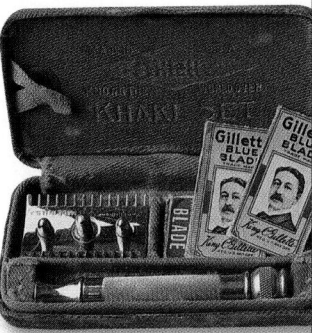

In 1917 American soldiers began marching off to war, carrying items such as this trench shaving kit.

Draftees and Volunteers At the time of Pershing's request, American troop strength fell far short of needs. When the United States entered World War I, the armed forces numbered only 120,000 enlisted men and 80,000 National Guardsmen. Thus, in May 1917 Congress passed a Selective Service Act, authorizing a draft of young men for military service.

During the Civil War, the draft had sparked riots. Now, however, the general feeling that this would be the "war to end all wars" resulted in wide acceptance for the program. By November 1918, over 24 million men had registered for the draft. From those, a lottery picked three million draftees. Volunteers and National Guardsmen made up the remainder of what was called the **American Expeditionary Force** (AEF).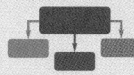

Included in this American force was a new group of people—women. Eleven thousand women volunteered to serve in uniform as nurses, drivers, clerks, and telephone operators. Another 14,000 women served abroad as civilians working for the government or in private agencies. As Addie Hunton and Kathryn Johnson, two of the few African American women who made it to the front, later wrote: "We had the greatest opportunity for service that we have ever known."

The Convoy System In addition to building a fighting force, the War Department also had to worry about getting troops and supplies

---

1. FOCUS

Connecting to the Big Idea

See page 368B. Point out that the United States quickly became fully involved in the war. Ask what roles Americans played abroad. What were the results of American efforts in the war?

Objectives
● Describe the limited role Americans at first envisioned for themselves in World War I.
● Describe how the role of the United States in the war quickly expanded.
● Explain how American military involvement helped to turn the tide of the war.

Bellringer

Are allies automatically equals? Can allies exist without a common enemy? Ask students what relationship allies share.

Reading Strategy

Predicting Content Ask students to skim Section 3, list the main headings and subheadings, and write a sentence or phrase under each heading that predicts the content that follows. When they have finished reading the section, ask students to test their predictions against the actual text.

Reproducible Lesson Plan found in the Unit 3 folder, p. 77, provides a summary of the Section 3 lesson plan content.

Alternate Lesson Plan: Learning Styles found in the Alternate Lesson Plans folder, p. 102, helps students use maps and other information to describe United States participation in the war in Europe and is especially useful for visual learners.

Guided Reading and Review found in the Unit 3 folder, p. 84, provides a structure for reading and mastering the key concepts and reviewing the key terms for Section 3. (Guided Practice)

Primary Source Activity Women on the War Front, found in the Unit 3 folder, p. 97, shows how African American women came to contribute to the war effort through an excerpt from Addie Hunton and Kathryn Johnson's *Two Colored Women with the American Expeditionary Forces*.

Explain/Discuss

Ask students to estimate the original number of U.S. troops sent to Europe with General Pershing (*14,500*) and the total number who eventually served overseas (*two million*). Write the actual numbers on the chalkboard. Ask students to account for the huge disparity between the two numbers. Work with students to list the steps required to create an army large enough to fight a war on that scale.

Ask students to locate on a map the major battles of the war involving American troops.

Analyze

Ask students to analyze Pershing's insistence on keeping the American troops separate from the Allied forces. Why did Pershing want to keep the Americans under American command? Why did some American troops wish to be transferred to French command?

Answer to ...

MAKING CONNECTIONS

Possible answer: The treatment of African Americans was inconsistent with the claim to be making the world safe for democracy, since that rationale seemed to imply that full democracy existed in the United States.

In Depth

Multicultural Perspectives

In 1919, when the 369th United States Infantry marched triumphantly through New York, its sixty-piece band, led by Lieutenant James Europe, switched to jazz when it reached Harlem. The band had played the same music to wildly enthusiastic crowds in Britain, France, Belgium, and Germany.

overseas. Toward this end, officials developed a system that protected merchant and troop ships from German U-boats by surrounding American ships with a convoy of small destroyers. The speed of the destroyers enabled them to mount counterattacks against U-boats or scare them off altogether. Between April and December 1917, merchant marine losses dropped by half.

American Soldiers in Europe "I don't know what the war's about, But I guess, by heck, I'll soon find out!" So went a popular World War I song that expressed the thoughts of the 2 million soldiers who eventually crossed the Atlantic Ocean. Infantrymen were called **doughboys**, a term that originated during the Civil War in reference to the dumpling-shaped buttons on Union infantry uniforms. ⊕

Once the American soldiers had arrived on foreign shores, Pershing did not integrate them with Allied troops, who in Pershing's view had become too accustomed to defensive action. He wanted to save his men's strength for offensive moves.

Segregation occurred not only between the American and Allied troops, but also within the American ranks. The more than 300,000 African Americans who volunteered or were drafted into service were kept separate from white troops. Though many African Americans fought with distinction and 3,925 died or were wounded, most never saw combat. The marines refused to accept African Americans

altogether, and the navy used them for menial tasks only. The army, too, used African Americans mostly for manual labor.

These assignments distressed many African Americans. The 369th Infantry Regiment, who came to be known as the Harlem Hell Fighters, was especially eager to fight. Its members convinced their white officers to loan them to the French, who did not practice segregation. Because of their distinguished service, the French awarded the entire regiment their highest combat medal, the *Croix de Guerre.*

MAKING   CONNECTIONS

Consider Wilson's justification for entering the war, which was discussed in Section 2. Is the military's treatment of African Americans consistent with this justification? Explain.

AMERICAN PROFILES

Mary E. Gladwin

Many women did not wait for American entry into the war to find ways to serve. As early as the fall of 1914, women traveled to Europe as volunteers for the Red Cross, YWCA, or other service organizations. One such volunteer was Mary E. Gladwin.

Gladwin had become a nurse in her thirties after a career in teaching. She served as an American Red Cross volunteer in Georgia,

African American soldiers endured segregation overseas. But that did not keep the 369th Infantry, pictured here, from fighting valiantly and winning recognition for their bravery. ✪

▶ RESOURCE DIRECTORY

Teaching Resources

✪ **Literature Activity** A War Song, found in the Unit 3 folder, p. 99, highlights "Hinky Dinky Parlay-Voo," a song popular with the American Expeditionary Force, to demonstrate the soldiers' outlook during that time.

✪ **American Profiles Activity** found in the Unit 3 folder, p. 91, profiles Henry Johnson, the most famous African American soldier of World War I.

Puerto Rico, and the Philippines during the Spanish-American War, and in Hiroshima, Japan, during the Russo-Japanese War of 1905. After a major flood in Dayton, Ohio, in 1913, she supervised a staff of 110 nurses there.

Gladwin was fifty-three years old when she responded to a call to assist in Europe. As chief nurse in a unit of three doctors and twelve nurses, she set sail on a freighter on September 13, 1914. Her ultimate destination was Belgrade, the capital of Serbia. Awaiting an Austrian occupation, the city was almost deserted.

Gladwin's unit set itself up in a walled hospital complex that stood on a bluff overlooking the Danube and Sava rivers. Aside from the picturesque setting, the situation at the hospital was desperate. Every window had been blown out by the fighting. The volunteers arrived to find no food or equipment and 250 patients waiting for help. Gladwin threw herself into her rounds. With an interpreter, she worked her way through the confusing mixture of German, French, Serbian, and Russian tongues spoken by those at the hospital. Wrote Gladwin,

> I used to tumble into bed at two or three o'clock in the morning, and hear those men. They begged and prayed . . . for help. They swore, they tore their bandages and the nights when I got up (it took all my strength of mind to stay in bed), I knew exactly what I would find . . . the men in their agony tearing off the dressings, the dark streams of blood on the floor.

The hospital lacked blankets and coal for heat. Fleas and lice were everywhere. Pneumonia, pleurisy, scarlet fever, typhoid, and tetanus raged among patients and staff. In March 1915, three nurses and two physicians had to return home. Chief surgeon Dr. Edward Ryan contracted typhus.

The American Red Cross set a date for the recall of all its overseas medical units—October 1, 1915. As the date approached, however, Gladwin's unit was pinned down by fighting in the area and could not move. Although she finally left in November, a year later she was back on the eastern front. For the remainder of the war, she served with the Serbian Red Cross, now from a station in Salonika, Greece. In 1920 the Red Cross awarded her the Florence Nightingale Medal.

Red Cross units had their critics. Before the United States entered the war, some asked what business American volunteers such as Gladwin had in a European war. By helping to heal soldiers and returning them to the front, were they not prolonging the conflict? But when the United States finally entered the war, the experience of people such as Gladwin would greatly assist the work of the Army Medical Corps in saving American lives.

New Factors in the War

As the United States was expanding its involvement in the war, a major development occurred within the alliance. In November 1917, Vladimir Lenin led a new government to power in Russia.

Prior to his takeover, Lenin had been living in Switzerland and had promised to make peace with Germany if he ever gained control in Russia. Thus, Germany had helped arrange his return to Russia in April 1917. By November, Lenin had taken over the country.

Lenin's new regime immediately faced opposition from within the country. When civil war broke out, Lenin made peace with Germany on March 3, 1918.

Russia's exit from the war freed the Germans from the two-front war they had been forced to fight. From March through May 1918, German forces turned all their energies toward pounding at the French and British lines. They finally broke through, and by June 3, they were a mere 56 miles from Paris.

American forces came to the rescue. Marching out from Paris, the men received this word from their leader, Brigadier General James G. Harbord: "We dig no trenches to fall back on. The Marines will hold where they stand." And

The efforts of American women like Mary Gladwin and the nurse shown above saved lives and contributed to the Allies' success. According to the Women's Overseas Service League, 348 women died during the war from bombardments or disease.

Activity

Question and Answer

Ask students in small groups to write *who*, *what*, *where*, *when*, and *why* questions for the section content. After groups exchange question sheets, they should continue to work together to answer the questions.

Enrichment

Ask students to locate the lyrics for some of the songs popular with troops and civilians alike during the war. Possibilities include "Over There," "Tipperary," and "Pack Up Your Troubles."

In Depth

Then and Now

When the war broke out, Wilson asked Americans to be "impartial in thought as well as in action." Even after declaring war against Germany, Wilson saw America as a mere "associate" on the allied side. In the 1990s, the United States assumes much more of a leadership role in global conflict resolution. In January 1991, the United States under President Bush led a coalition including French, British, and Middle Eastern forces against Iraq's Saddam Hussein, who had invaded Kuwait. Of 700,000 troops assembled by the allies, 540,000 were Americans.

Caption Answer to ...

 Interpreting Maps

The Central Powers had made the greatest territorial gains in the east.

3. ASSESS

Section 3 Review Answers

1. (a) American Expeditionary Force, see p. 379, (b) armistice, see p. 383

2. doughboy, see p. 380

3. The convoy system, in which destroyers protected merchant and troop ships from submarine attack; the use of tanks and airplane bombers in the last months of the war.

4. About eleven thousand wore the uniform of the AEF, working primarily as nurses, telephone operators, drivers, and clerks. Another fourteen thousand volunteered for service organizations throughout the war, even before the United States entered the conflict.

 In Depth

Interdisciplinary

One of the inventions that revolutionized twentieth-century warfare was the tank. By mounting the body of an armored car onto a tractor, the British improvised the first armored, tracked vehicle in July 1915. The prototype tank, called "Little Willie," was quickly succeeded by "Big Willie." The new weapon proved itself at the Battle of Cambrai in late1917, where 474 British tanks breached German lines. But the tanks were too slow to exploit the victory, necessitating the development of faster armored vehicles.

they did. At a loss of over half of their forces, they saved Paris, blunted the edge of the German advance, and began to turn the tide of the war.

Allied Counterattack The German command was astounded. "Nerves of the Americans are still unshaken," a general wrote to his headquarters. After turning back Germany at Paris, the Allied counteroffensive began in earnest in July. Using British tanks, a new machine that gave troops protection as well as mobility, the Allies began to break the German lines. On August 8, the battle of Amiens stopped the German advance once and for all. On August 11, German general Erich von Ludendorff sensed that the end was near. He advised Kaiser Wilhelm to seek terms for ending the war with the Allies.

The Allies, however, were not interested in any agreement in which Germany could win concessions from the Allies in return for peace.

They wanted total surrender. In September some 500,000 American troops, assisted by 100,000 French, began to hit the final German strongholds. Soon after the Germans were in full retreat.

The Allies also began to use airplanes to drop bombs. Aerial dogfights already had taken place. Each side had its "aces," such as the American captain Eddie Rickenbacker, who took down twenty-six enemy fighters. Now, Colonel Billy Mitchell organized a fleet of over 1,400 bomb-carrying planes. Although not very effective in this first attempt, aerial bombing raids would be devastating in future warfare.

Armistice The final Allied assault came on September 26. Over a million AEF troops began the drive to expel the Germans from France and cut their supply lines. Many individual acts of heroism shone during these final

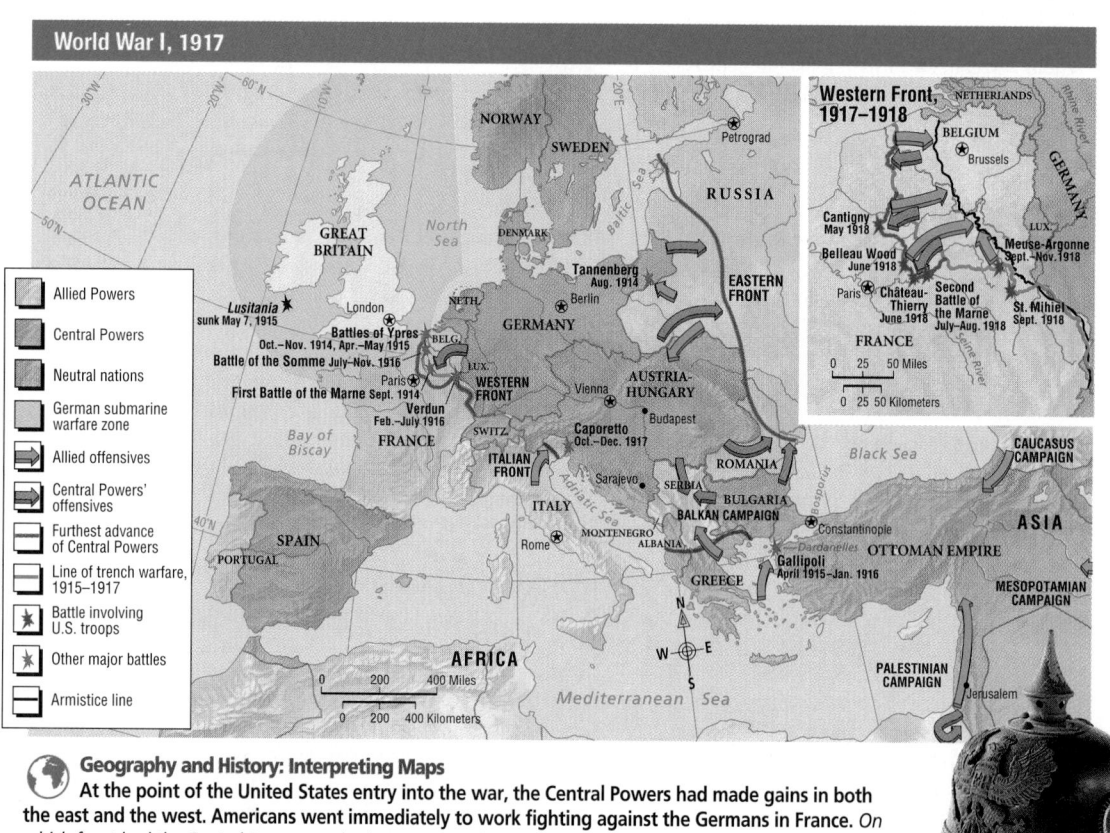

World War I, 1917

 Geography and History: Interpreting Maps
At the point of the United States entry into the war, the Central Powers had made gains in both the east and the west. Americans went immediately to work fighting against the Germans in France. *On which front had the Central Powers made the greatest gains?*

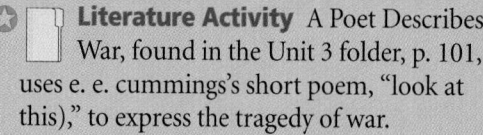 **RESOURCE DIRECTORY**

Teaching Resources

Literature Activity A Poet Describes War, found in the Unit 3 folder, p. 101, uses e. e. cummings's short poem, "look at this)," to express the tragedy of war.

105-horsepower, six-cylinder engine

Driver

Commander

One of four Lewis machine guns

One of two 57-mm pedestal-mounted guns

Armor plating

Pressed steel track plate

months. Sergeant Alvin York of Tennessee, for example, saved an entire platoon by picking off machine gunners with his rifle and then, armed only with a pistol, captured 132 prisoners.

The Allies pressed on against their enemy. The German commanders begged for peace, but still hoped to dictate some terms. The Allies refused. Revenge was too sweet. By the time **armistice,** or a cease-fire, came, the Kaiser had fled. On November 11, the guns finally fell silent.

The War's Toll More than 50,000 American soldiers died in battle, and many more died of disease. The physical scars—and the mental scars—ran deep. Twenty-one-year-old Corporal Elmer Sherwood of Indiana wrote after one bloody battle in August 1918:

> Hundreds of bodies of our brave boys lie on Hill 212, captured with such a great loss of blood. We will never be able to

explain war to our loved ones back home even if we are permitted to live and return. It is too gigantic and awesome for expression through words.

American losses were minute in comparison to those suffered by the Europeans. The total death toll of 8 million soldiers and sailors is only an estimate. The French alone suffered over 1 million war dead and 4,000 towns destroyed. Great Britain lost 900,000 troops and suffered 2 million wounded. As mentioned earlier, Russian deaths also were high. Across Europe, the war killed 20 million civilians during and immediately after the fighting, from starvation, disease, or related injuries.

This terrible slaughter took place on the battlefields of Europe. But the war also was "fought" on other fronts, as well. The next section discusses the impact of World War I on the American home front.

The tank was another new weapon introduced in World War I. The British and the Americans collaborated on designing and building tanks like the one shown above.

SECTION 3 REVIEW

Key Terms, People, and Places
1. Define (a) American Expeditionary Force, (b) armistice.
2. Identify doughboy.

Key Concepts
3. What were some of the military innovations introduced during World War I?
4. In what ways did American women serve in World War I?

5. How did American troops help turn the tide of the war on the battlefield?
6. How many people were killed and wounded as a result of World War I?

Critical Thinking
7. **Demonstrating Reasoned Judgment** The United States failed in its original plan to be a mere "associate" in the war. Do you think it is possible to be anything less than a "full partner" in a war? Explain.

 Quiz found in the Unit 3 folder, p. 85, covers the main ideas in this section as well as the key terms.

Media and Technology

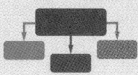 **Transparency**
The Way It Works, H-17

SECTION 4

On the Home Front

Connecting to the Big Idea

See page 368B. Point out that World War I brought many changes at home, including unprecedented government control of the economy and of news and information. Ask how the government's actions changed American life.

Objectives

● Describe the financial and managerial efforts required on the home front to support the war effort.

● Explain how an atmosphere of war hysteria enabled the United States government to control and manipulate information and to repress free speech.

● Identify the significant cultural and social changes caused by the war.

Bellringer

Ask students what the term *home front* implies about the nature of life in the United States during the war. Why could life not continue normally while the nation was involved in a "total" war?

Reading Strategy

Reading for Evidence Ask students to find evidence as they read to support the following statement on page 384: "Waging war required many sacrifices at home." Ask students to list as many kinds of sacrifices made by Americans as they can.

SECTION PREVIEW

World War I was fought at home, too. To win that war, the government took control of the economy—and of people's minds—to an extent never before attempted.

Key Concepts

• Waging World War I involved tremendous financial and managerial efforts on the home front.

• The atmosphere of war hysteria enabled the United States government to control and manipulate information and to repress free speech.

• The war spurred significant cultural and social changes.

Key Terms, People, and Places

Liberty Bond, Industrial Workers of the World

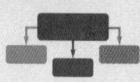

The United States government whipped up sentiment against the "Huns"—the Germans—with posters such as this.

W aging war required many sacrifices at home. Despite the efforts of the preparedness movement, the economy was not ready to meet the demands of modern warfare. In this era, war required huge amounts of money and personnel. As President Wilson explained, now "there are no armies . . . ; there are entire nations armed."

Financing the War

As those in Congress who had argued for peace had made clear, preparedness was costly. Taxes went up. Most of the money for the war, however, came from patriotic private citizens. The government launched a vigorous campaign to raise money from the American people, a plan created by Secretary of the Treasury William Gibbs McAdoo. By selling **Liberty Bonds** to enthusiastic Americans, McAdoo raised millions of dollars, which he then loaned to the Allies at low interest rates. People who purchased the bonds could later redeem them, collecting what they paid for the bonds plus interest.

Teams of salespeople across the country sold the bonds to the "patriotic people." Responding to the slogan "Every Scout to Save a Soldier," Boy Scouts and Girl Scouts set up booths on street corners and sold bonds. The government hired popular commercial artists to draw colorful posters and recruited famous screen actors to host bond rallies. An army of 75,000 "four-minute men" gave brief (four-minute) speeches before films, plays, and school or union meetings to persuade audiences to buy bonds.

Managing the Economy

The government also needed industry to convert to the production of war goods. In 1918 Wilson won authority to set up a huge bureaucracy to manage this process. Business leaders—so-called "dollar-a-year" men and women—gave their service for a token salary and flocked to Washington to take up posts in thousands of new agencies.

New Government Agencies A War Industries Board, headed by financier Bernard Baruch, oversaw the whole war effort. The board's control was almost dictatorial. It doled out raw materials, told manufacturers what and how much to produce, and even fixed prices. A Fuel Administration introduced gasless days and daylight saving time, which increased the number of daylight hours and thus lowered fuel consumption. A War Trade Board licensed foreign trade and punished firms suspected of dealing with the enemy.

A National War Labor Board, set up in April 1918 under former President Taft, mediated those labor disputes that might hinder the war effort. Labor leader Samuel Gompers promised to limit labor strife in war production industries. A separate War Labor Policies Board, headed by Harvard law professor Felix

RESOURCE DIRECTORY

Teaching Resources

Reproducible Lesson Plan found in the Unit 3 folder, p. 78, provides a summary of the Section 4 lesson plan content.

Alternate Lesson Plan: Critical Thinking Recognizing Cause and Effect, found in the Alternate Lesson Plans folder, p. 103, helps students practice this skill through examining the changes World War I brought to the American home front.

Guided Reading and Review found in the Unit 3 folder, p. 86, provides a structure for reading and mastering the key concepts and reviewing the key terms for Section 4. (Guided Practice)

Literature Activity Selling the War, found in the Unit 3 folder, p. 100, uses an excerpt from the propaganda booklet *Why America Fights Germany* to show how the government galvanized public sentiment against Germany.

Frankfurter, standardized wages, hours, and working conditions in the war industries. Labor unions won limited rights to organize and bargain collectively.

Regulating Food Consumption Using the slogan "food will win the war," the government began regulating food consumption. Under the leadership of engineer and future President Herbert Hoover, a Food Administration (1917) worked to increase agricultural output and reduce waste. Opposed to price controls and rationing, Hoover hoped that voluntary restraint and increased efficiency would accomplish these goals.

Women, assumed to be in charge of America's kitchens, were a key part of his program. Writing to women in August 1917, Hoover preached a "Gospel of the Clean Plate."

*S*top, before throwing any food away, and ask "Can it be used?" . . . Stop catering to different appetites. No second helpings. Stop all eating between meals. . . . Stop all refreshments at parties, dances, etc. . . . One meatless day a week. One wheatless meal a day. . . . No butter in cooking: use substitutes.

"The American woman and the American home," he concluded, "can bring to a successful end the greatest national task that has ever been accepted by the American people." Eager for a chance to play a purposeful part in the war, women across the country responded to this patriotic challenge.

A Progressive Victory? Thanks to the war, some aspects of progressive-era visions had come to pass. Government now regulated American economic life to an extent most progressives had never dreamed possible. When regulation spilled over into more private areas of life, however, some progressives wondered if the growth in public power had become excessive. In addition, regulation had not lessened the power of the corporate world. Indeed, during the war, the government relaxed its pursuit of antitrust suits, the influence of business leaders grew, and corporate profits tripled.

FOOD WILL WIN THE WAR
You came here seeking Freedom
You must now help to preserve it
WHEAT is needed for the allies
Waste nothing
UNITED STATES FOOD ADMINISTRATION

Using Historical Evidence
This poster served a dual purpose. It encouraged Americans to save food and also promoted patriotism among immigrants. *What symbols and ideas in this poster are aimed at immigrants?*

MAKING CONNECTIONS

How does the involvement of the federal government in the regulation of business during World War I differ from government policies toward business in the late 1800s? What factors account for this change?

Controlling Hearts and Minds

News and information also came under federal control during World War I. George Creel, a Denver journalist and former muckraker, headed a Committee on Public Information, the country's first propaganda machine. Creel's office coordinated the production of short propaganda films, pamphlets explaining war aims, and posters selling recruitment and Liberty Bonds. Study plans distributed to teachers from Creel's office put the entire blame for the war on Germany. ✪

Enforcing Loyalty As in all wars, fear of spies and sabotage was widespread. A few months after the sinking of the *Lusitania*, a staff

SOURCE READINGS

Source Readings on p. 398 will connect literature selections and primary source excerpts to historical events discussed in this section.

Media and Technology
Transparency
Critical Thinking, I-13

---

2. INSTRUCT

Explain/Discuss

Have the students first brainstorm a list of changes in American life caused by the war and then put the changes into categories.

Ask students how the War Industries Board controlled industry. Have students compare the operations of a small manufacturing company before the war with its operations during the war. Students should consider such activities as obtaining raw materials, negotiating with workers, and deciding how much of a given product to produce at what price. Ask in what ways the War Labor Policies Board controlled workers. Why did business and labor cooperate with these boards? Would business and labor have cooperated with them in peacetime? Why?

Caption Answer to . . .

Using Historical Evidence

The words on the base of the Statue of Liberty refer to the United States as a land that welcomes all people. The words on the poster remind immigrants that the United States has welcomed them and that they thus owe their allegiance in return.

Answer to . . .

MAKING CONNECTIONS

Government's heavy involvement in the regulation of business differs sharply with the laissez-faire policies of the late 1800s and early 1900s. Explanations for this change include the changing attitudes brought by the progressive era and the wartime need for more drastic government intervention.

Analyze

Analyze the way in which war hysteria led to the suppression of civil liberties. Tell students that in 1929, Herbert Hoover said, "Absolute freedom of the press to discuss public questions is a foundation stone of American liberty." How would Woodrow Wilson have responded if Hoover had made that statement in 1917? Do students agree with Hoover or with Wilson?

Activity

Teaching Heterogeneous Groups

As President Wilson exclaimed, "there are no armies. . . , there are entire nations armed," Americans mobilized their talents and efforts to support the war. To help students understand the consequences of this mobilization, divide the class into small groups. Have groups list as many jobs on the home front as possible that were essential to the war effort. Then have students list who would fill those jobs. **LEP**

Enrichment

For decades after the war, American schoolchildren memorized the poem "In Flanders Field," written by John McCrae, a Canadian physician killed in action. After helping students find the poem in an anthology, ask them to read it and then write a short report on its message.

3. ASSESS

Section 4 Review Answers

1. Industrial Workers of the World, see p. 386

2. Through higher taxes and the sale of Liberty Bonds.

3. They set up numerous agencies to regulate and control many aspects of the economy, including production, fuel usage, trade, labor relations, and food consumption. Boards included the War Industries Board, the War Trade Board, the Fuel Administration, the National War Labor Board, and the Food Administration.

---

member of the German embassy left his briefcase on a train. In it were plans for undermining pro-Allied sentiment and disrupting the American economy. Henceforth, the government was on the alert for sabotage.

Once the United States declared war, this alertness approached hysteria. Nativism revived, this time more vigorously than before. Having won its battle for preparedness, the National Security League began to preach "100 Percent Americanism." In 1917 the League finally got Congress to pass, over Wilson's veto, a literacy test for immigrants. This test excluded those who could not read or write a language—relatively few immigrants, as it turned out. Limits on immigration would become more severe after the war.

"Hate the Hun!" The war also spurred hostility toward Germans, who were called Huns in reference to an Asiatic people who brutally invaded Europe in the fourth and fifth centuries. German composers and musicians were banned from symphony concerts. German measles became "liberty measles," a hamburger

"I am afraid we are going to have a good many instances of people roughly treated on very slight evidence of disloyalty," wrote Secretary of War Newton Baker. Indeed, as this 1917 photograph shows, anti-German feeling in the United States led to the arrest of many citizens of German descent.

a "liberty sandwich." The California Board of Education condemned German as a language that spread "the ideals of autocracy, brutality and hatred." Yet it was a brutal mob of Americans that, in April 1918, lynched German-born citizen Robert Prager near St. Louis, in spite of the fact that Prager had tried to enlist in the navy. This act was but one of numerous wartime attacks on people of German descent.

Repression of Civil Liberties Wilson had claimed that the United States was now fighting for liberty and democracy. Many Americans, including women still denied the vote, found the claim ironic. It was particularly galling to those who suffered from wartime restrictions on their civil liberties.

When Wilson addressed Congress on the war resolution, he had warned that disloyalty would be "dealt with with a firm hand of repression." Accordingly, Congress passed the Espionage Act (1917), which made it illegal to interfere with the draft. This was followed by the Sedition Act (1918), which made it illegal to obstruct the sale of Liberty Bonds or to discuss anything "disloyal, profane, scurrilous, or abusive" about the American form of government, the Constitution, or the army and navy.

The government imposed censorship on the press and banned some publications from the mails. It pursued more than 1,500 prosecutions and won over 1,000 convictions. Socialist and former presidential candidate Eugene Debs drew a ten-year jail sentence for criticizing the American government and business leaders and urging people to "resist militarism." From prison he ran again for President in 1920 and won nearly a million votes. The victor in that race, Warren G. Harding, pardoned him in 1921.

Controlling Political Radicals Socialists such as Debs argued that the war was merely a quarrel among imperialist capitalists. This view became a rallying point for antiwar sentiment. In the elections of 1917 in New York, Ohio, and Pennsylvania, socialists made impressive gains. The **Industrial Workers of the World,** a radical labor organization seeking the overthrow of capitalism, also gained new supporters. The IWW (also known as the "Wobblies") was

---

▶ RESOURCE DIRECTORY

Teaching Resources

⭐ 📄 **Visual Learning Activity** Women's Roles in World War I, found in the Unit 3 folder, p. 103, uses recruitment posters from the United States to illustrate the roles promoted for women during World War I.

founded in 1905. Unlike the labor movement Samuel Gompers led, the IWW focused on unskilled workers. It consisted mostly of western miners, lumbermen, migrant farm workers, and some eastern textile workers.

The views of socialists and the IWW distressed moderate labor leaders like Gompers, who had pledged union cooperation with the war effort. The police hounded the IWW. Raids in September 1917 led to the conviction of nearly two hundred members in trials held in Illinois, California, and Oklahoma. Vigilante groups, citizens who take the law into their own hands, lynched and horsewhipped others.

Cultural and Social Changes

Despite American criticism of Germany for its militarism, American patriotism and war fever made military styles and activities acceptable at home. Scouting programs, which for both boys and girls involved military-style uniforms, marching, and patriotic exercises, grew in popularity. Military drill became part of many school programs. By the summer of 1918, all able-bodied males in colleges and universities became army privates, subject to military discipline.

Social Mobility for Women and Minorities

Americans turned against militarism after the war. But other social changes had more lasting implications. ✪

The war propelled certain people into higher paid work. As the war cut off the flow of immigrants from Europe, factories that used to discriminate against African Americans and Mexican Americans now actively recruited them. The Women's Land Army put women to work on farms. White women moved into jobs previously closed to them, such as telegraph messenger, elevator operator, and letter carrier. Middle-class white women moved into management positions.

As a result of the war, about 400,000 women joined the industrial work force for the first time. In 1917 a speaker for the Women's Trade Union League exulted, "At last, after centuries of disabilities and discrimination, women are coming into the labor and festival of life on equal terms with men." In 1919 a study appeared with the optimistic title, "A New Day for the Colored Woman Worker." These pronouncements, while premature, celebrated what seemed to be major change.

Prohibition Finally Passes In 1917 the temperance movement was almost a century old. In that year, Congress proposed prohibition. The Eighteenth Amendment was passed less out of concern for the health of alcoholics and their families than to show patriotism. Because of the war, the grain that used to make alcohol would now make bread to meet needs at home and overseas. The states ratified the amendment in 1919.

The IWW gained strength during World War I. They also became the target of government crackdowns, part of a wider effort to control political radicals.

SECTION 4 REVIEW

Key Terms, People, and Places
1. Identify Industrial Workers of the World.

Key Concepts
2. How did the United States finance its involvement in World War I?
3. In what ways did the government try to control the economy?
4. By what means did the government try to convince Americans to support the war?

5. Whose civil liberties were sacrificed in this effort to win the war?
6. What were some social and cultural changes that took place as a result of the war?

Critical Thinking
7. **Recognizing Ideologies** The federal government went to great lengths to control public opinion. What do these actions suggest about government's view of public opinion and its role in the war effort?

Quiz found in the Unit 3 folder, p. 87, covers the main ideas in this section as well as the key terms.

4. The government convinced Americans to support the war with both carrot and stick: The Committee on Public Information disseminated propaganda urging support; restriction of civil liberties, such as outlawing criticism of the army and navy, made not supporting the war difficult or dangerous.

5. So-called hyphenated Americans, such as German Americans; anyone who spoke up against the draft; radicals, such as the IWW; and the radical press.

6. Militarism gained popularity, as evidenced in scouting programs and military drill in schools; women and minorities made gains in social mobility; and after almost a century of struggle, the temperance movement finally won prohibition.

7. Possible answer: The American people's support was viewed as crucial to the success of the war effort.

Reteach

Ask students to read and correct each of the following statements:
● Most of the money to pay for the war came from taxes.
● The purpose of the War Industries Board was to run the nation's businesses so that their profits could help pay for the war.
● The Food Administration used price controls and rationing to make Americans conserve food supplies.
● The Committee on Public Information encouraged Congress to introduce a literacy test for immigrants.
● The Sedition and Espionage acts limited the rights of workers to bargain collectively.

4. CLOSE

Reinforcing the Big Idea

To support the war effort, the government took unprecedented control of the economy and of news and information. The next section describes the difficult task of shaping the peace that ended the war.

SECTION 5

Global Peacemaker

See page 368B.

1. FOCUS

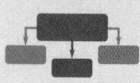

Connecting to the Big Idea

See page 368B. Explain that President Wilson's vision of postwar peace, summarized in his Fourteen Points, was not shared by the Allies. Nor did the United States Congress accept the final treaty ending the war. Ask what Wilson's Fourteen Points were. What were the provisions of the Versailles Treaty?

Objectives

● Describe the reception President Wilson's peace plan received from the Allies.

● Describe the reaction at home to Wilson's peace plan and to the Versailles Treaty.

● Identify the immediate postwar years as marred by disillusionment, and economic disorder.

Bellringer

Ask students to consider and explain the expression "At what cost peace?" How could this expression be applied to other wars the United States had fought?

Reading Strategy

Reinforcing Key Ideas Ask students to take notes as they read the section listing the steps involved in the creation of the Versailles Treaty and the decision of the United States Senate to withhold ratification of the treaty.

SECTION PREVIEW

President Wilson's lofty vision for peace was brought back to earth by contentious allies and Congress. Meanwhile, many Americans experienced keen disappointment over postwar conditions at home.

Key Concepts
- At the postwar peace talks, Wilson's grand vision for peace was welcomed—but not wholeheartedly embraced.
- In the United States, reaction to the Versailles Treaty and to Wilson's proposal for a League of Nations was cool.
- The immediate postwar years in the United States were marred by disillusionment and economic disorder.

Key Terms, People, and Places
Fourteen Points, self-determination, League of Nations, reparations, Versailles Treaty

Enthusiasm for the war effort, demonstrated by this game board cover, gave way to despair in the postwar years.

W ith the fighting in Europe over, the nations involved in the conflict began the difficult task of shaping the peace. President Wilson, who feared that the failure to craft a treaty acceptable to all parties would lead to future wars, was determined to play a large role in this effort. But the postwar world—in Europe and at home—seemed almost as divided as before the war.

Wilson's Vision for Postwar Peace

On January 8, 1918, President Wilson delivered a peace program to Congress, which came to be called the **Fourteen Points** for the number of provisions it included. Among the program's key points were a call for an end to secret alliances, the restoration of freedom of the seas, and a reduction in armaments. The plan called for European colonial powers to handle all claims to each other's colonies with respect for the native populations. Wilson also demanded that Austria-Hungary allow its several ethnic groups to determine their own futures, a principle called **self-determination.** Finally, he called for an association of nations to join together in a single organization to secure world peace.

Wilson hoped that these points would form the basis of peace negotiations. At first, the Allies appeared to cooperate. After a while, as new political realities intervened, the fourteen points began to unravel.

The Paris Peace Conference In January 1919 an international peace conference met in Paris. Wilson decided to head the United States delegation himself. He also chose not to name any Republicans or senators to the group, a snub that would not be forgotten.

When Wilson arrived in Paris, Parisians threw flowers in his path and greeted the American President as a conquering hero. Wilson claimed he was not interested in gaining rewards for the United States, but sought only the establishment of a permanent agency to guarantee international stability. As he had said two years earlier, "There must be not a balance of power, but a community of power; not organized rivalries, but an organized common peace."

Wilson Is Forced to Compromise All would not go Wilson's way. First, the Allies *were* interested in reward. In particular, they wanted to divide up Germany's colonies. The French, determined never to be invaded again, wanted the total humiliation if not destruction of Germany. Russia, although absent from the conference, was on everyone's mind. In March, civil war had erupted there. British, French, and American forces had become involved in the fray on the side of Lenin's opponents. Would

---

RESOURCE DIRECTORY

Teaching Resources

Reproducible Lesson Plan found in the Unit 3 folder, p. 79, provides a summary of the Section 5 lesson plan content.

Alternate Lesson Plan: Learning Styles found in the Alternate Lesson Plans folder, p. 104, extends students' understanding of the armistice through role-playing a press conference at the Treaty of Versailles and is especially effective for kinesthetic learners.

Guided Reading and Review found in the Unit 3 folder, p. 88, provides a structure for reading and mastering the key concepts and reviewing the key terms for Section 5. (Guided Practice)

Lenin's government collapse or prevail? Would it press for war claims?

From the start of the conference, Wilson was forced to compromise on his plans. He had to give up, for example, on the idea of self-determination for Germany's colonies, agreeing that the Allied powers could take them over.

Wilson did, however, get the other powers to postpone further discussion of Germany's fate and to move directly to his ideas for collective security. After ten days of hard work, he produced a plan for the **League of Nations,** an organization in which the nations of the world would join together to ensure security and peace for all members. Wilson then left for home, hoping to persuade Congress and the nation to accept his ideas.

Article 10 For Wilson, the heart of his proposal for the League of Nations was "Article 10." This provision pledged members to regard an attack on one as an attack on all. Since the League would not have any military power, the force of the article was moral only. Nevertheless, thirty-nine Republican senators or senators-elect signed a statement rejecting it, fearing the loss of American diplomatic independence.

MAKING   CONNECTIONS

Were Wilson's goals for the peace process, as outlined in his Fourteen Points, consistent with his stated reasons for entering the war? Explain.

The Peace Treaty

In March, Wilson returned to the peace conference. The Big Four—Britain, France, Italy, and the United States—dominated the proceedings. Though the Allies accepted Wilson's plan for the League of Nations, French premier Georges Clemenceau used Wilson's embarrassment over American opposition to the League to exact harsh conditions against Germany. These included a fifteen-year French control of the mineral resources in Alsace-Lorraine. Wilson feared that this decision would lead to future wars, but he could not get Clemenceau to budge.

Viewpoints
On the League of Nations

Joining the League of Nations would involve a major commitment for the United States. The wisdom of making such a commitment was discussed from every angle. *On what basis does each speaker below support or oppose American entry into the League?*

For Joining the League of Nations

"The United States will, indeed, undertake . . . to 'respect and preserve as against external aggression the territorial integrity and existing political independence of all members of the League,' and that engagement constitutes a very grave and solemn moral obligation. But it is a moral, not a legal, obligation, and leaves our Congress absolutely free to put its own interpretation upon it."

President Woodrow Wilson, testifying before
the Foreign Relations Committee, August 19, 1919

Against Joining the League of Nations

"Shall we go there, Mr. President, to sit in judgment, and in case that judgment works for peace join with our allies, but in case it works for war withdraw our cooperation? How long would we stand as we now stand, a great Republic commanding the respect and holding the leadership of the world, if we should adopt any such course?"

Senator William Borah (Idaho), testifying in the Senate,
November 19, 1919

Wilson had to compromise elsewhere. Self-determination for the peoples of Austria-Hungary proved hard to apply. Central Europe was (and still is) an ethnic mixture of monumental complexity. As the map on page 390 shows, the conference created the new nations of Czechoslovakia and Yugoslavia, more nearly following ethnic lines than before the war. But these arrangements failed to resolve all ethnic tensions, which in the early 1990s contributed to the breakup of these nations.

War Guilt and Reparations Wilson met his greatest defeat when he gave in to French insistence on German war guilt and financial responsibility. The French wanted to cripple Germany. The British wanted **reparations**—payment from its enemy for the economic injury suffered in the war. In 1921 a Reparations

---

Viewpoints Activity On the League of Nations, found in the Unit 3 folder, pp. 92–93, expands on opinions both favoring and opposing the establishment of the League.

Answer to . . .

Wilson supports joining the League to attain collective security; Borah views League membership as an excuse for drawing the United States into foreign quarrels and, therefore, foreign wars. For a more thorough examination of the League of Nations issue, see the Resource Directory below.

Answer to . . .

MAKING   CONNECTIONS

Possible answer: Yes. Wilson entered the war with the goal of making the world safe for democracy. His Fourteen Points expressed his desire to have all nations respect one another's integrity.

2. **INSTRUCT**

Explain/Discuss

Explain that Wilson made several political mistakes that cost him support for his peace plan. Ask why the loss of Republican support hurt Wilson's efforts to negotiate and fulfill his promise to "make the world safe for democracy."

Discuss why such harsh conditions were imposed on Germany. How do students think the German people reacted to the treaty? Ask students whether they agree that the seeds of World War II were sown in the Versailles Treaty. Why or why not?

Discuss the problems caused by the sudden return of the troops from overseas. What did the returning veterans need? How did their return affect women workers?

Analyze

Ask students to explain why Americans were disillusioned at the start of the 1920s. What ideals had been shattered by the war? In what ways did the nation's successes during the war—in battle, in building support for the war, and in reorganizing the economy—contribute to the disillusionment that followed the war?

The new map includes several new nations, for example, Poland, Czechoslovakia, and Yugoslavia. These nations resulted in part from Wilson's demand for self-determination.

Activity
Debate

Ask students to prepare arguments for or against United States membership in the League of Nations. Ask for pairs of volunteers to present their arguments at three-minute intervals. Ask one or two students to summarize the arguments on the chalkboard.

Enrichment

Ask students to research and report on the history of the League of Nations. How effective was it? What actions did it take? When was it dissolved? What organization eventually replaced it?

 In Depth

Did You Know?

Many historians have shared German criticism of the terms of the Versailles Treaty on the grounds that it was unusually punitive and led to the growth of totalitarianism. Yet in March 1918 (see page 381), the Germans themselves had imposed just as harsh terms on the Russian Bolsheviks. Under the Treaty of Brest-Litovsk, the Bolsheviks yielded all of Poland, Lithuania, the Ukraine, Finland, the Baltic provinces, and neighboring territories. All told, they gave up the source of 90 percent of Russia's coal and 80 percent of its iron.

Europe After World War I

New nations

Allied-occupied zones

Geography and History: Interpreting Maps
The peace process helped lead to the transformation of the map of Europe.
In what ways does this map of Europe differ from the map on page 371?

Committee ruled that Germany owed the Allies $33 billion, an amount far beyond its ability to pay. As Wilson had feared, Germany never forgot or forgave this humiliation.

Signing the Treaty The Allies presented the treaty to the Germans on May 7, 1919. Insisting that the treaty violated the Fourteen Points, the Germans at first refused to sign. They soon gave in, however, when threatened with a French invasion. On June 28 the powers signed the treaty at Versailles, the former home of the French kings outside of Paris. Thus, the treaty is known as the **Versailles Treaty.**

Seeking Approval at Home

On July 8, treaty in hand, Wilson returned home to great acclaim. But many legislators had doubts. Some senators, called the "irreconcilables," opposed the treaty because it included American commitment to the League of Nations. Irreconcilables argued that joining the League would weaken American independence.

Senator Henry Cabot Lodge, chair of the Foreign Relations Committee, led another group called the "reservationists." This group wanted to impose reservations on American participation in the League. In particular they wanted a guarantee that the Monroe Doctrine would remain in force. Wilson's point that compliance with League decisions was "binding in conscience only, not in law," failed to persuade them.

Wilson Barnstorms the Country Determined to win grass roots support for the League, Wilson took to the road. In twenty-three days he delivered three dozen speeches. In the midst of this tremendous effort, he suffered a stroke that paralyzed one side of his body. He would remain an invalid, isolated from his cabinet and visitors, for the rest of his term.

In his illness, Wilson grew increasingly inflexible. Congress would accept the treaty and the League as he envisioned it, or not at all. In November the Senate voted on the treaty with Lodge's reservations included. The vote was 39 for, 55 against. When the treaty came up without the reservations, it went down again, 38 to 53. In the face of popular dismay at this outcome, the Senate reconsidered the treaty in March, but once again the treaty failed to win approval.

A Formal End to Hostilities On May 20, 1920, Congress voted to declare the war officially over. Steadfast to his principles, Wilson vetoed it. Finally, on July 2, 1921, another joint resolution to end the war passed. By that time a new President, Warren Harding, was in office and signed it. Congress ratified separate peace treaties with Germany, Austria, and Hungary that October.

Difficult Postwar Adjustments

The biggest winners from the war were American business and financial interests. The United States was now the world's richest creditor. In 1922 a Senate debt commission calculated that Europe owed the United States $11.5 billion.

 RESOURCE DIRECTORY

Teaching Resources

Primary Sources Activity Mrs. Wilson's Role, found in the Unit 3 folder, p. 98, illustrates how First Lady Edith Wilson became the "voice" of President Wilson after her husband suffered a stroke.

The return to peace caused problems for the general population, however. There was no plan for reintegrating returning troops into society. The federal agencies that had controlled the economy during the war abruptly cancelled war contracts. By April 1919, about 4,000 servicemen a day were being mustered out of the armed forces. But jobs proved scarce. The women who had taken men's places in factories and offices also faced readjustment. Late in 1918, Mary Van Kleeck, head of the Women in Industry Service, reported that "the question heard most frequently was whether women would now retire from industry." Many women did, either voluntarily or because they were fired.

Postwar Despair Many artists and intellectuals in the United States faced the postwar years with disillusionment. Some progressives had been encouraged by the government-business collaboration during the war. But for most other reformers, the war years marked the end of an era of optimism.

This disillusionment was not unique to artists and intellectuals. Wrote Alice Lord O'Brian, a military post exchange director from Buffalo who was twice decorated,

W̶e all started out with high ideals . . . after being right up here almost at the front line . . . I cannot understand what it is all about or what has been accomplished by all this waste of youth.

African American Troops at Home Like white troops, African American soldiers

Weariness and fear line the face of Corporal Johnson of the 58th Regiment as he rests during a pause in battle. The experience of war left deep scars in the bodies and minds of many Americans.

came home heroes. When the soldiers went to find jobs, however, the reception was quite different.

W.E.B. Du Bois, editor of the NAACP's magazine, the *Crisis,* had supported the war. In July 1918 he had written, "Let us, while this war lasts, forget our special grievances and close our ranks . . . with our white citizens and the allied nations that are fighting for democracy." A year later, after more lynchings of African Americans, including some still in uniform, his message became defiant. "This country of ours, despite all its better souls have done and dreamed, is yet a shameful land," he wrote in May 1919. "It **lynches**. . . . It steals from us. . . . It insults us. . . . We **return.** We **return from fighting.** We **return fighting.**"

Du Bois's views, shared by many, heralded a new era in the struggle for equality. Indeed, the entire United States was on the threshold of a stormy era—the 1920s.

SECTION 5 REVIEW

Key Terms, People, and Places
1. Describe (a) self-determination, (b) League of Nations, (c) reparations, (d) Versailles Treaty.

Key Concepts
2. What were Wilson's Fourteen Points, and what were its key elements?
3. What factors forced Wilson to compromise on his plans at the Paris peace conference?

4. What was the American reaction to the Treaty of Versailles and the League of Nations?
5. What factors contributed to the difficult postwar adjustment in the United States?

Critical Thinking
6. **Expressing Problems Clearly** It is often said that Wilson won the war but "lost the peace." Explain your understanding of this statement.

 Quiz found in the Unit 3 folder, p. 89, covers the main ideas in this section as well as the key terms.

 Chapter Test Forms A and B are found in the Unit 3 folder, pp. 104–109.

 Answer Keys found in the Unit 3 folder, pp. 116–126, provide answers to all student activities.

Media and Technology

 **Transparency**
Graphic Organizer, G-4

🎧 **Guided Reading Audiotapes** (English and Spanish)

 **Computer Test Bank**

Understanding Key Terms, People, and Places

Terms

Students should refer to the definitions of the key terms in the chapter to write sentences that show the relation of each word to the outbreak of World War I, United States involvement in the war, or events that followed the conflict.

True or False

1. false, Allies
2. false, Industrial Workers of the World
3. false, reparations
4. true
5. false, Fourteen Points

Reviewing Main Ideas

1. Before 1914, the treaty system created a fragile balance of power. In 1914, however, the complex system of treaties and alliances brought most of Europe into a war that began as a dispute between Serbia and Austria-Hungary.

2. Because military leaders were not experienced in fighting with modern weaponry, no one was able to achieve victory. The mounting death toll that resulted led to loss of morale and acts of desperation.

3. Some American business leaders saw the war as an opportunity for economic expansion. Others pushed for neutrality, and some also urged preparedness, so that the United States would be ready to protect its commercial interests.

4. Americans developed an anti-German attitude because of German submarine warfare, British propaganda, and the revelation of the Zimmerman note.

5. Germany resumed its unrestricted submarine warfare.

6. Reasons included pressure from commercial interests and wide popular support, shaped in part by British propaganda.

7. At first, Americans envisioned themselves as playing only a supporting role in the war, but the Allies demanded that the United States send troops to help boost morale. The Allies' military needs also led to greater American involvement.

8. General Pershing at first sought to keep his troops separate from other Allied troops. Within American ranks, African Americans were segregated from white troops.

9. Holding firmly to their positions, American troops were able to save Paris and blunt the edge of the German advance.

Chapter Review

Understanding Key Terms, People, and Places

Key Terms
1. Central Powers
2. Allies
3. U-boat
4. *Lusitania*
5. Zimmerman note
6. American Expeditionary Force
7. armistice
8. Liberty Bond
9. Industrial Workers of the World
10. Fourteen Points
11. self-determination
12. League of Nations
13. reparations
14. Versailles Treaty

People
15. Kaiser Wilhelm
16. autocrat
17. doughboy

Terms For each term above, write a sentence that explains its relation to the outbreak of World War I, United States involvement in the war, or events that followed the conflict.

True or False Determine whether each statement is true or false. If it is true, write "true." If it is false, change the underlined term to make the statement true.

1. At the outbreak of World War I, the <u>Central Powers</u> consisted of Russia, France, and Great Britain.
2. The <u>American Expeditionary Force,</u> a radical labor organization, sought the overthrow of capitalism.
3. After the war, the European Allies demanded harsh <u>self-determination</u> from Germany.
4. Americans bought <u>Liberty Bonds</u> to help finance the war.
5. Wilson's peace program came to be called the <u>Zimmerman note</u>.

Reviewing Main Ideas

Section 1 (pp. 370–373)
1. How did the role of secret European treaties shift in 1914?
2. Why did troops fighting in the war resort to acts of desperation?
3. What position did businesses in the United States take regarding the war?

Section 2 (pp. 375–378)
4. For what reasons did many Americans develop an anti-German attitude?
5. Why was Wilson unable to keep his campaign promise to maintain neutrality?
6. In addition to Germany's refusal to respect American claims to neutrality, name two other reasons why the United States entered the war.

Section 3 (pp. 379–383)
7. Describe how Americans envisioned their role when they first entered the war. What led to the expansion of the American role in World War I?

8. What types of segregation occurred during the war?
9. Explain how the Allies were able to turn the tide of the war.

Section 4 (pp. 384–387)
10. Describe the changes in American life brought about by the War Industries Board, the National War Labor Board, and other new government agencies.
11. What was the result of news and media coming under government control during the war?
12. In what ways were people's civil liberties limited during the war?
13. Name some positive effects of the war.

Section 5 (pp. 388–391)
14. What was the response of the French and British to Wilson's peace plan?
15. Briefly describe congressional opposition to the League of Nations.
16. Describe the postwar adjustment for African Americans.

10. Answers include gasless days, daylight savings time, punishment for firms suspected of dealing with the enemy, and the mediation of labor disputes that might hinder the war effort.

11. The government was able to control the public's response to the war through propaganda.

12. The federal government actively attacked dissent with strict, harsh laws. Also, nativist sentiment was unleashed against German Americans, leading to much abuse.

13. The war propelled certain people into higher paid work and temporarily diminished discrimination against African Americans, Mexican Americans, and women.

14. They wanted harsher treatment for Germany.

15. The Reservationists wanted a guarantee that the Monroe Doctrine would remain in force.

16. Despite a triumphant return, African Americans again faced unemployment, discrimination, and even lynchings on their return home.

Thinking Critically

1. **Recognizing Ideologies** When the United States entered World War I, it hoped to play a supporting role as an "associate." What does this assumption suggest about the country's view of itself at the time?

2. **Identifying Central Issues** In what ways did World War I differ from previous wars involving the United States?

3. **Checking Consistency** Many members of Congress worried that the League of Nations would limit the independence of the United States. Based on what you have read about World War I, how independent was the United States from the affairs of Europe?

Making Connections

1. **Evaluating Primary Sources** Review the primary source excerpt on page 383. How would you expect such attitudes to affect soldiers returning from World War I?

2. **Understanding the Visuals** Examine the cartoon and the newspaper clippings on page 376. Do the cartoon and the clipping on the left support or refute each other? Explain your answer.

3. **Writing About the Chapter** Imagine that World War I has recently ended. Write a statement to Congress in which you express your opinion of President Wilson's proposal for the League of Nations. First, create a list of what you see as the positive aspects of Wilson's plan. Then, list the negative features. Note any suggestions you have for improvements. Next, write a draft of your statement in which you offer your ideas. Revise your statement, making certain that each idea is clearly explained. Proofread your statement and draft a final copy.

4. **Using the Graphic Organizer** This graphic organizer uses a modified flow map to organize information about the events leading to World War I and about early responses to the war on the part of Americans. Flow maps can show both a sequence of events or what happened as the result of an event. (a) Based on the chart, what was the cause of Americans becoming increasingly alarmed about the war? (b) What was the effect of American alarm? (c) On a separate sheet of paper, create your own flow map about American involvement in World War I in Europe and on the home front, using this graphic organizer as an example.

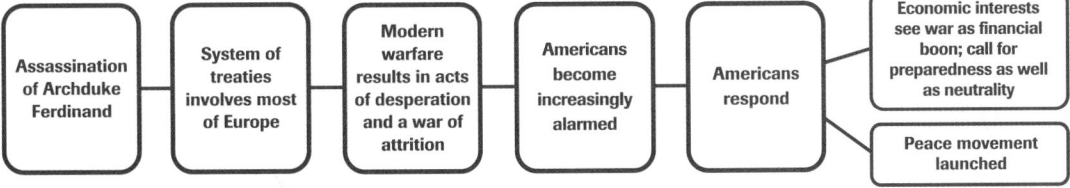

Alternative Assessment

Final Evaluation
Use the following guidelines to evaluate student projects:

• **Evidence of mastery of content** To what extent do projects demonstrate knowledge and understanding of chapter content?

• **Evidence of thoughtfulness** To what extent do projects demonstrate an understanding of the importance and significance of events?

• **Evidence of outside research** To what extent do projects use outside research materials?

Thinking Critically

1. The United States considered itself independent of the affairs of Europe.

2. It differed in the number of countries and regions involved, the fact that the war was fought entirely outside North America, and the effect of new weapons of mass destruction.

3. Possible answer: The fact that the United States was drawn into World War I indicates that the United States could never keep itself completely independent of European affairs.

Making Connections

1. Possible answer: Returning soldiers might face difficulty finding meaning in their war experience and readjusting to life during peacetime.

2. The visuals refute each other. Although the cartoon illustrates an uncaring and unconcerned Germany, the newspaper clipping shows that Germany did take some measures to warn the public not to board the *Lusitania*.

3. Statements should contain students' opinions of both positive and negative aspects of the League, as well as specific ideas for improvements.

Tell students that contemporary African American poet Margaret Walker calls the South the "sorrow home." Ask students why thousands of African Americans left their homes and communities to move to the cities of the North.

Ask students to scan the images in the American Album feature and to classify them into two categories. First have students identify those items that represent conditions in the South that pushed African Americans toward migration. (*doll, record book, home school, plow*) Then ask them to identify those that represent the attraction pulling African Americans to the North. (*job poster, soldiers*) Discuss the significance of the suitcase and the Bibles in terms of the community the migrants had to leave.

Explain to students that in 1940 and 1941, African American artist Jacob Lawrence painted a series of sixty panels, called "The Migration of the Negro," that tell the story of the extraordinary movement of people from South to North. Ask students to work in groups to plan a mural depicting items or conditions—such as those displayed in the American Album—that reflect an African American family's decision to leave their home in the rural South. Students should prepare a brief description of each panel in the mural.

American Album
ARTIFACTS FROM EXHIBITIONS AND COLLECTIONS AT THE SMITHSONIAN INSTITUTION
NATIONAL MUSEUM OF AMERICAN HISTORY

FROM FIELD TO FACTORY

Beginning in 1915, hundreds of thousands of African Americans moved from the rural South to the cities of the North. Most African Americans made this "Great Migration" to take advantage of job opportunities in the North. Others, however, moved to escape the poverty and discrimination they faced in the Jim Crow South. This migration changed the lives of the African Americans who made the journey, and it changed the nature of race relations in the North. *How did the lives of African Americans change when they moved from the fields of the South to the factories of northern cities?*

▲ HANDMADE DOLL
Cash-poor African Americans made or grew much of what they used in the South. This doll had its own handmade cradle and blankets.

▲ STORE OWNER'S RECORD BOOK The southern store owner kept track of sharecroppers' debts and payments in a ledger like this. Few African American sharecroppers ever made enough money to pay what they owed the store owner.

▲ PLOW More than two thirds of the African Americans living in the South were sharecropping farmers. Farming was back-breaking work for the whole family and seldom yielded more than survival. Farmers walked behind a mule-drawn plow like this one to break the land.

LABORERS WANTED AT HOG ISLAND GOVERNMENT SHIPBUILDING 35¢ AN HOUR $3.85 A DAY A CHANCE TO LEARN A GOOD TRADE AND GET HIGHER WAGES

▼ SUITCASE AND BIBLES African Americans in the South had strong community ties, which centered around the local church. Leaving this community, even to escape hardships, was difficult.

▲ JOB OPPORTUNITIES Because of World War I, industries could not get new laborers from Europe. Also, many native-born workers were drawn into the armed forces. African Americans streamed north to fill these open jobs.

◄ HOME SCHOOLING There were few schools for African Americans in the rural South, and the ones that existed were poor. Parents frequently were forced to be their children's teachers.

WORLD WAR I SOLDIERS ▶ Many African Americans learned about the opportunities in the North when they served as soldiers during World War I. For most soldiers, this was the first time they traveled more than a few miles from home.

Tell students that the death toll in World War I is estimated at 8 million soldiers, which is roughly equal to the population of the entire state of Ohio. In addition, 20 million civilians were killed or died during or immediately following the war; this figure is slightly more than the population of the entire state of New York. Remind students that new weapons used in combination with old fighting tactics resulted in these huge figures. Tell students that soldiers fighting on the battlefronts are the best source of information on what it was like to endure such a war, day after day. Explain to students that the source readings will help them develop an understanding of soldiers' war experiences and will show them one way soldiers boosted their spirits.

INSTRUCT

Ask students to review the excerpt and songs from the viewpoint of a World War I historian. Ask: What information about World War I can you gain from the excerpt and songs? What information can you discern from them about the emotions and morale of the American troops? How reliable are the songs as historical evidence? What questions would a historian need to answer before using the songs to learn about World War I? What questions should a historian ask about *All Quiet on the Western Front*?

CHAPTER 11

SOURCE READINGS

All Quiet on the Western Front

Erich Maria Remarque

 *Literature*

INTRODUCTION Erich Maria Remarque was wounded in action several times during World War I. In 1929 he wrote *All Quiet on the Western Front*, an autobiographical account of the war which became the most celebrated novel of its time. In the frontispiece to the book, Remarque writes, "This book is to be neither an accusation nor a confession, and least of all an adventure, for death is not an adventure to those who stand face to face with it. It will try simply to tell of a generation of men who, even though they may have escaped its shells, were destroyed by the war." Remarque emigrated to the United States in 1939 after his books were banned by the Nazis and his citizenship abolished. In the excerpt below, the book's main character, a soldier in whose voice the novel is told, describes a visit home on a leave. The selection opens just after the soldier has arrived by train in his hometown.

VOCABULARY Before you read the selection, find the meaning of these words in a dictionary: garrison, apoplexy, parapet, tremulous, brimstone.

Walking down the street I know every shop, the colonial warehouses, the chemist's, the tobacconist's. Then at last I stand before the brown door with its worn latch and my hand grows heavy. I open the door and a wonderful freshness comes out to meet me, my eyes are dim.

The stairs creak under my boots. Upstairs a door rattles, someone is looking over the railing. It is the kitchen door that was opened, they are cooking potato-cakes, the house reeks of it, and to-day of course is Saturday; that will be my sister leaning over. For a moment I am shy and lower my head, then I take off my helmet and look up. Yes, it is my eldest sister.

"Paul," she cries, "Paul—"

I nod, my pack bumps against the banisters; my rifle is so heavy.

She pulls a door open and calls: "Mother, Mother, Paul is here."

I can go no further—Mother, Mother, Paul is here.

I lean against the wall and grip my helmet and rifle. I hold them as tight as I can, but I cannot take another step, the staircase fades before my eyes, I support myself with the butt of my rifle against my feet and clench my teeth fiercely, but I cannot speak a word, my sister's call has made me powerless, I can do nothing, I struggle to make myself laugh, to speak, but no word comes, and so I stand on the steps, miserable, helpless, paralysed, and against my will the tears run down my cheeks.

My sister comes back and says: "Why, what is the matter?"

Then I pull myself together and stagger on to the landing. I lean my rifle in a corner, I set my pack against the wall, place my helmet on it, and fling down my equipment and baggage. Then I say fiercely: "Bring me a handkerchief."

She gives me one from the cupboard and I dry my face. Above me on the wall hangs the glass case with the coloured butterflies that once I collected.

Now I hear my mother's voice. It comes from the bedroom.

"Is she in bed?" I ask my sister.

"She is ill—" she replies.

I go in to her, give her my hand and say as calmly

as I can: "Here I am, Mother."

She lies still in the dim light. Then she asks anxiously:

"Are you wounded?" and I feel her searching glance.

"No, I have got leave."

My mother is very pale. I am afraid to make a light.

"Here I lie now," says she, "and cry instead of being glad."

"Are you sick, Mother?" I ask.

"I am going to get up a little to-day," she says and turns to my sister, who is continually running to the kitchen to watch that the food does not burn: "And put out the jar of preserved whortleberries—you like that, don't you?" she asks me.

"Yes, Mother, I haven't had any for a long time."

"We might almost have known you were coming," laughs my sister, "there is just your favourite dish, potato-cakes, and even whortleberries to go with them, too."

"And it is Saturday," I add.

"Sit here beside me," says my mother.

She looks at me. Her hands are white and sickly and frail compared with mine. We say very little, and I am thankful that she asks me nothing. What ought I to say? Everything I could have wished for has happened. I have come out of it safely and sit here beside her. And in the kitchen stands my sister making the evening bread and singing.

"Dear boy," says my mother softly.

We were never very demonstrative in our family; poor folk who toil and are full of cares are not so. It is not their way to protest what they already know. When my mother says to me "dear boy," it means much more than when another uses it. I know well enough that the jar of whortleberries is the only one they have had for months, and that she has kept it for me; and the somewhat stale cakes that she gives me too. She has taken a favourable opportunity of getting a few and has put them all by for me.

Two soldiers fire at the enemy from a trench. They wear masks to protect themselves against poison gas.

I sit by her bed, and through the window the chestnut trees in the beer garden opposite glow in brown and gold. I breathe deeply and say over to myself:—"You are at home, you are at home." But a sense of strangeness will not leave me, I can find nothing of myself in all these things. There is my mother, there is my sister, there my case of butterflies, and there the mahogany piano—but I am not myself there. There is a distance, a veil between us.

I go and fetch my pack to the bedside and turn out the things I have brought—a whole Edam cheese, that Kat provided me with, two loaves of army bread, three-quarters of a pound of butter, two tins of liver-sausage, a pound of dripping and a little bag of rice.

"I suppose you can make some use of that—"

They nod.

"Is it pretty bad for food here?" I enquire.

"Yes, there's not much. Do you get enough out there?"

I smile and point to the things I have brought. "Not always quite so much as that, of course, but we fare reasonably well."

Erna goes out to bring in the food. Suddenly my mother seizes hold of my hand and asks falteringly: "Was it very bad out there, Paul?"

Mother, what should I answer to that! You would not understand, and never realize it. And you never should realize it. Was it bad, you ask.—You, Mother,—I shake my head and say: "No, Mother, not so very. There are always a lot of us together so it isn't so bad."

"Yes, but Heinrich Bredemeyer was here just lately and he said it was terrible out there now, with the gas and all the rest of it."

It is my mother who says that. She says: "With the gas and all the rest of it." She does not know what she is saying, she is merely anxious for me. Should I tell

Have students read Remarque's book *All Quiet on the Western Front.* Ask students to write a critique of the book in which they compare the description of the war in the book to that found in Chapter 11 of their texts. In their critiques students should also comment on the effectiveness of Remarque's writing and how it differs from a first-person account written by a soldier who was in the war, such as that found on page 383. What are the pros and cons of each type of writing?

As an alternative, students can find other World War I songs or songs from World War II or the Vietnam War. Students should write a brief essay comparing and contrasting the songs. The essay should answer this question: How do the songs reflect the spirit of the times and American attitudes toward each war?

SOURCE READINGS

her how we once found three enemy trenches with their garrison all stiff as though stricken with apoplexy? Against the parapet, in the dug-outs, just where they were, the men stood and lay about, with blue faces, dead.

"No, Mother, that's only talk," I answer, "there's not very much in what Bredemeyer says. You see for instance, I'm well and fit—"

Before my mother's tremulous anxiety I recover my composure. Now I can walk about and talk and answer questions without fear of having suddenly to lean against the wall because the world turns soft as rubber and my veins become brimstone.

My mother wants to get up. So I go for a while to my sister in the kitchen. "What is the matter with her?" I ask.

She shrugs her shoulders: "She has been in bed two months now, but we did not want to write and tell you. Several doctors have been to see her. One of them said it is probably cancer again."

THINKING ABOUT THE SELECTION

1. Why does the author begin to cry when his sister calls to his mother that he is there?
2. Why does the author stress the strangeness of having his mother ask him about the horrors of the war?

Critical Thinking
3. **Identifying Central Issues** Why does the author have to keep repeating to himself that he is home and why does he feel a distance from his family and home?

Songs of World War One 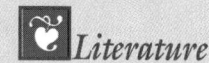 *Literature*

INTRODUCTION The popular songs about World War I played an important role in boosting the moral of both American soldiers abroad and civilians at home. As one soldier said, "Music keeps us from getting blue. We all have a country, a home and a girl, and music talks about these things without making you say anything." George M. Cohan was perhaps one of the most famous songwriters of the time. His song "Over There" expressed the patriotic spirit of citizens on the home front. It was also a favorite marching song of the men in the American Expeditionary Force. In 1940, Congress presented Cohan with a special medal for the song. Songs like Geoffrey O'Hara's "K-K-K-Katy," helped civilians and soldiers alike to rally their spirits and gave them hope for the future.

Over There
George M. Cohan

Johnnie get your gun, get your gun, get your gun,
Take it on the run, on the run, on the run;
Hear them calling you and me;
Every son of liberty.
Hurry right away, no delay, go today,
Make your daddy glad, to have had such a lad,
Tell your sweetheart not to pine,
To be proud her boy's in line.

ANSWERS TO

Thinking About the Selection
1. He begins to cry because the familiarity of home, with its smells, sights, and sounds, is so powerful to him, and he has dreamed of it so often. His sister's calling to his mother that "Paul is here" must seem like a dream that he never thought would come true.

2. The horrors of the war seem so separate from his home and his mother that he cannot seem to conceive of her even asking about the war. It is impossible for her to ever understand what he has experienced.

3. He has dreamed so often and so longingly of being allowed to return home, and of living to return home, that he is almost unable to comprehend that it has actually happened. The familiarity of his surroundings is enveloping him. Yet he himself has changed so drastically while at war that he cannot fit himself back into the old picture.

Chorus:
Over there, over there,
Send the word, send the word over there,
That the Yanks are coming, the Yanks are coming,
The drums rum-tumming everywhere.
So prepare, say a prayer,
Send the word, send the word to beware,
We'll be over, we're coming over,
And we won't come back till it's over over there.

Johnnie get your gun, get your gun, get your gun,
Johnnie show the Hun,[1] you're a son-of-a-gun,
Hoist the flag and let her fly,
Like true heroes do or die.
Pack your little kit, show your grit, do your bit,
Soldiers to the ranks from the towns and the tanks,
Make your mother proud of you,
And to liberty be true.

---
[1] A derogatory nickname for the Germans

World War I songs and posters such as this inspired patriotic feelings in Americans.

K-K-K-Katy

Geoffrey O'Hara

Jimmy was a soldier brave and bold,
Katy was a maid with hair of gold,
Like an act of fate,
Kate was standing at the gate,
Watching all the boys on dress parade.
Jimmy with the girls was just a gawk,
Stuttered every time he tried to talk,
Still that night at eight
He was there at Katy's gate,
Stuttering to her this lovesick cry:

"K-K-K-Katy, beautiful Katy,
You're the only g-g-g-girl that I adore;
When the m-moon shines over the cowshed,
I'll be waiting at the k-k-k-kitchen door."

No one ever looked so nice and neat,
No one could be just as cute and sweet.
That's what Jimmy thought,
When the wedding ring was bought;
Now he's off to France, the foe to meet.

Jimmy thought he'd like to take a chance,
See if he could make the Kaiser dance,
Stepping to a tune,
All about a silvery moon —
This is what they hear in far-off France:

"K-K-K-Katy, beautiful Katy,
You're the only g-g-g-girl that I adore;
When the m-moon shines over the cowshed,
I'll be waiting at the k-k-k-kitchen door."

THINKING ABOUT THE SELECTION

1. Which lines in "Over There" reflect the American commitment to preserving freedom?
2. In the second song, what is meant by the lines "Jimmy thought he'd like to take a chance, /See if he could make the Kaiser dance"?

Critical Thinking
3. **Recognizing Ideologies** What basic beliefs underlie the sentiments expressed in these two songs? How do you think Americans during World War I felt when they heard songs like these?

ANSWERS TO

Thinking About the Selection
1. The lines that reflect the American commitment to preserving freedom are: "Hear them calling you and me;/Every son of liberty" and "Make your mother proud of you,/And to liberty be true."
2. The lines refer to Jimmy's decision to enlist in the military in order to fight against the "Kaiser," meaning Kaiser Wilhelm, the ruler of Germany, and the Germans in general, in World War I.

3. The songs express a belief in fighting to preserve liberty when necessary, pride in serving one's country, respect for one's parents, religious faith, determination to finish a job, patriotism, idealistic love, and appreciation of home. Americans during World War I probably felt proud of their country and their fighting troops, determined to succeed against the Central Powers, frightened about losing loved ones and about the future, and anguished at the pain and suffering of those they loved and others in the war.

Boom Times to Hard Times
1919–1938

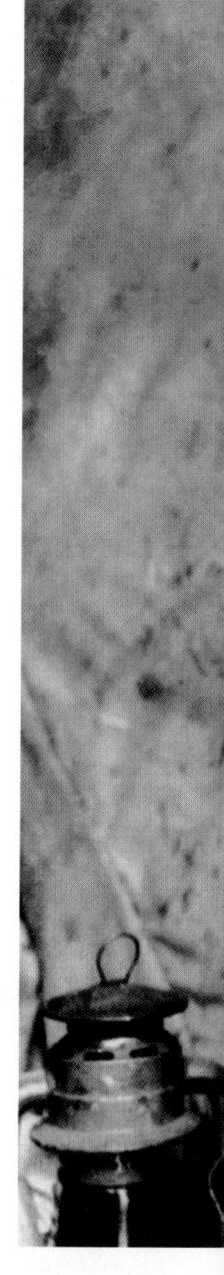

Introducing the Unit

Interpreting the Visual In March 1936, Dorothea Lange (1895–1965) made the photograph on pages 400–401 for the Farm Security Administration (FSA), a New Deal agency for which she took photographs from 1935 to 1939. "I saw and approached the hungry and desperate mother as if drawn by a magnet." Lange's evocative images of migrant farm families suffering terrible hardships during the Depression had great political impact, inspiring support for government relief programs. The FSA compiled the largest archive of Depression photographs, some 216,000 in all.

Herbert Hoover's words on page 400 provide an ironic contrast to Lange's photograph. Read the quote from Hoover to the class and ask students to determine which occurred first, the scene in the photograph or the quote.

Divide the class into two groups. Ask one group to write questions that they would like to ask the woman in the photograph. Ask the other half to pretend that they are the woman and to write questions for President Hoover about the country's economy.

Ask students to compare Lange's photograph to images of victims of poverty, war, and natural disasters appearing today in newspapers and newsmagazines. What gave Lange's work such impact?

Establishing Chronology Remind students that the previous chapter focused on the period of World War I, which ended in 1918. Explain that Unit 4 covers the two decades between the world wars. During the 1920s, the nation's economy soared, only to collapse in 1929. The 1930s were the bleak years of the Great Depression and the attempts of FDR's New Deal to restore the nation's vitality.

"We in America today are nearer to the final triumph over poverty than ever before."
—Herbert Hoover, 1928

*W*hen President Herbert Hoover spoke these words, he expressed the optimism and faith in business and technology that characterized the United States in the 1920s. Following the stock market crash of October 1929, however, the fragile prosperity of the decade gave way to a period of severe economic distress known as the Great Depression. In the election of 1932, voters chose Franklin Delano Roosevelt for President, a choice that marked a turning point in the way Americans would view their Presidents.

 RESOURCE DIRECTORY

Teaching Resources

Local History Activity "Down and Out in Newark" and the Local Focus research topic suggestions, found in the Local History Resources folder, pp. 21–23, are designed to help students understand how history affects all lives.

★ **Themes in American History Posters** Wall-size, illustrated posters, found in the Teaching Resources package, illustrate the four unit themes.

Unit Test Forms A and B are found in the Unit 4 folder, pp. 110–115.

During the Great Depression, poverty and suffering were constant traveling companions to families like the one above, forced to move from town to town to look for work.

Media and Technology

Visions of America: Scenes of an Era To introduce students to the main idea and events covered in this unit, play "Scenes of an Era: Boom Times to Hard Times, 1919–1938" (length: 2.5 minutes). This selection can be located on side 3 of the videodiscs. This selection can also be located on videotape 4. Lesson plans for "Scenes of an Era" can be found in the Visions of America Teacher's Guidebook.

Using Multimedia Technology This folder contains instructional tools and strategies for using technology in the classroom.

Transparency Binder Contains full-color transparencies with lesson suggestions. From a large collection divided into twelve categories, specific transparencies are referenced throughout the chapter at appropriate points of use. For this unit, see American Photo, B-7; Fine Art, D-18; Cause and Effect, F-9; The Way It Works, H-18; Links Across Time, J-7; and Political Cartoon, K-7.

Themes in American History

Teachers may wish to discuss specific historical events in the context of historical themes. Here are four suggestions for Unit 4.

Diversity *Throughout its history America has been made up of a gathering of many peoples from throughout the world. Americans have both benefited from and encountered problems with this diversity.*

● Immigration from southern and eastern European countries, which had been increasing since the late 1800s, was abruptly halted in the 1920s because of restrictive quotas.
● Many African Americans moved from the South to northern cities. They found opportunities, but also faced discrimination and violence.

American Culture *In every period of their history, Americans gave special expression to their views through art, literature, films, music, manners, and morals.*

● The 1920s experienced a rapid shift in fashions, music, manners, and morality that marked a dramatic break with the past. African Americans experienced a "black renaissance."
● A revolution in communications led to a period of bigger-than-life heroes and a growth in consumer products.

Economics *Americans have searched for new and better ways to make a living and have struggled to define government's role in this pursuit.*

● Americans demanded that their government take an active role to relieve the despair and suffering of the Depression. New Deal programs provided relief.

Environment *The geography and available resources of the continent have affected the actions of Americans. Similarly, the actions of Americans have affected the environment and physical landscape.*

● Unwise farming practices in the Great Plains and an extended drought caused the area to become a dust bowl.
● Massive public projects built dams to harness hydroelectric power and to control flooding.

Chapter 12 A Stormy Era
1919–1929

📁 Teaching Resources (See Unit 4 Folder)

	Instruction	Enrichment
Section 1 **Postwar Adjustments** (pp. 404–407)	Reproducible Lesson Plan, p. 3 Alternate Lesson Plan, p. 106 Guided Reading and Review, p. 8 Quiz, p. 9	History Might Not . . . Activity, Lobbying for Indian Immigration, pp. 18–19
Section 2 **Social and Political Developments** (pp. 410–414)	Reproducible Lesson Plan, p. 4 Alternate Lesson Plan, p. 107 Guided Reading and Review, p. 10 Quiz, p. 11	Primary Source Activity, Growing Up Black, pp. 26–27 Literature Activity, The Weary Blues, p. 31 American Profiles Activity, Bessie Smith, p. 20
Section 3 **New Manners, New Morals** (pp. 415–418)	Reproducible Lesson Plan, p. 5 Alternate Lesson Plan, p. 108 Guided Reading and Review, p. 12 Quiz, p. 13	Critical Thinking Activity, Testing Conclusions, p. 25 American Profiles Activity, Lillian Moller Gilbreth, p. 21 Historian's Toolbox Activity, Analyzing Advertisements, p. 24
Section 4 **Creating a Shared Culture** (pp. 420–423)	Reproducible Lesson Plan, p. 6 Alternate Lesson Plan, p. 109 Guided Reading and Review, p. 14 Quiz, p. 15	Visual Learning Activity, Advertising Techniques of the 1920s, p. 33 Primary Source Activity, Teens and Cigarette Smoking, p. 28
Section 5 **Stemming the Tide of Change** (pp. 424–427)	Reproducible Lesson Plan, p. 7 Alternate Lesson Plan, p. 110 Guided Reading and Review, p. 16 Quiz, p. 17 Chapter Test, Forms A & B, pp. 34–39	Viewpoints Activity, On the Eighteenth Amendment, pp. 22–23 Visual Learning Activity, The Ku Klux Klan, p. 32 Literature Activity, Tales of the Jazz Age, pp. 29–30

📁 Additional Chapter Resources

Resource Organizer, p. 2
Alternate Lesson Plan, p. 105
Answer Keys, pp. 116–128

Bibliography

For the Teacher

Delany, Sarah Louise and Annie Elizabeth. *Having Our Say: The Delany Sisters' First 100 Years.* Kodansha,1993. (History as lived by the Delany sisters—from Jim Crow, through Harlem migration and Depression, to the present day.)

Lemann, Nicholas. *The Promised Land, The Great Black Migration and How It Changed America.* Alfred A. Knopf, Inc., 1991. (A recent study of African American migration.)

Prentice Hall Literature Excerpts from *The American Experience,* 1994, including Hurston, Zora Neale. *Dust Tracks on a Road.* HarperCollins,1970 edition.

THE BIG IDEA

The Big Idea for the chapter and how the main ideas in each section relate to the Big Idea are graphically displayed below. Comprehension of this chapter's Big Idea is critical to students' understanding of United States history and how we as a nation got where we are today.

Media and Technology

- Visions of America: History Might Not Have Happened This Way Game

- Fine Art, D-16, D-17; Our Multicultural Heritage, C-12

- The Way It Works, H-18

- Graphic Organizer, G-3

- Guided Reading Audiotapes (English and Spanish)

- Computer Test Bank

For the Student

Bogart, Max, ed. *The Jazz Age.* Macmillan, 1969. (An anthology of literature of the 1920s.)

Willis-Braithwaite, Deborah. *Van Der Zee.* Harry N. Abrams, 1993. (Harlem in its heyday as seen by its most famous photographer.)

CHAPTER 12

American society changed in many ways following World War I. Conflict existed between those Americans ready to adopt new manners and new ways and those Americans who tried to resist the forces of change.

SECTION 1

After World War I, fear of radicals and communism turned many Americans against progressive ideas of reform.

SECTION 2

After the war, important social and political developments included women's suffrage and the Great Migration north by African Americans. During this time Republicans gained national support.

SECTION 3

The Jazz Age introduced a variety of new styles, tastes, and manners; and popular media spread the new image.

SECTION 4

Population movement and developments in communication and transportation helped to create a national culture as Americans throughout the country began to share the same information and experiences.

SECTION 5

Some Americans tried to slow the pace of change that followed the war. Whether through prohibition or through the terrorism of the Ku Klux Klan, such attempts were generally unsuccessful.

402B

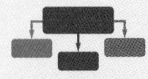

A Stormy Era
1919-1929

A Stormy Era
1919-1929

The Relevance of the Big Idea

Tell students that in the 1920s, Americans were divided over issues such as the ones discussed in this chapter. Manners and styles changed quickly after World War I. Young urban Americans in particular adopted the new styles and manners, while some other Americans tried to stop what they saw as the nation's moral decay.

Structure a class discussion on the following topic: What are the issues about which Americans of different generations disagree? Have students generate a list of issues, such as fashions, hairstyles, movies, television programming, and music, and explain why these issues have become subjects of generational controversy.

"My candle burns at both ends . . . " wrote poet Edna St. Vincent Millay in 1920, a phrase that can be used to symbolize a divided nation during the entire decade. Some people wanted to put aside the horrible memories of war and so embraced anything new, be it product, attitude, or behavior. Others wanted to shield their eyes from the responsibility that came with being a new global power and tried to pull the nation back to attitudes and behaviors that were known and "safe."

In Depth

Global Connections

After the devastation of the war in Europe and the deaths of more than 100,000 Americans out of two million who had been shipped "over there," Americans worked to withdraw from world affairs and focus on improving their lives at home. Material dreams, not the idealistic dreams that sent Americans to fight in Europe, were the important ones. Coolidge defined business as "one of the great contributing forces to the moral and spiritual advancement of the race."

Events in the United States

Events in the World

	1919	1920	1921	1922	1923
Events in the United States	**1919** Attorney General Palmer begins raids on suspected radicals. • Chicago race riot occurs.	**1920** Warren Harding elected President. • The first commercial radio broadcast is made.		**1922** T. S. Eliot publishes "The Wasteland."	**1923** Harding dies; Calvin Coolidge takes office. • Bessie Smith records her first jazz album.
Events in the World		**1920** The Treaty of Versailles ends World War I. • The League of Nations is formed.	**1921** Takashi Hara, Premier of Japan, is assassinated.		**1923** Adolf Hitler fails in an attempted coup in Germany.

▶ RESOURCE DIRECTORY

Teaching Resources

📄 **Alternate Lesson Plan: Demonstrating the Big Idea** found in the Alternate Lesson Plans folder, p. 105, provides a lesson strategy to instruct students about the Big Idea that the 1920s were years of change as well as resistance to change.

📄 **Alternative Assessment Handbook** provides information, guidance, and strategies for alternative methods of assessment. It includes an essay on new trends in assessment, guidance and strategies for developing performance tasks and portfolios, scoring rubrics, and sample evaluation forms.

Pages 404–407
Postwar Adjustments
With the shadow of World War I finally lifting, some Americans hoped the way toward progressive-style reform would be relighted. Others, however, began to view such ideas for change with suspicion and fear.

 Pages 410–414
Social and Political Developments
After the war, women and African Americans faced a world of new opportunities and old disappointments. In the political realm, Republicans won Americans' support—and votes.

 Pages 415–418
New Manners, New Morals
From rising hemlines to the energetic sounds of jazz, the 1920s daringly broke with tradition. New social freedoms created opportunity—and dilemmas—for women. But beneath it all lay a nagging question: How much had really changed?

 Pages 420–423
Creating a Shared Culture
People in city apartments, country farmhouses, and everywhere in between were connected in new ways in the 1920s. Such links allowed sweeping changes to envelop the entire nation.

 Pages 424–427
Stemming the Tide of Change
Jazz music, moving pictures, fast cars—American life moved at a dizzying pace in the 1920s. All the motion left some people feeling queasy, and they sought to slow the pace of change.

| 1925 The Charleston becomes a dance craze. • John Scopes is tried for teaching evolution. | 1927 Charles Lindbergh flies solo across the Atlantic Ocean. • Ford begins production of the Model A. | 1928 Republican Herbert Hoover is elected President. | 1929 Ten million families own radios. |

1924	1925	1926	1927	1928	1929

| 1924 V. I. Lenin, founder of the Soviet Union, dies. • France hosts the first Winter Olympics. | 1926 Ibn Saud becomes king of Saudi Arabia. • French painter Claude Monet dies. | 1928 Chiang Kai-shek becomes president of China. | 1929 The term apartheid is introduced in South Africa. |

Media and Technology
 Transparencies
Time Lines, E-6; Historical Maps, L-5

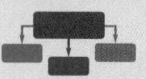

1. FOCUS

Connecting to the Big Idea

See page 402B. Tell students that after the war Americans tried to return to their normal lives. While progressives hoped to continue the prewar era of reform, many Americans viewed proposals for change with fear and suspicion. Ask students what events caused Americans to grow anxious about change.

Objectives

● Describe the postwar economic adjustments and labor unrest that troubled the nation after World War I.
● Describe the causes and results of the "red scare."
● Show how the United States limited immigration and foreign entanglements in the 1920s.

Bellringer

Write the word *optimism* on the board. Ask students to jot down a definition and to think about what the word might have to do with the climate in the United States during the early postwar years.

Reading Strategy

Reading for Evidence As they read the section, ask students to find evidence that some Americans looked on proposals for changing and improving society with "suspicion and fear" as stated on page 404.

2. INSTRUCT

Explain/Discuss

Review with students the progressives' belief that solutions could be found for the problems of the nation and of its citizens. Why did progressives think that the problems of the nation could be solved?

SECTION 1

Postwar Adjustments

SECTION PREVIEW

With the shadow of World War I finally lifting, some Americans hoped the way toward progressive-style reform would be relighted. Others, however, began to view such ideas for change with suspicion and fear.

Key Concepts
• Postwar economic adjustments and labor unrest troubled the nation.
   • Fears that the ideas of the Russian Revolution would spread led to a "red scare" in the United States.
   • Efforts to limit immigration and foreign entanglements won wide support in the 1920s.

Key Terms, People, and Places
communist, red scare, general strike; Vladimir I. Lenin, Nicola Sacco, Bartolomeo Vanzetti

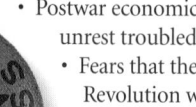

After the Russian Revolution, many Americans saw the Communist hammer and sickle as a symbol of a threat to the United States.

World War I was over. Now was the time, progressive reformers thought, to relaunch plans for economic and social change, such as unemployment insurance and housing initiatives, put on hold during the war.

The times, however, were less ripe for change than reformers hoped. The unprecedented brutality of the war had wounded the nation's spirit. Europe, once the model of enlightened civilization, was now viewed with disgust. Fear about the worldwide effects of revolution in Russia swept the country. And as the United States endured a bumpy transition back to peacetime, many Americans began to view proposals for changing society with suspicion and fear.

Postwar Economic Adjustments

During the war, American factories geared up to meet the demand for ships, guns, food, and other goods. When this demand dropped after the war, the economy entered a difficult period of adjustment. Returning veterans faced unemployment. When they got their jobs back, they did so by taking those that had been filled by women and minorities. In addition, food prices and rents shot up in the spring of 1919, and by 1920 the cost of living was more than double what it had been before the war. Farmers suffered as wartime orders declined and European farmers began producing crops again. Prices for wheat, corn, and hay dropped by half.

Labor unrest became increasingly common. From 1916 through 1920, the United States experienced between 3,350 and 4,450 strikes a year, most caused by disputes over wages and hours. When factory owners discovered that the absence of unions in the South helped make southern labor costs much lower than those in the North, many moved their businesses south, leaving northern mill towns to die. Union members responded with outrage.

The Russian Revolution Causes a Red Scare

The end of World War I did not bring an end to the turmoil overseas. As the fighting in Europe entered its final months, Russia erupted in revolution. Few foreign events would have as long-lasting an impact on the United States.

In March 1917, revolutionary forces overthrew the Russian monarchy headed by Czar Nicholas II and set up a representative form of government. Under the leadership of Aleksandr Kerensky, a lawyer who had defended opponents of the czarist regime, the new government pledged to continue in the European war. This pledge hurt Kerensky's standing with Russia's hungry workers and peasants, to whom the war seemed remote and unrelated.

Revolutionary leader **Vladimir I. Lenin** soon undermined Kerensky's power with

---

RESOURCE DIRECTORY

Teaching Resources

Reproducible Lesson Plan found in the Unit 4 folder, p. 3, provides a summary of the Section 1 lesson plan content.

Alternate Lesson Plan: Critical Thinking Recognizing Cause and Effect, found in the Alternate Lesson Plans folder, p. 106, is an alternate lesson plan that helps students clearly recognize cause and effect through construction of a graphic organizer.

Guided Reading and Review found in the Unit 4 folder, p. 8, provides a structure for reading and mastering the key concepts and reviewing the key terms for Section 1. (Guided Practice)

promises of "peace, land, and bread." This message offered hope to Russia's weary people.

Although in the minority, Lenin and his followers believed that they represented all of Russia's workers. They therefore took the name *Bolsheviks*, the Russian word for *the majority*. They also adopted the red flag as their emblem.

In November 1917, the Bolsheviks overthrew Kerensky. Their new state, which eventually became the Union of Soviet Socialist Republics, made peace with Germany. It adopted socialism, a political and economic system in which all of society—represented by the government—jointly owns all property. Lenin also referred to his new regime as **communist**, a term that comes from the writings of German philosopher Karl Marx. It describes the revolutionary system that exists when workers have taken over a society and proclaimed an end to all differences between social and economic classes.

Lenin's ideas appealed to many poor Russians. But others resisted violently, and in early 1918, Russia erupted in civil war. Soldiers from Britain, France, Japan, and the United States intervened militarily on the side of Lenin's opponents to protect their countries' investments in the former Russia.

Lenin's "Reds" eventually won the civil war in 1920, and they resolved to fulfill Marx's ideology by spreading communism to other nations. From then on, the United States regarded the Bolshevik Reds as the world's villain.

National Unrest Is Blamed on the Reds In the United States, a rash of labor strikes and terrorist acts convinced many that the Reds were about to take over. A **red scare**—the fear of communism, socialism, or other so-called extreme ideas—gripped the nation.

One major strike took place in Seattle in January 1919. Shipworkers walked off their jobs and later were joined by workers in other industries. This action, one in which many unions participate as a show of worker unity, is known as a **general strike**. The Seattle strike paralyzed industry, trade, and the delivery of essential services in the area for five days. It also convinced many Americans that the United States was on the brink of revolution.

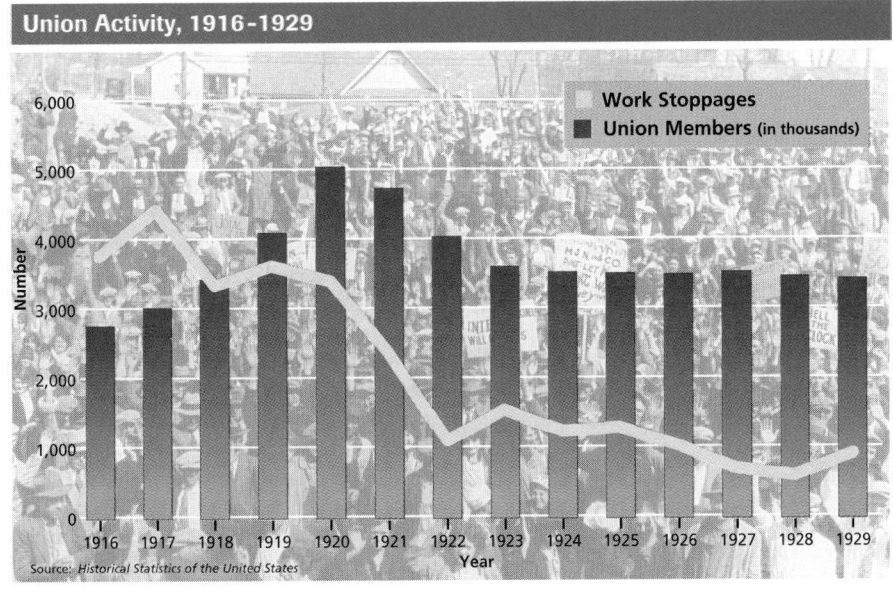

Union Activity, 1916-1929

Legend: Work Stoppages; Union Members (in thousands)

Y-axis: Number (0, 1,000, 2,000, 3,000, 4,000, 5,000, 6,000)
X-axis: Year (1916–1929)

Source: *Historical Statistics of the United States*

 Interpreting Graphs
The post–World War I years were stormy ones for labor and business. The number of annual strikes was high and union membership also rose slightly. *Based on this information, how would you summarize the condition of organized labor in the 1920s?*

Discuss with students how a long, brutal war might have changed people's view of the world. Encourage discussion with questions such as: How did postwar economic adjustments make Americans anxious? Why did demand lessen for the products of American factories and farms? Why did labor disputes increase? Why did many factory owners move their operations to the South?

Analyze

Have students analyze Americans' fear of communism. In what ways did the communist government established in Russia by Lenin differ from the government of the United States? Why did Lenin encourage communist revolutions in other countries?

Have students define the red scare and tell how it affected reform proposals. How did events such as the Palmer raids and the Sacco and Vanzetti trial affect legislation regarding immigration?

Caption Answer to ...

 Interpreting Graphs

Union membership declined slightly and reached a more or less stable level. The remaining union workers struck far less often than they had in the postwar years.

 In Depth

Did You Know?

Radio became a popular medium for evangelists in the 1920s. The best known of these was Billy Sunday, a one-time professional baseball player. His nativist views were heard by thousands throughout the country. When 249 aliens were deported to Russia on December 21, 1919, Sunday preached, "If I had my way with these ornery wild-eyed Socialists and I.W.W.'s, I would stand them up before a firing squad and save space on our ships."

Such fears set the stage for violent attacks on unions. In September, steelworkers in Gary, Indiana, and several other cities struck over hours, wages, shop conditions, and company recognition of their union. Claiming that the strike was the work of communists, the United States Steel Corporation used force to break it, killing eighteen and beating hundreds more.

Also that fall, Boston's police force tried to win their first pay raise since the start of World War I. When the police commissioner fired nineteen officers for union activity, the whole force voted to strike.

Many Bostonians were frightened and outraged by the police strike. But Massachusetts governor Calvin Coolidge responded quickly, proclaiming, "There is no right to strike against the public safety by anybody, anywhere, anytime." He received national attention for his firm response to the police walkout.

The case of Sacco and Vanzetti, who are pictured below, inspired much protest, including this piece of folk art.

The Palmer Raids Convinced by the events of 1919 that the country was about to fall to radicals, many Americans grew anxious. Attorney General A. Mitchell Palmer, a man with political ambitions combined with a genuine fear of the communist threat, responded with enthusiasm. He set up an antiradical division to raid organizations suspected of so-called radical activity. These included communist and anarchist groups.

Thousands of individuals, mostly foreign-born and many innocent of any crime, were jailed as a result of the raids. Eventually, over five hundred people were deported without being formally charged with or convicted of any crimes. The army's chief of staff recommended that they be sent away on "ships of stone with sails of lead," and preacher Billy Sunday recommended a firing squad to save money on the ships.

The antiradical campaign then sputtered out, in part because some of its followers went too far. For example, in January 1920 the New York State Assembly voted to expel five socialist members, even though they had been legally elected and had violated no rules or laws. The assembly's defiance of the democratic process aroused wide protests.

Although the red scare faded, fear of revolution lingered. Indeed, these fears put a halt to reformers' postwar plans. Skillful use of terms such as *un-American* or *Bolshevik* by reform opponents was enough to denounce any proposal. Plans for state-supported housing initiatives, health and unemployment insurance, and a social-security system received little support.

MAKING   CONNECTIONS

The United States Constitution is designed to protect expression of most ideas—even those that are unpopular. Did the Palmer raids violate this design? At what point is it acceptable to limit political speech?

The Sacco and Vanzetti Case

The red scare played a part in one of the most controversial events in United States history. The story began on April 15, 1920, when gunmen robbed and killed the guard and paymaster of a South Braintree, Massachusetts, shoe factory. A few weeks later, police arrested two Italian immigrants, shoemaker **Nicola Sacco** and fish peddler **Bartolomeo Vanzetti**, in connection with the crimes. Both were carrying guns at the time of their arrest, and Sacco's was the same model used in the crime. They were convicted and sentenced to die.

At the time, many Americans felt that the trial of Sacco and Vanzetti was unfair. The two admitted to being anarchists, and it seemed clear that their political views—as well as their

Italian heritage—had played a bigger role in their conviction than had any evidence against them. Appeals went on for years, but the original decision stood. In 1927, the two men were electrocuted.

The Sacco and Vanzetti case divided the country and provoked an international outcry. Some thought they were innocent. Others felt that, regardless of the pair's guilt or innocence, they had not been fairly tried. The two men, dignified to the end, went to their deaths comforted only by the thought that their fate would spark wider discussion of important issues. A writer who visited Vanzetti two days before his execution reported him as saying,

> This is our career and our triumph. Never in our full life could we hope to do such work for tolerance, for justice, for man's understanding of man as we now do by accident.

Renewed Isolationism and Nativism

Hostility to foreign people and ideas in the 1920s found expression in a renewed isolationism. The League of Nations was, as President Warren G. Harding said, "as dead as slavery." As for concerns about the security and safety of European countries, many Americans decided Europe would have to deal with them alone.

Nativism, a movement to limit immigration, first appeared in the 1800s. Not surprisingly, it revived after the war. Nativists now claimed that people from foreign countries could never be fully loyal to the United States.

When immigration swelled after the war, Congress reacted. In 1921, it limited annual immigration to 350,000 and set up quotas for certain nationalities. In 1924 it passed a law slashing immigration to 164,000. In addition to excluding Asians entirely, the law set quotas for each country at 2 percent of the total number of that country's immigrants living in the United States in 1890. The goal was to reduce immigration from southern and eastern Europe, for few immigrants from those countries had arrived in the United States before 1890. Nativists had long regarded these immigrants as undesirable, in part because of such cultural characteristics as their Catholic religion. (See Chapter 7.) As Washington congressman Albert Johnson declared in 1927,

This song, written in the 1920s, expressed the anti-immigration sentiment of the era.

> The United States is our land. . . . We intend to maintain it so. The day of unalloyed [pure] welcome to all peoples, the day of indiscriminate acceptance of all races, has definitely ended.

Distrust of people and things "un-American," like the concerns over strikes and the spread of communism, contributed to a political climate that was hostile to reformers in the postwar years. But while the nation held firm against the invasion of ideas and people from abroad, individuals within the country were transforming the nation's political and social landscape.

SECTION 1 REVIEW

Key Terms, People, and Places
1. Define (a) communist, (b) general strike.

Key Concepts
2. How did the difficult postwar economic adjustments in the United States affect workers?
3. Who were the Bolsheviks?
4. What was the red scare?

5. Who were Sacco and Vanzetti, and why are they remembered?
6. Why did Congress restrict immigration in the 1920s?

Critical Thinking
7. **Expressing Problems Clearly** Summarize the obstacles facing those who wished to reintroduce reforms in the postwar United States.

Quiz found in the Unit 4 folder, p. 9, covers the main ideas in this section as well as the key terms.

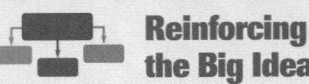

The Decision to Restrict Immigration

Focus Congress's passage of laws restricting immigration provides a vivid illustration of the postwar desire to curb the forces of change, to protect the United States from alien ideas, and to restore the United States to the kind of "normalcy" it enjoyed before the war. Students are asked to evaluate the congressional decisions to restrict immigration in the 1920s and to predict some of the consequences.

Instruct In order to give students a chronological framework for the material, ask them to make entries on a time line showing the changes in immigration law that are discussed in the text.

To check student understanding of the facts of immigration restriction, provide the following dates: 1913, 1926, 1967. Ask students which year or years each of the following would-be immigrants would most likely *not* have been admitted to the country.

• A Russian Jew, literate in two languages, but not in English, skilled at clock making and clock repair (*1926*)
• A Japanese teacher, literate in English (*1913, 1926*)
• An Italian chef (*1926*)
• An agricultural specialist from Nigeria (*1913, 1926*)

Review the arguments for and against immigration restriction. Ask volunteers to participate in a role-play of the congressional debate in 1924.

Extend To extend the activity, have students explore current trends in immigration, researching the latest census figures on the national origins of immigrants, their settlement patterns, and current discussions about immigration restriction.

The Decision to Restrict Immigration

Time Frame:	1917–1924
Place:	Washington, D.C.
Key People:	Members of United States Congress
Situation:	When some citizens strongly expressed their fear that new immigrants were threatening American character and institutions, Congress debated whether or not to control who would be allowed to enter the United States.

Congress has debated immigration policy every year since its first meeting in 1790. During World War I and in the years immediately after, the debate heated up. Congress faced strong pressure from the public to create an immigration policy that would severely restrict the numbers of newcomers from abroad.

Background to the Decision

Until the mid 1800s, most immigrants coming to the United States quickly blended in with old, established residents. Most of these immigrants to the United States came from western and northern Europe. They were culturally similar in many ways to the native-born descendants of America's first white settlers.

The "New" Immigrants Between 1880 and 1920 more than 23 million people left Europe to come to the United States. These "new" immigrants, as they were called, came from southern and eastern European countries such as Italy, Poland, and Russia. Their unfamiliar clothing, customs, and languages seemed "foreign" to many. Their religions were Catholicism, Orthodox Christianity, or Judaism—not Protestantism like most of the old immigrants. Many did not read or write any language, and few spoke English.

The new immigrants crowded into the cities. Some people blamed the growth of urban slums, the political corruption of cities, and other problems on the new immigrants. Others feared that they would take jobs away from "Americans."

The new immigrants, argued some, came from the most unstable parts of Europe—the places where the war had started and communism had been born. If newcomers did not already carry dangerous political ideas, many believed they were certainly vulnerable to these ideas. Furthermore, a number of respected scholars spread false notions that southern and eastern Europeans were inferior to other white people.

In Favor of Immigration Not everyone opposed immigration. To many, the United States was a "golden door" that all who wished to better themselves could enter.

THE ONLY WAY TO HANDLE IT.

 ## RESOURCE DIRECTORY

Teaching Resources

History Might Not ... Activity Lobbying for Indian Immigration, found in the Unit 4 folder, pp. 18–19, shows how J. J. Singh, an Indian immigrant himself, successfully lobbied Congress to revoke laws that obstructed Indian immigration to the United States.

Others believed that the poverty and illiteracy of the new immigrants showed a lack of opportunity, not a lack of ability. They pointed to the thousands of immigrants in the past who had contributed greatly to the growth of the country.

DECISION	Should immigration to the United States be restricted?				
ARGUMENTS OF PEOPLE FAVORING RESTRICTIONS	Immigrants are too "different."	Immigrants are creating slums.	Immigrants corrupt democracy.	Immigrants bring radical ideas.	Immigrants are inferior.
ARGUMENTS OF PEOPLE OPPOSED TO RESTRICTIONS	The U.S. represents hope to people all over the world.	Open immigration is an American tradition.	Immigrants bring needed talent to U.S.	Restriction would be discriminatory.	With opportunity, immigrants would contribute to America.

Congress Chooses Immigration Restriction

In 1924 the debate in Congress was not about open immigration, but about restricting immigration from some parts of Europe. Non-European immigration was already restricted. In 1882 Congress had banned Chinese immigration. A 1908 agreement with the Japanese government had halted Japanese immigration.

The crisis created by World War I gave immigration restriction a push forward. The fear of foreigners increased because of the communist revolution in Russia. A wave of terrorism also made many citizens nervous. In 1917 Congress passed a series of laws restricting immigration. The new laws barred political radicals and "undesirables," including those who could not read.

After the war, immigration from war-torn Europe began to rise again. Fears rose that the cities would fill with jobless, desperate, foreign radicals. In response, Congress passed new immigration laws in both 1921 and 1924. These immigration acts established a quota system based on national origins. The cartoon at left comments on the 1921 law, which set quotas at 3 percent of each country's white immigrants living in the United States in 1910.

Immigration Laws Since 1924

The decision to enact restrictive immigration laws in 1921 and 1924 reflected an American fear of diversity in the 1920s. Since then, Congress has continued to debate immigration. In the 1950s and 1960s, Americans closely examined their views on immigration and diversity, in large part because of the African American struggle for civil rights. Congress recognized that the immigration laws written in the 1920s discriminated against immigrants from most parts of the world. It passed new legislation in 1952, which greatly changed the quotas for each country. For the first time, individuals from any country in the world could enter the United States. In 1965 a new immigration act eliminated quotas altogether.

Immigration policy continues to be debated in Congress. The debate focuses on jobs, the country's ability to absorb new immigrants, and to what extent the United States should be a refuge for people seeking freedom. After twenty-five years, the Immigration Act of 1990 was passed. This law favors immigrants who are close relatives of American citizens and those who have skills that are in short supply. The new law also excludes some individuals: for example, criminals and drug abusers. No provisions of the current law, however, limit the entry of immigrants based on national origin.

EVALUATING DECISIONS

1. What caused many Americans to change their attitudes about immigration after 1880?
2. How did World War I and its aftermath create a mood favorable to immigration restriction?

Critical Thinking

3. **Predicting Consequences** How do you think the immigration acts of 1921 and 1924 affected the way that people from eastern and southern Europe viewed the United States?

Media and Technology

Visions of America: History Might Not Have Happened This Way Game

To encourage students to explore pivotal moments in United States history, have students use the Visions of America software. Refer to the Visions of America Teacher's Guidebook for viewing objectives, activities, game instructions, and discussion questions.

Answers

1. Immigration increased from southern and eastern Europe, where cultures differed from that of native-born Americans. Immigrants were blamed for social ills, political corruption, and radicalism. According to popular racist theories, the "new" immigrants were inferior and could not participate equally in American life.

2. World War I heightened patriotic fervor and suspicion of foreigners. In its aftermath, unrest in Europe and the fear of political radicals in America convinced many that renewed immigration after the war endangered the country.

3. Answers will vary but are likely to include: Eastern and southern Europeans did not like the United States as much; they would be less likely to follow American foreign policy; they viewed Americans as hypocrites.

SECTION 2

Social and Political Developments

1. FOCUS

Connecting to the Big Idea

See page 402B. Point out that important political and social developments changed the United States during the 1920s. Ask students how women's suffrage and the northward migration of African Americans affected the country.

Objectives

- Describe the impact of women's suffrage on American politics in the 1920s.
- Explain why many African Americans migrated to the North during the 1920s.
- Describe the Harlem Renaissance.
- Describe the candidates and issues of the presidential election of 1928.

Bellringer

Ask students if they have ever moved, and if so, for what reasons their family moved. Then ask students to decide which state or region of the country they think currently provides the best opportunity for good jobs and advancement. Have students consider why their family might have to move to this or another area.

Reading Strategy

Reinforcing Key Ideas Ask students to note this sentence on page 410: "Out of the postwar climate of fear of things foreign or new came several important political and social developments." As they read, ask students to list and briefly describe the political and social developments discussed in this section.

SECTION PREVIEW

After the war, women and African Americans faced a world of new opportunities and old disappointments. In the political realm, Republicans won Americans' support—and votes.

Key Concepts

- The newly won women's vote did not lead to widespread change in American politics.
- Many African Americans moved to the North; some experienced repression and others, a renaissance.
- The Republican party controlled national politics.

Key Terms, People, and Places

Harlem Renaissance, Teapot Dome; Marcus Garvey, Warren G. Harding, Calvin Coolidge, Herbert Hoover

Performers such as Louis Armstrong helped jazz find a home in northern cities.

O
ut of the postwar climate of fear of things foreign or new came several important political and social developments. Women looked to flex their political muscles after securing the right to vote. Southern African Americans sought greater opportunity in the North. Meanwhile, the nation's ailing economy began to show signs of improvement in the early 1920s, and voters gave the credit to the Republican party.

The Women's Movement Fades

Having won the right to vote in 1920, women voters now faced the daunting challenge of fulfilling their promises to themselves and the nation. Would women vote in significant numbers? Would men give women equality in political parties? These questions worried those who had fought for women's rights.

The Impact of Suffrage In fact, women did not flock to the polls in huge numbers. This was partly because the percentage of voter turnout continued a decline that had begun more than twenty years before. Because women's suffrage was new, however, observers focused more attention on how few women voted than on how many did.

In addition, women's votes did not seem to change politics as much as suffragists had hoped. In national elections especially, women voted in patterns similar to men. Only in local contests did women seem to have a noticeable impact.

After gaining the right to vote, many women joined the Republican and Democratic parties and sought central roles in them. But men who ran these parties gave women only minor posts and rarely nominated women for office. Women therefore continued working largely from behind the scenes or in groups such as the League of Women Voters that were not connected to any political party. A few women became active in the newly formed National Woman's party, which was founded by militant

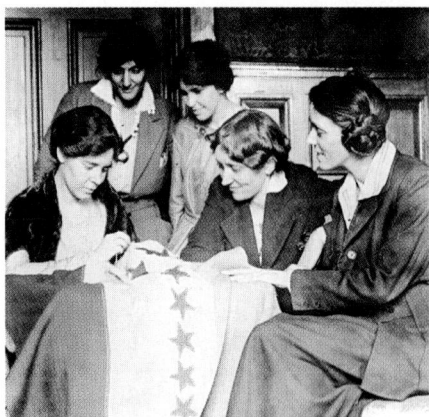

To celebrate the passage of the Nineteenth Amendment in 1920, Alice Paul adds the "ratification star" to the flag of the National Woman's Party.

▶ RESOURCE DIRECTORY

Teaching Resources

Reproducible Lesson Plan found in the Unit 4 folder, p. 4, provides a summary of the Section 2 lesson plan content.

Alternate Lesson Plan: Cooperative Learning found in the Alternate Lesson Plans folder, p. 107, is an alternate lesson plan that provides guidance for having students collectively produce a newspaper on the major issues of the 1920s.

Guided Reading and Review found in the Unit 4 folder, p. 10, provides a structure for reading and mastering the key concepts and reviewing the key terms for Section 2. (Guided Practice)

Primary Source Activity Growing Up Black, found in the Unit 4 folder, pp. 26–27, profiles Daisy Bates—a child of the South of the 1920s. The effects of segregation on seven-year-old Daisy and her neighbors—both African American and white—are described in Daisy's autobiography.

suffragist Alice Paul. Among the party's causes was an unsuccessful campaign for an Equal Rights Amendment (ERA) to the Constitution.

The Successes of Suffrage Suffrage did lead to some immediate gains for women. Polling places moved out of saloons and into more neutral public spaces, and women in twenty-one states began to serve on juries. National victories included the Sheppard-Towner Act (1921), which allocated federal money for pre-natal and infant health care. Also, the Cable Act (1922) allowed women who married foreigners to keep their United States citizenship. But perhaps more important than any concrete legislative or political success, suffrage marked an important first step for women on which they would base future gains in jobs, civil rights, and politics.

African Americans and the Great Migration

Throughout the early 1900s, jobs for African Americans, most of whom lived in the South, were scarce and low paying. Many factory jobs simply were closed to them. Opportunities for education were inadequate. In addition, lynchings and other forms of racial violence claimed the lives of dozens of innocent African Americans each year and terrorized countless others.

During World War I, factories in the North expanded production to meet the demands of the war, and many white factory workers left their jobs to join the battle overseas. These two developments created many new employment opportunities for African Americans in the North.

As a result of conditions in the South and new job opportunities in the North, half a million African Americans made the move to northern states by 1920, as the map below shows. Hundreds of thousands more followed later in the decade.

The trip from the South to the North was no small undertaking. The *Chicago Defender*, an African American newspaper, received thousands of letters like this one from a New Orleans man in 1917:

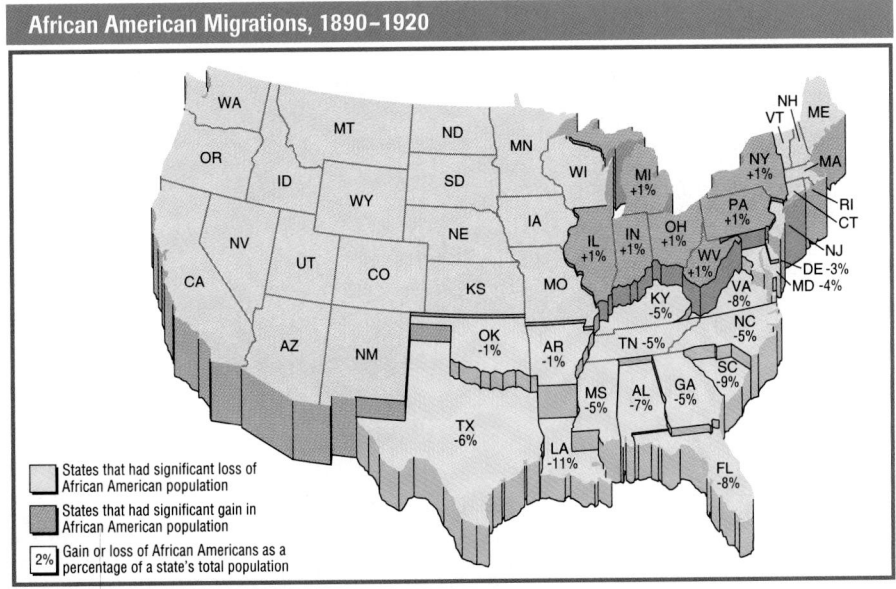

African American Migrations, 1890–1920

- States that had significant loss of African American population
- States that had significant gain in African American population
- 2% Gain or loss of African Americans as a percentage of a state's total population

Map labels: WA, MT, ND, MN, NH, VT, ME, OR, ID, SD, WI, MI +1%, NY +1%, MA, RI, CT, WY, IA, PA +1%, NE, IL +1%, IN +1%, OH +1%, WV +1%, NJ, NV, UT, CO, KS, MO, KY -5%, VA -8%, DE -3%, MD -4%, CA, AZ, NM, OK -1%, AR -1%, TN -5%, NC -5%, SC -9%, MS -5%, AL -7%, GA -5%, TX -6%, LA -11%, FL -8%

Geography and History: Interpreting Maps
The migration of African Americans from the South to the North helped alter the populations of both regions. *Which states lost the most population?*

Media and Technology

Transparency
Fine Art, D-16

2. INSTRUCT

Discuss
Discuss with students the impact of suffrage on the politics of the country. Ask how the newly gained right to vote affected the number of women holding elective office, voting patterns, location of polls, membership on juries, and reform bills. Have students identify the reasons many African Americans migrated from the South to the North. In reviewing the Chicago race riot of 1919 and its causes, ask students what conditions prompted the rapid spread of violence.

Analyze
Ask students to think about whether African Americans found more and better opportunities in the North and in what ways their desires to advance were frustrated. How did the writers and artists of the Harlem Renaissance and the Garvey movement inspire pride in African American culture?

Caption Answer to ...

Interpreting Maps

States that lost the most population were Louisiana, Florida, Texas, Alabama, South Carolina, and Virginia.

In Depth
Did You Know?
The first woman governor was elected in 1924 in Wyoming. Nellie Tayloe Ross served one energetic term before being defeated by a male opponent. She refused to be stereotyped and when movie cameramen requested to film her making bread or sweeping the floor, she refused to cooperate. Although Ross served only one term as governor, she was named director of the U.S. Mint in 1933.

Activity
Role Play—Voting Preference

Ask students to summarize the issues in the 1928 election. Play the part of a roving reporter, while students role-play the following voters: heir to a large furniture manufacturing company, Irish immigrant chauffeur, African American teacher, midwestern farmer and Roman Catholic head of a temperance movement in a small midwestern city. Ask the "voters" to explain their preference in the upcoming election.

In Depth
Multicultural Perspectives

The Harlem Renaissance inspired many artists to create masterpieces of language and tone. Claude McKay's "The Tropics in New York," Jean Toomer's "Cane," and Georgia Douglas Johnson's "Common Dust" are among the many works that express the feelings of both urban and rural African Americans. Langston Hughes's poem "I, Too" epitomizes the sense of possibility and the deep frustrations that African Americans felt at the time. Carl Van Doren, the editor of *Century* magazine and a Pulitzer winner for biography, observed: "What American literature decidedly needs at this moment is color, music, gusto, the free expression of gay or desperate moods. If the Negroes are not in a position to contribute to these items, I don't know what Americans are."

---

*I*f there is any way that you could get a pass please try and do that much for us as we are a party of four good working men the southern white are trying very hard to keep us from the north but still they wont give us no work to do.

The Reality of the North The North did offer more opportunities, but it was not a promised land, free of discrimination or hardship. Many African American women, for instance, found work as maids in white-owned homes. These jobs paid higher wages than most jobs in the South—but not enough to lift the women out of poverty. As one woman remarked in 1917, "They give you big money for what you do but they charge you big things for what you get." In addition, African American factory workers often met hostility from whites, who felt that the migrants threatened their jobs and wages.

African Americans also found that moving to the north did not ensure freedom from racial violence. Serious race riots occurred in 1917 in East St. Louis, Illinois, and in 1919 in Washington, D.C., and many other northern cities. ✪

Writers Langston Hughes (left) and Zora Neale Hurston (right) helped make Harlem a leading artistic center. Harlem was also a vital social hub in the 1920s.

Jazz singer Bessie Smith helped fill jazz nightspots in the North.

Perhaps the worst racial disturbance took place in Chicago. On Sunday, July 27, 1919, an African American youth went for a swim. New to town, he knew nothing of the invisible racial divisions that segregated the beach. When he drifted onto the "white" side, a white man threw a stone at him. The rock injured the youth, and he drowned. In retaliation, blacks began attacking whites. The riot left almost forty people dead, hundreds injured, and thousands homeless.

Racial tension clearly lay at the heart of the riots. But the fighting further unnerved a nation already troubled by the specter of radical violence and labor unrest. Attorney General Palmer even suggested that the rioting was the work of communists.

The Harlem Renaissance With the migration to northern cities, the number of African Americans living in New York's Harlem grew from 14,000 in 1914 to about 200,000 in 1930. At that time—prior to the economic devastation of the Depression in the 1930s—Harlem was a fashionable and exciting place to live. ✪

People flocked to Harlem nightspots to hear jazz, a musical form with roots deep in the African American South. With the Great

---

▶ **RESOURCE DIRECTORY** ✪

Teaching Resources

✪ **Literature Activity** *The Weary Blues*, found in the Unit 4 folder, p. 31, expresses the pain and frustration of Langston Hughes, a leading figure of the Harlem Renaissance, and serves as a pointed comparison to the indulgences of the flapper culture.

American Profiles Activity found in the Unit 4 folder, p. 20, profiles singer Bessie Smith whose life—from poverty, through migration, to success as a great interpreter of the blues—is a microcosm of the African American experience of the times.

Migration, jazz enjoyed a golden age. Singers Bessie Smith and Ma Rainey, pianist Duke Ellington, and trumpeter Louis "Satchmo" Armstrong became widely known performers.

Literary life among African Americans also flowered, part of a movement that came to be called the **Harlem Renaissance**. Publishers began printing novels and other writings by African American writers such as Countee Cullen, Zora Neale Hurston, Claude McKay, and Langston Hughes. Alain Locke's 1925 book titled *The New Negro* celebrated this development. Locke argued that being of both African and American heritage need not be a cause of conflict but rather of mutual enrichment.

The Garvey Movement New York City was home to another notable African American named **Marcus Garvey**. Garvey came to New York from his native Jamaica in 1916 to establish a new headquarters for his Universal Negro Improvement Association (UNIA). The UNIA sought to build up African Americans' self-respect. Its message of racial pride attracted masses of followers.

Garvey urged followers to return to "Motherland Africa." He also invested his followers' money in the Black Star steamship line. When Garvey oversold stock in this enterprise, he was jailed on fraud charges in 1925. The UNIA collapsed, but Garvey's ideas remained an inspiration to later "black pride" movements.

MAKING CONNECTIONS

Consider what you have read about postwar economic conditions in the United States. How might these conditions have contributed to the problems facing African Americans following their migration to the North?

A Decade of Republican Dominance

During the 1920s, the Republican party took a firm hold on the White House. One reason was that in the early 1920s, the economy began to rebound from the hard times that followed World War I. Industrial productivity soared, unemployment went down, and the number of strikes dropped. Voters gave the Republicans credit for the nation's recovery.

For the presidential election of 1920, Republican conservatives nominated **Warren G. Harding,** an Ohio senator. **Calvin Coolidge,** of the Boston police strike fame, was his running mate. The handsome, silver-haired Harding seemed the very picture of an American President, and many voters were attracted to his promise of a "return to normalcy." The Republicans overwhelmed the Democratic ticket of James Cox and Franklin D. Roosevelt.

A Scandal-Ridden Administration Harding, considered by many observers to be an "amiable second-rater," did make some good cabinet appointments, such as the highly regarded Herbert Hoover for secretary of commerce. Yet Harding also selected a number of unqualified friends for key posts. Some of these pals brought scandal down upon Harding's administration.

Harding himself did not have to deal with these troubles. He died on August 2, 1923, two-and-a-half years into his first term. By 1924, however, the full extent of the corruption in his administration was exposed. One Harding appointee had stolen government funds, others had taken payments in return for influence. Several other officials also were accused of wrongdoing, and two committed suicide.

The worst Harding scandal came to be known as **Teapot Dome**. It involved Harding's secretary of the interior, Albert B. Fall, who leased critical government oil reserves in Elk Hill, California, and Teapot Dome, Wyoming, to two private oil companies. In return, Fall received illegal payments and so-called loans that totaled over $300,000. Fall later went to jail for his role in the scandal.

The Democrats in 1924 tried to use public anger over the Teapot Dome affair to defeat the Republicans. The object below carried the Democratic message.

The Election of 1924 Voters apparently did not hold Vice President Calvin Coolidge responsible for these scandals. Following Harding's death, Coolidge completed the term. He then easily won his own election in 1924 over the Democratic ticket of John W. Davis and Charles Bryan and the Progressive candidate Bob La Follette.

Media and Technology

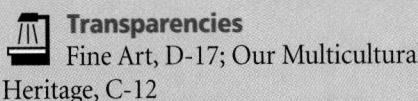

Transparencies
Fine Art, D-17; Our Multicultural Heritage, C-12

SOURCE READINGS

 Source Readings on p. 435 will connect literature selections and primary source excerpts to historical events discussed in this section.

Enrichment
Have students find a short poem or quotation from the works of one of the writers of the Harlem Renaissance such as Langston Hughes, Claude McKay, Arna Bontemps, Zora Neale Hurston, Countee Cullen, Jean Toomer, and Alain Locke. Encourage students to practice reading their selection aloud. Simulate a gathering of the Harlem Renaissance by having students read their selections and answer questions from the rest of the class.

Answer to …

MAKING CONNECTIONS

Competition for jobs and lagging wages might have led to hostility on the part of whites toward African Americans, whom whites have often perceived as a threat to jobs and their wages. Encourage students to explore the relationship between racial tensions and economic competition between whites and minority groups.

3. ASSESS

Section 2 Review Answers

1. (a) Harlem Renaissance, see p. 413, (b) Teapot Dome, see p. 413

2. (a) Marcus Garvey, see p. 413, (b) Warren G. Harding, see p. 413, (c) Calvin Coolidge, see p. 413, (d) Herbert Hoover, see p. 414

3. Women's suffrage did not bring about a purification of politics, huge voter turnouts, or a large number of women officeholders. Victories included moving polling places from saloons to more neutral public places, and allowing women jurors, although at first only in twenty-one of the forty-eight states.

4. They were seeking better jobs. Some northern cities experienced race riots. Others, like Harlem, had an entertainment and literary renaissance.

5. The economy seemed to be on its feet. The conservative policies, such as high tariffs and support for business, seemed to appeal to the voters.

6. Students might formulate questions about whether or not employment or overall earning rates increased in the North as compared to the South. They might also question whether African Americans experienced increases or decreases in poverty rates and incidents of racial violence.

Reteach

Tell students that the following statements are incorrect. Ask them to read and correct each of the statements and provide evidence from the section to support each correction.

● The women's vote had a major impact on American politics, since women voted in large numbers for Democrats.

● African Americans moving to the North found freedom from racial violence.

● *Harlem Renaissance* refers to the popularity of jazz in that part of New York City during the 1920s.

● In 1928 the Republicans appealed to those Americans who supported the repeal of prohibition.

● Democrat Al Smith was elected President in 1928.

Caption Answer to ...

Using Historical Evidence

The cartoon suggests that big business is quite happy with Coolidge. Big business is depicted as an energetic flapper who is enjoying dancing to Coolidge's music.

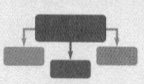

4. CLOSE

Reinforcing the Big Idea

The social and political changes examined in this section, women's suffrage, the northward migration of many African Americans, and the scandals of the Harding administration each changed the nation in different ways. The next section describes some of the changes in the social life, manners, and styles during the "roaring twenties."

Using Historical Evidence Calvin Coolidge, depicted here with a saxophone, was known for his support of big business. *What does this cartoon suggest about big business's reaction to Coolidge's policies?*

"Silent Cal" Coolidge, as he was nicknamed, was a shy man known for using few words. His other memorable trait was an uncritical support for the interests of American business, as the cartoon at left illustrates. "The chief business of the American people is business," he told a group of newspaper editors in 1925. Coolidge demonstrated his beliefs by raising tariffs. This helped American manufacturers by making foreign goods more expensive and American goods more attractive to buyers.

Coolidge was less willing to use the federal government to aid ordinary citizens. For example, he rejected aid for victims of a Mississippi River flood, saying that government had no duty to protect citizens "against the hazards of the elements."

The Election of 1928 As Coolidge neared the end of his first full term, he announced that he would not seek reelection in 1928. In his place, the Republicans nominated the well-respected **Herbert Hoover**. During and after World War I, Hoover achieved spectacular success running relief programs in Europe and the Food Administration in the United States. Later, he held cabinet posts in both the Harding and Coolidge administrations. Voters seemed to trust that he would provide sound leadership for the nation. Indeed, Hoover easily won election over the Democratic candidate, New York governor Al Smith.

In fact, the 1928 election returns did reveal some signs of weakness in the Republican armor, as you will read in Section 5. These political shifts, however, were subtle and hard to detect. Far more obvious were the dramatic changes in morals, manners, and fashion being flaunted by the energetic youth of the nation's growing urban centers.

SECTION 2 REVIEW

Key Terms, People, and Places
1. Define (a) Harlem Renaissance, (b) Teapot Dome.
2. Identify (a) Marcus Garvey, (b) Warren G. Harding, (c) Calvin Coolidge, (d) Herbert Hoover.

Key Concepts
3. What were some of the disappointments and successes of suffrage?
4. For what reasons did African Americans move north, and what was the result?
5. What factors helped lead to Republican success in the 1920s?

Critical Thinking
6. **Formulating Questions** What questions might you examine to determine whether or not African American migration in the early 1900s improved the lives of migrants generally?

 RESOURCE DIRECTORY

Teaching Resources

Quiz found in the Unit 4 folder, p. 11, covers the main ideas in this section as well as the key terms.

New Manners, New Morals

SECTION 3

New Manners, New Morals

From rising hemlines to the energetic sounds of jazz, the 1920s daringly broke with tradition. New social freedoms created opportunity—and dilemmas—for women. But beneath it all lay a nagging question: How much had really changed?

Key Concepts
• Many American youth were eager for social changes after the war.
• The Jazz Age introduced many new tastes and manners, especially for women.
• The changes were not as widespread as presented in popular media.

Key Terms, People, and Places
Jazz Age, flapper

F or many Americans, World War I was a watershed event. By bringing to a crashing close most of the monarchies of Europe, the war made the code of values and morals that they represented seem dreadfully old-fashioned. Many Americans longed to shed these old ideas and, with them, the horrors and disillusionment of World War I.

Young people were especially eager for change. They experimented with new social freedoms that took root first in the cities and then spread across the country. Yet, though the brash new ways of the urban youth became a symbol of the 1920s, many changes of the era turned out to be superficial.

Jazz Age Manners

Several factors contributed to the cultural changes taking place following World War I. As more youth finished high school and went on to college, they looked to each other rather than to their parents for standards of behavior. Soldiers returning home from the war brought new styles and habits to their hometowns.

Advances in communications rapidly spread the emerging culture. (See Section 4.)

Along with the great postwar African American migration from the South to the North came jazz, blues, and Dixieland music, which quickly found a home in northern urban nightspots. The wide availability of phonograph records and record players meant that people could play the music wherever they gathered. Jazz had such a strong influence on the tastes and manners of the age that the 1920s became known as the **Jazz Age.**

The exciting rhythms of jazz captivated young people and blossomed on dance floors. Dance marathons—in which couples competed to see who could stay on the dance floor longest—became a popular fad. Young Americans let off steam in other zany ways as well: Flagpole sitting and goldfish eating became crazes during the 1920s.

Like jazz itself, most American dance rages of the early 1900s came from African American culture. As Carl Van Vechten, an admirer of black culture in the twenties, explained, the dances would start on street corners in African American communities, move into saloons and nightclubs, and from there onto the music-hall stage and into the larger culture. "This has been the history of the Cake-Walk, the Bunny Hug, the Turkey Trot, the Charleston, and the Black Bottom," he wrote, referring to several dances of the early 1900s.

Older generations mocked the new dances. A writer in 1920 sneered about how the youth of his day "trot like foxes, limp like lame ducks, . . . all to the barbaric yawp of strange instruments. . . ." But by mid-decade, critics celebrated

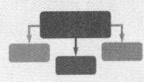

Jazz music, played on records and phonographs like these, lay at the heart of a dramatic change in fashion, manners, and morals.

1. FOCUS

Connecting to the Big Idea

See page 402B. Explain to students that the 1920s were the years of the flapper, the Jazz Age, new manners and new styles. Ask if changes in the social life, manners, and styles of urban youth marked a significant change in American life.

Objectives
● Explain why American youth were eager for social change after the war.
● Describe the new tastes and manners introduced during the Jazz Age.
● Show evidence that changes in the 1920s were not as widespread as presented by the media.

Bellringer

Ask students to list current fashions, music, fads, or pastimes that appeal to young people. Ask how these styles or activities are perceived by others of their generation or of their parents' generation.

In Depth

Biography

Margaret Sanger (1883–1966) established the first birth control clinic in the United States in Brooklyn, New York, in 1916. Within weeks, the police closed the clinic, arrested Sanger, and jailed her for thirty days. However, in 1921 she organized the first American Birth Control Conference and in 1923 the Clinical Research Bureau of New York. The merger of these two organizations in 1938 eventually became the modern-day Planned Parenthood Federation of America.

📄 **Reproducible Lesson Plan** found in the Unit 4 folder, p. 5, provides a summary of the Section 3 lesson plan content.

📄 **Alternate Lesson Plan: Critical Thinking** Making Comparisons, found in the Alternate Lesson Plans folder, p. 108, is an alternate lesson plan that provides a chart activity that helps students compare the social changes of the 1920s to those of the 1990s.

📄 **Guided Reading and Review** found in the Unit 4 folder, p. 12, provides a structure for reading and mastering the key concepts and reviewing the key terms for Section 3. (Guided Practice)

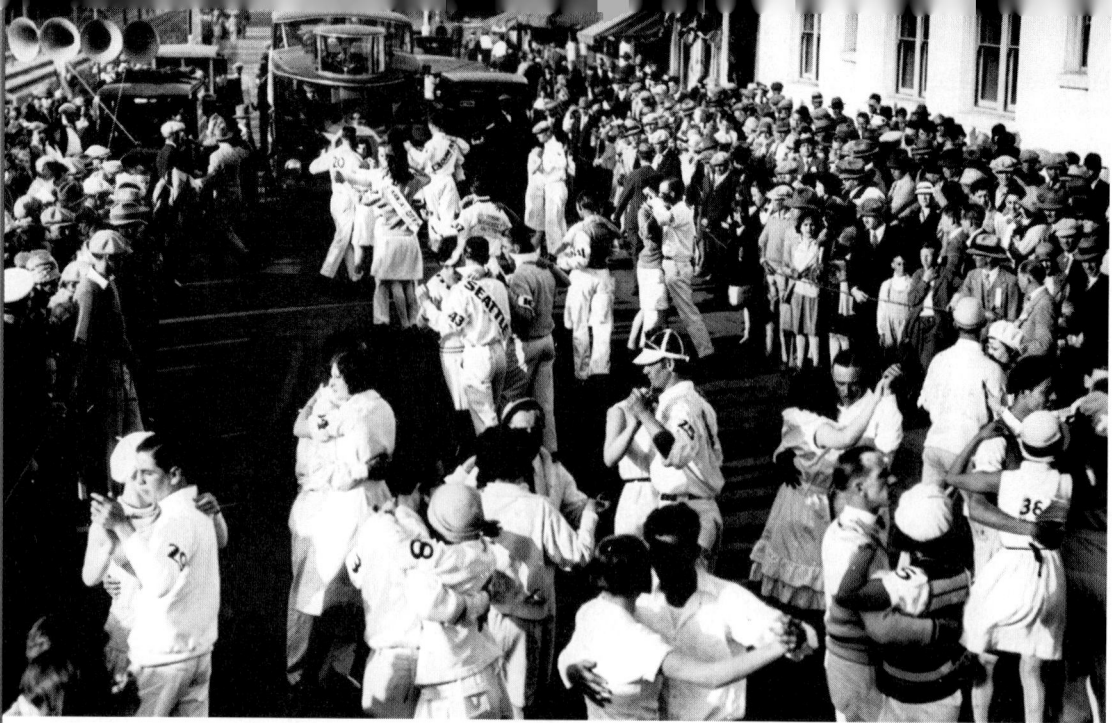

Reading Strategy

Finding Evidence Write the following statement on the board: In spite of new manners and trends, life continued much as usual. Ask students to find evidence of superficial changes in the 1920s.

2. INSTRUCT

Discuss

Tell students that the image of the 1920s as the "roaring twenties," the era of the flapper and the rake, is still prevalent. Why are these images popular with Americans? Do the gilded youth of the 1920s represent characteristics that Americans value? Why would young people want to embrace behaviors that were so different from those of their parents' generation?

Ask why the prevalence of the automobile brought about changes in manners and, perhaps, in morals.

Analyze

Discuss the fact that women went to work in large numbers in the 1920s. Ask students to decide if and how they think women's lives improved in the 1920s.

 Activity

Teaching Heterogeneous Groups

The desire for change and progress by youth during the Jazz Age was embodied in the flapper and the rake. Styles and manners today also illustrate the feelings and desires of youth. In small groups, have students name and describe three or four symbols to illustrate the styles and manners of today's youth culture. Have students compare these symbols to the symbols of the 1920s.

LEP

Enrichment

Ask students to research the life and writings of F. Scott Fitzgerald in order to determine if he invented the flapper.

During dance marathons in the 1920s, people frequently fainted from exhaustion. This 1928 marathon consisted of an 8-mile dance down the highway to a ballroom, where the marathon continued.

jazz as a positive force. Leopold Stokowski, a well-known symphony conductor, observed that jazz had "come to stay because it is an expression of the times, of the breathless, energetic, superactive times in which we are living."

Breaking Social Conventions in the Jazz Age

During the twenties, young men and women displayed growing freedom in their relations with one another. They dated without chaperones, talked slang, danced with their bodies touching, and in general defied the social conventions of the time. Poet Edna St. Vincent Millay voiced this youthful, some would say reckless, new spirit when she wrote:

*M*y candle burns at both ends;
*It will not last the night;
But ah, my foes, and, oh my friends—
It gives a lovely light.*
                                   "First Fig," 1920

Changes in fashion reflected the new morals and manners. Women's clothing became more revealing, exposing arms and knees. Makeup, once associated only with the stage and prostitutes, appeared on the faces of ordinary women for the first time.

The wider availability of cars in the 1920s shaped some aspects of youth behavior. Instead of meeting at a young woman's home, young men increasingly took their partners out on dates. In an automobile, they could escape all supervision. This development had far-reaching implications: Fearing a rise in sexually transmitted diseases and unwanted pregnancies, some teachers and social workers urged a more open discussion of sex.

The new freedoms, however, created a dilemma for many young women. In the twenties, women's behavior was still judged by stricter standards than men's. As a result, women were torn by conflicting social pressures that encouraged them both to adopt new standards of behavior and to adhere to old ones.

The Flapper The ultimate symbol of Jazz Age behavior was the youthful woman known as the **flapper**. The term came from a popular drawing of a dancing woman with her boots open and flapping. As author Preston Slosson

 RESOURCE DIRECTORY

Teaching Resources

Critical Thinking Activity Testing Conclusions: The Jazz Age, found in the Unit 4 folder, p. 25, provides a partial glossary of Jazz Age terms and expressions to help students test their conclusions on the values and mores of the era.

observed in his 1930 work *The Great Crusade and After,* the flapper was

> *breezy, slangy, and informal in manner; slim and boyish in form; covered in silk and fur that clung to her as close as onion skin; with carmined* [vivid red] *cheeks and lips, plucked eyebrows and close-fitting helmet of hair; gay, plucky and confident.*

Jazz Age men had their symbol, too—the "rake," with his careening automobile, reckless drinking, and irresponsible flirting. But the flapper became the more widely used symbol of the rebellious youth culture. Perhaps this was because standards of behavior for women had always been more constrained than for men. Thus, the new styles and manners seemed more startling when women adopted them.

MAKING CONNECTIONS

Compare the flapper to women from the suffrage or the abolition movements of the past or the feminist movement of recent years. In what ways are they similar and different?

How Widespread Was the New Youth Culture?

In reality, the urban youth culture represented by the flapper was not as widespread as the popular media suggested. Although the economy appeared healthy, deeply rooted problems, especially on the nation's farms, had many Americans worrying more about their economic survival than how to do the hottest new dance. Large numbers of young people did not rebel against traditional social and religious standards. Women everywhere experimented with cropped hair and short skirts, but many did so out of convenience rather than out of identification with flappers.

Reality for Women For women, especially, many of the new social freedoms turned out to be limited. Single women in large numbers moved into office, sales, and service jobs during the 1920s. Yet employers continued to assume that women were in the labor force only until they were married, and thus did not train them for advancement or pay them as well as men. Many hospitals and law firms refused to hire women physicians and lawyers.

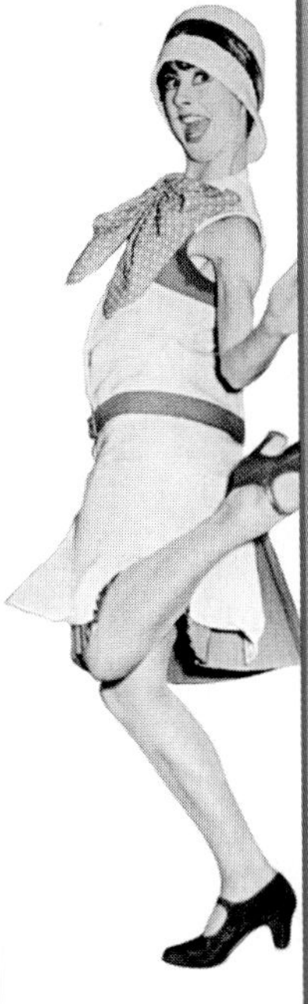

Flappers defined a whole new style of dress and behavior.

1650 1700 1750 1800 **Links Across Time** 1850 1900 1950 2000

Women's Fashions

The flappers of the 1920s broke the mold of traditional dress for women. Over the course of history, women's clothing has undergone many such changes. In the late 1800s, for example, many women took pains to present an "hourglass" figure. Because few women possessed the desirable tiny waist naturally, they often wore restrictive corsets that were reinforced with whalebone for added stiffness. Usually, a helper was needed to pull the laces of the corset tight enough to reduce the waist as much as possible. These corsets restricted the abdomen so much that they were blamed by physicians for contributing to many kinds of internal health problems.

Within a few years, young women wanted to achieve just the opposite look—a boyish, straight silhouette. Fashion changes in the 1920s reflected new morals and manners among the nation's youth. Ankle-length dresses and cotton stockings gave way to short, tight dresses worn with silk stockings rolled down to the knees. Young women bobbed their long hair into short, boyish styles, often to the horror of their more traditional mothers.

Following World War II, the desire for stability in the 1950s home contributed to another fashion shift toward longer skirts and a return to the hourglass figure ideal. But then the social revolution of 1960s youth led again to a fashion revolution. For the first time, slacks were considered acceptable garb for women and hemlines rose again—this time to the previously unseen heights of the miniskirt. ***What effects might accepted standards of beauty and fashion have on women?***

Answer to ...

Links Across Time

The *New York Times Magazine* of October 1993 described fifty years of women's fashion in the following way: "The salon trussed her. Advertising seduced her. Rock released her. Then the market indulged her, until just getting dressed became a complex but liberating challenge to her identity."

Answer to ...

MAKING CONNECTIONS

A possible response might be that unlike abolitionists and suffrage workers, flappers had no specific political agenda. Like feminists of recent years, flappers sought to redefine the social perception of women.

3. ASSESS

Section 3 Review Answers

1. flapper, see p. 416

2. Many Americans were anxious to shed old values and morals. A growing number of Americans were going to college and finding their own standards of behavior. Soldiers returning from the war brought new styles and habits that influenced young Americans.

3. Women's behavior was judged by stricter standards than that of men. Rebellion for them was thus more startling.

4. It was mainly an urban rebellion. Economic survival prevailed and though more women moved into the work force, the wage structure and other forms of discrimination held them back.

5. The developments of the decade seemed to offer new freedoms. At the same time, double standards still led to harsh judgments of many women's behavior, and technological improvements that were supposed to make women's work easier in fact created a new set of higher expectations.

Women still had many jobs to do, including sewing, vacuuming, ironing, cooking, and taking care of children. The woman reading the magazine advertisement also suggests that women were responsible for shopping and purchasing.

Reteach

Write the following phrases on the chalkboard: flappers and rakes; students and workers. Ask each student to write at least two generalizations about each phrase.

Alternative Assessment

Mid-Point Monitoring

Ask students if they have

- Chosen a format for their project
- Outlined the main ideas
- Begun outside research and preparation of the bibliography

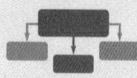**4. CLOSE**

Reinforcing the Big Idea

Many young Americans, eager for change after World War I, adopted the manners, styles, and customs of the Jazz Age and challenged the culture of their parents' generation. The next section describes how sweeping technological changes affected the entire nation.

Using Historical Evidence Thanks to new electrical appliances, the nature of housework changed, but the demands on women remained. *What does this ad suggest about the responsibilities of women?*

The number of married women combining work, careers, and family life also rose slowly during the 1920s. But married women's working lives remained restricted. Employers often fired white women when they became pregnant. African American women had different experiences. White employers expected—and their own economic need often required—that they work even after they became pregnant.

In spite of workplace inequalities, many women enjoyed the independence that came with a job. Yet many also felt the pull of traditional roles of wife and mother. Former suffragist Sue Shelton White expressed the dilemma as a choice "between the frying pan and the fire—both very uncomfortable." ⊙

The Impact of Technological Change For the majority of women, it was technological change more than flapperism or jazz that seemed to promise real liberation. Thanks to cars, women could more easily shop for food. As manufacturers lowered prices for electrical products and as merchants introduced installment-plan buying, more women bought sewing machines, vacuum cleaners, and other labor-saving devices.

These developments eased life, but by no means freed women from drudgery. In fact, they raised expectations of household work. Kitchens and clothes now could be—and thus had to be—spotless. "By Their Floors Ye Shall Judge Them," warned a floor-polisher ad. "It is written that floors are like unto a mirror, reflecting the character of the housewife."

Of course, technological change in the 1920s changed more than the ways women did housework. Enormous changes in communications technology helped to create a whole new culture.

SECTION 3 REVIEW

Key Terms, People, and Places
1. Define flapper.

Key Concepts
2. What factors led many Americans to challenge existing social norms following World War I?
3. Why did the Jazz Age changes in manners appear to have a greater impact on women than on men?

4. How far-reaching were Jazz Age changes? Explain.

Critical Thinking
5. **Demonstrating Reasoned Judgment** "The developments of the 1920s, including the changing manners and the technological developments of the era, were a mixed blessing for women." Explain the meaning of this statement.

**RESOURCE DIRECTORY**

Teaching Resources

⊙ **American Profiles Activity** found in the Unit 4 folder, p. 21, profiles Lillian Moller Gilbreth who raised twelve children while running a successful business and serving on several government committees on behalf of the less fortunate.

Quiz found in the Unit 4 folder, p. 13, covers the main ideas in this section as well as the key terms.

Analyzing Advertisements

Print advertisements—ads that appear as posters or in newspapers and magazines—offer important visual evidence about the consumer goods and services that were promoted during a historical period. Advertisements also can offer useful clues to the widely held ideas, attitudes, and values of the past. When using advertisements as historical evidence, however, it is important to bear in mind that advertisers rely on many different types of techniques in order to influence people's buying decisions. Ads may reflect certain lifestyles to which advertisers want consumers to aspire, rather than lifestyles that reflect reality for the majority of people during a certain historical period.

By the 1920s, the previously straightforward "what-it-is and what-it-does" mode of advertising was giving way to "situational" ads. These ads depicted not only the products, but also the ways in which those products might increase personal satisfaction or enhance the lives of typical consumers. One such advertisement from the 1920s appears at right.

Use the following steps to analyze the ad.

1. Identify the subject of the ad. (a) What product or service is being promoted? (b) What facts about the product does the ad provide? (c) What issue does this advertisement use to appeal particularly to men? To women?

2. Analyze the ad's reliability as historical evidence. (a) Do you think that the people depicted in the ad portray typical consumers of the 1920s? Explain. (b) What is the unstated message that the advertiser is using in this case to persuade people to buy the product?

3. Study the ad to learn more about the historical period. (a) What social or cultural values are being promoted in the advertisement? (b) In general, do you think that advertisements reflect consumers' desires for products or create the desire for such products? Explain.

 —and he wonders why she said "NO!"

Could he have read her thoughts he would not have lost her. A picture of neatness herself, she detested slovenliness. And not once, but many times, she had noticed his ungartered socks crumpling down around his shoe tops. To have to apologize to her friends for a husband's careless habits was too much to ask. So she had to say "NO"—and in spite of his pleading couldn't tell him WHY.

No SOX Appeal Without

 PARIS GARTERS

SINGLE GRIP   **NO METAL CAN TOUCH YOU**   DOUBLE GRIP
25c to $2
Dress Well and Succeed

Historian's Toolbox Activity Analyzing Advertisements, found in the Unit 4 folder, p. 24, uses an advertisement of the 1990s to assist students in analyzing visual evidence as a tool to research history; and as a guide to the social and cultural values of today.

SECTION 4

Creating a Shared Culture

1. FOCUS

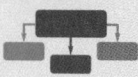

Connecting to the Big Idea

See page 402B. In the 1920s, the nation began to develop a truly national culture. Ask what changes helped to create this new culture.

Objectives

● Show how population movements and developments in communications and transportation helped create a common culture.

● Describe how developments in radio, movies, advertising, and the automobile industry furthered the process of creating a national culture.

Bellringer

Ask students to imagine that a new student joins your class from another part of the country. In what ways would they expect this new student to be different from other students? What might account for the new student's familiarity with the same slang, clothing, food, music, movies, and books?

Reading Strategy

Predicting Content Ask students to skim Section 4, list the main and subheadings, and write a sentence or phrase under each heading that predicts the content of each section. When they have finished reading the section, ask students to test their predictions against the actual text.

Caption Answer to ...

Interpreting Tables

Possible answers: There was also growth in broadcasting, as well as in all entertaining media that were carried on the radio, such as music and sports. Advertising also found a huge new market.

SECTION PREVIEW

People in city apartments, country farmhouses, and everywhere in between were connected in new ways in the 1920s. Such links allowed sweeping changes to envelop the entire nation.

Caps like this were worn by aviators in the 1920s. Heroes of aviation, as well as sports and movies, were products of the new entertainment media.

Key Concepts
• Population movements and new developments in communications and transportation helped create a culture common to many Americans.
• Developments in radio, movies, advertising, and the automobile industry furthered the process of creating a national culture.

Key Terms, People, and Places
Charles A. Lindbergh, Henry Ford

C hange—resisted by some and welcomed by others—remained a constant force during the 1920s. During this decade, 14.6 million Americans moved from rural to urban areas and from one state to another. This included the migration of African Americans described in Section 2.

As people moved, they interacted with people in other regions to an extent never before possible. In addition, expanding mass media and advances in transportation led to a wider sharing of tastes, values, and experiences among people all across the country.

Americans at Leisure

Partly as the result of decades of union campaigns for shorter hours, the average factory workweek in the mid-1920s was just over fifty hours, down from nearly sixty hours in 1900. Men and women began exploring new ways to spend their growing leisure time. Industry and commerce stood ready to meet this need.

The Radio In 1920, only about twenty thousand people using homemade sets were receiving wireless radio messages. As an experiment, Frank Conrad of the Westinghouse Company in East Pittsburgh began to broadcast recorded music and baseball scores over the radio. The response was so great that the company began broadcasting new programs on a regular basis. By the fall of 1920, the country had its first radio station operated as a commercial enterprise, Pittsburgh's KDKA.

By 1922, over five hundred stations had formed, with newspapers controlling about a quarter of them. Listeners could now hear music, news, sports events, and religious services over the air. To reach more people, networks such as the National Broadcasting Company (NBC) brought together many individual stations, and each station in the network played the same programming. Soon much of the country was sharing the same jokes, commercials, and music.

The Movies By 1917, the movies had become big business. Luxury movie theaters began to replace storefront nickelodeons. As with radio, corporate giants took control. The studios of

Households with Radios, 1920–1930

Year	Number of Households with Radio Sets
1920	20,000
1922	60,000
1924	1,250,000
1926	4,500,000
1928	8,000,000
1930	13,750,000

Source: *Historical Statistics of the United States*

Interpreting Tables
Radio—once the hobby of a few dedicated enthusiasts—soon became a household fixture. *What industries probably benefited from the growth in the number of household radios?*

▶ RESOURCE DIRECTORY

Teaching Resources

📄 **Reproducible Lesson Plan** found in the Unit 4 folder, p. 6, provides a summary of the Section 4 lesson plan content.

📄 **Alternate Lesson Plan: Learning Styles** found in the Alternate Lesson Plans folder, p. 109, is an alternate lesson plan that provides a group activity, especially effective for visual and auditory learners, around the theme of shared cultures.

📄 **Guided Reading and Review** found in the Unit 4 folder, p. 14, provides a structure for reading and mastering the key concepts and reviewing the key terms for Section 4. (Guided Practice)

⊛ 📄 **Visual Learning Activity** Advertising Techniques of the 1920s, found in the Unit 4 folder, p. 33, helps students understand how advertisers market their brands to specific groups of consumers; and how companies shape images to their own products.

Metro-Goldwyn-Mayer, Warner Brothers, and Columbia dominated the field. Talkies—movies with sound—arrived in 1927 with *The Jazz Singer,* starring stage performer Al Jolson. By 1930, patrons were buying 100 million movie tickets a week.

MAKING   CONNECTIONS

What leisure activities are important to young people today? In what ways are these activities similar to or different from the leisure activities of the 1920s?

The Worship of National Idols

The new entertainment media helped create national idols. The American people, eager for someone to look up to after the trauma of World War I, embraced them. From the movies, the ever-innocent Mary Pickford became America's Sweetheart; Clara Bow, the It Girl—a "good girl" who had "it," or sexual allure. Charlie Chaplin was the Little Tramp, and Rudolph Valentino, the Sheik.

Sports Heroes After the movie stars came sports figures. Among the most famous were Babe Ruth, the New York Yankee hitter of sixty home runs in 1927; prizefighters Jack Dempsey and Gene Tunney; and Gertrude Ederle, the first woman to swim the English Channel.

Lindbergh's Historic Flight The decade's ultimate hero, **Charles A. Lindbergh,** was from Minnesota. Lindbergh was a stunt flyer and air-mail pilot. In May 1927, the twenty-five-year-old competed for a $25,000 prize offered to the first aviator to fly nonstop across the Atlantic Ocean from New York to Paris. Except for a team of two flyers who landed in a sleepy Irish bog in 1919, everyone else attempting the crossing had crashed or disappeared.

Flying his *Spirit of St. Louis* with a dangerous overload of fuel, struggling through ice storms and fatigue, Lindbergh managed to cross the great ocean and land safely on May 21 at Le Bourget airfield near Paris. He became an instant hero. A poem in the *New York*

Sun ignored the industrial know-how that had made his flight possible and celebrated Lindbergh as the ultimate lone conqueror:

> *No kingly plane for him;*
> *No endless data, com-*
>   *rades, moneyed chums;*
> *No boards, no councils,*
>   *no directors grim—*
> *He plans ALONE and*
>   *takes luck as it comes."*

To many Americans, the tall, handsome, independent Lindbergh came to symbolize their national spirit. *The New Republic* declared, he is "ours. . . . He is no longer permitted to be himself. He is US personified. He is the United States."

Selling New Products and Ideas

While many Americans were adoring the same heroes, other aspects of their daily lives also became increasingly similar. Chain supermarkets spread, along with products known mostly by brand names. The A&P grocery chain, which had 5,000 stores in 1922, had 15,500 by 1929. The nation's first shopping center (in Kansas City) and first fast-food chain (A & W Root Beer) appeared in the twenties. Soon people across the country were shopping in the same stores for the same goods.

The advertising industry boomed, rising to the challenge of selling the country's many new products. Agents and salesmen grew from 11,000 in 1910 to 25,000 in 1920. Through advertising, products became synonymous with brand names. Paper hankies became "Kleenex," record players became "Victrolas."

In aggressive campaigns, advertisers convinced people that they needed to buy new products. When the Lambert Company discovered it could sell more Listerine as a cure for bad breath than as a general antiseptic, its advertising agents introduced the term *halitosis*—a new

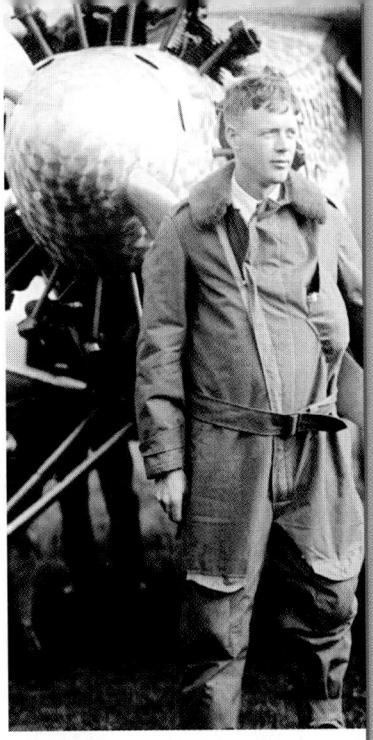

Daring Charles Lindbergh, who was the first aviator to fly nonstop across the Atlantic Ocean, embodied the American ideal of the lone conqueror.

Answer to . . .
MAKING   CONNECTIONS

Answers will vary, but students might note similar activities such as movies and dancing, and different activities such as computer and video games.

2. INSTRUCT

Explain/Discuss

Explain that the force of change continued to pervade American life. Many people moved, and improved means of communication allowed Americans around the country to share interests and experiences. Point out that these changes resulted in the creation of a national culture. Ask students how the invention of the radio contributed to this newly shared culture. What was the role of the advertising industry? Ask students how television programs, computer games, concert tours, and national chain stores create similarities among Americans today.

Analyze

Ask students to decide whether the advertising industry was the strongest force in building a national culture. What is the impact of television advertising on a national culture today?

In Depth

Did You Know?

"Lindbergh . . . has qualities of heart and head that all of us would like to possess," said the *New York Times.* On his flight across the Atlantic, Lindbergh seemed to carry the hopes and dreams of a nation struggling to come to grips with itself following World War I. It is estimated that 25,000 tons of newsprint alone were used to record his flight and five thousand poems were written to commemorate it.

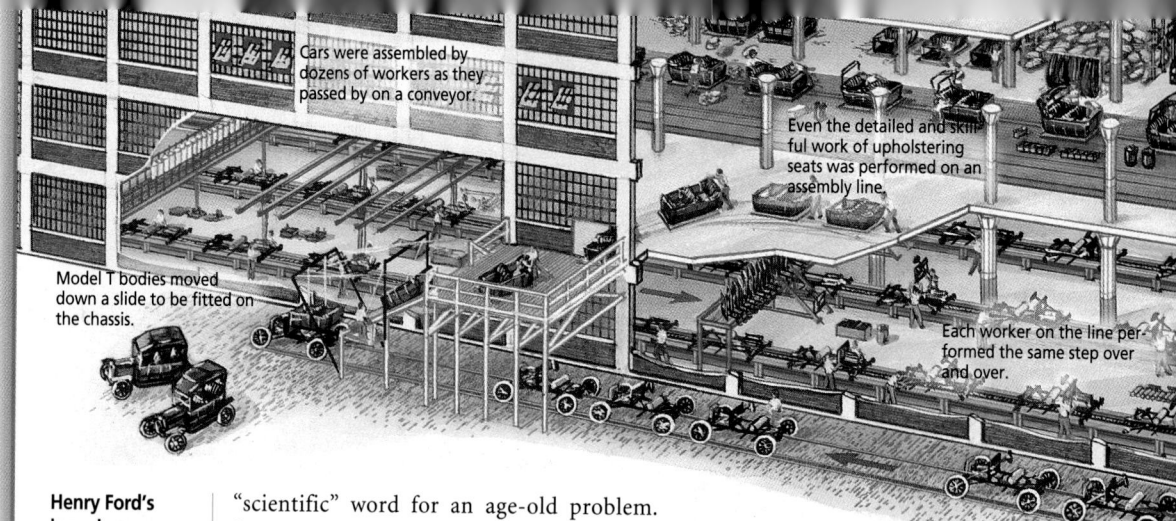

Cars were assembled by dozens of workers as they passed by on a conveyor.

Even the detailed and skillful work of upholstering seats was performed on an assembly line.

Model T bodies moved down a slide to be fitted on the chassis.

Each worker on the line performed the same step over and over.

Activity

Cooperative Learning

Time: One class period.
Activity: Create a movie idol.
Grouping: Groups of four students.
Purpose: Through the efforts of the entertainment media, national idols were created for the first time during the 1920s. Have groups select a movie character of the 1920s, and develop a campaign to make that character the newest movie idol. Students can refer to *The Story of Cinema* by David Shipman for ideas regarding movie characters of the decade.
Roles: Members of a media public relations group, such as writers, illustrators, marketing specialists.
Outcome: Students will portray the effects of the media and advertising in the 1920s.

Enrichment

Ask students to research the beginning of the national highway system and the construction of U.S. Highway 66. Ask them to include a map of the highway with their report.

In Depth

Historical Misconceptions

There is some debate about whether Henry Ford was oblivious to customer tastes regarding color. Ford biographer Robert Lacey says in *Ford: The Men and the Machine* that the only reason Ford's Model T was offered to customers in "any color so long as it's black" was because an engineer in the Ford plant discovered that black dried faster than any other color. Tin Lizzies originally came in green with a red stripe.

Henry Ford's ingenious production methods were based on two key ideas: the assembly line and uniformity of product. The assembly line, shown above, broke down car production into precise steps. Uniformity of product held that each car should be identical—an idea never before applied to such complicated machinery.

"scientific" word for an age-old problem. "What secret is your mirror holding back?" ads asked. "Even your best friend won't tell you."

Manufacturers put huge amounts of money into advertising. In 1922 Lambert's advertising budget came to $100,000. By 1928, it was spending $5 million and still raking in huge profits.

An Affordable Automobile

The automobile, invented in the 1890s, came of age in the 1920s. Over the decade, the number of registered automobiles rose from 8 million to over 23 million.

By freeing individuals to set their own schedules, automobiles individualized travel. People who were not wealthy traveled more often and over greater distances. To accommodate them, the government built new road systems, parks, and beaches for everyone, not just the rich. These developments had a powerful impact on the economy, stimulating the construction, rubber, gasoline and petroleum, advertising, and tourist industries. ⭐

The United States owed much of the boom in the auto industry to one man. His genius helped revolutionize industry at the same time that it changed the face of the nation itself.

AMERICAN PROFILES

Henry Ford

Henry Ford was born on a Michigan farm in 1863. Early in life he showed an aptitude for

things mechanical, and he seemed destined for a career working with machines.

In the late 1880s, while an engineer at the Detroit Illuminating Company, Ford began working on a horseless carriage powered by an engine. In 1896 he produced a "quadricycle," the lightest of the current gasoline-driven models. Ford started his own company in 1903 to manufacture automobiles. By 1910, he was selling over thirty thousand of his Model T's.

Pioneering Production Methods Ford had even higher ambitions. He wanted to "democratize the automobile," producing more cars at prices ordinary people could afford. Toward this end, he developed the revolutionary assembly line illustrated above.

Ford's system worked. By making large numbers of identical automobiles in an identical way, Ford could take advantage of the economy of scale to lower his costs for producing each car. In 1914, the first year his assembly line was fully operational, his company sold 248,000 cars at $490 each, almost half of what a car had cost in 1910. The following year he dropped the price to $390. By the early 1920s he was producing 60 percent of the nation's automobiles. He led the world market as well.

Others improved upon Ford's success. In the mid-twenties, General Motors surpassed Ford by introducing the Chevrolet in colors. Ford had failed to grasp the growing impor-

▶ RESOURCE DIRECTORY

Teaching Resources

⭐ **Primary Source Activity** Teens and Cigarette Smoking, found in the Unit 4 folder, p. 28, explains why attempts to regulate the tobacco industry in the 1920s targeted cigarette smoking among youth in particular.

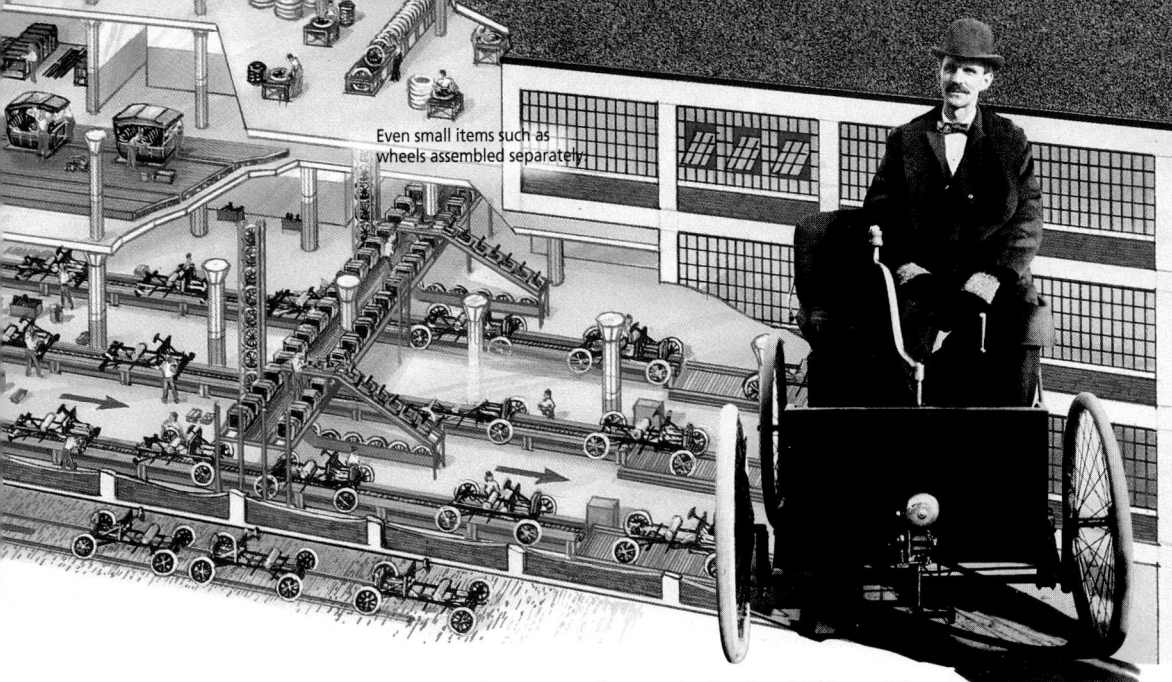
Even small items such as wheels assembled separately

tance of style and color to the American people. He joked that his customers could get their "Tin Lizzies" in any color they liked, as long as it was black. But in 1927, Ford began producing a new car, the Model A, in colors.

Running the Business In 1914, Ford had won praise by introducing the five-dollar-a-day pay rate for many of his workers, double what other factories paid. Yet Ford was not always well regarded by his workers. He was notorious for authorizing the use of spies and violence in an effort to combat unions in his plants.

Ford ruled his business like a dictator. "We expect the men to do what they are told," he explained in his 1922 book, *My Life and Work.*

The organization is so highly specialized and one part is so dependent upon another that we could not for a moment consider allowing men to have their own way. . . . Anyone who does not like to work in our way may always leave.

Ford's reputation also suffered when, in 1920, he allowed his newspaper, the *Dearborn Independent,* to engage in an anti-Semitic campaign. The attacks on Jews upset many people.

Ford's outbursts were a symptom of the age. Upset by social and moral changes of which he disapproved, Ford found a scapegoat in the Jews. As the next section discusses, he was not the only person to reach out for such simplistic solutions.

Henry Ford (above) began his career when horseless carriages like this were state of the art.

·SECTION 4 REVIEW·

Key Terms, People, and Places
1. Identify (a) Charles A. Lindbergh, (b) Henry Ford.

Key Concepts
2. How did commerce and industry respond to the increase in leisure time in the twenties?
3. How did the expanded advertising industry affect the American consumer?

4. What was the impact of easily available automobiles on American society?
5. What were the key features of Ford's assembly line?

Critical Thinking
6. **Recognizing Cause and Effect** How did the growth of mass media, such as radio and movies, lead to the creation of national heroes?

 Quiz found in the Unit 4 folder, p. 15, covers the main ideas in this section as well as the key terms.

Media and Technology

Transparency
The Way It Works, H-18

---

3. ASSESS

Section 4 Review Answers
1. (a) Charles A. Lindbergh, see p. 421, (b) Henry Ford, see p. 422
2. They increased radio broadcasting nationwide; created the movie industry and national idols; and speeded up the building of a national culture.
3. It created an identity between brand names and products and a new set of needs for the American public.
4. It liberated travel and thus speeded up the homogenization of American culture.
5. Making large numbers of automobiles in an identical way, and selling cars at affordable prices.
6. A possible answer is because the mass media can reach millions of people with the exact same message, and large numbers of people can share in events and information that help create heroes.

Reteach
Ask students to tell how each of the following helped create a national culture: migration from one state to another, the radio, the movies, the advertising industry, and the affordable automobile.

4. CLOSE

Reinforcing the Big Idea
Changes such as the population movement and developments in communication, transportation, industry, and the media worked to create a new national culture in America. The next section will describe how some Americans tried to slow down the fast pace of change.

Stemming the Tide of Change

SECTION 5

Stemming the Tide of Change

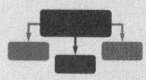

1. FOCUS

Connecting to the Big Idea

See page 402B. Explain to students that some Americans were alarmed by the ways in which American life and culture changed after World War I. They tried to slow down the pace of change. Ask how those Americans tried to halt what they considered the nation's moral and intellectual decay.

Objectives

● Evaluate the results of prohibition.
● Show how developments such as censorship and the growth of the Ku Klux Klan reflected a desire to slow changes in morals and manners in the 1920s.
● Describe how some artists responded to the changes in the nation with despair and self-exile.
● Describe how the election of 1928 revealed the social and political divisions in the United States.

Bellringer

Ask students to consider what might happen if the making, selling, transporting, importing, and exporting of soft drinks were made illegal. Do students think all Americans would stop drinking sodas? What undesirable effects might such a law have?

Reading Strategy

Structured Overview Ask students to write on their papers the following headings: Moral Controls, Controls on Beliefs, A Campaign of Political Action and Terror, and A Different Form of Social Protest. Have students scan the section and create subheadings under each of the headings. As students read, have them fill in details from the text.

SECTION PREVIEW

Jazz music, moving pictures, fast cars—American life moved at a dizzying pace in the 1920s. All the motion left some people feeling queasy, and they sought to slow the pace of change.

Key Concepts
• Prohibition, censorship, the growth of the Ku Klux Klan, and other developments reflected a desire to slow the changes in morals and manners in the 1920s.
• Some artists responded to the changes in the nation with despair and self-exile.
• The 1928 election dramatically demonstrated the social and political divisions in the United States.

Prohibition forced many beer companies to find new beverages to brew. Above are labels from such products.

Key Terms, People, and Places
speakeasies, bootlegging, fundamentalism, Scopes trial; T. S. Eliot, F. Scott Fitzgerald

---

The social and cultural changes taking place in the United States in the 1920s were exhilarating to many people. Other Americans, however, were quite alarmed at what they saw as the nation's moral and intellectual decay.

Moral Controls

Throughout United States history, various groups had worked for the prohibition of alcoholic beverages. In 1919, prohibitionists finally achieved their goal with the ratification of the Eighteenth Amendment to the Constitution. The amendment outlawed the making, selling, transporting, importing, or exporting of any intoxicating beverages.

Prohibition's supporters believed that the Eighteenth Amendment would stop people from drinking alcohol. They thought some of the most undesirable features of modern urban life might thus be curbed. As preacher Billy Sunday declared,

The reign of tears is over. The slums will soon be only a memory. We will turn our prisons into factories and our jails into storehouses and corncribs. Men will walk upright now. Women will smile and children will laugh. Hell will be forever for rent.

Prohibition in Practice The use of alcohol did decrease for a few years after 1919, especially among the poor. Prohibition, however, proved impossible to enforce. Congressman Thomas Spencer Crago of Pennsylvania had predicted that the attempt to enforce prohibition would breed "a discontent and disrespect for law in this country beyond anything we have ever witnessed before." He was right. For many, openly defying prohibition was almost fun. Others only pretended to comply, sneaking liquor into their homes or slinking off to **speakeasies,** bars where liquor was served illegally.

During prohibition, many crooks made fortunes **bootlegging**—smuggling liquor across the border from Canada, shipping it from the West Indies or Mexico, or distilling their own moonshine. Organized gangs, the most famous of which was Al Capone's in Chicago, fought to gain control over the illegal but highly profitable traffic in liquor. Designed to wipe out crime, prohibition created new ones. By decade's end, many people began to call for reform.

Morality at the Movies In an effort to draw bigger audiences, filmmakers in the early 1920s began to include more sexually explicit content. This development prompted a movement to control the industry. To avoid censorship from outside the movies, filmmakers decided to censor themselves. In 1922, they set up their own organization, which devised a production code

RESOURCE DIRECTORY

Teaching Resources

Reproducible Lesson Plan found in the Unit 4 folder, p. 7, provides a summary of the Section 5 lesson plan content.

Alternate Lesson Plan: Learning Styles found in the Alternate Lesson Plans folder, p. 110, is an alternate lesson plan especially effective for auditory learners that provides a team activity centered on a radio interview of a 1928 congressional candidate.

Guided Reading and Review found in the Unit 4 folder, p. 16, provides a structure for reading and mastering the key concepts and reviewing the key terms for Section 5. (Guided Practice)

for movies that limited the amount of love-making, bare skin, and crime a film could show.

Laws for the Dance Floor Considered a sign of the decay of modern morals, dancing to that "Unspeakable Jazz" aroused widespread criticism in the early 1920s. "Anyone who says that 'youths of both sexes can mingle in close embrace'—with limbs intertwined and torso in contact—without suffering harm lies," accused a writer in the *Ladies Home Journal* in 1921.

To discourage close dancing, respectable dance halls required couples to remain six inches apart and ceased moonlight dances—those with the lights turned low. By 1929, cities and states across the country passed over three hundred laws to control dancing and dance halls. Most were easily evaded.

MAKING CONNECTIONS

Consider some of the laws that regulate behavior today. Do you think these laws will still be enforced in one hundred years? Explain.

Controls on Beliefs

During the early twentieth century, the rising prestige of science, changing social roles for women, and social gospel reform movements challenged many traditional religious beliefs. In reaction, religious traditionalists published a series of pamphlets called *The Fundamentals*. These tracts, which appeared between 1909 and 1914, insisted that every word in the Bible was inspired by God, and that every biblical story was literally true. The pamphlets gave birth to a religious movement called **fundamentalism.**

The Scopes Trial In 1923 and 1924, fundamentalist legislators in at least twelve states introduced laws to ban the teaching of evolution in the public schools. *Evolution* is the name for Charles Darwin's theory, put forward in 1859, that holds that humans and all other species developed over time from lower to more complex forms. Fundamentalists argued that the theory of evolution contradicted biblical accounts of the creation of the world.

Viewpoints
On the Eighteenth Amendment

Flagrant violations of prohibition led to loud cries for reform, or repeal of the Eighteenth Amendment. The speakers below are addressing a Senate committee investigating violations of the law. *What basic value underlies each argument?*

For Reform or Repeal of the National Prohibition Act
"It is impossible to tell whether prohibition is a good thing or a bad thing. It has never been enforced in this country. . . . I will concede that the saloon was odious [offensive], but now we have delicatessen stores, pool rooms, drug stores, millinery shops, private parlors, and 57 other varieties of speakeasies selling liquor and flourishing."

New York congressman Fiorello La Guardia, 1926

Against Reform or Repeal of the National Prohibition Act
"Permit me to show another side of the picture, and propose that instead of lowering our standards, we urge that the law be strengthened. . . . The closing of the open saloon . . . has resulted in better national health, children are born under better conditions, homes are better, and the mother is delivered from the fear of a drunken husband."

Ella A. Boole, president of the
National Woman's Christian Temperance Union, 1926

Several states passed an antievolution law. The American Civil Liberties Union (ACLU), however, felt that the laws violated the Constitution. In 1925, the ACLU announced that it would defend any teacher willing to challenge the statutes. John T. Scopes, a young high school biology teacher from Dayton, Tennessee, accepted. He read to his class a description of Darwin's theory. His arrest followed.

Thanks to radio, the **Scopes trial** became a national sensation. Famed lawyer Clarence Darrow headed the ACLU defense team. Former presidential candidate William Jennings Bryan defended the antievolution law. The climax came when Bryan insisted that everything in the Bible was literally true. Darrow got Bryan to admit that even he interpreted figuratively some biblical stories and ideas. Bryan, widely ridiculed, died soon after the trial.

Because Scopes had violated the law, the trial jury convicted him and imposed a one-hundred

Viewpoints Activity On the Eighteenth Amendment, found in the Unit 4 folder, pp. 22–23, provides additional viewpoints and perspectives on the Eighteenth Amendment.

Answer to ...

Viewpoints

La Guardia emphasizes the unenforceability of the law; Boole argues that prohibition leads to a better economic and moral climate in the country. For a thorough understanding of the Eighteenth Amendment, see Resource Directory below.

Answer to ...

MAKING CONNECTIONS

Answers will vary. Students may cite generally accepted laws such as those regulating school attendance, or they may mention more controversial laws such as those concerning drug use. Encourage students to consider 1920s efforts at moral control in light of similar efforts today.

2. INSTRUCT

Explain/Discuss

Explain that many of the Americans who favored prohibition lived in small towns and on farms. Discuss the ways that the passing of a prohibition amendment and its failure to control the use of alcohol pointed up divisions in American society.

In Depth
Then and Now

In the 1920s, the Klan gained a foothold in the industrial Northeast as well as in the South, Midwest, and West. In a court battle pitting the Empire Knights of the Ku Klux Klan against the Southern Poverty Law Center, the Klan group agreed to surrender its name, its mailing list, and all its assets. The settlement followed a guilty verdict in a case involving a Klan-led attack on a group of African Americans in Georgia.

Ask students what other sorts of behavior those concerned about moral decay tried to regulate. Do students think censorship or related activities are desirable? Who should develop the standards for movies, rock concerts, or books available in the library?

Analyze

Ask students why John Scopes went to jail after the famous Scopes trial and what the lasting importance of the Scopes trial was.

How did the Ku Klux Klan try to halt what it saw as the nation's moral decline? Discuss why the actions of the Klan were illegal and immoral.

Caption Answer to ...

 Interpreting Maps

Strongest in the North Central and Southwest regions; weakest in the North Atlantic and Far West regions.

Activity

Teaching Heterogeneous Groups

For all students to understand censorship as a tool to regulate behavior, have them work in small groups and choose an industry, such as music, to censor. Have them select one criterion on which to censor that industry. Criteria for censorship might include language, behavior, or styles.

Enrichment

Tell students that in 1925 the first issue of *The New Yorker* magazine appeared, with a famous editorial statement vowing that the slick, expensive magazine of fiction, essays, cartoons, and reviews was not designed for "the old lady from Dubuque." Ask students to write a brief essay about the divisions in American society pointed up by that statement. What did the editors of *The New Yorker* see as the difference between the urbane elite they hoped would read their magazine and the middle class of rural America?

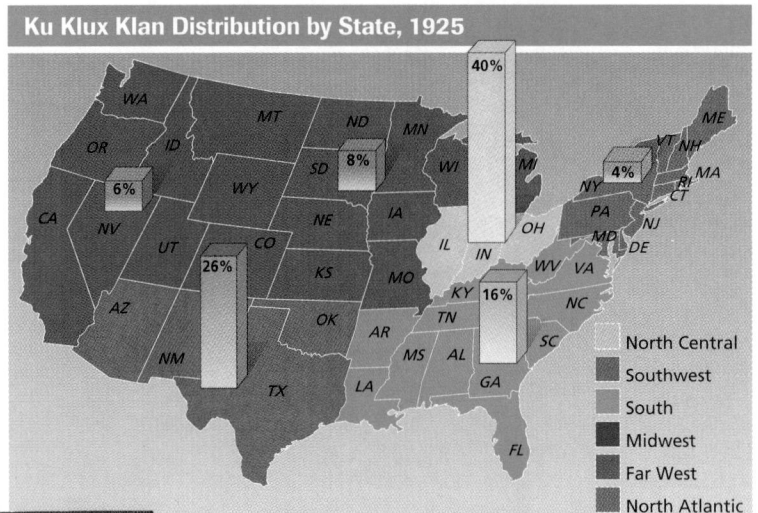

Ku Klux Klan Distribution by State, 1925

Legend:
- North Central
- Southwest
- South
- Midwest
- Far West
- North Atlantic

AMERICA for Americans

 **Geography and History: Interpreting Maps**
The resurgence of the Ku Klux Klan in the 1920s occurred in all corners of the country. *In which regions was the Klan the strongest? The weakest?*

dollar fine. The Tennessee Supreme Court threw out the fine—and a chance to test the law's constitutionality—on a technicality. The United States Supreme Court has since ruled, however, that similar laws violate the Constitution by promoting certain religious views. Nevertheless, debate over the proper place of evolution theory in American education continues today.

A Campaign of Political Action and Terror

In June 1920, the Ku Klux Klan (KKK), which had revived in 1915, launched a recruitment campaign using mass-marketing techniques of the advertising age. By October 1921, it had 85,000 new recruits. At its high point in the 1920s, the Klan boasted membership of between three and five million. ⭐

The Klan's political power extended across the country. In Oklahoma, Klan votes removed an anti-Klan governor. In Oregon, they dealt a blow to Catholic schools by getting a law passed requiring all children to attend public schools. In the South, they terrorized African Americans, and in the Southwest, pursued violators of prohibition. In the Northeast and West, they targeted Jews. They also went after Catholics, then 36 percent of the population and pre-

sumed by the Klan to be more loyal to their Pope than to the United States.

The Klan's goal was to restore white Protestants to a dominant place in American society and to halt the nation's so-called moral decline. According to the KKK's Imperial Wizard Hiram Wesley Evans, the Klan by 1926 was well on its way toward success. "When the Klan first appeared," he wrote, "the invasion of aliens and alien ideas" had brought about the destruction of cherished moral values. "After ten years of the Klan [the nation] is in arms for defense," Evans boasted.

The Klan movement of the 1920s collapsed suddenly under the weight of its violent nature. In 1928 the Grand Dragon of Indiana, David Stephenson, was jailed on second-degree murder charges. Stephenson took revenge on the politicians who failed to get him released by revealing the extent of Klan influence and political corruption in the state. Stephenson's revelations caused a scandal that broke the movement, at least for a time.

A Different Form of Social Protest

Efforts at moral, intellectual, and political control were not the only responses to the changes taking place in the United States in the 1920s. Some rebellious spirits were critical of their times for completely different reasons.

Before World War I, in urban artistic colonies such as New York City's Greenwich Village, artists and intellectuals had created hotbeds for discussion of new ideas in politics, theater, art, literature, and music. These thinkers felt themselves to be on the brink of artistic and intellectual triumph over nineteenth-century values and ideals. Then came World War I, a conflict of such brutality that belief in human progress seemed impossible to these artists. Following that came a period in which unconventional ideas were denounced as radical. Disillusioned, a whole group of artists turned

▶ RESOURCE DIRECTORY ⭐

Teaching Resources

⭐ **Visual Learning Activity** The Ku Klux Klan, found in the Unit 4 folder, p. 32, uses a 1923 drawing from *Life* magazine to enhance students' understanding of how symbols are used by artists to convey political viewpoints.

Literature Activity *Tales of the Jazz Age*, found in the Unit 4 folder, pp. 29–30, highlights the shallow, carefree rebellion of the flapper culture, and can be compared to the strong, poignant voices of *The Weary Blues*.

SOURCE READINGS

Source Readings on p. 432 will connect literature selections and primary source excerpts to historical events discussed in this section.

against their culture, depicting it in biting satires or choosing, instead, to flee from it altogether.

Poet Ezra Pound wrote of "a botched civilization." **T. S. Eliot's** "The Waste Land" became the symbolic poem of the generation. Novelist **F. Scott Fitzgerald** wrote of the youth of his times as "the beautiful and the damned." His 1925 masterpiece, *The Great Gatsby*, exposed what he saw as the shallow self-involvement and illusions of the Jazz Age rich. ★

To these disillusioned artists, old ideals no longer inspired faith. Progressivism and related reform ideas now seemed dull. "If I am convinced of anything," journalist H. L. Mencken wrote, "It is that Doing Good is in bad taste."

Rejecting the American mass culture and ethic of success, some artists went into self-exile, many to Paris. Soon, they found it just as hard to live there. Ironically, when they came back, some got jobs in advertising or the book trade, the very businesses they had earlier despised.

The Election of 1928 Reflects the Conflicts of the Era

No single event more dramatically reflected the divisions of the era than the presidential election of 1928. On the Democratic side was New York governor Al Smith, a Roman Catholic from a family of recent immigrants, and a "wet," or opponent of prohibition. Smith's formal education had ended at the eighth grade. But after New York's Democratic political machine, Tammany Hall, got him a seat in the New York State Assembly, Smith educated himself and became a champion of workers' rights. Because of his record in New York, Smith in 1928 had the support of many progressives—even though he was a product of Tammany Hall, which progressives despised.

The Republicans ran Herbert Hoover, a Protestant Quaker from West Branch, Iowa; a Stanford-educated friend of big business; and a "dry," or supporter of prohibition. In contrast to Smith, who was a fiery campaigner, Hoover was dull but polished. He was especially popular among women voters.

For the first time, radio played an extensive role in an election. Over the airwaves, Hoover came across as moderate, sensible, and trustworthy. In contrast, Smith's thick New York City accent made him sound uneducated and brash to many audiences. Smith also suffered the effects of an anti-Catholic propaganda campaign that sought to raise fears among voters about Smith's loyalty to the United States.

These factors—combined with the widespread though not entirely accurate belief that the economy was strong—gave Hoover a landslide victory. Yet Hoover's win did hide some dark clouds on the Republican horizon. Smith carried the nation's twelve largest cities, an important development in the increasingly urban United States. He also broke into the midwestern belt of unhappy, indebted farmers, who were experiencing economic hard times in spite of the nation's apparent prosperity.

From the vantage point of 1928, however, Hoover's victory seemed decisive. Indeed, with the election over, the roar of the 1920s seemed to quiet down. Yet it would not be long before it would rise again—this time driven by panic.

SECTION 5 REVIEW

Key Terms, People, and Places
1. Define (a) speakeasy, (b) bootlegging, (c) fundamentalism.

Key Concepts
2. For what reasons did Prohibition fail?
3. What attempts were made in the 1920s to control morals, and how successful were they?
4. Explain the facts and significance of the Scopes trial.

5. What were some of the goals of the Ku Klux Klan in the 1920s?
6. What group do T. S. Eliot and F. Scott Fitzgerald represent?

Critical Thinking
7. **Demonstrating Reasoned Judgment** In what ways did the 1928 election reflect the social and political divisions of the era?

Quiz found in the Unit 4 folder, p. 17, covers the main ideas in this section as well as the key terms.

Chapter Test Forms A and B are found in the Unit 4 folder, pp. 34–39.

Answer Keys found in the Unit 4 folder, pp. 116–128, provide answers to all student activities.

Media and Technology

Transparency
Graphic Organizer, G-3

Guided Reading Audiotapes
(English and Spanish)

Computer Test Bank

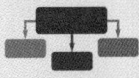

Understanding Key Terms, People, and Places

Terms Students should refer to the definitions of the key terms in the chapter to write sentences that show understanding of their relationship to the social and technological changes that took place in the 1920s.

Matching
1. speakeasies
2. flapper
3. bootlegging
4. Harlem Renaissance

True or False
1. false, Marcus Garvey
2. true
3. false, F. Scott Fitzgerald
4. false, Charles A. Lindbergh

Reviewing Main Ideas

1. Veterans faced unemployment; farmers suffered as prices for crops dropped; inflation was high; labor unrest increased.

2. Labor strikes and terrorist acts caused many people to believe that the fabric of society was tearing apart. Politicians' responses included the Palmer raids and the defeat of many progressive reforms.

3. Congress set quotas for each country at 2 percent of the total number of immigrants from that country living in the United States in 1890. The law reduced immigration from southern and eastern Europe.

4. Women did not vote in large numbers. Especially in national elections, women voted in patterns similar to men.

5. African Americans left the South to find work, but they were unable to substantially improve their standard of living. Also, discrimination and racial violence continued to plague them in the North. But many African Americans helped build vital new communities, such as Harlem in New York City.

6. Republicans capitalized on improvements in the economy to win each presidential election in the 1920s.

7. Fads such as dance marathons became popular. The young also displayed growing freedom in their social relations.

8. Women's clothing exposed arms and knees for the first time; ordinary women began to wear makeup.

9. Large numbers of women entered the work force, at lower pay than men. White women were often fired when they became pregnant; most African American women were forced by economic circumstances to keep working.

Chapter Review

Understanding Key Terms, People, and Places

Key Terms
1. communist
2. red scare
3. general strike
4. Harlem Renaissance
5. Teapot Dome
6. Jazz Age
7. flapper
8. speakeasies
9. bootlegging
10. fundamentalism
11. Scopes trial

People
12. Vladimir I. Lenin
13. Nicola Sacco
14. Bartolomeo Vanzetti
15. Marcus Garvey
16. Warren G. Harding
17. Calvin Coolidge
18. Herbert Hoover
19. Charles A. Lindbergh
20. Henry Ford
21. T. S. Eliot
22. F. Scott Fitzgerald

Terms For each term above, write a sentence that explains its relation to the social and technological changes that took place in the 1920s.

Matching Review the key terms in the list above. If you are not sure of a term's meaning, review its definition in the chapter. Then choose a term from the list that best matches each description below.
1. bars where liquor was served illegally
2. youthful woman symbolizing the spirit of the 1920s
3. smuggling or distilling liquor illegally
4. period when artistic life flowered among African Americans

True or False Determine whether each statement is true or false. If it is true, write "true." If it is false. change the underlined person or place to make the statement true.
1. <u>Warren G. Harding</u> sought to build up African Americans' self-respect and racial pride.
2. Many people believed that shoemaker <u>Nicola Sacco</u> had been unfairly tried because of his Italian heritage and political views.
3. <u>T. S. Eliot</u>'s novel *The Great Gatsby* exposed what he saw as the self-involvement of the Jazz Age.
4. <u>Bartolomeo Vanzetti</u> became a national hero after his solo flight across the Atlantic Ocean.

Reviewing Main Ideas

Section 1 (pp. 404–407)
1. Briefly describe conditions in the American economy in the first few years following World War I.
2. What events of 1919 led many Americans to fear that the Russian Revolution would spread to the United States? How did politicians respond?
3. How did Congress limit immigration in the 1920s?

Section 2 (pp. 410–414)
4. Why did women's votes fail to change politics as much as suffragists had hoped?
5. Describe the general experience of African American migrants to the North in the postwar years.
6. In what sense was the 1920s a "Republican decade"?

Section 3 (pp. 415–418)
7. In what ways did young people defy social conventions after World War I?

8. How did changes in fashion for women reflect the new morals and manners of the Jazz Age?
9. How were new social possibilities still limited for women during the Jazz Age?

Section 4 (pp. 420–423)
10. How did the growth of leisure time help lead to the creation of a national culture?
11. What role did chain supermarkets, advertisers, and fast-food chains play in creating a common culture?
12. How did Henry Ford "democratize the automobile"?

Section 5 (pp. 424–427)
13. Briefly describe some of the efforts to control Americans' morals and beliefs in the 1920s.
14. Why were many writers disillusioned in the 1920s?
15. In what ways did the election of 1928 reflect the divisions of the era?

10. Commerce and industry produced and sold new products such as the radio and automobile. Also the expanding communications industry led to a wide sharing of experiences among people throughout the country.

11. People across the country could shop in the same stores for the same products. Advertisers helped make brand names synonymous with certain types of products.

12. By applying the ideas of uniformity of product and the assembly line, Ford produced cars at prices that working people could afford.

13. Prohibition tried to outlaw the consumption of alcohol. The Ku Klux Klan tried to return white Protestants to a place of superiority. Fundamentalists helped push the passage of anti-evolution laws.

14. After the brutality of World War I, belief in human progress seemed impossible to many writers.

15. Smith, a Catholic of immigrant roots and an opponent of prohibition, represented one side of a number of the divisive issues of the decade. Hoover represented the opposite side of those issues.

1. **Recognizing Ideologies** During the 1920s, terms such as "un-American" and "Bolshevik" were used to ignite people's fears and obscure complex issues. Describe terms that play a similar role today.
2. **Demonstrating Reasoned Judgment** "For many African Americans, the migration to the North was a mixed success." Explain the meaning of this statement.
3. **Distinguishing False from Accurate Images** The flapper was a popular image of the 1920s that, in fact, represented only a small number of American women. Are there symbols that represent the present era? If so, what are they? What role does the media play in promoting this image? Who does the image truly represent?

1. **Evaluating Primary Sources** Review the primary source excerpt on page 423. If you were a business manager, what would be your opinion of this method of running a business? If you were a worker? If you were running a business, would you emphasize creativity or efficiency? What are the benefits and drawbacks of each approach?
2. **Understanding the Visuals** Write a short paragraph explaining how the information in the graph on page 405 and the photo of sheet music on page 407 are related.
3. **Writing About the Chapter** You are a newspaper editor in the early 1920s. Write an editorial in which you offer your opinion about the outcome of the Sacco and Vanzetti case. Before you begin, review the chapter for details about the red scare and the treatment of immigrants, and consider how these factors might have influenced the trial. As you write a draft of your editorial, consider the following questions: Is there any valid reason to consider Sacco and Vanzetti's political beliefs in their trial? What if Sacco and Vanzetti are in fact guilty—does it matter whether they received a fair trial? Proofread your work and draft a final copy.
4. **Using the Graphic Organizer** This graphic organizer uses a web to organize information about the changes in technology and culture that took place in the 1920s. Webs often can show connections between seemingly unconnected ideas. In this web, dotted lines are used to show these connections. (a) Based on what you have read in the chapter, what is the connection between increased leisure time and the rise in popularity of the radio and movies? (b) According to the graphic organizer below, what did chain stores and the auto industry have in common in the 1920s? (c) On a separate sheet of paper, create your own graphic organizer about the new manners and social freedoms that arose during the Jazz Age.

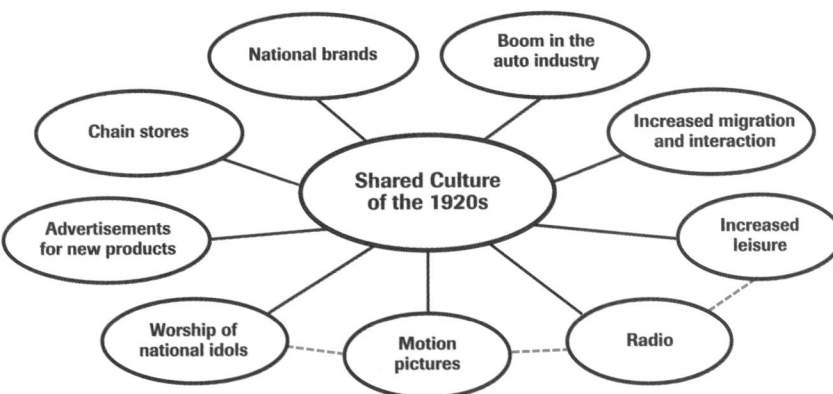

4. (a) When people began to enjoy more leisure time, commerce and industry produced new products and services such as radios and movies to meet this demand. Radio and motion pictures promoted certain figures such as sports figures and movie stars to large audiences across the country. (b) Both industries expanded rapidly. (c) Students' graphic organizers might include the rise of jazz and dance, changes in fashion, the flapper, automobiles, and developments in labor-saving devices.

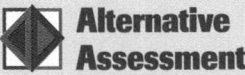 **Alternative Assessment**

Final Evaluation
Use the following guidelines to evaluate student projects:
- **Evidence of thoughtfulness** Did the student include the main topics from the chapter?
- **Evidence of outside research** To what extent did students use outside research materials for their projects?
- **Evidence of synthesis** Do projects demonstrate that students understand how topics are related?
- **Communication style** Does the project convey its purpose to an audience in a clear, appealing way?

Thinking Critically

1. Answers will vary. Students might respond that such terms as *communist, liberal, welfare state,* and *gay* are sometimes used today as negative labels.

2. African Americans who migrated North found some improvement in their lives, but not what many hoped for. But the Great Migration led to the flowering of African American culture in Harlem.

3. Answers will vary. Students may point to symbols of youth culture today, such as pencil-thin models and rock stars. Such images are promoted by the media and bear little resemblance to real lives.

Making Connections

1. From a business viewpoint, Ford's way is highly efficient. From the viewpoint of a worker, however, it might be dehumanizing. Students may offer ways of combining efficiency and creativity, perhaps by offering workers incentives for creative ideas.

2. When strikes and labor unrest broke out in the 1920s, many people blamed this on communism and feared an uprising in the United States. Such sentiments led to a fear of foreigners and renewed isolationism, which became so widespread that songs were written about it, such as this one, "O! Close the Gates."

3. Students' editorials should reflect serious thought about the purpose and meaning of the right to a fair trial.

Recall with students that the 1920s were referred to as the "Jazz Age," and whether Americans enjoyed or disapproved of jazz, the music and the idea were in the air.

Ask students to study the artifacts and to read the captions. Using the artifacts and captions as a basis for discussion, ask students why radio was important in making jazz familiar to the American public. Discuss how radio brought jazz to white audiences who were less likely to attend clubs where African American jazz musicians performed.

Ask students to compare the importance of jazz in the 1920s to the importance of rock music in all its many styles and varieties in the 1990s. Prompt discussion with questions such as: Is rock as prevalent as jazz was? Do people have more or less opportunity to hear rock as people did to hear jazz? Is rock as shocking to the older generation in the 1990s as jazz was in the 1920s?

Ask students to make a list of the artifacts they would include in an American Album display about the music of the 1990s. Tell them to choose items that illustrate the many aspects of life that rock touches.

If possible, play some jazz from the 1920s in the classroom. One good compilation is the *Smithsonian Collection of Classic Jazz*.

American Album
ARTIFACTS FROM EXHIBITIONS AND COLLECTIONS
AT THE SMITHSONIAN INSTITUTION
NATIONAL MUSEUM OF AMERICAN HISTORY

THE JAZZ AGE

No music was more important to an era than jazz was to the 1920s. This unique American music grew from the culture of southern African Americans and traveled north with them. Jazz was more than mere music, however. Much of the country's youth—African American and white—saw jazz as the symbol of their new generation.

Compare the importance of jazz in the 1920s with the importance of "rock and roll" to later generations.

▲1930s RADIO Radio, more than any other medium, made jazz familiar to the American public. The jazz heard on the radio was adapted by all-white bands to appeal to largely white audiences.

▲ DUKE ELLINGTON The jazz clubs of Harlem and Chicago were one of the few places where African American musicians could perform their music for white audiences. Duke Ellington, pictured on the sheet music of one of his famous compositions, became a Harlem headliner in 1923.

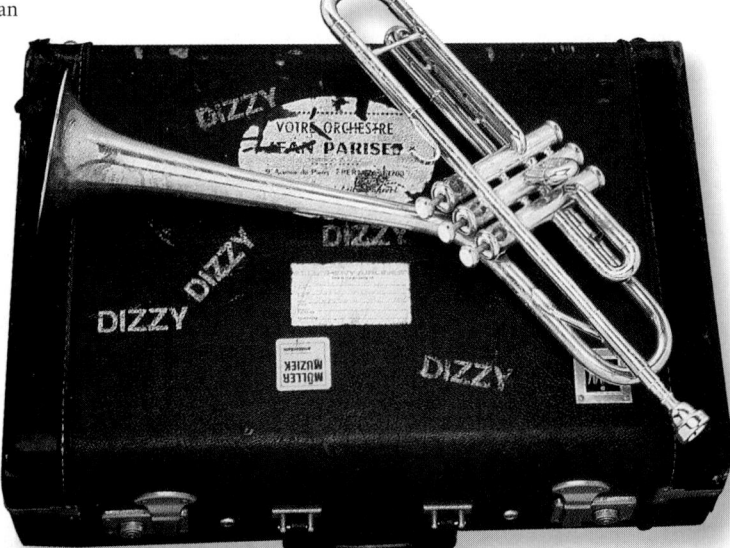

DIZZIE GILLESPIE'S ▶ TRUMPET Jazz musicians developed their own playing styles and unique signatures. Dizzy Gillespie, whose bent horn distinguished him from other trumpet players, pioneered the modern jazz and bebop styles. His career, which began in the 1930s, spanned seven decades.

◀ HYMIE SHERTZER
The well-known sax-
ophonist worked
with many bands
as well as in
recording
studios and
in radio.

FLAPPER'S DRESS ▶
AND BEADS The symbol of
the Jazz Age was the flapper
with her "jazz style" clothes. The
flapper's short skirts, silk stockings, and fake jewelry were new
and daring, shocking many in the
older generation. Flapper clothes
were a must for doing the newest
dances to jazz music.

◀
SHERTZER'S
SAXOPHONE
The saxophone
was invented in
Europe in 1840
but never became
a popular orchestral
instrument. Musicians
like Shertzer, however, made the sax's
smooth, easily blended sound one of the
major voices of the jazz band.

◀ BENNY GOODMAN'S
CLARINET Known as the "King of
Swing," Goodman began his jazz career in
1926. His "big band" helped make jazz
popular with white audiences, but he preferred small groups. Goodman's 1936
trio with African American musicians
Lionel Hampton and Teddy Wilson
was the first popular racially
mixed jazz group. Goodman
was also a classical performer
who made recordings with
leading symphony
orchestras.

◀ 1920s JAZZ BAND
Most jazz artists strug-
gled to earn a living and
remained anonymous.
This band, which was
photographed in St. Louis
in the 1920s, is unidenti-
fied. The band played the
New Orleans style jazz.

The Great Migration brought thousands of southern African Americans to northern cities by the 1920s. New York's Harlem, in particular, saw a blossoming of the arts based on the southern African American culture. Jazz thrived with great popularity, and the talent of African American writers emerged in a literary movement known as the Harlem Renaissance. For many other Americans, a desire to peer into areas previously unknown seemed to prevail. This, in part, can explain the sudden acknowledgment by white Americans of the literary merits of the Harlem Renaissance writers. It can also explain the interest of the American public in such works as *The Rich Boy*, which described the life of the very rich.

INSTRUCT

Have students review Chapter 12 for other examples of areas in which Americans explored uncharted territory in the 1920s. Students should point to such examples as African Americans moving to the North; new music such as jazz, blues, and Dixieland; new dances; new fashion styles for men and women; new technology for the home; daring new social standards. Students should also realize that Americans' fascination with Charles Lindbergh was part of this eager delving into new experiences. In a sense, so was the practice of frequenting speakeasies during Prohibition.

Remind students that another, equally strong force existed in the United States during the 1920s. This opposing force pulled Americans back to old morals, and even dragged the nation back down the road of racial prejudice and intolerance. Have students review the chapter for examples of these types of changes in the United States.

CHAPTER 12

SOURCE READINGS

The Rich Boy

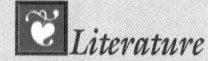 *Literature*

F. Scott Fitzgerald

INTRODUCTION The fiction of F. Scott Fitzgerald helped to define the wealthy people of the Jazz Age, at the same time exposing the shallowness and disillusionment that lurked on the fringes of their lives. Fitzgerald begins "The Rich Boy," a short story which was the first serious work he produced after *The Great Gatsby*, with this famous pronouncement: "Let me tell you about the very rich. They are different from you and me." Thus saying, Fitzgerald introduces the theme of the story and, in some sense, invites readers to share his own curiosity and fascination with the 1920s world of the very wealthy.

VOCABULARY Before you read the selection, find the meaning of these words in a dictionary: deference, feudal, brusque, débutante, dissipation, convivial, bawdy, avid, sardonic, emasculated, facetiousness.

Anson was the eldest of six children who would some day divide a fortune of fifteen million dollars, and he reached the age of reason—is it seven?—at the beginning of the century when daring young women were already gliding along Fifth Avenue in electric "mobiles." In those days he and his brother had an English governess who spoke the language very clearly and crisply and well, so that the two boys grew to speak as she did—their words and sentences were all crisp and clear and not run together as ours are. They didn't talk exactly like English children but acquired an accent that is peculiar to fashionable people in the city of New York.

In the summer the six children were moved from the house on 71st Street to a big estate in northern Connecticut. It was not a fashionable locality—Anson's father wanted to delay as long as possible his children's knowledge of that side of life. He was a man somewhat superior to his class, which composed New York society, and to his period, which was the snobbish and formalized vulgarity of the Gilded Age, and he wanted his sons to learn habits of concentration and have sound constitutions and grow up into right-living and successful men. He and his wife kept an eye on them as well as they were able until the two older boys went away to school, but in huge establishments this is difficult—it was much simpler in the series of small and medium-sized houses in which my own youth was spent—I was never far out of the reach of my mother's voice, of the sense of her presence, her approval or disapproval.

Anson's first sense of his superiority came to him when he realized the half-grudging American deference that was paid to him in the Connecticut village. The parents of the boys he played with always inquired after his father and mother, and were vaguely excited when their own children were asked to the Hunters' house. He accepted this as the natural state of things, and a sort of impatience with all groups of which he was not the centre—in money, in position, in authority—remained with him for the rest of his life. He disdained to struggle with other boys for precedence—he expected it to be given him freely, and when it wasn't he withdrew into his family. His family was sufficient,

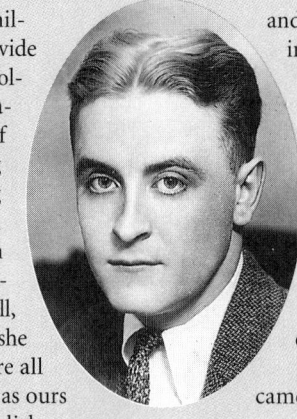

F. Scott Fitzgerald

for in the East money is still a somewhat feudal thing, a clan-forming thing. In the snobbish West, money separates families to form "sets."

At eighteen, when he went to New Haven, Anson was tall and thick-set, with a clear complexion and a healthy color from the ordered life he had led in school. His hair was yellow and grew in a funny way on his head, his nose was beaked—these two things kept him from being handsome—but he had a confident charm and a certain brusque style, and the upper-class men who passed him on the street knew without being told that he was a rich boy and had gone to one of the best schools. Nevertheless, his very superiority kept him from being a success in college—the independence was mistaken for egotism, and the refusal to accept Yale standards with the proper awe seemed to belittle all those who had. So, long before he graduated, he began to shift the centre of his life to New York.

He was at home in New York—there was his own house with "the kind of servants you can't get any more"—and his own family, of which, because of his good humor and a certain ability to make things go, he was rapidly becoming the centre, and the débutante parties, and the correct manly world of the men's clubs, and the occasional wild spree with the gallant girls whom New Haven only knew from the fifth row. His aspirations were conventional enough—they included even the irreproachable shadow he would some day marry, but they differed from the aspirations of the majority of young men in that there was no mist over them, none of that quality which is variously known as "idealism" or "illusion." Anson accepted without reservation the world of high finance and high extravagance, of divorce and dissipation, of snobbery and of privilege. Most of our lives end as a compromise—it was as a compromise that his life began.

He and I first met in the late summer of 1917 when he was just out of Yale, and, like the rest of us, was swept up into the sys-

tematized hysteria of the war. In the blue-green uniform of the naval aviation he came down to Pensacola, where the hotel orchestras played "I'm sorry, dear," and we young officers danced with the girls. Every one liked him, and though he ran with the drinkers and wasn't an especially good pilot, even the instructors treated him with a certain respect. He was always having long talks with them in his confident, logical voice—talks which ended by his getting himself, or, more frequently, another officer, out of some impending trouble. He was convivial, bawdy, robustly avid for pleasure, and we were all surprised when he fell in love with a conservative and rather proper girl.

Her name was Paula Legendre, a dark, serious beauty from somewhere in California. Her family kept a winter residence just outside of town, and in spite of her primness she was enormously popular; there is a large class of men whose egotism can't endure humor in a woman. But Anson wasn't that sort, and I couldn't understand the attraction of her "sincerity"—that was the thing to say about her—for his keen and somewhat sardonic mind.

Nevertheless, they fell in love—and on her terms. He no longer joined the twilight gathering at the De Soto bar, and whenever they were seen together they were engaged in a long, serious dialogue, which must have gone on several weeks. Long afterward he told me that it was not about anything in particular but was composed on both sides of immature and even meaningless statements—the emotional content that gradually came to fill it

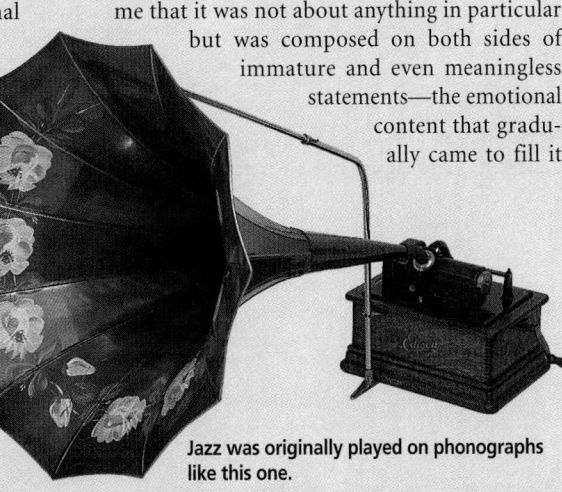

Jazz was originally played on phonographs like this one.

EXTEND

Have students think about a type of lifestyle in the United States today that is very different from their own and learn more about it. Examples might include the lives of those struggling with poverty, an urban lifestyle (if students live in a rural area), a rural lifestyle (if students live in an urban area), or life in a state like Alaska. Have students write a one-page essay about what they imagine life in the "unknown" area to be like. Then have them do research to compile a factual picture. Students should write a report on their findings and compare the facts with their earlier recorded perceptions.

grew up not out of the words but out of its enormous seriousness. It was a sort of hypnosis. Often it was interrupted, giving way to that emasculated humor we call fun; when they were alone it was resumed again, solemn, low-keyed, and pitched so as to give each other a sense of unity in feeling and thought. They came to resent any interruptions of it, to be unresponsive to facetiousness about life, even to the mild cynicism of their contemporaries. They were only happy when the dialogue was going on, and its seriousness bathed them like the amber glow of an open fire. Toward the end there came an interruption they did not resent—it began to be interrupted by passion.

Oddly enough, Anson was as engrossed in the dialogue as she was and as profoundly affected by it, yet at the same time aware that on his side much was insincere, and on hers much was merely simple. At first, too, he despised her emotional simplicity as well,

but with his love her nature deepened and blossomed, and he could despise it no longer. He felt that if he could enter into Paula's warm safe life he would be happy. . . . One evening after a dance they agreed to marry, and he wrote a long letter about her to his mother. The next day Paula told him that she was rich, that she had a personal fortune of nearly a million dollars.

THINKING ABOUT THE SELECTION

1. When did Anson first realize that his situation was different from that of many others?
2. Why was Anson uncomfortable at Yale?

Critical Thinking

3. **Recognizing Ideologies** Why does Anson's father not want to live in a fashionable area? What ideology does this reveal?

"Mother To Son" and "The Negro Speaks of Rivers"

 *Literature*

Langston Hughes

INTRODUCTION In the 1920s, writers, musicians, and artists began moving to Harlem to take part in the energy and excitement blossoming there. Langston Hughes, one of the most successful of the Harlem Renaissance writers, had this to say of his own arrival in Harlem in 1921: "At every subway station I kept watching for the sign 135th Street. When I saw it, I held my breath. . . . I went up the steps and into the bright September sun-

light. Harlem! I looked around . . . I took a deep breath and felt happy again." That same year "The Negro Speaks of Rivers" was published and Hughes began a career in which he put words to the struggles, pains, and triumphs of African Americans, striking a chord in all Americans as he did so. The powerful "Mother To Son" is from his second volume of collected poems. It was published in 1932.

Langston Hughes

ANSWERS TO

Thinking About the Selection

1. He first realized that his situation was different during his summers in Connecticut; the other boys treated him differently and their parents were excited when their children were invited to his house.
2. People mistook his independence for egotism and did not like his refusal to be awed by Yale; in addition, he was unhappy when he was not the center of attention, which was probably the case at Yale.

3. Anson's father does not want to live in a fashionable area because he wants to keep this "side of life" from his children. In other words, he does not wish them to know too early that they are rich, so that they will develop the ability to think for themselves and to be successful in their own right. His thinking reflects a belief that each person should make his or her own way in the world and not rely on the moneyed world of privilege and power.

"Mother To Son"

Well, son, I'll tell you:
Life for me ain't been no crystal stair.
It's had tacks in it,
And splinters,
And boards torn up,
And places with no carpet on the floor—
Bare.
But all the time
I'se been a-climbin' on,
And reachin' landin's,
And turnin' corners,
And sometimes goin' in the dark
Where there ain't been no light.
So, boy, don't you turn back;
Don't you set down on the steps
'Cause you find it kinder hard.
Don't you fall now —
For I'se still goin', honey,
I'se still climbin',
And life for me ain't been no crystal stair.

African American parents in the rural South often taught their children at home because there were few schools that would allow African Americans to enroll.

"The Negro Speaks of Rivers"

I've known rivers
I've known rivers ancient as the world and
        older than the flow of human blood in
        human veins.

My soul has grown deep like the rivers.

I bathed in the Euphrates when dawns were
        young.
I built my hut near the Congo and it lulled me
        to sleep.
I looked upon the Nile and raised the pyramids
        above it.
I heard the singing of the Mississippi when Abe
        Lincoln went down to New Orleans, and
I've seen its muddy bosom turn all
        golden in the sunset.

I've known rivers:
Ancient, dusky rivers.

My soul has grown deep like the rivers.

THINKING ABOUT THE SELECTION

1. What is the mother trying to tell her son in the first poem?
2. Who is the speaker in the second poem?
3. What has happened to the speaker's soul? Why?

Critical Thinking

4. **Making Comparisons** What comparison does Hughes develop in "The Negro Speaks of Rivers"? What does the comparison convey about African Americans?

ANSWERS TO

Thinking About the Selection

1. The mother is trying to tell her son that he must not give up when he becomes discouraged. She has had a hard life, but she has kept on trying to move forward in her life and she expects him to do the same.

2. The author, Langston Hughes, is the speaker. In this poem, he speaks for all African Americans.

3. The speaker's soul has "grown deep like the rivers." The poem implies that this has happened because the roots of African Americans go back so far into the past and they have experienced so much that it has deepened their souls.

4. The author compares the African race to rivers. The comparison conveys a sense that both are ancient, deep, and have experienced much.

Chapter 13 Crash and Depression
1929–1933

📁 Teaching Resources (See Unit 4 Folder)		
	Instruction	**Enrichment**

Section 1
 	
The Economy in the Late 1920s
(pp. 438–441)
	Reproducible Lesson Plan, p. 41
	Alternate Lesson Plan, p. 112
	Guided Reading and Review, p. 46
	Quiz, p. 47
		Critical Thinking Activity, Identifying Central
		  Issues, p. 65
		Visual Learning Activity, Hard Times
		  for Farmers, p. 73

Section 2
 	
The Stock Market Crash
(pp. 442–445)
	Reproducible Lesson Plan, p. 42
	Alternate Lesson Plan, p. 113
	Guided Reading and Review, p. 48
	Quiz, p. 49
		Literature Activity, The Stock Market
		  Crash, p. 69
		American Profiles Activity, Woody Guthrie,
		  p. 60
		Time and Place Activity, The Great Flood
		  of 1993, pp. 58–59

Section 3
 	
Social Effects of the Depression
(pp. 448–452)
	Reproducible Lesson Plan, p. 43
	Alternate Lesson Plan, p. 114
	Guided Reading and Review, p. 50
	Quiz, p. 51
		Literature Activity, The Psychological Effects
		  of the Depression, pp. 70–71
		Primary Source Activity, Hard Times
		  in Oklahoma, p. 66
		Historian's Toolbox Activity, Distinguishing
		  False from Accurate Images, p. 64

Section 4
 	
Surviving the Great Depression
(pp. 454–456)
	Reproducible Lesson Plan, p. 44
	Alternate Lesson Plan, p. 115
	Guided Reading and Review, p. 52
	Quiz, p. 53
		American Profiles Activity, Babe Didrikson
		  Zaharias, p. 61
		Primary Source Activity, The Forgotten Man,
		  pp. 67–68

Section 5
 	
The Election of 1932: A Turning Point in History
(pp. 457–461)
	Reproducible Lesson Plan, p. 45
	Alternate Lesson Plan, p. 116
	Guided Reading and Review, p. 54
	Quiz, p. 55
	Chapter Test, Forms A & B, pp. 74–79
		Visual Learning Activity, Veterans March on
		  Washington, p. 72
		Viewpoints Activity, On Ending the Depression,
		  pp. 62–63
		Turning Points Extension Activity, The Lasting
		  Impact of the Election of 1932, pp. 56–57

📁 **Additional Chapter Resources**	**Bibliography**

Resource Organizer, p. 40
Alternate Lesson Plan, p. 111
Answer Keys, pp. 116–128
	For the Teacher
	Watkins, T. H. *The Great Depression: America in the 1930s.*
	  Little, Brown, 1993. (Companion volume to the PBS video.)
	
	Prentice Hall Literature Excerpts from *The American*
	  Experience, 1994, including Wright, Richard. *Black Boy: A*
	  Record of Childhood and Youth. HarperCollins, 1993 edition.

THE BIG IDEA

The Big Idea for the chapter and how the main ideas in each section relate to the Big Idea are graphically displayed below. Comprehension of this chapter's Big Idea is critical to students' understanding of United States history and how we as a nation got where we are today.

Media and Technology

 Time Lines, E-6

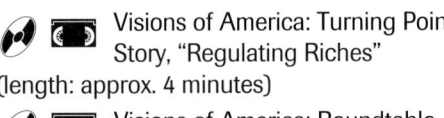 Visions of America: Turning Point Story, "Regulating Riches" (length: approx. 4 minutes)

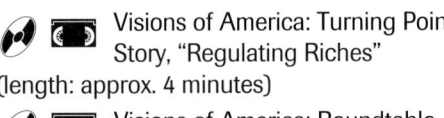 Visions of America: Roundtable Discussion on "Regulating Riches"

 Fine Art, D-18; Cause and Effect, F-9; Graphic Organizer, G-3

 Guided Reading Audiotapes (English and Spanish)

 Computer Test Bank

For the Student

The Great Depression. 420 minutes. PBS Video, 1993. Color. (Seven one-hour segments produced by Public Broadcasting Service.)

The Grapes of Wrath. 129 minutes. Zenger. Black-and-white film. (Dramatization of John Steinbeck's novel on the Depression.)

CHAPTER 13

When the high-flying 1920s crashed in 1929, the bleak years of the Great Depression began. Behind the headlines and photos of stock-buying frenzy and destitution grew a debate that cut to the very political, social, and economic fiber of the country and changed forever how Americans look at government.

SECTION 1

During the 1920s most Americans had great confidence in the country's economy. However, the seemingly booming economy was actually not healthy and there were signs of troubled times ahead.

SECTION 2

The stock market crashed in October 1929, bringing about a depression more severe than any the country had ever experienced.

SECTION 3

At first the Depression affected only certain Americans, but gradually it came to change the lives, and affect the physical and mental health, of almost all citizens.

SECTION 4

Life during the Great Depression was an unforgettable experience. In spite of the hard times, many Americans faced the future with courage.

SECTION 5

Republican President Hoover failed to control the Depression, and in 1932, for the first time in twelve years, voters elected a Democratic President who changed the concept of American government.

Crash and Depression
1929–1933

Crash and Depression
1929–1933

The Relevance of the Big Idea

Despite President Hoover's insistence that the economy was "fundamentally sound," and that "prosperity was just around the corner," business confidence failed in the late 1920s and unemployment became the norm. The Great Depression that followed brought a misery and fear that was unprecedented for most Americans. After taking office, President Roosevelt acted quickly to enact relief, recovery, and reform programs.

The stark policy differences between Hoover and FDR exemplified the political debate that has engaged all modern American Presidents: How best do we serve—with direct aid and intervention to the people or by encouraging business? Ask how policies of recent Presidents Bush (for an investment tax credit) and Clinton (for national health care) fit into this debate.

*T*he surface prosperity of the late 1920s hid deep faults in the American economy. When stock prices began to fall in October 1929, panic brought the economy crashing down. The United States sank into a long-lasting depression that brought widespread suffering. President Hoover's policies proved ineffective in turning the economy around, so Americans were eager to hear presidential candidate Franklin D. Roosevelt's proposals. In the 1932 election, voters chose Roosevelt, marking a major turning point in American history.

WORK-IS-WHAT-I WANT-AND-NOT-CHARITY WHO-WILL-HELP-ME-GET-A-JOB-7 YEARS-IN-DETROIT-NO-MONEY SENT-AWAY-FURNISH-BEST-OF-REFERENCES PHONE RANDOLPH 8381 Room #59.

In Depth

Global Connections

The breadlines symbolic of the Great Depression were common in most major industrial countries. Germany was racked by inflation, crippled industrially, and buried under war reparations debt. Newsreel cameras filmed consumers using carts to carry deutsche marks to market—inflation had made them so worthless that millions were needed just to buy a loaf of bread. As a leader rose in America promising "relief, recovery, and reform," a different kind of leader came to power in Germany. Within days of FDR taking office in 1933, Adolf Hitler became Germany's dictator.

Events in the United States

1928	1929	1930	1931
1928 The automobile, steel, rubber, glass, and housing industries are in recession.	**1929** Stock market hits record high in September, then crashes in October.		**1931** Empire State Building opens in New York, becoming the world's tallest skyscraper.

Events in the World

1928	1929	1930	1931
1928 Fifteen nations sign the Kellogg-Briand Pact renouncing war.		**1930** U.S., Britain, Japan, France, and Italy sign naval disarmament treaty.	**1931** Japanese troops occupy Manchuria. • Spain is declared a republic.

▶ RESOURCE DIRECTORY

Teaching Resources

Alternate Lesson Plan: Demonstrating the Big Idea found in the Alternate Lesson Plans folder, p. 111, provides a lesson strategy to instruct students about the Big Idea that the difficult years of the Great Depression led to dramatic changes in the American way of life.

Alternative Assessment Handbook provides information, guidance, and strategies for alternative methods of assessment. It includes an essay on new trends in assessment, guidance and strategies on developing performance tasks and portfolios, scoring rubrics, and sample evaluation forms.

Pages 438 – 441
The Economy in the Late 1920s
Optimism and faith in business continued throughout the 1920s. But while many were buying goods on credit and investing in the booming stock market, millions more had no share in the country's prosperity.

Pages 442–445
The Stock Market Crash
In 1929 the foundation of the seemingly prosperous economy was so unstable that the stock market crash in October led to a severe depression whose effects spread worldwide.

Pages 448 – 452
Social Effects of the Depression
Most people were not immediately affected by the 1929 stock market crash, but by the early 1930s, wage cuts and growing unemployment brought widespread suffering.

Pages 454 – 456
Surviving the Great Depression
Living through the Great Depression was an unforgettable experience. Despite the hard times, many Americans learned to face troubles together with courage and humor.

Pages 457–461
The 1932 Election: A Turning Point in History
As the Depression worsened, people came to blame Hoover and the Republicans for their misery. The 1932 presidential election brought a sweeping victory for Democrat Franklin D. Roosevelt, and a new direction for American government.

Pages 462–463
The Lasting Impact of the 1932 Election

1932	1933	1934	1935

1932 Veterans in the Bonus Army protest in Washington, D.C.

1933 Prohibition is repealed.
• Franklin D. Roosevelt is inaugurated as President.

1934 Farm families leave drought-stricken Great Plains and move west to California.

1932 Amelia Earhart is the first woman to fly solo across the Atlantic.

1934 Nationalists force communists under Mao Zedong into "Long March" across China.

Media and Technology

Transparency
Historical Maps, L-5

As an ongoing chapter project, students can create a local history project about the stock market crash and the Great Depression in their own community. Encourage students to analyze how the events and trends in their community compared to those nationwide.

Projects should contain a minimum of three of the following items:
• Interviews with relatives or community members who lived through the Great Depression
• Statistical information about the number of unemployed in the community for the years 1928–1940
• Information about industries that went out of business or started up during the Depression years
• Information about farming conditions during the Depression years
• Local history highlights in the arts, sports, politics, education, etc.

Interviews may be written or taped; statistics may be presented in a chart or a narrative; local highlights may be written, taped, or presented on a poster.

Projects will be evaluated according to the following guidelines:
• **Unacceptable** Activity not attempted; projects fail to meet basic requirements.
• **Limited/Acceptable** Three elements are completed and student attempts to compare local events and trends to those nationwide.
• **Extensive/Commendable** Three elements are completed and student makes general comparisons between local events and trends and those nationwide.
• **Extraordinary/Outstanding** Three elements are completed and student makes specific and general comparisons between local events and trends and those nationwide.

Encourage students to select pieces to include in their portfolios.

For information and guidance on alternative assessment trends and strategies, see the Alternative Assessment Handbook in the Resource Directory on page 436.

1. FOCUS

Connecting to the Big Idea

See page 436B. Explain to students that all three Presidents of the decade took a hands-off approach to government and the economy. As a result, stock market practices were largely unregulated. The stock market boomed in this climate, and many Americans thought prosperity was here to stay. Millions of other Americans, however, did not share in the good times, and that in fact was one of the signs of trouble to come. Ask what other signs pointed to serious flaws in the economy.

Objectives

● Relate Hoover's election in 1928 to voters' expectations of continuing prosperity.
● Explain why the government and many Americans believed that business prosperity was in the national interest.
● Analyze the increase of personal debt in the 1920s as an economic indicator.
● Identify farmers and industrial workers as groups not sharing in the prosperity of the 1920s.

Bellringer

Have students describe what happens when a consumer makes a purchase on credit. Suggest that they consider factors such as how a consumer gets credit, how buying on credit can add to the cost of the purchase, and consequences for those who are unable to pay for purchases made on credit.

Reading Strategy

Reading for Evidence As they read, ask students to look for reasons for optimism about the economy in the 1920s and also for reasons for concern about the economy.

SECTION 1

The Economy in the Late 1920s

SECTION PREVIEW

Optimism and faith in business continued throughout the 1920s. But while many were buying goods on credit and investing in the booming stock market, millions more had no share in the country's prosperity.

During the 1920s catalogs brimming with new goods tempted consumers to buy on credit.

Key Concepts

• Voters believed Herbert Hoover's administration would continue the good times.
• The government and many people believed that business prosperity served national interests.
• People went into debt to buy products and to invest in the stock market.
• Farmers and many industrial workers did not share in the general prosperity of the 1920s.

Key Terms, People, and Places

real wages, welfare capitalism, installment buying, speculation, buy on margin

T he mood of most Americans in the late 1920s was optimistic, and for good reason. Medical advances had greatly reduced deaths from whooping cough, diphtheria, and other serious diseases. Since 1900, the number of infant deaths had declined, and life expectancy had lengthened more than 10 years, to 59 years for men and 63 years for women.

The brightest hopes seemed to come from the economy. In his final message to Congress, President Calvin Coolidge said that the country could "regard the present with satisfaction and anticipate the future with optimism." His successor, Herbert Hoover, predicted that "poverty will be banished from this nation."

The Economy Inspires Trust

Coolidge chose not to run in 1928, but years of prosperity under the Republicans made victory easy for Hoover. A self-made millionaire, Hoover was widely admired for the way he had organized food relief in Europe during and after World War I. He had also been an effective secretary of commerce for Presidents Harding and Coolidge. People expected that the good times would get even better under Hoover.

"Wonderful Prosperity" The United States economy seemed to be in fine shape. In 1925, the market value of all stocks was $27 billion. Over the next few years, it soared: in 1928 alone, stock values rose by almost $11.4 billion. Because the stock market was widely regarded as the nation's economic weathervane, the *New York Times* could describe the year as one "of unprecedented advance, of wonderful prosperity." By early October 1929, stock values hit $87 billion.

Working people also seemed better off. Since 1914, **real wages**—what money could actually buy—had increased more than 40 percent. Although some industries were troubled, and some workers lost jobs to assembly-line machinery, unemployment in general averaged below 4 percent.

Even critics of capitalism made optimistic predictions. In 1928, former muckraker Lincoln Steffens wrote:

B ig business in America is producing what the Socialists held up as their goal: food, shelter and clothing for all. You will see it during the Hoover administration.

"Everybody Ought to Be Rich" People had unusually high confidence in the business world during the 1920s. For some, business success became almost a religion. One of the

---

▶ RESOURCE DIRECTORY

Teaching Resources

🗋 **Reproducible Lesson Plan** found in the Unit 4 folder, p. 41, provides a summary of the Section 1 lesson plan content.

🗋 **Alternate Lesson Plan: Cooperative Learning** found in the Alternate Lesson Plans folder, p. 112, is an alternate lesson plan that provides guidance for groups of students to prepare oral presentations on economic conditions of the 1920s.

🗋 **Guided Reading and Review** found in the Unit 4 folder, p. 46, provides a structure for reading and mastering the key concepts and reviewing the key terms for Section 1. (Guided Practice)

This car advertisement from 1927 reflects the apparent prosperity and optimism of those years.

"Higher Compression with *any* Gas!"

Plus Willys-Knight Silence, Velvet Smoothness, Graceful Lines, Rich Colors

BEAUTIFUL NEW COLORS
Your choice of many exquisitely distinctive new color combinations, both in lacquer and upholstery. Colors that are rich, harmoniously blended, lastingly attractive—outstanding ensembles of rare taste and artistry.

WILLYS·KNIGHT

$1295

---

decade's best-selling books was *The Man Nobody Knows* (1925). Written by Bruce Barton, an advertising executive, it told Jesus' life story in business terms. Barton portrayed Jesus as a managerial genius who "picked up twelve men from the bottom ranks of business and forged them into an organization that conquered the world."

Similarly, Americans trusted the advice of corporate leaders such as John J. Raskob. In a 1929 article, "Everybody Ought to Be Rich," he stated that savings of only $15 a week over twenty years could bring a $400-a-month income from investments. "And because income can do that," Raskob said, "I am firm in my belief that anyone not only can be rich, but ought to be rich."

The three Republican Presidents of the 1920s equated the interests of the nation with the interests of the business world. They, too, expressed great confidence in business. Although people in the late 1920s were wildly buying stocks with borrowed money, the Hoover administration did nothing to discourage such borrowing.

Welfare Capitalism Partly because workers' standard of living seemed to be improving, organized labor lost members during the 1920s. To counter moves by outside union organizers

and keep workers contented, companies met some of their workers' needs without prompting by unions. This new approach to labor relations was known as **welfare capitalism**. Employers raised wages and provided benefits such as paid vacations, health plans, and even English classes for recent immigrants.

MAKING CONNECTIONS

Although vacations and health plans were unusual benefits in the 1920s, more and more working people today expect them. What does this change show about the relative status of workers in the 1920s and 1990s?

Signs of Trouble

Despite the apparent prosperity, all was not well. Only later, however, did many people recognize the warning signs of an unsound economy.

Uneven Riches In reality, the economy of the 1920s was seriously out of balance. Despite some stock market success stories, it was mainly the rich who got richer. Huge corporations, rather than small businesses, dominated American industry. In 1929, 200 large companies controlled 49 percent of American industry.

Activity

Teaching Heterogeneous Groups

In the 1920s, farms and factories borrowed money to take advantage of new technology to increase production. Soon however, production exceeded demand. In order for students to understand how supply exceeded demand due to overproduction, divide the class into small groups representing farms and factories. Have students in each group list items required for production. For example, the auto industry would list rubber and steel. Then have students identify the other industries that might be affected should their industry overproduce and not be able to sell its goods, setting in motion a domino effect throughout the economy. **LEP**

Enrichment

Ask students to create a campaign poster or song for Herbert Hoover in the election of 1928, based on the Republican promise that Hoover would safeguard the nation's prosperity. Students might research some of the actual slogans used in the campaign.

 In Depth

Historical Misconceptions

The crash is usually seen as the result of bad business practices in the stock market and, therefore, avoidable. But the crash was, in the words of historian George Soule, "no easily preventable accident. While it is now possible to identify certain major infections that were developing, there seems to be no simple inoculation, the injection of which into the economic body would have maintained its health."

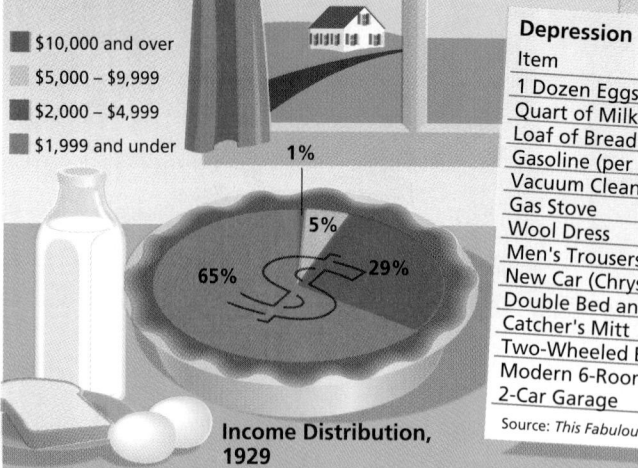

Income Distribution and Depression Era Prices

- ■ $10,000 and over
- ▨ $5,000 – $9,999
- ■ $2,000 – $4,999
- ■ $1,999 and under

1%

5%

65% $ 29%

Income Distribution, 1929

Source: *Historical Statistics of the United States*

Depression Era Prices

Item	Price
1 Dozen Eggs	$0.29
Quart of Milk	$0.10
Loaf of Bread	$0.05
Gasoline (per gallon)	$0.18
Vacuum Cleaner	$18.75
Gas Stove	$23.95
Wool Dress	$1.95
Men's Trousers	$2.00
New Car (Chrysler sedan)	$995.00
Double Bed and Spring Mattress	$14.95
Catcher's Mitt	$1.19
Two-Wheeled Bike	$10.95
Modern 6-Room House With 2-Car Garage	$2,800.00

Source: *This Fabulous Century*, Vol. IV, by Time-Life Books

This political cartoon, symbolic of the stock market frenzy, shows greedy brokers "fishing" for new clients from the top of the New York Stock Exchange building.

 Interpreting Graphs

The pie graph shows how unevenly the country's wealth was distributed in the 1920s. *What percentage of Americans earned less than $2,000 a year? Looking at the list of prices and assuming that you didn't buy on credit, find what you could have bought with that income—a monthly income of $165 or less.*

Similarly, personal wealth was concentrated in a tiny percentage of American families. (See the graph above.) In 1929, the richest Americans—24,000 families, or just 0.1 percent of the population—had incomes of more than $100,000. They also held 34 percent of the country's total savings. Of those families, 513 were millionaires. ✪

By contrast, 71 percent of American individuals and families earned less than $2,500 a year. About 21.5 million households—nearly 80 percent of all families—had no savings. Many people earned so little that almost everyone in a family, including children, had to work just to get by.

Buying on Credit Another sign of trouble was an increase in personal debt. Traditionally, Americans feared debt and resisted buying goods unless they had the cash to pay for them. In the 1920s, however, assembly-line production lowered the cost of many consumer items, making them affordable for more people. People also were eager to forget World War I. They flocked to buy radios, vacuum cleaners, refrigerators, and other exciting new products, whether or not they could afford them.

Advertising made new goods irresistible. Store owners also had enough confidence in the economy to let people buy goods "on time." **Installment buying** let people purchase expensive items such as automobiles and furniture and pay for them (with interest) over many months.

"Get Rich Quick" A "get-rich-quick" attitude prevailed during the 1920s. Stock prices were on a dizzy climb, and the press quickly reported success stories of ordinary people who had made fortunes.

Before World War I, only the wealthy played the stock market. Now, with stock prices rising, **speculation**—taking chances in the stock market—became widespread. Small investors entered the market, often with their life savings. If they could not afford to buy stocks at face value, stockbrokers let them **buy on margin**.

▶ RESOURCE DIRECTORY

Teaching Resources

✪ **Critical Thinking Activity** Identifying Central Issues: Signs of Trouble, found in the Unit 4 folder, p. 65, helps students to identify central issues by analyzing a graph on income distribution in the United States in 1929.

✪ **Visual Learning Activity** Hard Times for Farmers, found in the Unit 4 folder, p. 73, uses photographs and oral accounts to extend students' understanding of government attempts to draw attention to the plight of farmers during the Depression.

They paid a fraction of the price (10 to 50 percent) and borrowed the rest.

Brokers charged high interest and could demand payment of the loan at any time. But if the price of the stocks went up, the borrower could sell at a price high enough to pay off the loan and interest charges and still make money.

Too Many Goods, Too Little Demand By the late 1920s, the country's warehouses held piles of unbought consumer goods. Wages had risen, but not as fast as production. People could not afford to buy goods as fast as they were made.

Although the stock market kept rising, overproduction caused some industries to slow in the late 1920s. The automobile industry, which had helped create American prosperity, slumped after 1925. Industries that depended on it—steel, rubber, and glass—also were in recession. Housing construction fell by 25 percent between 1928 and 1929.

Hard Times Most farmers never shared in the 1920s prosperity. New machinery enabled them to grow more crops, but the huge postwar demand for food ended as European farmers recovered. As a result, crop prices in the United States fell so low that farmers could not pay what they owed for land and machinery. Rural banks suffered when loans were not repaid, and about 6,000 failed. "We were in the Depression before 1929, we just didn't call it that," recalled a rural Tennessean. ★

Outside agriculture, factory workers faced low wages and long hours. Conditions were especially bad in coal mines and southern

textile mills. In the rayon mills of Elizabethton, Tennessee, for instance, women worked 56-hour weeks, earning 16 to 18 cents an hour—about $10 a week.

To some observers, these factors—uneven wealth, rising debt, speculation in the stock market, overproduction, and hard times for many workers—clearly signaled trouble in the economy. In 1928, Belle Moskowitz, who had managed Al Smith's losing presidential campaign that year, predicted that "growing unemployment, business depression or some false step" would soon trigger a reaction against Hoover and his policies. Although the collapse did not come till the next year, she soon was proved right.

Farm families faced hard times in the 1920s. Many had to watch while their homes, land, and animals were sold at auction.

SECTION 1 REVIEW

Key Terms, People, and Places
1. Define (a) real wages, (b) welfare capitalism, (c) installment buying, (d) speculation, (e) buy on margin.

Key Concepts
2. Why was there so much optimism in the United States in the late 1920s?
3. How did most Americans regard the business world in the 1920s?

4. In what ways had many Americans gone deeply into debt? Why?
5. Which groups were experiencing hard times in the 1920s despite the general prosperity in the United States?

Critical Thinking
6. **Identifying Central Issues** Why did most people not realize that the economy in the 1920s was not as healthy as it seemed?

Quiz found in the Unit 4 folder, p. 47, covers the main ideas in this section as well as the key terms.

3. ASSESS

Section 1 Review Answers

1. (a) real wages, see p. 438, (b) welfare capitalism, see p. 439, (c) installment buying, see p. 440, (d) speculation, see p. 440, (e) buy on margin, see p. 440

2. Medical advances had increased human life expectancy by about ten years for both sexes. The booming stock market made it seem that the economy was very prosperous.

3. People had confidence in business prosperity and in business leaders; they believed people could achieve success.

4. They bought consumer goods on installment plans; they bought stocks on margin, borrowing from the broker. The mood was one of confidence and trust in business.

5. Farmers, industrial workers.

6. The economy appeared deceptively healthy because the stock market was rising, real wages had improved, and employers were giving more benefits. People also had confidence in business leaders and in Presidents Coolidge and Hoover; moreover, they wanted to forget problems and look to a bright future after World War I.

Reteach

Ask students to make two columns on a piece of paper. Ask them to list the 1920s economy's positive signs in the right-hand column and the negative signs in the left-hand column. Then ask them to write one or two sentences explaining the seriousness of the negative indications.

4. CLOSE

Reinforcing the Big Idea

Most Americans were optimistic about the continued growth of the economy in 1928 and early 1929. Certain key signs, however, showed that the economy was in trouble. The next section deals with the stock market crash in October 1929.

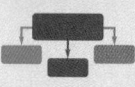

The Stock Market Crash

1. FOCUS

Connecting to the Big Idea

See page 436B. Explain to students that the stock market crash in October 1929 brought on a depression more severe than any the nation had ever experienced. Ask what the lasting effects of the Depression were on government, politics, and American thought.

Objectives

● Describe how a sudden fall in stock prices in late October 1929 brought on a stock market crash.

● Explain how the stock market crash led to a general decline in the United States economy.

● Account for the worldwide effects of the stock market crash.

Bellringer

Ask students to imagine themselves as a bank customer who wants to withdraw savings and is told by the bank teller that there is no money. What might be the cause of such a situation? What options would be available to the customer?

Reading Strategy

Predicting Content Ask students to skim Section 2, list the main headings and subheadings and write a sentence or phrase to predict the content of each section. When they have finished reading Section 2, ask them to review their predictions and test them against the actual text.

2. INSTRUCT

Explain/Discuss

Explain to students that the sense of prosperity described in the previous section came to a sudden halt as stock prices fell, investors began to sell, and prices fell even more. Ask students to explain how Richard

SECTION PREVIEW

The Long and the Short of it

Ticker-tape machines, which report stock market activity, brought both good news and bad to investors, as this drawing from a 1930 *Life* cover shows.

In 1929 the foundation of the seemingly prosperous economy was so unstable that the stock market crash in October led to a severe depression whose effects spread worldwide.

Key Concepts

• A sudden fall in stock prices in late October 1929 brought a wave of panic selling.

• The crash contributed to a severe decline in the overall United States economy.

• The results of the stock market crash were felt worldwide.

Key Terms, People, and Places

Dow Jones industrial average, Gross National Product (GNP), collateral

A fter Herbert Hoover's 1928 election, stock prices continued to climb. Early that year, the **Dow Jones industrial average**, an average of stock prices of leading industries, was 191. By inauguration day, March 4, 1929, it had risen another 122 points. Prices faltered in April, but brokers said, "Buy!" On September 3, the Dow Jones reached an all-time high of 381.

The Market Crashes

The rising stock market dominated the news. Keeping track of prices was almost as popular as counting Babe Ruth's home runs. Eager, nervous investors filled brokerage houses around the country to catch the latest news coming in on the ticker tape or posted on blackboards. Prices for many stocks soared far above their real value, in terms of the company's earnings and assets.

Black Thursday, Black Tuesday After the peak in September, stock prices fell slowly. Some brokers began to call in loans, but others loaned even more. Business leaders such as Charles E. Mitchell, head of the National City Bank of New York, assured the nervous public: "Although in some cases speculation has gone too far, . . . the markets generally are now in a healthy condition."

As the stock market closed on October 23, the Dow Jones average dropped 21 points in an hour. The next day, Thursday, October 24, worried investors began to sell, and stock prices fell. Falling prices panicked others, who also sold quickly—at any price. Investors who had bought General Electric stock at $400 a share sold it for $283 a share. U.S. Steel stock fell from 261 3/4 to 193 1/2.

Again, business and political leaders told the country not to worry. Colonel Leonard P. Ayres, a banking executive, said that only a nation as rich as the United States could "withstand the shock of a $3 billion paper loss on the Stock Exchange in a single day without serious effects to the average citizen." President Hoover announced: "The fundamental business of the country . . . is on a sound and prosperous basis."

To stop the panic, a group of bankers pooled their money to buy stock. Banker Richard Whitney, a Stock Exchange official, went to the floor and, in a few minutes, made offers for $20 to $30 million worth of stock. This action stabilized prices, but only for a few days. By Monday prices were falling again. Investors all over the country raced to get out of the stock market. On October 29, known as Black Tuesday, a record 16.4 million shares were sold, compared with 4 to 8 million shares a day, earlier in the year. ✪

The collapse continued. By November 13, the Dow Jones had fallen from its September high of 381 to 198.7. Overall losses amounted to $30 billion.

▶ RESOURCE DIRECTORY

Teaching Resources

 Reproducible Lesson Plan found in the Unit 4 folder, p. 42, provides a summary of the Section 2 lesson plan content.

Alternate Lesson Plan: Critical Thinking Predicting Consequences, found in the Alternate Lesson Plans folder, p. 113, is an alternate lesson plan that provides students with the skills to predict consequences by analyzing a newspaper stock market page.

Guided Reading and Review found in the Unit 4 folder, p. 48, provides a structure for reading and mastering the key concepts and reviewing the key terms for Section 2. (Guided Practice)

✪ **Literature Activity** The Stock Market Crash, found in the Unit 4 folder, p. 69, describes the mood on the floor of the New York Stock Exchange on Black Tuesday, October 29, 1929.

Coming to Terms It took time for people to recognize the extent of the disaster caused by the crash. Arthur Crew Inman, a wealthy Boston resident, lost heavily in the market. He wrote in his diary, "The profit in my little book melted yesterday to seven thousand. It is probably nil today. . . . My dreams of a million—where are they?" Inman, however, had a secure income of $12,000 a year. Although upset, he viewed the situation with wry humor, adding this mock prayer:

O *Stock Market, God of American gamblers, be merciful to me, a petty and insignificant worshipper at your shrine! If I have been greedy, forgive me! Leave me my remnants, O Stock Market!*

For people like Inman, whose entire wealth did not depend on the stock market, life went on much as before, with perhaps a few cutbacks. Others, even wealthy families, lost everything. Brokers and banks called in their loans, but people did not have cash to pay them.

When the stock market crashed, many investors—large and small—stockbrokers, bankers, and manufacturers fell too. As the economic slide got steeper, it took more and more ordinary people down with it. The graph below shows the fluctuations in the stock market from 1925 to 1933.

MAKING CONNECTIONS

Many people today use credit cards and charge accounts to buy on credit. Is it as dangerous now as it was in 1929? Why or why not?

The Crash Affects Millions

⭐ By 1929, about 4 million people, out of a population of 120 million, had invested in the stock market. They were the first to suffer from the crash, but it soon affected millions who had

As stock market prices fell, the ticker tape could not report market activity fast enough. Nervous investors crowded into Wall Street, hoping to hear the latest news.

Stock Prices,* 1925–1933

Price Index

*Standard and Poor's index of common stocks
Source: *Historical Statistics of the United States*

Interpreting Graphs
With only a few pauses, stock market prices climbed steadily during the 1920s. *According to this graph, when did market prices reach their lowest point before starting to rise again?*

⭐ **American Profiles Activity** found in the Unit 4 folder, p. 60, profiles folk song writer and singer Woody Guthrie, who used his considerable talent to chronicle the woes of ordinary Americans during the Depression.

The New York Times

NEW YORK, TUESDAY, OCTOBER 29, 1929.

STOCK PRICES SLUMP $14,000,000,000 IN NATION-WIDE STAMPEDE TO UNLOAD; BANKERS TO SUPPORT MARKET TODAY

Whitney and other bankers attempted to stop the panic, and what the outcome was.

Ask students to think about conditions in the United States on October 30, 1929, the day after the great stock market crash. Explain that much had changed, although few people really understood what had happened on the stock market. It took time for the effects of the crash to reach businesses and services. Ask students how a general economic failure would likely affect such employers as a zipper manufacturer, a restaurant in a small town, and a college.

Analyze

Have students examine the reasons for bank failures. Ask them to compare the plight of an investor who lost on the stock market and a worker who lost life savings.

Ask students to list and explain the underlying causes of the Great Depression. Ask why the government did not regulate the stock market.

Caption Answer to . . .

Interpreting Graphs

1932

Answer to . . .

MAKING CONNECTIONS

Answers may vary but are likely to reflect students' own experience or family background. Some students may know that nearly all credit cards place credit limits on buying but that people can still get into trouble with credit buying.

Activity

Cooperative Learning

Time: One class period.

Activity: Create a sequential chart that illustrates the effects of the stock market crash on different segments of the American economy.

Grouping: Groups of four to six students.

Purpose: In each group, let one student represent a given segment of the American economy. Each student should create an appropriate symbol for his or her segment. The group should create a flow chart showing the effects of the stock market on each segment and how each segment in turn affected all the others on the chart.

Roles: Assign the following roles: large manufacturing corporation, small manufacturing company, farm, American family, store owner, restaurant owner, etc.

Outcome: Students will demonstrate how the stock market crash affected different segments of the economy.

Enrichment

Suggest that students learn how to read the stock market reports in the daily newspaper. Ask them to pick one or two stocks that are traded on the New York Stock Exchange and chart the progress of their stocks for at least one week. Students might also be interested in writing to the corporations for annual reports. Addresses can be found in a business directory such as the one published by Standard & Poor's.

Caption Answer to ...

 Interpreting Graphs

(See page 445.) A domino effect had taken hold of the economy—income and profits fell, forcing businesses to close and unemployment to rise.

never owned a single share of stock. Eventually, like ripples from a stone thrown into a pond, its effects spread beyond the United States. The Great Depression had begun.

Workers and Farmers Lose Out As income and profits fell, American factories began to close. Week after week, thousands of workers lost their jobs or had their pay cut. In August 1931, Henry Ford shut down his Detroit automobile factories, putting at least 75,000 people out of work.

In several European countries, workers had government unemployment insurance, but the United States had no such program. By 1932, nearly 13 million were unemployed, about a quarter of the labor force (see graph on page 445). Others worked only part time or had their wages cut. The **Gross National Product (GNP)**—the total annual value of goods and services a country produces— was $103 billion in 1929. By 1933 it was only $56 billion.

The effects of the crash spread. Restaurants and other small businesses closed because customers could no longer afford to patronize them. Once-wealthy families dismissed household workers. Farm prices, already low, fell

even more, bringing final disaster to many families (see graph below). In 1929, a bushel of wheat had sold at the low price of $1.04; in 1932 it brought 38 cents. Cotton dropped from 17 to 6.5 cents a pound. In 1930 a severe drought parched farmlands in the Great Plains, a foretaste of the weather that would turn the area into a dust bowl. (See "Time and Place: The Black Blizzards," pages 446–447.)

Banks Close Unpaid farm loans already had ruined many rural banks. Now city banks were in trouble. Banks exist on the interest they earn from lending out their deposits. They assume that not everyone will claim their deposits at once. After the stock market crash, people with loans to repay as well as nervous depositors rushed to withdraw their money.

Thousands of banks closed their doors when they could not return their depositors' money or sell foreclosed properties. In just a few years, more than 5,500 banks failed. By 1933, the money from nine million savings accounts had vanished.

Worldwide Repercussions The crash would have been serious even if it had hurt only the United States. But by the 1930s, international banking, manufacturing, and trade had made nations interdependent. When the world's leading economy fell, the global economic system began to crumble.

After World War I, the United States had insisted that France and England, its wartime allies, repay their war debts. At the same time, Congress kept import taxes high, making it hard for European nations to sell goods in the United States. With economies weakened by the war and little chance of selling goods in the United States, the Allies had to rely on Germany's reparations payments for income.

As long as United States companies invested in Germany, reparations payments continued. But with the Depression, investments fell off. German banks failed, Germany suspended reparations, and the Allies in turn stopped

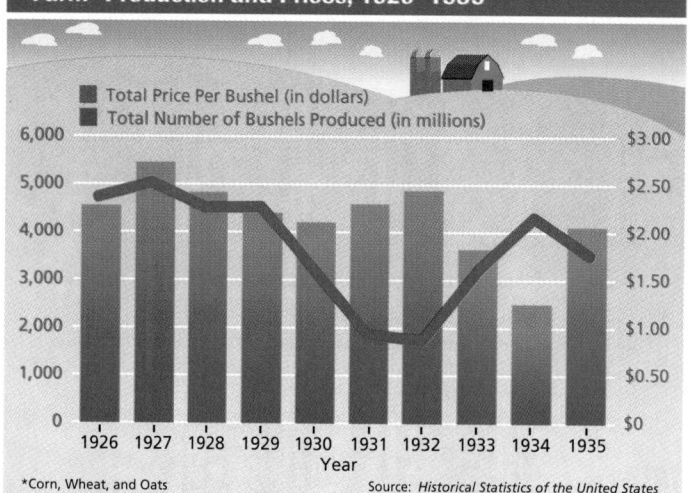

Farm* Production and Prices, 1926–1935

Total Price Per Bushel (in dollars)
Total Number of Bushels Produced (in millions)

*Corn, Wheat, and Oats

Source: *Historical Statistics of the United States*

 **Interpreting Graphs**
American farmers invested heavily to meet the postwar need for food, but demand suddenly fell—and crop prices dropped as a result. *In what year did farm prices drop the most?*

▶ RESOURCE DIRECTORY

Teaching Resources

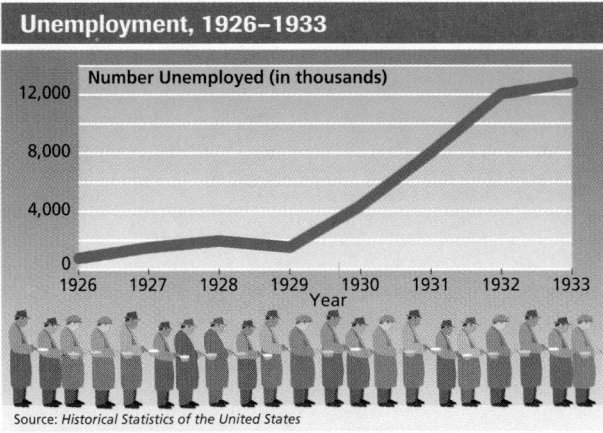

Unemployment, 1926–1933

Number Unemployed (in thousands)

12,000

8,000

4,000

0

1926 1927 1928 1929 1930 1931 1932 1933
Year

Source: *Historical Statistics of the United States*

Interpreting Graphs
The number of people without jobs increased each year after the crash. *What caused unemployment to rise sharply after 1929?*

paying their debts. Europeans no longer could afford to buy American-made goods. Thus the American stock market crash started a downward cycle in the global economy.

What Caused the Great Depression?

The stock market crash of 1929, though devastating to investors, was only the final push that toppled the fragile structure of the American economy. Deeper problems were the real underlying causes of the Great Depression.

Overspeculation During the 1920s, speculators bought stocks with borrowed money, then pledged those stocks as **collateral,** or security, for loans to buy more stocks. Brokers' loans went from under $5 million in mid-1928 to

$850 million in September 1929. Based on borrowed money and optimism instead of real value, the stock market boom was as unsteady as a house of cards. When investors lost confidence, it collapsed, taking them with it.

Government Policies Mistakes in monetary policy were also to blame. During the 1920s the Federal Reserve system, which regulates the amount of money in circulation, cut interest rates to spur economic growth. Then in 1929, worried about overspeculation, it introduced a tight-money policy, seeking to dry up credit. After the Crash, however, this meant that there was so little money in circulation that the economy was unable to recover.

An Unstable Economy Overall, the seemingly prosperous economy lacked a firm base. National wealth was unevenly distributed, with the most money in the hands of a few families, who tended to save or invest rather than buying goods. Industry produced more goods than most consumers wanted or could afford. While some people profited, most felt that their incomes had not kept up with prices. Farmers and many workers had not shared in the economic boom. The unevenness of the 1920s prosperity made rapid recovery impossible.

SECTION 2 REVIEW

Key Terms, People, and Places
1. Define (a) Dow-Jones industrial average, (b) Gross National Product, (c) collateral.

Key Concepts
2. What were the main events leading up to Black Tuesday in 1929?
3. Who were the first to feel the effects of the crash?
4. Why did banks fail?

5. What effect did the United States stock market crash have on the world economy?

Critical Thinking
6. **Identifying Assumptions** In the 1930s, the United States did not provide any type of unemployment insurance. What beliefs support the idea that government should provide workers with unemployment insurance?

 Quiz found in the Unit 4 folder, p. 49, covers the main ideas in this section as well as the key terms.

Media and Technology

Transparency
Time Lines, E-6

3. ASSESS

Section 2 Review Answers
1. (a) Dow Jones industrial average, see p. 442, (b) Gross National Product, see p. 444, (c) collateral, see p. 445

2. Stock prices reached an all-time high in September 1929, then began to slide. After a sudden drop on October 23, investors panicked and began to sell the next day. After a brief stabilization, prices fell drastically on Black Tuesday, October 29.

3. Investors who had speculated heavily, bought on margin, and risked all their assets and income.

4. Banks rely for profits on lending all but a portion of their deposits. When depositors tried to withdraw their savings all at once, the banks had no cash to pay them and had to close.

5. It stopped investment in Germany, which stopped paying reparations to the Allies, who in turn stopped paying war debts. European economies grew weaker, and international trade also slowed.

6. Answers may vary, but should touch on the question of whether government does or does not have some responsibility for citizens' well-being.

Reteach
Ask students to draw three concentric circles on a sheet of paper. Have them label the circles Causes of the Stock Market Crash, Immediate Effects of the Crash, and Later Effects of the Crash. Ask students to review the major sections of the chapter and to list three causes, one immediate effect, and three later effects of the crash.

4. CLOSE

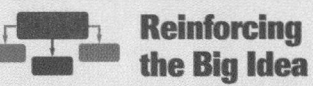 **Reinforcing the Big Idea**

The crash of the stock market in October 1929 brought on a depression more severe than any other in the nation's history. The Depression had repercussions around the world. The next section deals with some of the suffering endured by Americans in that bleak time.

The Black Blizzards

Focus Some of the most vivid images of the Great Depression are those of farms on the Great Plains, dust covered and abandoned, and those of Great Plains farm families on the road, headed for a new life. Their plight, vividly described in John Steinbeck's American classic *The Grapes of Wrath*, symbolized the misery of the Depression. The loss of their lands and the lessons of the Dust Bowl changed American farming.

In this section students will identify the natural and human causes of the Dust Bowl.

Instruct Explain to students that in the 1930s a great natural disaster—a series of terrible dust storms—destroyed many farms in the Great Plains. Point out that natural causes, as well as human actions, contributed to the disaster.

Before students read the feature, ask them to locate the Great Plains on a map of the United States.

Trace the history of farming on the Great Plains by creating a time line for the period between 1800 and 1950. Ask students to place the following events on the time line:
• Great Plains identified as desert.
• Richness of the Great Plains discovered.
• Hard winter wheat introduced.
• World War I causes rise in wheat prices.
• Four million acres under plow.
• Prices for wheat fall.
• First dust storms.
• Rain relieves drought.

Ask students to explain if it was a bitter coincidence that the dust storms came at the same time as the Depression or if the Depression helped to cause them. *(An early sign of the Depression was a drop in farm income, and farmers plowed up more land for wheat in an effort to survive.)*

Extend Ask students to explain how each of the following factors contributed to the Dust Bowl: extensive wheat farming on the Great Plains,

The Black Blizzards

Between 1933 and 1940, so much earth blew out of the central and southern Great Plains that the area became known as the Dust Bowl. What factors contributed to this environmental disaster?

The Great Plains is famous the world over as "America's breadbasket." Deep, fertile soils, a growing season long enough for most crops, and flat land give the region its farming advantage. But because the region is dry, farming on the plains is a risky undertaking.

The Plow that Broke the Plains

It was the dryness of the region that early settlers noticed first. For this reason, maps in the early 1800s referred to the Great Plains as the Great American Desert. By the late 1800s, however, farmers discovered the truth of the Great American Desert—when there was water, the Great Plains was one of the world's best farming regions.

Early farmers faced a major obstacle. The soils of the Great Plains were protected by a thick layer of native grasses with roots that were difficult to cut. To break the roots required expensive steel plows and months of hard labor. Yet, from the time that hard winter wheat was first introduced in central Kansas in the mid 1870s, farmers in the plains sank their plow blades into the sod and turned it over to make wheat fields.

In the early years of the twentieth century, wheat brought good prices, and farmers continually increased the acres of plowed land at the expense of the native grasses. In 1917 prices went even higher, spurred upward by the great demand caused by World War I. The price increases stimulated an even

greater fervor to plow more land to grow wheat: "Plant more wheat! Wheat will win the war!" was the slogan. By 1919 farmers plowed under nearly 4 million acres of grassland. Even after the war ended, the big plow-up continued.

It was new technology that allowed so much land to be plowed. Plowing with tractors allowed farmers to turn over far more acres in a day than they ever could have without those machines. When prices for wheat began to fall in the early 1920s, farmers responded by growing even more wheat. In the five years between 1925 and 1930 alone, more than 5 million additional acres of grassland disappeared, converted to wheat fields by the relentless plow blades.

Interaction: Drought and Human Activity Led to Dust Storms

At the time the first dust storms occurred in the early 1930s, farmers blamed them on the severe and lengthy drought that began and lasted until the end of the decade. While drought was a major factor in creating the Dust Bowl, it was not the only factor. Farming practices contributed as much as the weather to the disaster.

The plains region experiences great variations. Hot and humid tropical air masses move into the region from the Gulf of Mexico and cold polar air masses push southward from above the Arctic Circle. When these two air masses collide, powerful storms with fierce updrafts are created.

Violent winds picked up the dark, nutrient-rich topsoil and carried it eastward, sometimes for hundreds of miles, leaving behind barren, shifting dunes of grit and sand.

RESOURCE DIRECTORY

Teaching Resources

Time and Place Activity The Great Flood of 1993, found in the Unit 4 folder, pp. 58–59, explains the impact of human interaction with the environment by analyzing the great flood of the Mississippi River in 1993.

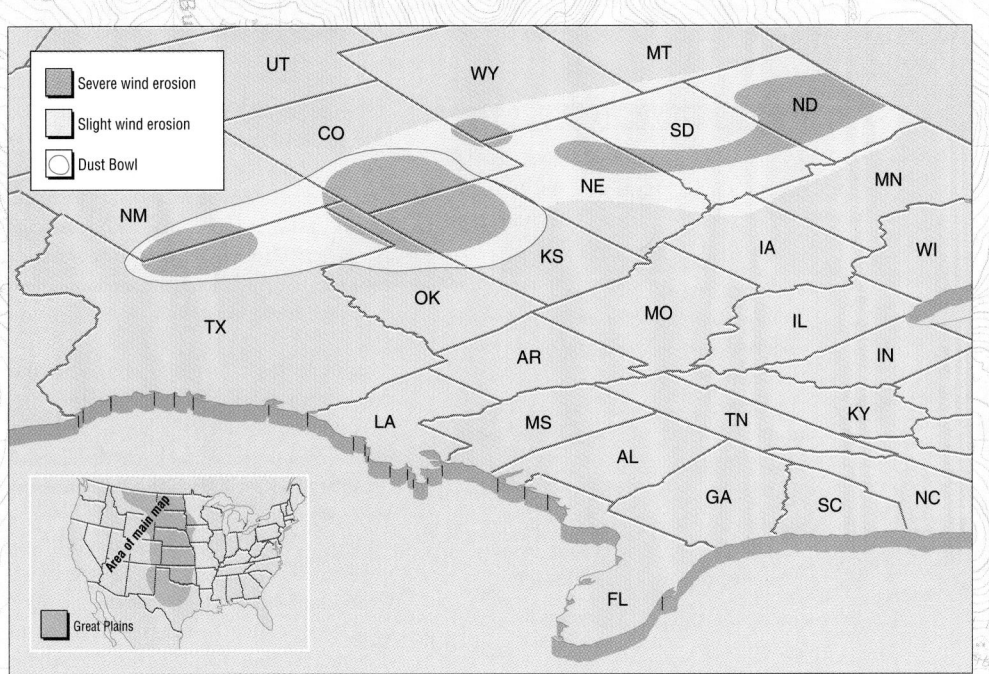

Severe wind erosion

Slight wind erosion

Dust Bowl

UT

WY

MT

ND

CO

SD

NE

MN

NM

KS

IA

WI

OK

MO

IL

IN

TX

AR

LA

MS

TN

KY

AL

GA

SC

NC

FL

Area of main map

Great Plains

Severe weather could not harm the environment as long as the thick layer of prairie grasses protected the topsoil. But when farmers stripped the soil of its natural protection by plowing the land, they opened the door to a major disaster.

Not Enough Rain

The most severe storms of the dry years were dubbed "black blizzards." Violent winds picked up the dark, nutrient-rich topsoil and carried it eastward, sometimes for hundreds of miles, leaving behind barren, shifting dunes of grit and sand. The map above shows the extent of soil erosion across the plains.

Time after time, dirt was sucked up off the parched plains and dropped by the ton over states and cities to the east. The dirt darkened the sky in New York City and Washington, D.C. It stained the snows of New England red and dropped on ships hundreds of miles off the Atlantic coast. The drought and winds persisted for more than seven years, bringing ruin to farmers.

The combination of terrible weather and very low prices for farm products caused 60 percent of the people in the Dust Bowl to lose their farms. Relief did not come until the early 1940s when the rains finally arrived and World War II drove farm prices up. By that time the damage was done. Driven by their need to grow more wheat to pay their growing debts, Dust Bowl farmers were the agents of their own destruction in the "Dirty Thirties."

GEOGRAPHIC CONNECTIONS

1. What caused the black blizzards of the 1930s?
2. (a) What features of land and climate make the Great Plains a good farming region? (b) What features make it a poor farming region?

Critical Thinking
3. **Identifying Alternatives** What might the farmers of the Great Plains do to prevent another Dust Bowl?

447

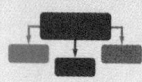

Connecting to the Big Idea

See page 436B. Explain to students that the effects of the stock market crash gradually filtered through all levels of American society. Ask how the Great Depression changed the way Americans lived.

Objectives

● Describe how wage cuts and unemployment affected all levels of American society.

● Show how those Americans already experiencing financial hardship, such as farmers, suffered even more.

● Explain how the Depression affected people's mental and physical health.

● Show how conditions for African Americans worsened during the Depression.

Bellringer

Ask students to describe how they would cut back on their expenses if their cash funds were limited. Have students describe how they might feel if this happened.

Reading Strategy

Predicting Content Before they read the section, have students predict which group of Americans suffered most from the Depression. Ask students to look for data to support their predictions as they read.

Social Effects of the Depression

SECTION PREVIEW

Most people were not immediately affected by the 1929 stock market crash, but by the early 1930s, wage cuts and growing unemployment brought widespread suffering.

Key Concepts

• Wage cuts and unemployment affected all levels of society, making many people homeless.

• Those groups already experiencing economic difficulty, such as farmers, faced harder times.

• The Depression affected people's mental and physical health.

• Conditions for African Americans worsened during the Depression.

Key Terms, People, and Places

Hooverville; Father Divine, Scottsboro Boys

"Apples 5 cents" became a familiar sign in many cities in the 1930s, as out-of-work people struggled to make a living.

Not everyone felt the impact of the crash immediately. Many thought the depression that followed would not last. For them, reality hit in 1931 or 1932. As hard times spread to all levels of society, a song from a 1932 Broadway revue became a theme song of the times:

*O*nce I built a railroad, made it run,
Made it race against time.
Once I built a railroad, now it's done.
Brother, can you spare a dime?

Brother, Can You Spare A Dime?

⭐ Imagine that the bank where you had a savings account suddenly closed. Your money was gone. Or your parents lost their jobs and could not pay the rent. One day you came home to find your furniture on the sidewalk—you had been evicted.

People at all levels of society faced these situations. Professionals and white-collar workers, who had felt more secure than laborers, were laid off suddenly with no prospects of finding another job. Those whose savings disappeared found it hard to understand why banks no longer had the money they had deposited for safekeeping.

"Hoovervilles" The hardest hit were those at the bottom of the economic ladder. Some unemployed laborers, unable to pay their rent, moved in with relatives. Others drifted. In 1931, census takers estimated the homeless in New York City alone at 15,000.

Homeless people sometimes built shanty towns, with shacks of tar paper, cardboard, or scrap material. These homes for the homeless came to be called **Hoovervilles,** mocking the President whom people blamed for the crisis. A woman living in Oklahoma visited one Hooverville:

*H*ere were all these people living in old, rusted-out car bodies. . . . There were people living in shacks made of orange crates. One family with a whole lot of kids were living in a piano box.

Farm Distress Farm families suffered as low food prices cut their income. When they could not pay their mortgages, they lost their farms to the banks, which sold them at auction. In the South, landowners expelled tenant farmers and sharecroppers. In protest against low farm prices, farmers dumped thousands of gallons of milk and destroyed other crops. These desperate actions shocked a hungry nation.

Migration from the Dust Bowl For thousands of farm families in the Dust Bowl, the harsh conditions of the Depression were made even worse by the drought and dust

---

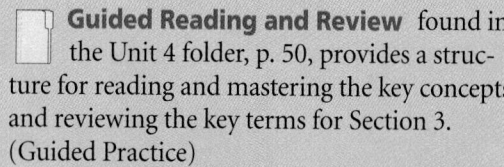

storms that took place in the Great Plains for much of the 1930s. (See "Time and Place: The Black Blizzards," pages 446–447.) In the face of low farm prices and terrible weather, many families lost or gave up their farms. More than 440,000 people left Oklahoma during the 1930s. Nearly 300,000 people left Kansas. Thousands of families in Oklahoma, Texas, Kansas, and other southwestern Plains states migrated to California. Many found work on California's farms as laborers. About 100,000 of the Dust Bowl migrants headed to cities, such as Los Angeles, San Francisco, and San Diego.

Hardships Create New Problems

As it wore on, the Depression had a serious physical and psychological impact on the entire nation. Unemployment and fear of losing a job caused great anxiety. People became depressed; many considered suicide, and some took their own lives.

Impact on Health "No one has starved," President Hoover declared, but some did, and thousands more went hungry. Those who could not afford food or shelter got sick more easily. Children suffered most from the long-term effects of poor diet and inadequate medical care. One boy tramp recalled:

All last winter we never had a fire except about once a day when Mother used to cook some mush or something. When the kids were cold they went to bed. I quit high school of course.

In the country, people grew food and ate berries and other wild plants. In cities, they sold apples and pencils, begged for money to buy food, and fought over the contents of restaurant garbage cans. Families who had land planted "relief gardens" to feed themselves or to barter food for other items.

Family Problems Living conditions declined as families moved in together, crowding into small houses or apartments. The divorce rate dropped because people could not afford separate households. Other couples postponed wedding plans. People gave up even small pleasures like an ice cream cone or a movie ticket.

Men who had lost jobs or investments often felt like failures because they could no longer provide for their families. If their wives or children were working, men thought their own status had fallen. It embarrassed them to be seen at home during normal work hours. They were ashamed to apply for relief or ask friends for help.

Women faced other problems. Those who worked at home and were used to depending

Makeshift huts were homes for homeless and the unemployed in this Hooverville in downtown New York.

⭐ 📄 **Primary Source Activity** Hard Times in Oklahoma, found in the Unit 4 folder, p. 66, focuses on Peggy Terry, a resident of Oklahoma City during the Depression, who describes in her own words how good times often accompanied the hard times.

SOURCE READINGS

Source Readings on p. 466 will connect literature selections and primary source excerpts to historical events discussed in this section.

Explain/Discuss

Explain to students that the effects of the 1929 crash took a while to reach all Americans, but the repercussions were powerful and long lasting. Point out that the crash immediately affected those with the least money.

Have students describe how the Depression affected each of the following segments of the population: farm families, men, women, African Americans in the North, African Americans in the South. Discuss with students how rural poverty differed from urban poverty. Ask students if they think they could have survived the Depression more easily in the country or in a large city. You might want to refer back to the Bellringer discussion about dealing with limited cash funds.

📥 In Depth

Biography

Gordon Parks, the first African American photographer on staff at *Life* magazine, joined the Civilian Conservation Corps (CCC)—one of the agencies set up during the New Deal to counteract the hopelessness of the breadlines. By 1936, Parks was working as a Pullman porter and during breaks looked through discarded magazines on the trains. Some had collections of photographs of the Farm Security Administration (FSA), an agency established to help starving farmers. The power of the FSA photographs of hungry migrants, both black and white, made Parks realize the power of the camera. He went on to take photographs for the FSA and then for *Life* and many other prestigious periodicals.

Analyze

Ask students to use the profile of Wilson Ledford on pages 451–452 to analyze the personality traits that helped people to survive in the Depression.

Answer to ...
MAKING CONNECTIONS

Answers may vary but are likely to reflect students' backgrounds and home experiences. Encourage students to note that while women today have much more legal protection and are more likely to be found in high-paying professional jobs, there is still a "glass ceiling" for professional women and a wage gap between men and women.

Answer to ...
Links Across Time

Answers will vary, but are likely to include social security, unemployment insurance, minimum wage laws, federal housing projects, and drug rehabilitation programs.

In Depth

Did You Know?

Although there are many familiar images of Wall Street brokers leaping to their deaths from skyscraper windows, most Depression-era suicides were ordinary people. In 1930, a Pennsylvania man caught stealing a loaf of bread for his children was so overcome by shame that he hanged himself. San Diego, California, had the highest suicide rate of any city in the country during these years.

---

on a husband's paycheck worried about feeding their hungry children. Working women were accused of taking jobs away from men. Even in the better times of the 1920s, Henry Ford had fired 82 married women. "We do not employ married women whose husbands have jobs," he explained. In the Depression, this practice became common. In 1931, the American Federation of Labor endorsed it. Most school districts would not hire married women teachers, and many fired those who got married.

Many women continued to find work, however, because poor-paying jobs such as domestic service, typing, and nursing were considered "women's work." The greatest job losses of the Depression were in industry and other areas that seldom hired women. Even on the same job, however, women usually were paid less than men.

MAKING CONNECTIONS

Depression attitudes and policies discriminated against working women. Have attitudes toward working women today changed? If so, how?

Discrimination Increases

African Americans continued to leave the South, though not as many as in the 1920s. They worked as janitors or porters in northern cities but soon lost even those jobs to whites. Black unemployment soared—56 percent of black Americans were out of work in 1932. Photographer Gordon Parks, who rode the rails to Harlem, later wrote:

> To most blacks who had flocked in from all over the land, the struggle to survive was savage. Poverty coiled around them and me with merciless fingers.

Because relief programs discriminated against African Americans, black churches and organizations like the National Urban League gave private help. The followers of M. J. Divine, a Harlem evangelist known as **Father Divine,** opened soup kitchens that fed hungry thousands every day.

Discrimination increased for African Americans in the South. Some white Americans declared openly that African Americans had no right to a job if whites were out of work. African Americans were denied civil rights such as access to education, voting, and health care. Lynchings increased.

The justice system often ignored black rights. In March 1931, near Scottsboro, Alabama, nine African American youths who had been riding the rails were arrested and accused of raping two white women on the train. Without being given the chance to hire a defense lawyer, eight of the nine were quickly convicted by an all-white jury and sentenced to die.

| 1650 | 1700 | 1750 | 1800 | Links Across Time | 1850 | 1900 | 1950 | 2000 |

Homelessness

So many homeless young men and women were riding freight trains and searching for work in 1933, that railroad officials often hired people to search the cars and remove the homeless they found there—by force, if necessary. Homelessness has become a growing problem in the 1990s as it was during the 1930s.

The economic conditions that brought about widespread unemployment during the Depression were a clear cause of homelessness. People point to a variety of reasons for the rapid increase in the number of homeless in the 1990s—unemployment, a decline in low-rent housing for the poor, changes in qualifications for government

disability payments, and the premature release of many patients from mental-health facilities. Experts estimate that about 20 percent of homeless people have jobs, 33 percent are families with children, and 10 percent are single women. *What assistance for the homeless is available in the 1990s that was not available in the 1930s?*

Poverty was especially hard on sharecroppers in the South, who had to live in improvised camps after being evicted from their farms by landowners.

Like the Sacco and Vanzetti case a few years earlier, saving the so-called **Scottsboro Boys** became a national cause. Eventually the Supreme Court decided the youths had not had a fair trial and ordered new trials.

AMERICAN PROFILES

Wilson Ledford

Americans survived the Depression in many ways. Here, Wilson Ledford, who was then a teenager in rural Tennessee, remembers the early years.

Wilson first felt the effects of the Depression in March 1930 when he was fifteen, living in Chattanooga with his mother and younger sister. Wilson had worked part time and after school in a grocery store since he was eleven. By 1930, his family could no longer afford Chattanooga. They moved back to Cleveland, Tennessee, a nearby small town where one of Wilson's brothers had left a house when he moved West. Like many farmhouses then, it had no running water or electricity.

Wilson's mother owned another house and 15 acres of land, which brought in $6 a month rent—except when the tenants were out of work. After taxes and insurance, the family had about a dollar a week to live on.

Wilson "swapped work with neighbors." He looked after the family horse and cow, chopped wood for the fireplace, tended the garden that provided family food, and raised corn to feed the animals:

> We had to raise most of what we ate since money was so scarce. . . . Sometimes I plowed for other people when I could get the work. . . . I got 15 cents an hour for plowing and I furnished the horse and plow.

Nothing was wasted. His mother kept chickens and traded eggs at the store for things they could not raise. Overalls cost 98 cents; shoes were $2. She bought a pig for $3 and raised it for meat, and made jelly from wild blackberries. Despite the family's own poverty, Wilson's mother gave extra milk and butter to

Activity

Teaching Heterogeneous Groups

During the Depression, people found ways to acquire, without money, the basic necessities to survive. For students to appreciate the cooperation and creativity necessary to survive during the Depression, have them list skills and resources they could have exchanged if they had lived during that time. In small groups, have students barter with each other. **LEP**

Enrichment

Ask students to choose a section from Studs Terkel's book *Hard Times*, Jeane Westin's *Making Do: How Women Survived the '30s*, or other collections of personal reminiscences from the Depression years. Students should present their selection to the class as either an oral reading or on audiotape.

3. ASSESS

Section 3 Review Answers

1. Hoovervilles, see p. 448

2. (a) Father Divine, see p. 450, (b) Scottsboro Boys, see p. 451

3. When banks failed, people lost their savings; when they lost their jobs, they couldn't pay mortgages or rent. Many became homeless.

4. Crop prices went even lower than they already had been in the late twenties. Many lost their land to bank foreclosures.

5. Men were depressed by losing their status as providers and were ashamed to ask for relief; women worried about their children and often lost their jobs. Families had to combine households; marriages and divorces both declined.

6. Conditions became worse; African Americans lost their jobs to white workers; they were discriminated against by relief agencies; in the South, civil rights violations increased.

7. Answers may vary but are likely to include how rural people worked and got by during the Depression; how they cooperated with one another and found ways to entertain themselves; and how hard it was to find work.

Have students work individually or in small groups to create a poster showing the effects of the Depression, including its impact on health and family problems, and its effect on women and African Americans.

Alternative Assessment

Mid-Point Monitoring

Ask students if they have
● Decided which materials they intend to include
● Located a subject and prepared questions for the interview
● Visited the local library and/or historical society to locate sources of information

4. CLOSE

Reinforcing the Big Idea

The Depression eventually touched the lives of nearly all Americans with wage cuts and unemployment. Those on the lowest end of the economic scale were most severely affected. The next section explains how some Americans made it through those difficult years.

In Depth

Did You Know?

Evictions were commonplace during the 1930s. In Chicago, an angry crowd in the street protested the eviction of an African American family. "All we want is to see that these people, our people, get back into their home," said one protestor. Those already marginalized before the Depression suffered heavily. Writer Langston Hughes observed, "[T]he Depression had brought everyone down a peg or two. And the Negroes had but a few pegs to fall."

"If they come to take my farm, I'm going to fight. I'd rather be killed outright than die by starvation." Although farm families were hard hit by the Depression, the fighting spirit represented by this quote was seen across the country.

"some poor people, a woman with three small children who lived in a one-room shack with a dirt floor."

Wilson never got to high school, "as survival was more important then than getting an education was, and I had to work to survive." The Ledfords had no radio, but he and his neighbors made their own entertainment. Wilson and some other boys cleaned the rocks off a field, graded it, and made a baseball diamond. Baseballs were precious. "You could buy a pretty good baseball for a quarter and a real good one for 50 cents. . . . If we lost a ball during the game, everyone had to go hunt for it."

In the summer of 1932, when he was seventeen, Wilson got a job in Chattanooga with another brother, delivering ice. At the end of the summer, the brother bought him a 1924 Model T Ford for $25. The next summer, too, Wilson hauled ice: "I worked twelve hours a day, six days a week and made $3.00 a week."

When the icehouse closed in the fall, Wilson hitchhiked throughout the Southeast looking for work, but never had any success. "I pumped up so many tires for people I rode with, I had blisters all in my hands. Finally I got back home."

In the next few years, Wilson bought a truck to haul coal, cotton, and oranges, then worked nights in a woolen mill while carrying ice during the day. Finally, "I got a call from Chickamauga Dam and I went to work there. That was a good job working on the dam, I made 60 cents an hour. Times were better by then, but did not start booming until World War II started."

SECTION 3 REVIEW

Key Terms, People, and Places
1. Define Hoovervilles.
2. Identify (a) Father Divine, (b) Scottsboro Boys.

Key Concepts
3. What were the earliest social effects of the Depression?
4. How did the Depression affect farmers?

5. How did the Depression affect family life?
6. How did conditions for African Americans change during the Depression?

Critical Thinking
7. **Determining Relevance** What can you learn about the Depression from Wilson Ledford's experiences?

 RESOURCE DIRECTORY

Teaching Resources

Quiz found in the Unit 4 folder, p. 51, covers the main ideas in this section as well as the key terms.

Distinguishing False from Accurate Images

Distinguishing false from accurate images means examining widely held beliefs about a person, a thing, or an event to determine whether or not those beliefs are based in fact. When studying history, you may uncover source materials such as newspaper and magazine articles that use stereotypes or that put forth misleading ideas. Learning to recognize the differences between false and accurate images will help you to reach your own conclusions about a statement.

The letter excerpted below was written to President Herbert Hoover during the early years of the Depression. Practice distinguishing between false and accurate images by using the following steps.

1. Summarize the main message of the passage. The first step in evaluating a piece of information is to understand what its central message is. Read the excerpt below and answer the following question: What is the main point of the letter?

2. Look for generalizations and overstatements in the passage. Generalizations are broad and oversimplified statements about people, events, or issues that are presented as being accurate in all cases. Overstatements exaggerate or stretch the truth. These techniques often signal claims that are unsupported by facts and, therefore, may indicate the use of false images. (a) What generalizations can you find in the letter? (b) What overstatements or unsupported claims do you find?

3. Look for supporting facts or evidence. Accurate statements are usually backed up by statistics, quotations, or other verifiable evidence. Facts can be fabricated and used in misleading ways, however, so always check them for accuracy. (a) What verifiable facts, if any, are given in the letter below? (b) Based on the use of facts in the letter, what can you conclude about the accuracy of its message?

Annapolis, Maryland
September 10, 1931

My dear Mr. Hoover,

In these days of unrest and general dissatisfaction it is absolutely impossible for a man in your position to get a clear and impartial view of the general conditions of things in America today. But, of this fact I am very positive, that there is not five per cent of the poverty, distress, and general unemployment that many of your enemies would have us believe. It is true, that there is much unrest, but this unrest is largely caused . . . by the excessive prosperity and general debauchery through which the country has traveled since the period of the war. The result being that in three cases out of four, the unemployed [person] is looking for a very light job at a very heavy pay, and with the privilege of being provided with an automobile if he is required to walk more than four or five blocks a day.

National Relief Director, Walter S. Gifford, and his committee are entirely unnecessary at this time, as it has a tendency to cause communities to neglect any temporary relief to any of their people, with the thought of passing the burden on to the National Committee. . . .

. . . Believe me to be one of your well wishers in this ocean of conflict.

Yours sincerely,
W. H. H.

Historian's Toolbox Activity Distinguishing False from Accurate Images, found in the Unit 4 folder, p. 64, uses President Clinton's presentation before Congress of his health-care plan to enhance students' application of this skill.

Surviving the Great Depression

1. FOCUS

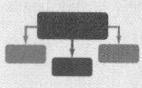

Connecting to the Big Idea

See page 436B. Explain to students that Americans who lived through the Great Depression never forgot the pain of that time, and their feelings about banks, business, government, and money changed forever. Ask what characteristics helped Americans to survive those troubled times.

Objectives

● Give examples of the lasting effects of the Great Depression on those who lived through it.
● Describe some of the positive experiences of life in the Depression.
● Explain why the Depression ended an era.

Bellringer

Ask students to recall a time in their lives when friends, neighbors, or strangers worked together to solve a problem or helped one another through an unpleasant situation.

Reading Strategy

Relating to Topic Ask students to think about the meaning of the two main subheadings of the section: Working Together for Change and Looking Ahead. Ask them to take note of the ways in which Americans worked together during the Depression and of the signs of change that gave them hope as they looked ahead.

Surviving the Great Depression

SECTION PREVIEW

Living through the Great Depression was an unforgettable experience. Despite the hard times, many Americans learned to face troubles together with courage and humor.

For the homeless of the Depression, this "kind-hearted woman" symbol on a sidewalk or fence in front of a house meant that the family inside would help provide food or clothing.

Key Concepts

• The Great Depression left a lasting impression on those who lived through it.
• People had good memories of working together and helping each other.
• The Depression ended the era of the 1920s.

Key Terms, People, and Places

Socialists, Twenty-first Amendment; Norman Thomas; Empire State Building

---

No one who lived through the Great Depression ever forgot it. It changed people's feelings about banks, business, government—and money. Even after the economy recovered, the "Depression generation" would continue to pinch and save before buying anything.

Working Together for Change

Not all the memories of the Depression were bad or despairing. Writing in 1932, reporter Gerald W. Johnson noted:

The great majority of Americans may be depressed. They may not be well pleased with the way business and government have been carried on, and they may not be at all sure that they know exactly how to remedy the trouble. They may be feeling dispirited. But there is one thing they are not, and that is—beaten.

People pulled together to help each other. Tenant groups formed to protest rent increases and evictions. Religious, political, and charitable groups set up soup kitchens and breadlines to feed the hungry. In some farm communities, people agreed to keep bids low when foreclosed farms were auctioned. Buyers then returned the farms to their original owners.

Many individual acts of kindness shone as people helped those they saw as worse off than themselves. One woman, Kitty McCulloch, remembered:

There were many beggars, who would come to your back door, and they would say they were hungry. I wouldn't give them money because I didn't have it. But I did take them in and put them in my kitchen and give them something to eat.

She also gave one beggar a pinstripe suit belonging to her husband, who, she explained, already had three others.

Moves to the Political Left As bad as conditions were, only a few called for radical political change. In Europe, economic problems had brought riots and political upheaval, but in the United States most citizens trusted in the democratic process to solve them. As writer William Saroyan observed in 1936:

Ten million unemployed continue law-abiding. No riots, no trouble, no multi-millionaires cooked and served with cranberry sauce, alas.

For some Americans, however, radical and reform movements offered new solutions to the country's problems, promising a fairer distribution of wealth. Membership in the Communist party, consisting mainly of intellectuals and labor organizers, was 14,000, and in the 1932 election, the Communist candidate polled just

---

 RESOURCE DIRECTORY

Teaching Resources

📄 **Reproducible Lesson Plan** found in the Unit 4 folder, p. 44, provides a summary of the Section 4 lesson plan content.

📄 **Alternate Lesson Plan: Critical Thinking** Formulating Questions, found in the Alternate Lesson Plans folder, p. 115, is an alternate lesson plan that provides an opportunity for students to learn to formulate questions by interviewing people who survived the Depression.

📄 **Guided Reading and Review** found in the Unit 4 folder, p. 52, provides a structure for reading and mastering the key concepts and reviewing the key terms for Section 4. (Guided Practice)

📄 **American Profiles Activity** found in the Unit 4 folder, p. 61, profiles Babe Didrikson Zaharias—an outstanding athlete whose gold-medal performances at the 1932 Olympic Games helped raise the spirits of a Depression-weary country.

over 100,000 votes. More people than the numbers suggest, however, also believed that the new Communist government in the Soviet Union might have the right answers.

Socialists, who called for gradual social and economic changes rather than revolution, did better politically. Their presidential candidate, **Norman Thomas,** won 881,951 votes in 1932, about 2.2 percent of the total vote. Others who might have supported Thomas voted for Franklin D. Roosevelt simply to defeat Hoover.

Voting figures and party membership do not reflect the widespread interest in radical and reform movements in the 1930s. Those who were part of those movements remember the decade as a high point of cooperation among different groups of Americans—students, workers, writers, artists, and professionals of all races. They worked together for social justice in cases such as that of the Scottsboro Boys.

MAKING CONNECTIONS

Third-party candidates, such as the Socialists, have almost no chance of winning presidential elections. Why, then, do they present candidates? What influence do minor parties have?

Looking Ahead

For the most part, Americans gritted their teeth and waited out the hard times. They looked for change and signs of hope. ✪

Depression Humor Wry jokes and cartoons kept people laughing through their troubles. The term "Hooverville" was at first a joke. People who slept on park benches huddled under "Hoover blankets"—old newspapers. Empty pockets turned inside out were termed "Hoover flags." When Babe Ruth was criticized for requesting a salary of $80,000—higher than President Hoover's—he joked, "I had a better year than he did." ✪

People fought despair by laughing at it. In 1929 humorist Will Rogers quipped, "When Wall Street took that tail spin, you had to stand in line to get a window to jump out of." A cartoon that showed two men jumping out of a

Above: To get a warm meal, many people—even those who had once been relatively prosperous—had to stand in breadlines or outside soup kitchens run by churches and community groups. *Below:* Showing the darker side of Depression humor, an end-of-the-year cartoon in *Life* magazine summed up the hopes and disasters of 1929.

window arm-in-arm was captioned "The speculators who had a joint account."

Prohibition Is Repealed In February 1933, Congress voted to repeal the ban on alcoholic beverages. The **Twenty-first Amendment** was ratified by the end of the year. Some people, including President Hoover, regretted the end of this social experiment limiting the sale of alcohol, but most welcomed repeal as an end to national hypocrisy and as a curb on gangsters who prospered from bootlegging.

✪ **Primary Source Activity** The "Forgotten Man," found in the Unit 4 folder, pp. 67–68, uses two letters written to President Hoover during the Depression to show the way many American workers viewed their President and the economic breakdown of the country.

Answer to ...

MAKING CONNECTIONS

Students should understand that many issues raised by third or minor parties have later been adopted by one of the two major parties. Third-party candidates often represent deeply felt ideologies or social policies that later enter the mainstream.

2. INSTRUCT

Discuss

Discuss with students how living through the Great Depression brought out characteristics of courage, kindness, charity, and humor in many Americans. Ask why they think crises bring out these characteristics. You might want to have students share their recollections from the Bellringer activity.

Discuss the signs of changing times that gave Americans hope. Ask students to explain the impact of the repeal of prohibition restrictions.

Analyze

Discuss the characteristics that defined the era of the 1920s. Ask students to explain why the Depression ended that era. Ask them to consider how Depression survivors might view savings banks, the stock market, or installment buying.

Activity

Creating Editorials

Ask students to draw an editorial cartoon about one of the following:
● Norman Thomas runs for President in 1932 (a brave crusade or a foolish gesture).
● Poor people call their shanty towns "Hoovervilles" (justified or unjustified slam at the President).
● Completion of the Empire State Building (marvelous accomplishment or questionable use of money).

The Empire State Building, the Chrysler Building, and Rockefeller Center were designed in the Art Deco style. Ask students to bring to class copies of photographs of some section of one of these buildings that illustrates the Art Deco style, and describe its prominent features.

3. ASSESS

Section 4 Review Answers

1. (a) Socialists, see p. 455, (b) Twenty-first Amendment, see p. 455

2. (a) Norman Thomas, see p. 455, (b) Empire State Building, see p. 456

3. The Socialist and Communist parties offered new answers to social problems.

4. People pulled together and helped each other through the hard times; Americans continued to believe in the democratic process; prohibition was repealed; "Depression humor" kept people's spirits up; the Empire State Building became a symbol of progress.

5. Sports heroes retired; Henry Ford lost popularity; the Lindbergh baby was killed; Coolidge died.

6. Answers will vary but may focus on daily life, search for jobs, bank closings, and similar topics.

Reteach

Have one student write on a piece of paper a sentence about how the Depression affected Americans or about signs that the Depression might end. Have another student add a sentence to the first. When the paper has circulated to all students, have a spokesperson read the resulting document aloud.

4. CLOSE

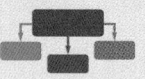
Reinforcing the Big Idea

The Depression changed the Americans who lived through it. Above all, an era ended. The next section shows the nation taking a new direction—through the exciting election of 1932.

Despite the economic hardships of the 1930s, American architects and developers raced to build the world's tallest building. Workers like the man shown above looked out over the rest of New York City as they labored to complete the Empire State Building.

The end of prohibition and return of legalized alcohol stimulated parts of the economy—grain growing, breweries and distilleries, even the pretzel industry. Control of alcohol returned to the states, eight of which chose to continue the ban on liquor sales.

The Empire State Building For many, a dramatic symbol of hope was the new **Empire State Building,** begun in 1930. John J. Raskob, the developer of the gleaming new skyscraper, won the race to build the world's tallest building.

One hundred and two stories high, the Empire State Building soared 1,250 feet into the sky and was topped with a mooring mast for blimps. Sixty-seven elevators, traveling 1,000 feet per minute, brought visitors to its observation deck. On the first Sunday after it opened, over 4,000 people paid a dollar each to make the trip.

The End of An Era By 1933, it was clear that an era was ending. One by one, symbols of the 1920s faded away. Gangster Al Capone went to prison for tax evasion. Boxer Jack Dempsey was defeated. Babe Ruth retired. The Depression-era labor policies of car-maker Henry Ford, once admired for his efficiency, made him labor's prime enemy.

In 1932 the nation was shocked when the infant son of aviation hero Charles Lindbergh and Anne Morrow Lindbergh was kidnapped and murdered. Somehow this tragedy seemed to echo the nation's woeful condition and its fall from the energy and heroism of the 1920s. Finally, eight weeks before Roosevelt's inauguration in 1933, former President Calvin Coolidge, a symbol of the age of prosperity, died.

SECTION 4 REVIEW

Key Terms, People and Places
1. Define (a) Socialists, (b) Twenty-first Amendment.
2. Identify (a) Norman Thomas, (b) Empire State Building.

Key Concepts
3. Why did radical political groups gain support in the early 1930s?

4. What Depression memories might some people remember as good?
5. What were signs that the 1920s era had ended?

Critical Thinking
6. **Formulating Questions** What questions could you ask people who lived in the Depression era in order to understand its effects on both their lives and their attitudes?

RESOURCE DIRECTORY

Teaching Resources

Quiz found in the Unit 4 folder, p. 53, covers the main ideas in this section as well as the key terms.

The Election of 1932: A Turning Point in History

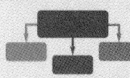

1. FOCUS

Connecting to the Big Idea

See page 436B. Recall with students that by 1932, President Hoover was unable to curb the ravages of the Depression. The 1932 presidential election presented an opportunity for change. Ask what the outcome of this election was. How did this administration change the direction of American government?

Objectives

● Explain how President Hoover hoped voluntary action would end the Depression.
● Describe the amount of governmental action and funds for relief provided under Hoover.
● Identify Franklin D. Roosevelt as the successful candidate for President who defeated Hoover in 1932.

Bellringer

Ask students to consider why elections are important and provide specific examples showing how elections are an avenue of change.

SECTION PREVIEW

As the Depression worsened, people came to blame Hoover and the Republicans for their misery. The 1932 presidential election brought a sweeping victory for Democrat Franklin D. Roosevelt, and a new direction for American government.

Key Concepts
• President Hoover hoped to use voluntary action to end the Depression.
• Federal government action and funds for relief were inadequate under Hoover.
• Promising a "new deal," the Democratic candidate, Franklin D. Roosevelt, won an overwhelming victory in the presidential election of 1932.

Key Terms, People, Places
Hawley-Smoot tariff, Reconstruction Finance Corporation; John Maynard Keynes, Bonus Army, Franklin Delano Roosevelt, Eleanor Roosevelt

---

Voluntary Action Fails Hoover believed deeply that voluntary controls in the business world were the best way to end the economic crisis. He quickly organized a White House conference of business leaders and got their promise to maintain wage rates. At first, many firms kept wages up. By the end of 1931, however, many quietly cut workers' pay.

Hoover meant well, but he held rigidly to this principle of voluntary action. A shy man, successful in business but inexperienced in politics, he could not make his plan attractive to the American people. After a year of misery, they began to blame him and the Republicans for the crisis.

The Government Acts Hoover then took more action. To create jobs, the government spent more on new public buildings, roads, parks, and dams. Boulder Dam (later renamed Hoover Dam) was begun in 1930. A President's Emergency Committee on Employment advised local relief programs.

Trying to protect domestic industries from foreign imports, in 1930 Congress passed the **Hawley-Smoot tariff,** the highest import tax in history. The tariff backfired. European countries raised their own tariffs, bringing a sudden slowdown in international trade. Hoover suspended the Allies' payments of their war debts, but Europe's economies grew weaker.

In 1932, Hoover set up the **Reconstruction Finance Corporation** (RFC), which gave government credit to banks so that they could extend loans. The RFC reflected the theory that prosperity at the top would help the economy as a whole. To many people, however, it seemed that the government was helping bankers while ordinary people went hungry.

The Democrats in 1932 based their campaign on the promise that Franklin Roosevelt would end the Depression.

F or a few months after the stock market crash, President Hoover, along with business leaders, insisted that the key to recovery was confidence. Hoover blamed the Depression on "world-wide economic conditions beyond our control"—not on problems in the United States economy.

Hoover Tries to End the Crisis

Taking Hoover's advice, business and government leaders tried to maintain public confidence in the economy. Even as factories closed and breadlines formed, Hoover administration officials insisted that things would get better soon.

In Depth

Interdisciplinary

Edward Hopper's (1882–1967) paintings reflected the character of the people and the land realistically and objectively. Hopper saw America as a lonely place, often silhouetted in harsh but true shades of light, as depicted in his paintings "Early Sunday Morning" (1930) or "Room in Brooklyn" (1932). In the midst of the Depression, Hopper's works achieved national recognition when New York's Museum of Modern Art mounted a one-man retrospective show in 1933.

 Reproducible Lesson Plan found in the Unit 4 folder, p. 45, provides a summary of the Section 5 lesson plan content.

Alternate Lesson Plan: Learning Styles found in the Alternate Lesson Plans folder, p. 116, is an alternate lesson plan, especially effective for auditory learners, that provides a structure for a radio debate on the differences between Hoover and FDR.

Guided Reading and Review found in the Unit 4 folder, p. 54, provides a structure for reading and mastering the key concepts and reviewing the key terms for Section 5. (Guided Practice)

Media and Technology

 Transparency
Fine Art, D-18

Reading Strategy

Problem Solving Ask students to imagine that it is 1932 and they will have an opportunity to vote in the upcoming presidential election. Ask them to gather data that will help them make the most educated choice. Suggest that they make two columns on a piece of paper and take notes about Hoover's attempts to end the Depression in one column, and about Roosevelt's campaign promises in the other.

Answer to ...

Answers may vary but should suggest that, since the Depression and the New Deal, the government has been more receptive to hearing "ordinary" people's opinions, and that there is more recognition and public appreciation of the rights of different groups.

In Depth

Multicultural Perspectives

Hardships for rural African Americans mounted during the Depression, often spurred by policies of the New Deal that were of benefit to the nation as a whole. Historian Jacqueline Jones writes in her book *The Dispossessed* that NRA (National Recovery Act) minimum-wage legislation spurred mechanization of the tobacco industry and put many African American men and women out of work. The crop-reduction programs of the AAA (Agricultural Adjustment Administration) severely cut demand for farm labor and provided ready cash for planters to invest in labor-saving machinery. The long-term effects of major development programs such as the TVA (Tennessee Valley Authority) are well known, but the fates of 841 Santee-Cooper (South Carolina) families living along the floodplain of a proposed dam are all but forgotten.

President Hoover's apparent inaction made people everywhere eager to blame him for their troubles, as this cartoon from 1931 shows.

Some government efforts helped, but not enough. Hoover wanted state and local governments to handle relief, but their programs never had enough money. Despite the RFC, banks continued to fail.

Hoover's Unpopularity Grows Many people blamed Hoover—not always fairly—for all their problems. "The 1932nd Psalm" was a popular take-off on Psalm 23:

> Hoover is my Shepherd, I am in want,
> He maketh me to lie down on
>   park benches,
> He leadeth me by still factories,
> He restoreth my doubt in the
>   Republican Party.

Hoover argued that direct federal relief would destroy people's self-respect and create a large bureaucracy. His refusal to help brought bitter public reaction and negative publicity.

Although his World War I relief work had made him the "Great Humanitarian," Hoover's attitude toward Depression relief made him seem cold and hard-hearted. While people went hungry, newspapers showed a photograph of him feeding his dog on the White House lawn. People booed when he said such things as "Our people have been protected from hunger and cold."

Private charities and local officials could not meet the demands for relief, as Hoover wanted. Finally in 1932, Hoover broke with tradition and let the RFC lend the states money for unemployment relief. But it was too little and too late.

As the Depression deepened, some economists backed the ideas of British economist **John Maynard Keynes.** He said that massive government spending could help a collapsing economy and encourage more private spending. This economic theory was not yet widely accepted, however.

Veterans March on Washington A low point for Hoover came in the summer of 1932, when 20,000 jobless World War I veterans and their families encamped in Washington, D.C. They wanted immediate payment of a pension bonus that had been promised for 1945. The House of Representatives agreed, but the Senate said no. Most of the **Bonus Army** then went home, but a few thousand stayed, living in shacks. ✪

Although the bonus marchers were generally peaceful, a few violent incidents prompted Hoover to call in the army. General Douglas MacArthur decided to use force to drive the marchers out of Washington. Armed with bricks and stones, the Bonus Army faced guns, tanks, and tear gas. Many were injured. Hoover was horrified but took responsibility for MacArthur's actions. In the next election, the lingering image of this ugly scene would help defeat him.

In recent decades, the government has actually helped protesters to hold marches in Washington. What reasons can you give for this difference in treatment?

 RESOURCE DIRECTORY

Teaching Resources

✪ **Visual Learning Activity** Veterans March on Washington, found in the Unit 4 folder, p. 72, especially effective for visual learners, enriches the section content by using a political cartoon.

World War I veterans from all parts of the country demonstrated on the steps of the Capitol in Washington, D.C., in 1932, hoping that their promised bonus would help them survive unemployment and homelessness.

A "New Deal" for America

"I pledge myself to a new deal for the American people," announced presidential candidate **Franklin Delano Roosevelt** as he accepted the Democratic party's nomination at its Chicago convention in July 1932. Delegates cheered, and an organ thundered out the song "Happy Days Are Here Again."

The Republicans, in June, had again named Hoover. As the presidential campaign took shape, the differences between the two candidates became very clear.

The Roosevelts In Franklin and **Eleanor Roosevelt,** the Democrats had a remarkable political couple to bring them victory. Franklin, nicknamed "FDR" by the press, was born in 1882. He graduated from Harvard University and took a job in a law firm, although his main interest was politics. He was elected twice to the New York State Senate, then became assistant secretary of the navy in President Woodrow Wilson's cabinet.

In 1920, FDR ran for Vice President but lost. The following summer, he came down with polio and he never walked without help again. He spent much of the 1920s recovering at Warm Springs, Georgia, but kept up his political interests.

Franklin and Eleanor Roosevelt (at right)—seen here a few years after their marriage—followed a family tradition of political and social activism.

Viewpoints

Hoover wanted to preserve the limited role of national government; Roosevelt proposed change through greater government involvement. For a more thorough examination of 1932 campaign issues, see the Resource Directory below.

Enrichment

Ask students to decide which of the following Presidents would have agreed with FDR and which would have supported Hoover on the issue of controls on business growth and power: Washington, McKinley, Theodore Roosevelt, Coolidge, Wilson. Ask students to explain their decisions based on evidence from the words and actions of the former Presidents.

3. ASSESS

Section 5 Review Answers

1. (a) Hawley-Smoot tariff, see p. 457, (b) Reconstruction Finance Corporation, see p. 457

2. (a) John Maynard Keynes, see p. 458, (b) Bonus Army , see p. 458, (c) Franklin Delano Roosevelt, see p. 459, (d) Eleanor Roosevelt, see p. 459

3. He hoped to wait it out, urged everyone to have confidence, and believed that voluntary actions would be enough.

4. It was intended to protect American industries, but actually caused higher European tariffs and a drop in trade.

5. Urban workers, coal miners, and recent immigrants of Catholic and Jewish descent; people voting against Hoover's policies.

6. Answers will vary but may point out that one person's policies and personality probably could not have compensated for the deep flaws in the economy. On the other hand, Hoover appeared cold and hardhearted, unwilling to provide enough government money either for relief or to stimulate industrial recovery.

TURNING POINTS

Eleanor Roosevelt, a niece of Theodore Roosevelt, was born in 1884 into a wealthy family. Educated in an English boarding school, she later worked at a social settlement house in New York City. She married her distant cousin Franklin in 1905 and they had six children.

By the 1920s, the marriage was shaky, but the couple stayed together. In New York state, Eleanor worked for legislation about public housing, state government reform, birth control, and better conditions for working women. By 1928, when FDR was persuaded to run for governor of New York, she was an experienced political worker and social reformer.

After FDR's success as governor of New York (1929–1932), his supporters believed him ready to try for the presidency. With his broad smile and genial manner, he represented a spirit of optimism that the country badly needed.

Unlike Hoover, FDR was ready to experiment with governmental roles. Though from a wealthy background, he had genuine compassion for ordinary people, in part because of his own struggle with illness. He was also moved by the great gap between the nation's wealthy and the poor.

As governor of New York, he had worked vigorously for Depression relief. In 1931, he set up an unemployment commission and a relief administration, the first state agencies to aid the poor in the Depression era. When, as a presidential candidate, FDR promised the country a "new deal," he had similar programs in mind.

Roosevelt and Hoover The two candidates and their proposed programs contrasted sharply. In October 1932, Hoover said:

Viewpoints
On Ending the Depression

Sharp philosophical differences characterized the presidential campaign of 1932. *How do both viewpoints below support what you know about the approach of Hoover and Roosevelt to ending the Depression?*

Against Drastic Measures
We are told by the opposition that we must have a change, that we must have a new deal. It is not the change . . . to which I object but the proposal to alter the whole foundations of our national life which have been built through generations of testing and struggle.

Herbert Hoover, speech at Madison Square Garden, October 31, 1932

For Drastic Measures
I have recounted to you in other speeches, and it is a matter of general information, that for at least two years after the crash, the only efforts made by the [Hoover administration] to cope with the distress of unemployment were to deny its existence.

Franklin D. Roosevelt, campaign address, October 13, 1932

This campaign is more than a contest between two men. . . . It is a contest between two philosophies of government.

Still arguing for voluntary aid, Hoover attacked the Democratic platform. If its ideas were adopted, he said, "this will not be the America which we have known in the past." He sternly resisted the idea of giving the national government more power.

Roosevelt, by contrast, called for "a reappraisal of values" and controls on business:

I feel that we are coming to a view through the drift of our legislation and our public thinking in the past quarter century that private economic power is . . . a public trust as well.

While statements like this showed FDR's new approach, probably any Democratic candidate could have beaten Hoover in 1932. Even long-time Republicans deserted him. Reserved by nature, Hoover became grumpy and isolated.

RESOURCE DIRECTORY

Teaching Resources

Viewpoints Activity On Ending the Depression, found in the Unit 4 folder, pp. 62–63, provides additional opinions and perspectives to extend students' understanding of the presidential campaign of 1932.

SOURCE READINGS

Source Readings on p. 468 will connect literature selections and primary source excerpts to historical events discussed in this section.

Mar. 4, 1933 THE NEW YORKER Price 15 cents

This *New Yorker* cover drawn for the inauguration clearly shows how people saw Roosevelt, the new President, in contrast with Hoover.

He gave few campaign speeches. Crowds jeered his motorcade.

FDR won the presidency by a huge margin—seven million popular votes. (See the map above.) Much of his support came from groups that had begun to turn to the Democrats in 1928: urban workers, coal miners, and immigrants of Catholic and Jewish descent. Some people did not really vote for Roosevelt, they

Election of 1932

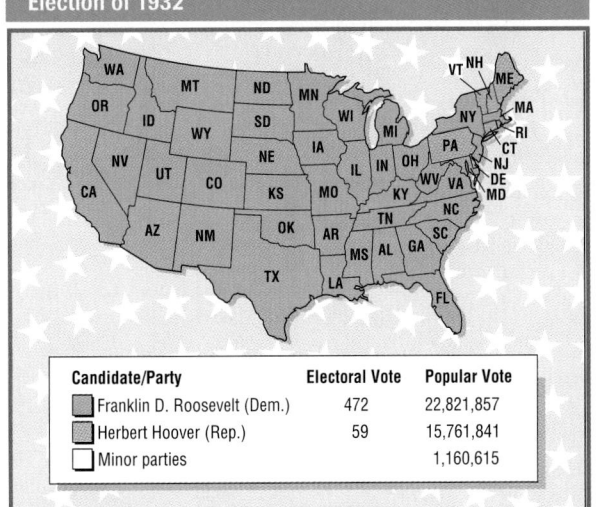

Candidate/Party	Electoral Vote	Popular Vote
Franklin D. Roosevelt (Dem.)	472	22,821,857
Herbert Hoover (Rep.)	59	15,761,841
Minor parties		1,160,615

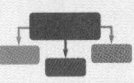 **Geography and History: Interpreting Maps**
Franklin D. Roosevelt and the Democratic party won the popular vote in 1932 as well as a huge margin of electoral votes. *Which states' electoral votes did Hoover win?*

simply voted *against* Hoover and the Republican policies. Still, the words of FDR's inaugural address gave most of the country renewed hope:

> *So first of all let me assert my firm belief that the only thing we have to fear is fear itself.*

With these words, Roosevelt reassured a frightened nation and began a journey into a new era of government involvement and presidential activism.

Caption Answer to ...

🌐 **Interpreting Maps**

Maine, New Hampshire, Vermont, Connecticut, Pennsylvania, Delaware

Reteach

Ask students to write an editorial for a 1932 newspaper. The editorial should summarize Hoover's major efforts to end the Depression, and either urge voters to reelect him or urge them to vote for Franklin D. Roosevelt.

4. CLOSE

Reinforcing the Big Idea

At first President Hoover tried to curb the Depression through voluntary controls. Hoover's later attempts at direct federal action and relief were inadequate. In 1932 voters swept in the Democratic candidate Franklin Delano Roosevelt and waited to see if he could indeed deliver a "New Deal."

SECTION 5 REVIEW

Key Terms, People, and Places
1. Define (a) Hawley-Smoot tariff, (b) Reconstruction Finance Corporation.
2. Identify (a) John Maynard Keynes, (b) Bonus Army (c) Franklin Delano Roosevelt, (d) Eleanor Roosevelt.

Key Concepts
3. How did President Hoover hope to end the Depression and its hardships?

4. What was the intent of the Hawley-Smoot tariff?
5. In the 1932 election, what groups supported Roosevelt?

Critical Thinking
6. **Distinguishing False from Accurate Images** Was Hoover's great unpopularity justified, or would the economic crisis have defeated anyone?

 Quiz found in the Unit 4 folder, p. 55, covers the main ideas in this section as well as the key terms.

 Chapter Test Forms A and B are found in the Unit 4 folder, pp. 74–79.

 Answer Keys found in the Unit 4 folder, pp. 116–128, provide answers to all student activities.

Media and Technology

📺 **Transparencies**
Cause and Effect, F-9; Graphic Organizer, G-3

🎧 **Guided Reading Audiotapes** (English and Spanish)

📖 **Computer Test Bank**

The Lasting Impact of the Election of 1932

Focus During FDR's administration, the federal government took on broad powers and responsibilities for regulating business and for promoting the welfare of all citizens. What has been the lasting impact of those powers and responsibilities?

Instruct Tell students that before FDR's administration, many familiar government programs such as social security, unemployment insurance, federal housing projects, and minimum wage laws did not exist. The federal government had never before taken the direct responsibility to see that each American enjoyed a minimum standard of living. Government was much smaller and much less expensive.

Review with students the reasons that Americans turned to the federal government in 1932 for relief from the Depression. What other sources of relief had failed? What government programs had been ineffective? Did citizens have any reason to expect that the federal government could end the Depression?

Ask students to discuss in small groups one critical current human problem such as homelessness or the spread of AIDS. Ask them to consider the following questions: Whose problems are these? What other institutions, groups, or segments of society are involved in attempts to solve these problems? Should the federal government take full responsibility for finding solutions and administering the programs that might correct these situations? What might be the harmful effects of such governmental action? Do students think that the federal government should take charge of solving such problems?

TURNING POINTS

The Lasting Impact of the Election of 1932

On a rainy day in 1933, FDR stood before a Depression-weary crowd and took the oath of office of President of the United States. As reporter Thomas Stokes observed, a stirring of hope moved through the crowd when Roosevelt began, "This nation asks for action and action now."

Phrases like this foreshadowed a sweeping change in the style of presidential leadership and government response to its citizens' needs. Ultimately, such changes altered the way many Americans viewed their government and its responsibilities.

A Revolutionary Change

In the depths of the Great Depression, many Americans had to give up cherished traditional beliefs in "making it on their own." They turned to the government as their only hope. Thus, the Roosevelt years saw the beginning of many programs that changed the role of the government in American society.

Presidential Activism In general, the Presidents since FDR—whatever their politics and personality—have carried on the tradition begun by Roosevelt and responded actively to people's needs. Harry Truman inherited the presidency when Roosevelt died in 1945. His domestic program extended the social welfare commitments that Roosevelt had made, such as social security and unemployment insurance. He also argued that government should provide medical care programs to its citizens.

Even supposedly nonactivist Presidents such as Dwight Eisenhower have acted when necessary. For example, in 1957 Eisenhower sent army troops to Little Rock, Arkansas, to protect black students entering a formerly all-white high school.

Government Involvement Continues In the 1960s, President Lyndon Johnson was even more successful at working with Congress than FDR had been. Johnson's proposal of programs like Medicare

1933 Roosevelt's inauguration begins a new age of activist Presidents.

1957 President Dwight Eisenhower sends troops to integrate Arkansas high school.

| 1930 | 1940 | 1950 |

1948 President Truman bans racial segregation in the military.

▶ RESOURCE DIRECTORY

Teaching Resources

Turning Points Extension Activity
The Lasting Impact of the Election of 1932, found in the Unit 4 folder, pp. 56–57, extends students' understanding of the Depression era by discussing the long-term impact of social programs that grew out of New Deal legislation.

and Medicaid, which offered health care benefits to the elderly and the poor, extended the ideas of social welfare.

Attempts at a More Limited Role Fail

During the 1970s and 1980s, several Presidents attempted to take a more limited role in social welfare. President Richard Nixon sought to scale back involvement in social issues, but because the American public had come to expect this commitment, he failed. At the same time, people began to complain about the "imperial presidency" as Nixon acted aggressively to maintain law and order at home.

Presidents Ford and Carter, too, fashioned a more modest role for themselves and the government during their presidencies, but found that without strong leadership, the American government could not operate effectively.

When Ronald Reagan took office in 1981, he waged a campaign against "entitlements"—those programs that provide basic support for elderly, unemployed, or impoverished people. Because these programs were taking the largest share of the federal budget, Reagan argued that they should be cut back, maintaining that the government should not be so involved in the social welfare of its citizens. But he still acknowledged the need for a basic safety net that would catch those who were unable to help themselves.

The People Choose Social Intervention

After such attempts to reduce government's role in people's lives, voters elected a President in 1992 who argued that the government has a responsibility to help citizens. President Bill Clinton acted on this belief often during his first year in office. When rain-swollen rivers flooded the Midwest in 1993, he authorized federal disaster funds and—as people expected—personally visited flooded towns and farmlands. He also presented a plan to Congress for a national health care program.

REVIEWING THE FACTS

1. How did Roosevelt's election affect people's expectations of the role of the President?
2. What actions has President Clinton taken that follow in President Roosevelt's footsteps?

Critical Thinking
3. **Expressing Problems Clearly** What are possible consequences of both a large government role in social welfare and a limited government role?

1971 President Richard Nixon imposes a freeze on wages and prices.

1984 President Reagan introduces programs to aid farmers.

1960   1970   1980   1990

1965 President Lyndon Johnson signs bills on Medicare and aid to education into law.

1993 President Bill Clinton visits flood-damaged areas in the Midwest.

Extend Ask students to review the presidential campaigns of 1992, 1988, 1984, and 1980. Which candidates proposed new governmental welfare programs? Which candidates vowed to cut back federal welfare programs? Did any candidates promise to do both?

Answers

1. After Roosevelt's election, people began to expect the President to take a more active role in the social welfare of the nation.
2. President Clinton approved relief for the Midwest after floods, personally visited towns there, and proposed to Congress a national health-care plan.
3. Answers will vary, but should indicate an understanding of the consequences of greater or lesser government involvement in social welfare issues. Greater government involvement might result in the creation and extension of programs such as health-care benefits. Lesser government involvement might be accompanied by an emphasis on areas such as foreign policy.

Understanding Key Terms, People, and Places

Terms
Students should refer to the definitions of the key terms in the chapter to write sentences that show understanding of the economy of the 1920s and the causes and effects of the Great Depression.

Matching
1. real wages
2. Gross National Product (GNP)
3. speculation
4. Reconstruction Finance Corporation

True or False
1. false, Father Divine
2. false, Bonus Army
3. true
4. false, Norman Thomas
5. false, John Maynard Keynes

Reviewing Main Ideas

1. People assumed that prosperity would continue under the Republicans, and the stock market seemed to be doing remarkably well.

2. A few people made fortunes, but generally, wealth remained concentrated in a small percentage of the population.

3. As European farmers recovered from World War I, crop prices in the United States fell. Farmers could not meet their payments on loans for land and machinery.

4. Worried investors began to sell, causing stock prices to fall. Falling prices caused a wave of panic selling.

5. The United States stopped investing in Germany; Germany could no longer meet its reparations payments to the Allies who in turn could no longer pay their debts or afford to buy American goods.

6. Some people moved in with relatives or lived in shanty towns; many became drifters.

7. When low crop prices resulting from the Depression cut their incomes, many farmers lost their farms to the banks.

8. African Americans lost jobs to whites; relief programs discriminated against them; civil rights violations grew worse in the South.

9. Examples include tenant groups forming to protest rent increases and evictions, groups setting up soup kitchens and breadlines, and people agreeing to keep bids low when foreclosed farms were sold.

Chapter Review

Understanding Key Terms, People, and Places

Key Terms
1. real wages
2. welfare capitalism
3. installment buying
4. speculation
5. buy on margin
6. Dow Jones industrial average
7. Gross National Product (GNP)
8. collateral
9. Hooverville
10. Socialists
11. Twenty-first Amendment
12. Hawley-Smoot tariff
13. Reconstruction Finance Corporation

People
14. Father Divine
15. Scottsboro Boys
16. Norman Thomas
17. John Maynard Keynes
18. Bonus Army
19. Franklin Delano Roosevelt
20. Eleanor Roosevelt

Places
21. Empire State Building

Terms For each term above, write a sentence that explains its relation to the economy of the late 1920s and the Great Depression.

Matching Review the key terms in the list above. If you are not sure of a term's meaning, review its definition in the chapter. Then choose a term from the list that best matches each description below.
1. what money can actually buy
2. the total annual value of goods and services a country produces
3. taking chances in the stock market
4. agency that gave government credit to banks so that they could extend loans

True or False Determine whether each statement is true or false. If it is true, write "true." If it is false, change the underlined name to make the statement true.
1. Herbert Hoover opened soup kitchens in Harlem during the Depression.
2. The Scottsboro Boys marched on Washington in the summer of 1932 to demand immediate payment of their pension bonuses.
3. Franklin Delano Roosevelt won the 1932 election by a huge margin.
4. In 1932 John Maynard Keynes ran for President on the Socialist ticket.
5. Father Divine supported massive government spending to revive the economy.

Reviewing Main Ideas

Section 1 (pp. 438–441)
1. Why did the economy of the 1920s inspire trust?
2. How did the rising stock market affect the way wealth was distributed in the United States?
3. Why did farmers fail to share in the 1920s prosperity?

Section 2 (pp. 442–445)
4. What were the results for investors when the Dow Jones average dropped suddenly?
5. Explain how the stock market crash started a downward cycle in the global economy.

Section 3 (pp. 448–452)
6. How did the Depression affect those at the bottom of the economic scale?

7. Why were farm families hit particularly hard by the Depression?
8. In what ways did the Depression affect African Americans more severely than white Americans?

Section 4 (pp. 454–456)
9. What were some ways in which people pulled together to help each other during the Depression?
10. In what ways did the end of Prohibition mark the end of an era?

Section 5 (pp. 457–461)
11. What government actions did Hoover finally take to try to end the Depression? Why did his program fail?
12. What programs had Roosevelt set up as governor of New York that foreshadowed his "new deal"?

---

10. The end of prohibition marked an end to a social experiment; it also ended a period of national hypocrisy, since many people drank anyway, thus encouraging gangsters and bootleggers.

11. Hoover set up the Emergency Committee on Employment to advise local relief programs, and tried to protect domestic industries with the Hawley-Smoot tariff. He also set up the Reconstruction Finance Corporation to give government credit to banks. These actions proved inadequate.

12. Roosevelt had set up an unemployment commission and a relief administration to provide Depression relief.

Thinking Critically

1. Answers will vary. Some students will point out that overspeculation, short-sighted government economic policies, and an unstable economy would have made it obvious that a depression was looming. Others will note that these warning signs were probably not as clear to people at the time as they are in retrospect.

2. Answers will vary. Some students will be aware that today the government spends much more money on social programs than it did before the Depression.

3. Answers will vary, but students should relate the general mood of the 1920s (Chapter 12) to these actions.

Final Evaluation
Allow students to present their portfolios during individual conferences. You might also want to display finished projects for students to observe and discuss.
  Use the following guidelines to evaluate students' projects:
● Type and variety of material included
● Evidence of synthesis
● Creativity of thought and presentation

Thinking Critically

1. **Predicting Consequences** If you had lived during the 1920s, what evidence would you have had of the coming Depression?
2. **Determining Relevance** During the Depression, some economists turned to the ideas of British economist John Maynard Keynes, who argued that massive government spending could help a collapsing economy. Do you agree with Keynes's approach? To what extent are Keynes's views still at work in the United States economy today?
3. **Recognizing Cause and Effect** Looking back, the stock market speculation and installment buying of the late 1920s may seem irresponsible. What reasons can you find for the way people were behaving at that time?

Making Connections

1. **Evaluating Primary Sources** Review the first primary source quotation on page 460. Do you agree with Hoover's assessment that the election of 1932 was a contest between two different philosophies of government? Explain your answer.
2. **Understanding the Visuals** Much of the "humor" of Depression jokes and cartoons is bitter rather than funny, like the cartoon on page 455. Look at the cartoons on pages 440 and 458 and answer the following questions: (a) What issues do they address? (b) What is the tone of the humor in each case?
3. **Writing About the Chapter** It is 1932. You want to preserve this period in history in a letter that your grandchildren can read in the 1990s. First list the main points you wish to make about events leading up to the Depression, daily life in difficult economic times, and the upcoming election. Note how your life has been permanently changed by the Depression. Then write a draft of a letter in which you explain your experiences and those of the people around you. Revise your letter, making sure that you have used enough detail to bring your experiences to life. Proofread your letter and draft a final copy.
4. **Using the Graphic Organizer** This graphic organizer uses a tree map to organize information about the social effects of the Depression. (a) Based on the graphic organizer below, what were the five social effects of the Depression? (b) According to the graphic organizer, which groups suffered increased discrimination due to the Depression? (c) On a separate sheet of paper, create your own graphic organizer about signs of trouble in the 1920s economy, using this graphic organizer as an example.

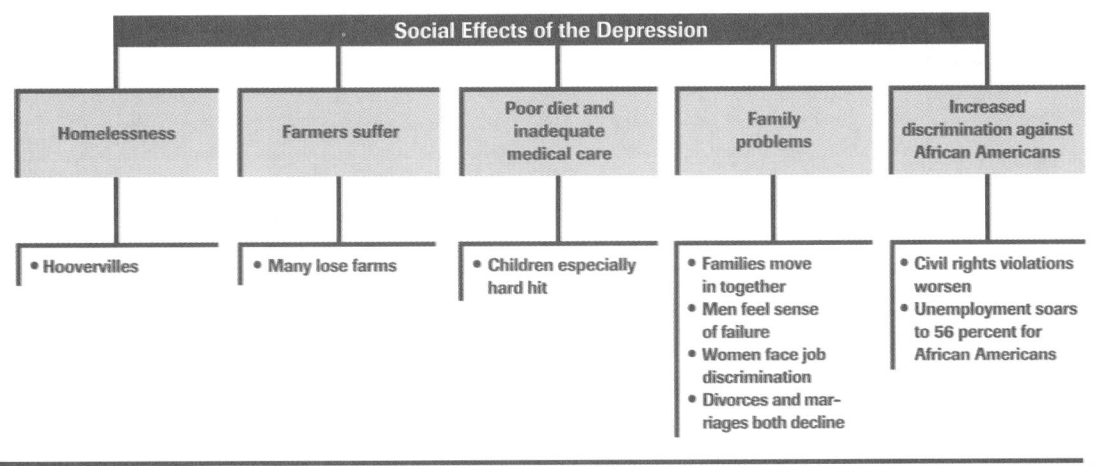

Social Effects of the Depression

Homelessness	Farmers suffer	Poor diet and inadequate medical care	Family problems	Increased discrimination against African Americans
• Hoovervilles	• Many lose farms	• Children especially hard hit	• Families move in together • Men feel sense of failure • Women face job discrimination • Divorces and marriages both decline	• Civil rights violations worsen • Unemployment soars to 56 percent for African Americans

Making Connections

1. Hoover believed that voluntary aid could solve the country's economic problems; he resisted the idea of a powerful central government. Roosevelt believed that government must play an active role in turning the economy around.

2. The cartoon on page 440 examines speculation on the stock market. Its tone is critical. The cartoon on page 458 examines public opinion about President Hoover. Its tone is accusatory.

3. Answers will vary. Students' letters should reflect a grasp of the causes and effects of the Depression. They should also mention some of the issues involved in the 1932 election.

4. (a) The five social effects were: homelessness, farmers suffer, poor diet and inadequate medical care, family problems, and increased discrimination against African Americans. (b) Women and African Americans. (c) Students' graphic organizers should include the increase in personal debt, overspeculation, overproduction, uneven distribution of wealth, and economic hard times for many workers.

"Going on relief" has always been viewed as something of a disgrace in the United States. That is why President Hoover waited so long to appropriate federal money to help end the Depression. It is also the reason that President Franklin Roosevelt tried so hard to find work for the nation's unemployed, instead of merely giving them handouts. His efforts were applauded by some, criticized by others. Still others were not eligible for any of his numerous "alphabet soup" programs and ended up on relief anyway, despite their hardest efforts. Tell students that the source readings will help them understand the extent of the suffering in the nation during the Great Depression.

INSTRUCT

Ask students to review the source readings and find evidence that the Depression affected people in varying degrees. Explain that not everyone was out of work and some people were even in a position to capitalize on the low prices of land and stocks and on the vulnerable positions of others.

Have students imagine that they are Russell Baker or Baker's mother. Students should then write the letter to the President or Mrs. Roosevelt that they imagine Baker or his mother would have written. Have some students read their letters aloud to the class.

CHAPTER 13

SOURCE
READINGS

Growing Up During the Depression

 Literature

Russell Baker

INTRODUCTION Single parents rarely have an easy life, but during the Depression they and their families' very survival was questionable. Because they were the sole caregivers for their children, they could not travel to look for work. Many found that they had no choice but to accept aid from the government. During hard times in the past, they had scraped by somehow, scorning government handouts. But this hard time was different. With some thirteen million people unemployed by 1932, the Depression dragged on and on and the collapsed economy took more and more people down with it. In the following excerpt from his 1982 autobiography, *Growing Up*, New York Times columnist Russell Baker remembers those difficult days and one trying day in particular.

VOCABULARY Before you read the selection, find the meaning of this word in a dictionary: ostentatious.

The paper route earned me three dollars a week, sometimes four, and my mother, in addition to her commissions on magazine sales, also had her monthly check coming from Uncle Willie, but we'd been in Baltimore a year before I knew how desperate things were for her. One Saturday morning she told me she'd need Doris and me to go with her to pick up some food. I had a small wagon she'd bought me to make it easier to move the Sunday papers, and she said I'd better bring it along. The three of us set off eastward, passing the grocery stores we usually shopped at, and kept walking until we came to Fremont Avenue, a grim street of dilapidation and poverty in the heart of East Baltimore.

"This is where we go," she said when we reached the corner of Fremont and Fayette Street. It looked like a grocery, with big plate-glass windows and people lugging out cardboard cartons and bulging bags, but it wasn't. I knew very well what it was.

"Are we going on relief?" I asked her.

"Don't ask questions about things you don't know anything about," she said. "Bring that wagon inside."

I did, and watched with a mixture of shame and greed while men filled it with food. None of it was food I liked. There were huge cans of grapefruit juice, big paper sacks of cornmeal, cellophane bags of rice and prunes. It was hard to believe all this was ours for no money at all, even though none of it was very appetizing. My wonder at this free bounty quickly changed to embarrassment as we headed home with it. Being on relief was a shameful thing. People who accepted the government's handouts were scorned by everyone I knew as idle no-accounts without enough self-respect to pay their own way in the world. I'd often heard my mother say the same thing of families in the neighborhood suspected of being on relief. These, I'd been taught to believe, were people beyond hope. Now we were as low as they were.

Pulling the wagon back toward Lombard Street, with Doris following behind to keep the edible proof of our disgrace from falling off, I knew my mother was far worse off than I'd suspected. She'd never have accepted such shame otherwise. I studied her as she walked along beside me, head high as always, not a bit bowed in disgrace, moving at her usual quick, hurry-up pace. If she'd given up on life, she didn't show it,

WORLD'S HIGHEST STANDARD OF LIVING

There's no way like the American Way

This photograph, taken at a relief center in Kentucky, offers an ironic comment on the Great Depression. The people standing on line are waiting for the same kind of supplies Russell Baker and his family picked up in Baltimore.

but on the other hand she was unhappy about something. I dared to mention the dreaded words only once on that trip home.

"Are we on relief now, Mom?"

"Let me worry about that," she said.

What worried me most as we neared home was the possibility we'd be seen with the incriminating food by somebody we knew. There was no mistaking government-surplus food. The grapefruit-juice cans, the prunes and rice, the cornmeal—all were ostentatiously unlabeled, thus advertising themselves as "government handouts." Everybody in the neighborhood could read them easily enough, and our humiliation would be gossiped through every parlor by sundown. I had an inspiration.

"It's hot pulling this wagon," I said. "I'm going to take my sweater off."

It wasn't hot, it was on the cool side, but after removing the sweater I laid it across the groceries in the wagon. It wasn't a very effective cover, but my mother was suddenly affected by the heat too.

"It is warm, isn't it, Buddy?" she said. Removing her topcoat, she draped it over the groceries, providing total concealment.

"You want to take your coat off, Doris?" asked my mother.

"I'm not hot, I'm chilly," Doris said.

It didn't matter. My mother's coat was enough to get us home without being exposed as three of life's failures.

THINKING ABOUT THE SELECTION

1. What had Baker learned about people who accepted government handouts?

2. How did Baker's mother handle the situation when the family needed to accept government help?

Critical Thinking

3. **Demonstrating Reasoned Judgment** What is your opinion about the self-respect of those who accepted government aid during the Depression? Today?

SOURCE READINGS

Letters from the Forgotten Man

Primary Source

INTRODUCTION The introduction to *Down and Out in the Great Depression: Letters from the Forgotten Man* begins with this quotation from an unemployed man in 1935: "We're about down and out and the only good thing about it that I see is that there's not much further down we can go." The letters that fill the book echo this sentiment, many written by citizens who are in despair; having exhausted all means they know to support themselves, they now turn to the government to ask for help, to voice their anger, and to merely inform the President of how things are going "out here." The President, with his conversational fireside chats and comforting manner, seemed like someone they could confide in; the First Lady was something of a mother figure. And so the letters poured in. Here are a few from that collection.

Troy, New York
January 2, 1935

Dear Mrs. Roosevelt,
About a month ago I wrote you asking if you would buy some baby clothes for me with the understanding that I was to repay you as soon as my husband got enough work. Several weeks later I received a reply to apply to a Welfare Association so I might receive the aid I needed. Do you remember?

Please Mrs. Roosevelt, I do not want charity, only a chance from someone who will trust me until we can get enough money to repay the amount spent for the things I need. As a proof that I really am sincere, I am sending you two of my dearest possessions to keep as security, a ring my husband gave me before we were married, and a ring my mother used to wear. Perhaps the actual value of them is not high, but they are worth a lot to me. If you will consider buying the baby clothes, please keep them (rings) until I send you the money you spent. It is very hard to face bearing a baby we cannot afford to have, and the fact that it is due to arrive soon, and still there is no money for the hospital or clothing, does not make it any easier. I have decided to stay home, keeping my 7-year-old daughter from school to help with the smaller children when my husband has work. The oldest little girl is sick now, and has never been strong, so I would not depend on her. The 7-year-old is a good willing little worker and somehow we must manage—but without charity.

If you still feel you cannot trust me, it is allright and I can only say I donot blame you, but if you decide and I can only say I donot blame you, but if you decide my word is worth anything with so small a security, here is a list of what I will need—but I will need it very soon.

 2 shirts, silk and wool. size 2
 3 pr. stockings, silk and wool, 4 1/2 or 4
 3 straight flannel bands
 2 slips—outing flannel
 2 muslin dresses
 1 sweater
 1 wool bonnet
 2 pr. wool booties
 2 doz. diapers 30 x 30—or 27 x 27
 1 large blanket (baby) about 45" or 50"
 3 outing flannel nightgowns

If you will get these for me I would rather no one knew about it. I promise to repay the cost of the layette as soon as possible. We will all be very grateful to you, and I will be more than happy.

Sincerely yours,
Mrs. H.E.C.

President Roosevelt,
Washington, D.C.

Dear President:
I am in debt needing help the worst in the world. I own my own little home and a few live stock. Nine (9) head of red white face cattle and a span of mules. I have them all mortgaged to a man and he is fixing to foreclose me.

I have done all I could to pay the note and have failed on everything I've tried. I fell short on my crop this time and he didn't allow me even one nickel out of it to feed myself while I was gathering it and now winter is here and I have a wife and three (3) little children, haven't got clothes enough to hardly keep them from freezing. My house got burned up three years ago and I'm living in just a hole of a house and we are in a suffering condition. My little children talking about Santa Claus and I hate to see Xmas come this time because I know it will be one of the dullest Xmas they ever witnessed.

I have tried to compromise with the man I am in debt to and he wont except nothing but the money or my stock and I can't borrow the money and I need my stock so I am asking you for help of some kind please.
So I remain,

Your humble servant,
N.S.

Sulphur Springs, Texas
P.S. That man won't even agree for me to have my stock fed.

Forest
February 24, 1936

Dear President Roosevelt,
You speak about the good neighbor idea and Mr. Farley speaks about the humane treatment the poor are receiving. Do you think it is humane to load a lot of old infirm men in steel bottom trucks—no protection from the storms or cold—send them 25 miles into the county and place them in the charge of tyrants and slave driver bosses, with no place to hang their coat or leave their dinner pails, only a snow bank and serve them dinner in a frozen state, also in a snow bank. Then if some have the misfortune to get sick and are sick 5 days cut them off from W.P.A. and relief for a month just because they happen to get sick. Is that humane? Is it right to give has-been Republicans all of the jobs as time-keepers and bosses whose cellars are full and who have farms, cows, pigs, chickens, and full and plenty to live on, leave us Democrats out in the cold. You pay them $65.00, $75.00, $90.00 and on up. You give us a starvation $48.00 and use us like dogs. You would be arrested if you treated a dog or any other dumb animal that way. Then Mr. Farley has the nerve to stand up and tell how humane we are being treated. You can remedy this by cutting the bosses' pay and giving us a little more so we can live as well as them. There is no reason they should be paid over $10.00 a month more than we are. Don't consider them skilled workmen because they are not. Out of every 1000 white collar jobs, how many Democrats will you find? No more than 10. Do you think us poor fools cannot see and understand what is going on? Oh yes, we can and don't blame us if we have to prove it when the time comes.

Yes, we realize you are trying to do your best and how you are being kept from doing it but we don't think you know what the men in charge of this W.P.A. and relief are doing. Will you try to change the program a little so there will not be so much dissatisfaction and starvation and unequalization?

A Poor Icicle

THINKING ABOUT THE SELECTION

1. What evidence can you find in the letters that shows these people have suffered much before finally appealing to the government for help?

2. What concerns does the author of the letter from Sulphur Springs, Texas, have?

Critical Thinking

3. Expressing Problems Clearly What complaint does "A Poor Icicle" have about the Republicans?

In the midst of the Depression, this unemployed Detroiter carried around a sign in the hopes of finding much-needed work.

Chapter 14 The New Deal
1933–1938

📁 Teaching Resources (See Unit 4 Folder)

	Instruction	Enrichment
Section 1 **Forging a New Deal** (pp. 472–478)	Reproducible Lesson Plan, p. 81 Alternate Lesson Plan, p. 118 Guided Reading and Review, p. 84 Quiz, p. 85	Primary Source Activity, A Fireside Chat: The NIRA, p. 98 Primary Source Activity, Providing Emergency Relief, pp. 96–97 Visual Learning Activity, Promoting the WPA, p. 102 Critical Thinking Activity, Recognizing Ideologies, p. 95
Section 2 **The New Deal's Critics** (pp. 479–483)	Reproducible Lesson Plan, p. 82 Alternate Lesson Plan, p. 119 Guided Reading and Review, p. 86 Quiz, p. 87	Literature Activity, In Search of Work: African Americans, p. 101 Visual Learning Activity, FDR Tries to Pack the Court, p. 103 Viewpoints Activity, On the New Deal, pp. 92–93 Historian's Toolbox Activity, Distinguishing Fact from Opinion, p. 94
Section 3 **Enduring Legacies of the New Deal** (pp. 485–489)	Reproducible Lesson Plan, p. 83 Alternate Lesson Plan, p. 120 Guided Reading and Review, p. 88 Quiz, p. 89 Chapter Test, Forms A & B, pp. 104–109	American Profiles Activity, Emma Tenayuca, p. 90 Literature Activity, In Search of Work: Migrant Farmers, pp. 99–100 American Profiles Activity, Jacob Lawrence, p. 91

📁 Additional Chapter Resources

Resource Organizer, p. 80
Alternate Lesson Plan, p. 117
Answer Keys, pp. 116–125

Bibliography

For the Teacher

Brinkley, A. *Voices of Protest: Huey Long, Father Coughlin, and the Great Depression.* Knopf, 1982.

Bunche, Ralph. *The Political Status of the Negro in the Age of F.D.R.* University of Chicago Press, 1975. (The view of an African American who served as ambassador to the United Nations.)

Lash, Joseph P. *Eleanor and Franklin: The Story of Their Relationship, Based on Eleanor Roosevelt's Personal Papers.* Norton, 1971.

Schraff, Anne E. *The Great Depression and the New Deal: America's Economic Collapse and Recovery.* Watts, 1990. (Includes an analysis of the impact of FDR's New Deal on American society.)

Prentice Hall Literature Excerpts from *The American Experience*, 1994, including Porter, Katherine Anne. "The Jilting of Granny Weatherall," from *Flowering Judas and Other Stories.* Harcourt Brace, 1958 edition.

The Big Idea for the chapter and how the main ideas in each section relate to the Big Idea are graphically displayed below. Comprehension of this chapter's Big Idea is critical to students' understanding of United States history and how we as a nation got where we are today.

Media and Technology

 Cause and Effect, F-9; Critical Thinking, I-11

 Critical Thinking, I-17

 Graphic Organizer, G-3

 Guided Reading Audiotapes (English and Spanish)

 Computer Test Bank

For the Student

Life History of the United States. Vol. 2. *New Deal and Global War.* 1964. (Illustrated account by the editors of *Life* magazine.)

Leuchtenburg, William E. *Franklin D. Roosevelt and the New Deal, 1932–1940.* Harper & Row, 1963. (An introduction to the New Deal.)

Warren, Robert Penn. *All the King's Men.* Random House, 1960. (A fictionalized account of the life of Huey Long.)

CHAPTER 14

President Roosevelt's New Deal—the name given to the vast collection of programs and policies formulated to combat the Depression—proved only a partial success at ending the nation's misery. Though critics were quick to point to the many failures, it was hard to argue against its resounding success in bringing hope to a weary nation. Moreover, the New Deal influenced the social, political, and cultural life and attitudes of Americans in ways that are still apparent six decades later.

SECTION 1

Roosevelt delivered on his promise of vigorous action. New Deal programs aided and uplifted millions and attacked root causes of the Depression. After the Supreme Court struck down key parts of the New Deal, the President pushed through a second set of programs.

SECTION 2

Not everyone was pleased with Roosevelt and the New Deal. Critics from all points on the political spectrum noted the President's failures or attacked his methods.

SECTION 3

The New Deal did not bring an end to the Depression. Yet the federal government's programs and policies helped transform the nation in lasting ways. Many physical, political, and cultural transformations are still evident today.

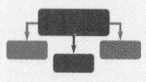

The New Deal
1933–1938

The New Deal
1933–1938

Franklin Roosevelt breezed into the White House, raising people's hopes with a promise to change the relationship between government and the economy. When the dust from FDR's first flurry of programs settled, critics were quick to point out the President's failures. Indeed, though the New Deal did help millions of Americans, it left many people out and failed to end the Depression. Still, the New Deal left permanent marks on American political, social, and cultural life—and on citizens' attitudes about their government.

The Relevance of the Big Idea

The Depression was a crisis that threatened the lives and security of millions of Americans. In response, President Roosevelt's New Deal instituted sweeping programs that changed the basic relationship between government and those it represented and governed.

Ask students what some of the major national issues are in the 1990s. Discuss issues such as health care, job retraining, AIDS research, the rights of minorities such as homosexuals, the breakup of the family, the inner-city underclass, foreign aid, drug abuse and rehabilitation, and education. What should the government's role be in any or all of these areas?

In Depth

Global Connections

The Great Depression had a catastrophic impact on the United States. But it was equally damaging to economies of other nations, whose fortunes were becoming ever more tightly interconnected. Japan's burden of a rapidly growing population and a lack of territorial resources was exacerbated by the economic depression. In response, militarist Japanese leaders promoted aggressive expansion into areas rich in natural resources, such as the northern Chinese province of Manchuria. The stage was thus being set for World War II, President Roosevelt's greatest challenge.

Events in the United States

1932	1933	1934	1935
1932 Franklin Delano Roosevelt is elected President of the United States.	**1933** Frances Perkins becomes the first woman cabinet member.	**1934** Congress passes the Indian Reorganization Act.	**1935** Congress passes the Social Security Act.

Events in the World

1932	1933	1934	1935
1932 Bolivia and Paraguay begin a three-year territorial war in which more than 100,000 people die.	**1933** Hitler and the Nazis take over Germany. • The Philippines gain independence from the United States.	**1934** Stalin launches the Great Purge in the Soviet Union.	**1935** Italy invades Ethiopia. • German Jews lose citizenship under Nuremburg Laws.

RESOURCE DIRECTORY

Teaching Resources

Alternate Lesson Plan: Demonstrating the Big Idea found in the Alternate Lesson Plans folder, p. 117, provides a lesson strategy to instruct students about the Big Idea that Roosevelt's New Deal, although it had many failures, influenced social, political, and cultural life for the next fifty years.

Alternative Assessment Handbook provides information, guidance, and strategies for alternative methods of assessment. It includes an essay on new trends in assessment, guidance and strategies for developing performance tasks and portfolios, scoring rubrics, and sample evaluation forms.

Pages 472–478

Forging a New Deal

FDR came to office with a breezy confidence—and no detailed plan of action. But act he did, pushing program after program to spur recovery and reduce misery. Not all of his ideas worked as planned, but they did manage to give the nation hope.

 Pages 479–483

The New Deal's Critics

For millions of Americans, the New Deal meant survival, security, and even opportunity. Others, including many women and minorities, noted its failures with bitterness. As the New Deal continued to disappoint, its critics accumulated large followings across the political spectrum.

 Pages 485–489

Enduring Legacies of the New Deal

The New Deal attacked the Great Depression with a barrage of programs and agencies. The Depression withstood this onslaught and refused to loosen its grip on the economy. Yet the New Deal was not without effect; it left a legacy that endures to this day.

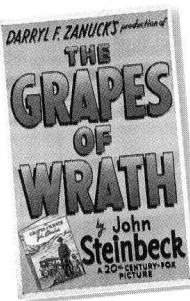

1936 President Roosevelt wins reelection in a landslide.
• Auto workers strike in Michigan.

1937 Roosevelt's attempt to pack the Supreme Court fails.

1938 The Fair Labor Standards Act bans child labor.
• Orson Welles's radio production of H. G. Wells's War of the Worlds causes national panic.

1939 Author John Steinbeck publishes The Grapes of Wrath.
• Hollywood releases The Wizard of Oz.

1936	**1937**	**1938**	**1939**	**1940**

1936 The Spanish Civil War begins.
• Olympic Games held in Berlin.

1937 Japan launches a full-scale war against China.

1938 Mexico nationalizes its oil fields.

1939 Germany and the Soviet Union sign the Nazi-Soviet Pact.
• World War II begins.

Media and Technology

 Transparency
Time Lines, E-7

 Alternative Assessment

As an ongoing chapter project, have students write three personal letters to President Franklin D. Roosevelt. Students should write the letters from the points of view of the following people:
• A beneficiary of a New Deal program living in the 1930s
• A critic of the New Deal living in the 1930s
• A recipient of social security benefits living in the 1990s

Students are free to choose which programs and aspects of the New Deal they want to write about. In all cases, however, the letters should be as specific and rich in detail as possible. In addition to the information provided in the textbook, students should seek information from newspapers, periodicals, biographies, and other sources. Students may also want to use primary sources such as interviews with relatives or neighbors who lived during the Depression. Students should submit a bibliography for their project.

Explain that projects will be assessed according to the following standards:
• **Unacceptable** Projects are not completed or fail to meet the requirements outlined.
• **Limited/Acceptable** Projects are based primarily on material from the textbook and present a limited view of the New Deal.
• **Extensive/Commendable** Projects are based on some outside resources as well as material from the textbook and present an in-depth picture of the period and its legacy.
• **Extraordinary/Outstanding** Projects are based on considerable outside research and present a detailed picture of the events, programs, and people of the time in the context of their relevance today.

For more information and guidance on alternative assessment trends and strategies, see the Alternative Assessment Handbook in the Resource Directory on page 470.

471

SECTION 1

Forging a New Deal

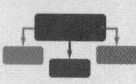

1. FOCUS

Connecting to the Big Idea

See page 470B. Explain that President Roosevelt promised action to combat the Depression and that he fulfilled that promise. Though the New Deal suffered setbacks, Roosevelt's attitude and programs uplifted the nation. Ask students to consider the ways in which the New Deal sought to overcome the Depression.

Objectives

● Explain how the Roosevelt administration restored the American people's optimism.

● Explain the results of the New Deal and determine why Roosevelt launched the Second New Deal.

In Depth

Did You Know?

With FDR's enactment of the New Deal, a horde of young, idealistic lawyers came to Washington eager to reform American society. These students and protégés of Harvard University's Felix Frankfurter—who were accordingly nicknamed "hot dogs"—incurred the disapproval of conservatives. One bureaucratic spokesperson complained of the "plague of young lawyers settled upon Washington."

Forging a New Deal

SECTION PREVIEW

FDR came to office with a breezy confidence—and no detailed plan of action. But act he did, pushing program after program to spur recovery and reduce misery. Not all of his ideas worked as planned, but they did manage to give the nation hope.

Key Concepts

• The Roosevelt administration restored the optimism of the American people.

• After achieving mixed results with his New Deal, Roosevelt launched the Second New Deal.

Key Terms, People, and Places

New Deal, hundred days, public works program, Wagner Act, Social Security Act; Frances Perkins, Mary McLeod Bethune

Many victims of the Depression found work and relief through such government programs as the Civilian Conservation Corps—the CCC.

When Franklin Roosevelt took office in 1933, he had big plans for the country—the so-called **New Deal.** Even Roosevelt himself, however, was not sure exactly how the New Deal would work. Nevertheless, the new President's personality and willingness to experiment won him the support of the American people. As humorist Will Rogers said, "The whole country is with him, just so he does something. If he burned down the capital we would cheer and say, 'Well, we at least got a fire started anyhow.' "

Restoring the Nation's Hope

Shortly after FDR took office, World War I veterans staged a second Bonus March on Washington. This time, the new administration provided campsites for the veterans. Even more astounding, Eleanor Roosevelt paid them a visit.

When she drove up, "They looked at me curiously and one of them asked my name and what I wanted," she recalled. By the time she left an hour later, the veterans were waving and calling out, "Good-by and good luck to you!" The First Lady later told reporters how polite the marchers had been. By this act she both soothed popular fears about renewed radical agitation and demonstrated the new administration's approach to unrest.

FDR also soothed the public. In his inaugural address of March 4, 1933, he tried to restore confidence: "Let me assert my firm belief that the only thing we have to fear is fear itself." The first Sunday after taking office, Roosevelt spoke to the nation over the radio in what became regular "fireside chats." His easy manner and confidence calmed his listeners. His words contained little of substance, but they made people feel better.

The First Hundred Days In campaigning for the White House, FDR had promised "bold, persistent experimentation." No one knew exactly what that experimentation would entail, only that someone was going to do something. As reporter Arthur Krock expressed it, Washington "welcomes the 'new deal,' even though it is not sure what the new deal is going to be."

Americans soon found out. From March to June 1933, during a period known as the **hundred days,** FDR feverishly pushed program after program through Congress to provide relief, create jobs, and stimulate economic recovery. Some of these programs were based on federal agencies that had controlled the economy during World War I, or on programs started under Hoover or by state governors. Former progressives figured prominently, inspiring New Deal legislation or administering programs.

Closing the Banks FDR's first step was to restore public confidence in the nation's banks. On March 6 he ordered all banks to close. He then pushed Congress to pass the Emergency

---

RESOURCE DIRECTORY

Teaching Resources

Reproducible Lesson Plan found in the Unit 4 folder, p. 81, provides a summary of the Section 1 lesson plan content.

Alternate Lesson Plan: Learning Styles found in the Alternate Lesson Plans folder, p. 118 is designed to help students create a graphic organizer identifying New Deal programs and agencies, as well as their goals and effects, and is particularly effective for visual learners.

Guided Reading and Review found in the Unit 4 folder, p. 84, provides a structure for reading and mastering the key concepts and reviewing the key terms for Section 1. (Guided Practice)

Banking Act, which authorized the government to inspect the financial health of all banks. Congress also established a Federal Deposit Insurance Corporation (FDIC) to insure deposits up to $5,000.

These acts reassured the American people, many of whom had been terrified by the prospect of losing all their savings in a bank failure. Government inspectors found that most banks were healthy, and two thirds had reopened by March 15. After the brief "bank holiday," deposits at last exceeded withdrawals.

Providing Relief and Creating Jobs FDR's next step was to replenish badly depleted local relief agencies. Harry Hopkins, a former social worker, directed a Federal Emergency Relief Administration (FERA) that sent funds to these agencies. He was in office barely two hours before he had given out $5 million. At the same time, Hopkins professed a strong belief in helping people find work. He said,

G*ive a man a dole* [handout], *and you save his body and destroy his spirit. Give him a job and pay him an assured wage and you save both the body and the spirit.*

The government also put federal money behind **public works programs**—government-funded projects to build public facilities. Its

President Roosevelt's manner both radiated and inspired confidence. At Hilltop Cottage in Hyde Park, New York, FDR chats with the caretaker's granddaughter in 1941.

first such effort along these lines was the Civil Works Administration (CWA), which gave the unemployed jobs building or improving roads, parks, airports, and other facilities. The CWA was a tremendous morale booster to its 4 million employees. As a former insurance salesman from Alabama remarked, "When I got that [CWA identification] card it was the biggest day in my whole life. At last I could say, 'I've got a job.'"
 FDR believed fervently in conservation of the environment. For this reason, the Civilian Conservation Corps (CCC), which put 2.5 million unmarried male workers into forest, beach, and

---

1650	1700	1750	1800	**Links Across Time**	1850	1900	1950	2000

Putting People to Work

W hen President Roosevelt took office in 1933, at least one of every four American workers was unemployed. Among FDR's first initiatives were programs to provide work—programs similar to ones Bill Clinton proposed during his presidential campaign in 1992.

New Deal programs created a variety of work agencies, such as the Civilian Conservation Corps (CCC), the Public Works Administration (PWA),

and the National Youth Administration (NYA). These organizations provided work to people who would otherwise have had none.

In 1993 Bill Clinton responded to high unemployment figures by proposing to invest $100 billion dollars in building and repairing roads, bridges, sewers, airports, and communication systems. He also proposed spending federal money on a job-training program that would

include classes and apprenticeships. Clinton hoped that his spending programs would provide work for unemployed Americans.

Roosevelt was able to put his plans into action. President Clinton hoped to use similar programs to help people learn skills and earn a living. ***Based on what you know about reactions to the New Deal, what do you think were the reactions to President Clinton's plan?***

SOURCE READINGS

 Source Readings on pp. 492 will connect literature selections and primary source excerpts to historical events discussed in this section.

Explain/Discuss

Explain that the Depression had deeply demoralized the nation by the time Roosevelt became President. Ask students to consider how prolonged joblessness with little prospect for relief might affect people. Ask how people might respond in such circumstances to the government programs that put people back to work and tried to address the root causes of such widespread unemployment and misery.

Explain that Roosevelt's New Deal was in many ways a revolutionary program; no President had ever attempted such far-reaching changes in the structure of the economy. Indeed, the Supreme Court found some New Deal programs unconstitutional. Ask students to identify the ways in which the Second New Deal addressed the shortcomings of the first New Deal.

Analyze

Ask students to analyze how the New Deal affected the relationship between the people and their government. As a result of the New Deal, would people expect more or less from government in future crises? Why?

The CCC gave young people jobs and preserved the nation's natural resources. This worker is planting seedlings in Montana.

NRA participants displayed the blue eagle label shown below.

park maintenance and restoration projects, was his favorite program. CCC workers earned only $1 a day but were boarded in camps and received job training. One participant commented that CCC work "gives a fellow self-confidence and teaches them how to get along by themselves." Thanks to Eleanor Roosevelt's intervention, from 1934 to 1937 the CCC funded similar programs for young women, though only 8,500 women benefited.

Public works programs also helped Native Americans. John Collier, FDR's commissioner of Indian affairs, used New Deal funds and Native American workers to build schools, hospitals, and irrigation systems. Native Americans also benefited from the Indian Reorganization Act of 1934, which ended the sale of tribal lands begun under the Dawes Act (1887) and restored ownership of unallocated lands to Native American groups.

A Helping Hand to Business The sharp decline of industrial prices in the early 1930s had caused many business failures—and also much unemployment. The National Industrial Recovery Act (NIRA) of June 1933 sought to bolster those prices and thus help businesses and individuals.

The NIRA allowed trade associations in many industries to draw up codes to regulate wages, working conditions, production, and even prices. The act also set a minimum wage and gave organized labor collective bargaining rights.

For a brief time, the codes stopped the tailspin of industrial prices. But by the fall of 1933, when higher wages went into effect, prices rose, too. Consumers stopped buying. The cycle of overproduction and underconsumption returned, and many businesses failed. Businesses soon complained that the codes were too complicated and that control by the National Recovery Administration (NRA) was too rigid. Critics joked that NRA really stood for "National Run Around" or "No Recovery Allowed."

The best part of the NIRA may have been its Public Works Administration (PWA). Directed by Secretary of the Interior Harold Ickes, the PWA launched projects ranging from the Grand Coulee Dam on the Columbia River in the state of Washington, to the causeway connecting Key West to the Florida mainland, to New York's Triborough Bridge.

Another New Deal act was less pleasing to business. A Federal Securities Act (May 1933) required full disclosure of information about stock offered for sale. The next year, Congress set up the Securities and Exchange Commission (SEC) to regulate the stock market. Congress also gave the Federal Reserve Board power to regulate the purchase of stock on margin—a practice that had contributed heavily to the crash.

Saving Homes and Farms The New Deal helped people keep their homes and farms. The Home Owners' Loan Corporation (HOLC) refinanced mortgages of middle-income home owners. An Agricultural Adjustment Administration (AAA) tried to raise farm prices. The AAA used proceeds from a new tax to pay farmers not to raise certain crops and animals. Lower production, it was hoped, would raise prices.

Under this program, some farmers also destroyed animals and plowed under growing crops. Many Americans, however, could not understand how the federal government could encourage the destruction of food while so many Americans were hungry.

Improving the Quality of Life One public works project proved especially popular. The Tennessee Valley Authority (TVA), created in May 1933, helped farmers and created jobs in one of the country's least modernized regions. By

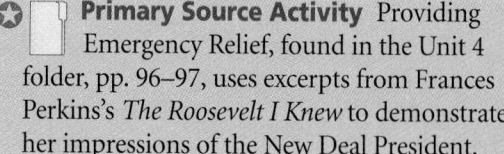

▶ **RESOURCE DIRECTORY**

Teaching Resources

⭐ **Primary Source Activity** A Fireside Chat: The NIRA, found in the Unit 4 folder, p. 98, provides an example of Roosevelt's use of radio to introduce and build support for his programs.

⭐ **Primary Source Activity** Providing Emergency Relief, found in the Unit 4 folder, pp. 96–97, uses excerpts from Frances Perkins's *The Roosevelt I Knew* to demonstrate her impressions of the New Deal President.

The Tennessee Valley Authority

Geography and History: Interpreting Maps
The TVA was a model of planning that linked together industry, agriculture, forestry science, and flood prevention. To many critics, however, the TVA was also the emblem of big government. *In how many states did the TVA provide service and benefits?*

reactivating a hydroelectric power facility started during World War I, the TVA provided cheap electric power, flood control, and recreational opportunities to the entire Tennessee River valley, as shown on the map above.

MAKING CONNECTIONS

What are the major differences between FDR's approach to the Depression and Hoover's?

New Deal Personnel

FDR surrounded himself with eager and hardworking advisers. Some, like Hopkins and Ickes, went directly into his cabinet or headed one of the new agencies. Others, such as Raymond Moley, Adolf A. Berle, and Rexford G. Tugwell, were part of a so-called brain trust, an informal group of intellectuals who helped Roosevelt devise policies. For the first time, a woman held a cabinet post. **Frances Perkins** became secretary of labor, a job she held until 1945. Perkins was one of almost thirty women who held key New Deal positions. ★

Eleanor Roosevelt Among FDR's most important colleagues was his wife, Eleanor Roosevelt. She threw herself into supporting New Deal programs and traveled widely for her husband, visiting coal mines, sewing rooms, and housing projects. She held her own press conferences, and in 1935 started her own newspaper column, "My Day," in which she drummed up support for the New Deal.

At times, ER took stands that embarrassed her husband. For example, in 1938 at a Birmingham, Alabama, meeting of the Southern Conference for Human Welfare, an interracial group, she knew she had to obey local Jim Crow laws that required African Americans and whites to sit in separate parts of the auditorium. In protest, she sat in the center aisle between the divided races. Her act

Eleanor Roosevelt surprised many Americans with her activism. In 1933 alone, she traveled 40,000 miles. Here, the First Lady emerges from an inspection of an Ohio coal mine.

SOURCE READINGS

 Source Readings on pp. 494 will connect literature selections and primary source excerpts to historical events discussed in this section.

Source Readings on pp. 494 will connect literature selections and primary source excerpts to historical events discussed in this section.

Activity
Teaching Heterogeneous Groups

During the first one hundred days of FDR's administration, many federal programs passed through Congress to provide relief, create jobs, and stimulate the economy. To understand the New Deal programs, have students create public works programs within their school. Divide students into small groups to develop a public works project. Each group should identify the goal of the project, the people who would qualify to work on it, and the way in which it would affect the school community.

Caption Answer to ...

 Interpreting Maps

Mississippi, Alabama, Georgia, Tennessee, North Carolina, Virginia, and Kentucky.

Answer to ...

MAKING CONNECTIONS

FDR was more willing to experiment with governmental programs. His willingness to try new ideas gave people hope that a solution would be found. Thus, he was a more effective leader of the people.

 In Depth

Biography

Frances Perkins (1882–1965), pushed for a minimum wage, a maximum work week, unemployment compensation for disabled workers, and a limit on the hiring of children under sixteen. Perkins said of the New Deal: "Its value was psychological. It made people feel better, and in that terrible period of depression they needed to feel better." Among her most notable achievements was the establishment of the Department of Labor and the Bureau of Labor Statistics.

received wide publicity, and no one missed its symbolism.

Many Americans were confused by ER's activities. In their view, a First Lady should take care of her husband and serve graciously at state dinners. Gradually, the public got used to ER, and many came to admire her for her idealism and humanity.

AMERICAN PROFILES

Mary McLeod Bethune

FDR's administration broke new ground by hiring African Americans to more than one hundred policy-making posts. One of Roosevelt's key appointments was **Mary McLeod Bethune** (1875–1955), who held the highest position of any black woman in the New Deal.

The President was not the first to recognize Bethune's talents. From the mid-1920s on, she had been one of the country's most influential spokespersons for African American concerns. Bethune achieved this status through her efforts in three areas: education, women's voluntary associations, and government.

Improving African American Education Born near Mayesville, South Carolina, Bethune was the fifteenth of seventeen children born to for-

"Your road may be somewhat less rugged because of the struggles we have made." So stated Mary McLeod Bethune of efforts in the New Deal era to further the interests of women and African Americans.

merly enslaved parents. With the help of a scholarship and money she earned by ironing, cooking, and cleaning, she received an education at the Scotia Seminary in Concord, North Carolina. Bethune's opportunity did not come without sacrifice. For example, during one period at Scotia, Bethune owned only one dress, which she washed out each night and wore again the next day.

In 1895 Bethune began training for missionary work in Africa, only to discover a year later that her church sent out only white missionaries. Undaunted, she turned her missionary spirit toward teaching, and in 1904 moved to Daytona Beach, Florida, determined to open a school for African American girls. Describing how she started this enterprise, Bethune later wrote:

> *On October 3, 1904, I opened the doors of my school, with an enrollment of five little girls, aged from eight to twelve, whose parents paid me fifty cents weekly tuition. . . . Though I hadn't a penny left, I considered cash money as the smallest part of my resources. I had faith in a living God, faith in myself, and a desire to serve.*

Later, Bethune moved her school to the site of an old dumping ground. She purchased the land with a five-dollar down payment, which she raised by selling ice cream and sweet-potato pies to local laborers.

That was how the Daytona Normal and Industrial Institute got started. Despite its humble beginnings, the school prospered. By 1918 Bethune had added a four-year high school. In 1923 it merged with Cookman Institute, a coeducational school in Jacksonville. This institution was renamed Bethune-Cookman College in 1929, and Bethune became its president.

Volunteerism Bethune was also active in voluntary groups, including the NAACP, National Urban League, and National Association of Colored Women. Assuming the presidency of this last group in 1924, Bethune developed international contacts to forge "a significant link between the peoples of color throughout the world." In 1935 she founded the National Council of Negro Women, which represented thirty African American women's organizations.

RESOURCE DIRECTORY

Teaching Resources

⭐ **Visual Learning Activity** Promoting the WPA, found in Unit 4 folder, p. 102, uses a poster created under the Works Project Administration to show how the agency simultaneously employed artists, historians, and others, and promoted public interest issues.

Serving in Government Also in 1935, the New Deal's National Youth Administration made her a consultant to its advisory council. This work eventually earned her an appointment to the post of director of the Division of Negro Affairs.

In her government posts, Bethune encouraged programs that aided African Americans. She also sought a share of New Deal posts for African Americans. "The White man has been thinking for us too long," she said, expressing her belief that African American officeholders would be more sensitive to African American concerns. She forged a united stand among black officeholders by organizing a Federal Council on Negro Affairs in August 1936. This unofficial group, known as the black cabinet, met weekly to hammer out priorities and to increase African American support for the New Deal.

At a time when no governmental commitment to the improvement of the lives of African Americans existed, Bethune helped create one. Recipient in 1935 of the NAACP's most prestigious award, the Spingarn Medal, and twelve honorary degrees, Bethune reached an extraordinary level of influence for women and for African Americans. Speaking about Bethune, Roosevelt once remarked, "I believe in her because she has her feet on the ground; not only on the ground but deep down in the plowed soil."

The End of the Honeymoon

The zeal and energy with which New Dealers attacked the Depression pleased most observers. But when the new programs failed to bring about significant economic improvement, criticism began to mount. Many worried about the increasing power that New Deal agencies were giving to the federal government. Former President Hoover warned against "a state-controlled or state-directed social or economic system. . . . That is not liberalism; it is tyranny," he said. Other criticisms of the New Deal are discussed in Section 2.

In 1935 the Supreme Court declared the NRA unconstitutional because it gave the President law-making powers and regulated local, rather than interstate, commerce. The following year, the Court ruled that the tax that funded AAA subsidies to farmers was also unconstitutional. The New Deal's most important programs had crumbled. It was time to reassess.

A Second New Deal

Meanwhile, most of the public remained behind Roosevelt. The midterm elections of 1934 showed stunning nationwide support for FDR's administration. In 1935 he launched a new, even bolder burst of legislative activity. Some have called this period the Second New Deal. In part, it was a response to his various critics. The Second New Deal included more social welfare benefits, stricter controls over business, stronger support for unions, and higher taxes on the rich.

New and Expanded Agencies New agencies attacked joblessness even more aggressively than before. The Works Progress Administration (WPA), an agency set up in 1935 and lasting eight years, provided work for more than eight million citizens. The WPA constructed or improved more than 20,000 playgrounds, schools, hospitals, and airfields, and supported the creative work of many artists and writers (see Section 3). ✪

The Second New Deal responded to the worsening plight of agricultural workers. The original AAA had ignored many of the farm workers who did not own land. In the Southwest, for example, Mexican American farm workers struggled to survive. Many were forced to return to Mexico; others tried to form unions, inspiring fierce resistance from farmer associations. In the South, landlords had pocketed AAA subsidies, taken land out of production, and left tenants and sharecroppers to shift for themselves.

In May 1935 Rexford Tugwell set up a Resettlement Administration that loaned money to owners of small farms and helped resettle tenants and sharecroppers on productive land. In 1937 a Farm Security Administration (FSA) replaced Tugwell's agency. It loaned more than $1 billion to farmers and set up camps for migrant workers.

New Labor Legislation Labor unions had liked the NIRA provision—known as 7a—that

Media and Technology

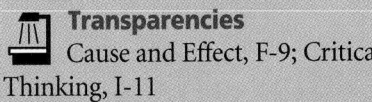
Transparencies
Cause and Effect, F-9; Critical Thinking, I-11

Section 1 Review Answers

1. (a) New Deal, see p. 472, (b) hundred days, see p. 472, (c) Wagner Act, see p. 478, (d) Social Security Act, see p. 478

2. Frances Perkins, see p. 475

3. FDR gave a stirring inaugural address and began proposing legislation to Congress at a feverish pace. Instead of driving the bonus marchers out of Washington, the government provided camp sites for them and Eleanor Roosevelt visited them.

4. After declaring a four-day bank holiday, FDR increased relief and created public works programs. He then launched a National Industrial Recovery Act, which did not work very well and was eventually declared unconstitutional. Farmers were somewhat helped by an Agricultural Adjustment Act, and agencies were created to help people refinance their mortgages. The Tennessee Valley Authority brought cheap electric power and flood control to one of the nation's poorest and least modernized areas. The CCC provided jobs and engaged in conservation projects.

5. She promoted African American education by founding a school, which later became a college. She worked on behalf of several African American volunteer associations. She also held a post in the New Deal administration, which she used to promote African American interests.

6. A Works Progress Administration, a National Youth Administration, the Wagner Act (which legalized unions), and the Social Security Act.

7. Possible answer: FDR gave the appearance of confidence. He also appeared willing to take whatever steps necessary to get results.

Reteach

Write the following questions on the chalkboard: Why was there a New Deal? Why was there a Second New Deal? Then ask students to formulate answers to these questions, and to give examples of how Roosevelt's goals were met.

Alternative Assessment

Mid-Point Monitoring

Ask students if they have

- Identified the programs and points of view on which their letters will be based
- Begun outside research on the New Deal
- Started drafts of their letters

 CLOSE

 **Reinforcing the Big Idea**

The New Deal uplifted millions by its vigorous response to the Depression. The next section explores some of the many criticisms that President Roosevelt and the New Deal provoked.

A major Second New Deal program was the Social Security Act, which provided a variety of benefits to many retired, disabled, and unemployed workers. The original social security program did not cover agricultural or domestic workers.

granted them the right to organize and bargain collectively. When the NIRA was declared unconstitutional, however, workers began to demand new legislation to protect their rights.

In July 1935, Congress responded. It passed a National Labor Relations Act, called the **Wagner Act** after its leading advocate, New York senator Robert Wagner. The Wagner Act legalized practices allowed only unevenly in the past, such as closed shops—in which only union members can work—and collective bargaining. It also outlawed spying on union activities and blacklisting—a practice in which employers agreed not to hire union leaders. The act also set up a National Labor Relations Board (NLRB) to enforce its provisions.

In 1938 a Fair Labor Standards Act banned child labor and established a minimum wage for all workers covered under the act. This law was a long-awaited triumph for progressive-era social reformers.

Social Legislation Congress also passed the **Social Security Act,** establishing a system that provided old-age pensions for workers; survivors' benefits for victims of industrial accidents; unemployment insurance; and aid for dependent mothers and children, the blind, and the physically disabled. The act was based

in part on models from European welfare states, and it was funded through contributions from employers and workers, which were then later paid out to people covered by the system who were not earning a wage.

Though the original Social Security Act did not cover many farm and domestic workers, it did help millions of beneficiaries feel more secure. Its importance to the American people has continued to grow, and its success has helped inspire numerous other social welfare programs. ○

The 1936 Election

No one expected the Republican presidential candidate of 1936, Kansas governor Alfred M. Landon, to beat FDR. But few predicted the extent of FDR's landslide. FDR carried every state except Maine and Vermont. Although Depression conditions had increased support for radical movements, no effective third party emerged to challenge the capitalist system. FDR buried Socialist Norman Thomas, who received fewer than 200,000 votes, and Communist candidate Earl Browder, who won only 80,000 votes.

Indeed, a broad cross section of the country's population supported the New Deal. Forming a new Democratic majority were farmers, recent immigrants, skilled and unskilled workers, northern African Americans, and women. Democrats also received support from the unions. Yet the New Deal was not without its critics, as the next section discusses.

SECTION 1 REVIEW

Key Terms, People, and Places
1. Describe (a) New Deal, (b) hundred days, (c) Wagner Act, (d) Social Security Act.
2. Identify Frances Perkins.

Key Concepts
3. What were some of the ways in which the Roosevelt administration restored hope to the nation?
4. What were some of the first New Deal programs?

5. In what ways did Mary McLeod Bethune seek to help African Americans?
6. What were the most important features of the Second New Deal?

Critical Thinking
7. **Drawing Conclusions** How do you explain the popularity of FDR with American voters?

 **RESOURCE DIRECTORY**

Teaching Resources

Critical Thinking Activity Recognizing Ideologies: The Role of Government, found in the Unit 4 folder, p. 95, helps students understand the ideology behind the implementation of the Social Security Act in 1935.

Quiz found in the Unit 4 folder, p. 85, covers the main ideas in this section as well as the key terms.

The New Deal's Critics

SECTION 2

The New Deal's Critics

SECTION PREVIEW

For millions of Americans, the New Deal meant survival, security, and even opportunity. Others, including many women and minorities, noted its failures with bitterness. As the New Deal continued to disappoint, its critics accumulated large followings across the political spectrum.

Key Concepts
• New Deal programs often treated women and minorities unfairly.
• The New Deal was criticized both for what it did and for what it did not do.

Key Terms, People, and Places
political right, political left, demagogue; Father Charles E. Coughlin, Huey Long

F ranklin Roosevelt's success at the polls in 1936 suggests overwhelming approval of his New Deal. Indeed, vast numbers of Americans benefited from the relief and employment programs of the New Deal. Letters thanking the President poured into the White House. One example read:

I 'm proud of our United States and every time I hear the "Star-Spangled Banner" I feel a lump in my throat. There ain't no other nation in the world that would have sense enough to think of WPA and all the other A's.

Yet the New Deal had its failures—and inspired its share of critics. Another letter to Roosevelt read:

I f you could get around the country as I have and seen the distress forced upon the American people, you would throw your darn NRA and AAA, and every other ... A into the sea.

The Limits of the New Deal

For all its success, the New Deal fell short of expectations. The Fair Labor Standards Act, for example, covered fewer than one quarter of all gainfully employed workers and set the minimum wage at twenty-five cents an hour—well below what most covered workers already made. New Deal agencies also were generally less helpful to women and minority groups than they were to white men.

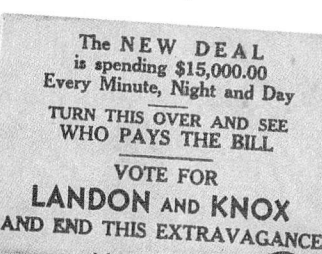

The NEW DEAL is spending $15,000.00 Every Minute, Night and Day

TURN THIS OVER AND SEE WHO PAYS THE BILL

VOTE FOR LANDON AND KNOX AND END THIS EXTRAVAGANCE

L. S. BONIME NEW YORK

Women Many aspects of New Deal legislation put women at a disadvantage. The NRA codes, for example, permitted lower wages for women's work in almost a fourth of all cases. In relief and jobs programs, men and boys received strong preference. Jobs went to male "heads of families," unless the men were unable to work. No New Deal provision protected domestic service, the largest female occupation. In 1942 an African American domestic worker in St. Louis pleaded with the President to ask the "rich people" to "give us some hours to rest in and some Sundays off and pay us more wages." Working fourteen-hour days, she earned only $6.50 per week. An official matter-of-factly wrote back,

S tate and Federal labor laws, which offer protection to workers in so many occupations, have so far not set up standards for working conditions in domestic situations. There is nothing that can be done ... to help you and others in this kind of employment.

African Americans In the South, federal relief programs reinforced racial segregation. No person of color received a job at a professional level. Segregation prevailed on public works

Millions of Americans benefited from the New Deal. But critics, including FDR's 1936 opponent Alf Landon, were quick to point out the program's problems and shortcomings.

Using Historical Evidence

All the people in the relief line are African American. The billboard, which trumpets the nation's high standard of living, features only white people.

2. INSTRUCT

Explain/Discuss

Explain that for all its successes, the New Deal did not solve the problems of many people. Ask students in what way the New Deal failed to address the problems of many women and African Americans.

Explain that other people objected to the New Deal because of what it did or did not do. Ask students to describe the opposition from the right and the left, respectively. Discuss the role of anti–New Dealers such as Huey Long and Father Coughlin, and ask students to consider why such demagogues are often effective critics. Then explore the Court-packing scheme. Ask how that episode provoked widespread public disapproval of Roosevelt and damaged his standing in Congress.

WORLD'S HIGHEST STANDARD OF LIVING

There's no way like the American Way

Using Historical Evidence This picture, taken at a relief center in Louisville, Kentucky, highlights the struggle of African Americans to overcome both the Depression and the effects of prejudice. *What elements of this picture contribute to its ironic effect?*

projects, and African Americans received lower pay than whites and were kept from skilled jobs on dam and electric power projects. Because the Social Security Act excluded both farmers and domestic workers, it failed to cover nearly two thirds of working African Americans.

African Americans in the North had not supported FDR in 1932. By 1936 they had joined his camp. Often the last hired and first fired, they had experienced the highest unemployment rates of any group during the Depression. They therefore appreciated many New Deal programs.

Yet the New Deal did nothing to end distressing discriminatory practices in the North. Especially troubling was the employment of only whites in white-owned businesses in black neighborhoods. In the absence of help from the federal government, African Americans took matters into their own hands. Protesters picketed and boycotted such businesses with the slogan "Don't shop where you can't work."

The early Depression also had seen an alarming rise in the number of lynchings. The federal government again offered no relief. In 1935 and 1938, bills to make lynching a federal crime went down to narrow defeat. NAACP head Walter White recalled in 1948 that FDR had given this explanation for his refusal to support these measures:

S outherners, by reason of seniority rule in Congress, are chairmen or occupy strategic places on most of the Senate and House committees. If I come out for the anti-lynching bill now, they will block every bill I ask Congress to pass to keep America from collapsing. I just can't take that risk.

Of course, FDR's record with African Americans was not all bad. FDR appointed more than a hundred African Americans to policy-making posts. The Roosevelts also conveyed an apparently genuine concern for the fate of African Americans. These factors help to explain FDR's wide support among black voters.

Criticism of the New Deal

African Americans may have supported FDR. But many others, at each end of the political spectrum, criticized the New Deal.

Criticism from the Right The **political right**—typically made up of those who want to preserve a current system or power structure—opposed Roosevelt. These critics included many wealthy people, who regarded FDR as their enemy. Early in the New Deal, they had disapproved of programs such as the TVA,

▶ RESOURCE DIRECTORY

Teaching Resources

 Literature Activity In Search of Work: African Americans, found in the Unit 4 folder, p. 101, uses the characters found in Zora Neale Hurston's novel *Their Eyes Were Watching God* to depict the lives of African American migrant workers.

which they considered to be socialistic. The Second New Deal gave them even more to hate, as FDR pushed through a series of higher taxes aimed at the rich.

The Social Security Act also aroused opposition from the right. Some people felt that it penalized successful, hardworking people. Other critics saw the assignment of social security numbers as the first step toward a militaristic, regimented society. They predicted that soon people would have to wear metal dog tags engraved with their social security numbers.

A group called the American Liberty League (1934) spearheaded much right-wing opposition to the New Deal. It was led by former Democratic presidential candidate Alfred E. Smith, the National Association of Manufacturers, and business figures such as John J. Raskob and the Du Pont family.

The league charged the New Deal with limiting individual freedom in an unconstitutional, "un-American" manner. To them, programs such as compulsory unemployment insurance smacked of "Bolshevism." They advised instead that people take responsibility for themselves and practice "thrift and self-denial."

Socialists and Progressives Others attacked the New Deal from the left. The **political left** generally seeks governmental change—sometimes radical change—as a means of helping the common people. These critics accused the New Deal of not going far enough in addressing the nation's ills.

In 1934 muckraking novelist and socialist Upton Sinclair ran for governor of California on the Democratic ticket. His platform, "End Poverty in California" (EPIC), called for a new economic system in which the state would take over factories and farms. EPIC clubs formed throughout the state, and Sinclair won the primary. Terrified, opponents used dirty tricks to discredit Sinclair. They produced fake newsreels showing people speaking in a Russian accent and endorsing Sinclair. Associated unfairly with Soviet communism, Sinclair lost the election.

The limited success of the New Deal in eliminating poverty helped lead to a revival of progressivism in Minnesota and Wisconsin. Running for the United States Senate, Wisconsin progressive Robert La Follette, Jr., argued that "devices which seek to preserve the unequal distribution of wealth . . . will halt the progress of mankind and, in the end, will retard or prevent recovery." His brother, Philip, also took a radical stand, calling for the redistribution of income. Philip's ideas persuaded the state Socialist party to join his progressives after he won the Wisconsin governorship in 1934.

Using Historical Evidence The artist who created this cartoon had little faith that FDR's New Deal programs were in the country's best interest. *What is it that has put the "patient" to sleep? What does the cartoon imply will happen when the "patient" wakes up?*

MAKING CONNECTIONS

Consider what you have read about the poverty caused by the Depression. Do you agree with the criticisms of the political left or the political right? Explain why.

UNCLE "GUINEA PIG"

Caption Answer to . . .

Using Historical Evidence

The patient (the country) has been put to sleep by government propaganda. The cartoon implies that when the country "wakes up," it will no longer tolerate the New Deal's experimental programs.

Answer to . . .

MAKING CONNECTIONS

Answers will vary. Encourage students to compare the political rhetoric of an era with the known facts.

Analyze

Ask students to analyze the difficulties of forging government programs that provide equal benefit and satisfaction to all citizens. Have students consider what limits the democratic process places on the ability of a government to implement broad new programs, such as universal health care.

 In Depth

Multicultural Perspectives

Many African Americans felt left out by the New Deal and turned to the Communist party. Hosea Hudson, for example, an African American farmer from rural Georgia, joined the party. Angered by the 1931 case of the Scottsboro Boys (see page 451), Hudson organized unemployed African Americans in Birmingham, Alabama, to meet weekly and discuss social issues. The Communist party's legal arm, the International Labor Defense (ILD) defended the Scottsboro Boys.

Activity
Creating a Political Advertisement

Ask students to create a political advertisement for a candidate opposed to President Roosevelt. The ad may identify particular or general criticisms. It may also identify specific actions the opponent hopes to take if elected.

Enrichment

Ask students to locate speeches given by 1936 Republican presidential candidate Alf Landon or by any other prominent New Deal critic. Have students summarize the messages of the speeches and analyze the strengths and weaknesses of all the arguments.

3. ASSESS

Section 2 Review Answers

1. (a) political right, see p. 480, (b) political left, see p. 481, (c) demagogue, see p. 482

2. (a) Father Charles E. Coughlin, see p. 482, (b) Huey Long, see p. 482

3. They permitted lower wages for women and gave job preferences to men. African Americans received lower pay and were kept from white-collar and skilled positions. The New Deal also failed to protect domestic workers.

4. Some, such as Upton Sinclair and progressives in the Midwest, criticized the New Deal for not going far enough in solving the nation's problems. Others—critics of social security, for example—feared that FDR had gone too far. Many deplored FDR's action in the Court-packing incident. And demagogues such as Father Coughlin and Huey Long also attacked Roosevelt for his policies.

Other New Deal Critics

Some New Deal critics were **demagogues**—charismatic leaders who manipulate people with half-truths, deceptive promises, and scare tactics. One such demagogue was **Father Charles E. Coughlin,** who used the radio to broadcast his message. In the early 1930s, the so-called Radio Priest was holding national audiences spellbound.

Coughlin achieved popularity in spite of the fact that his ideas were not consistent. Sometimes he advocated nationalizing the banks and redistributing wealth. At others, he defended the sanctity of private property. After first endorsing the New Deal, in 1934 he formed a "National Union for Social Justice," which denounced it. His increasing attacks on FDR grew reckless. In 1936 he called Franklin "Double-crossing" Roosevelt a "great betrayer and liar."

By the end of the 1930s, Coughlin was issuing openly anti-Semitic statements and showering praise on Adolf Hitler and Benito Mussolini, two menacing leaders who were then rising to power in Europe. Coughlin's actions alarmed many, and he lost some of his support. In the early 1940s, Roman Catholic officials ordered him to cease his broadcasts.

Huey Long—also known as the Kingfish—was a different type of demagogue. A country lawyer, he won the governorship of Louisiana in 1928 and became a United States senator in 1932. Unlike many other southern Democrats, Long never used racial attacks as the basis of his power. Instead, he worked to help the underprivileged, improving education, medical care, and public services. He also built an extraordinarily powerful and ruthless political machine.

Huey Long (below) achieved great popularity in the 1930s with his motto, "Every man a king." He had his eye on the presidency before his assassination.

Originally a supporter of FDR, he broke with him early in the New Deal. "Unless we provide for redistribution of wealth in this country, the country is doomed," he said. Calling his program "Share Our Wealth" (SOW) and using the motto "Every man a king," Long in 1934 proposed high taxes on large fortunes and inheritances, and grants of $5,000 to each American family.

Long's overly simplistic plan for helping all Americans achieve wealth attracted many followers. His success helped push FDR to propose new taxes on wealthy Americans in the Second New Deal. Meanwhile, Long began to eye the presidency. But in September 1935, the son-in-law of one of his political enemies shot and killed him.

Long and Coughlin never seriously threatened FDR or the New Deal. But their popularity warned Roosevelt that if he failed to spread the country's wealth more widely, he risked losing popular support.

The Court-Packing Scheme

⭐ Roosevelt received criticism not only for his programs, but also for his actions. No act aroused more opposition than his attempt to pack the Supreme Court.

Throughout the early New Deal, the Supreme Court had caused FDR his greatest frustration. The Court, which included four conservative justices, had invalidated the NRA, the AAA, and many state laws from the progressive era. In February 1937, FDR proposed a major court reform bill.

The Constitution had not specified the number of Supreme Court justices. Congress had last changed the number in 1869. But by Roosevelt's time, the number nine had become well established. Arguing dishonestly that he wanted to lighten the burden of the aging justices, FDR asked Congress to pass his reform, enabling him to appoint as many as six additional justices, one for each justice over seventy years of age. Most people understood Roosevelt's real intention. He wanted to "pack" the Court with judges favorable to the New Deal.

Negative reaction came swiftly from all sides. The President, critics raged, was trying to inject politics into the judiciary and was attacking the constitutional principle of separation of

▶ RESOURCE DIRECTORY

Teaching Resources

⭐ 📄 **Visual Learning Activity** FDR Tries to Pack the Court, found in the Unit 4 folder, p. 103, features a political cartoon mocking FDR's attempt to add more justices to the Supreme Court to illustrate a common response to the incident.

powers. With Hitler, Mussolini, and Stalin ruling as dictators in Germany, Italy, and the Soviet Union, the world seemed already to be tilting toward tyranny. If Congress let FDR reshape the Supreme Court, critics worried, the United States might follow. Sam E. Roberts of Kansas wrote his representative in Congress:

O ur liberty is much more important than any whim of the President's. He might be a kind dictator himself, but after the stage is set the next President might be a Hitler or Mussolini.

California's aging senator Hiram W. Johnson expressed the views of many legislators when he said:

S hall the Congress make the Supreme Court subservient to [subject to] the presidency? The implications of this are so grave and far-reaching, I can do but one thing, and that is, . . . oppose this extraordinary legislation.

FDR was forced to withdraw his reform. He also suffered much political damage. Southern Democrats and conservative Republicans united against further New Deal legislation. This alliance remained a force for years to come.

FDR did wind up with a liberal majority on the Court. Some older justices retired, allowing FDR to appoint his own justices. Even earlier, the Court had begun to uphold measures from the Second New Deal, including the Wagner Act—perhaps because the laws had been better thought out and drafted.

Viewpoints
On The New Deal

FDR's promise to improve life for all Americans with a New Deal did not win approval from all quarters. ***Why, according to the viewpoints below, were some people pleased and some displeased with the New Deal?***

For the New Deal

"Roosevelt is the only President we ever had that thought the Constitution belonged to the pore [poor] man too. . . . Yessir, it took Roosevelt to read in the Constitution and find out them folks way back yonder that made it was talkin' about the pore man right along with the rich one. I am a Roosevelt man."
Testimony by mill worker George Dobbin, 1939. Collected in *These Are Our Lives,* Federal Writers Project of the Works Progress Administration (1939).

Against the New Deal

"All the prosperity he had brought to the country has been legislated and is not real. Nothing he has ever started has been finished. My common way of expressing it is that we are in the middle of the ocean like a ship without an anchor. No good times can come to the country as long as there is so much discrimination practiced. . . . I don't see much chance for our people to get anywhere when the color line instead of ability determines the opportunities to get ahead economically."
Testimony by Sam T. Mayhew, 1939. Collected in *Such As Us* (1978).

SECTION 2 REVIEW

Key Terms, People, and Places
1. Define (a) political right, (b) political left, (c) demagogue.
2. Identify (a) Father Charles E. Coughlin, (b) Huey Long.

Key Concepts
3. How did New Deal programs discriminate against or neglect women and minorities?
4. Why did people criticize FDR and the New Deal?

5. What was Franklin Roosevelt's attitude toward African American concerns about lynching?

Critical Thinking
6. **Checking Consistency** The text says that Roosevelt had critics at both ends of the political spectrum during the New Deal. Yet Roosevelt was easily reelected in 1936. How do you explain these two apparently conflicting facts?

---

5. He told the head of the NAACP that he could not support federal antilynching bills for fear of losing the support of southern Democrats for New Deal programs.

6. Possible answer: Roosevelt had many critics, but the vast majority of people supported his ideas. In other words, Roosevelt's critics did not attract significant mainstream support.

Answer to . . .

Dobbin supports the New Deal because it addresses the problems of working people like himself; Mayhew thinks the New Deal legislation falls short of inclusion of African Americans. For a more thorough examination of New Deal legislation, see the Resource Directory below.

Reteach
Ask students to construct a two-column chart that identifies conservative critics of the New Deal in one column and the reasons behind their criticisms in the other; then have them create a similar chart identifying the liberals who criticized FDR and their reasons for doing so.

4. CLOSE

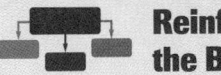
Reinforcing the Big Idea
President Roosevelt and the New Deal faced many criticisms, from all points along the political spectrum. The next section examines how the New Deal left a permanent mark on the United States in spite of its inability to end the Depression.

Critical Thinking
Distinguishing Fact from Opinion

Focus Analyze a speaker's use of facts and opinions in a political speech.

Instruct Divide students into small groups to examine the speech and identify the various facts and opinions used by the speaker. Ask each group to report its findings. If groups draw different conclusions about which statements are facts and which are opinions, have the whole class discuss the examples. Then ask students whether or not they think the speaker in this case has made an effective argument. What facts might he have used to strengthen his points? Which statements of opinion were effective? Why?

Extend See the Historian's Toolbox Activity in the Resource Directory below.

Answers

1. (a) The decisions of the Supreme Court are matters of public record and can thus be easily verified. (b) Possible answer: The statements about the growth of the national debt and the growth in the number of public officials are facts, which can be checked in public records.

2. (a) It winds up a sweeping accusation of the executive and the Congress. (b) Possible answer: The charge that the Congress has abandoned its responsibility and that New Deal developments have polluted the fountain of liberty are both opinions.

3. (a) He states that they were overthrown by the Supreme Court, the guardian of constitutional rights. (b) No, he gives no specific examples—just makes a sweeping accusation. (c) Students may be divided on how well or badly he has done, according to their own views of what government should and should not do.

Distinguishing Fact from Opinion

When you read historical materials—such as speeches, letters, and diaries—you will find that their authors express both facts and opinions. A fact is something that can be proved to be true by checking other sources. An opinion is a judgment that reflects beliefs or feelings—it may or may not be true.

To determine the soundness of an author's ideas, you need to be able to distinguish between fact and opinion. The ability to do so will help you evaluate what you read and reach your own conclusions about historical events.

Use the following steps to distinguish between fact and opinion in Herbert Hoover's criticism of the New Deal, excerpted from his speech to the Republican National Convention in 1936.

1. Determine which statements are facts. Remember that facts can be checked and confirmed by other sources. (a) For what reason is Hoover's first statement, about the Supreme Court, easily recognizable as a fact? (b) Choose two other statements of fact in the excerpt. Explain how you might prove that each statement is a fact.

2. Determine which statements are opinions. Sometimes authors signal opinions with phrases such as "I believe" or "I think," but often they do not. Other clues that indicate opinions are sweeping generalizations and emotion-packed words. (a) What indicates that the final sentence of the first paragraph is an opinion rather than a fact? (b) Choose two other statements of opinion, and explain what tells you that they are opinions.

3. Separate facts from opinions as you read. Generally, an opinion is more reliable when an author gives facts to support it. (a) How does Hoover support his opinion that many New Deal acts "were a violation of the rights of men and of self-government"? (b) Does he present any facts to support his statement that the Congress has "abandoned its responsibility"? (c) In your opinion, how good a job has Hoover done in supporting his opinions? Explain your answer.

> "The Supreme Court has reversed some ten or twelve of the New Deal major enactments. Many of these acts were a violation of the rights of men and of self-government. Despite the sworn duty of the Executive and Congress to defend these rights, they have sought to take them into their own hands. That is an attack on the foundations of freedom.
>
> More than this, the independence of the Congress, the Supreme Court, and the Executive are pillars at the door of liberty. For three years the word "must" has invaded the independence of Congress. And the Congress has abandoned its responsibility to check even the expenditures [spending] of money. . . .
>
> We have seen these gigantic expenditures and this torrent of waste pile up a national debt which two generations cannot repay. One time I told a Democratic Congress that "You cannot spend your way into prosperity." You recall that advice did not take then. It hasn't taken yet.
>
> Billions have been spent to prime the economic pump. It did employ a horde of paid officials upon the pump handle. We have seen the frantic attempts to find new taxes on the rich. Yet three-quarters of the bill will be sent to the average man and the poor. He and his wife and his grandchildren will be giving a quarter of all their working days to pay taxes. Freedom to work for himself is changed into a slavery of work for the follies of government. . . .
>
> We have seen the building up of a horde of political officials. We have seen the pressures upon the helpless and destitute to trade political support for relief. Both are a pollution of the very fountains of liberty."
>
> —Herbert Hoover, excerpted from
> *American Ideals Versus the New Deal*

 RESOURCE DIRECTORY

Teaching Resources

Historian's Toolbox Activity Distinguishing Fact from Opinion, found in the Unit 4 folder, p. 94, gives students further opportunity to apply this skill by evaluating President Bush's address to Congress after Iraq's 1990 invasion of Kuwait.

Enduring Legacies of the New Deal

SECTION PREVIEW

The New Deal attacked the Great Depression with a barrage of programs and agencies. The Depression withstood this onslaught and refused to loosen its grip on the economy. Yet the New Deal was not without effect; it left a legacy that endures to this day.

Key Concepts
• The New Deal did not resolve the economic problems of the Depression.
• The New Deal did leave a significant legacy that has affected the presidency, labor unions, and American cultural life.

Key Terms, People, and Places
national debt, Congress of Industrial Organizations, sit-down strike

T he New Deal did not attempt truly radical solutions to the problems of the American economy in the 1930s. Neither did it end the nation's suffering. It did, however, lead to some profound and lasting changes in American politics and social life.

FDR and the New Deal increased the public's expectations of the presidency. Voters began to expect a President to formulate programs and solve problems. Government now was authorized to intervene in major ways, and business could no longer resist regulation—or unionization—with claims about the sanctity of private property.

In addition to its effects on the economy, the New Deal also helped enhance American cultural life. Americans of the 1930s—and of future generations—were entertained and enriched due to programs aimed at helping artists.

The Recession of 1937

The New Deal did not put an end to the Great Depression. As predicted by economist John Maynard Keynes (see Chapter 13), the New Deal's massive government spending did lead to some economic improvement. But the economy collapsed again in August 1937, as you can see on the graph on page 486.

Reductions in consumer income from social security payroll deductions were partly to blame. Americans had less money in their pockets, and so bought fewer goods. Consumers also had less money because FDR had cut back on programs such as the WPA. The President— who campaigned in 1932 with a promise to balance the budget— had become distressed at the rising **national debt.** This is the total amount of money the federal government has borrowed and has yet to pay back. Because the government spent more than it took in, the debt rose from $21 billion in 1933 to $43 billion by 1940.

After 1937, Harry Hopkins and others convinced FDR to start up the suspended programs in 1938. Joblessness and misery slowly decreased. Still, hard times lasted well into the 1940s, until the nation's entry into World War II.

The Triumph of the Labor Unions

By legalizing unions, the New Deal permanently changed the relations between workers and employers in America. Union membership rose from 3 million in 1933 to 10.5 million by 1941, a figure representing 28 percent of the nonagricultural work force. By 1945, 36 percent were unionized, the high-water mark for unions in the United States.

A New Labor Organization Activism by powerful union leaders helped to increase membership. The cautious and craft-based American Federation of Labor (AFL) had done

The Depression era produced many lasting works of art, including the novel The Grapes of Wrath and the movie that was based on it.

Connecting to the Big Idea

See page 470B. Point out that the New Deal did not succeed in ending the Depression but that it did have a great impact on the nation's political, social, and cultural life. Ask students how that impact is felt today.

Objectives
● Explain that the New Deal did not resolve the economic problems of the Depression.
● Identify the ways in which the New Deal had a lasting effect on the presidency, labor unions, and American cultural life.

Bellringer
Write the words *federal government* on the chalkboard. Ask students to brainstorm a list of words they associate with the term. Explain that many modern attitudes and beliefs concerning the government stem from the New Deal era.

Reading Strategy
Structured Outline Have students take notes on the following topics as they read the section:
● The New Deal's impact on the Depression
● The New Deal and labor
● Cultural life in the 1930s
● Lasting monuments of the New Deal

Reproducible Lesson Plan found in the Unit 4 folder, p. 83, provides a summary of the Section 3 lesson plan content.

Alternate Lesson Plan: Cooperative Learning found in the Alternate Lesson Plans folder, p. 120, provides a strategy for groups of students to prepare presentations explaining the enduring legacy of the New Deal on different aspects of American life.

Guided Reading and Review found in the Unit 4 folder, p. 88, provides a structure for reading and mastering the key concepts and reviewing the key terms for Section 3. (Guided Practice)

2. INSTRUCT

Explain/Discuss

Explain that the New Deal did not by itself resolve the problems that were causing the Depression. Ask students what the Recession of 1937 revealed about the New Deal and the economy.

Discuss the real changes that the New Deal did introduce to the nation. Ask students to describe changes affecting labor unions. Ask them to consider the role of government in helping to make union gains possible.

Discuss government support for the arts as an important part of the New Deal. Ask students to discuss the benefits and drawbacks of government funding of art.

In Depth

Interdisciplinary

Technological developments changed the culture of this period. Specifically, the integration of sound with moving pictures revitalized the motion picture industry (see page 421). Adding sound was first accomplished by using a sound-on-film synchronization system, Phonofilm, patented by Lee DeForest in 1919. By 1933, when techniques had been developed to eliminate camera noise from recordings, improve microphones (so that actors could move while they spoke), and edit a soundtrack, all of the major studios had converted to sound, increasing their profits by 600 percent.

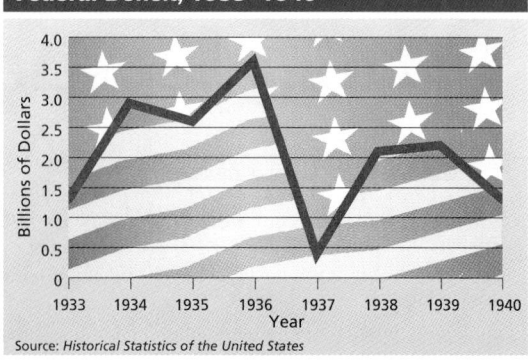

Federal Public Debt, 1933–1940

Federal Deficit, 1933–1940

Source: *Historical Statistics of the United States*

Interpreting Graphs
The New Deal was paid for by huge increases in government spending. Because of yearly deficits, the national debt expanded greatly during the Depression. *In which year was the deficit the greatest? The lowest?*

little to attract unskilled industrial workers during its half-century of existence. In 1935 United Mine Workers president John L. Lewis, whose bushy eyebrows made him a familiar front-page figure, joined with other AFL unions to create a Committee for Industrial Organizations (CIO) within the AFL. Though the AFL did not support its efforts, the CIO sought to organize the nation's unskilled workers. It sent organizers into steel mills, auto plants, and southern textile mills and welcomed all workers regardless of sex, color, or skill. The AFL suspended the CIO unions in 1936. Nevertheless, by 1938 the CIO had two million members. The group then changed its name to the **Congress of Industrial Organizations** and in November of that year it formed a new union.

An Era of Strikes The Wagner Act legalized collective bargaining and told management it had to bargain in good faith with certified union representatives. But the act could not force a company to accept

Thanks in part to the Wagner Act and the efforts of the CIO, union membership soared in the 1930s. By 1939, nearly 30 percent of nonagricultural workers belonged to unions.

union demands. Although the Wagner Act was designed to bring about industrial peace, in the short run it led to a wave of some of the country's most spectacular strikes. ⊘

Many of these work stoppages were known as **sit-down strikes,** in which workers stopped work and refused to leave the premises. Supporters outside then organized picket lines. Together the strikers and the picket line prevented the company from bringing in scabs, or substitute workers, and the business was paralyzed.

Sit-down strikes began in the rubber tire plants in Akron, Ohio. The most famous took place in the winter of 1936 to 1937 in Flint, Michigan. In this strike, workers associated with the United Auto Workers (UAW) occupied General Motors' Fisher body plants. GM executives turned off the heat and blocked entry to the plants so that the workers could not receive food. They also sent in police against picketers outside. Violence erupted. The wife of a striker then grabbed a bullhorn and urged other wives to join the picketers. The group became so large that the police could not control them. Women later organized food deliveries to supply the strikers, set up a speakers' bureau to present the union's position to the public, and formed a Women's Emergency Brigade to take up picket duty. Governor Frank Murphy of Michigan and President Roosevelt refused to use the militia against the strike. By

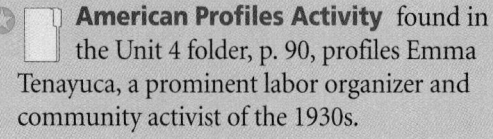
RESOURCE DIRECTORY

Teaching Resources

⊘ **American Profiles Activity** found in the Unit 4 folder, p. 90, profiles Emma Tenayuca, a prominent labor organizer and community activist of the 1930s.

⊘ **Literature Activity** In Search of Work: Migrant Farmers, found in the Unit 4 folder, pp. 99–100, uses an excerpt from John Steinbeck's *The Grapes of Wrath* to illustrate the plight of tenant farmers in the Depression and the harsh realities of a nation divided into economic classes.

early February, General Motors had given in.

Not all strikes were as successful. Henry Ford continued to resist unionism. In 1937 at a Ford plant near Detroit, his men viciously beat UAW officials when the unionists tried to distribute leaflets. Walter Reuther, a beating victim and future president of the UAW later testified,

> They picked me up about eight different times and threw me down on my back on the concrete. While I was on the ground they kicked me in the face, head, and other parts of my body. . . . I never raised a hand.

Like the Ford Company, Republic Steel Company refused to sign with steelworkers' unions until war loomed in 1941. At one bloody strike at Republic Steel on Memorial Day 1937, Chicago police killed ten picketers. Southern textile workers and clerical workers, both made up primarily of women, also remained unorganized in spite of New Deal efforts.

Cultural Life in the Thirties

Hard times stimulated a great release of creative energy in the United States during the Depression. In addition, Congress allocated federal funds to support the popular and fine arts. As a result, despite general unemployment among professionals, the arts not only thrived but created some enduring cultural legacies for the nation.

Literature Works of literature destined to become classics emerged during this period. Three examples are Pearl Buck's *The Good Earth* (1931), a saga of peasant struggle in China; John Steinbeck's *The Grapes of Wrath* (1939), a powerful tale about dust-bowl victims who travel to California; and Margaret Mitchell's fictional re-creation of the Old South, *Gone With the Wind* (1936). In 1936 Tennessee writer James Agee and photographer Walker Evans lived for a few weeks with sharecropper families in Alabama and produced a masterpiece of nonfiction literature, *Let Us Now Praise Famous Men* (1941). Folklorist Zora Neale Hurston wrote the classic *Their Eyes Were Watching God* (1937), a novel about an African American woman in Florida.

Radio and Movies Radio became the major medium of entertainment for most American families. In particular, comedy shows peaked in the thirties, producing stars such as Jack Benny, Fred Allen, George Burns, and Gracie Allen. The first soap operas—so called because they often were sponsored by soap companies—emerged in this period. These fifteen-minute stories designed to promote strong emotional responses were aimed at women who remained at home during the day. Symphony music and opera also thrived over the radio. By 1939 the country boasted 270 symphony orchestras.

By 1933 the movies had recovered from the initial setback caused by the early Depression. For a quarter, customers could see a double feature (introduced in 1931) or take the whole family to a drive-in (1933). Federal agencies used motion pictures to publicize their work. The Farm Security Administration, for example, produced classic documentaries of American agricultural life.

Some Hollywood studios concentrated on optimistic films about common people who

The successful sit-down strike at the Fisher body plant in the winter of 1936–37 demonstrated the effectiveness of the new technique. Here, workers guard a window during the strike.

triumphed over evil, such as Warner Brothers' *Mr. Smith Goes to Washington* (1939). In this era, the zany Marx Brothers produced such comic classics as *Monkey Business* (1931) and *Duck Soup* (1933). The greatest box-office hits were escapist, such as the gangster films that memorialized the prohibition era and the musicals featuring large orchestras and exquisitely choreographed dancers in luxurious costumes. No one understood the needs of Depression-era audiences better than Walt Disney, whose Mickey Mouse cartoons delighted moviegoers everywhere. Classics such as *Snow White and the Seven Dwarfs* (1937) and *The Wizard of Oz* (1939) came out in this period, as well as Charlie Chaplin's satire of capitalist society and its efficiency, *Modern Times* (1936).

In spite of the poverty of the Depression, cultural life bloomed in the 1930s. Charlie Chaplin's classic *Modern Times,* a satire about work in a modern factory, was released in 1936.

The WPA and the Arts FDR believed that the arts were not luxuries that people should give up in hard times. He thus earmarked WPA funds to support unemployed artists, musicians, historians, theater people, and writers. The Federal Writers' Project assisted more than six thousand writers, such as Richard Wright, Saul Bellow, Margaret Walker, and Ralph Ellison. Historians surveyed the nation's local government records, wrote state guidebooks, and collected life stories from about two thousand former slaves. Without this project, their stories would have been lost.

Other projects supported music and the visual arts. The Federal Music Project started community symphonies, organized free music lessons, and sent musicologists to lumber camps, prisons, and small towns to record a fast-disappearing folk heritage. The Federal Art Project hired artists to paint murals in the nation's public buildings. ✪

The Federal Theatre Project (FTP), directed by Vassar College professor Hallie Flanagan, was the most controversial. Flanagan used drama to create awareness of social problems. Her project launched the careers of many actors, playwrights, and directors who later became famous including Burt Lancaster, Arthur Miller, John Houseman, and Orson Welles.

Accusing the FTP of being a propaganda machine for international communism, the House of Representatives' Un-American Activities Committee (HUAC) investigated the project in 1938 and 1939. In July 1939 Congress killed the FTP appropriation.

MAKING CONNECTIONS

Americans still debate the role of government in funding the arts. In your opinion, should government pay to support art that criticizes it or offends certain taxpayers? Explain.

Lasting New Deal Monuments

The great public works of the Depression era—the bridges, dams, tunnels, public buildings, sewage systems, port facilities, and hospitals—remind us of this extraordinary period of government support for the national welfare. Constructed with great efficiency and durability, they stand to this day. In national and state parks and on mountain trails and oceanfront walks, Americans still reap advantages from the restoration and conservation work of the Civilian Conservation Corps.

Some of the federal agencies from the New Deal era have endured. The Tennessee Valley Authority remains a model of government planning. The Federal Deposit Insurance Corporation still guarantees bank deposits. The Securities and Exchange Commission continues to monitor the workings of the stock exchange. And in rural America, farmers still plant according to federal crop allotment strategies, which were put in place to conserve soil and reduce acreage after the Supreme Court struck down AAA crop reduction plans.

Social Security Almost everyone in the United States has come to depend on the social security system. Few people today seriously question its place in American society.

Over the years, however, social security has had many critics. You read about some of these critics in Section 2. Others attacked social security because, at first, payments were very low, and the program excluded millions of farmers, domestic workers, and the self-employed. For a long time the system discriminated against women. It assumed, for example, that the male-headed household was typical. A mother could lose benefits for her children if a man, whether providing support for her or not, lived in her house. Women who went to work when their children started school rarely stayed in the work force long enough or earned high enough wages to receive the maximum benefits from the system.

In addition, unlike every other industrialized country in the world except South Africa, the American social security system did not guarantee health insurance for all citizens. For decades this omission prompted calls for further legislation. Only recently has the executive branch of the government begun to tackle this problem.

A Legacy of Hope

In August 1939, Mrs. Renee Lohrback of San Antonio, Texas, wrote a sad letter to Eleanor Roosevelt. Lohrback was a typist who could not find work. Four children depended on her. The WPA had rejected her work application because she had a three-month-old baby to care for. The entire family lived in one damp basement room. Wrote Lohrback:

M rs. Roosevelt, I'm begging you with all my heart to please help me if you can. I love my babies dearly and won't sub-

mit to them being put in a home away from me. I would simply die apart from them.

This letter was typical of thousands both Eleanor and Franklin Roosevelt received daily in the late Depression era. As the letter indicates, personal suffering continued in the late 1930s, and people still despaired. But as the above letter also suggests, in their desperation people were now looking to their government for support. Indeed, government programs did mean the difference between survival and starvation for millions of Americans.

Shortly after Mrs. Lohrback wrote her letter, the event that would ultimately bring a lasting recovery to the United States was set in motion on the battlefields of Europe. Several years would pass before that recovery would reach the United States. When it did arrive, it came in the form of another tremendous test of the character of the United States: world war.

Government support for the arts led to many lasting works, including this mural painted by Thomas Hart Benton in 1930 for the New School of Social Research in New York City. Audrey McMahon, New York director of the WPA, said: "We did the best we could, and that best was very good."

SECTION 3 REVIEW

Key Terms, People, and Places
1. Define (a) national debt, (b) Congress of Industrial Organizations, (c) sit-down strike.

Key Concepts
2. What effect did the New Deal have on the American economy?
3. What factors contributed to the economic collapse of 1937?

4. In what sense did labor unions triumph in the thirties?
5. What was the impact of the New Deal on American cultural life?

Critical Thinking
6. **Identifying Central Issues** In your opinion, was the New Deal a success or a failure? Explain, citing information from the chapter.

 Quiz found in the Unit 4 folder, p. 89, covers the main ideas in this section as well as the key terms.

 Chapter Test Forms A and B are found in the Unit 4 folder, pp. 104–109.

 Answer Keys found in the Unit 4 folder, pp. 116–125, provide answers to all student activities.

Media and Technology
Transparency
Graphic Organizer, G-3

Guided Reading Audiotapes
(English and Spanish)

Computer Test Bank

Reteach

Ask students to identify and correct the errors in the sentences below:
- The New Deal brought an end to the Depression by the late 1930s.
- In spite of government support, unions failed to grow in the 1930s because of a lack of strong leadership.
- The New Deal helped Depression victims, but otherwise it had little impact on the nation.

4. CLOSE

Reinforcing the Big Idea

The New Deal failed to bring an end to the Depression. Yet it helped bring about many important developments, whose impact can still be felt.

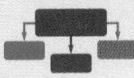 **In Depth**

Historical Misconceptions

It would be a mistake to assume that public confidence in FDR was unqualified. Many Americans considered FDR a power-hungry dictator who set a dangerous precedent by serving four terms, thus violating the unwritten rule against more than two terms. In 1947 the Eightieth Congress, which according to historian Daniel Boorstin "was really attacking the New Deal and the four-term President, FDR," passed the Twenty-second Amendment to limit any President to two terms in office.

Chapter Review

Key Terms
1. New Deal
2. hundred days
3. public works program
4. Wagner Act
5. Social Security Act
6. political right
7. political left
8. demagogue
9. national debt
10. Congress of Industrial Organizations
11. sit-down strike

People
12. Frances Perkins
13. Mary McLeod Bethune
14. Father Charles E. Coughlin
15. Huey Long

Terms For each term above, write a sentence that explains its relation to the New Deal or the legacies of the New Deal.

True or False Determine whether each statement is true or false. If it is true, write "true." If it is false, change the underlined term to make the statement true.
1. People on the <u>political right</u> accused Roosevelt's social programs of not going far enough in addressing the nation's problems.
2. The first <u>Congress of Industrial Organizations</u> employed the jobless to build or improve roads, parks, airports, and other public facilities.
3. Some critics of Roosevelt's programs were <u>demagogues</u> who manipulated people's emotions.
4. The <u>Social Security Act</u> legalized closed shops and collective bargaining.
5. President Roosevelt's <u>New Deal</u> programs provided jobs and improved the quality of life for some Americans.

Matching Review the key people in the list above. If you are not sure of a person's importance, review his or her significance in the chapter. Then choose a person from the list who best matches each description below.
1. a southern Democrat, known as the Kingfish, who called for the redistribution of wealth
2. the first woman to hold a cabinet post
3. the person who held the highest position of any African American woman in the New Deal
4. the radio broadcaster who first supported and then opposed the New Deal

Section 1 (pp. 472 – 478)
1. What characteristics of FDR's personality helped inspire hope in the American people?
2. Briefly describe the New Deal's public works programs and their purpose.
3. Explain how the Second New Deal differed from the original New Deal.

Section 2 (pp. 479 – 483)
4. For which groups in particular was the New Deal of limited success?
5. What was the basis of the political right's opposition to the New Deal?

6. Why did FDR want to pack the Supreme Court? Describe the consequences of his plan, citing details to support your statements.

Section 3 (pp. 485 – 489)
7. What did the Recession of 1937 indicate about the success of the New Deal?
8. What was the impact of the New Deal on the public's expectations of the presidency?
9. What permanent changes occurred for labor unions as a result of the New Deal?
10. Briefly describe the cultural impact of the New Deal, citing examples to support your description.

Thinking Critically

1. **Recognizing Ideology** What does the endurance and success of the Social Security Act suggest about the current attitudes of Americans toward government's role in their lives?
2. **Demonstrating Reasoned Judgment** You have read that voters were willing to follow the "bold, consistent experimentation" of the New Deal. What does this willingness suggest about the mood of the country when FDR was elected? Do you think that people would vote for bold experimentation today?
3. **Making Comparisons** Describe how Eleanor Roosevelt perceived her role as First Lady. How have the roles of more recent first ladies been similar to or different from that of Eleanor Roosevelt?

Making Connections

1. **Evaluating Primary Sources** Review the second primary source excerpt on page 483. Explain how the balance of power among the branches of government would be affected if Congress made the Supreme Court subject to the presidency.
2. **Understanding the Visuals** Skim through the chapter and find photographs, artwork, or other illustrations that both support and oppose the New Deal. Explain how each visual conveys its message of approval or disapproval.
3. **Writing About the Chapter** The New Deal tried to solve the nation's economic and social problems during the Depression. Write a proposal for a New Deal kind of program that would help end a social or economic problem today. First, choose a contemporary issue that you would like to see addressed. Then, jot down ideas for a government program that could help solve the problem. Include your ideas about how the program is to be financed. Next, write a draft of your proposal in which you explain your ideas. Revise your proposal, making certain that your solution is clearly explained, with as many details as possible about its implementation. Proofread your proposal and draft a final copy.
4. **Using the Graphic Organizer** This graphic organizer uses a tree map to organize main ideas and supporting details about the effects of the New Deal. (a) What were three main sources of entertainment during the 1930s, and what role did the government play in funding the arts? (b) If you were to travel throughout the United States today, what evidence of New Deal programs listed on the graphic organizer might you encounter? (c) On a separate sheet of paper, create your own tree map about the New Deal's critics, using this graphic organizer as an example.

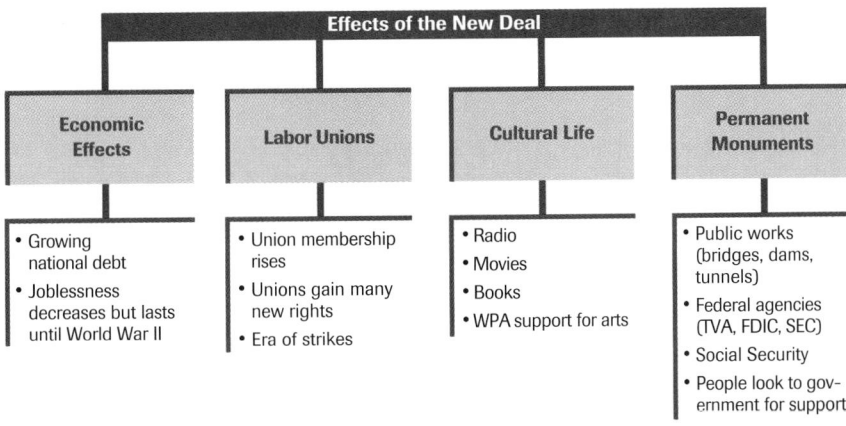

Effects of the New Deal

Economic Effects	Labor Unions	Cultural Life	Permanent Monuments
• Growing national debt • Joblessness decreases but lasts until World War II	• Union membership rises • Unions gain many new rights • Era of strikes	• Radio • Movies • Books • WPA support for arts	• Public works (bridges, dams, tunnels) • Federal agencies (TVA, FDIC, SEC) • Social Security • People look to government for support

Making Connections

1. There would no longer be a true balance of power, because the three branches of government would not be separate. The executive branch (the President) could simply alter the judicial branch if the courts did not support the President's program. There would be no judicial check on the executive's power.

2. Visuals that support the New Deal appear on the following pages: 470 (needle book and sheet music), 472, and 478. Visuals that disapprove of the New Deal appear on these pages: 470 (button), 479, and 481.

3. Students' proposals may deal with such challenges as homelessness, street violence, or environmental degradation. Government programs might, for example, provide housing, offer incentives for continuing education, or provide jobs in environmental protection. Programs could be financed by higher taxes, a special assessment to finance a particular program, cutbacks elsewhere, or by allowing a greater federal deficit.

4. (a) Sources of entertainment included radio, movies, and literature; many arts activities were supported with WPA funds. (b) You might encounter bridges, dams, and tunnels, as well as evidence of CCC restoration and conservation projects. (c) Students' graphic organizers should include information about the limits of the New Deal and the criticisms of women and minorities.

Connecting Literature and History

People in the United States had strong feelings about their President during the Depression. Franklin Roosevelt was the type of person whom people either loved or hated. People felt the same way about Roosevelt's New Deal programs. They loved them or they hated them. Explain to students that this controversy over the New Deal was part of its legacy; debates continued for years about whether the programs were good or bad for the nation, and whether Roosevelt acted too much like a dictator or whether he was the best President the nation ever had, one who was not afraid to take drastic action in a time that called for drastic changes.

Read students the following quotation in which an employee at the Emergency Relief Office in Michigan describes a typical day: "The little Golinski boy is worse. Pneumonia. . . . Yes, certainly we'll O.K. the drugstore order. . . . Ten more men for the highway project near Housetown. That's good news. Better have Elsie look over the list. That's her territory. Tell her not to forget that poor Collins chap. His wife is sick and his cow died and he's in an awful state of mind. . . . Yes, what did you want to see me about? Oh, you haven't been here before. Your landlord is going to evict you. Well, you leave your name

One Boy Remembers the New Deal

 *Literature*

Robert J. Hastings

INTRODUCTION After his mother's death, Robert Hastings found a collection of old newspaper clippings, letters, and photographs among her belongings. As he sifted through them, memories of the Great Depression began to come back to him so strongly that he decided to write them down. The result was *A Nickel's Worth of Skim Milk*, a book that describes, from the everyday viewpoint of a grade-school boy, the struggle and grind of those Depression days. After his book was published in 1972, people wrote him to say, "You were writing about my family, as much as your own. That's how I remember the 1930s, too." This excerpt tells how President Roosevelt's WPA was received by the people in Hastings's life.

VOCABULARY Before you read the selection, find the meaning of these words in a dictionary: intermittent, indelible.

President Franklin D. Roosevelt's "New Deal" used all twenty-six letters of the alphabet to identify the various government programs aimed at the economic crisis. There were, to name a few, the FERA, CCC, PWA, AAA, NRA ("We do our part"), NYA, and WPA.

Millions of dollars poured into direct welfare, surplus food, and government work projects, known first as the PWA (Public Works Administration) and later as the WPA (Works Progress Administration).

Eventually, eight million men worked on WPA projects during the Depression. In some areas the money was spent on public buildings, schools, bridges, and airports. Around Marion[1] most people felt it was wasted on "make-work" projects, so WPA was nicknamed "We Piddle Around." As I remember, it was road work for the most part—clearing right-of-way and opening up ditches—and a long-handled shovel was the standard tool.

To its credit, the WPA did construct 150,000 toilets. The design was so distinctive that "WPA toilet" still describes the conventional outdoor sanitary privy.

Like thousands of miners and other unemployed men in Southern Illinois, Dad applied for a WPA job. But he didn't like anything about it. He resented every day. He felt that the questionnaires were humiliating and that those who conducted the interviews were rude. When there was no WPA job, and he had to apply for welfare, he felt the same embarrassment. Whether this was his pride, or whether those lucky enough to get political jobs administering the government programs acted uppity, I don't know. Maybe a bit of both.

---

[1] Marion, Illinois, the town with a population of nine thousand in which the author grew up.

The National Recovery Administration adopted this label and the slogan "We Do Our Part."

This mural was painted by Thomas Hart Benton in 1930 for the New School of Social Research in New York City. Audrey McMahon, New York director of the WPA, said: "We did the best we could, and that best was very good."

WPA was intermittent—a few days' work and then a layoff when funds gave out. Top monthly pay was $44, but Dad seldom drew the full amount because of frequent layoffs or bad weather, especially in the winter. When a man was laid off, he was given Form 403, so the most feared news was, "Bill got his 403 today," or, "Henry says they're going to give all of us our 403's on Friday." It was almost like a death sentence.

WPA workers in and around Marion, with their long-handled shovels moving dirt that didn't necessarily need moving, dressed in long overcoats and with mufflers wrapped around their faces and necks—this is one of the indelible images of the Depression. To keep warm in the cold, muddy weather, Dad wore two or three pairs of socks and lined the thin bottoms of his shoes with newspaper or cardboard.

Dad was working on WPA in 1936 when my brother LaVerne died. When he went back to work, the men said, "Eldon, if you'd let us know, we'd have given our time and dug the grave." When he told Mom, she said, "I don't want no WPA shovel stuck in my boy's grave."

This was said, not out of ingratitude, but out of a deep pride that believed a mother and father should at least be able to bury their own son.

Welfare, or "relief," as it was known, was also intermittent. Occasionally we might get a "relief order" for groceries or an "order for coal"—these could be redeemed at the store or the mine but not converted into cash.

Then there was the surplus food—canned stew meat, powdered milk, and grapefruit. The powdered milk, unlike that of today, was hopeless. It wouldn't dissolve, but instead formed big lumps. Its taste and odor were beyond description. Mom did manage to use some of it in cooking, but most of it went to the chickens.

I had never tasted grapefruit until Dad brought home a sack from the relief office. I don't even remember having seen any in the stores. Everyone thought they were unbearably bitter and sour. Neighbors gave them to us by the peck, saying they were "not fit for a hog to eat." Mom solved the problem by slicing them in half the night before and sprinkling them with sugar, which filtered down into the fruit during the night, and then serving them for breakfast. We didn't throw any away.

We resented the welfare and the WPA, and especially the attitudes of those in Williamson County who administered the programs. At a time when we needed help most, we were made to feel undeserving, lazy, and shiftless. We knew better, but our pride hurt just the same.

THINKING ABOUT THE SELECTION

1. How does Hastings characterize the work that was done for the WPA?
2. Why did Hastings's father not like the WPA?

Critical Thinking

3. **Distinguishing Fact from Opinion** What facts does Hastings offer about the WPA? What opinions does he offer?

eyes are very bad. Yes, indeed, we'll be very glad to. Margaret, please make out an order for an office call to the oculist for this little boy. . . . Yes, what is it? Everybody gets work but you! Why, we mailed you a work card yesterday. You're to report on the city sidewalk project next Monday. Yes, absolutely sure. You'd better go home and watch for the postman." (Adapted from Louise V. Armstrong, *We Too Are the People*, Boston: Little, Brown, and Co., 1938.)

After reading the excerpt, discuss with students how the picture of federal relief painted by this employee is similar to or different from those painted by Robert Hastings and Gordon Parks. Students should see that this worker seems very busy and quite genuinely concerned about the people she is supposed to be helping. They should also note, however, that the description of one federal employee does not provide sufficient information to either dispute or support Hastings's or Parks's viewpoint.

Finally, ask students to comment on the power that a federal employee such as this held over many people's lives. Do students recognize the potential for abuse of that power? Tell students that there were many different experiences of FDR's New Deal programs, both positive and negative. All were valid experiences and historians have reviewed many accounts such as those given here in order to determine the overall effectiveness of Roosevelt's New Deal.

ANSWERS TO

Thinking About the Selection

1. He characterizes the work as "make-work"; in other words, the workers were given things to do that didn't really need to be done, just to keep them working.
2. Hastings's father was humiliated by the need to get government help and by the questionnaires and interviews that he had to endure in order to receive the help.
3. *Facts:* "Millions of dollars" went into New Deal programs; "eight million men worked on WPA projects during the Depression"; "in some areas the money was spent on public buildings, schools, bridges, and airports"; "Top monthly pay was $44"; "When a man was laid off, he was given Form 403."
Opinions: "Around Marion most people felt it was wasted on 'make-work' projects"; "As I remember, it was road work for the most part"; "the questionnaires were humiliating and that those who conducted the interviews were rude"; "At a time when we needed help most, we were made to feel undeserving, lazy, and shiftless."

Have student prepare skits in which
citizens come before President
Roosevelt one by one and present
their thoughts and opinions on one
of the New Deal programs. President
Roosevelt should react to each visitor
as the student playing him sees fit;
for example, he might argue with the
visitor and support his program, he
might ask for advice, or he might
suggest other avenues for the visitor
to look to for help. Students should
be broken into groups of five or six
and should decide within each group
who will play the President and who
will play the visitors. Students should
write out scripts before they actually
perform their skits. To gather information, they might consult biographies of President Roosevelt or
videotapes such as *The American
Parade: FDR, the Man Who Changed
America* (Phoenix/BFA Educational
Films). Sources on the New Deal
programs include *The New Deal* by
Paul Conkin and *Fifty Years Later:
The New Deal Evaluated* edited by
Howard Sitkoff.

As an alternative assignment, have
students interview teachers, parents,
or other adults in the community
about a current government program. Students can either ask about a
specific program or let the person
they are interviewing comment on
the program of their choice. Students
should ask such questions as: Do you
agree or disagree with this program?
How has this program affected your
life or the lives of others you know?
What would you like to tell the President about the program? If possible,
students should tape record the
interviews and play them back for
the class. Otherwise, they can write
up a transcript of the conversation
and read it aloud.

SOURCE READINGS

Working for the CCC

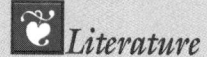 Literature

Gordon Parks

INTRODUCTION Gordon Parks was seventeen years old when the stock market crashed. During the Depression and years of recovery, he constantly searched for work and for a way to succeed. He held jobs from janitor to musi-cian to photographer, teaching himself how to take pic-tures with a secondhand camera. Since those days, Parks has become an accomplished photographer for *Life* maga-zine, a writer, composer, artist, and filmmaker. He has written about his life in his autobiography *Voices in the Mirror*. The excerpt below discusses Parks's days in the CCC, one of President Roosevelt's "alphabet soup" pro-grams for recovery.

VOCABULARY Before you read the selection, find the meaning of this word in a dictionary: impoverished, mali-ciously, cajole, wiles, dubious.

I was on the hustle again—trying for work at restau-rants, grocery stores, theaters, barbershops, pool halls, garages, amusement galleries, dance halls and even churches. I asked for a porter's job at a police sta-tion near Times Square. But it was always, "Sorry." As they said in Harlem, "Nothin' was shakin'." For that matter the same went for a lot of young men across the land. Joblessness and hunger were the words.

Thankfully, President Roosevelt did something about it. In March of that year, 1933, he reached out to the country's impoverished youth through the Civilian Conservation Corps, hoping to take them off the streets and bread lines. Two hundred and fifty thousand young men between the ages of eighteen and twenty-five were to be put to work at reforesta-tion, road construction and the prevention of soil erosion. The pay would be thirty dollars a month—approximately one dollar for a day's work. That was thirty dollars a month more than I could count on; furthermore, I was in debt to Mrs. Haskins for two months' back rent. After seeing the government notices posted at the Harlem YMCA, I pawned my white tailored suit, paid Mrs. Haskins off and, with several hundred others from Harlem, joined the CCC. Two mornings later we were transported by bus to Fort Dix, New Jersey. . . .

It was raining when we reached Camp Dix; acres of mud and rain-soaked tents stretched out before us. After we left the bus we were ushered into a line.

Michigan[1] then stepped forward, and with arrogant authority, scowled at us as though we were poisonous snakes. Behind him were six others struck in com-manding poses, and dressed in army surplus. We stood raggedly at attention.

"I'm Michigan Jones, your section leader! Behind me is Tate, my subsection foreman. Behind him are Marcus, Fats, Studs, Rufus and Barker! They are my assistants! I give the orders and they carry them out! Understand that?" In the quiet the sound of rain striking mud grew sharper. . . .

A friend I made during those first sullen days in Harlem had accompanied me into this ruthlessness. Bill Hunter was charming, bright, good-natured and an honor graduate of Columbia University—but like me he was down on his luck. He had majored in psy-chology, but that had very little to do with the job he was working when I met him. He was selling skinny hot dogs on Lenox Avenue. And it was doubtful that his honors would be of much use in this gloomy place where we had just arrived. En route we had made friends with a likable young man named Hubert Carter. Michigan Jones's greeting had left the three of us wanting to be someplace else. . . .

[Parks describes an evening in which he and Hunter entertain a large group of recruits in their tent. Michigan sees this as a threat to his power and demands that the two report for latrine duty the next morning. Instead, Parks and Hunter reported to the captain's tent.]

The captain looked up from his papers as we entered and saluted. "What can I do for you fellows?"

Bill's accented answer was straight from Oxford.

---

[1] Michigan was the name of one of the recruits who bullied the others into gambling their CCC checks away.

"Sir, we have been maliciously assigned to a duty we feel we don't deserve."

"And which duty is that?"

"The latrine, sir."

"Yessir—the latrine," I repeated.

"Well—who ordered you, and why?"

"Mr. Jones, sir. He seemed particularly annoyed because we took it upon ourselves to entertain some recruits in our tent last evening—some who, I might add, were in very low spirits."

"And your names?"

"I'm William C. Hunter, sir, and this is Gordon Parks."

"Low in spirits. Do you find that to be the general feeling around camp?"

"Forgive my frankness, sir, but I must say yes it is."

The captain's fingers were drumming his desk. "What's your background, Hunter—your schooling, I mean?"

"Columbia, sir. Psychology major."

"I see. Good school Columbia. I'm Princeton."

"A *very* good school also I must say."

The captain lit his cigar, puffed and blew out smoke. "Forget the latrine. I will have a word with Jones."

"We are quite thankful, sir."

"Good day."

"Good day, sir." The captain had been conned. A bit of intelligence had jarred his presence, and as far as I could see, Michigan's reign was nearing its end. It came two weeks later—when Bill was promoted to section leader, and I to subsection foreman. That meant fifteen dollars a month more to him and ten dollars more to me. It also meant that revenge would be staring at both of us every day. Without doubt, our company, the 235th, was the only one throughout the nation with two sets of leaders. That seemed to be the captain's only way out of his dilemma. But Bill

Many victims of the Depression found work and relief through such government programs as the Civilian Conservation Corps—the CCC. The worker above is planting seedlings in Montana.

Hunter was definitely in charge.

Eventually Michigan and his pack seemed to swallow their setback, while going on doing what they had come to do. They kept up the fleecings, but there was a big drop in the numbers of those who allowed themselves to be fleeced. And Bill, having the heart of a whale, furrowed on into the ranks of our enemies, cajoling them with his wiles. He even conned Michigan Jones into a dubious friendship. "Michigan," he said one morning, "I've organized a track meet this weekend, and it would sure please me if you would consent to handing out the prizes." Grudgingly, the ex-section leader gave his consent. . . .

Over two million men finally joined the corps—planting trees, building fish ponds, feeding wildlife and clearing areas for beaches and campsites; in all, forty-seven lost their lives fighting forest fires. We were earning our keep, but our time would be up in October. Depression still choked the country, and employment offices, park benches and hobo villages would be filled again. There was no more to return to now than what we had left a year before. But on the eighteenth of August, Bill posted a captain's bulletin that lifted everyone's spirits. President Roosevelt had extended the CCC camps for another six months.

THINKING ABOUT THE SELECTION

1. Why did Parks decide to join the Civilian Conservation Corps?
2. What kind of work did young men do in the CCC?

Critical Thinking

3. **Making Comparisons** Compare the experiences described by Gordon Parks and Robert Hastings. Are their viewpoints on the New Deal programs similar or different? Explain your answer.

Introducing the Unit

Interpreting the Visual In contrast to today, when television brings wars and battlefronts instantly into American living rooms, in World War II only press photographers, newspaper reporters, and radio journalists reported to the folks back home. Dwight Eisenhower, the supreme Allied commander, describes the natural conflict between the press and the military in his book *Crusade in Europe*: "Complete wartime . . . co-operation can never be achieved between the press and military authorities. For the commander, secrecy is a defensive weapon; to the press it is anathema."

Ask students to study the picture on pages 496–497. What can they learn from the picture and the caption alone about the course of the war at that moment? For example, how closely can they identify the region where the picture was taken?

Ask students to imagine being one of the soldiers in the picture and to write a letter home describing conditions during the last few months of the war.

Establishing Chronology Remind students that the previous chapter focused on the New Deal and the ending of the Great Depression. This unit focuses on World War II and the cold war years that followed. The war began in Europe in 1939, but the United States did not declare war until the Japanese bombed Pearl Harbor in December 1941. After the war ended in 1945 came fifteen "hot" cold war years, during which a nuclear war seemed all too possible.

Hot and Cold War
1939–1960

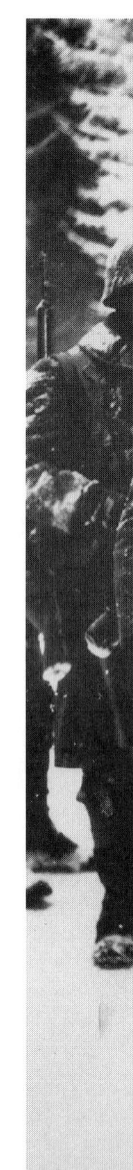

"We have to face the fact that either all of us are going to die together or we are going to learn to live together, and if we are to live together we have to talk."

—Eleanor Roosevelt, 1960

*M*any *Americans were determined to stay out of another European conflict, but Japan's attack on Pearl Harbor finally shattered their resolve and American isolationism ended forever. After the war, the nation barely had time to enjoy its hard-won peace before a "cold war" developed between the United States and the Soviet Union. That conflict and the threat of nuclear destruction cast a long shadow across the postwar era.*

 RESOURCE DIRECTORY

Teaching Resources

Local History Activity "Seattle at War" and the Local Focus research topic suggestions, found in the Local History Resources folder, pp. 24–26, are designed to help students understand how history affects all lives.

★ **Themes in American History Posters**
Wall-size, illustrated posters, found in the Teaching Resources package, illustrate the four unit themes.

Unit Test Forms A and B are found in the Unit 5 folder, pp. 140–145.

Weary American infantrymen line up in the cold for a meal. Despite the fatigue of the soldiers and the world, World War II would rage in Europe for another four months after this January 1945 photograph was taken.

Themes in American History

Teachers may wish to discuss specific historical events in the context of historical themes. Here are four suggestions for Unit 5.

Technology *Americans' ability to develop new skills and tools and to increase their knowledge of the physical world has greatly affected the way they live and work, and has led to a high standard of living.*

- The Manhattan Project to build the atomic bomb was the largest scientific project ever undertaken.
- American factories made a dramatic conversion to the production of war goods during World War II.

American Democracy *The concepts of democratic representation, equality under the law, and freedom from discrimination have been gradually broadened to include previously excluded groups.*

- Events on the home front stimulated a movement for equal rights for African Americans.
- The United States, believing that Japanese Americans posed a military threat on the West Coast, forcibly removed them to internment camps.

Unity and Conflict *Americans have developed unique political systems and laws that affirm a shared commitment to certain goals, such as individual rights and equality. Nevertheless, groups with differing views on how to achieve these goals have often clashed.*

- After more than a decade of economic depression, America's mood during the war turned to cooperation, unity, and resolve.
- Fear of communist subversives after the war led to attacks on the patriotism of many Americans.

The United States and the World *America's relationships with other countries have been influenced at different times by a sense of mission, by values, and by self-interest.*

- The Japanese attack on Pearl Harbor finally brought the United States into World War II.
- Relations between the United States and the Soviet Union broke down after the war, leading to a prolonged cold war.

Media and Technology

Visions of America: Scenes of an Era To introduce students to the main idea and events covered in this unit, play "Scenes of an Era: Hot and Cold War, 1939–1960 " (length: 2.5 minutes). This selection can be located on side 3 of the videodiscs. This selection can also be located on videotape 4. Lesson plans for "Scenes of an Era" can be found in the Visions of America Teacher's Guidebook.

Using Multimedia Technology This folder contains instructional tools and strategies for using technology in the classroom.

Transparency Binder Contains full-color transparencies with lesson suggestions. From a large collection divided into twelve categories, specific transparencies are referenced throughout the chapters at appropriate points of use. For this unit, see American Photo, B-8; Time Lines, E-7 and E-8; Cause and Effect, F-10; The Way It Works, H-19 and H-20; Links Across Time, J-8; and Political Cartoon, K-8.

Chapter 15 World War II
1939–1945

📁 Teaching Resources (See Unit 5 Folder)

	Instruction	Enrichment
Section 1 **Prelude to War** (pp. 500–505)	Reproducible Lesson Plan, p. 3 Alternate Lesson Plan, p. 122 Guided Reading and Review, p. 7 Quiz, p. 8	Visual Learning Activity, Books Are Weapons, p. 29
Section 2 **The Military Struggle** (pp. 506–512)	Reproducible Lesson Plan, p. 4 Alternate Lesson Plan, p. 123 Guided Reading and Review, p. 9 Quiz, p. 10	Visual Learning Activity, The North African Front, p. 30 Primary Source Activity, Guadalcanal, p. 23 American Profiles Activity, Navaho Code Talkers, p. 18 Literature Activity, Dispatches from the Battle Front, pp. 26–27
Section 3 **Americans on the Battle Fronts** (pp. 513–516)	Reproducible Lesson Plan, p. 5 Alternate Lesson Plan, p. 124 Guided Reading and Review, p. 11 Quiz, p. 12	American Profiles Activity, Jacqueline Cochran, p. 17 Critical Thinking Activity, Predicting Consequences, p. 22 Primary Source Activity, Experiences of an African American Soldier, pp. 24–25 Viewpoints Activity, On the Integration of the Military, pp. 19–20 Historian's Toolbox Activity, Examining Photographs, p. 21
Section 4 **Dropping the Atomic Bomb:** **A Turning Point in History** (pp. 518–521)	Reproducible Lesson Plan, p. 6 Alternate Lesson Plan, p. 125 Guided Reading and Review, p. 13 Quiz, p. 14 Chapter Test, Forms A & B, pp. 31–36	Literature Activity, Hiroshima, p. 28 Turning Point Extension Activity, The Lasting Impact of the Atomic Bomb, pp. 15–16

📁 Additional Chapter Resources

Resource Organizer, p. 2
Alternate Lesson Plan, p. 121
Answer Keys, pp. 146–160

Bibliography

For the Teacher
Roeder, George. *The Censored War: American Visual Experience During World War II.* Yale University Press, 1993.
(A collection of wartime photographs, many used for propaganda, and many from the National Archives.)

Prentice Hall Literature Excerpts from *The American Experience,* 1994, including "The Modern Age, 1915–1916."

The Big Idea for the chapter and how the main ideas in each section relate to the Big Idea are graphically displayed below. Comprehension of this chapter's Big Idea is critical to students' understanding of United States history and how we as a nation got where we are today.

Media and Technology

 Time Lines, E-7

 The Way It Works, H-19

 Critical Thinking, I-2

 Visions of America: Turning Point Story, "Atomic Cloud," (length: approx. 4 minutes)

 Visions of America: Roundtable Discussion on "Atomic Cloud"

 Graphic Organizer, G-5

 Guided Reading Audiotapes (English and Spanish)

 Computer Test Bank

For the Student
Hersey, John. *Into the Valley: A Skirmish of the Marines.* Knopf, 1942. (Eyewitness account of the battle for Guadalcanal.)
Selden, Kyoko and Mark Selden, eds. *The Atomic Bomb: Voices from Hiroshima and Nagasaki.* Sharpe, 1989.

CHAPTER 15

"The peace, freedom, and security of 90 percent of the population of the world is being jeopardized by the remaining 10 percent..." is the way President Roosevelt viewed the war raging in Europe. But many Americans did not want to intervene. After Pearl Harbor and the American entry into World War II, there was no question about the role of the United States in world affairs.

SECTION 1
After World War I, the aggression of the fascist allies—Italy, Germany, and Japan—led to conflict around the world, and eventually caused a second world war. After attempting to remain neutral, the United States entered the war when Japan bombed Pearl Harbor in Hawaii.

SECTION 2
World War II was a global war, fought on fronts in Europe, North Africa, and the Pacific. Success for the Allies required tremendous organization of people and resources.

SECTION 3
The 12 million Americans who fought in World War II endured terrible hardships. Women, African Americans, and members of other minority groups in the armed services helped to win the war, although discrimination reduced their effectiveness.

SECTION 4
In an attempt to hasten the end of the war, the United States dropped a devastating new weapon, the atomic bomb, on two Japanese cities in August 1945. Japan surrendered on August 14, 1945.

498B

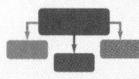
The Relevance of the Big Idea

As the war clouds massed over Europe and Asia, Americans debated their nation's role in the growing conflict. President Roosevelt helped the Allies in many ways short of engaging in combat until the bombing of Pearl Harbor propelled the nation into war.

Tell students that in the decade of the 1990s, the United States must balance requests and demands for military help in conflicts throughout the world—in such diverse places as Haiti, Somalia, and the former Yugoslavia—with its own political and economic needs.

In Depth

Global Connections

Between 1936 and 1939, Spain was consumed by civil war. Italian and German leaders aided Spanish General Francisco Franco's Nationalists in their effort to install a fascist state. Soviet leaders sent weapons and advisers to Spain's Republican government. Britain, France, and the United States did not officially take sides, but fear of fascism ran high, and many people from these countries volunteered to fight with "international brigades" on the Republican side. In December 1936 the first of 3,300 American volunteers sailed for Spain; sixteen hundred died. The Spanish Civil War was a battleground for European conflicts of the 1930s, and is often described as a prelude to World War II.

World War II
1939–1945

*I*n the 1930s a frightening series of events overseas showed that the world war Americans had fought from 1917 to 1918 had not succeeded in making the world "safe for democracy." As ruthless dictators devoured whole nations in Europe, northern Africa, and Asia, many Americans fervently hoped that the United States could remain uninvolved. This proved impossible, and in December 1941 the nation fully committed its material and human resources to a second global conflict that would end United States isolationism forever.

Events in the United States

1935 To keep the United States out of war in Europe, Congress passes Neutrality Acts.

1938 Severe recession hits the United States economy.

1935	1936	1937	1938	1939

Events in the World

1936 Spanish Civil War begins.

1939 German invasion of Poland sets off World War II.

RESOURCE DIRECTORY

Teaching Resources

Alternate Lesson Plan: Demonstrating the Big Idea found in the Alternate Lesson Plans folder, p. 121, provides a lesson strategy designed to instruct students in the Big Idea that the United States' involvement in World War II changed the country's status from an isolated nation to a world power.

Alternative Assessment Handbook provides information, guidance, and strategies for alternative methods of assessment. It includes an essay on new trends in assessment, guidance and strategies for developing performance tasks and portfolios, scoring rubrics, and sample evaluation forms.

Pages 500 – 505
Prelude to War
World War I had left deep scars in Europe. Wounded national pride and devastated economies laid the foundation for the rise of fascist dictators and a second global conflict.

 Pages 506 – 512
The Military Struggle
By December 1941, only an exhausted Britain stood between the Nazis and their dream of dominating the European continent. The United States finally cast its lot with the British—but was it already too late?

 Pages 513–516
Americans on the Battle Fronts
The grim reality of combat far from home was tough on all soldiers. Discrimination in the armed forces made the experience even more painful for many Americans.

 Pages 518–521
Dropping the Atomic Bomb:
A Turning Point in History
A collaboration of the top scientists in the world put a devastating secret weapon in American hands. Desperate to end the war as quickly as possible, the United States decided to unleash the terrible force of the atomic bomb on two unsuspecting Japanese cities.

Pages 522–523
The Lasting Impact of the Atomic Bomb

1940	1941	1942	1943	1944	1945
	1941 The United States enters World War II after Japanese attack on Pearl Harbor.	**1942** Japanese Americans are relocated to internment camps.	**1943** Nearly 400,000 coal miners go on strike. • Race riots break out in Detroit.	**1944** Roosevelt wins unprecedented fourth term as President.	**1945** President Roosevelt dies. • Harry S Truman becomes President.
1940 Germany, Italy, and Japan sign the Tripartite Pact.	**1941** Germany invades the Soviet Union.		**1943** The Allies invade Italy.	**1944** The Allies invade France at Normandy on D-Day.	**1945** Germany surrenders. • Japan surrenders after United States drops atomic bombs.

Alternative Assessment
As an ongoing project, students can work in groups to create an album of World War II in which they chronicle the steps leading up to the war, the major battles of the war, and the key events that brought the war to an end. In addition to the information provided in the textbook, outside resources such as texts, newspapers, and periodicals can be used. Students may also want to include pieces of oral history obtained through personal interviews. The World War II albums can be presented in written or oral form. Students are encouraged to include photographs, posters, political cartoons, or other visual pieces, as well as bibliographies.

Explain that projects will be assessed according to the following standards:

● **Unacceptable** Projects are not attempted or fail to meet requirements outlined.

● **Limited/Acceptable** Projects are based primarily on material from the textbook and present a view of the war in a limited way.

●**Extensive/Commendable** Projects are based on outside resources as well as material from the textbook and present an in-depth picture of the period.

●**Extraordinary/Outstanding** Projects are based on considerable outside research, include aspects of oral history, and present a detailed picture of events leading up to, during, and concluding the war.

For information and guidance on alternative assessment trends and strategies, see the Alternative Assessment Handbook in the Resource Directory on page 498.

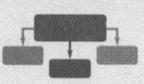

SECTION 1

Prelude to War

1. FOCUS

Connecting to the Big Idea

See page 498B. Fascist dictators seized control in several nations scarred by World War I, while military leaders in Japan insisted on a policy of expansion. Ask students how the United States responded to the growing worldwide conflict and what finally propelled the United States into the war.

Objectives

- Identify the aggressive nations of Europe and Asia and their leaders.
- Explain how the United States struggled to remain neutral while supporting the Allies with economic aid.
- Identify Japan's attack on Pearl Harbor as the aggressive action that propelled the United States into war.

Bellringer

Ask students to choose a current "hot spot," or place in the world where there is armed conflict, and to describe the United States' involvement in that area, if any. Ask them to consider under what conditions the United States should intervene in a conflict within another nation or between nations.

Reading Strategy

Graphic Organizer Ask students to make a concept map of this section by drawing three large circles on a piece of paper, labeled Fascism and Nazism in Europe, Japan Builds an Empire, and The American Response to Axis Aggression. Have students add supporting information in smaller circles, and draw lines connecting them to the appropriate large circles.

SECTION PREVIEW

World War I had left deep scars in Europe. Wounded national pride and devastated economies laid the foundation for the rise of fascist dictators and a second global conflict.

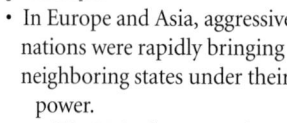

Nazis singled out Jews for persecution by forcing them to wear yellow Stars of David like this one.

Key Concepts

- In Europe and Asia, aggressive nations were rapidly bringing neighboring states under their power.
  - The United States at first struggled to stay out of the fighting abroad, while supporting the Allies with economic aid.
  - The Japanese attack on Pearl Harbor finally dragged the United States into the war.

Key Terms, People, and Places

fascism, Nazi party, anti-Semitism, appeasement, Lend-Lease Act; Benito Mussolini, Adolf Hitler, Winston Churchill; Rhineland, Manchuria, Pearl Harbor

---

Throughout the 1930s, Americans watched warily as dictators in Germany, Italy, and Japan sought to extend their power around the globe. Even so, most Americans wanted to stay out of the conflict. World War I had not made the world a better place; why, then, should they be eager to enter another foreign war? Besides, the American people had enough trouble at home, as the Depression stubbornly kept a grip on the economy. Yet as the struggle unfolded, it became clear that democracy everywhere was threatened by the dictators.

Fascism and Nazism in Europe

By the mid-1930s, Italian and German dictators had ruthlessly established their authority on the European continent. They took advantage of the humiliation felt by many Italians and Germans after World War I by promising to restore their nations to a position of glory.

Benito Mussolini was an Italian schoolteacher, journalist, and political activist who had been wounded in World War I. Along with many Italians, Mussolini felt that his country had been shortchanged in the peace settlement after the war. The few small territories Italy received from the former German and Turkish empires paled in comparison to those claimed by its fellow Allies, Britain and France. In 1919 Mussolini banded together with a group of war veterans, who also were dissatisfied, to found the revolutionary Fascist party.

The term *fascism* refers to a political philosophy that values the nation or the race above the individual. During World War II, Italy, Germany, and Japan all were ruled by fascist governments that wielded absolute power. The fascist powers each looked back in history to their nation's great and glorious past—a crucial difference between them and the communists, who looked forward to a transformation of society for a glorious new future.

Mussolini Becomes "the Leader" In 1922 Mussolini threatened a march on Rome unless his authority was recognized. King Victor Emmanuel III, who feared the disruption that could occur, asked him to become prime minister. Three years later, calling himself *Il Duce* ("the leader"), Mussolini declared a dictatorship that extended throughout the country.

Mussolini and the Fascists attempted to promote Italian power, in spite of the serious political and economic instability following World War I. Claiming that efficiency and order were necessary to make Italy as great as they felt it had been in the past, Mussolini and his party suspended elections, centralized the economy under state control, and began modernizing the armed forces. In order to supply

---

 RESOURCE DIRECTORY

Teaching Resources

Reproducible Lesson Plan found in the Unit 5 folder, p. 3, provides a summary of the Section 1 lesson plan content.

Alternate Lesson Plan: Learning Styles found in the Alternate Lesson Plans folder, p. 122, is particularly effective for auditory learners and is designed to guide students thorough a mock interview with world leaders of the World War II years.

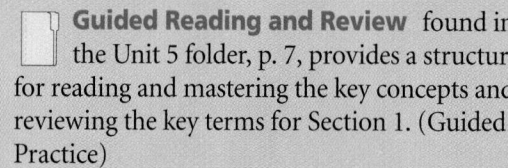 **Guided Reading and Review** found in the Unit 5 folder, p. 7, provides a structure for reading and mastering the key concepts and reviewing the key terms for Section 1. (Guided Practice)

colonies for his modern-day Roman Empire, he pursued an aggressive foreign policy. Under his direction, Italy invaded Ethiopia in 1935, and by the next year, it dominated that East African nation.

Hitler's Rise to Power At the same time, **Adolf Hitler,** a poorly educated Austrian who supported himself as a painter, rose to power in Germany. Hitler had been wounded and temporarily blinded in World War I. The war left him feeling enraged by Germany's defeat and by the degrading terms of the Treaty of Versailles.

In 1919 Hitler joined the forty-member German Workers' party. With his powerful public speaking, he soon became a leader in the growing party. In 1920 the group changed its name to the National Socialist German Workers' party, or **Nazi party**. In November 1923, by which time the party's membership had swelled to 55,000, Hitler and the Nazis attempted to seize power in the city of Munich.

Although many citizens of Munich supported Hitler, the rebellion was put down quickly. Hitler was found guilty of high treason and spent nine months in jail. During this time he began writing an autobiography titled *Mein Kampf* ("My Struggle"), in which he described his diagnosis of Germany's problems and how he planned to cure them.

Hitler and the Nazis continued their crusade throughout the 1920s and 1930s. They appealed to Germans ravaged by the Great Depression. Saddled with insurmountable war debts from World War I, Germany also faced terrible unemployment and massive inflation. Hitler promised to stabilize the country, rebuild the economy, and revive the German empire that had been shattered in the war.

As a result of such promises, Hitler won a large following. In addition, his tremendous personal magnetism swayed many to his views. One witness who observed Hitler speaking later recalled:

I cannot remember in my entire life such a change in the attitude of a crowd in a few minutes, almost a few seconds. There were certainly many who were not converted yet. But the mood of the majority

Adolf Hitler was once described as looking rather ordinary, "like a waiter in a railway station restaurant" (right). When he spoke, however, his passion and charisma electrified audiences.

abruptly changed. Hitler had turned them inside out, as one turns a glove inside out, with a few sentences. It had almost something of hocus-pocus, or magic about it.
Karl Alexander von Müller,
German historian

Hitler Becomes *Der Führer* In January 1933, the Nazi party was the largest group in the Reichstag (the German parliament), and Hitler was named chancellor. The next month he squelched his opposition in the Reichstag and suspended civil liberties. An act of parliament gave him dictatorial powers in the new government, known as the Third Reich. He was now *Der Führer* ("the leader").

Hitler appealed to a form of prejudice with a long and deep-rooted history in Western civilization: **anti-Semitism**, or the hatred of Jews. Hitler blamed Jews for Germany's problems and preached that so-called Aryans—blond, blue-eyed Germans—belonged to a dominant "master race." Anti-Semitism became a cornerstone of Hitler's program. He soon ordered the boycott of Jewish shops, the burning of books written by Jewish authors, and the imprisonment of Jews in concentration camps.

2. INSTRUCT

Explain/Discuss

Recall with students that the worldwide effects of the Great Depression were widespread and pervasive. Economic instability, inflation, and unemployment raged. Point out that the climate was ripe for the rise of dictators. Explain that dictators such as Mussolini and Hitler promised to restore economic strength.

Examine the similarities and differences between the two dominant dictatorships of this period: Communist Russia and Nazi Germany. Explore Hitler and the Nazi party's rise to power. Ask how and why the Jews became Hitler's scapegoat.

Analyze

Point out that it is believed that the United States became involved in World War II to support our allies against Nazi and fascist aggression and to respond to Japanese aggression in the Pacific.

 In Depth

Biography

Jesse Owens (1913–1980), the tenth child of African American sharecroppers in the South, gave an outstanding performance at the 1936 Olympic Games in Berlin, Germany. The Nazi dictator, Adolf Hitler, expected the Games to showcase German athletes' superiority since he believed that they were destined to rule "non-Aryan" or "inferior peoples." Before the eyes of the world, Owens proved Hitler wrong by winning four gold medals in track and field events. After the Games, Owens said, "I learned that the false leaders and sick movements of this earth must be stopped in the beginning, for they turn humanity against itself."

Historians have offered two other explanations: Roosevelt saw the war as a way to end the economic depression in the United States, and he knew that involvement in the war would guarantee the United States a key role in the postwar peace process. Have students discuss and explain how they might substantiate or refute such historical interpretation.

Activity

Cooperative Learning

Time: One class period.
Activity: Conduct a short, simulated debate between American interventionists and isolationists in 1939.
Grouping: Groups of four students.
Purpose: Ask the members of each group to review the section and to develop arguments for isolationism and for intervention in the European and Asian conflicts.
Roles: Two students in each group can act as research staff members for two student debaters.
Outcome: Students will understand the issues faced by America's leaders as they assessed their role in the global conflict.

Enrichment

Historian Geoffrey Perrett begins his book *Days of Sadness, Years of Triumph: The American People, 1939–1945* with the sentence: "The war came as a surprise that was expected." Ask students to explain this seemingly contradictory statement in a brief essay or speech.

Caption Answer to ...

 Interpreting Maps

The Axis powers have control over most of the European continent—including France—as well as North Africa. Britain and the Soviet Union are still fighting, but Germany has made great inroads into Russian territory.

Regions of Axis and Allied Control, 1941

- Axis powers
- Areas under Axis control, 1941
- Allies and areas under Allied control, 1941
- Neutral nations

Geography and History: Interpreting Maps
Millions of people like this Czechoslovakian woman, shown reluctantly saluting the Nazis in 1938, saw their homelands conquered by the Axis powers. *How does this map illustrate the dire situation of the Allies in 1941?*

Like Mussolini, Hitler saw foreign policy as a way to bolster national pride. He, too, was determined to return Germany to a dominant position in the world. In 1936 he marched troops into the **Rhineland**—a section of western Germany from which the Treaty of Versailles had excluded German forces since the end of World War I. (See the map above.) In that same year, Hitler formed an alliance with Mussolini, and Italy and Germany became known as the Axis Powers.

The German Empire Grows German aggression continued as the decade of the 1930s drew to a close. Early in 1938 Hitler annexed Austria. Later that year, he demanded possession of the Sudetenland, a section of Czechoslovakia inhabited by an ethnic German population.

The League of Nations, which had been organized after World War I to try to maintain international peace, proved powerless to resist German aggression. England and France, reluctant to become involved in another conflict after the devastation of World War I, adopted a policy known as **appeasement**. To *appease* means to "keep the peace by giving in to someone's demands." Over and over England and France allowed Hitler to seize control of European territories, on the assumption that he finally would be satisfied.

Their assumption was wrong. Hitler's appetite proved insatiable, and he moved relentlessly to take over all of Czechoslovakia. Then, in September 1939, after signing a nonaggression pact with the Soviet Union so he would not have to fear a Soviet assault, Germany invaded Poland. Two days after this attack, leaders in England and France decided they would appease Hitler no longer. Angry and frustrated over his steady encroachment on the European continent, they finally declared war on Germany.

Japan Builds an Empire

In Asia in the 1930s, Japan was every bit as eager as Germany and Italy to establish itself as a world power. Japan consisted of a chain of small islands in the Pacific and lacked the raw materials needed for a booming industrial economy. Military leaders who dominated the government resented their dependence on the United States and other nations for such necessary resources as iron, coal, and petroleum. High tariffs prevented Japan from enjoying a profitable export trade with the United States and led to a prolonged economic depression in Japan. To make Japan self-sufficient, its leaders were determined to incorporate part of the Asian mainland into what they called the Greater East Asia Co-Prosperity Sphere.

In 1931 Japan attacked **Manchuria**, a region in northern China rich in minerals. By the next year, Japan controlled Manchuria. It quickly established a puppet government and renamed the area Manchukuo. Despite condemnation by the League of Nations, Japan continued its aggression in China. In 1937 Japanese troops launched an attack and seized Shanghai, Nanjing, Beijng, and other Chinese cities.

Japanese aggression continued over the next few years. Ever hungry for more resources, raw materials, and markets, Japan also sought control of Southeast Asia, as the map below shows. In 1940 the island nation signed an alliance with Germany and Italy, known as the Tripartite Pact. Now all three of the world's major fascist powers were partners. Secure in that alliance, the Japanese invaded southern Indochina—then ruled by France—in the middle of 1941.

MAKING CONNECTIONS

How do you think different groups of Americans reacted to German and Japanese aggression? How might their memories of World War I have affected their responses? Compare your answers to the information that follows.

The American Response to Axis Aggression

The United States watched the storm clouds rising in Europe and Asia but hoped to remain uninvolved. Most Americans remained

Regions of Japanese Control, 1941

Areas under Japanese control, 1941

Geography and History: Interpreting Maps
The terrified baby at right somehow escaped harm during the 1937 bombing of a Shanghai train station by the Japanese. *Judging from this map, what regions in 1941 appear to have been in the greatest danger of being attacked next by Japan?*

In Depth

Did You Know?

On May 13, 1939, the Hamburg-American liner *St. Louis* left Germany bound for Cuba, carrying 930 Jewish refugees, 734 of whom were carrying United States immigration papers. When the *St. Louis* docked in Havana on May 27, however, the refugees were told that Cuban authorities would not allow them ashore. United States officials refused to waive quota restrictions then in effect, and the doomed vessel sailed back to Europe. Frantic workers from Jewish relief agencies finally persuaded four European countries to take in the refugees—but only those who settled in Britain remained free of Nazi persecution.

Section 1 Review Answers

1. (a) fascism, see p. 500, (b) Nazi party, see p. 501, (c) anti-Semitism, see p. 501, (d) appeasement, see p. 502, (e) Lend-Lease Act, see p. 504

2. (a) Benito Mussolini, see p. 500, (b) Adolf Hitler, see p. 501, (c) Winston Churchill, see p. 504

3. (a) Rhineland, see p. 502, (b) Manchuria, see p. 503, (c) Pearl Harbor, see p. 504

4. Hitler and Mussolini exploited the humiliation many people in Germany and Italy felt after defeat in World War I. Hitler also used anti-Semitic prejudices to his advantage. Japan invaded Manchuria and several other major population centers of China in order to gain influence and access to raw materials.

5. Most Americans wanted to stay out of the conflict. In the 1930s, Congress passed a series of Neutrality Acts to distance the United States from direct involvement in Europe and Asia.

In Depth

Historical Misconceptions

American isolationism in the late 1930s was quite significant. The America First Committee was not only vocal but also influential in gathering support from a cross-section of Americans *against* intervening in the war in Europe. Among the public figures who supported the America First Committee were former President Herbert Hoover, labor leader John L. Lewis, historian Charles Beard, architect Frank Lloyd Wright, chairman of Sears, Roebuck Robert Wood, and the most famous American of his generation—Charles Lindbergh.

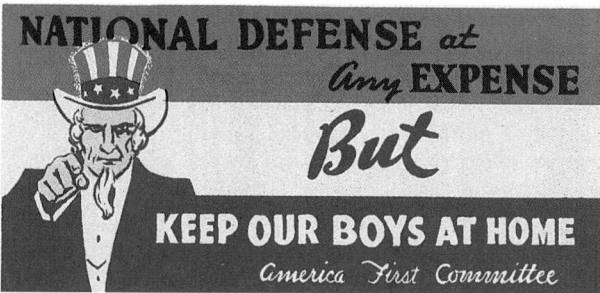

People opposed to the United States entering World War II voiced their opinions on bumper stickers such as the one above, or wore pins that read "America First" (below). Those who favored United States involvement in the war urged "Bundles [of supplies] for Britain" (below).

disillusioned by World War I; they had fought to make the world safe for democracy, but questioned later whether their actions had made any difference at all. Many Americans wanted to follow a policy of isolationism, believing that American interests could best be served by staying out of the quarrels of other nations entirely. Isolationists formed the America First Committee to denounce any move by the government toward involvement in the war.

Congress responded to isolationist sentiment in the 1930s by passing a series of three neutrality acts. Taken together, these laws declared that the United States would withhold weapons and loans from all nations at war and would sell other goods to warring powers only if they paid cash and picked up the goods themselves, a policy known as "cash and carry." The third and last of these acts was passed in 1937, thus completing American neutrality policy. In early 1941 a Gallup poll revealed that 88 percent of the American people still opposed entering the war.

Challenges to Neutrality Despite most Americans' desire for noninvolvement, the ominous events of the war convinced other Americans that the United States should help the Allies. Between September 1939 and June 1940, the Axis Powers in Europe defeated Poland, Norway, Denmark, Belgium, Luxembourg, and France. In Asia, Japan was swallowing up French and Dutch colonies. Unless something was done quickly, England—which was single-handedly resisting the Axis in Europe—might not survive. In May 1940, journalist William Allen White organized the Committee to Defend America by Aiding the Allies,

which worked vigorously to enlist the support of the American people.

The Arsenal of Democracy That same year, while seeking and winning a third presidential term, Roosevelt moved to help Great Britain directly. When British prime minister **Winston Churchill** asked for American destroyers to convoy supplies across the Atlantic, Roosevelt agreed to trade fifty old American ships in return for sites on which to build eight naval and air bases on British territory in the Western Hemisphere.

The next year, Roosevelt helped push the **Lend-Lease Act** through Congress. Britain desperately needed economic help to continue its struggle against the Axis. Under Lend-Lease, the United States would provide war supplies to Britain and worry about payment later. It was like lending a garden hose to a neighbor whose house was burning, Roosevelt said. You loaned it to him, and he returned it when the fire was out. With that commitment, the United States became, in FDR's words, "the great arsenal of democracy."

The Attack on Pearl Harbor

As the war in Europe unfolded, tensions between the United States and Japan increased. In 1940 the United States stopped selling airplanes to Japan, then moved to terminate a long-standing trade agreement. By mid-1940, the United States had ceased selling other crucial items, such as scrap metal and oil, to Japan. After Japan's attack on Indochina, it froze all Japanese financial assets in the United States. Desperate for oil in particular, Japan was determined to do whatever was necessary to attain its militaristic aims. The United States naval fleet based in Hawaii stood directly in the way of Japan's plans to dominate eastern Asia and the Pacific.

The Japanese took matters into their own hands. Hoping to knock out the United States Pacific Fleet before an all-out military conflict could begin, Japan launched a surprise attack on the American naval base at **Pearl Harbor**, Hawaii, on December 7, 1941. The attack destroyed five battleships, three cruisers, and

RESOURCE DIRECTORY

Teaching Resources

Visual Learning Activity Books Are Weapons, found in the Unit 5 folder, p. 29, enhances students' understanding of wartime propaganda and the power of the written word through a poster issued by the U.S. Office of War Information, depicting a Nazi book burning.

several smaller vessels, while wiping out almost 200 airplanes. Nearly 2,400 people died. Fortunately, the Pacific Fleet's aircraft carriers were on a mission elsewhere in the Pacific and so were spared destruction.

The attack stunned the American people. Then, in the wake of the initial shock, came a feeling of determination. A college student recalled hearing the news:

> I n an incredibly short time— it seemed to be almost a matter of moments—a wave of patriotism swept the country. As we drove home we felt, This is our country, and we're going to fight to defend it. When we got home that evening we were glued to the radio. "The Star-Spangled Banner" was played, and everyone in the room automatically rose. And we were disillusioned college students— the 1940s version of the 1960s kids.
>
> Dellie Hahne, a student at
> Santa Barbara State College, California

Anti-Japanese propaganda (right) kept the Pearl Harbor attack (above) fresh in Americans' minds.

In recent years Roosevelt had come to believe that the United States could not avoid involvement in World War II. The attack on Pearl Harbor meant that the nation could hesitate no longer. The day after the raid, in one of his most stirring speeches, the President told the Congress and the American people that December 7, 1941, was "a date which will live in infamy." He called on Congress to declare war against Japan. Congress quickly

complied. Three days later, Japan's allies, Germany and Italy, declared war on the United States. The American people now were committed to this war. Their contributions would make the difference between victory and defeat for the Allies.

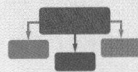

SECTION 1 REVIEW

Key Terms, People, and Places

1. Define (a) fascism, (b) Nazi party, (c) anti-Semitism, (d) appeasement, (e) Lend-Lease Act.
2. Identify (a) Benito Mussolini, (b) Adolf Hitler, (c) Winston Churchill.
3. Identify (a) Rhineland, (b) Manchuria, (c) Pearl Harbor.

Key Concepts

4. What steps did Italy, Germany, and Japan take early in 1935 to extend their power?

5. How did the United States respond to international upheaval in the 1930s?

Critical Thinking

6. **Testing Conclusions** "In the years leading up to the attack on Pearl Harbor, the United States was gradually becoming more and more involved in the war. Even if the attack had never happened, the United States would eventually have become involved in the fighting." Explain why you agree or disagree with this conclusion.

 Quiz found in the Unit 5 folder, p. 8, covers the main ideas in this section as well as the key terms.

Media and Technology

Transparency
Time Lines, E-7

---

6. Possible answers: Students may point out that it took the attack on Pearl Harbor to unite Americans behind the decision to enter World War II. On the other hand, some Americans had argued for joining the war long before Pearl Harbor.

Reteach

Ask students to identify the nation described in each statement below as Italy, Germany, Japan, or the United States.

- Benito Mussolini promised to restore this country's efficiency and order.
- This country's dictator blamed its problems on the Jews.
- Military leaders dominated the emperor of this country.
- This country bombed an American naval base on December 7, 1941.
- Britain and France declared war when this country invaded Poland.

4. CLOSE

Reinforcing the Big Idea

The United States overtly tried to remain neutral when the fascist powers began a second world war. However, the United States did give increasing amounts of aid to the Allies. When Japan bombed Pearl Harbor in 1941, the United States entered World War II. The next section describes the course of the war from that point.

SECTION 2

The Military Struggle

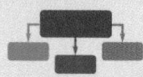

1. FOCUS

Connecting to the Big Idea

See page 498B. When the United States entered the war, the Allies were on the defensive. Ask students to consider how the Allies planned to win the war and shape the world during the postwar peace.

Objectives

● Identify American military strength as the ingredient that helped the Allies defeat their Axis foes.
● Explain why the Allies chose to concentrate on Europe and North Africa and then to focus on the Pacific.
● Define the Nazi holocaust and describe its terrors.

Bellringer

Ask students to decide what they consider the most basic human freedoms. Then have them compare their lists to President Roosevelt's: freedom of speech, freedom of worship, freedom from want, and freedom from fear.

In Depth

Multicultural Perspectives

The United States' "Good Neighbor policy" paid dividends during the war. The Latin American nations provided vital war materials—rubber, quinine, tin—along with naval and air bases. Brazil sent troops to Europe, and Mexico had an air squadron in the Pacific. The Mexican and Cuban navies patrolled the Caribbean for German submarines. In return, the United States provided military equipment and loans to these nations.

SECTION PREVIEW

By December 1941, only an exhausted Britain stood between the Nazis and their dream of dominating the European continent. The United States finally cast its lot with the British—but was it already too late?

This helmet was worn by General George Patton, whose brilliant use of tanks helped sweep the Germans out of France in 1944.

Key Concepts

• American military strength turned the tide of the war in favor of the Allies.
• The Allies decided to concentrate first on winning the war in Europe and North Africa and then focus on the Pacific.
• At the end of the war in Europe, the American public discovered the horrors of the holocaust.

Key Terms, People, and Places

blitzkrieg, Battle of the Bulge, holocaust; Douglas MacArthur, Dwight D. Eisenhower, Chester Nimitz, Joseph Stalin; Midway Island, Guadalcanal, Normandy

---

W orld War II was a global war in an even greater sense than World War I. With campaigns occurring on many fronts at the same time, the war required enormous coordination of people and resources. If they hoped to defeat their Axis foes, Allied military strategists had to look at the "big picture" formed by a mosaic of smaller objectives.

Allied War Aims

While the immediate objective was to win the war, the United States was from the start planning to shape the postwar peace. Months before the United States entered the war, Roosevelt had shared his vision of what the world should be like. In a speech to Congress in early 1941, the President spoke of the "four essential human freedoms"—freedom of speech, freedom of worship, freedom from want, and freedom from fear. That summer, he met with British prime minister Winston Churchill off the coast of Newfoundland, and the two leaders issued the Atlantic Charter. This document described their notion of a free and democratic postwar world. It demanded self-determination for all nations, so that people everywhere could decide what kind of government they wanted; equal trading rights for all, so that every country could share in the world's riches; and a system of general security to help keep peace.

While the four freedoms and the Atlantic Charter defined the United States' formal aims in the war, most Americans fought for more personal reasons. As soldiers huddled in filthy foxholes overseas, they dreamed of home and a cherished way of life. War correspondent John Hersey once asked a young marine on the Pacific front what he was fighting for. After reflecting for a moment, the soldier just sighed, "What I'd give for a piece of blueberry pie."

Early Danger

The Allies were in deep trouble by the time the United States entered the war. With fighting occurring around the globe, they found themselves on the defensive on virtually every front. To have any chance of victory, they had to determine military priorities. Soon after Pearl Harbor, Roosevelt and Churchill decided that they would concentrate on defeating Germany and its European supporters first, while waging a defensive war against Japan in the Pacific. Only after the Nazis had been defeated would they devote full attention to the Asian front.

The European and North African Fronts The situation was desperate in Europe and North Africa. The German **blitzkrieg** ("lightning war")—a series of sudden military attacks

---

RESOURCE DIRECTORY

Teaching Resources

Reproducible Lesson Plan found in the Unit 5 folder, p. 4, provides a summary of the Section 2 lesson plan content.

Alternate Lesson Plan: Learning Styles found in the Alternate Lesson Plans folder, p. 123, is especially effective for tactile learners and is designed to help students understand the military struggle of World War II.

Guided Reading and Review found in the Unit 5 folder, p. 9, provides a structure for reading and mastering the key concepts and reviewing the key terms for Section 2. (Guided Practice)

by land and air—had extended Germany's control across Europe. England had survived the Battle of Britain, a relentless air attack that lasted from July 1940 to June 1941, but the German bombings of cities like London had taken a heavy toll. Suspicious of Soviet intentions in eastern Europe, Hitler broke his nonaggression pact with the Soviet Union in early 1942. German troops drove deep into the Soviet Union, gaining substantial territory. In North Africa, a German army led by Field Marshal Erwin Rommel, known as the "Desert Fox" for his shrewd tactics, was equally successful.

The Pacific Front Conditions for the Allies were not much better in the Pacific. The attack on Pearl Harbor had destroyed much of the American fleet, although not its aircraft carriers. Japan already controlled a large part of eastern and southern Asia. After years of fighting, China had been ground down. India, a British colony, was threatened from east and west, and Australia, part of the British Commonwealth, was expecting a Japanese invasion soon.

After Pearl Harbor, Japan moved successfully against the Pacific islands of Guam and Wake and against the British colony of Hong Kong in China and the British naval base at Singapore, just south of the Malay Peninsula. (See the map below.) In the spring of 1942, Japanese forces defeated Filipino and American troops in the Philippines and drove General **Douglas MacArthur** from the islands. After the defeat on March 10, 1942, MacArthur promised the Filipinos and American soldiers: "I shall return."

Turnaround The situation began to improve toward the end of 1942. Despite initial German

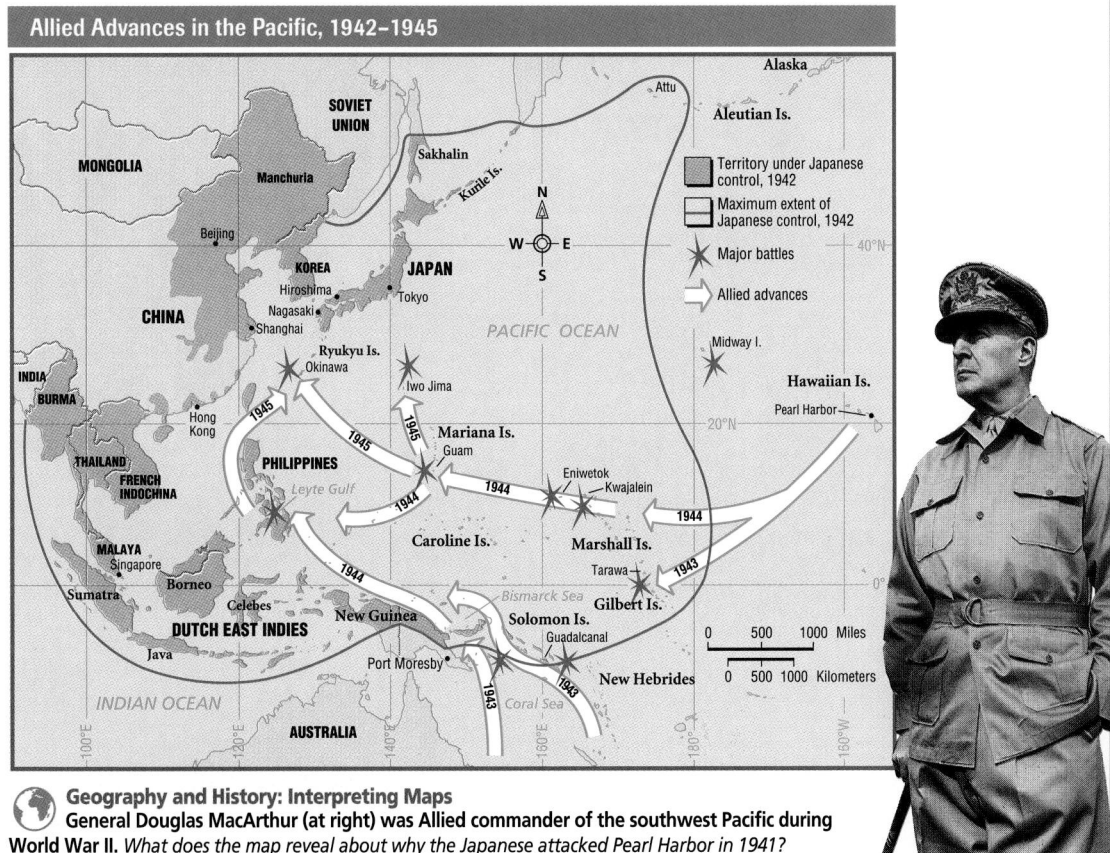

Allied Advances in the Pacific, 1942–1945

Territory under Japanese control, 1942
Maximum extent of Japanese control, 1942
★ Major battles
Allied advances

Geography and History: Interpreting Maps
General Douglas MacArthur (at right) was Allied commander of the southwest Pacific during World War II. *What does the map reveal about why the Japanese attacked Pearl Harbor in 1941?*

Structured Overview Have students create four columns on a sheet of paper and label them 1941, 1942, 1943, and 1944. In each column have them list the major battles and events in the European, North African, and Asian theaters of war for that year.

2. INSTRUCT

Explain/Discuss

Explain to students that the vision of a free and democratic postwar world posited by FDR and Churchill included the right of all nations to determine their own kind of government, to enjoy equal trading rights, and to live in peace. Discuss how the goals of the major wartime conferences support the conclusion that one of Roosevelt's main goals for entering the war was to ensure his role in the postwar peace talks.

Review the military strategy agreed upon by Churchill and Roosevelt. Ask students to describe the significance of Midway, Guadalcanal, Normandy, and the Battle of the Bulge. Have students describe how the use of radar and sonar equipment aided the Allies.

Ask students why the Soviet Union continually pressured the Allies to open a front in western Europe. Why did Churchill insist on attacking Germany through North Africa and Italy? What were the repercussions of this decision on future United States–Soviet relations?

Caption Answer to ...

🌐 **Interpreting Maps**

The arrows leading from the Hawaiian islands show that Pearl Harbor was the base from which Allied initiatives were launched in the Pacific.

Analyze

Ask why the holocaust was referred to as Hitler's "final solution." What was the impact of the discovery of the atrocities committed against millions of Jews and others whom the Nazis considered to be undesirable?

 Activity

Creating Maps

Ask students to work in groups to make a detailed map of one theater of the war, including lines of battle and the dates of important events.
LEP

Enrichment

Ask students to prepare a detailed report about one battle of World War II or about one military leader. Suggest that students locate old issues of *Yank* magazine in the library and read eyewitness accounts written by soldiers who actually participated in the battles.

Caption Answer to ...

 Interpreting Maps

The arrow labeled "1944" that crosses the English Channel into France represents the D-Day invasion; the arrows that cross North Africa and move through Sicily into Italy represent the "soft underbelly" strategy.

---

triumphs in the Soviet Union, the Soviets were helped by the fact that Hitler repeated the same mistake made by the French emperor Napoleon more than a hundred years earlier. German troops advanced into the Soviet Union far beyond their country's ability to support them, and they were not equipped to deal with harsh Russian winters. The Soviets managed to withstand a long and costly attack on the city of Stalingrad. In September 1942, the Germans began bombing the city, while 300,000 German soldiers waited to attack. The Soviets took up positions in the rubble left by the bombing. When the Germans advanced, the Soviets engaged them in bitter house-to-house fighting for the next four months. At the end of that time, the Germans had been repulsed. In the process of defending Stalingrad, however, the

Soviet Union suffered more casualties than the United States experienced in the entire war.

In the Atlantic, the Allies used radar (which had been crucial in the Battle of Britain) and sonar to find and destroy German submarines. Without that ability, troops would have been left without weapons or food, for the Germans had sunk 125 Allied ships in May 1942 alone.

⭐ Meanwhile, the Allies took the offensive in North Africa (see the map below). In early 1943, Roosevelt and Churchill met at Casablanca, in the North African nation of Morocco, to decide where to strike back. The Soviet Union, which was fighting alone on the eastern front, desperately wanted the other Allies to open up a second front in western Europe. Churchill, however, was determined not to launch a frontal invasion until he felt Germany was likely to fall.

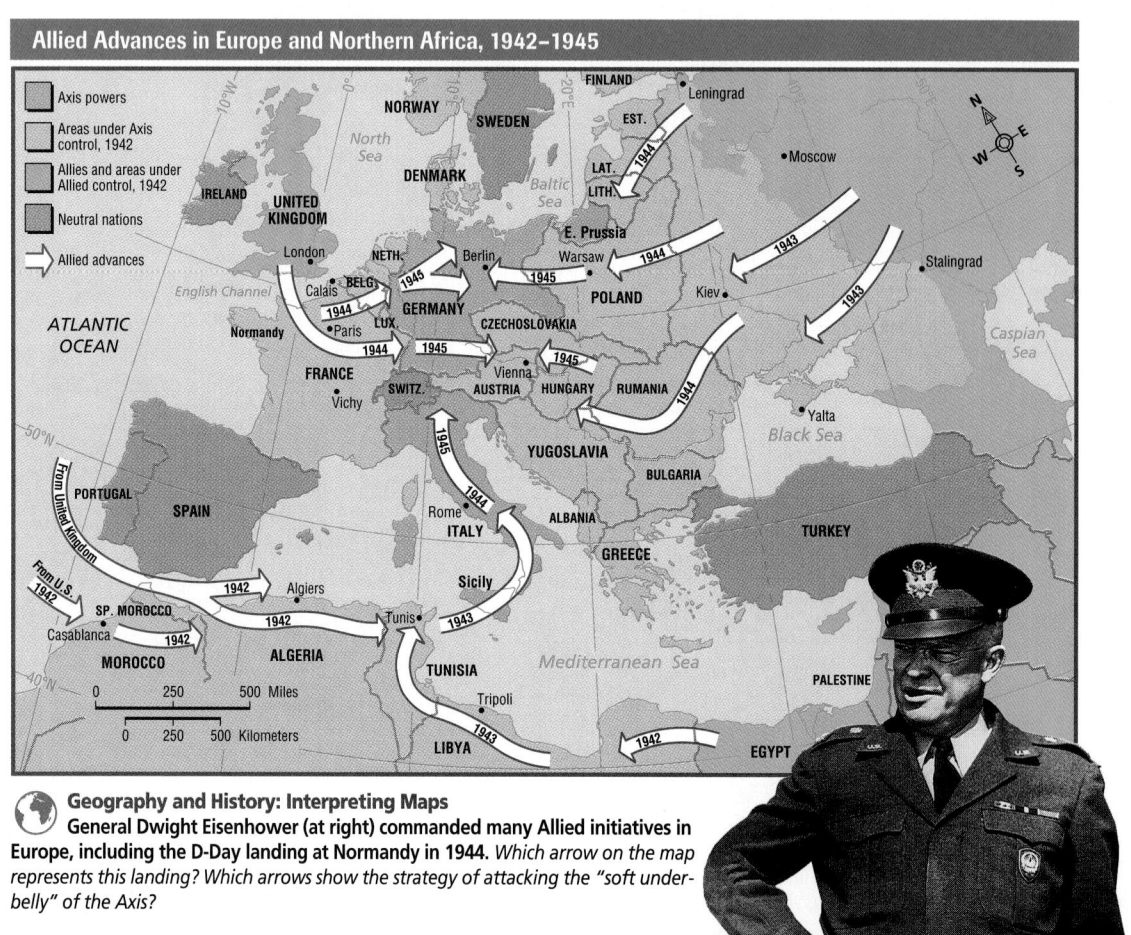

Allied Advances in Europe and Northern Africa, 1942–1945

 Geography and History: Interpreting Maps
General Dwight Eisenhower (at right) commanded many Allied initiatives in Europe, including the D-Day landing at Normandy in 1944. *Which arrow on the map represents this landing? Which arrows show the strategy of attacking the "soft underbelly" of the Axis?*

▶ **RESOURCE DIRECTORY**

Teaching Resources

⭐ **Visual Learning Activity** The North African Front, found in the Unit 5 folder, p. 30, uses information from the chapter and a photograph of American soldiers in Tunisia to challenge students' perception of detail.

⭐ **Primary Source Activity** Guadalcanal, found in the Unit 5 folder, p. 23, uses a passage written by Eleanor Roosevelt on the aftermath of the battle for Guadalcanal to express the sorrows of war and the ideals for which American soldiers died.

Instead, he persuaded Roosevelt to attack what he called the "soft underbelly" of the enemy, moving from North Africa to Sicily and Italy. The Soviets felt that by postponing the attack in western Europe, Britain and the United States "sacrificed" the Soviets in order to pursue their own war aims. Many thousands of Soviet soldiers died—and the German army was weakened—in the following months. Bitterness over this strategic decision would affect United States-Soviet relations in the postwar years.

Operation Torch, as the North African campaign was called, began in November 1942. It was a combined Anglo-American operation under the command of General **Dwight D. Eisenhower**. The Allied forces landed first in Morocco and Algeria, controlled by German puppet governments. The Allies easily triumphed, then moved east to Tunisia, where they encountered Rommel's Afrika Corps. In May 1943, the Axis forces in that region surrendered.

After their victory in North Africa, the Allies turned toward Italy. In July 1943, paratroopers of the 82nd Airborne Division jumped into Sicily, the island just off the "toe" of Italy; the invasion was a success. Next, Allied forces assaulted the Italian mainland and pushed toward Rome. The Italians overthrew Mussolini after the Sicily invasion and surrendered in September. German soldiers stationed in Italy dug in, though, and contested every mile of territory as the Allies moved up the Italian peninsula. In early 1944, the Allies landed, via sea, on the beaches of Anzio, and six months later they liberated the nearby city of Rome. The war was hardly over, but in the Italian campaign, the Allies had taken a major step forward. (See the map on page 508.)

MAKING   CONNECTIONS

What are some of the differences between fighting a war on your own soil and going somewhere else to fight?

Midway and Guadalcanal At about the same time, battles over two small but highly strategic islands in the Pacific shifted the balance of power between the Allies and Japan. Japanese admiral Isoroku Yamamoto wanted to engage the United States Navy at **Midway Island**, near Hawaii, in an attempt to destroy the aircraft carriers that the Pearl Harbor bombing had missed. When, in April 1942, Colonel James Doolittle launched a successful air raid on Tokyo from the carrier USS *Hornet*, which had departed from Midway, Japanese officials approved Yamamoto's plan.

Before the attack on Midway, the Japanese intended to secure their position around Australia by landing troops at Port Moresby in New Guinea. (See the map on page 507.) The United States had broken the Japanese military code, so American officials were aware of this strategy. In May 1942, in the Battle of the Coral Sea, planes launched from the American carriers *Lexington* and *Yorktown* fought a Japanese fleet for four days, finally forcing the enemy to turn back. This Allied victory slowed the Japanese drive toward Australia.

Americans wore pins like this one of General Eisenhower to show their support of the Allied military effort.

Americans again intercepted Japanese code messages and were prepared for the attack on Midway on June 4, 1942. Even so, the battle did not go well for the American forces at first. Most of the planes that Admiral **Chester Nimitz** sent from the island to attack the Japanese fleet were quickly shot down, as were those launched from American carriers. It was a bit of sheer luck that finally favored the Americans. At about 10:25 A.M., when the Japanese believed they had seen the last of the American fighter planes and were refueling for a final attack on the island, a group of dive-bombers that had gotten lost suddenly found their target. Three of the four Japanese carriers were swiftly demolished as fuel hoses and bombs on the Japanese ships exploded. The fourth was later destroyed while trying to escape. As a result of this tremendous blow to Japan's naval power, Midway would be the last Japanese offensive operation in the war.

 At this point, the Allies took the offensive in the Pacific. Their first goal would be to secure the island of **Guadalcanal**, in the Solomon Islands. (See the map on page 507.) United States marines landed on the island beginning on August 7, 1942. Japanese leaders deemed Guadalcanal "the fork in the road which leads

Answer to ...

MAKING   CONNECTIONS

Fighting on home territory means familiarity with the terrain and a very personal connection to the struggle. Soldiers fighting on foreign soil may not know the geography, feel no personal connection to the area, and may wonder if the conflict is worth dying for.

In Depth

Then and Now

The United Service Organizations (USO), founded in 1941, assembled volunteer touring companies of actors, comedians, bandleaders, singers, and dancers to entertain the armed forces overseas. USO camp shows performed wherever American troops were stationed—in the North African desert, in bombed-out opera houses in Italy, or in the steamy rain forests of New Guinea. The USO has toured in every American war zone since then. In the early 1990s, about forty thousand volunteers around the world keep USO active.

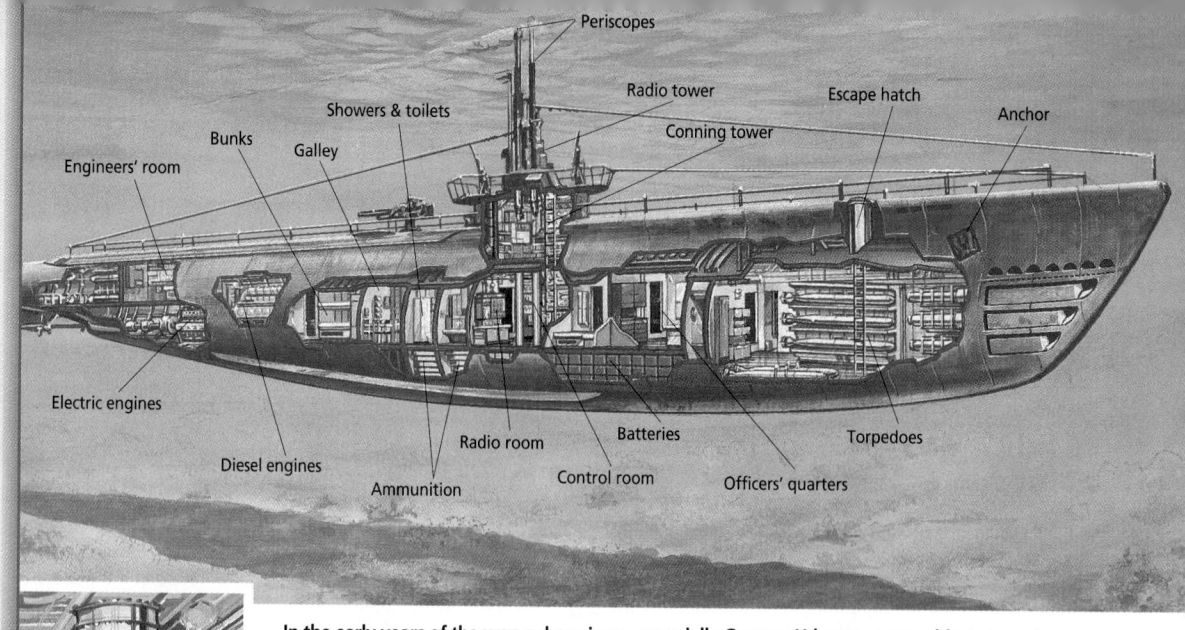

Periscopes
Radio tower
Escape hatch
Anchor
Showers & toilets
Conning tower
Bunks
Galley
Engineers' room
Electric engines
Diesel engines
Radio room
Batteries
Torpedoes
Ammunition
Control room
Officers' quarters

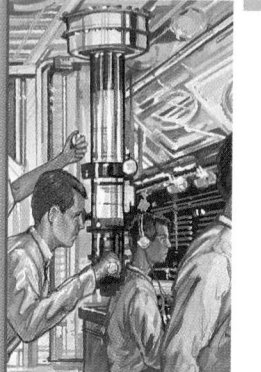

In the early years of the war, submarines—especially German U-boats—were able to terrorize surface ships with sneak attacks. They could approach other ships undetected, with their sailors viewing targets through the periscope (left). Later in the war, however, Allied aircraft equipped with radar were able to detect a submarine replenishing its supply of fresh air at the surface and alert destroyer ships to the submarine's location.

to victory for them or for us," so they made an all-out effort to recapture it.

Months of heavy fighting followed. In mid-November, the naval Battle of Guadalcanal ended with American control of the waters around the island, cutting off Japanese supply lines. In February 1943, American marines finally secured the island. From Guadalcanal, American forces would begin their strategy of "island-hopping," moving north through the Pacific by selectively attacking a few Japanese-held islands, their final objective being the Japanese homeland. The last two major battles in the Pacific war were fought on the small islands of Iwo Jima and Okinawa. The Japanese defended them fiercely, and both sides suffered heavy casualties before the Allies prevailed. ✪

The Road to Victory in Europe The Allies were ready to tighten the noose. In Europe they now looked to liberate Germany itself from the Nazis. Toward the end of 1943, Churchill, Roosevelt, and Soviet leader **Joseph Stalin** met together for the first time in Tehran, Iran. They

agreed that an invasion across the English channel should come next.

Air attacks throughout 1943 and 1944 softened German resistance. Yet even though the Allies destroyed military, industrial, and transportation facilities, the Nazis fought on.

Then came Operation Overlord, which aimed to drive the Germans out of France and defeat the Third Reich itself. D-Day began before dawn on June 6, 1944. It was the largest amphibious invasion—a landing by sea—in history. More than 150,000 Allied soldiers in 600 warships and 4,000 other vessels crossed the English channel and came ashore along 60 miles of the **Normandy** coast in northern France. (See the map on page 508.) The Germans knew an attack was coming, but they expected it near Calais, where the English channel was narrowest. Despite the advice of his generals to counterattack, Hitler hesitated, for he still feared a larger invasion at Calais. The Allies, under the command of General Dwight Eisenhower, were thus able to land safely on the beach. In the course of the first week, they placed 326,000 soldiers, 50,000 vehicles, and

In Depth

Interdisciplinary

Photography played a vital role in bringing the war to the American people at home. One acclaimed photograph, which became emblematic of the American effort in World War II, was Joe Rosenthal's study of six victorious marines hoisting the American flag on the captured isle of Iwo Jima. Rosenthal said of the shot: "I want[ed] to get at least *one* picture of an American flag on top of this hill." One writer later suggested that more people learned about the fight for Iwo Jima because of Rosenthal's photograph than because of any books or articles they have read on the subject. (For more on the role of photography in war see Historian's Toolbox on page 517.)

▶ RESOURCE DIRECTORY ✪

Teaching Resources

✪ **American Profiles Activity** Navaho Code Talkers, found in the Unit 5 folder, p. 18, profiles a corps of 420 radio operators who transmitted secret codes in the Navaho language during World War II.

✪ **Literature Activity** Dispatches from the Battle Front, found in the Unit 5 folder, pp. 26–27, features war correspondent Ernie Pyle's descriptions of the front lines of the European theater and the lives of the U.S. servicemen who fought there.

100,000 tons of supplies on the French coast. By the time the invasion of Normandy was over in July, the Allied forces had landed more than a million men.

⭐ Bitter fighting followed as the Allies pushed toward Paris. At the end of August, they liberated the French capital, then freed Brussels and Antwerp in Belgium a few days later.

The Germans launched a counterattack in Belgium and Luxembourg in December 1944, called the **Battle of the Bulge** because it caused a large bulge in the Allied line. When it sputtered out after one month, the way into Germany was clear. As Allied bombers continued to hammer major German cities, the Soviets pushed into Germany from the east, while American forces crossed the Rhine River and drove in from the west.

The Holocaust

As the Allies moved toward final victory, they discovered the horrors of what Hitler called the "Final Solution"—his effort to exterminate all Jews and other people he considered enemies of the Aryan state. For the duration of the war, the Nazis had engaged in a systematic campaign to liquidate the entire Jewish population of Europe. The extermination camps of Auschwitz, Maidanek, and Treblinka were located in Poland; Buchenwald and Dachau were in Germany. In these and other camps, the Nazis killed 6 million Jews in what we now call the **holocaust**, from the Greek term for "total destruction by fire." They also murdered another 5 million Slavs, Gypsies, and other people they considered undesirable—political enemies (especially communists), homosexuals, and the physically and mentally disabled.

Nazi doctors performed cruel experiments on their victims, often as an excuse to torture them as much as for any scientific purpose. Many victims were told to remove all their clothing and report to a bath house, which was actually a lethal gas chamber. Their bodies were then stripped of gold teeth, rings, and other valuables and burned in large ovens.

In liberating the concentration camps, American troops found the gaunt survivors who had somehow escaped death in the gas chambers and crematoriums. Second Lieutenant Dick Winters from Pennsylvania recorded the following impressions when he first saw Dachau:

1650   1700   1750   1800   1850   1900   1950   2000

Links Across Time

The "Final Solution" and "Ethnic Cleansing"

As Hitler and the Nazi party rose to power in Germany in the 1930s, they blamed Germany's recent economic and social troubles on the Jewish people and other minority groups.

Eventually, the Nazis decided on the "Final Solution" to what they termed the "Jewish problem." Their solution amounted to genocide, or systematic extermination of an entire ethnic group. When the realities of the "final solution" came to light, a horrified world community promised, "Never again."

In 1992 long-standing conflicts between Serb, Croat, and Muslim ethnic groups intensified in the former country of Yugoslavia. The Serbs wanted the areas they controlled to be the home of Serbians only, although Muslims had lived there for centuries. To bring about their aims, the Serbs followed a policy of "ethnic cleansing," including camps for the torture, rape, starvation, and execution of thousands of Slavic Muslim and ethnic Croat civilians. The United States State Department asserted that the Serbian abuse "dwarfs anything seen in Europe since the Nazis."

In 1993 the International Court of Justice in The Hague (in the Netherlands) implied that Serb aggression in Bosnia was "tantamount to genocide." The United Nations Security Council voted unanimously to establish a war crimes tribunal to bring to justice anyone found guilty of atrocities. ***What do you think are the responsibilities of the United States when faced with strong evidence of genocide in another country?***

Media and Technology

Transparency
The Way It Works, H-19

Answer to ...

Links Across Time

Possible answers: The United States should publicly protest genocide in another country, use its influence to protest in the United Nations, impose economic sanctions, and support a United Nations peacekeeping force.

3. ASSESS

Section 2 Review Answers

1. (a) blitzkrieg, see p. 506, (b) Battle of the Bulge, see p. 511

2. (a) Douglas MacArthur, see p. 507, (b) Dwight D. Eisenhower, see p. 509, (c) Chester Nimitz, see p. 509, (d) Joseph Stalin, see p. 510

3. (a) Midway Island, see p. 509, (b) Guadalcanal, see p. 509, (c) Normandy, see p. 510

4. The holocaust refers to the Nazi program of murdering Jews in concentration camps.

5. The United States' entry into the war allowed the Allies to keep the Japanese at bay in the Pacific while concentrating on dividing and conquering German forces in Europe and North Africa. The allies were then able to concentrate on defeating Japanese forces.

6. Possible questions: What are the strengths and weaknesses of both the Allies and the Axis powers? What are some possible strategies? How many Allied soldiers would be required to execute each strategy? What actions would most hurt enemy morale?

Ask students to use information in the section to correct the following incorrect statements.

● The Atlantic Charter declared the right of the United States to decide what kind of government nations would have after the war.
● The Allies decided to concentrate on defeating Japan while waging a defensive war in Europe.
● The Allied victory in the Philippines marked the last Japanese offensive operation in the war.
● The horrors of the holocaust were directed primarily at Muslims.
● The war in the Pacific ended before the war in Europe.

Alternative Assessment

Mid-Point Monitoring
Ask students if they have
● Divided responsibilities within the group
● Decided on an oral or written format for their album
● Obtained outside resources and found persons to interview

4. CLOSE

Reinforcing the Big Idea

In early 1941, the United States decided to join forces with the Allies, then on the defensive. Aided by American military strength, the Allies eventually gained control of Europe and North Africa. Germany at last surrendered, but the war in the Pacific continued. The next section describes life in the United States military during the war.

The memory of starved, dazed men, who dropped their eyes and heads when we looked at them through the chain-link fence, in the same manner that a beaten, mistreated dog would cringe, leaves feelings that cannot be described and will never be forgotten. The impact of seeing those people behind that fence left me saying, only to myself, "Now I know why I am here!"

Survivors of the Nazi holocaust were a chilling sight. Their bodies were emaciated from lack of food, and their eyes appeared haunted by memories of horrible torture.

The End of the War in Europe

In early 1945, Roosevelt, Churchill, and Stalin met again, this time at Yalta, a city in the Soviet Union near the Black Sea. After the "Big Three" Allied leaders had decided to split Germany into peacekeeping zones and to reorganize the government of Poland, the Soviets agreed to enter the war in the Pacific three months after the defeat of Germany.

The end of the European war was not far off. The Third Reich was in shambles. Hitler fulfilled a vow he had made in 1939: "I shall stand or fall in this struggle. I shall never survive the defeat of my people." On April 30, 1945, he committed suicide in a Berlin bunker. On May 8, Germany's unconditional surrender took effect, and the European war came to a close. American soldiers rejoiced, and civilians celebrated at home. But Japan still had to be defeated.

In the Pacific, the United States was embarking on a relentless drive toward the Japanese home islands. (See the map on page 507.) Pushing north from Australia and west through the islands of the central Pacific, American troops slowly gained control. Marines, with help from naval forces, took the islands of Tarawa, Kwajalein, and Guam. Meanwhile, MacArthur returned to the Philippines, as he had promised, with a dramatic landing on the island of Leyte. By the end of 1944, American bombers were close enough to attack the Japanese islands themselves and dropped hundred of tons of explosives on Japanese cities.

In one final meeting of the Big Three, Allied leaders met at Potsdam, Germany, in mid-1945. By this time Roosevelt was dead, and his successor, Harry S Truman, had to oversee the end of the war. The three heads of state warned the Japanese to surrender or face "prompt and utter destruction."

Around the same time, a meeting of delegates from fifty nations met in San Francisco to plan for an international organization to keep the peace. That conference created and approved the charter of the United Nations. While the conference was going on, however, there was still work to be done on the battlefields, carried out by the men and women who actually fought and won the war.

SECTION 2 REVIEW

Key Terms, People, and Places
1. Define (a) blitzkrieg, (b) Battle of the Bulge.
2. Identify (a) Douglas MacArthur, (b) Dwight D. Eisenhower, (c) Chester Nimitz, (d) Joseph Stalin.
3. Identify (a) Midway Island, (b) Guadalcanal, (c) Normandy.

Key Concepts
4. What was the holocaust?

5. How did the United States entry into the war affect the Allied position?

Critical Thinking
6. **Formulating Questions** Imagine that you are responsible for deciding Allied military strategy at the point when the United States entered World War II. Develop a list of questions that you would ask your military advisers before firming up your strategy.

 **RESOURCE DIRECTORY**

Teaching Resources

Quiz found in the Unit 5 folder, p. 10, covers the main ideas in this section as well as the key terms.

Americans on the Battle Fronts

SECTION 3

Americans on the Battle Fronts

SECTION PREVIEW

The grim reality of combat far from home was tough on all soldiers. Discrimination in the armed forces made the experience even more painful for many Americans.

Key Concepts

- Life for American soldiers on the war fronts was brutal and frightening.
- Several groups—including women, African Americans, Latino Americans, and Native Americans—served in the armed forces despite discrimination.
- While their families were interned at home, Japanese Americans bravely defended their country overseas.

Key Terms, People, and Places

GI, WAC

W orld War II changed the lives of the men and women who were uprooted from home and sent far away from loved ones to provide the military muscle that won the war. The 15 million Americans who served as soldiers, sailors, and aviators made their way through distant deserts, jungles, swamps, turbulent seas, and forbidding skies. Anxious to engage the enemy, fearful of what would happen when they did, for them the war was often a desperate struggle just to stay alive.

The GI War

American soldiers called themselves **GIs**, after the "Government Issue" stamp on all shoes, clothes, guns, and other equipment provided by the military. Thousands entered the service when they received their official draft notices: "Greetings. You are hereby ordered for induction into the Armed Forces of the United States. . . ." Even more rushed to volunteer after the attack on Pearl Harbor.

In the field, the war was hardly the romantic struggle portrayed in some books and films. The miserable conditions were described in the newspaper columns of Ernie Pyle, the popular war correspondent who lived with the enlisted men on the battle fronts and wrote about the war from their perspective. Pyle sent reports back to the United States six times a week until he died from a sniper's bullet in the Pacific campaign in 1945. He characterized the life of a typical soldier as follows:

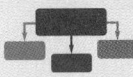

T he front-line soldier has lived like an animal for months and is a veteran of the cruel fierce world of death. Everything has been abnormal and unstable in his life for months. He has been filthy dirty, has eaten if and when, has slept on the hard ground without cover. His clothes have been greasy, he has lived in a constant haze of dust, pestered by flies and the heat, moving constantly, deprived of all the things that once meant stability. Things such as walls, chairs, floors, windows, faucets, shelves, Coca-Colas and the greatly important little matter of knowing you'll go to bed tonight in the same place you got up in this morning.

Written aboard a navy ship in the Allied invasion fleet headed for Sicily, July 16, 1943

The army Medal of Honor (above) paid tribute to gallantry in action above and beyond the call of duty. Fatigues (below) were standard wear for American soldiers.

AMERICAN PROFILES

Charles Rigaud, Marine

Ernie Pyle's description of combat life would have been all too familiar to Charles Alfred Rigaud. Marine Captain Rigaud was

---

Explain/Discuss

Explain to students that Americans on the battle front confronted perilous situations, miserable conditions, and loneliness. Discuss with students the characteristics, exemplified by Charles Rigaud, that made the American armed forces so efficient. (*Courage, fraternity, obedience, modesty, willingness to assume responsibility.*)

Ask students to tell how what they have read in the section supports or refutes the stereotype or typical Hollywood soldier described in the Bellringer activity.

Analyze

Some scholars trace the beginning of the civil rights movement to the experience of African Americans in the military during World War II. Which facet of this experience do students think was most important in beginning the movement for equality? Discuss the importance of leadership, the importance of experience in a large institution such as the military, and the significance of the contrast between the nation's stated goals and its discriminatory actions.

Activity

A Letter to Roosevelt

Explain that the average age of the typical soldier in World War II ranged from late teens to early twenties. Ask students to assume the role of a voting-age citizen during World War II. Have them write a letter to President Roosevelt explaining their views on one of the following topics: the role of women in the military; segregation in the armed forces; or the policy of separating army blood plasma by the race of the donor. Letters should respectfully suggest to Roosevelt a change the students feel is acceptable. Ask why they think the government did not change its policies at the time.

responsible for leading his men into battle against the Japanese on the island of Guadalcanal. John Hersey, another well-known war correspondent, was with Rigaud and his unit during the Third Battle of the Mataniko River. While this battle was not among the most famous of the war, Hersey's vivid account reveals that it was fraught with terror, death, heartache—and remarkable courage.

Rigaud's mission in the Third Battle was to push the Japanese, who were advancing toward the American camp, back across the Mataniko River. To reach the river, Rigaud's unit would have to pass through a jungle valley filled with Japanese snipers. Once there, they would face machine gun and mortar fire from established Japanese battle positions. Rigaud, the veteran marine in charge of this operation, looked to Hersey "like anything except a killer who took no prisoners. He had a boy's face. . . . His mustache was not quite convincing."

Charles Rigaud had grown up in Oriskany Falls, New York, almost ten thousand miles from the jungles of Guadalcanal. Back home he played the violin, both in orchestras and at square dances. Rigaud also loved the outdoors and he often went on hunting and trapping trips with a close friend.

Marine Captain Charles Rigaud was recommended for decoration after his brave fighting on the island of Tulagi in the Pacific.

Rigaud attended Syracuse University, where he joined ROTC (Reserve Officers' Training Corps) and graduated with a commission as a second lieutenant. He joined the marines just as the war began. In command in the field, he was responsible for his company. He had led them through other battles on Guadalcanal and on the nearby island of Tulagi. Success had come at no small cost—twenty-two of his men were dead.

Now, on October 8, 1942, Rigaud and his unit were slowly making their way through the jungle into another perilous situation. They walked single file down a narrow path, keeping five paces between them so that any snipers in

the area would not have a big target. Before they reached the river, one marine lay dead in the path, killed by a Japanese sharpshooter.

After hours of difficult marching, the trees began to thin and the river was in sight. Then a single "high flat snap [that] was easily recognizable as a Japanese sound" broke the silence. Within seconds the air was filled with sniper fire, followed quickly by machine gun and mortar fire from across the river. Rigaud's company had walked right into a Japanese trap.

Marines carrying machine gun parts came together in bunches to set them up. Under heavy fire from the Japanese, however, no more than two guns were ever assembled. As his men took cover and tried to fight back, Rigaud rushed about checking on all of them. The Japanese fire was terrifying, and before long, a desperate rumor began to circulate that the order to withdraw had been given. As his men headed back toward the jungle, Rigaud stood up and shouted, "Who . . . gave that order? . . . Where do you guys think you're going? . . . Get back in there." Soon, however, he did give the order for withdrawal. He knew they could not hold their position.

Rigaud and most of his men survived to fight another day. The Third Battle of the Mataniko River was won by other companies of marines who forced a Japanese retreat on October 9. John Hersey, when preparing to leave Guadalcanal, asked if he could do anything for Rigaud when he got back to the United States. Rigaud answered, "Well, if you go through a place called Oriskany Falls, wish you'd tell my folks you saw me."

Women in the Armed Forces

Not all soldiers were men. By the war's end, over 300,000 American women had served in the military. Faced with serious personnel needs, officials were willing to use women's help in virtually all areas except combat. ✪

Oveta Culp Hobby, director of the Women's Army Auxiliary Corps (WAAC—later shortened to **WAC**, Women's Army Corps), told potential recruits, "This is *your* war." Women

---

▶ RESOURCE DIRECTORY

Teaching Resources

✪ 📄 **American Profiles Activity** found in the Unit 5 folder, p. 17, profiles Jacqueline Cochran, veteran of the World War II Women's Air Force Service Pilots.

✪ 📄 **Critical Thinking Activity** Predicting Consequences: After the Army—What? found in the Unit 5 folder, p. 22, helps students to apply this skill by having them explore possible postwar lifestyle changes for returning servicewomen.

✪ 📄 **Primary Source Activity** Experiences of an African American Soldier, found in the Unit 5 folder, pp. 24–25, uses narrative by World War II veteran Timuel Black to illustrate some of the hardships and injustices faced by African American soldiers.

worked as typists and clerks, but also as control tower operators, radio operators, parachute riggers, and mechanics. The navy had a similar organization, the WAVES (Women Accepted for Volunteer Emergency Service). One quarter of all WAVES served in naval aviation. Women Air Force Service Pilots (WASPs) ferried planes around the country, and they towed targets for antiaircraft gunnery practice missions as well. ⭐

LIFE

AIR FORCE PILOT

JULY 19, 1943   **10** CENTS
YEARLY SUBSCRIPTION $4.50

Using Historical Evidence *How does this 1943 magazine cover demonstrate the new opportunities women had during World War II?*

MAKING   CONNECTIONS

How has the role of women in the United States military changed since World War II?

Equality in the Armed Forces

⭐ Although the military discriminated against African Americans, their participation as soldiers helped win the war. The all-African American 92nd Infantry Division, known as the Buffaloes, fought in the bloody Italian campaign of 1943 and 1944. The 333rd Field Artillery Battalion served with distinction with General George Patton's Third Army in France. These are only a few examples.

According to official policy, African Americans were not allowed to join either the air force or the marines. In the navy, they could only enlist in the messman's branch, which provided food services for the troops. The army, like the Red Cross, separated the blood plasma donated by African Americans.

Near the end of the war, however, shortages of soldiers led military officials to bend the

To defeat the Japanese in the Pacific, United States marines had to keep their strategies from the enemy. Navaho code talkers, using their native language for secret military communications, allowed the Allies to stay one step ahead of the Japanese.

Media and Technology

Transparency
Critical Thinking, I-2

Caption Answer to ...

Using Historical Evidence

The woman pictured on the cover is an air force pilot, operating in a field newly opened to women during the war. Her clothing (pantsuit) also suggests a wartime acceptance of new roles for women.

Answer to ...

MAKING   CONNECTIONS

In the years since World War II, the military has extended many more opportunities to women. They may now become officers and participate in most fields of duty. In 1993 women pilots were finally allowed to compete for assignments in combat missions.

Enrichment

Ask students to find out about, visit, and describe World War II memorials in your community. Students might interview a veteran of the war (possibly through contacting the local VFW post), and ask questions about his or her branch of service, locations of service, assignments, rank, and conditions experienced.

3. ASSESS

Section 3 Review Answers

1. (a) GI, see p. 513, (b) WAC, see p. 514

2. Rigaud's profile reveals that many American soldiers were ordinary men who became extraordinary leaders when faced with life-and-death situations.

3. Women served in all capacities except combat. They worked as typists, clerks, control tower operators, radio operators, parachute riggers, and mechanics.

4. African American participation helped win the war. For example, the "all-Negro" (as it was then called) 92nd Infantry Division fought in the Italian campaign of 1943 and 1944; the 333rd Field Artillery Battalion served with Patton's Third Army in France.

5. Possible answers: The United States was fighting for the liberties of those overseas, while the liberties of women and minorities were being curtailed at home.

Poage argues that keeping up the morale of the southern white volunteers is more important to winning the war than serving the interests of African Americans. A. Philip Randolph argues that the military is fighting for democracy—if it remains segregated, then the African American volunteers have won nothing. For a more thorough examination of the integration of the military, see the Resource Directory below.

Reteach

Write the following statements on the chalkboard and ask students to find details in the section to support each one:
• Americans serving on the war fronts suffered many hardships.
• Women served in the military in all areas except combat.
• The armed services segregated African American and Japanese troops.
• Minority groups helped to win the war despite discrimination.

4. CLOSE

Reinforcing the Big Idea

The stated goals the United States fought for during World War II were essentially inconsistent with its treatment of women and minorities. They suffered not only the hardships of war but also the added burden of discrimination. The next section describes the decision to use the atomic bomb to end the war.

Viewpoints
On the Integration of the Military

Discussion about desegregating the armed forces during World War II aroused strong feelings on both sides. Below are two opposing viewpoints. *What arguments does each side use to support its viewpoint?*

Against Integration
"In this hour of national crisis, it is much more important that we have the full-hearted co-operation of the thirty million white southern Americans than that we satisfy the National Association for the Advancement of Colored People. . . . If they be forced to serve with Negroes, they will cease to volunteer; and when drafted, they will not serve with that enthusiasm and high morale that has always characterized the soldiers and sailors of the southern states."
W. R. Poage, Texas state representative, 1941

For Integration
"Though I have found no Negroes who want to see the United Nations lose this war, I have found many who, before the war ends, want to see the stuffing knocked out of white supremacy. . . . If freedom and equality are not vouchsafed [granted] the peoples of color, the war for democracy will not be won. . . . We demand the abolition of segregation and discrimination in . . . [all] branches of national defense."
A. Philip Randolph, "Why Should We March?" November 1942

rules. An army program begun in January 1945 allowed 20,000 volunteers—including over 4,500 African Americans—to train for infantry duty. From March until the end of the war in Europe, African Americans fought alongside whites in these volunteer combat units. In 1944 the navy organized twenty-five supply ships with integrated crews. The marines finally invited African Americans to enlist in the corps in 1945.

Nearly 350,000 Mexican Americans served in the military during World War II, most enlisting in the army. Mexican American soldiers made up a quarter of the combat troops defending Bataan in the Philippines shortly after Pearl Harbor. They faced Erwin Rommel in North Africa and played a major role in the D-Day invasion of 1944. Guy Gabaldón, who had been raised by a Japanese American family in Los Angeles, earned the Silver Star for his actions in the Battle of Saipan, an island in the Marianas in the western Pacific. Using his language skills, he persuaded more than a thousand Japanese soldiers to surrender to the Allies. By the end of the war, seventeen Mexican Americans had earned the Congressional Medal of Honor.

Though Native Americans were denied the right to vote in three states, they were still eligible for the draft, and eventually 25,000 served in the army and other branches of the military. Ira Hayes, a Pima from Arizona, was one of three survivors at Mount Suribachi on Iwo Jima. Some Navahos worked as code talkers in the marines, using their unique language as a means of transmitting messages by radio and phone.

While tens of thousands of Japanese Americans were interned in camps in the United States (see Chapter 16, Section 4), others seized the opportunity offered them to fight. The 442nd Regimental Combat Team eventually fought in Italy under General Mark Clark and then moved into France. There, they took almost ten thousand casualties and became the most decorated unit in the war.

SECTION 3 REVIEW

Key Terms, People, and Places
1. Define (a) GI, (b) WAC.

Key Concepts
2. What does the profile of Charles Rigaud reveal about the soldiers who fought in the war?
3. Describe the roles that women played during World War II.

4. What contributions did African Americans make in the military during World War II?

Critical Thinking
5. **Checking Consistency** Were the goals the United States was fighting for in World War II consistent with its treatment of women and minorities? Explain why you answered yes or no.

RESOURCE DIRECTORY

Teaching Resources

Viewpoints Activity On the Integration of the Military, found in the Unit 5 folder, pp. 19–20, provides additional viewpoints and perspectives on the arguments for and against the integration of the military.

Quiz found in the Unit 5 folder, p. 12, covers the main ideas in this section as well as the key terms.

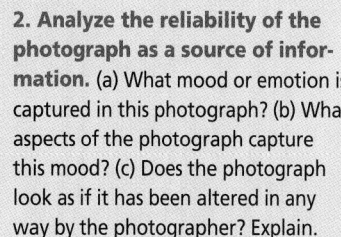

Examining Photographs

Photographs are a form of visual evidence that can provide valuable information about an event or historical period. They can show what people or places in recent history looked like and can document momentous occasions. Photographers, however, like other observers of events, have their own points of view. Therefore, you must analyze their photographs carefully.

By their choice of subject, lighting, and camera angle, photographers can influence what is seen and how it is perceived. They may choose to photograph a scene that strikes them as particularly interesting, dramatic, or revealing but that, in reality, is not typical or representative. Photographers may also distort the appearance of objects in their pictures to create an illusion or convey a particular mood. By making these choices, photographers affect what is learned from their pictures.

The photograph at right was taken during World War II on a Pacific island southeast of the Philippines that was the scene of bitter fighting during the fall of 1944. Use the following steps to analyze the photograph.

1. Study the photograph to identify the subject. Look at the photograph as a whole, then study the details. (a) What do you see in the picture? (b) What broad subject or issue does the photograph address? (c) Was the photograph likely taken before, during, or after a tough battle? Explain.

2. Analyze the reliability of the photograph as a source of information. (a) What mood or emotion is captured in this photograph? (b) What aspects of the photograph capture this mood? (c) Does the photograph look as if it has been altered in any way by the photographer? Explain.

(d) Does it seem as if the soldier posed or was unaware that he was being photographed?

3. Study the photograph to learn more about the historical period. Refer to the photograph and what you have read about World War II to answer the following questions. (a) What could you learn about the Pacific front if this photograph was your only source of information? (b) What can photographs such as this one contribute to a person's knowledge about an event that written sources cannot? (c) From what you have read in this chapter about the fighting on the Pacific islands during World War II, do you think this photograph presents a realistic picture of the war? Explain.

📄 **Historian's Toolbox Activity** Examining Photographs, found in the Unit 5 folder, p. 21, provides further opportunity for students to determine a photographer's intent and other information from a photograph.

Dropping the Atomic Bomb: A Turning Point in History

SECTION 4

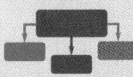

Dropping the Atomic Bomb: A Turning Point in History

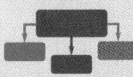

Dropping the Atomic Bomb: A Turning Point in History

1. FOCUS

Connecting to the Big Idea

See page 498B. To bring the war to an end as quickly as possible, the United States used a new weapon, the atomic bomb, against Japan. Ask students what was special or unique about the bomb and what were the results of its use.

Objectives

- Identify the Manhattan Project and the atomic bomb.
- Explain why President Truman chose to use the atomic bomb on Japan.
- Describe the results of the bombing of Hiroshima and Nagasaki.

Bellringer

Ask students to write one sentence describing what they think is the most important way the use of nuclear power has changed the world.

In Depth

Interdisciplinary

A number of factors helped win the war for the Allies; among them were the inventions of scientific tools. One of these was radar, an electronic tracking system. By 1943, airplanes using radar could locate submarines or direct ships to attack. In addition, navy ships using sonar, an apparatus that transmits high frequency sound waves through water, could detect distant propeller noises from objects such as submarines.

SECTION PREVIEW

A collaboration of the top scientists in the world put a devastating secret weapon in American hands. Desperate to end the war as quickly as possible, the United States decided to unleash the terrible force of the atomic bomb on two unsuspecting Japanese cities.

Key Concepts

- The top secret Manhattan Project, which began before the United States entered the war, took years to develop the atomic bomb.
  - Alternatives to using the bomb on Japan were considered, but President Truman believed that the bomb would actually save many lives.
  - Two atomic bombs demolished Hiroshima and Nagasaki; the long-term effects on survivors were unpredictable.

This watch was stopped and partially melted when an atomic bomb exploded over Hiroshima, Japan, in 1945.

Key Terms, People, and Places

Manhattan Project, Interim Committee; Albert Einstein, J. Robert Oppenheimer, Harry S Truman; Hiroshima, Nagasaki

W orld War II was a technological war. Aircraft were now more maneuverable and could fly longer distances without refueling. The aircraft carrier introduced a new type of naval battle at Midway: one in which the opposing vessels were never in sight of one another. Specialized landing craft and dive-bombers made amphibious landings such as the Normandy invasion possible. But the world could scarcely imagine the destructive capacity of the new bomb being secretly developed in the United States.

The Manhattan Project

A letter written by physicist **Albert Einstein** in August 1939 helped set in motion the process of developing this new kind of bomb in the United States. Einstein was known worldwide for developing the theory of relativity, which describes how time and space function in the universe. He speculated that enormous energy might be released if atoms could be split in a particular way. In his letter to President Roosevelt, he wrote, "It is conceivable . . . that extremely powerful bombs of a new type may . . . be constructed," and he hinted that the Germans were already trying to build such a weapon. Einstein's letter reached Roosevelt just as World War II was starting in Europe.

Intrigued with the possibility of a new weapon and concerned that Germany might develop it first, Roosevelt established an Advisory Committee on Uranium to look into the matter. After the United States entered the war, the venture was reorganized and became known as the **Manhattan Project**.

The Manhattan Project developed into one of the greatest engineering enterprises of all time. During the final three years of the war, this top secret undertaking involved the building of thirty-seven installations in the United States and Canada. It employed 120,000 people and cost $2 billion—an unimaginable sum at the time. Scientists already had succeeded in splitting the nucleus of the uranium atom. Now they needed to produce a self-sustaining atomic chain reaction, in which particles released from the splitting of one atom would cause another atom to break apart, and so on. In December 1942, a physicist working with Italian scientist Enrico Fermi at the University of Chicago placed a phone call including a coded message to be relayed to President Roosevelt:

RESOURCE DIRECTORY

Teaching Resources

Reproducible Lesson Plan found in the Unit 5 folder, p. 6, provides a summary of the Section 4 lesson plan content.

Alternate Lesson Plan: Critical Thinking Identifying Alternatives, found in the Alternate Lesson Plans folder, p. 125, is designed to help students apply this skill by charting and discussing President Truman's decision to drop the atomic bomb.

Guided Reading and Review found in the Unit 5 folder, p. 13, provides a structure for reading and mastering the key concepts and reviewing the key terms for Section 4. (Guided Practice)

"You'll be interested to know," the physicist said, "that the Italian navigator [Fermi] has just landed in the New World. The earth was not as large as he had estimated, and he arrived in the New World sooner than he had expected."

"Is that so?" he was asked. "Were the natives friendly?"

"Everyone landed safe and happy." The message meant that the chain reaction had been accomplished without blowing up the laboratory in the process. Next, scientists had to find ways to gather enough of a special kind of uranium—or produce a new element, plutonium—to mold into a bomb.

On July 16, 1945, they tested their effort. In the desert at Alamogordo, New Mexico, scientists detonated the world's first atomic device. It left a huge crater in the earth's floor and shattered windows 125 miles away. As he watched the first blast, physicist **J. Robert Oppenheimer**, who had spearheaded the entire project, remembered the words of the *Bhagavad Gita*, the Hindu holy book: "Now I am become Death, the destroyer of worlds."

The Decision to Drop the Bomb

Once the bomb was ready, American policymakers had to decide if and when to use it. The war in Europe was over, but the Pacific struggle still ground on. There were other courses of action besides dropping the bomb that might end the war. Allied planners had already worked out the details of a massive invasion of the Japanese islands. But this was a frightening prospect. Art Rittenberg, who joined the marines after he graduated from high school in 1942, describes the prospect of invading Japan from the point of view of an enlisted soldier:

M ake no mistake about it, the Japanese were great fighters and everyone respected . . . them and feared them. They fought like [crazy] for Iwo [Jima] . . . , a two-and-a-half-mile long piece of volcanic sand and rock. What are they going to fight like in the home islands?

The estimated cost of the invasion in American lives was as high as one million.

Using Historical Evidence This painting by Jacob Lawrence depicts a Hiroshima family after the atomic blast. *Why has the artist made the people's faces and the furniture look as they do?*

A naval blockade or continued bombing might also help defeat Japan. A demonstration on a deserted island might show the Japanese the bomb's awesome power. Some diplomats believed that Japan might surrender more quickly if the United States simply softened its insistence on "unconditional surrender" and guaranteed that the emperor could keep his throne.

American officials debated these possibilities in the **Interim Committee**, a group that included both government leaders and scientists. In the end, they were unwilling to choose any of the alternatives to dropping the bomb. They did not want to incur further casualties or let the long war drag on still longer. They did not want to suffer the embarrassment of a failed demonstration. Besides bringing Japan to its knees, some historians have speculated that the new bomb offered a dramatic display of

Activity

Teaching Heterogeneous Groups

On August 6, 1945, the United States dropped a uranium bomb on Hiroshima, Japan, killing thousands of people. Survivors later told stories about their terrifying experiences. Have students take the point of view of a survivor, possibly a child, mother or father, student, factory worker, or business owner, and write a fictional journal entry reflecting how the bombing affected that character on that day. Encourage students to describe what happened before, during, and after the explosion. **LEP**

Enrichment

Simulate a meeting of the Interim Committee by having students argue in favor of one of the following positions: a naval blockade or A-bomb demonstration; the invasion of Japan; immediate use of the atomic bomb; relaxation of the position on unconditional surrender. Students might research the opinions of a top policymaker—such as Henry L. Stimson, Ralph A. Bard, or James Frank—regarding the use of the atomic bomb.

Answer to ...
MAKING CONNECTIONS

Students may argue that a subtle racism contributed to the decision. Prejudice against Japanese Americans was clear, given the internment policy instituted earlier in the war. On the other hand, students may argue, since Allied forces had mercilessly bombed German cities just before Germany surrendered, the United States might well have used the atomic bomb there had it been ready in time.

Allied might and served as an example of American power to the Russians. Although they were allies during the war, the United States and the Soviet Union had very different ideas about the shape of the postwar world. The deployment of a new atomic weapon allowed the United States to flex its muscles before the eyes of its communist rival.

The Interim Committee therefore recommended dropping the new bomb. **Harry S Truman**, President for barely four months after Franklin Roosevelt's death in April 1945, would have had a difficult time arguing against using the weapon that had consumed so many resources over the past five years. Truman, however, had no intention of arguing. He recorded in his memoirs that he "regarded the bomb as a military weapon and never had any doubt that it should be used." Winston Churchill agreed. Speaking for the military and political leaders of the day, he explained, "The decision whether or not to use the atomic bomb to compel the surrender of Japan was never even an issue. There was unanimous, automatic, unquestioned agreement around our table."

Truman based his decision on two main factors. One was the fact that invading Japan would result in high casualty figures. Second was the bitterness Americans felt toward the Japanese in the first place. "You should do your weeping at Pearl Harbor," said Truman in 1963, "where thousands of American boys are underneath the waves caused by a Japanese sneak attack."

MAKING CONNECTIONS

Do you think Truman would have been more reluctant to use the atomic bomb on Germany or Italy, if they had not yet surrendered in August 1945, than he was to use it on Japan? Why or why not?

The Bombs in Japan

On August 6, 1945, an American plane dropped "Little Boy," a uranium bomb, on the Japanese city of **Hiroshima**. It killed 70,000

people immediately or soon thereafter and injured 70,000 more. Three days later, another plane dropped "Fat Man," a plutonium bomb, on the city of **Nagasaki**, killing 40,000 people and injuring a like number.

The bombs were a terrifying experience for those people who managed to escape instant death. Novelist Masuji Ibuse recalled the Hiroshima blast: "I saw a ball of blindingly intense light, and simultaneously I was plunged into total, unseeing darkness." Then followed the screams of pain as the city descended into chaos. The black cloud of dust that had instantly turned day into night soon formed a mushroom cloud over the region. People wandered around in confusion looking for friends and family or simply in shock. ★

Hiroshima was ablaze after the explosion. The bomb ignited fires near where it had detonated, and more fires began as hot wires were exposed in crumbling buildings. People suffering from terrible burns—many of whom would die within a few days—rushed to plunge themselves into one of Hiroshima's seven rivers. The white-hot blast had burned people's clothes off their bodies; some people had designs from their kimonos scorched into their flesh. Author Tatsue Urata pictured a victim in Nagasaki:

> The skin was peeling off his face and chest and hands. He was black all over—I suppose it was dirt that had stuck to him where the skin had peeled off; his whole body was coated with it and the blood trickling from his wounds made red streaks in the black.

People who survived the fires still had much to endure. Schoolchildren who had been outside when the bombs hit were so badly disfigured that they became social outcasts. Radiation poisoning—an effect that few people had even considered before the bomb was actually dropped—continued to produce unpredictable symptoms and to claim more victims in the years that followed.

Bombs in both cities demolished buildings, too. Hiroshima and Nagasaki were little more than mounds of rubble near where the bombs had hit. Similar damage had been done in

---

RESOURCE DIRECTORY

Teaching Resources

★ **Literature Activity** *Hiroshima*, an excerpt from the writings of war correspondent John Hersey, found in the Unit 5 folder, p. 28, helps students understand the experiences of six Japanese who survived the atomic blast over Hiroshima in 1945.

A moment before "Little Boy" leveled Hiroshima, the American GI above would have been standing in the midst of a thriving city. The photo at left shows the mushroom cloud that formed over Nagasaki when "Fat Man" exploded.

Tokyo and other cities by hundreds of conventional weapons, but this destruction had been caused by just one bomb.

The Japanese were dazed by the blasts. They were already considering surrender when the Soviet Union entered the war on the Chinese front two days after Hiroshima. Following the Nagasaki explosion, they sought to end the conflict any way they could. On August 14, 1945, Japanese leaders accepted American terms. The island nation formally surrendered on September 2, bringing the long and destructive war to a final end.

SECTION 4 REVIEW

Key Terms, People, and Places
1. Define Interim Committee.
2. Identify (a) Albert Einstein, (b) J. Robert Oppenheimer, (c) Harry S Truman.
3. Identify (a) Hiroshima, (b) Nagasaki.

Key Concepts
4. What was the purpose of the Manhattan Project, and what resources were required to accomplish this purpose?
5. What were some alternatives to dropping the atomic bomb on Japan?

Critical Thinking
6. **Demonstrating Reasoned Judgment** World War II veteran Art Rittenberg recalls that war propaganda "heavily influenced the way we viewed the Japanese. I never thought of them as people like myself who had gone to high school, who had gone to a dance, who had friends, who had parents. They were 'the Japs.' " List three reasons that such attitudes may have affected the decision to drop two atomic bombs on Japan and three reasons they may not have.

 Quiz found in the Unit 5 folder, p. 14, covers the main ideas in this section as well as the key terms.

 Chapter Test Forms A and B are found in the Unit 5 folder, pp. 31–36.

 Answer Keys found in the Unit 5 folder, pp. 146–160, provide answers to all student activities.

Media and Technology

 **Transparency**
Graphic Organizer, G-5

Guided Reading Audiotapes
(English and Spanish)

Computer Test Bank

3. ASSESS

Section 4 Review Answers
1. Interim Committee, see p. 519
2. (a) Albert Einstein, see p. 518, (b) J. Robert Oppenheimer, see p. 519, (c) Harry S Truman, see p. 520
3. (a) Hiroshima, see, p. 520, (b) Nagasaki, see p. 520
4. The Manhattan Project was established to research and develop a weapon that used a sustained nuclear reaction. The project involved thirty-seven sites in the United States and Canada, employed 120,000 people, and cost $2 billion.
5. Alternatives included an invasion, a blockade, a demonstration, or relaxation of the unconditional surrender formula.
6. Answers will vary, but students should support their answers with well-reasoned arguments.

Reteach
Ask students to complete each of the following statements, using information from the chapter section.
● The Manhattan Project was a top-secret plan to develop _____.
● The decision to drop the bomb was made by _____.
● The bomb was dropped on _____.
● The war in the Pacific ended eight days after _____.

4. CLOSE

Reinforcing the Big Idea
The United States ended the war with Japan by using a terrible new weapon, the atomic bomb. The war was finally over, but the world would never be the same again.

The Lasting Impact of the Atomic Bomb

Focus During World War II, the United States developed a secret weapon, the atomic bomb. In the summer of 1945, the United States made the momentous decision to use this new weapon against Japan in order to bring an end to the war. What has been the lasting impact of the development of atomic power?

Instruct Tell students that in the 1950s, schools regularly scheduled air raid drills and students practiced hiding under their desks and shielding their eyes in case of a nuclear attack. Many Americans built and stocked air raid shelters for their families. Families without shelters planned where to go along the evacuation routes out of major cities. As tension between the United States and the Soviet Union tightened or relaxed, people around the world lived above all with the threat that the world might suffer nuclear destruction.

Discuss the arms race with students. Why did Americans think that the way to prevent a nuclear war was to make more and better nuclear weapons? In what way can history prove them correct? What are some of the unforeseen problems of nuclear power that continue to await solutions?

Ask students to work in pairs to find out more about nuclear power and the arms race. Ask pairs to summarize their findings about the arms race and nuclear power plants and their impact on the environment.

Extend Ask students to bring in articles from newspapers, magazines, and other sources about new uses for nuclear power or about problems and proposed solutions concerning nuclear waste. You may want to display these pieces on a bulletin board.

The Lasting Impact of the Atomic Bomb

The atomic bomb did more than simply end the war. The nuclear technology developed by the Manhattan Project launched a wide range of political and economic changes in the postwar world. The Soviet Union tested its first atomic weapon in 1949, and the specter of nuclear war between the superpowers cast a dark shadow over international affairs.

The Arms Race

The arms race was on. The United States tested a new and even more destructive nuclear weapon, the hydrogen bomb, in 1952. The Soviets soon had their own hydrogen bomb. Besides increasing tension and fear between the superpowers, tests in the 1950s and 1960s produced large quantities of fallout, radioactive dust in the atmosphere that drifted down to earth and contaminated every-thing it touched. Water, milk, and all kinds of foods could become toxic. In response, the United States, the Soviet Union, and Great Britain—now also a member of the "nuclear club"—signed a treaty in 1963 banning above-ground testing of nuclear devices.

Both the United States and the Soviet Union continued to produce many thousands of nuclear devices. By 1983 the United States possessed about 26,000 nuclear warheads, a number closely matched by the Soviet stockpile. Despite the proliferation of weapons, however, leaders were in no hurry to spark a nuclear conflict. The possibility of "mutually assured destruction" acted as a strong deterrent. This situation meant that a country could not win a nuclear war because it would be destroyed by its opponent's defensive weapons.

The Soviet Union and the United States, as well as other countries, continued to devote much of

1945 *Physicist J. Robert Oppenheimer and General Leslie R. Groves oversee first atomic bomb test in New Mexico desert.*

1939 *Albert Einstein informs President Roosevelt that atomic weapons are possible.*

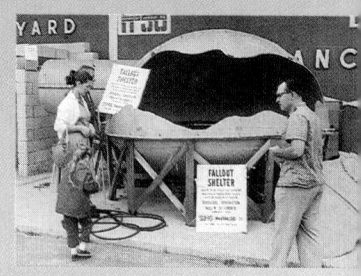

1900　1920　1940

RESOURCE DIRECTORY

Turning Points Extension Activity
The Lasting Impact of the Atomic Bomb, found in the Unit 5 folder, pp. 15–16, extends students' understanding of the postwar era by discussing the long-term impact of the arms race.

their defense budgets to the development of conventional (nonnuclear) weapons. Atomic weapons were a deterrent against atomic weapons, but "limited" wars employing conventional weapons still played a central role in the postwar world. The war between the United States and Iraq in 1991, called the Persian Gulf War, is a good example. This brief conflict introduced the sophisticated new Patriot missile, which is capable of seeking out and destroying incoming missiles in midair.

Peaceful Applications

Nuclear technology has other applications besides the machinery of war. In 1953 Britain harnessed the power of the atom to produce electricity, completing the first nuclear power plant. By 1957 the United States had an operating nuclear plant in Shippingport, Pennsylvania. Many more were to follow. But in the late 1960s and early 1970s, some citizens began to question the safety of nuclear power. The possibility of radiation leaks and the risks involved in storing atomic waste, which remains dangerously radioactive for tens of thousands of years, frightened many people. By 1978 orders for new nuclear power plants

had dropped to zero, and many plants under construction in the 1980s were abandoned before they were finished.

New technologies that have grown out of nuclear research have been useful in the medical field. For example, methods of isotope separation developed by the Manhattan Project have given birth to nuclear medicine, in which small amounts of radioactive chemicals can be injected into and traced throughout the body to diagnose certain diseases. The atom contains an awesome and terrifying force, but it can also be tamed for human benefit.

REVIEWING THE FACTS

1. Did nuclear weapons make conventional war obsolete? Explain your answer.
2. What are some of the peaceful applications of nuclear technology?

Critical Thinking
3. **Formulating Questions** If your local utility company were planning to build a nuclear power plant in your community, what questions would you want to ask a nuclear scientist about the plant?

1952 United States tests first megaton-class hydrogen bomb on Pacific island of Eniwetok.

1982 Nearly one million people join an antinuclear demonstration in New York City.

1990s A bone scan using radioisotope tracers can determine whether cancer in one part of the body has spread to the bones.

1960 **1980** **2000**

1950s American companies market backyard fallout shelters to families fearful of nuclear war.

1957 First American light-water nuclear power plant begins generating electricity in Shippingport, Pennsylvania.

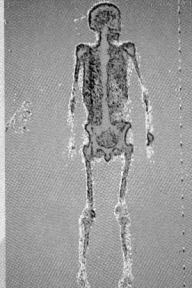

523

Chapter Review

Understanding Key Terms, People, and Places

Key Terms
1. fascism
2. Nazi party
3. anti-Semitism
4. appeasement
5. Lend-Lease Act
6. blitzkrieg
7. Battle of the Bulge
8. holocaust
9. GI
10. WAC
11. Manhattan Project
12. Interim Committee

People
13. Benito Mussolini
14. Adolf Hitler
15. Winston Churchill
16. Douglas MacArthur
17. Dwight D. Eisenhower
18. Chester Nimitz
19. Joseph Stalin
20. Albert Einstein
21. J. Robert Oppenheimer
22. Harry S Truman

Places
23. Rhineland
24. Manchuria
25. Pearl Harbor
26. Midway Island
27. Guadalcanal
28. Normandy
29. Hiroshima
30. Nagasaki

Terms For each term above, write a sentence that explains its relation to World War II.

Matching Review the key terms in the list above. If you are not sure of a term's meaning, review its definition in the chapter. Then choose a term from the list that best matches each description below.
1. a policy of keeping the peace by giving in to someone's demands
2. a series of sudden military attacks by land and air
3. the German counterattack in Belgium and Luxembourg in December 1944
4. the nickname for an American soldier
5. the group of American officials who studied alternative methods of ending the war in the Pacific

Word Relationships Three of the terms in each of the following sets of terms are related. Choose the term that does not belong, and explain why it does not belong.
1. (a) Albert Einstein, (b) Benito Mussolini, (c) J. Robert Oppenheimer, (d) Harry S Truman
2. (a) Chester Nimitz, (b) Douglas MacArthur, (c) Winston Churchill, (d) Dwight D. Eisenhower
3. (a) Pearl Harbor, (b) Rhineland, (c) Guadalcanal, (d) Midway Island

Reviewing Main Ideas

Section 1 (pp. 500 – 505)
1. What did Japan hope to gain by invading Manchuria and other parts of the Asian mainland?
2. How did the United States support the Allies with economic aid while staying out of the fighting?
3. Why did Japan attack Pearl Harbor?

Section 2 (pp. 506 – 512)
4. What events helped turn the tide of war in favor of the Allies?
5. What was Hitler's "Final Solution"?

Section 3 (pp. 513–516)
6. While some Japanese Americans were fighting the enemy overseas, what was happening to many of their families in the United States?
7. In what ways did the United States government discriminate against African Americans during World War II?
8. What unique contribution were Native Americans able to make to the American military effort?

Section 4 (pp. 518–521)
9. Why did the United States government reject the idea of invading Japan in order to end the war?
10. What were the immediate effects of using the atomic bomb on Hiroshima and Nagasaki?

Chapter Review Answers

Understanding Key Terms, People, and Places

Terms
Students should refer to the definitions of the key terms in the chapter to write sentences that show the relation of each word to World War II.

Matching
1. appeasement
2. blitzkrieg
3. Battle of the Bulge
4. GI
5. Interim Committee

Word Relationships
1. Mussolini, dictator of Italy during World War II, does not belong. Einstein and Oppenheimer were associated with the development of the atomic bomb and Truman with its deployment.
2. Churchill, the British prime minister, does not belong. Generals MacArthur and Eisenhower and Admiral Nimitz were American military leaders.
3. The Rhineland, one of the first areas occupied by Hitler in 1936, does not belong. Pearl Harbor, Guadalcanal, and Midway Island were all scenes of important battles in the Pacific.

Reviewing Main Ideas
1. Japan, a resource-poor chain of islands, hoped to gain access to raw materials and new markets.
2. In order to help the Allies, President Roosevelt traded American ships to convoy supplies across the Atlantic. The next year, in 1941, he supported the Lend-Lease Act to provide war supplies to Britain.
3. Japan hoped to knock out the U.S. Pacific Fleet so that nothing would stand in the way of Japanese control of the Pacific.
4. In Europe, the failed German invasion of the Soviet Union and the successful Allied offensives in North Africa and Italy helped turn the tide in favor of the Allies. In the Pacific, the Allies won key strategic victories on the islands of Midway and Guadalcanal.
5. The Nazis' "final solution" was to get rid of all Jews and other "undesirables" by gathering them in concentration camps and killing them.
6. Their families were interned in camps in the United States and not allowed to leave.
7. Official policy forced African Americans to fight in segregated units in the army. For most of the war, they were not allowed to join the air corps or the marine corps, and in the navy they could enlist only in the messman's branch.
8. The Navaho used their language to transmit secret messages by radio and telephone.
9. Because the Japanese were fierce fighters who would be defending their homeland, many people thought that the potential casualties of an invasion of Japan would be intolerable.
10. Buildings were demolished; seventy thousand people in Hiroshima and forty thousand in Nagasaki were killed; thousands more suffered terrible burns and radiation sickness; Japan finally agreed to surrender to the Allies.

Thinking Critically

1. Serious personnel shortages led military officials to bend the rules against women and African Americans in the military.
2. The United States and the Soviet Union had different ideas about what the postwar world should look like. The fact that the Soviet Union was excluded from the Manhattan Project showed a lack of trust and led to Soviet resentment. The United States deployed the atomic bomb in part to demonstrate America's strength to the Soviet Union.
3. Video games make war seem exciting and death seem unreal and impersonal. The actual experience of combat is numbingly terrifying; daily life is miserable and unstable.

- **Evidence of thoughtfulness** Did students include the major events presented in the chapter?
- **Evidence of outside research** To what extent did students use outside research materials?
- **Evidence of synthesis** Do the students' classification systems show how events are related? How complex are the relationships?
- **Communication style** Is the time line clear and easy to follow?

Thinking Critically

1. **Expressing Problems Clearly** What situation often motivated the armed forces to relax their discrimination against women and African Americans?
2. **Expressing Problems Clearly** The Soviet Union fought alongside the Allies during World War II, yet soon after became a bitter enemy of the United States. Give evidence to show that the seeds of conflict between the United States and the Soviet Union were already present during World War II.
3. **Distinguishing False from Accurate Images** Many popular video games deal with war. Do you think that the images of war presented in such games accurately portray the real experience of fighting in a war? Why or why not?

Making Connections

1. **Evaluating Primary Sources** Review the first primary source excerpt on page 520. Dwight Eisenhower disagreed with President Truman's decision to end the war by using the atomic bomb. Are Eisenhower's reasons convincing? Explain why or why not.
2. **Understanding the Visuals** Look through the chapter to find visuals that reveal the attitude of the United States toward the war before and after Pearl Harbor. Write a paragraph to accompany your choice of visuals, explaining what the attitude was and what change, if any, it underwent.
3. **Writing About the Chapter** Imagine that you are living in London during the Battle of Britain, the devastating German air attack that was most intense during the summer and fall of 1940. Write a letter to a relative in the United States, explaining your fears and uncertainties. First, review the chapter for details about the war. Next, write a draft of your letter, adding details from your imagination as you picture yourself living with the relentless bombing and the knowledge that much of Europe is under Nazi control. Revise your letter, making sure that it is written from the point of view of someone who does not know how the conflict will end. Proofread your letter and draft a final copy.
4. **Using the Graphic Organizer** This graphic organizer uses a multi-flow chart to organize information about the causes and effects of Britain and France's declaration of war on Germany in September 1939. Causes of that event appear in the boxes at left. Effects of the event are listed to the right. (a) According to the graphic organizer, what were two major causes of this event? (b) On a separate sheet of paper, create your own multi-flow chart. In the center box, write "Japanese bombing of Pearl Harbor draws U.S. into war." Add three causes and three effects of this event to the appropriate boxes.

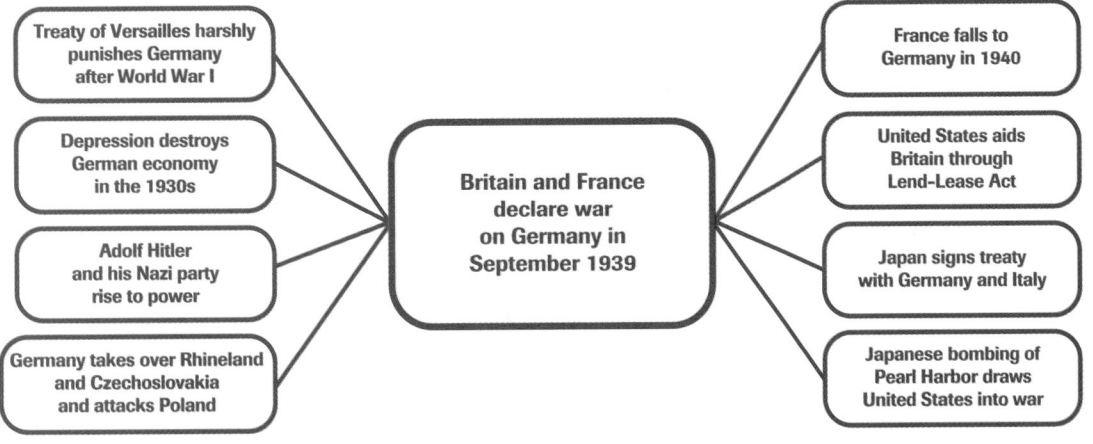

Making Connections

1. Answers will vary. Some students may argue that it was necessary to use the atomic bomb to ensure a quick end to the war; others may say that the United States should have tried other alternatives before using such a horrible weapon.

2. Students should use the visual "America First" on page 504 to demonstrate American isolationism before the war. To show the shift in the American attitude, they might use any of the photos or maps on pages 507, 508, 515, and 521. Students' paragraphs should demonstrate an understanding of the shift that the United States underwent from isolationism to interventionism.

3. Students' letters should be written from the viewpoint of someone living during the bombings and should reflect the uncertainty and fear of not knowing who will ultimately win the war.

4. (a) Answers should include two of the following: the Treaty of Versailles, depression in Germany, Hitler's rise to power, German aggression in Europe. (b) Causes may include American trade sanctions on Japan, Japanese desire for control over East Asia, and the threat of the Pacific Fleet to Japanese plans. Effects may include battles over tiny Pacific islands, anti-Japanese feelings in the United States, and the use of the atomic bomb.

Ordinary people become heroes during a war, saving lives, keeping calm, and enduring that which should never have to be endured. After the war, life slowly returns to normal, and those heroes go on with the ordinary business of living—but they are changed. Their experiences during the war color their perceptions of life and its events for the rest of their lives. Ask students to consider an event in their lives that they believe they will always remember. Have them write a paragraph that describes that event in as much detail as possible. Students should include a description of the surroundings in which the event took place, any smells in the air they can remember, the expressions on the faces of those with them, and so on.

INSTRUCT

Have students perform rehearsed conversations in front of the class in which they role-play Richard Glazar or Abraham Bomba, Joe McCarthy, and Jean Wood talking to each other about their experiences during the war. Form students into groups of three. Each student in the group should further research Treblinka, the liberation of Athens, or the London blitz. Then, group members should meet to select roles and write out scripts. Groups should craft their "conversations" to teach the rest of the class more about the three events, revealing the information in a way that is consistent with their character and showing appropriate reactions to the comments of the others. As part of their assignment, have students place the three events on a time line. The time lines can also include other events from World War II. Students should hand in the time lines with their scripts.

CHAPTER 15
SOURCE READINGS

Survivors of the Holocaust Remember

Primary Source

Claude Landzmann

INTRODUCTION From the horrors of the Holocaust, some words echo in our minds and bring a chill just by reading them on a page or hearing them spoken. The names of the concentration camps in which millions of Jewish people and others were murdered by the Nazis are words that evoke that terrible past: Auschwitz, Dachau, and Treblinka among others. At these camps, those prisoners who had skills that the Nazis found useful were spared. The rest, hundreds every day, were herded into vans or "showers" and killed with gas. The excerpts below are from the complete text of the 1985 film *Shoah, An Oral History of the Holocaust*. In the excerpts, two survivors describe their first hours at Treblinka, and the indescribable pain they endured when the realization surfaced that they and their entire families had been taken to a death camp. For many, the pain of knowing what their loved ones had endured, while they escaped, was too much to bear.

By the end of World War II, 800,000 Jewish men, women, and children had been murdered at Treblinka.

VOCABULARY Before you read the selection, find the meaning of these words in a dictionary: barracks, Yiddish.

Treblinka

Richard Glazar: We were taken to a barracks. The whole place stank. Piled about five feet high in a jumbled mass, were all the things people could conceivably have brought. Clothes, suitcases, everything stacked in a solid mass. On top of it, jumping around like demons, people were making bundles and carrying them outside. It was turned over to one of these men. His armband said "Squad Leader." He shouted, and I understood that I was also to pick up clothing, bundle it, and take it somewhere. As I worked, I asked him: "What's going on? Where are the ones who stripped?" And he replied: "Dead! All dead!"

But it still hadn't sunk in, I didn't believe it. He'd used the Yiddish word. It was the first time I'd heard Yiddish spoken. He didn't say it very loud, and I saw he had tears in his eyes. Suddenly, he started shouting, and raised his whip. Out of the corner of my eye I saw an SS man coming. And I understood that I was to ask no more questions, but just to rush outside with the package.

Abraham Bomba: At that time we started working in that place they called Treblinka. Still I couldn't believe what had happened over there on the other side of the gate, where the people went in, everything disappeared, and everything got quiet. But in a minute we find out, when we start to ask the people who worked here before us what had happened to the others, they said: "What do you mean, what happened? Don't you know that? They're all gassed, all killed." It was impossible to say anything—we were just like stones. We couldn't ask what had happened to the wife, to the kid. "What do you mean—wife, kid? Nobody is anymore!" How could they kill, how could they gas so many people at once? But they had a way to do it.

Richard Glazar: All I could think of then was my friend Carel Unger. He'd been at the rear of the train, in a section that had been uncoupled and left outside. I needed someone. Near me. With me. Then I saw him. He was in the second group. He'd been spared too. On the way, somehow, he had learned, he already knew. He looked at me. All he said was: "Richard, my father, mother, brother . . ." He had learned on the way there.

Your meeting with Carel— how long after your arrival did it happen?

It was . . . around twenty minutes after we reached Treblinka. Then I left the barracks and had my first look at the vast space that I soon learned was called "the sorting place." It was buried under mountains of objects of all kinds. Mountains of shoes, of clothes, thirty feet high. I thought about it and said to Carel: "It's a hurricane, a raging sea. We're shipwrecked. And we're still alive. We must do nothing . . . but watch for every new wave, float on it, get ready for the next wave, and ride the wave at all costs. And nothing else."

Abraham Bomba: That's how the day went through, without anything. Not drinking—we went twenty-four hours without water, without anything. We couldn't drink—we couldn't take anything into our mouths, because it was impossible to believe that just a minute, just an hour before, you were part of a family, you were part of a wife or a husband, and now all of a sudden everything is dead.

We went into a special barrack, where I was sleeping right next to the hallway. And over there, that night was the most horrible night for all the people, because of the memory of all those things that people went through with each other—all the joys and the happiness and the births and the weddings and other things—and all of a sudden, in one second, to cut through without anything, and without any guilt of the people, because the people weren't guilty at all. The only guilt they had was that they were Jewish.

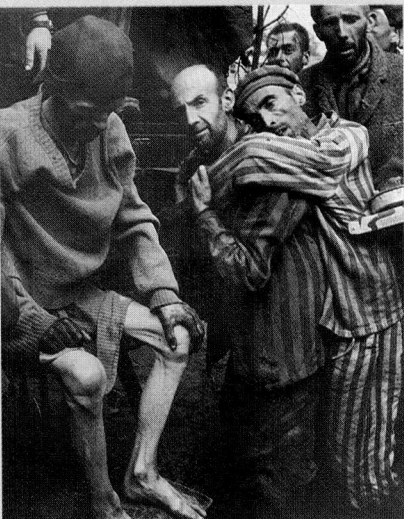

Allied soldiers discovered people like these— starved, sick, and dazed—when they liberated Nazi concentration camps.

Most of us were up all night, trying to talk to each other, which was not allowed. . . . We were not allowed to talk to each other or to express our views or our minds to each other. And till the morning at five o'clock we start going out from the barrack. In the morning when they had the appeal to go out from the barracks, from our group I would say at least four or five were dead. I don't know how that happened—they must have had with them some kind of poison and poisoned themselves. At least two of them were my close friends. They didn't say anything. We didn't even know they had poison with them.

Richard Glazar: Greenery—sand everywhere else. At night we were put into a barracks. It just had a sand floor. Nothing else. Each of us simply dropped where he stood. Half asleep, I heard some men hang themselves. We didn't react then. It was almost normal. Just as it was normal that for everyone behind whom the gate of Treblinka closed, there was death, had to be death, for no one was supposed to be left to bear witness. I already knew that, three hours after arriving at Treblinka.

THINKING ABOUT THE SELECTION

1. What were the belongings piled in the "sorting place"? To whom did they belong?
2. Why did the interviewer ask how long after arriving at the camp did Glazer meet his friend Carel?

Critical Thinking

3. **Identifying Central Issues** Why does Glazer tell his friend that "We must do nothing . . . but watch for every new wave, float on it, get ready for the next wave, and ride the wave at all costs. And nothing else"?

ANSWERS TO

Thinking About the Selection

1. They were shoes, clothing, and other articles that had belonged to the prisoners who were killed in the gas chambers.

2. He asks this in order to point out how little time it took for the Nazis to kill so many people. By the time Glazer found his friend— twenty minutes after arriving at the camp—hundreds of people, including their own families, had already been gassed.

3. He says this because in order to survive they could not resist, could not even think about the horrors they were witnessing and experiencing.

Political cartoons can reveal much
about the sentiments and conflicts of
a period. Have students compile a
collection of political cartoons from
World War II and provide a brief
analysis of each. You might have
some of the cartoons made into
overhead transparencies and share
them with the class, asking the student who found the cartoon to lead a
class analysis of its content. For
sources of political cartoons, students might use *The Ungentlemanly
Art* by Stephen Hess or *Years of
Wrath: Cartoon History, 1932–45* by
David Low.

SOURCE READINGS

The Liberation of Athens

Primary Source

Sergeant Joe McCarthy

INTRODUCTION "Liberation is getting to be old familiar stuff in Europe these days," wrote Sergeant Joe McCarthy in Athens, Greece, near the end of the war in Europe, "but the feeling that swept this great city when it found itself free of Germans was something extra special, in a class by itself." Indeed, the people of Athens had fought long and hard against the Germans. Their jubilant reception of the liberating troops is described here by McCarthy in an article he wrote for *Yank* magazine, the army weekly.

VOCABULARY Before you read the selection, find the meaning of this word in a dictionary: partisan

In every country village along the road, church bells were ringing and people pressed forward to our jeep, shaking our hands,
giving the thumbs-up salute and offering us bread, cakes and
fresh fruits even though food is scarce here. One woman handed a
large bundle to one of our men and was lost in the crowd before he
could give it back to her. He opened it later and found a large hand-
knitted blanket, two clean sheets and a pillowcase.

When we reached downtown Athens, it was impossible to drive
the jeep on until Greek Partisan soldiers opened a path for us
through the mobs of people. We finally managed to reach the
Grande Bretagne Hotel. When we climbed out of the jeep, the crowd
swallowed us up, and the next thing I knew I was being squeezed,
shaken, thumped, kissed and then picked up and carried down the
street on somebody's shoulders. Luckily I heard a boy near me
speaking English. I leaned down, shouting in his ear to make myself
heard above the roaring crowd, and asked him to get me off the
shoulders of these people and into the hotel across the street.

The army Medal of Honor, awarded for gallantry
in action above and beyond the call of duty.

THINKING ABOUT THE SELECTION

1. Why was the Greeks' offering of "breads, cakes and fresh fruits" especially touching?
2. Why does McCarthy say that liberation was becoming "old familiar stuff" in Europe at the time this article was written?

Critical Thinking

3. **Formulating Questions** What questions might you ask McCarthy to find out more about the Greek struggle in World War II?

Thinking About the Selection
1. Due to the war, food was scarce in Athens at
the time, so the people were giving away food
that they really needed themselves.
2. McCarthy says this because by that time the
Allies had already liberated many cities in
Europe.
3. Questions might include: What year did
Greece enter World War II? How many Greeks
were killed in the war? What happened to
Greek cities and the economy during the war?

A Londoner Describes Life During the Blitz

Primary Source

INTRODUCTION The excerpt below is from an oral account by Jean Wood, a Londoner who had four children during World War II. Wood's narrative appeared in *"The Good War": An Oral History of World War II*, by historian Studs Terkel. Here she describes the bombing of London and how people adapted to living with the constant fear and uncertainty of life in a city under siege.

VOCABULARY Before you read the selection, find the meaning of this word in a dictionary: staccato.

I never thought I could sit and read to children, say, about Cinderella, while you could hear the German planes coming. Sometimes a thousand a night came over, in waves. We had a saying, (says it staccato) I'm gonna getcha, I'm gonna getcha. That's how the planes sounded. You'd hear the bomb drop so many hundred yards that way. And you'd think, Oh, that missed us. You'd think, My God, the next one's going to be a direct hit. But you'd continue to read: "And the ugly sister said"—and you'd say "Don't fidget, dear." And you'd think, My God, I can't stand it. But you bore up. And I wasn't the bravest of people, believe me.

You had hunches. About half past three you'd say, "I won't sleep over there tonight. I'll put them all over here 'cause I have a hunch that that part of the wall will come down." Or what few neighbors were left would say, "Why don't you bring all the kids over to me tonight and let's all sing and play cards. We won't bother with Jerry[1] tonight." Now would it be safer that side of the road or this side? We'll go over there.

I did fire-watch. And that's frightening. You got up on the roof with a steel helmet on. You're supposed to have a protective jacket. The fire bombs were round balls. They'd come onto roofs and start fires. So the government gave you a bucket of sand and a shovel. Charming. (Laughs.) You stood there till the bomb fell. And you'd shovel it up quick and throw it into the bucket of sand. . . .

I had an aunt who was bombed out three times. My grandmother, who was eighty-odd, was bombed out and left clinging to the stairs, with her hair alight. The air-raid wardens got her out. She said, "I must go back for my hat." They took her in a truck with a lot of other elderly people to a safety zone.

I had to stay with my mother-in-law once. Sometimes the raids came before the siren went off, so you weren't down in the shelter. Land mines came down by parachute and laid whole streets low. It was like a bombed-out piece of land. This airplane was very low dropping the fire bombs, dropping them everywhere she was going. She did this terrific zigzag all across this field, hopping and leaping, hopping and leaping. Afterwards, people ran to get the parachute, 'cause with this parachute, we could make ourselves clothes. Clothes rationing was terribly strict. My husband got me a piece, and I made the children little dresses out of this nylon.

A lot of flowers grew on these bombed spaces, especially one in particular. It was a stalk with a lot of little red spots. It was like a weed, really. It was called London pride.

There was the blitz, when all London caught fire, except Saint Paul's Cathedral, thank God. That's why every time I go to Saint Paul's, I say, Oh, you're still there, thank God. Everything was in flames that night. It was like daylight, the flames.

---

[1] "Jerry" was a name used for the Germans during the war.

THINKING ABOUT THE SELECTION

1. Why did the Londoners gather up the parachutes from the bombs after they exploded?
2. Why might the flowers that grew on the bombed spaces have been called "London pride"?

Critical Thinking

3. **Drawing Conclusions** What does the excerpt show about Wood's personality that might have helped her cope with the bombings even though, as she says, she was not "the bravest of people"?

ANSWERS TO

Thinking About the Selection

1. They used the nylon cloth of the parachutes to make clothes because clothing was rationed during the war.

2. The name was probably a reference to the fact that, despite the hardship they endured, the Londoners survived and managed to keep their dignity. The flowers blooming in the desolation of a bombed area symbolized such steadfast determination.

3. The excerpt shows that Wood views the world with a strong sense of humor, which probably helped her get through those trying years.

Chapter 16 World War II at Home
1941–1945

📁 Teaching Resources (See Unit 5 Folder)

	Instruction	Enrichment
Section 1 **The Shift to Wartime Production** (pp. 532–535)	Reproducible Lesson Plan, p. 38 Alternate Lesson Plan, p. 127 Guided Reading and Review, p. 42 Quiz, p. 43	Visual Learning Activity, Campaign on the Home Front, p. 63 Critical Thinking Activity, Identifying Alternatives, p. 55
Section 2 **Daily Life on the Home Front** (pp. 536–539)	Reproducible Lesson Plan, p. 39 Alternate Lesson Plan, p. 128 Guided Reading and Review, p. 44 Quiz, p. 45	Literature Activity, How to Win Friends and Influence People, p. 59 Visual Learning Activity, The Nature of the Enemy, p. 62
Section 3 **Women and the War** (pp. 540–544)	Reproducible Lesson Plan, p. 40 Alternate Lesson Plan, p. 129 Guided Reading and Review, p. 46 Quiz, p. 47	Primary Source Activity, Working Conditions for Women of Color, pp. 57–58 Historian's Toolbox Activity, Identifying Assumptions, p. 54
Section 4 **The Struggle for Justice at Home** (pp. 546–551)	Reproducible Lesson Plan, p. 41 Alternate Lesson Plan, p. 130 Guided Reading and Review, p. 48 Quiz, p. 49 Chapter Test, Forms A & B, pp. 64–69	Literature Activity, Black Boy, pp. 60–61 American Profiles Activity, James Farmer, p. 50 American Profiles Activity, Daniel K. Inouye, p. 51 Viewpoints Activity, On Japanese American Internment, pp. 52–53 Primary Source Activity, Anti-Japanese Sentiment, p. 56

📁 Additional Chapter Resources

Resource Organizer, p. 37
Alternate Lesson Plan, p. 126
Answer Keys, pp. 146–160

Bibliography

For the Teacher
O'Neill, William L. *A Democracy at War: America's Fight at Home and Abroad in World War II.* Free Press, 1993.
Winkler, Allan M. *Home Front, U.S.A.: America During World War II.* Harlan Davidson, 1986. (A concise volume with a chapter devoted to ethnic minorities and women.)
Motley, Mary Penick, ed. *The Invisible Soldier: The Experience of the Black Soldier, World War II.* Wayne State University Press, 1975. (Personal accounts of African American soldiers during the war; illustrated with photographs and maps.)

Prentice Hall Literature Excerpts from *The American Experience,* 1994, "The Modern Age, 1915–1946."

The Big Idea for the chapter and how the main ideas in each section relate to the Big Idea are graphically displayed below. Comprehension of this chapter's Big Idea is critical to students' understanding of United States history and how we as a nation got where we are today.

Media and Technology

 Fine Art, D-18; Critical Thinking, I-10

 Graphic Organizer, G-3

 Guided Reading Audiotapes (English and Spanish)

 Computer Test Bank

For the Student

Frank, Miriam, et al. *The Life and Times of Rosie the Riveter.* Clarity, 1982. (Photographs and interviews provide a lively account of women and African American workers on the home front.)

Armour, John, and Peter Wright. *Manzanar.* Random House, 1988. (Uses text and photographs by Ansel Adams to tell the story of one Japanese internment camp.)

Harris, Mark Jonathan, et al. *The Home Front: America During World War II.* G. P. Putnam's Sons, 1984. (An informal anthology of interviews with ordinary citizens, including women and minorities, describing life during the war.)

CHAPTER 16

World War II affected every aspect of American life, from jobs and wages to the kind of food that appeared on the nation's dinner tables. Americans were asked to examine the ideals they were fighting for overseas and compare them with practices at home.

SECTION 1

World War II brought an end to the Great Depression as American factories and workers began to produce goods needed to win the war.

SECTION 2

Americans on the home front supported the war effort by conserving resources and coping with rationing.

SECTION 3

Thousands of American women took jobs in defense plants during the war.

SECTION 4

The need for workers during the war temporarily broke down some racial barriers in the job market. Japanese Americans, however, were treated with bitter prejudice and many were forced into internment camps.

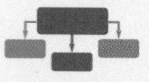

World War II at Home
1941–1945

CHAPTER 16

World War II at Home
1941–1945

The Relevance of the Big Idea

World War II required large numbers of American men to fight in Europe and Asia. At the same time, workers were needed in industries at home. As a result, a major change in the American workplace took place: Women and minorities entered the work force in unprecedented numbers—and in fields previously off-limits to them. Executive orders barred racial discrimination in government war production jobs, but African Americans continued to suffer from widespread discrimination. In the midst of the cheerfully portrayed flurry of the war effort at home, Japanese Americans were interned in remote camps and their civil rights suspended.

Discuss the contrast of these conditions with the ideals put forth as the reasons Americans were fighting the war. Tell students that the civil rights movement of the sixties and some aspects of the women's movement of the seventies have their roots during this period.

In Depth

Global Connections

The Great Depression ended with the start of World War II. By 1943, there was virtually no unemployment in the United States. The war fueled economic growth not only in the United States but also in the other countries involved in the war. Germany and Japan both entered the war hoping that their economies would get a much-needed boost. In Japan, 3.2 million people became employed during the war years. In Great Britain, the labor force grew by 2.9 million.

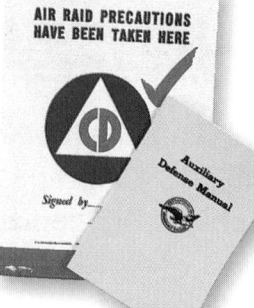

*A*s war clouds gathered over Europe and Asia in the late 1930s, the United States government faced an enormous challenge. How would it convert a depressed peacetime economy and a public that still remembered the horrors of World War I into an efficient war production machine? This massive organizational project required not only mobilizing American businesses but also "selling" the American public on the war. Families who had known terrible hardship during the Depression and who were sending their loved ones into combat would have to be convinced to sacrifice still more. With slogans such as "Remember Pearl Harbor" and "Don't You Know There's A War On?" the government launched a massive campaign that reminded people at every turn to conserve, participate, and sacrifice.

Events in the United States

1938	1939	1940	1941
	1939 Robert de Graff starts the Pocket Books company.	**1940** Roosevelt asks Congress to approve the production of 50,000 airplanes per year.	**1941** A. Philip Randolph suggests a march on Washington to end discrimination.

Events in the World

| | **1939** First evacuation of women and children from London. | **1940** Rationing begins in Britain. | |

▶ RESOURCE DIRECTORY

Teaching Resources

📄 **Alternate Lesson Plan: Demonstrating the Big Idea** found in the Alternate Lesson Plans folder, p. 126, provides a lesson strategy to instruct students about the Big Idea that the wartime economy involved unprecedented public effort in financing and participating in the massive war effort.

📄 **Alternative Assessment Handbook** provides information, guidance, and strategies for alternative methods of assessment. It includes an essay on new trends in assessment, guidance and strategies for developing performance tasks and portfolios, scoring rubrics, and sample evaluation forms.

Pages 532–535
The Shift to Wartime Production

Despite its horrors, World War II did bring an end to the Depression in America. Millions of workers streamed back into the factories to produce airplanes, tanks, and guns—and to receive a welcome paycheck.

Pages 536–539
Daily Life on the Home Front

While American soldiers crouched in foxholes overseas, friends and families supported their struggle on the home front. Rationing and conserving resources like gasoline, scrap metal, and rubber drew most of the country into the war effort.

Pages 540–544
Women and the War

During World War II, thousands of American women rolled up their sleeves and went to work in defense plants and shipyards. Adapting quickly to work usually done by men and overcoming a sometimes cold welcome from fellow male employees, they helped satisfy the Allies' urgent need for military goods.

Pages 546–551
The Struggle for Justice at Home

For many Americans, the war broke down racial barriers in the job market. Japanese Americans, however, fell victim to bitter prejudice at home as the United States battled Japan abroad.

1942	1943	1944	1945	1946
1942 Popular movies such as Casablanca glorify the war effort and inspire troops.	*1943* Race riots in Los Angeles. • Congress passes Smith-Connally Act limiting strikes.	*1944* The number of working women rises to over 19 million, up from 14.6 million in 1941.	*1945* Japanese Americans are released from internment camps.	
1942 Great Britain produces 23,671 aircraft, 8,611 tanks, and 173 major vessels.	*1943* Germans give up after 900-day siege of Stalingrad.	*1944* Anne Frank and her family arrested by Nazis in Amsterdam.	*1945* Hitler commits suicide in an underground bunker in Germany.	

Alternative Assessment

As an ongoing chapter project, students can demonstrate their understanding of the changes in American life during World War II by preparing a "Guide to Life on the Home Front" for returning veterans. Point out that many of the veterans have had little contact with home for several years. The guides should address all of the following topics:

● The economy and the shift to wartime production
● Daily life at home
● Women and the war
● The struggle for justice at home

Students may prepare a booklet, an audiotape, or an oral presentation. Guides should be interesting, easy to follow, and appropriately humorous. Explain that projects will be evaluated according to the following guidelines:

● **Unacceptable** Activity not attempted; guide does not describe topics as outlined above.
● **Limited/Acceptable** Guide provides a limited description of changes in each area and states causes.
● **Extensive/Commendable** Guide provides an extensive description of changes in each area with analysis of causes.
● **Extraordinary/Outstanding** Guide contains a lively, in-depth description of changes in each area with thoughtful analysis of causes and includes information from sources other than the textbook.

For information and guidance on alternative assessment trends and strategies, see the Alternative Assessment Handbook in the Resource Directory on page 530.

The Shift to Wartime Production

SECTION 1

The Shift to Wartime Production

The Shift to Wartime Production

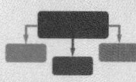

1. FOCUS

Connecting to the Big Idea

See page 530B. Explain to students that World War II changed American life by helping to end the Depression—putting Americans back to work. As factories shifted into wartime production, there were new opportunities for workers, businesses, and entrepreneurs. Ask students what these new opportunities were and how they changed life in America.

Objectives

- Describe the changes in the American economy as it converted to wartime production.
- Explain how World War II ended the Depression in the United States.
- Explain how the United States paid for the cost of the war.

In Depth

Did You Know?

When Coca-Cola was developed in 1885, it was sold as a cure for headaches. Concocted by John Pemberton, an Atlanta pharmacist, the original drink was a syrup made with wine, cocaine, and a few other ingredients. A year later, Pemberton took out the wine and cocaine, adding caffeine and kola nut extract for flavor. By 1889, drugstores sold drinks made of Coca-Cola syrup and carbonated water. By 1919, Coca-Cola was so popular that the company was sold for $25 million.

SECTION PREVIEW

Despite its horrors, World War II did bring an end to the Depression in America. Millions of workers streamed back into the factories to produce airplanes, tanks, and guns—and to receive a welcome paycheck.

Key Concepts

- During World War II, the American economy converted to producing materials for the war.
- World War II ended the Great Depression as millions joined the wartime labor force and, after the United States joined the war, the military.
- The war was paid for with taxes and by government borrowing.

Many advertisements linked their products to wartime patriotism.

Key Terms, People, and Places

cost-plus system, wildcat strike, deficit spending; John L. Lewis

---

At the start of World War II, supplying goods to the Allied forces helped boost the American economy. With the cloud of the Depression finally beginning to lift, companies were eager to start making cars, refrigerators, and washing machines again, and consumers were eager to buy them. The government would have to campaign vigorously to convince Americans to continue to sacrifice such items for the sake of the war effort.

Mobilizing the War Economy

President Roosevelt understood that the outcome of the war would ultimately depend on America's ability to produce war materials such as bombers, tanks, and uniforms. He knew that the government would have to take a firm hand in coordinating the production efforts of hundreds of American businesses used to pursuing their own interests. In May 1943 FDR organized the Office of War Mobilization under the direction of James F. Byrnes. A former Supreme Court justice, Byrnes was a skillful negotiator whose guidance made wartime production run smoothly.

Conversion of the Auto Industry After the bombing of Pearl Harbor, the nation was convinced of the need to produce large amounts of war materials. The automobile industry responded to this need by converting its factories to produce bombers. On February 10, 1942, as the last cars rolled off the assembly lines, workers began taking apart automobile machinery and packing it for storage.

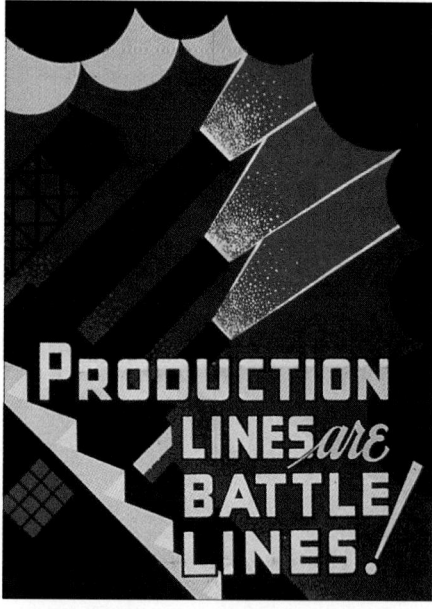

The government used posters such as this one, designed by Ches Cobb, to remind people on the home front of their responsibility to the war effort.

RESOURCE DIRECTORY

Teaching Resources

Reproducible Lesson Plan found in the Unit 5 folder, p. 38, provides a summary of the Section 1 lesson plan content.

Alternate Lesson Plan: Learning Styles found in the Alternate Lesson Plans folder, p. 127, is especially effective for visual learners and uses unnumbered graphs designed to extend students' understanding of how the war was financed.

Guided Reading and Review found in the Unit 5 folder, p. 42, provides a structure for reading and mastering the key concepts and reviewing the key terms for Section 1. (Guided Practice)

Visual Learning Activity Campaign on the Home Front, found in the Unit 5 folder, p. 63, uses government posters to help students understand the techniques used to "sell" Americans on making sacrifices for the war.

Passenger Car and Military Aircraft Production, 1939–1946

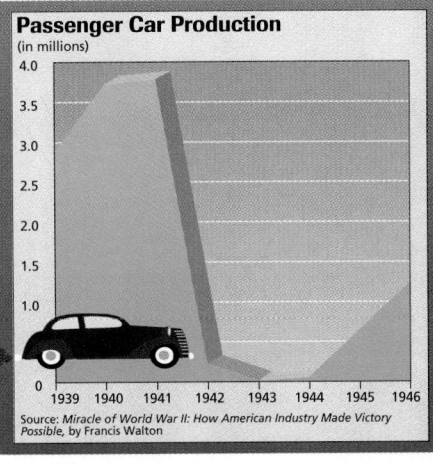

Passenger Car Production
(in millions)

Source: *Miracle of World War II: How American Industry Made Victory Possible*, by Francis Walton

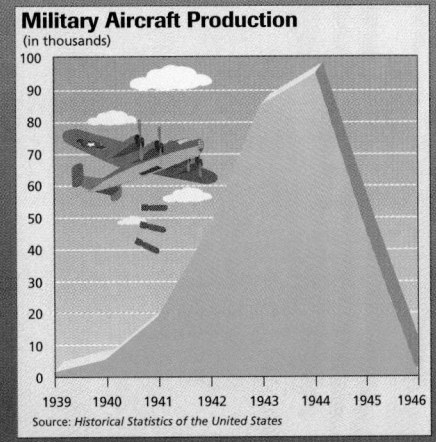

Military Aircraft Production
(in thousands)

Source: *Historical Statistics of the United States*

Interpreting Graphs
What overall trends in auto production and military aircraft production do these graphs show? Do you think the effect of assembly-line production on the aircraft industry can be judged from the information in the graph on the right? Explain your answer.

While many existing plants were being converted, Henry Ford was planning to build an immense new factory to produce B-24 Liberator bombers. Ford wanted to use assembly-line techniques, which had never before been applied in the aircraft industry, to produce planes faster and more efficiently. To achieve his goal, Ford conceived the huge Willow Run bomber plant near Ann Arbor, Michigan. Willow Run covered 975 acres with an assembly line that stretched a full mile across a flat meadowland. When operating at full capacity, the plant employed more than 42,000 people.

MAKING CONNECTIONS

How do you suppose the government encouraged businesses to undertake the expensive process of wartime conversion? Compare your response to the information that follows.

New Opportunities for Profit Secretary of War Henry L. Stimson understood that "if you are going to try to go to war, or to prepare for war, in a capitalist country, you have to let business make money out of the process or business won't work." To that end, the government established the **cost-plus system,** in which the government paid all development and production costs plus a percentage of those costs as profit on anything a company made for the war.

Thousands of business executives went to Washington to work in war agencies responsible for coordinating production. Many accepted token salaries of one dollar from the government while remaining on their own companies' payrolls. From inside war agencies, these "dollar-a-year men" helped to decide which firms would receive profitable contracts.

New Markets and Methods Entrepreneurs prospered during World War II. Some succeeded in creating profitable new markets for their products. Robert Woodruff, head of Coca-Cola, declared in December 1941: "We will see that every man in uniform gets a bottle of Coca-Cola for five cents wherever he is and whatever it costs [the company]." By the time the war was over, American troops had drunk five billion bottles of Coca-Cola. At the same time, Woodruff's company had established a new "army" of civilian consumers who had enjoyed the drink while in uniform.

Caption Answer to ...

Interpreting Graphs

A steep decline in auto production and a sharp increase in military aircraft. Assembly-line production may be one factor affecting the graph on the right, but the increased demand for military planes and the conversion of many more factories to their production are other factors.

Bellringer

Ask students to imagine themselves in President Roosevelt's shoes on December 8, 1941. Now that the United States is at war, what are the three most important things that must be done at once to help the country fight it?

Reading Strategy

Predicting Content Ask students to skim the section, looking at the illustrations and reading the headings. Ask them to predict the content of the section by completing the following sentences: During the war, American factories and businesses concentrated on making goods for _____. Union membership _____ during the war. The government paid for the war through taxes and _____.

Answer to ...

MAKING CONNECTIONS

Students may predict that the government provided financial incentives for businesses to convert to wartime production. In fact, as the text goes on to explain, the government started the cost-plus system and allowed business executives to influence the distribution of government contracts.

2. INSTRUCT

Discuss

Point out the slogan on the poster on page 532: "Production lines are battle lines." Ask students to restate the slogan in their own words. Have students list the types of goods that were needed, and describe the incentives used by the government to mobilize industries to produce them.

Ask students to explain the reduction in unemployment after the country entered the war.

Analyze

Ask students to explain why putting money into the economy by deficit spending would get the economy moving.

Activity

Teaching Heterogeneous Groups

War can bring new opportunities for business expansion. To illustrate this concept for all students, have them work in groups to design an ad campaign for a product to be sold during wartime. This product might be one that both soldiers and those on the home front can use, such as Coca-Cola or chewing gum. Suggest that students identify which of their product's features the ad should promote, as well as the audience that it is designed to reach.

Enrichment

Ask students to research some of the new products developed by the petrochemical industry during the war, such as artificial rubber, nylon, and plastics. Suggest that they find out why these new products were needed.

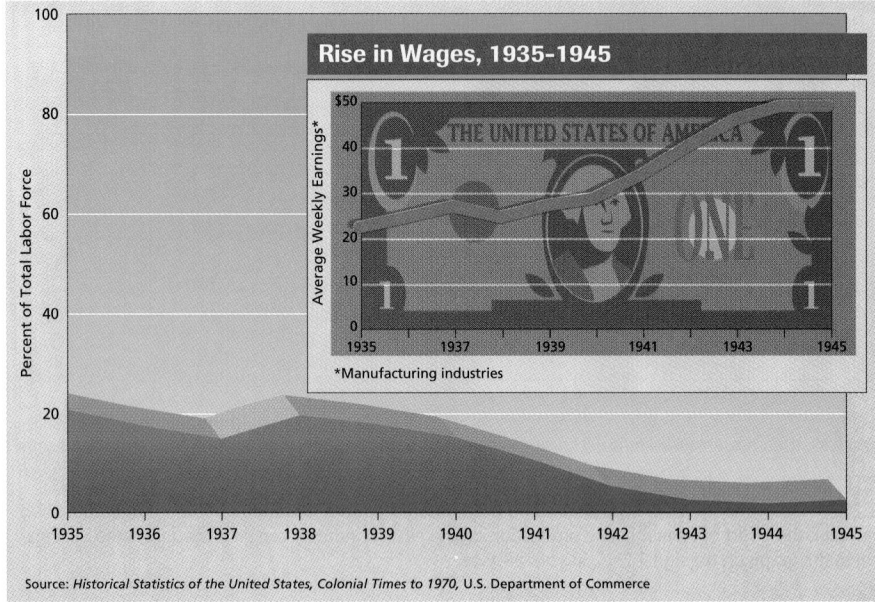

Percent of Labor Force Unemployed, 1935–1945

Rise in Wages, 1935-1945

*Manufacturing industries

Source: *Historical Statistics of the United States, Colonial Times to 1970*, U.S. Department of Commerce

 Interpreting Graphs
The conversion of the United States economy during the war brought businesses huge profits from government contracts. According to these graphs, in what two ways did workers benefit during the war?

Other entrepreneurs pioneered modern production methods. Henry J. Kaiser, for example, introduced mass production techniques to shipbuilding. The vessels that made him famous were called Liberty ships. In 1941 it took 355 days to build one Liberty ship. By the end of the war, Kaiser's shipyard located in Portland, Oregon, could assemble a ship in just 14 days.

Workers, the War, and Unions

Business owners were not the only group to benefit from war production. War production brought an end to the devastating unemployment of the 1930s. As the graph shows, by 1943 unemployment had fallen dramatically. Average weekly wages in manufacturing, adjusted for inflation, rose 27 percent in a little over three years.

With more people working, union membership rose. Between 1940 and 1941, the number of workers belonging to unions increased by 1.5 million. Union membership continued to rise sharply once the United States entered the war, from 10.5 million in 1941 to 14.8 million in 1945.

Two weeks after the attack on Pearl Harbor, labor and business representatives agreed to refrain from strikes and lockouts—a tactic in which an employer "locks" employees out of their jobs to avoid meeting their demands. The no-strike agreement became hard to honor, however, as the cost of living rose during the war and Pearl Harbor faded from memory. The government had to remind citizens continually of the importance of the agreement. Leonard Williamson, a superintendent for a large construction company, recalled the government's involvement in the building of a military base in New Jersey:

Welder Benny Chan gives the "V for Victory" sign.

▶ RESOURCE DIRECTORY

Teaching Resources

Critical Thinking Activity Identifying Alternatives: Mobilizing a Wartime Labor Force, found in the Unit 5 folder, p. 55, uses one of Roosevelt's fireside chats to help students apply this skill.

They started at one time to develop a strike there, and some big guy from the Pentagon came down, and he just laid the cards on the table: "There'll be no strikes." Everybody kind of buckled down, and we finished the thing in record time.

Still, the number of strikers doubled between 1942 and 1943, and it continued to rise in the last two years of the war. Some of the strikes were **wildcat strikes**—that is, they were organized by the workers themselves and not endorsed by the unions.

The most serious confrontations organized by unions occurred in the coalfields, where **John L. Lewis,** head of the United Mine Workers union, called strikes on four different occasions in 1943. Lewis and the miners, seeing industry profits soar while their wages stayed the same, demanded a pay raise to compensate for the rising cost of living. Secretary of the Interior Harold J. Ickes finally negotiated an agreement with Lewis. Meanwhile, Congress passed the Smith-Connally Act in June 1943 to place limits on future strike activity.

Financing the War

In World War II, the United States government was willing to spend whatever it cost to energize war production and maintain a "fighting" mentality at home. Federal spending increased from $9.4 billion in 1939 to $95.2 billion in 1945, and the gross national product more than doubled in that time.

A raise in taxes paid for approximately 41 percent of the cost of the war. The Revenue Act of 1942 increased the number of Americans who paid income taxes, levying a flat 5 percent tax on all incomes over $624 a year. The rest of the money was borrowed from banks, private investors, and the public. The United States Treasury launched a series of bond drives to borrow money from individual Americans, raising a total of $135 billion.

Massive wartime spending ended the Great Depression. In the 1930s most economists believed that the economy would fix itself if the government did not interfere. English economist John Maynard Keynes, on the other hand, argued that **deficit spending**—government spending of borrowed money—should be used to get a depressed economy moving again. Deficit spending during World War II turned the economy around overnight. Unfortunately, it also catapulted the nation into a habit of deficit spending, causing economic problems that continue to this day.

The results of wartime spending were stupendous. Each year the United States raised its production goals for military materials, and each year it met them. By the middle of 1945, the nation had produced 80,000 landing craft, 100,000 tanks and armored cars, 300,000 airplanes, 15 million guns, and 41 billion rounds of ammunition. The country had indeed become, in Franklin Roosevelt's words, the "arsenal of democracy."

Don't Let That Shadow Touch Them *Buy* WAR BONDS

This poster, designed to appeal to people's emotions, encouraged Americans to sacrifice and helped raise money for the war.

SECTION 1 REVIEW

Key Terms, People, and Places
1. Define (a) cost-plus system, (b) wildcat strike.
2. Identify John L. Lewis.

Key Concepts
3. What were the major problems involved in mobilizing the American economy in World War II?
4. How did World War II end the Great Depression?

5. How did deficit spending help the war effort?

Critical Thinking
6. **Formulating Questions** Imagine that you are a business owner in 1942, and that the government has asked you to produce materials for the war. Develop a list of questions that you would want to ask before you agreed to cooperate.

 Quiz found in the Unit 5 folder, p. 43, covers the main ideas in this section as well as the key terms.

Media and Technology

 **Transparencies**
Fine Art, D-18; Critical Thinking, I-10

---

3. ASSESS

Section 1 Review Answers
1. (a) cost-plus system, see p. 533, (b) wildcat strike, see p. 535
2. John L. Lewis, see p. 535
3. Businesses were reluctant to turn away customers now that the demand for consumer goods was on the rise; plants had to be retooled in order to make war materials.
4. The urgent need for war products created jobs for many Americans, and the new policy of deficit spending helped get the economy moving again.
5. Deficit spending—government spending of borrowed money—helped end the Depression and boost the economy.
6. Possible questions: How will production be financed? How will the product(s) be marketed? Who will supply the raw materials and machinery needed for production?

Reteach

Ask students to correct any of the following statements that are false:
- The coming of the war made the Depression worse because many workers lost their jobs.
- The government paid for goods and services needed to fight the war by borrowing money.
- During the war, factories switched from producing consumer goods to producing war materials.

4. CLOSE

Reinforcing the Big Idea

Involvement in the war stimulated the domestic economy and ended the Depression. The geared-up factories and industries needed workers. In the next section, students will learn who kept the assembly lines moving during the war.

Daily Life on the Home Front

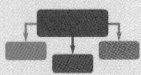

1. FOCUS

Connecting to the Big Idea

See page 530B. Explain to students that Americans at home were continually reminded of the war. Almost every American had a relative, friend, or neighbor overseas. Constant effort was required to support the war. Ask students how daily life in America changed as a result of these efforts.

Objectives

● Describe the mood on the American home front during the war.
● Explain the change in Americans' spending habits.
● Describe the shortages that plagued American consumers during the war.
● Explain how the government used public relations to maintain morale at home.

Bellringer

Ask students to think about how their lives would change if their family could buy only three gallons of gasoline a week—the amount that Americans were allowed under rationing during World War II.

Reading Strategy

Question Writing Ask students to read the section's three main headings and rewrite each as a question. Have them jot down answers to their questions as they read the chapter.

Daily Life on the Home Front

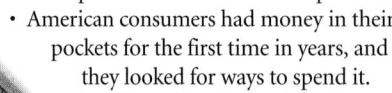

While American soldiers crouched in foxholes overseas, friends and families supported their struggle on the home front. Rationing and conserving resources like gasoline, scrap metal, and rubber drew most of the country into the war effort.

Key Concepts
• The mood on the American home front was one of cooperation and determined optimism.
  • American consumers had money in their pockets for the first time in years, and they looked for ways to spend it.
    • Shortages of many basic items, such as sugar, meat, and gasoline, plagued the wartime economy.
  • The government sought to maintain morale at home through various public relations campaigns.

Key Terms, People, and Places
rationing

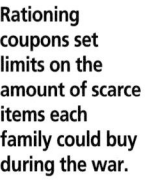

Rationing coupons set limits on the amount of scarce items each family could buy during the war.

The daily life of most Americans during World War II was filled with constant reminders of the war. To escape, many used the first extra cash they had earned since the Depression to purchase paperback books and go to the movies or baseball games, among other popular diversions. Rubber and aluminum drives, encouraged by the government, were designed to make most Americans feel part of the war effort.

Prosperity and Popular Culture

In the middle of the war, seven out of ten Americans felt that they had not had to make any "real sacrifices" because of the war. Morale was quite high as the Depression subsided. In 1941, 34 percent of all American families had incomes of less than $1000 a year, but new jobs created by the war brought that figure down below 20 percent by 1945. One measure of people's optimism was an increase in the birthrate. The population grew by 7.5 million between 1940 and 1945, nearly double the rate of growth for the 1930s. The so-called postwar baby boom that extended through the 1950s really began during the war.

Money to Burn As the wartime economy gathered speed, many Americans who had gone without steady paychecks for years suddenly found themselves earning more money than they needed just for basic necessities. They were hungry for ways to spend this extra income—they wanted new cars and trucks and appliances. Unfortunately, wartime conversion meant that most of these goods were unavailable, so they had to look for other ways to spend their money.

Among the items that people did buy were books. The new Pocket Books company, founded by Robert de Graff in 1939, developed a market for paperback books. De Graff believed that more Americans would read if books were more widely available and at lower prices. His instinct proved correct when he sold 34,000 copies of the first Pocket Book, titled *How to Win Friends and Influence People,* in two months. Soldiers carried Pocket Books with them into combat, and when the war was over, these men joined a sizeable new market for paperbacks. ✪

Approximately 85 million Americans, or 62 percent of the population, went to the movies each week during the war. Many of these films were in the "escapist" category: love stories, adventure tales, or light comedies that took audiences' minds off the serious business of war. Others dealt with the war directly and promoted themes of patriotism and American victory. Hollywood, too, was "doing its part" to contribute to the war effort.

▶ RESOURCE DIRECTORY

Teaching Resources

📄 **Reproducible Lesson Plan** found in the Unit 5 folder, p. 39, provides a summary of the Section 2 lesson plan content.

📄 **Alternate Lesson Plan: Critical Thinking** Determining Reasoned Judgment, found in the Alternate Lesson Plans folder, p. 128, extends students' application of this skill by completing a chart on the section content.

📄 **Guided Reading and Review** found in the Unit 5 folder, p. 44, provides a structure for reading and mastering the key concepts and reviewing the key terms for Section 2. (Guided Practice)

✪ 📄 **Literature Activity** *How To Win Friends and Influence People,* found in the Unit 5 folder, p. 59, introduces students to the spirit of the times with excerpts from Dale Carnegie's best-seller.

Baseball and Popular Music Though more than 4,000 of the 5,700 major and minor league players were in the military services, Americans still flocked to baseball games during the war. Ball clubs had to scramble to make up for the losses in their ranks. To fill their rosters, many had to place want ads in newspapers:

> I f you are a free agent and have previous professional experience, we may be able to place you to your advantage on one of our clubs. We have positions open on our AA, B, and D classification clubs. If you believe you can qualify for one of these good baseball jobs, tell us about yourself.
> *Sporting News,* February 25, 1943

Women ball players also took to the fields to lift the spirits of war-weary Americans. In 1943 Philip Wrigley founded the All-American Girls' Softball League, which became the All-American Girls' Baseball League in 1945. Women who played for teams such as the Rockford (Illinois) Peaches and the South Bend (Indiana) Blue Sox had to attend charm school and wear impractical skirted uniforms. But they endured such inconveniences for the chance to play professional ball, and they attracted scores of devoted fans.

As in World War I, many popular songs during World War II were written to inspire hope and patriotism. Frank Loesser's "Praise the Lord and Pass the Ammunition"—based on a true story—told of a navy chaplain who took over an anti-aircraft gun at Pearl Harbor after several of his fellow sailors had been killed. "There's a Star-Spangled Banner Waving Somewhere" was one of the best-selling records of 1942 and 1943. "White Christmas," from the 1942 film *Holiday Inn,* was the sentimental favorite, both for soldiers overseas and for civilians at home.

Shortages and Controls

The war brought its share of problems along with increased prosperity and a high-spirited popular culture. Although they had money to spend, Americans had to live with shortages and disruptions throughout the war.

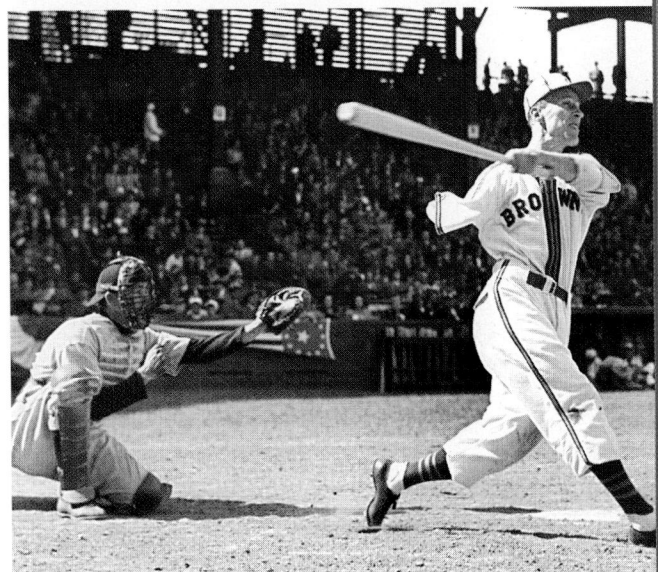

Pete Gray, a one-armed outfielder, did his part for the war effort by playing for the St. Louis Browns and giving the "troops" at home a lift.

Some consumer items were simply unavailable. Metal to make zippers was used for guns; rubber for girdles went into tanks and trucks; fabric for dresses became military uniforms instead. In an effort to save cloth, government regulations required the elimination of vests, patch pockets, and cuffs in men's suits. They also limited the length and width of women's skirts, which grew shorter and narrower during the war period. Two-piece bathing suits for women—considered somewhat shocking in the 1920s and 1930s—could now be justified on the basis of military need because they required less fabric.

Some foods were also in limited supply during the war. Sugar became scarce when the major source of American imports, the Philippines, fell to the Japanese and shipping lanes from other countries were closed. Coffee could not be transported easily from Brazil. Meat and countless other items were likewise scarce.

Worried that shortages would lead to price increases, the government used tough measures to head off inflation.

2. INSTRUCT

Explain

Explain that during the war, jobs were plentiful and workers made good wages. Point out the subheading Money to Burn on page 696 and ask students to describe the forms of entertainment that Americans supported and enjoyed with their extra money. Also note that many basic necessities were not available. Have students explain why rationing was instituted and how, in essence, this policy was an example of home-front support.

Discuss

Discuss the many reasons the government wanted to maintain high morale among its citizens. Ask students to brainstorm reasons and then to rank them in order of importance.

Activity

Teaching Heterogeneous Groups

To help students understand the shortages and rationing during World War II, have them make a list of what they are wearing or what they might eat in the course of a day. Then have them identify the raw materials that make up the listed items. Finally, ask students to list what materials or food they would have had to sacrifice to support the war effort in the 1940s. **LEP**

Enrichment

Ask students to choose one year during the war and find the following information: the movie that won the Academy Award for best picture; a popular song and the artist who recorded it; the team that won a popular sports event; a best-selling book; the nation's GNP for the year. Encourage students to review their answers to see if they reflect common aspects of the wartime mood.

3. ASSESS

Section 2 Review Answers

1. (a) rationing, see p. 538

2. There were shortages of sugar, coffee, meat, butter, shoes, and gasoline. The OPA established a rationing system to conserve these resources, and government campaigns encouraged people to collect scrap metal, rubber, and other recyclable items.

3. Styles that used less cloth came into fashion, such as suits without vests for men and two-piece bathing suits for women.

4. Government campaigns were designed to foster a sense of home-front participation in the war as well as to use human and other resources wisely.

5. Answers will vary but some underlying beliefs might be that the American people needed to be "sold" on the war if they were not convinced the goals of fighting for freedom and democracy were enough; the belief that the cause of the war was a good enough one to launch the huge propaganda campaign; the belief that it is acceptable for a government to use propaganda on its own citizens in certain cases.

Children, too, did their part for the war effort. These boys in New York City used their powers of persuasion—and noisemaking—to urge their neighbors to contribute to an aluminum drive.

President Roosevelt created the Office of Price Administration (OPA) in mid-1941, and the following year he gave the agency the authority to freeze prices. In the middle of 1942, OPA began **rationing,** or distributing goods in a fixed amount by using coupons. It assigned point values to scarce items such as sugar, coffee, meat, butter, shoes, and gasoline. Consumers were issued coupons worth a certain number of points. Once they had used up their points, they were not allowed to buy any more of the rationed items until additional coupons were issued.

MAKING CONNECTIONS

What effect do you think wartime shortages and rationing had on people's morale? Do you suppose it made people feel angry at the government or more patriotic?

Campaigns at Home

The government understood the need to maintain morale. While making rationing seem fun was not an easy task, the government had to create a sense of patriotism and participation in the war effort while convincing citizens to conserve precious resources. ⭐

| 1650 | 1700 | 1750 | 1800 | **Links Across Time** | 1850 | 1900 | 1950 | 2000 |

Taking Care of the Troops

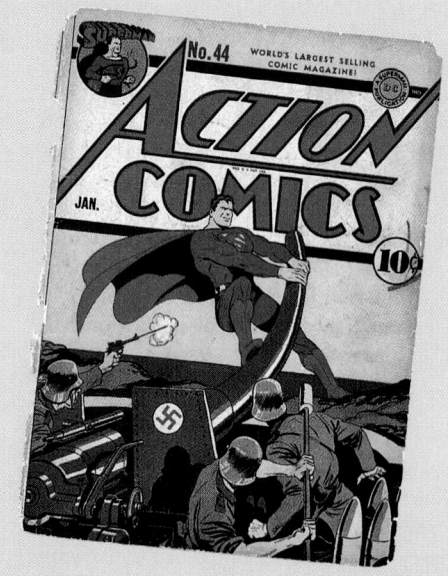

During wartime, America's businesses have always played their part by producing items designed specifically to boost the morale of those on the front lines. During World War II, special editions of certain comic books, such as Action Comics, were printed and sent to cheer up the soldiers overseas. Similarly, Hershey Foods developed a nonmelting chocolate bar for the troops in the Persian Gulf War of 1991 that was specially formulated "for desert or tropical conditions." *What product would you develop for our troops? Explain your reasoning.*

▶ RESOURCE DIRECTORY

Teaching Resources

⭐ **Visual Learning Activity** "The Nature of the Enemy," found in the Unit 5 folder, p. 62, presents a Nazi photo from an OWI exhibit in order to extend students' understanding of wartime propaganda.

In one campaign, Americans were asked to save scrap metal and other materials that could be used for war machinery. Huge drives collected tin cans, pots and pans, razor blades, old shovels, and even old lipstick tubes. In Virginia, collectors raised sunken ships from the James River; in Wyoming they took apart an old steam engine to use the parts. When rubber was in short supply, people collected rubber hoses, raincoats, and bathing caps. Americans were asked to save kitchen fats because the glycerin could be used to make powder for bullets or shells. Some historians have questioned whether the items collected were ever really used for their intended purpose. Whether they were or not, the collection process served another important purpose: it was another way the government kept the American public's attention focused on the war effort.

Another campaign encouraged Americans to buy savings bonds to finance the war. In the spring of 1941, Secretary of the Treasury Henry Morgenthau, Jr., decided "to use *bonds* to sell the *war,* rather than *vice versa.*" Morgenthau realized that selling war bonds would give people "a financial stake in American democracy—an opportunity to contribute toward the defense of that democracy."

"Play your part." "Conserve and collect." "Use it up, wear it out, make it do or do without"—these refrains echoed throughout the United States, constantly reminding Americans of their patriotic duty in the wartime campaign.

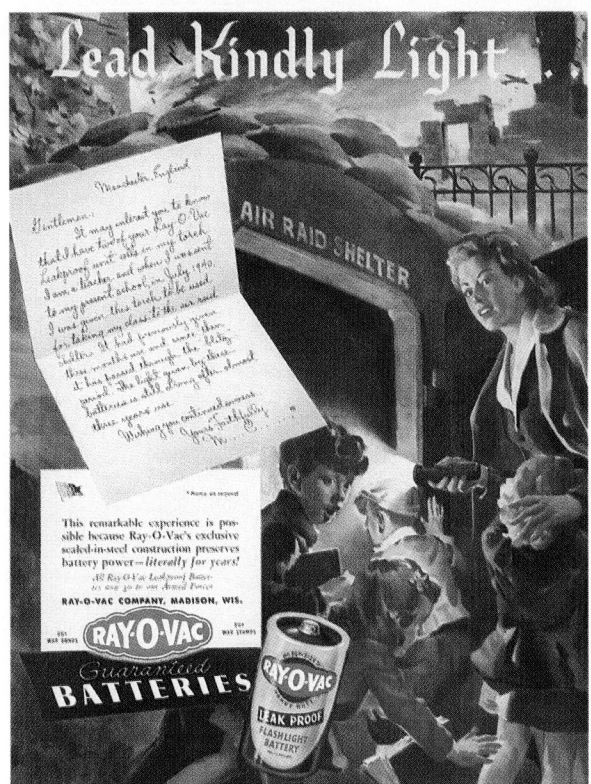

Using Historical Evidence Besides emphasizing quality and value, advertisers used a war-related setting and emotion to sell their products during the war. *How are all of those used in this ad?*

SECTION 2 REVIEW

Key Terms, People, and Places
1. Define rationing.

Key Concepts
2. What items were in short supply during the war, and how did the government respond to these shortages?
3. How did the scarcity of cloth during World War II affect clothing fashions?

4. What was the purpose of government campaigns such as the war bond campaign?

Critical Thinking
5. **Identifying Assumptions** What underlying beliefs was the United States government acting upon when it waged its massive effort to "sell" the war to Americans at home?

Quiz found in the Unit 5 folder, p. 45, covers the main ideas in this section as well as the key terms.

Ask students to read and complete the following sentences with a short phrase.
● During the war, many Americans used their extra income to buy

_____.
● In order to cope with shortages of items such as sugar and gasoline, the government began a policy of

_____.
● Americans collected scrap metal because _____.

Alternative Assessment

Mid-Point Monitoring
Ask students if they have
● Chosen a format for their guide
● Completed notes for each section

Caption Answer to ...

Using Historical Evidence

The poster shows a dramatic scene of an air raid in Britain during the war and tells the story of a schoolteacher who used a flashlight with Ray-O-Vac batteries to lead her young students to a shelter. The text of the poster claims that the batteries last a long time because of their "sealed-in-steel construction" and appeals to the parental concerns for safety.

4. CLOSE

Reinforcing the Big Idea

The war touched Americans at home in many ways. The next section describes the dramatic ways in which the war changed the lives of many American women.

SECTION 3

Women and the War

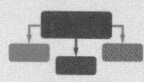

Connecting to the Big Idea

See page 530B. Explain that during the war, women responded to the urgent demand for workers in factories and shipyards. They quickly adapted to their new status and responsibilities. Just as quickly, most gave up their jobs when the war ended. Ask students what impact the war actually had on the lives of women.

Objectives

● Understand that American women of all ages went to work during World War II.
● Describe how women overcame hardships and discrimination to become successful at their new jobs.
● Explain why women were strongly encouraged to leave their jobs at the end of the war.

Bellringer

Have students list their hobbies, after-school activities, and responsibilities at home. Then ask them to imagine that they were of the opposite sex. How might their lists change? How might expectations of parents and others be different?

Reading Strategy

Predicting Content Ask students to look at the illustrations and skim the headings of this section. Ask them to predict as many ways as they can in which the lives of American women changed during World War II.

SECTION PREVIEW

During World War II, thousands of American women rolled up their sleeves and went to work in defense plants and shipyards. Adapting quickly to work usually done by men and overcoming a sometimes cold welcome from fellow male employees, they helped satisfy the Allies' urgent need for military goods.

The motto of the women's Auxiliary Reserve Pool (ARP) during World War II was "Prepared and Faithful."

Key Concepts

• During World War II, American women of all ages went to work.
• Women were successful in their new jobs despite the hardships and discrimination they faced.
• At the end of the war, women were strongly encouraged to leave their jobs, whether they wanted to or not.

Key Terms, People, and Places

Rosie the Riveter

A popular song during World War II paid tribute to a fictional young woman named **Rosie the Riveter,** who worked in a defense plant while her boyfriend Charlie served in the marines. The government used images of Rosie the Riveter in posters and propaganda films of the 1940s to attract women to the work force. In general, the Rosie created by the government was young, white, and middle class. Patriotism was her main motive for taking a war job—she wanted to do her part on the home front while her brother, husband, or boyfriend fought on the military front. In reality, the wartime economy made it essential for American women of all ages and ethnic and economic backgrounds to work. And, despite the ideals that the government set before them, they worked for a variety of reasons beyond patriotism.

Shifting Patterns of Employment

Before the war, most women who worked for wages were single and young. Even during the hard times of the Depression, most people disapproved of a married woman working outside the home to earn money. This social opposition was reinforced by the fear that working women took jobs away from unemployed men. According to a poll taken in 1936, 82 percent of Americans believed that a married woman should not work if her husband had a job. Nevertheless, by 1940 about 15.5 percent of all married women were working.

Women often worked as sales clerks and household servants because many other fields were closed to them. Men dominated the machinery, steel, and automobile industries, while women more commonly worked in industries that produced clothing, textiles, and shoes. In the jobs they did hold, women usually earned much less than men.

Like World War I, World War II brought many women into the work force. As men were drafted into the armed forces, a large number of factory jobs fell vacant. News of these well-paying job openings brought women who were already working in traditional women's jobs to take over these positions. But these women were not enough. So the Office of War Information launched a propaganda campaign to fill the rest of the positions with women who normally would not have considered working outside the home: older, married women.

Posters and advertisements told women that it was their patriotic duty to work for their country. "An American homemaker with the strength and ability to run a house and raise a family . . . has the strength and ability to take her place in a vital War industry," declared one government advertisement. As a result of this campaign, the number of working women rose from 14.6 million in 1941 to about 19.4 million in 1944. (See the graph on page 542.)

(See the graph on page 542.)

RESOURCE DIRECTORY

Teaching Resources

Reproducible Lesson Plan found in the Unit 5 folder, p. 40, provides a summary of the Section 3 lesson plan content.

Alternate Lesson Plan: Cooperative Learning found in the Alternate Lesson Plans folder, p. 129, gives students, in groups of six, guidance in creating a question-and-answer activity to summarize information on the effects of women workers on the labor force.

Guided Reading and Review found in the Unit 5 folder, p. 46, provides a structure for reading and mastering the key concepts and reviewing the key terms for Section 3. (Guided Practice)

More than half of all American women were employed at some point during the war; at its peak, women made up 36 percent of the total civilian labor force.

Along with growing numbers of women in the work force, the type of women who worked changed significantly during the war. Married women accounted for almost three quarters of the increase; for the first time in American history, they outnumbered single working women. More than two million women over the age of thirty-five found jobs, and by the end of the war, half of all women workers were over age thirty-five.

An even more striking change occurred in the kind of work women did. Increasingly they moved out of domestic service and into manufacturing, particularly the defense industries. Now women worked in airplane plants and shipyards as steelworkers, riveters, and welders. Rosie the Riveter—strong, determined, and capable—became the ideal to which American women were supposed to aspire.

This war worker is assembling one part of an aircraft in a California factory.

MAKING CONNECTIONS

Rosie the Riveter was the image of the working woman promoted by the government. Why did the government have to create a character such as Rosie the Riveter?

The Wartime Working Experience

Despite resistance in the past, employers were usually pleased to have women workers—although often for reasons many Americans find misguided today. Employers believed, for instance, that women could do certain welding tasks better than men, for they could squeeze into smaller places. They also made assumptions about women's mental abilities that led them to think that women could do simple, repetitive tasks more effectively than men.

Working Conditions for Women of Color

African American women had long worked in greater proportion than married white women, but they had been largely restricted to domestic work. In addition to gender stereotyping,

African American women often faced racial discrimination when they applied for defense jobs. Wanita Allen, who wanted to work at Murray Auto Body in Detroit, Michigan, described her experience this way:

I didn't have any problem getting in the training program. They said you have to have 300 hours to get a job in the plant, and I got my 300, 400, going on 500 hours, and was learning blueprint and everything else, but still no job. They would come in from the plant proper to pick women who'd maybe been there just a couple of days on the training program, and they would put them to work. But they were white women.

Allen later helped gather evidence for a lawsuit against the plant, and she and many other African American women were eventually hired at Murray Auto. Through lawsuits and other forms of protest, African American women changed their profile in the work force. Between 1940 and 1944, the proportion of African American women in industrial jobs

Discuss

Ask students to explain why women went to work during the war. Then have them provide examples of how women felt about their work experience, especially regarding working conditions, attitudes, employment benefits, stresses of family life, salaries, and discrimination against African American women. Ask students if attitudes regarding these issues have changed and, if so, how.

Answer to ...

MAKING CONNECTIONS

The government needed to convince women to take the factory jobs that were falling vacant as men were drafted into the armed forces. Rosie the Riveter introduced a new model for women's behavior, showing that during the war it was "right" for women to take jobs normally reserved for men.

In Depth

Then and Now

Almost 2,000 women flew non-combat air missions during World War II. The Women's Airforce Service Pilots, known as WASP, flew every airplane in the U.S. air arsenal, including the B-29 Super-fortress and the super-quick P-51 Mustang fighter. Although they were highly skilled, the women had to fight for advanced training and more challenging assignments. Even today there is still debate over the role of women in combat.

Analyze

Just as women were urged to join the work force during the war, they were urged to return home after the war. While some women were quite agreeable to these conditions, others were ambivalent about giving up what they had earned during the war. Ask students to identify the reasons for this ambivalence felt by many women.

Activity

Cooperative Learning

Time: One class period.
Activity: Produce a script for a newsreel for a particular event during World War II.
Grouping: Groups of four to six students.
Purpose: Have students work to research a topic related to the war front or the home front during World War II and to write a brief newsreel-style story about it. Possible subjects include a war hero, entertainment, movies, or clothes.
Roles: Have students assign the following roles: researchers, editors, broadcasters.
Outcome: Students will learn how newsreel stories were used as part of the government's propaganda campaign during World War II.

Enrichment

Ask students to read interviews with women in Studs Terkel's book *The Good War: An Oral History of World War II* or pertinent chapters in Richard R. Lingeman's *Don't You Know There's a War On? The American Home Front, 1940–1945.* Have them summarize what they read.

Caption Answer to ...

 Interpreting Graphs

The number of women employed rose during the war, but since the number of men in the labor force increased as well, the ratio of women to men stayed about the same.

These women welders at the Kaiser shipyard in Richmond, California, are working on the Liberty ship S.S. *George Washington Carver.*

increased from 6.8 percent to 18 percent, while the number working in domestic service dropped from 59.9 percent to 44.6 percent.

Benefits of Employment On the whole, women were delighted to be employed. To many, the money they earned made a difference in their lives. Josephine McKee, a Seattle mother of nine who worked at the Boeing Aircraft Company, was able to pay off debts from the Depression. Leola Houghland, also from Seattle, used her earnings at Associated

Shipyards to pay for her family's home. Other women simply found the work more exciting than what they had done before. Evelyn Knight described why she left a position as a cook to work in a navy yard: "After all, I've got to keep body and soul together, and I'd rather earn a living this way than to cook over a hot stove." Still other women took jobs for patriotic reasons. One rubber plant worker declared, "Every time I test a batch of rubber, I know it's going to help bring my three sons home quicker."

Many women also were eager to prove that they could do whatever their jobs required. Adele Erenberg left a position as a Los Angeles cosmetics clerk to work in a machine shop when the war began. The noisy atmosphere was intimidating at first, and it was two weeks before fellow employees spoke to her. Her response was: "Okay, . . . I'm going to prove to you I can do anything you can do, and maybe better than some of you."

AMERICAN PROFILES

Beatrice Morales Clifton

Beatrice Morales Clifton never imagined herself as Rosie the Riveter. In 1942 she was living in Pasadena, California, with her husband Julio and four children. Her teenage niece wanted to get a job, so Clifton took her to apply for work in the aircraft industry.

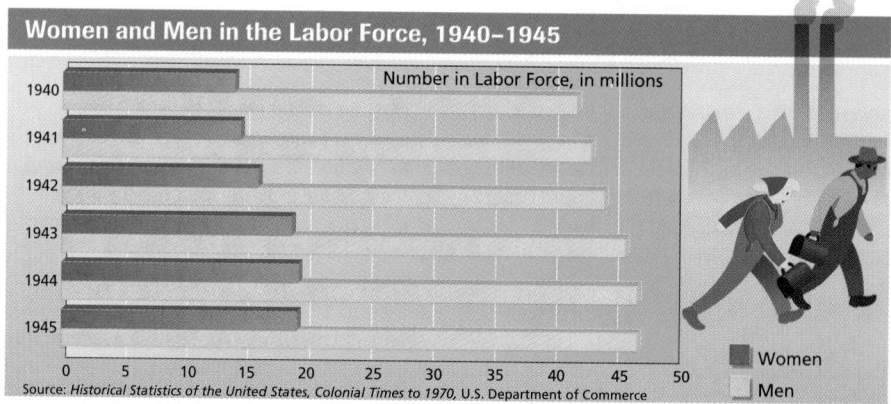

Women and Men in the Labor Force, 1940–1945

Number in Labor Force, in millions

1940
1941
1942
1943
1944
1945

0 5 10 15 20 25 30 35 40 45 50

Source: *Historical Statistics of the United States, Colonial Times to 1970,* U.S. Department of Commerce

■ Women
□ Men

 **Interpreting Graphs**
What was the overall trend in women's employment during World War II, according to this graph? Why did the ratio of women to men in the labor force remain about constant during the war?

▶ RESOURCE DIRECTORY

Teaching Resources

★ 📄 **Primary Source Activity** Working Conditions for Women of Color, found in the Unit 5 folder, pp. 57–58, profiles Sybil Lewis, an African American worker who tells of discrimination in the wartime work place.

Clifton was surprised when the man in the employment office suggested that she herself fill out an application; she had been married at age fifteen and had never considered looking for work outside the home. "But," she later explained, "the more I kept thinking about it, the more I said, 'That's a good idea.' " Her husband was initially opposed to her plan, but Clifton was determined. She told him, "I've made up my mind. I'm going to go to work."

⭐ Clifton was hired by Lockheed Aircraft in Los Angeles. When she arrived for her first day of work, she found the factory "exciting and scary at the same time." The male worker assigned to teach Clifton her job resented working women. When she made a slight slip with the rivet gun, he told her, "You're not worth the money Lockheed pays you."

With the support of her female co-workers, however, Clifton soon learned to enjoy her work. Her confidence grew as she mastered one skill after another. She later explained:

> I felt proud of myself and felt good [because] I had never done anything like that. I felt good that I could do something, and being that it was war, I felt that I was doing my part.
>
> I went from 65 cents to $1.05 [an hour]. That was top pay. It felt good and, besides, it was my own money. I could do whatever I wanted with it.

After leaving her wartime job for several years, Clifton returned to Lockheed in 1951. By the time she retired in 1978, she was a supervisor for about fifty other workers, half of them men. Asked how her work experiences affected her life, Clifton said,

> My life, it was changed from day to night. . . . The changes started when I first started working. They started a little bit, and from then on it kept on going. Because after I quit . . . at Lockheed, I wasn't satisfied. I started looking for ways of getting out and going to work. See, and before, I had never had that thought of going out.

Problems for Working Women

For all the positive aspects of employment, working women experienced a number of problems. Some faced hostile reactions from other workers, particularly in jobs previously held only by men. Restrictions imposed by managers who worried about mixing the sexes in their plants irritated other women. General Motors, for example, fired male supervisors and female employees found "fraternizing," or socializing with one another.

Many working women worried about leaving their children. More than half a million women with children under ten worked during the war, and day-care centers were scarce. Even when the government provided such facilities, most women preferred to have their children cared for by family members or friends, and this often required making complicated arrangements. Women were encouraged to work, but at the same time they continued to bear complete responsibility for both their children and for many of the chores in the home.

Women also earned significantly less than men doing the same jobs. Although the National War Labor Board declared in the fall of 1942 that women who performed "work of the same quality and quantity" as men should receive equal pay, the policy often was ignored. Women began at the bottom, with the lowest-paying jobs. Because they had less seniority, they frequently advanced more slowly. Their wages reflected these patterns. At the Willow Run plant in 1945, women earned a yearly average of $2,928, compared with $3,363 for men. Conditions improved toward the end of the war, but the gap never closed.

Beatrice Morales Clifton worked at Lockheed Aircraft during World War II.

MAKING CONNECTIONS

Women were encouraged to enter the work force and provided essential labor for the war effort, but they were never paid the same as men. What do you predict happened to these workers when the war ended?

Answer to ...
MAKING CONNECTIONS

Students may predict that since women remained second-class citizens in the wartime economy, they were expected to give up their jobs when servicemen returned from overseas.

3. ASSESS

Section 3 Review Answers

1. Rosie the Riveter, see p. 540

2. Women over thirty-five and married women entered the work force, taking jobs previously reserved for men.

3. Propaganda featuring Rosie the Riveter made defense jobs seem glamorous as well as patriotic. The government initially used Rosie to fill the jobs it needed to produce the materials to win the war, and later to remind women of their "proper" role as homemakers once the war was over.

4. Women encountered hostile reactions from men in the factories, received lower wages than men doing the same work, and had to juggle child care and domestic responsibilities with their factory work schedules.

In Depth
Did You Know?

"There was a passion for marriage in wartime America," observed historian William Tuttle in *Daddy's Gone to War,* that was almost absent in the 1930s. Two reasons help explain why.

Hope—As people went back to work, they felt better about themselves. That and rising wages made the proposal easier to consider.

Fear—War made young draftees and enlisted men face the question of survival: "As a soldier, will I even live through the war?" Young women faced a similar dilemma: "If I don't get married now, will I have a second chance?" Not wanting to hear "I won't," both rushed to the altar in record numbers to say "I do."

5. Women were pressured to leave their defense jobs. Some returned to their jobs as full-time homemakers. Others continued to work part-time or full-time despite the pressure to return home.

6. Some possible underlying beliefs are that women really belonged in the home and that it was more important for men to have jobs than for women.

Reteach

Have students construct a concept map of the section, with a central circle labeled Women Go to Work During WW II. Ask them to write statements in outer circles about changing patterns of employment, working conditions for women of color, advantages of employment, and problems for working women.

4. CLOSE

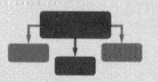

Reinforcing the Big Idea

World War II changed the lives of millions of American women who went to work outside their homes for the first time or moved into jobs previously held by men. The next section describes how African Americans, Mexican Americans, Native Americans, and Japanese Americans were involved in World War II.

Sisters under the apron—Yesterday's war worker becomes today's housewife.

What's Become of Rosie the Riveter?

Government propaganda aimed at women did an about-face once the war was over. Posters such as this one now urged women to give up their factory jobs and return to full-time homemaking.

The Postwar Push to "Demobilize" Women

The government propaganda campaign that urged women to report to the defense plants also assumed that when the war was over, women would leave their jobs and return to their homes. The following script excerpt from the recruitment film *Women of Steel*, produced by the Office of War Information, demonstrates this assumption.

> NARRATOR: *Women make good drivers, too. American girls raised to drive the family car have no trouble at all handling trucks and tractors. Edith Stoner's husband is in Alaska. She took this job for the duration. . . . How do you like your job, Mrs. Stoner?*

EDITH STONER: *I love it.*
NARRATOR: *How about after the war? Are you going to keep on working?*
EDITH STONER: *I should say not. When my husband comes back, I'm going to be busy at home.*
NARRATOR: *Good for you!*

At the war's end, many women in fact wanted to continue working, but the pressures to return home were intense. Servicemen wanted "their" jobs back, and they longed to return to the familiar family arrangements they had known before the war. A new campaign by industrialists and government officials now encouraged women to leave their jobs. Articles in women's magazines changed their tune after the war, too. Ammunitions worker Margaret Wright recalled:

> Y *ou know, during the war they [were] telling you to cook dishes that you could cook quick and get on to work. Now, they were telling you how to cook dishes that took a full day. There were more articles in there about raising your child. . . .*

During demobilization, twice as many women as men lost factory jobs.

Some women were tired of their defense jobs—which in many cases were not very fulfilling once the war's sense of urgency had ended—and looked forward to their work at home. Others, like Beatrice Clifton, would never again feel satisfied being full-time homemakers. After the war, many women continued to work part-time to supplement their families' incomes.

SECTION 3 REVIEW

Key Terms, People, and Places
1. Identify Rosie the Riveter.

Key Concepts
2. How did the profile of women in the work force change during World War II?
3. How did the government use Rosie the Riveter to accomplish its wartime goals?
4. What problems did women encounter as they worked?

5. What options did women defense workers have at the war's end?

Critical Thinking
6. **Recognizing Bias** At the end of the war, government and business responded to the need to provide jobs for returning soldiers by pressuring women to leave their jobs. What underlying beliefs does this response suggest?

 **RESOURCE DIRECTORY**

Teaching Resources

Quiz found in the Unit 5 folder, p. 47, covers the main ideas in this section as well as the key terms.

Identifying Assumptions

Identifying assumptions means recognizing the unstated beliefs that may underlie a statement or action. An assumption is an idea that a person takes for granted as true. In fact, it may prove either true or false, but in order to determine the accuracy of an assumption, you must first be able to recognize it as such.

Editorials, opinion pieces, and illustrations frequently contain many assumptions. Magazine covers, such as the one shown here, are often excellent sources of information about public attitudes toward historical events. At the same time, illustrations may be drawn in such a way that they also reveal assumptions of the artist.

By the time artist Norman Rockwell's portrayal of "Rosie the Riveter" appeared on the cover of *The Saturday Evening Post* in 1943, American women by the thousands were already making history. They were working in nontraditional factory jobs, assembling ships and airplanes for the country's war effort.

To examine the accuracy of the image portrayed in this painting, use the following steps to identify and evaluate the assumptions on which it may be based.

1. Determine the subject of the cover illustration. Study the illustration carefully and answer the following questions. (a) What is the woman in the illustration doing? (b) Who is "Rosie the Riveter" supposed to represent? (c) What general subject or issue does the illustration address? (d) What is the overall message of the illustration?

2. Define the artist's point of view. To help determine if the artist is presenting a particular viewpoint,

answer the following questions. (a) What seems to be the artist's purpose in creating this illustration? (b) How would you describe the artist's attitude toward the subject? (c) What aspects of the illustration clearly express this point of view? (d) Are there any elements in the illustration that contrast with each other? If so, what might the artist be trying to convey through these contrasts?

3. Identify the assumptions on which the artist's viewpoint is based and decide whether they are valid. To help decide if the artist's assumptions can be supported by facts, answer the following questions. (a) What assumptions, if any, does the artist make about the nature of the work performed by the woman in the illustration? Does the artist make any assumptions about why she holds this job? (b) What assumptions, if any, does the artist make about the women who work in nontraditional jobs? (c) Can any aspects of a person's physical appearance, such as clothes or posture, be reliably linked to his or her occupation? Explain. (d) How can you find out if the artist's apparent assumptions are valid?

Historian's Toolbox Activity Identifying Assumptions, found in the Unit 5 folder, p. 54, uses a recruitment brochure for the United States Air Force to help students apply this skill.

TOOLBOX

Critical Thinking
Identifying Assumptions

Focus Identify and evaluate assumptions in historical sources such as editorials, speeches, or works of art.

Instruct Ask students to brainstorm a list of adjectives that describe "Rosie the Riveter," the symbol of women workers during World War II. Have them work in small groups to identify the assumptions that underlie the lists they have generated. Compare their assumptions to those of Norman Rockwell's magazine cover. Ask why some of their assumptions might be different from Rockwell's.

Extend See the Historian's Toolbox Activity in the Resource Directory below.

Answers

1. (a) Taking a break from work to eat lunch. (b) American women during World War II. (c) Women in the workplace. (d) Women are capable of doing work that was traditionally done by men.

2. (a) To show support for women in the workplace. (b) He seems to admire women workers supporting the home front. (c) The woman looks strong, capable, and confident. (d) The woman's muscular body contrasts with her childish face, and her rough work clothes contrast with the dainty mirror in her pocket. The artist may be suggesting an inherent contradiction in a young woman doing a traditional "man's" job.

3. (a) The artist seems to assume that the work is physically demanding and "men's" work. The American flag background suggests that the woman has taken a factory job for patriotic reasons. (b) The artist seems to assume that women have had to give up their femininity and are somewhat masculine in appearance and/or attitude. (c) Answers will vary. Some students may think that a muscular appearance may mean that a person performs physically demanding work or that a person who wears a dress or suit must work in an office. Others may say that appearances are often wrongly interpreted as stereotypes and are in fact not reliable indicators. (d) Read biographies of women, or interview women, who lived during World War II.

The Struggle for Justice at Home

SECTION 4

The Struggle for Justice at Home

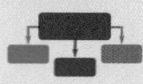

1. FOCUS

Connecting to the Big Idea

See page 530B. Point out to students that just as women were mobilized to support the war effort, Americans of different races and ethnic groups were also heavily recruited. Explain that in spite of this, discrimination continued at many levels. Ask students what impact the involvement in the war had on these Americans.

Objectives

● Explain how events on the home front stimulated the movement for equal rights for African Americans.

● Cite the effect of the war on the employment of Mexican Americans and Native Americans.

● Describe how many Japanese Americans were forced into internment camps during the war.

Bellringer

Write the words *injustice* and *inequality* on the chalkboard. Have students describe an incident that they associate with these words. Encourage students to explain why the incident serves as an example of injustice or inequality.

Reading Strategy

Reinforcing Key Concepts As they read, ask students to see how our policies at home toward women and minorities compared to our goals for fighting abroad.

SECTION PREVIEW

For many Americans, the war broke down racial barriers in the job market. Japanese Americans, however, fell victim to bitter prejudice at home as the United States battled Japan abroad.

Key Concepts

• Events on the home front helped stimulate the movement for equal rights for African Americans.

• Mexican Americans and Native Americans battled discrimination at home and entered the work force in greater numbers during the war.

• A large number of Japanese Americans were forced into internment camps by the United States government during the war, while others served courageously in the military.

Key Terms, People, and Places

"Double V" campaign, bracero, internment camp; A. Philip Randolph

Clinging to her most precious belongings, this little girl waits to be moved to an internment camp.

P resident Roosevelt, in his 1942 Columbus Day speech, expressed the need to set aside bigotry for the sake of the wartime effort:

> I n some communities employers dislike to hire women. In others they are reluctant to hire Negroes. We can no longer afford to indulge such prejudice.

In fact, the war did bring greater opportunities for a number of groups in America. But racial prejudice did not disappear during the war years. On the contrary, the war fanned the flames of many conflicts that had been smoldering for decades.

The Wartime Struggle Against Jim Crow

Although the effort to end discrimination toward African Americans had long been under way by the time the United States entered World War II, the Jim Crow system—which provided for the rigid separation of the races—remained firmly in place in the South. In the North, fewer laws enforcing segregation were on the books, but African Americans still were discriminated against in employment, education, and housing patterns. During the 1940s, over two million African Americans migrated from the South to northern and western cities (see map on page 547). There they found new opportunities, but they also found themselves concentrated in urban ghettos, or sections of a city in which many members of a particular minority group live due to economic pressure or discrimination. A survey taken in 1941 showed that 50 percent of all African American homes were substandard, versus only 14 percent of white homes.

When the war began, African American unemployment remained high—one out of five potential workers was unemployed. The United States Employment Service, a government agency created during the Depression to provide unemployed Americans with job counseling and placement, continued to honor employers' requests for "whites only," thereby continuing existing patterns of discrimination.

⭐ The war turned a spotlight on the injustice of racism in the United States. Alexander J. Allen, who worked for the Baltimore Urban League during the war, remarked, "It made a mockery of wartime goals to fight overseas against fascism only to come back to the same kind of discrimination and racism here in this country." One poignant example of this "mockery" occurred when a group of African American GIs was refused service by the owner of a lunch counter:

▶ RESOURCE DIRECTORY

Teaching Resources

Reproducible Lesson Plan found in the Unit 5 folder, p. 41, provides a summary of the Section 4 lesson plan content.

Alternate Lesson Plan: Learning Styles found in the Alternate Lesson Plans folder, p. 130, is especially effective for auditory learners, and gives students guidance in creating a television report on prejudice.

Guided Reading and Review found in Unit 5 folder, p. 48, provides a structure for reading and mastering the key concepts and reviewing the key terms for Section 4. (Guided Practice)

⭐ **Literature Activity** *Black Boy,* found in the Unit 5 folder, pp. 60–61, focuses on Richard Wright's novel about the struggle to survive in the segregated United States.

African American Migration, 1940–1950

WA
OR
ID
MT
ND
MN
SD
WY
NE
NV
UT
CO
KS
CA
AZ
NM
OK -1%
TX -2%
WI
MI +3%
IA
IL +3%
IN +1%
OH +2%
MO +3%
KY -2%
TN -2%
AR -4%
MS -5%
AL -4%
GA -6%
LA -4%
VT
ME
NY +3%
NH
MA
PA +2%
RI
CT
NJ +1%
DE
MD
WV
VA -5%
NC -3%
SC -7%
FL -7%

States that had significant loss of African American population

States that had significant gain in African American population

2% Gain or loss of African Americans as a percentage of a state's total population

 Geography and History: Interpreting Maps

All of their possessions loaded into the family car, these young people are moving north. *According to this map, what states lost the greatest percentage of their African American populations in the 1940s? How do you think the wartime economy affected African American migration?*

"Y ou know we don't serve coloreds here," the man repeated. . . .

We ignored him, and just stood there inside the door, staring at what we had come to see—the German prisoners of war who were having lunch at the counter. . . .

We continued to stare. This was really happening. It was no jive talk. The people of Salina would serve these enemy soldiers and turn away black American GIs.

Lloyd Brown, an American soldier stationed in Salina, Kansas

African Americans and others experienced discrimination not only at lunch counters. In the United States military, where men were risking their lives to defend their country, white and African American troops were strictly segregated.

Many white Americans, however, saw no problems in these racial practices. A 1942 poll

revealed that six out of ten whites felt that African Americans were satisfied with existing conditions and needed no additional opportunities. Mirroring the lack of concern felt by much of white America, the government did not seem eager to improve the situations of African Americans. Franklin Roosevelt, preoccupied with military matters, was not willing to disrupt the war effort to promote social equality. "I don't think, quite frankly," he said in late 1943, "that we can bring about the millennium [a period of human perfection] at this time."

African Americans disagreed with the President and began organizing for change on their own. The Pittsburgh *Courier*, an African American newspaper, launched a **"Double V" campaign:** *V* for victory in the war against the Axis powers, *V* for victory in the struggle for equality at home. **A. Philip Randolph**—head of the Brotherhood

Discuss

Although the war provided opportunities for African Americans, it did not put an end to discrimination at home. Have students list examples of continued discrimination, and describe efforts to promote racial equality. Then ask them to consider whether the advances outweighed the setbacks.

Caption Answer to . . .

Interpreting Maps

Virginia, South Carolina, Florida, Georgia, Mississippi; the concentration of wartime industries—and jobs—in the North attracted people to the region.

In Depth

Then and Now

The 99th Fighter Squadron, formed in 1942, were the first African Americans to fly in the Army Air Corps. They were known as the "Black Eagles" because of their success in escorting all-white bomber crews over Europe. The 99th was commanded by Benjamin O. Davis, Jr., the son of the man who became the first African American general. In 1991, Davis wrote about the exploits of the Black Eagles in his autobiography. By the early 1990s, 5,527 African American officers made up 5.6 percent of the officers in the United States Air Force.

Using Historical Evidence

While African Americans were fighting and dying in combat to preserve democracy worldwide, they did not enjoy equal rights in their own country.

Answer to ...

The war gave momentum to the civil rights movement because the fact that the United States was fighting for justice abroad brought injustice at home into sharper focus. On the other hand, the devotion of the nation's resources to the war effort made civil rights a lower priority.

In Depth

Biography

Adam Clayton Powell, Jr. (1908–1972), charismatic minister from Harlem, used the pulpit and his oratorical skills to mobilize frustrated African Americans into positive political action. He echoed tne sentiments of many fellow African Americans of his time when he said: "If the Negro is good enough to drive tanks on the battlefronts of Europe and Asia, he's good enough to work on the assembly lines of America." In 1944, Powell became one of only two African Americans in Congress and gained admiration for his "Powell Amendments"— attachments to bills that called for the cut-off of federal funds to any organization that practiced racial discrimination.

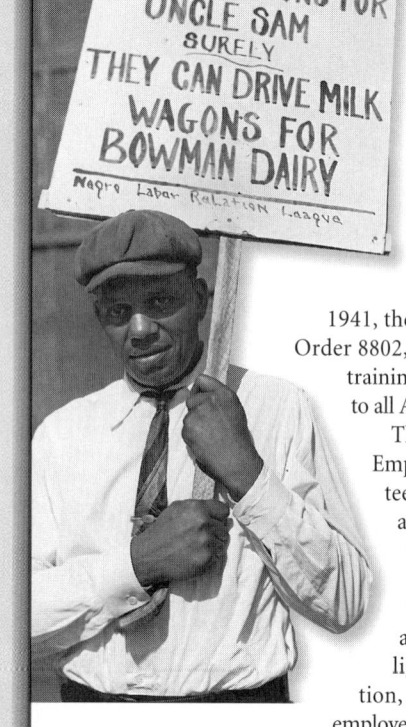

Using Historical Evidence This man is protesting outside a Chicago milk company in 1941. *How does the injustice the man is protesting conflict with the issues being fought for abroad during World War II?*

of Sleeping Car Porters, a labor union with a largely African American membership—proposed a massive march on Washington in early 1941 to demand an end to discrimination in all areas of American society. Worried about the possibility of violence in the nation's capital, Roosevelt tried to talk Randolph out of the march. Randolph agreed only when, on June 25, 1941, the President signed Executive Order 8802, which opened jobs and job training programs in defense plants to all Americans regardless of race.

The order also created the Fair Employment Practices Committee (FEPC) to hear complaints about job discrimination in defense industries as well as in the government. While the FEPC was only moderately successful, it did highlight the issue of discrimination, and it opened the way for employers to fill their job openings by hiring African Americans.

Meanwhile, African Americans were beginning to take direct action to promote equality. The Congress of Racial Equality (CORE), committed to using nonviolent techniques to end racism, was founded in Chicago in 1942. In May 1942 CORE organized its first sit-in at a restaurant called the Jack Spratt Coffee House. Groups of CORE members, each including at least one African American, filled the restaurant's counter and booths and refused to leave until everyone was served. They succeeded in ending Jack Spratt's discriminatory policies, and the sit-in technique quickly spread to CORE groups in other cities. These efforts paved the way for later civil rights activity but could not head off major race riots during the summer of 1943. Thirty-four people died in Detroit on June 16, and New York City was the scene of another riot on August 1 and 2. ✪

In what ways did the war speed up, and in what ways did it retard, the movement toward equal rights for African Americans?

Mexican Americans and Braceros During World War II

Like African Americans, Mexicans working in the United States and Mexican American citizens faced discrimination during the war. At the same time, the war did bring new employment opportunities for Mexican Americans. Planning for future needs, the Labor Department's Office of Education established vocational schools in a number of southwestern cities and provided training for rural Americans—including Mexican Americans—that eased the transition to war work.

Mexican Americans made major gains on the industrial front during World War II. By 1944, 17,000 were employed in the Los Angeles shipyards, where none had worked three years before. Mexican Americans also found jobs in shipyards and aircraft factories elsewhere in California and in Washington, Texas, and New Mexico. Some headed for other war production centers in places such as Detroit, Chicago, Kansas City, and New York.

The Bracero Program On the agricultural front, a shortage of farm laborers led the United States to seek help from Mexico. In 1942 an agreement between the two nations provided for transportation, food, shelter, and medical care for thousands of **braceros** (Spanish for "workers"), Mexican farm laborers brought to work in the United States. Between 1942 and 1947, more than 200,000 braceros participated in the program. When their contracts expired, however, they were quickly transported back to Mexico.

Despite their vital contributions to the war effort, Mexicans and Mexican Americans continued to suffer discrimination. Braceros endured miserable working conditions, and employers sometimes withheld their wages. Industrial workers occasionally received lower

▶ RESOURCE DIRECTORY

Teaching Resources

✪ **American Profiles Activity** found in the Unit 5 folder, p. 50, profiles James Farmer, a conscientious objector during the war, and one of the leaders of the civil rights movement of the 1960s.

✪ **American Profiles Activity** found in the Unit 5 folder, p. 51, profiles Daniel K. Inouye—the first American of Japanese descent to serve in the United States Congress.

wages for the same work done by people of other ethnic backgrounds. Crowded cities often bred racial tensions. In Los Angeles, where many Mexican Americans lived, those tensions erupted in a bloody race riot in mid-1943.

Zoot Suit Riots Los Angeles was a popular city for sailors on leave from nearby military bases. In April and May 1943, street fighting broke out between sailors and residents of Mexican descent. Many Mexican American men wore a popular style of clothing known as the "zoot suit," which had baggy pants and a long jacket. Gangs of sailors roamed the streets looking for men wearing such suits, whom they attacked and humiliated. Although one Spanish newspaper, *La Opinión,* encouraged the victims not to respond with more violence, some Mexican American youths took revenge on the sailors when they had the chance.

The fighting turned into a full-scale riot during the first weeks of June 1943. Local newspapers usually blamed Mexican Americans for the violence. Police often arrested the victims rather than the sailors who had initiated the attacks. Finally, army and navy officials intervened by restricting soldiers' off-duty access to Los Angeles. By mid-June the riots had subsided.

Native Americans and the War at Home

Despite their history of oppression by the United States government, Native Americans behaved patriotically during World War II. Thousands enlisted in the armed forces or migrated to urban centers to work in defense plants. Government propaganda held up these Native Americans as models of loyal service.

Nearly fifty thousand Native Americans worked in war industries around the country. Over two thousand Navaho helped build a large supply depot in New Mexico. Iroquois worked in aluminum plants and mining operations in New York state. Other Native Americans constructed airplanes on the West Coast and made tanks and ships in other war production centers.

Thousands of Native Americans who left reservations to take military or industrial jobs

had to adapt quickly to white culture. At the end of the war, Native Americans who had served abroad or worked in industrial centers in the United States were less likely to return home. For some Native Americans, the cultural transition brought a sense of alienation and rootlessness that left lasting scars.

The Japanese American Internment

 Japanese Americans suffered the worst discrimination during the war. In late 1941, they comprised a tiny minority in the United States. Numbering but 127,000—or one tenth of one percent of the entire population—they were concentrated on the West Coast, where prejudice against them had been festering for decades. About two thirds of the Japanese Americans had been born in the United States and were therefore American citizens, but their citizenship mattered little in the heat of war. ✪

Anti-Japanese sentiment grew stronger after Japan attacked Pearl Harbor. Rumors of sabotage on the West Coast spread quickly. One report that reached President Roosevelt's desk, while noting that the Japanese Americans there were almost all loyal citizens, went on to say that "there are still Japanese in the United States who will tie dynamite around their waist and make a human bomb out of themselves." The report also suggested that "dams could be blown and half of California could actually die of thirst."

Mexican American "zoot suiters" were the target of attacks in 1943, but they themselves were often blamed by police for the violence.

SOURCE READINGS

Source Readings on pp. 556 will connect literature selections and primary source excerpts to historical events discussed in this section.

In Depth

Multicultural Perspectives

In 1942, the U.S. government forced thousands of Italian and German immigrants to leave their homes in California. (Among those evacuated were the parents of baseball star Joe DiMaggio.) These people, perceived as a threat to American security, were taken to guarded army camps in the interior of the country. Four months later, the government realized its mistake and allowed the Italian and German aliens to return home. Japanese Americans, nevertheless, remained in internment camps for the entire war.

Answer to ...
Viewpoints

Lippmann: Under certain conditions, peoples' constitutional rights can be suspended. Murphy: The internees had the right to be protected under the Constitution. For a more thorough examination of the issue of Japanese internment, see the Resource Directory below.

3. ASSESS

Section 4 Review Answers

1. (a) "Double V" campaign, see p. 547, (b) bracero, see p. 548, (c) internment camp, see p. 550

2. A. Philip Randolph , see p. 547

3. African Americans used the "Double V" campaign, the March on Washington movement, and peaceful demonstrations to demand equal rights during the war.

4. The war brought new employment opportunities for Mexican Americans, but it also saw racial tensions erupt into race riots in Los Angeles in 1943.

5. Thousands of Native Americans worked in war industries; for some the war also sped the process of their assimilation into white culture.

6. The belief that some Japanese Americans were cooperating with Japan and that Japanese people were fanatical and would even sacrifice their lives to sabotage the West Coast laid the groundwork for the policy of internment.

7. Answers will vary. Students may suggest that since Japanese Americans were such a small minority and looked physically different from the Caucasian population, it was easier for white Americans to believe the wild rumors about them and to make them scapegoats.

Reteach

Ask students to make four columns on a piece of paper, with the headings African Americans, Mexican Americans, Native Americans, and Japanese Americans. Ask them to summarize under each heading the major effects of the war on members of that group.

Viewpoints
On the Internment of Japanese Americans

The forced internment of Japanese Americans produced strong feelings on both sides of the issue. Two views are given below. *How does each of these viewpoints address the issue of constitutional rights?*

For Internment

"It is a fact that the Japanese navy has been reconnoitering [investigating] the Pacific Coast. . . . It is [a] fact that communication takes place between the enemy at sea and enemy agents on land. The Pacific Coast is officially a combat zone: some part of it may at any moment be a battlefield. Nobody's constitutional rights include the right to reside and do business on a battlefield."

Walter Lippmann, American columnist,
February 12, 1942

Against Internment

"Racial discrimination in any form and in any degree has no justifiable part whatever in our democratic way of life. . . . All residents of this nation are kin in some way by blood or culture to a foreign land. Yet they are primarily and necessarily a part of . . . the United States [and are] . . . entitled to all rights and freedoms guaranteed by the Constitution."

Supreme Court Justice Frank Murphy's dissenting opinion,
Korematsu v. *United States*, 1944

The press capitalized on people's fears. Headlines such as "Jap Boat Flashes Message Ashore" and "Japanese Here Sent Vital Data to Tokyo" gave newspaper readers the feeling that Japanese spies were everywhere. *Time* and *Life* magazines told readers how to tell the Chinese, who were allies, from the Japanese, who were enemies: "The Chinese expression is likely to be more placid, kindly, open; the Japanese more positive, dogmatic, arrogant." ⭐

As a result of these fears and prejudices, the government decided to remove all Japanese from the West Coast. On February 19, 1942, President Roosevelt signed Executive Order 9066 authorizing the secretary of war to establish military zones and to remove "any or all persons" from such zones. The War Relocation Authority (WRA) was created to move 110,000 Japanese Americans—citizens and noncitizens alike—to ten **internment camps** in remote areas across the country.

The relocation process took place hastily, and Japanese Americans had little time to secure their property before they left for the camps. Many lost their businesses, homes, and other property. Henry Murakami, a resident of California, remembers losing the $55,000 worth of fishing nets that had been his livelihood:

> When we were sent to Fort Lincoln [in Bismarck, North Dakota] *I asked the FBI men about my nets. They said, "Don't worry. Everything is going to be taken care of." But I never saw the nets again, nor my brand-new 1941 Plymouth, nor our furniture. It all just disappeared. I lost everything.*

Japanese Americans had no idea where they were going when they boarded the buses for the internment camps. Monica Sone, who lived in Seattle before the war, imagined her camp would be "out somewhere deep in a snow-bound forest, an American Siberia. I saw myself plunging chest deep in the snow, hunting for small game to keep us alive." She and her family packed winter clothes, only to end up in Camp Minidoka, on the sun-baked prairie of central Idaho. Normal July temperatures there are about 90 degrees Fahrenheit.

All of the internment camps were located in desolate areas. They consisted of wooden barracks covered with tar paper and were protected by barbed wire and armed guards. Rooms inside the barracks had only cots, blankets, and a light bulb. Toilet, bathing, and dining facilities were communal.

Despite these injustices, more than 17,000 Japanese Americans served in the armed forces. About 1,200 of the Japanese Americans who volunteered for service did so from relocation centers. Many more volunteers came from Hawaii, where no internment had taken place. The 442nd Regimental Combat Team, composed entirely of Japanese Americans, won more medals for bravery than any other unit in United States history.

RESOURCE DIRECTORY

Teaching Resources

Viewpoints Activity On Japanese American Internment, found in the Unit 5 folder, pp. 52–53, provides additional viewpoints and perspectives on the internment of Japanese Americans during the war.

Primary Source Activity Anti-Japanese Sentiment, found in the Unit 5 folder, p. 56, profiles Mary Tsukamoto, who experienced anti-Japanese sentiment in the United States firsthand.

Although the vast majority of Japanese Americans abided by the policy of internment, a few did challenge it in the courts. Four cases eventually reached the Supreme Court, which in each case upheld the constitutionality of the wartime relocation. In one case, California resident Fred Toyosaburo Korematsu was convicted of violating Executive Order 9066 because he failed to report to an assembly center for relocation. The Supreme Court ruled in *Korematsu* v. *United States* (1944) that "Korematsu was not excluded from the Military Area because of hostility to him or his race," but that "the military urgency of the situation demanded that all citizens of Japanese ancestry be segregated from the West Coast temporarily." The dissenting opinion, however, labeled the policy "an obvious racial discrimination."

Finally, early in 1945, all Japanese Americans were allowed to leave the camps. Some were able to return to their homes and resume their lives. Others, finding that their property had been seized, had no place to go. It was not until 1988 that the United States government took responsibility for this gross violation of civil liberties. At that time Congress passed and President Ronald Reagan signed a law awarding each surviving Japanese American internee a tax-free payment of $20,000. These monetary reparations could not undo the damage that had been done decades earlier, but the law at least acknowledged the injustice.

Using Historical Evidence Tags with family identification numbers were attached to each piece of luggage and each family member at assembly centers for Japanese Americans. Permitted to take only a few possessions with them, many tried to sell their belongings but were forced to abandon what they could not carry or sell. *How do you think each person in this photo is feeling about the situation?*

SECTION 4 REVIEW

Key Terms, People, and Places
1. Define (a) "Double V" campaign, (b) bracero, (c) internment camp.
2. Identify A. Philip Randolph.

Key Concepts
3. What strategies did African Americans use in their struggle for equal rights during World War II?
4. What were the major effects of World War II on the lives of Mexican Americans?
5. What impact did World War II have on the lives of Native Americans?

6. What fears and prejudices led to the internment of Japanese Americans during World War II?

Critical Thinking
7. **Recognizing Cause and Effect** Although some German Americans and Italian Americans were relocated from the West Coast during the war, this action was on a much smaller scale than the internment of Japanese Americans. What do you think caused the harsher treatment of Japanese Americans?

 Quiz found in the Unit 5 folder, p. 49, covers the main ideas in this section as well as the key terms.

 Chapter Test Forms A and B are found in the Unit 5 folder, pp. 64–69.

 Answer Keys found in the Unit 5 folder, pp. 146–160, provide answers to all student activities.

Media and Technology

Transparency
Graphic Organizer, G-3

Guided Reading Audiotape
(English and Spanish)

Computer Test Bank

---

4. CLOSE

Reinforcing the Big Idea

World War II hastened the demand for and the rate of social change on the home front. Although minority groups broke through some racial barriers during the war, discrimination and injustice continued to affect many Americans.

Caption Answer to ...

Using Historical Evidence

Answers will vary but may include the following: The elderly man is proud, attempting to maintain his dignity; the children are innocent and uncertain.

 In Depth

Historical Misconceptions

There is debate about how much of a surprise the attack on Pearl Harbor really was. Some historians suggest that Roosevelt deliberately exposed the Pacific Fleet in Hawaii to provoke a Japanese attack. Fleet commanders *had* been put on war alert, but never anticipated the bombing of Pearl Harbor. Most felt that before attacking American bases, the Japanese would strike closer to home. Planes approaching Pearl Harbor were seen on radar but were thought to be American, although the radar indicated a flight path from the north, not the east—the likely direction for an American approach. Eleven months before the attack, the American ambassador to Japan heard a rumor that the Japanese were planning a surprise attack on Pearl Harbor. No action was taken.

Understanding Key Terms, People, and Places

Terms
Students should refer to the definitions of the key terms in the chapter to write sentences that show the relation of each word to America during World War II.

True or False
1. true
2. false, wildcat strikes
3. true
4. false, braceros
5. false, "Double V" campaign

True or False
1. true
2. false, John L. Lewis
3. false, A. Philip Randolph

Reviewing Main Ideas

1. President Roosevelt established the Office of War Mobilization and appointed James F. Byrnes its director. The government also established the cost-plus system so that businesses could make money on what they produced for the war.

2. Robert Woodruff of Coca-Cola and Philip K. Wrigley created new markets for their products. Other entrepreneurs, including Henry Ford and Henry J. Kaiser, introduced new methods such as mass production to their companies.

3. More workers in the work force resulted in more union members. The rise in the cost of living during the war, coupled with increased union membership, led to more frequent strikes despite agreements to refrain from striking.

4. Deficit spending turned the economy around and helped finance the war. Unfortunately it also created huge debts, causing economic problems that continue to this day.

5. With the Depression over, people were able to find new jobs and had money in their pockets for the first time in many years. In addition, the government waged a massive propaganda war to encourage a sense of cooperation. Participation in the war effort also contributed to the mood of optimism.

6. People spent their free time and newly earned money buying and reading the new paperback books created by the Pocket Book company, going to movies, watching professional baseball (both women's and men's leagues), and listening to popular music.

7. The government froze prices and began a rationing program. It tried to

---

Chapter Review

Understanding Key Terms, People, and Places

Key Terms
1. cost-plus system
2. wildcat strike
3. deficit spending
4. rationing
5. "Double V" campaign
6. bracero
7. internment camp

People
8. John L. Lewis
9. Rosie the Riveter
10. A. Philip Randolph

Terms For each term above, write a sentence that explains its relation to World War II in the United States, from 1941 to 1945.

True or False Determine whether each statement is true or false. If it is true, write "true." If it is false, change the underlined term to make the statement true.
1. During World War II, Japanese citizens and noncitizens alike were sent to <u>internment camps</u> in remote areas of the country.
2. <u>Braceros</u> are organized by workers themselves and not endorsed by the union.
3. A government program called <u>rationing</u> distributed scarce goods among consumers by using a point value system and issuing coupons.

4. In 1942 a shortage of farm labor led the United States to seek help from Mexican <u>wildcat strikes.</u>
5. African Americans launched the <u>cost-plus system</u>, with the goals of victory against the Axis powers and victory in the struggle for equality.

True or False Determine whether each statement is true or false. If it is true, write "true." If it is false, change the underlined name to make the statement true.
1. <u>Rosie the Riveter</u> was a fictional defense plant worker in World War II.
2. <u>A. Philip Randolph</u> called strikes in 1943 to demand pay raises.
3. <u>John L. Lewis</u> proposed a massive march on Washington in 1941 to demand an end to discrimination.

Reviewing Main Ideas

Section 1 (pp. 532–535)
1. How did the United States government help businesses convert to wartime production?
2. Give examples to show how entrepreneurs were able to profit during the war.
3. What effect did the increased work force during the war have on union membership?
4. Describe the positive and negative effects of deficit spending during World War II.

Section 2 (pp. 536–539)
5. What factors accounted for the mood of optimism on the home front?
6. Name several new ways in which people spent their free time and newly earned money during the war.
7. How did the government deal with wartime shortages?
8. What campaigns did the government undertake to encourage Americans to participate in the war effort?

Section 3 (pp. 540–544)
9. What changes took place in the kinds of jobs women held before and during World War II?
10. How did their new jobs benefit women?
11. Why did government campaigns strongly encourage women to return home after the war?

Section 4 (pp. 546–551)
12. Explain how the war turned a spotlight on the injustice of racism in American society.
13. Describe some of the opportunities and some of the problems encountered by Mexican Americans during the war.
14. How did the war speed the process of assimilation for Native Americans?
15. What factors influenced the government's decision to intern Japanese Americans on the West Coast during World War II?

---

maintain morale by encouraging patriotism and a sense of participation in the war effort.

8. One campaign asked Americans to conserve resources by saving items such as scrap metal and rubber. Another encouraged Americans to buy savings bonds.

9. Before the war women often worked as sales clerks or household servants. During the war many women took jobs in manufacturing, especially in the defense industry.

10. Women were able to make their own money. Many felt that their lives became more exciting and enjoyed a new sense of accomplishment.

11. The government assumed that women's proper role was in the home. In addition, men wanted

"their" jobs back and wanted to return to home life as it had been before the war.

12. During the war many people realized the incongruity of fighting fascism overseas while ignoring racism and discrimination at home.

13. During the war Mexican Americans were able to find jobs in defense industries that had been closed to them before. As they moved to cities like Los Angeles to take advantage of these opportunities, however, they often encountered racial prejudice that sometimes led to violence and rioting.

14. Native Americans who left reservations to take military or industrial jobs had to adjust quickly to white culture. This transition brought with it a sense of alienation for some Native Americans.

Thinking Critically

1. **Making Comparisons** Many entrepreneurs prospered during the war. What did Robert de Graff's Pocket Books company have in common with Robert Woodruff's Coca-Cola company?
2. **Predicting Consequences** At the end of the war, government propaganda urged women to resume their traditional roles as homemakers. How do you think this campaign influenced family patterns and women's self-perception in the postwar years?
3. **Identifying Assumptions** Explain the assumptions underlying the 1942 poll that revealed that six out of ten whites felt that African Americans were satisfied with existing conditions and opportunities (page 547).

Making Connections

1. **Evaluating Primary Sources** Review the primary source excerpts on page 543. What long-term effects did joining the work force during the war have for some women?
2. **Understanding the Visuals** Write a short paragraph explaining the contradiction demonstrated by the poster on page 532 and the photos on pages 548 and 551. Find a primary source excerpt in Section 4 that supports your explanation.
3. **Writing About the Chapter** Write a letter from the viewpoint of an American teenager in the early 1940s to a soldier who is serving in World War II. In your letter explain how your life and the lives of people around you have changed because of the war, including the lives of women, minorities, and local entrepreneurs. First, make a list of the changes that are affecting your life such as shortages and rationing. Note new ways in which you spend your leisure time. Write a draft of your letter, in which you describe your present life. Revise your letter, making sure that you have presented a detailed and interesting picture of life on the home front. Proofread your letter and draft a final copy.
4. **Using the Graphic Organizer** This graphic organizer uses a tree map to organize information about daily life on the home front during the war. Tree maps can help classify main ideas and supporting details. (a) According to the tree map, what are two factors that contributed to the mood of optimism and cooperation on the home front? (b) What supporting details could be included under a new main idea on the tree map: "Entrepreneurs profited from the war"? (c) On a separate sheet of paper, create your own graphic organizer about the struggle for justice among minorities during the war, using this graphic organizer as an example.

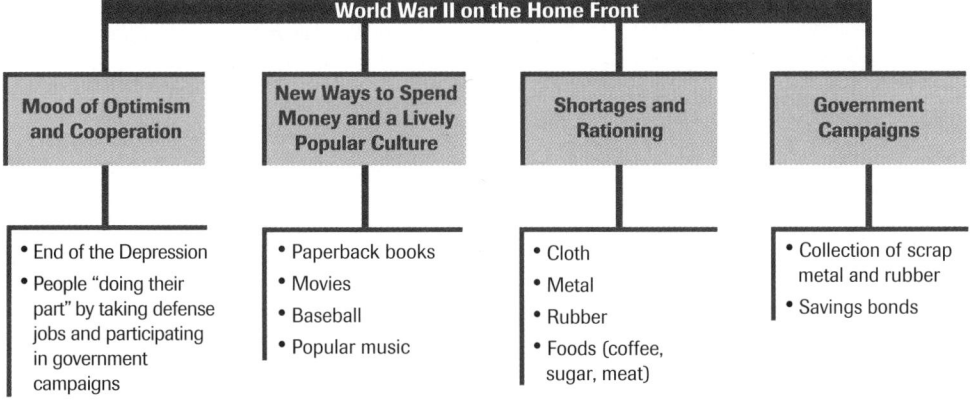

World War II on the Home Front

Mood of Optimism and Cooperation	New Ways to Spend Money and a Lively Popular Culture	Shortages and Rationing	Government Campaigns
• End of the Depression • People "doing their part" by taking defense jobs and participating in government campaigns	• Paperback books • Movies • Baseball • Popular music	• Cloth • Metal • Rubber • Foods (coffee, sugar, meat)	• Collection of scrap metal and rubber • Savings bonds

15. Some of the factors included prejudice against Japanese Americans that had existed for many years on the West Coast; wild rumors, supported by the press, that suggested Japanese Americans were assisting Japan in the war; the attack on Pearl Harbor that shocked and infuriated Americans; and a report to President Roosevelt that outlined the possibilities for sabotage in the United States.

Thinking Critically

1. Both entrepreneurs created new markets for their products among American GIs. Woodruff sent Coca-Cola overseas and de Graff lowered the price of books and made them more widely available so that soldiers could carry them into combat.

2. Answers will vary. Students may predict that the homemaker image promoted for women led to an idealization of the nuclear family consisting of a wife who stayed at home while her husband worked, and that women—even those who attended college—did not see themselves as destined for lifelong careers outside the home.

3. The attitude expressed in the poll assumes that African Americans did not want or were unable to take advantage of the same opportunities available to white Americans. It also suggests that some white Americans believed that the hierarchy of race that existed in the United States was somehow "natural" or inevitable.

Making Connections

1. Although many women had to leave their jobs after the war, the numbers of women who joined the work force during the war sowed the seeds for women to work outside the home in the future. The movement of women into jobs traditionally reserved for men also encouraged women to seek better, more challenging jobs than they had in the past.

2. The poster on page 532 seems to convey that "we're all in this together" and reminds citizens that their work in the factories is needed to help win the war. The photographs on pages 548 and 551 demonstrate the inequalities that still existed in American society at the time. Students' explanations should show an understanding of the contradiction between what the government was asking its citizens to do and how it treated some segments of society. Primary source excerpts that support this idea can be found on pages 546 and 547 (Alexander J. Allen and Lloyd Brown).

3. Possible answers: reading paperback books; attending movies; playing and attending baseball games; saving aluminum and rubber; shortages of foods such as sugar and meat; clothing styles that conserve cloth; wartime songs, slogans, and posters; women in the work force; minorities in the work force; their struggle for justice.

4. (a) The tree map cites the end of the Depression and the introduction of defense jobs and participation in wartime campaigns as factors that contributed to the mood of the home front. (b) Possible answers: Robert Woodruff's sending Coca-Cola to troops overseas, Robert de Graff's establishing a market for paperback books, and Henry Kaiser's applying mass production techniques to shipbuilding. (c) Answers will vary. Students' graphic organizers should show an awareness of the main ideas and supporting details that explain these struggles.

Alternative Assessment

Final Evaluation

Display written guides and allow students to present their taped or spoken guides.

Use the following criteria to evaluate students' projects:
- Extensiveness of their description of changes
- Effectiveness of their analysis of the causes for change

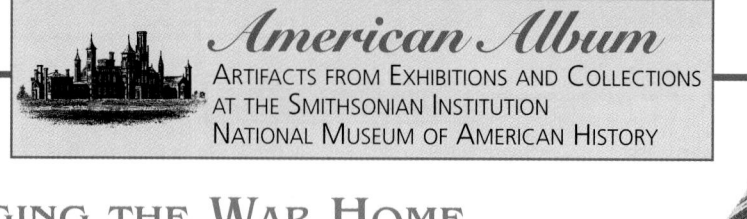

American Album
ARTIFACTS FROM EXHIBITIONS AND COLLECTIONS
AT THE SMITHSONIAN INSTITUTION
NATIONAL MUSEUM OF AMERICAN HISTORY

Review with students the ways in which the United States government attempted to bolster morale and enlist support for the war effort. Recall the ways in which the government appealed to the conscience of every American.

Using the images and captions highlighted in the American Album as a basis for discussion, ask why the propaganda campaigns were important and necessary for American victory in World War II. Point out that campaigns, rationing, slogans, posters, songs, and movies delivered a powerful message during the war. Have students identify the different segments of the population targeted by the various campaigns through a study of the various artifacts.

Ask students how messages are delivered to Americans today. Discuss the role of television in advertising. Ask how "infomercials" help create images for political candidates. Have students identify other forms of advertising. Ask how billboards, posters, and magazine photographs are used by clothing, tobacco, and other manufacturers to appeal to specific groups. Discuss the ways in which radio programming and videos appeal to Americans of different generations.

You might want to have students bring to class examples of advertising artifacts of the 1990s.

BRINGING THE WAR HOME

Americans living and working "stateside" seldom forgot about the war overseas. Almost everyone had relatives and close friends who faced constant danger from the fighting. Besides, the government wouldn't let Americans forget about the war. Rationing, pleas for conservation, a steady stream of patriotic messages, even requests to donate the family dog to the army— all this and more reminded Americans that their country was in a life-and-death struggle against totalitarian dictatorships. *What effect do you think these reminders had on the morale of soldiers and on Americans living in the United States?*

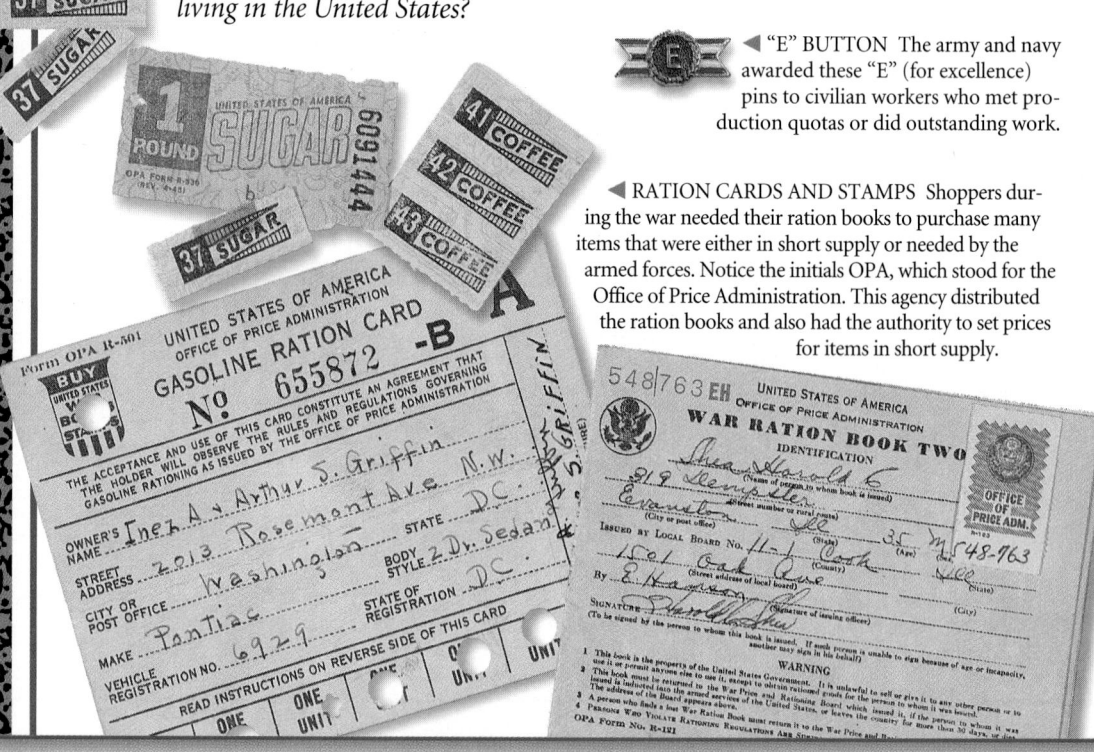

▲ LABEL ON MILK BOTTLE This label conveyed the message that conserving resources was every American's patriotic duty. The recycling effort included hundreds of products, especially those made with metal or rubber.

◄ "E" BUTTON The army and navy awarded these "E" (for excellence) pins to civilian workers who met production quotas or did outstanding work.

◄ RATION CARDS AND STAMPS Shoppers during the war needed their ration books to purchase many items that were either in short supply or needed by the armed forces. Notice the initials OPA, which stood for the Office of Price Administration. This agency distributed the ration books and also had the authority to set prices for items in short supply.

▲ HITLER AND UNCLE SAM This button used gallows humor to ask everyone to "pull" together to win the war. The need to put aside disagreements among Americans was a common government message.

◀ WAR RELIEF EFFORT While the American economy boomed during the war, Europe and Asia were devastated. Americans proudly wore pins like this one to indicate that they had contributed money to help people in other countries.

VICTORY ▶ BUTTON The letter *V*, for victory, was the most common symbol of the war effort. Many businesses used the *V* and the American flag to send a patriotic and a promotional message.

UNITED STATES WAR SAVINGS BONDS

U.S. WAR BONDS MEAN The AMERICAN WAY of LIFE BUY THEM HOLD THEM

PROTECT your valuable papers by storing them in one of our Safe Deposit Boxes.
PREVENT loss by fire or petty thievery. Your papers are always here when you want them.
MANITOWOC SAVINGS BANK
MANITOWOC, WISCONSIN
MEMBER FEDERAL DEPOSIT INSURANCE COMPANY

◀ DOGS FOR DEFENSE The armed forces needed dogs for sentry duty, to sniff out explosives, and for many other tasks. Citizens who donated dogs to the military could proudly wear this button.

SLEEVE FOR U.S. WAR BONDS ▲
The government borrowed an incredible 135 billion dollars from individual Americans to finance the war effort. These War Savings Bonds not only helped finance the war, but they gave thousands of Americans a personal and financial stake in the outcome of the war and preserving "the American way of life."

PROPAGANDA POSTERS No matter where they went—at work, on the street, at the movies—Americans saw wonderfully creative posters reminding them that their way of life depended on the outcome of the war. The posters shown at right encouraged people to work hard at their jobs to win the war. The posters used images of happy families to stir up even more support for the war effort. ▶

SOURCE READINGS

Farewell to Manzanar

Primary Source

Jeanne Wakatsuki Houston and James D. Houston

INTRODUCTION The internment of Japanese Americans during World War II tore people from their communities, destroyed lives and careers, and profoundly affected young Americans who suddenly found themselves removed from their schools and friendships. Jeanne Wakatsuki, born in California, was one such child. She was seven years old when she and her family were relocated to Manzanar, an internment camp in eastern California. Wakatsuki remained at Manzanar until she was eleven years old. At college she met her husband, James D. Houston, a novelist. Together they wrote *Farewell to Manzanar*, published in 1973, which describes life in the camp. This excerpt tells how her mother had to part with precious belongings because they were not allowed at the camps, the bus ride to the camp, and finally, the camp itself.

VOCABULARY Before you read the selection, find the meaning of these words in a dictionary: intact, abate, alleviate.

The secondhand dealers had been prowling around for weeks, like wolves, offering humiliating prices for goods and furniture they knew many of us would have to sell sooner or later. Mama had left all but her most valuable possessions in Ocean Park, simply because she had nowhere to put them. She had brought along her pottery, her silver, heirlooms like the kimonos Granny had brought from Japan, tea sets, lacquered tables, and one fine old set of china, blue and white porcelain, almost translucent. On the day we were leaving, Woody's car was so crammed with boxes and luggage and kids we had just run out of room. Mama had to sell this china.

One of the dealers offered her fifteen dollars for it. She said it was a full setting for twelve and worth at least two hundred. He said fifteen was his top price. Mama started to quiver. Her eyes blazed up at him. She had been packing all night and trying to calm down Granny, who didn't understand why we were moving again and what all the rush was about. Mama's nerves were shot, and now navy jeeps were patrolling the streets. She didn't say another word. She just glared at this man, all the rage and frustration channeled at him through her eyes.

He watched her for a moment and said he was sure he couldn't pay more than seventeen fifty for that china. She reached into the red velvet case, took out a dinner plate and hurled it at the floor right in front of his feet.

The man leaped back shouting, "Hey! Hey, don't do that! Those are valuable dishes!"

Mama took out another dinner plate and hurled it at the floor, then another and another, never moving, never opening her mouth, just quivering and glaring at the retreating dealer, with tears streaming down her cheeks. He finally turned around and scuttled out the door, heading for the next house. When he was gone she stood there smashing cups and bowls and platters until the whole set lay in scattered blue and white fragments across the wooden floor.

The name Manzanar meant nothing to us when we left Boyle heights. We didn't know where it was or what it was. We went because the government ordered us to. And, in the case of my older brothers and sisters, we went with a certain amount of relief. They had all heard stories of Japanese homes being attacked, of beatings in the streets of California towns. They were as frightened of the Caucasians as the Caucasians were of us. Moving, under what appeared to be government protection, to an area less

---

directly threatened by the war seemed not such a bad idea at all. For some it actually sounded like a fine adventure.

Our pickup point was a Buddhist church in Los Angeles. It was very early, and misty, when we got there with our luggage. Mama had bought heavy coats for all of us. She grew up in eastern Washington and knew that anywhere inland in early April would be cold. I was proud of my new coat, and I remember sitting on a duffel bag trying to be friendly with the Greyhound driver. I smiled at him. He didn't smile back. He was befriending no one. Someone tied a numbered tag to my collar and to the duffel bag (each family was given a number, and that became our official designation until the camps were closed), someone else passed out box lunches for the trip, and we climbed aboard.

Japanese Americans bused to internment camps during World War II had no idea where they were going. Like the family group here, each wore a tag bearing an identification number of a camp.

I had never been outside Los Angeles County, never traveled more than ten miles from the coast, had never even ridden on a bus. I was full of excitement, the way any kid would be, and wanted to look out the window. But for the first few hours the shades were drawn. Around me other people played cards, read magazines, dozed, waiting. I settled back, waiting too, and finally fell asleep. The bus felt very secure to me. Almost half its passengers were immediate relatives. Mama and my older brothers had succeeded in keeping most of us together, on the same bus, headed for the same camp. I didn't realize until much later what a job that was. The strategy had been, first, to have everyone living in the same district when the evacuation began, and then to get all of us included under the same family number, even though names had been changed by marriage. Many families weren't as lucky as ours and suffered months of anguish while trying to arrange transfers from one camp to another.

We rode all day. By the time we reached our destination, the shades were up. It was late afternoon. The first thing I saw was a yellow swirl across a blurred, reddish setting sun. The bus was being pelted by what sounded like splattering rain. It wasn't rain. This was my first look at something I would soon know very well, a billowing flurry of dust and sand churned up by the wind through Owens Valley.

We drove past a barbed-wire fence, through a gate, and into an open space where trunks and sacks and packages had been dumped from the baggage trucks that drove out ahead of us. I could see a few tents set up, the first rows of black barracks, and beyond them, blurred by sand, rows of barracks that seemed to spread for miles across this plain. People were sitting on cartons or milling around, with their backs to the wind, waiting to see which friends or relatives might be on this bus. As we approached, they turned or stood up, and some moved toward us expectantly. But inside the bus no one stirred. No one waved or spoke. They just stared out the windows, ominously silent. I didn't understand this. Hadn't we finally arrived, our whole family

abandoned their Japanese culture completely and may be unhappy about that. The Nisei might defend their decision to try to fit in with American culture.

After several groups of students have had a chance to role-play in front of the class, lead a discussion about the positive and negative aspects of the American "melting pot." Help students to understand that it is important to support and feel a part of American culture. Explain that the citizens of the United States cannot become segregated into distinct groups based on race, religion, or other factors, but must all work together to keep the nation strong. At the same time, students should realize that members of particular ethnic backgrounds value the cultures of their ancestors and they should try to preserve that cultural heritage. Becoming an American citizen does not require the new citizen to abandon their backgrounds, but rather to share that background with others and to use it to enrich the collective heritage of the United States.

Have students visit the local public library to look in newspapers from 1942 to see what sorts of reactions were being printed after the announcement that Japanese Americans would be relocated. Ask them to write a report on their findings, using quotations from articles or letters to the editor. Students should also note other events that were taking place in the nation and in the world at the same time. Do they see any connections between these other events and Japanese American internment? Ask students to look for evidence of hostility toward other groups, such as German Americans or Italian Americans. Finally, ask students to note in their reports any information they learned about the internment that they did not know before.

intact? I opened a window, leaned out, and yelled happily "Hey! This whole bus is full of Wakatsukis!"

Outside, the greeters smiled. Inside there was an explosion of laughter, hysterical, tension-breaking laughter that left my brothers choking and whacking each other across the shoulders.

We had pulled up just in time for dinner. The mess halls weren't completed yet. An outdoor chow line snaked around a half-finished building that broke a good part of the wind. They issued us army mess kits, the round metal kind that fold over, and plopped in scoops of canned Vienna sausage, canned string beans, steamed rice that had been cooked too long, and on top of the rice a serving of canned apricots. The Caucasian servers were thinking the fruit poured over rice would make a good dessert. Among the Japanese, of course, rice is never eaten with sweet foods, only with salty or savory foods. Few of us could eat such a mixture. But at this point no one dared protest. It would have been impolite. I was horrified when I saw the apricot syrup seeping through my little mound of rice. I opened my mouth to complain. My mother jabbed me in the back to keep quiet. We moved on through the line and joined the others squatting in the lee of half-raised walls, dabbing courteously at what was, for almost everyone there, an inedible concoction.

After dinner we were taken to Block 16, a cluster of fifteen barracks that had just been finished a day or so earlier—although finished was hardly the word for it. The shacks were built of one thickness of pine planking covered with tarpaper. They sat on concrete footings, with about two feet of open space between the floorboards and the ground. Gaps showed between the planks, and as the weeks passed and the green wood dried out, the gaps widened. Knotholes gaped in the uncovered floor.

Each barracks was divided into six units, sixteen by twenty feet, about the size of a living room, with one bare bulb hanging from the ceiling and an oil stove for heat. We were assigned two of these for the twelve people in our family group; and our official family "number" was enlarged by three digits—16 plus the number of this barracks. We were issued steel army cots, two brown army blankets each, and some mattress covers,

which my brothers stuffed with straw.

The first task was to divide up what space we had for sleeping. Bill and Woody contributed a blanket each and partitioned off the first room: one side for Bill and Tomi, one side for Woody and Chizu and their baby girl. Woody also got the stove, for heating formulas.

The people who had it hardest during the first few months were young couples like these, many of whom had married just before the evacuation began, in order not to be separated and sent to different camps. Our two rooms were crowded, but at least it was all in the family. My oldest sister and her husband were shoved into one of those sixteen-by-twenty foot compartments with people they had never seen before—two other couples, one recently married like themselves, the other with two teenage boys. Partitioning off a room like that wasn't easy. It was bitter cold when we arrived, and the wind did not abate. All they had to use for room dividers were those army blankets, two of which were barely enough to keep one person warm. They argued over whose blanket should be sacrificed and later argued about noise at night—the parents wanted their boys asleep by 9:00 P.M.—and they continued arguing over matters like that for six months, until my sister and her husband left to harvest sugar beets in Idaho. It was grueling work up there, and wages were pitiful, but when the call came through camp for workers to alleviate the wartime labor shortage, it sounded better than their life at Manzanar. They knew they'd have, if nothing else, a room, perhaps a cabin of their own.

THINKING ABOUT THE SELECTION

1. According to the author, why did some Japanese Americans view the relocation with relief?
2. What was the author's attitude on reporting to the pickup point and during the bus ride to the camp?

Critical Thinking
3. **Demonstrating Reasoned Judgment** Given the government's reason for relocating Japanese Americans, why do you think the shades on the bus were drawn during the first part of the trip?

ANSWERS TO

Thinking About the Selection
1. They had heard of Japanese homes being attacked and Japanese people being beaten in the streets and they thought that they were being taken to the camps for their own protection.
2. The author was in good spirits, looked forward to the prospect of a journey, and was excited about going to a new place.

3. The shades were probably drawn so that the occupants of the bus would not know where they were going. The government wanted to keep their destination secret from the Japanese Americans.

"In Response to Executive Order 9066: All Americans of Japanese Descent Must Report to Relocation Centers"

Dwight Okita

Literature

A Japanese American girl on her way to an internment camp.

INTRODUCTION Dwight Okita's mother was interned during World War II, and he wrote the poem below from her perspective. In it, Okita shows another side of the experience: the pain and confusion many felt when former friends began to view them with suspicion and fear. Okita was born in Chicago in 1958.

Dear Sirs:
Of course I'll come. I've packed my galoshes
and three packets of tomato seeds. Janet calls them
"love apples." My father says where we're going
they won't grow.

I am a fourteen-year-old girl with bad spelling
and a messy room. If it helps any, I will tell you
I have always felt funny using chopsticks
and my favorite food is hot dogs.
My best friend is a white girl named Denise—
we look at boys together. She sat in front of me
all through grade school because of our names:
O'Connor, Ozawa. I know the back of Denise's head
     very well.
I tell her she's going bald. She tells me I copy on tests.
We are best friends.

I saw Denise today in Geography class.
She was sitting on the other side of the room.
"You're trying to start a war," she said, "giving
     secrets away
to the Enemy, Why can't you keep your big mouth
     shut?"

I didn't know what to say.
I gave her a packet of tomato seeds
and asked her to plant them for me, told her
when the first tomato ripened
she'd miss me.

THINKING ABOUT THE SELECTION

1. Who is the speaker of the poem? To whom is the poem addressed?
2. What is the author trying to say with the lines "If it helps any, I will tell you/I have always felt funny using chopsticks/and my favorite food is hot dogs./My best friend is a white girl named Denise"?

Critical Thinking

3. **Making Comparisons** Compare the sentiments of the speaker in this poem to those of the author in *Farewell to Manzanar* as each readies for her journey. How are they similar? How are they different?

ANSWERS TO

Thinking About the Selection
1. The speaker is a fourteen-year-old girl of Japanese descent. The poem is addressed to the writers of Executive Order 9066. The author treats the executive order as an invitation to all Japanese Americans. The poem is the acceptance of the invitation.
2. The author is showing how eager this girl was to prove that she is an American girl; she wishes to downplay her differences and to point out the ways in which she is similar to American girls. She makes a point of saying that her best friend is white. The author's underlying point is that people were influenced by the internment and made to feel that being of Japanese descent meant that they were inferior to white people.
3. Both girls are hurt by the actions and comments of others, but in the first piece Wakatsuki shows mixed sentiments about internment. She looked upon the trip to the camp as an adventure of sorts. The speaker in the poem, on the other hand, although she is cooperative, tries to prove that she is an American and should not be imprisoned as the enemy.

Chapter 17 The Cold War and American Society
1945–1960

📁 Teaching Resources (See Unit 5 Folder)

	Instruction	Enrichment
Section 1 **Origins of the Cold War** (pp. 562–565)	Reproducible Lesson Plan, p. 71 Alternate Lesson Plan, p. 132 Guided Reading and Review, p. 75 Quiz, p. 76	Primary Source Activity, Uncle Joe, p. 89 Visual Learning Activity, What They Fear Most, p. 95 Historian's Toolbox Activity, Recognizing Cause and Effect, p. 87
Section 2 **Containment** (pp. 567–571)	Reproducible Lesson Plan, p. 72 Alternate Lesson Plan, p. 133 Guided Reading and Review, p. 77 Quiz, p. 78	American Profiles Activity, George F. Kennan, p. 83 Viewpoints Activity, On Joining NATO, pp. 85–86 Critical Thinking Activity, Identifying Central Issues, p. 88
Section 3 **The Cold War in Asia, the Middle East, and Latin America** (pp. 572–576)	Reproducible Lesson Plan, p. 73 Alternate Lesson Plan, p. 134 Guided Reading and Review, p. 79 Quiz, p. 80	American Profiles Activity, Marguerite Higgins, p. 84 Visual Learning Activity, Civilian Control of the Military, p. 96 Literature Activity, The Ugly American, p. 92
Section 4 **The Cold War in the United States** (pp. 577–581)	Reproducible Lesson Plan, p. 74 Alternate Lesson Plan, p. 135 Guided Reading and Review, p. 81 Quiz, p. 82 Chapter Test, Forms A & B, pp. 97–102	Primary Source Activity, The Rise of Joseph McCarthy, pp. 90–91 Literature Activity, The Hunt for Witches and Communists, pp. 93–94

📁 Additional Chapter Resources

Resource Organizer, p. 70
Alternate Lesson Plan p. 131
Answer Keys pp. 146–158

Bibliography

For the Teacher

Gimbel, John. *The Origins of the Marshall Plan.* Stanford University, 1976.

Kennan, George F. *Memoirs: 1925–1959.* Pantheon, 1983. (A personal view of the era by the definitive statesman of the policy of "containment.")

McCullough, David. *Truman.* Simon & Schuster, 1992. (A comprehensive biography of the cold war President.)

Prentice Hall Literature Excerpts from *The American Exprience,* 1994, including Momaday, N. Scott. "A Vision Beyond Time and Place." *Life,* 1971.

The Big Idea for the chapter and how the main ideas in each section relate to the Big Idea are graphically displayed below. Comprehension of this chapter's Big Idea is critical to students' understanding of United States history and how we as a nation got where we are today.

Media and Technology

 Cause and Effect, F-10

 Critical Thinking, I-2

 Graphic Organizer, G-5

 Guided Reading Audiotapes (English and Spanish)

 Computer Test Bank

For the Student

Macridis, Roy C., and Steven L. Burg. *Introduction to Comparative Politics: Political Regimes and Political Change.* HarperCollins, 1991.

Orwell, George. *Nineteen Eighty-Four.* Buccaneer, 1982. (A haunting, futuristic indictment of the totalitarian state.)

Solzhenitsyn, Aleksandr I. *One Day in the Life of Ivan Denisovich.* Bantam, 1984. (A famous Russian dissident's moving account of life in a Soviet prison camp.)

White, Theodore H. *In Search of History: A Personal Adventure.* Harper and Row, 1978. (A well-known writer's personal look at the unfolding of United States history.)

CHAPTER 17

American foreign policy after World War II remained consistent with the nation's wartime activities: force would be used to oppose authoritarian regimes that the United States considered a threat to the free world. At home the federal government would use strong, and sometimes questionable, measures to counter what it perceived to be threats to the nation's internal security.

SECTION 1

World War II forced communist and capitalist nations into a temporary alliance. In the postwar era, however, they began to compete for power and territory.

SECTION 2

To counter possible communist influence in Europe, the United States embarked on a foreign policy strategy known as containment.

SECTION 3

As communist movements arose outside Europe, the United States extended its policy of containment to Asia, the Middle East, and Latin America.

SECTION 4

The United States launched a cold war at home, embarking on an ugly crusade to root out suspected communists among its own citizens.

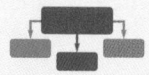

The Cold War and American Society

1945–1960

The Relevance of the Big Idea

War costs money—even a cold war. The cold war between the superpowers lasted for more than forty years. It affected the political systems and economies of nearly every nation on earth. We are still paying the costs of that war.

With the end of the cold war in the late 1980s, Americans began a long debate over how to spend the "peace dividend," the money saved from cuts in the defense budget that could be used in other programs.

Ask students to list ways in which the government could spend the peace dividend. List their responses on the chalkboard. Have students work in small groups to rank the items listed in order of importance. Compare the groups' lists, noting similarities and differences. Ask students what the results reveal about American values.

In Depth

Global Connections

At the end of World War II, Europe was in political disarray and economic ruin. In war-torn France and Italy, Soviet-backed Communist parties began to gain strength. Civil war broke out in Greece, where the right-wing government came under fire from communist rebels. The growing tension between the United States and the Soviet Union added to the political uncertainty and in turn impeded economic recovery. It also made maintenance of Europe's security in the face of Soviet domination the central focus of the cold war.

The Cold War and American Society

1945–1960

*T*he United States and the Soviet Union temporarily ignored their differences during World War II. After the war, however, these differences began to pull the two nations apart again. Soon the world was divided into two camps, formed around communist and capitalist beliefs. The bitterness of the conflict affected both international relations and relations among Americans at home. In its effort to counteract communism around the world, the United States government contributed to a frenzied mood of fear and suspicion within its own borders.

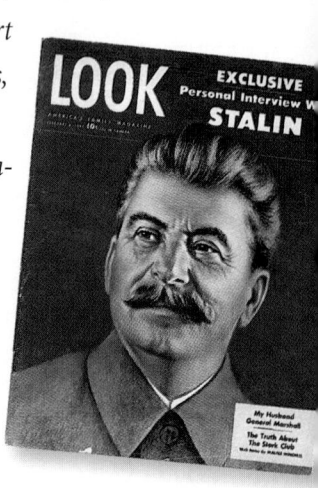

Events in the United States

Events in the United States	1945 Fifty nations adopt the United Nations charter in San Francisco.	1946 Winston Churchill gives his famous "iron curtain" speech in Fulton, Missouri.	1948 George Orwell's frightening novel 1984 is published.	1949 North Atlantic Treaty Organization (NATO) is established.	1952 Dwight D. Eisenhower is elected President.
1945	**1947**		**1949**	**1951**	
Events in the World			1948 The Berlin airlift begins. • Israel is founded.	1949 Communists seize control of China. • Soviet Union tests its first atomic bomb.	1950 The Korean War begins.

RESOURCE DIRECTORY

Teaching Resources

Alternate Lesson Plan: Demonstrating the Big Idea found in the Alternate Lesson Plans folder, p. 131, provides a lesson strategy to instruct students about the big idea that the wartime alliance of the capitalist United States and the communist Soviet Union crumbled into an increasingly hostile ideological struggle affecting both international and domestic affairs.

Alternative Assessment Handbook provides information, guidance, and strategies for alternative methods of assessment. It includes an essay on new trends in assessment, guidance and strategies for developing performance tasks and portfolios, scoring rubrics, and sample evaluation forms.

 Pages 562–565
Origins of the Cold War

During World War II, a common enemy forced communist and democratic nations together in a shaky alliance. Once the shooting stopped, however, political and economic differences divided the globe along new lines.

 Pages 567–571
Containment

The United States government viewed Soviet communist influence as a disease that was rapidly spreading around the globe. Foreign policy in the postwar years focused on preventing any more capitalist nations from becoming "infected."

 Pages 572–576
The Cold War in Asia, the Middle East, and Latin America

The policy of containment had been created with the aim of maintaining European stability. As communist movements developed in Asia, the Middle East, and Latin America, however, the United States extended the policy to meet challenges around the world.

 Pages 577–581
The Cold War in the United States

The effort to contain communism abroad made Americans fear subversion at home. The nation became swept up in an ugly campaign to expose suspected communists among its own citizens.

1953	1955	1957	1959	1961
1953 The Rosenbergs are executed for espionage.	**1954** Nationally televised McCarthy hearings lead to Joseph McCarthy's downfall.	**1957** President Eisenhower formulates a plan to protect the Middle East from communism.	**1959** The United States cuts diplomatic ties with Cuba after Fidel Castro seizes power.	
	1954 The Vietnamese defeat the French at Dien Bien Phu.	**1956** The Soviet Union crushes a popular uprising in Hungary.	**1957** The African nation of Ghana wins independence.	**1959** Revolutionary leader Fidel Castro overthrows dictatorship in Cuba.	**1960** The Soviet Union shoots down a United States spy plane.

Media and Technology

 Transparency
Time Lines, E-8

Alternative Assessment

As an ongoing chapter project, students can role-play reporters for Radio Free Europe, which the United States government established in 1950 to broadcast news reports into communist Eastern Europe, where news was heavily censored. Their job will be to write factually accurate news reports that show capitalism and democracy at its best. The more sophisticated reports will also fulfill Radio Free Europe's mission to broadcast propaganda—material that specifically promotes the advantages of capitalism and democracy.

Students' reports may include straight news, mock interviews, profiles, on-the-scene reports, and editorials. Projects should include at least four broadcasts, based on the topics discussed in the chapter, and additional research. Students may choose to submit the scripts or do a live "broadcast" of one script in class. They may also choose to tape-record their performance.

Projects will be evaluated according to the following guidelines:

● **Unacceptable** Projects are not attempted or fail to meet requirements outlined.

● **Limited/Acceptable** Projects include four factually accurate reports based primarily on material from the textbook.

● **Extensive/Commendable** Reports incorporate some outside research and demonstrate an understanding of the arguments in favor of democratic capitalism.

● **Extraordinary/Outstanding** Reports incorporate considerable outside research, are written in a lively style, and successfully fulfill Radio Free Europe's propaganda mission.

For information and guidance on alternative assessment trends and strategies, see the Alternative Assessment Handbook in the Resource Directory on page 560.

SECTION 1

Origins of the Cold War

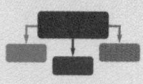

1. FOCUS

Connecting to the Big Idea

See page 560B. Having defeated a common enemy in World War II, the United States and the Soviet Union then became enemies. Ask students what both sides sought to gain after the war.

Objectives

● Summarize the relationship between the United States and the Soviet Union during World War II.
● Explain why relations between the United States and the Soviet Union broke down after World War II.
● Identify the main goals of the superpowers in the postwar period and explain why those goals were in conflict.

Bellringer

Write the following questions on the chalkboard and ask students to jot down an answer: What do you think a "cold war" is? Why was this war considered "cold" and not "hot"? What made it a war?

Reading Strategy

Reading for Evidence Explain that the United States and the Soviet Union went from being allies to being enemies in a very short period of time. Ask students to identify turning points in this process as they read, and find reasons for the rapid political shift.

SECTION PREVIEW

During World War II, a common enemy forced communist and democratic nations together in a shaky alliance. Once the shooting stopped, however, political and economic differences divided the globe along new lines.

Key Concepts

• The Soviet Union and the United States suppressed their disagreements during World War II.
• Diplomatic relations between the United States and the Soviet Union quickly broke down after the war.
• The beliefs of communism and capitalism created different goals for the two superpowers in the postwar period.

The mass media helped spread tension during the cold war years. This 1947 comic book described how the Soviets might be planning to conquer and enslave the people of the United States.

Key Terms, People, and Places

cold war, proletariat, totalitarian, iron curtain

The **cold war** was the bitter state of indirect conflict that existed between the United States and the Soviet Union for more than four decades after the end of World War II. This conflict developed out of long-standing disagreements between the two nations. After the Russian Revolution of 1917, the United States had refused to extend formal diplomatic recognition to the new communist nation until 1933. Americans were angered when the Soviet Union signed a nonaggression pact with Germany in 1939, but found themselves on the same side as the Soviets when Hitler broke the agreement and attacked the Soviet Union in 1941. The Allies pulled together to defeat the Axis powers, but by the end of the war, relations between the United States and Britain on the one hand and the Soviet Union on the other became increasingly tense.

Wartime Problems

At Tehran in 1943 and at Yalta in 1945, President Franklin Roosevelt had met with British prime minister Winston Churchill and Soviet leader Joseph Stalin to work out disagreements about the future of Germany and Poland. The three leaders had finally agreed to partition Germany into four zones—one American, one British, one French, and one Soviet. They also had agreed that in Poland a government sympathetic to the Soviet Union should control postwar policy. This new Polish government should, however, include representatives sympathetic to the West, and democratic elections should be held in the future. In diplomatic fashion, these agreements were left vague so that everyone could agree to them. Their imprecise terms, however, left room for disputes in the future.

Adding to this tension over Germany and Poland, the Soviet Union blamed the United States for delaying the opening of a western front in Europe during the war. While the Allies attacked the "soft underbelly" of the Axis Powers in southern Europe, the Soviets sustained heavy losses fighting the Germans alone on the eastern front. The Soviets were on their own for two years before Operation Overlord finally took some of the pressure off in June 1944.

Tension also arose during the development of the atomic bomb. The United States had relied on British help in the Manhattan Project while consciously excluding the Soviet Union. President Truman, Stalin, and Churchill had met at the Berlin suburb of Potsdam in 1945 to discuss ending the war in Japan and postwar plans for Europe. At that time, Truman hinted to Stalin that the United States had a new weapon of extraordinary force, but he said nothing more about it. Stalin, who knew about the bomb from Soviet spies in New Mexico, simply nodded and said that he hoped it would be put to good use. Stalin's casual manner hid, for

▶ RESOURCE DIRECTORY

Teaching Resources

Reproducible Lesson Plan found in the Unit 5 folder, p. 71, provides a summary of the Section 1 lesson plan content.

Alternate Lesson Plan: Critical Thinking Recognizing Ideologies, found in the Alternate Lesson Plans folder, p. 132, is designed to provide students with the skills to identify ideologies by focusing on ideologies in conflict during the cold war.

Guided Reading and Review found in the Unit 5 folder, p. 75, provides a structure for reading and mastering the key concepts and reviewing the key terms for Section 1. (Guided Practice)

Primary Source Activity "Uncle Joe," found in the Unit 5 folder, p. 89, presents excerpts from Svetlana Stalin's memoirs to afford students a personal glimpse of her father, Joseph Stalin.

the moment, the Soviets' resentment over being left out of the atom bomb project.

The Allies Follow Separate Postwar Paths

Americans became increasingly disillusioned with the Soviet Union as the war drew to a close. During the struggle, they had viewed the Soviets sympathetically. Newspapers and magazines encouraged support for the Americans' long-suffering ally. Journalist Joseph Goulden, who grew up in Texas during the war, recalled how he and his friends had played war games and pretended to be Soviet soldiers:

> We assembled new sabotage devices with fingers stiffened by the subzero temperatures of Mother Russia—old soup cans hand-packed with dirt and cinders—and climbed back up the embankment. . . . Another successful sabotage by Russian guerrillas. Under cross-examination none of the band could have distinguished a Communist from a logarithm. But we did know from movies that the Russians were brave and skilled partisans; in our minds their heroic stand at Stalingrad was equal to the defense of the Alamo.

Franklin Roosevelt affectionately referred to Stalin as "Uncle Joe." *Time* magazine even chose the Soviet leader as "Man of the Year" in 1940. But near the end of the war, the gaping divide between the two nations' postwar goals could be ignored no longer. ✪

American Aims The United States fought in World War II to protect its vision of the American dream. The nation hoped to share with the world the essential elements of a democratic life—liberty, equality, and representative government. The United States also sought to create a world in which its own economic interests would be served by worldwide markets for its products. As a major contributor to victory in the war, the United States was determined to see its vision survive in the postwar world.

HOLLYWOOD'S FIRST DRAMA OF RUSSIA'S YOUNG HERO

THE BOY FROM STALINGRAD

with BOBBY SAMARZICH · CONRAD BINYON · MARY LOU HARRINGTON
SCOTTY BECKETT · STEVEN MULLER · Screen Play by Ferdinand Reyher
Produced by COLBERT CLARK · Directed by SIDNEY SALKOW
A COLUMBIA PICTURE

MAKING CONNECTIONS

How would communism, a system in which private property does not exist and resources are shared by everyone, present a threat to American capitalism?

The Soviet Stance The Soviets approached the postwar world very differently from the United States. Communism predicted that through a process of class struggle, the workers of the world would eventually triumph. The first step toward that triumph involved removing the resources necessary for production from the hands of private business owners. If this happened, then members of the **proletariat**—working-class men and women—would join together for the common good, sharing resources equally among themselves. 🔲

Until the proletariat established a true communist state, however, a strong central government would control the society's resources. In practice, the Soviet state under Stalin was vastly different from the ideal state under communism. He created a **totalitarian** dictatorship in which the central government ruled by terror and held absolute control over its citizens' lives.

The 1943 film advertised in this poster promoted a heroic image of our Soviet allies. When World War II was over, however, Hollywood portrayed the "Commies" as sly and dangerous enemies.

SOURCE READINGS

 Source Readings on p. 584 will connect literature selections and primary source excerpts to historical events discussed in this section.

Source Readings on p. 584

Explain/Discuss

Discuss how the personalities of two successive American Presidents affected relations with the Soviet Union. Remind students that President Roosevelt felt that he could "handle" Joseph Stalin, while Truman saw Stalin as evil and power-hungry.

Ask students how they think the change in attitudes from Roosevelt to Truman affected postwar talks between the two countries. What was Truman's strategy in mentioning to Stalin that the United States had a powerful new weapon?

Analyze

Have students analyze the difference between a capitalist economy and a communist one. List key differences on the chalkboard.

Answer to . . .

MAKING CONNECTIONS

Communist nations would not provide markets for goods produced by the American capitalist economy. If many nations adopted communism, the United States would not have many opportunities for foreign trade.

Activity

Cooperative Learning

Time: One class period.
Activity: Reenact the meeting between President Truman and the Soviet foreign minister, Molotov.
Grouping: Four to six students.
Purpose: Every group should assign two students to role-play the officials, and students to act as coaches. Each official/coach team should develop a list of overall goals and specific demands for the meeting. Students should consider the desires, fears, and political system of their respective countries.
Roles: Officials, coaches, researchers, moderator.
Outcome: Students will understand the political perspective of each official and nation.

The map shows how the Soviet Union secured compliant nations along its European borders.

Enrichment

Have students write an essay in response to this question: Had the United States and the Soviet Union been able to avoid the deep split that made them enemies and instead remain allies, what benefits might have resulted?

3. ASSESS

Section 1 Review Answers

1. (a) cold war, see p. 562, (b) proletariat, see p. 563, (c) totalitarian, see p. 563, (d) iron curtain, see p. 565

2. There were disagreements over the fate of Germany and Poland. The Soviet Union was also irritated at having been left out of the effort to develop the atomic bomb.

3. The United States wanted to keep foreign markets open for the benefit of its own capitalist economy. Thus, it supported governments sympathetic to capitalism around the world. The Soviet Union demanded communist regimes along its western borders for its own security.

4. Americans went from considering the Russians brave allies to thinking of the Soviet Union as a harsh dictatorship that repressed its people and could not be trusted to cooperate with the United States.

5. Capitalism rests on a free market system in which private owners of resources make their own decisions on how to use the resources. Communism is predicated on a future proletarian state in which people will forgo their selfish goals to promote the common good; in the meantime, a powerful central government controls economic resources and makes decisions for everyone.

The Cold War in Europe

0   200   400 Miles

0   200   400 Kilometers

"Iron curtain"

Communist nations

Capitalist nations

⊛ Capital cities

Geography and History: Interpreting Maps
This map shows the territories controlled by communist and capitalist countries. After World War II, the Soviet Union was every bit as concerned about protecting its national security as was the United States. *How does this map illustrate the policy pursued by the Soviet Union to protect itself from its capitalist rivals in Europe?*

After losing twenty million people—about as many as live in New York state today—and suffering the destruction of cities such as Stalingrad in the war, the Soviet Union was determined to rebuild on its own terms. One part of that rebuilding required having friendly nations along the western borders of the Soviet Union. Several times in the past century and a half, the Soviet Union had faced attack from the west. Having repelled first Napoleon and then Hitler, the Soviets wanted regimes in Eastern Europe sympathetic to their own aims.

Postwar Clashes The United States and the Soviet Union clashed first over Poland. The loosely worded Yalta agreement called for a new Polish government influenced strongly by the Soviet Union but including a few representatives sympathetic to the West. President Truman met with Soviet foreign minister Vyacheslav Molotov on April 23, 1945, and told him that "the United States Government . . . could not agree to be a party to the formation of a Polish government which was not representative of all Polish democratic elements." Truman insisted that the Soviets were not keeping their part of the Yalta agreement, and he demanded bluntly that the Soviets do exactly as they were told. Molotov protested, "I have never been talked to like that in my life." "Carry out your agreements and you won't get talked to like that," Truman retorted.

The next evening President Truman received an answer from Molotov's boss. Stalin sent a message in which he emphasized that because Poland bordered the Soviet Union, the Soviets must be allowed to have a strong influence there. He said that securing friendly neighbors along Soviet borders was "demanded by the blood of the Soviet people abundantly shed on the fields of Poland," and he concluded:

I am ready to fulfill your request and do everything possible to reach a harmonious solution. But you demand too much of me. In other words, you demand that I renounce the interests of security of the Soviet Union, but I cannot turn against my country.

It was clear from the determined tone of Stalin's message that there was to be no such "harmonious solution" to the Poland problem.

American and British officials were not the only ones grappling with the alarming actions of their former ally. Polls reflected the American public's shifting views of the Soviet Union. A poll in September 1945 found that 54 percent

RESOURCE DIRECTORY

Teaching Resources

⭐ **Visual Learning Activity** What They Fear Most, found in the Unit 5 folder, p. 95, uses a 1952 cartoon to illustrate fears on both sides of the cold war.

of the respondents trusted the Soviets to cooperate with Americans in the postwar period. Two months later, the number fell to 44 percent, and by February 1946, it had dropped still further to 35 percent.

As they soured on the Soviet Union, Americans began to transfer their wartime hatred of Nazi Germany to the communist Soviet Union. Both nations, according to authors, journalists, and government officials, were totalitarian regimes whose leaders had absolute control and the ability to eliminate any opposition. George Orwell's haunting novel *1984,* published in the United States in 1949, described a frightening future world in which a totalitarian state, represented by the ever-present face of "Big Brother," monitors and controls every aspect of people's lives. *Life* magazine called Big Brother a mating of Hitler and Stalin. Truman himself declared the next year that "there isn't any difference between the totalitarian Russian government and the Hitler government."

Declaration of the Cold War While there was no formal declaration of war, two speeches marked the onset of the struggle. In 1946 Stalin declared his confidence in the ultimate triumph of the Soviet system. The Soviet Union would strengthen its military forces and do whatever was necessary to ensure its survival in a struggle with the West.

Winston Churchill, now out of office, responded that same year. Speaking in Fulton, Missouri, Churchill said that "from Stettin in the Baltic to Trieste in the Adriatic, an iron curtain has descended across the [European] Continent." This so-called **iron curtain**, the new battlefront of the cold war, sharply divided the

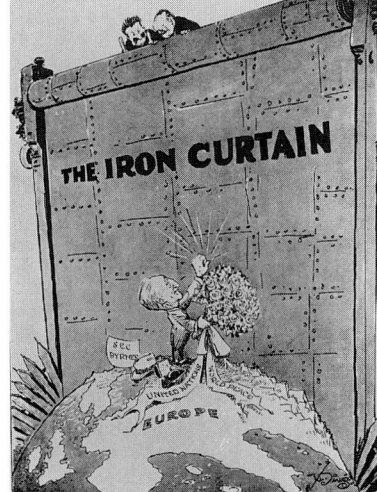

Using Historical Evidence Winston Churchill (right) is shown making the 1946 speech in which he introduced the idea of the iron curtain. *In the cartoon (left), why is United States secretary of state James Byrnes portrayed as a determined suitor? Whom is he courting? How does the cartoonist rate his chances of success?*

capitalist West from the communist East. The map on page 564 shows these divisions. In his speech, Churchill stressed that the English-speaking peoples had to work together to stop the Soviet Union from closing the iron curtain around any more nations.

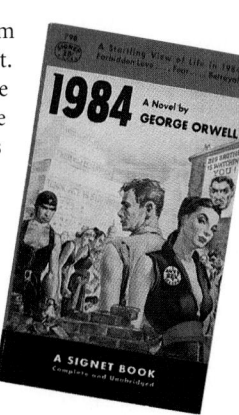

Orwell's *1984*—a story of "forbidden love and terror in a world many of us may live to see"—painted a dismal picture of life under a communist dictatorship.

SECTION 1 REVIEW

Key Terms, People, and Places
1. Define (a) cold war, (b) proletariat, (c) totalitarian, (d) iron curtain.

Key Concepts
2. What wartime issues paved the way for the cold war?
3. How did American aims and Soviet aims for the postwar period differ?

4. How did American public opinion about the Soviet Union change after World War II ?

Critical Thinking
5. **Identifying Central Issues** What are the main points that separate the capitalist from the communist vision of society?

Quiz found in the Unit 5 folder, p. 76, covers the main ideas in this section as well as the key terms.

Media and Technology

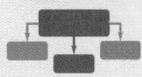 **Transparency**
Cause and Effect, F-10

Reteach

Ask students to explain what the iron curtain was. Have students list facts about life on both sides of the iron curtain.

 **4. CLOSE**

Reinforcing the Big Idea

Deep and bitter divisions emerged between the United States and the Soviet Union after World War II. The next section describes how the Soviets' dream of spreading communism soon fueled a massive American effort to stop it.

Critical Thinking

Recognizing Cause and Effect

Focus Distinguish between causes and effects; recognize multiple causes and effects.

Instruct Present this quotation from Harry Truman: "There is nothing new in the world except the history you do not know." Why, then, is it important to study the causes and effects of historical events?

Ask students to cite causes of the cold war. Discuss events in the world today that are similar to those that caused the cold war, such as the tensions caused by the spread of nuclear technology to developing countries.

Extend See the Historian's Toolbox Activity in the Resource Directory.

Answers

1. (a) Statements A and B. (b) Statement A cause: President Roosevelt believed that postwar cooperation with the Soviet Union was possible. Effect: He viewed Stalin as a partner—if not an ally—in formulating a Great Powers peace. Statement B cause: President Truman was persuaded by advisers that the Soviet Union would become a "world bully" after the war. Effect: He adopted a "get tough" policy whose aim was to block any possibility of Soviet expansion. (c) *Because* signals cause. *As a result* signals effect.

2. (a) Cause: mounting distrust between the United States and the Soviet Union. Effects: Peace negotiations were viewed as opportunities to test each other's global objectives. Negotiations on Poland, the former German satellite states, and the occupation of Germany were used as tests. (b) Effect: the cold war. Causes: mounting distrust; negotiations viewed as opportunities to test global objectives; negotiations used as tests; defensive positions seen as aggressive stances.

3. Distrust between the United States and the Soviet Union mounted. ➔ Peace negotiations were viewed as an opportunity to test the other's global objectives. ➔ Negotiations on Poland, the former German satellite states, and the occupation of Germany were used as tests. ➔ Defensive positions of each power were viewed as aggressive stances by the other. ➔ The cold war began.

Recognizing Cause and Effect

History is more than a list of events; it is a study of the relationships among events. Recognizing cause and effect means examining how one event or action brings about others. If you can understand how events or ideas relate to and affect each other, you can begin to formulate workable solutions to problems.

Follow the steps below to practice recognizing cause and effect.

1. Identify the two parts of a cause-effect relationship. A cause is an event or action that brings about an effect. As you read, look for key words that signal a cause-effect relationship. Words such as *because, due to,* and *on account of* signal causes. Words such as *so, thus, therefore,* and *as a result* signal effects. Read statements A through C at right, and answer the following questions. (a) Which statements contain both a cause and an effect? (b) Which is the cause and which is the effect in each statement? (c) What words, if any, signal the cause-effect relationship?

2. Remember that an event can have more than one cause and more than one effect. Several causes can lead to one event. So, too, can a single cause have several effects. Read statement D at right, and respond to the following. (a) Find an example of a cause that has more than one effect. (b) Find an example of an effect that has more than one cause.

3. Understand that an event can be both a cause and an effect. A cause can lead to an effect, which in turn can be the cause of another event. In this way, causes and effects can form a chain of related events. You can diagram the following statements to show such a chain: The United States feared Soviet expansion in Europe. ➔ The United States began a military buildup. ➔ The Soviet Union began a military buildup. ➔ An arms race between the two countries began. Now read statement D below, and using arrows, draw a diagram of the causes and effects that shows the chain of related events.

Statements

A Because President Roosevelt believed that postwar cooperation with the Soviet Union was necessary, he viewed Stalin as a partner—if not an ally—in formulating a peace.

B Unlike Roosevelt, President Truman was persuaded by advisers that the Soviet Union would become a "world bully" after the war. As a result, he adopted a "get tough" policy whose aim was to block any possibility of Soviet expansion.

C The Soviets, for their part, believed that the United States was intent on global domination and meant to encircle the Soviet Union with anticommunist states.

D Due to mounting distrust between the United States and the Soviet Union, each power came to view the postwar peace negotiations as an opportunity to test the other's global objectives. Thus, negotiating the status of Poland became the first such test. Other tests included the plans for former German satellite states and the policies for the occupation of Germany. Each power regarded its own positions in these negotiations as essentially defensive, but each viewed the other's stances as aggressive and expansionist. Together these tests and stances produced the cold war, an armed and dangerous truce that lasted for forty-five years.

RESOURCE DIRECTORY

Historian's Toolbox Activity Recognizing Cause and Effect, found in the Unit 5 folder, p. 87, helps students apply this skill by focusing on the end of the cold war.

Containment

SECTION PREVIEW

The United States government viewed Soviet communist influence as a disease that was rapidly spreading around the globe. Foreign policy in the postwar years focused on preventing any more capitalist nations from becoming "infected."

Key Concepts

• American foreign policy in the postwar years was summed up by the term *containment*, which meant preventing nations around the world from adopting communism.
• Containment was spelled out in a series of speeches, plans, and documents.
• Despite talk of liberating the nations dominated by the Soviet Union during the 1950s, containment continued to shape American foreign policy under President Eisenhower.

Key Terms, People, and Places

United Nations, containment, Truman Doctrine, Marshall Plan, Berlin airlift, NATO, NSC-68, satellite nation; George C. Marshall, Mao Zedong

T he founding of the United Nations in 1945 ignited new hope for international peace and understanding. Deep differences between Western democracy and communism, however, made it difficult for the UN to fulfill its great promise. Afraid of Soviet communist expansion, American leaders developed programs aimed at preventing the Soviets from extending their influence any further.

The United Nations

Near the end of World War II, diplomats hoped to create a new international peacekeeping organization. The League of Nations, founded at the end of World War I, had failed, largely because the United States had refused to join. This time, American policymakers succeeded in securing the support of the United States Congress for the **United Nations.**

In April 1945, delegates from fifty nations met in San Francisco to adopt a charter, or document setting down official rules, for the new organization. The United Nations charter pledged that member countries would seek to settle their disagreements peacefully. It also committed them to try to stop wars from occurring and to end those that did break out. All member nations belonged to the General Assembly. Eleven countries sat on the Security Council. Five of those—the United States, the Soviet Union, Great Britain, France, and China—had permanent seats and a chance to veto any policies under consideration. This veto power, exercised by both communist and capitalist powers, limited the UN's ability to take action in the early postwar years and led the United States to explore other approaches to controlling the Soviet Union.

On June 26, 1945, after the UN charter had been signed by representatives from all fifty nations, Harry Truman delivered a speech to the assembly. He said,

T he Charter of the United Nations which you have just signed is a solid structure upon which we can build a better world. History will honor you for it. Between the victory in Europe and the final victory in Japan, in this most destructive of all wars, you have won a victory against war itself.

The Policy of Containment

Despite the hopeful sentiments expressed in Truman's speech to the UN and the fact that the Soviet economy was in ruins following World War II, American leaders still perceived a serious threat to United States interests from the Soviet Union. To address their concerns, officials developed a policy known as **containment.**

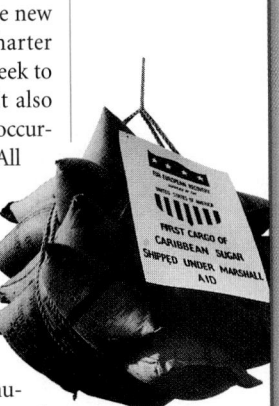

After World War II, the Marshall Plan provided United States aid to European nations. Some of this aid went to purchase food, such as this load of sugar.

Reproducible Lesson Plan found in the Unit 5 folder, p. 72, provides a summary of the Section 2 lesson plan content.

Alternate Lesson Plan: Learning Styles found in the Alternate Lesson Plans folder, p. 133, is especially effective for visual learners and helps students to understand containment and how it influenced United States international relations.

Guided Reading and Review found in the Unit 5 folder, p. 77, provides a structure for reading and mastering the key concepts and reviewing the key terms for Section 2. (Guided Practice)

1. FOCUS

Connecting to the Big Idea

See page 560B. Fearing the further spread of communism in Europe, the United States developed a new foreign policy goal called containment. Ask students how this policy was carried out.

Objectives

● Describe the goals of the United States policy of containment.
● Explain how the containment policy was carried out.
● Explain why the United States settled for a policy of containing communism instead of eliminating it.

Bellringer

Write on the chalkboard, "The buck stops here." Ask students if they know what this famous quotation means. Tell them that President Truman kept it on his desk, and that it was emblematic of the policy that Truman advocated to fight communism.

Reading Strategy

Structured Overview Have students write the heading Containment at the top of a piece of paper, followed by the subheadings Action and Result. As they read, they should list under Action the steps taken by the United States to combat communism and indicate under Result the success or failure of each action.

Explain/Discuss

Explain to students that during the course of the cold war, there were several flashpoints in hostilities between the United States and the Soviet Union. One took place in Berlin, Germany, in 1948–49. The news that the Soviets had blockaded West Berlin, a Western-controlled area surrounded by East Germany, raised world tensions.

Discuss with students why they think the blockade of one city caused so much anxiety to people around the world. Why did the West see the action as provocation? What might the Soviets have hoped to gain by such a move? Why is the incident a good example of the cold war and of the policy of containment?

Analyze

Ask students to identify the major United States foreign policy efforts discussed in this section. Then have them analyze those actions and decide whether each was aimed more at confrontation or at peacemaking. Students should support their analysis with specific facts from the text.

Answer to ...

MAKING CONNECTIONS

Vandenberg advised Truman to scare Americans into supporting the Truman Doctrine, which Truman did by describing the Soviet Union as a threat to the rights of "free peoples." Similarly, Reagan used his "evil empire" rhetoric to rally public support for increasing the military budget.

At its birth, the United Nations was hailed by President Harry Truman as "a victory against war itself." In this photograph, Truman and representatives from other member nations look on as Secretary of State Edward Stettinius signs the UN charter in June 1945.

The definition of containment came from George Kennan, a top-ranking American diplomat stationed in Moscow. In early 1946, he sent an eight-thousand-word telegram back to the State Department analyzing Soviet policy. The Soviet Union was not going to yield, he believed, and the United States needed to remove any opportunities for its enemy to establish communist governments in other countries. ✪

The Truman Doctrine Truman was an unassuming man, with a straightforward approach to the job he inherited from Franklin Roosevelt. He had a chance to apply the policy of containment in early 1947. When Great Britain informed the United States that it could no longer continue to provide Greece and Turkey with economic and military aid, Truman was afraid that those two nations might embrace communist strategies to ease their economic troubles. The State Department therefore developed a program for American assistance and then had to sell the plan to Congress. Undersecretary of State Dean Acheson told congressional leaders that "like apples in a barrel infected by one rotten one, the corruption of Greece would infect Iran and all to the east."

This sign, which sat on Truman's desk, expressed his belief that the President of the United States cannot "pass the buck"—or shirk responsibility for tough decisions.

Meanwhile, Truman followed the advice of Senator Arthur Vandenberg of Michigan. The President, a Democrat, was determined to enlist Republicans in his foreign policy initiatives, and Vandenberg was the ranking Republican in this area. Vandenberg told Truman that if he wanted his program passed to assist Greece and Turkey, he had to generate public support—and that meant he had to "scare the hell out of the country." In his speeches, Truman warned the American people about the serious threat to national security posed by Soviet influence abroad. In a statement to Congress that came to be called the **Truman Doctrine,** he said, "I believe that it must be the policy of the United States to support free peoples who are resisting attempted subjugation [conquering] by armed minorities or by outside pressures." Responding to his plea, Congress appropriated $400 million for Turkey and Greece.

MAKING CONNECTIONS

In the 1980s, President Ronald Reagan referred to the Soviet Union as "the evil empire." How does this compare to Arthur Vandenberg's advice to President Truman?

The Marshall Plan By 1947, Communist parties were growing stronger in a number of countries, and American policymakers were afraid that the Soviet Union might intervene to support local communist movements. At the same time, they were eager to open new markets for American goods. That year, Secretary of State **George C. Marshall** carried containment a step further with a plan to address both concerns.

Marshall unveiled his plan in a speech at Harvard University in June 1947. The **Marshall Plan** called for the nations of Europe—including the Soviet Union and other communist countries—to draw up a program for economic recovery from the war. The United States would then support the program with financial aid.

The Soviet Union and its Eastern European neighbors (under Soviet pressure) did not participate. Soviet foreign minister Molotov called the plan "nothing but a vicious American scheme for using dollars to buy its way" into European affairs. Sixteen Western European

▶ RESOURCE DIRECTORY

Teaching Resources

✪ **American Profiles Activity** found in the Unit 5 folder, p. 83, profiles George F. Kennan, the diplomat and scholar who developed the containment doctrine on which the United States based its postwar foreign policy.

nations, however, hammered out a plan requesting $17 billion over a four-year period. In 1948 Congress approved the Marshall Plan, also called the European Recovery Program. The United States sent over $13 billion in aid to Europe over the next four years. The Western European economy was quickly restored to health, and the United States was rewarded with strong trading partners in that region of the world.

One of the nations to benefit from the Marshall Plan was West Germany. At the end of World War II, Germany had been split into four zones occupied by the Soviet Union, France, Britain, and the United States. The city of Berlin, located in the Soviet zone, was likewise divided among the four Allies. When the Western powers united the French, British, and American zones to form West Germany and introduced a West German currency in the western part of Berlin, the Soviets reacted by blockading all ground and water routes to West Berlin in June 1948.

Truman did not want to risk starting a war with the Soviet Union by forcing open the transportation routes; nor did he want to give up West Berlin to the Soviets. Instead he began the **Berlin airlift,** moving supplies into West Berlin by plane. Food, coal, and other vital supplies were flown into the city every day for over a year. The Soviets finally ended the blockade in May 1949, and the airlift ended the following September. By this time the Marshall Plan had resulted in progress toward economic stability in the capitalist nations of Western Europe, including West Germany. Nevertheless, the tension that resulted from the airlift helped convince the Western powers that they needed to form a peacetime alliance for security against the Soviet threat.

NATO In 1949 the United States helped to establish the North Atlantic Treaty Organization—**NATO**—shown on the map on page 570. The twelve nations in the alliance—Belgium, Britain, Canada, Denmark, France, Iceland, Italy, Luxembourg, the Netherlands, Norway, Portugal, and the United States—vowed that an attack against one would be viewed as an attack against all. Dropping its opposition to military treaties with Europe for the first time since the American Revolution, the United States was now actively involved in European affairs.

Two disturbing events in 1949 prompted more drastic action from the United States. In April of that year, Chinese nationalists led by General Chiang Kai-shek lost control of their country to **Mao Zedong** and his communist followers. Civil war between these two factions had torn China since the early part of the century, and not even the need to fight off a common enemy—Japan—during World War II could unite the nation.

Despite support from the United States in the postwar years, Chiang was unable to stop Mao from steadily taking over control of China. Now, in mid-1949, Roosevelt's intended "anchor" of democracy in East Asia had turned into a communist dictatorship. Chiang was forced to retreat to the island of Taiwan off the southeast coast of China. The United States continued to

Viewpoints
On Joining NATO

Debates over whether or not the United States should join the North Atlantic Treaty Organization (NATO) were held in Congress and in the press. *What fears underlie the following arguments for and against the United States joining this peacetime alliance?*

For Joining NATO

"From now on, no one will misread our motives or underestimate our determination to stand in defense of our freedom. . . . The greatest obstacle that stands in the way of complete recovery [from World War II] is the pervading and paralyzing sense of insecurity. The treaty is a powerful antidote to this poison. . . . With this protection afforded by the Atlantic Pact, western Europe can breathe easier again."
Senator Tom Connally (Texas), Chairman, Committee on Foreign Relations, address before the United States Senate, 1949

Against Joining NATO

"This whole program in my opinion is not a peace program; it is a war program. . . . We are committing ourselves to a policy of war, not a policy of peace. We are building up armaments. We are undertaking to arm half the world against the other half. We are inevitably starting an armament race. . . . The general history of armament races in the world is that they have led to war, not to peace."
Senator Robert A. Taft (Ohio), address before the United States Senate, 1949

Viewpoints Activity On Joining NATO, found in the Unit 5 folder, pp. 85–86, encourages discussion of the North Atlantic Treaty Organization and helps students evaluate predictions.

Section 2 Review Answers

1. (a) containment, see p. 567,
(b) Truman Doctrine, see p. 568,
(c) Marshall Plan, see p. 568, (d) Berlin airlift, see p. 569, (e) NATO, see p. 569,
(f) satellite nation, see p. 571

2. (a) George C. Marshall, see p. 568,
(b) Mao Zedong, p. 569

3. (a) The UN sought to settle disagreements between nations peacefully and to put an end to wars. (b) The veto power exercised by both capitalist and communist nations in the UN Security Council made it difficult for the body to reach any agreements.

4. The Truman Plan and the Marshall Plan, both of which provided aid to foreign countries thought to be vulnerable to communist takeover, expressed the determination of the United States to prevent communism from spreading.

5. NSC-68 recommended that the United States triple its defense budget.

6. Eisenhower exercised caution because he did not want to involve the United States in a full-scale shooting war with the Soviet Union.

7. Over the course of its history, Russia had suffered terrible losses in successive attacks by hostile European neighbors. After World War II, the Soviet Union hoped to insulate itself from possible future invasion by controlling the neighbors along its borders.

Caption Answer to ...

 Interpreting Maps

After almost two hundred years of isolationism, the United States finally formed peacetime ties with European nations. The United States recognized that its interests now extended around the world.

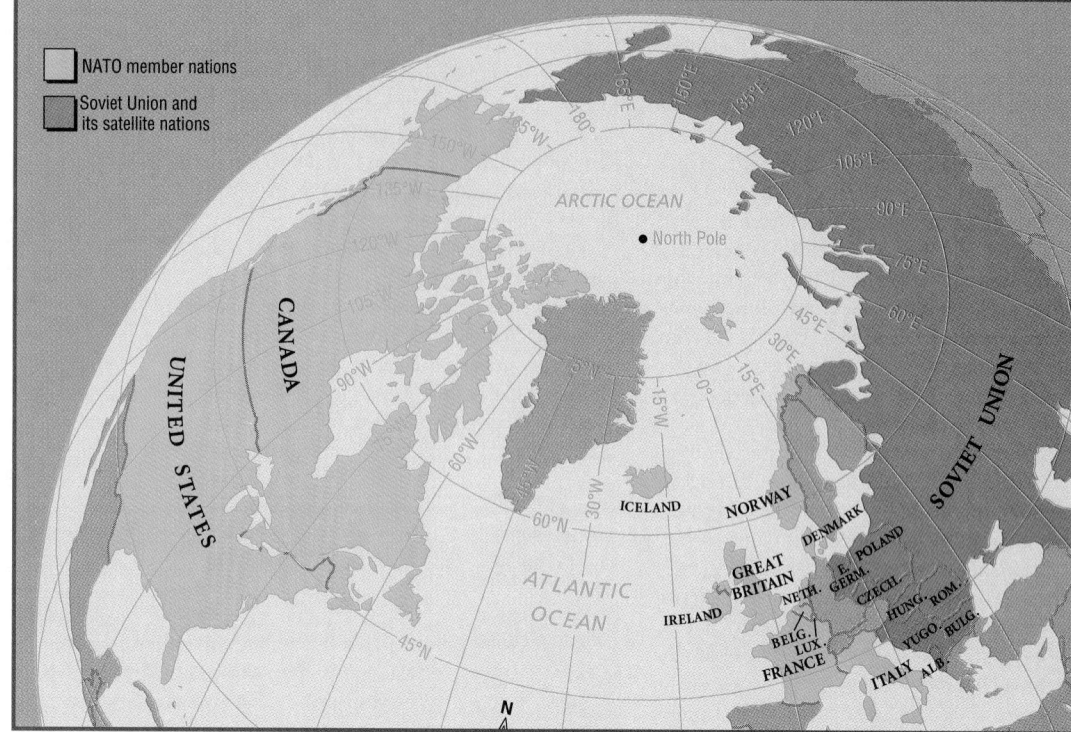

The NATO Alliance, 1949

NATO member nations

Soviet Union and its satellite nations

Geography and History: Interpreting Maps
This map shows the nations that sided with the United States during the cold war and those that aligned with the Soviet Union. *How does the map illustrate the new global perspective gained by American leaders after World War II?*

recognize Chiang's government (now located on Taiwan) as the official government of all China, but Chiang would never regain control from the communists. The "loss of China" would become, in the minds of many Americans, a stain on the record of the Truman administration. The desire to prevent other nations in Asia from following the same path would be used to justify many future cold war policies, including involvement in the Korean and Vietnam wars.

More bad news surfaced later in 1949. On September 23, Truman made a brief but terrifying announcement to the nation: "We have evidence that within recent weeks an atomic explosion occurred in the USSR." Years sooner than some officials expected, the Soviet Union had broken the West's monopoly on nuclear weapons.

NSC-68 In response to these events, the National Security Council spelled out American policy in a document known as **NSC-68.** The National Security Council had been created in 1947 to develop broad policy concepts on which the President could build specific strategies.

NSC-68 outlined several policies that the United States might adopt in light of the current state of international affairs. The paper said, however, that only one of these policies could be seriously considered. It stated that the United States should triple its defense budget—and some leaders suggested quadrupling it from about $13 billion to $50 billion annually. This unprecedented level of peacetime defense spending was justified by NSC-68 and its supporters on the basis of the new demands of global security. According to this policy, only a vigorous

 RESOURCE DIRECTORY

Teaching Resources

Critical Thinking Activity Identifying Central Issues: Cold War Policy, found in the Unit 5 folder, p. 88, uses a speech by Christian A. Herter, undersecretary of state in 1957, to help students apply this skill in examining the nation's cold war policy.

defense effort could keep communism in check and ensure the survival of the free world.

Containment in the 1950s

 When Dwight Eisenhower succeeded Harry Truman in 1953, the Republican party redefined American foreign policy. Secretary of State John Foster Dulles was a deeply religious person who hated communism because it denied the existence of God. Containment, he believed, was too cautious an approach to the communist threat. Instead, he proposed a policy of liberation, to roll back communism where it had already taken hold.

This approach proved impossible to put into practice. Eisenhower, who had helped keep the Allies together during World War II, understood the need for caution in dealing with the Soviet Union. Less rigid than his secretary of state, he recognized that the United States could not change the governments of Soviet **satellite nations**—countries controlled politically and economically by the Soviet Union—in Eastern Europe. When East Germans demonstrated against the Soviet Union in 1953, the United States merely stood back and watched. Three years later, when freedom fighters in Hungary rose up against Soviet domination, the United States again kept its distance as Soviet soldiers crushed the uprising. President Eisenhower recognized that any other response by the United States might have led to a larger war, and he wanted to avoid that at all costs.

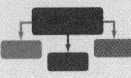

On November 4, 1956, newspaper headlines announced that Soviet tanks had attacked Budapest and other cities in Hungary to squash the resistance of anticommunist rebels. Hungarian premier Imre Nagy was taken prisoner; Joseph Cardinal Mindszenty, the Roman Catholic bishop of Hungary, took refuge with the American diplomatic staff in Budapest.

 Throughout the 1950s, despite talk of liberating Soviet satellite nations, the policy of containment remained in effect. Containment itself proved difficult enough. Before long the United States would be putting to use some of the weapons NSC-68 had recommended it build.

SECTION 2 REVIEW

Key Terms, People, and Places

1. Define (a) containment, (b) Truman Doctrine, (c) Marshall Plan, (d) Berlin airlift, (e) NATO, (f) satellite nation.
2. Identify (a) George C. Marshall, (b) Mao Zedong.

Key Concepts

3. (a) What were the goals of the United Nations in 1945? (b) What prevented the UN from achieving these goals?
4. How were the Truman Doctrine and the Marshall Plan expressions of the containment policy?

5. What did NSC-68 recommend that the United States do to defend against the communist threat?
6. Why did President Eisenhower not follow the advice of John Foster Dulles and attempt to "roll back communism" in Germany and Hungary?

Critical Thinking

7. **Recognizing Cause and Effect** In 1946 George Kennan described "the traditional and instinctive Russian sense of insecurity" on which the Soviet view of world affairs was based. What events in Russian history may have caused such insecurity?

Quiz found in the Unit 5 folder, p. 78, covers the main ideas in this section as well as the key terms.

Media and Technology

Transparency
Critical Thinking, I-2

SOURCE READINGS

 Source Readings on p. 586 will connect literature selections and primary source excerpts to historical events discussed in this section.

Reteach

Have students trace the steps that the United States took to counter communism from 1945 to 1949. Then have them discuss as a group how the nation's foreign policy began to shift after Truman's announcement in 1949.

Alternative Assessment

Mid-Point Monitoring

Ask students if they have
● Decided on the types of broadcasts they will include
● Researched the main ideas for each report
● Started drafting some of the items for their broadcasts

4. CLOSE

Reinforcing the Big Idea

The United States launched its containment strategy to prevent the further spread of communism in Europe. The next section describes how it broadened that strategy to include other potential communist "hot spots" around the globe.

In Depth

Did You Know?

Successful Soviet development of a nuclear bomb created widespread fear of a "sneak" attack by the Soviets. The Civil Defense Administration (CDA) was set up to oversee warning, evacuation, and communications systems. Thousands of Americans built backyard bomb shelters, while schoolchildren learned to "duck and cover." In 1955, the CDA staged the first nationwide nuclear air raid drill, dubbed "Operation Alert '55," in which sixty cities underwent mock hydrogen bomb attacks and were evacuated.

The Cold War in Asia, the Middle East, and Latin America

SECTION 3

The Cold War in Asia, the Middle East, and Latin America

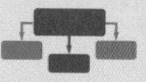

1. FOCUS

Connecting to the Big Idea

See page 560B. In the postwar era, countries in Asia, the Middle East, and Latin America began to lean toward the communist model of government. Ask what the United States did in response.

Objectives

- Explain why the United States became involved in the affairs of Korea and Vietnam.
- Identify the factors that complicated United States containment policy in the Middle East.
- Describe the superpowers' struggle for control in Latin America.

Bellringer

Set up a row of dominos in the front of the classroom. Knock over the first domino so that it causes the whole line to fall. Ask students to explain what this "domino effect" has to do with containing communism in the 1950s.

Reading Strategy

Reinforcing Key Ideas Read the following sentence on page 572: "As communist movements developed in Asia, the Middle East, and Latin America, however, the United States extended the policy to meet challenges around the world." As students read the section, they should list the incidents that drew the United States into other countries' affairs.

SECTION PREVIEW

The policy of containment had been created with the aim of maintaining European stability. As communist movements developed in Asia, the Middle East, and Latin America, however, the United States extended the policy to meet challenges around the world.

This cover illustration from a 1959 *Newsweek* magazine shows that the fate of the world hung on the uneasy balance of power between Khrushchev and Eisenhower, each of whom commanded many nuclear warheads.

Key Concepts

- Both the Korean War and early American involvement in Vietnam stemmed from cold war tension.
- The United States juggled oil interests and political sympathies in the Middle East while trying to control communist influence there.
- In Latin America, the United States and the Soviet Union struggled for control in unstable countries.

Key Terms, People, and Places

38th parallel, domino theory, 17th parallel; Ho Chi Minh, Fidel Castro; Indochina

---

The policy of containment soon was broadened to apply not only to Europe but also to Asia, the Middle East, Latin America—in short, anywhere United States government and military officials perceived a communist threat. Political struggles in countries that had seemed to have little impact on the United States before 1945, such as Korea, Vietnam, Iran, and Cuba, became vital issues of national security when viewed through the lens of the cold war. Each "minor" war in which the United States took part reflected the delicate balance between its two major foreign policy objectives: avoiding another world war and keeping a tight lid on communism.

The Korean War

The policy followed by the Allies at the very end of World War II created the context for the Korean War. Korea, which had been occupied by Japan for decades, hoped for its independence once the Japanese finally were defeated. The war ended, however, before careful plans could be worked out, and the Allies resorted to a short-term solution. Soviet soldiers accepted the surrender of Japanese troops north of the **38th parallel,** the latitude line that runs through Korea at 38°N; American forces did the same south of the parallel. While the dividing line was never intended to be permanent, the Soviet Union set up and supported a government in the north, and the United States did the same in the south. The major powers left Korea but continued to support the regimes they had created.

Both North and South Korea hoped to unify the country, but each wanted to do so on its own terms. In June 1950, the North Korean army moved across the 38th parallel intending to bring about this unification. The United States felt certain—wrongly, it turned out—that the maneuver had been directed by the Soviets. Faced with what he viewed as a clear case of aggression, Truman was determined to respond. He recalled in his memoirs:

> In my generation, this was not the first occasion when the strong had attacked the weak. I recalled some earlier instances: Manchuria, Ethiopia, Austria. I remembered how each time that the democracies failed to act it had encouraged the aggressors to keep going ahead. . . . If this was allowed to go unchallenged, it would mean a third world war, just as similar incidents brought on the second world war.

 RESOURCE DIRECTORY

Teaching Resources

Reproducible Lesson Plan found in the Unit 5 folder, p. 73, provides a summary of the Section 3 lesson plan content.

Alternate Lesson Plan: Cooperative Learning Activity found in the Alternate Lesson Plans folder, p. 134, helps students work together to understand U.S. foreign policy in Asia, the Middle East, and Latin America during the cold war.

Guided Reading and Review found in the Unit 5 folder, p. 79, provides a structure for reading and mastering the key concepts and reviewing the key terms for Section 3. (Guided Practice)

American Profiles Activity found in the Unit 5 folder, p. 84, profiles Marguerite Higgins, a journalist who became a frontline war correspondent in Korea, despite the opposition she faced as a woman.

Rather than respond alone, the United States went to the UN Security Council. With the new People's Republic of China excluded and the Soviet delegation absent in protest of that exclusion, the United States gained unanimous approval for resolutions branding North Korea the aggressor and calling on UN member states to assist in restoring peace.

⭐ General Douglas MacArthur planned a bold strategy to drive the North Koreans out of South Korea. In September 1950, while most North Korean troops were fighting near Pusan in the southeast, marines landed at the western port city of Inchon. The landing allowed UN forces to cut off North Korean supply lines through Inchon and to sandwich enemy troops between MacArthur at Inchon and the other UN troops at Pusan.

MacArthur's strategy was an overwhelming success. UN troops pushed the North Koreans back across the 38th parallel and continued into the north. With these early victories behind them, they hoped to unify the country on South Korea's terms. As they approached China's border, however, the Chinese warned them against going any farther. MacArthur ignored the warning, and in October 1950 Chinese troops entered the war. In fierce fighting, the Chinese and North Koreans pushed the UN forces back into the south (see the map at right).

As the war bogged down, Truman found himself in conflict with his most colorful general. MacArthur wanted to teach the Chinese a lesson, and proposed using atomic weapons or blockading the Chinese mainland. Truman wanted to do everything he could to keep the conflict limited and refused to expand the war.

⭐ MacArthur would not back down, however. In March 1951 he sent a letter to Joseph W. Martin, the minority leader of the House of Representatives, that contained a thinly veiled attack on the Truman administration's failure to see the gravity of the situation in Asia. After Martin read the letter in the House on April 5, Truman fired MacArthur for insubordination.

MacArthur returned home to a hero's welcome. When he addressed a joint session of Congress on April 19, his speech was often interrupted by bursts of applause. Finally, he said an emotional farewell:

*S*ince I took the oath at West Point, the *hopes and dreams [of youth] have all vanished. But I still remember the refrain of one of the most popular barracks ballads of that day, which proclaimed most proudly that old soldiers never die, they just fade away.*
And like the old soldier of that ballad, I now close my military career and just fade away, an old soldier who tried to do his duty as God gave him the light to see that duty.
Good-bye.

Once tempers had cooled, MacArthur did, in fact, fade from view, and Truman was able to proceed with his plan to keep the war limited. The struggle dragged on for two more years. Finally, a truce was signed in 1953, leaving the

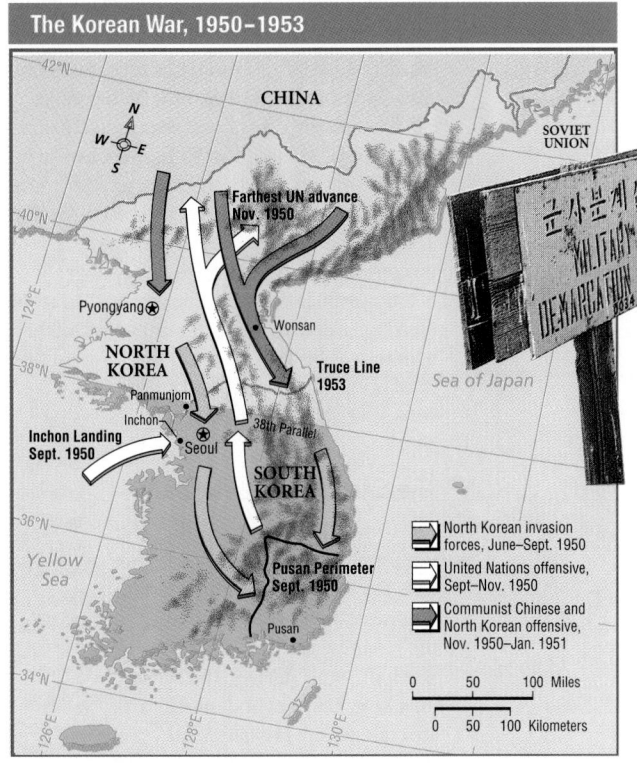

The Korean War, 1950–1953

CHINA

SOVIET UNION

Farthest UN advance Nov. 1950

Pyongyang

Wonsan

NORTH KOREA

Truce Line 1953

Sea of Japan

Panmunjom

Inchon

38th Parallel

Inchon Landing Sept. 1950

Seoul

SOUTH KOREA

Yellow Sea

Pusan Perimeter Sept. 1950

Pusan

North Korean invasion forces, June–Sept. 1950

United Nations offensive, Sept.–Nov. 1950

Communist Chinese and North Korean offensive, Nov. 1950–Jan. 1951

0   50   100 Miles

0   50   100 Kilometers

🌐 **Geography and History: Interpreting Maps**
This map shows the major battles of the Korean War. The sign shown above marked the final truce line in Korea, near the 38th parallel. *How does the map illustrate the back-and-forth nature of the war? What did MacArthur accomplish by landing his troops at Inchon rather than Pusan?*

⭐ 🗒 **Visual Learning Activity** Civilian Control of the Military, found in the Unit 5 folder, p. 96, uses a cartoon to present one view of Truman's controversial firing of General MacArthur during the Korean War.

2. INSTRUCT

Explain/Discuss
Explain that in its efforts to fight communist aggression, the United States engaged in its own aggressive policies. Ask students to identify United States actions that other countries saw as aggressive. Discuss whether those actions were justified in order to contain communism. Encourage students to support their opinions with facts and reasoning.

Caption Answer to ...

🌐 **Interpreting Maps**

The arrows on the map show the first North Korean offensive, which pushed the South Koreans to the Pusan perimeter; the counterattack of UN forces, which extended almost to the Chinese border; and the final push of the Chinese and North Koreans back to the 38th parallel. MacArthur was able to open up another front by landing at Inchon, thus sandwiching the North Koreans between Inchon and Pusan.

In Depth

Multicultural Perspectives

Following President Truman's 1948 order to desegregate the military, the Korean War was the first in which African American and white soldiers fought side by side. A 1951 NAACP investigation, however, unearthed a striking disparity in military justice. It found that of thirty-four soldiers convicted of misconduct in combat, two were white and received minimal sentences. The thirty-two convicted African Americans received extremely harsh sentences including one death sentence and fifteen life sentences.

In this oft-repeated scene from the war, South Korean civilians flee from North Korean invaders while United States troops advance to meet the enemy.

country divided at almost exactly the same place as before the war, near the 38th parallel.

The Korean War caused enormous frustration at home. Americans wondered why 54,000 of their soldiers had been killed, and far more had been wounded, for such limited results. They also wondered whether their government was serious about wanting to stop the spread of communism. Meanwhile, the war also led to an ever-larger defense budget, just as NSC-68 had demanded. By 1950 the military took up one third of the total federal budget. Ten years later, it consumed one half.

The Early War in Vietnam

At the same time, another war was unfolding in **Indochina.** France had long controlled this part of Southeast Asia, which had fallen to the Japanese during World War II. Vietnam, one part of Indochina, now sought independence in a struggle led by **Ho Chi Minh,** the leader of the Indochina Communist party. Although Ho was sympathetic to the principles of communism, he was really more of a Vietnamese nationalist than a

Soviet sympathizer. In his battle for Vietnamese independence, he used the American Revolutionary War as his model for independence. Ho and his political organization, the Viet Minh, established the Democratic Republic of Vietnam in 1945. He then had to fight France, which was determined to reclaim its empire.

An ugly war unfolded and attracted the attention of American officials. The United States needed the assistance of France for its policy of containment in Europe. American leaders doubted that France could survive a long colonial war in Asia without help. While Ho Chi Minh did not have close ties with the Soviet Union, he was still dedicated to the ideas of Karl Marx, and Americans were persuaded that communism was the same everywhere and had to be resisted wherever it surfaced. The United States therefore provided France with large amounts of economic aid for reconstruction at home, and that assistance allowed France to use its own resources in Vietnam. By 1954 the United States was giving France aid amounting to more than three fourths the cost of the war. ✪

Even so, the war was not going well. France's position deteriorated at about the time Eisenhower took over the presidency, and in 1954 the Vietnamese defeated France in a major battle at Dien Bien Phu, an outpost in northern Vietnam. This worried Eisenhower, who believed in the **domino theory.** This theory

ON BEHALF OF VIETNAM GOVERNMENT AND PEOPLE I BEG TO INFORM YOU THAT IN COURSE OF CONVERSATIONS BETWEEN VIETNAM GOVERNMENT AND FRENCH REPRESENTATIVES THE LATTER REQUIRE THE SECESSION OF COCHINCHINA AND THE RETURN OF FRENCH TROOPS IN HANOI STOP MEANWHILE FRENCH POPULATION AND TROOPS ARE MAKING ACTIVE PREPARATIONS FOR A COUP DE MAIN IN HANOI AND FOR MILITARY AGGRESSION STOP I THEREFORE MOST EARNESTLY APPEAL TO YOU PERSONALLY AND TO THE AMERICAN PEOPLE TO INTERFERE URGENTLY IN SUPPORT OF OUR INDEPENDENCE AND HELP MAKING THE NEGOTIATIONS MORE IN KEEPING WITH THE PRINCIPLES OF THE ATLANTIC AND SAN FRANCISCO CHARTERS

RESPECTFULLY

HOCHIMINH

Ho Chi Minh (left) sent this urgent telegram to President Truman in October 1945 asking for United States support of Vietnamese independence. Not wanting to jeopardize relations with France, Truman ignored Ho's plea.

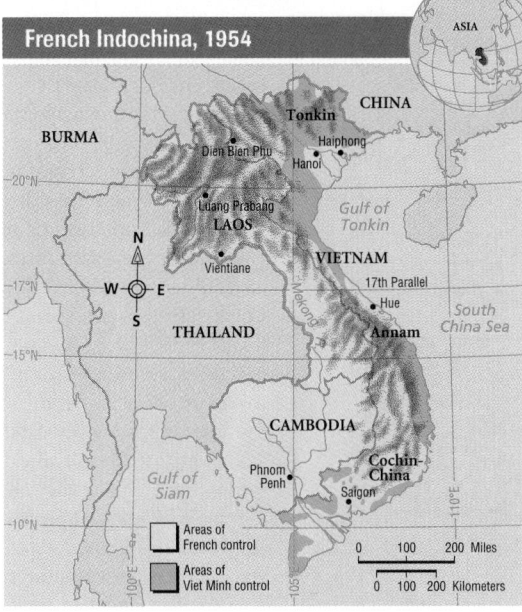

French Indochina, 1954

CHINA
BURMA
Tonkin
Dien Bien Phu
Haiphong
Hanoi
Luang Prabang
LAOS
Gulf of Tonkin
Vientiane
VIETNAM
17th Parallel
Hue
THAILAND
Annam
South China Sea
CAMBODIA
Phnom Penh
Cochin-China
Gulf of Siam
Saigon

Areas of French control

Areas of Viet Minh control

0   100   200 Miles
0   100 200 Kilometers

ASIA

Geography and History: Interpreting Maps
Reread Ho Chi Minh's telegram on page 574. *What did the French demand in 1945? According to this map, how many of their objectives had the French achieved by 1954?*

compared countries to dominos and held that "you have a row of dominos set up, you knock over the first one, and what will happen to the last one is the certainty that it will go over very quickly." Thus, if one country in Indochina fell to communism, other countries in the area would soon follow. Still, Eisenhower did not want the United States to become further involved.

Instead, an international conference in Geneva decided to draw a dividing line, similar to the ones drawn in Germany and Korea following World War II. Vietnam would be divided along the **17th parallel,** with Ho Chi Minh holding power in the north and an anti-communist government in charge in the south.

For the time being, the United States provided military aid to the South Vietnamese government but resisted greater involvement. That course would change in the next decade.

The Middle East

The cold war was also played out in the Middle East. This area had strategic importance because of its large supplies of oil. During World War II, the Allies had occupied Iran, a large nation just south of the Soviet Union. After the war, the United States and Britain departed; the Soviet Union did not. The United States became increasingly concerned as Soviet tanks rumbled toward the Iranian border, and threatened vigorous American action unless the Soviets pulled back. In the face of that determined stance, the Soviets withdrew.

Two years later, in 1948, the UN divided Palestine into an Arab state and a Jewish state. Zionist Jews had for years hoped to establish a Jewish nation in Palestine, but it was not until World War II, when thousands of European Jews immigrated to the region, that the Jewish population was large enough to form a new state. Tensions between Palestinian Jews and Arabs erupted with the UN announcement of the new Jewish state, called Israel, on May 14, 1948. The United States and the Soviet Union immediately recognized Israel, but Israel was soon invaded by surrounding Arab states. Israel defeated those states and annexed most of the Palestinian territory, as shown on the map on page 576. While sympathetic to Israel, the United States tried to maintain ties with the oil-rich Arab nations of the region and to prevent them from falling into the Soviet orbit.

MAKING CONNECTIONS

What conflicts over oil-rich Middle East nations has the United States been drawn into in recent years?

The Cold War in Latin America

The cold war likewise affected United States policy in Latin America. For decades the United States had dominated economic affairs in this part of the world. By the mid-1920s, the United States had gained control over the economies of ten Latin American countries.

Caption Answer to ...

Interpreting Maps

That Ho surrender Cochin-China and Hanoi. By 1954, the French occupied much of Cochin-China (southern Vietnam) and also controlled a large area around Hanoi.

Answer to ...

MAKING CONNECTIONS

In 1991 the United States entered the Persian Gulf War in part to defend its oil interests in Kuwait, which had been invaded by neighboring Iraq.

3. ASSESS

Section 3 Review Answers

1. (a) 38th parallel, see p. 572, (b) 17th parallel, see p. 575

2. (a) Ho Chi Minh, see p. 574, (b) Fidel Castro , see p. 576

3. Indochina, see p. 574

4. A temporary dividing line at the 38th parallel, established at the end of World War II, endured and led to a split between North and South Korea. The North's invasion in 1950 was an attempt to unify the country.

5. The United States wanted French support for its containment policy in Europe. America also perceived communism in any form or location as a threat to its national security. The United States was thus willing to aid France in its war against Vietnam.

6. The Middle East contained large supplies of oil to which the United States needed access.

7. Both the Guatemalan and Cuban governments had seized American property in these countries. The United States wanted to restore that property and generally to protect its economic interests in Latin America.

8. The theory that once the West lost control of one part of a region, the rest would fall to the communists like a row of dominos was based on the assumption that the Soviet Union would expand its sphere of influence wherever the United States did not actively prevent it from doing so.

Ask students to write the column headings Problem and Solution on a piece of paper. In the first column have them list the problems faced by the United States in Asia, the Middle East, and Latin America, and in the second have them write the solutions the United States attempted to carry out.

Caption Answer to ...

 Interpreting Maps

The fact that the Soviet Union lies next to Iran and very close to the rest of the Middle Eastern nations may have fueled U.S. concerns that it could easily gain control over the oil in this region.

 **4. CLOSE**

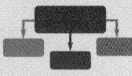 **Reinforcing the Big Idea**

In an expansion of its containment policy, the United States battled communism in smaller countries throughout the world. The next section describes how America's fear of communism would eventually lead it to suspect its own citizens.

 In Depth

Biography

The bloody fighting between Arabs and Jews that erupted after Israel's declaration of independence in 1948 ended with a truce in 1949. The chief mediator of that truce was UN diplomat Ralph J. Bunche (1904–1971). Formerly a U.S. State Department official, Bunche joined the United Nations at its inception and later oversaw UN peacekeeping operations in the Suez, the Congo, and Cyprus. For his mediation of the Arab-Israeli war, Bunche became the first African American to be awarded the Nobel Peace Prize.

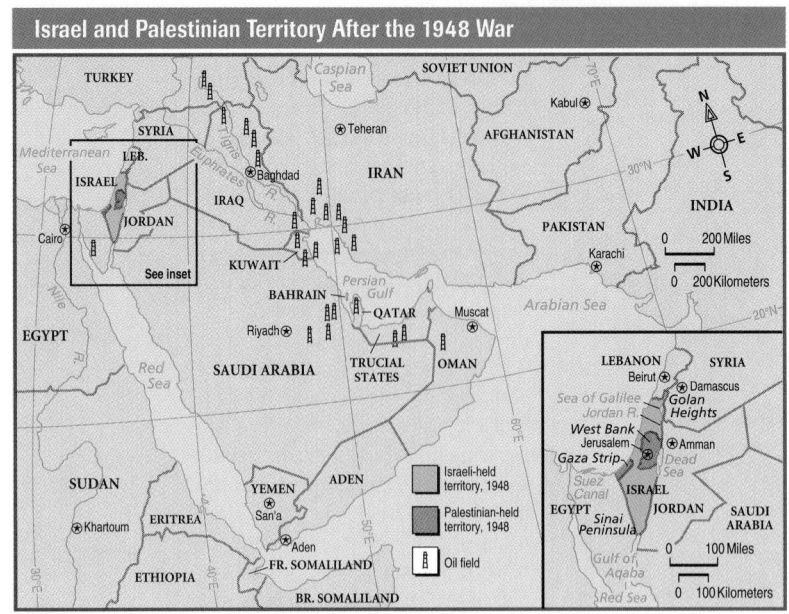

Israel and Palestinian Territory After the 1948 War

Israeli-held territory, 1948
Palestinian-held territory, 1948
Oil field

Geography and History: Interpreting Maps
After the 1948 war, Palestinian-held territory was annexed by Egypt and Jordan. *How might the location of the Soviet Union in relation to that of Middle Eastern countries have fueled concerns in the United States?*

American troops also had invaded Honduras and Nicaragua to prop up leaders who supported United States interests. After World War II, the fear of Soviet communist influence led the United States government to protect Latin American nations where United States corporations had large financial investments.

In 1954 the United States feared possible communist activity in Guatemala. As a result, the Central Intelligence Agency (CIA) helped to overthrow Jacobo Arbenz Guzmán, a reform-minded leader, on the grounds that he was sympathetic to radical causes. The CIA takeover restored the property of an American corporation called the United Fruit Company, which had been seized by the government in Guatemala. This action also demonstrated that where it sensed a communist threat, the United States would do almost anything to restore stability and to install leadership it found more sympathetic. Such actions also fueled the Soviet perception that the United States was escalating the cold war.

In 1959 another crisis occurred as revolutionary leader **Fidel Castro** overthrew a long-standing dictatorial regime in Cuba. Although some Americans recognized the need for social reform in Latin America, others were more shortsighted. When Castro seized American property in Cuba, the United States responded by severing diplomatic ties and cutting off exports. In response, Cuba turned to the Soviet Union for economic and military support. Even when Soviet aid dried up several decades later, the United States refused to deal more closely with its Caribbean neighbor because Cuba remained a communist nation.

SECTION 3 REVIEW

Key Terms, People, and Places
1. Define (a) 38th parallel, (b) 17th parallel.
2. Identify (a) Ho Chi Minh, (b) Fidel Castro.
3. Identify Indochina.

Key Concepts
4. How were the seeds of the Korean War planted at the end of World War II?
5. What was the connection between the war in Vietnam and the cold war in Europe?

6. Why was the United States especially concerned about the possibility of communist control in the Middle East?
7. What economic factors led the United States to intervene in Guatemala and Cuba?

Critical Thinking
8. **Determining Relevance** Explain how Eisenhower's "domino theory" expressed the basic assumptions of American cold war policy.

 RESOURCE DIRECTORY

Teaching Resources

Quiz found in the Unit 5 folder, p. 80, covers the main ideas in this section as well as the key terms.

The Cold War in the United States

SECTION 4

The Cold War in the United States

SECTION PREVIEW

The effort to contain communism abroad made Americans fear subversion at home. The nation became swept up in an ugly campaign to expose suspected communists among its own citizens.

Key Concepts
- The fear of subversion by communist sympathizers in the United States led President Truman to create the Federal Employee Loyalty Program.
- A congressional committee investigated "un-American activity" in the late 1940s and 1950s.
- Senator Joseph McCarthy led a vicious crusade against American radicals that destroyed the careers and lives of many citizens.

Key Terms, People, and Places
House Un-American Activities Committee (HUAC); Alger Hiss, Julius and Ethel Rosenberg, Joseph R. McCarthy

D uring the Great Depression, tens of thousands of Americans had joined the Communist party, which was a legal organization. They were looking for answers to the question of why the American economic system no longer seemed to work. After World War II, some of these citizens were still Communist party members, although most had withdrawn. Now, in an atmosphere of cold war fears, their past came back to haunt them.

In the administrations of both Harry Truman and Dwight Eisenhower, concern over the growing appeal of communism around the world led to wholesale violations of civil liberties at home. The fear of subversion, or conspiracy to overthrow the government, launched a crusade that persecuted not only people who had ties to the Communist party but also anyone whose views leaned toward the left. The political left is made up of people who generally want to see the existing political system changed—sometimes radically—to benefit the common person. The political right is composed of people who generally wish to preserve the current system. During the late 1940s and 1950s, people were afraid to make statements that could in any way identify them with the political left. The government's loyalty program removed the left from power while effectively silencing any real political debate in the United States.

Truman's Loyalty Program and HUAC

As the Truman administration pursued support for its containment program, it pictured the cold war struggle in life-or-death terms. In his speeches, the President declared that the issue facing the world was whether "tyranny or freedom" would win out. Godless communism was a "threat to our liberties and to our faith," Truman said. It had to be stopped at all costs.

Administration officials feared that communism was infiltrating the United States. Exposure of a number of wartime spy rings in 1946 increased American anxiety. When the Republican party made significant gains in the midterm congressional elections that year, Truman became concerned that his political opponents would use the loyalty issue for their own ends. He therefore began his own investigation. He established a Federal Employee Loyalty Program in early 1947.

Under the terms of this program, the FBI was to check its files for individuals who might be engaged in suspicious activity. Cases would then move to a new Loyalty Review Board. While civil rights were supposed to be safeguarded, in fact those accused of disloyalty to

Anticommunist films like *The Red Menace* (1949) played on Americans' fear of communist activity in the United States. Such films also gave Hollywood studios a chance to prove their loyalty and patriotism.

1. FOCUS

Connecting to the Big Idea

See page 560B. In its effort to uncover communist spies and revolutionaries at home, the United States government embarked on an anticommunist purge. Ask students what dangers resulted from this red scare.

Objectives
- Describe President Truman's Federal Employee Loyalty Program.
- List the outcomes of congressional investigations of "un-American activity" in the 1940s and 1950s.
- Explain Senator Joseph McCarthy's role in the anticommunist crusade.

Bellringer

Ask students to list three elements that define loyalty. Does criticism of one's country constitute disloyalty?

Reading Strategy

Predicting Content Ask students to read the first paragraph of Section 4 and skim the headings and subheadings in the section. Have them predict the main idea and possible conclusion of the section. When they have finished reading the section, ask students to test their predictions against the actual text.

Reproducible Lesson Plan found in the Unit 5 folder, p. 74, provides a summary of the Section 4 lesson plan content.

Alternate Lesson Plan: Learning Styles found in the Alternate Lesson Plans folder, p. 135, guides students in an activity to identify reasons for the anticommunist crusade in the United States and is particularly helpful for auditory learners.

Guided Reading and Review found in Unit 5 folder, p. 81, provides a structure for reading and mastering the key concepts and reviewing the key terms for Section 4. (Guided Practice)

Explain/Discuss

Explain to students that in the name of patriotism, the United States in the early 1950s embarked on a crusade that deprived citizens of their constitutional rights. Why, in the end, did this witch hunt threaten democracy more than any communist plots? Why is it important for the United States to allow dissent?

Analyze

Many people knew that Senator McCarthy's claims were exaggerated at best. Why, then, was he able to gain so much power and ruin the lives of so many people?

Activity

Teaching Heterogeneous Groups

In the late 1940s and early 1950s, the film and television industries were often a target of investigation by the House Un-American Activities Committee (HUAC). Have students work in small groups to list three activities by the film and television industry today that might be considered un-American, and three activities that would be considered "good" for Americans.

In Depth

Then and Now

The Alger Hiss controversy was refueled in 1992 when the chairman of the Russian Military Intelligence Archives announced that, based on his review of Soviet archives, the espionage charges against Hiss were groundless. The official subsequently admitted that he could not fully clear Hiss; given the size and complexity of Soviet archives, perhaps no one could. The debate thus remains very much alive.

Actor Humphrey Bogart (top) flew to Washington, D.C., in 1947 to protest the congressional committee's actions against other actors. He then had to launch a public relations campaign to clear his own name. *Red Channels* (bottom), an index of blacklisted actors, was published in 1950.

their country often found themselves under attack with little chance to defend themselves. Rather than being innocent until proven guilty, they found that the accusation alone made it difficult for them to clear their names.

Although the Truman loyalty program examined several million employees, it only dismissed several hundred. Still, it helped create a dangerous climate of suspicion throughout the country.

Meanwhile, Congress began its own loyalty program. The **House Un-American Activities Committee (HUAC)**, which had been established a decade earlier to investigate disloyalty on the eve of war, now began a probe of the motion picture industry. It argued that films had tremendous power to corrupt the American public and suggested that numerous Hollywood figures had left-wing inclinations that compromised their work.

Many stars protested the procedures. Singer Judy Garland urged Americans to "write your Congressman a letter" denouncing the campaign. Actor Frederic March asked Americans to consider the question: "Who's next? . . . Is it you, who will have to look around nervously before you can say what's on your mind? . . . This reaches into every American city and town!" But HUAC pressed on. ⭐

AMERICAN PROFILES

The Hollywood Ten

In October 1947, HUAC called nineteen Hollywood figures to testify. According to rumors, all were either members of, or had close associations with, the Communist party. These Hollywood personalities—writers, directors, producers, actors—were a distinguished lot. Ring Lardner, Jr., had shared an Academy Award for writing *Woman of the Year* in 1942; Howard Koch had coauthored *Casablanca* that same year. Others too were responsible for some of the best films of the previous ten years.

Facing the committee, the celebrities who stood accused had no chance to defend themselves. Chairman J. Parnell Thomas first called friendly witnesses (those whose views were in line with the committee's), allowing them to make accusations and to slander whomever they chose. Then he turned his attention to the Hollywood activists themselves. Over and over the committee asked, "Are you now or have you ever been a member of the Communist party?" When some of the writers attempted to make their own statements, Thomas denied them the floor. Ten of the accused refused to answer his question by invoking rights guaranteed by the First Amendment. This amendment protects individuals, as the Supreme Court recently had ruled in *West Virginia Board of Education* v. *Barnette* (1942), against government officials who try to "prescribe what shall be orthodox in politics, nationalism, religion, or other matters of opinion." The committee responded by threatening prison terms if the Hollywood Ten failed to testify, but they held their ground. When the committee likewise stood firm, the Ten went to jail for contempt of Congress and served sentences ranging from six months to a year.

Worse still, Hollywood gave in totally to the committee. The day Congress voted the contempt citations, fifty motion picture executives held a meeting at the Waldorf-Astoria Hotel in New York. They announced that the Hollywood Ten had "been a disservice to their employers" and had "impaired their usefulness to the industry." They were discharged without compensation until they had "purged" themselves, or demonstrated their loyalty in some undefined way. So began the blacklist—a list of persons who would not be allowed to work. The blacklist included not only the Hollywood Ten but also many others who seemed in some way "subversive."

The hearings had a powerful impact on American films. In the immediate postwar years, the industry had been willing to make movies dealing with controversial subjects such as racism and anti-Semitism. Now studios resisted all films dealing with social problems and emphasized "pure entertainment" instead.

RESOURCE DIRECTORY

Teaching Resources

⭐ **Primary Source Activity** The Rise of Joseph McCarthy, found in the Unit 5 folder, pp. 90–91, provides students with an insider's description of how the stage was set for the McCarthy hearings with a chapter from Senator Charles E. Potter's book, *Days of Shame.*

Spy Cases Inflame the Nation

Several spy cases at the start of the cold war helped fuel suspicion of a communist conspiracy in the United States. In 1948, HUAC investigated **Alger Hiss,** who had been a high-ranking State Department official before he left government service. Whittaker Chambers, a former Communist who had become a successful *Time* magazine editor, accused Hiss of having been a Communist in the 1930s. Hiss denied the charge and sued Chambers for libel. Chambers then went one step further and declared that Hiss had been a Soviet spy.

After two trials, Hiss was convicted of perjury—too much time had passed for the espionage charge to be pressed—and in 1950 he went to prison for four years. Not all Americans were convinced he was guilty—indeed, even today Americans still debate the Hiss case—but for most people at the time the case seemed to prove that there was a real communist threat in the United States.

Several months after Hiss's conviction, **Julius and Ethel Rosenberg,** a husband and wife who held radical views, were accused of passing atomic secrets to the Soviets during the war. While opinion about the Rosenbergs' guilt was split, they were nonetheless convicted of espionage and executed in the electric chair in 1953. Like the Hiss case, the Rosenberg trial focused attention on a possible internal threat and inflamed anticommunist passions.

The McCarthy Era

Joseph R. McCarthy, a Republican senator from Wisconsin, took the anticommunist crusade even further. Through his skillful use of the media and his willingness to make wild accusations about almost anyone, he quickly landed himself on center stage.

McCarthy's Rise to Power McCarthy attracted attention in early 1950 with a speech in Wheeling, West Virginia. He would be up for reelection in two years, and he figured that he could gain support by identifying himself as a leader in the fight against communism in the United States government. So he claimed he

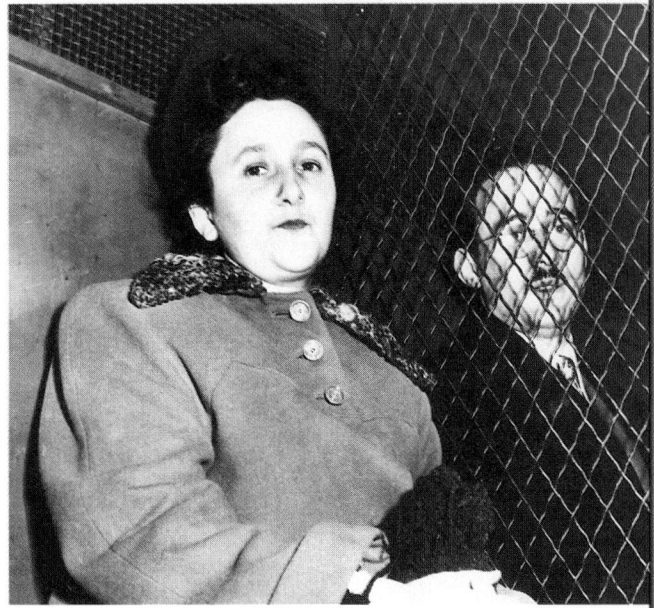

held in his hand a list with the names of 205 known Communists in the State Department. In fact he had no such list, simply names of people accused of disloyalty under the Federal Employee Loyalty Program and still in their jobs. But such minor complications never stopped McCarthy. When pressed for details, he declared that he would show his list to the President; then he reduced the number from 205 to 57.

McCarthy soon took on other targets. He lashed out at Dean Acheson, the current secretary of state, calling him a "pompous diplomat in striped pants," and at George Marshall, a former secretary of state, referring to him as "a man steeped in falsehood" for his inability to prevent the fall of China to the communists. Marshall was a national hero and a man of unquestioned integrity, but McCarthy made the incredible claim that he was involved in "a conspiracy so immense and an infamy so black as to dwarf any such previous venture in the history of man."

McCarthy gained support through these tactics because Truman's loyalty program had planted fears in the minds of many Americans about the supposed communist threat at home. But McCarthy also succeeded because he knew how to give journalists what they needed for newspaper stories. He knew when their deadlines

Ethel and Julius Rosenberg, shown above just after her conviction in 1951, were the first U.S. civilians to be executed for espionage. They were accused of passing top-secret data on nuclear weapons to the Soviets.

In Depth

Historical Misconceptions

Joseph McCarthy was not solely responsible for the wave of anticommunist hysteria that swept the nation in the 1950s. There is a long tradition of antiradicalism in the United States that goes back to the late nineteenth and the early twentieth centuries. This sentiment surfaced in the red scare of 1919. It also fueled the decision not to grant formal recognition to the Bolshevik regime of the new Soviet Union until 1933, a decade and a half after the Russian Revolution. Thus Joseph McCarthy was not the first to prey on and magnify fears and suspicions about communists, though he created perhaps the most serious upheavals with his irresponsible charges. Journalist Walter Lippmann was a relentless critic of what he called McCarthy's "cold, calculated, sustained and ruthless effort to make himself feared." (See Key Events in the Reference Section.)

Caption Answer to ...

Using Historical Evidence

Welch looks dazed and frustrated, probably unable to comprehend McCarthy's relentless attack on his associate, Fred Fisher.

Answer to ...

MAKING CONNECTIONS

Students may suggest that certain segments of the media, such as tabloid newspapers, are able to make unsupported claims about people and thus shape public opinion about their subjects.

Answer to ...

Links Across Time

Possible answers: Fear verging on hysteria is an emotion commonly associated with both the witch trials and McCarthy's hunt for communists.

In Depth

Interdisciplinary

The ritualism and quasireligious fervor of McCarthy's anticommunist crusade were mirrored in *The Crucible,* Arthur Miller's allegorical dramatization of the Salem witch trials. Miller, who later became the target of a HUAC hearing, created a parable of American society under McCarthyism in his play. It was poorly received when it opened on Broadway in 1953 but went on to become Miller's most frequently produced play. (See Literature Activity in the Resource Directory.)

Using Historical Evidence Army counsel Joseph Welch (seated at table) listens to Senator McCarthy discuss communist infiltration with the aid of a giant map. *How does this photo show Welch's reaction to McCarthy's tactics?*

occurred and recognized that they needed stories for their editors. He provided material at just the right time. When he had nothing to report, he would call a press conference to announce that new disclosures would be coming soon.

Some Republican politicians, who hoped McCarthy's campaign would damage the reputation of the Democratic administration in the eyes of voters, encouraged McCarthy. Robert Taft, a senator from Ohio, told his colleague, "If one case doesn't work, try another." McCarthy did.

The public responded favorably to McCarthy's attacks. By the end of 1953, 50 percent of the sample in one Gallup poll had a positive opinion of McCarthy, with only 29 percent holding an unfavorable view.

MAKING CONNECTIONS

McCarthy had the power to ruin a person's reputation with a mere accusation. What people or institutions today have a similar power?

McCarthy's Fall McCarthy finally overreached himself when he took on the United States Army. In 1953 the army drafted McCarthy's assistant G. David Schine. When the military refused the request of Roy Cohn, another influential McCarthy assistant, to give Schine special treatment, McCarthy decided to investigate army security. Congress then began to examine the complaint.

⭐ The Army-McCarthy hearings began in April 1954, were televised nationally, and lasted for thirty-six days. They reached a climax when McCarthy charged that Fred Fisher, an assistant to army counsel Joseph Welch, had been a member of an organization sympathetic to the

| 1650 | 1700 | 1750 | 1800 | **Links Across Time** | 1850 | 1900 | 1950 | 2000 |

The Hunt for Witches and Communists

Between June and September of 1692, fourteen women and five men were hanged in Salem, Massachusetts, as witches. Those who "confessed" to witchcraft were spared; many who maintained their innocence were hanged. Historians today compare Salem in 1692 to the United States in the 1950s. The Puritans had recently resisted hostile Native Americans in King Philip's War and outlasted all challenges to their religious beliefs. Instead of feeling secure, however, the Puritans suddenly saw the devil in the very heart

of their community. Similarly, the United States in the 1950s had just defeated its enemies in World War II and recovered from the Depression. Yet, many Americans feared that evil forces within their community posed a grave threat. Senator Joseph R. McCarthy seized upon this fear to start a "witch-hunt" of his own.

The stress of the cold war with the Soviet Union frightened Americans. On very little evidence, they began to suspect a strong communist conspiracy to take over the United States. In what has been called "the

McCarthy terror," thousands of innocent people were accused of being communists or communist sympathizers. At numerous public hearings, those who refused to answer questions were treated as guilty.

In 1954, after being condemned by the Senate for his activities, McCarthy's reign of terror ended. As in Salem more than two centuries earlier, the witch-hunt was over. *What emotion seems to have allowed both the Salem witch trials and the McCarthy hunt for communists to happen?*

 RESOURCE DIRECTORY

Teaching Resources

⭐ **Literature Activity** The Hunt for Witches and Communists, found in the Unit 5 folder, pp. 93–94, focuses on *The Crucible,* Arthur Miller's play about the Salem witch trials of 1692, which he wrote in response to the McCarthy hearings.

Communist party. Welch, an eloquent Boston lawyer, was furious:

> *U*ntil this moment, Senator, I think I never really gauged your cruelty or your recklessness. . . . If it were in my power to forgive you for your reckless cruelty, I would do so. I like to think I am a gentleman, but your forgiveness will have to come from someone other than me. . . . Let us not assassinate this lad [Fisher] *further, Senator. You have done enough. Have you no sense of decency, sir, at long last? Have you left no sense of decency?*

The Senate, once frightened by McCarthy's power, now condemned him for his reckless attacks. Although he remained in office, his strength was gone. He died three years later, a broken man.

McCarthy's Impact In his peak years in power, though, McCarthy had a powerful impact on American society. He, and the others who participated in the anticommunist crusade, generated a sense of fear and suspicion that filtered down to all levels. In the late 1940s and early 1950s, it seemed impossible to dissent in the United States. Civil servants, government workers, teachers, and writers all came under attack and found their right to defend themselves restricted. Often an accusation alone was enough to end a person's career.

Examples of abuse extended throughout American life. Subway workers in New York were fired for refusing to answer questions about their political beliefs and actions. A fire

department officer in Seattle was dismissed just forty days before reaching twenty-five years of service (and gaining retirement benefits) because, although he denied that he was a current member of the Communist party, he declined to speak about his past involvement. Investigations of university faculties in 1952 and 1953 led to dismissals of professors who refused to cooperate with hostile congressional committees. Navaho in Arizona and New Mexico were denied all government assistance during one brutal winter on the grounds that their communal way of life was un-American. Latino workers sometimes faced deportation for belonging to unions that seemed radical.

Eventually, this second red scare, like the first one following World War I, subsided. But for a time it created widespread fear and confusion in the United States. Some of the victims were fortunate enough to reclaim their careers. Others suffered for years to come. The entire nation suffered from the era's suppression of free speech and honest debate.

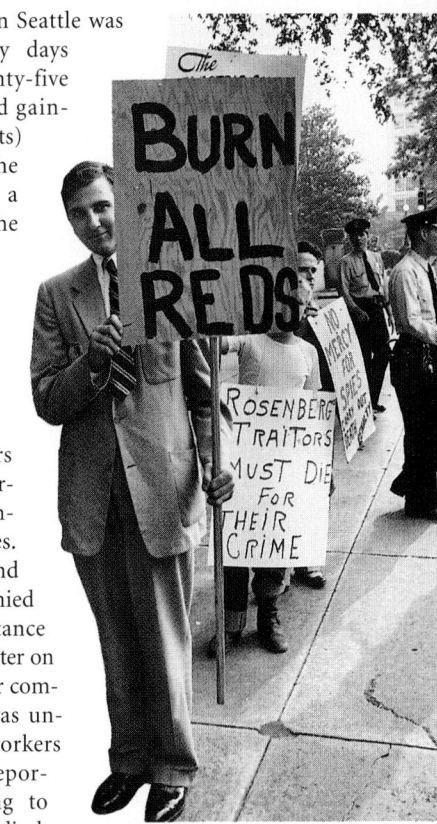

These demonstrators show the depth of anticommunist feeling among many Americans in the postwar period.

SECTION 4 REVIEW

Key Terms, People, and Places
1. Identify (a) Alger Hiss, (b) Julius and Ethel Rosenberg, (c) Joseph R. McCarthy.

Key Concepts
2. Why did Harry Truman launch his Federal Employee Loyalty Program?
3. What was the HUAC and why did it make Hollywood a specific target of its investigations?

4. How did Senator McCarthy create an atmosphere of suspicion and paranoia in the United States?

Critical Thinking
5. **Identifying Assumptions** HUAC forced Americans to answer the question "Are you now or have you ever been a member of the Communist party?" What assumptions was this question based on?

 Quiz found in the Unit 5 folder, p. 82, covers the main ideas in this section as well as the key terms.

 Chapter Test Forms A and B are found in the Unit 5 folder, pp. 97–102

 Answer Keys found in the Unit 5 folder, pp. 146–158, provide answers to all student activities.

Media and Technology

Transparency
Graphic Organizer, G-5

Guided Reading Audiotapes
(English and Spanish)

Computer Test Bank

Understanding Key Terms, People, and Places

Terms
Students should refer to the definitions of key terms in the chapter to create sentences that show an understanding of their relation to the post–World War II period.

Matching
1. 38th parallel
2. domino theory
3. cold war
4. iron curtain

True or False
1. false, Alger Hiss
2. false, Joseph R. McCarthy
3. false, Ho Chi Minh
4. true

Reviewing Main Ideas

1. The United States and the Soviet Union suppressed their disagreements and worked together in a shaky alliance against their common enemy.

2. The Soviet Union wanted to create a Polish government sympathetic to Soviet interests. The United States demanded a democratic government in Poland—one that would be friendly to American interests. This conflict over the loyalty of foreign governments would become a pattern in United States–Soviet relations during the cold war.

3. The two countries' goals differed in part because of their different economic and political systems. The Soviet Union looked forward to the collapse of capitalism worldwide and wanted to establish friendly foreign governments along its borders. The United States wanted to open as many foreign markets as possible.

4. Containment meant that the United States would take action to prevent the Soviet Union from extending its influence beyond the satellite nations it controlled in 1946.

5. The Truman Doctrine declared the United States responsible for helping "free peoples" resist communist influence. The Marshall Plan provided American money to rebuild Western European economies, thus preventing the Soviets from exerting their influence there. NSC-68 proposed tripling the peacetime defense budget to allow the United States to fight communism worldwide.

Chapter Review

Understanding Key Terms, People, and Places

Key Terms
1. cold war
2. proletariat
3. totalitarian
4. iron curtain
5. United Nations
6. containment
7. Truman Doctrine
8. Marshall Plan
9. Berlin airlift
10. NATO
11. NSC-68
12. satellite nation
13. 38th parallel
14. domino theory
15. 17th parallel
16. HUAC

People
17. George C. Marshall
18. Mao Zedong
19. Ho Chi Minh
20. Fidel Castro
21. Alger Hiss
22. Julius and Ethel Rosenberg
23. Joseph R. McCarthy

Places
24. Indochina

Terms For each term above, write a sentence that explains its relation to the post–World War II period.

Matching Review the key terms in the list above. If you are not sure of a term's meaning, review its definition in the chapter. Then choose a term from the list that best matches each description below.
1. division line between North and South Korea
2. belief that if one country falls to communism, neighboring countries will fall as well
3. state of indirect conflict between the United States and the Soviet Union after World War II
4. division between the capitalist West and the communist East in Europe

True or False Determine whether each statement is true or false. If it is true, write "true." If it is false, change the underlined name to make the statement true.
1. After two trials, Joseph R. McCarthy went to prison for four years on perjury charges.
2. George C. Marshall rose to power by accusing people of disloyalty to the United States.
3. Fidel Castro led the struggle for independence in Vietnam.
4. After their conviction on charges of espionage, Julius and Ethel Rosenberg were executed in 1953.

Reviewing Main Ideas

Section 1 (pp. 562–565)
1. Describe the relationship between the United States and the Soviet Union during World War II.
2. How did the issue of Poland's government cause diplomacy between the United States and the Soviet Union to break down after World War II?
3. Why did the United States and the Soviet Union have different goals for the postwar period?

Section 2 (pp. 567–571)
4. Summarize the policy of containment pursued by the United States during the cold war.
5. How were the Truman Doctrine, the Marshall Plan, and NSC-68 expressions of containment policy?
6. How did President Eisenhower and Secretary of State Dulles differ in their views of foreign policy?

Section 3 (pp. 572–576)
7. What two foreign policy objectives did Presidents Truman and Eisenhower have to balance in their handling of the Korean War and the early Vietnam War?
8. What conflicts did the United States face in shaping foreign policy in the Middle East?
9. How did the cold war affect United States policy in Latin America?

Section 4 (pp. 577–581)
10. What were the purpose and effects of Truman's Federal Employee Loyalty Program?
11. What accusations did HUAC make against the nineteen Hollywood figures that it called in to testify?
12. What impact did Senator McCarthy's anticommunist crusade have on American society?

---

6. Dulles wanted to liberate other nations from communism. Eisenhower followed a more cautious approach, favoring containment instead.

7. Truman and Eisenhower had to balance the foreign policy objectives of containing the spread of communism while avoiding another world war.

8. While sympathetic to the new Jewish state of Israel, the United States also wanted to remain friendly with the oil-rich nations of the Middle East in order to prevent them from falling under Soviet influence.

9. Fear of communist activity led the United States to take decisive action to protect its economic interests in Latin America. For example, the United States helped overthrow Jacobo Arbenz Guzmán of Guatemala on the grounds that he was sympathetic to communism.

10. The Federal Employee Loyalty Program was established to investigate government workers for possible ties to the Communist party. The program created an atmosphere of fear and suspicion throughout the country.

11. HUAC accused the Hollywood figures of membership in or association with the Communist party.

12. The anticommunist crusade generated fear and suspicion on all levels of society. People found that dissent was nearly impossible, that their rights to defend themselves were curtailed, and that accusations alone could end their careers.

Making Connections

1. Possible questions: Will the Truman Doctrine be modified if support for capitalist governments is leading to world war? Where will the money come from to finance this support? Will the United States support repressive governments that resist communism? Will support be financial, humanitarian, or military?

2. Students' paragraphs should observe that the United States was reluctant to provoke the Soviet Union into a conflict that might involve nuclear weapons.

3. Students' statements should reflect an understanding of McCarthyism and the atmosphere of suspicion that it created.

4. (a) The Marshall Plan restored the European economy and created new markets for American goods in Europe in order to head off communist involvement. In doing so, it took action on a much larger scale than Truman had taken in Greece and Turkey. (b) The communist takeover of China and the Soviet explosion of an atomic bomb led to the recommendation in NSC-68 to increase defense spending. (c) Students' graphic organizers should demonstrate an understanding of the origins of the cold war, including the reasons diplomatic relations between the United States and the Soviet Union broke down after World War II and how communism and capitalism represented a mutual threat.

Thinking Critically

1. Making Comparisons You have read about the different political and economic ideas that motivated the United States and the Soviet Union during the cold war. How were the foreign policy aims of the two countries similar?

2. Drawing Conclusions During the cold war, fear and hostility toward communism were the driving forces behind many of the social and foreign policies in the United States. How much of this fear actually was grounded in reality?

3. Identifying Alternatives Imagine that you are an adviser to President Eisenhower. The President has asked you to draw up a list of alternatives to help him decide on his policy about the emerging conflict in Vietnam. What alternatives can you propose? Which alternative will you advise the President to use?

Making Connections

1. Evaluating Primary Sources Review the statement of the Truman Doctrine on page 568. Create four questions that, if answered, would help explore what Truman's statement meant for foreign policy in the future.

2. Understanding the Visuals Look at the image in the section preview showing Khrushchev and Eisenhower on page 572, and then at the photograph on page 571. Write a short paragraph explaining how the illustration of the two cold war leaders explains one reason why the United States was reluctant to become involved in the event shown in the photograph on page 571.

3. Writing About the Chapter You have been accused by HUAC of participating in a communist conspiracy. Write a statement in which you defend yourself against these charges. First create a list of the reasons why the accusation is false. Note ways in which the anticommunist hysteria of the times has contributed to your false accusation. Then write a draft of your statement in which you respectfully but firmly defend yourself. Revise your statement, making certain that each point is clearly explained. Proofread your statement and draft a final copy.

4. Using the Graphic Organizer This graphic organizer uses a modified flow map to outline developments on the policy of containment during the 1940s and 1950s. Large boxes show main developments; smaller boxes add details. (a) Based on your reading of the chapter and this graphic organizer, explain how the Marshall Plan implemented the Truman Doctrine and took it a step further. (b) According to the flow map, what events led to the NSC-68 recommendation for a massive increase in defense spending? (c) On a separate sheet of paper, create your own graphic organizer about the origins of the cold war, using this graphic organizer as an example.

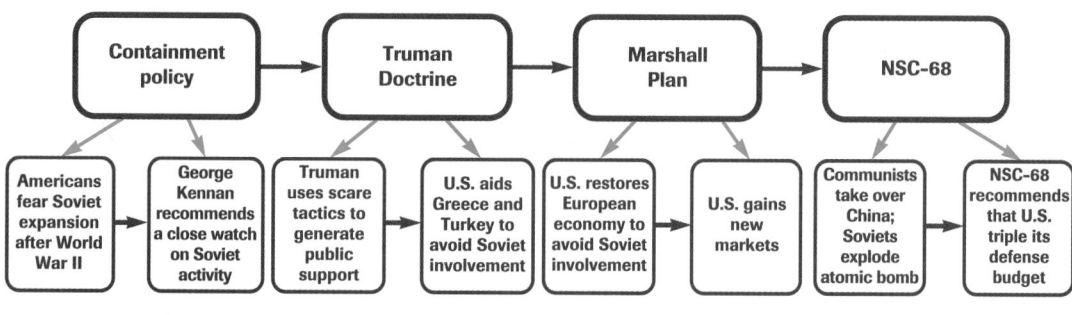

Thinking Critically

1. Both the Soviet Union and the United States were trying to create a global context in which their respective political and economic systems could flourish.

2. On the one hand, the Soviet Union had refused to relinquish control in countries such as Poland, where the Allies had agreed on a temporary presence. Also, the Soviets believed that communism would one day spread throughout the world. Thus some fear was justified. On the other hand, Senator McCarthy's anticommunist campaign led to a hysteria that was quite out of proportion to the actual threat.

3. Alternatives include a "get tough" policy against Ho Chi Minh and an attempt to negotiate a settlement between France and the Viet Minh. Students' advice should take into account what was believed about Soviet aggression at the time, rather than what is known in hindsight.

 Alternative Assessment

Final Evaluation
Use the following guidelines to evaluate student projects:

● **Evidence of mastery of content** Do students' reports reflect at least one main idea from each of the sections in the chapter?

● **Evidence of outside research** To what extent did students use outside research materials for their reports?

● **Evidence of synthesis** Do students' reports demonstrate that they understand the overall significance of the topics they chose?

● **Communication style** Do the reports convey their purpose to an audience in a clear, appealing way?

Allow interested students to present their "broadcasts" to the class.

Tell students that the Soviet Union under communism was ruled by a series of totalitarian dictators who demanded complete control over the citizens of the country. The secret police, called the KGB, were the agents of maintaining this control, and they did so by imprisoning, torturing, and killing any opponents to the central government. Explain to students that when the people of the United States became embroiled in the cold war, they were reacting to this atmosphere and to the Soviet's aggression in taking control of various nations of the world.

INSTRUCT

Point out to students that more than ten years passed between the publication of George Orwell's *1984* and Eisenhower's farewell address. Ask students to analyze the speech. What can they tell about the progression of the cold war by reading it?

Have students think about Joseph McCarthy's attack on supposed communists in the United States. Ask: Compare this era in American history to the type of world described in George Orwell's *1984*. Do you see any similarities? Differences?

1984

Literature

George Orwell

INTRODUCTION From the first sentence of George Orwell's novel, *1984*, the reader knows they have entered another world. The clock is just striking thirteen and the city is readying itself for Hate Week. Yet, although this world is much different from that of 1949, when it was written, or from today, it is not far from the imaginings of the people of the United States at the start of the cold war. British author George Orwell successfully captured the fears and concerns of much of the Western world when he wrote of a government that monitored all actions, taught people to hate, and dealt out death sentences for any thoughts or beliefs that were not specifically authorized. To the minds of many, the communist government in the Soviet Union was headed in precisely that direction. The timing of Orwell's novel was such that it contributed to the anti-communist feeling in the United States by painting a vivid picture of what life under communist rule might be like.

VOCABULARY Before you read the selection, find the meaning of these words in a dictionary: sanguine, scrutinize.

It was a bright cold day in April, and the clocks were striking thirteen. Winston Smith, his chin nuzzled into his breast in an effort to escape the vile wind, slipped quickly through the glass doors of Victory Mansions, though not quickly enough to prevent a swirl of gritty dust from entering along with him.

The hallway smelt of boiled cabbage and old rag mats. At one end of it a colored poster, too large for indoor display, had been tacked to the wall. It depicted simply an enormous face, more than a meter wide: the face of a man of about forty-five, with a heavy black mustache and ruggedly handsome features. Winston made for the stairs. It was no use trying the lift. Even at the best of times it was seldom working, and at present the electric current was cut off during daylight hours. It was part of

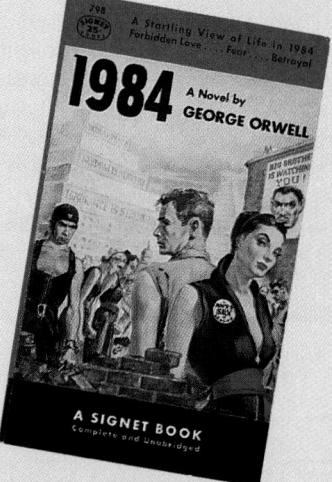

Shown above is a copy of *1984*. Visible on the front cover —posted on the wall at the right—is one of the book's most famous slogans, "Big Brother Is Watching You.

the economy drive in preparation for Hate Week. The flat was seven flights up, and Winston, who was thirty-nine and had a varicose ulcer above his right ankle, went slowly, resting several times on the way. On each landing, opposite the lift shaft, the poster with the enormous face gazed from the wall. It was one of those pictures which are so contrived that the eyes follow you about when you move. BIG BROTHER IS WATCHING YOU, the caption beneath it ran.

Inside the flat a fruity voice was reading out a list of figures which had something to do with the production of pig iron. The voice came from an oblong metal plaque like a dulled mirror which formed part of the surface of the right-hand wall. Winston turned a switch and the voice sank somewhat, though the words were still distinguishable. The instrument (the telescreen, it was called) could be dimmed, but there was no way of shutting it off completely. He moved over to the window: a smallish, frail figure, the meagerness of his body merely emphasized by the blue overalls which were the uniform of the Party. His hair was very fair, his face naturally sanguine, his skin roughened by coarse soap and blunt razor blades and the cold of the winter that had just ended.

Outside, even through the shut window pane, the world looked cold. Down in the street little eddies of wind were whirling dust and torn paper into spirals, and though the sun was shining and the sky a harsh blue, there seemed to be no color in anything except the posters that were plastered everywhere. The black-mustachio'd face gazed down from every commanding corner. There was one on the house front immediately opposite. BIG BROTHER IS WATCHING YOU, the caption said, while the dark eyes looked deep into Winston's own. Down at street level another poster, torn at one corner, flapped fitfully in the wind, alternately covering and uncovering the single word ING-SOC.[1] In the far distance a helicopter skimmed down between the roofs, hovered for an instant like a bluebottle, and darted away again with a curving flight. It was the Police Patrol, snooping into people's windows. The patrols did not matter, however. Only the Thought Police mattered.

Behind Winston's back the voice from the telescreen was still babbling away about pig iron and the overfulfillment of the Ninth Three-Year Plan. The telescreen received and transmitted simultaneously. Any sound that Winston made, above the level of a very low whisper, would be picked up by it; moreover, so long as he remained within the field of vision which the metal plaque commanded, he could be seen as well as heard. There was of course no way of knowing whether you were being watched at any given moment. How often, or on what system, the Thought Police plugged in on any individual wire was guesswork. It was even conceivable that they watched everybody all the time. But at any rate they could plug in your wire whenever they wanted to. You had to

[1]Orwell defines this as English Socialism.

live—did live, from habit that became instinct—in the assumption that every sound you made was overheard, and, except in darkness, every movement scrutinized.

Winston kept his back turned to the telescreen. It was safer; though, as he well knew, even a back can be revealing. A kilometer away the Ministry of Truth, his place of work, towered vast and white above the grimy landscape. . . .

The Ministry of Truth—Minitrue, in Newspeak[2]—was startlingly different from any other object in sight. It was an enormous pyramidal structure of glittering white concrete, soaring up, terrace after terrace, three hundred meters into the air. From where Winston stood it was just possible to read, picked out on its white face in elegant lettering, the three slogans of the Party:

WAR IS PEACE

FREEDOM IS SLAVERY

IGNORANCE IS STRENGTH.

[2] Newspeak was the offical language of Oceania. Orwell describes its purpose in the Appendix to *1984* as "not only to provide a medium of expression for the world-view and mental habits proper to the devotees of Ingsoc, but to make all other modes of thought impossible." In other words, freedom of expression and even thought would be ended by making it impossible to find the word to describe concepts such as democracy or liberty.

THINKING ABOUT THE SELECTION

1. What was the telescreen, and how was it used by the government?
2. What was the government trying to accomplish by hanging Big Brother posters everywhere? What did the slogan on the posters mean?

Critical Thinking

3. **Distinguishing False from Accurate Images**
   Reread the three slogans of the Ministry of Truth. How do these slogans contradict the name of the ministry? How might such contradictions affect a society?

ANSWERS TO

Thinking About the Selection

1. The telescreen was like a television screen, except that it both transmitted and received a signal. One was put in every citizen's home in order to feed government propaganda into the home and to monitor the people's actions.

2. The posters were meant to remind people of the ever-watchful eye of the government. Their presence kept people from acting in ways that were against government rules by reminding them that their actions were being watched at all times. The slogan on the poster was meant

to have a double meaning. It reminded the people that they were being watched and it also was meant to comfort them, to make them believe that Big Brother, or the government, was looking out for their best interests.

3. Although the ministry is called the Ministry of Truth, the slogans are lies, or distortions of the truth. The constant bombardment of a society by such contradictions or lies would no doubt produce a psychologically damaged society, capable of doing anything the government demands, because there would no longer be any truth against which to measure what they were being told.

Ask students to consider this question: Do you think the abuse of power that Eisenhower is warning the nation about in his speech could actually happen? Form the class into groups of five or six students each and then pair the groups. Assign one group in each pair to debate the "pro" side of this question and the other to debate the "con" side. Students should conduct research and prepare at least four points with which to argue their side of the debate. Schedule the debates for several days and give each group the date on which they will present their arguments. Hold the debates in a formal way, with each side being given a chance to present one argument, the opposing side being given a chance to rebut the argument and so on. Grade students on the extent of their research, their understanding of the issue of the power of the military-industrial complex, the soundness of their arguments, and their ability to articulate those arguments.

As an alternative assignment, have students take another issue from Chapter 17 and explore the most far-reaching consequences that could have evolved from that issue, as Orwell did with his novel. Students can write a short play, a poem, or draw a poster depicting a future world in which something that began in the 1950s went out of control. For example, students might examine the policy of containment gone awry or the House Un-American Activities Committee with too much power.

SOURCE READINGS

Eisenhower's Farewell Address

Primary Source

Dwight D. Eisenhower

INTRODUCTION "Our arms must be mighty, ready for instant action," stated President Dwight Eisenhower as he left office in 1961. Yet, he goes on to say, we must be careful not to allow the makers of our military weapons and military strategies to become too powerful, for that would lead to the destruction of democracy. Eisenhower knew that the creation of an industrial group devoted solely to military purposes—never before necessary in the United States but necessary for the first time in the 1950s due to the pressures of the cold war—carried with it the potential for grave misuse of power. So he left office with these words of warning to the people he had served for over fifty years.

VOCABULARY Before you read the selection, find the meaning of these words in a dictionary: atheistic, insidious, transitory, provocation, predecessor, conjunction, allocations, insolvent.

My fellow Americans:

Three days from now, after half a century in the service of our country, I shall lay down the responsibilities of office as, in traditional and solemn ceremony, the authority of the Presidency is vested in my successor. . . .

We now stand ten years past the midpoint of a century that has witnessed four major wars among great nations. Three of them involved our own country. Despite these holocausts America is today the strongest, the most influential and most productive nation in the world. Understandably proud of this pre-eminence we yet realize that America's leadership and prestige depend, not merely upon our unmatched material progress, riches and military strength, but on how we use our power in the interests of world peace and human betterment.

Soviet leader Nikita Krushchev (left) and President Eisenhower (right) perch on a seesaw balanced on top of a nuclear warhead in this 1959 *Newsweek* cover that illustrated the balance of power between the Soviet Union and the United States.

Throughout America's adventure in free government, our basic purposes have been to keep the peace; to foster progress in human achievement, and to enhance liberty, dignity and integrity among people and among nations. To strive for less would be unworthy of a free and religious people. Any failure traceable to arrogance, or our lack of comprehension or readiness to sacrifice would inflict upon us grievous hurt both at home and abroad.

Progress toward these noble goals is persistently threatened by the conflict now engulfing the world. It commands our whole attention, absorbs our very beings. We face a hostile ideology—global in scope, atheistic in character, ruthless in purpose, and insidious in method. Unhappily the danger it poses promises to be of indefinite duration. To meet it successfully, there is called for, not so much the emotional and transitory sacrifices of crisis, but rather those which enable us to carry forward steadily, surely, and without complaint the burdens of a prolonged and complex struggle—with liberty the stake. Only thus shall we remain, despite every provocation, on our charted course toward permanent peace and human betterment. . . .

A vital element in keeping the peace is our military establishment. Our arms must be mighty, ready for instant action, so that no potential aggressor may be tempted to risk his own destruction.

Our military organization today bears little relation to that known by any of my predecessors in peacetime, or indeed by the fighting men of World War II or Korea.

Until the latest of our world conflicts, the United States had no armaments industry. American makers of plowshares could, with time and as required, make swords as well. But now we can no longer risk emergency improvisation of national defense; we have been compelled to create a permanent armaments industry of vast proportions. Added to this, three and half million men and women are directly engaged in the defense establishment. We annually spend on military security more than the net income of all United States corporations.

This conjunction of an immense military establishment and a large arms industry is new in the American experience. The total influence—economic, political, even spiritual—is felt in every city, every statehouse, every office of the federal government. We recognize the imperative need for this development. Yet we must not fail to comprehend its grave implications. Our toil, resources, and livelihood are all involved; so is the very structure of our society.

In the councils of government, we must guard against the acquisition of unwarranted influence, whether sought or unsought, by the military-industrial complex. The potential for the disastrous rise of misplaced power exists and will persist.

We must never let the weight of this combination endanger our liberties or democratic processes. We should take nothing for granted. Only an alert and knowledgeable citizenry can compel the proper meshing of the huge industrial and military machin-ery of defense with our peaceful methods and goals, so that security and liberty may prosper together.

Akin to, and largely responsible for the sweeping changes in our industrial-military posture, has been the technological revolution during recent decades.

In this revolution, research has become central; it also becomes more formalized, complex, and costly. A steadily increasing share is conducted for, by, or at the direction of, the federal government. . . .

The prospect of domination of the nation's scholars by federal employment, project allocations, and the power of money is ever present—and is gravely to be regarded.

Yet, in holding scientific research and discovery in respect, as we should, we must also be alert to the equal and opposite danger that public policy could itself become the captive of a scientific-technological elite.

It is the task of statesmanship to mold, to balance, and to integrate these and other forces, new and old, within the principles of our democratic system—ever aiming toward the supreme goals of our free society.

Another factor in maintaining balance involves the element of time. As we peer into society's future, we—you and I, and our government—must avoid the impulse to live only for today, plundering, for our own ease and convenience, the precious resources of tomorrow. We cannot mortgage the material assets of our grandchildren without risking the loss also of their political and spiritual heritage. We want democracy to survive for all generations to come, not to become the insolvent phantom of tomorrow.

THINKING ABOUT THE SELECTION

1. What is Eisenhower referring to when he mentions "the conflict now engulfing the world"?
2. What does Eisenhower say is the "vital element in keeping the peace"?

Critical Thinking

3. **Identifying Central Issues** Why does Eisenhower believe that Americans need to be warned about the potential dangers of the military-industrial complex?

ANSWERS TO

Thinking About the Selection
1. He refers to the cold war.
2. The vital element is our military establishment.
3. He believes Americans need to be warned because the military-industrial complex is new to the country, and Americans might not realize the potential dangers of such a powerful organization.

Chapter 18 The Postwar Years at Home
1945–1960

📁 **Teaching Resources** (See Unit 5 Folder)

	Instruction	Enrichment
Section 1 **The Postwar Economy** (pp. 590–594)	Reproducible Lesson Plan, p. 104 Alternate Lesson Plan, p. 137 Guided Reading and Review, p. 108 Quiz, p. 109	American Profiles Activity, Ray A. Kroc, p. 120 Visual Learning Activity, The Miracle of Television, p. 133 Historian's Toolbox Activity, Evaluating Magazine Advertisements, p. 124
Section 2 **The Mood of the 1950s** (pp. 596–599)	Reproducible Lesson Plan, p. 105 Alternate Lesson Plan, p. 138 Guided Reading and Review, p. 110 Quiz, p. 111	Literature Activity, Conformity in the 1950s, pp. 129–130 Critical Thinking Activity, Determining Relevance, p. 125 Literature Activity, Nonconformity in the 1950s, p. 131 Viewpoints Activity, On Rock and Roll, pp. 122–123 Time and Place Activity, Edge Cities, pp. 118–119
Section 3 **Domestic Politics and Policy** (pp. 602–607)	Reproducible Lesson Plan, p. 106 Alternate Lesson Plan, p. 139 Guided Reading and Review, p. 112 Quiz, p. 113	Visual Learning Activity, Auto Strike, 1950, p. 132 Primary Source Activity, Harry Truman: Off the Record, pp. 126–127
Section 4 **The Continuing Struggle for Equality** (pp. 608–611)	Reproducible Lesson Plan, p. 107 Alternate Lesson Plan, p. 140 Guided Reading and Review, p. 114 Quiz, p. 115 Chapter Test, Forms A & B, pp. 134–139	Primary Source Activity, Enforcing Brown v. Board of Education, p. 128 American Profiles Activity, Maria Latigo Hernandez and Pedro Hernandez, p. 121 History Might Not . . . Activity, Integrating the University of Georgia, pp. 116–117

📁 **Additional Chapter Resources**

Resource Organizer, p. 103
Alternate Lesson Plan, p. 136
Answer Keys, pp. 146–158

Bibliography

For the Teacher
Halberstam, David. *The Fifties.* Villard Books, 1993. (A comprehensive look at the social, political, economic, and cultural history of the 1950s.)
Handlin, Oscar. *Fire-Bell in the Night: Crisis in Civil Rights.* Little, Brown, 1964. (A study of the racial crises of the 1950s.)

Prentice Hall Literature Excerpts from *The American Experience,* 1994, including Ellison, Ralph. "Hidden Name and Complex Fate," from *Shadow and Act.* Random House, 1953.

THE BIG IDEA

The Big Idea for the chapter and how the main ideas in each section relate to the Big Idea are graphically displayed below. Comprehension of this chapter's Big Idea is critical to students' understanding of United States history and how we as a nation got where we are today.

CHAPTER 18

Emerging from World War II, the nation momentarily reveled in its triumph of good over evil. The American Dream of having a secure job, owning a house, and using labor-saving appliances came within reach of many after the war. The economy, fueled by the postwar baby boom, rocketed in the late 1940s and 1950s. The dividends of the triumph of democracy eluded many, however. The civil rights movement gained momentum as it brought into focus the democratic principles that the United States had fought for in World War II.

SECTION 1

During the postwar years, the economy of the United States had one of its greatest periods of expansion, as Americans began families, purchased brand-new homes, and spent their wartime savings.

SECTION 2

The American Dream—a life of wealth, success, and leisure time—seemed more accessible than ever before during the 1950s; but critics claimed that the dream encouraged conformity and was sterile.

SECTION 3

President Truman concentrated on helping the nation adjust to peacetime and tried to continue the New Deal spirit of reform. The next President, Dwight D. Eisenhower, believed in more limited presidential power and attempted to reduce the size and authority of government.

SECTION 4

The civil rights movement gained fresh momentum and new victories in the courts and through boycotts and protests.

Media and Technology

 Historical Maps, L-5

 Critical Thinking, I-4

 The Way It Works, H-20

 Visions of America: History Might Not Have Happened This Way Game

 Graphic Organizer, G-2

 Guided Reading Audiotapes (English and Spanish)

 Computer Test Bank

For the Student

Ellison, Ralph. *Invisible Man.* Random House, 1989. (Awarded the 1952 National Book Award for fiction, uses the experiences of an idealistic young African American to depict the alienation of American society.)

Time-Life Books editors. *This Fabulous Century. Vol. 6, 1950–1960.* Time-Life Books, 1969. (Richly illustrated and comprehensive study of the 1950s.)

588B

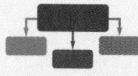

The Relevance
of the Big Idea

Much of the way of life familiar to Americans in the 1990s took shape in the 1950s. Mass media, especially television, created a national culture; radio offered teenagers their own music; advertising defined the American Dream; franchise businesses sprouted in shopping centers in the suburbs, "bedroom communities" near large cities and towns. People who had previously lived in either crowded cities or on isolated farms now moved to these new towns. More and more people wore white rather than blue collars to work, similar to the 1990s, and began to grapple with many of the social issues—urban flight to suburbs, the changing roles of women, continuing discrimination in various forms, and lasting pockets of poverty—that exist within an affluent society.

Discuss aspects of these social issues that remain in the forefront of life in America in the 1990s.

In Depth

Global Connections

After World War II, as demands for independence increased, European countries—most notably Britain—gradually began to quit colonial possessions in Asia and Africa. In 1947, the former British colony of India was partitioned into two independent countries, India and Pakistan, signaling the dissolution of the British Empire, the largest in history. As two centuries of British world dominance ended, the United States rose to superpower status in the West.

The Postwar Years
at Home
1945–1960

*A*mericans had dreamed of peace and prosperity through sixteen grueling years of economic depression and world war. After the war, they expected to enjoy the benefits of their new standing as a military and economic superpower. People embraced a wide array of technological developments that promised to make their lives easier, and they relished the chance to live more comfortably than their parents had. While not all groups shared in the prosperity, most Americans now were able to buy the homes, cars, and other items that they had once only imagined owning.

Events in the United States

1945	1947	1949	1951

1947 Jackie Robinson becomes the first African American to play major league baseball.

1948 Scientists invent the transistor. • President Truman desegregates the armed forces.

1951 J. D. Salinger publishes his novel The Catcher in the Rye.

Events in the World

1945 The British Labour party nationalizes major industries after winning power.

1947 India is divided into India and Pakistan. • Japan adopts a new constitution.

1948 South African Alan Paton's Cry the Beloved Country examines racial segregation in his country.

1951 United States occupation of Japan ends.

▶ RESOURCE DIRECTORY

Teaching Resources

Alternative Lesson Plan: Demonstrating the Big Idea found in the Alternate Lesson Plans folder, p. 136, provides a lesson strategy to instruct students about the Big Idea that many Americans benefited from postwar prosperity, but not all could enjoy these middle-class advantages, and the civil rights movement thus gained momentum.

Alternative Assessment Handbook provides information, guidance, and strategies for alternative methods of assessment. It includes an essay on new trends in assessment, guidance and strategies for developing performance tasks and portfolios, scoring rubrics, and sample evaluation forms.

Pages 590–594

The Postwar Economy

The American Dream—a home in the suburbs, a car in the garage—materialized for many people in the postwar years.

Pages 596–599

The Mood of the 1950s

After World War II, many Americans were blessed with wealth, success, and leisure. Conformity seemed the order of the day, although some groups made it their business to avoid the popularly accepted lifestyles of the 1950s.

Pages 602–607

Domestic Politics and Policy

The postwar period created many challenges for American leaders—including the conversion back to a peacetime economy and the debate over the proper role of government in the nation's economic and social affairs. Presidents Harry Truman and Dwight Eisenhower used two very different styles of leadership to meet these challenges.

Pages 608–611

The Continuing Struggle for Equality

The events of World War II—including the fight against fascism abroad and the African American migration at home—breathed new life into the civil rights movement. The actions of many courageous Americans brought significant results in the postwar years.

1953 Two thirds of all families in the United States own televisions.

1954 Supreme Court issues Brown v. Board of Education ruling desegregating schools.

1955 Ray Kroc opens his first McDonald's fast-food restaurant.
• Montgomery bus boycott begins.

1957 First commercial nuclear power plant opens in Shippingport, Pennsylvania.

1960 Gross National Product reaches $504 billion, more than double that of 1945.

1953	1955	1957	1959	1961

1953 Soviet leader Joseph Stalin dies.

1955 Juan Perón is deposed as dictator of Argentina.
• Soviet Union forms Warsaw Pact.

1957 The Soviet Union launches Sputnik satellite.

1960 Organization of Petroleum Exporting Countries (OPEC) is formed.

Media and Technology

Transparency
Time Lines, E-8

SECTION 1

The Postwar Economy

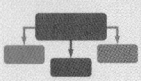

Connecting to the Big Idea

See page 588B. The nation's economy boomed during the postwar years. Ask students how economic growth changed the jobs available to Americans and the communities they lived in.

Objectives

● Describe how the nation's economy grew after World War II.
● Give examples of technological advances, such as atomic energy and computers, that spurred economic growth and altered American life.
● Explain why the economy was increasingly driven by the needs and wants of affluent consumers prepared to buy on credit.

Bellringer

Have students think of inventions that would be totally new to a person from the 1930s who was suddenly transported to the 1990s.

Reading Strategy

Reading for Evidence Have students note the statement on page 590 that after the war, the United States "embarked on one of the greatest periods of economic expansion in its history." Ask students to find evidence to support this statement as they read the section, including information on each of the following topics: corporations, technology, changes in the work force, farm work and life, suburbs, and consumer credit.

SECTION PREVIEW

The American Dream—a home in the suburbs, a car in the garage—materialized for many people in the postwar years.

Even some children's games in the 1950s reflected the ideal middle-class life. These game pieces are from "Merry Milkman," in which players delivered milk, eggs, and butter to suburban homes.

Key Concepts
• After World War II, the American economy grew rapidly. People could buy more with their money and created new ways of organizing businesses.
• Technological advances such as atomic energy and computers altered American life.
• The economy was increasingly driven by the needs and wants of affluent consumers.

Key Terms, People, and Places
per capita income, real purchasing power, diversified conglomerate, franchise, agribusiness, baby boom, GI Bill; William J. Levitt

---

W hen American soldiers returned from the battlefields, they wanted nothing more than to put the horrors of the war behind them and enjoy the comforts of home and family. As large numbers of young people married and started families, they wanted homes, furniture, and other household items. During the war, when most items were rationed or not produced at all, many people had simply put their money into savings. Now most Americans were eager to acquire everything the war—and before that, the Depression—had denied them.

Thus the United States embarked on one of the greatest periods of economic expansion in its history. The Gross National Product (GNP) more than doubled, jumping from $212 billion in 1945 to $504 billion in 1960. During the same period, **per capita income**—the average income per person—increased from $1,526 to $2,788. **Real purchasing power**—what people actually could buy with their money—grew by about 22 percent. The United States was now the richest nation in the world.

Corporations Create New Jobs

Major corporate expansion accompanied economic growth. In the 1950s, a few huge firms dominated many industries. General Motors, Ford, and Chrysler overshadowed all competitors in the automobile industry; General Electric and Westinghouse enjoyed similar positions in the electrical business. Giant corporations, fearful after the Depression of investing all their resources in one business, became **diversified conglomerates.** They acquired companies that produced entirely different goods and services, so that if one area of the economy failed, their investments in another area would be safe. International Telephone and Telegraph, for example, purchased Avis Rent-a-Car, Sheraton Hotels, Hartford Fire Insurance, and Continental Baking.

At the same time, another kind of expansion took place. In 1954 Ray Kroc, who sold milk-shake machines called Multimixers, was amazed when two brothers who owned a restaurant in San Bernardino, California, ordered their tenth Multimixer. With ten machines, the restaurant could make fifty milk shakes at once. Because of the restaurant's fast, efficient service and its prime location along a busy highway, it was enjoying great success. Intrigued by the possibilities, Kroc purchased the two brothers' idea of assembly-line food production. He also acquired the name of the brothers' restaurant: McDonald's. Kroc took his fast food nationwide by selling **franchises**—the right to open McDonald's restaurants using the same system—to other eager entrepreneurs. Hundreds of other restaurant franchises, such as Burger King and Kentucky Fried Chicken, followed. ⬢

The franchise system flourished in the 1950s. It worked so well that it was applied to

---

RESOURCE DIRECTORY

Teaching Resources

📄 **Reproducible Lesson Plan** found in the Unit 5 folder, p. 104, provides a summary of the Section 1 lesson plan content.

📄 **Alternate Lesson Plan: Learning Styles** found in the Alternate Lesson Plans folder, p. 137, is especially effective for visual learners and helps students understand the effects of economic and social change in the postwar period through the creation of a graphic organizer.

📄 **Guided Reading and Review** found in the Unit 5 folder, p. 108, provides a structure for reading and mastering the key concepts and reviewing the key terms for Section 1. (Guided Practice)

⬢ 📄 **American Profiles Activity** found in the Unit 5 folder, p. 120, profiles Ray A. Kroc, founder of the McDonald's fast-food restaurant chain.

other kinds of businesses, such as clothing stores and automobile muffler shops. The system's advantage lay in the fact that an individual with only a few thousand dollars could own a small business that enjoyed the support—especially in terms of national advertising—of a multimillion-dollar parent company. The system also created countless low-paying jobs across the nation. But with the growth of the franchise system, many small, unique stores with ties to the local community were replaced by nationwide chains that were the same everywhere in the country.

Technology Transforms Life

New developments in technology also spurred industrial growth. An entirely new industry—the generation of electrical power through the use of atomic energy—resulted from the research that had produced the atomic bomb. In 1956 film producer Walt Disney voiced Americans' hopes and fears about atomic power in his book and film *Our Friend the Atom.* Disney began with a story about a fisherman who found a sealed bottle. When the fisherman opened the bottle, a genie escaped and threatened to kill him. The fisherman got the genie back into the bottle and would only open it again when the genie promised to grant him three wishes. "The story of the atom is like that tale," Disney explained:

T*he fable . . . has a happy ending; perhaps our story can, too. Like the Fisherman we must bestir our wits* [think carefully before we act]. *We have the scientific knowledge to turn the Genie's might into peaceful and useful channels.*

The next year, Navy captain Hyman G. Rickover oversaw the development of the first commercial nuclear power plant in Shippingport, Pennsylvania. The new plant promised the peaceful use of atomic energy that Walt Disney had imagined.

The Computer Industry At the same time that Americans were looking forward to inexpensive energy from nuclear reactors, they reached out to embrace the computer industry. Wartime research led to the development of ever more powerful calculators. Grace Hopper, a research fellow at Harvard University's computation laboratory, led the way in the creation of the software that runs computers. She also introduced the term *debugging,* which was born when she removed a moth caught in a relay switch that had caused a large computer to shut down. Today the term means "ridding a computer program of errors."

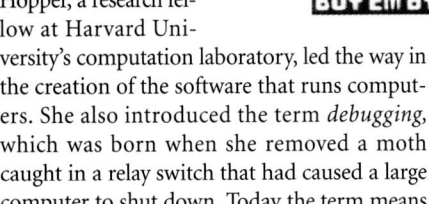

This sign at the original fast-food restaurant in San Bernardino, California, advertised the McDonald brothers' mass-produced hamburgers.

In 1947 scientists at Bell Laboratories invented the transistor, a tiny circuit that did the work of a much larger vacuum tube. Because of the transistor, giant machines that once filled whole rooms could now fit on a desk. Calculations that had taken hours could now be computed in fractions of a second. The Census Bureau purchased one of the first computer systems to tally the 1950 census. Soon hotels, airlines, and countless other industries used computers to keep track of their customers.

MAKING CONNECTIONS

Today the government and many businesses use computers to create files with information on every American. How might this use of computers threaten people's right to privacy?

Television Americans fell in love with another invention in the 1950s: television. Developed in the 1930s, television became enormously popular after World War II. By 1953 two thirds of all American families owned TVs.

In 1955 the average American family watched television four to five hours a day. Children grew up on such programs as "Howdy Doody Time" and "The Mickey Mouse Club." Teenagers danced to the rock-and-roll music played on "American Bandstand," a predecessor of today's MTV. Other viewers followed situation comedies like "I Love Lucy" and "Father Knows Best."

Television networks raised the money to broadcast these shows by selling advertising

---

 Visual Learning Activity The Miracle of Television, found in the Unit 5 folder, p. 133, uses a 1949 advertisement to enhance students' understanding of the impact the introduction of television had on American life.

SOURCE READINGS

Source Readings on p. 616 will connect literature selections and primary source excerpts to historical events discussed in this section.

Media and Technology

Transparency
Historical Maps, L-5

Explain/Discuss

Discuss how the end of the war also marked the end of the Great Depression. However, fear of another depression governed many economic decisions of the time.

Discuss how a technological advance such as the development of commercial nuclear power or of the computer industry creates jobs.

Ask students why a credit-driven economy moves faster than a cash-only economy. What industries profit from credit use?

Analyze

The baby boom was both a result of increased economic growth and the cause of more growth. Ask how babies created what syndicated economics writer Sylvia Porter called "the biggest, boomiest boom ever known in history."

Answer to . . .

MAKING CONNECTIONS

Computers make it easy both to collect and store information and to transfer it from one place to another. Thus, confidential information may be available to anyone with a modem or other means of accessing computer data.

In Depth

Interdisciplinary

The new nuclear technology had few detractors and fewer restrictions. From the 1940s to the early 1970s, the federal government exposed as many as 1,800 people to radiation in experiments that provided little or no medical benefit. In early 1994, Congressman Ed Markey (D–Massachusetts) said that "the appalling truth is that in some cases American citizens were used as nuclear calibration instruments."

Links Across Time

 Activity

Teaching Heterogeneous Groups

Today we take business franchises for granted, but after World War II the franchise was a new concept, designed to address the growing consumer demand in the United States. Divide students into small groups and have them list as many franchises as possible in five minutes. Discuss with students how the increasing number of franchises contributed to the growing economy after World War II. Then have the groups list two positive and two negative effects of franchises. **LEP**

Enrichment

Invite students to watch episodes from some children's television series of the 1950s, such as "Kukla, Fran, and Ollie," "Howdy Doody," "The Lone Ranger," "Hopalong Cassidy," or "The Mickey Mouse Club." Some of these programs are broadcast on cable networks, and some are available on video. Students may compare the subject matter, format, types of people and groups represented, and level of sophistication of these programs with current children's television programs.

| 1650 | 1700 | 1750 | 1800 | **Links Across Time** | 1850 | 1900 | 1950 | 2000 |

The Incredible Shrinking Computer

In their early days, computers filled entire rooms and performed calculations at a snail's pace (left). Over the years, improvements in technology have reduced the size of computers—such as the laptop model above—to fit almost anywhere. Computers now have the power to do many complex operations at lightning speed. *How has the computer revolution increased the pace of life for all Americans?*

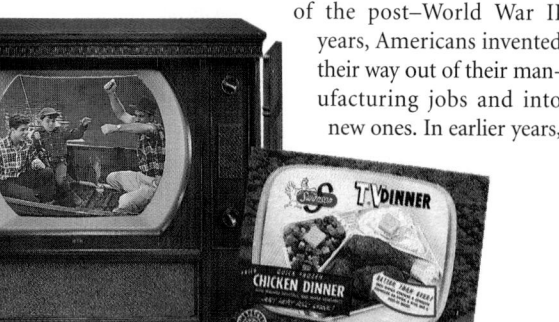

Situation comedies like "Leave It to Beaver" (TV inset) entertained audiences while promoting the family values of the 1950s. Frozen foods allowed TV viewers to cook dinner during commercial breaks.

time. Television commercials gave Americans constant exposure to products they supposedly needed to live a comfortable life. Children grew up singing lyrics to commercials, which they sometimes knew even better than popular songs. Companies got their money's worth from advertising dollars: millions of viewers were persuaded to buy the items they saw on television commercials.

Changes in the Work Force

Using the nearly miraculous technology of the post–World War II years, Americans invented their way out of their manufacturing jobs and into new ones. In earlier years, most Americans made a living as blue-collar workers, or those who produce goods. After the war, however, new machines performed many of the jobs previously done by people. By 1956 a majority of all American workers held white-collar jobs, in which they no longer produced goods but instead performed services for others, working at counters or in offices.

The new white-collar workers felt encouraged by the working conditions they found: clean, bright offices rather than the dark, often dangerous factories of the recent past. But they soon realized that office jobs had drawbacks as well. Work in large corporations was often impersonal. White-collar workers sometimes never saw the products that their companies made. Employers might pressure employees to dress, think, and act alike. Some workers felt they sacrificed individuality for the sake of the corporation. Sociologist C. Wright Mills had this scathing comment: "When white-collar people get jobs, they sell not only their time and energy but their personalities as well."

For those who kept their blue-collar jobs, working conditions and wages improved during the 1940s and 1950s. Labor unions continued to work for change, and their strength reached an all-time high as the war ended. In 1955 the two largest unions, the American Federation of Labor (AFL) and the Congress of Industrial Organizations (CIO) merged. The AFL-CIO, a new and more powerful organization, remains a major force today. Workers won gains that we now take for granted, such as guaranteed cost-of-living increases.

Changes in Farm Work and Life

The world of American agriculture was also transformed in the postwar period. Technological improvements made planting and harvesting easier. Fertilizers, fungicides, and pesticides promoted and protected plant growth. As farming became more profitable, it underwent the same kind of consolidation experienced by industry.

Once again, Americans had invented themselves out of their old jobs. Hundreds of thousands of small farmers who could no longer compete with farms using high-tech machinery abandoned rural America in search of new lives in the cities and suburbs. They left their farms behind to be bought up by big businesses. Americans called this new industry **agribusiness.**

Americans Move to the Suburbs

With so many people working and making a better living than ever before, the **baby boom** that had begun during World War II continued. The birthrate, which had fallen to 19 births per one thousand people during the Depression, soared to more than 25 births per thousand in its peak year of 1947. (See the graph at right.)

Large families seeking new houses and wanting to enjoy the benefits of a booming economy retreated from the aging cities to suburbs that ringed the urban areas. World War II veterans enjoyed the benefits of the Servicemen's Readjustment Act of 1944, commonly known as the **GI Bill,** which gave them low-interest mortgages to purchase their new homes.

Developers like **William J. Levitt** built new communities in the suburbs. He pioneered mass-production techniques in home building by buying precut and preassembled materials and building houses in weeks instead of

months. Proud of his creations, Levitt gave his name to the new towns. Soon there was a Levittown in New York, another in Pennsylvania, and a third in New Jersey. Others quickly adopted Levitt's techniques, and new communities sprang up all over the United States.

The houses were affordable, but they all bore a monotonous resemblance to one another. Folk singer Malvina Reynolds expressed her revulsion for the new communities with these words from "Little Boxes," a popular song of the era:

Little boxes on the hillside
Little boxes made of ticky-tacky
Little boxes on the hillside
Little boxes all the same.
There's a green one and a pink one
And a blue one and a yellow one
And they're all made out of ticky-tacky
And they all look just the same.

Suburban growth depended on automobiles and roads. To meet the demand, auto makers produced up to 8 million new cars each year in the 1950s. The 1956 Interstate Highway Act provided $26 billion to build an interstate highway

As reported in a 1953 article in *Life* magazine, "Every day, including Saturdays and Sundays, is moving day in Los Angeles." Four hundred people a day moved into the suburbs around that city in the 1950s.

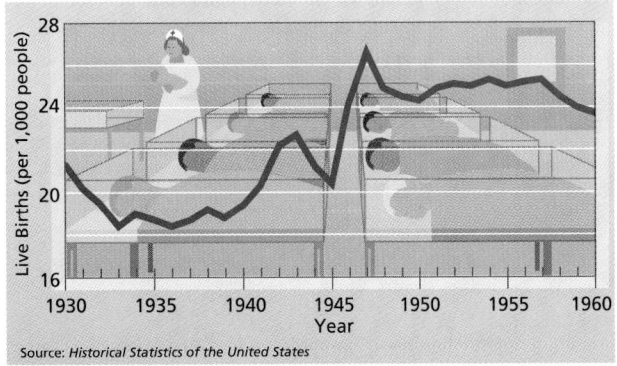

Birth Rate, 1930–1960

Live Births (per 1,000 people) — Year 1930 to 1960

Source: *Historical Statistics of the United States*

 Interpreting Graphs
What was the overall trend in the birth rate after World War II? How might the lack of consumer goods during the war have contributed to this trend?

3. ASSESS

Section 1 Review Answers

1. (a) per capita income, see p. 590, (b) real purchasing power, see p. 590, (c) baby boom, see p. 593, (d) GI Bill, see p. 593

2. William J. Levitt, see p. 593

3. The diversified conglomerate led to the formation of giant corporations that owned businesses in many different areas of the economy. The franchise system meant that unique local businesses were sometimes pushed out of business by chains that were uniform throughout the country. Agribusiness shifted much control of the nation's farms from individual farmers to large corporations.

4. Atomic generation of electrical energy, computer technology, and television-related industries had a powerful impact on Americans after World War II.

5. Suburbs developed because of urban decay; an increase in population due to the postwar baby boom; cheap, plentiful housing; improved roads; and availability of automobiles and fuel.

6. Americans were eager to buy everything they were denied during the Depression and the war.

Caption Answer to ...

Interpreting Graphs

The overall trend was that the birth rate increased dramatically. The unavailability of consumer goods during World War II meant that families saved more money, which made the expense of raising a family after the war more manageable. Thus, people began to have more children.

 Interpreting Graphs

Consumer credit increased by a factor of six—about $2.5 billion to about $15 billion—between 1945 and 1950. It increased by about $20 billion between 1950 and 1958.

Reteach

Ask students to write one or two sentences showing how each of the following developments changed American life during the postwar period: corporate expansion, technological advances, changes in the work force, changes in farm work and life, the move to the suburbs, and consumer credit.

 CLOSE

Reinforcing the Big Idea

After World War II, the nation's economy boomed. Many Americans enjoyed a comfortable lifestyle, with a new house in the suburbs and a car to drive to work. In the next section, students will learn why some critics claimed that conformity was the cost of comfort.

In Depth

Then and Now

Between 1947 and 1951 William Levitt built more than 17,000 nearly identical 800-square-foot houses in Levittown, New York, which sold for as little as $6,990 —with no down payments for veterans. "I'm not here just to build houses," Levitt said in 1952. "To be perfectly frank, I'm looking for a little glory, too." By the 1990s, these houses were selling for more than $150,000.

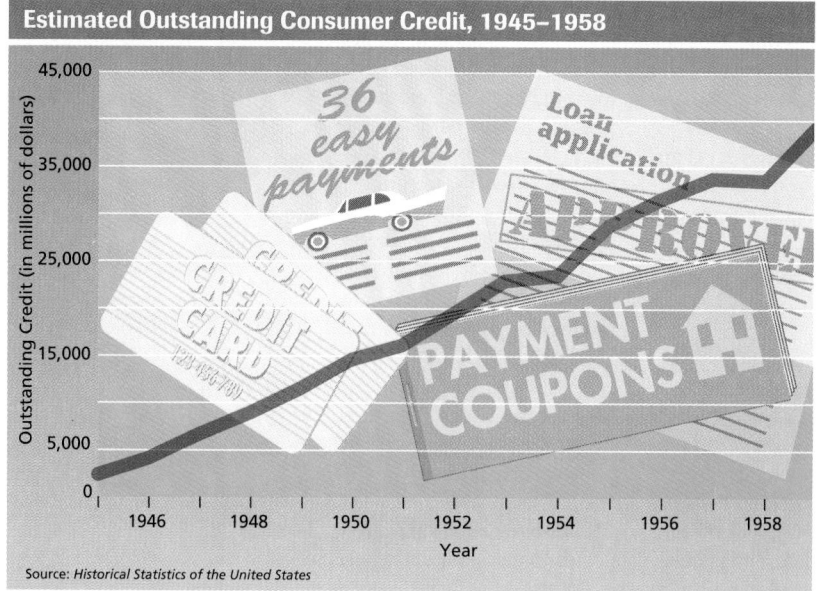

Estimated Outstanding Consumer Credit, 1945–1958

Source: *Historical Statistics of the United States*

Consumer Credit Finances Growth

The postwar American economy required enormous consumption of goods to remain healthy. The increase in real purchasing power helped pay for some consumer goods but not all. After years of depression and war, Americans willingly went into debt to make up the difference, as the graph at left shows. Lending agencies created new ways to make borrowing easy, such as the credit card. The Diner's Club credit card appeared in 1950, followed at the end of the decade by the American Express card, and then by the BankAmericard (later called Visa).

Interpreting Graphs
The consumer credit shown in this graph includes automobile and home loans as well as credit card debts. *By approximately what factor did consumer credit increase between 1945 and 1950? How many more dollars worth of consumer credit was accumulated between 1950 and 1958?*

system more than 40,000 miles long. The project provided a national web of new roads and allowed the evacuation of major cities in the event of nuclear attack. As President Eisenhower noted,

> The total pavement of the system would make a parking lot big enough to hold two thirds of all the automobiles in the United States. The amount of concrete poured to form these roadways would build . . . six sidewalks to the moon.

Advertisers persuaded consumers that only by buying new products could they attain status and success. Americans responded by using their credit to purchase washing machines, vacuum cleaners, and television sets. The United States had become, in the words of economist John Kenneth Galbraith, "the affluent society."

A decade before, the nation had faced the problems of scarcity and want. Now it would have to deal with the consequences of abundance.

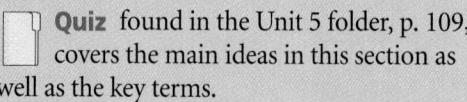 SECTION 1 REVIEW

Key Terms, People, and Places

1. Define (a) per capita income, (b) real purchasing power, (c) baby boom, (d) GI Bill.
2. Identify William J. Levitt.

Key Concepts

3. How did the diversified conglomerate, the franchise system, and agribusiness each change the American economy after World War II?

4. What technological advances had an important impact on Americans in the decade after World War II?
5. What factors contributed to suburban development from 1945 to 1960?

Critical Thinking

6. **Recognizing Cause and Effect** In what ways did the Depression and World War II contribute to the postwar economic boom of the 1950s?

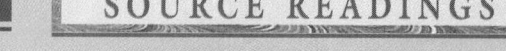

RESOURCE DIRECTORY

SOURCE READINGS

Teaching Resources

Quiz found in the Unit 5 folder, p. 109, covers the main ideas in this section as well as the key terms.

Source Readings on p. 619 will connect literature selections and primary source excerpts to historical events discussed in this section.

Evaluating Magazine Advertisements

Magazine advertisements can be a rich and colorful source of evidence about the past. Because popular weekly or monthly magazines are aimed at a broad audience, advertisements frequently reflect a society's prevailing attitudes and values. Remember, though, that every ad also reflects the purpose of the company whose products are being advertised—namely, to sell their products. Therefore, an ad may present a slanted view of the desirable American life, designed to make people want to buy certain products.

Use the following steps to evaluate the advertisement at right, which appeared in the *Saturday Evening Post* in April 1958.

1. Identify the nature of the advertisement. (a) What is the point of this advertisement? What does it encourage readers to do? (b) What company created this ad? What product does the company make? (c) What other products are shown in the ad? (d) Who is the intended audience for the advertisement?

2. Study the advertisement to evaluate the underlying messages it contains. (a) What things seem to make the people shown in the advertisement happy? (b) Does this ad suggest a preference for suburban life or city life? Explain why you think so. (c) What does this ad suggest is the "good life" toward which Americans should strive?

3. Study the advertisement to learn more about the historical period. Use the information in the ad to help you answer the following questions. (a) Based on what you see in this ad, how closely linked were happiness and material wealth in the minds of many Americans in the 1950s?

(b) Would everyone in the 1950s have been able to afford to buy the items shown in the ad? What reasons does the ad suggest for why credit cards became so popular during this period? (c) Are your conclusions consistent with what you already know about the United States in the 1950s? Explain.

Historian's Toolbox Activity Evaluating Magazine Advertisements, found in the Unit 5 folder, p. 124, encourages students to apply this skill in a modern setting, using a 1993 magazine ad for the sporting goods retailer L. L. Bean.

The Mood of the 1950s

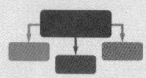

Connecting to the Big Idea

See page 588B. In the 1950s, many Americans enjoyed unprecedented prosperity and security. Ask students if this comfort was worth the price of conformity and frustration.

Objectives

- Describe the value assigned to comfort and security by middle-class Americans in the 1950s.
- Explain how the media and society fostered expectations about the proper roles for men and women.

Bellringer

Ask students to decide what they consider the "proper" roles for men and women in today's society. Have them consider how their views of gender-based roles might differ from those of their parents or grandparents.

Reading Strategy

Reinforcing Key Ideas Ask students to write two headings on a piece of paper: Conformity and Nonconformity. As they read the section, students should note relevant information in the appropriate column. When they have finished, ask students to write one sentence explaining whether conformity or nonconformity was more prevalent in the 1950s than in their present life.

Explain/Discuss

Ask students how people behave when they want to fit into a group. Ask why Americans wanted to fit in after the war. How did the Great Depression and World War II affect Americans' need for comfort and security?

The Mood of the 1950s

SECTION PREVIEW

After World War II, many Americans were blessed with wealth, success, and leisure. Conformity seemed the order of the day, although some groups made it their business to avoid the popularly accepted lifestyles of the 1950s.

Key Concepts

- Middle-class Americans valued comfort and security during the 1950s.
- Expectations about the proper roles for men and women were fostered by the media and society.

Key Terms, People, and Places

beatniks; Benjamin Spock, Betty Friedan, J. D. Salinger

In the 1950s, the "happy house-wife" portrayed in the media used state-of-the-art appliances to cook and clean, and she looked glamorous while doing so. Poodle skirts (below) were part of the uniform for teenage girls.

Middle-class Americans were comfortable during the 1950s. Most did not question whether the images of prosperous, suburban white families frequently seen on television represented "typical" American experiences. They valued the apparent harmony that minimized differences between individuals and groups in the United States. Compromise, rather than conflict, was the way disagreements could be settled. After the deprivations of depression and war, people wanted to enjoy their newly won prosperity and provide even better opportunities for their children.

Americans Value Conformity

The 1950s were years of conformity in the United States. Throughout the country, members of middle-class society seemed to want to imitate those around them rather than search out unique experiences. Even the descendants of the immigrants of the early 1900s seemed to value American middle-class culture above their own diverse cultural heritages.

In the past, sociologist David Riesman observed, Americans had valued individuality. Now they strained to conform. Riesman cited *Tootle the Engine,* a children's story in the popular Little Golden Book series. Tootle, a young train engine, found it was more fun to play in the fields than it was to stay on the tracks. His fellow citizens in "Engineville" worked hard to break him of the habit. Tootle finally absorbed the lesson of his peers: "Always stay on the track no matter what." The story, Riesman believed, was a powerful parable for the young people of the 1950s.

Some called the middle-class youth of the 1950s the "silent generation." The silent generation seemed to have little interest in the problems and crises of the larger world; its members were content to let other people worry about such issues. Instead, many middle-class young people appeared to devote their energies to joining fraternities and sororities, organizing parties and pranks, and generally pursuing entertainment and fun.

Movies generally portrayed the girls of the silent generation in poodle skirts and bobby socks and the boys in letter sweaters. The image of 1950s youth as cheerleaders and football heroes was not entirely accurate, however. Many young people rejected the values of their parents and felt misunderstood and alone. A few films, such as *Rebel Without a Cause* in 1955, captured these feelings of alienation.

Religion Revives in the United States In the 1950s Americans who had drifted away from religion in earlier years flocked back to their churches or synagogues. Evangelists like Billy Graham used radio and television to spread

---

▶ RESOURCE DIRECTORY

Teaching Resources

📘 **Reproducible Lesson Plan** found in the Unit 5 folder, p. 105, provides a summary of the Section 2 lesson plan content.

📘 **Alternate Lesson Plan: Critical Thinking** Making Comparisons, found in the Alternate Lesson Plans folder, p. 138, helps students use this skill to identify the values of middle-class Americans in the 1950s and compare and contrast them to those of the 1990s.

📘 **Guided Reading and Review** found in the Unit 5 folder, p. 110, provides a structure for reading and mastering the key concepts and reviewing the key terms for Section 2. (Guided Practice)

⭐📘 **Literature Activity** Conformity in the 1950s, found in the Unit 5 folder, pp. 129–130, uses an excerpt from Sloan Wilson's novel *The Man in the Gray Flannel Suit* to provide students with a perspective on the shortcomings of unquestioned conformity.

Thousands gathered to hear evangelist Billy Graham preach. He conducted large-scale crusades in major American cities, including this one in New York in 1957.

their messages to more people than ever before. The new interest in religion stemmed in part from the cold war struggle against "godless communism," in part from an effort to find hope in the face of the threat of nuclear war, and in part from a desire to do what everyone else seemed to be doing.

Evidence of the newfound commitment to religion was everywhere. In 1954 Congress added the words "under God" to the Pledge of Allegiance, and the next year it required the phrase "In God We Trust" to appear on all American currency. Religion also became commercial. Those in need could Dial-a-Prayer for the first time, and new slogans such as "The family that prays together stays together" became commonplace. By the end of the 1950s, 95 percent of all Americans felt linked to some formal religious group, even if they never attended services.

Women's and Men's Roles Americans in the post-World War II years were keenly aware of the roles that they were expected to play as men and women. Men were supposed to go to school and then find jobs to support wives and children. Theirs was the public sphere, the world away from home where they earned money and made important political, economic, and social decisions. Men of this time often judged themselves and others by what they could buy with the money they earned.

Women in the 1950s were expected to play a supporting role for their husbands' lives in the public sphere. They kept house, cooked meals, and raised children. Many women had enjoyed working outside the home during World War II and were reluctant to give up good jobs. But propaganda from both employers and the government made it clear that women were expected to give their jobs to returning soldiers. In 1947 *Life* magazine recorded women's frustration in a photo essay titled "The American Woman's Dilemma."

By the 1950s the dilemma seemed solved. Most middle-class women settled into the demands of raising children and decorating their suburban homes. In 1956 *Life* produced a special edition on women that carried a very different message from the issue of nine years before. In a story entitled "Busy Wife's Achievements," *Life* profiled Marjorie Sutton, a happy housewife who had married at the age of sixteen, had four children, and now kept busy with the PTA, Campfire

These Chicago-area commuters may have identified with the characters in *The Man in the Gray Flannel Suit*. The 1955 novel told the story of a couple who seemed to be living the American dream but who felt strangely discontented with their lives.

Discuss other factors in American life that led to increased conformity. Recall that corporations expected their employees to accept and follow the company code. Explain that the postwar fear of communism and the related fear of being branded a communist or communist sympathizer also contributed to the desire to conform and blend in.

Analyze

Ask students to consider this statement by Annie Dillard about her young life in *An American Childhood*: "Every woman stayed alone in her house in those days, like a coin in a safe. Amy [Dillard's sister] and I lived alone with our mother most of the day." What is the mood of Dillard's statement? What image does she create of a woman's life in the 1950s?

In Depth

Did You Know?

Embracing the postwar view that "a woman's place is in the home," Future Homemakers of America was founded in 1945. Its aim was to teach girls how to cook, sew, decorate a home, and raise children. In the last two decades, Future Homemakers has broadened its focus to appeal to both sexes, stressing communications and family management skills as much as cooking and cleaning. As a result, boys now make up 16 percent of the group's membership; and the president of Future Homemakers of America in 1993 was a boy.

Cooperative Learning

Time: One class period.
Activity: Prepare questions and select potential subjects for interviews about life in the 1950s.
Grouping: Four to six students.
Purpose: Have students work in groups to brainstorm topics concerning life in the 1950s, write questions for potential interviews, and select possible subjects to interview. Students may focus their interview questions on a specific population, for example, women.
Roles: Topic specialists, writers, editors, interviewers, spokesperson.
Outcome: Students will identify significant aspects of life in the 1950s and learn about them through first-person accounts.

Enrichment

Have students work in groups to prepare a dramatic presentation based on an excerpt of their choice from J. D. Salinger's *The Catcher in the Rye*.

Caption Answer to ...

 Interpreting Graphs

More women were joining the work force; approximately 5 million between 1950 and 1960.

3. ASSESS

Section 2 Review Answers

1. beatniks, see p. 599

2. (a) Benjamin Spock, see p. 598,
(b) Betty Friedan, see p. 598,
(c) J. D. Salinger, see p. 599

3. Conformity was in evidence in the bureaucratic workplace, schools, churches, and in the acceptance of traditional gender roles.

Girls, and charity causes. She served as "home manager, mother, hostess, and useful civic worker," and even found time to exercise twice a week "to help preserve her size 12 figure."

Pediatrician **Benjamin Spock** assured American families that mothers should stay home with their young children. In his *Common Sense Book of Baby and Child Care*, published in 1946 and still selling today (though in revised form), he advised a mother to remain with her children if she wanted them to grow up stable and secure. Adlai Stevenson, Democratic candidate for President in 1952 and 1956, reinforced this message when he told a group of female college students that "the assignment for you, as wives and mothers, you can do in the living room with a baby in your lap or in the kitchen with a can opener in your hand."

Despite such expectations, more women than ever before—many of them married with children—held paying jobs in the 1950s. Besides the satisfaction of earning their own money, women wanted to be able to buy the items that were part of the media image of "the good life"—automobiles, electric appliances, and so on.

In 1950, 22 percent of all married American women had jobs; by 1960 the figure had risen to 31 percent. Married women with jobs had first begun to outnumber unmarried women with jobs near the end of World War II; in the postwar years, the gap grew even larger. The graph below shows these trends.

In 1963 **Betty Friedan** published an explosive critique of the 1950s ideal of womanhood. Friedan had graduated with top honors from Smith College in 1942 but had given up her career as a journalist to become a full-time homemaker and mother. In her book *The Feminine Mystique*, Friedan lashed out at the culture that denied creative roles to women:

> I t was unquestioned gospel [in the 1950s] that women could identify with nothing beyond the home—not politics, not art, not science, not events large or small, war or peace, in the United States or the world,

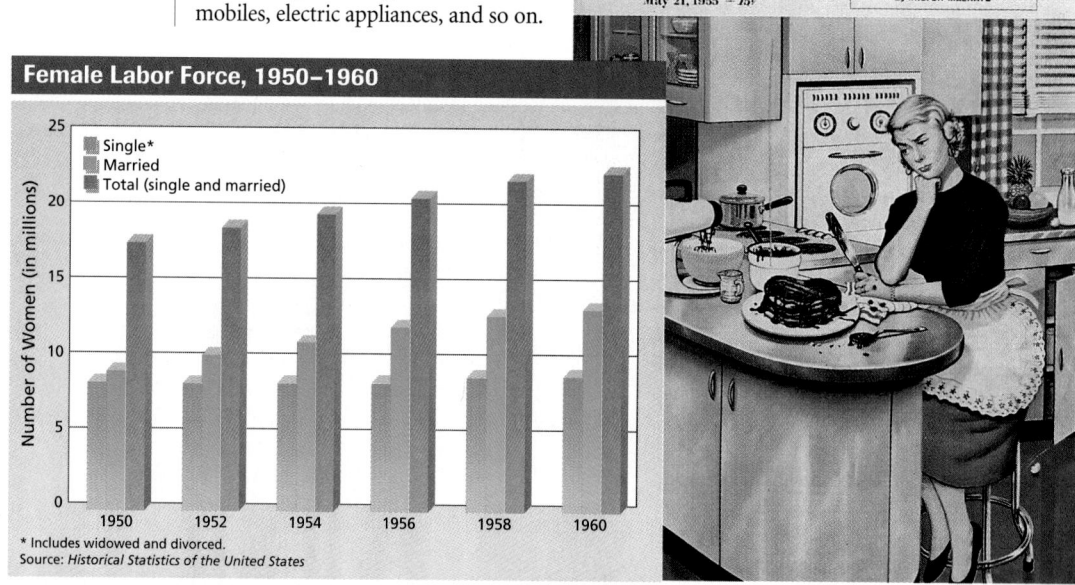

Female Labor Force, 1950–1960

* Includes widowed and divorced.
Source: *Historical Statistics of the United States*

Interpreting Graphs
As the *Post* cover (above right) suggests, women in the 1950s were encouraged to link their self-esteem to their success in the kitchen and home. *According to the graph, what was actually happening to American women during this period? How many women joined the work force between 1950 and 1960?*

▶ RESOURCE DIRECTORY

Teaching Resources

Critical Thinking Activity Determining Relevance: Wages, Hours, and Unions, found in the Unit 5 folder, p. 125, uses graphs of wages, working hours, and union membership in the United States between 1900 and 1960 to help students apply this skill.

Literature Activity Nonconformity in the 1950s, found in the Unit 5 folder, p. 131, features a passage from the novel *On the Road* by Jack Kerouac, the author whose work and life are often considered synonymous with the "Beat Generation" counterculture.

*unless it could be approached through
female experience as a wife or mother
or translated into domestic detail!*

Millions of women, Friedan charged, were frustrated with their roles in the 1950s.

MAKING CONNECTIONS

In what ways are women and men today pressured to conform to social standards?

Pockets of Nonconformity Appear

Occasional challenges to the rigid expectations of 1950s society did erupt. Holden Caulfield, the main figure in **J. D. Salinger's** 1951 novel *The Catcher in the Rye*, was troubled by the hypocrisy of the "phonies" he saw at boarding school and in the world at large. His effort to preserve his own integrity despite the fierce pressure to conform was an experience to which many readers could relate.

Members of the "Beat Generation," called **beatniks** by middle-class observers, launched a different kind of challenge. Beatniks, some of them writers, some artists, some simply participants in the movement, stressed spontaneity and spirituality instead of apathy and conformity. They challenged traditional patterns of respectability and shocked other Americans with their more open sexuality and their use of illegal drugs.

Author Jack Kerouac, the spiritual leader of the beatniks, gathered with others in coffee houses in San Francisco, California, where they shared ideas and experiences. The unconventional Kerouac typed his best-selling novel *On the Road*, published in 1957, on a 250-foot roll of paper. The novel's lack of standard punctuation and paragraph structure was meant to reflect an open approach to life.

Such challenges to conformity were not the norm. Most Americans were willing to seize the comfort offered by the postwar economy and preferred to live their lives in the relative safety of the suburbs. Many people pleased with this lifestyle eventually began to expect the government to ensure that the "good life" continued.

Viewpoints
On Rock-and-Roll Music

When the defiant beat of rock and roll burst onto the American scene in the mid-1950s, few people remained impartial about its sound or its impact. **What does each viewpoint below say about the relationship between rock music and delinquency?**

Against Rock and Roll

"Rock 'n' roll . . . is sung, played and written for the most part by [mentally deficient] goons and by means of its almost imbecilic repetition and sly, lewd, in plain fact, dirty lyrics . . . it manages to be the [warlike] music of every sideburned delinquent on the face of the earth."
  Singer Frank Sinatra, The *New York Times*, January 12, 1958

For Rock and Roll

"If my kids are home at night listening to my radio program, and get interested enough to go out and buy records and have a collection to listen to and dance to, I think I'm fighting delinquency."
  Radio disc jockey Alan Freed, The *New York Times*, January 12, 1958

---

4. Men were supposed to acquire an education, hold a good job, and concern themselves with politics, economics, and social policy; women were supposed to remain in the home to serve as wives, mothers, and housekeepers.

5. Both the beatniks of the 1950s and the rebellious middle-class youth of the 1920s rejected the values of their respective parents' generations, used illegal drugs (alcohol in the 1920s; marijuana and others in the 1950s), and expressed their sexuality more openly than the older generation did.

Answer to . . .

Viewpoints

Frank Sinatra implies that only delinquent people are attracted to rock music, because it is repetitive and dirty. Alan Freed maintains that the music gives kids something wholesome to do and keeps them out of trouble. For a more thorough examination of the impact of rock-and-roll music, see the Resource Directory below.

Answer to . . .

MAKING CONNECTIONS

Students may mention pressures to be successful at school or work, to make a lot of money, to dress a certain way, to have a certain body type, and so on.

Reteach

Have students create an editorial cartoon about the 1950s, focusing on the need and desire to conform or on the challenges to conformity posed by beatniks.

SECTION 2 REVIEW

Key Terms, People, and Places
1. Define beatniks.
2. Identify (a) Benjamin Spock, (b) Betty Friedan, (c) J. D. Salinger.

Key Concepts
3. In what aspects of American life was conformity most visible during the period between 1945 and 1960?

4. What social and economic roles were men and women expected to play in the 1950s?

Critical Thinking
5. **Making Comparisons** In what ways was the "Beat Generation" of the 1950s similar to or different from the rebellious youth of the 1920s?

Viewpoints Activity On Rock and Roll, found in the Unit 5 folder, pp. 122–123, provides a basis for discussion of censorship of free speech and artistic expression.

Quiz found in the Unit 5 folder, p. 111, covers the main ideas in this section as well as the key terms.

Media and Technology

Transparency
Critical Thinking, I-4

4. CLOSE

Reinforcing the Big Idea

Middle-class Americans prized comfort and security in the 1950s, and most also valued conformity. The next section focuses on the attempts of government to maintain prosperity and security.

The Suburban Explosion

Focus Before the postwar building boom, only the wealthy could afford to live in the suburbs, although many Americans longed to escape life in dingy city apartments and crowded houses. After the war, prosperity and government programs to finance mortgages started a suburban building spree that changed the way many Americans lived.

Instruct Using an overhead projector, show students a fairly detailed map of the nearest large city and its surrounding suburbs. Ask students to point out the core city, beltways, and "edge cities" near suburban shopping malls.

Ask students to list ways in which the development of suburban housing changed American life. Ask them to consider each of the following aspects:
• The family: How did suburban housing encourage nuclear, as opposed to extended, families?
• The environment: What impact did the growth of suburbs have on wildlife, quality of air and water, amount of farmland, and so on?
• Integration: Did the growth of suburbs encourage or discourage integration of housing and schools?

Extend Many observers thought that the suburban shopping mall would become the "community center" of the suburbs, filling the roles of Main Street, the town common, the city square, and the neighborhood playground. Ask students how successful they think shopping malls have been in creating a sense of community. What activities other than shopping, such as eating meals or snacks, taking an exercise class, or going to a movie, are available in shopping malls?

The Suburban Explosion

After World War II, American cities rapidly expanded outward as people moved into suburbs that first housed them and then became major centers for shopping, working, and recreation. What factors contributed to this suburban explosion?

Both nature and people can change a place. Changes in the landscape, such as those caused by a hurricane or drought, often are dramatic. The changes that people make in the environment can be just as striking. At no time in United States history were these changes more evident than in the decades following World War II.

Movement: Railroads and Streetcars Lead to Suburban Growth

The largest cities in the United States in the 1700s were commercial centers situated at key waterfront locations. This was because goods and people could move much more rapidly and easily on water than over land. Workplaces in these cities were clustered near the waterfront, while residences crowded nearby, so working people could walk between their homes and jobs.

These compact, circular-shaped cities began to expand when railroads first cut paths outward from the centers. In the decades before and after the Civil War, small residential communities sprouted around railroad stations that were situated six or more miles from the central cities, as the map of Newport in 1775 shows. These small communities provided quiet, pastoral settings for those with sufficient money to afford daily rail trips to and from their jobs in the city.

Even more urban residents could consider moving away from the city centers after the late 1880s, when electric-powered streetcar lines reached into the surrounding countryside. Many of the newer dwellings accessible by streetcar were larger than city homes and sat in the middle of pleasant yards. By World War I, some of the larger cities extended out as far as ten miles from their centers, where most people still worked and shopped. Because streetcar lines did not extend as far in some directions as in others, the overall shape of the cities were star-like, shown in the map of Detroit in 1920.

Population Growth, Automobiles, and Highways Continue the Trend

The Great Depression and World War II required most Americans to defer their desire for new, larger houses in pleasant settings. Once the war ended, however, millions of people returned to the nation's cities, where they married, produced children in record numbers, and searched for bigger homes. Available housing within cities filled quickly, but the automobiles that many veterans purchased permitted them to consider locations outside cities. The GI Bill made money readily available for housing. The result was construction at a rate unprecedented in the nation's history. Between 1947 and 1965, at least 1.25 million new houses were built each year, with more than one half of those units in the expanding suburbs.

In the first decade after the war ended, the number of automobiles owned by city dwellers increased dramatically. In 1956 the federal government established an interstate highway system to connect

After the nation's first enclosed, climate-controlled shopping center opened in 1956, the suburban mall became the new mecca for American consumers.

▶ RESOURCE DIRECTORY

Teaching Resources

Time and Place Activity Edge Cities, found in the Unit 5 folder, pp. 118–119, focuses on the "third wave" of the suburban explosion, when job opportunities followed retail businesses and residential developments out of the center cities, creating altogether new—and different—cities.

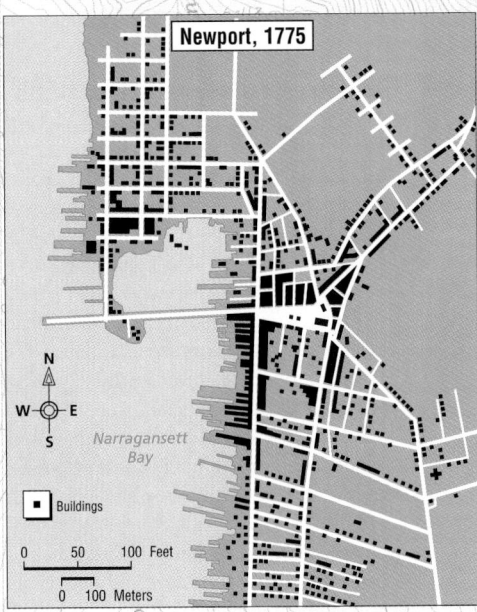

Newport, 1775

Narragansett Bay

N W E S

■ Buildings

0   50   100 Feet
0   100 Meters

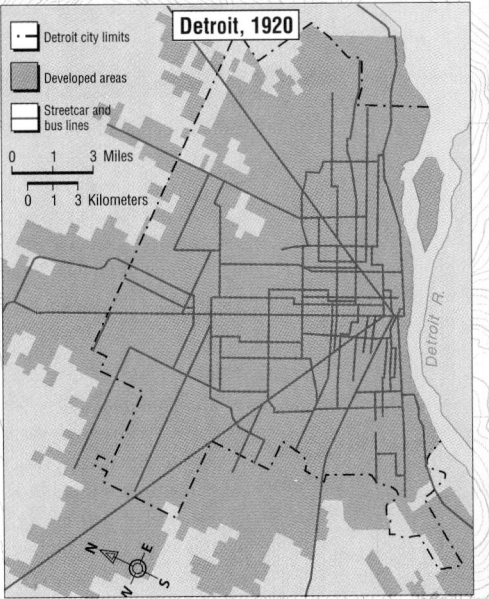

Detroit, 1920

- - - Detroit city limits
         Developed areas
         Streetcar and
         bus lines

0   1   3 Miles
0   1   3 Kilometers

N W E S

Detroit R.

major cities. In addition to highways radiating out from city centers, engineers constructed "beltways" that circled cities at distances ranging from six to twenty miles from the core. The result was a dramatic reshaping of metropolitan areas.

Stores and Jobs Follow

As suburban neighborhoods grew, traveling to stores in the city center was no longer convenient. Store owners soon recognized this and built new establishments in suburban locations. Starting in the early 1950s, groups of stores began to cluster together in shopping centers surrounded by large parking lots. After the nation's first enclosed, climate-controlled shopping center opened in 1956, the suburban mall became the new mecca for American consumers.

A major reason for the success of suburban shopping malls was their easy access from freeways. Such locations also were recognized as ideal sites for offices, factories, service providers, and many other forms of economic activity. These businesses grouped themselves in dozens of low buildings straddling heavily traveled freeways and streets and formed what journalist Joel Garreau has called "edge cities."

The growth of edge cities was not without its difficulties. As suburbs became more densely settled, they began to experience the same pollution, crime, and other problems formerly associated with central cities. Of greatest concern to the people who worked, shopped, and lived in edge cities was the increasing traffic congestion. The easy access that attracted so many people to the suburbs was becoming a distant memory. Urban observers today wonder what new forms of transportation will evolve to move people and goods more quickly and easily—and how those new forms once again will transform the geography of American cities.

GEOGRAPHIC CONNECTIONS

1. Why did the earliest large cities develop in waterfront locations?
2. What factors contributed to the boom in suburban housing construction after World War II?

Critical Thinking

3. **Predicting Consequences** Many cities have considered banning cars from downtown streets. How would this affect both cities and suburbs?

Answers

1. Major cities were located on waterways because people and goods could be moved more quickly and easily over water than they could over land.

2. After the war millions of military personnel returned to the nation's cities, married, had families, and looked for housing. The shortage of urban housing, the availability of government-guaranteed bank loans, and the increased availability of automobiles allowed people to buy new, larger homes farther from the cities where they worked.

3. A ban on automobile transportation would force many more suburban commuters to use public transportation such as buses and trains and would probably mean that fewer people would be willing to commute into the city to work. More businesses might relocate to the suburbs as a result, thus contributing to the further growth and problems of "edge cities." The decreased congestion and pollution in the city cores, however, might make them more attractive for shoppers, city residents, and tourists.

SECTION 3

Domestic Politics and Policy

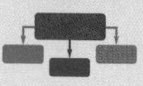
**Connecting to
the Big Idea**

See page 588B. Presidents Truman and Eisenhower presented Americans with different approaches to government and to the challenges facing the postwar nation. Ask students in what ways Eisenhower and Truman disagreed about the proper role of government and the way to solve the nation's social problems.

Objectives

● Identify Truman's main task as President as converting the nation to a peacetime economy.
● Describe Truman's Fair Deal as a continuation of the principles of the New Deal.
● Describe Eisenhower's modern Republicanism.

Bellringer

Ask students to think of someone in a leadership position whom they admire, for example, a teacher, school administrator, coach, or member of the clergy. Ask students to describe that person's leadership style and explain why they think it is effective.

Reading Strategy

Problem Solving Ask students to imagine that they must evaluate Presidents Truman and Eisenhower for their administrations' handling of domestic affairs. As they read, students should note positive and negative points about the administration of each President. Have students write a brief analysis of both Presidents and use it to give each a grade. Students should give specific reasons for the grades.

SECTION PREVIEW

The postwar period created many challenges for American leaders—including the conversion back to a peacetime economy and the debate over the proper role of government in the nation's economic and social affairs. Presidents Harry Truman and Dwight Eisenhower used two very different styles of leadership to meet these challenges.

Key Concepts

• Truman's main task as President was converting a powerful wartime economy to peacetime production.
  • Truman wanted to advance the principles of the New Deal through his own Fair Deal.
  • In 1952 Americans favored Dwight Eisenhower's modern republicanism, which encouraged expansion without destroying the economic and social programs of the 1930s.

Key Terms, People, and Places

Taft-Hartley Act, modern republicanism, *Sputnik*; Adlai Stevenson, Richard M. Nixon

Enthusiastic Eisenhower supporters during the 1952 election campaign could add this colorful scarf to their wardrobe.

I n the postwar years, political events reflected the economic and social patterns of the country. Middle-class Americans, who grew more numerous all the time, pressured the government to help maintain the nation's newly won prosperity. Democrat Harry S Truman first struggled with the problems of reconversion to a peacetime economy, then fought for a reform program blocked repeatedly by Congress. Republican Dwight D. Eisenhower took a more low-key approach to the presidency. His genial, reassuring manner made him one of the most popular Presidents in the years following World War II.

Reconversion and the Fair Deal

Harry Truman wanted to follow in Franklin Roosevelt's footsteps, but he often appeared ill-prepared for the presidency. He seemed to have a scattershot approach to governing, offering a different batch of new proposals in every speech. People wondered where his focus lay.

Truman's first priority was reconversion—the social and economic transition from wartime to peacetime. Soldiers wanted to return home, and politicians were flooded with messages that warned, "No boats, no votes." Truman responded quickly and got most soldiers home by 1946.

Lifting the economic controls that had kept wartime inflation in check proved a more difficult challenge. Americans had done without thousands of consumer goods during World War II. Now they wanted those goods, and they wanted them right away. The government eased the controls, and prices soared, in the words of one political cartoonist, "over the moon!" Since wages failed to keep up with prices, many people still could not enjoy the fruits of their years of sacrifice.

Meanwhile, angry workers demanded wage increases that they had forgone for the sake of the war effort. In 1946, 4.6 million workers went on strike, more than ever before in the United States. Strikes hit the automobile, steel, electrical, coal, and railroad industries and affected nearly everyone in the country. ✪

Though Truman agreed that workers deserved high wages, he thought that their demands were inflationary—that is, he believed that such increases would push the prices of goods still higher. In his view, workers failed to understand that big wage increases might destroy the health of the economy.

Angry at the disruptions, Truman threatened to draft some striking workers and order them as soldiers to stay on the job. Truman's White House took other steps as well. When

---

▶ RESOURCE DIRECTORY

Teaching Resources

📁 **Reproducible Lesson Plan** found in the Unit 5 folder, p. 106, provides a summary of the Section 3 lesson plan content.

📁 **Alternate Lesson Plan: Critical Thinking** Drawing Conclusions, found in the Alternate Lesson Plans folder, p. 139, provides a structure for students to analyze the Truman and Eisenhower administrations.

📁 **Guided Reading and Review** found in Unit 5 folder, p. 112, provides a structure for reading and mastering the key concepts and reviewing the key terms for Section 3. (Guided Practice)

✪ 📁 **Visual Learning Activity** Auto Strike, 1950, found in the Unit 5 folder, p. 132, uses a photograph of United Auto Workers members preparing for a strike to illustrate the continuing rift between workers and management.

John L. Lewis and his United Mine Workers defied a court order against a strike, the Truman administration asked a judge to serve Lewis with a contempt of court citation. The court fined Lewis $10,000 and his union $3.5 million.

Congress went even further than Truman. In 1947 it passed the **Taft-Hartley Act.** This act allowed the President to declare an eighty-day cooling-off period, during which strikers in industries that affected the national interest had to return to work while the government conducted a study of the situation. Reflecting the widespread anticommunist paranoia gripping the United States at the time, the measure also required union officials to sign noncommunist oaths. Furious union leaders complained bitterly about the measure, and Truman vetoed it. Congress passed the act over Truman's veto.

MAKING CONNECTIONS

Why might Congress have been especially concerned about possible communist ties among union officials?

Truman's Fair Deal Truman had supported Roosevelt's New Deal, and now, playing on the well-known name, he devised a program he called the Fair Deal. The Fair Deal extended the New Deal's goals.

Truman agreed with FDR that government needed to play an active role in securing economic justice for all American citizens. As the war ended, he introduced a twenty-one point program that included legislation designed to promote full employment, a higher minimum wage, greater unemployment compensation for workers without jobs, housing assistance, and a variety of other items. Over the next ten weeks, Truman added more proposals. By early 1946 he had asked for a national health insurance program and legislation to control atomic energy.

In attempting to promote his program, Truman ran into tremendous political opposition. A coalition of conservative Democrats and Republicans opposed him at every turn.

As the 1946 midterm elections approached, Truman seemed little more than another bungling bureaucrat. Some people commented,

"You just sort of forget about Harry until he makes another mistake." Others adapted a well-known saying: "To err is Truman." Truman's support in one poll dropped from 87 percent just after he assumed the presidency to 32 percent in November 1946. In the 1946 elections, Republicans won majorities of both houses of Congress.

The 80th Congress battered the President for the next two years. Under the leadership of conservative Republican senator Robert A. Taft of Ohio, commonly known as "Mr. Republican," the Republican party did whatever it could to reduce the size and the power of the federal government, to decrease taxes, and to stymie Truman's liberal goals.

The Election of 1948 Truman decided to seek another term as President in 1948. He had no reason to expect victory, however, because even in his own party, his support was disintegrating. The southern wing of the Democratic party, protesting a moderate civil rights plank in the party platform, split off from the main party. These segregationists formed the States' Rights, or Dixiecrat, party and nominated

Some supporters of the Truman-Barkley ticket in 1948 attached this sign to their cars' license plates.

In 1948 Truman became the first President ever to campaign in Harlem. The button at left announced his commitment to the civil rights cause.

2. INSTRUCT

Explain/Discuss

Almost as quickly as the nation had mobilized for war, it needed to demobilize once the war was over. Discuss with students the tasks that needed to be accomplished to return the nation to a peacetime footing, including bringing the troops home; lifting wartime economic controls, such as price restrictions and rationing; controlling inflation; and finding jobs for returning troops whose jobs had been taken by women during the war. Ask students to assess how well Truman carried out each of these tasks and show how Truman was a New Dealer in his view of the appropriate role of government in American life. In which of his policies did Truman follow in the footsteps of Franklin Roosevelt?

Ask students to compare Eisenhower's view of government with Truman's. What other Presidents would have agreed with Eisenhower's policy of "modern republicanism"? Ask students to explain the significance of Eisenhower's willingness to accept the welfare programs of the New Deal.

Analyze

Ask students to compare the personalities of Truman and Eisenhower. Ask how Eisenhower's personality helped him win the election of 1952. Encourage students to use what they know about the 1950s to explain how Eisenhower's style fit the mood of the country at the time.

Answer to ...

MAKING CONNECTIONS

The demands and tactics of union leaders often went against the interests of big business. Their activities pointed out the failure of capitalism to meet the needs of workers, which may have been interpreted as a "communist" point of view.

Election Press Conference

Ask students to prepare for the role of either Stevenson or Eisenhower in a press conference during the election of 1952. Students should prepare to answer questions about their candidate's experience, record, goals, style, and view of government as part of the role-play.

Ask each student to write one question for the press conference and put it in a bowl or box. Choose random pairs of students to role-play the two candidates, and ask for volunteers to select and read the questions to them. Any student may object to an answer presented by one of the "candidates" and present an alternative answer; he or she then must take over as the "candidate" and continue answering new questions. Ask students to evaluate both answers in that event.

In Depth

Historical Misconceptions

Far from being a passive President, as was the common perception at the time, historians today argue that Dwight Eisenhower was an astute behind-the-scenes policymaker who only gave the appearance of not being involved. He kept Secretary of State John Foster Dulles in check and refused to intervene on the side of the French when they faced defeat in Vietnam. He once joked, when asked how he would answer questions about a delicate issue at a press conference, that he would simply confuse the audience if that issue arose. Ike's public style reflected later generations' perception of the 1950s—there was a lot more underneath than met the eye.

Governor J. Strom Thurmond of South Carolina for President.

Meanwhile, the left wing of the Democratic party deserted Truman to follow Henry Wallace, who had been Roosevelt's third Vice President. Many Democrats believed that Wallace was the right person to carry on the ideas begun by Franklin Roosevelt. Most recently Wallace had served as Truman's secretary of commerce. Wallace had resigned, however, because he did not support Truman's cold war policies.

Running against Republican Thomas E. Dewey, governor of New York, Truman crisscrossed the country by train, campaigning not so much against Dewey as against the Republican Congress, which the President repeatedly mocked as the "do-nothing" 80th Congress. Truman's campaign style was electrifying. In off-the-cuff speeches, he challenged all Americans: "If you send another Republican Congress to Washington, you're a bigger bunch of suckers than I think you are." "Give 'em hell, Harry," the people yelled as Truman got going. And he did. ●

Among other things, Truman vehemently attacked Congress's farm policy. In the past, a federal price-support program permitted farmers to borrow money to store surplus crops until someone bought the produce. Recently, however, Congress had failed to provide additional storage bins, just as a good harvest loomed on the horizon. Truman told the farmers:

The *Chicago Tribune* was so certain of Truman's defeat that it printed this edition before the final election results were tallied. Truman was delighted to see the headline proved wrong.

RESOURCE DIRECTORY

Teaching Resources

● **Primary Source Activity** Harry Truman: Off the Record, found in the Unit 5 folder, pp. 126–127, uses excerpts from the private papers of the former President to provide students with an additional perspective on the issues of that era.

The Republican Congress has already stuck a pitchfork in the farmers' backs. . . . When you have to sell your grain below the support price because you have no place to store it, you can thank this same Republican Congress.

On election day, although virtually all experts and polls picked Dewey to win, Truman scored an astounding upset. He now stepped out of FDR's shadow to claim the presidency in his own right, with a chance to push further for his liberal legislative goals. But over the next four years, the Fair Deal scored only occasional successes, and on balance was disappointing compared to the New Deal the decade before. Truman decided not to run for reelection in 1952. Instead, the Democrats chose **Adlai Stevenson,** governor of Illinois, as their presidential candidate.

Dwight Eisenhower and the Republican Approach

Running against Stevenson for the Republicans was Dwight Eisenhower. As a public figure, Eisenhower's approach to politics differed from Harry Truman's. Whereas Truman was a scrappy fighter, Ike—as the people affectionately called Eisenhower—had always been a talented diplomat. During World War II, Eisenhower forged agreements among Allied military commanders; now his easy-going charm gave Americans a sense of security.

By 1952, Americans across the land chanted, "I Like Ike." The Republicans used a "K_1C_2" formula for victory, which focused on the three problems of Korea, communism, and corruption. Eisenhower promised to end the Korean War, and the Republican party guaranteed a tough approach to the communist challenge. Eisenhower's vice-presidential running mate, Californian **Richard M. Nixon,** hammered on the topic of corruption in government.

The Checkers Speech In spite of his overwhelming popularity, Eisenhower's candidacy hit a snag in September 1952. Newspapers accused Richard Nixon of having a special fund, set up by rich Republican supporters.

"Secret Nixon Fund!" and "Secret Rich Man's Trust Fund Keeps Nixon in Style Beyond His Salary," screamed typical headlines. In fact, Nixon had done nothing wrong, but the accusation that he had received illegal gifts from political friends was hard to shake.

Soon, cries arose for Eisenhower to dump Nixon from the ticket. Eisenhower decided to allow Nixon to save himself, if he could. On September 23, Nixon went on television to explain the situation in his own words. With Ike joining a national audience, Nixon delivered one of the most memorable speeches in recent political history. He emotionally denied wrongful use of campaign funds. He gave a detailed account of his personal finances, including his $4,000 life insurance policy and the $38,500 debt on his house and other items. In response to the charge that he was living above his means, he described his wife, Pat, as wearing a "good old Republican cloth coat."

The emotional climax of the speech came when Nixon admitted that he had, in fact, received one gift from a political supporter:

I t was a little cocker spaniel dog. . . . Black and white spotted. And our little girl— Tricia, the six-year-old—named it Checkers. And you know the kids love that dog and I just want to say this right now, that regardless of what they say about it, we're going to keep it.

At the end of his speech, Nixon requested that the American people contact the Eisenhower campaign headquarters to register their opinions as to whether or not he should stay on the Republican ticket. The response was overwhelming. People from all across the nation called, wired, and wrote to Eisenhower, demanding that Nixon continue as his running mate. Nixon had turned a political disaster into a public relations bonanza.

In the election, Democratic candidate Adlai Stevenson never had a chance. Ike got 55 percent of the popular vote and swept into office with a Republican Congress as well.

Four years later, despite a number of serious illnesses during his first term in office, the American people wanted Ike back. Eisenhower won reelection—again over Stevenson—with almost 58 percent of the vote. After 1952, however, the Democrats regained control of Congress.

Modern Republicanism

In domestic matters, the President was determined to slow the growth of the federal government. He also wanted to limit the President's power and raise the legislature's and the courts' authority.

Ike's priorities included cutting spending, reducing taxes, and balancing the budget. He called this approach to government "dynamic conservatism" or **"modern republicanism."** He intended to be "conservative when it comes to money, liberal when it comes to human beings."

Ike's natural inclination was to work behind the scenes. One writer has described his style as the "hidden hand." "I am not one of those desk-pounding types that likes to stick out his jaw and look like he is bossing the show," Eisenhower said. Critics misinterpreted his apparent lack of leadership, joking about an Eisenhower doll— you wound it up and it did nothing for eight years. But the American people approved of Ike's style. Eisenhower defended his approach, declaring,

N ow, look, I happen to know a little about leadership. I've had to work with a lot of nations, for that matter, at odds with each other. And I tell you this: you do not lead by hitting people over the head. . . . I'll tell you what leadership is. It's persuasion—and conciliation—and education—and patience. It's long, slow tough work. That's the only kind of leadership I know or believe in—or will practice.

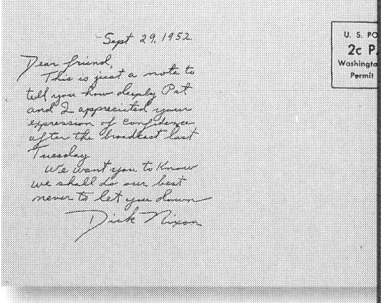

Using Historical Evidence Richard Nixon thanked the voters who had shown their support after his "Checkers" speech with this postcard. *What image of Nixon does the photograph promote?*

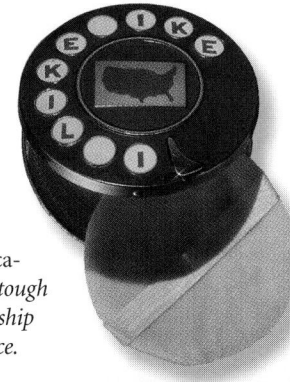

The "I Like Ike" message was seen everywhere in 1952, even on women's compacts.

In Depth

Biography

The period of history that this chapter covers has many truly heroic figures, but none more memorable than Thurgood Marshall. The great-grandson of a freed slave, Thoroughgood (he later changed the name to Thurgood) Marshall (1908–1993) spent more than twenty years challenging institutional racism as the NAACP's chief legal counsel. In 1967, President Johnson appointed Marshall the Supreme Court's first African American associate justice. Marshall maintained a staunchly liberal presence on what soon became an increasingly conservative Court. He opposed the death penalty and favored affirmative action and other remedies for discrimination. By the time he retired in 1991 he had become, in the words of one Harvard Law School professor, "the great dissenter . . . part of the conscience of the Court." (See Section 4.)

Section 3 Review Answers

1. (a) Taft-Hartley Act, see p. 603, (b) modern republicanism, see p. 605

2. (a) Adlai Stevenson, see p. 604, (b) Richard M. Nixon, see p. 604

3. Truman's main problem was releasing the American economy from wartime price controls, which created postwar inflation.

4. The Fair Deal included legislation designed to promote full employment, a higher minimum wage, greater unemployment compensation for workers without jobs, housing assistance, and a variety of other items. Truman later added other proposals: a national health insurance program and legislation to control atomic energy.

5. *Sputnik* was the first artificial satellite to orbit the earth. When the Soviet Union launched it in 1957, the United States awoke from its dream of scientific superiority with a rude shock and began taking steps to catch up with the Soviets in that area. Legislation provided incentives for people to become teachers and funds for schools to build science and foreign language facilities.

In Depth

Then and Now

Eisenhower's Atoms for Peace program was an attempt to ease cold war tensions by promoting the commercial uses of nuclear power. By the time Eisenhower left office in 1960, three nuclear power plants were operating in the United States with a total generating capacity of 350 megawatts. (A megawatt equals one million watts or 10,000 100-watt light bulbs.) In the 1990s, nuclear power is America's second-largest provider of electricity (after coal). Over ninety nuclear power plants, representing a total capacity of over 85,000 megawatts, supply 13 percent of the nation's electricity.

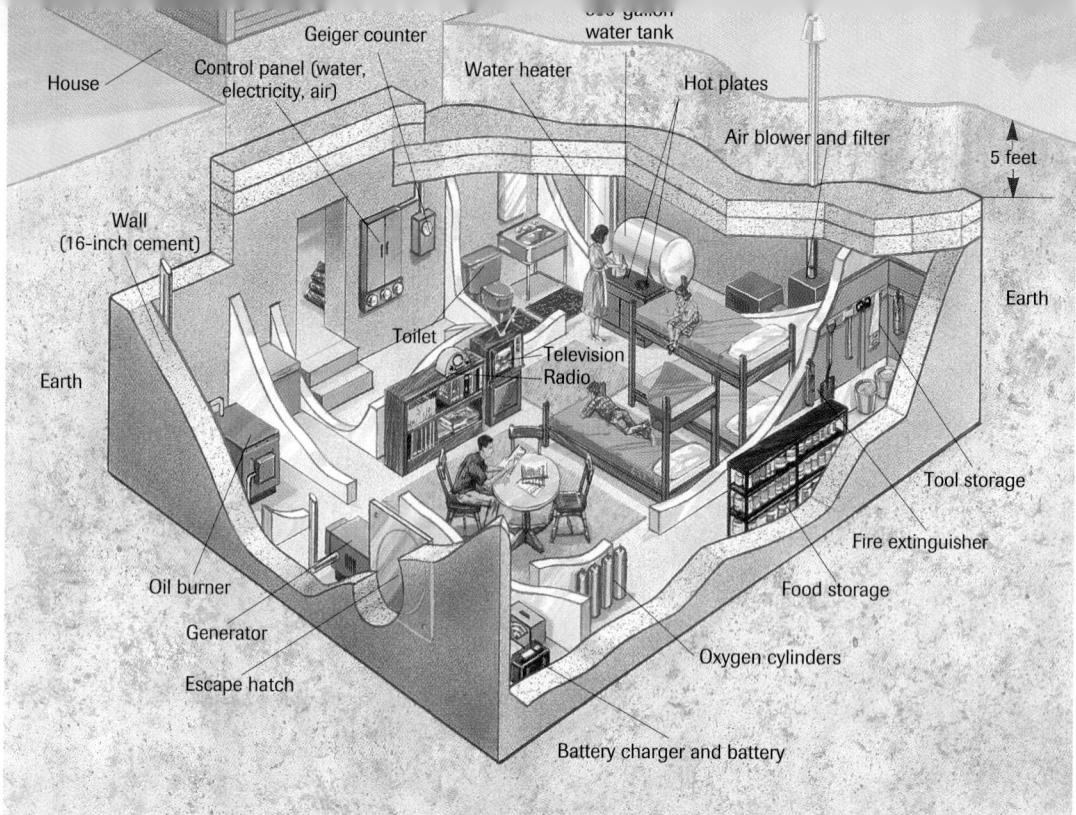

Sputnik sparked real fears of nuclear attack. Many Americans hoped they could survive a nuclear war in a basement fallout shelter. After an atomic explosion, radioactive particles attach themselves to dust in the atmosphere, which continues to rain down upon the earth for as long as two weeks. In the shelter shown above, an air filter protects people from breathing radioactive dust, and a Geiger counter tells them when the radioactivity outside has returned to a safe level.

In the tradition of past Republican Presidents such as Coolidge and Hoover, Eisenhower favored big business. His cabinet was composed mostly of successful businessmen, plus one union leader, which prompted critics to charge that the cabinet consisted of "eight millionaires and a plumber." For secretary of defense he chose Charles E. Wilson, former president of General Motors, who believed that "what was good for our country was good for General Motors, and vice versa."

Modern republicanism did everything possible to aid corporate America. It transferred control of about $40 billion worth of offshore oil lands from the federal government to the states so that the states could lease oil rights to corporations. The administration also tried to end government competition with big business. For example, Eisenhower sought to eliminate the Tennessee Valley Authority, the New Deal enterprise that provided electrical energy to the public at low cost. Though he failed, in this effort Ike revealed his preference for private power companies.

Ike's attempt to balance the budget backfired. His cuts in government spending caused the economy to slump. When that happened, tax revenues dropped, and the deficit grew larger instead of smaller. Economic growth, which had averaged 4.3 percent between 1947 and 1952, fell to 2.5 percent between 1953 and 1960. The country suffered three economic recessions during Eisenhower's presidency, from 1953 to 1954, from 1957 to 1958, and again from 1960 to 1961.

▶ RESOURCE DIRECTORY

Teaching Resources

Eisenhower's Achievements Despite economic troubles, Eisenhower helped maintain a mood of stability in America. He also underscored the basic commitment the government had made during the New Deal to ensure the economic security of all Americans. For example, in 1954 and 1956 Social Security was extended to make eligible 10 million additional workers. In 1955 the minimum wage was raised from 75 cents to one dollar an hour.

Sputnik* Shocks Americans** In 1957 the Soviet Union launched ***Sputnik, the first artificial satellite to orbit the earth. *Sputnik* sped around the world every 96 minutes at a rate of 18,000 miles per hour. The United States, which had viewed itself as the world's foremost scientific power, was mortified. Worse yet, the United States' own rocket, rushed to the launching pad before it was ready, rose only a foot before crashing to the ground.

Critics charged that the apparent stability and security of the United States was, in fact, only smugness and self-satisfaction. Perhaps the institutions most vulnerable to critics' attacks were the nation's schools. Americans questioned whether their children were learning to read, write, and calculate well enough to succeed in an increasingly competitive world.

Another fear prompted by *Sputnik* was the possibility of nuclear attack. The Soviet rocket that launched the satellite might also be used to send a hydrogen bomb to American shores. In one response to anxiety about a nuclear attack, millions of Americans constructed bomb shelters in their basements. The art on page 606 shows a typical bomb shelter of the 1950s.

Less than a year after the launching of *Sputnik* shredded Americans' confidence, Congress passed and President Eisenhower signed into law the National Defense Education Act of 1958. The act provided millions of dollars in low-cost loans to college students and significant reductions in repayments if they ultimately became teachers. The federal government also granted millions to state schools for building science and foreign language facilities.

Besides the jolt to their confidence caused by *Sputnik,* Americans had other reasons to doubt the health of the nation in the postwar years. Some people began to wonder whether the inequalities in American society might be just as dangerous to the United States as threats from foreign nations. The people still liked Ike, but deep troubles were becoming more and more visible.

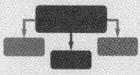

The blow that *Sputnik* delivered to American self-assurance is reflected in this "Space Race" card game from the 1950s, in which those dealt the *Sputnik* card would lose two turns.

SECTION 3 REVIEW

Key Terms, People, and Places
1. Define (a) Taft-Hartley Act, (b) modern republicanism.
2. Identify (a) Adlai Stevenson, (b) Richard M. Nixon.

Key Concepts
3. What problem did Harry Truman face in reconverting the nation to a peacetime economy after World War II?

4. What were some of the goals of Harry Truman's Fair Deal program?
5. What was *Sputnik,* and what impact did it have in the United States?

Critical Thinking
6. **Recognizing Ideologies** How did Truman's and Eisenhower's approaches to the role of the federal government in solving domestic problems differ?

 Quiz found in the Unit 5 folder, p. 113, covers the main ideas in this section as well as the key terms.

Media and Technology

Transparency
The Way It Works, H-20

---

6. Truman believed in an active, positive role for the federal government in social and economic matters; Eisenhower wanted to curb the role of the federal government in these matters.

Reteach

Write the following sentences on the chalkboard and ask students to decide which of them apply to President Truman and which to President Eisenhower.
● He stood by his running mate in 1952 despite accusations that the vice-presidential candidate had accepted illegal gifts.
● His victory in 1948 was a surprise to experts and pollsters.
● He failed to get his social program through Congress.
● He thought government should aid business.
● Although he wanted to reduce the size of government, he accepted FDR's welfare state.

◆ Alternative Assessment

Mid-Point Monitoring
Ask students if they have
● Decided on a format for their projects
● Begun their outside research
● Started drafting portions of their projects

4. CLOSE

Reinforcing the Big Idea

The Presidents of the 1950s, Truman and Eisenhower, differed greatly in style and political philosophy. The next section presents material on the growth of a great social movement that grew during both of their administrations—the civil rights movement.

SECTION 4

The Continuing Struggle for Equality

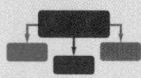

Connecting to the Big Idea

See page 588B. The civil rights movement took on a new momentum in the years following World War II. Ask what methods Americans used in the struggle to attain racial justice.

Objectives

● Describe the changes in American society that led African Americans to demand more equality between the races.
● Identify the methods used by African Americans to wage their battle for racial justice.
● Explain how other minority groups began to follow the example of the African American movement for equality.

Bellringer

Ask students to consider the role of sports in American life. Ask if sports stars should be considered heroes. Is there a difference between a "star" and a "hero"? What qualities does a "hero" possess? Ask students who their heroes are. Why?

Reading Strategy

Reading for Evidence Note with students the opening sentence on page 608: "The events of World War II . . . breathed new life into the civil rights movement." Ask students to look for evidence to support that statement and to describe the change as they read the section.

SECTION PREVIEW

The events of World War II—including the fight against fascism abroad and the African American migration at home—breathed new life into the civil rights movement. The actions of many courageous Americans brought significant results in the postwar years.

Key Concepts

• World War II caused changes in American society that led African Americans to demand more equality between the races.
• African Americans used the courts and a protest movement to wage their battle for racial justice.
• Other minorities began to follow the example set by the African American movement.

Key Terms, People, and Places

termination policy; Jackie Robinson, Thurgood Marshall, Martin Luther King, Jr.

The NAACP was one organization devoted to fighting racial injustice in the United States. In the South, African Americans had to use separate facilities at all public places.

B efore and during World War II, African Americans were not treated as equals by a large portion of American society. After the war, however, the campaign for civil rights began to accelerate. Thousands of African Americans had served their country during the war and felt this service was a mockery if they were not allowed equal rights in their own country. Hundreds of thousands had moved to northern cities during the war and experienced a new sense of freedom there, in spite of poor living conditions. Millions more simply believed that the time had come to demand that the nation live up to its creed that all are equal before the law.

President Truman, while holding in private many of the racial prejudices he had learned growing up in the South, recognized that as President he had to take action. In 1948 he wrote in a letter to a friend,

---

I am not asking for social equality, because no such things exist, but I am asking for equality of opportunity for all human beings, and, as long as I stay [in the White House], I am going to continue that fight.

In July 1948 Truman banned discrimination in the hiring of federal employees. He also ordered an end to segregation and discrimination in the armed forces. Real change came slowly, however. Only with the onset of the Korean War in 1950 did the armed forces make significant progress in ending segregation.

AMERICAN PROFILES

Jackie Robinson

The battle against racial segregation was taken up not only in the military but on the professional baseball diamond as well. For years, major league baseball had banned African Americans, forcing them to play in the separate Negro Leagues. In 1946 Branch Rickey, general manager of the Brooklyn Dodgers, decided to challenge the ban. (See "History Might Not Have Happened This Way," page 612.)

Rickey selected **Jackie Robinson** (1919–1972) to be the first African American to break the color line. Robinson had grown up in Pasadena, California, and attended the University of California in Los Angeles. In college Robinson earned letters in football, basketball, baseball, and track and was also a superb golfer, swimmer, and tennis player.

Robinson had a record of standing up against racial injustice. While he was in the army during World War II, a bus driver had snarled at him, "Get in the back where you belong or there'll be trouble." Robinson knew that buses on the army post were not segregated, so he stood his ground. Although he had not broken any rules, Robinson had to undergo a court-martial before clearing his name.

RESOURCE DIRECTORY

Teaching Resources

Reproducible Lesson Plan found in the Unit 5 folder, p. 107, provides a summary of the Section 4 lesson plan content.

Alternate Lesson Plan: Cooperative Learning found in the Alternate Lesson Plans folder, p. 140, provides a strategy for groups of students to identify contributions of African Americans to the postwar struggle for racial equality.

Guided Reading and Review found in the Unit 5 folder, p. 114, provides a structure for reading and mastering the key concepts and reviewing the key terms for Section 4. (Guided Practice)

After his brilliant first season with the Brooklyn Dodgers, Jackie Robinson was featured in baseball magazines such as the one above, issued in 1951.

The mental toughness that Robinson acquired from such experiences and his ability to rise above the injustices he encountered served him well during his baseball career. He faced prejudice from fans, opponents on the field, and even his own teammates. Robinson later recalled his first interview with Branch Rickey:

I am a normal man with the feelings of any normal man. If anything, my competitive instincts are so sharp that I will eagerly challenge any man who challenges me. But Mr. Rickey made entirely clear to me that day that I could not behave normally. . . . On my ability to measure up to the challenge would depend not only my future but the future of my race in baseball.

Despite many instances of prejudice, Robinson behaved with dignity and had a sparkling first season. He was Rookie of the Year in 1947 and kept improving with time. Just as important, Robinson fostered pride in African Americans around the country and opened the way for other African Americans to follow him into professional sports.

MAKING CONNECTIONS

In the 1990s Charles Barkley, an African American professional basketball player, insisted, "I am not a role model!" How might the American public have reacted if Jackie Robinson had made that statement in 1947?

Brown v. Board of Education

Beginning in the 1930s, the National Association for the Advancement of Colored People, NAACP, launched a series of court cases aimed at overturning the 1896 *Plessy* v. *Ferguson* Supreme Court decision. *Plessy* v. *Ferguson* held that segregation of the races in public institutions and accommodations was constitutional as long as facilities were "separate but equal."

In 1951 Oliver Brown sued the Topeka, Kansas, Board of Education to allow his eight-year-old daughter Linda to attend a school that only white children were allowed to attend. She passed the school on her way to the bus that took her to a distant school for African Americans. After appeals, the case reached the Supreme

Linda Brown (inset) was at the center of the landmark *Brown* v. *Board of Education* case. African American students like Elizabeth Echford of Little Rock, Arkansas, (below) still had to endure the insults of white students who disagreed with the Court's decision.

Answer to ...

MAKING CONNECTIONS

Because Robinson was the first African American in the major leagues, he was under constant scrutiny, especially from those who disapproved of the integration of baseball. If he had not been willing to lead a "model" life, his critics would have had more ammunition against him.

2. INSTRUCT

Explain/Discuss

Compare with students the Supreme Court's rulings in the 1896 *Plessy* v. *Ferguson* and the 1954 *Brown* v. *Board of Education* decisions. Ask students why the Supreme Court sometimes reverses its own decisions. How do social factors affect the way the Supreme Court decides a case?

Discuss with students why African Americans in Montgomery chose to boycott the bus system. Ask what sacrifices African Americans had to make to maintain the boycott. What did African Americans gain by the bus boycott?

Discuss why the civil rights movement spread to other minority groups. Ask students to think of the factors that might have motivated other groups to follow the lead of African Americans in the 1950s.

Analyze

Analyze President Eisenhower's role in the school integration of Little Rock. Why did Eisenhower try to avoid action? What presidential role was he taking when he federalized the Arkansas National Guard? What other actions might Eisenhower have taken?

Activity

Teaching Heterogeneous Groups

Beginning in the 1930s the NAACP took action by bringing a series of court cases aimed at overturning the 1896 Supreme Court decision that segregation in public institutions was constitutional as long as facilities were "separate but equal." To illustrate the inherent unfairness of this decision, divide students into small groups. Have each group design, justify, and implement a "separate but equal" seating chart for the classroom. For example, students might segregate the classroom according to clothing color. Have students who were segregated tell how they felt in that role. **LEP**

Enrichment

Martin Luther King, Jr., was one of the nation's great orators and writers. Ask students to assemble a collection of quotations from King's speeches and writings. Students should arrange their quotes by date or theme, preparing their collections in pamphlet form.

Caption Answer to ...

Using Historical Evidence

It showed that groups could peacefully force change by straining an institution's pocketbook.

3. ASSESS

Section 4 Review Answers

1. termination policy, see p. 611

2. (a) Jackie Robinson, see p. 608,
(b) Thurgood Marshall, see p. 610,
(c) Martin Luther King, Jr., see p. 610

3. (a) Thousands of African Americans had served their country during World War II and felt they had earned the right to equality. Hundreds of thousands now living in northern cities experienced a new sense of freedom. (b) Marches and boycotts.

Court. There a brilliant African American lawyer named **Thurgood Marshall** argued on behalf of Brown and against segregation in America's schools.

On May 17, 1954, in *Brown* v. *Board of Education of Topeka, Kansas,* the Supreme Court issued its ruling. It declared unanimously that "separate facilities are inherently unequal." The "separate but equal" doctrine was no longer permissible in public education. President Eisenhower, who privately disagreed with the *Brown* ruling, refused to take a stand, saying only that "the Supreme Court has spoken and I am sworn to uphold the constitutional processes in this country; I will obey." A year later, the Court ruled that local school boards should move to desegregate "with all deliberate speed."

The ruling in *Brown* v. *Board of Education* caused fear and angry resistance in many southern whites. The worst confrontation came at Central High School in Little Rock, Arkansas. Just before the start of the 1957 school year, Governor Orval Faubus declared that he could not keep order if integration occurred. He posted the Arkansas National Guard at the school, and guardsmen turned away nine African American students who tried to enter.

Eisenhower could no longer avoid the issue of segregation. Faubus's actions were a direct challenge to the Constitution and to his own authority as President. Eisenhower therefore placed the National Guard under federal command. With paratroopers and other soldiers on guard in Arkansas to protect the nine African American children, the long, slow process of school integration began. ✪

The Montgomery Bus Boycott

In December 1955, in Montgomery, Alabama, Rosa Parks, a seamstress who had been secretary of the Montgomery NAACP for twelve years, took a seat in the middle section of a bus, where both African Americans and whites usually were allowed to sit. When a white man got on at the next stop and had no seat, however, the bus driver ordered Parks to give up hers. She refused. Even when threatened with arrest, she held her ground. At the next stop, police seized her and ordered her to stand trial for violating the segregation laws.

African American civil rights officials in Montgomery made the most of the incident. Fifty African American leaders met and, after Jo Ann Robinson of the Women's Political Council (WPC) suggested the idea, decided to organize a boycott of the entire bus system. Robinson and other members of the WPC wrote and distributed leaflets announcing the boycott. **Martin Luther King, Jr.,** the twenty-six-year-old minister of the Baptist church where the original boycott meeting took place, eventually became the spokesperson for the protest movement. He proclaimed:

> There comes a time when people get tired . . . tired of being segregated and humiliated, tired of being kicked about by the brutal feet of oppression. We have no alternative but to protest.

Using Historical Evidence These participants in the Montgomery bus boycott seemed not to mind getting a little wet as they walked to work. *How did the boycott demonstrate the effectiveness of applying economic pressure to promote social change?*

▶ RESOURCE DIRECTORY ✪

Teaching Resources

✪ **Primary Source Activity** Enforcing *Brown* v. *Board of Education,* found in the Unit 5 folder, p. 128, uses excerpts from an Eisenhower press conference in 1957 to illustrate the federal government's role in enforcing the integration of public schools in the South.

✪ **American Profiles Activity** Maria Latigo Hernandez and Pedro Hernandez, found in the Unit 5 folder, p. 121, profiles two Mexican immigrants who sought relief in the United States from Mexico's famine and chaos in the early twentieth century.

The morning of the first day of the boycott, King prowled the streets of Montgomery anxiously to see how many African Americans would participate. Here are excerpts from his account of that morning:

*D*uring the rush hours the sidewalks were crowded with laborers and domestic workers, many of them well past middle age, trudging patiently to their jobs and home again, sometimes as much as twelve miles. They knew why they walked, and the knowledge was evident in the way they carried themselves. And as I watched them I knew that there is nothing more majestic than the determined courage of individuals willing to suffer and sacrifice for their freedom and dignity.

Over the next year, fifty thousand African Americans in Montgomery walked, rode bicycles, or joined car pools to avoid the city buses. Despite losing money, the bus company refused to change its policies. Finally, the Supreme Court ruled that bus segregation, like school segregation, was unconstitutional.

The Montgomery bus boycott produced a new generation of leaders in the African American community, particularly Martin Luther King, Jr. In addition, it introduced nonviolent protest as a means of achieving equality for minority groups in the United States.

Other Voices of Protest

⭐ Mexican Americans also demanded equal rights after World War II. A court case in Texas involving a funeral home that refused to bury a

Mexican American war casualty led to the soldier's burial in Arlington National Cemetery in Washington, D.C. Groups like the Community Service Organization and the Asociación Nacional México-Americana found that peaceful protest could slowly bring about some of the results Mexican Americans desired.

Native Americans faced discrimination unique to their situation. The federal government managed the reservations where most Native Americans lived. In 1953, however, the government adopted a new approach, known as "termination," which sought to eliminate Native American reservations altogether. The administration used its **termination policy** to promote assimilation of Native Americans into the mainstream of American life.

Such assimilation did more harm than good. A 1954 Seminole petition to President Eisenhower eloquently stated the Native Americans' pride in their heritage:

*W*e are not White Men but Indians, do not wish to become White Men but wish to remain Indians, and have an outlook on all things different from the outlook of the White Man.

In time the federal government discarded the termination policy. Yet the problems of the Native Americans remained: poverty, discrimination, and little real political representation. For Native Americans, the civil rights advances of the 1950s were mere tokens of the real gains that were needed.

This young protester was part of a 1958 Tuscarora picket in New York. The Native Americans were attempting to block a state power project on their reservation.

4. The main principle underlying the decision was that there can be no such thing as "separate but equal"; segregated facilities are by definition not equal.

5. Mexican American groups used peaceful protest to demand equal rights. Native Americans protested the federal government's termination policy, which threatened to destroy their culture, and eventually the policy was abandoned.

6. Eisenhower believed it was his duty as President to uphold constitutional processes, including enforcement of Supreme Court decisions. The Court had ordered integration of public schools, but Faubus used his state's resources to block the Court's ruling. Eisenhower was therefore forced to respond to Faubus's challenge.

Reteach

Ask students to use the information in the section to correct each of these following incorrect statements.
● The civil rights movement slowed after World War II.
● In *Brown* v. *Board of Education* the Supreme Court ruled that separate schools for African Americans were constitutional.
● The Montgomery bus boycott introduced Jackie Robinson as a new leader of the civil rights movement.
● The purpose of the termination policy of the federal government was to end the demands of Native Americans for advances in civil rights.

4. CLOSE

 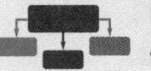

Reinforcing the Big Idea

The civil rights movement accelerated quickly following World War II. African Americans worked for their rights through the courts and on the streets in nonviolent protests, and other minority groups also began to demand equal rights.

SECTION 4 REVIEW

Key Terms, People, and Places
1. Define termination policy.
2. Identify (a) Jackie Robinson, (b) Thurgood Marshall, (c) Martin Luther King, Jr.

Key Concepts
3. (a) For what reasons did the civil rights movement accelerate after World War II? (b) What avenues of protest did civil rights activists use in their struggle?

4. What was the principle behind the Supreme Court's ruling in *Brown* v. *Board of Education?*
5. How did Mexican Americans and Native Americans assert their rights in the 1950s?

Critical Thinking
6. **Determining Relevance** Why did Eisenhower feel bound to respond to the use of the National Guard to prevent school integration in Little Rock?

 Quiz found in the Unit 5 folder, p. 115, covers the main ideas in this section as well as the key terms.

 Chapter Test Forms A and B are found in the Unit 5 folder, pp. 134–139.

 Answer Keys found in the Unit 5 folder, pp. 146–158, provide answers to all student activities.

Media and Technology

Transparency
Graphic Organizer, G-2

Guided Reading Audiotapes
(English and Spanish)

Computer Test Bank

The Decision to Integrate Major League Baseball

Focus Branch Rickey's decision to hire Jackie Robinson for the Brooklyn Dodgers, integrating major league baseball, preceded the great civil rights struggles of the 1950s and 1960s. However, as the English believed that "The battle of Waterloo was won on the playing fields of Eton," so some part of the civil rights struggle was won on the ball diamonds, courts, and fields of this nation.

Robinson signed with the Dodgers in 1945. In 1946 he played with the Montreal Royals, a Dodgers' farm team, against the New York Giants. It was the Giants' first game since the end of the war. Robinson grounded out his first time at bat. His second time up, he hit a home run over the left-field fence.

Instruct Ask students to review Rickey's options, to integrate or not, and to speculate about the results of each option in both the long and short term.

Ask students to list the circumstances that came together to make Rickey's decision possible, starting with Rickey himself. (*Rickey's motivation to integrate big league baseball, his ability to hire Robinson, Robinson's spectacular ability, willingness to sign on, and ability to withstand abuse.*)

Extend Ask students to find out when other sports were integrated, including professional football, basketball, and the United States Davis Cup tennis team. Have students examine issues of racial barriers today, including the lack of African American football coaches, sport executives, and team owners.

The Decision to Integrate Major League Baseball

Time Frame	1945
Place	New York City
Key People	Branch Rickey, general manager of the Brooklyn Dodgers baseball team, and Jackie Robinson, an African American athlete
Situation	Branch Rickey wanted to hire the first African American baseball player in the major leagues and prove that integration was possible. His decision could further African American civil rights in sports and other areas.

Unbelievable as it may seem today, in 1945 African American baseball players were not allowed to play in the major leagues. Many people at the time were beginning to fight for African American civil rights, and the situation in professional baseball attracted their attention. African Americans pointed with pride to athletes like Joe Louis, who was the world heavyweight boxing champion, and Jesse Owens, who won an unprecedented four gold medals in track and field in the 1936 Olympic games. Civil rights activists wanted to see the integration of baseball as well. Branch Rickey, the general manager of the Brooklyn Dodgers, recognized the possibilities integration offered to baseball. Jackie Robinson, a spectacular African American athlete from California, was the man Rickey identified as he considered his options. Rickey began to wonder whether the time had come to end segregation in baseball. As he considered the sensitive issue of integration, Rickey could have chosen any one of several possible avenues.

To Integrate or Not, and If So, How?

One possible avenue Rickey could have chosen was to drop the idea of integrating the major leagues altogether. Although baseball commissioner Kenesaw Mountain Landis declared in 1942 that "There is no rule, formal or informal, or any understanding—unwritten, subterranean, or sub-anything—against the hiring of Negro players by the teams of organized ball," baseball remained rigidly segregated. Most owners and other leaders of the game wanted to keep it that way. Many white Americans agreed.

Another option was to try to enlist the support of other teams before attempting to hire an African American player. Rather than working alone, Rickey knew that persuading other important baseball figures of the merits of opening the major leagues to African Americans would make it more likely that integration would succeed.

A third option was to find a superb African American athlete, such as Robinson, who could endure the taunts and jeers he was certain to receive when he took the field, and to work with him to show other teams—and American society as a whole—that integrated baseball could work.

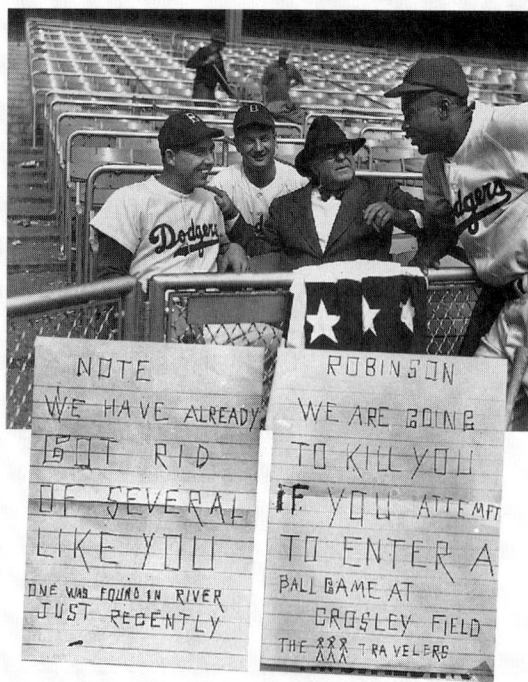

RESOURCE DIRECTORY

Teaching Resources

History Might Not . . . Activity
Decision Making: Integrating the University of Georgia, found in the Unit 5 folder, pp. 116–117, provides students an opportunity to role-play decision makers and those who influenced them in the decision of Charlayne Hunter and Hamilton Holmes to push for admittance to, and thus integration of, the University of Georgia.

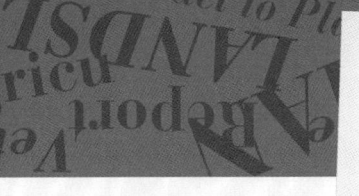

Possible Repercussions

Rickey knew that the safest course was to leave the situation alone and abandon the idea of integration. Major league baseball was prospering, and many people were reluctant to rock the boat. African American players had their own Negro Leagues, such people reasoned, so they had a chance to play. Taking no action was the best way to ensure stability on the field.

Seeking support from other teams, Rickey believed, would backfire. Baseball commissioner Landis and other top officials already had derailed the efforts of Bill Veeck, Jr., the bold young son of the former president of the Chicago Cubs, to buy the Philadelphia Phillies and hire black players. The more people who were involved, the more likely any integration plan was to fail.

Rickey also realized that the final option, simply hiring Jackie Robinson, might well erupt in violence both on and off the field. White ballplayers might refuse to play with Robinson. Fans might stay away from the game. Robinson himself might be hurt.

Rickey's Decision

Rickey decided that he would take what was in some ways the riskiest option: he would hire Jackie Robinson to play for the Brooklyn Dodgers.

Rickey called Robinson into his office on August 28, 1945 and told the ballplayer of his plan. Then, in a calculated move to test how Robinson would respond to the pressure he was likely to face, Rickey acted the part of those who might try to discourage him. He roared insults at Robinson, abused him, and threatened him with violence. "Mr. Rickey," Robinson finally said, "do you want a ballplayer who's afraid to fight back?" Rickey answered, "I want a player with guts enough not to fight back."

Rickey's decision paid off. Robinson played first for the Montreal Royals, a minor league team, then joined the Brooklyn Dodgers to become the first African Ameri-

Goal	To integrate major league baseball		
Possible Actions	Do nothing and hope integration would eventually take place	Enlist the support of other baseball teams	Hire an African American player
Possible Results	• Continue the tradition of segregated baseball, as integration was not likely to occur without some major impetus	• Unlikely to succeed in integrating the major leagues, because strong resistance to integration existed in the baseball community	• Might convince baseball leaders and society in general that integration could work, but might lead to violence both on and off the field

can to play in the major leagues. The photograph at left shows Rickey, seated and wearing a suit, and Robinson (far right). At first, he did have to endure much abuse, including threatening letters like the one on page 612. Robinson's wife, Rachel, worried about him:

> At the end of his first season in baseball, I became extremely worried about Jack. I knew nobody could go along day after day, week after week, month after month bottling up his emotion. . . . He couldn't eat, and at night he'd toss constantly in his sleep. . . . But Jack wouldn't give it up.

Robinson's bravery and Branch Rickey's willingness to take a chance paved the way for future African American baseball players.

EVALUATING DECISIONS

1. Why did Branch Rickey choose not to work with other teams in bringing African Americans into major league baseball?
2. What did Rickey want Jackie Robinson to do when taunted by other players and fans?

Critical Thinking

3. **Predicting Consequences** What do you think Rickey hoped would happen if Jackie Robinson proved to be a success? What might have happened if he had failed?

Media and Technology

Visions of America: History Might Not Have Happened This Way Game
To encourage students to explore pivotal moments in United States history, have students use the Visions of America software. Refer to the Visions of America Teacher's Guidebook for viewing objectives, activities, game instructions, and discussion questions.

Answers

1. Because baseball commissioner Landis and other top officials already had derailed efforts to hire black players. The more people who were involved, Rickey believed, the more likely any integration plan was to fail since strong resistance to integration existed in the baseball community.

2. Rickey wanted Robinson to "turn the other cheek," or practice nonresistance.

3. Rickey probably hoped that Robinson's success would lead to the entrance of many other black athletes into professional baseball and other sports and that this change would eventually lead to more equality for African Americans in society in general. If he failed, the negativity of the situation might drag the African American civil rights movement backward.

Understanding Key Terms, People, and Places

Terms
Students should refer to the definitions of key terms in the chapter to create sentences which show an understanding of their relation to the postwar years in the United States.

True or False
1. false, termination policy
2. false, franchises
3. true
4. false, real purchasing power
5. false, modern republicanism

Matching
1. Thurgood Marshall
2. Adlai Stevenson
3. Richard M. Nixon
4. William J. Levitt
5. Betty Friedan

Reviewing Main Ideas

1. After the war, people who had put their money into savings were eager to buy everything that the war and the Depression had denied them. In addition, new technological advances spurred the economy.

2. After the war, giant corporations organized themselves into diversified conglomerates. In addition, franchises began to flourish.

3. The work force shifted from a blue-collar to a white-collar majority. This change occurred because machines now did the work once done by people; thus fewer people were needed to produce goods and instead performed services.

4. The middle class generally valued comfort, security, and conformity.

5. *Life* magazine produced a special edition featuring a happy housewife. Benjamin Spock advised mothers to remain home with their children. Adlai Stevenson told female college students that their "assignment" was to care for children and to cook.

6. Beatniks challenged traditional patterns of respectability. Authors J. D. Salinger and Jack Kerouac wrote novels whose themes challenged 1950s conformity.

7. Truman's first priority was to accomplish the transition from wartime to peacetime by bringing soldiers home from abroad and lifting controls on the economy.

8. Truman was concerned about controlling inflation, and he believed that wage increases demanded by workers would inflate the prices of consumer goods.

Chapter Review

Understanding Key Terms, People, and Places

Key Terms
1. per capita income
2. real purchasing power
3. diversified conglomerate
4. franchise
5. agribusiness
6. baby boom
7. GI Bill
8. beatniks
9. Taft-Hartley Act
10. modern republicanism
11. *Sputnik*
12. termination policy

People
13. William J. Levitt
14. Benjamin Spock
15. Betty Friedan
16. J. D. Salinger
17. Adlai Stevenson
18. Richard M. Nixon
19. Jackie Robinson
20. Thurgood Marshall
21. Martin Luther King, Jr.

Terms For each term above, write a sentence that explains its relation to the postwar years in the United States.

True or False Determine whether each statement is true or false. If it is true, write "true." If it is false, change the underlined term to make the statement true.
1. The <u>Taft-Hartley Act</u> sought to eliminate Native American reservations.
2. Ray Kroc started the first <u>diversified conglomerate</u>.
3. The launching of <u>*Sputnik*</u> embarrassed the United States, which viewed itself as the world's greatest scientific power.
4. <u>Per capita income</u>, what people actually could buy with their money, grew by about 22 percent in the postwar period.
5. President Eisenhower called his approach to government <u>agribusiness</u>.

Matching Review the key people listed above. If you are not sure of a person's significance, review his or her importance in the chapter. Then choose a name from the list that best matches each description below.
1. African American lawyer who argued on the side of Oliver Brown in *Brown* v. *Board of Education*
2. Democratic candidate for President in 1952 and 1956
3. accused of receiving illegal gifts from political friends
4. pioneered mass-production techniques in home building
5. author of a book that criticized society for limiting the roles of women

Reviewing Main Ideas

Section 1 (pp. 590–594)
1. Why did the United States economy grow so rapidly after World War II?
2. What changes occurred in American business after the war?
3. What changes took place in the work force after World War II? What accounts for this change?

Section 2 (pp. 596–599)
4. What values did middle-class Americans cherish most during the 1950s?
5. Give examples showing how the media fostered expectations about the proper role of women.
6. What challenges to the rigid expectations of the period arose during the 1950s?

Section 3 (pp. 602–607)
7. What was President Truman's first priority after World War II?
8. Why did Truman oppose the demand of labor for higher wages?
9. What were Eisenhower's goals for the presidency? How successful was he in achieving these goals?

Section 4 (pp. 608–611)
10. What steps did President Truman take that helped African Americans achieve racial justice?
11. How did African Americans use the courts and nonviolent protest in their battle for equality?
12. Why did Native Americans protest against the federal government's termination policy in the 1950s?

---

9. Eisenhower wanted to cut spending, reduce taxes, and balance the budget. He was largely unsuccessful in achieving these goals, because his cuts in government spending caused the economy to slump.

10. Truman banned discrimination in the hiring of federal employees and ordered an end to segregation and discrimination in the military.

11. The NAACP launched a series of court cases that culminated in the Supreme Court's *Brown* v. *Board of Education* decision overturning the "separate but equal" doctrine. African Americans also successfully used nonviolent protest in the Montgomery bus boycott.

12. The federal government's termination policy promoted the assimilation of Native Americans and in the process undermined their tribal society.

Thinking Critically

1. Answers will vary. Students may point out that television has been blamed for such problems as obesity, violence, and consumerism; computers have become ordinary elements of daily life, changing the nature of work and recreation; and atomic weapons have altered whole generations' outlooks on the future.

2. Positive effects include a higher standard of living for more people. Negative effects include materialism and preoccupation with wealth.

Thinking Critically

1. **Demonstrating Reasoned Judgment** Which technological advance of the 1950s—atomic energy, computers, or television—do you think has had the most far-reaching impact on the way Americans live? Explain why you think so.

2. **Drawing Conclusions** During the 1950s the United States became, in the words of economist John Kenneth Galbraith, "the affluent society." What might be some of the consequences, both positive and negative, of this abundance?

3. **Making Comparisons** During the 1990s many politicians, religious leaders, and ordinary citizens have called for a return to "family values." What do these family values have in common with the values of the 1950s?

4. **Predicting Consequences** In 1957, the launch of the Soviet satellite *Sputnik* jolted Americans' sense of stability and security. Do you think that a major scientific breakthrough by another nation would have the same effect today?

Making Connections

1. **Evaluating Primary Sources** Review the primary source excerpt on page 611. What assumptions did the federal government make when it created the termination policy to promote Native American assimilation into mainstream American culture?

2. **Understanding the Visuals** Examine the visuals on pages 590, 593, and 594 and describe how the issues represented may have contributed to the dilemma faced by women in the 1950s.

3. **Writing About the Chapter** You have read that in 1956, *Life* magazine published a photo essay titled "Busy Wife's Achievements" about a happy full-time mother of four. Write the text for a *Life* magazine photo essay about a working mother's life in the 1990s. First make a list describing some of the activities in a typical working mother's day, noting her job, number of chil-

dren, and responsibilities. Next, write a draft of your essay in which you describe the typical working mother today, including her achievements and the challenges she faces. Revise your essay, making certain that each idea is clearly explained. Proofread your essay and draft a final copy. If you wish, you may include ideas for photos and captions to accompany the text.

4. **Using the Graphic Organizer** This graphic organizer uses a double web to compare and contrast the presidencies of Harry Truman and Dwight Eisenhower. (a) Based on the information in the web, how were Truman and Eisenhower similar as Presidents? (b) How does the web contrast Truman's personality with Eisenhower's? (c) Create your own graphic organizer comparing and contrasting the concerns of men and women in the 1950s.

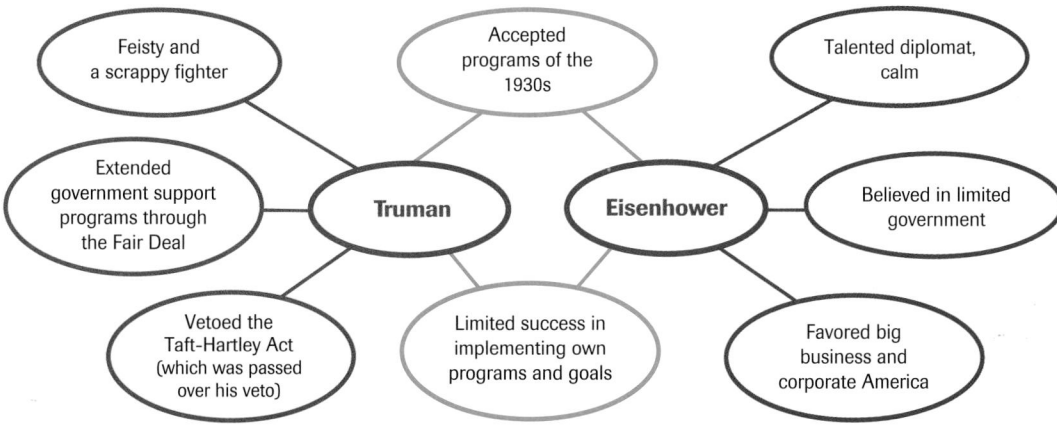

Feisty and a scrappy fighter

Accepted programs of the 1930s

Talented diplomat, calm

Extended government support programs through the Fair Deal

Truman

Eisenhower

Believed in limited government

Vetoed the Taft-Hartley Act (which was passed over his veto)

Limited success in implementing own programs and goals

Favored big business and corporate America

Alternative Assessment

Final Evaluation

Use the following guidelines to evaluate student projects:

● **Evidence of mastery of content** To what extent do the projects demonstrate knowledge and understanding of chapter content?

● **Evidence of thoughtfulness** To what extent do the projects present a personal assessment of the period with evidence to support it?

● **Evidence of outside research** To what extent are the projects based on materials and information from outside research materials?

● **Communication style** Do the projects convey a purpose in a clear appealing way?

---

4. (a) Both embraced the programs of the 1930s but had some difficulty implementing their own programs. (b) Whereas Truman was a scrappy fighter in the political arena, Eisenhower was diplomatic and affable. (c) Students' graphic organizers should indicate that men and women shared the values of home and family and the acquisition of material goods, although their roles were very different.

---

3. "Family values" share with some 1950s values the notion that women should stay at home as full-time mothers, emphasizing the well-being of children and the importance of religion.

4. Answers will vary. Students may point out that since the end of the cold war has opened the global marketplace for ideas and technology, a major scientific breakthrough by another country today would not only be less devastating than *Sputnik,* it would probably be a positive development.

Making Connections

1. The federal government assumed that Native Americans wanted to give up their culture and be like "white men."

2. The images depict suburban houses and an increasing birth rate, representing home and family, which women were supposed to consider their sole domain, even though many had held jobs during the war; increased consumer spending also presented women with a dilemma, since without a job they could not make money of their own.

3. Students' essays should show an awareness of the complexity and stresses of the lives of many women today as they struggle to balance work and family responsibilities.

Ask students to tell by a show of hands how many of them ate at a fast-food restaurant in the last month. Chances are that nearly every student will raise his or her hand. Tell students that the idea of fast-food restaurants was created by Dick and Maurice McDonald, and that they will read about how the brothers developed their idea in the first source reading.

INSTRUCT

Tell students that some events have obvious connections to one another, such as the connection between the Triangle Shirtwaist fire in 1911 and the subsequent enactment of stricter worker safety laws. Some seemingly unrelated events, upon closer inspection, are connected as well. Explain to students that before the fast-food restaurant was invented, people visited drive-in restaurants, where carhops waited on customers who remained in their cars. Discuss with students how the rise of the drive-in restaurant might have been connected to Henry Ford's assembly line.

Ask students to recall how two events described in the second excerpt were related: the proliferation of bomb shelters and the Soviet launching of *Sputnik*.

CHAPTER 18

SOURCE
READINGS

The Origin of McDonald's  *Literature*

David Halberstam

INTRODUCTION Mass production and later, the franchise, marked the McDonald brothers as groundbreakers in the food-service industry. In addition, the brothers created a part of the national identity that will forever be associated with the end of the "good old days" and the beginning of the new fast-paced, hectic rush of life in the United States. In the excerpt below from his book, *The Fifties*, journalist

David Halberstam tells the story behind the origin of McDonald's and the McDonald brothers' uncommon success.

VOCABULARY Before you read the selection, find the meaning of these words in a dictionary: periphery, collateral, carhop, impediment, venerable, tryst, deluge.

Two brothers, who, in the beginning, failed at almost everything they did, were among the first to understand that the fundamental changes taking place in American society concerning where people lived and worked would also affect how they ate. It was then that the luck of Dick and Maurice (Mac) McDonald took a startling turn for the better. The McDonald brothers moved to California from their native New Hampshire in 1930, driven by the grim economy that had forced textile and shoe factories to close throughout the Northeast. . . . They had never liked working for large companies and had often talked of running a place of their own. They had good reason to distrust big companies: their father, Pat McDonald, had worked in a shoe factory in Manchester, New Hampshire, for forty-two years in an age when there were no pensions or vacations. In his last year he was called in by his boss and told, "Pat, I think you've outlived your usefulness to us. We think we've had your best years. I'm afraid we don't need you here anymore."

At the height of the Depression, the brothers opened a small movie theater, but it quickly went bust. As far as they could tell, the only business making money at the time was a nearby hot-dog stand run by a man named Walker Wiley. So in 1937 they opened a stand near the Santa Anita racetrack; they

did well from the start, but when the racing season ended, business would dry up.

Finally, Mac McDonald decided they should build a bigger place in San Bernardino, a growing blue-collar city of perhaps 100,000 people. "We weren't going to sell to the country club set," noted Dick McDonald. The problem was financing: It was going to take $7,500, they estimated. They approached various banks, only to be asked again and again how much collateral they had. Collateral? thought Dick McDonald. All we have is our smiles. Finally, in desperation, they went to the one they were sure would turn them down, because it was so big: the Bank of America. Unlike the others, S.P. Bagley, the manager, listened carefully and asked them to come back in a week so that he could take their proposal to the bank's finance committee. A week later they nervously reappeared. The finance committee, he reported, was far from enthusiastic, "but sometimes I like to play a hunch, and I have a hunch that McDonald's is going to make it and make it big," he said. "I can't give you the full $7,500, but what about a loan of $5,000?" So it was in 1940 they opened a small drive-in restaurant in San Bernardino.

Somewhat to their own surprise, they were an immediate hit and were soon making a profit of

$40,000 a year. Their customers came in two varieties, they decided: teenage boys, with their first patched-up used cars, who liked the place as a hangout to flirt with the cute carhops, and young families, in which sometimes both parents worked, who ate there because it was

The McDonald's restaurant chain of today traces its origin to the first fast-food restaurant, opened by the McDonald brothers in 1940. The sign at the original restaurant appears above.

relatively fast and cheap. Obviously, the brothers wanted to encourage the second group and discourage the first.

The McDonalds figured they needed even greater speed. On the average, customers had to wait some twenty minutes for their food. "My God, the carhops were slow," remembered Dick McDonald. "We'd say to ourselves there had to be a faster way. The cars were jamming up the lot. Customers weren't demanding it, but our intuition told us they would like speed. Everything was moving faster. The supermarkets and dime stores had already converted to self-service, and it was obvious the future of drive-ins was self-service."

The McDonalds had understood an important new trend in American life: Americans were becoming ever more mobile and living farther from their workplaces than ever before. As they commuted considerable distances, they had less time and always seemed to be in a rush. Life in America was surging ahead and one of the main casualties was old-fashioned personal service. Their customers wanted to eat quickly.

Therefore, the brothers began to look for the weaknesses in their operation that caused the delays. Obviously, the carhops would have to go, but to their surprise the McDonalds discovered another impediment to faster service as well: Their menu was surprisingly large, including hamburgers, hot dogs, barbecue, and all manner of sandwiches. However, when the McDonalds checked their receipts, they found that 80 percent of their sales consisted of hamburgers. "The

more we hammered away at the barbecue business, the more hamburgers we sold," Dick McDonald said later. So they decided to get rid of the labor-intensive barbecue and sandwiches and narrow the menu to the venerable American hamburger. That would allow them to mechanize the food-preparation process as well. . . .

Suddenly, the McDonalds found themselves blossoming as brilliant innovators in the one thing they knew: fast food. In the fall of 1948 they closed down for several months, fired all their carhops, and began to reinvent the process. They replaced their small three-foot cast-iron grill with two stainless steel six-footers; the new grills were custom-designed, and the stainless steel was not only easier to clean, it held the heat better (if they had put too many hamburgers on the cast-iron grill, it lost heat). They replaced the plates and silverware, which had a tendency to disappear anyway, with paper bags, wrappers, and paper cups. That eliminated the need for the dishwasher. They cut the menu from twenty-five items to nine, featuring hamburgers and cheeseburgers, and they made the burgers a little smaller—ten hamburgers from one pound of meat instead of eight. The McDonalds, rather than their customers, chose the condiments: ketchup, mustard, onions, and two pickles (condiment stations had always been an eyesore, as far as they were concerned—slopped ketchup was everywhere). . . .

Under the new system, if a customer wanted something different on his hamburger, he faced a major delay in service. The McDonalds believed choices meant delays and chaos. After some experimentation—regular heat lamps had failed—they figured out that they could keep the hamburgers hot with infrared lights. "Our whole concept was based on speed, lower prices, and volume," Dick McDonald

SOURCE READINGS

said. In front of the drive-in they erected a sign with a chef whose name was Speedy. McDONALD'S FAMOUS HAMBURGERS, said the sign. BUY 'EM BY THE BAG. And larger than the letters of the name was the price: 15 cents.

To the McDonalds' surprise, business fell off at first. Deprived of their trysting spot, some of the old carhops and teenage boys came back and heckled them. For a time the McDonalds had to tell employees to park their cars in the parking lot so that it would look like they always had a few customers. But as the McDonalds added milkshakes and french fries, they began to be more successful than ever. By 1950, the teenagers had departed to more tolerant hangouts and were replaced by working-class families, who, thanks to the McDonalds' low prices, could afford to feed their families restaurant meals for the first time. . . .

What the McDonald brothers were doing with food was, as John Love[1] pointed out, what Henry Ford had done to automobile manufacturing (and what Bill Levitt had done with housing): They turned their kitchen into an assembly line. Because they were pioneers, they had to invent much of their own kitchen equipment. In this they were greatly aided by Ed Toman, a local friend who had a small machine-tool shop and no previous experience in the world of food, save inventing a small device to grind orange peels for marmalade. His San Bernardino shop was primitive, with no air-conditioning; the heat seemed to overwhelm all but Toman. He helped design the lazy Susan (stainless steel, of course) on which to prepare two dozen hamburger buns with condiments; a larger, stronger stainless-steel spatula; and the one-squeeze stainless-steel pump that shot just the right amount of mustard or ketchup onto the burger and which, John Love noted, Toman failed to patent, thus costing him a chance to be a millionaire.

Inside the kitchen, everything was mechanized: There were three grill men, who did nothing but cook patties; two milkshake men; two french-fries men; two dressers (who wrapped the hamburgers); and out

[1] Love was the author of *McDonald's: Behind the Arches*, published in 1986.

After World War II, the concept of fast food appealed to Americans who were more mobile than ever before and looking for faster ways to enjoy a meal out.

front were three countermen, who took the orders. Much of the food was preassembled; the slack time between the rush hours was used to prepare food for the next onslaught.

Here was the perfect restaurant for a new America, and it was a smashing success. There were long lines at rush hour, and by 1951, the gross annual receipts were $227,000, some 40 percent higher than in the old premechanized days. By the mid-fifties, the brothers were sharing profits of $100,000 a year, a dazzling figure for men selling items that cost fifteen cents apiece. Soon all kinds of would-be competitors were studying them, trying to figure out how to repeat their formula for success.

THINKING ABOUT THE SELECTION

1. Why were the McDonald brothers distrustful of big corporations?
2. What did the McDonald brothers decide their customers wanted the most? On what facts did they base their decision?

Critical Thinking

3. **Predicting Consequences** The McDonalds did away with plates and silverware in favor of paper bags, wrappers, and paper cups. What public issue arose in subsequent years that revealed a problem with this decision? Could the McDonald brothers have foreseen this problem?

ANSWERS TO

Thinking About the Selection

1. Their father had been fired after forty-two years of service with a big company because he had "outlived [his] usefulness" to them.
2. They decided their customers wanted fast service. They based their decision on changes in American society at the time: supermarkets and other stores had begun to convert to self-service; everything was moving faster in general.

3. The issue of landfills becoming full and Americans producing an excessive amount of garbage arose in subsequent years. If the McDonald brothers had looked at the issue, they probably could have foreseen this problem, as their idea spread and more and more restaurants began doing the same thing. In addition, other packaging began to be disposable. However, at the time, there probably did not seem to be any reason to worry about how much garbage was being created.

A "Boom Baby" Describes Fifties Life

Primary Source

Steve McConnell

INTRODUCTION Steve McConnell, born in 1947 during the baby boom, started out in the city and then moved with his family to the suburbs. That was a common experience for many American families in the 1950s as were several others that McConnell remembers. Historian Studs Terkel interviewed McConnell in 1981 in Washington. Part of their conversation is reprinted here.

VOCABULARY Before you read the selection, find the meaning of these words in a dictionary: provisions, imminent.

I always had a sense that our generation was bigger and better than any that had come before. And probably bigger and better than any that would follow. Every time we turned around, something was happening that we felt we had control over. We had the feeling that somehow we were the chosen, we were gonna make the world right. We were gonna invent the better mousetrap.

Everybody was havin' a good time, hangin' out at the milkshake parlors and the drive-ins. We were all drivin' souped-up cars. We had the run of things. We carried that into college.

I was in the class of '65. With our sense of power, along came uncertainty. Lots of things were changing. We were faced with a war[2] that nobody really understood. We were a generation brought up not to think that war was a good thing. Something was going on that we didn't like. . . .

We had no sense of the Depression before World War Two. Parents talked about it, but it had no meaning. There was no sense of World War Two, either. It was distant. One reason the Vietnam War came home to us, it hit us directly, fast. . . .

We went throught the bomb-shelter era in the late fifties. I remember it as kind of fun. You could go into a shopping center and at the corner of the parking lot was one of these bomb shelters. Gee, that was neat. Mom, can't we get a bomb shelter in the back yard and store up? Get some great provisions, like campin' out? But there was that sense of nagging that maybe this was more than just fun. Nothing serious was imminent, but . . . there was talk. They'd sell 'em. It was a big marketing thing. They were selling bomb shelters like they were selling lawn mowers. There'd be big displays. Each company would have a little fancier one than the other. It was another consumer item. (Laughs.)

We had drills in school. The alarms would go off and you'd hit the floor and put your back to the windows and cover your head. You were mostly afraid of getting hit by glass. What most of us didn't realize was that that would be the least of our problems. (Laughs.)

Along came Sputnik in '57. That has brought the technology drive to our generation. There was this great push to get people trained in engineering. The thing, next to being an athlete, was to be an astronaut. That was hot stuff, cool.

---

2 McConnell is referring to the Vietnam War.

THINKING ABOUT THE SELECTION

1. What were schools preparing students for when they had drills?
2. When McConnell describes the drills they had in school, what does he mean when he says "What most of us didn't realize was that [the glass] would be the least of our problems"?

Critical Thinking

3. **Recognizing Cause and Effect** How were the underlying fears and concerns of the youth of the fifties related to the surge in the sales of bomb shelters and to Sputnik?

ANSWERS TO

Thinking About the Selection

1. They were preparing them for the possibility of a nuclear attack.

2. He was referring to the fallout that would accompany a nuclear attack, which would be much more dangerous than glass from breaking windows.

3. Their underlying fears and concerns were the possibility of war and nuclear attack. The fears were brought on by World War II and the dropping of atomic bombs on Hiroshima and Nagasaki. Such fears also prompted manufacturers to produce, and families to buy, bomb shelters in the event of a nuclear attack. The push to get people trained in engineering was in response to the fear that the Soviets were outdistancing the United States technologically. This fear was prompted by *Sputnik*.

The Upheaval of the Sixties
1960–1975

UNIT 6

The Upheaval of the Sixties
1960–1975

Introducing the Unit

Interpreting the Visual The 1960s and early 1970s were years of unrest and change. John F. Kennedy's inauguration as President marked the political shift of a new generation. His words on page 620 form a concise summary of the nation's mood over the next two decades. Many Americans, determined to reform the nation, worked to bring change quickly; other Americans resisted their efforts. The energy and confidence of the marchers in the photograph reprinted on pages 620–621 constitute an apt image for the spirit and determination of the civil rights movement, the first of the social struggles of the sixties.

John Lewis, one of the marchers at Selma, recalls his feelings in these words: "You didn't get tired, you really didn't get weary, you had to go. It was more than an ordinary march. . . . It was the sense of community moving there."

Ask students to think of a title for this photograph that appropriately conveys its mood and feeling.

Establishing Chronology Remind students that the previous chapter focused on the postwar years at home. This unit covers the tumultuous years from 1960 to 1975. From 1960 to 1968, a strong civil rights movement worked for equality at home, equality which the previous generation of African Americans had hoped to gain after their valiant participation in World War II. From 1960 to 1975, other movements for social change emerged. The Vietnam War defined these years by challenging the nation's military ability and by leading antiwar activists to challenge the nation's values.

"Today our concern must be with the future. For the world is changing. The old era is ending. The old ways will not do."
—John F. Kennedy, 1960

*W*hen John F. Kennedy became President in 1961, Americans sensed a new era was dawning. Buoyed by the promise of change, African Americans pushed hard to end a century of inequality. Inspired by the civil rights movement, women, Latinos, Native Americans, and others also pressed for equality. Although much progress was achieved in the sixties, the promise that began this turbulent decade was shattered by a series of assassinations, a wave of urban riots, and a controversial war in Southeast Asia.

 RESOURCE DIRECTORY

Teaching Resources

📄 **Local History Activity** "The Second Battle of Atlanta" and the Local Focus research topic suggestions, found in the Local History Resources folder, pp. 27–29, are designed to help students understand how history affects all lives.

⭐ **Themes in American History Posters** Wall-size, illustrated posters, found in the Teaching Resources package, illustrate the four unit themes.

📄 **Unit Test** Forms A and B are found in the Unit 6 folder, pp. 140–145.

Inspired by the righteousness of their cause, civil rights workers march toward a better future in this 1965 voter registration drive in Selma, Alabama.

Media and Technology

Visions of America: Scenes of an Era To introduce students to the main idea and events covered in this unit, play "Scenes of an Era: The Upheaval of the Sixties, 1960–1975" (length: 2.5 minutes). This selection can be located on side 4 of the videodiscs. This selection can also be located on videotape 5. Lesson plans for "Scenes of an Era" can be found in the Visions of America Teacher's Guidebook.

Using Multimedia Technology This folder contains instructional tools and strategies for using technology in the classroom.

Transparency Binder Contains full-color transparencies with lesson suggestions. From a large collection divided into twelve categories, specific transparencies are referenced throughout the chapters at appropriate points of use. For this unit, see American Photo, B-9; Our Multicultural Heritage, C-15; Fine Art, D-20; Links Across Time, J-9; and Political Cartoon, K-9.

Teachers may wish to discuss specific historical events in the context of historical themes. Here are four suggestions for Unit 6.

Reform Movements *People in the United States have frequently taken action in grass-roots movements to right perceived wrongs and to secure improvements in the quality of life.*

● African Americans used the courts and nonviolent protests to win reforms.
● The women's movement urged the end of all discrimination based on gender.

Environment *The geography and available resources of the continent have affected the actions of Americans. Similarly, the actions of Americans have affected the environment and physical landscape.*

● Rachel Carson's book *Silent Spring* spurred the modern environmental movement.
● The Environmental Protection Agency (EPA) was established by Congress to be the nation's watchdog against polluters.

American Culture *In every period of their history, Americans gave special expression to their views through art, literature, films, music, manners, and morals.*

● The 1950s saw the growth of suburbs and consumerism—the purchase of consumer goods to achieve success and status.
● The counterculture in the 1960s and early 1970s advanced new attitudes about personal relationships, drugs, and music.

The United States and the World *America's relationships with other countries have been influenced at different times by a sense of mission, by values, and by self-interest.*

● During the Cuban missile crisis, the world came closer than ever before to nuclear war.
● The United States became involved in Vietnam in an effort to contain communism, but soon became bogged down in a war that American citizens did not understand.

Chapter 19 The Kennedy and Johnson Years
1960–1968

📁 **Teaching Resources** (See Unit 6 Folder)

	Instruction	Enrichment
Section 1 **The New Frontier** (pp. 624–627)	Reproducible Lesson Plan, p. 3 Alternate Lesson Plan, p. 142 Guided Reading and Review, p. 6 Quiz, p. 7	Visual Learning Activity, Creating Images of the Candidates, p. 26 American Profiles Activity, Dr. Frances Kelsey, p. 14 Literature Activity, A Grieving Nation, pp. 23–24 Historian's Toolbox Activity, Exploring Oral History, p. 18
Section 2 **The Great Society** (pp. 629–633)	Reproducible Lesson Plan, p. 4 Alternate Lesson Plan, p. 143 Guided Reading and Review, p. 8 Quiz, p. 9	Primary Source Activity, President Johnson's Thanksgiving Address, p. 20 Critical Thinking Activity, Recognizing Cause and Effect, p. 19 Visual Learning Activity, The Job Corps, p. 27 Literature Activity, The Invisible Poor, p. 25 History Might Not . . . Activity, Building an International Manned Space Station, pp. 12–13
Section 3 **Foreign Policy in the 1960s** (pp. 636–643)	Reproducible Lesson Plan, p. 5 Alternate Lesson Plan, p. 144 Guided Reading and Review, p. 10 Quiz, p. 11 Chapter Test, Forms A & B, pp. 28–33	Primary Source Activity, Cuban Missile Crisis, pp. 21–22 American Profiles Activity, Robert F. Kennedy, p. 15 Viewpoints Activity, On the Cold War, pp. 16–17

📁 **Additional Chapter Resources**

Resource Organizer, p. 2
Alternate Lesson Plan, p. 141
Answer Keys, pp. 146–160

Bibliography

For the Teacher

Hodgson, Godfrey. *America in Our Time: From World War II to Nixon, What Happened and Why.* Vintage Books, 1976. (Includes the New Frontier, civil rights movement, and Vietnam.)

Miller, Merle. *Lyndon: An Oral Biography.* Ballantine, 1987. (Lyndon Johnson's presidency by people who knew him.)

Reeves, Richard. *President Kennedy: Profile of Power.* Simon & Schuster, 1993. (A study of Kennedy written thirty years after his death.)

White, Theodore H. *The Making of the President, 1960: A Narrative History of American Politics in Action.* Macmillan, 1988. (Comprehensive coverage of the 1960 presidential campaign of John F. Kennedy.)

Prentice Hall Literature Excerpts from *The American Experience,* 1994, "Contemporary Writers, 1946–Present."

The Big Idea for the chapter and how the main ideas in each section relate to the Big Idea are graphically displayed below. Comprehension of this chapter's Big Idea is critical to students' understanding of United States history and how we as a nation got where we are today.

Media and Technology

 Our Multicultural Heritage, C-3

 Critical Thinking, I-13

 Visions of America: History Might Not Have Happened This Way Game

 Graphic Organizer, G-4

 Guided Reading Audiotapes (English and Spanish)

 Computer Test Bank

For the Student

Brown, Claude. *Manchild in the Promised Land.* Macmillan, 1965. (Autobiography of an African American youth from poverty in Harlem to a law degree from Howard University.)

Kennedy, Robert F. *Thirteen Days.* Norton, 1971. (Gripping account of the Cuban missile crisis by the President's brother and closest adviser, who served as attorney general of the United States.)

Schlesinger, A. M., Jr. *A Thousand Days.* Houghton Mifflin, 1965. (The Kennedy presidency as viewed by members of the White House staff.)

CHAPTER 19

The contrast between the presidencies of John Kennedy and Lyndon Johnson is striking. While Kennedy articulated plans for domestic reform, few of his programs actually advanced through Congress, perhaps because he was preoccupied with foreign affairs. When Johnson took office after Kennedy's death, he used his legislative skills to push through Congress some of the most significant social programs in the nation's history.

SECTION 1

Young, energetic, and popular, President Kennedy proposed a New Frontier for the United States but was unable to move his program through Congress before his assassination.

SECTION 2

President Johnson hoped to create a "Great Society," and pushed an extraordinary number of social reform bills through Congress.

SECTION 3

Both Presidents Kennedy and Johnson continued to wage the cold war. Both Presidents reacted boldly to communist challenges, bringing the nation into serious confrontations and threatening world peace.

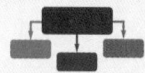

The Relevance of the Big Idea

For the baby-boom generation born right after World War II, the Kennedy style was full of youth, humor, and vigor. "For those who lived during his times," wrote journalist Richard Reeves, "Kennedy seemed to be the beginning of the new."

The promise of the new was actually fulfilled by Lyndon Johnson, who lacked Kennedy's appeal but had a style very much his own. A master builder of coalitions, he used these skills to pass some of the most lasting social legislation of this century—Medicare, the Voting Rights Act, the Civil Rights Act, Head Start, and many others.

Discuss with students the extent to which the Great Society legislation affects their lives.

In Depth

Global Connections

"From Korea to Berlin to Cuba to Vietnam, the Truman Doctrine governed America's response to the Communist world," was how Senator Fulbright explained the United States' foreign policy in the 1960s. By then, however, the economic position of the United States relative to the rest of the world was slowly declining. And the war-shattered Soviet Union had rebuilt its military strength, thus making it possible for the Soviets to challenge the United States in Cuba.

CHAPTER 19

The Kennedy and Johnson Years
1960-1968

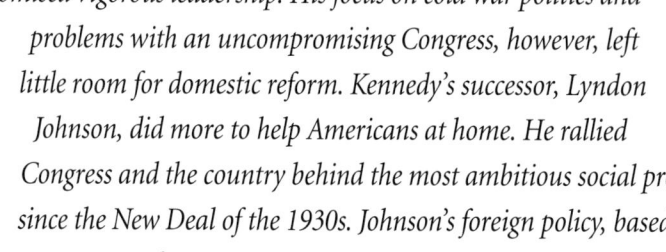

*B*old phrases such as "the New Frontier" and "the Great Society" captured the spirit of optimism that energized the United States in the early 1960s. John F. Kennedy, the youngest President ever elected, promised vigorous leadership. His focus on cold war politics and problems with an uncompromising Congress, however, left little room for domestic reform. Kennedy's successor, Lyndon Johnson, did more to help Americans at home. He rallied Congress and the country behind the most ambitious social program since the New Deal of the 1930s. Johnson's foreign policy, based on the assumption that communists were determined to take over the world, led the nation into conflicts with other countries.

Events in the United States

1960 John F. Kennedy and Richard Nixon appear in the first televised presidential debates.	**1961** President Kennedy establishes the Peace Corps. • Bay of Pigs invasion in Cuba fails.	**1962** The Cuban missile crisis occurs.	**1963** President Kennedy is assassinated. • Lyndon Johnson becomes President.

1960	1961	1962	1963

Events in the World

1960 The Soviets shoot down U.S. spy plane. • The Congo gains independence from Belgium.	**1961** The Soviets build the Berlin Wall. • Soviet cosmonaut is first to orbit the earth.

RESOURCE DIRECTORY

Teaching Resources

Alternate Lesson Plan: Demonstrating the Big Idea found in the Alternate Lesson Plans folder, p. 141, provides a lesson strategy to instruct students about the Big Idea that Kennedy focused primarily on dealing with the cold war abroad while Johnson pushed a broad domestic agenda through Congress.

Alternative Assessment Handbook provides information, guidance, and strategies for alternative methods of assessment. It includes an essay on new trends in assessment, guidance and strategies for developing performance tasks and portfolios, scoring rubrics, and sample evaluation forms.

Pages 624 – 627
The New Frontier

President John F. Kennedy's first years in office did not bear the legislative fruit he promised in his inspiring campaign speeches. More interested in foreign affairs than in affairs at home, Kennedy did not shepherd his proposals along the legislative path. Congress, which fought him at every step, contributed to the lack of progress.

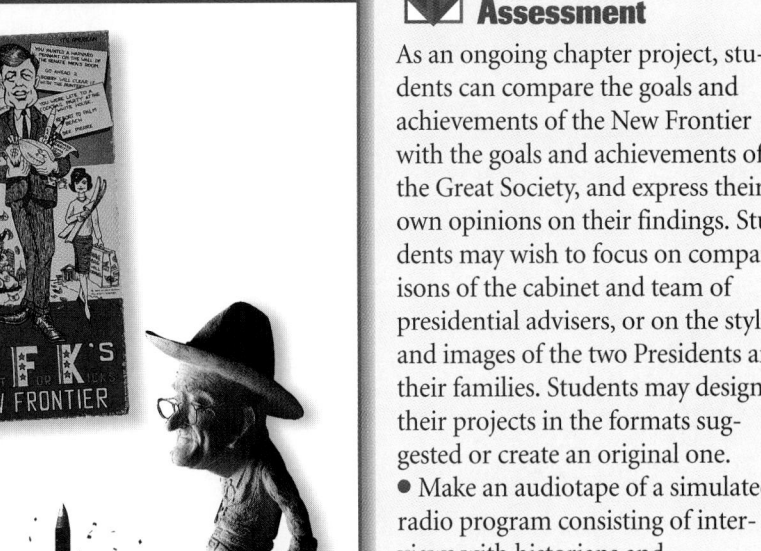

Pages 629 – 633
The Great Society

Lyndon Johnson picked up the domestic agenda after John Kennedy's death. In the greatest triumph of social legislation since Franklin Roosevelt's New Deal, he launched a remarkable reform program that offered something for everyone and for a time promised to ease the inequalities in American life.

Pages 636 – 643
Foreign Policy in the 1960s

The drama and seriousness of events on the world stage beckoned Kennedy more than did the problems at home. He performed boldly on several foreign policy issues, with decisions grounded in familiar cold war assumptions about the intentions of the Soviet Union. When Johnson took office, he saw foreign affairs as something of a nuisance, but continued Kennedy's policies.

1964	1965	1966	1967	1968
1964 Congress passes the Civil Rights Act.	*1965* Congress passes the Voting Rights Act and establishes Medicare and Medicaid.	*1966* Miranda v. Arizona *ruling establishes that suspects must be informed of their rights before questioning.*		
1964 Khrushchev is removed from power in the Soviet Union. • The military leads coup in Brazil.	*1965* Ferdinand Marcos becomes president of the Philippines.	*1966* Chinese Cultural Revolution begins. • Indira Gandhi becomes Indian prime minister.	*1967* Israel defeats Arab states in Six-Day War. • Civil war breaks out in Nigeria.	*1968* Student uprising shakes France. • The Soviet Union invades Czechoslovakia.

SECTION 1

The New Frontier

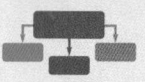

Connecting to the Big Idea

See page 622B. During the close-fought election of 1960, John F. Kennedy promised new programs of reform. Ask what those programs were. Why did few of them make it through Congress?

Objectives

● Identify John F. Kennedy and describe his popular image.
● Describe Kennedy's proposed domestic program, including a tax cut, the space program, and direct aid to the poor.
● Explain why Kennedy's legislative proposals on domestic policy suffered defeat in Congress.

Bellringer

Ask students to imagine a political campaign for President waged without television appearances, interviews, or campaign commercials. How would voters learn about the candidates? What do voters learn about candidates from television? How valuable is this information?

Reading Strategy

Structured Overview Ask students to write two column headings on a piece of paper: Kennedy's Image and Kennedy's Actual Domestic Accomplishments. Ask students to take notes in the appropriate column as they read the section.

SECTION PREVIEW

President John F. Kennedy's first years in office did not bear the legislative fruit he promised in his inspiring campaign speeches. More interested in foreign affairs than in affairs at home, Kennedy did not shepherd his proposals along the legislative path. Congress, which fought him at every step, contributed to the lack of progress.

Key Concepts

• The youthful President Kennedy created a popular image that appealed to Americans eager for change.
• Kennedy's program included the space program, a tax cut to restore prosperity, and, near the end of his presidency, direct aid to the poor.
• Kennedy's legislative proposals on domestic policy suffered defeat in Congress.

Key Terms, People, and Places

liberal consensus, mandate, New Frontier, Warren Commission; John F. Kennedy, Earl Warren

Images of the new President and his family flooded popular culture in the early 1960s, appearing even in board games such as the one shown above.

P resident Eisenhower had steered the nation along a moderate course through the 1950s. In an era of conformity, the popular Eisenhower had presided over a consensus, or general agreement, within the government that the United States was in good shape.

When **John F. Kennedy** took office, he adopted this **liberal consensus** view. According to this view, held by many in government and the public, capitalism was the best economic system and the United States was threatened more by communism abroad than by domestic problems such as poverty and racial injustice. Only at the end of his time in office, when he could no longer ignore the signs that the fabric of American society was being torn apart, did Kennedy earnestly move toward addressing these domestic problems.

The Election of 1960

Kennedy, a Massachusetts Democrat who had served in the United States House of Representatives and Senate, faced serious obstacles in his quest for the presidency. He was only forty-three years old, and many questioned whether he had the experience needed for the nation's highest office. His Roman Catholic religion also seemed a potential problem to some. No Catholic had ever been elected President, and some feared he would be controlled by the Catholic church in Rome. Kennedy defused the religion issue in the primary campaign, when he won in the largely Protestant state of West Virginia. With that hurdle behind him, he campaigned hard, with promises to spur the sluggish economy. During the Eisenhower administration, the Gross National Product (GNP) had grown very slowly, and the economy had suffered several recessions. Kennedy proclaimed that it was time to "get America moving again." Television played a key role in the election. Kennedy and Republican candidate Richard Nixon, who was Eisenhower's Vice President, squared off in the first televised debates ever held. Television sets now glowed in a majority of American households, and the debates made a major difference in the outcome of the election. Both candidates expressed their views well, but Kennedy, who had hired professional television consultants to help him with makeup and clothes, looked more polished and relaxed. While Nixon looked out at the studio audience, Kennedy looked directly at the camera and thus into the eyes of every television viewer. At the end of the first debate, momentum had shifted Kennedy's way. A CBS poll estimated that 57 percent of the people voting in November felt that the debates had affected their choice.

RESOURCE DIRECTORY

Teaching Resources

Reproducible Lesson Plan found in the Unit 6 folder, p. 3, provides a summary of the Section 1 lesson plan content.

Alternate Lesson Plan: Learning Styles found in the Alternate Lesson Plans folder, p. 142, is especially useful for visual or tactile learners and is designed to help students identify reasons for Kennedy's popularity and explain the New Frontier program.

Guided Reading and Review found in the Unit 6 folder, p. 6, provides a structure for reading and mastering the key concepts and reviewing the key terms for Section 1. (Guided Practice)

Visual Learning Activity Creating Images of the Candidates, found in the Unit 6 folder, p. 26, shows how the candidates in the 1960 presidential campaign tried to manipulate their images with buttons, T-shirts, and other items.

In the election, Kennedy won by an extraordinarily close margin. Though the electoral vote was 303 to 219, Kennedy won by only 120,000 popular votes out of more than 34 million cast. If but a few thousand voters in Illinois or Texas had cast ballots for Nixon, the Republicans would have won. The razor-thin victory would affect policy decisions when Kennedy took office. With only borderline support, he did not have a **mandate,** or the backing of voters, to push his more controversial measures through Congress.

The Promise of Camelot

 No matter how slim his margin of victory, Kennedy was now President. In ringing phrases he declared in his inaugural address that "the torch has been passed to a new generation of Americans." He pledged the United States to defend the interests of western democracies at any cost:

> *L et every nation know, whether it wishes us well or ill, that we shall pay any price, bear any burden, meet any hardship, support any friend, oppose any foe to assure the survival and the success of liberty.*
>
> Inaugural Address, January 20, 1961

The new administration was buoyant and energetic. Jacqueline Kennedy, the President's attractive young wife, charmed the country with her grace. Nobel Prize winners visited the White House. The Kennedys and their friends loved to play touch football on the lawn or take long hikes. The administration, which seemed full of idealism and youth, earned the nickname Camelot after a 1960 Broadway musical that portrayed the legendary kingdom of the British king Arthur. Arthur dreamed of transforming medieval Britain from a country in which "might makes right"—or the strong always get their way—into one where might, or power, would be used to achieve right. The sentimental idealism of Broadway's *Camelot* seemed the perfect image for President Kennedy.

Jacqueline and John Kennedy dazzled the nation with their beauty, glamour, and youth.

MAKING CONNECTIONS

In what ways might an image of youthful energy help—and hurt—a new President?

Kennedy's Economic Program

In a speech early in his administration, Kennedy said that the nation was poised at the edge of a **New Frontier,** and the name stuck to the reform programs he proposed. The proposals focused on the economy, aid to the poor, and the space program.

Concerned about the continuing recession, Kennedy hoped to work with the business community to restore prosperity to the nation. Often, however, he faced resistance from executives who were suspicious of his plans. The worst fears of business leaders were realized in the spring of 1962. When the U.S. Steel Company announced that it was raising the price of steel by $6 a ton, other firms did the same. Worried about inflation, Kennedy called the price increase unjustifiable and charged that it showed "utter contempt for the public interest." He ordered a federal investigation into the possibility of price-fixing. Under that pressure, U.S. Steel and the other companies backed down. But business

Media and Technology

Transparency
Our Multicultural Heritage, C-3

SOURCE READINGS

 Source Readings on p. 646 will connect literature selections and primary source excerpts to historical events discussed in this section.

Source Readings on p. 646 will connect literature selections and primary source excerpts to historical events discussed in this section.

2. INSTRUCT

Explain/Discuss

Discuss the importance of a "mandate for change" for a reform-minded President. Ask how lack of such a mandate hampered Kennedy. Who were his opponents in Congress?

Ask which of the powers of the presidency Kennedy used to "encourage" U.S. Steel and other companies to comply with his voluntary limits on price hikes. What did this action reveal about Kennedy's view of the presidency? Students might compare JFK's handling of business interests such as U.S. Steel with Teddy Roosevelt's handling of the trusts.

Analyze

One way to analyze JFK's presidency is to evaluate his performance in each of these roles: chief of state; chief administrator; chief diplomat; commander in chief of the armed forces; chief legislator; leader of his political party; and representative of all the people. Ask students to find references to as many of the roles as they can in the section.

Answer to ...

MAKING CONNECTIONS

Such an image might give people a feeling of hope for progressive change, thus increasing the President's chances of public support for new programs. On the other hand, a young President might appear inexperienced or naive and thus lose public confidence.

Eighteen percent. The graph shows that most Americans were not wealthy; Harrington said that one fifth of the population could be classified as poor.

Activity

Cooperative Learning

Time: Two class periods.
Grouping: Groups of four to six students.
Activity: Create an oral history of the Kennedy assassination.

First day: preparation for interviews. Students should create a list of open-ended questions about people's memories of and reactions to Kennedy's assassination.

Outside class: interviews and preparation of finished project. Each group member should use the questions to interview one or two adults over the age of forty.

Second day: presentations. Students may present the results of their interviews in a magazine-type collage, or in the form of a television newsmagazine segment.
Purpose: To study the impact of the Kennedy assassination on the American public.
Roles: Interviewers, designers, writers, editor, broadcasters, director.
Outcome: Students will compile an oral history of the Kennedy assassination and understand its impact at the time.

Enrichment

Ask students to research and report on the folk revival in popular music in the early 1960s (focusing on artists such as Joan Baez and Bob Dylan) and its relation to increasing demands for social reform in the nation.

Caption Answer to ...

 Interpreting Graphs

About $800 million. After *Sputnik,* NASA funding increased significantly, because the United States wanted to remain competitive with the Soviets.

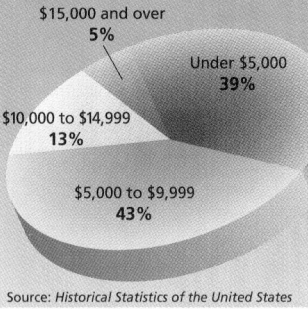

Distribution of Families, by Annual Income, 1962

- $15,000 and over **5%**
- Under $5,000 **39%**
- $10,000 to $14,999 **13%**
- $5,000 to $9,999 **43%**

Source: *Historical Statistics of the United States*

 **Interpreting Charts**
What percentage of American families in 1962 had an annual income of $10,000 or more? How does the pie chart support what Michael Harrington wrote in The Other America?

Federal Funding of NASA* Research and Development, 1950–1965

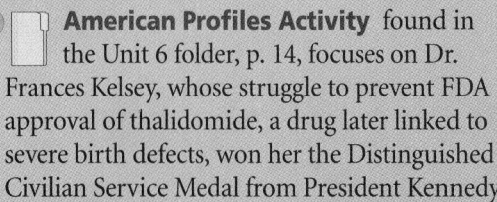

Millions of Dollars

Launching of *Sputnik,* 1957

Year

*National Aeronautics and Space Administration
Source: *Historical Statistics of the United States*

 **Interpreting Graphs**
Approximately how much federal funding did NASA receive in 1961, the year Alan Shepard flew in space? How does the graph illustrate the influence of the Soviet Union's Sputnik on United States policy?

leaders remained angry, and the stock market fell in the steepest drop since the Great Crash of 1929.

On the larger issue of ending the economic slump, Kennedy proposed cutting taxes. In 1963 the President called for a $13.5 billion cut in taxes over three years. The measure would reduce government income and create a budget deficit at first, but Kennedy believed that the extra cash in taxpayers' wallets would stimulate the economy and bring added tax revenues in the end. Many people, both conservative and liberal, vigorously opposed the policy. Economist John Kenneth Galbraith claimed that the deficit would cause frivolous spending without addressing serious national problems:

> I am not sure what the advantage is in having a few more dollars if the air is too dirty to breathe, the water too polluted to drink, the commuters are losing out on the struggle to get in and out of the cities, the streets are filthy, and the schools are so bad that the young, perhaps wisely, stay away, and hoodlums roll citizens for some of the dollars that they save in taxes.

The tax-cut proposal, like many others Kennedy made, was soon bottled up in a congressional committee and stood little chance of passage.

Kennedy also was eager to take action against poverty. In his first two years in office, Kennedy hoped that he could help the poor simply by stimulating the economy. With his privileged background, Kennedy was out of touch with the brutal realities of poverty. In 1962 author Michael Harrington publicized this problem in a book he called *The Other America.* Harrington revealed that while middle-class Americans were enjoying the prosperity of the 1950s, a shocking one fifth of the population was living below the poverty line. The chart at left shows income distribution in the United States in 1962. Kennedy, who had seen poverty firsthand during the 1960 campaign, read Harrington's book and realized that the situation demanded direct aid to the poor. Despite his concern, however, Kennedy acted to address the poverty problem too late in his presidency, and he never succeeded in pushing legislation through Congress.

Kennedy was more successful in his effort to breathe life into the space program. As astronaut Alan Shepard was launched 115 miles into space in 1961, Kennedy committed the United States to landing a man on the moon before the end of the decade. As the graph at left shows, Congress increased National Aeronautics and Space Administration (NASA) funding for this project.

Camelot in Perspective

⭐ Kennedy energized the country with his eloquent call for action, but his legislative record was mixed at best. Foreign policy, covered in Section 3, really concerned Kennedy the most, and his domestic vision was not as focused. He also wanted to avoid making enemies in Congress by pushing unpopular programs; such enemies might refuse to give him the votes he

▶ **RESOURCE DIRECTORY** ⭐

Teaching Resources

⭐ **American Profiles Activity** found in the Unit 6 folder, p. 14, focuses on Dr. Frances Kelsey, whose struggle to prevent FDA approval of thalidomide, a drug later linked to severe birth defects, won her the Distinguished Civilian Service Medal from President Kennedy.

⭐ **Literature Activity** A Grieving Nation, found in the Unit 6 folder, pp. 23–24, features a detailed account of JFK's funeral from William Manchester's *Death of a President* to help students understand the impact of Kennedy's assassination throughout the nation and the world.

needed to progress on foreign policy. Kennedy's lack of experience as a legislative leader further eroded his effectiveness. Finally, the Congress, though Democratic, was determined to follow its own agenda and seemed to thwart Kennedy at every turn. For all these reasons, most of Kennedy's proposals died in Congress. Measures that did finally work their way into law, like a modest increase in the minimum wage, barely made a dent in the nation's problems.

The Nation Mourns Still, Kennedy pressed on. On November 22, 1963, as he looked ahead to reelection the following year, he went to Texas to mobilize support. As he rode through Dallas in an open car, shots rang out. Fatally wounded, President Kennedy was pronounced dead soon after his arrival at a nearby hospital.

The country was shattered. Jimmy Carter, a Georgia farmer who later became President, had just gotten down from his tractor when he heard the news: "I wept openly for the first time in ten years, for the first time since my own father died." Millions of Americans remained glued to their television sets for the next four days as the impact of the tragedy sank in. Just as members of an earlier generation remembered where they had been when the Japanese attacked Pearl Harbor, Americans would always recall vividly what they were doing in 1963 when they learned that their President had been shot. ★

The Assassination Debate Shortly after Kennedy's death, a commission headed by Chief Justice **Earl Warren** was formed to investigate the crime. Despite the fact that the prime

suspect, Lee Harvey Oswald, was himself gunned down two days after Kennedy was killed, the **Warren Commission** declared that Oswald had worked alone in shooting the President. Since then, however, some people have argued that Oswald was involved in a larger conspiracy, and that he was killed in order to protect others who had helped plan Kennedy's murder.

For a time the assassination embellished the Kennedy myth. The myth began to fade with time, but Lyndon Johnson, who succeeded Kennedy as President, made good use of the spirit of hope and the desire for change that Kennedy had inspired. He saw enacted much of the legislation that his predecessor had failed to push through Congress.

Millions of Americans watched President Kennedy's funeral on television. *Inset:* A *Life* magazine cover shows Jacqueline Kennedy and her children during the funeral.

SECTION 1 REVIEW

Key Terms, People, and Places
1. Define (a) liberal consensus, (b) mandate, (c) New Frontier, (d) Warren Commission.
2. Identify (a) John F. Kennedy, (b) Earl Warren.

Key Concepts
3. How did President Kennedy hope to stimulate the economy?
4. Why was the Kennedy administration nicknamed Camelot?

5. (a) What did Kennedy try to accomplish in his domestic program? (b) How successful was he?

Critical Thinking
6. **Drawing Conclusions** Kennedy remarked that in the 1960 election, "it was TV more than anything else that turned the tide." Do you think that television may have given Kennedy an unfair advantage over Nixon, or did it provide voters with information they needed to make an intelligent decision?

📖 **Quiz** found in the Unit 6 folder, p. 7, covers the main ideas in this section as well as the key terms.

3. ASSESS

Section 1 Review Answers
1. (a) liberal consensus, see p. 624, (b) mandate, see p. 625, (c) New Frontier, see p. 625, (d) Warren Commission, see p. 627

2. (a) John F. Kennedy, see p. 624, (b) Earl Warren, see p. 627

3. In 1963 Kennedy proposed cutting taxes by $13.5 billion over three years.

4. The youth, vigor, and idealism that the Kennedy administration exuded was compared with the idealistic and energetic reign of the legendary King Arthur, portrayed in the 1960 Broadway musical hit *Camelot*.

5. (a) Kennedy's domestic proposals focused on the economy, aid to the poor, and the space program. (b) With the exception of the space program, his record was not very successful at all. Most legislative proposals were stymied by Congress.

6. Possible answers: Kennedy did gain an unfair advantage because his skill in presenting himself to a television audience said little about his ability to govern; voters were able to see the candidates in an impromptu speaking situation and could evaluate how each performed under pressure.

Reteach
Ask students to correct the following incorrect statements.
● Kennedy defeated Nixon by a wide margin in 1960.
● Kennedy was able to move most of his New Frontier legislation through Congress.
● Kennedy was killed at the end of his fourth year as President.

4. CLOSE

Reinforcing the Big Idea
John F. Kennedy inspired and invigorated the nation, but he was unable to get many of his reform bills through Congress. The next section describes how Lyndon Johnson pushed much new legislation through Congress.

Historical Evidence

Exploring Oral History

Focus Students will analyze the content of oral history excerpts.

Instruct Ask students to work in groups to consider the following: Twenty Americans have been selected to answer questions about the presidency of John Kennedy. Ask each group to write questions about the characteristics of the twenty citizens that might provide useful information when historians try to evaluate their testimony. (Questions might include age, level of political activity, level of education.) Ask why such information is critical.

Extend See the Historian's Toolbox Activity in the Resource Directory below.

Answers

1. (a) John Lewis, Atlanta city council member and civil rights leader. (b) 1983 (c) He loved and admired President Kennedy and was saddened by his assassination. (d) No. Lewis's admiration has not lessened over time.

2. (a) Answers will vary, but Lewis worked closely with Kennedy on difficult issues. It is likely that his views are accurate, not sentimentalized. (b) Lewis likely sees Kennedy as instrumental in the passage of civil rights legislation that occurred after his death. If successful legislation had not been passed, he may have viewed Kennedy in a different light. (c) They reveal that he favored government intervention on domestic issues such as civil rights, and that he believed government should be accessible to the people.

3. (a) Lewis believes that Kennedy was a sincere and caring President and that he gave people, especially African Americans, feelings of hope that his administration cared about the American people and would work on domestic issues such as civil rights. (b) Lewis's account indicates that Kennedy may not have been universally admired as a President, but that many people felt for the first time that there was a friend in the White House.

Exploring Oral History

Oral history is made up of people's verbal accounts and recollections of former times and events. As historical evidence, it is one of the oldest and most universal methods by which people have acquired information about the past.

Historians preserve oral history by interviewing people and recording their words on audio- or videotape or in written transcripts. Historians may gather oral history at the time an event takes place or at some later date, perhaps years or even decades later.

Historians often seek out oral histories because they give a unique perspective on the past. Oral histories are a type of primary source and therefore are more valuable to historians than secondary sources. Oral histories record not only facts about the past, but also people's opinions, feelings, and impressions—all important to a historian in putting together a picture of the past.

The excerpt at right is taken from a 1983 interview with John Lewis, an Atlanta city council member, on the twentieth anniversary of President Kennedy's death. In 1963 Lewis was chairperson of the Student Nonviolent Coordinating Committee and one of the leaders of the civil rights March on Washington.

Read the oral account at right and then use the following steps to analyze its content.

1. Identify the nature of the oral account. (a) Who was interviewed?

(b) When did the interview take place? (c) What was Lewis's attitude toward Kennedy at the time of his death? (d) Did that attitude change in any way over time?

2. Determine the reliability of the evidence. (a) How might Lewis's role in the events being recollected affect his interpretation of those events? (b) How might events after Kennedy's

death have affected the account? (c) What do Lewis's views reveal about his political perspective?

3. Study the evidence to learn more about the historical event. (a) What impact does Lewis think Kennedy's presidency had on government policy and the nation? (b) What can you learn about Kennedy's presidency from Lewis's account?

An Interview with John Lewis:
Remembering President Kennedy's Assassination

"I was living in Atlanta then, but I had gone back to Nashville for a trial. I was getting into a car to go to the Nashville airport when I heard it on the radio. And to me, it was the saddest moment in my life. I had grown up to love and to admire President Kennedy. I remember crying on the plane.

I saw him as a sort of guy that listened. Sincere. Caring. People argue and say that he didn't really do anything. But he did listen, and during that period from 1961 to 1963, I'll tell you, I think probably for the first time in modern American history, we felt, "Well, we have a friend in the White House." On some things we disagreed. We'd call them up and argue and debate with them on some issue, and we said a lot of different things, and sometimes it was harsh. But we saw the Kennedy administration during that period as a sympathetic referee in the whole struggle for civil rights.

His campaign had created a sense of hope, a sense of optimism for many of us. When someone asked him about the civil rights sit-ins that year, he said, 'By sitting down, these young people are standing up for the very best in American tradition.' "

—*Newsweek,* November 28, 1983

RESOURCE DIRECTORY

Teaching Resources

Historian's Toolbox Activity Exploring Oral History, found in the Unit 6 folder, p. 18, provides a further example of what oral history can reveal about public affairs in a *U.S. News & World Report* interview with President Clinton using readers' questions on health care.

The Great Society

SECTION PREVIEW

Lyndon Johnson picked up the domestic agenda after John Kennedy's death. In the greatest triumph of social legislation since Franklin Roosevelt's New Deal, he launched a remarkable reform program that offered something for everyone and for a time promised to ease the inequalities in American life.

Key Concepts

- Lyndon Johnson was a skillful politician who used his forceful personality to get measures passed in Congress.
- Johnson's Great Society included a tax cut, a "war on poverty," health-care legislation, aid to education, and other proposals.
- Supreme Court decisions in the 1960s supported the Great Society, but the program also had many critics.

Key Terms, People, and Places

Great Society, Volunteers in Service to America (VISTA), Medicare, Immigration Act of 1965; Lyndon B. Johnson

L yndon B. Johnson succeeded where Kennedy had failed. Vice President under JFK, Johnson found himself elevated to the presidency when Kennedy was assassinated. Once in office, he used all the talents he had developed as Senate majority leader to push through Congress an extraordinary program of reforms on domestic issues.

LBJ's Path to the White House

Lyndon B. Johnson arrived in Congress in 1937 as a New Deal Democrat from Texas. Johnson took a conservative stance in order to appeal to more Texas voters during his quest for a Senate seat. He won the seat in 1948 by a tiny margin of only eighty-seven votes and was promptly dubbed "Landslide Lyndon"—a

nickname that stuck for the rest of his career. In the Senate, Johnson demonstrated both his talent and his ambition by winning leadership posts. In the six years from 1954 to 1960, he became famous for his ability to manipulate the political system to accomplish his goals.

Johnson was a forceful, energetic man. He was "not a very likable man," as former Secretary of State Dean Acheson once told him, but Johnson was more concerned with accomplishment than popularity, and his single-minded intensity enabled him to get his way. Other senators marveled at the "Johnson treatment," in which he carefully researched a bill, then approached in a hallway or office the legislator whose vote he needed. If he thought it was the best way to persuade the legislator, he would attack, "his face a scant millimeter from his target, his eyes widening and narrowing, his eyebrows rising and falling," according to columnists Rowland Evans, Jr., and Robert Novak. He might grab his victim by the lapels or by the shoulders, flattering, cajoling, shouting in turn. And without fail he got the vote.

Johnson was a master of behind-the-scenes dealing in the Senate, but John Kennedy knew more about how to win a presidential nomination. When Johnson's bid for the Democratic nomination failed in 1960, he accepted Kennedy's invitation to run for the vice presidency. Once in office, however, Johnson suffered miserably. He was uncomfortable with the Kennedy crowd, whose Ivy League educations made him feel intellectually inferior. He also was frustrated with the powerlessness of the vice presidency and upset at being away from Congress, where he had been so effective. Then came the assassination, and suddenly he was President.

Johnson sensed the profound shock gripping the nation. He knew that millions of Americans viewed him as the wrongful heir to the Kennedy tradition. He also was aware that he had less than a year to convince the American

The fiberglass sculpture above, which was a gift to President Johnson, portrays him as a rough-and-ready Texan.

1. FOCUS

Connecting to the Big Idea

See page 622B. Lyndon Johnson, taking office after Kennedy's assassination, moved many reform bills through Congress as part of his goal of achieving a "Great Society." Ask what Johnson's most important reform bills were. Why did some Americans criticize Johnson's program?

Objectives

- Describe the qualities that allowed Lyndon Johnson to move his programs through Congress.
- Identify some of the major proposals that made up the Great Society legislation.
- Explain why criticism of the Great Society came from many different segments of American society.

Bellringer

Ask students what they think is great about American society. Was it as great or less so in Johnson's time? What differences are evident?

Reading Strategy

Reading for Evidence As they read, students should look for evidence that "Lyndon B. Johnson succeeded where Kennedy had failed," as stated on page 629.

📄 **Reproducible Lesson Plan** found in the Unit 6 folder, p. 4, provides a summary of the Section 2 lesson plan content.

📄 **Alternate Lesson Plan: Critical Thinking** Determining Relevance, found in the Alternate Lesson Plans folder, p. 143, helps students identify the impact of various aspects of the Great Society programs and the role of Supreme Court decisions during this time.

📄 **Guided Reading and Review** found in the Unit 6 folder, p. 8, provides a structure for reading and mastering the key concepts and reviewing the key terms for Section 2. (Guided Practice)

2. INSTRUCT

Explain/Discuss

Discuss with students why LBJ was able to succeed where Kennedy had failed. Remind students that Congress, as well as LBJ, wanted to pass legislation proposed by the slain President as a memorial and as a way of reassuring the country. Ask students to what extent LBJ's political experience helped him move legislation through Congress.

Ask students to list the programs instituted by LBJ. What areas of American life did they touch? Ask students to consider what sort of bureaucracy was required to keep such programs going. Do students see any potential for overlapping programs in the list of legislation? Read students the following comment by Sargent Shriver, head of the Office of Economic Opportunity and chief administrator of the War on Poverty, concerning the multitude of programs: "It's like we went down to Cape Kennedy and launched a half dozen rockets at once."

In Depth

Multicultural Perspectives

The war on poverty is continuing into the late twentieth century. The focal point of poverty, however, is not predominantly among African Americans in the North and in urban areas, as popular perception might have it. The 1990 census data shows that poor whites (21 million) outnumber poor African Americans (9 million) by more than two to one. However, African Americans do bear a disproportionate burden of poverty—28 percent compared to 8.8 percent of the white population.

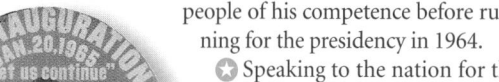

When Lyndon Johnson was elected President in 1964, he renewed his pledge to follow through on Kennedy's programs.

Despite strong publicity efforts, including advertising on bars of soap, Republican candidate Barry Goldwater's run for the presidency in 1964 was unsuccessful. It did signal the beginnings of a conservative movement in the United States, however.

people of his competence before running for the presidency in 1964.

Speaking to the nation for the first time after Kennedy's death, Johnson expressed his grief at the loss. "All I have," he declared in this address, "I would have given gladly not to be standing here today." He went on to convey his determination to carry on where the slain President had left off. Johnson's theme was "Let us continue," and he asked Congress to pass the measures that Kennedy had sought.

The Great Society

Congress, also aware that the American people needed some action that would heal the wound caused by the loss of their President, responded to Johnson's appeal. Swift passage of Kennedy's civil rights and tax-cut bills followed. Soon Johnson branched out and sought laws to aid public education, provide medical care for the elderly, and eliminate poverty. By the spring of 1964, he had begun to use the phrase **"Great Society"** to describe his goals. In a speech at the University of Michigan in May 1964, he told students:

> Your imagination, your initiative, and your indignation will determine whether we build a society where progress is the servant of our needs, or a society where old values and new visions are buried under unbridled [unrestrained] growth. For in your time we have the opportunity to move not only toward the rich society and the powerful society, but upward toward the Great Society.

Johnson's early successes paved the way to a true landslide victory over Republican Barry Goldwater in the election of 1964. Goldwater, a senator from Arizona, held views that seemed frighteningly radical to many Americans. For example, he

opposed civil rights legislation, and he believed that military commanders should be allowed to use nuclear bombs as they saw fit on the battlefield. The Johnson campaign capitalized on voters' fears of nuclear war and aired a television commercial in which a little girl's innocent counting game turned into the countdown for a nuclear explosion. Johnson received 61 percent of the popular vote and an overwhelming 486 to 52 tally in the Electoral College. Democratic majorities were established in both houses of Congress: 295 to 140 in the House of Representatives and 68 to 32 in the Senate. Landslide Lyndon now had the mandate to move ahead even more aggressively.

The Tax Cut Johnson accepted the idea that had been supported by Kennedy that carefully controlled budget deficits could bring about prosperity. To gain conservative support for Kennedy's tax-cut bill, he agreed to cut spending. Once that was done, the measure passed, and it worked just as planned. As the tax cut went into effect, the Gross National Product (GNP) rose 7.1 percent in 1964, 8.1 percent in 1965, and 9.5 percent in 1966. The deficit, which many people feared would grow, shrank, while the revival of prosperity generated new tax revenues. Unemployment fell, and inflation remained in check.

The War on Poverty Next, LBJ pressed for the poverty program that Kennedy had begun to consider. In his 1964 State of the Union message he vowed, "This administration today, here and now, declares unconditional war on poverty in America." The Economic Opportunity Act, passed in the summer of 1964, created **Volunteers in Service to America (VISTA)**, which sent volunteers to help people in poor communities. The act also set up "community action programs" to give the poor a voice in defining housing, health, and education policies in their own neighborhoods. Poor people were to participate in decisions about the distribution of government money and resources. ●

Medicare Johnson also focused attention on the increasing cost of medical care. Twenty years before, Harry Truman had proposed a

▶ RESOURCE DIRECTORY

Teaching Resources

Primary Source Activity President Johnson's Thanksgiving Address, found in the Unit 6 folder, p. 20, includes portions of the first national speech LBJ made as President—after only seven days in office.

Critical Thinking Activity Recognizing Cause and Effect, found in the Unit 6 folder, p. 19, helps students apply this skill with a graph showing trends in poverty and the economy from 1948 to 1987.

Federal Dollars to Public Schools,* 1959–1971

Millions of Dollars

School Year	
1959–60	
1961–62	
1963–64	
1965–66	
1967–68	
1969–70	
1970–71	

4,000 / 3,500 / 3,000 / 2,500 / 2,000 / 1,500 / 1,000 / 500 / 0

* Elementary and secondary
Source: *Digest of Education Statistics*

Interpreting Graphs
Congress passed President Johnson's Elementary and Secondary Education Act in 1965. *How does the graph illustrate the overall effect of this legislation? By how much did the federal education budget increase between the 1963–1964 and 1965–1966 school years?*

medical assistance plan as part of his Fair Deal program, but it had never been passed into law. Johnson provided the necessary leadership by tying **Medicare**—which would provide health care for the elderly—to social security and confining the new approach to people over the age of sixty-five. "No longer will older Americans be denied the healing miracle of modern medicine," Johnson declared. "No longer will illness crush and destroy the savings that they have so carefully put away." Another program, called Medicaid, met the needs of poor Americans of any age who could not afford their own private health insurance. This broad-based health care program was the most important piece of social welfare legislation since the passage of the Social Security Act in 1935. It demonstrated the government's commitment to provide help to those Americans who needed it.

Aid to Education Johnson was equally successful in his effort to provide funds for elementary and secondary education. Kennedy had fought for a bill to aid public education but

was defeated when Catholics insisted on equal support for parochial, or private Catholic, schools. Bending over backwards to prove that his own Catholicism was not influencing policy decisions, Kennedy had opposed the Catholics, saying that such a provision would be a violation of the separation of church and state. In the process he had lost the entire bill. Johnson endorsed a measure to provide aid to states based on the number of children from low-income homes. That money could then be distributed to public as well as private schools, including parochial schools. The bill passed, and Johnson signed it into law in the small Texas school he had attended as a child. The graph above shows federal aid to schools from 1959 to 1971.

Other Measures As a result of White House prodding, Congress passed a measure to give rent supplements to the poor. It created a new Department of Housing and Urban Development, thus elevating the importance of housing issues. It provided substantial aid to colleges

Media and Technology

 Transparency
Critical Thinking, I-13

The overall effect of the law was to increase federal spending for public schools. The budget increased by approximately $1.1 billion between the 1963–64 and 1965–66 school years.

Analyze

Ask students to analyze the criticisms leveled against Great Society legislation. Ask which, if any, of the criticisms seem justified.

 Activity
Drawing a Political Cartoon

Ask students to draw a political cartoon illustrating either a criticism of Johnson's Great Society legislation or a response to LBJ's critics.

Enrichment

Three Supreme Court cases, *Gideon* v. *Wainwright*, *Escobedo* v. *Illinois*, and *Miranda* v. *Arizona*, dealt with the rights of individuals accused of crimes. Ask students to work in groups to write dialogue for a drama in which police officers, suspects, and lawyers refer to these cases and discuss instances in which the rights of the accused may have been violated.

 In Depth

Then and Now

An enduring legacy of LBJ's aid to education is Head Start—a program begun in 1965 to prepare economically disadvantaged preschoolers for school. Now administered by the Department of Health and Human Services, Head Start works through local communities to provide nutritious lunches, medical and family services, and educational preparation. Head Start receives bipartisan support in Congress, and serves over 11 million children, mostly under age five.

Interpreting Graphs

An increase in immigration from Asia and from southern and eastern Europe and a decrease in immigration from northwestern Europe. It eliminated some of the restrictions on immigration from areas outside northwestern Europe.

3. ASSESS

Section 2 Review Answers

1. (a) VISTA, see p. 630, (b) Medicare, see p. 631, (c) Immigration Act of 1965, see p. 632

2. Lyndon B. Johnson, see p. 629

3. Johnson invoked Kennedy's memory and asked legislators to pass the bills Kennedy had supported.

4. The Great Society included bills guaranteeing civil rights, providing medical care for the aged (and poor), and mandating a tax cut. It also organized an antipoverty program, offered aid to education, and gave federal support to artists and scholars.

5. Middle-class Americans felt the burden of aiding the poor. Conservatives argued that Great Society programs went too far. Radicals argued that they didn't go far enough.

 In Depth

Biography

In 1965, lawyer Marian Wright Edelman (b. 1939) became the first African American woman admitted to the Mississippi bar. Edelman is the founder and president of the Children's Defense Fund, an advocacy group that promotes the health and welfare of children. Edelman summarizes the Fund's philosophy as follows: "Children cannot eat rhetoric and they cannot be sheltered by commissions. I don't want to see another commission that studies the needs of kids. We need to help them."

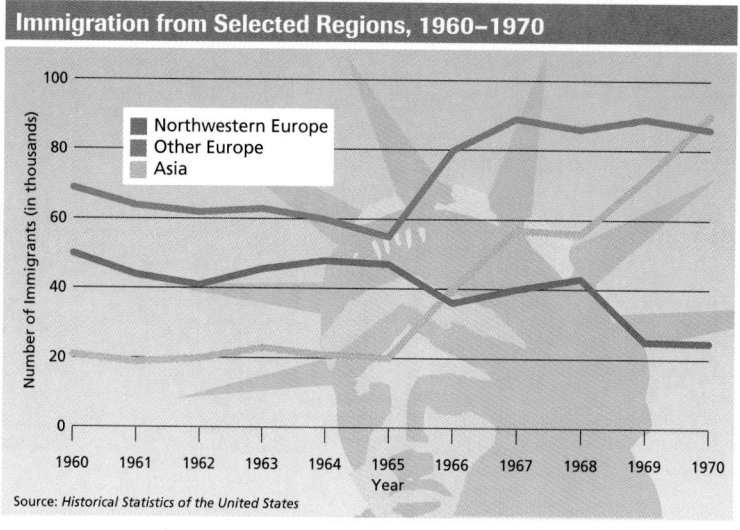

Immigration from Selected Regions, 1960–1970

Source: *Historical Statistics of the United States*

Interpreting Graphs
What general trends in immigration during the 1960s are shown by the graph? How did the Immigration Act of 1965 contribute to these trends?

and universities. It offered grants to artists through a new National Endowment for the Arts and to scholars through a similar National Endowment for the Humanities. This was the first assistance for such groups since the Works Progress Administration of the New Deal.

The Great Society also reformed the restrictive immigration policy that had been in place since 1924. The **Immigration Act of 1965** eliminated the quotas that had discriminated against all immigrants from areas outside northern and western Europe. It now had a much more flexible limit of 170,000 people from the Eastern Hemisphere and 120,000 from the Western Hemisphere. Family members of United States citizens were exempted from the quotas, as were political refugees. In the 1960s approximately 350,000 immigrants entered the United States each year; in the 1970s the number rose to more than 400,000 a year. ★

Supreme Court Support

The Supreme Court under Chief Justice Earl Warren supported the actions of Johnson's Great Society in the 1960s. The 1954 *Brown* v. *Board of Education* decision outlawing school segregation signaled that the Warren Court was prepared to play an active role in politics. As the Johnson administration made good on its promise to promote civil rights, the Court backed up this program. It upheld all measures aimed at guaranteeing African American rights and demonstrated that discrimination would no longer be tolerated.

The Supreme Court handed down several decisions protecting the rights of persons accused of crimes. In the *Gideon* v. *Wainwright* case in 1963, the Court ruled that suspects in criminal cases who could not afford a lawyer had the right to free legal aid. In *Escobedo* v. *Illinois*, 1964, the justices said that accused individuals had to be given access to an attorney while being questioned. In 1966 the Court ruled, in *Miranda* v. *Arizona*, that a suspect must be warned of his or her rights before being questioned. Police must now read all suspects a Miranda warning, which informs accused persons that they have the right to remain silent and that anything they do say may be used against them in court.

In 1965 the Court struck down a Connecticut law that prohibited the use of birth control devices and prevented doctors from sharing information about contraceptives, even with married couples. *Griswold* v. *Connecticut* held that such a law violated a couple's right to privacy. Although the Constitution does not explicitly mention a right to privacy, the Court ruled that such a right was implied because without it, the rights that are specifically guaranteed would be meaningless.

In *Baker* v. *Carr,* 1962, the Court declared that congressional districts had to be apportioned on the basis of "one person, one vote." This prevented the party in power from gerrymandering electoral districts—drawing the lines that established the districts in unfair ways to give themselves more votes. In another area, the Court ruled that religious prayer in public schools was unconstitutional

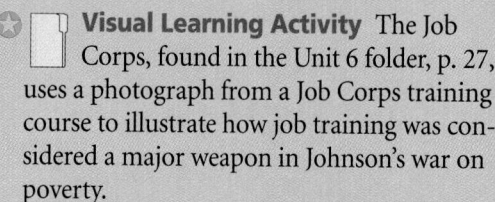 **RESOURCE DIRECTORY** ★

Teaching Resources

★ **Visual Learning Activity** The Job Corps, found in the Unit 6 folder, p. 27, uses a photograph from a Job Corps training course to illustrate how job training was considered a major weapon in Johnson's war on poverty.

★ **Literature Activity** The Invisible Poor, found in the Unit 6 folder, p. 25, features an excerpt from Michael Harrington's bestseller, *The Other America*, which inspired Kennedy and shocked middle-class Americans into supporting action against poverty.

according to the First Amendment principle of separation of church and state. In yet another significant decision, the Court decreed that obscenity laws could not restrict material that might have some "redeeming social value."

The Supreme Court's decisions in the 1960s were controversial. Some conservatives argued that the justices had gone too far and began a long struggle to turn back the new decisions.

MAKING CONNECTIONS

Is the Supreme Court any less political—any less affected by its members' liberal or conservative views—than Congress? Should it be?

Challenges to the Great Society

At first the Great Society seemed enormously successful. Opinion polls taken after Johnson's speech of May 22, 1964, in which he introduced his vision of the Great Society, showed Johnson more popular than Kennedy had been at a comparable point in his presidency. Pressed by Johnson, Congress had passed Kennedy's tax-cut bill early in 1964, and, as detailed on page 778, the state of the economy improved significantly.

Soon, however, criticisms began to surface. New programs raised expectations, and disillusionment followed when not all demands could be met. Middle-class Americans complained that too many of their tax dollars were being spent on poor people. Other critics argued that Great Society programs put too much authority in the hands of the federal government, which could not possibly respond well to the particular needs of local communities across the nation.

At the same time, others complained that the Great Society did not fundamentally alter the distribution of wealth and power in a capitalist economy. Some critics charged that the program sought simply to maintain the middle class and to provide the poor with middle-class values, but not middle-class incomes. Antipoverty measures were criticized for not allotting enough money to carry out their stated goals. Michael Harrington, who had helped focus attention on poverty with his book *The Other America*, argued that the amount of money the government spent was not nearly enough: "What was supposed to be a social war turned out to be a skirmish and, in any case, poverty won."

Before his death, John Kennedy had been more concerned about foreign affairs than domestic; when Johnson took office, he placed the emphasis on the latter. The next section describes Kennedy's actions on the world stage and, after his death, the beginnings of a conflict in Southeast Asia that began to consume the resources that Johnson had hoped to spend on his programs at home. His inability to keep that conflict under control undermined and finally ended the Great Society.

Johnson was both criticized and praised for his Great Society but to him, the programs were all good—"major accomplishments without equal or close parallel in the present era."

SECTION 2 REVIEW

Key Terms, People, and Places
1. Define (a) VISTA, (b) Medicare, (c) Immigration Act of 1965.
2. Identify Lyndon B. Johnson.

Key Concepts
3. How did Lyndon Johnson mobilize support for his domestic programs when he became President?
4. What were the key elements of the Great Society?

5. What were some criticisms of the Great Society?

Critical Thinking
6. **Determining Relevance** What role did the principle of judicial interpretation—the power of the courts to interpret the law—play in the 1965 Supreme Court case *Griswold* v. *Connecticut*? Would the case have been decided differently if the Court did not have this power?

Quiz found in the Unit 6 folder, p. 9, covers the main ideas in this section as well as the key terms.

6. Judicial interpretation allowed the court to extrapolate the right of privacy (not expressly written in the Bill of Rights) from the existence of other guaranteed rights. It may have been harder for the court to rule as it did in *Griswold* without this interpretation, and the effects of the ruling would not have been as far-reaching.

Reteach

Have students locate the key concepts on page 629. Ask each student to write one question based on each of the key concepts. Have students exchange papers with a classmate and answer the questions. Pairs of students can work together to correct their answers.

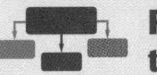

Alternative Assessment

Mid-Point Monitoring
Ask students if they have
● Decided on a format for their finished project
● Started taking notes about the topic
● Begun their outside research

Answer to ...

MAKING CONNECTIONS

The Court's decisions are certainly affected by the political views of its members. Since the justices are not elected but are appointed for life, they probably feel less political pressure than members of Congress do. Most people would argue that the Supreme Court should be as apolitical as possible.

4. CLOSE

Reinforcing the Big Idea

Lyndon Johnson moved an astonishingly comprehensive reform program through Congress in an attempt to build a "Great Society" and wage a war on poverty. The next section discusses foreign affairs during the Kennedy and Johnson administrations.

Kennedy's Decision to Send an American to the Moon

Focus Ask students which of the following programs they would recommend cutting from the nation's budget in order to reduce government spending:

• Preschool programs and food supplements for children at risk

• Repairs to highways, bridges, harbors, and other parts of the transportation system

• Research on AIDS

• Space programs, including a program to land astronauts on the surface of Mars

• Hazardous waste cleanup programs at government installations

Tally student responses. Allow students to debate their decisions briefly and to explain their reasons for choosing a particular program to cut. Point out that the debate over the value of space exploration began decades ago and continues today.

Instruct Explain that in 1969, when American astronauts actually landed on the moon, many Americans were not convinced that the tremendous outlay of money and talent devoted to the space program was worthwhile.

In the July 7, 1969, issue of *Newsweek,* several Americans voiced negative opinions regarding the upcoming moon walk. Ralph Abernathy, then president of the Southern Christian Leadership Conference, said that United States society had "failed to use its ability to rid itself of the scourges of racism, poverty and war, all of which were brutally scarring the nation even as it mobilized for the assault on the solar system." (*Newsweek*, July 7, 1969, p. 60.)

The tribal secretary of the Laguna Pueblos in Paguate, New Mexico, said: "What we could do with that money!" Others favored the project, such as the physicist who hoped, "This seemingly lifeless moon may tell us about the origins of life on the earth . . .a feeling of intense excitement grips the scientific community."

Kennedy's Decision to Send an American to the Moon

Time Frame:	November 1960—May 1961
Place:	Washington, D.C.
Key People:	President John F. Kennedy, physicist Jerome Wiesner, NASA head James Webb
Situation:	When John F. Kennedy was elected President, the Soviet Union was rapidly widening its lead in space exploration. The United States needed to find a way to catch up and, if possible, surpass the Soviets in space.

When the Soviet Union launched *Sputnik*, the first artificial satellite, in 1957, a shocked American public worried that the Soviets were gaining a dramatic lead in space. Senator Henry Jackson captured the dismay of many Americans when he declared that *Sputnik* represented "a devastating blow to the prestige of the United States as the leader of the scientific and technical world."

When Kennedy took office in 1960, he assigned a task force, headed by MIT physicist Jerome Wiesner, to evaluate the future direction of the space program. Wiesner's team concluded that the potential scientific payoffs of sending astronauts into space were not worth the enormous costs. They recommended that NASA concentrate on exploratory missions without human crews.

In April 1961, however, Soviet Yuri Gagarin became the first person to complete an orbital flight around the earth. Gagarin's flight rekindled Americans' fears that the United States was falling behind the Soviet Union. Under fire for neglecting his campaign promise to revitalize the space program, the President began to press his advisers for ways to beat the Soviets in space.

Lunar Politics

In the early 1960s, many experts remained skeptical about the scientific merits of sending human beings into space. Sending a person to the moon seemed particularly foolish, both because the moon held little scientific interest and because robots and other instruments could explore it without risking human life.

Financial considerations made the goal of landing a person on the moon even more problematic. Estimates placed the cost of a 10-year project to send an American to the moon at $30 billion to $40 billion. Opponents of the plan questioned the wisdom of diverting so much money and energy to a high-stakes project of questionable scientific value. They pointed to the nation's need for greater spending on public education and social welfare programs. As President Eisenhower bluntly put it, "Anybody who would spend $40 billion in a race to the moon for national prestige is nuts."

Yet a growing number of politicians and scientists—including Vice President Lyndon Johnson and NASA head James Webb—supported sending a person to the

▶ RESOURCE DIRECTORY

Teaching Resources

History Might Not . . . Activity Decision Making: Building an International Manned Space Station, found in the Unit 6 folder, pp. 12–13, provides a structure for groups of students to understand the interests involved, weigh the pros and cons, and debate the issues while simulating a congressional subcommittee hearing on the decision to fund a manned space station.

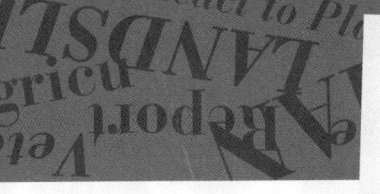

GOALS	Prevent the Soviets from taking control of space; protect American prestige and security		
POSSIBLE ACTIONS	Continue current uncrewed program of space exploration	Begin crewed space program to land an American on the moon within 10 years	Begin crewed program to land on the moon when space technology makes it safe to do so
POSSIBLE RESULTS	• Enable NASA to emphasize scientific discovery at a much lower cost • United States will have more money to spend on domestic problems • Soviet Union may increase lead in space, thus winning greater international prestige	• Project will fail, causing great embarrassment and, possibly, loss of life • Project will succeed, keeping Soviets from dominating space • Project will prove more costly and less scientifically valuable than an uncrewed space program	• Domestic problems will worsen as funds go to space program • Project will lose momentum and never be completed • Project will succeed, putting American space program ahead and advancing scientific knowledge

moon. They believed that the risks could be addressed by careful engineering and that a human could gather much more information than a robot.

The supporters of a crewed space program believed that the race to the moon represented an important battle in the cold war. If the Soviets won in space, the rest of the world might see it as a victory of communism over capitalism. The United States would have to resign itself, as the Vice President put it, "to going to bed each night by the light of a Communist moon."

People who favored a crewed flight to the moon also believed that there were economic benefits to this approach. The race to the moon meant huge contracts and thousands of new jobs for the aerospace industry. In the view of those who supported such a race, science, industry, and education also would profit from technological advances made by a crewed space program.

Some scientists who supported sending people into space favored a third approach. They believed that NASA should wait until space technology was further advanced before attempting to send a person to the moon. They recognized that this emphasis on safety meant it might take several decades to land an American on the moon rather than the relatively short space of ten years.

Kennedy's Decision

Despite the objections, President Kennedy came to believe that a highly visible space program would distract attention from problems at home and abroad. "I am tired of the headlines," he told an aide. "All they describe is crisis, and they give the impression that we have our backs against the wall everywhere in the world." A successful lunar program could erase that impression.

On May 5, 1961, as part of Project Mercury, Alan Shepard became the first American to travel in space. The public's enthusiastic response convinced Kennedy that it was time to submit the moon launch proposal.

In his May 25 special message to the Congress, the President issued a bold challenge to the nation. Rather than continuing an uncrewed space program or taking a go-slow approach in the moon race, he said, the United States "should commit itself to achieving the goal, before this decade is out, of landing a man on the moon." Kennedy's decision finally yielded results on July 20, 1969, when astronaut Neil Armstrong became the first person to set foot on the moon.

EVALUATING DECISIONS

1. What were some reasons in favor of starting a project to put an American on the moon?
2. Why did some people oppose the moon program?

Critical Thinking

3. **Determining Relevance** Lyndon Johnson said that "control of space means control of the world." To what extent was this idea behind Kennedy's decision to send an astronaut to the moon? What other factors contributed to his decision?

Media and Technology

Visions of America: History Might Not Have Happened This Way Game

To encourage students to explore pivotal moments in United States history, have students use the Visions of America software. Refer to the Visions of America Teacher's Guidebook for viewing objectives, activities, game instructions, and discussion questions.

Foreign Policy in the 1960s

SECTION 3

Foreign Policy in the 1960s

1. FOCUS

Connecting to the Big Idea

See page 622B. The foreign policies of Presidents Kennedy and Johnson were grounded in the cold war. Ask how Kennedy reacted to communist challenges. How did Johnson intervene in South American countries?

Objectives

● Identify the Peace Corps and describe its purpose.

● Explain how Kennedy's commitment to the cold war and inexperience in foreign affairs affected his handling of foreign policy.

● Describe the events of the Cuban missile crisis of 1962.

● Describe President Johnson's attitude toward foreign affairs.

Bellringer

Ask students to think about foreign policy—the way the United States pursues relationships with other countries. Ask them to list what they think should be the goals of our foreign policy.

Reading Strategy

Structured Overview Before students begin reading the section, ask them to write two column headings on a piece of paper: Kennedy's Trouble Spots and Johnson's Trouble Spots. As they read the section, students should list each of the foreign affairs crises discussed in the section in the appropriate column and briefly describe the crisis and its resolution.

SECTION PREVIEW

The drama and seriousness of events on the world stage beckoned Kennedy more than did the problems at home. He performed boldly on several foreign policy issues, with decisions grounded in familiar cold war assumptions about the intentions of the Soviet Union. When Johnson took office, he saw foreign affairs as something of a nuisance, but
• continued Kennedy's policies.

Key Concepts

• Kennedy promoted a new program called the Peace Corps.

• Kennedy's commitment to the cold war and his inexperience in foreign affairs showed in his handling of an invasion of Cuba and in his dealings with the Soviet Union.

• The Cuban missile crisis brought the United States and the Soviet Union perilously close to nuclear war.

• President Johnson continued the cold war against communism abroad.

Key Terms, People, and Places

Peace Corps, Berlin Wall, Cuban missile crisis, Limited Test Ban Treaty; Nikita Khrushchev; Bay of Pigs

Long-range missiles capable of carrying nuclear explosives heightened cold war tension. The Soviet Union and the United States could launch nuclear attacks against each other with the push of a button.

While Presidents Kennedy and Johnson promised to seek a "new frontier" and a "great society" in domestic affairs, their foreign policy stayed strictly within the limits of the cold war. Communist challenges and the Presidents' reactions to them led to confrontations that seriously threatened world peace.

Kennedy's Approach to Foreign Policy

The rhetoric of Kennedy's inaugural address proclaimed that the United States would do anything to uphold its version of freedom

---

throughout the world. By this, the new President was referring to defending United States interests against the Soviet Union and its allies.

The Alliance for Progress One focus of Kennedy's foreign policy was the promotion of "peaceful revolution" in developing countries around the world. In other words, he wanted to promote changes in foreign countries that would serve the capitalist interests of the United States in order to prevent those countries from aligning with the Soviet Union. To counter procommunist revolutionary movements, the United States wanted to help countries in Latin America, Asia, and Africa. To do so, Kennedy believed that modern transportation and communication systems and stable governments sympathetic to the United States were necessary. Two months after taking office, Kennedy called on

all the people of the hemisphere to join in a new Alliance for Progress—Alianza para Progreso—a vast cooperative effort, unparalleled in magnitude and nobility of purpose, to satisfy the basic needs of the American people for homes, work and land, health and schools.
Address to Latin American diplomats, March 13, 1961

The administration devoted $100 billion to public and private funding to promote economic development and social reform and to sidetrack revolution before it occurred. All citizens in the Western Hemisphere, Kennedy declared, had "a right to social justice," and that included "land for the landless, and education for those who are denied education." Soon, however, Latin Americans began to question whether what was good for the United States was necessarily good for their countries. Because of such doubts, the Alliance for Progress never lived up to Kennedy's expectations.

▶ RESOURCE DIRECTORY

Teaching Resources

Reproducible Lesson Plan found in the Unit 6 folder, p. 5, provides a summary of the Section 3 lesson plan content.

Alternate Lesson Plan: Learning Styles found in the Alternate Lesson Plans folder, p. 144, helps students identify Kennedy's cold war policies around the world by locating "hot spots" on a world map—especially helpful for tactile and auditory learners.

Guided Reading and Review found in the Unit 6 folder, p. 10, provides a structure for reading and mastering the key concepts and reviewing the key terms for Section 3. (Guided Practice)

One answer to such charges that the United States was more interested in its own agenda than it was in helping other countries was the **Peace Corps.** This new program of JFK's would send volunteers abroad to help developing nations around the world. It would, aide Arthur M. Schlesinger, Jr., declared,

> *replace protocol-minded, striped-pants officials [with] reform-minded missionaries of democracy who mixed with the people, spoke the native dialects, ate the food, and involved themselves in local struggles against ignorance and want.*

AMERICAN PROFILES

Paul Cowan

Paul Cowan was one such "reform-minded missionary." After college in 1963 he worked in the civil rights movement tutoring African American children in Maryland. In 1965 Cowan and his wife, Rachel, joined the Peace Corps and prepared to work in Ecuador in South America. After a training program at the University of New Mexico, they went to the city of Guayaquil to do community development work. Their task would be to raise the standard of living in poor areas by pressuring local governments to provide services such as garbage disposal and clean water.

The job turned out to be far more complicated and frustrating than the Cowans had anticipated. An inefficient bureaucracy constantly hampered their work. The local government was almost as poor as the people it served, and its lack of funds made it essentially powerless. "From the day we moved into the *barrio* [neighborhood]," Paul Cowan later recalled, "the question we were most frequently asked by the people we were supposed to be organizing was whether we would leave them our clothes when we returned to the States."

The Peace Corps bureaucracy, which was too often insensitive to the local culture in which the volunteers were

Paul Cowan volunteered for the Peace Corps in Ecuador.

immersed, also frustrated the couple. Cowan returned home upset, like so many students of his generation, with the slow pace and the twisted path toward progress. Yet, as he looked back on his experience, he wrote:

> *After all the tragedies and frustrations of this past decade, I still believe that someday we will create an America which realizes, with the great Cuban revolutionary José Martí, that "los niños son la esperanza del futuro del mundo" [the children are the hope of the future of the world] and create a society based on that homily.*

A Series of Global Crises

The Peace Corps program was one for which Kennedy was, in general, praised. Other actions of his on the foreign scene were viewed less positively. Kennedy's first serious problem arose in Cuba, an island approximately 90 miles off the Florida coast.

The Bay of Pigs The United States had worried about Cuba ever since revolutionary leader Fidel Castro had seized power there in 1959.

The executive order that created the Peace Corps stated, "They will live at the same level as the citizens of the countries which they are sent to, doing the same work, eating the same food, speaking the same language." The Peace Corps volunteer above is teaching sewing skills to women in Sri Lanka.

Explain/Discuss

Explain to students that in the first three years of the Peace Corps, ten thousand Americans volunteered for duty. During the program's first twenty years, some eighty thousand volunteers served in eighty-eight countries. The Peace Corps, like the Alliance for Progress, had an underlying political goal: to build goodwill in developing nations and to prevent them from forming ties with the Soviet Union. Ask students why Kennedy was so concerned with winning the favor of developing nations. How successful do students think he was in South America and in other parts of the world?

Discuss the Bay of Pigs fiasco. Why was the United States concerned about Castro? Why did Kennedy agree to support the invasion?

Have students make a time line of the Cuban missile crisis events on the chalkboard. Ask them to identify the most critical time period of the crisis. Ask students to explain the following statement by Secretary of State Dean Rusk at the moment the first Soviet ships began to turn back: "We're eyeball to eyeball, and I think the other fellow just blinked."

Ask students to compare the actions taken by Presidents Kennedy and Johnson in South America with Kennedy's stated goals for the Alliance for Progress. How do students think the gap between the actions and the rhetoric could be bridged?

Links Across Time

Possible answers: In Panama, the United States took action because of Noriega's involvement in drug trafficking and because he had refused to heed his country's democratic election by stepping down. All of the previous United States invasions were prompted by fears of the spread of communism in the Western Hemisphere.

Analyze

Ask students to think of other ways in which Kennedy's goals for the Alliance for Progress might have been reached.

Activity

Teaching Heterogeneous Groups

Foreign policy during the Kennedy and Johnson administrations consisted of maintaining safety from nuclear threat by blocking the establishment of communist governments in other—particularly neighboring—countries. To help students relate to this concept, have them describe their neighborhoods. Then ask them to list characteristics of their neighborhoods that make them feel safe and those that make them feel threatened. **LEP**

Many Cubans had supported Castro because he promised to improve the lives of poor people who were being exploited by wealthy Cubans and by United States companies operating in Cuba. Castro had taken over private property, including that of the United States corporations that had dominated the Cuban economy for decades. He also developed ties to the Soviet Union, particularly after the United States broke diplomatic relations and refused to accept him as the legitimate leader of Cuba. United States officials feared that he could become a model for revolutionary upheaval throughout Latin America.

When Kennedy became President, he learned that President Eisenhower had approved a plan in 1960, in which the Central Intelligence Agency (CIA) was providing military training for Cuban opponents of Castro in Guatemala, a nearby Central American country. When training was complete, an invasion of Cuba at a place called the **Bay of Pigs** was planned. With the expectation that when the invasion began, the Cuban people would use the opportunity to overthrow Castro, Kennedy gave the CIA the go-ahead.

Resistance to the plan soon surfaced, however. When Senator J. William Fulbright, Democratic chairman of the Foreign Relations Committee, learned of the scheme, he called it an "endless can of worms" and declared:

> To give this activity even covert [secretive] support is of a piece with the hypocrisy and cynicism for which the United States is constantly denouncing [condemning] the Soviet Union in the United Nations and elsewhere. This point will not be lost on the rest of the world—nor on our own consciences. . . . The Castro regime is a thorn in the flesh; but it is not a dagger in the heart.
> Memorandum to President Kennedy, March 29, 1961

Despite such reservations and those of some military leaders, Kennedy accepted the advice of the Joint Chiefs of Staff to push ahead.

1650 1700 1750 1800 **Links Across Time** 1850 1900 1950 2000

Intervention in Latin America

When the United States invaded Cuba at the Bay of Pigs in 1961, it was neither the first time nor the last that the United States invaded a Latin American country. The United States has often intervened militarily in Latin America to protect its own interests.

Plans for the invasion of Cuba were, in fact, modeled on an invasion of Guatemala, in Central America, that took place in 1954 during the Eisenhower administration. The CIA had backed a group of guerrillas who opposed the elected, procommunist president, Jacobo Arbenz Guzmán. Concerned that Guatemala would become a communist foothold in Latin America, the United States funded a military coup that overthrew the government. Only later did people learn of the CIA's role in the coup.

More recently, the United States invaded both Grenada, an island nation off the coast of Venezuela, and Panama, in Central America. After Grenada's leader, Maurice Bishop, was killed by procommunist members of his own party in October 1983, President Ronald Reagan sent a force of 6,000 United States troops and 300 from several Caribbean countries to Grenada. They removed the leaders of the coup and returned power to the country's original anticommunist government.

Six years later, in 1989, the United States launched an invasion of Panama to oust Manuel Noriega, the head of the Panamanian military. Noriega was indicted in the United States in 1988 on charges of drug trafficking. Although Noriega lost an election in 1989, he disregarded election results and declared himself "maximum leader." At first the United States supported Panamanians who wanted to overthrow Noriega. When their attempt failed, President George Bush ordered an invasion. Noriega surrendered to United States authorities early in 1990, after 24,000 United States troops invaded Panama to ensure his arrest. *How did the reasons for the invasion of Panama differ from those in Cuba, Guatemala, and Grenada?*

The Bay of Pigs Invasion, 1961

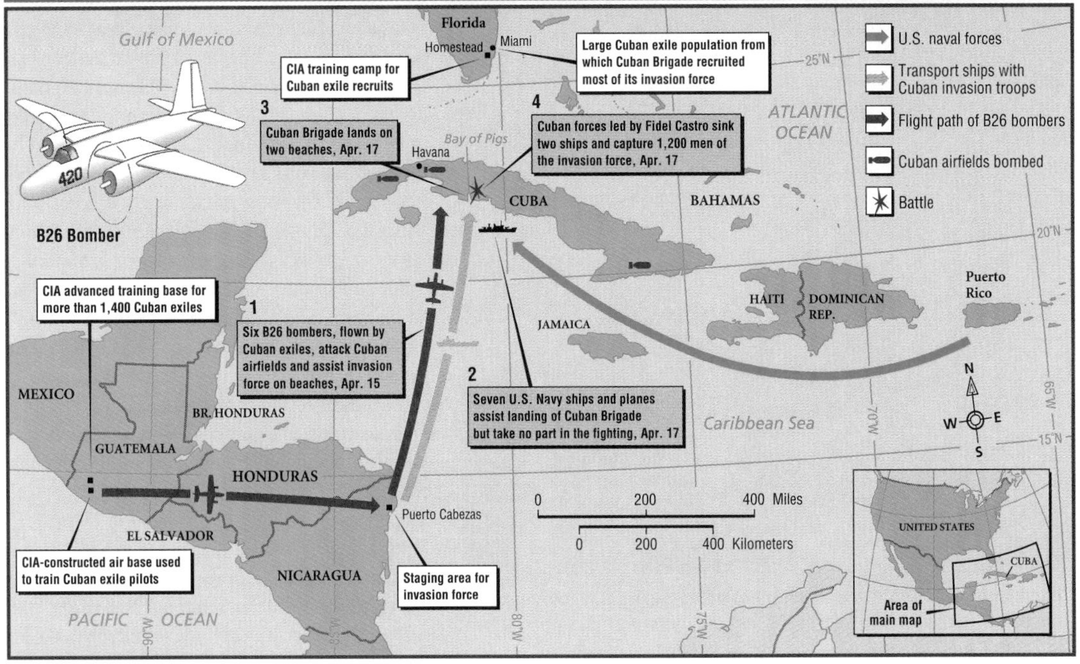

Gulf of Mexico
Florida
Homestead
Miami
CIA training camp for Cuban exile recruits
Large Cuban exile population from which Cuban Brigade recruited most of its invasion force
3
Cuban Brigade lands on two beaches, Apr. 17
4
Cuban forces led by Fidel Castro sink two ships and capture 1,200 men of the invasion force, Apr. 17
Bay of Pigs
Havana
ATLANTIC OCEAN
25°N
CUBA
BAHAMAS
20°N
B26 Bomber
420
CIA advanced training base for more than 1,400 Cuban exiles
1
Six B26 bombers, flown by Cuban exiles, attack Cuban airfields and assist invasion force on beaches, Apr. 15
JAMAICA
HAITI
DOMINICAN REP.
Puerto Rico
2
Seven U.S. Navy ships and planes assist landing of Cuban Brigade but take no part in the fighting, Apr. 17
MEXICO
BR. HONDURAS
GUATEMALA
HONDURAS
Caribbean Sea
70°W
65°W
15°N
EL SALVADOR
Puerto Cabezas
CIA-constructed air base used to train Cuban exile pilots
NICARAGUA
Staging area for invasion force
PACIFIC OCEAN
90°W
80°W
75°W
0 200 400 Miles
0 200 400 Kilometers
U.S. naval forces
Transport ships with Cuban invasion troops
Flight path of B26 bombers
Cuban airfields bombed
Battle
N
W
E
S
UNITED STATES
CUBA
Area of main map

Geography and History: Interpreting Maps
This map outlines the ill-fated Bay of Pigs invasion authorized by President Kennedy in 1961. *How were Guatemala and Nicaragua involved in the plan? How does the map show why the United States would want to maintain friendly governments in Latin American nations?*

The invasion, depicted in the map above, took place on April 17, 1961, and was a total disaster. An air strike failed to destroy Cuba's air power. Castro was therefore able to stop the United States–supported troops from coming ashore. When advisers urged Kennedy to use United States planes to provide air cover for the soldiers, he refused. Rather than continue a hopeless effort, he chose simply to cut his losses and accept defeat.

The United States lost a great deal of prestige in the disastrous attack. The nation's illegal effort to overthrow a legitimate government was exposed to the world. The United States faced anger from other countries in Latin America for violating agreements not to interfere in the rest of the Western Hemisphere. And the invasion itself was clumsy and incompetent. European leaders, who initially had high hopes for the new President, were concerned about the kind of leadership he planned to provide.

The Berlin Crisis Upset by the experience at the Bay of Pigs, Kennedy was now even more determined to respond firmly to what he perceived as a growing communist threat. Unfortunately, his first meeting with Soviet leader **Nikita Khrushchev** was another disaster.

This time the issue was Germany. After World War II, the Allies had divided Germany into zones, with the United States, Great Britain, the Soviet Union, and France each controlling one sector of the country. While the original intention was that the zones would be temporary, the lines had hardened as cold war tensions pitted the former Allies against each other. In time the western regions had been combined into one, creating the nation of West Germany, while the sector controlled by the Soviet Union became East Germany. The city of Berlin, lying inside East Germany, had been likewise divided. The Soviet effort to cut off access to Berlin in 1948 had failed as a result of President Truman's

Caption Answer to ...

Interpreting Maps

Friendly governments in nations such as Guatemala and Nicaragua allowed the CIA to establish bases from which to prepare for the invasion. Such sympathetic governments were thus essential to United States foreign policy in the region.

Enrichment

The threat of a nuclear holocaust was very real in the 1960s. Ask students to use the *Reader's Guide to Periodical Literature* to locate and report on contemporary magazine articles about building, stocking, and maintaining fallout shelters.

In Depth

Then and Now

When the Berlin Wall that divided East and West Germany for thirty years was torn down on November 9, 1989, a witness said that protesters "seemed to be drawn by the sense that . . . the barrier of concrete and steel that had figured so prominently in the history of this city and the world, might soon be relegated to history." And the reunification of Germany one year later proved to be just part of the collapse of the monolithic "iron curtain."

SOURCE READINGS

Source Readings on p. 648 will connect literature selections and primary source excerpts to historical events discussed in this section.

Caption Answer to ...

Using Historical Evidence

The Berlin Wall was a symbol of the "unfriendly neighbor" status of nations in Eastern and Western Europe; it also represented the ideological wall that kept East and West from communicating with each other.

Using Historical Evidence A West Berlin resident walks along his side of the Berlin Wall. *Why was the wall an appropriate symbol of the cold war?*

successful Berlin airlift. Now the Soviets made another effort to resolve problems in Berlin on their own terms. They demanded a peace treaty that would make the division of the city permanent and cut off the flow of East Germans into West Germany, particularly through Berlin.

Kennedy feared that the Soviet effort in Germany was part of a larger plan to take over the rest of Europe. Despite his need to establish himself as a leader in the international community, Kennedy's first conversation with Khrushchev in Vienna, Austria, in June 1961 went poorly. Kennedy felt bullied by the Soviet leader, and he knew he came off second best.

Upon returning home, Kennedy decided to show the Soviets that the United States would not be intimidated. He asked Congress for a huge increase of more than $3 billion for defense. He requested more men for the army, navy, and air force. He doubled the number of young men being drafted into the armed services, and he called up reserve forces for active duty. At the same time, he sought over $200 million for a program to build fallout shelters across the country, with the argument that the United States had

to be prepared if the confrontation over Berlin led to a nuclear war. Kennedy appeared on television to tell the American people that West Berlin was "the great testing place of Western courage and will, a focal point where our solemn commitments . . . and Soviet ambitions now meet in basic confrontation." The United States, he said, would not be pushed around: "We do not want to fight—but we have fought before." This address, strategic analyst Michael Mandelbaum later declared, was "one of the most alarming speeches by an American President in the whole, nerve-wracking course of the cold war."

The Soviets responded by building a wall in Berlin. It effectively sealed East Berliners in their region of the city (and in East Germany) and so ended the immediate crisis. The **Berlin Wall** became an enduring symbol of East-West conflict for the next three decades.

The Cuban Missile Crisis Kennedy had a chance to regain his prestige in another confrontation in Cuba. The Soviet Union, disturbed by the attempted invasion at the Bay of Pigs, had pledged to support Cuba. In October 1962, photographs taken from a United States spy plane revealed that the Soviets were placing offensive missiles on Cuban soil. Khrushchev may have been trying to bolster Soviet standing in the international community by positioning missiles so close to the United States. He may have been trying to show that the Soviets would not allow their Cuban allies to be shoved around. In any event, the missiles did not alter the overall strategic balance, for the Soviets could already inflict serious damage on the United States from missile bases within their own country. But Kennedy was convinced that the missiles in Cuba presented a direct challenge to which he must respond. ✪

The President quickly convened his top advisers in a series of secret meetings. His brother Robert, serving as the nation's attorney general and his most influential adviser, argued against an air strike to knock out the missiles. It seemed, he said, too much like the Japanese attack on Pearl Harbor that had started World War II. Nonetheless, President Kennedy ordered United States forces on full alert. Bombers and missiles were armed with nuclear weapons. The

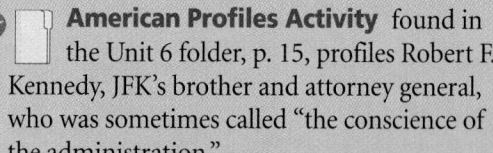

fleet was ready to move. Soldiers were prepared to invade Cuba at a moment's notice.

Kennedy's advisers in the National Security Council realized the dangerousness of the situation in this **Cuban missile crisis,** especially with nuclear warheads poised ready for use. At one point former Secretary of State Dean Acheson joined the deliberations and declared that the United States had to knock out the Soviet missiles. He was then asked what would happen next. The following conversation records his response.

> ACHESON: *I know the Soviet Union well. I know what they are required to do in the light of their history and their posture around the world. I think they will knock out our missiles in Turkey.*
> AN NSC ADVISER: *Well, then what do we do?*
> ACHESON: *I believe under our NATO treaty . . . we would be required to respond by knocking out a missile base inside the Soviet Union.*
> ANOTHER ADVISER: *Then what do they do?*
> ACHESON: *That's when we hope that cooler heads will prevail, and they'll stop and talk.*

After preparing his forces, Kennedy went on television to tell the public about the missiles and to demand that the Soviets remove them. The United States, he said, would not shrink from the risk of nuclear war. He then announced a naval "quarantine" around Cuba to prevent the Soviets from bringing in more missiles. He was careful not to call the action a "blockade," because a blockade is an act of war.

For two days the two most powerful nations in the world stood teetering on the brink of disaster. Soviet ships steamed toward the quarantine line. United States forces were ready to respond as soon as the line was crossed. Then Khrushchev called the ships back, though work on the missile sites inside Cuba continued. A few days later Khrushchev sent Kennedy a long letter in which he pledged to remove the missiles if Kennedy promised that the United States would end the quarantine and stay out of Cuba. A second letter demanded that the United States remove its missiles from Turkey

in exchange for the withdrawal of Soviet missiles in Cuba. The United States accepted the terms of the first note and ignored the second. With that, the crisis was over. As Secretary of State Dean Rusk observed to President Kennedy, "We have won a considerable victory. You and I are still alive."

In the Cuban missile crisis, the world was closer than ever before to nuclear war. Far more powerful hydrogen bombs had replaced the first atomic weapons, and this was the closest the superpowers had come to using them. For a time, Kennedy emerged from the confrontation as a hero. He had stood up to the Soviets and shown that the United States would not be pushed around. His reputation, and that of the Democratic party, improved, and popular support

Viewpoints Activity On the Cold War, found in the Unit 6 folder, pp. 16–17, presents an expanded discussion of different views of the cold war and the policies proposed for battling communism.

Viewpoints
On the Cold War

The fear of Soviet communist expansion continued to concern the United States and its allies in the decades following World War II. *How does each of the speakers below propose to battle communism?*

For Coexistence with the Soviet Union
"Some may object that, as a practical matter, the fire spread by communism can be fought effectively only with fire. I disagree. . . . Our duty is to show that between communism and the flickering old order, the United States recognizes a third choice—permissive societies whose central purpose is to embody [represent and act on] the peoples' will and the peoples' needs."
 Senator J. W. Fulbright of Arkansas in an address to the United States Senate, June 29, 1961

For Aggression Against the Soviet Union
"It is our purpose to win the cold war, not merely wage it in the hope of attaining a standoff. . . . [I]t is really astounding that our government has never stated its purpose to be that of complete victory over the tyrannical forces of international communism. . . . We need a declaration that our intention is victory. . . . And we need an official act, such as the resumption of nuclear testing, to show our own peoples and the other freedom-loving peoples of the world that we mean business."
 Senator Barry Goldwater of Arizona in an address to the United States Senate, July 14, 1961

Answer to . . .
Viewpoints

Fulbright favors trying to encourage democracies around the world; Goldwater seeks a stated policy of armed aggression to crush communism. For a more thorough examination of the cold war, see the Resource Directory below.

In Depth
Historical Misconceptions

Although the outcome of the Cuban missile crisis seemed to limit the Soviet role there, the removal of Soviet missiles from Cuba in 1962 did not in fact lessen Soviet influence nor rid Cuba of dictatorship. "There is a good deal of unfinished business in Cuba," said Kennedy. "[Castro] still remains a major danger to the United States." Castro was still in power more than thirty years later when the breakup of the Soviet Union led to the departure of Russian troops in 1993.

3. ASSESS

Section 3 Review Answers

1. (a) Peace Corps, see p. 637, (b) Berlin Wall, see p. 640, (c) Limited Test Ban Treaty, see p. 642

2. Nikita Khrushchev, see p. 639

3. Bay of Pigs, see p. 638

4. The confrontation over Berlin showed Kennedy's willingness to do anything to avoid being pushed around. When Kennedy felt bullied by Khrushchev at their first meeting in Vienna, he responded by calling for more troops and for civil defense measures to show he was ready for war.

5. Satellite photography revealed that the Soviet Union was developing a missile base in Cuba, which the United States interpreted as a threatening gesture. Both sides talked of aggressive action. Khrushchev backed down. Faced with the American quarantine, he called Soviet ships back and agreed to remove offensive missiles from Cuba if the United States ended the blockade and promised not to invade Cuba.

6. Johnson's approach to foreign affairs differed from Kennedy's. Kennedy had been most interested in foreign affairs: Johnson considered them something of a nuisance. Both leaders agreed, however, in the view that the Soviet Union was trying to spread communism and in responding aggressively to any perceived threat.

The tongue-in-cheek slogan on this bumper sticker refers to the Soviet missiles in Cuba, which marked the presence of the enemy only 90 miles off the Florida coast.

helped with mid-term congressional elections just weeks away. In time, however, critics came to suggest that what Kennedy felt was his finest hour was actually a rash and extreme response to a situation that could have been handled more rationally. Kennedy had not used traditional diplomatic channels to try to defuse the crisis, but rather had proclaimed his willingness to move to the brink of nuclear war and even beyond. He avoided disaster, Dean Acheson later observed, by "plain dumb luck."

The Cuban missile crisis did lead to a number of efforts to reduce the risk of nuclear war. Once the confrontation was over, Kennedy and Khrushchev established a "hot line" between their two nations to a'low for immediate discussion in the event of a future crisis. In the summer of 1963, they also signed the first nuclear treaty since the development of the atomic bomb. The **Limited Test Ban Treaty** banned nuclear testing above the ground, and so eliminated the radioactive fallout that was threatening to contaminate human, animal, and plant life. It still permitted underground testing, and scientists proved

After coming close to war with the Soviets early in his presidency, Kennedy signed the Limited Test Ban Treaty in 1963. In a nationwide television address following the signing, Kennedy said, "Let us, if we can, step back from the shadows of war and seek out the way of peace."

resourceful in creating bigger and better bombs that way, but it was nonetheless, as Kennedy noted, "an important first step toward peace, a step toward reason, a step away from war."

Yet despite such steps, turmoil still afflicted the relationship between the United States and the Soviet Union. In Southeast Asia, conflict between communist North Vietnam and United States–backed South Vietnam was escalating. In the years ahead, it would lead the United States into war.

LBJ and Foreign Affairs

Whereas Kennedy had been passionately concerned with the world abroad, President Johnson was preoccupied with domestic policy. Johnson was convinced that he could cajole foreign leaders with the same ease with which he controlled policymakers at home. His dismissive attitude toward smaller countries led the United States into some large and costly conflicts.

Trouble in Panama Johnson was frustrated by what he called those "piddly little" countries in Latin America. Soon after he had assumed the presidency, Panama asked for a renegotiation of the treaty Theodore Roosevelt had signed in 1903 guaranteeing the United States access to the Canal Zone. The symbolic issue of which flag—the United States or the Panamanian—should fly in the zone led to a riot and loss of life. Johnson phoned the Panamanian leader and helped cool the situation, then authorized discussions that eventually led to a new treaty.

Invasion of the Dominican Republic In the Dominican Republic, Johnson acted more aggressively. In 1965 he heard that the military rulers in this Caribbean nation close to Cuba had been attacked by rebels, and that the

Teaching Resources

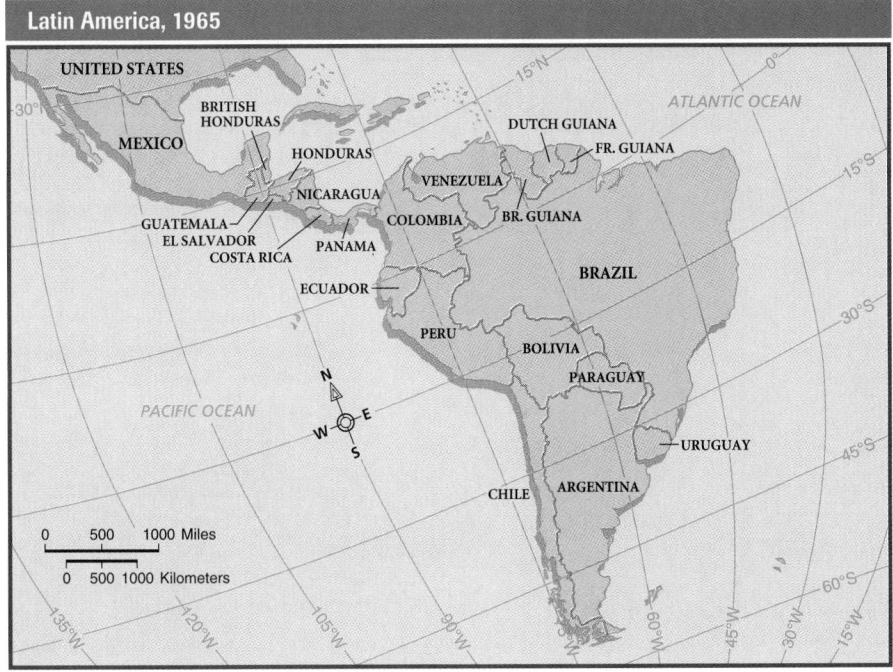

Latin America, 1965

Geography and History: Interpreting Maps
President Johnson often felt annoyed when faced with problems in Latin America that took his attention away from domestic policy. *In the context of the cold war, why did United States leaders consider it important to maintain a strong presence in this part of the world?*

disruption might endanger United States citizens living there. LBJ was livid. Arguing (wrongly, it turned out) that communist elements were causing the disruption, he sent 22,000 marines to the Dominican Republic. The presence of the United States forces tipped the balance away from the rebels. Johnson's action promoted stability in the Dominican Republic, but only at the cost of supporting a repressive military government.

Meanwhile, the Vietnam War began and soon consumed more and more resources. Johnson tried to take the same approach in Vietnam as he had in the Dominican Republic. As will be discussed in Chapter 22, his policy there had much more disastrous results.

SECTION 3 REVIEW

Key Terms, People, and Places
1. Define (a) Peace Corps, (b) Berlin Wall, (c) Limited Test Ban Treaty.
2. Identify Nikita Khrushchev.
3. Identify Bay of Pigs.

Key Concepts
4. What was the significance of Kennedy's confrontation with Khrushchev over Berlin?
5. What was the Cuban missile crisis, and how did it end?

6. Was President Johnson's approach to foreign affairs similar to or different from Kennedy's? Explain your answer.

Critical Thinking
7. **Demonstrating Reasoned Judgment** Dean Acheson called Kennedy's success in the Cuban missile crisis a result of "plain dumb luck." Do you agree or disagree with this opinion? Give reasons to support your answer.

Quiz found in the Unit 6 folder, p. 11, covers the main ideas in this section as well as the key terms.

Chapter Test Forms A and B are found in the Unit 6 folder, pp. 28–33.

Answer Keys found in the Unit 6 folder, pp. 146–159, provide answers to all student activities.

Media and Technology

Transparency
Graphic Organizer, G-4

Guided Reading Audiotapes
(English and Spanish)

Computer Test Bank

7. Answers will vary. Students may cite Kennedy's lack of experience and his failure to use normal diplomatic channels to deal with the crisis as evidence to support Acheson's claim. Others may suggest that Kennedy instinctively sensed that the only way to deal with Khrushchev was to bully him, as Khrushchev had bullied Kennedy in Vienna.

Caption Answer to ...

🌐 **Interpreting Maps**

During the cold war, United States leaders sought to contain communist influence all over the world. Communist governments in Latin America seemed especially threatening because this region was so close to the United States.

Reteach

Ask students to identify the following cold war crises by writing the name of the country in which each occurred.

● The United States and the Soviet Union came close to war over a buildup of Soviet missiles here.
● When the Soviets demanded a peace treaty that permanently divided this city, Kennedy responded forcefully.
● The bungled invasion here by opponents of Fidel Castro was organized by the United States.
● President Johnson sent troops to this country in 1965 to put down a rebellion.

4. CLOSE

Reinforcing the Big Idea

President Kennedy acted boldly to maintain United States strength in the cold war, at times bringing the nation perilously close to war. President Johnson, though little interested in foreign affairs, sent United States troops to quell a rebellion in the Dominican Republic.

Chapter Review Answers

Understanding Key Terms, People, and Places

Terms
Students should refer to the definitions of the key terms in the chapter to write sentences that show the relation of each word to domestic and foreign policy during the presidencies of John F. Kennedy and Lyndon B. Johnson.

True or False
1. false, Great Society
2. false, Peace Corps
3. false, Limited Test Ban Treaty
4. false, Medicare
5. false, Immigration Act of 1965

Matching
1. Earl Warren
2. John F. Kennedy
3. Lyndon B. Johnson

Reviewing Main Ideas

1. In the legendary kingdom of Camelot, King Arthur wanted to transform Britain into a country where strength was used to achieve right. Americans saw the Kennedy administration as symbolizing a similar idealism.

2. Kennedy wanted to stimulate the economy with a large tax cut, which he thought would help the poor indirectly. Later he proposed direct aid to the poor. He also expanded the space program.

3. Kennedy lacked a mandate from the electorate and was unable to push his programs through Congress. In addition, he addressed the problem of poverty too late in his presidency.

4. (a) The nation was shattered. Millions of Americans mourned as they watched the tragedy unfold on television. (b) The Warren Commission was formed to investigate the crime.

5. Johnson was forceful, energetic, and ambitious. His ability to win people over to his point of view helped him to get the votes he needed to pass the legislation he supported.

6. The Great Society was Johnson's program to increase the social well-being of all Americans. This program aimed to create a truly humane society that was more than simply rich and powerful.

7. In *Gideon* v. *Wainwright* (1963), the Supreme Court upheld the rights of persons accused of crimes by defending the right to free legal aid. *Escobedo* v. *Illinois* (1964) guaranteed defendants access to an attorney during questioning, and *Miranda* v. *Arizona* (1966) held that a

suspect must be informed of his or her rights before questioning. In *Griswold* v. *Connecticut* (1965) the Court upheld a couple's right to privacy.

8. Middle-class Americans felt that too many of their tax dollars were being spent on the poor; critics argued that the federal government could not respond appropriately to the needs of local communities; radicals argued that programs did not go far enough; conservatives argued that they went too far.

9. Kennedy initiated the Peace Corps to help people in developing nations.

10. These incidents revealed that Kennedy was firmly anticommunist, inexperienced in foreign affairs, and willing to take great risks.

11. He saw the missiles as a direct threat to national security requiring an immediate response.

12. Johnson was more interested in domestic than foreign policy. However, he was militantly anticommunist, as he demonstrated when he sent United States forces to fight rebels in the Dominican Republic who he thought were backed by communists.

13. Johnson's contemptuous attitude toward smaller foreign nations resulted in costly conflicts for the United States. Foreign affairs diverted Johnson's attention from Great Society programs, as well as the money to support them.

Chapter Review

Understanding Key Terms, People, and Places

Key Terms
1. liberal consensus
2. mandate
3. New Frontier
4. Warren Commission
5. Great Society
6. Volunteers in Service to America
7. Medicare
8. Immigration Act of 1965
9. Peace Corps
10. Berlin Wall
11. Cuban missile crisis
12. Limited Test Ban Treaty

People
13. John F. Kennedy
14. Earl Warren
15. Lyndon B. Johnson
16. Nikita Khrushchev

Places
17. Bay of Pigs

Terms For each term above, write a sentence that explains how it relates to domestic and foreign policy during the presidencies of John F. Kennedy and Lyndon B. Johnson.

True or False Determine whether each statement is true or false. If it is true, write "true." If it is false, change the underlined term to make the statement true.
1. Lyndon Johnson's <u>New Frontier</u> focused on domestic policy.
2. President Kennedy's <u>Medicare</u> program sent American volunteers abroad to help people in developing countries.
3. The <u>Warren Commission</u> prohibited above-ground nuclear testing.
4. <u>VISTA</u> was designed to provide medical care for older Americans.
5. <u>The Limited Test Ban Treaty</u> eliminated quotas that had discriminated against immigrants from areas outside northern and western Europe.

Matching Review the key people in the list above. If you are not sure of a person's significance, review that person in the chapter. Then choose a name from the list that best matches each description below.
1. the head of the group that investigated the Kennedy assassination
2. the leader who ordered United States forces on full alert during the Cuban missile crisis
3. the creator of the Great Society

Reviewing Main Ideas

Section 1 (pp. 624–627)
1. Explain why the Kennedy administration was compared to the Broadway musical *Camelot*.
2. What domestic programs did Kennedy propose?
3. Why was Kennedy's domestic policy largely unsuccessful?
4. (a) How did the nation react to Kennedy's assassination in 1963? (b) What later actions were taken to investigate his death?

Section 2 (pp. 629–633)
5. How did Lyndon Johnson's personality help him advance his political career?
6. Explain Johnson's statement to University of Michigan students that they had the opportunity to move "upward toward the Great Society."

7. Describe three Supreme Court decisions of the 1960s that supported the ideals of the Great Society.
8. What criticisms of the Great Society surfaced?

Section 3 (pp. 636–643)
9. For what reasons did President Kennedy initiate the Peace Corps?
10. What did the invasion at the Bay of Pigs and the Berlin crisis reveal about President Kennedy's foreign policy?
11. How did President Kennedy interpret the presence of Soviet missiles in Cuba?
12. What was Johnson's approach to foreign policy?
13. How did foreign affairs affect Johnson's Great Society programs?

1. **Making Comparisons** Describe the programs you would implement if you were to create a Great Society today. In what ways would they be similar to the programs of Johnson's Great Society?

2. **Predicting Consequences** How did the beliefs of Kennedy and Johnson about the spread of communism abroad lead to United States involvement in the Vietnam War?

Making Connections

1. **Evaluating Primary Sources** Review the first primary source excerpt on page 641. What does this conversation reveal about the way in which ideologies—fundamental political beliefs—determined the actions of the United States and Soviet governments during the cold war?

2. **Understanding the Visuals** Look at the tables on page 626. How might the facts illustrated in the table on income distribution have affected President Kennedy's ability to influence Congress to change NASA spending, as shown in the second table?

3. **Writing About the Chapter** You are a top adviser to President Kennedy when photos from a United States spy plane reveal the presence of Soviet missiles in Cuba. Write a memo advising the President on how to handle the situation. First, make a list of the various actions that the President might take. Note both the positive and negative aspects of each. Next,

write a draft of your memo in which you offer each possibility, describe its pros and cons, and finish with your recommendation for the best course of action. Revise your memo, making certain that each possible course of action is clearly explained. Proofread your memo and draft a final copy.

4. **Using the Graphic Organizer** This graphic organizer uses a tree map to organize information about foreign policy in the 1960s. (a) Based on the information in the tree map, what earlier event may have caused President Kennedy to need to regain the respect of the international community during the Cuban missile crisis? (b) What was the Soviet response to Kennedy's declaration that West Berlin was a testing ground for Western resolve? (c) On a separate sheet of paper, create your own tree map about the Great Society, using this tree map as an example.

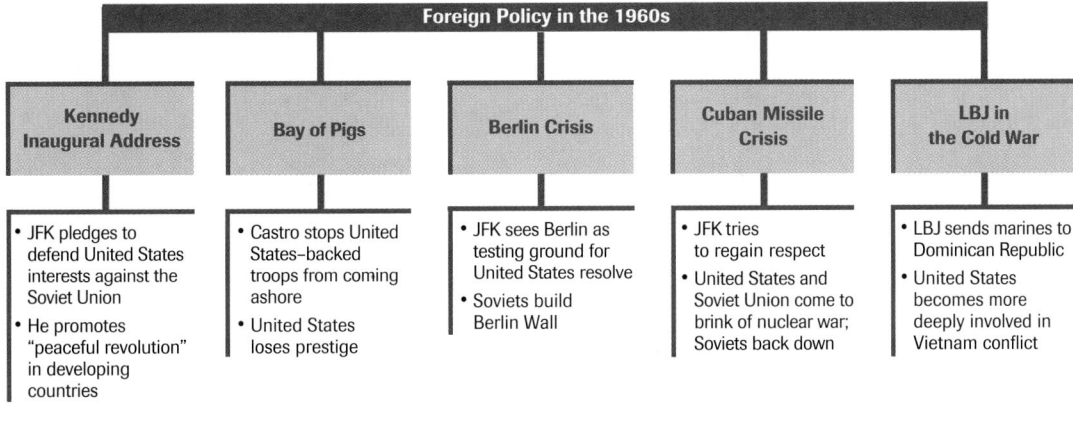

Foreign Policy in the 1960s

Kennedy Inaugural Address	Bay of Pigs	Berlin Crisis	Cuban Missile Crisis	LBJ in the Cold War
• JFK pledges to defend United States interests against the Soviet Union • He promotes "peaceful revolution" in developing countries	• Castro stops United States–backed troops from coming ashore • United States loses prestige	• JFK sees Berlin as testing ground for United States resolve • Soviets build Berlin Wall	• JFK tries to regain respect • United States and Soviet Union come to brink of nuclear war; Soviets back down	• LBJ sends marines to Dominican Republic • United States becomes more deeply involved in Vietnam conflict

3. Students' memos should mention alternative solutions to the crisis such as ignoring the Soviet missiles, negotiation, and economic or political pressure. They should also mention the pros and cons of each and conclude with a recommendation for a course of action.

4. (a) The flow map indicates that the United States lost prestige during the Bay of Pigs affair. (b) The Soviets' response was to build the Berlin Wall. (c) Students' graphic organizers should include information about Johnson's tax cut, his war on poverty, health care legislation, aid to education, and other proposals.

Alternative Assessment

Final Evaluation
Use the following guidelines to evaluate student projects:
● **Evidence of mastery of content** To what extent do projects show knowledge and understanding of chapter content?
● **Evidence of thoughtfulness** To what extent do projects reflect a personal position?
● **Evidence of outside research** To what extent do projects reflect outside research?

Thinking Critically

1. Students may propose a variety of social welfare programs to combat such contemporary problems as homelessness and unemployment. Students may mention that while the focus has shifted somewhat, many of the issues of the 1960s, such as civil rights and affordable medical care, are still unresolved.

2. Both Kennedy and Johnson were convinced that communism needed to be fought wherever it turned up, or else the Soviet Union and its allies would take control of the world. Thus they were willing to send United States troops to fight the forces of Ho Chi Minh in Vietnam.

Making Connections

1. Both superpowers had an almost blind, irrational fear of the threat each nation posed to the other. Thus, a United States strike in Cuba would "require" the Soviet Union to hit missile sites in Turkey, and so on. The cold war made honest diplomatic talks seem a last resort rather than an obvious first step toward solving disputes.

2. Because of the huge expense of the space program—especially compared with Americans' salaries—members of Congress were probably under pressure from constituents not to increase spending on such programs. Thus, Congress was likely to make it difficult for Kennedy to pass legislation increasing spending on NASA.

Read this quotation to students: "Ask not what your country can do for you—ask what you can do for your country." Ask students whether they have ever heard this quotation before and lead a discussion about its meaning. Tell students that these famous words come from John F. Kennedy's inaugural address.

Then, read students this quotation: "I am well aware of the fact that many American families will bear the burden of these requests. . . . But these are burdens which must be borne if freedom is to be defended. Americans have willingly borne them before, and they will not flinch from the task now." Ask students how this quotation might be related to the first. Help students understand that both quotations ask Americans to support their country. Tell the class that the author of this quotation is also John Kennedy, and he spoke these words in July 1961, six months after he took office. Have students make educated guesses about what the world situation might have been when Kennedy made the second speech. Then tell them that the speech preceded the building of the Berlin Wall in Germany.

Have students use their textbooks to make a time line of the events in the United States between 1961 and 1963. Then discuss whether the hopes that Kennedy expresses in his inaugural address were realized during his term in office. Point out to students Kennedy's belief that "All this will not be finished in the first one hundred days. Nor will it be finished in the first one thousand days, nor in the life of this administration, nor even perhaps in our lifetime on this planet." Discuss with them whether any of these hopes have been realized in the years since Kennedy's death.

CHAPTER 19
SOURCE READINGS

President Kennedy's Inaugural Address

 *Primary Source*

INTRODUCTION When John F. Kennedy gave his bold inaugural address on a cold, windy day in January 1961, it seemed to many Americans to signal a fresh new start for the country. In the address, Kennedy spoke to the American people, to the friends of the United States, and to the nation's most threatening foe—the Soviet Union. He spoke sternly of the nation's intent to "pay any price, bear any burden, meet any hardship" in order to ensure the survival of democracy and freedom in the world. But he also stretched out his hand to the communist nation, asking that "both sides begin anew the quest for peace."

VOCABULARY Before you read the selection, find the meaning of these words in a dictionary: forebears, asunder, belabor, eradicate, tribulation.

We observe today not a victory of party but a celebration of freedom—symbolizing an end as well as a beginning—signifying renewal as well as change. For I have sworn before you and Almighty God the same solemn oath our forebears prescribed nearly a century and three-quarters ago.

The world is very different now. For man holds in his mortal hands the power to abolish all forms of human poverty and all forms of human life. And yet the same revolutionary beliefs for which our forebears fought are still at issue around the globe—the belief that the rights of man come not from the generosity of the state but from the hand of God.

We dare not forget today that we are the heirs of that first revolution. Let the word go forth from this time and place, to friend and foe alike, that the torch has been passed to a new generation of Americans—born in this century, tempered by war, disciplined by a hard and bitter peace, proud of our ancient heritage—and unwilling to witness or permit the slow undoing of those human rights to which this nation has always been committed, and to which we are committed today at home and around the world.

Let every nation know, whether it wishes us well or ill, that we shall pay any price, bear any burden, meet any hardship, support any friend, oppose any foe to assure the survival and the success of liberty.

This much we pledge—and more.

To those old allies whose cultural and spiritual origins we share, we pledge the loyalty of faithful friends. United, there is little we cannot do in a host of co-operative ventures. Divided, there is little we can do—for we dare not meet a powerful challenge at odds and split asunder.

To those new states whom we welcome to the ranks of the free, we pledge our word that one form of colonial control shall not have passed away merely to be replaced by a far more iron tyranny. We shall not always expect to find them supporting our view. But we shall always hope to find them strongly supporting their own freedom—and to remember that, in the past, those who foolishly sought power by riding the back of the tiger ended up inside. . . .

Finally, to those nations who would make themselves our adversary, we offer not a pledge but a request: that both sides begin anew the quest for peace, before the dark powers of destruction unleashed by science engulf all humanity in planned or accidental self-destruction.

We dare not tempt them with weakness. For only when our arms are sufficient beyond doubt can we be certain beyond doubt that they will never be employed.

But neither can two great and powerful groups of nations take comfort from our present course—both sides overburdened by the cost of modern weapons, both rightly alarmed by the steady spread of the deadly atom, yet both racing to alter that uncertain balance of terror that stays the hand of mankind's final war.

So let us begin anew—remembering on both sides that civility is not a sign of weakness, and sincerity is always subject to proof. Let us never negotiate out of fear. But let us never fear to negotiate.

Let both sides explore what problems unite us instead of belaboring those problems which divide us.

Let both sides, for the first time, formulate serious and precise proposals for the inspection and control of arms—and bring the absolute power to destroy other nations under the absolute control of all nations.

Let both sides seek to invoke the wonders of science instead of its terrors. Together let us explore the stars, conquer the deserts, eradicate disease, tap the ocean depths, and encourage the arts and commerce.

Let both sides unite to heed in all corners of the earth the command of Isaiah—to "undo the heavy burdens . . .[and] let the oppressed go free."

And if a beachhead of co-operation may push back the jungle of suspicion, let both sides join in creating a new endeavor,

President John F. Kennedy and First Lady Jacqueline Kennedy pause on their way to a White House function.

not a new balance of power, but a new world of law, where the strong are just and the weak secure and the peace preserved.

All this will not be finished in the first one hundred days. Nor will it be finished in the first one thousand days, nor in the life of this administration, nor even perhaps in our lifetime on this planet. But let us begin.

In your hands, my fellow citizens, more than mine, will rest the final success or failure of our course. Since this country was founded, each generation of Americans has been summoned to give testimony to its national loyalty. The graves of young Americans who answered the call to service surround the globe.

Now the trumpet summons us again—not as a call to bear arms, though arms we need—not as a call to battle, though embattled we are—but a call to bear the burden of a long twilight struggle, year in and year out, "rejoicing in hope, patient in tribulation"—a struggle against the common enemies of man: tyranny, poverty, disease, and war itself.

Can we forge against these enemies a grand and global alliance, North and South, East and West, that can assure a more fruitful life for all mankind? Will you join in that historic effort?

In the long history of the world, only a few generations have been granted the role of defending freedom in its hour of maximum danger. I do not shrink from this responsibility—I welcome it. I do not believe that any of us would exchange places with any other people or any other generation. The energy, the faith, the devotion which we bring to this endeavor will light our country and all who serve it—and the glow from that fire can truly light the world.

Using a source such as the Department of State Bulletins, have students locate and read the full text of Kennedy's 1961 inaugural address. Then have them locate and read the full text of President Clinton's inaugural address, given in 1993. Students should then write a paper that compares the tone, content, and style of the two addresses. It should also use the text of the addresses to explain the different world and domestic situations facing the nation in 1961 and 1993.

As an alternative assignment, have students look up newspapers from July 26, 1961, the day after Kennedy's speech on the Berlin crisis. Students should team up with three or four others to prepare a news broadcast that demonstrates to the class the public reaction to Kennedy's speech and that relates other events happening in the world at the time. Students might include the Kennedy speech as their top story and interview political analysts and members of the public for reactions to the speech. Students might then give brief reports on other leading news stories for that day, including sports events and weather forecasts if they like. The source for the news program should be newspapers from that day; thus, all broadcasts should be an actual reporting of the facts. Have students write scripts and perform their news program for the class. If possible, videotape the presentations for other classes to watch.

SOURCE READINGS

And so, my fellow Americans: ask not what your country can do for you—ask what you can do for your country.

My fellow citizens of the world: ask not what America will do for you, but what together we can do for the freedom of man.

Finally, whether you are citizens of America or citizens of the world, ask of us here the same high standards of strength and sacrifice which we ask of you. With a good conscience our only sure reward, with history the final judge of our deeds, let us go forth to lead the land we love, asking His blessing and His help, but knowing that here on earth God's work must truly be our own.

THINKING ABOUT THE SELECTION

1. What "dark powers of destruction" does Kennedy refer to several times in his speech?
2. What five proposals does Kennedy make to "those nations who would make themselves our adversaries"?

Critical Thinking

3. **Testing Conclusions** "The United States was in the midst of the cold war when Kennedy took office in 1961." Find evidence from the excerpt to support or refute this statement.

Kennedy's Report on the Berlin Crisis

 *Primary Source*

INTRODUCTION Just over six months after President Kennedy took office, actions by Soviet leaders seemed to indicate that the Communists intended to refuse the invitation of peace that he had extended to them in his inaugural address. Instead, Premier Nikita Khrushchev chose to test Kennedy's determination to protect freedom and democracy throughout the world by threatening to take over the city of Berlin. On July 25, 1961, Kennedy appeared on television and gave a most alarming speech, one that set the tone for many more years of cold war.

VOCABULARY Before you read the selection, find the meaning of this word in a dictionary: timidity.

July 25, 1961

Seven weeks ago tonight I returned from Europe to report on my meeting with Premier Khrushchev and the others. His grim warnings about the future of the world, his aide memoire on Berlin, his subsequent speeches and threats which he and his agents have launched, and the increase in the Soviet military budget that he has announced have all prompted a series of decisions by the administration and a series of consultations with the members of the NATO organization. In Berlin, as you recall, he intends to bring to an end, through a stroke of the pen, first, our legal rights to be in West Berlin and, secondly, our ability to make good on our commitment to the 2 million free people of that city. That we cannot permit.

We are clear about what must be done—and we intend to do it. I want to talk frankly with you tonight about the first steps that we shall take. These actions will require sacrifice on the part of many of our citizens. More will be required in the future. They will require, from all of us, courage and perseverance in the years to come. But if we and our allies act out of strength and unity of purpose—with calm determination and steady nerves, using restraint in our words as well as our weapons—I am hopeful that both peace and freedom will be sustained. . . .

Let me remind you that the fortunes of war and diplomacy left the free people of West Berlin in 1945 110 miles behind the Iron Curtain. . . .

ANSWERS TO

Thinking About the Selection

1. Kennedy refers to nuclear war and destruction several times in his speech.

2. He proposes: (1) that both sides explore the problems that they can solve together; (2) that both sides formulate a plan for arms control and inspection; (3) that both sides work to develop positive scientific advances, rather than destructive ones; (4) that both sides work to help the oppressed of the world; and (5) that both sides help to create a world of justice.

3. The evidence supports this statement. Specific examples include Kennedy's statement of strength and warning, meant for the Soviet Union, that we will fight to preserve democracy in the world; his reference to the "dark powers of destruction" (the atomic bomb) and the need to prevent a nuclear war; his assertion that the nation must remain strong militarily; his reference to the "steady spread of the deadly atom"; his use of the term "balance of terror" in place of the traditional cold war term "balance of power."

It would be a mistake for others to look upon Berlin, because of its location, as a tempting target. The United States is there, the United Kingdom and France are there, the pledge of NATO is there, and the people of Berlin are there. It is as secure, in that sense, as the rest of us, for we cannot separate its safety from our own. . . .

We do not want to fight, but we have fought before. And others in earlier times have made the same dangerous mistake of assuming that the West was too selfish and too soft and too divided to resist invasions of freedom in other lands. Those who threatened to unleash the forces of war on a dispute over West Berlin should recall the words of an ancient philosopher: "A man who causes fear cannot be free from fear."

We cannot and will not permit the Communists to drive us out of Berlin, either gradually or by force. . . .

In the days and months ahead, I shall not hesitate to ask the Congress for additional measures or exercise any of the Executive powers that I possess to meet this threat to peace. Everything essential to the security of freedom must be done; and if that should require more men, or more taxes, or more controls, or other new powers, I shall not hesitate to ask them. The measures proposed today will be constantly studied, and altered as necessary. But while we will not let panic shape our policy, neither will we permit timidity to direct our program. . . .

And let me add that I am well aware of the fact that many American families will bear the burden of these requests. Studies or careers will be interrupted; husbands and sons will be called away; incomes in some cases will be reduced. But these are burdens which must be borne if freedom is to be defended. Americans have willingly borne them before, and they will not flinch from the task now.

We have another sober responsibility. To recognize the possibility of nuclear war in the missile age without

The Berlin Wall was built in August, 1961. It stood until 1989, when the East German government opened the border to the West.

our citizens' knowing what they should do and where they should go if bombs begin to fall would be a failure of responsibility. In May I pledged a new start on civil defense. . . . Tomorrow I am requesting of Congress new funds for the following immediate objectives: to identify and mark space in existing structures—public and private—that could be used for fallout shelters in case of attack; to stock those shelters with food, water, first-aid kits, and other minimum essentials for survival; to increase their capacity; to improve our air-raid warning and fallout detection systems, including a new household warning system which is now under development; and to take other measures that will be effective at an early date to save millions of lives if needed.

In the event of an attack, the lives of those families which are not hit in a nuclear blast and fire can still be saved—if they can be warned to take shelter and if that shelter is available. We owe that kind of insurance to our families—and to our country. In contrast to our friends in Europe, the need for this kind of protection is new to our shores. But the time to start is now. In the coming months I hope to let every citizen know what steps he can take without delay to protect his family in case of attack. I know that you will want to do no less.

THINKING ABOUT THE SELECTION

1. Why is Kennedy's speech so alarming?
2. What actions does Kennedy pledge to take to ready the nation for nuclear war?

Critical Thinking

3. **Predicting Consequences** One consequence of Kennedy's speech was a debate in the United States about the pros and cons of the large-scale construction of fallout shelters. What might some of those pros and cons be?

ANSWERS TO

Thinking About the Selection

1. The speech is alarming because Kennedy seems to expect the situation to escalate; he feels it is serious enough to ask the American people to be ready to make sacrifices to defend freedom.

2. He pledges to request funds from Congress to set up fallout shelters, to increase the capacity of existing fallout shelters, to improve the nation's air-raid warning system, and "other measures" that he does not specify.

3. *Pros:* millions of lives would be saved in the event of a nuclear attack; the construction of shelters would help calm people's fears by making them feel they would have protection in the event of a nuclear attack. *Cons:* the construction of shelters might increase the possibility of nuclear war by creating the perception that the country could survive a nuclear war and thus making the decision to begin a nuclear war less frightening; the money spent constructing fallout shelters would largely be wasted because there is no real protection against all-out nuclear attack.

Chapter 20 The Civil Rights Movement
1960–1968

📁 Teaching Resources (See Unit 6 Folder)

	Instruction	Enrichment
Section 1 **Leaders and Strategies** (pp. 652–657)	Reproducible Lesson Plan, p. 35 Alternate Lesson Plan, p. 146 Guided Reading and Review, p. 39 Quiz, p. 40	American Profiles Activity, Thurgood Marshall, p. 50 Viewpoints Activity, On School Integration, pp. 51–52 Visual Learning Activity, Passive Resistance, p. 61 Literature Activity, SNCC Workers, pp. 58–59 Historian's Toolbox Activity, Using Autobiography and Biography, p. 53
Section 2 **Nonviolent Confrontation: A Turning Point in History** (pp. 659–663)	Reproducible Lesson Plan, p. 36 Alternate Lesson Plan, p. 147 Guided Reading and Review, p. 41 Quiz, p. 42	American Profiles Activity, Sidney Poitier, p. 49 Primary Source Activity, Protecting the Freedom Riders, p. 55 Turning Points Extension Activity, The Lasting Impact of Nonviolent Confrontation, pp. 47–48
Section 3 **The Political Response** (pp. 666–670)	Reproducible Lesson Plan, p. 37 Alternate Lesson Plan, p. 148 Guided Reading and Review, p. 43 Quiz, p. 44	Primary Source Activity, Registering to Vote in Mississippi, pp. 56–57 Visual Learning Activity, A White House Demonstration, p. 62
Section 4 **The Challenge of Black Power** (pp. 671–675)	Reproducible Lesson Plan, p. 38 Alternate Lesson Plan, p. 149 Guided Reading and Review, p. 45 Quiz, p. 46 Chapter Test, Forms A & B, pp. 63–68	Literature Activity, Sins of the Fathers, p. 60 Critical Thinking Activity, Demonstrating Reasoned Judgment, p. 54

📁 Additional Chapter Resources

Resource Organizer, p. 34
Alternate Lesson Plan, p. 145
Answer Keys, pp. 149–159

Bibliography

For the Teacher
Branch, Taylor. *Parting the Waters: America in the King Years, 1954–1963.* Simon & Schuster, 1988. (Chronicles the times from Eisenhower to Kennedy.)
Davis, Flora. *Moving the Mountain: The Women's Movement in America Since 1960.* Simon & Schuster, 1991. (Blends archival material with interviews to trace the movement from the 1960s to the early 1990s.)

Prentice Hall Literature Excerpts from *The American Experience,* 1994, including Walker, Alice. "Everyday Use," from *In Love and Trouble: Stories of Black Women.* Harcourt Brace, 1967.

The Big Idea for the chapter and how the main ideas in each section relate to the Big Idea are graphically displayed below. Comprehension of this chapter's Big Idea is critical to students' understanding of United States history and how we as a nation got where we are today.

Media and Technology

  Visions of America: Turning Point Story, "Nonviolent Solutions" (length: approx. 4 minutes)

  Visions of America: Roundtable Discussion of "Nonviolent Solutions"

 Critical Thinking, I-17; Graphic Organizer, G-3

 Guided Reading Audiotapes (English and Spanish)

 Computer Test Bank

For the Student
"Eyes on the Prize." PBS Video. (Comprehensive six-part series on the history of the civil rights movement from 1954.)
Raines, Howell. *My Soul Is Rested: Movement Days in the Deep South Remembered.* Penguin, 1983 edition. (First-person accounts of participants in major civil rights events.)

CHAPTER 20

The 1960s were a time of great progress and great frustration for African Americans. Through nonviolent protests and an extremely focused civil rights struggle, African Americans ended institutional segregation and secured voting rights in the South. Lack of progress in economic issues, especially in urban areas, however, drove some to vent their anger through bitter violence.

SECTION 1

The civil rights movement was diverse in its tactics but united in its goal of halting segregation.

SECTION 2

Nonviolent protests—on segregated buses and at whites-only lunch counters— brought both violence and victories and revealed the courage of ordinary Americans in standing up for their convictions.

SECTION 3

As the voices of protest grew, politicians could no longer ignore the issue of civil rights.

SECTION 4

Not content with limited progress and continuing discrimination, African American frustration turned to violence—and the civil rights movement split on its response to discrimination.

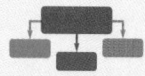

The Civil Rights Movement
1960–1968

The Relevance of the Big Idea

The civil rights movement of the 1990s is similar to the 1960s movement in some significant ways—progress and frustration are still its major characteristics. African Americans are no longer fighting for the right to vote; they are steadily increasing their representation in legislative bodies across the country. Yet they still face problems of housing and job discrimination, as well as high poverty and mortality rates. The impoverished ghettos of urban America and starkly poor rural communities still simmer—and sometimes boil over, as witnessed in the Los Angeles riots of 1992.

Ask students to list ways in which African Americans today are trying to call attention to the inequities that they suffer. Discuss the goals of each method.

In Depth

Global Connections

While the civil rights movement of the 1960s forced the American people to turn inward, the nation was also experiencing a revolution in international communications. In 1965, the first operational communications satellite, *Early Bird,* was launched; and by the late 1960s, satellite telecasts could be seen by 500 million viewers in thirty nations. The war in Vietnam, civil rights marches, and riots in the street all appeared on the nation's TV screens at home. This leap forward in communications has been compared to the 1866 opening of the first transatlantic telegraph link.

The Civil Rights Movement
1960–1968

After scoring major legal victories through the 1950s, the civil rights movement enjoyed a groundswell of popular support in the 1960s. African Americans and others focused their attention on ending segregation and securing voting rights in the South. The battle against inequality was a bitter and often violent one, but it yielded significant results by the middle of the decade. Once desegregation was under way, the movement began to address the more subtle issues of economic injustice that plagued the nation's urban centers.

Events in the United States				
		1961 Freedom Riders challenge segregation on interstate buses.	**1962** James Meredith becomes the first African American student to attend the University of Mississippi.	**1963** Martin Luther King writes his "Letter from a Birmingham Jail." • The March on Washington takes place.
	1960	**1961**	**1962**	**1963**
Events in the World	**1960** Congo and Nigeria win independence. • South Africa bans the African National Congress.	**1961** Mao Zedong's economic plan, the Great Leap Forward, ends in China.	**1962** Algeria and Uganda win independence. • The Soviet Union removes missiles from Cuba.	**1963** The Organization of African Unity is founded.

▶ RESOURCE DIRECTORY

Teaching Resources

Alternate Lesson Plan Demonstrating the Big Idea, found in the Alternate Lesson Plans folder, p. 145, provides a strategy to instruct students about the Big Idea that a highly focused civil rights movement in the 1960s resulted in some progress, but frustration and disagreement eventually split the movement.

Alternative Assessment Handbook provides information, guidance, and strategies for alternative methods of assessment. It includes an essay on new trends in assessment, guidance and strategies for developing performance tasks and portfolios, scoring rubrics, and sample evaluation forms.

Pages 652–657
Leaders and Strategies

Civil rights groups in the 1960s were as diverse as the people in the movement. Each group had its own priorities, but all spoke up against violence and unfair treatment of African Americans with a clear, strong voice that said, "No more."

Pages 659–663
Nonviolent Confrontation: A Turning Point in History

"We Shall Overcome," sang civil rights protesters, revealing both their spirit of nonviolence and their steadfast commitment to the cause. Acts such as sitting at "whites only" lunch counters brought vicious responses, but also showed the courage and determination of the protesters.

Pages 664–665
The Lasting Impact of Nonviolent Confrontation

Pages 666–670
The Political Response

For politicians in the early 1960s, taking a firm stand in favor of civil rights was a risky business. As the decade wore on, however, the rising voice of protest no longer could be ignored in Washington.

Pages 671–675
The Challenge of Black Power

During the civil rights movement, change happened slowly and at times appeared to have ground to a halt. The response from some African Americans was a call for self-defense—even if it meant using violence.

1964	1965	1966	1967	1968
1964 Congress passes the Civil Rights Act. • Three young civil rights activists are killed in Mississippi.	**1965** Congress passes Voting Rights Act. • Malcolm X is assassinated. • Watts riot occurs.	**1966** The militant Black Panther party is founded. • Splits develop in civil rights movement.		**1968** The Kerner Commission publishes its report on civil disobedience.
1964 The Beatles achieve international fame as rock musicians. • Palestine Liberation Organization is founded.		**1966** The Cultural Revolution begins in China.	**1967** First successful human heart transplant takes place in South Africa. • Israel defeats Arabs in Six-Day War.	**1968** Japanese novelist Kawabata Yasunari wins Nobel Prize in literature.

Media and Technology

Transparency
Fine Art, D-19

As an ongoing chapter project, students can compile a *Who's Who in the Civil Rights Movement* based on people mentioned in this chapter and others they can find out about through research. Students should research and write short biographies of eight to ten leaders. The selection should include both men and women, African Americans and whites. Students may include an interesting quotation by or anecdote about each leader. Students might choose to illustrate their books with a time line or chart, pictures or sketches of leaders, or photos of protest marches. They might use other relevant visuals to create an interesting cover.

Explain that projects will be evaluated according to the following guidelines:
- **Unacceptable** Projects are not attempted, or fail to meet the guidelines outlined.
- **Limited/Acceptable** Projects include biographies of people relevant to the civil rights movement and meet basic requirements of the project.
- **Extensive/Commendable** Biographies are written in an engaging manner; the book includes some visuals.
- **Extraordinary/Outstanding** Biographies are of high interest and are well integrated with visuals, reflecting an understanding of the variety of people, ideas, and strategies within the civil rights movement.

For more information and guidance on alternative assessment trends and strategies, see the Alternative Assessment Handbook in the Resource Directory on page 650.

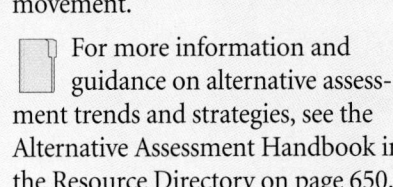

1. FOCUS

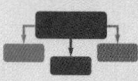

Connecting to the Big Idea

See page 650B. Explain to students that the civil rights movement was not a monolithic organization under the sway of one leader. The groups were as diverse as the people in the movement. Ask students to note in what ways it was diverse and in what ways it was united.

Objectives

● Describe the variety of opinions and goals within the civil rights movement.

● Identify Martin Luther King, Jr., and explain his role in the civil rights movement.

Bellringer

Ask students to think of ways in which people can protest without resorting to violence. What advantages do these tactics have?

Reading Strategy

Question Writing Ask students to read the section headings and subheadings and formulate a question pertaining to each. Then have them answer the questions they have written as they read.

SECTION 1

Leaders and Strategies

SECTION PREVIEW

Civil rights groups in the 1960s were as diverse as the people in the movement. Each group had its own priorities, but all spoke up against violence and unfair treatment of African Americans with a clear, strong voice that said, "No more."

The Congress of Racial Equality was one of many civil rights groups committed to improving the status of African Americans. This hat was designed to be worn at the 1963 March on Washington.

Key Concepts

• The civil rights movement consisted of many separate groups, each with a slightly different aim within the larger goal of social equality.

• Martin Luther King, Jr., was a Southern Baptist minister who became a leader in the civil rights movement through his powerful speaking and commitment to nonviolent resistance.

Key Terms, People, and Places

interracial, Congress of Racial Equality (CORE), Southern Christian Leadership Conference (SCLC), Student Nonviolent Coordinating Committee (SNCC)

T he civil rights movement was composed of ordinary citizens whose courage and determination to end racial injustice in the United States brought remarkable changes to the nation. As in all grassroots movements, the motivation for change came from the experiences and beliefs of a large number of people at the local level, not from a central organization directing activities. Several groups did form, however, out of the need to share information and coordinate activities within the movement. Each of the groups described in this section had its own goals and concerns, but all of them helped to focus the energies of thousands of Americans committed to securing civil rights for all citizens.

The NAACP Focuses on Legal Issues

By the time the civil rights movement began to make its impact felt in the 1960s, the National Association for the Advancement of Colored People (NAACP) was one of the oldest civil rights organizations in the United States. It had been founded in 1910 to promote equality, remove obstacles to voting for all Americans, and secure full legal equality. W.E.B. Du Bois, a prominent African American scholar who had been one of the founding members, summarized the NAACP's goals in a memo to its board of directors:

> T he main object of this association is to secure for colored people, and particularly for Americans of Negro descent, free and equal participation in the democracy of modern culture. This means the clearing away of obstructions to such participation, effort toward fitting these people for this participation, and it means also the making of a world democracy in which all men may participate.

The NAACP was **interracial**—it consisted of both African Americans and white Americans working together for the common goal of equality. Du Bois, who was the first African American to receive a doctoral degree from Harvard University, served as director of publicity and research. He also edited the NAACP magazine, the *Crisis*.

One major focus of NAACP activity was to put an end to lynching. The organization's efforts succeeded in getting two antilynching bills passed by the House of Representatives in the 1930s. Southern leaders in the Senate prevented these bills from becoming law, but the NAACP kept the issue of lynching in the public eye.

The NAACP was more successful in its court battles. In the 1920s and 1930s, it had won a number of legal battles in the areas of

▶ RESOURCE DIRECTORY

Teaching Resources

Reproducible Lesson Plan found in the Unit 6 folder, p. 35, provides a summary of the Section 1 lesson plan content.

Alternate Lesson Plan: Cooperative Learning found in the Alternate Lesson Plans folder, p. 146, helps groups of students focus on the goals and strategies of civil rights activists through writing speeches for civil rights leaders.

Guided Reading and Review found in the Unit 6 folder, p. 39, provides a structure for reading and mastering the key concepts and reviewing the key terms for Section 1. (Guided Practice)

American Profiles Activity found in the Unit 6 folder, p. 50, profiles Thurgood Marshall, the first African American justice on the U.S. Supreme Court, whose remarkable legal career was devoted to championing civil rights.

In its efforts to desegregate public schools, the NAACP leadership frequently met with civil rights leaders in the South, where school segregation was especially entrenched. In a 1955 meeting in Atlanta, Georgia, NAACP leaders met with African American leaders from southern states to discuss the latest Supreme Court ruling that public school desegregation begin "with all deliberate speed." Seated at the table second from the left is Thurgood Marshall, NAACP chief counsel.

2. INSTRUCT

Discuss

Ask students to read the quotation by Martin Luther King, Jr., at the top of page 655. Then discuss these questions: Do you agree with King's view that the failure to fight oppression made African Americans guilty of cooperating with evil? What values and beliefs did King hold that caused him to view the struggle this way?

Analyze

Ask students to respond to this question: Why did the civil rights movement splinter into many factions instead of uniting as one?

housing and education and scored a major victory in the 1954 *Brown* v. *Board of Education* decision. (See Chapter 18, Section 4.)

Although the NAACP appealed primarily to middle- and upper-class African Americans, it also welcomed the support of whites in the effort to end social and political discrimination. Sometimes, in its emphasis on achieving legal equality for all races, the organization appeared out of touch with the more basic issues of economic survival faced by many African American citizens.

Other organizations emerged to fill that gap. The National Urban League, founded in 1911, sought to assist people moving to major American cities. It helped African Americans moving out of the South find homes and jobs and made sure that they received fair treatment at work. Urban League workers looked for migrant families on ship docks and at train stations. They placed them in apartments they had inspected, and they insisted factory owners and union leaders teach African American workers the skills that could lead to better jobs. Urban League activities complemented those of the NAACP.

CORE Continues Its Fight

The **Congress of Racial Equality (CORE)** took another approach. It had been founded in 1942 by pacifists dedicated to bringing about change through peaceful confrontation. It too was interracial, including both African American and white members. During World War II, CORE had organized demonstrations against segregation in cities including Baltimore, Chicago, Denver, and Detroit.

In the years after World War II, CORE director James Farmer worked without pay in order to keep the organization alive. The growing interest in civil rights in the 1950s gave him a new base of support and allowed him to turn CORE into a national organization. It would soon play a major role in the confrontations that lay ahead.

SCLC: A Southern Group Emerges

Another key organization in the civil rights movement was the **Southern Christian Leadership Conference (SCLC).** It was founded in 1957 by Martin Luther King, Jr.,

In Depth

Biography

Baptist minister Jesse Jackson (b. 1941) was a close aide to Martin Luther King, Jr. Jackson headed Operation Breadbasket, a Southern Christian Leadership Conference (SCLC) program to expand educational and job opportunities for African Americans, until 1971. He then founded People United to Save Humanity (PUSH), which grew to a membership of 80,000. PUSH brought Jackson into the national spotlight. In 1984, he unsuccessfully ran for the Democratic presidential nomination, but his candidacy spurred African American voter registration. "Hands that picked cotton in 1884," said Jackson, "will pick the President in 1984."

Answer to . . .

Kennedy expresses frustration at the slow course of change in the civil rights area of school integration; Wallace symbolizes the intransigence of the South. For a more thorough examination of the school integration issue, see the Resource Directory below.

In Depth

Historical Misconceptions

Dorothy Cotton, a leader of the Southern Christian Leadership Conference (SCLC), found that internally the group fell short of its egalitarian goals and was instead more of a microcosm of society at large. "I'm conscious of the fact that I did have a decision-making role," she states. "But I'm also very conscious of the male chauvinism that existed within the Movement. I was on the executive staff, and that's where a lot of the decisions got made, but I'm also aware that like any other place . . . historically, where there was a female sitting, she was always asked to go get the coffee and take notes."

Viewpoints
On School Integration

In parts of the Deep South, the battle for equal rights continued to be fought at the nation's schoolhouse doors each September, even after the Supreme Court ordered schools to desegregate in 1954. *How do the viewpoints below reflect the course of the civil rights movement of the 1960s?*

For School Integration

"Nearly nine years have elapsed since the Supreme Court ruled that state laws requiring or permitting segregated schools violate the Constitution. That decision represented both good law and good judgment—it was both legally and morally right. Since that time it has become increasingly clear that neither violence nor legalistic measures will be tolerated as a means of thwarting court-ordered desegregation."

President John F. Kennedy,
message to Congress, February 28, 1963

Against School Integration

"I draw the line in the dust and toss the gauntlet before the feet of tyranny and I say segregation today, segregation tomorrow, segregation forever."

Governor George Wallace (Alabama),
inaugural address, January 14, 1963

and other African American clergymen after their success in the Montgomery bus boycott (see Chapter 18). Initially, sixty African Americans from ten states convened in Atlanta, Georgia, and agreed that they needed to coordinate their efforts. They urged African Americans "to assert their human dignity" and to refuse "further cooperation with evil." A month later, one hundred African American ministers took the next step they had agreed on and met in New Orleans, Louisiana. Later they elected King president of what came to be called the Southern Christian Leadership Conference. In its first official statement, SCLC called on African Americans

to understand that nonviolence is not a symbol of weakness or cowardice, but as Jesus demonstrated, nonviolent resistance transforms weakness into strength and breeds courage in the face of danger.

It was SCLC that shifted the focus of the civil rights movement to the South. Other civil rights organizations had been dominated by northerners. Now southern African American church leaders moved into the forefront of the struggle for equal rights.

Martin Luther King Leads a Movement
King used his post at SCLC to become a leader in the national civil rights movement. He had been born in Atlanta and raised in a prominent Baptist family. Both his father and his grandfather were ministers, and he followed in their footsteps. King grew up memorizing biblical passages and watching members of his family fight for African American rights. He went to Morehouse College in Atlanta, then received a divinity degree from the Crozer Theological Seminary in Pennsylvania. He later earned his Ph.D. from Boston University. He preached to his first congregation in Montgomery, Alabama. Before he was thirty years old, King was playing a central role in the civil rights movement as a result of his articulate leadership of the bus boycott.

King was influenced by the beliefs of Mohandas Gandhi. Gandhi was a great Indian leader who had won a fierce struggle to gain his country's independence from Great Britain in 1947. Gandhi preached that nonviolence was the only way to achieve victory against much stronger foes. It would not help to fight violence with violence. Rather, those who fought for justice must peacefully refuse to obey unjust laws and must remain nonviolent—regardless of the violent reaction such peaceful resistance might provoke. ⬡

Nonviolence Training As the Montgomery boycott came to a successful conclusion, King began training followers for what they might expect in the months ahead. Films describing Gandhi's activities were shown regularly in African American congregations. Songs and theatrical skits served to underscore the success of passive resistance in India. A leaflet urged bus boycotters to follow seventeen rules for maintaining a nonviolent approach as they prepared to ride newly desegregated vehicles. Among those rules were:

RESOURCE DIRECTORY

Teaching Resources

Viewpoints Activity On School Integration, found in the Unit 6 folder, pp. 51–52, presents extended quotations from the debate on school desegregation, reflecting the course of the civil rights movement of the 1960s.

Visual Learning Activity Passive Resistance, found in the Unit 6 folder, p. 61, uses a poster to spur discussion on nonviolence and passive resistance, ideals shared by Martin Luther King, Jr., and Mohandas Gandhi.

*P*ray *for guidance and commit yourself to complete nonviolence in word and action as you enter the bus. . . . Be loving enough to absorb evil and understanding enough to turn an enemy into a friend. . . . If cursed, do not curse back. If pushed, do not push back. If struck, do not strike back, but evidence love and goodwill at all times. . . . If another person is being molested, do not arise to go to his defense, but pray for the oppressor and use moral and spiritual force to carry on the struggle for justice. . . . Do not be afraid to experiment with new and creative techniques for achieving reconciliation and social change. . . . If you feel you cannot take it, walk for another week or two* [rather than ride the bus].

Nonviolent protest was a practical strategy in the civil rights struggle, but it also represented a moral philosophy. "To accept passively an unjust system is to cooperate with that system; thereby the oppressed become as evil as the oppressor," King said. "Noncooperation with evil is as much a moral obligation as is cooperation with good." King's message, eloquently delivered, told African Americans that they would be victorious in the end. At the same time, it forced whites to confront the difficulties African Americans faced and persuaded many of them to offer their support to the movement for change.

MAKING CONNECTIONS

What do you think are some of the strengths and weaknesses of nonviolent protest as a means to bring about social change? Do you think this approach would be effective in the 1990s?

SNCC Breaks Away

The **Student Nonviolent Coordinating Committee (SNCC,** pronounced "snick") was originally part of SCLC. In the spring of 1960, as the movement was heating up, SCLC executive director Ella Baker organized a conference

for students active in the struggle. Baker believed that the NAACP and SCLC had not kept up with the demands of young African Americans, and she wanted to provide a way for them to play an even greater role in the movement. More than two hundred students showed up for her meeting in North Carolina. Most came from southern communities, but some northerners attended as well.

Baker delivered the opening address. "The younger generation is challenging you and me," she told the adults present. "They are asking us to forget our laziness and doubt and fear, and follow our dedication to the truth to the bitter end." Martin Luther King spoke next and called the civil rights movement

a revolt against the apathy and complacency of adults in the Negro community; against Negroes in the middle class who indulge in buying cars and homes instead of taking on the great cause that will really solve their problems; against those who have become so afraid they have yielded to the system.

At the end of the meeting, the participants organized a temporary coordinating committee. A month later, fifteen student leaders met with Baker and other SCLC and CORE leaders and

On the night of April 26, 1960, burning crosses—the symbol of the Ku Klux Klan—appeared in the front yards of many African American residents of Atlanta. Above, Martin Luther King, Jr., removes a cross from his lawn as his young son looks on.

Activity

Teaching Heterogeneous Groups
The civil rights movement comprised disparate groups with different priorities within the larger goal of social equality. To help students understand this, divide the class into three groups. Have groups organize for the common goal of social equality for all young adults. Have each group state its own aims, create an acronym for itself, and describe one way they will organize to achieve that aim. Discuss how groups might support each other in their aims. **LEP**

Enrichment

Students can explore and compare the philosophies and leadership of Mohandas K. Gandhi and Martin Luther King, Jr. On which of Gandhi's experiences did King draw? How did King blend those ideas with his own Christian beliefs and tailor them to the political situation in the United States?

Answer to . . .

MAKING CONNECTIONS

Strengths: Nonviolent protest preserves the moral integrity of the protesters because they refuse to use violence against their oppressors; in this way, they may also win the respect and support of other people. Weaknesses: Nonviolent protesters who receive violent treatment have no way to protect themselves. Students may give examples of nonviolent demonstrations in the 1990s in which people have protested laws and situations that they consider unfair.

Section 1 Review Answers

1. (a) interracial, see p. 652, (b) CORE, see p. 653, (c) SCLC, see p. 653, (d) SNCC, see p. 655

2. The National Urban League addressed the concerns of poor African Americans living in urban areas, unlike the NAACP, which was geared mostly to upper- and middle-class people.

3. King was committed to the notion of nonviolence and counseled nonviolent direct action to attain the movement's goals. In this kind of passive resistance, people were asked to turn the other cheek in response to violence.

4. SNCC gave the movement a younger focus and energized it. Its members were idealistic activists who pushed for social change and forced others to confront their demands.

5. Possible answers: The oppressed are not as evil as the oppressors because their role is passive rather than active and because they live under the constant threat of brutal retaliation from a stronger force if they resist their own oppression. The oppressed are just as evil, because the lack of self-respect that allows a person to put up with injustice is just as evil as the lack of respect for others that allows another person to act unjustly.

Reteach

Have students list the key organizations and people mentioned in this section and describe the contributions of each to the civil rights movement.

Robert Moses helped train SNCC volunteers in Ohio in 1964. His low-key style was well suited to SNCC, which strove for democracy rather than rigid leadership. SNCC member Jane Stembridge summed up the philosophy: "Finally it all boils down to human relationships. . . . Love alone is radical. Political statements are not."

One focus of SNCC activities was African American voter registration in the South. Those involved were jailed, beaten, and even killed for their efforts.

voted to maintain their independence from other civil rights groups. By the end of the year, the Student Nonviolent Coordinating Committee was a permanent and separate organization.

SNCC filled its own niche in the civil rights movement. It gave young African Americans a chance to make decisions about priorities and tactics, and it shifted the focus away from church leaders alone. SNCC was also more militant, or willing to resort to more extreme measures to achieve immediate change, than were most of the older organizations committed to gradual change.

Robert Moses was one of the most influential leaders of SNCC. He had been a mathematics teacher in Harlem, a largely African American section of New York City, as the civil rights movement developed. Like many others, he wanted to be involved. He first went to work for SNCC in Atlanta, and later headed for Mississippi to encourage other African

American students to come to SNCC meetings. While Martin Luther King spoke with eloquence and passion, Moses was much more soft spoken. He took time to gather his thoughts, and then he spoke slowly. Todd Gitlin, a white student activist leader, later noted that Moses was loved and trusted *"precisely because* he seemed humble, ordinary, accessible." Gitlin went on to describe Moses's style:

> He liked to make his points with his hand, starting with palm down-turned, then opening his hand outward toward his audience, as if delivering the point for inspection, nothing up his sleeve. The words seemed to be extruded [thrust forth], with difficulty, out of his depths. What he said seemed earned. . . . To teach his unimportance, he was wont [accustomed] to crouch in the corner or speak from the back of the room, hoping to hear the popular voice reveal itself.

AMERICAN PROFILES
Anne Moody

⭐ Anne Moody was one of the many young Americans who became involved in the civil rights movement in the 1960s. As a child in the rural Mississippi town of Centreville, Moody grew up wondering what "the white folks' secret" was. "Their homes were large and beautiful with indoor toilets and every other convenience that I knew of at the time," she observed. "Every house I had ever lived in was a one- or two-room shack with an outdoor toilet." When fourteen-year-old Emmett Till, visiting from Chicago, was killed in Mississippi, supposedly because he had whistled at a white woman, Moody was horrified. She became increasingly disturbed as she noticed how the African Americans she knew passively accepted constant humiliation by white southerners. "I began to look upon Negro men as cowards," she said. "I could not respect them for smiling in a white man's face, addressing him as Mr. So-and-So, saying yessuh and nossuh when after they were

▶ RESOURCE DIRECTORY

Teaching Resources

⭐ 📄 **Literature Activity** SNCC Workers, found in the Unit 6 folder, pp. 58–59, features an excerpt from *Coming of Age in Mississippi*, in which Anne Moody describes what it was like to be an African American in Mississippi in the 1960s.

home behind closed doors" they would curse that same man.

Because she was bright and did well in school, Moody became the first member of her family to go to college. She completed her sophomore year at a small school called Natchez Junior College, then spent her last two years at Tougaloo College near Jackson, Mississippi. At Tougaloo she became involved in the civil rights movement. She joined the NAACP and also worked with CORE and SNCC. The professor who coordinated NAACP activities at Tougaloo asked Moody to take part in the first sit-ins in Jackson in 1963. She agreed to lead groups of students in still more sit-ins to desegregate local businesses, and she gave self-defense workshops for demonstrators.

Moody was amazed at the violent reaction she and other demonstrators—both African American and white—provoked when they sat down at a Woolworth's lunch counter in Jackson. (See photo on page 660.) After three hours of being humiliated—screamed at, beaten, and smeared with ketchup and mustard—Moody went back to the NAACP office. She sat there and reflected on her experience:

> *All I could think of was how sick Mississippi whites were. They believed so much in the segregated Southern way of life, they would kill to preserve it. . . . Before the sit-in, I had always hated the whites in Mississippi. Now I knew it was impossible for me to hate sickness. The whites had a disease, an incurable disease in its final stages.*

Like so many other students in the 1960s, Moody was jailed for taking part in civil rights demonstrations. The jail cells in Jackson were segregated, and she and her African American friends were separated from their white colleagues. Facilities for the African Americans were crude, with no curtain around the shower.

Worse was the reaction from her family at home. Her mother, afraid for the lives of her relatives, begged Moody to end her involvement with the civil rights movement. The local sheriff had warned that Moody should never return to her hometown. Her brother had been beaten up and almost lynched by a group of white boys. Moody's sister angrily told her that her activism was threatening the life of every African American in Centreville.

Against all that resistance, Moody persevered. She participated in demonstrations, helped force the desegregation of facilities, and remained determined to do everything she could to make the South a better place for African Americans. But it was never easy, and the gains came at tremendous personal cost. Like many other Americans committed to changing their society through nonviolent means, Moody learned that challenging white supremacy often provoked an ugly and violent reaction.

Anne Moody joined a SNCC voter registration drive during her first year at Tougaloo College. She said of her fellow SNCC workers, "I had never known people so willing and determined to help others."

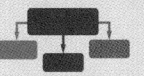

4. CLOSE

Reinforcing the Big Idea

The civil rights movement was made up of many groups that differed on tactics but agreed on the urgent need to halt segregation. As the next section describes, the first battle lines were drawn on the whites-only buses and lunch counters of the South.

SECTION 1 REVIEW

Key Terms, People, and Places
1. Define (a) interracial, (b) CORE, (c) SCLC, (d) SNCC.

Key Concepts
2. What function did the National Urban League perform for African Americans?
3. What was Martin Luther King, Jr.'s, contribution to the civil rights movement?
4. What role did SNCC play in the movement?

Critical Thinking
5. **Demonstrating Reasoned Judgment** Martin Luther King, Jr., said, "To accept passively an unjust system is to cooperate with that system; thereby the oppressed become as evil as the oppressor." Drawing on your knowledge of the section, give a concrete example of what this statement means, and explain why you do or do not agree with it.

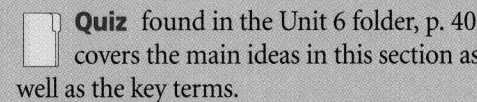

Quiz found in the Unit 6 folder, p. 40, covers the main ideas in this section as well as the key terms.

In Depth

Multicultural Perspectives

After the death of Martin Luther King, Jr., in 1968, his widow Coretta Scott King (b. 1927) remained active in various civil rights issues. In the 1993 edition of her book, *My Life with Martin Luther King, Jr.,* she wrote: "One reason so many young people became involved in the Movement was television. The Movement began in Montgomery just when the electronic era was beginning. Students were educated about social issues through the nightly news."

Historical Evidence
Using Autobiography and Biography

Focus Use autobiography and biography as sources of clues about society at a given time.

Instruct Ask students to read the feature and work through the questions. Discuss their responses. Then divide students into groups and ask each group to use the library to choose an important figure in American history for whom they can locate both a biography and an autobiography. Suggest that students focus on one important event in the person's life. Ask students to use the questions in the feature as a guide to compare the sources and decide which is more reliable.

Extend See the Historian's Toolbox Activity in the Resource Directory below.

Answers

1. (a) An autobiography, as evidenced by the use of the first person. (b) He is describing the events surrounding the nonviolent struggle for civil rights in the 1960s. This can be determined by his references to nonviolence, arrests, and Martin [Luther King].

2. (a) He was right on the scene, training the protesters in nonviolent tactics. (b) He operates from a firm belief in the justice of the civil rights cause and is a partisan of it. (c) Students will probably find his account quite accurate; he was an eyewitness, his tone is matter-of-fact, and his presentation does not seem exaggerated.

3. (a) Whites who resist the civil rights movements and African Americans who support it. (b) Physical attacks with billy clubs, fists, rocks, and bottles attest to a high degree of violence. (c) They are willing to act violently in the midst of it. (d) They are willing to withstand the physical abuse to further their cause.

Using Autobiography and Biography

Autobiography and biography are two major sources of evidence about a historical period. An autobiography is an account of a person's life as written by that person. A biography is an account of a person's life written by someone else. Both sources offer clues—revealed in the narrative—of what society was like at the time the person lived. As well as describing the person's life, an autobiography or biography also describes the kind of conditions under which people lived, how they reacted to those conditions, and the attitudes and values prevailing at that time.

An autobiography can be especially helpful in capturing a moment in time because it is a firsthand account. But both autobiography and biography must be judged on their reliability. How objective is the writer about the facts presented? Do the facts seem colored by the writer's desire to cast the person profiled in a good or bad light? Or do the facts seem straightforward and believable?

Use the following steps to analyze an excerpt from *And the Walls Came Tumbling Down*, by Ralph Abernathy. Abernathy was a civil rights leader who worked with Martin Luther King, Jr., in organizing the Montgomery bus boycott and who later founded the SCLC with King.

1. Identify the kind of account and the subject of the profile. (a) Is the excerpt from an autobiography or a biography? How can you tell? (b) What events is Abernathy describing? How can you tell?

2. Analyze the source's reliability as historical evidence. (a) How well acquainted is the writer with the facts he describes? (b) What is his point of view toward them? (c) How accurate do you judge his report to be? Explain why.

3. Search for clues that tell what the historical period was like. (a) What groups are in conflict and why? (b) What can you learn about the level of violence that exists in some parts of society? (c) What is the attitude of certain whites to the struggle? (d) What is the attitude of the African Americans involved?

> Though we knew that our people could follow the path of nonviolence while in control of themselves, we also knew that in moments of sudden anger almost anybody could be tempted to strike back—and one injured policeman could nullify the work of weeks. So we took particular care to teach our people to count to ten before they responded in any way to verbal or physical abuse.
>
> We also showed them how to march along bent over, elbows guarding their stomachs and hands covering their ears and temples. We devised this technique for use in the event that we were bombarded with rocks and bottles while demonstrating. We also taught a modified version of the same maneuver for use while being beaten with fists or billy clubs.
>
> Then, too, we told everyone to go limp when anyone laid hands on them during an arrest. In the first place, it signaled to the arresting officer that he would encounter no active resistance; hence there was no need for excessive force. But equally important, a limp body was harder to handle, took more time to haul into a paddy wagon, and therefore limited the efficiency of the police. . . .
>
> It is surprising how many of the situations we would later face were actually anticipated and discussed in these Saturday workshops. By the time we reached the end of our years together, Martin and I had seen people assaulted with fists, clubs, bottles, and rocks and were moved by the manner in which they endured such abuse. Almost without exception they behaved exactly as we taught them to behave. They protected themselves from the full force of blows, but they didn't strike back, even when their lives were endangered; and for the most part they replied with courtesy and charity.
>
> —From *And the Walls Came Tumbling Down*, by Rev. Ralph David Abernathy, 1989

 RESOURCE DIRECTORY

Historian's Toolbox Activity Using Autobiography and Biography, found in the Unit 6 folder, p. 53, provides students further practice in this skill with a passage written by Elizabeth Dole in 1988.

Nonviolent Confrontation: A Turning Point in History

SECTION PREVIEW

"We Shall Overcome," sang civil rights protesters, revealing both their spirit of nonviolence and their steadfast commitment to the cause. Acts such as sitting at "whites only" lunch counters brought vicious responses, but also showed the courage and determination of the protesters.

Key Concepts
- The sit-in technique, pioneered by CORE in the 1940s, became a popular and effective tool among civil rights activists in the 1960s.
- Nonviolent protest took the form of Freedom Rides in 1961, when activists bravely desegregated the interstate bus system.
- The violence that erupted during peaceful marches in Birmingham, Alabama, shocked the nation and created sympathy for the civil rights movement.

Key Terms, People, and Places
sit-in, Freedom Rides, Albany Movement

B uilding on the success of the Montgomery bus boycott, African American students took the next step in the campaign for equal rights. With quiet dignity, they insisted on fair treatment in facilities that had been segregated for decades. When their peaceful protests caused angry whites to strike back violently, they refused to respond with violence. Throughout the early 1960s, they maintained their commitment to passive resistance and in the process generated nationwide support for their goals. ⊕

Sit-Ins Test the Limits of Inequality

The Congress of Racial Equality (CORE) created the **sit-in** in 1943 when it desegregated the

Jack Spratt Coffee House in Chicago. (See Chapter 16, Section 4.) The sit-in technique meant that African American CORE members, often accompanied by white members, simply sat down in a segregated establishment and refused to leave until they were served or accommodated. By testing the limits of segregation policies and putting business owners' profits at risk by causing a disruption, CORE brought an end to segregation in the facilities it targeted. Sit-ins became common practice for many groups participating in the civil rights movement.

On January 31, 1960, Ezell Blair, Jr., an African American freshman at the Agricultural and Technical College in Greensboro, North Carolina, asked his parents if they would be troubled if he caused a disturbance in the community. They were puzzled by the strange question and wanted to know why. "Because," he said, "tomorrow we're going to do something that will shake up this town."

The next day, Blair and three other African American students from the college walked into a Woolworth's store in Greensboro and purchased a few items. Then they sat down at a lunch counter reserved for "whites only." When a surprised waitress wanted to know what they were doing, one of them answered, "We believe since we buy books and papers in the other part of the store, we should get served in this part."

The manager refused to allow them to be served. Rather than leave, Blair and his friends simply remained where they were until the store closed. The next day, twenty students returned to participate in a sit-in at the store. Members of the press poured into Greensboro, and the publicity led to other sit-ins across the state.

John Lewis, an African American activist who participated in sit-ins in Nashville, Tennessee, reflected on his experience in a similar store:

This student picketed a restaurant in Georgia that refused to serve African Americans unless they stood up at the lunch counter.

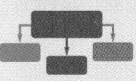

1. FOCUS

Connecting to the Big Idea

See page 650B. Explain that as civil rights activists put the philosophy of nonviolence into action, protests began to sweep the South. Ask students to describe what happened as a result of these protests.

Objectives
- Describe the sit-in technique and explain why it was an effective form of protest.
- Explain the significance of the Freedom Rides.
- Analyze how white violence against nonviolent protesters affected public opinion.

Bellringer

Read aloud the quotation by John Lewis on page 660. Then ask students to weigh carefully this question: Could you have endured what the lunch-counter protesters did without either fleeing or defending yourself? Ask what motivated Lewis and the other protesters to suffer the abuse of the white segregationists.

Reading Strategy

Problem Solving Explain to students that the "weapons" of civil rights protesters differed greatly from those of their opponents. Ask students to list as they read the nonviolent "weapons" (that is, tactics) of the freedom fighters and the methods that were used to try to stop them.

Reproducible Lesson Plan found in the Unit 6 folder, p. 36, provides a summary of the Section 2 lesson plan content.

Alternate Lesson Plan: Learning Styles found in the Alternate Lesson Plans folder, p. 147, guides pairs of students to create a simulated radio broadcast about an event from this section and is especially helpful for auditory or kinesthetic learners.

Guided Reading and Review found in the Unit 6 folder, p. 41, provides a structure for reading and mastering the key concepts and reviewing the key terms for Section 2. (Guided Practice)

American Profiles Activity found in the Unit 6 folder, p. 49, profiles Sidney Poitier, whose movies in the 1950s and 1960s dramatically portrayed the evils of racism in United States society.

Discuss

Discuss with students what issues made the civil rights movement so unstoppable. Ask students to consider the following factors in their examination of the movement: the particular people involved; the tactics; the moral philosophy of the movement; the reactions of whites; television and newspaper images of the violence.

Analyze

After students have read the statement by Assistant Attorney General Burke Marshall on page 661, ask them to analyze why, indeed, whites reacted as they did to the Freedom Rides. What was at stake from the point of view of white segregationists? Why did African Americans riding a bus alongside whites seem so threatening to them?

Answer to ...

MAKING CONNECTIONS

Possible answers: Anti-abortion groups have used sit-ins to try to block the entrances to clinics. In some cases these protesters have temporarily succeeded, but their actions have also been treated as criminal violations, as well as generating anger among their opponents. In addition, some anti-abortion activists have not adhered to the principle of nonviolence.

TURNING POINTS

John Salter, Jr., Joan Trumpauer, and Anne Moody (left to right) held a sit-in at a Jackson, Mississippi, lunch counter in May 1963. A hostile crowd registered their response by mocking and pouring food on the three activists.

*I*t was a Woolworth in the heart of the downtown area, and we occupied every seat at the lunch counter, every seat in the restaurant. . . . A group of young white men came in and they started pulling and beating primarily the young women. They put lighted cigarettes down their backs, in their hair, and they were really beating people. In a short time police officials came in and placed all of us under arrest, and not a single member of the white group, the people that were opposing our sit-in, was arrested.

But the students persisted, and soon thousands were involved in the campaign. The sit-ins gained the support of SCLC. Martin Luther King told students that arrest was a "badge of honor." In the next year, some 70,000 students participated in the sit-ins, and 3,600 served time in jail. The protests failed to change southern customs immediately, but they began a process of change that could be contained no longer.

MAKING CONNECTIONS

What groups in recent times have used nonviolent protests such as sit-ins to affect public policy? Have their tactics been effective?

Freedom Rides

In the spring of 1961, CORE led an effort to test a recent Supreme Court decision. In *Boynton* v. *Virginia,* 1960, the Court had expanded on an earlier ruling that prohibited segregation on buses traveling across state lines. As a result of the *Boynton* decision, waiting rooms and dining facilities that served interstate travelers now could not be segregated, either. The **Freedom Rides,** organized by CORE with aid from SNCC, placed groups of African American and white activists on interstate buses heading south and stopping at terminals on the way, as the map on page 661 shows.

At first the Freedom Riders encountered little trouble. When they reached the Deep South, however, they faced a ferocious response. In Anniston, Alabama, a bus was met by a mob of white men at the terminal. They carried weapons—guns, knives, blackjacks, chains—all clearly visible and meant to intimidate. The Freedom Riders decided not to test the facilities there and prepared to move on. James Farmer described what happened next:

*B*efore the bus pulled out, however, members of the mob took their sharp instruments and slashed tires. The bus

RESOURCE DIRECTORY

Teaching Resources

Primary Source Activity Protecting the Freedom Riders, found in the Unit 6 folder, p. 55, uses an excerpt from a letter written by Robert Kennedy to Governor John Patterson of Alabama citing the reasons for federal protection of the Freedom Riders.

got to the outskirts of Anniston and the tires blew out and the bus ground to a halt. Members of the mob had boarded cars and followed the bus, and now with the disabled bus standing there, the members of the mob surrounded it, held the door closed, and a member of the mob threw a firebomb into the bus, breaking a window to do so. Incidentally, there were some local policemen mingling with the mob, fraternizing with them while this was going on.

The riders escaped before the bus burst into flames, but many were beaten by the mob as they stumbled, choking on the smoke, out of the vehicle. They had anticipated trouble, and indeed, their strategy was meant to provoke a confrontation. But the level of violence took them by surprise.

As a result of the savage response, CORE director James Farmer contemplated calling the project off. But SNCC leaders begged to be allowed to continue. When Farmer warned,

"You know that may be suicide," student activist Diane Nash answered, "If we let them stop us with violence, the movement is dead! . . . Your troops have been badly battered. Let us pick up the baton and run with it."

Photographs of the charred and battered bus in Anniston, with flames and black smoke rising from its smashed windows, horrified the country. Burke Marshall, Assistant Attorney General, expressed astonishment "that people—presumably otherwise sane, sensible, rational—would have this kind of reaction simply to where people were sitting on a bus." His boss, Attorney General Robert Kennedy, who initially had been reluctant to lend federal support to the protest, finally assigned federal marshals to protect the Freedom Riders. Kennedy and the Justice Department also pressured the Interstate Commerce Commission to issue a ruling prohibiting segregation in interstate transportation, and the federal government forced local communities to follow the new regulations. ☆

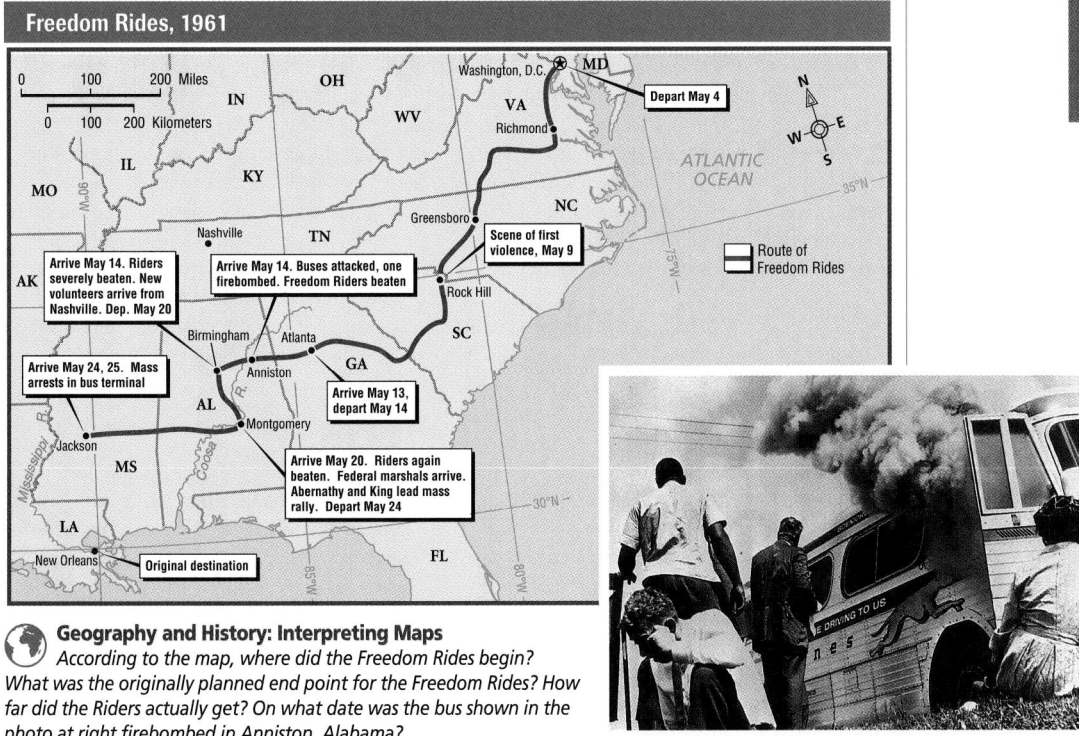

Freedom Rides, 1961

Geography and History: Interpreting Maps
According to the map, where did the Freedom Rides begin? What was the originally planned end point for the Freedom Rides? How far did the Riders actually get? On what date was the bus shown in the photo at right firebombed in Anniston, Alabama?

Media and Technology

Visions of America: Turning Point Story To enhance students' understanding of the Turning Point topic in this section, play "Nonviolent Solutions," a story about the role of nonviolent action in the civil rights movement (length: approximately 4 minutes). This selection can be located on side 4 of the videodiscs. This selection can also be located on videotape 5. Lesson plans for Turning Point stories can be found in the Visions of America Teacher's Guidebook.

Visions of America: Roundtable Discussion To introduce students to different and differing viewpoints on the Turning Point topic in this section, play all or part of the Roundtable Discussion on "Nonviolent Solutions," remarks by respected historians and social commentators. This selection can be located on side 4 of the videodiscs. This selection can also be located on videotape 5.

Side 4, Chapter 33

Side 4, Chapter 34

Activity

Cooperative Learning
Time: One class period.
Activity: Make a collage depicting the civil rights movement.
Grouping: Groups of three students.
Purpose: Have each student in the group find or make three images relating to the civil rights movement to include in the collage. The group should decide on a title for the artwork, perhaps borrowing a film or television series title (*Mississippi Burning* or "Eyes on the Prize"), using a line from a speech ("I Have a Dream"), or making up a title. One student from each group should present the finished collage to the class.
Roles: Art designers, caption writers, presenters.
Outcome: Students will identify images that express the goals, attitudes, controversies, and sentiments surrounding the civil rights movement in the 1960s.

Caption Answer to . . .

Interpreting Maps

The route was supposed to begin in Washington, D.C., and end in New Orleans, Louisiana. The riders made it as far as Jackson, Mississippi, where they were arrested. The firebombing took place on May 14, 1961.

Enrichment

Ask students to compare the civil rights movement in the United States with the African independence movements of the late 1950s and early 1960s. Suggest that students present their findings in either narrative or chart form. Encourage them to research the leaders, goals, and respective challenges of the movements, as well as any inspirational symbols, slogans, or songs. Ask them to conclude with a paragraph addressing this question: How did events in Africa challenge America's image as the protector of democracy?

In Depth

Interdisciplinary

Most Americans in the early 1960s were more focused on President-elect Kennedy's New Frontier and its faith in a future based on science and technology than on civil rights activism. In January 1961, *Time* magazine chose fifteen scientists as its "Men of the Year" with the following glowing testimonial: "Statesmen and savants, builders and even priests are their servants . . . . Science is at the apogee of its power."

TURNING POINTS

Police in Birmingham, Alabama, used high-powered hoses to break up civil rights marches in 1963. Television coverage of this brutal treatment of peaceful demonstrators prompted widespread sympathy for the movement.

The Albany Movement

The Freedom Rides exacted a heavy toll from civil rights workers, but the campaign did lead to significant gains in the desegregation of interstate bus travel. A campaign that began soon after the Freedom Rides did not fare so well.

In October 1961, African Americans in Albany, Georgia, who had joined together and called themselves the **Albany Movement,** began a year-long campaign of protest marches. They demanded the desegregation of bus terminals, and they wanted to open talks with white community leaders to address racial injustices. In December, Martin Luther King arrived in Albany, hoping to lead the movement toward its goals.

While King's presence did inspire many African Americans to join the demonstrations, it also irritated some local civil rights leaders, who resented the way King seemed to swoop in and take charge of the movement. The Albany police chief, Laurie Pritchett, also did not help the movement. He shrewdly kept the national press from seeing and reporting on the worst violations of civil rights committed by his forces. Once he even joined a group of demonstrators in prayer before they were carted off to jail. His tactic of "nonviolent" opposition to the civil rights protests kept the Albany Movement from stirring up the same nationwide sympathy that the Freedom Rides had created.

King was jailed at one point but promptly released when Albany authorities learned that volunteers were mobilizing to protest the arrest. As the campaign seemed to be failing, King began to turn his attention elsewhere. The Albany Movement had largely fizzled out by the end of 1962, with few real accomplishments to show for a difficult year.

The Integration of Ole Miss

In September of 1962, James Meredith had better success in his personal quest for civil rights. The African American air force veteran was a student at Jackson State College but wanted to transfer to the all-white University of Mississippi (known as Ole Miss). When he was denied entrance on racial grounds, he sued and carried his case to the Supreme Court, which upheld his claim. Mississippi governor Ross Barnett had other ideas. He declared that Meredith would not be allowed to enroll, whatever the Court declared, and at one point personally blocked the way to the admissions office.

With the lines of confrontation drawn, a major riot began. One angry resident tried to drive a bulldozer into the administration building. Agitated whites destroyed vehicles bringing marshals to campus. Tear gas covered the grounds. Two men died and hundreds were hurt. Army troops sent by President Kennedy finally restored order, and Meredith entered the university with troops to guarantee his safety. He remained until he graduated in 1963.

The Birmingham Confrontation

In late 1962 Fred Shuttlesworth, head of the Alabama Christian Movement for Human Rights in Birmingham, Alabama, decided that his city would be the perfect site for another nonviolent campaign. Birmingham, which was 40 percent African American, was rigidly segregated. Victory there could serve as a model for future resistance elsewhere. Shuttlesworth therefore invited Martin Luther King to visit the city in April 1963.

RESOURCE DIRECTORY

Teaching Resources

Local business leaders, afraid of the money they would lose if King's visit touched off demonstrations throughout the city, tried to negotiate with Shuttlesworth to call off the plan. These negotiations did not go very far, however, and King arrived on schedule.

Civil rights activists faced Eugene "Bull" Connor, the Birmingham police commissioner who was committed to crushing the protest. When reporters wanted to know how long King planned to stay, King drew on a biblical story and told them he would remain until "Pharaoh let his people go." Bull Connor replied, "I got plenty of room in the jail."

Activists, still committed to their peaceful approach, challenged discriminatory hiring practices and segregated public facilities. City officials declared that protest marches violated a regulation prohibiting parades without a permit and arrested King. When a group of white clergy criticized the campaign as an ill-timed threat to law and order, King responded from his cell. In his "Letter from a Birmingham Jail," he defended his tactics and his timing:

> For years now I have heard the word "Wait!" It rings in the ear of every Negro with a piercing familiarity. . . . But when you have seen vicious mobs lynch your mothers and fathers at will and drown your sisters and brothers at whim; when you have seen hate filled policemen curse, kick, brutalize and even kill your black brothers and sisters with impunity; . . . when you have to concoct an answer for a five-year-old son who is asking in agonizing pathos: "Daddy, why do white people treat colored people so mean?" . . . then you will understand why we find it difficult to wait.

After more than a week, King posted bail and emerged from jail. Soon after, he decided to allow children to participate in the campaign to test the conscience of the Birmingham authorities and the nation. As they marched with the adults, Bull Connor arrested more than 900 of the children. Police turned high-pressure fire hoses, able to tear the bark from trees, on the demonstrators. They also brought out trained police dogs that attacked the arms and legs of marchers. When protesters fell to the ground, policemen beat them with clubs and took them off to jail.

Television cameras recorded the scenes of appalling violence for people around the country. Even those unsympathetic to the civil rights movement were revolted. As reporter Eric Sevareid observed, "A newspaper or television picture of a snarling police dog set upon a human being is recorded in the permanent photo-electric file of every human brain."

In the end, the protesters won. A compromise arranged by Assistant Attorney General Burke Marshall led to desegregation of city facilities, fairer hiring practices, and organization of a biracial committee to keep channels of communication open. The success of the Birmingham marches was just one example that proved the effectiveness of nonviolent protest. While the technique did not always work—or worked only slowly—nonviolent confrontation as a means to social change had earned itself a place of honor in the history of civil rights in the United States.

SECTION 2 REVIEW

Key Terms, People, and Places
1. Define (a) sit-in, (b) Freedom Rides, (c) Albany Movement.

Key Concepts
2. What was the significance of the sit-in movement?
3. What was the point of the Freedom Rides?
4. What was the aim of the Birmingham campaign?

Critical Thinking
5. **Drawing Conclusions** In May 1961, an article in *The New York Times* encouraged the Freedom Riders to call off their program, arguing, "Non-violence that deliberately provokes violence is a logical contradiction." Explain why you agree or disagree with this statement as it applies to the Freedom Rides.

Quiz found in the Unit 6 folder, p. 42, covers the main ideas in this section as well as the key terms.

SOURCE READINGS

Source Readings on pp. 678 will connect literature selections and primary source excerpts to historical events discussed in this section.

---

3. ASSESS

Section 2 Review Answers
1. (a) sit-in, see p. 659, (b) Freedom Rides, see p. 660, (c) Albany Movement, see p. 662

2. The sit-ins mobilized students in the civil rights movement. They also generated tremendous publicity around the country, which helped the larger movement gain momentum.

3. The Freedom Riders hoped to test a recent Supreme Court decision calling for an end to segregation in interstate transportation.

4. Martin Luther King, Jr., wanted to bring about the integration of public facilities and to end discrimination in hiring practices. He also wanted to use Birmingham as a model for the desegregation of other southern cities.

5. Answers will vary. Encourage students to support their responses with examples.

Reteach
Ask students to create a three-column chart listing the locations of major civil rights protests, immediate purposes, and the outcomes of each.

Alternative Assessment
Mid-Point Monitoring
Ask students if they have
● Chosen the subjects for their biographical entries
● Begun to collect information
● Decided what visuals to include

4. CLOSE

Reinforcing the Big Idea
Nonviolent protests sparked violent responses but caught the attention and sympathy of the nation. In the next section students will read about how politicians, slow to acknowledge the civil rights issue, finally were forced to take action.

The Lasting Impact of Nonviolent Confrontation

Focus It is difficult for young people today to imagine living in a world in which segregation was the law and a person could be arrested for sitting in the wrong seat. It is equally difficult for them to comprehend how baffling southerners found the rapid changes in civil rights legislation.

In this section students will learn how nonviolent protests brought about the transformation of the South. They will also see how both the gains and the continuing battles today are rooted in the struggles of the 1960s.

Instruct On the chalkboard, make a flow chart consisting of these terms: *colored, Negro, black, Afro-American, African American*. Explain that the preferred term for Americans of African descent has changed over the years. Ask students what these name changes indicate. Then ask them to read this feature and discuss the questions at the end.

Extend Ask students to list and/or draw examples of how African American pride is expressed today. Have volunteers share their examples.

The Lasting Impact of Nonviolent Confrontation

The nonviolent, direct-action campaigns of the early 1960s marked the beginning of a new chapter in the African American struggle for equal rights. The sit-ins, the Freedom Rides, and the marches forced a shift in American attitudes and created a climate within which reform could take place.

Prior to the movement, most Americans had taken white supremacy for granted. Most white southerners were not significantly different from Melton McLaurin, who grew up in the rural town of Wade, North Carolina, in the 1950s. "Like many such families in small southern towns," he later recalled, "we assumed that the blacks of the village were in residence primarily to serve us, and we used their labor to support our comfortable lifestyle." The civil rights movement of the 1960s, however, brought a shift in perspective that made McLaurin

different from his parents. Returning home for a visit in 1984, he watched his father deliver a gift to an African American family at Christmas. It was a gracious gesture from a 65-year-year-old man who accepted changes without fully understanding them. At the same time, McLaurin observed, his father "remained, spiritually, emotionally, a resident of the Wade I had left and to which I could never return."

African Americans themselves experienced even more dramatic changes. In the late 1960s, Henry Louis Gates, a high school student from West Virginia, applied for admission to Yale University in Connecticut. In his application, which earned him a spot at the school, he described how the civil rights movement had brought changes in his own life: "My grandfather was colored; my father was Negro; and I am black." In other words, the movement

1960s African American students around the nation demand that their colleges create Black Studies programs.

| 1965 | 1970 | 1975 |

1960s African Americans' pride in their heritage is shown in the popularity of traditional African clothing.

RESOURCE DIRECTORY

Teaching Resources

Turning Points Extension Activity
The Lasting Impact of Nonviolent Confrontation, found in the Unit 6 folder, pp. 47–48, provides background and structure for groups of students to work on task forces promoting nonviolence today.

brought a shift in African Americans' sense of identity and in the way they wanted to be viewed by the larger culture. African Americans looked back toward their African roots, and with that rediscovery came a powerful pride in their ethnic identity. Some African American students began wearing *dashikis*—brightly colored African shirts—while others stopped straightening their hair and wore it longer in a style called the Afro.

Those were surface changes, to be sure, but they reflected larger cultural shifts. In the course of the next several decades, as you will read in the following chapters, the civil rights movement itself shifted course. African Americans refused to accept the second-class citizenship that had been forced upon them for the past one hundred years. They discovered that beyond segregation lay more subtle forms of discrimination, and they continued the fight to secure their full rights.

In time, however, their efforts sparked an opposing reaction on the part of previously sympathetic whites, who felt that change was coming too quickly and often at their expense. For example, Americans were divided on the issue of affirmative action programs, which sought to make up for past discrimination by requiring employers to make a special effort to hire African Americans. The civil rights movement, so passionate in the 1960s, has today lost some of its steam. But the results remain visible. And the struggle to attain equality continues, especially in the economic sphere.

REVIEWING THE FACTS

1. How did the civil rights movement change the way some African Americans perceived their own identity?
2. What obstacles did the movement toward full equality for African Americans face after the 1960s?

Critical Thinking

3. **Formulating Questions** Imagine that you are conducting a study on how far the civil rights movement has come as of the 1990s. Create a list of questions that your study would seek to answer. Some of the questions may involve statistics, while others may deal with how African Americans and others perceive the situation today.

Answers

1. The movement gave African Americans growing pride in and respect for their heritage. Changes in terminology, such as the change from *colored* to *Negro* to *black,* signaled a shift both in how African Americans viewed themselves and in how they were viewed by others.

2. The movement faced a backlash from people who felt that changes were happening too quickly. Also, the problem of economic inequality persisted.

3. Questions will vary, but students should focus on issues of economic equality, job opportunities, racist attitudes in popular culture, and so on.

1970s The women's rights movement employs nonviolent protests like those of the civil rights movement.

1992 Spike Lee's film Malcolm X *marks a renewed interest in the slain civil rights leader.*

| 1980 | 1985 | 1990 |

1980s Multicultural curriculums reflect the growing diversity in American classrooms.

SECTION 3

The Political Response

Connecting to the Big Idea

See page 650B. Explain to students that few politicians of the early 1960s were willing to risk taking a strong stand for civil rights. Ask students to note what forced them to change their minds.

Objectives

- Characterize John F. Kennedy's response to civil rights at the beginning of his presidency.
- Summarize Kennedy's efforts on the civil rights issue.
- Identify the key civil rights accomplishments of Lyndon B. Johnson.

Bellringer

Ask students if they plan to vote when they are of age. Why or why not? How many students would vote if it meant facing possible harassment or violence? Explain that protection of voters' rights was an important aspect of the civil rights movement.

Reading Strategy

Finding Evidence Ask students to look for evidence as they read the section to support this statement: As nonviolent protests continued, civil rights became not only a moral issue but also a political one.

SECTION PREVIEW

For politicians in the early 1960s, taking a firm stand in favor of civil rights was a risky business. As the decade wore on, however, the rising voice of protest no longer could be ignored in Washington.

Key Concepts
- At the start of his presidency, John F. Kennedy was hesitant to embrace the civil rights cause.
- Kennedy finally took a moral stand for civil rights but was unable to secure passage of his bill.
- Lyndon Johnson succeeded in gaining passage of the Civil Rights Act of 1964 and the Voting Rights Act of 1965.

Key Terms, People, and Places
March on Washington, Civil Rights Act of 1964, Voting Rights Act of 1965

When President Kennedy avoided committing himself to the politically charged civil rights struggle, students demanded leadership from the White House.

The protest activities of the early 1960s forced a political response. At first President John F. Kennedy, worried about his narrow electoral victory, hoped to avoid getting involved in the struggle. Finally, when the violence became extreme, he provided the moral leadership that President Eisenhower had not and committed himself to full support for a civil rights bill. The bill remained bottled up in a congressional committee when he died late in 1963, however. Kennedy's successor, Lyndon B. Johnson, harnessed a wave of popular sympathy after Kennedy's assassination and made the cause his own. Through LBJ's efforts, the civil rights movement reached its high point in the middle of the decade.

John Kennedy's Reaction

Kennedy had sought to straddle the fence at the start of his presidency. As a member of Congress, he had voted for civil rights measures but never embraced the cause wholeheartedly. In his presidential campaign, he had sought and won many African American votes with bold rhetoric. In 1960 he proclaimed, "If the President does not himself wage the struggle for equal rights—if he stands above the battle—then the battle will inevitably be lost." He also declared that a "stroke of the pen" could eliminate racial discrimination in federal housing.

In October 1960, just weeks before the election, Kennedy had an opportunity to make a powerful gesture of goodwill toward African Americans. Martin Luther King had been arrested in Alabama and sentenced to four months of hard labor. His family feared for his life in the prison camp. Kennedy called Coretta Scott King, Dr. King's wife, and said, "If there is anything I can do to help, please feel free to call on me." Then Robert Kennedy called the Alabama judge who had sentenced King and persuaded the judge to release him on bail. Word of the Kennedys' actions spread quickly through the African American community, and many switched their votes from Nixon to Kennedy. These votes were crucial in Kennedy's slim margin of victory in the election.

Once in office, though, Kennedy moved slowly. He did not want to alienate southern senators, whose votes he would need to achieve his foreign policy goals, by taking a strong stand on civil rights. He appointed a number of African Americans to prominent positions. Thurgood Marshall, for example, joined the United States Circuit Court and later became the first African American Supreme Court justice. But at the same time, Kennedy named a number of segregationists to federal courts. He also conveniently forgot about his pledge to end housing discrimination.

But Kennedy was deeply disturbed by the scenes of violence in the South that were flooding the media. The race riots surrounding the Freedom Rides in 1961 had been an embarrassment

▶ RESOURCE DIRECTORY

Teaching Resources

Reproducible Lesson Plan found in the Unit 6 folder, p. 37, provides a summary of the Section 3 lesson plan content.

Alternate Lesson Plan: Learning Styles found in the Alternate Lesson Plans folder, p. 148, highlights the responses of Kennedy and Johnson to the civil rights movement and is particularly effective for visual learners.

Guided Reading and Review found in the Unit 6 folder, p. 43, provides a structure for reading and mastering the key concepts and reviewing the key terms for Section 3. (Guided Practice)

to Kennedy when he met with Nikita Khrushchev in Vienna. To observers around the world, the upheaval in Birmingham looked even more like the beginning of a revolution. Aware that he had to do something, Kennedy spoke to the American people on nationwide television. He called the quest for equality "a moral issue" and underscored the need for action:

> We preach freedom around the world, and we mean it, and we cherish our freedom, here at home, but are we to say to the world, and much more importantly, to each other that this is a land of the free except for the Negroes? . . . The time has come for this nation to fulfill its promise.

Several months earlier, Kennedy had proposed a modest civil rights bill to help support African American voting rights and to aid schools beginning to desegregate. The Birmingham crisis pushed him further. He introduced a far stronger bill that would prohibit segregation in public places, ban discrimination wherever federal funding was involved, and advance the effort to desegregate schools. It was the most comprehensive civil rights measure ever endorsed by a United States President. The public stood behind Kennedy; a Gallup poll soon after his televised speech showed that 61 percent of the nation approved of the way he was doing his job. But Congress, still dominated by white southerners, proved resistant and kept the bill from coming up for a vote.

The March on Washington

Civil rights leaders proposed a march on Washington to lobby for passage of Kennedy's civil rights bill. Like Franklin Roosevelt when he was faced with a similar march in 1941, Kennedy tried to sidetrack the proposal. He feared it would simply alienate Congress and might result in serious racial violence in the United States capital. But his efforts to get organizers to call off the demonstration failed. Vice President Johnson warned civil rights leaders that the march might

backfire, and that it was time instead for political deal making in Congress. But Martin Luther King noted, "I have never engaged in any direct action movement which did not seem ill-timed." In the end, Kennedy bowed to the inevitable and supported the march.

The **March on Washington** took place in August 1963. More than 200,000 people came from all over the country to call for jobs and freedom. Prominent African American celebrities were present: government official Ralph Bunche, author James Baldwin, entertainer Sammy Davis, Jr., singer Harry Belafonte, baseball player Jackie Robinson. Many of the leading folk singers of the early 1960s were also there. Peter, Paul, and Mary; Joan Baez; and Bob Dylan all sang songs like "Blowin' in the Wind" and "We Shall Overcome," which had become the unofficial anthem of the struggle. The leaders of the major civil rights organizations all addressed the crowd.

At the march, Martin Luther King delivered what was to become his best-known address. With power, eloquence, and passion, he spoke to the demonstrators and to the nation at large:

> I have a dream that one day this nation will rise up and live out the true meaning

"Jobs and Freedom" was the official slogan for the March on Washington in 1963. Thousands like the young woman in the inset turned out to show their support for the civil rights movement.

2. INSTRUCT

Discuss

Explain to students that John Kennedy was from Massachusetts and Lyndon Johnson was from Texas. Discuss Kennedy's and Johnson's reactions to the civil rights crisis. Was one of them more genuinely concerned about the issue than the other? How might each man's origins have played a role in his handling of civil rights issues?

Analyze

Ask students to reread the passage from the famous speech by Martin Luther King, Jr., on pages 667 and 668. Have them identify the moral, political, and religious ideas his words reflect and consider why the speech is regarded as one of the most powerful in American history. Encourage students to consider both substance and style.

In Depth

Then and Now

In August 1993, 75,000 people— far fewer than the 250,000 who came in 1963—gathered in Washington, D.C., for the 30th anniversary of the March on Washington. The theme of the 1993 march, "Jobs, Justice and Peace," was chosen by African American leaders to focus on the gap between the promise of 1963 and the reality thirty years later. "When we were segregated, we said, if we could sit all over the bus, things would be all right," said one civil rights leader. "We have since discovered the bus has flat tires and burned out pistons. We have got to rebuild the bus."

Activity

Creating a Symbol

Symbols of unity were an important inspiration to the civil rights movement. Ask students to create a logo, song, poem, or slogan that represents the moral tone of the struggle and the bravery of its participants.

Answer to ...

MAKING   CONNECTIONS

As students will recall from Chapter 19, Johnson was a master of political deal making in Congress, and so it was natural for him to use that method—rather than the unpredictable and uncontrollable March on Washington—to get civil rights legislation passed.

Caption Answer to ...

Interpreting Graphs

Approximately two million new voters registered between 1960 and 1970.

In Depth

Then and Now

The struggle for equal rights is an ongoing one. Assistant Attorney General for Civil Rights Deval L. Patrick, appointed by President Clinton in 1994, defined the issue of race in a 1993 commencement address at Milton Academy in Massachusetts. "As a nation, we are still not free. For it is undoubtedly true that legions of African Americans feel less of a sense of opportunity, less assured of our equality, and less confident of fair treatment today than we have in many, many years. . . . We lack a national consensus on civil rights today. More ominously, in my view, we lack the national interest to build one."

---

of its creed, "We hold these truths to be self-evident, that all men are created equal." I have a dream that one day on the red hills of Georgia, sons of former slaves and the sons of former slave owners will be able to sit down together at the table of brotherhood. . . . I have a dream that my four little children will one day live in a nation where they will not be judged by the color of their skin, but by the content of their character. . . . When we allow freedom to ring, when we let it ring from every village and every hamlet, from every state and every city, we will be able to speed up that day when all of God's children, black men and white men, Jews and Gentiles, Protestants and Catholics, will be able to join hands and sing in the words of the old Negro spiritual: "Free at last. Free at last. Thank God Almighty, we are free at last."

King's words echoed around the country. President Kennedy, watching the speech on television, was impressed with King's skill. But still the civil rights bill remained stalled in Congress.

MAKING   CONNECTIONS

Why do you think Vice President Johnson preferred to use politics to get the civil rights bill passed rather than relying on demonstrations?

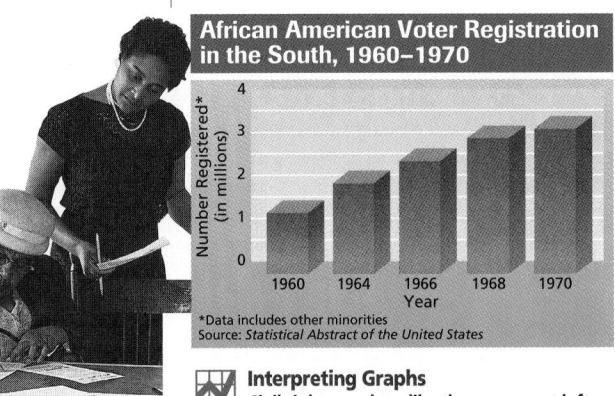

African American Voter Registration in the South, 1960–1970

*Data includes other minorities
Source: Statistical Abstract of the United States*

Interpreting Graphs
Civil rights workers like the woman at left had already begun registering African Americans years before the Voting Rights Act of 1965. *How many new African American voters registered between 1960 and 1970?*

RESOURCE DIRECTORY

Teaching Resources

Primary Source Activity Registering to Vote in Mississippi, found in the Unit 6 folder, pp. 56–57, uses the testimony of Fannie Lou Hamer to show why hundreds of civil rights workers volunteered to spend the summer of 1964 with the Mississippi Summer Project.

Lyndon Johnson's Role

Three months after the March on Washington, President Kennedy was dead and his civil rights bill was not much closer to passage. Lyndon Johnson was finally able to move the legislation along. Although he had voted against civil rights measures early in his congressional career, as Senate majority leader Johnson had worked to get a civil rights bill passed in 1957. Upon becoming President, he was eager to use his political skills to build support for Kennedy's bill. In his first public address, he told Congress and the country that nothing "could more eloquently honor President Kennedy's memory than the earliest possible passage of the civil rights bill." Johnson promised African American leaders that he would push for the measure "with every energy [he] possessed," and he made good on that commitment.

Johnson let Congress know that he would accept no compromise on civil rights. After the House of Representatives passed the bill, the Senate became caught in a lengthy filibuster, in which southern members exercised their privilege of unlimited debate. Johnson finally enlisted his old colleague, Republican minority leader Everett Dirksen, to support cloture—a two-thirds vote to cut off debate. Never before had such a procedure been used for a civil rights measure. In June 1964 the Senate voted for cloture. Soon after, it passed the bill.

The **Civil Rights Act of 1964** banned discrimination in all public accommodations and gave the Justice Department authority to act more vigorously in school segregation and voting rights cases. It also included an equal-opportunity provision that prohibited discriminatory hiring on the basis of race, sex, religion, or national origin in companies with more than twenty-five employees, as shown in the chart on page 669.

Johnson was satisfied, but the struggle moved on with a momentum of its own. In 1964 leaders of the major civil rights groups organized a voter registration drive in Mississippi. About a thousand African American and white volunteers, most of them college students, went to Mississippi to participate in what came to be called Freedom Summer. The

Civil Rights Act of 1964	
Title I	Prohibits different registration standards for white and African American voting applicants
Title II	Prohibits discrimination in the use of public accommodations
Title III	Guarantees equal access to and treatment in all public-owned and -operated facilities
Title IV	Authorizes the federal government to provide technical and financial aid to all school districts in the process of desegregation
Title V	Extends tenure of Civil Rights Commission until January 31, 1968
Title VI	Guarantees that no individual will be subjected to racial discrimination in any program that is receiving federal financial aid
Title VII	Prohibits discrimination by employers or unions with more than 100 employees or members during the first four years the Act is in effect, and thereafter for more than 25 employees or members Establishes a commission to investigate and to mediate charges of discrimination
Title VIII	Directs the Census Bureau to compile voting statistics by race in regions designated by the Civil Rights Commission
Title IX	Allows higher federal courts to prevent lower federal courts from remanding a civil rights case to a state or local court
Title X	Establishes a Community Relations Service in the Department of Commerce to mediate racial disputes at the local level
Title XI	Guarantees the right of jury trial in criminal contempt cases that grow out of any part of the Act, except for Title I Provides that the Civil Rights Act cannot be invalidated as a whole even if a single portion of it is invalidated

Source: *The Negro Almanac: A Reference Work on the Afro American*

STUDENT NONVIOLENT
WE SHALL OVERCOME
COORDINATING COMMITTEE

 Interpreting Tables
One of the landmark achievements of the Johnson administration was the passage of the Civil Rights Act of 1964. *Which provision of the act allows the federal government to assist in school desegregation with money or other forms of aid?*

Ku Klux Klan held rallies to intimidate the volunteers. In August FBI agents found the bodies of three civil rights workers—James Chaney, Andrew Goodman, and Michael Schwerner—who had been murdered by opponents. This violence was only part of the turbulence seen that summer. Civil rights leaders reported three deaths, thirty-five shootings, thirty firebombings, and eighty mob attacks. A thousand volunteers were arrested.

In order to claim their full political rights, newly registered Mississippi voters, along with members of SNCC, organized the Mississippi Freedom Democratic party. The MFDP sent delegates to the Democratic National Convention in the summer of 1964. These delegates argued that they, rather than segregationist politicians, were the rightful representatives of the state.

Fannie Lou Hamer, a timekeeper on a cotton plantation who had lost her job when she tried to register to vote, addressed the convention in a speech carried on national television. She related the treatment she had received in one voter drive:

> I began to scream, and one white man got up and began to beat me on my head and tell me to "hush." . . . All of this on account we want to register, to become first class citizens. [If] the Freedom Democratic Party is not seated now, I question America. ⭐

Lyndon Johnson offered a compromise to the Freedom party: he would seat two MFDP delegates of his own choosing, and he promised that the rules of the convention would be

Enrichment

Encourage interested students to examine the book or video version of "Eyes on the Prize" or another source of firsthand information on the civil rights movement. Then ask them to write a short essay addressing these questions: Was it right for "outsiders" (northern African Americans and whites) to come to southern towns to spark confrontations over civil rights? Were some southern whites and African Americans justified in accusing these activists of "meddling" by inflaming hatred and igniting violence with their nonviolent actions?

Caption Answer to ...

Interpreting Tables

Title IV

In Depth

Did You Know?

Southerners were caught off guard when Representative Charles Weltner (D–Georgia) voted in favor of the Civil Rights Act of 1964, arguing, "We can offer resistance and defiance, with their harvest of strife and tumult. We can suffer continued demonstrations, with their wake of violence and disorder. Or, we can acknowledge this measure as the law of the land. We can accept the verdict of the Nation. . . . I would urge that we at home now move on to the unfinished task of building a new South. We must not remain forever bound to another lost cause."

Section 3 Review Answers

1. (a) March on Washington, see p. 667, (b) Civil Rights Act of 1964, see p. 668, (c) Voting Rights Act of 1965, see p. 670

2. Having won the presidency by a very narrow margin, JFK was afraid of alienating white southerners, whose votes he needed to support other measures. He soon decided to back stronger civil rights legislation.

3. After making passage of Kennedy's civil rights bill his first priority upon assuming the presidency, Lyndon Johnson threw his support behind another measure aimed at securing voting rights.

4. The United States was probably not ready for the Civil Rights Act and the Voting Rights Act in the 1940s. The nation was fighting a world war and had little energy left to focus on civil rights. The march might have had some impact, but most likely Randolph decided to settle for Roosevelt's promise to form the FEPC because he knew it was about the best possible outcome at the time.

Reteach

Have students review the section by listing ways in which politicians responded to the civil rights conflict. Next to each item, have students grade each type of response as *strong* or *weak*.

Reinforcing the Big Idea

Politicians belatedly joined the issue of civil rights. Yet their efforts left many wrongs unrighted, and some African Americans became disillusioned with nonviolence as a solution to continuing discrimination. The next section describes the reactions of those African Americans.

When Fannie Lou Hamer registered to vote in her home state of Mississippi, the owner of the plantation where she lived promptly evicted her. She told her story at the 1968 Democratic National Convention (right), reaching a television audience of millions.

changed in 1968 so there would be no more discrimination in the Mississippi delegation. The MFDP rejected the compromise. Johnson went on to win reelection in a landslide, but he knew he had to do something about the issue of voting rights for African Americans.

In early 1965 Johnson addressed a joint session of Congress and a national television audience. He was at his most eloquent as he spoke about the right to vote: "The command of the Constitution is plain. There is no moral issue. It is wrong—deadly wrong—to deny any of your fellow Americans the right to vote in this country."

At one point in his speech, Johnson paused, raised his arms, and repeated the words that had become the marching song of the civil rights movement: "And . . . we . . . shall . . . overcome." Johnson got the response he wanted. After turning back another filibuster, Congress passed the **Voting Rights Act of 1965.**

The Voting Rights Act authorized the attorney general to appoint federal examiners to register voters where local officials prevented African Americans from exercising their constitutional right. The act singled out the South, for six states and part of another did not pass the test of having 50 percent of the voting-age population registered in 1964. In the year following passage, over 400,000 African Americans registered to vote in the Deep South, as shown by the chart on page 668. By 1968 the number reached 1 million. This act changed the nature of southern politics. It created an entirely new voting population, and it led to African American representation at local, state, and national levels.

The Civil Rights Act and the Voting Rights Act were landmarks in the history of civil rights in the United States, and they had a real impact. For some African Americans, however, these legislative accomplishments were not nearly enough. Impatient with the slow pace of progress, many African Americans turned a receptive ear to radical leaders who voiced the fury born of centuries of oppression. Pride and power, rather than peaceful resistance, were the watchwords for this new outgrowth of the civil rights movement.

SECTION 3 REVIEW

Key Terms, People, and Places
1. Define (a) March on Washington, (b) Civil Rights Act of 1964, (c) Voting Rights Act of 1965.

Key Concepts
2. Why was Kennedy initially reluctant to support civil rights wholeheartedly? How did his position change?
3. What role did Lyndon Johnson play in the passage of civil rights legislation?

Critical Thinking
4. **Demonstrating Reasoned Judgment** Reflect on the struggle for civil rights up to 1965. Then explain why you agree or disagree with the following statement: "If A. Philip Randolph had gone ahead with his plans for the 1941 March on Washington, legislation such as the Civil Rights Act and the Voting Rights Act would have been passed twenty years earlier."

▶ RESOURCE DIRECTORY

Teaching Resources

 **Visual Learning Activity** A White House Demonstration, found in the Unit 6 folder, p. 62, enriches students' understanding of the pressure on Washington to pass the Voting Rights Act with a 1965 photo of a civil rights demonstration.

Quiz found in the Unit 6 folder, p. 44, covers the main ideas in this section as well as the key terms.

SOURCE READINGS

Source Readings on pp. 680 will connect literature selections and primary source excerpts to historical events discussed in this section.

The Challenge of Black Power

SECTION PREVIEW

During the civil rights movement, change happened slowly and at times appeared to have ground to a halt. The response from some African Americans was a call for self-defense—even if it meant using violence.

Key Concepts

• The anger felt by many African Americans was expressed in the words of writer James Baldwin, activist Malcolm X, and others.
• Malcolm X preached that African Americans could expect nothing from white society in the United States and therefore needed to create a separate society.
• Street riots erupted in some cities in the late 1960s.

Key Terms, People, and Places

de jure segregation, de facto segregation, Nation of Islam, Black Power; James Baldwin, Malcolm X

A fter passage of the two civil rights acts in 1964 and 1965, the movement shifted course. Racial discrimination continued, both in the North and in the South. African Americans became frustrated at the slow and sometimes halting pace of change. Their growing anger found expression in the speeches and essays of a number of critics, who challenged the nonviolent approach that had guided the movement in the early 1960s. More militant calls for reform changed the nature of the struggle and led to increasing division in the movement and in the United States as a whole.

African American Anger

James Baldwin was a gifted writer who described the African American experience in his works and became a spokesperson for the civil rights movement. In his *Notes of a Native*

Son, a collection of essays published in 1955, he told of the damaging effects of segregation in the United States. He attacked not simply **de jure segregation**—the rigid pattern of separation dictated by law in the South—but also **de facto segregation**—the separation that resulted from the ghetto conditions in many northern cities. This pattern is shown on the map below. In 1963, in his best seller *The Fire Next Time*, Baldwin argued that these conditions could not continue. African American anger was ready to erupt. In one essay he described the horrors of the recent past—

this past, the Negro's past, of rope, fire, torture, castration, infanticide, rape; death and humiliation; fear by day and night; fear as deep as the marrow of the bone; doubt that he was worthy of life, since everyone around

A raised fist became the symbol of the Black Power movement, a militant outgrowth of the earlier civil rights movement.

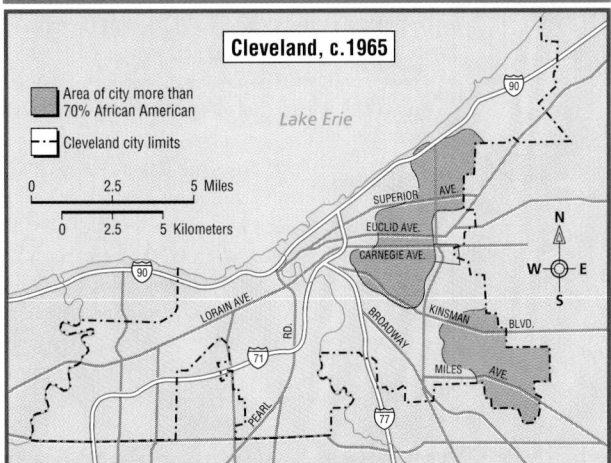

De Facto Segregation in the North, c. 1965

Cleveland, c.1965

Area of city more than 70% African American

Cleveland city limits

Lake Erie

0   2.5   5 Miles
0   2.5   5 Kilometers

SUPERIOR AVE.
EUCLID AVE.
CARNEGIE AVE.
LORAIN AVE.
BROADWAY
KINSMAN BLVD.
MILES AVE.
PEARL RD.

Geography and History: Interpreting Maps
This map shows the areas of Cleveland, Ohio, with the highest concentrations of African Americans in the 1960s. *What social and economic factors may have contributed to this pattern of settlement?*

1. FOCUS

Connecting to the Big Idea

See page 650B. Explain to students that nonviolent protests earned early gains, but that progress subsequently seemed to stall. Ask students how African Americans reacted to continuing discrimination.

Objectives

• Identify the figures who expressed the rage that many African Americans felt during the 1960s.
• Summarize the main ideas preached by Malcolm X.
• Describe how nonviolence gave way to violent protests in the late 1960s.

Bellringer

Ask students what kinds of activities go on in school that are officially against the rules. Then explain the difference between the terms *de jure* and *de facto*.

Reading Strategy

Structured Overview Have students make a two-column chart headed Problems and Solutions. As they read, they should write in the appropriate columns the problems African American leaders identified and the solutions that they advocated.

Caption Answer to ...

Interpreting Maps

The fact that African Americans were discriminated against in the work force meant that many had to accept low-paying jobs and could not afford to live in affluent neighborhoods. African Americans also may not have been able to buy homes in white neighborhoods because of prejudice on the part of realtors and white residents.

Reproducible Lesson Plan found in the Unit 6 folder, p. 38, provides a summary of the Section 4 lesson plan content.

Alternate Lesson Plan: Critical Thinking Making Comparisons, found in the Alternate Lesson Plans folder, p. 149, encourages students to apply this skill by examining the evolution of various civil rights groups.

Guided Reading and Review found in the Unit 6 folder, p. 45, provides a structure for reading and mastering the key concepts and reviewing the key terms for Section 4. (Guided Practice)

Literature Activity Sins of the Fathers, found in the Unit 6 folder, p. 60, uses an essay from Eldridge Cleaver's *Soul on Ice* to show Cleaver's view that there could be mutual respect between the races if "white youth" could repudiate the evils of the past.

Answers will vary but students can be encouraged to research and report on the extent of equal access for disabled students in their school cafeterias, classrooms, and libraries, for example.

2. INSTRUCT

Discuss

Point out President Johnson's comment on page 675. Then discuss with students the answers to his and the following questions: Why, after so much progress on civil rights, did so much anger and violence erupt? Why did African Americans become cynical about the goal of nonviolent integration pursued by Martin Luther King, Jr.?

Analyze

Have students analyze why de facto segregation was so much harder to identify and extinguish than de jure segregation. How did the Black Power movement seek to solve the problem of de facto segregation?

Equal Rights Movements

The civil rights movement of the 1960s resulted in federal laws that forbade discrimination against African Americans. The success of the civil rights movement has inspired other minority groups to fight for equal rights. Latinos, Asian Americans, women, children, the elderly, and people with disabilities are among those groups who have also used demonstrations and sit-ins, court challenges, and legislative pressure to demand their constitutional guarantee of equal rights.

Victory was gained by one group when President Bush, in his 1990 State of the Union message, spoke of the need for a "better America" where "for the first time, the American mainstream includes all our disabled citizens." In July 1990 the Americans with Disabilities Act was finally approved by both houses of Congress. This law was the result of a long struggle by physically or mentally disabled people to ensure equal access to employment, transportation, telecommunications, and public accommodations.

Businesses that employ twenty-five or more workers are now forbidden to refuse to hire or promote a qualified disabled job applicant. In addition, nearly all businesses are required to provide access for people with disabilities. For example, aisles in stores must be wide enough for a wheelchair.

Railroads, bus lines, mass transit systems, and public school bus companies are required to ensure that all new vehicles are accessible to disabled persons. Telephone companies must provide services so that hearing- or voice-impaired people can use their systems. *What facilities and programs in your school ensure equal access for disabled students?*

---

him denied it; sorrow for his women, for his kinfolk, for his children, who needed his protection, and whom he could not protect; rage, hatred, and murder, hatred for white men so deep that it often turned against him and his own, and made all love, all trust, all joy impossible.

In this essay and others published in the popular press, Baldwin warned Americans that unless change occurred soon, the nation could expect uncontrollable violence.

Malcolm X

Another leader who expressed the deeply felt anger of many African Americans was **Malcolm X.** He was born Malcolm Little in Omaha, Nebraska, in 1925. His father, a Baptist minister, spread the "back-to-Africa" message of Marcus Garvey but died when Little was a child. Little was raised in ghettos in Detroit, Boston, and New York, where he spent his youth involved in various criminal activities. At age twenty, he was arrested for an attempted burglary and served seven years in prison. While in jail he read widely and became interested in a group called the **Nation of Islam.**

The Nation of Islam was founded in 1933 in Chicago by Elijah Muhammad. He taught that Allah, the God of Islam, would bring about a "Black Nation" composed of all the nonwhite peoples of the world. According to Elijah Muhammad, one of the keys to self-knowledge was knowing one's enemy, and the enemy of the Nation of Islam was the white man and white supremacy. Members of the Nation of Islam did not seek change through political means but waited for Allah to create the Black Nation. In the meantime, they led a righteous life and worked hard to become economically self-sufficient.

Released from prison in 1952, Malcolm Little converted to the Nation of Islam, changed his name to Malcolm X, and became a disciple of Elijah Muhammad. He spent the next twelve years spreading the gospel of his new faith.

Malcolm X disagreed with both the tactics and the goals of the early civil rights movement. He called the March on Washington the "Farce on Washington" and voiced his irritation at "all of this non-violent, begging-the-white-man kind of dying . . . all of this sitting-in, sliding-in, wading-in, eating-in, diving-in, and all the rest." He preached that integration would not work and that African Americans had to take their destiny into their own hands:

No sane black man really wants integration! No sane white man really wants integration! No sane black man really believes that the white man ever will give the black man anything more than token integration. No! The Honorable Elijah Muhammad teaches that for the black man in America the only solution is complete separation from the white man .... The American black man should be focusing his effort toward building his own businesses, and decent homes for himself. As other ethnic groups have done, let the black people, wherever possible, however possible, patronize their own kind, hire their own kind, and start in those ways to build up the black race's ability to do for itself. That's the only way the American black man is ever going to get respect.

Before long Malcolm X had attracted a wide following. By 1963 Elijah Muhammad had become increasingly jealous of the attention that Malcolm X was receiving. When Elijah Muhammad objected to a remark Malcolm X had made about the Kennedy assassination, Malcolm X left the Nation of Islam and formed his own religious organization, called Muslim Mosque, Inc. He then made a pilgrimage to Mecca, the holy city of Islam in Saudi Arabia. When he returned, he proclaimed that he had been wrong to preach the hatred of white people. Malcolm X was assassinated in February 1965; three members of the Nation of Islam were charged with the murder. But his message lived on, and it attracted the attention of many of the young workers in SNCC.

MAKING CONNECTIONS

The Nation of Islam had its historical roots in the ideas of Marcus Garvey's "back-to-Africa" movement. How were the ideas behind each movement related to each other?

Black Power Rages

One of the SNCC leaders influenced by Malcolm X was Stokely Carmichael. He had

been born in Trinidad, in the West Indies, and came to the United States at the age of eleven. He grew up interested in political affairs and involved in African American protest. At Howard University in Washington, D.C., he and other students took over the Washington chapter of SNCC. He was beaten and jailed for his participation in demonstrations and finally got tired of civil disobedience. Carmichael called on SNCC workers to carry guns for self-defense. He also argued that African Americans should cease deferring to whites and make SNCC into an exclusively African American organization. His election as head of the organization in 1966 was a reflection of SNCC's growing radicalism.

A turning point in the civil rights movement came in June 1966, at a march that took place in Greenwood, Mississippi. As Martin Luther King's followers sang "We Shall Overcome," Carmichael's supporters drowned them out by singing "We Shall Overrun." Then Carmichael, just out of jail, jumped into the back of an open truck to address the group:

This is the twenty-seventh time I have been arrested, and I ain't going to jail no more! . . . The only way we gonna stop them white men from whuppin' us is to take over. We been saying freedom for six years—and we ain't got nothin.' What we gonna start saying now is "Black Power!"

Elijah Muhammad (above left) called African Americans "the lost-found Nation of Islam in the wilderness of North America." Malcolm X (above right) was a leading minister of the Nation of Islam until 1963.

Activity

A Panel Debate
Stage a mock panel debate between supporters of nonviolent protest, such as Martin Luther King, Jr., and Black Power advocates, such as Malcom X or Stokely Carmichael, in 1966. Panel members on both sides should become familiar with the moral, social, and political arguments of their positions and try to refute the arguments of the opposition.

Enrichment

Ask students to locate protest poems, prose, songs, and art from the 1960s and to include several in a notebook. Suggest that they begin by examining the writings of James Baldwin and Malcolm X.

Answer to ...

MAKING CONNECTIONS

Both Marcus Garvey and Elijah Muhammad preached that African Americans could succeed only by separating themselves from white society.

In Depth

Multicultural Perspectives

In 1975, congressional committees in the House and Senate began inquiries into the infiltration activities of the Federal Bureau of Investigation (FBI) into certain civil rights groups. The government found, according to scholar Howard Zinn, that "[t]he FBI had sent forged letters, engaged in burglaries (it admitted to ninety-two between 1960 and 1966), opened mail illegally, and, in the case of Black Panther leader Fred Hampton, seems to have conspired in murder."

Section 4 Review Answers

1. (a) de jure segregation, see p. 671,
(b) de facto segregation, see p. 671,
(c) Nation of Islam, see p. 672,
(d) Black Power, see p. 674

2. James Baldwin was a writer whose essays described the experience of African Americans growing up in a white-dominated culture. He predicted that the anger engendered by centuries of unjust treatment of African Americans would soon explode into violence if it were not addressed seriously.

3. Malcolm X argued that integration was not sufficient and insisted that African Americans had to develop a sense of racial pride and a willingness to help themselves. He also declared that the moderate civil rights movement would not help them achieve their ends, so African Americans would have to create their own separate society within the United States.

4. African Americans remained frustrated, despite gains made. Small gains only whetted their appetite for more progress, but some whites felt that too much had already been done. These bitterly opposed viewpoints eventually erupted into violence in areas where African Americans and whites lived close together.

5. Possible answers: Separate communities would reject King's dream of "sitting down together at the table of brotherhood," and would probably be difficult to maintain on a practical level. Separate communities might decrease African American frustration, in line with Malcolm X's warning that African Americans ought not to expect anything more than "token integration" from the white establishment.

As he repeated "We . . . want . . . Black . . . Power!" the audience responded with the same words in a thunderous echo. Carmichael's idea of **Black Power** called on African Americans "to unite, to recognize their heritage, to build a sense of community . . . to begin to define their own goals, to lead their own organizations and support those organizations."

In the fall of 1966, a number of African American militants founded a new political party—the Black Panthers. The Panthers wanted African Americans to lead their own communities and demanded that the federal government rebuild the nation's ghettos in repayment for years of discrimination. Huey Newton, one of the founders of the group, repeated the words of Chinese leader Mao Zedong: "Power flows from the barrel of a gun." At the same time, the organization had a gentler side and developed day-care centers, health-care facilities, and free breakfast programs in communities where it took hold.

Black Power gave rise to the "Black Is Beautiful" slogan that helped foster a sense of racial pride. It also led to a serious split in the civil rights movement, as radical groups like SNCC and the Black Panthers moved away from the NAACP and other more conservative organizations. ⊗

Riots in the Streets

Riots in a number of American cities were symptoms of the continuing poor conditions under which many African Americans were forced to live in the mid-1960s. There were no "whites only" signs above water fountains in northern cities, but more subtle forms of discrimination kept African Americans living in poverty. African Americans were kept out of well-paying jobs, job training programs, and suburban housing. Police officers assigned to ghetto neighborhoods were viewed by African American residents as dangerous oppressors rather than upholders of justice. James Baldwin remarked that a white police officer in one of these neighborhoods was "like an occupying soldier in a bitterly hostile country."

Riots ravaged Rochester, New York; New York City; and several cities in New Jersey in 1964. One of the most violent riots began in the Watts neighborhood of Los Angeles on August 11, 1965. On that steamy summer day, police pulled over a twenty-one-year-old African American man for drunk driving. At first the interaction was friendly between the police, the suspect, and the crowd of Watts residents that had gathered around. When the suspect resisted arrest, however, one police officer panicked and began swinging his riot baton. The crowd was outraged, and the scene touched off six days of rioting. Thousands of people filled the streets, burning cars and stores, stealing merchandise, and sniping at fire fighters. When the national guard and local police finally gained control, thirty-four people were dead and more than a thousand were injured.

Violence spread to other cities in 1966 and 1967. Cries of "Get Whitey" and "Burn, Baby, Burn" replaced the gentler slogans of the earlier civil rights movement. The

Members of the Black Panther party marched through the streets of New York City in 1968 to protest the trial of one of their leaders, Huey P. Newton.

 RESOURCE DIRECTORY

Teaching Resources

⊗ **Critical Thinking Activity** Demonstrating Reasoned Judgment: How to Respond, found in the Unit 6 folder, p. 54, presents passages from four of America's most powerful civil rights leaders to help students apply this skill.

National Advisory Commission on Civil Disorders, known as the Kerner Commission, noted in a report in 1968: "The nation is rapidly moving toward two increasingly separate Americas."

The Legacy of the Movement

African Americans and whites both wondered at times whether progress in civil rights was possible. Anne Moody felt frustrated when the movement failed to bring the quick change activists sought. As she listened to others sing civil rights songs during one demonstration, she found herself unable to forget the suffering that continued. "We Shall Overcome" echoed around her, but all she could think was, "I wonder. I really wonder."

Lyndon Johnson was devastated by the violence that exploded near the end of his presidency. "How is it possible," he asked, "after all we've accomplished? How could it be? Is the world topsy turvy?" While the measures passed by his administration had brought good results, they were not nearly enough.

Despite the need for further progress, the movement had brought tremendous change. Segregation was now illegal. African Americans were assured the right to vote, and the power they wielded changed the nature of American political life. Between 1970 and 1975, the number of African American elected officials rose by 88 percent. African Americans served as mayors in large cities like Atlanta, Detroit, Los Angeles, and Newark and served in Congress in larger numbers as well. Black studies courses

began to appear in high schools and colleges. African Americans had a new sense of identity and pride in their ethnic heritage.

African American congresswoman Barbara Jordan noted the impact of the movement:

The civil rights movement called America to look at itself in a giant mirror. . . . Do the black people who were born on this soil, who are American citizens, do they really feel that this is the land of opportunity, the land of the free. . . . America had to say no.

The response to that question was the first step toward making the United States a fairer society for all.

The rallying cry "Burn, Baby, Burn" became a nightmarish reality in the streets of Los Angeles in 1965. After fire fighters quenched the flames in buildings all over Watts, crowds of looters moved in to carry off the spoils.

SECTION 4 REVIEW

Key Terms, People, and Places
1. Define (a) de jure segregation, (b) de facto segregation, (c) Nation of Islam, (d) Black Power.

Key Concepts
2. How did James Baldwin give voice to African American anger?
3. When Malcolm X belonged to the Nation of Islam, what did he preach about the future of race relations in the United States?

4. Why was there rioting in many cities across the United States in the late 1960s?

Critical Thinking
5. **Drawing Conclusions** The Nation of Islam and the Black Power movement both taught that African Americans should seek to establish their own communities separate from white Americans. Explain why you do or do not believe that such a goal is possible.

Quiz found in the Unit 6 folder, p. 46, covers the main ideas in this section as well as the key terms.

Chapter Test Forms A and B are found in the Unit 6 folder, pp. 63–68.

Answer Keys found in the Unit 6 folder, pp. 146–159, provide answers to all student activities.

Media and Technology

Transparencies
Critical Thinking, I-17; Graphic Organizer, G-3

Guided Reading Audiotapes (English and Spanish)

Computer Test Bank

Reteach
Have students make a chart illustrating the key occurrences in the chain of events that led from nonviolent protests to the ghetto riots.

 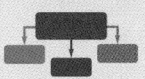
4. CLOSE

Reinforcing the Big Idea
Delays in achieving full equality caused increasing frustration among some African Americans, whose anger boiled over into violence.

In Depth
Then and Now

In January 1994, activist Tom Hayden, then a state senator and gubernatorial candidate in California, looked back on the 1960s. "We made long strides in a short time: ending segregation, reforming presidential primaries, the eighteen-year-old vote, the birth of the environmental and women's movements. It may have caused the Nixon reaction, but it also made Clinton-Gore possible."

Understanding Key Terms, People, and Places

Terms

Students should refer to the definitions of the key terms in the chapter to write sentences that show the relation of each word to the civil rights movement.

Matching

1. Freedom Rides
2. SNCC
3. Civil Rights Act of 1964
4. Nation of Islam
5. Albany Movement

Matching

1. James Baldwin
2. Malcolm X

Reviewing Main Ideas

1. The NAACP emphasized legal equality, while CORE was dedicated to effecting change through peaceful confrontation.

2. King favored nonviolent resistance; he was influenced by the ideas implemented by Mohandas Gandhi during India's struggle for independence from Britain.

3. SNCC was made up of young people and was more radical than the SCLC.

4. Sit-ins were effective because they demonstrated the unfairness of segregationist policies and put business owners' profits at risk.

5. Activists placed groups of African Americans and whites on Freedom Rides to the South. After the Freedom Riders were attacked at many bus terminals, the federal government finally stepped in and forced local authorities to uphold desegregation policies for interstate travelers.

6. The violence shocked people throughout the country and created sympathy for the civil rights movement.

7. On the one hand, Kennedy talked boldly about the need for civil rights; on the other hand, he was careful not to alienate white southern leaders in Congress by taking effective action.

8. Besides being an organizer of the march, King, always an eloquent and inspiring speaker, delivered his best-known and most inspiring address on this occasion.

9. Johnson used his skills as a political consensus builder and played on the nation's sorrow over Kennedy's death to ensure passage of the Civil Rights Act of 1964 and the Voting Rights Act of 1965.

10. Baldwin warned that violence would erupt if change did not come soon.

Chapter Review

Understanding Key Terms, People, and Places

Key Terms

1. interracial
2. Congress of Racial Equality
3. Southern Christian Leadership Conference (SCLC)
4. Student Nonviolent Coordinating Committee (SNCC)
5. sit-in
6. Freedom Rides
7. Albany Movement
8. March on Washington
9. Civil Rights Act of 1964
10. Voting Rights Act of 1965
11. de jure segregation
12. de facto segregation
13. Nation of Islam
14. Black Power

People

15. James Baldwin
16. Malcolm X

Terms For each term above, write a sentence that explains its relation to the civil rights movement.

Matching Review the key terms in the list above. If you are not sure of a term's meaning, review its definition in the chapter. Then choose a term from the list that best matches each description below.

1. bus trips on which groups of African American and white activists traveled south to protest segregation on interstate transportation facilities
2. an organization that grew out of a conference for students active in the civil rights struggle
3. the legislation that banned discrimination in all public accommodations
4. a religious group whose members believed that Allah would create a Black Nation
5. a group of African Americans who joined together in Georgia for a year-long campaign of protest marches

Matching Review the key people in the list above. Then choose a name from the list that best matches each description below.

1. an author who wrote about the damaging effects of segregation in his book *Notes of a Native Son*
2. a member of the Nation of Islam who preached that neither African Americans nor whites wanted integration

Reviewing Main Ideas

Section 1 (pp. 652–657)

1. How did CORE differ from the NAACP in its approach?
2. What methods did Martin Luther King, Jr., favor to achieve equality, and where did these methods originate?
3. How did SNCC differ from SCLC?

Section 2 (pp. 659–663)

4. Why was the sit-in strategy effective in ending segregation policies?
5. How did activists desegregate the interstate bus system?
6. Describe the effect of the violence that erupted during the 1963 Birmingham marches, explaining both its local and national impact.

Section 3 (pp. 666–670)

7. In what ways did President Kennedy straddle the fence in his civil rights policies?
8. What role did Martin Luther King, Jr., play in the March on Washington?
9. How did Lyndon Johnson secure passage of major civil rights legislation during his presidency?

Section 4 (pp. 671–675)

10. What did author James Baldwin warn might happen if change in the area of civil rights did not occur quickly?
11. What message for African Americans did Malcolm X preach as a member of the Nation of Islam?
12. What were the underlying causes of the riots that occurred in many cities in the mid- to late 1960s?

---

11. Malcolm X preached that African Americans must create a separate society.

12. Continuing discrimination against African Americans that kept many from gaining access to economic opportunities fueled the anger that erupted in street riots across the nation.

Thinking Critically

1. Possible questions: Why did you join the civil rights movement? What was your family's response to your participation in the civil rights movement? How did your opinions of race relations change as a result of your participation? Do you agree that the use of nonviolent confrontation is the most effective way of achieving equality?

2. Answers will vary, but students may suggest issues related to racial or other forms of injustice or to the environment and land development. Alternatives to nonviolent protest include working through established political channels, voting for candidates sympathetic to one's position, and letter-writing campaigns.

1. **Formulating Questions** Create four questions to ask civil rights activist Anne Moody that would, if answered, lead to a deeper understanding of what participating in the civil rights movement of the early 1960s was like.
2. **Identifying Alternatives** What issues could provoke a sit-in or other nonviolent protest in your community? What other options for effecting change are available to members of your community?
3. **Distinguishing Fact from Opinion** Malcolm X once said that for African Americans, "The only solution is complete separation from the white man." Explain why you think this statement is a fact or an opinion.

1. **Evaluating Primary Sources** Review the primary source excerpt on pages 667–668. In what ways has Martin Luther King's dream come closer to being a reality? In what ways is it still a dream for the future? Use as many specific examples as possible, from both your personal experience and your knowledge of current events, to support your conclusions.
2. **Understanding the Visuals** In the primary source excerpt on page 663, Martin Luther King says, "For years now I have heard the word 'Wait!'" Find visuals in the chapter that illustrate why the people who fought for civil rights found it impossible to "wait" any longer to be treated fairly.
3. **Writing About the Chapter** It is the spring of 1960. SCLC executive director Ella Baker has asked you, a young African American, to attend a meeting of a new organization, the Student Nonviolent Coordinating Committee (SNCC). Write a letter in which you reply to Baker's invitation, explaining why you will or will not attend this meeting. First, create a list of what you see as the potential benefits of SNCC. Then list its possible negative features. Note any suggestions you have for the new organization. Next, write a draft of your reply to Baker's invitation in which you offer your ideas. Revise your letter, making sure that each idea is clearly expressed. Proofread your letter and draft a final copy.
4. **Using the Graphic Organizer** This graphic organizer uses a tree map to organize information about nonviolent confrontation during the civil rights movement. A tree map shows how details support a main idea. On this tree map, blue entries show the results of various events. (a) What was the result of each of the protests mentioned on the chart? (b) Which method of protest listed was the most effective as a nonviolent protest? (c) On a separate sheet of paper, create your own tree map about the challenge of Black Power, using this graphic organizer as an example.

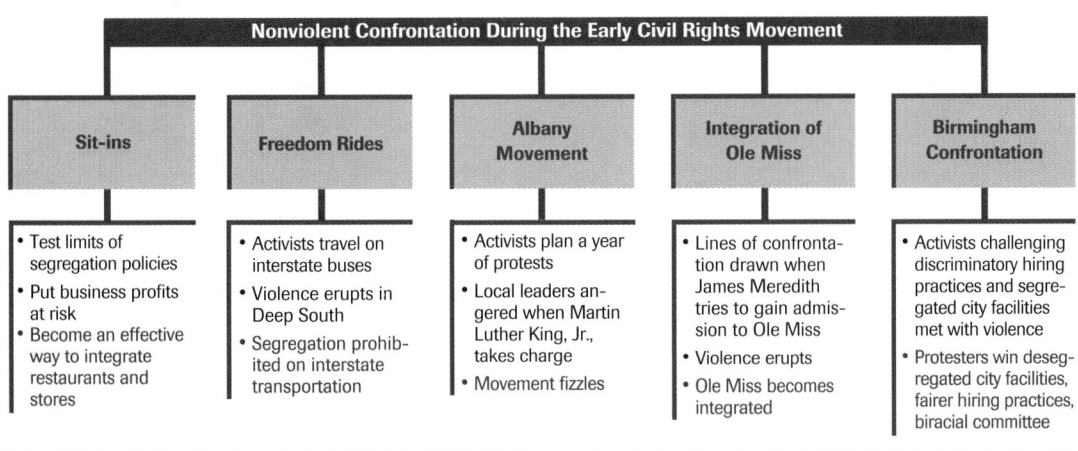

Nonviolent Confrontation During the Early Civil Rights Movement

Sit-ins	Freedom Rides	Albany Movement	Integration of Ole Miss	Birmingham Confrontation
• Test limits of segregation policies • Put business profits at risk • Become an effective way to integrate restaurants and stores	• Activists travel on interstate buses • Violence erupts in Deep South • Segregation prohibited on interstate transportation	• Activists plan a year of protests • Local leaders angered when Martin Luther King, Jr., takes charge • Movement fizzles	• Lines of confrontation drawn when James Meredith tries to gain admission to Ole Miss • Violence erupts • Ole Miss becomes integrated	• Activists challenging discriminatory hiring practices and segregated city facilities met with violence • Protesters win desegregated city facilities, fairer hiring practices, biracial committee

4. (a) Successes include the integration of many stores and restaurants, the prohibition of segregation on interstate transportation, the integration of Ole Miss, and the desegregation of city facilities and fairer hiring practices in Birmingham. (b) The sit-ins seem to have been the most effective nonviolent means of protest, as most of the other nonviolent tactics degenerated into violence. (c) Students' graphic organizers should include details that illustrate the influence of Black Power during the mid- and late 1960s.

 Alternative Assessment

Final Evaluation
Use the following guidelines to evaluate student projects:
● **Evidence of thoughtfulness** Did students include significant leaders of the civil rights movement?
● **Evidence of outside research** To what extent did students use outside research materials for their projects?
● **Evidence of synthesis** Do projects demonstrate that students understand the relationships among the subjects and their spheres of influence?
● **Communication style** Do projects convey their purpose to an audience in a clear, appealing way?

Allow interested students to present their finished projects to the class.

3. The statement is an opinion; it expresses Malcolm X's conclusion about the complex problem of race relations in the United States, but other conclusions are possible.

Making Connections

1. Answers will vary but should demonstrate an awareness that although progress has been made toward achieving equality, much still remains to be done.

2. Students may cite any of the following visuals to illustrate the injustices faced by African Americans: lynching on page 653, burnt cross in King's yard on page 655, sit-in on page 660, violence of Freedom Rides indicated on map on page 661, firemen directing hoses at people on page 662, de facto segregation shown on map on page 671.

3. Answers will vary, but letters should demonstrate an awareness of the goals of SNCC.

FOCUS

Connecting Literature and History

Throughout history leaders have used the spoken word to gain followers, to reason with opponents, and to inform the ignorant. Until we read their words, we often do not have a real understanding of what made a particular person great, or loved, or influential. Tell students that the source readings for this chapter shed some light on the personalities and the crusades of two great men.

INSTRUCT

Ask students whether they believe it is important to have the right to vote. After reaching general agreement that it is important, lead students in a discussion as to the reasons why. Students should understand that being able to vote means being able to elect the representatives to government who most closely agree with one's own political beliefs. Thus, by voting we are exercising our right to have a voice in government. In order to illustrate why this is important, ask students to consider this scenario: A representative in Congress has just proposed a new amendment to the Constitution that would ban any person below the age of twenty-one from purchasing any music on compact disc without the written consent of an adult. Because voter turnout in the age group 18 to 21 has historically been low, that group is underrepresented in Congress. Thus, the bill stands a better chance of being passed than it would if this age group had elected a sizable proportion of the Congress with its votes. Explain to students that without the ability to elect representatives to local, state, and national posts, African Americans were essentially powerless to effect change in American politics.

SOURCE READINGS

Letter from Birmingham Jail

Primary Source

Martin Luther King, Jr.

INTRODUCTION In 1963 the Reverend Martin Luther King, Jr., and the Southern Christian Leadership Conference staged a mass protest in Birmingham, Alabama. Long the site of troubled race relations, in recent years Birmingham had seen eighteen racial bombings and many crosses burning on the lawns of African American citizens. King was arrested for his participation in the protest, and he wrote the following letter from his jail cell. The letter was his answer to eight Birmingham clergymen who had condemned the demonstration and claimed King was in their city as an "outside agitator."

VOCABULARY Before you read the selection, find the meaning of these words in a dictionary: deplore, superficial, unduly, ominous, abyss, complacency, incorrigible, emulate, solace, manifest.

My Dear Fellow Clergymen:

You deplore the demonstrations taking place in Birmingham. But your statement, I am sorry to say, fails to express a similar concern for the conditions that brought about the demonstrations. I am sure that none of you would want to rest content with the superficial kind of social analysis that deals merely with effects and does not grapple with underlying causes. It is unfortunate that demonstrations are taking place in Birmingham, but it is even more unfortunate that the city's white power structure left the Negro community with no alternative. . . .

We know through painful experience that freedom is never voluntarily given by the oppressor; it must be demanded by the oppressed. Frankly, I have yet to engage in a direct-action campaign that was "well timed" in the view of those who have not suffered unduly from the disease of segregation. For years now I have heard the word "Wait!" It rings in the ear of every Negro with piercing familiarity. This "Wait!" has almost always meant "Never." We must come to see, with one of our distinguished jurists, that "justice too long delayed is justice denied."

We have waited for more than 340 years for our constitutional and God-given rights. The nations of Asia and Africa are moving with jetlike speed toward gaining political independence, but we still creep at horse-and-buggy pace toward gaining a cup of coffee at a lunch counter. Perhaps it is easy for those who have never felt the stinging darts of segregation to say, "Wait." But when you have seen vicious mobs lynch your mothers and fathers at will and drown your sisters and brothers at whim; when you have seen hate-filled policemen curse, kick, and even kill your black brothers and sisters; when you see the vast majority of your twenty million Negro brothers smothering in an airtight cage of poverty in the midst of an affluent society; when you suddenly find your tongue twisted and your speech stammering as you seek to explain to your six-year-old daughter why she can't go to the public amusement park that has just been advertised on television, and see tears welling up in her eyes when she is told that Funtown is closed to colored children, and see ominous clouds of inferiority beginning to form in her little mental sky, and see her beginning to distort her personality by developing an unconscious bitterness toward white people; when you have to concoct an answer for a five-year-old son who is asking: "Daddy, why do white people treat colored people so mean?"; when you take a cross-country drive and find it necessary to sleep night after night in the uncomfortable corners of your automobile because no motel will accept you; when you are humiliated day in and day out by nagging signs reading "white" and "colored"; when your first name becomes "nigger," your middle name becomes "boy" (however old you are) and your last name becomes "John," and your wife and mother are never given the respected title "Mrs."; when you are harried by day and haunted by night by the fact that you are a Negro, living constantly at tiptoe stance, never quite knowing what to expect next, and are plagued with inner fears and outer resentments; when you are forever fighting a degenerating sense of "nobodiness"— then you will understand why we find it difficult to wait. There comes a time when the cup of endurance runs over, and men are no longer willing to be plunged into the abyss of despair. I hope, sirs, you can understand our legitimate and unavoidable impatience. . . .

As shown in this picture, Martin Luther King, Jr., experienced racial hatred firsthand. As his son looks on, King removes a cross—a symbol of the Ku Klux Klan—set on fire in front of his home in Atlanta, Georgia, in 1960.

You speak of our activity in Birmingham as extreme. At first I was rather disappointed that fellow clergymen would see my nonviolent efforts as those of an extremist. I began thinking about the fact that I stand in the middle of two opposing forces in the Negro community. One is a force of complacency, made up in part of Negroes who, as a result of long years of oppression, are so drained of self-respect and a sense of "somebodiness" that they have adjusted to segregation; and in part of a few middle-class Negroes who, because of a degree of academic and economic security and because in some ways they profit by segregation, have become insensitive to the problems of the masses. The other force is one of bitterness and hatred, and it comes perilously close to advocating violence. It is expressed in the various black nationalist groups that are springing up across the nation, the largest and best-known being Elijah Muhammad's Muslim movement. Nourished by the Negro's frustration over the continued existence of racial discrimination, this movement is made up of people who have lost faith in America, who have absolutely repudiated Christianity, and who have concluded that the white man is an incorrigible "devil."

I have tried to stand between these two forces, saying that we need emulate neither the "do-nothingism" of the complacent nor the hatred and despair of the black nationalist. For there is the more excellent way of love and nonviolent protest. I am grateful to God that, through the influence of the Negro church, the way of nonviolence became an integral part of our struggle.

If this philosophy had not emerged, by now many streets of the South would, I am convinced, be flowing with blood. And I am further convinced that if our white brothers dismiss as "rabble-rousers" and "outside agitators" those of us who employ nonviolent direct

Have students draw a picture or a political cartoon, or write a ten-minute play that relates to the struggle for civil rights in the 1960s. Alternatively, students can research whether any polls were taken during the 1960s that gauge public opinion on civil rights for African Americans. Gallup polls would likely be a good source for students to begin their search; students should be able to find *The Gallup Poll: Public Opinion 1935–1971* in their public libraries. Newspapers and newsmagazines such as *Newsweek* or *Time* would also be likely sources for such information. Students should compile the statistics they find to report to the class.

SOURCE READINGS

action, and if they refuse to support our nonviolent efforts, millions of Negroes will, out of frustration and despair, seek solace and security in black-nationalist ideologies—a development that would inevitably lead to a frightening racial nightmare.

Oppressed people cannot remain oppressed forever. The yearning for freedom eventually manifests itself, and that is what has happened to the American Negro. Something within has reminded him of his birthright of freedom, and something without has reminded him that it can be gained.

THINKING ABOUT THE SELECTION

1. According to King, why can African Americans no longer wait for their freedom?
2. Why does King find fault with the criticism leveled against him by the Birmingham clergy?

Critical Thinking

3. **Recognizing Ideologies** What two ideologies does King describe in the African American community? Where does he place himself in relation to these two ideologies?

President Johnson Calls for the Voting Rights Act

 Primary Source

Lyndon Johnson

INTRODUCTION When you are sixteen or seventeen years old, thirty years seems like a long period of time. But when you consider that many aspects of American society were the same in the early 1960s as they are today—we had automobiles, telephones, computers, women were entering the work force in greater and greater numbers, and on and on—it is quite surprising to realize that only thirty years ago, African Americans in many areas of this country were not allowed to vote. On March 15, 1965, President Lyndon Johnson addressed Congress and the nation and asked that a Voting Rights Act be passed so that this essential right could no longer be denied to any citizen. Part of that speech follows.

Mr. Speaker, Mr. President, Members of the Congress:

I speak tonight for the dignity of man and the destiny of democracy. I urge every member of both parties, Americans of all religions and of all colors, from every section of this country, to join me in that cause. . . .

Our mission is at once the oldest and the most basic of this country; to right wrong, to do justice, to serve man.

In our time we have come to live with the moments of great crisis. Our lives have been marked with debate about great issues, issues of war and peace, issues of prosperity and depression. But rarely in any time does an issue lay bare the secret heart of America itself. Rarely are we met with a challenge, not to our growth or abundance, or our welfare or our security, but rather to the values and the purposes and the meaning of our beloved nation.

The issue of equal rights for American Negroes is such an issue. And should we defeat every enemy, and should we double our wealth and conquer the stars and still be unequal to this issue, then we will have failed as a people and as a nation.

For with a country as with a person, "What is a man profited, if he shall gain the whole world, and lose his own soul?"

There is no Negro problem. There is no Southern problem. There is no Northern problem. There is only an American problem. And we are met here tonight as Americans, not as Democrats or Republicans, we are met here as Americans to solve that problem.

ANSWERS TO

Thinking About the Selection

1. They can no longer wait because they have suffered for 340 years. King poignantly describes this suffering and says "Oppressed people cannot remain oppressed forever. The yearning for freedom eventually manifests itself."

2. He disagrees with the criticism because he thinks the clergy should be more concerned about the conditions in Birmingham that brought about the protest than about the protests themselves.

3. King describes the "complacent," those who are willing to let segregation continue, and the "black nationalists," who are willing to use violence to overcome segregation. He places himself between these two groups as a force that is trying to find an approach between the "do-nothing" and the violent.

This was the first nation in the history of the world to be founded with a purpose. The great phrases of that purpose still sound in every American heart, North and South: "All men are created equal"—"government by consent of the governed"—"give me liberty or give me death." Those are not just clever words. Those are not just empty theories. In their name Americans have fought and died for two centuries, and tonight around the world they stand there as guardians of our liberty, risking their lives.

A poster from the 1960s urges African Americans to register and vote.

Those words are a promise to every citizen that he shall share in the dignity of man. This dignity cannot be found in a man's possessions. It cannot be found in his power or in his position. It really rests on his right to be treated as a man equal in opportunity to all others. It says that he shall share in freedom, he shall choose his leaders, educate his children, provide for his family according to his ability and his merits as a human being.

To apply any other test—to deny a man his hopes because of his color or race, or his religion, or the place of his birth—is not only to do injustice, it is to deny America and to dishonor the dead who gave their lives for American freedom. . . .

Many of the issues of civil rights are very complex and most difficult. But about this there can and should be no argument. Every American citizen must have an equal right to vote. There is no reason which can excuse the denial of that right. There is no duty which weighs more heavily on us than the duty we have to ensure that right.

Yet the harsh fact is that in many places in this country men and women are kept from voting simply because they are Negroes.

Every device of which human ingenuity is capable has been used to deny this right. The Negro citizen may go to register only to be told that the day is wrong, or the hour is late, or the official in charge is absent.

And if he persists and if he manages to present himself to the registrar, he may be disqualified because he did not spell out his middle name or because he abbreviated a word on the application. And if he manages to fill out an application he is given a test. The registrar is the sole judge of whether he passes this test. He may be asked to recite the entire Constitution, or explain the most complex provisions of state laws. And even a college degree cannot be used to prove that he can read and write.

For the fact is that the only way to pass these barriers is to show a white skin. . . .

In such a case our duty must be clear to all of us. The Constitution says that no person shall be kept from voting because of his race or his color. We have all sworn an oath before God to support and to defend that Constitution. We must now act in obedience to that oath. . . .

A century has passed, more than a hundred years since equality was promised. And yet the Negro is not equal.

A century has passed since the day of promise. And the promise is unkept.

The time of justice has now come. I tell you that I sincerely believe that no force can hold it back. It is right in the eyes of man and God that it should come. And when it does, I think that day will brighten the lives of every American.

THINKING ABOUT THE SELECTION

1. According to President Johnson, whose problem is the lack of voting rights for African Americans?
2. What strategies have been used to keep African Americans from voting?

Critical Thinking

3. **Drawing Conclusions** What argument does Johnson use to convince Congress and the nation to pass the Voting Rights Act?

ANSWERS TO

Thinking About the Selection

1. The lack of voting rights for African Americans is every American's problem. It is not the problem of one section of the country or solely of African Americans themselves, but rather it is of concern to every American because it is a violation of the basic beliefs on which the nation was founded.

2. Officials have changed the day or hour when registration to vote can take place, pretended that the person who is in charge of voter registration is absent; disqualified applicants for not spelling out their middle name or using an abbreviation on the application.

3. Johnson uses the argument that voting rights for all citizens is an issue at the root of the beliefs on which the nation was founded. He emphasizes that to deny this right to anyone is to fail as a nation.

Chapter 21 Continuing Social Revolution
1960–1975

📁 Teaching Resources (See Unit 6 Folder)		
	Instruction	**Enrichment**
Section 1 **The Women's Movement** (pp. 684–689)	Reproducible Lesson Plan, p. 70 Alternate Lesson Plan, p. 151 Guided Reading and Review, p. 74 Quiz, p. 75	Literature Activity, A Changing Sense of Self, p. 93 Primary Source Activity, The Equal Rights Amendment, p. 90 Viewpoints Activity, On Working Mothers, pp. 86–87 Historian's Toolbox Activity, Recognizing Bias, p. 88
Section 2 **Ethnic Minorities Seek Equality** (pp. 691–695)	Reproducible Lesson Plan, p. 71 Alternate Lesson Plan, p. 152 Guided Reading and Review, p. 76 Quiz, p. 77	Literature Activity, Perspectives by Women of Color, p. 95 American Profiles Activity, Delores Huerta, p. 84
Section 3 **Native American Struggles** (pp. 696–700)	Reproducible Lesson Plan, p. 72 Alternate Lesson Plan, p. 153 Guided Reading and Review, p. 78 Quiz, p. 79	Visual Learning Activity, Changing Attitudes Toward Native Americans, p. 96 American Profiles Activity, Vine Deloria, Jr., p. 85 Critical Thinking Activity, Identifying Assumptions, p. 89 Literature Activity, Native American Voices, p. 94
Section 4 **Environmental and Consumer Movements** (pp. 701–703)	Reproducible Lesson Plan, p. 73 Alternate Lesson Plan, p. 154 Guided Reading and Review, p. 80 Quiz, p. 81 Chapter Test, Forms A & B, pp. 98–103	Primary Source Activity, The Desecration of America, pp. 91–92 Visual Learning Activity, Preserving the Environment, p. 97 Time and Place Activity, The Costs of Environmental Protection, pp. 82–83

📁 Additional Chapter Resources	**Bibliography**
Resource Organizer, p. 69 Alternate Lesson Plan, p. 150 Answer Keys, pp. 146–159	**For the Teacher** Carson, Rachel. *Silent Spring.* Houghton Mifflin, 1962. (Classic, ground-breaking book on environmental awareness.) Friedan, Betty. *The Feminine Mystique.* Dell, 1984 edition. (A critique of postwar inequities and discrimination against women.) *Voices from Wounded Knee.* Akwesasne Notes, 1973. (Anthology of critically praised expressions of Native American militancy during the late 1960s and early 1970s.) ***Prentice Hall Literature*** Excerpts from *The American Experience,* 1994, including Lopez, Barry H. *Arctic Dreams: Imagination and Desire in a Western Landscape.* Charles Scribner's Sons, 1986.

The Big Idea for the chapter and how the main ideas in each section relate to the Big Idea are graphically displayed below. Comprehension of this chapter's Big Idea is critical to students' understanding of United States history and how we as a nation got where we are today.

Media and Technology

 Fine Art, D-20

 Our Multicultural Heritage, C-15

 Critical Thinking, I-9

 Graphic Organizer, G-3

 Guided Reading Audiotapes (English and Spanish)

 Computer Test Bank

For the Student

Darling, Frank Fraser. *Wilderness and Plenty.* Houghton Mifflin, 1970. (On shrinking natural resources, the effects of accelerated technology, and conservation.)

Momaday, N. Scott. *House Made of Dawn.* New American Library, 1969. (The Pulitzer Prize–winning novel of a young Native American caught between the white world and the ways of his people; written by an Oklahoma Kiowa.)

Time-Life Books editors. *This Fabulous Century, Vol. 7, 1960–1970.* Time-Life Books, 1970. (Illustrated and comprehensive study.)

CHAPTER 21

Inspired by the civil rights movement, women, Latino Americans, Asian Americans, and Native Americans struggled to achieve equality in the 1960s and early 1970s through protests. The movement for social change affected almost every aspect of American society—from the environment to consumer awareness.

SECTION 1

The civil rights movement encouraged many American women to face their own inequality in society. These women worked to end discrimination based on gender and experienced considerable success.

SECTION 2

The civil rights movement also inspired Latino Americans and Asian Americans to work for equality.

SECTION 3

In the 1960s and early 1970s, Native Americans worked to gain equality and control over their own lives and land.

SECTION 4

Activists in the environmental and consumer movements used tactics introduced by the civil rights movement to bring about changes in public awareness, attitudes, and public policy.

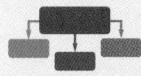

Continuing Social Revolution
1960–1975

The Relevance of the Big Idea

In the 1990s advertising agencies, school administrators, movie producers, book publishers, and politicians strive to attain "political correctness" (p.c.), or calculated inoffensiveness. Those who maintain a high level of p.c. try to avoid offending groups working against discrimination. Support for the environment is also considered politically correct. Concerned observers note that p.c. can be superficial and hypocritical. Real gains, which cannot be lost when the next political or advertising fashion comes along, must come from the courts, the legislatures, and through significant social change.

Have students discuss briefly what they think are real gains and changes for the better in American society over the last twenty years.

In Depth

Global Connections

The youth revolution was just as powerfully expressed in Europe as in the United States. In 1963, the irreverent, working-class Beatles, heavily influenced by American pop and rock music, were the first of a number of British groups to find wide appeal in the youth-dominated popular music markets in both Europe and America. From clothes to politics, the youth cultures across the Atlantic were similar. In 1968, as the Democratic National Convention in Chicago was besieged by protesters, university sit-ins in France played a major role in the demise of the French government.

Continuing Social Revolution
1960–1975

*C*hange. Upheaval. Action. These words describe the social revolution of the 1960s and early 1970s. Far from occurring in a vacuum, the 1960s civil rights movement breathed new life into other issues. Women, Latinos, Asian Americans, and Native Americans adapted civil rights tactics to achieve their own goals of equality. Similar tactics helped launch movements to protect the environment and improve the quality and safety of certain consumer goods.

	1960 Asian Americans represent Hawaii in Congress.	1962 Biologist Rachel Carson publishes Silent Spring.	1963 Feminist Betty Friedan publishes The Feminine Mystique.	1965 César Chávez organizes farm workers. • Ralph Nader publishes Unsafe at Any Speed.	1966 The National Organization for Women is founded.
Events in the United States					

1960	1962	1964	1966

Events in the World				
	1961 The Berlin Wall is built to divide East and West Berlin.		1964 Jomo Kenyatta becomes president of independent Kenya.	1966 Indira Gandhi becomes prime minister of India.

▶ RESOURCE DIRECTORY

Teaching Resources

Alternate Lesson Plan: Demonstrating the Big Idea found in the Alternate Lesson Plans folder, p. 150, provides a lesson strategy to instruct students about the Big Idea that the movement for social change affected almost every aspect of American life.

Alternative Assessment Handbook provides information, guidance, and strategies for alternative methods of assessment. It includes an essay on new trends in assessment, guidance and strategies for developing performance tasks and portfolios, scoring rubrics, and sample evaluation forms.

Pages 684–689
The Women's Movement

For generations, many American women had realized they were being treated as second-class citizens. Encouraged by the gains of the civil rights movement, women united behind the goal of ending discrimination based on gender.

 Pages 691–695
Ethnic Minorities Seek Equality

Inspired by the civil rights movement, Latinos and Asian Americans launched their own movements to overcome racial discrimination. Each group faced different obstacles in its struggles for equal treatment.

 Pages 696–700
Native American Struggles

Most Native Americans in the 1960s were living under conditions that were the result of centuries of discrimination and constantly changing government policies. They too took their cue from the civil rights movement to work for self-determination.

 Pages 701–703
Environmental and Consumer Movements

The mood of protest in the 1960s energized movements to preserve the environment and challenge the safety of certain consumer products.

1968 Activists found American Indian Movement (AIM).

1970 The federal government sets up the Environmental Protection Agency.

1972 Ms. magazine is founded.

1973 Native Americans stage a protest at Wounded Knee, South Dakota.

1975 Congress passes the Indian Self-Determination and Education Assistance Acts.

| 1968 | 1970 | 1972 | 1974 | 1976 |

1969 Golda Meir becomes prime minister of Israel.

1970 Salvador Allende is elected president of Chile.

1972 Bangladesh becomes an independent nation.

1974 Haile Selassie is deposed as ruler of Ethiopia.

1975 Margaret Thatcher becomes head of Britain's Conservative party.

Media and Technology

 Transparency
Time Lines, E-9

 ## Alternative Assessment

As an ongoing chapter project, students can select one of the major movements discussed in the chapter—the women's movement, Latino American movement, Asian American movement, Native American movement, environmental movement, or consumer movement—and present a report about its major activities in their community between 1960 and 1975. Student reports may be written or tape-recorded.

Explain that finished projects will be assessed according to the following standards:

- **Unacceptable** Projects are not attempted or fail to meet requirements outlined.
- **Limited/Acceptable** Projects present some information about the activities of one movement in the community based on limited outside research.
- **Extensive/Commendable** Projects present information about the activities of one movement in the community based on some outside research. Reports attempt to relate local activities to the national movement's goals and activities.
- **Extraordinary/Outstanding** Projects present detailed information about one movement in your community based on extensive outside research. Reports effectively relate local activities to the national movement's goals and activities.

For information and guidance on alternative assessment trends and strategies, see the Alternative Assessment Handbook in the Resource Organizer on page 682.

SECTION 1

The Women's Movement

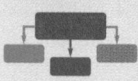

Connecting to the Big Idea

See page 682B. Women were among the first groups to note the successes of the civil rights movement and to apply them to the inequalities of their own lives. Ask students how the women's movement affected American society.

Objectives

- Describe ways in which American society discriminated against women economically and socially in the 1950s.
- Explain how women learned legal and political techniques to fight discrimination from the civil rights movement.
- Describe how feminist leaders organized groups to advocate women's rights.
- Describe the backlash the feminist movement provoked among those who wanted to preserve traditional roles.

Bellringer

Write the terms *feminist* and *women's libber* on the chalkboard. Ask students to list five words that help describe each. Have them rank the words in order from most positive to most negative.

Reading Strategy

Structured Overview Ask students to write the following three column headings on a piece of paper: Social Conditions for Women in the 1950s, Steps Taken by Feminists to Change Conditions, and Backlash Against the Feminist Movement. As students read the section, ask them to note relevant information in the appropriate column.

SECTION PREVIEW

For generations, many American women had realized they were being treated as second-class citizens. Encouraged by the gains of the civil rights movement, women united behind the goal of ending discrimination based on gender.

Key Concepts

- American society in the 1950s discriminated against women economically and socially.
- From the civil rights movement, women learned legal and political techniques to fight discrimination.
  - Feminist leaders organized groups to advocate women's rights.
  - The feminist movement produced a backlash among some who wanted to preserve traditional roles.

Key Terms, People, and Places

feminism, feminist, National Organization for Women (NOW), Equal Rights Amendment (ERA); Gloria Steinem, Phyllis Schlafly

The new women's movement chose symbols for its cause that represented power.

The African American struggle for civil rights made other citizens keenly aware of inequalities in American life. Women, though not a minority in numbers, recognized certain disadvantages they had accepted for years and were determined to do something about them. From working in civil rights and other movements, many women had learned techniques that would help them gain a more equal role in American life.

The women's movement of the 1960s, although influenced by the civil rights movement, was not a new development in the nation's history. In the 1800s, particularly, women had worked for the right to vote and for equality in education and in jobs. The term **feminism** first came into recorded use in 1895 as a word to describe the theory of political, economic, and social equality of men and women. **Feminists** were those who believed in or acted on behalf of this theory.

Social Conditions Set the Stage for the Feminist Movement

The women's movement of the 1960s sought to change the style of American life that had been accepted for decades. Society expected women always to put home and family first.

During and after World War II, however, more and more women entered the labor force. As described in Chapter 18, the popular image of the 1950s put women at home, married, and raising children, but in fact more and more married women were employed. By the beginning of the 1960s, about half of all women held jobs.

Working women, however, earned less than working men doing similar or even the same jobs. In 1963, for example, women, on average, were paid only 63 cents for each dollar that men earned. By 1973 this figure had dropped to 57 cents. This financial inequality created a growing sense of frustration among women and led to demands for change.

In those same years, more and more women were going to college. In 1950 only 25 percent of all Bachelor of Arts degrees had gone to women. Twenty years later, in 1970, it was 41 percent. Better-educated women had high hopes for the future but often were discouraged by the discrimination they faced when they looked for jobs or tried to advance in their professions. Many employers, for example, acting under the belief that home and family should be a woman's only responsibility, denied women job opportunities for which they were qualified. Women who did enter the work force often found themselves underemployed, performing jobs and earning salaries far below their abilities. The graph on page 685 shows median incomes of men and women from 1950 to 1975. Now this generation of women was ready to act to change these conditions.

▶ RESOURCE DIRECTORY

Teaching Resources

Reproducible Lesson Plan found in the Unit 6 folder, p. 70, provides a summary of the Section 1 lesson plan content.

Alternate Lesson Plan: Critical Thinking Identifying Central Issues and Demonstrating Reasoned Judgment, found in the Alternate Lesson Plans folder, p. 151, helps students practice these skills in examining the growth of and reaction to the feminist movement.

Guided Reading and Review found in the Unit 6 folder, p. 74, provides a structure for reading and mastering the key concepts and reviewing the key terms for Section 1. (Guided Practice)

The Impact of the Civil Rights Movement

While social conditions set the scene for the women's movement, the civil rights movement provided a model for techniques and an inspiration for action. Black and white women joined in the struggle for civil rights, but they often found that they were expected to make coffee and do clerical work while men made most of the policy decisions.

At the same time, women gained valuable skills from their work in the movement. They learned the value of direct action and the usefulness of political pressure in making society respond. They saw the importance of strong publicity in making others understand the conditions they were trying to change.

The civil rights movement also provided women with legal tools to fight discrimination. One important piece of legislation was the 1964 Civil Rights Act (see Chapter 20).

Originally, the section of the act called Title VII prohibited discrimination based on race, religion, or national origin. When Congress debated the bill, however, some opponents of civil rights added an amendment to outlaw discrimination on the basis of gender. This action was a strategy to make the entire bill look ridiculous, so that it would fail in the final vote. To the dismay of its opponents, both the amendment and the bill passed. The new Civil Rights Act now had a provision that gave women a legal framework to use to fight discrimination.

Even with the added boost of the new legislation, progress took time. Women soon discovered that the Equal Employment Opportunity Commission (EEOC) set up by the bill took women's claims less seriously than those of African Americans. Nevertheless, Title VII would be tremendously important as the women's movement gained steam.

Women's Groups Raise "Consciousness"

As the 1960s unfolded, women began to meet together to compare experiences. Civil rights workers met to look for ways in which they could play a larger role in the struggle.

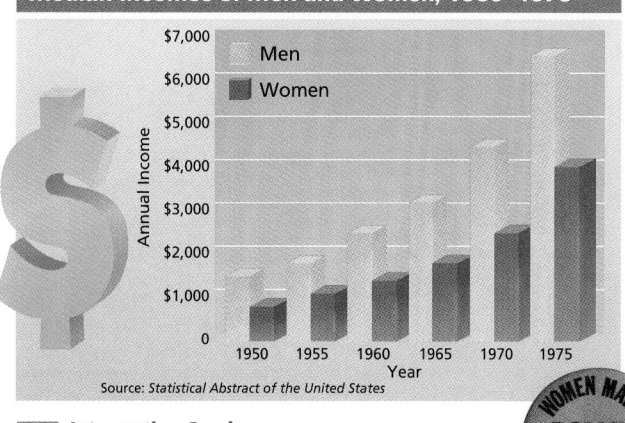

Median Incomes of Men and Women, 1950–1975

Source: *Statistical Abstract of the United States*

Interpreting Graphs
Women's incomes continued to lag behind men's earnings, partly because many low-paying fields were traditionally considered "women's work." *Did the gap increase or decrease between 1950 and 1975?*

Soon they went beyond politics, exploring other aspects of their lives. The growing movement drew women who were active in other forms of protest and reform—student radicals, opponents of the draft, and workers for welfare rights and other social issues.

Another important influence was Betty Friedan's 1963 book *The Feminine Mystique* (see Chapter 18). Friedan described the cultural patterns that prevented women from achieving their full potential. Many readers recognized what she called "the problem that has no name"— the despair that came from trying to be the perfect wife and mother, the only roles society granted women.

Meeting in kitchens and living rooms, women in "consciousness-raising" groups began to talk about their lives in new ways. One participant, Nancy Hawley, a community activist in Boston, Massachusetts, was troubled by patterns she saw in her work for other social issues. "Though many of us were working harder than the men," she noted, "we realized we were not listened to and often ignored."

Betty Friedan voiced many women's feelings in her influential book *The Feminine Mystique*.

Caption Answer to ...

Interpreting Graphs

The gap increased, from about $700 in 1950 to more than $2,000 in 1975.

2. INSTRUCT

Explain/Discuss

Discuss with students the conditions in American society that feminists wanted to change. Ask students to list the ways in which employers discriminated—and in some cases continue to discriminate—against women.

Ask students to list the kinds of action taken by feminists to improve conditions for women. Which actions do students think were most successful? How strong do students consider the subsequent backlash against the women's movement to be?

In Depth

Did You Know?

In the late 1960s and early 1970s, women created a vast network of health clinics, legal centers, newspapers, counseling centers, and professional caucuses for their needs. But since "men and institutions resisted radical challenges," according to one historian, women found it difficult to break through the "glass ceiling" in business. Women with college degrees were earning half as much as men with similar education, and one third of all working women held clerical jobs. Even by the late 1970s, very few women were executives or upper-level managers.

Students are likely to agree that people today expect women to have a job or career, whereas people in the 1950s expected that women would stay home, raise children, and keep house. You might want to contrast media images such as popular television programs from the two periods.

Analyze

Tell students that the following states did not ratify the Equal Rights Amendment: Alabama, Arkansas, Arizona, Florida, Georgia, Illinois, Louisiana, Missouri, Mississippi, Nevada, Oklahoma, North Carolina, South Carolina, Utah, Virginia. Have them locate these states on a map and then ask what generalizations students can make about them.

In Depth

Biography

In 1970 Betty Friedan (b. 1921) helped create the National Women's Political Caucus, and led a national Women's Strike for Equality. Friedan continually stirred women "to march, to picket, and to speak up for equal rights." A frequent target of her attacks was the advertising industry, which she claimed promoted an image of women as the "weaker sex." In her 1981 book *The Second Stage,* Friedan assumed a more moderate stance, and criticized earlier feminists for trying to emulate the male realm rather than "affirm the differences between men and women." (See Key Events in the Reference Section.)

Women from different backgrounds shared their stories in informal meetings and found they had common experiences.

Throughout the country, more and more women recognized the negative attitudes directed toward them. In New Orleans, Louisiana, civil rights activist Cathy Cade mentioned that her boyfriend had made fun of her for going to a "women's meeting." Others in her group began to tell stories of being teased or ridiculed for coming to a women's group. Such lack of support outside the group made their bond stronger within the group. As Cade put it:

> One thing became clear: that in the black movement I had been fighting for someone else's oppression and now there was a way that I could fight for my own freedom, and I was going to be much stronger than I ever was.

In San Francisco, Mimi Feingold, also a veteran of the civil rights and draft resistance movements, felt the same sense of exhilaration at her group's first meeting:

> It was something that we had all been waiting for, for a long time. It was a really liberating experience for all of us. . . . This was finally permission to look at our own lives and talk about how unhappy we were.

MAKING   CONNECTIONS

What is the popular image of women today, and how does it differ from the image of women in the 1950s?

Women Organize NOW

In 1966 a small group of women decided to form an organization to pursue their goal of achieving equality. These women were frustrated that existing women's groups were unwilling to pressure the Equal Employment Opportunity Commission to take women's grievances more seriously. Twenty-eight professional women, including Betty Friedan, established the **National Organization for Women (NOW)** "to take action to bring American women into full participation in the mainstream of American society *now.*"

NOW sought fair pay and equal job opportunities. It attacked the "false image of women" in the media, such as advertising that used sexist slogans or photographs. In one such ad in the 1960s, for example, an oven manufacturer asked, "Can a woman ever feel right cooking on a dirty range?" thus reinforcing the popular notion that a woman's sole contribution was to be a homemaker. NOW also called for more balance in marriages, with men and women sharing parenting and household responsibilities. A year after NOW was founded, it had 1,000 members.

On August 26, 1970, the anniversary of the passage of the constitutional amendment on women's suffrage, thousands of women left jobs and household chores to observe "Women's Equality Day."

 **RESOURCE DIRECTORY**

Teaching Resources

Literature Activity A Changing Sense of Self, found in the Unit 6 folder, p. 93, describes the early steps taken in the women's movement, in an excerpt from *Our Bodies, Ourselves.*

Four years later there were 15,000. Today, about 280,000 women belong to NOW.

For some women, NOW seemed too extreme; for others it was not extreme enough. Some saw NOW—and the women's movement in general—as mainly for the benefit of white, middle-class women. Nonetheless, NOW served as a rallying point in the movement to end sex discrimination and promote greater equality for all women.

The Impact of Feminism

The women's movement came of age in the early 1970s. Songs were one expression of the energy of the struggle. In 1971 pop singer Helen Reddy recorded a song that was soon broadcast on radio stations around the country. Delivered in the ringing, forceful style of an anthem, Reddy's hit song proclaimed:

I am woman, hear me roar
In numbers too big to ignore,
And I know too much to go back
*   and pretend. . . .*

Yes, I've paid the price
But look how much I gained.
If I have to, I can do anything.
I am strong, I am invincible,
I am woman.

Reddy's lyrics reflected a new sense of women's self-confidence and a strength that drove the movement on.

⭐ Books and magazines likewise promoted the cause. *Our Bodies, Ourselves,* a handbook published by a women's health collective in Boston, encouraged women to understand their own health issues. It sold 200,000 copies in the first several years after its publication and three million by 1990. In 1972 journalist **Gloria Steinem** and several other women founded *Ms.* magazine, which was devoted to feminist issues and provided women with viewpoints that were decid-

edly different from those in *Good House-keeping, Ladies' Home Journal,* and other women's magazines of the day. The preview issue of 300,000 copies sold out in eight days, and by 1973 *Ms.* had nearly 200,000 subscribers. While not all readers considered themselves feminists, they became familiar with the arguments of the movement from the magazine.

Slowly the women's movement brought a shift in attitudes. For example, a survey of first-year college students revealed a significant change in career goals. In 1970, men interested in fields such as business, law, engineering, and medicine outnumbered women by eight to one. Five years later, the margin had dropped to three to one. More women entered law school and medical school. They were finally admitted to military academies and trained as officers. The graph on page 688 clearly illustrates this trend in women's career paths.

Feminist Issues on the National Stage

Despite many shared concerns, the women's movement continued to be divided on its goals. In 1972 *Time* magazine observed, "The aims of the movement range from the modest, sensible amelioration [betterment] of the female condition to extreme and revolutionary visions." The more radical feminists emphasized the need to end male domination, sometimes rejecting men, marriage, and childbearing.

The cover at left from the first edition of *Ms.* magazine, begun by Gloria Steinem (above), shows the many roles women had to fill.

In Depth

Then and Now

Some of the lasting effects of the social movements of the 1960s and 1970s were in the areas of environmental awareness and health education. When DDT manufacturers fought back against Rachel Carson, it was just one of many occasions in American history when businesses gave profits a higher priority than safety. Until well into the 1990s, tobacco companies refused to accept evidence showing that cigarette smoking can cause cancer. Sometimes companies cover up facts they have discovered; in the early 1990s, Dow Corning was cited for ignoring evidence that their silicone breast implants might be harmful to women.

Caption Answer to ...

 Interpreting Graphs

The smallest increase was in doctoral degrees.

3. ASSESS

Section 1 Review Answers

1. (a) feminism, see p. 684, (b) feminist, see p. 684, (c) National Organization for Women (NOW), see p. 686, (d) Equal Rights Amendment (ERA), see p. 688

2. (a) Gloria Steinem, see p. 687, (b) Phyllis Schlafly, see p. 689

3. The civil rights movement made women realize that they too could fight back against long-standing discrimination; it trained them in techniques of resistance and political action. Title VII of the 1964 Civil Rights Act prohibited sex discrimination.

4. NOW fought for equal pay, equal job opportunities, the end of false media images, more equality in marriages, and a woman's right to abortion.

5. She was describing the frustration of trying to live up to traditional mother/wife roles and the limitations they placed on women.

6. Some men rejected the idea; some women defended traditional roles, while others opposed what they claimed would be the effects of the ERA.

7. Possible answers: the realization that many attitudes and practices were unfair, that women were underpaid, and that society's expectations prevented them from realizing their ambitions.

Reteach

Ask students to correct the following incorrect statements.
● In the 1960s, women workers were paid the same wages as male workers.
● The civil rights movement learned techniques and tactics from the women's movement.
● The 1964 Civil Rights Act was passed in response to demands from NOW and other women's groups.
● The ERA was ratified in 1973.
● American women welcomed the advances brought by the women's movement.

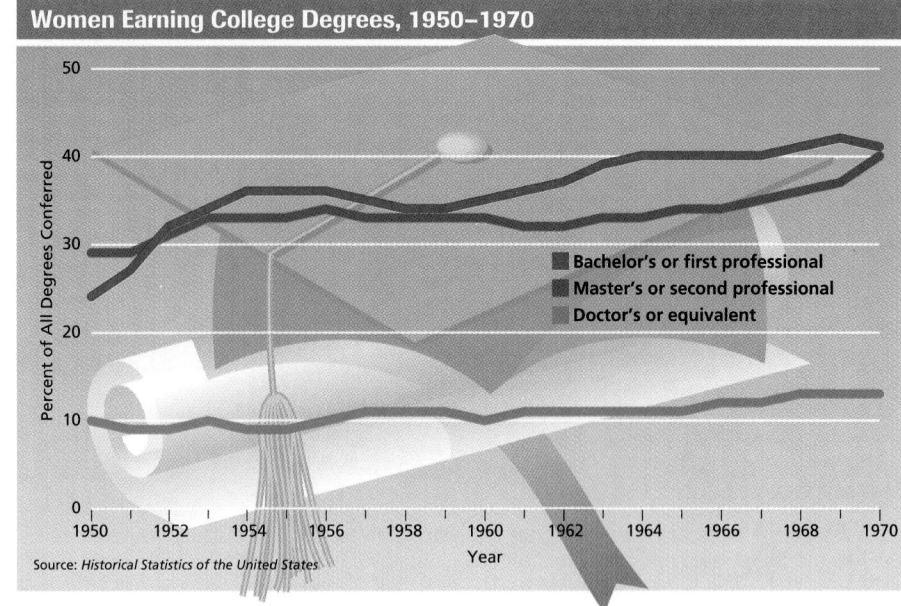

Women Earning College Degrees, 1950–1970

Legend:
■ Bachelor's or first professional
■ Master's or second professional
■ Doctor's or equivalent

Source: Historical Statistics of the United States

(y-axis: Percent of All Degrees Conferred; x-axis: Year, 1950–1970)

 Interpreting Graphs
As women's educational levels rose, so did their expectations of good jobs and fair salaries. *At which degree level—bachelor's, master's, or doctoral—did women gain the least?*

The Equal Rights Amendment NOW and other groups pressed for equal employment opportunities and facilities like day-care centers to make life more manageable for working parents. An even wider group took part in the campaign for constitutional change. In 1972 Congress passed the **Equal Rights Amendment (ERA)** to the Constitution:

> Equality of rights under the law shall not be denied or abridged by the United States or by any State on account of sex.

To become law, the amendment had to be ratified by thirty-eight states. Thirty states complied quickly, then a few others, and approval at first seemed certain. Strong opposition surfaced, however, and the struggle for ratification went on until 1982 and then died. ✪

Roe v. Wade NOW also worked to reform the laws governing a woman's right to choose an abortion instead of continuing an unwanted pregnancy. Many states outlawed or severely restricted access to abortion. Women who could afford to travel to another state could usually find legal medical services, but poorer women turned to abortion methods that were not only illegal but frighteningly unsafe. A landmark social change came in 1973, when the Supreme Court legalized abortion in the controversial *Roe* v. *Wade* decision. The justices based their decision on a constitutional right to personal privacy, but they still allowed states to restrict abortions.

Backlash Against the Women's Movement

Many men at first were hostile to the feminist movement, which became known as "women's liberation" or "Women's Lib." Nor were all women sympathetic. Some responded by stressing their desire to remain at home and raise children and their satisfaction with traditional roles.

Marabel Morgan, a housewife from Florida, was one of those who argued that a woman's highest purpose in life should be to stay home

▶ RESOURCE DIRECTORY

Teaching Resources

✪ 📄 **Primary Source Activity** The Equal Rights Amendment, found in the Unit 6 folder, p. 90, uses Congresswoman Shirley Chisholm's 1969 speech proposing the ERA to Congress as an example of the arguments in its favor.

and help her husband. In her book *The Total Woman*, published in 1973, she said:

> It is only when a woman surrenders her life to her husband, reveres and worships him, and is willing to serve him, that she becomes really beautiful to him. She becomes a priceless jewel, the glory of femininity, his queen!

Morgan suggested the "4A" approach: accept, admire, adapt, appreciate. She advised women readers how to make their marriages move from "fizzle to sizzle." Her tactic of defining a woman's self-worth in terms of beauty won her an approving audience. Two years after publication, her book had sold 500,000 copies.

Conservative political activist **Phyllis Schlafly** led a national campaign to block ratification of the ERA, saying:

> It won't do anything to help women, and it will take away from women the rights they already have, such as the right of a wife to be supported by her husband, the right of a woman to be exempted from military combat, and the right . . . to go to a single-sex college.

Schlafly also helped spread false ideas about the supposed effects of the ERA, such as coed bathrooms and the end of alimony. Women already had legal backing for their rights, she argued. Eventually, such arguments would prevent the ERA from being ratified within the time limit.

Viewpoints
On Working Mothers

The paragraphs below are from two of the books most widely read by women in the years from 1950 to 1975. ***What argument does each author use to support his or her opinion?***

Against Working Mothers

"To work or not to work? *Some mothers* have to work to make a living. Usually their children turn out all right, because some reasonably good arrangement is made for their care. But others grow up neglected and maladjusted. . . . It doesn't make sense to let mothers go to work making dresses in a factory or tapping typewriters in an office, and have them pay other people to do a poorer job of bringing up their children."

Benjamin Spock, M.D., *Baby and Childcare*, 1957 edition, first published in 1945

For Working Mothers

"At the present time, one can say anything—good or bad—about children of employed mothers and support the statement by some research finding. But there is no definitive evidence that children are less happy, healthy, adjusted, because their mothers work. The studies that show working women to be happier, better, more mature mothers do not get much publicity. Since juvenile delinquency is increasing, and more women work or 'are educated for some kind of intellectual work,' there is surely a direct cause-and-effect relationship, one says. Except that evidence indicates there is not."

Betty Friedan, *The Feminine Mystique*, 1963

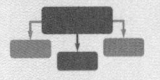

Answer to . . .

Viewpoints

According to Benjamin Spock, some children are harmed because their mothers work; therefore, it would be better if they did not work. According to Betty Friedan, there is no proven cause-and-effect relationship between working mothers and maladjusted children. For a more thorough examination of the subject of working mothers, see the Resource Directory below.

4. CLOSE

Reinforcing the Big Idea

American women were encouraged by the successes of the civil rights movement to work for greater equality for their sex. The women's rights movement made some significant gains but produced a backlash among those who wished to preserve traditional roles. As students will read in the next section, other groups also learned from the civil rights movement.

SECTION 1 REVIEW

Key Terms, People, and Places

1. Define (a) feminism, (b) feminist, (c) National Organization for Women (NOW), (d) Equal Rights Amendment (ERA).
2. Identify (a) Gloria Steinem, (b) Phyllis Schlafly.

Key Concepts

3. How did the civil rights movement influence the women's movement?
4. What were some goals of NOW?

5. What did Betty Friedan identify as "the problem that has no name"?
6. What opposition did the women's movement encounter?

Critical Thinking

7. **Identifying Assumptions** What beliefs prompted many women to join the women's movement and groups such as NOW in the 1960s?

 Viewpoints Activity On Working Mothers, found in the Unit 6 folder, pp. 86–87, presents several facets of the debate about the effect of working mothers on children.

Quiz found in the Unit 6 folder, p. 75, covers the main ideas in this section as well as the key terms.

Media and Technology

Transparency
Fine Art, D-20

Critical Thinking

Recognizing Bias

Focus Students will practice recognizing bias in two written selections.

Instruct After students have read the selections, ask them to analyze this quote using the questions presented in the feature.

"As radical feminists we recognize that we are engaged in a power struggle with men. . . . For while we realize that the liberation of women will ultimately mean the liberation of men from their destructive role as oppressor, we have no illusion that men will welcome this liberation without a struggle."

Extend See the Historian's Toolbox Activity in the Resource Directory below.

Answers

1. (a) Excerpt A: Black women distrust Women's Lib because it is white, and see white women as a racist enemy. Excerpt B: Passing the Equal Rights Amendment will solve the problem of legal discrimination against women. (b) Both excerpts A and B.

2. (a) Excerpt A: The phrase "faces of those white women hovering behind that black girl at the Little Rock school in 1957." Excerpt B: The text of the Fourteenth and Fifteenth amendments; Susan B. Anthony's arrest, trial, and conviction for voting in 1872; the number of legal discriminations against women contained in state statutes in 1969; and the text of the Equal Rights Amendment. (b) Yes. In excerpt A, the writer presents as facts her own opinions of black women's attitudes toward Women's Lib, white feminist organizations, and white women.

3. Excerpt A: All black women have the same distrustful view of Women's Lib, white feminist organizations, and white women; all white women share the racism apparent in the expressions of a few white women in Little Rock in 1957. Excerpt B: Women are not now protected by the Constitution.

4. Excerpt B is the less biased, although it favors both legal equality for women and passage of the ERA.

Recognizing Bias

Recognizing bias means being aware of information and ideas that are one-sided or that present only a partial view of a subject. Knowing how to recognize bias is important because this skill helps you to better understand not only historical events, but also current issues. Campaign speeches, debates on controversial topics, and opinions expressed in the media all contain elements of bias. The ability to spot bias will help you analyze information about the present and the past.

Bias often is attached to issues that have an impact on people's emotions. One such issue is the women's movement, which questions the role of women in American life. Both of the excerpts on this page were taken from articles written during the reappearance of the women's movement in the 1960s and early 1970s. Use the following questions to help you determine whether either of these writings is biased.

1. Decide whether the excerpt presents only one side of an issue, while suggesting it covers all sides. Writing from a single viewpoint signals imbalance—and bias. (a) What is the overall message of each excerpt? (b) Which presents only one side of the issue while suggesting that it is a complete picture?

2. Determine whether the issue as described is supported by opinions or verifiable facts. Sometimes what appear to be facts are actually opinions disguised as facts. (a) Which details presented in the excerpts can be checked for accuracy? (b) Are any opinions presented as though they were facts? Give an example from the excerpts.

3. Examine the excerpts for hidden assumptions or generalizations that are not supported by facts. What hidden assumptions or generalizations does excerpt A contain? Excerpt B?

4. Analyze the excerpts for bias. Which excerpt is the least biased? Explain your answer.

A "What do black women feel about Women's Lib? Distrust. It is white, therefore suspect. They don't want to be used again to help somebody gain power—a power that is carefully kept out of their hands. They look at white women and see them as the enemy—for they know that racism is not confined to white men. . . . The faces of those white women hovering behind that black girl at the Little Rock school in 1957 do not soon leave the retina of the mind."

—Toni Morrison, "What the Black Woman Thinks About Women's Lib," *The New York Times Magazine*, August 22, 1971

B "The 14th and 15th amendments, written in 1868 and 1870, said: "ALL PERSONS BORN OR NATURALIZED IN THE U.S. ARE CITIZENS AND HAVE THE RIGHT TO VOTE."

Susan B. Anthony, considering herself to be a person, registered and voted in 1872. She was arrested, brought to trial, convicted of the crime of voting—because she was a woman, and the word PERSONS mentioned in our Constitution *DID NOT MEAN WOMEN.* . . . If she were alive today, Susan B. Anthony might vote, but she would still see 1000 legal discriminations against women upon various state statute books. . . .

The solution of the problem of giving women 100 per cent protection of the Constitution . . . is the adoption of the Equal Rights for Women Amendment which reads: "EQUALITY OF RIGHTS UNDER LAW SHALL NOT BE DENIED OR ABRIDGED BY THE UNITED STATES OR BY ANY STATE ON ACCOUNT OF SEX."

—Marjorie Longwell, "The American Woman—Then and Now," *Delta Kappa Gamma Magazine*, Fall 1969

 RESOURCE DIRECTORY

Teaching Resources

Historian's Toolbox Activity Recognizing Bias, found in the Unit 6 folder, p. 88, uses both statements and questions about the women's movement to help students identify bias.

Ethnic Minorities Seek Equality

SECTION PREVIEW

Inspired by the civil rights movement, Latinos and Asian Americans launched their own movements to overcome racial discrimination. Each group faced different obstacles in its struggles for equal treatment.

Key Concepts

- Latinos used tactics from the civil rights movement to overcome discrimination.
- Education and cultural pride were the major goals of the Latino movement.
- The United Farm Workers, led by César Chávez, sought better conditions for Mexican American farm workers.
- Asian Americans faced racial discrimination, particularly during World War II and the cold war.
- Asian Americans made economic and political gains in the 1960s and 1970s.

Key Terms, People, and Places

Latino, Anglo, *barrio,* migratory farm workers, United Farm Workers, Japanese American Citizens League; César Chávez

T he United States is home to many ethnic and racial groups. Throughout the country's history, each group has faced different kinds of prejudice and discrimination. Latinos and Asian Americans have lived in the United States for many years. Yet both have had to fight for equality in mainstream American society.

The Latino Population

Spanish-speaking Americans, or **Latinos,** come from many places, although they share the same language and some elements of culture. But whether they come from Puerto Rico, Cuba, Mexico, or other parts of the Americas, Latinos often have been seen as outsiders and denied equal opportunities in many aspects of life, including employment, education, and housing.

In the 1960s and early 1970s, more and more people arrived from Central America and South America. Between 1970 and 1980, census figures for people "of Spanish origin" rose from 9 million to 14.6 million. Different groups tended to settle in certain areas. Americans of Cuban descent concentrated in Florida, Puerto Rican in the Northeast, and Mexican in the West and Southwest. As their population grew, Latinos throughout the country found and expressed a new pride in their heritage. ✪

Mexican American Protests

Mexican Americans, often known as Chicanos, always have been the most numerous Latinos in the United States. In the 1960s, they began to organize against discrimination in education, jobs, and the legal system, leading to *el Movimiento Chicano*—the Chicano movement.

Cultural Identity Activists began encouraging pride in Mexican American culture and its dual heritage from Spain and the ancient cultures of Mexico. In 1967 Rodolfo "Corky" Gonzales, a Denver activist, wrote a long poem that raised Mexican Americans' self-awareness nationwide. *Yo Soy Joaquin* ("I am Joaquin") expresses the importance of cultural identity in Mexican history and the modern world. It begins:

I am Joaquin
lost in a world of confusion
caught up in the whirl of a gringo [white]
   society,
confused by the rules,
scorned by attitudes,
suppressed by manipulation
and destroyed by modern society.

Nationwide boycotts made the United Farm Workers' symbol, the eagle, well known.

Connecting to the Big Idea

See page 682B. Inspired by the civil rights movement, other ethnic minorities such as Latino Americans and Asian Americans began to struggle for greater equality. Ask how their struggles were different.

Objectives

- Describe how Latino Americans used tactics from the civil rights movement to overcome discrimination.
- Identify César Chávez and describe his efforts to obtain better conditions for Mexican American farm workers.
- Describe the types of discrimination faced by Asian Americans during World War II and the cold war.
- Identify the political and economic gains made by Asian Americans in the 1960s and 1970s.

Bellringer

Ask students to consider the dilemma faced by all ethnic Americans from the early days of mass immigration: whether to assimilate or to try to retain their native culture and language. Ask students to note what is gained and what is lost by assimilation.

Reading Strategy

Structured Overview Ask students to make a chart on a piece of paper comprising two vertical columns, headed Latino Americans and Asian Americans, and two horizontal rows, headed Reasons for Protest and Results of Protest. Ask students to fill in the chart as they read the section.

Reproducible Lesson Plan found in the Unit 6 folder, p. 71, provides a summary of the Section 2 lesson plan content.

Alternate Lesson Plan: Learning Styles found in the Alternate Lesson Plans folder, p. 152, helps students identify and compare discrimination faced by Latinos and Asian Americans, and is especially helpful for visual learners.

Guided Reading and Review found in the Unit 6 folder, p. 76, provides a structure for reading and mastering the key concepts and reviewing the key terms for Section 2. (Guided Practice)

✪ **Literature Activity** Perspectives by Women of Color, found in the Unit 6 folder, p. 95, personalizes the hopes of women of color with a poem by Puerto Rican–born poet Judith Ortiz Cofer.

Explain/Discuss

Discuss how cultural differences among different groups of Latinos have led to many Latino movements rather than a single unified effort for equality in American society. Read this comment by Daniel Villanueva, a TV executive: "We need a Spanish Bobby Kennedy or Martin Luther King. Right now he's just not there." Discuss what a "Spanish Martin Luther King" might have been able to do that César Chávez did not do.

Ask how differences in language and culture affect any unified Asian American movement. Discuss why the admission of Hawaii to the Union was a step forward for Asian Americans throughout the United States.

Analyze

Ask students to analyze the success of the grape boycott and compare it with the Montgomery bus boycott. What made them different? Have students compare the work and tactics of César Chávez with those of Martin Luther King, Jr.

In Depth

Historical Misconceptions

The 1989 movie *Stand and Deliver* chronicled a true story belying the common assumption that young Americans from low-income areas plagued by drugs and gang violence have nowhere to go but down. A high school math teacher, Jaime Escalante, inspired his class of unprepared, predominantly Latino students from Garfield High School in East Los Angeles to become a team of motivated mathematicians. In 1982, eighteen of Escalante's students passed the Advanced Placement calculus exam, and Garfield High attained high national ranking in math. One student said of Escalante, "He made us feel powerful, that we could do anything."

Gonzales emphasized that **Anglos**—English-speaking, non-Latinos—had undermined Mexican Americans' control over their lives. Gonzales said that Anglos had done this through economic pressure and through institutions such as the schools, the Roman Catholic church, and the media.

Education Many Chicanos wanted changes in education. Schools in the *barrios,* or Latino neighborhoods, were crowded and run-down, with high dropout rates. In March 1968, ten thousand Mexican American students walked out of five such Los Angeles high schools to protest their unequal treatment. Students in Colorado, Texas, and other parts of California followed their example. Students demanded better courses and facilities and Latino teachers and counselors.

As leader of the United Farm Workers, César Chávez once said the "truest act of courage . . . is to sacrifice ourselves for others in a totally nonviolent struggle for justice."

AMERICAN PROFILES

César Chávez

César Chávez (1927–1993), founder of the United Farm Workers, became a hero to millions of Americans, both Latino and Anglo. He was born in Yuma, Arizona, where his family had farmed for three generations. During the Great Depression, they lost their adobe farmhouse because they could not afford the taxes. Moving to California, they became **migratory farm workers,** who make a living moving from farm to farm to provide the labor needed to plant, cultivate, and harvest crops.

Chávez later remembered how his family fostered a powerful sense of independence:

> I don't want to suggest we were that radical, but I know we were probably one of the strikingest families in California, the first ones to leave the fields if anyone shouted "Huelga!" — which is Spanish for "Strike!"

As he grew up among farm workers, Chávez gradually came to believe that unions were a way to resist employers' economic power. Migratory farm workers were some of the most exploited workers in the country, spending long hours doing backbreaking work for little pay. In the 1960s Chávez began to organize Mexican field hands into what became the **United Farm Workers (UFW)**. He and a group of loyal followers went from door to door and field to field. By 1965 the union had 1,700 members. ✪

The UFW's first target was the grape growers of California. Chávez, like Martin Luther King, Jr., believed in nonviolent action. In 1967, when growers refused to grant more pay, better working conditions, and union recognition, Chávez organized a successful nationwide consumer boycott of grapes picked on nonunion farms. Later boycotts of lettuce and other crops also won consumer support.

Chávez's efforts created many angry enemies and even brought him death threats. He responded by saying:

> It's not me who counts, it's the Movement. And I think that in terms of stopping the Movement—this one or other movements by poor people around the country—the possibility is very remote. . . . The tide for change now has gone too far.

In 1975 California passed a measure that required collective bargaining between growers and union representatives. Workers now had a legal basis to ask for better working conditions. Chávez's efforts not only made him a national hero but also brought migratory farm workers into the broader movement for civil rights.

Other Latino Protests

Mexican Americans had other heroes too. Some formed organizations that took a militant approach, while others used political action.

Brown Berets In East Los Angeles, David Sanchez and other young Mexican Americans formed a community action group that took

---

RESOURCE DIRECTORY

Teaching Resources

✪ **American Profiles Activity** found in the Unit 6 folder, p. 84, profiles Delores Huerta, who cofounded the United Farm Workers and worked for social justice.

A mural in Los Angeles illustrates Mexican American pride.

Divide students into groups and assign each group a region of the United States. Distribute outline maps of the United States, or ask students to sketch or trace such maps. Students can use almanacs or Census Bureau documents to find statistics about the number of Latino Americans in each state. Have students find or calculate the percentage of Latino Americans in their state and display that information on their maps.

Then ask students to compare this information with the percentage of African Americans in their state's population.

on a semi-military style. Known as the Brown Berets, they later started branches in other cities. The group regarded itself as "defensive," protecting Mexican Americans against police and other authorities and sometimes acting outside the law. Sanchez said:

> We're not a violent or a nonviolent organization . . . we are an emergency organization. . . . If we see a cop beating up a Chicano, we move in and stop the cop, we try to be ready for every emergency.

Political Action Some Latinos worked within mainstream politics. In 1961 voters in San Antonio, Texas, elected Henry B. González to Congress. Another Texan, Elizo "Kika" de la Garza, went to the House of Representatives in 1964, while Joseph Montoya of New Mexico was elected to the Senate.

New political groups formed to support Latino interests. For example, José Angel Gutiérrez brought together Mexican American groups in Crystal City, Texas, leading to the formation of the political party *La Raza Unida* in 1970. The new party worked for better housing and jobs and backed Mexican American political candidates.

Another leader, Reies López Tijerina, argued that the Anglo culture had stolen the Chicanos' land and heritage. To call attention to broken treaties, in 1966 his *Alianza Federal de Mercedes* (Federal Alliance of Land Grants) marched on the New Mexico state capital. At about the same time, the Mexican American Legal Defense and Educational Fund (MALDEF), was founded. It has provided legal aid to help Mexican Americans gain civil rights and encouraged Mexican American students to become lawyers.

MAKING CONNECTIONS

Different regions of the United States are home to larger numbers of certain ethnic groups. What ethnic groups are prominent in your area and what discrimination do they face, if any?

Answer to . . .

MAKING CONNECTIONS

Answers will vary depending on the ethnic composition of the area, but should indicate an awareness of their own and other groups' status and position in the community. In many places, large numbers of students may themselves be members of minority groups.

In Depth

Biography

Writer Amy Tan was born in Oakland, California, in 1952. Her childhood typifies the difficulties inherent in cultural assimilation in the United States during the 1950s and 1960s. Her mother always spoke to her in Mandarin, but Amy would always answer in English. As Tan explains, "With assimilation you have a dominant culture and the underlying message is you have to reject your other culture." Drawing from her experiences, Tan has written successful novels, including *The Joy Luck Club* and *The Kitchen God's Wife,* about Asian American life in the United States.

Media and Technology

 Transparency
Our Multicultural Heritage, C-15

SOURCE READINGS

Source Readings on p. 708 will connect literature selections and primary source excerpts to historical events discussed in this section.

Ask students to research the Congressional Hispanic Caucus. Who are its members? What are its goals? How successful has the caucus been in reaching its goals?

3. ASSESS

Section 2 Review Answers

1. (a) Latino, see p. 691, (b) Anglo, see p. 692, (c) *barrio*, see p. 692, (d) migratory farm workers, see p. 692, (e) United Farm Workers, see p. 692, (f) Japanese American Citizens League, see p. 694

2. César Chávez, see p. 692

3. It emphasized Mexican American self-identity in history and the modern world.

4. He formed the United Farm Workers in order to win better conditions for migratory workers. By winning in California, he drew national attention to the cause.

5. Chicano high school students walked out of schools; organizations like the Brown Berets engaged in defensive patrol actions; others joined mainstream politics or used the court system.

6. World War II and the communist takeover in China increased prejudices.

7. It gave them political influence in Congress.

8. Answers should point out that Asian Americans are physically distinguishable from those of European ancestry and that they are often perceived as having closer ties to the countries from which their ancestors came.

Reteach

Ask students to list the goals, tactics, and gains of Latinos and Asian Americans, based on information from the section.

Caption Answer to ...

 Interpreting Maps

Japan and China sent the most immigrants in the 1950s, Korea and the Philippines in the 1970s.

Asian Americans Fight Discrimination

Ever since their arrival in the United States, Americans of Chinese and Japanese ancestry have faced racial discrimination. Prejudice against Japanese Americans reached a peak during World War II, and the communist takeover of China in 1949 influenced attitudes toward Chinese Americans. In general, the years after the war brought many hopeful and positive changes for Asian Americans.

Japanese Americans After the War A major issue for Japanese Americans was compensation for the losses they had suffered during their wartime internment in the 1940s. As discussed in Chapter 16, Japanese American citizens living along the West Coast were forced to relocate to internment camps after the government decided they were a risk to American security once the nation declared war on Japan. Not only had their lives been disrupted, but they had lost hundreds of millions of dollars in homes, farms, and businesses. The main voice for Japanese Americans, the **Japanese American Citizens League** (JACL), in 1948 won passage of the Japanese American Claims Act, under which Congress eventually paid relatively small amounts for property losses. JACL also worked for changes in anti-Asian immigration laws.

About two thirds of Japanese Americans who had been relocated returned to the Pacific Coast, but others moved to cities east of the Rockies. Their new communities were more a part of mainstream society than the prewar *nihonmachis*—"Japantown"—had been.

Economic Changes Although Asian Americans as a group were well educated, in 1960 they earned less than white Americans. In California, for example, for each $51 a white male was paid, a Chinese man would earn $38 and a Japanese man, $43. College graduates faced prejudice in attempting to move into management jobs.

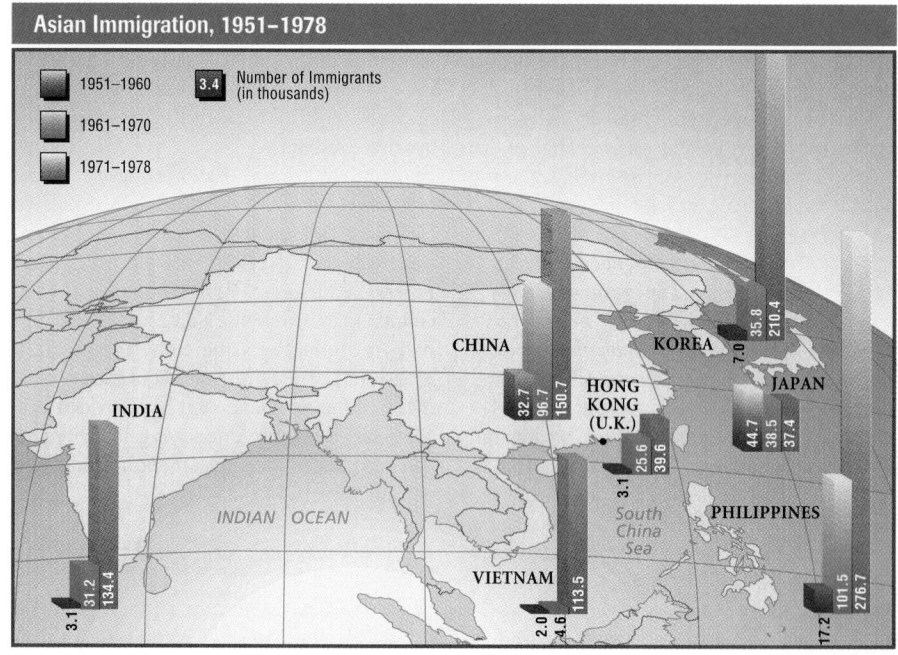

Asian Immigration, 1951–1978

1951–1960
1961–1970
1971–1978

3.4 Number of Immigrants (in thousands)

CHINA
KOREA
HONG KONG (U.K.)
JAPAN
INDIA
PHILIPPINES
INDIAN OCEAN
South China Sea
VIETNAM

 **Geography and History: Interpreting Maps**
Patterns of immigration from Asia changed dramatically in the 1950s, 1960s, and 1970s. *Which two countries sent the greatest number of people in the 1950s? In the 1970s?*

▶ RESOURCE DIRECTORY

Teaching Resources

Statehood for Hawaii created, for the first time, a state in which most voters were of Asian or part-Asian ancestry. Members of Congress from the new state, such as Daniel Inouye (above), reflected the islands' cultural diversity.

As a group, Asian Americans in the 1960s and 1970s were making economic gains faster than other minorities. Nonetheless, they still faced discrimination and relied on the example of the civil rights movement to push for gains. Some Chinese American community activists in the 1970s asked for federal help in overcoming problems of unemployment, health, and language barriers. Another development in the 1970s was an increase in immigration from other Asian countries, especially Korea, India, and Vietnam, as illustrated by the map on page 694.

Political Representation A major step forward for Asian Americans' self-image was the granting of statehood to Hawaii in 1959. The new state sent Hiram Leong Fong, a Chinese American, to the Senate, and Daniel K. Inouye, a Japanese American, to the House of Representatives. Other Asian American lawmakers have since been elected from Hawaii and California.

SECTION 2 REVIEW

Key Terms, People, and Places

1. Define (a) Latino, (b) Anglo, (c) *barrio*, (d) migratory farm workers, (e) United Farm Workers, (f) Japanese American Citizens League.
2. Identify César Chávez.

Key Concepts

3. What was the importance of the poem *Yo Soy Joaquin*?
4. What role did César Chávez play in the Chicano struggle for equal rights?

5. What were other forms of Chicano protest?
6. What world events influenced prejudice against Asian Americans?
7. Why was Hawaiian statehood significant for Asian Americans?

Critical Thinking

8. **Recognizing Bias** What factors might have made prejudice against Asian Americans last longer than discrimination against people of European ancestry?

 Quiz found in the Unit 6 folder, p. 77, covers the main ideas in this section as well as the key terms.

SECTION 3

Native American Struggles

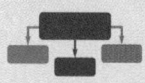

Connecting to the Big Idea

See page 682B. As a result of discrimination and shifting governmental policies, most Native Americans lived in poverty in the 1960s. Ask how Native Americans tried to change government policy and win more self-determination.

Objectives

● Explain why Native Americans faced unique problems of poverty and discrimination.
● Describe how many Native American activists worked to maintain their traditional culture and identity as a people.
● Identify the focus of the American Indian Movement as urban problems and protests.
● Cite gains in self-determination achieved by Native Americans through protests and legal challenges.

Bellringer

Ask students to write a definition for *self-determination.* Ask them to what extent they think that they themselves are now self-determining. In what areas do they not make decisions for themselves? When do students think they might become completely self-determining?

Reading Strategy

Predicting Content Before students begin reading the section, write the main headings from the section on the chalkboard: Native Americans Face Unique Problems, Roots of Native American Activism, Confronting the Government. Ask students to formulate at least two questions for each heading and to look for answers to their questions as they read.

SECTION PREVIEW

Most Native Americans in the 1960s were living under conditions that were the result of centuries of discrimination and constantly changing government policies. They too took their cue from the civil rights movement to work for self-determination.

A Sioux woman joins a protest against federal policies for Native Americans.

Key Concepts

• Native Americans faced unique problems in terms of poverty and discrimination.
• Many Native American activists worked to maintain their traditional culture and identity as a people.
• The American Indian Movement focused on urban problems and spearheaded protests.
• Protests and legal challenges won Native Americans more self-determination.

Key Terms, People, and Places

American Indian Movement (AIM); Dennis Banks, Russell Means; Alcatraz

---

Native Americans were another minority who were inspired by the civil rights movement to seek equality and control over their own lives. Overall, Native Americans were perhaps the country's most troubled nonwhite group, in part because of government policies. Activists used legal challenges and direct action to reach their goals.

Native Americans Face Unique Problems

As the original inhabitants of North America, Native Americans have occupied a unique social and legal position. Although their cultures and languages are varied, white society has seen "Indians" as one group. The Constitution excluded them from citizenship, and Congress assumed the right to supervise them.

From the 1800s on, government agencies limited self-government for Native Americans and often worked to erase their traditional lifestyles. Until 1924, many Native Americans did not have full citizenship rights. Today they are citizens of both the United States and their own nations or tribal groups.

As a whole, Native Americans have routinely been denied equal opportunities. They have had higher rates of unemployment, alcoholism, and suicide, as well as a shorter life expectancy, than white Americans. Poverty and poor living conditions were once common in their communities. Like other nonwhite groups, Native Americans were the victims of centuries-old stereotypes, reinforced by the way movies and other media depicted them. ✪

Native Americans also had some grievances that were unique. **Dennis Banks,** a Chippewa, explained why he became an activist:

> I t was a question of this government being responsible to me, and not seeing to it that I had an opportunity to lead a decent life, or to own a piece of land, or to find a good job, like they had promised my ancestors in all these treaties. They broke all of those promises. They stole everything from them and wrecked their way of life— which was a good way.

Roots of Native American Activism

An important part of the Native Americans' way of life was their tie to the land and what it stood for. "Everything is tied to our homeland," declared D'Arcy McNickle, a Native American anthropologist, in 1961. Yet, many years after pioneers first moved onto Indian territory, state and federal governments continued to take over traditional tribal lands. Protecting what was left became a major goal of Native Americans.

▶ RESOURCE DIRECTORY

Teaching Resources

Reproducible Lesson Plan found in the Unit 6 folder, p. 72, provides a summary of the Section 3 lesson plan content.

Alternate Lesson Plan: Cooperative Learning found in the Alternate Lesson Plans folder, p. 153, helps groups of students focus on the goals of Native American activists by writing headlines and brief articles.

Guided Reading and Review found in the Unit 6 folder, p. 78, provides a structure for reading and mastering the key concepts and reviewing the key terms for Section 3. (Guided Practice)

✪ **Visual Learning Activity** Changing Attitudes Toward Native Americans, found in the Unit 6 folder, p. 96, portrays attempts made in the 1960s and 1970s to challenge stereotypes about Native Americans.

Native American Pride and Sports Team Names

The Native American movement of the 1960s and early 1970s influenced changes in more areas than one might expect. One example of the effects of the reawakening of Native American pride can be found in the sports world, where Native American names and images often have been used as team names and mascots. Arguing that using Native American names in such a way is degrading and racially offensive and that other races are not used for the same purpose, Native Americans began to request that some teams change their names. In response,

in 1969 Dartmouth College, in New Hampshire, changed its team name from the Indians to the Big Green to avoid racial insensitivity. In 1972, Stanford University, in California, whose team name was also the Indians, likewise changed its name. Stanford chose the Cardinal to replace its previous name. Syracuse University followed suit not much later, abandoning its original mascot, the Saltine Warrior, for an orange with arms and legs.

The attitudes that prompted these changes have affected professional sports teams as well. In 1991

the Atlanta Braves sparked considerable debate over both their name and their rallying cry, the "Tomahawk Chop." The same year, controversy over the Washington Redskins reached fever pitch with the introduction of a bill before Congress. Senator Ben Nighthorse Campbell of Colorado proposed that no federal land be allotted for the Redskins' new stadium until the team changed its name. Thus far, the name change has not taken place. ***What other popular names or symbols might some groups find offensive?***

Land Claims A government project in New York state triggered one early protest. According to a 1794 treaty, the Seneca Nation held the land on its Allegany reservation. The federal government, however, had long planned to build a dam there as part of a flood control project. The Kinzua Dam would affect 10,000 acres of hunting and fishing land, as well as homes and sacred sites.

In 1956 Congress held hearings, which did not include the Seneca, and appropriated funds for the dam. After legal appeals failed, the Seneca in 1961 went to President John Kennedy, but he supported the government claim. Once the dam was built, Congress agreed to pay $15 million in damages, but this did not restore the land.

Other Native Americans responded to this decision by bringing lawsuits for violations of treaty rights and failure to make promised payments. Court rulings supported many claims. For example, in 1967 the Court of Claims ruled that the federal government had forced the Seminole to give up Florida lands in 1823 for an unreasonably low price. The court directed the government to pay more to the Seminole community.

The American Indian Movement One of the leading activist movements began in Minneapolis in 1968, led by Dennis Banks and George Mitchell, both Chippewa. At a meeting of 250 people representing twenty Native American organizations, Banks set forth the goals: "Let's get a new organized effort going, a new coalition that will fight for Indian treaty rights and better conditions and opportunities for our people."

The new organization came to be called the **American Indian Movement (AIM).** It originally focused on the special problems of Native Americans living in cities. Following the example of militant black groups, AIM set up Indian patrols to monitor street activity. It also began survival schools to encourage racial and cultural pride in young people. ⬚

Many people, both white and Native American, criticized AIM's militant approach. On the group's second anniversary, however, Banks repeated its goals:

We must commit ourselves to changing the social pattern in which we have been forced to live. . . . The government and churches have demoralized, dehumanized, massacred, robbed, raped,

---

SOURCE READINGS

⬚ Source Readings on p. 710 will connect literature selections and primary source excerpts to historical events discussed in this section.

---

2. INSTRUCT

Explain/Discuss

Discuss with students how the federal government came to make special treaties with Native Americans. Recall that for years, Native Americans were considered members of tribal nations with whom the United States negotiated as with a foreign country.

Ask students to discuss the problems of contemporary Americans who think they own land that by treaty belongs to a group of Native Americans. If the government returns the land to the Native Americans, how should the "owners" be compensated?

Discuss what Native Americans accomplished at Alcatraz and Wounded Knee. Then ask what they accomplished through legal battles. Which route do students think was more effective?

In Depth

Biography

During the turbulent decade of the sixties, Northern Cheyenne Ben Nighthorse Campbell (b. 1933) channeled an angry adolescence into the study of martial arts. It eventually earned him the captaincy of the 1964 United States Olympic Judo Team at the Tokyo games. In 1982, Campbell became the first Native American to serve in Congress since the 1930s. In 1992, he was elected to represent Colorado in the United States Senate.

Answer to ...

Analyze

The protesters at Wounded Knee were armed. By the end of the siege, two AIM participants had been killed and others had been injured. Ask students to compare the methods used by AIM and those used in protests led by Martin Luther King, Jr., and César Chávez. How did the goals of these protests differ? Did they differ in their results?

In Depth

Multicultural Perspectives

Attempts to correct injustices against Native Americans often created other problems. When the Chippewa in Minnesota sued the government in 1975 to regain 100,000 acres that they claimed had been taken, in the words of one sympathetic historian, "through theft, trickery, ignorance, or for failing to pay taxes that were, in fact, illegal," it hurt white farmers who had bought the land in good faith. Because of the pending claims, banks wouldn't lend these farmers money to buy machinery, and no one would buy the land.

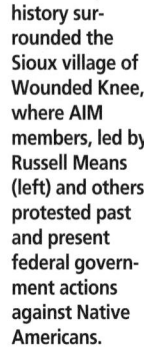

Echoes of past history surrounded the Sioux village of Wounded Knee, where AIM members, led by Russell Means (left) and others, protested past and present federal government actions against Native Americans.

promised, made treaty after treaty, and lied to us. . . . We must now destroy this political machine that man has built to prevent us from self-determination.

MAKING CONNECTIONS

One goal of Native American activists has been to force the federal government to honor treaties made in the 1800s. Why were so many treaties made—and then broken?

Confronting the Government

Trying to call attention to issues long ignored, Native Americans staged several standoffs with the federal government. In 1972, demonstrators formed the Broken Treaties Caravan, traveled to Washington, D.C., and occupied the federal government's Bureau of Indian Affairs' offices for six days. Other protests were even more dramatic.

The Occupation of Alcatraz In November 1969, seventy-eight protesters from several Native American groups landed on

Alcatraz, an island in San Francisco Bay on which stood an abandoned federal prison. They claimed the 13-acre rock under the terms of the Fort Laramie Treaty of 1868, which allowed male Native Americans to file homestead claims on federal lands. The occupation also was a protest against the policies and methods of the Bureau of Indian Affairs.

⭐ Others joined the original group, planning to turn the deserted island into an educational and cultural center. In March 1970, author Vine Deloria, Jr., a Standing Rock Sioux, wrote hopefully about the project in the *New York Times:*

> *By making Alcatraz an experimental Indian center operated and planned by Indian people, we would be given a chance to see what we could do toward developing answers to modern social problems. Ancient tribalism can be incorporated with modern technology in an urban setting. Perhaps we would not succeed in the effort. . . . It just seems to a lot of Indians that this continent was a lot better off when we were running it.*

The occupation failed to achieve the desired results. Federal marshals eventually removed

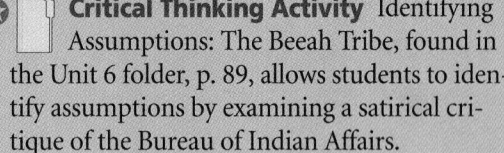
RESOURCE DIRECTORY

Teaching Resources

⭐ **American Profiles Activity** found in the Unit 6 folder, p. 85, profiles Vine Deloria, Jr., who through his books emerged as a leading spokesman for Native American nationalism.

⭐ **Critical Thinking Activity** Identifying Assumptions: The Beeah Tribe, found in the Unit 6 folder, p. 89, allows students to identify assumptions by examining a satirical critique of the Bureau of Indian Affairs.

Activity

Teaching Heterogeneous Groups
Cultural pride and education were very important tools for gaining self-determination. For students to understand the importance of cultural heritage and the ways in which it is taught, have them list as many aspects as possible of their cultural heritage and recall briefly how they learned about them. **LEP**

Enrichment
A number of Native American groups have opened gambling casinos on their reservations. Ask students to prepare a report explaining the casino openings, their financial success, and why some Native American leaders oppose them.

3. ASSESS

Section 3 Review Answers

1. American Indian Movement, see p. 697

2. (a) Dennis Banks, see p. 696,
(b) Russell Means, see p. 699,
(c) Alcatraz, see p. 698

3. They faced poverty, high unemployment, alcoholism, suicide, and low life expectancy.

4. Native Americans followed African American groups' example of direct action and militant tactics; they worked to instill racial and cultural pride.

5. It focused on Native Americans in cities.

the last protesters after a year and a half. But the episode dramatized Native American grievances and gained important national exposure.

Confrontation at Wounded Knee An even more dramatic confrontation came in 1973 at the Oglala Sioux village of Wounded Knee, South Dakota. There, in 1890, the army's Seventh Cavalry had massacred more than two hundred Sioux men, women, and children.

The Pine Ridge reservation around the village was one of the country's poorest, with half its families living on welfare. In February 1973, AIM leaders **Russell Means** and Dennis Banks and some two hundred AIM members took over the village. AIM sought to draw attention to conditions on the reservation and to the 371 treaties it said the government had broken over the years.

Other Native American leaders came out in support of the occupation. Onondaga Chief Oren Lyons, speaking for the Iroquois, said:

W e support the Oglala Sioux Nation or any Indian Nation that will fight for its sovereignty. . . . The issue here at Wounded Knee is the recognition of the treaties between the United States Government and the sovereign nations that were here before.

Federal marshals and FBI agents then surrounded the village, allowing only occasional shipments of supplies. From time to time, gunfire broke out. As the siege went on, agents arrested some three hundred people, including news reporters and outside supporters.

By the time the standoff finally ended in May, two AIM members had been killed and about a dozen people hurt, including two federal marshals. The government agreed to reexamine treaty rights. ✪

The Government Responds Native American activism brought some responses from the government. The Kennedy and Johnson administrations in the 1960s tried to bring jobs and income to some reservations by encouraging industries to locate there and leasing reservation lands to energy and development corporations. But many Native Americans worried about the effects

AIM leader Dennis Banks leads a protest march at Mount Rushmore, South Dakota.

Media and Technology

 Transparency
Critical Thinking, I-9

6. They wanted to assert their claims to lands that were important to them, to gain redress for treaties the government had broken in past years, and have more control over their own communities.

7. Possible answer: Native Americans struggled to claim certain sovereign rights granted to them through treaty with the United States government; African Americans for the most part fought to gain rights granted to U.S. citizens by the Constitution.

Reteach

Ask students to work in pairs or groups of three to develop a set of five questions about the section content. Each group should have a question beginning with *who, what, why, when,* and *how.* Have groups exchange question sheets and decide on consensus answers.

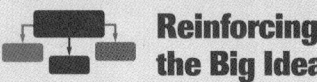

Reinforcing the Big Idea

Native Americans in the 1960s continued to suffer poverty and discrimination, largely the result of long standing government policies. Native Americans worked for self-determination through protests and court cases. The next section describes the efforts of the environmental and consumer movements.

Many Native American groups went to court to win back land and other rights. Wearing traditional ceremonial dress, George Crows Fly High and Martha Grass, along with civil rights leader Ralph Abernathy, seek a meeting with Supreme Court justices.

these projects would have on the land. In the 1970s, the Navaho, Crow, Northern Cheyenne, and others sought to renegotiate or cancel many of the leases.

Pressure by Native Americans also led to their inclusion in "Great Society" programs dealing with housing, health, and education. Government agencies made resources available and let Native Americans plan and run their own programs and, in some places, their own schools.

A number of laws passed in the 1970s favored Native American rights. The Indian Education Act of 1972 gave parents and tribal councils more control over schools and school programs. The Indian Self-Determination and Education Assistance Acts of 1975 upheld Native American autonomy and let local leaders administer federally supported social programs for housing and education.

Native Americans also continued to win legal battles to regain land, mineral, and water rights. For example, in 1971 the Alaska Federation of Natives was given $1 billion and 40 million acres of land. In 1970, after rejecting a cash settlement, the Taos in New Mexico won back Blue Lake, a religious shrine, as well as 48,000 acres of land. A Taos representative said:

W*e don't have gold temples in this lake, but we have a sign of a living God to whom we pray—the living trees, the evergreen and spruce . . . and the lake itself. . . . We are taking that water to give us strength so we can gain in knowledge and wisdom.*

SECTION 3 REVIEW

Key Terms, People, and Places
1. Define American Indian Movement.
2. Identify (a) Dennis Banks, (b) Russell Means, (c) Alcatraz.

Key Concepts
3. What problems were typical of Native American communities in the 1960s?
4. How did the African American civil rights movement influence the tactics of Native American groups?

5. What group was the original focus of the American Indian Movement?
6. What did Native Americans hope to accomplish by lawsuits?

Critical Thinking
7. **Making Comparisons** How was the social and political situation of Native Americans different from that of African Americans?

 **RESOURCE DIRECTORY**

Teaching Resources

Literature Activity Native American Voices, found in the Unit 6 folder, p. 94, presents a poem that expresses the hope of Native Americans in the 1970s.

Quiz found in the Unit 6 folder, p. 79, covers the main ideas in this section as well as the key terms.

Environmental and Consumer Movements

SECTION PREVIEW

The mood of protest in the 1960s energized movements to preserve the environment and to challenge the safety of certain consumer products.

Key Concepts
- The activism of minorities in the 1960s spurred environmentalists and consumers to take action.
- The modern environmental movement was triggered by Rachel Carson's *Silent Spring*.
- Ralph Nader was a major figure in beginning the movement for consumers' rights.

Key Terms, People, and Places
Environmental Protection Agency (EPA);
Rachel Carson, Ralph Nader

I n the 1960s and early 1970s, the mood of protest surrounding the civil rights movement inspired a number of other movements. Environmentalists demanded actions that would preserve and restore the earth's environment and resources. Similarly, consumers and vigilant consumer advocates used proven protest techniques to ensure that American industries would be accountable to their customers and workers. Their efforts brought changes in public attitudes and public policy—changes that affect the lives of Americans to this day.

The Environmental Movement

Like the women's movement, the environmental movement did not spring up in the 1960s but had roots in the American past. In the late 1890s and early 1900s, progressives had worked to make public lands and parks available for the people. New Deal programs of the 1930s included tree-planting projects in an effort to put people back to work—as well as to conserve forests and farmlands.

Rachel Carson The modern environmental movement stemmed even more directly, however, from the work of marine biologist **Rachel Carson.** She had once hoped to become a writer but initially followed her interest in zoology. In the 1930s and 1940s, however, she combined her talents and began to write about scientific subjects for general audiences. In 1951 Carson published *The Sea Around Us,* which was an immediate best seller. Her major—and most influential—book was *Silent Spring,* published in 1962.

In *Silent Spring,* Carson attacked the use of chemical pesticides, particularly DDT, which had increased agricultural productivity but killed various plants and animals other than the insect pests that were its target:

Environmental activists battled for a variety of issues in the 1960s.

> T he most alarming of all man's assaults upon the environment is the contamination of air, earth, rivers, and sea with dangerous and even lethal materials. This pollution is for the most part irrecoverable. . . . In this now universal contamination of the environment, chemicals are the sinister and little-recognized partners of radiation in changing the very nature of the world.

As Carson explained, chemicals sprayed on crops entered into living organisms and moved from one to another in a chain of poisoning and death. Specifically, the lingering effects of DDT threatened to destroy many species of birds and fish, including the national symbol, the bald eagle.

📋 **Reproducible Lesson Plan** found in the Unit 6 folder, p. 73, provides a summary of the Section 4 lesson plan content.

📋 **Alternate Lesson Plan: Learning Styles** found in the Alternate Lesson Plans folder, p. 154, is useful for many types of learners and helps students identify and describe issues and concerns raised by environmental and consumer groups.

📋 **Guided Reading and Review** found in the Unit 6 folder, p. 80, provides a structure for reading and mastering the key concepts and reviewing the key terms for Section 4. (Guided Practice)

1. FOCUS

Connecting to the Big Idea

See page 682B. Inspired by other protest movements, environmentalists and consumer advocates demanded action to preserve the environment and protect the buyers and users of products in America. Ask students what triggered the environmental and consumer movements. How successful were they?

Objectives
- Explain how the activism of minorities in the 1960s spurred environmentalists and consumers to take action.
- Identify Rachel Carson's *Silent Spring* as the trigger for the modern environmental movement.
- Identify Ralph Nader as the major figure in the early movement for consumer rights.

Bellringer

Ask students to recall how many purchases they made on each day of the past week and how long they spent shopping. Have them use the information to estimate how much money and how much time a year they spend as consumers. Discuss the importance of consumers in our economy.

Reading Strategy

Reading for Evidence Note the statement on page 701 that the efforts of environmentalists and consumerists " . . . brought changes in public attitudes and public policy— changes that affect the lives of Americans to this day." Ask students to look for evidence to support this statement as they read.

Explain/Discuss

Explain that many environmental problems grew out of the rapid development of technology, industry, and transportation after World War II.

Have students list some voluntary measures that people undertake to preserve the environment. Next ask how big a role they think the federal government should play in regulating our care of the environment. Should government determine how communities dispose of trash and regulate speed limits, or how manufacturers package items?

Analyze

Ask students why *Silent Spring* and *Unsafe at Any Speed* had such immediate impact and produced such far-reaching effects. Ask what conditions came together for Carson's and Nader's books to attract the immediate attention of the nation.

Answer to ...

MAKING CONNECTIONS

Answers will vary depending on local events and activism, as well as on students' own families' interest in the environment and conservation.

Activity

Cooperative Learning

Time: One class period.
Activity: Create an Earth Day celebration.
Grouping: Four to six students.
Purpose: The first Earth Day was celebrated in 1970. Have groups decide on a focus, theme, or goal for an Earth Day celebration and plan a day's schedule, including entertainment, speakers, and other events coordinated with the focus.
Roles: Community committee members, each responsible for one aspect of the celebration.
Outcome: Students will identify ways in which the community can celebrate the preservation of the environment.

Disturbed by the changes she saw in her environment, biologist Rachel Carson sounded a trumpet call to action in her book *Silent Spring*, inspiring others to join a strong environmental movement.

Silent Spring was a bombshell. The chemical industry fought back vigorously, arguing that Carson confused the issues and left readers "unable to sort fact from fancy." The public was not persuaded by this attack. So great was national concern that a special presidential advisory committee was appointed. It called for continued research and warned against the widespread use of pesticides. Eventually DDT was banned in the United States, and other chemicals were controlled more strictly. For more information about the impact of *Silent Spring*, see the feature "Time and Place: A Geographic Perspective" on page 704.

⚫ It was not only DDT that worried people. They became more conscious of poisonous fumes in the air, oil spills on beaches, and toxic wastes buried in the ground. In the mid-1960s, President Lyndon Johnson's administration addressed environmental concerns as part of the "Great Society." Johnson hoped for "an environment that is pleasing to the senses and healthy to live in." Environmental legislation was part of his broader reform program.

Nuclear Power Another issue arose toward the end of the 1960s, as environmentalists focused on the problems of nuclear power plants built to generate electricity. While nuclear plants caused less air pollution than coal-burning plants, they produced steam that was then discharged into local waterways. The steam raised water temperatures, killing fish and plant life. People also worried about the possibility of nuclear plant accidents.

Public Response Grassroots environmental movements sprang up in many places, supporting conservation efforts and opposing actions such as the building of new nuclear plants. In 1970 Americans celebrated the first Earth Day, which would become a yearly observance aimed at heightening awareness of environmental issues and marked by day-long activities to clean up pollution and litter. Besides Rachel Carson, other scientists were alarmed by environmental problems. For example, in his 1971 book *The Closing Circle*, biologist Barry Commoner warned about rapid increases in pollution.

The efforts of the environmentalists helped spur the federal government to create new policies. Responding to public concerns about air and water pollution, in 1970 Congress passed the Water Quality Improvement Act and the Clean Air Act. Also in 1970, President Richard Nixon's administration established the **Environmental Protection Agency (EPA).** The EPA combined existing federal agencies concerned with air and water pollution. As the nation's watchdog against polluters, the EPA today monitors and reduces air and water pollution and regulates the disposal of solid waste and the use of pesticides and toxic substances. ⚫

MAKING CONNECTIONS

Do you think that concern for the environment has increased or decreased since the 1970s? What evidence have you seen?

The Consumer Movement

The consumer movement was yet another outgrowth of the 1960s protests. It too had roots

RESOURCE DIRECTORY

Teaching Resources

⚫ **Primary Source Activity** The Desecration of America, found in the Unit 6 folder, pp. 91–92, features excerpts from a 1961 *Atlantic Monthly* article by Vance Packard in which he examines the state of the countryside with dismay.

⚫ **Visual Learning Activity** Preserving the Environment, found in the Unit 6 folder, p. 97, helps students understand and visually express specific environmental issues.

in earlier years. The Pure Food and Drug Act of 1906, for example, was one early effort to maintain standards and protect the public. In the 1960s and early 1970s, however, the movement grew far stronger and involved more people.

Attorney **Ralph Nader** spearheaded the new consumer effort. Nader had been a serious activist all his life. While a student at Princeton University in the early 1950s, Nader protested the spraying of campus trees with DDT. His interest in automobile safety began at Harvard Law School and continued into his law practice in Hartford, Connecticut. In 1964 Daniel Patrick Moynihan, then assistant secretary of labor, hired Nader as a consultant on the issue of automobile safety regulations.

The government report Nader wrote soon became a book, *Unsafe at Any Speed: The Designed-in Dangers of the American Automobile.* It began:

> F or over half a century the automobile has brought death, injury, and the most inestimable sorrow and deprivation to millions of people. With Medea-like intensity, this mass trauma began rising sharply four years ago reflecting new and unexpected ravages by the motor vehicle. A 1959 Department of Commerce report projected that 51,000 persons would be killed by automobiles in 1975. That figure will probably be reached in 1965, a decade ahead of schedule.

Like the muckrakers of the Progressive era, Nader used facts to support his passionate argument that car manufacturers would be responsible for many of these deaths. He called many cars "coffins on wheels," pointing to dangers such as a tendency to flip over. The industry, he charged,

knowingly continued to build over one million cars before confronting the safety problems.

Nader's book was a sensation, and in 1966 he testified before Congress about automobile hazards. That year, Congress passed the National Traffic and Motor Vehicle Safety Act. The *Washington Post* noted that, "Most of the credit for making possible this important legislation belongs to one man—Ralph Nader. . . . A one-man lobby for the public prevailed over the nation's most powerful industry."

Nader broadened his efforts and investigated the meatpacking business, helping to secure support for the Wholesome Meat Act of 1967. He next looked into consumer problems in other industries. Scores of volunteers, called "Nader's Raiders," signed on to help. They turned out report after report and inspired consumer activism. As ordinary Americans began to stand up for their rights, consumer protection offices had to respond to a flood of complaints.

Concern for the earth and its health prompted Earth Day rallies and clean-ups, including such events as a roadway "lie-down" by 5,000 people to protest car fumes in Italy and a Cheyenne ceremony at dawn outside Bozeman, Montana.

SECTION 4 REVIEW

Key Terms, People, and Places
1. Define Environmental Protection Agency.
2. Identify (a) Rachel Carson, (b) Ralph Nader.

Key Concepts
3. What was the target of Rachel Carson's book *Silent Spring*?

4. What role did Ralph Nader play in the consumer movement?

Critical Thinking
5. **Recognizing Cause and Effect** What were some of the results of Rachel Carson's book *Silent Spring*?

---

3. ASSESS

Section 4 Review Answers

1. Environmental Protection Agency, see p. 702

2. (a) Rachel Carson, see p. 701, (b) Ralph Nader, see p. 703

3. It focused attention on chemical pesticides, particularly DDT, and alerted Americans to the problems they caused.

4. He first investigated automobile safety and made people aware of unsafe cars; he and his volunteers helped mobilize support for consumer legislation in other fields as well.

5. Answers should indicate that the book did not just cause public concern over pesticides but aroused awareness of other environmental issues.

Reteach

Write the following two column headings on the chalkboard: The Environmental Movement and The Consumer Movement. Then make three horizontal rows, labeled Started By, Goals, and Results. Ask students to fill in the chart with information from the section.

4. CLOSE

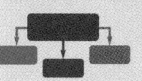 **Reinforcing the Big Idea**

The environmental and consumer movements started in the 1960s and used some of the techniques of the civil rights movement to change public attitudes and public policy.

After *Silent Spring*

Focus Tell students that when *Silent Spring* appeared in 1962, *ecology* was not a familiar word in the vocabularies of most Americans. There was virtually no way for Americans to recycle glass, paper, metal, or plastic. The Environmental Protection Agency did not exist. Few Americans considered the environment when they went shopping; fewer still would refuse to purchase an item because of its excessive packaging. Most Americans did not know about the ozone layer, much less worry about it when buying hair spray or air conditioners; and store clerks would have cast strange looks at a shopper who wanted to reuse grocery bags. When did Americans start learning about the environment? When did "environmentally conscious" become a compliment? When did *green* start to mean a lifestyle as well as a color? A trend such as the environmental movement seldom begins at one specific time, but the publication of *Silent Spring* marks the moment when the American public began to learn about the choices required to safeguard the earth.

Instruct Divide the class into small groups. Ask students to discuss the information on DDT presented in the feature and to brainstorm as many groups as possible who were hurt in any way by restrictions on the use of DDT. *(Farmers who lost crops, manufacturers, suppliers, stockholders, employees, etc.)* Then make a list of these groups with the whole class and ask students to decide if the benefit to the world as a whole from the banning of DDT outweighed the cost to the groups on the list. Ask who makes such cost-benefit decisions. *(Individuals; federal, state, and local governments; the courts.)*

After *Silent Spring*

Although many of her concerns were shared by other scientists, Rachel Carson's book Silent Spring *was a landmark in the environmental movement. Why did Carson's book have such an impact?*

The publication of Rachel Carson's book *Silent Spring* in 1962 is usually described as a landmark event in the history of the environmental movement. Carson, concerned about the disappearance of songbirds from America's towns and cities, blamed the immensely successful and widely used pesticide DDT. Scientists already were beginning to weigh the environmental costs of DDT against its proven benefits in controlling insects. Their voices, however, tended to be overridden by the chemical companies and the agricultural lobby, both of which favored continued DDT use.

What Carson did was to plant in the mind of the general public an important concept: that humans are a part of a living ecological system, not outside of it or dominant over it. Geographers and other scientists had long been interested in the concept that people, plants, and animals are all part of the same ecosystem. After *Silent Spring*, however, a growing awareness of the theme of interaction between humans and the environment led to a national movement that continues to this day.

What Carson did was to plant in the mind of the general public an important concept: that humans are a part of a living ecological system, not outside of it or dominant over it.

some time, at first in Europe, and much later in the United States. This was the concern that "progress" in science and technology was a two-edged sword. Such progress, people worried, might bring about negative as well as positive outcomes, and unintended as well as intended consequences. One such worry focused on the massive increase in the number of automobiles. While cars made it possible for many Americans to live outside of the cities where they worked, their use also brought increased air pollution. By the end of the 1960s, cars and trucks were identified as being the sources of more than half the air pollution in the United States.

It was into this troubled decade that Rachel Carson brought the environmental movement in 1962. During the 1960s, the environmental movement grew to a mass movement, partly because of court cases against the use of DDT brought late in the decade by the Environmental Defense Fund, one of many activist groups. At the close of the decade, the movement won official government recognition with the founding of the Environmental Protection Agency in 1970.

Human and Environmental Interaction: Background to a Movement

By pointing out that DDT not only poisoned insects, but also killed birds that ate the poisoned insects, Carson questioned humankind's relationship with the natural world. Her views were part of a much larger concern that had been building for

DDT: A Case Study of a Shift in Ideology

Until the 1960s, most Americans generally accepted the idea that humans should use the natural world for their own ends. Science and technology were the tools that let them do so. A case in point was the use of DDT by large-scale commercial farmers. Many important and profitable American

▶ RESOURCE DIRECTORY

Teaching Resources

Time and Place Activity
The Costs of Environmental Protection, found in the Unit 6 folder, pp. 82–83, discusses more recent concerns about the environment and encourages understanding of the link between economics and conservation.

A Shift in Public Opinion: The Environment

"Which of these problems would you like to see government devote most of its attention to in the next two years? — Gallup Poll question

Issue	Percent of Public Mentioning Item		
	1965	1970	Five-Year Change
Reducing amount of crime	41	56	15%
Reducing pollution of air and water	17	53	36%
Improving public education	45	31	-14%
Helping people in poor areas	32	30	-2%
Conquering "killer" diseases	37	29	-14%
Improving housing, clearing slums	21	27	6%
Reducing racial discrimination	29	25	-4%
Reducing unemployment	35	25	-10%
Improving highway safety	18	13	-5%
Beautifying America	3	5	2%

Source: *The Politics of Environmental Concern*, by Walter A. Rosenbaum

farm crops came originally from Europe and Asia, bringing their own insect pests with them. By the early 1900s, farmers were ready to use any easy-to-use, inexpensive method to kill insects that gobbled up corn, wheat, and other crops.

Farmers turned enthusiastically to chemical insecticides, but many of these poisons contained metals such as lead or arsenic that were deadly to humans. Against this background, DDT—which was apparently not toxic to humans even in massive doses—seemed like a wonderful solution.

By the 1960s, however, new research findings caused some people to question the assumption that humans should freely exploit nature. Rachel Carson brought some of that new research to light. She based her book on observations of the negative effect of DDT caused by massive spraying in American urban areas in an attempt to protect Dutch Elm trees from insect pests. As it turned out, DDT was a poison that remained in the ecosystem long after it had destroyed insect pests. It built up in the fatty tissues of birds and fish that ate the poisoned insects, and its long-term effects could be fatal. In birds, for example, DDT weakened shell formation so that young birds did not hatch. Predator birds

high in the food chain, such as hawks and eagles, reached the crisis stage first because they ate smaller birds, fish, and rodents.

Silent Spring sparked a debate that in 1972 resulted in the banning of almost all uses of DDT in the United States. Even more significantly, by questioning the popular ideology that nature exists for the benefit of humanity, Carson and other scientists and historians helped introduce a new ideology. Within a decade, environmentalism grew from something that interested only a small number of geographers and scientists to a nationwide movement embraced by a majority of citizens.

GEOGRAPHIC CONNECTIONS

1. Why were American crops such as wheat and corn susceptible to insect pests?
2. How did farmers' use of DDT affect other parts of the environment?

Critical Thinking

3. **Recognizing Ideologies** How did people's beliefs about their relationship with the natural environment change during the 1960s?

Chapter Review

Chapter Review Answers

Understanding Key Terms, People, and Places

Terms

Students should refer to the definitions of the key terms in the chapter to write sentences that show the relation of each word to consumer activism and the social revolution of the 1960s and early 1970s.

Matching

1. feminism
2. *barrio*
3. Environmental Protection Agency
4. Anglos
5. migratory farm workers

True or False

1. false, Rachel Carson
2. false, Ralph Nader
3. false, Betty Friedan
4. true

Reviewing Main Ideas

1. The only long-term role considered acceptable for women was that of wife and mother. Women who did work outside the home earned less than men, even when they held similar or identical jobs. They also often faced discrimination by employers who denied them job opportunities for which they were qualified.

2. Women learned the value of direct action, political pressure, and the importance of publicity in making others understand their positions.

3. Women organized local feminist groups as well as the national organization for women's rights, NOW. They also promoted the cause through publications like *The Feminine Mystique, Our Bodies, Ourselves,* and *Ms.* magazine. They supported the Equal Rights Amendment and worked to reform the laws that governed abortion.

4. Beliefs that women would lose existing rights, such as the right to be supported by a husband, and fears about coed bathrooms and the end of alimony eventually prevented ratification.

5. The goals of the Chicano movement were to instill cultural pride, improve education for Chicanos, and fight discrimination.

6. The profile of César Chávez reveals that Latino Americans used nonviolent tactics, such as boycotts, borrowed from the civil rights movement.

7. Japanese Americans were eventually paid some compensation for property losses incurred because of forced relocation during World War II. In addition,

---

Understanding Key Terms, People, and Places

Key Terms
1. feminism
2. feminist
3. National Organization for Women (NOW)
4. Equal Rights Amendment (ERA)
5. Latino
6. Anglo
7. *barrio*
8. migratory farm workers
9. United Farm Workers (UFW)
10. Japanese American Citizens League
11. American Indian Movement (AIM)
12. Environmental Protection Agency (EPA)

People
13. Gloria Steinem
14. Phyllis Schlafly
15. César Chávez
16. Dennis Banks
17. Russell Means
18. Rachel Carson
19. Ralph Nader

Places
20. Alcatraz

Terms For each term above, write a sentence that explains its relation to citizen activism and the social revolution of the 1960s and early 1970s.

Matching Review the key terms in the list above. If you are not sure of a term's meaning, review its definition in the chapter. Then choose a term from the list that best matches each description below.

1. the theory of the political, economic, and social equality of men and women
2. a Latino neighborhood
3. the nation's watchdog against polluters
4. English-speaking, non-Latino Americans
5. people who make a living moving from place to place to plant, cultivate, and harvest crops

True or False Determine whether each statement is true or false. If it is true, write "true." If it is false, change the underlined name to make the statement true.

1. Gloria Steinem began the environmental movement by writing *Silent Spring*.
2. César Chávez spearheaded the consumer effort by attacking automobile safety.
3. In *The Feminine Mystique,* Dennis Banks described the cultural patterns that prevented women from reaching their full potential.
4. The American Indian Movement leader Russell Means helped take over the village of Wounded Knee as a protest against the American government.

Reviewing Main Ideas

Section 1 (pp. 684–689)
1. Describe how society in the 1950s discriminated against women.
2. What political skills did women learn from their work in the civil rights movement?
3. Name at least three of the ways in which women tried to fight discrimination during the 1960s and early 1970s.
4. Describe the beliefs and fears that eventually prevented ratification of the ERA.

Section 2 (pp. 691–695)
5. Describe the goals of the Chicano movement.
6. What does the profile of César Chávez reveal about the tactics used by Latinos to overcome discrimination?
7. What positive changes did the years after World War II bring for Asian Americans?

Section 3 (pp. 696–700)
8. How did the United States government contribute to the discrimination faced by Native Americans?
9. What was the major issue over which Native American activists confronted the federal government?
10. Describe some of the tactics used by the American Indian Movement.
11. How successful was Native American activism in achieving its goals?

Section 4 (pp. 701–703)
12. What were the goals of the consumer movement?
13. Describe how Rachel Carson's *Silent Spring* initiated the environmental movement.
14. What were two of the targets of Ralph Nader's consumer movement?

Asian Americans as a group made faster gains than other minorities. Politically, Asian American pride was boosted by Hawaiian statehood.

8. Native Americans were excluded from citizenship by the Constitution and did not have full citizenship rights until 1924. Government agencies limited self-government and often worked to erase Native American traditions.

9. Activists wanted to protect what was left of traditional tribal lands, such as the Senecan lands on which the Kinzua Dam was built, and protested the government's many broken treaties.

10. AIM set up patrols to monitor street activity and began survival schools to encourage racial and cultural pride.

11. Activism was somewhat successful. In the 1960s the federal government tried to bring jobs to reservations. Native Americans were also included in President Johnson's Great Society programs; and a number of laws passed in the 1970s favored Native American rights.

12. The consumer movement wanted to hold American industries accountable to their customers and workers and to ensure the safety of consumer products.

13. *Silent Spring* initiated the environmental movement by calling attention to the dangers of pesticides in the environment.

14. Nader targeted automobile safety and the meat-packing industry.

Thinking Critically

1. **Drawing Conclusions** During the l960 and l970s, César Chávez's United Farm Workers organized boycotts of grapes, lettuce, and other crops. Explain the purpose of these boycotts. What issues might lead you to join in a boycott?

2. **Demonstrating Reasoned Judgment** Think of a local concern that affects your community, such as a new housing development that threatens to destroy your favorite patch of trees or the need for increased recycling in your neighborhood. Following the examples of any of the activists you have read about in the chapter—such as Gloria Steinem, César Chávez, Rachel Carson, or Ralph Nader—what could you do to champion your cause?

Making Connections

1. **Evaluating Primary Sources** Review the second primary source excerpt on page 689. What assumptions is Phyllis Schlafly making when she explains her arguments against the ERA?

2. **Understanding the Visuals** Look at the graph of median incomes for men and women on page 685. What does this graph tell you about the legitimacy of the drive for passage of the Equal Rights Amendment?

3. **Writing About the Chapter** Choose one of the following characters: a woman, a Chicano, a Native American, or an Asian American during the 1960s. As your chosen character, you are to testify to a congressional subcommittee regarding the discrimination faced by you and your group. First, create a list of examples illustrating the discrimination you face. Note any historical explanations for this discrimination and any suggestions you have for improving the situation. Next, write a draft of your testimony in which you explain your experiences and those of your group. Revise your testimony, making sure that each example, explanation, and suggestion is clearly explained. Proofread your testimony and draft a final copy.

4. **Using the Graphic Organizer** This graphic organizer uses a tree map to organize information about the women's movement. (a) According to the graphic organizer, how did the women's movement benefit from legal action? (b) What was the connection between consciousness-raising and women's groups? (c) On a separate sheet of paper, create your own graphic organizer about Native American struggles against discrimination, using this graphic organizer as an example.

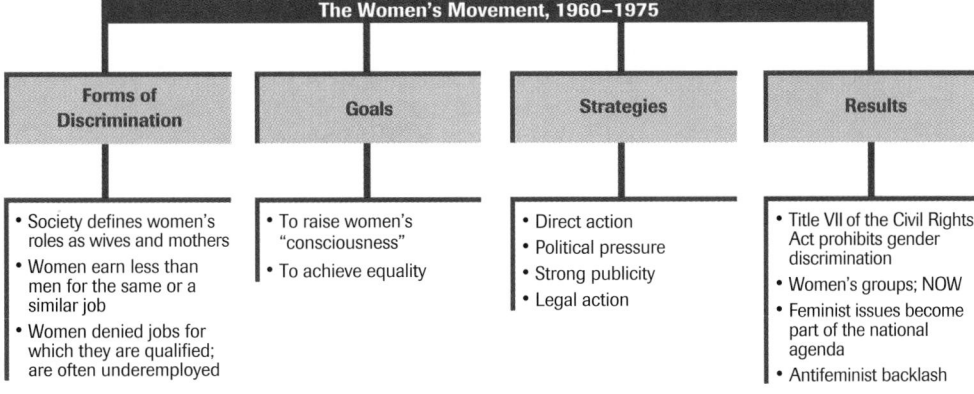

The Women's Movement, 1960–1975

Forms of Discrimination	Goals	Strategies	Results
• Society defines women's roles as wives and mothers • Women earn less than men for the same or a similar job • Women denied jobs for which they are qualified; are often underemployed	• To raise women's "consciousness" • To achieve equality	• Direct action • Political pressure • Strong publicity • Legal action	• Title VII of the Civil Rights Act prohibits gender discrimination • Women's groups; NOW • Feminist issues become part of the national agenda • Antifeminist backlash

 Alternative Assessment

Final Evaluation
Use the following criteria to evaluate student projects:

• **Evidence of mastery of content** To what extent do reports demonstrate knowledge and understanding of chapter content?

• **Evidence of thoughtfulness** To what extent do reports relate the selected movement's local activities to the national movement's goals and successes?

• **Evidence of outside research** To what extent do projects demonstrate students' outside research?

Thinking Critically

1. Boycotts were organized to show support for the United Farm Workers union. Students might join in boycotts related to a variety of social, political, and environmental concerns.

2. Possible answers: speak and write to inform people about the issue, organize boycotts, propose legal challenges, and carry out more militant actions such as sit-ins.

Making Connections

1. She is assuming that other women will see the conditions she mentions—wives supported by husbands, women exempted from combat, and female students attending all-female colleges—as rights.

2. The graph shows that women consistently make less money than men, justifying the need for the Equal Rights Amendment.

3. Students' responses should demonstrate an understanding of the origins and nature of discrimination against their chosen group, and suggest ways to end such discrimination.

Tell students that when one person or group stands up to fight against injustice, their actions often have more far-reaching consequences than they originally intended. Ask students to identify Anita Hill and Clarence Thomas. After they have done so, have a brief discussion about the fact that the allegations that Hill brought against Thomas as he was being considered for the post of Supreme Court justice resulted in greater national awareness and debate about the issue of sexual harassment. Tell students that, in much the same way, the African American struggle for civil rights resulted in a greater national awareness about the issue and prompted other groups who also felt discriminated against to work for equal rights. Tell students that these groups included women, Latinos, Native Americans, and Asian Americans. The source readings concern two of these groups, Latinos and Native Americans.

INSTRUCT

Have students write a list of questions that they would ask Woody Guthrie or Vine Deloria, Jr., if they had the opportunity to interview them. Tell students that their goal is to learn more about the person's life and why he spoke out against the injustices he saw in American society.

CHAPTER 21
SOURCE
READINGS

Plane Wreck at Los Gatos (Deportee)

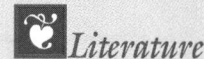 Literature

Woody Guthrie

INTRODUCTION As discussed in Chapter 21, the United Farm Workers formed during the 1960s to improve working conditions for migratory farm workers. Then, as now, migrant workers included people of Mexican descent, some of them American citizens but some of them Mexican residents working illegally in the United States. After the harvesting season was over, Mexican workers were not allowed to remain in the United States but instead were returned to Mexico. Quite frequently, the same workers made their way back to the United States the following year. Mexican farm workers risked illegal border crossings in order to find jobs; although pay on the American farms was low, it was often lower in Mexico.

The ballad below was written in 1961 by folk singer and songwriter Woody Guthrie to focus attention on the Mexican residents who made up most of the population of migratory farm workers. The song tells the story of a plane crash in California in 1948, in which twenty-eight Mexicans were killed while being deported to Mexico. By focusing on this event and protesting the system under which it occurred, Guthrie provided a boost to the United Farm Workers movement as well as to the Chicano movement.

VOCABULARY Before you read the selection, find the meaning of these words in a dictionary: creosote, deportee.

Mexican American labor leader César Chávez organized migratory farm workers using techniques developed by civil rights activists.

The crops are all in and the peaches are rott'ning,
The oranges are piled in their creosote dumps;
You're flying them back to the Mexican border
To pay all their money to wade back again.

Refrain:
Goodbye to my Juan, Goodbye Rosalita;
Adiós mis amigos, Jesús y Maria,
You won't have your names when you ride the big
*   airplane:*
All they will call you will be deportees.

My father's own father he waded that river;
They took all the money he made in his life;
My brothers and sisters come working the fruit
    trees
And they rode the truck till they took down
    and died.

Some of us are illegal and some are not wanted,
Our work contract's out and we have to move on;

A Mexican American mural in Los Angeles, California.

Six hundred miles to that Mexico border,
They chase us like outlaws, like rustlers, like thieves.

We died in your hills, we died in your deserts,
We died in your valleys and died on your
    plains;
We died 'neath your trees and we died in your
    bushes,
Both sides of this river we died just the same.

The sky plane caught fire over Los Gatos
    Canyon,
A fireball of lightning and shook all our hills.
Who are all these friends all scattered like dry
    leaves?
The radio says they are just deportees.

Is this the best way we can grow our big orchards?
Is this the best way we can grow our good fruit?
To fall like dry leaves to rot on my top soil
And be called by no name except deportees?

THINKING ABOUT THE SELECTION

1. What does Guthrie mean in the lines "You won't have a name when you ride the big airplane:/All they will call you will be deportees"?

2. What river is Guthrie referring to in stanza 4? What does he mean by this reference?

Critical Thinking

3. **Drawing Conclusions** At the end of the song, Guthrie poses several questions. To whom are the questions addressed? What point is Guthrie trying to make by ending the song this way?

ANSWERS TO

Thinking About the Selection

1. He is referring to poor treatment of the migrant workers by their employers in the United States and by American society in general. He says the workers are not even considered to be individual people with names, they are just "deportees," unwanted and considered to be of little value.

2. He is referring to the Rio Grande, which forms part of the border between the United States and Mexico. He is saying that the Mexican workers are human; they are the same on either side of the border. They do not cease to be human when they cross over to the United States.

3. The questions are addressed to the owners of the large farms that employ the Mexicans. The point he is trying to make is that there must be a better way to harvest crops in the United States than mistreating people in order to do it.

Have students research the life of Woody Guthrie or Vine Deloria, Jr., and write a biography about the person. As part of their research, students should read Woody Guthrie's autobiography *Bound for Glory* or *Custer Died for Your Sins* by Vine Deloria, Jr. If the equipment is available for student use, have them create a videotape documentary about either of these men. A videotape on Woody Guthrie, for example, might play some of his songs while showing pictures of Guthrie and some of the things he writes about in his lyrics. It might also show interviews with adults who remember him and can talk about what his music meant to them.

After completing this assignment, students should be very familiar with one of these subjects. Have students return to the list of questions they compiled in the "Instruct" section of this lesson. Ask students to go to the front of the room in pairs, one student acting as the interviewer and the other student playing the part of Guthrie or Deloria. The interviewers can ask some of the questions on their list. The second student answers in the way he or she believes Guthrie or Deloria would have answered.

SOURCE READINGS

Custer Died for Your Sins  *Literature*

Vine Deloria, Jr.

INTRODUCTION For many years, Vine Deloria, Jr., has been fighting for equal rights for Native Americans and for a more realistic, rather than an idealistic or stereotypical, understanding of their background and their ways. In this excerpt from his 1969 book *Custer Died for Your Sins*, Deloria, with some bitterness, tries to expose some stereotypes about Native Americans that he has encountered among white people. He also points out with searing logic the harsh treatment often meted out to nonwhites in the United States. Deloria is a Sioux from the Pine Ridge Reservation in South Dakota. He speaks from his own and his people's experience.

VOCABULARY Before you read the selection, find the meaning of these words in a dictionary: quandary, nebulous, blatantly, foreordained, contemptuous.

One of the finest things about being an Indian is that people are always interested in you and your "plight." Other groups have difficulties, predicaments, quandaries, problems, or troubles. Traditionally we Indians have had a "plight."

Our foremost plight is our transparency. People can tell just by looking at us what we want, what should be done to help us, how we feel, and what a "real" Indian is really like. Indian life, as it relates to the real world, is a continuous attempt not to disappoint people who know us. Unfulfilled expectations cause grief and we have already had our share.

Because people can see right through us, it becomes impossible to tell truth from fiction or fact from mythology. Experts paint us as they would like us to be. Often we paint ourselves as we wish we were or as we might have been.

The more we try to be ourselves the more we are forced to defend what we have never been. The American public feels more comfortable with the mythical Indians of stereotype-land who were always THERE. These Indians are fierce, they wear feathers and grunt. Most of us don't fit this idealized figure since we grunt only when overeating, which is seldom.

Indian reactions are sudden and surprising. One day at a conference we were singing "My Country 'Tis of Thee" and we came across the part that goes:

> *Land where our fathers died*
> *Land of the Pilgrims' pride . . .*

Some of us broke out laughing when we realized that our fathers undoubtedly died trying to keep those Pilgrims from stealing our land. In fact, many of our fathers died because the Pilgrims killed them as witches. We didn't feel much kinship with those Pilgrims, regardless of who they did in.

We often hear "give it back to the Indians" when a gadget fails to work. It's a terrible thing for a people to realize that society has set aside all nonworking gadgets for their exclusive use.

American blacks had become recognized as a species of human being by amendments to the Constitution shortly after the Civil War. Prior to emancipation they had been counted as three-fifths of a person in determining population for representation in the House of Representatives. Early Civil Rights bills nebulously state that other people shall have the same rights as "white people," indicating there were "other people." But Civil Rights bills passed during and after the Civil War systematically excluded Indian people. For a long time an Indian was presumed incapable of initiating an action in a court of law, of owning property, or of giving testimony against whites in court. Nor could an Indian vote or leave his reservation. Indians were America's captive people without any defined rights whatsoever.

Then one day the white man discovered that the Indian tribes still owned some 135 million acres of land. To his horror he learned that much of it was very valu-

The American Indian Movement (AIM) held a protest in 1973 at the Oglala Sioux village of Wounded Knee to draw attention to the poverty-stricken Pine Ridge reservation, where Vine Deloria, Jr., was born. Inset: AIM leader Russell Banks prepares to lead the protest.

able. Some was good grazing land, some was farm land, some mining land, and some covered with timber.

Animals could be herded together on a piece of land, but they could not sell it. Therefore it took no time at all to discover that Indians were really people and should have the right to sell their lands. Land was the means of recognizing the Indian as a human being. It was the method whereby land could be stolen legally and not blatantly.

Once the Indian was thus acknowledged, it was fairly simple to determine what his goals were. If, thinking went, the Indian was just like the white, he must have the same outlook at the white. So the future was planned for the Indian people in public and private life. First in order was allotting them reservations so that they could sell their lands. God's foreordained plan to repopulate the continent fit exactly with the goals of the tribes as they were defined by their white friends.

It is fortunate that we were never slaves. We gave up land instead of life and labor. Because the Negro labored, he was considered a draft animal. Because the Indian occupied large areas of land, he was considered a wild animal. Had we given up anything else, or had anything else to give up, it is certain that we would have been considered some other thing.

Whites have had different attitudes toward the Indians and the blacks since the Republic was founded. Whites have always refused to give non-whites the respect which they have been found to legally possess. Instead there has been a contemptuous attitude that although the law says one thing, "we all know better."

Thus whites steadfastly refused to allow blacks to enjoy the fruits of full citizenship. They systematically closed schools, churches, stores, restaurants, and public places to blacks or made insulting provisions for them. For one hundred years every program of public and private white America was devoted to the exclusion of the black. It was, perhaps, embarrassing to be rubbing shoulders with one who had not so long before been defined as a field animal.

The Indian suffered the reverse treatment. Law after law was passed requiring him to conform to white institutions, Indian children were kidnapped and forced into boarding schools thousands of miles from their homes to learn the white man's ways. Reservations were turned over to different Christian denominations for governing. Reservations were for a long time church operated. Everything possible was done to ensure that Indians were forced into American life. The wild animal was made into a household pet whether or not he wanted to be one.

THINKING ABOUT THE SELECTION

1. According to Deloria, why did white people decide that Native Americans were, after all, human beings and not animals?

2. How does Deloria compare the treatment of African Americans and Native Americans by white Americans?

Critical Thinking

3. **Recognizing Bias** Do you find any evidence of bias or stereotyping in Deloria's piece? Explain your answer.

ANSWERS TO

Thinking About the Selection

1. The white man realized that Native Americans owned a good deal of valuable land. Therefore, he had to acknowledge that they were human beings with the right to sell their land. In this way, the white people were able to obtain much Native American land, so the recognition was to the white man's advantage and the Native Americans' disadvantage.

2. He says that African Americans were at least given full citizenship after the Civil War; no such rights were ever expressly granted to Native Americans. However, he also points out that white Americans then prevented African Americans from exercising those rights for many years. At the same time that white people were excluding African Americans from society in this way, they were treating Native Americans in a way exactly opposite, by forcing them to join white American society and to be like white Americans against the Native Americans' will.

3. Students should note that Deloria seems to lump all white Americans together and does not allow that some white Americans have also fought for Native American rights and had nothing to do with their mistreatment.

Chapter 22 The Vietnam War and American Society 1960–1975

📁 Teaching Resources (See Unit 6 Folder)

	Instruction	Enrichment
Section 1 **The War in the 1960s** (pp. 714–717)	Reproducible Lesson Plan, p. 105 Alternate Lesson Plan, p. 156 Guided Reading and Review, p. 110 Quiz, p. 111	American Profiles Activity, Colin Powell, p. 120

Section 2
The Brutality of the War
(pp. 718–721)
	Reproducible Lesson Plan, p. 106
	Alternate Lesson Plan, p. 157
	Guided Reading and Review, p. 112
	Quiz, p. 113
		Literature Activity, Experiences of a Young
		    Soldier in Vietnam, pp. 129–130
		Primary Source Activity, An Army Nurse
		    Remembers, p. 126

Section 3
Student Protest
(pp. 722–725)
	Reproducible Lesson Plan, p. 107
	Alternate Lesson Plan, p. 158
	Guided Reading and Review, p. 114
	Quiz, p. 115
		American Profiles Activity, Joan Baez, p. 121
		Visual Learning Activity, Antiwar
		    Demonstrations, p. 132
		Historian's Toolbox Activity, Checking
		    Consistency, p. 124

Section 4 **The Counterculture** (pp. 727–730)	Reproducible Lesson Plan, p. 108 Alternate Lesson Plan, p. 159 Guided Reading and Review, p. 116 Quiz, p. 117	Visual Learning Activity, Reflections of the Counterculture, p. 133 Literature Activity, The Flower Children, p. 131

Section 5
The End of the War
(pp. 731–735)
	Reproducible Lesson Plan, p. 109
	Alternate Lesson Plan, p. 160
	Guided Reading and Review, p. 118
	Quiz, p. 119
	Chapter Test, Forms A & B, pp. 134–139
		Primary Source Activity, LBJ Withdraws from
		    the Race, pp. 127–128
		Viewpoints Activity, On the Tragedy of Kent
		    State, pp. 122–123
		Critical Thinking Activity, Drawing
		    Conclusions, p. 125

📁 Additional Chapter Resources

Resource Organizer, p. 104
Alternate Lesson Plan, p. 155
Answer Keys, pp. 146–159

Bibliography

For the Teacher

Fitzgerald, Frances. *Fire in the Lake: The Vietnamese and the Americans in Vietnam.* Random House, 1989 edition. (Considered the classic history of the war.)

Severo, Richard, and Lewis Milford. *The Wages of War: When America's Soldiers Came Home—From Valley Forge to Vietnam.* Simon & Schuster, 1989. (A social history of America's returning soldiers.)

Sheehan, Neil. *A Bright Shining Lie: John Paul Vann and America in Vietnam.* Random House, 1989. (The war seen through the story of one American officer.)

Prentice Hall Literature Excerpts from *The American Experience,* 1994, including Jarrell, Randall. "The Death of the Ball Turret Gunner," and "Losses," from *The Complete Poems.* Farrar, Straus and Giroux, 1969 edition.

The Big Idea for the chapter and how the main ideas in each section relate to the Big Idea are graphically displayed below. Comprehension of this chapter's Big Idea is critical to students' understanding of United States history and how we as a nation got where we are today.

Media and Technology

 Critical Thinking, I-13

 Critical Thinking, I-12; Graphic Organizer, G-4

 Guided Reading Audiotapes (English and Spanish)

Computer Test Bank

For the Student

Kovic, Ron. *Born on the Fourth of July.* McGraw-Hill, 1976. (A personal account by a disillusioned Vietnam veteran; later made into an Academy Award–winning film.)

O'Brien, Tim. *The Things They Carried.* Viking Penguin, 1991. (A blending of fact and fiction on coming to terms with Vietnam.)

Rottmann, Larry, Jan Barry, and Basil T. Paquet, eds. *Winning Hearts and Minds: War Poems by Vietnam Veterans.* 1st Casualty Press, 1972.

Vietnam: A Television History. PBS Video. (Award-winning thirteen-hour history of the war.)

CHAPTER 22

The 1960s and 1970s were decades of deep division and turmoil in the United States. Under Presidents Kennedy and Johnson, the country became increasingly involved in stopping a communist takeover in Vietnam. As the war continued to cost more and more in lives and money while achieving little apparent success, many Americans began to question their government's role there. At the same time, a youthful counterculture arose, criticizing the traditional values of many Americans.

SECTION 1

When communists threatened to take over South Vietnam in the 1960s, Presidents Kennedy and Johnson sent thousands of American troops to fight them, supporting repressive but anticommunist governments in Indochina.

SECTION 2

Americans at home learned from televised broadcasts, and American soldiers learned while trying to fight a hidden enemy, that the war was a brutal guerrilla struggle lacking clear objectives.

SECTION 3

Students, already primed by activists on behalf of civil rights and the free speech movement, were among the first to protest against the Vietnam War.

SECTION 4

In the 1960s, many young Americans rejected the traditional norms of American life in favor of the counterculture, experimenting with alternative lifestyles.

SECTION 5

The antiwar movement finally grew strong enough to persuade the government to find a way out of Vietnam, and in 1973, a cease-fire was proclaimed.

The Relevance of the Big Idea

For most Americans, the name *Vietnam* connotes tragedy, failure, doubt, and confusion. By the 1970s, the Vietnam War had become the longest, most expensive war in American history—and the least successful. The war split the nation into "hawks" and "doves," and returning GIs bore much of the bitterness of the nation's failure.

To help students understand the relevance of this conflict, point out that failure in Vietnam dimmed the nation's view of its own power. However, it also led to demands for more openness and accountability in government, and Congress limited the powers of the President to commit United States troops abroad.

In Depth

Global Connections

President Eisenhower claimed Vietnam was like the first in a row of "standing dominoes." If communists toppled it over, the other dominoes, the neighboring countries, would also fall to communism. The Central Intelligence Agency supplied anticommunist guerrillas with arms in Laos as early as 1962 to ensure that Laos would not fall into communist hands. By 1975, however, Laos had been taken over by communists. In 1970, American and South Vietnamese forces crossed the Cambodian border to destroy North Vietnamese supply bases there. Soon after, Cambodia too was plunged into civil war, and in 1975 its government fell to the communist Khmer Rouge.

*T*he Vietnam War was one of the most tragic events of the cold war. United States Presidents from Eisenhower to Nixon spent billions of dollars and sent half a million soldiers to Vietnam. Over time, as the war consumed more and more resources, many Americans questioned whether the United States should remain involved in this faraway conflict. The Vietnam War was only one of many issues that divided American society in the 1960s, but it cut deep and left lasting scars.

	Events in the United States				
	1960 Student activists establish Students for a Democratic Society (SDS).	**1963** President Kennedy is assassinated. • The Bob Dylan song "The Times They Are A-Changin'" is a hit.	**1964** Lyndon Johnson wins reelection to the presidency.	**1965** President Johnson rapidly increases the number of American troops in Vietnam.	**1967** Antiwar protesters march on the Pentagon
	1960	**1962**	**1964**	**1966**	
	Events in the World				
		1963 South Vietnamese leader Diem is assassinated. • Kenya wins independence.	**1964** Civil war escalates in Vietnam. • United Nations troops restore order in the Congo.	**1965** European Common Market nations eliminate industrial tariffs.	**1967** Israel defeats the Arabs in the Six-Day War. • Civil war begins in Nigeria

▶ RESOURCE DIRECTORY

Teaching Resources

Alternate Lesson Plan: Demonstrating the Big Idea found in the Alternate Lesson Plans folder, p. 155, provides a lesson strategy to instruct students about the Big Idea that the Vietnam War not only consumed many lives and billions of dollars but also deeply wounded the American psyche.

Alternative Assessment Handbook provides information, guidance, and strategies for alternative methods of assessment. It includes an essay on new trends in assessment, guidance and strategies for developing performance tasks and portfolios, scoring rubrics, and sample evaluation forms.

Pages 714–717

The War in the 1960s

Determined to defeat Ho Chi Minh's communist forces, Presidents Kennedy and Johnson supported dictatorships and sent thousands of American soldiers to fight and die in Vietnam.

 Pages 718–721

The Brutality of the War

Vietnam was the first war that Americans witnessed on their television screens. They were not prepared for the awful violence they saw, but neither were those who experienced the war firsthand.

 Pages 722–725

Student Protest

"The times they are a-changin'," folksinger Bob Dylan sang in the 1960s. Student activists demanded many changes during this period, but the Vietnam War took center stage in the protest movement.

 Pages 727–730

The Counterculture

In the 1960s, a youth culture that stressed freedom and individuality created for some people a promising new "space" in which to explore themselves. At the same time, it filled others with fear and disgust.

 Pages 731–735

The End of the War

The antiwar movement finally convinced politicians in Washington that it was time to pull out of Vietnam, but American troops withdrew very slowly, and the fighting was far from over.

1968 Richard Nixon is elected United States President.

1970 Rock stars Janis Joplin and Jimi Hendrix die of drug overdoses.
• Four students are shot at Kent State.

1972 Nixon is reelected.

1973 The United States withdraws final troops from Vietnam.

1968	1970	1972	1974	1976

1969 Golda Meir becomes prime minister of Israel.

1970 The Aswan Dam is completed in Egypt.

1971 East Pakistan becomes the independent nation of Bangladesh.

1972 Ferdinand Marcos declares martial law in the Philippines.

1974 Argentinian dictator Juan Perón dies.

1975 The South Vietnamese government surrenders to North Vietnam.

◆ Alternative Assessment

As an ongoing chapter project, students can create a local history project about the Vietnam War and their community. Encourage students to relate local events and opinions prevalent in the community to those throughout the nation.

Projects should include a variety of the following items:
● Interviews with relatives or community members who served in Vietnam, as well as with those who participated in antiwar protests
● Statistics concerning the number of local residents who served in Vietnam and the number who were killed or wounded there
● Articles about community protests, vigils, and antiwar demonstrations
● A narrative tracing the level of support for the war through the editorial pages of the local newspaper, including letters to the editor
● Images and captions about local Vietnam memorials

Interviews and narratives may be written or taped; statistics may be presented in chart or narrative form. Students should include posters, drawings, or other illustrations where appropriate.

Explain that finished projects will be assessed according to the following standards:
● **Unacceptable** Projects are not attempted or fail to meet requirements outlined.
● **Limited/Acceptable** Projects make a reasonable attempt to compare local events and opinions with those nationwide.
● **Extensive/Commendable** Projects include general comparisons between local events and opinions and those nationwide.
● **Extraordinary/Outstanding** Projects draw specific and general comparisons between local events and opinions and those nationwide.

For more information and guidance on alternative assessment trends and strategies, see the Alternative Assessment Handbook in the Resource Directory on page 712.

SECTION 1

The War in the 1960s

1. FOCUS

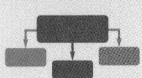

Connecting to the Big Idea

See page 712B. Explain that in the 1960s, Presidents Kennedy and Johnson were determined to maintain South Vietnam under an anticommunist government. Ask why the United States became involved in Vietnam. How did the American presence in Vietnam escalate?

Objectives

● Explain why the United States supported the repressive regime of Ngo Dinh Diem.
● Describe how President Kennedy increased American involvement in Vietnam in the early 1960s.
● Describe how President Johnson used the Gulf of Tonkin incident to intensify the war.

Bellringer

Ask students to brainstorm words, phrases, and images that come to mind when they hear the word *Vietnam.*

Reading Strategy

Structured Overview Ask students to write the following column headings on a piece of paper: Background of the War, John Kennedy's Policy in Vietnam, and Lyndon Johnson's War. Ask students to take notes in the appropriate column as they read the section.

SECTION PREVIEW

Determined to defeat Ho Chi Minh's communist forces, Presidents Kennedy and Johnson supported dictatorships and sent thousands of American soldiers to fight and die in Vietnam.

Key Concepts
• Fearing that communist forces would take over Vietnam, the United States supported the repressive government of Ngo Dinh Diem in southern Vietnam.
  • President Kennedy increased American involvement in the early 1960s by sending military advisers to South Vietnam.
  • President Johnson used the Gulf of Tonkin incident as an excuse to begin bombing North Vietnam and sending thousands more American troops to the country.

Key Terms, People, and Places
Viet Cong, Gulf of Tonkin Resolution, escalation, Tet Offensive; Ngo Dinh Diem; Saigon

The fates of three nations—Vietnam, the United States, and France—became interwoven in the struggle for control over Vietnam.

By the mid-twentieth century, Vietnam had a history of nationalism that extended back nearly 2,000 years. Two Vietnamese sisters, Trung Trac and Trung Nhi, organized the first major revolt against Chinese oppressors in A.D. 39. The Vietnamese continued to resist Chinese domination for centuries afterward. In the 1800s, France established itself as a new colonial power in Vietnam. Ho Chi Minh, the leader of the Vietnamese independence movement after World War II, continued his country's tradition of nationalism in his resistance to Chinese and French control. Policy makers in the United States, however, saw Ho merely as a communist and therefore an enemy in the cold war. As the independence movement in Vietnam turned into a civil war in the 1960s, the United States was

determined to support the anticommunist government it had helped create in the south.

Background of the War

The United States became involved in Vietnam because of the demands of the cold war. As discussed in Chapter 17, American policy makers supported the French effort to crush Ho Chi Minh's independence movement because they needed French support to make the policy of containment work in Europe. The French attempt to reestablish control over its former colony failed in 1954. After the French were defeated at Dien Bien Phu, a conference was held in Geneva, Switzerland, to discuss the situation in Indochina. The conference included representatives of Ho Chi Minh, Vietnamese emperor Bao Dai, Cambodia, Laos, France, the United States, the Soviet Union, China, and Britain.

As a result of the Geneva Conference, Vietnam was divided into two separate nations in 1954. Ho Chi Minh, a nationalist leader sympathetic to communist ideas, controlled North Vietnam. **Ngo Dinh Diem,** a former official in Bao Dai's government who had been living in exile in the United States and Europe, became the premier of South Vietnam, with the support of the United States. In 1955, Diem became the president. France and North Vietnam agreed that elections would be held in 1956 to unify the country. Diem and his United States supporters, however, did not commit to the elections, which they feared would remove Diem from power. The elections never took place.

John Kennedy's Policy in Vietnam

President Eisenhower gave his firm support to Diem's South Vietnamese government, providing some 675 United States military advisers to assist in the continuing struggle against the north. When President Kennedy took office, he decided to do even more.

▶ **RESOURCE DIRECTORY**

Teaching Resources

  Reproducible Lesson Plan found in the Unit 6 folder, p. 105, provides a summary of the Section 1 lesson plan content.

  Alternate Lesson Plan: Critical Thinking Recognizing Cause and Effect, found in the Alternate Lesson Plans folder, p. 156, helps students identify the sequence of events leading to the military escalation in Vietnam and analyze the United States' role in terms of cold war policy.

  Guided Reading and Review found in the Unit 6 folder, p. 110, provides a structure for reading and mastering the key concepts and reviewing the key terms for Section 1. (Guided Practice)

Kennedy was a cold warrior, like most other United States leaders after World War II. He was determined to prevent the spread of communism at all costs. Early in his term, Kennedy sent Vice President Lyndon Johnson to Vietnam to assess the situation. Referring to the great British leader of World War II, Johnson called Diem "the Winston Churchill of Southeast Asia." He argued that if South Vietnam was to survive, it needed even more aid. In response, Kennedy increased the number of American military advisers to Vietnam. By the end of 1963, that number had grown to more than 16,000.

But military aid by itself could not ensure success. The problem was that Diem lacked support in his own country. He imprisoned people who criticized his government in "re-education centers." He filled many powerful government positions with members of his own family. United States aid earmarked for economic reforms went instead to the military and into the pockets of corrupt officials. Diem launched an enormously unpopular program to move peasants from their ancestral lands to "strategic hamlets"—government-run farming communities that isolated the peasants from communist influences seeping into South Vietnam. On top of everything else, Diem was a Catholic in a largely Buddhist country, and he often dismissed the religious concerns of others.

When Diem insisted that Buddhists obey Catholic religious laws, serious opposition developed. In June 1963, a Buddhist monk doused himself with gasoline and burned himself to death. Photographs showing his silent, grisly protest appeared on the front pages of newspapers around the world. Other monks followed the example, but their martyrdom did not budge Diem. Kennedy finally realized that Diem would never reform and acknowledged that the struggle against communism in Vietnam could not be won under Diem's rule.

United States officials told South Vietnamese military leaders that the United States would not object to Diem's overthrow. With that encouragement, Vietnamese troops struck in early November 1963, assassinated Diem, and seized control of the government.

Lyndon Johnson's War

Three weeks after Diem's assassination, Kennedy himself was dead, and the new military government in South Vietnam was already in trouble. While the ruling generals bickered among themselves and failed to direct the South Vietnamese army effectively, communist guerrillas in the south, known as **Viet Cong,** gained control over more territory and earned the loyalty of an increasing number of South Vietnamese. Throughout the struggle, the Viet Cong received assistance from Ho Chi Minh and the North Vietnamese.

Lyndon Johnson, the new United States President, was as much of a cold warrior as Kennedy, and he was equally suspicious of the communist

Media and Technology

Transparency
Critical Thinking, I-13

sympathies of Ho Chi Minh. He commented about the continuing need for containment:

> The Communists' desire to dominate the world is just like the lawyer's desire to be the ultimate judge on the Supreme Court or the politician's desire to be President. You see, the Communists want to rule the world, and if we don't stand up to them, they will do it. And we'll be slaves. Now I'm not one of those folks seeing Communists under every bed. But I do know about the principles of power, and when one side is weak, the other steps in.

Just after he assumed office, Johnson met with Henry Cabot Lodge, United States ambassador to South Vietnam. Lodge told the new President that if he wanted to save Vietnam, he faced some tough choices. Johnson was determined to do whatever necessary to win the war. "I am not going to lose Vietnam," he said. Referring to the communist takeover of China in 1949, he went on: "I am not going to be the President who saw Southeast Asia go the way China went."

In his campaign for reelection as President in 1964, Johnson posed as a man of peace. "We are not about to send American boys nine or ten thousand miles away from home to do what Asian boys ought to be doing for themselves," he declared. He called Barry Goldwater, his Republican opponent in the election, a

General William Westmoreland (below) believed he could win the war with enough American troop strength, but he and President Johnson vastly underestimated the determination of the communist forces operating throughout Vietnam.

warmonger. He attacked critics who suggested using American bombs in Vietnam.

Intensifying the War Meanwhile, however, war planning was under way. During the election campaign, LBJ cleverly secured congressional authorization for deepening American involvement in Vietnam. He did so in August 1964 by announcing that North Vietnamese torpedo boats had attacked United States destroyers in the international waters of the Gulf of Tonkin, thirty miles from North Vietnam. He did not mention that the United States ships appeared to the North Vietnamese to be participating in combat raids against North Vietnam, nor that the commander of one United States ship was not sure that an attack really had taken place. Despite the confusion over these details, Johnson asked for and obtained a resolution giving him authority to "take all necessary measures to repel any armed attack against the forces of the United States and to prevent further aggression."

Congress passed this **Gulf of Tonkin Resolution** by a vote of 416 to 0 in the House of Representatives and 88 to 2 in the Senate. Johnson had been waiting for some time for an opportunity to propose the resolution, which, he noted, "covered everything." The President now had nearly complete control over what the United States did in Vietnam—without Congress ever officially declaring war.

After his reelection, Johnson began a drastic military **escalation,** or expansion, of the war by devoting more and more American money and personnel to the conflict. In February 1965, after a Viet Cong attack at Pleiku in South Vietnam killed eight Americans and wounded 126, Johnson authorized retaliatory bombing of North Vietnam. Two weeks after the Pleiku attack, General William Westmoreland, the commander of United States forces in Vietnam, asked Johnson to send two battalions of marines to protect the American airfield at Danang. Johnson heeded the request, beginning a rapid buildup of American troops. At the start of 1965, nearly 25,000 American soldiers were stationed in Vietnam; by the end of the year, the number rose to 184,000. That number had climbed to 385,000 by 1966, to 485,000 by 1967, and to 543,000 by 1968. ⭐

Initially, United States soldiers had gone to Vietnam to advise the South Vietnamese. Now they took responsibility for trying to prop up the South Vietnamese government. Led by military men Nguyen Van Thieu and Nguyen Cao Ky, the new government was more effective than Diem's but remained dictatorial. Despite the large United States presence in Vietnam, the communist forces only intensified their efforts.

The Tet Offensive On January 30, 1968, the North Vietnamese mounted a major offensive during Tet, the Vietnamese new year. The **Tet Offensive,** shown in the map at right, included strikes on numerous provincial and district capitals and other towns in South Vietnam. In **Saigon,** the South Vietnamese capital, the Viet Cong attacked the American embassy, Tan Son Nhut air base, and the presidential palace. Even though they were turned back, the Viet Cong won a psychological victory. In contrast to official reports that claimed the North Vietnamese were on the verge of surrender, the Tet Offensive dramatically demonstrated that the Viet Cong could launch a massive attack on targets throughout South Vietnam. Furthermore, as images of

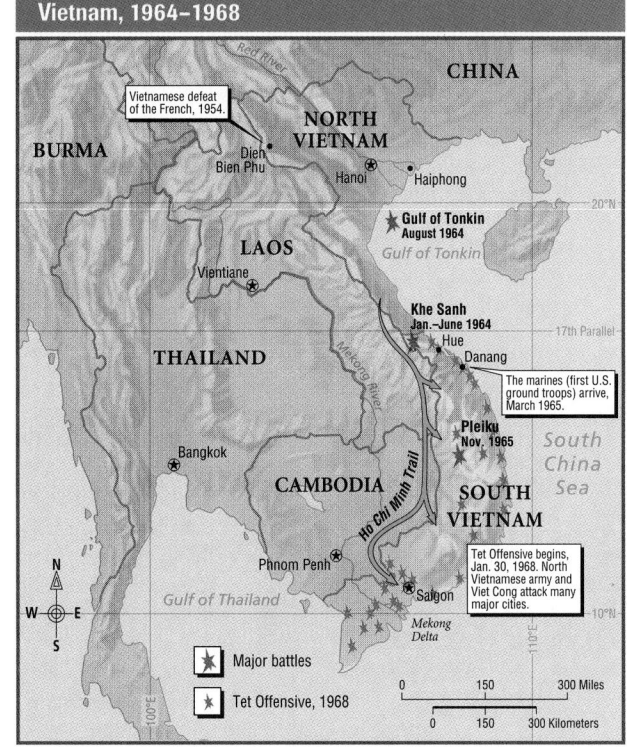

Vietnam, 1964–1968

Vietnamese defeat of the French, 1954.

Gulf of Tonkin August 1964

Khe Sanh Jan.–June 1964

The marines (first U.S. ground troops) arrive, March 1965.

Pleiku Nov. 1965

Tet Offensive begins, Jan. 30, 1968. North Vietnamese army and Viet Cong attack many major cities.

 Major battles

 Tet Offensive, 1968

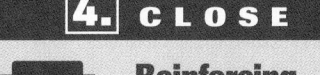

Geography and History: Interpreting Maps
The Ho Chi Minh Trail, shown in the map above, was a supply route from North Vietnam through Laos and Cambodia into South Vietnam. *How might the Ho Chi Minh Trail have contributed to the execution of the Tet Offensive?*

the fighting flooded American television, many people at home began to express reservations about United States involvement in Vietnam.

SECTION 1 REVIEW

Key Terms, People, and Places
1. Define (a) Viet Cong, (b) Gulf of Tonkin Resolution, (c) escalation, (d) Tet Offensive.
2. Identify Ngo Dinh Diem.
3. Identify Saigon.

Key Concepts
4. Why did the United States support the government of Ngo Dinh Diem in South Vietnam?
5. How did President Kennedy increase United States involvement in Vietnam's civil war in the early 1960s?

6. How did President Johnson use the Gulf of Tonkin incident to further his goals in the Vietnam conflict?

Critical Thinking
7. **Checking Consistency** Based on what you have read about Ngo Dinh Diem's government in South Vietnam, do you think that supporting this government was consistent with the stated aim of United States foreign policy: to defend freedom around the world? Explain why or why not.

Quiz found in the Unit 6 folder, p. 111, covers the main ideas in this section as well as the key terms.

5. Kennedy sent Vice President Lyndon Johnson to South Vietnam, then dramatically increased the number of United States military advisers there.

6. Just after North Vietnamese torpedo boats supposedly attacked American ships in the Gulf of Tonkin, Johnson convinced Congress to give him broad powers to control United States actions in the war.

7. Since Diem's government oppressed the South Vietnamese people, supporting it seems to have contradicted America's foreign policy aim of defending freedom. United States leaders at the time, however, believed that by preventing the spread of communism they were defending freedom in a fundamental sense.

Reteach

Ask students to write one or two sentences describing the level of United States involvement in the Vietnam War under Presidents Eisenhower, Kennedy, and Johnson, respectively.

Caption Answer to ...

🌐 **Interpreting Maps**

The Ho Chi Minh Trail allowed the North Vietnamese government to provide the Viet Cong with ammunition and other supplies for use in the Tet Offensive.

4. CLOSE

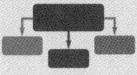 **Reinforcing the Big Idea**

Attempting to keep communism out of Vietnam, Presidents Kennedy and Johnson supported dictatorships and sent thousands of American troops to Southeast Asia. The next section describes the brutality of the war.

SECTION 2

The Brutality of the War

1. FOCUS

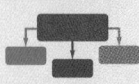

Connecting to the Big Idea

See page 712B. American soldiers were not prepared for the brutality of the fighting in Vietnam, and Americans at home were not prepared for the violence they were to witness on their television screens. Ask why American forces had little success in Vietnam. How did the war affect Vietnamese civilians?

Objectives

● Describe the effect of the war on the morale of American troops.
● Describe how the war affected Vietnamese civilians.
● Explain the effects of the My Lai massacre on Americans.

Bellringer

Ask students to consider how they would define a "just" war. Is any war just? Does the way the war is waged, including the type of weapons and damage inflicted, determine whether or not it can be considered just?

Reading Strategy

Reading for Evidence Have students read the first paragraph of the section, which states that American soldiers and Vietnamese civilians suffered during the war. Then ask students to list as they read, the different ways in which the soldiers and the civilians suffered.

SECTION PREVIEW

Vietnam was the first war that Americans witnessed on their television screens. They were not prepared for the awful violence they saw, but neither were those who experienced the war firsthand.

Images of brutality and bloodshed, such as this one of a Vietnamese child wounded in the war, made American television viewers question United States involvement in Vietnam.

Key Concepts

• Many American soldiers went to Vietnam eager to do their patriotic duty, but they quickly learned that fighting the Viet Cong was a cruel and nerve-wracking ordeal.
• Vietnamese civilians were under constant attack from the air and the ground by United States troops, who could not distinguish them from Viet Cong or North Vietnamese soldiers.
• The massacre at My Lai brought the horrifying reality of the war home to many Americans.

Key Terms, People, and Places

My Lai massacre

T he Vietnam War was a long, brutal struggle. American soldiers were fighting a guerrilla war against a hidden enemy, and so they were often unable to tell friendly South Vietnamese peasants from Viet Cong soldiers waiting for an opportunity to attack them. As buddies fell before sniper bullets, land mines, and booby traps, GIs grew increasingly frustrated by the demands of a war that seemed to be accomplishing few clear objectives. Meanwhile, Vietnamese civilians in both the north and the south suffered heavy casualties in the ferocious destruction of their land and way of life.

The American Soldiers' War

Many American soldiers went to war enthusiastic about the job they were being asked to do. Many, like Ron Kovic of Long Island, had dreamed of being heroes when they grew up. Television characters such as the Lone Ranger and the Cisco Kid—rugged heroes of the American West—shaped their ideas about what it meant to be an American. They learned patriotism by watching actor John Wayne perform daring deeds in his movie roles.

Kovic, like many Americans, worried about the communist threat and was afraid that communists "were infiltrating our schools, trying to take over our classes and control our minds." After high school, he joined the marines to do his part to defend his country. He proudly served a tour in Vietnam and signed up for a second tour. This second tour of duty would take a terrible toll on Kovic's body and mind.

He and other soldiers were finding the war confusing and disturbing. They were trying to defend the freedom of the South Vietnamese, but the population, reared in an altogether different political tradition, seemed indifferent to their effort. "We are the unwilling working for the unqualified to do the unnecessary for the ungrateful," Kit Bowen of the First Infantry Division wrote to his father in Oregon.

⭐ Fighting conditions were also different from those they had seen in films. Carrying sixty-pound packs, they had to walk through jungles of ten-foot-tall elephant grass and across flooded rice paddies. Much of the time they fought leeches, fever, and jungle rot—a tropical fungus that infected the skin. Racial tensions within the American ranks destroyed morale. Death always lurked around the corner. American troops never knew what to expect next, and they never could be sure who was a friend and who was an enemy. The Vietnamese woman selling soft drinks by the roadside might be a Viet Cong ally, counting enemy soldiers as they

▶ RESOURCE DIRECTORY

Teaching Resources

Reproducible Lesson Plan found in the Unit 6 folder, p. 106, provides a summary of the Section 2 lesson plan content.

Alternate Lesson Plan: Cooperative Learning found in the Alternate Lesson Plans folder, p. 157, guides groups of students in preparing and presenting scripts for a mock radio or TV broadcast describing the war from the perspective of various people in Vietnam.

Guided Reading and Review found in the Unit 6 folder, p. 112, provides a structure for reading and mastering the key concepts and reviewing the key terms for Section 2. (Guided Practice)

 Literature Activity Experiences of a Young Soldier in Vietnam, found in the Unit 6 folder, pp. 129–130, relates the Vietnam experiences of Charles Coe in an excerpt from his book *Young Man in Vietnam*.

passed. A child peddling candy might be concealing a live grenade.

The Viet Cong lacked the sophisticated equipment of the United States troops, so they avoided head-on clashes. Instead they used guerrilla warfare tactics, working in small groups to launch sneak attacks and practice sabotage. They were skilled in setting clever traps. For example, they might bury a land mine in a path that they expected a platoon of marines to take. When a soldier stepped on the mine, platoon leaders and others would gather around the wounded man, and Viet Cong snipers would have their guns aimed at the spot, ready to kill them.

Angel Quintana, an American soldier, described life in Vietnam:

An infantryman almost never sleeps. Even if you have time to sleep, you can't because you have all these memories in your head. If you're near a fire-support base, then you sleep even less with the noise of the cannons—the 155s, the 105s, the 4.2s, all firing at the same time. It's like an earthquake. And when you're in the jungle, you're afraid. As macho as you may be, you feel it. You know that death is behind you. You don't know whose turn it is. There are times when you lose the fear because something happens, like they kill a friend of yours. For five or six days it goes away because you're so shook up from losing your friend that life means nothing to you. Then it passes, and you start to be interested in life again.

 Ron Kovic confronted his fears by making an aggressive effort to be a good soldier. But the horrors of war came to haunt him after he accidentally killed a United States corporal. Later, he shot at shadowy figures in a village hut, only to learn that his unit had killed and wounded innocent children. The final blow came when a sniper's bullet entered his spine. As his spinal column was severed and he lost all sensation in his legs, all he could feel was "the worthlessness of dying right here in this place at this moment for nothing." He was paralyzed from the chest down, after which he felt, in his words, "like a big clumsy puppet with all his strings cut."

MAKING CONNECTIONS

In what ways were the experiences of American soldiers who served in Vietnam and in the Pacific theater during World War II similar? How were they different?

Vietnamese Civilians and the War

The war was even more devastating for Vietnamese civilians in both the north and the south. Because American soldiers were never sure who might be sympathetic to the Viet Cong, civilians suffered as much as soldiers. As the struggle intensified, the destruction worsened. Saturation bombing—air raids that dropped thousands of tons of explosives over large areas—tore North Vietnam apart. The fragmentation bombs used in these raids, which threw pieces of their thick metal casings in all directions when they exploded, were not confined to the north alone; they were also used in the south, where they killed and maimed countless civilians.

United States forces also used chemical weapons against the Vietnamese. In order to expose Viet Cong hiding places, an herbicide known as Agent Orange was dropped on jungle landscapes, causing the leaves to fall off trees. Agent Orange also killed crops, and later it was discovered to cause health problems in humans and livestock. (See "History Might Not Have Happened This Way," pages 800–801.) Another destructive chemical used in Vietnam was called napalm. This jellylike substance, dropped from planes, burned uncontrollably as it stuck to people's bodies and seared off their flesh.

The war touched everyone in Vietnam. As Le Thanh, a North Vietnamese child in the 1960s, recalled,

Nobody could get away from the war. It didn't matter if you were in the countryside or the city. While I was living in the country I saw terrible things. . . . I saw children who had been killed, pagodas and churches that had been destroyed, monks and priests dead in the ruins, schoolboys who were killed when schools were bombed.

SOURCE READINGS

 Source Readings on p. 740 will connect literature selections and primary source excerpts to historical events discussed in this section.

2. INSTRUCT

Explain/Discuss

Ask students to explain how a guerrilla war differs from a conventional war. Discuss why the superior firepower and technology of the American forces was not more successful against the Viet Cong guerrillas.

Ask students whether the Vietnam War meets the definition of "total war," one in which destruction of property and civilian life is carried out to persuade the enemy that continuing the conflict is not worth the cost. Ask students to describe American attempts at total warfare and to explain why these efforts were not successful.

Answer to . . .

MAKING CONNECTIONS

The jungle fighting conditions were similar, but in Vietnam, American soldiers never knew whom they were fighting—it was often impossible for them to tell friendly South Vietnamese from the Viet Cong.

In Depth

Interdisciplinary

As American herbicides destroyed crops in the South Vietnamese countryside, in the United States the Environmental Protection Agency (EPA) ordered a near-total ban on the pesticide dichlorodiphenyltrichloroethane (DDT). Although the use of DDT had resulted in dramatically increased crop yields, it was suspected to be a carcinogen and a possible cause of birth defects in humans and animals. DDT was banned in the United States and most other industrialized countries in the early 1970s.

Analyze

Explain that thousands of Vietnamese civilians were killed in the war. Ask students what made the My Lai massacre stand out. Why was it so shocking to Americans at home?

Activity

Researching War Images

Ask students to find illustrated books and magazines about the Vietnam War and to select one image that they think best represents the entire war. Students may present their chosen image to the class with a description and explanation of why they chose it.

Enrichment

Present to the class the following quotation by an American army officer after the total destruction of the village of Ben Tre in January 1968: "It became necessary to destroy the town in order to save it." Then ask students to explain why those opposed to the war frequently quoted this statement.

3. ASSESS

Section 2 Review Answers

1. My Lai massacre, see p. 721

2. American soldiers never knew who among the Vietnamese were enemies and who were friends. The fighting conditions in the jungle climate were also difficult.

3. Vietnamese civilians suffered heavy casualties as they watched their land and traditional way of life destroyed.

4. Over a hundred Vietnamese villagers were massacred by United States troops at My Lai. Reports of the massacre horrified Americans at home and made them wonder what kind of war their government was waging in Vietnam.

5. Many GIs probably felt that bringing Western culture to other people meant enlightenment and a better life for those people. The Vietnamese, however, were happy with their own way of life and did not want to see it overshadowed by Western culture with all of its "bewildering machines."

Although death was a constant presence in the war, few could harden their hearts against it. From the medic trying in vain to save a dying comrade, to the marine finally giving in to anguished tears in a lonely barracks, the war left few untouched. ✪

The situation was similar in the south. Near the village of My Thuy Phuong, one peasant remembered this incident:

> One day I was walking back home from the ricefield, carrying tools on my shoulder. Then behind me I heard a large, loud noise. A very bad noise. I looked back and saw an American helicopter following me, shooting down the path toward me. I was very scared, so [I] jumped into the water by the side. Just one moment later, the bullets went right by. So scary.

AMERICAN PROFILES

Le Ly Hayslip

Born in a tiny village in the northern part of South Vietnam, Le Ly Hayslip now lives in the United States and is an American citizen. Like other Vietnamese, as a child she learned "to love God, my family, our traditions, and the people we could not see: our ancestors." Then, when she was twelve years old, American helicopters came to Ky La, and the war intruded on her life.

For the next three years Le Ly fought for the Viet Cong. She and others were taught to follow Uncle Ho—Ho Chi Minh—in the struggle against the South Vietnamese government. For them, " 'Western culture' meant bars, brothels, black markets, and *xa hoi van minh*—bewildering machines—most of them destructive."

Life for Le Ly was never safe. Because she had ties to the Viet Cong, she always had to be alert to the moves of South Vietnamese soldiers. They often "took out their frustration on us: arresting nearby farmers and beating or shooting them on the spot, or carting anyone who looked suspicious off to jail." Captured by the South Vietnamese, she was questioned and then released. Later she was detained again, and this time tortured. Though she was fortunate enough to be freed once again, she now found herself suspected by the Viet Cong, since they could not understand why she had been released twice. She was caught in the middle. "If the [South

▶ RESOURCE DIRECTORY

Teaching Resources

Primary Source Activity An Army Nurse Remembers, found in the Unit 6 folder, p. 126, provides insight into the lives of women who served in Vietnam through the remembrances of army nurse Grace Barolet O'Brien.

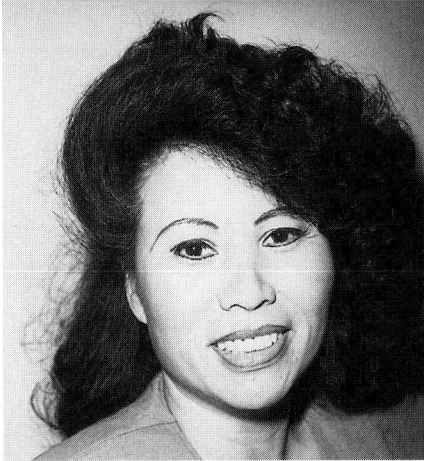

Le Ly Hayslip endured both physical and emotional pain during the Vietnam War.

Vietnamese] were like elephants trampling our village," she observed, "the Viet Cong were like snakes who came at us in the night."

After the Viet Cong sentenced her to death, Le Ly's life was filled with the terror of being discovered. She realized she could not stay in Ky La. She also realized that her life had changed forever: "From now on, I promised myself, I would only flow with the strongest current and drift with the steadiest wind—and not resist."

Determined to leave Vietnam, Le Ly began to spend time with American soldiers and civilians. Eventually she met Ed Hayslip, a civilian contractor, who wanted to marry her and take her and her son back to the United States.

Le Ly accepted his proposal and became an immigrant to the United States. Still a young woman, she had seen more than most people see in a lifetime. For her, the war would never go away, and she devoted her life to trying to break down the barriers between the old world where she had been raised and the new world where she now lived.

The My Lai Massacre

In March 1968, the brutality of the war came into sharp focus in a massacre at My Lai, a small village in South Vietnam. In response to word that the community was sheltering 250 members of the Viet Cong, a United States infantry company moved in to clear out the village. Rather than enemy soldiers, the company found women, children, and old men. The American troops already had suffered heavy combat losses. They were worn down by the uncertainties and terrors of fighting a guerrilla war. Some lost control.

Lieutenant William L. Calley, Jr., was in charge. He first ordered, "Round everybody up," and then gave the order for the prisoners to be killed. One soldier, Private Paul Meadlo, later described what happened:

> We huddled them up. We made them squat down. . . . I poured about four clips [about 68 shots] into the group. . . . The mothers kept hugging their children. . . . Well, we kept right on firing. . . . I still dream about it. About the women and children in my sleep. . . . Some nights, I can't even sleep. I just lay there thinking about it.

Stories of the horrible **My Lai massacre,** in which more than a hundred Vietnamese were slaughtered, shocked Americans at home. This was more than the nation had bargained for when it went to war.

Reteach

Ask students to write two or three sentences about the hardships and dangers confronting American soldiers in Vietnam and two or three sentences about the hardships and dangers that the war brought to Vietnamese civilians.

 Alternative Assessment

Mid-Point Monitoring

Ask students if they have
● Decided which materials to include
● Begun to locate sources of information

4. C L O S E

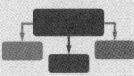 **Reinforcing the Big Idea**

The Vietnam War took an enormous toll both on the American soldiers who tried to fight it and on the Vietnamese civilians who tried to survive it. The televised images of the war shocked Americans at home. The next section describes how the student protest movements of the time developed into the antiwar movement.

SECTION 2 REVIEW

Key Terms, People, and Places
1. Define My Lai massacre.

Key Concepts
2. Why was the war so hard on American troops?
3. How did the war affect Vietnamese civilians?
4. What happened at My Lai, and how did it affect Americans' perception of the war?

Critical Thinking
5. **Making Comparisons** Le Ly Hayslip and her fellow Viet Cong were willing to fight and die to keep "Western culture" out of Vietnam. How did their perception of American values differ from that of the GIs who grew up watching the Lone Ranger on television?

Quiz found in the Unit 6 folder, p. 113, covers the main ideas in this section as well as the key terms.

SECTION 3

Student Protest

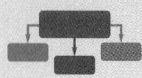

Connecting to the Big Idea

See page 712B. Explain that during the 1960s, college campuses erupted in student protest. The most dramatic, and perhaps the most effective, student protests were against the war in Vietnam. Ask why college students became activists during the 1960s.

Objectives

● Explain why the United States was ripe for change in the early 1960s and describe how college students at that time challenged the foundations of American life.
● Identify the Vietnam War as the focus of the protest movement in the 1960s.
● Describe the methods used by student protesters to voice their opinions.

Bellringer

Ask students whether the decade in which they are living seems to have a particular theme or identity. Ask them to suggest adjectives that might describe its general tone and spirit. What was the tone and spirit of the 1960s and early 1970s?

Reading Strategy

Structured Overview Ask students to write the main headings Student Activism and Changing Times and Resistance to War in the center of a piece of paper. Ask them to add important details from the relevant part of the section to support each main idea.

SECTION PREVIEW

"The times they are a-changin'," folksinger Bob Dylan sang in the 1960s. Student activists demanded many changes during this period, but the Vietnam War took center stage in the protest movement.

This 1969 poster advertised one of many antiwar demonstrations that shook the nation during the Vietnam War era.

Key Concepts
• The United States was ripe for change in the early 1960s, and students began to challenge the foundations of American life.
• The Vietnam War became the focus of the protest movement in the 1960s.
• Student protesters used peaceful demonstrations, teach-ins, educational campaigns, and sometimes violence to voice their opinions.

Key Terms, People, and Places
Students for a Democratic Society (SDS), New Left, teach-in, conscientious objector

---

In June 1971, the *New York Times* published the first in a series of articles based on a classified government study of United States involvement in the Vietnam War. The Pentagon Papers, as the study came to be called, revealed that government officials, including President Johnson, had lied to Congress and the American public about the war. Although many were shocked by these revelations, others had long suspected that there were ugly truths hiding behind the optimistic statements of politicians and military leaders. In fact, opposition to the war had been growing steadily since the early 1960s.

Students were in the forefront of the antiwar movement, and their activism undermined support for the war in the population at large. Still, many Americans remained patriotically devoted to their country's involvement in Vietnam, and the issue created deep rifts within the United States.

Student Activism and Changing Times

Student activism began in the early 1960s. When members of the baby boom generation graduated from high school, college and university enrollments swelled with more students than ever before. Unlike previous generations of students, who needed to work after high school, members of this generation had time to experiment before they went out into the world.

Change was in the air. Even in the conformist years of the 1950s, popular culture—including rock-and-roll music and rebellious youths on the movie screen—had indicated that many young Americans were not satisfied with the values of their parents. The early 1960s saw a widening of this generation gap. In 1963 folksinger Bob Dylan captured the new mood in a song entitled "The Times They Are A-Changin' ":

Come mothers and fathers
Throughout the land
And don't criticize
What you can't understand
Your sons and your daughters
Are beyond your command
There's a battle
Outside and it's ragin'
It'll soon shake your windows
And rattle your walls . . .
For the times they are a-changin'.

The civil rights movement, discussed in Chapter 20, was a stepping-stone to other movements for change. Civil rights activists were among those who organized **Students for a Democratic Society (SDS)** in 1960. Its manifesto, the Port Huron Statement, appeared

---

in 1962. It was written largely by Tom Hayden, a student at the University of Michigan. The statement declared:

> We are people of this generation, bred in at least modest comfort, housed now in universities, looking uncomfortably at the world we inherit.
>   When we were kids the United States was the wealthiest and strongest country in the world. . . . As we grew, however, our comfort was penetrated by events too troubling to dismiss. . . . We would replace power rooted in possession, privilege, or circumstance by power and uniqueness rooted in love, reflectiveness, reason, and creativity. As a social system we seek the establishment of a democracy of individual participation.

Although it was but a tiny organization at the start, SDS was a major force in the development of a new political movement that came to be called the **New Left**. Members of the New Left believed that radical changes were the only way to solve problems such as poverty and racism in the United States.

MAKING CONNECTIONS

The Port Huron Statement rejected a system of "power rooted in possession, privilege, or circumstance." What other social movements have you read about that criticized similar aspects of American society?

The Free Speech Movement The first blow of the student revolution came at the University of California at Berkeley in September 1964. Civil rights workers became angry when the university refused to allow them to distribute leaflets outside the main gate of the campus. The students, who had fought for equal rights in the South, argued that their right to free speech was being challenged, and they resisted the university's effort to restrict their political activity. When police came to arrest one of their leaders, students surrounded the police car and kept it from moving. The free speech movement was under way.

Eventually the administration tried to find a compromise. Then, however, the governing board that had the final word over university policy decided to hold student leaders responsible for their actions and filed charges against some. Irate students took over Sproul Hall, the main administration building. Student leader Mario Savio declared that the university was no more than a vast, impersonal bureaucracy:

> There comes a time when the operation of the machine becomes so odious [hateful], makes you so sick at heart, that you can't take part, you can't even tacitly [silently] take part. And you've got to put your bodies upon the gears and upon the wheels, upon the levers, upon all the apparatus, and you've got to make it stop.

⭐ Students wore buttons echoing the instructions on their university registration cards and protesting the impersonal treatment they received from the school. "I am a U.C. Student," the buttons read. "Do not Fold, Bend, or Mutilate." Folksinger Joan Baez came to the school and sang "We Shall Overcome," the marching song of the civil rights movement. When police arrested students in Sproul Hall, other students, supported by the faculty, went on strike and stopped attending classes to show their support for the free speech demonstrators.

Berkeley remained the most radical campus, but the agitation there spread to other campuses across the United States. In the spring of 1965, activists challenged regulations they felt unfairly curbed their freedom, such as restrictions on the hours when women and men could visit each others' dorms. Students also sought greater involvement in college

In October 1964, Berkeley student Mario Savio stood atop a police car to address a crowd of protesters demanding free speech (above). The building in the background is Sproul Hall.

2. INSTRUCT

Explain/Discuss

Note that the Port Huron Statement on page 723 begins with a generational identification: "We are people of this generation." Ask students why they think Hayden began the statement with those words.

Discuss how the civil rights movement strengthened students' belief in their ability to bring about change. Ask students to explain why student activists, trained in the civil rights movement, began to work to change their schools and to stop the Vietnam War.

Ask students to describe the various forms of protest used by antiwar activists. Ask them which method they think was probably most effective and to explain their choice.

Analyze

Ask students to consider the options open to young men of draft age during the Vietnam War and the possible consequences of each course of action. Now ask students to imagine they are male high school graduates in excellent health in 1965. What do they propose to do about the draft? What would they advise a friend to do?

Answer to ...

MAKING CONNECTIONS

Students may cite the progressive movement of the late 1800s and the civil rights movement of the 1950s and 1960s.

Activity

Cooperative Learning

Time: Two class periods.
Activity: Students should create and administer a questionnaire about the 1960s to people who were of college age during that time.
Grouping: Four to six students.
Purpose: The questionnaire should ask open-ended but focused questions about college attendance, work, attitudes toward SDS and other protest movements, feelings about the Vietnam War, and participation in or opposition to the antiwar movement.
Roles: Researchers, question writers, analysts.
Outcome: Students will understand the primary concerns of Americans of college age during the 1960s.

Enrichment

Dr. Benjamin Spock, author of the perennial best-selling child care manual, *Baby and Child Care*, joined the antiwar movement when LBJ ordered the bombing of North Vietnam. Ask students to research the activities of Spock, Daniel Berrigan, Philip Berrigan, Jane Fonda, or William Sloane Coffin in the antiwar movement.

Caption Answer to ...

 Interpreting Graphs

There were approximately 185,000 American troops in Vietnam in 1965 and 485,000 in 1967. As the 1960s progressed, the increasing number of both draftees and casualties fueled antiwar protest. The Tet Offensive took place in 1968—the peak year for American troops in Vietnam. The fact that the offensive could happen despite the presence of so many troops there pointed to the hopelessness of the American war effort; after 1968, the number of troops began to decline.

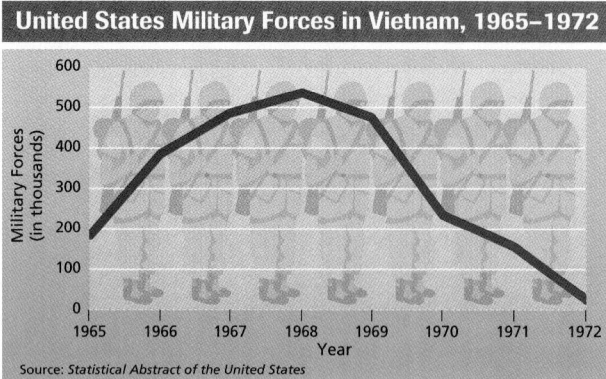

United States Military Forces in Vietnam, 1965–1972

Source: *Statistical Abstract of the United States*

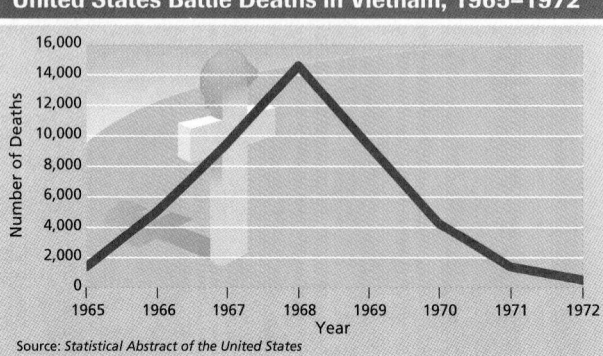

United States Battle Deaths in Vietnam, 1965–1972

Source: *Statistical Abstract of the United States*

Interpreting Graphs
How many United States soldiers were in Vietnam in 1965? In 1967? How do the graphs show some reasons for antiwar protest, especially among students? Explain how the top graph might relate to the Tet Offensive (January 1968) and its effect on public opinion in the United States.

affairs. SDS recruited some of these discontented students to work in campaigns to improve conditions in the cities of the United States.

The Teach-in Movement Then the Vietnam War intervened. As escalation began, students were among the first to protest American involvement in the war. Some opposed what they regarded as American imperialism. Others questioned American interests in a civil war. All called for withdrawal. The Tet Offensive in early 1968 finally turned a majority of Americans against the war, but the student protest movement had been registering many young people's disapproval for years. The graphs above give some indication of the statistics students found disturbing.

The first **teach-in** took place at the University of Michigan in March 1965. When a small group of faculty members planned a strike to protest the war, the Michigan legislature threatened to fire them. Instead, an even larger group decided to make a public statement. Fifty or sixty professors decided to teach a special night session in which issues concerning the war could be aired. To their surprise, several thousand people showed up and made the evening a monumental success. Soon other teach-ins followed at colleges around the country. Both supporters and opponents of the war appeared at the early teach-ins, but soon antiwar voices dominated the proceedings.

Resistance to War

At about the same time that the first teach-ins were taking place, resistance to the military draft was beginning to sweep the country. A selective service act allowing the government to draft men between the ages of eighteen and twenty-six had been in place since 1951. As more and more young men were being called into service and sent to fight in Vietnam, Americans began to question the morality and fairness of the draft. College students could receive deferments, which meant they did not have to go to war, but those who could not afford college did not have this avenue open to them. Many other young men tried to avoid the draft by leaving the country or by claiming that they were **conscientious objectors**—they opposed fighting in the war on moral grounds.

SDS grew by leaps and bounds as it embarked on a campaign against the draft. Leaders encouraged men to refuse to report for duty. The organization also launched attacks on campus units of the Reserve Officers' Training Corps (ROTC), on CIA recruiters, and on companies producing napalm and other tools of destruction. "Hey, hey, LBJ. How many kids did you kill today?" marchers chanted during demonstrations around the country. In 1967 some 300,000 opponents of the war marched in New York City, while 100,000 tried to close down the Pentagon, home of the Defense Department, near Washington, D.C. In 1969 the National Chicano Moratorium Committee staged its own antiwar

 RESOURCE DIRECTORY

Teaching Resources

Visual Learning Activity Antiwar Demonstrations, found in the Unit 6 folder, p. 132, shows two pictures of protesters to illustrate the way the antiwar movement won broad support in late 1969.

demonstrations. These protesters argued that Vietnam was a racial war, with black and brown Americans being used against their brothers and sisters in developing nations.

Protest became a way of life. In the first six months of 1968, more than 200 major demonstrations erupted at colleges and universities around the country. The most dramatic confrontation came at Columbia University in New York. There the issues of civil rights and the war were closely related. An SDS chapter sought to get the university to cut its ties with a research institute that did work for the military. At the same time, an African American students' organization tried to halt construction of a gymnasium that would encroach upon an adjacent neighborhood. Together, these two groups took over the president's office. Finally the president called the police, and hundreds of students were arrested. A student sympathy strike followed, and the university closed early that spring.

Sometimes the radical movement turned violent. Activists in one SDS faction called themselves the Weathermen, after a line in a Bob Dylan song—"You don't need a weatherman to know which way the wind blows." They were determined to bring about a revolution immediately. In October 1969, the group converged on Chicago. Members dressed in hard hats, boots, and work gloves rampaged through the streets wielding pipes, clubs, rocks, and chains. They tangled with police (as they had planned), regrouped, and came back for still another confrontation.

Bo Burlingham, a participant from Ohio, explained why he had joined in the attack:

This antiwar protest took place in San Francisco in 1967. ⭐

*W*hy did we do it? The status quo meant to us war, poverty, inequality, ignorance, famine and disease in most of the world. To accept it was to condone and help perpetuate it. We felt like miners trapped in a terrible poisonous shaft with no light to guide us out. We resolved to destroy the tunnel even if we risked destroying ourselves in the process.

The violent measures of groups like the Weathermen represented the extreme expression of youthful discontent in the 1960s. The spirit of change led most members of the counterculture to work for reforms in peaceful ways, but that same spirit led others simply to "drop out" of the traditional culture they were rejecting.

SECTION 3 REVIEW

Key Terms, People, and Places
1. Define (a) SDS, (b) New Left, (c) teach-in, (d) conscientious objector.

Key Concepts
2. What were the roots of student activism in the 1960s?
3. What was the role of SDS in the growing protest movement?
4. How did the Vietnam War affect the student protest movement?

5. What did activists hope to accomplish, and what methods did they use?

Critical Thinking
6. **Distinguishing False from Accurate Images** Mario Savio described the university as a huge machine with gears and wheels. Explain why you think that this image does or does not accurately reflect the nature of any large institution.

📄 **Quiz** found in the Unit 6 folder, p. 115, covers the main ideas in this section as well as the key terms.

3. ASSESS

Section 3 Review Answers

1. (a) SDS, see p. 722, (b) New Left, see p. 723, (c) teach-in, see p. 724, (d) conscientious objector, see p. 724

2. Baby boomers in college had time to experiment before getting jobs, and they were dissatisfied with the traditional values of their parents. The model of the civil rights movement helped spark other movements for change.

3. SDS formed the core of the New Left, and it led the protest against the draft as the Vietnam War progressed. Some radical SDS members formed the Weathermen, who used violent methods of protest.

4. The Vietnam War took center stage in the student protest movement as more and more young men were drafted.

5. Activists hoped to challenge the corporate values that had defined the 1950s and, more specifically, to change unfair university policies and to stop the Vietnam War. Their methods included draft resistance, protest marches, and strikes.

6. Possible answers: The machine image works well because each person plays a small part in achieving a larger purpose, even though they may not be happy as tiny parts of huge machines that are out of their direct control. The machine image is inaccurate because the human element in institutions will always keep them more dynamic and changeable than mere machines.

Reteach

Ask students to describe the goals and methods of the free speech movement, draft resistance, and antiwar protest.

4. CLOSE

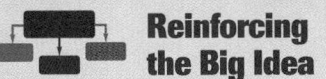 **Reinforcing the Big Idea**

Student protesters demanded many changes during the 1960s, but the primary focus of their protest became the Vietnam War. The next section describes the development of the counterculture.

Critical Thinking

Checking Consistency

Focus Students check for consistency between what they have read about the Vietnam era and the passages provided.

Instruct Divide the class into pairs and ask students to work with their partners to answer the questions in the feature. Ask for a show of hands to indicate how many find the passages in Item A inconsistent. Do the same for Item B. Then ask for volunteers to explain the inconsistency they find. Ask those who find the items consistent to explain their reasoning.

Extend See the Historian's Toolbox Activity in the Resource Directory below.

Answers

1. (a) The First Amendment of the Constitution, which guarantees freedom of the press. (b) Johnson's highly sympathetic depiction of the North Vietnamese in 1965 suggested policy objectives geared toward peaceful settlement rather than military victory in Vietnam. (c) Johnson's language and imagery, used in support of a policy of peace, can serve as the basis of comparison with his language, imagery, and policy objectives on the same subject at a later date.

2. (a) The U.S. Supreme Court turned down the government's request to keep two newspapers from publishing "The Pentagon Papers." (b) The ruling meant that the newspapers were free to publish the material, which they probably did. (c) In 1966 Johnson's depiction of the North Vietnamese in harsh, flatly threatening terms suggested policy objectives geared toward a military victory rather than a peaceful settlement in Vietnam. He now painted a menacing, inhuman picture of the North Vietnamese.

3. (a) The Supreme Court's ruling against the government agreed with the constitutional requirement of the First Amendment that no law interfere with the freedom of the press. (b) No, it was not consistent. In 1965 Johnson's policy objective was portrayed as a peaceful settlement with the North Vietnamese. In 1966 it was portrayed as a military victory over the North Vietnamese.

Checking Consistency

Checking consistency means determining whether ideas that should agree—or follow logically one from the other—actually do. Government actions, for example, should always agree with the Constitution. Where no such overriding rules apply—in the creation of foreign policy, for instance—policy objectives are expected to be consistent with past decisions on similar issues. Checking for consistency will help reveal whether the government is in fact operating as it should.

Use the following steps and what you have read about the Vietnam era to check for consistency in the examples at right.

1. Identify the principle or other factor to be used as the baseline for checking consistency. You should expect certain facts, ideas, or actions to agree—either with one another or with an overriding principle. Read the information in Items A and B at right. (a) What rule or principle serves as the baseline for checking consistency in Item A? (b) In Item B, what did Johnson's description of the North Vietnamese in 1965 suggest about the goals of his policy in Vietnam at the time? (c) How can Johnson's statement serve as the baseline for checking his consistency in other statements about Vietnam?

2. Note the corresponding action or idea to be checked for consistency. (a) In Item A, what action did the Supreme Court take? (b) What probably happened as a result of this action? (c) In Item B, what did Johnson's description of the North Vietnamese (the "Communists") in 1966 suggest about the goals of his policy in Vietnam at the time?

3. Check for consistency between the principle or baseline factor and the corresponding action or idea. In the examples below, compare the second action or idea against the baseline you have identified to see if the two ideas are consistent with or contradict each other. (a) In Item A, did the action taken by the Supreme Court agree or conflict with the constitutional requirement of the First Amendment? Explain your answer. (b) In Item B, was Johnson's statement of his policy objective in 1966 consistent with the statement he had made in 1965? Explain your answer.

A "Congress shall make no law . . . abridging the freedom of speech, or of the press. . . ."

—First Amendment, United States Constitution

In 1971 the United States Supreme Court denied the government's request to prohibit two newspapers from publishing "The Pentagon Papers," a highly classified documentary history of United States involvement in Vietnam through May 1968.

B "This war, like most wars, is filled with terrible irony. For what do the people of North Vietnam want? They want what their neighbors also desire: food for their hunger, health for their bodies, . . . an end to the bondage of material misery. . . . Neither independence nor human dignity will ever be won by arms alone. It also requires the works of peace."

—President Lyndon B. Johnson, address at Johns Hopkins University (April 7, 1965)

"Aggression is on the march and the enslavement of free men is its goal. . . . If we allow the Communists to win in Vietnam, it will become easier and more appetizing for them to take over other countries in other parts of the world. . . . That is why it is vitally important to every American family that we stop the Communists in South Vietnam."

—President Lyndon B. Johnson, Honolulu Conference (February 6, 1966)

 RESOURCE DIRECTORY

Teaching Resources

Historian's Toolbox Activity Checking Consistency, found in the Unit 6 folder, p. 124, provides passages in which students can practice this skill by determining whether words and actions follow a given principle.

The Counterculture

SECTION PREVIEW

In the 1960s, a youth culture that stressed freedom and individuality created for some people a promising new "space" in which to explore themselves. At the same time, it filled others with fear and disgust.

Key Concepts

• Rejecting the conventional lifestyles of older Americans, many young people in the 1960s became part of a counterculture that sought to promote freedom and creativity.
• The counterculture advanced new attitudes about personal relationships, drugs, and music.
• Many Americans were shocked by the new values of the counterculture.

Key Terms, People, and Places

counterculture, hippie, psychedelic drug, Woodstock

I n the 1960s, many Americans began to look for alternatives to traditional patterns of living. Young people in particular were involved in what became known as the **counterculture.** Drawing on the example of the Beat Generation of the 1950s, members of the counterculture rejected conventional customs. They experimented with new forms of dress, different attitudes toward sexual relationships, and the use of drugs. Some members of the counterculture were politically involved; most were not. But their challenge to traditional norms was visible both in the political protests of the 1960s and in the changing social patterns of American life.

Reflections of the Counterculture

People's appearances reflected the changes that were taking place. The **hippies** of the 1960s—men and women who self-consciously rejected conventional norms—tried to look different. Women chose freer fashions, such as miniskirts and loose-fitting dresses. Men let their hair grow long and wore beards. Many hippies adopted the dress of working people, which seemed somehow more "authentic" than the school clothes of middle-class youth. Therefore, men and women wore jeans, muslin (plain-woven cotton) shirts, and other simple garments that were intended to look handmade.

The Sexual Revolution The new views about sexual behavior advanced by the counterculture were labeled "the sexual revolution." The young people who led this revolution demanded more freedom to make personal choices. Some argued that sex should be separated from its traditional ties to family life. Lynn Ferrin, who moved to San Francisco to become part of the counterculture in California, remembered her feelings at the time:

> I was among the women in that whole vanguard of sexual freedom who were very excited by being free women. . . . In my circles, you wouldn't think of getting married, settling down with one person. The suburbs and the station wagon full of Cub Scouts became something you didn't want anything to do with.

The sexual revolution in the counterculture led to more open discussion of sexual subjects. Newspapers, magazines, and books published articles that might not have been printed, even in the recent past. The 1962 book by Helen Gurley Brown, *Sex and the Single Girl*, became a best-seller. In 1966 William H. Masters and Virginia E. Johnson shocked many people when they published *Human Sexual Response*, a report on their scientific studies of sexuality.

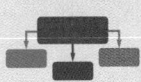

One way in which 1960s youth expressed themselves was by turning everyday objects into works of art. Country Joe McDonald of the popular rock group Country Joe and the Fish decorated his guitar (above) with antiwar symbols. Others decorated their clothing with colorful embroidery. ⭐

Explain/Discuss

Discuss the aspects of American life that hippies rejected. What sort of life did hippies want to build for themselves?

Discuss the reactions of other Americans to hippies and would-be hippies. Why did hippies attract so much attention? Why did some more conservative Americans feel threatened by the hippie lifestyle? Ask students what aspects of the counterculture were dangerous.

Answer to ...

MAKING CONNECTIONS

Young people in the 1960s may have been trying to escape the lives of conformity and materialism their parents were living—as well as all of the normal problems that accompany growing up. Today, many young people also seek to escape problems through experimentation and rebellion.

In Depth

Historical Misconceptions

The common belief concerning antiwar sentiments during this period was that they were held exclusively by the young and the highly educated. But a May 1971 Gallup Poll found that 75 percent of those with only a grade school education opposed the war, against 66 percent of college graduates. "A careful review of public opinion data over the last seven years [1965–72]," stated a 1972 University of Michigan Survey Research Center study, "shows that on most war-related issues, the greatest opposition to continued American involvement has come from the least educated parts of the population."

This group of hippies lived together in the New Buffalo Commune. They turned out for the 1968 Fourth of July parade in El Rito, New Mexico, in their outrageously painted bus.

Novels like D. H. Lawrence's *Lady Chatterly's Lover,* which had been banned in the United States since 1928 for being too explicit, now became available.

Many men and women also experimented with new living patterns. Some hippies rejected traditional relationships and lived together in communal groups. More and more people simply lived together as couples, without getting married.

The Drug Scene Also part of the 1960s counterculture were **psychedelic drugs,** which are drugs that cause the brain to behave abnormally. As a result, the brain produces hallucinations and other altered perceptions of reality. The beatniks had experimented with drugs a decade before, but they had been in the minority. Now drug use became more widespread among the nation's youth.

One early proponent of psychedelic drug use was researcher Timothy Leary, who worked at Harvard University with Richard Alpert on the chemical compound lysergic acid diethyl amide, commonly known as LSD. The two men were fired from their research posts for using undergraduates in experiments with the drug. Leary then began to preach that drugs could help free

the mind. He advised listeners, "Tune in, turn on, drop out."

Soldiers who had used drugs in Vietnam brought them home when their tours of duty were completed. Marijuana became common among middle-class college students. Todd Gitlin, a radical activist who became president of SDS, explained that "the point was to open up a new space, an *inner* space, so that we could *space out,* live for the sheer exultant point of living."

On the other side of the drug issue, however, was serious danger. Overdoses and deaths from accidents that occurred while under the influence of drugs caused concern in many quarters. Three leading musicians—Janis Joplin, Jim Morrison, and Jimi Hendrix—died of complications from drug overdoses. They were not the only ones. Their deaths represented the tragic excesses to which some people were driven by their reliance on drugs as an escape.

MAKING CONNECTIONS

What might some young people in the 1960s have been trying to escape by seeking a spiritual "inner space"? In what ways do young people today seek similar escapes?

▶ RESOURCE DIRECTORY

Teaching Resources

 Literature Activity The Flower Children, found in the Unit 6 folder, p. 131, uses lyrics from the song "San Francisco (Be Sure to Wear Flowers in Your Hair)" to describe the group of young people who called themselves "flower children."

The Music World

 Music likewise reflected and contributed to the cultural changes. The rock and roll of the 1950s and the folk music of the early 1960s gave way to a new kind of rock. The Beatles, a group of performers from England, heavily influenced the music of this period, taking first England and then the United States by storm. Mick Jagger of the Rolling Stones was an aggressive, sometimes violent showman on stage. Janis Joplin was a hard-driving, hard-drinking singer whose powerful interpretations of classic blues songs catapulted her to superstardom before her death in 1970.

Woodstock The diverse strands of the counterculture all came together at the Woodstock Music and Art Fair in upstate New York in August 1969. About 300,000 people gathered for several days in a large pasture in Bethel, New York, to listen to the major bands of the rock world. Despite brutal heat and bursts of rain, those who attended **Woodstock** recalled the festival with something of a sense of awe for the fellowship they experienced there. Tom Law, one participant at Woodstock, commented on the mood:

> The music had very little to do with it. The music was great and it was there and kept everybody focused on that. But the event was so much bigger than the music. It was a phenomenon. It was absolutely a phenomenon. And it was also the most peaceful, civilized gathering that was probably happening on the planet at the time.

The weekend was trouble-free. Police avoided confrontations with those attending by choosing not to enforce drug laws. The crowd remained under control. After the festival, many supporters spoke about the "Woodstock Nation" as a model for the new and better world to come.

Other Americans, however, viewed both the festival and the mood it reflected with distaste. Even as older people began growing their hair

Links Across Time

1650   1700   1750   1800   1850   1900   1950   2000

Music: The Sound of Rebellion

The 1960s were not the first time that Americans were shocked by the music their children were listening to. In the 1920s, the jazz sound of Louis Armstrong and the Hot Five (left) was too hot for many older listeners—but the young flappers and rakes loved it. The performances of rock bands in the 1960s (above) were similarly lost to the older generation. *Does any of the music you listen to today leave the older people you know baffled?*

Analyze

Ask students to analyze what ultimately happened to the 1960s counterculture. Why did most hippies melt back into the middle class, and why had many who protested against capitalistic values in the 1960s become business executives by the 1980s? What aspects of American life were permanently changed by the counterculture?

Activity
Teaching Heterogeneous Groups

In protest against conventional lifestyles, many young people in the 1960s adopted alternative ways of dressing and behaving. To understand the purpose of this form of expression, divide students into small groups to define today's counterculture in terms of dress and behavior. In order to do this, each group must first describe the conventional customs that this counterculture rejects. Students should then state what change today's counterculture seeks to realize. **LEP**

Enrichment

Ask students to research the various kinds of communes that were formed in the 1960s. Ask students to present a brief report on their findings to the class.

Answer to ...

Links Across Time

Answers will vary but should reflect an understanding that trends in music often evolve along generational lines.

Section 4 Review Answers

1. (a) hippie, see p. 727, (b) psychedelic drug, see p. 728, (c) Woodstock, see p. 729

2. The counterculture rejected the conformity and traditional values that had marked the 1950s. Instead, it emphasized freedom and individuality.

3. The counterculture valued individual freedom and experimentation; its members tried new types of sexual relationships, experimented with mind-altering drugs, and enjoyed new forms of rock music.

4. Many outside the counterculture viewed it with distaste because it seemed childish and vulgar and rejected time-honored values.

5. The assumption is that marriage is boring and restricting. Students may agree with this view, or they may point out that marriage allows for a kind of personal growth that living without commitment does not.

Reteach

Ask students to read and correct each of the following statements and to provide evidence from the section to support their correction.
- The counterculture began as an attempt by older Americans to halt the spreading student protest movement.
- The term *sexual revolution* refers to women's demands for equality with men in the workplace.
- LSD is a kind of music that was popular in the 1960s.
- The rock festival at Woodstock was marred by violence.

4. CLOSE

Reinforcing the Big Idea

In the 1960s, many young Americans traded traditional patterns of living for a counterculture that stressed freedom and individuality. The next section describes the success of the antiwar movement in bringing an end to the Vietnam War.

The young people who attended the Woodstock Music and Art Fair in 1969 reflected the new fashions and social values of their times.

longer and wearing more colorful clothes, they were not interested in the more fundamental changes they saw occurring around them. Some young people also disliked these changes. In particular, opponents deplored the drugs, sex, and nudity they saw at the Woodstock festival and around the country. To them, the counterculture represented a rejection of morals and honored values and seemed a childish reaction to the problems of the era.

Altamont The fears of those who criticized Woodstock came true at another rock festival that took place at the Altamont Speedway in California in December 1969. There, 300,000 people gathered for a concert concluding an American tour by the Rolling Stones. When promoters of the concert failed to provide adequate security, the Stones hired a band of Hell's Angels, the infamous and lawless motorcycle gang, to keep order. The cyclists battered any people who annoyed them and ended up beating one man to death when he ventured on stage.

The violence at the Altamont concert was not the only sign of contradictions within the counterculture. Despite their celebration of simple lifestyles, most hippies were children of the comfortable middle class, and they melted right back into it when the counterculture fell apart. American corporations seized on the opportunity to market items such as blue jeans and stereo equipment to members of the counterculture, who eagerly bought the products. By the 1980s, many baby boomers who had protested the capitalistic values of the 1950s and 1960s would be holding executive positions in the same corporations they had once denounced.

SECTION 4 REVIEW

Key Terms, People, and Places
1. Define (a) hippie, (b) psychedelic drug, (c) Woodstock.

Key Concepts
2. Describe the values that were rejected and those that were embraced by the counterculture of the 1960s.
3. How was the counterculture reflected in the sexual values, drug use, and music of its members?
4. How did Americans outside the counterculture view the movement?

Critical Thinking
5. **Identifying Assumptions** Lynn Ferrin recalled being part of a group of women in the 1960s "who were very excited by being free women" and "wouldn't think of getting married, settling down with one person." What assumptions about marriage are revealed in this statement? Explain why you think these assumptions are or are not valid.

 **RESOURCE DIRECTORY**

Teaching Resources

Quiz found in the Unit 6 folder, p. 117, covers the main ideas in this section as well as the key terms.

The End of the War

SECTION PREVIEW

The antiwar movement finally convinced politicians in Washington that it was time to pull out of Vietnam, but American troops withdrew very slowly, and the fighting was far from over.

Key Concepts
- Growing opposition to the war convinced Lyndon Johnson not to run for reelection and helped Richard Nixon to become President in 1968.
- Nixon gradually replaced American troops with South Vietnamese, but at the same time he began a new bombing assault on Cambodia that enraged antiwar protesters.
- A cease-fire was finally signed in 1973, but by 1975 North Vietnamese leaders had taken control of the entire country.
- The war left permanent scars in the Vietnamese countryside as well as in the hearts of Vietnamese and Americans.

Key Terms, People, and Places
Vietnamization; Kent State University

T he antiwar movement created serious opposition to American involvement in Vietnam. It also polarized the United States. Deep rifts in the Democratic party and in the country as a whole forced Lyndon Johnson to leave the presidency at the end of his term and paved the way for the election of Republican Richard Nixon in 1968. Nixon made good on a pledge to withdraw the United States from the Southeast Asian struggle, but only after expanding the war outside Vietnam and creating even more violent protest at home.

Mounting Opposition

By 1968 the antiwar movement was in full swing. Political activists drew on all of their resources to mount the most extensive resistance campaign in American history. Marchers took to the streets, while artists, authors, and musicians contributed their talents to the antiwar crusade.

Years of protest and a growing list of American casualties had steadily increased public opposition to the war. In a 1965 Gallup poll, 62 percent of those interviewed felt that the United States was handling the war in Vietnam "as well as could be expected." In 1966 only 41 percent approved of Johnson's Vietnam policy; that figure dropped to 35 percent in 1968. At the same time, disapproval of Johnson's actions increased from 37 percent in 1966 to 50 percent in 1968. In 1968, 49 percent of those polled felt that the United States had made a mistake in sending troops into the war. Details on these statistics can be found in the table on page 732.

Johnson finally succumbed to the opposition. As resistance to the war mounted, his own popularity fell accordingly. After the Tet Offensive, when the North Vietnamese demonstrated that they still had the resources to carry out a broad-based attack in South Vietnam, Johnson recognized that American public opinion had shifted in such a way that he could not win another election.

The Vietnam Women's Memorial in Washington, D.C., shows two nurses helping a wounded soldier. The memorial sculpture was erected in 1993 to honor the thousands of women who had served in the war.

Reproducible Lesson Plan found in the Unit 6 folder, p. 109, provides a summary of the Section 5 lesson plan content.

Alternate Lesson Plan: Critical Thinking Testing Conclusions, found in the Alternate Lesson Plans folder, p. 160, is designed to help students apply this skill by citing evidence to support or refute a set of statements.

Guided Reading and Review found in the Unit 6 folder, p. 118, provides a structure for reading and mastering the key concepts and reviewing the key terms for Section 5. (Guided Practice)

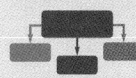

1. FOCUS

Connecting to the Big Idea

See page 712B. Explain that antiwar protests grew in strength and frequency until finally President Nixon managed to bring the war to a close. Ask how opposition to the war affected the election of 1968. How did the war finally end?

Objectives
- Explain how growing opposition to the war persuaded Lyndon Johnson not to run for reelection and helped Richard Nixon become President in 1968.
- Explain how Nixon gradually replaced American troops with South Vietnamese forces but also initiated a bombing assault on Cambodia in 1970.
- Explain how American involvement in Vietnam finally ended in 1973 and describe the takeover of South Vietnam by North Vietnamese leaders.
- Describe the permanent scars left by the war in Vietnam.

Bellringer

Ask students whether it is possible for a United States President to continue a course of action strongly opposed by most of the American people. In what ways can the people make their opinions known to the President?

Reading Strategy

Predicting Content Ask students to skim the section, list the main headings and subheadings, and write a sentence or phrase predicting the content under each one. When they have finished reading the section, ask students to test their predictions against the actual text.

Explain/Discuss

Ask students to list the reasons for growing opposition to the war. Ask why Lyndon Johnson could not end the war. What steps finally led to the cease-fire and withdrawal of American forces? Why did Nixon's escalation of the bombing and the invasion of Cambodia cause such outrage? Tell students that Nixon's adviser Henry Kissinger hoped that "jugular diplomacy" would force the North Vietnamese into making some concessions at the negotiating table.

Analyze

Explain that once President Nixon had determined that the United States should no longer seek victory in Vietnam, he tried to find a way to gain "peace with honor." Ask students how the Vietnamization policy seemed to placate both antiwar protesters and conservatives who did not think the United States should abandon Vietnam to its fate. Then ask students to determine how successful the policy was as a military strategy.

Caption Answer to ...

Interpreting Tables

In December 1965, 56 percent of those polled approved of Johnson's handling of the war; by February 1968, that number had dropped to 35 percent. Between May 1966 and February 1968, the percentage of people who thought the United States had made a mistake in sending troops to Vietnam increased from 36 percent to 49 percent.

Answer to ...

Answers will vary, but students should note that the American public obtains information from a variety of sources, including print, radio, television, on-line computer services, and others. The topic choices these media sources make, their analysis of issues, and their heavy use of poll-takers all influence public opinion.

Public Opinion of United States Involvement in Vietnam

"Do you approve or disapprove of the way President Johnson is handling the situation in Vietnam?"

	Approve	Disapprove	No opinion
December 1965	56%	26%	18%
May 1966	41%	37%	22%
April 1967	43%	42%	15%
July 1967	33%	52%	15%
December 1967	39%	49%	12%
February 1968*	35%	50%	15%

* During Tet Offensive

"In view of the developments since we entered the fighting in Vietnam, do you think the United States made a mistake sending troops to fight in Vietnam?"

	Yes, made mistake	No, did not	No opinion
May 1966	36%	49%	15%
April 1967	37%	50%	13%
July 1967	41%	48%	11%
February 1968†	49%	41%	10%

† After Tet Offensive

Source: *The Gallup Poll: Public Opinion 1935–1971*, by George H. Gallup

Interpreting Tables

What percentage of those polled in 1965 approved of Lyndon Johnson's handling of the war? What percentage approved in 1968? Between 1966 and 1968, what happened to the percentage of people who thought the United States should never have entered the war?

Johnson rarely left the White House near the end of his presidency for fear of being assaulted by angry, shouting crowds of protesters. He felt like "a jackrabbit in a hailstorm, hunkering up and taking it."

After watching the campaign of antiwar candidate Eugene McCarthy gain momentum in the Democratic primaries, President Johnson declared dramatically in a nationally televised speech that he would not run for another term as President. He knew that he had lost his base of support. He hoped that by ordering a pause in the relentless bombing of Vietnam he could encourage peace talks to end the war and so restore unity in the United States as he left public life. ★

The media—especially television—strongly influenced public opinion during the Vietnam War. What are the major issues facing the people of the United States today, and how are people's opinions on these issues affected by the media?

Richard Nixon's Approach

Eugene McCarthy's campaign faltered, and Robert Kennedy, who likewise challenged Johnson, was assassinated (see Chapter 23). Another candidate, Hubert Humphrey, eventually was nominated by the Democrats. For the Republicans, Richard Nixon ran for the presidency with the claim that he had a secret plan to end the war in Vietnam. He never divulged the details, and critics doubted that a plan really existed, but his pledge still helped secure his election over Humphrey. Once in the White House, Nixon dedicated himself to a policy of **Vietnamization,** which involved removing American forces and replacing them with South Vietnamese soldiers. Between 1968 and 1972, American troop strength dropped from 543,000 to 39,000, and opposition to the war among people in the United States declined.

Even as he moved to bring American soldiers home, Nixon himself became caught up in the war. As much as he wanted to defuse antiwar sentiment at home, he was determined not to lose the war, either. And so, as he withdrew American troops, he resumed bombing raids, keeping his actions secret from his critics. The map on page 733 shows the major targets of those bombing raids.

President Nixon also widened the war beyond the borders of Vietnam. In April 1970, he announced that United States and South Vietnamese forces were moving into neighboring Cambodia to clear out communist camps there, from which the enemy was mounting attacks on South Vietnam. The United States, he asserted, would not stand by like "a pitiful helpless giant" while the Viet Cong attacks from Cambodia went on:

▶ RESOURCE DIRECTORY

Teaching Resources

Primary Source Activity LBJ Withdraws from the Race, found in the Unit 6 folder, pp. 127–128, describes the reasons behind President Johnson's decision to withdraw from the 1968 presidential race, in a passage from his memoirs.

We take this action not for the purpose of expanding the war into Cambodia but for the purpose of ending the war in Vietnam and winning the just peace we all desire. We have made and we will continue to make every possible effort to end this war through negotiation at the conference table rather than through more fighting on the battlefield.

His actions belied his words, however, and the move brought chaos and civil war in Cambodia and a fresh wave of protests at home.

Renewed Protests

Nixon's invasion of Cambodia in 1970 reignited the protest movement on college campuses in the United States. At **Kent State University** in Ohio, students reacted angrily to the President's action. On the weekend following his speech, they broke windows in the business district downtown and burned the army ROTC building on campus, which had become a hated symbol of the war.

In response, the governor of Ohio ordered the National Guard to Kent State. Tension mounted. When students threw rocks and empty tear gas canisters at them, the soldiers loaded their guns and donned gas masks. They knelt down and aimed their rifles at the students, as if warning them to stop. Then the guardsmen retreated to another position. At the top of a hill, they suddenly turned and began firing on the students below.

Tom Grace was a sophomore crossing campus just before the outburst. He was more than 150 feet away and thought he was keeping a safe distance from the disturbance. He was wrong:

When the National Guardsmen got to the top of the hill, all of a sudden there was just a quick movement, a flurry of activity, and then a crack, or two cracks of rifle fire, and I thought, Oh my God! I turned and started running as fast as I could. I don't think I got more than a step or two, and all of a sudden I was on the ground. It was just like somebody had come over and given me a body blow and knocked me right down. The bullet had entered my left heel and had

literally knocked me off my feet. I tried to raise myself, and I heard someone yelling, "Stay down, stay down! It's buckshot!" . . . The bullet blew the shoe right off my foot, and there was a bone sticking through my green sock. It looked like somebody had put my foot through a meat grinder.

Grace was relatively lucky. After just thirteen seconds of firing, four students lay dead, with nine others wounded. Two of the dead had been demonstrators more than 250 feet away from the soldiers. The other two were bystanders, almost 400 feet away.

A similar attack occurred at Jackson State University in Mississippi. Policemen and highway patrolmen fired into a women's dormitory there without warning. Two people were killed, and more were wounded.

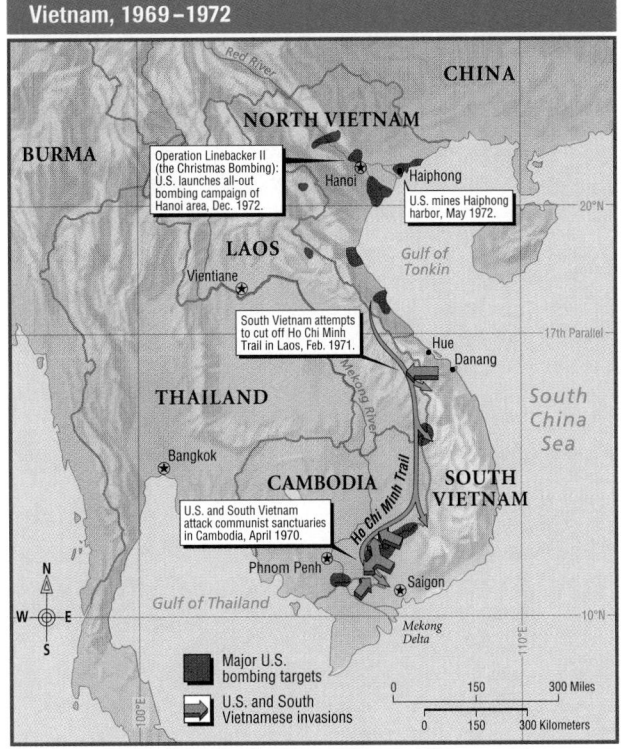

Vietnam, 1969–1972

Operation Linebacker II (the Christmas Bombing): U.S. launches all-out bombing campaign of Hanoi area, Dec. 1972.

U.S. mines Haiphong harbor, May 1972.

South Vietnam attempts to cut off Ho Chi Minh Trail in Laos, Feb. 1971.

U.S. and South Vietnam attack communist sanctuaries in Cambodia, April 1970.

Major U.S. bombing targets

U.S. and South Vietnamese invasions

Geography and History: Interpreting Maps
According to this map, in what areas were United States bombing raids concentrated during the later years of the war? What do you think these bombing raids were supposed to accomplish?

Activity
Making a Time Line

Ask students to make time lines identifying the major dates in the Vietnam War, starting their time lines in 1960.

Enrichment

The fate of the Americans taken prisoner during the war in Vietnam (POWs), and those missing in action (MIAs), was of great concern for years after the hostilities ended. Ask students to find out how many POWs were held in Vietnam, how many were released, and how many remained unaccounted for in the 1990s. Ask students also to find out how many MIAs are still unaccounted for.

Caption Answer to ...

 Interpreting Maps

The later bombing raids were concentrated on the Vietnam-Cambodia border and in the Hanoi area. One goal of these raids was to cut off supplies being carried along the Ho Chi Minh Trail to the Viet Cong.

 In Depth

Multicultural Perspectives

Of Americans who served in Vietnam, including professional military personnel and volunteers, the greatest percentage were draftees from minority and low-income families. In Lawrence Baskir and William Strauss's *Chance and Circumstance: The Draft, the War and the Vietnam Generation,* S. L. A. Marshall, a military historian, is quoted as saying that "in the average rifle company, the strength was 50 percent composed of Negroes, Southwestern Mexicans, Puerto Ricans, Guamians, Nisei, and so on. But a real cross-section of American youth? Almost never."

The mother accuses the government of initiating the violence; the wife accuses the students of threatening the National Guard and making the violence inevitable. For a more thorough examination of the Kent State tragedy, see the Resource Directory below.

3. ASSESS

Section 5 Review Answers

1. Vietnamization, see p. 732

2. Kent State University, see p. 733

3. President Johnson decided not to run for reelection in 1968.

4. Nixon planned to gradually replace United States troops with Vietnamese troops. At the same time, he was determined not to lose the war.

5. The United States withdrew from the war in 1973. The South Vietnamese army could not hold back the North Vietnamese on their own, and the communists took control of the country in 1975.

In Depth

Then and Now

"I felt like Lady Macbeth. I couldn't get the blood of Vietnam off my hands," remembers Jean Fury, who served as a nurse in the war. "Part of me had held on, hoping that I'd be proven right, that all those sacrifices were worth something." On Veterans' Day, 1993, Fury was one of the 11,500 women who had served in Vietnam to be honored with a permanent tribute in the form of a bronze statue of two service-women in action. "I didn't realize how much your sacrifice equaled and even exceeded that of the men," said General Colin Powell at the groundbreaking ceremony for the memorial in July 1993. (See page 731.)

Viewpoints
On the Tragedy of Kent State

In May 1970, four students were killed at Kent State University when the National Guard opened fire on a crowd of antiwar protesters. *How do the following viewpoints reflect the issues that tore apart American society at that time?*

From the mother of a student

"President Nixon wants people to believe Jeff turned to violence. That is not true. What kind of sympathy is this? When four kids are dead he gave no comfort. Nixon acts as if the kids had it coming. But shooting into a crowd of students, that is violence. They say it could happen again if the Guard is threatened. They consider stones threat enough to kill children. I think the violence comes from the government."

Mother of Jeffrey Glenn Miller, one of four students killed at Kent State, quoted in *Life* magazine, May 15, 1970

From the wife of a Guardsman

"They didn't go to Kent State to kill anyone. I know he'd rather have stayed home and mowed the lawn. He told me so. He told me they didn't fire those shots to scare the students off. He told me they fired those shots because they knew the students were coming after them, coming for their guns. People are calling my husband a murderer; my husband is not a murderer. He was afraid."

Wife of a member of the National Guard, quoted in *Newsweek* magazine, May 18, 1970

Americans were horrified by these attacks. They had hoped that the rifts of the past few years between the youth of the United States and those in positions of power were starting to heal. Now the wounds were opened even wider than before.

The United States Withdraws

The war dragged on as Nixon ran for a second term as President in 1972, and South Vietnam refused to accept a proposed settlement. To reassure the South Vietnamese of continuing American concern, Nixon ordered the most intense bombing campaign of the war in the spring of 1972. The United States bombed Hanoi, the North Vietnamese capital, and mined North Vietnamese harbors. Just days before the election, National Security adviser

Henry Kissinger announced, "Peace is at hand." In January 1973, after Nixon was reelected, a cease-fire was finally signed, and United States involvement in the war came to an end.

But the civil war continued for another two years in Vietnam. After the withdrawal of United States forces, South Vietnamese soldiers steadily lost ground to their North Vietnamese enemies. In the spring of 1975, the North Vietnamese launched a campaign of strikes against strategic cities throughout South Vietnam, the final objective being the seat of government in Saigon. South Vietnamese forces crumpled in the face of this campaign. On April 29, with communist forces surrounding Saigon, the United States carried out a dramatic last-minute evacuation. More than 1,000 Americans and nearly 6,000 Vietnamese were taken from the city by helicopter to aircraft carriers waiting offshore. On April 30, the Saigon government officially surrendered to the North Vietnamese.

Legacy of the War

The Vietnam War was the longest and least successful war in which the United States had ever participated. It resulted in 58,000 Americans dead and about 300,000 wounded. It cost more than $150 billion and disrupted the American economy in the process. The costs of the war were even higher in Vietnam itself. The Vietnamese were bombarded by more bombs than had fallen on all Axis powers during World War II. The number of dead and wounded Vietnamese soldiers ran into the millions, with countless civilian casualties. The landscape itself would long reveal the scars of war. ⊙

In the United States, the war also fractured the liberal consensus that had guided the nation during and after World War II. Americans had believed that they could defend the world from communism anywhere, at any time. American technology and money, they assumed, could always bring victory. That assumption was proved false in Vietnam, and the United States now had to reassess its global mission.

RESOURCE DIRECTORY

Teaching Resources

Viewpoints Activity On the Tragedy of Kent State, found in the Unit 6 folder, pp. 122–123, provides extended comments on the 1970 shooting of student protesters.

Critical Thinking Activity Drawing Conclusions: Military Spending, found in the Unit 6 folder, p. 125, charts the increase in military spending that many people thought was prolonging the Vietnam War.

The legacy of the war lingered on long after the last bomb had been dropped. Soldiers came home to a different reception than their fathers and grandfathers had in World War II. The war had been so unpopular that some of the outrage felt by antiwar Americans was transferred to the GIs who had fought in Vietnam. It was often hard for returning soldiers to rationalize their participation in Vietnam, and it was harder still to integrate themselves back into American life. Ron Kovic, who was paralyzed in the war, summed up his feelings about his smashed dreams and body in a haunting poem. He had been born on the fourth of July, a date that had once underscored his patriotism. Now it seemed a bitter joke.

*I am the living death
the memorial day on wheels
I am your yankee doodle dandy
your john wayne come home
your fourth of july firecracker
exploding in the grave*

The Vietnam Veterans Memorial in Washington, D.C., was created to recognize the courage of American GIs during the Vietnam ordeal and to help heal the wounds the war had caused. An open competition, announced in 1980, specified that the memorial should be a quiet, contemplative structure that included a list of the war dead. It was won by Maya Ying Lin, a twenty-two-year-old Chinese American architecture student.

The memorial is a starkly beautiful structure, elegant in its simplicity. It consists of two long black marble slabs, intersecting in a V shape, with all the names of the known dead inscribed chronologically according to date of death. In 1993 a Vietnam Women's Memorial was unveiled near the wall to honor the more than 11,000 women who served in Vietnam.

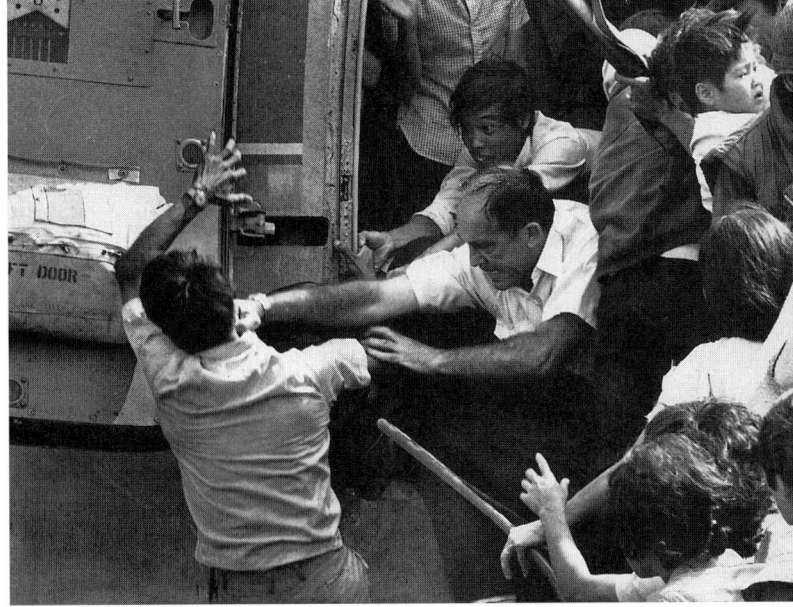

In 1975 Nha Trang in South Vietnam was evacuated just before communist troops took over. The man above was punched by an American official as he tried to board the last plane out, which was already overcrowded with fleeing refugees.

SECTION 5 REVIEW

Key Terms, People, and Places
1. Define Vietnamization.
2. Identify Kent State University.

Key Concepts
3. What were the political effects of growing public disapproval of the war in 1968?
4. What was Richard Nixon's approach to the war in Vietnam?
5. How did the war in Vietnam finally end?

6. What was the lasting impact of the war in Vietnam and in the United States?

Critical Thinking
7. **Determining Relevance** The counterculture of the 1960s was despised by many Americans who saw it as a senseless rejection of time-honored values. Explain how such feelings might have played a part in the violence that erupted at Kent State University in 1970.

 Quiz found in the Unit 6 folder, p. 119, covers the main ideas in this section as well as the key terms.

 Chapter Test Forms A and B are found in the Unit 6 folder, pp. 134–139.

 Answer Keys found in the Unit 6 folder, pp. 146–159, provide answers to all student activities.

Media and Technology

 Transparencies
Critical Thinking, I-12; Graphic Organizer, G-4

Guided Reading Audiotapes (English and Spanish)

Computer Test Bank

6. Vietnam suffered millions of casualties and the destruction of its land. The United States lost 58,000 soldiers and would never again feel as confident about its ability to defeat communism around the world.

7. Possible answer: National Guard members who felt hostile toward the counterculture may have been more likely to fire upon antiwar demonstrators.

Reteach

Ask students to explain the significance of each of the following events in the 1960s: the 1968 presidential election, Nixon's policy of Vietnamization, the invasion of Laos, the antiwar protest at Kent State University.

 **4. CLOSE**

 **Reinforcing the Big Idea**

The Vietnam War finally ended in 1973, but the war left deep scars in both the United States and Vietnam.

In Depth

Then and Now

In February 1994 President Bill Clinton lifted the nineteen-year trade embargo on Vietnam. Senator John McCain (R–Arizona), a former prisoner of war in Vietnam, and Senator John Kerry (D–Massachusetts), a thrice-wounded, decorated Vietnam veteran, were chief sponsors of the Senate resolution to lift the trade ban. "I have made the judgment," said Clinton to critics of the action, "that the best way to ensure cooperation from Vietnam, and to continue getting the information Americans want on POWs and MIAs, is to end the trade embargo."

Understanding Key Terms, People, and Places

Terms

Students should refer to the definitions of the key terms in the chapter to write sentences that show the relation of each word to the Vietnam War or to American society during the 1960s.

True or False

1. true
2. false, escalation
3. false, New Left
4. false, Tet Offensive
5. true

Matching

1. Saigon
2. Kent State University
3. Ngo Dinh Diem

Reviewing Main Ideas

1. Diem's government was repressive, corrupt, and did not enjoy popular support.

2. A committed cold warrior, Kennedy increased American involvement in the war by sending military aid.

3. Johnson used the Gulf of Tonkin incident as an excuse to devote increasing amounts of American money and personnel to the war and to bomb North Vietnam.

4. Many American soldiers were worried about the communist threat and wanted to do their patriotic duty. They thought that the war would be as exciting as the battles they had seen in the movies. In reality, the war was dangerous, disturbing, confusing, and frustrating.

5. Americans used saturation bombing and chemical weapons, such as Agent Orange and napalm, which had a destructive effect on civilian life in both North and South Vietnam.

6. The My Lai massacre shocked Americans at home into the realization that the course of the war was out of control.

7. Many young Americans rejected the conservative values of their parents.

8. Students demanded free speech and an end to poverty and racism. Their primary demand, however, was an end to the Vietnam War.

9. Women rejected confining clothing in favor of freer fashions; men let their hair grow long and wore beards. People wore jeans, "working people's" clothes, and colorful garments intended to convey their sense of individuality.

Chapter Review

Understanding Key Terms, People, and Places

Key Terms

1. Viet Cong
2. Gulf of Tonkin Resolution
3. escalation
4. Tet Offensive
5. My Lai massacre
6. Students for a Democratic Society (SDS)
7. New Left
8. teach-in
9. conscientious objector
10. counterculture
11. hippie
12. psychedelic drug
13. Woodstock
14. Vietnamization

People

15. Ngo Dinh Diem

Places

16. Saigon
17. Kent State University

Terms For each term above, write a sentence that explains its relation to the Vietnam War or to American society during the 1960s.

True or False Determine whether each statement is true or false. If it is true, write "true." If it is false, change the underlined term to make the statement true.

1. People who attended Woodstock remembered the sense of fellowship they experienced there.
2. After his reelection, Johnson began the Vietnamization of the war.
3. Members of a new political movement called the Viet Cong believed that radical change was the only way to solve poverty and racism in the United States.
4. The Gulf of Tonkin Resolution included strikes on provincial and district capitals and other towns in South Vietnam.
5. The use of psychedelic drugs, which alter perceptions of reality, was part of the 1960s counterculture.

Matching Review the key people and places in the list above. If you are not sure of their significance, review the information given in the chapter. Then choose a person or place from the list that best matches each description below.

1. the site of major strikes during the Tet Offensive
2. the site of violent protests against the American invasion of Cambodia
3. the repressive prime minister of South Vietnam

Reviewing Main Ideas

Section 1 (pp. 714–717)

1. Describe the government of Ngo Dinh Diem.
2. What was President Kennedy's policy toward Vietnam in the early 1960s?
3. Describe how the Vietnam War escalated under President Johnson.

Section 2 (pp. 718–721)

4. Explain why many American soldiers were eager to go to Vietnam. Why did many feel different once they actually began to fight?
5. Why was the war so devastating for Vietnamese civilians?
6. Explain how the My Lai massacre affected the attitudes of Americans at home toward the Vietnam War.

Section 3 (pp. 722–725)

7. What was the source of the 1960s "generation gap"?

8. What were some of the changes that student activists demanded during the 1960s?

Section 4 (pp. 727–730)

9. How did the styles of dress in the 1960s reflect counterculture values of freedom and individuality?
10. Why did many Americans view the counterculture with shock and dismay?

Section 5 (pp. 731–735)

11. Why did Lyndon Johnson decide not to run for reelection in 1968?
12. Why did Richard Nixon authorize the invasion of Cambodia in 1970?
13. What happened in Vietnam after the United States withdrew?
14. What is the purpose of the Vietnam Veterans Memorial in Washington, D.C.?

---

10. They saw the counterculture as a rejection of traditional morals and values.

11. Johnson had become so unpopular because of continuing American involvement in the Vietnam War that he could not possibly win an election.

12. Nixon bombed Cambodia in order to destroy North Vietnamese bases there.

13. North Vietnam took over South Vietnam.

14. The purpose of the memorial is to honor the American GIs who died in the war, to recognize the courage of those who returned only to become scapegoats for public anger toward government policies during the war, and to help heal the wounds that the war caused.

Thinking Critically

1. Students' answers should demonstrate an understanding that many people's views changed from acceptance to strong disapproval over the course of the war. Factors that influenced this shift in opinion included television coverage of the brutality of war and student protests.

2. The warning cautions against becoming involved in distant conflicts that are difficult to pull out of, that consume great amounts of money and numbers of lives, and that are probably doomed to failure.

3. Possible questions: Was the reality of the war what you expected? Did you feel that you were fighting for a worthwhile cause? How were you received when you returned home?

Thinking Critically

1. **Demonstrating Reasoned Judgment** If you had been a student during the Vietnam War, do you think that your views of the conflict would have changed or remained the same throughout the course of the war? What factors might have influenced your views?

2. **Expressing Problems Clearly** Since the end of the Vietnam War, government officials have advised caution in global affairs so that the United States does not get involved in "another Vietnam." Explain what is meant by this warning.

3. **Formulating Questions** Create three questions that you might ask a soldier who fought in Vietnam that, if answered, would give some idea of what participating in the war was like.

Making Connections

1. **Evaluating Primary Sources** Review the primary source excerpt on page 716. What underlying beliefs are revealed in Johnson's statement? Did history prove his beliefs to be correct?

2. **Understanding the Visuals** A protest sign carried in a 1967 antiwar demonstration in San Francisco read, "No war on children." Find an image in the chapter that might have inspired such a slogan. In general, how do the visuals in the chapter support the idea that the 1960s were a turbulent and confusing era?

3. **Writing About the Chapter** It is 1968. Write a letter to the editor of your school newspaper explaining why you will or will not participate in the upcoming student demonstration against the Vietnam War. First, create a list of the reasons why you do or do not support the war. Note your opinion about peaceful demonstrations as a way to effect change. Next, write a draft of your letter in which you explain your point of view. Revise your letter, making certain that each idea is clearly explained. Proofread your letter and draft a final copy.

4. **Using the Graphic Organizer** This graphic organizer uses a flow map to show the sequence of events leading to the end of the Vietnam War. (a) According to the map, what was one result of Nixon's bombing of Cambodia? (b) What contradiction in Nixon's policy toward Vietnam is shown by the flow map? (c) On a separate sheet of paper, create your own flow map about the beginnings of the Vietnam War, using this graphic organizer as an example.

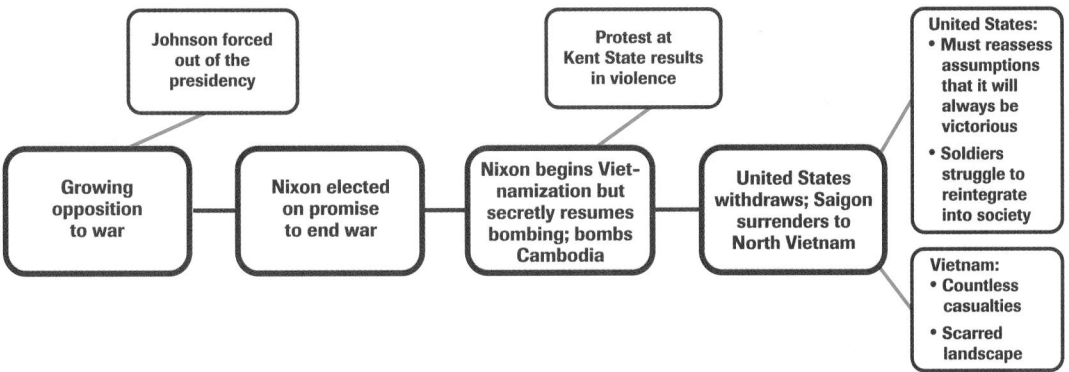

Making Connections

1. Johnson believed that communists would take over the world if the United States did not stand up to them. The collapse of communism in the Soviet Union and Eastern bloc in the early 1990s proved Johnson's assumptions wrong.

2. Possible answer: The image of the wounded Vietnamese child on page 718. The visuals in the chapter—photographs and posters of antiwar protest, a memorial sculpture, a medic trying in vain to save a dying soldier, an anguished marine, the counterculture on display at Woodstock—support the idea that the 1960s were a turbulent and confusing era.

3. Students' responses should consider reasons for supporting the war, such as stopping the threat of communism, or reasons for opposing the war, such as loss of American lives and brutality toward Vietnamese civilians.

4. (a) The bombing of Cambodia sparked protest at Kent State, which resulted in violence. (b) Nixon seemed to be pulling the United States out of the war with his policy of Vietnamization while at the same time he secretly resumed bombing raids and expanded the war beyond the borders of Vietnam by bombing Cambodia. (c) Students' graphic organizers should contain information about United States support of Ngo Dinh Diem and about the policies of Kennedy and Johnson toward Vietnam.

The United States' involvement in the Vietnam War divided the country into two angry camps: those who opposed the war and those who supported it. When the war ended and Saigon fell to the North Vietnamese, many Americans felt strongly that the years of agony and the loss of life had been in vain. Vietnam veterans returned to face anger and confusion, not the honor and gratitude of their country. Some vets were asked about the children they had killed or about their lack of success in the war. Many veterans suffered physically and mentally from the effects of the violence they had witnessed during the war. The indifference of the nation to their sacrifices only increased their stress and difficulty in becoming rehabilitated.

A change in attitude was evident when the Vietnam Veterans Memorial was unveiled in 1982 in Washington, D.C. Ask students to read the feature and to look at the personal memorials left at the "Wall." Ask students to focus on various images and discuss the significance of each to a combat soldier or to a member of a soldier's family.

Ask students to compare the items belonging to soldiers who fought in Vietnam with the artifacts from the Civil War shown on pages 220–221. Then ask students to list similar experiences common to veterans of both conflicts.

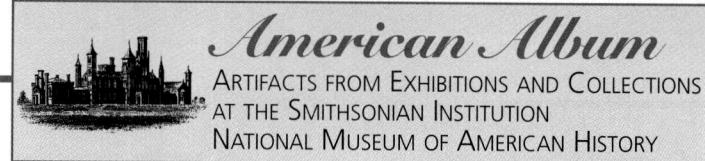

PERSONAL LEGACY

The V-shaped Vietnam Veterans Memorial, unlike most other monuments in Washington, D.C., is built on a small, human scale. Visitors find themselves drawn to its two polished black-granite walls, on which are inscribed more than 58,000 names of Americans killed and missing in the war. When this memorial opened in 1982, something unusual and unexpected began to occur: visitors left personal tokens at the base of the walls to honor and remember the soldiers who fought the war. This practice continues today. The usual gifts of flowers, wreaths, and small American flags mix with the most common items of a soldier in Vietnam—helmets, combat boots, and dog tags. Some mourners leave the items that gave soldiers comfort, such as favorite magazines, beverages, and items of clothing. A few visitors leave things, such as notes, jewelry, and stuffed animals, that carry memories of the bond between soldier and mourner. This practice continues today, and the National Park Service collects and preserves the artifacts. *What do the objects shown here tell you about the life of a combat soldier in Vietnam?*

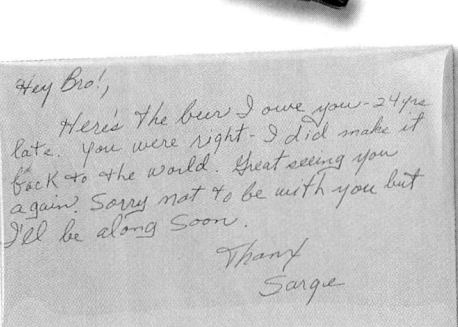

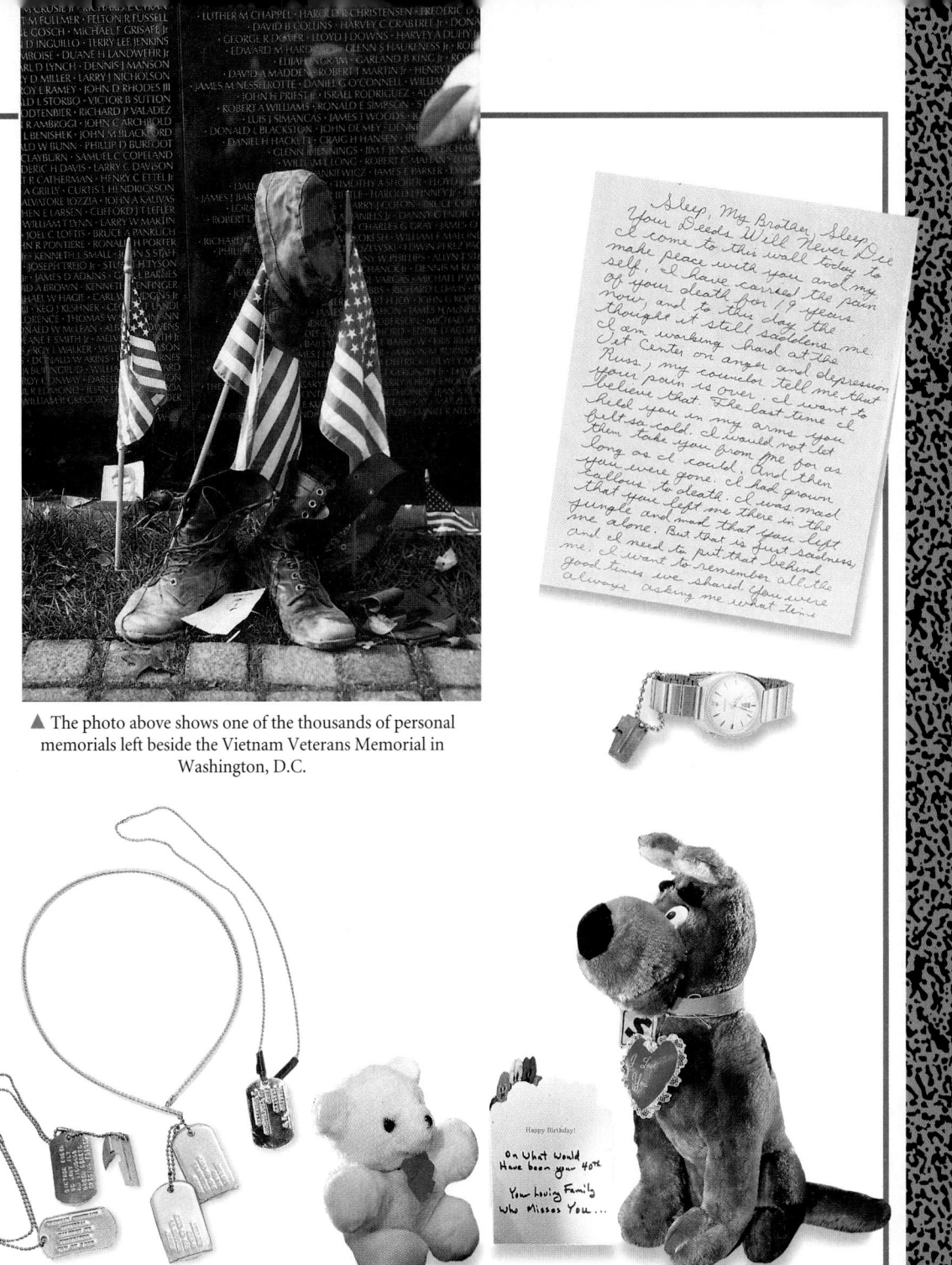

▲ The photo above shows one of the thousands of personal memorials left beside the Vietnam Veterans Memorial in Washington, D.C.

Tell students that invisible lines linked Vietnam soldiers and their families and friends during the war. These invisible lines were the international and United States mail routes, on which most people depended to keep in contact with each other.

INSTRUCT

Tell students to imagine they are historians sifting through a pile of letters from soldiers during the Vietnam War. They are using the letters as historical evidence to try to learn more about the war and how it affected those who fought it. Have students read the letters in the source readings and then analyze them to see what factual information they can glean from them.

After completing this activity, read the following statement to students: "Soldiers in the Vietnam War reacted to the dangers constantly surrounding them by becoming more and more suspicious of anyone they encountered, including the friends with whom they fought. The war resulted in a soldier who cared for no one and who fought for nothing but his own survival." Ask students to use the facts they collected above and the letters to find evidence that either supports or refutes this statement.

CHAPTER 22
SOURCE READINGS

Letters Home from Vietnam Primary Source

INTRODUCTION "With the possible exception of his rifle, nothing was more important to an American in Vietnam than his mail," writes William Broyles, Jr., in the foreword to *Dear America: Letters Home from Vietnam.* Letters from home provided the American soldier in Vietnam with a link to reality, something that often seemed to recede during the long days of war. Writing from Vietnam to loved ones provided many soldiers with a way to voice the feelings they were experiencing, a way to release the powerful emotions of fear, despair, pride, and bravery that brought them through their tours of duty.

17 Sept. 69

Red,

Thanks for the letter, but now you've made me self-conscious about my writing. . . .

Yesterday we took to the bush to recon[1] a river crossing on one of Charlie's[2] major supply routes coming in from Laos. . . . It was an uneventful patrol, but I committed the mortal sin of small-unit patrolling: I broke contact with the man in front of me and split the patrol into two elements, something that could easily prove fatal in the event of contact with the enemy. We'd just crossed the river at a ford to join the team reconning the other bank and were going through fairly green stuff when the man in front of me dropped his lighter. I bent to pick it up and by the time I straightened up he was out of sight and hearing. Had we been hit then, it would have been a bad situation made worse by my stupidity. I've picked up most of the patrolling tricks—taping metal parts to prevent their making noise during movement, wearing bandoliers so the magazines are on your chest and stomach and form makeshift body armor, and other tricks that stretch the odds a little more in your favor and give you a little more of an edge in combat—but I'm still new and yesterday I really loused up. . . .

The fact of the matter is that I was afraid—which I am most of the time over here—but I allowed my fear to interfere with the job at hand, and when that happens to someone, he ceases to be a good soldier. It's all right to be afraid, but you can't allow that fear to interfere with the job because other people are depending on you and you've got responsibility to them and for them. From now on I'll be keeping that in mind and I won't louse up so badly again. Had that happened under fire, people might have died unnecessarily due to me.

One other impression from that patrol is that anyone over here who walks more than 50 feet through elephant grass should automatically get a Purple Heart. Try to imagine grass 8 to 15 feet high so thick as to cut visibility to one yard, possessing razor-sharp edges. Then try to imagine walking through it while all around you are men possessing the latest automatic weapons who desperately want to kill you. You'd be amazed at how such a man can age on one patrol.

George

1 reconnoiter
2 a term for the Viet Cong

Dear Mom & Dad,

Sunday
July 3rd [1966]

I don't know how I can say this without alarming you, but I know I'll have to tell you about it because NBC News was there and I'm afraid you might have seen me on film or read about the dreadful fighting.

When I think about [what] I've been through the last few days, I can't help but cry and wonder how I am still alive. My company suffered the worst casualties—I believe something close to 50 dead and wounded. Friends who I took training with at Ft. Polk have been killed, and some are seriously wounded. In my squad of nine men, only four of us survived.

This was the worst battle as far as losses are concerned that this company has experienced. I'm not able to go into details now. I'm still in a slight state of shock and very weary and shaken from the last three days.

I just wanted you to know that I'm OK. How I made it I don't know. Perhaps you didn't read about it, but in case you did I just wanted to tell you I'm OK.

I can't help crying now because I think about the horror of those three days. I was carrying the bodies of wounded and dead onto helicopters that were in a clearing when I saw, I believe, Ron Nessen, of NBC, and they were taking pictures.

Yesterday (I thought they'd never come for us) we were evacuated from that area by helicopter. The area is less than two miles from Cambodia, where VCs[3] have regiments, and they ambushed us.

I received your letter dated June 25th and will answer at a later date. Try to hold up. By the time you receive this, I hope to be somewhat recovered and at ease.

Love,
Kenny

---
[3] Viet Cong

Dear Mom and Dad,

29 January 68

I guess by now you are worried sick over my safety. Khe Sanh village was overrun, but not the combat base. The base was hit and hit hard by artillery, mortars, and rockets. All my gear and the rest of the company's gear was destroyed. Right now we are living in bunkers just like the Marines at Con Thien did last fall.

I am unhurt and have not been touched. I skinned my knee on the initial assault, but other than that I am OK. My morale is not the best because my best buddy was killed the day before yesterday. I was standing about 20 feet from him and a 60-mm mortar exploded next to him. He caught a piece of shrapnel in the head. I carried him over to the aid station where he died. I cried my eyes out. I have seen death before but nothing as close as this. Junior, my buddy, had 67 days left in country and then he was to return to his wife and daughter. His death really hit me hard. . . . I think that with all the death and destruction I have seen in the past week I have aged greatly. I feel like an old man now. I am not as happy-go-lucky as before, and I think more maturely now. Payback for my buddies is not the uppermost thought in my mind. My biggest goal is to return to you and Dad and Ann in June or July. . . .

Please pray for us all here at Khe Sanh and also for my buddy Junior Reather. I hope he is happy where he is. Take care and God Bless.

Your Son & Marine,
Kevin

After returning from a mission in which he risked his life trying to save a mortally wounded soldier, this marine broke down in tears, grief-stricken by the death of his fellow soldier.

Have students conduct a poll to determine the general feeling today about United States involvement in the Vietnam War. Students should ask parents, neighbors, or teachers the following question: Do you think the United States should or should not have been involved in the Vietnam War? To gauge the person's basis for answering the question as well as to learn how many people were directly influenced by the war, students should also ask: Do you know anyone who fought in the Vietnam War? Students should each poll at least five people. Then, as a class, compile the results and form a conclusion as to current public opinion about the war and how many people in your community were directly affected by the conflict.

Tuesday, Sept. 6, 1966

Dear Mom,

. . . You'll probably be hearing about us again. Yesterday my platoon had six injured and one killed. We had a fire fight that lasted nine hours. We killed a lot of VC on this operation we're on now, but we also have had a lot killed. . . .

Well, Mom, I don't have much time, and I just wanted you to know I'm all right.

When you go to church, I want you to give all the people you see this address and tell them to send anything they can, like old clothes and anything.

I went down to this orphanage the other day, and these little kids are pitiful. They sleep on plain floors and don't get hardly anything to eat.

The reason I want you to tell everyone to help them is because I feel I may have killed some of their parents and it makes me feel sick to know they have to go on with nothing. Address: Mang-Lang Orphanage, Le-Loi Street, Tuy Hoa, Vietnam.

Love, Your son,
Dan

[January 1968]

To Cub Scout Pack 508
Saratoga, California

I don't know how to thank you for the wonderful gifts you sent to me and my buddies.

We are located on top of a hill, and it is isolated. The only way in is by chopper, so you can see we don't get many treats such as you sent. After eating C-rations, the popcorn, cake and candy were like gold. The biggest hit was the plastic Christmas tree.

Last week I had a fever and had to spend three days in the medic tent. In the tent sleeping next to me was a 12-year-old Vietnamese boy who had shrapnel in his elbow and shoulder. He was hiding in a bunker with his parents when a grenade exploded, killing all his family. I became friends with him and tried to converse with him in our different languages. When I shared with him the present you sent, he smiled for the first time. He sure got a kick out of the game.

We all hear of protests and riots and get mad. When our buddies die, we wonder why, but we also think of the boys of Den I and Den V and know why this must be done, and we know how lucky we are to live in America.

I pray that none of you will ever have to put on a uniform for hostile reasons.

Your friend,
David Hockett

Dear Family,   January 7th, 1971

I got all the Xmas packages—at least I think I did. The tree was a huge success. I brought it with me to a small fire base where I spent Christmas Eve and Christmas. We rigged up the lights with dry-cell batteries, and it was the only "formal" tree in the small camp.

Christmas out here was really something. I can hardly tell everything since there was a certain emotion that belies words. At midnight on Xmas Eve, the mortars and tracks and tanks and all the 1st Cavalry artillery sent up an absolutely thunderous barrage of high-altitude flares—all red and green star clusters. Since we were in a valley ringed by 1st Cav positions, it was quite a show. The Cavalry gunners topped it off with a crown of white phosphorus shells fired at an extreme altitude. I believe few people have seen fireworks like these.

Then, when all had quieted and the flares had gone out, the whole area calmed and hushed and we could just hear one of the fire bases start singing "Silent Night." Then it was picked up by the other positions around us and by everyone. It echoed through the valley for a long time and died out slowly. I'm positive it has seldom been sung with more gut feeling and pure homesick emotion—a strange and beautiful thing in this terribly death-ridden land. It is something I will always remember. . . .

Love,
Pete

(Above) A medic works bravely to save a dying comrade. (Left) This helmet is one of the many items that have been left at the Vietnam Veterans Memorial in Washington, D.C.

THINKING ABOUT THE SELECTION

1. Why does George feel so badly about the mistake he made while on patrol?
2. Why does Dan feel responsible for the children in the orphanage at Mang-Lang?

Critical Thinking

3. **Recognizing Cause and Effect** How did the presence of television affect the relationship between soldiers and their families back home?

ANSWERS TO

Thinking About the Selection

1. He feels that he was responsible for the well-being of others and he let them down. He knows that his mistake could well have cost one of his comrades his life.

2. He feels responsible for the children because he thinks he may have killed some of their parents in the line of duty. He is trying to help them make up for the loss that he feels he has inflicted upon them.

3. The presence of television meant that the soldiers were always wondering whether their families had heard reports of what was happening to them. Many soldiers seemed to feel concerned about the worry that this would inflict upon their families and so tried to write quickly after a battle to let them know they had survived the fighting.

Continuity and Change
1968–Present

Introducing the Unit

Interpreting the Visual Continuity and change are key features of American government and politics. At regular intervals, Americans have the opportunity to choose another President, to elect new legislators, and thus to change the party in power. Despite these changes, however, the government continues to function in an orderly manner, and the new President and legislators must abide by the Constitution and the traditions of government.

In 1993, when Bill Clinton, a Democrat opposed to the policies of his two Republican predecessors, Reagan and Bush, took the oath of office, the ritual of orderly transfer of power was repeated and the strength of the Republic once again reaffirmed.

Ask students to imagine that they must explain the significance of the photograph reproduced on pages 744–745 to a citizen of a nondemocratic nation. In their explanations, students should answer the following questions:
● Why is the inauguration a time for festivity and celebration?
● Why does the outgoing President attend the inauguration?
● Who can become President?

Establishing Chronology Remind students that the previous chapter focused on the politically divisive years of the Vietnam War. This unit covers four distinct political periods since 1968, beginning with the election of Richard Nixon, who resigned amid the disgrace of Watergate in 1974. From 1974 to 1980, the nation tried to recover from the damage of Watergate. Conservative Republicans again held the White House from 1980 until 1992, when Democrat Bill Clinton was elected. In the 1994 mid-term election, the Republican party gained control of Congress for the first time in over 40 years.

Continuity and Change 1968–Present

"In this present crisis, government is not the solution to our problem; government is the problem."
—Ronald Reagan, 1981

*B*y 1968 many Americans were tired of the turmoil of the sixties. The election of Richard Nixon as President that year marked the emergence of a Republican majority that lasted, with one brief exception, for more than twenty years. A long recession following the election of George Bush in 1988, however, created growing dissatisfaction with Republican policies. When Democrat Bill Clinton defeated Bush in the 1992 presidential election, Americans seemed ready to head in a new direction.

RESOURCE DIRECTORY

Teaching Resources

Local History Activity "'Boom and Bust' in Houston" and the Local Focus research topic suggestions, found in the Local History Resources folder, pp. 30–32, are designed to help students understand how history affects all lives.

★ Themes in American History Posters Wall-size, illustrated posters, found in the Teaching Resources package, illustrate the four unit themes.

Unit Test Forms A and B are found in the Unit 7 folder, pp. 137–142.

With a handshake and a smile, presidential power passed from Republican George Bush to Democrat Bill Clinton on a sunny day in January 1993.

Media and Technology

Visions of America: Scenes of an Era To introduce students to the main idea and events covered in this unit, play "Scenes of an Era: Republican Revival and Decline, 1968–Present" (length: 2.5 minutes). This selection can be located on side 4 of the videodiscs. This selection can also be located on videotape 5. Lesson plans for "Scenes of an Era" can be found in the Visions of America Teacher's Guidebook.

Using Multimedia Technology This folder contains instructional tools and strategies for using technology in the classroom.

Transparency Binder Contains full-color transparencies with lesson suggestions. From a large collection divided into twelve categories, specific transparencies are referenced throughout the chapters at appropriate points of use. For this unit, see American Photo, B-10; Our Multicultural Heritage, C-3; Links Across Time, J-10; Political Cartoon, K-10; and Historical Maps, L-5.

Teachers may wish to discuss specific historical events in the context of historical themes. Here are four suggestions for Unit 7.

Values *A variety of religious, ethical, and moral beliefs have propelled and guided the quest of Americans for a just and ordered society.*

● President Carter introduced a foreign policy based on a moral commitment to human rights, freedom, and democracy.
● The issue of abortion stirred a debate over morality, religious beliefs, and freedom of choice.

Economics *Americans have searched for new and better ways to make a living and have struggled to define government's role in this pursuit.*

● The energy crisis of the 1970s and high rates of inflation created an unstable economy.
● Presidents Carter, Reagan, and Bush all moved toward deregulation, reducing or removing controls on industry.

Diversity *Throughout its history America has been made up of a gathering of many peoples from throughout the world. Americans have both benefited from and encountered problems with this diversity.*

● New immigrants from Asia and Latin America added to America's cultural diversity.
● The debate over multiculturalism heightened Americans' awareness of the country's diversity.

American Democracy *The concepts of democratic representation, equality under the law, and freedom from discrimination have been gradually broadened to include previously excluded groups.*

● Shock at the unethical actions represented by Watergate forced President Nixon's resignation and some reform of the presidential election process.
● The civil rights movement grew to include Latinos, Native Americans, and gays.

Section		

Section 1
1968: A Turning Point in History
(pp. 748–751)
	Reproducible Lesson Plan, p. 3
	Alternate Lesson Plan, p. 162
	Guided Reading and Review, p. 7
	Quiz, p. 8
		Primary Source Activity, Selling Candidate
		    Nixon, pp. 23–24
		Turning Points Extension Activity, The Lasting
		    Impact of the Year 1968, pp. 15–16

Section 2
The Nixon Administration
(pp. 754–759)
	Reproducible Lesson Plan, p. 4
	Alternate Lesson Plan, p. 163
	Guided Reading and Review, p. 9
	Quiz, p. 10
		Visual Learning Activity, The Imperial
		    President, p. 29
		Critical Thinking Activity, Predicting
		    Consequences, p. 22
		American Profiles Activity, Maggie Kuhn, p. 17

Section 3 **Nixon's Foreign Policy** (pp. 760–764)	Reproducible Lesson Plan, p. 5 Alternate Lesson Plan, p. 164 Guided Reading and Review, p. 11 Quiz, p. 12	Primary Source Activity, The Trip to China: Diplomacy and Publicity, p. 25

Section 4
The Watergate Scandal
(pp. 765–770)
	Reproducible Lesson Plan, p. 6
	Alternate Lesson Plan, p. 165
	Guided Reading and Review, p. 13
	Quiz, p. 14
	Chapter Test, Forms A & B, pp. 31–36
		Visual Learning Activity, Wanted, p. 30
		American Profiles Activity, John J. Sirica, p. 18
		Literature Activity, Unraveling the Story of
		    Watergate, pp. 26–28
		Viewpoints Activity, On Nixon's Impeachment,
		    pp. 19–20
		Historian's Toolbox Activity, Analyzing
		    Presidential Records, p. 21

Additional Chapter Resources

Resource Organizer, p. 2
Alternate Lesson Plan, p. 161
Answer Keys, pp. 143–156

Bibliography

For the Teacher

Hersh, S. M. *The Price of Power: Kissinger in the Nixon White House.* Summit Books, 1983. (A critical study of Nixon's secretary of state.)

Lukas, J. Anthony. *Common Ground: A Turbulent Decade in the Lives of Three American Families.* Random House, 1986. (A study of the impact of school busing on three economically diverse families.)

Wills, Garry. *Nixon Agonistes: The Crisis of the Self-Made Man.* Houghton Mifflin, 1970. (A critical and probing analysis of Richard Nixon and his most famous crisis.)

Prentice Hall Literature Excerpts from *The American Experience,* 1994, including Oates, Joyce Carol. "Journey," from *The Poisoned Kiss and Other Stories from the Portuguese.* Vanguard, 1975.

The Big Idea for the chapter and how the main ideas in each section relate to the Big Idea are graphically displayed below. Comprehension of this chapter's Big Idea is critical to students' understanding of United States history and how we as a nation got where we are today.

Media and Technology

  Visions of America: Turning Point Story, "Yearbook 1968" (length: approx. 4 minutes)

  Visions of America: Roundtable Discussion on "Yearbook 1968"

 Time Lines, E-9

 Critical Thinking, I-14

 Graphic Organizer, G-4

 Guided Reading Audiotapes (English and Spanish)

 Computer Test Bank

For the Student

The Right Stuff. Warner Communications, 1983. Film/Video. (Award–winning look at astronauts, based on Tom Wolfe's best-seller.)

All the President's Men. Warner Home Video, 1976. Video. (Fast-paced depiction of *Washington Post* reporters Bob Woodward and Carl Bernstein and the story they uncovered about the Watergate break-in.)

CHAPTER 23

A series of tumultuous events in 1968 helped pave the way for the presidency of Richard Nixon and a twenty-year era of almost uninterrupted Republican control of the White House. The new President's domestic and foreign policies marked a shift in national politics. But Nixon's leadership style led to scandal and his own shattering downfall.

SECTION 1

In 1968, events in Vietnam and assassinations at home ripped the nation and the Democrats apart. Nixon and the Republicans took advantage of the chaos to win the White House.

SECTION 2

Nixon adopted a conservative approach to domestic policies. From the economy, to crime, to race relations, Nixon tried to take the nation in a new direction.

SECTION 3

Nixon used his credentials as a tough anticommunist to forge new, positive relationships with China and the Soviet Union. The President relied heavily on adviser Henry Kissinger.

SECTION 4

The President's willingness to exploit presidential power for personal political aims led to scandal. Nixon himself was tainted and forced to resign.

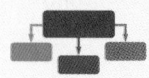

The Relevance of the Big Idea

In 1968, voters in the United States elected Richard Nixon, ushering in an era of Republican dominance in national politics. Nixon's policies at home and abroad marked a shift from the Democratic policies that began with the New Deal and continued through most of the 1960s. Though Nixon himself was undone by his personal failings, his Republican successors generally followed a similar political line.

In the 1990s, the nation appears to be considering another shift in political direction. In 1992, voters put Democrat Bill Clinton in the White House; it remains to be seen whether this election marks a lasting shift similar to the one the nation experienced in 1968. Ask students if they can identify a significant change in the direction of the country in the 1990s compared with the 1980s.

In Depth

Global Connections

Richard Nixon forged an active and bold foreign policy. Besides rebuilding relations with China and making peace in Vietnam, he turned his attention to the explosive Middle East. During the Arab-Israeli war of 1973, Secretary of State Henry Kissinger helped engineer a cease-fire, then traveled back and forth between countries trying to work out a peace treaty. The success of this "shuttle diplomacy" was limited but it did result in Egypt and Israel's agreement to pull back their troops and establish a buffer zone between them. By the 1990s, shuttle diplomacy had become an established way of negotiating disputes between nations.

The Nixon Years
1968–1974

*A*merican politics shifted dramatically in 1968, as violence and confrontation divided the country. Republican Richard Nixon capitalized on the disruption to gain the presidency. In office, Nixon was mainly interested in foreign affairs, and he took bold steps in changing relations with China and the Soviet Union. The Watergate scandal, involving Nixon's 1972 reelection campaign, angered Americans and forced Nixon to an action never before taken by a United States President.

Events in the United States

1968 Martin Luther King, Jr., and Robert Kennedy are assassinated. • Violence disrupts the Democratic National Convention.

1969 Richard Nixon is sworn in as President. • United States astronauts land on the moon.

1970 Four Kent State University students are killed by the Ohio National Guard at an antiwar protest.

1971 The Supreme Court allows school busing for desegregation.

| 1968 | 1969 | 1970 | 1971 |

Events in the World

1968 Pierre Trudeau is elected prime minister of Canada.

1969 Civil war continues in Nigeria.

1971 China is admitted to the United Nations. • Idi Amin seizes power in Uganda and begins a reign of terror.

▶ RESOURCE DIRECTORY

Teaching Resources

Alternate Lesson Plan: Demonstrating the Big Idea found in the Alternate Lesson Plans folder, p. 161, provides a lesson strategy to instruct students about the Big Idea that Republican President Richard Nixon's policies signaled a shift in national politics, but Nixon's leadership style ultimately led to scandal and personal ruin.

Alternative Assessment Handbook provides information, guidance, and strategies for alternative methods of assessment. It includes an essay on new trends in assessment, guidance and strategies for developing performance tasks and portfolios, scoring rubrics, and sample evaluation forms.

Pages 748–751

1968: A Turning Point in History

A crisis-filled year of assassinations, antiwar protest, and violence polarized the country in 1968. The turmoil paved the way for the election of Richard Nixon and the emergence of a Republican majority in national politics.

Pages 752–753

The Lasting Impact of the Year 1968

Pages 754–759

The Nixon Administration

Having gained the presidency, Richard Nixon was determined to maintain his power at all costs. He kept tight control of his administration and took a conservative direction on the national front.

Pages 760–764

Nixon's Foreign Policy

Nixon's main interest was in foreign affairs, where he made significant changes. Working closely with Henry Kissinger, he took dramatic steps toward new relationships with both China and the Soviet Union.

Pages 765–770

The Watergate Scandal

Richard Nixon was willing to use presidential power to do whatever was necessary to remain in the White House. Eventually this approach compromised the presidency itself. The resulting Watergate scandal angered the nation and moved Nixon to take drastic steps.

MR. PRESIDENT:
**RELEASE
the
TAPES!**

1972 Nixon visits China.
• Break-in at Democratic headquarters sets off the Watergate scandal.

1973 The Senate begins investigating the Watergate affair.
• Spiro Agnew resigns as Vice President.

1974 Nixon resigns the presidency.
• Vice President Gerald Ford becomes President.

1975 White House aides go to jail for Watergate crimes.

1972   **1973**   **1974**   **1975**   **1976**

1972 SALT I treaty between the United States and the Soviet Union limits nuclear weapons.

1973 The fourth Arab-Israeli war begins on Yom Kippur.
• OPEC places embargo on oil shipments.

1974 Writer Alexander Solzhenitsyn is exiled from the Soviet Union.

1975 Civil war begins in Lebanon.
• Mozambique wins independence from Portugal.

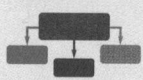

SECTION 1

1968: A Turning Point in History

1. FOCUS

Connecting to the Big Idea

See page 746B. Explain to students that in 1968 the American people endured a series of traumatic shocks, shaking the nation's faith in itself. Americans seemed interested in changing direction politically. Ask students how the Republicans and Richard Nixon took advantage of these changing attitudes.

Objectives

● Identify the Tet Offensive and its impact on American attitudes toward the Vietnam War.
● Explain the impact of the assassinations of Dr. Martin Luther King, Jr., and Robert Kennedy.
● Describe the events at the Democratic National Convention in Chicago and their effect on Democrats.
● Explain how public reaction against violence helped Republican Richard Nixon win the presidency.

Bellringer

Ask students to imagine the following situation: The United States is losing a war and violence is breaking out in cities across the country. How might the nation react under such circumstances? Who would be held responsible for the state of affairs?

SECTION PREVIEW

A crisis-filled year of assassinations, antiwar protest, and violence polarized the country in 1968. The turmoil paved the way for the election of Richard Nixon and the emergence of a Republican majority in national politics.

LBJ's political career is crushed in "The Time Machine," shown in this 1967 British cartoon.

Key Concepts
• The Tet Offensive increased protests over American involvement in Vietnam.
• The assassinations of Dr. Martin Luther King, Jr., and Robert Kennedy increased divisions in the country.
• Violence at the Democratic presidential convention polarized people politically and caused disunity in the party.
• Reaction against violence helped Republican Richard Nixon win the presidency.

Key Terms, People, and Places
Poor People's Campaign; Robert F. Kennedy, Eugene McCarthy, Hubert Humphrey, George C. Wallace, Richard M. Nixon, Spiro Agnew

I n the troubled decade of the 1960s, perhaps the most shattering year was 1968. A series of tragic events hit with such force that, month by month, the nation seemed to be coming apart. In the midst of the turmoil—and, in part, as a result of it—the way was paved for the election of Richard Nixon and the emergence of a Republican majority in national politics that would last for the next twenty years. The nation experienced an emotional shift as well as a political one. Against a backdrop of domestic violence, chaos, and confrontation, many Americans saw as hopeless the chance of achieving peaceful social change through political activism.

The Tet Offensive Increases Antiwar Sentiment at Home

The Vietnam War continued to rage in 1968. One encounter during the war had a profound effect on the American people and made 1968 a turning point in the conflict.

Beginning on January 30, the Viet Cong launched a massive three-week surprise attack against South Vietnam. While the Tet Offensive, as this attack was called, ended in military defeat for North Vietnam, it caused more and more Americans to question whether winning the Vietnam War was possible. After three years of escalation under the Johnson administration, many Americans wondered what had been achieved if the enemy could mount such a blistering offensive. Television news coverage of Tet increased the impact the attack had on the American public. Millions watched as news anchor Walter Cronkite, known for his objective viewpoint, said in February, "It now seems more certain than ever that the bloody experience in Vietnam is to end in stalemate."

After Tet, public opinion polls showed that a majority of Americans opposed the war. From a military perspective, Tet was a major defeat for the Viet Cong. But from a political perspective, it was a major defeat for the United States—and for the Johnson administration.

Popular Leaders Fall to Violence

For many Americans, the memory of President John F. Kennedy's assassination in 1963 was still vivid and haunting five years later. They looked to other leaders to carry on the spirit and idealism of the Kennedy years. But in 1968, people's hopes were again shattered by the burst of bullets from assassins' guns.

Tragedy Strikes The major spokesperson for African Americans in the decade after 1955 was Martin Luther King, Jr. By the mid-1960s,

King, convinced that poverty bred violence, broadened his crusade to attack all economic injustice.

In 1968 King began the **Poor People's Campaign,** planning a march on Washington like that in 1963. Traveling around the United States to mobilize support, he went to Memphis, Tennessee, in early April to support striking garbage workers seeking better working conditions. On April 3, King spoke eloquently, referring to threats made against his life:

*W*e've got some difficult days ahead. But it doesn't matter with me now, because I've been to the mountain top. And I don't mind. Like anybody, I would like to live a long life. . . . But I'm not concerned about that now. I just want to do God's will. And He's allowed me to go up to the mountain. And I've looked over. And I've seen the promised land.

The next day, as King stood on the balcony of his motel, a shot from a high-powered rifle ripped through his jaw. An hour later, King was dead.

King's assassination sparked violent reactions across the nation. In an outburst of rage and frustration, some African Americans rioted, setting fires and looting stores in 124 cities. Riots and police responses left forty-five people dead. President Johnson ordered flags on federal buildings to be flown at half-mast to honor King, but it took more than 5,500 troops to quell the violence. For many Americans of all races, the death of King eroded faith in the idea of nonviolent change.

Another Leader Falls **Robert F. Kennedy,** who had served his brother John as attorney general, was now running for President himself. Earlier in the year, in March, Senator **Eugene McCarthy** of Minnesota had come out against the war and challenged Lyndon Johnson in the New Hampshire Democratic primary. When McCarthy did well—42 percent to the President's 49 percent—Kennedy saw that

Seconds after shots ring out, Martin Luther King lies mortally wounded, while companions point frantically to the direction from which the shots were fired.

TURNING POINTS

Johnson was vulnerable and entered the campaign himself. Kennedy's bid received a critical boost later that month when, on March 31, LBJ addressed the American people on television. After announcing that he had ordered a reduction in the bombing of North Vietnam as a step toward furthering peace negotiations, Johnson stunned the nation by saying he would not run for a second term as President.

In the years since his brother's death, Bobby Kennedy had reached out to many Americans—Chicanos in the California fields, Native Americans in the Southwest, African Americans in the Mississippi delta, poor white families in New York tenements. Morally and politically opposed to the Vietnam War, he condemned the killing of both Americans and Vietnamese. And he criticized the Johnson administration for financing a war instead of the programs needed to help the poor and disadvantaged at home.

Kennedy spent the spring of 1968 battling McCarthy in the Democratic primary elections. In June he won a key victory in California's primary. But on the evening of the primary, after giving his victory speech, Robert Kennedy was shot by an assassin and died a day later.

When the shooting was reported, several campaign workers who had watched the speech

---

2. INSTRUCT

Explain/Discuss

Explain that the 1960s was a time of great political and social upheaval. Discuss the impact of the Tet Offensive. Encourage discussion by asking students why Tet made many Americans feel that they had been misled about the struggle in Vietnam.

Ask students to explain why the deaths of Robert Kennedy and Martin Luther King, Jr., led many to feel that their hopes for the future were disappearing. Why were these acts of violence a signal to many of a major social development?

Analyze

Ask students to examine the election of 1968 and explain how the Republicans benefited from the events taking place in the United States and in the Democratic party. Ask students if they think people generally hold a political party responsible for events in the country.

Activity

Writing a Letter to the Editor

Ask each student to assume the role of a Republican party official in 1968 and to write a letter to a newspaper editor encouraging voters to support Republican candidates in the 1968 elections.

Media and Technology

Visions of America: Turning Point Story To enhance students' understanding of the Turning Point topic in this section, play "Yearbook 1968," a story about the turbulent year of 1968 (length: approximately 4 minutes). This selection can be located on side 4 of the videodiscs. This selection can also be located on videotape 5. Lesson plans for Turning Point stories can be found in the Visions of America Teacher's Guidebook.

Side 4, Chapter 38

Visions of America: Roundtable Discussion To introduce students to different and differing viewponts in the Turning Point topic in this section, play all or part of the Roundtable Discussion on "Yearbook 1968," remarks by repected historians and social commentators. This selection can be located on side 4 of the videodiscs. This selection can also be located on the videotape 5.

Side 4, Chapter 39

In Depth

Multicultural Perspectives

The civil rights movement helped
transform the role of African

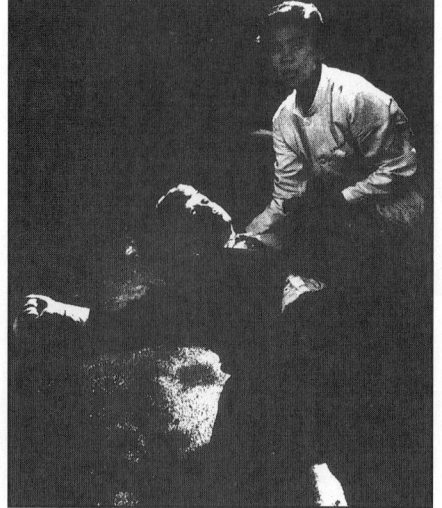

Busboy Juan Romero was the first to reach Robert Kennedy after he was shot in a hotel kitchen just after winning the California primary.

on TV were waiting for Kennedy in his Los Angeles hotel room. One of them, civil rights leader John Lewis, later said, "We all just fell to the floor and started crying. To me that was like the darkest, saddest moment." In a 1987 statement, Lewis also described the funeral journey to Arlington National Cemetery and reflected on the killings that had shattered the country:

> All along the way, you saw people coming up to the train crying and these hand-made signs saying, "We love you, Bobby," "Goodbye, Bobby," "God bless you, Bobby," and so forth. . . . Something was taken from us. The type of leadership that we had in a sense invested in, that we had helped to make and to nourish, was taken from us.

Kennedy's death ended many people's hopes for reform or reconciliation.

MAKING CONNECTIONS

Many people who lived through the 1960s would agree with John Lewis that the country lost its sense of hope after the assassinations. Do you think that people in the United States today have regained a sense of hope?

The 1968 Democratic Convention

By the time the Democrats convened in Chicago that summer, the party was in shreds. Eugene McCarthy was still a prominent antiwar candidate, but party regulars thought he was too far from the mainstream. They supported Vice President **Hubert Humphrey,** who had long been a strong advocate of social justice and civil rights.

Humphrey, however, was hurt by his support of administration policies on Vietnam. In the face of growing antiwar protest, he hardly seemed the one to bring the party together. Robert Kennedy, the one candidate who might have succeeded, was dead.

"The Whole World Is Watching" The prospect of thousands of demonstrators at the Democratic convention—radicals, peace marchers, hippies—enraged Chicago mayor Richard J. Daley. He had the convention hall protected by barbed wire and chain-link fencing. He also ordered police to clear out protesters gathered in Lincoln Park along the lake shore. As the police went in with tear gas and clubs, several violent confrontations took place.

The climax came as the delegates voted down a peace resolution and seemed ready to nominate Humphrey. As thousands of protesters gathered for a rally near the convention hotel, the police moved in, using their nightsticks to club anyone on the street, including passersby, hotel guests, and reporters.

Historian Theodore H. White, the even-handed chronicler of presidential elections, recorded the scene this way:

> Slam! Like a fist jolting, like a piston exploding from its chamber, comes a hurtling column of police . . . into the intersection, and all things happen too fast: first the charge as the police wedge cleaves through the mob; then screams, whistles, confusion . . . And as the scene clears, there are little knots in the open clearing—police clubbing youngsters, police dragging youngsters, police rushing them by the elbows, their heels dragging, to patrol wagons.

Much of the violence took place in front of television cameras, while crowds chanted "The whole world is watching." As convention delegates voted, Senator Abraham Ribicoff of Connecticut denounced the "Gestapo tactics on the streets of Chicago," provoking an angry scene with Daley. Humphrey was nominated, but the party had been torn apart.

Wallace Woos Voters Adding to the Democrats' problems was a third-party candidate in the race. Alabama governor **George C. Wallace** had gained national fame for playing on racial tensions among southerners. Now he turned to blue-collar voters in the North who resented campus radicals and liberal antiwar forces. Wallace won support by attacking "left-wing theoreticians, briefcase-totin' bureaucrats, ivory-tower guideline writers, bearded anarchists, smart-aleck editorial writers and pointy-headed professors."

The Election of 1968

The Republicans chose **Richard M. Nixon,** who had narrowly lost to John Kennedy in 1960. In his campaign, Nixon backed law and order and claimed to have a secret plan to end the war in Vietnam. Earlier, Nixon had often seemed harsh and angry, but this time he let his running mate, Governor **Spiro Agnew** of Maryland,

Determined to stop protests at the 1968 Democratic Convention, Chicago police and National Guardsmen used nightsticks, tear gas, and rifles against demonstrators and others who were caught up in the violence.

deliver nasty rhetoric, such as calling Humphrey "squishy soft" on communism.

Nixon's campaign was well run and well financed. Late in the campaign, Humphrey began to catch up. But even though President Johnson stopped the bombing of North Vietnam on October 31, it was too late. Many disillusioned Democrats stayed home on election day, voting for no one.

In the popular vote, Nixon squeaked by with only 43.4 percent—less than one percentage point ahead of Humphrey's 42.7 percent. Wallace won the rest. Although Democrats kept control of both houses of Congress, the Republicans were back in the White House.

TURNING POINTS

SECTION 1 REVIEW

Key Terms, People, and Places
1. Define Poor People's Campaign.
2. Identify (a) Robert F. Kennedy, (b) Eugene McCarthy, (c) Hubert Humphrey, (d) George C. Wallace, (e) Richard M. Nixon, (f) Spiro Agnew.

Key Concepts
3. How did the Tet Offensive contribute to the turbulence of 1968?

4. What were some aftereffects of the assassination of Martin Luther King, Jr.?
5. From what groups did Wallace try to attract support?
6. What issues did Nixon emphasize in his campaign?

Critical Thinking
7. **Recognizing Cause and Effect** How did the assassination of Robert Kennedy affect the chances of the Democrats in the 1968 presidential election?

Quiz found in the Unit 7 folder, p. 8, covers the main ideas in this section as well as the key terms.

Media and Technology
Transparency
Time Lines, E-9

3. ASSESS

Section 1 Review Answers
1. Poor People's Campaign, see p. 749
2. (a) Robert F. Kennedy, see p. 749, (b) Eugene McCarthy, see p. 749, (c) Hubert Humphrey, see p. 750, (d) George C. Wallace, see p. 751, (e) Richard M. Nixon, see p. 751, (f) Spiro Agnew, see p. 751

3. Since the enemy was able to mount such a successful attack in spite of escalation during the Johnson administration, many Americans began to question the possibility of winning the war. Also, television news coverage of Tet increased the awareness of the American public.

4. It destroyed people's confidence in the possibility of peaceful reform, convinced many African Americans that nonviolence did not work, and caused angry riots in many American cities.

5. White conservative southerners, northern blue-collar Democrats.

6. He tried to appeal to conservatives and blue-collar workers, emphasizing law and order and an end to unrest; he promised a plan to end the war in Vietnam.

7. It hurt Democratic chances; antiwar supporters found it hard to support Humphrey; Kennedy was probably the only candidate who could have united the party.

Reteach

Have students create a time line of the events of 1968. Students should be able to explain the significance of each event they include.

4. CLOSE

Reinforcing the Big Idea

The traumatic events of 1968 revealed the deep divisions in the nation and helped clear the way for a Republican victory. The next section examines the domestic policies introduced by President Richard Nixon as he sought to lead the country in a more conservative direction.

CHAPTER 23 SECTION 1   **751**

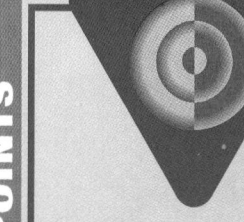
The Lasting Impact of the Year 1968

Focus Events of the year 1968 helped lead to a shift in the direction of the nation's domestic and foreign policies. Attitudes toward the nation's use of military power changed dramatically, and the government sharply reduced its commitment to social programs. Ask students to describe how the events of 1968 helped to shape the political world in which they live today.

Instruct Remind students that the war in Vietnam had resulted from an aggressive policy, which many Americans supported, of resisting communist expansion around the world. The failure of the United States in Vietnam gave the nation reason to question that policy. The failure also caused people to question the authority of the President alone to commit the nation to armed conflict. Ask students to review Article I, Section 8, Clause 11, and Article II, Section 2, Clause 1, of the Constitution. In what ways do these two clauses leave open the question of whether or not a President alone can commit the nation to war?

Review also with students massive government programs such as the New Deal and the Great Society, which greatly expanded government's role in people's lives. Following the election of 1968, the federal government slowly retreated from some of those programs. After Ronald Reagan was elected President in 1980, many social programs were drastically cut. Ask students to discuss current attitudes toward government support for programs such as welfare, social security, or health care.

Extend Have students work in pairs to research and prepare a report on the War Powers Act. Students should research the congressional debate on this act, and examine the ongoing debate over the constitutionality of the War Powers Act, particularly in the Reagan and Bush administrations. Students can present their findings in an oral or written report.

The Lasting Impact of the Year 1968

The year 1968 was a turning point in American political life, bringing a shift in the direction of both foreign and domestic policies. The turmoil of the year also had a psychological impact on many people.

Foreign Policy Attitudes

The turbulence sparked by Vietnam, which reached a peak in 1968, destroyed the nation's consensus on foreign policy. Now many Americans wondered whether they could—or should—support the aims of the United States around the world. Questions about Vietnam would haunt the country for decades.

Presidential War Powers Opposition to the war also brought a challenge to the President's powers as commander in chief. Many Americans were disturbed by the way Lyndon Johnson had maneuvered the United States into Vietnam and by Nixon's order to bomb Cambodia, thereby escalating the war. The War Powers Act, passed over Nixon's veto in 1973, required the President to notify Congress quickly if troops were sent overseas. The act then required congressional approval of such troop movements.

The war powers issue continued to cause controversy. In the Reagan administration, for example, members of Congress filed lawsuits to stop military actions in Central America and on the island of Grenada. The question arose again in 1990 when President George Bush sent American troops to Kuwait after the Iraqi invasion. Bush finally asked for—and got—Congress's approval of the Persian Gulf War.

1977 When Jimmy Carter won the presidency, he served as a lone Democrat in the midst of over twenty years of Republicans in the White House.

| 1980 | 1982 | 1984 |

1984 Despite protests from members of Congress, President Reagan orders military action in Grenada.

RESOURCE DIRECTORY

Teaching Resources

Turning Points Extension Activity
The Lasting Impact of the Year 1968, found in the Unit 7 folder, pp. 15–16, focuses on the election of President Nixon as a turning point in U.S. relations with communist powers.

Changes at Home

In domestic affairs, the events of 1968 brought significant change, both political and social. As the war eroded many "Great Society" programs, conservative Americans challenged the entire liberal approach toward government assistance for those in need. Since Franklin Roosevelt's New Deal in the 1930s, the range of social programs had grown. Few people wanted to eliminate programs like social security or Medicare, but Republicans were committed to cutting back the role of government. Winning the White House in 1968 gave them the chance to do so. Their successors went even further—in particular, the Reagan administration in the 1980s drastically cut funds for social programs.

The 1968 election also brought an end to the Democratic domination of national politics that had lasted for more than thirty years. Joined together by President Roosevelt in 1936, the party included working-class Americans, first- and second-generation immigrants, and African Americans. The events of 1968 split that group. What followed was seen by some analysts as an emerging Republican majority. Although a Democrat won the White House in 1976, Republicans won the presidency in every other election from 1980 to 1988. In congressional politics, Republicans encouraged the growth of a new conservative movement, reflected in legislation and in several significant decisions by the Supreme Court.

Emotionally, the violence of 1968 also left its mark on the nation, ending what for many had been an era of idealism. After Bobby Kennedy's death, civil rights worker John Lewis said:

> There are people today who are afraid, in a sense, to hope or to have hope again, because of what happened in 1963, and particularly what happened in 1968.

REVIEWING THE FACTS

1. What groups were included in the old Democratic party?
2. What was the significance of Richard Nixon's victory in 1968?

Critical Thinking

3. **Identifying Assumptions** Why did Congress believe it was necessary to pass the War Powers Act in 1973?

1980s Republicans continued their push for a new conservative movement with Supreme Court nominations that moved the Court to the right.

1991 The question of presidential war powers arose again when President George Bush sent troops to the Persian Gulf.

1986   1988   1990

1989 As social programs were cut back during the years of Republican government, homelessness and other local problems increased.

Answers

1. It included working-class Americans, first- and second-generation immigrants, African Americans, and women.

2. It marked the end of the Democratic coalition that had governed since the 1930s and signaled a shift in the course of both foreign and domestic policy.

3. Congress felt that it needed to reassert its control of war making, because President Johnson had maneuvered the country into deep involvement in Vietnam and Nixon had ordered the bombing of Cambodia without Congress's approval.

The Nixon Administration

The Nixon Administration

1. FOCUS

Connecting to the Big Idea

See page 746B. Explain that as President, Nixon employed a closed, secretive style in his effort to steer the nation in a more conservative direction than had his Democratic predecessors. Ask how Nixon's style influenced his presidency.

Objectives

• Describe Nixon's reserved, secretive style and how it influenced his administration.
• Explain how Nixon sought to take a more conservative stance with regard to economic policies and crime.
• Explain how Nixon tried to slow the pace of civil rights advances as part of an effort to win white support in the South.

Bellringer

Write the word *leadership* on the chalkboard. Ask students to brainstorm a list of words and ideas they associate with this term. Explain that Nixon, upon taking office, exercised a new type of leadership.

Reading Strategy

Reinforcing Key Ideas Have students write two column headings on a piece of paper: Nixon's Personality and Nixon's Domestic Policies. As they read the section, students

SECTION PREVIEW

Having gained the presidency, Richard Nixon was determined to maintain his power at all costs. He kept tight control of his administration and took a conservative direction on the national front.

Key Concepts

• Nixon's reserved, secretive personality influenced his staff and his style of governing.
  • Nixon tried to take a more conservative stance in dealing with the economy and with issues such as law and order.
    • Nixon slowed the advancement of civil rights with his policies, aimed in part at winning support in the South.

Key Terms, People, and Places

imperial presidency, Organization of Petroleum Exporting Countries (OPEC), embargo, busing; Henry A. Kissinger, H. R. Haldeman, John Ehrlichman, John Mitchell

This crocheted replica of the presidential seal was sent to President Nixon by a well-wisher early in his presidency.

R ichard Nixon had struggled hard during a twenty-year political career mixed with setbacks and successes. He suffered a number of bitter defeats but came back to national politics each time. Having worked hard to gain the presidency, he was determined to maintain strict control over his administration.

Nixon in Person

Richard Nixon was a shy and remote man. Although uncomfortable with people, he put up a front when he campaigned, and he used new techniques such as television to good advantage. He often seemed stiff and lacking in humor and charm, however. Many Americans respected Nixon for his abilities and his skillful handling of the vice presidency under Eisenhower, but many others neither trusted nor liked him.

Nixon's family was poor, and he never got over his sense of being an outsider. In 1963 he described how that feeling drove him to achieve:

> W hat starts the process really are laughs and slights and snubs when you are a kid. Sometimes it's because you're poor or Irish or Jewish or Catholic or ugly or simply that you are skinny. But if you are reasonably intelligent and if your anger is deep enough and strong enough, you learn that you can change those attitudes by excellence, personal gut performance.

According to Pat Buchanan, then a Nixon speech writer, there was "a mean side to his nature." He was willing to say or do anything to defeat his enemies. Adlai Stevenson, who ran

Despite his shy personality, Nixon knew how to play a crowd and often put on an "imperial" aspect when appearing in public.

unsuccessfully for the presidency twice in the 1950s, spoke of a place called "Nixonland—a land of slander and scare, of sly innuendo, of a poison pen, the anonymous phone call, and hustling, pushing, shoving—the land of smash and grab and anything to win."

Nixon had few close friends, insulating himself from people and the press. He took support and security from his family—his wife, Pat, and their two daughters. Away from the White House, he secluded himself at his estates in Florida and California, both lavishly redone at government expense. He dreamed of what historian Arthur Schlesinger, Jr., has called an **imperial presidency,** meaning an executive branch that dominates the branches of government to an extreme degree. By his own choice, his administration reflected a closed, secretive style. ⭐

Nixon's Top Staff People

Nixon's staff gave him support and loyalty. His cabinet members were all wealthy, white, male Republicans, sympathetic to his views. Yet Nixon generally worked around his cabinet and more often relied on a few other key appointees for advice.

One was **Henry A. Kissinger,** a Harvard government professor, who joined the Nixon administration as head of the National Security Council and in 1973 became Nixon's secretary of state. He played a major role in shaping foreign policy, both as an adviser to the President and in behind-the-scenes diplomacy.

Two influential staff members shielded Nixon from the outside world and carried out his orders. **H. R. Haldeman,** an advertising executive who had campaigned tirelessly for Nixon, became chief of staff. He once observed, "I get done what he wants done and I take the heat instead of him."

The Oval Office in the White House saw many meetings of Nixon and his inner circle of close advisers— here, left to right, are Kissinger, Ehrlichman, the President, and Haldeman.

Lawyer **John Ehrlichman** served first as legal counselor, then rose to the post of chief domestic adviser. He and Haldeman framed issues and narrowed options for the President. Together they became known as the "Berlin Wall" for the way they protected Nixon's privacy.

Finally, there was **John Mitchell,** a lawyer who had worked with Nixon in New York and then managed his campaign. He was named attorney general and wielded great influence, speaking with Nixon several times a day. White House staff members called Mitchell "El Supremo" for his stature as a top aide.

MAKING CONNECTIONS

A President's personality can greatly affect the style and actions of an administration. What kind of personalities have recent Presidents such as Reagan, Bush, and Clinton had?

Domestic Policy Issues: A Different Direction

The Vietnam War and domestic issues had both been important in the 1968 political campaigns. Domestically, Nixon took a different course than his Democratic predecessors.

Economic Problems The economy was shaky when Nixon took office. Largely because of spending for the Vietnam War, inflation had doubled between 1965 and 1968. At the same time, unemployment continued to grow. Nixon's first priority was to halt inflation. He felt that federal spending had gotten out of control and wanted to cut back, even if it led to further unemployment.

At the same time, he was determined to avoid economic controls. He had seen such controls in action while working for the Office of Price Administration during World War II. "I will not take the nation down the road of wage and price controls, however politically expedient they may seem," he said in 1970.

During his first few years in office, however, controlling spending proved difficult. Both unemployment and inflation continued to rise. Lawrence O'Brien, head of the Democratic National Committee, called the new situation "Nixonomics":

> *All the things that should go up—the stock market, corporate profits, real spendable income, productivity—go down, and all the things that should go down— unemployment, prices, interest rates—go up.*

Although Republicans traditionally aimed for a balanced budget, Nixon began to consider deficit spending—spending beyond the budget in order to stimulate the economy. This was the approach that English economist John Maynard Keynes had called for during the Depression and that many Democrats had supported. "I am now a Keynesian in economics," Nixon announced in 1971, to the surprise of many.

⭐ To slow the high rate of inflation, shown in the graph below, he imposed a ninety-day freeze on wages, prices, and rents, but then pressure from business and labor led him to lift controls. Inflation soared again.

Unrest in the Middle East brought more disruptions to the troubled economy. Americans depended on cheap, imported oil for about a third of their energy needs. But in 1973, Israel and the Arab nations of Egypt and Syria went to war. When the United States backed its ally Israel, the Arab members of the **Organization of Petroleum Exporting Countries** (OPEC) angrily responded by imposing an **embargo,** or restriction, on oil shipped to the United States. OPEC, a group of nations that sets oil prices and production, also quadrupled its prices. Oil prices soared, even after the embargo ended in 1974. The map on page 757 shows the nations that belong to OPEC.

The oil crisis affected everyone. A loaf of bread that had cost twenty-eight cents earlier in the 1970s now was eighty-nine cents. Americans

Because Americans depended so heavily on oil from the Middle East for gasoline and heating fuel, Arab oil producers had an effective weapon in the threat of raising prices.

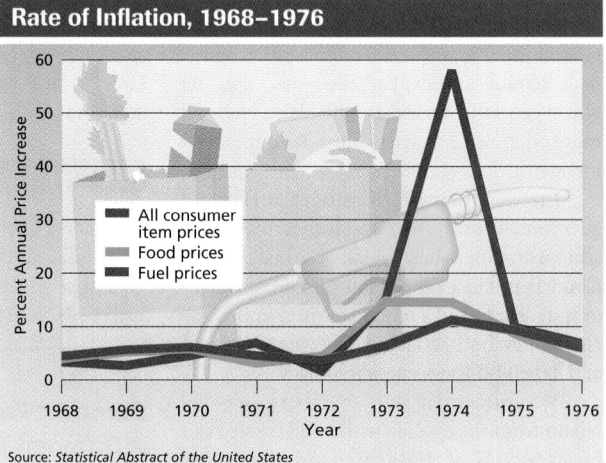

Rate of Inflation, 1968–1976

Percent Annual Price Increase (y-axis: 0, 10, 20, 30, 40, 50, 60)

Legend:
■ All consumer item prices
■ Food prices
■ Fuel prices

Year (x-axis): 1968, 1969, 1970, 1971, 1972, 1973, 1974, 1975, 1976

Source: *Statistical Abstract of the United States*

Interpreting Graphs
Rising oil prices in the 1970s had a strong impact on all parts of the American economy. *When did oil prices reach their peak? How long did high prices last?*

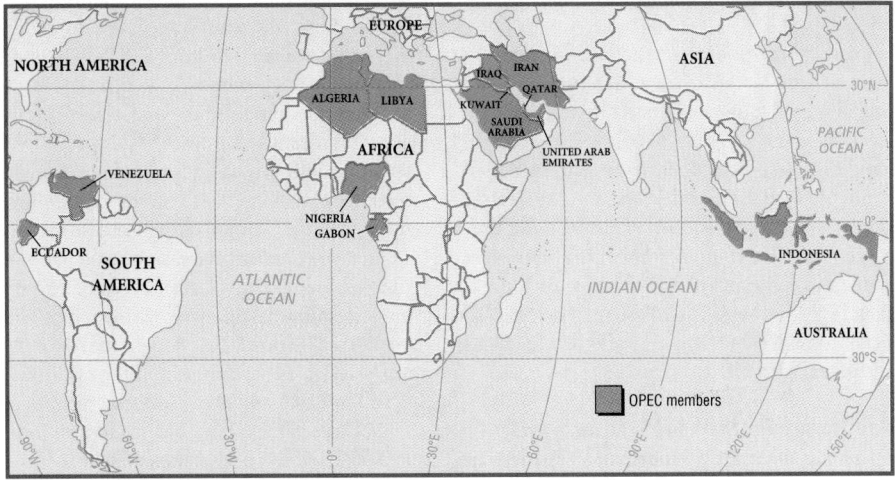

Organization of Petroleum Exporting Countries (OPEC), c. 1970

OPEC members

 Geography and History: Interpreting Maps
OPEC brought together the world's major oil producers. *In what region of the world are many of these nations concentrated? What political effects did this have? What oil-producing nations are located in the Americas?*

who were used to paying twenty-five cents a gallon for gas now paid sixty-five cents. Higher energy prices fueled inflation, which in turn led consumers to cut back on spending. The result was another recession. Unemployment reached 9 percent, the highest rate since the 1930s.

Social Programs Meanwhile, Nixon was trying to stop the growth of government spending on social programs that were part of Lyndon Johnson's Great Society. Critics claimed that the programs were wasteful, encouraged "welfare cheaters," and discouraged people from seeking work.

Nixon had exploited that frustration in his campaign, but he now faced a dilemma. On the one hand, he wanted to please conservative voters in the South who demanded cutbacks. On the other hand, he hoped to appeal to traditionally Democratic blue-collar voters, who wanted to keep the programs that benefited them.

The administration suggested a work-incentive program that would give families a basic minimum income, while requiring them to register for job training and accept a job when one was found. The Family Assistance

Plan failed to pass the Senate but did gain Nixon political points with some voters.

Law and Order Another important campaign issue had been the need to restore "law and order" in the country. President Nixon recognized that a strong backlash had developed against student radicals, antiwar protesters, and the youth counterculture in general. Many older working-class and middle-class Americans held those groups responsible not only for demonstrations in the streets but also for rising crime, growing drug use, and permissive attitudes toward sex.

 To strengthen his position on law and order, Nixon's strategy was to discourage any kind of protest. In speeches, he lashed out at all demonstrators, once calling students "bums." After National Guardsmen shot and killed student protesters at Kent State University, Nixon implied that the students themselves had caused the tragedy. Speaking at Kansas State University later in 1970, he said:

The time has come for us to recognize that violence and terror have no place in a free society. Whatever the purported

Media and Technology

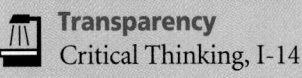 **Transparency**
Critical Thinking, I-14

Enrichment
To help students gain a better insight into the racial climate during the Nixon administration, ask them to research the history of busing as a means of integrating schools. Students should prepare a brief report demonstrating the successes and failures of busing. Reports may take the form of a photo or video montage.

Caption Answer to ...

Interpreting Maps

Africa and the Middle East; strained relations between the United States and these countries; Venezuela and Ecuador.

In Depth

Interdisciplinary

In July 1969, after nine years of preparation, Americans set out to land on the moon. Manned by astronauts Collins, Armstrong, and Aldrin, *Apollo 11* (see pages 634–635) successfully completed its mission. It was not only an unprecedented scientific and technical achievement, but it also diverted attention from the social unrest rocking the United States at the time. Part of the lunar module remains on the moon with a plaque that, rather than boasting of an American achievement, proclaims the hope of the world: "Here men from the planet earth first set foot upon the moon, July 1969, A.D. We came in peace for all mankind."

[supposed] *cause of the perpetrators may be . . . no cause justifies violence.*

Other members of the administration backed him up. Attorney General Mitchell stepped up the Justice Department's campaign against crime. Using his gift for colorful rhetoric, Vice President Spiro Agnew called student protesters and professors an "effete corps of impudent snobs," *effete* meaning they were weak and *impudent* meaning they were rude and disrespectful. Unhappy with press coverage of the White House, Agnew also accused television reporters and producers of distorting administration actions.

The "Southern Strategy" Nixon felt that he had little to gain by supporting advances in civil rights. Few African Americans had voted for him in the 1960 race against John Kennedy, and in 1968 he had gotten just 12 percent of the black vote. Besides, he reasoned, any attempt to court the black electorate could threaten the white southern vote in a reelection bid. Thus, while there were some civil rights gains in the Nixon years, the record was generally weak.

Explaining his position, Nixon once observed that "there are those who want instant integration and those who want segregation forever. I believe that we need to have a middle course between those two extremes." Given the strong resistance to change that persisted in many places, this meant a slowdown in desegregation.

Nixon's aim was to find the proper "southern strategy" to win over the Democratic white South. Senator Strom Thurmond of South Carolina, who had left the Democratic party in 1948, was now a Republican and became Nixon's strongest southern supporter. To keep him and his colleagues happy, Nixon sought to reduce the appropriation needed for enforcing fair housing, and he eased guidelines for desegregation.

The Justice Department, headed by John Mitchell, tried to prevent the extension of the Voting Rights Act of 1965, which had greatly increased the number of African Americans who could vote in the South. Congress went ahead with the extension, but Nixon had made his point to white southern voters.

Another controversial issue was the use of **busing** to end school segregation. In several cities, federal courts ordered school systems to

| 1650 | 1700 | 1750 | 1800 | **Links Across Time** | 1850 | 1900 | 1950 | 2000 |

To Coin a Phrase

The language of American politics gained a new entry when Spiro Agnew uttered the phrase "effete corps of impudent snobs" in a speech he made in 1969. American political language has had a long and colorful past. Since the early republic, American politicians have invented their own words and phrases or borrowed them from other people, such as journalists or members of the military. Some of the terms and phrases coined by politicians from the past to the present include:

silk stocking A wealthy person; dates back to colonial times when only the rich could afford to wear silk stockings.

cookie pusher A diplomat who spends time attending social teas rather than doing any real work; dates from the 1940s.

fishing expedition An investigation with no specific goal, usually made by one political party into the business of another; popularized in the 1940s.

pooh-bah A self-important high official; a popular term in American politics since the 1950s.

nervous Nellies People who become easily disturbed or upset; popularized by President Johnson,

who used the term to describe some critics of his policy in Vietnam.

waxworks The honored guests at a political dinner who sit on a raised platform, so named because of the frozen, or waxen, smiles they keep on their faces; dates from the late 1960s.

break all the china To obey an order regardless of the obstacles; a favorite Nixon phrase.

FOB Friend of Bill's; a phrase meant to describe a personal friend of President Clinton, popularized in the press since Clinton's inauguration.

How might a term or a phrase coined by a politician become commonly used by Americans?

bus students to other schools to end the pattern of all-black or all-white schools. Particularly in northern cities, such as Detroit and Boston, some white students and their parents met incoming black students with boycotts or violent protests.

In 1971 guidelines for busing were laid down by a Supreme Court decision that went against Nixon's views. A federal judge in North Carolina had ruled that voluntary integration efforts were not working. In *Swann* v. *Charlotte-Mecklenburg Board of Education,* the Court agreed, saying that busing was one possible option for ending school desegregation.

Nixon had long been opposed to busing. He now went on national television to say that he would ask Congress to halt it. He also allowed the Department of Health, Education, and Welfare to restore federal funding to school districts where segregation persisted. Although busing continued in some places, Nixon's position was clear to voters in the South.

Nixon and the Supreme Court

During the campaign, Nixon had criticized the Supreme Court as too liberal and soft on criminals. In his first term, four justices died, resigned, or retired, giving him the extraordinary opportunity to name four new justices and thus reshape the Court. He first named Warren Burger as Chief Justice, replacing Earl Warren. Burger was a moderate who was easily confirmed by the Senate.

Later nominations reflected Nixon's southern strategy and conservative views. The Senate rejected his first nominees from the South: Clement Haynsworth of South Carolina and G. Harrold Carswell of Florida. Opponents

These demonstrators expressed their unhappiness with busing by burying a school bus and erecting the following epitaph nearby: "Here lies a school bus/No mourning from us./No more fuming/No more fussing/May this be the end of busing."

charged that both choices showed racial bias. Haynsworth was also suspected of conflict of interest in some court rulings, while Carswell was seen as intellectually mediocre. Bitterly, Nixon told the press, "I cannot successfully nominate to the Supreme Court any federal appellate judge from the South who believes as I do in the strict construction of the Constitution." Eventually Nixon appointed Harry A. Blackmun, Lewis F. Powell, Jr., and William H. Rehnquist, all qualified jurists, who generally tilted the Court in a more conservative direction.

While Nixon developed domestic policies to "bring Americans together again," as he said in his inaugural speech, he took a greater interest in what he could do to shape foreign policy. The outcome of his plans to play an important role in world affairs is discussed in the next section.

SECTION 2 REVIEW

Key Terms, People, and Places
1. Define (a) imperial presidency, (b) OPEC, (c) embargo, (d) busing.
2. Identify (a) Henry A. Kissinger, (b) H. R. Haldeman, (c) John Ehrlichman, (d) John Mitchell.

Key Concepts
3. What steps did Nixon take to fix the economy?

4. Why did Nixon strongly advocate law and order?
5. What was Nixon's "southern strategy"?

Critical Thinking
6. **Determining Relevance** How did Nixon's background and philosophy influence his style of governing?

Quiz found in the Unit 7 folder, p. 10, covers the main ideas in this section as well as the key terms.

Reteach
Ask students to review the lists and notes they created during the Reading Strategy exercise for this section. Have students use the information they gathered to describe briefly the key features of Nixon's staff and the administration's domestic policy.

Alternative Assessment

Mid-Point Monitoring
Ask students if they have
● Created an outline for their profile
● Identified materials to incorporate into their profile
● Begun research on Nixon's presidency

 **4. CLOSE**

Reinforcing the Big Idea
In the domestic sphere, Nixon tried to take the nation in a new, more conservative direction than Johnson and Kennedy before him. The next section examines Nixon's efforts in the foreign policy field.

Nixon's Foreign Policy

SECTION PREVIEW

Nixon's main interest was in foreign affairs, where he made significant changes. Working closely with Henry Kissinger, he took dramatic steps toward new relationships with both China and the Soviet Union.

Key Concepts

• Henry Kissinger played an important role in shaping the foreign policy of the Nixon administration.

• Nixon took bold steps in relaxing international tensions.

• Nixon reversed American policy in relations with the People's Republic of China.

• The United States and the Soviet Union moved toward arms control.

Key Terms, People, and Places

realpolitik, détente, Strategic Arms Limitation Talks (SALT)

This panda bear was one of two given to the people of the United States from the People's Republic of China on the occasion of President Nixon's visit there in 1972.

A s President, Nixon's greatest achievements were in the field of foreign policy. "I've always thought this country could run itself domestically without a President," he once observed. He understood the implications of strategic planning and diplomacy in foreign affairs, and took a creative approach that helped ease the tensions of the cold war. Aided by the skillful diplomacy of Henry Kissinger, Nixon opened the way to establishing relations with China and crafted a better relationship with the Soviet Union.

AMERICAN PROFILES

Henry Kissinger

While Nixon had an astute grasp of foreign policy, he still relied heavily on Henry Kissinger in charting his course. The German-born Kissinger quickly gained the President's confidence and became a dominant figure in the administration.

Henry (originally Heinz) Kissinger came from a Jewish family that fled Nazi Germany in 1938 when he was fifteen. The Kissingers settled in New York City that same year. In New York, Kissinger worked during the day at a shaving brush company, finished high school at night, and then attended City College. He was drafted in 1943, and an army teacher and historian encouraged him to go to Harvard University at the end of the war. There he completed both undergraduate and graduate degrees and wrote his doctoral dissertation on Klemens von Metternich, a nineteenth-century Austrian statesman and diplomat who helped maintain stability in Europe in the face of liberal change. Kissinger's studies gave him an admiration for *realpolitik,* a German term for "practical politics" based on achieving power.

On the faculty at Harvard, Kissinger rose quickly through university positions, gaining a reputation for being brilliant but arrogant and abrasive. By 1962 he was a full professor of government.

Outside the university, Kissinger soon became a recognized expert on foreign relations. His first book, *Nuclear Weapons and Foreign Policy,* published in 1957, argued that President Eisenhower's doctrine of massive retaliation was a mistake, and that a limited nuclear war could be fought successfully. He also worked with Nelson Rockefeller, governor of New York, who recommended him to Nixon.

Kissinger understood how to deal with the insecure President. Nixon needed to be flattered, and he liked people who could talk tough. Kissinger was willing to accommodate him and soon became the man Nixon talked to most. "Henry, of course, was not a personal friend," Nixon later said, but the two spoke five

Henry Kissinger was a major architect of American foreign policy in the 1970s.

or six times a day, sometimes in person, sometimes by phone, and often for hours at a time.

Kissinger's actual influence in shaping American foreign policy was broader than his official roles—first as national security adviser and then as secretary of state. He knew how to frame questions in ways the President wanted. He could distill foreign policy issues into briefing papers that gave Nixon options for making decisions. In his memoirs, Kissinger wrote:

> N ixon could be very decisive. Almost invariably during his Presidency his decisions were courageous and strong and often taken in loneliness against all expert advice. But wherever possible Nixon made these decisions in solitude on the basis of memoranda or with a few very intimate aides.

Kissinger saw to it that he was with the President when such decisions were made.

Both men were suspicious and secretive. Together, they took an almost conspiratorial approach to foreign policy. "They tried not to let anyone else have a full picture, even if it meant deceiving them," Lawrence Eagleburger, a State Department official, observed.

Kissinger also had a remarkable ability to manipulate the press. Journalists depended on him for stories and were wary of antagonizing him. A *Time* magazine reporter noted how Kissinger worked: "You know you are being played like a violin, but it's still extremely seductive."

His efforts in ending the Vietnam War and easing cold war tensions made Kissinger a celebrity. He shared the 1973 Nobel Peace Prize with North Vietnam's Le Duc Tho (who refused it), appeared on twenty-one *Time* covers, and in 1973 was first in a Gallup Poll listing the most-admired Americans. He left a lasting mark on American foreign policy.

Superpower Tensions Relax

Nixon's greatest accomplishment was in bringing about **détente,** a relaxation in the tensions between the superpowers. This role was ironic, for in the 1950s Richard Nixon had been one of the most bitter and active anticommunists in government. He had made his reputation as someone willing to demand extraordinary action in response to the communist threat. As President, however, Nixon dealt imaginatively with both China and the Soviet Union. Bypassing Congress, and often bypassing his own advisers, he and Kissinger reversed the direction of postwar American foreign policy.

Nixon drew on Kissinger's understanding that foreign affairs were more complex than a simple standoff between the United States and the threat of communism. Kissinger pointed out that there were deep rifts in the communist world itself, noting, "The deepest international conflict in the world today is not between us and the Soviet Union but between the Soviet Union and Communist China."

A New Approach to China

The most surprising policy shift was toward China. When the communist revolution ended in 1949, establishing the People's Republic of China, Americans saw all communists in Asia

Explain/Discuss

Discuss the role of Henry Kissinger in shaping Nixon's foreign policy. What skills made Kissinger such a valued aide? What did he offer Nixon that other advisers could not?

Tell students that United States–China relations were tense during Nixon's presidency. Ask how Nixon's reputation as a strong anticommunist enabled him to approach China. Ask what might have happened had a President with weaker anticommunist credentials attempted a similar maneuver.

Analyze

Analyze Nixon's effort to play one communist country off against the other. Ask how such efforts would improve the position of the United States. Help students see that Nixon believed that if the United States became friendly with China, the Soviet Union would grow insecure and more willing to get closer to the United States.

In Depth

Then and Now

By the 1990s détente no longer defined United States foreign policy. But traditional alliances have prolonged the civil war in Bosnia-Herzegovina (see Chapter 26, pages 847–848) and increased the dangers of prolonged conflict. Russia has sided with its old allies and fellow Slavs, the Serbs, while the United States and its Western allies have sided with the Serbs' Muslim and Croat enemies.

The President and First Lady Pat Nixon head a group touring the Great Wall of China on this historic first visit to the People's Republic of China.

as part of a united plot to dominate the world. Ignoring reality, the United States did not extend formal diplomatic recognition to the new Chinese government—in effect, officially pretending instead that it did not exist. Even when a Chinese-Soviet alliance crumbled, the United States clung to its rigid position. It insisted that the government of Chiang Kai-shek, set up on the island of Taiwan when the Nationalists fled the Chinese mainland, was the rightful government of all China.

Quietly, Nixon began to prepare the way for change. In his inaugural address in 1969, he referred indirectly to China when he declared, "We seek an open world . . . a world in which no people, great or small, will live in angry isolation." His first foreign policy report to Congress in 1970 began:

> T he Chinese are a great and vital people who should not remain isolated from the international community. . . . United States policy is not likely soon to have much impact on China's behavior, let alone its

ideological outlook. But it is certainly in our interest, and in the interest of peace and stability in Asia and the world, that we take what steps we can toward improved practical relations with Peking [Beijing].

The next year, the administration relaxed some regulations toward China. Then the Chinese invited an American table-tennis team to visit the mainland, and the United States began to ease some trading restrictions. In July 1971, after extensive secret diplomacy by Kissinger, Nixon made the dramatic announcement that he planned to visit China the following year. He would be the first United States President to travel to that country.

Nixon understood that the People's Republic was an established government and would not simply disappear. Other nations had recognized the new government, and it was time for the United States to do the same. Similarly, other countries wanted to give China's seat in the United Nations to the People's Republic, and the United States could no longer muster international opinion against this change.

Nixon had other motives as well. He recognized that he could use Chinese friendship as a bargaining chip in his negotiations with the Soviet Union. Press coverage of the trip would give him a boost at home. Also, he believed that he could take the action without political damage, because of his past reputation as a strong anticommunist.

✪ Nixon traveled to China in February 1972. He met with Mao Zedong, the Chinese leader who had spearheaded the revolution in 1949. He spoke with Premier Zhou Enlai about international problems and ways of dealing with them. He and his wife, Pat, toured the Great Wall and other Chinese sights, all in front of television cameras that sent historic pictures home. When he returned to the United States, he waited in his plane until prime time so his return would be seen by as many television viewers as possible. Formal relations were not yet restored—that would take a few more years—but the basis for diplomatic ties had been established.

Strengthening Ties with the Soviet Union

At the same time that he was dealing with China, Nixon turned his attention to the Soviet Union. He and Kissinger hoped to play off one communist state against the other. In 1971 he outlined his aim for East-West relations in Europe:

E ast-West conflict in Europe springs from historical and objective causes, not transient [changing] moods or personal misunderstandings. For 25 years Europe has been divided by opposing national interests and contrary philosophies. . . . To relax tensions means a patient and persistent effort to deal with specific sources and not only with their manifestations [obvious appearances]. . . . We in the West are convinced by the history of the postwar period that a détente that does not apply equally to Eastern and Western Europe will be inherently [basically] unstable.

Several months after his China trip, Nixon visited the Soviet Union. He was welcomed as warmly in Moscow as he had been in Beijing. In a series of cordial meetings with Premier Leonid Brezhnev, the two nations negotiated a weapons pact, agreed to work together to explore space, and eased long-standing trade limits.

MAKING CONNECTIONS

What are the relations between the United States and Russia today? How have they changed since the 1970s?

The Superpowers Agree to Limit Weapons

Nixon saw arms control as part of the process in tying the various strands of his foreign policy program together. Like many Americans, he was worried about the wide-

As reporters catch the event for the world, Chinese premier Zhou Enlai and President Richard Nixon congratulate each other on the new ties between their nations.

spread proliferation of nuclear weapons. The Limited Test Ban Treaty of 1963 had ended atmospheric testing of new bombs, but underground testing continued. Bigger and better bombs were being made all the time, and some people feared that the world might be destroyed unless these weapons were brought under control.

Nixon was determined to address the nuclear threat and to deal creatively with the Soviet Union at the same time. He had entered office intent on achieving superiority over the Soviet Union, but came to recognize that superiority made little sense in an era in which each nation had more than enough weapons to

In Depth

Interdisciplinary

In the 1970s, the Soviet Union's rise as a nuclear superpower intensified the cold war. In 1971, for the first time, the Soviet Union passed the United States in total number of land- and submarine-based nuclear missiles. A confident Foreign Minister Andrei Gromyko boasted that in world affairs, "No question of any significance . . . can now be decided without the Soviet Union or in opposition to it."

1. (a) *realpolitik*, see p. 760, (b) détente, see p. 761, (c) Strategic Arms Limitation Talks (SALT), see p. 764

2. Officially, he was initially national security adviser, then secretary of state. Actually, he was one of Nixon's closest advisers, playing a major role in formulating foreign policy.

3. Kissinger used the press shrewdly so that they generally gave the public a favorable picture of the administration.

4. Nixon recognized that the People's Republic was solidly established as the legitimate government of China. He saw that the rest of the world had recognized the government; he felt it was a good move politically.

5. He visited the Soviet Union in 1972 and signed the SALT I treaty, and made agreements to collaborate on space exploration and to ease trading restrictions.

6. It was the first real joint step toward arms control on the part of the United States and the USSR.

Reteach

Have students create a campaign document that could be used to inform voters about key components of Nixon's foreign policy. Ask students to highlight people and strategies employed by Nixon during his administration.

Reinforcing the Big Idea

Nixon's efforts in the field of foreign

The Cold War warmed slightly as Soviet premier Leonid Brezhnev and President Nixon met and SALT I was signed.

destroy their enemies many times over. This ability is known as overkill. Balance between the superpowers was what the nuclear age demanded. The United States and the Soviet Union therefore began **Strategic Arms Limitation Talks,** known as SALT. Once again,

Kissinger kept tight control of the negotiating process. In 1971 Nixon noted:

> Perhaps for the first time, the evolving strategic balance allows a Soviet-American agreement which yields no unilateral [one-sided] advantages. The fact [that] we have begun to discuss strategic arms with the USSR is in itself important. Agreement in such a vital area could create a new commitment to stability, and influence attitudes toward other issues.

Thirty months of talks culminated in an important pact to limit offensive nuclear weapons, ready to be signed when Nixon went to Moscow.

The SALT I treaty included a five-year interim agreement that held the number of intercontinental ballistic missiles (ICBMs) and submarine-launched ballistic missiles at 1972 levels. The treaty also included an agreement restricting the development and deployment of defensive antiballistic missile systems.

SALT I was a diplomatic triumph and an important step forward. But it did little to limit the number of warheads the two nations possessed or to stop them from improving nuclear weapons systems in other ways. The practical Kissinger called for respecting the limits imposed while improving defenses. "The way for us to use this freeze is for us to catch up," he said soon after the summit. "If we don't do this we don't deserve to be in office." Still, SALT I showed that arms control agreements were possible, paving the way for more progress in the future.

SECTION 3 REVIEW

Key Terms, People, and Places
1. Define (a) *realpolitik*, (b) détente, (c) Strategic Arms Limitation Talks (SALT).

Key Concepts
2. What were Henry Kissinger's official and actual roles in the Nixon administration?
3. What was Kissinger's relationship with the press?
4. How did Nixon alter American relations with the

People's Republic of China? Why did he believe it was important to effect such changes?
5. What actions did President Nixon take toward the Soviet Union?

Critical Thinking
6. **Demonstrating Reasoned Judgment** Considering its weaknesses, how important was the SALT I treaty?

The Watergate Scandal

SECTION PREVIEW

Richard Nixon was willing to use presidential power to do whatever was necessary to remain in the White House. Eventually this approach compromised the presidency itself. The resulting Watergate scandal angered the nation and moved Nixon to take drastic steps.

Key Concepts
• The Nixon White House operated in an atmosphere of suspicion.
• Nixon and his supporters were willing to take extreme measures to win the 1972 election.
• When the Watergate break-in was traced to the White House, the President himself became involved in trying to cover it up.
• Nixon's involvement in Watergate made his impeachment likely, causing him to resign.

Key Terms, People, and Places
Watergate, Pentagon Papers, perjury; Plumbers, Daniel Ellsberg, John J. Sirica

L ooking toward the 1972 election, Nixon was determined to win an overwhelming mandate for a second term. Fiercely loyal aides were prepared to do anything for him, even if it meant breaking the law. When Nixon tried to hide their actions, he implicated himself in what became known as **Watergate,** a scandalous series of events that ended his presidency and threatened the foundations of American government.

Suspicion and Deceit at the White House

Reflecting Nixon's suspicious mind, the White House operated as if it was in a state of siege, surrounded by enemies. Nixon's staff responded to the President's attitude by trying to protect him at all costs from anything that might weaken his position.

One result of this mind-set was what became known as the "enemies list." Special counsel Charles W. Colson helped develop a list of prominent people unsympathetic to the administration. It included politicians such as Senator Edward Kennedy, members of the media such as reporter Daniel Schorr, and a number of outspoken performers including comedian Dick Gregory and actors Jane Fonda and Steve McQueen. Aides then considered how to harass these White House "enemies." One idea, for example, was to arrange income tax investigations of people on the list.

Despite his dedication to a domestic policy of law and order, Nixon was sometimes willing to take illegal actions more serious than the activities they were meant to control. For example, when he suspected that news stories were being leaked by the National Security Council, he ordered Kissinger to wiretap the phones of his own staff. When stories began to circulate about the secret bombing of Cambodia, Nixon had reporters' phones tapped, too.

At the same time, he sought tighter coordination of American intelligence activities. Both the FBI and the CIA were already illegally monitoring radical activists by tapping their phones and opening mail. In mid-1970 Nixon's staff proposed a plan for wiretaps and other investigations that was so far outside the law that even FBI director J. Edgar Hoover rejected the plan.

The White House then organized its own unit—nicknamed the **Plumbers**—to stop government security leaks. The group included E. Howard Hunt, a spy novelist and former CIA agent, and G. Gordon Liddy, once an FBI agent. In the spring of 1971, **Daniel Ellsberg,** a

THE WHITE HOUSE
WASHINGTON

August 9, 1974

Dear Mr. Secretary:

I hereby resign the Office of President of the United States.

Sincerely,

Richard Nixon

11:35 AM

The Honorable Henry A. Kissinger
The Secretary of State
Washington, D.C. 20520

MR. PRESIDENT: RELEASE the TAPES!

After persistent public demands for the release of the tapes containing information about Watergate, President Nixon finally complied—then resigned three days later. His resignation letter is shown above.

📄 **Reproducible Lesson Plan** found in the Unit 7 folder, p. 6, provides a summary of the Section 4 lesson plan content.

📄 **Alternate Lesson Plan: Critical Thinking** Drawing Conclusions, found in the Alternate Lesson Plans folder, p. 165, encourages students to use this skill in identifying the abuses of power that led to the Watergate scandal, and the effect that had on the Nixon presidency.

📄 **Guided Reading and Review** found in the Unit 7 folder, p. 13, provides a structure for reading and mastering the key concepts and reviewing the key terms for Section 4. (Guided Practice)

---

1. FOCUS

Connecting to the Big Idea

See page 746B. Tell students that Nixon's suspicious nature and his willingness to use his presidential power for partisan political ends set in motion a series of events that compromised the presidency itself. Ask students how the people of the United States reacted to presidential wrongdoing.

Objectives
● Describe the atmosphere of suspicion that existed in the Nixon White House.
● Explain that Nixon and his team went to extreme lengths to secure his reelection.
● Describe Nixon's efforts to cover up his involvement in the Watergate break-in.
● Explain that Nixon's involvement led to the likelihood of his impeachment, and thus his resignation.

Bellringer

Ask students how they would feel if they discovered that the President might have broken the law. Ask them to discuss the impact of such a piece of news, and the symbolic role of the President.

Reading Strategy

Graphic Organizer Tell students that the Watergate scandal involved several causes and effects. Have students make a cause-and-effect chart of this section comprising three columns on a piece of paper. They should head the first column Causes of the Break-In, the second The Break-In, and the third Effects of the Break-In. Have students write notes in the appropriate column as they read.

former Defense Department official, had given the *New York Times* the **"Pentagon Papers"**—a huge, secret Pentagon study of the Vietnam War. The *New York Times* began to publish the Pentagon Papers in June 1971. The documents showed that the executive branch often had deceived the Congress and American people about the real situation in Vietnam and had deliberately escalated the conflict. Intent on stopping further leaks, Nixon approved the plan to create the Plumbers. With approval from White House chief domestic adviser John Ehrlichman, the undercover unit broke into the office of Ellsberg's psychiatrist in an effort to discover damaging information about Ellsberg's private life.

The Watergate scandal began when security guard Frank Willis (above) discovered a door left ajar by CREEP "burglars" trying to break in and install wiretaps in the Democratic party headquarters.

MAKING CONNECTIONS

Other than its illegality, what problem can you see with a President assuming as much power as did Nixon?

Nixon's Campaign for Reelection

Determined to ensure Nixon's victory in 1972, the Committee to Reelect the President—known as CREEP—used other questionable tactics. Headed by John Mitchell, CREEP launched a fund-raising campaign to collect as much money as possible before a new law made it necessary to report such contributions. The money would fund both routine campaign activities and "dirty tricks" kept hidden from the public.

CREEP funded a variety of questionable actions. For example, people on its payroll leaked a fabricated letter to a conservative New Hampshire newspaper to discredit presidential contender Edmund Muskie, a Democratic senator from Maine. Charging Muskie with making insulting remarks about French Canadians living in the state, the letter was timed to arrive two weeks before the New Hampshire primary. The normally calm and composed Muskie responded by breaking down in tears in front of television cameras, which seriously damaged his reputation. Other "dirty tricks" carried out by CREEP included sending hecklers to disrupt Democratic campaign meetings and assigning undercover "spies" to join the campaigns of major candidates.

"Dirty Tricks" at the Watergate Complex An intelligence branch within CREEP, which included "Plumbers" Liddy and Hunt, masterminded outlandish plans. One elaborate scheme called for the wiretapping of top Democrats to try to compromise them at their convention. Twice Mitchell refused to go along, not because the plan was illegal, but because it was too risky and expensive. Finally in 1972 he approved another idea: tapping the phones at Democratic National Committee headquarters in the Watergate apartment complex in Washington, D.C.

⭐ The first break-in to install illegal listening devices failed. A second attempt, on the night of June 16, 1972, ended with the arrest of the five men involved. One suspect was James McCord, a former CIA officer working for CREEP as a security officer. The Watergate "burglars" carried money that could be traced to CREEP and thus implicated Nixon's reelection campaign.

Top officials, including Nixon himself, had to decide what to do to conceal the incident. When the FBI traced the money carried by the Watergate burglars to CREEP, Nixon authorized the CIA to call off the FBI on the grounds that the matter involved "national security." Though he had not been involved in planning the break-in, the President was now part of the illegal cover-up.

As the Watergate case went on, the White House became more deeply involved. Nixon authorized the payment of hush money to keep Hunt and others quiet. Top officials, including Mitchell, committed **perjury**—lying under oath—in court to shield the President and others.

The 1972 Presidential Election Still, Watergate had barely reached the public's notice. In the 1972 presidential election, the Democrats ran George McGovern, a liberal senator from South Dakota, who lost to Nixon by a landslide. Nixon won a popular majority of 47 million to 29 million votes and swamped the Electoral College by a tally of 520 to 17. He had the mandate he wanted, though he did not get a Republican majority in either house of Congress.

The Watergate Story Continues

Despite Nixon's victory, the Watergate case refused to disappear. Nixon himself had proclaimed publicly that "no one in the White House staff, no one in this administration, presently employed, was involved in this very bizarre incident." At the trial in early 1973, the Watergate burglars either pleaded guilty or were found guilty. At sentencing time, however, Judge **John J. Sirica** was not convinced that he had gotten to the bottom of the matter. Criticizing the prosecution, he said:

> I have not been satisfied, and I am still not satisfied that all the pertinent facts that might be available—I say might be available—have been produced before an American jury. . . . I would hope that the Senate committee is granted the power by Congress . . . to try to get to the bottom of what happened in this case.

To prompt the burglars to talk, Sirica sentenced them to long prison terms.

Meanwhile, *Washington Post* reporters Bob Woodward and Carl Bernstein were following a trail of leads. Even before the election, they had learned about the secret funds at CREEP and had begun to write about the political intelligence effort and the sabotage campaign. As they began to realize who was involved, they called Mitchell and asked him to verify their story. He denied it angrily.

Investigative reporters Bob Woodward (left) and Carl Bernstein (right) persisted in tracking down information to uncover the Watergate story. ★

SOURCE READINGS

Source Readings on p. 774 will connect literature selections and primary source excerpts to historical events discussed in this section.

Source Readings on p. 774 will connect literature selections and primary source excerpts to historical events discussed in this section.

Analyze

Tell students that the televised investigation of the President was a first in American history. Not since Andrew Johnson in the 1860s had a President come under such heavy suspicion. Ask students to consider the American state of mind during Nixon's final days.

In Depth

Historical Misconceptions

The 1972 Republican campaign was not devoid of support from young people, as might be assumed from Nixon's and Agnew's assaults on youth in general (see pages 757–758) and the still-fresh memories of Kent State (see pages 732–734). Young Republicans, according to *Life* magazine in September 1972, comprised "the nation's largest bloc of first-time voters, 2.5 million of them, mostly 18–24-year-olds." By early fall 1972, "Young Voters for the President" claimed 10,000 college volunteers on more than ninety campuses—many established far ahead of McGovern's youth workers. On election day Nixon got 52 percent of the votes cast by those under thirty.

A Watergate Chronology

1972

June Five members of CREEP are arrested for breaking into Democratic National Committee headquarters in the Watergate Office Building. Two former Nixon aides are also arrested.

1973

January All seven men arrested plead or are found guilty.

April Nixon denies knowledge of the break-in.

May Nixon appoints special prosecutor Archibald Cox. The Senate establishes a Select Committee on Presidential Campaign Activities, which begins Watergate hearings.

June John Dean tells the Select Committee that Nixon authorized a cover-up.

July The Select Committee learns that Nixon had been secretly recording presidential conversations since 1971 and asks Nixon to release certain tapes. Nixon refuses.

Dean testifies before the Select Committee.

August Cox sues Nixon for the tapes. Judge John J. Sirica orders Nixon to release the tapes. Nixon appeals, but the appeals court supports Sirica.

October Nixon offers summaries of the tapes, which Cox rejects. Nixon has Cox fired, setting off a series of firings and resignations known as the "Saturday Night Massacre." The House of Representatives begins steps to impeach Nixon. Nixon finally releases the tapes, but investigators find two are missing.

The tapes become the center of the controversy.

November An eighteen-and-a-half minute gap is found on one of the tapes. The White House blames accidental erasure, but later investigation proves that the tape was deliberately erased.

1974

January Nixon claims "executive privilege."

April Attorney Leon Jaworski, the new special prosecutor, and the House Judiciary Committee subpoena Nixon to surrender tapes and related documents. Nixon supplies 1,254 pages of edited transcripts. Jaworski sues Nixon for the originals.

July The Supreme Court orders Nixon to give Jaworski the tapes and documents. The House Judiciary Committee recommends three articles of impeachment.

August Nixon releases additional transcripts, which show that he learned of the break-in as early as June 23, 1972 and ordered the cover-up. Nixon resigns August 9.

Nixon leaves Washington, D.C.

The Senate Investigates At the same time, a Senate Select Committee on Presidential Campaign Activities began to investigate the Watergate affair. James McCord, one of the convicted Watergate burglars, responded to his lengthy prison sentence by testifying before the committee, giving members a sense of what had gone on. The newspaper stories by Woodward and Bernstein helped the investigation, while leads from the Senate committee in turn aided the reporters.

As rumors grew that the White House was involved, Nixon tried to protect himself. In April 1973 he fired Haldeman and Ehrlichman, his two closest aides. On national television, he proclaimed that he would take final responsibility for the mistakes of others, for "there can be no whitewash at the White House."

Still the investigation ground on. In May 1973 the Senate committee, chaired by Senator Sam Ervin of North Carolina, began televised public hearings on Watergate. Millions of Americans watched, fascinated, as the story unfolded like a mystery thriller. John Dean, seeking to save himself, testified that Nixon knew about the cover-up. Other staffers described the various illegal activities undertaken in the White House.

The most dramatic moment came when one aide revealed the existence of a secret taping system in the President's office that recorded all meetings and telephone conversations—supposedly to provide a historical record of Nixon's presidency. Now those tapes could show whether or not Nixon had actually been involved in the cover-up.

The "Saturday Night Massacre" In an effort to prove his honesty, Nixon agreed to the appointment of a special Watergate prosecutor in the Justice Department. Archibald Cox, a Harvard law professor, took the post and immediately asked for the tapes. Nixon refused to release them. When Cox persisted, Nixon ordered him fired during the weekend of October 20, 1973, triggering a series of resignations and firings that became known as the "Saturday Night Massacre."

An Administration in Jeopardy By this time, Nixon was in serious trouble. His public

RESOURCE DIRECTORY

SOURCE READINGS

Source Readings on p. 776 will connect literature selections and primary source excerpts to historical events discussed in this section.

approval rating plummeted. After Cox's firing, *Time* magazine declared "The President Should Resign."

Nixon appointed another special prosecutor, Leon Jaworski of Texas, who also asked for the tapes. Nixon then tried to show his innocence by releasing edited transcripts of some of his White House conversations. He carefully excised the most damaging evidence, but many people were angry and disillusioned when they read the actual words of some of the conversations in the Oval Office.

There was a subplot in the troubled White House. Vice President Spiro Agnew, accused of evading income taxes and taking bribes, resigned in disgrace early in October 1973, just ten days before the "Saturday Night Massacre." To succeed him, Nixon named Gerald R. Ford, the House minority leader. For nearly two months, until the Senate confirmed Ford, the nation had a President in trouble—and no Vice President.

Impeachment Ahead? Nixon had to do something. After the "Saturday Night Massacre," Congress had begun the process that could lead to impeachment—bringing charges and holding a trial to determine whether he should remain in office. In July 1974, the House Judiciary Committee, which included twenty-one Democrats and seventeen Republicans, began to hold hearings to determine if there were adequate grounds for impeachment.

This debate, like the earlier hearings, was televised nationally. The country watched anxiously as even Republicans deserted the President. Representative M. Caldwell Butler of Virginia spoke for many of them when he said:

> For years we Republicans have campaigned against corruption and misconduct. . . . But Watergate is our shame. Those things have happened in our house and it is our responsibility to do what we can to clear it up. . . . It is a sad chapter in American history, but I cannot condone what I have heard; I cannot excuse it; and I cannot and will not stand for it.

By sizable tallies, the House Judiciary Committee voted to impeach the President on

 **Viewpoints Activity** On Nixon's Impeachment, found in the Unit 7 folder, pp. 19–20, presents several excerpts from impeachment hearings to further the discussion on presidential conduct.

Viewpoints
On Nixon's Impeachment

In July 1974, the House Judiciary Committee conducted its televised debate on the possible impeachment of President Richard Nixon. **What attitudes about Nixon's impeachment are expressed in the two statements below?**

For Impeachment

"My faith in the Constitution is whole, it is complete, it is total. I am not going to sit here and be an idle spectator to the diminution [lessening], *the subversion* [overthrow], *the destruction of the Constitution. . . . The Framers confided in the Congress the power if need be to remove . . . a President swollen with power and grown tyrannical."*

Representative Barbara Jordan, Democrat (Texas)

Against Impeachment

"As the trust is placed in Congress to safeguard the liberties of the people through the awesome and extraordinary powers to remove a President, so must Congress's vigilance be fierce in seeing that the trust is not abused. . . . Not only do I not believe that any crimes by the President have been proved beyond a reasonable doubt, but I do not think the proof even approaches the lesser standards of proof which some of my colleagues, I believe, have injudiciously [with poor judgment] *suggested we apply."*

Representative Edward Hutchinson, Republican (Michigan)

Americans were fascinated but dismayed by the conversations taped in the Oval Office. This cartoonist saw Nixon as a man trapped by his own plots.

In Depth
Then and Now

When Richard Milhous Nixon died on April 22, 1994, at age eighty-one, biographer Garry Wills wrote of him: "In some areas of politics, he seemed to know almost everything about anything—except about himself. His strengths and weaknesses fed upon each other. He was a small bitter man and a very grand diplomat. Who can read that riddle? Some of us have spent much of our lives trying to read it, with little better success than his own."

Section 3 Review Answers

1. (a) Watergate, see p. 765, (b) Pentagon Papers, see p. 765, (c) perjury, see p. 767

2. (a) Plumbers, see p. 765, (b) Daniel Ellsberg, see p. 765, (c) John J. Sirica, see p. 767

3. To monitor Democratic party headquarters activities.

4. Money carried by the burglars was traced back to CREEP (the Committee to Reelect the President), involving campaign manager John Mitchell, the former attorney general.

5. Nixon became involved in the cover-up when he authorized the CIA to call off the FBI investigation on the grounds that national security was involved and when he approved the payment of hush money to keep the burglars quiet.

6. It was clear that he would be impeached if he did not resign.

7. While the upheaval in leadership was unusual for the United States and had many repercussions, the transition was legal and peaceful, and the basic structure of government and law remained intact.

Reteach

Have students use information from this section to answer the following questions in one or two sentences:
• Who were Nixon's "enemies"?
• What methods did Nixon use to win reelection?
• Where were the Watergate burglars captured and arrested?
• Why did Nixon fire special prosecutor Archibald Cox?
• How did Nixon respond to the threat of impeachment?

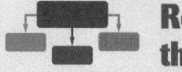

4. CLOSE

Reinforcing the Big Idea

Nixon's White House was one of suspicion and abuse of power. His efforts to use the presidency for his own political gain led to scandal—and to the end of his presidency.

In the midst of the Watergate hearings, a worn Nixon finds the energy to shake hands with some sightseers at the White House.

charges of obstruction of justice, abuse of power, and refusal to obey a congressional order to turn over his tapes. To remove him from office, the full House of Representatives would have to vote for impeachment, and the Senate would have to hold a trial. The outcome seemed obvious in this case.

Nixon Resigns from Office On August 5, after a brief delay, Nixon finally obeyed a Supreme Court ruling and released the tapes. Despite a disturbing gap of eighteen and a half minutes where the conversation had been mysteriously erased, the tapes gave clear evidence of Nixon's involvement in the cover-up. Three days later, Nixon appeared on national television and painfully announced that he would resign the office of the President the next day. On August 9, Nixon resigned, the first President ever to do so. In a smooth constitutional transition, Vice President Gerald Ford was sworn in, telling the country "our long national nightmare is over."

Why Watergate?

Watergate raised many questions about the use and abuse of power. Richard Nixon was committed to winning in 1972 at any cost. He had gone further than his predecessors in creating an "imperial presidency," surrounding himself with subordinates who believed he could do no wrong. Though many of them were lawyers, they did not let the law stand in their way. They paid a high price, for most of them spent time in prison because of the Watergate cover-up. Nixon himself was never indicted and remained free by virtue of a presidential pardon granted by Gerald Ford.

SECTION 4 REVIEW

Key Terms, People, and Places
1. Define (a) Watergate, (b) Pentagon Papers, (c) perjury.
2. Identify (a) Plumbers, (b) Daniel Ellsberg, (c) John J. Sirica.

Key Concepts
3. Why did the White House undertake illegal wiretaps?
4. How was the Watergate break-in linked to the White House?

5. How did Richard Nixon become involved in the Watergate cover-up?
6. What was the ultimate reason for Nixon's resignation?

Critical Thinking
7. **Determining Relevance** In what way did the ending of the Watergate affair demonstrate the strength of the Constitution?

RESOURCE DIRECTORY

Teaching Resources

Quiz found in the Unit 7 folder, p. 14, covers the main ideas in this section as well as the key terms.

Chapter Test Forms A and B are found in the Unit 7 folder, pp. 31–36.

Answer Keys found in the Unit 7 folder, p. 143–156, provide answers to all student activities.

Media and Technology

Transparency
Graphic Organizer, G-4

Guided Reading Audiotapes (English and Spanish)

Computer Test Bank

Analyzing Presidential Records

Presidential papers record a President's time in office. Letters, memorandums, notes on meetings, speeches, transcripts of press conferences—nearly every word the President utters seems to find its way into these papers. Thus, they provide a good source of information when trying to piece together historical evidence about the past.

In more recent times, technology has added new forms of "papers" as historical evidence—audio- and videotapes. President Nixon's audiotapes, recorded in the Oval Office, loomed large in the Watergate affair. In fact, it was a tape that finally ended the affair—a recording of a conversation that took place just a few days after the Watergate break-in on June 16, 1972. Not released until August 5, 1974, it proved that Nixon knew of the cover-up all along.

Use the following steps to analyze excerpts from this tape.

1. Identify the source by asking *who, when, where,* **and** *what.*
(a) Who are the speakers on the tape?
(b) Who else is mentioned in it?
(c) When did the conversation take place? (d) Where? (e) What is the major topic?

2. Identify the main points of information in the excerpts.
(a) Why is Haldeman concerned about the FBI? (b) What recommendation does he put forward about using the CIA to end the investigation? (c) How does President Nixon respond to the recommendation?

3. Study the tape to find clues to the historical period. (a) What can you infer about the extent of the powers that Nixon believed he had over FBI and CIA operations? (b) What can you infer about Nixon's sense of priorities at the time the recording was made? (c) What can you infer about the extent of Haldeman's influence?

CAST OF CHARACTERS
PRESIDENT NIXON
H. R. HALDEMAN, *Chief of Staff*
PAT GRAY, *Acting FBI Director*
JOHN MITCHELL, *Chairman of CREEP*
VERNON WALTERS, *Deputy CIA Director*

June 23, 1972

HALDEMAN Now, on to the investigation, you know the Democratic break-in thing. We're back in the problem area because the FBI is not under control, because Gray doesn't exactly know how to control it and . . . their investigation is now leading into some productive areas—because they've been able to trace the money. . . . Mitchell's recommendation [is] that the way to handle this now is for us to have Walters call Pat Gray and just say, "Stay . . . out of this—this is ah, business here we don't want you to go any further on it." That's not an unusual development, and ah, that would take care of it.

NIXON What about Pat Gray—you mean Pat Gray doesn't want to?

HALDEMAN Pat does want to. He doesn't know how to, and he doesn't have any basis for doing it. Given [Walters' call], he will then have the basis.

NIXON Yeah.

HALDEMAN [Gray will] say, "We've got this signal from across the river [the CIA] to put a hold on this." And that will fit rather well because the FBI agents who are working the case, at this point, feel that's what it is.

NIXON They've traced the money [the money that was found on the Watergate burglars]? Who'd they trace it to?

[Haldeman describes various people who contributed to CREEP and Nixon wonders if these people will say that the burglars, not CREEP, asked for the money.]

HALDEMAN Well, if they will. But then we're relying on more and more people all the time. That's the problem and they'll stop if we could take this other route.

NIXON All right.

HALDEMAN And you seem to think the thing to do is get [the FBI] to stop?

NIXON Right, fine.

Excerpted from *The New York Times,* Tuesday, August 6, 1974

Historian's Toolbox Activity Analyzing Presidential Records, found in the Unit 7 folder, p. 21, focuses on the inaugural address of President Clinton for further examination of presidential documents as historical evidence.

Chapter Review

Understanding Key Terms, People, and Places

Terms

Students should refer to the definitions of the key terms in the chapter to write sentences that show the relation of each word to the events of 1968 or the Nixon years.

True or False

1. true
2. false, *realpolitik*
3. false, Poor People's Campaign
4. false, embargo
5. true

Word Relationships

1. (b) does not belong. Humphrey, Wallace, and Nixon all ran for President in 1968. Kissinger was Nixon's national security adviser and secretary of state.

2. (a) does not belong. Haldeman, Ehrlichman, and Mitchell were members of Nixon's staff; McCarthy, an antiwar candidate, ran for the Democratic nomination in the 1968 election.

3. (c) does not belong. The Plumbers were men organized by the White House to stop security leaks. They broke into the office of Ellsberg's psychiatrist after Ellsberg released the "Pentagon Papers"; and Sirica investigated their burglary of the Democratic party headquarters at the Watergate complex. Kennedy was assassinated while running for President in 1968.

Reviewing Main Ideas

1. Americans' beliefs in nonviolent change were threatened; and many people felt disillusioned. Some African Americans showed their frustration and rage by rioting; 124 cities experienced riots after King's death.

2. The party was in disarray because of differing attitudes toward the Vietnam War, the lack of a candidate who could draw the party together, and the propensity of counterculture groups to annoy the establishment.

3. Voters were reacting against the recent assassinations of King and Kennedy and the violence at the Democratic convention.

4. Nixon's staff was fiercely loyal and willing to go to any lengths to protect him or to help him achieve his goals.

5. Nixon took a more conservative stance, although he eventually resorted to deficit spending and ninety-day freezes. He also tried to stop increased government spending on social programs.

Understanding Key Terms, People, and Places

Key Terms
1. Poor People's Campaign
2. imperial presidency
3. Organization of Petroleum Exporting Countries (OPEC)
4. embargo
5. busing
6. *realpolitik*
7. détente
8. Strategic Arms Limitation Talks (SALT)
9. Watergate
10. Pentagon Papers
11. perjury

People
12. Robert F. Kennedy
13. Eugene McCarthy
14. Hubert Humphrey
15. George C. Wallace
16. Richard M. Nixon
17. Spiro Agnew
18. Henry A. Kissinger
19. H. R. Haldeman
20. John Ehrlichman
21. John Mitchell
22. Plumbers
23. Daniel Ellsberg
24. John J. Sirica

Terms For each term above, write a sentence that explains its relation to the events of 1968 or to the Nixon years.

True or False Determine whether each statement is true or false. If it is true, write "true." If it is false, change the underlined term to make the statement true.

1. In the spring of 1971, newspapers published the <u>Pentagon Papers,</u> a huge, secret government study of the Vietnam War.
2. Henry Kissinger was an admirer of <u>détente,</u> or politics based on achieving power.
3. In 1968 Martin Luther King, Jr., began the <u>Strategic Arms Limitation Talks.</u>
4. Because the United States supported Israel in the war in the Middle East, Saudi Arabia imposed a <u>perjury</u> on oil shipments.
5. Oil prices soared when members of <u>OPEC</u> quadrupled their prices.

Word Relationships Three of the people in each of the following sets are related in terms of their activities and accomplishments. Choose the person who does not belong and explain why he does not belong.

1. (a) Hubert Humphrey, (b) Henry A. Kissinger, (c) Richard M. Nixon, (d) George C. Wallace
2. (a) Eugene McCarthy, (b) John Ehrlichman, (c) John Mitchell, (d) H. R. Haldeman
3. (a) Plumbers, (b) Daniel Ellsberg, (c) Robert F. Kennedy, (d) John J. Sirica

---

Reviewing Main Ideas

Section 1 (pp. 742–751)
1. How did the assassinations of Martin Luther King, Jr., and Robert Kennedy affect Americans?
2. Why was the Democratic party in such a state of disunity and disarray at the 1968 convention?
3. How did Nixon's law and order stance help him win the presidency?

Section 2 (pp. 754–759)
4. Describe Nixon's relationship to the key members of his staff.
5. How did Nixon differ from his predecessors on issues of the economy and social programs?
6. Describe Nixon's civil rights policies and their effect on the civil rights movement.

Section 3 (pp. 760–764)
7. Explain why Henry Kissinger left a lasting mark on American foreign policy.
8. Describe how Nixon reversed United States policy toward China.
9. What was the result of Nixon's negotiations with the Soviet Union on arms control?

Section 4 (pp. 765–770)
10. What measures did the Committee to Reelect the President take to win the 1972 election?
11. Describe Nixon's involvement in the Watergate cover-up.
12. What were the impeachment charges brought against Nixon? Why was he not impeached?

---

6. Nixon opposed busing and did not support reform to advance the status of minorities; his policies slowed the civil rights movement.

7. Kissinger worked to ease cold war tensions and to end the Vietnam War.

8. Nixon reversed the policy of refusing to give diplomatic recognition to the communist government of China by relaxing some regulations and finally becoming the first American President to visit the country.

9. The result was the SALT I treaty, which was an important first step in limiting nuclear weapons.

10. The Committee to Reelect the President (CREEP) lied to discredit opposition candidates. For example, it falsely charged presidential contender Edmund Muskie with making insulting remarks about French Canadian residents of New Hampshire just two weeks before the New Hampshire primary. CREEP also sent hecklers to disturb Democratic campaign meetings. And a special unit within CREEP, the Plumbers, tried to wiretap the Democratic party headquarters at the Watergate complex in Washington, D.C.

11. Nixon tried to protect himself by firing his closest aides; he at first refused to release tapes from his secret taping system, then released edited transcripts of the tapes with the most damaging evidence excised; he fired special prosecutor Archibald Cox when Cox demanded the release of the tapes.

Thinking Critically

1. **Testing Conclusions** Some commentators have observed that only a Republican veteran of the cold war like Richard Nixon would have been able to reestablish relations with China. Do you agree, or do you feel that a Democratic President might have been equally successful?

2. **Demonstrating Reasoned Judgment** Should Nixon have been pardoned? Explain your reasoning.

3. **Predicting Consequences** What kind of President do you think Americans were looking for after Watergate and the Nixon resignation?

4. **Distinguishing False from Accurate Images** Adlai Stevenson described "Nixonland" as a place where the President would do "anything to win." Do you agree or disagree with Stevenson's observation? Explain your answer.

Making Connections

1. **Evaluating Primary Sources** Review the primary source excerpt on page 754. What does this statement reveal about Nixon's motivations? What other possible responses might someone have to being an outsider? Can you think of anyone with whom you are familiar in your personal life or from your reading whose ambition stems from anger?

2. **Understanding the Visuals** On page 754, Nixon is described as a shy and remote man who put up a front when he campaigned for office. The picture on page 754 shows Nixon on the campaign trail. Based on this picture, what conclusions can you make about the public side of Nixon's personality?

3. **Writing About the Chapter** You have been asked to write a preface to a new biography of Richard Nixon, in which you evaluate his presidency. First,

make a list of the positive accomplishments of the Nixon administration. Then, make a list of the negative aspects of Nixon's presidency. Note which events you think have had the most lasting impact. Next, write a draft of your preface in which you summarize your conclusions. Revise your preface, making sure that each idea is clearly explained. Proofread your preface and draft a final copy.

4. **Using the Graphic Organizer** This graphic organizer uses a flow map to show the sequence of events in 1968. (a) What was the result of the 1968 Democratic convention? (b) List three factors that contributed to Nixon's victory in the 1968 election. (c) On a separate sheet of paper, create your own flow map about the Watergate scandal, using this graphic organizer as an example.

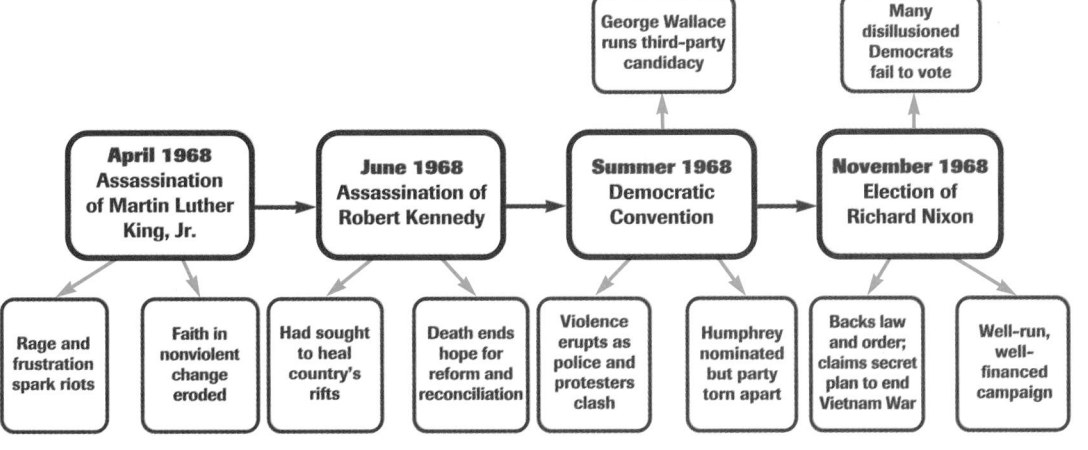

---

12. Nixon was charged with obstruction of justice, abuse of power, and refusal to obey a congressional order to turn over his tapes. He resigned before he could be impeached.

Thinking Critically

1. Students' responses should demonstrate an awareness that a hard-liner like Nixon was less likely to encounter conservative opposition than a Democrat.

2. Some students may believe that Nixon should have been imprisoned, as were many of his subordinates. Others may feel that the healing gesture suggested by the pardon was more important than censure.

3. Americans were probably looking for a President who could instill trust in the government.

4. Students should find ample evidence to support Stevenson's statement. Besides Watergate, Nixon's domestic policies on law and order and his "southern strategy" were both designed to win votes; in foreign policy, his trip to China was partly arranged to give him a boost at home.

Making Connections

1. Nixon was motivated by anger at being an outsider. Being an outsider could, for example, make someone more compassionate toward other outsiders or wish to educate others about acceptance of differences. The ambition of many dictators is thought to stem from anger.

2. The picture shows Nixon standing on the hood of a car with his arms stretched out high over his head in an effusive, triumphant gesture. Students should conclude that, based on this image, the public side of Nixon's personality was outgoing and exuberant.

3. Positive accomplishments include Nixon's foreign policy achievements; negative aspects include Watergate and Nixon's civil rights policies. Watergate had a lasting impact on the issue of trust in government, and Nixon's policy of détente had a lasting effect on foreign relations.

4. (a) Hubert Humphrey was nominated, but the party was torn apart. (b) Nixon backed law and order and claimed a secret plan to end the Vietnam War; his campaign was well run and well financed; the Democrats were not united behind Humphrey. (c) Students' graphic organizers should include events leading to the Watergate break-in, Nixon's involvement in the cover-up, and Nixon's resignation.

Alternative Assessment

Final Evaluation
Use the following guidelines to evaluate student projects:

● **Evidence of thoughtfulness** To what extent do projects demonstrate an understanding of Nixon's policies and his successes and failures?

● **Evidence of outside research** To what extent do projects reflect use of outside research materials?

● **Sensitivity** To what extent do projects reflect an increased awareness of the role of Nixon's personality and personal style in his successes and failures as President?

FOCUS

Connecting Literature and History

Ask students how powerful they think the President of the United States is. What do they think would happen if a President was elected who planned to turn the United States democratic system into a dictatorship? Ask students what prevents this from happening. Students should point out that the American system of checks and balances is designed to stop any one person from gaining too much power. Tell students that this is one of the very circumstances that the framers of the Constitution were trying to avoid when they devised the system of checks and balances. Tell students that the illegal deeds of the White House were brought to light by security guard Frank Willis, Washington Post reporters Bob Woodward and Carl Bernstein, and the Senate Select Committee on Presidential Campaign Activities. Point out that freedom of the press as well as checks and balances worked to remove a President from power who was abusing the office.

SOURCE READINGS

The Impact of the Watergate Transcripts

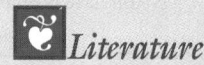 *Literature*

Sam Ervin, Jr.

INTRODUCTION Senator Sam Ervin, Jr., of North Carolina was chosen as the chairperson of the Senate Select Committee to investigate the Watergate affair. As the hearings unwound the scandal before a disappointed public, it became increasingly clear that the choice had been an excellent one. Ervin strove to uphold the principle that all people are equal before the law. Later, he stated that "the only security America has against anarchy on the one hand and tyranny on the other is . . . the Constitution" of the United States. It was that Constitution that President Nixon had so gravely abused. In the excerpt that follows

from his book, *The Whole Truth*, Ervin explains how the White House, after refusing to release the tapes, finally agreed to release a transcript of those tapes. It was filled with inaccuracies, but despite this last desperate attempt at a cover-up, the transcript still managed to discredit the Nixon administration.

VOCABULARY Before you read this selection, find the meaning of these words in a dictionary: decipher, replete, awry, ambiguous, besieged, exonerate, disreputable, vacillate.

On April 30 the White House delivered to the House Judiciary Committee and released to the public more than 1,200 pages of hastily deciphered and heavily edited White House transcripts of private conversations President Nixon had with his principal aides about Watergate between September 15, 1972, and April 27, 1973.

The transcripts omitted some passages appearing on the original tapes, whose revelation was critical to a full understanding of Nixon's connection with Watergate. The transcripts assigned as the reason for the omissions that the passages were "unrelated to Watergate" or "unrelated to Presidential actions."

The transcripts were replete with notations that words on the tapes were "inaudible" or "unintelligible," and the expression "expletive deleted," which the editors used to camouflage the foul language President Nixon employed in his private conversations with his aides. Some of the conversations on the tapes were twisted awry by the transcripts, and their real meanings were thereby distorted.

The transcripts were also ambiguous in spots. It is not surprising that this was so. They undertook to transcribe the taped recordings of the intimate conversations of a troubled President and his perplexed aides, who believed they were besieged by enemies, and were seeking some way to escape the peril the truth about Watergate posed for them.

Several hours before it delivered the White House transcripts to the House Judiciary Committee and made them public, the White House released to the press what it claimed was a 50-page summary of them. The thesis of the summary was that the White House transcripts would discredit Dean's[1] testimony before the Senate Select Committee and exonerate President Nixon of any criminal behavior in the Watergate affair.

The White House transcripts did not support the White House summary of them. Despite their ambiguities, inaccuracies, and omissions, the White House transcripts convinced multitudes of Americans for

---

[1] John Dean, White House counsel under Nixon

the first time that Dean testified truthfully when he charged Nixon with participating in the cover-up of Watergate and thereby aiding in the obstruction of justice. In addition, multitudes of others were disillusioned by the picture of Nixon which the transcripts presented.

For these reasons, the White House transcripts boomeranged, and Nixon's remaining support among the people, the press, and the politicians dwindled rapidly. A few incidents indicate the erosive impact of the transcripts on former supporters of Nixon. Two of his former champions among the press, the Chicago *Tribune* and the Omaha *World Herald*, forthwith demanded that he resign. In so doing, the Chicago *Tribune* said:

> We saw the public man in his first administration and we were impressed. Now in about 300,000 words we have seen the private man, and we are appalled.
>
> He is preoccupied with appearances rather than substance. His aim is to find a way to sell the idea that disreputable schemes are actually good, are defensible for some trumped-up cause. He is humorless to the point of being inhumane. He is devious. He is vacillating. He is profane. He is willing to be led. He displays dismaying gaps in knowledge. He is suspicious of his staff. His loyalty is minimal. His greatest concern is to create a record that will save him and his administration. The high dedication to grand principles that Americans have a right to expect from a President is missing from the transcript record.

After crediting Nixon with achievements in foreign affairs, the Omaha *World Herald* stated:

The Watergate scandal raised strong feelings in American citizens. This cartoon portrays Nixon caught up in a web of tapes and lies.

Important as these accomplishments are, they are overshadowed now by the appallingly low level of political morality in the White House, as indicated in a variety of ways in recent months and confirmed now in damning detail by the White House tapes.

The transcripts have diminished the President's image from that of a moral man surrounded by underlings who had betrayed him to that of an amoral man who compounded his troubles by withholding for more than a year the shocking truth about the mess he and his administration were in.

. . . On the day following its receipt of the White House transcripts, the House Judiciary Committee met in closed session to determine what response it should make to the President. After hours of sometimes heated debate, it voted 20 to 18 to notify the President that it refused to accept the transcripts as substitutes for the forty-two subpoenaed tapes, and demanded that he deliver the tapes to it forthwith in obedience to its subpoena.

THINKING ABOUT THE SELECTION

1. What did Ervin think about the quality of the transcripts when compared to the tapes themselves?
2. What might the Nixon White House have been attempting to accomplish by using these transcripts?

Critical Thinking

3. **Demonstrating Reasoned Judgment** Ervin says the White House transcripts "boomeranged." What does he mean by this description?

SOURCE READINGS

Tapes and Transcripts

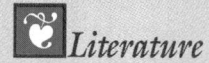 Literature

John Ehrlichman

INTRODUCTION John Ehrlichman served as chief domestic advisor to President Nixon. When the Watergate scandal came to light, his role was immediately questioned, because he was one of the men closest to the President. He was found guilty of participating in the cover-up of Watergate and served several years in jail. *Witness to Power* is the book he wrote after his release, and it describes the Nixon years from his insider's perspective. The following excerpt centers on Ehrlichman's view of the secret tapes documenting White House conversations concerning the Watergate burglary, its cover-up, and Nixon's reelection efforts.

VOCABULARY Before you read this selection, find the meaning of these words in a dictionary: innuendo, fidelity, syntax, advocate.

There is some question as to what I knew about the President's taping system. The fact is I was totally unaware it existed. Because one of the tapes has me referring to the President's recording of a conversation with John Dean, some commentators deduced that I knew about the whole system. In fact, Bob Haldeman, alluding to Nixon's fear that he might have said something self-incriminating to Dean in one of their March 1973 meetings, had just told me, "We have Dean on tape in that one." I didn't dream that everything I'd been saying and hearing in the President's office for years had been recorded.

My reaction to the news that there was a taping system is perhaps a measure of how little I understood of Watergate. "That's great," I said to a reporter on my front lawn when he informed me of Alex Butterfield's disclosure[2]. "Now all the innuendoes and questions will be answered with some hard evidence." I was confident the tapes would help, not hurt.

I was convicted in two criminal trials. In the months between them, the Special Prosecutor was required by law to let my lawyers and me listen to any and all of the tapes that might be used in the second trial. (No tapes had been played during the first Fielding break-in trial.)

My lawyers, William Frates and Andrew Hall, tried to listen to some of the tapes, but they simply couldn't understand them. The prosecution said it had called upon electronic experts to assemble the finest available playback equipment, but even with the most sensitive earphones it was nearly impossible at times to guess what people were saying.

The prosecution and the FBI had prepared written "transcripts" of the tapes, copies of which were given to us to read along with the tapes. I knew the voices and had been present during some of the conversations, so I was elected by my lawyers to monitor the tapes in order to evaluate the accuracy of the transcripts. Some passages I replayed a dozen times, fast and slowly.

The fidelity of the tapes was terrible. If Judge John Sirica had required the jury to listen to them without benefit of written transcripts, those poor people could not have had a clue to what was being said or done. Moreover, as I sat in

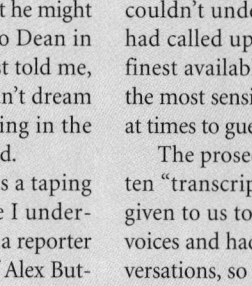

The White House tapes became the center of the Watergate controversy when Nixon refused to release all of the tapes to the Senate Select Committee.

---

2 Alex Butterfield was the White House aide who informed the Senate Select Committee about Nixon's taping system.

the Special Prosecutor's listening room looking at the written text and playing the tapes, I immediately understood that the authors of the transcript didn't know the players. The text often attributed Haldeman's words to me, Nixon's to Haldeman, Dean's to Haldeman and many phrases to "unknown."

I had been listening to Richard Nixon for years; I knew his voice and I also knew his syntax and speaking rhythm. It was obvious that the transcribers did not.[3] Also, literally dozens of phrases the FBI put into the transcript were not to be heard on the tapes.

There is a conversation taped the afternoon of March 22, 1973, involving five people. The transcript indicates I said the classic phrase "It's a modified limited hang-out." Writers on Watergate have pointed to the passage as evidence I proposed that the President make a sham disclosure. In fact, all through that meeting, as attested by the tapes, I was advocating that everything except a few FBI summaries be included in a report by Dean to be published or turned over to Senator Sam Ervin. But at page 287 of the transcript, I suddenly seem to shift to a "modified limited hang-out." In fact I am not the person who speaks those phrases. (The voice in question isn't mine; I believe it is Bob Haldeman's.) The FBI transcripts are full of important errors of that kind.

As I sat in the Special Prosecutor's hot little listening room, playing the hard-to-hear passages over and over, I experienced a kind of revelation. I heard how people had talked about me in the President's office when I wasn't there; for example, I heard the President tell people to keep secrets from me. And I heard

Henry Kissinger, John Ehrlichman, and H. R. Haldeman made up the inner circle of President Nixon's advisors during his administration. They are pictured here with the President in the Oval Office.

Nixon agree with Haldeman that there must be a meeting with the CIA's Richard Helms and Vernon Walters on June 23, 1972, to try to block an FBI investigation.

THINKING ABOUT THE SELECTION

1. What problems does Ehrlichman find with the quality of the tapes and transcripts?
2. How might such problems have resulted in a faulty perception on the part of a jury?

Critical Thinking

3. **Drawing Conclusions** Based on the points Ehrlichman makes in this excerpt, do you think he pleaded innocent or guilty to charges of being involved in the Watergate conspiracy? Explain your answer.

---

[3] The problem is not limited to listening. In a handwriting-analysis book published during Watergate, the author deeply analyzes Richard Nixon's character from "his" writing. The only trouble is that the Nixon samples are my writing, not Nixon's. [Footnote is from original source.]

ANSWERS TO

Thinking About the Selection

1. He writes that the tapes were very hard to understand, even with the most sophisticated listening equipment, and that the transcripts often attributed comments to the wrong person.
2. The jury might have believed that Ehrlichman said some things that he, in fact, did not ever say.

3. Based on Ehrlichman's point about the problems with the tapes and the transcripts, as well as his point about his revelation on hearing the tapes ("I heard how people had talked about me in the President's office when I wasn't there; for example, I heard the President tell people to keep secrets from me."), it seems fairly certain that Ehrlichman would have continued to claim his innocence.

Chapter 24 The Post-Watergate Period
1974–1980

📁 Teaching Resources (See Unit 7 Folder)

	Instruction	Enrichment
Section 1 **The Ford Administration** (pp. 780–784)	Reproducible Lesson Plan, p. 38 Alternate Lesson Plan, p. 167 Guided Reading and Review, p. 42 Quiz, p. 43	Literature Activity, A Search for Roots, pp. 61–63 Primary Source Activity, 1976: The Bicentennial Year, p. 58
Section 2 **The Carter Transition** (pp. 785–788)	Reproducible Lesson Plan, p. 39 Alternate Lesson Plan, p. 168 Guided Reading and Review, p. 44 Quiz, p. 45	American Profiles Activity, Patricia Roberts Harris, p. 52 Primary Source Activity, A Crisis of Confidence, pp. 59–60
Section 3 **Carter's Foreign Policy** (pp. 789–793)	Reproducible Lesson Plan, p. 40 Alternate Lesson Plan, p. 169 Guided Reading and Review, p. 46 Quiz, p. 47	American Profiles Activity, Andrew Young, p. 53 Visual Learning Activity, The Hostage Crisis as a Media Event, p. 64 Historian's Toolbox Activity, Recognizing Ideologies, p. 56
Section 4 **Carter's Domestic Problems** (pp. 795–799)	Reproducible Lesson Plan, p. 41 Alternate Lesson Plan, p. 170 Guided Reading and Review, p. 48 Quiz, p. 49 Chapter Test, Forms A & B, pp. 66–71	Critical Thinking Activity, Formulating Questions, p. 57 Visual Learning Activity, Responding to the Energy Crisis, p. 65 Viewpoints Activity, On Nuclear Energy, pp. 54–55 History Might Not . . . Activity, Helping to Heal a War-Torn Nation, pp. 50–51

📁 Additional Chapter Resources

Resource Organizer, p. 37
Alternate Lesson Plan, p. 166
Answer Keys, pp. 143–156

Bibliography

For the Teacher
Lasch, C. *The Culture of Narcissism: American Life in an Age of Diminishing Expectations.* Warner Books, 1979.
Lasky, Victor. *Jimmy Carter: The Man and the Myth.* Marek, 1979. (An analysis of the Carter presidency.)
Sheehan, Neil. *After the War Was Over: Hanoi and Saigon.* Vintage, 1993. (A look at Vietnam's recovery in the 1990s.)
Terkel, S. *Working: People Talk About What They Do All Day and How They Feel About What They Do.* Pantheon, 1974, and *American Dreams: Lost and Found.* Pantheon, 1980. (Oral histories on the American Dream in the seventies and eighties.)

Prentice Hall Literature Excerpts from *The American Experience,* 1994, including Walker, Alice. "Everyday Use," from *In Love and Trouble: Stories of Black Women.* Harcourt Brace Jovanovich, 1973 edition.

The Big Idea for the chapter and how the main ideas in each section relate to the Big Idea are graphically displayed below. Comprehension of this chapter's Big Idea is critical to students' understanding of United States history and how we as a nation got where we are today.

Media and Technology

 Visions of America: History Might Not Have Happened This Way Game

 The Way It Works, H-21; Critical Thinking, I-5; Graphic Organizer, G-3

 Guided Reading Audiotapes (English and Spanish)

 Computer Test Bank

For the Student

Colby, Anne, and William Damon. *Some Do Care: Contemporary Lives of Moral Commitment.* The Free Press, 1993. (Profiles individuals who have made lifetime commitments to social change.)

Kidder, Tracy. *The Soul of a New Machine.* Little, Brown, 1981. (A study of the growth of the computer industry in the 1970s.)

Nader, Ralph. *Civics for Democracy: A Journey for Teachers and Students.* Essential Books, 1993. (Teaches citizenship by profiling students across the country working to improve their communities, and covers a history of the civil rights and women's rights movements.)

CHAPTER 24

The political scandal dubbed *Watergate* profoundly shook the people's faith in their leaders. Coming on the heels of the turbulence of the 1960s, the scandal's reach into the highest, most trusted offices of the government seemed to confirm the country's worst fears about the abuse of power. It was no surprise, then, when an outsider to Washington politics, Jimmy Carter, was elected President.

SECTION 1

When Nixon resigned, Vice President Gerald Ford, a modest and popular politician, became President. Ford's presidency was lackluster in addition to being plagued by economic stagnation and an undefined foreign policy. Ford's pardon of Nixon for any Watergate crimes was extremely unpopular.

SECTION 2

In 1976 Jimmy Carter, former governor of Georgia, was elected President. Carter, who had campaigned as an outsider to the world of Washington politics, discovered that his inexperience in and unfamiliarity with the federal government made it difficult for him to get his programs enacted.

SECTION 3

Carter had some great successes in foreign affairs by emphasizing negotiations, peacemaking, and human rights; however, his approach also brought about some serious crises, one of which played a central role in his failure to win reelection.

SECTION 4

Carter was generally unsuccessful in creating domestic programs and working with Congress to see them enacted.

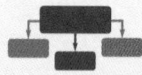

The Post-Watergate Period
1974–1980

The Relevance of the Big Idea

After the Watergate scandal, the American people and the press began to scrutinize the nation's leaders and political candidates more closely than ever. Any hint of potential scandal became headline news. Almost all presidential candidates since Watergate have had to explain (some with more success than others) an embarrassing skeleton dug out of their closet. Tell students that in 1994, President Clinton and First Lady Hillary Rodham Clinton were challenged on their investment in the Whitewater real estate venture, which formed part of a confusing series of financial dealings carried out when Clinton held office in his home state of Arkansas.

Ask students to list minimum standards of conduct that should apply to all public officials.

In Depth

Global Connections

Early in his presidency Jimmy Carter made human rights a cornerstone of American foreign policy. He condemned the Soviet Union's treatment of dissidents and South Africa's policy of apartheid; and he also chastised South Korea, Ethiopia, and several Latin American nations for repressive policies. But Carter found it necessary to reconcile his convictions about human rights with pledges of support for repressive anticommunist regimes. He praised Iran under the dictatorship of the shah, for example, as an "island of stability."

778

CHAPTER 24

The Post-Watergate Period
1974–1980

The upheaval from the Watergate scandal continued to disrupt American society even after Richard Nixon resigned. People wondered whether any President could heal the rifts that tore the country apart. Gerald Ford, the man who took Nixon's place, tried to revive the confidence that had sustained the United States through past troubles. But after two years in office, he lost the presidency to a little-known Democrat, Jimmy Carter, who promised the country honesty and morality.

Events in the United States

1973 Henry Kissinger wins the Nobel Peace Prize. • Congress enacts the War Powers Act.	**1974** Gerald Ford becomes President after Nixon resigns.		**1976** Americans celebrate their bicentennial. • Jimmy Carter is elected President.

| **1973** | **1974** | **1975** | **1976** |

Events in the World

1973 President Allende of Chile is killed in a military coup.	**1974** Giscard d'Estaing becomes president of France.	**1975** The Khmer Rouge takes power in Cambodia.	**1976** Chinese leader Mao Zedong dies.

▶ RESOURCE DIRECTORY

Teaching Resources

Alternate Lesson Plan: Demonstrating the Big Idea found in the Alternate Lesson Plans folder, p. 166, provides a lesson strategy to instruct students about the Big Idea that the Watergate scandal had far-reaching consequences in American politics, hampering Ford's attempts to lead after Nixon and enabling Carter, with his promises of honest government, to be elected.

Alternative Assessment Handbook provides information, guidance, and strategies for alternative methods of assessment. It includes an essay on new trends in assessment, guidance and strategies for developing performance tasks and portfolios, scoring rubrics, and sample evaluation forms.

Pages 780–784
The Ford Administration

Gerald Ford faced difficulties with the presidency he inherited. Although he wanted to help the nation recover from the Watergate affair, he never managed to step forward as a strong leader or deal effectively with problems that dogged the economy.

Pages 785–788
The Carter Transition

The Watergate scandal continued to influence the nation's political decisions as the people chose a Democrat, Jimmy Carter, for President in 1976. Carter tried to bring a new spirit of trust and honesty to Washington.

Pages 789–793
Carter's Foreign Policy

Carter's religious beliefs led him to emphasize peacemaking and human rights in foreign affairs, resulting in some outstanding successes. Those same beliefs also played a part in preventing his reelection.

Pages 795–799
Carter's Domestic Problems

In addition to crises overseas, domestic issues brought more trouble for the Carter presidency. The administration could not effectively create and pass legislation, dooming Carter's energy program and efforts to stabilize the economy.

1977	1978	1979	1980	1981

Above timeline:

1977 President Carter establishes the Department of Energy. • The Panama Canal treaties are signed.

1978 President Carter visits Nigeria and Liberia. • Egyptian and Israeli leaders meet at Camp David.

1979 Americans are taken hostage in Iran. • A nuclear accident occurs at Three Mile Island in Pennsylvania.

1980 Jimmy Carter loses the presidency to Ronald Reagan.

Below timeline:

1977 South Africa declares the black homeland of Bophuthatswana independent.

1978 Civil war begins in Nicaragua.

1979 Egypt and Israel sign a peace treaty. • Margaret Thatcher becomes British prime minister.

1980 War begins between Iran and Iraq.

Alternative Assessment

As an ongoing chapter project, students can assume the role of a curator of exhibits at the presidential library of either Ford or Carter. Students should collect and interpret information for a display about the administration of their chosen ex-President. Presentations should include a minimum of three of the following display sections:

- A biography of the President
- Campaign material such as posters, banners, and buttons
- Chart identifying cabinet and important judicial appointments
- Significant quotations from the President at key events during his administration
- Political cartoons about the President and his policies
- Data regarding foreign affairs, including maps of crisis locations, and a summary of events abroad
- Statistics on inflation rates, unemployment, and productivity

Explain that finished projects will be assessed according to the following standards:

- **Unacceptable** Projects are not attempted or fail to meet requirements outlined.
- **Limited/Acceptable** Projects present some information that illustrates the times and administration of the President.
- **Extensive/Commendable** Projects present significant information from a variety of sources illustrating the times and administration of the President.
- **Extraordinary/Outstanding** Projects present carefully researched information that highlights the key events and significant trends of the times and administration of the President in a creative and sophisticated manner.

For information and guidance on alternative assessment trends and strategies, see the Alternative Assessment Handbook in the Resource Directory on page 778.

The Ford Administration

The Ford Administration

1. FOCUS

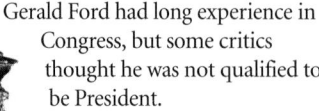

Connecting to the Big Idea

See page 778B. Explain that when Vice President Ford stepped up to the presidency after Nixon resigned in 1974, Americans were cheered by his honesty and simplicity. However, his administration proved mediocre. Ask what problems plagued the Ford administration.

Objectives

● Describe Gerald Ford's congressional experience and explain why some critics questioned his qualifications for President.
● Describe the economic troubles of the mid-1970s.
● Describe Ford's foreign policy.

Bellringer

Ask students to think of a time when they excused, or forgave, a friend, classmate, or family member. What does offering a pardon imply about the guilt or innocence of the person pardoned?

Reading Strategy

Relating to Topic Ask students to think about the meaning of the subheading on page 780, "A Ford, not a Lincoln." Then ask them to note the various failings of the Ford presidency described in the section.

SECTION PREVIEW

Gerald Ford faced difficulties with the presidency he inherited. Although he wanted to help the nation recover from the Watergate affair, he never managed to step forward as a strong leader or deal effectively with problems that dogged the economy.

Key Concepts

• Gerald Ford had long experience in Congress, but some critics thought he was not qualified to be President.
• Neglected during Watergate, the economy was in trouble by the mid-1970s.
• Ford continued the foreign policies initiated under Nixon.

This ornate soup tureen was a gift from Queen Elizabeth II of Great Britain to President Ford to commemorate the American bicentennial.

Key Terms, People, and Places

stagflation, Helsinki Accords; Gerald R. Ford, Nelson Rockefeller

T he new President, **Gerald R. Ford,** was a decent man who faced a difficult job. He had to help the United States emerge from its worst political scandal at a time when the economy was in trouble and the war in Vietnam was ending in defeat. Ford began on the wrong foot, with a well-meant pardon for Richard Nixon that outraged many. In the months that followed, he never managed to provide the leadership the country needed.

"A Ford, not a Lincoln"

Gerald Ford was one of the most popular politicians in Washington when he was appointed Vice President in October 1973, after Spiro Agnew resigned in disgrace for accepting bribes. In a long career in Congress, Ford had risen to become minority leader of the House of Representatives, where he was well-liked by members of both parties. He was an unassuming, midwestern Republican from Michigan, who believed in traditional American virtues such as hard work and self-reliance. His stands on the issues of the day reflected these beliefs. Over the years, he had opposed federal aid to education, the antipoverty program, and government funds for mass transit. He supported measures for law and order and defense spending.

Nixon chose Ford as a noncontroversial figure who might bolster his own support from Congress. When Ford was confirmed, Congress and the public were interested mainly in his honesty and stability, not his qualifications for the presidency. In fact, during his years in Washington, Ford had often been the target of jokes. One was attributed to President Lyndon Johnson, who could be cruel when fighting political opponents. Knowing that Ford had played football on the University of Michigan championship team in the 1930s, Johnson remarked that perhaps he had played too long without a helmet.

While the choice of Ford as Vice President was generally well received, it brought new criticism of the man from those concerned about his qualifications for taking over the presidency should the need arise. Journalist Richard Rovere wrote in *The New Yorker*:

That he is thoroughly equipped to serve as Vice President seems unarguable; the office requires only a warm body and occasionally a nimble tongue. However . . . neither Richard Nixon nor anyone else has come forward to explain Gerald Ford's qualifications to serve as Chief Executive. He altogether lacks administrative experience. If his knowledge of foreign affairs

 RESOURCE DIRECTORY

Teaching Resources

Reproducible Lesson Plan found in the Unit 7 folder, p. 38, provides a summary of the Section 1 lesson plan content.

Alternate Lesson Plan: Critical Thinking Determining Relevance, found in the Alternate Lesson Plans folder, p. 167, identifies the issues Ford confronted and analyzes his approach to problem solving.

Guided Reading and Review found in the Unit 7 folder, p. 42, provides a structure for reading and mastering the key concepts and reviewing the key terms for Section 1. (Guided Practice)

exceeds that of the average literate citizen, the fact has yet to be demonstrated.

Ford acknowledged his own limitations when he was sworn in, saying, "I am a Ford, not a Lincoln."

When Nixon resigned eight months later, Ford became the first nonelected President. Other Vice Presidents who had moved into the White House had at least been elected to the vice presidency as part of the national ticket. To fill the vice-presidential vacancy, Ford named former New York governor **Nelson Rockefeller**—creating the unique situation of having both a President and a Vice President who had been appointed, but not elected.

MAKING CONNECTIONS

The Twenty-fifth Amendment to the Constitution, which allows the President to appoint a replacement when the vice presidency is vacant, was passed in 1967, only a few years before Watergate. Is this the best way to fill such a high office? What other method would you suggest?

The Nixon Pardon

Ford became President in the midst of what he called "our long national nightmare." The nation was embittered by Watergate and did not look forward to the prospect of an impeachment trial—which would be only the second in United States history. Many Americans wondered whether the Constitution would survive such seeming disrespect from the nation's leaders. When Ford assumed the presidency, the nation needed a leader who could take it beyond the ugliness of Watergate.

In response to this public mood, President Ford declared that it was a time for "communication, conciliation, compromise and cooperation." Americans were on his side. *Time* magazine noted "a mood of good feeling and even exhilaration in Washington that the city had not experienced for many years."

All too quickly, however, Ford lost that popular support. Barely a month after Nixon had

resigned, Ford pardoned the former President for "all offenses" he might have committed, preventing further prosecution. On national television, Ford explained that he had looked to God and his own conscience in deciding "the right thing" to do about Nixon and "his loyal wife and family":

> Theirs is an American tragedy in which we have all played a part. It could go on and on and on, or someone must write the end to it. I have concluded that only I can do that, and if I can I must. . . . My conscience tells me that only I, as President, have the constitutional power to firmly shut and seal this book. My conscience tells me that it is my duty not merely to proclaim domestic tranquillity but to use every means that I have to ensure it.

Ford knew critics would surface, but he thought, "Most Americans will understand." He was wrong. While many of Nixon's loyalists

Betty Ford described her husband as "an accidental Vice President, and an accidental President, and in both jobs he replaced disgraced leaders." One of Ford's first presidential acts—pardoning Richard Nixon—stirred up a storm of controversy.

2. INSTRUCT

Explain/Discuss

Review the constitutional requirements for the office of President and discuss Ford's qualifications. What about Ford made him suitable as Nixon's Vice President, but less suitable as President?

Discuss Ford's reasons for pardoning Nixon. Then review the public reaction to Ford's well-intentioned action.

Discuss the efforts of the Ford administration to control inflation and increase productivity. Ask students to consider the results of these efforts. Why was the WIN program such a disaster for Ford?

Answer to . . .

MAKING CONNECTIONS

Students may suggest that Congress should have the right to appoint a new Vice President, that there be a special election, or that some other person in the executive branch be automatically next in line.

In Depth

Historical Misconceptions

The popular image of Gerald Ford as a bumbling, guy-next-door, caretaker politician is far from the truth. Social critic Michael Medved writes: "The guy next door doesn't spend sixteen hours a day and twenty-five years of his life in a nonstop quest for votes, power, and admiration. Like most politicians, Ford is a driven man."

Analyze

Ask students to analyze the concept of presidential leadership. Everett Carl Ladd, executive director of the Roper Center for Public Opinion Research, observes in his book *American Polity*: "At its best, presidential leadership moves the nation as far as possible in the directions the public favors, by means that are acceptable given prevailing values and institutional requirements." When did Ford act according to Ladd's definition of presidential leadership? Which of the methods Ford tried to use to solve problems were in opposition to prevailing values?

In Depth

Did You Know?

In the mid-1970s, Ford's case-by-case clemency offer to thousands of Vietnam-era draft resisters and military deserters was as controversial as his presidential pardon of Nixon. The Clemency Board found that though thousands had been either prosecuted and punished, or officially forgiven, the question remained "whether the American people will continue to condemn them."

faced prison for their role in Watergate, the former President walked away without a penalty. Ford's generous gesture backfired, making people wonder what kind of bargain had been made when Nixon resigned. They questioned the new President's judgment and ability as he tried to move ahead. Ford found himself booed when he made public speeches, just as Johnson and Nixon had been. He, too, had to leave speaking engagements from back doors to avoid angry demonstrators.

Ford Tries to Move Ahead

Recovery from Watergate was not the only difficult issue Ford had to face. While focused on the scandal, the nation seemed to have stood still, but some conditions had grown worse. Now, at a time when the country needed direction, the new administration seemed unclear about what course to take.

Problems with inflation and unemployment prompted one cartoonist to send President Ford this comment on the issue.

The Economy Stagnates Preoccupation with Watergate had hurt Nixon's ability to deal with the economy, and it was still in sorry shape. Inflation hovered around 11 percent a year, significantly higher than it had been in the past, while unemployment climbed to 5.3 percent, as the graph on page 783 shows. Home building, usually a sign of a healthy economy, stalled as interest rates rose. The fears of worried investors brought a drop in stock prices.

In the past, economists had believed that a moderate rise in inflation could help control the rate of unemployment. Conversely, rising unemployment would counterbalance an increase in inflation. Federal policy makers had sought to strike a satisfactory balance between the two. Now, however, inflation and unemployment both rose, while the economy remained stalled and stagnant. Economists named this new situation **stagflation,** but giving it a name did not make it go away. Nixon's preoccupation with Watergate had compromised his effort to deal with economic difficulties. By the time Ford assumed the presidency, the situation had reached crisis levels. Not since Franklin Roosevelt took office during the Great Depression had a new President faced such harsh economic troubles.

Ford's approach—like Herbert Hoover's in the early 1930s—was to try to restore public confidence. The centerpiece of his economic program was the "Whip Inflation Now," or "WIN," campaign. The President asked Americans to wear red and white "WIN" buttons, to save a portion of their incomes, and to plant vegetable gardens to challenge rising prices in the stores. This effort to manage the economy by coordinating the everyday actions of millions of people was doomed from the start. The plan had no real incentives and soon faded away.

Eventually, Ford's administration recognized that the government must act, but its initial attempts backfired. A policy to curb inflation by controlling the money supply led to the worst recession since the 1930s, with widespread job layoffs. Unemployment soared to 9 percent in 1975. Congress then backed an antirecession spending program, and Ford, reversing his previous course, backed an increase in unemployment benefits and a multibillion dollar tax cut. The economy recovered slightly, but inflation and unemployment remained high and the deficit increased.

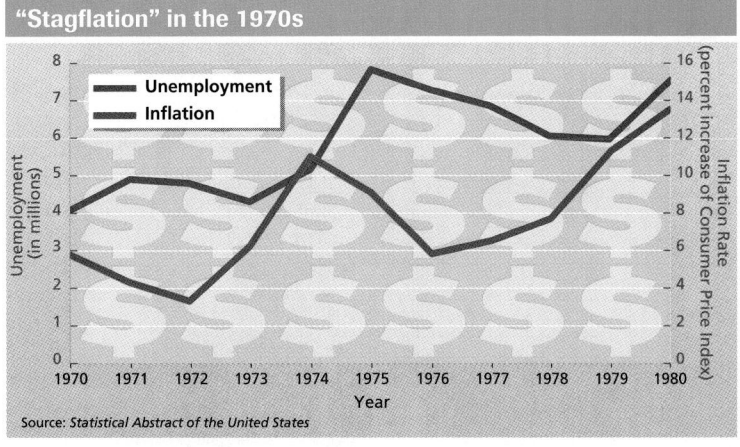

"Stagflation" in the 1970s

Source: Statistical Abstract of the United States

Interpreting Graphs
Upon assuming office, President Ford declared war on inflation, calling it "Public Enemy No. 1." Ford's administration, however, saw the worst economic slump in the United States since the Great Depression. *In what year did the highest consumer prices coincide with the second highest level of unemployment in the decade?*

Conflicts with Congress In spite of having served many years in the House of Representatives, President Ford was often locked in combat with the Democratic Congress. His basic dilemma was that he believed in limited government at a time when strong executive leadership was needed to get the nation on its feet. Jerold F. terHorst, his first press secretary, once noted how Ford's own sense of decency came into conflict with his view of presidential power:

> I f he saw a schoolkid in front of the White House who needed clothing, he'd give him the shirt off his back, literally. Then he'd go right in the White House and veto a school-lunch bill.

Ford vetoed bills to create a consumer protection agency and to fund programs for education, housing, and health care. Congress responded by overriding a higher percentage of presidential vetoes than it had since the presidency of Franklin Pierce in the 1850s.

Foreign Policy Actions In foreign policy, Ford followed the basic outlines of Nixon's approach, keeping Henry Kissinger on as secretary of state. During the Ford years, the United States continued forging ties with China, freeing the country from its involvement in Vietnam, and refocusing its attention on Europe.

Congress asserted itself on foreign policy as it did on domestic policy. Irritated at the growth of the "imperial presidency," it had passed the War Powers Act in 1973 over Nixon's veto. This law let Congress either approve or disapprove the President's sending troops overseas and bringing forces home. Congress now used its power to stop new United States military action in Southeast Asia as the North Vietnamese strengthened control over all Vietnam in 1975. It also refused to become involved in political unrest in Turkey and Angola.

Despite Congress's effort to play a greater role in foreign affairs, the Ford administration did initiate some foreign policy actions. In mid-1975, soldiers from communist Cambodia captured the *Mayaguez,* an American merchant ship cruising in Cambodian waters. When protests went unanswered, Ford sent 250 marines to rescue the ship's crew. The rescue succeeded, but 41 Americans were killed—probably needlessly, as later investigations showed that the Cambodian government apparently was preparing to return both ship and crew. For Ford and Kissinger, however, the incident was a chance to counteract the impression that Vietnam had weakened the United States internationally.

Section 1 Review Answers

1. (a) stagflation, see p. 782,
(b) Helsinki Accords, see p. 784

2. (a) Gerald R. Ford, see p. 780,
(b) Nelson Rockefeller, see p. 781

3. He had long experience in Congress and was well liked but had no experience as an executive or leader; he lacked foreign policy experience and knowledge.

4. Unemployment and inflation were both high; Ford's WIN program was ineffective. Efforts to control money brought a recession and higher unemployment.

5. Ford retained Kissinger as secretary of state; they continued the initiatives begun in the Nixon years.

6. Ford's good relationship with Congress deteriorated after he became President.

7. Whether or not they agree with Ford's decision to grant the pardon, students should demonstrate an understanding both of Ford's wish to bring Watergate to an end and of the widespread negative public reaction to his decision.

Reteach

Ask students to assess President Ford's effectiveness in healing the wounds of Watergate, restoring the health of the economy, and maintaining peace and good relationships with other nations.

 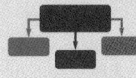

Reinforcing the Big Idea

Since President Ford's administration failed to develop and carry out coherent policies, Ford was not perceived as a strong leader. The next section describes the presidential campaign of 1976 and Carter's approach to the presidency.

"Uncle Sam" leads a joyful parade in honor of the 200th anniversary of the Declaration of Independence. All across the country, bicentennial celebrations drew people together and stirred up feelings of national pride. ✪

On other foreign policy fronts, Ford's record was stronger. Ford continued Strategic Arms Limitation Talks (SALT) and held out hope for further nuclear disarmament. He also signed the **Helsinki Accords**, a series of agreements made at a summit meeting in Finland. There, thirty-five nations, including the Soviet Union, pledged to cooperate economically and to promote human rights. As revolutions in Africa and elsewhere around the world toppled colonial governments, the administration took steps toward developing relationships with the new regimes.

Foreign policy in the Ford years was mainly a reaction to outside events. Still, the United States remained at peace, avoided major confrontations, and continued the difficult process of redefining its role abroad.

The Country Celebrates a Birthday

Amidst lingering recession and the memory of Watergate, Americans seized the chance to forget their problems at a nationwide birthday party. July 4, 1976, marked the bicentennial, or two hundredth anniversary, of the Declaration of Independence. Across the country, people in small towns and great cities celebrated with parades, concerts, air shows, political speeches, and fireworks. ✪

The climax of the national party was the Fourth of July itself. In New York City, more than two hundred sailing ships, including majestic "tall ships," sailed into the harbor while millions watched from the shore. Other cities competed to have the most spectacular fireworks display or the longest parade. Many observers saw the bicentennial mood as an optimistic revival after years of gloom.

SECTION 1 REVIEW

Key Terms, People, and Places
1. Define (a) stagflation, (b) Helsinki Accords.
2. Identify (a) Gerald R. Ford, (b) Nelson Rockefeller.

Key Concepts
3. What were Ford's strengths and weaknesses as President?
4. What problems did the economy face during the Ford administration? How did President Ford attempt to address those problems?

5. What was the direction of Ford's foreign policy?
6. What was the relationship like between President Ford and Congress?

Critical Thinking
7. **Demonstrating Reasoned Judgment** Should Gerald Ford have pardoned Richard Nixon? Why or why not? Consider both the explanations that Ford gave and your own assessment of what the pardon did and did not accomplish.

▶ **RESOURCE DIRECTORY** ✪

Teaching Resources

✪ **Literature Activity** A Search for Roots, found in the Unit 7 folder, pp. 61–63, describes Alex Haley's search for his ancestral identity, in an excerpt from his book *Roots*, published in 1976.

Primary Source Activity 1976: The Bicentennial Year, found in the Unit 7 folder, p. 58, presents quotations from various demographic groups commenting on issues important in contemporary American society.

Quiz found in the Unit 7 folder, p. 43, covers the main ideas in this section as well as the key terms.

The Carter Transition

The Watergate scandal continued to influence the nation's political decisions as the people chose a Democrat, Jimmy Carter, for President in 1976. Carter tried to bring a new spirit of trust and honesty to Washington.

Key Concepts
- Gerald Ford did not appear "presidential" to many voters in the 1976 election.
- Jimmy Carter's campaign emphasized his trustworthiness and his status as a Washington outsider.
- Carter's small-town background and deep religious beliefs influenced his style and policies as President.

Key Terms, People, and Places
James Earl Carter, Jr.

I n a reaction against the Watergate scandal and economic woes, voters elected a Democrat, Jimmy Carter, as President in 1976. **James Earl Carter, Jr.,** a businessman and former naval officer who had been governor of Georgia, promised to bring a fresh approach to the White House. At first Carter enjoyed his status as a "Washington outsider," but in time that position lessened his ability to lead effectively.

The Election of 1976

Although Gerald Ford initially said that he would not seek election to the office he had inherited, by 1976 he had changed his mind. But as he campaigned to win the nation's approval, a number of personal liabilities continued to hurt his chances for success.

In the public's perception, Ford did not appear "presidential," and while people liked him, he never completely captured their confidence. He was a wooden speaker, and, as

described by the English journalist Alistair Cooke, "always seemed to be battling gamely with a language he had only recently acquired." At the Republican convention, Ford narrowly won the nomination against a strong challenge from Ronald Reagan, a former actor and governor of California, who represented the conservative wing of the party.

Ford faced Jimmy Carter, who, as governor of Georgia, had worked against racial discrimination in his state. Nationally, Carter began as a virtual unknown, with a broad smile and soft southern accent. In addition to his political activities, he also owned a successful peanut farm in Georgia. In a skillful primary campaign, he appealed to a wide audience and easily won the Democratic nomination. His running mate was Walter Mondale, a progressive senator from Minnesota.

Carter played on the backlash that followed Watergate. Over and over, he stressed that he was not part of the Washington establishment and so would bring a different perspective to the nation's capital. He distanced himself from many involved in the scandal by pointing out that he was not a lawyer but just "a peanut farmer."

Carter presented himself as honest and straightforward. In *Why Not the Best?*—an autobiography published in 1975—he said, "There is no need for lying. Our best national defense is the truth." In a later memoir, he recalled his campaign approach:

> I ran as though I would have to govern— always careful about what I promised, and determined not to betray those who gave me their support. Sometimes I irritated my opponents and the news reporters by firmly refusing to respond to questions to which I did not know the answers. And

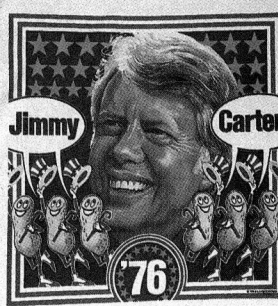

Jimmy Carter's smile was famous. One writer described it as **"the biggest grin of any President since TR."**

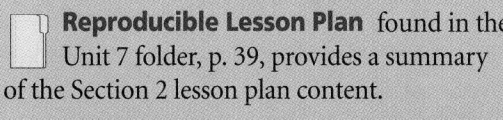

Reproducible Lesson Plan found in the Unit 7 folder, p. 39, provides a summary of the Section 2 lesson plan content.

Alternate Lesson Plan: Cooperative Learning found in the Alternate Lesson Plans folder, p. 168, helps groups of students describe Jimmy Carter's approach to the presidency by preparing materials for his campaign.

Guided Reading and Review found in the Unit 7 folder, p. 44, provides a structure for reading and mastering the key concepts and reviewing the key terms for Section 2. (Guided Practice)

Connecting to the Big Idea

See page 778B. Explain that in 1976, Jimmy Carter, former governor of Georgia, was elected President. Ask what promises Carter made to the American people.

Objectives
- Describe how Ford's inability to project a presidential image affected his showing in the 1976 election.
- Describe how Jimmy Carter's campaign emphasized his trustworthiness and his status as a Washington outsider.
- Explain how Carter's small-town background and deep religious beliefs influenced his style and policies as President.

In Depth

Biography

Barbara Jordan (b. 1933) represented the "New South" that the Carter presidency brought to national prominence. Elected to the Texas Senate in 1966, she was the first African American to sit in that body since 1883 and became one of its most articulate members. Jordan was elected to the United States House of Representatives in 1972, where she served for three terms. She delivered the keynote address at the Democratic convention in 1976, warning: "This is the great danger America faces. That we will cease to be one nation and become instead a collection of interest groups: city against suburb, region against region, individual against individual. Each seeking to satisfy private wants."

Bellringer

Ask students how they would rate the honesty of the current President and administration. Ask if they can envision any situation in which a President should be less than completely open and honest with the public.

Reading Strategy

Structured Overview Ask students to write the name *Jimmy Carter* in the center of a piece of paper and to note important details about Carter around his name as they read the section.

2. INSTRUCT

Explain/Discuss

Discuss how Ford's failure to convey a "presidential" image on television affected the election of 1976. Ask students which recent President they think had the strongest "presidential" image, and whether that President was also a good leader.

Ask students whether they think a campaign such as that waged by Carter tells voters what they really need to know about a candidate.

Discuss how Carter's outsider status, and his choice of other outsiders as his key advisers, hampered his ability to work with Congress.

Answer to ...

MAKING CONNECTIONS

Students should note that a vein of public distrust of officials and politicians runs through American political history, and that being an "outsider" separates a candidate from people's current discontent.

Caption Answer to ...

 Interpreting Maps

Ford was from the Midwest himself. His belief in traditional American values would appeal to many voters in this traditionally conservative area of the country.

---

repeatedly I told supporters, "If I ever lie to you, if I ever make a misleading statement, don't vote for me. I would not deserve to be your President."

Carter's appeal succeeded. The basic issue in 1976 was trust, and he used it superbly. Patrick Caddell, a public opinion pollster, noted:

> W ithout the trust thing, he couldn't have made it. . . . Most people would really rather trust other people than distrust them, except in politics; most people have a reason to distrust most candidates. Jimmy was a stranger in town. They had no reason to distrust him and he didn't give them one.

Carter began the campaign with a lead, then nearly lost it as voters wondered whether he could really govern. Ford hurt his own cause with a number of embarrassing mistakes, such as declaring in a television debate that the Soviets did not dominate Eastern Europe. One observer

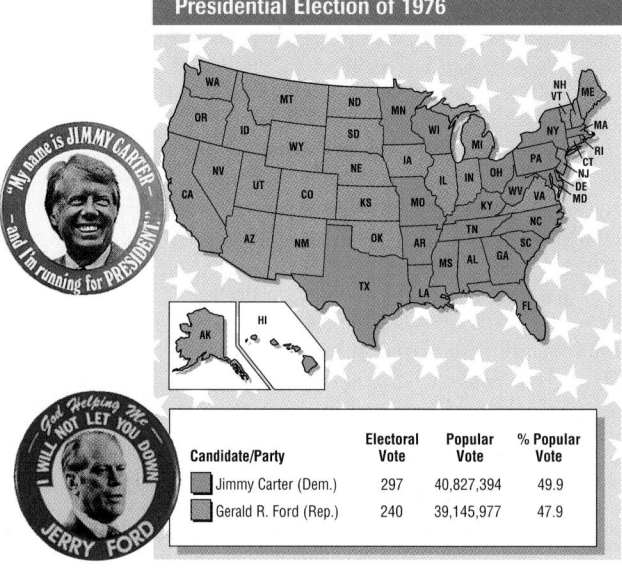

Presidential Election of 1976

Candidate/Party	Electoral Vote	Popular Vote	% Popular Vote
Jimmy Carter (Dem.)	297	40,827,394	49.9
Gerald R. Ford (Rep.)	240	39,145,977	47.9

Geography and History: Interpreting Maps
This map shows that Ford captured the vote of most of the Midwest. *What do you know about Ford's background that might help to explain this?*

---

commented that the campaign was like the Indianapolis 500, the nation's largest auto race, with people watching to see who would crash next.

In the end, Carter gained the support of most elements of the old Democratic coalition. He was successful with blue collar, African American, and some Catholic voters. He also won most of the South. Though Democrats in races for Congress and local contests generally swept the election, Carter's own margin was narrow: he won 50 percent of the popular vote to Ford's 48 percent. The electoral vote, 297 to 240, was also close. The map below left shows these election results.

MAKING CONNECTIONS

Like Jimmy Carter, candidates for Congress and the presidency often point out that they are "Washington outsiders," not part of the establishment. Why do you think this argument appeals to some voters?

The President from Plains, Georgia

Jimmy Carter—a southerner with a short career in politics—*was* different from his recent predecessors in the White House. His family had lived for generations in the rural South; the population of his hometown of Plains was six hundred. After graduating in 1946 from the United States Naval Academy, where he was trained as an engineer, he served on nuclear submarines. Later he took over management of his family's prosperous peanut farm and warehouse. He did not enter Georgia state politics until 1962.

Carter's deeply felt religious faith dominated his view of the world and led to considerable curiosity and questioning from reporters. He was a born-again Baptist, who noted that his life had been "shaped in the church." He relied on the Bible and read it daily—often in Spanish to improve his skill with the language. His faith, he believed, would keep him from taking on "the same frame of mind that Nixon or Johnson did—lying, cheating and distorting the truth."

On the other hand, Carter believed strongly in personal freedom. In Georgia, for instance, he had rejected calls for prayer in the public

▶ RESOURCE DIRECTORY

Teaching Resources

⭐ 📄 **American Profiles Activity** Patricia Roberts Harris, found in the Unit 7 folder, p. 52, profiles the woman who, in addition to being the head of Carter's Department of Housing and Urban Development, was also the first African American woman to head a law school and the first to serve as an American ambassador.

Refusing the traditional limousine ride, President Jimmy Carter takes an inaugural stroll with his wife, Rosalynn, and daughter, Amy.

schools. Despite his strong religious beliefs, he would not use the presidency as a "pulpit" to promote them.

Personal Abilities Carter was thoughtful, able, and precise. Alistair Cooke called him the "most intelligent" and "best-informed" President the nation had known in years. Yet, Cooke said, Carter

unfortunately used his intelligence to identify, and articulate, 12 sides to every question. . . . He wound up bearing a distressing resemblance to a stalled centipede. All the feelers were wiggling, but the body itself was immobile.

Approach to the Presidency In the first months of Carter's presidency, he appeared to be a reform Democrat. When he accepted his party's nomination, he demanded "an end to discrimination because of race or sex," challenged the established "political and economic elite," and suggested new welfare and health-care programs.

⭐ He began by appointing significantly more women and minorities to his staff than previous administrations had done. Of 1,195 full-time appointees, 12 percent were women, 12 percent were African American, and another 4 percent were Hispanic. In nominating federal judges, he chose four times as many women as had all previous Presidents combined.

In other areas, however, Carter began to look more conservative. As a result, his support from his own party gradually began to dwindle. He had won in 1976 by a narrower margin than other Democratic candidates, who consequently felt that they owed him less than if he had won a sweeping victory that carried them into office as well. The press, too, became more critical as the Carter presidency seemed to lose its momentum.

Staff Problems The "outsider" role became a disadvantage in the White House, too. Carter surrounded himself with southern, mostly Georgian, advisers, who had little sense of how crucial it was for the President to work with Congress. Carter himself was uneasy with congressional expectations and demands, and found it difficult to bargain effectively to pass legislation. Without any congressional experience, he lacked the kind of ability that Lyndon Johnson had to wheel and deal and win over reluctant politicians.

Carter also suffered from hints of scandal in an administration that took pride in being pure. Banker Bert Lance, the director of the Office of Management and Budget, was an old friend from Georgia on whom the President relied. When Lance was accused of allowing large bank overdrafts and other irregularities in

---

SOURCE READINGS

 Source Readings on p. 804 will connect literature selections and primary source excerpts to historical events discussed in this section.

Analyze

Explain that Carter won nearly 90 percent of the African American and Mexican American vote in the 1976 election. President Ford did best among middle- and upper-middle class voters. Ask students to analyze these results in terms of each political candidate's party, and in terms of the problems of the economy under President Ford.

Activity

Preparing a Press Release

In order to have students understand the central issues of the 1976 presidential campaign, ask students to prepare a brief press release. Present to the class one of the broad themes of either the Carter or Ford campaign. Members of the class, acting as the press, may address questions to each "press official."

Enrichment

Ask students to research and report on the controversial role of Rosalynn Carter as her husband's most trusted adviser and on the major activities of the presidential spouses since Carter.

In Depth

Then and Now

A legacy of the Carter era is the link between human rights and diplomacy. As Winston Lord, assistant secretary of state for East Asian and Pacific affairs, described the post–cold war 1990s: "There are still security considerations but increasingly the thrust of the debate in foreign policy today is economics versus human rights. . . . I find myself going from a meeting with Amnesty International or Asia Watch in the morning to one with the Chamber of Commerce in the afternoon."

1. James Earl Carter, Jr., see p. 785

2. Ford failed to convince people that he was "presidential" or a strong leader; also, many Americans were still reacting against the Republicans because of Watergate.

3. Carter chose advisers who were also outsiders; both he and they lacked skills and experience in establishing relations with Congress and passing legislation.

4. He tried at first to move away from the imperial presidency to a more casual, simple style. People liked it at first, but some critics charged that he was not being presidential enough.

5. Voters may have concluded that a sincerely religious person would bring honesty and integrity to act as an "antidote" to Watergate.

Reteach

Ask students to write either a newspaper editorial endorsing Carter for President in 1976 or an editorial column analyzing why Ford lost.

Alternative Assessment

Mid-Point Monitoring

Ask students if they have
- Selected a presidential subject
- Decided which materials to include
- Begun to locate sources of information

Reinforcing the Big Idea

In 1976 American voters selected Jimmy Carter, a Washington outsider and former governor of Georgia, as the nation's new President. Carter, who had a small-town background and strong religious beliefs, vowed to bring honesty to government. The next section focuses on Carter's foreign policy.

The Carters brought a folksy style to the presidency, a style some people criticized as undignified. In spite of the President's low-key image, he was known among friends as a "super-achiever." One friend called Carter "the most disciplined person I've ever seen."

his bank in the past, Carter came strongly to his defense but finally had to conclude that Lance must resign.

Carter's brother Billy posed other problems. He was a flamboyant, irreverent character who relished the attention he received as part of the presidential family. His careless, sometimes anti-Semitic, comments were embarrassing, and his acceptance of $200,000 in "loans" from friends in Libya made it look as if family business was entwined with foreign affairs.

A Question of Style Finally, Carter's image suffered from his attempt to discard the aloof, ceremonial style of the presidency for one of greater simplicity. At first, people responded warmly to his informal, "down home" approach. They loved it when he and his wife, Rosalynn, dismissed the limousine and strolled down Pennsylvania Avenue after the inauguration. Carter wore jeans in the White House and spoke to the nation on television wearing a cardigan sweater instead of a business suit. Critics, however, soon complained about the lack of dignity and ceremony. ⊙

Carter finally discarded his low-key approach. After a few months, he let the band play "Hail to the Chief" on "special occasions," noting, "I found it to be impressive and enjoyed it." The honesty that prompted the President to make this comment also influenced his decisions in foreign policy, as the next section shows.

SECTION 2 REVIEW

Key Terms, People, and Places
1. Identify James Earl Carter, Jr.

Key Concepts
2. What problems during Ford's first term plagued him in the 1976 election?
3. How did Carter's "outsider" image hurt his effectiveness in office?

4. What was Carter's presidential style? How did the American people react to this style?

Critical Thinking
5. **Determining Relevance** How might Carter's outspokenness about his religious beliefs have affected the 1976 election?

▶ RESOURCE DIRECTORY

Teaching Resources

 Primary Source Activity A Crisis of Confidence, found in the Unit 7 folder, pp. 59–60, presents an excerpt from a televised address in which President Carter talked about what he saw as "threatening to destroy the social and the political fabric of America."

Quiz found in the Unit 7 folder, p. 45, covers the main ideas in this section as well as the key terms.

Carter's Foreign Policy

SECTION PREVIEW

Carter's religious beliefs led him to emphasize peacemaking and human rights in foreign affairs, resulting in some outstanding successes. Those same beliefs also played a part in preventing his reelection.

Key Concepts
- Carter's peacemaking efforts helped bring some stability to the Middle East.
- Carter's beliefs also guided his actions in Latin America and Africa.
- Relations with the Soviet Union worsened because of Carter's stand on certain issues.
- A hostage crisis in Iran gravely damaged the Carter presidency.

Key Terms, People, and Places
shuttle diplomacy, Camp David Accords, dissident; Anwar el-Sadat, Menachem Begin, Cyrus Vance, Shah Mohammad Reza Pahlavi, Ayatollah Ruholla Khomeini

P resident Carter achieved his greatest successes in foreign policy. Although he had little diplomatic experience when he took office, he brought the standards that governed his personal life into foreign affairs. While that approach brought notable achievements, it also complicated the relationship of the United States with some nations and ultimately hurt his chance for reelection.

Human Rights Diplomacy

Carter was unwilling to compromise his powerful sense of morality. This trait guided his approach to foreign policy. In his inaugural speech, he declared, "Our commitment to human rights must be absolute. . . . We can never be indifferent to the fate of freedom elsewhere." Support for human rights became the cornerstone of his foreign policy.

Carter later wrote, "Our country has been strongest and most effective when morality and a commitment to freedom and democracy have been most clearly emphasized in our foreign policy." But since the Truman era, he went on, the country had not kept to that standard:

> I nstead of promoting freedom and democratic principles, our government seemed to believe that in any struggle with evil, we could not compete effectively unless we played by the same rules or lack of rules as the evil-doers. . . . When I announced my candidacy in December 1974, I expressed a dream: "That this country set a standard within the community of nations of courage, compassion, integrity, and dedication to basic human rights and freedoms."

MAKING CONNECTIONS

Jimmy Carter set certain standards for foreign policy. Do you think foreign policy today is based on some or all of those principles? Should it be? Why or why not?

A Step Toward Middle East Peace

Carter's commitment to finding ethical solutions to prickly problems was most visible in the Middle East question, and there he had the greatest success. In that unstable region, conflicts between Israel and the Arab nations had existed for nearly thirty years, most recently in 1967 and 1973. After the last Arab-Israeli war, Henry Kissinger had undertaken **shuttle diplomacy**, moving back and forth between nations in an attempt to arrange peace in the region, but conflicts continued.

At first, Carter hoped to call an international conference on the Middle East. Then leader

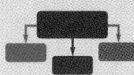

Yellow ribbons became the symbol of hope for the safe return of the Americans held hostage in Iran. The ribbons seemed to decorate every available space when the hostages finally were freed.

1. FOCUS

Connecting to the Big Idea

See page 778B. Point out that President Carter's greatest successes were in the area of foreign policy. Ask what those successes were. How did Carter's stand on certain issues create problems with other nations?

Objectives
- Describe how Carter's peacemaking efforts brought some stability to the Middle East.
- Identify Carter's major actions in Latin America and Africa and show how they related to his emphasis on human rights and peacemaking.
- Explain how Carter's stance on human rights and the Soviet invasion of Afghanistan led to a worsening of relations with the Soviet Union.
- Describe the Iran hostage crisis and explain how it damaged the Carter presidency.

Bellringer

Ask students to list the rights that they would include in a definition of the term *human rights*.

Reading Strategy

Structured Overview Ask students to write the names of the following countries on a piece of paper: Israel, Egypt, Panama, China, Africa, Soviet Union, Iran. Ask students to take notes on Carter's major dealings with each country as they read the section.

Answer to ...

MAKING CONNECTIONS

Answers will vary, but this is a good starting point for discussion of the role of human rights in United States foreign policy.

Reproducible Lesson Plan found in the Unit 7 folder, p. 40, provides a summary of the Section 3 lesson plan content.

Alternate Lesson Plan: Learning Styles found in the Alternate Lesson Plans folder, p. 169, is especially effective for auditory learners as it guides pairs of students in creating interview questions that help describe President Carter's foreign policy and analyze the causes and implications of the Iran hostage crisis.

Guided Reading and Review found in the Unit 7 folder, p. 46, provides a structure for reading and mastering the key concepts and reviewing the key terms for Section 3. (Guided Practice)

Explain/Discuss

Ask students to create a definition of *human rights*, using their thoughts from the Bellringer activity above. Ask them to compare their definitions with that of the Carter administration.

Ask why boycotting the Olympic Games was a serious demonstration of dissatisfaction with the Soviet invasion of Afghanistan. Tell students that, in addition, Carter imposed a grain embargo preventing the Soviet Union from importing grain from the United States. Ask how such an embargo hurt the Soviet Union. How would it hurt the United States?

Review the events leading up to the Iran hostage crisis. Ask what other measures Carter might have taken to free the hostages. Why was the situation so frustrating for Americans?

In Depth

Interdisciplinary

While at Harvard, An Wang (1920–1990) started his own business, Wang Laboratories, in 1951. During the 1970s and early 1980s, the company became a $3 billion operation. He also helped fund a student exchange program between the United States and China and was awarded the Medal of Liberty at the relighting of the Statue of Liberty in 1986. (See the Resource Directory on page 812.)

A jubilant President Carter congratulates Egypt's President Sadat (left) and Israeli prime minister Begin (right) on the signing of the Camp David Accords, a historic step toward peace in the Middle East.

Anwar el-Sadat of Egypt made a historic visit to Israel, beginning negotiations with Prime Minister **Menachem Begin.** The two men had such different personalities, however, that they had trouble compromising. Carter intervened, sending Secretary of State **Cyrus Vance** to invite them to Camp David, the rustic presidential retreat in the Maryland hills. In such a setting, he hoped that he could smooth their differences and move the peace process forward.

Carter knew it was a bold step. In his diary entry for July 31, 1978, he wrote, "We understand the political pitfalls involved, but the situation is getting into an extreme state." He and the two Middle Eastern leaders maintained tight secrecy about the coming conference.

At Camp David in September 1978, Carter assumed the role of peacemaker and practiced highly effective personal diplomacy to bridge the gap between Sadat and Begin. They finally agreed on a framework for peace that became known as the **Camp David Accords.** Under the resulting peace treaty, Israel would withdraw from the Sinai peninsula, which it had occupied in 1967. Egypt, in return, became the first Arab country to recognize Israel's existence as a nation.

The Camp David Accords, of course, did not solve all the problems of the Middle East. Foremost was the question of what to do about the Palestinians, many of whom had fled their homes when Arab nations declared war on Israel immediately after that country was established in 1948. Still, as Secretary of State Vance noted:

> The Camp David Accords rank as one of the most important achievements of the Carter administration. First, they opened the way to peace between Egypt and Israel, which transformed the entire political, military, and strategic character of the Middle East dispute. Genuine peace between Egypt and Israel meant there would be no major Arab-Israeli war, whatever the positions of [other Arab groups].

Moreover, Vance pointed out, the agreement also let negotiators focus on the Palestinian question and established a process for future talks.

Foreign Policy Takes New Directions

Carter's foreign policy team took new steps in other parts of the world as well. Often these reflected the President's own philosophy.

The Panama Canal Another diplomatic milestone was Carter's successful fight to have the Senate ratify treaties returning the Panama Canal to Panama by the year 2000. Once again, his morality guided his approach to foreign policy.

In the early 1900s, President Theodore Roosevelt was proud of the way he had gained control of Panamanian land for the canal. Now Panama and other Latin American countries were increasingly unhappy with the continuing United States presence. It was time to give up some control over that region.

Returning the canal caused bitter debate in Congress, but the Senate finally accepted the pacts by a close margin of one vote. While agreeing to return the canal, the United States reserved the right to intervene militarily, if necessary, to keep it open. The pacts gave the United States security while improving relations with Latin America.

Recognition of China Building on Nixon's initiative in Asia, Carter took the next step and established diplomatic relations with the People's Republic of China as of January 1979. The Chinese wanted American technology and expertise in modernizing their country, while the United States hoped that closer ties with China would keep the Soviet Union on guard. Businesses in the United States also were eager to open the Chinese market of nearly a billion people.

▶ RESOURCE DIRECTORY

Teaching Resources

⊗ 📄 **American Profiles Activity** found in the Unit 7 folder, p. 53, profiles Andrew Young, President Carter's ambassador to the United Nations.

New African Nations Great changes were taking place in Africa, as countries that had been dominated by colonial powers revolted and became independent nations. Under Carter, relations with many nations in Africa improved, guided by Andrew Young, United States ambassador to the United Nations.
⭐ Young, a minister and civil rights leader who had served in Congress, shared many of Carter's views. He convinced the President that the United States should not interfere with African leaders as they shaped new governments. When Carter visited Nigeria and Liberia in March 1978, the popularity of this approach was shown as thousands cheered him in the streets.

Soviet-American Relations

Several issues complicated the relationship between the United States and the Soviet Union. Détente—a relaxation of the tensions between the superpowers—was at a high point when Carter took office. In his first year, he declared optimistically that the United States would forge even closer ties with the Soviet Union.

Then Carter's commitment to human rights alienated Soviet leaders, undermining efforts to work together. The Soviets were annoyed when the President verbally supported **dissidents,** Soviet writers and other activists who opposed the actions of their government.

SALT II In particular, this situation slowed efforts to reach further agreement on arms control. Negotiations were already underway for a second Strategic Arms Limitation Treaty (SALT II). Misjudging the Soviets, Carter offered new weapons reduction proposals that went further than earlier agreements. The Soviets, already suspicious of Carter because the United States had recognized China and was vocally supporting human rights, balked at the proposals.

Finally, Carter and Soviet president Leonid Brezhnev signed the new treaty in Vienna in June 1979. More complicated than SALT I, it limited the number of nuclear warheads and missiles each power retained. SALT II still had to be ratified by the Senate, however.

Andrew Young (left) believed strongly in black majority rule in Africa. In 1981 he would be elected mayor of Atlanta, Georgia.

Afghanistan SALT II seemed to have little chance of passage when the Soviet Union invaded Afghanistan, a country on its southern border. To end agitation against the Soviet-supported government there, Soviet troops invaded in December 1979.

Carter reacted by calling Brezhnev on the "hot line," the open telephone line between Washington and Moscow, and telling him that the invasion was "a clear threat to the peace." He also added, "Unless you draw back from your present course of action, this will inevitably jeopardize the course of United States–Soviet relations throughout the world."

Carter took other steps to emphasize United States disapproval of Soviet aggression. Realizing that SALT II surely would be turned down, he postponed sending it to the Senate. He also imposed a boycott on the summer Olympic Games scheduled to be held in Moscow in 1980. Eventually, some sixty other nations joined the boycott. Détente was effectively dead.

Iran Holds Americans Hostage

The worst foreign policy crisis that Carter faced occurred in Iran, on the Persian Gulf. For years the United States had supported the rule of **Shah Mohammad Reza Pahlavi,** who had taken many steps to modernize Iran.

Section 3 Review Answers

1. (a) shuttle diplomacy, see p. 789, (b) Camp David Accords, see p. 790, (c) dissident, see p. 791

2. (a) Anwar el-Sadat, see p. 790, (b) Menachem Begin, see p. 790, (c) Cyrus Vance, see p. 790, (d) Shah Mohammad Reza Pahlavi, see p. 791, (e) Ayatollah Ruholla Khomeini, see p. 792

3. Egypt was the first Arab nation to recognize Israel's existence and make peace with it; the agreement would discourage other Arab countries or groups from going to war; it was an important first step.

4. Carter believed that morality had to govern foreign policy, and that concern for human rights everywhere must be integral to foreign policy. He respected the rights of developing nations to make their own policies.

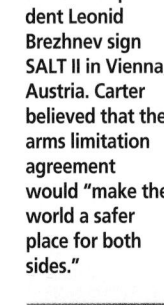

In Depth

Then and Now

In 1976 women won an important equal rights victory when Congress passed a bill authorizing the admission of women to military academies. Eight years later, in 1984, Kristine Holderied became the first woman to graduate, at the top of her class, from the United States Naval Academy in Annapolis, Maryland. As late as 1994, however, legal action was required to compel The Citadel, a South Carolina military college, to allow its first female student, Shannon Faulkner, to attend classes.

Americans overlooked the corruption and harsh repression of the shah's government because he was a reliable supplier of oil and a pro-Western force. Carter himself praised the shah in a visit to Tehran, Iran's capital, in late 1977.

In January 1979, revolution broke out in Iran, led by Muslim fundamentalists who wanted to bring back old ways, and liberal critics who wanted political and economic reform. The shah fled the country and was replaced by an elderly Islamic leader, the **Ayatollah Ruholla Khomeini,** who had been in exile. Khomeini and his followers were aggressively anti-Western, determined to make Iran a strict Islamic state.

In October, in what was intended as a humanitarian gesture, Carter let the exiled shah enter the United States for medical treatment. Many Iranians were outraged. On November 4, angry students seized the American embassy in Tehran and took sixty-six Americans hostage. Though a few were soon released, more than fifty were held for over a year, creating bitter animosity between the United States and Iran.

President Carter and Soviet president Leonid Brezhnev sign SALT II in Vienna, Austria. Carter believed that the arms limitation agreement would "make the world a safer place for both sides."

AMERICAN PROFILES

Kathryn Koob

One of the American hostages was Kathryn Koob, a diplomat. The eldest of six daughters

who grew up on an Iowa farm, she loved to travel. After graduating from Wartburg College in Iowa and earning a master's degree at the University of Denver, she joined the Foreign Service. She became a diplomat, working to promote American aims abroad.

Kate Koob arrived in Iran in July 1979, when the revolution was in full swing. She was director of the Iran-American Society, which promoted cultural exchange. On November 4, her staff heard that students had occupied the American embassy. The next day, she herself was taken hostage.

It was a brutal experience. During the day, zealous young women revolutionaries were her guards, while the "brothers" came at night with threats and questions. "The next day passed, and the next, and the next," she later wrote, "with more interrogations, more comings and goings. And always, the ever-present chanting of the mob outside the gates."

Sometimes imprisoned alone, sometimes with other women, she never knew whether any of them would survive:

> The biggest fear was not knowing what the future held and not knowing what was happening to my colleagues. And then there was the undercurrent: threats of trials and executions.

Usually she could maintain her resolve:

> A they're-not-going-to-get-us attitude began to set in. . . . Each day we survived was to our benefit. I decided the challenge each morning was to get through the day.

Sometimes, though, fear broke through, intensified by thoughts of her worried family and by constant stress:

> And the sounds outside the embassy were nerve-wracking. . . . There seemed to be a continuous crowd of people shouting anti-American slogans, listening to the exhortations [cries] of the students and mullahs [clergymen] who were always on hand. In addition to the crowd noises,

---

▶ RESOURCE DIRECTORY

Teaching Resources

⭐ **Visual Learning Activity** The Hostage Crisis as a Media Event, found in the Unit 7 folder, p. 64, demonstrates, in a political cartoon by Mark Alan Stamaty of the *Village Voice*, the perception that the media sometimes overshadow the story they are trying to cover.

there were three or four loud-speakers blaring newscasts. . . . As I sat confined in my chair I thought, I can't take this, I just can't take this.

The Hostage Crisis Ends

The ordeal of Kate Koob and the other hostages continued for 444 days. They were blindfolded and moved from place to place. Some were tied up and beaten. Others spent time in solitary confinement and faced mock executions intended to keep them constantly afraid. Meanwhile, the American public became increasingly frustrated and impatient for the hostages' release. Nightly newscasts made the crisis a national issue. ⭐

People expected the President to secure the hostages' freedom. When his efforts failed, his hopes for reelection were doomed. Carter broke diplomatic relations with Iran and froze all Iranian assets in the United States. Khomeini held out, insisting that the shah be sent back. Under pressure, Carter finally authorized a daring commando rescue mission, but it ended in disaster when several helicopters broke down in the desert sands and eight American soldiers were killed. The government was humiliated, and Carter's popularity dropped even further.

Carter was torn apart by the crisis. At one point, just weeks after the Americans had been taken prisoner, he confided his feelings to Hamilton Jordan, one of his closest aides:

You know, I've been worried all week about the hostages as a problem for the country and as a political problem for me. But it wasn't until I saw the grief and hope on the faces of their wives and mothers and fathers that I felt the personal responsibility for their lives. It's an awesome burden.

After months of secret talks, in early 1981 the Iranians agreed to release the 52 hostages. Not until the day Carter left office, however, were they allowed to come home. Buses carried them, blindfolded, to the airport where—almost in disbelief—they saw the airplanes that would take them out of Iran. Because Carter was not reelected, however, it was his successor, Ronald Reagan, who greeted them as they arrived on American soil.

In spite of the sentiments of anti-American Iranians (left), personnel from the United States embassy in Teheran, Iran, reach freedom after being held as hostages for more than a year (above). Among them is Katherine Koob (second from bottom).

SECTION 3 REVIEW

Key Terms, People, and Places
1. Define (a) shuttle diplomacy, (b) Camp David Accords, (c) dissident.
2. Identify (a) Anwar el-Sadat, (b) Menachem Begin, (c) Cyrus Vance, (d) Shah Mohammad Reza Pahlavi, (e) Ayatollah Ruholla Khomeini.

Key Concepts
3. What was the significance of the Egypt-Israel agreements made at Camp David?

4. How did Carter's personal beliefs affect his actions in Latin America and Africa?
5. What factors led to the worsening of relations with the Soviet Union?
6. How did Carter respond to the Iran hostage crisis?

Critical Thinking
7. **Making Comparisons** How did Carter's commitment to acting on moral principles compare with Nixon and Kissinger's emphasis on *realpolitik*?

📄 **Quiz** found in the Unit 7 folder, p. 47, covers the main ideas in this section as well as the key terms.

---

5. Carter's support for Russian dissidents angered Soviet leaders; he strongly criticized the Soviet invasion of Afghanistan; SALT II was not ratified.

6. He broke diplomatic relations, seized Iranian assets in the United States, and later authorized a rescue raid that failed. Secret talks finally won the hostages' release.

7. Students should note the increasing emphasis on human rights and self-determination under Carter, in contrast to the maneuvering for power that characterizes *realpolitik*.

Reteach
Ask students to describe the major events of Carter's administration affecting each of the following countries: Israel, Egypt, Panama, China, Soviet Union, Iran.

4. CLOSE

Reinforcing the Big Idea

Carter tried to emphasize human rights and peacemaking in his foreign policy, but his actions complicated United States relationships with the Soviet Union and Iran. The hostage crisis in Iran cost Carter much support in the United States. The next section describes Carter's domestic problems.

Critical Thinking

Recognizing Ideologies

Focus Students will learn the importance of recognizing the ideology of a speaker or writer.

Instruct After students have read and discussed the feature, ask if they think that President Theodore Roosevelt, who said, "Speak softly and carry a big stick," shared the ideology of Senator Thurmond or of President Carter.

Ask students to work in small groups to identify several current issues and to draft a list of questions about those issues designed to reveal a presidential candidate's ideologies.

Extend See the Historian's Toolbox Activity in the Resource Directory below.

Answers

1. (a) Whether or not treaties should be ratified that would turn control and operation of the Panama Canal over to the Panamanians. (b) Passage A: Senator Strom Thurmond in opposition; Passage B: President Jimmy Carter in support. (c) Thurmond: legislative branch; Carter: executive branch. (d) Thurmond: Republican; Carter: Democratic.

2. (a) The Panama Canal belongs to the United States, not to Panama, so it is our right to retain it. It would show weakness to give it up. (b) It is in our national interest, and it is the right and fair thing to do.

3. (a) They take precedence over everything else. We bought and paid for the canal, and therefore it is ours. (b) Strength, with never a sign of weakness. (c) It should take precedence—Panama is a sovereign country and we should respect that sovereignty. (d) Fairness and honor toward smaller countries; generosity, as well as strength.

Recognizing Ideologies

An ideology might be defined as the beliefs that underlie the actions or statements of a person, a group, or a culture. An important critical thinking skill is being able to identify such beliefs. If you can recognize ideologies, you can better understand why certain actions are taken or statements are made.

Use the following steps to help you recognize the ideologies that underlie two opposing statements made during the debate over the Panama Canal treaties.

1. Identify the main topic of the statements and the people who made them. (a) What is the subject under debate in these statements? (b) Who made each statement? (c) In which branch of government does each speaker serve? (d) To what party does each belong?

2. Locate the major points that each speaker makes. (a) What reasons does Speaker A give for rejecting the proposed change? (b) What reasons does Speaker B give for accepting it?

3. Identify the beliefs that underlie the reasons given. (a) What does Speaker A believe about the rights of property with regard to the Panama Canal? (b) What attribute of the national character does he believe should guide United States foreign policy on this issue? (c) What does Speaker B believe about the role of fairness with regard to the canal? (d) What attributes of national character does he think should guide United States foreign policy?

Passage A

The case for rejecting the proposed treat[ies] . . . begins with one crucial point: The Panama Canal is United States property, and the Canal Zone is United States territory. According to the terms of the 1903 treaty with Panama, we acquired sovereign rights over the Canal Zone "in perpetuity" [forever]. The Supreme Court upheld our exercise of sovereignty in 1907. . . . Moreover, the maps of the world show the Canal Zone as part of the United States.

Thus, it is clear that the burden of proof rests on those who favor the treaties; those who oppose them are merely standing up for American rights. Proponents must show that it is in the national interest to dispose of American property which, in addition to its strategic and economic value, represents a cumulative investment of roughly $7 billion.

. . . Would we give up Alaska to the Russians if they were suddenly to demand it? Such weakness is entirely contrary to our national character and heritage.

—Strom Thurmond, Republican (South Carolina), "Why the U.S. Should Keep the Panama Canal," *The Christian Science Monitor*, September 13, 1977

Passage B

The most important reason, the only reason, to ratify the treaties is that they are in the highest national interest of the United States and will strengthen our position in the world. Our security interest will be stronger; our trade opportunities will be improved. We will demonstrate that as a large and powerful country we are able to deal fairly and honorably with a proud but smaller sovereign nation.

. . . We Americans want a more humane and stable world. We believe in goodwill and fairness as well as strength. This agreement with Panama is something we want because we know it is right.

. . . If Theodore Roosevelt were to endorse the treaties, as I'm quite sure he would, it would be mainly because he could see the decision as one by which we are demonstrating the kind of great power we wish to be. . . . In this historic decision, he would join us in our pride for being a great and generous people with a national strength and wisdom to do what is right for us and what is fair to others.

—President Jimmy Carter, televised speech, February 1, 1978

 RESOURCE DIRECTORY

Teaching Resources

Historian's Toolbox Activity Recognizing Ideologies, found in the Unit 7 folder, p. 56, helps students apply the skill by analyzing two opposing viewpoints on the topic of taxing America's richer people to alleviate the federal deficit.

Carter's Domestic Problems

SECTION PREVIEW

In addition to crises overseas, domestic issues brought more trouble for the Carter presidency. The administration could not effectively create and pass legislation, dooming Carter's energy program and efforts to stabilize the economy.

Key Concepts

- The Carter administration had trouble getting its domestic programs through Congress.
- Economic policy under Carter was inconsistent and ineffective.
- Congress blocked Carter's ambitious energy conservation goals.
- Carter gave stronger support to civil rights than Nixon or Ford had done.

Key Terms, People, and Places

Nuclear Regulatory Commission, deregulation, amnesty; Allan Bakke; Three Mile Island

While Jimmy Carter had several triumphs in foreign affairs, he had little success in programs at home. He could not find a way to work effectively with Congress and its leaders, which stalled his plans in many areas, especially energy and the economy. Looking back, he wrote, "I quickly learned that it is a lot easier to hold a meeting, reach a tentative agreement, or make a speech than to get a controversial program through Congress."

That was not the only problem. As *New York Times* columnist Tom Wicker observed, Carter "never established a politically coherent administration." His strategies were not clearly defined. Public support, which had been with him at first, faded as his programs floundered.

The Economy Wobbles

Carter inherited an unstable economy and had trouble finding a way to balance inflation and growth. Inflation also had been a problem for Ford, but had seemed under control after the recession that lasted from 1974 to 1976. To prevent another recession, Carter tried to stimulate growth with government deficit spending. As deficits grew, the Federal Reserve Board increased the money supply, but inflation then rose to about 10 percent.

To stop inflation, Carter tried to slow the economy and reduce the deficit by cutting spending. Cuts fell mostly on social programs, angering reform-minded Democrats. At the same time, the slowdown in the economy increased unemployment and the number of business failures.

Things got worse in 1980, when the new federal budget showed continued high spending. In reaction, bond prices fell and interest rates soared. Borrowers were angry at having to pay high interest rates—sometimes over 20 percent, which is about 3 times higher than they are today—for mortgages and other loans.

People lost confidence in Carter and his economic advisers. The administration's vacillating efforts—trying first one approach, then another—gave the impression that it had no idea what was happening or how to fix it. When Carter left the White House, economist Robert J. Samuelson commented:

> *What was most consistent about the Carter administration was its inability to make a proposal in January that could survive until June. . . . The Carter administration never projected a clear economic program or philosophy because it never had one.*

A Carter Crusade: Saving Energy

Carter made energy conservation a major goal, but he had trouble winning support from Congress and the public. Despite earlier

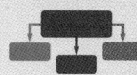

When a revolution in Iran caused oil shortages at home, American drivers faced long lines at the gas pumps—when gas was available at all.

Explain/Discuss

Discuss Carter's various attempts to regulate the economy and the results of each attempt. Ask students to test Samuelson's comment on page 795 by trying to find a clear relationship among the attempts they have listed.

Ask why energy conservation became especially important during the Carter presidency. Discuss Carter's various energy proposals and ask students to identify those that became law. Ask students to classify the complaints about nuclear power plants into two categories: environmental concerns and financial concerns.

Discuss the *Bakke* case and ask students to define *reverse discrimination* in their own words. Ask them if the Supreme Court decision in the *Bakke* case is consistent with their own ideas of fairness.

Analyze

Ask students to state the connection between the high cost of imported oil and the high inflation rate during Carter's presidency.

Answer to ...

Links Across Time

Answers will vary according to students' perceptions of former Presidents' visibility.

In Depth

Did You Know?

Jimmy Carter reflected thus on his presidency: "I have found it much more difficult to be a leader in a time of calm than in a time of crisis. Leaders are very popular in a time of crisis because it is easy to arouse support for the interest of those who are concerned with the crisis itself. But to take action to prevent a future crisis that can't be easily detected nor proved is a very difficult task indeed."

embargoes and shortages, Americans still depended heavily on imported oil. In the late 1970s, more than 40 percent of the oil used in the United States was imported. Some thought the country should be energy self-sufficient instead of depending on supplies from other countries.

OPEC, the Organization of Petroleum Exporting Countries, had been raising oil prices steadily since 1973. People grumbled about rising prices, shortages, and long lines at the gas station. Although Carter was not responsible for oil prices or shortages, he often was the focus of people's complaints. ✪

In April 1977, Carter presented his comprehensive energy program to Congress and the people. He asked people to save fuel by driving less and keeping homes and offices cooler. He also created a new cabinet department, the Department of Energy, to bring together a variety of federal programs promoting conservation and looking for new energy sources. But when he called the need for conservation the "moral equivalent of war," critics seized on the acronym MEOW (from the first letter of each word) to make fun of it.

The energy proposals bogged down in Congress for months, opposed fiercely by representatives from states that produced oil and gas. Eventually, however, the National Energy Act taxed "gas-guzzling" cars, required utilities to use coal rather than oil, removed price controls on domestic oil and natural gas, and allowed tax credits and research funds for alternative energy sources such as solar energy and synthetic fuels. ✪

Three Mile Island Nuclear power seemed one exciting alternative energy source, but serious questions persisted about its costs and safety. Since the 1960s, grassroots activists and some scientists had been criticizing the nuclear power industry. In March 1979, people's doubts and fears seemed to be confirmed by an accident at the nuclear power plant at **Three Mile Island,** near Harrisburg, Pennsylvania.

A small leak through a faulty seal in the cooling system stopped the pumps that circulated the coolant. Temperatures in the reactor core rose, but plant operators misread the symptoms and shut down an emergency cooling system. A partial meltdown of the core occurred, releasing some radiation.

| 1650 | 1700 | 1750 | 1800 | **Links Across Time** | 1850 | 1900 | 1950 | 2000 |

Carter's Commitment to Public Service

Jimmy Carter had entered public service years before he became President in 1976 (near right). After he lost the presidency to Ronald Reagan in 1980, Carter remained committed to public service. Among other activities, Carter is a leading member of Habitat for Humanity (far right), which volunteers its members' time and energy to build houses for the homeless. *Can you think of any Presidents since Carter who have continued their involvement in public life?*

▶ RESOURCE DIRECTORY

Teaching Resources

✪ **Critical Thinking Activity** Formulating Questions: Prices at the Pump, found in the Unit 7 folder, p. 57, helps students practice this skill by analyzing the 1970s oil shortage.

✪ **Visual Learning Activity** Responding to the Energy Crisis, found in the Unit 7 folder, p. 65, illustrates one solution to the problem of dwindling natural resources in a poster issued by the Hawaii Department of Planning and Natural Resources.

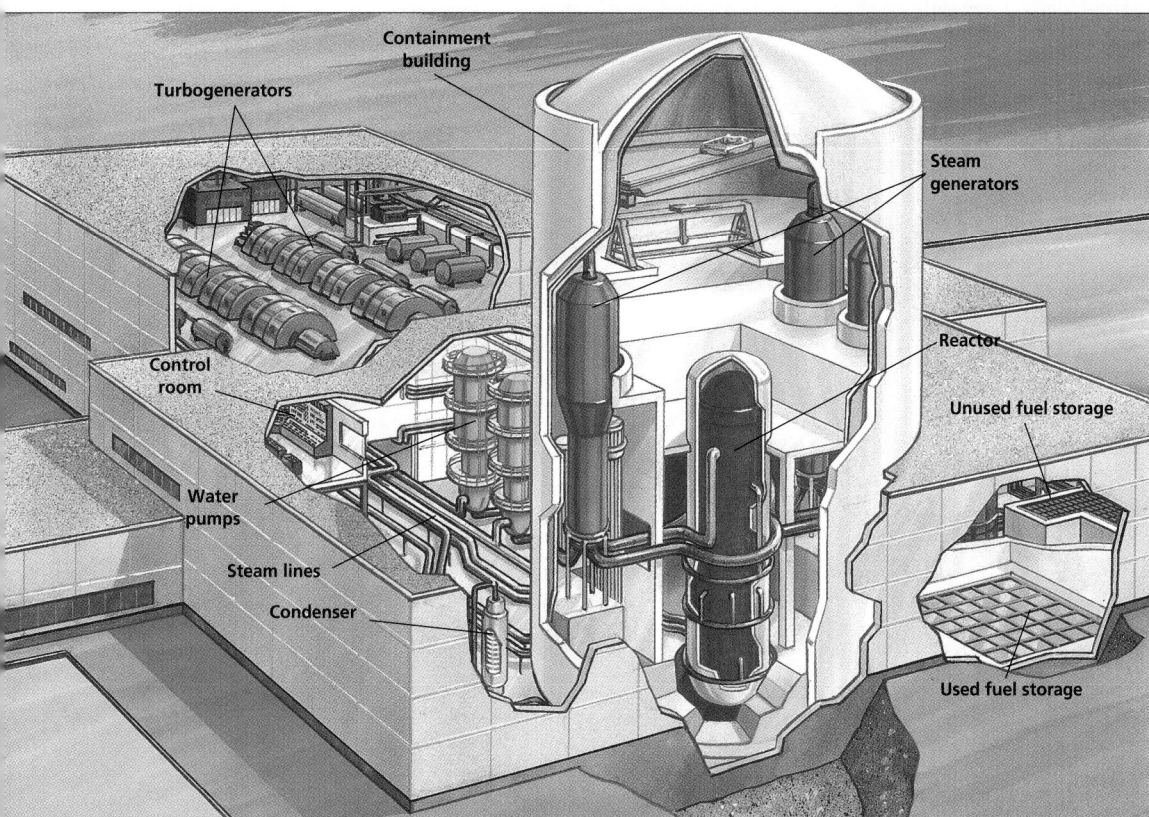

Turbogenerators

Containment building

Steam generators

Reactor

Unused fuel storage

Control room

Water pumps

Steam lines

Condenser

Used fuel storage

Nuclear energy generates enormous amounts of heat, which then is used to make steam. The steam then produces electricity. To make heat, the reactor splits the nuclei of uranium or plutonium in half. Despite the strides made in understanding such reactions, scientists have not yet been able to make use of the full potential of nuclear energy, which could supply the world's electricity for millions of years.

People near the plant were terrified by the idea of a radioactive leak, and 140,000 people fled their homes. Panic increased when the film *The China Syndrome*—in which the plot centers on a fictional reactor meltdown—opened in town. As reporters flocked to Three Mile Island, the story made headlines around the world.

The Future of Nuclear Power Carter named a commission to investigate the accident at Three Mile Island. Its report identified operator errors that had made the initial problem worse. In his response to the report, Carter noted "very serious shortcomings in the way that both the Government and the utility industry regulate and manage nuclear power." He proposed reorganizing the **Nuclear Regulatory Commission,** the

agency in charge of nuclear power, and called on utility companies to improve standards:

> The steps that I am taking today will help to assure that nuclear power plants are operated safely. Safety, as it always has been and will remain, is my top priority. . . . I challenge our utility companies to bend every effort to improve the safety of nuclear power.

In spite of Carter's efforts, the nuclear industry fell on hard times. People were angry at cost overruns in building new plants, often reflected in their electric bills. Protesters blocked building sites. Orders for new plants were canceled, and some construction was halted.

Media and Technology

Transparencies
The Way It Works, H-21; Critical Thinking, I-5

SOURCE READINGS

Source Readings on p. 806 will connect literature selections and primary source excerpts to historical events discussed in this section.

Activity
Responding to a Poll

Ask students the following question, used in a 1988 Harris poll: "I'd like to ask you about the last nine Presidents of the United States. Please keep in mind Roosevelt, Truman, Eisenhower, Kennedy, Johnson, Nixon, Ford, Carter, and Reagan. If you had to choose one, which President do you think was best on domestic affairs? best on foreign affairs? was least able to get things done? most inspired confidence? set the lowest moral standards? was the most likely to be viewed by history as the best over all?" Compile and display the class responses. Tell the class that 46 percent of those polled at the time chose Carter as the least able to get things done, and that Ford came in second, with 15 percent. Only 1 percent of those polled chose either Carter or Ford as the President "most likely to be viewed by history as the best over all."

Enrichment

In 1976, writer Tom Wolfe proclaimed the 1970s as the "me decade," a comment on the high level of interest in self-improvement. Ask students to research and report on both the human-potential movement and the fascination with health and physical fitness of the 1970s.

Answer to ...
Viewpoints

McClure argues that nuclear energy is tied to the economic growth, or future well-being, of the United States; Caldicott pleads for restraint, on the grounds that a nuclear meltdown would have disastrous effects on people in every way. For a more thorough examination of the nuclear energy issue, see the Resource Directory below.

Answer to ...
MAKING CONNECTIONS

Answers will vary. Examples of concern might include recycling, the marketing of "green" products, efforts to promote mass transport, production of fuel-efficient cars, and so on.

In Depth
Multicultural Perspectives

The Voting Rights Act of 1965 (see page 670), a landmark in civil rights history, has been extended through amendments four times —in 1970, 1975, 1982, and 1992. In 1975 literacy requirements were abolished for any state or county where more than 5 percent of the population of voting age included persons of Spanish heritage, Native Americans, Asian Americans, and Alaskan Natives. In such areas, all ballots and official election materials must be printed both in English and in the language of the minority or minorities involved. In 1992 minority provisions were amended: they now apply to any community that has a minority-language population of 10,000 or more.

Viewpoints
On Nuclear Energy

The need to reduce the dependence of the United States on foreign oil prompted viewpoints strongly for and against nuclear power. **What concerns do the following viewpoints address?**

For Nuclear Energy

"When you debate the issue of nuclear energy, you are actually debating the issue of growth. Growth will be the key issue for the remainder of this century, and it is the resolution of that issue which will determine the lifestyles of most Americans for generations to come. . . . Economic growth has been inextricably linked to the growth of the supply of energy throughout history."
Senator James A. McClure (Idaho), address before the National Conference on Energy Advocacy, February 2, 1979

Against Nuclear Energy

"If this country . . . continues to rely more and more on nuclear power a meltdown disaster is almost predictable, and when it does occur, disaster and chaos from the medical and psychological effects as well as the shutdown of electricity from all nuclear power plants will be the result. For years now, the utilities and nuclear power industry have refused to listen to scientific logic and reasoning concerning the dangers of this technology. . . . Perhaps it is time for emotion and for passion and for commitment to stir our souls and our hearts and our minds once again into action."
Dr. Helen Caldicott, in *Nuclear Madness, What You Can Do!* 1980

MAKING CONNECTIONS

Carter tried to emphasize the importance of using energy wisely and conserving oil. Are many Americans today concerned about this issue? What examples can you give?

Steps Toward Deregulation

Carter also moved toward **deregulation,** or reducing or removing government controls, in several industries. In the late 1800s and early 1900s, agencies such as the Interstate Commerce Commission had been established to regulate rates and business practices in certain industries. Over the years, regulations had multiplied, and now Carter argued that they hurt competition and increased consumer costs.

Carter's energy plan included proposals to take controls off oil and natural gas prices. He also took steps to deregulate railroads, trucking, and airlines.

Many liberal Democrats and consumer groups were upset. They argued that regulation was a way of assuring that businesses would be accountable to the public. Critics also worried that companies would not maintain safety standards and that airlines and railroads, for example, would cut service to less profitable areas of the country. Deregulation continued during the next two administrations, both Republican, though not always with the promised benefits to consumers.

Other Domestic Issues

Concern for moral values influenced the President's approach to domestic questions as well as foreign policy. Some of his actions were controversial. Once in office, for example, Carter carried out his promise to grant **amnesty**—a general pardon—to those who had evaded the draft during the Vietnam War. Because the war still divided Americans, reactions were mixed.

Civil Rights Carter was more sympathetic to the goal of equal rights than either Ford or Nixon had been. During the 1976 campaign, he had won African American support with what columnist David Broder called "an eloquence, a simplicity, a directness that moved listeners of both races."

Carter also tried to move beyond the civil rights battles of the 1950s and 1960s. As a white southerner himself, he understood the South's need to overcome the negative images of the past decades:

> The most important [message] was that we in the South were ready for reconciliation, to be accepted as equals, to rejoin the mainstream of American political life. This yearning for what might be called political redemption was a significant factor in my successful campaign.

Carter won the approval of African Americans with his staff appointments, particularly to

RESOURCE DIRECTORY

Teaching Resources

Viewpoints Activity On Nuclear Energy, found in the Unit 7 folder, pp. 54–55, provides different opinions on the issue of nuclear power.

visible, prestigious posts such as the United Nations ambassadorship for Andrew Young. On the other hand, African Americans were disappointed by his weak support of social programs and his concentration on economic problems and foreign affairs instead of on civil rights.

The Bakke Case In 1978 the Supreme Court ruled on a case that had important implications for civil rights and affirmative action policies. **Allan Bakke,** who was white, applied to the medical school at the University of California at Davis in 1973 and 1974. After being turned down twice, he sued the school for "reverse discrimination." Bakke charged that the policy of reserving sixteen of one hundred class spaces for minority group applicants violated both the Civil Rights Act of 1964 and the Constitution.

In a complex ruling in *Regents of the University of California v. Bakke*, the justices wrote six separate opinions. While the Court ordered Bakke's admission to the California medical school, it also upheld the consideration of race as one factor in admission decisions, though it did not allow actual quotas. The decision supported the concept of affirmative action, but the case signaled the start of a white backlash against the policy.

Evaluating the Carter Presidency

Historians continue to assess Jimmy Carter's presidency. Some explain it as mainly a reaction to Watergate, a brief period of Democratic rule in a long period of Republican dominance. They also find serious flaws in the administration itself, mainly in its inability to create and stick

Allan Bakke took his case against affirmative action all the way to the Supreme Court when he claimed to be a victim of reverse discrimination. People argued both sides of the issue and some marched to voice their views.

with a consistent policy or to display strong leadership. After Carter's defeat in 1980, economist Robert J. Samuelson observed that Charles Schultze, retiring head of the Council of Economic Advisers, was typical of the entire team :

> I n many ways, Schultze symbolizes the puzzle of the departing Carter administration: that a lot of good people went into government four years ago, and a government of good people didn't produce a good government.

SECTION 4 REVIEW

Key Terms, People, and Places
1. Define (a) Nuclear Regulatory Commission, (b) deregulation, (c) amnesty.
2. Identify Allan Bakke.
3. Identify Three Mile Island.

Key Concepts
4. What were the problems with Carter's economic policy?

5. What were Carter's energy goals?
6. What developments in civil rights took place during the Carter administration?

Critical Thinking
7. **Recognizing Cause and Effect** Carter won the presidency on the strength of being a Washington "outsider." How did this ultimately hurt his administration?

 Quiz found in the Unit 7 folder, p. 49, covers the main ideas in this section as well as the key terms.

 Chapter Tests Forms A and B are found in the Unit 7 folder, pp. 66–71.

 Answer Keys found in the Unit 7 folder, pp. 143–156, provide answers to all student activities.

Media and Technology

 Transparency
Graphic Organizer, G-3

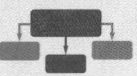 **Guided Reading Audiotapes**
(English and Spanish)

Computer Test Bank

---

might not have
History Happened This Way

The Decision to Reveal the Effects of Agent Orange

Focus Before students read the feature, ask them to consider to what extent they think one average citizen can change policy. Encourage them to evaluate Maude de Victor's decision to expose the effects of Agent Orange, and the future impact of her decision, as they read.

Instruct Ask students to read the feature. Play the part of the roving reporter, interviewing students role-playing the following citizens: Vietnam veteran with no visible effects of Agent Orange, Vietnam veteran with disease attributable to Agent Orange exposure, taxpayer, VA official. Ask the "citizens" to explain how Maude de Victor's decision to reveal the effects of Agent Orange will affect each of their lives.

Discuss with students the role of the media in American society. How were the media instrumental in getting compensation for veterans damaged by Agent Orange?

Ask students to consider how Jimmy Carter would respond to Maude de Victor's decision. What do students think Carter would have advised de Victor to do? Why?

The Decision to Reveal the Effects of Agent Orange

Time Frame:	1977–1978
Place:	Chicago, Illinois
Key People:	Maude de Victor, Ethel Owens, Bill Kurtis
Situation:	Veterans Administration counselor Maude de Victor found evidence that mysterious illnesses among Vietnam veterans were due to exposure to the chemical Agent Orange, but had to decide what to do about her discovery.

During and after the Vietnam War, the federal Veterans Administration (the VA) was faced with helping a new generation of veterans who were troubled by the physical and psychological aftereffects of a confusing and unpopular war. Many Vietnam veterans could not find work or resume a normal life, for they had come home emotionally shattered, alcoholic, or addicted to drugs. In addition, many developed mysterious ailments. Some blamed these health problems on exposure to Agent Orange, a chemical used by the American military to destroy vegetation in Vietnam. The photograph at right shows a before-and-after shot of one area in Vietnam that was treated with the chemical. The VA rejected the claims against Agent Orange, but one dedicated VA employee became convinced that it had harmed many soldiers.

Looking for the Truth

Maude de Victor was a benefits counselor at the VA in Chicago. She had been a corpsman at a naval hospital from 1959 to 1961, then joined the VA. Perhaps because of her work on an experimental program in radiation therapy while in the navy, she contracted breast cancer in 1976. She was still recovering from treatment when she began to hear complaints about Agent Orange from Vietnam veterans.

In 1977 Ethal Owens called de Victor to say that her husband Charlie, a thirty-year air force veteran, was dying of cancer. Charlie, Ethel said, had once told her that if he died of cancer, "it was because of the chemicals used in Vietnam." De Victor sent Owens's file to Washington but was told the illness had nothing to do with Vietnam. When Owens died, the VA did not pay full benefits, saying his death was not service related.

De Victor began to track down military and chemical company records. She learned about Operation Ranch Hand, the program to defoliate Vietnamese forests and crops by spraying chemical herbicides from the air. One chemical, Agent Orange, contained a type of dioxin considered highly toxic. Between 1965 and 1970, nearly 12 million gallons of Agent

 RESOURCE DIRECTORY

Teaching Resources

History Might Not . . . Activity Decision Making: Helping to Heal a War-Torn Nation, found in the Unit 7 folder, pp. 50–51, helps students apply this skill through the story of Jan Scruggs, the initiator of the Vietnam Memorial in Washington.

POSSIBLE ACTIONS	Drop the investigation as ordered by superiors	Apply pressure for action within the VA	Take the information outside the VA	Publicize the situation through the news media
POSSIBLE RESULTS	• Victims of Agent Orange will be ignored, and VA policy will not change. • The VA will eventually recognize the claims of Agent Orange victims and help them.	• The VA will not change its position, and veterans will not receive help. • The VA will, in time, take responsibility for helping Agent Orange victims.	• Officials will protect the military's image. • Some politicians may take up the cause of Agent Orange victims but fail to change VA policy. • Sympathetic politicians will act to change the VA policy.	• The media will not pursue the story. • The media will publicize, but the public will not respond. • Publicity will prompt public outrage, but no results. • Publicity and outrage will bring help for victims.

Orange were sprayed on Vietnam. Soldiers in helicopters flew through clouds of the defoliant, while chemical fog drifted down onto troops and Vietnamese civilians on the ground.

De Victor talked to veterans who had a variety of bizarre illnesses—rashes, headaches, strange lumps and sores, mood swings, or cancers. Others told her of their children's birth defects or their wives' miscarriages. Mapping the use of Agent Orange in Vietnam, she found that these ailing veterans had served in the areas sprayed with the chemical.

By early 1978, she had more than fifty case histories showing a link between Agent Orange and medical problems. She also had evidence that the government knew the dangers of Agent Orange. She showed her data to her superiors at the VA, but the they dismissed her findings and ordered her to stop her investigation.

Disobeying Orders

At that point, Maude de Victor could have dropped the investigation as she had been told to do. She understood why the VA would not admit the dangers of Agent Orange—the government feared a flood of disability claims and lawsuits from sick veterans and Vietnamese survivors, as well as condemnation from the world community. But she decided that getting help for sick veterans and their families was important.

Again, there were choices. She could go on applying pressure within the VA. Or she could risk her job and go to officials elsewhere in government. Both courses could be slow—and possibly useless. She wanted the world to know the story—so she turned to the news media.

Bill Kurtis, a Chicago news anchor, put on an hour-long documentary about her findings. "Agent Orange: The Deadly Fog" aired on March 23, 1978, and drew a torrent of calls from journalists, politicians, and Vietnam vets. The VA did not let de Victor take the calls and transferred her to another department, but she continued to discuss the issue. Claims related to Agent Orange began to pour into the VA, which still denied its harmful effects.

De Victor lost her job at the VA in 1984, but she had started a movement. Veterans formed lobbying organizations and filed a class action suit against chemical companies. They turned up evidence that the government and manufacturers had known the risks of using Agent Orange. In 1984 Vietnam veterans injured by Agent Orange were awarded millions of dollars in compensation.

EVALUATING DECISIONS

1. Why did Maude de Victor go to the media with her findings?
2. What was the impact of de Victor's decision to publicize the harmful effects of Agent Orange?

Critical Thinking

3. **Determining Relevance** What element of de Victor's personal life may have contributed to her commitment to the Agent Orange cause?

Visions of America: History Might Not Have Happened This Way Game

To encourage students to explore pivotal moments in United States history, have students use the Visions of America software. Refer to the Visions of America Teacher's Guidebook for viewing objectives, activities, game instructions, and discussion questions.

Answers

1. The VA refused to take any action in response to what she had learned, and her other options for gaining a response seemed slow and uncertain.

2. Many veterans learned why they were sick; organizations formed to fight for Agent Orange victims' rights; veterans took their cases to court and gained recognition of and compensation for their suffering.

3. The fact that her own cancer may have been caused by the work she did while in the navy may have made her particularly sympathetic to other veterans in similar circumstances.

Understanding Key Terms, People, and Places

Terms
Students should refer to the definitions of the key terms in the chapter to write sentences that show the relation of each word to the events of the Ford or Carter administrations.

Matching
1. amnesty
2. dissident
3. stagflation
4. Helsinki Accords
5. deregulation

True or False
1. false, Alan Bakke
2. false, Shah Mohammad Reza Pahlavi
3. true

Reviewing Main Ideas

1. A midwestern Republican, Ford believed in traditional values such as hard work and self-reliance. In Congress he had opposed federal funds for education and mass transit, and the antipoverty program. He supported law and order and defense spending. Critics cited his lack of administrative and foreign policy experience.

2. Ford inherited the problems of healing the country after the Watergate scandal and nagging problems in the economy, including inflation and unemployment (stagflation).

3. Ford's rescue of the *Mayaguez* succeeded in sending a message of American strength, although probably with needless loss of life. He continued the SALT talks, signed the Helsinki Accords, and took steps toward new relationships with African nations. The nation remained at peace, although Ford's foreign policy was mainly a reaction to outside events.

4. Carter presented himself as trustworthy and honest; he also emphasized his status as a Washington outsider.

5. Carter was deeply religious but also believed strongly in personal freedom of conscience. His personal style was low-key and unassuming. He was intelligent, well informed, and precise. Sometimes, however, his focus on all sides of a question made him unable to make decisions.

6. Carter sent Cyrus Vance to invite Sadat and Begin to Camp David in order to move the peace process forward. While at Camp David, Carter assumed the role of peacemaker and practiced personal diplomacy to bridge the gap between the two leaders.

Chapter Review

Understanding Key Terms, People, and Places

Key Terms
1. stagflation
2. Helsinki Accords
3. shuttle diplomacy
4. Camp David Accords
5. dissident
6. Nuclear Regulatory Commision
7. deregulation
8. amnesty

People
9. Gerald R. Ford
10. Nelson Rockefeller
11. James Earl Carter, Jr.
12. Anwar el-Sadat
13. Menachem Begin
14. Cyrus Vance
15. Shah Mohammad Reza Pahlavi
16. Ayatollah Ruholla Khomeini
17. Allan Bakke

Places
18. Three Mile Island

Terms For each term above, write a sentence that explains its relation to the events of the Ford or Carter administrations.

Matching Review the key terms in the list above. If you are not sure of a term's meaning, review its definition in the chapter. Then choose a term from the list that best matches each description below.
1. a general pardon
2. a writer or other activist who opposes the actions of his or her government
3. a condition in which the economy remains stalled during a period of high inflation and rising unemployment
4. a series of agreements in which thirty-five nations pledged to cooperate economically and to promote human rights
5. the process of reducing or removing government controls

True or False Determine whether each statement is true or false. If it is true, write "true." If it is false, change the underlined name to make the statement true.
1. In 1978 <u>Nelson Rockefeller</u> sued the University of California at Davis for "reverse discrimination."
2. <u>Menachem Begin</u> took many steps to modernize Iran, but his government was corrupt and repressive.
3. Egyptian leader <u>Anwar el-Sadat</u> made a historic visit to Israel to try to establish peace between the two countries.

Reviewing Main Ideas

Section 1 (pp. 780 – 784)
1. Briefly describe Gerald Ford's beliefs and his voting record in Congress. Why did some critics feel that he was not qualified to be President?
2. Describe two major challenges that Ford inherited when he took office.
3. Briefly describe the successes and failures of Ford's foreign policy.

Section 2 (pp. 785 – 788)
4. Why did Jimmy Carter's candidacy appeal to voters eager to recover from the Watergate scandal?
5. Describe Carter's personal beliefs, his personal style, and his special abilities.

Section 3 (pp. 789 – 793)
6. What was President Carter's role in establishing the Camp David Accords?

7. Describe President Carter's policy toward Africa.
8. In Carter's first year, he said that the United States would forge closer ties with the Soviet Union. Why did his statement prove to be premature?
9. Why did the Iran hostage crisis damage Carter's presidency?

Section 4 (pp. 795 – 799)
10. What problems did Carter experience in his dealings with Congress?
11. You have read columnist Tom Wicker's observation that Carter "never established a politically coherent administration." How can this observation be applied to Carter's economic policies?
12. Explain why Americans faced oil shortages and high prices in the late 1970s. Why was Carter unable to reach his energy conservation goals?

---

7. Persuaded by Andrew Young, U.S. ambassador to the United Nations, Carter did not interfere with the newly emerging nations of Africa.

8. Ties between the United States and the Soviet Union actually worsened under Carter because of Carter's insistence on human rights and the sanctions he adopted following the Soviet invasion of Afghanistan.

9. People expected Carter to secure the hostages' release. In addition, the country was humiliated when a rescue mission failed, killing eight Americans.

10. Carter did not find a way to work effectively with Congress, which stalled his plans for energy conservation and the economy.

11. The Carter administration continually shifted its economic policies as new problems arose, thus appearing to have no coherent economic program. For example, Carter tried to stimulate growth with deficit spending. When an increase in the money supply resulted in inflation, he then tried to reduce the deficit through cuts in government spending, including social programs.

12. OPEC had been raising prices since 1973. Carter was unable to reach his energy goals because he had trouble winning support from Congress and from the public.

Thinking Critically

1. **Testing Conclusions** Both Ford and Carter were branded as ineffective leaders by their critics. Yet both inherited serious economic and social problems from previous administrations. To what extent do you think the ineffectiveness of these Presidents was due to inherited problems and to what extent was it due to inadequate leadership?

2. **Demonstrating Reasoned Judgment** Do you think that Jimmy Carter would have been a more effective or a less effective President if he had been less concerned with moral values? Give evidence from the chapter to support your point of view.

3. **Checking Consistency** Although people complained about gas lines and fuel shortages during the 1970s, many did not back Carter's energy policies. How do you account for this discrepancy?

4. **Identifying Central Issues** You have read that in the election of 1976 the most important issue was trust. What do think is the most important issue for voters today when electing a President?

 ## Alternative Assessment

Final Evaluation
Use the following guidelines to evaluate student projects:
- **Evidence of thoughtfulness** To what extent do projects demonstrate an understanding of the presidency?
- **Evidence of outside research** To what extent do projects use outside research materials?
- **Evidence of synthesis** To what extent do projects demonstrate an understanding of relationships among topics?
- **Communication style** Do projects convey their purpose to an audience in a clear, appealing way?

Making Connections

1. **Evaluating Primary Sources** Review the primary source excerpt on page 789. Based on your reading of the chapter, to what extent was Carter able to live up to his ideals in his foreign and domestic policies?

2. **Understanding the Visuals** Look at the map on page 786. How did your state vote in the 1976 election? Is this consistent with its voting pattern today?

3. **Writing About the Chapter** You are running as a third-party candidate in the presidential election of 1976. You want to combine the best aspects of both Carter and Ford while avoiding their weaknesses. Write a speech in which you announce your candidacy and the reasons why you should be elected. First, create a list detailing Ford's and Carter's positions on important issues. Note how your positions will

improve upon theirs. Next, write a draft of your speech in which you explain your positions. Revise your speech, making sure that your ideas are clearly explained, then proofread and draft a final copy.

4. **Using the Graphic Organizer** This graphic organizer uses a tree map to organize main ideas and supporting details about Carter's foreign policy. (a) One reason for the breakdown of détente in the Carter years was due to Carter's commitment to human rights. According to the map, what was a second reason? (b) According to the map, what events led to the capture of American hostages in Iran? (c) Create your own tree map about Carter's domestic policy, using this graphic organizer as an example.

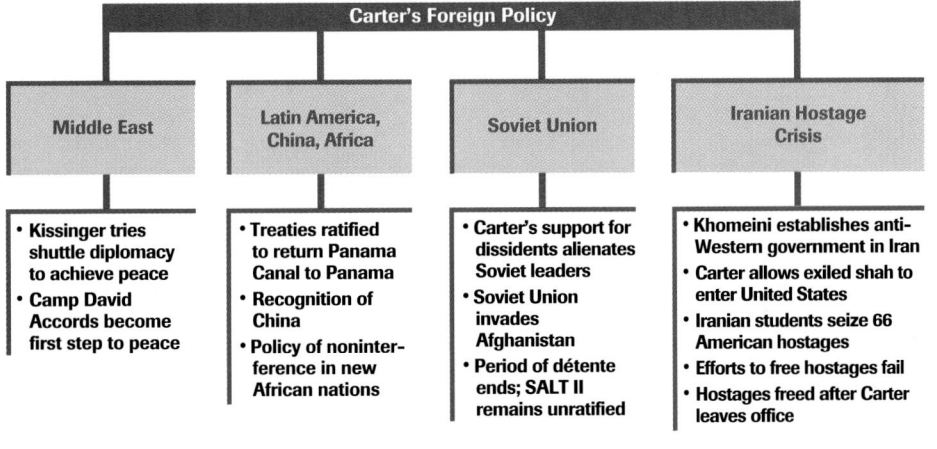

Carter's Foreign Policy

Middle East	Latin America, China, Africa	Soviet Union	Iranian Hostage Crisis
• Kissinger tries shuttle diplomacy to achieve peace	• Treaties ratified to return Panama Canal to Panama	• Carter's support for dissidents alienates Soviet leaders	• Khomeini establishes anti-Western government in Iran
• Camp David Accords become first step to peace	• Recognition of China	• Soviet Union invades Afghanistan	• Carter allows exiled shah to enter United States
	• Policy of noninterference in new African nations	• Period of détente ends; SALT II remains unratified	• Iranian students seize 66 American hostages
			• Efforts to free hostages fail
			• Hostages freed after Carter leaves office

Thinking Critically

1. Responses should consider the economic and social effects of Watergate inherited by Ford and the continuing economic problems inherited by Carter.

2. Responses should consider, for example, the worsening relations with the Soviet Union caused by Carter's stand on human rights.

3. Possible answers: Carter did not effectively promote his energy policies; Americans might have been unwilling to make sacrifices under any circumstances, despite inconvenience and high prices.

4. Possible answer: The ability to solve economic and social problems.

Making Connections

1. Responses should consider the areas of foreign policy in which Carter successfully carried out his ideals of promoting peace and compassion, such as the Camp David Accords. They should also consider the compromises the President was forced to make in cutting social programs in order to lower the deficit.

2. Answers will vary.

3. Students' speeches should consider Ford's and Carter's respective positions on and goals for the economy and foreign affairs as well as their qualifications for the presidency.

Ask students to recall President Nixon and the Watergate scandal of the early 1970s. Then ask: what sort of person do you think Americans would be likely to elect to the presidency following such a scandal? After some discussion, students will probably realize that a President who seemed uninterested in power, who seemed honest, informal, and accessible, would be the nation's likely choice. Tell students that, as the first source reading reveals, this is just the sort of person the people found in Jimmy Carter.

If there is a nuclear power plant near your community, ask students what they have heard from parents and others about the plant. Do people seem comfortable with having the plant nearby? If a nuclear power plant is not located anywhere nearby, ask students how they think the community would react if they learned that plans were in the works to build one. Explain to students that many of the fears and concerns relating to nuclear power stem from the 1979 accident at Three Mile Island in Pennsylvania.

Why We Chose to Walk: Carter's Inauguration

Primary Source

Jimmy Carter

INTRODUCTION Jimmy Carter wrote his memoirs, *Keeping Faith*, the year after he left office. In them, he remained true to the honest, everyday aspect of his personality that had so endeared him to the American people. The following quotation, taken from his book, typifies his unpretentiousness: "Even though I had been preparing to be President, I was genuinely surprised when in the benediction, the Bishop from Minnesota referred to 'blessings on President Carter.' Just the phrase, 'President Carter,' was startling to me." In this President, the people had found someone they could relate to, someone they could trust. In this President, it seemed, they had found a friend.

VOCABULARY Before you read the selection, find the meaning of these words in a dictionary: revelation, tangible, imperial, precipitate, consummate, affectation.

The inaugural parade route stretched before us with tens of thousands of people lining the streets. I leaned forward and told the Secret Service driver to stop the automobile, then touched Rosalynn's hand and said, "Let's go!" The security men looked all around, saw only friendly faces, and opened the doors of the long black limousine. As we stepped into the street, the people seemed anxious and concerned about us. They obviously thought something was wrong with the car. Then our three sons and their wives joined us as we began to walk down the center of the broad avenue.

It seemed that a shock wave went through the crowd. There were gasps of astonishment and cries of "They're walking! They're walking!" The excitement flooded over us; we responded to the people with broad smiles and proud steps. It was bitterly cold, but we felt warm inside. Even our nine-year-old daughter Amy got the spirit, walking in front of our family group and carefully placing her small feet on the white centerline. We were surprised at the depth of feeling from our friends along the way. Some of them wept openly, and when I saw this, a few tears of joy ran down my cold cheeks. It was one of those few perfect moments in life when everything seems absolutely right. . . .

Many people have asked why we chose to walk. A few weeks before the inauguration, Senator William Proxmire had suggested in a letter that it would set a good example for the nation's physical fitness program if a new President would walk the entire 1.2 miles from the U.S. Capitol to the White House. The idea seemed rather silly, and I discarded it immediately. Later, however, I began to realize that the symbolism of our leaving the armored car would be much more far-reaching than simply to promote exercise. I remembered the angry demonstrators who had habitually confronted recent Presidents and Vice Presidents, furious over the Vietnam war and later the revelations of Watergate. I wanted to provide a vivid demonstration of my confidence in the people as far as security was concerned, and I felt a simple walk would be a tangible indication of some reduction in the imperial status of the President and his family.

I had told few people about my decision. The leader of my Secret Service detail had been somewhat

President Jimmy Carter set the tone for his administration when he decided to walk the inaugural parade route rather than ride in a limousine.

startled by the idea, but then concluded there would be no objections, provided we could keep the plan secret. I agreed with our security men that any publicity in advance could precipitate an incident or threat which might make such a walk impossible. Besides, I wanted it to be a dramatic moment. . . .

Now I strolled hand in hand with Rosalynn, our family around us. She and I had discussed the idea of walking to the White House, just as she had worked with me on the themes of my inaugural speech. We had been married for thirty-one years and were full partners in every sense of the word. . . .

After completing our walk and reviewing the parade from a pavilion in front of the White House, Rosalynn and I entered the mansion grounds, alone together for the first time since we had begun our official day. As we quietly approached our new home, I told Rosalynn with a smile that it was a nice-looking place. She said, "I believe we're going to be happy in the White House." We were silent for a moment, and then I replied, "I just hope that we never disappoint the people who made it possible for us to live here." Rosalynn's prediction proved to be correct, and I did my utmost for four solid years to make my own hope come true. . . .

On that first day, I tarried in the living quarters only a few minutes, eager to get to the Oval Office. Where I would work was much more interesting to me than where we would be sleeping.

When the elevator reached the ground floor, the security men were waiting. Not certain how to find my office, I said as casually as possible, "I'm just going to the Oval Office" and followed the lead agent. We walked along the ground-floor corridor, left the mansion proper, proceeded west about forty-five paces under the south arcade, turned left, and arrived at the entrance. As soon as I entered, the security agents closed the doors and I was alone.

Only once before had I visited the Oval Office, quite briefly—about a month after the election, when Rosalynn and I came to pay a courtesy call on President and Mrs. Ford. The room was mine now and for the first minute or two I savored my solitude. . . . In my uncertainty I hesitated a few seconds, wondering if it was all right for me to disturb anything. Then I boldly pulled aside the window drapes and examined the beautiful south grounds in the late afternoon sunlight.

THINKING ABOUT THE SELECTION

1. Why did the Carters decide to walk in the inaugural parade, rather than riding in a limousine?
2. Why did the Carters keep their decision to walk secret from the public?

Critical Thinking

3. **Checking Consistency** In his final days in office, Carter wrote, "Rosalynn and I expressed our personal thanks to more than fifty thousand people in our country. We enjoyed remembering the pleasant and productive friendships we had formed with so many Americans." Is this statement consistent with the ideals at the basis of the Carters' decision to walk in the inaugural parade? Explain why or why not.

INSTRUCT

Read students the following quotation, adapted from Chapter 24 of their textbooks: "A government of good people [doesn't] produce a good government." Ask students whether they agree or disagree with this statement and why. Ask them what qualities they will look for in a presidential candidate when they are eligible to vote.

Have students pretend they lived in Middletown, Pennsylvania when the accident occurred at Three Mile Island. Have them write their "recollections" of the event from the perspective of a high-school student, an employee at Metropolitan Edison (the company that operated the plant), or another personality. Select some students to read their pieces aloud to the class.

ANSWERS TO

Thinking About the Selection

1. The Carters decided to walk in order to show the American people that they were trusted and to reduce the imperial aspect of the presidency. Jimmy Carter wanted to show that he was accessible to the people.
2. They kept the decision secret in order to avoid any threats or the possibility that someone might take the opportunity to harm the President or his family.

3. Yes, the statement is consistent with the ideals at the basis of the Carters' decision to walk in the inaugural parade. The statement shows that the Carters remained accessible to the public and that they did not consider themselves "above" making friends with many Americans.

Have students poll members of the
community on their feelings toward
an existing or potential nuclear
power plant in the area. Each student
should ask five people how they feel
about the nuclear power plant
nearby, or how they would feel if
they learned a power plant was going
to be built in their town. Compile the
results as a class and discuss the community's perception of the safety of
nuclear power.

In addition, hold a class debate
with one side taking the pro–nuclear
power position and the other side
taking a position opposing nuclear
power. Students should research both
sides of the issue so that they can
effectively counter the opposing
side's arguments.

SOURCE READINGS

Voices from Three Mile Island

Primary Source

Robert Leppzer

INTRODUCTION After the accident at Three Mile Island nuclear power plant near Harrisburg, Pennsylvania, the Nuclear Regulatory Commission concluded that the plant came within thirty to sixty minutes of a full meltdown. The consequences of such a meltdown would have been the immediate deaths of thousands of people, later death or sickness for hundreds of thousands of others from leukemia, cancer, and birth defects, and the contamination of an area as large as the entire state of Pennsylvania for over one hundred years.

The partial meltdown that did occur was enough to seriously affect the lives of those who lived nearby. In the following excerpts from *Voices from Three Mile Island*, by Robert Leppzer, some of those people express what happened on the day of the accident and the fear they have been living with ever since. Bill Whittock was a seventy-four-year-old civil engineer who lived one mile from Three Mile Island; Bob Reid was the mayor of Middletown, where the plant is located, and a high school teacher; Vickie DiSanto was born and raised in Middletown and lived less than one mile from the plant with her husband and two children.

Bill Whittock:

The accident occurred around four o'clock in the morning on Wednesday, March 28. I was sleeping and became aware of this explosive release of steam over at the plant. There was a roar, a *terrific* roar. It woke me up and I jumped out of bed. I looked across the river and saw the column of steam that was escaping. It roared for about five minutes. It stopped and then it started to roar again.

After the second time, it eased off until there was just a relatively small column of steam which just kept hissing pretty near all morning. I went back to sleep because the plant had erupted about ten times before and I thought it was just an ordinary disturbance like we've been going through for the last several years.

About seven o'clock when I got up I heard on the radio that there had been a radioactive release. Then I went uptown to get the mail. I could sense a metallic taste in the air when I got outside. I asked up at the marina if the people up there had sensed this taste. Two of them did.

About nine-thirty a helicopter came in and landed up here in the field. There was a TV crew that came down. That was when I began to realize that it was pretty serious.

Mayor Bob Reid:

I was called by my civil defense director who told me it was an accident. I asked him, "Well, what kind of accident is it, Butch?" And he said, "Well, all we've gotten so far is an *on-site emergency.*"

We had no concrete information that we could go on. We had a television set in our communication center but each channel gave us different information. We had a radio but each station gave us different information. We didn't know what to do. So I called the home office of Metropolitan Edison Company. They told me that "Yes, there was an accident" and tried to explain to me just exactly what took place. I said, "Well look, I don't want to hear the technical aspects of this darn thing because I don't understand it. What about radiation?" I knew that. He said, "Oh, no radiation was released. You don't have to worry about that. No radiation was released and no one was injured." I said, "Great!"

So I told Butch, "Well look, I'm going back to school. If anything else happens let me know." I turned my radio on in the car and the first thing the announcer said was that radiation was released. I'd just talked to an official from the plant at eleven o'clock. At four o'clock in the afternoon the same man called me and said, "Bob, I'd like to update our conversation." I said, "You're going to tell me now that radiation was released." He said, "Yes." I said, "Well, I guess we're in for a lot of malarkey from you people." And lo and behold, boy, there it was. . . .

Friday was the day. When they said there was a hydrogen bubble and the possibility of an explosion, people went haywire and left town. We estimated that between 30 and 35% of the people left. The schools were in a panic. A lot of the kids thought about dying and wrote their last wills and testaments. *Fifth* and *sixth* grade kids! People were concerned. You could tell they were afraid because a lot of people who left town left their doors wide open, unlocked. They just put anything in the car and took off. They had to run to the bank to get money to go where they were going. It was just a mess.

The news media was all over the place, trying to talk to people. And people were trying to get away from them, trying to get out of town. People didn't understand why these people were *coming* when everyone else was trying to *leave*! The news media would talk to them and people would say, "Well look, I don't have time to talk to you now—I'm trying to get out of here."

Vickie DiSanto:

Back in September I had the most miserable dreams about running and running. I could always see the towers behind me when I was running. I'd try to go into a house and they'd say, "No, you can't come in here." And I'd run to the next place but everybody would tell me, "No, you can't come in." It was like I was running from it because I knew it was dangerous, but there was just no place to go. And I had that dream for three or four nights in a row. The funny

The towers of the Three Mile Island nuclear power plant rise ominously above a farm in Middletown, Pennsylvania. The March 1979 accident at the plant stirred the fears of Americans and touched off demands for better safety regulations.

thing was I mentioned to a friend of mine that I had been having dreams about TMI. And he said, "I have too." We compared them and they were the same.

On the surface, we have very normal lives here in Middletown, but underneath there's always this presence. It's always with us. I usually think about it at least once a day. There are some nights every now and then when I would just lie in bed and it would strike me and I would cry and cry because I'm worried about my children.

There have been times before when we would have been able to ignore the fact that the towers were down there, but now you can't see them without thinking something. We don't know what to teach our son. We used to go out for bike rides all summer long—he and I—and he'd ask about different things and what they were. And, of course, there were always the towers. I didn't know what to tell him. I don't want to scare him, at two years old. But finally we settled on yucky towers and that's what he calls them now.

THINKING ABOUT THE SELECTION

1. Why was Bill Whittock not concerned when he heard the explosion and saw columns of steam escaping from the plant?
2. What sort of dreams did Vickie DiSanto have following the accident? What feelings might DiSanto be expressing through such dreams?

Critical Thinking

3. **Expressing Problems Clearly** Find evidence in the excerpts that shows that it was difficult to get information about what had really happened at the plant and that the public was receiving conflicting information.

ANSWERS TO

Thinking About the Selection

1. He was not concerned because there had been accidents on about ten other occasions in the past and they had not been reported as serious. He thought this was another of the same type of problem.
2. She dreamed that she was running and could see the towers of the nuclear power plant in the background. When she tried to take shelter in people's houses, no one would let her in. The dream might be her way of expressing her fears about the plant and the ever-present possibility of another accident. As in the dream, if such an accident, or a worse one, should occur, it would be difficult to find a safe place of refuge.
3. Evidence exists in the excerpt from Mayor Reid. He states that the television and radio reports were all conflicting and that when he called the plant he was told one thing and then later another. It is especially significant that he was the mayor and still could not find conclusive answers about the accident.

Chapter 25 High Tide of the Conservative Movement 1980–1992

📁 Teaching Resources (See Unit 7 Folder)

	Instruction	Enrichment
Section 1 **The Conservative Revolution** (pp. 810–814)	Reproducible Lesson Plan, p. 73 Alternate Lesson Plan, p. 172 Guided Reading and Review, p. 77 Quiz, p. 78	American Profiles Activity, An Wang, p. 87 Visual Learning Activity, Passing the Economy Buck, p. 100 Primary Source Activity, Speaking for the President, p. 93
Section 2 **Republican Policies at Home** (pp. 815–819)	Reproducible Lesson Plan, p. 74 Alternate Lesson Plan, p. 173 Guided Reading and Review, p. 79 Quiz, p. 80	American Profiles Activity, Sandra Day O'Connor, p. 88 Literature Activity, In Pursuit of Health and Happiness, p. 96 Historian's Toolbox Activity, Demonstrating Reasoned Judgment, p. 91
Section 3 **The Halting Pace of Reform** (pp. 821–825)	Reproducible Lesson Plan, p. 75 Alternate Lesson Plan, p. 174 Guided Reading and Review, p. 81 Quiz, p. 82	Viewpoints Activity, On the Legacy of the Civil Rights Movement, pp. 89–90 Visual Learning Activity, Wages for Housework, p. 99 Critical Thinking Activity, Recognizing Ideologies, p. 92 Time and Place Activity, Infectious Disease: Escherichia coli, pp. 85–86
Section 4 **The United States in a New World** (pp. 828–831)	Reproducible Lesson Plan, p. 76 Alternate Lesson Plan, p. 175 Guided Reading and Review, p. 83 Quiz, p. 84 Chapter Test, Forms A & B, pp. 101–106	Literature Activity, Operation Desert Storm, pp. 97–98 Primary Source Activity, An Explanation of Iran-Contra, pp. 94–95

📁 Additional Chapter Resources

Resource Organizer, p. 72
Alternate Lesson Plan, p. 171
Answer Keys, pp. 143–156

Bibliography

For the Teacher

Atkinson, Rick. *Crusade: The Untold Story of the Persian Gulf War.* Houghton Mifflin, 1993. (A *Washington Post* reporter looks at the war three years later.)

Evans, Rowland, and Robert Novak. *The Reagan Revolution.* Dutton, 1981. (Account of Ronald Reagan's political and economic ideas.)

Hunter-Gault, Charlayne. *In My Place.* Vintage, 1993. (A successful journalist remembers her youth as one of the first two African American students at the University of Georgia.)

Prentice Hall Literature Excerpts from *The American Experience,* 1994, including Beattie, Ann. "Imagined Scenes," from *Distortions.* International Creative Management, 1976.

The Big Idea for the chapter and how the main ideas in each section relate to the Big Idea are graphically displayed below. Comprehension of this chapter's Big Idea is critical to students' understanding of United States history and how we as a nation got where we are today.

Media and Technology

 Critical Thinking, I-3

 Critical Thinking, I-11

 Graphic Organizer, G-1

 Guided Reading Audiotapes (English and Spanish)

 Computer Test Bank

For the Student

Ashe, Arthur, and Arnold Rampersad. *Days of Grace: A Memoir.* Random House, 1993. (Reflections by the African American tennis champion and activist who died of AIDS.)

Erdrich, Louise. *Love Medicine: New and Expanded Version.* HarperCollins, 1993. (Updated version of the author's first novel of Native American life.)

Salzman, Marian, and Ann O'Reilly. *War and Peace in the Persian Gulf: What Teenagers Want to Know.* Peterson's Guides, 1991.

CHAPTER 25

The 1980s followed a decade of political, social, and economic turmoil and ushered in a decade of disclosures of abuse of power at home and diminishing American stature abroad. Elected on a tidal wave of conservatism, Ronald Reagan and the New Right took direct aim at liberal government programs and won enormous support.

SECTION 1

By 1980 an alliance of various special-interest groups formed a conservative coalition that scored a major electoral victory and succeeded in changing the course of American politics.

SECTION 2

Republican administrations in the 1980s moved aggressively to implement conservative goals in their domestic policy, cutting social welfare programs and widening the gap between the rich and the poor.

SECTION 3

The movement toward greater equality for women and minority groups slowed during the 1980s and early 1990s as the conservative administrations of Reagan and Bush refused to extend rights to these groups and even attempted to reverse earlier gains.

SECTION 4

The world changed dramatically in the 1980s and early 1990s as the cold war came to an end, and Americans had to learn to operate in a "new world order."

CHAPTER 25

High Tide of the Conservative Movement
1980–1992

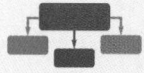

High Tide of the Conservative Movement
1980–1992

The Relevance of the Big Idea

In the 1980s, conservatives, still rooted in the anticommunist fervor of the 1950s, revived popular agendas—cutting back on the domestic economic front, increasing military spending, and flexing American muscle abroad easily and often. In the early 1990s, however, the world changed dramatically. The Soviet Union crumbled, and the cold war ended.

To help students understand how the post–cold war world rendered a great deal of conservative ideology outdated, discuss with students what factors stand in the way of American well-being today. *(Possible answers: trade deficits, unemployment, lack of health care, slow retraining of the work force, drug problems, and a high crime rate.)*

*I*n 1980 the Republican party—now controlled by conservatives—scored a major electoral victory. Under the leadership of Ronald Reagan and then George Bush, the Republicans rolled back the liberal agenda that had shaped national policy ever since the New Deal of Franklin D. Roosevelt. The Republicans' main thrust was an attempt to revive the moral values of the nation, which conservatives felt had eroded in an increasingly permissive society.

Building on America's Strength
GEORGE BUSH
PRESIDENT

Events in the United States

	1979 Religious conservatives found the Moral Majority.	1980 Republican Ronald Reagan defeats Democrat Jimmy Carter for the presidency.	1982 The Equal Rights Amendment fails to win ratification.	1984 Democrat Geraldine Ferraro becomes the first woman to run for the vice presidency on a major party ticket.
	1978	**1980**	**1982**	**1984**

Events in the World

1979 The Soviet Union invades Afghanistan.	1980 Rhodesia, in Africa, is renamed Zimbabwe.	1982 Britain and Argentina engage in the Falklands War.	1984 South African archbishop Desmond Tutu receives the Nobel Peace Prize.

In Depth

Global Connections

In the early 1980s, Britain and the United States were both faced with economies that suffered from inflation and national attitudes of self-doubt. They also had political leaders with similar goals. Former Secretary of State Henry Kissinger said of former British prime minister Margaret Thatcher: "During the Reagan administration, she achieved an influence over American decisions, especially with respect to NATO and arms control policy, not seen since Churchill's day."

RESOURCE DIRECTORY

Teaching Resources

Alternate Lesson Plan: Demonstrating the Big Idea found in the Alternate Lesson Plans folder, p. 171, provides a lesson strategy to instruct students about the Big Idea that with Ronald Reagan's victory in 1980, the Republican party began to roll back the liberal agenda that had shaped national policy since the New Deal, attempting to institutionalize conservative social values as well as economic ones.

Alternative Assessment Handbook provides information, guidance, and strategies for alternative methods of assessment. It includes an essay on new trends in assessment, guidance and strategies for developing performance tasks and portfolios, scoring rubrics, and sample evaluation forms.

Pages 810–814
The Conservative Revolution

The elections of 1980 brought a conservative President to the White House and a Republican majority to the Senate. Behind these changes was a well-organized union of several diverse groups who sought to reverse many of the policies and programs of the preceding decades.

 Pages 815–819
Republican Policies at Home

The 1980s were years in which the rich became even richer, while the poor and many of those in the middle saw few benefits from the nation's apparent prosperity. Presidents Reagan and Bush cut back on social programs and followed a conservative agenda.

 Pages 821–825
The Halting Pace of Reform

The movement toward greater equality for women and minority groups slowed during the administrations of Presidents Reagan and Bush. Because many conservatives opposed extending more rights to such groups, the government sometimes adopted policies that reversed earlier gains.

 Pages 828–831
The United States in a New World

After more than forty years of the cold war, in the early 1990s the United States watched as communist governments crumbled. The foreign policies of Reagan's first years in office became outdated as the nation faced new possibilities and problems.

1986 *The Iran-contra affair becomes public.*

1987 *The Senate rejects Robert Bork's nomination to the Supreme Court.*

1988 *Vice President George Bush wins the presidential election.*

1990 *A severe economic recession deepens.*

1991 *The United States and United Nations troops defeat Iraq in the Persian Gulf War.*

1986   1988   1990   1992

1986 *Corazon Aquino is elected president of the Philippines.*

1987 *Syrian troops invade Lebanon.*
• *Riots break out in Israel's West Bank territory.*

1988 *Civil wars sweep Ethiopia and the Sudan.*
• *Pakistan elects Benazir Bhutto president.*

1989 *The Berlin Wall is torn down.*
• *Japanese emperor Hirohito dies.*

1990 *Violetta Chamorro is elected president of Nicaragua.*
• *Namibia becomes an independent state.*

1992 *Somalia is torn by war and famine.*

 Alternative Assessment

As an ongoing chapter project, students can create a project entitled "The Conservative Movement, 1980–1992: How It Changed the Country." Students should illustrate the impact of conservatism on American society in the 1980s and early 1990s. Research may involve examining published sources, viewing documentaries, and conducting interviews. Students may use the suggestions that follow or come up with an original format.

• Create a collage of newspaper and magazine photographs.
• Write and perform a skit in the format of a talk show.
• Develop the script for a television documentary of the period.
• Tape actual interviews with leading conservatives in your town or city.

Explain that finished projects will be assessed according to the following standards:

• **Unacceptable** Projects are not attempted or fail to meet the requirements outlined.
• **Limited/Acceptable** Projects are based on material from the textbook and reflect an effort to show the impact of the conservative movement on American society.
• **Extensive/Commendable** Projects are based on some outside research, show the impact of the conservative movement, and reflect the student's own position.
• **Extraordinary/Outstanding** Projects are based on considerable outside research, show the impact of the conservative movement in a creative and effective way, and reflect the student's own position.

For more information and guidance on alternative assessment trends and strategies, see the Alternative Assessment Handbook in the Resource Directory on page 808.

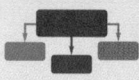

1. FOCUS

Connecting to the Big Idea

See page 808B. Explain that the 1980 election ushered in an era of conservatism in politics. A well-organized coalition of groups sought to reverse many of the policies and programs of the preceding decades. Ask how these groups, known as the New Right, influenced politics in the 1980s.

Objectives

● Describe the roots of the new conservative movement.

● Explain how groups with conservative economic, social, and religious views overturned the liberal programs of the New Deal and the Great Society.

● Identify the techniques conservatives used to promote their views.

Bellringer

Ask students to define the word *conservative*. Discuss its meaning in relation to style, behavior, and values. Ask students what the word might have to do with politics in the United States during the 1980s.

Reading Strategy

Question Writing Have students read the section's main headings and then ask them to formulate questions about each one, filling in the answers as they read.

The Conservative Revolution

SECTION PREVIEW

The elections of 1980 brought a conservative President to the White House and a Republican majority to the Senate. Behind these changes was a well-organized union of several different groups who sought to reverse many of the policies and programs of the preceding decades.

Key Concepts

• The new conservative movement had its roots partly in the anticommunist politics of the 1950s.

• Groups with conservative economic, social, and religious views worked together to overturn the liberal programs of the New Deal and the Great Society.

• Conservatives used television and other techniques very effectively to promote their views.

Key Terms, People, and Places

New Right, coalition, televangelism; Ronald Reagan, George Bush

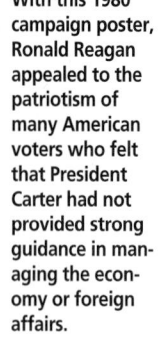

With this 1980 campaign poster, Ronald Reagan appealed to the patriotism of many American voters who felt that President Carter had not provided strong guidance in managing the economy or foreign affairs.

I n the presidential election of 1964, the Republicans nominated Senator Barry Goldwater, an extreme conservative. This nomination signaled the growing influence of a new conservative movement. By 1980 this movement had created an alliance of various special-interest groups to form what became known as the **New Right.** Not only had conservatives gained influence within the Republican party; they had, through the effective use of the media, found supporters elsewhere as well. By the early 1980s, members of the New Right had succeeded in electing many conservative candidates in state, local, and national elections.

Foremost among these conservative politicians was **Ronald Reagan,** who was elected to the presidency in 1980. A former movie and television actor, Reagan was an ideal New Right candidate. Likable, photogenic, genial—and committed to conservative ideals—Reagan as President had little trouble winning support for cutbacks in many liberal social programs created by previous administrations.

Background of the "New" Conservatives

The New Right had its political roots in the anticommunism of the 1950s, although many conservative Americans also looked back to earlier social values. In the late 1940s and early 1950s, as the cold war began and Soviet power increased, fear of communism was widespread. Some conservatives viewed federal social programs—even popular ones such as social security—as evidence of communist influence within the United States government. Moderate Republicans like President Dwight D. Eisenhower accepted most of these programs, but others in the party did not.

After Lyndon Johnson's crushing defeat of Barry Goldwater in 1964, some analysts concluded that conservative views could never succeed in United States politics. Goldwater had, for example, opposed federal civil rights and antipoverty efforts and supported a buildup of weapons against an expected Soviet attack. But his candidacy did show that anticommunist fear, combined with conservative views, still persisted. In 1968 Richard Nixon, who had begun his political career with a "tough-on-communism" stance in the 1940s and 1950s, was able to bring the Republicans back to the White House.

After the Watergate scandal ended Nixon's administration in disgrace, Democrat Jimmy Carter won the presidency in 1976. Four years later, spiraling inflation and a frustrating hostage situation in Iran made Carter appear ineffective. The Republican party was ready to take over again.

RESOURCE DIRECTORY

Teaching Resources

Reproducible Lesson Plan found in the Unit 7 folder, p. 73, provides a summary of the Section 1 lesson plan content.

Alternate Lesson Plan: Critical Thinking Recognizing Ideologies, found in the Alternate Lesson Plans folder, p. 172, provides students with practice in this skill as they explain the ideas and principles of the conservative movement.

Guided Reading and Review found in the Unit 7 folder, p. 77, provides a structure for reading and mastering the key concepts and reviewing the key terms for Section 1. (Guided Practice)

The Conservative Coalition

The New Right derived its power from the support of many groups with a wide range of political, economic, and social concerns. These groups formed a **coalition**—a union of several groups that work together to achieve a common goal. The groups in the new conservative coalition did not always agree with one another, but they all contributed to the broad-based strength of the movement. Middle-class Americans were particularly supportive of the cause.

Some in the conservative coalition were most concerned with the role of government in the economy. These conservatives argued that the nation was faced with enormous inefficiency and waste. Productivity was falling while prices were rising. They believed it was time to reduce the size of government, cut taxes, and get rid of the regulations that limited economic competition. The United States would prosper only if the free market was allowed to function without serious restriction. This group charged that liberal policies that spent large sums of money on social problems had failed. Such programs should be cut, they maintained, as part of a massive effort to balance the budget.

Ronald Reagan, who would bring this ideology to the White House in the 1980s, revealed its spirit in his own slogan: "Government is not the solution to our problem. Government is the problem." The answer, he said, was traditional American free enterprise:

*T*he competitive free enterprise system has given us the greatest standard of living in the world, produced generation after generation of technical wizards who consistently lead the world in invention and innovation, and has provided unlimited opportunities enabling industrious Americans from the most humble of backgrounds to climb to the top of the ladder of success.

Some groups in the conservative movement wanted to restore what they considered Christian values to society. They objected to attitudes and ways of behaving that had become more widely accepted in the 1970s, including sexual freedom, legalized abortion, "Women's Lib," some forms of rock music, and the movement for gay and lesbian rights. Overall, they wanted to root out what they believed were the liberalizing tendencies in American life and restore a more traditional morality. The Moral Majority, a group led by a Baptist minister from Virginia named Jerry Falwell, was founded in 1979 to focus the efforts of religious conservatives. It was part of a larger movement to revive moral values in the United States.

Other conservatives demanded an end to many government-supported social programs. Those who were part of the backlash against civil rights activism (Chapter 23) criticized the policy of affirmative action. This program was one result of the civil rights movement of the 1960s. First designed for African Americans, its intent was to make up for past discrimination. Affirmative action required certain employers to give special consideration to the hiring of women, blacks, and members of other minority groups. It also gave special preference to women, blacks, and other minorities for admission to college and professional schools. Affirmative action extended this special consideration even though women and minority applicants were not necessarily better qualified than others. Some conservatives called affirmative action a form of reverse discrimination, favoring one group over another on the basis on race or gender. This issue was one that attracted some traditionally Democratic blue-collar workers to the new conservatism.

MAKING CONNECTIONS

In what ways did the New Right resemble the progressive movement of the early 1900s? In what ways was it different?

Conservatives Find Effective Tactics

Conservatives used the latest political techniques to win over new supporters. Jerry Falwell and a number of other evangelists used the power of television brilliantly to reach millions of people. In a format that became known as **televangelism,** they appealed to viewers to contribute money to their campaign against sin.

SOURCE READINGS

 Source Readings on p. 834 will connect literature selections and primary source excerpts to historical events discussed in this section.

Explain/Discuss

Remind students that the conservative revolution represented a backlash against policies that some Americans felt were destroying the United States. Discuss the conservative reaction to the society that was created after World War II. What political, social, and economic values did the conservatives want to restore?

Answer to ...

MAKING CONNECTIONS

Both movements were coalitions of groups with different but related goals that worked together to achieve common political ends. Unlike the progressives, the New Right worked within the existing Republican party. The New Right also sought a return to "traditional" values, while the progressives looked for new solutions.

In Depth

Multicultural Perspectives

Economist Thomas Sowell is one of the most vocal African American conservatives. His views on affirmative action mirror the Reagan administration's position: "What affirmative action has done is to destroy the legitimacy of what had already been achieved, by making all black achievements look like questionable accomplishments, or even outright gifts. Here and there, this program has undoubtedly caused some individuals to be hired who would otherwise not have been hired—but even that is a doubtful gain in the larger context of attaining self-respect and the respect of others."

Analyze

Have students analyze the conservatives' appeal to the American public in the late 1970s and early 1980s. Why were the conservatives able to win so much support at this particular time in American history? How did Reagan's down-to-earth style of communication contribute to his popularity?

Activity

Role-Play a Reporter

Ask students to take on the role of a television or newspaper reporter. Each student should prepare six questions to ask during an interview with a political candidate from the New Right and from a liberal organization. Students can pose their questions to other students who take the roles of political candidates and answer the questions.

Enrichment

Assist students in locating some of the books written about Ronald Reagan that claim to reveal what the President was really like. Ask them to read sections of their choice from the books and to deliver an oral report on them to the class.

Televangelists delivered fervent sermons on specific political issues and used the money they raised to back conservative politicians.

Conservative strategists also used television effectively, with brief, powerful television images that conveyed their message visually. Speeches were crafted to contain "sound bites"—short, memorable statements that would be repeated on the evening news. Strategists also pioneered in using "spin doctors" to give a candidate's comments the best possible interpretation for the public. For example, conservative columnist George Will helped Ronald Reagan prepare for a debate with President Carter in the 1980 campaign. In the TV coverage immediately following the debate, Will appeared as a political analyst. Hoping to influence viewers who might not have made up their own minds yet, Will declared Reagan the winner in the debate.

⭐ Similarly, conservatives led the way in using direct mail to raise huge sums of money for conservative candidates. Mass mailings of requests for donations were sent to individuals who were likely to support conservative causes. This effort reached out to people who might ignore generalized appeals such as television ads.

AMERICAN PROFILES

Richard Viguerie

Richard A. Viguerie (1933–) was at the cutting edge in developing the conservative coalition's new fund-raising techniques. Originally from near Houston, Texas, Viguerie had graduated from college but dropped out of law school before the end of his first year. His real interest was politics, especially conservative politics, and he spent much of his spare time working for the Republican party. He was a campaign worker for Eisenhower in 1952 and 1956, and he served as a county chairman in the Young Republicans organization.

Viguerie's big break came in 1961, when he responded to an advertisement in the prominent conservative magazine *National Review*. He was hired as executive secretary of Young Americans for Freedom, a conservative youth group. Viguerie began to approach wealthy contributors for funds to pay off the group's

huge debt, but he soon found that he was more comfortable writing them letters. This experience led him to start his own direct-mail organization in 1964.

Viguerie began by going to the office of the clerk of the House of Representatives, where he copied down the names and addresses of contributors who had given fifty dollars or more to Barry Goldwater's presidential campaign. His first list of 12,500 conservative contributors was the basis for later lists with millions of names.

Next, Viguerie began to sell his services to conservative political candidates. Using his list to run direct-mail campaigns, he helped Robert Griffin win a Senate race in Michigan in 1966. In 1969 he assisted Phil Crane in an upset victory in an Illinois congressional race. After the Watergate scandal, tighter limits were imposed on campaign contributions. Now it was even more important to be able to tap small contributors, and Viguerie's services were in great demand. The graph on page 813 shows the results of these new methods.

Viguerie firmly believed that the country was ready for a conservative revival. "The plain truth is that more and more Americans are sick of liberalism—and aren't afraid to say so," he argued. He believed that the real job for conservatives

Conservative activist Richard Viguerie recognized the enormous potential of direct mail as a political fund-raising tool.

 ## RESOURCE DIRECTORY

Teaching Resources

⭐ **American Profiles Activity** An Wang, found in the Unit 7 folder, p. 87, profiles the founder of Wang Laboratories, who developed the magnetic core memory that helped fuel the computer revolution.

⭐ **Visual Learning Activity** "Passing the Economy Buck," found in the Unit 7 folder, p. 100, reveals two cartoonists' suggestions of why successive administrations were unable to control government waste and inefficiency.

Political Campaign Spending,* 1952–1988

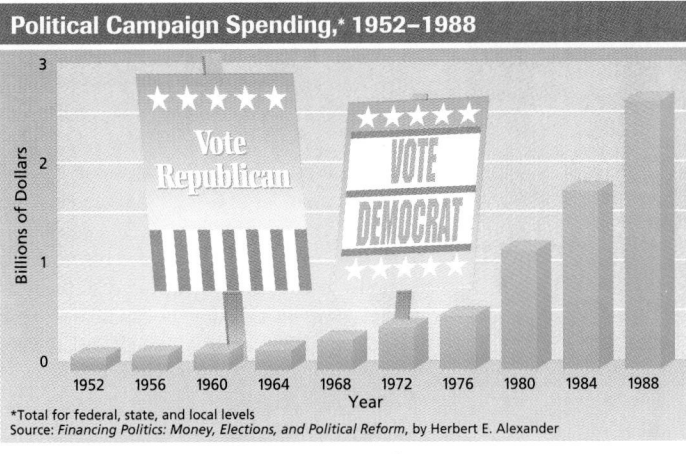

*Total for federal, state, and local levels
Source: *Financing Politics: Money, Elections, and Political Reform*, by Herbert E. Alexander

 Interpreting Graphs
In what year shown on the graph did campaign spending first increase significantly? How might the activities of Richard Viguerie and other conservatives have affected these statistics?

was to seize control of the Republican party, and he devoted all his energies to that goal.

Reagan Brings Conservatism to the White House

Ronald Reagan, who came to politics late in life, became the most influential spokesperson for the conservative cause. He began as a radio broadcaster and then embarked on a career as a movie actor in Hollywood. When he stopped acting in films, he served as a spokesperson for General Electric. Adopting the conservative point of view, he made speeches praising capitalism and corporate leaders and criticizing government regulation.

Reagan's personality, visibility, and skill in articulating conservative ideas helped him become governor of California in 1966. In 1976, with the support of Republican conservatives, he challenged Gerald Ford for the presidential nomination but lost by a narrow margin. By 1980, however, the growing strength of conservatives in the party gave Reagan the nomination.

⭐ In his campaign, Reagan attacked the incumbent Jimmy Carter, saying he offered little more than a "litany of broken promises." He entertained voters with his down-to-earth humor while criticizing Carter's economic record: "A recession is when your neighbor loses his job. A depression is when you lose yours. A recovery is when Jimmy Carter loses his."

The continuing hostage crisis in Iran, as well as other issues, worked against Carter, and Reagan won a landslide victory. He gained 51 percent of the popular vote to Carter's 41 percent. (John Anderson, member of Congress from Illinois, ran as a third-party candidate.) The Republicans gained control of the Senate for the first time in twenty-five years.

Reagan Seeks a Second Term Four years later, Reagan ran for a second term. This time the Democrats picked Senator Walter Mondale, who had been Carter's Vice President. In an unusual move, Mondale chose Geraldine Ferraro, a member of Congress from New York, as his running mate. Ferraro was the first woman ever to be nominated on a major party's presidential ticket. While the nomination appealed to many voters, it also created a backlash among some voters who believed women should remain in traditional roles.

The ticket was not strong enough to overcome Reagan's popularity and an economy that appeared strong despite growing deficits. Reagan won 59 percent of the popular vote, and Mondale won the electoral votes of only the District of Columbia and his home state of Minnesota.

While hosting the popular "G. E. Theater" in the 1950s, young Ronald Reagan sharpened his communication skills and gained valuable exposure to the American television audience.

SOURCE READINGS

Source Readings on p. 836 will connect literature selections and primary source excerpts to historical events discussed in this section.

Caption Answer to ...

 Interpreting Graphs

Campaign spending more than doubled in 1980, from just over $500 million to approximately $1.2 billion. Viguerie's direct-mail fund-raising, televangelism, and other conservative techniques contributed to this trend.

In Depth

Then and Now

The ideology of the New Right was first articulated in the late 1970s by disenchanted liberal thinkers in the quarterly journal *Public Interest*. While accepting many features of the New Deal, these critics were dismayed by what they saw as a decline of standards in every sphere of American life. The many Democrats who voted for Ronald Reagan and the emergence of a more conservative Democratic party in the 1990s may attest to the pervasive effect of the New Right's ideas on the United States.

Section 1 Review Answers

1. (a) New Right, see p. 810, (b) coalition, see p. 811, (c) televangelism, see p. 811

2. (a) Ronald Reagan, see p. 810, (b) George Bush, see p. 814

3. The conservative movement traced its roots to the anticommunism of the 1950s, when liberal programs were viewed by extreme conservatives as evidence of communist influence in the United States government.

4. The coalition included economic conservatives who opposed big government spending, conservative Christians, and conservatives who opposed liberal social programs such as affirmative action.

5. Techniques included televangelism, using sound bites and "spin doctoring," and direct-mail fund-raising.

6. Politicians and televangelists used television skillfully to shape public opinion and to elicit financial contributions. Direct-mail fund-raising techniques also gained attention and raised money for conservative causes. The New Right brought conservative groups and their money resources together to win political campaigns in the 1980s.

Reteach

Ask students to write one or two paragraphs explaining the seemingly incongruous phrase "the conservative revolution."

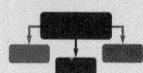

4. CLOSE

Reinforcing the Big Idea

The conservatives asserted their dominance over American politics through elections in the 1980s. The next section discusses how successive Republican administrations carried out a conservative domestic policy.

When debating Democratic challenger Michael Dukakis (right) in the 1988 presidential campaign, George Bush raised questions in voters' minds about Dukakis's plans for the economy.

In his second term, Reagan continued to win over the country. He was a skillful communicator who used television the way Franklin Roosevelt had used radio fifty years before, talking soothingly about concerns everyone shared. He was a talented storyteller, often using anecdotes to make his points. ○

In spite of problems during his presidency, Reagan enjoyed enormous popularity. One critic gave him the name "Teflon President" because, like pans with a nonstick coating, nothing stuck to him. He made mistakes and misstatements, often seemed uninterested in governing, and occasionally fell asleep during meetings. He delegated a great deal of authority to others and sometimes was unclear about policy decisions made in his name. A number of his aides and associates were charged and convicted of illegal and unethical actions. None of these blunders lessened his personal approval ratings, however. In 1989, when Reagan left office, 63 percent of the American people approved of his overall performance.

Bush Continues the Agenda

The conservative movement seemed safe when Reagan's Vice President, **George Bush,** sought the presidency. The son of a well-to-do Connecticut senator, Bush had begun his career in the Texas oil industry, then served in government as a member of Congress, as an envoy to China, and as head of the CIA. The public initially saw him as a weak candidate, without Reagan's charm, but the prosperity of the Reagan years was on his side. The candidate for the Democrats, Governor Michael Dukakis of Massachusetts, was at a disadvantage as he tried to convince voters of the need for a change. The campaign was marked by personal attacks and negative advertising.

Although Bush and his running mate, Senator Dan Quayle, won nearly 54 percent of the popular vote, Bush still lacked the mandate Ronald Reagan had enjoyed eight years earlier. Moreover, many Republican congressional candidates lost in the elections, giving Democrats control of both the Senate and the House of Representatives.

As President, Bush projected an image of cheerful energy and optimism, calling for cooperation and an end to dissension between Congress and the White House. While people were aware of problems in his handling of many issues, they generally felt that he was trying to do his best. Bush's personal approval rating remained at a remarkably high 67 percent after his first year and a half and rose even higher during the Persian Gulf War in 1991 (see Section 4 of this chapter). His popularity began to drop only when the economy faltered late in his term.

SECTION 1 REVIEW

Key Terms, People, and Places
1. Define (a) New Right, (b) coalition, (c) televangelism.
2. Identify (a) Ronald Reagan, (b) George Bush.

Key Concepts
3. What roots did the conservative movement have in the 1950s?
4. What groups formed the conservative coalition?

5. What techniques did the conservative movement use to promote its ends?

Critical Thinking
6. **Recognizing Cause and Effect** How did new fund-raising techniques help the conservative movement to achieve political power in the 1980s?

 RESOURCE DIRECTORY

Teaching Resources

○ **Primary Source Activity** Speaking for the President, found in the Unit 7 folder, p. 93, highlights the writings of Peggy Noonan, who worked as a speech writer for Ronald Reagan and George Bush.

Quiz found in the Unit 7 folder, p. 78, covers the main ideas in this section as well as the key terms.

Republican Policies at Home

SECTION PREVIEW

The 1980s were years in which the rich became even richer, while the poor and many of those in the middle saw few benefits from the nation's apparent prosperity. Presidents Reagan and Bush cut back on social programs and followed a conservative agenda.

Key Concepts
- Reagan's economic plan reduced government spending, except in the area of defense.
- Reagan and Bush's Supreme Court appointments made the Court more conservative.
- Although the economy prospered in the 1980s, the gap between rich and poor increased.

Key Terms, People, and Places
supply-side economics, S & L, new federalism; Sandra Day O'Connor, Clarence Thomas

R epublican administrations in the 1980s took a three-part approach to domestic policy. First, they hoped to revive the economy. Second, they wanted to cut back on costly social welfare programs. Third, they sought to restore the traditional values held by conservative Christians.

Reagan's Domestic Program

Reagan was most concerned with promoting economic recovery. Achieving this goal, he believed, meant reforming tax policy, cutting back on the role of government, and shifting responsibility for many programs from the federal government to city and state governments. At the same time, however, he greatly increased spending for defense.

Tax Reform Reagan's recovery program, which became known as "Reaganomics," rested on the theory of **supply-side economics.** This theory reversed earlier policies, based on the ideas of

John Maynard Keynes, which argued that it was necessary to increase people's purchasing power to improve the economy. This meant giving them more money, whether through jobs, grants, or lower taxes. By contrast, "supply-siders" wanted to lower taxes to put more money in the hands of businesses and investors—those who supplied the goods for consumers to buy. The theory assumed they would then hire more people and produce more goods and services, making the economy grow. Prosperity would "trickle down" from the top to those at the lower levels of the economy.

In February 1981 Reagan presented to Congress his proposals to cut spending, lower taxes, and eliminate unnecessary government regulations. The administration pushed through the new tax policy. A 5 percent tax cut went into effect in October 1981, followed by 10 percent cuts in 1982 and 1983. The new cuts benefited wealthy Americans the most.

Then, in 1986, Congress passed the most sweeping tax reform measure in American history. It closed loopholes in the law that had allowed some Americans to avoid paying their fair share of taxes, and it expanded the tax base. Yet it still benefited the rich most of all, cutting the maximum tax rate—the rate on the highest incomes—from 70 percent to 28 percent.

MAKING CONNECTIONS

How was Reaganomics similar to the economic policies of Presidents Harding and Coolidge in the 1920s?

This doll suggests that while Reagan's economic policies benefited the very rich, many other Americans "lost their shirts"—along with their jobs—in the 1980s.

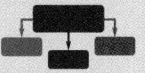 **Connecting to the Big Idea**

See page 808B. Explain that during the 1980s, Presidents Reagan and Bush followed a conservative domestic agenda. Ask what the goals of their Republican administrations were. How did they set about achieving them?

Objectives
- Describe the goals of Reagan's economic plan.
- Explain how the Supreme Court appointments made by Reagan and Bush affected the Court.
- Explain how, as the economy prospered, the gap between the rich and the poor widened in the 1980s.

Bellringer

Ask students to explain how they balance their own budget. Then ask them to suggest how they might balance the United States budget.

Reading Strategy

Reading for Evidence Ask students to find evidence as they read the section to support the statement on page 815 that Republican administrations in the 1980s had a three-part goal to revive the economy, cut back on social welfare programs, and restore traditional values.

Answer to ...

MAKING CONNECTIONS

Both Reagan and his Republican predecessors in the 1920s believed that by helping the wealthiest segment of the economy, the overall economy would improve, creating prosperity that would eventually trickle down to the poor.

Discuss

Discuss Republican domestic policies during the 1980s. Ask how Reagan planned to revive the economy. How did Reaganomics reverse earlier gains made under FDR and LBJ in the area of social welfare? In what ways did Bush continue to pursue conservative goals?

Caption Answer to ...

Interpreting Graphs

The defense budget under Reagan more than doubled, from approximately $130 billion to $290 billion. Under Bush it increased slightly, although it dropped between 1989 and 1991.

In Depth

Interdisciplinary

Christa McAuliffe, a teacher from Concord, New Hampshire, was chosen from a pool of 11,000 applicants to be the first "citizen observer" on a space shuttle flight. "I really hope the students get excited about the Space Age," said McAuliffe, "because they see me as an ordinary person up there in space." On January 28, 1986, the shuttle *Challenger* exploded in a fiery ball before a horrified nation watching the historic launch on television. At the funeral for the seven *Challenger* astronauts, President Reagan said, "Christa McAuliffe . . . dared to fly because she realized that without actions, dreams are meaningless."

Cuts in Social Programs Both philosophy and practicality guided Reagan's efforts to cut back social programs. He challenged the assumption held since the New Deal that the federal government had the responsibility to assist people directly. While he said that his administration would maintain a "safety net" for truly needy people, he also was committed to the idea that *anyone* who really tried could succeed in the United States.

Reagan's economic policy also dictated saving money at the federal level wherever possible. The federal government was collecting less in taxes and, as the graph below shows, spending more on defense. To make up the difference, he cut back public service jobs, unemployment payments, welfare benefits, and food stamp allocations. Elderly Medicare patients had to pay a larger share of their own medical bills. College students had to take out loans instead of getting federal grants. Spending for social welfare programs dropped by billions of dollars.

Deregulation Reagan, like President Jimmy Carter before him, was in favor of removing government regulations that stifled competition in the free-market economy. While Carter had begun deregulation by focusing on the oil

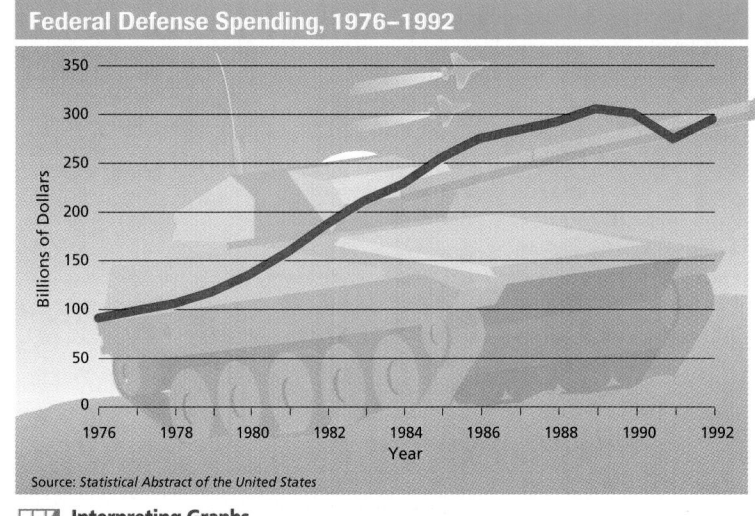

Federal Defense Spending, 1976–1992

Source: *Statistical Abstract of the United States*

Interpreting Graphs
Notice the change in defense spending in the early 1980s. *By how much did the defense budget increase during Reagan's two terms in office? What happened to defense spending during the Bush administration?*

and transportation industries, Reagan sought to remove government controls from virtually all areas of the economy.

The Reagan approach to deregulation removed both rules that limited competition and those that protected the public. It targeted agencies like the Environmental Protection Agency and the Occupational Health and Safety Administration, which enforced standards for controlling pollution or maintaining safe workplaces. Always the emphasis was on eliminating regulations that the administration believed were inefficient and expensive, but that others saw as protecting workers, consumers, and the environment.

The S & L Scandal One crucial area of deregulation was banking and finance, particularly the "thrift institutions" or savings and loan banks, often called **S & Ls.** These generally small, stable banks historically had concentrated on making home mortgage loans to individuals. The aim of deregulation was to allow these banks to make riskier but more profitable investments.

Officials at a number of unregulated S & Ls took advantage of the new laws to make huge fortunes for themselves while driving their banks into failure. When the banks failed, it was not the bank officials or even most depositors who lost money. Because bank accounts are insured by the federal government, taxpayers had to make up the millions of dollars in bad investments. Although a number of banking officials were indicted for their dishonest actions, the money was gone.

The New Federalism While he moved to cut back the role of the federal government, Reagan sought to give more responsibility to state and local governments. Borrowing a term from the Nixon administration, Reagan called this plan the **new federalism.** By eliminating funding for federal programs and instead giving the states sizable grants that they could spend as they chose, he hoped to

▶ RESOURCE DIRECTORY

Teaching Resources

⭐ **American Profiles Activity** found in the Unit 7 folder, p. 88, profiles Sandra Day O'Connor, the first woman appointed to serve on the United States Supreme Court.

encourage local governments to take the lead in meeting community needs.

Unfortunately, the policy did not work as planned. A recession early in Reagan's presidency left a number of cities and states nearly bankrupt, for they now had responsibility but not enough money for programs formerly funded from Washington.

Social Issues Reagan also took a conservative approach to social issues, endorsing the goals of such groups as the Moral Majority. He spoke out on issues like the need for prayer in public schools, which the Supreme Court had earlier ruled unconstitutional.

Bush Continues Conservatism

When he challenged Reagan for the Republican nomination in 1980, George Bush criticized Reagan's economic plan, calling it "voodoo economics." But after he lost his own bid for the presidency and accepted the vice-presidential slot, Bush adhered to Reagan's approach. While running for the presidency himself in 1988, he played on voters' fears that his Democratic opponent, Michael Dukakis, would raise taxes. Bush became known for his own promise: "Read my lips: no new taxes." As President, however, he went back on that promise when the budget deficit soared out of control.

Bush also continued to cut spending for social programs. Democratic majorities in both houses of Congress passed measures to assist people caught in a serious recession—such as one extending benefits for unemployed workers—but Bush used his veto power again and again to defeat these bills.

Bush was even more outspoken than Reagan in his support for conservative social goals. Conservatives once had questioned Bush's commitment to their program for moral renewal. As President, he reassured them by coming out directly against abortion. He tried to further their other demands as well.

The Supreme Court

Conservative ideals got further help from a series of Republican appointments to the

Supreme Court. As justices retired, Reagan and Bush had the chance to nominate five new justices—more than half the Court. In 1981 Reagan appointed **Sandra Day O'Connor,** the first woman justice on the Supreme Court. Her conservative views led her to vote often with other conservatives, such as William Rehnquist and Warren Burger. Rehnquist, the most conservative member of the Court, became Chief Justice when Burger retired in 1986. Reagan chose another conservative, Antonin Scalia, to take the spot on the Court that Rehnquist had vacated.

Reagan's next choice, judge and former law professor Robert Bork, displayed a narrow view of civil liberties and civil rights that worried many members of Congress as well as the public. The Senate rejected his nomination in 1987. Reagan then nominated Douglas Ginsberg, but Ginsberg soon withdrew himself from consideration amid charges of having used marijuana in the past. Finally, Reagan nominated Anthony Kennedy, a moderate conservative who was quickly approved by the Senate.

The Thomas Hearings George Bush made two appointments to the Court. The first, in 1990, was David Souter of New Hampshire, a relative unknown who proved to be fairly moderate. The second, in 1991, was **Clarence Thomas,** who became one of the Court's most conservative justices. Although Thomas was approved by the Senate, his confirmation hearings brought a storm of public debate.

When Thomas first appeared before the Senate Judiciary Committee, questions arose about

Sandra Day O'Connor became the first woman on the United States Supreme Court in 1981. President Reagan took her conservative views into account when selecting her as a nominee.

Analyze

Have students analyze the continuing conservative influence on American society. How do changes made during the Reagan-Bush era still affect the poor in the United States? How do conservatives continue to influence social values?

Activity
Teaching Heterogeneous Groups

Supply-side economics put more money in the hands of businesses and investors in the hope that increased production of goods and services would result in increased wealth for everyone. Selling an increased supply, however, required new markets. To help all students understand supply-side economics, divide the class into small groups, or "companies." Each company should choose a product or service of which it will increase production, and increase market share to absorb the increased supply. Companies should then explain how their increased profits will "trickle down" to the rest of society.

In Depth

Then and Now

In late 1993, during the Clinton administration, Ruth Bader Ginsburg (b. 1933) became the second woman to serve on the United States Supreme Court. Judge Ginsburg said at the confirmation hearings: "What a distance we have traveled from the day President Thomas Jefferson told his secretary of state the appointment of women to public office is an innovation for which the public is not prepared; 'Nor,' Jefferson added, 'am I.'" (See Key Events in the Reference Section.)

Enrichment

To help students gain some perspective on the federal budget deficit, have them first research the figures for the deficit during the period 1960–1993 and then plot them on a line graph using five-year intervals. Ask them to make generalizations regarding the trends they observe.

3. ASSESS

Section 2 Review Answers

1. (a) supply-side economics, see p. 815, (b) S & L, see p. 816, (c) new federalism, see p. 817

2. (a) Sandra Day O'Connor, see p. 818, (b) Clarence Thomas, see p. 818

3. Their appointments made the Court more conservative.

4. Reagan slashed taxes to give wealthy Americans more money to spend and invest, believing that their increased prosperity would "trickle down" to everyone else. At the same time, he cut spending on social programs that directly helped poor and elderly Americans.

5. The gap between rich and poor widened, and enormous federal debts accrued.

6. Reagan's policy of cutting taxes while increasing defense spending meant that the government was spending much more money than it was taking in. As a result of this yearly increase in the deficit a huge national debt accumulated over the course of the 1980s that would have to be paid off for many years after Reagan and Bush left office.

Anita Hill (below left) faced a panel of white male senators in October of 1991 to testify that she had been sexually harassed by Supreme Court nominee Clarence Thomas (inset). The scene itself—along with the senators' ultimate rejection of her testimony—symbolized for many Americans the continuing problem of sexism.

his commitment to civil liberties and his stand on crucial issues such as abortion rights and affirmative action. By the time Thomas was to be considered by the full Senate, however, these matters were overshadowed by charges made against him by a former co-worker. In a surprise statement, University of Oklahoma law professor Anita Hill alleged that Thomas had sexually harassed her when he was her supervisor at the Equal Employment Opportunity Commission (EEOC).

During several days of televised Senate hearings, committee members questioned Thomas, Hill, and numerous witnesses for each side. Millions of Americans watched and made their own judgments. Although Hill's charges did not prevent Thomas's confirmation, the hearings brought the issue of sexual harassment into the spotlight, sparking dialogue across the nation.

Attacks on *Roe* v. *Wade* While not all Republican choices for the Supreme Court were equally conservative, they clearly created a different consensus. Gone was the liberal Court of the 1950s and 1960s. The new Court was far less likely to take such an active role in social policy and far more likely to reconsider and limit rights granted in the past. One area in which the Court showed its more conservative nature was in its rulings on abortion. After the Court made abortion legal in the 1973 *Roe* v. *Wade* decision, antiabortion forces concentrated their efforts on overturning the ruling. While the Court continued to uphold the basic principle of *Roe* v. *Wade,* in several later cases, it allowed states to impose some restrictions. In a 1989 Missouri case, *Webster* v. *Reproductive Health Services,* the Court said that state legislatures could impose rather severe restrictions on the right to abortion. In *Planned Parenthood* v. *Casey,* in 1992, the Court reaffirmed the essential right to choose an abortion, but it allowed the state of Pennsylvania to impose certain restrictions, such as a twenty-four-hour waiting period and a requirement that minors have permission from a parent or judge before ending a pregnancy.

Impact of the Reagan-Bush Era

⭐ Republican policies on the domestic front brought an end to the recession that Reagan had inherited when he first took office and ushered in the prosperous, materialistic decade of the 1980s. While the United States experienced an economic boom from 1983 to 1990, however, the next decade began with another devastating recession. Corporate profits dropped, and large companies began to lay off workers. In mid-1991, the unemployment rate reached 7 percent, the highest rate in almost five years.

A small group of people prospered in the 1980s. Political analyst Kevin Phillips described this new class of "upper America."

> The 1980s were the triumph of upper America—an ostentatious [showy] celebration of wealth, the political ascendancy of the rich and a glorification of capitalism, free markets and finance. . . . No parallel upsurge of riches had been seen since the late 19th century, the era of the Vanderbilts, Morgans and Rockefellers. It was the truly wealthy, more than anyone else, who flourished under Reagan. . . . The truth is that the critical concentration of wealth in the United States was developing at higher levels—decamillionaires, centimillionaires, half-billionaires and

---

 RESOURCE DIRECTORY

Teaching Resources

⭐ 📄 **Literature Activity** In Pursuit of Health and Happiness, found in the Unit 7 folder, p. 96, presents an excerpt from a self-help book that personifies the self-focus of many Americans during the Reagan-Bush era.

billionaires. Garden variety million-aires had become so common that there were about 1.5 million of them by 1989.

Meanwhile, less fortunate Americans were hurting. Particularly in the cities, a permanent "underclass" of those who could never escape poverty seemed to be developing. Homeless people living on the street became a common and distressing sight. At the same time, blue-collar workers witnessed high-paying industrial jobs disappear. Scores of farmers watched banks foreclose on their farms.

The Deficit Soars Beginning with Reagan's presidency, Americans began to feel greater confidence about the nation's future. Still, one problem was of great concern—the federal deficit. The huge increase in military spending, combined with Reagan's tax-cutting policies, meant that the government was spending far more than it was taking in.

The 1980s saw the annual deficit soar out of control. It rose from $60 billion in 1980 to $221 billion in 1986. As a result of those yearly short-falls, the national debt rose from $914 billion in 1980 to $3.1 trillion in 1990.

Alarmed, George Bush worked out a deal with Congress in 1990 to cut the deficit. The deal included raising taxes, thus breaking a promise Bush had made when running for office (page 941). Even with the agreement, the deficit continued to climb—and even worse, the economy entered a recession. These economic problems led to Bush's defeat in 1992.

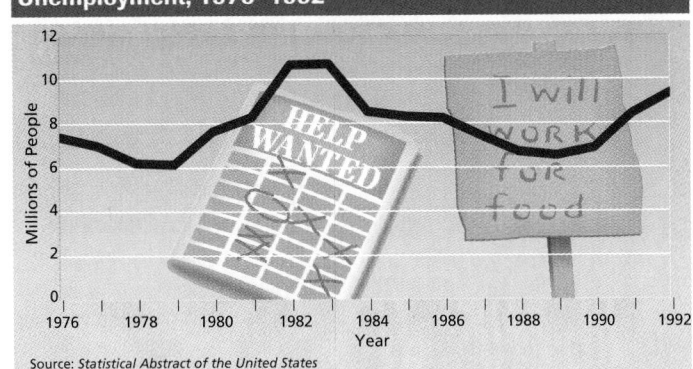

Unemployment, 1976–1992

Millions of People (y-axis: 0, 2, 4, 6, 8, 10, 12)
Year (x-axis: 1976, 1978, 1980, 1982, 1984, 1986, 1988, 1990, 1992)

Source: *Statistical Abstract of the United States*

 Interpreting Graphs
Examine the graph above showing unemployment statistics from 1976 to 1992. *What was the general trend in unemployment during Bush's term? What effect might these statistics have had on his campaign for reelection in 1992?*

The Reagan-Bush Legacy Bill Clinton's election as President (see Chapter 35) seemed at the time to signal an end to the Reagan-Bush era. As it turned out, the legacy of their presidencies endures. The Republicans' sweeping victory at the polls in 1994 suggested that voters wanted to continue the policies of cutting government spending as well as reducing the role of government in daily life. With the Republicans gaining control of Congress for the first time in over 40 years, there was new interest in such measures as a balanced budget amendment to the Constitution. Recognizing that future generations will have to bear the monumental interest payments on the national debt, Congress seemed determined to tackle the thorny issue with new resolve.

SECTION 2 REVIEW

Key Terms, People, and Places
1. Define (a) supply-side economics, (b) S & L, (c) new federalism.
2. Identify (a) Sandra Day O'Connor, (b) Clarence Thomas.

Key Concepts
3. How did the appointments made by Reagan and Bush change the character of the Supreme Court?

4. Describe Reagan's economic plan.
5. What were the results of the economic policies followed by the federal government in the 1980s?

Critical Thinking
6. **Expressing Problems Clearly** Explain how Reaganomics created enormous deficits and a mounting national debt that would burden future generations of taxpayers.

Quiz found in the Unit 7 folder, p. 80, covers the main ideas in this section as well as the key terms.

Ask students to create a cause-and-effect chart in which they state the Republicans' conservative domestic policy and its effects.

◆ **Alternative Assessment**
Mid-Point Monitoring
Ask students if they have
● Chosen a format for their project
● Outlined the main ideas
● Begun outside research

4. CLOSE

Reinforcing the Big Idea
Republican Presidents Reagan and Bush instituted conservative domestic policies that had far-reaching consequences for the United States. The next section discusses the effects of their policies on the movement for greater equality for women and minority groups.

Caption Answer to ...

Interpreting Graphs

During the Bush administration (1989–1993), the number of unemployed Americans rose from approximately 6.5 million to 9.4 million. Students may predict that these statistics were a serious problem for Bush in his bid for reelection.

Critical Thinking

Demonstrating Reasoned Judgment

Focus Analyze a passage on preventing drug abuse to judge its validity.

Instruct After students have read the passage, have them identify the main thrust of the statement. Then have them list key pieces of evidence that support the main message. Ask students if the writer includes any information that does not support the main message. Point out that sometimes a writer or speaker will include information that does not necessarily support an argument and that it is important to be able to recognize this when making reasoned judgments.

Extend See the Historian's Toolbox Activity in the Resource Directory below.

Answers

1. (a) Ramsey Clark (b) October 16, 1989 (c) In *Nation* magazine. (d) As a former U.S. attorney general, presumably he would know about crime, drugs, and law enforcement. (e) Since he served in a Democratic administration, he may have a somewhat partisan view of a Republican proposal.

2. (a) and (b) He says that these strategies have not worked in the past. (c) He cites the fact that expenditures for law enforcement and more prisons have already skyrocketed, to no effect; and he recalls the Vietnam War as proof of the impossibility of making foreign countries do what the United States wants. (d) He wants increased efforts to improve living standards, education, and job opportunities.

3. (a), (b), and (c) Answers will vary.

Demonstrating Reasoned Judgment

Making connections between ideas is the basis for reasoned judgment. This critical thinking skill enables you to analyze the merits of a statement or opinion and so to reach your own conclusions about its validity.

During the Reagan and Bush administrations, the use of illegal drugs in the United States reached historic highs, and both Presidents sought to end drug abuse. In September 1989, President Bush declared an all-out "War on Drugs." The administration's major weapon in this war, he declared, would be strengthened law enforcement—more police, more prisons, more and longer prison sentences for drug offenders—and military intervention in stopping the shipment of drugs into the United States from other countries. The passage at right represents one person's response to this plan.

Read the passage. Then use the following steps to analyze the response and to test the reasonableness of both the writer's judgment and your own.

1. Examine the source and nature of the evidence by asking *who, when, where,* and *what.*
(a) Who wrote the response?
(b) When? (c) Where did the response appear? (d) What are the writer's qualifications for knowing about the subject he is addressing? (e) Might the writer have any personal biases that affected his view of the drug policies pursued by Reagan and Bush?

2. Identify the major points in the response. (a) Why does the writer of this passage think that expanded legal measures will not work? (b) Why does he think that military action is doomed to failure as well? (c) What evidence does he offer that both are bound to fail? (d) What steps does he think should be taken to solve the problem?

3. Evaluate the evidence offered and the writer's reasoning.
(a) How convincing do you find his arguments? Explain why. (b) How possible do you think it is to achieve the solution he suggests? Explain why. (c) What grade—from A down to F (failing)—would you give the writer on how well he demonstrates reasoned judgment? Why?

Police, prosecutors, courts and prison, not to mention the military, can do little to prevent crime, including drug abuse.

. . . Expenditures for law enforcement have been increasing at a rate four times greater than those for education. Only recognition of the truth and effective action based on it can free us from the human tragedy of drug abuse. A first truth in the war on drugs, as on crime generally, is that the enemy is us, or more precisely, our children, hence our future.

The population of our prisons is already greater than that of Washington, D.C. Inmates are overwhelmingly young, male and from minorities. Is it possible that a country that talks of freedom, equality and justice and claims any sense of responsibility, decency or a degree of intelligence would offer more prisons as a solution to anything . . . ?

. . . The Vietnam War should have taught us the impossibility of controlling foreign conduct by military intervention. This includes the impossibility of stopping the production of cocaine, heroin and other drugs in foreign countries by military action. . . .

In a real fight against drugs, we must work with our young people. To reduce crime and drug abuse we must work for adequate housing and assistance to families; good health care; an education for a full life, including the truth about drugs; meaningful jobs and commitment to freedom, equality and justice. Children born and raised healthy, in loving families among people aspiring to those ideals, will rarely abuse drugs, or hurt one another.

—Ramsey Clark, U.S. attorney general under President Johnson, 1967–1969, quoted in *Nation* magazine, October 16, 1989

 RESOURCE DIRECTORY

Teaching Resources

Historian's Toolbox Activity Demonstrating Reasoned Judgment, found in the Unit 7 folder, p. 91, helps students apply this skill by analyzing Clinton's ideas on the federal government's role in education.

The Halting Pace of Reform

SECTION PREVIEW

The movement toward greater equality for women and minority groups slowed during the administrations of Presidents Reagan and Bush. Because many conservatives opposed extending more rights to such groups, the government sometimes adopted policies that reversed earlier gains.

Key Concepts
- More African Americans voted and were elected to public office during the 1980s than in previous years, but the conservative agenda did not generally support extending civil rights.
- The women's movement faced a backlash from conservatives but still pressed forward.
- Latinos became a more visible presence in politics in the 1980s.
- Native Americans became more involved and influential in their own businesses and educational institutions.

Key Terms, People, and Places
acquired immunodeficiency syndrome (AIDS); Henry Cisneros

I n the 1980s and early 1990s, minority groups continued to push for equality in American life. But progress came more slowly than in the past. The economic climate, with its periodic downturns, made life more difficult for many middle-class Americans, who began to think that enough had been done already to assist minority groups. Meanwhile, the Reagan and Bush administrations did little to encourage change.

Civil Rights in the 1980s

Real gains in civil rights were visible as the 1980s began. The federal commitment to extend voting rights had given the vote to millions of African Americans who had been denied it for years. These new voters, helped by a greater openness in people's attitudes, elected an increasing number of African American candidates to office.

Voters in some of the nation's largest cities, including those in New York, Los Angeles, Chicago, and Cleveland, elected African American mayors. In 1989 Douglas Wilder of Virginia became the first African American to be elected governor of a state. Thousands of other African Americans served in state legislatures and other state offices.

At the national level, the number of African American representatives in Congress doubled from twelve in 1971 to twenty-four in 1989. In the 1984 and 1988 elections, the Reverend Jesse Jackson, once an aide to Martin Luther King, Jr., ran for the presidency. At first, Jackson found himself on the fringe of the Democratic party. The second time around, he moved into the mainstream and dominated the primary campaign. He received 7 million votes and won nearly 1,200 delegates. While he did not win the nomination, he demonstrated that an African American candidate could be a serious contender at the national level.

Yet at the same time, administration policies opposed many of the programs that had helped to achieve these gains. Reagan, like Nixon, opposed the policy of busing students to achieve

Jesse Jackson (at the Democratic Convention in Atlanta, below) tried to build a "Rainbow Coalition" of supporters from differing backgrounds in his bids for the presidential nomination in 1984 and 1988.

Explain/Discuss

Discuss the slow progress in the area of social equality for women and minorities during the administrations of Reagan and Bush. Ask what the Reagan and Bush administrations did to weaken some of the gains made by women and minorities during the 1960s and 1970s. Despite a lack of government support for their goals, how were African Americans, Latinos, and Native Americans actually successful in achieving increased social equality during the 1980s and early 1990s?

Analyze

Ask students to analyze the reaction of conservatives to the women's movement and to the gay and lesbian rights movement. Why did conservatives feel threatened by these groups in particular? How did these groups challenge the values of conservative Christians? Why did some women oppose the ERA?

Answer to ...

Viewpoints

Barth thinks that African Americans are more hopeful and more visible in society in the 1990s; Lewis sees less promise of integration than when Dr. King was alive. For a more thorough examination of the civil rights movement, see the Resource Directory below.

Answer to ...

MAKING CONNECTIONS

Seeing all of the problems that persisted into the 1990s, African Americans might feel that the song's promise remained unfulfilled.

Viewpoints
On the Legacy of the Civil Rights Movement

Decades after the civil rights movement demanded racial justice in the United States, problems persisted. *What does each of the viewpoints below say about the impact of the movement on race relations in the early 1990s?*

Substantial Progress
"Before the civil rights movement, there was a very wide separation between blacks and whites. I don't think the separation is as great today. There has been more speaking out. Blacks now let themselves open up and say how they feel in no uncertain terms. I think there are friendships between blacks and whites that didn't exist before. In spite of everything, I think the racial situation is healthier than it was before. Blacks are no longer invisible."
　　Eileen Barth, retired social worker and child care professional, quoted in Studs Terkel, *Race,* 1992

Little or No Progress
"The country is more segregated today than it was when [Martin Luther] King and [Robert] Kennedy were alive. What Dr. King and Bobby were fighting was segregation and discrimination imposed by law, by the state. . . . All of that has changed. . . . But in the North, everybody knows what's happened in the cities. At universities, there's much more black withdrawal into separate communities. I grew up thinking we were going to have an integrated society, not just an end to official racism."
　　Anthony Lewis, columnist for the *New York Times,* quoted in *Life,* April 1993

racial balance in public schools, and his position signaled a general shift in direction. The administration worked to end some affirmative action programs. Reagan tried to prevent the extension of the Voting Rights Act of 1965, which had sparked African American political gains, and only backed off when faced with intense criticism from both Democrats and Republicans. He also weakened the Civil Rights Commission by appointing members who did not support its major goals.

As federal judges appointed by Reagan and Bush took office, the federal courts did less in the area of civil rights. The courts stopped pressing for school desegregation and in some cases approved patterns of racial separation. In

---

the spring of 1992, the Supreme Court's decision in the *Freeman* v. *Pitts* case released a suburban Atlanta school board from a desegregation order. The Court argued that it was not permissible to use federal policy to undo the effects of population shifts.

Many African Americans were troubled by the changes they saw taking place. Joseph Lattimore, a fifty-year-old insurance broker from Chicago, reflected on what he had seen in the years since he had moved north from Mississippi. "Some things are better today and some things are worse," he told author Studs Terkel in the early 1990s. Lattimore felt frustrated with the slow pace of change:

> As far as integrating with you [white Americans]—we have sang "We Shall Overcome," we have prayed at the courthouse steps, we have made all these gestures, and the door is not open. I'm just tired. Pretty soon I'll have grandkids and they will want to sing "We Shall Overcome." I will say, "No, we have sang that long enough." We should not make a lifetime of singing that song. I refuse to sing it anymore.

MAKING CONNECTIONS

Why might the song "We Shall Overcome," which had inspired civil rights activists in the 1960s and 1970s, cause a feeling of disappointment for African Americans in the 1990s?

The Women's Movement Meets a Backlash

The women's movement, too, had made progress but now occasionally met with setbacks. Conditions had clearly improved in the two decades during which the movement had been under way. In 1982, in the tenth anniversary issue of *Ms.* magazine, founding editor Gloria Steinem noted, "Now, we have words like 'sexual harassment' and 'battered women.' Ten years ago it was just called 'life.'"
⊕ The women's movement, however, had also met with a backlash, or counterreaction. One focus of the backlash was the Equal Rights

---

RESOURCE DIRECTORY

Teaching Resources

Viewpoints Activity On the Legacy of the Civil Rights Movement, found in the Unit 7 folder, pp. 89–90, provides differing perspectives on the topic of race relations in the 1990s.

Visual Learning Activity Wages for Housework, found in the Unit 7 folder, p. 99, illustrates in a poster by Betsy Warrior the backlash from women who felt that their traditional role in the home was being unfairly devalued by the women's movement.

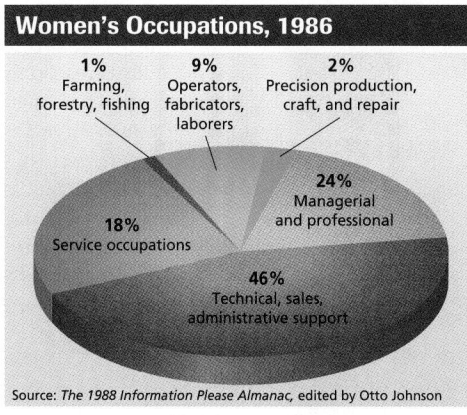

Women's Occupations, 1986

- 1% Farming, forestry, fishing
- 9% Operators, fabricators, laborers
- 2% Precision production, craft, and repair
- 24% Managerial and professional
- 18% Service occupations
- 46% Technical, sales, administrative support

Source: *The 1988 Information Please Almanac, edited by Otto Johnson*

 Interpreting Charts
The chart above shows a one-year snapshot of occupations held by women. *What percentage of women in 1986 held managerial or professional jobs? What kinds of jobs were held by the largest share of women? How do you think a pie chart for men's occupations would be different?*

Amendment to the Constitution, which banned discrimination on the basis of gender. Though its ratification seemed assured after Congress passed the amendment in 1972, its momentum faltered and opposition increased—both from women who felt threatened by social changes and from conservative members of Congress who were similarly uncomfortable with the women's movement. Conservative activist Phyllis Schlafly organized a letter-writing campaign to legislators, claiming that passage of the ERA would lead to such changes as the drafting of women into the armed forces and the decline of the traditional family. By mid-1982 it was clear that too many state legislatures would reject the amendment, and the ERA died.

Economically, more women gained access to good jobs and the professions, but most remained concentrated in lower-paying, traditionally "female" jobs—secretaries, nurses, waitresses, or cashiers. The graph above shows the percentage of women in various occupations in 1986. Even when they got jobs formerly reserved for men, they faced barriers to promotions and executive positions. Wage differences continued: in 1985 full-time working women still earned only about sixty-four cents for every dollar earned by men.

In the 1980s and 1990s, support for feminism declined. Despite challenges and conditions that still warranted improvement, some women found their energies focused on other concerns. Many young women, taking advantage of the gains already made, simply wanted to get ahead. As Beverly Stephen, a reporter for the *New York Daily News*, noted:

> They are so busy learning to play games mother never taught them that they are not aware that only a decade ago they would not have been allowed to play.

Thus, despite all challenges, the women's movement continued to flourish. The hard-won victories of the 1960s and 1970s paved the way for future progress.

The Gay and Lesbian Rights Movement

In the progressive climate of the 1960s and 1970s, some homosexual men and women became more open about their sexual orientation and about the discrimination they often encountered. One crucial event was a 1969 riot following a police raid on the Stonewall Inn, a gay bar in New York City, which sparked a new sense of activism. The movement to secure rights and protection for gay men and lesbian women took many forms, from quiet political action to deliberately outrageous behavior. But, even more than the women's movement, it brought an emotional backlash from people who were uncomfortable with the challenge to traditional sexual norms.

The appearance of **acquired immuno-deficiency syndrome (AIDS)** in 1981 contributed to the backlash. Caused by a virus that attacks the body's immune system, AIDS as yet has no cure. At first, most of its victims were intravenous drug users and gay men. Some conservatives therefore viewed AIDS as a curse that punished certain people for their habits and lifestyles. By the early 1990s, however, the number of cases in the United States had reached 200,000, and the disease had spread into the larger community. AIDS could no longer be viewed as strictly a gay issue—it was an epidemic, nationally and internationally.

The struggle over the ERA was intense, and the issues it addressed continue to be the center of heated debate. Have students research the views of conservative Phyllis Schlafly and a leading feminist, such as Gloria Steinem. Then have students take a position regarding equal rights for women and support it in a short essay.

3. ASSESS

Section 3 Review Answers

1. AIDS, see p. 823

2. Reagan opposed busing to achieve racial balance in schools, tried to block the extension of the Voting Rights Act of 1965, weakened the Civil Rights Commission, and appointed federal judges whose decisions were in line with his own thinking on these issues.

In Depth

Biography

Wilma Mankiller (b. 1946) was the first elected female leader of a major Native American tribe, the 94,460-member Cherokee Nation of Oklahoma. She was also chief executive of Cherokee Nation Industries, a multimillion-dollar business that channels its profits from factories, gift shops, and other concerns into Cherokee social programs. "If you look at data over the last twenty years," says Chief Mankiller, who would not seek reelection in 1995, "we've had an impact in infant mortality and the educational attainment level, [but] we're nowhere near where we need to be on any of those issues, nowhere near, but we're headed in the right direction."

The AIDS quilt is a personal memorial to Americans who have died of the disease. Friends and family members contribute patches that celebrate the lives of their loved ones. In 1992 the quilt was displayed before the Capitol. It contained 26,000 panels—only one sixth of the total number of Americans who had succumbed to AIDS by that time.

"Time and Place," on pages 826–827, contains a full discussion of the AIDS epidemic.

The Movement for Latino Rights

Latinos continued to make political gains in the 1980s and 1990s. **Henry Cisneros** was elected mayor of San Antonio, Texas, while Federico Peña was elected to the same post in Denver, Colorado. In New Mexico, Governor Toney Anaya referred to himself as the nation's highest elected Hispanic American. Nationwide, more and more Latinos won elective office, and more Latino administrators were appointed at all levels of government. In 1988 Lauro Cavazos was named secretary of education, becoming the first Latino to serve in the President's cabinet.

Outside government, the number of Latino college and university faculty members more than doubled in the decade ending in 1980. Appointments to prestigious positions, like that of Manuel T. Pacheco as president of the University of Arizona in 1991, promised to lead to future gains for Latinos.

Yet Latinos also faced continuing problems in the United States. In 1987 only 60 percent of all Latino high school students graduated, and only 31 percent were enrolled in courses preparing them for college. Of those who went on to higher education, only 7 percent completed their course of study. In many cases, these figures were due to lack of encouragement in school, combined with discrimination in counseling and class assignments.

Native Americans Take Action

On their own, Native Americans made considerable gains in the 1980s and early 1990s. They gave particular attention to increasing their education and to developing their business and legal skills. ✪

Many tribal communities founded their own colleges. In the decade after Congress passed the Tribally Controlled Community College Assistance Act in 1978, twenty tribally controlled colleges received financial support. In the early 1960s, only a few hundred Native Americans in the entire country attended college, but in the 1980s, the number rose to the tens of thousands.

Another approach involved the development of business skills, although many business values and ethics contradict traditional Native American attitudes. Dale Old Horn, department head at Little Big Horn College in Montana, explained the problem of clashing values:

T *he Crow Indian child is taught that he is part of a harmonious circle of kin relations, clans and nature. The white child is taught that he is the center of the circle. The Crow believe in sharing wealth, and whites believe in accumulating wealth.*

Nonetheless, a number of Native American groups started business ventures in an effort to improve their communities' prosperity. Iola Hayden, executive director of Oklahomans for

▶ RESOURCE DIRECTORY

Teaching Resources

 Critical Thinking Activity Recognizing Ideologies: Oglala Lakota College, found in the Unit 7 folder, p. 92, helps students apply this skill by analyzing an account of a Native American community college.

Henry Cisneros was one of many Latinos elected to prominent government positions in the 1980s and 1990s.

Indian Opportunity, described a new willingness to be involved in commercial ventures:

> I grew up with the liberal thinking that big business was bad, and we had been treated in such a way that kept us out of the enterprise arena. Now we're beginning to realize that, if we want to be self-sufficient, we're going to have to become entrepreneurs ourselves. It's a painfully slow process because we . . . don't have a generation of entrepreneurs to look back on as an example. We are the generation to develop that.

The Choctaw in Mississippi are an example of one group that made an aggressive effort to develop skills as entrepreneurs. By the middle of the 1980s, they owned all or part of three businesses on their reservation. They employed a thousand people and cut their unemployment rate in half.

Native Americans continued to fight in the courts for their land and their rights. An Office of Economic Opportunity program established in 1968 helped the University of New Mexico Law School start a Native American scholarship program that educated thirty-five to forty Native American lawyers each year. Graduates of this program, along with other attorneys, successfully argued for tribal jurisdiction in cases concerning reservations. Court cases around the country upheld long-ignored treaty rights.

SECTION 3 REVIEW

Key Terms, People, and Places
1. Define AIDS.

Key Concepts
2. How did President Reagan try to curtail some of the civil rights gains of the 1960s and 1970s?
3. By the 1980s, what had the women's movement achieved, and what obstacles did women still face?
4. Who was Henry Cisneros, and why was his career in public office significant?

5. How did Native Americans use economics and the law to promote their interests?

Critical Thinking
6. **Formulating Questions** Imagine that you are preparing a report entitled "How Much Have Women Gained Since the 1960s?" Create a list of questions on which you would base your investigation before writing the report.

 Quiz found in the Unit 7 folder, p. 82, covers the main ideas in this section as well as the key terms.

Media and Technology

 **Transparency**
Critical Thinking, I-11

---

3. The women's movement had raised people's awareness of sexism and had changed some attitudes and practices. At the same time, the ERA failed to gain ratification, and women still had not achieved economic equality with men by the 1990s.

4. Henry Cisneros was elected mayor of San Antonio, Texas. He was one of a growing number of Latinos in prominent and powerful positions.

5. Some Native Americans began learning entrepreneurial skills in order to become financially self-sufficient; others became lawyers and fought for their rights in the courts.

6. Questions will vary but should address changes in women's economic status—such as average yearly earnings compared to men—and in their social status—how they are viewed and treated by the rest of society.

Reteach

Ask students to write a sentence or two explaining the significance of the following in relation to the movement for greater equality for women and minority groups: Jesse Jackson's presidential candidacy, the ERA, Henry Cisneros, Tribally Controlled Community College Assistance Act.

4. CLOSE

Reinforcing the Big Idea

Although the pace of reform slowed in the 1980s because conservative ideas dominated the government, women and minority groups continued to push for equality in American society. The next section discusses the ebb of the conservatives' hold on government as the United States faced a new world.

The AIDS/HIV Pandemic

Focus Explain that until recently AIDS was considered by many to be a disease affecting only homosexual men and intravenous drug users. Only after an increasing proportion of the heterosexual population began to contract AIDS did Americans come to view it as a threat to all humankind.

In this feature students will learn about the origins and spread of AIDS. **Instruct** Point out that since 1982, AIDS-related deaths among young adults have risen dramatically. Today AIDS is the second leading cause of death among men aged twenty-five to forty-four and the sixth leading cause of death among women in the same age group. Explain that there is no known cure for the disease.

After students have read the feature, ask them to look at the map on page 827. Explain that the map provides a three-dimensional view of AIDS incidence rates over the period from 1981 to 1990. Ask students to use the information in the map key to calculate the incidence of AIDS in one area, such as southern Florida. *(2 cm X 310 cases per 100,000 people = 620 cases per 100,000 people.)*

To be sure students understand the vulnerability of all Americans to AIDS, create a chart illustrating the three phases of the spread of the disease in the United States (1981–1985, 1985–1987, 1987–1990). Ask students to indicate the correct column for each of the following:
• Smaller counties close to big cities experience the most rapid growth in AIDS cases.
• Occurrence confined to large cities and to homosexual men and intravenous drug users.
• Rapid increase in AIDS cases both in cities and surrounding counties.
• About 2,500 new AIDS cases reported annually.

The AIDS/HIV Pandemic

With no cure and no vaccine, the only strategy to curb the spread of the deadly disease of AIDS and the HIV virus is through prevention. But what patterns can we detect in the movement of the disease? How can we use that information to prevent the disease from spreading further and to find a cure?

With its enormous impact on our society today, it is hard to imagine that little more than ten years ago, acquired immunodeficiency syndrome (AIDS) was unknown. The first cases of AIDS were reported at the Centers for Disease Control (CDC) in June 1981. During the 1980s, more than 65,000 people died from the disease. As of September 1993, a total of 328,392 AIDS cases had been reported to the CDC, of which 201,775 had died. Globally, reliable statistics are difficult to obtain, but estimated numbers of AIDS cases range from 400,000 to 1 million. With no cure and no vaccine in sight, the number of people with AIDS continues to rise. Moreover, it is no longer an epidemic confined to certain limited populations. AIDS has become a pandemic—a disease that threatens the lives of the entire human population around the world.

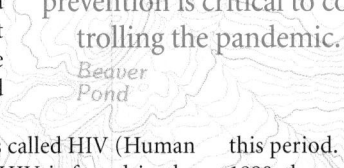

Education, especially of teenagers, about AIDS and its prevention is critical to controlling the pandemic.

AIDS is caused by a virus called HIV (Human Immunodeficiency Virus). HIV is found in the blood and other bodily fluids of infected people, and it is transmitted by sexual intercourse, intravenous drug use, exposure to contaminated blood, or from mother to fetus. So far, the only way to halt further spread of the pandemic is to change the behaviors that transmit the virus.

Movement of AIDS and the HIV Virus

The origins and spread of a disease are important in understanding the disease. Thus, examining the geographic theme of movement in relation to AIDS is important in uncovering clues in the search for cures and prevention strategies.

The AIDS pandemic in the United States went through three phases in the 1980s. The years before 1985 represent an initial phase when the occurrence of AIDS was mainly confined to large urban areas and to certain risk groups such as homosexual men and intravenous drug users. San Francisco, New York, the District of Columbia, and Miami were the major epicenters in this early phase. About 2,500 new cases were reported nationally each year during this period.

The second phase, from 1985 to 1987, was characterized by a rapid increase in AIDS cases along with greater public awareness. AIDS incidence increased significantly both in the epicenters themselves and in the counties surrounding these epicenters. About 17,000 new cases were added each year in this period. During the third phase, from 1988 to 1990, the number of new AIDS cases rose to 33,000 each year. More important, the pattern of the pandemic changed. Smaller counties close to big cities experienced the fastest growth in AIDS, most of them in the Midwest, West Virginia, and rural Florida. Additionally, a steady increase in AIDS in the heterosexual population, low-income classes, and ethnic minority groups was reported.

The map on page 827 is a three-dimensional perspective on AIDS incidence rates by county for the period 1981 to 1990. The geographical pattern is shaped like a horseshoe, with high AIDS rates on the

Teaching Resources

 Time and Place Activity Infectious Disease: *Escherichia coli*, found in the Unit 7 folder, pp. 85–86, focuses on the pathway of this bacteria in several recent outbreaks.

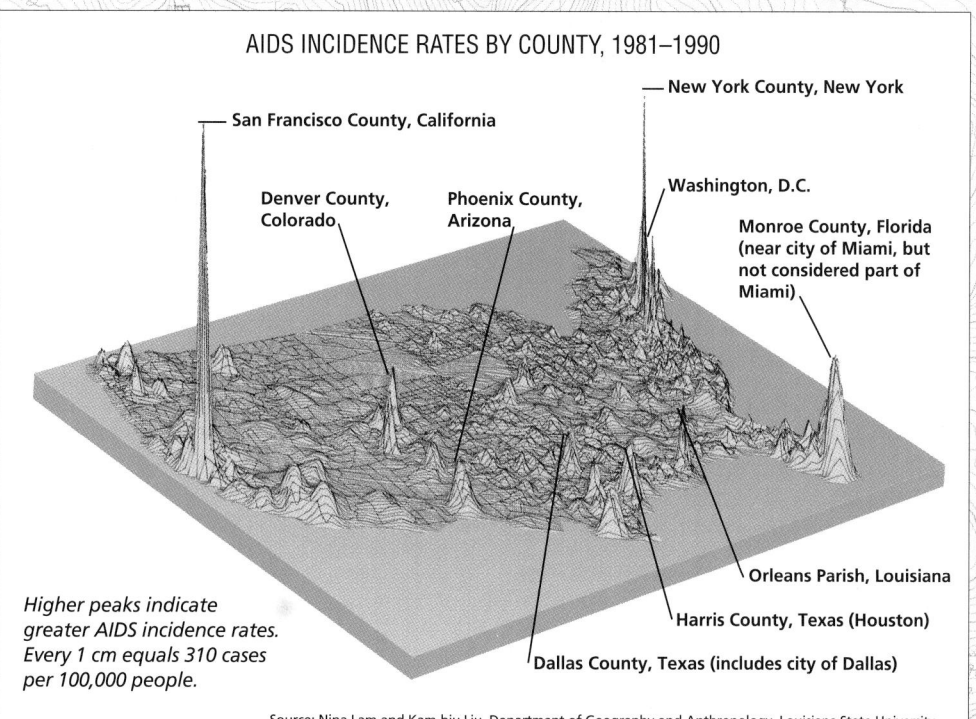

AIDS INCIDENCE RATES BY COUNTY, 1981–1990

San Francisco County, California

New York County, New York

Denver County, Colorado

Phoenix County, Arizona

Washington, D.C.

Monroe County, Florida (near city of Miami, but not considered part of Miami)

Orleans Parish, Louisiana

Harris County, Texas (Houston)

Dallas County, Texas (includes city of Dallas)

Higher peaks indicate greater AIDS incidence rates. Every 1 cm equals 310 cases per 100,000 people.

Source: Nina Lam and Kam-biu Liu, Department of Geography and Anthropology, Louisiana State University

East and West coasts and in the South, forming a ring around the United States on three sides. High concentrations occur in metropolitan areas; the interior section of the country generally has much lower AIDS rates. San Francisco and New York continue to be the dominant epicenters. Chicago and a number of midwestern cities, by contrast, have lower rates than might be expected for urban areas of their size. In 1990 Florida became the third-highest infected state, following New York and California.

Controlling the Pandemic: A Continuing Challenge

The HIV/AIDS pandemic will continue to pose a serious threat to society in the twenty-first century. It is important to remember that the disease is no longer confined to certain groups; the entire population is at risk. More and more cases are found in rural areas and among poor people, ethnic minorities, women, children, and heterosexual people.

Education, especially of teenagers, about AIDS and its prevention is critical to controlling the pandemic.

Scientists are working together to find a vaccine and a cure. Systematic collection of HIV/AIDS data will be crucial in the 1990s. By carefully examining this data and learning about the movement of the disease, we can predict future trends and allocate limited health resources more efficiently.

GEOGRAPHIC CONNECTIONS

1. Where in the United States did the fastest growth in AIDS occur in the late 1980s?
2. How is the disease spread? What geographic patterns has the spread of AIDS followed?

Critical Thinking

3. **Identifying Alternatives** What do you think the government should do to control the pandemic effectively, given the country's limited health resources?

SECTION 4

The United States in a New World

The United States in a New World

1. FOCUS

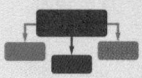

Connecting to the Big Idea

See page 808B. Explain that in the 1980s and early 1990s, the world changed dramatically. The cold war ended after more than forty years, and the Soviet Union crumbled. Aggressively anticommunist foreign policies became outdated as the nation faced a new world. Ask what possibilities and challenges this new world presented to the United States.

Objectives

- Explain how the collapse of the Soviet Union ended the cold war.
- Explain why President Bush organized military action against Iraq in 1991.
- Describe how the United States responded to the internal struggles of neighboring Latin American countries.

Bellringer

Ask students if they think the United States is as powerful today as it was during the cold war.

Reading Strategy

Predicting Content Ask students to skim the section, list the main headings and subheadings, and write a sentence or phrase to predict the content under each one. When they have finished reading the section, ask them to test their predictions against the actual text.

SECTION PREVIEW

After more than forty years of the cold war, in the early 1990s the United States watched as communist governments crumbled. The foreign policies of Reagan's first years in office became outdated as the nation faced new possibilities and problems.

Key Concepts

- The collapse of the Soviet Union brought an end to the cold war.
- The United States and Iraq went to war after Iraq invaded its neighbor Kuwait.
- The United States intervened in countries in Latin America and the Caribbean.

Key Terms, People, and Places

Strategic Defense Initiative (SDI), Intermediate-Range Nuclear Forces (INF) Treaty, Persian Gulf War, Iran-contra affair; Mikhail Gorbachev, Boris Yeltsin, Saddam Hussein, Sandinista, contras

American poet Robert Frost once wrote, "Something there is that doesn't love a wall," and the people of East Germany would no doubt agree. This concrete slab came from the dismantling of the hated Berlin Wall in 1989.

In the 1980s and early 1990s, the world changed dramatically. Ronald Reagan was intent on defending the United States against what he termed an "evil empire"— the Soviet Union. Yet by the end of George Bush's term, the cold war that had dominated international politics for more than forty years was over. American policy makers had to rethink traditional assumptions and learn to operate in what George Bush called a "new world order."

Reagan's Defense Policies

Ronald Reagan took office in 1981 determined to defend United States interests in the cold war. He believed in a tough approach toward the Soviet Union and wanted not only to strengthen conventional military forces but also to increase the supply of nuclear weapons.

The costs of such a buildup were enormous, contributing to the growing budget deficit. Over a five-year period, the administration sought a military budget of $1.5 trillion, an amount far higher than ever before.

In March 1983 Reagan proposed an altogether new program of missile defense. The **Strategic Defense Initiative (SDI)**, popularly called "Star Wars," involved a satellite shield in outer space that would intercept incoming Soviet missiles. It would cost an estimated $30 billion and, according to many scientists, might never work. Still, Reagan remained committed to funding research on the initiative.

While proposing increased spending for defense, the Reagan administration continued arms control discussions. It abandoned SALT II, the arms reduction plan negotiated but never ratified under Jimmy Carter. As new negotiations bogged down, the arms race escalated and military budgets soared.

The Cold War Comes to an End

Surprising events in the Soviet Union changed the direction of American foreign policy. **Mikhail Gorbachev,** who became the new Soviet leader in 1985, made daring reforms in his country. He proposed a program of *perestroika*—restructuring the economy— and *glasnost*—political openness. These new policies paved the way toward better relations with the United States. Summit meetings led to the **Intermediate-Range Nuclear Forces (INF) Treaty** in 1987. Under the INF treaty, 2,500 Soviet and American nuclear missiles in Europe would be destroyed.

Later, talks between Bush and Gorbachev in 1989 and 1990 brought agreements limiting the buildup of both nuclear and chemical weapons. The two leaders signed the Strategic Arms Reduction Treaty (START) in 1991. START dramatically decreased the number of long-range weapons that the superpowers had stockpiled.

RESOURCE DIRECTORY

Teaching Resources

Reproducible Lesson Plan found in the Unit 7 folder, p. 76, provides a summary of the Section 4 lesson plan content.

Alternate Lesson Plan: Learning Styles found in the Alternate Lesson Plans folder, p. 175, is designed to help students, particularly auditory and visual learners, identify foreign policy challenges in the Reagan-Bush era and explain the Iran-contra affair.

Guided Reading and Review found in the Unit 7 folder, p. 83, provides a structure for reading and mastering the key concepts and reviewing the key terms for Section 4. (Guided Practice)

Post–Cold War Europe, 1994

Geography and History: Interpreting Maps
In the late 1980s the Eastern bloc shattered into a jigsaw puzzle of diverse republics. *What kinds of problems do you think might follow the break-up of such a large nation as the Soviet Union?*

Upheaval in Russia The arms control agreements were one indication that the cold war was ending. Changes accelerated within the Soviet Union, where Gorbachev began moves toward democracy, including free elections. He faced opposition on both sides, however—from conservatives in the Soviet government and from those who wanted faster reforms.

Boris Yeltsin had been elected president of Russia, the largest and most heavily populated of the Soviet republics. He now emerged as the new Soviet leader. With a speed that shocked the world, the Soviet Union itself fell apart, as reformers pressed for more gains. The various republics, shown in the map above, proclaimed their autonomy. Most joined Russia in a loose Commonwealth of Independent States (CIS).

Eastern Europe The changes in the Soviet Union echoed throughout Eastern Europe. In November 1989 the Communist party leader in East Germany suddenly announced that people could travel freely to West Germany. As the border guards—who in the past had shot people

trying to leave—stepped aside, East Germans flooded into West Berlin.

The fall of the Berlin Wall was heard all over Eastern Europe. In Poland, Lech Walesa's ten-year-old Solidarity movement finally triumphed over the communist government and assumed power. In Czechoslovakia, the forces of freedom were similarly victorious, and playwright Vaclav Havel became president. New regimes took charge in Bulgaria, Hungary, Romania, and Albania as well.

The transition was not always easy. Czechoslovakia soon broke into two states, the Czech Republic and Slovakia. A brutal civil war broke out in Yugoslavia when the central government collapsed and rival ethnic groups went to war with each other. The map above shows Europe in the aftermath of these changes.

World Trouble Spots

The end of the cold war did not bring peace outside Europe either. Conflict broke out in many places, and terrorism brought unexpected

Caption Answer to ...

Interpreting Maps

Possible answer: Ethnic conflicts might arise between groups vying for power in the new governments; economic resources might be fought over.

2. INSTRUCT

Discuss

Discuss the challenges faced by the United States after the cold war. Ask how the end of the cold war forced a change in American foreign policy. How did the United States respond to trouble spots in the Middle East?

Analyze

Ask students to consider why the United States chose to intervene in some conflicts and not others. For instance, why did it withdraw from Lebanon but pursue an aggressive policy against Iraq?

Activity
Cooperative Learning

Time: One class period.
Activity: Create a poster illustrating a new world image for the United States.
Grouping: Groups of four to six students.
Purpose: To define a post–cold war role for the United States after the breakup of the Soviet Union and the dissipation of the communist threat.
Roles: Members of a public relations and graphic design group, such as researchers, writers, publicists, illustrators, and designers.
Outcome: Students will portray the changing role of the United States in the post–cold war world.

Enrichment

The dramatic changes that have occurred in the world in recent years have produced much talk about a "new world order." Ask students to research the speeches of George Bush and then write a one-page statement expressing their own vision of the new world order.

3. ASSESS

Section 4 Review Answers

1. (a) SDI, see p. 828, (b) INF treaty, see p. 828, (c) Persian Gulf War, see p. 830, (d) Iran-contra affair, see p. 831

2. (a) Mikhail Gorbachev, see p. 828, (b) Boris Yeltsin, see p. 829, (c) Saddam Hussein, see p. 830, (d) Sandinista, see p. 831, (e) contras, see p. 831

3. The Soviet Union disintegrated in the wake of Gorbachev's economic and political reforms; a number of arms control treaties improved relations with the United States; communist countries in Eastern Europe began to collapse.

4. The United States sought to defend Kuwait because, besides being an unjustified act of aggression, Iraq's invasion of Kuwait threatened to cut off the supply of Middle Eastern oil to the West.

5. Reagan administration officials funded the contras with money from the illegal sale of arms to Iran. When this information became public, Reagan faced scandal.

6. Answers will vary but should reflect an understanding of the intertwined relationship between economics, politics, and the military rivalry of the United States and the Soviet Union.

In Depth

Interdisciplinary

In late 1993, the Geological Society of America found that the Persian Gulf War "caused severe and lasting damage to Kuwait's desert, economic resources and ecosystems." Marine life still shows the acute toxicity from oil deliberately spilled into the gulf by Iraqis; and wildlife and vegetation will suffer the effects for decades.

| 1650 | 1700 | 1750 | 1800 | **Links Across Time** | 1850 | 1900 | 1950 | 2000 |

The Wall: Its Rise and Fall

Begun in 1961, the Berlin Wall was still being reinforced by East German workers—under the watchful eyes of armed border patrols—in 1967 (left). When the border finally opened in 1989, Berliners celebrated with a joyous all-night party (above). *Do you think it would be possible for a barrier such as the Berlin Wall to keep a city permanently divided?*

---

tragedies. The Middle East remained a place of religious tension and chaos.

Lebanon Some of the problems in the Middle East centered in Lebanon, a country caught up in the hostilities between Israel and the Palestine Liberation Organization (PLO). In 1982 President Reagan sent several thousand marines into Beirut, the capital, as part of a peacekeeping force. Early in 1983, an explosive-filled truck blew up the American embassy in Beirut, killing more than sixty people.

Then, on a Sunday morning in October 1983, another terrorist truck loaded with explosives crashed through the gates of a marine barracks, killing 241 Americans. Many Americans demanded an immediate withdrawal from Lebanon, and by the following February, all the troops left.

The Persian Gulf War In August 1990, **Saddam Hussein,** the dictator of Iraq, invaded neighboring Kuwait, a small nation rich in oil. Now Americans worried that Iraq's action might threaten the flow of oil to the West. They also were shocked by the open aggression.

Bush responded strongly. In an open letter to college students, he declared:

There is much in the modern world that is subject to doubts or questions—washed in shades of gray. But not the brutal aggression of Saddam Hussein against a peaceful, sovereign nation and its people. It's black and white. The facts are clear. The choice unambiguous—right vs. wrong.

Working through the United Nations, the United States mobilized an alliance of twenty-eight nations. When the UN deadline for Iraqi withdrawal passed in mid-January 1991, an international army of half a million troops struck at Iraq in "Operation Desert Storm."

The **Persian Gulf War** was over quickly. Iraqi rockets fell on cities in nearby Saudi Arabia, Israel, and Bahrain, while the UN forces struck back from the air. Despite Hussein's promise of victory, UN forces overwhelmed the Iraqis in just forty-two days. Iraqi casualties numbered in the tens of thousands, while only 240 UN troops were killed. Bush's approval rating in the United States soared to an unprecedented 91 percent.

Though compelled to leave Kuwait, Hussein remained in power. His ruthless armies continued to crush opponents within his own country. Fearful of getting involved in another situation like Vietnam, Bush was unwilling to send in

---

▶ RESOURCE DIRECTORY

Teaching Resources

Literature Activity Operation Desert Storm, found in the Unit 7 folder, pp. 97–98, dramatically illustrates the events surrounding the Allied action in Kuwait in an excerpt from General Norman Schwarzkopf's autobiography, *It Doesn't Take a Hero.*

Primary Source Activity An Explanation of Iran-Contra, found in the Unit 7 folder, pp. 94–95, presents an excerpt from President Reagan's televised address on March 4, 1987, to demonstrate how he defended his involvement in the scandal.

more United States forces. Public opinion also favored bringing American troops home.

MAKING CONNECTIONS

Reread the excerpt from Bush's letter. How does his description of Saddam Hussein echo the cold war speeches of earlier Presidents?

Policy in Latin America

Like earlier administrations, Reagan and Bush often intervened in the internal struggles in neighboring Latin America. The policies of these two Presidents reflected the fear that left-wing or Marxist governments would gain power in the Americas. As a result, the United States, as in the past, sometimes supported repressive dictators as a way of opposing communism.

In El Salvador the United States aided a repressive conservative regime in resisting guerrillas, some of whom were Marxists. In neighboring Nicaragua, the administration tried to undermine the Marxist **Sandinista** government. Working through the CIA, the United States armed and trained guerrilla fighters known as **contras** (from the Spanish for "counterrevolutionaries"). The official reason for this aid was that the contras would stop the flow of weapons from Cuba to the guerrillas in El Salvador.

Congress, however, thought that Reagan also wanted to help the contras overthrow the Sandinistas. In 1982 Congress forbade using federal funds for this purpose, and in 1984 it

voted to stop the CIA or any other agency from giving the contras any military aid.

Some members of the Reagan administration still believed that aid to the contras was justified to prevent communist forces from controlling Latin America. When the contras' war floundered, some members of the National Security Council sent money from the illegal sale of weapons to Iran to the contras. ⭐ When this action became public in the fall of 1986, Oliver North, the marine colonel who had made the arrangements, took the blame. Most Americans realized, however, that North was not acting on his own. Investigations of the **Iran-contra affair,** as the incident came to be called, suggested that both President Reagan and Vice President Bush had known more about the plan than they admitted. The Iran-contra scandal brought the most serious criticism faced by the Reagan administration.

Using Historical Evidence
Women soldiers, like the two Americans above, played a significant role in the Persian Gulf War. *How do you think a World War II soldier in the 1940s would have reacted to this photograph?*

SECTION 4 REVIEW

Key Terms, People, and Places
1. Define (a) SDI, (b) INF treaty, (c) Persian Gulf War, (d) Iran-contra affair.
2. Identify (a) Mikhail Gorbachev, (b) Boris Yeltsin, (c) Saddam Hussein, (d) Sandinista, (e) contras.

Key Concepts
3. How did the cold war end?
4. Why did the United States become involved in the Persian Gulf War?

5. Why did the Reagan administration's support for Nicaraguan rebels lead to scandal?

Critical Thinking
6. **Demonstrating Reasoned Judgment** "The cold war could not have lasted long after 1990. If the Soviet economic and political system had not failed when it did, the United States economy would have collapsed under the weight of the soaring defense budget." Explain why you agree or disagree with this statement.

 Quiz found in the Unit 7 folder, p. 84, covers the main ideas in this section as well as the key terms.

 Chapter Test Forms A and B are found in the Unit 7 folder, pp. 101–106.

 Answer Keys found in the Unit 7 folder, pp. 143–156, provide answers to all student activities.

Media and Technology

 **Transparency**
Graphic Organizer, G-1

Guided Reading Audiotapes
(English and Spanish)

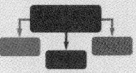 **Computer Test Bank**

Understanding Key Terms, People, and Places

Terms
Students should refer to the definitions of the key terms in the chapter to write sentences that show the relation of each word to the social and political changes that took place during the conservative movement of the 1980s and early 1990s.

Matching
1. supply-side economics
2. Strategic Defense Initiative
3. S & Ls
4. new federalism

True or False
1. false, Ronald Reagan
2. false, Clarence Thomas's
3. false, Saddam Hussein
4. true

Reviewing Main Ideas

1. Conservatives were the driving force behind the anticommunist crusade of the 1950s, and some of them viewed social programs as evidence of communism within the federal government. This negative view of social programs continued to shape the conservative political agenda in the 1980s.

2. Goals include reducing the size of government, restoring Christian values to American society, and ending government-supported social programs.

3. Christian evangelists used television to appeal to viewers to donate money (televangelism). Other conservatives pioneered the use of "sound bites" in speeches and "spin doctors" to give a candidate's comments the best possible interpretation. They also used direct mail to raise money for political causes.

4. Reagan wanted to put more money in the hands of businesses and investors who would then hire more people and produce more goods and services, thus making the economy grow. This overall growth was supposed ultimately to benefit every level of the economy.

5. Reagan and Bush favored business-oriented economics, "less government" politics, and traditional social values, thus appealing to a broad range of conservative groups.

6. According to Kevin Phillips, no similar upsurge of wealth had been seen since the late nineteenth century. However, at the same time banks foreclosed on farms, high-paying industrial jobs disappeared, and the gap between rich and poor widened.

Chapter Review

Understanding Key Terms, People, and Places

Key Terms
1. New Right
2. coalition
3. televangelism
4. supply-side economics
5. S & L
6. new federalism
7. acquired immuno-deficiency syndrome (AIDS)
8. Strategic Defense Initiative (SDI)
9. Intermediate-Range Nuclear Forces (INF) Treaty
10. Persian Gulf War
11. Iran-contra affair

People
12. Ronald Reagan
13. George Bush
14. Sandra Day O'Connor
15. Clarence Thomas
16. Henry Cisneros
17. Mikhail Gorbachev
18. Boris Yeltsin
19. Saddam Hussein
20. Sandinista
21. contra

Terms For each term above, write a sentence that explains its relation to the social and political changes that took place during the conservative movement.

Matching Review the key terms in the list above. If you are not sure of a term's meaning, review its definition in the chapter. Then choose a term from the list that best matches each description below.
1. the theory that predicts lower taxes will stimulate the economy by putting more money in the hands of businesses and investors
2. a satellite shield intended to intercept incoming missiles
3. generally small, stable banks that historically made home mortgage loans to individuals
4. the policy of shifting the focus of government from the federal to the state level

True or False Determine whether each statement is true or false. If it is true, write "true." If it is false, change the underlined name to make the statement true.
1. A former actor, <u>George Bush</u> was tremendously popular during his two terms as President.
2. <u>Sandra Day O'Connor's</u> nomination hearings brought a storm of public controversy when charges were filed by a former co-worker.
3. Brutal dictator <u>Henry Cisneros</u> remained in power after the Persian Gulf War.
4. <u>Boris Yeltsin</u> emerged as the new Russian leader after the break-up of the Soviet Union.

Reviewing Main Ideas

Section 1 (pp. 810–814)
1. What were the roots of the conservative movement?
2. Describe three goals of the conservative coalition.
3. What techniques did conservatives use to win support for their political agenda?

Section 2 (pp. 815–819)
4. Explain President Reagan's theory that prosperity would "trickle down" from the top of the economy.
5. What conservative goals did Reagan and Bush support?
6. How did the policies of Reagan and Bush affect the distribution of wealth in the United States?

Section 3 (pp. 821–825)
7. How did conditions for African Americans change under Reagan and Bush?

8. Describe the backlash against the women's movement during the 1980s.
9. Give evidence to show that Latinos continued to make political gains during the 1980s and 1990s.
10. What changes occurred for Native Americans during the Reagan and Bush era?

Section 4 (pp. 828–831)
11. What was Reagan's defense policy when he took office in 1980?
12. What events in the Soviet Union and Eastern Europe changed the direction of American foreign policy during the 1980s and early 1990s?
13. What was the outcome of the Persian Gulf War?

7. Although increasing numbers of African Americans were elected to public office, the Reagan and Bush administrations did little to strengthen civil rights.

8. Some women, as well as conservative male legislators, felt threatened by the rapid social changes created by the women's movement. The ERA died after opposition from these groups increased.

9. An increasing number of Latinos, for example Henry Cisneros, were elected to public office and appointed at all levels of government. The number of Latino college and university faculty members more than doubled.

10. Native Americans made substantial gains in education and in developing business and legal skills.

11. Reagan took a tough stance toward the Soviet Union and pursued a considerable buildup of conventional and nuclear forces.

12. The cold war ended and the Soviet Union broke apart. The communist governments in Eastern Europe collapsed.

13. The United States forced Saddam Hussein to retreat from Kuwait. He remained in power in Iraq, however.

Thinking Critically

1. **Demonstrating Reasoned Judgment** You have read that Ronald Reagan enjoyed a 68 percent approval rating when he left office, despite his many mistakes and misstatements. How do you account for Reagan's popularity?
2. **Making Comparisons** Native Americans experienced some positive changes during the 1980s and early 1990s. From what you have read about the experience of African Americans at the time, do you think that Native Americans were helped in their efforts by the Reagan and Bush administrations?
3. **Predicting Consequences** What opportunities and challenges for the United States do you think were created by the end of the cold war?
4. **Determining Relevance** If Reagan and Bush had attended the Constitutional Convention in 1787, how might they have advised the Framers as to the proper role of the federal government?

Making Connections

1. **Evaluating Primary Sources** Review the primary source excerpt on page 811. What does Reagan assume about the free enterprise system? Are there factors that can hinder an individual's success even if he or she is industrious?
2. **Understanding the Visuals** Reread the Kevin Phillips quotation on pages 818 to 819. How does the Reaganomics doll on page 815 illustrate what Phillips calls "upper America"? How does it illustrate what is on the other side of the prosperity of the 1980s?
3. **Writing About the Chapter** It is 1990. *Time* magazine has asked you to write a retrospective essay about the 1980s, focusing on either the social, political, or economic changes that occurred in the United States during the decade. First, review the chapter and make a list of the points you plan to cover. Next, write a draft of your essay in which you describe life in the 1980s. Revise your essay, making certain that each idea is clearly explained. Proofread your essay and draft a final copy.
4. **Using the Graphic Organizer** This graphic organizer uses a web map to organize information about Republican policies during the 1980s and early 1990s. In this web, dotted lines are used to show connections between seemingly unconnected ideas. (a) What is the connection between tax reform, increased spending for defense, and cuts in social programs? (b) How do both deregulation and the new federalism demonstrate a similar view of the role of the government? (c) On a separate sheet of paper, create your own web map about the conservative movement using this graphic organizer as an example.

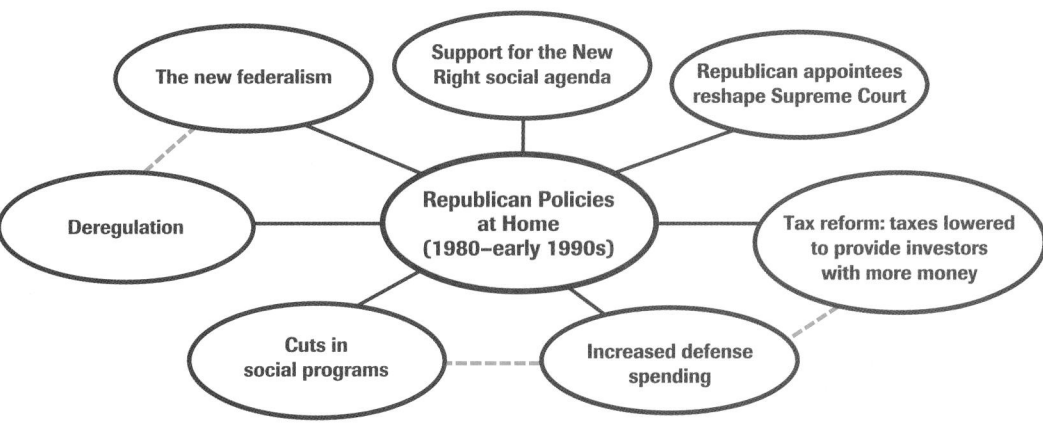

Thinking Critically

1. Responses should consider Reagan's enormous personal appeal and communication skills, as well as the conservative views of many Americans.

2. Based on the fact that African Americans were not helped by the Reagan and Bush administrations to extend their civil rights, students may conclude that Native Americans likewise received little active help from the federal government during these years.

3. Possible answer: The opportunity to cooperate politically and economically with former communist states and the challenge of dealing with the problems caused by the breakdown of the Eastern bloc.

4. In line with their conservative beliefs, Reagan and Bush would probably have advocated an extremely limited role for the federal government in economic and social matters but would have suggested allowing for an aggressive role in foreign affairs.

Making Connections

1. Reagan attributes the economic success of the United States to free enterprise and implies that anyone who is industrious can achieve success. He rejects the idea that factors such as racial or gender discrimination or other circumstances beyond an individual's control can hinder success despite the opportunities afforded by free enterprise.

2. "Upper America" is represented by Reagan wearing a tuxedo and a contented smile. On the "demand side" of the doll is an American who has not fared so well—perhaps he has lost his farm or his job during the 1980s.

3. Students' essays should demonstrate an understanding of the social, political, and economic changes that took place as a result of the influence of the conservative movement.

4. (a) Because of increased defense spending and decreased federal revenue due to tax cuts, the government had less money and therefore had to cut social programs. (b) Both demonstrate the view that the federal government should have a limited role in business regulation and economic affairs. (c) Students' graphic organizers should include information about the composition of the conservative movement, the views of the various members of the conservative coalition, and the role of television and other techniques for promoting conservative ideas.

◆ Alternative Assessment

Final Evaluation
Use the following guidelines to evaluate student projects:
● **Evidence of thoughtfulness** Did students include the main topics from the chapter?
● **Evidence of outside research** To what extent did students use outside research materials for their project?
● **Evidence of synthesis** Do projects demonstrate an understanding of how topics are related?
● **Communication style** Do projects convey their purpose to an audience in a clear, appealing way?

Encourage students to present their finished projects to the class.

The split in American politics has traditionally been between Democrats and Republicans, with the Democrats favoring more liberal government and the Republicans siding with conservative choices. This split reached an all-time extreme, however, with the advent of Ronald Reagan on the political scene. Apple pie, baseball, patriotism, and pride in the United States of America became fashionable again under Reagan after long years of national self-doubt and criticism following Vietnam, Watergate, and economic downturns. Reagan reminded the people that America was founded on great ideals and that the freedom of democracy was worth the inevitable conflicts and pain it sometimes precipitated. Along with his conservative ideals, Reagan was able to gain support for increases in defense spending, cuts in social welfare and other programs, and a withdrawal of government regulations in favor of allowing the American system of capitalism to expand, unfettered by the government.

INSTRUCT

Have students review the Noonan excerpt, making a list of the values that she expresses. Discuss these values in class. Ask students whether they see evidence of these ideas toward government in their own communities and in the nation in general.

Ask students to read President Reagan's speech and answer the following questions: What opinion does Reagan hold about the policy of isolationism? What does Reagan think about the use of force? What does Reagan think is worth dying for? For what purpose does Reagan say United States military forces remain in Europe?

CHAPTER 25

SOURCE READINGS

Why I Became a Conservative

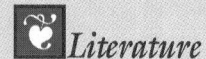 *Literature*

Peggy Noonan

INTRODUCTION Peggy Noonan (1950–) worked as a speechwriter for President Ronald Reagan from 1984 to 1986 and for President George Bush from 1984 to 1989. Her memoir of that time, *What I Saw at the Revolution,* is, in her words, "about politics in its most essential sense: who 'the people' are and what they want," and about Reagan, who "was to popular politics what Henry James was to American literature: He was the master." In this excerpt, Noonan tells why she rejected the liberal viewpoint and became a conservative while still in college.

VOCABULARY Before you read the selection, find the meaning of these words in a dictionary: assuage, chronic, gulag.

My friend Kathy's mother was sick with heart disease, and when I used to go over to her house, I'd hear her mother yelling at the TV upstairs, "You tell 'em, Bill! Tell that big jerk!" She was watching William F. Buckley, Jr. . . .

Every few weeks she received a magazine called *National Review.* Kathy told me, "You should read it. You don't know it, but you think like my mother." I started reading *NR,* and it sang to me. They saw it the way I was seeing it: America is essentially good, the war[1] is being fought for serious and valid reasons, the answer to every social ill is not necessarily a social program, when you let government get too big you threaten your own liberties—and God is real as a rock. I was moved, and more. It assuaged a kind of loneliness. Later I found that half the people in the Reagan administration had as their first conservative friend that little magazine.

People always ask me how I came from my generation and became a conservative. It's hard to pinpoint where the rebellion began, but I can tell you the moment I knew I wasn't of the left.

I was going to a big antiwar demonstration in Washington. I think it was the spring of '71, and I think we were going to shut the government down. Early that evening, before we got in the buses that would take us down the Jersey Turnpike, we went to a rally in the student union and a guy got up and made a speech. . . . He said words to the effect of, Let's face it, man, this is a country that's greatest contribution to humanity is Coca-Cola, which we make in a lab, sell on TV, and force down the bloated throats of Third World children who are dying of malnutrition.

Hooray, everyone said.

I listened to the kids on the bus. They were very earnest. I listened to the grown-ups, women with intense faces and men who were starting to wear beads and medallions. Everybody's liberal parents, hurtling down the turnpike toward mayhem.

I couldn't get into the spirit, into the swing. I kept observing. There was contempt for the nineteen-year-old boys who were carrying guns in the war or in the Guard[2]. It was understood that they were uneducated, and somewhat crude. There was contempt for America.

---

[1] in Vietnam

[2] the National Guard

A 1969 poster advertising a march against the Vietnam War similar to the demonstration Noonan attended in 1971.

—What can you expect of a culture that raises John Wayne[3] to the status of hero?

—We were founded on violence and will meet our undoing in violence. . . .

—We're a racist, genocidal nation with an imperialistic lust for land that isn't ours, and . . . and . . .

And get me off this bus! I looked around, and I saw those mouths moving and shrank in my seat. What am I doing with these people? What am I doing with these intellectuals or whatever they are, what am I doing with this—this contemptuous elite? . . . *And what was the Democratic party doing on the side of these people?*

That was the moment it changed for me, that was the day I got skeptical. I never again assumed the young had pure motives, never again thought intellectuals had the answers, never again thought the people who write for the papers and talk on TV knew more than the rest of us, never again assumed that just because people talk loud they care.

I always come back to the war as the formative political experience of my life because it involved one of the most painful political injustices of our time. I still think that America's attempt to help another people in a country far away resist a Communist takeover was not proof of America's cynicism but an illustration of that peculiar American mix, one part idealism and one part strategic calculation, which may have been wrong but at least had a point.

The grunt work of the war was fought by the grunts of American society; and while they were fight-

[3] a popular movie actor who often starred in war movies

ing, their more advantaged brothers and sisters were back home giving interviews to Eric Sevareid on the Concord Bridge. When the veterans returned, they were sometimes patronized by the privileged—and I mean privileged not only in money but in gifts, in standing, in background—who, as the vets were going back to pumping gas on Route 80, went on to become the professionals and news producers and opinion leaders of the baby-boom generation, where they have, some of them, devoted a considerable amount of time to talking about the lessons of Vietnam, which is to say: the lessons we taught you by not going, the painful lessons you learned because you did.

But I'm not sure the gifted lucky ones got a clean getaway. The characters they invent on *thirtysomething* and *L.A. Law* will probably never say, "You know, that war, I look at what happened after we left and we were wrong, we should have stayed," and they are probably not going to write columns saying, "What the Communists did was terrible, and we should have known what they were going to do." But I think I perceive an unease, the chronic unease of the person whose instinct it is to be honest but who has trouble acknowledging a painful fact: that our protests and the politicians' withdrawal from the war and the manner in which they withdrew helped produce the boat people, the Cambodian holocaust, a gulag called Vietnam, and an untold increase in horror for the people of that part of the planet. That chronic unease: That's the real big chill.

THINKING ABOUT THE SELECTION

1. Reread the second paragraph of the selection. How are views expressed by Noonan similar to the conservative viewpoint described on page 811 of the chapter?

2. Briefly describe Noonan's experience on the way to the antiwar rally. Why was this experience a turning point for her?

Critical Thinking

3. **Determining Relevance** Why do you think Noonan called the Vietnam War the "formative political experience" of her life?

ANSWERS TO

Thinking About the Selection

1. Noonan's comments are supported by the text on page 811, which outlines the conservative ideology of the early 1980s. This ideology included a push to end many government-supported social programs, a desire to reduce the size of government, and an attempt to restore Christian values to society.

2. The bus was filled with liberal intellectuals who seemed to Noonan to be belittling the soldiers who were fighting in Vietnam and, worst of all, belittling the United States itself. It was a turning point for her because she listened to their criticisms of the United States and decided that she did not agree with them at all.

3. The war was an issue on which many of the beliefs of both liberals and conservatives were called into question. The country was split by such questions as whether we had a legitimate reason to be in the war, what our motives were, what our attitude toward the soldiers fighting the war should be, and so on. Noonan probably considered it to be the "formative political experience" of her life because no other political event raised such profound questions about the nation as did the Vietnam War.

SOURCE READINGS

"These Are the Boys of Point du Hoc"

Primary Source

Ronald Reagan

Introduction On June 6, 1984, President Reagan gave a speech at Point du Hoc, France, on the occasion of the fortieth anniversary of D-Day—the day the Allies launched an invasion of German-occupied France along Normandy, France's northern coast. Peggy Noonan worked with Reagan on the Point du Hoc speech, one of Reagan's most memorable. Both elegant and powerful, it reminded Americans of the nation's effort to stop totalitarianism and promote democracy. Reagan's Point du Hoc speech also showcases his ability as a communicator and his presidential style—unassuming, personable, and candid.

VOCABULARY Before you read the selection, find the meaning of these words in a dictionary: desolate, deter, valor.

We're here to mark that day in history when the Allied armies joined in battle to reclaim this continent to liberty. For four long years, much of Europe had been under a terrible shadow. Free nations had fallen, Jews cried out in the camps, million cried out for liberation. Europe was enslaved, and the world prayed for its rescue. Here in Normandy the rescue began. Here the Allies stood and fought against tyranny in a giant undertaking unparalleled in human history.

President Reagan and Nancy Reagan laying flowers at the graves of American soldiers killed in the 1944 Normandy invasion.

We stand on a lonely, windswept point on the northern shore of France. The air is soft, but forty years ago at this moment, the air was dense with smoke and the cries of men, and the air was filled with the crack of rifle fire and the roar of cannon. At dawn, on the morning of the 6th of June, 1944, 225 Rangers jumped off the British landing craft and ran to the bottom of these cliffs. Their mission was one of the most difficult and daring of the invasion: to climb these sheer and desolate cliffs and take out the enemy guns. The Allies had been told that some of the mightiest of these guns were here and they would be trained on the beaches to stop the Allied advance.

The Rangers looked up and saw the enemy soldiers—at the edge of the cliffs shooting down at them with machine guns and throwing grenades. And the American Rangers began to climb. They shot rope ladders over the face of these cliffs and began to pull themselves up. When one rope was cut, a Ranger would grab another and begin his climb again. They climbed, shot back, and held their footing. Soon, one by one, the Rangers pulled themselves over the top, and in seizing the firm land at the top of these cliffs, they began to seize back the continent of Europe. Two hundred and twenty-five came here. After two days of fighting, only ninety could still bear arms.

Behind me is a memorial that symbolizes the Ranger daggers that were thrust into the top of these cliffs. And before me are the men who put them there.

These are the boys of Point du Hoc. These are the men who took the cliffs. These are the champions who helped free a continent. These are the heroes who helped end a war. . . .

Forty summers have passed since the battle that you fought here. You were young the day you took these cliffs; some of you were hardly more than boys, with the deepest joys of life before you. Yet, you risked everything here. Why? Why did you do it? What impelled you to put aside the instinct for self-preservation and risk your lives to take these cliffs? What inspired all the men of the armies that met here? We look at you, and somehow we know the answer. It was faith and belief; it was loyalty and love.

The men of Normandy had faith that what they were doing was right, faith that they fought for all humanity, faith that a just God would grant them mercy on this beachhead or on the next. It was the deep knowledge—and pray God we have not lost it—that there is a profound moral difference between the use of force for liberation and the use of force for conquest. You were here to liberate, not to conquer, and so you and those others did not doubt your cause. And you were right not to doubt.

You all knew that some things are worth dying for. One's country is worth dying for, and democracy is worth dying for, because it's the most deeply honorable form of government ever devised by man. All of you loved liberty. All of you were willing to fight tyranny, and you knew the people of your countries were behind you. . . .

When the war was over, there were lives to be rebuilt and governments to be returned to the people. There were nations to be reborn. Above all, there was a new peace to be assured. These were huge and daunting tasks. But the Allies summoned strength from the faith, belief, loyalty, and love of those who fell here. They built a new Europe together. . . .

In spite of our great efforts and successes, not all that followed the end of the war was happy or planned. Some liberated countries were lost. The great sadness of this loss echoes down to our own time in the streets of Warsaw, Prague, and East Berlin. Soviet troops that came to the center of this continent did not leave when peace came. They're still there, uninvited, unwanted, unyielding, almost forty years after the war. Because of this, allied forces still stand on this continent. Today, as forty years ago, our armies are here for only one purpose—to protect and defend democracy. The only territories we hold are memorials like this one and graveyards where our heroes rest.

We in America have learned bitter lessons from two world wars: It is better to be here ready to protect the peace, than to take blind shelter across the sea, rushing to respond only after freedom is lost. We've learned that isolationism never was and never will be an acceptable response to tyrannical governments with an expansionist intent.

But we try always to be prepared for peace; prepared to deter aggression; prepared to negotiate the reduction of arms; and yes, prepared to reach out again in the spirit of reconciliation. In truth, there is no reconciliation we would welcome more than a reconciliation with the Soviet Union, so, together, we can lessen the risks of war, now and forever.

It's fitting to remember here the great losses also suffered by the Russian people during World War II: 20 million perished, a terrible price that testifies to all the world the necessity of ending war. I tell you from my heart that we in the United States do not want war. We want to wipe from the face of the earth the terrible weapons that man now has in his hands. And I tell you, we are ready to seize that beachhead. We look for some sign from the Soviet Union that they are willing to move forward, that they share our desire and love for peace, and that they will give up the ways of conquest. There must be a changing there that will allow us to turn our hope into action. . . .

Here, in this place where the West held together, let us make a vow to our dead. Let us show them by our actions that we understand what they died for. . . . Strengthened by their courage, heartened by their valor, and borne by their memory, let us continue to stand for the ideals for which they lived and died.

Thank you very much, and God bless you all.

THINKING ABOUT THE SELECTION

1. What did President Reagan mean when he said that some European countries were "lost" after World War II?
2. Based on your reading of the chapter, what step did the United States and the Soviet Union take to "wipe from the face of the earth the terrible weapons that man now has in his hands"?

Critical Thinking

3. **Checking Consistency** President Reagan believed in a strong military to protect the nation's interests. He also strongly opposed communism. How does the Point du Hoc speech reflect these beliefs?

ANSWERS TO

Thinking About the Selection

1. President Reagan refers to the fact that some countries were taken over by the Communist Soviet Union after World War II and thus were "lost" to communism.

2. In 1987 the United States and the Soviet Union signed the Intermediate-Range Nuclear Forces (INF) Treaty, which provided for the destruction of 2,500 Soviet and American nuclear missiles in Europe. In 1991 President George Bush and Soviet leader Mikhail Gorbachev signed the Strategic Arms Reduction Treaty (START). This treaty dramatically decreased the number of long-range weapons that both superpowers had stockpiled.

3. His speech praises the military for its bravery during World War II and condemns the Soviet Union for refusing to leave Europe following the war. In addition, Reagan talks of the lessons learned by the United States during two world wars: "It is better to be here ready to protect the peace, than to take blind shelter across the sea, rushing to respond only after freedom is lost." This is an argument for preparedness and a strong military.

Chapter 26 The Promise of Change
1992–Present

📁 Teaching Resources (See Unit 7 Folder)

	Instruction	Enrichment

Section 1
The Clinton Administration
(pp. 840–845)
	Reproducible Lesson Plan, p. 108
	Alternate Lesson Plan, p. 177
	Guided Reading and Review, p. 111
	Quiz, p. 112
		Visual Learning Activity, The Year of the
		  Woman, p. 129
		American Profiles Activity, Henry Cisneros,
		  p. 117
		Primary Source Activity, Defining Economic
		  Goals, pp. 123–124
		Critical Thinking Activity, Drawing
		  Conclusions, p. 122
		Viewpoints Activity, On Health-Care Reform,
		  pp. 119–120

Section 2 **The United States and the World** **in the 1990s** (pp. 846–851)	Reproducible Lesson Plan, p. 109 Alternate Lesson Plan, p. 178 Guided Reading and Review, p. 113 Quiz, p. 114	Visual Learning Activity, Clinton and Foreign Affairs, p. 130

Section 3
American Society in the 1990s
(pp. 852–856)
	Reproducible Lesson Plan, p. 110
	Alternate Lesson Plan, p. 179
	Guided Reading and Review, p. 115
	Quiz, p. 116
	Chapter Test, Forms A & B, pp. 131–136
		American Profiles Activity, Amy Tan, p. 118
		Primary Source Activity, Trying to Break the
		  Cycle of Crime, p. 125
		Literature Activity, Living in a New World,
		  pp. 126–128
		Historian's Toolbox Activity, Predicting
		  Consequences, p. 121

📁 Additional Chapter Resources

Resource Organizer, p. 107
Alternate Lesson Plan, p. 176
Answer Keys, pp. 143–156

Bibliography

For the Teacher
Bell, Derrick. *Faces at the Bottom of the Well: The Permanence of Racism.* Basic, 1993. (Attitudes toward race revealed through dialogues and myths.)
Glickman, Rose L. *Daughters of Feminists.* St. Martin's Press, 1993. (Reports on fifty women raised by feminist mothers.)
Takaki, Ronald. *A Different Mirror: A History of Multicultural America.* Little, Brown, 1993. (An attempt to view all of American history from a multicultural perspective.)

Prentice Hall Literature Excerpts from *The American Experience,* 1994, including McElroy, Colleen J. "For My Children," from *What Madness Brought Me Here: New and Selected Poems, 1968–1988.* University Press of New England, 1990.

THE BIG IDEA

The Big Idea for the chapter and how the main ideas in each section relate to the Big Idea are graphically displayed below. Comprehension of this chapter's Big Idea is critical to students' understanding of United States history and how we as a nation got where we are today.

CHAPTER 26

As the twentieth century drew to a close, the United States found itself on the brink of a new era. The end of the cold war rendered the rules that had governed international relations for decades obsolete. New information technology created "highways" that linked individuals and nations with unprecedented speed. At home, the demographics of American society were once again changing with the arrival of record numbers of immigrants from Latin America and Asia.

SECTION 1

In the early 1990s, American voters were ready for a change. In 1992 they elected Democrat Bill Clinton as President. Clinton and his wife Hillary—his most trusted adviser—quickly immersed themselves in the complex issue of health-care reform.

SECTION 2

The end of the cold war and the disintegration of the Eastern bloc changed the nature of foreign relations in the 1990s. Although Clinton's primary focus was on domestic affairs, his administration needed to find ways to help mitigate crises in a number of hot spots around the world.

SECTION 3

Greater ethnic diversity in the United States sparked debate about how best to integrate many different groups of Americans to form a unified nation. As always, the United States would have to cope with the problems, as well as the benefits, of being a nation of immigrants.

Media and Technology

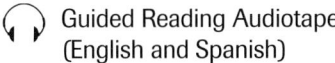 Historical Maps, L-5; Our Multicultural Heritage, C-3, C-14; Graphic Organizer, G-1

Guided Reading Audiotapes (English and Spanish)

Computer Test Bank

For the Student

Ashabranner, Brent. *An Ancient Heritage: The Arab American Minority.* HarperCollins, 1993. (Personal reflections on the experience of being Arab American.)

Cisneros, Sandra. *The House on Mango Street.* Arte Publico, 1989. (A short story collection by a Mexican American writer.)

Santiago, Esmeralda. *When I Was Puerto Rican.* Addison-Wesley, 1993.

Smith, Jessie Carney. *Black Firsts: 2,000 Years of Extraordinary Achievement.* Visible Ink Press, 1994. (Chronicles the "firsts" among people of color.)

The Promise of Change
1992–Present

The Relevance of the Big Idea

Like every other period in the nation's history, the 1990s presented a unique set of challenges to the United States government and to the American people. Students have studied the circumstances, problems, and fresh ideas that have grown out of each era in the nation's past. They should understand by now that at each point in history, the choices people make are based on their best guesses about how their actions will affect the future—but that there is never any certainty as to how the future will unfold. The present era is no exception. Even when people try to act in a way that is likely to have beneficial results, it is impossible to predict what far-reaching effects any action might have. Ask students to list some of the situations they have heard about in the news recently in which the outcome of events is highly uncertain. Ask them what they know about how the government is dealing with these situations.

In Depth

Global Connections

After more than four decades of cold-war orientation, the United States was set on a new course. The redefinition of its superpower role would set the tone for the twenty-first century. In 1994, President Clinton said: "I am often troubled as I try hard here to create a new sense of common purpose. . . . We oftentimes get so caught up in the battle of the moment, the heat of the moment . . . that sometimes we forget that we are all in this because we are seeking a good that helps all Americans."

The Promise of Change
1992–Present

*I*n 1993 Democrat Bill Clinton ended twelve years of Republican rule in the White House when he became the forty-second President of the United States. The 1990s would present a unique set of challenges to the new administration. With the end of the cold war abroad and a rapidly changing cultural climate at home, President Clinton and the American people would need to find creative solutions to many complex problems.

Events in the United States

1990 Congress passes the Immigration Act of 1990.

1992 Democrat Bill Clinton defeats Republican George Bush in the presidential election.

1989	1990	1991	1992

Events in the World

1991 Yugoslavian republics of Slovenia and Croatia declare their independence.
• The Haitian president is overthrown.

1992 The European Community drops many trade barriers between members.
• Boris Yeltsin is elected president of Russia.

RESOURCE DIRECTORY

Teaching Resources

Alternate Lesson Plan: Demonstrating the Big Idea found in the Alternate Lesson Plans folder, p. 176, provides a lesson strategy to instruct students about the Big Idea that as the twentieth century drew to a close, the United States faced new challenges in technology, foreign affairs, and culture.

Alternative Assessment Handbook provides information, guidance, and strategies for alternative methods of assessment. It includes an essay on new trends in assessment, guidance and strategies for developing performance tasks and portfolios, scoring rubrics, and sample evaluation forms.

Pages 840–845

The Clinton Administration

After twelve years of Republican rule, the American public cast a vote for change in 1992. Democrat Bill Clinton promised a plan for universal health care and help for the ailing economy. As President, he made a quick start at tackling these complex and deep-rooted problems.

Pages 846–851

The United States and the World in the 1990s

The end of the cold war in the 1990s left the Clinton administration struggling to find its way through uncharted waters in international relations. The collapse of communism and the increase in ethnic tensions in various parts of the world created new problems for the nation.

Pages 852–856

American Society in the 1990s

By the 1990s, the face of the United States had changed. With an increase in the number of immigrants and a rise in minority birth rates, a much larger percentage of the population than ever before was African American, Latino, Asian American, or Native American. The United States needed to find new ways to deal with this ethnic and cultural diversity.

1993 President Clinton appoints Ruth Bader Ginsburg to the Supreme Court.
• Congress passes the North American Free Trade Agreement.

1994 President Clinton pushes for reform of the health-care and welfare systems.

1993	1994	1995	1996	1997

1993 Israel and the Palestine Liberation Organization sign a peace treaty.

1994 War continues between Serbia and Bosnia-Herzegovina.
• The Winter Olympics are held in Lillehammer, Norway.

Alternative Assessment

As an ongoing chapter project, students may imagine that they are part of a task force collecting information about one of the complex issues faced by the Clinton administration. They should provide information that would affect either health-care reform; foreign policy in the Middle East, Bosnia-Herzegovina, or another "hot spot"; or the debate over multiculturalism. Possible formats for presenting information include the following:

• Audiotaped interviews with citizens who have opinions about the issue
• Role-plays depicting possible outcomes of policy decisions
• Oral presentations exploring potential policies, with charts or maps
• Scrapbooks containing newspaper clippings related to the issue
• Analyses comparing a current issue with a similar situation in the past, with a description of past policies and their effects

Explain that projects will be evaluated according to the following guidelines:

• **Unacceptable** Projects are not attempted or fail to address a relevant issue.
• **Limited/Acceptable** Project incorporate information from the chapter and show a limited understanding of the chosen issue.
• **Extensive/Commendable** Projects show evidence of outside research and present information in a well-organized and interesting fashion.
• **Extraordinary/Outstanding** Projects demonstrate a clear understanding of the issue based on extensive research and present policy options in an original and thought-provoking manner.

Students may choose to include finished work in their portfolios.

For information and guidance on alternative assessment trends and strategies, see the Alternative Assessment Handbook in the Resource Directory on page 838.

The Clinton Administration

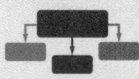

1. FOCUS

Connecting to the Big Idea

See page 838B. Explain to students that in 1992, after twelve years of Republican administrations, voters hoping for change elected Democrat Bill Clinton. Ask students to describe how Clinton differed from Bush and what specific changes he promised.

Objectives

• Identify the changes Bill Clinton promised to bring to the United States.
• Describe Hillary Rodham Clinton's role in the new administration.
• Explain how Clinton's cabinet reflected a commitment to diversity.

Bellringer

Ask students to imagine that they are preparing to vote in the 1992 presidential election. Conservative Republicans have controlled the White House for twelve years. Based upon the issues at the time, what might they be looking for in a new President?

Reading Strategy

Question Writing Ask students to write *who, what, when, where,* and *why* questions for the section content and to answer them as they read the text.

The Clinton Administration

SECTION PREVIEW

After twelve years of Republican rule, the American public cast a vote for change in 1992. Democrat Bill Clinton promised a plan for universal health care and help for the ailing economy. As President, he made a quick start at tackling these complex and deep-rooted problems.

Democratic nominees Bill Clinton and Al Gore went "on the road to change America" in 1992, making a bus tour of the country to win voters' support.

Key Concepts

• Bill Clinton, elected President in 1992, promised to revive the economy and renew the nation's sense of community.
• Hillary Rodham Clinton, the new First Lady, was a trusted adviser to the President and headed a task force to devise a national health insurance plan.
• President Clinton made an effort to appoint members of underrepresented groups to his cabinet and the Supreme Court.

Key Terms, People, and Places

Bill Clinton, Hillary Rodham Clinton, Al Gore

I n November 1992, voters faced an unusual choice among three major presidential candidates. The current President had presided over the third term of a Republican era, and he hoped to extend it another four years. His Democratic challenger, the youthful governor of Arkansas, proposed a more active role for the government in solving the nation's economic and social problems. The third candidate, a billionaire businessman, promised to shun traditional party politics and bring common-sense thinking to Washington.

The Election of 1992

⭐ The election of 1992 reflected transformations both at home and abroad. As the cold war came to an end, voters wanted the government to address the huge federal deficit and related economic difficulties with the same intensity it had shown in resisting communism since the end of World War II.

On the Republican side, George Bush sought a second term as President. Conservative journalist Patrick Buchanan, who had worked as a speech writer for Richard Nixon and Ronald Reagan, challenged Bush for the Republican nomination. Bush survived that test, but Buchanan's popularity among many voters in the primary campaign persuaded Bush that he had to take a more conservative stance in order to win broad support.

On the Democratic side, **Bill Clinton** was the surprise victor in a crowded field of candidates. During the campaign, he had to overcome a label that some journalists in Arkansas had used to describe his political style: "Slick Willie." The name suggested that Clinton would say whatever he needed to say—regardless of the complete truth—to get what he wanted. His statements to the press about his avoidance of the draft during the Vietnam War seemed evasive, and critics saw Slick Willie at work. Despite such criticisms, Clinton managed to regain his control over the primary elections, and he gave himself a new nickname: the "Comeback Kid."

Clinton reached out to the large population of voters who had been born during the postwar baby boom. A baby boomer himself who had reached maturity during the 1960s, Clinton argued that it was time for a new generation to take over. At the age of forty-six, he provided a stark contrast to the sixty-eight-year-old Bush, who had come of age during World War II.

The third candidate was Ross Perot, a wealthy Texan who had made his fortune in computer data processing. Perot offered to use his business skills to cut the budget, revive the economy, and give the country leadership. He organized a large network of volunteers who collected the necessary signatures from all fifty states to get his name on the ballot.

The campaign was fought largely on television. Presidential and vice-presidential debates gave the candidates formal exposure to the voters. Far more important for molding public opinion, however, were informal appearances on talk shows and interview programs. Ross Perot was a frequent guest on "Larry King Live." Bill Clinton played his saxophone on the "Arsenio Hall Show" and appealed to younger voters with appearances on MTV.

On election day, Clinton won 43 percent of the popular vote, versus 38 percent for Bush and 19 percent for Perot. In the Electoral College, Clinton gained 357 votes, versus 168 votes for Bush and none for Perot. The Democrats kept control of both houses of Congress, with more women and minority members than ever before.

Bill Clinton's Early Years

Bill Clinton was born in the small town of Hope, Arkansas, in 1946. He attended public schools in Arkansas, where he was a hardworking and competitive student. As a high school senior, he participated in Boys State, a summer camp in which students learn about politics. From there, Clinton was elected as one of Arkansas's delegates to Boys Nation. He traveled to Washington, D.C., and met his idol, President John Kennedy. The experience convinced him that he should pursue a career in politics.

Wanting to spend more time in the nation's capital while preparing himself for a political career in Arkansas, Clinton attended Georgetown University in Washington. After earning a bachelor's degree in international government, he spent two years studying at Oxford University in England on a Rhodes scholarship. Then he accepted a scholarship to Yale Law School, where he earned his law degree in 1973.

Clinton won his first political campaign in 1976, when he was elected Arkansas state attorney general. Two years later, at age thirty-two, he became the youngest governor in the United States. One of Clinton's top priorities was education reform. He appointed his wife, **Hillary Rodham Clinton,** to chair an Education Standards Committee of the Arkansas State Board of Education. This committee recommended a

Bill Clinton loved music as much as he loved politics. After meeting President Kennedy at age seventeen, however, he was swayed toward politics. Arkansas newspaper columnist John Brummet has mused, "One can only wonder what might have happened if young Billy . . . had met Elvis Presley instead of JFK that summer." In 1992 Clinton demonstrated on the "Arsenio Hall Show" that his skills on the saxophone were still sharp.

new set of requirements for high school graduation so that students in the state would be better prepared when they left the public school system. Improving Arkansas's schools would remain high on Clinton's agenda throughout his time as governor.

Before his run for the presidency, Clinton had heard political science professor William A. Galston speak about the need for citizens to balance rights and responsibilities. It was not enough for people to wait for government to provide things for them; they had obligations to fulfill as well. When he won the presidency in 1992, Clinton embraced Galston's approach. He spoke about the need for the nation to operate on the basic principle that both individuals and government have responsibility to each other. President Clinton called this philosophy a "New Covenant."

Discuss

Review the three candidates in the 1992 election. How were they different from each other? How did each candidate use television to reach voters?

Ask students to describe Bill Clinton's background. What office did he hold before becoming President? Have students explain Hillary Rodham Clinton's role in her husband's political career. What employment experience did she have prior to being appointed to head the task force on national health-care reform? Review the two major objectives of the Clinton administration discussed in the section. How did Clinton hope to cut the budget deficit? Why and how did he want to change the health-care system in the United States?

Analyze

Hillary Rodham Clinton's strong and highly visible presence in the Clinton White House came under public scrutiny. Ask students why they think she might be viewed as a controversial figure, and how attitudes about men's and women's proper roles in society may have contributed to this image.

Kennedy and Clinton were both Democrats who believed that the government should take an active role in caring for its citizens. At the same time, Kennedy's inaugural message and Clinton's "New Covenant" emphasized citizens' responsibility to give something back to their country.

Activity

Cooperative Learning

Time: One class period.

Activity: Role-play a press conference featuring the three candidates in the 1992 election. Three students should prepare to act as the candidates, while other group members develop lists of questions about the economy that they, as reporters, might ask the candidates.

Grouping: Groups of four to six students.

Purpose: To research each candidate's views on the economy.

Roles: Bill Clinton, George Bush, Ross Perot, reporters.

Outcome: Students will develop an understanding of the economic issues that dominated the 1992 election. **LEP**

Enrichment

Maya Angelou wrote and recited the first inaugural poem in thirty-two years in 1993. Students can read the poem "On the Pulse of Morning" at the end of the chapter in Source Readings. Help students locate a copy of "The Gift Outright," the poem Robert Frost read at John F. Kennedy's inauguration in 1961. Ask them to compare and contrast the poems. How does each reflect a spirit of patriotism or love for the United States? Whom does each poem include in its definition of Americans—to whom do the words *we* and *us* refer in each poem? How does each poem treat Native Americans?

MAKING CONNECTIONS

President Kennedy, in his inaugural address, encouraged Americans to "ask not what your country can do for you—ask what you can do for your country." How did Bill Clinton's "New Covenant" reflect Kennedy's influence?

AMERICAN PROFILES

Hillary Rodham Clinton

Clinton was aided immeasurably in his political career by his wife, Hillary Rodham Clinton. She had grown up in Park Ridge, Illinois, a suburban community not far from Chicago. After graduating from high school, she attended Wellesley College, just outside Boston. She majored in political science, developed a reputation for her ability to analyze problems clearly, and in her senior year, served as president of the college government.

Rodham attended law school at Yale University, where she met Bill Clinton. Following graduation, she worked for the Children's Defense Fund in Boston for a few months, and then took a job with the House Judiciary Committee in Washington, which was investigating the possible impeachment of President Nixon during the Watergate affair. When Nixon resigned in 1974, she decided to join Clinton in Arkansas. She taught at the University of Arkansas Law School in Fayetteville and then joined a law firm in Little Rock when Clinton, now her husband, was elected state attorney general.

From 1983 to 1987, Hillary Rodham Clinton chaired the Arkansas Education Standards Committee. For this job, she traveled to each of the state's seventy-five counties, attending public meetings to discuss education reform. She also helped create a program in which the state sent aides into the homes of preschool children whose parents did not have the resources to prepare them for success in school. Many conservatives objected to this program, believing that the state should not interfere in family life.

Hillary Rodham Clinton was often criticized for her outspoken stance. Columnist

Describing her commitment to public service, Hillary Rodham Clinton has said, "It [is] very hard for me to see the waste and the damage and the hurt that occur every day [in this world]. I can't help wanting to do something about it."

Anna Quindlen noted that, to some observers, "Hillary Clinton was seen as abrasive, power-hungry and unfeminine when to some of us she seemed merely smart, outspoken and hard-working." During the 1992 campaign, she carefully played a more subdued role in order to avoid drawing such criticism. Once Bill Clinton was in office, however, it became clear how much he relied on her judgment and advice.

Hillary Rodham Clinton was more than an informal adviser. Her husband asked her to head the effort to define a new approach to national health care. Drawing on her experience with education reform in Arkansas, she led a task force of five hundred people and traveled throughout the country to speak with all concerned groups. Her work led to the development of the Clinton administration's massive health-care reform package, which she and her husband hoped would extend medical benefits to all American citizens.

Clinton's White House Team

As he assembled his political team, President Clinton vowed that his cabinet appointees would "look like the rest of America." (See the chart on page 843.) In 1993 Clinton chose four women, four African Americans, and two Latinos to be part of his cabinet. He chose Janet Reno as the first woman attorney general. He appointed African Americans Jesse Brown in Veterans Affairs, Ronald Brown in Commerce, and Mike Espy in Agriculture. Henry Cisneros in Housing and Urban Development and Federico Peña in Transportation gave Latinos more representation than ever before. ○

Clinton's first appointment to the Supreme Court also reflected his commitment to diversity. Ruth Bader Ginsburg became the second woman justice in 1993, joining Sandra Day O'Connor and the seven male justices.

Clinton's First Year in Office

Clinton swept into office on a wave of positive feelings. Maya Angelou, a prominent

---

▶ RESOURCE DIRECTORY

Teaching Resources

○ **American Profiles Activity** found in the Unit 7 folder, p. 117, profiles Henry Cisneros, Clinton's secretary of housing and urban development.

○ **Primary Source Activity** Defining Economic Goals, found in the Unit 7 folder, pp. 123–124, presents a speech by Bill Clinton to an economic conference shortly after his election outlining national economic goals.

○ **Critical Thinking Activity** Drawing Conclusions: Comparing Budget Categories, found in the Unit 7 folder, p. 122, helps students apply this skill by analyzing brief descriptions of parts of the 1995–1996 budget submitted to Congress by President Clinton.

African American poet, reflected the optimism in a poem she wrote especially for his inauguration:

*H*ere, on the pulse of this
new day,
You may have the grace to
look up and out
And into your sister's eyes
and into
Your brother's face, your
country,
And say simply,
Very simply,
With hope,
Good morning.

Clinton was committed to acting quickly. He and his aides wanted to move aggressively at the start, as Franklin Roosevelt had done in 1933, and create enough momentum to continue to the end of his term. "I know I can pass a sweeping package of legislation during the first 100 days of my administration," Clinton had declared before the election. "It will be the most productive period in modern history." Clinton's statement reflected a very optimistic view of what he could achieve as President. Once in office, he found the going a bit tougher and slower than he had imagined.

Economic Initiatives The economy clearly needed help. The recession that had struck near the end of George Bush's term lingered. The massive deficit, meanwhile, was squelching new initiatives, which required increased spending. During the campaign, Clinton's proposed solution was to cut the deficit and stimulate the economy at the same time. Over and over, he spoke of the need to "grow the economy" to get the country moving again. All too soon, however, his economic stimulus package went down to defeat at the hands of Congress. ✪

He was more successful with his first budget, but even this plan just barely squeaked by Congress. Budget cuts, along with tax increases, were necessary to reduce the deficit. Yet neither cuts nor taxes were popular with the public. The gas tax that was finally proposed—4.3 cents per gallon—was the result of a difficult compromise and continued to cause some complaints. New income taxes and taxes on social security benefits were met with similar discontent. The tax increases fell most heavily on the wealthiest Americans but still caused irritation among people who had to pay anything more. As they sought to gauge public opinion, legislators in both houses of Congress were reluctant to approve cuts that affected their own constituents.

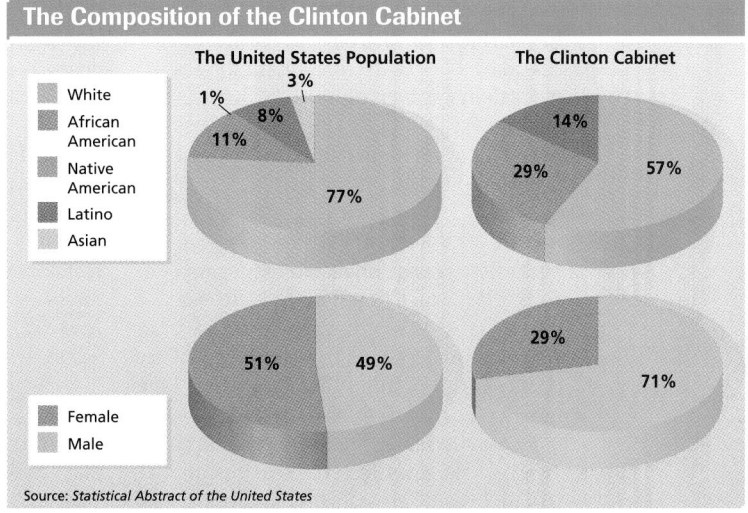

The Composition of the Clinton Cabinet

The United States Population

White — 77%
African American — 11%
Native American — 1%
Latino — 8%
Asian — 3%

The Clinton Cabinet

57%
29%
14%

Female 51% / Male 49%

Female 29% / Male 71%

Source: *Statistical Abstract of the United States*

Interpreting Charts
Clinton pledged to appoint a cabinet that "looked like the rest of America." *According to the pie charts, how well did Clinton succeed in this plan—in terms of both ethnicity and gender?*

Bill Clinton asked Maya Angelou to compose an official inaugural poem. She read her poem, "On the Pulse of Morning," at the January 1993 ceremony, as Vice President Al Gore (bottom right) looked on.

SOURCE READINGS

 Source Readings on p. 862 will connect literature selections and primary source excerpts to historical events discussed in this section.

In Depth

Interdisciplinary

President Clinton promised to prepare young Americans for the challenges of the twenty-first century. Teaching problem-solving skills is key to that preparation, and Bob Moses is doing it. In the mid-1960s, Bob Moses organized voting rights activists in Mississippi for SNCC (Student Nonviolent Coordinating Committee) and was one of the most prominent civil rights activists. (See Chapter 20, page 656.) In 1992 Moses returned to Mississippi as creator and director of Algebra Project, a groundbreaking method of teaching algebra to grade school students. "It's our version of Civil Rights 1992," says Moses. "But this time, we're organizing around literacy. . . . The question we asked then was: What are the skills people have to master to open the doors to citizenship? Now math literacy holds the key."

Section 1 Review Answers

1. (a) Bill Clinton, see p. 840, (b) Hillary Rodham Clinton, see p. 841, (c) Al Gore, see p. 844

2. In addition to formal televised debates, the major presidential candidates made informal appearances on television—from talk shows to MTV—in their efforts to reach a broad range of voters.

3. Hillary Rodham Clinton served informally as an adviser to her husband and also headed the task force to develop the administration's plan for health-care reform.

4. Clinton's pledge was to appoint a diverse group of people to his cabinet—one that reflected the diversity of the American people. His appointees included four women, four African Americans, and two Latinos.

5. Clinton's first major goals were to pass an economic stimulus package and develop a plan for health-care reform.

6. Winning only 43 percent of the popular vote, Clinton did not have a clear mandate. Therefore, Congress did not feel obligated to go along with all of the legislation proposed by the new President.

Reteach

Write the following names and phrases on the chalkboard: Ross Perot, George Bush, John F. Kennedy, Arkansas, Hillary Rodham Clinton, "look like the rest of America," "grow the economy," Al Gore, health-care reform. Ask students to state briefly how each one is connected to President Bill Clinton.

Caption Answer to …

 Interpreting Tables

Unemployed workers would have their health-care costs paid by the government under the new plan.

The final votes could not have been closer. In the House of Representatives, the budget passed by a 218 to 216 margin. In the Senate, the margin was even slimmer. With fifty senators voting for and fifty against, Vice President **Al Gore,** the presiding officer, had to break the tie to pass the measure.

Health-Care Reform As President Clinton pushed for passage of his economic program, Hillary Rodham Clinton directed the work of the task force on health-care reform. It was an enormous undertaking that consumed all her attention in the administration's first nine months. For years Americans had sought a more comprehensive health-care system. Harry Truman was the first President to propose national health insurance as part of his Fair Deal program at the end of World War II. Like much of his program, however, it failed to gain passage partly because of Republican resistance to extending social welfare goals.

In the 1950s and early 1960s, as other nations experimented with national health programs, the American Medical Association led the opposition to any plan that limited doctors' independence. Meanwhile, health care grew increasingly expensive and was often out of reach of the poorest Americans. Lyndon Johnson finally broke the logjam with the passage of Medicare, for the elderly, and Medicaid, for the poor, in 1965. These efforts helped for a time. But by the 1990s, the system was more expensive and less efficient than ever before. Approximately 37 million Americans lacked even the most limited health-care coverage.

In September 1993, Clinton appeared on national television and spoke on behalf of his administration's new health-care package. He told Congress and the entire country:

T*his health-care system of ours is badly broken, and it is time to fix it. Despite the dedication of literally millions of talented health-care professionals, our health care is too uncertain and too expensive, too bureaucratic and*

Clinton's Health-Care Plan, 1994

Basic Provisions	Types of Care	Costs	Administration	Financing of Reform
• Doctors' services • Preventive care • Ambulance services, hospitalization • Long-term care, home health care, hospice care • Eye and ear care, dental care (children) • Laboratory work • Physical therapy • Prescription drugs • Mental health/substance abuse care • Health education	• Health maintenance organizations (HMOs) offer a variety of services under one roof for a monthly fee • Fee-for-service plans require full payment for each particular service (20% paid by the individual, 80% by the insurer) • "Hybrid," or "blended" plans offer features of both	• Businesses will pay at least 80% of the costs; employees will pay remainder. The federal government will subsidize costs for small businesses. • The self-employed will pay 100%, but that cost will be 100% tax-deductible. • The unemployed will have their costs paid by the government.	• Health alliances, formerly known as "health-insurance purchasing cooperatives," will pool the purchasing power of consumers, defined by region or state, enabling them to purchase insurance at bulk rates. Large businesses may form their own alliances.	• Medicare savings • Medicaid savings • Revenue gains • Sin taxes • Medicare and Medicaid recipients who would join health alliances • Other federal program savings

 Interpreting Tables
Hillary Rodham Clinton traveled around the country gathering information, opinions, and ideas for national health-care reform. At right, she meets an elderly woman who would be affected by the reforms. *How would the new plan help unemployed workers?*

▶ RESOURCE DIRECTORY

Teaching Resources

too wasteful. It has too much fraud and too much greed. At long last, after decades of false starts, we must make this our most urgent priority: giving every American health security, health care that can never be taken away, health care that is always there.

Clinton stated that all citizens would be covered by the new program, outlined in the table on page 844. Each state would create health alliances to pay health claims. Health plans, consisting of networks of doctors, hospitals, and insurers, would work with the alliances to provide health care.

Many people, including Republican leaders, criticized Clinton's health-care package. Following Clinton's State of the Union Address in January 1994, in which the President vowed to veto any health-care legislation that did not guarantee coverage for all Americans, Senate minority leader Bob Dole appeared on television to respond to the address. Voicing the concerns of many Americans, Dole said that the Clinton plan would "put a mountain of bureaucrats between you and your doctor" and lead to "more cost . . . less choice . . . more taxes . . . less quality . . . more government control." Republicans argued that the administration had not come up with a way to finance the costly plan, which they estimated would create a deficit of at least $918 billion in its first six years. These were serious criticisms, which Clinton would need to address. Still, his proposal had forced serious debate on the future of health care in the United States.

Viewpoints
On Health-Care Reform

In November 1993, as he presented his detailed health-care plan to Congress, President Clinton promised he would sign only a law that "guarantees every single American a comprehensive package of health benefits . . . that can never be taken away." **Compare and contrast the following statements on the subject.**

Against the Clinton Plan

"There is good reason to believe the Clinton plan will dilute health-care delivery in the United States. . . . Based on past performance, neither the federal government nor the insurance industry can be trusted to be solely responsible for America's health coverage. That's why the only solution to the crisis lies in a public-private partnership, one that maintains and enhances a high level of quality health care, that transcends partisan differences and special interests and keeps pace with technological advances and clinical skills. Unfortunately, on this Thanksgiving day that kind of solution lies somewhere between Plymouth Rock and the Congress of the United States."

Benjamin Lipson, insurance agent and editor of The Lipson Letter, a column in the *Boston Globe*, November 25, 1993

For the Clinton Plan

"There are moral, ethical, social, political, and economic reasons why we must ask to take on this [health-care] system, to fix what is broken and to preserve and enhance what does work so well for those of us able to access the system. . . . The status quo is unacceptable and . . . marginal changes are also unacceptable as to what the basic building blocks of health care reform must be. . . . Individuals have to take more responsibility for their own health. And . . . we have to responsibly fund our health-care system."

Hillary Rodham Clinton, address to a forum on health care at the World Trade Center, December 1993

Answer to . . .

Viewpoints

Both Lipson and Clinton believe that the positive aspects of the present health-care system must be maintained. Lipson believes that putting health care under the control of the federal government will decrease the quality of care; Clinton, however, thinks that the government can "fix what is broken" and improve health care overall with a new federal plan.

4. CLOSE

Reinforcing the Big Idea

With his experience in state government, Bill Clinton was more comfortable tackling the problems of domestic reform than those of foreign affairs. A flood of calamitous events in the post–cold war world, however, demanded his attention from the very beginning of his presidency. In the next section, students will learn about some of these events.

SECTION 1 REVIEW

Key Terms, People, and Places

1. Identify (a) Bill Clinton, (b) Hillary Rodham Clinton, (c) Al Gore.

Key Concepts

2. What part did television have in the 1992 presidential election?

3. What role did Hillary Rodham Clinton have in the new administration?

4. What did President Clinton mean when he pledged

to appoint a cabinet that "looked like the rest of America"? How did he fulfill this pledge?

5. What were the two main goals of the Clinton administration at the beginning of his presidency?

Critical Thinking

6. **Determining Relevance** Did Bill Clinton receive a clear mandate from voters in the 1992 election? How might the election results have affected his ability to pass his legislative measures in Congress?

Viewpoints Activity On Health-Care Reform, found in the Unit 7 folder, pp. 119–120, presents different opinions on Clinton's proposed health-care plan.

Quiz found in the Unit 7 folder, p. 112, covers the main ideas in this section as well as the key terms.

The United States and the World in the 1990s

Connecting to the Big Idea

See page 838B. Point out that some of the most dramatic changes of the 1990s occurred not in the United States but in the Soviet Union, Eastern Europe, Africa, Mexico, and other regions of the world. Ask what these changes were and how the Clinton administration responded to them.

Objectives

• Explain how the Clinton administration supported Boris Yeltsin in his efforts to bring reform to Russia.
• Explain the agreement signed by Israel and the Palestine Liberation Organization in 1993 and the problems that grew out of it.
• Describe changes that occurred in South Africa and Somalia in the early 1990s.
• Explain the basic provisions of the North American Free Trade Agreement.

Bellringer

Ask students to recall some of the political systems already mentioned in the text, such as socialism, communism, welfare capitalism, and so on. Invite students to predict some possible consequences in a nation undergoing a major change in its political system; for example, from communism to capitalism, or from minority rule to constitutional democracy.

Reading Strategy

Reinforcing Key Terms Have students copy the list of key terms, people, and places on a piece of paper and, as they read the section, write down to which part of the world each one is connected, and how.

846 CHAPTER 26 SECTION 2

The United States and the World in the 1990s

SECTION PREVIEW

The end of the cold war in the 1990s left the Clinton administration struggling to find its way through uncharted waters in international relations. The collapse of communism and the increase in ethnic tensions in various parts of the world created new problems for the nation.

Key Concepts

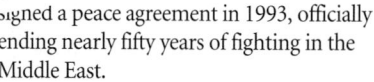

• The Clinton administration supported Russian president Boris Yeltsin in his efforts to bring reform to the former Soviet Union.
• Israel and the Palestine Liberation Organization signed a peace agreement in 1993, officially ending nearly fifty years of fighting in the Middle East.
• While South Africa moved toward justice for its African majority population, the United States became involved in civil war in Somalia.
• An agreement signed by Mexico, the United States, and Canada in 1993 promised more open trade between these North American neighbors.

Key Terms, People, and Places

apartheid, sanctions, North American Free Trade Agreement (NAFTA); Slobodan Milosevic, Yitzhak Rabin, Yasir Arafat, Frederik W. de Klerk, Nelson Mandela

... in a mission dubbed Operation Restore Hope, the United States helped distribute truckloads of food and other vital supplies in the famine-stricken East African country of Somalia.

I n the 1990s, the United States faced a radically different world. The cold war was now over, but the collapse of communism and the rise of religious, racial, and ethnic tensions around the globe created new problems. The United States struggled to support the efforts of many nations to create more democratic societies. At the same time, American leaders tried to keep the United States on top of a changing world economy. ★

The United States and the Former Soviet Union

As the Soviet empire crumbled, United States leaders tried to promote the move toward Western-style democracy in the former republics. Boris Yeltsin was elected president of Russia, the largest of the republics. American policy makers quickly voiced their support for his initiatives. The United States, Clinton declared, "supports the historic movement toward democratic political reform in Russia. President Yeltsin is the leader of that process."

Yet Yeltsin faced serious difficulties. The transition to a free market economy, after decades of rigid controls, could not happen overnight. The United States offered a $2.5 billion aid package to help ease the process, but even that was not enough. Goods were still in short supply, and the economy remained unstable. In the fall of 1993, when the Russian parliament resisted reforms that Yeltsin argued were necessary, he dissolved the parliament and called for a new legislature to be chosen in December elections. A group of one hundred legislators resisted Yeltsin's move and continued to meet in the parliament building. Two weeks later, in early October, government tanks stormed the building. More than 150 people were killed in the process, and more than 1,500 people, including the legislators, were placed under arrest. Yeltsin meanwhile strengthened his own authority by increasing censorship and removing his opponents from the government.

The December elections, however, did not provide Yeltsin with the popular mandate he

RESOURCE DIRECTORY

Teaching Resources

Reproducible Lesson Plan found in the Unit 7 folder, p. 109, provides a summary of the Section 2 lesson plan content.

Alternate Lesson Plan: Critical Thinking Predicting Consequences, found in the Alternate Lesson Plans folder, p. 178, helps pairs or groups of students analyze a world hot spot of the early 1990s and apply this skill to the resolution of conflicts there.

Guided Reading and Review found in the Unit 7 folder, p. 113, provides a structure for reading and mastering the key concepts and reviewing the key terms for Section 2. (Guided Practice)

Visual Learning Activity Clinton and Foreign Affairs, found in the Unit 7 folder, p. 130, uses a cartoon to illustrate President Clinton's preference for domestic policymaking being overpowered by the world's trouble spots.

wanted for his reforms. Instead of filling the new parliament with representatives who favored reform, Russians cast nearly 25 percent of their votes for the right-wing party headed by Vladimir Zhirinovsky. Yeltsin's party received less than 15 percent. Voters approved a new constitution granting President Yeltsin wider powers, but Yeltsin would face an uphill battle against antireform leaders.

Zhirinovsky's success in the election was a sign of trouble to many observers around the world. Like the fascist leaders of the 1930s, Zhirinovsky appealed to voters by promising an end to economic hardship and a return to national greatness. He also blamed many of Russia's woes on "foreigners" and Jews. When asked if he would run for president in 1996, when Yeltsin's term expired, Zhirinovsky replied, "Certainly."

The United States and the Former Yugoslavia

The fragmentation of the Soviet Union was felt throughout Eastern Europe. Former satellite nations threw off communist rule. Poland, Czechoslovakia, Bulgaria, Hungary, Romania, and Albania all established new regimes. In Yugoslavia, ethnic hostilities that had been suppressed for years resurfaced when the nation's central government collapsed.

Yugoslavia, shown in the map on page 848, had long been a powder keg. A political spark there had ignited World War I almost eighty years before. After World War II, only a strong communist dictatorship bound together the various republics, composed of different ethnic groups.

During the 1980s, political leaders with strong nationalist feelings rose to power in each of Yugoslavia's republics. **Slobodan Milosevic**— a leader of the largest ethnic group, the Serbs— wanted to preserve the union of Yugoslavia and ensure that Serbs had a powerful voice in governing the country. When the republics of Slovenia and Croatia declared their independence in 1991, many ethnic Serbs living in those regions feared repression by the new governments. Fighting soon broke out among Serbs, Croats, and Muslims. The powder keg had been ignited, and violence quickly spread to the neighboring republic of Bosnia-Herzegovina.

| 1650 | 1700 | 1750 | 1800 | **Links Across Time** | 1850 | 1900 | 1950 | 2000 |

Sarajevo Then and Now

Before the breakup of Yugoslavia, Sarajevo was a bustling modern city (above). With the outbreak of civil war in 1991, however, Sarajevo found itself under siege by Serbian forces. Much of the city was reduced to rubble, including the Bosnian National Library—where an undaunted Sarajevo Orchestra rehearsed in 1993 (left). *What might such destruction mean for the people of a city?*

Explain/Discuss

Explain that no government ever has the support of all of its citizens. Remind students of the debate that accompanied the formation of the United States government in the late eighteenth century and of the many movements for change that have altered the nation's laws and policies since then. Discuss what might happen when a federal system of government is suddenly dissolved, as happened in the former Soviet Union or the former Yugoslavia; when a leader is overthrown, as in Haiti; or when different groups within a country struggle to maintain control over their own destinies, as in Israel or South Africa. Ask students to explain why hostilities between various ethnic or religious groups might intensify during times of political turmoil.

Analyze

Have students analyze the nature of a good government. What guarantees does such a government provide to its citizens? Who decides which people will be subject to a particular government, or determines the borders that divide an area into separate political entities? Why are debates over such issues often accompanied by violence?

Answer to ...

Links Across Time

When libraries and other buildings are destroyed, part of the city's and the nation's history is lost with them. In addition, the destruction of a city means physical danger for its citizens and creates an atmosphere of chaos and instability that takes a heavy psychological toll on the entire country.

Activity

Writing a Radio News Report

Ask students to imagine that they are foreign correspondents for a radio news program. Divide students into groups and assign each group one of the regions discussed in the chapter. Groups should consult recent newspaper and magazine articles to learn what is happening in their assigned region currently and then prepare a background report from that region for broadcast in the United States.

LEP

Enrichment

The world leaders discussed in this section all followed different paths to power and each exercises power in different ways. Have each student select one leader and gather biographical information for a short essay on that person.

Caption Answer to ...

Interpreting Maps

The map shows that, after the dissolution of a strong central government, many groups formerly within that nation often compete for political power and control over land. The former Yugoslavia is just one example of an Eastern bloc country that experienced such problems at the end of the cold war.

The Former Yugoslavia, 1994

Boundary of the former Yugoslavia

Portion of Bosnia Herzegovina under Muslim control

Portion of Bosnia Herzegovina under Serbian control

Portion of Bosnia Herzegovina under Croatian control

Geography and History: Interpreting Maps
This map shows the regions of Bosnia-Herzegovina controlled by various groups in 1994. *How does it demonstrate the problems in many former communist nations after their governments collapsed in the late 1980s and early 1990s?*

When the Muslim and Croatian majority in Bosnia-Herzegovina decided to secede from Serbian-dominated Yugoslavia in 1992, Serbian forces in those regions were ready to resist. Backed by Milosevic and the republic of Serbia, these forces began a siege of the city of Sarajevo. They also embarked on a vicious "ethnic cleansing" campaign to eliminate Croatian and Muslim inhabitants from Serb-controlled areas of Bosnia-Herzegovina. Killing took place on both sides of the conflict, as Croat and Muslim forces mercilessly slaughtered Serbs.

The world watched in horror as the violence in Bosnia-Herzegovina worsened. In the spring of 1993, Clinton pledged to send American troops as part of a peacekeeping force, but when the American public proved reluctant to become involved, he backed off from his pledge. Meanwhile, negotiators plunged into the complex process of trying to craft a peace treaty that could provide some balance among the warring groups. In March 1994, Croats and Muslims signed a pact that would politically unite their territories in Bosnia-Herzegovina and, it was hoped, encourage Bosnian Serbs to agree to a peaceful settlement.

The United States and the Middle East

More progress in the quest for stability came in the Middle East. The patient diplomacy of the Bush administration had failed to bring the long-sought peace settlement to the region. Then, in September 1993, the world learned that the Palestine Liberation Organization (PLO) and Israel had been engaged in secret negotiations of their own and were almost ready to sign a peace treaty recognizing Israel's right to exist and ending more than fifty years of hostility.

The agreement provided for Palestinian self-rule in the Gaza Strip, between Israel and the Sinai Peninsula, and in the town of Jericho, on the West Bank of the Jordan River. (See the map on page 849.) Israel had seized both regions from the Palestinians in the Six-Day War of 1967 and controlled them ever since. Over the years, violence between Palestinians and Israeli occupying forces had made the regions into virtual war zones. Weary of the constant fighting, PLO and Israeli leaders finally committed themselves to negotiating a workable solution.

Peacemaking was a prickly process, particularly between people who had been enemies for so long. But, as Israeli prime minister **Yitzhak Rabin** observed, "Peace is not made with friends. Peace is made with enemies." As events moved quickly forward, the United States joined the peace process. On September 13, 1993, in a ceremony held on the White House lawn, PLO head **Yasir Arafat** and Yitzhak Rabin shook hands after signing the agreement.

In the months that followed the historic handshake, radical Palestinian groups and some Israelis showed their disapproval of the accord with renewed violence. Arafat's authority was challenged by radicals within the PLO who killed a number of Israelis in terrorist attacks.

In February 1994, a Jewish settler in the West Bank walked into a crowded mosque in the town of Hebron and opened fire on the Palestinians who were kneeling in prayer there. More than forty people were killed and many others wounded, and riots that followed the massacre led to more casualties.

In addition to the problems caused by violence, the accord had left many issues unsettled. Arafat and Rabin argued over who would control border crossings around the new Palestinian territories. Months after the deadline for withdrawal of Israeli troops had passed in December 1993, the future of Israeli-Palestinian relations hung in a highly uncertain balance.

The United States and Africa

Meanwhile, the United States became more involved in Africa. Americans, like people around the world, hailed the effort to overturn **apartheid**—the systematic separation of the races—in South Africa. Throughout the twentieth century, the white minority (which was only 15 percent of the population) had segregated and suppressed the African majority. In the mid-1980s, the United States Congress voted to impose economic **sanctions** to try to topple the repressive regime. Economic sanctions are actions taken by one or more countries against another country to restrict that nation's trade by boycotting, blockading shipping, or other means. The sanctions against South Africa included a rule prohibiting new American investments in the country. In 1990 South African prime minister **Frederik W. de Klerk** recognized that he

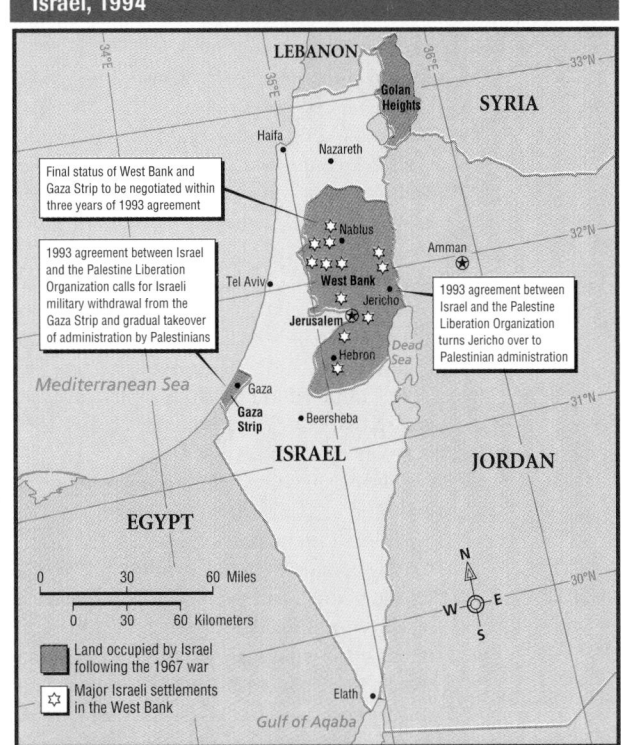

Israel, 1994

Final status of West Bank and Gaza Strip to be negotiated within three years of 1993 agreement

1993 agreement between Israel and the Palestine Liberation Organization calls for Israeli military withdrawal from the Gaza Strip and gradual takeover of administration by Palestinians

1993 agreement between Israel and the Palestine Liberation Organization turns Jericho over to Palestinian administration

■ Land occupied by Israel following the 1967 war

☆ Major Israeli settlements in the West Bank

Geography and History: Interpreting Maps
President Clinton presided over the signing of the 1993 peace accord between Israel's Yitzhak Rabin (above left) and the PLO's Yasir Arafat (above right). *How did the accord affect the West Bank and Gaza Strip?*

could not control the forces of change; he released seventy-one-year-old **Nelson Mandela,** a leader in the struggle to end apartheid, who had spent the last twenty-seven years in jail.

Mandela made a triumphant tour of the United States and the world. His organization, the African National Congress (ANC), spearheaded the negotiations with the ruling white regime to create a smooth transition to a biracial democracy.

Mandela and de Klerk both received the 1993 Nobel Peace Prize, an honor that reflected their common commitment to ending apartheid in South Africa. In 1993 Mandela called for an end to international economic sanctions in South Africa, in recognition of the country's new beginning. But the legacy of apartheid continued to cause serious problems. President de Klerk had called for the country's

Caption Answer to ...

🌍 **Interpreting Maps**

The agreement committed Israel to turn over the city of Jericho in the West Bank to Palestinian control and called for Israel to withdraw its military presence in the Gaza Strip. The final status of the West Bank and Gaza Strip was to be negotiated over the next three years.

In Depth

Multicultural Perspectives

"I think Alex Haley . . . did connect a lot of us to Africa," said George Curry, editor of the African American newsmagazine *Emerge.* "It's where we came from, it's where civilization started. How can we turn our backs on it?" He spoke for many African Americans who have followed the bitter course of South African history with interest and support. A 1994 news article on the April elections in South Africa commented that African Americans look on South Africans as "a sea of black faces that mirror their own, the faces of a proud people one huge step away from wielding the power African-Americans still strive for." In May 1994, Nelson Mandela was inaugurated as president after a landslide victory in South Africa's first democratic, "all-race" election.

Americans vividly remember the tragic results of United States involvement in the Vietnam War—especially the many assurances from the government and military leaders that "peace was at hand," as more and more troops were committed. A desire not to repeat the mistakes of the past influences the United States' approach to foreign policy in the present.

Caption Answer to . . .

Using Historical Evidence

It has exacerbated the devastating poverty of many of its citizens.

3. ASSESS

Section 2 Review Answers

1. (a) apartheid, see p. 849, (b) sanctions, see p. 849, (c) NAFTA, see p. 851

2. (a) Slobodan Milosevic, see p. 847, (b) Yitzhak Rabin, see p. 848, (c) Yasir Arafat, see p. 848, (d) Frederik W. de Klerk, see p. 849, (e) Nelson Mandela, see p. 849

3. The United States supported the move toward Western-style democracy in the former republics and backed Russian leader Boris Yeltsin.

4. When Israel and the PLO were nearly ready to sign a peace agreement, the United States supported the plan.

5. Mandela called for an end to economic sanctions against South Africa in 1993, and de Klerk announced that multiracial elections would take place in 1994. Several groups threatened to boycott the elections.

6. NAFTA removed trade barriers between the United States, Mexico, and Canada, opening up new markets for products from all three nations.

7. In both Israel and the former Yugoslavia, ethnic groups fought for control over territory and demanded self-rule. In Israel, a long history of border strife and violence intensified after the 1993 signing of a peace agreement that was unpopular among radicals on both sides. Ethnic violence in the former Yugoslavia broke out after the dissolution of a strong central government.

first multiracial elections to be held in April 1994. The ANC registered to become a political party in February, but more radical white and African groups planned to boycott the elections.

The Freedom Alliance, which included both proapartheid whites and African nationalists, feared the ANC would win the elections and impose a communist dictatorship. The alliance demanded changes in the constitution that would ensure greater independence for regions within South Africa. As the April elections approached, negotiations between the government and the various political groups followed a twisting and uncertain path. Violence continued to flow from conflict between the ANC and African nationalist groups, leading to many deaths.

At the same time, the United States became embroiled in East Africa. Following a severe drought, the nation of Somalia suffered from a terrible famine. After thousands of people had starved to death and many more were in danger of starving, President Bush sent American troops into Somalia as part of a United Nations relief effort. By June 1993, when food and medicine had been successfully distributed to many Somalis, the number of United States troops had dwindled from 28,000 to 5,000.

That June, however, the situation took a turn for the worse. A number of American soldiers were killed or taken hostage. The UN envoy to Somalia offered a reward for the capture of Mohammed Farrah Aidid, the leader believed to be behind the increased violence toward UN troops. As the hunt for Aidid went on, the American public recalled how the United States gradually had been drawn deeper and deeper into the Vietnam War. They demanded withdrawal from Somalia before it was too late. In October 1993, President Clinton increased the number of American troops but vowed that they would all return home by the following April.

MAKING CONNECTIONS

How does the Vietnam War continue to affect United States foreign policy in the 1990s?

The United States in the Western Hemisphere

The 1990s saw a mixture of hope and frustration in the dealings of the United States with its Western Hemisphere neighbors. In

Using Historical Evidence A group of Haitian children stands in front of the shantytown where they live. *What does this photograph tell you about the effects of political instability in Haiti?*

 RESOURCE DIRECTORY

Teaching Resources

Haiti, located on a Caribbean island 600 miles off the Florida coast, the United States supported exiled president Jean-Bertrand Aristide. This democratically elected president was forced out of power in 1991 by a military coup. The United States helped negotiate a plan for military leaders to step down and allow Aristide to resume control, but then found it impossible to enforce the agreement. Guerrilla hit men terrorized the nation, assassinating officials from the Aristide government and others who opposed military rule. Neither diplomacy nor economic sanctions by the United States seemed to help the situation, and the people of Haiti suffered from vicious terrorism and stifling poverty.

One reflection of the effort to foster cooperation in the Western Hemisphere was the **North American Free Trade Agreement (NAFTA),** which sought to promote free trade between Canada, Mexico, and the United States. The table above shows the provisions of NAFTA. The agreement inspired heated debate in the United States between groups that predicted the different effects NAFTA might have on the economy.

NAFTA was negotiated during the Bush administration, but Clinton had to get it ratified by Congress. He threw his support behind the pact, only to face sustained opposition from labor unions that feared NAFTA might lead to

the loss of American jobs. Despite the opposition, the Senate finally approved the NAFTA treaty in November 1993.

The next month, representatives from the United States and 116 other nations agreed to expand the General Agreement on Tariffs and Trade (GATT). Pending approval by Congress and other legislatures, GATT would eliminate a broad range of international tariffs, thus removing long-standing barriers to world trade. The new agreement also would create a new World Trade Organization (WTO), which would enforce GATT rules and settle trade disputes between countries. President Clinton praised GATT, expressing his belief that it would boost the global economy: "No wealthy country in the world today can hope to ... raise incomes unless there are more customers for its goods and services."

| The North American Free Trade Agreement (NAFTA), 1994 |||
The Agreement	The Result	The Controversies
The United States, Canada, and Mexico will remove tariffs and most other mutual trade restrictions over the next 15 years.	The resulting free-trade zone will form a single market similar to, but much larger than, the European Community.	Despite NAFTA's "side agreements" and other provisions, concern remains over its potential effects on the environment and on the United States job market.

Interpreting Tables
President Clinton called NAFTA "more than a trading bloc—it's a building block in our efforts to assert America's global leadership on behalf of American jobs and opportunity." *According to the table, what new trading opportunities does NAFTA provide?*

SECTION 2 REVIEW

Key Terms, People, and Places
1. Define (a) apartheid, (b) sanctions, (c) NAFTA.
2. Identify (a) Slobodan Milosevic, (b) Yitzhak Rabin, (c) Yasir Arafat, (d) Frederik W. de Klerk, (e) Nelson Mandela.

Key Concepts
3. How did the United States respond to the disintegration of the Soviet Union?
4. What role did the United States play in helping to further peace in the Middle East?

5. What changes occurred in South Africa in the first part of the Clinton administration?
6. What was the purpose of the North American Free Trade Agreement?

Critical Thinking
7. **Making Comparisons** Israel and the former Yugoslavia were two regions that experienced ethnic violence in the early 1990s. In what ways were the circumstances of this violence similar and different in these two places?

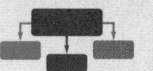
Quiz found in the Unit 7 folder, p. 114, covers the main ideas in this section as well as the key terms.

SECTION 3

American Society in the 1990s

1. FOCUS

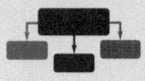

Connecting to the Big Idea

See page 838B. As the number of nonwhite Americans continued to rise in the early 1990s, the nation confronted the question of how to accommodate this diversity. Ask what factors led to increasing ethnic diversity and how multicultural education aimed to address this issue.

Objectives

● Explain how the overall profile of immigrants to the United States changed in the 1980s and 1990s.
● Identify the factors that led to increasing ethnic diversity in the United States.
● Describe two opposing viewpoints in the debate over multicultural education.

Bellringer

Discuss with students the fact that it is usually easier to maintain the uniformity of a group of people similar to oneself then to expand one's community to include people who have different backgrounds. Ask them why they think clusters of communities of specific groups, like "little Italy" or Chinatown, are formed in larger cities.Why do settlement patterns happen?

Reading Strategy

Problem Solving Ask students to skim the section, to list the main headings and subheadings, and to write a sentence or phrase under each heading that predicts what problems it will raise. Students should check their predicted problems against the actual text when they have finished reading the section, and identify possible solutions.

SECTION PREVIEW

By the 1990s, the face of the United States had changed. With an increase in the number of immigrants and a rise in minority birth rates, a much larger percentage of the population than ever before was African American, Latino, Asian American, or Native American. The United States needed to find new ways to deal with this ethnic and cultural diversity.

Though known as a "nation of immigrants," the United States still had problems dealing with the many people who sought to immigrate in the 1990s. This California road sign warns drivers to be on the lookout for undocumented aliens who might have crossed the border from Mexico.

Key Concepts

• In the 1980s and 1990s, more immigrants came to the United States from parts of the world other than Western Europe.
• Several factors combined to change the ethnic and cultural composition of the United States.
• Many Americans supported the attempt to include all groups in the definition of the nation, but others worried that this effort could be taken to extremes.

Key Terms, People, and Places

bilingual education, multiculturalism

A s the United States shifted course in both domestic and foreign affairs, the makeup of the nation itself changed. Although the 1990 census revealed that during the 1980s the population had increased from 228 million to about 250 million, the growth rate was one of the lowest in United States history. More important was the changing composition of the population. By the early 1990s, the number of Americans with non-European roots had risen dramatically. This increased ethnic diversity forced the United States to take a fresh look at itself as a nation of immigrants.

New Immigration Patterns and Policies

Immigration patterns changed in the 1980s and 1990s. The Immigration Act of 1965, which was part of Lyndon Johnson's Great Society, altered quotas that favored Western Europeans and allowed the freer acceptance of people from all parts of the world. The Immigration Reform and Control Act of 1986 sought to curb illegal immigration while permitting aliens who had lived in the United States since 1982 to register to become citizens. The Immigration Act of 1990 went even further. This law increased immigration quotas by 40 percent and eased restrictions that had denied entrance to many people in the past.

In the 1980s, 37 percent of all legal immigrants came from Asia and 47 percent came from Mexico, the Caribbean, and Latin America. (See the pie chart on page 853.) The same patterns continued in the 1990s. The so-called Sun Belt, stretching from Florida to California, felt the impact of this immigration most of all. In cities such as Los Angeles, numerous new arrivals—Koreans, Vietnamese, Cambodians, Filipinos, Samoans, Taiwanese—competed for jobs and apartments with Mexicans, African Americans, and Anglos. This was the same kind of competition found among different groups in New York City a century before.

The adjustment was not always easy for the recent immigrants. The new arrivals often strained public services. "We just can't keep up," declared Los Angeles board of education president Jackie Goldberg:

> *O ften we get the child without the parent. How do they come? I think most come on a bus, after walking a long time. They come with whatever money their parents can spare and a piece of paper with a name and address. We get kids of 11 or 12 who have never been to school.*

 ### RESOURCE DIRECTORY

Teaching Resources

Reproducible Lesson Plan found in the Unit 7 folder, p. 110, provides a summary of the Section 3 lesson plan content.

Alternate Lesson Plan: Learning Styles found in the Alternate Lesson Plans folder, p. 179, guides class debate on differing viewpoints of multiculturalism in education, and is especially effective for auditory learners.

Guided Reading and Review found in the Unit 7 folder, p. 115, provides a structure for reading and mastering the key concepts and reviewing the key terms for Section 3. (Guided Practice)

American Profiles Activity found in the Unit 7 folder, p. 118, profiles Amy Tan, author of the best-selling novel *The Joy Luck Club,* which depicts life in America from the perspective of Chinese American women.

Language posed a particular problem for the nation's schools. The pros and cons of **bilingual education,** in which students are taught in both their native language and English, were hotly debated. Amelia McKenna, director of Los Angeles's bilingual education program, observed, "We have between 84 and 90 languages in our district. Nearly 40 percent of our students—242,000 children—are limited in English."

As native-born Americans struggled with hard times, they became less sympathetic to new immigrants than they had been before. A *Newsweek* cover story in August 1993 noted that while a majority of those polled felt that immigration had been a good thing in the past, a mere 29 percent thought it was good in the present, and 60 percent said that it was harmful to the United States today. A poll in the newspaper *USA Today* that same summer found that 65 percent of the people questioned wanted to see immigration cut back.

Some people felt that immigrants took jobs from working Americans, drained taxpayer dollars, and threatened the stability of American culture. "They bring different values and that's why we have more crime and drug problems," declared Mary Goldsmith, a homemaker from Kentucky who was one of those surveyed by *USA Today.* Once again, as in the past, the United States had to deal with opposition to immigration.

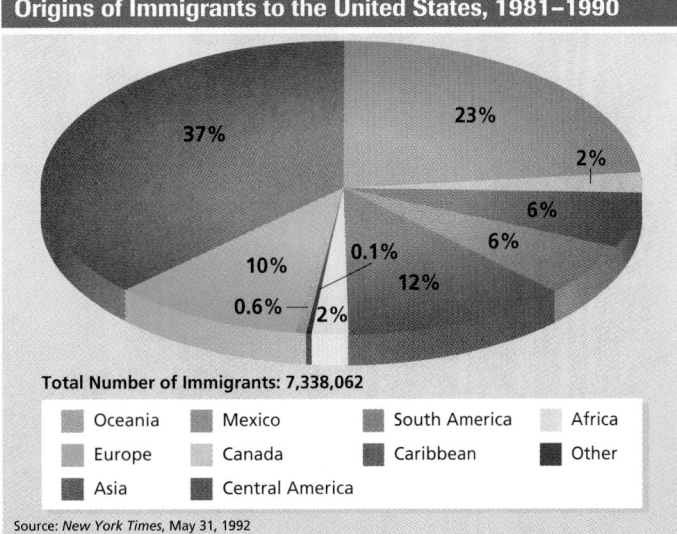

Origins of Immigrants to the United States, 1981–1990

37%
23%
2%
6%
6%
0.1%
12%
10%
0.6%
2%

Total Number of Immigrants: 7,338,062

- Oceania
- Europe
- Asia
- Mexico
- Canada
- Central America
- South America
- Caribbean
- Africa
- Other

Source: *New York Times,* May 31, 1992

 Interpreting Charts
Which group comprised the largest percentage of immigrants to the United States in the 1980s? What was the second largest group? How would you expect these statistics to affect the overall ethnic composition of the United States over several decades?

856 shows, an all-time high of 23 percent of the population in 1990 was African American, Latino, Asian American, or Native American, up from 20 percent ten years before. Now the nation included 30 million African Americans (11 percent of the population), 22.4 million Latinos (8 percent of the population), 7.3 million Asian Americans (3 percent of the population), and 2 million Native Americans (just under 1 percent of the population). The United States was entering a new age. It was becoming, in the words of writer Ben J. Wattenberg, "the first universal nation." ✪

African Americans continued to make major strides forward. They were increasingly visible in national politics as a result of the elections of 1992. Carol Moseley-Braun of Illinois became the first African American woman ever to serve in the United States Senate. In the House of Representatives, the number of African Americans rose from twenty-six to thirty-nine. In the field of education, Condoleezza Rice became the first African American woman to hold the position of provost, or chief academic officer, at Stanford University in California.

MAKING CONNECTIONS

During what other periods of United States history have Americans disapproved of immigrants moving into their communities? Why did they object to immigration?

Ethnic and Cultural Diversity

In the 1980s and 1990s, as immigration increased and minority birth rates soared, the number of Americans with roots outside Europe rose dramatically. As the chart on page

Media and Technology

Transparencies
Historical Maps, L-5; Our Multicultural Heritage, C-14

SOURCE READINGS

Source Readings on p. 864 will connect literature selections and primary source excerpts to historical events discussed in this section.

Discuss
Ask students how patterns of immigration to the United States changed in the 1980s and 1990s. How did these new patterns affect the composition of the population as a whole? Ask students to cite evidence from the section to show both the progress and the continuing problems of minority groups in the 1990s.

Have students summarize the arguments for and against multiculturalism that are outlined in the section.

Analyze
Ask students to explore the possibility of a middle ground between Eurocentrism—a perspective on history that focuses on the experiences of European Americans to the exclusion of other groups—and multiculturalism—an approach criticized by historian Arthur M. Schlesinger, Jr., as "ethnic cheerleading." Have students describe how they might tell the story of the United States from such a middle-ground perspective.

Caption Answer to ...

Interpreting Charts

Asians were the largest group, with Mexicans in second place. Students may predict an increase in the percentage of Asian Americans and Mexican Americans in the overall population.

Answer to ...

MAKING CONNECTIONS

Possible answer: During the late nineteenth century, the United States experienced a massive influx of immigrants. People already living in the United States often shunned these immigrants and worried that they would take jobs away from them.

Using Historical Evidence

The man represents African Americans. The civil rights movement has led to changes in laws and in many people's attitudes that have helped overcome racial inequality. He faces yet another hard climb out of a second pit, representing the economic injustice that has only begun to be addressed. The cartoon reflects the circumstances of many African Americans in the 1990s.

 Activity

Teaching Heterogeneous Groups

Tell students that one kind of diversity that exists within any classroom is the diversity of learning styles. Have students work in small groups to come up with a list of alternate ways a class might study United States history other than by reading textbooks and taking written tests. **LEP**

 In Depth

Biography

Dr. Lori Cupp (b. 1950) is the first Navaho woman to become a surgeon. Cupp took Native American studies at Dartmouth before graduating from Stanford University Medical School in 1990. "In the [Navaho] religion and culture, there is an emphasis on how you relate to everything around you," said Cupp during an interview in 1994. "Everything has to be measured, weighed and harmonious. We call it *nizhoni*—walking in beauty—and I believe what I do as a surgeon fits into this philosophy. I know my actions directly alter the course of people's lives."

Using Historical Evidence *Whom does the man in the cartoon represent? In what ways has he climbed out of the pit of racial inequality? What new obstacle does he face as he emerges from the first pit? What circumstances in the United States of the 1990s does the cartoon reflect?* ⭐

Senator Ben Nighthorse Campbell (below) was elected to represent his home state of Colorado in the election of 1992.

⭐ Latinos made similar gains. In Congress, the number of representatives rose from thirteen to nineteen in the election of 1992. This was the largest Latino delegation in United States history. In the past, most Latinos in Congress were Mexican Americans. Now Cubans, Puerto Ricans, and other groups were represented. They were ready to help the nation move in new directions. As Nydia M. Velázquez, a Puerto Rican member of Congress from New York, noted, "Many of the new members were elected on [the promise of] changing business as usual. The message and mandate from voters was clear. We have to change and put partisanship [party politics] aside."

Native Americans, too, became increasingly visible and vocal. Ben Nighthorse Campbell of Colorado became the first Native American in the Senate in more than sixty years when he assumed his seat in 1993. Outside of Congress, some Native Americans pressed long-standing claims for land that had been taken from them years before. The Oglala Lakota, for example, struggled to regain possession of the Black Hills of South Dakota, and turned down a $300,000 cash settlement offered by the government in an effort to get them to drop their claim. Elsewhere, a number of Native American groups fought to keep the landscape from being despoiled. In 1991 the Hualapais in Arizona defeated plans to build a uranium strip mine near the lip of the Grand Canyon. A growing sense of pride and self-determination among Native Americans made it possible for them to fight such developments, even when some Native Americans viewed industrial growth as the way to overcome poverty and unemployment in their communities.

Women, too, contributed to increasing cultural diversity in the United States. In the 1992 Congress, the Senate included six women and the House forty-eight—both new records. Women who had demanded equal pay for equal work in the past now began to argue that they should receive equal pay for *comparable* work, so that employees in jobs traditionally relegated to women might still earn a fair wage. Legal cases dealing with this question of comparable work began to make their way through the courts.

Gay men and lesbians began to assert their identities and fight for their rights more aggressively in the 1990s. President Clinton, while compromising on a campaign promise to lift the ban on homosexuals in the military, supported homosexual rights and appointed an openly lesbian woman, Roberta Achtenberg, as an assistant secretary of housing and urban development. A few gay and lesbian characters began to appear on television and in movies, demonstrating a gradually increasing tolerance of and sensitivity to homosexuality in the mainstream culture.

In the spring of 1993, one of the largest marches in United States history took place in

 **RESOURCE DIRECTORY**

Teaching Resources

⭐ **Primary Source Activity** Trying to Break the Cycle of Crime, found in the Unit 7 folder, p. 125, gives the text of a pledge introduced by Jesse L. Jackson to high school students in the Washington, D.C., area.

⭐ **Literature Activity** Living in a New World, found in the Unit 7 folder, pp. 126–128, describes the life of a new immigrant in New York through an excerpt from *When I Was Puerto Rican*, by Esmeralda Santiago.

Washington, D.C., where hundreds of thousands of Americans gathered to demand homosexual rights. The march was an inspiring experience for many gays and lesbians who were both happy to see the large turnout and astonished at the diversity of people within the homosexual community itself. Some Americans, on the other hand, were shocked by the same realizations, and continued to believe that a homosexual lifestyle was morally wrong.

The increasing diversity in the United States was reflected in still other ways. In the religious realm, many new houses of worship arose. The number of Muslim mosques in the New York area and in other cities around the country rose dramatically. Asian groups brought their own temples and shrines to the United States. Meanwhile, groups with long histories in the United States continued to grow.

Multiculturalism and Education

As various groups within the United States began to develop a greater sense of pride in their individual cultural identities, many people began to criticize the way that American history was written and taught. The perspective of history books and school curriculums, critics charged, was biased toward the cultural heritage of Western Europe while ignoring African American, Latino, Asian American, Native American, and other cultures. The desire to embrace rather than exclude minority cultures led to the concept of **multiculturalism.** "The key to multiculturalism," writes professor of education Jaime S. Wurzel, "is awareness"—awareness that one's own way of thinking is shaped by culture, and awareness that there are other, equally valid cultures in the world. Wurzel defines the goal of a multicultural education as follows:

In the 1993 march for gay and lesbian rights in Washington, D.C., some gay men and lesbians marched with their parents. Many others turned out to show their support—including Jesse Jackson (near center, holding banner).

The multicultural style of thinking and feeling is tolerant of cultural differences, the ambiguities of knowledge, and variations in human perspective. It rejects simple answers and fosters inquiry. The multicultural person questions the arbitrary nature of his or her own culture and accepts the proposition that others who are culturally different can enrich their experience. Thus, to be multicultural is to be aware and able to incorporate and synthesize different systems of cultural knowledge into one's own.

Some advocates of multicultural education took the definition of multiculturalism a step further than awareness and tolerance of other cultures. They insisted that for minority students to develop self-esteem, they needed historical role models from their own ethnic groups. Therefore, textbooks in the United States would need to recognize and celebrate the contributions of people from all groups in the shaping of the nation's history.

Others disapproved of this approach. One historian and former adviser to President

Enrichment

Have students imagine that they are history teachers preparing to teach a lesson on this chapter in this textbook. Ask students to locate additional materials that would make the lesson truly multicultural. Suggest that they research materials suitable for students visiting from other countries. Ask them to describe the materials they would choose and why.

3. ASSESS

Section 3 Review Answers

1. (a) bilingual education, see p. 853, (b) multiculturalism, see p. 855

2. In the 1980s and 1990s, more immigrants than ever before came from Asia, Mexico, the Caribbean, and Latin America.

3. The percentage of African Americans, Latinos, Asian Americans, and Native Americans increased while the percentage of white Americans declined.

4. Possible answer: As the multiculturalism movement gains influence, some groups whose members disagree with its goals may find it difficult to express their views or may not have their opinions taken seriously because they fall outside the mainstream.

In Depth

Multicultural Perspectives

The debate on multiculturalism and inclusion in American society is not a wholly new one. In his book *A Different Mirror: A History of Multicultural America,* Ronald Takaki writes: "As Americans we originally came from many different shores, and our diversity has been at the center of the making of America. While our stories contain the memories of different communities, together they inscribe a larger narrative."

 **Interpreting Charts**

Asian Americans will triple their share of the population—from 3 percent to 9 percent—according to the projected figures. The white population will decline as a percentage of the total, from 77 percent to only 60 percent.

Reteach

Have students revise and correct each of the following incorrect statements.
- In the 1980s and 1990s, the percentage of immigrants from Asia and Latin America decreased.
- New immigration patterns had no effect on the overall population of the United States.
- African Americans no longer faced economic inequality in the 1990s.
- Multiculturalism was an effort to increase the number of immigrants from places other than Western Europe.

4. CLOSE

Reinforcing the Big Idea

Increasing diversity within the United States presented new challenges to the "nation of immigrants" in the 1990s.

In Depth

Did You Know?

Representative Maxine Waters (D–Calif.) predicts the course of the 1990s as follows: "The two most profound possibilities for the nineties are the advancements in high technology and of women in significant positions and roles in society. It will be a decade of relearning how to live—the way you pay your bills, the way you communicate, the way your children learn in school, and the way you interact with this diversity."

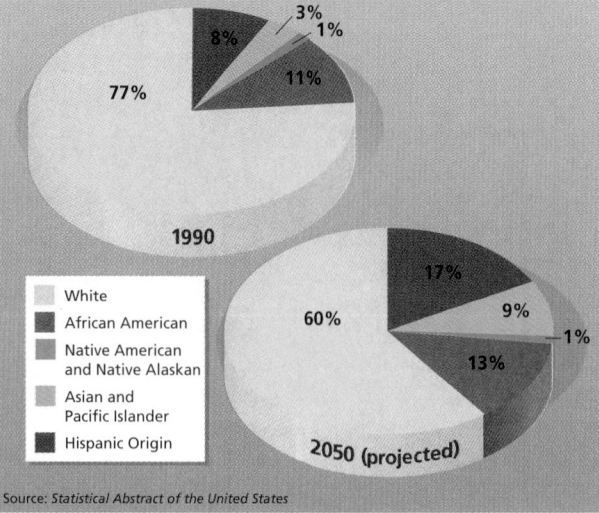

The Changing Ethnic Composition of the United States

3%
1%
8%
11%
77%
1990

White
African American
Native American and Native Alaskan
Asian and Pacific Islander
Hispanic Origin

17%
9%
60%
1%
13%
2050 (projected)

Source: *Statistical Abstract of the United States*

 **Interpreting Charts**
According to the charts, which group in the United States will experience the most dramatic rate of growth between 1990 and 2050? What will happen to the white population as a percent of the total population?

Kennedy, Arthur M. Schlesinger, Jr., criticized what he called "ethnic cheerleading"—using history to make people feel good about themselves rather than to discover the truth about the past. In his book *The Disuniting of America*, Schlesinger pointed out that many great leaders had found inspiration in the lives and writings of people from other ethnic groups. Martin Luther King, Jr., for example, was named after the sixteenth-century monk Martin Luther, who sparked the Protestant Reformation in Europe, and King's ideas about nonviolent resistance were shaped by the work of Indian leader Mohandas Gandhi.

Schlesinger and others worried that extreme interpretations of multiculturalism could work to undermine American society by emphasizing the differences between groups rather than the shared values and experiences of all Americans. Peggy Noonan, once a speech writer for President Reagan, declared that immigrants especially needed to be taught "the great unifying myths that define the dreams, characteristics, and special history of America." Schlesinger elaborated on this point:

O ur task is to combine due appreciation of the splendid diversity of the nation with due emphasis on the great unifying Western ideas of individual freedom, political democracy, and human rights. These are the ideas that define the American nationality—and that today empower people of all continents, races, and creeds.

The debate over multiculturalism was but a new wrinkle in the uniquely American question of how to create a unified society from a nation of diverse immigrants. As author Michael Dorris noted, "Our dynamic American landscape of fabulously interwoven ethnicities has struggled for generations to devise a workable definition of itself." The motto of the United States declared the nation's ongoing commitment to achieve that goal: *E pluribus unum*— "Out of many, one."

SECTION 3 REVIEW

Key Terms, People, and Places
1. Define (a) bilingual education, (b) multiculturalism.

Key Concepts
2. What changes occurred in immigration in the 1980s and 1990s?
3. How did the ethnic composition of the United States change in the 1980s and early 1990s?

Critical Thinking
4. **Predicting Consequences** The movement toward multiculturalism is an attempt to allow all groups to have a voice in American history and policy making. How might the movement actually have the opposite effect on some groups, for example by making it difficult or uncomfortable for some people to speak up?

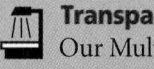 **RESOURCE DIRECTORY**

Teaching Resources

Quiz found in the Unit 7 folder, p. 116, covers the main ideas in this section as well as the key terms.

Chapter Test Forms A and B are found in the Unit 7 folder, pp. 131–136.

Answer Keys found in the Unit 7 folder pp. 143–156, provide answers to all student activities.

Media and Technology

 Transparencies
Our Multicultural Heritage, C-3; Graphic Organizer, G-1

 Guided Reading Audiotape
(English and Spanish)

Computer Test Bank

Predicting Consequences

Many social scientists, especially those who work for the government, try to look into the future. They study what has happened in the past, and on the basis of that, they try to predict what might happen next.

Every ten years the government takes a census of the national population. Social scientists study the evidence from the census to see what they can predict from it. For example, what has been the rate of population growth over the past decades? What does this suggest about the rate of population growth we might expect in the next few years? Which groups are likely to grow faster and which slower?

The table at right focuses on census information on the changing number of families in three ethnic groups in the United States and family income in those groups over a fifteen-year period. Use the following steps to analyze the information in the table and draw on your understanding of history to predict possible trends in the 1990s and beyond.

1. Identify the kinds of information in the table. (a) What does this table tell you about the number of families in various ethnic groups in the United States? (b) By what percentage did the number of Latino families increase between 1975 and 1980? (c) The median income for a given group represents the center of the income distribution—in each group, exactly half of the families earn more and half earn less than the median income. What does it mean if one group has a lower median income than another group?

2. Analyze the rate of change. (a) Which group of families is growing at the fastest rate? (b) Which group's median income has grown at the fastest rate? (c) Which group or groups seem the most economically vulnerable—that is, which have the least stable median incomes?

3. Use your knowledge of history to predict the consequences that your findings might have in the future. You have read in the chapter that the Immigration Act of 1965 allowed more people from places other than Western Europe to immigrate to the United States, and that the Immigration Act of 1990 further increased immigration quotas by 40 percent. (a) How might the table illustrate the consequences of the 1965 law? (b) What consequences might the 1990 law have by the year 2000? (c) If there were an economic recession or boom in the late 1990s, which group or groups might reflect such changes in their median incomes? How do you think the median incomes in the three groups might be affected in these scenarios? (d) What changes in the trends shown on the table would have to take place in order to alter your predictions?

Change in Number of Families and Median Income,* by Selected Ethnic Groups, 1975–1990

	Year	Number of Families (in thousands)	Percent Change (over past 5 years)	Median Income (dollars)	Percent Change (over past 5 years)
White Families	1975	49,873	—	34,662	—
	1980	52,710	+5.7	34,743	+0.2
	1985	54,991	+4.3	35,410	+1.9
	1990	56,803	+3.3	36,915	+4.3
African American Families	1975	5,586	—	21,327	—
	1980	6,317	+13.1	20,103	−5.7
	1985	6,921	+9.6	20,390	+1.4
	1990	7,471	+7.9	21,423	+5.1
Latino Families	1975	2,449	—	23,303	—
	1980	3,235	+29.5	23,342	+0.6
	1985	4,206	+30.0	23,112	−1.0
	1990	4,981	+18.4	23,431	+1.4

* In 1990 dollars

Source: *Statistical Abstract of the United States*

📘 **Historian's Toolbox Activity** Predicting Consequences, found in the Unit 7 folder p. 121, helps students apply the skill by identifying trends and possible consequences of those trends as revealed by an age distribution graph of the United States for the years 1992–2050.

Chapter Review

Understanding Key Terms, People, and Places

Understanding Key Terms, People, and Places

Key Terms
1. apartheid
2. sanctions
3. North American Free Trade Agreement (NAFTA)
4. bilingual education
5. multiculturalism

People
6. Bill Clinton
7. Hillary Rodham Clinton
8. Al Gore
9. Slobodan Milosevic
10. Yitzhak Rabin
11. Yasir Arafat
12. Frederik W. de Klerk
13. Nelson Mandela

Terms For each term above, write a sentence that explains its relation to the Clinton administration, American society in the 1990s, or the relationship of the United States to the rest of the world during the 1990s.

Matching Review the key terms in the list above. If you are not sure of a term's meaning, review its definition in the chapter. Then choose a term from the list that best matches each description below.
1. a systematic separation of the races
2. the treaty promoting free trade between Canada, Mexico, and the United States

True or False Determine whether each statement is true or false. If it is true, write "true." If it is false, change the underlined name to make the statement true.
1. Serbian leader <u>Yitzhak Rabin</u> wanted to preserve the union of Yugoslavia.
2. Weary of constant fighting, PLO leader Yasir Arafat and Israeli prime minister <u>Nelson Mandela</u> committed themselves to negotiating peace in the Middle East.
3. <u>Al Gore</u> led the effort to define a new American health-care system.

Terms

Students should refer to the definitions of the key terms in the chapter to write sentences that show the relation of each word to the Clinton administration, American society in the 1990s, or the relationship of the United States to the rest of the world during the 1990s.

Matching

1. apartheid
2. North American Free Trade Agreement (NAFTA)

True or False

1. false, Slobodan Milosevic
2. false, Yitzhak Rabin
3. false, Hillary Rodham Clinton

Reviewing Main Ideas

1. American voters wanted the government to address the huge federal deficit and related economic difficulties.

2. Clinton had to overcome the public perception that he would say whatever he needed to say to get what he wanted, regardless of whether or not it was the truth.

3. The profile reveals her interests in education and health care and her ability to head an important task force and advise the President.

4. He appointed the Court's second woman justice, Ruth Bader Ginsburg.

5. He wanted to offer affordable health care to all Americans.

6. Yeltsin faced both the challenge of converting to a free market economy after decades of rigid controls and right-wing opposition from Vladimir Zhirinovsky.

7. Zhirinovsky's promises to Russians to end economic hardship and bring a return to national greatness were not unlike those made by fascist leaders in the 1930s. Also, he blamed many of Russia's problems on "foreigners" and Jews.

8. Ethnic hostilities that had been suppressed for years broke out when the republics of Slovenia and Croatia declared independence in 1991. Many Serbs living in those regions were afraid of repression, and fighting broke out among Serbs, Croats, and Muslims.

9. Israel and the Palestinian Liberation Organization signed a peace agreement in 1993. Extremist Israelis and Palestinians impeded the peace process with renewed violence; many issues, such as who would control border crossings

Reviewing Main Ideas

Section 1 (pp. 840–845)
1. What issues did American voters want the federal government to address in 1992?
2. What public perception did Bill Clinton have to overcome in his race for the presidency?
3. What does the profile of Hillary Rodham Clinton reveal about her interests and abilities?
4. How did President Clinton's first appointment to the Supreme Court reflect his commitment to diversity?
5. What were President Clinton's objectives in reforming the health-care system?

Section 2 (pp. 846–851)
6. What challenges faced Boris Yeltsin in 1993?
7. Why were many people around the world concerned by the number of votes won by Zhirinovsky in elections held in Russia in 1993?
8. What caused fighting to break out in Yugoslavia in 1991?

9. What progress did Israel and the Palestinian Liberation Organization make toward peace in the early 1990s? What forces impeded this progress?
10. Explain why the United States became involved in the civil war in Somalia. What was the reaction of the American public to this involvement?
11. What arguments were made in favor of and in opposition to NAFTA?

Section 3 (pp. 852–856)
12. How was the Sun Belt affected by immigration during the 1980s and 1990s?
13. Describe the Immigration Act of 1990 and tell how it differed from the Immigration Reform and Control Act of 1986.
14. What factors led to change in the ethnic and cultural composition of the United States?
15. How have Americans responded to multiculturalism?

around the new Palestinian territories, were left unsettled.

10. When Somalia suffered a famine, George Bush sent American troops as part of a United Nations relief effort; in Clinton's first year in office, a number of Americans were killed or taken hostage. Recalling Vietnam, the American public demanded withdrawal from Somalia.

11. In favor: NAFTA would open up free trade between Mexico, the United States, and Canada. In opposition: the pact would lead to loss of jobs.

12. Many new immigrants—especially those from Asian countries such as Korea and Vietnam—moved into the Sun Belt. They often competed with other residents for jobs and strained public services.

13. The Immigration Act of 1990 increased immigration quotas by 40 percent and eased restrictions that had denied entrance to many people in the past.

14. An increase in immigration from non-European regions and a rise in minority birthrates led to ethnic and cultural change.

15. Many Americans supported multiculturalism, while others complained that attempts to recognize the contributions of every group were extreme.

Thinking Critically

1. **Identifying Assumptions** Columnist Anna Quindlen commented that to some observers Hillary Rodham Clinton was seen as "abrasive, power-hungry and unfeminine" while to others she seemed "smart, outspoken and hard-working." How do you account for these opposing points of view?

2. **Identifying Central Issues** If President Clinton appointed you to head a task force to make recommendations about health-care reform, what steps would you take in order to investigate the issue?

3. **Determining Relevance** What changes, if any, have occurred in the ethnic and cultural composition of your community in recent years? What factors might account for these changes? If your community has not experienced change, how do you explain the lack of change?

Making Connections

1. **Evaluating Primary Sources** Review the primary source excerpt on page 843. Why was the poem appropriate for Bill Clinton's inauguration? For what other twentieth-century President might this poem have been appropriate?

2. **Understanding the Visuals** Look at the pie charts on pages 853 and 856. How is the information in the two charts related? Explain how you might use one of the charts to predict the information shown in the other one.

3. **Writing About the Chapter** Write a television script entitled "The First Years of the Clinton Presidency in Review." First, create a list of what you see as the accomplishments of Clinton's presidency. Then make a list of the challenges that still remain and the ways in which the President might be able to meet them. Next write a draft of your script in which you explain your ideas and note what kinds of images—such as photographs or television news footage—could be used to illustrate your points. Revise your script, making certain that each idea is clearly explained. Proofread your script and draft a final copy.

4. **Using the Graphic Organizer** This graphic organizer uses a web map to organize international events during the early years of the Clinton administration. (a) Which events show a trend toward peace and global unity? (b) Which regions present challenges during the 1990s? (c) On a separate sheet of paper, create your own web map about American society in the 1990s using this graphic organizer as an example.

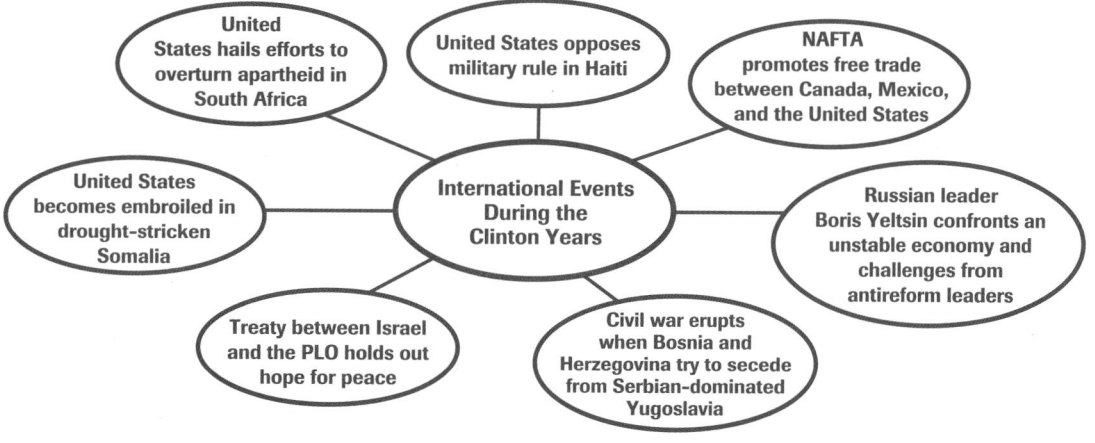

- United States hails efforts to overturn apartheid in South Africa
- United States opposes military rule in Haiti
- NAFTA promotes free trade between Canada, Mexico, and the United States
- United States becomes embroiled in drought-stricken Somalia
- **International Events During the Clinton Years**
- Russian leader Boris Yeltsin confronts an unstable economy and challenges from antireform leaders
- Treaty between Israel and the PLO holds out hope for peace
- Civil war erupts when Bosnia and Herzegovina try to secede from Serbian-dominated Yugoslavia

Thinking Critically

1. Judgments rest on people's expectations of women's roles. For some people an assertive woman can seem abrasive and power-hungry while a man in the same role would be seen as appropriately hard-working.

2. Possible answers: study health-care systems in other countries, investigate health-care costs in the United States, investigate how many people in the United States are without health care, investigate the costs of a universal health-care system, poll health-care providers.

3. Answers will vary according to students' individual communities. Factors that account for change include immigration and higher birthrates among minority groups. Reasons for lack of change include living in a rural area or outside the Sun Belt.

Making Connections

1. The poem is appropriate because it captures the mood of optimism and renewal and the sense of community that the American people hoped for with the election of Bill Clinton. The poem might also have been appropriate for the inauguration of Franklin Delano Roosevelt or John F. Kennedy.

2. The percentage of immigrants from various parts of the world (page 853) will affect the ethnic composition of the nation (page 856). Because the percentages of immigrants from Asia, Mexico, Central America, and South America are high, it makes sense to predict an increase in the percentage of Asian Americans and Americans of Hispanic origin in the coming years. The chart on page 856 makes just such a prediction.

3. Students' scripts should mention Clinton's budget battle, his health-care plan, the tobacco industry, and events in the former Soviet Union, the Middle East, Africa, Eastern Europe, and North America.

4. (a) Peace treaty between the PLO and Israel, efforts to overturn apartheid, NAFTA. (b) Haiti, Somalia, former Yugoslavia, former Soviet Union. (c) Students' graphic organizers should contain information about immigration and multiculturalism.

 **Alternative Assessment**

Final Evaluation
Use the following guidelines to evaluate student projects:

- **Evidence of thoughtfulness** Did the students select an appropriate topic from the chapter to research?
- **Evidence of outside research** Did the students gather relevant information from a variety of sources?
- **Evidence of synthesis** Do projects demonstrate an understanding of the factors that influence government policy? Have students pulled together information from various sources in a coherent presentation?
- **Communication style** Do projects convey information in a clear, purposeful, and appealing way?

Explain that the 1990s have often been referred to as the "information age." Ask students to scan pages 860–861, noting the images and reading the captions. As a group, discuss how the objects help illuminate or present information.

After students have read the feature, ask them to list as many occasions as they can in which they could either use computers or are affected by their use. Point out that a revolutionary invention such as the computer usually fosters the rapid development of other inventions and products. Ask students to find pictures of other objects used to send or process information to add to the feature. Students should write short captions explaining what each item is and how it works.

Discuss with students how new computer and information technology will continue to change American lives. For example, many Americans already use their computers, telephones, and other equipment to link them to a distant office—while they work at home.

Allow students to suggest other ways in which new information technology will change their daily lives.

THE INFORMATION AGE

Ever since people began recording and exchanging information, they've asked four practical questions: What is the best way to store the information? How much information can be put in a space of a certain size? How can later users of the information retrieve it? How can the information be sent to people in other places? You hold one of the best and earliest answers to these questions in your hands—a book. Starting in the last century, people began to develop new forms of communication—the telegraph, the telephone, and the radio. In the last few decades, many more ways to store, retrieve, and transmit information have created an information explosion. *How does each object shown here help send or process information?*

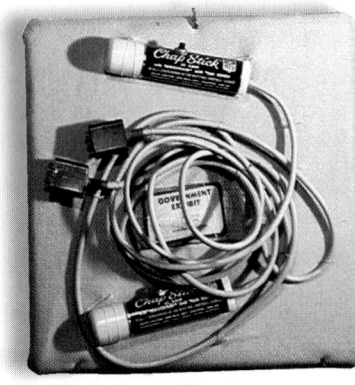

▲ WATERGATE BUGS The burglars who broke into the Democratic National Committee headquarters carried these "bugs." The ability to listen in on private conversations and invade privacy is an unwelcome by-product of the information age.

▼ COMMUNICATIONS SATELLITE Telstar was the world's first communications satellite, relaying signals from one part of earth to another. On the day it was launched, July 10, 1962, it transmitted the first live television pictures from the United States to Europe.

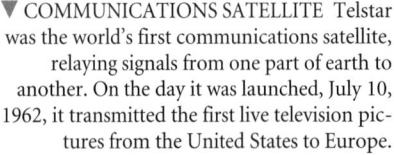

◄ FIBER–OPTIC CABLE Hair-thin glass fibers can carry sound and data long distances using coded light pulses. Cables made of these optical fibers are lighter, cost less to use, and can carry much more information than metal cables.

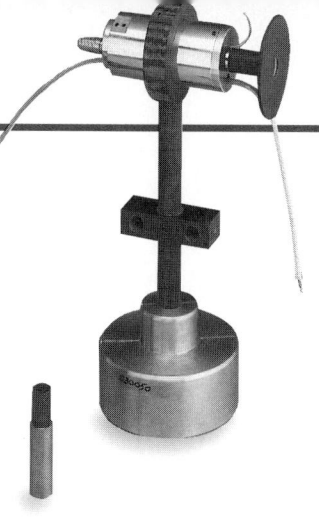

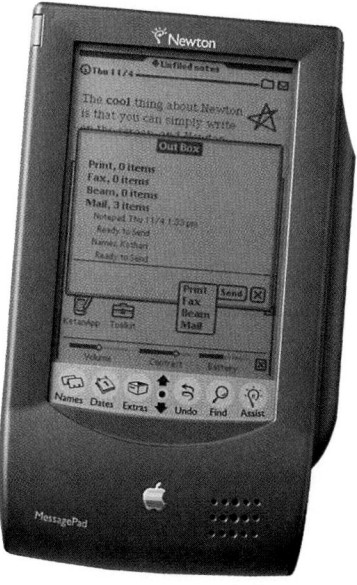

▶ COMPUTER PIONEER
Grace Murray Hopper stands next to the UNIVAC, one of the earliest computers. Hopper pioneered the compiler—the link between a computer's circuits and the computer program. Her work also served as a foundation for COBOL, the most widely used computer language for business applications.

▲ LASER HEAD Theodore Maiman developed this early laser in 1960. Laser light can carry more information than radio waves. Laser light is used to decode information stored on CD-ROM and compact audio disks.

◀ HAND-HELD COMPUTER
The ability of a single silicon chip to store and process information has shrunk the size of the computer. A person can carry this computer anywhere and operate it at any time with a small stylus.

▶ SILICON CHIP
The miracle of the information age is this chip of impure silicon—a microprocessor. Computers with silicon chips are more complex, faster, and can handle many times more information than the original room-size computers that used vacuum tubes and transistors.

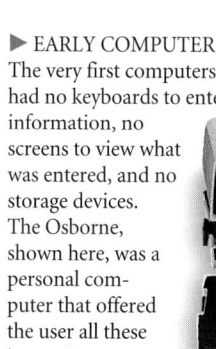

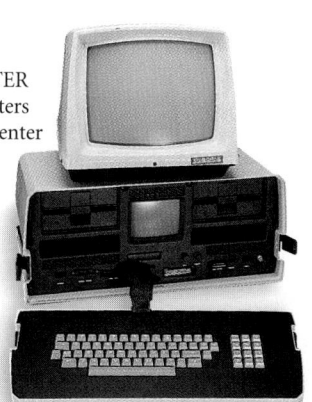

▶ EARLY COMPUTER
The very first computers had no keyboards to enter information, no screens to view what was entered, and no storage devices. The Osborne, shown here, was a personal computer that offered the user all these improvements.

▲ BAR CODES *Mad Magazine* makes fun of bar codes—lines of varying thickness carrying information that can be read by laser light.

FOCUS

Connecting Literature and History

Remind students of the title of their history book: *America: Pathways to the Present*. Ask them what they think is meant by this title. Lead a discussion about the importance of history in shaping the present. Tell students that Maya Angelou's poem has several themes and that one of them is history as the pathway to the present. Ask students to look for this theme as they read the poem.

Then ask students what they think when they hear someone who cannot speak English well. Ask them to write down the words that come into their mind to describe this person. Then, after students have read Amy Tan's piece, ask them whether it made them feel any differently.

INSTRUCT

Divide the class into ten groups and give each group a stanza or two from Maya Angelou's poem to analyze. Ask students to discuss within their groups the possible meaning of their stanzas and then to report back to the class. After every group has reported its findings, discuss the meaning of the entire poem as a class.

Create a composite picture of the class, or all the history classes you teach, by listing on the board the number of African Americans, white Americans, Native Americans, Asian Americans, and Hispanic Americans in the class. Help students calculate the percentage of the total that each of these groups represents. Then, have students turn to the graph at the end of Chapter 26 to examine how the class statistics compare with those of the nation. Discuss any similarities or differences. For example, if your sample has significantly fewer Asian Americans than the national, discuss with students any reasons they can think of for this difference.

On the Pulse of Morning

 Literature

Maya Angelou

INTRODUCTION Maya Angelou is a writer of autobiography, fiction, song, and verse. She is probably best known for her autobiographical work *I Know Why the Caged Bird Sings*, an account of her childhood in segregated Arkansas. She was chosen by Bill Clinton to write a poem to mark the occasion of his inauguration to the office of President in January 1993.

Maya Angelou

The poem she wrote is both a gentle rebuke and an welcoming trumpet call to a better, brighter, more peaceful future for all Americans.

VOCABULARY Before you read the selection, find the meaning of these words in a dictionary: mastodon, sojourn, haven, siege, yoked, brutishness, mendicant.

A ROCK. A RIVER. A TREE
Hosts to species long since departed,
Marked the mastodon.
The dinosaur, who left dry tokens
Of their sojourn here
On our planet floor,
Any broad alarm of their hastening doom
Is lost in the gloom of dust and ages.

BUT TODAY, THE ROCK CRIES OUT TO US, CLEARLY,
forcefully,
Come, you may stand upon my
Back and face your distant destiny,
But seek no haven in my shadow.
I will give you no hiding place down here.

YOU, CREATED ONLY A LITTLE LOWER THAN
The angels, have crouched too long in
The bruising darkness,
Have lain too long
Face down in ignorance.
Your mouths spilling words
Armed for slaughter.
The Rock cries out to us today,
you may stand upon me,
But do not hide your face.

ACROSS THE WALL OF THE WORLD,
A River sings a beautiful song,
It says, come, rest here by my side.

EACH OF YOU A BORDERED COUNTRY,
Delicate and strangely made, proud,
Yet thrusting perpetually under siege.
Your armed struggles for profit
Have left collars of waste upon
My shore, currents of debris upon my breast.
Yet, today I call you to my riverside,
If you will study war no more. Come.
Clad in peace and I will sing the songs
The Creator gave to me when I and the
Tree and the Rock were one.
Before cynicism was a bloody sear across your
Brow and when you yet knew you still
Knew nothing.
The River sang and sings on.

THERE IS A TRUE YEARNING TO RESPOND TO
The singing River and the wise Rock.
So say the Asian, the Hispanic, the Jew
The African, the Native American, the Sioux.
The Catholic, the Muslim, the French, the Greek
The Irish, the Rabbi, the Priest, the Sheikh.

The Gay, the Straight, the Preacher,
The privileged, the homeless, the Teacher.
They all hear
The speaking of the Tree.

THEY HEAR THE FIRST AND LAST OF EVERY TREE
Speaks to humankind today. Come to me, here
    beside the River.
Plant yourself beside the River.

EACH OF YOU, DESCENDANT OF SOME PASSED
On traveller, has been paid for.
You, who gave me my first name, you
Pawnee, Apache, Seneca, you
Cherokee Nation, who rested with me, then
Forced on bloody feet, left me to the
    employment of
Other seekers—desperate for gain,
Starving for gold.
You, the Turk, the Arab, the Swede, the
    German, the Eskimo, the Scot . . .
You the Ashanti, the Yoruba, the Kru, bought
Sold, stolen, arriving on a nightmare
Praying for a dream.
Here, root yourselves beside me.
I am that Tree planted by the River,
Which will not be moved.
I, the Rock, I the River, I the Tree
I am yours—your Passages have been paid.
Lift up your faces, you have a piercing need
For this bright morning dawning for you.
History, despite its wrenching pain,
Cannot be unlived, and if faced
With courage, need not be lived again.

LIFT UP YOUR EYES UPON
This day breaking for you.
Give birth again
To the dream.

LIFT UP YOUR EYES UPON
This day breaking for you.

Give birth again
To the dream.

WOMEN, CHILDREN, MEN,
Take it into the palms of your hands.
Mold it into the shape of your most
Private need. Sculpt it into
The image of your most public self.
Lift up your hearts
Each new hour holds new chances
For new beginnings.
Do not be wedded forever
To fear, yoked eternally
To brutishness.

THE HORIZON LEANS FORWARD.
Offering you space to place new steps of
    change.
Here, on the pulse of this fine day
You may have the courage
To look up and out and upon me, the
Rock, the River, the Tree, your country.
No less to Midas than the mendicant.
No less to you now than the mastodon then.

HERE ON THE PULSE OF THIS NEW DAY
You may have the grace to look up and out
And into your sister's eyes and into
Your brother's face, your country
And say simply
Very simply
With hope
Good morning.

THINKING ABOUT THE SELECTION

1. How is this poem a gentle rebuke?
2. What message does Angelou want to convey about history and its effect on the present?

Critical Thinking

3. **Recognizing Ideologies** Judging by this poem, what beliefs about humankind does Angelou hold?

ANSWERS TO

Thinking About the Selection

1. The poem gently rebukes humankind for "crouching too long in the bruising darkness"; i.e., for fighting with one another and hurting one another.

2. She wants to convey that history is important, but that we must not be immobilized by it. In other words, we must not feel that because something has happened one way in the past it must always happen that way. In addition, we must learn about history in order that we do not repeat the same mistakes that were made in the past.

3. Angelou seems to believe that every human has worth and that a person should not be judged by others but rather accepted and welcomed into society as they are.

SOURCE READINGS

Mother Tongue

Amy Tan

👤 *Literature*

INTRODUCTION Amy Tan was born in 1952, the daughter of Chinese immigrants. As she was growing up, she found that her scores on aptitude tests and in her schoolwork were consistently higher in math and science than they were in English. Surprisingly, she later earned a master's degree in linguistics and went on to write several best-selling novels. Looking back, she attributes her poor performance in English to the fact that the English she heard at home was different from that taught in school. In the piece below, she explores the effect of those different "Englishes" on her life and her mother's life, and wonders whether other Asian Americans have encountered the same difficulty. In a nation that is becoming more and more ethnically diverse, the questions Tan raises may also apply to all Americans.

VOCABULARY Before you read the selection, find the meaning of these words in a dictionary: evoke, wrought, nominalize, belies, empirical, guise, impeccable.

Amy Tan

I am a writer. And by that definition, I am someone who has always loved language. I am fascinated by language in daily life. I spend a great deal of my time thinking about the power of language—the way it can evoke an emotion, a visual image, a complex idea, or a simple truth. Language is the tool of my trade. And I use them all—all the Englishes I grew up with.

Recently, I was made keenly aware of the different Englishes I do use. I was giving a talk to a large group of people, the same talk I had already given to half a dozen other groups. The nature of the talk was about my writing, my life, and my book, *The Joy Luck Club*. The talk was going along well enough, until I remembered one major difference that made the whole talk sound wrong. My mother was in the room. And it was perhaps the first time she had heard me give a lengthy speech, using the kind of English I have never used with her. I was saying things like, "The intersection of memory upon imagination" and "There is an aspect of my fiction that relates to thus-and-thus"—a speech filled with carefully wrought grammatical phrases, burdened, it suddenly seemed to me, with nominalized forms, past perfect tenses, conditional phrases, all the forms of standard English that I had learned in school and through books, the forms of English I did not use at home with my mother.

Just last week, I was walking down the street with my mother, and I again found myself conscious of the English I was using, the English I do use with her. We were talking about the price of new and used furniture and I heard myself saying this: "Not waste money that way." My husband was with us as well, and he didn't notice any switch in my English. And then I realized why. It's because over the twenty years we've been together I've often used the same kind of English with him, and sometimes he even uses it with me. It has become our language of intimacy, a different sort of English that relates to family talk, the language I grew up with.

So you'll have some idea of what this family talk I heard sounds like, I'll quote what my mother said during a recent conversation which I videotaped and then transcribed. During this conversation, my mother was talking about a political gangster in Shanghai[1] who had the same last name as her family's, Du, and how the gangster in his early years wanted to be adopted by her family which was rich by comparison. Later, the gangster became more powerful, far richer than my mother's family, and one day showed up at my mother's wedding to pay his respects. Here's what she said in part:

"Du Yusong having business like fruit stand. Like off the street kind. He is Du like Du Zong—but not Tsung-ming Island people. The local people call putong, the river east side, he belong to that side local people. That man want to ask Du Zong father take him in like become own family. Du Zong father wasn't look

---

[1] a seaport in eastern China

down on him, but didn't take seriously, until that man big like become a mafia. Now important person, very hard to inviting him. Chinese way, come only to show respect, don't stay for dinner. Respect for making big celebration, he shows up. Mean gives lots of respect. Chinese custom. Chinese social life that way. If too important won't have to stay too long. He come to my wedding. I didn't see, I heard it. I gone to boy's side, they have YMCA dinner. Chinese age I was nineteen."

You should know that my mother's expressive command of English belies how much she actually understands. She reads the *Forbes*[2] report, listens to "Wall Street Week,"[3] converses daily with her stock-broker, reads all of Shirley McLaine's[4] books with ease—all kinds of things I can't begin to understand. Yet some of my friends tell me they understand 50 percent of what my mother says. Some say they understand 80 to 90 percent. Some say they understand none of it, as if she were speaking pure Chinese. But to me, my mother's English is perfectly clear, perfectly natural. It's my mother tongue. Her language, as I hear it, is vivid, direct, full of observation and imagery. That was the language that helped shape the way I saw things, expressed things, made sense of the world.

Lately, I've been giving more thought to the kind of English my mother speaks. Like others, I have described it to people as "broken" or "fractured" English. But I wince when I say that. It has always bothered me that I can think of no way to describe it other than "broken," as if it were damaged and needed to be fixed, as if it lacked certain wholeness and soundness. I've heard other terms used, "limited English," for example. But they seem just as bad, as if everything is limited, including people's perceptions of the limited English speaker.

I know this for a fact, because when I was growing up, my mother's "limited" English limited my perception of her. I was ashamed of her English. I believed that her English reflected the quality of what she had to say. That is, because she expressed them imperfectly her thoughts were imperfect. And I had plenty of empirical evidence to suport me: the

---

[2] a magazine of business and finance

[3] a weekly television program that reports business and investment news

[4] an American actress who has written several books

fact that people in department stores, at banks, and at restaurants did not take her seriously, did not give her good service, pretended not to understand her, or even acted as if they did not hear her.

My mother has long realized the limitations of her English as well. When I was fifteen, she used to have me call people on the phone to pretend I was she. In this guise, I was forced to ask for information or even to complain and yell at people who had been rude to her. One time it was a call to her stockbroker in New York. She had cashed out her small portfolio and it just so happened we were going to go to New York the next week, our very first trip outside California. I had to get on the phone and say in an adolescent voice that was not very convincing, "This is Mrs. Tan."

And my mother was standing in the back whispering loudly, "Why he don't send me check, already two weeks late. So mad he lie to me, losing the money."

And then I said in perfect English, "Yes, I'm getting rather concerned. You had agreed to send the check two weeks ago, but it hasn't arrived."

Then she began to talk more loudly. "What he want, I come to New York tell him front of his boss, you cheating me?" And I was trying to calm her down, make her be quiet, while telling the stockbroker, "I can't tolerate any more excuses. If I don't receive the check immediately, I am going to have to speak to your manager when I'm in New York next week." And sure enough, the following week there we were in front of this astonished stockbroker, and I was sitting there red-faced and quiet, and my mother, the real Mrs. Tan, was shouting at his boss in her impeccable broken English.

THINKING ABOUT THE SELECTION

1. Why did Tan make phone calls pretending to be her mother? Why was such an action necessary?
2. What conclusion did Tan draw about her mother because of her "broken" English when she was growing up? How did she later revise that conclusion?

Critical Thinking
3. **Recognizing Bias** How do differences in speech, clothing, and appearances in general affect the treatment of individuals? How might such treatment affect the self-esteem of those individuals?

ANSWERS TO

Thinking About the Selection

1. She did so in order that people might pay attention to what was being said and act on any requests being made. When Tan's mother made the phone calls herself, she was not treated with respect because of her poor English.

2. She thought that the ideas her mother was expressing had less value because they were expressed imperfectly. She later realized that her mother's way of speaking did not mean she was less intelligent or that her ideas had less merit.

3. Individuals are often mistreated because they speak or dress differently from the majority of people around them. This treatment might make such people feel they are less worthwhile as human beings.

A Nation Looks Ahead

In the 1990s, the United States is struggling with issues that have colored its history for hundreds of years. The campaign to deal with the budget deficit and revive the economy is part of an ongoing effort to promote national prosperity. The crusade to accommodate cultural diversity is the result of discussions in the past about how to integrate millions of immigrants into American society. The battle to better the lives of citizens who still face discrimination is rooted in the reform movements that have gradually extended the American dream.

On the foreign front, the need to adjust to an ever-changing world is likewise anchored in the past. The debate about how best to deal with the collapse of communism is related to discussions about the role of the United States in foreign affairs that began in the early days of the republic. These discussions and the decisions that follow from them will expand the scope of United States interests across the North American continent and then well beyond American shores.

As the nation heads toward the twenty-first century, it is trying to revive its sense of purpose. Many citizens are seeking to recover the sense of community that has sustained the United States at key points in the past. They hope that the fundamental values Americans hold in common will bring the nation together to work for a better future. But serious differences of opinion on many issues make consensus hard to come by. The United States, like other nations, has long grappled with the question of how best to deal with conflict over public policy. Sometimes disputes degenerate into violence. More often they are resolved in heated debates in Congress and other arenas where all competing groups can have their say.

In the 1990s Americans sometimes find themselves pitted against one another as they try to decide how to reform the health-care system; under what circumstances—if any—to permit abortion; and what to do about preserving the natural environment. The tone of debate often is shrill, but the discussion itself is a testament to the power of democracy as a means of settling disputes.

Despite the enduring value of democracy as a political foundation, the nation faces tough times as it looks ahead. The economy remains sluggish. Families sometimes cease hoping they can get ahead and resign themselves to trying not to fall behind. Children wonder whether they will be able to do as well as their parents did when they set off on their own.

Still, Americans in the 1990s look ahead with a sense of hope. In spite of its many problems, the United States has tremendous assets to use in confronting the challenges of the modern world. First among these assets are the American people themselves, who have proven themselves capable not only of economic miracles but also of acts of inspiring generosity. Both abilities will be needed as the world enters the twenty-first century.

The challenges that face the country in the 1990s seem both familiar and strange as we head into the future from our vantage point of knowing the past. And we know that, like the immigrants to Ellis or Angel islands in the late 1800s and early 1900s, like the ordinary citizens who struggled through the Great Depression, like the Native Americans rebuilding their communities in the late twentieth century, and like the politicians debating whether to send the country to war in 1990, our paths will be full of decisions and unexpected turns. As we choose our way among the paths of the present, we, too, are shaping the nation's future.

From Sea to Shining Sea by Jacqueline Paton, Merrimack, New Hampshire.

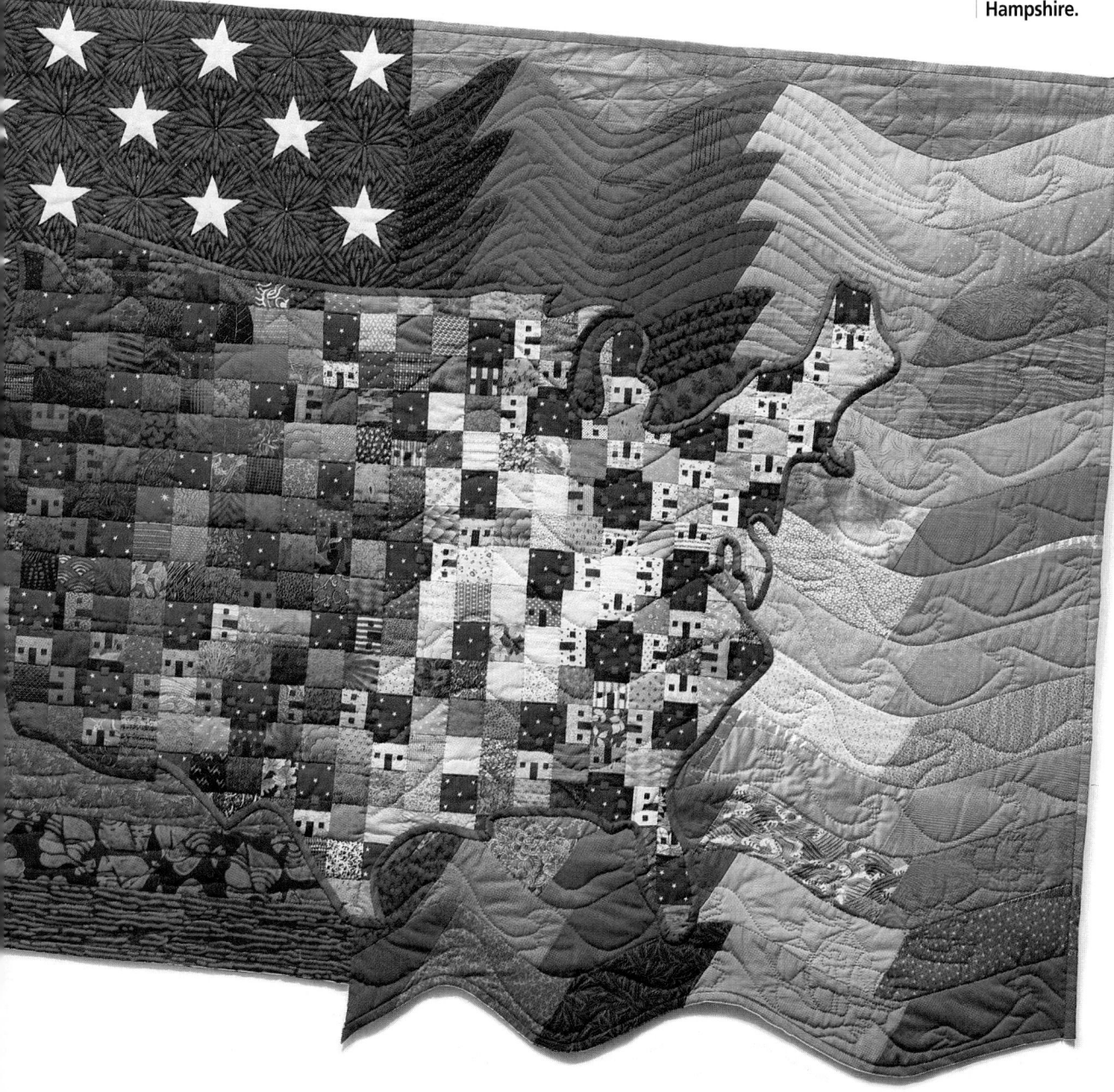

Reference Section

A Correlation to
Prentice Hall Literature
The American Experience (© 1994)

Chapter	Author	Title	Genre
UNIT ONE The Nation's Beginnings to 1840			
1 **Encounters and Colonies to 1754**	Pima	"From the Houses of Magic" Page 26	oral tradition
2 **The Revolutionary Era, 1754–1783**	Thomas Paine	From *The Crisis*, Number 1 Page 122	essay
3 **The Constitution of the United States, 1783–1789**	Michel-Guillaume Jean de Crèvecoeur	From *Letters from an American Farmer* Page 148	literary letter
4 **From Jefferson through Jackson, 1789–1840**	Abigail Adams	"Letter to Her Daughter From the New White House" Page 142	letter
UNIT TWO The United States, 1815–1915			
5 **Reform and Expansion, 1815–1860**	Henry David Thoreau	From *Civil Disobedience* Page 262	essay
6 **Civil War and Reconstruction, 1848–1877**	Frederick Douglass	From *My Bondage and My Freedom* Page 364	autobiography
7 **Changing Frontiers, 1860–1910**	Bernard Malamud	*The First Seven Years* Page 822	autobiography
8 **Cultural and Social Transformations, 1870–1915**	Mark Twain	From *Life on the Mississippi* Page 438	narrative account
UNIT THREE The United States on the Brink of Change, 1890–1920			
9 **Becoming a World Power, 1890–1913**	Ambrose Bierce	*An Occurrence at Owl Creek Bridge* Page 464	short story
10 **The Era of Progressive Reform, 1890–1920**	Carl Sandburg	"Chicago" Page 742	poem
11 **The World War I Era, 1914–1920**	Ernest Hemingway	*In Another Country* Page 580	short story

Continued on page 870

LITERATURE CORRELATION

A Correlation to Prentice Hall Literature *The American Experience* (continued)

Chapter	Author	Title	Genre
UNIT FOUR Boom Times to Hard Times, 1919–1938			
12 **A Stormy Era, 1919–1929**	John Dos Passos	*Tin Lizzie* Page 670	biography
13 **Crash and Depression, 1929–1933**	F. Scott Fitzgerald	*Winter Dreams* Page 588	short story
14 **The New Deal, 1933–1938**	Carl Sandburg	From "The People, Yes" Page 740	poem
UNIT FIVE Hot and Cold War, 1939–1960			
15 **World War II, 1939–1945**	Randall Jarrell	"The Death of the Ball Turret Gunner" Page 979 "Losses" Page 980	poems
16 **World War II at Home, 1941–1945**	W. H. Auden	"The Unknown Citizen" Page 783	poem
17 **The Cold War and American Society, 1945–1960**	Ezra Pound	"In a Station of the Metro" Page 700 "The River-Merchant's Wife: A Letter" Page 701 "Canto 13" Page 703	poems
18 **The Postwar Years at Home, 1945–1960**	Joan Didion	*On the Mall* Page 916	essay
UNIT SIX The Upheaval of the Sixties, 1960–1975			
19 **The Kennedy and Johnson Years, 1960–1968**	Robert Hayden	"Frederick Douglass" Page 1004	poem
20 **The Civil Rights Movement, 1960–1968**	Colleen McElroy	"For My Children" Page 1010	poem
21 **Continuing Social Revolution, 1960–1975**	N. Scott Momaday	*A Vision Beyond Time and Place* Page 924	essay
22 **The Vietnam War and American Society, 1960–1975**	Carson McCullers	*The Mortgaged Heart* Page 902	essay
UNIT SEVEN Continuity and Change, 1968–Present			
23 **The Nixon Years, 1968–1974**	John Updike	*The Slump* Page 854	short story
24 **The Post-Watergate Period, 1974–1980**	Simon Ortiz	"Hunger in New York City" Page 1020	poem
25 **High Tide of the Conservative Movement, 1980–1992**	Sandra Cisneros	*Straw Into Gold: The Metamorphosis of the Everyday* Page 930	essay
26 **The Promise of Change, 1992– Present**	Amy Tan	*Mother Tongue* Page 946	essay

LITERATURE CORRELATION

The Declaration of Independence

In Congress, July 4, 1776

THE UNANIMOUS DECLARATION OF THE THIRTEEN UNITED STATES OF AMERICA,

When in the Course of human events, it becomes necessary for one people to dissolve the political bands which have connected them with another, and to assume among the Powers of the earth, the separate and equal station to which the Laws of Nature and of Nature's God entitle them, a decent respect to the opinions of mankind requires that they should declare the causes which impel them to the separation.

We hold these truths to be self-evident, that all men are created equal, that they are endowed by their Creator with certain unalienable Rights, that among these are Life, Liberty and the pursuit of Happiness. That to secure these rights, Governments are instituted among Men, deriving their just powers from the consent of the governed, That whenever any Form of Government becomes destructive of these ends, it is the Right of the People to alter or to abolish it, and to institute new Government, laying its foundation on such principles and organizing its powers in such form, as to them shall seem most likely to effect their Safety and Happiness. Prudence, indeed, will dictate that Governments long established should not be changed for light and transient causes; and accordingly all experience hath shown, that mankind are more disposed to suffer, while evils are sufferable, than to right themselves by abolishing the forms to which they are accustomed. But when a long train of abuses and usurpations, pursuing invariably the same Object evinces a design to reduce them under absolute Despotism, it is their right, it is their duty, to throw off such Government, and to provide new Guards for their future security.—Such has been the patient sufferance of these Colonies; and such is now the necessity which constrains them to alter their former Systems of Government. The history of the present King of Great Britain is a history of repeated injuries and usurpations, all having in direct object the establishment of an absolute Tyranny over these States. To prove this, let Facts be submitted to a candid world.

He has refused his Assent to Laws, the most wholesome and necessary for the public good.

He has forbidden his Governors to pass Laws of immediate and pressing importance, unless suspended in their operation till his Assent should be obtained; and when so suspended, he has utterly neglected to attend to them.

He has refused to pass other Laws for the accommodation of large districts of people, unless those people would relinquish the right of Representation in the Legislature, a right inestimable to them and formidable to tyrants only.

He has called together legislative bodies at places unusual, uncomfortable, and distant from the depository of their Public Records, for the sole purpose of fatiguing them into compliance with his measures.

He has dissolved Representative Houses repeatedly, for opposing with manly firmness his invasions on the rights of the people.

He has refused for a long time, after such dissolutions, to cause others to be elected; whereby the Legislative powers, incapable of Annihilation, have returned to the People at large for their exercise; the State remaining in the mean time exposed to all the dangers of invasions from without, and convulsions within.

He has endeavored to prevent the population of these States; for that purpose obstructing the Laws for Naturalization of Foreigners; refusing to pass others to encourage their migration hither, and raising the conditions of new Appropriations of Lands.

He has obstructed the Administration of Justice, by refusing his Assent to Laws for establishing Judiciary powers.

He has made Judges dependent on his Will alone for the tenure of their offices, and the amount and payment of their salaries.

He has erected a multitude of New Offices, and sent hither swarms of Officers to harass our people and eat out their substance.

He has kept among us in time of peace, Standing Armies, without the Consent of our legislature.

He has affected to render the Military independent of and superior to the Civil power.

He has combined with others to subject us to a jurisdiction foreign to our constitutions, and unacknowledged by our laws; giving his Assent to their Acts of pretended Legislation:

For Quartering large bodies of armed troops among us:

For protecting them, by a mock Trial, from Punishment for any Murders which they should commit on the Inhabitants of these States:

For cutting off our Trade with all parts of the world:

For imposing taxes on us without our Consent:

For depriving us in many cases, of the benefits of Trial by Jury:

For transporting us beyond Seas to be tried for pretended offenses:

For abolishing the free System of English Laws in a neighbouring Province, establishing therein an Arbitrary government, and enlarging its Boundaries so as to render it at once an example and fit instrument for introducing the same absolute rule into these Colonies:

For taking away our Charters, abolishing our most valuable Laws, and altering fundamentally the Forms of our Governments;

For suspending our own Legislature, and declaring themselves invested with Power to legislate for us in all cases whatsoever.

He has abdicated Government here, by declaring us out of his Protection, and waging War against us.

He has plundered our seas, ravaged our Coasts, burned our towns, and destroyed the lives of our people.

He is at this time transporting large armies of foreign mercenaries to compleat the works of death, desolation and tyranny, already begun with circumstances of Cruelty and perfidy scarcely paralleled in the most barbarous ages, and totally unworthy the Head of a civilized nation.

He has constrained our fellow Citizens taken Captive on the high Seas to bear Arms against their Country, to become the executioners of their friends and Brethren, or to fall themselves by their Hands.

He has excited domestic insurrections amongst us, and has endeavored to bring on the inhabitants of our frontiers the merciless Indian Savages, whose known rule of warfare, is an undistinguished destruction of all ages, sexes, and conditions.

In every stage of these Oppressions We have Petitioned for Redress in the most humble terms. Our repeated Petitions have been answered only by repeated injury. A Prince, whose character is thus marked by every act which may define a Tyrant, is unfit to be the ruler of a free People.

Nor have We been wanting in attentions to our British brethren. We have warned them from time to time of attempts by their legislature to extend an unwarrantable jurisdiction over us. We have reminded them of the circumstances of our emigration and settlement here. We have appealed to their native justice and magnanimity, and we have conjured them by the ties of our common kindred to disavow these usurpations, which, would inevitably interrupt our connections and correspondence. They too have been deaf to the voice of justice and of consanguinity. We must, therefore, acquiesce in the necessity, which denounces our Separation, and hold them, as we hold the rest of mankind, Enemies in War, in Peace Friends.

We, therefore, the Representatives of the united States of America, in General Congress, Assembled, appealing to the Supreme Judge of the world for the rectitude of our intentions, do, in the Name, and by the Authority of the good People of these Colonies, solemnly publish and declare, That these United Colonies are, and of Right ought to be Free and Independent States; that they are Absolved from all Allegiance to the British Crown, and that all political connection between them and the State of Great Britain, is and ought to be totally dissolved, and that as Free and Independent States, they have full Power to levy War, conclude Peace, contract Alliances, establish Commerce, and to do all other Acts and Things which Independent States may of right do. And for the support of this Declaration, with a firm reliance on the protection of Divine Providence, we mutually pledge to each other our Lives, our Fortunes and our sacred Honor.

JOHN HANCOCK
President of the Continental Congress 1775–1777

NEW HAMPSHIRE
- Josiah Bartlett
- William Whipple
- Matthew Thornton

MASSACHUSETTS BAY
- Samuel Adams
- John Adams
- Robert Treat Paine
- Elbridge Gerry

RHODE ISLAND
- Stephan Hopkins
- William Ellery

CONNECTICUT
- Roger Sherman
- Samuel Huntington
- William Williams
- Oliver Wolcott

NEW YORK
- William Floyd
- Philip Livingston
- Francis Lewis
- Lewis Morris

NEW JERSEY
- Richard Stockton
- John Witherspoon
- Francis Hopkinson
- John Hart
- Abraham Clark

DELAWARE
- Caesar Rodney
- George Read
- Thomas McKean

MARYLAND
- Samuel Chase
- William Paca
- Thomas Stone
- Charles Carroll of Carrollton

VIRGINIA
- George Wythe
- Richard Henry Lee
- Thomas Jefferson
- Benjamin Harrison
- Thomas Nelson, Jr.
- Francis Lightfoot Lee
- Carter Braxton

PENNSYLVANIA
- Robert Morris
- Benjamin Rush
- Benjamin Franklin
- John Morton
- George Clymer
- James Smith
- George Taylor
- James Wilson
- George Ross

NORTH CAROLINA
- William Hooper
- Joseph Hewes
- John Penn

SOUTH CAROLINA
- Edward Rutledge
- Thomas Heyward, Jr.
- Thomas Lynch, Jr.
- Arthur Middleton

GEORGIA
- Button Gwinnett
- Lyman Hall
- George Walton

Source: Documents of American History, Volume I

The Constitution of the United States of America

PREAMBLE

We the people of the United States, in order to form a more perfect union, establish justice, insure domestic tranquility, provide for the common defense, promote the general welfare, and secure the blessings of liberty to ourselves and our posterity, do ordain and establish this Constitution for the United States of America.

The Preamble, or opening paragraph of the Constitution, establishes the fundamental assumption of American government: that government derives its power from the people. "We the people" are the most important words in the Constitution, as President Abraham Lincoln emphasized in 1863 when he called the United States a "government of the people, by the people, and for the people" in his Gettysburg Address. Presidents and other politicians today regularly invoke "the people" as the source of their power when making important speeches.

The Preamble also states, however, that the purpose of the Constitution is to create an orderly, stable, and just society. The authors of the Constitution were worried about the impact of too much democracy in the new American nation, fearing that what "We the people" wanted would not always lead to "a more perfect union" or insure "domestic tranquility." In fact, the tension between the desire for democracy and the wish for a stable social order is one of the most important and enduring themes in American history.

Article I
LEGISLATIVE BRANCH
Section 1 *Legislative Powers; The Congress*

All legislative powers herein granted shall be vested in a Congress of the United States, which shall consist of a Senate and House of Representatives.

SECTION 1 The Constitution outlines the legislative branch first, for this part of the federal government is the closest and most directly responsible to the people. The men who wrote the Constitution deliberately established a bicameral, or two-part, legislative branch, whose two houses would not only balance each other but also modify the impact of "the people." All legislation requires the approval of both the House of Representatives and the Senate.

Section 2 *House of Representatives*

1. Election of Members The House of Representatives shall be composed of members chosen every second year by the people of the several states, and the electors in each state shall have the qualifications requisite for electors of the most numerous branch of the state legislature.

CLAUSE 1 The Founding Fathers wanted the House of Representatives to be the part of the federal government most responsive to the will of the people. They made sure that voters could change the membership of the House frequently by requiring every member to run for office every two years. Today, the House is the only part of the federal government the people could change in one election; if the people wished, they could replace all 435 members of the House every two years.

2. Qualifications No person shall be a representative who shall not have attained to the age of twenty-five years, and been seven years a citizen of the United States, and who shall not, when elected, be an inhabitant of that state in which he shall be chosen.

CLAUSE 2 The purpose of these requirements was to make certain that representatives actually live among the people whom they represent. The authors of the Constitution wanted to avoid absentee legislators—representatives who did not actually live in their districts—something that happened frequently in the British Parliament. They wanted to ensure direct contact between the people and their representatives.

3. Apportionment Representatives ~~and direct taxes~~* shall be apportioned among the several states which may be included within this Union, according to their respective numbers, ~~which shall be determined by adding to the whole number of free persons, including those bound to service for a term of years and excluding Indians not taxed, three fifths of all other persons.~~ The actual enumeration shall be made within three years after the first meeting of the Congress of the United States, and within every subsequent term of ten years, in such manner as they shall by law direct. The number of representatives shall not exceed one for every thirty thousand, but each state shall have at least one representative; ~~and until such enumeration shall be made, the state of New Hampshire shall be entitled to choose three, Massachusetts eight, Rhode Island and Providence Plantations one, Connecticut five, New York six, New Jersey four, Pennsylvania eight,~~

---

* The black lines indicate portions of the Constitution altered by subsequent amendments to the document or that no longer apply.

Note: Spelling and capitalization have been modernized.

Source: Documents of American History, Volume I

THE CONSTITUTION

~~Delaware one, Maryland six, Virginia ten, North Carolina five, South Carolina five, and Georgia three.~~

CLAUSE 3 As a result of this provision, the United States government must conduct a census of the population every ten years. The primary purpose of the census is to determine how many members of Congress each state will have. The decision to count only three fifths of the total number of enslaved persons was a compromise between southerners, who wanted the total number to be counted in order to have more members in Congress, and northerners, who wanted southerners to have fewer representatives and consequently less influence in the legislature. This clause became controversial in the 1800s when abolitionists and slaveholders began to argue about whether the Constitution sanctioned slavery. Notice that the language is very vague. The word *slaves* does not appear, just "other persons." The Thirteenth Amendment effectively repealed this clause when it made slavery illegal in 1865 following the Civil War.

4. Filling Vacancies When vacancies happen in the representation from any state, the executive authority thereof shall issue writs of election to fill such vacancies.

CLAUSE 4 This clause allows the governor of each state to call special elections to replace members of Congress who die or resign in the middle of their terms.

5. Officers; Impeachment The House of Representatives shall choose their speaker and other officers; and shall have the sole power of impeachment.

CLAUSE 5 Both the British Parliament and the colonial legislatures had fought long and hard to obtain the right to control their own affairs, meaning that the members rather than a king or president would choose their officers. Imagine how much more power the President of the United States would have in Congress if he or she could simply appoint the Speaker of the House and other officials. Another cherished right was the power to impeach, or accuse, government officials of committing crimes or abusing their offices. Impeachment proceedings against a federal official or judge must always begin in the House.

Section 3 *Senate*

1. Composition; Term The Senate of the United States shall be composed of two senators from each state ~~chosen by the legislature thereof,~~ for six years; and each senator shall have one vote.

CLAUSE 1 By giving each state two senators, the authors of the Constitution sought to prevent large states with bigger populations from dominating smaller states. To make the Senate less directly responsive to the people's wishes, senators were to have six-year terms and be chosen by state legislators. The people did not directly elect senators until the Seventeenth Amendment was ratified in 1913.

2. Classification; Filling Vacancies Immediately after they shall be assembled in consequence of the first election, they shall be divided as equally as may be into three classes. The seats of the senators of the first class shall be vacated at the expiration of the second year, of the second class at the expiration of the fourth year, and of the third class at the expiration of the sixth year, so that one third may be chosen every second year; ~~and if vacancies happen by resignation, or otherwise, during the recess of the legislature of any State, the executive thereof may make temporary appointments until the next meeting of the legislature, which shall then fill such vacancies.~~

CLAUSE 2 This clause ensures that the membership of the Senate, unlike that of the House, cannot be changed in one election. In the Senate, terms are staggered, so it would take three elections and six years to replace all 100 senators. Longer terms tend to make the Senate a more independent body than the House; its members are a little more likely to vote the way they wish rather than the way they think people might want them to vote.

3. Qualifications No person shall be a senator who shall not have attained to the age of thirty years, and been nine years a citizen of the United States, and who shall not, when elected, be an inhabitant of that state for which he shall be chosen.

CLAUSE 3 This clause is meant to ensure that senators will not be absentees, that they will represent the people and places they know. When politicians who have grown up in one state run for the Senate in another state, they are often accused of being outsiders. Massachusetts native Robert F. Kennedy overcame this charge when he was elected senator from New York in 1964, but Connecticut-born George Bush could not do so when he ran for the Senate from Texas and lost in 1970.

4. President of the Senate The Vice President of the United States shall be president of the Senate, but shall have no vote, unless they be equally divided.

CLAUSE 4 During the first few decades of the republic, the Vice President generally attended the meetings of the Senate. Now he usually attends only on ceremonial occasions or when the Senate is equally divided over a bill.

5. Other Officers The Senate shall choose their other officers, and also a president pro tempore, in the absence of the Vice President, or when he shall exercise the office of the President of the United States.

CLAUSE 5 This sentence ensures that no other officials, such as the President, can exercise undue influence in the Senate by controlling the selection of its officers.

6. Impeachment Trials The Senate shall have the sole power to try all impeachments. When sitting for that purpose, they shall be on oath or affirmation. When the President of the United States is tried, the Chief Justice shall preside: and no person shall be convicted without the concurrence of two thirds of the members present.

CLAUSE 6 If the House votes to impeach, or indict, a federal official, the Senate becomes a court to try that person. The senators are like members of a jury. They listen to lawyers present evidence for and against the accused and then vote to convict or acquit. To make sure that an official is not impeached for frivolous or partisan reasons, the Constitution requires a two thirds vote in the Senate in order to convict someone. In 1974 President

Richard Nixon resigned the presidency when he realized that more than 67 senators would vote to convict him.

7. Penalty on Conviction Judgment in cases of impeachment shall not extend further than to removal from office, and disqualification to hold and enjoy any office of honor, trust or profit under the United States: but the party convicted shall nevertheless be liable and subject to indictment, trial, judgment and punishment, according to law.

CLAUSE 7 Under the Constitution, the only punishment for officials who are impeached and convicted is that they can no longer be part of the United States government. The regular criminal court system must determine all jail terms, fines, and other punishments. In 1974 President Gerald Ford pardoned Richard Nixon for all illegal acts he may have committed as President, even though Nixon was never actually convicted of any specific crime.

Section 4 *Elections and Meetings*

1. Election of Congress The times, places and manner of holding elections for senators and representatives, shall be prescribed in each state by the legislature thereof; but the Congress may at any time by law make or alter such regulations, except as to the places of choosing senators.

CLAUSE 1 The states decide how and when to choose members of Congress, although Congress reserves the right to change the ways in which they do it. In 1842 Congress required that elections be held on the first Tuesday after the first Monday in November in even-numbered years.

2. Sessions The Congress shall assemble at least once in every year, and such meeting shall be on the first Monday in December, unless they shall by law appoint a different day.

CLAUSE 2 This clause guarantees that Congress will meet on a regular basis. A few decades before the American Revolution, kings and royal governors had called legislatures into session and dismissed them at their pleasure. In the 1630s, King Charles I refused to call Parliament and tried to govern England without a legislature. The Constitution makes certain that this cannot happen in the United States. Congress, not the President, decides when it will meet. In 1933 the Twentieth Amendment set the annual opening date as January 3, rather than the first Monday in December.

Section 5 *Legislative Proceedings*

1. Organization Each house shall be the judge of the elections, returns and qualifications of its own members, and a majority of each shall constitute a quorum to do business; but a smaller number may adjourn from day to day, and may be authorized to compel the attendance of absent members, in such manner, and under such penalties, as each house may provide.

2. Rules Each house may determine the rules of its proceedings, punish its members for disorderly behavior, and, with the concurrence of two thirds, expel a member.

CLAUSES 1 AND 2 These clauses were also designed to ensure that Congress would maintain control of its activities. They protect the integrity of the people's representatives from interference by the President or judges.

3. Record Each house shall keep a journal of its proceedings, and from time to time publish the same, excepting such parts as may in their judgment require secrecy; and the yeas and nays of the members of either house on any question, shall, at the desire of one fifth of those present, be entered on the journal.

CLAUSE 3 The Founders recognized that the people needed some sort of record of what their representatives said and how they voted in order to hold them accountable for their actions. Although the Constitution requires Congress to maintain a journal—today published as the *Congressional Record*—it also gives Congress the power to keep some matters secret. For example, representatives might not want to publish their debates on an issue involving national security.

4. Adjournment Neither house, during the session of Congress, shall, without the consent of the other, adjourn for more than three days, nor to any other place than that in which the two houses shall be sitting.

CLAUSE 4 Some of the Constitution's clauses may seem strange today. Why, for example, would the men who wrote the Constitution care about adjournments? The answer lies in colonial and British history. Sometimes one house of Parliament or a colonial legislature would leave or adjourn in order to prevent some legislation from passing or to hold up proceedings. This clause guarantees that, while they may not always agree with each other, the two houses of Congress must deal with each other. One house cannot adjourn unless the other agrees to an adjournment.

Section 6 *Compensation, Immunities, and Disabilities of Members*

1. Salaries; Immunities The senators and representatives shall receive a compensation for their services, to be ascertained by law, and paid out of the treasury of the United States. They shall, in all cases, except treason, felony and breach of the peace, be privileged from arrest during their attendance at the session of their respective houses, and in going to and returning from the same; and for any speech or debate in either house, they shall not be questioned in any other place.

CLAUSE 1 Imagine what would happen if members of Congress could be arrested for what they say. This idea may seem ridiculous now, but it actually happened in the 1600s and 1700s. If Presidents or judges could arrest members of Congress, they could directly interfere with their proceedings. This clause essentially guaranteed that members of Congress did not have to worry about arbitrary interference by the executive and judicial branches.

2. Restrictions on Other Employment No senator or representative shall, during the time for which he was elected, be appointed to any civil office under the authority of the United States, which shall have been created, or the emoluments whereof shall have been increased during such time; and no person holding any office under the United States shall be a member of either house during his continuance in office.

Section 7 *Revenue Bills, President's Veto*

1. Revenue Bills All bills for raising revenue shall originate in the House of Representatives; but the Senate may propose or concur with amendments as on other bills.

2. How a Bill Becomes a Law; the Veto Every bill which shall have passed the House of Representatives and the Senate, shall, before it become a law, be presented to the President of the United States; if he approve he shall sign it, but if not he shall return it, with his objections to that house in which it shall have originated, who shall enter the objections at large on their journal, and proceed to reconsider it. If after such reconsideration two thirds of that house shall agree to pass the bill, it shall be sent, together with the objections, to the other house, by which it shall likewise be reconsidered, and if approved by two thirds of that house, it shall become a law. But in all such cases the votes of both houses shall be determined by yeas and nays, and the names of the persons voting for and against the bill shall be entered on the journal of each house respectively. If any bill shall not be returned by the President within ten days (Sundays excepted) after it shall have been presented to him, the same shall be a law, in like manner as if he had signed it, unless the Congress by their adjournment prevent its return, in which case it shall not be a law.

3. Resolutions Passed by Congress Every order, resolution, or vote to which the concurrence of the Senate and House of Representatives may be necessary (except on a question of adjournment) shall be presented to the President of the United States; and before the same shall take effect, shall be approved by him, or being disapproved by him, shall be repassed by two thirds of the Senate and House of Representatives, according to the rules and limitations prescribed in the case of a bill.

Section 8 *Powers of Congress*

The Congress shall have power

1. To lay and collect taxes, duties, imposts and excises, to pay the debts and provide for the common defense and general welfare of the United States; but all duties, imposts and excises shall be uniform throughout the United States;

2. To borrow money on the credit of the United States;

3. To regulate commerce with foreign nations, and among the several states, and with the Indian tribes;

4. To establish an uniform rule of naturalization, and uniform laws on the subject of bankruptcies throughout the United States;

another attempt to create uniform economic regulations throughout the United States.

5. To coin money, regulate the value thereof, and of foreign coin, and fix the standard of weights and measures;

6. To provide for the punishment of counterfeiting the securities and current coin of the United States;

CLAUSES 5 AND 6 These two clauses ensure that there is only one kind of money in the United States. Without such regulation, the states or private institutions could issue their own money. The members of the Constitutional Convention included these clauses to create a stable and predictable medium of exchange throughout the United States.

7. To establish post offices and post roads;

CLAUSE 7 Just as Congress has the power to regulate commerce—the exchange of goods—so, too, it has the power to regulate the exchange of information and news through the mails. Without this power, Americans might have to contend with fifty different postal services in the United States.

8. To promote the progress of science and useful arts, by securing for limited times to authors and inventors the exclusive right to their respective writings and discoveries;

CLAUSE 8 This clause gives Congress the power to regulate the exchange of knowledge in the United States. Congress, not the states, issues patents and copyright protection to people who come up with new ideas or technology.

9. To constitute tribunals inferior to the Supreme Court;

CLAUSE 9 This brief clause grants Congress an important power—the right to create the federal court system below the level of the Supreme Court. Because the Constitution itself does not explain the judicial system in great detail, Congress has had enormous leeway in the creation of this system.

10. To define and punish piracies and felonies committed on the high seas and offenses against the law of nations;

11. To declare war, grant letters of marque and reprisal, and make rules concerning captures on land and water;

CLAUSES 10 AND 11 Congress also has the power to regulate international relations, particularly any matters concerning war.

12. To raise and support armies, but no appropriation of money to that use shall be for a longer term than two years;

CLAUSE 12 Although Congress can form armies to defend American interests, it can only pay for them for two years at a time. This clause reflects the deep fear the Founders and other former colonists had about standing, or professional, armies. They worried that government officials might use permanent armies to stifle opposition and take away liberties, as kings had done in the past.

13. To provide and maintain a navy;

CLAUSE 13 Following a British constitutional tradition, the delegates at the Constitutional Convention felt no need to restrict naval expenditures to two years. They viewed the navy as far less of a threat to civil authority than the army.

14. To make rules for the government and regulation of the land and naval forces;

CLAUSE 14 These rules are spelled out in the Uniform Code of Military Justice, passed by Congress in 1950.

15. To provide for calling forth the militia to execute the laws of the Union, suppress insurrections and repel invasions;

16. To provide for organizing, arming, and disciplining, the militia, and for governing such part of them as may be employed in the service of the United States, reserving to the states respectively, the appointment of the officers, and the authority of training the militia according to the discipline prescribed by Congress;

CLAUSES 15 AND 16 The National Defense Act of 1916 made each state's militia part of the National Guard. Under normal circumstances, each state's governor is in charge of that state's National Guard; however, the President has the power to call into federal service any or all National Guard units when necessary, as President George Bush did during the 1991 Persian Gulf War.

17. To exercise exclusive legislation in all cases whatsoever, over such district (not exceeding ten miles square) as may, by cession of particular states, and the acceptance of Congress, become the seat of the government of the United States, and to exercise like authority over all places purchased by the consent of the legislature of the state in which the same shall be, for the erection of forts, magazines, arsenals, dockyards, and other needful buildings; and

CLAUSE 17 This clause provides for what would become the nation's capital, Washington, D.C., and for federal establishments in the states. Without this provision, Philadelphia or some other large city might have become the nation's permanent capital.

18. To make all laws which shall be necessary and proper for carrying into execution the foregoing powers, and all other powers vested by this Constitution in the government of the United States, or in any department or officer thereof.

CLAUSE 18 No other clause in the Constitution has been used more often by judges and federal officials to increase the power of the federal government. Read loosely, the "necessary and proper," or "elastic," clause says that Congress may take any steps not otherwise prohibited by the Constitution to guarantee that the other provisions of the Constitution are carried out.

Section 9 *Powers Denied to Congress*

1. The Slave Trade ~~The migration or importation of such persons as any of the states now existing shall think proper to admit, shall not be prohibited by the Congress prior to the year one thousand eight hundred and eight, but a tax or duty may be imposed on such importation, not exceeding ten dollars for each person.~~

CLAUSE 1 Although the Constitution outlawed the importation of enslaved persons into the United States, this provision did not take effect until two decades after the ratification of the document. Notice again how careful the language is. The word "slave" does not appear, only "such persons as any of the States now existing shall think proper."

2. Writ of Habeas Corpus The privilege of the writ of habeas corpus shall not be suspended, unless when in cases of rebellion or invasion the public safety may require it.

CLAUSE 2 The writ of habeas corpus directs a sheriff, public official, or other person who is holding citizens against their will to produce them so that the legality of their detention can be determined. This clause protects American citizens from being held in prison without being formally charged with a crime. Without the writ, the government could simply put people it did not like in jail and hold them there without explanation. President Abraham Lincoln, who called the Civil War a rebellion, did suspend the writ of habeas corpus and imprison people without showing cause.

3. Bills of Attainder; *Ex Post Facto* **Laws** No bill of attainder or ex post facto law shall be passed.

CLAUSE 3 A bill of attainder is a legislative act that punishes a person without a trial in court. An ex post facto law is a retroactive one; it declares that an action is a crime after it has been committed. These important provisions prevent the government from arresting and punishing people without due process of law.

4. Apportionment of Direct Taxes No capitation, ~~or other direct,~~ tax shall be laid, unless in proportion to the census or enumeration herein before directed to be taken.

CLAUSE 4 This provision outlawed all direct taxes on individuals until the Sixteenth Amendment (1913) gave Congress the power to tax personal incomes.

5. Taxes on Exports No tax or duty shall be laid on articles exported from any state.

CLAUSE 5 Congress cannot tax anything sent out of a state, although it does have the power to tax imported goods.

6. Special Preference for Trade No preference shall be given by any regulation of commerce or revenue to the ports of one state over those of another: nor shall vessels bound to, or from, one state, be obliged to enter, clear, or pay duties in another.

CLAUSE 6 These specific restrictions on the states keep them from trying to regulate trade outside their own boundaries. Interstate trade is solely the business of the national government.

7. Spending No money shall be drawn from the treasury, but in consequence of appropriations made by law; and a regular statement and account of the receipts and expenditures of all public money shall be published from time to time.

CLAUSE 7 Like many other parts of the Constitution, this paragraph reflects eighteenth-century fears about corruption and power. The purpose of the clause was to prevent Presidents or other officials from thwarting the will of Congress and the people by spending money in secret on projects prohibited by Congress. It is a significant check on presidential power. The Iran-contra scandal involved government officials who attempted to raise and spend money in support of the contras in Nicaragua, an activity that Congress had made illegal.

8. Titles of Nobility No title of nobility shall be granted by the United States: and no person holding any office of profit or trust under them, shall, without the consent of the Congress, accept of any present, emolument, office, or title, of any kind whatever, from any king, prince or foreign state.

CLAUSE 8 The Founders included this provision to prevent the establishment of an aristocracy in the United States. The clause was also designed to discourage foreign nations from attempting to bribe or otherwise corrupt government officials. Today, exceptions are made, usually in the case of retired officials. Presidents Ronald Reagan and George Bush, for example, received formal recognition from the government of Great Britain after their public careers were over.

Section 10 *Powers Denied to the States*

1. Unconditional Prohibitions No state shall enter into any treaty, alliance, or confederation; grant letters of marque and reprisal; coin money; emit bills of credit; make any thing but gold and silver coin a tender in payment of debts; pass any bill of attainder, ex post facto law, or law impairing the obligation of contracts, or grant any title of nobility.

2. Powers Conditionally Denied No state shall, without the consent of the Congress, lay any imposts or duties on imports or exports, except what may be absolutely necessary for executing its inspection laws: and the net produce of all duties and imposts, laid by any state on imports or exports, shall be for the use of the treasury of the United States; and all such laws shall be subject to the revision and control of the Congress.

3. Other Denied Powers No state shall, without the consent of Congress, lay any duty of tonnage, keep troops, or ships of war in time of peace, enter into any agreement or compact with another state, or with a foreign power, or engage in war, unless actually invaded, or in such imminent danger as will not admit of delay.

CLAUSES 1, 2, AND 3 These three clauses specifically prohibit the states from getting involved in foreign affairs or interstate commerce. Their purpose is to limit the power of the states to internal affairs. Anything that affects more than one state, economically or militarily, is properly the business of the national government.

Article II
EXECUTIVE BRANCH
Section 1 *President and Vice President*

1. Chief Executive; Term The executive power shall be vested in a President of the United States of America. He shall hold his office during the term of four years, and, together with the Vice President, chosen for the same term, be elected, as follows:

CLAUSE 1 The Founders deliberately left the duties of the President vague. During the past century, Presidents have assumed great power, in part because the Constitution does not put many specific restrictions on the office. Although the presidential term is four years, many members of the Constitutional Convention expected incumbents to be reelected more than once. In fact, they thought most Presidents would serve for a long time. But after Franklin Roosevelt was elected to four terms between 1932 and

1944, the Twenty-second Amendment (1951) restricted Presidents to two terms. There is no such limit on Vice Presidents.

2. Electoral College Each state shall appoint, in such manner as the legislature thereof may direct, a number of electors, equal to the whole number of senators and representatives to which the state may be entitled in the Congress: but no senator or representative, or person holding an office of trust or profit under the United States, shall be appointed an elector.

CLAUSE 2 This clause establishes what we call the Electoral College, the group of people who elect the President. State legislatures decide how electors for that state will be chosen. The number of electoral votes each state has is equal to the number of its senators and representatives added together.

3. Former Electoral Method ~~The electors shall meet in their respective states, and vote by ballot for two persons, of whom one at least shall not be an inhabitant of the same state with themselves. And they shall make a list of all the persons voted for, and of the number of votes for each; which list they shall sign and certify, and transmit sealed to the seat of the government of the United States, directed to the president of the Senate. The president of the Senate shall, in the presence of the Senate and House of Representatives, open all the certificates, and the votes shall then be counted. The person having the greatest number of votes shall be the President, if such number be a majority of the whole number of Electors appointed; and if there be more than one who have such majority, and have an equal number of votes, then the House of Representatives shall immediately choose by ballot one of them for President; and if no person have a majority, then from the five highest on the list the said House shall in like manner choose the President. But in choosing the President, the votes shall be taken by states, the representation from each state having one vote; a quorum for this purpose shall consist of a member or members from two thirds of the states, and a majority of all the states shall be necessary to a choice. In every case, after the choice of the President, the person having the greatest number of votes of the electors shall be the Vice President. But if there should remain two or more who have equal votes, the Senate shall choose from them by ballot the Vice President.~~

CLAUSE 3 The Twelfth Amendment (1804) replaced this paragraph, which is no longer in force.

4. Time of Elections The Congress may determine the time of choosing the electors, and the day on which they shall give their votes; which day shall be the same throughout the United States.

CLAUSE 4 Congress has established the Tuesday after the first Monday in November every fourth year as the time to choose electors. By law, the electors cast their ballots on the Monday after the second Wednesday in December.

5. Qualifications for President No person except a natural-born citizen, ~~or a citizen of the United States at the time of the adoption of this Constitution,~~ shall be eligible to the office of President; neither shall any person be eligible to that office who shall not have attained to the age of thirty-five years, and been fourteen years a resident within the United States.

CLAUSE 5 This provision ensures that the President of the United States will be a mature person, who is not only a natural-born citizen of the United States but has also lived in the nation for at least fourteen years.

6. Presidential Succession ~~In case of the removal of the President from office, or of his death, resignation, or inability to discharge the powers and duties of the said office, the same shall devolve on the Vice President,~~ and the Congress may by law provide for the case of removal, death, resignation or inability, both of the President and Vice President, declaring what officer shall then act as President, and such officer shall act accordingly, until the disability be removed, or a President shall be elected.

CLAUSE 6 The Twenty-fifth Amendment (1967) supersedes the first half of this provision, more clearly explaining when and how a Vice President becomes President.

7. Salary The President shall, at stated times, receive for his services, a compensation, which shall neither be increased nor diminished during the period for which he shall have been elected, and he shall not receive within that period any other emolument from the United States, or any of them.

CLAUSE 7 This clause prohibits Congress from changing a President's salary while he or she is in office. The authors of the Constitution were afraid that Congress might use its power to corrupt or punish a President. Without this clause, for example, Congress could threaten to lower a President's salary to prevent him or her from vetoing a bill. Today, the President of the United States is paid $200,000 a year, plus $50,000 in a taxable expense account. Additional benefits include residence in the White House, Secret Service protection, and means of transportation. Congress cannot give a President a valuable gift ("an emolument") while he or she is in office.

8. Oath of Office Before he enter on the execution of his office, he shall take the following oath or affirmation:—"I do solemnly swear (or affirm) that I will faithfully execute the office of the President of the United States, and will to the best of my ability, preserve, protect and defend the Constitution of the United States."

CLAUSE 8 Note that the President swears to uphold the Constitution, not the United States. When Presidents take the oath of office, they commit themselves to the form of government outlined in this document. Remember that people in the 1780s and 1790s did not assume that the Constitution would be permanent; after all, the Articles of Confederation had lasted only a decade. The oath commits the President to this Constitution and no others.

Section 2 *Powers of the President*

1. Military Powers The President shall be commander in chief of the army and navy of the United States, and of the militia of the several states, when called into the actual service of the United States; he may require the opinion, in writing, of the

THE CONSTITUTION

principal officer in each of the executive departments, upon any subject relating to the duties of their respective offices, and he shall have power to grant reprieves and pardons for offenses against the United States, except in cases of impeachment.

CLAUSE 1 Even though the President is a civilian, he or she is the supreme commander of the military. The phrase "require the opinion, in writing" is one of the few places in which the Constitution refers to what is called the cabinet, the heads of the executive departments. The President's power to grant pardons is limited to federal crimes.

2. Treaties; Appointments He shall have power, by and with the advice and consent of the Senate, to make treaties, provided two thirds of the senators present concur; and he shall nominate, and by and with the advice and consent of the Senate, shall appoint ambassadors, other public ministers and consuls, judges of the Supreme Court, and all other officers of the United States, whose appointments are not herein otherwise provided for, and which shall be established by law: but the Congress may by law vest the appointment of such inferior officers, as they think proper, in the President alone, in the courts of law, or in the heads of departments.

CLAUSE 2 To make major agreements with foreign countries or to appoint major public officials, the President has to seek the advice and consent of the Senate. The aim of this provision is to prevent the President from conducting personal diplomacy, committing the United States to something only he or she wants, and from appointing only his or her friends to judgeships and federal offices.

3. Temporary Appointments The President shall have power to fill up all vacancies that may happen during the recess of the Senate, by granting commissions which shall expire at the end of their next session.

CLAUSE 3 This clause simply allows the President to make temporary appointments when Congress is not in session.

Section 3 *Duties of the President*

He shall from time to time give to the Congress information of the state of the Union, and recommend to their consideration such measures as he shall judge necessary and expedient; he may, on extraordinary occasions, convene both houses, or either of them, and in case of disagreement between them, with respect to the time of adjournment, he may adjourn them to such time as he shall think proper; he shall receive ambassadors and other public ministers; he shall take care that the laws be faithfully executed, and shall commission all the officers of the United States.

SECTION 3 This paragraph lists the specific duties and responsibilities of the President. He must give a State of the Union address occasionally (usually once a year). In addition, he may call special sessions of Congress, adjourn Congress if the two houses are divided about it, receive ambassadors, and commission officers. Finally, he must see "that the laws [of the United States] be faithfully executed." These are important duties. But notice how general they are and how few in number. Compare them with the lengthy list of specific things the Congress can and

cannot do. The members of the Constitutional Convention were not as sure of what the office of the presidency would be as they were of Congress. Much of the job has been defined by the men who have held the office.

Section 4 *Impeachment*

The President, Vice President and all civil officers of the United States, shall be removed from office on impeachment for, and conviction of, treason, bribery, or other high crimes and misdemeanors.

SECTION 4 If the President goes too far in assuming powers and breaks the law in the opinion of a majority of the members of the House of Representatives, he can be impeached and tried by the Senate. This event has happened once in American history. President Andrew Johnson was impeached by the House of Representatives in 1867. Although a majority of senators voted that he was guilty, more than a third had doubts, so Johnson remained in office. In 1974 the House Judiciary Committee voted to recommend the impeachment of President Richard Nixon, but he resigned before the full House was able to vote on the recommendation.

Article III
JUDICIAL BRANCH
Section 1 *Courts, Terms of Office*

The judicial power of the United States, shall be vested in one Supreme Court, and in such inferior courts as the Congress may from time to time ordain and establish. The judges, both of the Supreme and inferior courts, shall hold their offices during good behavior, and shall, at stated times, receive for their services, a compensation which shall not be diminished during their continuance in office.

SECTION 1 Although the Constitution makes provisions for a federal court system to hear and decide cases, it only specifically creates the Supreme Court. Acts of Congress have created all other federal courts, as well as established the number of Supreme Court justices. In order to preserve the integrity and independence of judges from both the executive and legislative branches, federal judges serve "during good behavior," which basically means as long as they live, and cannot have their salaries reduced.

Section 2 *Jurisdiction*

1. Scope of Judicial Power The judicial power shall extend to all cases, in law and equity, arising under this Constitution, the laws of the United States, and treaties made, or which shall be made, under their authority;—to all cases affecting ambassadors, other public ministers and consuls;—to all cases of admiralty and maritime jurisdiction;—to controversies to which the United States shall be a party;—to controversies between two or more states;— between a state and citizens of another state;—between citizens of different states;—between citizens of the same state claiming lands under grants of different states, and between a state, or the citizens thereof, and foreign states, citizens or subjects.

CLAUSE 1 This paragraph lists the kinds of cases federal courts can hear and decide on. They have jurisdiction over cases relating to the Constitution, federal laws, treaties, and diplomatic officials. They also have jurisdiction over cases involving disputes between the United States and someone else, between two states, or between citizens of different states. The Eleventh Amendment (1795) substantially restricted the jurisdiction of federal courts in cases involving states.

2. Supreme Court In all cases affecting ambassadors, other public ministers and consuls, and those in which a state shall be a party, the Supreme Court shall have original jurisdiction. In all the other cases before mentioned, the Supreme Court shall have appellate jurisdiction, both as to law and fact, with such exceptions, and under such regulations as the Congress shall make.

CLAUSE 2 Under this clause, the Supreme Court has both original and appellate jurisdiction. That is, the Court is first to hear and decide cases involving foreign ambassadors and individual states. But it also has appellate jurisdiction, meaning people can appeal the decisions of lower courts to the Supreme Court.

3. Trial by Jury The trial of all crimes, except in cases of impeachment, shall be by jury; and such trial shall be held in the state where the said crimes shall have been committed; but when not committed within any state, the trial shall be at such place or places as the Congress may by law have directed.

CLAUSE 3 In reaction to cases in English constitutional history, the members of the Constitutional Convention guaranteed American citizens the right to trial by jury in federal cases and the right to have the trial in the place where the crime supposedly occurred. The Founders feared the power of government to take defendants to distant places to try them quickly and without a jury.

Section 3 *Treason*

1. Definition Treason against the United States shall consist only in levying war against them, or in adhering to their enemies, giving them aid and comfort. No person shall be convicted of treason unless on the testimony of two witnesses to the same overt act, or on confession in open court.

CLAUSE 1 The definition of treason is very specific because the authors of the Constitution wanted to make certain that people were not imprisoned or punished simply for criticizing the government. The crime of treason can apply only to citizens or resident aliens, and even then only in time of war.

2. Punishment The Congress shall have power to declare the punishment of treason, but no attainder of treason shall work corruption of blood, or forfeiture except during the life of the person attained.

CLAUSE 2 Although the United States has never executed anyone for treason, death remains the maximum punishment for someone convicted of this charge. The minimum punishment, by act of Congress, is five years in prison and/or a $10,000 fine. The phrase "corruption of blood, or forfeiture" means that punishment for treason affects only the person convicted of it; neither the traitor's family nor descendants can be punished.

Article IV
RELATIONS AMONG THE STATES
Section 1 *Full Faith and Credit*
Full faith and credit shall be given in each state to the public acts, records, and judicial proceedings of every other state. And the Congress may by general laws prescribe the manner in which such acts, records and proceedings shall be proved, and the effect thereof.

SECTION 1 In this clause, the authors of the Constitution were again asserting the supremacy of the federal government. Congress would have responsibility for making sure that each state respected the legal actions of the others.

Section 2 *Privileges and Immunities of Citizens*
1. Privileges The citizens of each state shall be entitled to all privileges and immunities of citizens in the several states.

CLAUSE 1 The Constitution ensures that states cannot discriminate against people from other states. The federal government will make certain that citizens of the United States enjoy their full rights in every part of the nation.

2. Extradition A person charged in any state with treason, felony, or other crime, who shall flee from justice, and be found in another state, shall on demand of the executive authority of the state from which he fled, be delivered up, to be removed to the state having jurisdiction of the crime.

CLAUSE 2 The legal term for this process is *extradition*. If someone commits a crime in Minnesota, for example, and then flees to Montana, the governor of Montana must arrange to transport the alleged criminal back to Minnesota for trial if the governor of Minnesota requests this action. Although governors sometimes delay complying with such requests for political reasons, the federal government has the power to force governors to comply.

3. Fugitive Slaves ~~No person held to service or labor in one state, under the laws thereof, escaping into another, shall, in consequence of any law or regulation therein, be discharged from such service or labor, but shall be delivered up on claim of the party to whom such service or labor may be due.~~

CLAUSE 3 This clause was nullified by the Thirteenth Amendment in 1865, which made slavery illegal throughout the United States.

Section 3 *New States and Territories*
1. New States New states may be admitted by the Congress into this Union; but no new states shall be formed or erected within the jurisdiction of any other state, nor any state be formed by the junction of two or more states, or parts of states, without the consent of the legislatures of the states concerned as well as of the Congress.

CLAUSE 1 Only the federal government can create new states. Congress decides on the rules and procedures for admitting new states to the Union. It cannot, however, make new states out of old ones unless the legislature of a particular state agrees to this course of action. Since 1789 Congress has created thirty-seven states. Five of these—Vermont, Kentucky, Tennessee, Maine,

THE CONSTITUTION

and West Virginia—were originally parts of other states. One—Texas—was an independent republic. One—California—was part of Mexico before it became a state. The other thirty states have become parts of the United States after first being territories. The Northwest Ordinance of 1787 outlines the process by which a territory becomes a state.

2. Federal Lands The Congress shall have power to dispose of and make all needful rules and regulations respecting the territory or other property belonging to the United States; and nothing in this Constitution shall be so construed as to prejudice any claims of the United States, or of any particular state.

CLAUSE 2 Simply put, this clause gives Congress the power to govern all federal territory and other property as it sees fit. In theory, state governments have no say when it comes to the regulation or disposal of federal lands. This clause led to controversy in the 1800s because Congress had the power to abolish slavery on federal property if it wished. Controversy has continued in the 1900s because of the question of how to handle the vast acreage in national parks and other preserves owned and operated by the federal government, particularly in western states.

Section 4 *Protection Afforded to States by the Nation*
The United States shall guarantee to every state in this Union a republican form of government, and shall protect each of them against invasion; and on application of the legislature, or of the executive (when the legislature cannot be convened) against domestic violence.

SECTION 4 The federal government is the most powerful government in the United States. Not only will it protect the states from all enemies, foreign and domestic, it will ensure that each state has a "republican form of government." Officials and judges today assume that "republican" means a representative government. But the Constitution leaves it up to Congress to decide what is "republican" and what is not.

Article V
PROVISIONS FOR AMENDMENT
The Congress, whenever two thirds of both houses shall deem it necessary, shall propose amendments to this Constitution, or, on the application of the legislatures of two thirds of the several states, shall call a convention for proposing amendments, which, in either case, shall be valid to all intents and purposes, as part of this Constitution, when ratified by the legislatures of three fourths of the several states, or by conventions in three fourths thereof, as the one or the other mode of ratification may be proposed by the Congress; provided that no amendment which may be made prior to the year one thousand eight hundred and eight shall in any manner affect the first and fourth clauses in the ninth section of the first Article; and that no state, without its consent, shall be deprived of its equal suffrage in the Senate.

ARTICLE V One of the most democratic features of the Constitution is its ability to be changed. Amendments to the Constitution are essentially revisions of the original document.

While the authors of the Constitution wanted the people to be able to change this document, they did not want it changed for frivolous reasons. Consequently, they made sure that the process of amending the Constitution would take a great deal of consensus as well as time. Proposing an amendment to the Constitution requires either a two thirds vote in each house of Congress or the approval of a national convention called by two thirds of the state legislatures. After an amendment has been proposed, either the legislatures or special conventions of three fourths of the states must approve the amendment before it can become law. All twenty-seven amendments to the Constitution have originated in Congress.

Article VI
NATIONAL DEBTS, SUPREMACY OF NATIONAL LAW, OATH
Section 1 *Validity of Debts*
All debts contracted and engagements entered into, before the adoption of this Constitution, shall be as valid against the United States under this Constitution, as under the Confederation.

SECTION 1 One of the major reasons some Americans supported the Constitution was because this document would enable the new nation to pay off the huge debts contracted during the American Revolution. Under the Articles of Confederation, Congress had lacked the power to tax; to pay for the war effort, it had been forced to borrow millions of dollars. Once the Constitution went into effect, this clause promised creditors of the United States that the new government would pay all bills contracted under the Articles of Confederation.

Section 2 *Supremacy of National Law*
This Constitution, and the laws of the United States which shall be made in pursuance thereof; and all treaties made, or which shall be made, under the authority of the United States, shall be the supreme law of the land; and the judges in every state shall be bound thereby, anything in the constitution or laws of any state to the contrary notwithstanding.

SECTION 2 This is the "supremacy clause." In very general terms, it says that federal laws rank above state or local laws. No other government in the United States can make or enforce any law that is in conflict with the Constitution, acts of Congress, diplomatic treaties, or orders issued by the executive branch. In other words, the federal government is supreme in the United States.

Section 3 *Oaths of Office*
The senators and representatives before mentioned, and the members of the several state legislatures, and all executive and judicial officers, both of the United States and of the several states, shall be bound by oath or affirmation, to support this Constitution; but no religious test shall ever be required as a qualification to any office or public trust under the United States.

SECTION 3 This clause simply reinforces the supremacy clause. It requires that everyone holding office within the borders of the United States swear to uphold the Constitution.

The Framers of the Constitution specifically forbid the exclusion of anyone from government office for religious reasons. Americans take this right for granted today, but in the 1700s it was a relatively novel idea. In Great Britain, people who were not members of the Church of England could not hold office until the 1800s; Catholics, Jews, and Protestant Dissenters were effectively barred from government service.

Article VII
RATIFICATION OF CONSTITUTION

The ratification of the conventions of nine states shall be sufficient for the establishment of this Constitution between the states so ratifying the same.

ARTICLE VII The Framers required only nine of thirteen states to approve the Constitution, in large part because they knew it would be extremely difficult to win unanimous approval. Because they also had doubts about whether state legislatures would approve their new government, they provided for specially elected conventions to make the decision.

Done in convention by the unanimous consent of the states present the seventeenth day of September in the year of our Lord one thousand seven hundred and eighty-seven, and of the independence of the United States of America the twelfth. *In Witness* whereof we have hereunto subscribed our names.

ATTEST:
William Jackson, SECRETARY
George Washington, PRESIDENT
and deputy from Virginia

NEW HAMPSHIRE
John Langdon
Nicholas Gilman

MASSACHUSETTS
Nathaniel Gorham
Rufus King

CONNECTICUT
William Samuel Johnson
Roger Sherman

NEW YORK
Alexander Hamilton

NEW JERSEY
William Livingston
David Brearley
William Paterson
Jonathan Dayton

PENNSYLVANIA
Benjamin Franklin
Thomas Mifflin
Robert Morris
George Clymer
Thomas Fitzsimons
Jared Ingersoll
James Wilson
Gouverneur Morris

DELAWARE
George Read
Gunning Bedford, Jr.
John Dickinson
Richard Bassett
Jacob Broom

MARYLAND
James McHenry
Dan of St. Thomas Jennifer
Daniel Carroll

VIRGINIA
John Blair
James Madison, Jr.

NORTH CAROLINA
William Blount
Richard Dobbs Spaight
Hugh Williamson

SOUTH CAROLINA
John Rutledge
Charles Cotesworth Pinckney
Charles Pinckney
Pierce Butler

GEORGIA
William Few
Abraham Baldwin

THE CONSTITUTION

AMENDMENTS

The supporters of the Constitution had to agree to several changes in order to win the approval of the required nine states. The first ten amendments to the Constitution—or the Bill of Rights—incorporate most of the revisions called for by critics of the Constitution. Basically, the Bill of Rights protects the hard-won rights of citizens from a powerful national government. These amendments were originally meant to restrict only the federal government; however, the Supreme Court on occasion has held that most of them also apply to the states. The justices have based this extension on the due process clause of the Fourteenth Amendment. The amendments in the Bill of Rights were proposed by Congress on September 25, 1789, and ratified by December 15, 1791.

FIRST AMENDMENT (1791) *Freedom of Religion, Speech, Press, Assembly, and Petition*

Congress shall make no law respecting an establishment of religion, or prohibiting the free exercise thereof; or abridging the freedom of speech, or of the press; or the right of the people peaceably to assemble, and to petition the government for a redress of grievances.

FIRST AMENDMENT The First Amendment prohibits Congress from restricting five basic liberties—the right of the people to practice their religion as they wish; the right of the people to speak, publish, and express their views; and the right of the people to join together publicly with others to discuss issues and to petition, or ask, their government to change laws they think are unfair. Although most Americans now take these basic rights for granted, they are a vital part of the democratic system of government established by the Founders.

SECOND AMENDMENT (1791) *Bearing Arms*

A well-regulated militia being necessary to the security of a free state, the right of the people to keep and bear arms shall not be infringed.

SECOND AMENDMENT Although Congress must allow each state to maintain a militia, or national guard, for its protection, all state governments regulate the possession and use of firearms by private citizens. In the eighteenth century, when people were very distrustful of powerful governments, the right to bear arms was a cherished liberty. After all, the American Revolution began in April 1775 when men grabbed muskets and rifles to resist a British army marching from Boston to Concord, Massachusetts. Today, however, this amendment is more controversial. Some Americans continue to think of the right to bear arms as an essential right; others argue that because our times are so different from the late 1700s, the amendment is outdated.

THIRD AMENDMENT (1791) *Quartering of Troops*

No soldier shall, in time of peace be quartered in any house, without the consent of the owner, nor in time of war, but in a manner to be prescribed by law.

THIRD AMENDMENT It was a common practice for governments in the 1700s to house troops in private homes in order to save money on food and shelter. Before the American Revolution, the British government frequently quartered, or housed, troops in the homes of Americans. The colonists resented the practice, and it was one of the major grievances with Great Britain listed in the Declaration of Independence. Determined to prevent the practice in the United States, many Americans demanded and won this amendment to the Constitution. As a result, the United States government cannot quarter troops in private homes.

FOURTH AMENDMENT (1791) *Searches and Seizures*

The right of the people to be secure in their persons, houses, papers, and effects, against unreasonable searches and seizures, shall not be violated, and no warrants shall issue, but upon probable cause, supported by oath or affirmation, and particularly describing the place to be searched, and the persons or things to be seized.

FOURTH AMENDMENT This amendment protects another "right of the people" from a potentially intrusive government. No one can search for or seize evidence in an American citizen's house or arrest a citizen without a court order issued for "probable cause." The Supreme Court has reinforced this right with the "exclusionary rule," which holds that illegally obtained evidence cannot be used against a person in a court of law.

FIFTH AMENDMENT (1791) *Criminal Proceedings; Due Process; Eminent Domain*

No person shall be held to answer for a capital, or otherwise infamous crime, unless on a presentment or indictment of a grand jury, except in cases arising in the land or naval forces, or in the militia, when in actual service in time of war or public danger; nor shall any person be subject for the same offense to be twice put in jeopardy of life or limb; nor shall be compelled in any criminal case to be a witness against himself, nor be deprived of life, liberty, or property, without due process of law; nor shall private property be taken for public use, without just compensation.

FIFTH AMENDMENT This amendment, like the others in the Bill of Rights, provides people with protection from a powerful government. It outlines the ways in which the United States government must treat its citizens, even when it suspects them of criminal activity. For example, people cannot be tried unless they have been formally indicted, or accused, by a grand jury. They cannot be tried twice for the same crime. They cannot be required to give evidence against themselves. And they are entitled to "due process of law." If the government takes their property, it must pay them for what it took. In other words, government officials cannot behave in an unfair or arbitrary manner. By respecting due process in dealing with alleged criminals, the Constitution respects and protects the rights of all Americans.

SIXTH AMENDMENT (1791) *Criminal Proceedings*

In all criminal prosecutions, the accused shall enjoy the right to a speedy and public trial, by an impartial jury of the state and district wherein the crime shall have been committed, which district shall have been previously ascertained by law, and to be informed of the nature and cause of the accusation; to be confronted with the witnesses against him; to have compulsory process for obtaining witnesses in his favor, and to have the assistance of counsel for his defense.

SIXTH AMENDMENT This amendment guarantees that even citizens who stand accused of a crime have rights when dealing with their government. They have the right to a relatively quick and open trial before a jury of their peers. They also have the right to be represented by an attorney, to know the charges against them, to examine witnesses, and to present evidence in their own defense.

SEVENTH AMENDMENT (1791) *Civil Trials*
In suits at common law, where the value in controversy shall exceed twenty dollars, the right of trial by jury shall be preserved, and no fact tried by a jury shall be otherwise re-examined in any court of the United States, than according to the rules of the common law.

SEVENTH AMENDMENT This amendment applies only to civil cases—that is, cases heard in federal courts that involve the rights of private individuals and involve no criminal behavior. People have a right to a jury trial in cases involving more than twenty dollars, a fairly large amount of money in the 1700s, unless both parties agree to waive, or give up, that right.

EIGHTH AMENDMENT (1791) *Punishment for Crimes*
Excessive bail shall not be required, nor excessive fines imposed, nor cruel and unusual punishments inflicted.

EIGHTH AMENDMENT Bail is the sum of money that a person accused of a crime may be required to post, or deposit with the court, in order to guarantee his or her appearance before the court at the proper time. Governments in the United States may require bail. They may also punish people convicted of crimes. The purpose of this amendment is to make certain that both bail and punishments are reasonable and fair. For example, executing someone for stealing a small amount of money would be unreasonable; however, the question of what constitutes a fair and reasonable punishment is not always easy to determine. Today, for example, many Americans disagree about whether capital punishment, or the execution of a convicted criminal, is by definition a "cruel and unusual" punishment.

NINTH AMENDMENT (1791) *Unenumerated Rights*
The enumeration in the Constitution, of certain rights, shall not be construed to deny or disparage others retained by the people.

NINTH AMENDMENT The Constitution lists many, but not all, of the rights enjoyed by the people. In other words, because a right is not spelled out in the Constitution does not necessarily mean that the people do not have this right. The point of this amendment was to prevent governments from denying people a right simply because it was not specifically listed in the Constitution.

TENTH AMENDMENT (1791) *Powers Reserved to the States*
The powers not delegated to the United States by the Constitution, nor prohibited by it to the States, are reserved to the states respectively, or to the people.

TENTH AMENDMENT The states are free to exercise whatever powers are not specifically given to the federal government or denied the states by the Constitution. In other words, states can do whatever they wish, as long as the Constitution does not prohibit the activity or reserve it solely for the federal government.

ELEVENTH AMENDMENT (1798) *Suits Against States*
The judicial power of the United States shall not be construed to extend to any suit in law or equity, commenced or prosecuted against one of the United States by citizens of another state, or by citizens or subjects of any foreign state.

ELEVENTH AMENDMENT People from other states or from foreign countries may not sue a state in federal court. For example, a resident of Pennsylvania, a citizen of France, or the government of France may not sue the state of Ohio in federal court.

Proposed by Congress March 4, 1794; ratified February 7, 1795; officially announced January 8, 1798.

TWELFTH AMENDMENT (1804) *Election of President and Vice President*
The electors shall meet in their respective states, and vote by ballot for President and Vice President, one of whom, at least, shall not be an inhabitant of the same state with themselves; they shall name in their ballots the person voted for as President, and in distinct ballots the person voted for as Vice President, and they shall make distinct lists of all persons voted for as President, and of all persons voted for as Vice President, and of the number of votes for each, which lists they shall sign and certify, and transmit sealed to the seat of the government of the United States, directed to the president of the Senate; the president of the Senate shall, in the presence of the Senate and the House of Representatives, open all the certificates and the votes shall then be counted;—the person having the greatest number of votes for President shall be the President, if such number be a majority of the whole number of electors appointed; and if no person have such a majority, then from the persons having the highest numbers not exceeding three on the list of those voted for as President, the House of Representatives shall choose immediately, by ballot, the President. But in choosing the President, the votes shall be taken by states, the representation from each state having one vote; a quorum for this purpose shall consist of a member or members from two thirds of the states, and a majority of all the states shall be necessary to a choice. And if the House of Representatives shall not choose a President whenever the right of choice shall devolve upon them, before the fourth day of March next following, then the Vice President, shall act as President, as in the case of the death or other constitutional disability of the President.—The person having the greatest number of votes as Vice President, shall be the Vice President, if such number be a majority of the whole number of electors appointed, and if no person have a majority, then from the two highest numbers on the list, the Senate shall choose the Vice President; a quorum for the purpose shall consist of two thirds of the whole number of senators, and a majority of the whole number shall be necessary to a choice. But

no person constitutionally ineligible to the office of President shall be eligible to that of Vice President of the United States.

TWELFTH AMENDMENT This amendment was a response to the election of 1800. Article II, Section 1, Clause 3 stated that each member of the Electoral College should vote for two people for President of the United States; the one with the most votes would win, and the person who finished second would become Vice President. In 1800, however, Thomas Jefferson and Aaron Burr ended up with the same number of electoral votes. To prevent another tie, the Twelfth Amendment separates the voting for the two offices. Each elector now casts one vote for President and another for Vice President.

The Twentieth Amendment (1933) changed inauguration day from March 4 to January 20, mainly because of the sense of national emergency during the Depression and the problems created by Franklin Roosevelt having to wait from November to March to become President.

Proposed by Congress December 9, 1803; ratified June 15, 1804.

THIRTEENTH AMENDMENT (1865) *Slavery and Involuntary Servitude*
Section 1 *Outlawing Slavery*
Neither slavery nor involuntary servitude, except as a punishment for crime whereof the party shall have been duly convicted, shall exist within the United States, or any place subject to their jurisdiction.

Section 2 *Enforcement*
Congress shall have power to enforce this article by appropriate legislation.

THIRTEENTH AMENDMENT With the addition of this amendment following the North's victory in the Civil War, the Constitution forbade the practice of slavery anywhere in the United States. American citizens may not be held against their will unless they have been convicted of a crime. Section 2 simply gave Congress the power to enforce the abolition of slavery.

Proposed by Congress January 31, 1865; ratified December 6, 1865.

FOURTEENTH AMENDMENT (1868) *Rights of Citizens*
Section 1 *Citizenship*
All persons born or naturalized in the United States, and subject to the jurisdiction thereof, are citizens of the United States and of the state wherein they reside. No state shall make or enforce any law which shall abridge the privileges or immunities of citizens of the United States; nor shall any state deprive any person of life, liberty, or property, without due process of law; nor deny to any person within its jurisdiction the equal protection of the laws.

SECTION 1 Until the Civil War, constitutional amendments had been directed primarily at restricting the power of the national government. The Fourteenth Amendment, on the other hand, protects citizens against the states. Congress passed this amendment during the Reconstruction era, when some northerners were angry about the attempts by southern states to evade or ignore legislation dealing with the rights of African Americans.

This section of the amendment defines citizenship. People are citizens of the United States if they are born within its territorial borders or if they have been naturalized through the legal process. States can neither deprive American citizens of any of their rights and privileges without "due process of law," nor discriminate against them. They are entitled to "equal protection of the laws" simply because they are citizens of the United States. The purpose of this amendment was to protect former enslaved persons from state governments, many of which were trying to restrict their rights. Here the federal government is no longer viewed as the potential enemy of the people, as it had been in most of the first thirteen amendments. Now it is an ally of the people against potentially oppressive state governments.

It would be difficult to overestimate the importance of this section of the Fourteenth Amendment in the history of the United States. Through the "due process" provision, the Supreme Court has extended to the state governments the restrictions on government action listed in the first eight amendments.

Section 2 *Apportionment of Representatives*
Representatives shall be apportioned among the several states according to their respective numbers, counting the whole number of persons in each state, excluding Indians not taxed. But when the right to vote at any election for the choice of electors for President and Vice President of the United States, representatives in Congress, the executive and judicial officers of a state, or the members of the legislature thereof, is denied to any of the male inhabitants of such state, being twenty-one years of age, and citizens of the United States, or in any way abridged, except for participation in rebellion, or other crime, the basis of representation therein shall be reduced in the proportion which the number of such male citizens shall bear to the whole number of male citizens twenty-one years of age in such state.

SECTION 2 The first sentence replaces Article I, Section 2, Clause 3. From this point forward, all people were to be counted equally in the census.

Section 3 *Former Confederate Officials*
No person shall be a senator or representative in Congress, or elector of President and Vice President, or hold any office, civil or military, under the United States, or under any state, who, having previously taken an oath, as a member of Congress, or as an officer of the United States, or as a member of any state legislature, or as an executive or judicial officer of any state, to support the Constitution of the United States, shall have engaged in insurrection or rebellion against the same, or given aid or comfort to the enemies thereof. But Congress may, by a vote of two thirds of each house, remove such disability.

SECTION 3 This paragraph concerns the pardoning of the men who led the Confederate States of America during the Civil War. Many members of Congress were upset with President Andrew Johnson's liberal pardon policy. This provision essentially gave

THE CONSTITUTION 887

Congress the power to pardon former Confederates. Congress repealed this section in 1898.

Section 4 *Public Debt*

The validity of the public debt of the United States, authorized by law, including debts incurred for payment of pensions and bounties for services in suppressing insurrection or rebellion, shall not be questioned. But neither the United States nor any state shall assume or pay any debt or obligation incurred in aid of insurrection or rebellion against the United States, or any claim for the loss or emancipation of any slave; but all such debts, obligations and claims shall be held illegal and void.

SECTION 4 According to this section, the public debt of the United States, including that incurred in fighting the Civil War, was legal and would be paid. The public debt of the Confederate States of America, however, was illegal and would not be paid. No one could recover any money they loaned the Confederacy or any expense they had incurred in supporting the South during the Civil War. Nor could they receive compensation for the loss of enslaved persons. This section was simply a punishment designed to hurt those who had engaged in, or supported, rebellion against the Union.

Section 5 *Enforcement*

The Congress shall have power to enforce, by appropriate legislation, the provisions of this article.

SECTION 5 Congress may do what is necessary to make sure Americans obey the provisions of the Fourteenth Amendment.

Proposed by Congress June 13, 1866; ratified July 9, 1868.

FIFTEENTH AMENDMENT (1870) *Right to Vote—Race, Color, Servitude*

Section 1 *Extending the Right to Vote*

The right of citizens of the United States to vote shall not be denied or abridged by the United States or by any state on account of race, color, or previous condition of servitude.

Section 2 *Enforcement*

The Congress shall have power to enforce this article by appropriate legislation.

FIFTEENTH AMENDMENT Like the Fourteenth Amendment, the purpose of the Fifteenth Amendment was to protect African Americans from the attempts of southern states to restrict their rights. As a result of this amendment, no state could deny persons the right to vote on the basis of race or color or because they had once been enslaved.

Proposed by Congress February 26, 1869; ratified February 3, 1870.

SIXTEENTH AMENDMENT (1913) *Income Tax*

The Congress shall have power to lay and collect taxes on incomes, from whatever source derived, without apportionment among the several states, and without regard to any census or enumeration.

SIXTEENTH AMENDMENT This amendment gives Congress the right to collect an income tax. Both the United States and its gov-

ernment had grown larger and more expensive to run, and the purpose of the income tax was to ensure a fair and regular source of income. The amendment modified Article I, Section, 2, Clause 3 and Section 9, Clause 4.

Proposed by Congress July 12, 1909; ratified February 3, 1913.

SEVENTEENTH AMENDMENT (1913) *Popular Election of Senators*

Section 1 *Method of Election*

The senate of the United State shall be composed of two senators from each state, elected by the people thereof, for six years; and each senator shall have one vote. The electors in each state shall have the qualifications requisite for electors of the most numerous branch of the state legislatures.

SECTION 1 Repealing parts of Article I, Section 3, Clauses 1 and 2, this amendment provides for the direct election of United States senators. As a result, voters, rather than state legislatures, choose their senators. Any person who is qualified to vote for state representatives can vote for United States senators.

Section 2 *Vacancies*

When vacancies happen in the representation of any state in the Senate, the executive authority of such state shall issue writs of election to fill such vacancies: provided, that the legislature of any state may empower the executive thereof to make temporary appointments until the people fill the vacancies by election as the legislature may direct.

SECTION 2 If a senator dies or resigns while in office, the governor of that state may appoint someone to serve until an election can be held, if the legislature of his or her state grants the governor such power.

Section 3 *Those Elected Under Previous Procedure*

~~This amendment shall not be so construed as to affect the election or term of any senator chosen before it becomes valid as part of the Constitution.~~

SECTION 3 Anyone who was serving in the Senate when this amendment was passed by Congress could complete his or her term.

Proposed by Congress May 13, 1912; ratified April 8, 1913.

EIGHTEENTH AMENDMENT (1919) *Prohibition of Intoxicating Liquors*

Section 1 *Ban on Alcohol*

~~After one year from the ratification of this article, the manufacture, sale, or transportation of intoxicating liquors within, the importation thereof into, or the exportation thereof from the United States and all territory subject to the jurisdiction thereof for beverage purposes is hereby prohibited.~~

Section 2 *Enforcement*

~~The Congress and the several states shall have concurrent power to enforce this article by appropriate legislation.~~

Section 3 *Method of Ratification*

~~This article shall be inoperative unless it shall have been ratified as an amendment to the Constitution by the legislatures of the~~

NINETEENTH AMENDMENT (1920) *Women's Suffrage*

The right of citizens of the United States to vote shall not be denied or abridged by the United states or by any state on account of sex.

Congress shall have power to enforce this article by appropriate legislation.

TWENTIETH AMENDMENT (1933) *Commencement of Terms; Sessions of Congress; Death or Disqualification of President-Elect*

Section 1 *Beginning of Terms*
The terms of the President and Vice President shall end at noon on the 20th day of January, and the terms of senators and representatives at noon on the 3d day of January, of the years in which such terms would have ended if this article had not been ratified; and the terms of their successors shall then begin.

Section 2 *Congressional Sessions*
The Congress shall assemble at least once in every year, and such meeting shall begin at noon on the 3d day of January, unless they shall by law appoint a different day.

Section 3 *Presidential Succession*
If, at the time fixed for the beginning of the term of the President, the President-elect shall have died, the Vice President-elect shall become President. If a President shall not have been chosen before the time fixed for the beginning of his term, or if the President-elect shall have failed to qualify, then the Vice President-elect shall act as President until a President shall have qualified; and the Congress may by law provide for the case wherein neither a President-elect nor a Vice President-elect shall have qualified, declaring who shall then act as President, or the manner in which one who is to act shall be selected, and such person shall act accordingly until a President or Vice President shall have qualified.

Section 4 *Elections Decided by Congress*
The Congress may by law provide for the case of the death of any of the persons from whom the House of Representatives may choose a President whenever the right of choice shall have devolved upon them, and for the case of the death of any of the persons from whom the Senate may choose a Vice President whenever the right of choice shall have devolved upon them.

Section 5 *Date of Implementation*
Sections 1 and 2 shall take effect on the 15th day of October following the ratification of this article.

Section 6 *Ratification Period*
This article shall be inoperative unless it shall have been ratified as an amendment to the Constitution by the legislatures of three fourths of the several states within seven years from the date of its submission.

TWENTY-FIRST AMENDMENT (1933) *Repeal of Prohibition*

Section 1 *Repeal*
The eighteenth article of amendment to the Constitution of the United States is hereby repealed.

Section 2 *State Laws*
The transportation or importation into any state, territory, or possession of the United States for delivery or use therein of intoxicating liquors, in violation of the laws thereof, is hereby prohibited.

Section 3 *Ratification Period*
This article shall be inoperative unless it shall have been ratified as an amendment to the Constitution by conventions in the several states, as provided in the Constitution, within seven years from the date of the submission hereof to the states by the Congress.

TWENTY-FIRST AMENDMENT This amendment, the only one submitted to state conventions rather than to legislatures, repealed the Eighteenth Amendment and marked the failure of prohibition. Section 2 does give states power to regulate the distribution and use of intoxicating beverages in ways that would be unconstitutional with any other commodity.

Proposed by Congress February 20, 1933; ratified December 5, 1933.

TWENTY-SECOND AMENDMENT (1951) *Presidential Tenure*
Section 1 *Two-Term Limit*
No person shall be elected to the office of the President more than twice, and no person who has held the office of President, or acted as President for more than two years of a term to which some other person was elected President shall be elected to the office of the President more than once. ~~But this article shall not apply to any person holding the office of President when this article was proposed by the Congress, and shall not prevent any person who may be holding the office of President, or acting as President, during the term within which this article becomes operative from holding the office of President or acting as President during the remainder of such term.~~

Section 2 *Ratification Period*
~~This article shall be inoperative unless it shall have been ratified as an amendment to the Constitution by the legislatures of three fourths of the several states within seven years from the date of its submission to the States by the Congress.~~

TWENTY-SECOND AMENDMENT Written in reaction to Franklin Roosevelt's four terms as President, this amendment limited future Presidents (after President Harry Truman, who was in office at the time) to two terms. If a Vice President succeeded a President when the latter was more than halfway through his term, then that Vice President could run for two more terms. For example, Lyndon Johnson became President during President Kennedy's third year in office; Johnson ran for President in 1964 and won. He could have run again in 1968, if he had chosen to do so. But no President can serve more than ten years. In the nation's history, only Franklin Roosevelt has been President for more than eight years; he served a little more than twelve.

Proposed by Congress March 24, 1947; ratified February 27, 1951.

TWENTY-THIRD AMENDMENT (1961) *Presidential Electors for the District of Columbia*
Section 1 *Determining Number of Electors*
The district constituting the seat of government of the United States shall appoint in such manner as the Congress may direct:

A number of electors of President and Vice President equal to the whole number of senators and representatives in Congress to which the district would be entitled if it were a state, but in no event more than the least populous state; they shall be in addition to those appointed by the states, but they shall be considered, for the purposes of the election of President and Vice President, to be electors appointed by a state; and they shall meet in the district

and perform such duties as provided by the twelfth article of amendment.

Section 2 *Enforcement*
The Congress shall have power to enforce this article by appropriate legislation.

TWENTY-THIRD AMENDMENT Until this amendment became law in 1961, residents of Washington, D.C., could not vote for President of the United States. The Twenty-third Amendment gives them that right. The District has three electoral votes; it cannot have more than any state. Residents of Washington still do not have voting representatives in the United States Senate or in the House of Representatives. In fact, Congress governed the capital city until 1968, when it granted residents the right to elect their own mayor and city council.

Proposed by Congress June 16, 1960; ratified March 29, 1961.

TWENTY-FOURTH AMENDMENT (1964) *Right to Vote in Federal Elections—Tax Payment*
Section 1 *Poll Tax Banned*
The right of citizens of the United States to vote in any primary or other election for President or Vice President, for electors for President or Vice President, or for senator or representative in Congress, shall not be denied or abridged by the United States or any state by reason of failure to pay any poll tax or other tax.

Section 2 *Enforcement*
The Congress shall have the power to enforce this article by appropriate legislation.

TWENTY-FOURTH AMENDMENT Some states used poll taxes in order to keep African Americans and poor Americans from voting in elections. This amendment made it illegal to require people to pay a tax in order to vote for a federal officeholder. Like the Reconstruction amendments (Thirteenth to Fifteenth), its purpose is to keep states from infringing on the rights of any of their citizens.

Proposed by Congress September 14, 1962; ratified January 23, 1964.

TWENTY-FIFTH AMENDMENT (1967) *Presidential Succession, Vice Presidential Vacancy, Presidential Inability*
Section 1 *President's Death or Resignation*
In case of the removal of the President from office or of his death or resignation, the Vice President shall become President.

SECTION 1 Written shortly after the assassination of President John F. Kennedy, this section simply clarified Article II, Section 1, Clause 6. It followed the precedent established by Vice President John Tyler when he became President upon the death of President William Henry Harrison in 1841.

Section 2 *Vacancies in Vice Presidency*
Whenever there is a vacancy in the office of the Vice President, the President shall nominate a Vice President who shall take office upon confirmation by a majority vote of both houses of Congress.

SECTION 2 The purpose of this paragraph was to outline a procedure for filling a vacancy in the office of Vice President. After the assassination of President Kennedy in November 1963, the United States did not have a Vice President until January 1965. The vacancy marked the sixteenth time in American history that such a situation had occurred. This section provided a procedure for choosing a new Vice President; it has been used only twice. The first time occurred in 1973, when Spiro T. Agnew resigned the vice presidency. President Richard Nixon nominated and Congress confirmed Gerald R. Ford as Vice President. In 1974, when President Nixon resigned, Ford became President and chose Nelson Rockefeller to be the Vice President.

Section 3 *Disability of the President*

Whenever the President transmits to the president pro tempore of the Senate and the Speaker of the House of Representatives his written declaration that he is unable to discharge the powers and duties of his office, and until he transmits to them a written declaration to the contrary, such powers and duties shall be discharged by the Vice President as acting President.

SECTION 3 This section provides for a situation in which a President is too sick, too mentally incapacitated, or too gravely wounded to carry out the duties of his office.

Section 4
Vice President as Acting President

Whenever the Vice President and a majority of either the principal officers of the executive departments or of such other body as Congress may by law provide, transmit to the president pro tempore of the Senate and the Speaker of the House of Representatives their written declaration that the President is unable to discharge the powers and duties of his office, the Vice President shall immediately assume the powers and duties of the office as acting President.

Thereafter, when the President transmits to the president pro tempore of the Senate and the Speaker of the House of Representatives his written declaration that no inability exists, he shall resume the powers and duties of his office unless the Vice President and a majority of either the principal officers of the executive department or of such other body as Congress may by law provide, transmit within four days to the president pro tempore of the Senate and the Speaker of the House of Representatives their written declaration that the President is unable to discharge the powers and duties of his office. Thereupon Congress shall decide the issue, assembling within forty-eight hours for that purpose if not in session. If the Congress, within twenty-one days after receipt of the latter written declaration, or, if Congress in not in session, within twenty-one days after Congress is required to assemble, determines by two thirds vote of both Houses that the President is unable to discharge the powers and duties of his office, the Vice President shall continue to discharge the same as acting President; otherwise, the President shall resume the powers and duties of his office.

SECTION 4 This section creates the procedure whereby somebody other than the President determines whether he or she is incapable of performing his or her duties. Initiating such an action requires the agreement of the Vice President and a majority of the cabinet. This procedure has never been used.

Proposed by Congress July 6, 1965; ratified February 10, 1967.

TWENTY-SIXTH AMENDMENT (1971) *Right to Vote—Age*
Section 1 *Lowering of Voting Age*

The right of citizens of the United States, who are eighteen years of age or older, shall not be denied or abridged by the United States or by any state on account of age.

Section 2 *Enforcement*

The Congress shall have the power to enforce this article by appropriate legislation.

TWENTY-SIXTH AMENDMENT In response to the size and influence of the "baby boom" generation, Congress lowered the minimum age to eighteen for voting in elections in the United States. A state could, if it wished, make the minimum age even lower.

Proposed by Congress March 23, 1971; ratified July 1, 1971.

TWENTY-SEVENTH AMENDMENT (1992) *Congressional Pay*

No law, varying the compensation for the services of the senators and representatives, shall take effect until an election of representatives shall have intervened.

TWENTY-SEVENTH AMENDMENT Congress can vote an increase in the pay of its members, but that increase may not take effect until after the next election. In other words, it gives "the people" a chance to express their opinion on the subject before it becomes law.

Proposed by Congress September 25, 1989; ratified May 18, 1992.

THE CONSTITUTION

Illustrated Data Bank

The maps, tables, and graphs that make up this Illustrated Data Bank are designed as reference materials to help you in your study of United States history. The first eight pages present data that is organized chronologically. This page and the facing page show a demographic picture of the nation in 1790. A table on pages 894 and 895 presents a summary of selected wars between Native American groups and the United States government. Pages 896 and 897 show three maps that describe the United States population in 1890 and territorial growth. Page 898 compares birth rate and median age over time and page 899 presents a demographic picture of the United States in 1990. The last five pages of the Illustrated Data Bank contain a physical-political map of the United States, a world political map, and a table of the fifty states.

Wherever possible, maps, tables, and graphs present data on three years: 1790, 1890, and 1990. This makes it possible to make comparisons among the different sets of data. For example, you can compare the population density maps to see how the nation's population changed from 1790 to 1890 to 1990. You can also compare data presented for the same year; for example, you can compare the map on this page with the table on the next page.

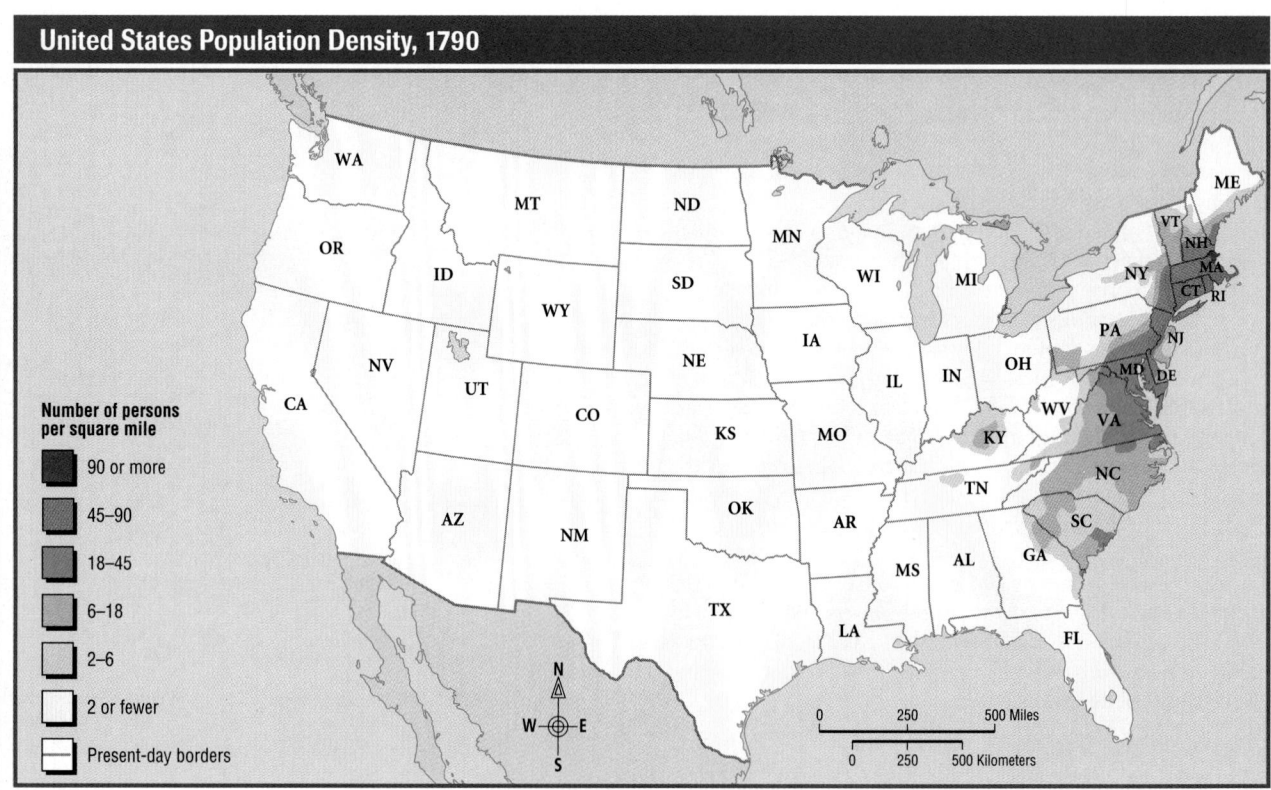

United States Population Density, 1790

Number of persons per square mile
- 90 or more
- 45–90
- 18–45
- 6–18
- 2–6
- 2 or fewer
- Present-day borders

United States Ethnic Groups, 1790

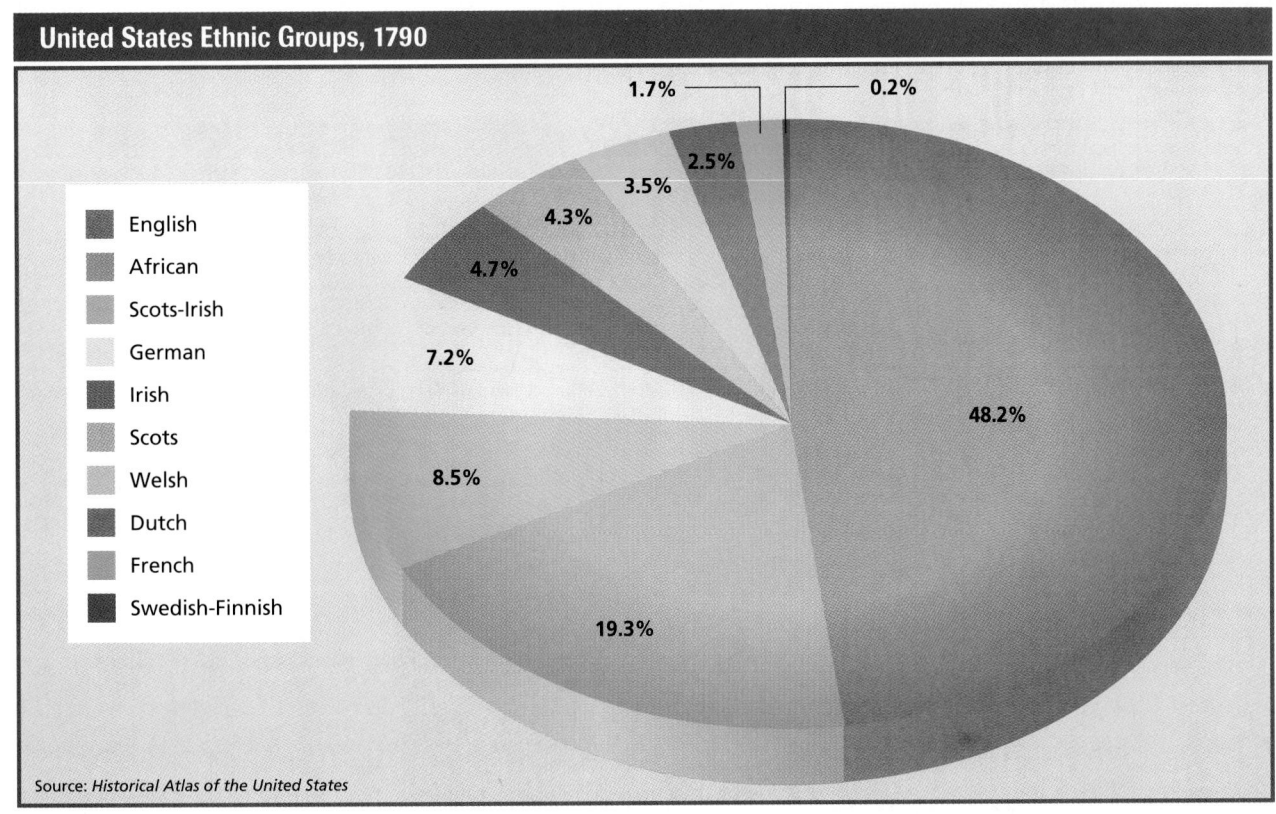

Legend:
- English
- African
- Scots-Irish
- German
- Irish
- Scots
- Welsh
- Dutch
- French
- Swedish-Finnish

48.2%
19.3%
8.5%
7.2%
4.7%
4.3%
3.5%
2.5%
1.7%
0.2%

Source: *Historical Atlas of the United States*

Enslaved Population of the United States, 1790

State	Total Population	Enslaved Population	Percent Enslaved
Connecticut	237,946	2,648	1.11
Delaware	59,096	8,837	14.95
Georgia	82,548	29,624	35.89
Maryland	319,728	103,036	32.33
Massachusetts	475,307	0	0.00
New Hampshire	141,885	157	0.11
New Jersey	184,139	11,423	6.20
New York	340,120	21,193	6.23
North Carolina	393,751	100,783	25.60
Pennsylvania	434,373	3,707	0.85
Rhode Island	68,825	958	1.39
South Carolina	249,073	107,094	43.00
Virginia	747,600	292,627	39.14

Source: *Historical Statistics of the United States*

Selected Major Indian Wars, 1794–1890

In the first column, states in parentheses refer to present-day states.
All casualty figures are estimates.

Old Northwest Territory

Battle of Fallen Timbers, 1794 (Ohio)	General Anthony Wayne and his 2,000 soldiers defeated a force of nearly 2,000 Miami led by Chief Little Turtle near what is now Toledo, Ohio. Wayne's victory forced the Native Americans to give up land in present-day Ohio and Indiana.
Battle of Tippecanoe, 1811 (Indiana)	A 1,000-man army led by William Henry Harrison defeated Shawnee chief Tecumseh and his alliance of Native Americans at present-day Battle Ground, Indiana.
War of 1812	During the war, many Native American groups joined the British to fight against the Americans.
Battle at River Raisin, 1813 (Ohio)	On the River Raisin, Tecumseh's alliance and British forces attacked and defeated the Kentucky militia.
Black Hawk's War, 1832 (Illinois, Wisconsin)	Led by Chief Black Hawk, Sauk and Fox resisted white demands, initiating a short war that consisted mainly of the outnumbered Native Americans trying to escape from the United States Army.
• Battle of Stillman's Run, 1832 (Illinois)	A force of about 40 Native Americans routed a 274-man militia commanded by Major Isaiah Stillman.
• Battle of Wisconsin Heights, 1832 (Wisconsin)	Fifty warriors held off 500 soldiers while the Sauk and Fox crossed the Wisconsin River.
• Bad Axe River, 1832 (Wisconsin)	The Army severely defeated Black Hawk's group, ending Native American resistance in the Northwest Territory. Hundreds of men, women, and children were shot or drowned as they crossed the Mississippi River.

Southeast

Creek War, 1813–1814 (Alabama, Georgia, Mississippi)	Moved to action by the encroachment of white settlers and the warnings of Shawnee leader Tecumseh, the Creek launched attacks in Alabama, Georgia, and Mississippi.
• Fort Mims Massacre, 1813 (Alabama)	In a surprise attack, the Creek attacked Fort Mims in Alabama and massacred more than 350 settlers.
• Battle of Horseshoe Bend, 1814 (Alabama)	General Andrew Jackson, aided by friendly Creek and Cherokee, virtually annihilated 1,000 Creek warriors. Jackson's victory forced the Creek to give up about two thirds of their land in Alabama.
First Seminole War, 1818 (Florida)	Seminole in northern Florida rose against whites, prompting General Jackson to invade Florida with a force of 3,000 men. Many Seminole were forced onto reservations.
Second Seminole War, 1835–1842 (Florida)	War began when the United States tried to move Seminole from Florida. Most of the Seminole surrendered in 1842.
• Dade's Massacre, 1835 (Florida)	Seminole warriors ambushed and defeated Major Francis Dade's force of 150 soldiers sent to reinforce Fort King. One soldier survived and 149 died.
• Battle of Okeechobee, 1838 (Florida)	About 400 Seminole ambushed General Zachary Taylor's 1,000-man army and were defeated by Taylor's superior numbers.
Third Seminole War, 1848–1858 (Florida)	Over ten years of raids and battles, the remaining Seminole were forced out of Florida and moved to reservations in Arkansas.

Northern Plains

Northern Plains Wars, 1854–1890	As white settlers spread farther into Native American territory, the Sioux, Cheyenne, and Shoshoni fought against American soldiers who sought to force the Indians to live on reservations.
• Minnesota Sioux War, 1862–1863	Angered over reservation conditions, the Sioux launch attacks in August 1862, on several settlements in Minnesota, including New Ulm and Fort Ridgely. The army put down the Sioux within a few months.

Selected Major Indian Wars, 1794–1890 (continued)

Northern Plains

• Colorado Cheyenne Wars, 1864–1869 (Colorado)	The Second Colorado Cavalry attacked a peaceful village of Cheyenne at Sand Creek in present-day Colorado. United States soldiers killed an estimated 450 men, women, and children, setting off the Colorado Cheyenne Wars.
• Fetterman Massacre, 1866 (Wyoming)	Crazy Horse and a group of Sioux successfully lured Caption William Fetterman and 80 troops out of Fort Kearny in present-day Wyoming. Fetterman's men rode directly into a force of 1,500 to 2,000 Sioux and were killed to a man.
Battle of the Rosebud, 1876 (Montana)	Led by Crazy Horse, a force of Sioux and Cheyenne defeated General George Crook and an army of about 1,100 men on the banks of the Rosebud River in present-day southern Montana.
Battle of Little Big Horn, 1876 (Montana)	General George Custer attacked a force of 2,000 to 3,000 Sioux and Cheyenne camped in the Little Big Horn valley. Custer and his regiment of over 260 men died.
Massacre at Wounded Knee, 1890 (South Dakota)	As the Seventh Cavalry attempted to disarm a Sioux village camped along the Wounded Knee River, an unidentified shot caused the soldiers to fire. More than 200 unarmed Sioux , including women and children, were killed.

Southern Plains

Pueblo Wars, 1847(New Mexico)	The Taos Pueblo attacked Americans in present-day New Mexico, setting off a short-lived war. The army defeated the Pueblo within a few weeks, killing more than 160 and hanging six of the leaders.
Navaho Wars, 1846–1864 (New Mexico)	Navaho attacks on white settlers increased with the start of the Civil War. Kit Carson led an army that defeated a Navaho stronghold in Canyon de Chelly in present-day New Mexico and forced the Navaho onto reservations.
Meeker Massacre, 1879 (Colorado)	A Ute revolt began when Ute killed N. C. Meeker, a government agent. The fighting ended when Chief Ouray returned from a hunting trip and restrained his people. This was the last Ute war.
Red River War, 1874 (Texas)	In 1874, almost 4,000 Cheyenne, Kiowa, and Comanche left their reservations and moved into Texas. The army forced the Native Americans to return to their reservations in a campaign led by Lieutenant General Philip Sheridan.
Apache Wars, 1822–1890 (Texas, New Mexico, Arizona, and Mexico)	Leaders such as Mangas Coloradas and Geronimo led Apache raids against American Mexican settlements. After about 40 years of Apache hostilities, the government launched a campaign to kill Apache men and capture the women and children. Survivors were then forced onto reservations. Geronimo and his force surrendered at Skeleton Canyon, Arizona, in 1886, and were shipped to reservations.

Northwest

Cayuse War, 1847–1850 (Washington and Oregon)	Missionaries Marcus and Narcissa Whitman and eleven others were murdered by Cayuse in present-day Washington. The massacre sparked a bitter war. The local militia virtually destroyed the Cayuse as a people.
Rogue River War and Yakima War, 1855–1856 (Oregon)	The Rogue River Indians and Yakima both fought the movement of Americans into their territory and went to war in 1855. The army easily defeated both groups in separate wars, moving each to reservations.
Modoc War, 1872–1873 (Oregon, California)	The Modoc of southern Oregon and northern California left their reservation in northern California to return to their former hunting grounds. At the Battle of the Lava Beds at Tule Lake, California, a small group of Modoc warriors held off an army of 1,000 for months until the Modoc surrendered.
Nez Percé War, 1877 (Oregon, Idaho, Washington, Montana, Colorado)	The Nez Percé War started when a group of Nez Percé attacked white settlers in the Wallawa Valley. Chief Joseph of the Nez Percé led a retreat to Montana, but at Big Hole Basin, United States soldiers attacked. Chief Joseph later surrendered about 40 miles from the Canadian border.

United States Population Density, 1890

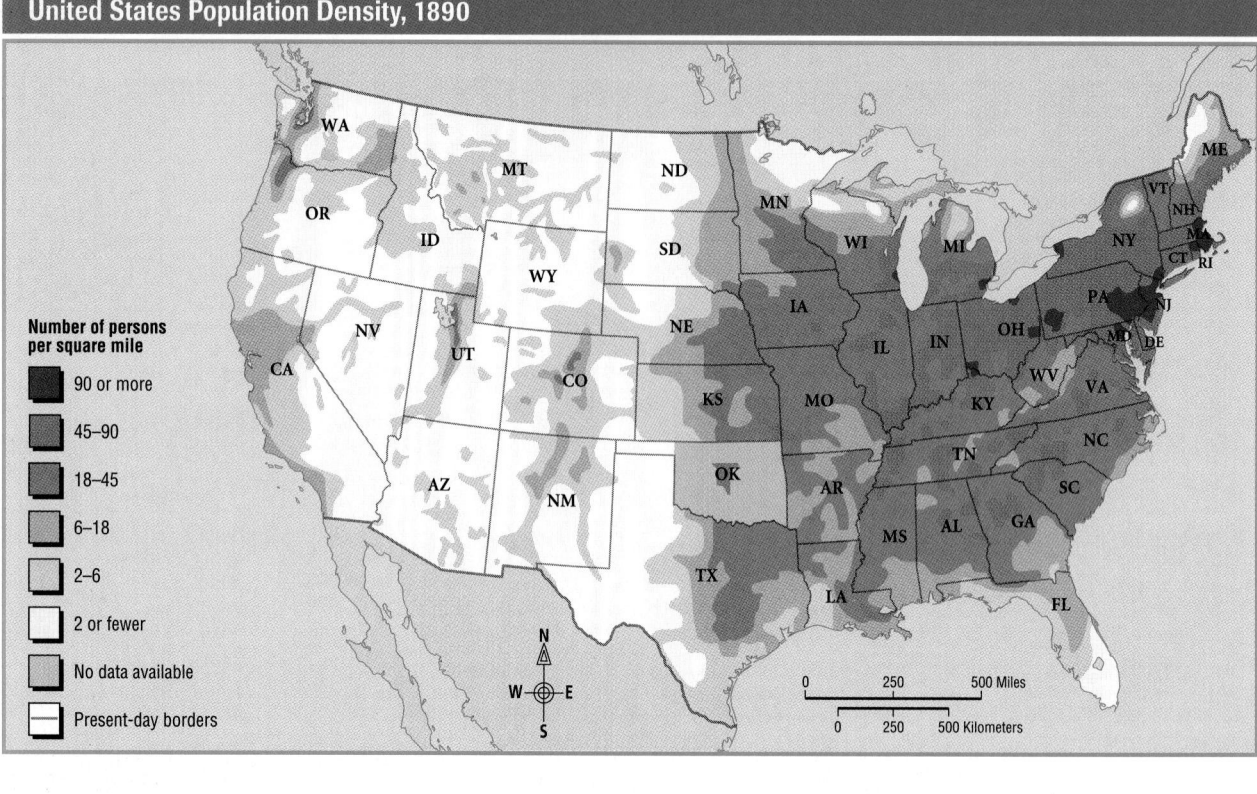

Number of persons per square mile

- 90 or more
- 45–90
- 18–45
- 6–18
- 2–6
- 2 or fewer
- No data available
- Present-day borders

0   250   500 Miles
0   250   500 Kilometers

United States Foreign-Born Population, 1890

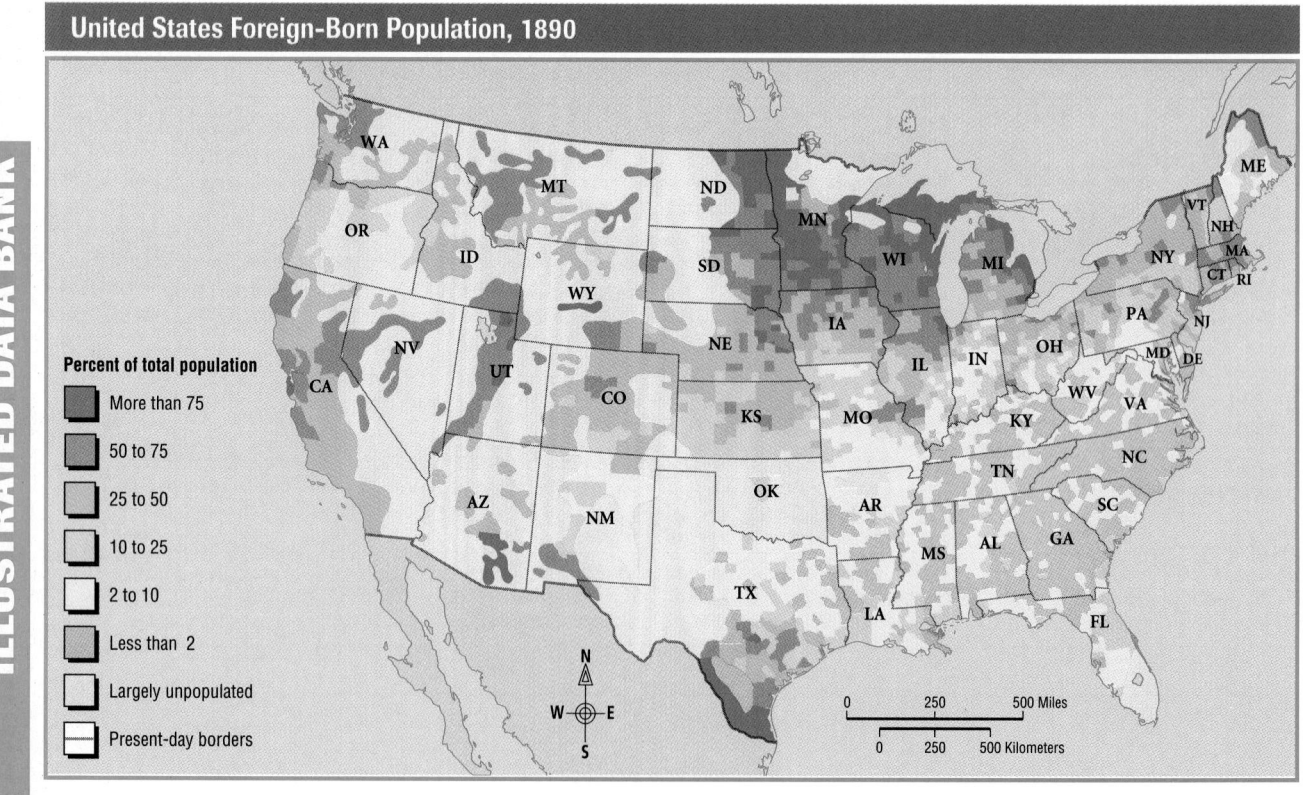

Percent of total population

- More than 75
- 50 to 75
- 25 to 50
- 10 to 25
- 2 to 10
- Less than 2
- Largely unpopulated
- Present-day borders

0   250   500 Miles
0   250   500 Kilometers

United States Territorial Growth

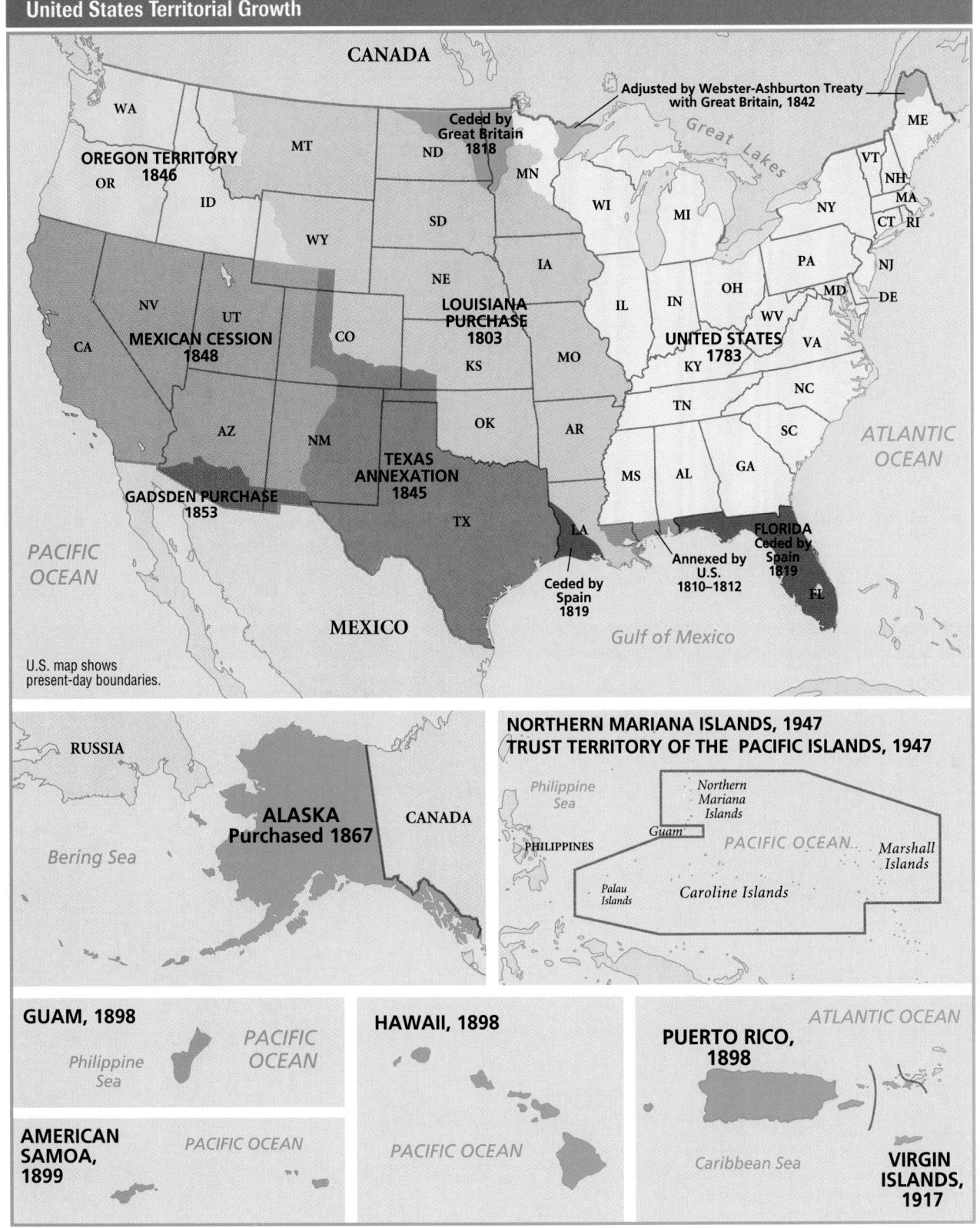

CANADA

WA

OREGON TERRITORY
1846

OR

ID

MT

ND

Ceded by
Great Britain
1818

MN

Adjusted by Webster-Ashburton Treaty
with Great Britain, 1842

Great Lakes

ME

VT

NH

MA

WI

MI

NY

CT RI

SD

WY

NE

IA

PA

NJ

NV

UT

CO

LOUISIANA
PURCHASE
1803

IL

IN

OH

WV

MD

DE

CA

MEXICAN CESSION
1848

KS

MO

UNITED STATES
1783

VA

KY

AZ

NM

OK

AR

TN

NC

SC

GADSDEN PURCHASE
1853

TEXAS
ANNEXATION
1845

MS

AL

GA

ATLANTIC
OCEAN

PACIFIC
OCEAN

TX

LA

FLORIDA
Ceded by
Spain
1819

Ceded by
Spain
1819

Annexed by
U.S.
1810–1812

FL

MEXICO

Gulf of Mexico

U.S. map shows
present-day boundaries.

RUSSIA

ALASKA
Purchased 1867

CANADA

Bering Sea

NORTHERN MARIANA ISLANDS, 1947
TRUST TERRITORY OF THE PACIFIC ISLANDS, 1947

Philippine
Sea

Northern
Mariana
Islands

PHILIPPINES

Guam

PACIFIC OCEAN

Marshall
Islands

Palau
Islands

Caroline Islands

GUAM, 1898

PACIFIC
OCEAN

Philippine
Sea

HAWAII, 1898

PACIFIC OCEAN

ATLANTIC OCEAN

PUERTO RICO,
1898

AMERICAN
SAMOA,
1899

PACIFIC OCEAN

PACIFIC OCEAN

Caribbean Sea

VIRGIN
ISLANDS,
1917

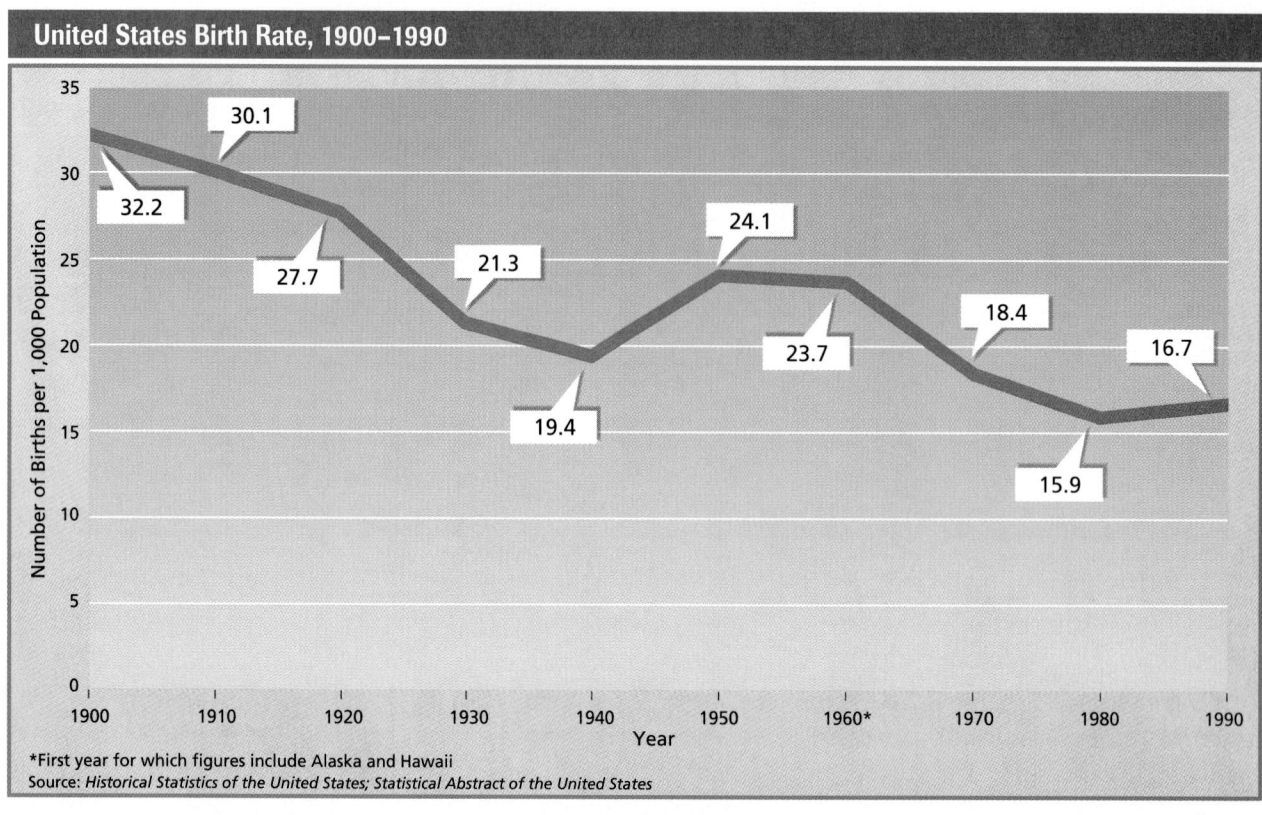

United States Birth Rate, 1900–1990

Number of Births per 1,000 Population

32.2
30.1
27.7
21.3
19.4
24.1
23.7
18.4
15.9
16.7

Year

*First year for which figures include Alaska and Hawaii
Source: *Historical Statistics of the United States; Statistical Abstract of the United States*

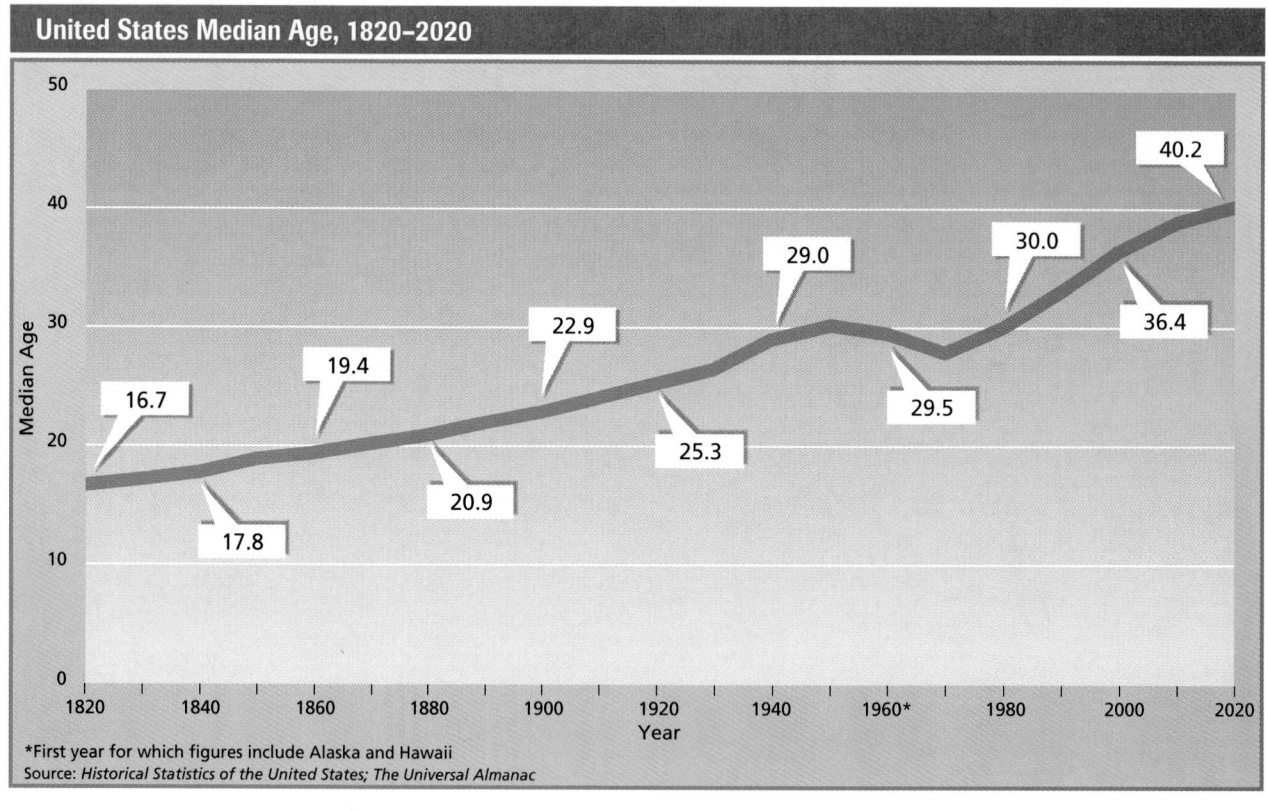

United States Median Age, 1820–2020

Median Age

16.7
17.8
19.4
20.9
22.9
25.3
29.0
29.5
30.0
36.4
40.2

Year

*First year for which figures include Alaska and Hawaii
Source: *Historical Statistics of the United States; The Universal Almanac*

United States Population by Race, 1990

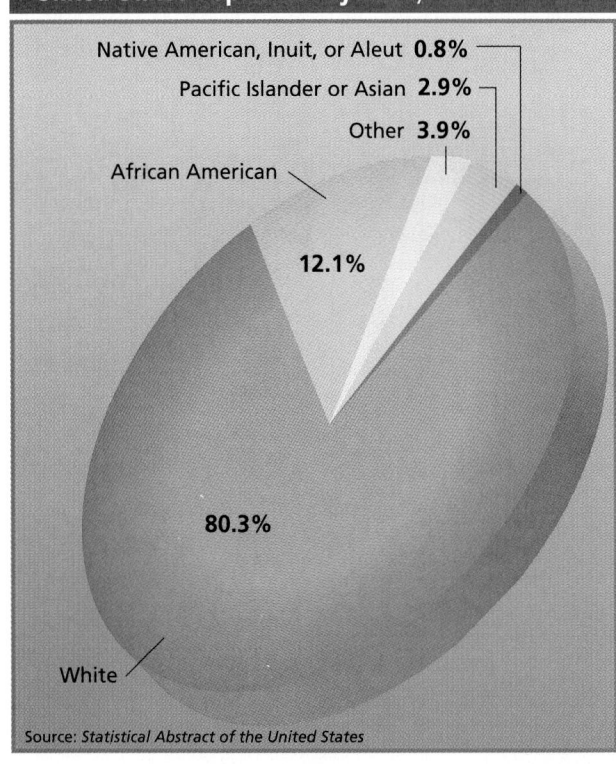

Native American, Inuit, or Aleut **0.8%**
Pacific Islander or Asian **2.9%**
Other **3.9%**
African American
12.1%
White
80.3%

Source: *Statistical Abstract of the United States*

United States Latino Population, 1990

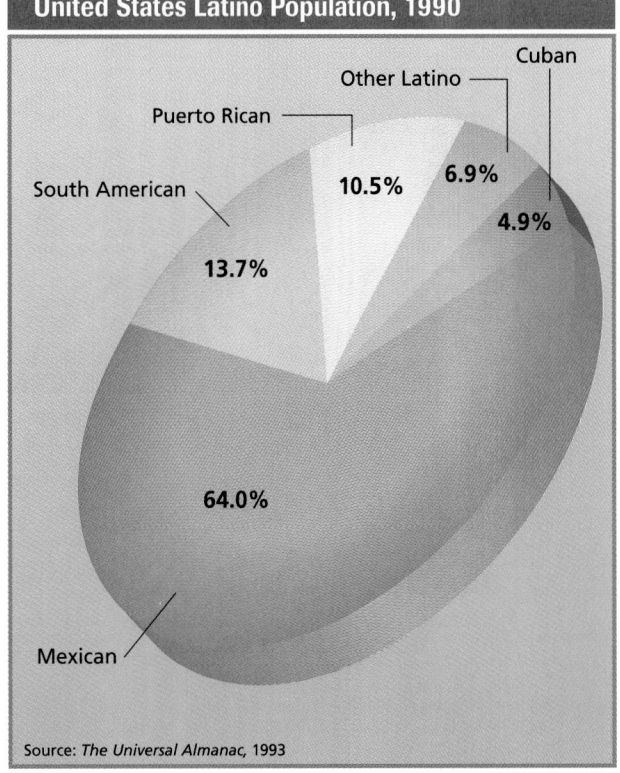

Cuban
Other Latino
Puerto Rican
South American
10.5% **6.9%**
4.9%
13.7%
64.0%
Mexican

Source: *The Universal Almanac,* 1993

United States Population Density, 1990

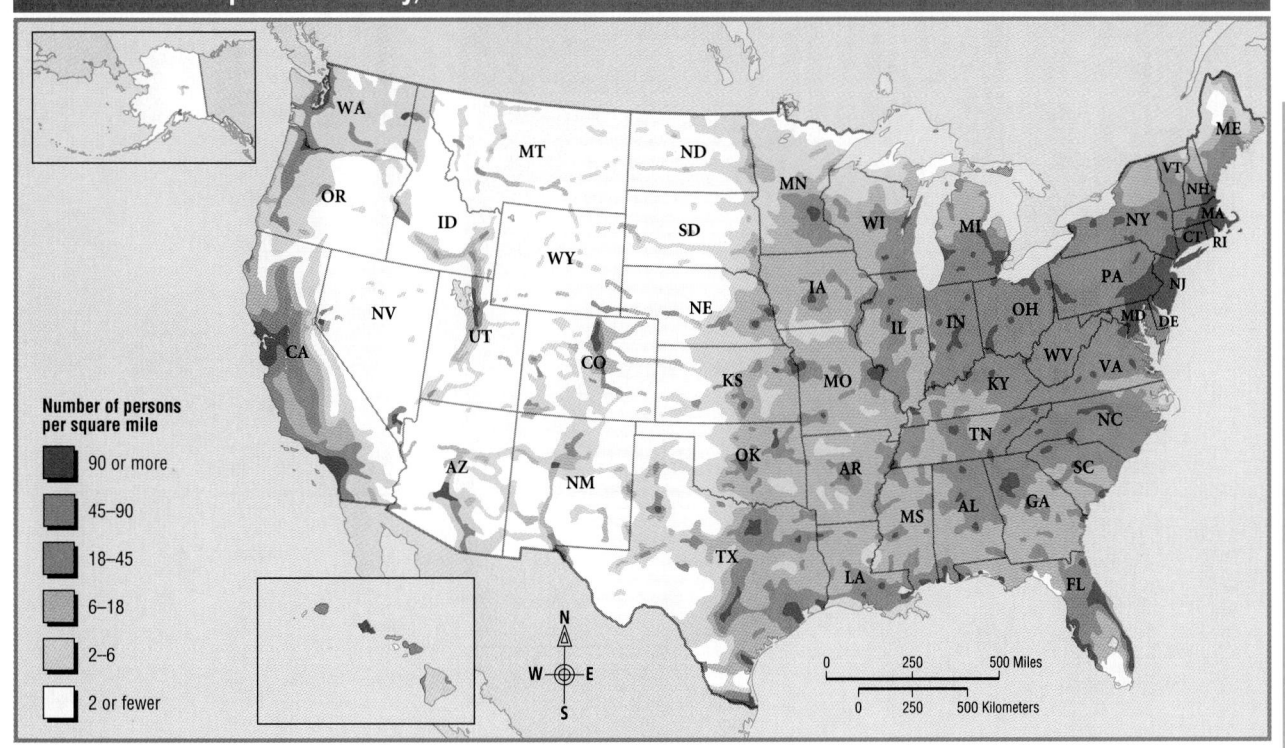

Number of persons per square mile

- 90 or more
- 45–90
- 18–45
- 6–18
- 2–6
- 2 or fewer

0   250   500 Miles
0   250   500 Kilometers

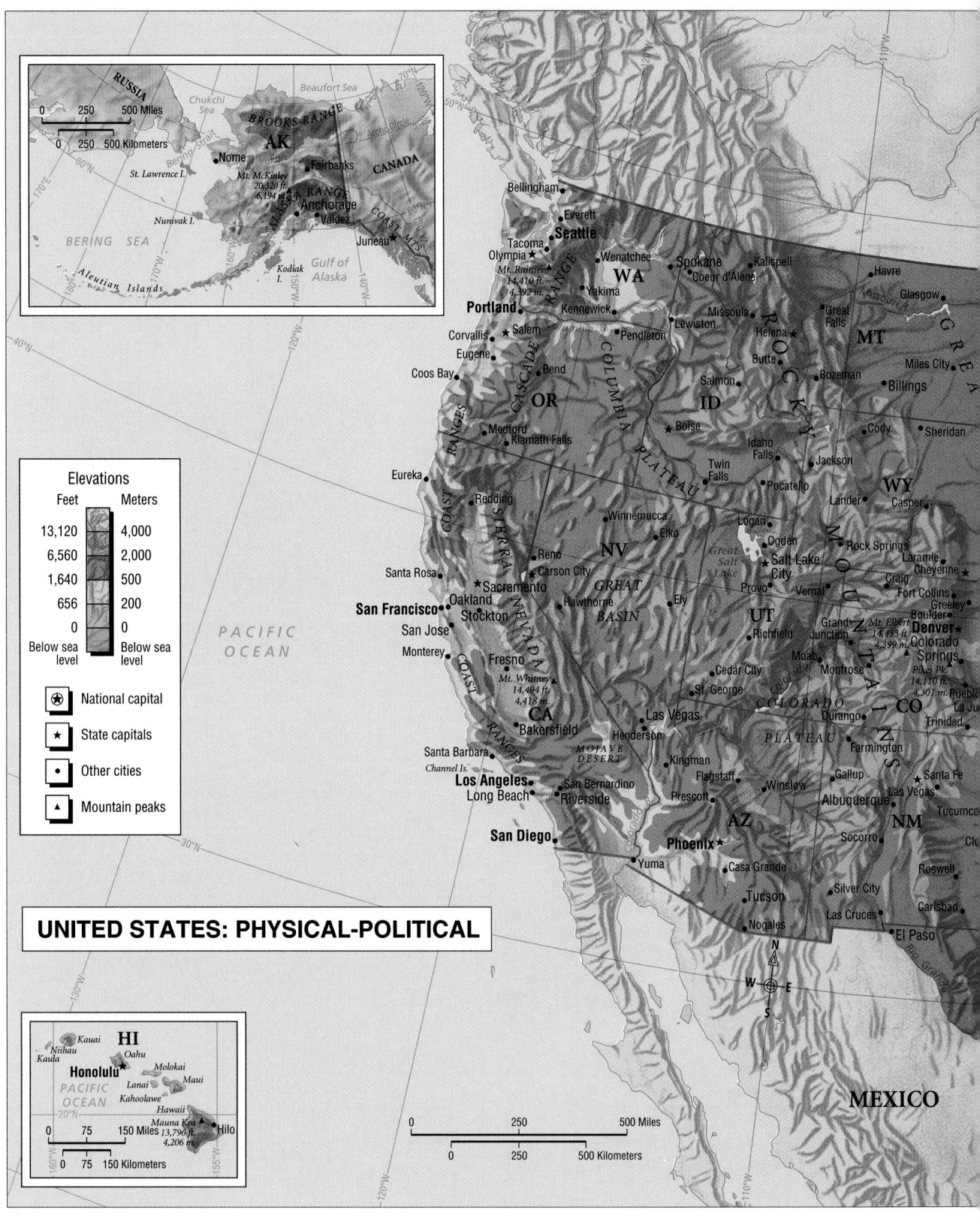

Elevations

Feet		Meters
13,120		4,000
6,560		2,000
1,640		500
656		200
0		0
Below sea level		Below sea level

⊛ National capital

★ State capitals

• Other cities

▲ Mountain peaks

UNITED STATES: PHYSICAL-POLITICAL

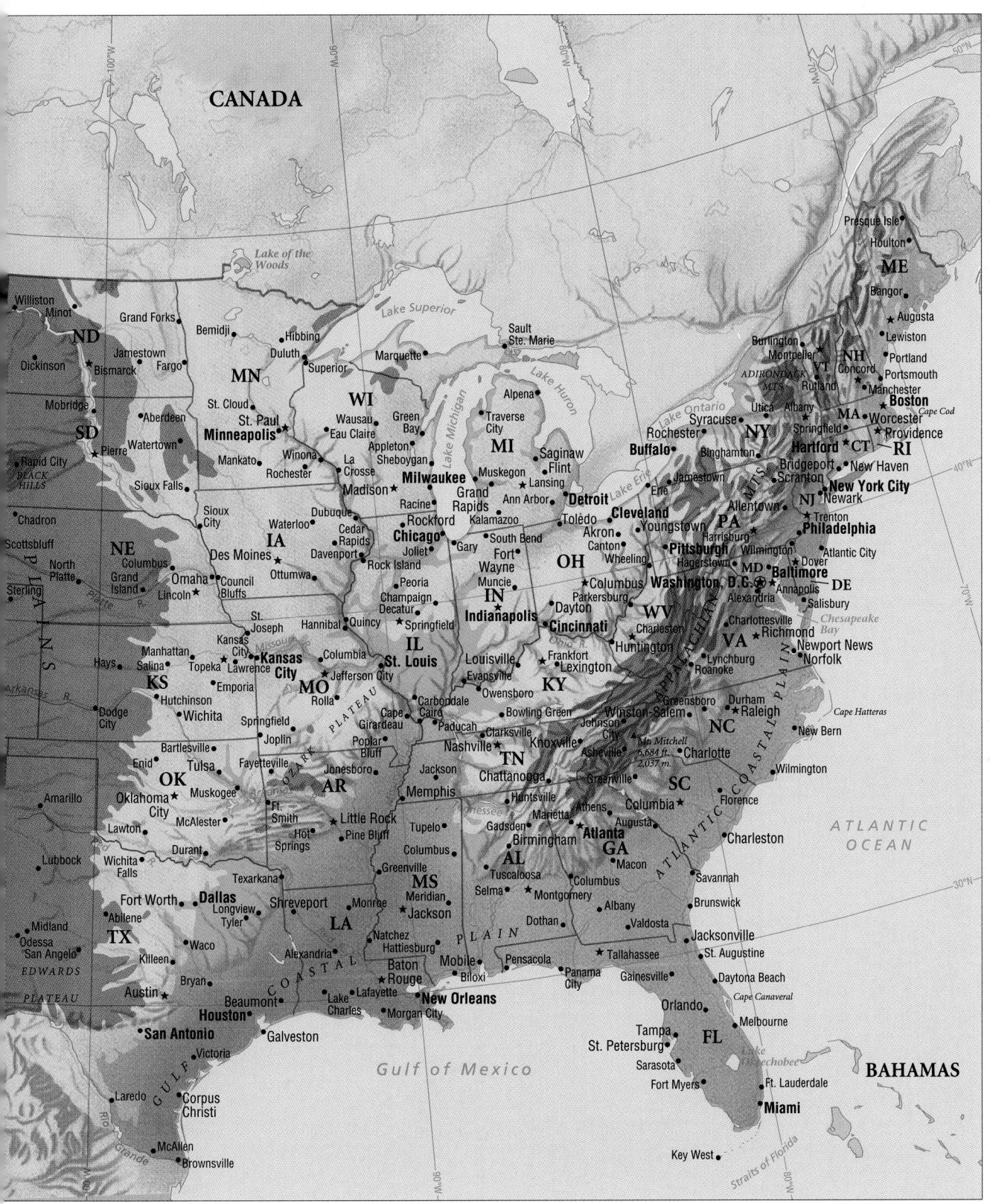

CANADA

Williston
Minot
ND
Dickinson
Bismarck
Fargo
Grand Forks
Jamestown
Bemidji
Hibbing
Duluth
Lake of the Woods
Lake Superior
Marquette
Sault Ste. Marie

Mobridge
SD
Rapid City
BLACK HILLS
Pierre
Watertown
Aberdeen
St. Cloud
MN
Minneapolis
St. Paul
WI
Wausau
Green Bay
Appleton
Eau Claire
Alpena
Traverse City
Lake Michigan
MI
Saginaw
Lake Huron

Chadron
Scottsbluff
North Platte
Sterling
NE
Columbus
Grand Island
Lincoln
Omaha
Council Bluffs
Sioux City
Sioux Falls
IA
Des Moines
Waterloo
Dubuque
Cedar Rapids
Davenport
Rockford
Madison
Milwaukee
Racine
Mankato
Rochester
Winona
La Crosse
Sheboygan
Grand Rapids
Kalamazoo
Muskegon
Flint
Lansing
Ann Arbor
Detroit
Toledo
Erie
Lake Erie
Cleveland
Akron
Canton
Youngstown

St. Joseph
Manhattan
Salina
Hays
Topeka
Lawrence
KS
Hutchinson
Wichita
Dodge City
Emporia
Kansas City
Kansas City
MO
Columbia
Jefferson City
Springfield
Rolla
Hannibal
Quincy
IL
Peoria
Champaign
Decatur
Springfield
St. Louis
Joliet
Chicago
Gary
South Bend
Fort Wayne
Muncie
IN
Indianapolis
Dayton
Cincinnati
OH
Columbus
Parkersburg
Wheeling
Pittsburgh
Harrisburg
PA
Hagerstown
Charleston
Huntington
WV

Amarillo
Lubbock
Lawton
OK
Oklahoma City
McAlester
Muskogee
Tulsa
Bartlesville
Enid
Joplin
Fayetteville
AR
Jonesboro
Ft. Smith
Poplar Bluff
Cape Girardeau
Cairo
Carbondale
Paducah
Clarksville
Nashville
Louisville
Evansville
Owensboro
Bowling Green
KY
Frankfort
Lexington

Midland
Odessa
San Angelo
EDWARDS PLATEAU
TX
Abilene
Waco
Killeen
Bryan
Austin
Fort Worth
Dallas
Longview
Tyler
Durant
Wichita Falls
Texarkana
Shreveport
LA
Alexandria
Monroe
Greenville
MS
Meridian
Jackson
Natchez
Hattiesburg
Columbus
Tupelo
Memphis
Jackson
Selma
Tuscaloosa
Montgomery
AL
Birmingham
Gadsden
Atlanta
Marietta
Athens
GA
Macon
Columbus
Dothan
Albany
Valdosta

Lubbock
Laredo
Corpus Christi
Victoria
Galveston
Beaumont
Houston
San Antonio
McAllen
Brownsville
Rio Grande
GULF COASTAL PLAIN
Lake Charles
Lafayette
Morgan City
New Orleans
Baton Rouge
Biloxi
Mobile
Pensacola
Panama City
Tallahassee
Gainesville
St. Augustine
Jacksonville
Daytona Beach
Cape Canaveral
Orlando
Melbourne
Tampa
St. Petersburg
Sarasota
Fort Myers
Ft. Lauderdale
Miami
Key West
FL
Lake Okeechobee
Gulf of Mexico
Straits of Florida
BAHAMAS

Presque Isle
Houlton
ME
Bangor
Augusta
Lewiston
Portland
Portsmouth
Burlington
Montpelier
VT
NH
Concord
Manchester
Boston
Cape Cod
ADIRONDACK MTS.
Rutland
Worcester
Providence
MA
RI
Utica
Albany
Springfield
Rochester
Syracuse
Binghamton
Jamestown
NY
Hartford
CT
Bridgeport
New Haven
Scranton
Allentown
NJ
Newark
New York City
Trenton
Philadelphia
Wilmington
Atlantic City
Baltimore
MD
Dover
DE
Annapolis
Washington, D.C.
Alexandria
Salisbury
Charlottesville
Chesapeake Bay
Richmond
VA
Lynchburg
Roanoke
Newport News
Norfolk
Greensboro
Winston-Salem
Durham
Raleigh
New Bern
Cape Hatteras
Johnson City
Mt. Mitchell 6,684 ft. 2,037 m.
Asheville
Greenville
Charlotte
NC
Wilmington
Knoxville
TN
Chattanooga
SC
Columbia
Florence
Augusta
Charleston
Savannah
Brunswick

APPALACHIAN MTS.
ATLANTIC COASTAL PLAIN
ATLANTIC OCEAN
Lake Ontario

ROCKY PLAINS
GREAT PLAINS
OZARK PLATEAU
Arkansas R.
Missouri R.
Platte R.
Tennessee R.

THE WORLD: POLITICAL

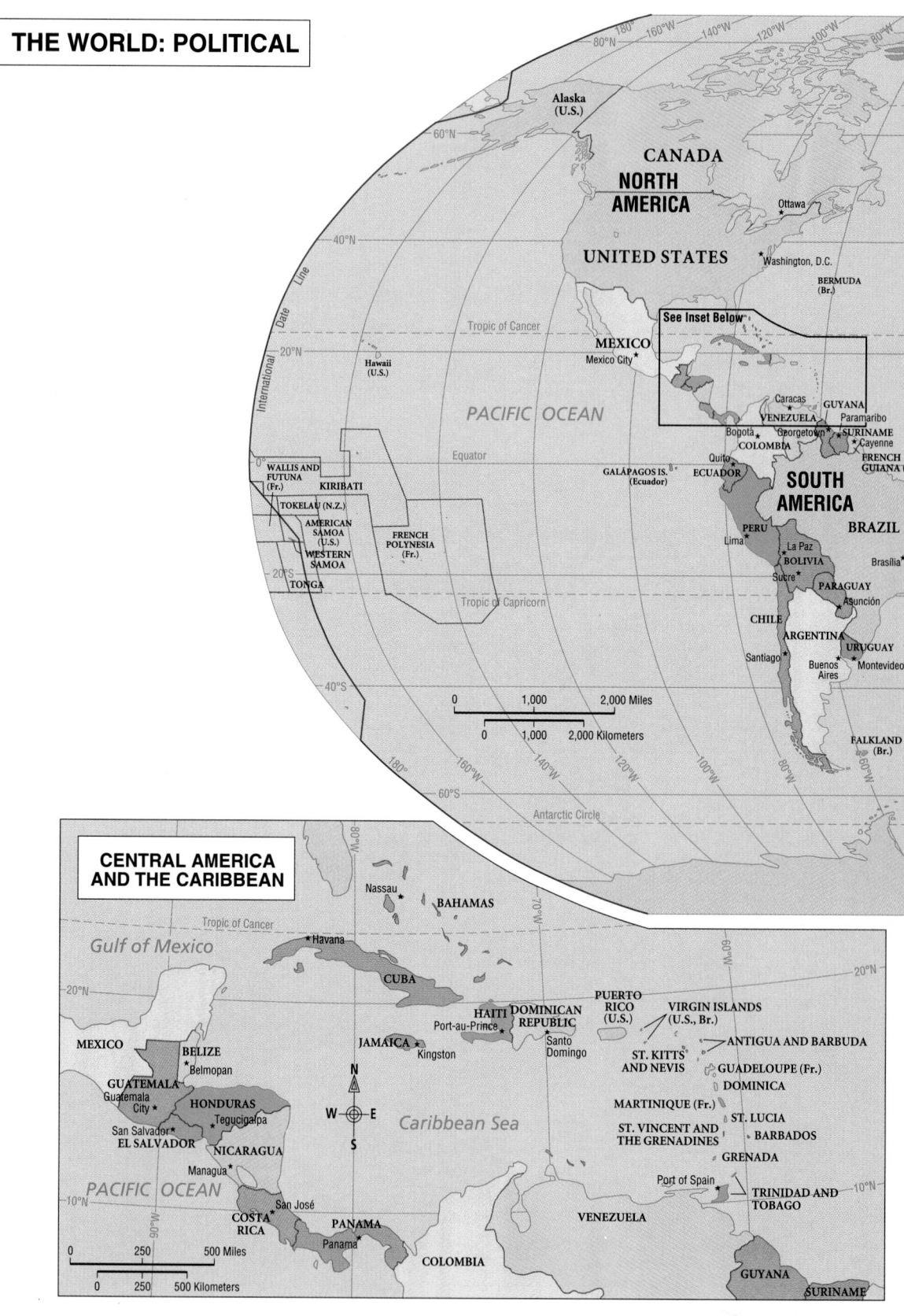

CANADA

NORTH AMERICA

Ottawa ★

UNITED STATES

★ Washington, D.C.

BERMUDA
(Br.)

Alaska
(U.S.)

60°N

80°N

40°N

Tropic of Cancer

20°N

See Inset Below

MEXICO
Mexico City ★

Hawaii
(U.S.)

PACIFIC OCEAN

Equator

Caracas ★
VENEZUELA GUYANA
Bogotá ★ Georgetown ★ Paramaribo
COLOMBIA ★ SURINAME
★ Cayenne
Quito ★ FRENCH
ECUADOR GUIANA (Fr.)

GALÁPAGOS IS.
(Ecuador)

**SOUTH
AMERICA**

WALLIS AND
FUTUNA
(Fr.) KIRIBATI

TOKELAU (N.Z.)

AMERICAN
SAMOA
(U.S.)

FRENCH
POLYNESIA
(Fr.)

WESTERN
SAMOA

20°S

TONGA

Tropic of Capricorn

PERU
Lima ★
La Paz ★
BOLIVIA
Sucre ★

BRAZIL

Brasília ★

PARAGUAY
Asunción ★

CHILE
ARGENTINA
Santiago ★
Buenos
Aires ★

URUGUAY
★ Montevideo

40°S

0	1,000	2,000 Miles

0	1,000	2,000 Kilometers

FALKLAND IS.
(Br.)

60°S

Antarctic Circle

180° 160°W 140°W 120°W 100°W 80°W 60°W 40°W

CENTRAL AMERICA AND THE CARIBBEAN

Nassau ★
BAHAMAS

Tropic of Cancer

Gulf of Mexico

★ Havana
CUBA

20°N

MEXICO

BELIZE
★ Belmopan

GUATEMALA
Guatemala
City ★
HONDURAS
★ Tegucigalpa
San Salvador ★
EL SALVADOR
NICARAGUA
Managua ★

JAMAICA ★
Kingston

HAITI DOMINICAN
REPUBLIC
Port-au-Prince ★ ★ Santo
Domingo

PUERTO
RICO
(U.S.)

VIRGIN ISLANDS
(U.S., Br.)

ANTIGUA AND BARBUDA

ST. KITTS
AND NEVIS
GUADELOUPE (Fr.)
DOMINICA
MARTINIQUE (Fr.)
ST. LUCIA
ST. VINCENT AND
THE GRENADINES
BARBADOS
GRENADA

Caribbean Sea

N
W E
S

PACIFIC OCEAN

10°N

COSTA
RICA
★ San José
PANAMA
Panama ★

VENEZUELA

Port of Spain ★
TRINIDAD AND
TOBAGO

10°N

COLOMBIA

GUYANA

SURINAME

0	250	500 Miles

0	250	500 Kilometers

ILLUSTRATED DATA BANK

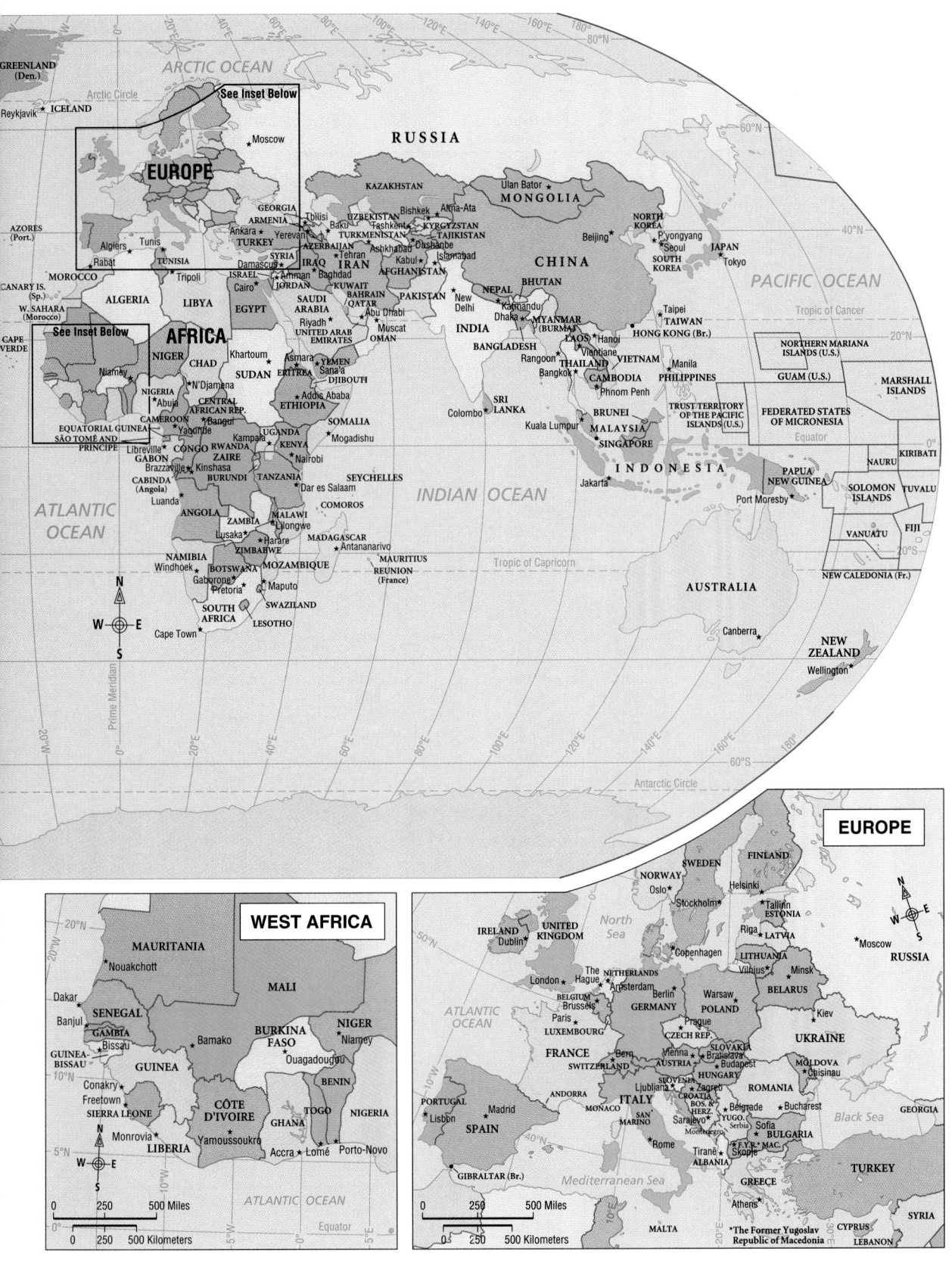

ARCTIC OCEAN

GREENLAND (Den.)

Arctic Circle

Reykjavik ★ ICELAND

See Inset Below

EUROPE

Moscow ★

RUSSIA

AZORES (Port.)

CANARY IS. (Sp.)

Algiers ★ Tunis ★
Rabat ★ TUNISIA

MOROCCO

W. SAHARA (Morocco)

See Inset Below

AFRICA

ALGERIA   LIBYA

CAPE VERDE

NIGER   CHAD

Niamey ★

NIGERIA ★ Abuja

EQUATORIAL GUINEA

SÃO TOMÉ AND PRINCIPE

CAMEROON ★ Bangui

Libreville ★ CONGO

GABON   ZAIRE

Brazzaville ★ ★ Kinshasa

CABINDA (Angola)

Luanda ★

ATLANTIC OCEAN

ANGOLA   ZAMBIA

Lusaka ★

NAMIBIA

Windhoek ★

Gaborone ★

BOTSWANA

Pretoria ★

SOUTH AFRICA

Cape Town ★

N W E S

GEORGIA
ARMENIA
ANKARA ★ Yerevan ★
TURKEY
SYRIA
Damascus ★
ISRAEL
Cairo ★
EGYPT

Tbilisi ★
Baku ★
AZERBAIJAN
IRAQ ★ Baghdad
JORDAN
Amman ★

UZBEKISTAN
Bishkek ★ Alma-Ata ★
Tashkent ★ KYRGYZSTAN
TURKMENISTAN
Ashkhabad ★ Dushanbe ★ TAJIKISTAN
Tehran ★
IRAN
Kabul ★
AFGHANISTAN
KUWAIT
BAHRAIN
QATAR
Abu Dhabi ★
UNITED ARAB EMIRATES
Muscat ★
OMAN

KAZAKHSTAN

Islamabad ★
PAKISTAN

NEPAL
New Delhi ★
INDIA
Kathmandu ★
Dhaka ★

Khartoum ★
SUDAN
Asmara ★
ERITREA
N'Djamena ★
CENTRAL AFRICAN REP.
Yaoundé ★
UGANDA
RWANDA
Kampala ★
BURUNDI
Nairobi ★
KENYA
TANZANIA
Dar es Salaam ★

Addis Ababa ★
ETHIOPIA
SOMALIA
Mogadishu ★

Sana'a ★
YEMEN
DJIBOUTI

MALAWI
Lilongwe ★
ZIMBABWE
Harare ★
MOZAMBIQUE
Maputo ★
SWAZILAND
LESOTHO

SEYCHELLES

COMOROS

MADAGASCAR
Antananarivo ★

MAURITIUS
REUNION (France)

INDIAN OCEAN

Ulan Bator ★
MONGOLIA

RUSSIA

Beijing ★

CHINA

BHUTAN
MYANMAR (BURMA)
Rangoon ★
BANGLADESH

SRI LANKA
Colombo ★

NORTH KOREA
Pyongyang ★
Seoul ★
SOUTH KOREA

JAPAN
Tokyo ★

Taipei ★
TAIWAN
HONG KONG (Br.)

LAOS ★ Hanoi
Vientiane ★
VIETNAM
THAILAND
Bangkok ★
CAMBODIA
★ Phnom Penh

Manila ★
PHILIPPINES

BRUNEI
MALAYSIA
Kuala Lumpur ★
SINGAPORE

Jakarta ★

INDONESIA

PACIFIC OCEAN

Tropic of Cancer

NORTHERN MARIANA ISLANDS (U.S.)

GUAM (U.S.)

TRUST TERRITORY OF THE PACIFIC ISLANDS (U.S.)

FEDERATED STATES OF MICRONESIA

Equator

NAURU

PAPUA NEW GUINEA
Port Moresby ★

KIRIBATI

MARSHALL ISLANDS

SOLOMON ISLANDS

TUVALU

VANUATU

FIJI

NEW CALEDONIA (Fr.)

AUSTRALIA

Canberra ★

NEW ZEALAND
Wellington ★

Tropic of Capricorn

ATLANTIC OCEAN

Antarctic Circle

WEST AFRICA

MAURITANIA

Nouakchott ★

Dakar ★
SENEGAL
Banjul ★
GAMBIA
Bissau ★
GUINEA-BISSAU

MALI

Bamako ★

GUINEA

Conakry ★
Freetown ★
SIERRA LEONE

Monrovia ★

LIBERIA

CÔTE D'IVOIRE

Yamoussoukro ★

BURKINA FASO
Ouagadougou ★

GHANA

Accra ★

NIGER
Niamey ★

BENIN

TOGO

Lomé ★ Porto-Novo ★

NIGERIA

N W E S

0   250   500 Miles

0   250   500 Kilometers

ATLANTIC OCEAN

Equator

EUROPE

NORWAY
Oslo ★

SWEDEN

FINLAND
Helsinki ★

Stockholm ★

North Sea

IRELAND
Dublin ★

UNITED KINGDOM

London ★

ATLANTIC OCEAN

The Hague ★ NETHERLANDS
Amsterdam ★
BELGIUM
Brussels ★
Paris ★
LUXEMBOURG

Berlin ★
GERMANY

FRANCE

Bern ★
SWITZERLAND
Vienna ★
AUSTRIA

ANDORRA

PORTUGAL
Lisbon ★

MONACO

SPAIN
Madrid ★

SLOVENIA
Ljubljana ★
CROATIA
BOS. & HERZ.
Sarajevo ★
Montenegro

ITALY

SAN MARINO

Rome ★

Tallinn ★
ESTONIA
Riga ★
LATVIA

Moscow ★

RUSSIA

LITHUANIA
Vilnius ★
Minsk ★
BELARUS

Copenhagen ★

Warsaw ★
POLAND

Prague ★
CZECH REP.
SLOVAKIA
Bratislava ★
Budapest ★
HUNGARY

Kiev ★

UKRAINE

MOLDOVA
Chisinau ★

Zagreb ★
Belgrade ★
YUGO.
Serbia

ROMANIA
Bucharest ★

Black Sea

GEORGIA

BULGARIA
Sofia ★

Tirane ★
ALBANIA
F.Y.R. MAC.
Skopje ★

GREECE
Athens ★

Mediterranean Sea

GIBRALTAR (Br.)

MALTA

CYPRUS

TURKEY

SYRIA

LEBANON

*The Former Yugoslav Republic of Macedonia

0   250   500 Miles

0   250   500 Kilometers

N W E S

The Fifty States

State	Capital	Entered Union	Population (1990 Census)	Population Rank	Land Area (Square Miles)	Land Area Rank
Alabama	Montgomery	1819	4,040,587	22nd	51,705	29th
Alaska	Juneau	1959	550,043	49th	591,004	1st
Arizona	Phoenix	1912	3,665,228	24th	114,000	6th
Arkansas	Little Rock	1836	2,350,725	33rd	53,187	27th
California	Sacramento	1850	29,760,021	1st	158,706	3rd
Colorado	Denver	1876	3,294,394	26th	104,091	8th
Connecticut	Hartford	1788	3,287,116	27th	5,018	48th
Delaware	Dover	1787	666,168	46th	2,044	49th
Florida	Tallahassee	1845	12,937,926	4th	58,664	22nd
Georgia	Atlanta	1788	6,478,216	11th	58,910	21st
Hawaii	Honolulu	1959	1,108,229	41st	6,470	47th
Idaho	Boise	1890	1,006,749	42nd	83,564	13th
Illinois	Springfield	1818	11,430,602	6th	56,345	24th
Indiana	Indianapolis	1816	5,544,159	14th	36,185	38th
Iowa	Des Moines	1846	2,776,755	30th	56,275	25th
Kansas	Topeka	1861	2,477,574	32nd	82,277	14th
Kentucky	Frankfort	1792	3,685,296	23rd	40,409	37th
Louisiana	Baton Rouge	1812	4,219,973	21st	47,751	31st
Maine	Augusta	1820	1,227,928	38th	33,265	39th
Maryland	Annapolis	1788	4,781,468	19th	10,460	42nd
Massachusetts	Boston	1788	6,016,425	13th	8,284	45th
Michigan	Lansing	1837	9,295,297	8th	58,527	23rd
Minnesota	St. Paul	1858	4,375,099	20th	84,402	12th
Mississippi	Jackson	1817	2,573,216	31st	47,689	32nd
Missouri	Jefferson City	1821	5,117,073	15th	69,697	19th
Montana	Helena	1889	799,065	44th	147,046	4th
Nebraska	Lincoln	1867	1,578,385	36th	77,355	15th
Nevada	Carson City	1864	1,201,833	39th	110,561	7th
New Hampshire	Concord	1788	1,109,252	40th	9,279	44th
New Jersey	Trenton	1787	7,730,188	9th	7,787	46th
New Mexico	Santa Fe	1912	1,515,069	37th	121,593	5th
New York	Albany	1788	17,990,455	2nd	49,108	30th
North Carolina	Raleigh	1789	6,628,637	10th	52,669	28th
North Dakota	Bismarck	1889	638,800	47th	70,703	17th
Ohio	Columbus	1803	10,847,115	7th	41,330	35th
Oklahoma	Oklahoma City	1907	3,145,585	28th	69,956	18th
Oregon	Salem	1859	2,842,321	29th	97,073	10th
Pennsylvania	Harrisburg	1787	11,881,643	5th	45,308	33rd
Rhode Island	Providence	1790	1,003,464	43rd	1,212	50th
South Carolina	Columbia	1788	3,386,703	25th	31,113	40th
South Dakota	Pierre	1889	696,004	45th	77,116	16th
Tennessee	Nashville	1796	4,877,185	17th	42,144	34th
Texas	Austin	1845	16,986,510	3rd	266,807	2nd
Utah	Salt Lake City	1896	1,722,850	35th	84,899	11th
Vermont	Montpelier	1791	562,758	48th	9,614	43rd
Virginia	Richmond	1788	6,187,358	12th	40,767	36th
Washington	Olympia	1889	4,866,692	18th	68,138	20th
West Virginia	Charleston	1863	1,793,477	34th	24,231	41st
Wisconsin	Madison	1848	4,891,769	16th	56,153	26th
Wyoming	Cheyenne	1890	453,588	50th	97,809	9th

Source: *The Universal Almanac*, 1993

ILLUSTRATED DATA BANK

Name	Party	State*	Entered Office	Vice President(s)
1 George Washington (1732-1799)	Federalist	Virginia	1789	John Adams
2 John Adams (1735-1826)	Federalist	Massachusetts	1797	Thomas Jefferson
3 Thomas Jefferson (1743-1826)	Dem-Rep	Virginia	1801	Aaron Burr/George Clinton
4 James Madison (1751-1836)	Dem-Rep	Virginia	1809	George Clinton/Elbridge Gerry
5 James Monroe (1758-1831)	Dem-Rep	Virginia	1817	Daniel D. Tompkins
6 John Q. Adams (1767-1848)	Dem-Rep	Massachusetts	1767	John C. Calhoun
7 Andrew Jackson (1767-1845)	Democrat	Tennessee (SC)	1829	John C. Calhoun/Martin Van Buren
8 Martin Van Buren (1782-1862)	Democrat	New York	1837	Richard M. Johnson
9 William H. Harrison (1773-1841)	Whig	Ohio (VA)	1841	John Tyler
10 John Tyler (1790-1862)	Democrat	Virginia	1841	. . . .
11 James K. Polk (1795-1849)	Democrat	Tennessee (NC)	1845	George M. Dallas
12 Zachary Taylor (1784-1850)	Whig	Louisiana (VA)	1849	Millard Fillmore
13 Millard Fillmore (1800-1874)	Whig	New York	1850	. . . .
14 Franklin Pierce (1804-1869)	Democrat	New Hampshire	1853	William R. King
15 James Buchanan (1791-1868)	Democrat	Pennsylvania	1857	John C. Breckinridge
16 Abraham Lincoln (1809-1865)	Republican	Illinois (KY)	1861	Hannibal Hamlin/Andrew Johnson
17 Andrew Johnson (1808-1875)	Democrat	Tennessee (NC)	1865	. . . .
18 Ulysses S. Grant (1822-1885)	Republican	Illinois (OH)	1869	Schuyler Colfax/Henry Wilson
19 Rutherford B. Hayes (1822-1893)	Republican	Ohio	1877	William A. Wheeler
20 James A. Garfield (1831-1881)	Republican	Ohio	1881	Chester A. Arthur
21 Chester A. Arthur (1830-1886)	Republican	New York (VT)	1881	. . . .
22 Grover Cleveland (1837-1908)	Democrat	New York (NJ)	1885	Thomas A. Hendricks
23 Benjamin Harrison (1833-1901)	Republican	Indiana (OH)	1889	Levi P. Morton
24 Grover Cleveland (1837-1908)	Democrat	New York (NJ)	1893	Adlai E. Stevenson
25 William McKinley (1843-1901)	Republican	Ohio	1897	Garret A. Hobart/Theodore Roosevelt
26 Theodore Roosevelt (1858-1919)	Republican	New York	1901	. . . ./Charles W. Fairbanks
27 William H. Taft (1857-1930)	Republican	Ohio	1909	James S. Sherman
28 Woodrow Wilson (1856-1924)	Democrat	New Jersey (VA)	1913	Thomas R. Marshall
29 Warren G. Harding (1865-1923)	Republican	Ohio	1921	Calvin Coolidge
30 Calvin Coolidge (1872-1933)	Republican	Massachusetts (VT)	1923	. . . ./Charles G. Dawes
31 Herbert Hoover (1874-1964)	Republican	California (IA)	1929	Charles Curtis
32 Franklin Roosevelt (1882-1945)	Democrat	New York	1933	John N. Garner/Henry A. Wallace/ Harry S Truman
33 Harry S Truman (1884-1972)	Democrat	Missouri	1945	. . . ./Alben W. Barkley
34 Dwight D. Eisenhower (1890-1969)	Republican	NY-PA (TX)	1953	Richard M. Nixon
35 John F. Kennedy (1917-1963)	Democrat	Massachusetts	1961	Lyndon B. Johnson
36 Lyndon B. Johnson (1908-1973)	Democrat	Texas	1963	. . . ./Hubert H. Humphrey
37 Richard M. Nixon (1913-1994)	Republican	New York (CA)	1969	Spiro T. Agnew/Gerald R. Ford
38 Gerald R. Ford (1913-)	Republican	Michigan (NE)	1974	Nelson A. Rockefeller
39 James E. Carter (1924-)	Democrat	Georgia	1977	Walter F. Mondale
40 Ronald W. Reagan (1911-)	Republican	California (IL)	1981	George H.W. Bush
41 George H.W. Bush (1924-)	Republican	Texas (MA)	1989	J. Danforth Quayle
42 William J. Clinton (1946-)	Democrat	Arkansas	1993	Albert Gore, Jr.

* State of residence when elected; if born in another state that state in parentheses.

Key Events That Shaped the Nation

In addition to the seven "Turning Point" events discussed in detail in this book, the list that follows describes seventy-six events (arranged in chronological order) that have shaped the United States. Like all such lists, this one is biased—representing the personal opinions of this textbook's authors. The list is not intended to include every event of lasting importance. If it were, the result would be a list many times longer. You are invited to think about the events on this list, debate their significance with your classmates, and add events of your own.

1607 Jamestown and Tobacco

Jamestown, the first permanent English settlement in the Americas, teetered on the edge of ruin for the first decade of its existence. The colony was saved, however, when John Rolfe recognized that tobacco, which was highly prized in Europe, thrived in the climate and soil of Virginia. The lure of wealth from tobacco farming ensured the colony a steady stream of colonists. At the same time, Jamestown provided England with a foothold in North America and helped inspire further attempts at colonization.

1619 The Arrival of Enslaved Africans in North America

In 1619, Dutch traders sold twenty Africans to the English colonists in Jamestown. Unfamiliar with the concept of slavery, the colonists treated the Africans the same way they treated English indentured servants, who were freed after working off debts incurred in their passage to North America. It was not until the 1680s that the use of enslaved Africans became widespread. By 1760 about 325,000 enslaved Africans labored in England's North American colonies.

1651 The Navigation Acts

In the 1600s, England and the Netherlands clashed over which nation would control trade in Europe and the Americas. This economic competition caused the English government to enact a series of Navigation Acts beginning in 1651. These acts sought to cut the Dutch out of the profitable colonial trade by forcing the English colonies to limit their trade in certain goods to England alone. As the result of a series of wars between the two European powers, the English captured and retained the prosperous Dutch colony of New Amsterdam in 1664, renaming it New York. New York City became one of the most profitable commercial centers in the English colonies.

1670 The Founding of South Carolina

Planters from the island of Barbados founded Charleston in 1670, establishing what in 1701 would become the colony of South Carolina. These planters brought enslaved Africans with them, and, using the Africans' knowledge of rice farming, developed a plantation economy based upon rice cultivation. Slavery became so heavily established in South Carolina that by 1720 the African enslaved population outnumbered the white population by two to one. This lopsided ratio created an undercurrent of fear among white Americans that would lead to further repressive measures against the enslaved people.

1680 Popé's Rebellion

In an attempt to gain a firm hold on their colony in New Mexico, the Spanish ruthlessly exploited the native Pueblo people. Not only were the Pueblo forced into slavery, but they were also subject to the Spaniards' brutal attempts at destroying native religious practices. Popé, a Pueblo religious leader, led a rebellion in 1680. Under his leadership, the Pueblo drove the Spanish completely out of New Mexico. The Spanish returned twelve years later, but they never again attempted to enslave the Pueblos and gave some measure of respect to Pueblo cultural identity.

1720s–1760s The Great Awakening

A series of religious revivals swept through the colonies between 1720 and 1760, igniting religious fervor with an emphasis on achieving salvation. The so-called Great Awakening reached its peak in 1739, thanks to the preaching of George Whitefield. The twenty-four-year-old Whitefield, an Anglican priest, won converts by the thousands with his dramatic sermons. The Great Awakening helped shape the colonists' commitment to religious pluralism and equality, which later would help to shape their commitment to revolution against the British Empire.

1759 The Fall of Quebec

After five long years of defeat in the French and Indian War, the British finally turned the tides in 1759. Brigadier General James Wolfe decided to attempt the capture of Quebec, the capital of New France. Wolfe surrounded the fortress, eventually drawing out the French commander, Montcalm, into open battle. When the conflict was over, Wolfe and Montcalm lay dead, and the British controlled Quebec. This victory foreshadowed an overall French defeat in the war and the loss of all the French holdings in North America.

1765 The Stamp Act

In an attempt to raise money and pay the cost of an army to protect the colonies, Parliament passed the Stamp Act in 1765. This law required colonists to buy official stamps—in effect, pay a tax—for items such as legal documents. The British had had such a tax for 100 years, and Parliament felt justified requiring it in the colonies. But Parliament underestimated colonial reaction to the act. The direct taxation of the Stamp Act outraged and united the colonies. Colonial assemblies passed resolutions claiming the sole right to pass taxes, and riots broke out in numerous port cities. Colonial sentiment against Great Britain deepened.

1775 Lexington and Concord

As relations between colonists and the British worsened, colonists began collecting weapons in preparation for war. On April 19, 1775, General Thomas Gage, the British military commander in Boston, sent about 700 British soldiers on a raid to seize weapons in nearby Concord. Warned in advance, colonial militiamen assembled on the village green in Lexington, a town through which the British would pass on their way to Concord. Upon arriving in Lexington, the British ordered the colonials to disperse. An unknown person then fired a shot, and both sides began shooting. When the smoke cleared, eight colonials lay dead. Marching on to Concord, the British found a much larger force of armed colonists waiting. After a battle in Concord, the British retreated toward Boston. Along the way, colonists fired on the British from the roadside, inflicting 273 casualties. The Revolutionary War had begun.

1776   The Declaration of Independence

The Second Continental Congress established a committee of five men to write a declaration of American independence. The committee insisted that Thomas Jefferson, a young Virginian, write the original draft. The Continental Congress approved the document, with some revisions, and on July 4, the thirteen colonies declared their independence from Great Britain.

1787   The Northwest Ordinance

The United States faced a serious problem after the Revolutionary War: sorting out land claims in its huge territory west of the Appalachian Mountains. States with large land claims in this territory insisted they be given the land; states with no claims argued for congressional control of the territory. Congress passed the Northwest Ordinance to solve these problems. This act reduced tensions over land claims, granted settlers the right to form their own territorial governments, and provided for an orderly admission of the new territories into statehood. This act guaranteed Americans in the new states equal representation in government, which set the stage for the rapid expansion of the United States.

1787   The Constitutional Convention

The weak American government created under the Articles of Confederation had become a serious concern to a powerful group of American leaders. The very survival of the republic seemed at stake. So when Congress called a convention to reform the Articles, the delegates quickly decided to go beyond their assigned task and form an entirely new government. The result of their efforts was the Constitution. In 1788 the Constitution was ratified, creating a new, powerful central government that would alter the nature of American democracy.

1793   The Invention of the Cotton Gin

Although it is a matter of some debate who invented the cotton gin, Eli Whitney gained credit for the machine. The simple box contraption separated seeds from cotton fifty times faster than could be done by hand. The gin helped make possible a great expansion in cotton production. Increasing cotton production led to an increase in the practice of slavery in the South. Cotton and cotton products were the most important American exports until 1839, helping to fuel the expanding American economy.

1803   Marbury v. Madison

In the final hours of his presidency, John Adams appointed William Marbury to a judicial post. When President Jefferson took office, however, he declared that Marbury's appointment would not be honored. Marbury sued, taking the case to the Supreme Court. Chief Justice John Marshall denied Marbury's argument on a technicality. In the process, Marshall held that the courts have the power to declare acts of Congress unconstitutional. This landmark

decision established the principle of judicial review, which gave great authority to the Supreme Court.

1803   The Louisiana Purchase

President Jefferson and the Senate nearly doubled the size of the nation by purchasing the Louisiana territory from France. The Louisiana territory was an enormous area of land that extended from the Mississippi River to the Rocky Mountains and from the Louisiana coast to Canada. The United States paid about $15 million for more than 800 million acres of land, a cost of about 1.8 cents per acre. Territory from the Louisiana Purchase created all or part of thirteen states.

1820   The Missouri Compromise

In 1819 the United States consisted of eleven free states and eleven slave states. "Free" Maine and "slave" Missouri were seeking statehood. At this point, Representative James Tallmadge introduced an amendment providing for gradual emancipation in Missouri. This sparked off a round of bitter debate. Henry Clay offered a compromise. Missouri would be slave and Maine free. And, in cases of territories seeking statehood in the future, land north of latitude 36° 30' would be free, and land south of the line would be open to slavery. The compromise temporarily quieted congressional debate over slavery and preserved the balance between the opposing sides in Congress.

1825   The Opening of the Erie Canal

The Erie Canal opened in 1825 after seven years of construction. The canal was a marvel of engineering: 40 feet wide and 364 miles long. Its closest competitor was only 28 miles long. The canal greatly improved shipping between the Great Lakes region and New York City. The Erie Canal encouraged commerce and economic growth all along its route, and it also made New York City a vital center for western trade. The Erie Canal's success represented the transportation revolution in the United States that accelerated the growth of the economy.

1830   The Indian Removal Act

President Andrew Jackson supported the Indian Removal Act, which made provisions for the relocation of Native Americans living in the Southeast to what is today Oklahoma. In spite of the act, however, most of the Cherokee people living within the borders of Georgia and other states remained in their homes. But in 1837 and 1838, the United States Army forcibly moved the Cherokee west. The event came to be known as the "Trail of Tears," because as many as one quarter of the 15,000 Cherokee who made the trek died. The removal opened up vast tracts of land in the Southeast for white settlement, but Native Americans paid a terrible price.

1831   Nat Turner's Revolt and Garrison's Liberator

In 1831 the southern slaveholding culture suffered two powerful attacks. William Lloyd Garrison made a fiery appeal for the immediate end to slavery in the first issue of his abolitionist publication, *The Liberator*. Eight months later, African American Nat Turner led a slave revolt that stunned southern white society. Turner presented himself as a prophet ordained by God to free his people. With a small band of followers, he launched a revolt that was quickly crushed. Shaken by the verbal attacks by Garrison and the physical attacks of Turner, white southerners sought to tighten their control over enslaved people and heightened sectional tensions.

1832 The Nullification Crisis

South Carolina grew increasingly fearful of the federal government's power in the wake of spreading abolitionist views. Vice President John C. Calhoun, a South Carolinian, developed the doctrine of nullification, which held that a state had the right to nullify any law harmful to its interests. This doctrine struck at the heart of the dispute over the rights of the states versus the power of the federal government. President Andrew Jackson threatened to use force if South Carolina defied federal law. Meanwhile, Congress worked out a compromise that temporarily ended the standoff. The debate over states' rights, however, remained unresolved and would be decided only by the Civil War.

1834 – early 1850s The Settlement of the Oregon Country

The Oregon Country, home to numerous Native American groups for centuries, extended from northern California to the southern border of Alaska. Ignoring the Native Americans who already lived there, the United States and Britain signed a treaty in 1818 agreeing to joint occupation. Starting off from Independence, Missouri, settlers traveled along the Oregon Trail, a 2,000-mile trek across the Great Plains and the Rocky Mountains. Between 1842 and 1848, approximately 11,500 pioneers migrated to Oregon. In 1846, the United States and Britain agreed to divide the Oregon Country along the 49th parallel.

1836 The Founding of the Texas Republic

In 1822 Stephen Austin founded a colony of about 300 settlers in Texas, which then belonged to Mexico. By 1835 more than 30,000 Americans and 3,000 enslaved African Americans lived in Texas. In March 1836, supporters of a Texas independence movement formally declared the founding of the Republic of Texas. Mexico's leader, General Santa Anna, led an army of several thousand men to subdue the rebellion. At the Alamo, a former mission in San Antonio, fewer than 200 Texans held off 4,000 Mexican troops but ultimately were defeated. At the Battle of San Jacinto in April 1836 the Texas rebels routed Mexican troops and later forced Santa Anna to sign a treaty recognizing the republic. With almost no help from the United States government, Texas settlers had succeeded in gaining a large piece of territory from Mexico.

1848 The Discovery of Gold at Sutter's Mill, California

No event was more important in attracting settlers to the West than the discovery of gold at Sutter's Mill near the city of Sacramento in California in 1848. Lured by the promise of gold, people rushed west by the thousands. California had 14,000 residents in 1848; within a year its population was 100,000, and by 1852 the number had reached 200,000. The gold rush had a tremendous impact on life in California. Native Americans were forced to work in the mines, and disease and forced labor greatly reduced their population. While the gold rush devastated the Native Americans, it also brought growth to Pacific coast cities.

1848 The Treaty of Guadalupe Hidalgo

The Treaty of Guadalupe Hidalgo ended the Mexican War, which took place between 1846 and 1848 over a dispute between the United States and Mexico about the southern border of Texas. Under the terms of the Treaty of Guadalupe Hidalgo, Mexico ceded the United States one third of its territory, including present-day California, New Mexico, Nevada, Utah, and Arizona. The territorial acquisition, however, once again sparked bitter controversy over the extension of slavery and the balance of slave and free states in Congress.

1857 Dred Scott v. Sandford

Dred Scott, an enslaved African American living in Missouri, filed suit against his owner. He argued that because he and his wife, Harriet, had once been taken into states and territories where slavery was illegal, the couple was in fact free. The case reached the Supreme Court, and, in one of its most controversial rulings, the justices ruled against the Scotts. The Court held that as an African American, Scott was not a citizen and could not sue anyone. The Court also held that, because enslaved persons were property, Congress had to protect the rights of the slave owner. This decision stayed in force until the passage of the Fourteenth Amendment, which in 1868 guaranteed citizenship to African Americans.

1861 The Secession of the South

The election of Republican Abraham Lincoln to the presidency in the 1860 election demonstrated to the white South that northerners had the ability to elect a purely regional—and antislavery—candidate. Within a matter of months, seven southern states seceded and formed the Confederate States of America. Calmer heads on both sides sought to avoid the crisis, but events had proceeded beyond their control. The decisive incident came on April 12, 1861, when Confederate forces bombarded and captured the federal garrison of Fort Sumter in South Carolina, starting the Civil War. The United States had run out of peaceful compromises, and as a result over 600,000 Americans would die.

1863 The Emancipation Proclamation

President Lincoln issued the Emancipation Proclamation on New Year's Day, 1863. Lincoln had long said that the purpose of the Civil War was to save the Union. But he now realized that the war must also be a crusade against slavery. Critics noted that the declaration did not physically free a single enslaved person. The proclamation changed the nature of the war for the Union, however, adding to the war's purpose the freeing of enslaved people. The pronouncement also helped the Union politically by reducing the likelihood that Great Britain, which hated slavery, would support the South.

1863 The Battle of Gettysburg

In the summer of 1863, General Robert E. Lee led a Confederate army into the North. Lee thought he could end the Civil War by defeating a Union army on its own soil, which would compel the war-weary Union to recognize Confederate independence. Lee's army met the Union forces under General George Meade at Gettysburg, a small Pennsylvania town. The bloody fighting ended with Lee withdrawing his mauled army. The three days of battle cost nearly 50,000 casualties on both sides. Lee's shattered Confederate army never recovered and Union victories mounted. America's most costly war ended in 1865, with the Confederacy's surrender.

1865 African American Higher Education

Reconstruction offered African Americans an era of new promise. The African American community saw a great need for a core of educated leaders. Responding to this need, the American Missionary Association, the African Methodist Episcopal Church, and numerous other religious groups and philanthropists founded educational institutions throughout the country. Out of these efforts emerged the nation's leading black institutions of higher education, including Howard, Fisk, Atlanta, Dillard, Tougaloo, Morehouse, and Spelman. These colleges and universities were invaluable to African Americans, nurturing future political and social leaders.

1865–1870 The Reconstruction Amendments

The Thirteenth, Fourteenth, and Fifteenth amendments to the Constitution represented the central efforts of the Radical Republicans to benefit African Americans in the post–Civil War era. The Thirteenth Amendment abolished forever the institution of slavery. The Fourteenth and Fifteenth amendments guaranteed African Americans full citizenship and stated that the right to vote could not be denied on the basis of color or creed. After 1877, however, northern apathy for the issue of African American rights enabled southern states to deny African Americans many protections of the Fourteenth and Fifteenth amendments. Not until the 1960s were these injustices remedied.

1867 The Purchase of Alaska

When Russia expressed its desire to sell Alaska to the United States, William H. Seward, President Andrew Johnson's secretary of state, persuaded Congress to appropriate the asking price of $7.2 million. Initially mocked as "Seward's Folly," the purchase was to prove its asking price many times over. Thirty years later, an Alaskan gold rush yielded millions of dollars worth of gold. With this acquisition of Alaska, Russian influence in North America was eliminated and the United States gained a huge new territory.

1869 The Founding of the Knights of Labor

Originally founded as a secret labor society in 1869, the Noble Order of the Knights of Labor became a national, public organization in 1879. Terrence Powderly, the Knights' leader, sought reforms such as an eight-hour day and better wages. The Knights also attempted to form a political party by running candidates for political office, though their attempts were largely unsuccessful. Although the organization faded from significance by the end of the 1900s, the Knights of Labor was the most important representative of American labor into the 1890s.

1869 The Transcontinental Railroad

During the Civil War, the Union government promoted the building of railroads by offering generous land grants. One such project was a railroad that would link the West Coast with the East. The line was to be built by two different companies: the Central Pacific and the Union Pacific. In 1869, the two lines linked up in Utah, completing the first transcontinental railroad. The railroads promoted settlement of the West and helped create a nationwide transportation system that sparked tremendous growth in the American economy.

1869 Women's Suffrage in the Wyoming Territory

Western territories, with their rugged life styles and small populations, depended on women to take roles in social and political life that were unavailable to them in the eastern United States. In 1869 the Wyoming Territory passed into law a bill that granted women the right to vote and fully participate in national politics. This set a trend followed by many of Wyoming's neighbors. By 1914 every state in the western third of the nation, except New Mexico, had passed women's suffrage bills. The trailblazing of these western states helped pave the way for the ratification of the Nineteenth Amendment, which guaranteed all women the right to vote, in 1920.

1876 The Invention of the Telephone

On March 10, 1876, Alexander Graham Bell uttered the words, "Mr. Watson, come here. I want you." These few words, transmitted over a Bell invention called the telephone, altered communications technology forever. In the years ahead, Bell's American Telephone and Telegraph Company (AT&T) organized telephone line service and made widespread use of the telephone practical. By 1899 about one million telephones were operating in the United States. That number had grown to ten million by 1915. The telephone created a reliable, nationwide communication system that would play a vital part in American economic expansion.

1882 The Opening of the First Power Plant

Thomas Edison opened the first electric power plant in 1882. The plant generated energy that made electric lights glow throughout the Wall Street district in New York City. The display so impressed the public that investors poured money into construction of new power plants. Within sixteen years, nearly 3,000 stations provided power to businesses and the public. By 1929 two thirds of American families had electricity, and electric generators supplied 80 percent of industrial power needs.

1886 AF of L Formed

As the Noble Order of the Knights of Labor foundered in the 1890s, a new organization emerged to replace it as the leading national labor union. In 1886 Samuel Gompers organized the American Federation of Labor (AF of L). Gompers and the AF of L focused on such issues as a shorter workday, better wages, and safer working conditions. By 1900 the AF of L had one million members, and was the most important national union.

1887 The Dawes Severalty Act

Native American people in the West suffered greatly as settlers moved onto their lands. Reformers concerned with the fate of the Native Americans believed strongly that only by adopting the customs and values of white civilization could Native Americans be saved. Toward this end, Congress passed the Dawes Severalty Act. The law broke up tribal lands and allotted land parcels to individuals. Government officials hoped that individual land ownership would encourage Native Americans to farm like white

Americans. In reality, relatively few Native Americans were able or willing to farm on their individual plots. Many sold their land to whites. As a result, Native American land holdings dwindled.

KEY EVENTS

1890 The Formation of the National American Woman Suffrage Association

As the drive for women's suffrage heated up in the late 1800s, two leading woman suffrage groups joined forces to form the National American Woman Suffrage Association (NAWSA). NAWSA coordinated the efforts of state suffrage groups and utilized pressure tactics to convince legislators to vote for suffrage bills. The group's efforts finally paid off in 1920, when the Nineteenth Amendment was ratified.

1893 The First Automobiles

Inventors first developed prototypes of automobiles in 1893. This mode of transportation did not become common, however, until the 1910s and 1920s. It was then that Henry Ford's car company began to mass-produce cars at a cost low enough for working people to afford. By 1929 there were almost 27 million registered cars in the United States. The automobile industry became a dominant force in the American economy. Cars, trucks, and buses revolutionized American transportation and helped to spur the continued growth of the suburbs.

1896 Plessy v. Ferguson

By the 1880s, the United States government clearly had retreated from its commitment to African American equality. Southern state and local governments passed laws that segregated public facilities. The Supreme Court ruled on the constitutionality of these laws in the landmark case *Plessy* v. *Ferguson*. In its ruling, the Court held that "separate but equal" facilities did not violate the Fourteenth Amendment. Until the 1950s, southern states continued their systematic segregation of southern society and denial of African American voting and civil rights.

1898 The Spanish-American War and the Annexation of Hawaii

A powerful group of Americans sought to expand United States' influence beyond its own shores in the late 1890s. The Cuban revolt from Spain provided an opportunity, as public sentiment turned against the Spanish. In addition to its alleged mistreatment of the Cuban people, Spain was blamed for the mysterious sinking of the American battleship *Maine* in Havana harbor. The Spanish-American War lasted for three months, and victory gave the United States control of Puerto Rico and Guam. The United States also annexed the Philippines. Meanwhile, in Hawaii, an 1893 coup by American planters led to the overthrow of the Hawaiian government, and the islands were annexed by the United States government in 1898.

1909 The Founding of the NAACP

A prominent group of white and African American reformers joined together in 1909 to form the National Association for the Advancement of Colored People (NAACP). This organization fought important battles for voting rights and against segregation and lynching. In 1915 the NAACP scored its first major victory when the Supreme Court declared so-called grandfather clauses unconstitutional. These laws had been used throughout the South as part of an effort to deny African Americans their voting rights. The NAACP continued to fight discrimination and white violence and remains a leading civil rights organization today.

1914 The Opening of the Panama Canal

The Isthmus of Panama was an ideal location for a quick route between the Atlantic and Pacific oceans. After supporting a Panamanian revolt against Colombia in 1903, the United States received a permanent grant of a 10-mile-wide Canal Zone across the isthmus. Construction began in 1904 and ended ten years later. At a cost of $400 million, the United States now had easy access between two oceans and a greater ability to extend its power to other parts of the world.

1917 The United States Entry into World War I

After several years of claiming neutrality in World War I, the United States finally entered the war on the side of the Allies in 1917. American forces delivered an Allied victory, but after the war, revenge-minded Allied leaders frustrated Wilson's visions for postwar peace and security, opting instead to humiliate the defeated Germans. The Germans never forgot nor forgave their treatment at the hands of the Allies. The treaty contained the seeds of future conflict between the powers of Europe.

1929 The Stock Market Crash

In October 1929, stock prices plummeted. The stock market crash helped push the American economy into a deep downward cycle that would come to be known as the Great Depression. Unregulated speculation on the stock market, overvalued stocks, bad government policy, and a decline in purchasing power all contributed to the downturn. The Depression caused thousands of banks to close. By 1932 median income had been cut in half. Unemployment remained high throughout the 1930s, ranging from 20 to 38 percent. More than merely an economic crisis, the Depression shattered many Americans' faith in government and business.

1935 The Social Security Act

During the Depression, President Franklin Roosevelt initiated reforms to ensure that no future depression would have such a devastating effect on the nation. The Social Security Act grew out of these efforts. This act provided income for retired workers, compensation to the unemployed, and assistance for dependent children. The program was funded by joint employee-employer contributions. The Social Security Act was a landmark piece of legislation that helped to create the foundation for the modern welfare state.

1935 The Wagner Act

Prior to 1935, President Roosevelt had not been interested in extending labor protections through new legislation. But when the Supreme Court struck down existing legislation that included key protections for labor, Roosevelt gave his support to the National Labor Relations Act, commonly known as the Wagner Act. This act outlawed blacklisting—by which employers conspired not to hire certain workers—and guaranteed labor the right to organize and bargain collectively. After decades of outright hostility toward unions, the United States government now officially recognized the right of labor unions to exist and represent workers in their relations with employers.

1941 The Attack on Pearl Harbor

On December 7, 1941, a Japanese force launched a surprise attack upon the American naval base at Pearl Harbor, Hawaii. Japanese leaders believed that the United States was blocking Japanese expansion in the Pacific, and they decided a lightning thrust would disable the American navy. The attack killed over 2,335 American soldiers and 68 civilians and destroyed 19 ships and 150 planes. On December 8, Congress voted in favor of a declaration of war against Japan, and the United States entered World War II.

1944 The Normandy Invasion

The Normandy invasion was the beginning of the end of World War II. With a force of 175,000 soldiers, 600 warships, and 11,000 planes, combined American and British forces landed on the northern coast of German-controlled France in June 1944. Within one month, over a million Allied troops had moved into France, and the defeat of Germany took less than a year. The Soviet Union, the United States wartime ally, never forgave the late date of the invasion, because the Soviets had been suffering terribly at the hands of the Germans since 1942. This contributed to postwar American-Soviet hostility.

1944 The Serviceman's Readjustment Act

In gratitude for the service of World War II veterans, Congress passed the Serviceman's Readjustment Act, commonly known as the GI Bill, in 1944. The act granted returning veterans job guidance, priority for jobs, loans, mortgage assistance, technical training, and educational benefits. This bill contributed to the peacetime success of World War II veterans, who as a group earned 40 percent more than nonveterans. Few women and minorities, however, received full benefits under the act.

1945 The Formation of the United Nations

Near the end of World War II, diplomats hoped to create a new international peacekeeping organization. In April 1945, delegates from fifty nations met in San Francisco to adopt a charter for the new organization, called the United Nations (UN). Members pledged to settle their disagreements peacefully and to try to prevent wars from occurring and stop those that did break out. The formation of the UN provided new hope for an era of international peace and understanding.

1947 The Desegregation of Major League Baseball

After World War II, African Americans began to make louder demands for equality. Mild-mannered Jackie Robinson proved to be one of the trailblazers. In 1947 Robinson took the field for the Brooklyn Dodgers, thus ending the exclusion of African Americans from major league baseball. Within a few years, more African American players entered professional baseball, football, and basketball. In coming years, athletes such as Hank Aaron, Lawrence Taylor, and Michael Jordan would rise to the top of their respective sports.

1947 The Truman Doctrine

The years after World War II witnessed increasing hostility between the United States and the Soviet Union. Postwar American policy came to be dominated by the goal of resisting communist expansion. This policy was first expressed officially in the Truman Doctrine. In 1947, Truman announced that it was the duty of the United States to protect the "free peoples" of the world from "subjugation by armed minorities or outside pressures." If America failed in this duty, Truman warned, communism could take over the world. The Truman Doctrine helped shape a United States foreign policy that contributed to the tensions of the cold war.

1949 The Formation of the North Atlantic Treaty Organization

The United States committed its economic resources to rebuild war-torn Western Europe, partially in an effort to prevent communist gains there. To provide military protection for Western Europe, the United States created a military alliance known as the North Atlantic Treaty Organization (NATO) in 1949. Twelve nations joined NATO, pledging mutual military protection. The United Sates provided military aid to all the members. NATO ensured that Western Europe would be protected from Soviet invasion and provided the United States with a cold war weapon that could be used to contain any threat of communist aggression.

1954 The Army-McCarthy Hearings

The tense cold war atmosphere of the 1950s in the United States produced a widespread, exaggerated fear of Soviet infiltration. In this atmosphere, Wisconsin senator Joseph McCarthy won fame with his wild accusations of communist infiltration of American government. His attacks continued for four years, while producing little evidence of communist activity in the government. McCarthy's accusations against the army led to televised hearings, in which Americans for the first time recognized the reckless and ruthless nature of his tactics. Defeated and censured by his colleagues in Congress, McCarthy lost his influence. His anticommunist crusade, however, contributed to the cold war fears in the United States.

1954 Brown v. Board of Education of Topeka

Civil rights leaders in the 1950s determined that they had to overturn the "separate but equal" doctrine established by *Plessy v. Ferguson* in 1896. The NAACP's Legal Defense Fund fought segregation in the courts, and in 1951 it helped Oliver Brown sue the Topeka, Kansas, school board for not allowing his daughter to attend a nearby white school. The Supreme Court ruled on May, 17, 1954, that "separate facilities are inherently unequal." A year later, the court ordered desegregation of public schools to begin "with all deliberate speed." Though the South resisted integration for years, the *Brown* decision proved to be a major legal victory for the civil rights movement.

1955 The Montgomery Bus Boycott

Life in racially segregated Montgomery, Alabama, was radically altered in December 1955 when Rosa Parks, a seamstress and

NAACP secretary, refused to move from the "whites-only" section of a public bus. Parks' defiance led to her arrest and unified the city's black community. African Americans began a campaign to boycott the public bus system. The boycott reduced the bus system's gross revenue by 65 percent. Meanwhile, the NAACP tested the legality of bus segregation, and in 1956 the Supreme Court ruled it unconstitutional. This victory gave strength to a broader civil rights movement, and Martin Luther King, Jr., emerged as a leading spokesperson for civil rights.

1960 Kennedy-Nixon Debate on Television

In the first televised presidential debate, Democratic candidate John F. Kennedy debated Republican candidate Richard Nixon. Kennedy took advantage of the power of television, projecting a charismatic, vigorous image. Polls showed that those who listened to the debate on the radio thought Nixon had won, while those who watched the debate on television believed Kennedy had triumphed. In future political elections, candidates' television images would be groomed as carefully as their stands on issues.

1962 The Cuban Missile Crisis

In 1962 Cuban leader Fidel Castro secretly secured Soviet aid to install Soviet-made nuclear missiles in Cuba, well within striking distance of the United States. American officials learned of the missiles when American spy planes took pictures of the missile sites. After considering options that included a military attack on Cuba, President Kennedy opted to set up a blockade around the island to turn back any Soviet ships. Kennedy's strong stance placed the United States at the very brink of war with the Soviet Union. The Soviets however, pulled back, agreeing to remove the missiles. The event intensified the cold war and the arms race between the United States and Soviet Union.

1962 The Publication of Silent Spring

Marine biologist Rachel Carson almost singlehandedly started the environmental movement with the publication of her 1962 book, Silent Spring. The book claimed that while the chemical pesticide DDT increased crop production, it also released deadly chemicals into the food chain. Silent Spring rocked the nation, and public concern eventually led to a government ban against the use and sale of DDT. Carson had succeeded in encouraging an awareness in American society of the concept of human-environmental interaction.

1963 The Assassination of President John F. Kennedy

On November 22, 1963, President John F. Kennedy was struck by an assassin's bullets while riding through the streets of Dallas, Texas. The wounds were fatal and the stunned nation was plunged into mourning. Authorities arrested and charged Lee Harvey Oswald with the assassination, but two days later night-club owner Jack Ruby murdered Oswald. Despite the official government report of the Warren Commission that Oswald had acted alone in the assassination, many Americans continued to believe that the murder was the product of a conspiracy of some sort. The assassination of President Kennedy, who had invigorated the nation with his youth and enthusiasm, inflicted a serious blow to the spirit of the nation.

1963 The Publication of The Feminine Mystique

After World War II, the United States witnessed a strong resurgence of the ideal of the woman as domestic homemaker. Betty Friedan did as society expected: she gave up a career in psychology to raise a family. Unhappy with the role that society had defined for women, she wrote The Feminine Mystique. In her book, Friedan charged that women were expected to find total personal satisfaction from being housewives. She claimed that women needed other ways to gain fulfillment, such as forming an identity separate from the home. The Feminine Mystique gave rise to a renewed women's movement that continues today.

1964 The Civil Rights Act

The 1964 Civil Rights Act outlawed discrimination in public places and in employment practices, and empowered the attorney general to bring suit against offenders. The Supreme Court upheld the legislation. The American government finally had taken strong action toward guaranteeing African Americans their civil rights.

1964 The Gulf of Tonkin Resolution

President Lyndon B. Johnson was determined not to allow South Vietnam to fall under the control of communist North Vietnam. Toward this end, he sought a way to strengthen the United States commitment to South Vietnam. Johnson saw his opportunity when American ships, in North Vietnamese waters to aid South Vietnamese raids, were attacked by North Vietnamese torpedo boats. Johnson described the incident as a confirmed example of North Vietnamese aggression. He persuaded Congress to pass the Gulf of Tonkin Resolution, which gave him broad powers in applying military force. Johnson eventually would use the resolution to send more than 500,000 troops to Vietnam.

1965 The Voting Rights Act

The Civil Rights Act of 1964 had gaps that made possible the continued disenfranchisement of African Americans by southern states. Further peaceful protest by civil rights activists helped force the federal government to address this issue. Congress passed the Voting Rights Act in 1965. The act outlawed devices, such as literacy tests, used to deny African Americans the vote. It also empowered the federal government to oversee elections. By 1968 one million African Americans had registered to vote, a force that would come to have a strong impact upon elections.

1966 The Formation of the National Organization for Women

A small group of professional women, dissatisfied with existing women's groups, formed the National Organization for Women (NOW) in 1966. NOW sought equal pay for equal work, partnership in marriage, and changes in the representation of women in the media. Within five years the organization had 15,000 members and served as a powerful voice for women disenchanted with their status in American society. NOW helped to revolutionize the way Americans thought about and treated women.

1969 The Moon Landing

The Soviet advantage in space technology in the early 1960s spurred President John F. Kennedy to invest heavily in an American space program. Throughout the 1960s the space program made rapid progress. On July 20, 1969, the Apollo 11 lunar module landed on the moon. The nation watched as Commander Neil Armstrong took the first steps outside the spacecraft. Humankind had made a giant stride in the exploration of space, the last great frontier.

1972–1974 The Watergate Scandal

The Committee to Re-Elect the President (CREEP) was determined to win the 1972 reelection of President Richard Nixon. Toward this goal, a group of men tried to break into the Democratic National Headquarters in the Watergate building in order to install a listening device. The break-in led to the burglars' arrest. President Nixon claimed to have had no prior knowledge of the break-in, but he did participate in a cover-up of the incident. Though Nixon was overwhelmingly reelected, the investigation of Watergate continued, and it became clear the President was involved. Facing certain impeachment, Nixon became the first President to resign from office.

1973 Roe v. Wade

The National Organization for Women (NOW) made the reform of abortion laws a priority in the early 1970s. Existing laws made it difficult for women to obtain abortions, and the procedure was illegal in many states. NOW argued that the individual woman, not the state, should have the right to decide if abortion was appropriate. The issue went before the Supreme Court, which held that a woman's right to privacy gave her the right to obtain an abortion and that the state could regulate abortions only after a certain point in the pregnancy. This decision was a major victory for women's rights activists, but it inspired strong opposition by antiabortion groups. In the years after *Roe* v. *Wade,* the abortion debate has become a leading political issue.

1973 AIM Occupies Wounded Knee, South Dakota

The American Indian Movement (AIM), organized in 1968, occupied the town of Wounded Knee, South Dakota, to protest reservation conditions and to bring public attention to the history of broken treaties between the United States and Native Americans. The government reacted to the armed occupation of the town with force, firing upon Native Americans who sought to bring supplies to AIM. The standoff ended with the government agreeing to examine treaty rights. Native American actions such as this pressured the government to reevaluate its policy toward Native Americans.

1975 The United Farm Workers' Grape Boycott

César Chávez and his union of migratory farm workers confronted the grape growers of California, demanding better wages, working conditions, and the right to collective bargaining. The growers refused the demands of the workers. In response, Chávez organized a nationwide consumer boycott of grapes. The boycott was successful, and several growers came to terms with Chávez's group, now called the United Farm Workers. In 1975 the California legislature passed a law that required growers to bargain collectively with the agricultural workers' unions.

1981 The Appointment of Sandra Day O'Connor to the Supreme Court

President Ronald Reagan appointed Sandra Day O'Connor to the Supreme Court in 1981. Following her confirmation by the Senate, she became the first woman to sit on the Supreme Court. Her appointment marked an important symbolic achievement for American women, who continued to make gains in their access to leadership positions at all levels of government. In 1993 O'Connor was joined on the Supreme Court bench by Ruth Bader Ginsberg, who was appointed by President Bill Clinton.

1981 The Discovery of the AIDS Virus

In 1981 medical researchers discovered a fatal new disease, known as acquired immunodeficiency syndrome (AIDS). The disease, scientists learned, was caused by a virus that damages the body's ability to fight infection. Research also showed that the disease is transmitted through sexual contact with an infected person or by the sharing of contaminated intravenous needles. As yet, no cure for the disease nor means of immunization against the virus has been found. By March 1994, about 200,000 Americans had died of AIDS-related complications.

1987 The Intermediate-Range Nuclear Forces Treaty

After meeting several times to discuss arms control, President Ronald Reagan and Soviet premier Mikhail Gorbachev signed a treaty to limit the number of intermediate-range nuclear weapons. The INF treaty helped pave the way for the Strategic Arms Reduction Talks in 1991, which decreased the number of long-range nuclear missiles. These two treaties marked a significant warming in the relationship between the United States and the Soviet Union.

1991 The Collapse of the Soviet Union

Mikhail Gorbachev could not control the forces he had unleashed in the Soviet Union through his democratic, *perestroika* reforms. In the closing days of 1991, the Soviet Union dissolved, and the republics that once made up the Soviet Union became independent countries. In 1991, Boris Yeltsin leader of the Russian republic, declared a final end to the cold war, which had dominated American and Soviet foreign policy for over forty years.

KEY EVENTS

Glossary

This Glossary defines all key terms listed in section previews. The page number at the end of each entry indicates the text page on which the term appears in boldface. Key people are defined in the Biographical Dictionary on pages 925–931.

abolition Movement to ban, or abolish, slavery; began in the early 1800s and continued through the Civil War (p. 154)

acquired immunodeficiency syndrome (AIDS) Incurable, fatal disease that appeared in 1981; transmitted through the bodily fluid of an infected individual (p. 823)

administration A President's term in office, or the group of officials that makes up the executive branch, including the President (p. 93)

agribusiness Method of producing agricultural goods in which corporations run large farms using high-tech machinery (p. 513)

Albany Movement Largely unsuccessful protests against racial inequality in Albany, Georgia, in 1961 and 1962; led by Martin Luther King, Jr. (p. 662)

Allies The combination of Russia, France, Great Britain, and later the United States in World War I; opponents of the Central Powers (p. 370)

American Expeditionary Force (AEF) United States troops in World War I, including draftees, volunteers, and the National Guard (p. 379)

American Indian Movement (AIM) Native American rights group organized in 1968; organized protests and participated in the occupation at Wounded Knee in 1973 (p. 697)

American Revolution The war and the social and political changes that accompanied the creation of the United States of America (p. 52)

American System Economic policy proposed in 1825 by John Q. Adams and others under which the federal government would support business by passing protective tariffs and making internal improvements such as roads and canals (p. 132)

amnesty General pardon for those guilty of a certain crime; granted by President Jimmy Carter to draft evaders during Vietnam War (p. 798)

Anaconda Plan Civil War plan formed by the North to blockade the South and cut off its foreign trade (p. 200)

anarchist Political radical who opposes all government because it limits individual liberty and serves the wealthy, ruling classes (p. 240)

Anglo A white, non-Latino, English-speaking American (p. 692)

annexation Addition of a new territory to an existing country (p. 308)

Anti-Federalist Those who opposed the new Constitution between 1787 and 1789 on the grounds that the central government it would create would be too powerful (p. 88)

anti-Semitism Hostility toward or discrimination against Jews (p. 501)

apartheid Systematic separation and inequality of races in South Africa enforced by whites during the 1900s (p. 849)

appeasement Act of giving in to someone's demands in order to keep the peace; unsuccessful policy of England and France toward Nazi Germany before World War II (p. 502)

arbitration Process of settling disputes in which both sides accept the legally binding decision of an impartial third party; often used in labor conflicts (p. 345)

armistice Cease-fire during a war, particularly at the end of World War I in 1918 (p. 383)

Articles of Confederation Agreement establishing a form of government among the states in 1781 (p. 66)

Atlantic World The encounter and exchange among the people of the Americas, Africa, and Europe that began in 1492 (p. 24)

autocrat Ruler with unlimited governing power (p. 372)

baby boom Increase in birth rate that began in World War II and continued into the 1950s (p. 593)

balance of trade Difference in value between a country's imports and exports over a given period of time (p. 36)

barrio City neighborhood inhabited by Spanish speakers (p. 310, 692)

Battle of the Bulge Battle fought from December 16, 1944 to January 16, 1945, between the Allies and Nazi forces in Belgium (p. 511)

beatnik Member of the "Beat Generation" in the 1950s who protested the pressure to conform through writing, art, and unconventional living (p. 599)

Berlin airlift The emergency program undertaken by the United States to deliver supplies to West Berlin in 1948 and 1949 after the Soviet Union blocked other access routes (p. 569)

Berlin Wall Barrier built by the Soviets in 1961 to keep people of East Berlin from escaping to the West; symbol of the cold war; torn down in 1989 (p. 640)

bicameral legislature Executive branch with two houses or groups of representatives, as in the United States Congress (p. 68)

bilingual education Education in which students with little knowledge of English are taught in both their native language and English (p. 853)

Black Power An African American movement seeking unity, self-determination, and economic and political power (p. 674)

black codes Laws intended to keep African Americans under white authority, especially following the Civil War (p. 114)

blitzkrieg "Lightning war"; German tactic employed at the beginning of World War II, based upon overwhelming the enemy with a series of sudden attacks by land and air (p. 506)

blue laws Laws that regulate work, business, or entertainment on Sunday (p. 252)

bonanza farms Large farms owned by big businesses and managed by professionals (p. 247)

Bonus Army Group of World War I veterans who marched to Washington in 1932 asking to receive their pension bonus early (p. 458)

bootlegging Supplying liquor illegally during prohibition (1920–1933) by producing or smuggling it (p. 424)

boycott A means of protest based on refusing to buy products or use services (p. 53)

bracero Spanish term for "worker," particularly applied to the thousands of Mexican farm workers who migrated into the United States during World War II, most of whom were sent back after the war (p. 548)

Bull Moose party Name for the Progressive party, organized to run Theodore Roosevelt for President in 1912 (p. 351)

busing Program begun in the 1960s to end racial segregation in schools by redistributing students (p. 758)

buy on margin Practice of buying stocks by paying 10 to 50 percent of the full price and borrowing the rest; common in the 1920s before the stock market crash of 1929 (p. 440)

cabinet Heads of the major departments of the United States government who advise the President (p. 92)

Camp David Accords Framework for peace between Israel and Egypt; signed in 1978 (p. 790)

canister Projectile used in a cannon that opens up after firing and sprays bullet-sized shot (p. 199)

capital Supply of wealth used to produce goods and profits (p. 121)

capitalism Economic system in which manufacturing is controlled by private corporations and individuals competing for profits (p.121)

capitalist Person using capital to produce goods or services for profit (p. 126)

carpetbagger Northern Republican who moved to the South during Reconstruction to profit from unstable social conditions (p. 215)

cartel Loose association of businesses supplying the same product, often formed secretly; its members agree to limit supplies to keep prices high (p. 232)

Central Powers Combination of Germany and Austria-Hungary in World War I; opponents of the Allies (p. 370)

centralize To locate tasks or responsibilities so that they all happen in one place (p. 122)

Civil Rights Act of 1964 Law prohibiting discrimination in public accommodations and job opportunities (p. 668)

Civil War Armed conflict between the northern and southern states between 1861 and 1865 (p. 190)

clan Type of kinship network; consists of a group of families descended from a common ancestor (p. 18)

coalition Union of several groups who work together toward a common political, social, or economic goal (p. 811)

cold war Condition of indirect conflict that existed between the United States and the Soviet Union from World War II through the late 1980s (p. 562)

collateral Something pledged as security for a loan that can be claimed by the lender if the loan is not repaid (p. 445)

collective bargaining Negotiation between employers and workers, usually through a labor union (p. 238)

colony An area settled by immigrants who continue their ties with the parent country (p. 28)

commodity Something that can be bought and sold (p. 121)

communist Economic system in which manufacturing is controlled by the workers (p. 405)

Compromise of 1850 Agreement reached between northern and southern states in an effort to end dispute over the extension of slavery to the western territories (p. 191)

confederation An alliance of states formed to coordinate defense and their relations with foreign governments (p. 66)

congregacion Spanish colonial village where Native Americans were forced to worship as European Catholics and to farm (p. 29)

Congress of Industrial Organizations (CIO) Labor group that split off from the American Federation of Labor in 1938 and organized unskilled steel, auto, and other workers (p. 486)

Congress of Racial Equality (CORE) Civil rights organization started in 1942; active in sit-ins and demonstrations during the 1950s and 1960s (p. 653)

conquistador Spanish term for "conqueror" in North and South America during the period of conquest after the opening of the Atlantic World (p. 28)

conscientious objector Person who opposes fighting in a war on moral or religious grounds (p. 727)

containment Cold war policy of the United States intended to prevent communist power from expanding beyond its geographical boundaries after World War II (p. 567)

contra Rebel fighting the Marxist Sandinista government of Nicaragua in the 1980s (p. 831)

contraband Property of the enemy seized during wartime; applied during the Civil War to enslaved African Americans set free by the Union army (p. 207)

cost-plus system System devised during World War II to allow profits from war production, in which the government paid for basic manufacturing costs, plus a percentage for profit (p. 533)

counterculture A cultural movement in the 1960s formed mostly of young people who rejected conventions and experimented with new practices in dress, sexual relationships, and drug use (p. 724)

Cuban missile crisis Dispute between the United States and the Soviet Union in 1962 over Soviet missile bases in Cuba (p. 641)

cult of domesticity The widespread belief in the early to mid-1800s in the importance of women's work in the home (p. 161)

de facto discrimination Discrimination caused by conditions rather than by law; common in the North for African Americans after the Civil War (p. 282)

de facto segregation Segregation in the North and elsewhere caused by ghetto conditions rather than by law (p. 671)

de jure segregation Segregation enforced by laws; common in the South through the 1960s (p. 671)

debt peonage Labor system common in the South after the Civil War in which debt was used to keep farm workers on the land (p. 216)

Declaration of Independence Document published in 1776 declaring the independence of the United States from British rule (p. 56)

deficit spending Economic policy in which the government spends more than it receives in taxes, making up the difference by borrowing money (p. 535)

deflation Period of gradually dropping prices, generally brought on by the decrease in the supply of available money (p. 248)

demagogue Charismatic leader who manipulates people with half-truths, false promises, and scare tactics (p. 482)

Democratic party Political party descended from Jeffersonian Democrat-Republicans and Jacksonian Democrats (p. 191)

depression Severe economic slump during which stock values, business activity, and employment decline severely or remain at very low levels (p. 53)

deregulation Policy of reducing or removing government controls on industry (p. 798)

détente Relaxation of strained relations between nations, especially among the United States, the Soviet Union, and China in the 1970s and late 1980s (p. 761)

direct primary Election system in which voters rather than political bosses select nominees for elections (p. 344)

dissident An opponent of the established government, especially in the Soviet Union (p. 791)

diversified conglomerate Extremely large corporation formed of other corporations of many types (p. 590)

dollar diplomacy Policy of increasing United States investments abroad to keep foreign societies stable; adopted by President William Howard Taft in the early 1900s (p. 323)

domino theory Political theory common during the cold war that if one country fell to communism, countries nearby would also quickly become communist (p. 547)

"Double V" campaign Civil rights movement by African Americans during World War II, calling for victory both in the war and in the struggle for equality at home (p. 547)

doughboy Nickname for an infantryman in World War I (p. 380)

Dow Jones industrial average An average of the prices of the stock of leading industries that gauges the health of the stock market (p. 442)

draft Legal means of forcing people to serve in the armed forces (p. 205)

Dred Scott **v.** *Sandford* Supreme court case in 1857 that refused to recognize African Americans as citizens and overturned the Missouri Compromise (p. 193)

Electoral College Body of electors chosen by voters in each state to elect the President and Vice President (p. 85)

Emancipation Proclamation Declaration by President Abraham Lincoln that as of January 1, 1863, all enslaved people in areas in rebellion against the Union would be considered free by the North (p. 206)

embargo A policy of restricting trade with a nation (p. 756)

encomienda **system** Social system in which Native Americans were required to work for an individual Spaniard, who was supposed to care for their well-being in return (p. 28)

entrepreneur Businessperson who takes risks for the sake of large profits (p. 121)

Environmental Protection Agency (EPA) Government agency established in 1970 to curb air and water pollution; now also regulates solid waste disposal, pesticides, and toxic substances (p. 702)

Equal Rights Amendment (ERA) Constitutional amendment to ensure equal rights for women; passed by Congress in 1972 but never ratified by the required number of states (p. 688)

escalation An increase or expansion, especially of war (p. 716)

evangelical movement Christian religious movement that emphasizes preaching instead of rituals, and stresses that salvation is possible only for those who believe in Christ (p. 116)

excise Tax on an item manufactured within a country (p. 107)

executive branch The part of a government that executes, or carries out, laws (p. 67)

faction Separate subgroup within a political system (p. 88)

fascism A political philosophy that values the nation or race over the individual, autocratic over democratic rule, and rigid control of society and the economy over a free society and market (p. 500)

Federalist Supporter of the new United States Constitution in the 1780s; also a member of a party that favored a strong federal government in the 1790s and early 1800s (p. 88)

feminism Theory of political, economic, and social equality of men and women (p. 684)

feminist Person who advocates the political, economic, and social equality of men and women (p. 684)

first American party system Earliest political party system in the United States; composed of Jeffersonian Republicans and Federalists (p. 106)

flapper A type of young woman having a straight, slim silhouette and a fondness for dancing and brash actions; a symbol of the Jazz Age (p. 416)

Fourteen Points Peace program proposed by President Woodrow Wilson in 1918, intended to prevent wars like World War I (p. 388)

franchise The right to open a restaurant or other business using a system developed by and a name owned by a parent company (p. 590)

Freedmen's Bureau Federal bureau in operation after the Civil War that helped former enslaved people and war refugees with food, medical, and other aid as well as schooling (p. 213)

Freedom Rides Campaign by African American and white civil rights workers in 1961 to protest segregated southern bus facilities by riding through the Lower South on buses (p. 660)

fundamentalism Christian religious movement based on pamphlets issued between 1909 and 1914; holds that every word in the Bible was inspired by God and is literally true (p. 425)

Gadsden Purchase United States purchase of southern New Mexico and Arizona from Mexico for $10 million in 1853 (p. 178)

gag rule Rule passed in 1836 by southern representatives in Congress that prevented antislavery petitions from being considered by the House for eight years (p. 157)

general strike A strike in which many unions participate in order to show worker unity (p. 405)

gentry People, generally landowners, wealthy enough to afford others to work for them (p. 38)

Gettysburg Address Speech by President Abraham Lincoln at a Gettysburg cemetery dedication in 1863; redefined the meaning of the United States (p. 209)

GI Bill Common name for Servicemen's Readjustment Act of 1944, which provided veterans' benefits such as low-interest mortgages (p. 593)

GI United States soldier serving during World War II (p. 513)

Gilded Age The period between 1877 and 1900; also called the Tragic Era and the Dreadful Decades (p. 251)

grandfather clause A part of a law that exempts a group from the law if they met certain conditions before the law was passed; used in the South in the late 1800s and early 1900s to ensure that white voting rights were not affected by literacy tests intended to screen out African American voters (p. 281)

Great Awakening Religious revival in the American colonies, 1730s–1740s (p. 41)

Great Compromise Agreement of 1787 that created a bicameral legislature in the Constitution; it established that representation in one house was to be proportional to population in one house and equal among states in the other (p. 82)

Great Society The legislative program proposed by President Lyndon Johnson in the 1960s; included civil rights laws, federal aid to education, elderly medical care, and poverty programs (p. 630)

Gross National Product (GNP) Total amount of goods and services a nation produces; used to gauge economic strength (p. 444)

guerrilla Soldier who fights irregular warfare, especially one using surprise tactics to harass and sabotage the enemy (p. 313)

Gulf of Tonkin Resolution Resolution passed by Congress in 1964 that gave the President authority to use "necessary" military force in Vietnam (p. 716)

gunboat Type of steam-driven boat used during the Civil War that was fitted with cannons and, sometimes, iron armor; it was able to navigate shallow rivers (p. 201)

Harlem Renaissance Period in the early 1900s during which the literary, musical, and artistic expression of African Americans blossomed in Harlem (p. 413)

Hawley-Smoot tariff Import tax levied in 1930, the highest in United States history; produced the opposite of its intended effect when international trade slowed (p. 457)

Helsinki Accords Agreement reached in the 1970s by a group of nations, including the United States and the Soviet Union, to cooperate economically and promote human rights (p. 784)

hierarchy Social system of many levels in which each level has power over the levels beneath it (p. 19)

hippie A member of the counterculture during the 1960s (p. 727)

holding company A corporation that controls other companies by holding their stocks (p. 346)

holocaust Nazi execution of six million Jews and five million others during World War II in extermination camps (p. 511)

home rule Municipal reforms in the late 1800s and early 1900s that gave cities limited self-rule, rather than state rule (p. 339)

Homestead Act Law passed in 1862 that offered certain settlers 160 acres of land if they built a house and farmed for five years (p. 244)

Hooverville Towns of makeshift houses built by homeless people during the Great Depression (p. 448)

horizontal consolidation Process of creating one giant business by bringing together smaller firms in the same field (p. 232)

House Un-American Activities Committee (HUAC) Committee of the House of Representatives active during the 1940s and 1950s that investigated supposed communist influence in the film and other industries (p. 578)

household economy Economic system common before the 1800s in which people's business consisted of maintaining households by growing food and making clothes and other necessities (p. 121)

hundred days First one hundred days of President Franklin D. Roosevelt's term of office (p. 472)

Immigration Act of 1965 A law that changed quotas favoring northern and western Europeans and expanded the number of people allowed to immigrate (p. 632)

impeach To formally charge a public official with misconduct; brought by the lower house in a legislative body (p. 215)

imperial presidency The type of presidency sought by President Richard Nixon, in which the executive branch would gain more power than allowed by the Constitution (p. 775)

imperialism A policy by which stronger nations attempt to create empires by dominating weaker nations economically, politically, or military; also called expansionism (p. 308)

indentured servant Person who contracts to work for another for a period of time (usually seven years), especially in return for travel costs or food and shelter (p. 31)

Industrial Revolution A period of major economic change that began during the late 1700s with the introduction of machines using sources of power other than humans or animals (p. 115)

Industrial Workers of the World (IWW) Radical labor organization of the early 1900s that sought the overthrow of the capitalist system; also known as the Wobblies (p. 386)

inflation A steady increase in prices and loss of value of currency that reduces people's ability to buy goods; usually results from an increase in the amount of money and credit available (p. 64)

installment buying A method of paying for an expensive item over many months in installments and including interest (p. 440)

Interim Committee Group of government leaders and scientists who studied the question of using the atomic bomb to force Japan's surrender during World War II (p. 519)

Intermediate-Range Nuclear Forces (INF) Treaty Nuclear arms reduction treaty signed by President Ronald Reagan and Soviet president Mikhail Gorbachev in 1987 (p. 828)

internment camp A camp in which people are confined or isolated, especially during a time of war (p. 550)

interracial Including two or more racial groups (p. 652)

Interstate Commerce Act Law passed in 1887 to curb rate-setting abuses by railroads and regulate other interstate business (p. 254)

Iran-contra affair A scandal during the administration of President Ronald Reagan in which money from illegal Iran arms sales was given to Nicaraguan contras to fight Sandinistas (p. 831)

iron curtain The imaginary line separating communist countries allied with the Soviet Union in eastern Europe and the allies of the United States in western Europe during the cold war (p. 565)

Jacksonian Democrats Name given to the Democratic party during the period from the 1820s to the 1850s; supported Andrew Jackson's policy of discouraging federal involvement in the United States economy (p. 132)

Japanese American Citizens League Organization that helped Japanese Americans after World War II (p. 694)

Jazz Age Term for the 1920s, a period marked by the great popularity of jazz music, which was linked to changes in manners, morals, and fashions (p. 415)

jazz Music that grew out of "raggy" rhythms and call-and-response forms for singers and instruments in New Orleans in the 1890s (p. 279)

Jeffersonian Republicans Name given to the Democratic party in the first American party system by historians seeking to distinguish it from the modern-day Republican party (p. 106)

Jim Crow System of laws in the late 1800s that segregated African Americans and forced them to use separate, inferior facilities (p. 281)

jingoism The swelling of national pride and desire for an aggressive foreign policy in late 1800s and early 1900s; resulted in the Spanish-American War and other expansionist activity (p. 313)

judicial branch The part of a government that decides if laws have been broken (p. 67)

Kansas-Nebraska Act Act of 1854 establishing that the people of a territory should decide whether slavery would be allowed there (p. 191)

kinship network Type of social organization consisting of relatives, or kin, such as parents, children, grandparents, aunts, uncles, cousins, and those who marry into the family (p. 17)

Ku Klux Klan Organization formed in the South in 1866, which used lynching and violence to intimidate and control African Americans and others (p. 217)

laissez-faire Economic policy under which government takes a hands-off approach to economic matters and plays a limited role in business (p. 251)

Latino People whose roots lie in Spanish-speaking lands to the south of the United States, including Mexico, Central and South America, and many islands of the Caribbean (p. 691)

League of Nations Organization proposed by President Woodrow Wilson after World War I in the hopes of joining nations together for peace and security (p. 389)

legislative branch The part of a government that makes the laws (p. 67)

Lend-Lease Act Law allowing United States loans to Great Britain early in World War II, without specified time of payment; helped Britain resist attacks before the United States entered the war (p. 504)

liberal consensus View widely held in the 1950s and 1960s that capitalism was the best economic system and that the United States was threatened more by communism abroad than by domestic issues like poverty (p. 624)

Liberty Bonds Certificates issued by the United States to raise money to loan to the Allies during World War I (p. 384)

Limited Test Ban Treaty Agreement reached by the United States and the Soviet Union in 1963 banning nuclear testing above ground (p. 642)

lineage Kinship network in which the members trace their descent from a common ancestor (p. 21)

literacy tests Tests in which would-be voters have to demonstrate certain knowledge before they can vote; once used in several states to prevent certain groups from voting (p. 281)

Loyalists American colonists who remained loyal to Britain during the American Revolution (p. 59)

Lusitania British passenger ship sunk by German U-boats in 1915 (p. 375)

lynching The illegal capture and execution of a person by a mob (p. 282)

mandate Wishes of constituents, as expressed in the election of a candidate by a large majority of voters (p. 625)

Manhattan Project Secret project that created the first atomic bomb in 1945 for use in World War II (p. 518)

manifest destiny Belief that the United States has a divine right to expand its territory; used to support imperialist expansion in the late 1800s (p. 176)

March on Washington Civil rights demonstration in Washington, D.C., led by Martin Luther King, Jr., in 1963 (p. 667)

Market Revolution Shift in the United States economy from home-based to market-based industries (p. 120)

Marshall Plan Program of European economic recovery after World War II, financed by the United States (p. 568)

Medicare Public health-care plan that funds medical care for the elderly (p. 631)

mercantilism European economic theory of the 1600s whereby a nation's economy can be strengthened by the use of protective tariffs, trade monopolies, and a balance of exports over imports (p. 36)

Middle Passage Section of the triangular trade from Africa to the Americas that transported enslaved persons (p. 40)

migratory farm workers Laborers who move from farm to farm planting, cultivating, and harvesting crops (p. 692)

minstrel show Theatrical show of the late 1800s in which white actors wore blackface and parodied African American music, dance, and humor (p. 278)

minutemen Colonists who fought British forces in the American Revolution; pledged to volunteer military service at a minute's notice (p. 52)

Missouri Compromise Agreement of 1820 that admitted Missouri into the Union as a slave state and Maine as a free state; set a precedent that continued until the Civil War (p. 115)

modern republicanism President Eisenhower's term for an approach to government that was "conservative when it comes to money, liberal when it comes to human beings" (p. 605)

monopoly Control of a commodity or service extending to the elimination of competition and the fixing of prices (p. 232)

Morrill Land-Grant Act Federal grant of 1862 that gave 140 million acres of western land to state governments, which then could sell the land to fund agricultural colleges (p. 244)

most-favored nation Trade status granting a nation the same trading privileges as other nations (p. 309)

muckraker Journalist of the late 1800s to early 1900s who tried to alert the public to alleged wrongdoing by politicians and big business (p. 341)

multiculturalism Social and educational movement that tries to embrace rather than exclude minority cultures (p. 855)

My Lai massacre The slaughter of more than a hundred

unarmed Vietnamese peasants in March 1968 by United States forces during the Vietnam War (p. 721)

Nation of Islam African American religious group founded in 1933 that believes in the religion of Islam, self-sufficiency, self-discipline, and the creation of a black nation (p. 672)

National Association for the Advancement of Colored People (NAACP) African American civil rights organization founded in 1910; fought for civil rights through demonstrations, lawsuits, and other means throughout the 1900s (p. 283)

national debt Total debt of the federal government (p. 485)

National Organization for Women (NOW) Feminist group founded in 1966 to pursue equal rights for women (p. 686)

National Republicans Political party of the 1820s that favored strong federal government and a national bank; supported John Q. Adams and opposed the Jacksonian Democrats (p. 132)

Nationalist Member of a 1780s political group advocating strong national government to control the states (p. 68)

NATO North Atlantic Treaty Organization; alliance of ten European nations, the United States, and Canada that pledged mutual assistance in the event of an attack on any member nation (p. 569)

Nazi party National Socialist Workers party; fascist political party that controlled Germany from 1933 until it was abolished in 1945; led by German dictator Adolf Hitler (p. 501)

New Deal Proposals and programs adopted by President Franklin Roosevelt in response to the Great Depression; included social and economic programs and changes in government regulation (p. 472)

new federalism Replacement of federal programs by federal grants to cities and states (p. 816)

New Freedom Political platform of Woodrow Wilson in the 1912 presidential election that criticized both big business and big government (p. 352)

New Frontier President John F. Kennedy's reform programs; included economic measures, aid to the poor, and the space program (p. 625)

New Jersey Plan Constitutional Convention proposal for a federal government having a unicameral legislature with equal representation for each state regardless of population (p. 82)

New Left Political movement of the 1960s advocating the need for radical change to solve the social problems of the United States (p. 723)

New Right Alliance of conservative special-interest groups in the Republican party from the 1960s to the 1990s (p. 810)

New Nationalism Program of progressive reforms proposed by President Theodore Roosevelt in 1910; included more regulation of business, welfare legislation, and other measures (p. 351)

nomad Person who migrates continually rather than living permanently in one place (p. 168)

North American Free Trade Agreement (NAFTA) International agreement in 1993 between Mexico, Canada, and the United States designed to promote free trade (p. 851)

NSC-68 National Security Council document of the cold war that suggested tripling the defense budget in an effort to contain communism (p. 570)

Nuclear Regulatory Commission Agency overseeing the operation of nuclear power plants in the United States (p. 797)

Open Door policy United States efforts to develop a trade relationship with China in the late 1800s to early 1900s; urged European nations with spheres of influence in China to not restrict trade in those areas (p. 317)

Organization of Petroleum Exporting Countries (OPEC) Group of Arab nations controlling prices and production of oil for export (p. 756)

paradox of power Combination of contradictory attitudes toward a powerful country (p. 329)

patriarchal society Male-dominated social organization (p. 19)

Patriots American fighting forces in the War for Independence (p. 59)

Peace Corps Federal program that trains and sends volunteers to aid people of developing countries (p. 637)

Pendleton Act Legislation of 1883 that established a Civil Service Commission to control government hiring, ending the patronage system (p. 254)

Pentagon Papers Secret study by the Defense Department on the Vietnam War; leaked to the *New York Times* in 1971 (p. 766)

per capita income Average income per person; used to compare income of states, countries, etc. (p. 590)

perjury Lying under oath (p. 767)

Persian Gulf War War between Iraq and United Nations forces led by the United States over Iraq's annexation of oil-rich Kuwait in 1991 (p. 830)

Pinkertons Private police force of the late 1800s and early 1900s; hired by companies to break strikes (p. 240)

Plumbers Secret White House group under President Richard M. Nixon; created to stop security leaks to the press (p. 765)

political boss Leader of a political machine (p. 261)

political left Those who wish to change the current social and political system or power structure (p. 481)

political machine Unofficial city organization designed to keep a particular party or group in power (p. 261)

political party Group actively involved in the political process; seeks to elect candidates to public office in order to control government policies (p. 106)

political right Those who wish to preserve the current social and political system or power structure (p. 480)

poll tax A tax (now unconstitutional) paid in some states before a person was allowed to vote (p. 281)

Poor People's Campaign Movement organized in 1968 by civil rights leader Martin Luther King, Jr., to attack economic injustice (p. 749)

popular sovereignty Belief that people can and should govern themselves (p. 56)

Populists Followers of the People's party of 1892 who sought radical reforms in United States economic and social policies; supported a silver standard, increased money supply, and a graduated income tax (p. 249)

precedent Custom arising from previous practice rather than a written law (p. 108)

presidio Spanish fort built in the American southwest to protect Spanish holdings and missions (p. 28)

progressivism Political and social reform movement of the late 1800s and early 1900s; included socialism, the labor movement, municipal reform, prohibitionism, the settlement house movement, and other reform movements (p. 339)

proletariat Members of the working class (p. 563)

psychedelic drug Drug that produces hallucinations and other altered perceptions of reality (p. 728)

public works programs Government-funded projects to build public facilities; central to President Franklin Roosevelt's New Deal job programs (p. 473)

Puritans Members of the Protestant Church of England of the 1600s and 1700s who wanted to reform, or purify, the church; some migrated to New England in the 1600s (p. 33)

ragtime Style of music consisting of complex syncopated rhythms played over a steady beat; developed by African American musicians in the 1880s (p. 278)

ratify Formally approve a suggested action (p. 89)

rationing Distribution of goods in a limited amount in times of scarcity (p. 538)

real wages Value of income adjusted to account for inflation; used to compare wages in different time periods (p. 438)

real purchasing power Value of money adjusted to account for inflation; used to compare economic conditions in different time periods (p. 590)

realpolitik Foreign policy theory based on efficiency rather than ethics; from the German term for "practical politics" (p. 760)

Reconstruction Period from 1865 to 1877 when the states of the Confederacy were controlled by the federal government before being readmitted to the Union (p. 212)

Reconstruction Finance Corporation Government corporation set up by President Herbert Hoover in 1932 that gave government loans to banks (p. 457)

red scare Fear of communism, socialism, or other so-called extreme ideas (p. 405)

Reformation Religious movement in Western Europe in the 1500s originally aimed at reforming the Roman Catholic church; resulted in the formation of Protestant churches (p. 32)

religious toleration Idea that people of different religions should live together in peace (p. 33)

reparations Payments for economic injury exacted from a defeated enemy (p. 389)

Republican party Political party organized in the 1850s to oppose southern interests; gave rise to today's Republican party (p. 192)

Roosevelt Corollary Extension of the Monroe Doctrine by President Theodore Roosevelt whereby the United States would use force to prevent other foreign powers from intervening in the affairs of Western Hemisphere countries (p. 321)

Rosie the Riveter Fictional defense plant worker portrayed in government propaganda films and posters to attract women to the work force during World War II (p. 540)

S & L Savings and loan bank (p. 816)

salutary neglect Great Britain's colonial policy of not interfering in colonial politics and economy as long as such neglect served Britain's economic interests (p. 37)

sanction Coercive measure, such as a boycott, taken by a group to enforce demands (p. 849)

Sandinistas Marxist Nicaraguan revolutionaries who took control of the Nicaraguan government in 1979 (p. 831)

satellite nation Country controlled politically and economically by a powerful nation, especially by the Soviet Union during the cold war (p. 571)

scab Slang for a person hired to replace a striking worker (p. 240)

scalawag Southern white who became a Republican during Reconstruction to profit from unstable social conditions in that area (p. 215)

Scopes trial Tennessee trial of 1925 that challenged the law against teaching evolution in public schools (p. 425)

Scottsboro Boys Nine African American youths accused and unfairly tried and convicted of raping two white woman in Alabama in 1931; gained national support and received new trials by order of the Supreme Court (p. 451)

secede Formally withdraw from a political organization; southern states seceded from the United States to form the Confederacy in late 1860 and early 1861 (p. 135)

second American party system The political parties that developed out of the election of 1828; the National Republicans and Jacksonian Democrats (p. 132)

Second Great Awakening Wave of religious revivals in the United States during the early 1800s (p. 116)

section Region distinguished from others in United States geography by economic and cultural differences (p. 124)

secularize Transfer control from the church to the state (p. 171)

self-determination Freedom of a group of people to determine their own political status; proposed by President Wilson for ethnic groups in Austria-Hungary after World War I (p. 388)

separation of powers Constitutional provision that separates the powers of the federal government into legislative, executive, and judicial branches (p. 84)

17th parallel Latitude line established after World War II that divided North Vietnam from South Vietnam (p. 575)

sharecropper Farmer who grows crops on land owned by someone else and gives a share of the crops produced to the landowner in return for use of the land and supplies (p. 216)

shell Hollow cannon ball that explodes in the air or as it hits; developed during the Civil War (p. 199)

shuttle diplomacy Diplomatic negotiations conducted by an official mediator traveling frequently to the nations involved; used by Henry Kissinger in the 1970s to promote peace in the Middle East (p. 789)

sit-down strike Work stoppage in which workers refuse to leave the premises until their demands are considered or met (p. 586)

sit-in Organized demonstration in which protesters seat themselves in segregated establishments to protest racial discrimination; became a common practice for many civil rights groups during the 1960s (p. 659)

social Darwinism Application of Charles Darwin's "survival of the fittest" theory to human society; used by the great industrialists of the late 1800s to discourage government interference in business (p. 231)

social welfare program Government program that helps ensure a basic standard of living; includes unemployment, accident, and health insurance and social security programs (p. 340)

social gospel movement Social movement of the early 1900s that applied the Christian gospel to social problems (p. 263)

Social Security Act Legislation of 1935 that established a social welfare system funded by employee and worker contributions; included old-age pensions, survivor's benefits for victims of industrial accidents, and unemployment insurance (p. 478)

socialism The economic and political philosophy that advocates collective ownership of factories and property (p. 236)

socialist A person who advocates the principles of socialism (p. 454)

Southern Christian Leadership Conference (SCLC) Civil rights organization founded in 1957 by Martin Luther King, Jr.; employed nonviolent means of protest and helped shift the focus of the civil rights movement to the South (p. 653)

speakeasy Establishment that illegally sold and served liquor during prohibition (p. 424)

speculation Undertaking risk on stocks or real estate for the chance of profit (p. 440)

sphere of influence Area of economic control exerted by a foreign power, especially in China during the late 1800s (p. 317)

Sputnik First artificial satellite to circle Earth; launched by the Soviet Union in 1957, beginning the space race (p. 607)

stagflation Slow economic growth coupled with high rates of inflation and unemployment (p. 782)

Strategic Defense Initiative (SDI) Satellite-operated defense system proposed by President Ronald Reagan in 1983; popularly called "Star Wars" (p. 858)

Strategic Arms Limitation Talks (SALT) Negotiations between the United States and the Soviet Union from 1971 to 1973 to limit offensive nuclear weapons (p. 764)

Student Nonviolent Coordinating Committee (SNCC) Student civil rights organization begun in 1960 to address the concerns of young African Americans; originally part of the Southern Christian Leadership Conference (p. 655)

Students for a Democratic Society (SDS) New Left political group organized in 1960 to work for radical change in United States society; heavily involved in Vietnam War protests (p. 722)

suburb Residential community on the outskirts of a city (p. 260)

suffrage The right to vote (p. 160)

supply-side economics Theory that the economy can be stimulated by increasing the availability of money for investments, achieved by reducing taxes on the rich; called "Reaganomics" in the 1980s (p. 815)

system of checks and balances United States system of government in which the power of each of the three branches of government is limited by that of the others (p. 85)

Taft-Hartley Act Legislation of 1947 that allows a President to order striking workers in crucial industries back to work while the government investigates the dispute (p. 603)

Tammany Hall Political machine controlling New York City politics from the 1860s to the 1920s (p. 261)

tariff Tax on imports or exports (p. 107)

teach-in Extended lecture on a controversial issue; arose in the 1960s to protest the Vietnam War (p. 724)

Teapot Dome Scandal during the administration of President Warren G. Harding involving the lease of public oil reserves to private companies in exchange for illegal payments (p. 413)

televangelism Television broadcasts conducted by evangelists; often used to raise money and support for churches and political movements (p. 811)

temperance movement Campaign against alcohol consumption; began as part of the middle-class reform movements of the 1800s (p. 153)

tenant farmer Farmer who pays cash for rental of land (p. 216)

termination policy United States government policy of the 1950s to eliminate reservations and assimilate Native Americans into mainstream American life (p. 611)

Tet Offensive Attack by the Viet Cong in South Vietnam in 1968 during Tet, the Vietnamese lunar new year; turned the United States public against United States involvement in the Vietnam War (p. 717)

Three-fifths Compromise Constitutional Convention agreement to count three fifths of a state's enslaved population when establishing state populations for representation in the House of Representatives (p. 83)

38th parallel Latitude line established after World War II that divided North Korea, which was allied with the Soviet Union, from South Korea, which was allied with the United States (p. 572)

Tories Majority party in the British Parliament during the American Revolution; also the name for American colonists still loyal to the crown (p. 59)

total war Warfare in which opponents attack civilians and the economic system of the enemy in addition to its soldiers (p. 209)

totalitarian Relating to a form of dictatorship or central government that has total control over all aspects of life and that suppresses all political and cultural expression of opposition (p. 563)

Trail of Tears Forced march of 15,000 Cherokee from their homes in the southeast to western reservations from 1837 to 1838 (p. 135)

Transcendentalism Intellectual and philosophical movement of the mid-1800s asserting that the nature of reality can be learned only by intuition rather than through experience (p. 152)

Treaty of Paris Agreement of 1783 that ended the War for Independence (p. 64)

triangular trade Trade between the Americas, Europe, and Africa in the 1700s; supported New England economies (p. 38)

Truman Doctrine Cold war policy, established by President Harry S Truman, pledging United States support for "free peoples" resisting communism (p. 568)

trust Combination of companies that turn over their assets to a board of trustees to control prices and competition in a particular industry (p. 232)

Twenty-first Amendment Constitutional amendment of 1933 repealing the Eighteenth Amendment, thus ending prohibition (p. 455)

U-boat Submarine of the German navy; introduced during World War I (p. 375)

unicameral legislature Government having a single legislative house (p. 68)

Union United States of America as a national unit, especially during the Civil War; the North and its forces in the Civil War (p. 190)

United Farm Workers (UFW) Group organized in the early 1960s to help migratory farm workers gain better pay and working conditions (p. 692)

United Nations International organization formed in 1945 to promote peace, security, and economic development among nations (p. 567)

vaudeville Theatrical performances of the late 1800s characterized by slapstick and song-and-dance routines (p. 277)

Versailles Treaty Agreement in 1919 ending World War I; included huge war reparations to be paid by Germany (p. 390)

vertical consolidation Control of all phases of a product's development, from raw materials to delivery of the finished products (p. 232)

veto Overturn a law or decision by using the constitutionally granted power of one branch of government to block legislation made by another; the President can veto a bill passed by Congress (p. 82)

Victorianism Moral ideas associated with Britain's Queen Victoria in the nineteenth century; characterized by strict moral codes (p. 279)

Viet Cong Communist guerrillas of South Vietnam during the Vietnam War (p. 715)

Vietnamization Nixon's Vietnam War policy to replace United States troops in Vietnam with South Vietnamese troops (p. 732)

Virginia Plan Constitutional Convention proposal for a federal government having a bicameral legislature with representation based on population (p. 82)

Volunteers in Service to America (VISTA) Federal program that sends volunteers to aid poor communities in the United States (p. 630)

Voting Rights Act of 1965 Legislation that gave the federal government the power to register voters in areas where local officials prevented African Americans from voting (p. 670)

WAC Women's Army Corps; organization of women who volunteered for military service in World War II; a member of the Women's Army Corps (p. 514)

Wagner Act National Labor Relations Act of 1935; legalized union practices such as collective bargaining and the closed shop and outlawed certain antiunion practices such as blacklisting (p. 478)

War for Independence War fought between American colonists and Great Britain from 1775 to 1783, resulting in an independent United States of America (p. 52)

war of attrition Warfare in which a weaker army inflicts small but continuous losses of soldiers and material that gradually add up to an unbearable burden for the enemy (p. 199)

Warren Commission Group headed by Chief Justice Earl Warren; formed to investigate President John Kennedy's assassination (p. 627)

Watergate Scandal of President Richard M. Nixon's administration that began in 1972 when leading Nixon supporters burglarized Democratic National Party Headquarters at the Watergate office building in Washington, D.C. (p. 765)

welfare capitalism Industrial policy of meeting workers' needs with increased pay and benefits for the purpose of preventing labor union organization (p. 439)

Whiskey Rebellion Pennsylvanian revolt against a whiskey tax in 1794; demonstrated that the federal government would use force to make citizens obey federal law (p. 107)

wildcat strike A workers' strike not authorized by their union (p. 535)

Wilmot Proviso Proposal of 1846 that slavery not be allowed in territory acquired from the Mexican War; defeated by Congress, but opened debate between the North and South on slavery in the western territories (p. 178)

woman question Wide-ranging debate of the early 1900s on the social role of women (p. 286)

Woodstock Rock music festival of 1969 that became a symbol of counterculture music and behavior (p. 729)

yellow journalism Newspaper coverage that sensationalizes stories to increase circulation; inflamed anti-Spanish sentiment in the United States before and during the Spanish-American War (p. 278)

Zimmerman note Telegram intercepted from a German official proposing an alliance with Mexico and offering to help Mexico regain Texas, New Mexico, and Arizona if the United States entered World War I; increased pressure on the United States to enter the war (p. 377)

Biographical Dictionary

The Biographical Dictionary identifies key people listed in section previews. The page number at the end of each entry indicates the text page on which the name appears in boldface. Presidents of the United States are also listed in the Biographical Dictionary.

Pronunciations given here are based on those given in *Webster's Biographical Dictionary*. To determine the pronunciation of the symbols used, compare them with the following examples.

ā	fāte		ī	īce
ā	chāotic		ĭ	ĭll
â	câre		i̇	di̇rect
ă	făt		к	like *ch* in German *ich*
ă	ăccount		ō	ōld
ä	ärm		ō	ōbey
ȧ	ȧsk		ô	ôrb
a	sofa		ŏ	ŏdd
ē	ēve		o͞o	fo͞od
ē	ēvent		o͝o	fo͝ot
e	end		th	then
e	silent		ŭ	ŭp

´ accent

• syllable break

Adams, Abigail First Lady, 1797–1801; as the wife of Patriot John Adams, she urged him to promote women's rights at the beginning of the American Revolution (p. 56)

Adams, John Quincy Sixth President of the United States, 1825–1829; proposed greater federal involvement in the economy through tariffs and improvements such as roads, bridges, and canals (p. 130)

Adams, John Second President of the United States, 1797–1801; worked to relieve increasing tensions with France; lost reelection bid to Jefferson in 1800 as the country moved away from Federalist policies (p. 108)

Addams, Jane Cofounder of Hull House, the first settlement house, in 1889; remained active in social causes through the early 1900s (p. 263)

Agnew, Spiro Vice President under President Richard Nixon until forced to resign in 1973 for crimes committed before taking office; known for his harsh campaign attacks (p. 751)

Arafat, Yasir (ār´ä•făt, yä´sĭr) Palestinian leader; gave up terror-ist tactics and signed a peace agreement with Israelis in 1993 (p. 848)

Arthur, Chester A. Twenty-first President of the United States, 1881–1885; signed 1883 Pendleton Act, which instituted the Civil Service (p. 253)

Austin, Stephen Leader of first American group of Texas settlers in 1822; worked for Texan independence (p. 172)

Stephen Austin

Bakke, Alan Student who won a suit against the University of California in 1978 on the grounds that the affirmative action program had kept him out (p. 799)

Baldwin, James African American author and spokesperson for the civil rights movement during the 1960s (p. 671)

Banks, Dennis Native American leader in 1960s and 1970s; helped organize American Indian Movement (AIM) and the 1973 Wounded Knee occupation (p. 696)

Beecher, Catharine Author whose 1841 book *Treatise on Domestic Economy* supported the cult of domesticity (p. 160)

Beecher, Lyman Revivalist during the Second Great Awakening; feared the rise of individualism in the United States (p. 152)

Begin, Menachem (bĕ´•gēn´, mä•nä´hĕm) Israeli leader during the 1970s; began the Middle East peace process by reaching the 1978 Camp David Accords with Egypt (p. 790)

Bellamy, Edward Author of the novel *Looking Backward* (1888), which proposed nationalizing trusts to eliminate social problems (p. 338)

Bethune, Mary McLeod African American educator, New Deal worker; founded Bethune Cookman College in the 1920s, advised the National Youth Administration (p. 476)

Beveridge, Albert J. Indiana senator in the early 1900s; saw United States imperialism as a duty owed to "primitive" societies (p. 311)

Brown, John Abolitionist crusader who massacred proslavery settlers in Kansas before the Civil War; hoped to inspire slave revolt with 1859 attack on Virginia arsenal; executed for treason against the state of Virginia (p. 193)

Bryan, William Jennings Advocate of silver standard and proponent of Democratic and Populist views from the 1890s through the 1910s; Democratic candidate for President in 1896, 1900, and 1908 (p. 249)

Buchanan, James Fifteenth President of the United States, 1857–1861; supported by the South; attempted to moderate fierce disagreement over expansion of slavery (p. 192)

Bush, George H. W. Forty-first President of the United States, 1989–1993; continued Reagan's conservative policies; brought together United Nations coalition to fight the Persian Gulf War (p. 814)

Calhoun, John C. Statesman from South Carolina who held many offices in the federal government; supported slavery, cotton exports, states' rights; in 1850 foresaw future conflicts over slavery (p. 130)

Carnegie, Andrew Industrialist who made a fortune in steel in the late 1800s through vertical consolidation; as a philanthropist, he gave away over $350 million (p. 231)

Carson, Rachel Marine biologist, author of *Silent Spring* (1962), which exposed harmful effects of pesticides and inspired concern for the environment (p. 701)

Carter, James Earl, Jr. Thirty-ninth President of the United States, 1977–1981; advocated concern for human rights in foreign policy; assisted in mediating the Camp David Accords (p. 785)

Castro, Fidel (käs′trō, fĕ•thĕl′) Revolutionary leader who took control of Cuba in 1959; ally of Soviet Union through the 1980s (p. 576)

Catt, Carrie Chapman Woman suffrage leader in the early 1900s; helped secure passage of Nineteenth Amendment in 1920; headed National American Woman Suffrage Association (p. 357)

Chávez, César (chä′vāz, sā′sär) Latino leader from 1962 to his death in 1993; organized the United Farm Workers (UFW) to help migratory farm workers gain better pay and working conditions (p. 692)

Churchill, Winston Leader of Great Britain before and during World War II; powerful speechmaker who rallied Allied morale during the war (p. 504)

Henry Cisneros

Cisneros, Henry Latino mayor of San Antonio; he was made head of Housing and Urban Development in 1993 under President Bill Clinton (p. 824)

Clark, William Leader, with Meriwether Lewis, of expedition through the West in 1804; brought back scientific samples, maps, and information on Native Americans (p. 167)

Clay, Henry Senator from Kentucky; accused by Jackson of giving votes to John Q. Adams in return for post as secretary of state; endorsed the American System to promote economic growth; advocate of Compromise of 1850 (p. 131)

Cleveland, Grover Twenty-second and twenty-fourth President of the United States, 1885–1889, 1893–1897; supported railroad regulation and a return to the gold standard (p. 254)

Clinton, Bill Forty-second President of the United States, 1993–; defeated George Bush after overcoming numerous political obstacles; advocated economic and health-care reform (p. 840)

Clinton, Hillary Rodham First Lady, 1993– ; lawyer; head of United States health-care reform team (p. 841)

Columbus, Christopher Explorer whose voyage for Spain to North America in 1492 opened the Atlantic World (p. 23)

Coolidge, Calvin Thirtieth President of the United States, 1923–1929; promoted big business and opposed social aid (p. 413)

Coughlin, Father Charles E. "Radio Priest" who supported and then attacked President Franklin Roosevelt's New Deal; prevented by the Catholic church from broadcasting after he praised Hitler (p. 482)

Coxey, Jacob S. Populist who led Coxey's Army in a march on Washington, D.C., in 1894 to seek government jobs for the unemployed (p. 255)

Custer, George Armstrong General who directed army attacks against Native Americans in the 1870s; commanded army forces killed in 1876 at Little Bighorn in Montana (p. 246)

de Klerk, Frederick W. Prime minister of South Africa who began the process of ending apartheid in the early 1990s (p. 849)

Dewey, George Officer in United States Navy, 1861–1917; led a surprise attack in the Philippines during the Spanish-American War that destroyed the entire Spanish fleet (p. 314)

Dinh Diem, Ngo (dĭn′zē′ĕm, nō′) Leader of South Vietnam, 1954–1963; supported by United States, but not by Vietnamese Buddhist majority; assassinated in 1963 (p. 714)

Dix, Dorothea Advocate of prison reform and of special institutions for the insane in Massachusetts before the Civil War (p. 154)

Douglass, Frederick African American abolitionist leader who spoke eloquently for abolition in the United States and Britain before the Civil War (p. 156)

Du Bois, W.E.B. (dōō•bois′) African American scholar and leader in early 1900s; encouraged African Americans to attend colleges to develop leadership skills (p. 275)

Ehrlichman, John Adviser on domestic policy to President Richard Nixon; deeply involved in Watergate (p. 755)

Einstein, Albert Physicist whose theory of relativity led to harnessing nuclear energy; proposed development of the atomic bomb in 1939 (p. 518)

Eisenhower, Dwight D. Thirty-fourth President of the United States, 1953–1961; leader of Allied forces in World War II; as President, he promoted business and continued social programs (p. 509)

Eliot, T. S. Poet; his work "The Waste Land" described the struggle of youth in the 1920s (p. 427)

Ellsberg, Daniel Defense Department official; leaked Pentagon Papers to the *New York Times* in 1971, showing government lies to public about Vietnam (p. 765)

Father Divine African American minister; his Harlem soup kitchens fed the hungry during the Great Depression (p. 450)

Fillmore, Millard Thirteenth President of the United States, 1850–1853; promoted the Compromise of 1850 to smooth over disagreements about slavery in new territories

Fitzgerald, F. Scott Novelist who depicted the United States and the world during the 1920s in novels such as *The Great Gatsby* (p. 427)

Ford, Gerald R. Thirty-eighth President of the United States, 1974–1977; succeeded and pardoned Nixon; failed to establish strong leadership (p. 780)

Ford, Henry Manufacturer from the 1910s through the 1940s; made affordable cars for the masses using assembly line and other production techniques (p. 422)

Friedan, Betty Feminist author; criticized limited roles for women in her 1963 book *The Feminine Mystique* (p. 598)

Betty Friedan

Garfield, James A. Twentieth President of the United States, 1881; his assassination by a disappointed office seeker led to the reform of the spoils system (p. 253)

Garrison, William Lloyd White leader of radical abolition movement based in Boston; founded *The Liberator* in 1831 to work for an immediate end to slavery (p. 155)

Garvey, Marcus African American leader from 1919 to 1926 who urged African Americans to return to "motherland" of Africa; provided early inspiration for "black pride" movements (p. 413)

George III King of England during American Revolution (p. 53)

George, Henry Author of *Progress and Poverty* (1879) linking land speculation and poverty; proposed a single tax based on land value (p. 338)

Gorbachev, Mikhail (gôr´bǎ•chěv, myĭ•ĸǔ•ēl´) Soviet leader whose bold reforms led to the breakup of the Soviet Union in the late 1980s (p. 828)

Gore, Al Senator from Tennessee; Vice President under President Bill Clinton, 1993– (p. 844)

Grant, Ulysses S. Eighteenth President of the United States, 1869–1877; commander of Union forces who accepted Lee's surrender in 1865 (p. 201)

Haldeman, H. R. Chief of staff under President Richard Nixon; deeply involved in Watergate (p. 755)

Hamilton, Alexander Officer in the War for Independence; delegate to the Constitutional Convention; Federalist and first secretary of treasury (p. 93)

Harding, Warren G. Twenty-ninth President of the United States, 1921–1923; presided over a short administration marked by corruption (p. 413)

Harrison, Benjamin Twenty-third President of the United States, 1889–1893; signed 1890 Sherman Antitrust Act later used to regulate big business (p. 255)

Harrison, William Henry Ninth President of the United States, 1841; died of pneumonia after only a month in office (p. 136)

Hayes, Rutherford B. Nineteenth President of the United States, 1877–1881; promised to withdraw Union troops from the South in order to end dispute over his election; attacked spoils system (p. 217)

Hearst, William Randolph Newspaper publisher from 1887 until his death in 1951; used "yellow journalism" in the 1890s to stir up sentiment in favor of the Spanish-American War (p. 313)

Hiss, Alger Former State Department official investigated as a possible communist spy by House Un-American Activities Committee after World War II; convicted of perjury in 1950 (p. 579)

Hitler, Adolf German leader of National Socialist (Nazi) party 1933–1945; rose to power by promoting racist and nationalist views (p. 501)

Ho Chi Minh (hō´ chē´ mǐn´) Leader of the Communist party in Indochina after World War II; led Vietnamese against the French, then North Vietnamese against the United States in the Vietnam War (p. 574)

Hoover, Herbert Thirty-first President of the United States, 1929–1933; worked to aid Europeans during World War I; responded ineffectively to 1929 stock market crash and Great Depression (p. 414)

Houston, Sam Leader of Texas troops in war for independence from Mexico in 1836; elected first governor of independent Texas (p. 173)

Humphrey, Hubert Democratic presidential candidate in 1968; lost narrowly to Nixon in an election bid hurt by support for the Vietnam War and by third-party candidate George Wallace (p. 750)

Hussein, Saddam (hŏŏ•sǐn´, sǎd•dǎm´) Iraqi dictator; invaded Kuwait in 1990, setting off Persian Gulf War (p. 830)

Jackson, Andrew Seventh President of the United States, 1829–1837; supported minimal government and the spoils system; vetoed rechartering of the national bank; pursued harsh policy toward Native Americans (p. 113)

Jackson, Stonewall Confederate general known for his swift strikes against Union forces; earned nickname Stonewall by holding his forces steady under extreme pressure at the First Battle of Manassas (p. 199)

Jefferson, Thomas Third President of the United States, 1801–1809; main author of the Declaration of Independence; a firm believer in the people and decentralized power; reduced the federal government (p. 56)

Johnson, Andrew Seventeenth President of the United States, 1865–1869; clashed with Radical Republicans on Reconstruction programs; was impeached, then acquitted, in 1868 (p. 213)

Johnson, Lyndon B. Thirty-sixth President of the United States, 1963–1969; expanded social assistance with his Great Society program; increased United States commitment during Vietnam War (p. 629)

Joseph, Chief Leader of Nez Percé; forced to give up his home by United States army, fled toward Canada; captured in 1877 (p. 246)

Kelley, Florence Progressive reformer active from 1886 to 1920; worked in state and federal government for laws on child

Chief Joseph

labor, workplace safety, and consumer protection (p. 341)

Kennedy, John F. Thirty-fifth President of the United States, 1961–1963; seen as youthful and inspiring; known for his firm handling of the Cuban missile crisis; assassinated in 1963 (p. 624)

Kennedy, Robert F. Attorney general under his brother, President John Kennedy, in the early 1960s; supported civil rights; assassinated while running for President in 1968 (p. 749)

Keynes, John Maynard British economist who believed that government spending could help a faltering economy; his theories helped shape New Deal legislation (p. 458)

Khomeini, Ayatollah Ruholla (kō•mā´nē, ĭ•yä•tŏl´lȧ rōō•hŏl´lȧ) Islamic fundamentalist leader of Iran after the 1979 overthrow of the Shah; approved holding of American hostages (p. 792)

King, Martin Luther, Jr. African American civil rights leader from the mid-1950s until his assassination in 1968; used nonviolent means such as marches, boycotts, and legal challenges to win civil rights (p. 610)

Kissinger, Henry Secretary of state under Presidents Richard Nixon and Gerald Ford; used *realpolitik* to open relations with China, to end the Vietnam War, and to moderate Middle East conflict (p. 755)

Khrushchev, Nikita (кrōōsh´chôf, nyĭ•kyē´tŭ) Soviet leader from 1953 to 1964; opposed President Kennedy in the Cuban missile crisis (p. 639)

Lafayette, Marquis de (lä´fī•ĕt´, mär•kē´dĕ´) French officer who assisted American forces in the War for Independence (p. 63)

Lee, Robert E. Brilliant general of Confederate forces during the Civil War (p. 202)

Lenin, Vladimir I. Revolutionary leader in Russia; established a communist government in 1917 (p. 404)

Levitt, William J. Built new communities in the suburbs after World War II, using mass-production techniques (p. 593)

Lewis, John L. Head of United Mine Workers through World War II; used strikes during the war to win pay raises (p. 535)

Lewis, Meriwether Leader with William Clark of expedition through the West in 1804; brought back scientific samples, maps, and information on Native Americans (p. 167)

Lincoln, Abraham Sixteenth President of the United States, 1861–1865; known for his effective leadership during the Civil War and his Emancipation Proclamation declaring the end of slavery in Confederate-held territory (p. 194)

Lindbergh, Charles A. Aviator who became an international hero when he made the first solo flight across the Atlantic Ocean in 1927 (p. 421)

Lodge, Henry Cabot Massachusetts senator of early 1900s; supported United States imperialism (p. 311)

Long, Huey Louisiana politician in 1930s called the Kingfish; suggested redistributing large fortunes by means of grants to families; assassinated in 1935 (p. 482)

Low, Juliette Founder of American Girl Scouts in 1912 (p. 329)

MacArthur, Douglas United States general during World War II and Korean War; forced by Truman to resign in 1951 (p. 507)

Madison, James Fourth President of the United States, 1809–1817; called the Father of the Constitution for his leadership at the Constitutional Convention (p. 80)

Mahan, Alfred T. Author who argued in 1890 that the economic future of the United States rested on new overseas markets protected by a larger navy (p. 310)

Malcolm X African American leader during the 1950s and 1960s; eloquent spokesperson for African American self-sufficiency; assassinated in 1965 (p. 672)

Mandela, Nelson African anti-apartheid leader in South Africa beginning in the 1960s; imprisoned 1962–1989 (p. 849)

Mann, Horace School reformer and supporter of public education before the Civil War; devised an educational system in Massachusetts later copied by many states (p. 153)

Mao Zedong (mou´ dzŭ´ dŏŏng´) Leader of communists who took over China in 1949; remained in power until his death in 1976 (p. 569)

Marshall, George C. Secretary of state under President Harry Truman; assisted economic recovery in Europe after World War II and established strong allies for the United States through his Marshall Plan (p. 568)

Marshall, Thurgood First African American Supreme Court justice; as a lawyer, won landmark school desegregation case *Brown* v. *Board of Education* in 1954 (p. 610)

McCarthy, Eugene Candidate in the 1968 Democratic presidential race who opposed the Vietnam War; convinced President Lyndon Johnson not to run again through his strong showing in the primaries (p. 749)

McCarthy, Joseph R. Republican senator from Wisconsin in the late 1940s and early 1950s; led a crusade to investigate officials he claimed were communists; discredited in 1954 (p. 579)

McClellan, George Early Union army leader in the Civil War; careful organizer and planner who moved too slowly for northern politicians; ran against President Abraham Lincoln in the election of 1864 (p. 200)

McKinley, William Twenty-fifth President of the United States, 1897–1901; supported tariffs and a gold standard; expanded the United States by waging the Spanish-American War (p. 256)

Means, Russell Native American leader of 1960s and 1970s; helped organize American Indian Movement (AIM) and 1973 Wounded Knee occupation (p. 699)

Metacom Leader of Pokanokets in Massachusetts; also known by his English name, King Philip; led Native Americans in King Philip's War, 1675–1676 (p. 33)

Milosevic, Slobodan (mē•lôsh´ĕ•vĭk, slō´bä•dän) Leader of Serbs in civil war that started in 1991 after the breakup of Yugoslavia; accused of genocide of Croats and Muslims (p. 847)

Mitchell, John Attorney general under President Richard Nixon; deeply involved in Watergate scandal (p. 755)

Mohammad Reza Pahlavi, Shah Leader of Iran, from 1941 until his overthrow in 1979; supported by the United States; brought modernization to his country along with repression and corruption (p. 791)

Monroe, James Fifth President of the United States, 1817–1825; acquired Florida from Spain; declared Monroe Doctrine to keep foreign powers out of the Americas (p. 130)

Mott, Lucretia Women's rights leader; helped organize first women's convention in Seneca Falls, New York, in 1848 (p. 162)

Mussolini, Benito (mōō′sō•lē′nĕ, bā•nē′tō) Italian fascist leader from 1925 through 1945; called *Il Duce* — "the leader"; known for his brutal policies (p. 500)

Nader, Ralph Consumer advocate; published *Unsafe at Any Speed* in 1965 criticizing auto safety and inspiring new safety laws (p. 703)

Nimitz, Chester Leader of United States troops in World War II battle of Midway Island, during which much of the Japanese navy was destroyed (p. 509)

Nixon, Richard M. Thirty-seventh President, 1969–1974; known for his foreign policy toward the Soviet Union and China and for illegal acts he committed in the Watergate affair that forced his resignation (p. 604)

Sandra Day O'Connor

O'Connor, Sandra Day First woman Supreme Court justice; appointed by Reagan in 1981 (p. 817)

Oppenheimer, J. Robert Physicist; headed Manhattan Project in World War II to develop first atomic bomb (p. 519)

Paine, Thomas Author of political pamphlets during 1770s and 1780s; wrote *Common Sense* in 1776 (p. 56)

Paul, Alice Woman suffrage leader of early 1900s; her Congressional Union used aggressive tactics to push the Nineteenth Amendment (p. 357)

Perkins, Frances Secretary of labor 1933–1945 under President Franklin Delano Roosevelt; first woman cabinet member (p. 475)

Pierce, Franklin Fourteenth President of the United States, 1853–1857; signed the Kansas-Nebraska Act, which renewed conflicts over slavery in the territories

Polk, James K. Eleventh President of the United States, 1845–1849; led expansion of United States to southwest through war against Mexico (p. 176)

Popé (pō•pā′) Medicine man who led Pueblos and Apaches against Spanish rule in the Revolt of 1680 (p. 29)

Powhatan Native American leader of Pamunkey people in Chesapeake Bay region of Virginia in late 1500s and early 1600s (p. 30)

Pulitzer, Joseph Early 1900s newspaper publisher; used "yellow journalism" to stir up public sentiment in favor of the Spanish-American War (p. 313)

Rabin, Yitzhak (rä•bēn′, yĭtz′äk) Israeli prime minister who signed a peace agreement with Palestinians in 1993 (p. 848)

Randolph, A. Philip Civil rights activist from the 1930s to the 1950s; planned the Washington march that pressured President Franklin Delano Roosevelt into opening World War II defense jobs to African Americans (p. 547)

Reagan, Ronald Fortieth President of the United States, 1981–1989; conservative leader who promoted supply-side economics and created huge budget deficits (p. 810)

Robinson, Jackie Athlete who in 1947 became the first African American to play baseball in the major leagues (p. 608)

Rockefeller, Nelson Vice President appointed by President Gerald Ford in 1974; the nation's only nonelected Vice President to serve with a nonelected President (p. 781)

Roosevelt, Eleanor First Lady 1933–1945; tireless worker for social causes, including women's rights and civil rights for African Americans and other groups (p. 459)

Roosevelt, Franklin D. Thirty-second President of the United States, 1933–1945; fought the Great Depression through his New Deal social programs; battled Congress over Supreme Court control; proved a strong leader during World War II (p. 459)

Roosevelt, Theodore Twenty-sixth President of the United States, 1901–1909; fought trusts, aided progressive reforms, built Panama Canal, and increased United States influence overseas (p. 319)

Rosenberg, Julius and Ethel Husband and wife convicted and executed in 1953 for passing atomic secrets to the Soviet Union; their guilt is still debated (p. 579)

Sacajawea (săk′ä•jä•wē•ä) Shoshone woman who served as guide and translator for Lewis and Clark on their exploratory journey through the West in the early 1800s (p. 167)

Sacco, Nicola (säk′kō, nē•kô′lä) Immigrant and anarchist executed for a 1920 murder at a Massachusetts factory, though believed to be innocent by many (p. 406)

Sadat, Anwar el- (sà•dat′, än•wär′ ĕl) Egyptian leader in the 1970s; began the Middle East peace process by reaching the 1978 Camp David Accords with Egypt (p. 790)

Salinger, J. D. Author of 1951 novel *The Catcher in the Rye*, which criticized 1950s pressure to conform (p. 599)

Schlafly, Phyllis Conservative activist; led campaign during the 1960s and 1970s to block the Equal Rights Amendment (p. 689)

Sirica, John J. Washington judge who presided over the Watergate investigation in the 1970s; gave tough sentences to convicted participants and ordered President Richard Nixon to release secret tapes (p. 767)

Smith, Joseph Founder of Church of Jesus Christ of Latter-day Saints, or Mormons, in New York in 1830; killed by a mob in Illinois in 1844 (p. 178)

Spock, Benjamin Pediatrician and author of *Common Sense Book of Baby and Child Care* (1946), which encouraged mothers to stay home with their children rather than work (p. 598)

Jackie Robinson

Stalin, Joseph Leader of the Soviet Union from 1924–1953; worked with Roosevelt and Churchill during World War II but afterwards became an aggressive participant in the cold war (p. 510)

Stanton, Elizabeth Cady Women's rights leader in the 1800s; helped organize first women's convention; wrote the *Declaration of Sentiments* on women's rights in 1848 (p. 162)

Starr, Ellen Gates Cofounder of Chicago's Hull House, the first settlement house, in 1889 (p. 263)

Steinem, Gloria Journalist, women's rights leader since 1960s; founded *Ms.* magazine in 1972 to cover women's issues (p. 687)

Stevenson, Adlai Senator from Illinois and Democratic candidate for President in 1952 and 1956 against Eisenhower (p. 604)

Taft, William Howard Twenty-seventh President of the United States, 1909–1913; continued progressive reforms of President Theodore Roosevelt; promoted "dollar diplomacy" to expand foreign investments (p. 323)

Taylor, Zachary Twelfth President of the United States, 1849–1850; tried to avoid slavery issues

Thomas, Clarence Conservative African American Supreme Court justice appointed in 1991; during his confirmation hearings he was charged with sexual harassment (p. 817)

Thomas, Norman Socialist party leader and candidate for President in the 1920 and 1930s; won 2 percent of the vote in 1932 (p. 455)

Thoreau, Henry David Transcendentalist author known for his work *Walden* (1854) and other writings (p. 152)

Truman, Harry S Thirty-third President of the United States, 1945–1953; authorized use of atomic bomb; signed Marshall Plan to rebuild Europe (p. 520)

Truth, Sojourner Abolitionist and women's rights advocate before the Civil War; as a formerly enslaved person, she spoke effectively and authentically to white audiences on abolition issues (p. 163)

Sojourner Truth

Tubman, Harriet "Conductor" on the underground railroad that helped enslaved persons escape to freedom before the Civil War (p. 156)

Turner, Frederick Jackson Historian who wrote an essay in 1893 emphasizing the western frontier as a powerful force in the formation of the American character (p. 250)

Turner, Nat African American preacher who led a slave revolt in 1831; captured and hanged after the revolt failed (p. 128)

Tweed, William Marcy Boss of Tammany Hall political machine in New York City; convicted of forgery and larceny in 1873 and died in jail in 1878 (p. 261)

Tyler, John Tenth President of the United States, 1841–1845; accomplished little due to quarrels between Whigs and Jacksonian Democrats (p. 136)

Van Buren, Martin Eighth President of the United States, 1837–1841; Jacksonian Democrat; was voted out of the executive office after the Panic of 1837 brought widespread unemployment and poverty (p. 136)

Vance, Cyrus Secretary of state under President Jimmy Carter; invited Israelis and Egyptians to Camp David in 1978 to begin Middle East peace process (p. 790)

Vanzetti, Bartolomeo (văn•zĕt´ĭ, bär´tŏ•lōmâ´ō) Immigrant and anarchist executed for a 1920 murder at a Massachusetts factory, though believed to be innocent by many (p. 406)

Vesey, Denmark African American who planned 1822 South Carolina slave revolt; captured and hanged after revolt failed (p. 128)

von Steuben, Baron Prussian officer who trained Washington's troops in the winter at Valley Forge (p. 63)

Walker, Madam C. J. African American leader and businesswoman in the early 1900s; she spoke out against lynching (p. 284)

Wallace, George C. Third-party candidate for President in 1968; focused his campaign on issues of blue-collar anger in the North and racial tension (p. 751)

Warren, Earl Chief Justice of Supreme Court 1953–1968; led in many decisions that protected civil rights, rights of the accused, and right to privacy (p. 627)

Washington, Booker T. African American leader from the late 1800s until his death in 1915; founded Tuskegee Institute in Alabama; encouraged African Americans to learn trades (p. 275)

Washington, George First President of the United States, 1789–1797; led American forces in the War for Independence; set several federal precedents, including the two-term maximum for presidential office (p. 52)

Whitney, Eli Inventor; developed the cotton gin in 1793, which rapidly increased cotton production in the South and led to a greater need for slave labor (p. 115)

Wilhelm, Kaiser (vĭl´hĕlm, kī´zêr) Emperor of Germany during World War I; symbol to the United States of German militarism and severe efficiency (p. 372)

Wilson, Woodrow Twenty-eighth President of the United States, 1913–1921; tried to keep the United States out of World War I; proposed League of Nations (p. 351)

Yeltsin, Boris (yĕlt´sĭn, bŭ•ryēs´) Leader of Russia in late 1980s and early 1990s; took over from Mikhail Gorbachev as reforms continued and Communist party control ended (p. 829)

Young, Brigham Mormon leader who supervised migration to Utah beginning in the 1840s; first governor when Utah became a United States territory (p. 179)

Index

Note: Entries with a page number followed by a *c* indicate a chart or graph on that page; *m* indicates a map; and *p* indicates a picture.

INDEX

INDEX

INDEX

Acknowledgments

Cover Design Martucci Studio, Alison Anholt-White, and L. Christopher Valente

Front Cover Engraving "The Brooklyn Bridge," engraving by the Shugg Brothers after the original by R. Schwartz, 1883. Museum of the City of New York.

Back Cover Photo Larry Fisher/Masterfile

Book Design DECODE, Inc.

Epilogue and Prologue Design Alan Lee

Picture Research Pembroke Herbert and Sandi Rygiel/Picture Research Consultants, Inc.

Time & Place Contributing Writers Carol Barrett, Department of Geography, University of Wisconsin at River Falls, River Falls, WI; Tom Baerwald, Program Director of Geography and Regional Science, National Science Foundation, Washington, D.C.; Peter Hugill, Department of Geography, Texas A&M University, College Station, TX; Nina Lam, Department of Geography and Anthropology, Louisiana State University, Baton Rouge, LA

Maps

GEO Systems, A Unit of R.R. Donnelly & Sons, Co.: 14, 119, 155, 159, 173, 175, 176, 201, 202, 211, 309, 318, 321, 325, 359, 371, 382, 390, 475, 694, 892, 896, 897, 899, 900–901, 902–903

Horizon Design/Sanderson Associates: 17, 29, 37, 43, 62, 115, 195, 214, 229, 245, 314, 322, 327, 346, 411, 447, 461, 502, 503, 507, 508, 547, 564, 570, 573, 575, 576, 601, 639, 643, 661, 671, 757, 786, 823, 848, 849

Illustration

Peter Brooks: 54–55, 768

Function Thru Form: 26, 67, 84, 113, 126, 153, 154, 165, 240, 252, 273, 274, 283, 310, 372, 405, 420, 426, 440, 443, 444, 445, 486, 533, 534, 542, 593, 598, 626, 631, 632, 668, 685, 688, 756, 783, 813, 816, 819, 827, 843, 853, 856, 893, 894–895, 898, 899, 904

Paul Gagnon: 45, 73, 91, 97, 132, 137, 139, 178, 183, 193, 200, 216, 219, 265, 282, 293, 313, 331, 344, 347, 352, 354, 363, 393, 429, 465, 491, 525, 553, 583, 615, 645, 669, 677, 705, 707, 773, 803, 833, 844, 851, 857, 859

Matthew Pippin: 18, 116, 125, 422–423, 606, 797

Photography

Abbreviation Key LOC = Library of Congress; U/B = UPI/Bettmann Archives; RH/LS = photo by Rob Huntley/Lightstream; NA = National Archives; PRC = Picture Research Consultants, Inc.; FRENT = Collection of David J. and Janice L. Frent; BB = Brown Brothers; CP = Culver Pictures; WW = Wide World Photos; GL = Gamma Liaison; WC = Woodfin Camp & Associates; C&G = Chermayeff & Geismar/MetaForm photo by Karen Yamauchi; BS = Black Star; MP = Magnum Photos; SI = Smithsonian Institution; OPPS = Office of Printing and Photographic Services, Smithsonian Institution. NPS = Courtesy of the National Park Service

Prologue xxii, CP; **1 T**, Harper's Weekly, May 26, 1883; **1 B**, U/B; **2 TL, B**, Rensselaer Polytechnic Institute; **2 M**, The Metropolitan Museum of Art. The Edward W.C. Arnold Collection of New York Prints, Maps and Pictures. Bequest of Edward W.C. Arnold; **4 T**, Bernard Gotfryd/WC; **4 INSET**, Andy Levin/Photo Researchers; **6**, © 1992 Jon Feingersh/The Stock Market; **7 BL**, FPG; **7BM,** © 1993, Ted Horowitz/ The Stock Market;

7 background, FPG; **7 TR,** RH/LS; **8 TR,** TWA; **8 BR,** San Diego Historical Society; **9 BR,** McDonald's Corporation; **9 BL,** FPG; **10 T,** Missouri Historical Society. Block Brothers photograph; **10 INSET,** © Fredericks/The Image Works; **11,** Museum of Modern Art Film Still Archive.

Unit Openers Pages **12–13,** "Election Day in Philadelphia" by John Lewis Krimmel, 1815. (detail) Courtesy, Winterthur Museum; **148–149,** "Excursion Party at Devil's Gate Bridge, Utah" by A. J. Russell. (detail) Courtesy of the Oakland Museum History Department; **304–305,** New York & Cuba Mail Steamship Company Dock scene. (detail) U/B; **400–401,** "Mother and Child" by Dorothea Lange (detail). LOC; **496–497,** "Chow is served to American Infantrymen on their way to La Roche, Belgium, 347th Inf. Reg. January 13, 1945."(detail) NA #1075; **620–621,** "Selma March" March 1965 (detail) by James H. Karales; **744–745,** Clinton Inauguration, January 1993 (detail) U/B.

American Album Pages **98–99,** *Jug,* Eric Long, SI; *Gridiron,* OPPS; *Sampler,* Eric Long, SI; *Suit,* Eric Long, SI; *Respect,* Library of Congress; *Toys,* OPPS; *Dairying,* Courtesy of Princeton University Library, Dept of Rare Books and Special Collections; *Anvil & Hammer,* Eric Long, SI; *Gravestones,* Dane Penland, SI; **220–221,** *Shoulder Plate, Knife, Tins, Cutlery, Hard Tack,* all by Rick Vargas and Richard Strauss, SI; *Uniform,* Dane Penland, SI; *Flag,* Alfred Harrell and Andrew Wynn, SI; *Quinine,* Dane Penland, SI; FIELD HOSPITAL, OPPS; *Muskett,* Rick Vargas, SI; **294–295,** *Football Player, Baseball Music,* Larry Gates, SI; *Skiing, Football Pants, Baseball,* all by Rick Vargas, SI; SKATING, Jim Wallace, SI; *Bicycle,* Alfred Harrell, SI; *Cyclist,* Collection of Sally Fox; **394–395,** *Record Book,* Dane Penland, SI; *Doll,* Eric Long, SI; *Plow,* Jeff Tinsley, SI; *Suitcase,* Eric Long, SI; *Soldiers,* Courtesy of the National Archives and Records Administration; *Home Schooling,* Library of Congress; *Jobs,* Jeff Tinsley, SI; **430–431,** *Duke,* Courtesy of John Hasse; *Radio,* Dane Penland, SI; *Hymie,* Danny Thompson, SI; *Saxophone,* Dane Penland, SI; *Dress,* Jeff Tinsley, SI; *Clarinet,* Dane Penland, SI; *Trumpet,* Jeffrey Ploskonka, SI; *Band,* Missouri Historical Society, Block Brothers Photo; **554–555,** Jeff Tinsley, SI all with the exception of; *Propaganda Posters,* Richard Strauss, SI; **738–739,** *Boots, Helmut, Letter, Watch, Letter to Gary,* Eric Long, SI, NPS; *Dogtags,* Rick Vargas, SI, NPS; *Stuffed Animals,* Richard Strauss, SI, NPS; *Vietnam Memorial,* Sandra Rogers, SI; **860–861,** *Satellite,* OPPS; *Watergate,* Margaret McCullough, SI, courtesy of the National Archives and Records Administration; *Laser Head,* OPPS, SI; *Grace Hopper,* Danny Thompson, SI; *Hand Held Computer,* Courtesy of Apple Computer, Inc.; *Early Computer,* Eric Long, SI; *Barcodes,* MAD's UPC symbol cover is © E.C. Publications, Inc., 1978. Used with permission from MAD Magazine.; *Chip,* Copyright of Motorola, Inc. Used by permission. *Fiber-Optic,* Courtesy of Intel Corporation; Jeff Tinsley, SI.

Chapter 1 Page **14 L,** National Maritime Museum, Greenwich, England; **14 R,** Museum of Early Southern Decorative Arts; **16 inset,** Courtesy of the National Museum of the American Indian/ Smithsonian Institution #S:1514; **19,** Giraudon/Art Resource, NY; **21 T, B** Photograph by Jeffrey Ploskonka, National Museum of African Art, Eliot Elisofon Archive, Smithsonian Institution; **22,** "Arrival at Tomboctou from Barth", from *Travels in Central Africa,* 1857. Rare Book and Manuscripts Division, The New York Public Library, Astor, Lenox and Tilden Foundations; **23,** National Maritime Museum. Photo © Michael Holford; **24,** "Portuguese Caravels" from *America* by Theodore De Bry 1594. (detail) Rare Book and Manuscript Division, The New York Public Library, Astor, Lenox and Tilden Foundations; **25 TR,** Aztec drawing of smallpox victim from the Flortine Codex, v. 4, Book 12 (detail). Courtesy of Biblioteca Medicea Laurenziana, Florence. Photo by Alberto Scardigli; **25 BL,** Courtesy of Magellan Systems Corporation; **25 BR,** London Science Museum. Photo © Michael Holford; **28** Courtesy of South Florida Science Museum, Photo by Randy Smith; **32,** "The Mason Children: David, Joanna, and Abigail" 1670 attributed to the

Freake-Gibbs painter. Fine Arts Museums of San Francisco, Gift of Mr. & Mrs. John D. Rockefeller 3rd; **33**, Courtesy of the National Museum of the American Indian/ Smithsonian Institution, #4662, #4663; **34**, "Landing of Negroes at Jamestown, 1619" Free Library of Philadelphia; **36**, Norwich textile sample book. Courtesy, The Winterthur Library: Joseph Downs Collection of Manuscripts and Printed Ephemera; **38 T**, John Lewis Stage; **38 B**, Colonial Williamsburg Foundation; **39**, "The First, Second, and Last Scenes of Mortality" by Prudence Punderson ca. 1783, Connecticut Historical Society; **40**, Collection of Roddy and Sally Moore; **42**, "Rev. George Whitefield" by J. Wollaston, 1742. Courtesy of the National Portrait Gallery, London; **49**, Library Company of Philadelphia.

Chapter 2 **50 TL, BL**, Nichipor Collection, Courtesy of Minuteman National Historical Park. RH/LS; **50 R**, Lexington Historical Society. Photo © Rob Huntley/Lightstream; **52**, Colonial Williamsburg Foundation; **53**, LOC; **55**, The Bostonian Society/Old State House; **57**, Mass. Historical Society; **59**, Lexington Historical Society. RH/LS; **60**, Courtesy Minuteman National Historical Park, RH/LS; **61**, "Attack on Bunker Hill, with the Burning of Charlestown" unknown artist. Gift of Edgar William and Bernice Chrysler Garbisch, ©1994, National Gallery of Art, Washington, D.C.; **62 both**, Courtesy Minuteman National Historical Park, RH/LS; **63**, "Tarleton's Cavalrymen after the Battle of Cowpers" by William Ranney. Collection of the State of South Carolina. Photo by Hunter Clarkeson, Alt Lee, Inc.; **64**, New York Historical Society; **65 T**, LOC; **65 B**, Independence National Historical Park, Philadelphia; **66**, Yale University Art Gallery, Mabel Brady Garven Collection; **67**, "General Washington's Resignation" by Alonzo Chappel. Chicago Historical Society; **68**, Eric P. Newman Numismatic Education Society. RH/LS; **69**, *Popular History of the United States* by William Cullen Bryant, 1881 p. 98. LOC; **71**, CP.

Chapter 3 **78 BR**, Independence National Historic Park, Philadelphia; **78 TR**, NA. Photo © Rob Huntly/Lightstream; **80**, Independence National Historic Park, Philadelphia (detail); **81**, "James Madison" by Charles Willson Peale, 1783. LOC; **82**, "Independence Hall" by William Birch, 1790. Rare Book Department, Free Library of Philadelphia; **83**, "Signing of the Constitution" by Thomas Prichard Rossiter, 1872. Independence National Historic Park, Philadelphia; **86**, "Washington at Verplancke's Point" by John Trumbull, 1790. Courtesy, Winterthur Museum; **88**, "The Federal Ship Union" from AMERICAN MUSEUM, 1787, Philadelphia. Vol 4, p. 61. American Antiquarian Society; **90**, American Antiquarian Society; **92**, Museum of American Political Life; **93**, "Washington Taking the Oath" by H.A. Odgen. LOC; **94 T**, "The Republican Court" 1861 by Daniel Huntington. (detail) The Brooklyn Museum 39.536.1, Gift of the Crescent-Hamilton Athletic Club; **94 B**, Museum of American Political Life; **95 TL**, LOC; **95 TR**, Fred J. Maroon.

Chapter 4 **104 L**, Shelburne Museum; **104 R**, West Virginia State Museum, photo by Michael Keller; **106**, Henry Ford Museum and Greenfield Village; **108**, "John Adams" by John Trumbull, 1793. National Portrait Gallery, Smithsonian Institution, Washington, D.C./Art Resource N.Y.; **109**, U/B; **110 both**, Museum of American Political Life. Photo by Sally Anderson-Bruce; **111 both**, U/B; **112**, Peabody and Essex Museum; **114**, *The National Archives of the United States* by Herman Viola. Publisher, Harry N. Abrams, Inc. Photo by Jonathan Wallen; **117**, Dukes County Historical Society, photo by Robert Schellhammer; **120**, Lowell Historical Society; **121**, CP; **123**, Old Sturbridge Village; **124**, Museum of American Textile History. Photo Rob Huntley/Lightstream; **130**, FRENT; **131**, The New York Historical Society; **133**, The New York Historical Society; **134**, "Webster's Reply to Haynes" by G.P.A. Healy. City of Boston Art Commission; **135**, Museum of the City of New York; **136**, FRENT; **140**, LOC; **143** "Lazell, Perkins and Co., Bridgewater, Ma." 1858 by J. P. Newell. The Cocoran Gallery of Art, Mary E. Maxwell, Fund.

Chapter 5 **150 TL**, New York State Historical Association; **150 BL, TR**, Collection of Mrs. Elizabeth Waldo Dentzel; **152**, Mass. Historical Society; **154 T**, "Daguerreotype of Emerson School" 1855 by Southworth and Hawes. The Metropolitan Museum of Art, Gift of I.N. Phelps Stokes, Edward S. Hawes, Alice Mary Hawes, Marion Augusta Hawes, 1937; **154**

B, Boston Athenaeum; **156**, National Portrait Gallery, Smithsonian Institution/ Art Resource, N.Y.; **157**, Sophia Smith Archives, Garrison Collection; **158**, ©Louis Psihoyos/Contact Press Images; **160**, American Antiquarian Society; **161**, Schlesinger Library, Radcliffe College; **162 L**, "Elizabeth Cady Stanton" by Harriet Stanton de Forest, 1860. Courtesy National Woman's Party, Washington, D.C. Photo by Jeff Mathewson; **162 R**, Women's Rights Collection, Sophia Smith Archives; **163**, Courtesy of Special Collections, Vassar College Libraries; **164**, "Colonel and Mrs. James A Whiteside, Son Charles and Servants" by James Cameron. Hunter Museum of Art, Chattanooga TN. Gift of Mr. and Mrs. Thomas B. Whiteside; **167**, Roberta Campbell Lawson Collection, Philbrook Museum of Art, Tulsa, OK; **168**, "Migration of the Pawnees" by Alfred Jacob Miller, 1837. Collection of Western Americana, Beinecke Rare Book and Manuscript Library, Yale University; **169**, "Buffalo Chase, A Single Death" by George Catlin. National Museum of American Art, Smithsonian Institution. Gift of Mrs. Joseph Harrison, Jr./ Art Resource N.Y.; **170 B**, Courtesy of The Oakland Museum History Dept.; **170 TL**, Courtesy Museum of New Mexico, Neg. #11329; **170 TR**, Lowell Georgia Photography; **172**, "Stephen F. Austin" by Brand. Archives Div.-Texas State Library; **173**, Courtesy of the Texas Memorial Museum, Univer. of Texas at Austin; **174**, Boot Hill Collection, photo by Henry Groskinsky; **179**, p 1983.20 California Forty-Niner c. 1850, 1/4 plate daguerreotype with applied color. Amon Carter Museum, Fort Worth, TX; **186**, California State Library.

Chapter 6 **188 TL**, Museum of the Confederacy; **188 BL**, Confederate Memorial Hall, New Orleans. From ECHOES OF GLORY; ARMS & EQUIPMENT OF THE CONFEDERACY. Photo by Larry Sherer ©1991 Time-Life Books, Inc.; **188 TR**, Smithsonian Institution. From THE CIVIL WAR; TWENTY MILLION YANKEES. Photo by Larry Sherer ©1985 Time-Life Books, Inc.; **188 BR**, C. Paul Loane Collection, From ECHOES OF GLORY; ARMS & EQUIPMENT OF THE UNION. Photo by Larry Sherer ©1991 Time-Life Books, Inc.; **190**, LOC; **191**, "The Little Giant–in the Character of the Gladiator" 1858. Chicago Historical Society; **192 TL**, Collection of PRC; **192 TR**, Grant Heilman; **194**, LOC; **196**, "Dred Scott" by Louis Schultze, 1881. Missouri Historical Society; **198**, Collection of David & Kevin Kyle; **201**, Collection of Michael J. McAfee. Courtesy William Gladstone. Photo by Seth Goltzer; **205**, West Point Museum Collections. Courtesy William Gladstone. Photo by Seth Goltzer; **206**, LOC; **207**, Moorland-Spingarn Research Center; **208**, "Give Them Cold Steel" painting by Don Troiani. Photo courtesy Historical Art Prints, Southbury, CT 06488; **210**, "Sherman's March to the Sea" engraving after F.O.C. Darley. Photo by Ben Lourie. Collection of David M. Sherman, Washington, D.C.; **212, 213**, Collection of William Gladstone. Photo by Seth Goltzer; **223**, "Bombardment of Sumter" Harpers Weekly, 1861. LOC; **224**, Museum of American Political Life.

Chapter 7 **226**, Courtesy of the Panhandle-Plains Historical Society, Canyon, TX; **228**, Division of Community Life, Smithsonian Institution; **229**, Lightfoot Collection; **230 BL**, Div. of Political History, Smithsonian Institution, #75-2343; **230 BR**, Courtesy Picture Tel; **231**, LOC; **233**, Urban Archives, Temple Univ.; **235**, "The Protectors of Our Industries." Puck. Feb. 7, 1883. LOC; **236**, Collection of Ralph J. Brunke; **227 TR**, PRC; **237 TL**, "Underground Lodging for the Poor" by Paul Frenzeny. Harper's Weekly, Feb. 20, 1869. LOC; **240**, "Haymarket Riot May 4, 1886" by Thure De Thulstrup (detail) Harper's Weekly, May 15, 1886. LOC; **241**, BB; **242 BR**, Minnesota Historical Society/ St. Paul Daily News; **242 BL**, LOC; **242 M**, Franklin D. Roosevelt Presidential Library; **275 BL**, U/B; **275 BR**, Courtesy International Brotherhood of Teamsters; **244**, The Oakland Museum History Department; **246**, LOC; **247**, State Historical Society of Wisconsin; **248** East Carolina Manuscript Collection, J.Y. Joyner Library, East Carolina Univ.; **249**, LOC; **250**, Buffalo Bill Historical Center, Cody WY; **251**, Division of Political History, Smithsonian Institution, #93-3020; **253 BL, 253 INSET, 255, 256**, LOC; **257**, Collection of PRC RH/LS; **258**, BB; **259**, LOC; **261**, BB; **262**, C&G; **263 TR**, LOC; **263 INSET**, California Museum of Photography WX5266; **267**, © Justin Kerr, 1989; **668**, National Park Service, Gift of Angelo Forgione.

Chapter 8 270 **BL**, Collection of John Craig. RH/LS; 270 **TL**, Radcliffe College Archives, Schlesinger Library; 270 **R**, Museum of the City of New York, Gift of Aaron & Abby Shroeder; 272, Collection of Sue and Lars Hotham; 273, Nebraska State Historical Society; 274, Sophia Smith Collection; 275 **both**, BB; 276, Collection of Sally Fox; 277 **TR**, LOC; 277 **INSET**, California Museum of Photography #X55458; 278 **TL**, Chicago Historical Society; 278 **B**, UPI/Bettman; 278 **INSETS**, Artwork from Wood River Gallery, Mill Valley, CA; 279 **BL**, LOC; 279 **BR**, Peter Menzel/Stock Boston; 280, Chicago Historical Society; 281, Old Court House Museum, Vicksburg, Mississippi; 283, U/B; 284, The Walker Collection of A'Lelia Perry Bundles, Alexandria, VA; 285, Museum of American Political Life; 286, 287 **T**, Collection of PRC RH/LS; 287 **INSET**, Courtesy Maytag Co.; 288 **TR**, Kansas Historical Society; 288 **INSET**, State Historical Society of Wisconsin.

Chapter 9 306 **TR**, Granger Collection; 306 **BR**, Museum of American Political Life. Photo by Sally Anderson-Bruce; 306 **L**, Courtesy Deere & Company; 308, The Oakland Museum History Dept.; 310, 311, LOC; 312, Collection of PRC. Photo by Lightstream; 314 **TL**, Chicago Historical Society; 314 **INSET**, CP; 315, NA; 316, California Museum of Photography; 317, Courtesy of the Liliuokalani Trust and the Bishop Museum (detail); 319, Museum of American Political Life; 320 **TL**, LOC; 320 **INSET**, BB; 322, "The World's Constable" by Dolrymple, JUDGE 1905, LOC; 323, "William Howard Taft" (detail) White House Historical Assoc.; 324, U/B; 326, "Goddess of Liberty Weathervane" by L.W. Cushing, 1870. Courtesy of Fred and Kathryn Giampietro; 329 **both**, Courtesy Archives of the Girl Scouts of the U.S.A.

Chapter 10 336 **L**, Division of Political History, Smithsonian Institution, #79-1002; 336 **R**, Collection of PRC RH/LS; 337 **TR**, 338, Boston Athenaeum; 339, Labor-Management Documentation Center, Cornell University; 340 **B**, International Museum of Photography, George Eastman House; 340 **INSET**, LOC; 341, CP; 342, U/B; 337 **TL**, 343, Courtesy of the Decorative & Industrial Arts Collection of the Chicago Historical Society: 1978.154.4; photo by John Alderson; 345 **TL**, CP; 345 **TR**, Bob Daemmrich/Stock Boston; 348 **BR**, Museum of the City of New York; 348 **INSET**, Stock Montage, Inc.; 337 **M**, 350, Museum of American Political Life; 351, "Goodness Gracious I Must Have Been Dozing" by Joseph Keppler from PUCK. Theodore Roosevelt Collection, Harvard College Library; 352, 353, 337 **B**, 355, FRENT; 356, Courtesy of the League of Women's Voters of the US; 358 **T**, Sophia Smith College Archives; 358 **B**, LOC; 360 **BL**, Radcliffe College Archives, Schlesinger Library; 360 **BR**, The New York Historical Society; 360 **M**, NA #44-2A-229; 361 **T**, **B**, Collection of Bettye Lane. RH/LS; 361 **BR**, U/B; 365, LOC.

Chapter 11 368 **TL**, 368 **BL**, Collection of Sue and Lars Hotham. RH/LS; 368 **TR**, 368 **BR**, 369 **TR**, 370 **T**, Collection of Colonel Stuart S. Corning, Jr. RH/LS; 370 **B**, CP; 372, Bayerisches Haupstaatsarchiv; 373, CP; 375, Granger Collection; 369 **TL**, 376 **TR**, Boston Athenaeum; 376 **TL**, LOC; 377, "Wilson" by Edmund Charles Tarbell, 1921. National Portrait Gallery, Smithsonian Institution/Art Resource, NY; 378, U/B; 379, Collection of Colonel Stuart S. Corning, Jr. RH/LS; 380, 369 **MR**, 381 **T**, NA #111-SC-25026, #111-SC-14129; 381 **INSET**, 382, Collection of Colonel Stuart S. Corning, Jr. RH/LS; 369 **ML**, 384, LOC; 385, Collection of PRC; 386, U/B; 387, Wayne State University, Archives of Labor and Urban Affairs; 388, The Michael Barson Collection/Past Perfect. RH/LS; 369 **B**, 391, NA #111-SC-25026.

Chapter 12 402 **TL**, FRENT; 402 **R**, Courtesy Ford Archives; 402 **BL**, Collection of Col. Stuart S. Corning, Jr. Photo by Lightstream; 404, FRENT; 405, Archives of Labor and Urban Affairs, Wayne State Univ.; 406 **BL**, FRENT; 406 **TL**, U/B; 403 **TR**, 407, C&G; 408, 410 **BR**, LOC; 410 **TL**, Collection of Frank Driggs; 403 **TL**, 412, **B INSET**, U/B; 412 **R INSET**, Beinecke Library, Yale University; 412 **L INSET**, Cartier Bresson/MP; 413, FRENT; 414 **TL**, LIFE magazine December 10, 1925; 403 **MR**, 415, Nipper's Choice Phonographs, Keene, NH. Photo by Wright Studio; 415 **TR**, LOC; 416, 417, U/B; 418, Collection of PRC RH/LS; 419, Saturday Evening Post, June 30, 1928, Curtis Archives; 420, Nancy Gewirz, Antique Textile Resource, Bethesda, MD RH/LS. Collection of Joseph Benjamin Shuff; 421, U/B; 403 **ML**, 423, Courtesy Ford Archives; 403 **B**, 424, Michael Barson Collection/Past Perfect RH/LS; 426, C&G; 432, BB.

Chapter 13 436 **TL**, **BL**, FRENT; 436 **R**, Detroit News; 437 **T**, 438, Courtesy of Speigel; 439, Artwork from Wood River Gallery, Mill Valley, CA; 440, Boston Athenaeum; 441, U/B; 442, LOC; 443 **B**, U/B; 443 **BL**, Copyright © 1929 by The New York Times Company; 448, U/B; 449 **T**, Museum of the City of New York. Photograph by Bernice Abbott, Federal Arts Project; 437 **TM**, 451, U/B; 452 **TL**, LOC; 437 **BM**, 455 **T**, 456 **T**, U/B; 455 **B**, CP; 437 **B**, 457, FRENT; 458, Reprinted from the Albany Evening News 6/7/31, with permission of the Times Union, Albany, N.Y.; 459 **T**, U/B; 459 **B**, CP; 461, FDR Library; 462 **BL**, **TR**, U/B; 462 **TL**, FRENT; 462 **TL**, Nixon Presidential Materials; 463 **BL**, Lyndon Baines Johnson Presidential Library; 463 **TR**, **BR**, Roy Roper and Diana Walker/GL.

Chapter 14 470 **ALL**, FRENT; 471 **T**, 472, LOC; 473, FDR Library; 474 **T**, US Forest Service; 474 **B**, U/B; 475, BB; 476, "Mary McLeod Bethune" by Betsy G. Reyneau (detail). National Portrait Gallery, Smithsonian Institution/Art Resource N.Y.; 478, LOC; 472 **M**, 479, FRENT; 480, Margaret Bourke-White LIFE Magazine © Time Warner; 481, FDR Library; 482, U/B; 472 **B**, 485, The Oakland Museum History Dept.; 486 **B**, 487, LOC; 488, Museum of Modern Art Film Still Archive; 489, James Prigoff.

Chapter 15 498 **TL**, Collection of Chester Stott RH/LS; 498 **BL**, Nancy Gewirz, Antique Textile Resource, Bethesda, MD RH/LS; 498 **R**, Collection of Col. Stuart S. Corning Jr. RH/LS; 499 **TL**, 500, US Holocaust Memorial Museum; 501 **TL**, Bilderdienst Suddeutscher Verlag; 501 **TR**, NA #242-HMA-2773; 502 **INSET**, 503, NA, *War & Conflict*, #993, #1131; 504 **T**, Herbert Hoover Presidential Library; 504 **B**, Collection of Col. Stuart S. Corning, Jr. RH/LS; 505 **TR**, US Navy; 505 **INSET**, NA #179-WP-936; 499 **TR**, 506, Collection of Major General George S. Patton RH/LS; 507, 508, U/B; 509, Collection of Col. Stuart S. Corning, Jr. RH/LS; 512, US Holocaust Memorial Museum; 513 **B**, Collection of Chester H. Stott, RH/LS; 513 **T**, US Dept of Defense; 514, 515 **B**, NA #127-PX-227672, #127-GR-137; 515 **T**, Peter Stackpole © Time Warner; 499 **M**, 517, U/B; 499 **B**, 518, NA; 519, HIROSHIMA SERIES, 1983. No. 2: "The Family". Gouache on paper 23"x17 1/2". Courtesy of Jacob Lawrence and Francine Seders Gallery Ltd.; 521 **TL**, NA#127-GR-137; 521 **TR**, 522 **TR**, U/B; 522 **BL**, LOC; 522 **BR**, Archive Photos; 523 **TL**, Department of Energy; 523 **M**, **BR**, Leif Skoogfors, Howard Sochurek/WC.

Chapter 16 530 **BL**, Collection of Chester Stott RH/LS; 530 **TL**, Collection of Picture Research Consultants, Inc. RH/LS; 530 **R**, Collection of Jeff Ikler RH/LS; 531 **TR**, NA *War & Conflict* #830; 532 **T**, Private Collection RH/LS; 532 **B**, 534, 535, NA, #127-GR-137, #208-MP-1-DDD-5, #44-PA-124; 536, 531 **TL**, National Museum of American History, Smithsonian Institution; 537 **T**, U/B; 537 **B**, LOC; 538 **BR**, Michael Barson Collection/Past Perfect © 1943, DC Comics RH/LS; 538 **BL**, Courtesy Hershey Foods Corp.; 538 **T**, WW; 539, Collection of Jeff Ikler RH/LS; 531 **MR**, 540, Collection of Col. Stuart S. Corning, Jr. RH/LS; 541, LOC; 542, NA #208-NP-1-HHH-5; 543, Rosie the Riveter Revisited Project, Oral History Program, California State Univer. Long Beach; 544, Ellen Kaiper Collection, Oakland; 545, Courtesy of the Norman Rockwell Family Trust and Curtis Archives; 531B, 546, 547 **T**, 548, 549, LOC; 573 **B**, Collection of Jeff Ikler RH/LS; 551, NA #210-GC-160.

Chapter 17 560 **ALL**, 561 **T**, 562, 563, 565 **B**, The Michael Barson Collection/Past Perfect. Photo by Rob Huntley/Lightstream; 565 **TR**, U/B; 565TL, Courtesy of the J.N. Ding Darling Foundation; 567, U/B; 568 **T**, **B**, Harry S. Truman Presidential Library; 561 **TM**, 571 **INSET**, Copyright © 1956 by The New York Times Company; 571 **T**, ©Stern/BS; 561 **BM**, 572, © 1959 Newsweek Inc. All rights reserved. Reprinted by permission; 573 **INSET**, 574 **BR**, Reni Burri/MP; 574 **INSET**, NA #210-GC-160; 574 **T**, U/B; 577, 578 **TL**, 561, **& INSET**, The Michael Barson Collection/Past Perfect RH/LS; 579, BB; 580, U/B; 581, Elliot Erwitt/MP.

Chapter 18 588 **L**, Collection of PRC RH/LS; 588 **R**, Bill Ray LIFE

Magazine © Time Warner; **589 T, 590**, Collection of Robert and Bonnie Pope RH/LS; **591**, McDonald's Corp.; **592 TL**, Courtesy IBM Archives; **592 TR**, "Big Computers in Little Packages" ©1993 by Consumers Union of U.S. Inc., Yonkers, NY 10703-1057. Reprinted by permission from Consumer Reports, November 1993; **592 BL**, National Museum of American History, Smithsonian Institution. #90-15751; **592 INSET**, Photofest; **592 BR**, Courtesy Campbell Soup Company; **593**, J.R. Eyerman LIFE Magazine © Time Warner; **595**, Collection of PRC RH/LS; **596 T**, The Michael Barson Collection/Past Perfect RH/LS; **589 TR, 596 B**, Collection of Nancy Gewirz, Antique Textile Resource, Bethesda, MD RH/LS; **597 T**, Ralph Morse LIFE © Time Warner; **597 B**, Dan Weiner, Courtesy Sandra Weiner; **598**, Curtis Archives; **589 ML, 602**, Museum of American Political Life, photo by Steve Laschever; **603 T**, FRENT; **603 B, 604** U/B; **589 MR, 603, INSET, 605 T**, FRENT; **605 B**, Division of Political History, Smithsonian Institution, #91-13778; **607 TR**, The Michael Barson Collection/Past Perfect RH/LS; **607 B**, Copyright © 1957 by The New York Times Company; **608 T**, Bob Adelman/MP; **608 INSET**, FRENT; **609 TL**, The Michael Barson Collection/Past Perfect RH/LS; **589 B, 609, INSET**, Carl Iwasaki LIFE Magazine © Time Warner; **609 BR**, WW; **610**, Grey Vielet LIFE Magazine © Time Warner; **611**, WW; **612 ALL**, U/B.

Chapter 19 **622 TL, BL, R, 623 T, 624**, FRENT; **625**, JFK Presidential Library; **627 T**, © Charles Harbutt/Actuality Inc.; **627 INSET**, LIFE Magazine Cover December 6, 1963. Photo by Fred Ward/BS; **623 M, 629**, Lyndon Baines Johnson Presidential Library. Photo by Henry Groskinsky; **630 BOTH**, FRENT; **631**, © Bob Daemmrich; **633**; Lyndon Baines Johnson Presidential Library; **634**, NASA; **623 B, 636**, Courtesy Boeing Defense & Space Group; **637 T & INSET**, Courtesy of the Peace Corps; **637 B**, Fred W. McDarrah; **640**, U/B; **642 T**, FRENT; **642 B**, WW.

Chapter 20 **650 L**, Dan Budnick/WC; **650 R, 651T, 652**, Art and Artifacts Division, Schomburg Center for Research in Black Culture, The New York Public Library, Astor, Lenox and Tilden Foundations; **653, 655**, U/B; **656 T**, Steve Shapiro/BS; **656 B**, FRENT; **657**, Dial Juvenile Books, 1968, a Division of Penguin Books USA, Inc.; **651 ML, 659**, Don Uhrbrock LIFE Magazine © Time Warner; **660**, State Historical Society of Wisconsin; **661**, U/B; **662, 664 BL**, Charles Moore/BS; **664 BR**, Jack O'Connell/The Boston Globe; **665 M**, Nancy Pierce/BS; **665 BL**, Steve Northrup/TIME Magazine; **665 BR**, © Largo Int./Shooting Star International; **651 TR, 666**, Robert Phillips LIFE Magazine ©Time Warner; **667 T**, Fred Ward, **667 INSET**, Steve Schapiro, both BS; **668**, Eve Arnold/MP; **669**, FRENT; **670**, U/B; **651B, 671 TR**, WW; **673**, Eve Arnold/MP; **674**, U/B; **675**, Co Rentmeester LIFE Magazine © Time Warner.

Chapter 21 **682 L**, Museum of American Political Life. Photo by Sally Anderson-Bruce; **682 TR**, M. Abramson/BS; **682 BR**, Collection of Michael McCloskey; **683 TL, 684, 685 TR**, Al Freni LIFE Magazine © Time Warner; **685 B**, © 1993 Jill Krementz; **685 INSET**, FRENT; **686 T**, © Bettye Lane; **686 B**, Radcliffe College Archives, Schlesinger Library; **687 INSET**, Courtesy Lang Communications; **687 TR**, © Bettye Lane; **688**, Collection of PRC; **689 TR & BR**, Al Freni LIFE Magazine © Time Warner; **691 T & B**, FRENT; **683 TR, 692**, Paul Fusco/MP; **693**, Craig Aurness/WC; **695 TL**, George Bacon Collection, Hawaii State Archives; **695 TR**, WW; **683 M, 696**, Eddie Adams/TIME Magazine; **698 B & BL**, Dirck Halstead/TIME Magazine; **699 T**, Rick Smolan/Against All Odds; **699 B**, FRENT; **700**, U/B; **683 B, 701**, FRENT; **702 INSET**, Collection of PRC; **702 TR**, Alfred Eisenstaedt LIFE Magazine © Time Warner; **703 TR**, Ken Regan/Camera 5.

Chapter 22 **712 R**, Forest McMullin/BS; **712 L**, The Image Works Archive; **713 T, 714 TL**, Courtesy United Nations. RH/LS; **715 TL**, Howard Sorhurek LIFE Magazine © Time Warner; **715 TR**, U/B; **716**, WW; **718 INSET**, Philip Jones Griffiths/MP; **713 ML, 718 L**, Zenith Electronics Corporation; **720 TL**, Catherine Leroy/AP, print courtesy Time Inc. Picture Collection; **720 INSET**, Larry Burrows LIFE Magazine © Time Warner; **721**, Courtesy of Le Ly Hayslip; **713 MR, 722**, FRENT; **723**, The Bancroft Library, University of California; **725**, © Lisa Law/The Image Works; **713 BL, 727 TL & TR**, The Oakland Museum History Department; **728**, © Lisa Law/The Image Works; **729 BL**, Frank Driggs Collection/MP; **729 BR**, Elliott Landy/MP; **730**, © Fredericks/The Image Works; **713 BR, 731**, Brad Markel/GL; **735**, Thai Khad Chuon/U/B.

Chapter 23 **746 T & B**, FRENT; **747 T, 748**, "The Time Machine" by Leslie Illingworth. Sept. 13, 1967 in *Punch*. Courtesy of the Lyndon B. Johnson Presidential Library; **749**, Joseph Louw LIFE Magazine © Time Warner; **750**, Bill Eppridge LIFE Magazine © Time Warner; **751 B (ALL)**, FRENT; **751 T**, U/B; **752 BR**, Jean Louis Atlan/Sygma; **752 BL**, Arthur Grace/Sygma; **753 BR**, J. Langevin/Sygma; **753 M**, U/B; **753 BL**, Jim Pickerell; **754 TL**, Richard Nixon Library. Photo © Henry Groskinsky; **747 MR, 754 BR**, Roddey E. Mims/U/B; **755**, Nixon Presidential Materials Project; **756**, Courtesy Draper Hill, Memphis, Tenn © The Commercial Appeal, Memphis; **759**, Ted Cowell/BS; **760**, Courtesy National Zoological Park, photo by Jessie Cohen; **761**, Gerald R. Ford Presidential Library; **762**, Nixon Presidential Materials Project; **747 ML, 763**, John Dominis LIFE Magazine © Time Warner; **764**, J.P. Laffont/Sygma; **747 B, 765 INSET**, FRENT; **765 TR**, Nixon Presidential Materials Project; **766**, Dennis Brack/BS; **767**, U/B; **768 T**, Fred Ward/BS; **768 M**, "Watergate" by Tony Auth, 1973. Reprinted by permission: Tribune Media Services; **769**, "Nixon Caught in a Web of Tapes" by Robert Pryor. Courtesy of John Locke Studios, Inc.; **770**, Nixon Presidential Materials Project.

Chapter 24 **778 L**, Gerald R. Ford Presidential Library. Photo by Henry Groskinsky; **778 R**, Jimmy Carter Presidential Library. Photo by Henry Groskinsky; **780**, Courtesy Gerald R. Ford Presidential Library; **781 TR**, WW; **779 T, 781 INSET**, Copyright © 1974 by The New York Times Company; **782**, "Inflation" by Frank Interlandi. Courtesy Gerald R. Ford Presidential Library; **784**, Matthew Naythons/GL; **779 ML, 785, 786 BL & BR**, FRENT; **787**, Jimmy Carter Presidential Library; **788**, Dennis Brack/BS; **789**, FRENT; **779 MR, 790**, Jimmy Carter Presidential Library; **792**, Alex Webb/MP; **793**, U/B; **793 TR**, Peter Marlow/MP; **793 TL**, Alain Mingam/GL; **779 B, 795, 796 L & R**, Dennis Brack/BS; **799**, U/B; **800**, WW; **807**, © Dan Miller, 1979, WC.

Chapter 25 **808 L & R, 809 T, 810**, FRENT; **811**, Steve McCurry/MP; **812**, Dennis Brack/BS; **813**, U/B; **814**, Larry Downing/WC; **809 TM, 815**, FRENT; **817**, White House Photo/BS; **818 B & INSET**, Dennis Brack/BS; **809 BM, 821 T**, Division of Political History, Smithsonian Institution #2061-167; **821 B**, Wally McNamee/WC; **824**, © 1987 Matt Herron; **825**, Dennis Brack/BS; **809 B, 828, 830 TL & TR**, U/B; **831**, David Turnley/BS; **836**, Courtesy, The Reagan Library.

Chapter 26 **838 L**, Photograph by Mark Seliger from *Rolling Stone*, December 9, 1993. By Straight Arrow Publishers, Inc. 1993. All Rights Reserved. Reprinted by Permission. **838 R**, FRENT; **839 T, 840**, Dennis Brack/BS; **841 INSET**, John C. Sykes Jr.; **841 TR**, WW; **842**, Sygma; **843**, Jacques M. Chenet/GL; **844**, John Harrington/BS; **846**, © 1992 Klaus Reisinger/BS; **847 BL**, AFP Photo; **847 BR**, Leonard Freed/MP; **839 M, 849, 850**, Les Stone/Sygma; **839 B, 852**, JB Pictures Ltd.; **854 B**, Brad Markel/GL; **854 T**, David Horsey/Reprinted courtesy of the Seattle Post-Intelligencer; **855**, Porter Gifford/GL; **864**, The Putnam Publishing Group/The Robert Foothorap Co.

Epilogue **866**, "From Sea to Shining Sea" Quilt by Jacqueline Paton. From the Permanent Collection of the Museum of American Folk Art.

Primary Source Bibliography

Chapter 1 **Chief Joseph:** McLuhan, T. C. *Touch the Earth: A Self-Portrait of Indian Existence.* Simon and Schuster, 1971, p. 54; **anonymous poet:** Furnivall, F. J., ed. *Ballads from Manuscripts, Vol. 1, 1868–1872.* Ballad Society Series, 1873; **Christopher Columbus:** Morison, Samuel Eliot. *Admiral of the Ocean Sea: A Life of Christopher Columbus.* Little Brown, 1942, p. 231; **Inca Garcilaso:** Garcilaso de la Vega, El Inca. *The Royal Commentaries of Peru, La Florida Del Inca.* Fondo de Cultura Económica, 1956, pp. 220, 229; **Adriaen Van der Donck:** Jennings, Francis. *The Ambiguous Iroquois Empire.* W.W. Norton & Company, 1984,

p. 47; **Miantonomo:** Cronin, William. *Changes in the Land: Indians, Colonists, and the Ecology of New England.* Hill and Wang, 1983, p. 139; **Jonathan Edwards:** Kupperman, Karen Ordahl, ed. *Major Problems in American Colonial History: Documents and Essays.* D.C. Heath, 1993, p. 369; **George Whitefield:** Gaustad, Edwin Scott. *The Great Awakening in New England.* Quadrangle Books, 1957, p. 27.

Chapter 2 Declaration of Independence; Abigail Adams: Brown, Richard D., ed. *Major Problems in the Era of the American Revolution, 1760–1791, Docments and Essagys.* D. C. Heath, 1992, p. 302.; **anonymous Englishman:** Wallace, Willard M. *Appeal to Arms: A Military History of the American Revolution.* Quadrangle/The New York Times Book Co., 1975, p. 43; **Michael Graham:** Dann, John C., ed. *The Revolution Remembered: Eyewitness Accounts of the War for Independence.* The University of Chicago Press, 1980, p. 50; **Thomas Paine:** Foot, Michael and Isaac Kramnick, eds. *Thomas Paine Reader.* Penguin Books, 1987, p. 116; **Sarah Osborn:** Dann, p. 245; **Joseph Plumb Martin:** Brown, pp. 223–224; **Fisher Ames:** Wood, Gordon S. *The Creation of the American Republic,1776–1787.* W. W. Norton & Company, 1969, p. 411; **Richard Price:** Wood, p. 396; **Benjamin Rush:** Wood, p. 466.

Chapter 3 United States Constitution; United States Constitution; Thomas Jefferson: Kammen, Michael, ed. *The Origins of the American Constitution: A Documentary History.* Penguin, 1986, p. 91; **French ambassador:** Harwell, Richard. *Washington.* Charles Scribner's Sons, 1968, p. 567; **Convention member:** Parton, James. *Life of Thomas Jefferson.* Da Capo, 1971, quoted in Barbash, Fred. *The Founding: A Dramatic Account of the Writing of the Consitution.* Simon and Schuster, 1987, p. 77.

Chapter 4 Margaret Bayard Smith: Morris, Richard B. and James Woodress. *Voices from America's Past, Vol. 1: The Colonies and the New Nation.* E. P. Dutton, 1963, p. 194; **Thomas Jefferson:** Peterson, Merrill D., ed. **Thomas Jefferson.** Library of America, 1984, p. 494; **Mason Weems:** Weems, Mason. *The Life of George Washington.* The Belknap Press of Harvard University Press, 1962, p. xv; **From *The Life of Washington* :** Weems, p. 12; **Methodist women:** Davis, David Byron. *Antebellum American Culture: An Interpretive Anthology.* D. C. Heath, 1979, p. 267; **Denmark Vesey:** Freehling, William W. *Prelude to the Civil War: The Nullification Controversy in South Carolina, 1816–1836.* Harper and Row, 1966, p. 54; **Edwin C. Holland:** Freehling, p. 59; **John Quincy Adams:** Wilentz, Sean, ed. *Major Problems in the Early Republic, 1778–1848.* D.C. Heath, 1992, p. 341; **President Jackson:** Wilentz, p. 388; **Cherokee:** Van Every, Dale. *Disinherited: The Lost Birthright of the American Indian.* William Morrow and Company, 1966, pp. 135–136.

Chapter 5 Abraham Lincoln: Davis, David Brion. *Antebellum American Culture: An Interpretive Anthology.* D. C. Heath, 1979, p. 407; **William Lloyd Garrison:** Wilentz, Sean, ed. *Major Problems in the Early Republic, 1787–1848.* D. C. Heath, 1992, p. 477; **Catharine Beecher:** *A Treatise on Domestic Economy.* T. H. Webb, 1842, pp. 26–34, 36–38; **Elizabeth Cady Stanton:** Stanton, Elizabeth Cady, et al. *History of Woman Suffrage, Vol. 1.* Fowler and Wells, 1889, pp. 58–59; **Sojourner Truth:** Ripley, Peter, ed. *Witness for Freedom: African Voices on Race, Slavery, and Emancipation.* University of North Carolina Press, 1993, p. 102; **President Jefferson:** Brown, Richard C., ed. *The Human Side of History.* Ginn and Co., 1970, p. 73; **James R. Walker:** Walker, James R. *Lakota Society.* University of Nebraska Press, 1982, p. 74; **Wilkis:** Grinnell, George Bird. *When Buffalo Ran.* University of Oklahoma Press, 1966, p. 46; **William Travis:** Ramsdell, Charles. "The Storming of the Alamo," *American Heritage,* Vol. XII, No. 2, February 1961, p. 91; **anonymous:** Unruh, John D., Jr. *The Plains Across.* University of Illinois Press, 1979, p. 414; **Reverend Walter Colton:** *Three Years in California.* S.A. Rollo, 1850, pp. 242–253.

Chapter 6 Abraham Lincoln: *Selected Speeches and Writings.* The Library of America, 1992, p. 131; **John Brown:** Oates, Stephen B. *To Purge This Land with Blood: A Biography of John Brown.* Harper Torchbooks, 1970, p. 351; **Tennessee soldier:** McPherson, James. *Battle Cry of Freedom: The Civil War Era.* Oxford University Press, 1988, p. 413; ***New York Herald* reporter:** *New York Herald,* July 18, 1863; **Union officer:** Wheeler, Richard. *The Siege of Vicksburg.* Thomas Y. Crowell, 1978, p. xii; **Abraham Lincoln's Gettysburg Address; white northerner:** Foner, Eric. *Reconstruction: America's Unfinished Revolution 1863–1877.* Harper and Row, 1988, p. 109; **Fourteenth Amendment:** United States Constitution.

Chapter 7 Andrew Carnegie: Carnegie, Andrew. *The Empire of Business.* Doubleday, 1902, pp. 138–140, quoted in Kirkland, Edward Chase. *Dream and Thought in the Business Community, 1860–1900.* Cornell, 1956, p. 156–157; **Frederick Winslow Taylor:** Taylor, Frederick W. *The Principles of Scientific Management.* W.W. Norton and Company, 1911, p. 39; **factory manager:** Massachusetts Bureau of the Statistics of Labor. *Thirteenth Annual Report,* 1883; **Samuel Gompers:** Gompers, Samuel. *Labor and the Employer.* Ayer Company Publishers, 1971, p. 118; **George Baer:** Roy, Andrew. *A History of Coal Miners of the U.S.* J.L. Trauger, 1906, p. 424; **August Spies:** Kogan, B.R. "The Chicago Haymarket Riot," 1959 (a reproduction of the circular in the Chicago Historical Society collection); **Howard Ruede:** *Sod-House Days. Letters from a Kansas Homesteader, 1877–1878.* Columbia University Press, 1937, p. 28; **Chief Joseph:** Utley, Robert M. *The Indian Frontier of the American West, 1846–1890.* University of New Mexico Press, 1984, p. 193; **anonymous:** Kutler, Stanley I. *Looking for America: The People's History, Vol. 2.* W.W. Norton & Company, 1979, p. 178; **Fiorello LaGuardia:** *The Making of an Insurgent.* J.B. Lippincott Co., 1948, pp. 64–65; **Eleanor McMain:** "Behind the Yellow Fever in Little Palermo: Housing Conditions Which New Orleans Should Shake Itself Free From Along with the Summer's Scourge," *Charities and the Commons,* Vol. 15, 1905, pp. 152–159.

Chapter 8 Pauli Murray: *Proud Shoes.* Harper and Row, 1956, pp. 269–270; **notice to performers:** Royle, Edwin Milton. "The Vaudeville Theatre," *Scribner's Magazine,* Vol. XXVI, October 1899, pp. 485–495; **Madam C. J. Walker:** Hine, Darlene Clark et al., eds. *Black Women in America. An Historical Encyclopedia,* Vol. 2. Carlson Publishing, 1993, pp. 1209–1214; **Edward H. Clarke:** *Sex in Education; or a Fair Chance for the Girls.* Ayer Co. Publishers, 1972 (reproduction of the 1873 edition).

Chapter 9 James G. Blaine: LaFeber, Walter. *The New Empire: An Interpretation of American Expansion, 1860–1898.* Cornell University Press, 1963, p. 165; **Albert J. Beveridge:** *The Meaning of the Times and Other Speeches.* Books for Libraries Press, 1908, pp. 84–85; **Hearst newspaper:** LaFeber, p. 230; **Theodore Roosevelt:** Hart, Albert Bushnell and Herbert Ronald Ferleger, eds. *Theodore Roosevelt Cyclopedia.* Roosevelt Memorial Association, 1941, p. 407; **Lucia Mead:** Crapol, Edward P., ed. *Women and American Foreign Policy: Lobbyists, Critics, and Insiders.* Greenwood Press, 1987, p. 72; **Carl Schurz:** "The Policy of Imperialism," 1899 address by Carl Schruz to Anti-Imperialist Conference in Chicago, October 17, 1899; **Bishop Alexander Walters:** "Wisconsin Weekly Advocate," August 17, 1899, quoted in Gatewood, Willard B., Jr. *Black Americans and the White Man's Burden, 1898–1903.* University of Illinois Press, 1975, p. 200; **Carl Schurz:** Lasch, Christopher. "The Anti-Imperialists, the Philippines, and the Inequality of Man," *Journal of Southern History,* August 1958, p. 115.

Chapter 10 Edward Bellamy: *Looking Backward.* River City Press, 1888, p. 56; **Jane Addams:** "Why Women Should Vote." *Ladies Home Journal,* Vol. XXVII, January 1910, pp. 21–22; **Upton Sinclair:** *The Jungle.* Doubleday, 1906, pp. 96–97; **Justice David J. Brewer:** Muller v. Oregon, quoted in Kerber, Linda J., and Jane De Hart, eds. *Women's America: Refocusing the Past.* Oxford University Press, 1987, p. 541; **Elizabeth Cady Stanton:** Flexner, Eleanor. *Century of Struggle: The Woman's Rights Movement in the United States.* The Belknap Press of Harvard University Press, 1975, p. 177; **Carrie Chapman Catt:** Flexner, p. 176.

Chapter 11 Richard Harding Davis: New York *Tribune,* August 1914; **Arthur Zimmerman:** Leckie, Robert. *The Wars of America.* Harper and Row, 1968, p. 628; **Woodrow Wilson:** Cooper, John Milton, Jr. *Pivotal Decades: The United States, 1900–1920.* W.W. Norton and Company, 1990, p. 265; **Mary Gladwin:** Dock, Lavinia L., et al. *A History of Ameri-*

can Red Cross Nursing. Macmillan, 1922, p. 179; **Corporal Elmer Sherwood:** Berger, Dorothy and Josef, eds. *Diary of America.* Simon and Schuster, 1957, p. 536; **Herbert Hoover:** "Gospel of the Clean Plate" *Ladies Home Journal,* August 1917, p. 25; **Alice Lord O'Brian:** *No Glory: Letters from France, 1917–1919.* Airport Publishers, 1936, pp. 8, 141, 152–153.

Chapter 12 Bart Vanzetti: Stong, Phil, "The Last Days of Sacco and Vanzetti," in Leighton, Isabel, ed. *The Aspirin Age, 1919–1941.* Simon and Schuster, 1949, p. 188; **Albert Johnson:** Daniels, Roger. *Coming to America: A History of Immigration and Ethnicity in America.* HarperCollins, 1990, p. 284; **New Orleans citizen:** "Additional Letters of Negro Migrants of 1916–1918." *Journal of Negro History,* April 4, 1919, p. 451; **Edna St. Vincent Millay:** "First Fig." *Edna St. Vincent Millay: Selected Poems.* HarperCollins, 1991, p. 19; **Preston Slosson:** *The Great Crusade and After, 1914–1928.* Macmillan, 1929, p. 157; **New York Sun:** Ward, John William. "The Meaning of Lindbergh's Flight." *American Quarterly,* Vol. X (Spring 1958), p. 1; **Henry Ford:** *My Life and Work.* Doubleday, 1923, p. 251; **Billy Sunday:** Sinclair, Andrew. *Era of Excess: A Social History of the Prohibition Movement.* Harper and Row, 1964, p. 248.

Chapter 13 Lincoln Steffens: Leuchtenberg, William. *The Perils of Prosperity, 1914–1932.* University of Chicago Press, 1958, p. 202; **Arthur Crew Inman:** Aaron, Daniel, ed. *The Inman Diary: A Public and Private Confession.* Harvard University Press, 1985, p. 401; **Broadway show tune:** Words by E. Y. Harburg, music by Jay Gorney. Harms, Inc., 1932. Renewed, permission from Warner Brothers Music. **Oklahoma woman:** Terkel, Studs. *Hard Times: An Oral History of the Great Depression.* Pantheon Books, 1970, p. 50; **Woody Guthrie:** *Bound for Glory.* E. P. Dutton, 1968, p. 189; **boy tramp:** Minehan, Thomas. *Boy and Girl Tramps of America.* Holt, Rinehart, and Winston, 1934, pp. 21–23, 53–54, 62–64; **Gordon Parks:** *Voices in the Mirror: An Autobiography.* Doubleday, 1990; **Wilson Ledford:** "How I Lived During the Depression." Interview taped and transcribed by Reuben Hiatt, November 7, 1982. Quoted in Snell, William R. ed., *Hard Times Remembered: Bradley County and the Great Depression.* Bradley County Historical Society, 1983, pp. 117–121; **Gerald W. Johnson:** "The Average American and the Depression." *Current History,* February 1932; **Kitty McCulloch:** Terkel, Studs. *Hard Times: An Oral History of the Great Depression.* Pantheon Books, 1970; **William Saroyan:** *Inhale and Exhale.* Random House, 1936, p. 81; **The 1932nd Psalm:** E. J. Sullivan. Quoted in McElvaine, Robert S., ed. *Down and Out in the Great Depression: Letters from the Forgotten Man.* University of North Carolina Press, 1983, p. 34; **Herbert Hoover:** Myers, William S., ed. *The State Papers and Other Public Writings of Herbert Hoover.* Doubleday, Doran and Company, Inc., Vol. II, 1934, pp. 408–413; **Franklin D. Roosevelt:** *New York Times,* September 24, 1932; **Roosevelt:** Inaugural Address, March 4, 1933.

Chapter 14 Harry Hopkins: Dawley, Alan. *Struggles for Justice: Social Responsibility and the Liberal State.* Harvard University Press, 1991, p. 367; **Mary McLeod Bethune:** "Faith That Moved a Dump Heap." *Who, The Magazine About People,* January 3, 1941, pp. 31–35, 54; **Letters to Roosevelt:** Editors of Time Life. *This Fabulous Century: Sixty Years of American Life, 1930–1949.* Time Life Books, Vol. IV, 1969, p. 136; f**ederal offficial:** Markowitz, Gerald, and David Rosner, eds. "Slaves of the Depression." *Workers' Letters About Life on the Job.* Cornell, 1987, p. 154; **Walter White:** *A Man Called White: The Autobiography of Walter White.* Viking Press, 1948, pp. 179–180; **Sam E. Roberts:** Duram, James C. and Eleanor A. "Congressman Clifford Hope's Correspondence With his Constituents: A Conservative View of the Court-Packing Fight of 1937." *Kansas Historical Quarterly* 37/1 (Spring 1971), p. 71; **Hiram W. Johnson:** Barnes, William R., and A. W. Littlefield. *The Supreme Court Issue and the Constitution, Comments Pro and Con by Distinguished Men.* Barnes & Noble, 1937, p. 49; **Walter Reuther:** Madison, Charles A. *American Labor Leaders, Personalities and Forces in the Labor Movement.* Ungar, 1950, p. 382; **Mrs. Renee Lohrback:** Blackwelder, Julia Kirk. *Women of the Depression: Caste and Culture in San Antonio, 1929–1939.* Texas A&M

Press, 1984.

Chapter 15 Karl Alexander von Müller: Flood, Charles Bracelen. *Hitler: The Path to Power.* Houghton Mifflin Company, 1989, p. 493; **Dellie Hahne:** Harris, Mark Jonathan, et al. *The Homefront: America During World War II.* G. P. Putnam's Sons, 1984, p. 27; **Dick Winters:** Ambrose, Stephan. *Band of Brothers: E. Company, 506th Regiment, 101st Airborne: From Normandy to Hitler's Eagle's Nest.* Simon & Schuster, 1992, p. 270; **Ernie Pyle:** Nichols, David. *Ernie's War: The Best of Ernie Pyle's World War II Dispatches.* Random House, 1986, p. 141; **Art Rittenberg:** Lidz, Richard. *Many Kinds of Courage: An Oral History of World War II.* G. P. Putnam's Sons, 1980, p. 243; **Eisenhower:** Carroll, James. "The monster that adds a chill to the August air." *The Boston Globe,* August 17, 1993; **Tatsue Urata:** Winkler, Allan M. *Life Under a Cloud, American Anxiety About the Atom.* Oxford University Press, 1993, p. 23.

Chapter 16 Leonard Williamson: Hoopes, Roy. *Americans Remember the Home Front: An Oral Narrative.* Hawthorn Books, 1977, p. 115; **Want ad:** *Sporting News,* February 25, 1943; **Wanita Allen:** Frank, Miriam, Marilyn Ziebarth, and Connie Field. *The Life and Times of Rosie the Riveter.* Clarity Educational Productions, 1982, p. 57; **Beatrice Clifton:** Gluck, Sherna Berger. *Rosie the Riveter Revisited: Women, the War, and Social Change.* Twayne Publishers, 1987, pp. 211, 219; **from the film Women of Steel:** Frank, Miriam, et al. *The Life and Times of Rosie the Riveter.* Clarity Educational Productions, 1982, p. 100; **Margaret Wright:** Frank et al., p. 94; **Roosevelt:** Columbus Day speech, 1942; **Lloyd Brown:** Blum, John Morton. *V Was for Victory: Politics and American Culture During World War II.* Harcourt Brace Jovanovich, 1976, p. 191; **Henry Murakami:** Harris, Mark Jonathan, et al. *The Homefront: America During World War II.* G. P. Putnam's Sons, 1984, p. 113.

Chapter 17 Joseph Goulden: *The Best Years, 1945–1950.* Atheneum, 1976; **Joseph Stalin:** Truman, Harry S *Memoirs, Volume I: Year of Decisions.* Doubleday & Company, Inc., 1955, p. 86; **Harry Truman:** Truman, p. 289; **Truman:** Truman, *Memoirs, Volume I;* **MacArthur:** Phillips, Cabell. *The Truman Presidency: The History of a Triumphant Succession.* The Macmillan Company, 1966, p. 348; **Joseph Welch:** Lately, Thomas. *When Even Angels Wept: The Senator Joseph McCarthy Affair—A Story Without a Hero.* William Morrow & Company, Inc., 1973, pp. 587–588.

Chapter 18 Walt Disney: Winkler, Allan M. *Life Under a Cloud: American Anxiety About the Atom.* Oxford University Press, 1993, p. 140; **Malvina Reynolds:** Winkler, Allan M. *Modern America: The United States from World War II to the Present.* HarperCollins, 1985, p. 86; **Eisenhower:** *Mandate for Change, 1953–1956.* Doubleday and Company, Inc., 1963, p. 548; **Betty Friedan:** *The Feminine Mystique.* Norton, 1963; **Harry Truman:** Winkler, p. 70; **Richard Nixon:** Wicker, Tom. *One of Us: Richard Nixon and the American Dream.* Random House, 1991, p. 98; **Eisenhower:** Holbo, Paul S., and Robert W. Sellen, eds. *The Eisenhower Era.* Dryden Press, 1974, p. 113; **Jackie Robinson:** Henderson, Edwin B. *The Black Athlete: Emergence and Arrival.* Publisher's Agency under the auspices of the Association for the Study of Afro-American Life and History, 1976, p. xii; **Martin Luther King, Jr.:** Sitkoff, Harvard. *The Struggle for Black Equality: 1954–1980.* Hill and Wang, 1981, p. 50; **Martin Luther King, Jr.:** *Stride Toward Freedom: The Montgomery Story.* Harper and Row, 1958, pp. 53–55; **Seminole petition to Eisenhower:** Josephy, Alvin M., Jr. *Now That the Buffalo's Gone: A Study of Today's American Indians.* Alfred A. Knopf, 1982, p. 28.

Chapter 19 John F. Kennedy: Inaugural Address. January 20, 1961; **John Kenneth Galbraith:** Winkler, Allan M. *Modern America: The United States from World War II to the Present.* HarperCollins, 1985, p. 125; **Lyndon B. Johnson:** Speech at the University of Michigan, May 1964; **Tom Hayden:** Winkler, Allan M. *The Recent Past: Readings on America Since World War II.* Harper and Row, 1989, p. 164; **John F. Kennedy:** Address to Latin American diplomats, March 13, 1961; **Arthur M. Schlesinger, Jr.:** Nash, Gary. *The American People. Volume Two, Since 1865: Creating a Nation and a Society.* Harper and Row, 1986,

p. 963; **Paul Cowan:** *The Making of an Un-American: A Dialogue with Experience.* Viking Press, 1970, dedication page; **Senator J. William Fulbright:** Schlesinger, Arthur M. *A Thousand Days: John F. Kennedy in the White House.* Houghton Mifflin, 1965, p. 251; **Dean Acheson:** Winkler, Allan M. *Life Under a Cloud: American Anxiety About the Atom.* Oxford University Press, 1993, pp. 173–174.

Chapter 20 W. E. B. DuBois: Aptheker, Herbert, ed. *Pamphlets and Leaflets by W. E. B. DuBois.* Kraus-Thomason Organization Limited, 1986, p. 116; **Southern Christian Leadership Conference:** Sitkoff, Harvard. *The Struggle for Black Equality.* Hill and Wang, 1981, p. 65; **SCLC leaflet:** Sitkoff, p. 59; **Martin Luther King, Jr.:** Sitkoff, p. 92; **Todd Gitlin:** *The Sixties: Years of Hope, Days of Rage.* Bantam Books, 1987, pp. 148–149; **Anne Moody:** *Coming of Age in Mississippi.* Dell, 1968; **John Lewis:** Hampton, Henry, et al. *Voices of Freedom: An Oral History of the Civil Rights Movement from the 1950's Through the 1980's.* Bantam Books, 1990, p. 58; **James Farmer:** Hampton, p. 78; **Martin Luther King, Jr.:** "Letter From a Birmingham Jail." *Essay Series.* A. J. Muste Memorial Institute, p. 18; **John F. Kennedy:** Radio and Television Report to the American People on Civil Rights, June 11, 1963; **Martin Luther King, Jr.:** "I Have a Dream." Speech in Washington, D.C., August 1963. In Winkler, Allan M. *The Recent Past: Readings on America Since World War II.* Harper and Row, 1989, p. 275; **Fannie Lou Hamer:** Harley, Sharon, et. al. *The African American Experience: A History.* Globe Book Company, 1992, p. 336; **James Baldwin:** *The Fire Next Time.* Dial Press, 1963, p. 132; **Malcolm X**: *The Autobiography of Malcolm X.* Ballantine Books, 1990, pp. 245–246; **Stokely Carmichael:** Nash, Gary B., et al., eds. *The American People.* Harper and Row, 1986, p. 1001; **Barbara Jordan:** Harley, et al., p. 343.

Chapter 21 Cathy Cade: Evans, Sara. *Personal Politics: The Roots of Women's Liberation in the Civil Rights Movement and the New Left.* Alfred A. Knopf, 1979, p. 205; **Mimi Feingold:** Evans, p. 204; **Helen Reddy:** "I Am Woman." Words by Helen Reddy, music by Ray Burton. Irving Music, Inc. and Buggerlugs Music Co., 1971; **Equal Rights Amendment to the Constitution, 1972; Marabel Morgan:** *The Total Woman.* Simon and Schuster, 1973, pp. 96–97; **Phyllis Schlafly:** Nash, Gary B. *The American People: Creating a Nation and a Society.* Harper and Row, 1986, p. 1008; **Rodolfo Gonzales:** Hammerback, John C., Richard J. Jensen and Jose Angel Gutierrez. *A War of Words: Chicano Protest in the 1960's and 1970's.* Greenwood Press, 1985, p. 59; **César Chávez:** Levy, Jacques E. *César Chávez: Autobiography of La Causa.* W.W. Norton, 1975; **César Chávez:** Levy, p. 293; **David Sanchez:** Vigil, Maurilio. *Chicano Politics.* University Press of America, 1977, p. 173; **Dennis Banks:** Zimmerman, Bill. *Airlift to Wounded Knee.* Swallow Press, 1976, p. 117; **Dennis Banks:** Dewing, Rolland. *Wounded Knee: The Meaning and Significance of the Second Incident.* Irvington Publishers, Inc., 1985, p. 41; **Vine Deloria, Jr.:** "This Country Was a Lot Better Off When the Indians Were Running It." *New York Times Magazine,* March 8, 1970; **Onondaga Chief Oren Lyons:** *Voices from Wounded Knee: The People Are Standing Up.* Akwesasne Notes, 1974, p. 96; a **Taos representative:** Debo, Angie. *A History of the Indians of the United States.* University of Oklahoma Press, 1977, p. 419; **Rachel Carson:** *Silent Spring.* Houghton Mifflin, 1962, p. 6; **Ralph Nader:** *Unsafe at Any Speed: The Designed-in Dangers of the American Automobile.* Grossman Publishers, 1972, preface.

Chapter 22 Lyndon B. Johnson: Kearns, Doris. *Lyndon Johnson and the American Dream.* Harper and Row, 1976, p. 316; **Angel Qunitana:** Maurer, Harry. *Strange Ground: Americans in Vietnam, 1945–1975, An Oral History.* Henry Holt and Company, 1989, p. 171; **Le Thanh:** Chanoff, David, and Van Toai Doan. *Portrait of the Enemy.* Random House, 1986, pp. 62–63; **Vietnamese peasant:** Trullinger, James Walker, Jr. *Village at War: An Account of Revolution in Vietnam.* Longman, 1980, p. 118. **Private Paul Meadlo:** *New York Times,* November 25, 1969, p. 16; **Bob Dylan:** "The Times They Are A-Changin.' " Words and music by Bob Dylan. Warner Brothers, 1963; **Tom Hayden:** Students for a Democratic Society, *Port Huron Statement.* Quoted in Winkler, Allan. *The*

Recent Past: Readings on America Since World War II. Harper and Row, 1989, pp. 218–219; **Mario Savio:** Winkler, Allan M. *Modern America: The United States from World War II to the Present.* HarperCollins, 1985, p. 153; **Bo Burlingham:** Obst, Lynda Rosen, ed. *The Sixties: The Decade Remembered Now by the People Who Lived It Then.* Random House Rolling Stone Press, 1977, p. 300; **Lynn Ferrin:** Morrison, Joan and Robert K. *From Camelot to Kent State: The Sixties Experience in the Words of Those Who Lived It.* Times Books, 1987, p. 176; **Tom Law:** Makower, Joel. *Woodstock: The Oral History.* Doubleday, 1989, p. 333; **Richard Nixon:** Address to the Nation on the Situation in Southeast Asia. April 30, 1970; **Tom Grace:** Morrison, et al., pp. 332–333; **Ron Kovic:** *Born on the Fourth of July.* Pocket Books, 1989.

Chapter 23 Martin Luther King, Jr.: Kaiser, Charles. *1968 in America: Music, Politics, Chaos, Counterculture, and the Shaping of a Generation.* Weidenfeld and Nicolson, 1988, p. 144; **John Lewis:** Morrison, Joan, and Robert K. *From Camelot to Kent State: The Sixties Experience in the Words of Those Who Lived It.* Times Books, 1987, pp. 34–35; **Todd Gitlin:** Obst, Lynda Rosen, ed. *The Sixties: The Decade Remembered Now by the People Who Lived It Then.* Random House Rolling Stone Press, 1977; **Richard Nixon:** Wicker, Tom. *One of Us: Richard Nixon and the American Dream.* Random House, 1991, p. 9; **Lawrence O'Brien:** Siegal, Frederick F. *Troubled Journey: From Pearl Harbor to Ronald Reagan.* Hill and Wang, 1984; **Richard Nixon:** Ambrose, Stephen E. *Nixon: Volume Two: The Triumph of a Politician, 1962–1972.* Simon and Schuster, 1989, p. 376; **Henry Kissinger:** *White House Years.* Little, Brown and Company, 1979, p. 45; **Richard Nixon:** *The Memoirs of Richard Nixon.* Grosset and Dunlap, 1978, p. 545; **Richard Nixon:** *Public Papers of the Presidents of the United States: Richard Nixon.* United States Government Printing Office, 1972, p. 237; **Richard Nixon:** *Public Papers of the Presidents of the United States: Richard Nixon,* p. 320; **John J. Sirica:** Bernstein, Carl and Bob Woodward. *All the President's Men.* Warner Paperback Books, 1975, p. 268; **M. Caldwell Butler:** Burns, James MacGregor. *The Crosswinds of Freedom.* Alfred A. Knopf, 1989, p. 507.

Chapter 24 Richard Rovere: Reeves, Richard. *A Ford, Not a Lincoln.* Harcourt Brace Jovanovich, 1975; **Gerald Ford:** *A Time to Heal: The Autobiography of Gerald R. Ford.* Harper and Row, 1979, pp. 177–178; **Jerold F. terHorst:** "How Good a President?" *Newsweek,* October 18, 1976, p. 31; **Jimmy Carter:** *Keeping Faith: Memoirs of a President.* Bantam Books, 1982, p. 65; **Patrick Caddell:** Wooten, James. *Dasher: The Roots and the Rising of Jimmy Carter.* Weidenfeld and Nicolson, 1978, p. 356; **Alistair Cooke:** "On Language." *New York Times Magazine,* July 19, 1981; **Jimmy Carter:** Carter, pp. 142–143; **Cyrus Vance:** *Hard Choices: Critical Years in America's Foreign Policy.* Simon and Schuster, 1983, pp. 228–229; **Kathryn Koob:** *Guest of the Revolution.* Thomas Nelson Publishers, 1982, pp. 57, 64, 73; **Jimmy Carter:** Jordan, Hamilton. *Crisis: The Last Year of the Carter Presidency.* G. P. Putnam's Sons, 1982, p. 54; **Robert J. Samuelson:** "Good People, but Not Very Good Government." *The Eugene Register-Guard,* January 19, 1981; **Jimmy Carter:** Public address; **Jimmy Carter:** Carter, p. 22; **Robert J. Samuelson:** Samuelson, January 19, 1981.

Chapter 25 Ronald Reagan: *An American Life.* Simon and Schuster, 1990, p. 135; **Kevin Phillips:** "Reagan's America: A Capital Offense." *New York Times Magazine,* June 24, 1990; **Joseph Lattimore:** Terkel, Studs. *Race: How Blacks and Whites Think and Feel About the American Obsession.* The New Press, 1992, p. 138; **Gloria Steinem:** Gibbs, Nancy. "The War Against Feminism." *Time,* March 9, 1992, p. 57; **Dale Old Horn:** Sahagun, Louis. "Crow Tribe: Heavy Price of Tradition." *Los Angeles Times,* December 22, 1986; **Iola Hayden:** Gorman, Tom. "Choctaws Retain Culture as Their Business Thrives." *Los Angeles Times;* **George Bush:** "Open Letter to College Students on the Persian Gulf Crisis," January 9, 1991.

Chapter 26 Maya Angelou: Inaugural poem "On the Pulse of the Morning"; **Bill Clinton:** Address to Congress and the Nation on Health Care Reform. September, 1993; **Jackie Goldberg:** Gore, Rick. "L.A.'s

Rainbow Road." *National Geographic*, June 1992, pp. 40–69; **Jaimie S. Wurzel:** *Toward Multiculturalism: A Reader in Multicultural Education.* Intercultural Press, Inc. 1988, p. 10; **Arthur M. Schlesinger, Jr:** *The Disuniting of America.* W.W. Norton and Company, 1992.

Source Readings Acknowledgments

Chapter 1 "Song Concerning a Dream of the Thunderbirds": Reprinted from *Teton Sioux Music*, Bureau of American Ethnology Bulletin 61. By Frances Desmore (Washington, D.C., Smithsonian Institution Press), "Song Concerning a Dream of the Thunderbirds." By permission of the publisher. Copyright 1918. **The Captivity of Mary Rowlandson:** From *Journeys in New Worlds: Early American Women's Narratives*, edited by William L. Andrews, Sargeant Bush, Jr., Annette Kolodny, Amy Schrager Lang, and Daniel B. Shea. © Copyright 1990 (Madison: The University of Wisconsin Press). Reprinted by permission of the publisher. **The Diary of a Colonial Gentleman:** Reprinted by permission of The Putnam Publishing Group from THE GREAT AMERICAN GENTLEMAN WILLIAM BYRD by Louis B. Wright and Marion Tinling. Copyright © 1963 by Louis B. Wright and Marion Tinling.

Chapter 2 April Morning: From *April Morning* by Howard Fast. Copyright 1961 by Howard Fast. Copyright renewed 1989 by Howard Fast. Reprinted by permission of Crown Publishers, Inc.; **A Young Woman's War-Time Diary:** From *Root of Bitterness: Documents of the Social History of American Women* edited, with a new foreword, by Nancy F. Cott. Copyright 1972 by Nancy F. Cott. Reprinted with the permission of Northeastern University Press, Boston.

Chapter 3 Miracle at Philadelphia: From *Miracle at Philadelphia* by Catherine Drinker Bowen. Copyright 1966 by Catherine Drinker Bowen. By permission of Little, Brown and Co.; **Benjamin Franklin Campaigns for the Constitution:** Reprinted by permission from The Putnam Publishing Group from DEBATES OF THE CONSTITUTIONAL CONVENTION 1787 edited by Gaillard Hunt. Copyright © 1903; **Journal of a Senator:** E.S. Maclay, ed. *Journal of William Maclay.* New York, 1890. Reprinted in *Diary of America*, edited by Josef and Dorothy Berger (New York: Simon and Schuster, 1957).

Chapter 4 The Monroe Doctrine: Adapted from James D. Richardson. *A Compilation of the Messages and Papers of the Presidents, Vol. II.* (New York: Bureau of National Literature. Inc., ©1897 by James Richardson); **President Jackson's Letter to the Seminoles:** Adapted from "President Andrew Jackson's Letter to the Seminoles," in *History of the Indian Wars*, ed. Henry Trumbull, 1841; **"To a Locomotive in Winter":** Walt Whitman. "To a Locomotive in Winter" in *Walt Whitman Complete Poetry and Collected Prose.* (New York, NY: Literary Classics of the United States, Inc., 1982).

Chapter 5 Incidents in the Life of a Slave Girl: Written by Herself: Harriet Ann Jacobs. *Incidents in the Life of a Slave Girl: Written by Herself.* (Cambridge, MA: Harvard University Press, 1987); **The Pioneer Chinese:** Betty Lee Sung. "The Pioneer Chinese," from *Mountain of Gold: The Story of the Chinese in America.* (New York: Macmillan, 1967).

Chapter 6 Diary of a Southern Woman: Mary Boykin Chesnut. *A Diary from Dixie*, edited by Ben Ames Williams. (Boston: Houghton Mifflin, 1945); **Gettysburg Address:** Abraham Lincoln. Gettysburg Address, in Henry Steele Commager, ed. *Documents of American History*, 8th ed. (New York: Appleton-Century-Crofts, 1968). **Saving the Union:** Abraham Lincoln. Discussion of War Aims, in *The Annals of America*, Volume 9 (Encyclopaedia Britannica, Inc., 1968).

Chapter 7 Talks with Otoe Chiefs: U.S. National Archives, Office of Indian Affairs. Letters Sent: Otoe Agency (1856–1876); **Where Is America?:** Anzia Yezierska. *Hungry Hearts.* Permission granted by Ayer Company Publishers.

Chapter 8 Separate but Equal: *Plessy* v. *Ferguson*, 163 U.S. 537 (1896); **The Ethics of Living Jim Crow: An Autobiographical Sketch:** Selected excerpts from "The Ethics of Living Jim Crow" from *Uncle Tom's Children* by Richard Wright. Copyright 1937 by Richard Wright. Copyright renewed 1965 by Ellen Wright. Reprinted by permission of HarperCollins Publishers, Inc.

Chapter 9 "The United States Looking Outward": Adapted from Alfred T. Mahan, "The United States Looking Outward," Boston, MA: *Atlantic Monthly*, December 1890; **"To Theodore Roosevelt":** Reprinted from FORTY POEMS TOUCHING ON AMERICAN HISTORY, edited by Robert Bly, Beacon Press, Boston, 1970. Reprinted with permission of Robert Bly.

Chapter 10 Children at Work: John Spargo. *The Bitter Cry of the Children.* (New York: Macmillan, 1906); **Suffragists on a Hunger Strike:** Reprinted from *Jailed for Freedom* by Doris Stevens, by permission of Liveright Publishing Corporation. Copyright 1920 by Boni & Liveright. Copyright renewed 1949 by Liveright Publishing Corporation.

Chapter 11 *All Quiet on the Western Front*: All Quiet on the Western Front by Erich Maria Remarque. "Im Westen Nichts Neues", ©1928 by Ullstein A.G.; © renewed 1956 by Erich Maria Remarque. "All Quiet on the Western Front", ©1929, 1930 by Little, Brown, and Co.; © renewed 1957, 1958 by Erich Maria Remarque. All rights reserved; **Songs of World War One:** "Over There" from *Those Wonderful Years: 1900–1920*, compiled by Dick Stern (New York: Big Three Music Corp). Song by George M. Cohan © 1917, renewed 1945 by Leo Feist, Inc., New York. "K-K-K-Katy" by Geoffrey O'Hara © 1918, renewed by Leo Feist, Inc., New York.

Chapter 12 The Rich Boy: F. Scott Fitzgerald. "The Rich Boy," in *The Stories of F. Scott Fitzgerald* (New York: Charles Scribner's Sons, 1951); **"Mother to Son":** From SELECTED POEMS by Langston Hughes. Copyright 1926 by Alfred A. Knopf, Inc., and renewed 1954 by Langston Hughes. Reprinted by permission of the publisher. **"The Negro Speaks of Rivers":** From SELECTED POEMS by Langston Hughes. Copyright 1926 by Alfred A. Knopf, Inc., and renewed 1954 by Langston Hughes. Reprinted by permission of the publisher.

Chapter 13 Growing Up During the Depression: Adapted from Russell Baker. *Growing Up.* (New York: Congdon & Weed, Inc., 1982); **Letters from the Forgotten Man:** Reprinted from DOWN AND OUT IN THE GREAT DEPRESSION: LETTERS FROM THE "FORGOTTEN MAN," edited by Robert S. McElvaine. Copyright © 1983 by The University of North Carolina Press. Used by permission of the publisher.

Chapter 14 One Boy Remembers the New Deal: "Sour Grapefruit and WPA," pp. 19–22, from *A Nickel's Worth of Skim Milk: A Boy's View of the Great Depression*, by Robert J. Hastings. Copyright 1972 by the Board of Trustees, Southern Illinois University; **Working for the CCC :** From *Voices in the Mirror* by Gordon Parks. Copyright 1990 by Gordon Parks. Used by permission of Doubleday, a division of Bantam Doubleday Dell Publishing Group, Inc.

Chapter 15 Survivors of the Holocaust Remember: From *Shoah: An Oral History of the Holocaust*, by Claude Lanzmann. Copyright © 1985 by Claude Lanzmann. Reprinted with permission of Georges Borchardt, Inc.; **The Liberation of Athens:** "Liberation of Athens" by Sgt. Joe McCarthy, edited by Franklin S. Forsberg, from *The Best from Yank, the Army Weekly* by Franklin S. Forsberg, editor. Copyright 1945 by Franklin S. Forsberg. Used by permission of Dutton Signet, a division of Penguin Books USA Inc. **A Londoner Describes Life During the Blitz:** Studs Terkel. From *The Good War: An Oral History of World War II* by Studs Terkel. Copyright © 1984 by Studs Terkel. Reprinted by permission of Pantheon Books, a division of Random House, Inc.

Chapter 16 Farewell to Manzanar: From *Farewell to Manzanar* by James D. Houston and Jeanne Wakatsuki Houston. Copyright 1973 by James D. Houston. Reprinted by permission of Houghton Mifflin Co. All rights reserved. **"In Response to Executive Order 9066: All Americans of Japanese Descent Must Report to Relocation Centers":** Copyright 1992 by Dwight Okita. Reprinted with permission of Tia Chucha Press.